NEW CATHOLIC ENCYCLOPEDIA

An International Work of Reference on the Teachings, History, Organization, and Activities of the Catholic Church, and on All Institutions, Religions, Philosophies, and Scientific and Cultural Developments Affecting the Catholic Church from Its Beginning to the Present.

Prepared by an Editorial Staff at The Catholic University of America, Washington, District of Columbia.

McGRAW-HILL BOOK COMPANY NEW YORK ST LOUIS

Volume III

Can to Col

NEW CATHOLIC ENCYCLOPEDIA

SAN FRANCISCO TORONTO LONDON SYDNEY

Nihil Obstat:
John P. Whalen, M.A., S.T.D.
Censor Deputatus

Imprimatur:
✠ Patrick A. O'Boyle, D.D.
Archbishop of Washington
August 5, 1966

NEW CATHOLIC ENCYCLOPEDIA

Library of Congress Catalog Card Number: 66-22292

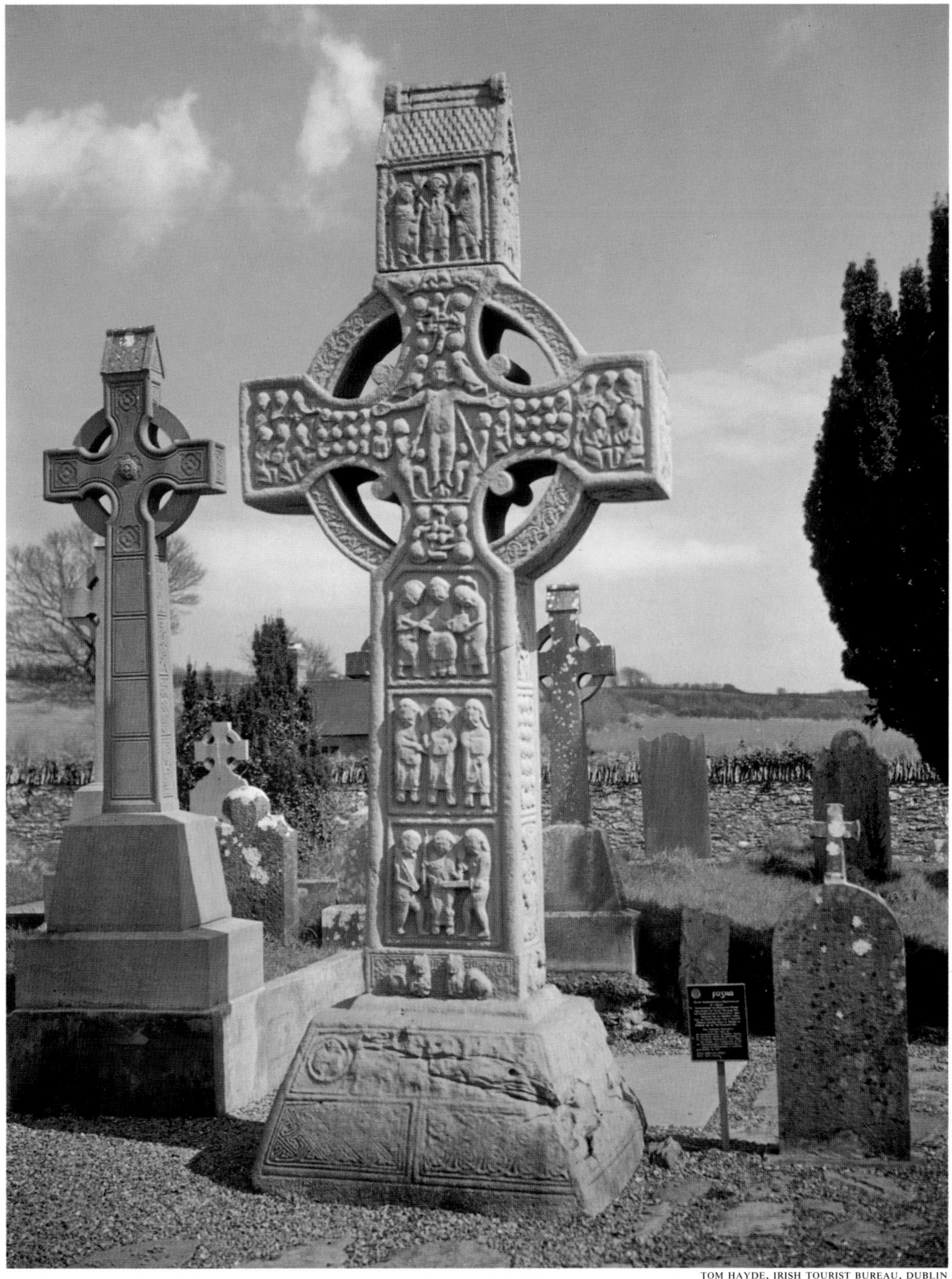

TOM HAYDE, IRISH TOURIST BUREAU, DUBLIN

The early 10th-century "Cross of Muiredach" at Monasterboice, County Louth, Ireland. Almost 18 feet high, the cross, one of the chief examples of its type, is carved with high-relief scenes of the Passion of Christ.

C

CANA CONFERENCE

A Catholic family movement founded in St. Louis, Mo., in response to expressed needs of Catholic couples. Having heard of *retreats for married couples conducted in various cities by John P. Delaney, SJ (1894–1956), a St. Louis group requested a similar retreat, which was conducted by Edward Dowling, SJ (1898–1960), on Oct. 15, 1944, in honor of Our Lady of Cana and called by him a Cana Conference. Three characteristics distinguished this Cana Conference from the retreats previously given. First, in Father Dowling's words, it was intended to consider "not so much spiritual things, as things spiritually"; that is, it was an attempt to apply religious principles to integrate the mundane aspects of marital life; second, the conference material was directed to the 20th-century American mentality; third, the conferences, unlike those of a retreat, were held in a hall in an atmosphere of informality and relaxation.

The Cana Conference exceeded the original expectations of the couples. In addition to personal benefits, it instilled a sense of community, a family spirit that led to mutual aid and to participation in the social apostolate on a wider scale. Thus, the conferences for married couples assisted the start of a movement that resulted in the appointment of family life directors in most dioceses and in the enlistment of thousands of priests and lay persons in the conduct and extension of the movement. The Cana movement was carried by missionaries to foreign lands. The first institute for Cana Conference directors was held at The Catholic University of America, Washington, D.C., in 1947; this was followed in later years by study weeks and workshops.

In addition to conferences for married couples, the movement reaches out to many before and after marriage. It has inspired courses in high schools and given rise to a Triune Conference for parents and teenagers. Pre-Cana Conferences for engaged couples have gained widespread acceptance. Discussion clubs, variously known as Cana Clubs or Mr. and Mrs. Clubs, enable those who have attended Cana Conferences to continue their common study-prayer activities more frequently; these clubs meet in homes of participants with a chaplain when the latter is available. In recent years, similar clubs have been formed for the widowed, and are called variously Post-Cana Clubs or Naim Conferences (after the Biblical widow). These groups of widowed persons also hold retreats, days of recollection, and educational and recreational events, frequently on an interclub basis. A deep sense of community and mutual support has resulted. The most recent development has been the Bethany Conference for single people; conferences for separated persons are under consideration in several dioceses. Also, the Cana movement, which sprang from the couples' retreat movement, has become one of the most active promoters of retreats for families.

Bibliography: W. R. Clark, *One in Mind, One in Heart, One in Affections* (pa. Providence, R.I. 1950). A. H. Clemens, *The Cana Movement in the U.S.* (Washington 1953). Cana Conference, *The Cana Conference Proceedings,* v.1–2 (Chicago 1949–50). W. J. Imbiorski, ed., *The Basic Cana Manual: Cana Conference of Chicago* (Chicago 1963).

[A. H. CLEMENS]

CANA OF GALILEE, the home town of Nathaniel (Jn 21.2), where Jesus changed water into wine at a wedding feast (Jn 2.1–11), and where later a Jewish royal official came to Jesus and asked Him to cure his son at Capharnaum (Jn 4.46). This town is certainly distinct from the Cana (modern Qanah) in the tribe of Aser (Jos 19.28), near Sidon. Tradition since 1600 locates it at modern Kefr Kenna on the road from Nazareth to Tiberias. Older tradition locates it, with greater probability, at modern Khirbet Qanah, 10 miles north of Nazareth.

Bibliography: Abel GéogrPal 2:412–413. C. Kopp, *The Holy Places of the Gospels* (New York 1963) 143–154. R. Schnackenburg, *Das erste Wunder Jesu* (Freiburg 1951).

[J. E. WRIGLEY]

CANAAN AND CANAANITES

The term "Canaanite" is historically, geographically, and culturally synonymous with "Phoenician." For convenience, Canaanite is used to designate the Northwest Semitic people and culture of Palestine and Western Syria before 1200 B.C., while Phoenician refers to the same people and culture after that date.

The origin of the term Canaanite, which first appears in 15th- and 14th-century texts from Egypt, Alalakh, Nuzi, and Ugarit, is not certain. Derivation from a lost Semitic word *kn',* "murex," with later meanings of merchant or purple merchant is possible. The etymology of

Phoenician is uncertain also, but since the murex shellfish, which yielded purple dye, was abundant along the Syrian coast, so that Phoenicia became the center of the manufacture of purple dye, the Greek name "Phoenicia" probably refers to this industry (φοῖνιξ, purple or crimson).

Canaanite territory included most of Palestine west of the Jordan and the Lebanon-Syrian coast as far north as Ugarit near modern Latakia. Just how far inland this latter region extended cannot be determined with precision.

History. The Canaanites may have settled in these areas as early as the 4th millennium. This inference is based on the Canaanite names of towns founded before 3000 B.C., such as Jericho, Beth Yerakh, and Megiddo. The coastal cities such as *Accho (Acre), *Tyre, *Sidon, and *Ugarit have names that are Semitic and in some instances specifically Canaanite. Since there is no clear evidence to show that these names supplanted earlier non-Semitic names, it becomes difficult to accept the theory of S. Moscati [*I Predecessori d'Israele* (Rome 1956) 40–41] that the Canaanites migrated into these parts around 2000 B.C.

Early Period. In the 3d millennium Canaan was in close commercial and political contact with Egypt. In fact, Egypt claimed political suzerainty over Canaan, and *c.* 2600–2200 B.C. *Byblos was virtually an Egyptian colony. After two centuries of decline and anarchy in Egypt, matched by similar developments in Canaan, there arose the powerful Twelfth Dynasty in Egypt (1991–1786 B.C.), which once again brought Canaan into the Egyptian orbit. The Egyptian execration texts from 1950–1850 B.C. reveal that a new wave of Semitic nomads had moved into Palestine bearing Amorrite names. Though Egypt claimed political control over Palestine, revolts were not infrequent. The second half of the 18th century saw the rise of the Hyksos who ruled Canaan and the Delta of Egypt *c.* 1710–1580 B.C. Further study in the history of the *Hyksos shows that most of the known Hyksos names are certainly or probably Canaanite or Amorrite, not Hurrian nor Hittite, as formerly believed. Concurrent with the Hyksos movement was a great migration of Hurrian and Indo-Iranian tribes from the northeast into Syria and Palestine, so that by the 15th century many cities in Palestine, such as Megiddo, Ascalon, and Jerusalem, were ruled by princes with non-Semitic names (*see* HURRIANS). It follows that the Canaanites of the Late Bronze Age (*c.* 1550–1230 B.C.) were a much more mixed people than their ancestors of the Middle Bronze Age. The Late Bronze Age is characterized as a period of vigorous commercial activity and trade with the Aegean regions, interior Syria, and Egypt. As a result of wealth gathered by trade, Canaanite prosperity—that of *Ugarit is a good example—reached an unprecedented level.

Late Period. In the course of the 13th century the Canaanites lost most of their territory to the Israelites who conquered the hill country of Palestine, and to the *Philistines who, driven away from the Delta by Ramses III, settled along the coast from *Gaza to south of *Jaffa (Joppe). Several decades later, Aramaean tribesmen from the Syrian desert occupied the hinterland of Phoenicia from Hauran to the Eleutherus Valley. Phoenicia was thus reduced to the coast and the immediate hinterland from the Ladder of Tyre to just north of Arvad, a distance of about 120 miles. The Phoenicians, however, were later able to extend their southern border as far as Jaffa. Their cities included Tyre, Sidon, Sarepta, Byblos, *Arvad, and Amrit. In the early Iron Age, the most important were Byblos and Sidon, but later Tyre assumed the ascendancy (Ez 27). In the Bible (Dt 3.9; Is 23.2) and in Homer's Odyssey the Phoenicians are called Sidonians.

Phoenicia's commercial expansion began in the 11–10th century, when her traders penetrated to all parts of the Mediterranean coast, setting up colonies by 900 B.C. in Cyprus, Sicily, Sardinia, Africa, and Spain. In the late 8th and early 7th century Assyrian expansion put an end to the independence of Sidon, while at the same time the rise of Greek colonization weakened Phoenician commerce in the Mediterranean. In 572 B.C., after a siege of 13 years, the Chaldeans destroyed Tyre and with it all serious Phoenician maritime activity. The Greeks and the Punic colonies would fill the void created by the passing of the mainland powers. *See* CARTHAGE.

Culture. Phoenician art was essentially synthetic; it borrowed and combined motifs from Egypt and Mesopotamia, as is evident in the groups of Phoenician ivories found at *Mageddo (Megiddo), Enkomi in Cyprus, Nimrud, *Samaria, and Arslan Tash, as well as from the silver bowls discovered in Greece and Cyprus. The chief cultural contribution of the Phoenicians was the invention, sometime before 1500 B.C., of the linear *alphabet from which are derived Hebrew, Syriac, Arabic, Amharic, and numerous other Oriental scripts. Though there is still some dispute, 800 B.C. is the probable date when the Greeks borrowed the Phoenician alphabet and thus began its spread throughout the West.

Before the hundreds of inscribed clay tablets dating to the 15th and 14th century B.C. were discovered at Ugarit beginning in A.D. 1929, the principal sources of knowledge of the Canaanite language were the Hebrew Bible, since Biblical Hebrew is a Canaanite dialect, and the scores of Phoenician inscriptions, which, though generally brief and formulaic, sufficed to give a substantial idea of the nature of the language. The Azitawwadu Inscription from Karatepe in southern Turkey, discovered in 1946 and dating to the late 8th century B.C., contains 63 lines and is thus the longest and linguistically perhaps the most informative Phoenician inscription yet found.

See also AMORRITES.

Bibliography: E. A. SPEISER, "The Name *Phoinikes*," *Language* 12 (1936) 121–126. B. MAISLER, "Canaan and the Canaanites," BullAmSchOrRes 102 (1946) 7–12. J. GRAY, *The Legacy of Canaan: The Ras Shamra Texts and Their Relevance to the Old Testament* (VetTest Suppl 5; 2d ed. 1964). W. F. ALBRIGHT, "The Role of the Canaanites in the History of Civilization," *The Bible and the Ancient Near East*, ed. G. E. WRIGHT (New York 1961) 328–362. J. C. L. GIBSON, "Observations on Some Important Ethnic Terms in the Pentateuch," JNEastSt 20 (1961) 217–238.

[M. J. DAHOOD]

CANADA

A sovereign state of the British Commonwealth, comprising all the northern half of the North American Continent and adjacent islands, except Alaska, a state of the U.S. Its area (3,851,800 square miles, of which 291,571 square miles is fresh water) is greater than that of any other country except the U.S.S.R. Its southern boundary coincides with the northern boundary of the U.S. over a distance of 4,000 miles, while its northern, western, and eastern boundaries are formed, respectively, by the Canadian Arctic Islands, the Pacific Ocean, and the Atlantic Ocean. Canada is divided into 10 provinces, the Yukon Territory, and the Northwest Territories. Ontario is the largest and most populous of the principally English provinces, while the Province of Quebec, mostly French, is second in both population and industrial production. Ranging from 42° to 83° north latitude, the principal regions of Canada lie almost entirely within the Temperate Zone, with only the northernmost portions of the territories inside the Frigid Zone.

From 12,500,000 at the end of World War II, the population of Canada had increased to about 18,250,000 by 1961. Of these about 44 per cent were Catholic, 20.5 per cent were United Church, 14.7 per cent Church of England, 5.6 per cent Presbyterian, 3.7 per cent Baptist, 3 per cent Lutheran, 1.5 per cent Jews, and 7 per cent of other denominations. During the decade from 1950 to 1960 Canada received more than 1½ million immigrants. The population includes 11,000 Eskimos and 160,000 Indians, the latter living, for the most part, on reservations. Approximately 30 per cent of the total population are French-speaking and the greater part of these are settled in the Province of Quebec, forming more than 80 per cent of the population there.

Discovery and Colonization. About the 11th century Norsemen from Greenland under Leif Ericson explored the American shores, probably of present-day Canada. In 1497 John Cabot, sailing from Bristol, England, reached the coast of either Cape Breton Island or Newfoundland. Thereafter numbers of European fishermen were attracted to the banks of Newfoundland and to the coasts of the mainland. In 1534 Jacques Cartier of Saint-Malo, France, reached the Gaspé Peninsula and on July 24 planted a cross, taking possession of Canada in the name of King Francis I. The following year he explored the interior of the country, visiting both Stadaconé (Quebec) and Hochelaga (Montreal), and preaching to the Indians with the help of interpreters. With François Roberval, he planned a settlement but war interfered and for the next 60 years no colonization was effected, although some attention was given to the fisheries and fur trade.

French Rule. In 1603 Samuel de Champlain visited Canada briefly. Upon his return in 1604 the first settlement was made on Sainte-Croix Island, a site chosen by Pierre de Monts over Champlain's preference for the Saint Lawrence area. Half of the expedition died of scurvy during the first winter, and so when help arrived from France in June 1605 the colony moved to Port Royal, Acadia (Annapolis, Nova Scotia). There Father Nicolas Aubry devoted himself to the conversion of the Indians until he was replaced in 1610 by Jesse Fléché, who had been brought to the colony by Jean de Poutrincourt, successor of De Monts. When Fléché died in 1611 the Jesuits Pierre Biard and Ennemond Massé took up the missionary work, devoting themselves particularly to the Micmacs. Unfortunately, in 1613 an English vessel under Samuel Argall attacked Port Royal and also destroyed the colony the Jesuits had begun at Mount Desert Island on the New England coast, whereupon the Acadian missions were abandoned and the missionaries sent back to France.

Meanwhile, in 1608 Champlain had founded Quebec to which he brought the Franciscans (Récollets) and from which he made several explorations of the interior. Four friars, Denys Jamet, Joseph Le Caron, Jean Dolbeau, and Brother Pacifique Duplessis gave themselves to the education of the young and spared no effort in behalf of the Indians of Lower Canada. Accompanying Champlain to the Great Lakes, they brought the Gospel to the Hurons whose daily life they shared. In need of assistance, the friars issued a call to the Jesuits and in 1625 Fathers Charles Lallemant, Jean de Brébeuf, and Ennemond Massé arrived at Quebec. Brébeuf proceeded immediately to Huron country and 2 years later received support from the Company of One Hundred Associates (Company of New France), formed to settle the area. Meanwhile Quebec prospered; it had about 100 inhabitants when it was captured by Scottish-English forces under the Kirke brothers on July 19, 1629. However, after the Treaty of Saint-Germain-en-Laye (1632), which restored France's possessions in America, the French resettled Acadia and colonization of Quebec began again. The Capuchins sent to Acadia by Cardinal Richelieu at this time proved zealous missionaries until 1755, when the inhabitants of the colony were dispersed by English conquerors. However, 2,800 of them avoided exile and when London in 1764 authorized the return of former inhabitants to Acadia, a number of those who had taken refuge in Canada, Newfoundland, and the U.S. made their way back.

In 1632 when Richelieu failed to get either the Capuchins or the Franciscans for the colony at Quebec, he sought the help of the Jesuits. That same year Fathers Paul Lejeune, Anne de Nouë, Antoine Daniel, Ambroise Davost, and Brother Gilbert Burel arrived in Quebec and within a year had reopened the missions. In August 1634 the missionaries set themselves up at Trois-Rivières, founded by M. de Laviolette a month earlier, and established a college at Quebec in 1635, the first north of Spanish America. The missionaries worked among the Indian tribes from the shores of the Atlantic to the Illinois and the Mississippi. Their success in preaching the Gospel to the Hurons aroused the ire of the Iroquois, resulting in the death of the eight *North American martyrs, canonized by Pius XI on June 29, 1930. The Jesuits received help from Champlain, and at Quebec where the Duchess of Aiguillon founded the Hotel Dieu under the direction of the Augustinians from Dieppe, and the Ursulines established a convent, directed by *Marie of the Incarnation.

Main French Settlements. From 1632 to 1659 Quebec, Trois-Rivières, and Montreal formed the three important centers of the French colony. Montreal was settled under the aegis of the Society of Our Lady of Montreal, founded in Paris in 1640 by Jerome Royer de la Dauversière and the Sulpician, Jean Olier. It was not until May 17, 1642, however, that Paul Chomédy de Maisonneuve succeeded in establishing Montreal with a company of 66 persons. On that occasion a Mass was celebrated by Barthélemy Vimont, SJ. The founder of the Hotel Dieu at Montreal, Jeanne Mance, was also a member of the society. In 1653 Marguerite Bourgeois arrived and 5 years later founded the Sisters of the Congregation of Our Lady for the education of girls. In 1657 the Society of Ville-Marie sent the first four Sulpicians to Montreal. About this time the Church of New France received a leader in the person of François de Montmorency *Laval, who was consecrated bishop of Pétrée on Dec. 8, 1658, and reached Quebec in June 1659. He hastened to establish a seminary of foreign missions, affiliated with that of Paris (1663) and a secondary school at Quebec (1668) in which the students followed the curriculum of the Jesuit college there. By 1665 the settlement included 18 secular priests, 31 Jesuits, 10 Ursulines, 23 hospitallers, and 4 Sisters of the Congregation. In 1674 Laval succeeded in having Quebec established as a diocese responsible directly to the Holy See.

The colonies had a threefold struggle against the Indians, the English coastal colonies, and the self-interest of the commercial companies that controlled the settlements under royal grant. In 1663, however, the King appointed an administrator in addition to the governor and set up an independent council. The Sulpicians ministered to the new colony set up at Kingston (1672), and constructed a church and seminary at Montreal. After 40 years absence the Franciscans returned to the country in 1670 and set themselves up in Quebec, Montreal, Detroit, the Gaspé, Cape Breton, and Newfoundland. The Iroquois agreed to receive Jesuits missionaries; it was through the latter that Kateri *Tekakwitha was converted to Christianity. Claude *Allouez, SJ, the first missionary to the Ottawas, founded at the extreme western end of Lake Superior the Mission of the Holy Ghost, from which Father Jacques *Marquette and Louis Jolliet left in 1673 for their exploration of the Mississippi.

During a visit to France in 1674, Laval resigned his see but returned to Canada where he died in 1708. His successor, Jean Baptiste de la Croix· Chevrières de *Saint-Vallier, was consecrated in Paris on Jan. 25, 1688, and arrived in Quebec August 15. His administration was disturbed by trouble with the civil authorities, the clergy, and the religious orders. In 1700 during a journey to France, he was captured and imprisoned by the English and did not return to Canada until 1713. Before his death in 1727, he founded the general hospital at Quebec and convoked the diocesan synods, the first of which met in 1690. A later occupant of the see, Henri Marie Dubreuil de Pontbriand, who arrived in Quebec in 1741, restored and enlarged the cathedral, reorganized the clergy retreats, twice traveled throughout his immense diocese, and wrote a considerable number of circulars and pastoral letters. He took a personal interest in the missions of the Louisiana Territory and Detroit. In 1755 he sanctioned the Institute of Mme. d'*Youville, the Sisters of Charity of the General Hospital of Montreal (*Grey Nuns). Later, when Quebec was bombarded during the Seven Years' War and the cathedral was destroyed, he retired to Montreal and died on June 8, 1760.

French Losses of Territory. Although France, by the Treaty of Utrecht in 1713, ceded to England all of Hudson's Bay, Newfoundland, and Acadia, French explora-

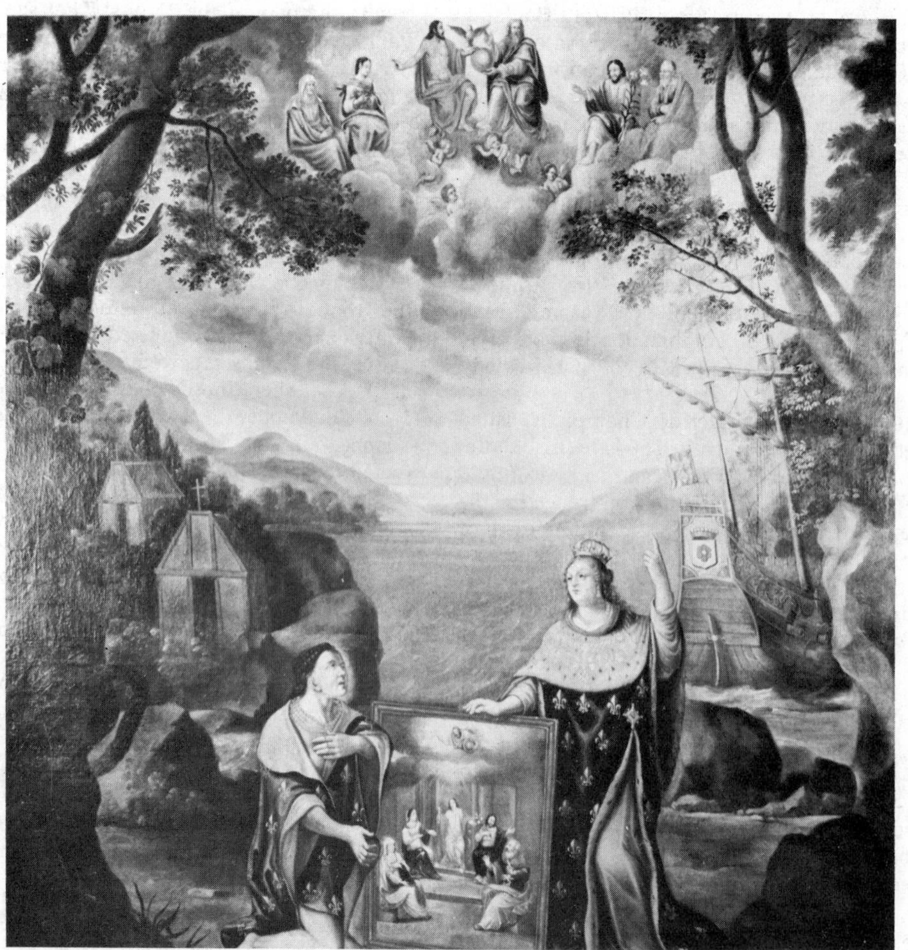

Fig. 2. "France Bringing Faith to the Indians of the New World," painting, c. 1671, by the Franciscan Frère Luc, in the convent of the Ursulines at Quebec.

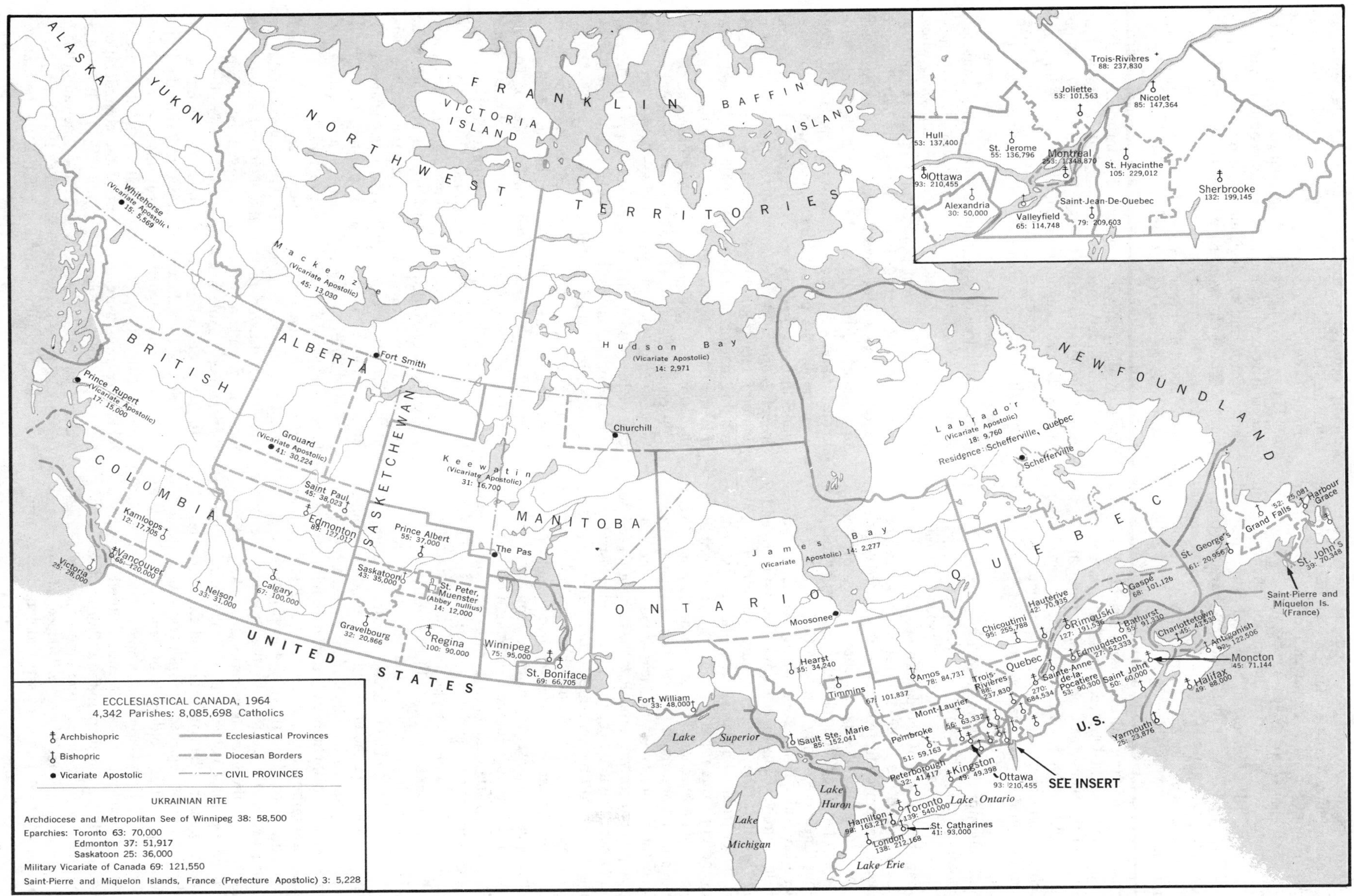

Fig. 1. Ecclesiastical jurisdictions in Canada, 1964.

tion attempted to extend the boundaries westward from the coast. Pierre Gaultier de *La Vérendrye reached Lake Winnipeg in 1733. However, the English colonists took advantage of the Seven Years' War, 1756–63, to make themselves master of the city of Quebec, which fell on Sept. 18, 1759, and of Montreal, which held out until Sept. 8, 1760. By the Treaty of Paris, Feb. 17, 1763, England acquired Canada, Acadia, and the eastern part of Louisiana, leaving France only the islands of Saint-Pierre and Miquelon.

By this time the Catholic population of Canada had increased to 65,000, all of French origin, distributed among the cities of Quebec, Trois-Rivières, and Montreal, and the well-organized parishes along the banks of the Saint Lawrence. Each city had its own institutions of charity and elementary schools conducted by nuns, while the rural schools were entrusted to the Sisters of the Congregation of Our Lady, or to lay teachers under the direction of the clergy. In addition, the Jesuits had their college at Quebec and the Sulpicians their apostolic works at Montreal. Missionaries pursued their ministry among the Indians of the eastern and central portions of Canada and the Louisiana Territory. At the fall of Canada the Church there lacked a bishop; its 196 priests, 88 parishes, and 6 religious communities of women passed to the direct control of the English, whose laws at that time were openly hostile to Catholics.

English Rule. After 1763 when Canada became a British colony, Canadians enjoyed religious freedom only "insofar as the laws of England" permitted it. Thus all control from Rome was illegal and correspondence with the pope was forbidden. A shortage of priests resulted when a number chose to return to France. After the death of Pontbriand in 1760, the chapter had reaffirmed the authority of the vicars-general and a third was appointed for the Trois-Rivières area. In 1764 Joseph Olivier Briand, vicar-general and administrator of Quebec, went to London armed with a letter from Gov. James Murray. After 18 months he succeeded in getting a promise that the English government would not actively oppose his consecration. The ceremony took place on March 16, 1766, with the intervention of the nuncio at Paris. Later Briand obtained permission from London for a coadjutor with the right of succession and in 1772 he consecrated Louis Philippe Mariaucheau d'*Esglis, the first Canadian to become a bishop. Although at first the bishop and his coadjutor were regarded simply as "overseers of the Roman Church," the British eventually gave in and in 1811 the crown lawyers submitted that it would be difficult to deny the bishop the use of his title. Later the bishops of Quebec were accorded the honorary title of archbishop until, in 1844, Abp. Joseph Signay became the first to bear the title of metropolitan.

The Quebec Act. Just before the American Revolution, in which the Canadians refused to take part, England passed the Quebec Act (1774), which returned to the Canadians their civil and religious liberties. A civil government replaced the military and an oath of loyalty replaced the old oath of renunciation of the Catholic faith. Thus Catholics became eligible for public office and freedom of religion was assured, the single restrictive clause "obedient to the authority of the King" being added to calm the fanatics and to reserve the right to install a Protestant bishop at Quebec. However, the Canadians were still not fully satisfied with the act, principally because of the unpopularity of the legislative council. In 1791, therefore, two new constitutional governments were created: one for Lower Canada and one for Upper Canada, each with its own governor aided by a legislative council and an executive council chosen by the governor, and by a legislative assembly elected by the people. These changes proved beneficial to the Church as did also the French Revolution, for between 1791 and 1802, about 45 French priests in exile in England were permitted to emigrate to Canada.

In 1818 Bp. Joseph Octave *Plessis, desiring to divide his huge diocese, which stretched from the Atlantic to the Pacific, regrouped his 500,000 Catholics into four units: the vicariate apostolic of Halifax (1817); Montreal in Lower Canada; Upper Canada, where the Catholics were becoming more numerous; and the Red River area. When Plessis set out for London and Rome in 1819 to obtain approval for his plan, he did not know that Rome had already designated Quebec an archdiocese (Jan. 12, 1819), and had established a vicariate apostolic for Upper Canada and New Brunswick, whose titulary was the vicar-general of Quebec. Opposition from Lord Bathurst, Colonial Secretary, led Plessis to renounce his plan for several dioceses and to agree not to assume the title of archbishop, which would have made him senior to the Protestant bishop. He did, however, obtain the government's permission for two regional bishops: Jean Jacques Lartigue for Montreal and Joseph Norbert *Provencher for the Red River. But in point of fact, four bishops had been named in 1819 and this state of affairs was eventually sanctioned. After that the Church grew rapidly, due in no small part to the efforts of Bp. Ignace *Bourget of Montreal who enlisted the help of several religious communities in France, established them locally, worked for the education of his people, and took an active part in the missionary movement both in Canada and among the Canadians who had emigrated to the U.S.

In 1826 Alexander MacDonell became bishop of Kingston and Angus MacEachern bishop of Charlottetown in 1829. There followed the Dioceses of Toronto (1841) and Bytown (1847), the Ottawa of today. After that the sees multiplied rapidly in Upper Canada, which, having welcomed a group of Scottish Catholics in 1807, continued to attract various non-English immigrants. The Church expanded also into the western part of the country. In 1845 the Oblates of Mary Immaculate went to the Red River country and under the leadership of Bp. Alexandre *Taché (later archbishop of St. Boniface), the Church made rapid progress among the native tribes even in the northernmost regions.

Confederation. Meanwhile, the movement for a union of all the provinces from the Atlantic to the Pacific slowly gained favor. In 1864 the decision for federation was finally made and London approved the plan by the British North America Act. The confederation came into being on July 1, 1867, under the name of The Dominion of Canada, comprising at that time the Provinces of Ontario, Quebec, New Brunswick, and Nova Scotia, with Ottawa as the capital city. Subsequently other provinces were made part of the confederation: Manitoba (1870), British Columbia (1871), Prince Edward Island (1873), Alberta and Saskatchewan (1905), the Yukon and Northwest Territories (1912), and Newfoundland, including Labrador (1949). By the Statutes

Fig. 3. Canada: (a) Quebec in 18th century, engraving by Thomas Johnston. (b) Modern Montreal.

of Westminster (1931) Canada received full and complete independence, with no tie to Britain other than her voluntary allegiance to the Crown.

Under the British North America Act, Canada is a two-culture country, and French and English are both official languages in the Canadian Parliament. The country is governed by a governor-general, representing the Crown and appointed by it, by a parliament composed of a House of Commons (legislative assembly) elected by the people, and an upper house (the Senate) whose members are appointed for life by the governor with the advice and consent of his cabinet. In each of the 10 provinces there is a local government modeled on the national plan but with unicameral legislative bodies, except in the case of Quebec, which has retained the upper house. The provinces are completely autonomous in such things as education, civil law, property rights, exploitation of natural resources, and other matters of local interest. The federal government has jurisdiction in things of national concern, e.g., postal service, customs, shipping, navigable rivers, criminal law, and military service.

20th Century. In international affairs Canada is an active member of the United Nations, where she has several times rendered service as a mediator. Geography and history have worked to establish a firm bond between Canada and the U.S.; tradition and a common heritage have caused them to adopt standards of value similar in many respects. The great ideological conflicts of the 20th century forced them to become partners in the defense of North America. The Saint Lawrence Seaway and its hydroelectric installations, completed in 1959, exemplify the accomplishments resulting from their close collaboration. Differences between the two countries have always been resolved by peaceful means.

By the first half of the 20th century, Canada had attained full industrial and national maturity. In 1959 Georges Vanier became governor-general, the second Canadian and the first Catholic to hold this office. The period after 1900 was also one in which the Canadian Church came of age. In 1908 it was removed from the jurisdiction of the Congregation for the Propagation of the Faith, signifying that it was no longer regarded by the Holy See as a missionary territory. This recognition of the adulthood of the Canadian Church had been foreshadowed in 1899 by the establishment of an apostolic delegation and the naming of Canada's first cardinal in the person of Abp. Elzéar *Taschereau of Quebec.

Church-State Relations. There is no State religion in Canada; all beliefs enjoy complete freedom. Relations between the civil authority and the Catholic Church are both proper and cordial. In several matters the State collaborates closely with the Church. On the other hand, Catholics have had to contend with injustices, especially in the realm of education; the laws of several provinces discriminated against Catholic schools and failed to provide them an equal share of financial support. However, by mid-20th century this situation was being gradually rectified.

Present Situation. By 1963 Catholics were prominent in all walks of life in the country: in the magistracy, including the Supreme Court of Canada, in business, in the various professions, in education, in the state universities, and in politics. Several Canadian Catholics have become prime ministers, and one has become the governor-general.

Fig. 4. Shrine church of Sainte Anne de Beaupré, Quebec.

The Church's vitality appears in its numerous clergy, its prosperous religious communities, its agencies for religious and social work, and its numerous colleges and universities. It can count two cardinals, one of the French tongue, the other English, and a score of Canada's sons are bishops in missionary regions. Canadian missionaries can be found in all areas of missionary endeavor and they have initiated a very important effort for the aid of the countries of Latin America.

The Latin Church has 14 metropolitan sees: *Edmonton, *Halifax, *Kingston, *Moncton, *Montreal, *Ottawa, *Quebec, *Regina, *Rimouski, *St. Boniface, *St. John's, Newfoundland, *Sherbrooke, *Toronto, and *Vancouver; and 1 archdiocese, *Winnipeg, which has no suffragans and is immediately subject to the Holy See. The Eastern Church has four exarchates, Manitoba, Edmonton, Saskatoon, and Toronto, suffragans of the Ukrainian-rite Archeparchy of *Winnipeg. The archbishop of Quebec, the primate of Canada, is at the head of the military vicariate.

Bibliography: A. Shortt and A. G. Doughty, eds., *Canada and Its Provinces,* 23 v. (Toronto 1914–17). J. Bruchési, *Histoire du Canada pour tous,* 2 v. (Montreal, v.1, 5th ed.; v.2, 4th ed., 1946). W. P. Bull, *From Macdonnell to McGuigan: The History of the Growth of the Roman Catholic Church in Upper Canada* (Toronto 1939). Canada Bureau of Statistics, *Canada Year Book 1960* (Ottawa 1906–). Canadian Catholic Historical Association, *Report* (Ottawa 1933–). P. F. X. de Charlevoix, *History and General Description of New France,* tr. J. G. Shea, 6 v. (New York 1866–72). Dominique de Saint-Denis, *L'Église catholique au Canada* (6th ed. Montreal 1956), Fr. and Eng. É. M. Faillon, *Histoire de la colonie française en Canada,* 3 v. (Montreal 1865–66). A. H. Gosselin, *L'Église du Canada après la conquête,* 2 v. (Quebec 1916–17). L. M. Le-Jeune, *Dictionnaire général . . . du Canada,* 2 v. (Ottawa 1931). *The Makers of Canada Series,* 12 v. (New York 1926). A. G. Morice, *History of the Catholic Church in Western Canada: From Lake Superior to the Pacific, 1659–1895,* 2 v. (Toronto

1910). G. L. NUTE, ed. and tr., *Documents Relating to Northwest Missions 1815–1827* (St. Paul 1942). G. SAGARD-THÉODAT, *Histoire du Canada et voyages que les Frères mineurs recollects y ont faicts pour la conversion des infidèles depuis l'an 1615,* 4 v. (Paris 1866). A. TESSIER, *Histoire du Canada,* 2 v. (3d ed. Quebec 1959) v.1 *Neuve France, 1524–1763.* H. TÊTU and C. O. GAGNON, eds., *Mandemants, lettres pastorales et circulaires des èvêques de Québec,* 2 v. (NS, Quebec 1889–90). **Illustration credits:** Fig. 2. Quebec Film Bureau. Driscoll. Fig. 3*a.* New York Public Library, Phelphs Stokes Collection. Fig. 3*b.* Armour Landry, Montreal. Fig. 4. Archives of Quebec.

[G. CARRIÈRE]

CANADA, CATHOLIC ELEMENTARY AND SECONDARY EDUCATION IN

Catholic elementary and secondary education in Canada follows very much the same pattern as the public school system, although the Province of Quebec has a few characteristic differences that make it somewhat atypical (see the accompanying chart). On the elementary level there are ungraded rural and graded urban schools; on the secondary level, both the academic and vocational type of school, which together operate on either a 8–4, 6–3–3, or 6–3–4 plan leading from the first grade to the university; i.e., 8 or 6 years of elementary education followed by 4 or 3 years on the secondary level and 3 or 4 years of higher education in a classical college. In Quebec, four differences in the concept of education stand out: the belief that (1) the school should cooperate in preserving the French language and those customs relating to their national origin, (2) religion should form an integral part of education, (3) boys and girls should be educated separately, and (4) those who terminate the 8 years of elementary schooling are capable of choosing an occupation or profession.

Organization. Canada has, in effect, 11 school systems, since each of the 10 provinces is autonomous in educational affairs and the national government also has an interest in schools for federal wards (Indians and Eskimos in the north) and for children of military personnel at some bases. Within these systems, the status of Catholic schools varies greatly, some having full support of public monies and others being entirely privately financed. Administratively, Catholic schools with public financing are generally established under public statutes, while those that are private are under self-appointed directorates of various kinds.

Several main patterns are to be found. The predominantly French-speaking and Catholic Province of Quebec has tax-supported denominational schools for Catholics and Protestants. The Atlantic island-province of Newfoundland also has a publicly supported denominational system, but quite different from Quebec's. Ontario, Saskatchewan, and Alberta have legislation that allows Catholic or Protestant minorities to withdraw from the majority public system and set up their own "separate" tax-supported schools.

The three provinces on the Atlantic seaboard—New Brunswick, Nova Scotia, and Prince Edward Island—have, on the other hand, legal provisions only for public schools. However, many of these, by "gentlemen's agreements," are in fact acceptable to Catholics in communities that are mainly Catholic. British Columbia and Manitoba also provide only for public systems. But unlike the Atlantic provinces, British Columbia has no Catholic schools except private ones supported by parents who also must pay taxes to the public schools. In Manitoba, some of the public schools in French-speaking areas are in fact Catholic. In other areas there are private or parochial Catholic schools, whose supporters are also subject to public school taxes.

In the Yukon and Northwest Territories, in systems evolved through cooperation of federal and territorial authorities with Church groups, Catholic elementary schools for the sparse Indian, Eskimo, and white populations have full government and local tax support.

Administration. Each province has a governmental department of education with jurisdiction and responsibility in all major fields of education, such as curriculum development, teacher training and certification, examination of students, and administration of public funds. The general pattern is for Catholics to share in these fields where that is legally possible, or at least to measure up to the public standards in the case of private Catholic schools. In Quebec, for example, there are Catholic teacher-training institutions. In the other provinces, Catholics, whether they are going to teach in public or Catholic schools, follow the general courses in provincial universities or teachers' colleges. At these, special instruction for Catholics in such matters as the teaching of religion is usually extra, or even extracurricular.

Because of the complexity of these systems, overall national statistics are not available for Catholic schools or for Catholics in schools of all types. In Quebec, where both religious and language differences are taken into account, by far the greater number of elementary schools—more than 7,500, with more than 780,000 pupils—are Catholic, a minority of them English-speaking. Protestant schools in Quebec, by comparison, are mainly English-speaking, and total some 380 with 115,000 students.

Operating under a very different system, all schools in Newfoundland are considered public schools, although administered by denominational boards. In addition to Catholic schools, full recognition and public funds are accorded to Church of England, United Church, Salvation Army, and Pentecostal Assembly schools. There are also amalgamated interdenominational schools in some areas. Catholic schools enroll the largest number—about 45,000 out of 120,000 at the elementary level.

Ontario's Catholic "separate" schools, with public tax support, total about 1,425 with nearly 330,000 pupils. In locations where there are no such schools, Catholic pupils are among the 900,000 listed as attending the 5,133 public schools. By present law, Catholic separate schools enroll only the eight elementary and two lower secondary grades. For the three upper secondary grades, 100 private Catholic schools have some 30,000 students. Catholic secondary students well in excess of this number, however, are enrolled in public collegiates and high schools.

The prairie provinces of Saskatchewan and Alberta have legislation for "separate" Catholic schools similar to Ontario's, but these are largely confined to the major urban centers. Hence Alberta's 40,000 students in Catholic schools and Saskatchewan's 20,000 represent only a portion of the total of Catholic students. In the other provinces where there are no Catholic schools except for a few private ones, well under half of all Catholic students are in Catholic schools as such.

The fact that some provinces have systems that are more favorable to Catholics than others means that the

Elementary — Secondary — Post-Secondary — Higher

1964

Trade Schools

Music and Art Schools
Agriculture Colleges
Technical Institutes

Composite Schools

Technical Schools

Commercial Schools

Academic Schools

Elementary School

Junior High School

Senior High School

Junior Colleges

Teacher Training

Nurses Training

Arts and Science
Agriculture
Architecture
Commerce
Dentistry
Education
Physical Education
Engineering
Applied Science
Forestry
Home Economics
Law
Library Science
Medicine
Nursing
Optometry
Pharmacy
Social Work
Theology
Veterinary Science
Etc.

Articulation of the English-Language School System, All Provinces.

Elementary — Secondary — Post-Secondary — Higher

Forestry

Business Schools

General Course

Commercial Course

Family Institutes

Hospital Schools

Institutes of Technology

Normal Schools (B & C)

Normal Schools (A)

Schools of Fine Arts

Commerce

Academic Course

Elementary School

Science Mathematics

Science

Science-Letters

Classical Colleges

Agriculture

Trades-Apprenticeship

Home Economics

Hospital Science
Sciences
Military College
Commerce, Accountancy
Agriculture, Fisheries
Pedagogy and Guidance
Optometry
Veterinary Medicine
Domestic Science
Forestry, etc.
Letters
Arts
Law
Medicine
Music
Philosophy
Social Sciences
Theology
Psychotherapy
Hospital Science
Etc.

Articulation of the French-Language School System in Quebec

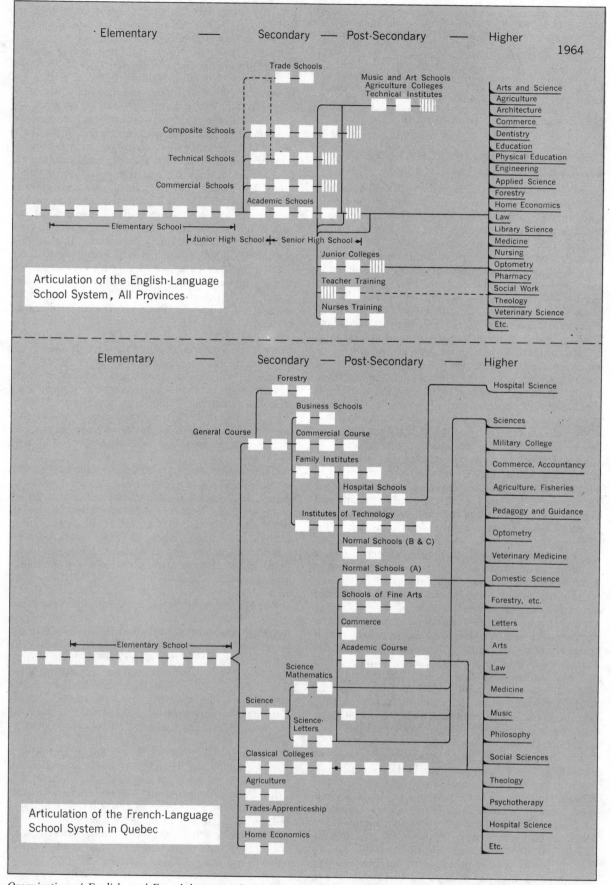

Organization of English- and French-language elementary and secondary school systems in Canada.

overall situation for Catholic education in Canada is very dynamic. In Manitoba, for example, there is a long history of public striving on the part of Catholics to win for their schools public support similar to that enjoyed in neighboring provinces. Within other systems, there is evolution to meet present-day needs and ideas, so that Canada can be called a laboratory of experiments in Church-State relations in the field of education.

Curriculum. In the 17th and 18th centuries, education at the elementary level in parish, charity, and private venture schools consisted of reading, writing, and numbers, which were considered to be adequate to satisfy the needs of the majority. On the secondary level, education was either college preparatory in Latin grammar schools or terminal in academies and limited to a select few. When in the 19th century education became compulsory between the ages of 6 and 14, Catholic schools largely followed the same courses of studies offered in the public schools with religion as an integral part of the program. In addition to academic or classical education on the secondary level, opportunities were provided for vocational education in technical schools, arts and trade schools, and other specialized institutions. A typically Catholic feature of secondary education is the classical college modeled on the early Jesuit college established in Quebec in 1635 or the Sulpician college founded in Montreal in 1767. These colleges comprise 8 years of study after grade 7 and lead to a bachelor's degree granted by either Laval University in Quebec or the University of Montreal. In fact, they constitute the universities' Faculty of Arts. Their curriculum is based on religion, philosophy, the Greco-Latin humanities, and science. To receive their degree, students take the baccalaureate examination set by the university with which the college is affiliated. In 1965 there were 32 classical colleges for men and 9 for women affiliated with Laval University and 27 colleges for men and 6 for women affiliated with the University of Montreal.

Bibliography: UNESCO WorldSurvEd 1:140–152, bibliog. 147–148; 2:200–217, bibliog. 212–213; 3:317–337, bibliog. 328–329. *Bilan du Monde* (1964) 2:202. J. G. ALTHOUS, *Structure and Aims of Canadian Education* (Toronto 1950). J. K. KATZ, *Canadian Education Today: A Symposium* (Toronto 1956) 243. D. O'BRIEN, "Education in Canada: The Varying Position of Catholic Schools," *Tablet* 218 (June 1964) 632–634. **Illustration credit:** Information Division, Department of External Affairs, Ottawa.

[B. M. DALY]

CANADA, CATHOLIC HIGHER EDUCATION IN

Higher education in Canada falls into three groups: church-related institutions—Roman Catholic, Anglican, and Baptist; government supported (provincial); and independent, although at one time denominational.

Historical Background. The history of Catholic higher education in Canada has its roots in the Collèges des Jésuites, founded in Quebec in 1635, and the Séminaire de Québec, founded in 1663, from which developed *Laval University (1852), which in turn gave rise to the University of *Montreal (1876).

In time, classical French-speaking colleges, affiliated with the universities, appeared in areas of French concentration. English-speaking non-Catholic colleges began to appear shortly after the American Revolution when loyalists from the American colonies, who had poured into Canada, sought to provide education for their children. They established the so-called "King's Colleges," the first of which, founded at Windsor, Nova Scotia, in 1789, and later transferred to Halifax, is now associated with Dalhousie University.

In 1961–62 nineteen Catholic colleges and universities in Canada held charters empowering them to grant degrees. Their enrollment was slightly under 25,000, with another 10,000 students, mainly in Quebec, attending affiliated colleges, making a total of 35,000 students, or approximately 30 per cent of the total registration in all Canadian colleges and universities.

As these figures indicate, Catholic colleges and universities play a major role in higher education in Canada. The significance of this role, however, varies greatly from one province to another, with little resemblance between the four regions: Atlantic Provinces, Quebec, Ontario, and Western Canada.

Atlantic Provinces. There are nine Catholic institutions in the Atlantic Provinces, some of them of long standing, but, five of these have an enrollment between 200 and 300 and, consequently, generally limit their offerings to a liberal arts program. The other four provide additional professional courses: St. Dunstan's University, Charlottetown (est. 1855), under diocesan control; Mount St. Vincent, Halifax (est. 1925), conducted by the Sisters of Charity; St. Mary's University, Halifax (est. 1841), directed by the Jesuits; and *St. Francis Xavier University, Antigonish (est. 1853), also diocesan and the largest of these institutions with a worldwide reputation for its leadership in the cooperative and adult education movement in Nova Scotia.

Quebec. *Laval University did not receive a royal charter until 1852 but is acknowledged to be the oldest Catholic university in Canada since it derives from the Seminary of Quebec, which was established in 1663. Originally the University buildings were closely associated with those of the Seminary, but in 1952 the University began to transfer professional faculties to a campus on the outskirts of Quebec. Although Laval receives grants from the province, its control is diocesan, a description that however does not precisely apply to the same extent to the University of *Montreal, independently established with a provincial charter in 1920 after 40 years of affiliation with Laval. Although the University of Montreal maintains a strongly religious character, it comes closer to filling the role of a provincial university than any other institution in Quebec. The University of *Sherbrooke has a similar charter granted in 1954. The two Jesuit colleges in Montreal, Loyola, which is English-speaking, and Jean-de-Brébeuf, have enrollments of 1,100 and 700 respectively. They grant arts degrees through the University of Montreal but had applications for independent charters pending in 1961.

Ontario. The University of *Ottawa, Canada's first bilingual university, has been conducted by the Oblate Fathers since its beginnings in 1848. Its structure combines many of the features of both the French and English pattern, and since the end of World War II, it has rapidly expanded the variety of its offerings. St. Michael's College (est. 1852), a federated arts college within the University of Toronto, is the prototype of an educational compromise, which has been much discussed in other parts of Canada. In the federation, a Catholic arts college retains a certain measure of independence but offers its degrees through the provincial

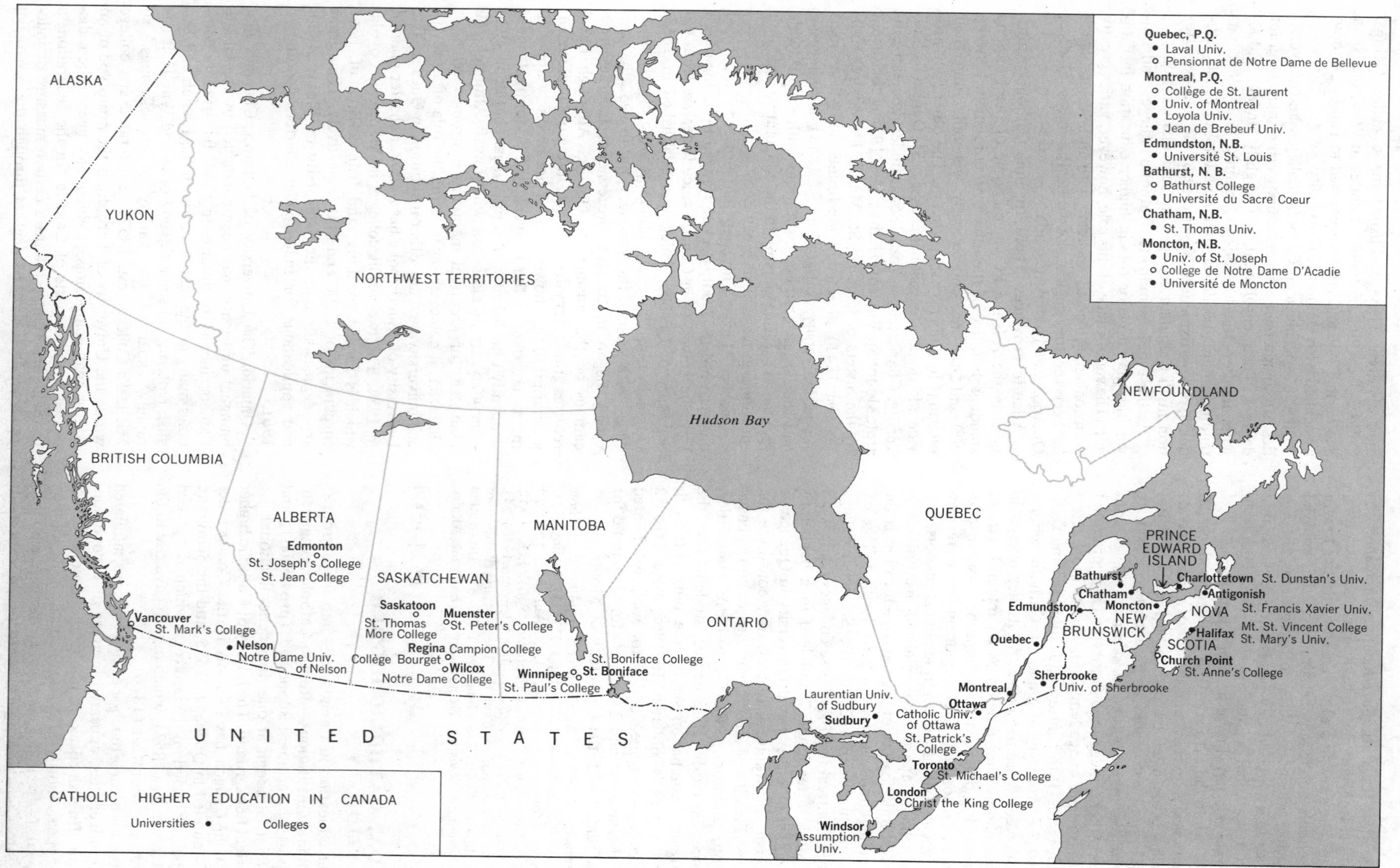

Quebec, P.Q.
● Laval Univ.
○ Pensionnat de Notre Dame de Bellevue
Montreal, P.Q.
○ Collège de St. Laurent
● Univ. of Montreal
● Loyola Univ.
● Jean de Brebeuf Univ.
Edmundston, N.B.
● Université St. Louis
Bathurst, N. B.
○ Bathurst College
● Université du Sacre Coeur
Chatham, N.B.
● St. Thomas Univ.
Moncton, N.B.
● Univ. of St. Joseph
○ Collège de Notre Dame D'Acadie
● Université de Moncton
ALASKA
YUKON
NORTHWEST TERRITORIES
BRITISH COLUMBIA
ALBERTA
SASKATCHEWAN
MANITOBA
ONTARIO
QUEBEC
NEWFOUNDLAND
Hudson Bay
PRINCE EDWARD ISLAND
NEW BRUNSWICK
NOVA SCOTIA
Edmonton
St. Joseph's College
St. Jean College
Vancouver
St. Mark's College
Nelson
Notre Dame Univ. of Nelson
Saskatoon
St. Thomas More College
Muenster
St. Peter's College
Regina
Campion College
Collège Bourget
Wilcox
Notre Dame College
Winnipeg
St. Boniface
St. Boniface College
St. Paul's College
Laurentian Univ. of Sudbury
Sudbury
Catholic Univ. of Ottawa
Ottawa
St. Patrick's College
Toronto
St. Michael's College
London
Christ the King College
Windsor
Assumption Univ.
Montreal
Quebec
Sherbrooke
Univ. of Sherbrooke
Edmundston
Bathurst
Chatham
Moncton
Charlottetown
St. Dunstan's Univ.
Antigonish
St. Francis Xavier Univ.
Halifax
Mt. St. Vincent College
St. Mary's Univ.
Church Point
St. Anne's College
UNITED STATES
CATHOLIC HIGHER EDUCATION IN CANADA
Universities ● Colleges ○

university. Assumption University in Windsor, conducted by the Basilian Fathers, attained independent university status in 1953, but placed its degree granting powers, except in theology, in abeyance in 1963, to federate with the new nondenominational University of Windsor. It began as Assumption College, founded in 1857 and was subsequently long affiliated with the University of Western Ontario. Its constitution allows cooperation with secular organizations and with other religious bodies, and there was consequently much interest in the success of its unique affiliations with Essex College (secular) and Canterbury College (Anglican), arrangements on the part of a Catholic university that were evidently without parallel in any other country. A similar experiment has also been initiated at the Laurentian University of Sudbury, established in 1960 as a development of a college conducted by the French Jesuits since 1913, with Huntington University (United Church) in formal federation.

Western Canada. The development of higher education in Western Canada has been marked by the maintenance of a degree granting monopoly for a single institution in each province with no other charters granted by legislatures. Consequently there are no independent Catholic colleges or universities in Western Canada, but there is an interesting variety of affiliation with each provincial institution depending on local circumstances: St. Paul's College (Jesuit) offers an affiliated arts course on the campus of the University of Manitoba; St. Thomas More College (Basilian) gives a considerable part of the arts course as a federated college on the campus of the University of Saskatchewan, on the St. Michael's pattern; St. Joseph's College (Basilian), a student residence on the campus of the University of Alberta, has a staff authorized to offer several courses in scholastic philosophy for university credit; and St. Mark's College (Basilian), adjacent to the campus of the University of British Columbia, has a staff whose members have received direct appointment from the University to such departments as classics, history, and philosophy.

Summary. Since Catholic colleges and universities have not yet secured independent charters in Great Britain and Australia, and since they are rarely eligible for state or Federal grants in the U.S., the educational situation in Canada, where both concessions have been made, has aroused great interest among these nations. Particular attention has been given in England and in the U.S. to the enterprising departures associated with the Basilian Fathers, who developed the arts college federated with a provincial university in Ontario and Saskatchewan, and who successfully experimented with original arrangements permitting affiliation of secular or Protestant colleges with a Catholic university, as in Windsor.

The wide variety of situations in which Catholic colleges and universities are operating in Canada makes broad generalizations impossible, but it would be a valid assertion that these institutions have attained a high level of academic competence and are clearly entering upon a period of great expansion.

Bibliography: National Conference of Canadian Universities, *Canadian Universities and Colleges,* 1964 (Ottawa, n.d.), biennial. Association of Universities of the British Commonwealth, *Commonwealth Universities Yearbook, 1965* (London 1914), annual.

[J. F. LEDDY]

CANADA, UNITED CHURCH OF

A union of Canadian Methodist, Presbyterian, and Congregational Churches formed in 1925 (*see* METHODISTS IN NORTH AMERICA; PRESBYTERIANS IN NORTH AMERICA; CONGREGATIONALISTS; PROTESTANISM IN CANADA).

History. Most of the denominational differences that the Protestant settlers of Canada inherited from the Old World were political, not doctrinal. In 1875 four sections of Presbyterians became The Presbyterian Church in Canada; in 1884 four sections of Methodists became The Methodist Church; and in 1906 The Congregational Union of Canada was formed from various Congregational Churches. These internal unions set the stage for interdenominational cooperation and union and by 1908 a Joint Union Committee, made up of representatives of the three churches, had agreed on a "Basis of Union." After approval by the supreme courts of the three churches, it was referred to the lower courts and the memberships. In 1914 the name United Church of Canada was approved but the war postponed final action. In 1924 the Dominion Parliament passed the United Church of Canada Act, and on June 10, 1925, the union of the three churches was solemnly inaugurated.

Doctrine. The basic doctrines of the United Church of Canada are set down in 20 articles and constitute the first section of the "Basis of Union." In setting forth the substance of the Christian faith as commonly held among them, it states that:

> we build upon the foundation laid by the apostles and prophets, Jesus Christ Himself being the chief corner-stone. We affirm our belief in the Scriptures of the Old and New Testaments as the primary source and ultimate standard of Christian faith and life. We acknowledge the teaching of the great creeds of the ancient Church. We further maintain our allegiance to the evangelical doctrines of the Reformation, as set forth in common in the doctrinal standards adopted by the Presbyterian Church in Canada, by the Congregational Union of Ontario and Quebec, and by the Methodist Church.

The United Church of Canada holds only to the two sacraments of baptism and the Lord's Supper. The Lord's Supper is a reception "after a spiritual manner" of the body and blood of the Lord Jesus Christ. Referring to the Church, art. 15 states:

> We acknowledge one holy Catholic Church, the innumerable company of saints of every age and nation, who being united by the Holy Spirit to Christ their Head are one body in Him and have communion with their Lord and with one another. Further, we receive it as the will of Christ that His Church on earth should exist as a visible and sacred brotherhood, consisting of those who profess faith in Jesus Christ and obedience to Him, together with their children, and other baptized children, and organized for the confession of His name, for the public worship of God, for the administration of the sacraments, for the upbuilding of the saints, and for the universal propagation of the Gospel; and we acknowledge as a part, more or less pure, of this universal brotherhood, every particular Church throughout the world which professes this faith in Jesus Christ and obedience to Him as divine Lord and Saviour.

The United Church acknowledges that "the Supreme and only Head of the Church is the Lord Jesus Christ; that its worship, teaching, discipline, and government should be administered according to His will by persons chosen for their fitness and duly set apart to their office" (art. 18).

Forms and Methods of Worship. The forms and methods of worship used in the United Church of Canada are for the most part the same as those used by the individual churches before the union. However, in accordance with the tendency throughout Protestantism, there has been a movement toward increased ritualism. After the union, there was also a general tendency to raise standards of worship to those held by the more meticulous. The communion service, in general, is a distribution of the bread and wine in individual portions to the congregations by the minister aided by elders, deacons, or laymen. It is usually held four times a year. A new hymnal and "book of orders" was prepared soon after union for those who cared to use them.

Organizational Structure. The pastoral charge is the basic unit of organization. In it the individual member finds opportunity for work, worship, and financial support. The Presbytery is an important court of the church. The Presbyterians meet several times a year, receive and supervise candidates for the ministry, determine pastoral charge boundaries, deal with calls, induct ministers, and cultivate pastoral charges according to programs adopted by the higher courts. The Conference is the next higher court; it meets annually and elects a president each time. All ministers are members, together with an equal number of laymen, elected by the Presbyteries. The Conference ordains and settles ministers, and oversees the religious life of the church. The General Council meets every 2 years. It has an equal number of ministers and laymen as its members. An elected moderator holds office until the next General Council meets. The secretary and treasurer are permanent officials. The General Council is the supreme legislative body of the church and carries on its work through a number of boards and committees.

Developments. Discussions and negotiations between the United Church of Canada and the Anglican Church in Canada have been going on since 1943, but no definite plans for organic union have been settled. The coolness of the 1948 *Lambeth Conference toward Anglican participation in the formation of the Church of *South India caused some hesitation. The success of the Anglican World Congress held (1954) in Minneapolis, Minn., caused the Anglicans in Canada to look more toward a world Anglican fellowship. And there seemed to be a hesitancy on the part of some Anglican bishops about the orders held by United Church ministers. The United Church was held back for a time by some who were not willing to accept the episcopacy in any stronger form than that of Methodist bishops. The subsequent success of Anglican-Methodist discussions in Great Britain, however, led to higher hopes for Canada. In the 1960s Committees of Ten of the Anglican and United Churches were carrying on discussions and negotiations which seemed to be bringing these two churches toward organic union.

Bibliography: G. K. A. BELL, ed., *Documents on Christian Unity* (New York 1955), a selection from the 1st and 2d series, 1920–30; 3d ser. 1930–48 (1948); 4th ser. 1948–57 (1958). J. DOW, *This is Our Faith: An Exposition of the statement of faith of the United Church of Canada* (Toronto 1944). J. R. NELSON, ed., *Christian Unity in North America: A Symposium* (St. Louis 1958). R. ROUSE and S. C. NEILL, eds., *A History of the Ecumenical Movement, 1517–1948* (Philadelphia 1954). C. E. SILCOX, *Church Union in Canada* (New York 1933). *The Manual of the United Church of Canada: Constitution and Government* (rev. ed. Toronto 1960). E. M. HOWSE, "The United Church of Canada: Perils of Ecclesiasticism," *Christian Century* 80.32 (Aug. 7, 1963) 976–979. "Survey of Church Union Negotiations 1961–63," *The Ecumenical Review* 16.4 (1964) 436.

[G. R. SPOONHOUR]

CANADIAN ART

This article presents the general development of Canadian art from the early European settlement of the country up to the new vitality following World War II.

The earliest Canadian paintings were in the French colonial period from the mid-17th century. The patrons were the churches, and the artists were frequently in religious orders. They reflected a naive provincial French style; the exception was Frère Luc (1614–85), whose paintings were of high professional quality. Most of these paintings remain in private collections of religious houses in Quebec Province, notably in the Ursuline convent and Hôtel Dieu in the city of Quebec and at Sainte Anne de Beaupré. These are not readily accessible to the public. There are also numerous *ex voto* paintings of imagination and originality in provincial parish churches.

Perhaps of greater significance was the production of wood carving, primarily for churches, in the 17th and 18th centuries. Although it reflected provincial French art, it was frequently of a high level of competence and sophistication. Usually executed in a conservative baroque manner, it occasionally employed rococo coloring such as creamy white, blue, and pink, which was in keeping with contemporary fashions of interior decoration. Much of the sculpture is still in its original locations, but significant pieces can now be seen in major galleries in Canada and in the Detroit Museum of Fine Arts.

Although French influence continued to the end of the 18th century, French Canada remained aloof to the influences of neoclassicism. This may have been due in part to the religious patrons who were unsympathetic to a style they associated with the French Revolution and the anticlericalism experienced in France.

Painters of nonreligious subjects became active in the early 19th century. With the English settlement of Upper Canada after the American Revolution, the English tradition of landscape painting became popular, and landscape was to dominate art for more than a century, reaching high levels of achievement in the descriptive paintings of Paul Kane (1810–71) and the narrative and genre landscapes of Cornelius Krieghoff (1815–72) and culminating in the distinctly national styles of the "Group of Seven" and Quebec landscape painters. While in the 19th century painting in Canada was a reflection of contemporary British painting, in the 20th century the influence of Paris was dominant. Canadian artists went to Europe for training (usually Paris); impressionist colors and *art nouveau* patterns were adapted to Canadian scenery to produce a new expression for Canadian art. Prominent painters at that time were Tom Thomson, J. E. H. MacDonald, Lawren Harris, Jackson, Lismer, Varley, Carmichael, Casson, Morrice, Milne, Fitzgerald, Cullen, and Gagnon. The great period of Canadian landscape painting was in the 1920s.

By the end of World War II the international styles of art had drawn younger Canadian artists away from the landscape tradition into new forms of abstraction.

Fig. 1. "The Three Shipwrecked at Levis, 17 June 1754," votive painting attributed to Paul Beaucourt, oil on panel, 12¾ by 20½ inches, one of many similar ex voto paintings in the basilica of Sainte Anne de Beaupré, Quebec.

Leadership came from painters in Montreal, notably Riopelle, Dumouchel, Pellan, De Tonnancour, and Borduas. Later, younger artists in Toronto who also took a prominent lead were Coughtry, Urquhart, Town, and Ronald.

The art of western Canada had a distinctive regional development. Early artists were frequently army engineers concerned with surveying and with building railroads. Their sketches were detailed descriptive scenes. After this the most influential painter was Emily Carr (1871–1945), who was the first to paint the rain forests of the coast. After World War II a younger group of artists painted in a style that synthesized the local landscape and the Indian heritage with abstract expressionist techniques, a unique contribution to Canadian art. Outstanding were Jack Shadbolt, Gordon Smith, and John Korner. Apart from this tradition was B. C. Binning with a gay, lyrical, decorative style using local imagery in abstraction.

The prairie provinces emerged after 1960, giving a new vitality to the art of the country, principally in an international style.

Encouragement for the development of Canadian art came with the establishment of art societies, schools, and galleries in the late 19th and early 20th centuries, but more specifically from the assistance and leadership offered by the National Gallery of Canada and by the Canada Council after World War II. The former instituted a program of exhibitions for national circulation, a biennial exhibition of Canadian painting, and a plan for extensive purchases of contemporary art. The Canada Council provided scholarships enabling artists to travel and paint abroad. Added to this is a program of government commissions. The result has been a genuine development in interest in Canadian art since 1945. (See illustrations on following pages.)

Bibliography: C. M. Barbeau, *Cornelius Krieghoff* (Toronto 1934). D. W. Buchanan, *The Growth of Canadian Painting* (London 1950). W. G. Colgate, *Canadian Art: Its Origin and Development* (Toronto 1943). J. R. Harper, ed., *Canadian Paintings in Hart House* (Toronto 1955). L. S. Harris, "The Group of Seven in Canadian History," *Report of the Canadian Historical Association* (1948) 28–38. R. H. Hubbard, ed., *National Gallery of Canada Catalogue of Paintings and Sculpture,* v.3 *Canadian School* (Ottawa 1960). **Illustration credits:** Fig. 1, Photo by courtesy of the Art Gallery of Toronto, Canada, Figs. 2, 4, 5, 6, 7, 8, 9, and 10, The National Gallery of Canada, Ottawa. Fig. 3, The National Gallery of Canada, Ottawa, gift of Miss Geneva Jackson.

[I. MC NAIRN]

CANADIAN LITERATURE

The Treaty of Paris in 1763 made official the British rule that had actually begun 3 years before. The treaty provided, however, for the maintenance of the French language, which shares official status with English in the province of Quebec, in the parliament of Canada, and in the law courts. Approximately 30 per cent of the total population of 18 million use French as their home language. The following survey deals with Canadian literature in French and Canadian literature in English.

1. French

French-Canadian literature developed under difficult conditions, and made very slow progress until the middle of the 19th century. After 150 years of colonization by the French, Canada had a population of only 70,000, predominantly rural and scattered over a vast territory.

Fig. 2. *Paul Kane, "Blackfoot Chief and Subordinates," canvas, 25 by 30 inches.*

Fig. 5. *Arthur Lismer, "Road Through the Bush," canvas, 40½ by 31½ inches, 1914.*

CANADIAN ART

Fig. 3. *Cornelius Krieghoff, "The Ice Bridge at Longueuil," canvas, 23 by 29 inches, c. 1847.*

Fig. 6. *Emily Carr, "Heida," canvas, 51 by 36 inches, 1928.*

Fig. 4. *J. E. H. MacDonald, "Batchawana Rapid," canvas, 28 by 36 inches, 1920.*

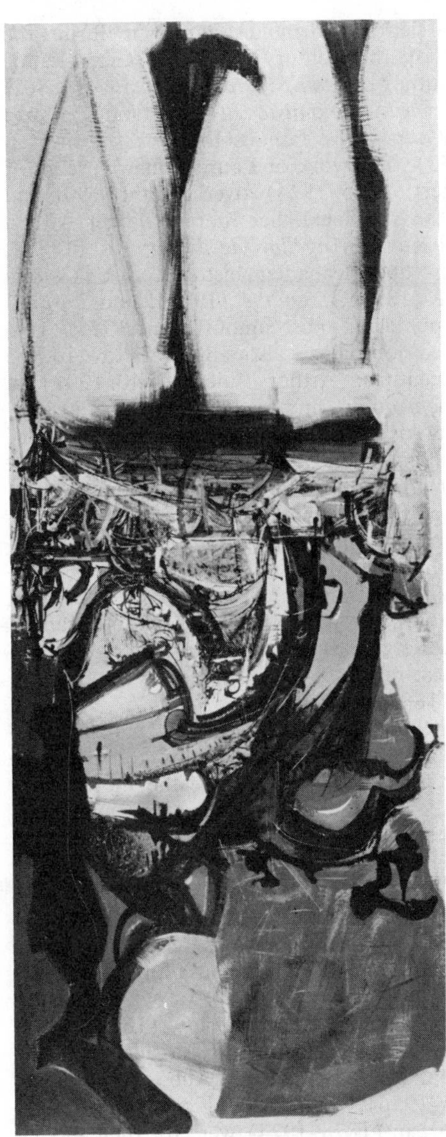

Fig. 7. Harold Town, "Dead Boat Pond," canvas, 95½ by 38 inches, 1956.

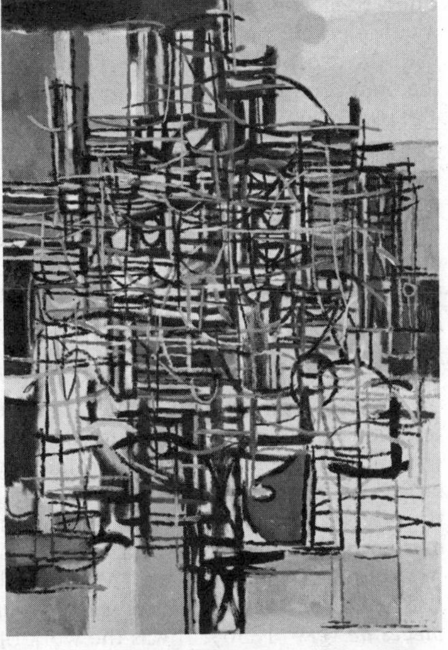

Fig. 8. Gordon Smith, "Structure with Red Sun," canvas, 40 by 28 inches, 1955.

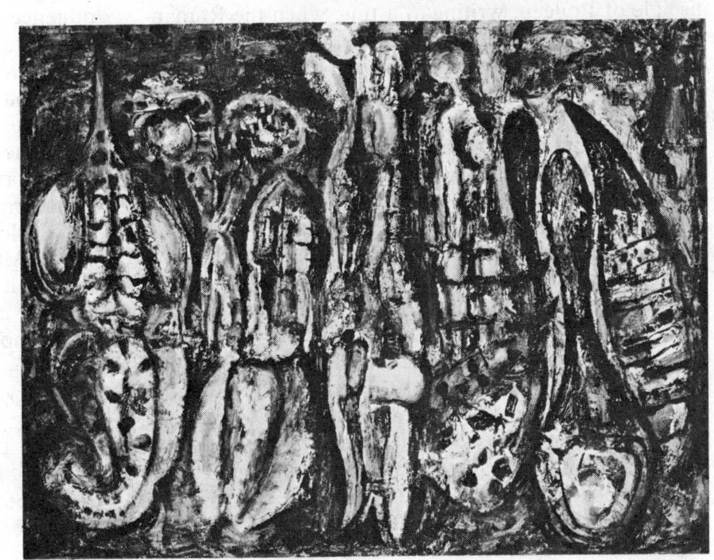

Fig. 9. Albert Dumouchel, "Les Bubons du Soleil sont Allongés," canvas, 27½ *by* 37¾ *inches*, 1953.

Fig. 10. B. C. Binning, "Theme Painting," canvas, 28 by 50 inches, 1953.

Educational opportunities were extremely limited, and a considerable proportion of the small educated class, with the exception of the clergy, moved to France after the final conquest of the country by the British (1763). The works written about Canada by early French explorers, travelers, government officials, and missionaries cannot properly be considered as literature. Their purpose was obviously instructional—to provide information about geography, the history of the country's discovery and settlement, and the life and customs of its inhabitants. Furthermore, in the absence of printing presses in the colony during the French regime, these works were all published in France.

First Stirrings of Literature (1760–1860). During the first 70 years of British rule, whatever feeble manifestations of literary life occurred were limited to the writing of verse of very mediocre quality, and of prose largely of a political character printed in newspapers, the great majority of which had a most precarious existence. The first book of a literary nature published by a French-Canadian was Michel Bibaud's (1782–1857) *Épîtres, Satires, Chansons, Épigrammes et autres pièces de vers* (1830). It was the work of an uninspired disciple of Boileau, writing at a time when the Romantic school was flourishing in France, but it nevertheless marked an important moment in the history of French Canadian literature, mainly because it encouraged other Canadians to write. In 1837, Philippe Aubert de Gaspé *fils* published *Le Chercheur de trésors: Ou l'Influence d'un livre,* the first novel to appear in French Canada. Within the next decade, three more works of fiction appeared: Joseph Doutre's *Les Fiancés de 1812* (1844), Patrice Lacombe's *La Terre paternelle* (1846), and P. J. O. Chauveau's *Charles Guérin* (1846). One writer of truly superior talent during the decade 1840–50 was François Xavier *Garneau, whose *Histoire du Canada* (3 v., 1845–48) has remained a classic. By showing conclusively that, contrary to the impression of many English Canadians, French-Canadians had a glorious history, Garneau aroused in them a feeling of pride and self-confidence that was to lead to the founding of what was later called the patriotic school of Quebec.

Real Beginnings (1860–1900). The first writer to reflect the new spirit was Octave *Crémazie, a Quebec bookseller who, although too much influenced by the French Romantics and too inclined to rhetoric, raised Canadian poetry to a level of respectability. His close association with the early history of the school of Quebec is noteworthy. From the mid 1850s until 1862, when business difficulties forced him to move to France, his bookshop was the rendezvous of intellectuals and writers such as the Abbé Henri Raymond *Casgrain; the journalist Étienne Parent; the historians François Xavier Garneau and Jean Baptiste Ferland; and the novelists and short story writers P. J. O. Chauveau, Hubert La Rue, Joseph Charles Taché, and Antoine Gérin-Lajoie. Casgrain, after being assigned to the cathedral of Quebec in 1860, soon became the leader of the movement and exerted a most decisive influence upon the future course of French-Canadian literature by insisting that it should draw its inspiration from the dual source of religion and patriotism, a view that was strictly adhered to until the end of the 19th century and continued to be reflected in the subject matter treated by a majority of authors until the 1930s.

Fiction. In fiction two names stand out during the second half of the century: Antoine Gérin-Lajoie (1824–82), author of *Jean Rivard le défricheur* (1862) and *Jean Rivard économiste* (1864), and Philippe Aubert de *Gaspé *père,* famous for *Les Anciens Canadiens* (1863). The work of Laure Conan (pseud. of Félicité Angers, 1845–1924) overlaps the 19th and 20th centuries. She began her literary career with a psychological novel, *Angéline de Montbrun* (1884), and then drew upon Canadian history for *A l'Oeuvre et à l'épreuve* (1891), *L'Oublié* (1900), and *La Sève immortelle,* published posthumously in 1925. Two highly talented journalists also appeared toward the end of the century: Arthur Buies (1840–1901), a master of the *chronique;* and Jean Paul Tardivel (1851–1905), a vigorous polemist and a forceful defender of Catholic teaching.

Poetry. Of the poets who attained distinction between 1860 and the beginning of the 20th century, four deserve special mention: Alfred Garneau (1836–1904), Pamphile Le May (1837–1918), Louis *Fréchette, and William Chapman (1850–1917). Fréchette, in spite of a marked tendency to triteness and grandiloquence, was the greatest French-Canadian poet of his time. He is best remembered for his epic, *La Légende d'un peuple* (1887).

Period of Maturation (1900–39). By 1890, intellectual life, in danger of being stifled by too great an adherence to tradition, began to breathe more freely as education became more widespread and interest in literature more general. In this new cultural climate the École littéraire de Montréal came into existence in 1895. Although this group is always referred to as a school, it was in reality more of a club, since its membership comprised poets of various tendencies, upon whom no attempt was made to impose any set of doctrines.

Poetry. While Jean Charbonneau (1875–1960), founder of the École, Arthur de Bussières (1877–1913), Lucien Rain (pseud. of Abbé Joseph Mélançon, 1877–1956), Émile Nelligan (1879–1941), and Albert Lozeau (1878–1924) went for their models

Émile Nelligan.

either to the French Parnassians or the French Symbolists—some of them were, as a matter of fact, influenced by both schools. Gonzalve Désaulniers (1863–1934) and Charles Gill (1871–1918) were great admirers of the French Romantics, especially of *Lamartine. Albert Ferland (1872–1943), Louis Joseph Doucet (1874–1959), and Englebert Gallèze (pseud. of Lionel Léveillé, 1875–1955), however, found their inspiration in scenes from the Canadian *terroir* or country life. (*See* PARNASSIANISM; SYMBOLISM, LITERARY; FRENCH LITERATURE, 5.) The most celebrated member of the École was Émile *Nelligan, a consummate artist and a supreme master of imagery, whose extraordinarily promising career was suddenly cut short when, at 19, he was committed to a mental institution, where he spent the rest of his life. Outside the École, the writers who brought to French-Canadian poetry greater originality and technical virtuosity were Louis Dantin (pseud. of Eugène Seers, 1865–1945), René Chopin (1885–1953), Robert Choquette (b. 1905), and especially Paul Morin (1889–1963), who is recognized as a supreme craftsman.

A number of poets more conservative in technique and in choice of subject matter were satisfied with describing country life and customs. The best representatives of this school are Nérée Beauchemin (1850–1931), Blanche Lamontagne-Beauregard (1889–1960), and Alfred Desrochers (b. 1901); the last is the most talented of the group.

Fiction. The novel showed considerable vitality during the first 3 decades of the 20th century, some 200 works being published. These manifested great diversity of form and content, although the writers' principal source of inspiration continued to be country life, which they undoubtedly wished to describe before it was too radically changed by rapid industrialization. Although none of the works of fiction produced between 1900 and 1930 was of sufficient stature to win the attention of critics and readers outside Canada, the following deserve mention for their skillful handling of plot and style: Adjutor Rivard (1868–1945), Damase Potvin (1878–1964), Abbé Lionel Groulx (b. 1878), Harry Bernard (b. 1898), and Robert de Roquebrune (b. 1899). Although one might have the temptation to annex to Canadian literature Louis Hémon's masterpiece *Maria Chapdelaine,* first published serially in the Parisian *Temps* in 1914, the fact is that this novel with a Canadian background and written in Canada was the work of a Frenchman who died there in 1913, after a residence of less than 2 years.

One has to wait until the decade immediately preceding World War II to find three novelists of truly superior talent: Claude Henri Grignon (b. 1894), author of *Un Homme et son péché* (1933), a powerful portraiture of a miser; Ringuet (pseud. of Philippe *Panneton), who wrote *30 Arpents* (1938), a vividly realistic study of the disintegration of a peasant family; and Georges Bugnet (pseud. of Henri Doutremont, b. 1879), whose narrative *La Forêt* (1935) is a remarkable treatment of the power and mystery of the Canadian woods, a theme that until then had remained strangely untouched.

Other significant literary activities between 1900 and 1939 include the work of Msgr. Camille *Roy and Louis Dantin (pseud. of Eugène Seers, 1865–1945), the most eminent literary critics French Canada has had; and the labors of Abbé Lionel Groulx (b. 1878), who, as professor of Canadian history at the University of Montreal and as writer and lecturer, exerted a profound influence upon the younger generation of French-Canadian intellectuals.

The Scene after 1939. French-Canadian society, essentially rural in 1900, had by the early 1930s become predominantly urban. With the further industrialization that took place during World War II, French Canada, which, as a measure of self-preservation, had always been most reluctant to accept change, was forced to enter the mainstream of modern life. Literature lost most of the moralizing and didacticism that had hitherto characterized it. The scope of the writer's observations was broadened, and subjects previously shunned began to be treated.

Anne Hébert.

Fiction. The first novels to gain wide acclaim during this period were Gabrielle Roy's *Bonheur d'occasion* (1945), and Roger Lemelin's *Au Pied de la pente douce* (1944), and *Les Plouffe* (1948), works dealing with the life of French Canadians in the urban centers of Montreal and Quebec. The emancipation of fiction from the old themes, begun with Grignon, Ringuet, and Bugnet, and carried further by Lemelin and Mlle. Roy, has now run its full course. The psychological novel is represented by Robert Charbonneau (b. 1911), Robert Élie (b. 1915), André Giroux (b. 1916), Jean Filiatrault (b. 1919), Eugène Cloutier (b. 1921), Jean Paul Pinsonneault (b. 1923), and André Langevin (b. 1927). The French school of the *nouveau roman* has found disciples in Marie Claire Blais (b. 1939), Claire Martin (pseud. of Claire Faucher), Diane Giguère, and Claude Jasmin. Other notable writers of fiction include Albert Laberge (1871–1960), René Ouvrard (b. 1894), Germaine Guèvremont (pseud. of Germaine Grignon, b. 1896), Abbé Félix Antoine Savard (b. 1896), Jean Jules Richard (b. 1911), Aimé Pelletier (b. 1914), Yves Thériault (b. 1915), Pierre Baillargeon (b. 1916), Jean Simard (b. 1916), Claire France (pseud. of Claire Morin, b. 1918), Gérard Bessette (b. 1920), and Adrien Thério (b. 1925).

Poetry. A conservative approach to poetry that, in 1939 and in the years immediately following World War II still marked the compositions of Simone Routier (b. 1900), Roger Brien (b. 1910), Clément Marchand (b. 1912), and Jeannine Bélanger (b. 1915), was soon to give way before new trends of a truly radical nature. Metaphysical anguish and abstract style, first found in

Hector de Saint-Denys *Garneau's *Regards et Jeux dans l'espace* and *Les Solitudes* (1935–38), have given French-Canadian poetry of the period much of its essential tonality. Alain Grandbois (b. 1900), François Hertel (b. 1905), Rina Lasnier (b. 1915), and Anne Hébert (b. 1916) became French Canada's leading poets. Jean Guy Pilon (b. 1930) was generally acknowledged by critics as the most talented of the younger generation.

Bibliography: S. BAILLARGEON, *Littérature canadienne-française* (3d ed. Montreal 1962). M. LEBEL, *D'Octave Crémazie à Alain Grandbois: Études littéraires* (Quebec 1963). C. ROY, *Nos Origines littéraires* (Quebec 1909). G. SYLVESTRE, *Anthologie de la poésie canadienne-française* (4th ed. Montreal 1963). G. TOUGAS, *Histoire de la littérature canadienne-française* (2d ed. Paris 1964). A. VIATTE, *Histoire littéraire de l'Amérique française des origines à 1950* (Quebec 1954). **Illustration credit:** Fig. 2, Canadian Consulate General, New York City.

[J. M. CARRIÈRE]

2. ENGLISH

The making of Canadian history by explorers, trappers, traders, and missioners has left records of courage and sacrifice but no literature as such. Life in the raw young country was too challenging during the first 300 years to foster interest in creative writing. English-speaking Canadians came into their own politically in 1763 when Britain took Canada from the French, but their interests remained British and imperial for some time. The most important influence on future Canadian literature came after the American Revolution. Almost 40,000 Loyalists moved to Canada and together with large numbers of British immigrants created the Anglo-Saxon Protestant culture that has dominated English-Canadian literature.

The main writing in these years appeared in journals and letters, with some backwoods poetry modeled on that of Robert Burns and the popular broadsides of the 18th century. The first noteworthy fictional work was Thomas Chandler Haliburton's *The Clockmaker* (1836), stories about one Sam Slick, an itinerant Yankee clock peddler. In nonfiction, the best work was Susanna Moodie's *Roughing It in the Bush* (1852), a still-vigorous and human account of frontier life in Upper Canada.

Awakening Nationalism. The Canadian national consciousness that emerged at the end of the war with the U.S. in 1812 became politically more evident with the confederation of the eastern provinces in 1867. The awakening spirit of nationalism was reflected in the rise of such regional writers as the romantic novelists Sir William Kirby (1817–1906), and Ralph Connor (Charles W. Gordon, 1860–1937), but Canada's first signs of literary maturity took the form of poetry. A small group of poets born in the 1860s produced a significant body of minor poetry in the 1890s. Sir Charles G. D. Roberts and his cousin Bliss Carman, both of New Brunswick, and an Ontario trio, Archibald Lampman, Wilfred Campbell, and D. C. Scott, published a considerable body of nature poetry. The group possessed visual power, but their attempts to philosophize on nature resulted in pale reflections of Emersonian transcendentalism (*see* TRANSCENDENTALISM, LITERARY).

Poetry after World War I. The romantic heritage was abandoned in the decades following World War I. Paradoxically, the greatest poet of the period belonged to no school or popular movement. This was Edwin J. Pratt (1883–1964), an elder statesman of Canadian letters, who published his first volume, *Newfoundland Verse,* in 1923, and from then on went his own way, putting fresh life into traditional forms while his contemporaries were experimenting in modern styles. His narrative poems, of which *Brébeuf and His Brethren* (1940) and *Dunkirk* (1941) are the most powerful, have made Pratt one of the few writers to win attention outside Canada.

A body of significant poetry came from a group of poets influenced by the work of Pound, Eliot, and Yeats. A. J. M. Smith, F. R. Scott and A. M. Klein wrote intellectually passionate verse, often metaphysical and symbolic, interpreting the chaotic world of their day. Irving Layton is eminent among the younger contemporaries, notably for his gift of vividly dramatizing human experience. *A Red Carpet for the Sun* (1959) contains the best poems of his 12 volumes published between 1942 and 1958.

Development of Fiction. English-Canadian fiction was born in the late 1920s. In his sketches and essays, Stephen Leacock (1869–1944) humorously preserves a warm feeling for the human spirit and a healthy irreverence for organizations that tend to submerge it. Three novelists appeared soon after World War I. Mazo de la Roche (1885–1961) began a long series of romantic novels with *Jalna* (1927), and Frederick Philip Grove (1872–1948) wrote Hardyesque novels about the Canadian prairies in *Our Daily Bread* (1928) and *Fruits of the Earth* (1933). Neither was of the stature of Morley Callaghan (1903–), whose first novel, *Strange Fugitive,* was published in 1928. His later novels, *The Loved and the Lost* (1951), *The Many Colored Coat* (1960), and *A Passion in Rome* (1961), are perhaps his best. Callaghan was part of the Hemingway circle in Paris in the 1920s, but his style remains distinctive and personal. He is the first Catholic writer of any stature in English-speaking Canada.

Fine fiction has been written by Hugh MacLennan (1907–) and the rural novelists, W. O. Mitchell, Sinclair Ross, and Ernest Buckler; Mordechai Richler (1931–) has produced five volumes that mark him as the most promising of Canada's younger novelists. Ironically, the most impressive recent fiction has been produced by two newcomers to Canada, Malcolm Lowry (1909–57) and Brian Moore (1921–).

It is interesting to note that the two writers who won the greatest reputation in the English-speaking world of their day were humorists, Haliburton and Leacock. The world has paid little attention to Canada's poetry, somewhat more to her fiction. Since 1940, there has been a rapid development in the complexity of Canadian poetry and more experimentation in fiction. English-Canadian writing is becoming something more than a reflection of European and American literatures. But the challenge of transforming private vision into public meaning remains the main problem of English-Canadian writers.

Bibliography: D. PACEY, *Creative Writing in Canada* (2d ed. Toronto 1961), with bibliog. E. A. MCCOURT, *The Canadian West in Fiction* (Toronto 1949), with bibliog. W. EGGLESTON, *The Frontier and Canadian Letters* (Toronto 1957). C. F. KLINCK and R. E. WATTERS, eds., *Canadian Anthology* (Toronto 1955), poems and prose, with bibliog. and biog. material. A. J. M. SMITH, ed., *The Book of Canadian Poetry: A Critical and Historical Anthology* (3d ed. Toronto 1957), comprehensive bibliog. to 1956. "Letters in Canada," *University of Toronto*

Quarterly (April 1936–). *Canadian Literature* (1959–), a quarterly of criticism and review that publishes an annual checklist of all books published each year. C. F. KLINCK, ed., *Literary History of Canada* (Toronto 1965); the first comprehensive history, with bibliog. and notes.

[C. P. CROWLEY]

CANAL, JOSÉ DE LA, historian and apologist; b. Uciedo, Spain, Jan. 11, 1768; d. Madrid, April 17, 1845. He became an Augustinian in 1785 and a priest in 1792. He taught philosophy at Burgos, Salamanca, Toledo, and Madrid. When religious houses in Spain were dissolved in 1809 under the French, he translated several French works in defense of the Church. He was attacked for some of them, replied in 1814, and was confined in a monastery at Ávila for a year. He was released by Ferdinand VII and appointed, with Antolin Merino, to continue the *España Sagrada,* v. 43–44 (*see* FLÓREZ, ENRIQUE). In volumes 45 to 47 Canal treated the dioceses of Gerona and Lérida. He wrote a number of religious works and was director of the Real Academia de la Historia until his death.

Bibliography: G. DE SANTIAGO VELA, *Ensayo de una biblioteca ibero-americana de la Orden de San Agustín,* 7 v. in 8 (Madrid 1913–31) 1:570–595. A. C. VEGA, *La España sagrada y los Agustinos en la Real Academia de la historia* (El Escorial 1950). A. ORTIZ, DHGE 11:698–700. R. BÄUMER, LexThK[2] 2:913.

[F. ROTH]

CANALETTO (ANTONIO CANALE), Italian painter of views; b. Venice, Oct. 18, 1697; d. Venice, April 20, 1768. He began his life's career as a *vedutista* by painting stage scenery with his father and brother in Venice and in Rome. When he saw the work of the many Dutch realists then in Rome, he broke away from the extravagant perspective of scene painting and turned to painting sensitive landscapes. Some early works seem actually to have been painted out-of-doors. He soon achieved success, especially among English travelers, who took Canaletto's views of Venice back with them as mementos of their tours. Canaletto, in fact, went to England and stayed there from 1746 to 1755. It is often claimed that the visit injured his style, hardening it and causing a loss of breadth and freedom. However, the change to more precisely drawn and less atmospheric painting had begun as early as 1730 as a result of the pressure of numerous commissions and his own desire for greater objectivity.

Canaletto, "The Square of Saint Mark's," c. 1740, oil on canvas, 45 by 60½ inches.

Bibliography: K. T. PARKER, *The Drawings of Antonio Canaletto* (Oxford 1948). F. J. B. WATSON, ed., *Canaletto* (New York 1949). V. MOSCHINI, *Canaletto* (London 1955). W. G. CONSTABLE, *Canaletto,* 2 v. (Oxford 1962). **Illustration credit:** National Gallery of Art, Gift of Mrs. Barbara Hutton.

[T. BUSER]

CANARY ISLANDS, a chain of seven mountainous and volcanic islands, situated in the Atlantic Ocean off the northwest coast of *Africa, extending westward 250 miles, and 2,807 square miles in area. Known in ancient times as the Fortunate Islands because of their mild climate and fertility, they were rediscovered around the 11th century. During the Middle Ages various navigators from Genoa and Catalonia made expeditions to the Canaries. The Portuguese came in the 14th century, but made no permanent settlement. The Spanish conquest of the islands began in 1401 and was complete by 1496. Eventually the surviving indigenous, Berber-speaking population was assimilated by the colonizing Andalusians. In the trade of Spain with Asia, Africa, and South America, the Canaries occupied an important place, but their economy depends nowadays on agricultural exports and tourism. The islands form two provinces of Spain. In 1964 the population, almost entirely Catholic, totaled nearly 1 million. The few Protestant chapels are mainly for tourists.

The Basilica of Nuestra Señora de Candelaria, on the island of Tenerife in the Canary Islands.

The Portuguese sent bishops in the 14th century, and in 1351 mention was made of a "bishop of the Canaries," named by the pope and resident in Majorca in the Balearic Islands. Spanish Franciscans have been responsible for the methodical evangelization of the archipelago, beginning *c.* 1400. The antipope Benedict XIII created a bishopric suffragan to Seville at Rubicon on the island of Lanzarote in 1404. Later the see was transferred to Fuerteventura, and in 1483 to Las Palmas on Grand Canary Island. In 1819 the Diocese of San Cristobal de la Laguna was established on the island of Tenerife; it was suppressed in 1851 and reestablished definitively in

1876. In 1963 the archipelago had two dioceses, suffragan to *Seville in Spain. The Diocese of the Canary Islands, with its seat in Las Palmas on Grand Canary Island, had jurisdiction also over the islands of Fuerteventura and Lanzarote. It then had 454,000 Catholics, 115 parishes, 191 secular and 65 religious priests, 102 seminarians, 120 religious men in 12 houses, and 640 religious women in 42 houses. The Diocese of San Cristobal de la Laguna, for the islands of Tenerife, Gomera, Hierro, and Las Palmas, had 506,000 Catholics, 119 parishes, 154 secular and 88 religious priests, 150 religious men in 15 houses, and 733 religious women in 47 houses. The island of Tenerife has the celebrated Marian sanctuary of Nuestra Señora de Candelaria, whose fame was spread by Spanish and Portuguese navigators.

Bibliography: S. Ruiz, DHGE 11:702–712. G. Caraci and G. Pou y Marti, EncCatt 3:506–507. EncRelCat 2:356–359. J. Vincke, LexThK² 5:1276. For additional bibliography and map, *see* AFRICA. **Illustration credit:** Spanish National Tourist Office, New York City.

[J. BOUCHAUD]

CAÑAS Y CALVO, BLAS, Chilean founder of homes for children; b. Santiago, Feb. 3, 1827; d. there, March 23, 1886. He was the son of José Antonio Cañas and Mercedes Calvo and came from a family that had many priests, among them the first Chilean archbishop, Manuel Vicuña, who baptized him. In 1836 he entered the seminary in Santiago, where he was a brilliant and pious student. He was ordained Sept. 22, 1849. Subsequently he was professor at the seminary, joining the faculty of theology in 1859. He preached in the capital in a powerful but simple style, dogmatic yet evangelical. He served as a chaplain for nuns and held several other minor ecclesiastical positions. He acquired a reputation for sanctity and was known for his great love for the poor. On Aug. 15, 1856, he founded La Casa de María, a place of asylum and education for girls of poor families, and established a congregation of nuns to run it. A pontifical congregation since 1941, this group had 50 nuns in 1964 and conducted similar houses in Santiago, Valparaíso, and Mendoza (Argentina). In 1872 he founded a similar institution for boys, Patrocinio de San José, which is now under the care of the Salesians. Cañas y Calvo was expert in obtaining alms for his houses; his humility elicited them even from non-Christians. He shunned honors, and against his will the government presented his name to Rome for the bishopric of Concepción. However, he died before any appointment was made.

Bibliography: C. Fernández Freite, *Don Blas Cañas el Vicente de Paul chileno* (Santiago 1936). M. A. Román, *Vida del señor D. Blas Cañas* (Santiago 1887).

[F. ARANEDA BRAVO]

CANBERRA AND GOULBURN, ARCHDIOCESE OF (CAMBERRENSIS ET GULBURNENSIS), in *Australia, since 1948 immediately subject to the Holy See, without suffragan sees. It was created a diocese in 1862 as a suffragan of *Sydney. Its 33,560 square miles embrace some of the country's richest pastoral and agricultural land, its highest mountain area, and the Federal Capital Territory of approximately 900 square miles, including Canberra, the capital. Its archbishop in 1964 was Eris M. O'Brien, who resided at Canberra; its auxiliary bishop was John

SS. Peter and Paul cathedral, Goulburn, Australia.

Cullinane, who resided at Goulburn. Predecessors were Bps. Bonaventure Geoghegan, who died in 1864 before taking possession of the see, William Lanigan (1867–1900), John Gallagher (1900–23), John Barry (1924–38), and Terence McGuire, first archbishop of Canberra and Goulburn (1948–57). In a population of 250,000 (1963), Catholics numbered 71,789; there were 49 parishes, 163 churches, 105 diocesan and 46 religious priests, 72 brothers, 600 sisters, 3 hospitals, 4 charitable institutions, and 74 schools with 18,270 pupils (*see* AUSTRALIA for further statistics and map).

Bibliography: *The Official YearBook of the Catholic Church of Australasia* (Sydney 1963–64). AnnPont (1964) 90.

[J. G. MURTAGH]

CANDIDO, VINCENZO, moral theologian; b. Syracuse, Sicily, 1572 or 1573; d. Rome, Nov. 7, 1654. He became a Dominican at Rome in 1593. Owing to his piety and prudence, he was elected provincial of the Sicilian Province in 1609 and of the Roman Province in 1633. Three times he was prior of the Minerva; twice (1642, 1649), vicar-general of the Order; and intermittently from 1617 to 1642, penitentiary at St. Mary Major. In 1645 Innocent X appointed him Master of the Sacred Palace. His theological opinions expressed about Jansenism and those in his *Illustriorum disquisitionum moralium* (1637–43) have often been classed as laxist. (*See* LAXISM.)

Bibliography: Taurisano Hier 57–58. P. Mandonnet, DTC 2.2:1506.

[J. A. FARREN]

CANDIDUS OF FULDA (BRUUN), hagiographer, theologian; d. Fulda 845. He entered Fulda under its second abbot, Baugulf (779–802), and was sent by Abbot Ratgar (802–817) for literary and artistic study under *Einhard. He was ordained after his return, but seems to have played no part in the canonical deposition of Ratgar. He enjoyed the confidence of Abbot Eigil (818–822) who assigned him to paint the apse of the new basilica where the remains of St. Boniface were placed. Bruun was a teacher, but it is not certain that he became head of the monastery school after *Rabanus Maurus was elected abbot (822–842). His chief literary work was a *Life of St. Eigil* in two books, one in prose (MGS 15:221–33) and one in verse (MGPoetae 2:96–

117). The work, written *c.* 840 with the encouragement of Rabanus, is valuable for the internal history of Fulda. A life of Baugulf, suggested by Eigil, if actually written, remains unknown.

It is another "Candidus," Wizo, the Anglo-Saxon disciple and confidant of *Alcuin who is almost certainly the author of the first section, *De imagine Dei,* of the *Dicta Candidi* (MGEp 5:615), long attributed to Bruun. This section, on man's soul as bearing the image of the Trinity, was taken in part from the *Libellus de dignitate conditionis humanae,* Ch. 2. The rest of the passage is that which is known also as the *Dicta* of Alcuin. Unfortunately, the origin of the *Libellus de dignitate* itself is obscure; but since it was already quoted as a supposed work of St. Ambrose *c.* 790, it is strongly suggested that both parts of Wizo's passage, *De imagine Dei,* are excerpts from this earlier *Libellus.* When B. Hauréau published the *Dicta Candidi* [*Hist. de la phil. scolastique* (Paris 1872) 1:134–137], he included 11 other items along with the above section, treating all 12 entries as a single treatise; hence, the rise of the misnomer *XII Dicta Candidi.* Special interest has centered on No. XII as an early example of rational argument for the existence of God. However, the actual provenance of these 11 items must still be explored before their place in the history of early medieval speculation and scholastic method can properly be assessed. Like the first *Dicta* of Wizo, with which they appear as anonymous items in the earliest MS tradition, these last 11 dicta undoubtedly belong to a period before 800 A.D.

There is an *Opusculum de passione Domini* (PL 106: 57–104), a series of Holy Week homilies for a monastic community, and a letter entitled "Whether Christ could see God with His bodily eyes" (MGEp 4:557–561) that are both by the same author; but critical opinion is divided as to which "Candidus" it is.

Bibliography: Manitius 1:660–663. F. ZIMMERMANN, "Candidus . . . Geschichte der Frühscholastik," DivThomF 7 (1929) 30–60. H. LÖWE, "Zur Geschichte Wizos," DeutschArch 6 (1943) 363–373. P. SCHMITZ, *Histoire de l'ordre de saint Benoît* (Maredsous 1942–) 2:109–110. Wattenbach–Levison 233. S. HILPISCH, LexThK² 2:736.

[J. J. RYAN]

CANDLEMAS. A feast celebrated on February 2, with blessing of candles and procession, to commemorate the presentation of Christ in the temple at Jerusalem and the legal purification of Mary 40 days after His birth (Lk 2.22–38).

The feast, first recorded in the 4th-century diary of Etheria, spread through the East under the name *Hypapante* (*Occursus Domini,* or meeting of the Lord and Simeon), and the Emperor Justinian (d. 565) ordered it observed throughout the Empire. Rome must have accepted the feast very early. The ancient antiphonary [ed. R. J. Hesbert, *Antiphonale Missarum septuplex* (Brussels 1935) 29] proves that both procession and feast were kept at Rome before the reign of Sergius I (d. 701).

The procession seems to have originated at Rome, perhaps before the feast itself was accepted. Apparently the procession took the place of the pagan *amburbale,* a lustral procession around the city at the beginning of February. Though it cannot be proved, this hypothesis explains the penitential nature of the procession and the fact that it was always held on February 2, even when the feast itself was transferred.

Representatives of religious communities offering large candles to Pius XII on the feast of Candlemas.

According to Cyril of Scythopolis [*ante* 565; ed. E. Schwarz, *Kyrillos von Skytopolis* (Leipzig 1939) 236], the use of candles was introduced in about 450 in Jerusalem by a certain Ikalia, a Roman matron. This supports the theory that the procession with lights is indeed of Roman origin. The penitential procession with candles is first described in the 8th-century Roman Ordinal 20 (Andrieu OR 3:235–236); the blessing of candles, with the antiphon *Lumen ad revelationem* and the *Nunc Dimittis,* is first mentioned in the Romano-Germanic Pontifical of the 12th century (Andrieu Pont 1:206–209). Since the 18th century it has been customary for dignitaries to present ornate candles to the pope on this day.

Though originally Christological, the feast soon acquired a Marian character, perhaps because the procession in both East and West terminated at a Marian church. The texts of the Office and the antiphons of the procession are Marian, while the Mass (except the Offertory and Postcommunion) is Christological.

All penitential vestiges in the procession were suppressed by the 1961 Code of Rubrics: white vestments are worn instead of purple, and the antiphon *Exsurge* is no longer sung. It is no longer possible for the procession and the feast to be observed on different days. Though the feast pertains to the sanctoral, in a sense it concludes the Christmas cycle. The Marian antiphon of the Office and the seasonal Mass of Our Lady change on this day.

Bibliography: J. Löw, EncCatt 10:341–345. Miller FundLit. A. G. MARTIMORT, ed., *L'Église en prière* (Tournai 1961). D. DE BRUYNE, "L'Origine des processions de la Chandeleur et des Rogations, à propos d'un sermon inédit," RevBén 34 (1922) 14–26. Righetti. **Illustration credit:** Fotografia Pontificia Felici.

[C. SMITH]

CANDLES

Though not used in the Jewish worship of the Old Testament, candles were used by the Romans—not only for necessary lighting but also for veneration of the gods, of the dead, and of the emperor (*see* LIGHT, LITURGICAL USE OF).

From the earliest Christian times candles were used for the *Lucernarium* (the 2d-century ceremonial light for evening prayer, the ancestor of the paschal candle); borne in funeral processions; burned at the tombs of the dead, especially of the martyrs (from the 3d century); and lighted before relics of the saints and sacred images (4th–5th centuries). From the same period candles in great numbers were used to give splendor in churches and particularly around the high altar.

From the 7th century there is evidence of the use of candles at Mass. They were borne in procession to the altar, carried for the chanting of the Gospel, and placed around the altar. Only in the 11th century did they make their appearance *on* the altar table. From the early 17th century came legislation making obligatory the use of candles at Mass and determining their number.

Present legislation concerns the quality and number of candles for different occasions. Candles must be of pure beeswax *saltem ex maxima parte* (reckoned as at least 65 per cent) for the paschal candle and for Mass, and beeswax in "notable quantity" (reckoned as at least 25 per cent) for all other candles burned *on* the altar. Because of local shortages a decree of the Congregation of Rites, given in December 1957, allows the episcopal conference of any country to determine what is "a becoming part" of beeswax for altar candles if it is difficult to obtain. Altar candles are normally of bleached wax, but unbleached wax is used for Requiem functions. At least two candles must burn at low Mass, six at festal solemn Mass, and seven for a festal pontifical Mass of the living celebrated by the ordinary. At solemn Mass two candles are borne in procession and for the chanting of the Gospel, and two or more are carried as torches for the Consecration. Two candles are lighted on the altar whenever the Blessed Sacrament is taken from the tabernacle; if it is solemnly exposed 20, or at least 12, are used. At Baptism, Anointing of the Sick, and the Churching of Women, one candle is needed. Candles are lighted on the altar for the chief hours of the Divine Office.

A blessing has been in use for candles since the 15th century. There is no obligation to bless candles for liturgical use except the paschal candle and the candles used for the liturgy of *Candlemas (February 2), but it is more becoming that they be blessed. The Roman Ritual (9.8.1) gives a form of blessing.

Bibliography: S. Marsili, EncCatt 3:519–521. G. Carandente, EncCatt 7:868–870. J. B. O'Connell, *Church Building and Furnishing* (Notre Dame, Ind. 1955) 208–210. Righetti 1:325–327. P. Radò, *Enchiridion liturgicum,* 2 v. (Rome 1961). F. Cabrol, DACL 3.2:1613–22. Miller FundLit 205–206; 108.

[J. B. O'CONNELL]

CANISIUS, HEINRICH, canonist and historian; b. Nijmegen in Geldern, 1548; d. Ingolstadt, Sept. 2, 1610. He was a nephew of St. Peter *Canisius. He studied at Louvain and received his doctorate in both Canon Law and civil law. From 1590 until his death, he taught Canon Law at Ingolstadt, eight times serving also as rector of the academy there. He suffered a stroke during Mass on Aug. 21, 1610, and died a few days later.

Among his principal works are the *Summa iuris canonici in libros quatuor institutionum contracta* (Ingolstadt 1594), *Disputationes de immunitate ecclesiastica* (1597), *Reputatio trium tractatum de judice causarum matrimonialium quas Heidelbergensis quidam Ictus sub nomine Marsilii de Padua et Guil. Occam anno MDIIC edidit* (1599), *Commentarius in regulas iuris libri VI Decret.* (1600), and *De differentiis iuris canonici et civilis* (1620). His canonical works were collected and published by Andreas Desvellius as *Opera quae de iure canonico Canisius reliquit* (Louvain 1644–49).

In his historical research, Canisius discovered many previously unedited documents relating to Church history. He published the results of his research as *Antiquae lectiones seu antiqua monumenta ad historiam Maedii Aetatis illustrandam, nunquam edita* (6 v., Ingolstadt 1601–08) with a supplement, *Promptuarium Ecclesiasticum* (1608). The work lacked systematic arrangement and uncritically mixed important documents with documents of little worth. A complete, critical revision was published by Basnage under the title *Thesaurus monumentorum ecclesiasticorum* (7 v., Antwerp 1725).

Bibliography: J. Denis, DDC 2:1282–83. Hurter Nomencl 3:516–517. V. Rotmarus and J. Engerd, *Annales Ingolstadiensis Academiae,* continued J. N. Mederer, 4 pt. (Ingolstadt 1582) 2:119, 121, 123, 130, 139, 162, 167, 172, 180, 192, 198. Schulte 3.1:130–131.

[C. M. ROSEN]

CANISIUS, PETER, ST.

Jesuit theologian, writer, apostle, and Doctor of the Church (in the vernacular more properly Kanijs, not de Hondt); b. Nijmegen, Netherlands, May 8, 1521; d. Fribourg, Switzerland, Dec. 21, 1597 (feast, April 27).

Canisius was born of an aristocratic family of Nijmegen, which belonged to the duchy of Gelderland and was thus at the time still subject to the constitution of the German Empire. His father, a graduate of the University of Paris, became the instructor of the princes in the court of the Duke of Lorraine and was nine times appointed mayor of his native town. Against the will of his father, Canisius chose to take up the study of theology. In Cologne (1536–46, except for the years 1539–40, which he spent in Louvain) he became closely acquainted with a circle of learned and devout priests who labored to effect a reform within the Church and who were influenced by the spirit of German mysticism and of the *Devotio Moderna, especially of Nikolaus van Esche, and Gerard Kalckbrenner and Johannes Justus *Lanspergius, prior and subprior respectively of the Carthusians of St. Barbara. Canisius' career as a writer, which won him the honor of being one of the creators of a Catholic press and the first of the literary Jesuits, began early. The Cologne 1543 edition of Tauler, edited by "Petrus Noviomagnus," was attributed to Canisius by Braunsberger and Tesser, but this is open to doubt (according to Streicher and Brodrick). However, Canisius is certainly the author of the two-volume edition of the "Fathers of the Church," (Cologne 1546), which contains texts from Cyril of Alexandria and Leo I. This first work of Canisius is at the same time the first book ever published by a Jesuit.

In the meantime, after attending a retreat that (Bl.) Peter Faber, one of the first six companions of Ignatius Loyola, gave in Mainz in April and May 1543, Canisius joined the Society of Jesus, which had been confirmed by Paul III in 1540. While in Cologne Canisius became the center of the first Jesuit foundation on German soil. In their controversy with the elector and archbishop, Hermann von Wied, who was inclined to Protestantism, Canisius was chosen to be spokesman for the Catholic clergy and the citizens; and, in 1545, he was called upon

St. Peter Canisius, engraving of the 17th century.

three times to represent the rights of the city of Cologne before Emperor Charles V. On one of these occasions Canisius attracted the attention of Cardinal Otto Truchsess of Waldburg, Bishop of Augsburg, and was called by him to the Council of Trent as his theological consultant. When the Council moved to Bologna, Canisius went with it. In September 1547, Ignatius Loyola summoned him to Rome. Canisius was sent to Messina where he taught in the first Jesuit School from spring 1548 to July 1549. Recalled to Rome, he made his solemn profession on Sept. 4, 1549, thus becoming the eighth Jesuit to be professed.

Canisius was called by Leo XIII the "Second Apostle of Germany after Boniface." It was during the 3 decades following his return to Germany after his profession that he labored for the reestablishment of the Catholic Church in Germany, which had been greatly shaken by the Reformation. He sought to restore and to renew the Catholic faith by teaching and preaching, especially in Ingolstadt, Vienna, Augsburg, Innsbruck, and Munich. He exercised great influence upon the whole ecclesiastical situation in Germany, which grew continuously more favorable owing to his activity.

In June 1556 Canisius was appointed by Ignatius Loyola to be the first superior of the German Province of the Society; in 1562, the Austrian section was separated to form the Austrian Province, but Canisius continued as provincial in South Germany (except for two short interruptions) until 1569. The development of the three already existing colleges of Ingolstadt, Vienna, and Prague was due largely to him, as was also the establishment of new ones in Munich, Innsbruck, Dillingen, Tyrnau, Hall (Tyrol). He also took a leading part in the founding of several Jesuit colleges in the North German Province.

In spite of difficulties and misunderstandings Canisius remained faithful to the Society during his life. The contrary opinion of Protestant biographers lacks historical justification and is in contradiction to the evidence.

His personal reputation contributed much to attract new vocations from the native population to religious life in the Society. By developing the organization of the Jesuits, Canisius created the necessary basis for a permanent and regular apostolate through which the Society of Jesus in Germany became an important and leading force in the Counter Reformation.

Canisius' influence on the hierarchy and on the general situation of the Church became more and more important. He was in contact with almost all the Catholic leaders of his time and aided in the awakening of a new self-assurance among the German Catholics. Evidence of this is clear in the letters of the Saint, of which about 1,400 are known, and of these 1,310 have been published. Only a small number are private letters; most of them deal with reforms within the Church, with questions concerning Church government and religious life. He was the adviser of Emperor Ferdinand I (at whose personal wish Canisius was made administrator of the Diocese of Vienna, 1554–55), and of Pius IV, Pius V, and Gregory XIII. He participated in the discussion between Catholic and Protestant divines at Worms (1557), aided in the solution of the crisis in the Council (1562–63), and was consulted in the Reichstag Sessions (1566, 1576). Moreover, Canisius was the adviser of the nunciatures and the papal legates assigned to Germany. Several times the popes conferred special missions upon him. He came forth with numerous admonitions concerning Church reforms and severely criticized the attitude of a large part of the clergy in Germany, including the bishops. For the clergy he demanded better selection and education, and he advocated closer ties between Rome and the Church in Germany. The importance of his recommendations appeared in decisions later taken in Rome under Gregory XIII. The number of nunciatures was increased, papal seminaries were founded in Germany, and the Collegium Germanicum in Rome was enlarged and consolidated. Canisius' suggestion for the abolition of the privileges of the aristocracy with regard to elections to canonries and episcopates failed, however, due to the circumstances of the time.

Writings. Canisius exerted his widest and most permanent influence through his writings. Of primary importance are his catechisms, which appeared in three different forms. The *Summa Doctrinae Christianae,* first published anonymously in Vienna in 1555, contained 213 questions and answers, a number that increased in the post-Tridentine edition of 1566 to 223. It was intended to be a compendium for universities and graduating classes of Jesuit schools. On the request of Canisius a collection of sources and texts to support the catechism was published in four volumes by Petrus *Busaeus (de Buys), SJ, *Authoritatum sacrae Scripturae et Sanctorum Patrum, quae in Summa Doctrinae Christianae Doctoris Petri Canisii theologi S. I. citantur . . .,* pars 1, etc. (Cologne 1569–70). In 1556 at Ingolstadt, Canisius' short catechism was printed as a supplement of a Latin grammar, with the title *Summa doctrinae christianae per questiones tradita et ad captum rudiorum accomodata.* It asks 59 questions and gives short answers, thus representing a short summary of the Catholic doctrine intended for the use of the first religious instruction to children. The third edition, with the title *Catechismus Minor seu parvus Catechismus Catholicorum,* first printed in Vienna in 1558 or 1559, appeared in later editions also under the title *Catechismus Catholicus* or *Institutiones christianae pietatis.* It contains, besides a detailed calendar with feasts and saints, 124 questions and short answers, and was introduced into secondary schools as a textbook for religious instruction. All these editions have a certain common format in that they contain concise questions and answers. This method was not invented by Canisius but it was one to which he adhered strictly. Very often illustrations were added to the editions of the catechisms. The "Illustrated Catechism" (published by Christoph Plantin, Antwerp 1589) deserves special attention because of its excellent format.

Though Canisius made no claim to the originality of his ideas and was without literary ambition, his catechisms are his most ingenious achievement. In use throughout Europe and in mission countries, they went through 200 editions even during his lifetime, and were translated into many languages. Hundreds of editions were published from the 17th to the 19th centuries. The fact that until the 19th century the name "Canisius" in German was synonymous with "catechism" is proof of the popularity and importance of his catechetical work.

Moreover, there were exegetical, apologetic, ascetical, and hagiographical works, in which Canisius, obviously not gifted in speculative thought, nevertheless showed learning in the field of Holy Scripture and the writings of the Fathers of the Church.

Last Years. Misunderstandings arose between him and his successor, Paul Hoffaeus. According to reports of Canisius' stepbrother Theodore and others, Canisius' insistence upon extreme accuracy, his tendency to perfectionism, and his careful attention to completeness of documentation seemed to Hoffaeus to lay too heavy a burden upon the province. Hoffaeus therefore reported the case to Rome, hoping to have Canisius relieved of the responsibility of continuing his writing against the *Centuriators of Magdeburg, with which he had been charged by Pius V. This was done in 1578. Further misunderstandings arose about lending money at interest, which was a very controversial issue at that time: Hoffaeus favored the licitness of taking interest under the so-called *contractus germanicus* (see Brodrick). Canisius did not, and his opposition led to his transfer to Fribourg (Switzerland), where the task of the development of the newly erected college was assigned to him. He gathered the funds, selected the site, and superintended the erection of a college. His main work in Fribourg was preaching, though he continued writing until his death.

The "Spiritual Testament" written during the last years of his life at the end of his "Spiritual Diary," although it survives only in fragments, shows features characteristic of Canisius.

He was indefatigable, strong in faith and in his attitude toward the pope and the Church. Nevertheless he was fully aware of the shortcomings in the lives of ecclesiastics of his time, and he criticized them with a severity and a frankness nearly unprecedented. In his writings one finds such characteristic statements as "Peter sleeps, but Judas is awake." The worship of relics, the doctrine of indulgences, pilgrimages, and the cult of the saints were subject to distortion and abuse, and the awareness of this spurred Canisius continually to do what he could to correct it. Canisius never showed signs of despair or even of discouragement. On the contrary, he encouraged the timid. The secret of his confidence in God was his imperturbable faith of which the following passage of a letter (written in March or April 1561) may be quoted as an example: "The fear of many people is greater than necessary, because they look for human and not for divine help; they act in despair instead of praying with holy confidence for the oppressed Church." Judging from the fragments of his diary, he lived in constant union with God, and this influenced and connected his multiple activities. His religious life was according to the pattern of Christian humanism as this was practiced in his native country. The influence of the Devotio Moderna is discernible to him. His knowledge of Holy Scripture and of the Fathers of the Church was profound. He enjoyed certain privileges of a mystical kind. Although he was often maliciously defamed and vituperated by his adversaries, his language, severe though it appears to us, was remarkably mild when compared to the asperity common in controversy of his time, and he tried also to have his friends use moderation. He clarified the distinction between culpable apostasy and a mere matter-of-fact separation from the Church that did not, in his opinion, necessarily imply fault. When in Rome, Canisius emphasized his conviction that there was no question of formal apostasy in the case of many Protestants. He refused to accept the new scientific principles of humanism. As is apparent from his hagiographic and historical writings, he lacked the competence of a critical observer of history. This uncritical attitude, furthermore, is to be seen very often in his manner of dealing with cases of personal revelation, obsession, and sorcery. He was intransigent in his views regarding the lawfulness of taking interest for loans; he did not take the changing circumstances of the times sufficiently into account. Nevertheless, these shortcomings do not diminish the importance of his versatile genius for the Church in Germany. His historical greatness lies in the fact that he was entirely aware of the tasks of his time, and with indefatigable zeal he sought to cope with them, devoting his entire life to the work without thought of personal advantage or self-interest.

Soon after his death the veneration of the first German Jesuit began within the German Jesuit provinces, in Switzerland, in the Tyrol, and in South Germany, and it was principally through his catechisms that he remained in the memory of the people. In 1614 the first biography was published by Matthaeus Rader, followed in 1616 by F. Sacchini's, which was appreciated even by L. Ranke. The process of beatification started soon after the publication of these biographies but was interrupted by the suppression of the Jesuit Order. Canisius was beatified in 1864 and canonized by Pius XI in 1925, when he was also declared a Doctor of the Church, an honor that emphasized the importance of his catechisms. He is buried in St. Michael's Church in Fribourg.

Bibliography: *B. Petri Canisii epistulae et acta,* ed. O. BRAUNSBERGER, 8 v. (Freiburg 1896–1923); *S. Petri Canisii catechismi latini et germanici,* ed. F. STREICHER, 2 v. (Rome 1933–36). Sommervogel 2:617–688; 8:1974–83; 12:988. J. BRODRICK, *St. Peter Canisius: 1521–97* (Baltimore 1950). J. H. M. TESSER, *Petrus Canisius als humanistisch geleerde* (Amsterdam 1932). F. STREICHER, "De spirituali quodam libro diurno S. Petri Canisii," ArchHistSocJesu 2 (1933) 56–63. B. SCHNEIDER, "Petrus Canisius und Paulus Hoffaeus," ZKathTh 79 (1957) 304–330. A. DE PELSEMACHER, "St. Pierre Canisius: La Spiritualité d'un apôtre," RevAscMyst 35 (1959) 167–193. J. LECLER, "Die Kirchenfrömmigkeit des hl. Petrus Canisius," *Sentire Ecclesiam,* ed. J. DANIÉLOU and H. VORGRIMLER (Freiburg 1961) 304–314.

[B. SCHNEIDER]

CANISIUS COLLEGE OF BUFFALO

A liberal arts college that was founded in New York in 1870 by the German province of the Society of Jesus. At its beginning, the College offered two courses, Latin and business, and in its first year had a student body of 34. On Jan. 11, 1883, the College was incorporated by the Board of Regents of the University of the State of New York, with the power to confer baccalaureate degrees and academic honors. In 1887 the College conferred its first advanced degree, an M.A.

Established as a day and boarding institution, besides the Latin and commerce college courses, Canisius maintained a high school department, which was separated in 1913 when the College moved from its location in downtown Buffalo to its present site in the north central part of the city. The College continued as a day school, however, from 1913 to 1963, when it opened a student residence.

In 1914 the founders' original concept of a College of Arts was extended when Canisius added a science program, leading to the B.S. degree. In 1919 the College inaugurated its evening division; in 1926 it introduced into the day division undergraduate programs in business, which were subsequently offered in the evening division as well; and in 1958 established the School of Business Administration. During the 1930s the College conducted graduate courses on a limited basis in arts and sciences and in education, and in 1938 announced an accredited program leading to an M.A. in English and in history and an M.S. in chemistry and in education. In 1943 the College inaugurated a joint program with two Buffalo hospitals providing for training of student nurses, and in 1963 began a joint graduate program with St. Mary's School for the Deaf, under state auspices, to provide qualified teachers of the deaf. The College also offers a summer session on both the graduate and undergraduate level.

Although founded as an institution for men, the College is coeducational in all divisions. An accredited member of the Middle States Association of Colleges and Secondary Schools, it is on the list of registered colleges and universities of the Board of Regents of the University of the State of New York. It holds membership in the American Council on Education, Association of American Colleges, National Catholic Educational Association, Jesuit Educational Association, Conference of Catholic Schools of Nursing, Association of Colleges and Universities, Middle Atlantic Association of Colleges of Business Administration, and the Association of Urban Universities.

The College is governed by a board of trustees made up of members of the Jesuit community attached to the College. In 1964 the full-time faculty had 36 priests and 118 laymen, the latter constituting more than 70 per cent of the total faculty. They held 56 doctoral, 6 professional, and 77 master's degrees. Student enrollment, which originally numbered 34, totaled 1,542 full-time and 1,500 part-time students, including 500 on the graduate level in the regular session and 1,339 in the summer session.

The College of Arts and Sciences, the School of Business Administration and the Evening Division offer the B.A. and B.S. degrees. The graduate division grants M.A. degrees in English and history and M.S. degrees in chemistry and education. The College offers a special honors program for qualified undergraduates.

In 1958 the College erected a library that in 1964 housed 102,000 volumes, received 1,000 periodicals, and maintained an annual growth of 7,000 volumes. In addition to Christ the King Chapel, Loyola Hall (a residence for the Jesuit community), and a classroom building, facilities include an administration building (1960) and a student center and residence hall (1963).

A 1963 alumni survey revealed that more than 55 per cent of Canisius graduates had gone on for professional or graduate study. Since 1955 about 10 per cent of all undergraduates have received graduate aid through graduate scholarships, assistantships, and fellowships.

[F. L. P. KELLY]

CANNIZZARO, STANISLAO, Italian chemist, who brought the importance of *Avogadro's hypothesis to the attention of the chemists of the world after it had been ignored for almost half a century; b. Palermo, July 13, 1826; d. Rome, May 10, 1910. His father was inspector general of police in Sicily. At 15, he began the study of medicine at the University of Palermo, then turned to chemistry at Pisa and Naples. In 1848 Cannizzaro joined the revolutionists and was chosen deputy to the newly organized Sicilian parliament. The revolution proved abortive and he fled to France, studying in the laboratory of Michel *Chevreul, where he prepared cyanamide (1851). On his return to Italy, he became professor of chemistry at the National College of Alessandria. Four years later he occupied the chair of chemistry at the University of Genoa.

In 1860 Cannizzaro joined *Garibaldi. In the midst of this campaign he received an invitation to attend a congress of chemists at Karlsruhe. Here he eloquently championed the hypothesis Avogadro had advanced in 1811, emphasized the difference between an atom and a molecule, and clarified the concept and determination of atomic weights. He distributed to the assembled chemists his *Outline of a Course in the Philosophy of Chemistry* based on Avogadro's theory. For this work he was awarded the Copley Medal of the Royal Society of London in 1891.

He continued his political activities while teaching, and became a member of the Senate in 1871 and later vice president of this body. Cannizzaro was also an organic chemist of considerable eminence. Of the 80 papers he wrote, 56 were in this field. The best known concerns the Cannizzaro reaction (1881), which established the self oxidation-reduction of aromatic aldehydes in the presence of an alkali, forming equal molecules of alcohol and acid.

Bibliography: S. CANNIZZARO, *Scritti vari e lettere* (Rome 1926). T. E. THORPE, *Essays in Historical Chemistry* (3d ed. London 1923). N. SPETER and B. VANZETTI, "Cannizzaro," *Das Buch der grossen Chemiker,* ed. G. BUGGE, 2 v. (Berlin 1929–30) 2:173–189.

[B. JAFFE]

CANNON, JAMES, Southern Methodist bishop and militant social reformer; b. Salisbury, Md., Nov. 13, 1864; d. Chicago, Ill., Sept. 6, 1944. After preparation at Randolph-Macon College, Ashland, Va. (A.B. 1884), and Princeton University, N.J. (B.D. 1888; M.A. 1889), he entered the ministry (1888) and spent 6 years in pastorates, 24 as college president, 20 as bishop, and 6 in active retirement. Concurrently he promoted numerous extracurricular projects, including development of a summer assembly; edited religious periodicals and a "dry" newspaper; headed Virginia's Anti-Saloon League and, later, the national organization; and fostered temperance and social service in his church and then through the World League Against Alcoholism. He was chairman of several interchurch commissions and participated regularly in world ecumenical gatherings. Criticism of Cannon's business and lobbying methods reached a climax in 1928, when he successfully marshaled Southern Democrats to vote against Alfred E. *Smith because of his advocacy of repeal of the Prohibition Amendment and because of his Roman Catholic faith. While efforts to discredit Cannon undoubtedly reduced his influence, maligning newspapers settled his damage suits favorably to him, a civil court cleared him of alleged "corrupt practices," and a Methodist investigating committee found no cause for trial.

Bibliography: Bishop Cannon's Papers, Duke University Library. J. CANNON, *Bishop Cannon's Own Story,* ed. R. L. WATSON, JR. (Durham, N.C. 1955). V. DABNEY, *Dry Messiah: The Life of Bishop Cannon* (New York 1949).

[R. STOODY]

CANO, ALONSO, distinguished painter, sculptor, and architect, master of Spanish baroque; b. Granada, March 19, 1601; d. Granada, September 1667. In 1614, his family moved to Seville; he was apprenticed (1616) to the painter Francisco Pacheco and met Velázquez, whose influence appears in his "San Francisco de Borja" (Seville Museum, 1624) and "Ecclesiastic" (Hispanic Society of America, New York). The Seville period (1624–38) includes "St. Agnes" (destroyed, formerly in Berlin) and "St. John Evangelist" (London, Wallace Collection); they display idealism and beautiful draftsmanship. Cano created also polychrome wood sculpture, his masterpiece being the high altar of Santa María, Lebrija (1629–31). During the Madrid period (1638–52), study of Venetian masters in the royal collection and renewed friendship with Velázquez transformed his color and technique, notably in the "Immaculate Conception" (Vitoria Museum), "Miracle of the Well" (Prado), and "Descent into Limbo" (Los Angeles County Museum). Wrongly accused of murdering his wife, Cano fled to Valencia (1644–45). He was accepted as prebendary of Granada Cathedral and remained there after 1652 except for his return to Madrid (1657–60) over his dispute with the canons. Certain late masterpieces display increasingly baroque form: the seven canvases of the "Life of the Virgin" (Granada Cathedral), "Immaculate Conception" (cathedral oratory), "Holy Family" (Convento del Angel), and the "Madonna of the Rosary" (Málaga Cathedral). His wood sculpture of this period created the Granada school. To the "Immaculate Conception" and "Madonna of Bethlehem" (Granada Cathedral) he gave an innocent charm, whereas the Franciscan saints (palace of Charles V) are ascetic and intensely contemplative. His architectural masterpiece is his design for the Granada Cathedral façade (1667). *See* BAROQUE ART.

Alonso Cano, "Madonna of Bethlehem," Granada Cathedral.

Bibliography: H. E. WETHEY, *Alonso Cano: Painter, Sculptor, Architect* (Princeton 1955); EncWA 3:56–57. **Illustration credit:** Photo MAS, Barcelona.

[H. E. WETHEY]

CANO, MELCHIOR

Spanish Dominican and theologian; b. Tarancón (Cuenca), Jan. 6, 1509; d. Toledo, Sept. 30, 1560. His *De locis theologicis* entitles him to be regarded as the founder of modern *fundamental theology. After entering the *Dominican Order in 1523, he studied from 1527 to 1531 under Francis de *Vitoria at *Salamanca. Cano always remained grateful to his old master, who inspired him to attempt a new, methodical treatment of theology, based on the sources and expressed in literary language.

In 1533 his brilliant but stormy career began with his appointment as a lecturer in philosophy at the Dominican College of St. Gregory in Valladolid. There too he obtained the second chair in theology in 1536, having for his senior colleague Bartholomew *Carranza. From this period dates the rivalry between these two utterly incompatible characters, which ended only with Cano's death. His outstanding ability won for him the principal professorship of theology at the University of *Alcalá in 1542 and the succession to De Vitoria at Salamanca in 1546. Two of his courses from this period (1546–52), the *Relectio de sacramentis in genere* and the *Relectio de paenitentia,* were printed in 1550. His reputation as a theologian was enhanced during his attendance (1551–52) at the Council of *Trent as theologian of the Emperor *Charles V. He was rewarded with the bishopric of the Canary Islands, but he did not take up

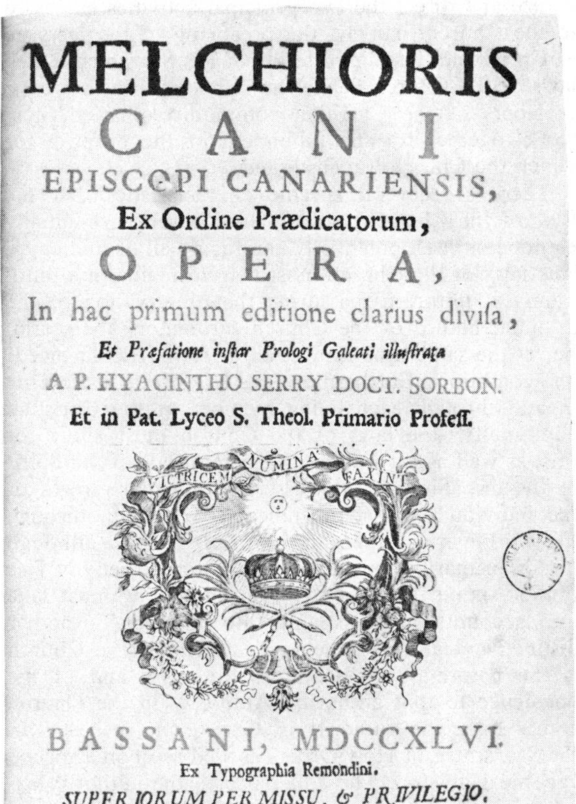

MELCHIORIS
CANI
EPISCOPI CANARIENSIS,
Ex Ordine Prædicatorum,
OPERA,
In hac primum editione clarius divisa,
Et Præfatione instar Prologi Galeati illustrata
A P. HYACINTHO SERRY DOCT. SORBON.
Et in Pat. Lyceo S. Theol. Primario Profess.

BASSANI, MDCCXLVI.
Ex Typographia Remondini.
SUPERIORUM PERMISSU, & PRIVILEGIO.

Title page from an edition of the "Collected Works," of Melchior Cano printed in 1746.

residence and resigned the see in 1554. He then became involved in the religious politics of the Spanish court, and his impetuous disposition gained him many enemies. As the theological adviser of *Philip II in his dispute with Pope Paul *IV, he fell into deep disfavor at Rome. Further causes of contention were his implacable hostility to the newly founded Society of Jesus and his campaign against the immunities and privileges of powerful cathedral chapters. Although twice (1557, 1559) elected provincial of the Castile Dominicans, he was denied confirmation in office by Rome until 1560, after the death of Paul IV. The leader of the opposition against him among the Spanish Dominicans was his old rival Carranza, since 1557 archbishop of Toledo. Less brilliant as a theologian and more tolerant of new currents in spirituality, Carranza differed also from Cano in his esteem for the *Jesuits and papal theologians. Carranza's *Commentarios sobre el Catecismo Cristiano* (Antwerp 1588) brought him into conflict with the *Inquisition, and Cano was charged to examine the book. He produced two long lists of censured propositions. His attitude in this unhappy affair is still a matter of controversy.

Cano's epoch-making and influential treatise on theological method, the *De locis theologicis,* was first printed posthumously in 1563. Book 1 is introductory; bks. 2 to 11 deal with the authority of the 10 *loci,* or sources of theology: Scripture, oral tradition, the Catholic Church, the councils, the Roman Church, Fathers, theologians, natural reason, philosophers, and human history. Book 12 treats of the use of the *loci* in scholastic disputation; bks. 13 and 14 were planned to discuss their use in the exposition of Scripture and in controversy with adversaries of the Catholic faith; these, however, were never written. The work is a skillful application to theology of the methodological principles expounded by Rudolf *Agricola in his *De inventione dialectica* (Cologne 1548).

Bibliography: The *De locis theologicis* has had about 30 editions, most recently in J. P. MIGNE, *Theologiae cursus completus,* 28 v. (Paris 1837–66) 1:58–716; since the Cologne edition of 1605 the two *Relectiones* have been included. F. A. CABALLERO, *Melchior Cano,* v.2. of his *Conquenses ilustres,* 4 v. (Madrid 1868–75). Quétif-Échard 2.1:176–178. P. MANDONNET, DTC 2.2:1537–1540. DTC, Tables générales 513–514. A. LANG, *Die Loci Theologici des Melchior Cano und die Methode des dogmatischen Beweises* (Munich 1925); LexThK² 2:918. E. MARCOTTE, *La Nature de la théologie d'après M. Cano* (Ottawa 1949). A. DUVAL, *Catholicisme* 2:465–467.

[F. COURTNEY]

CANON, BIBLICAL, the official list of the inspired books that constitute Sacred Scripture. Since divine inspiration pertains to the realm of the supernatural, the fact of inspiration can be known only through divine revelation. According to Catholic doctrine, the proximate criterion of the Biblical canon is the infallible decision of the Church. This decision was not given until rather late in the history of the Church (at the Council of *Trent). Before that time there was some doubt about the canonicity of certain Biblical books, i.e., about their belonging to the canon. Books that were always accepted as inspired by all are known as protocanonical (belonging to the "first" or undisputed canon); books whose canonicity was once doubted or disputed but later defined are called deuterocanonical (belonging to the "second" or later-defined canon). For Catholics all the books of both groups are of equal value. The canon of the NT is the same for all Christians, Protestants as well as Catholics. For the OT, however, Protestants follow the Jewish canon; they have only the OT books that are in the Hebrew Bible. Catholics have, in addition, seven "deuterocanonical" books of the OT, which are also in the Greek Bible (the Septuagint): Tobit, Judith, Wisdom, Sirach, Baruch, 1 and 2 Machabees. Protestants rank these books among the Apocrypha. For a fuller treatment of the Biblical canon and its history, *see* BIBLE, III (CANON).

Bibliography: J. SCHILDENBERGER et al., LexThK² 5:1277–84. G. RICCIOTTI, EncCatt 2:1547–51. A. JEPSEN, RGG³ 1:1123–26. L. VISCHER, RGG³ 3:1119–22. EncDictBibl 308–314.

[L. F. HARTMAN]

CANON LAW

The term Canon Law is used to designate the body of law constituted by legitimate ecclesiastical authority for the proper organization and government of the Church as a visible society. In its essential notion, "law" is common to all societies (*see* LAW, PHILOSOPHY OF). The term canon is used to designate the body of law that is proper to the Roman Catholic Church. A single law of the Church also is popularly referred to as an ecclesiastical law, and the laws of the *Code of Canon Law are frequently referred to as the canons of the Code.

The term canon comes from the Greek word κανών, basically meaning a rule, norm, measure. It has had various applications—the "canon of Sacred Scripture," meaning the list of those books accepted as inspired; the "rule of faith" according to which Christians are to live (Gal 6.16); the "norm of the Christian life" (Phil 3.16); the "norm for the liturgical life" of the early Church (First Epistle of St. Clement to the Corinthians 1.44; *Ancient Christian Writers* 1:36).

The Council of Nicaea I (325) referred to the complex of ecclesiastical regulations in disciplinary matters as the "ecclesiastical canon." There were other terms used in the early Church to designate ecclesiastical laws: the law of heaven (*ius poli*), divine law (*ius divinum*), sacred law (*ius sacrum*). During the early Middle Ages the complex of ecclesiastical laws was known as the canonical order (*ordo canonica*); and the canonical collections, particularly those from the 10th to the 12th centuries, referred to the laws of the Church as the sacred canons (*sacri canones*). *See* CANONICAL COLLECTIONS BEFORE GRATIAN. The term canon law (*ius canonicum*) was popular among canonical writers (the *decretists and *decretalists) of the late 12th and 13th centuries. A trend began in the 15th century to reserve the term canon for the dogmatic decrees of councils; however, it was common to refer also to the norms of the **Corpus Iuris Canonici* as Canon Law, and this was the term adopted by the Code of Canon Law of 1917.

Nature and Function of Canon Law. The Church is not to be identified with its laws and legal institutions. Nevertheless, law and legal institutions constitute an essential part of the nature and mission of the Church as it was established by Jesus Christ. Those who are baptized into the life of Christ form a society: "For in one Spirit we were all baptized into one body" (1 Cor 12.13). The essential nature and characteristics of law, the general juridic principles, are valid for Canon Law and all other legal systems alike. In actual fact the history of Canon Law is the history of continual borrowing and adaptation from various legal systems, and especially from that of the Roman Empire (*see* CANON LAW, INFLUENCE OF ROMAN LAW ON; CANON LAW, HISTORY OF). However the legal system of the Church always has had, and will have, its own distinctive nature and characteristics by reason of the distinctive nature and mission of the society that it serves.

The external, visible organization of the Church is not to be considered separate from its interior, supernatural structure. According to Vatican Council II, "as the assumed nature inseparably united to Him [Christ] serves the divine Word as a living organ of Salvation, so, in a similar way, does the visible structure of the Church serve the Spirit of Christ, who vivifies it, in the building up of the body" [*Constitution on the Church,* Nov. 21, 1964; NCWC ed. (Washington) 8]. However, even though the legal organization of the Church comes under the guidance of the Holy Spirit, this does not automatically ensure its perfection as a legal system. Canon Law, like everything else in the Church that is constituted with the cooperation of men, is and will be in a state of perfectibility until the final coming of Christ. It is the task of canonists to use their talents to perfect the juridic system of the Church, and thus to contribute to the "building up of the body of Christ . . . to perfect manhood, to the mature measure of the fulness of Christ" (Ephesians ch. 4, 12).

The ultimate purpose of Canon Law is to assist the Holy Spirit, who is working in and through the visible organization of the Church. Canon Law helps to organize and direct the two principal activities entrusted to the Church, namely, the preaching of the message of Christ and the administering of His Sacraments. The laws of the Church define the rights and duties of the members of the Christian community, that all may work together for the fulfillment of the purpose for which the Church was instituted.

There are several specific characteristics that the laws of the Church possess. The Church is essentially catholic, at least potentially embracing all of humanity. The laws of the Church must help to maintain a minimum of uniformity, assuring the preservation of the essential nature of the Church throughout the world; but at the same time it must allow for particular needs and conditions. Furthermore, the Holy Spirit is working in and through each living member of the Christian community: the laws of the Church must allow for this, as well as for putting the inspirations of the Spirit to the test. Similarly the essential spiritual growth of the individual Christian comes from within, through the workings of grace and the Spirit: thus, although law is primarily concerned with external activity [*see* PUBLIC ORDER (CANON LAW)], Canon Law must take into account the Christian's "life in grace." Another distinctive feature of the legal system of the Church is the nature of the Church's authority and of the obedience to that authority. Authority in the Church comes from the authority of Christ, and is based on the Sacrament of Holy Orders as well as upon a special canonical mission. The adherence to the authority exercised in the Church is based on faith and charity, and it is freely assumed.

From the point of view of the individual Christian, the laws of the Church fulfill various purposes. They enable him to best use the means of salvation instituted by Christ. They help to ensure the fruitfulness of his activity on behalf of Christ, preserving him from self-centered activity and orientating him toward the Christian community. Furthermore, even though the goal of Christian perfection is not the observance of law, nevertheless the laws of the Church point to that perfection and outline the practical norms within which the individual must operate. The manner in which one observes the laws of the Church can be a measure of his perfection. The perfection of the Christian consists in his living the life of Christ in and through the Christian community, in dying to self-love and growing in the love of others (Jn 13.35). The more perfect the growth in the life of Christ, the more perfect will be the union with the Mystical Body of Christ. This is accomplished not by the individual's own efforts, but by reason of the strength of Christ in him. Thus St. Augustine states: "Now to the end the law commands, that it may admonish us what faith should do; that is he to whom the command is given, if he is as yet unable to perform it, may know what he is to ask for. But if he has at once the ability, and is obedient to the command, he ought also to acknowledge from whose gift the ability comes" (*De spiritu et littera* 3.22; PL 44:214).

Approaches to Canon Law. Canon Law may be examined in many ways, but principally according to its history, since it is a science, and according to its sources.

The scientific study of the history of Canon Law is of relatively recent origin. Canonists of the Middle

Ages were more concerned with the practical application of the law than with its origin. The "father" of the study of the history of Canon Law is generally considered to have been an Oratorian priest named Ludovicus Thomassinus (d. 1697). A proper understanding and appreciation of the history of Canon Law is essential to a full understanding of the nature of Canon Law in general, and of individual laws and canonical institutes. The study of the history of Canon Law is generally divided into the history of the laws and institutes of the Church, the history of the science of Canon Law, and the history of the sources of Canon Law.

The science of Canon Law is the methodical and coordinated knowledge of the law of the Church. The popularly acclaimed "father" of the science of Canon Law is the Camaldolese monk named Gratian (d. 1140). *See* GRATIAN, DECRETUM OF. The science of Canon Law attempts to reduce all ecclesiastical laws to a system, serving as a basis for methodical study and giving rise to general theories. It shares in the basic juridic principles that are accepted by juridical science in general, but it differs from all other juridical sciences by reason of the object and specific nature of the laws of the Church. As a sacred science it is related to dogmatic theology, formulating the practical rules toward which theology tends (thus it is sometimes called practical theology). It is related to moral theology because it deals with the actions of Christians, but differs from moral theology in that it treats of these actions not as they appear before the law of God, but specifically as they appear before the law of the ecclesiastical society. Jurisprudence is an outgrowth of the science of Canon Law, and it is concerned with showing the true sense and application of the laws of the Church.

The sources of Canon Law are principally divided into constitutive sources (*fontes iuris essendi, constituendi, existendi*), namely, those that constitute Canon Law and give it its force (i.e., the legislators), and the documentary sources (*fontes iuris cognoscendi, cognitionis*), namely, the monuments and written records by which Canon Law is made known.

The only ones with authority to make law, in the strict sense, are those who possess supreme authority in a society. In the ecclesiastical society, this authority and duty, according to the institution by Christ, rests solely with the pope and with the universal episcopacy acting in union with the pope. As successors of the apostolic college, with Peter at its head, they inherit the duty and office imposed by Christ to go forth to the whole world, preach the message of Christ, baptize men, make disciples of them, and teach them to observe all that Christ has commanded (Mt 26.19–20). Moreover, they inherited also the authority and power of the apostolic college to carry this mission out, namely, the "keys of the kingdom of heaven" on earth, to bind and loose. This role of the pope and the episcopacy is essentially one of service: they are to be shepherds of the flock of Christ. As Vatican Council II stressed, they are endowed with a sacred power to serve their brethren, the "People of God," to enable all to cooperate in the achievement of their common goal (*Constitution on the Church;* NCWC ed. n.18). They must guide and direct those who have been "reborn in Christ" in their earthly pilgrimage toward eternal happiness (*ibid.* n.21). They do this not only by preaching, exhortation, counsel, but also by the making of laws for the government of the universal ecclesiastical society. This office rests with both the pope alone, as successor of St. Peter at the head of the college, and with the universal episcopacy acting in union with their head (*ibid.* n.22). This authority to legislate for the universal Church can therefore take the form of papal law (instituted by the pope alone) or of conciliar law (instituted by an ecumenical council). All other individuals and organizations in the Church have only that authority to make laws which has been delegated to them.

The principal documentary sources of Canon Law are the Code of Canon Law, principally for the "Latin" Church; the *Oriental Codes of Canon Law; the **Acta Apostolicae Sedis;* and special publications containing laws regarding *concordats and the sacred liturgy.

The sources of Canon Law may be understood also as those elements from which the material for the law was drawn. Thus ecclesiastical laws can be based on prescriptions of the divine positive and natural laws; they can be drawn from laws of other societies; they can originate by means of a *custom of the ecclesiastical community. These become ecclesiastical law, part of Canon Law, when they are in some way adopted, formulated, or sanctioned by the legislators in the Church.

Principles of Canon Law. According to the strict sense of the term, a law may be defined as a regulation in accordance with reason promulgated by the head of a community for the sake of the common good (ST 1a2ae, 90.4). Applying this to the Church, an ecclesiastical law may be described as a norm regulating the activity of Christians, instituted permanently by legitimate ecclesiastical authority, for the common good of the ecclesiastical society.

Ecclesiastical law is a guiding and directive principle, established to ensure the proper enjoyment of the rights and privileges of the members of the Church and to direct them in the fulfillment of their duties and obligations. It is a binding norm of action, not merely a counsel or directive.

The Church is regulated in its activity by the divine positive and natural laws (*see* LAW, DIVINE POSITIVE). The law established by God cannot be changed by the Church. However, the Church is entrusted with the practical formulation of divine law, and the Church can change this (for example, the practical formulation of the command of Christ to "do penance"). Furthermore, the Church can change substantially those laws that are not based on the divine positive and natural law. The laws of the Church are intended to be of a permanent nature, as a stable norm of action. But they must be based on and in accord with actual conditions if they are to be effective. A law is said to be abrogated when it is totally suppressed, without replacement; obrogated, when the old law is absorbed into a new one; derogated, when it is modified by a new law. The authority to abrogate, derogate, or obrogate an ecclesiastical law is the same as the authority to constitute it: that of the pope or an ecumenical council, for a law for the whole Church or for a law for a particular segment of the Church of which they are the author (CIC cc.218, 227); the plenary council, for a law made for several ecclesiastical provinces (CIC c.281); the provincial council, for a law concerning one province

(CIC c.283); the local ordinary, for a law concerning the diocese (CIC c.335). For a vacant see the vicar capitular (CIC cc.431, 432) or the administrator (CIC c.427) has the authority of the bishop in this matter [*see* ADMINISTRATOR, DIOCESAN (VICAR CAPITULAR)].

A law is made in view of the good of all the members of the society, and not for the private good of an individual. The law must be necessary, or at least useful, for the attainment of the purpose for which the Church exists. The universal Church is the primary subject of ecclesiastical law. Segments of the universal Church also may be the subject of ecclesiastical law: according to the rites (*see* RITES, CANONICAL), for the Latin, Ukrainian, Greek, etc., Churches; according to dioceses; according to constitutions for particular classes of persons in the Church, e.g., religious, clergy, laity. It is disputed whether or not an individual parish can be the subject of an ecclesiastical law.

Divisions of Ecclesiastical Law. According to the manner by which a law binds, it is called either territorial or personal. Territorial laws bind irrespective of territorial limits. The principle enunciated by CIC c.8.2 is that an ecclesiastical law is presumed to be territorial and not personal, unless there are positive indications to the contrary.

According to their extension, the laws of the Church are classified as universal and particular. Universal laws are those that are to be observed all over the world by those to whom they pertain (CIC c.13.1); particular laws oblige a designated community in a designated territory. The Code of Canon Law uses also other terms in this regard: for universal, the term general is used (CIC cc.13.1, 20, 22, 71); for particular, the Code uses also peculiar, special, or singular (CIC cc.6.1, 22, 83, 319, 324, 1501).

Ecclesiastical laws may be designated also as supraritual, ritual, and interritual, as they bind members of all rites in the Church, or only the members of a particular rite, or members of a certain group of rites, respectively.

According to their effect, ecclesiastical laws are divided into invalidating laws and merely prohibitory laws. Invalidating laws stipulate certain requirements that are to be fulfilled; and if they are not fulfilled, the act is inefficacious (CIC cc.53, 642, 1094). Invalidating laws are further subdivided into directly invalidating and incapacitating laws, as they directly affect the act or the person: in both cases the effect is the same, namely, the act is null. The general principle of the Code is that laws do not render acts invalid unless the law expressly or equivalently so states (CIC c.11).

According to subject matter, ecclesiastical laws may be divided into five general categories: (1) laws having to do with general juridic principles of the Church, the institution and interpretation of law, custom, rescripts, and privileges (CIC, bk. 1); (2) those concerning physical and moral persons in the Church, their rights, and their duties (CIC, bk. 2); (3) those concerned with various institutions in the Church, such as the Sacraments, sacred places and times, the teaching office (includes preaching, schools, censorship), administration of Church property (CIC, bk. 3); (4) laws concerning ecclesiastical procedures in formal investigations (CIC, bk. 4); (5) and laws concerning crimes and penalties in the Church (CIC, bk. 5).

According to whether regulations issued by ecclesiastical superiors fulfill certain requirements or not, they are divided into ecclesiastical laws in the strict sense and precepts (*see* PRECEPTS, CANONICAL). A precept is a command given by a superior, with either jurisdictional or dominative power, to an individual or group of individuals, for a limited time or for an indefinite period.

Another division according to subject matter is that of ecclesiastical law into public and private law. There has been considerable discussion as to the precise basis for this distinction. According to the most common conception, public law of the Church embraces all laws—divine and human—according to which the Church is constituted as a perfect society. Private law is that law constituted by ecclesiastical authority for the discipline and government of individual members of the Church. Public law is subdivided into external and internal law, as it concerns the relationship of the Church to the state or to other lesser societies within itself. Public law is generally studied as a separate discipline, and is closely allied to dogmatic theology.

Institution of Ecclesiastical Law. There are several phases in the institution of an ecclesiastical law, the final and most important one being its promulgation. This is the official publication of the law, whereby it is fully established and officially made known to the community it is to bind. According to the Code of Canon Law, laws enacted by the pope are to be promulgated by their publication in the *Acta Apostolicae Sedis* (CIC cc.8.1, 9). Papal laws do not ordinarily become binding until 3 months after announcement in the *Acta.* In the same manner, acts of councils do not bind in the external forum until they have been officially promulgated by the pope (CIC cc.227, 1323). In regard to laws enacted by bishops or by plenary and provincial councils, the method of promulgation is to be determined by the authors of the laws (CIC c.335).

The laws of the Church that have been fully established are not retroactive; however, the law may make provision for special retroactive effects (CIC c.10). The primary effect of the law, the moral obligation, can never be retroactive. Furthermore, the general rule is that all acts are to be judged according to the law that was in force at the time when they were completed. In exceptional cases the law may provide for certain effects in the external forum that can be legally considered to be retroactive. For example, the Code of Canon Law provides for the application of the milder penalty in case of a change in a penal law, even though, strictly speaking, the penal act (delict) ought to be punished according to the penalty stipulated for that act at the time when the crime was committed (CIC c.2226.2).

Cessation of Ecclesiastical Law. Ecclesiastical laws can cease to exist as law without any positive intervention by legitimate authority in two cases: (1) if the circumstances become such that the law becomes positively harmful or unreasonable; (2) if the purpose of the law has entirely ceased for the community. According to CIC c.21, a law passed to guard against a common danger remains binding even in individual cases in which the danger does not exist (CIC cc.199, 409.1, 422, 1028).

Ecclesiastical laws may cease to exist by a positive act of legitimate authority. The promulgation of a new law can revoke a former law in various circumstances (CIC c.22): If the later law is equal in extension to the former law, making it impossible for the two to stand together, or if it deals entirely with the subject matter of the former law. If the later law is universal and the former law is particular, the later law must expressly mention the former in order to repeal it. However, in cases of doubt, the later and former laws are to be considered as still binding and are to be reconciled if possible (CIC c.23).

Obligation of Ecclesiastical Laws. In order that a person be bound by merely ecclesiastical laws, four conditions must be present: he must be baptized; he must have the use of reason; he must have attained 7 years of age; the law must be in force in the place where he is. In theory the Church has jurisdiction over all baptized persons, since it is by Baptism that they are incorporated into the Church (CIC c.87). However, baptized non-Catholics are expressly exempt from ecclesiastical law in certain matters (CIC cc.1099, 1070), and in most other cases they are excused from the observance of Church law by reason of their inculpable ignorance and good faith.

In regard to the age requirement, the general rule is that ecclesiastical laws begin to bind only after the completion of the 6th year of age (or on the 7th birthday), and continue to bind until death (CIC c.12). However, there are exceptions to this rule. Ecclesiastical laws based on divine law begin to bind when the use of reason is acquired (e.g., laws regarding reception of Sacraments in danger of death and the fulfillment of the Easter duty; CIC cc.854.2, 859.1, 906, 940). The law of fasting binds only after the completion of the 21st year and before the inception of the 60th year (CIC c.1254.2). And penal laws that have automatically applicable (i.e., *latae sententiae*) penalties attached to them do not bind before the 14th year (CIC c.2230). Finally, the ecclesiastical law must actually be in force in the place where the individual is (CIC cc.13, 14). This does not pertain to personal laws that bind everywhere. It does have application in regard to a universal law that is not in force in a particular place, for example, when the law of Friday abstinence is dispensed within a given diocese. This principle has special application in the case of particular laws (i.e., laws for a local area). The particular laws of a person's own territory do not bind a person when he is outside his own territory, unless the transgression of such a law would cause harm in his own territory. Furthermore, persons who are visiting a place where there are particular laws are not bound by these laws, except in the following cases: (1) if they have no permanent residence (domicile or quasi-domicile) in any place; (2) if the local laws have to do with legal formalities for judicial acts; (3) if the laws concern the maintenance of public order.

The laws of the Church bind in conscience those subject to them. The obligation to follow a law carries with it the obligation to take the ordinary means (according to one's state) necessary to know and fulfill the law. Not all the laws of the Church have the same gravity of obligation. This is determined by: (1) the matter prescribed by the law, which is measured by the needs of the community, the purpose of the act, etc. (e.g., the obligation of hearing Mass on Sunday is grave by reason of its relationship to the obligation of the Church to worship God); (2) the will of the legislator, manifested in the formulation of the law.

In order to fulfill the obligation of an ecclesiastical law, one must place a "human act," that is, a deliberately willed act. Thus one cannot fulfill his obligation by mere physical presence at Mass. It is not necessary to intend specifically to satisfy the obligation; for example, when attending Mass, one need only to intend to hear Mass. Nor does one have to intend what the law intends him to accomplish by the act prescribed, even though this would be the more virtuous act (e.g., attending Mass to avoid loss of reputation, instead of desiring to worship God). Moreover, if one cannot fulfill the entirety of what the law prescribes, he is obliged to fulfill as much of the law as he can. In regard to the effect of time on the fulfillment of one's obligation, a distinction is necessary. If the time limit expressed in the law was intended to mark the limit for the fulfillment of the obligation (e.g., Lenten fast), the law ceases to bind once the time has elapsed. If the time was stipulated only to urge the fulfillment of the obligation (e.g., Easter duty), the obligation remains even after the time has elapsed. *See* TIME (IN CANON LAW).

Cessation of the obligation in a particular case can take place by reason of an excusing cause intervening or by reason of a *dispensation granted by competent authority. In both cases the act remains in force, but ceases to bind an individual or group of individuals. A person is excused from the observance of merely ecclesiastical laws by reason of moral or physical impossibility. Moral impossibility is present when the observance of the law would constitute a grave inconvenience for the individual. This must be in proportion to the gravity of the law in question, extrinsic to the obligation itself (e.g., the inconvenience of getting up and going to Mass), and provided the act does not bring about scandal or contempt for religion. Other factors excusing one from the observance of ecclesiastical law are ignorance, insanity, and error. At times it is possible that one may be in a state of doubt concerning his obligation. If the doubt concerns the existence, force, extension, or cessation of the law itself, it is called a doubt of law. If it concerns some fact that may or may not bring a given situation under the law, it is called a doubt of fact. The general principle is that if there is a true doubt of law—based on real obscurity of the text or on disputes among canonical writers—the law ceases to oblige. If it is a doubt of fact, the ordinary can dispense as long as it concerns a matter in which the Holy See is accustomed to grant a dispensation (CIC c.15).

It is disputed among canonists whether the Church can bind her subjects to purely internal acts. The common opinion is that it cannot, in that the purpose of the Church's legislative authority is to regulate the external organization and actions of the Christian people.

Interpretation of Ecclesiastical Law. Interpretation of law is the declaration or explanation of the true meaning of the law. There are three main types of interpretation: (1) authentic, that which comes from the one who issued the law (or from his delegate); (2) customary, as the law is interpreted by its practical application; (3) doctrinal, that which is made by anyone with knowledge of the law. Canons 17 to 20 of the Code of Canon Law present various principles regarding interpretation of ecclesiastical law.

Canon 17 gives three general rules regarding authentic interpretation: (1) it is to be made by the legislator or one to whom the authority has been delegated; (2) if the interpretation extends or restricts the law, it must be treated as a new law, requiring promulgation; (3) if it is given by means of a judicial sentence or by means of a particular *rescript, it does not have the force of law and binds only those for whom it was given. In regard to the authentic interpretation of pontifical law, Benedict XIV created a commission of cardinals to interpret the Code authentically.

General principles regarding doctrinal interpretation of ecclesiastical law are given in CIC cc.18 and 19. The primary rule is that they are to be understood first of all in their own proper signification, according to their text and context. If the meaning of the text is obscure, recourse is then to be had to the following: parallel passages of the Code; the purpose and circumstances of the law; and, if possible, the mind of the legislator. The purpose of the law is the reason or motive intended by the law, and not the subjective intention the legislator had in mind. Recourse to the mind of the legislator is had by either examining the practice of the Holy See in similar matters or even by direct consultation with the Code commission.

Canon 19 enumerates three classes of laws that are to receive strict interpretation, that is, a restrictive, narrowing interpretation: (1) laws to which there is attached a canonical sanction, even of an indeterminate nature; (2) laws that limit the free exercise of rights; (3) laws that constitute an exception to the general law.

Canon 20 lists four sources from which a norm may be drawn when the situation is not covered by existing legislation: (1) laws enacted in similar matters, that is, dealing with correlative or equivalent situations; (2) the general principles of law, drawn from the "*rules of law" and jurisprudence, applied with canonical equity; (3) the style and practice of the Roman Curia; (4) the common and consistent teaching of recognized canonists. These norms are ordinarily referred to as "supplementary sources of law," even though a norm established by means of them is not a law in the strict sense of the term.

Bibliography: Principal periodicals. *Apollinaris.* ArchKathK Recht. *Archivio di diritto ecclesiastico* (Rome 1939–). *Il diritto ecclesiastico* (Rome 1890–). EphemIC. *Jurist. Il monitore ecclesiastico* (Rome 1876–). *Monitor ecclesiasticus* (Rome 1876–). PeriodicaMorCanLiturg. RevEspDC. RevDr Can.

General works. Abbo. C. A. Bachofen (C. Augustine), *A Commentary on the New Code of Canon Law,* 8 v. (St. Louis 1918–31), various editions. Bousc-Ellis. A. G. Cicognani, *Canon Law,* tr. J. M. O'Hara and F. Brennan (2d ed. Philadelphia 1934). É. Jombart, *Summary of Canon Law,* tr. R. Bégin (New York 1960). R. Metz, *What Is Canon Law?,* tr. M. Derrick (New York 1960). Michiels Norm. M. Ramstein, *A Manual of Canon Law* (Hoboken 1948). Van Hove, v.1–2. M. Cabreros de Anta et al., *Commentarios al Código de derecho canónico* (BiblAutCrist 223, 225; 1963). DDC. Wernz-Vidal. Woywod-Smith.

Special studies. P. Fedele, "La teoria generale del diritto canonico nella letteratura dell'ultimo decennio," EphemIC 19 (1963) 2–52. B. Frison, *The Retroactivity of Law* (CUA CLS 231; 1946). J. L. Hammill, *The Obligations of the Traveler according to Canon 14* (CUA CLS 160; 1942). M. Huftier, "La Loi ecclésiastique: Sa valeur et son obligation," AmiDuCl 74 (1964) 375–382. C. Kemmeren, "Recent Trends in the Science of Canon Law towards a Theology of Canon Law," *Jurist* 25 (1965) 24–45. J. A. McCloskey, *The Subject of Ecclesiastical Law according to Canon 12* (CUA CLS 165; 1942). C. Lefebvre, "Le Droit naturel et le droit canonique," DDC 6:986–990; "Lois ecclésiastiques: Interpretation," *ibid.* 659–677. R. Naz, "Lois ecclésiastiques," *ibid.* 635–659; "Doute," DDC 4:1437–45; "Droit canonique," *ibid.* 1446–95. L. de Naurois, "Qu'est ce que le droit?" RevDrCan 8 (1958) 164–184, 253–269. L. Örsy, "The Constitutional Law of the Church," Greg 46 (1965) 89–95; "The Life of the Church and the Renewal of Canon Law," *Jurist* 25 (1965) 46–65. V. de Reina, "Eclesiologia y derecho canónico: Notas metodologicas," Rev EspDC 19 (1964) 342–366. E. G. Roelker, *Invalidating Laws* (Paterson, N.J. 1955); *Precepts* (Paterson, N.J. 1955). A. de la Hera and C. Munier, "Le Droit public ecclésiastique à travers ses définitions," RevDrCan 14 (1964) 32–63. J. Salaverri, "El derecho en el mistero de la Iglesia" in *Investigación y elaboración del derecho canónico: Trabajos de la quento Semana de derecho canónico, 1956* (Barcelona 1956). R. E. Rodes, "Canon Law as a Legal System: Function, Obligation, and Sanction," *Natural Law Forum* 9 (1964) 45–94. K. Mörsdorf and A. Hollerbach, LexThK² 6:245–252. F. della Rocca, *Manual of Canon Law,* tr. A. Thatcher (Milwaukee 1959).

[J. M. BUCKLEY]

CANON LAW, HISTORY OF

The nature of the Church as a visible society existing in the world demands that there be a formal legal structure guiding and coordinating the faithful to the attainment of a common goal. The body of these ecclesiastical laws is called *Canon Law. Since there is continual change in society, there is constant change in Canon Law. The history of Canon Law is, in fact, the history of continual borrowing from and adaptation to the milieu in which the Church found herself. The discussion in this article is treated under the following main headings: (1) Early Church, (2) Carolingian Era, (3) False Decretals to Gratian, (4) Classical Period, (5) The Corpus Iuris Canonici to the Council of Trent, (6) The Council of Trent to the Code of Canon Law, and (7) The Code of Canon Law to the Present.

1. Early Church

From the beginning of the 3d century at least, the local Christian community—wherever it was established—possessed adequate and necessary machinery for its government. It had certain stable and universal characteristics: oneness of faith, of ethics, and of cult (especially Baptism and the Eucharist), a monarchial and indivisible episcopacy, the notion of apostolic succession, the distinction between clergy and laity, and finally an awareness of the principle of a *ius ecclesiasticum* (ecclesiastical law). There were as well factors that assured coordination among Christian communities and promoted supralocal unity: the consecration of the bishop by several neighboring bishops; episcopal assemblies; the drawing up of the constitutions of the Church; exchange of episcopal letters; collections of conciliar canons; and, after the advent of the Roman Emperor *Constantine I (313), the support of imperial power. Although it cannot be said that a juridical society in the strict sense existed as yet (for in fact the code of laws was concerned mainly with matters of worship), the bases of the organization of a community were ready at hand in NT writings (cf. Mt 16.18–19; 18.18; 28.18; Jn 10.21; 21.15–17), where the beginnings of a regulatory system can be seen: the Apostolic Council of Antioch of 51 (Acts 15.23–29), matrimonial legislation, excommunication, justice within a community (Mt 18.15–18; 1 Corinthians 5–7).

The internal organization of Christian communities before the end of the 3d century must be reconstructed from sources not specifically juridical: the NT, apocryphal and antiheretical literature of the 2d century, and the writings of the apostolic Fathers and apologists. The most important of these are the letter of the Roman community to the community of Corinth, known as the *Prima Clementis* (Rome, *c.* 96), the Epistle of *Barnabas (Alexandria, 96 to 130), the apocryphal apocalypse known as the *Shepherd of *Hermas* (Rome, *c.* 96 to 140), the letters of *Ignatius of Antioch (d. *c.* 110), and the letter of *Polycarp of Smyrna (d. 167?) to the community of Philippi.

With the 3d century, the Africans Tertullian and Cyprian molded the framework and the vocabulary of Western Law (*institutio, disciplina, regula, successio, sacramentum, ordo, plebs, ius, primatus, cathedra,* etc.). Besides, there were the pseudo-Apostolic Constitutions of the Church, juridico-didactic or juridico-liturgical documents. Written primarily in Greek, these constitutions were soon translated into Arabic, Syriac, Ethiopian, Coptic, and Latin, and constantly corrected and reedited. They were widely diffused and became the foundation of the discipline of the communities. They included the *Doctrina XII Apostolorum* or the *Didache (*c.* 100), which originated in Syria or Palestine; the *Traditio Apostolica* of *Hippolytus of Rome (*c.* 218), which is fundamental for the cult and discipline of the Church of Rome (again written in Greek) and which is the basis for subsequent constitutions; the **Didascalia Apostolorum* (*c.* 250 or 300, Syria or Palestine), the first attempt at a canonical corpus; the *Constitutiones Apostolorum* in eight books (*c.* 400, Syria or Palestine), whose influence was widespread despite subsequent reprobation of *Quinisext, the Council in Trullo (691); the 30 *Canones ecclesiastici Apostolorum* (*c.* 300, Syria or Egypt); the 85 *Canones Apostolorum* (which are books of *Constitutiones Apostolorum*), the first 50 of which are known in the West (notwithstanding their rejection by the *Decretum Gelasianum*); the 38 *Canones Hippolyti,* which were an enlargement of the *Traditio Apostolica* of Hippolytus; the 9 *Canones pseudo-synodi Antiochenae apostolorum* (*c.* 350 to 400, Palestine? Antioch?); the *Constitutiones per Hippolytum* or *Epitome* (post-5th-century); the *Testamentum Domini* (400 to 500, Syria); the 18 and the 25 *Canones paenitentiales apostolorum* (4th century); the *Octateuchus Clementis* (512 or 518? 8th-century Syriac version).

Development of Canon Law in the East to the 7th Century. The first Greek canonical collection preserved in the original text was the *Synagoge Canonum* in 50 titles by John the Scholastic III (*c.* 570). The Oriental collections before this date are accessible only in reconstructions from Latin or Syriac versions. These are conciliar texts that became sources of law by reason of the authority attributed to them by the Churches. Including translations, the Oriental collection prior to the 6th century consists of the following documents: (1) The first deposit embraces the decrees of the Councils of *Ancyra (314), *Neocaesarea (314–325), *Gangra (341–342), Antioch (*c.* 341), and *Laodicea (343–380), compiled under Bishop Meletios of Antioch (*c.* 342–381), and known as the *Corpus canonum* of Antioch. To this were subsequently added (2) the canons of the Councils of *Nicaea I (325) and *Constantinople I (381); this is the collection to which the Fathers of *Chalcedon (451) referred. (3) Finally, after 451, the canons of *Chalcedon were added to the above mentioned documents. The whole collection (1, 2, 3) is known as the **Syntagma canonum Antiochenum,* or the primitive foundation upon which all the ancient collections rested. In about 500 the *Syntagma* was translated into Syriac at Mabbug. During the 6th century (soon after 519), the canons of the Councils of Ephesus (431), Africa (419), and *Sardica (343) and the 85 *Canones Apostolorum* were added. The Council in Trullo, or the *Quinisext Council (691), limited the sources of law to the general and local councils, the Patristic canons, and the Canon of Cyprian (c.2). It is, indeed, this list in the *Collectio Trullana* that constitutes the common foundation of Oriental law.

After the era of Constantine, the emperors often legislated on ecclesiastical matters, as protectors of the Church (e.g., in the *Codex Theodosianus* of 438, bks. 3, 9, and 16). But it was Justinian who exercised a capital, formal, and decisive influence on the development of Canon Law by his religious legislation in the *Corpus Iuris Civilis,* from which excerpts or summaries were soon drawn for the special use of the Church. The imperial laws were added as appendixes to the systematic canonical collections, such as the *Collectio LX titulorum* (*c.* 535) and the *Collectio L titulorum* of John the Scholastic (*c.* 570), to make up mixed collections that prepared the way for a new type of collection, the **Nomocanon.* These latter were collections *utriusque iuris,* combining civil laws and conciliar canons on the same subject.

Pre-Carolingian Law in the West. In the West the history of the most ancient canonical collections is mixed up with the history of the versions. Very early (probably under Julius I, 337–352? and Innocent I, 401–417?), the canons of Nicaea (325) and of Sardica were translated and gathered in the collection *Vetus Romana,* which certainly was in use at the beginning of the 5th century. The so-called *Isidoriana,* or *Hispana Collectio-Versio,* known in three recensions, was probably prepared in Rome between *c.* 419 and 451. The so-called *Prisca,* or *Itala Collectio-Versio,* differs from the *Isidoriana* with respect to the ordering of the canons.

Under the pontificates of Gelasius I (492–496) and his successors until Hormisdas (514–523), there was a fruitful and original juridical activity, born of the Gelasian renaissance. The work no longer consisted merely of translations, but was an ordering of the councils and decretals into a single corpus, with the purpose of unifying and coordinating legislation under the authority of the Roman pontiff and of making it universally obligatory. The most famous work is the *collectio-versio* of *Dionysius Exiguus, the so-called *Dionysiana,* known in at least three editions: the *Prima* (*c.* 497–500), the *Secunda* (beginning of 6th century), and the *Tertia* (before 523). The same Dionysius completed his *collectio-versio* with a *Collectio decretalium* (*c.* 498–514), consisting of decretals from Siricius (384–399) to Anastasius II (496–498), taken either from the archives of the Lateran or from earlier collections. The two Dionysian works, known also as *Liber canonum* and *Liber decretorum* (Zacharias to Pepin in 747) are now called the **Dionysiana Collectio.* Together with the *Dionysiana,* in the same period are (*c.* 495–500) the **Quesnelliana Collectio,* known especially in France, the Freising Collection (after

495), the *Vaticana* (under Hormisdas), the *Sanblasiana,* and the *Teatina* or *Collectio Ingilrami* (soon after 523), all of which pursue the same goal as the *Dionysiana* with varying degrees of success, i.e., the collecting of ancient law and the unifying of it.

The researches of W. H. Peitz call into question the history of the earlier collections up to the 6th century. According to Peitz (1) all the ancient versions, with the exception of the *Vetus Romana,* were prepared by Dionysius Exiguus. The *Prisca* and the *Isidoriana* were thus successive corrections of the same work by the same author. (2) Before Dionysius, there was no collection at all, in either Greek or Latin. Even the *Syntagma canonum antiochenum* is a work of Dionysius circulating in the East. The same applies to the *Corpus canonum* of the African Church. (3) Collections such as the *Frisingensis* or the *Quesnelliana* derive from the *Dionysiana* in varying degrees. If these conclusions are accepted, they will necessitate the rewriting of the history of the sources anterior to the 6th century.

The Italian collections subsequent to the Gelasian renaissance (*Dionysiana*) and prior to the Carolingian renaissance (*Dionysio-Hadriana*) are of minor importance, except for the following collections of decretals: the *Thessalonicensis* (*c.* 531), the **Avellana* (*c.* 555) and the *Mutinensis* (*c.* 601).

Canon Law in the Spanish Church. Juridical activity in Spain was characterized from its origins by a concern for unification. Few documents (versions, decretals) have survived from the period before the Visigothic invasion. Beginning with the conversion of Recaredo (586), close ties were forged between the civil power and the hierarchy, favoring the establishment of solid institutions. With the Council of *Toledo (589) there began a conciliar activity unique in the Church for its regularity and conservatism. It resulted in the *Collectio Hispana chronologica,* the so-called *Isidoriana* (falsely attributed to Isidore of Seville, d. 636). Based on the *Dionysiana,* this collection was drawn up at the Council of Toledo (633); between then and the 17th Council of Toledo (694) it was increased by 104 decretals (from Damasus, 366–384, to Gregory I, 604). To facilitate its use, a *Tabula* (systematic summary) was composed, followed later by *Excerpta* along the same lines. When the extracts in the *Excerpta* were replaced by complete texts from the *Collectio,* the *Hispana chronologica* then became what is known as the *Hispana systematica* (in Spain, end of 7th century; or in Gaul, *c.* 800).

Systematic Collections of the African Church. The African Church, particularly in the persons of Tertullian and Cyprian, molded the vocabulary of law. Versions were always held in honor there, such as the *Caeciliani Versio* (beginning of 5th century) and the two versions established at the time of the Apiarian controversy: the *Attici Versio* and the *Cyrilli Versio.* The *Corpus canonum orientale* was translated for the first time in Africa (*Corpus canonum Africanum*). Among the canonical collections there may be noted the *Breviarium* of Hippo (393) and the *Collectio concilii Cartaginensis* 17 (419), known also as the *Codex canonum Ecclesiae Africanae.* Both the West and the East owed their acquaintance with African canons to the text of this collection. The Vandal invasion and persecution (after 429) put an end to the vitality of the African Church; even after the restoration of the hierarchy under Justinian (534), conciliar activity did not revive. Production was confined to systematic compilations: the *Breviatio canonum* of Fulgentius Ferrandus in 232 chapters (*c.* 546), and the *Concordia canonum* attributed to a bishop, Cresconius, but actually compiled in the 6th or 7th century. The latter is a systematic classification of the chronological collections of Dionysius Exiguus (according to Peitz, this would in fact be one of Dionysius' works). The Arabian invasion permanently destroyed the African Church.

Gallic Collections. In Gaul, as in the Spanish Church but with less continuity and centralism, the conciliar activity was active until the end of the 7th century (Council of Saint-Jean-de-Losne, 673–675). During the troubled years of the accession to power of the mayors of the Palace of Austrasia (the future Carolingians) toward 740, the Frankish Church went through a period of profound decadence. The Gallic collections up to the Carolingian renaissance are as follows: the **Statuta Ecclesiae antiqua* (*c.* 476–485), the *Collectio Arelatensis* or the (pseudo) Council of Arles II (442–506), the *Andegavensis* I (after 450), and perhaps the *Quesnelliana.* In the 6th century there was the *Liber auctoritatum,* or *Liber canonum,* of the Church of Arles (*c.* 560–595), as well as various collections: the *Corbeiensis,* the *Coloniensis,* the *Albigensis,* the *Lugdunensis,* the *Remensis I,* the *Lauresheimensis* (Lorsch), the *Pithouensis,* the *Bigotiana,* the *Collectio S. Mauri,* and the Collection of Saint-Amand. To the period immediately preceding the Carolingian period belong the Andegavensis II, which is relatively well ordered, and the *Herovalliana* (*c.* 740), which is badly ordered and corrupt. Neither collection was of a quality to arrest in any way the deterioration that law was undergoing.

Decline and Decentralization of Discipline. In fact, from the end of the paleo-Christian era (late 6th century) until the Carolingian renaissance (from the 2d half of the 8th century), a period of anarchy and decadence reigned in the Church, as a result of the breaking up of the *Imperium* after the invasions, and of the progressive and turbulent rise of the national kingdoms. The sources of law reflect this situation: there are local peculiarities and a confusion in discipline and in worship.

From the time of the invasions the new law of the conquerors had been juxtaposed to Roman law. However, because of the personal character of the Roman laws, the *Lex romana* continued to be applied to the persons and things of the Church, which were considered as "Roman." Hence special collections were compiled for the use of persons subject to Roman law: the *Lex romana Visigothorum* or the *Breviarium* of Alaric (*c.* 506), the *Edictum Theodorici* (beginning of the 6th century), the *Lex romana Burgundionum* (beginning of 6th century), and the *Lex romana Curiensis* or *Raetica* (8th century). *See* LEGES ROMANAE BARBARORUM.

From the 6th to the 12th centuries Germanic law contributed increasingly to the formation of Canon Law, because of the ascendancy of the Franks and later of the Empire in the life of the Church. The collections of Germanic law, which were all composed after the conversion of the peoples to Christianity, already reflected the influence of the Church: the *Lex Salica* (*c.* 500, and versions until *c.* 750), the *Lex Ripuaria* (6th–

8th centuries), the *Lex Francorum Chamavorum* (c. 802 or 803), the *Lex barbara Burgundionum* or *Lex Gundobaldi* (end of 5th century), the *Lex Alamannorum* (beginning of 7th century), the *Lex Baïwarorum* (c. 750), the *Lex Frisonum* (8th or 9th century), the *Lex Saxorum* (beginning 9th century), the *Lex Thuringorum* or *Lex Anglorum* (beginning 9th century), the *Lex barbara Visigothroum* (466 or 485–649 or 672), the *Leges Langobardorum* (whose first collation of 643 is known as the *Edictum Rothari*).

To these documents should be added the acts emanating from the royal power, such as the *Capitularies and the *Diplomata.* A very concrete source of law is provided by the *Formularies, collections of formulas used for the authentic production of civil or ecclesiastical acts. Such for example were the 400 *Formulae* of the Ostrogothic Kingdom collected by Cassiodorus *c.* 537 under the name of *Variae,* and the *Formulae* of Marculf (*c.* 660). All the other collections of Formulae, including the famous **Liber diurnus Romanorum Pontificum* (from 590 to 795) are not from this period.

Penitentials. From the Insular Churches (i.e., those of the British Isles: England, Wales, Scotland, Ireland), where there prevailed juridical peculiarities in organization and discipline, a penitential system based on a scale of penances, and differing from the ancient *Paenitentia* of the Church, spread to the Continent through missionary monks and the numerous *libri paenitentiales* that appeared from the 6th century onward. These *penitentials contain catalogues of sins and the corresponding scales of penances and were of great importance both for penitential discipline and for the history of morals and customs. The penitentials were also an effective instrument of civilization through their regulations on hygiene and food.

Bibliography: Maassen. Fournier-LeBras. Kuttner. I. A. Zeiger, *Historia iuris canonici,* 2 v. (Rome 1940–47). B. Kurtscheid and F. A. Wilches, *Historia iuris canonici,* 2 v. (Rome 1941–43). Van Hove. Stickler. W. M. Plöchl, *Geschichte des Kirchenrechts,* 3 v. (Vienna 1953–59). H. E. Feine, *Kirchliche Rechtsgeschichte,* v.1, *Die Katholische Kirche* (3d ed. Weimar 1955). J. Gaudemet, *L'Église dans l'Empire romain* (Paris 1958). J. J. Ryan, "Observations on the Pre-Gratian Canonical Collections," *Actes du Congrès de Droit Canonique médiéval* (Louvain 1958). W. M. Peitz, *Dionysius Exiguus-Studien,* ed. H. Foerster (Berlin 1960). A. Coussa, *Epitome praelectionum de iure ecclesiastico orientali,* 3 v. (Grottaferrata-Rome 1948–50; suppl. 1958). G. Le Bras et al., eds., *Histoire du droit et des institutions de l'Église en Occident* (Paris 1955–) v.1, *Prolégomenès.* E. Schwartz, ZSavRGKan 25, 56 (1936) 1–114.

[C. VOGEL]

2. Carolingian Era

In about the middle of the 8th century, the Franks began to take over the protection of the Latin Church. Spain was Arab, England isolated, and the Eastern Roman Empire, alienated from the Western Church after the Trullan Council (692) and weakened by the iconoclast controversy, had quarreled with the papacy, which in turn sought support among the Franks against the Lombards. The consolidation of the Frankish Church had been intimately connected with the development of the Austrasian Carolingians. Imbued as he was with Germanic notions of a private church, the major-domo Charles Martel (d. 741) had parceled out Church lands and offices to laymen; he did indeed support missionary activity (of Willibrord, Pirmin, Boniface), but he did not trouble himself with Canon Law or constitutions. The last known conference of bishops had been in about 680, and there was no longer any metropolitan organization.

When he took over the duties of a king, Martel's son Pepin (742–768), together with his brother Carloman until 747, and in accord with the ideas of the Pope, set about strengthening ecclesiastical organization. Though Pepin may have disappointed the Pope after his acquisition of the royal title in 751, a title and legitimation for which he had the Pope to thank, he did lay the groundwork of a Rome-oriented Canon Law, and this was of importance for the future.

Canon Law of the Merovingian Period. Under the Merovingians, the independence of the national churches had come strongly to the fore, both in the field of liturgy and in the field of Canon Law; the universal collections (e.g., **Dionysiana,* later **Hispana*) had been supplemented since as early as the 6th century (perhaps stemming from Arles) by works of a more local coloring. There had indeed been attempts to combine the two principles, the universal and the local [cf. the *Collectio Andegavensis,* probably initiated by Leodegar of Autun (d. 679 or 680) and the *Herovalliana* from the first half of the 8th century]. But hope of success was assured only when the Monarch began to interest himself in a unification of Canon Law. Pepin himself requested from Pope Zacharias a rescript on Canon Law in 747.

The insular *penitentials, brought by the Irish-Scottish and Anglo-Saxon missionaries, exercised an influence on the Frankish Church, independently of the general collections. With their highly developed casuistry and their tendency to replace protracted mild penances by short strict ones (redemption principle), these insular penitentials became widely disseminated and began to supplant the comparatively meager penitential instructions of the ancient Church.

Carolingian Ecclesiastical Reform. The aim of the Carolingian ecclesiastical reform initiated by Pepin was to reduce the divergent institutions and tendencies of Canon Law into a unity dictated by the Carolingian monarchy and supported by the clergy and imperial nobility. Anyone who, like U. Stutz or H. E. Feine, speaks of an "irruption of Germanism into canon law" and a period of "Germanically cast canon law" extending down to Gratian (1140), simply because the lower echelons of the Church were being reorganized according to the idea of the private church is looking at a broad reform in a way that narrows it to a mere portion of itself and then regards it from a merely modern legal-dogmatic point of view. For the ecclesiastical organization as a whole was restored; every diocese was given a bishop to whom monasteries and foundations were subordinated; the metropolitan constitution was renewed—so that Charlemagne (768–814) could already list 21 metropolitans in the Empire as a whole in his testament of 811.

Implementation. The monarchs used reform councils and legislation to raise the level of ecclesiastical life; the bishops used diocesan synods and *capitula episcoporum.* The series of reform councils began in Austrasia with the *Concilium Germanicum* (probably 743), continued in Neustria (Soissons) in 744 and by 745–747 embraced the entire Empire. The important reform councils were: imperial Councils of Heristal (779) and Frankfurt (794), where Charlemagne tackled questions of dogmatic theology and recognized the institution of the private church; the Council of Aachen (816–817), which newly defined the status of canons; the Council of Paris (829).

On many occasions, ecclesiastical *capitularies were promulgated in connection with the conciliar decisions. The *Admonitio generalis* of 798 was of fundamental importance for the discipline of the Church; and the *Capitulare* of 802, for the program of the new Emperor. There appears to have been no official collection of the numerous capitularies. From 829 it was customary to refer in the capitularies to the private collection of Abbot St. *Ansegis of Fontenelle (d. 833), which had come into existence shortly before but which included barely 30 per cent of the capitularies from the preceding 50 years; the Pseudo-Isidorean collection of capitularies of *Benedict the Levite claimed to be a continuation of this Ansegis collection. Of importance for the life and practice of the Church were the *capitula episcoporum,* episcopal instructions to the diocesan clergy that often exerted an influence far beyond the time and diocese of the promulgator (*Theodulf of Orléans, Chaerbald of Lüttich, Hincmar of Reims).

Collections of Canon Law. When ecclesiastical regulations had been unified, the general collections regained prestige. This no doubt was due to their practicability and suitability, as well as to a newly awakened esteem for ecclesiastical authority, particularly that of the ancient plenary councils and papal decretals. Capitularies and councils made extensive reference to the general collections, and Pope Adrian I delivered to Charlemagne in 774 a model code that contained the councils and the collection of Decretals of *Dionysius Exiguus (i.e., *Dionysio-Hadriana*). The **Quesnelliana* can be traced in Carolingian capitularies in 755 (MG Cap 14); from 789 (MGCap 22), and perhaps even from 779, until about 830 the *Dionysio-Hadriana* or the *Dionysiana* was the almost exclusive source; in West Frankish capitularies, the *Hispana* appeared before the middle of the 9th century. Similarly in the councils after 800, the *Dionysio-Hadriana* was evidently the standard collection (Aachen 836, perhaps also the **Dacheriana*); but it is doubtful whether the **Hadriana* was granted official recognition at the Council of Aachen of 802. Pope Nicholas I (858–867) certainly spoke of the *Hadriana* as the *Codex Canonum* (Jaffé E 2785). *Dacheriana* was compiled about the year 800(?) from the *Hadriana* and the *Hispana,* and is considered to be the real achievement of the Frankish reform, whose efforts slackened about 830. Among the reform collections must finally be listed the *False Decretals (Pseudo-Isidorean forgeries), which, however, together with the Roman law brought to light in the 9th century, had but little influence on Carolingian Canon Law.

With the return to the ancient Canon Law, there was a corresponding revision of the penitential regulations. The provincial synods of Reims, Arles, Châlon-sur-Saône, and Tours were held at the command of Charlemagne in 813 and their decisions were officially compiled (this being the only known instance of a systematic collection of decisions of Carolingian reform synods). They were attempting to counteract the confusion created by the various contradictory penitentials, and to direct attention back to the general collections. In 829 a direct order was given to do away with the penitentials, and attempts were made to replace them with new ones. Witness to this reform effort is the penitential of Bp. Haltigar of Cambrai (817–831), compiled probably about 829. *Rabanus Maurus (d. 856), whose special concern was the canonical instruction of the clergy, compiled two penitentials of a similar character (841–847; 853), based mainly on the *Hadriana* and the *Hispana.* But the influence of the old penitentials could not be eradicated, and the attempt as well to reinstate the *poenitentia publica* that had been supplanted by private confessional practice had only a short-lived success.

Carolingian Theory of Canon Law. There was no ecclesiastical jurisprudence as such in Carolingian days. A start was made on a theory of the sources of law, but there was a lack of theoretical and systematic investigation and of scholarly institutions. Writings on Canon Law were occasioned usually by ecclesiastical and political controversies; and it is significant that it was precisely men involved in politics and in theological controversy who occupied themselves with Canon Law.

The older generation (centering around Charlemagne), under the stimulus of newly flourishing theology, began to devote attention to the role of authority (*auctoritas*) and reason (*ratio*), and was chiefly interested in reform, thereby collaborating with the monarch. The Spanish-born Bp. *Theodulf of Orléans (d. 821), a man well informed in legal process, produced influential capitularies; Bp. Remedius of Chur (d. *c.* 806) attempted in his *Capitula* to effect a synthesis of Roman, Germanic, and Frankish penal law; Bp. Ghaerbald of Lüttich (d. 809), put the instructions of Charlemagne into practice.

The faltering regime of Louis the Pious and numerous lay encroachments divided the empire into factions. Some men, e.g., the theologically trained Bp. Jonas of Orléans (d. 843), felt themselves protectors and guides of the King; Jonas remained loyal to Emperor Louis when the Emperor's elder sons rose against him. On the opposing side stood Abp. Agobard of Lyons (d. 840), a representative of "Carolingian rationalism." He called upon Emperor Louis to extend the law of the Franks to the entire Empire in order to eliminate the multiplicity of indigenous tribal laws (principle of personal law). For him, to act against the canons meant to act against God, and he earnestly called for the restitution of all ecclesiastical property held by laymen. Agobard supported Louis's sons and lost his archdiocese, in which, however, his faithful assistant, Deacon Florus (d. *c.* 860), a man thoroughly familiar with Canon Law and Roman law, continued to be active. He was certainly echoing his master when he demanded the *privilegium fori* for clerics and episcopal jurisdiction. The most prolific scholar in questions of Canon Law seems indeed to have been Abp. *Hincmar of Reims (d. 882). Despite the considerable number of his writings on the subject of Canon Law, he does not present an accurate picture of the Canon Law of that time. His chief concern was to strengthen the power of metropolitans and synods, and it was only reluctantly that he allowed Pope Nicholas I the last word in their controversy. The achievement of the Carolingian canonists was that they again enhanced the prestige of the canonical traditions of the ancient Church. They did indeed mold tradition according to their ideas, but without them the Latin Church might have dissolved into individual churches; at least the ties of unity would have been dangerously loosened.

Bibliography: General. Maassen. É. LESNE, *La Hiérarchie épiscopale . . . 742–882* (Lille 1905); *Histoire de la propriété ecclésiastique en France,* 6 v. in 8 (Lille 1910–43), v.2. A. WERMINGHOFF, *Verfassungsgeschichte der deutschen Kirche im Mittelalter* (2d ed. Leipzig 1913). H. VON SCHUBERT, *Geschichte der christlichen Kirche im Frühmittelalter* (Tübingen 1921). R. SOHM, *Das altkatholische Kirchenrecht und das Dekret Gratians,* ed. E. JACOBI and O. MAYER (Munich 1918). Fournier-LeBras. E. RÖSSER, *Göttliches und menschliches, unveränderliches und veränderliches Kirchenrecht . . . bis zur Mitte des 9. Jahrhunderts* (Paderborn 1934). Van Hove v.1. Stickler. Wattenbach-Levison suppl. *Die Rechtsquellen,* ed. R. BUCHNER (1953). G. LE BRAS et al., eds., *Histoire du droit et des institutions de l'Église en Occident* (Paris 1955–) v.1 *Prolégomènes.* G. LE BRAS, *Institutions ecclésiastiques de la chrétienté médiévale* (Fliche-Martin 12; 1959). W. M. PLÖCHL, *Geschichte des Kirchenrechts,* v.1 (2d ed. Vienna 1960). H. E. A. FEINE, *Kirchliche Rechtsgeschichte* (4th ed. Cologne 1964–) v.1. J. J. RYAN, "Observations on the Pre-Gratian Canonical Collections: Some Recent Work and Present Problems," *Congrès de Droit Canonique Médiéval Louvain et Bruxelles, 22–26 Juillet* (Louvain 1959) 88–103.

8th Century. E. LOENING, *Geschichte des deutschen Kirchenrechts,* 2 v. (Strasbourg 1878) v.2. F. ZEHETBAUER, *Das Kirchenrecht bei Bonifatius* (Vienna 1910). H. NOTTARP, "Sachkomplex und Geist des kirchlichen Rechtsdenkens bei Bonifatius" in *Sankt Bonifatius: Gedenkgabe zum zwölfhundertsten Todestag* (Fulda 1954). T. SCHIEFFER, *Winifried-Bonifatius und die christliche Grundlegung Europas* (Freiburg 1954). G. LE BRAS, "Pénitentiels," DTC 12.1:1160–79. J. T. MCNEILL and H. M. GAMER, trs., *Medieval Handbooks of Penance* (New York 1938). L. BIELER, ed., *The Irish Penitentials,* app., D. A. BINCHY (Scriptores Latini Hiberniae 5; Dublin 1963).

Reform. U. STUTZ, "Das Karolingische Zehntgebot," ZSavRG Germ 29 (1908) 180–224. H. FICHTENAU, *Das karolingische Imperium* (Zurich 1949). É. DELARUELLE, "Charlemagne et l'Église," RevHistEglFrance 39 (1953) 165–199. H. BARION, *Das fränkisch-deutsche Synodalrecht des Frühmittelalters* (Bonn 1931). C. DE CLERCQ, *La Législation religieuse franque . . .,* 2 v. (Paris-Antwerp 1936–58). J. SEMMLER, "Reichsidee und kirchliche Gesetzgebung," ZKirchgesch 71 (1960) 37–65. F. L. GANSHOF, *Was waren die Kapitularien?* (Weimar 1961). H. HÜRTEN, "Alkuin und der Episkopat im Reiche Karls des Grossen," HistJb 82 (1963) 22–49. W. A. ECKHARDT, *Die Kapitulariensammlung Bischof Ghaerbalds von Lüttich* (Göttingen 1955). J. RAMBAUD-BUHOT, "Une Collection canonique de la réforme carolingienne," RevHistDrFranÉtr 33 (1956) 50–73.

Theory. For individual authors, see Wattenbach-Levison, with extensive bibliog. J. FLECKENSTEIN, *Die Bildungsreform Karls des Grossen* (Freiburg 1953). L. WALLACH, *Alcuin and Charlemagne* (Ithaca, N.Y. 1959), reviewed by H. LÖWE in GöttGel Anz 214 (1962) 144–153. H. DÖRRIES, "Die geistigen Voraussetzungen und Folgen der Karolingischen Reichsteilung 843" in *Der Vertrag von Verdun 843,* ed. T. MAYER (Leipzig 1943). J. DEVISSE, *Hincmar et la loi* (Dakar 1962). H. BACHT, "Hinkmar von Reims" in *Unio Christianorum: Festschrift für Erzbischof Dr. Lorenz Jaeger* (Paderborn 1962).

[H. FUHRMANN]

3. False Decretals to Gratian

The Carolingian reform had striven to unify and restore Canon Law: composite collections had been for the most part eliminated; and the return to the ancient texts of the universal law, approved by the Church of Rome (Dionysio-Hadriana) had restored to their place of honor the traditional rules respecting the ecclesiastical hierarchy, penitential discipline, the institution of marriage, and judicial order. However, the Church was still undergoing many trials: seizure of ecclesiastical property by secular rulers, abuses of the privilege of the forum, and all sorts of obstacles to the exercise of episcopal power.

It was in this context that the Isidorian forgeries (*False Decretals) were put into circulation (847–857) alleging incontestable authorities for texts decreeing much needed reforms. Generally faithful to traditional law, the False Decretals innovated on certain points and exercised a considerable influence on canonical literature. They reinforced the episcopal power, generalized the principle of appeal to Rome in important cases, broadened the privilege of the forum, regularized judicial procedure (*Spoliatus ante omnia est restituendus*), and reemphasized the sacred character of ecclesiastical property.

From the 10th to the middle of the 11th century, Canon Law underwent a period of decline; it suffered, in effect, from the weakening of the authority of the Holy See, which resulted from the interference of the Roman aristocracy and the Germanic emperors. It was characterized by an extreme fragmentation, as was the political power of the day, which was bound up with the parceling out of feudal lands, the contemporary culture, which was then sheltered in monasteries, and the economy itself, which was essentially tied to the land and was domestic and stagnant. The Church and its law were narrowly dependent on these concrete conditions; it underwent a partial laicization through the system of private churches (*Eigenkirchen*) and had to depend on the local authorities to carry out its moral mission, slowly and with difficulty. This latter function had to be accomplished in the most diverse areas: in struggles against superstition, immorality and violence; in the defense of the lower classes; etc. Progress was neither uniform nor constant, often being compromised by upheavals, wars, primitive customs, and such calamities as famines and epidemics.

In the absence of an active and respected central power, the most noteworthy canonical works of this era were the local collections, of limited scope, composed by private authors. These generally manifest no critical sense in the choice of texts, which they treat with extreme liberty (by interpolations, false attributions, composition of apocrypha) with a view to adapting them to local needs or their own reforming intentions. In the midst of an abundant but uneven output, several works merit particular mention: in Italy, the collection called **Anselmo dedicata, Collectio,* dedicated to Abp. Anselm of Milan (882–896) and the *Collectio libri quinque* (1015–20); in Germany, the *Libri duo de synodalibus causis et disciplinis ecclesiasticis,* dedicated by *Regino of Prüm (d. 915) to Abp. Atto of Mainz; in France, the Collection of *Abbo of Fleury (988–996), addressed to King Hugh and King Robert. But the most celebrated work of this period is the *Decretum* of *Burchard, Bishop of Worms (1000–25), which sets forth the principles that should govern imperial reform. A protegé of Emperor Henry II, Burchard relied on the support of the secular powers for reorganizing the Church and maintaining the discipline of the clergy and of the Christian people.

The Gregorian Reform. The optimism of Burchard nonetheless lacked foresight, for a true reform of Christian society could not be effectively brought about unless it was begun from the very center, free from self-interested interventions of secular powers, and carried out in line with the spiritual mission of the Church.

Such would be the principles animating the *Gregorian reform: the primacy of the Holy See, the independence of the Church, and fidelity to tradition. The decree of Nicholas I (1059) confining papal elections to the cardinals constituted a decisive step in the emancipation of pontifical power. Now that the Church was free at the summit and the supreme authority of the sovereign pontiff was restored, indispensable reforms could be progressively extended to all Christendom.

Gregorian teaching made the sovereign pontiff the primary source of ecclesiastical law (*Dictatus Papae* 17). He exercises authority through councils, over which he presides and whose decisions he approves, and through written responses (decretals), which he gives whenever he is consulted on a disputed point. The pope also guarantees the authority of the texts expressing the common law of the Church. In order to restore to honor the authentic sources of a canonical tradition that they claimed was continuous, the Gregorians carried out research in libraries and archives in Rome and throughout Italy. They unearthed a great number of new fragments, favorable to the rights of the Roman Church (**Liber Diurnus, Ordines Romani,* and, above all, decretals, collected in the *Britannica*) or capable of providing support for reforming measures [ancient councils, patristic texts, Roman law (the *Authentica* and *Pandecta*)]. These texts supplemented the Gregorian collections, the best known of which are the **Dictatus Papae,* attributed to Gregory VII; the *Breviarium* of *Atto of Vercelli; the *Collectio Libri Duo;* the *Collection of *Seventy-four Titles;* and the collections of *Anselm II of Lucca and of Cardinal Deusdedit (*Deusdedit Collectio).

The controversies over the burning issues of the day (the power of the papacy, the validity of Sacraments conferred by simoniacal clergy, law investiture, oaths, reordination, etc.) provoked an abundant polemical literature. Many theological questions are treated in these writings, and the argumentation is rarely objective and dispassionate, but the discussions favored the progress of canonical science. Authorities are discussed, compared, interpreted; their particular force is evaluated and related to the jurisdictional primacy of Rome.

Urban II to Gratian. After the reign of Gregory VII (1073–85), precisely because the principle of the primacy had triumphed to such an extent that it had obscured the original doctrinal aspects of the reform, it became possible to moderate the overly rigorous measures of the Gregorian reform by the frequent use of dispensations and the reconciliation of guilty clerics, particularly in the pontificates of Urban II (1088–99) and Paschal II (1099–1118). But the initial indulgence of Urban II was not approved by some, such as *Bonizo of Sutri, who in his *Liber de vita christiana* (1089–95) showed himself a partisan of the rigorist Gregorian position, or by the anonymous author of the *Britannica* (*c.* 1090).

On the other hand, the **Polycarpus* of Cardinal Gregory (1104–13), while Gregorian in tendency, reflects the more conciliatory influence of *Ivo, Bishop of Chartres (1091–1116), the classic representative of the French canonical tradition. Favorable to reform, respectful of the papal primacy, Ivo was no less careful to maintain peaceful relations between Church and State, with prudence, moderation, and realism. He accepted lay investiture on condition that it be limited to temporalities and conferred only after legitimate election and consecration; he suggested thereby the solution that had been adopted in England (1102) and in France (1107), and which at Worms (1122) would reestablish peace between the papacy and the Empire. An enlightened pacifist, Ivo wanted to limit recourse to war and to extend the machinery of peace (*Peace of God), while admitting the right of recourse to arms to defend rights unjustly violated. The divorce of King Philip I (1092) and other cases that were submitted to him gave him an opportunity to develop more precisely the doctrine of marriage (*Decretum,* VIII–IX; *Panormia* VI–VII). With regard to ecclesiastical law, Ivo counseled tempering strict justice with mercy, for the supreme law of ecclesiastical government is of the pastoral order: the salvation of souls and the building up of the kingdom of God in charity, which is the fulfillment of the law (*Prologue,* PL 161:47C, 58D). The *Liber de misericordia et de justitia* of *Alger of Liège (*c.* 1105) expressed the same ideal.

A conservative and moderate spirit, Ivo did not reject indiscriminately the traditional texts of the methodical collections (the *Decretum* of *Burchard and the *penitentials) condemned by the Gregorians, but strove to bring them into harmony with the new trends and authorities, drawing inspiration from and adapting rules laid down by *Bernold of Constance. The latter (1054–1100) had set forth excellent principles on the sources of Canon Law and the rules of interpretation and concordance of texts. He urged canonists to reject apocrypha, analyze each fragment according to circumstances of time, place, and persons that occasioned its composition; then to determine the nature of the rule laid down, its permanent or temporary character. To these rules, as adopted and developed by the prologue of Ivo (PL 161:47–60), the preface to Abelard's *Sic et Non* (PL 178:1339–49), *c.* 1115–17, added remarks of a semantic and dialectic order that were to profit canonists and theologians alike. In this manner, canonical science was gradually organized, arming itself with a method suitable for resolving the conflicts of authorities. The choice of texts and arguments became rigorous, and juridical rules were formulated with more precision. Besides, the renaissance of Roman law at Bologna at the end of the 11th century exerted a happy influence on canonists. (*See* ROMAN LAW, HISTORY OF, 7.)

Byzantine Law to 1054. From the 7th century until the break of July 16, 1054, the history of the Canon Law of the Byzantine Church was dominated by three factors: the fixing of legislation, the composition of systematic collections, and the growth of canonical science.

In 691–692 the *Quinisext Synod (in Trullo) met at Constantinople to revise and complete the legislation of the fifth and sixth ecumenical councils (Constantinople, 553, 680–681). The 102 canons then promulgated were for the most part a repetition of previous legislation, but canon 2 was of decisive importance for the Canon Law of the Oriental Churches; it enumerated the sources of this law to the exclusion of all other documents, so much so that the collections produced according to its specifications constitute the common *fontes* of Oriental Canon Law. After the councils of Nicaea (787) and Constantinople (869) the Orient had no general councils; ecclesiastical questions were henceforth decided by the patriarch of Constantinople (with his synod of bishops located in, or visiting, the capital), or by the secular authorities (legislation of the basilicas).

The composition of systematic collections, begun *c.* 535 with the *Collection in 60 Titles* and the various

Nomocanones, was continued in new collections. The most important of these collections is the *Nomocanon in 14 Titles,* composed *c.* 630 by the jurisconsult Enantiophanes. As its name indicates, the work resembles both the civil laws (third part) and ecclesiastical documents (second part); the first part gives the titles that divide the canonical material. A second edition of this work dates from 883; it is generally attributed to the patriarch *Photius (857–886) and was recognized in 920 as the official collection of the Church of Constantinople. It was brought up to date by Theodore Bestès in 1080. (*See* NOMOCANON.)

The canonical science of the Oriental Church is noteworthy for the composition of systematic commentaries, expounding the ensemble of legislation then in force, both canonical and imperial. The first commentator seems to have been Theodore Prodramus (8th century); the most famous are John *Zonaras, Alexis Aristenes (beginning of the 12th century), and Theodore *Balsamon. The method followed by these authors was inspired by the rules of jurisprudence of Justinian. After the paraphrase, giving the general sense of the text, come the *scholia:* explanations of difficult terms, and circumstances of composition. Then the author compares, if need be, decisions relative to the same topic and points out their application. He proposes questions and cases and gives their solutions, illustrated by patriarchal decrees and imperial constitutions. It is incontestable that the canonical science manifested by the great Oriental commentators surpasses that of contemporary Western canonists, who were still seeking a properly scientific method.

Bibliography: Fournier-LeBras 1:127–456; 2:1–352. Van Hove 1:157–164, 216–233, 293–342. Stickler 67–72, 117–195, 407–410. S. KUTTNER, "Liber Canonicus: A Note on Dictatus Papae c. 17," StGreg 2 (1947) 387–401. MGLibLit. Sacred Congregation for the Eastern Church, *Codificazione canonica orientale: Fonti* (Vatican City 1930–), ser.1, fasc.8. *Studi storici sulle fonti del diritto canonico orientale.* C. DE CLERCQ, DDC 2:1170–84. A. WUYTS, *Catholicisme* 3:1109–16. *Traditio,* an annual with summary of recent bibliog.

[C. MUNIER]

4. CLASSICAL PERIOD

The time from the *Decretum* of *Gratian (*c.* 1140) to the death of the canonist *Joannes Andreae (1348) was the classical period in the history of Western Canon Law; for the scientific study of the canons of the Church was begun by Gratian and reached its climax in the works of Joannes Andreae. During this period the Church, for the first time, promulgated official collections of universally binding laws: the *Decretals of *Gregory IX* in 1234; the **Liber Sextus* in 1298; and the **Clementinae* in 1317. These remained the only authenticated collections of decretal legislation and became the center of the **Corpus Iuris Canonici* that governed the Western Church from 1582 until the *Code of Canon Law of 1917.

Before the *Concordia discordantium canonum* or *Decretum* of Gratian there was available the confusing wealth of written traditions described in the preceding sections of this article. Time and again efforts had been made to reform and unify this tradition (*see* CANONICAL COLLECTIONS BEFORE GRATIAN), most strikingly in the *Decretum* of *Burchard of Worms (*c.* 1023), but none of these was regarded as adequate by the reforming party that came to the fore in the Church of the 11th century. Coherence and universality were lacking, and the reformers turned to more ancient sources (*see* GREGORIAN REFORM). However, the preoccupations of these reformers led them to suppress as contradictory of papal authority a great portion of the Franco-Germanic tradition. This led to greater confusion. Most of the *Decretum* of Burchard reappeared in the influential *Decretum* (*c.* 1096) of *Ivo of Chartres; the situation was complicated by competition between varying types of collections and by numerous contradictions between texts appealed to by champions of reform and those advanced by their opponents. At the turn of the 11th century, as the fires of the investiture controversy died away and the reformers began to understand that the enforcement of full reform would be impossible in practice, there was a search for a workable system of interpretation of texts that would at once make for unity within the Church and allow a reconciliation between the Roman and the suspect Franco-Germanic traditions. The chief figures in this movement were *Bernold of Constance (*De excommunicatis vitandis, c.* 1091), Ivo of Chartres (prologue "De consonantia canonum" to his *Panormia, c.* 1096), and *Alger of Liège (*Liber de misericordia, c.* 1105). Adapting certain principles of Biblical and rhetorical hermeneutics to the study of the canons, they separated precept from counsel and principles of eternal validity from those affected by conditions of time, place, or person.

This quest of a sure way through the thickets of canonical tradition was paralleled by efforts of theologians with respect to their sources; as had been made clear by *Lanfranc in his criticism of the Eucharistic theology of *Berengarius of Tours, the problem of the authenticity, reconciliation, and interpretation of sources was crucial also to theology. It was, in fact, a theologian who gave the final sheen to the rules of interpretation and principles of textual criticism adumbrated by Bernold and Ivo and practiced to some extent by Alger. About 1115 to 1117 Peter *Abelard developed these principles in a theological setting in the preface of his *Sic et Non* (PL 178:1344–49), a treatise in which patristic texts are played off dialectically against one another in order to arrive at a balanced, coherent tradition. A method of scientific theology was now set, and it was claimed at once for the canonical field. Whether or not Gratian decided in or about 1120, independently of Abelard, to compile a rigorous *summa* of canonical tradition along the lines suggested by his predecessors, he undoubtedly received a stimulus at some point from Abelard's incisive rendering of their principles, and in particular from Abelard's insistence, apparently original, on working out from context, phraseology, etc., the precise meaning of a term or an idea in a given text. Applying Abelard's dialectical method to the mass of texts provided by existing collections, Gratian proposed texts for and against chosen propositions and sought to penetrate textual divergences by defining terms and applying relentlessly the rules of interpretation. The result (*c.* 1140) was his *Concordia discordantium canonum,* the foundation of the classic law of the Church. To arrive at this first scientific formulation of the teaching of the canons, Gratian doubtlessly was spurred on by the presence in Bologna of a vigorous school of civil law, which, under *Irnerius, had since 1100 contributed to the revival of the study of classical Roman law. Gratian then demonstrated in the *Decretum* that it was possible to mold a seemingly amorphous mass of canons into a system of jurisprudence that could compare with the enviable order of the civilian corpus.

Stages of the Classical Period. As a synthesis of the patristic, conciliar, and papal teaching on the organization of the Church (the hierarchy, clerical discipline, excommunication), on the social structure of Christianity (matrimony, usury, relations of spiritual and secular authorities), and on the Sacraments, worship, and liturgy, the *Decretum* provided canonists with a mine of solid information and provided the Church with sure bases on which to build an ordered array of institutions. By 1150 it was in use in schools and synods; although never "received" by the Church as an authentic collection, from the time of Alexander III (1159–81) onward it was the manual of the Roman Curia. The first impact of the *Decretum* was on the scholastic centers. Commentaries and glosses on and summaries of the *Decretum* began to appear, first at Bologna, then in France and England (*see* DECRETISTS), notably, to mention only a few, from *Paucapalea, Gratian's own disciple; Roland Bandinelli (*Alexander III); *Stephen of Tournai; *Rufinus; *Sicardus of Cremona; also many anonymous authors (e.g., the *Summa Parisiensis, Summa Monacensis*); and *Huguccio (Hugh of Pisa). If the *Decretum* set in motion a wave of canonistic writing, it no less occasioned a flood of questions. On many points the solutions Gratian offered were fragmentary or hesitant and called for development; in some areas of Europe confusion was caused by a lack of harmony between local custom and the tradition of the Church as represented in the *Decretum.* The papacy, as a result of the Gregorian Reform and of the tradition mirrored in the *Decretum* itself, had emerged as the undisputed guardian and master of Church law, and was now called upon to offer solutions to these problems. From the mid-12th century onward thousands of replies to cases appeared from the papal chancery, particularly between 1159 and 1216 (from Alexander III through Innocent III); in the meantime the masters in the schools posed new questions, suggested solutions other than those advanced by Gratian, and provided the papacy with arguments upon which to draw.

This papal and canonistic activity introduced the second phase of the classical period. In order to implement the *Decretum* and to continue its *concordia,* canonists began about 1160 to make collections of papal, conciliar, and patristic material overlooked by or unknown to Gratian and, in particular, of the new papal replies or *decretals. These collections of *Decretales extravagantes* (i.e., circulating distinct from the *Decretum*) were put together in most parts of Europe, the best known coming from Spain, Portugal, France, Italy, and England (*see* DECRETALS, COLLECTIONS OF). Many were of a private nature and loosely ordered; the first semisystematic collection was that of Bernard of Pavia between 1177 and 1179 (*Collectio Parisiensis II*), covering decretals from Honorius II (1127–30) to Alexander III. After the Third Lateran Council more systematic collections made their appearance, notably, in England (*Appendix Concilii Lateranensis III*), France (*Bambergensis*), and Italy (*Lipsiensis*). The high point was reached (1191–92) when Bernard of Pavia published his *Breviarium extravagantium,* an arrangement in five books of about 900 decretals issued between 1140 and 1191; the headings given the books, *iudex, iudicium, clerus, connubia, crimen,* originally were a mnemonic aid for memorizing the main subject of the books. This was soon accepted by the schools as a definitive collection and became the *Compilatio Prima* of the **Quinque Compilationes Antiquae.*

The third phase of classic canonistics began with canonists who, in preference or in addition to making glosses on the *Decretum,* composed commentaries on the "new" decretals of the *Compilatio Prima* and kindred compilations. *Peter of Spain wrote an apparatus on Bernard of Pavia's collection as early as 1193, the Englishman *Richard de Mores 4 or 5 years afterward, and Bernard himself in 1198. Apparatuses followed from *Alanus Anglicus, *Lawrence and *Vincent of Spain, *Tancred, *John of Wales, etc., and were joined by writings on the later compilations. Although there was a lull in decretist activity as such after 1191–92, studies on Gratian's *Decretum* resumed with a new vigor when it was perceived that a harmony had to be established between the *Decretum* and the new compilations, glosses, and apparatuses. The period from 1210 to 1220 was in fact one of intense decretist as well as decretalist production at Bologna, many of the decretalists mentioned above being the authors also of decretalist writings, e.g., Alanus Anglicus, Lawrence of Spain, and John of Wales. It proved to be the final, brilliant moment of the decretist epoch. In 1216

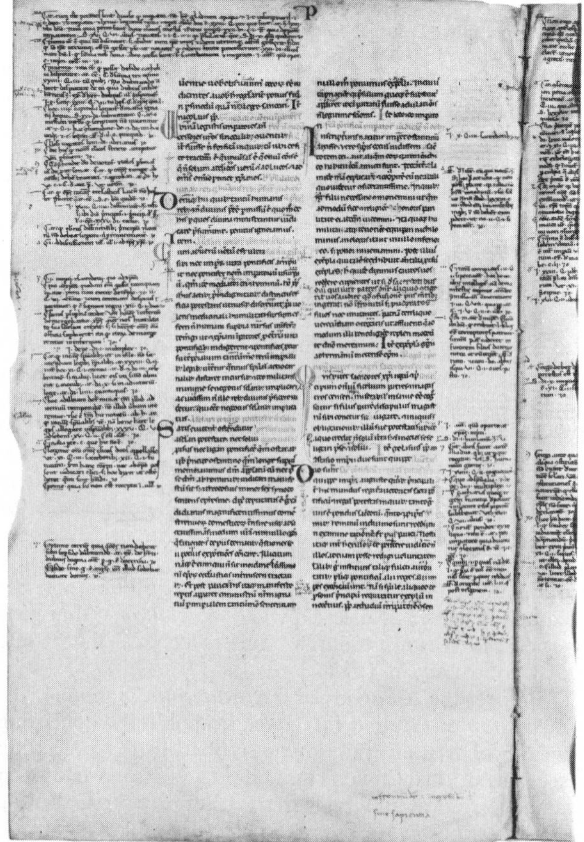

"Glossa ordinaria" of Joannes Teutonicus on Decretum 96, in a 13th-century MS (MS Pal. lat. 624, fol. 69v).

*Joannes Teutonicus, the author also of an apparatus on the *Compilatio tertia antiqua* and one on *Compilatio quarta antiqua,* published the gloss on the *Decretum* that became the *ordinaria.* Summing up more than a half-century of decretist learning, this gloss announced in effect the end of the period of canonistic research. The range of the decretal legislation of Innocent III (1198–1216) and of the constitutions of the Fourth Lateran Council (1215) had shown once and for all that there was now a living law of the Church and that this called for the same canonistic attention that hitherto had been given to the traditions enshrined in the work of Gratian.

It was also becoming clear that the time had come for a new *concordia*—not, as in Gratian's day, of *discordantium canonum,* but of *collectionum discordantium.* By 1230 there was such a profusion of decretals and variety of collections that Gregory IX commissioned and then authenticated (1234) a definitive collection of decretals not included in or coming after Gratian's *Decretum* (*see* GREGORY IX, DECRETALS OF). Gratian's *Decretum,* however, retained its place, and *Bartholomew of Brescia brought the *glossa ordinaria* of Joannes Teutonicus into line with the "new" universal law from about 1240 to 1245. The spread of a uniform law of the Church was now possible and henceforth juridical activity concentrated on the consolidation of a strongly hierarchical, centralized, closely regulated society. There was a great flowering in the next half-century of glosses, commentaries, *summae, lecturae,* and *reportoria* on the decretals, chiefly from Sinibaldus Fieschi (*Innocent IV), *Godfrey of Trani, *Bernard of Parma (*glossa ordinaria,* before 1241), *Bernard of Montmirat (*Abbas antiquus*), *Hostiensis, and William *Duranti the Elder (*see* DECRETALISTS).

Of course decretal legislation was continued after 1234: Gregory IX himself published decretal letters, as did most of the succeeding popes. Besides, the two Councils of Lyons (1245, 1274) published constitutions. From time to time collections of this new material were made (e.g., three collections of his own decretals by Innocent IV), and special glosses were composed (e.g., by *Bernard of Compostella the Younger on the *Novellae* of Innocent IV; by Duranti the Elder on the *Novellae* of Gregory X); but until the *Liber Sextus* (also called the 'Sext') of Boniface VIII cleared the air in 1298, there was an ever-increasing problem of the relationship of these new decretals to the universal legislation established by Gregory IX. A great part of the Sext was legislation especially composed to meet new needs or in mitigation of decretal and conciliar legislation since 1234. Canonical science, which had tended to rest on its laurels after the masterly *Summa* (1253) and the exhaustive *Lectura* (*c.* 1270) of Hostiensis and *Speculum iudiciale* of Duranti the Elder (1272; 1287), now stirred itself once more. With the Sext, in fact, the classical period of Canon Law entered its final phase. Although the **Clementinae,* promulgated some 19 years later by John XXII, also occasioned much canonical activity, the Sext was in effect the last great collection of the classical age, and it led to a flow of brilliant glosses, apparatuses, etc., from such canonists as *Guido de Baysio, *John Le Moine, *William of Mont Lauzun, *Zenzelinus de Cassanis, Petrus Bertrandus, and *Alberic of Rosate.

With Joannes Andreae the golden age of canonistic scholarship came to an end. The great Bolognese lay canonist produced, among other works, two *glossa ordinaria* (one on the Sext, *c.* 1301, and on the *Clementinae,* 1322). Moreover, in his *Novella Commentaria* on the *Decretals* of Gregory IX, completed in 1338, Joannes Andreae surveyed the whole of decretalist literature from the *Quinque Compilationes Antiquae* onward and arranged a century of glosses on the decretals into a coherent, enduring apparatus. The classical period was at an end, and in Joannes it had its last representative and its first literary historian. The *Black Death, which claimed Joannes Andreae in 1348, thinned the ranks of canonists and of scholarship in general; and the Great Schism soon disrupted that unity of Christendom that the classic age had labored to build. Canonical science never quite recovered afterward.

Aspects of the Classical Period. The ideal of a *concordia discordantium canonum* so succesfully pursued by Gratian at Bologna soon attracted a following all over Europe. By the end of the 12th century there were flourishing schools of Canon Law in France (especially at Paris) and in England (chiefly at Oxford, where John of Tynemouth, Simon of Southwell, and Master Honorius were the leaders, but also to some extent at Northampton and in the cathedral schools of Exeter and Lincoln). From the early 13th century on a faculty of Canon Law was a normal part of the *studia generalia* then coming to life in France (Orleans, Angers, Montpellier, Toulouse), and Spain (Palencia, Salamanca, Valladolid), and Italy (Padua, Vercelli, Siena, and Piacenza). Bologna, the nursery of canonists, never yielded her position, although powerful centers (e.g., Padua in the 14th century) were to constitute a challenge. Bologna's fertility is best seen, perhaps, around 1200, when a host of decretists and decretalists—Italians, Germans, Spaniards, Anglo-Normans, Welsh—worked side by side to produce numerous collections and apparatuses.

For most of the 13th century the *Decretum* was the basic or ordinary text in these schools, and lectures on it took place in the morning period. When the *Decretals of Gregory IX* appeared, they were read *extraordinarie* in the afternoon sessions and generally did not achieve the "ordinary" status of the *Decretum* until the Sext (1298) and *Clementinae* (1317) were introduced as "extraordinary" books. In some studia, however, e.g., Oxford, there was a changeover from the *Decretum* to decretals before 1300, the *Decretum* being relegated to the former "extraordinary" place of the decretals. Lectures on the ordinary text were given by professors and regent doctors; but when regent doctors were scarce, exceptional bachelors might be enlisted to conduct "quasi-ordinary" lectures; as a rule, the extraordinary texts were entrusted to the bachelors. In some universities there were endowed chairs, or at least a fixed stipend, for the ordinary teachers, but in others each professor had to negotiate a contract with his students as a body; bachelors, however, were not entitled at any point to a fee. The course for the license to lecture *extraordinarie* or *cursorie* (baccalaureate) generally comprised 3 years of civil law, 2 years on the *Decretum,* and a complete study of the decretals; for the doctorate a further 3 or 4 years were required, during which the

The "Novella" of Joannes Andreae (d. 1348), book 2, in a Bolognese manuscript (MS Vat. lat. 1456, fol. 179r, detail). The miniature is signed by the artist Nicholas of Bologna and is dated June 3, 1353.

bachelor *extraordinarie,* engaged in public disputations, and stood in as *ordinarius* at least once for each regent doctor. After the final doctorate examination there was a compulsory period, normally 2 years in duration, of ordinary teaching as a regent doctor.

The statutes of Canon Law faculties generally echo those of the faculties of the older (though to canonists, inferior) science of civil law. Canon Law, indeed, owed an immense debt to Roman law; civilians, on the other hand, armed with a code of laws stabilized in the 6th century, depended little on canonists, although they did not ignore the principles underlying Canon Law and ecclesiastical institutions. Classic Roman law had enjoyed the favor of the Roman Curia from the earliest days, and in time many popes came to look on it as part of their heritage. However, the use to which it was put by imperial jurists, such as Peter Crassus during the investiture contest, occasioned a certain ecclesiastical reserve, which is to some extent reflected in Gratian's *Decretum.* But as glosses and commentaries multiplied on the *Decretum,* canonists often found it to their advantage to adopt techniques from the civilian glossators; and as questions increased and situations grew more complex, it became widely recognized that the classic Roman law could be profitably exploited in the interests of the public law of the Church for its theory of laws, its approach to justice, its teaching on contracts and pacts, its sense of the privileges of priesthood and of sacred places, its maxims and reflex principles. By 1220 canonists were studying Roman law as a matter of course; by mid-century the complete canonist was a *doctor utriusque iuris;* by 1300 a civil law degree was desirable before proceeding to Canon Law studies. With the development of ecclesiastical courts a knowledge of civil law procedures became imperative (*see* ORDINES JUDICIARII), and from 1170 onward various summaries and expositions of procedure were written for canonists, the most influential being those of Tancredus (1214–16; later adapted by Bartholomew of Brescia about 1236), *William of Drogheda (Oxford 1239), and William Duranti the Elder (*Speculum iudiciale,* 1272, 1287; later reworked by Joannes Andreae, Baldus, and others). The spread of the universal law, the growth of papal provisions, the development of episcopal curias, etc., naturally created a demand for canonists well versed in both laws. To counter career-seeking, Honorius III prohibited in 1219 the study of civil law to monks, priests, and beneficed clerks, but papal dispensations were not too difficult to obtain afterward. The ordinary canonist who attended Roman law schools probably would not be more than a simple clerk at the time, and would not come under the ban.

Relations between Canon Law and theology were on another footing. At the beginning of the 12th century the canons were regarded as a part of theology, and Gratian himself taught them at Bologna as "external theology." But in establishing Canon Law as a science, Gratian, for all the theological source material in his *Decretum,* opened the way not only to a distinction of the science of Canon Law from that of theology, but also to a separation. There were, of course, decretists in the early period who were both canonists and theologians: Roland Bandinelli (Alexander III), Gandulpus, *Laborans, Huguccio (the latter a prime source for the theological learning of his day). Toward the end of the 12th century, however, canonists and theologians alike contributed to a widening gap between the two fields. If Sicardus of Cremona abandoned a discussion of the Eucharist "to the theologians," there were theologians who omitted to speak of Matrimony (on which there had been a cascade of decretals from Alexander III) and of Orders. From 1200 onward canonistic science concentrated more and more on institutional aspects of the Church, deriving little from the vigorous theological speculation that began to sweep Europe. The theologians, for their part, seemed content to allow that Canon Law govern worship, the administration of the Sacraments, the functioning of the ecclesial body. Richard Fishacre, who wrote the first commentary on Peter Lombard's *Liber Sententiarum* at Oxford (*c.* 1240–43), borrowed freely from Raymond of Peñafort; St. Albert and St. Thomas were indebted to the *Decretum* and decretals.

One genre of canonical literature to which the classic age gave rise was to play a large part in the emergence of later moral theology. Through *summae* of penitential practice (later called *Summae confessorum*), the decrees of popes and councils and the doctrines developed by canonists on all aspects of domestic, social, and economic life were made available to priests often far removed from scholastic circles. The movement began about 1210 with *Robert of Flamborough, an English penitentiary at St. Victor in Paris, and grew in strength after the pastoral reforms of the Fourth Lateran Council (1215). Its greatest exponents were the Dominicans *Raymond of Peñafort (*Summa de casibus, c.* 1225; revised *c.* 1234) and *John of Freiburg (*Summa confessorum,* 1298). These *Summae* in turn inspired a host of manuals of the general pastoral care and of sacramental practice, such as the *Oculus sacerdotis* of *William of Pagula (*c.* 1320), the *Manipulus curatorum* of Guido de Monte Richerii (1333), and the *Summa praedicantium* of John of *Bromyard (1348). All these contributed in no small way to the spread of a knowledge of the universal law of the Church and to its universal observance.

Bibliography: G. LeBras, "Canon Law," in *The Legacy of the Middle Ages,* ed. C. G. Crump and E. F. Jacob (Oxford 1926) 321–361; *Institutions ecclésiastiques de la Chrétienté médiévale* (Fliche-Martin 12; 1959) 21–119. Fournier-LeBras 2:334–352. Van Hove 1:343–377, 412–465. Stickler 1:188–268. C. Munier, *Les Sources patristiques de droit de l'Église du VIIIe au XIIIe siècle* (Strasbourg 1957). Kuttner. S. Kuttner, *Harmony from Dissonance: An Interpretation of Medieval Canon Law* (Latrobe, Pa. 1960); "Papst Honorius III. und das Studium des Zivilrechts," *Festschrift für Martin Wolff,* ed. E. von Caemmerer (Tübingen 1952); "Bernardus Compostellanus Antiquus," *Traditio* 1 (1943) 277–340; "Notes on a Projected Corpus of Twelfth-Century Decretal Letters," *ibid.* 6 (1948) 345–351. S. Kuttner and E. Rathbone, "Anglo-Norman Canonists of the Twelfth Century," *ibid.* 7 (1949–51) 279–358. C. Duggan, *Twelfth-Century Decretal Collections and Their Importance in English History* (London 1963). S. Kuttner's introduction to repr. ed. of Joannes Andreae, *In quinque decretalium libros novella commentaria,* 5 v. in 4 (Venice 1581; repr. Turin 1963). B. Kurtscheid, "De utriusque iuris studio saeculo XIII," in *Acta Congressus iuridici internationalis Romae, 1934,* v.2 (Rome 1935) 315–324. H. Rashdall, *The Universities of Europe in the Middle Ages,* ed. F. M. Powicke and A. B. Emden, 3 v. (new ed. Oxford 1936) 1:87–175, 585–589. E. Fournier, "L'Enseignement des décrétales à la Faculté de Paris au moyen âge," appendix to *L'Origine du vicaire-général et des autres membres de la curie diocésaine* (Paris 1940) 367–375. Ghellinck Mouv 416–510. A. M. Landgraf, "Diritto canonico e teologia nel secolo XII," *Studia Gratiana* 1 (1953) 373–413. S. Stelling-Michaud, *L'Université de Bologne et la pénétration des droits romain et canonique en Suisse aux XIIIe et XIVe siècles* (Geneva 1955). C. G. Mor, "Il 'miracolo' bolognese: La diffusione del metodo scientifico della scuola di Bologna nel secolo XII," *Studi e memorie per la storia dell'Università di Bologna,* N.S. 1 (1956) 161–171. P. Michaud-Quantin, *Sommes des casuistique et manuels de confession au Moyen Âge (XII–XIV siècle)* (Louvain 1962). L. E. Boyle, "The Curriculum of the Faculty of Canon Law at Oxford in the First Half of the 14th Century," in *Oxford Studies Presented to Daniel Callus* (Oxford 1964) 135–162. P. Legendre, *La Pénétration du droit romain dans le droit classique de Gratien à Innocent IV* (Paris 1964). Valuable bibliogs. and notes in the *Bulletin of the Institute of Research and Study in Medieval Canon Law in Traditio* 11– (1955–). G. Le Bras et al., *L'Age classique, 1140–1378. Sources et théorie du droit* (Histoire du droit et des institutions de L'Église en Occident 7; Paris 1965). **Illustration credits:** Biblioteca Apostolica Vaticana.

[L. E. BOYLE]

5. The Corpus Iuris Canonici to the Council of Trent

The publication of the **Clementinae* and **Extravagantes Ioannis XXII* during John XXII's lifetime and of the *Extravagantes Communes* at the end of the 15th century opened up a new field of study to canonists, who had already written several works on the other collections of **Corpus Iuris Canonici*. Many of these new publications stem from the study of law pursued in the great university centers of Europe as well as at the University of the Pontifical Curia. Thus originated the *commentaria, summae, quaestiones, repetitiones, consilia* or *responsa,* etc. The didactic and practical nature of the works contributed to the lack of originality of the majority of canonists of this period.

Besides the usual commentaries or works of a practical nature, the literary output is marked by the publication of works that reflect the problems of the time. Treatises on schism appeared in order to prove the legitimacy of a specific pope or the supremacy of the sovereign pontiff or of the general councils, during the crucial phase of *conciliarism. The reports of civil and ecclesiastical authorities on the modality of the origin of the power of the emperor or of kings in relation to the pope were notable; so were those that dealt with the independence of kings from the emperor, with corollaries on the so-called ecclesiastical liberties. In addition to the treatises there appeared several works that were concerned with international law. They were occasioned by the wars of conquest against the Saracens in Africa and against the Turks, and the discovery of new, distant lands, such as India and America.

Councils of Constance and Pisa. Many canonists wrote on schism, taking a stand either for or against the pope. Besides his commentaries on the *Decretales* of Gregory IX and the *Clementinae, Repetitiones,* and *Consilia,* Cardinal Francis *Zabarella, legate to the Council of Constance, wrote *De schismate,* which was published in several editions and later forbidden by the Council of Trent. Petrus de Ancherano, legate to the same Council and author of commentaries on the *Decretales* of Gregory IX, *Liber Sextus,* and *Consilia,* had participated in the Council of Pisa, where he wrote the *Repetitio* on the war on the infidels against *Hostiensis and composed the *Allegationes iuris pro Concilio Pisano.* Antonius de Butrio, author of commentaries on the *Decretales of Gregory IX* and *Liber Sextus,* and of *Consilia, Repertoria iuris, De iure patronatus, De symonia,* and *De acquisitionibus,* besides being engaged by pontifical commission in negotiations for the extirpation of schism, wrote a treatise on the subject in 1408.

Among the writers participating in the Council of Constance who wrote on schism and the general councils was Master André Dias with treatises on: *De schismatibus, Gubernaculum conciliorum,* and *De civitate ecclesiastica,* and the canonical-pastoral works *Confessio generalis maior, Confessio generalis minor* or *Modus confitendi, De decimis,* and *Lumen confessorum.* Jean Gerson and Pierre d'Ailly wrote theologico-juridical works and treatises on the supremacy of a council over the pope. Paulus Vladimirus, Rector of the University of Cracow, presented to the Council his *Demonstratio Cruciferis de Prussia seu Ordini Teutonico opposita Infideles armis et bello non esse ad Christianam fidem convertendos.* He also wrote *Tractatus de potestate papae et imperatoris respectu infidelium.* Defending the opposite side was the treatise *De bello* by the contemporary Iacobus episcopus Laudensis.

An important treatise on the schism is that of Ioannes de Lignano, commentator on the *Decretum, Decretales* of Gregory IX, and *Clementinae,* and author of *De bello, De pace, Repetitiones, Concordantia decreti et decretalium,* etc. Like Baldus de Ubaldi he wrote twice in defense of Urban VI. Against J. Lignano's treatise *De fletu Ecclesiae*, St. Vincent Ferrer wrote *De moderno Ecclesiae schismate,* in which he defended the antipope Clement VII. Baldus, having lectured on the three first books of the *Decretales* of Gregory IX, after his first *Allegationes* in favor of Urban VI, published under the title *Quaestio Baldi de schismate,* wrote *Allegationes secundae pro Urbano VI.* Ioannes de Imola, lawyer, canonist and author of commentaries on the *Decretales* of Gregory IX, *Liber Sextus,* and *Clementinae, Consilia* and *Repetitiones,* produced also a *Tractatus super schismate.* Bartholomew de Saliceto, civil lawyer, left a *Consilium pro Urbano VI;* and Nicholas de Fakenham, the *Determinatio pro Urbano VI.* Concerning Clement VII and Benedict XIII, Jean Le Fèvre wrote *Tractatus de schismate,* or *De planctu bonorum;* the works of Cardinal Petrus Flandrin and Peter Barriere were directed against Ioannes de Lignano; and Boniface Ferrer issued his *Tractatus pro defensione Benedicti XIII.* Cardinal Petrus Amelii wrote a treatise against the calling of a council to dissolve the schism; and Laurentius Ridolfi, a Florentine canonist, wrote a *Consilium* and *Allegationes* to justify the Council of Pisa. Robertus de Fronzola and Iacobus de Camplo, compiler of *Decisiones novae* of the Sacred Rota, also wrote the treatises *De schismate* concerning the Council of Pisa. Besides the tract on the legitimacy of his election, Benedict XIII wrote a reply to William d'Ortolan's treatise written to refute the first mentioned.

Council of Basel-Ferrara-Florence. Various canonists who took part in the Council of Basel-Ferrara-Florence produced works on Canon Law. John de Torquemada, commentator on the *Decretum,* was the first to appear in defense of the pope against the Council in his *Summa de Ecclesia, Tractatus in favorem Eugenii IV contra decreta Concilii Constantiensis et contra gesta in Concilio Basiliensi,* and *Tractatus de potestate papae et Concilii generalis auctoritate.* Nicholas de Tudeschis, the King of Aragon's ambassador at the Council of Basel, has a place among the best canonists of his time for his commentaries on the *Decretum, Decretales* of Gregory IX, *Liber Sextus, Clementinae,* and *Flores utriusque iuris.* Rodrigo Sanchez de Arevolo wrote *Defensorium Ecclesiae et status ecclesiastici, De libera et irrefragabili auctoritate Romani Pontificis, De conciliis generalibus, De origine ac differentia principatus imperialis et regalis, De pace et bello,* etc. Of no small importance was St. John Capistran's *Tractatus de papae et concilii sive Ecclesiae auctoritate,* as well as his commentaries on the *Decretales* of Gregory IX and *Extravagantes* and his work of a pastoral nature, *Speculum conscientiae.* Petrus de Monte, defender of the pope against the Council of Basel, wrote *De potestate papae et concilii.* Joannes de Podio, author of *Lectura super decretales,* also wrote *De potestate Summi Pontificis et concilii;* and Marcus Mantuanus, *Dialogus de concilio.*

Church and State. Besides the common commentaries and works already mentioned, which refer to war, the spread of the gospel, and the power of the pope in relation to civil authority, one should remember the *Consilia* on the legitimacy of the Portuguese war against the Saracens, by Antonio de Pratovecchio and Antonio Rosellis. Rosellis, author of commentaries on the *Decretales* of Gregory IX, *Repetitiones,* and *Tractatus legitimationum,* issued also the *Monarchia seu Tractatus de potestate Imperatoris et Papae.* The same subjects are treated by Petrus Quesvel in *Directorium iuris;* Joannes Quaglia, in *De Civitate Christi:* Master Adam, in *Defensorium Ecclesiae;* Alvarus Pelagii, in *Speculum Regum* and *De planctu Ecclesiae;* Ludovicus de Cividale, in *Dialogus de papali potestate;* Aeneas Silvii Piccolomini, in *Tractatus de ortu et auctoritate Imperii Romani;* Franciscus Zoanettus, in *De Romano Imperio ac eius iurisdictione;* Guillelmus de Monserrat, in *Tractatus de successione regum;* Restaurus Cataldus Perusinus, in *De imperatore;* Michael Ulcurrunus, in *Opus imperiale;* and Alphonsus Alvares Guerreiro, in *Thesaurus Christianae Religionis et Speculum Sacrorum Summorum Pontificum, Imperatoris ac regum.* Antonius Corsetus Siculus was the author of *Repetitiones* and *De potestate et excellentia regia.* Aegidius Bellamera commented on the *Decretum, Decretales* of Gregory IX, and *Clementinae* and authored *Consilia,* which copies the statements made by Oldrado de Ponte on the total independence of kings from the emperor. These arguments are treated, though not always *ex professo,* by Petrinus Belli Albensis in *De re militari;* by Joannes Lupi Segobiensis, in *De bello;* by Paris a Puteo, in *De re militari;* or by Martinus Laudensis, in *De bello.*

General Commentaries. Other commentators on one collection or other of the *Corpus Iuris Canonici* not yet mentioned were Guido de Baysio, Henricus Bohic, Dominicus de Sancto Geminiano, Joannes Fantuzzi, Marianus Socinus, Benedictus Capra de Benedictis, Bonifatius de Vitalinis, Paulus de Aretio, Guilelmus Bonte, Philipus Franchus de Franchis, Ioannes de Prato, Alexander de Nevo, Angelus de Castro, Franciscus de Accoltis, Ioannes Antonius de Sancto Georgio, Laurentius de Pinu, Ioannes Franciscus de Pavinis, Stephanus Costa, Felinus Sandeus, Augustinus Beroius, Prosdocimus de Comitibus, Andreas Alciati, Iacobus de Zocchis de Ferraria, Andreas de Barbatia, Ioannes de Anaia, Laurentius Puldericus, Andreas Tartagnus, Decius, Iacobus Ioannes de Canis, Ioannes de Vico Mercato, Ioannes de Palaciis Rubeis, Iacobus Radwicz, Guido Papa, Ludovicus Gomesius, and Ioannes Koelnet de Vanckel. Several authors developed both Canon and civil law, and some indicated their points of contact and their differences; e.g., Bartolo di Sassoferrato, in his *Tractatus inter ius canonicum et civile;* Ioannes Baptista de S. Blasio, in his *Contradictiones iuris civilis cum canonico;* Galvanus de Bettino de Bononia, in *Contrarietates et diversitates seu differentiae inter ius canonicum et romanum;* Ioannes Milis, in *Repertorium utriusque iuris;* Ioannes Berberius, in *Viatorium utriusque iuris;* Felinus Sandeus; Franciscus de Accoltis; Antonius Corsetus; Iacobus Fontanus; and Petrus Maurocenus, author of *Concordantiae iuris civilis et canonici.*

The pastoral aspect of canonist publications is represented in *Summae confessorum,* or cases of conscience, such as *Summa Astesana* by Astesano, OFM, brought up to date in regard to sources of law by Gomes de Lisboa; the *Summa Pisana,* by Bartolomew a Sancto Concordio, OP, and added to by Nicolaus ab Auximo, OFM; the *Summa,* by Saint Antonine of Florence, OP; the *Summa iuris,* by Antonio de Bitonto; the *Summa Angelica,* by Angelus de Clavasio, OFM; the *Summa Rosella,* by Ioannes Baptista Trovamala, OFM; the *Summa Tabiena,* by Ioannes Cagnazzo de Tabia; the *Summa Sylvestrina,* by Sylvester Prierias, OP; and the *Summa Armilla,* by Bartholomeus a Fumo, OP. Finally, worth recalling in the beginning of the 16th century are the merit and influence of Ioannes de Chapuis and Vitalis de Thebis on future editions of the *Corpus Iuris Canonici.*

Bibliography: Van Hove 1:466–481. R. H. TRAME, *Rodrigo Sánchez de Arévalo, 1404–1470* (Washington 1958). A. D. DE SOUSA COSTA, *Canonistarum doctrina de Judaeis et Saracenis tempore Concilii Constantiensis* (Rome 1965). N. DEL RE, "Il 'Consilium pro Urbano VI' di Bartolomeo da Saliceto," StTest 219 (1962) 213–263.

[A. D. DE SOUSA COSTA]

6. THE COUNCIL OF TRENT TO THE CODE OF CANON LAW

The decrees of the Council of Trent had the controlling influence on the Canon Law of the Church until the promulgation of the *Code of Canon Law in 1917. New canonical institutes that developed in the period had their foundation in the reform in the Church that the Council inspired.

Council of Trent. The Council of Trent (19th ecumenical, 1545–63) laid the dogmatic and canonical bases for the internal reform of the Church, anchoring the Church still more in the papacy. It gave the Church a new direction in its development, toward being no longer the Western Church but rather the Catholic Church. Tridentine Canon Law did not abolish the older Canon Law but rather restored, supplemented, and renewed it, and thereby created the basis for the modern development. Dogma and discipline were discussed together. The reform decrees were primarily canonical in content, dealing with the position and duties of clerics, regulations on ordinations, benefices and patronages, religious orders, criminal proceedings and penitential discipline, synods, and, in a particularly detailed fashion, marriage.

These regulations concentrated ecclesiastical faculties in the hands of the pope and in the hands of the bishop with regard to the diocesan clergy. But the implementation of the reform decrees encountered opposition in individual states, which led to legal confusion and legal disparities, especially for Catholics in Protestant territories where the council decrees were not recognized at all. Since many points of the agenda had not been completed at the Council, certain important matters were left to the personal regulation of the pope: Creed, Index, catechism, Missal, editions of the Bible, Breviary.

Since the interpretation, implementation, and dispensation of the council decrees had been entrusted to the pope, the Congregatio Cardinalium Concilii Tridentini Interpretum (now Congregation of the Council) was established in 1564.

In order to cope with all the assignments, the Roman *Curia was expanded and thoroughly reformed. The college of cardinals (which since 1586–87 included 70 members, of whom 6 were cardinal bishops, 50 were cardinal priests, and 14 were cardinal deacons) began the reform. Congregations of cardinals (initially 15 in number) were established to supplement the old curial offices, and each of these new congregations had its own area of competency; this entailed a fundamental and systematic reorganization of the curial administration. Thus there came into existence the Congregation of the Index (1571), the Congregation of the Inquisition (1542, 1564; later Holy Office), the Congregation of the Consistory (1587), the Congregation of Bishops and Regulars (1601), Propaganda (1622), etc. The work of codifying Canon Law was begun under Gregory XIII (1572–85). The text of the *Corpus Iuris Canonici* was reviewed by a commission of cardinals and *periti* (*Correctores Romani*), and an official Roman edition was published (1580–82). Clement VIII (1592–1605) had all the scattered decretals of the remaining common Canon Law collected into a Liber Septimus of the *Corpus;* but this book was not approved, because some states did not recognize all the regulations of Canon Law. Only the most important canonist among the popes, Benedict XIV (1740–58), had his decrees collected and published (1746, 1751) as authentic sources of Canon Law.

Missions. The discovery of new continents with heathen inhabitants and the defection of entire peoples of the Old World from the Catholic Church made necessary an organizational separation of the areas that had remained Catholic from the countries that were only gradually to be encompassed by the missions to the heathens and Protestants (*terrae missionis*). Of radical importance for the organization of the missions was the institution of the Congregation for the Propagation of the Faith (1622) as a central Roman office. The area of the missions (organizational forms were mission stations, mission parishes, apostolic prefectures, apostolic vicariates, missionary dioceses) was placed under the Congregation, whose prefect (the "red pope") acquired extensive plenary powers.

Diocesan Constitution. Trent strengthened the position of bishops by giving them papal plenary powers as ordinary jurisdictional powers in their capacity as *delegati sedis apostolicae.* The *Pontificale Romanum* prescribed for bishops an oath of obedience to the pope. The jurisdictional power of the ordinary over cathedral and collegiate chapters and monasteries was restored. The orderly episcopal constitution that had been breached before the Council by exemptions was again implemented.

The Council deprived the office of archdeacon of all ordinary jurisdiction; all disputes were to be referred to the episcopal court. The archdeacon was replaced in judicial matters by the *officialis and in matters of administration by the *vicar-general. The episcopal visitation rights were strengthened. The auxiliary *bishop came to the fore as the assistant to the bishop, especially when the bishop was encumbered with political duties.

The Council of Trent ordered that provincial synods be held every 3 years and diocesan synods annually, but the command was never implemented. The parish clergy was bound to the bishop because the *approbatio pro cura* was granted for only a limited time. The ordinary was given supervision of the clergy and their theological training to ensure that ecclesiastical offices were filled worthily. There was an intensification of the parochial pastorate, a strict enforcement of celibacy and residence requirement, a limitation of plurality of benefices (only one benefice could be awarded to each cleric), and a reorganization of the law on patronage and incorporation.

Religious Institutes. Religious life acquired new importance because of the new orders and congregations that were founded. These were the Theatines (1524), the Capuchins (1528), and the Jesuits (1534) with their monarchically centralist constitution and sterner obligation to obedience. There was a general reform of the old orders and the foundation of numerous congregations, adapted by specialized assignments to the individualism of the modern age. They constituted a mobile element in ecclesiastical assignments in virtue of the disappearance of the cloister, the concept of stability, and the profession of solemn vows. The papal rights of supervision over exempt monasteries were delegated by Trent to the bishops.

Marriage Law. The Council of Trent's decree **Tametsi* established exact norms for the form of marriage, namely, the solemnization of the marriage before the pastor and two witnesses. It corrected the abuses that had arisen through clandestine marriages and prescribed the entry of the marriage in ecclesiastical marriage registries. These regulations were not uniformly implemented; they came into force only in the parishes in which they were officially proclaimed, and they were not proclaimed uniformly everywhere.

The papal decree **Ne temere* (1907–08) declared that the decree *Tametsi* was universally binding and made the participation of the pastor active rather than passive; i.e., he was to obtain the consent of the bridal couple. A new impediment to marriage, that of *mixed religion, arose as a result of the Protestant Reformation.

Procedure and Penal Law. In procedural Canon Law, the *iudices in partibus* appeared as the court of third appellate instance, instead of a papal court; and the competency of circuit courts was renewed. The old procedure for accusations gradually gave way to the inquisitorial procedure. In official procedure there developed the office of the public prosecutor (*promotor fiscalis*), modeled on French trial law (*procureur du roi*).

In penal law the *Cenacle* bull collated the censures reserved to the pope, and these were raised in 1568 to the status of penal law with legal force in perpetuity. The Protestants were still considered members of the Catholic Church, but they were held to be heretical and therefore excommunicate. The necessity of daily coexistence led to the ban from all communication with only those excommunicated by name (*excommunicati vitandi*).

Currents dangerous to the papal system arose within the Church in the 17th century in France in *Gallicanism and *Jansenism. Gallicanism was a form of national State-Church sovereignty supporting *conciliarism, and had a basis in the canonicodogmatic and religiotheological area. A general assembly of Catholic clergy (1682) set the four slogans of Gallicanism: (1) princes are unlimited in matters of secular government; (2) the pope is limited in matters of spiritual government by the general council (in accord with decrees of the Council of Constance); (3) the pope is specially limited by the Gallican privileges; (4) in matters of faith, the pope is limited by the episcopate as a whole. These articles were condemned by Pope Alexander VIII in 1690, but it had descendants in the *Febronianism founded by Nicholas of Hontheim in 1763 and *Josephinism in Austria and Belgium. These theories formed, together with the theory of natural law of the Enlightenment, the bases for the system of State-Church sovereignty. According to this system, the State claims the right to make the Church subject to the power of the State (*iura circa sacra*): *ius advocatiae, ius inspectionis, ius cavendi, ius placeti, ius exclusivae, ius appellationis ab abusu, ius dominii supremi, ius reformandi.* The radical tendencies of the Enlightenment led during the French Revolution to the legal abolition of Christianity.

Neither the French Revolution nor the Napoleonic era led to the collapse of the Church; rather they contributed to its spiritual renewal. The papacy centralized in itself, in ever-increasing measure, all ecclesiastical power. The episcopalistic currents of the *ancien régime* receded in favor of the common law. With many European states concordats were concluded that mitigated State-Church sovereignty. Conferences were held by the bishops in individual states to discuss improvement of the state of the Church and the means to a universal implementation of the Canon Law. The Church's desire to strengthen its rights so as to attain independence for the fulfillment of its divine commission led to the convocation of Vatican I (20th ecumenical council, 1869–70). The definition of the universal papal primacy and papal infallibility in matters of faith anchored the Canon Law on the infallible supreme episcopacy of the pope; political conditions prevented the Council from concluding its deliberations on the place of the bishop in the Church. Thus the question of the reform of Canon Law remained unresolved.

It was not until the reign of Pius X (1903–14) that this thought was revived. In 1904 a commission of cardinals was established to elaborate a draft of a code of Canon Law. Meanwhile, difficult and urgent areas had been regulated experimentally: rights of religious orders and pastors, appointment of bishops, solemnization of marriages, penal and procedural law, election of the pope, and reorganization of the Roman Curia. After intensive work over several years, the *Codex Iuris Canonici* was promulgated by Benedict XV on Pentecost Sunday (May 27) 1917, opening a new phase of the history of Canon Law.

Bibliography: R. NAZ, DDC 4:1446–1520. A. M. STICKLER, LexThK² 5:1296–1300. H. E. FEINE, *Kirchliche Rechtsgeschichte,* v.1 *Die katholische Kirche* (4th ed. Cologne 1964). A. M. KOENIGER, *Grundriss einer Geschichte des Katholischen Kirchenrechts* (Cologne 1919). W. PLÖCHL, *Geschichte des Kirchenrechts,* 3 v. (Vienna 1953–59; 2d ed. 1960–) v.3. P. HINSCHIUS, *Das Kirchenrecht der Katholiken und Protestanten in Deutschland,* 6 v. (Berlin 1869–97; repr. Graz 1959). R. VON SCHERER, *Handbuch des Kirchenrechts,* 2 v. (Graz 1886–98). U. STUTZ, "Kirchenrecht" in *Encyklopädie der Rechtswissenschaften,* ed. F. VON HOLTZENDORFF and J. KOHLER, 5 v. (2d ed. Berlin 1913–15) 5:279–390. Schulte, v.3. Stickler. Van Hove.

[P. LEISCHING]

7. The Code of Canon Law to the Present

At the Council of Trent, voices were raised in vain to demand a general codification of Church law, as the last official collection of law, the *Clementinae,* had been promulgated in 1317. Complaints became particularly pressing when Vatican Council I of 1869 was announced. The untimely interruption of the Council made it impossible even to consider the plans for codification.

It was Pius X who undertook the difficult and delicate task left undone by his predecessors. In the motu proprio *Arduum sane munus,* March 19, 1904 [ActApS 36 (1904), 549] he announced the plan for codification and indicated the broad outlines of its realization. General responsibility was entrusted to a commission of cardinals, and the actual work was done by a council of consultors presided over by Cardinal P. Gasparri, who was the guiding spirit of the undertaking. All bishops and Catholic universities were invited to collaborate in the work. As the various portions were completed (1912, 1913, 1914), they were sent to the bishops and to the major superiors for their judgment. The new collection of Church laws, which was given the title of *Codex Iuris Canonici* (CIC), was practically completed by the end of 1914, and was promulgated by Benedict XV on Pentecost, May 27, 1917, in the constitution *Providentissima Mater Ecclesia.* It went into effect on Pentecost, May 19, 1918.

The Code was drawn up in short articles, called canons, following the method inaugurated early in the 19th century and adopted by all modern states for the codification of their legislation. Despite certain defects, which are amply compensated by the Code's qualities, the CIC is a work of real value.

Interpretation of the Code. The official interpretation of the CIC was entrusted to a permanent commission, instituted on Sept. 17, 1917 (motu proprio *Cum juris canonici*), known as the Commission for the Authentic Interpretation of the *Code of Canon Law. This commission was given a twofold mission: to declare the authentic meaning of the canons presenting difficulties, and to watch over the structure of the Code, making necessary modifications without changing the numbers of the canons. The commission has competence over the CIC to the exclusion of the other Roman Congregations. Thanks to these measures, the fundamental aspect of the CIC has not been materially modified. Only a few canons have undergone minor changes, the elimination of a few words: CIC cc.1097.2, 2099.2, 2319.1n1; the substitution of a few terms for others: CIC cc.160, 534.1. This does not mean that after 1917 the legislative activity of the Church ceased. On the contrary, it has been intense. The popes, the Roman Congregations, and also the Code Commission have issued many decrees and instructions, which have clarified and complemented the text of the CIC in the most varied areas: the pontifical election, marriage, Communion, Confirmation, secular institutes, military chaplaincies, procedure, and so on.

The canonists have made private interpretations of the CIC, and stimulated the activity of official organizations.

Post-Code Collections. The **Acta Apostolicae Sedis,* which appears approximately every 20 days, constitutes the official bulletin of the Acts of the Apostolic See. Thus it is the most important source of present Church law, for it is through the publication of the *Acta* that pontifical laws are regularly promulgated. The Rota publishes annually a volume of *Decisiones* making it possible to follow the jurisprudence of the Roman tribunal.

Two collections are related to the CIC. One contains the sources that have served in the elaboration of the Code: *CIC Fontes,* 9 volumes, published from 1923 to 1939, by P. Gasparri, and afterward by I. Seredi. The other, *CIC Schemata,* begun in 1940 by F. Roberti, gives the *schemata* (successive drafts) of the various canons of the Code. By 1964 only one volume had appeared (cc.1556–1924).

Among the notable private collections of canonical works published by faculties or institutes, there are, in addition to the publications of the Roman universities: *Canon Law Studies* (Catholic University, Washington 1916– ; more than 400 volumes), *Münchener Theologische Studien, Kanonistische Abteilung* (Munich 1951–).

Revision of the Code. Contemporary events, especially World War II, caused such profound changes that a complete revision of the Code of Canon law became necessary. That is why John XXIII, soon after his advent to the pontificate, decided upon "the expected and desired modernization of the Code of Canon Law" [ActApS 51–68 (1959)]. He made known his decision in the famous allocution of Jan. 25, 1959, addressed to 18 cardinals assembled in an extraordinary consistory in the Monastery of St. Paul Outside-the-Walls. He called it to mind in the encyclical *Ad Petri cathedram,* (ActApS 51:511). The Rule of the inter-session of Vatican Council II specified that "everything concerning the future revision of the Code would be entrusted to a competent Commission." On March 28, 1963, John XXIII announced officially that he had just constituted the Commission for the revision of the Code of Canon

Law. This commission includes members (cardinals) appointed by the pope (29 were named immediately), and consultors, designated by the president. As early as June 22, 1963, Paul VI revealed that he would continue "the work to revise the Code" begun by his predecessor (ActApS 55:572), and in November 1963, he increased the membership of the Commission to 41.

Oriental Canon Law. The Oriental Churches were not subject to the legislation of the CIC (c.1). Each Church had its own law, a situation that brought about great diversity. In order to achieve a certain unity, Pius XI took the initiative in calling for the elaboration of a Code of Oriental Canon Law for the entire group of these Churches. At the end of 1929, a commission of cardinals was assigned the task of preparing the new codification (ActApS 21:669). By 1930, two working commissions had been organized. One was to prepare drafts of canons for the future code; the other, composed of scholars belonging to all the rites, was to collect and publish the sources of the law of the various Oriental Churches. This second commission published more than 40 volumes from 1930 to 1964, divided into three series, under the general title *Fonti Codificazione canonica orientale*. The work is not yet completed (1964), and the publication of the sources continues. On July 17, 1935, the preparatory commission was transformed into the *Commissio pontificia ad redigendum "Codicem juris canonici orientalis"* (ActApS 27: 306). Before promulgation, the texts of the new Code were to be sent to the Oriental bishops for their judgment.

In contrast to the Latin Code, the Oriental Code is published in successive parts. Each portion is promulgated as it is completed. In chronological order, the following parts have been promulgated: matrimonial law, motu proprio *Crebrae allatae*, Feb. 22, 1949 (ActApS 41:89); the law of procedure, motu proprio *Sollicitudinem nostram*, Jan. 6, 1950 (ActApS 42:5); the law of religious, of temporal goods, the definition of terms, motu proprio *Postquam apostolicis litteris*, Feb. 9, 1952 (ActApS 44:63); the law of rites and persons, motu proprio *Cleri sanctitati*, Jan. 2, 1957 (ActApS 49:433). While giving an important place to local variations, the Oriental Code is conceived on the model of the Latin Code and written in Latin. *See* ORIENTAL CODES (CANON LAW).

Bibliography: Collection of decisions. E. F. REGATILLO, *Interpretatio et iuris prudentia codicis iuris canonici* (Santander 1958). S. MAYER, *Neueste Kirchenrechts-Sammlung*, 4 v (Freiburg in Br. 1953–62). Bousc-O'Connor. Commentaries. Abbo. M. CONTE A CORONATA, *Institutiones iuris canonici*, 5 v. (Turin 1950–61), various eds. E. EICHMANN, *Lehrbuch des Kirchenrechts*, ed. K. MÖRSDORF, 3 v. (9th ed. Paderborn 1959–60). R. NAZ, ed., *Traité de droit canonique*, 4 v. (2d ed. Paris 1955). Pospishil PersOr. A. COUSSA, *Epitome praelectionum de iure ecclesiastico orientali*, 3 v. (v.1. Grottaferrata 1948; v.2, Rome 1942, v.3, 1950). C. PUJOL, *De religiosis orientalibus ad normam vigentis iuris* (Rome 1957). F. GALTIER, *Le Mariage* (Beirut 1950); *Code Oriental de procédure ecclesiastique* (Beirut 1951).

[R. METZ]

CANON LAW, INFLUENCE OF ROMAN LAW ON

The development of the Church in the West put its law and institutions in contact with other legal systems and institutions, which could not fail to exercise a profound influence on the Church itself.

Reception of Secular Law. Among the secular systems with which the Church came in contact from the 5th to the 14th century, Roman law occupies an eminent place. Its form and content, tested by 1,000 years of experience, made Roman law, notwithstanding certain errors, a legislative monument of human reason. Comparison with the laws of the barbarous peoples assured Roman law an advantage that was admitted by these peoples themselves. Finally, its intimate union with the Church and ecclesiastical institutions strengthened its position even more.

Thus, the renaissance of Roman law favored its reception on the part of the rising legislation of the Church, which canonized various provisions of Roman law. These outnumbered the provisions received from laws of Germanic origin, which had a rather tolerated status, or the rules of other more recent secular systems, which the Church accepted in concordats (*see* ROMAN LAW, HISTORY OF, 6).

Influence of the Scholastic Method. The renaissance of Roman law soon emphasized the importance of Bologna and of the scholastic method that flourished there. Bologna, made illustrious by Pepo, by *Irnerius, and then by the Four Doctors, was, from the end of the 12th to the beginning of the 13th century, the juridical center of Europe. It relegated to the background those centers where Lombard law was still taught. And by attracting English, Spanish, and, a fortiori, French, German, and Italian scholars, Bologna secured for the law that it cultivated an exclusive role. Due allowance being made for Bologna's relations with the Emperor and for its constitution as a commune, the fame of its teaching was such that it attracted authorities and forces that increased even more its prestige as the city of law: the popes addressed their decretals to its university and entrusted important missions to its jurists such as *Huguccio, *Tancred, Sinibaldus Fieschi (*Innocent IV), and *Hostiensis (*see* ROMAN LAW, HISTORY OF, 7).

As *mater legum,* Bologna was therefore the center where canonists acquired their reputation; however, the sacred canons interested them only in the light of Roman law as taught by Azon, Accursius, and James Baudouin.

Furthermore, the scholastic method and its application in the juridical field also were held in honor in Bologna. Paris was perhaps the place of origin of this method, but juridical problems needed precision and clearness for their solution and for the interpretation of juridical texts. A comparison of the method used in Orléans, which was inspired mostly by Paris, with the method followed in Bologna shows that reasoning was not pressed in Bologna to the extent of its use by James of Revigny or Peter of Belleperche. But the juridical text, even if represented only by a gloss, was more fully examined in Bologna, and the great glossators, by using this method, showed special care in seeking, most of all, the law as the legislator had intended it. Obviously, even in Bologna as in Paris and Orléans, we find *argumenta* and *notabilia, quaestiones* and *distinctiones,* but these exercises and the commentaries that followed them were closely connected with the expression of the will of the legislator. This method, carried to an extreme by the postglossators who compared the gloss with the legal text, received an influx of new blood with *Bartolo of Sassaferrato and *Baldus de Ubaldis; it was hardly capable of judicious adaptation, without being corrected in its fundamental elements. The scholastic excesses of Bartolo's followers marked the end of an era of scholars who were far too separated from the text.

Thus, for 2 centuries Bologna and the method there advocated focused attention on Roman law: either through the juridical formation given, or through the lacunae that it filled in temporal matters, Roman law was eventually "received" by Canon Law. It assured Canon Law a scientific structure and modified it in such a way as to adapt it to the society of that time. However, Roman law was not the only law taken into consideration. The gloss, following the principles inherited from Germanic law with Martinus, did not neglect Lombard law, or general or particular customs, or statutory laws. *Bernard of Parma and Hostiensis, following certain decretals, did the same. Thus the *utrumque ius* began to take shape, a manifestation of a synthesis that was to be fruitful.

Canonization of Secular Rules. Besides general approval granted to Roman law as a whole, approval that was denied to other legislations, Canon Law "canonized" certain provisions either of Roman law or of other secular systems. This "canonization" consisted in the legal weight explicitly granted to certain rules. Through this recognition, they obtained the same binding force as canonical rules. The rules implied an intervention of the legislator himself and made their appearance either as insertions in canonical rules covering legal impositions, or by express reference to a secular rule.

It followed as a consequence that many provisions of Roman law, and also of Lombard or feudal or statutory law, inserted in the *Decretum* of *Gratian or in decretals, passed into Canon Law. But the manner in which this "canonization" was put into effect sometimes leaves us somewhat doubtful in respect to the extent it was received. Furthermore this integration into the canonical system was accomplished under condition of conformity not only with the natural and divine positive law but also with the general principles of the canonical order. It was in this manner that certain penalties as well as general norms regulating domicile, contracts, procedure, and infamy were admitted into Canon Law.

Concordats. The agreements entered into between the Holy See, an episcopacy, or simply a bishop and the secular power probably adopted a similar attitude. Their contractual character, although sometimes called in question, indicates that a concession on the part of the secular power was accompanied by a concession of the same nature on the part of the ecclesiastical authority. It is of little significance that these concessions are called privileges or agreements. In actual fact the Church accepted into its own laws, at least for specified regions, norms that could be contrary to the spirit of its own law, *normae exorbitantes* as they were then called, as a counterpart to the advantages, at least in fact, granted by secular power.

Thus, during the early Middle Ages the bishops of Gaul and Karloman agreed that the king's subjects to whom secularized goods of the Church had been assigned could keep them for their own use, but could not consider themselves other than as holders of a *precaria.*

During the course of the 12th and 13th centuries the number of concordats increased. As usual their main objective was to assure freedom for the Church or even to obtain the preservation or the grant of privileges in favor either of the ecclesiastical hierarchy, or of property, or finally of judiciary power.

In exchange the Church conceded some benefits: a council could not be convoked in a city where the sovereign was staying without the latter's consent; the appointment of bishops was subject to a right of veto on the part of the king, or the king even reserved the right of consent for the election of prelates before their enthroning.

By a policy of toleration, the Church, far from accepting certain secular norms, bore with them, while waiting for the opportune time to suppress them. Such toleration manifested itself in matters of secondary importance when there was no danger of sin being committed, and therefore in matters concerning the acquisition or administration of property. The observance of such laws did not entail any sin; indeed, observance was demanded in order to avoid greater evils.

Thus, some customs of Germanic law were tolerated, like the accumulation of benefices and the acknowledgment that the receiver of the benefice did not have to fill its conditions, since he could have others do what he could not do himself. The Church struggled for a long time against appropriation of private churches, but such appropriation was finally accepted. Some bishops and even some monasteries came to own private churches as a part of their temporalities. Enfeoffed tithes also were tolerated, while the collection of the revenues from property belonging to bishoprics or vacant monasteries was tacitly balanced by the royal protection granted to the Church. Certain texts of the *Decretum* afforded the gloss an opportunity of indicating some cases of toleration, though some experts believe that there is question in those cases of dissimultation. The decretals were not less explicit in respect to the cumulation of benefices (CorpIurCan X 3.5.18), and, for example, with reference to the distribution of the fruits of a benefice (CorpIurCan X 3.5.21).

Reception of Roman Law. While councils exhibited considerable force and action in the West as well as in the East, Roman law continued to exercise its influence although weakened by barbarous customs. From time to time it had resurgences before the renaissance of the 12th century. This is clear from an examination of the life of the Church and from the collections that were made in the West, particularly during the Middle Ages.

Following the invasions of the barbarians Roman law was preserved thanks to a twofold factor: it remained territorial law, since it had been promulgated by the Roman emperors, and it adhered to the principle of personal law in matters of private law for those who were of Roman origin and for the Church.

However, with the exception of the collections of the Eastern councils and of the *Avellana* (*c.* A.D. 555), the Roman law employed in Gaul and Spain was the *Breviarium* of Alaric or *Liber Aniani,* promulgated in 506, and the Theodosian Code. The former was a summary of the *Sentences of Paul,* the *Epitome* of Gaius, the Gregorian and Hermogenian Codes, the Theodosian Code and its Novels, and selections from Papinian. In Spain the *Breviarium* was abrogated by the Visigoths in 654. But in Gaul it was called *Lex romana* and applied solely to clerics of Roman origin in matters of the secular as well as of the ecclesiastical forum.

At that time, of Justinian's law only the *Epitome* of Julian was known. Thus the councils of Orléans (537 and 547) and of Tours (567) referred only to the *Breviarium* of Alaric. But in Burgundy after the fall of the monarchy, both the *Lex romana Burgundiorum* and Justinian law—the latter modified by custom—were in use, as the council of Macon (583) exemplifies. At a later date Gregory III is reported to have sent the Justinian Code to Charles Martel, and Charlemagne seems to have recognized the *Breviarium* of Alaric as having the force of law. When the councils had recourse to Roman law, they acted under the influence of a system of law that was no longer familiar. Knowledge of the law came only with the intervention of scholars, whose contribution began to increase with *Hincmar of Reims. The latter made considerable use of the Justinian legislation as well as of the *Brevarium* of Alaric and the Theodosian Code.

In the British Isles the vestiges of Roman law are very rare. Only one text of Roman law, relative to fiscal immunity of churches, seems to have been cited (Council of Calart, 787).

In Italy, on the contrary, while Lombard law represented the territorial law, from Luitprand and especially after the invasion by the Franks, Justinian law became the personal law of Romans and clerics, although occasionally the *Breviarium* of Alaric was applied, since the *Lex romana Curiensis* shows that Theodosian law was maintained. In central Italy the territorial law was Justinian law modified by custom, even though Lombard law played, at least in Rome, an important role in personal law. Indeed, after Pelagius I (492–496) and Gregory I (590–604) who, according to Hincmar, *ex integro contexuit de imperialibus legibus,* John VIII (872–882) observed that some Roman laws were considered canonical simply because the Church had so decided. Eugene II (824–827), Leo IV (847–855), and Nicholas I (858–867) had recourse to Roman law respecting prescription and Sunday rest. In the 10th century and in the first part of the 11th century the popes made less use of Roman law; however, its renaissance was about to occur.

Collections of Roman Law. It must be pointed out that the availability of collections of Roman law facilitated its influence on Canon Law.

In fact, besides the Gregorian Code (about 294), the Hermogenian Code (about 314–24), and the *Fragmenta Vaticana* (372–438), the Roman Empire left a *Collatio legum mosaicarum et romanarum* (394–408), the Theodosian Code (438), and a collection of Novels. Justinian's work (Code 529, 534; Digest 533; Institutes 533) was promulgated for the West on Aug. 13, 554, and completed by the *Authenticum* or Novels (556), and by the *Epitome* of Julian (582).

From the time of the invasions some collections were promulgated by the kings for their Roman subjects: the edict of Theodoric (beginning of the 6th century) was promulgated in Italy; so too was the *Lex romana Wisigothorum,* called mostly the *Breviarium* of Alaric or *Liber Aniani* (506), which attained great importance. The *Lex romana Burgundiorum* or *Liber Papianus,* at the beginning of the 6th century, was an adaptation of the Theodosian Code and Novels. The *Lex romana Curiensis* was a paraphrase of the *Lex romana Wisigothorum* of later composition (2nd half of the 8th century). Other collections used had a more pronounced Roman character: an *Epitome Pandectarum* (before 1080), and some abstracts, now lost, from the Code and the Institutes, called *Lex romana* (end of the 8th century), *Lex Iustiniana* (9th century), and *Lex Beneventana* (9th century).

From the *Lex romana* came the *Lex romana canonice compta* for the use of the clergy (after 825), when the *Excerpta Bobiensia* (*c.* 825) took up again the religious elements of the Code of Justinian and of the *Epitome* of Julian.

In Gaul the *Epitome* of Julian made the Novels of Justinian known, while the *Constitutions* of Sirmond, the *Breviarium* of Alaric, and the Theodosian Code did the same for Theodosian law. In the middle of the 11th and in the 12th century, the Pandects, the Institutes, and the Code—through some abstracts—became known. Thus Justinian law replaced Theodosian law. The *Liber Tubingensis,* and then the *Book of Ashburnham,* the *Book of Gratz,* the *Exceptiones Petri legum romanarum,* and likewise the *Brachylogus* (1110 or 1125–50) were for the most part abstracts from the Institutes.

Roman Law in Canonical Collections. Beginning with the 9th century numerous extracts from the Roman law were included in canonical collections. The *Collectio *Anselmo dedicata* (882–896) counted 238 of them, and the *Collectio novem librorum* (910–925) had several, while the *Collectio Quinque librorum* (*c.* 1020) included 38 fragments from the *Epitome* of Julian on ecclesiastical matters.

In Gaul the *Collecta ex lege et canone* by Florus of Lyons (813–843) established the rights of the Church on Roman law, and the *Capitula Angilramni* (*c.* 850) borrowed from the Theodosian Code. The capitularies of Benedict the Deacon (*c.* 850) contained many extracts but noted that they were not to be considered binding if they were against the canons. Even false decretals had recourse to them. It was Hincmar of Reims (806–882) who exercised a strong influence by using bk. 16 of the Theodosian Code. The *Libri duo de synodalibus causis* of *Regino of Prüm (d. 915) and the *Canones ad Hugonem et Robertum* (988–996) of *Abbo of Fleury were to borrow extracts from it also.

In Italy the influence was marked, since the impact of the *Decretum* of *Burchard of Worms (1008–12) in Germany had weakened the influence of Roman law. The Collection in *Seventy-four Titles, influenced by Hildebrand, followed both Hincmar of Reims and the Theodosian Code. These texts passed into the works of *Anselm of Lucca (1083) and *Deusdedit (1088–93), but Bonizo of Sutri (1085) rarely mentions them. Some texts concerning secular matters were taken from the Digests and the Institutes. The *Collectio Britannica* (1090) cites some from an epitome prior to 1080, as does the **Polycarpus* (1104–06) and the *Liber ordinis romani vel canonum* (1104–10), followed by the *Caesaraugustana* (1110–20; first recension).

In France, after the *Exceptiones Petri* and the *Brachylogus,* the works of *Ivo of Chartres cite Justinian law.

Gratian's Decretum. In its first part, the *Decretum* rarely makes reference to Justinian law as found in manuscripts; in the third part, no mention is found at all. However, the second part and first distinction, *De poenitentia,* frequently employ it. Little was taken from prior canonical collections; bks. 5, 6, 10, and others of the Code were not utilized, nor was the *Infortiatum*. The Institutes were hardlly used, while the Novels come from Ivo of Chartres (*Decretum*) and from the *Polycarpus,* except Novel 23. According to J. Rambaud-Buhot, isolated texts of Roman law represent additions that are subsequent to the first redaction; the small treatises are probably later also.

Decretal Collections. The **Liber Sextus* and the **Clementinae* relied heavily on Roman law, at least indirectly by reporting the numerous doctrines inspired by Roman law. This is true particularly of the decretals of Innocent III. However, opposition to Roman law was emphasized also. The decretals were one of the chief means by which Roman law passed into medieval law.

Classical Canon Law, either general or particular, was profoundly influenced by secular law represented either by Roman law, which exerted its action by means of Theodosian law and later by Justinian law, or by the various laws of Germanic origin. These elements were blended in the systematization accomplished by decretals and doctrines, and thereby assimilated.

Bibliography: A complete bibliog. can be found in VAN HOVE v.1 and G. LE BRAS et al., eds., *Histoire du droit et des institutions de l'Église en Occident,* v.7 *L'Âge classique (1140–1378): Sources et théorie du droit* (Paris 1965).

[C. H. LEFEBVRE]

CANONESSES

The term *canonica* (*mulier religiosa, femina Deo devota, ancilla Dei*) meant in the Eastern Church from the 4th century, and in the Western Church from the 8th century, a pious woman who performed some function in a church, in whose register (canon) she was inscribed. Soon the same designation was employed for virgins and widows who desired a fervent religious life according to the *canones synodales* of the bishops, but who were unable to enter a convent. As early as 742 the Concilium Germanicum distinguished between the *ancillae Dei monasteriales* (*virgines velatate,* or nuns) and the *ancillae Dei canonicae* (*virgines non velatae*).

Secular Canonesses. The *virgines non velatae* (virgins who did not wear a veil) were obliged to live in communities under a milder rule than that of the *velatae* (who wore veils). Both groups were ruled by abbesses. The *canonicae,* already known in England to Egbert of York (d. 766) as an old institution, had no relationship to *beguines and other groups of noncanonical common life. The Council of Chalons in 813 and that of Aachen in 816 promulgated rules for the *moniales canonice viventes* (nuns living according to canonical rule) and for *sanctimoniales qui se canonicas vocant* (women living a devout life, who call themselves canonesses). These canonesses (a late medieval form of *canonica*) were allowed to keep their personal properties. Rome regarded them with suspicion, refused to recognize them, and even forbade them, but was not effective against the wishes of emperors and princes who protected the abbeys of the canonesses because they provided refuge for their daughters. In deference to the Roman Curia, these canonesses often pretended to be Benedictine nuns or, later, canonesses regular.

In Germany, France, and the Netherlands there were flourishing abbeys, centers of scholarship and medieval Christian culture, such as those of Essen, Quedlinburg, Gandersheim, Zurich Fraumünster, Ratisbon Ober- and Niedermünster, Hohenburg, Remiremont, Nivelles, Andenne, Thorn, Mons Sainte-Waudru, Andlau, Maubeuge, and others. Some of the abbesses were princesses of the German Empire. Abbeys such as those just mentioned were reserved for ladies of royal blood and higher nobility; smaller ones were destined for daughters of knights. In the later centuries only the abbess was obliged to remain in residence and to profess vows. Most of the canonesses dwelt in their own houses around the abbey church, which usually was also a parish church. The ladies wore no religious habit, but a suitable garb was uniform in each abbey. At ecclesiastical solemnities they wore a special sign, such as a medal or a scarf. They professed no vows at all and were allowed to leave and to marry. The abbess was consecrated by the bishop according to a formula similar to that of the deaconesses. She was authorized to participate in provincial and diocesan synods and to have her own chapter of canons and honorary chaplains, whom she appointed. In addition the offices in the abbey were analogous to those of a monastery of canons, including a *scholastica* (teacher) who ran the often famous abbey school. From the 16th to the 18th centuries such "abbeys" were still found in Germany and in Austria, but they were simply residences for ladies of nobility. To some degree they still exist. Some abbeys of secular canonesses in north Germany, even some convents of nuns, became Protestant and continue to flourish as Evangelische Fräuleinstifte.

Regular Canonesses. The great renewal of clerical life under Gregory VII in the 11th century aimed to regularize all the clergy living in canonical communities, by prescribing the Rule of St. Augustine (*see* AUGUSTINE, RULE OF ST.). Some houses of canonesses followed suit, adopting the rule and taking the vow of poverty. For the most part, however, the origin of canonesses regular is due to the fact that the various congregations of canons regular of the 11th and 12th centuries, such as those of *Saint-Victor and Sainte-Geneviève at Paris, and later those of *Windesheim, created double *monasteries where the community of female religious followed the same rule and wore the same habit as the canons. Their life was contemplative, they professed vows, and were always considered as true *sanctimoniales,* or nuns. For a long time many of their houses did not belong to any organized congregation. They were ruled by abbesses or prioresses, by *magistrae,* in addition to the provost, and in Germany even by provostesses. Their habit was generally white. The main branches of the Canonesses Regular of St. Augustine (and allied groups) are the following.

The Canonesses of the Congregation of the Lateran. In 1964 they had four houses in Italy, where they conduct schools in Rivoli, Rome, Caldarola, and Spoleto.

The Canonesses of Windesheim. Some of their old houses still exist but are attached to the Congregation of the Lateran. They are Nazareth at Brugge, Zoeterbeek, and St. Oedenrode in the Low Countries; and Newton Abbot, Haywards Heath, and Hoddesdon in England. They all conduct schools, and in 1930 they formed the English Union.

The Canonesses of the Congregation of Notre Dame. They were founded in 1598 by St. Peter *Fourier and Bl. Alix *Le Clerc for the instruction of girls. Their religious life has only a few of the traditional canonical elements. The congregation is divided into three groups:

the Roman Union, with about 900 members (1964); the Jupille Union (Belgian), with about 400; and the German Union. In England there are houses at Hull, St. Leonards (Hastings), and Westgate. In Canada and the U.S. the Sisters of the *Congregation de Notre Dame were established in 1658 on a similar pattern by Bl. Marguerite *Bourgeoys at Montreal.

The Missionary Canonesses of St. Augustine. They were begun in Belgium in 1897 by Mother Marie Louise *De Meester. In more recent years they became known as *Missionary Sisters of St. Augustine; in 1964 there were more than 1,300 members.

Independent Houses of Canonesses Regular of St. Augustine. Eleven abbeys exist in Spain at Astigarraga, Perelada, Palencia, Palma de Mallorca, Valencia, Placencia de las Armas, Hernani, Arceniega, Ibiza, Medina del Pomar, and Alicante. There is a federation of German houses that numbers four institutes. Goldenstein near Salzburg is attached to the Austrian Congregation of Canons Regular of St. Augustine. Three convents that formerly belonged to the Congregation of Saint-Victor still exist in Belgium at Roesbrugge, Waasmunster, and Neerpelt. The English house of Victorine Canonesses, formerly at Paris, was moved to London in 1904. The branches of Augustinian Hospitaller Canonesses, founded in France and in Belgium in the 17th and 18th centuries, had (1964) 46 houses with more than 2,300 sisters. Included among these were 3 foundations in England, 7 in South Africa, and 14 in Canada. In 1946 the houses in France, England, and South Africa formed a federation under one superior general residing in France. The Canadian foundations remained independent. There are also several convents of Premonstratensian Canonesses, strictly cloistered nuns who constitute the second order of the *Premonstratensians.

Bibliography: P. Torquebiau, DDC 3:448–500. R. Piacentini, *Les Chanoinesses régulières, hospitalières de la Miséricorde de Jésus* (Kortrijk 1935). *The Canonesses Regular of St. Augustine* (Haywards Heath, Eng. 1946). P. Frank, *Canonicorum regularium sodalitates* (Vorau 1954). M. Schmid, LexThK[2] 5:1288–89.

[N. BACKMUND]

CANONICAL COLLECTIONS BEFORE GRATIAN

Three main periods are distinguished in the history of the sources of Canon Law prior to the *Code of Canon Law: (1) the collections prior to the **Corpus Iuris Canonici,* (2) the formation of the *Corpus Iuris Canonici,* and (3) the collections between the *Corpus Iuris Canonici* and the Code of Canon Law. The first period extends from the beginnings of the Church to the *Decretum* of *Gratian (about 1140) and contains a great number of collections of the most varied sort and structure: those of universal and regional law; collections whose norms owe their origin and authority to councils, popes, secular legislators; those containing genuine and spurious statutes ascribed to their real or alleged authors; collections that arrange the material chronologically or systematically. All these are to be considered as private collections in the technical sense of the word.

Pseudoapostolic Collections. The exigencies of the first years of the Church's history gave rise to the pseudoapostolic collections that contain, together with other material, disciplinary decrees that in one way or another go back to the apostolic tradition or appeal to it. The content is to a large extent genuine, but the ascription to the apostles is spurious. Of particular significance among such collections are the *Didache, the **Didascalia Apostolorum,* the *Constitutiones* and the 85 *Canones Apostolorum,* and also the *Tradito Apostolica* of *Hippolytus, all of which have been subjected to more or less numerous reworkings and imitations.

Regional Collections. A further group of collections came into existence from the 4th to 6th centuries in various regions: in the Orient, the **Syntagma Canonum Antiochenum,* or *Corpus Canonum Orientale,* containing the norms of the general and local Oriental councils; in Africa, the *Codex Canonum Ecclesiae Africanae* (419); in Gaul, the **Statuta Ecclesiae Antiqua* (in the last quarter of the 5th century, probably by Gennadius of Marseilles) and various translations of the canons of the Greek councils and collections of papal decretals (*Arelatensis, *Quesnelliana Collectio*); in Italy, the various editions of the famous **Dionysiana Collectio,* containing canons and papal decretals, of the end of the 5th and early 6th centuries, as well as far less important ones such as the *Coll. Frisingensis* (after 495), *Vaticana,* etc. In Spain, there was a merging of the collections of Italy, Africa, and Gaul. In all these collections, despite their regional variety, is expressed the uniform Catholic legal code.

Regional-National Collections. In the mid-6th century, a political fragmentation and particularization began, bringing with it a variety of national and regional disciplines and a plethora of collections expressing regional particularism. This situation lasted until the end of the 7th century. In the East the individual churches developed their own codes which were used in conjunction with the latest edition of the *Syntagma.* Among these there were notable systematic collections, in particular the *Collectio L titulorum* (550–570) of John Scholasticus and the **Nomocanon* (amalgamation of civil and ecclesiastical laws). In Africa there was the *Breviatio Canonum Fulgentii Ferrandi* (mid-6th century) and the *Concordia Canonum Cresconii* (6th–7th century). The only Italian collection of substantial importance is the *Avellana* (*c.* 555), containing papal decrees. In the most widely scattered dioceses and provinces of Gaul, a plethora of *libri canonum* appeared. The *penitentials (above all the *Columbani, Cumeani, Theodori Cantauriensis*) gave expression to the discipline prevailing in the insular churches (Ireland and England); from these churches at this period came only a few collections in the wider sense, e.g., the *Collectio *Hibernensis* (*c.* 700). But the Church of Spain continued the ancient tradition of universal disciplinary norms especially in the continually supplemented *Hispana* (*chronologica* and later also *systematica*), containing conciliar canons and papal decretals.

Collections of the Frankish Reform. Efforts at reform in the territory of the politically unified Frankish kingdom and its sphere of influence led to a compilation drive that initially effected the acceptance of the large ancient collections of universal and papal norms: the *Dionysio-Hadriana* (transmitted in 774 by Pope Adrian I to Charlemagne as an expression of the Roman discipline) and the **Hispana Collectio,* as well as the combination of the two, the **Dacheriana Collectio* (*c.* 800). There were also new penitentials of this sort and the episcopal capitularies. This authentic reform movement was partially successful. It was followed by the efforts of a group of reformers in France to use collections in order to assure the victory of a rather genuine ecclesiastical discipline. At this time there appeared the so-called *False Decretals (Pseudo-Isidorean Forgeries) of mid-9th century: the *Hispana* of Autun, the *Capitula Angilramni,* the *Capitularia Benedicti Levitae,* the *Decretales Pseudo-Isidorianae.* (*See* BENEDICT THE LEVITE.)

Collections from the Frankish to the Gregorian Reform. In the transitional period of the late 9th century and the 10th century there were, aside from the smaller collections, in Germany the *Libri duo de synodalibus causis* of *Regino of Prüm (*c.* 906), in France the *Collectio* of *Abbo of Fleury (988–996), in Italy the *Collectio Anselmo dedicata* (*c.* 882). In the wake of the reform of the first half of the 11th century, supported by bishops and princes, new collections were made; they included two of special importance: in Italy, the *Collectio V Librorum* (between 1015 and 1020); in Germany, the *Decretum* of *Burchard in 20 books (1020–25).

Gregorian Reform Collections. The Gregorian Reform based itself deliberately, as a disciplinary reform, on new collections that stressed the appropriate norms of the past and the prerequisite of a central ecclesiastical authority, the Roman primacy. The most important of these numerous collections were: in Italy, the *Collection of *Seventy-Four Titles* (*c.* 1175), the *Collectio canonum* of Anselm of Lucca (*c.* 1082), the collection of *Deusdedit in 4 books (between 1083 and 1086), the *Liber de vita christiana* of Bonizo of Sutri (*c.* 1090), the *Coll. Britannica* (*c.* 1090), the **Polycarpus* of Cardinal Gregory (*c.* 1104–06); in France, the *Liber Tarraconensis* (between 1085 and 1090), and above all, continuing the reform in a manner aimed at compromise, the important *Collection of *Ivo of Chartres: Tripartita, Decretum, Panormia;* in Spain was compiled the *Collectio Caesaraugustana* (between 1110 and 1120). This same period produced numerous compilations of lesser importance.

Collections Immediately before Gratian. The great number of the above-mentioned collections and especially the variety of the norms they contained occasioned canonical uncertainty that had inconvenient consequences. Efforts to harmonize the norms therefore became more and more pronounced. They expressed themselves not only in the elaboration of rules of interpretation and concordance, such as the *Prologus* of Ivo of Chartres and the *Sic et Non* of Abelard, but also in concordance treatises and collections such as that of *Bernold of Constance (end of the 11th century), the *Liber de misericordia et iustitia* (*c.* 1105) of Alger of Liège, and the *Sententiae Sidonenses* (between 1130 and 1135). All these prepared the way for Gratian's work, which not only brought together the past norms in one collection, but also harmonized them one with another and so became the *terminus ad quem* of the preceding and the *terminus a quo* of the subsequent canonical collections.

Bibliography: B. LIJDSMAN, *Introductio in ius canonicum,* 2 v. (Hilversum 1924–29). B. KURTSCHEID and F. A. WILCHES, *Historia iuris canonici,* 2 v. (Rome 1941–43). Van Hove v.1. Stickler. Massen. Fournier-LeBras. G. LE BRAS: et al., eds., *Histoire du droit et des institutions de l'Église en Occident* (Paris 1955–) v.1. Wattenbach-Levison, Suppl: *Die Rechtsquellen.* G. D' ERCOLE, EncCatt 3:1967–73. A. M. STICKLER, LexThK[2] 6:253–256. J. J. RYAN, "Observations on the Pre-Gratian Canonical Collections," in *Actes du Congrès de Droit canonique mediéval, 1958* (Louvain 1959) 88–103. *Bulletin of the Institute of Research and Study* in *Traditio* 12 (1956) 616–620; 13 (1957) 510–513; 14 (1958) 510–511; 15 (1959) 500–504; 16 (1960) 564–571; 17 (1961) 545–552; 18 (1962) 482–490; 19 (1963) 538–553; 20 (1964) 513–524.

[A. M. STICKLER]

CANONIZATION OF SAINTS (HISTORY AND PROCEDURE)

Canonization is an act or definitive sentence by which the pope decrees that a servant of God, member of the Catholic Church and already declared blessed, be inscribed in the book of saints and be venerated in the universal Church with the cult given to all saints.

History. The faithful of the primitive Church believed that martyrs were perfect Christians and saints since they had shown the supreme proof of love by giving their lives for Christ; by their sufferings, they had attained eternal life and were indefectibly united to Christ, the Head of the Mystical Body. These reasons induced the Christians, still oppressed by persecution, to invoke the intercession of the martyrs. They begged them to intercede before God to obtain for the faithful on earth the grace to imitate the martyrs in the unquestioning and complete profession of faith.

The remembrance of the martyrs had, from its very beginning, the characteristics typical of a true veneration. It was distinguished clearly from the memory of other deceased persons in that the date and place of martyrdom or of the martyr's burial were held sacred not only by his relatives but by the whole Christian community, and their anniversary was entered in the public calendar. Furthermore, whereas the usual commemoration of the dead was dominated by a sense of mourning and intercession for their eternal rest, in the memory of the martyrs a feeling of joy prevailed as well as the conviction that they, being united with Christ, could intercede in behalf of the living.

Toward the end of the great Roman persecutions, this phenomenon of veneration, which had been reserved to martyrs, was extended to those who, even without dying for the faith, had nonetheless defended it and had suffered for it (confessors of the faith, *confessores fidei*). Within a short time, this same veneration was extended to those who had been outstanding for their exemplary Christian life, especially in austerity and penitence, as well as to those who had excelled in Catholic doctrine (doctors), in apostolic zeal (bishops and missionaries), or in charity and the evangelic spirit.

Episcopal Canonization. Between the 6th and 10th centuries, the number of deceased who received the cult of saints notably increased. The faithful were often satisfied with the reputation of a holy life or with a great spirit of charity, and most of all with the fame of miracles. New names were added to the calendars and martyrologies; the number of feasts rapidly grew; lives, often legendary, were written. As a result, abuses arose that had to be suppressed. The urgent need of regulating this important matter gradually brought about a certain uniformity of practice.

In the first centuries the popular fame or the *vox populi* represented in practice the only criterion by which a person's holiness was ascertained. A new element was gradually introduced, namely, the intervention of the ecclesiastical authority, i.e., of the competent bishop. However, the fame of sanctity, as a result of which the faithful piously visited the person's tomb, invoked his intercession, and proclaimed the thaumaturgic effects of it, remained the starting point of those enquiries that culminated with a definite pronouncement on the part of the bishop. A biography of the deceased person and a history of his alleged miracles was presented to the bishop. Following a judgment of approval, the body was exhumed and transferred to an altar. Finally, a day was assigned for the celebration of the liturgical feast within the diocese or province.

Papal Canonization. The transition from episcopal to papal canonization came about somewhat casually. The custom was gradually introduced of having recourse to the pope in order to receive a formal approval of the canonization. This practice was prompted obviously because a canonization decreed by the pope would necessarily have greater prestige, owing to his supreme authority. The first papal canonization of which there are positive documents was that of St. Udalricus in 973.

The pope's action was initially confined to giving his consent for a solemn transfer of the remains of a saint and the introduction of cult, but the frequent travels of the popes in the 11th and 12th centuries gave the popes the opportunity to be present and perform the ceremonies of canonization in person.

Through a gradual multiplication of the interventions of the Roman pontiffs, papal canonization received a more definite structure and juridical value. Procedural norms were formulated, and such canonical processes became the main source of investigation into the saint's life and miracles. Under Gregory IX, this practice became the only legitimate form of inquiry (1234). From this time on, papal canonization acquired an exclusive and more distinguished value. Further and important phases of this historicodoctrinal development were realized by the provisions of Sixtus V, in the constitution *Immensa aeterni Dei* (1588). In it the Pope drew the guidelines for an organic division of the work of the Roman Curia, established the dicasteries that would take charge of papal affairs, and entrusted to the Congregation of Rites the task of preparing papal canonizations. The Congregation developed its own method of action and adopted a stable and uniform practice. This period of orientation and settlement lasted from 1588 through the entire pontificate of Urban VIII. In 1642 Urban VIII ordered the publication, in one volume, of all the decrees and subsequent interpretations issued on the canonization of saints during his pontificate. The work appeared under the title *Urbani VIII Pont. O. M. Decreta servanda in canonizatione et beatificatione sanctorum.*

In the following century, when Benedict XIV wrote his masterly treatise *De Servorum Dei beatificatione et Beatorum canonizatione,* he relied heavily on the experience of the Congregation of Rites. He illustrated, in a clear and definitive manner, all the elements that had been used in these processes and clarified the fundamental concept of the heroic degree of virtue.

In recent times, the division of the Congregation of Rites into two sections (the liturgical section and the section for causes of canonization), decreed by Pius X in 1914, and the establishment by Pius XI of the historical section for historical causes (1930) represent a notable improvement.

Procedure. The *Code of Canon Law became effective on May 19, 1918. Book 4 of the Code brought together in one place the various judicial and administrative processes to be used in the Church. Canons 1999 to 2141 contain the norms to be followed in the beatification and canonization of saints.

Ordinary Process. Following the death of a person who has lived an exemplary Christian life, the so-called "fame of sanctity" or "fame of martyrdom" may spread in an ever-increasing manner, together with the conviction that by appealing to his intercession, special favors will be granted by God. The bishop of the diocese where the person died, may, if he deems it opportune, institute a process. A tribunal is established to interrogate witnesses in order to gather evidence of a juridical character, which the Congregation of *Rites will use in ascertaining whether or not there exists *de facto* a fame of sanctity and, if so, its foundation and extent.

This process on the repute of sanctity or martyrdom is called ordinary, because it is instituted by authority of the ordinary of the place. It is said to be informative, since it furnishes the Holy See with the information necessary to determine the advisability of formally introducing the cause, in order to verify whether the servant of God exercised virtues in a heroic manner or whether he died for the faith. The original acts of this process are preserved in the archives of the diocese; and a faithful copy of them, called *transumptum,* duly authenticated and subsequently sealed, is transmitted to the Congregation of Rites.

For the advancement of the cause, it is necessary to ascertain whether purity of doctrine exists in the writings of the servant of God. In addition, it must be verified that public cult was never accorded him. For this twofold purpose, the bishop must conduct a thorough search of all the writings of the servant of God and institute a process aimed at establishing the absence or presence of a public cult.

Introduction of the Cause. The actors of the cause operate before the Congregation of Rites through the postulator, who has the duty of presenting and discussing the cause with the competent judges. In his study, presentation, and defense of the cause, the postulator avails himself of one of the advocate-procurators of the Congregation of Rites. It is the duty of the advocate to prepare a brief, based on the testimonies and documents available, aimed at proving the existence of a true reputation for sanctity and the advisability of introducing the cause. The brief must prove that the cause contains the elements required to proceed to further inquiries on the virtues or martyrdom of the servant of God. The advocate's work, composed of two parts, the *informatio* and the *summarium depositionum,* undergoes a thorough examination by the Congregation, following which the general promoter of the faith proposes his *animadversiones,* namely, objections to what the advocate has attempted to prove. The postulator then has the task of demanding an adequate answer of the advocate to the objections advanced.

A printed volume, technically called *Positio* and containing all the material thus far described, is presented to the cardinals of the Congregation of Rites and to the official prelates of the same Congregation. After due examination, they express their judgment in the course of a discussion (ordinary congregation) in the Vatican palace or in the residence of the cardinal *ponens* or relator.

Pope Pius II canonizes St. Catherine of Siena, fresco by Pinturicchio (1454–1513), in the Piccolomini Library, Siena.

The Holy Father, having been informed of the outcome of the discussion, then decrees, if he deems it opportune, the so-called introduction of the cause.

Apostolic Process. By the decree of introduction, the cause passes from the competency of the bishop to the exclusive jurisdiction of the Apostolic See. Following a decree of the Congregation of Rites, the apostolic process on the heroic practice of virtue or martyrdom is instituted.

The judges for the process are delegated by the Holy See. The general and particular questions for the interrogation of the witnesses are prepared by the general promoter of the faith, who is represented before the tribunal by a subpromoter.

In addition to the witnesses already interrogated during the informative process, new witnesses may be presented, summoned, and interrogated. At the conclusion of the process, an authenticated volume of the acts is sent to Rome and is officially opened and, if necessary, translated into one of the official languages.

A copy of the whole process is consigned to the postulator, who then assumes the responsibility of preparing, together with the advocate, a new study that will serve as a basis for discussions on the heroic practice of virtues or martyrdom.

Decree on the Validity of the Processes. The Church does not authorize a discussion on the important topic of the servant of God's heroic practice of virtues or martyrdom unless the lawfulness and validity of the acts, on which the discussion will be based, are first guaranteed by a special decree. The Congregation of Rites conducts, therefore, a careful study in order to determine whether all the juridic formalities that give the proceedings the elements of veracity and the probative value that represent the logical requirement before initiating more important discussions, have been faithfully observed. Such investigation on the validity of the processes will be repeated also for the inquiries of juridical character that take place in the examination of the miracles. As a conclusion to this investigation, a decree is issued on the validity of all the acts of the processes. This guarantees their legitimate use.

Heroic Practice of Virtues or Martyrdom. When the validity of the processes, both ordinary and apostolic, has been ascertained, the postulator and the advocate, using the probative elements contained in the proceedings, prepare and present to the Congregation of Rites an outline composed of (1) an information, i.e., a systematic and clear exposition of the life of the servant of God and of his virtues or martyrdom, and (2) a summary of the depositions of the witnesses interrogated specifically on these points during the course of the processes. This outline has the purpose of demonstrating, if the cause is about a nonmartyr, that his life was so profoundly inspired by Christian charity toward God and men that, in the actual occurrences of daily living, he practiced all Christian virtues in a truly perfect, exemplary, and heroic manner. If the cause is about a martyr, the report is intended to prove that the servant of God was killed *in odium fidei* and that he accomplished, therefore, the supreme sacrifice of love for Christ and the Church.

This study is presented and carefully examined by the Congregation of Rites. The general promoter of the faith formulates his doubts, raises objections or *animadversiones* against the conclusions drawn, and solicits a reply on the part of the postulator and advocate. Their answers are inserted into a printed volume, containing all the materials described above (*informatio, summarium, animadversiones, responsiones*). Copies of this volume are distributed among the Congregation's officials and consultors, who, after due examination of the contents of this *positio super virtutibus* or *positio super martyrio,* pronounce their judgment at the Antepreparatory Congregation.

Difficulties and reservations, advanced in the course of the discussion, are assembled by the promoter of the faith into a fascicle that appears under the title of *novae animadversiones.* Then the postulator and the advocate prepare their answers, which represent the basis for the second discussion by the Preparatory Congregation in the presence of cardinals, officials, and consultors.

Following this second meeting, further difficulties, the *novissimae animadversiones,* are raised, which, together with the relative answers, are the object of the last discussion, that of the General Congregation, sometimes called Congregation *coram Sanctissimo* because it takes place in the presence of the Holy Father.

Historical Section. It is a proved fact that some causes, of themselves indeed worthy of consideration, have faced almost insuperable obstacles because of insufficient juridical evidence represented by depositions of eyewitnesses. The consideration of this situation strongly emphasized the need of making a more ample recourse, whenever necessary, to documents of historical character. Indeed, in many cases, historical documents have been indispensable in order to bring light to some controverted points and thus to permit several causes to progress toward the final goal. By the adoption of this integrative method of inquiry, a beginning was given to the movement that culminated in the establishment of the historical section of the Congregation of Rites, instituted by Pius XI with the motu proprio *Già da qualche tempo* of Feb. 6, 1930 (ActApS 22:87–88).

With regard to causes of canonization, the task assigned to this section is that of studying and publishing documents for historical causes, namely, those causes that no longer have witnesses *de visu;* and hence the servant of God is known only through archival documents or literary studies. The section must also prepare historical essays relative to controverted questions concerning recent causes. It is directed by a general relator, assisted by a vice relator, by a suitable number of *aiutanti di studio,* and by a group of consultors, ecclesiastical as well as lay, chosen from the best scholars of historical sciences.

Miracles. Even when the severest investigation and discussions have brought the conclusion that a servant of God practiced all Christian virtues in a heroic manner, the Church prudently demands a confirmation in the form of miracles before proceeding to beatification.

In fact, these extraordinary interventions of divine omnipotence, so numerous in the life of Our Lord, were announced and promised by Him as signs that would accompany and distinguish throughout the centuries His Church, and in particular her faithful children, who believed in and lived according to the principles of the gospel.

For this reason, miracles constitute an unequivocable proof of the approval given by God to the person and life of the future *beatus* or saint. When miracles are performed by God in connection with the fact that some faithful have turned in prayer to a servant of God and invoked his intercession, being fully convinced that he is not only in heaven, but also a powerful intercessor before God in virtue of his merits, then it is evident that miracles indicate that God does not deny such conviction; indeed He confirms it. In fact, God confirms with signs only what corresponds to truth and reality.

The inquiries that are conducted, especially in cases that show characteristics of miracles, are aimed at establishing (1) whether God truly performed a miracle and (2) whether the miracle is to be ascribed to the intercession of a determinate servant of God who has been invoked.

These processes follow a procedural pattern that, in the preparatory stage as well as in the phase of discussion, is substantially similar to that illustrated above. They nevertheless possess an element of distinction: in addition to questions of a theological, juridical, and historical character, many problems of a strictly scientific nature and questions of medical science must be examined, since miraculous medical recoveries are often under examination. Investigations of this kind are conducted with the utmost rigor, and both in performing and in estimating them, the Church avails itself of the help of experts in the sciences related to the question at issue.

Beatification. Once the discussion on the miracles is favorably concluded, the way is open to beatification. Nonetheless, a final General Congregation is required to be held in the presence of the pope for the purpose of determining "whether it is possible to safely proceed to the beatification of the Servant of God." Having heard the opinion of the consultors, of the officials, and of the cardinals, if and when he deems it opportune, the pope orders the publication of the decree called *de tuto.* A day is then selected for the solemn celebration in the Vatican basilica of the formal beatification.

The ceremonies begin with the promulgation of the Apostolic brief by which the pope grants the venerable servant of God the title and allows attribution of those acts of veneration that are reserved to the blessed. Subsequently the image of the newly beatified is unveiled; a solemn *Te Deum* of thanksgiving is sung, and a Pontifical Mass is celebrated, representing the first act of worship toward the blessed. In the late afternoon, the pope descends into the Vatican basilica to venerate the new blessed.

From Beatification to Canonization. The Holy See presents the new blessed to the faithful as an example to imitate. It allows veneration of him, but restricts it to a city, a diocese, a region, or a religious family. Accordingly, the Apostolic See authorizes a special prayer, a Mass, and a proper Divine Office.

If, following beatification, information is received about further miracles obtained through the intercession of the blessed, the cause is resumed, that is, again taken into consideration, with a view to canonization, which constitutes the final goal of every cause. New processes or inquiries are made on the alleged miracles, and the cases are discussed along the procedural lines described above.

Only when it is proved, by means of various discussions and examinations, that God operated miracles through the intercession of the blessed, does the Holy See proceed to his solemn canonization. This constitutes the final and definitive sentence by which veneration of the new saint is extended to the universal Church. The sentence, which infallibly declares the exemplariness of the saint's life and exalts his sublime function of heavenly intercessor, is contained in the bull of canonization.

The ceremonies of canonization have a character of extraordinary solemnity. Certain ceremonies have been in existence for centuries: the procession that precedes the pope descending to St. Peter's (in this procession it is customary to carry a standard bearing the image of the new Saint); the triple petition *instanter, instantius, instantissime,* directed to the pope, asking him to canonize the blessed; the singing of *Veni Creator Spiritus,* an invocation to the Holy Spirit to enlighten the pope; the reading of the bull of canonization; the solemn singing of *Te Deum,* followed by a solemn Pontifical Mass celebrated by the pope; and the offering of symbolic gifts to the pope at the Offertory of the Mass.

Equivalent Canonization. In addition to the formal beatification and canonization, regulated by precise procedural norms just now described, there exist also the so-called equivalent beatification and canonization, which are granted the same recognition and effects as the formal beatification and canonization. However, no fixed procedure is determined by law for this kind of proceeding. In such cases, the investigation, conducted by the historical section of the Congregation of Rites, is intended primarily to ascertain the existence, origin, and continuation of a true ancient cult, which, once adequately proved, is officially confirmed by the pope.

Bibliography: L. HERTLING, DictSpirAscMyst 2:77–85. H. DELEHAYE, *Les Origines du culte des martyrs* (2d ed. Brussels 1933); *Sanctus: Essai sur le culte des saints dans l'antiquité* (Brussels 1927). F. GAGNA, *De processu canonizationis a primis ecclesiae saeculis usque ad Codicem iuris canonici* (Rome 1940). G. GIAQUINTA, *Ricerche sull'istituto giuridico della canonizzazione dalle origini alle decretali di Gregorio IX* (Rome 1947). L. HERTLING, "Materiali per la storia del processo di canonizzazione," Greg 16 (1935) 170–195. F. SPEDALIERI, *De Ecclesiae infallibilitate in canonizatione sanctorum: Quaestiones selectae* (Rome 1949). S. INDELICATO, *Le basi giuridiche del processo di beatificazione: Dottrina e giurisprudenza intorno all'introduzione delle cause dei servi di Dio* (Rome 1944); *Il processo apostolico di beatificazione* (Rome 1945). D. J. BLAHER, *The Ordinary Processes in Causes of Beatification and Canonization* (CUA CLS 268; 1949). F. ANTONELLI, *De inquisitione medico-legali super miraculis in causis beatificationis et canonizationis* (Rome 1962). J. BROSCH, *Der Heiligsprechungsprozess per viam cultus* (Rome 1938). A. P. FRUTAZ, *La sezione storica della Sacra Congregazione dei Riti: Origine e metodo di lavoro* (2d ed. Vatican City 1964). Congregation of Sacred Rites, *Index ac status causarum beatificationis servorum Dei et canonizationis beatorum* (Vatican City 1962). C. SALOTTI and J. LÖW, EncCatt 2:1090–1100; 3:569–607. **Illustration credit:** Alinari-Art Reference Bureau.

[P. MOLINARI]

CANONIZATION OF SAINTS (THEOLOGICAL ASPECT)

The solemn act by which the pope, with definitive sentence, inscribes in the catalogue of saints a person who has previously been beatified. By this act he declares that the person placed on the altar now reigns in eternal glory and decrees that the universal Church show him the honor due to a saint. The formulas used indicate that the pope imposes a precept on the faithful; e.g., ". . . We decide and define that they are saints and inscribe them in the catalogue of saints, stating that their memory should be kept with pious devotion by the universal Church" [ActApS 39 (1947) 209]. Public cult primarily

The nave of St. Peter's Basilica illuminated for the canonization of St. Bernadette Soubirous, 1933.

consists of a Mass and Office in the saint's honor, but there are other forms, e.g., selecting him to be the titular patron of churches and venerating his relics in public procession.

Permissive or Preceptive. The pope may permit the Mass and Office of a blessed to be used by a diocese, region, or religious institute as an effect of *beatification. If the pope commands that he be venerated as a saint, then such honor is due him everywhere in the Church. This is the proper effect of canonization. Local and universal canonization are terms occasionally substituted for the terms permissive and preceptive canonization, respectively.

Formal and Equivalent. Formal canonization terminates a canonical process in the Sacred Congregation of Rites that establishes juridically the heroism of a person's virtues, as well as the truth of the miracles by which God has manifested this heroism. This definitive sentence, official notification to Rome and the world, is proclaimed by the pope in the fullness of his apostolic teaching power amid solemn ceremonies that manifest its importance.

Equivalent canonization is the pope's definitive sentence to honor as a saint one for whom a canonical process has not been introduced but who for more than 100 years has been the object of a public cult. His heroic virtue, along with miracles worked before or after his death, need not be juridically proven but must be historically credible. Mere permission for a Mass and Office or insertion of the name in the Roman Martyrology is not equivalent canonization.

Baptized babies who have died are not canonized. They were free from sin, yet they could not perform those deliberate acts that are the fruit of heroic virtue. Saints are canonized not only to intercede before the throne of God but also to afford those on earth models of perfection. The Holy Innocents fall into a unique category because of their role in the life of the infant Savior.

Infallibility. The dogma that the saints are to be venerated and invoked as set forth in the profession of faith of Trent (Denz 1867) has as its correlative the power to canonize. Otherwise the faithful would not know whom to invoke as their intercessors or whom to take as their models in Christian virtue. St. Thomas Aquinas says, ". . . Honor we show the saints is a certain profession of faith by which we believe in their glory, and it is to be piously believed that even in this the judgment of the Church is not able to err" (*Quodl.* 9.8.16). The pope cannot by solemn definition induce errors concerning faith and morals into the teaching of the universal Church. Should the Church hold up for universal veneration a man's life and habits that in reality led to damnation, it would lead the faithful into error.

It is now theologically certain that the solemn canonization of a saint is an infallible and irrevocable decision of the supreme pontiff. God speaks infallibly through His Church as it demonstrates and exemplifies its universal teaching in a particular person or judges that person's acts to be in accord with its teaching.

May the Church ever uncanonize a saint? Once completed, the act of canonization is irrevocable. In some cases a person has been popularly "canonized" without official solemnization by the Church. A blessed whose cult is permitted in a diocese, region, or religious institute may have great popularity in the Church at large even to the extent of having a Mass and Office. Yet any act short of solemn canonization by the Roman pontiff is not an infallible declaration of sanctity. Should circumstances demand, the Church may limit the public cult of such a person popularly "canonized."

See also CANONIZATION OF SAINTS (HISTORY AND PROCEDURE); SAINTS, INTERCESSION OF; TEACHING AUTHORITY OF THE CHURCH (MAGISTERIUM); VENERABLE.

Bibliography: T. ORTOLAN, DTC 2.2:1634–42. E. DUBLANCHY, *ibid.* 4.2:2186–87. DTC, Tables générales 1:516–517. G. OESTERLE and R. KLAUSER, LexThK[2] 5:142–144. BENEDICT XIV, *De servorum Dei beatificatione et beatorum canonizatione,* 4 v. (Prato 1839–42). I. SALAVERRI, SacTheolSumma BAC 1.3:705, 724–726. J. DOUILLET, *What Is a Saint?,* tr. D. ATTWATER (New York 1958) 84–91. **Illustration credit:** Leonard Von Matt.

[A. E. GREEN]

CANONS, CHAPTER OF (CANON LAW)

A chapter is a college of clerics, called canons, whose primary function is to give God solemn worship in a cathedral or collegiate church (CIC c.391). This purpose is common to all chapters, but a cathedral chapter has the added purpose of assisting the bishop as his council.

History. The word chapter is found for the first time in pontifical documents of the 12th century, although it was already used in the correspondence of the popes and in private documents. The word indicates the function of serving as the bishop's counselor. In the primitive Church the bishop, priests, and deacons took part in the government of the cathedral church, which was the only church in the diocese. Later, with the increase in the number of priests and churches, it became necessary for the priests of the episcopal city, and in particular for those of the cathedral church, to participate more closely in the government of the church together with the bishop. They were readily available on occasions of solemn liturgical ceremonies performed at the cathedral.

It was the cathedral clergy who assumed the government of the diocese during vacancy of the see and elected the new bishop. Until the 12th century the laity participated with the clergy in the election, but the Church soon reserved the election exclusively to the clergy of the cathedral. The chapter came to claim wider powers: to impose excommunications and interdicts; to confer benefices; to require the bishop to consult it; and to participate in provincial councils. This prompted the councils, and in particular the Council of Trent, to intervene in order to correct abuses and exaggerations. The primary sources of historical information concerning chapters are therefore the decrees of the councils and in particular the decretals. From them derives the present structure of the Code of Canon Law.

Canonical Legislation. According to the Code (CIC cc.392, 248), the power to establish, innovate, or suppress a chapter of canons is reserved to the Consistorial Congregation. One must distinguish first between foundation and establishment. When a chapter is founded, lands, estates, and benefices are created as sources of revenues and prebends for the canons. When a chapter is established, it is given status as an ecclesiastical, collegiate, moral person. An innovation is any change in the legal status of a chapter. When a chapter is suppressed, it suffers a *de jure,* but not *de facto,* loss of its benefices or its members for a certain period.

Certain members within a chapter have honorary titles that involve both rights and duties (CIC c.394.2). The titles of these "dignitaries" may vary from chapter to chapter, but the most common is dean or provost, given to the one serving as president of the council. All dignitary titles are conferred by the Holy See (CIC c.396.1). Titular canons, the only appointed members of a chapter, are appointed by the bishop on the advice of the chapter (CIC c.403). With regard to the number, a chapter is generally not allowed to have more canons than the number of prebends, i.e., parts of the income of the benefice. After consulting the chapter, the bishop may appoint some honorary canons; these do not have any voice in the chapter, but enjoy the right of participating in choir at the recitation of the Divine Office and of wearing the insignia and vestments proper to the chapter. Canons *emeriti,* declared such by indult from Rome, remain members of the chapter but without any duty whatsoever (CIC c.422). Every cathedral chapter must have a canon theologian, charged with the duty of delivering, at prescribed times, public lectures on Sacred Scripture (CIC c.398). Whenever possible there should also be a canon penitentiary with ordinary jurisdiction to hear confessions and absolve from censures reserved to the bishop (CIC cc.398, 399).

Each regularly appointed member of a chapter, either dignitary or canon, has a right to the income of the benefice, under the form of prebends or daily distributions, and to the privileges (CIC cc.405, 409, 411). Besides a right of special precedence (CIC c.408), the principal right of the chapter is that of taking part in the government of the diocese. In fact, *sede plena,* its counsel or advice is often required by the code either for the validity or licitness of the decisions of the ordinary. *Sede vacante,* it assumes the entire government and all the powers of the ordinary, but must elect, within 8 days, a vicar capitular, who will administer the diocese in its behalf. *Sede impedita* and in default of others, it will assume the government (CIC c.492.2). It also participates in the government of the ecclesiastical province, since it is by law invited to the provincial council (CIC c.286).

The main obligation of the chapter consists in the presence in choir for the recitation of the Office and the celebration of the conventual Mass. Choir attendance admits, however, numerous exceptions (CIC cc.414, 420).

As a benefice and moral person capable of owning, acquiring, and administering goods, the chapter must provide for the upkeep and administration of its endowments (CIC c.415). In an ordinary assembly convoked by the dean, the chapter must, at the very beginning, vote on a number of statutes for itself. These statutes are approved by the ordinary (CIC c.410.2), and they establish rules of procedure for deliberations and other norms concerning liturgical and administrative functions (CIC c.416). Besides this, the cathedral chapter will have to participate in extraordinary assemblies, convoked by the bishop, in order to give him advice and consent.

Diocesan Consultors. In the U.S. there exists no cathedral chapter. At the end of the last century, the American bishops did not deem it opportune to petition for the establishment of such chapters, but at the Second and Third Councils of Baltimore they decreed the institution of diocesan *consultors. The Consistorial Congregation later recognized this institution and the Code of Canon Law included it in the universal legislation (CIC cc.423, 428).

In Canada there are cathedral chapters, but imperfect ones. In fact, by indult these chapters are dispensed from the obligation of choir Office and conventual Mass and do not constitute a benefice. They enjoy the privilege of wearing some insignia and special vestments as well as the right to participate in the government of the diocese.

Bibliography: H. A. AYRINHAC, *Constitution of the Church in the New Code of Canon Law* (New York 1925). D. BOUIX, *Tractatus de capitulis* (3d ed. Paris 1882). P. TORQUEBIAU, DDC 3:530–595, contains a complete bibliog.

[R. LATRÉMOUILLE]

CANONS REGULAR OF ST. AUGUSTINE

One of the largest monastic families of the medieval Church; called also Austin Canons.

Origin. Unlike that of so many other religious orders, the origin of the Austin canons was not closely tied to the work of a single saint or the work of a single house, but was the result of a complex process. After his conversion St. *Augustine displayed an immense attachment to the full *common life, and when bishop of Hippo he insisted that the clergy living at his cathedral should live under a common rule and hold no private property. The disordered condition of the times prevented his example having considerable immediate effect, but records of his deep interest in the religious life were preserved for posterity in his writings and in his biography written by *Possidius.

The continuous existence of the regular canons as an organized body is now known to date from the middle decades of the 11th century and to have begun with the adoption of what was in effect a monastic regime by certain communities, largely communities of clergy, in Italy and southern France. To the often neglected obligation of *celibacy, and the equally neglected life with a common dormitory and refectory, both of which ancient canons had demanded of clergy living in collegiate or cathedral churches, there was now added acceptance of an obligation to hold no private possessions, i.e., to follow apostolic precedent and "be of one heart and mind and have all things in common." Inevitably this radical form of life struck some clerics as both novel and questionable, and its legitimacy was hotly challenged. The matter was brought up at the Lateran Synod of 1059 by no less a person than Hildebrand, the future Pope *Gregory VII, who, like so many leaders of the *Gregorian reform, saw the value of the movement in an age of considerable ecclesiastical corruption. The synod gave this form of clerical life full approval, though it was not made in any way compulsory; this decision was confirmed in almost identical wording at the Lateran Synod of 1063. Surviving evidence does not give a complete and precise list of the houses that first followed the form of life thus approved, but it is certain that it was early adopted at Rome and in Tuscany, where *Lucca seems to have soon become a major center of the new way of life. Other houses were to be found in certain parts of northern Italy and southern France, the former owing something to the influence of the *Camaldolese and *Vallombrosans. Especially important in these early stages were the houses of San Frediano at Lucca, San Lorenzo of Ulcio near Turin, and Saint-Ruf near Avignon. *Peter Damian gave the order vigorous and valuable support at this time.

Early Expansion. In the last decades of the 11th century and in the early 12th century, the new order made very considerable progress in western Europe, the chief areas of expansion being Lombardy, Tuscany, Burgundy, Aquitaine, and northeastern France, where the Province of Reims was a major center. Important foundations of this period included Santa Croce, Mortara; Santa Maria in Porto (Ravenna); *Great Saint Bernard; Rottenbuch, *Reichersberg; *Toulouse Cathedral; *Saint-Quentin in Beauvais; and Mont-Saint-Elois. *Altman, Bishop of Passau (1091), had been an early pioneer and a keen reformer in southern Germany and Austria, but major progress came only in the early 12th century, notably with the support of Abp. Conrad of Salsburg (d. 1147). The effective spread of the order in England began under King *Henry I (1100–35) and proceeded rapidly, as it did also in Ireland but on a smaller scale somewhat later. In Scotland little progress was made for local reasons; expansion in the Spanish peninsula and Scandinavia was also limited. But by the mid-13th century the total number of houses of regular canons in Europe was certainly very considerable. It cannot be precisely estimated, and in any case houses of the order varied so greatly in size that any such figure by itself would be misleading. But in England alone about 206 houses had been founded by the late 13th century.

The Adoption of the Rule of St. Augustine. In the early years of the regular canons it was not regarded as necessary for any monastic order to adopt a specific rule, but experience quickly showed the value of this practice. At first regular canons appealed to the "apostolic life," but for legal and other reasons and by an obscure and piecemeal evolution they fairly quickly came to adopt the so-called Rule of St. *Augustine. The first major signs of this adoption are to be found mostly in France, about the time of Pope *Urban II (1088–99); by the second quarter of the 12th century the rule seems to have been almost universally adopted by the order. The Rule of St. Augustine itself has a very complex history, which has not yet been fully revealed despite much modern research. Most of the document is a masculine version of a number of precepts given by St. Augustine *c.* 423 to a community of nuns of which his sister was superior, but to these precepts was prefixed a short list of injunctions of a very practical nature generally known as the *Ordo monasterii.* The date and authorship of the latter and that of the adaptation of Augustine's *Letter 211* are in dispute, but not a few authorities regard both as having been drawn up by a follower of Augustine shortly after, or possibly just before, the saint's death (430). The early regular canons found much of the *Ordo monasterii* archaic, and it is clear that from the early 12th century they abbreviated the text of the Rule in the interests of practicality.

The Observances of the Order. The early regular canons found no ready made corpus of observances completely suitable for their purpose but gradually built up their own from a variety of sources. The Rule of St. Augustine was very brief and largely concerned with spiritual precepts. It was to some extent augmented by the *Institutio canonicorum* drawn up in 816–817 for houses of canons throughout the Carolingian Empire, though these latter were seculars not regulars and so their rules were not completely suitable. The customs of the *Benedictines, built up over the centuries, proved a valuable quarry for the new order; a section of the order drew also on the observances of the new contemporary orders, notably the *Cistercians. For long there was no very close uniformity of observance within the order, individual houses picking and choosing fairly freely, subject only to the approval of the local ordinary. But the leading houses of the order soon compiled observances that were widely adopted, the more influential customs being those of Saint-Quentin at Beauvais, Saint-Ruf, *Saint-Victor of Paris, and *Marbach. As time went on, attempts were made to secure a greater uniformity of detail. Thus, in the late 13th century the General Chapters of the English Austin Canons, after much effort, produced a uniform code of observances for their members, the Statutes of Healaugh Park (*Statuta de Parco*), though their adoption was slow and partial. Furthermore, at an early date individual congregations of canons had developed their own particular customs, which in certain cases were much more severe than those followed by the rest of the order, principally owing to the influence of the Cistercians. Then in 1339 Pope *Benedict XII promulgated a code of observances for the order in the bull *Ad decorem.*

Basically, however, most of the regular canons had adopted from early times observances whose temper, they claimed, was a *via media* between that of the clergy and the monks. In effect they did not differ greatly from many Benedictine observances, though they were somewhat less exacting over silence, fasting, and the length of Matins.

Organization. The regular canons were clerical in origin and always generally retained this quality of personnel, lay brethren forming only a minor element in the order. Their houses were normally subject to visitation by the ordinary, only a small minority aquiring the privilege of *exemption from episcopal inspection. On the Continent a fair sprinkling of houses ranked as abbeys, but in England almost all were *priories. The Cistercians having early demonstrated the utility of general chapters, these were instituted for all orders not already possessing them by *Lateran Council IV (1215). Those of the regular canons were subsequently organized on a regional basis normally meeting every 3 years.

An important if not large minority of medieval regular canons early belonged to independent congregations that had their own customs and an independent machinery of government. One of the first of these, the Order of the Holy Sepulcher of Jerusalem, begun by 1114, gave extensive powers to the motherhouse, in imitation of the venerable Order of *Cluny, but later congregations usually adopted a system of general chapters of their own on Cistercian lines. Most of these formal orders of regular canons were small, with some widely scattered houses that tended to drift away as time went on. The various independent orders were mostly in their heyday in the 12th century. The Order of Arrouaise, originating *c.* 1090, followed a severe, contemplative regime; that of Saint-Victor of Paris, whose motherhouse was founded in 1108 by Abelard's teacher *William of Champeaux, was closely connected with the rise of the University of *Paris and produced an important group of writers that included *Hugh of Saint-Victor and *Richard of Saint-Victor. The *Premonstratensians, whose motherhouse of *Prémontré near Laon was founded in 1120 by *Norbert of Xanten, showed great vitality from the first; some of its houses were contemplative, others were early involved in missionary work, notably in eastern Germany. The Order of the Holy Sepulcher of Jerusalem, which owed its existence to the crusading movement, declined when this collapsed. In the Spanish peninsula the Order of *Santa Cruz (Coimbra), begun in 1132, was of some importance and owed much in its origin to the Order of Saint-Ruf near Avignon, whose own reputation was considerable. The Order of Sempringham (the *Gilbertines), the only medieval order of English origin, was not of more than local importance, and had double *monasteries. Its motherhouse was founded in 1131, but the Augustinian Rule was not followed for some years.

Houses of Austin Canons in the Middle Ages and long after varied greatly in size. Few of them rivaled the largest Benedictine houses, but many were of moderate size. For largely unavoidable reasons, the order was early saddled with a sizable minority of very small houses, whose lack of resources and personnel rendered their life liable to considerable strains and were a cause of anxiety to those in authority. As time went on a number of these were either suppressed or made cells of larger houses. A number of houses, especially in early times, were founded in parochial or collegiate churches, but later it was often found preferable to establish them either just outside residential areas or more rarely in "places remote from human habitation," like Cistercian houses. A notable feature of the order was its connection with *hospitals, including those of the Great Saint Bernard, and of St. Bartholomew's and St. Thomas' in London.

Recent research strongly suggests that the earliest regular canons seldom tried to carry out pastoral work in the modern sense: such activity would have interfered greatly with the complex liturgical regime they early adopted. Occasionally one of the brethren might serve a parish in, or near, the conventual church, and a house was usually authorized to put a canon in charge of souls at any of its churches provided he were living in community with other brethren. But generally speaking, regular canons in charge of souls in the Middle Ages were not numerous, though their number seems to have increased somewhat after the *Black Death of 1347-50. Like the Benedictines, the medieval regular canons gradually established some contacts with medieval universities, but these were not, on the whole, very vigorously exploited.

Recent History. By the end of the Middle Ages the regular canons were reduced in number and influence, though signs of continued vitality were not lacking, notably the foundation of the Congregation of *Windesheim in Holland, whose motherhouse was founded in 1386 under the influence of the mystic Gerard *Groote and which flourished in Germanic lands. Its most famous member was *Thomas à Kempis, the probable author of the **Imitation of Christ*. Rather later came the Congregation of the Lateran, begun at Fregionaia, near Lucca, under *Bartholomew of Rome. Confirmed by the Pope in 1421, its brethern were given charge of the Lateran Basilica by Pope *Eugene IV but were replaced there by seculars in 1471.

The religious changes of the 16th century led to considerable numbers of houses of the order being suppressed, and the secularizations of the 18th and 19th centuries caused much further damage. As time went on old machinery was modified; e.g., the French houses of the order were regrouped to form a French congregation. Austria and Switzerland were the only major areas where the order's life went on without interruption: in 1907 the surviving houses in Austria were formed into the Austrian Congregation of Canons Regular; in Switzerland the venerable house of SS. Nicholas and Bernard, the Great Saint Bernard Hospice, despite much adversity, continues as the head of a congregation, as does the other leading Swiss house of the order, *Saint-Maurice. Also maintaining continuity with the medieval world are the Canons Regular of the Holy Cross, originally founded in Belgium *c.* 1210, and the Military Order of the Red Star Crucifers, which long worked extensively in eastern Europe (*see* BRETHREN OF THE CROSS). The largest of the medieval orders today, however, is that of the Premonstratensians. The Canons Regular of the Immaculate Conception, founded by Dom Adrien Gréa in 1871, now have their chief house in Rome. The modern regular canons are engaged in a very wide range of pastoral, educational, and social activities. Recently the smaller congregations have been considering coordinating their common activities.

Bibliography: E. AMORT, *Vetus disciplina canonicorum regularium et saecularium,* 2 v. (Venice 1747), old but valuable. Heimbucher 1:392–455, with useful bibliogs. J. C. DICKINSON, *The Origins of the Austin Canons and Their Introduction into England* (London 1950). P. FRANK, *Canonicorum regularium sodalitates* (Vorau, Austria 1954). C. DEREINE, DHGE 12:353–405; "Coutumiers et ordinaires de chanoines réguliers," *Scriptorium* 5 (1951) 107–113; 13 (1960) 244–246. *La vita commune del clero nei secoli XI e XII,* 2 v. (Università cattolica del S. Cuore; Milan 1962).

[J. C. DICKINSON]

CANOSSA, MADDALENA GABRIELLA, BL., foundress of the Daughters of Charity of Canossa; b. Verona, Italy, March 2, 1774; d. there, April 10, 1835 (feast, April 10). After the death in 1779 of her father, a wealthy marquis, her mother Marchesa Teresa Szluha remarried (1781). Maddalena, who was then raised by an uncle, was given a good private education. In 1799 she dedicated herself to caring for poor girls and in 1800 she began to house some of them. In 1803 she opened a charity school, but when she attempted in 1805 to dwell there herself she was constrained to return to her family. In 1808 she founded her religious congregation, dedicated to educational and hospital work. By the time of her death the Canossian Sisters had five houses. Maddalena was beatified Dec. 7, 1941 (*see* CHARITY, DAUGHTERS OF).

Bibliography: I. GIORDANI, *Maddalena di Canossa* (4th ed. Brescia 1957). G. STOFELLA, EncCatt 3:610–611. Butler Th Attw 2:309–311. T. PICCARI, *Sola con Dio* (Milan 1965).

[A. MENATO]

CANOVA, ANTONIO, Italian neoclassic sculptor; b. Passagno, Italy, Nov. 1, 1757; d. Venice, Oct. 12, 1822. As early as age 5, Antonio Canova had the tools of a stonecutter in his hand, since this was the trade of his grandfather and also of his guardian. By age 14, when his talent was recognized, he began study under a mediocre sculptor, Torritti. He then studied in Venice

Antonio Canova, monument of Pope Clement XIV, in the church of the Santi Apostoli, Rome, 1784–87.

where he sculptured his first commission, "Orpheus and Eurydice" (1773–76). Soon he was called to Rome (1779) under the auspices of the Venetian ambassador to copy ancient statues for the embellishment of Venice; but the young sculptor, being a creative artist, blossomed forth as one of the first to produce subjects in the spirit of the ancients rather than in imitation of them. His first group, "Theseus and the Minotaur" (1781), secured international fame bringing him commissions from England, France, and Austria, as well as from Rome. He was soon so busy that it was necessary to have assistants mechanically reproduce his plaster sketches in marble, which accounts somewhat for the dry impression of the finished product. His works included tomb sculpture (Clement XIV, 1784–87), Christian subjects ("Dying Mary Magdalene"), and female Greek types ("Three Graces," 1789). Perhaps most popular were his portraits, especially of Napoleon and his family.

Bibliography: A. C. Quatremère De Quincy, *Canova et ses ouvrages* (Paris 1834). E. Bassi, *Canova* (Rome 1943). E. Lavagnino and M. Praz, EncWA 3:57–62. **Illustration credit:** Alinari-Art Reference Bureau.

[R. Kavesh]

CANTATA

A concert setting of a secular or sacred text, with instrumental accompaniment. The term was first used by Alessandro Grandi (d. 1630) in his *Cantade et avie a voce sola* (1620). The solo (secular) chamber cantata (*a camera*), which reached its greatest period of development between 1650 and 1725, is essentially an Italian form, being an outgrowth of early-17th-century Italian monody. Although tentative cantata-like works appeared earlier (e.g., in the Monteverdian madrigal), the Roman composers Luigi Rossi and G. Carissimi first perfected the technique of alternating recitatives and arias, a technique associated with all later cantatas, sacred and secular. The composers Francesco Provenzale (1627–1704), A. Scarlatti (who composed over 500 cantatas), and Handel are the most important representatives of this period. From the end of the 17th century to the end of the 18th, the Italian cantata and the individual opera scene were very similar in musical form.

In the late 17th century the Italian cantata spread to other countries, and as it spread it took on more characteristics of the *oratorio, often utilizing chorus and orchestra as well as soloists. In France cantata composition reached a high level during the 18th century, especially in the art of Destouches (1672–1749), Clérambault, Campra, and Rameau. English composers such as Henry Purcell were composing cantatas, but calling them something else (e.g., Pindaric odes), until Handel introduced the term itself.

The German Protestant church cantata is a special development, one connected only tenuously with the Italian cantata. There are examples of church cantatas in Germany as early as the mid-17th century, but the cantata reached its fullest development only during the time of Buxtehude and J. S. Bach. The fundamental difference between the German (Protestant) cantata and the Italian is that in the Protestant cantata the chorale was used extensively, in addition to the usual arias, recitatives, and choruses. The Protestant cantata, whose average timing was 20 minutes, had a definite liturgical function in the Lutheran service. It was often performed between the Credo and the sermon, the Gospel of the day usually serving for its subject matter. When the cantata had two parts, the second part was performed after the sermon. All German Protestant composers of Bach's time were prolific composers of cantatas; Bach himself turned out about 300 (of which some 200 are extant). By the end of the century cantatas ceased to be anything but special works written for ceremonial occasions. Mozart and Beethoven, among others, created works of this type.

First page of an autograph fragment of the score of Handel's "Cantata for One Voice and Instruments."

The 19th century inspired few additions to the cantata literature. This is not surprising since, with the impact of Beethoven's Ninth Symphony, most composers preferred massive choral groups singing over huge orchestras; thus Berlioz, Liszt, and Mahler, and later, Vaughan Williams and Stravinsky, all composed choral symphonies. Brahms's smaller choral works with orchestral accompaniment, e.g., *Song of Destiny* (1871) and *Nänie,* (1881), may, however, be considered as part of the cantata genre. The growth in popularity of choral festivals in England and oratorio societies in America during the latter half of the century failed to produce works of lasting merit. The many choral works, large and small, of C. H. H. Parry, C. V. Stanford, and J. Stainer—with the possible exception of Stainer's *Crucifixion* (1887)—enjoyed instant success and equally instant oblivion.

Composers of the 20th century have thus far shown more interest in instrumental than in choral composition. William Walton's *Belshazzar's Feast* (1931) is probably 20th-century England's most notable addition to the literature of the dramatic cantata. This work, Vaughan Williams's *Sancta Civitas* (1926) and *Dona nobis pacem* (1936), and Benjamin Britten's *Rejoice in the Lamb* (1943) and *St. Nicholas* (1948) form a small but interesting corpus of contemporary cantata-like compositions. Influential smaller choral works have come from the pens of Bartók (*Cantata profana,* 1930), Anton Webern (*Cantata No. 1,* 1940, and *Cantata No. 2,* 1943), and Stravinsky (*Cantata,* 1952, *Canticum Sacrum,* 1955, and *Threni,* 1957–58). Compositions by such American composers as Wallingford Riegger (*The Raising of Lazarus,* 1931), William Schuman (*Cantata No. 1,* 1940, and *Cantata No. 2,* 1942), Norman dello Joio (*Song of Affirmation,* 1944), and Samuel Barber (*Prayers of Kierkegaard,* 1954) stand as ample evidence that, although choral composition may hardly be considered a major concern of the best contemporary composers, the cantata tradition is reemerging in exciting new shapes and sonorities.

Opening page of the autograph manuscript of Igor Stravinsky's "Canticum Sacrum," in the Library of Congress.

Bibliography: M. Lange, *Die Anfänge der Kantate* (Dresden 1938). E. Schmitz, *Geschichte der weltlichen Solokantate* (2d ed. Leipzig 1955). H. Engel et al, MusGG 7:553–611. E. J. Dent, Grove DMM 2:45–46. Apel HDMus 114–116. Young ChorTrad. **Illustration credits:** Fig. 1, Manuscript Division, New York Public Library. Fig. 2, Courtesy of Igor Stravinsky. Copyright 1956 by Boosey & Hawkes, Inc. Reproduced by permission of the copyright owner.

[W. C. HOLMES]

CANTERBURY, ANCIENT SEE OF

Principal metropolitan see of England, founded by *Augustine of Canterbury *c.* 600. Pope St. *Gregory the Great had envisaged *London as the ecclesiastical metropolis of southern England, but Augustine chose instead the capital of Kent, the most powerful and civilized Anglo-Saxon kingdom of the time, whose King *Ethelbert had become a Christian. Canterbury was itself a Roman city, and in ecclesiastical organization, architecture, and church-dedications (e.g., *see* SAINT AUGUSTINE, ABBEY OF) it was a small replica of Rome. The See of Canterbury has always been small in extent: eastern Kent with several "peculiars" elsewhere; but the Province of Canterbury came to include the whole of England south of the Humber, along with Wales. Before his death (*c.* 604), Augustine had founded the suffragan Sees of *Rochester and London.

History. Until 653 Canterbury was ruled by Augustine and his Italian companions: *Lawrence, *Mellitus, *Justus, and *Honorius. The first Anglo-Saxon archbishop was Frithonas (Deusdedit of Canterbury, 655–664). A new impulse was given to the Church in England by Archbishop Theodore (668–690), who held councils; appointed bishops to new sees, even in the north; and placed Irish missionary centers under episcopal control. With the African monk *Hadrian, he refounded the Canterbury school, which trained scholars and future bishops and outshone the Irish schools of the time.

In 753 *York, in accordance with Gregory the Great's plan, became a metropolitan see. About 40 years later King *Offa of Mercia tried to make Lichfield a Midland metropolitan see, but in 802–803, the supremacy of Canterbury was confirmed by both the Pope and a provincial council. After the disasters of the 9th-century Danish invasions the see recovered under Odo of Canterbury and *Dunstan, who worked in close association with the Kings of the time. In the later Danish invasions, Canterbury gained its first martyr, St. *Alphege, archbishop from 1005 to 1012.

After the Conquest, *Lanfranc, who replaced the simoniacal *Stigand, worked very closely with King *William I at the reform of the English church. *Simony, and eventually marriage for the higher clergy (*see* CELIBACY, HISTORY OF) were abolished, the monasteries were reformed by the introduction of Norman abbots and a more vigorous intellectual and spiritual life, and monks sometimes replaced canons as chapters of cathedrals. This latter practice, almost unique in Christendom, had already started under Dunstan. Soon after his death the *cathedral chapter of Christ Church, Canterbury, had become monastic, and under Lanfranc its observances, codified in his *Monastic Constitutions,* and its literary and artistic activities strongly influenced other monasteries. Lanfranc also regained lost Canterbury estates from *Odo of Bayeux and established a temporary ascendancy over the northern province of York. However, in spite of *Eadmer's claims and the Canterbury forgeries, Lanfranc's position was reversed by a papal decision in 1121, and York regained permanent independence.

The disputes over *investiture between Abp. *Anselm of Canterbury and King *William II and King *Henry I brought importance to Canterbury and exile to the most original theological thinker ever to occupy Augustine's chair. The dispute over the Constitutions of *Clarendon, including the treatment of criminous clerks and the right of appeal to Rome, between Thomas *Becket and *Henry II culminated in the former's martyrdom. This shocked all Europe and a cult of the archbishop rapidly sprang up over most of Europe, while in England the pilgrimage to Becket's tomb retained its immense popularity throughout the Middle Ages.

The later 12th century was marred by disputes between archbishops, who wanted to establish a collegiate church at Hackington whence archbishops might draw trained curialists for administering the diocese, and monastic chapters whose monks regarded this projected church as their rival. The monks were successful in the prolonged litigation that followed, though at a high cost, financially and in diminution of religious spirit.

Archbishops from 1200 to the Reformation. The disputed election of 1205 to 1207, which ended in the nomination of *Stephen Langton by Pope Innocent III, was the most famous in English ecclesiastical history. After the end of the interdict that followed King *John's rejection of Langton, Canterbury enjoyed a series of remarkably able and intellectual bishops for most of the 13th century. These included St. *Edmund of Abingdon, *Boniface of Savoy, *Robert Kilwardby, *John Peckham, and *Robert of Winchelsea who put into effect the decrees of the reforming Councils of the *Lateran and of *Lyons. They visited the province as well as the diocese systematically and efficiently, and promulgated a code of laws about clerical discipline, administration of the Sacraments, and preaching.

The 14th- and 15th-century archbishops were generally civil servants or canon lawyers rather than scholars; often their promotion reflected the growing control of the Church by the crown. *Simon of Sudbury (1375–81), e.g., was killed by the mob in the Peasants' Revolt as the King's principal reactionary adviser. These archbishops, often of aristocratic families, took a prominent part in politics and sometimes were translated by the Pope at the King's request to remote and unimportant sees in punishment for their political activities.

Through most of the Middle Ages England was remarkably free from heresy, but when the *Lollards arose Archbishops William *Courtenay, Thomas *Arundel, and Henry *Chichele were zealous in suppressing them with the help of the secular arm. However, they excluded the *Inquisition.

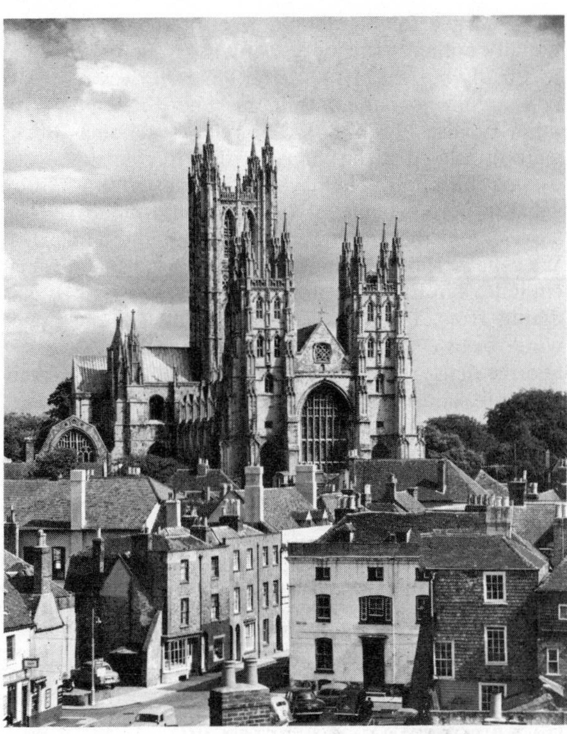

Canterbury cathedral, the west front as seen over the rooftops of the city.

From the 12th century, archbishops of Canterbury were so frequently papal *legates that they enjoyed the name of *legatus natus.* A few were promoted to be cardinals in Rome, but John *Kemp, *Bourgchier, and *Morton (1452–1500) were all cardinals while remaining archbishops of Canterbury. William *Warham (1503–32) was a friend of *Colet and *Erasmus, and toward the end of his reign the crisis began that was to lead to the Reformation in England. Thomas *Cranmer (1533–56), tool of *Henry VIII, pronounced the king's marriage with *Catherine of Aragon null after its validity had been upheld by the Pope, and rejected papal supremacy, substituting for it the novel and heretical doctrine that the king was supreme head of the Church in England. Under Cranmer, all the monasteries and chantries and several hospitals were suppressed, four of the diocesan manors were ceded to the King, the relics of Thomas Becket were destroyed and his name, together with that of the Pope, was removed from all the service books.

The accession of *Mary Tudor brought reconciliation with Rome and the appointment of Cardinal Reginald *Pole as archbishop and legate (1556–58). But the deaths of Mary and of Pole on the same day ended all hope of a permanent Catholic restoration. Under *Elizabeth I the Acts of Supremacy and *Uniformity were renewed, England became Protestant, and Canterbury was made the headquarters of the Anglican Church (*see* ANGLICANISM).

Cathedral. The first cathedral of Canterbury, begun by Augustine and completed by his successors, had been burned in 1067. Eadmer describes it as a miniature of Old St. Peter's, Rome. It was rebuilt by Lanfranc on a much bigger scale with a nave of nine bays, but a choir of only two. From 1100 to 1130, under Anselm and priors Ernulf and Conrad, the eastern limb was rebuilt and enlarged for processions and the display of exceptionally numerous relics of Canterbury saints. This part was badly burned in 1174, and the choir was rebuilt by two architects named William, one French and the other English (1174–84). The relics of Thomas Becket were translated to the chapel of the Holy Trinity, to the east of this choir. The nave was rebuilt from 1379 onward in perpendicular style under the architect Henry Yevele, and the fine tower ("Bell Harry") under John Wastell, *c.* 1500. Architecturally, it is one of the finest cathedrals in England, and it is enriched by stained glass dating from 1180 to 1280, especially the theological windows of Old and New Testament types and antitypes and the martyrdom of St. Thomas. There are also many tombs of saints and archbishops. A Norman crypt and part of the monastic buildings survive.

Bibliography: BEDE, *Eccl. Hist.,* i, 25–33; ii, 5–8; iv, 1–2 and *passim.* H. SPELMAN, ed., *Councils and Ecclesiastical Documents Relating to Great Britain and Ireland,* ed. A. W. HADDAN and W. STUBBS, 3 v. (Oxford 1869–78) v.3. Registers of archbishops of Canterbury pub. by Canterbury and York Society. I. J. CHURCHILL, *Canterbury Administration,* 2 v. (New York 1933). W. A. PANTIN, "The Pre-Conquest Saints of Canterbury," *For Hilaire Belloc,* ed. D. WOODRUFF (New York 1942); DHGE 11:785–812. R. WILLIS, *The Architectural History of Canterbury Cathedral* (London 1845). **Illustration credit:** British Travel Association, New York City.

[H. FARMER]

CANTICLE OF CANTICLES

The Canticle of Canticles, or Song of Songs, is a canonical book of the OT. The title means "the greatest song," and the book is the first of the *m^egillôt* or "scrolls" used in the liturgy of the Synagogue. This article treats of its author, date, and canonicity; its literary structure; its content; and its interpretation.

Authorship. The authorship is unknown; the mention of Solomon in 3.7; 8.11 probably is a reason why this postexilic work was ascribed to him. Although some of the songs are doubtless preexilic (as suggested by the reference to Thersa, the early capital of the Northern Kingdom, in 6.4), the form of the language, as a whole, suggests a late date. Early Jewish tradition indicates that there was some opposition before the first Christian century to its inclusion in the canon [see W. Rudolph, ZATWiss 18 (1942–43) 189–199]. Among Christians, Theodore of Mopsuestia is alleged to have opposed the work; but the condemnation of Theodore at Chalcedon V in 553 is aimed at his views concerning the inspired character of the book, not at the so-called naturalistic interpretation attributed to him [see R. E. Murphy, CathBiblQuart 15 (1953) 502–503; A. Brunet, *Études et Recherches* 9 (Ottawa 1955) 155–170]

Literary Structure. Although there are refrains in the work (2.7; 3.5; 8.4; etc.), there has been no general agreement on the division into poetic units. A. Bea finds 7; the CCD has 24 subheadings. As the book now stands, several songs have been combined into a loose unity. Some scholars (e.g., F. Delitzsch) have interpreted it as a drama, with two leading characters, Solomon and the Sulamite girl (cf. Ct. 7.1). Others (e.g, H. Ewald; W. Pouget–J. Guitton) have recognized three characters: the girl, her rustic lover, and Solomon, whose blandishments the girl resists. But the dramatic interpretation has not been able to overcome its own subjective and arbitrary explanations. There is no example of any drama in all of ancient Semitic literature, and in this book any conflict between the alleged suitors necessary for true drama seems to be absent. The truth in this view is that the Canticle is in a certain sense dramatic, since it is a dialogue, as the ancients recognized and as the Hebrew text itself makes clear; hence, modern translations (e.g., CCD) supply marginal rubrics to indicate the speakers.

Contents. As a collection of love lyrics, this book is not easy to summarize. The poems follow no logical sequence; rather, they express the various moods of love: the joy of union, the pain of separation. There are protestations of love and fidelity, reminiscences of courtship, descriptions of each other's beauty. The mood of mutual love is sustained throughout, but a highpoint is reached in 8.6–7, "Set me as a seal on your heart . . . ." The imagery is spontaneous and varied: gazelles and hinds, pomegranates and mandrakes, myrrh and spices, vineyards and wine. The rich use of geographical references suggests the disparate origins of the lyrics: Cedar, Engaddi, Lebanon, etc.

Interpretation. If identifying the literary structure is difficult, the interpretation of the meaning is more so. Both Christian and Jewish interpretations have agreed on a religious meaning: this book describes the love of Yahweh and Israel (or Christ and the Church) in terms of human marriage, thus continuing the theme inaugurated by Osee (ch. 1–3) and echoed in many later prophets (Is 1.21–22; 62.5; Jer 3.1–10; Ezechiel ch. 16, 23).

As Parable or Allegory. In detail, this interpretation is worked out as a parable, or as an allegory. The parabolic view is presented by D. Buzy, who claims that the work as a whole deals with the covenant relationship under the guise of human marriage. One should not press the details here; they serve to create the marriage atmosphere and to carry on the theme. Others argue that the Canticle is an allegory; the details have each a transferred meaning, referring to various aspects of Yahweh's dealings with Israel. This approach was first given a strong philological and exegetical basis by P. Joüon, and it has been supported by the method of *style anthologique,* applied by A. Robert. The "anthological style" refers to the Biblical practice (e.g., in Prv ch. 1–9, Sir, Wis) of composing a work in phrases and diction borrowed from earlier Biblical works; presumably the allusions to the previous books betray the intention of the writer of this book.

As Cultic Songs. Another interpretation, by such scholars as T. Meek, M. Haller, H. Ringgren, H. Schmökel, finds in this book cultic songs of the pagan myth of Tammuz and Ishtar. Presumably these could have been sung in the temple (e.g., during the reign of Manasse) and might later have entered the Passover liturgy. But the contacts that are pointed out between the Canticle and the myth are not sufficient to establish this interpretation. Nor can one easily imagine that Israel would have glossed over such origins in eventually accepting the poems into the canon. Any similarity is more easily explained by the influence that popular beliefs might have had on the love poetry and the wedding imagery of the Israelites themselves.

As Extolling Human Love. In recent times several Catholic scholars have criticized both the allegorical and parabolic approach. The principal reason for this criticism is that the obvious meaning of the Canticle is human love. When human love is used in the prophetical writing as referring to Yahweh and Israel, the

Illustrated page from the block-book edition of the Latin version of the Canticle of Canticles, printed in the Netherlands c. 1471. Passages are quoted (or adapted) from the Canticle: "Your words [verba *for* ubera, *'breasts'*] *will be like clusters of the vine, and the fragrance of your breath like apples" (7.9); "My lover is for me a sachet of henna from the vineyards of Engaddi" (1.13); "You are an enclosed garden, my sister, my bride, an enclosed garden, a fountain sealed" (4.12); "You are a garden fountain, a well of water flowing fresh from Lebanon" (6.15); "Arise, north wind! Come, south wind! Blow upon my garden, that its perfumes may spread abroad" (4.16).*

explanation of the symbolism is always given. Hence we may not presume that the intent of this book goes beyond the obvious and direct meaning. The use made by the prophets is usually in terms of Israel as the adulterous spouse (Os 2.18–22; Is 62.5; etc. are clear exceptions), but the Canticle presents a picture of idyllic love. The elaborate use of anthological style by A. Robert and A. Feuillet has not convinced many, especially for the reason that there is no indication in the Canticle of alleged mercy toward an unfaithful spouse.

There is a strong trend among recent Catholic scholars to agree with many of their Protestant colleagues (H. H. Rowley, W. Rudolph, etc.) that the literal sense of this book is the extolling of love and fidelity between man and woman; so say J. P. Audet, A. Dubarle (at the Louvain *journées bibliques* of 1963), M. van den Oudenrijn, and others. Comparison of this book with the love poems of the ancient Near East, especially Egypt, shows a common atmosphere and similarity of theme. The Canticle would be the "voice of the bridegroom" and the "voice of the bride" mentioned in Jer 7.34 (Audet). Such praise of love is entirely consonant with inspiration, since God himself is the author of that love (Gn 1.27).

In line with this deeper understanding of love, these scholars also allow that a higher sense, fuller or typical, can be found here. Human love is a participation in divine love, to which it is oriented; the family reflects the people of God. Here exegesis would join the age-old interpretation that sees in the Canticle the description of the love between God and his People. Christian tradition has developed this theme, already found in the NT (Eph 5.23–25, marriage compared to the relationship between Christ and his Church). The famous medieval writers, such as St. Bernard, and the mystical writers, such as St. John of the Cross, have exploited the richness of this interpretation.

Bibliography: For surveys, see R. E. MURPHY, "Recent Literature on the Canticle," CathBiblQuart 16 (1954) 1–11. H. H. ROWLEY, *The Servant of the Lord and Other Essays on the Old Testament* (London 1952). A complete and up-to-date bibliography is to be found in the two recent commentaries: A. ROBERT et al., eds. and trs., *Le Cantique des cantiques* (ÉtBibl; Paris 1963) 29–39 and G. GERLEMAN, *Ruth, Das Hohelied* (Biblischer Kommentar: Altes Testament 18.2; Neukirchen 1963) 85–92. D. BUZY, ed. and tr., *Le Cantique des Cantiques* (Paris 1950). T. MEEK, *The Song of Songs,* InterBibl 5:91–148. W. RUDOLPH, *Das Buch Ruth, Das Hohe Lied, Die Klagelieder* (Kommentar zum Alten Testament 17:1–3; Gütersloh 1962). For comparisons with ancient Near Eastern literatures, cf. the excursus in the volume by Robert, et al. 339–421. A history of interpretation is to be found in F. OHLY, *Hohelied-Studien* (Wiesbaden 1958). Two important articles are: A. M. DUBARLE, "L'Amour humain dans le Cantique des cantiques," RevBibl 61 (1954) 67–86. J. P. AUDET, "Le Sens du Cantique des cantiques," RevBibl 62 (1955) 197–221. **Illustration credit:** The Pierpont Morgan Library.

[R. E. MURPHY]

CANTICLES, BIBLICAL, liturgical hymns taken from the books of the Bible other than the Book of Psalms and resembling the Psalms in form and content. The use of the Biblical canticles in the Christian liturgy began in the East, where it may have been borrowed from a Jewish custom; but it was known in the West as early as the 4th century. In some Biblical MSS (e.g., the Codex Alexandrinus) the canticles are inserted immediately after the Book of Psalms. According to the Roman rite, three NT canticles are used each day in the Divine Office: the *Benedictus or Canticle of Zachary (Lk 1.68–79) at Lauds; the *Magnificat or Canticle of the Blessed Virgin Mary (Lk 1.46–55) at Vespers; and the *Nunc Dimittis or Canticle of Simeon (Lk 2.29–32) at Compline. The Roman rite uses several OT canticles as the fourth "psalm" at Lauds, two different ones for each day of the week, one for "first" Lauds (on most days) and another for "second" Lauds (on penitential days). These are (in the order of the Bible): the first Canticle of Moses, also known as the Canticle of *Mariam (Miriam; Ex 15.1–18), second Lauds of Thursday; the second Canticle of *Moses (Dt 32.1–43), second Lauds of Saturday (but since 1960 only Dt 32.1–18); the Canticle of *Anna (1 Sm 2.1–10), second Lauds of Wednesday; the Canticle of David (1 Chr 29.10–13), first Lauds of Monday; the Canticle of Tobit (Tobias; Tb 13.1–8), first Lauds of Tuesday; the Canticle of *Judith (Jdt 16.13–17), first Lauds of Wednesday; the Canticle of Sirach (Sir 1.1–13), first Lauds of Saturday; the first Canticle of Isaia (Is 20.1–6), second Lauds of Monday; the second Canticle of Isaia (Is 45.15–25), first Lauds of Friday; the Canticle of Ezechia (Is 38.10–20), second Lauds of Tuesday; the Canticle of Jeremia (Jer 31.10–14), first Lauds of Thurs-

Illuminated capital letter D at the beginning of the canticle in the third chapter of the Book of Habacuc, in the 12th-century English "Saint Alban Psalter" preserved in the cathedral treasury at Hildesheim, Germany.

day; the *Benedicite Dominum or the Canticle of the Three Youths in the Fiery Furnace (Dn 3.52–88), divided into two hymns—Dn 3.52–57, second Lauds of Sunday, and Dn 3.57–88, first Lauds of Sunday; and the Canticle of Habacuc (Hab 3.2–19), second Lauds of Friday. The Biblical text of some of the canticles has been somewhat altered for use in the Divine Office.

Bibliography: P. ALBRIGI, EncCatt 3:621–624. L. KUNZ, Lex ThK² 2:922. EncDictBibl 314–315. H. SCHNEIDER, *Die altlateinischen biblischen Cantica* (Beuron 1938); "Die biblischen Oden im christlichen Altertum," *Biblica* 30 (1949) 28–65, 239–272, 432–452, 479–500. **Illustration credit:** University of London, The Warburg Institute.

[L. F. HARTMAN]

CANTON, ARCHDIOCESE OF (COAMCEUVENSIS), metropolitan see since 1946, in southeast *China. The city of Canton (Kuang-chou) is the civil capital of Kwangtung (Kuang-tung) province. Statistics for 1950, the latest available, showed the see to be 16,730 square miles in area with 44 secular and 17 religious priests, 94 women in 12 convents, and 20,000 Catholics in a population of 5 million; it is 16,730 square miles in area. Its six suffragan sees (all created in 1946) are *Hong Kong, Mei-hsien (Kaying), Chiang-men (Kongmoon), Pakhoi, Shao-kuan (Suichow), Shan-t'ou (Swatow). In 1950 the last five of these sees had 170 priests, 176 sisters, and 82,000 Catholics in a population of 19 million.

St. Francis *Xavier died on Sancian Island off the coast of Kwangtung (1552), and Jesuits, including Matteo *Ricci, labored in Canton from 1582. Kwangtung was administered as part of the See of *Macao by Pierre *Lambert de la Motte (1659) and formed part of the Diocese of *Nanking (1690), but did not become a vicariate in 1696, as did many Chinese provinces. In 1706 there were seven chapels in Canton, from which missionaries were expelled in 1724; the area by then formed part of the Diocese of Macao. The Prefecture Apostolic of Kwangtung, established in 1850, comprised the Provinces of Kwangtung and Kwangsi, the island of Hainan, and French Kwangchou and Fort Bayard. In 1875 Kwangsi (*see* NANNING) was detached, and in 1914 Kwangtung became a vicariate called Canton (1914–46), from which were created other vicariates in 1915 and 1924.

Bibliography: *Annuaire de l'Église catholique en Chine* (Shanghai 1950). MissCattol 384–388. A. PUCCI, EncCatt 3:643–644.

[J. KRAHL]

CANTOR, GEORG, mathematician; b. St. Petersburg, Russia, March 3, 1845; d. Halle, Germany, Jan. 6, 1918. Cantor's father was a Jewish convert to Protestantism; his mother was a Catholic. He entered the University of Berlin in 1863 to study theoretical mathematics under E. Kummer, L. Kronecker, and K. Weierstrass. Cantor's doctoral thesis (1867) was on the solution of the indeterminate equation $ax^2 + by^2 + cz^2 = 0$, where *a, b, c* are integers, a point unsolved by Gauss in *Disquisitiones arithmeticae*. Cantor spent most of his academic career at the University of Halle (Wittenberg), becoming ordinary professor in 1879. He made his greatest achievements in mathematical research from 1871 to 1884. He published many articles now considered classics on the theory of numbers, Fourier series, and the theory of irrationals. His study of trigonometric series became the basis for his theory of sets (*Mengenlehre*).

Cantor took the attributes of equal, greater than, and less than and applied them to infinite quantities. His definition of infinite classes rests on the paradox that the whole is no greater than any of its parts. The classes that could be put into one-to-one correspondence with the natural numbers he symbolized by the first letter in the Hebrew alphabet, *aleph,* with a subscript zero, since he suspected a hierarchy of *alephs.* These new classes he called transfinite because they differed from finite cardinals. After showing that rational numbers were dense, he proved them denumerable by the ingenious method known as the Cantor diagonal process. Though this process was considered controversial from an operational point of view, it became a model for many mathematical demonstrations. Cantor proved that algebraic numbers (those that are roots of algebraic equations, $a_0x^n + a_1x^{n-1} + \cdots + a_{n-1}x + a_n = 0$) are countable by the method of heights (sum of the absolute values of coefficients plus the degree of the equation less one), hailed by mathematicians as the triumph of ingenuity. He also proved that the set of rational numbers in the interval $0 < x < 1$ and the class of transcendentals are not only infinite but also not countable. As a consequence, the class of all real numbers is nondenumerable.

Cantor's theory of sets was neglected during his lifetime, but at present there is no writer on analysis who does not refer directly or indirectly to the concept of sets, which has clarified and generalized the fundamental concepts of mathematics.

The last 17 years of his life Cantor suffered from nervous disorders; he died in a psychiatric clinic in Halle.

Bibliography: R. C. ARCHIBALD, "Outline of the History of Mathematics," *American Mathematical Monthly* 56 (Jan. 1949) supp. C. B. BOYER, *The Concepts of the Calculus* (New York 1939). G. PRASAD, *Some Great Mathematicians of the Nineteenth Century,* v.2 (Benares City, India 1934). D. J. STRUIK, *A Concise History of Mathematics,* 2 v. (New York 1948).

[T. À K. KLOYDA]

CANTOR IN CHRISTIAN LITURGY

The role of cantor as the solo singer of Jewish prayer tunes has a venerable history in Hebrew music and came to achieve official recognition in the Christian liturgy also, but not until the 4th century, and then somewhat obscurely. Until the 4th century there had been only a lector; the forms of worship had not been fixed; and there is no trace of the present alternation of chants with liturgical elements, but only of cantillated readings, psalms, and prayers. The faithful heard them from the mouth of the deacon or the bishop (*Apostolic Tradition* of St. *Hippolytus, ch. 26); the lector had an equally important role. At home the faithful chanted psalms (Pliny, letter 97, A.D. 110). There are numerous references to lectors, but only one of them (who died at 18) had trained "all" the faithful "in singing psalms and reading holy books," according to an epitaph whose veracity may have been sacrificed to literary style (cited by H. Leclercq).

4th Century and After. The cantor appears in the collection of Laodicea (343–381), whose canon 15 states that only a cantor who has been canonically chosen may ascend to the ambo to read "from the parchment"; and in canons 23 and 24 cantors are forbidden to patronize inns and wear the stola (Mansi 2:564). St. John Chrysostom (347–407) observes that in church the lector speaks alone and even the seated bishop listens in silence; in the same way the cantor chants alone, and when all reply they sound as a single voice (*Hom. in 1 Cor* 36.6). During this period, references to holy men who have sung in church and become priests grow more numerous in epitaphs and other sources; these men are not, however, expressly designated as cantors.

These changes reflect the spread of Christianity. The faith was extended, the liturgy acquired elements of the spectacular and began to be unified. Some of the musical compositions newly introduced were difficult to perform. An experienced singer was indispensable, especially for the vocalise of the Alleluia, called the jubilus, whose origin is still obscure. St. Jerome mentions it as a difficult piece (letter 38) and St. Augustine speaks at length of the wordless vocalise that expresses what words cannot—the ineffable (see *In psalm.* 32.3, PL 36:283; *In psalm.* 99, PL 37:1272; *Serm.* 152.9, PL 38:1176; and elsewhere). This experienced soloist, alone at the ambo, is known through a text of Victor de Vite, dated between 450 and 470 (MGAuctAnt 3.1.1.41:10). From this time on the references to cantors are more frequent.

Role of St. Gregory. In this development of ceremonies and participants there were abuses; e.g., a priest might be chosen because of his voice rather than his character. In one decree, Pope (St.) *Gregory I prohibited priests from singing anything but the Gospel; the Psalms and the other readings were chanted by the subdeacons and the lesser clergy, and there is no mention at all of cantors (year 595, Mansi 10:434). In this period the only clear traces of a **schola cantorum* are in the East, and even there only in Greece (Corbin, 168).

The Group of Cantors. At the end of the 7th century there is mention of a leader of the cantors (Duchesne LP 1:371), which suggests that there was an organized group, the future *schola cantorum.* But the question arises: Were these cantors necessarily priests? The texts are equivocal; a cantor is only very rarely named in the lists of the orders [except in the Gelasian Sacramentary; see Wilson's edition (1894) 145]. The ambiguity is such that, on one hand, frequently laymen are forbidden to sing liturgical compositions (year 688, Mansi 12:25), and on the other, cantors are reproached for their vanity and for the time lost in their training. They learned their repertory by heart until the invention of the clef in the 11th century and spent more than 10 years in the process. From the 9th century, according to the *solfège* of the *Musica Enchiriadis,* some of them specialized in polyphonic *organum.

Separation of Title and Function. It was thus as the result of a perfectly natural evolution that the honorific title of cantor was separated from the duties that had become so taxing that they created special qualifications. From the 11th century the title was reserved for a dignitary of the chapter who was entitled to a prebend, the actual function being performed by carefully chosen specialists. From such experienced personnel and the challenge of polyphonic music evolved the polyphonic choirs, which originated with the first organa of the Winchester Troper (*see* MUSIC, SACRED, HISTORY OF, 3) and an increase in the number of singers.

Oriental Churches. In the East the deacon and cantor are often, but not necessarily, one and the same person. Usually the cantor is entrusted with carefully determined selections and must make the responses to the deacon. As during the Middle Ages in the West, the trainee cantor in the East learns his art by ear, listening to an older singer. The cantor sits in the center of the group and sings a psalm on a simple formula. The children learn first to hold the *ison* (the modal tonic sustained throughout a chant), thus achieving the effect of polyphony. By degrees they learn the final cadence of the psalm. When the master reaches this cadence, the children join in little by little, depending on how capable they are. Then they learn the words and sing the entire psalm. The whole repertory is learned in this manner, and it is a slow process. The Eastern cantor is considered with great respect, even if he himself is not in Holy Orders. His talent is to a certain extent hereditary; families of singers are known, in which the skill and the office have been passed from father to son.

Bibliography: H. LECLERCQ, DACL 3.1:344–365. J. QUASTEN, *Musik und Gesang in den Kulten der heidnischen Antike und christlichen Frühzeit* (LiturgQuellForsch 25; 1930). T. GÉROLD, "Les Pères de l'Église et la musique," RevHistPhilRel 11 (1931) 409–418. W. GURLITT, *Zur Bedeutungsgeschichte von "Musicus" und "Cantor" bei Isidor von Sevilla* (Akademie der Wissenschaften und der Literatur. Abhandlungen der Geistes- und sozialwissenschaftlichen Klasse 7; Mainz 1950) 543–558. S. CORBIN, *L'Église à la conquête de sa musique* (Paris 1960) ch. 7–8.

[S. CORBIN]

CANTOR IN SYNAGOGUE SERVICE

The prayer leader, called *ḥazzān* in Hebrew, in Jewish liturgical services. Originally the term *ḥazzān* meant supervisor, and it was applied both to the janitor in the school and to the bailiff of the court who executed punishments, especially flogging. In ancient times, therefore, the *ḥazzān* of the synagogue was a sort of beadle. According to the Talmud his function was to take out from the holy ark the Torah (Pentateuch) scroll, open it at the appointed reading for the week, call the weekly portion, and return it to the ark after the service was completed. The oldest mention of the *ḥazzān,* though not by this name, is in Lk 4.20, where he is called a ὑπηρέτης (attendant). For a long time the *ḥazzān* continued to fulfill the modest duties of a factotum around the synagogue, but little by little, especially in smaller congregations, he attained more importance, as he assumed the functions of a preacher, judge, and schoolmaster. He had, however, no right to read the weekly portion from the Pentateuch without special permission from the elders of the synagogue. In the measure that the knowledge of the Hebrew language declined and the ordinary worshiper was no longer able to read the unvocalized text of the Torah, official readers were appointed, often the *ḥazzān* himself, while the individual worshiper recited only the benedictions.

With the development of the synagogical service, particularly by the addition of an evergrowing liturgical poetry, the congregation required the guidance of a professional cantor. In the gaonic period after the 5th century, the reading from the Torah and the recitation of the prayers were as a rule duties of the cantor, who in this function was called the *sheliaḥ tzibbur* (agent of the congregation). The poetical pieces called **piyyuṭim* stimulated the creation of complicated musical compositions that no lay precentor was able to execute. The musical performance became so demanding that the *ḥazzān* had to be assisted by other singers called *tomechim* (supporters), especially on festival days. This applied to rich communities. Poorer ones, unable to afford two officials, gave preference to a *ḥazzān* rather than to a rabbi, according to the directive given by Asher ben Yehiel (*c.* 1250–1327), one of the leading rabbinical authorities of his time. Nevertheless, both in late medieval and in early modern times, in the measure that the authority of the rabbi was in ascendancy in the synagogue as against the former lay leadership, there was a tendency to relegate the *ḥazzān* to a position completely under the rabbi's control. The rabbis demanded that all candidates be examined for piety as well as for voice and insisted that piety and learning count above musical distinction. The *ḥazzān* enjoyed much liberty in his musical performance and frequent complaints were made against him for using too elaborate melodies and thus lengthening the service inordinately. Beginning from the 17th century, especially in the Yiddish-speaking congregations, the *ḥazzān* became solely an artist, without retaining any of the tasks historically associated with his office.

"Shavuoth," painting by the 19th-century Jewish artist Moritz Oppenheim. The cantor is shown fulfilling his original function of taking the Torah scroll from the ark.

See also JEWISH LITURGY; MUSIC, HEBREW.

Bibliography: I. ELBOGEN, UnivJewishEnc 3:17–18. A. KAISER, JewishEnc 6:284–287. A. Z. IDELSOHN, EncJudaica 9:888–902; *Jewish Music in Its Historic Development* (New York 1929; repr. 1946). A. M. ROTHMÜLLER, *The Music of the Jews* (London 1953; repr. Gloucester, Mass. 1962). **Illustration credit:** Photo Archives, Jewish Theological Seminary of America, F. J. Darmstaedter. Oscar Gruss Collection, New York.

[M. J. STIASSNY]

CANTÙ, CESARE

Historian with strong Catholic principles, litterateur, polygrapher, patriot, and statesman; b. Brivio (Como), Italy, Dec. 5, 1804; d. Milan, March 11, 1895. He was born in a poor, pious family and studied for the priesthood for a short time. His education left an indelible mark on his spiritual formation. He steadfastly opposed political clericalism and narrow religious bigotry. At 18 he began teaching literature in the Gymnasium of Sondrio, and later in those of Como and Milan. Meanwhile, he devoted himself to historical scholarship.

An indefatigable worker, he wrote extensively on religion and country, earning the reputation of having been the first and the last among the staunchest partisans of *Neo-Guelfism. His interest in the Catholic Church and in the Middle Ages resulted in his *Storia della città e della diocesi di Como* (1830–31), a typical historical monograph on a city. From this study he evolved the principle that characterized all his historical writings: "a commune and a saint: herein are the elements on which the Italians have always based their liberty."

In 1832 he came under the influence of *Manzoni, for whose *Promessi Sposi* Cantù wrote a historical commentary entitled *Ragionamenti sulla storia lombarda del secolo XVIII.*

As an enemy of all forms of conspiracy and a strong supporter of the Neo-Guelf party, Cantù aimed to educate Italians in the Christian tradition. In 1835 the suspicions of the Austrian police caused his imprisonment for 10 months. He was released for want of legal evidence. However, he had compromised himself, and as a result suffered many vexations, including loss of

Cesare Cantù.

employment. Forced to write to earn a living, he published the well-known novel *Margherita Pusterla* (1838), which enjoyed wide popularity. Its pronounced ethical, religious aims obscured the historical background of the subject.

After Cantù's release from prison, Pomba, a publisher, invited him to write the monumental *Storia Universale,* published in 35 volumes (1838–46). In it Cantù contended that history is the constant and perennial work of divine Providence, who watches over, guides, and judges men and institutions; and that through Christianity man may attain peace, brotherhood, cultural and social elevation. The work contains many factual errors and is partial in its judgments and purposely moralist in tone. Cantù did not possess a solid basis for his historical ideas, although he was convinced that Neo-Guelfism meant a widespread, universal return of civilized society to Christianity.

Among his more than 500 writings are: *Storia di cento anni* (1851); *L'abate Parini e la Lombardia del secolo passato* (1854); *Beccaria e il diritto penale* (1862); *Gli eretici d'Italia* (1865–66); *Alcuni italiani contemporanei* (1868); *Il conciliatore e i carbonari* (1878); *Monti e l'età che fu sua* (1879); and *Reminiscenze su A. Manzoni* (1882), which provoked heated discussions. His writings were popular despite his frequent inaccuracies and lack of profound scholarship.

Bibliography: A. VISMARA, *Cantù bibliografia* (Milan 1896). F. BERTOLINI, *Cesare Cantù e le sue opere* (Florence 1896). B. CROCE, *Storia della storiografia italiana nel secolo XIX,* 2 v. (2d ed. Bari 1930) v.1. P. DALLA TORRE, EncCatt 3:646–649.

[H. R. MARRARO]

CANTUS FIRMUS, a borrowed or newly composed melody used as the basis for constructing a polyphonic composition. The use of preexistent melodic material is important from the earliest beginnings of polyphony. **Organum,* which was first described in the 9th century, used *Gregorian chant melodies as its foundation. The school of St. Martial (*see* MUSIC, SACRED, HISTORY OF, 3, 4) placed the chant melody in the bottom voice of a two-voice composition, and lengthened the notes so much that the chant became almost unrecognizable, while a fast-moving freely invented voice soared above. During the *ars antiqua* (13th century), the school of Notre Dame based its *organa* and *clausulae* on plainchant melodies. The use of a plainchant as *cantus firmus* for *Masses and *motets was almost universal during the 13th and 14th centuries. In the 15th century secular songs, such as *L'homme armé,* and freely invented melodies drawn from the hexachord, were used as the basis for Masses, appearing especially in the tenor voice. Palestrina's Mass *Ut Re Mi Fa So La* is an example of this. Another type of *cantus firmus,* called *soggetto cavato,* is derived from a literary sentence, transforming its vowels into corresponding syllables of the hexachord. Thus the *cantus firmus* for *Desprez's Mass *Hercules Dux Ferrarie* is: *re-ut-re-ut-re-fa-mi-re.* Certain keyboard works in the 16th century, such as those for the organ by Schlick, *Cabezón, Redford, and Titelouze and for the virginal by Bull, *Byrd, and Morley, are another category of *cantus firmus* compositions, of which later manifestations are the chorale preludes of *Buxtehude, Pachelbel, and J. S. *Bach.

Bibliography: E. H. SPARKS, *Cantus Firmus in Mass and Motet, 1420–1520* (Berkeley 1963). F. H. SAWYER, "The Use and Treatment of Canto Firmo by the Netherlands School of the Fifteenth Century," *Proceedings of the Musical Association* 63 (1937) 97–116. Reese MusMA. Reese MusR.

[L. J. WAGNER]

CANTWELL, JOHN JOSEPH, first archbishop of *Los Angeles, Calif.; b. Limerick, Ireland, Dec. 1, 1874; d. Los Angeles, Oct. 30, 1947. He was the son of Ellen (O'Connell) and Patrick Cantwell. After attending Sacred Heart College, Crescent, Limerick, and St. Patrick's College, Thurles, he was ordained on June 19, 1899. He then went to the U.S., where he was stationed at Berkeley, Calif., from 1899 to 1904. While assistant at St. Joseph's Church there, he founded the Newman Club at the University of California. From 1905 to 1914 he was secretary to Abp. Patrick Riordan of San Francisco, Calif., and in 1914 was made vicar-general. Having been appointed bishop of Monterey–Los Angeles on Sept. 21, 1917, he was consecrated and installed that December. With the separation of Monterey–Fresno on June 1, 1922, Cantwell's see became Los Angeles–San Diego. He was made metropolitan of the new Province of Los Angeles on July 11, 1936.

Cantwell's 30-year episcopate in Los Angeles coincided with a phenomenal growth in the area. In 1917 the population of Los Angeles was less than 500,000; at his death it exceeded 2,000,000. The number of Catholics in 1917 was estimated at 178,233; in 1947, even after two dioceses had been detached, the Los Angeles see had 600,000 Catholics. They were served by 2 auxiliary bishops and 688 priests, of whom 362 were diocesan; there were 217 parishes with resident pastors, 2 diocesan seminaries, 3 seminaries for religious, 4 colleges, 35 high schools, and 115 parochial schools with 42,877 pupils. The Confraternity of Christian Doctrine was organized in 1922, and from 1943 on it utilized released time authorized by the state at the archbishop's request. At the archbishop's invitation, 14 communities of priests, 6 of lay brothers, and 36 of nuns established themselves in his see. Despite the 1929 Depression and the 1933 earthquake, progress continued as Catholic hospitals and charitable institutions were founded or enlarged.

Under Cantwell, synods were held in 1927 and 1942. In 1931 he received the Golden Rose of Tepeyac in gratitude for hospitality to exiled Mexican bishops and their flock during persecution. His solicitude for aliens led to the foundation of Mexican, Italian, Portuguese, Chinese, Russian, and Maronite chapels. Cantwell also inspired the organization of a Catholic Actors' Guild, the Thomas More Club for lawyers, and the Bellarmine group for industry and labor. The Legion of Decency (1934) grew out of Cantwell's appeal for a curb on abuses in the movie industry.

Bibliography: Archives, Los Angeles Chancery. J. B. CODE, *Dictionary of American Hierarchy* (New York 1940). M. P. O'DONNELL, *Effect of John J. Cantwell's Episcopate On Catholic Education in California* (Washington 1952).

[N. C. EBERHARDT]

CANUTE IV, KING OF DENMARK, ST., reigned 1080 to July 10, 1086; b. *c.* 1043; d. Odense, Denmark (feast, Jan. 19, July 10). He was the son of King Sweyn Estrithson and the grandnephew of King *Canute the Great of England and Denmark. Before succeeding his brother Harold Hen to the throne, Canute had spent his youth in Viking expeditions to England and the Baltic countries. He proved to be an energetic, reforming king, seeking to extend the royal tax laws at home and to challenge *William the Conqueror's hold on England. After his marriage to a Flemish princess, Adele, he attempted to organize the Danish Church on a Continental pattern (*see* DACIA). His donation to the cathedral of Lund is the first recorded act of a Danish king. He established an abbey of English Benedictines at Odense. The rural aristocracy resented his fiscal policy, and in 1085 a revolt broke out as he was about to sail for England. He was captured and killed in the church he had founded in Odense (today, Sankt-Knud). Miracles at the tomb of this "martyr" led King Erik Evergood to request his canonization, and this was granted in 1099 by Pope Paschal II. The monks at Odense fostered his veneration and wrote his life. Traditionally the patron of Denmark, he was also popularly regarded as the patron of numerous guilds until eclipsed by *Canute Lavard. His relics are still at Odense in a 12th-century wooden reliquary. Canute was the father of Bl. Charles the Good, Count of Flanders.

Bibliography: M. C. GERTZ, *Vitae sanctorum danorum,* (new ed. Copenhagen 1908–12) 27–168, 531–558; *Knud den Helliges Martyrhistorie* (Copenhagen 1907). B. SCHMEIDLER, "Eine neue Passio S. Kanuti regis et martyris," *Gesellschaft für altere deutsche Geschichtskunde/Neues Archiv* 37 (1911–12) 67–97. P. D. STEIDL, *Knud den Hellige* (Copenhagen 1918). Butler Th Attw 1:121. T. GAD, *Kulturhistorisk Leksikon for nordisk Middelalder,* ed. J. DANSTRUP (Copenhagen 1956–) 8:596–600.

[L. MUSSET]

CANUTE, KING OF ENGLAND AND DENMARK, 1016 (1018 for Denmark) to Nov. 12, 1035; b. *c.* 995; d. Shaftesbury, England. The younger son of King Sweyn "Forkbeard" of Denmark, Canute (Cnut) the Great joined his father's attack on England in 1013, and upon Sweyn's death (Feb. 3, 1014) he was elected ruler by the fleet. He was soon driven back to Denmark, to which his brother Harold had succeeded and from which he prepared a fresh invasion. In 1015 he returned to England, and after the death of King Ethelred II (April 23, 1016), defeated Ethelred's son Edmund "Ironside" at Assandûn (Ashington?), Essex. A treaty left Edmund in possession of Wessex while Canute was acknowledged king of the regions

Canute and his Queen, Aelfgyfu (Emma), placing a gold cross upon the altar at Winchester, in a registry and martyrology from Winchester, c. 1016–20 (Stowe MS 944).

north of the Thames; but when Edmund died suddenly on November 30, Canute was formally chosen king of all England. His position was strengthened in July 1017 by his marriage to Emma (Aelfgyfu), Ethelred's widow. In 1018, when Harold died, Canute succeeded as king of Denmark; and 10 years later, having defeated *Olaf II Haroldsson, he gained control of Norway. These holdings, a veritable northern empire, put Canute second only to the Holy Roman Emperor (*see* HOLY ROMAN EMPIRE) in power and stature in western Europe. He was a generous patron of the church and in 1026–27 made a pilgrimage to Rome. He is buried at Winchester. His son Harold "Harefoot" succeeded briefly and contrary to plan in England while Harthacnut, his son by Emma, became king of Denmark and later (1040–42) king of England.

Bibliography: Sources. EngHistDoc 1:308–312, 414–430. J. EARLE and C. PLUMMER, eds., *Two of the Saxon Chronicles Parallel,* 2 v. (Oxford 1892–99), under years 1013–35. Literature. L. M. LARSON, *Canute the Great* (New York 1912). F. M. STENTON, *Anglo-Saxon England* (2d ed. Oxford 1947) 380–414.
Illustration credit: Courtesy of the Trustees of the British Museum.

[R. D. WARE]

CANUTE LAVARD, ST., Danish noble; b. Roskilde, *c.* 1096; d. Haraldsted, Jan. 7, 1131 (feast, Jan. 7; June 25). Son of the Danish King Erik Evergood, he was baptized Gregory. The surname "Lavard" is equivalent to the English "Lord." As a youth he was at the court of Saxony with the future Emperor *Lothair III. His uncle, King Niels (Nicholas), named him Duke of Schleswig *c.* 1115. Through the protection of Lothair he became, *c.* 1129, Prince (Knés) of the Wends in eastern Holstein, whom he tried to evangelize. Put forward as eventual successor to King Niels, he constituted a rival to the latter's son, Magnus, whose entourage assassinated Canute at Haraldsted, near Ringsted, Denmark. This crime brought on a civil war that lasted until the accession of Canute's son, Waldemar I the Great. Reports of miracles at Canute's tomb at Ringsted led to the building of a chapel on the site of the murder. Pope Alexander III canonized Canute in 1169; the solemn translation of his remains took place June 25, 1170. Canute became the patron saint of the Danish guilds, and his cult spread throughout Denmark and Schleswig. His present tomb at Sankt-Bendt church, Ringsted, dates only from the 17th century.

Bibliography: *Vitae sanctorum danorum,* ed. M. C. GERTZ (new ed. Copenhagen 1908–12) 169–247. L. WEIBULL, *Nordisk historia* 2 (1948) 415–432. Butler Th Attw 1:49. T. GAD, *Kulturhistorisk leksikon for nordisk middelalder,* ed. J. DANSTRUP (Copenhagen 1956–) 8:600–603, with bibliog.

[L. MUSSET]

CAODAISM

The religion of the modern Vietnamese sect, Cao Dai. It is more properly called the Third Amnesty (Dispensation) of God. Caodaism is based essentially upon a synthesis of Confucianism, Taoism, Buddhism, Catholicism, theosophy, and occultism, religions current in Vietnam. It originated in one of the numerous Vietnamese groups influenced by French culture that gave up the traditional occult practices of late Taoism and adopted the more "modern" and Western methods of spiritualism. During a seance of table moving in 1925, Phu Ngo-Van-Chien, an official of the French administration in Indo-China, received the order to announce —on the authority of the God, who called himself by the Taoist name Cao Dai (Supreme Palace)—the third revelation. The first and second revelations had been those of Buddha and Lao-tzu in the East, and of Moses and Christ in the West. There would seem to be an allusion to the revelation of the Paraclete promised in the Gospels, but according to the official declaration of the sect, "instead of coming in human form, God has adapted his teaching to the progress of the mind and has manifested himself in our times through a medium, since he does not wish to grant to any mortal the honor of presenting himself as the founder of Caodaism."

At first, before the conversion of a person of importance, Le Van Trung, the Third Amnesty was known as the doctrine of only a small group. Le Van Trung soon became the head of the movement and inaugurated its extraordinary spread. The sect, officially founded at Tayninh in 1926, within a few years numbered 1½ million members, among them many leading persons in the state. It owed its success to the syncretism mentioned. From Confucianism it borrowed its legal code; from Buddhism, its teaching on reincarnation and karma; from Taoism, occult practices; from Catholicism, the ideal of universal love, hierarchical organization, and the symbol of God represented as an Eye in a triangle; and from the old national religion, its ancestor worship. The sect's moral precepts are Buddhist and Confucianist, and its division into proper and simple religious adherents was suggested by Buddhism. But syncretism went further, for the cult includes great saints, among whom are found Pericles, Julius Caesar, Li Thai Po, Joan of Arc, Voltaire, Victor Hugo, J. Jaurès, Sun Yat Sen, and similar figures.

Through its strong hierarchical organization, Cao Dai soon developed into a state, with Tayninh as its capital, and it introduced social and agricultural reforms. During the Japanese occupation, the sect received arms from the conquerors and created an army of 20,000 men. Following the end of the war, it first supported the Vietminh party, and then the French. In a struggle with the rival sects, Hoa Hao and Binh Xuhan, Cao Dai, under the leadership of its "supreme pontiff" Pham Cong Tak and generals Nguyen Thanh Phuong and Trinh Minh Thé, gained political control of South Vietnam and forced Bao Dai out of office. It contributed to the seizure of power by Ngo Dinh Diem, but then revolted against him. In February 1956 Ngo Dinh Diem occupied Tayninh and incorporated the armed forces of Cao Dai into the army of South Vietnam. Pham Cong Tak took refuge in Cambodia, and the political role of Cao Dai was suppressed. The sect, however, continues to be an important religious element in the nation; its membership probably exceeds 2 million.

Bibliography: J. DORSENNE, "Naissance d'une religion: Le Cao-Daïsme," *Revue de Paris* 40 (1933) 663–676. G. GOBRON, *Histoire du caodaïsme: Bouddhisme rénové, spiritisme annamite, religion nouvelle en Eurasie* (Paris 1948). L. M. CADIÈRE, *Croyances et pratiques religieuses des Vietnamiens* (Paris 1957). E. THIEL, et al., StL 8:266–275, with good bibliog.

[C. REGAMEY]

CAPACCINI, FRANCESCO, cardinal, papal diplomat; b. Rome, Aug. 14, 1784; d. there, June 15, 1845. After ordination (1807) he taught astronomy at the University of Naples. In September 1815 he was appointed an official (*minutante*) of the papal secretariat of state, and became chief collaborator of Cardinal Ercole *Consalvi in politicoecclesiastical affairs. Capaccini was named in 1824 substitute (*sostituto*) to the secretariat of briefs. According to Christian *Bunsen, the secretariat of state thereby lost "the only man who understood affairs." At the end of 1826 Capaccini was delegated with Cardinal Bartolomeo Cappellari (later Pope Gregory XVI) to negotiate the concordat with the Low Countries. In 1828 Capaccini was sent to the Low Countries and appointed (1829) as internuncio. He went in 1830 to London to attend the conference on the independence of Belgium. Returning to Rome he assumed the post of *sostituto* in the *secretariat of state from Oct. 26, 1831, until the end of 1844. From July 1836 until November 1837 he was also secretary of the Congregation for *Extraordinary Ecclesiastical Affairs. On June 12, 1837, he left on an official mission to Vienna, and from there he went to Berlin. In May 1839 he was sent to Naples as internuncio extraordinary and plenipotentiary. He was appointed again internuncio to the Low Countries (April 1841) and extraordinary and apostolic delegate to Portugal (November 1841). After being created a cardinal *in petto* (June 22, 1844), he was publicly announced as such on April 21, 1845, a few weeks before his death. He was named auditor of the Apostolic Camera (February 1844) and arrived in Rome on Nov. 14, 1844. Capaccini was one of the most highly regarded papal diplomats of the 19th century.

Bibliography: H. BASTGEN, *Forschungen und Quellen zur Kirchenpolitik Gregors XVI,* 2 v. in 1 (Paderborn 1929), v.1. A. SIMON, *Biographie nationale de Belgique,* v.30, suppl. 2.1 (1958) 262–264. L. JADIN, DHGE 11:821–823.

[L. PÁSZTOR]

CAPE COAST, ARCHDIOCESE OF (LITORIS CAPITIS), metropolitan see since 1950, on the Gulf of Guinea, south *Ghana, west Africa. In 1963 it had 23 parishes, 82 priests (23 Ghanaians), 41 sisters (10 Ghanaians), and 230,600 Catholics in a population of 1,355,000; it is 18,792 square miles in area. Accra, Keta, Kumasi, and Tamale became suffragan sees in 1950, Navrongo in 1956, and Wa in 1959. All sees are under the Congregation for the *Propagation of the Faith. Cape Coast was the center of the British colony from 1664 to 1877, when Accra became the capital.

Originally under the Portuguese *Order of Christ and the Dioceses of Funchal (1514) and *São Tomé (1534), Ghana, which had a mission at Elmira as early as 1482, was part of the Vicariate of the Two Guineas (1842). It became the Prefecture of the Gold Coast (1879), entrusted to the Society of African Missions of Lyons; from it were detached the Prefecture of the *Ivory Coast (*Abidjan) in 1895 and other prefectures and vicariates (now suffragans) since 1923. The Gold Coast Vicariate (1901) was called Cape Coast when made an archbishopric (1950). Native secular clergy also work in the diocese, which publishes a weekly newspaper and a monthly magazine.

Bibliography: MissCattol 112–114. R. M. WILTGEN, *Gold Coast Mission History, 1471–1880* (Techny, Ill. 1956). AnnPont (1965) 92.

[R. M. WILTGEN]

CAPE TOWN, ARCHDIOCESE OF (CAPETOWNENSIS), metropolitan see since 1951, on the Atlantic Ocean in the Republic of *South Africa. In 1962 it had 40 parishes, 46 secular and 44 religious priests, 113 men in 13 religious houses, 492 women in 36 convents, and 67,755 Catholics (39,207 non-Europeans) in a population of 916,922 (548,606 non-Europeans); it is 11,928 square miles in area. Its four suffragans, which had 165 priests, 945 sisters, and 71,722 Catholics in a population of 2,507,000, were: Aliwal, Oudtshoorn, Port Elizabeth, and Queenstown (all created in 1951). The province includes the Prefecture of De Aar. The city of Cape Town, founded by the Dutch (1652) and occupied by the English (1795), is the legislative capital of the Republic of South Africa. Calvinism kept Catholicism out of the area until a small church was established under the Vicariate of *Mauritius (1819). A resident bishop, Patrick *Griffith, arrived with the creation of the Vicariate of the Cape of Good Hope (1837), which was divided into east and west vicariates (1847); the latter, called Cape Town (1939), became the archdiocese. St. Mary's Cathedral was built (1841–51). Hottentots in Namaqualand were evangelized in 1884, and a Central Prefecture (1872–82) was restored in 1922 and called Oudtshoorn (1939). There has been an Anglican archbishopric in Cape Town since 1853. Salesians, Redemptorists, Dominicans, Franciscans, and Capuchins work with the secular clergy in the archdiocese. Owen McCann, archbishop since 1951, became a cardinal in 1965.

Bibliography: MissCattol 162–163. AnnPont (1965) 92.

[J. E. BRADY]

CAPE VERDE ISLANDS, a chain of 14 volcanic islands in the Atlantic off the coast of *Africa, 300 miles west of Senegal, 1,557 square miles in area. Discovered in 1460 and colonized by the Portuguese and their Negro slaves, the islands were strategic in Portugal's trade with Africa, Asia, and South America. Until 1951 they were a colony; since then they have been an overseas territory of Portugal. Of the estimated 215,000 inhabitants in 1964, more than 60 per cent were mulattoes and the rest were Negroes, except for a few thousand Europeans. Almost the entire population was Catholic. The non-Catholics included about 1,000 Protestants.

Franciscans were the first to minister on the islands. In 1532 the Diocese of Santiago de Cabo Verde was created; it is still the see for all the islands and is a suffragan of *Lisbon. Originally its jurisdiction extended to the African coast from Gambia River to Cape Palmas (in modern Liberia); this seriously hindered its development. From the 17th to the 19th century the mission languished. Twice for long periods (1646–72, 1826–45) there was no resident bishop. A minor seminary was established in 1866, but Portugal's anticlerical government closed it in 1910. In 1940 the islands were separated from Portuguese *Guinea. The arrival of Holy Ghost Fathers in 1941 started a renewal of the diocese. Capuchins came in 1946, followed by Salesians, to work among a population described as dechristianized. In 1963 there were 17 secular and 33 religious priests, 8 brothers, 22 sisters, and 68 Catholic schools with 4,600 students.

Bibliography: "A religião em Cabo Verde," in *Portugal em Africa* 13 (1956) 151– . J. PEREIRA DE OLIVEIRA, "Actividades dos padres do Espirito Santo em Cabo Verde," *ibid.* 14 (1957) 303– . "A acção dos padres do Espirito Santo em Cabo Verde," *Boletim Geral do Ultramar* 392 (Lisbon 1958) 111–115. R. PATTEE, *Portugal na África contemporânea* (Coimbra 1959) with full bibliography. *Bilan du Monde* 2:205–206. A. MENDES PEDRO, *Anuário Católico do Ultramar Portugues (1960): Annuaire Catholique de l'Outre-Mer. Portugais* (Estudos de ciências políticas e sociais 57; 1962), Fr. and Port. on opposite pages. Centro de Estudos Políticos e Sociais, Lisbon. Missão para o Estudo da Missionologia Africana, *Atlas missionário português* (Lisbon 1962). AnnPont (1965) 400. For further bibliography *see* AFRICA.

[R. PATTEE]

CAPECELATRO, ALFONSO, cardinal, author; b. Marseilles, Feb. 5, 1824; d. Capua, Italy, Nov. 14, 1912. He was born in France, whence his father Francesco, Duke of Castelpagano, had gone into exile to escape the tyranny of Ferdinand I, King of the Two Sicilies. In 1830, the family returned to Italy, residing at S. Paolo Belsito, Province of Nola. In 1840 Alfonso entered the *Oratorians in Naples. Shortly after ordination (1847), he was chosen pastor of St. Philip Neri parish in Naples, devoting himself to studies and religious duties. He was of great service to the Oratorians when he succeeded in having the church of the Girolomini, with its cloisters and rich library, declared a national monument with all the privileges and guarantees appertaining thereto. Leo XIII appointed him assistant librarian of the Vatican Library (1879). He became archbishop of Capua (1880), cardinal (1885), and prefect of the Vatican Library (1899). His close relations with the royal court, and his support of *Tosti may account for his not receiving the See of Naples in 1898. Capecelatro's vast literary production includes several biographies distinguished for their historical and scholarly qualities, wealth of information, and classical style. These qualities are especially evident in his *Storia di S. Caterina da Siena* (1856). He also published *Newman e la religione cattolica in Inghilterra* (1859); several well-known prayer books; a life of Christ; biographies of SS. Peter Damian, Alphonsus Liguori, and Philip Neri. The last work has appeared in English. Capecelatro published also his autobiography *I miei venticinque anni di episcopato* (1905). His *Carteggio* contains the correspondence he exchanged with outstanding men of the period.

Bibliography: G. FALLANI, EncCatt 3:659–660.

[H. R. MARRARO]

ČAPEK, KAREL, Czech novelist, essayist, and playwright; b. Svatoňovice, eastern Bohemia, Jan. 9, 1890; d. Dobříš, near Prague, Dec. 25, 1938. He was the son of a country physician, and constantly handicapped by poor health; at Charles University, Prague, he concentrated on philosophy and journalism. While working on Prague newspapers, he began writing stories but soon turned to the novel and the drama. In this development he was encouraged by his brother Josef, a painter, who also collaborated with him on some dramatic works.

Karel Čapek.

Čapek's formation was not Christian, nor did he ever proclaim adherence to Christian doctrine. Nevertheless, he developed a philosophy that closely resembled that of the Christian tradition. His first book, *Trapné povídky* (Embarrassing Stories), written during World War I, differed greatly in its bitter irony from the tenets of the pragmatic philosophy he then professed. Much of the same bitterness pervaded the play *Ze života hmyzu* (1920, From the Life of the Insects), an immediate success. The same tone prevailed in his works even later, whenever he touched the evil elements in man's heart. The power of military dictators, for instance, provoked the play *Bílá nemoc* (1937, White Sickness), and the same bitter tone is in the prophetical novel *Válka s mloky* (1936, War with the Newts).

Most of Čapek's later works grew from a distinctly Chestertonian attitude that recognized man's spiritual propensity and his need for the absolute. The absolute, in Čapek's concept, was no certainty, but rather a mysterious postulate. In *RUR* (1921, Rossum's Universal Robots), perhaps his most famous play, the essential opposition between mechanical perfection and the possibility of joyous laughter engages the playwright's probing attention. Judging from *Povětroň* (1934, Meteor), a masterful report on a seemingly purposeless life and death, and in the *Povídky z jedné kapsy* (1929, Stories From One Pocket), the mystery of human life seems to have puzzled and challenged the author with ever-increasing force. Čapek, who had foreseen the horrors of totalitarian domination even before he experienced its reality, died frustrated in heart on the verge of his country's humiliation by the Nazis. Most of his works have appeared in English.

Bibliography: O. ELTON, *Essays and Addresses* (London 1939). W. E. HARKINS, *Karel Čapek* (New York 1962). **Illustration credit:** Columbia University Press. I. KLÍMA, *Karel Čapec* (Prague 1962).

[B. CHUDOBA]

CAPELLE, BERNARD, liturgist; b. Namur, Belgium, Feb. 8, 1884; d. Louvain, Oct. 12, 1961. Born to a family of magistrates and baptized Paul, he followed the course of studies at the Collège Notre Dame de la Paix at Namur. In 1906 he was ordained for the Diocese of Namur and for 6 years served as assistant pastor at Gembloux. He then went to Rome where he earned doctorates in philosophy and theology at the Gregorian University, and in 1912 received the first doctorate bestowed by the Biblical Institute. His dissertation concerned the text of the Latin psalter in Africa. On Oct. 14, 1918, he entered the Abbey of Maredsous and made his profession on Oct. 15, 1919. He was immediately given the direction of the library and charged with editing the *Revue Bénédictine*. In 1922 he was assigned by his Abbot, Dom Columba Marmion, to teach dogmatic theology at the Abbey of Mont-César in Louvain. So great was the enthusiasm with which the monks there received the new professor, that they chose him on Jan. 23, 1923, as coadjutor abbot to Abbot Robert de Kerchove (1846–1942).

Bernard Capelle.

Mont-César had retained since 1909 the leadership of the liturgical movement in Belgium. Capelle strengthened this leadership by his energetic collaboration on the abbey's review, *Questions liturgiques et paroissiales,* and through the influence he exercised over many liturgical study weeks and circles. From 1936 to 1956 he occupied the chair of liturgy at the University of Louvain and later taught for the Institut Supérieur de Liturgie at Paris. He was consultor for the Congregation of Rites, a member of the Henry Bradshaw Society and the preparatory liturgical commission of Vatican Council II.

An erudite historian of ancient Christian liturgies, he was also a popular writer and preacher. Most of his writings have been gathered into three volumes of *Travaux liturgiques de doctrine et d'histoire* (Louvain 1955, 1962; v. 3 is still in preparation).

Bibliography: F. VANDENBROUCKE, RHE 56 (1961) 1024–25; "Dom Bernard Capelle," EphemLiturg 76 (1962) 43–49. A. G. MARTIMORT, *Maison-Dieu* 68 (1961) 203–207. RevBén 71 (1961) 231–232.

[N. N. HUYGHEBAERT]

CAPÉRAN, LOUIS, theologian; b. Saint-Gaudens, France, April 15, 1884; d. Toulouse, Jan. 9, 1962. He was named canon at the Cathedral of Toulouse. At first, he wrote works that pertained to contemporary thought such as: *Foi laïque et foi chrétienne: La Question du surnaturel* (Paris 1938); *L'Anticléricalisme et l'affaire Dreyfus (1897–1899)* (Paris 1948); *Histoire contemporaine de la laïcité française* (La Roche-sur-Yon 1957); *France nouvelle et Action Catholique* (Toulouse 1942). Then, his books concerning practical evangelization were published: *La Méthode du prêtre: Leçons et lectures sur les preuves de la religion* (Toulouse no date); *Manuel à l'usage des écoles, des catéchismes et des mouvements de jeunesse* (Paris no date). He also made translations of the Gospel for the use of the faithful: *Évangile de Saint Jean: La Lumière et la vie* (Paris 1950); *Évangile de Saint Luc: Le Sauveur des hommes* (Paris 1951); *Évangile de Saint Marc: Le Fils de Dieu* (Paris 1951); *Évangile de Saint Matthieu: Le Roi Messie* (Paris 1951).

[G. MOLLAT]

CAPETIAN DYNASTY

The third family of kings to rule France, whose skill in solving problems of succession, finance, and administration was instrumental in creating the French nation. The dynasty contained 14 kings who reigned from 987 to 1328. The family, descended from Robert the Strong, Count of Anjou (d. 866), claimed three earlier kings, the Robertians, and is named after Hugh Capet (987–996).

Hugh Capet, eldest son of Hugh the Great, Count of Paris, owed his throne to his own energy and to the support of *Adalbero, Bishop of Reims and to Gerbert (*see* SYLVESTER II). Adalbero declared the crown elective and quickly crowned Hugh after the death without issue of Louis V, the last Carolingian king of France. Because of this ecclesiastical support Hugh was a loyal son of the Church, interested in clerical reform and in liturgical ceremonies. His surname "Capet" is of uncertain origin.

Before 987 disputes over succession were frequent since the throne was elective and the kingdom divisible. By electing his son Robert as king-designate in December 987, Hugh Capet initiated a procedure that by 1200 made the kingship indivisible, hereditary, and subject to primogeniture.

The Capetians controlled initially little more than the Île de France, but, by insisting on their feudal rights and by annexing what lands they could, they gained the revenues and fiefs necessary to overawe their vassals and to expand their authority. Particularly important here are the reigns of *Louis VI (1108–37), *Philip II Augustus (1180–1223), *Louis VIII (1223–26), and *Philip III (1270–85).

Philip Augustus and his successors also developed a paid bureaucracy to replace the feudal nobles and royal household retainers who had previously ruled. Central departments for handling correspondence, justice, and finance grew from the King's Council, and in the provinces, royal bailiffs and seneschals tried to increase the King's power. New concepts of public authority appeared; and while it would be wrong to consider the Capetians anything but feudal in outlook, it is nevertheless true that these developments laid the foundations of the modern French nation-state.

The Capetians were generally loyal sons of the Church, active in the *Crusades, and zealous in the maintenance of the faith. One of them, *Louis IX (1226–70), has been canonized, and his reign is a model of medieval kingship. The University of *Paris, center of scholastic theology, was supported by these kings, who were equally generous in their encouragement of the *Gothic in ecclesiastical art. The story ends unhappily, however, since *Philip IV's battles with *Boniface VIII led not only to that Pontiff's death, but also to the "Babylonian Captivity" (*see* AVIGNON PAPACY).

Bibliography: F. LOT, *Études sur le règne de Hugues Capet* (Paris 1903). C. PETIT-DUTAILLIS, *The Feudal Monarchy in France and England from the Tenth to the Thirteenth Century,* tr. E. D. HUNT (London 1936). J. L. A. CALMETTE, *Le Réveil capétien* (Paris 1948). F. LOT and R. FAWTIER, eds., *Histoire des institutions françaises au moyen âge,* 3 v. (Paris 1957–62) v.2, 3. R. FAWTIER, *The Capetian Kings of France, tr.* L. BUTLER and R. J. ADAM (New York 1960). P. E. SCHRAMM, *Der König von Frankreich,* 2 v. (2d ed. Weimar 1960).

[C. T. WOOD]

CAPGRAVE, JOHN, historian, theologian; b. Lynn, Norfolk, England, April 21, 1393; d. Lynn, Aug. 12, 1464. Probably the most important of the English *Augustinians, Capgrave became a doctor of theology at Cambridge *c.* 1430 and served as Augustinian provincial of England from 1453 to 1457. His *Chronicle of England* to 1417 (ed. F. C. Hingeston, RollsS), dedicated to King Edward IV, was the first history of England not written in Latin. In his same Norfolk dialect he also wrote *Ye solace of pilgrimes* (ed. C. A. Mills, London 1911), an excellent description of classical and Christian Rome done in 1450; the *Lives of St. Augustine, St. *Gilbert of Sempringham* and a *Sermo* (EEng TSoc 1910); and the metrical lives of *St. *Catherine of Alexandria* (EEngTSoc 1893) and *St. *Norbert* (not yet edited). In Latin he wrote commentaries on almost all the books of the Bible, of which only those on Genesis, Exodus, and Acts of the Apostles are extant in MS; the *De fidei symbolis;* and the *Liber de illustribus Henricis* (ed. F. C. Hingeston, RollsS), dedicated to King *Henry VI; as well as other works now lost, such as a life of *Humphrey of Gloucester, his chief patron. The *Nova legenda Anglie* (London 1901), Capgrave's most famous work, is actually only a rearrangement of the *Sanctilogium* of John of Tynemouth, OSB.

Bibliography: E. M. THOMPSON, DNB 3:929–931. W. DIBELIUS, "John Capgrave und die englische Schriftsprache," *Anglia* 23 (1901) 153–194, 323–375, 427–472; 24 (1901) 211–263, 269–308. A. DE MEIJER in *Augustiniana* 5 (1955) 400–440; 7 (1957) 118–148, 531–575, bibliog. A. KURVINEN, "The Source of Capgrave's *Life of St. Katharine of Alexandria*," *Neuphilologische Mitteilungen* 61 (1960) 268–324. Emden Cambr. 121–122.

[A. DE MEIJER]

CAPHARNAUM, town in Galilee, at site of modern Tell Ḥûm. The name comes from the Aramaic or late Hebrew *k*ᵉ*par-nāḥûm,* "village of Nahum." Capharnaum was "by the sea, in the territory of Zabulon and Nephthalim" (Mt 4.13), about 3 miles southwest of the Jordan's entrance into the Sea of Galilee. Although unmentioned in the OT, it is referred to 16 times in the Gospels. Using it as the center for much of His ministry, Jesus worked many miracles there. It was there, too, that St. Matthew, the publican, was called to follow Jesus. Because of its unbelief (Mt 11.23; Lk 10.15), Jesus threatened severe judgment on Capharnaum. It is mentioned also by Flavius Josephus, who was brought there when he was wounded in a battle near the Jordan.

In 1921 G. Orfali excavated the impressive remains of a *synagogue at Tell Ḥûm, which dates from the 2d or 3d Christian century. It may have replaced the synagogue in which Jesus preached. Also found were the remains of an octagonal church, which had been built probably on the traditional site of the house of St. Peter. There is evidence that in very early times the Judeo-Christians converted the house of Peter into a place of worship.

Bibliography: G. ORFALI, *Capharnaum et ses ruines . . .* (Paris 1922).

[S. MUSHOLT]

CAPILLAS, FRANCIS DE, BL., Dominican protomartyr of China; b. Bacquerin de Campos, Spain, Aug. 18, 1607; d. Fukien, China, Jan. 15, 1648 (feast, Jan. 15). From Spain he went to Manila (1631), where he was ordained and was active from 1633 to 1641 in Cagayan and Babuyanes. In 1642 he was sent to China via Formosa, joining Francisco Diaz OP, a missionary returning to his former work in Fukien. They arrived just at the time that the Manchu Tartars were overthrowing the Ming dynasty. During the Tartar invasions heavy demands were made on the Dominicans, and it was difficult to maintain the peace. Christianity was outlawed on Aug. 9, 1647. Francis, apprehended by mistake on the following day in Fukien, was beaten, and his ankles were stretched on the rack. He was suspected of sorcery because of his patience in suffering. Later he was beheaded as "the leader of the traitorous Christians." His body was eventually taken away by his followers; his head is still venerated at the Dominican house in Valladolid. The process for beatification was begun immediately; resumed in 1901, it was completed Sept. 2, 1909.

Bibliography: J. RECORDER DE DORDA, *Vida del protomartir de China, beato Francisco de Capillas* (Avila 1909). J. M. GONZÁLEZ, *Historia de las misiones dominicanas de China,* v.1 (Madrid 1964). Butler Th Attw 1:98–99. C. TESTORE, EncCatt 3:663. B. M. BIERMANN, *Die Anfänge der neueren Dominikanermission in China* (Münster 1927).

[B. M. BIERMANN]

CAPITAL PUNISHMENT

The execution of a criminal under death sentence imposed by competent public authority. Unlike the act of a private person exacting revenge for a wrong done to himself or to his family, this penalty manifests the community's will to vindicate its laws and system of justice. Among some primitive peoples, a popular assembly might order death not only to retaliate for murder or treason, but also to appease spirits offended by sorcery, incest, or sacrilege.

Ancient Practices. Capital punishment existed in the legal codes of the ancient Middle Eastern kingdoms. These codes commonly prescribed death for homicide and for some religious or sexual offenses. Thus, for Israel, it was declared that "whoever sheds the blood of man, by man shall his blood be shed" (Gn 9.6) and further that "you shall not let the sorceress live. Anyone who lies with an animal shall be put to death. Whoever sacrifices to any god, except to the Lord alone, shall be doomed" (Ex 22.17–19). The law of the Israelites at one time or another listed as capital crimes homicide, bearing false witness in a capital charge, kidnapping, insult or injury to a parent, sexual immorality, witchcraft or magic, idolatry, blasphemy, and sacrilege. Hebrew law clearly distinguished between voluntary and involuntary manslaughter: "When a man kills another after maliciously scheming to do so, you must take him even from my altar and put him to death" (Ex 21.14). It likewise embraced the *lex talionis:* "If injury ensues, you shall give life for life, eye for eye, tooth for tooth, hand for hand" (Ex 21.23–24). It is generally understood that this principle of retribution was enunciated not only to sanction stern penalties, but also to protect offenders from excessive punishments. When death was prescribed, the sentence was more often carried out by stoning, although hanging, beheading, strangulation, and burning were also used. Among the Babylonians, the Code of *Hammurabi distinguished between manslaughter and willful homicide and also proclaimed the *lex talionis.* Death and mutilation were frequent penalties. The Assyrian Code likewise mentioned death and mutilation, but it remains questionable how often such penalties were inflicted. In the Hittite kingdom, death was reserved mainly for crimes committed by slaves or for special crimes against the king.

The term capital punishment derives from *caput,* a word used by the Romans variously to mean the head, the life, or the civil rights of an individual. *Roman law also knew the death penalty as the *summum supplicium.* In addition to death, Roman law looked on perpetual hard labor and banishment (*interdictio aquae et ignis et tecti*—denial of fire, water, and shelter) as lesser capital punishments. Banishment meant in effect a grave loss of one's civil rights or status (*deminutio capitis*). During the Republic, death was imposed mainly for crimes among the military. Under the emperors, it became increasingly common as the penalty for a much wider range of offenses. Rome early embraced the *lex talionis* in its Law of the Twelve Tables (450 B.C.). Ancient Greece and Rome generally looked on homicide, treason, and sacrilege as capital offenses. Later Roman law put other crimes, such as arson and false coining, in the same category. The Greeks imposed death in several ways, e.g., sometimes a free man would be permitted to take poison, and a slave would be beaten to death. Roman usages included strangulation, exposure to wild beasts, crucifixion, and the *culeus* (drowning a condemned man tied up in a sack with a cock, a viper, and a dog).

Catholic Recognition of Capital Punishment. Two patterns of grave punishment emerged in Europe before the Middle Ages. The law of Germanic peoples generally, and of a few countries such as Ireland, tended to see homicide and attacks on person or property chiefly as wrongs done to individuals. The proper penalty in such cases came to be a fine paid to the injured party or his heirs. Capital punishment was employed elsewhere, however. From the Middle Ages on, Britain, France, and the Latin peoples decreed death for a variety of crimes. Moreover, the method took on added refinements of brutality and degradation, as in death by pressing, burning at the stake, or hanging and quartering.

Throughout this period in Europe, pronouncements of the Church contained at least tacit recognition of the *state's competence to execute criminals; insistence that the death penalty be imposed with due regard for justice, prudence, and mercy; and expressions of the Church's own horror of bloodshed. Ancient Israel had prescribed capital punishment for some crimes, but the Old Testament spoke also of divine mercy: "As I live, says the Lord God, I swear I take no pleasure in the death of the wicked man, but rather in the wicked man's conversion, that he may live" (Ez 33.11). Few took these words, however, as a restriction on the community's power to execute a justly condemned criminal. The same proved true of Christ's new teaching on the *lex talionis:* "You have heard that it was said, 'An eye for an eye,' and, 'A tooth for a tooth.' But I say to you not to resist the evildoer; on the contrary, if someone strike thee on the right cheek, turn to him the other also" (Mt 5.38–39). Christians have tended to hear in these words an exhortation to be quick to waive lawful rights out of love even for an erring neighbor. Along with it, however, they have recalled St. Paul's defense of civil authority: "For it is God's minister to thee for good. But if thou dost what is evil, fear, for not without reason does it carry the sword. For it is God's minister, an avenger to execute wrath" (Rom 13.4).

The essence of this traditional concept of the state as the upholder of justice and of its competence to punish with measures it deems necessary and reasonable was defended by *Pius XII, who, in an address to Italian Catholic jurists on Feb. 5, 1955, repeated an earlier assertion that "the Church in her theory and practice has maintained this double type of penalty (medicinal and vindicative), and that this is more in conformity with what the sources of revelation and traditional doctrine teach regarding the coercive power of legitimate human authority. It is not sufficient reply . . . to say that these sources contain only thoughts which correspond to historical circumstances . . . of the time, and that a general and abiding validity cannot therefore be attributed to them. The reason is that . . . the sources and the living teaching power do not refer to the specific content of individual juridical prescriptions or norms (cf. particularly Rom 13.4), but rather to the very foundation of penal power and of its intrinsic finality. This, in turn, is as little determined by circumstances of time and culture as the nature of man and the human society decreed by nature itself" [*Resta ora;* ActApS 47 (1955) 81–82].

Not all early Christian writers felt compelled to reconcile the teachings of the Old and New Testaments. *Tertullian and *Lactantius held that there could be no exception to God's law against taking human life. St. *Augustine, commenting on Rom 13.4, defended severity for the sake of social order, but praised the Christian instinct to temper such juridical sternness. Pope *Leo I in the 5th century and *Nicholas I in the 9th insisted that the Church itself shunned the use of the sword. Councils such as *Toledo (675) and Fourth *Lateran (1215) forbade clerics to take any part in a juridical process or sentence on a capital charge. At times this spirit made itself felt in secular practices, as when, during the later Middle Ages, the custom spread of permitting an offender to perform a pilgrimage to some famous religious shrine in place of another penalty for murder or other grave crime.

On the theoretical plane, in medieval times, St. *Thomas Aquinas made his classic defense of the death penalty on the ground that "if a man be dangerous and infectious to the community, on account of some sin, it is praiseworthy and advantageous that he be killed in order to safeguard the common good" (ST 2a2ae, 64.2). Citing Aristotle, he argued that "by sinning man departs from the order of reason and . . . falls into the slavish state of the beasts" (ST 2a2ae, 64.2 ad 3). Aquinas, however, also proposed as a working jurisprudential norm that "in this life penalties should rather be remedial than retributive" (ST 2a2ae, 66.6). Thus, while upholding capital punishment in principle on grounds of retribution, social defense, and deterrence, he sounded an interestingly modern note by the priority he gave to rehabilitation as a penal aim. Through the Middle Ages and the rise of the national state, the countries of Europe in practice invoked the death penalty more frequently and against more offenses as the old social order disappeared or heresies appeared to threaten new national unity. English law, for instance, from the 16th to the 18th century piled up more than 200 capital crimes, ranging from high treason to the theft of property worth a few shillings.

Modern Challenges to Capital Punishment. The churches continued to stress the need for just and reasonable penalties and for prudence in imposing them. But few at the time seriously contested the state's right to execute criminals or the essential reasonableness of capital punishment. It was a young Italian, Cesare *Beccaria, who opened the modern debate on the institution itself with his essay *Dei delitti e delle pene* (1764). On the basis of his own theory of society, he rejected the state's right to take a citizen's life. Far more influential, however, was his critique of the death penalty as cruel, unreasonable, and ineffective. Within 2 years his essay had appeared in French translation and had become known all over Europe. Beccaria spoke of Montesquieu's influence on his thought, but he himself merits the title of father of modern penal reform.

Many trace the abolition of capital punishment in Tuscany (1786) and Austria (1787) to Beccaria's challenge to "enlightened" rulers. His essay also stimulated Samuel Romilly and other leaders of the crusade to reform England's penal code, a movement that reduced British capital offenses to four crimes by 1861. In the U.S. at the end of the 18th century, Dr. Benjamin Rush and others led a campaign for the abolition of capital punishment in Pennsylvania and elsewhere. By the dawn of the 20th century, abolition was a fact in Portugal, the Netherlands, and Belgium (*de facto* from 1867); and these are among the European nations that remain abolitionist today. Brazil, Costa Rica, Ecuador, and Venezuela, which are still among the Latin American abolitionist nations, renounced the death penalty before 1900. In the U.S. several states also experimented with abolition during the 19th century. Of those that completely, or almost completely, were without the death penalty in 1965, Maine, Wisconsin, Michigan, and Rhode Island followed laws passed before 1900. Other abolitionist states in 1965 included Alaska, Hawaii, Iowa, Minnesota, North Dakota, Oregon, Vermont, and New York. In Europe, in the same year, aside from Communist lands, only France, Ireland, Greece, and Spain still retained the death penalty. After decades of political debate, England had in 1964 and 1965 taken major steps toward total abolition.

More significant than the growing number of nations or states that have abolished capital punishment has been the sharp drop in actual executions for capital offenses in jurisdictions that retain the death penalty. In the U.S., for example, executions averaged more than 150 annually between 1930 and 1940, but executions under all state and Federal laws in 1964 totaled only 15. In the West, only Communist countries did not participate in the general trend toward *de facto* abolition. With the U.S.S.R. in the lead, several Communist nations in the early 1960s began to impose the death penalty for grave economic crimes such as black-marketing or currency speculation. (A comprehensive survey of present use of the death penalty, based on data from more than 65 nations, was published in 1962 by the United Nations Economic and Social Council.)

Debate over capital punishment has continued on several levels since World War II. Discussion of basic human rights has led to new questions on the humaneness of the death penalty, its potential abuse as an instrument of *genocide, and possible inequities in its administration that work against the socially or economically disadvantaged. Sociologists have tested and subsequently called into question the validity of a classic claim advanced by most advocates of capital punishment, namely, its alleged deterrent effect. Finally, many religious and humanitarian groups have joined the Quakers and other pioneers in pressing for abolition on sociological, philosophical, and theological grounds. In the U.S., for instance, many Protestant synods and assemblies have denounced the death penalty as unnecessary and unjust.

Relatively few Roman Catholics in the U.S. or elsewhere have been active in these debates. When Catholic theologians have dealt with the topic, they have tended to repeat affirmations of the state's competence to inflict death as a penalty, at least when it can be said to be necessary for social defense or as a deterrent. It should be noted, however, that Pius XII, in his extensive statements on crime and punishment, never explicitly defended or denied the state's right to impose the death sentence, even while he defended its right to have a retributive intention in its penal administration. Any further Catholic thought on the topic will undoubtedly reflect a new emphasis on the notion of the inalienable rights of the human person as set forth in recent authoritative documents such as John XXIII's **Pacem in terris*. It may also reveal reliance on a dynamic conception of natural law and of the nature of man and society that has been manifested in the deliberations on the Church in the modern world by Vatican Council II. At that point, the state of the question may come to embrace not merely the relative effectiveness or social necessity of capital punishment, but also the basic right of the state to employ it as a matter of normal social policy.

See also CRIME; CRIMINOLOGY; PENOLOGY; PUNISHMENT.

Bibliography: H. A. BEDAU, *The Death Penalty in America* (pa. New York 1964), useful bibliog. United Nations, Dept. of Economic and Social Affairs, *Capital Punishment* (New York 1962), world survey. J. T. SELLIN, *The Death Penalty* (Philadelphia 1959). J. A. FARRER, *Crimes and Punishments, including a New Translation of Beccaria's 'Dei delitti e delle pene'* (London 1880). PIUS XII, "Nous croyons que très" (address, Oct. 3, 1953) ActApS 45 (1953) 730–744, Eng. *Catholic Mind* 52 (1954) 107–118, to the 6th International Congress of Penal Law; "Accogliete" (address, Dec. 5, 1954) ActApS 47 (1955) 60–85, Eng. *ibid.* 53 (1955) 364–384, to the Italian Assoc. of Catholic Jurists.

[D. R. CAMPION]

CAPITALISM

Although the term capital—the principal of a debt—derives from Roman law, the term capitalism is of recent origin. It seems that it was first used by Louis Blanc (1811–82) in his *Organisation du travail:* "Capitalism means a system in which some appropriate capital at the exclusion of others" (5th ed. Paris 1850, 161). Karl *Marx (1818–83) called his three-volume analysis of capitalism *Das Kapital,* and in it, as well as in the *Communist Manifesto,* he speaks of capitalists and the capitalist mode of production but does not use the abstract noun capitalism. The Marxian labor movement and its propaganda freely used the word, generally in an invidious sense. For decades, however, academic economists, especially in English-speaking countries, took little note of either Marx or the term. In 1902 W. Sombart (1863–1941) published his monumental work *Modern Capitalism,* and a little later Max Weber (1864–1920) published his famous study *The Protestant Ethic and the Spirit of Capitalism.* This gave the term capitalism academic respectability, and thereafter R. H. Tawney (1880–1962), J. A. Schumpeter (1883–1950), A. P. Usher, Talcott Parsons, and many others accepted it.

As long as the classical economists regarded free enterprise as the only system that corresponded to the nature of man and society, there was little likelihood that capitalism would be recognized as a historical and transient phenomenon. Their adoption of the word capitalism with its implicit recognition of the historical character of the capitalist system was, therefore, a signal departure from tradition.

Differences in Definition. But use of the term by economists did not bring agreement among them on its definition. There is little agreement even on the meaning of the more basic term capital. Eugen von Böhm-Bawerk's (1851–1914) brilliant survey of doctrines of capital and interest amply illustrates the confusing variety of definitions. They range from one taking material cost as its criterion (capital equals the produced means of production) through Marx's definition of capital as "surplus value hatching value" and the psychological interpretation of the marginalist school to the functional definition dating from Jevons and dominating today. The functional concept is preferred in this article: capital is the present value of actually or presumably recurrent returns discounted at the prevailing rate of interest.

Distinction in Forms of Term. What, then, is the relationship of capital to the terms capitalist and capitalism? Scholars of high rank, among them the historians Tawney and Georg von Below (1858–1927), have doubted the usefulness of the term capitalist, since all historically known societies used capital. According to Von Below, if the term is to make any sense at all, capitalist societies must be those using more capital than others. This suggestion is clearly unacceptable; it would make the Soviet system capitalist.

Obviously, the owner of capital may properly be called a capitalist. In this sense there were capitalists long before there was capitalism. For example, in late medieval and Renaissance Florence, Genoa, Venice, Siena, Augsburg, Bruges, and Cahors, there were merchants, manufacturers, and financiers (not the least those of the *camera apostolica*); but nobody called them capitalists, because they were exceptions in a precapitalist environment. Neither feudalism nor mercantilism permitted its "capitalists" to shape the economic system. Under the former, tradition, and under the latter the absolute monarch, gave the economy its characteristic tone. When the Enlightenment and liberalism, its offspring, did away with the remnants of medieval institutions and royal absolutism, the stage was set for capitalism, that is, for an economic system organized and controlled by capitalists. In contradistinction to a primitive market society emphasizing commodities as commodities and functioning according to the formula commodity → money → commodity (to use Marxian symbols), there arose a system that functioned, $M \rightarrow C \rightarrow M +$: a sum of money is invested in marketable commodities for the purpose of exchanging them for a sum greater than the original investment, that is, for profit. Capitalism, then, is a system controlled by private owners of capital whose operations are directed toward net returns with a view to reinvesting surpluses.

Schumpeter's analysis emphasizes a further aspect—the dynamic nature of the capitalist process. The energy is generated by the entrepreneurs, the free agents operating within the system who, using bank credit as a source of investment funds, break through the "circular flow" of economic relations by innovations in process and products. These innovations, when occurring in clusters, release "a gale of creative destruction." Traditional ways of doing things are made obsolete by new or better production functions, new products, new markets, etc. The drive behind the innovations is the profit motive, but the profits that accrue to particular successful innovations gradually disappear through pressures from competing innovations.

Capitalism as a Historical Phenomenon

Capitalism as a historical phenomenon has its cycle of birth, growth, and decline. It began in Great Britain and spread to the Continent and the U.S., achieving in England the status of a fully developed system only about the middle of the 19th century. Why did it rise in the Western world and why so late?

Some Unitary Explanations. Marx found the reason in the advent of the machine age with its destruction of traditional methods of production and distribution. According to his theory of economic materialism, the new social stratification and new political forms followed the change in technology. The rising bourgeoisie unleashed productive forces that, through the dialectic inherent in the capitalist system, would in turn also destroy it in a final underconsumption, overproduction crisis.

Quite different is Max Weber's analysis. In his *Protestant Ethic and the Spirit of Capitalism* he emphasizes the role of Calvinism and of the Puritan ethic in particular. Thus he raises a hitherto ignored issue that Tawney was to take up later in his *Religion and the Rise of Capitalism.* Although Tawney insists that a capitalist spirit, the drive for more and more, is a general human propensity, he finds that Puritanism in its secularized phase was "milk for lions" to the emerging business world.

Alfred Mueller-Armack discusses these questions on an even broader historical and analytical basis than Weber and Tawney. A Lutheran, well versed in the controversial theology of the 19th century, he makes a convincing case for the profound influence of theology and morals on the rise of the capitalist spirit and capitalism. H. M. Robertson in his *Rise of Economic Individualism* denies any such influence. W. Sombart believes that the financiers among the Jews and the "rational" moral theology of the Scholastics were strong contributing factors to the emergence of capitalism.

For Schumpeter the whole controversy is irrelevant, "a typical instance of what may be termed Spurious Problems" (*History of Economic Analysis,* New York 1954, 80). When an "ideal" feudal man is contrasted with an "ideal" capitalist, there is a problem of explaining how the first became the second. But it is a problem of the investigator's own creation arising from the substitution of abstract, simplified types for the complex historical realities. The problem vanishes when attention is paid to historical detail. Not wholly different is B. W. Dempsey's position (208): "there is no such a thing as capitalism. The word is incapable of scientific definition. . . . It should be used only with great reluctance since it is largely a creation of [the] socialist interpretation of economic history . . .. Preoccupation with capitalism as an abstract concept has inhibited study (at least in Catholic circles) of institutions as they are."

W. P. Webb, in *The Great Frontier,* has proposed a controversial thesis. The prime cause for the emergence of capitalism was the discovery and exploitation of three continents that gave Europe new frontiers, the monetary basis for economic evolution, a wide variety of new products, and almost limitless opportunities. These continents also offered an environment where personal freedom and democracy could grow; the pioneers, settlers, and trappers were "caught in the trap of freedom" and urged to a democratic life. Moreover the migration of Calvinism to the new world with its settlers permitted it to grow into a world power as that world developed. Webb here has made a point that is all too frequently overlooked or insufficiently appraised. His explanation of capitalism's failure to develop in Central and South America complements the Weber-Tawney thesis. The absence of the kind of institutional disintegration in Latin America that facilitated the rise of capitalism elsewhere he would trace to the rigid inner character of Catholicism. "The rigidity and stability of the Catholic Church has done more to frustrate the atomizing influence of the frontier than any other single factor operating in the New World."

Today the consensus recognizes no specific factor as responsible for the advent of capitalism, but traces it to a multiplicity of causes and circumstances. There remains, however, the question as to the priority and weight of these multiple causes and circumstances.

Some Theories of Capitalist Evolution. Once economists had identified capitalism as a historical phenomenon, they were confronted with the problem of identifying and explaining its phases or stages. W. Sombart identifies three states: early capitalism, beginning in the Middle Ages; high capitalism, covering, roughly speaking, the 19th century; and late capitalism. Schumpeter has a similar sequence. He distinguishes the liberal laissez-faire, free-trade era of the 19th century from the maturity phase that followed and sees the latter leading over into the erosion of the elements of capitalism, the crumbling of its protecting walls, and finally ending in socialism.

The most recent work in this field is W. W. Rostow's *The Stages of Economic Growth.* For Rostow the capitalistic evolution begins with the decline of the pre-Newtonian traditional society that was characterized by a ceiling on attainable per capita output because the potentialities of modern technology were not available or were not systematically utilized. Then follows a period of transition that begins largely as a result of "some external intrusion by more advanced societies" and of the rise of the "effective national state." Then follows the take-off. "The forces making for economic progress, which yielded limited bursts and enclaves of modern activity, expand and come to dominate the society. Growth becomes its normal condition. Compound interest becomes built, as it were, into its habits and institutional structure" (7). After this phase (some 60 years after the take-off begins) follows maturity, that stage "in which an economy demonstrates the capacity to move beyond the original industries which powered its take-off and to absorb and to apply efficiently over a very wide range of its resources—if not the whole range—the most advanced fruits of [their] modern technology" (9). In this stage "an economy demonstrates that it has the technological and entrepreneurial skills to produce not everything but anything that it chooses to produce" (10). The next stage is high mass consumption.

In the U.S. this stage probably opened with Ford's moving assembly line (1913–14), but it reached its full development only in the 1920s and in the decade from 1946 to 1956. In the 1950s Western Europe and Japan appeared to have entered this stage, and the Soviet Union was technically ready for it. These stages, Rostow assures, "have an inner logic and continuity. They have an analytic bone structure, rooted in a dynamic theory of production" (12).

Space prohibits the entering of a detailed dissent or extended comment on the filiation of Rostow's ideas from the 18th century's belief in nature, reason, and progress. Acknowledgment, however, should be accorded the important vision gained from Rostow's combination of the historical and analytical approach. He deserves credit for having introduced a remarkable degree of articulation, sense, and meaning into the complexity of historical events and economic fact. And this he achieved without falling into the trap of economic determinism that ensnared Marx. He has made a contribution to an anti-Communist manifesto—a pronouncement long overdue in an age that has grown familiar with the grisly reality of communism in action.

Economic Liberalism. The historical nature of capitalism, however, cannot be fully appreciated apart from its frame of reference, economic liberalism, one branch of the great ground swell called *liberalism that slowly arose out of nominalism, Pelagianism, rationalism, and secularism (*see* LIBERALISM, ECONOMIC).

Philosophy. Economic liberalism views the individual as the agent of economic life. He is free in his economic decisions, therefore, responsible for his actions and hence self-interested; and since all individuals are thus motivated, competition rules. In fact, its rule is indispensable because it is the balancing wheel of the economic society. For Adam Smith, the natural system of economic liberty is like a trading company in which everybody is "as it were a trader." Society conceived as a market society expects everybody—including propertyless workers—to behave as traders in their commodities.

This philosophy entrusted social welfare exclusively to the operation of individual self-interest and competitive forces. To the extent that philosophy influenced practice, justice was discarded as an operational norm under the assumption that the market mechanism made it unnecessary. No social minima were accepted as criteria for economic action or omission, with the result that no social institutions were devised for keeping self-interest and competition within proper limits. Entrepreneurs were thus encouraged, often with good conscience, to make the most of whatever favorable opportunities were available, whether arising from superior performance or from the accident of superior bargaining position. Thus there followed a drift toward submarginal standards in both business practices and labor relations. Questionable competitive practices, submarginal methods of hiring and firing, excessive working hours, oppressive employment of women and children in mines and mills gave industrial capitalism the reputation from which it still suffers.

Effects. The misery, destitution, and often subhuman working and living conditions of the early generation of industrial workers were notorious. But caution is needed in assessing this fact. Industrial capitalism was not the cause but the inheritor of this pauperism. Poverty in Europe was a fact of long standing. The statutes of Elizabeth I had used the term "laboring poor" or "poor laborers" in referring to the working people. In fact, St. Thomas Aquinas in the 13th century had characterized the peripheral group of propertyless workers of his time as those "who are poor and therefore earn their living from their daily work." The capitalist employers, it is true, benefited from the surplus labor accumulated over centuries as they transformed the "laboring poor" into jobholders and wage earners; but the material cause of the social misery accompanying the rise of capitalism was the disparity between capital formation and labor supply. Nor has communism, despite its pose as the workers' paradise, escaped this problem or its consequences.

Communism, although it has always made and still makes its bid for power by holding out glowing promises to the poor, once power has been won, accumulates capital by imposing a burden on the working population that exceeds anything that was known in the starkest days of early capitalism. By any standard the poor of mid-18th century England were better off. They could protest, they could strike, they could riot; and they did so. When their lot aroused the compassion and indignation of socially minded churchmen, statesmen, intellectuals, and not a few employers, these groups could use the forum of public opinion and the free press to demand reform; and they did so. Misinformation about industrial capitalism's "feeding on the misery of the laboring poor" seems to circulate more readily than information about the misery that accompanies the rise of industrial communism.

There is no desire to exculpate this era. The claim of exemption from integral ethics was capitalism's original sin. Once the consequences of this exemption turned up in social misery, revolts, and anticapitalist ideologies, the time was ripe for social reform and control. But as Schumpeter has aptly remarked, the time was ripe because the rapidly rising productivity of the capitalist system afforded the means for remedial action. Nor is there any suggestion here that capitalism, even in its "tamed form," is above criticism, and this least of all if the mind and heart of society lose awareness of man's third dimension—that of eternity.

Savings and Investment and the Rise of Capitalism. Economic liberalism and the freedom it won for the entrepreneur was a necessary condition for the emergence of capitalism. Two complementary factors, a supply of uncommitted savings seeking profitable investment and corresponding investment opportunities, were needed to transform the liberal principles into the capitalist reality. Without discussing the theories concerning the source of investment funds, it may be noted that scarcely any accumulation of savings had survived from the Middle Ages and that, Schumpeter's objections notwithstanding, there is merit in Webb's observation that the flow of precious metals from Central and South America gave a mighty impetus to capital accumulation.

The industrial revolution provided the investment opportunities. The steam engine, steam-driven machine tools, new process of iron smelting, and new methods of transportation, to name but a few innovations, offered opportunities for investment that returned profits that seemed, and at times were, fantastic. These profits, in turn, afforded a source of funds for reinvestment. Each investment, of course, had its element of uncertainty and risk, and losses were not infrequent. Savings, however, when compared with investment opportunities and available labor, were in short supply even in England and to a greater extent in other European countries. In North America labor as well as savings was scarce, but natural resources abounded. Exploitation of these resources offered investment opportunities and attracted mass inflows of both people and capital.

Three Phases of Capitalist Evolution

If the view is correct that capitalism is a historical phenomenon and that liberalism is its frame of reference, there remains the task of explaining the capitalist evolution in terms of the interaction of capitalism and the underlying liberal principles. It is here submitted that capitalism first moved through a stage dominated by laissez-faire liberalism; and that this phase was succeeded—at first slowly but later on at an accelerated rate—by one characterized by elements of monopoly and socio-economic institutions, such as cartels, trade associations, and other organized interest groups, and by government intervention in the form of social legislation; and that this intermediate stage was in turn followed by a third, the present existing pluralistic economy and society.

First Phase. In its laissez-faire phase capitalism first busied itself with removing obsolete institutions that had survived the Middle Ages and the mercantilist era, thus opening the way for the full play of self-interest and competition. Trade and industries were remodeled according to the requirements of the oncoming machine age, and social structures adjusted themselves correspondingly. The new industrial classes first challenged and then surpassed the landed gentry in prestige and power. Many traditional crafts and small enterprises, hard pressed by the competition of the new production methods, disappeared from the scene. Markets were expanded, widening the radius of competition, and as they expanded they created a new factor market, the labor market, destroying at the same time many local employment opportunities and causing the traditional relations between master and servant to disintegrate. The process was essentially the same everywhere, but it developed at varying degrees of speed and intensity that reflected differences in national and regional circumstances and in economic, political, and social conditions. In the U.S. capitalism could spread out over a continent that abounded in natural resources. Since labor was scarce and job opportunities were ample, except during depressions, there occurred the twin phenomena of mass immigration and vast capital imports. Continental countries adopted capitalism with a time lag and with modifications reflecting national traditions and environment. In general the farther east capitalism extended, the slower was its progress. Remnants of feudal institutions and political structures, a scarcity of savings, and a relative or complete absence of a middle class retarded its growth. Interspersed in the basically agricultural economy of eastern Europe were a few industrial undertakings developed by estate owners on the basis of surplus agricultural products, or coal and ore mines and iron smelters exploiting mineral resources.

Governmental Non-Intervention. The basic feature of liberalism, nonintervention of government including free trade, was carried further and lasted longer in Great Britain and the Netherlands than elsewhere. In France, Germany, and other European countries the period of free trade was relatively short, extending from about 1860 to the end of the 1870s. Although the U.S. was committed to protectionism from the beginnings of the Republic, the intervention of government in economic affairs in other respects was relatively slight at first and grew slowly. Among the exceptions to this general rule of nonintervention were the government's policy with respect to money and credit (reflecting the Jacksonian era's response to the perennial shortage of investment funds), its subsidies for transportation facilities (turnpikes, canals, and railroads) and its land policies, such as the Homestead Act, both of which were a response to the needs and opportunities of the open spaces west of the Alleghenies. The relative scarcity of labor, coupled with the abundance of arable land, favored large-scale farming that, as the Middle West opened, called for a mass production technology.

With the introduction of machinery in agricultural production there arose a need for agricultural credits. More than in any European country, large sectors of American agriculture increasingly acquired the stamp of capitalist enterprise. Thus the U.S. offered the unique example of capitalist production methods in both industrial and agricultural sectors.

The Gold Standard. A further feature of the laissez-faire period was the adoption and spread of the gold standard. Great Britain had returned to gold in 1816 after the Napoleonic Wars and Peel's Act of 1844 closely tied the issue of bank notes to the Bank of England's gold reserve. As the industrial revolution progressed in other countries, those engaging in international trade and finance found it advisable to base their currency on gold, since London's position in the international money markets as the world's financier and broker was undisputed. Compared with London the other money and credit markets were more or less regional. A stable exchange rate was a prime requirement for doing business with Great Britain. Germany and France adopted the gold standard in the 1870s; and Russia, in the 1890s. In that same decade the U.S. closed its long era of monetary uncertainty by also turning to gold.

In summary it may be said that the era of liberal capitalism generated production methods, market horizons, and economic institutions that more or less validated the promises of Adam Smith's natural system of economic liberty. It released productive forces of magnitudes undreamed of and widened men's economic outlook beyond the most imaginative speculations of prior periods. This was the achievement of the trader's world. But men are not born traders, and human society is not a trading company. An economic system geared to the requirements of trading and the virtues of the trader released, for want of an integral ethic and corresponding institutions, submarginal pressures against traditional values and ways of life. Social protest emerged almost at once, first among the groups hardest hit by the exigencies of the society conceived as a trading company, and later on even among the social groups for whom such a society originally was cut to measure.

Second Phase. The second phase of the capitalist evolution was marked, as already noted, by increasing social legislation and by the gradual development of monopolistic elements in the economy—socioeconomic institutions, such as cartels, trade associations, and other organizations.

Social Legislation. In England some elements of reform appeared relatively early. Following a mild relaxation in 1824 of the Conspiracy Acts of the 18th century, which had practically outlawed worker's associations, some cautious social legislation was enacted, such as protective measures for women and children working in certain industries, the outlawing of payments in kind, and later factory inspection acts. In 1846 a 10-hour law for children was passed.

In the U.S. social legislation, viewed as a function of the police power and thus under the jurisdiction of the states, developed slowly, especially in the South. The decision of the Massachusetts Supreme Court in *Commonwealth v. Hunt* (1842), legalizing a limited range of union activities, became a landmark and was followed more or less closely by the courts in other jurisdictions. Details aside, it may be said that in all industrialized countries the increasing need for a minimum of social legislation came to be recognized. As the century wore on there was a quickening of the social conscience, stimulated by the labor movement and inspired by both Christian charity and socialist ideology.

The failure of the attempts of some employers to assume social responsibility for their working forces and of others to admit any such responsibility was a great disappointment to many social idealists. Paternalism failed because it applied precapitalist ethos patterns in an environment of competitive pressures and because the awakening labor movement, for reasons of its own, would have none of it. In Europe this left but two potential forces for social improvement, the government and the labor movement. In the U.S. the organized farm movements periodically constituted a third force. Governments entered the uncharted field of social action with caution and reluctance, but pressed by the rising tide of protest they grew bolder and more assertive.

In the area of social legislation Bismarck's social security program of the 1880s became a landmark to be imitated by other countries. Great Britain adopted a somewhat similar program in 1911, but in the U.S. social security legislation, with the exception of workmen's compensation, awaited the New Deal of the 1930s.

Interest Groups. Trade unions at the outset operated under the threefold handicap of legal restrictions, employer resistance, and worker indifference. As the legal restrictions came to be relaxed, the craft union, which had the advantage of the strong craft consciousness among artisans of the same trade and a more favorable market position, made headway during periods of business prosperity. Unskilled workers, long thought incapable of unionization because of the ready substitutability of one worker for another, experienced their first success in the London dockers' strike of 1889. Broadly speaking, the ebb and flow of union strength and achievement and the growth of social legislation mirrored the course of business prosperity. Both union achievements and the prospects for and the probable success of social legislation are to a great extent dependent on favorable business conditions.

Laissez faire, both as doctrine and practice, was losing ground even in business circles. The need for rules clarifying what was permissible in pricing, in wage setting, in business and employer practice came more and more to be recognized. The issue of justice, which liberalism had regarded as obsolete, was being revived by the claims of interest groups that as a rule were raised in the name of justice. However, it was partisan justice that was being proclaimed, "justice for us"—for trade unions, the farming community, and business sectors. These groups were insisting on the right to define justice and their just demands in the light of their several interests. Emerging in an era of economic liberalism, they adapted their principles of actions to the prevailing individualistic ethos patterns. With this development an important change had taken place. Instead of individuals acting in self-interest, the group had become the agent.

To the extent that group demands and social legislation implied increased costs, business had to meet them, and did so in a variety of ways, especially by increasing productivity. Business drew heavily on scientific research and applied its results to old and new industries. Investment requirements grew apace. In the U.S. the rise of powerful corporations in the steel, electrical, glass, railroad, and finance industries evidenced the change in the industrial structure of the country. The big corporations enhanced their power by a variety of devices, such as, until passage of the Sherman Act in 1890, overt price and market arrangements between different firms and, after passage of that legislation, interlocking directorates, outright mergers, cleverly arranged pricing agreements, and suggestive cost calculations publicized by trade journals and trade associations. The Sherman Act of 1890 turned out to be a somewhat inadequate instrument in the fight against restraint of trade.

The spread and the rapid growth of corporations contributed to the expansion of markets. Large corporations had to plan ahead, to make long-run provision for prime materials, tools, and credit. The normally competitive spot market was insufficient and uncertain; more efficient devices had to be found to meet the conditions of new, large, and concentrated industries. Vertical and horizontal concentration began to emerge as a dominant characteristic of industry. Trusts, holding companies, and interlocking directorates proved useful for the purposes of control. Price leadership in oligopolistic industries and basing point systems in the U.S. substituted in some fashion for the functions filled by cartels in Europe. In the U.S. consumers became alarmed in this unfamiliar world of business giants, and at their urging "trust-busting" again became an issue during the Theodore Roosevelt and Woodrow Wilson administrations. This second phase also witnessed a wave of imperialism; in both Asia and Africa colonial expansion was a response to the need of a mature capitalism for ever-widening markets.

Third Phase. With the shift of liberal capitalism to its second phase the fragmented society began a process of regrouping. "The people" took refuge against the vicissitudes of the market in a multitude of interest organizations that, accelerated by war and the depression, soon spread over the whole contour of national life. War economies seemed to have shown that economic life could be managed and directed for national ends to a surprising extent. The question naturally arose: If governments are so powerful a factor in war economy, why not draft them for social reform? Government and social forces joined for ambitious social programs. Consonant with this change was a mutation in the meaning of democracy as well as a new status for government. Since time immemorial democracy had been a form of government; now it was turned into a creed, into a way of life. Government now appeared either as a clearinghouse for conflicting interest groups (as in the U.S.) or as a junior partner of powerful groups (as in Sweden), or even as the instrument of a dominant single group (as the British Labor Party between 1945 and 1951). The spheres of economic and political life seemed to interpenetrate, if not to merge.

Shift In Power Structure. Paul P. Harbrecht calls the existing economic society paraproprietal and considers its characteristic note to be the fact that independence, security, and power in society are no longer conferred by ownership of property but that contractual arrangements (seniority, pensions, welfare programs, etc.) offer security and power derives from position in the institutions that control productive property. Where the individual "was once master of a domain . . . he now looks to a complex of contracts, equities and expectancies over which he has very little control. . . . Institutions that determine a man's relationship to productive property and to other men are the structuring elements of today's society insofar as it is given form by economic relationships. Thus we conclude that *a man's relationship to things—material wealth—no longer determines his place in society* (as it did in a strong proprietary system) *but his place in society now determines his relationship to things.* This is the consequence of the separation of control over property from individual ownership" [P. P. Harbrecht, *Pension Funds and Economic Power* (Twentieth Century Fund, New York 1959) 286–287].

Forces Effecting Transition. There is merit in these observations, but they are not the whole story. Outside forces invited this development. After World War II long pent-up consumer wants, in some countries supported by substantial savings accumulated during the war, created a sellers' market for consumer goods. This high-level demand lasted long enough to create a pattern of continuing rising expectations among producer groups. As their demands were met, the keener became their expectations. Success became habit forming and brought about an important change in the character of these groups. From a position of being dependent variables in the economic structure whose achievements reflected business conditions, some of the stronger of the interest groups became relatively independent and began to influence the course of business. Cost structures resulting from collective bargaining or from parity prices for agricultural products had to be validated by the central banks. That the pressures of cost inflation were held in check was due in large part to the wartime wave of innovations that came to be applied to the peacetime economy. But unions and firms in highly progressive industries, or in those with highly inelastic demand schedules, more or less absorbed the benefits of innovation in profits and improved labor conditions. The remaining inflationary impact fell as a heavy burden on social groups that were unable to exert political and economic pressure.

The whole story would also have to tell of the power structure that affects the process of distribution, the pressure powers of social groups accommodated by government. The differentials in economic and political power combined with the groups' propensity to hold government responsible for full employment, for "fair" profits, for income parity levels, and for easy credit reveal the inherent weakness of the pluralistic economic society. Its focus is the divorce of group demand and group action from social responsibility. Liberal capitalism, it is true, had tied responsibility too closely to individual actions and behavior, especially for the workers and periodically for the farmers. Today, however, the divorce of group policy from group responsibility and the shift of the latter from the groups to government results in an anonymity of responsibility. The locus of responsibility has become indeterminate.

Future of Capitalism. The third phase of capitalism has become an era of trouble and uncertainty. Cold war and brush fires at the rim of the global economy appear to be the lot of the present generation. The balance of power between capitalism and communism is precarious. Webb would maintain that he was right, that since there are no longer wide-open frontiers, the Western nations are faced with the end of capitalism.

Marx, as is well known, prophesied that the forces inherent in capitalism would destroy it. The great disparity between the productive potential of the capitalist technology and the limited purchasing power of the masses condemned to subsistence wages would cause recurrent overproduction, underconsumption crises, climaxing in a cataclysmic crisis, heralding revolution, the end of capitalism, and a dictatorship of the proletariat. Schumpeter, the most distinguished nonsocialist economist to deal with this matter at any length, is also pessimistic about the future of capitalism but for far different reasons. Capitalism, he asserts, is doomed not because of its failure but because of its outstanding success. The capitalist process has created an amazingly efficient economic structure and technology. It has, for practical purposes, institutionalized the processes of innovation and progress. In so doing it has rendered obsolete the key figure of capitalist society, the entrepreneur—the captain of industry who had the capacity of marshaling resources, the foresight to recognize opportunities, and the daring to undertake the risks that were inherent in progress. But a system that has been thoroughly institutionalized is also readily socialized, especially in a polity of universal suffrage.

There are also optimists, of course, among whom J. K. Galbraith is well known in the U.S. In his *American Capitalism* he defends the thesis that capitalism in the U.S., because it operates in a system of countervailing forces, will survive. In such a system the appearance and exercise of power begets a countervailing force, and the operation of countervailing forces disciplines capitalism and causes it to preserve a degree of adaptability that argues for its survival. He fails to recognize that the countervailing forces are unneeded during periods of depression—market forces would exert the necessary discipline—where during inflation the countervailing forces, as he concedes, would be ineffective; the interest groups would strike bargains among themselves, shifting the burden of inflation to other groups or to government.

Neoliberals of the type of L. von Mises, F. von Hayek, G. Haberler, Edward H. Chamberlin, M. Friedman, F. Machlup, and W. Roepke are likewise optimists, but they more or less advocate a return to effective market competition with its definite allocation of responsibilities. They recognize that the competitive process must be softened by a social frame of reference, with a variable minimum of social control. The almost miraculous rehabilitation of the German economy after the war gives support to their view.

Capitalism and Communism. The debate about the future of capitalism still continues, and its answer lies with the future. Two points, however, may be made. The first is a question of semantics. Is the system that now exists in the Western world properly called capitalism, or has capitalism already been supplanted by a new system? There is in the existing system, it may be conceded, a degree and kind of government intervention that more resembles mercantilism or, as some would have it, socialism than capitalism. Yet there exists a larger sector of small- and medium-sized business, that, together with parts of agriculture, is undoubtedly capitalist. There is still a good deal of individual self-determination, self-responsibility, self-interest, and competition, overt or inverted. Much the greater part of business investment is made by privately owned firms—giant corporations, it is true—and is motivated by profit. This matter of semantics in itself is unimportant, although the terms capitalism and communism, charged as they are with emotional bias, will long be symbols of the titanic struggle between East and West. It may be that the term capitalism for emotional reasons is today a liability, but no one can doubt that it still serves its purposes, if rightly interpreted.

The second point is that this system, whatever it is called, has shown an astonishing flexibility and power of survival. It has accepted the fact that economic laws and business enterprise presuppose respect for the laws of social life, for eternal laws ordering and regulating human society. Capitalism has demonstrated also that it can cope with a load of social overhead never carried by any other economic system. Communism does it the honor of adapting its know-how, its technology, and its economic and administrative structures. On the other hand, it is no secret that in the Soviet system black markets and black practices make up some of the deficiencies of central planning. Thus an element of free enterprise, although operating in an underground fashion, also asserts itself as a complement of the Soviet economy. And there is some evidence that the Communist economic system, at least as exemplified by the U.S.S.R., is itself subject to change.

The Challenge. There is a paradox in the different treatment that the Church has accorded liberalism on the one hand and capitalism on the other. Seeing the former as a resurgence of ancient heresies in a strange confraternity with a secularized Calvinism, the Holy See has frequently condemned it. Capitalism, although founded on liberalism, has never been condemned as such. This fact argues that the Church has judged that the system, as Bp. Wilhelm von Ketteler had pointed out in 1867, is morally and socially redeemable. Pius XI called attention to the fact that "Leo XIII's whole endeavor was to adjust this economic regime to the standards of true order. Whence it follows that the system is not to be condemned. And surely it is not vicious of its very nature" (*Quadragesimo anno,* 101).

Today the Catholic doctrine of state and society has its historic chance. Both laissez-faire liberalism, to which most of the errors of primitive capitalism may be traced,.and communism have lost glamour and appeal. In the wake of the struggle between them, the Western world has been encumbered with a chaotic pluralism of institutions and policies, and the institutions themselves have developed vested interests. If interest associations are "dams and dykes" (Sidney Webb) built into the dynamic expansion of the capitalist economy to keep it from engulfing society, if they draw their strength from the vitality of capitalism itself, then these power groups have a vital stake in the preservation of capitalism. The danger is that the superstructure, in seeking only its own interests to the exclusion of the larger common good, will undermine the foundations on which it stands.

The Church, in censuring economic liberalism's claim to be a sufficient principle for directing economic activity, has never denied that individual responsibility, self-interest, and competition have a vital economic function. Indeed the principal of subsidiarity, which Pius XI called a fundamental principle of social philosophy, calls for individual responsibility within a framework of social premises. The present situation, with its confused response to its complex of problems, offers Catholic social doctrine an unparalleled opportunity and a crucial test. To seize the opportunity and meet the test it must reassess the application of its principles to the historic, contingent, and changing facts. Here lies its challenge.

Bibliography: J. H. CLAPHAM, *An Economic History of Modern Britain,* 3 v. (Cambridge, Eng. 1926–38). B. W. DEMPSEY, "Capitalism," *Social Order* 4 (1954) 199–208. J. K. GALBRAITH, *American Capitalism* (pa. Boston 1956); *Affluent Society* (New York 1961). F. A. VON HAYEK, ed., *Capitalism and the Historians* (Chicago 1954). L. C. A. KNOWLES, *The Industrial and Commercial Revolutions in Great Britain During the 19th Century* (New York 1921). P. J. MANTOUX, *The Industrial Revolution in the 18th Century,* tr. M. VERNON (New York 1928; rev. ed. 1961). W. A. ORTON, *The Economic Role of the State* (Chicago 1950). H. M. ROBERTSON, *Aspects of the Rise of Economic Individualism: A Criticism of Max Weber and His School* (New York 1933). W. RÖPKE, *The Social Crisis of our Time,* tr. A. and P. S. JACOBSOHN (5th ed. Chicago 1950). J. A. SCHUMPETER, *Essays* (Cambridge, Ind. 1951); "Capitalism in the Postwar World," *Postwar Economic Problems,* ed. S. E. HARRIS (New York 1943) 113–126; *Capitalism, Socialism and Democracy* (3d ed. New York 1950). W. SOMBART, *Der moderne Kapitalismus* (Berlin 1955). R. H. TAWNEY, *Religion and the Rise of Capitalism* (pa. Baltimore 1947; New York 1958). W. P. WEBB, *Great Frontier* (Boston 1952). M. WEBER, *The Protestant Ethic and the Spirit of Capitalism,* tr. T. PARSONS (London 1930). THOMAS WILSON, *Modern Capitalism and Economic Progress* (New York 1950). W. W. ROSTOW, *The Stages of Economic Growth* (Cambridge, Eng. 1960).

[G. A. BRIEFS]

CAPITANIO, BARTOLOMEA, ST., cofoundress of the Sisters of *Charity of Lovere; b. Lovere (Lombardy), Italy, Jan. 13, 1807; d. Lovere, July 26, 1833 (feast, July 26). At the age of 11 she entered the convent of the *Poor Clares in Lovere, but she returned to her family in 1824, and in her home opened a school for youth. She received spiritual and practical guidance from Don Angelo Bosio. Her inclination toward an active apostolate of charity toward all classes led her to forgo entering the Poor Clares. At Lovere in 1826 she started a hospital, where she was prodigiously active as directress and in other positions, even tending the sick in their own homes. By her letters, about 300 of which are extant, she continued to counsel the youth of Lovere and neighboring towns. Local pastors esteemed this correspondence very highly. Her writings include also many devotional pieces; programs for pious associations; prayers for various feasts; and norms for life, even for priests. In the spiritual combat she fought especially against pride. Bartolomea conceived a religious institution dedicated to all types of charitable work. After she and Vincenza *Gerosa had dedicated themselves completely to God (Nov. 21, 1832), they founded the first house of the new congregation. The youngest among religious foundresses, she died the following year. She was beatified May 30, 1926; and canonized, together with Vincenza Gerosa May 22, 1950.

St. Bartolomea Capitanio.

Bibliography: L. MAZZA, *Della vita e dell'Istituto della venerabile Bartolomea Capitanio,* 5 v. (Modena 1905). A. STOCCHETTI, *Le Sante Bartolomea Capitanio e Vincenza Gerosa* (Vicenza 1950).

[M. C. BIANCHI]

CAPITO, WOLFGANG, Swiss reformer; b. Hagenau in Alsace, 1478; d. Strassburg, Nov. 4, 1541. Capito (Köpfel) was educated at Ingolstadt, Freiburg, and Basel, where he was professor of theology and cathedral preacher (1515–20). He held degrees in law, theology, and medicine and was in addition a distinguished Hebraist. From 1520 to 1523 he was chaplain and chancellor to the archbishop of Mainz. After his arrival in Strassburg in May 1523 he worked tirelessly for the propagation of the Reformation in the city. Some of the ideas and emphases in his early theology approximate to a striking degree those of the *Anabaptists, with a few of whom he was on friendly terms, but this unusually sympathetic position altered after 1532, and in a vernacular pamphlet of 1534 he repudiated the Anabaptists decisively.

Bibliography: J. W. BAUM, *Capito und Butzer (Leben und ausgewählte Schriften der Väter und Begründer der Reformirten Kirche,* ed. K. R. HAGENBACH, v.3, Elberfeld 1860). O. E. STRASSER, *La Pensée théologique de Wolfgang Capiton dans les dernières années de sa vie* (Neuchâtel 1938). *The Mennonite Encyclopedia,* 4 v. (Scottdale, Pa. 1955–60) 1:512–516. R. STUPPERICH, RGG^3 1:1613.

[C. GARSIDE, JR.]

CAPITULARIES, IMPERIAL AND ECCLESIASTICAL

The name given to the body of legislation, in the form of short articles (*capitula*), issued by the Carolingian kings and emperors during the second half of the 8th and 9th centuries. The term *capitulare* for such a royal or imperial ordinance occurs in contemporary sources.

Capitularies were sometimes concerned with one particular matter, e.g., church organization or defense, but more often they dealt with a variety of topics; some articles were in the nature of true legislation, others were of a more administrative and executive kind. The capitularies are the hallmark of the Carolingian attempt at ordered government.

Area and Period. Most capitularies were issued for people of all of the lands under Frankish rule; some, for the Franks or the Lombards only ("Frankish" and "Italian" capitularies); and some for certain ethnic groups only, such as the Salic Franks or the Bavarians. Their validity was on a personal basis and its duration is hard to generalize. They sometimes contained specific references to duration, e.g., the capitulary of Quierzy (A.D. 877), which was to be in force only during the Italian expedition of Charles the Bald. But usually there was no explicit indication; duration depended on the nature of the capitulary and the circumstances of its promulgation. Capitularies of a real legislative character had permanent validity unless expressly changed or abolished; those inspired by temporary situations naturally had only a temporary validity. There are some extant capitularies from the time of Carloman and Pippin III, but the main body comes from the period of Charlemagne and Louis the Pious. After the division of 843 there were no more capitularies in the East Frankish kingdom, or in the realm of Lothair I, except for Italy where they continued until the late 9th century (A.D. 898). In the West Frankish kingdom capitularies continued to be issued to a considerable extent until the death of Charles the Bald (877); they stopped altogether after A.D. 884.

Promulgation and Conservation of the Text. Although sometimes sent out in the form of official circular letters, capitularies were not usually drafted in official full texts by the royal chancery, but were notes or title lists set down to recall the contents of royal commandments made orally; hence, the allusive and elliptical character of most of them. The form was often that of orders and prohibitions. Since there was no one authoritative text, manuscript tradition shows an exceptional number of variant readings.

The royal *bannum,* i.e., the ruler's right to command, was the basis of the authority of the capitulary. The spoken word of the prince was the ultimate legal basis for his contemporaries. Consultation with and consent given by lay and ecclesiastical magnates was a feature of annual meetings though the impact of this advice and consent differed from time to time. The real meaning of the consent has been much discussed. It may be assumed that until the reign of Louis the Pious the term meant little more than a formal recognition of the validity of the royal edicts, and a promise to stand by them and see to their execution. This is clear in texts where people are to be ordered to "consent" to certain capitularies. Certainly there is no textual evidence to warrant a theory of the necessity of popular consent for the validity of royal legislation, let alone a theory of popular sovereignty. During the latter part of Louis the Pious's reign and after it, the aristocracy gained power from the weakening of royal authority and turned their "consent" into something that could be withheld and could, therefore, be a factor of real importance in the promulgation of the capitulary.

When the prince issued a new set of capitularies they were distributed throughout the realm either by royal envoys (*missi dominici*) or by the counts in their respective domains (*pagi*). Copies were made and preserved not only in the royal archives but throughout the realm. From the beginning individuals made collections of capitularies for practical purposes, often combining them with other legal material in a single manuscript. Most copies of capitularies that have come down to us (from the 9th, 10th, and 11th centuries) are of that nature; no original text has been preserved. One of the most influential collections was made under Louis the Pious by Abbot Ansegisus of Saint-Wandrille. It follows a systematic order, and was frequently in official use. The so-called Benedict the Levite, well-known through the False Decretals, made a collection of capitularies as a continuation of those gathered by Ansegisus, probably in 847–852. Benedict's collection contains many spurious elements.

Contents and Types. Capitularies dealt with diverse matters: legal, ecclesiastical, military, fiscal, administrative, and commercial. Even though matters in several of these categories were often treated in the same set of capitularies, it is nevertheless possible to distinguish certain types on the basis of their form or contents. The distinction between *ecclesiastica* and *mundana* is made in the texts; the former deal with church matters, the latter, with a variety of legal, military, and administrative topics. *Capitula mundana* are further divided into: (1) *capitula legibus addenda,* or capitularies adding some legislation to various existing national bodies of law, such as the *Lex Salica;* (2) *capitula per se scribenda,* or autonomous royal edicts; and (3) *capitula missorum,* or instructions given to royal envoys on their departure from the royal palace. This threefold division goes back to Carolingian times.

Capitularies dealt with monastic and canonical organization and discipline: such liturgical topics as stipulations concerning church chant and computation of the date of feast days; access to Holy Orders; and the veneration of (new) saints and image worship. They were valid in areas where Church and civil law might both claim some jurisdiction such as: restoration of church buildings and the benefices of their incumbents; church tithes; wandering monks and pilgrims; competence of courts, procedure, and punishment of criminous clerks; crimes committed by laymen for which church courts were competent; protection of churches and churchmen. They also treated of the role of the *advocatus,* i.e., the layman responsible for various temporal functions of ecclesiastical institutions; the special attention to be given in the law courts to actions brought by churches; the belief in ordeals; and numerous other religious and ecclesiastical matters.

All preserved capitularies are in Latin, although very imperfect Latin, and it is improbable that any were written in other languages. The Latin is interspersed with Germanic or Romance words and is sometimes very difficult to understand precisely. The capitularies were conceived in one of the Germanic or Romance dialects of the time and then literally translated into Latin. They present the phenomenon of vernacular thought and speech patterns using Latin words. The situation improved under Louis the Pious as a consequence of the so-called Carolingian Renaissance, and the Italian capitularies were always better written than the Frankish ones. The absence of a precise technical language was particularly felt in legal matters where there was little or no influence of Roman law.

Editions. The capitularies have often been edited. The best critical edition available is that in MGL 2. This edition does not altogether meet present critical requirements, and a new one would be most welcome.

Bibliography: F. L. GANSHOF, *Was waren die Kapitularien?* (Weimar 1961), contains a complete list of capitularies. G. SEELIGER, *Die Kapitularien der Karolinger* (Munich 1893). For the ecclesiastical legislation: C. DE CLERCQ, *La Législation religieuse Franque . . .,* 2 v. (Paris-Antwerp 1936–58). R. BUCHNER, "Die Rechtsquellen," Wattenbach-Levison (1953) Beiheft, a recent survey of editions and literature.

[R. C. VAN CAENEGEM]

CAPITULATIONS, agreements by electors limiting in advance the powers of a prelate to be chosen from among themselves. Such capitulations were frequently entered into by episcopal electors in the Middle Ages, although Pope *Nicholas III in 1280 declared invalid any oath by which a future prelate bound himself to fufill conditions that were "illicit or impossible or contrary to the liberty of the church" (CorpIurCan VI° 2.11.1). The most important capitulations were those by which the cardinals sought, from the 14th century onward, to limit the powers of future popes. The right of the cardinals to be sole electors of the pope was established by a canon of 1179. Subsequently their role in the general work of ecclesiastical government became increasingly important and, in the 13th century, it was commonly maintained that the *sacred college was a divinely established element in the government of the Church. The election capitulations of the 14th and 15th centuries brought this development to a climax, for they were essentially attempts to establish an oligarchic headship for the Church in place of a papal monarchy. In laying down conditions to be observed by future popes, the cardinals were especially concerned with enhancing their own status. The first recorded capitulations (1352) stated that the number of cardinals was to be limited to 20 and that no new ones were to be created until the number had fallen to 16. No cardinal was to be deposed or excommunicated without the unanimous consent of the others, and none appointed without the consent of two-thirds of them. Similarly, consent of two-thirds of the cardinals was required for any alienation of church property by the pope, and, finally, half the revenues of the papacy were to be assigned to the sacred college. *Innocent VI, who was elected in this conclave of 1352, subsequently denounced the pact as contrary to the provisions of the canon *Ubi periculum,* which had regulated the conduct of the election of *popes (1274), and as an illicit infringement of the pope's plenitude of power. During the *Western Schism cardinals of both obediences swore that, if elected, they would seek to end the schism, by resigning if necessary. Subsequently, detailed capitulations were drawn up at the conclaves of 1431, 1458, and 1464. During the 1460s the theologian Teodoro de' Lelli and the canonist Andreas de *Barbatia denounced the recent capitulations as contrary to the divinely willed *primacy of Peter's successor. Nevertheless the practice continued into the 15th and 16th centuries. All pacts and promises among the cardinals during election *conclaves were forbidden by Pius IV in the bull *In eligendis* (1562) and again by Gregory XV in the bull **Aeterni Patris* (1621).

Bibliography: J. LULVÈS, "Die Machtbestrebungen des Kardinalkollegiums gegenüber dem Papsttum," MitteilIÖG 35 (1914) 455–483. W. ULLMANN, "The Legal Validity of the Papal Electoral Pacts," EphemIC 12 (1956) 246–278. Jedin Trent 1:76–100.

[B. TIERNEY]

CAPPA Y MANESCAU, RICARDO, Spanish priest and historian; b. Madrid, Oct. 25, 1839; d. there, Nov. 8, 1897. He was a seaman and served as navy lieutenant in the Spanish armada sent to the Pacific to demand reparation from Peru and Chile for the injuries to Spanish subjects. He entered the Society of Jesus on March 18, 1866, in Cádiz. After completing his ecclesiastical studies in Spain and France, he was sent to Quito in 1872 as professor of cosmography and astronomy at the polytechnic school. Afterward he went to Lima. During the War of the Pacific (1878) he was a volunteer chaplain of the Peruvian army; as a teacher at the Immaculata School, he began a series of important historical publications. One, *Historia compendiada del Peru,* caused so much controversy that Cappa fled to Bolivia in 1887 and later returned to Spain, where he lived until his death. There he reedited his books and added more on Hispanic-America. The definitive edition (Madrid 1889–97) contains 20 volumes with the general title *Estudios críticos acerca de la dominación española en América,* valuable because of its deep historical knowledge. Volumes 1 to 4 treat of Columbus, the discovery of America, and the conquest of Peru, without disguising a sound apologetic judgment; 5 and 6, agriculture and cattle industry; 7, 8, and 9, manufacturing and mechanical industry; 10, 11, and 12, naval industry; 13 and 14, fine arts; 15 to 20, Old and New Worlds. He also discussed the influence of Christianity on the civilization of the American peoples.

Bibliography: F. MATEOS, *Jesuítas españoles en el Perú contemporáneo, siglo XIX* (Madrid 1946).

[F.MATEOS]

CAPPONI, GINO, Italian writer, historian; b. Florence, Sept. 13, 1792; d. there, Feb. 3, 1876. Descended from a prominent Florentine family, Capponi was a leader among 19th-century liberal Italian Catholics and clearly understood the link between the political and religious problems posed by the *Risorgimento. From an early age he enjoyed foreign contacts, and he spent some years at the Austrian court. Subsequently he journeyed throughout Italy, England, the Low Countries, Germany, and Switzerland. After 1825 he settled in Florence to a life of study, interrupted by brief interludes of political activity. In 1848 he headed the ministry of Tuscany for 70 days, and in 1860 he became a senator of the Kingdom of Italy. Capponi contributed much to the spiritual and cultural revival of Italian life and to *Neo-Guelfism. He supported the establishment of the periodicals *Antologia* (1821), *Giornale agrario toscano* (1827), *Guida dell'Educatore* (1836), and *Archivio storico italiano* (1842). Despite his blindness after 1840, Capponi enjoyed an international circle of friends and wrote on many subjects. Most of his numerous works remain incomplete except for his two-volume *Storia della Republica di Firenze* (1875). His best writings are those on education, which were probably the most original composed in Italy on the subject between 1800 and 1850. Capponi believed that education, a sound family life, and sincere religious faith should form the bases for any reform movement.

Bibliography: G. CAPPONI, *Scritti inediti,* ed. G. MACCHIA (Florence 1957), includes most up-to-date bibliog. of all Capponi's writings and letters. "Capponi's History of the Republic of Florence," *Edinburgh Review* 143 (1876) 474–510. G. GENTILE, *Gino Capponi e la cultura toscana del secolo decimonono* (3d ed. Florence 1942). A. GAMBARO, ed., *La critica pedagogica di G. Capponi* (Bari 1956), contains all C.'s works on education. M. PETROCCHI, EncCatt 3:712–713.

[E. P. NOETHER]

CAPRANICA, DOMENICO AND ANGELO, brothers, notable in the ecclesiastical life of the 15th century.

Domenico, humanist and cardinal; b. Capranica (near Palestrina), Italy, May 31, 1400; d. Rome, Aug. 14,

1458. After being educated at Padua and Bologna, he entered papal service where he won the admiration of *Poggio and other humanists. *Martin V created him bishop of Fermo (1425) and cardinal (1426; published November 1430). He failed to receive his hat before Martin's death. Excluded from the conclave, he was driven from Rome to plead his cause before the Council of *Basel. *Eugene IV recognized him as cardinal (1434). His intelligence, integrity, and wholehearted service made him the confidant of *Nicholas V, who appointed him grand penitentiary; he was also a stern critic of the *nepotism of *Callistus III. His zeal and generosity found expression in the foundation (1458) of the Collegio Capranicense for poor scholars in theology and Canon Law.

Angelo, bishop and cardinal; b. Capranica, *c.* 1400; d. Rome, July 3, 1478. Educated in philosophy and law, he was appointed archbishop of Siponto-*Manfredonia (1438) and bishop of Ascoli (1447). He played a significant role in the canonization of *John Capistran. He was appointed bishop of Rieti in 1450. *Pius II made him governor at Bologna (1458), where he displayed both personal integrity and ability as an administrator and diplomat. Created cardinal (1460), he labored unceasingly for the revival of the religious life and the improvement of clerical education.

Bibliography: J. Toussaint, DHGE 11:932–941. R. Mols, *ibid.*, 11:928–932. J. Wodka, LexThK² 2:930, recent literature.

[J. G. ROWE]

CAPRARA, GIOVANNI BATTISTA, cardinal, papal diplomat; b. Bologna, May 29, 1733; d. Paris, June 21, 1810. He owed his rapid rise to noble birth and competence in Canon Law. After serving as vicelegate to Bologna (1758–66), he went as titular archbishop of Iconium and nuncio to Germany (1767–75), where he had to contend with the *Febronianism of *Hontheim; combat the prince-bishops of Cologne and Mainz who were hostile to the nuncio's religious action and to the interventions of Rome; and face resistance to the application of Clement XIV's brief, *Dominus ac Redemptor* (1773), suppressing the Jesuits. His period as nuncio to Lucerne (1775–85) was happier. He was then (1785–93) promoted to the nunciature of Vienna at the request of Catholic Austria. Careful to avoid a rupture between Austria, with its *Josephinism, and the Holy See, Caprara was patient to the point of weakness. This accounted for his passivity when the Congress of *Ems (1786) voted the famous Punctation challenging papal authority and when the Diet of Frankfort (1791) imposed on the new Emperor Leopold II a capitulation contrary to the rights of the sovereign pontiff. He waited 8 days after the close of the Diet to raise an ineffectual protest. Created cardinal (1792), he returned to Rome (1793) in disgrace with Pius VI because of his failure at Vienna and the Jacobin tendencies that were attributed to him as a result of his admonitions concerning the policy to be adopted toward the French Revolution.

*Napoleon I, aware of this, demanded Caprara as papal legate *a latere* to regulate the application of the *Concordat of 1801. The cardinal arrived in Paris (Oct. 4, 1801), although the Concordat was not promulgated until April 18, 1802. The legate anticipated the use of his powers to obtain the resignation of bishops and to establish a new division of dioceses. In this delicate, complex situation he had to resolve with the French minister *Portalis the many problems connected with the reorganization of the Church in France. Counseled by *Bernier, who acted as his adviser and duped him in the process, he wanted to be above all else a peacemaker. Rome reproached him for giving way and permitting constitutional bishops to be named to the new sees set up by the Concordat; for the retractions by bishops and priests who had supported the *Civil Constitution; for not preventing the *Organic Articles; and for having taken an oath to the First Consul, although the version attributed to him differed from the one he actually made.

Caprara participated in the negotiations for the Italian Concordat and Bonaparte's coronation in Paris. He received the See of Josi in 1800 and that of Milan in 1802. As archbishop of Milan he crowned Napoleon King of Italy. His policy of conciliation placed him more and more in the bad graces of Pius VII, who resolved in 1806 to resist caesaropapism. Caprara was excluded from the negotiations undertaken in 1807 and confided to Cardinal de Bayanne. Despite the papal order (December 1807) that he ask for his passport, Caprara remained in Paris. In 1809 he made one last effort to obtain concessions from the Pope, who was imprisoned at Savona. Ill, deaf, almost blind, he died at Paris. Napoleon had him buried in the Pantheon.

Bibliography: R. Mols, DHGE 11:944–957.

[J. A. M. LEFLON]

CAPREOLUS, JOHN, scholastic theologian; b. Rodez, France, *c.* 1380; d. Rodez, April 6, 1444. Little is known of this most celebrated Thomist of the Middle Ages. He entered the Dominican Order at Rodez for the province of Toulouse, and in 1407 was assigned by the Dominican general chapter at Poitiers to lecture on the *Sentences* of Peter Lombard at the University of Paris. In 1408 and 1409 he composed the first part of his *Libri defensionum theologiae divi Thomae de Aquino,* familiarly called the *Defensiones.* He took his degree at the University of Paris (1411 and 1415) in theology. He was made regent of studies at Toulouse, but by 1426 was back at Rodez, where he spent the rest of his life.

Capreolus completed parts two, three, and four of the *Defensiones,* his only known work, in 1426, 1428, and 1433, respectively. Although it is cast in the form of a commentary on the *Sentences,* the content is a penetrating exposition and defense of Thomistic teaching. Isidore de Isolanis (d. 1528), who summarized the work, honored Capreolus no less than Aquinas, and he was then and later known as "the soul of St. Thomas" and the "prince of Thomists." With clarity and erudition he systematically defended the Thomistic doctrine against *Duns Scotus, *Henry of Ghent, *John of Ripa, Ockham (*see* OCKHAMISM), and lesser theologians.

After his death his work was published at Venice in four folio volumes (1483, 1514, 1519, 1589); the first volume was edited by Thomas de St. Germain, a colleague of Capreolus. Isidore de Isolanis, Paul Soncinas (d. 1494), and Sylvester Prierias (d. 1523) published abridgments, and a modern edition in seven quarto volumes was published in Tours (1900–07), edited by Ceslaus Paban and Thomas Pègues.

Bibliography: Quétif-Echard 1:795–796. Copleston v.3. T. M. Pègues, "Capréolus 'Thomistarum Princeps' à propos de la nouvelle édition de ses oeuvres," RevThom 7 (1899) 63–81; "La Biographie de Jean Capréolus," *ibid.* 317–334; "Pouvons nous sur cette terre arriver à connaître Dieu," *ibid.* 8 (1900) 50–76;

"Théologie Thomiste d'après Capréolus: De la voie rationelle que nous conduit à Dieu," *ibid.* 288–309; "L'idée de Dieu en nous," *ibid.* 505–530. M. GRABMANN, "Johannes Capreolus O.P. der 'Princeps Thomistarum' († 1444), und seine Stellung in der Geschichte der Thomistenschule," *Mittelalterliches Geistesleben,* v.3 (Munich 1956) 370–410.

[J. A. WEISHEIPL]

CAPTIVITY EPISTLES

Term applied to four Epistles of St. Paul written while he was in prison. In his second letter to the Corinthian community, written *c.* A.D. 57, Paul referred to the "imprisonments" that he had already suffered (1 Cor 6.5), and he added that he had, in fact, been imprisoned more frequently than his detractors (11.23). Although a certain amount of literary hyperbole may be admitted in the two passages, it seems that behind these assertions there was more than the overnight detention in the Philippian prison described in Acts 16.19–40, which is the only imprisonment explicitly mentioned by Luke up to this time (*c.* A.D. 51). Scholars ask, therefore, whether there were not other imprisonments before A.D. 57 not recorded by the author of Acts. The problem is compounded somewhat by the fact that Clement of Rome, writing toward the end of the 1st century, explicitly stated that Paul was imprisoned seven times.

Paul's Various Imprisonments. From the Acts it is known that Paul had two long imprisonments, one at *Caesarea in Palestine from 58 to 60 (Acts 23.22–26.32) and the other at Rome for the 2 following years (Acts 28.16–31). If one can suppose a second Roman imprisonment, as suggested by the *Pastoral Epistles (e.g., 2 Tm 1.12; 4.6–8, 16–18), this brings only to four the number of Paul's imprisonments recorded in the NT. Some scholars have argued for other imprisonments on the basis of bits of evidence in Acts and Paul's letters. The one suggestion that has received the greatest attention and consideration is that there was an imprisonment at *Ephesus. The passage in Acts 19.23–40 indicates the fierce opposition to the Apostle and to "the Way" encountered in Ephesus, and Paul himself speaks of "fighting with beasts at Ephesus" (1 Cor 15.32) and of severe "affliction," of being "crushed beyond measure," and of being "delivered" from such great perils in Asia (2 Cor 1.8–10).

Provenance of Captivity Epistles. The time and place of these imprisonments are of prime importance for a better understanding of the so-called Captivity Epistles, i.e., those Pauline letters that were written while he was detained in prison. These are Ephesians (see Eph 3.1; 4.1; 6.20), Colossians (see Col 4.3, 10, 18), Philippians (see Phil 1.7, 12–17), and Philemon (see Phlm 1, 9, 10, 13, 23). The question is asked which imprisonment is involved in each of these four cases. Traditionally the common opinion has been that they were all written from Rome, although there were some dissenting voices even among the Fathers. But it is only with the development of literary criticism that serious internal arguments have been proposed for a Caesarean or an Ephesian provenance of one or more of the Captivity Epistles. Moreover, the marked similarity of style and content noted in Ephesians and Colossians argues in favor of their having been written at the same time. And since Tychicus, who was the letter-bearer for these two (Eph 6.21–22; Col 4.7–8), was accompanied by the same *Onesimus (Col 4.9) who is the object of the letter to Philemon (Phlm 10), that letter, too, is associated with the other two. We can thus consider these three together. The historical references in the letters are not sufficient to argue conclusively to any one imprisonment.

Caesarean Provenance. The least likely provenance for the three letters is Caesarea in Palestine. Apparently Paul did not have the semifreedom in his Caesarean imprisonment that these letters seem to suppose. Moreover, it could hardly be supposed that Onesimus, the runaway slave whom Paul converted at this time had fled from *Colossae in western Asia Minor to Caesarea in Palestine.

Ephesian Provenance. For arguments in favor of an Ephesian provenance for Philippians, *see* PHILIPPIANS, EPISTLE TO THE. It can be added that the references in Philippians to "the *praetorium" (Phil 1.13) and "Caesar's household" (4.22) would fit an Ephesian provenance as much as a Roman one. Moreover, in the references to his imprisonment Paul implies that his arrest was caused by his preaching the gospel (1.7, 12–17), whereas the Caesarean imprisonment (and consequently the Roman one) resulted from a false charge of having violated the Temple by bringing Gentiles into it (Acts 21.28–30; 24.6). Although these arguments are not conclusive, they make an Ephesian provenance of at least Philippians quite likely. The only argument in favor of such a provenance for the other three letters is the fact that Onesimus, who was converted by Paul while the Apostle was in this imprisonment (Phlm 10), would have fled from Colossae to the nearby metropolis of Ephesus much more probably than to the distant city of Rome.

Roman Provenance. In favor of a Roman provenance of the letters the weakest argument is that deduced from Paul's age. In Phlm 9 he speaks of himself as an "old man." But the year of his birth is unknown, and the earliest possible date for his Ephesian imprisonment (*c.* A.D. 54) would be only 9 years before the end of his first Roman imprisonment (A.D. 63). A stronger argument for a Roman provenance of the letters is from Luke's presence with him (Col 4.14; Phlm 24). From the so-called "we-sections" of the *Acts of the Apostles it can be argued that Luke was in Caesarea and in Rome while Paul was in prison in these cities, whereas it would seem from the lack of the "we" form in Acts ch. 19 that Luke did not assist Paul in his Ephesian ministry.

The strongest argument in favor of a Roman provenance of the letters comes from their doctrinal nature. Even if Philippians were written during an Ephesian imprisonment of Paul, the other three letters were apparently written during a later imprisonment, which would probably be Paul's first one in Rome. Philippians can be easily distinguished from Ephesians and Colossians. Its personal and digressive nature reveals no attempt to propose definitive teaching on any one point. It is a letter that could have been written almost anytime during Paul's missionary career. The same is not true of Ephesians and Colossians, where the doctrine is so clearly expressed that as late a date as possible would be supposed for their composition.

In these two Epistles is reflected the fruit of much of Paul's thinking that is given in a more embryonic form in his major Epistles (Romans, 1 and 2 Corinthians, and Galatians). In this respect one can note the emphasis on the cosmic aspect of Redemption and on the πλήρωμα (fullness: Eph 1.23; 3.19; 4.13; Col 1.19; 2.9). Also, there is a fuller development of the doctrine of the Mystical Body of Christ, since only in these two letters is Christ explicitly called the head of the body that is the Church universal. There is, moreover, a clearer exposition of the great "mystery" [*see* MYSTERY (IN THE BIBLE)] reflecting more mature thinking on the whole plan of salvation as revealed in Christ. Finally, one finds more explicit statements on the preexistence of Christ in these two letters. In all of this there is a continuity of thought with ideas expressed in the major Epistles, but in these two the ideas are given a synthesis that could be the result of only more mature reflection. The same progressive and organic continuity can be noted in Colossians and Ephesians, the latter Epistle manifesting a less impassioned and more thoughtful expression of the Apostle's views on the Church universal. Indeed, it is only in Ephesians and Colossians that the word Church is applied so regularly to the universal, not to the local body of believers. These arguments, then, would favor a time of composition later than that of the major Epistles, and since Romans was composed after the Ephesian sojourn, one can conclude that Ephesians, Colossians, and Philemon were probably written by Paul in Rome during his first imprisonment there.

See also COLOSSIANS, EPISTLE TO THE; EPHESIANS, EPISTLE TO THE; PHILEMON, EPISTLE TO.

Bibliography: Commentaries. M. MEINERTZ and F. TILLMAN (4th ed. Bonn 1931). J. HUBY (Paris 1935). P. ALTHAUS et al. (5th ed. Göttingen 1949). P. BENOIT (BJ; 1949). K. STAAB and J. FREUNDORFER (Regensburg 1950). K. STAAB (Würzburg 1954). P. BONNARD and C. MASSON (Neuchâtel-Paris 1951–53). M. DIBELIUS and H. GREEVEN (3d ed. Tübingen 1953).

Studies. A. COTTER, "The Epistles of the Captivity," CathBibl Quart 11 (1949) 370–380. J. SCHMID, *Zeit und Ort der Gefangenschaftsbriefe* (Freiburg 1931). W. MICHAELIS, *Die Gefangenschaft des Paulus in Ephesus* (Gütersloh 1925). T. DA CASTEL SAN PIETRO, EncCatt 10:1–3. K. STAAB, LexThK[2] 4:578–579. Enc DictBibl 320–322.

[E. H. MALY]

CAPUA, ARCHDIOCESE OF (CAPUANUS)

Metropolitan see since 966, in south Italy. In 1963 it had 127,100 Catholics in 64 parishes, 103 secular and 16 religious priests, 19 men in 6 religious houses, and 350 women in 46 convents; it is 193 square miles in area. Its five suffragans, which had 268,172 Catholics, 411 priests, and 367 sisters, were: Caiazzo (founded in the 7th century), Calvi and Teano (both 5th century, united in 1818), Caserta (1113), Isernia and Venafro (both 5th century, united 1032–1207 and since 1852), and Sessa Aurunca (*c.* 500).

Christianity must have come very early to Capua, whose martyrs included Priscus, Lupus, Marcellus, Rufus, Augustine, and Felicita. The first known bishop, Proterius, attended councils of Rome (313) and Arles (314). Vincent, papal legate to the Council of Nicaea I (325), was bishop of Capua (341–372). The Vandal Genseric destroyed Capua (456). Lombards took the city while the North African Priscus was bishop (555–560) and held it as part of the duchy of *Benevento until 787, when Charlemagne ceded it to the patrimony of St. Peter at the request of Pope Adrian I. Except for that of John VIII, however, papal authority remained nominal. After Saracens destroyed Capua (842), bishop and count built a new city a few miles away on the Volturno. In 847 Capua came under the rule of the duchy of *Salerno, separated from Benevento, but Count Landon and especially his brother Bishop Landolfo I (852–879), who built a cathedral, soon became masters of Campania with the support of Emperor Louis II. In 879 John VIII recognized rival episcopal claimants in old and new Capua, but in 882 Bishop Landolfo II, the nephew of Landolfo I, seized new Capua from bishop and count. With Byzantine aid the Saracens were expelled from Campania (915). The princes of Capua ruled Benevento (899–980), but in 1047 the German emperors reasserted their authority in the area.

In 1062 the Normans ended Lombard rule in Capua, doing homage for the fief to popes in 1059, 1061, and 1080, but receiving investiture from Henry IV in 1082. Despite papal protests they extended their rule over Campania. In 1098 they did homage to Roger I of Sicily, and in 1139 Innocent II recognized Roger II of Sicily as king. Nearby *Monte Cassino, which had suffered from Lombards and Saracens, in the 10th century built near Capua a number of monasteries that gave rise to difficulties with Norman rulers and bishops as late as the 12th century. After Sicilian rule, Capua came under the kingdom of Naples until 1860, when it became part of united Italy.

Portal of the church of S. Marcello in Capua. The painting is of later date than the carved doorframe, which is probably of 12th-century workmanship.

The first council of Capua (391–392) was concerned with the *Meletian schism, the heretical Bishop Bonoso of Sardica, disciplinary measures against the transferring of bishops from see to see, and rebaptism. The council of 1087 confirmed the election of Desiderius of Monte Cassino (Victor III) as successor to Pope Gregory VII. The council of 1118 under Gelasius II (also from Monte Cassino) excommunicated Emperor Henry V and his antipope Gregory VIII. St. Robert *Bellarmine was bishop of Capua (1602–05), as was Bp. Alfonso *Capecelatro (1880–1912), scholar and historian.

Most of Capua's ancient and medieval sacred monuments were destroyed in the 18th century or in World War II. The 11th-century cathedral has been rebuilt since its destruction during World War II. The church of S. Angelo in Formis dates from the 11th century and that of S. Marcello from the 12th.

Bibliography: Gams. Eubel HierCath. H. LECLERCQ, DACL 2.2:2064–84. D. MALLARDO, EncCatt 3:729–732. L. JADIN, DHGE 11:888–907 with list of bishops. AnnPont (1964) 93, 1413. **Illustration credit:** Alinari-Art Reference Bureau.

[G. A. PAPA]

CAPUTIATI, members of a religious confraternity of laymen organized *c.* 1182 in the neighborhood of Le Puy, France, to restore peace by combating roving bands of mercenaries who were ravaging the countryside. Their name derived from the white hood (*caputium*) worn by the members, to which was attached a picture or medal of the Virgin and Child, bearing the inscription *Agnus Dei qui tollis peccata mundi dona nobis pacem.* The founder of the movement, Durand Chaduiz, was a woodcutter or carpenter who claimed to have received his mission from the Blessed Virgin in a vision. The brethren bound themselves to refrain from cursing and swearing, gaming, drunkenness, and ostentation in dress. They undertook to live in harmony and to proceed against disturbers of the peace. The movement spread rapidly through Auvergne and the neighboring provinces and received support from the clergy. It succeeded in pacifying Auvergne and in reducing the exactions of feudal lords from their subjects. In 1183, with the assistance of the army of King Philip II, the Caputiati massacred a great number of mercenaries. They are said to have subsequently developed revolutionary and heretical ideas, demanding absolute liberty and equality for all. Whatever the truth of these charges, within a year or two they were ruthlessly suppressed by the feudal nobility assisted by the hated mercenaries.

Bibliography: E. SEMICHON, *La Paix et la trève de Dieu,* 2 v. (2d ed. Paris 1869). A. MENS, DHGE 11:970–973. G. MARSOT, Catholicisme, 2:520. A. BORST, LexThK[2] 2:932.

[F. COURTNEY]

CARABANTES, JOSÉ DE, Spanish Capuchin missionary; b. June 27, 1628; d. April 11, 1694. He entered the order on Oct. 11, 1645, and was ordained on Sept. 21, 1652. In 1657 he went to the missions in Venezuela and in 1660 went into the interior to catechise the cannibal Indians. After 9 years of intense and effective work he returned to Spain to report to the Council of the Indies about the mission and the Indians. A year later he personally presented to the Pope the submission of five caciques, written in the Chaima language. Unable to return to his favorite field of missions among the pagans, he dedicated the rest of his days to preaching the gospel in Spain, working great wonders and accomplishing many spiritual rejuvenations, which gained him the title of Apostle of Galicia. He was also a successful writer, publishing books for spiritual reading and many volumes of sermons, homilies, and instructions. Of particular importance is *Práctica de las misiones* (2 v. León-Madrid 1674–78), from which modern missiologists have taken methods for the conversion of the pagans. Also attributed to him is *Arte y vocabulario de la lengua de los caribes de Nueva Andalucía.* In 1666 in Seville he published an account of his missionary work in Venezuela. He died with a reputation of sanctity, and a movement for his beatification began in 1729. The cause was introduced in 1910, and in 1920 the apostolic processes began.

Bibliography: A. DE VALENCINA, *Vida del V. P. José de Carbantes* (Seville 1908). P. M. DE MONDREGANES, *Problemas misionales* (Madrid 1960). B. DE CARROCERA, *Los primeros historiadores de las misiones capuchinas en Venezuela* (Caracas 1964).

[I. DE VILLAPADIERNA]

CARACAS, ARCHDIOCESE OF (CARACENSIS)

The first diocese in Venezuela was founded in Coro in 1531. The see was transferred to Caracas in 1638. In 1804 it became an archbishopric. In 1964 its territory included the Federal District and the state of Miranda, and the archdiocese included six suffragan dioceses: Barquisimeto (1863), Calabozo (1863), Coro (1922), Guanare (1954), Maracay (1958), and Valencia (1922); and the prelature *nullius* San Fernando de Apure (1958).

STATISTICS (1964)

Area	Population	Catholics (per cent)	Parishes	Clergy Sec.	Clergy Reg.
Caracas	1,749,864	99	102	171	372
Barquisimeto	664,431	94	58	52	58
Calabozo	244,966	97	33	22	9
Coro	340,450	97	26	22	20
Guanare	203,707	98	15	11	10
Maracay	313,274	98	31	27	31
Valencia	500,000	99	48	36	61
San Fernando de Apure	117,877	87	12	2	17

Originally Caracas was the only diocese in the area that is now modern Venezuela. The eastern provinces of Cumaná, Margarita, and Trinidad depended on the bishop of Puerto Rico, and the Andean provinces depended on the See of Santafé de Bogotá. When the archdiocese was created, all this territory was made part of the ecclesiastical province. It remained the sole archbishopric until 1923. In 1964 there were three archdioceses in Venezuela.

The See of Caracas has been one of great influence in the development of the religious life of the country. From it missionaries went out to found Indian pueblos, which were taken over by the secular clergy as soon as they were ready to be organized as parishes. The see has had 26 bishops and 12 archbishops. Only one of the

The church of Santa Teresa in Caracas, Venezuela.

bishops during the period of Spanish control was a native Venezuelan, Francisco Ibarra, who became the first archbishop.

The bishops of Caracas have been a force in the cultural as well as the religious development of the area. Bishop Juan J. de Escalona y Calatayud founded the Pontifical University of Santa Rosa de Caracas in 1721; it later became a cultural and civic center. Antonio González de Acuña planned and built with Church funds the first aqueduct for Caracas. Diego de Banos y Sotomayor called a synod in 1687, whose constitutions served for a century and a half to maintain excellent Church discipline. Mariano *Martí traveled extensively over his Venezuelan territory and wrote an account of his visit. Zealous defenders of the rights of the Church against the infringements of the civil authority were Abps. Ramón I. Méndez (1827–39) and Silvestre Guevara y Lira (1852–76). Archbishop Juan B. Castro (1904–15) fostered devotion to the Blessed Sacrament and founded a religious order of women, the Servants of the Blessed Sacrament, dedicated to perpetual adoration. The old pontifical university was taken over by the civil power after Venezuela achieved its independence and was secularized. In 1954, in response to a request of the episcopacy, the Jesuits founded the Catholic University of Andrés Bello in memory of the distinguished humanist.

In the see city of Guanare is the shrine of the Santísima Virgen de Coromoto, in memory of the apparition of 1652. Since she is the patroness of the country, the image has been canonically crowned.

In 1964 the ecclesiastical province had 263 schools with an enrollment of over 72,000 pupils; some 400 were enrolled in the seminaries. Almost 800 members of male religious orders and over 2,000 sisters of various congregations were working in the area.

See also VENEZUELA.

Bibliography: I. ALONSO et al., *La Iglesia en Venezuela y Ecuador* (Madrid 1962). **Illustration credit:** Pan American Airways.

[P. P. BARNOLA]

CARACCIOLO

Perhaps the oldest of the Neapolitan noble families. Its history in *Naples dates back to the 8th or 9th century. For the most part its members are noteworthy for their loyalty to the rulers of Naples and to the Church. Outstanding figures include *Sergianni,* or Giovanni (d. Naples, 1431), who fought under King Ladislaus of Naples in 1411 and became the seneschal of his successor, Joanna II (*see* ANJOU, HOUSE OF). Out of favor and then returned to power, he oppressed the nobles and acted arrogantly toward the Queen. He was murdered, probably at her orders. *Giovanni* (b. 1487; d. Susa, 1550) was a general in Florence in 1529, then marshal of Kings *Francis I and Henry II of France. *Galeazzo* (b. Naples, 1517; d. Geneva, 1586), a nephew of Pope *Paul IV, was influenced by the new religious teachings and in 1551 became a follower of Calvin in Geneva, where he remained. *Domenico* (b. in Spain, 1715; d. Naples, 1789) was educated at the Caracciolo College in Naples. After brief diplomatic experiences in Florence and Paris, he represented Naples at Turin (1754–64). Advanced to the major courts of London (1764–71) and Paris (1771–81), he was well liked and praised by the French. In 1781 he was appointed viceroy of Sicily, where his reforms were the finest work of his career, according to Croce. In 1786 he was recalled to be the chief minister in Naples, an office he held until his death. *Francesco* (b. Naples, 1752; d. Naples, 1799) obtained naval experience by serving on a British ship, fighting the pirates of North Africa, participating in the Battle of Toulon, and commanding a Neapolitan ship that supported the English blockade of the French coast (1795). When Ferdinand IV and Maria Carolina fled from Naples to Sicily at the approach of the French army, December 1798, Francesco commanded one of the ships, Nelson the other. In January, Francesco obtained permission to return to Naples, where he joined the Republicans. During Cardinal Fabrizio *Ruffo's siege of Naples in June, Francesco escaped from the city but was captured and turned over to Nelson by the cardinal. He was tried and hanged on board ship, and his body was thrown into the sea, June 29, 1799.

The cardinals in the family (the first date given being that of their cardinalate) included *Bernardo* (1244; d. 1255) and the Dominican theologian *Nicolò* (1378; d. 1389). *Marino* (1535; d. 1538) represented the Duke of Milan at Lateran Council V (1515) and later Pope *Leo X, first at Augsburg (1518), then at Worms (1521). During Pope *Clement VII's pontificate he favored a league with Emperor *Charles V against King Francis I of France. Charles V appointed him governor of Milan in 1536. *Innico* (1667; d. 1685) was an energetic archbishop of Naples. His nephew *Innico* (1715; d. 1730) spent 33 years as bishop of Aversa. *Nicolò* (1715; d. 1728) was nuncio to Florence and vicegerent of Rome. *Giovanni Costanzo* (1759; d. 1780) was a member of several congregations in Rome. *Diego Innico*

(1800; d. 1820) accompanied Pope *Pius VI into exile and remained with him until he died. He negotiated a concordat with Naples in 1818.

Landolf (d. 1351) was a distinguished Franciscan theologian. The Augustinian *Giacomo* (d. 1357) was a philosopher, theologian, and preacher. *Roberto* (d. 1495), a Franciscan Conventual, was perhaps the greatest preacher of the school of *Bernardine of Siena. St. *Francis Caracciolo* (d. 1608) founded the Congregation of Clerks Minor Regular (Caracciolini) in 1588.

Bibliography: F. DE'PIETRI, *Cronologia della famiglia Caracciolo* (Naples 1605). Moroni 9:231–235. P. LITTA, *Famiglie celebri italiane,* 11 v. (Milan 1819–99); 2d ser., 78 fasc. (Turin 1902–23), fasc. 6. M. SAGLIOCCO, *Compendio delle virtù del cardinale I. Caracciolo già vescovo d'Aversa* (Rome 1738). B. CROCE, *Uomini e cose della vecchia Italia,* 2 ser. (Bari 1927), ser. 1, 143–182; ser. 2, 83–112. M. SCHIPA, *Nel regno di Ferdinando IV Borbone* (Florence 1938) 77–323. H. M. ACTON, *The Bourbons of Naples, 1734–1825* (New York 1958) 92–94, 198–206, 364–366, 398–401. I. CECCHETTI et al., EncCatt 3:737–741. G. FUSSENEGGER et al., LexThK[2] 2:933–934.

[M. L. SHAY]

CARACCIOLO, FRANCIS, ST.

Cofounder of the Congregation of Clerks Regular Minor; b. Villa Santa Maria, Abruzzi, Italy, Oct. 13, 1563; d. Agnone, Italy, June 4, 1608 (feast, June 4). The early life of Francis (baptized Ascanio) Caracciolo del Leone o Pisquizi was exemplary, and after being miraculously cured of a kind of elephantiasis, then called leprosy, the 22-year-old youth vowed himself to an ecclesiastical life. He quietly slipped off to Naples, and in 1587 was ordained there. He joined the Confraternity of the White Robes of Justice organized to give spiritual assistance to condemned criminals, but in 1588 he mistakenly received a letter addressed to an uncle also named Ascanio Caracciolo. Father John Augustine Adorno, former Genoese ambassador to Spain, and Father Fabricius Caracciolo Marsicovetere of the Church of St. Mary Major in Naples, were begging Ascanio's participation in the founding of a new religious institute. Young Ascanio accepted the invitation as providentially meant for himself and helped to formulate the rules of the Clerks Regular Minor approved by Sixtus V (July 1, 1588) and confirmed by Gregory XIV (Feb. 18, 1591) and Clement VIII (June 1, 1592). The members of the congregation took a fourth vow not to aspire to ecclesiastical dignities. Their ministry comprised numerous works of charity, and one of their distinctive characteristics was their practice of perpetual adoration of the Blessed Sacrament. The original intention was to honor the Mother of God with the title of Clerks Regular Marian, but Sixtus V, a Friar Minor, preferred Clerks Regular Minor, and so the name remained.

At his profession Ascanio took the name of Francis. Adorno had been superior of the new community, but upon his death in 1591, the office devolved on Francis. He remained rector general until 1598. During his administration, the Clerks Regular Minor became established in Rome and in Spain. He personally founded the house and Church of St. Joseph in Madrid and of the Annunciation in Valladolid, as well as a house of studies near the University of Alcalá. As rector general, then as novice master, local superior, and vicar-general in Italy, Francis was distinguished for humility, mortification, unflagging toil, purity, and devotion to the Eucharist and the Blessed Virgin. In 1607 Francis was finally relieved of administrative offices. He begged for an obscure room under a staircase, and there he devoted himself anew to contemplation and redoubtable penances. He interrupted his retirement to negotiate with the Oratorians for the transfer of one of their houses in Agnone to the Clerks Regular Minor. He went to Agnone by way of Loretto, where he spent an entire night in prayer, seemingly with a premonition of his end. After a brief illness he died at Agnone. His body had to be transferred secretly to Naples because the popular cult of Francis Caracciolo had already begun.

Caracciolo's extant writings include some letters and a work of devotion, *Le sette stazioni sopra la Passione di N.S. Gesu Christo* (Rome 1710). He was beatified by Clement XIV in 1769 and canonized by Pius VII, May 24, 1807. In 1838 St. Francis Caracciolo was chosen patron of the city of Naples; and in 1925 patron of Eucharistic Congresses held in Abruzzi. The Pia Unione Famiglia Caracciolo was organized in 1925. Comprising representatives of all the branches of the ancient noble Caraccioli, the union serves as a lay auxiliary organization of the Clerks Regular Minor; propagates devotion to the Holy Eucharist and to St. Francis Caracciolo; and sponsors the review, "S. Francesco Caracciolo," which appears several times during the year.

Bibliography: A. B. FRASSONI, *La gente e la famiglia di S. Francesco Caracciolo* (Rome 1943). G. ROSSI, *Il precursore dell'adorazione perpetua* (4th ed. Rome 1951). I. FELICI, *Il principe mendicante* (Rome 1959). Butler Th Attw 2:470–472.

[M. P. TRAUTH]

CARACCIOLO, LANDOLF

Franciscan theologian, *Doctor collectivus;* b. Naples, *c.* 1287; d. Amalfi, 1351. He studied arts probably at the University of Naples, *c.* 1305 to 1310, and theology at the University of Paris, *c.* 1315, where he commented on the *Sentences, c.* 1322, and later became master. He returned to Naples, where he became minister provincial, 1324–25. In 1326 he was sent to Bologna as the legate of Robert of Naples. On Aug. 21, 1327, he was consecrated bishop of Castellammare, but was transferred on Sept. 20, 1331, to the See of Amalfi. From 1343 onward he was frequently entrusted with diplomatic missions by Queen Johanna I of Anjou (d. 1382), for which he was honored with the titles of *Logotheta* and *Protonotarius* of the Kingdom of Naples.

At least 35 MSS of his *Commentary on the Sentences* are known to be extant [Stegmüller RS 1:n.514; V. Doucet, "Supplement," ArchFrancHist 47 (1954) 58]. He also wrote *Commentaria moralia in quatuor Evangelia* (ed. Naples 1637), *Postilla super Evangelia dominicalia* (Florence MS Laurenziana, Plut.8 dext. 12, fol. 5–98v), *Sermones, Tractatus de arte sermocinandi* (Cracow, Univ. Library MS 1295, fol. 294–308), and lost commentaries on Zacharias and on Hebrews (Stegmüller RB 3:nn.5365–67). The *Tractatus de Conceptione B. M. V.* attributed to him is unauthentic, and the *Extracta ex Landulphi de Immaculata Conceptione B. M. V.* is a posthumous version of his doctrine (*In 3 sent.* 3).

*Peter of Candia, later Alexander V, enumerated him with *Francis of Meyronnes and *Francis of Marchia as the most notable followers of *Duns Scotus in the first half of the 14th century. Caracciolo himself declares that he follows the Subtle Doctor in many points: "Doctorem Subtilem ut plurimum sequimur" (Naples, Bibl. Naz. MS VII. C. 49). Nevertheless, in the same MS there are several marginal notations indicating that the doctrine proposed is contrary to that of Scotus: "Loquitur contra Scotum." Similarly an Assisi MS (Bibl. Munic. 199) of Peter of Candia's lectures contains a marginal note expressing amazement that Caracciolo should thus deviate from the Subtle Doctor, whom he always follows (fol. 13r).

In *In 3 sent.* 3 Caracciolo defends the *Immaculate Conception in a way that suggests the doctrinal development between 1320 and 1325. Although he adopted many of the ideas and arguments in favor of the privilege from Scotus and *William of Ware and opposed the Dominican view proposed by *John of Naples, he is often too oratorical and lacking in critical judgment. More notable in his teaching are the "quinque regulae" for disputing with an opponent both from authority and from reason; in this he seems to have been influenced by the treatise *Nondum erant abyssi* of *Peter Aureoli (ed. Quaracchi 1904, 78–94).

Caracciolo's writings notably influenced later theologians, such as *Peter of Aquila, Alphonsus of Toledo (fl. 1344), *William of Vaurouillon, St. *Bernardine of Siena, John Vitalis (fl. 1390), Juan de *Torquemada, Ludovicus a Turre (fl. 1486), and Bernardine of Busti (fl. 1490).

Bibliography: A. EMMEN, "Testimony of Landulf Caracciolo on Scotus' dispute in favour of the Immaculate Conception," *Doctor Subtilis* ('s Hertogenbosch, Netherlands 1946) 92–129. Sbaralea 3:163–165. Eubel HierCath 1:84, 462. D. SCARAMUZZI, *Il pensiero di Giovanni Duns Scoto nel Mezzogiorno d'Italia* (Rome 1927) 67–75; "L'Immacolato Concepimento di Maria," *Studi Francescani* 28 (1931) 33–69. H. MAISONNEUVE, DHGE 11:980. E. CAGGIANO, EncCatt 3:739.

[A. EMMEN]

CARACCIOLO, ROBERTO, noted Franciscan preacher; b. Lecce, Kingdom of Naples, 1425; d. there, May 6, 1495. The son of a noble family, he entered the Friars Minor of the Observance, but left to join the Friars Minor Conventual *c.* 1453. Following the school of St. Bernardine of Siena, he was for about 50 years the most celebrated preacher in Italy, and was sometimes referred to as a "second Paul." He was enthusiastically acclaimed by the common people, and also highly esteemed by popes and kings. Callistus III made him papal nuncio to Milan to preach the collection of tithes for a crusade against the Turks; Paul II named him preacher apostolic; King Ferdinand I of Naples made him preacher of the realm; and his son and successor, Alphonse, chose Caracciolo as royal confessor. In 1475 he was made bishop of Aquila, but in 1477 he was transferred to the See and title of Aquino. After 1485 he acted as bishop of Lecce, but retained the title of Aquino. Although he was a controversial figure among Franciscans of his time, his sermons powerfully aroused the feelings of his listeners and were avidly read by his contemporaries. They were printed in various places at various times in numerous editions under different titles. Some of his earlier publications were gathered together in his *Opera varia* (Venice 1479), and more complete collections later appeared, including editions at Venice in 1496 and at Lyons in 1503.

Bibliography: S. BASTANXIO, *Fra Roberto Caracciolo* (Isola 1947). Hain-Copinger 1:106–107. Hurter Nomencl 4:915. J. HEERINCKX, DictSpirAscMyst 2.1:120–121. F. DIOTALLEVI, Enc Catt 3:740–741.

[J. C. WILLKE]

CARAFA (CARAFFA)

A noble Neapolitan family that first came into notice during the 14th century, and in its several branches has had a remarkable history in the annals of the Church. Almost exclusively during the 16th and 17th centuries it provided prelates for Naples and Aversa, exerting great influence there and throughout Europe. The apex of its fame was the elevation of Gian Pietro Carafa to the papacy as Paul IV (1555–59), followed soon after in the reign of Pius IV by the lowest ebb of its fortunes, the trial and execution of Paul IV's nephews Cardinal Carlo and Giovanni, Duke of Paliano, for treason and other crimes.

Oliviero. Diplomat; b. Naples, 1430; d. Rome, Jan. 20, 1511. He descended from the counts of Maddaloni (Caserta), became a jurist, was consecrated archbishop of Naples on Dec. 29, 1458, and created a cardinal on Nov. 18, 1467, at the insistence of King Ferdinand of Naples, whom he had served faithfully as president of his council of state and as special envoy. He helped end the war between Ferdinand and Sixtus IV and was sent to draw up the peace treaty. He founded the magnificent crypt chapel in the cathedral of Naples and had the body of St. Januarius (San Gennaro) brought there from Montevergine. Oliviero became cardinal bishop of Ostia, Nov. 29, 1503, and dean of the Sacred College. A generous and pious patron of literature and the arts, he erected for his family the chapel of St. Thomas Aquinas in the church of Santa Maria sopra Minerva at Rome and commissioned Filippino *Lippi to decorate it with frescoes, one of which depicts the saint presenting the cardinal to the Virgin. Another monument is the cloister

Oliviero Carafa, engraving of the 17th century.

of Santa Maria della Pace, built by Donato *Bramante in 1504. Oliviero's palace at Rome, alongside of which stood the statue of Pasquino, was a circumspect retreat for artists and writers. In its cultured atmosphere Oliviero's nephew, Gian Pietro, the future Paul IV, received his education.

Carlo. Adventurer; b. Naples, 1517; d. Rome, March 4, 1561. He was the youngest son of Gian Alfonso, Count of Montorio, and nephew of Paul IV, and he was made a cardinal, June 7, 1555. A debauched and scheming military adventurer without even the requisite education for a simple clerk, he rapidly acquired influence over his uncle and was the guiding spirit of the anti-Spanish policy, which ended in an unsuccessful war against Philip II. While the Pope was pursuing with fierce energy the work of Church reform, unknown to him his nephew was leading a dissipated life in the pontifical court. Only toward the end of his reign did Paul IV learn of his immorality, crimes, and double-dealing with the foreign powers. Indignant, he banned the cardinal and his brothers with their families from Rome on Jan. 27, 1559. This ban undermined the prestige of the Carafa and led to their downfall in the next pontificate. At the death of Paul IV Carlo believed that he could regain his position in the Curia by working for the election of Cardinal de' Medici. Once elected, however, Pius IV arrested the nephews of his predecessor (June 7, 1560), probably yielding to pressure from certain cardinals and Philip II. Following the murder of the Duchess of Paliano, Carlo's sister-in-law, by members of the Paliano family who suspected her of infidelity, an inquest was held in which Carlo's devious political career was investigated. He and his brother Giovanni, Duke of Paliano, and others were condemned to death for high treason. The cardinal was executed by strangulation in the Castel Sant' Angelo. His reputation was at least formally rehabilitated in a consistory held Dec. 26, 1567, by Pius V, early intent on restoring the prestige of his revered predecessor's family. It is to be noted that only the charges of *laesa maiestas* and *fellonia* were examined and revised, not that of murder.

Antonio. Scholar; b. Naples, March 25, 1538; d. Rome, Jan. 13, 1591. He was the cousin of Carlo and a learned Greek scholar who had as his teacher Cardinal Guglielmo *Sirleto. He received a canonry at St. Peter's from his uncle, Paul IV, but was deprived of his benefice when other members of his family were exiled. He was eventually recalled to Rome by Pius V, restored to his canonry, and created a cardinal in 1568. Prefect of the Congregation of the Council, he was also a member of the congregations charged with the correction of the Missal, the Breviary, and the Vulgate. Gregory XIII appointed him *bibliothecarius* (librarian) of the Vatican Library. He prepared an edition of the Septuagint published at Rome in 1586. He left some manuscript notes of an apologetic nature on the life of Paul IV, later used by Antonio Caracciolo in his *Collectanea historica de vita Pauli IV*.

Alfonso. Librarian; b. Naples, 1540; d. there, Aug. 26, 1565. As the favorite nephew of Paul IV, he was made a cardinal when 17 years old (March 15, 1557) and named *bibliothecarius* of the Vatican Library. Alfonso was the only member of the family whom Pius IV allowed near him after the expulsion of the Carafas from Rome. His promising career was ended by an early death. He is the subject of an important recent study by De Maio, who complains that Alfonso has been altogether neglected by biographers or confused with his cousin Antonio, a later *bibliothecarius*.

Carlo II, Ven. Social apostle; b. Mariglianella (Naples), 1561; d. Naples, Sept. 8, 1633. After a short stay with the Jesuits he entered the Spanish military service. Although a brilliant officer, his earlier interest, the religious life, again took hold of him. From the time of his ordination in Naples, Jan. 1, 1599, he dedicated himself to an apostolate among the masses. After giving his possessions to the poor, he and eight companions organized missions for the people (1601) and in 1606 opened a house at Naples for his *Pii Operarii* (Pious Workers), the origin of the congregation surviving to the present. After his death several miracles were attributed to him. His cause was reintroduced at Rome in 1894–95.

Vincenzo. Jesuit general; b. Andria, May 9, 1585; d. Rome, June 8, 1649. The third son of the Duke of Andria, he entered the Jesuit novitiate on Oct. 4, 1604. After his ordination he taught philosophy and engaged in social works. Under his direction the congregation of the nobles at Naples became a center of social action for the diffusion of charity. He was provincial of Naples when elected to succeed Mutius Vitelleschi on Jan. 7, 1646, as seventh general of the society. His firmness in governing was tempered by his charity for the sick and poor, suggesting the ways of St. Ignatius. During the famine and plague that ravaged Rome (1648–49) he personally saw to the feeding of thousands for 2 months. The plagues provided him the opportunity of fulfilling a vow made in 1624, to dedicate himself to the care of the plague-ridden. In their service he contracted the disease from which he died. Under the pseudonym of Luigi Sidereo he left a series of ascetic writings: *Fascetto di Mirra* (Rome 1635) and *Camino del cielo* (1641). He instituted in all the churches of his order the confraternity of **Bona Mors* (A Good Death), at once approved and favored by the popes and still in existence today.

Pierluigi. Papal nuncio; b. Naples, July 31, 1581; d. Rome, July 15, 1655. After studies in Venice, Rome, and a doctorate in law from the University of Naples, he became vice legate to Ferrara, governor of Fermo, and bishop of Tricarico (Potenza) on March 29, 1624. As nuncio to Cologne he effected reforms, founded colleges throughout lower Germany and a university at Münster, and introduced the Capuchins and Jesuits into the Palatinate and the Dioceses of Trier, Fulda, and Constance. He returned to his diocese and rebuilt the cathedral. When he received the cardinalate in 1645 he resigned his see to become legate to Bologna and prefect of the Congregation of the Council. He died during the conclave that elected Alexander VII.

Carlo III. Papal nuncio; b. place and date uncertain; d. April 1644. He became bishop of Aversa (Naples) on July 19, 1616, and then nuncio to the imperial court (1621), where he became well acquainted with the religious problems in Germany and Bohemia. He aided Emperor Ferdinand II in selecting candidates for sees, reforming colleges, and arranging for the restitution of churches and abbeys taken by the Protestants. He published the *Commentaria de Germania sacra restaurata* in 1641.

Carlo IV. Papal nuncio; b. Naples, 1611; d. Rome, Oct. 19, 1680. He was the nephew of Carlo III and succeeded to the See of Aversa, then was made nuncio to Switzerland (1653), Venice (1654), and the court of Emperor Leopold (1658–64). When he was created cardinal (1664), he renounced his see to his brother, Paolo, a Theatine.

Rosa di Traetto, Ven. Franciscan tertiary; b. Naples, April 6, 1832; d. there, May 2, 1890. She was a descendant of the dukes of Traetto, a branch of the Carafas, and joined the Order of the Servants of the Sacred Heart (Franciscan Tertiaries), founded by Caterina Volpicelli. Her life was marked by continual, painful illness and extraordinary gifts of prayer. She won many vocations to her order by her example and direction. The cause of her beatification was introduced on Aug. 28, 1907.

For Gian Pietro Carafa, *see* PAUL IV, POPE.

Bibliography: L. JADIN, DHGE 11:986–995, bibliog. E. MANGENOT and A. PALMIERI, DTC 2.2:1709. P. AUVRAY et al., *Catholicisme* 2:524–527. F. SCANDONE, "I Carafa di Napoli" in *Famiglie celebri italiane* of P. LITTA et al, 2d ser., 2 v. (Naples 1902–23). For Carlo I see Pastor v.14 *passim;* 15:131–178, 415–429. For Alfonso and contemporaries R. DE MAIO, *Alfonso Carafa, Cardinale di Napoli 1540–1565* (StTest 210; Vatican City 1961), bibliog. and documentation.

[H. H. DAVIS]

CARAMUEL LOBKOWITZ, JUAN, Cistercian bishop, moral theologian, and mathematician; b. Madrid, Spain, May 23, 1606; d. Vigevano, Italy, Sept. 8, 1682. He studied philosophy at Alcalá, entered the Cistercians at Palencia in 1623, continued his sacred studies at Salamanca, and taught for 3 years in monasteries of his order. He was missioned to the monastery of Dunes, Spanish Flanders, and in 1638 he received his doctorate in theology from the University of Louvain.

He then became titular abbot of Melrose, Scotland, and vicar for the Cistercian abbeys of Ireland, England, and Scotland. Later named abbot of Dissembourg in the Diocese of Mayence, he drew much attention by his preaching and became suffragan to the bishop of Mayence. The King of Spain then sent him to the court of the Emperor, Ferdinand III, who gave him the Benedictine Abbeys of Montserrat and Vienna. At the same time he became vicar general to the archbishop of Prague. During a siege he organized the ecclesiastics and was praised for helping to defend the city.

In 1655 he was cited to Rome to answer for some of his writings but is said to have satisfied and amazed Pope Alexander VII with his learning. He became bishop of Compagna-Satriano in the Kingdom of Naples in 1657. This see he resigned in 1673; he was then named bishop of Vigevano (Pavia) in central Italy.

Caramuel was a man of extraordinarily broad learning. He spoke 24 languages and wrote more than 250 works in grammar, poetry, mathematics, astronomy, physics, politics, Canon Law, logic, metaphysics, theology, and asceticism. However, he had a penchant for the singular and even the bizarre. In dogma he engaged in speculation that was regarded as temerarious, and a number of his works were put on the Index. In moral theology he tried to reduce everything to mathematical formulas, and he maintained that even the most difficult problems relating to grace could be resolved with ruler and compass. He appeared to use probabilism as a means of attenuating the obligation of law and was dubbed by St. Alphonsus Liguori with the unenviable title, "Prince of Laxists." The restless energy of his mind and laxity of his moral thought are illustrated in the following passage from his *Theologia fundamentalis:*

> I am a man of sharp and fervid intelligence. One moment I am in the heavens, the next in the depths. A fly cannot move in chapel without distracting me. . . . I do not avoid distractions; they come by the thousands and sometimes they are voluntary. Yet I suffer no scruple on that account, for I reasonably suppose that I am obliged to no internal activity [in prayer]. . . . To have it is good, yet to lack it involves not even a slight fault. [n.442; cited by D. Prummer, *Manuale Theologiae Moralis* (Freiburg im Br. 1928) 2.302.]

Bibliography: V. OBLET, DTC 2.2:1709–12. R. BROUILLARD, *Catholicisme* 2:527–528. L. F. O'NEIL, CE 3:329–330. Hurter Nomencl 4:604–610.

[P. F. MULHERN]

CARAVAGGIO, MICHELANGELO MERISI DA

A major painter and personality of the Italian baroque period; b. Caravaggio, Sept. 28, 1573; d. Port'Ercole, July 18, 1610. He was the effective creator of "realism" in Italian painting at a time when the theories of late *mannerism dominated the cultural scene in Rome. Caravaggio arrived in the capital about the age of 20. His apprenticeship was spent in Milan (1584–90) under Simone Peterzano. The two basic influences on his work were mannerist stylization and the humble realism of Lombard painting of the 16th century (*Lotto, Savoldo, Moretto, the Campi).

The artist's fractious temperament brought him into frequent conflict with authority; he was involved in brawls, lawsuits, and arrests throughout his violent life. In 1606 he was charged with manslaughter and fled Rome. The next 4 years he worked feverishly in Naples, Malta, Syracuse, and Messina. Finally, after a series of desperate misadventures, he died prematurely, of malarial fever, on a deserted beach near Grosseto.

Caravaggio's "antimythic" attitude was at once apparent in the early work "Bacchus" (*c.* 1594), ironically modeled by a fellow painter. Both still life and figure are scrupulously rendered in a clear, factual light. Caravaggio's credo that a good painter should know how to imitate natural things outraged his opponents.

Cardinal del Monte was his first serious patron and got him the commission for the stories of St. Matthew in S. Luigi dei Francesi (Contarelli chapel, 1598–1600) that launched his career. There, and in the altarpieces of St. Paul in S. Maria del Popolo (Cerasi chapel, 1600–01), his emphasis on plain settings and plebeian models offended the conventional sense of decorum, but making a mysterious light act as protagonist brought out as never before the gospel's power to cleanse and transfigure (*see* PAUL, APOSTLE, ST.). Like other commissions, the "Death of the Virgin" (Louvre 1606) was refused by the brothers of S. Maria della Scala and became a *cause célèbre.* In the stark late works that he executed in Malta and Sicily, he achieved the summit of his power to elicit empathy. In the "Raising of Lazarus" (Messina Museum, 1608–09) the blaze of faith uniting the small figures prevails against the undefined menace of a gloomy background.

Caravaggio perfected a vigorous mode of pictorial evangelism. His mature art, on the surface simple and straightforward, was complex in its values and references. He studied many painters of his time and of the past, as well as works of antiquity. In his paintings, staged like tableaux in a hushed and solemn atmosphere,

Fig. 1. "Bacchus," oil on canvas, 39 by 34 inches, c. 1594, in the Uffizi at Florence.

CARAVAGGIO

Fig. 2. "Resurrection of Lazarus," oil on canvas, 12 feet 5⅝ inches by 9 feet ½ inch, 1608–09, in the National Museum at Messina, Italy.

Fig. 3. "Death of the Virgin," oil on canvas, 12 feet 1¼ inches by 8 feet ½ inch, 1606, in the Musée du Louvre, Paris.

his themes are made tense by the probing light, which functions to bring them dramatically to a climax. The "action" is mainly psychological, interior, and must be resolved in the heart of the beholder. This vital art, essentially misunderstood by Caravaggio's patrons and public, intrigued numerous artists and helped to change the course of 17th-century European painting.

See also BAROQUE ART.

Bibliography: R. P. HINKS, *Michelangelo Merisi da Caravaggio* (London 1953). R. LONGHI, ed., *Il Caravaggio* (Milan 1952). B. BERENSON, *Caravaggio, His Incongruity and His Fame* (London 1953). C. BARONI ed., *All the Paintings of Caravaggio,* tr. A. F. O'SULLIVAN (New York 1962). W. F. FRIEDLÄNDER, *Caravaggio Studies* (Princeton 1955). S. SAMEK LUDOVICI, *Vita del Caravaggio dalle testimonianze del suo tempo* (Milan 1956). A. BERNE-JOFFROY, *Le Dossier Caravage* (Paris 1959). R. JULLIAN, *Caravage* (Paris 1961). **Illustration credits:** Figs. 1 and 2, Alinari-Art Reference Bureau. Fig. 3, Giraudon, Paris.

[R. M. ARB]

CARAYON, AUGUSTE, bibliographer; b. Saumur (Maine-et-Loire), France, March 31, 1813; d. Poitiers (Vienne), France, May 15, 1874. After ordination, he joined the Jesuits (1841) and spent his life as a procurator and librarian. Despite weak eyesight, he loved books and manuscripts. In addition to reediting some books on asceticism and ecclesiastical history, he edited a list of 4,370 works on the Society of Jesus in *Bibliographie historique de la Compagnie de Jésus* (1864) and a collection of *Documents inédits concernant la Compagnie de Jésus* (23 v. 1863–70, 1874–86).

Bibliography: Sommervogel 2:714–718. Koch JesLex 299.

[M. DIERICKX]

CARBONARI

One of the most influential of the numerous secret societies in 19th-century Italy aiming at political and social betterment.

Origin, Organization, Membership. Many obscurities remain concerning the Carbonari (literally charcoal burners). Legends have connected them with Philip of Macedonia (383–336 B.C.), with St. Theobald, an 11th-century monk who was proclaimed patron of the Carbonari, with a medieval benevolent group of German charcoal workers, and with the Good Cousins, a late medieval association in France. It is doubtful, however, that the Carbonari anteceded the late 18th century, and it is possible that the society was introduced to Naples early in the 19th century by returning exiles or by French troops. In rites and organization the Carbonari resembled the *charbonnerie* of Franche-Comté. Native Italian secret societies of the 18th century or the Illuminati in Germany are also possible forerunners. *Freemasonry influenced the Carbonari, perhaps in its origin; but significant differences existed between the two in their type of members, program, and religious outlook. Most Carbonari were middle-class, military, petty bureaucrats, or peasants. Their aim was to win national independence, institute constitutional and democratic reforms, and broaden the franchise. Professedly they were Christians, although anticlerical, and they utilized Christian symbolism.

The Carbonari were organized into numerous local cells, each one being bound in obedience to a central hierarchy. Individual members referred to one another as *buoni cugini* (good cousins) and to their opponents as *pagani* (heathens). Meetings were held in a *baracca* (hut), whose interior was referred to as the *vendita* (shop), whereas the surroundings were designated as the *foresta* (forest). The hierarchy consisted of a regent, two assistants, an orator or preacher, a secretary, a treasurer, and an archivist. Periodic general or partial assemblies met to implement policy and to preserve discipline. Carbonari were joined regionally in a *vendita madre* and an *alta vendita*. Organization, rites, and aims differed widely according to place and time. Originally there were, it seems, only two grades, apprentices and masters. No limits appear to have been placed on the number of apprentices who could be admitted. In their initiation ceremony, some pious generalities were uttered and an oath of secrecy was imposed. The role of apprentices was that of disciplined, obedient fieldmen. The initiation rites of a master involved a pseudoreligious ceremony, during which Jesus Christ was revealed as the first victim of tyranny and as the "great carbonaro." The candidate for master, in imitation of Christ, had to submit to a mock trial that ended with Pilate's washing of his hands. New Testament expressions were used frequently during these proceedings. Little information is available concerning the higher ranks of the Carbonari. There is some indication that the ceremony for a grand master, or cavalier of Thebes, included a mock crucifixion. Perfect masters were obligated to destroy Caesar, Herod, and Judas, the murderers of Christ, who may have been taken as figures for lay tyrants, autocratic ecclesiastics, and malefactors of wealth, the political and religious enemies of the Carbonari. As many as seven or nine grades may have existed, but even their names are a source of some confusion. Detailed knowledge of conspiratorial aims seems to have been reserved for the higher echelons.

History. By 1802 mention was made of Carbonari. Joachim *Murat wrote to Napoleon I in 1809 that they existed in the chief Italian cities. They were especially strong in Abruzzi and Calabria and sought first to end the French dominance there (1808–14). After the restoration of the Bourbon monarchy in the Kingdom of Naples, they pressed for constitutional reforms, but Ferdinand I issued instead a stringent edict (April 14, 1814) against them and backed up the measure with arrests, imprisonments, and even executions. When Carbonari forged a papal document approving them, Pius VII put an end to rumors by issuing an edict condemning them. Some members then fled throughout the Mediterranean area, especially to France, Spain, or Portugal, taking the society's aims with them. Other splinter groups emerged, such as the *Confederazione Latina,* the *Adelfia,* and the *Guelfia.* Meanwhile Carbonari had infiltrated the Neapolitan army and took part in minor uprisings in 1816 and 1817. When mutiny erupted at Monteforte (July 1, 1820), the Neapolitan Carbonari encouraged rebellion for "God, King, Constitution." At that time Carbonari membership in the Kingdom of Naples alone was reputed to be 100,000; and for all Italy, perhaps 300,000 or even 640,000.

In northern Italy the organization's headquarters were in Genoa. The rise of Austria to dominance in the Italian peninsula after 1815 roused the resentment of many nationalists in the *States of the Church and in Lombardy. Most prominent leaders of the *Risorgimento were Carbonari at one time or another. Thus the Carbonari were implicated in an uprising in Piedmont (March 1821) that Austrian troops had to suppress. The Holy See continued its opposition in more stringent terms. In the constitution *Ecclesiam* (Sept. 13, 1821) Pius VII condemned the society specifically and applied to its members the penalty of excommunication and the other censures contained in earlier disapprovals of Freemasonry. In reply to inquiries by some Neapolitan bishops, the Sacred Penitentiary stated that the teachings and proceedings of the Carbonari were prohibited and that the condemnation was to be rigorously enforced (Nov. 8, 1821). These strictures were confirmed by Leo XII in the constitution *Quo graviora* (March 13, 1825). To counteract the Carbonari within the States of the Church, the *Sanfedists were employed.

Despite this, the Carbonari remained strong. Around 1830 they were directed from Paris by a veteran revolutionary and Freemason, Filippo Buonarrotti (1761–1837), who had founded the Perfect Sublime Masters to coordinate the revolutionary activities of all secret societies throughout Italy and Europe. Rebellions fomented by Carbonari in the States of the Church (in Romagna and the Marches) and in the Duchies of Parma and Moderna (1831) were again repressed by Austrian arms. This led to the society's rapid decline. Giuseppe *Mazzini, a carbonaro since 1827, questioned the Carbonari aims and methods and organized a rival secret society, *Young Italy. The two movements occasionally concerted their action, especially during uprisings in the Romagna (1843) and at Rimini (1845). Pius IX, however, condemned both societies in the encyclical *Qui pluribus* (Nov. 9, 1846). Carbonari groups probably participated in the revolutionary movements of 1848, 1860, and 1870. Leo XIII renewed all previous condemnations in the encyclical *Humanum genus* (April 20, 1884). The *ipso facto* excommunication reserved to the Holy See, which is directed in the Code of Canon Law (c.2335) against masonic and other societies that plot against the Church and legitimate civil authority, applies also to the Carbonari.

Outside of Italy the Carbonari proved something of a threat in France until 1830. A revival of the society in Portugal (1907) was partially responsible for the establishment there of a republic. On the whole the Carbonari never posed the threat to public order that *Metternich claimed. For the most part they did not go beyond seeking national independence and moderate constitutional reforms. Only in the Papal States and in Lombardy, where *anticlericalism was strong, is there evidence that the society might have sought the destruction of religion and civil authority. The significance of the Carbonari was less in the realm of actual, immediate accomplishment than in the field of catalytic revolutionary action.

Bibliography: A. Luzio, *Giuseppe Mazzini Carbonaro* (Turin 1920). E. Morelli, *Giuseppe Massini: Saggi e Ricerche* (Rome 1950), esp. 5–25, "Mazzini nella recente storiografia: Note ed appunti." E. L. Eisenstein, *The First Professional Revolutionist: Filippo Michele Bounarroti, 1761–1837* (Cambridge, Mass. 1959). R. J. Rath, "The Carbonari: Their Origins, Initiation Rites and Aims," AmHistRev 69 (1964) 353–370. F. S. Maranca, EncIt 8:962–963. P. Pirri, EncCatt 3:765–770.

[M. P. TRAUTH]

CARCHEMISH (CHARCHAMIS), ancient city on the right bank of the upper Euphrates. Its ruins are on the southern border of Turkey, just north of the modern town of Jerablus on the northern border of Syria, about 60 miles northeast of Aleppo. Carchemish (Assyrian *karkamiš,* Hebrew *kark*ᵉ*mîš*) was strategically situated at the northern end of the Syrian plain where the important road that ran from *Assyria and *Haran crossed the Euphrates and there divided into one road running further west into Asia Minor and another running south into Syria, Palestine, and Egypt. The excavations made at the site of the ruins by English archeologists from 1876 to 1879 and (under C. L. *Woolley and T. E. Lawrence) in 1912, 1914, and 1920 revealed a city relatively large for ancient times with walls about 8,000 feet in circumference. In the 16th century B.C. Carchemish became one of the most important cities in the *Hittite Empire. Although *Thutmose (Tuthmose) III (1490–1436) boasted that, on his raid into Syria, he went as far as "the country of Carchemish" (Pritchard ANET[2] 241), the city remained thereafter in Hittite hands for several centuries. In the 9th century B.C. the neo-Hittite city-state of Carchemish, under King Sangara, was the head of a league of similar small kingdoms in northern Syria that came into conflict with the advancing Assyrians under *Assurnasirpal II (884–860) and *Salmanasar (Shalmaneser) III (859–825; see *ibid.* 275–279). In 717 B.C. Carchemish was captured and devastated by *Sargon II of Assyria (722–706), an event that the Assyrian boasts of in Is 10.9. In 605 B.C. *Nechao (Necho) of Egypt was defeated by *Nabuchodonosor (Nebuchadrezzar) of Babylon at Carchemish (2 Chr 35.20) in a decisive battle that is vividly described in Jer 46.2–12.

Bibliography: C. L. Woolley and T. E. Lawrence, *Carchemish,* 3 v. (London 1914–52). H. T. Bossert, "Zur Geschichte der Stadt Karkamis," *Studi Classici e Orientali* 1 (1915) 36–68. O. R. Gurney, *The Hittites* (2d ed. Penguin Bks. Baltimore 1961). A. Kleinhans, EncCatt 3:770–771. EncDictBibl 348.

[J. A. GRISPINO]

CARDANO, GERONIMO (GIROLAMO), physician and mathematician; b. Pavia, Italy, Sept. 24, 1501; d. Rome, Sept. 20, 1576. He was the illegitimate son of a jurist, Facio Cardano. From 1520 to 1526, he studied at the Universities of Pavia and Padua, receiving from the latter the degree of Doctor of Medicine. After 6 years as country doctor at Sacco, he held chairs of mathematics and medicine at Milan (1534–52), Pavia (1559–62), and Bologna (1562–70), obtaining this last post through the mediation of Charles Borromeo. After a false accusation of heresy and brief imprisonment, he spent his last days in Rome pensioned by Pope Gregory XIII.

Cardan's greatest achievements are in mathematics: his masterpiece, the *Ars Magna* (1545), a pioneer work in the theory of algebraic equations, contains valuable contributions that were somewhat obscured by the notoriety he received for publishing Tartaglia's solution of the cubic equation. His works in other fields include *De Subtilitate Libri XXI* (1550), and *De Rerum Varietate Libri XVII* (1557). His *Omnia Opera* (10 v.) was edited by Sponius (Lyons 1663).

See also TARTAGLIA, NICCOLÓ.

Bibliography: J. Cardan, *The Book of My Life,* tr. J. Stoner (New York 1930). H. Morley, *The Life of Girolamo Cardano,* 2 v. (London 1854). J. Eckman, "Jerome Cardan," *Bulletin of the History of Medicine,* suppl. 7 (1946) 1–120. O. Øystein, *Cardano: The Gambling Scholar* (Princeton 1953).

[M. S. M. VAN RYZIN]

CÁRDENAS, BERNARDINO DE

Bolivian Franciscan missionary, writer, and bishop of Paraguay; b. La Paz, 1579; d. near Santa Cruz de la Sierra, Bolivia, Oct. 20, 1668. In 1594 he entered the Jesuit Colegio de San Martín in Lima and later entered the Franciscan Order in that city. Cárdenas grew up speaking Spanish and two Indian languages, Quechua and Aymará. This advantage combined with his zeal helped him become a noted missionary. In 1621 he almost lost his life working among the tribes to the east of La Paz. In 1624–25, he was able to quell a dangerous rebellion of the Indians who were threatening La Paz itself. In 1629 the bishops of the province of Bolivia in provincial council named Cárdenas official delegate and visitor to all the Indians of their jurisdictions, a task that he completed with great zeal and to almost universal approval. One result of this experience was his noteworthy *Memorial y relación verdadera . . . de cosas del Reyno del Perú* (Madrid 1634). His success moved Pedro Villagómez, then Bishop of Arequipa, to name him visitor to the important mining center of Cailloma. There, as in Bolivia, Cárdenas's condemnation of the sale of coca and alcoholic beverages to the Indians brought the censure of some and the approval of many. By Feb. 27, 1638, the King had presented Cárdenas for the bishopric of Paraguay; the Holy See approved on Aug. 13, 1640. Impatient to get to work, Cárdenas did not await the arrival of his bulls and was consecrated in Tucumán on Oct. 14, 1641, an act that the Holy See later judged valid, even though illicit. His enemies had declared that he was not a bishop. The Jesuit *Reductions were the most important institutions in the bishopric. In the beginning, relations between Cárdenas and the Jesuit superiors were cordial, but by the end of 1644 a scandalous disagreement broke out that resulted in violence on both sides and lasted until Cárdenas was finally driven from his see in 1651. After long litigation the Council of the Indies disapproved of the actions against him and in 1660 ordered that he be escorted to his see. However, he was too old to return, and in 1662 he was transferred to the See of Santa Cruz de la Sierra, where he died in the sanctuary of Araní, the common opinion being that he was a saint.

The figure of Cárdenas has become a symbol of controversy similar to that of Bishop *Palafox of Mexico, of whom he was a contemporary. At the time of the expulsion of the Jesuits, their enemies at court published three volumes of the memorials and countermemorials of the case. In the 19th century the Peruvian priest *Vigil resurrected Cárdenas's reputation as a bishop, and in the 20th century Augusto Guzmán wrote a novelized version of his life. The Jesuits still continue their defense of their actions. Cárdenas's life has not yet received objective treatment. Yet his pectoral cross, smashed by a bullet fired while he was besieged in his cathedral by the Indians of the Reductions and still carefully preserved with due authentication, is mute testimony that the bishop had many opponents.

Bibliography: A. Guzmán, *El kolla mitrado: Biografía de un obispo colonial, fray Bernardino de Cárdenas* (2d ed. La Paz 1954). A. Ybot Léon, *La iglesia y los eclesiásticos españoles en la empresa de Indias,* 2 v. (Barcelona 1954–63). P. Pastells, ed., *Historia de la Compañía de Jesús en la provincia del Paraguay,* 8 v. in 9 (Madrid 1912–49).

[L. G. CANEDO]

CÁRDENAS, JUAN DE, Jesuit moral theologian; b. Seville, 1613; d. there, June 6, 1684. He entered the Society of Jesus at the age of 14, and for many years he held various administrative offices, including those of novice master, rector, and provincial. He wrote many short ascetical treatises, but his fame comes chiefly from his work in moral theology. His *Crisis theologica bipartita* (Lyons 1670) examined many of the moral opinions prevalent at his time, especially those involving laxism and rigorism. This work was strongly attacked by the French Dominican James of St. Dominic, and in the 1680 edition Cárdenas reasserted his position in a supplement that defended moderate probabilism. Although he presented a clear and strong line of argumentation, and although his opinions were moderate and sound, the work was weakened by constant digressions referring to his rigorist adversaries, who included Vincent *Baron and Jean Baptiste *Gonet. The Venetian editions of 1694, 1700, and 1710 contained also an explanation of the 65 propositions condemned by Pope Innocent XI in 1679. This part was also published as a separate volume entitled *Crisis theologica in qua plures selectae difficultates ex morali theologia ad lydium veritatis lapidem revocantur ex regula morum posita a SS. D.N. Innocentis XI P.M. . . .* (Seville 1687). Cárdenas holds an important place in the history of casuistry and of probabilism.

Bibliography: P. Bernard, DTC 2.2:1713–14. Hurter Nomencl 2.1:231. Sommervogel 2:734–737.

[F. C. LEHNER]

CARDIEL, JOSÉ, missionary and geographer of Paraguay; b. La Guardia, Spain, March 18, 1704; d. Faenza, Italy, Dec. 6, 1781. He entered the Jesuit Society on April 8, 1720, and was already a priest when he arrived in Buenos Aires in 1729. Two years later he was sent to the Guaraní Reductions. (*See* REDUCTIONS OF PARAGUAY.) He took part in various attempts to establish new missions among the Mocoví, Abipón, Charrua, Pampa, and Serrano tribes, and also explored the Patagonian Coast. In 1768 he was deported to Italy where he lived until his death, preparing studies and maps for the history and geography of Paraguay. His cartographic work has been almost completely reproduced and analyzed by G. Furlong (*Cartografía jesuítica del Río de la Plata,* 2 v. Buenos Aires 1936). Cardiel's most important writings are *Carta-relación* (1747), *Declaración de la verdad* (1758), and *Breve relación* (1771).

Bibliography: G. Furlong, *José Cardiel, S.J., y su Carta-relación (1747)* (Buenos Aires 1953).

[H. STORNI]

CARDIFF, ARCHDIOCESE OF (CARDIFFENSIS), metropolitan see since 1916, in south *Wales. Its 2,188 square miles embrace Glamorganshire in Wales, and Monmouthshire and Herefordshire in England. Its sole suffragan since 1916 has been Menevia. The growth of the city of Cardiff after 1800 accompanied its rise as a port and as a center of the coal and iron industries. There were two Catholics in Cardiff in 1801. Irish immigration after the 1847 famine laid the basis of the present Catholic population in south Wales. In 1840 the English Vicariate of the Western District was split into two vicariates, with

Wales, Monmouthshire, and Herefordshire constituting one of them. Glamorganshire and the other five counties of south Wales, Monmouthshire, and Herefordshire became the Diocese of Newport and Menevia (1850–95). When the Vicariate Apostolic of Wales was created (1895), it included all Wales except Glamorganshire; this same area has formed the Diocese of Menevia since 1898. The Diocese of Newport and Menevia, minus five of its original Welsh counties, was called the Diocese of Newport (1896–1916) and the Archdiocese of Cardiff since 1916. The seat of the diocese moved from Newport to Cardiff in 1916. This territory was suffragan to Westminster (1850–1911) and to Birmingham (1911–16); after that Wales constituted a separate ecclesiastical province. In 1911, when John Cuthbert *Hedley was bishop of Newport, the see had 50,000 Catholics. The first archbishop of Cardiff was Francis Mostyn. Archdiocesan synods met in 1947 and 1957. The former abbeys of *Tintern, Margam, Neath, and Ewenny are in the archdiocese, as are the pre-Reformation shrine and well of Our Lady of Penrhys and the tomb of Bl. David *Lewis at Usk. In 1964 the archdiocese had 98,000 Catholics in a population of 1,802,000, 136 secular and 77 religious priests, 84 men in 20 religious houses, 440 women in 30 convents, 20,794 pupils in 82 Catholic schools (58 parochial, 10 secondary, 13 independent, and one special), 4 hospitals, 3 orphanages, and 3 homes for unwed mothers. In 1963 there were 4,896 baptisms of children up to 7 years of age, 1,633 Catholic marriages, and 362 adult conversions.

Bibliography: G. ALBION, DHGE 11:1021–22. *Catholic Directory of England and Wales,* (London 1838–), annual. Ann Pont (1965) 94.

[C. M. DANIEL]

CARDINAL, I (HISTORY OF)

The designation borne by members of the Sacred College, the "senators" of the Church. From the 15th century onward, there has been no common understanding of the origin and meaning of the term. Etymology stood at the crux of this disagreement. On the evidence of classical precedent and of parallels in civil government, some scholars held that *cardinalis* in an ecclesiastical context derived from *cardo* (hinge), and that consequently it referred to a principal officer or church on whose functions much of the administration was said to "turn." Hence, from various related arguments it appeared that *cardinalis* originally designated a permanent administrative officer in a given church, or the incumbent of a major church on the parish, diocesan, or provincial level, or by extension the principal officer of any church.

Other scholars, however, have judged that the term followed a development in the Church quite independent of its usages in other contexts, and, indeed, that it had derived not from *cardo,* but from *incardinare,* a term first known from the *Letters* of *Gregory I. The term was invented apparently to describe the action of *incardination. According to this opinion, the name cardinal was used to designate men in the three major orders serving a church other than the one in which they were ordained. Though set forth long ago, this interpretation was first fully stated by S. Kuttner. As modified by M. Andrieu and, on balance, accepted by K. Ganzer, it represents a tentative consensus of contemporary canonistic specialists. The title "Cardinal" appears to have achieved currency during the barbarian invasions of western Europe, especially in the 6th century. At that time *cardinalis* designated those bishops whose sees had been overwhelmed by insurrection or invasion, and whom Gregory the Great had translated to vacant sees. If the sees of the translated prelates were extinguished, the bishops remained permanently in the new sees; but if their own churches revived, they were returned to them. In this way the canons against episcopal pluralism were satisfied.

Among the Germanic peoples the term gradually assumed the very different meaning based on its supposed derivation from *cardo.* Cardinal clergy were understood to be the clergy of churches directly subject to a bishop, especially of baptismal and cathedral churches, as distinct from private chapels and *proprietary churches. This usage remained relatively stable. But in the 10th and 11th centuries several important churches (Magdeburg, Trier, Cologne, and Santiago de Compostela) began, as a special privilege, to exercise the right of having "cardinal" clergy "in the fashion of the Roman Church"; and from the 12th century onward there was a tendency to align current terminology with Roman usage. In the interval since Gregory the Great that usage had seemingly combined the meaning of *cardinalis* in Gregory's letters with the early Germanic sense.

By the time of *Stephen III (768–772) at the latest, the bishops of Ostia, Albano, Palestrina, Porto, Silva Candida, Gabii, and Veletri had received liturgical duties in the *Lateran Church and had thus become "cardinal" bishops, since they performed these duties outside their own sees. By the same time the "title" churches of Rome increased from 25, a number unchanged since the 6th century, to 28, and seven of these "parish" churches were subjected to each of the four greater basilicas of Rome, viz, St. Peter's, St. Paul's, St. Lawrence's, and S. Maria Maggiore. The senior priests of these "title" churches were likewise "cardinals" because of their obligation to participate in specified services in the basilicas. This organization established a loosely knit but distinct body of privileged clergy in Rome, and in the 11th century the Sacred College achieved institutional form when reforming popes assigned to cardinal bishops and priests administrative as well as liturgical functions in the Roman Church, and when they elevated non-Romans, such as *Humbert of Silva Candida, to the cardinalate in their effort to create an administrative corps.

From the pontificate of *Leo IX onward the cardinal bishops and priests were the principal counselors and assistants of the popes; by the *papal election decree of 1059 in the pontificate of *Nicholas II they became the papal electors as well. By 1084 deacons had joined the cardinals in their deliberations, and though the development is obscure, it is clear that seven deacons bore the title "cardinal" in the pontificate of *Urban II, and 18 in that of *Paschal II. By that time the meaning of *cardinalis* had undergone such change that Urban wrote, in a tenor exactly the reverse of Gregory I's sense, that cardinal bishops were those elected by the dioceses in which they presided, as distinct from translated prelates. It seems most likely that the cardinal clergy of Rome were similarly thought to be the permanent clergy of the greater churches in that see. The nomination of prelates in distant countries to the cardinalate, a practice that

A cardinal receives his red hat from Pope John XXIII at a consistory in Rome held on March 22, 1962.

began in the late 11th century, did not impair this position, although the men so elevated could seldom, if ever, discharge the liturgical functions formerly expected of cardinal clergy.

As the temporal power of the papacy increased from the time of Leo IX, the power of the Sacred College also grew; already in the late 11th century the claim was advanced that the cardinals were the true representatives, the *cardines,* who ruled and directed God's people, and that the powers of St. Peter belonged not to the pope alone, but collectively to the pope and the cardinals. Later developments in canonistic thought further enhanced the authority of the Sacred College and led, in the 13th century, to the assertions that during a vacancy of the Roman see the papal powers rested among the cardinals, and that under any circumstances the Sacred College was the effective head of the see of St. Peter. These claims were most fully expressed in the conflict between *Boniface VIII and the *Colonnas.

Bibliography: J. Schnitzer, *Die Gesta Romanae Ecclesiae des Kardinals Beno und andere Streitschriften der schismatischen Kardinäle wider Gregor VII.* (Bamberg 1892). J. Lulvès, "Die Machtbestrebungen des Kardinalkollegiums gegenüber dem Papsttum," MitteilIöG 35 (1914) 456–483. H. W. Klewitz, "Die Entstehung des Kardinalkollegiums," ZSavRGKan 25 (1936) 115–221; repr. in H. W. Klewitz, *Reformpapsttum und Kardinalkolleg* (Darmstadt 1957). K. Jordan, "Die Entstehung der römischen Kurie," ZSavRGKan 28 (1939) 97–152. S. Kuttner, "*Cardinalis:* The History of a Canonical Concept," *Traditio* 3 (1945) 129–214. M. Andrieu, "L'Origine du titre de cardinal dans l'église romaine," MiscMercati 5:113–144. F. Merzbacher, "Wandlungen des Kirchenbegriffs im Spätmittelalter: Grundzüge der Ekklesiologie des ausgehenden 13., des 14. und 15. Jahrhunderts," ZSavRGKan 39 (1953) 274–361. K. Ganzer, *Die Entwicklung des auswärtigen Kardinalats im hohen Mittelalter: Ein Beitrag zur Geschichte des Kardinalkollegiums vom 11. bis 13. Jahrhundert* (Tübingen 1963).

[K. F. MORRISON]

CARDINAL, II (CANON LAW OF)

An ecclesiastical title used to designate the members of the college of cardinals, who assist the pope in governing the Catholic Church. As the principal counselors of the pope, it is the duty of cardinals to assist the supreme pontiff in guiding and directing the affairs of the Catholic Church throughout the world. The word is derived from the Latin word *cardo* meaning "hinge," and in the words of Pope Eugene IV, "as the door of a house turns on its hinges, so on the cardinalate does the Apostolic See, the door of the whole Church, rest and find support."

Number. Prior to the pontificate of Pope John XXIII, the maximum number of ecclesiastics who could enjoy this dignity at any one given time was 70, a number fixed by Pope Sixtus V in 1586. Rarely was this maximum number reached. Of the 70 cardinals, 6 were designated as cardinal bishops, and they were the bishops of the dioceses that surround the city of Rome, namely, Ostia, Albano, Frascati, Porto-Santa Rufina, Valletri, and Palestrina. There were 50 designated as cardinal priests; the majority of this group were bishops of various dioceses throughout the world who had been elevated by the pope to the cardinalitial dignity. The third designation was that of cardinal deacon. There were 14 of these, and they were usually priests associated with the various administrative offices of the Vatican.

Pope John XXIII abrogated the previous legislation that had set the maximum number of cardinals at 70. He at one time during his pontificate had the number of cardinals in the 80s. Pope Paul VI has followed the tradition of Pope John. Consequently, there is no limit to the number who could at any given time comprise the college of cardinals. Moreover, after creating a number of cardinal deacons who were not bishops, Popes John XXIII and Paul VI immediately consecrated them as bishops. According to present legislation one must be at least a priest in order to be eligible for this high dignity. Prior to the promulgation of the Code of Canon Law in 1917, this dignity was often conferred on laymen. The last cardinal who was not a priest at the time he was elevated was Giacomo Antonelli (1806–76).

Creation of Cardinals. When new cardinals are created, the pope calls a secret consistory of the cardinals in and around Rome and announces to them the names of the men he has decided to honor. The individuals so selected are then notified and if possible come to Rome to be officially invested with the red biretta and the red cloak or mantle. This was previously done at a secret consistory, but Paul VI made it a public ceremony. If the cardinal is not in Rome, the biretta is carried to him by a legate appointed for this specific purpose. Should the newly appointed cardinal pertain to a Catholic country, then the duly appointed ruler of that state imposes the red biretta on the new cardinal.

The conferring of the red hat also takes place at the public consistory. At the death of a cardinal this red hat must be placed at the foot of the catafalque, and afterward it is suspended from the ceiling of his cathedral church. At this same public consistory, the pope bestows the ring upon the new cardinal and may assign one of the churches of the city of Rome as his titular church or deaconry church. Oriental patriarchs do not usually have a titular church.

Duties and Privileges. Cardinals are in charge of the various congregations of the Roman *Curia. An analogy can be drawn between these cardinals and the various department heads who comprise the cabinet of the president of the United States. When referred to as the "senate" of the Roman Catholic Church, it should be noted that they enjoy a dignity similar to that of American senators but differ from them in that they have no legislative power or authority.

One of the chief privileges of the college of cardinals is to elect a successor following the death of the pope. For this purpose they must convene in Rome within 15 days and in *conclave (a Latin word meaning "locked in") vote upon a successor. A two-thirds majority is required for election. They have enjoyed this privilege since the reign of Pope Alexander III (1159–81). *See* POPES, ELECTION OF.

Cardinals enjoy the privilege of being directly addressed as "Eminence"; in English, usually "Your Eminence" and "His Eminence." Also when addressing a cardinal in writing, custom has sanctioned the practice of inserting the word cardinal between the first and family names (e.g., "His Eminence, Francis Cardinal Spellman). Besides the privileges of dress and address, cardinals enjoy many privileges not accorded by church law to lesser ecclesiastics. These are listed in CIC c.239 and ClerSanc c.185.

Bibliography: H. G. HYNES, *Privileges of Cardinals* (CUA CLS 217; 1945). C. A. BACHOFEN (C. Augustine), *A Commentary on the New Code of Canon Law,* 8 v. (St. Louis 1919–23) v.2, 6. P. A. BAART, *The Roman Court* (2d ed. New York 1895). M. BELARDO, *De iuribus S. R. E. cardinalium in titulis* (Vatican City 1939). Beste. A. G. CICOGNANI, *Canon Law,* tr. J. O'HARA and F. BRENNAN (rev. ed. Westminster, Md. 1947). P. FAGNANUS, *Commentaria in primum [-quintum] librum decretalium,* 5 v. in 3 (Venice 1697). N. HILLING, *Procedure at the Roman Curia* (New York 1907). J. A. NAINFA, *Costume of Prelates of the Catholic Church, according to Roman Etiquette* (2d ed. Baltimore 1926). J. PIATTI, *De cardinalis de dignitate et officio: Hieronymi Plati e Societate Jesu,* ed. A. SPADA (Rome 1836). A. REIFFENSTUEL, *Ius canonicum universum,* 7 v. (Paris 1864–70). J. B. SÄGMÜLLER, *Die Thätigkeit und Stellung der Cardinäle bis Papst Bonifaz VIII* (Freiburg 1896). F. SCHMALZGRUEBER, *Ius ecclesiasticum universum,* 5 v. in 12 (Rome 1843–45). S. KUTTNER, "*Cardinalis:* The History of a Canonical Concept," *Traditio* 3 (1945) 129–214.

[H. G. HYNES]

CARDINAL CUSHING COLLEGE. A liberal arts college for women founded in 1952 at Brookline, Mass., at the request of Cardinal Richard Cushing, it is one of five colleges conducted by the Sisters of the Holy Cross of Notre Dame, Ind., whose work in education in the U.S. began in 1844. Cardinal Cushing College opened in September 1952, with 2-year terminal programs in the liberal arts, business secretarial arts, and medical secretarial science. Since September 1956, the College has offered 4-year programs leading to the B.A. degree. Majors are offered in the natural sciences, elementary education, English, French, history, mathematics, sociology, theology, and American studies. The College avails itself of the rich historic and literary traditions of New England for its interdepartmental program in American studies. Associate degrees are conferred in business secretarial arts, liberal arts, and medical secretarial science. This combination of 2- and 4-year programs gives Cardinal Cushing College its distinct character among Catholic colleges for women in the area. While constantly developing and enriching its 4-year curricula, the College has maintained its original purpose of providing an integrated humanistic-vocational preparation for students who wish to devote only 2 years to college studies.

The College is administered by a board of trustees consisting of the archbishop of Boston, the superior general of the Sisters of the Holy Cross, the assistant superior general, the provincial superior, the president of the College, and three other members. The College operates on the two-semester plan. A limited number of scholarships are awarded annually on the basis of scholastic achievement and financial need. In 1964, the administration and faculty included 18 sisters, 2 priests, and 18 laymen. The staff held 4 doctorates and 23 master's degrees. Enrollment totaled 240, with students from 11 states and 7 foreign countries. Total capacity is 500 students. On the 7½-acre campus, four residence halls accommodate 92 students. The central campus building is Trinity Hall, housing administrative offices, classrooms, science and language laboratories, the assembly hall, and the library, which contains approximately 15,540 volumes and receives 138 periodicals.

The College is authorized by the Board of Collegiate Authority of the Commonwealth of Massachusetts. It is affiliated with The Catholic University of America and holds membership in the National Catholic Educational Association.

[J. A. DONAHUE]

CARDINAL STRITCH COLLEGE

Founded in Milwaukee, Wis., in 1937 as St. Clare College for the education of the Sisters of St. Francis, the College was incorporated that same year by the laws of Wisconsin as a degree-granting institution. In 1946 the name was changed to Cardinal Stritch College in recognition of the interest and direction given by Cardinal Samuel Stritch, then archbishop of Milwaukee, and thenceforth laywomen were admitted. A coeducational graduate division was opened in 1956. In 1962 the College moved from its original location near the motherhouse to an independent campus in Fox Point. In 1963 the six newly constructed buildings could accommodate more than 450 students.

The mother general and four counselors serve as the board of trustees, and 15 professional laymen constitute the advisory board. The administrative staff is composed of the president, dean, dean of students, registrar, and business officer. In 1964 the 52-member faculty, composed of priests, religious, and laymen, held 13 doctorates and 28 master's degrees. Approximately 225 full-time students were undergraduates and 254 were in the graduate division.

The College confers B.A. and M.A. degrees. At the undergraduate level, there are 11 areas of concentration embracing the liberal arts, fine arts, and science. Two seminars (directed reading and coordinating seminar) scheduled in the junior and senior years, offer opportunity for independent study. Although emphasis in the undergraduate program is on the liberal arts, several departments afford professional preparation for careers as dietitians, medical technologists, and teachers. The teacher program is approved by the Wisconsin Department of Public Instruction on both the primary and secondary levels. Two areas of specialization in the master's program prepare the student as a reading specialist or teacher of the mentally handicapped. Pupil demonstration and observation are conducted at the Cardinal Stritch College clinic and at the St. Coletta School, Jefferson, Wis. In 1964 the library totaled 29,750 volumes and subscribed to 281 periodicals.

The College is accredited by the North Central Association of Colleges and Secondary Schools, the University of Wisconsin, the American Association for Colleges of Teacher Education, and the National Council for Accreditation of Teacher Education. It is affiliated with The Catholic University of America and is on the U.S. Attorney General's List for Foreign Students. It has the approval of the American Medical Association for premedical training and holds membership in the leading educational organizations.

[M. F. LOCHEMES]

CARDINAL VICAR, title belonging to the cardinal appointed by the holy father to rule with full powers the main part of the pope's own Diocese of Rome. His full title is *Sanctissimi Domini Nostri Vicarius Generalis in Urbe, Romanae Curiae eiusque Districtus Judex Ordinarius.* The supreme pontiff's solicitude for all Churches, and therefore his worldwide duties, prevent him from attending daily to the ordinary diocesan affairs of Rome, and this is why ever since 1558 the popes have entrusted all necessary ordinary jurisdiction to a cardinal vicar, whose office does not expire with the pope's death, as would a vicar-general's of any other diocese. Thus the pastoral care of the Roman faithful is permanently ensured. The cardinal vicar is assisted by a titular archbishop (until recently often a titular patriarch) called vicegerent of Rome, who also enjoys ordinary jurisdiction, but in subordination to the cardinal vicar. After the synod of Rome held by John XXIII (1960), the cardinal vicar was given two auxiliary bishops as well. In certain cases the holy father may also name a cardinal provicar with authority similar to that of the cardinal vicar. The diocesan offices of the Eternal City are known as the Vicariate of Rome. Exempt from the cardinal vicar's authority in the Diocese of Rome are the Vatican Basilica (which has its own ordinary in the person of the cardinal archpriest of St. Peter's) as well as, since 1929, the Vatican City State, which is pastorally administered by the pope's sacristan, a titular bishop, who is vicar of his holiness for Vatican City and has his own vicariate.

[P. C. VAN LIERDE]

CARDOSO, MANOEL, leading Portuguese composer; b. Fronteira (between Portalegre and Estremoz), Portugal, 1566 (baptized Dec. 11); d. Lisbon, Portugal, Nov. 24, 1650. He was enrolled *c.* 1575 by his father in the Colégio dos Moços do Coro at Evora, where he came under the influence of two important composers, Cosme Delgado (*c.* 1532–96), cathedral chapelmaster, and Manuel Mendes (*c.* 1547–Sept. 24, 1605), instructor of the boy choristers. On July 1, 1588, he was clothed as a Calced Carmelite, and on July 5, 1589, he was professed in the Convento do Carmo at Lisbon, where he spent the rest of his life, except for a journey to conduct the royal choir at Madrid in 1631 and a possible earlier visit to Vila Viçosa to instruct the next Portuguese king, João IV, in music. His first published music, a book of Magnificats (Lisbon 1613), was followed by three books of Masses and, finally, a book of Holy Week music (1648), in all of which he combined *singular erudicão* with the utmost expressiveness. Every parody Mass in his first book was founded on compositions by *Palestrina; in his second book he acknowledged João IV's patronage by parodying only royal motets; in his third book a single motet, *Ab initio ante secula creata sum,* ascribed to Mateo Romero's royal pupil, Philip IV, serves as model for the parodies. Called the cynosure of his epoch by Manuel Rodrigues Coelho, composer of the first printed Portuguese keyboard collection, *Flores de Música* (Lisbon 1620), Cardoso was succeeded in the public esteem by two other Portuguese Calced Carmelites considered the best composers in Spain during *Velázquez's era—Francisco de Santiago (b. Lisbon; paternal name Vega; chapelmaster at Seville, April 5, 1617, until his death, Oct. 5, 1644) and Manuel Correa [b. Lisbon; chapelmaster at Saragossa (Seo), Sept. 13, 1650, until his death, Aug. 1, 1653)].

Bibliography: *Liber primus missarum,* tr. and ed. J. A. ALEGRIA (Lisbon 1962–), v.1 of projected *Opera omnia.* D. BARBOSA MACHADO, *Bibliotheca Lusitana historica, critica, e cronologica,* 4 v. (2d ed. Lisbon 1930–35) 3:210–211. M. DE SAMPAYO RIBEIRO, in *Diccionario de la música Labor,* ed. J. PENA and H. ANGLÉS, 2 v. (Barcelona 1954) 1:449; "No tricentenário da Morte del-Rei D. João Quarto," *Ocidente* 51 (1956) 172–178; *Frei Manuel Cardoso* (Lisbon 1961). E. GAMA, "O assento do baptismo de frei Manuel Cardoso," *Arte musical* 13–14 (1961) 460–471.

[R. STEVENSON]

CARDUCCI, GIOSUÈ

Italian poet and scholar; b. near Pietrasanta, July 27, 1835; d. Bologna, Feb. 16, 1907. He received his secondary education in Florence and attended the University of Pisa. In 1856 he began teaching at San Miniato al Monte; 2 years later he moved to Florence, and in 1859 became professor of Greek at the Pistoia *lycée.* In 1860 he took the chair of Italian literature at the University of Bologna—a post he held until illness forced him to retire in 1904. In 1906 he was awarded the Nobel Prize for literature. Some of his early work was written under the name Enotrio Romano.

Amazingly active, Carducci edited texts of Italian classics, wrote much criticism, and published volumes of poems. A nonconformist, and a sincere admirer of the heroic ages, he educated generations of Italian intellectuals. As an avowed classicist, he rejected the late Romantics and anything he considered morbid or decadent. His independence in politics (even when it

Giosuè Carducci.

wore the labels of republicanism or anticlericalism), made him oppose all forms of weakness and corruption; he found in history the ideals that the new generations should espouse.

His best critical essays are those on Cino da Pistoia, Dante, Politian, Ariosto, Parini, and Alfieri—the last two being in many ways his direct masters. He began to write verse early, and continued this work until 1899. His first volumes reflect well his volcanic, polemical temperament, but his best work may be found in the two mature collections: *Odi barbare* (1877–89), and *Rime nuove* (1889). The *Odi barbare* (so called because they attempt in Italian the Greek and Latin meters with resulting rhythms that would sound "barbarous" to the ancients) evoke the splendor of Rome and the freedom of the medieval city states. Beneath their passionate eloquence, a reader may sense the poet's nostalgia.

A virile melancholy is the overt inspirer of *Rime nuove,* probably Carducci's best work. Its most impressive poems sing of the things nearest to his heart: the sudden and seductive apparition of his childhood projected against the harshness of adult reality in "Davanti San Guido"; the sense of emptiness created by the death of his child in "Pianto antico," a poem worthy of ancient Greece; the landscape of his youth in "Idillio maremmano." Although the last volume, *Rime e ritmi* (1899), contains some excellent selections, it is not as significant as *Odi barbare* and *Rime nuove.*

Carducci wrote and taught during the post-**risorgimento* era, which was constantly in danger of falling prey to self-gratification, and in need of a guide. He was such a guide; more than that, he was a poet.

Bibliography: G. CARDUCCI, *Edizione nazionale delle opere,* 30 v. (Bologna 1935–44); *Lettere,* 21 v. (Bologna 1938–60); *Carducci: A Selection of His Poems,* tr. G. L. BICKERSTETH (London 1913); *Odi barbare,* tr. W. F. SMITH (New York 1950). J. C. BAILEY, *Carducci* (Oxford 1926). S. E. SCALIA, *Carducci: His Critics and Translators in England and America, 1881–1932* (New York 1937). B. CROCE, *Giosuè Carducci: Studio critico* (2d ed. Bari 1927). L. RUSSO, *Carducci senza retorica* (Bari 1957). F. FLORA, *La poesia e la prosa di Giosuè Carducci* (Pisa 1959). **Illustration credit:** Italian Information Center, New York City.

[G. CECCHETTI]

CAREY, HENRY CHARLES, economist, social scientist, publisher; b. Philadelphia, Pa., Dec. 15, 1793; d. Philadelphia, Oct. 13, 1879. He was the son of Mathew Carey, the noted publisher, and became one of the most important American economists of the 19th century. He entered his father's business at the age of 12, and from his experience there became well educated. In 1834 he ended a successful career as a publisher to become a voluminous and eclectic writer. Originally a defender of free trade, he became an ardent and influential advocate of protectionism. He rejected the then accepted theses of the iron law of wages, the law of diminishing returns, the Malthusian population theory, and the Ricardian theory of rent. He developed a dynamic teleological system of total societal change, in which a "harmony of interests" between man and nature causes capital and population to increase most rapidly and makes profits highest where wages are highest. Carey exerted a powerful influence on U.S. businessmen and young German economists, who found in his writings a justification for protectionism and nationalism. Carey married Martha Leslie in 1819; they had no children.

Bibliography: A. D. KAPLAN, *Henry Charles Carey* (Johns Hopkins University Studies in Historical and Political Science, ser. 49, 4; Baltimore 1931).

[J. J. MURPHY]

CAREY, MATHEW

Author, economist, and publisher; b. Dublin, Ireland, Jan. 28, 1760; d. Philadelphia, Pa., Sept. 16, 1839. A fall in infancy crippled him for life, and this condition limited his formal education. He nevertheless developed a talent for writing, and while an apprentice printer published a militant protest against British maltreatment of Irish Catholics. To save him from a fine or worse, his family sent him to Paris for a year, where he met Benjamin Franklin. Back in Ireland, Carey incurred the political wrath of the Duke of Rutland, Lord-Lieutenant of Ireland. After a brief sentence in Newgate Prison, he sailed to the U.S. in 1784. Arriving in Philadelphia, he was given financial help by the Marquis de *Lafayette, a debt repaid 40 years later when the aging French aristocrat was in need.

In 1785 Carey began the *Pennsylvania Herald,* which reported in detail the sessions of the State's Legislature. A bitter political controversy with a Colonel Oswald led to a duel, in which Carey was painfully wounded. In 1791 he married Bridget Flahanen; nine children were born to this union, of whom three died while young.

In 1792 Carey borrowed money to establish himself as a bookseller and publisher, a venture that prospered after several years of uncertainty. He helped found the Hibernian Society dedicated to the relief of Irish immigrants, was elected (1802) a director of the Bank of Pennsylvania, and was one of the few Jeffersonian Republicans in Philadelphia to press for the renewal (1810) of the charter of the first Bank of the United States. His *Olive Branch* (1814) strove to compromise the widening differences between Federalists and Republicans, occasioned by the War of 1812. Fearing that U.S. economic growth would be injured by English "dumping" of finished goods on the American market at low prices, he helped initiate a "protectionist" policy, and became a charter member of the Philadelphia Society for the Promotion of National Industry. Most of the Society's protectionist arguments were developed by Carey, who, next to Alexander Hamilton, was most influential in shaping a distinctly nationalist school of economic theory.

Carey's own writings were mainly on economic themes and include *Essays on Banking* (1816) and *An Appeal to the Wealthy of the Land* (1836). From 1789 to 1822 he published 26 Catholic doctrinal and devotional books. His *Holy Bible* (1790) was the first American Douay edition. *See* BIBLE, IV (TEXTS AND VERSIONS) 22. As a publisher he maintained friendly relations with Fielding *Lucas, Jr., of Baltimore; as a bookseller he carried over 2,500 titles in stock as early as 1794. His practice of reprinting English novels has been judged a deterrent to American authorship and an indirect cause for the development of the American short story. In 1822 his firm became Carey and Lea; its publications were of a general, nonreligious nature.

See also IRISH IN THE UNITED STATES.

Bibliography: M. CAREY, *Autobiography* (New York 1942). K. W. ROWE, *Mathew Carey: A Study in American Economic Development* (Baltimore 1933). E. P. WILLGING, "Mathew Carey," *Books on Trial* 15 (1957) 237–240, 284–285.

[G. L. A. REILLY]

CAREY, WILLIAM, Baptist missionary pioneer; b. Paulers Pury, Northamptonshire, England, Aug. 17, 1761; d. Serampore, India, June 9, 1834. Born in humble circumstances and baptized an Anglican, he was apprenticed to a shoemaker (1779), and during this period became a Baptist. He was ordained and supplemented a meager income as a pastor by making shoes and teaching school. Impressed with the importance of giving the gospel to the non-Christian world, he stimulated the organization of the Baptist Missionary Society (1792). Under its appointment he went to India (1793), where he became eminent as a missioner, linguist, translator, educator, and scientist. To make a living and to avoid deportation by the East India Company, then opposed to missions, he was for a time manager of an indigo plantation. Gaining a foothold in Serampore, at that time a Danish possession, he and two colleagues translated the Bible in whole or in part into 44 Indian languages and dialects. By means of a press, which they established at Serampore, copies were manufactured and distributed. Carey also translated some of the Sanskrit classics into English. He and his colleagues established schools and capped them with a degree-granting college. As recreation he developed a botanical garden and won fame in India and Europe as a naturalist.

Bibliography: F. D. WALKER, *William Carey* (London 1926). Latourette 4, 6.

[K. S. LATOURETTE]

CARIATH-JARIM, ancient Palestinian town, about 8 miles northwest of Jerusalem. Before the Israelite invasion it was one of the towns of the Gabaonite league (Jos 9.17; *see* GABAON); after the conquest it belonged to the tribe of Juda (Jos 15.60; see also Jgs 18.12), although located on the border of Benjamin (Jos 18.15). The *Ark of the Covenant remained here in the house of Abinadab for several years after its recovery from the Philistines (1 Sm 6.21). The men of this town chose Eleazar, son of Abinadab, to guard the ark (1 Sm 7.1–2). Later David transported it from Cariath-Jarim to Jerusalem (2 Samuel ch. 6; 1 Chronicles ch. 13). The Prophet Uria, put to death by King *Joachin, was a native of Cariath-Jarim (Jer 26.20–23). Apparently the original name of the town was Cariath-Baal, "town of Baal" (Jos 15.60), or simply Baala (Jos 15.9). Because of Israelite opposition to the Canaanite god *Baal, its name was changed to Cariath-Jarim (Heb. *qiryat y^{e}ārîm*), "town of the woods." Its site, now called Tell el-Azhar, is near Qariat el-'Enab (Abu Gosh).

Bibliography: EncDictBibl 323–324. Abel GéogrPal 2:419–421. A. PENNA, EncCatt 3:790–791. R. NORTH, LexThK^{2} 6:306–307. R. DE VAUX and A. M. STEVE, *Fouilles à Quaryet el-'Enab Abū Gôsh, Palestine* (Paris 1950).

[L. DANNEMILLER]

CARILEFFUS, ST., hermit; b. Aquitaine; d. *c.* 540 (feast, July 1). According to the two 9th-century lives, the only written evidence, Carileffus was a monk at the Abbey of Ménat or at the Abbey of *Micy. He set out with a companion, *Avitus, and he was ordained by Maximin of Micy (d. 520), Bishop of Orléans. Leaving Avitus, he adopted a solitary life in the Diocese of Le Mans on the river Anille. The Abbey of Anille, later *Saint-Calais, from evidence in royal charters of the 8th century, seems to have been built in his honor. It took his name perhaps in the 9th century when his cult is well attested. A diploma of 760 suggests that his body was buried at Saint-Calais, where, after its translation to Blois during the course of the Norman invasions, it was again returned in 1663.

Bibliography: MGSrerMer 3:386–394, earliest life, fragments only. Mabillon AS 1:621–633. A. M. ZIMMERMANN, LexThK^{2} 2:941. BHL 1:1568–72. Zimmermann KalBen 2:389. R. AIGRAIN, *Catholicisme* 2:369–370. J. HAVET, *Questions mérovingiennes,* 6 pts. in 1 v. (Paris 1885–90) pt. 4 *Les Chartes de Saint-Calais,* 5–58, 209–247.

[V. I. J. FLINT]

CARISSIMI, GIACOMO, Italian composer; b. Marino, April 18, 1605; d. Rome, Jan. 12, 1674. Nothing definite is known about his early training. After having served as a singer and organist at the cathedral in Tivoli and as *maestro di cappella* at the cathedral in Assisi, he became *maestro di cappella* on Dec. 15, 1629, at the church of San Apollinare (attached to the German College) in Rome, where he remained until his death. He was also active at the Oratory of San Marcello and, in July 1656, was named *maestro di cappella del concerto di camera* at the Roman court of *Christina of Sweden. Such eminent musicians as M. A. *Charpentier, Bernhard, *Kerll, and *Colonna were his students, and the wide dissemination of his music, especially in Germany and France, won him an international reputation. Attempts were made to persuade him to work in Venice and in the Low Countries,

Autograph MS of a solo cantata "Cantabo Domino" by Giacomo Carissimi (Brit. Mus. Add. MS 37027, fol. 19r).

but Carissimi refused to leave Rome. He was influential in introducing into sacred music techniques of the *stile moderno* employed in secular music, thus hastening the demise of the *stile antico*. Very little of his liturgical music (Masses, motets, psalms, *sacrae contiones*) is available in modern editions, but the use of *concertato* devices and monody is seen in the few examples that are at hand. His contribution to the nonliturgical Latin *oratorio was of fundamental importance for that form, which he was the first to make artistically significant. (In fact *Handel borrowed whole scenes from his work.) His 16 oratorios are not only important historically, they are also excellent music.

Bibliography: F. GHISI, MusGG 2:842–845. Eitner QuellLex **2**:332–335. J. LOSCHELDER, "Neue Beiträge zu einer Biographie Giacomo Carissimis," *Archiv für Musikforschung* 5 (1940) 220–229. Buk MusB 123–126. Láng MusWC. A. C. LEWIS, Grove DMM 2:70–73. Young ChorTrad. T. CULLEY, *A Documentary History of the Liturgical Music at the German College in Rome, 1573–1674* (Doctoral diss. unpub. Harvard U. 1965). **Illustration credit:** Courtesy of the Trustees of the British Museum.

[T. CULLEY]

CARITAS CHRISTI, a secular institute of pontifical right that aims to provide the Church with laywomen who have been trained to combine the contemplative and apostolic spirit in every walk of life. It originated in France (1937), where it was encouraged by the bishop of Marseilles. In 1950 the Holy See permitted its erection as a secular institute of diocesan right; following its spread to other countries it was recognized in 1955 as of pontifical right. In 1964 it numbered more than 1,000 members throughout 37 countries of the world. The members seek to acquire a high degree of the Christian virtues, especially through prayer, penance, and the works of the apostolate. They keep their membership in the institute discreetly hidden and follow a rule that requires a vow of chastity and promises of poverty and obedience, but without detriment to their life in the world. Monthly studies on the rule, meetings with sponsors and chaplains, days of recollection, and an annual retreat are arranged for members. Their apostolate is preferably an organized one, carried on wherever they find themselves. The institute is remarkable for its emphasis on living the spirit of the Gospel, and for its close union with the hierarchy in carrying out its apostolate.

Bibliography: J. E. HALEY, *Apostolic Sanctity in the World* (Notre Dame, Ind. 1957). P. M. J. CLANCY, "A Secular Institute: Caritas Christi," CrossCrown 13 (1961) 176–185. J. M. PERRIN, *Caritas Christi: A Secular Institute* (3d ed. River Forest, Ill. 1961).

[P. M. J. CLANCY]

CARLETON, WILLIAM

Irish novelist; b. Prillisk, County Tyrone, 1794; d. Dublin, Jan. 30, 1869. He was the son of peasants; his mother was a traditional singer in the Gaelic mode, and in the Tyrone of that period Carleton had access to the tales and folklore still alive around the firesides in the Gaelic-speaking parts of Ireland. In an unfinished autobiography that is one of the best pieces of his writing, he tells of lazy golden days in the Clogher Valley, days disturbed only by the leaden echo from the "first year of liberty" (and the worst year of repression and horror)—1798. He had clerical ambitions, later perhaps comically parodied in his delightful short novel *Denis O'Shaughnessy Going to Maynooth.* Young Carleton went to Munster as a poor scholar in search of Latin, but while resting at Grehan's Inn in Granard, County Longford, he dreamed of a roaring bull and was so terrified—he does not say why—that he headed for home. It could have been a Freudian or a papal bull, but it is more likely that the young man preferred his lazy life to that of a poor scholar. Relatives who reproached him for his idle ways finally drove him from his valley. He had read Le Sage in Smollett's translation, and in the spirit of Gil Blas he set off walking to Dublin, visiting on the way both the Jesuits at Clongowes and the secular clergy at Maynooth, and picking up the original of what was to become one of his most vivid tales of bloodshed and burning in an unsettled and discontented land, *Wildgoose Lodge.*

Carleton arrived in Dublin in 1818 and stayed there until his death. He lived for a time in Hogarthian slums and even spent a night in a beggar's cellar, an experience he vividly described in his autobiographical sketch. He eked out a precarious living by teaching school and, with the improvidence that characterized him and his people, married (Jane Anderson, 1820). It is significant that she was a Protestant; that, with Catholic Emancipation only 9 years away, religious controversy in Ireland was at its most poisonous; and that 9 years after his marriage Carleton was to meet and be encouraged by that remarkable Protestant clergyman Rev. Caesar Otway (1768–1842). Otway was a scholar and antiquarian whose books *Sketches in Ireland* (1827) and *Sketches in Erris and Tyrawley* (1841) are of perennial value. He was, too, the master of a lucid, distinguished prose, but on one matter, the Church of Rome—particularly as manifest in Ireland—scholarship and lucidity deserted him, and he saw only the scarlet of Babylon; and the manifestation of the Church in Ireland that affected his eyesight most was the Lough Derg pilgrimage (*see* PATRICK, ST.). Yeats said of Otway that he "felt no reverence for the grey island consecrated by the verse of Calderon and the feet of 12 centuries of pilgrims"; and to say simply

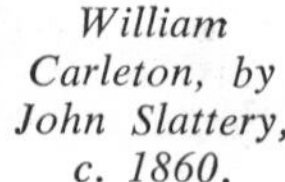

William Carleton, by John Slattery, c. 1860.

that he felt no reverence is a considerable understatement. When Otway and Carleton met, Carleton related to him that he had read *Sketches in Ireland* and agreed with much that Otway had said about Lough Derg; Carleton in his youth had made the pilgrimage. At any rate, acting on Otway's suggestion, Carleton wrote the sketch *The Lough Derg Pilgrim,* whose words still breathe and live and laugh. Otway revised and published this in his periodical, the *Christian Examiner,* and the revisions, mostly inserted diatribes against the whore of Babylon (in his view, the Church of Rome), can be readily recognized.

This was Carleton's start as a writer even if, because of the state of the country and Carleton's own impulsive nature, it placed him in an uneasy position between the faith of his fathers and the church established by law and the Protestant Ascendancy. Carleton was later to remove himself from the influence of Otway and come under the sanative influence of Thomas Davis (1814–45), cofounder of the *Nation* and leader of the Young Ireland movement, even though Carleton could never think of the revolutionary doctrine of Young Ireland as anything but a lunatic rant. But it was Otway who put him into print and set him going so that he was able, in the *Traits and Stories of the Irish Peasantry,* to preserve the life he had known in the Clogher Valley. The first series of that great work appeared in 1830 in two volumes. Shane Leslie has said of Carleton that he "caught his types before Ireland made the greatest plunge in her history and the famine had cleaned her to the bone." Those types are in *Traits;* in the major novels, *The Emigrants of Ahadarra, Fardorougha the Miser* (1839), *Valentine McClutchy* (1845); in his apocalyptic picture of the famine, *The Black Prophet* (1847); and in several other works. Lesser works, that appeal only to the specialist, are *Jane Sinclair, The Fawn of Springvale, The Double Prophecy, The Trials of the Heart,* and *Father Butler.*

Yeats as a young man had found that Carleton was "the great novelist of Ireland by right of the most Celtic eyes that ever gazed from under the brow of storyteller." The history of a nation, Yeats conceived, was to be found "not in parliaments and battlefields, but in what the people say to each other on fair-days and high days, and in how they farm and quarrel and go on pilgrimage." Carleton recorded these things, and in his longer novels Yeats found a "clay-cold melancholy" that made the author and his characters kin with the animals in Milton's *Paradise,* "half-emerged only from the earth and its brooding."

Bibliography: D. J. O'Donoghue, ed., *The Life of William Carleton,* 2 v. (London 1896). B. Kiely, *Poor Scholar* (New York 1947). **Illustration credit:** National Gallery of Ireland, Dublin.

[B. KIELY]

CARLISLE, ANCIENT SEE OF, English bishopric established by Henry I in 1133 with its seat at Carlisle, county Cumberland (Latin, *Carleolensis*). Originally the area was part of the kingdom of Strathclyde, having been Christianized by St. *Ninian and other Celtic missionaries from Glasgow. Later it was placed under the jurisdiction of the bishops of *Lindisfarne. Considerably impoverished during the Scandinavian invasions, it was then captured by King *William II (Rufus) in 1092 and placed under the archbishopric of *York. This aroused opposition from the bishops of both *Glasgow and *Durham, which may have prompted Henry I to establish Carlisle as a separate diocese. Henry's visit to Carlisle in 1122 was followed by a series of royal endowments for the priory of *canons regular, which he had founded there in 1102; in 1133 the *priory was raised to *cathedral status, the King's confessor, Aethelwulf, being consecrated as its first bishop.

The cathedral at Carlisle as seen from the southwest.

As a frontier see between England and Scotland it had a later history that was frequently turbulent, its bishops often being called upon to settle border disputes. Nevertheless, much construction work was carried on under great bishops such as John de Halton (1292–1324) and Thomas Appleby (1363–95), as their diocesan constitutions show. Among the religious orders introduced into the diocese were the Benedictines at Wetheral (1106–12) and St. Bees (1120), the Cistercians at Calder (1134) and Holmcultram (1150), another house for the canons regular of St. Augustine at Lanercost (1169), and the Premonstratensians at Preston, Kendal, *c.* 1180. As for the Mendicants, both the Franciscans and Dominicans arrived in Carlisle in 1233; the Carmelites, in Appleby in 1281; and the Augustinian friars, in Penrith by 1300. There were also six hospitals and two colleges in the diocese.

The Wars of the Roses, and later the Anglo-Scottish wars, contributed considerably to the spiritual decline of the diocese. The dissolution of its monasteries was completed with some difficulty between 1536 and 1540, but in general neither the religious nor the secular clergy offered much resistance to the ecclesiastical reforms of *Henry VIII, who refounded the see in 1541. Its present cathedral is one of the smallest in England.

Bibliography: *The Victoria History of the County of Cumberland,* ed. J. Wilson (London 1901–) v.2, basic. H. Dauphin, DHGE 11:1050–58, adds modern history of see up to 1946. J. C. Dickinson, *The Origins of the Austin Canons and Their Introduction into England* (London 1950) 245–251. Knowles-Hadcock 132. F. Powicke and E. B. Fryde, *Handbook of British Chronology* (2d ed. London 1961) 212–214. **Illustration credit:** L. Herbert Felton.

[L. MACFARLANE]

CARLOMAN, Frankish mayor of the palace; b. before 714; d. Vienne, France, Aug. 17, 754. The assembly of nobles accepted *Charles Martel's division of the Frankish kingdom between his eldest son Carloman, who received Austrasia, Alamannia, and Thuringia, and his younger son *Pepin III, who ruled in Neustria, Burgundy, and Provence, and the two brothers soon united to dispossess Grifo (d. 753), an illegitimate son of their father, of his rather meager inheritance. They then reduced revolts in Aquitaine and Bavaria and collaborated against rebellions of Aquitanians, Alans, Bavarians, and Saxons. They crowned the last Merovingian, the so-called son of Theuderich IV (d. 737), who became *Childeric III. Carloman took the initiative in supporting the reform of the Church in Gaul, which was carried out by St. *Boniface, and he established bishoprics in Würzburg, Erfurt, and Eichstätt. He arranged for reforming councils in 742 and 743 and secured metropolitan dignity for Boniface. The opposition of the nobles and the perils of war made it impossible for him to restore the church property confiscated by his father, but he gave new lands to the Church and endowed the Abbey of *Fulda for Boniface. In 747 Carloman entrusted his lands and his children to his brother Pepin and went to Rome to become a monk. He built the monastery of St. Sylvester on Mt. Soracte, but later retired to *Monte Cassino to escape the attentions of affectionate Frankish pilgrims. Later when *Aistulf, King of the *Lombards, menaced the safety of Rome, Pope *Stephen II, having asked in vain for aid from the eastern Roman Emperor *Constantine V, turned to Pepin, who had with papal support declared himself king of the Franks. To counteract this appeal, Aistulf sent Carloman (whether willing or not is unknown) to intervene in his behalf or to rouse his former subjects in opposition to Pepin's policy of papal alliance. As Monte Cassino lay in the territory of the Duke of Benevento, a vassal of the Lombard King, it is probable that Carloman was under pressure to perform this difficult mission. He was entirely unsuccessful, however, as Pepin forced him into a monastery at Vienne, where he died the next year. His sons were deprived of their inheritance and were also confined to a monastery. Carloman was buried at Monte Cassino, and he was considered a saint during the centuries immediately following his death. He is still remembered in the *Benedictine calendar on August 17.

Bibliography: MGS 1:292, 329; 7:581. Duchesne LP 1:448. PL 173:498. G. DRIOUX, DHGE 11:1058–60, with extensive bibliog. Gebhardt-Grundmann 1:125–27. T. SCHIEFFER, LexThK[2] 5: 1362–63; *Winfrid-Bonifatius und die christliche Grundlegung Europas* (Freiburg 1954); "Angelsachsen u. Franken," *Abhandlungen der Akademie der Wissenschaften und der Literatur Mainz* 20 (1950) 1431–1529. Zimmermann KalBen 2:584–586. R. MACAIGNE, *L'Église mérovingienne et l'état pontifical* (Paris 1929) 287–292. Mabillon AS 4:112–118. J. DUBOIS, *Catholicisme* 2:561–562.

[C. M. AHERNE]

CARLYLE, THOMAS

English essayist, historian, and social critic; b. Ecclefechan, Scotland, Dec. 4, 1795; d. London, England, Feb. 5, 1881. He was the eldest of nine children of James Carlyle by his second wife, Margaret Aiken. After local schooling he attended the University of Edinburgh (1809–14), where, reading Gibbon, Hume, and Voltaire, he lost the Calvinist faith of his parents and abandoned his studies for the ministry. To support himself he tutored and taught school at Annan (1814–16) and at Kirkcaldy (1816–18). For the next 16 years he struggled to find a new faith and a career suited to his special talents, inconclusively studying law and civil engineering. Carlyle met Jane Baillie Welsh in 1821, and shortly thereafter underwent a partly psychological but essentially spiritual conversion that enabled him to conquer his old doubts and fears, which in *Sartor Resartus* (1833–34) he called the "Everlasting No," and to

Thomas Carlyle, portrait by J. E. Millais.

evolve gradually a new, positive faith, his "Everlasting Yea." He married Jane Welsh in 1826.

Carlyle introduced German *transcendentalism into England by translating Goethe's *Wilhelm Meister* (1824), writing a biography of Schiller (1825), and contributing numerous articles to the *Edinburgh Review* and other journals. In 1828 he and his wife left Edinburgh to spend the next 6 years at Craigenputtock, a desolate farm in the moorlands of Dumfriesshire. There he read widely, meditated, and wrote *Sartor Resartus* and the essays on Burns, Goethe, Novalis, Richter, Schiller, Boswell, Voltaire, Diderot, and others. Emerson's visit in 1833 testifies to the growing influence of Carlyle's writings; but in 1834, unable to sell *Sartor* as a book and wanting to write a history of the French Revolution, he settled permanently in London.

The remainder of Carlyle's career falls into three periods: (1) 1834 to 1850, his initial success in London with the publication of the *French Revolution* (1837), *Chartism* (1839), *Critical and Miscellaneous Essays* (1839), *Heroes and Hero-Worship* (1841), *Past and Present* (1843), and *Cromwell* (1845); (2) 1850 to 1867, his growing anger at the materialism and false optimism of the Crystal Palace era, in *Latter-Day Pamphlets* (1850), *Frederick the Great* (1852–65), and "Shooting Niagara" (1867); and (3) 1867 to 1881, his grief following his wife's death in the same year that he had been appointed rector of Edinburgh University (1866), and despair at the course England was taking, expressed in his *Reminiscences* (1881), letters, and journals, but in no major work.

Carlyle's intuitions eventually hardened into dogma. In the early essays "Signs of the Times" (1829) and

"Characteristics" (1831), he had diagnosed his age with remarkable acuteness as mechanical and godless. *Sartor* distinguished, in an age of change, the transience of social institutions from the permanence of spiritual realities and warned that a society whose values are merely utilitarian cannot last. His *French Revolution* illuminated with lightning flashes the chaos that England faced. His prophecy of her eventual decline was given added force in *Past and Present* with its sharp contrast between the disordered present and Abbot Samson's 12th-century world. Abbot Samson, with his wise but firm rule, was the kind of hero England needed, and Carlyle's antidote to galloping democracy. *Frederick* is a heroic, if unsuccessful, attempt to prove that only a hero can bring order to the modern world; the clearest proof that Carlyle was no proto-fascist is that long before the work was completed he knew Frederick was not, in fact, a true hero.

Carlyle had divined the greatness in Cromwell, Boswell, and Burns and had exposed the causes of pauperism and the "Hungry Forties." When, finally, his intuitions failed him, it was his earlier impact on the Victorian conscience and sensibility, his profound spiritual vision of man in society, the moral force of his social teachings, and his doctrine of work that claimed the reverence of his contemporaries and exerted so strong an influence on writers like Dickens, Ruskin, Kingsley, and Arnold.

Carlyle was always an artist, even when most anxious to teach. His work is never slipshod, and at its best is a powerful rendering of thought and image into language. For his characteristic style, "Carlylese," he has been both praised and blamed. This style, at once Biblical, Germanic, and Scottish, was his most natural expression, though we may see from the graceful *Life of Sterling* (1851) that he was also master of the orthodox manner. In all his works there is a rich vein of humor, sometimes comic, often satiric, at last so bitterly ironic that both humor and meaning were often missed, as in "The Nigger Question" and "Shooting Niagara."

Bibliography: T. CARLYLE, *Works,* ed. H. D. TRAILL, 30 v. (New York 1896–1901). I. W. DYER, *A Bibliography of Thomas Carlyle's Writings and Ana* (Portland, Maine 1928). J. A. FROUDE, *Thomas Carlyle: A History of the First Forty Years of His Life, 1795–1835,* 2 v. (London 1882); *Thomas Carlyle: A History of His Life in London, 1834–1881,* 2 v. (New York 1884). J. SYMONS, *Thomas Carlyle: The Life and Times of a Prophet* (New York 1952). C. MOORE, "The Persistence of Carlyle's 'Everlasting Yea,'" ModPhilol 54 (1957) 187–197. An edition of Carlyle's letters is in preparation under the editorship of C. R. SANDERS of Duke University, Durham, N.C. **Illustration credit:** National Portrait Gallery, London.

[C. MOORE]

CARMAN, HARRY JAMES, educator and social historian; b. Greenfield, N.Y., Jan. 22, 1884; d. New York, N.Y., Dec. 26, 1964. He began his teaching career in an upstate rural schoolhouse but entered Syracuse University, N.Y., in 1905 to complete his formal education. After serving as principal of Rhinebeck High School, N.Y. (1909–13), he returned to Syracuse for his M.A. and opened a career in college teaching that continued until his death. He received his Ph.D. from Columbia University, New York City (1919), and joined its history department, which became his permanent academic home.

At Columbia he pioneered the development first of general education and then of American social history. As secretary of the American Historical Association, he launched the first drive to underwrite historical research. For 24 years beginning in 1938, he served on the New York Board of Higher Education, the governing body

Harry James Carman.

of the municipal college system. He was also active in fostering opportunities for Negro students through the National Scholarship Fund and in encouraging study abroad for American students. As chairman of the John Hay Whitney Foundation's humanities division, he developed a program to help public school teachers pursue graduate degrees. He served also on numerous Federal, state, and city labor mediation boards and fostered union educational programs and scholarships.

In 1943 he was appointed dean of Columbia College, a post he held until 1950. His gifts as a teacher supplemented his talents as an administrator. Sensitive to the difficulties of the young, generous, and compassionate, he provided not only intellectual guidance but a moral example. His Roman Catholicism always emphasized its catholicism rather than parochialism. His example attracted into the teaching profession a host of men who subsequently reveled in the label "one of Carman's boys." Throughout his life he never lost contact with the rugged earth of his native upstate New York, priding himself in remaining always a "good farmer." His first wife, Cathryne M. Barrett, whom he married in 1910, died in 1943. In 1953 he married M. Margaret Carscadden.

Among his numerous historical works were *Jesse Buel, Agricultural Reformer* (1947), *Lincoln and the Patronage* (1943), and the *Guide to Principal Sources for American Civilization* (1960–62).

Illustration credit: Columbiana Collection, Columbia University.

[J. P. SHENTON]

CARMEL, MOUNT, mountain range stretching from Haifa, Israel, southeastward for about 15 miles and reaching a height of *c.* 1,800 feet above sea level. It separates the Plain of Saron (Sharon) on the south from the Plain of Aser on the north. The lofty headland of Carmel, with its church and Carmelite monastery, juts into the Mediterranean and can be seen for miles from a ship approaching the port of Haifa. Its Hebrew name *karmel* ordinarily means orchard, but here connotes a pleasant woodland. The range, which is still heavily wooded, but now mostly with scrub growth, was noted in antiquity for its magnificent forest (Am 1.2; Is 33.9; 35.2), symbolic of a land blessed by God (Jer 50.19).

Since antiquity Carmel has been regarded as a holy mountain. In the middle of the 2d millennium B.C. the geographical lists at Karnak called Carmel "the sacred cape"; Iamblichus (*De vita Pythagorica* 3.15) wrote that it was "the most holy of all mountains and forbidden of access to many," and Tacitus (*Hist.* 2.78) related that Vespasian, after offering sacrifice at Carmel's open-air altar, received the favorable oracle that hinted he would become emperor (see also Suetonius, *Lives of the Caesars* 8.5). This sacred mountain was chosen by Elia as the site for the altar in the contest between him and the prophets of *Baal (3 Kgs 18.17–46). Tradition locates the place of Elia's sacrifice on the rocky plateau of el-Muḥraqa on the southeast flank of the range. Carmel is now known in Arabic as Jebel Mâr Elyâs (Mountain of Lord Elia).

Bibliography: EncDictBibl 324–325. AbelGéogrPal 1:350–353. D. BALY, *The Geography of the Bible* (New York 1957) 136–137. M. DU BUIT, *Géographie de la Terre Sainte* (Paris 1958) 65–66, 107. M. AVI-YONAH, "Mount Carmel and the God of Baalbek," IsrExplorJ 2 (1952) 118–124.

[C. MC GOUGH]

Carmelite friars among the faithful paying homage to St. Peter, detail of a fresco by Filippino Lippi, Brancacci Chapel, Church of the Carmine, Florence.

CARMELITE SPIRITUALITY

The characteristic spirituality of the Carmelites is marked by the imprint of its origin. It began with the spiritual revival of the Latin Church in the East after the First Crusade and grew up under the evangelical movement which was promoted by the mendicants of the 13th century.

Beginnings. James of Vitry, Bishop of Acre from 1216 to 1228, said of the early Carmelites: "Some lived a solitary life in beehive monasteries of simple rooms, like bees of the Lord bringing forth honey of spiritual sweetness. Their model was the holy and solitary man, the prophet Elia. They were located on Mount Carmel, especially on the part of the mountain that overlooks the city of Porphiry, now called Cayphas, near what is known as the fountain of Elia, not far from the monastery of the Blessed V. Margaret" [*Historia orientalis,* ch. 52, ed. J. Bongars, *Gesta Dei per Francos* (Hanover 1611) 1075].

These hermits had asked the Latin Patriarch of Jerusalem (1206–14), Albert of Vercelli, for a rule in accordance with their proposals. Its primitive form, as it is transcribed by Philip Ribot in his *Decem libri* [*Speculum ordinis* (Venice 1507) fol. 29r–30r], gives an idea of the life of the hermits of Carmel before they accepted mendicant status under Innocent IV in 1247. In the prologue to the rule the essential aim of the Carmelite is said to be: "To live for the sake of Jesus Christ and to serve him with purity of heart and good conscience." The rhythm of Carmelite life is marked by collective and individual solitude, which creates an atmosphere in which union with God is achieved through continuous prayer. Fasting, perpetual abstinence, vocal prayer, and *missarum solemnia* are additional elements. The dynamism of those primitive Carmelites flowed from the practice of the theological virtues, the vows, the chapter of faults (in which the hermit submitted himself to a social criticism of his behavior), and the "spiritual armor," a technical term used by the Crusaders to designate a complexus of the moral virtues, manual work, and silence. All these things were done under the sign of the example of the Prophet Elia and consecration to the Blessed Mother, because of which the hermits were known as "Brethren of St. Mary."

A bull of Gregory IX dated April 6, 1229, imposed on them the observance of collective poverty and mendicancy [E. Monsignani, *Bullarium carmelitanum* (Rome 1715) 1.4]. By this change they embraced the mendicant life. When they moved to Europe their form of mendicancy forced upon them the care of souls [see R. W. Emery, "The Second Council of Lyons and the Mendicant Orders" in CathHistRev, 39 (1953–54) 257–271]. This situation compelled them to seek an adaptation of their rule, and Innocent IV by the apostolic letter *Quae honorem Conditoris* of Oct. 1, 1247, introduced these significant features: (1) a common refectory and (2) choral office in common. Moreover, they were permitted (3) to establish themselves in urban areas and (4) to have their cells, which were formally distinct hermitages, all in one house. Continual prayer was still in force, although its fulfillment was more difficult [*Ephemerides Carmeliticae,* 2 (1948) 11–16]. As a result of these changes, the spirituality of the new generation combined contemplative life with apostolic activity; thus there arose the perennial problem of sustaining an effective harmony between the two. During this metamorphic process some masters general of the order, such as Randolph Freysborn (d. 1277), Raymond de Isla (*c.* 1300), and John Alerio, went off to contemplative solitude [see B. Zimmerman, *Monumenta Historica Carmelitana* (Lérins 1907) 249–251].

Characteristics. John XXII put an end to the juridical evolution of the order by the bull *Sacer ordo vester* (1317), which allowed them any type of activity: teaching, preaching, spiritual direction, and the parochial apostolate (*Bullar. Carmel.* 1.57). No later documents determine the proper apostolate of the Carmelites, except for their Marian devotion [see V. Hoppenbrouwers, *Devotio mariana in ordine fratrum B. M. V. de Monte Carmelo* (Rome 1960)]. The only thing that remained inviolable was the preeminence of contemplation, the root of all activity.

The Elian-Marian form of Carmelite life is described in the book *De institutione primorum monachorum,* which first appeared in 1370 in the *Decem libri* by Philip Ribot. Perhaps because it was considered to be the primitive rule, which was summed up in the rule written by Patriarch Albert, it came to be the principal book for spiritual reading for all Carmelites and thus stamped them with their peculiar seal. Its numerous printings and editions, also its translations (English by Thomas Bradley; French by Thomas de Lemborch; Spanish, anonymous in the Codex of Avila), all of them in the 15th century, testify to its quick spread and its influence.

According to this book two things are characteristic of the Carmelites: purification and the acquistion of the virtues, and the consequent fruition of the presence of God, which is experienced in the well-disposed soul. There are four moments in the itinerary of purification: first, the leaving of one's own country and relatives; second, the mastering of one's passions; third, the achievement of interior solitude and purity of intention; fourth, the governing of self by perfect charity. If he would reach perfection quickly, the monk cannot tolerate even a slight incidence of sin in his life but must dedicate himself completely to attaining the height of perfection. Once the peak of the pure love of God and neighbor is achieved, the Carmelite can wait for the encounter with God, which will follow without fail (ch. 2–7).

This itinerary is between the eremitic ideal and the Elian activity, all under the mantle of the Blessed Virgin. The *Vivit Deus, in cuius conspectu sto* and the *Zelo zelatus sum* (contemplation and action) will always buoy up the spirit of the Carmelite whether he is fighting against heresy, as Thomas of Walden (d. 1430), or against the abuses of the cloister, as Bl. John *Soreth and St. Teresa.

Literary Activity until 1500. The literary activity of the Carmelites during this period, though slight, maintains the parallel between action and contemplation. The German Henry of Hane (d. 1299) wrote *Paradisus animae intelligentis* [ed. P. Strauch (Berlin 1919)]. Influenced by Meister *Eckhart, he centered his spirituality upon the presence of God in the center of the soul and the soul's consequent encounter with God, The Catalonian Guido Terrena wrote against the pseudo-mysticism that invaded the south of France and Catalonia [see B. Xiberta, *Guiu Terrena* (Barcelona 1923)]. Another Catalonian, Peter Riu (1372), wrote a mystical commentary on the *Miserere.* In Italy Michael Anguani of Bologna (d. 1400) wrote commentaries on the Bible, trying to couple activity with mysticism. In England Sibert of Beka presented a call to mysticism, basing the achievement of union with God upon pure love accompanied by certain experiential knowledge of the divine goodness (*Quodlibeta,* 1.6.3, in MS Vat. Borgh. 39).

The Carmelites reacted very slowly to the movement of spiritual renewal initiated by Gerard *Groote (d. 1384) with his Devotio Moderna. Carmel was gravely affected by the general decay that followed the black death. The renovation of piety, when it came, was somewhat rationalistic in the sense that the practice of meditation point by point limited the expansion of the spirit toward comtemplation.

The reform of the contemplative life of the Carmel was particularly noticeable in the reform of Mantua [see L. Saggi, *La Congregazione mantovana dei carmelitani* (Rome 1954)]. The contemplative tradition found its authentic expression in the *Vita dei santi et romiti del Monte Carmelo,* by Nicolá Calciuri [ed. Graziano di S. Teresa, *Ephemer. Carmelit.,* 6 (1955) 241–531]. The principal figure is Bl. Bautista of Mantua (1447–1516), both a true humanist and a genuine mystic [see Adelbertus Lokkers, "Baptista Mantuanus, asceta et mysticus," AnalOCarmC 13 (1948) 193–198].

Bl. John *Soreth (d. 1471), reformer of the order, was another leading representative of Carmelite life. In his *Expositio paraenetica in regulam carmelitarum* (ed. Paris 1894) he drew the ideal of the contemplative life from the rule, which, although mitigated under Eugene IV (1432), still breathed with the contemplative spirit of the early hermits. He accepted the meditation of the Devotio Moderna, but only as a stepping stone to contemplation. In Germany Mathias Fabri followed the same line in his *Lucerna fratrum* (MS München, Bibl. Stat. Clem. 4151).

The Devotio Moderna and Meditation. The influence of the Devotio Moderna can be seen in the introduction of meditation in common, which, after the 15th century, became more and more universal. In the province of Portugal, by the year 1424, there was an assembly for prayer twice a day, morning and afternoon [cf. José Pereyra de S. Ana, *Disertatio apologetica . . . legum provinciae Lusitaniae* (Venice 1757) 112; cf. AnalOCarmC 10 (1937–40) 77]. In 1481 the practice existed among the nuns of Mantua [cf. C. Catena, *Antiquae constitutiones monialium carmelit.,* AnalOCarmC 16 (1952) 237]. In Spain, by the year 1566, the Province of Andalucía had a daily hour of mental prayer. In 1571 the visitator Pedro Fernández, OP, introduced it in Castile, though only for 15 minutes twice a day. In Aragon the practice existed in 1573. Miguel de Carranza, in 1587, ordered an hour of meditation after Matins and a half hour after Compline. In the general chapter of Cremona (1593) it was imposed upon all the provinces for half an hour twice a day, after Prime and Vespers [cf. C. Catena, "La meditazione in comune nell'Ordine carmelitano," *Carmelus* 2 (1955) 315–350].

St. Teresa. While she was in the Monastery of the Incarnation at Avila, St. Teresa was supposed to have known nothing about mental prayer in common. But the text given in support of this reveals the opposite (*Vida,* 8.7). During the reform of Carmel many hours were devoted to mental prayer. At the beginning, however, the praying was done in private. In the constitutions of the discalced friars written in 1567, 3 hours of prayer were prescribed. And one of them, at least, was to be spent "reading aloud the point to be meditated on during the mental prayer that followed" [*Bibliotheca Mist. Carm.* 6 (Burgos 1919) 400]. This norm had its influence on the rest of the order, but it was not considered necessary to give as many hours to the practice as did the discalced, who were specifically contemplative. Spiritual literature, even among the calced friars, showed signs of renewal. Miguel de Carranza wrote *Camino del cielo en siete jornadas para los siete días de la semana* (Valencia 1601). And Juan Sanz excelled as a master of contemplation [J. Pinto de Vitoria, *Vida del V. M. Fr. Juan Sanz* (Valencia 1612)].

But the success of the reform of St. Teresa was the beacon that lighted new paths for Carmelite spirituality. When she began the reform of Carmel, Aug. 24, 1567, Teresa put before her eyes the model of the holy hermits from whom the Carmel took its origin (*Way of Perfection* 20.6), even though the structure adopted was cenobitic in form in conformity with the requirements of the Council of Trent [cf. Efrén de la Madre de Dios, "El ideal de S. Teresa en la fundación de San Jose," *Carmelus* 10 (1963) 227–230]. Having been formed in the doctrine of the *Institutio primorum monachorum,* Teresa's contemplative ideal came forth from the atmosphere of solitude, silence, and prayer as demanded by the rule. In her first book, written for the instruction of her discalced nuns, she centered the whole observance around mental prayer (*Way of Perfection,* 5.2). The mystical life described in her autobiography is based on personal experiences that occur when she "commits herself" totally to God (*Vida,* 10.8). She received advice from many confessors and learned men of the secular clergy and of different religious orders. They did not change her Carmelite spirit but rather contributed to it a kind of ecclesial dimension. From that time forward it was characteristic of Teresa to feel herself a "daughter of the Church" (*Way of Perfection,* 1.5).

St. John of the Cross. When the confessors and learned men were Teresa's own friars, their voice was familiar to her and it had the sound of her own traditions and of the doctrines and teachings of the *Institutio.* They, as men, illuminated the style of life they were following with dogmatic principles, and with the light of science and of the history of spirituality they gave an ecclesial context to the Carmelite family. One of them, St. John of the Cross, was a genius. He had studied the spirituality of Carmel in the light of patrology, history, and of the Bible "to draw out the substance of contemplation," as was said by his first biographer [José de Jesús Maria, *Historia . . . del V. P. Fr. Juan de la Cruz* (Brussels 1628) 1.4.37–38].

John of the Cross was not the inventor of a new doctrine but a wise man who framed his doctrine in principles so diaphonous that their ultimate consequences are seen at a glance to follow from them. For St. John the supernatural life pivots on two hinges, the soul and God. God is like a seed infused in the depths of the soul where He dwells and whence He governs the soul and with it the whole body, so that God and the soul constitute in a sense one thing, thus making it possible to say with St. Paul: "It is no longer I that live, but Christ lives in me" (Gal 2.20). The will is in charge of this supernatural metabolism. This transforming union takes place when the will submits itself completely to God's will. And it is achieved by an absolute "negation" of everything that does not come from God. Although this is spoken of as negation, it is positive in its significance, for it is made up of acts of the love of God. The Triune God is not an abstract concept but a spiritual reality implanted in the apex of the human spirit, which, in its turn, is surrounded by many corporal crusts, "like a dwarf fan-palm," to use the metaphor of St. Teresa (*Interior Castle,* 2.8). An elaborate analysis of the characteristics of the body and of the spirit or soul, whether intellectual or sensitive, is the starting point from which the Carmelite mystic begins his elaboration of the doctrine of perfect union of the soul with God. His philosophical concepts of sanctifying grace, soul, and spirit spring from the Neoplatonic sources that, from the apostolic era until the 16th century, through Clement of Alexandria, St. Augustine, the school of Saint-Victor, and St. Bonaventure, gave modes of expression to Christian thought. The abstract concepts of Aristotelian thought would have been an obstacle rather than a help to the clear exposition of spiritual realities that are vital in the sense that they are to be lived. The first fruit of the doctrinal influence of St. John of the Cross appears in the *Interior Castle* of St. Teresa. She tells of the opportune intervention of a learned man, who was John (4th Mansions, 1.8). The detailed analysis she makes of the soul, pointing out potencies, passions, imaginations, thoughts, soul and spirit, is a superb treatise that could well bear the signature of John of the Cross [(cfr. Efrén de la Madre de Dios, *San Juan de la Cruz y el misterio de la Santisima Trinidad en la vida espiritual* (Saragossa 1947)].

Influence of St. John of the Cross in the 17th Century. The first disciples of St. John of the Cross, unaffected by scholasticism, which was to prevail afterward, follow his trinitarian schema; e.g., Joseph of Jesus and Mary (Quiroga) in his *Subida del alma a Dios . . .,* (Madrid 1656–59) and Innocent of St. Andrew in his *Teología mistica y espejo de la vida eterna* (1515), and also the nun Cecilia of the Nativity (1570–1646), who wrote *De la transformación del alma en Dios* [cf. Emeterio de Jesús Maria in *El Monte Carmelo* (1946)].

Less close to St. John of the Cross than those mentioned above, but outstanding and influential figures, were John of Jesus and Mary (Araválles), author of *Tratado de oración* (ed. Toledo 1925) who gave an idea of the formation given to the Discalced Carmelites; and the great mystic John of Jesus and Mary (family name, Sampedro; 1564–1615), important for his contribution to spiritual formation in the Italian congregation [*Opera omnia,* 3 v., ed. Ildefonso de S. Luis (Florence 1771–74)]. More eclectic and somewhat influenced by St. John of the Cross was *Thomas of Jesus (Díaz Sánchez de Avila; 1564–1627), author of numerous and profound mystical treatises, such as *De contemplatione divina libri sex.* Gracián de la Madre de Dios, although without scientific pretensions, was a most effective interpreter of Carmelite spirituality. He was devoted to the eremitical origins of Carmel and fond of the "cave" of Pastrana. To his contemplative fervor he added an indefatigable zeal in preaching and writing [*Obras selectas,* 3 v. (Burgos 1933)]. At the request of the general Enrique Silvio, he wrote on the formation of the Calced Carmelites *Della disciplina regolare . . ., dell perfettione e spirito con che si ha de osservare la regola . . ., particolarmente quella sotto la quale vive l'Ordine della gloriosa Vergine del Carmine* (Venice 1600). This work had a wide diffusion among the Italian Carmelites, partly because of the interest Silvio took in it. For many years it was a refectory reading book.

St. John of the Cross also had eminent followers outside the Discalced Carmelites, especially Miguel de la Fuente (1574–1625), who borrowed his psychological structure in *Las tres vidas del hombre: corporal, racional y espiritual* (Toledo 1623). Pablo Ezquerra (1626–96) shows himself a follower of St. John of the Cross in his *Escuela de perfección, formada de espiritual doctrina de filosofía sagrada y mística teología* (Saragossa 1675; new edition, Barcelona 1965).

Touraine Reform. While Carmelite spirituality was flourishing in Spain and Italy, there was a new and powerful revival of interest in stricter observance at Rennes in France (*see* TOURAINE REFORM). This was led by Philip Thibault (1572–1638), who avoided using the word "reform" to prevent a schism, such as had occurred in Spain. The best exponent of this mystical revival in France was the laybrother *John of Saint-Samson (1571–1636). His principal works are: *Les Contemplations sur les mysterieux effets de l'amour divin; De l'effusion de l'homme hors de Dieu, et de sa refusion en Dieu par voye mystique; La Vraye espirit du Carmel; Le Miroir et les flammes de l'amour divin; De la souverain consommation de l'âme en Dieu par amour* (*Les Oeuvres spirituelles et mystiques du divin contemplatif fr. Jean de St. Samson,* Rennes 1658). His inspiration came from classic sources—the presence of the Trinity in the soul and the human form of God in Jesus Christ. Union with God is achieved through introversion, beginning by mastering the senses, until one gets to the spiritual potencies, whose apex is God's dwelling place. The following are some of the most important writers of this current and their works: Dominic of St. Albert (1596–1634), especially for his *Théologie mystique, Traicté de l'oraison mentale,* and *Formulaire de l'oraison unitive* [cf. E. Tonna, "De doctrina spirituali Dominici a S. Alberto," *Carmelus* 2 (1964) 44–80]; Leo of St. John (1600–71), who wrote *Théologie mystique* (Paris 1654) and *L'ouverture des trois cieux de S. Paul* (Paris 1633); Peter of the Resurrection, master of novices, author of *Le manuel des religieux profez pour servir à la conduite des seminaires et études des religieux de la province de Tourraine* (4 v. Nantes 1666), *De l'amour et de la connaissance de Jésus et de Marie* (2 v. Rennes 1664), *Le gouvernement des passions* (Nantes 1662); Maur of the Child Jesus (1618–90) who wrote *L'Entrée à la divine sagesse* (Bordeaux 1652), *Théologie chrétienne et mystique* (Bordeaux 1651); and *Le Royaume intérieur de Jésus-Christ dans les âmes* (Paris 1668). But the most outstanding of all, with the exception of John of Saint-Samson, was Michael of St. Augustin (1621–84), for his *Institutionum mysticarum libri quatuor,* especially where he treats *De introductione ad vitam mysticam et fruitiva praxis eiusdem,* which explains in depth the Marian spirituality of Carmelites (ed. Antwerp 1671).

Influence of Scholasticism. Meanwhile, in the discalced Carmel, a powerful school of Carmelite mysticism scholastically structured was being shaped. Defending St. John of the Cross and crediting him with the doctrine of St. Thomas, who after the Council of Trent was the oracle of Catholic doctrine, the Discalced Carmelites built up their master's mystical doctrine with the stones of Thomism. At the same time, they formed the three great *cursus:* the *Complutensis* (University of Alcalá de Henares) in philosophy and the **Salmanticenses* (University of Salamanca) in dogmatic and moral theology. Diego de Jesús (Salamanca; 1570–1621) edited the works of St. John of the Cross with luminous *Apuntamientos* (explanatory notes) justifying his doctrine. Nicolás de Jesús María (Centurión; d. 1655) defended it also in 1631 with his *Elucidatio theologica circa aliquas phrases et propositiones theologiae mysticae, in particulari V. P. N. Joannis a Cruce.* In a more positive form the Portuguese José del Espíritu Santo (Baroso; 1609–74) wrote *Cadena mística: Enucleatio mysticae theologiae S. Dionysii, Primera parte del camino espiritual de oración y contemplación,* etc. Antonio del Espíritu Santo, also a Portuguese, wrote *Directorium mysticum,* published in 1677, 3 years after its author's death. Antonio de la Anunciación (d. 1713) wrote *Manual de padres espirituales para almas que tratan de oración* (Alcalá 1679); *Disceptatio mystica de oratione et contemplatione* (1683); and *Quodlibeta mystica* (1712). In France Philip of the Blessed Trinity published his *Summa theologiae mysticae* (1656), and Cyprian of the Nativity (1605–80), his *Traité de l'oraison mentale* (1650). Honoratus of St. Mary (1652–1729), a learned and polemic writer, defended his mystical school with *Tradition des pères et des auteurs ecclesiastiques sur la contemplation.* In Italy Balthasar of St. Catherine wrote an excellent commentary on the *Interior Castle* of St. Teresa, illuminated with the doctrine of St. Thomas: *Splendori riflessi di sapienza celeste vibrati dá gloriosi gerarchi Tommaso d'Aquino e Teresa di Gesù* (Bologna 1671). In Spain Francis of St. Thomas made a summary of Carmelite mysticism in his *Médula mística, sacada de las divinas letras, de los santos padres y de los más clásicos doctores místicos y escolásticos* (1691). But the summit of this scientific ascent was achieved by the eminent Andalucian Joseph of the Holy Spirit (1667–1736) with his *Cursus theologiae mystico-scholasticae,* which remained incomplete because of its author's death. This work put an end to the scholastic cycle of the Carmelite mysticism. At this point, mystical writing had arrived at so insipid a conceptualistic analysis that it was necessary to abandon it and look for new horizons of greater relevance.

Postscholastic Development. The possibilities facing Carmelites since the scholastic influence has run its course have been two: either to defend the past, selecting texts and writing new commentaries, or to reopen the psychological route, which had been abandoned when the second generation of discalced mystics turned toward Thomistic scholasticism. Confronted with this dilemma, the renovation of Carmelite spirituality has suffered a crisis of indecision and almost of sterility [see *El estado actual de los estudios sobre espiritualidad entre los carmelitas,* Trabajos del I Congreso de espiritualidad (Salamanca 1954; Barcelona 1957); for the Discalced, see 337–383; for the Calced, see 321–336].

The scholastic form was very helpful at the beginning, but it soon became antiquated and focused on subtleties of little value. Although the Carmelite mystical school took on this form, it was never the essence of the school's traditions. More characteristic were the advances in the field of religious psychology made by St. John of the Cross and the first leaders of the reform he initiated. Modern developments in psychology have aroused new interest in the analysis of the human spirit found in the works of these Carmelites. This trend, reflected in the *Études Carmélitaines* of the French Carmelites, has marked the route that the new generation must follow in the best service of the Church and the culture of the spirit.

Bibliography: *Acta capitulorum generalium Ordinis fratrum B. V. de Monte Carmelo,* ed. G. Wessels, 2 v. (Rome 1914–34). *Bullarium carmelitanum,* 4 v. (Rome 1715–68). *Speculum Ordinis fratrum Carmelitarum* (Venice 1507). Daniel a Virgine Maria, *Speculum carmelitanum* (Antwerp 1680). C. de Villiers, *Bibliotheca carmelitana* (Orleans 1752; Rome 1927). *Ephemerides carmeliticae* (Florence 1947–). *Carmelus: Commentarii ab Instituto Carmelitano editi* (Rome 1954–). B. Zimmerman, *Monumenta historica carmelitana,* v.1 (Lérins 1907). *Élie le prophète,* 2 v. in *Études carmélitaines* 35 (1956). V. Hoppenbrouwers, *Devotio mariana in Ordine fratrum B. V. M. de Monte Carmelo a medio saeculi XVI usque ad finem saeculi XIX* (Rome 1960). L. Saggi, *La congregazione mantovana dei Carmelitani sino alla morte del B. Battista Spagnoli* (Rome 1954). O. Steggink, *La reforma del Carmelo español* (Rome 1965). Silverio de Santa Teresa, *Historia del Carmen Descalzo,* 15 v. (Burgos 1935–52). Crisógono de Jesús Sacramento, *La escuela carmelitana* (Avila 1923). C. Janssen, *Les Origines de la réforme des Carmes en France au XVII*[e] *siècle* (La Haye 1963). A. E. Steinmann, *Carmel vivant* (Paris 1963). T. Brandsma, *Carmelite Mysticism: Historical Sketches* (Chicago 1936). K. Healy, *Methods of Prayer in the Directory of the Carmelite Reform of Touraine* (Rome 1956). H. C. Graef, *The Light and the Rainbow* (Westminster, Md. 1959) 310–352. **Illustration credit:** Photo Alinari.

[EFRÉN DE LA MADRE DE DIOS; O. STEGGINK]

CARMELITES

The Brothers of the Blessed Virgin Mary of Mount Carmel (OCarm), one of the *mendicant orders, originated on Mount *Carmel in Palestine.

Origin and Development. The earliest certain witness to the Carmelites is their rule, written by St. *Albert, Patriarch of Jerusalem, between 1206 and 1214. Since the rule indicates that the religious were then living near the fountain of Elias and governed by a prior, one can justify placing their actual coming at an earlier date. *Jacques de Vitry, Bishop of Acre in the 13th century, described the settlement of Mount Carmel by devout pilgrims and religious men after the establishment of the Latin kingdom in the 12th century. The rule of Albert, a medieval rule that has been little noticed by historians, shows the Carmelites leading an eremitical life, and practicing perpetual abstinence, fasts, and silence. In the midst of the cells stood an oratory where the religious assisted at Mass "when this can conveniently be done." Those who could read recited the psalms that "the institutions of the holy fathers and the approved custom of the Church assigned to each hour."

The hermits dwelling on Mount Carmel had a particularly keen sense of the continuity of monasticism with the way of life of Elias and of others of the Old Testament. The statement prefixed to the constitutions of 1281 may be taken to reflect the viewpoint of the primitive Carmelites: "From the time when the prophets Elias and Eliseus dwelt devoutly on Mount Carmel, holy fathers both of the old and new testament... lived praiseworthy lives in holy penitence by the fountain of Elias in a holy succession uninterruptedly maintained" (*AnalOCarmC* XV, 208).

In 1226 Honorius III approved the Carmelite rule and in 1229 Gregory IX imposed the absolute poverty of the mendicant orders. With the decline of the Latin kingdom, the Carmelites after 1238 migrated to Cyprus, Messina, and Marseilles, and Aylesford and Hulne in England. Life on Mount Carmel was totally extinguished with the fall of Acre in 1291, but the province of the Holy Land, reduced to the houses on Cyprus, continued to exist until 1570, when the Turks took the island. The Discalced Carmelites returned to Mount Carmel in the 17th century and are there today. Excavations begun in 1958 uncovered the foundations of the monastery and chapel near the fountain of Elias.

In 1247 the rule was mitigated to permit foundations in cities, and the Carmelites began to engage in the apostolate after the manner of the mendicant orders. They managed to survive the Second Council of Lyons (1274) that abolished all mendicant orders, except the Franciscans and Dominicans, but granted provisional approval to the Carmelites and Augustinians. Later (1298), Boniface VIII extended unconditional approval to the latter two. In 1326 John XXII extended the *Super cathedram* of Boniface VIII to the Carmelites, thereby making them partakers of all the privileges and exemptions of the Franciscans and Dominicans. This act completed the gradual process by which the Carmelites became mendicants. Their original striped mantle was replaced by a white one in 1287.

By the end of the 13th century the order numbered over 150 houses, divided into 12 provinces scattered through Cyprus, Sicily, England, Scotland, Ireland, France, Italy, Germany, and Spain. During the 14th century the number of houses doubled, and the provinces reached a total of 21. In the 15th century the order underwent a final phase of expansion in Scandinavia, Eastern Europe, and Portugal.

Medieval Growth and Decline. The entry of the Carmelites into the ranks of the mendicants brought with it the need for learning. The constitutions of 1281 established a *studium generale* at Paris, but only in 1309 did the Carmelites move from Charenton (outside Paris) to the left bank of the Seine to a house provided by *Philip (IV) the Fair in the Place Maubert. By 1294 houses for philosophy were established in Toulouse, Montpellier, London, and Cologne. By 1324 the *studia generalia* included also Bologna, Florence, and Avignon. Oxford and Cambridge, though never officially designated *studia generalia,* were highly regarded, and drew students from overseas. The Carmelites arrived too late in the scholastic period to establish a distinct school. Noteworthy Carmelite scholastics were: Gerard of Bologna (d. 1317); Guy Terrena of Perpignan (d. 1342); *John Baconthorp; Michele *Aiguani; and Thomas *Netter of Walden, author of the *Doctrinale antiquitatum fidei Catholicae* against the Lollards.

The original oratory on Mount Carmel had been dedicated to the Blessed Virgin, and the Carmelites made their vows to God and Our Lady. In Europe, Carmelite devotion to Mary underwent rapid development and became characteristic of the order. Everywhere the Carmelites dedicated their new churches to the Blessed Virgin and established Marian confraternities. The Marian title of the order was often defended in the early writings of the Carmelites; the constitutions of 1294 declared that the order was to be identified by the name of the Blessed Virgin.

During the Western Schism (1378–1417) the Carmelites, like other religious orders, followed pope and antipope according to regional loyalty. The general of the time, Bernard Oller, a native of Minorca and residing with his curia in Avignon, followed Clement VII. The Urbanist portion of the order elected Michele Aiguani of Bologna in 1381. Both groups abided by the Council of Pisa (1409) and adhered to Alexander V

Fig. 1. Carmelites at the Fountain of Elias on Mount Carmel in Palestine, 14th-century panel by Pietro Lorenzetti in the Pinacoteca at Siena. The hermits are shown wearing the early habit of the order.

and John XXII. In 1411 the order was unified under one general, John Grossi.

In 1432 the rule underwent a second mitigation that authorized the use of meat 3 days a week and walking in the cloisters at suitable times. The regulations for fast and abstinence were later modified still further. Today the prior general has full powers in this matter.

By the 15th century religious observance had considerably declined. Reaction to abuses produced movements of reform, Observantine groups, typical of the times. Some time before 1413 the reform of Mantua arose in northern Italy. In the Rhineland and in the Low Countries reforms originated in the convents of Mörs (1441) and Enghien (*c.* 1447). These movements achieved official status with the election of Bl. John *Soreth, who issued new constitutions in 1462, eliminating the more serious abuses. In addition, his reform prescribed the renunciation of temporal goods and privileges, observance of the common life, curtailment of outside activity, and exclusion of seculars from the monastery. The reform of Soreth was effective especially in Germany, the Low Countries, and northern France.

Another pre-Tridentine reform was inaugurated in Albi by the reforming Bishop Louis d'Amboise in 1499. Under the leadership of Louis de Lire (d. *c.* 1522) it spread to the convents of Rouen and Melun and to the *studia generalia* of Paris and Toulouse. In Italy the reformed convent of Monte Oliveto, founded at Multedo (Pegli) near Genoa in 1514, followed the rule of 1247.

During the Renaissance the order produced a number of noteworthy humanists, including the Florentine painter Fra Filippo *Lippi; John Crastone (fl. 1475), author of an early Greek lexicon and psalter; and Bl. *Baptist of Mantua, whose many poems appeared in more than 500 editions.

The Protestant Reformation wiped out the provinces of Saxony, Denmark, England, Scotland, and Ireland. The remaining provinces of Germany, the Low Countries, and France suffered much from the wars of religion. Outstanding in the defense of the Catholic faith were Paul *Helgesen, in Denmark; Eberhard *Billick, in the Archdiocese of Cologne; and Andreas Stoss (d. 1540), son of Veit Stoss, the sculptor, in the Diocese of Bamberg (Germany). At the head of the order in those parlous times was Nicholas Audet, Prior General from 1524 to 1562. Besides his labors in doctrine and discipline at the Council of Trent, Audet carried on the reform of the order, neglected since the death of Soreth. In 1524 he published newly revised constitutions.

The Reforms of the Counter Reformation. Giovanni Battista Rossi (1507–88), better known by the Spanish form of his name, Rubeo, carried on the reform of the order in the spirit of Trent. In the quickened atmosphere of the Counter Reformation, with its strongly mystical bent, the order hearkened back to its eremitical origins. St. *Teresa of Avila, during her lifetime, founded convents where the cloistered contemplative life was led, and with the help of St. *John of the Cross, inaugurated a reform among the friars. The reform group became involved in a conflict with the order over jurisdictional rights, and was censured by the general chapter of 1575. Eventually peace was restored, and in 1593 the discalced friars became a separate order (*see* CARMELITES, DISCALCED).

In France, during the 17th-century spiritual revival, a movement emphasizing the contemplative ideal began in the convent of Rennes in the province of Touraine. Under the leadership of Philippe Thibault (1572–1638) it spread throughout the province and all of France, the Low Countries, and Germany. In Italy several independent movements arose: in northern Italy, the reform of Piedmont; in Naples, the reform of Santa Maria della Vita; in Sicily, the reforms of Santa Maria della Scala del Paradiso and of Monte Santo, trends which spread also to the Papal States. Reformed convents and provinces sprang up in Poland, Brazil, Portugal, and Spain. The general chapter of 1645 amalgamated all these convents under one discipline, called the Stricter Observance, to be ruled by uniform constitutions. These constitutions (1650), basically those of Touraine, emphasized the contemplative character of Carmelite life.

The renewed religious fervor gave the order new vitality. Old convents were repopulated and restored, and many new foundations were made, among them a number of hermitages. A flourishing spiritual literature was developed by such writers as *John of Saint-Samson, Michael of St. Augustine, *Mark of the Nativity, Maur of the Child Jesus, and Michael de la *Fuente. In the other theological sciences a number of *summae* and compendia were produced. An attempt to make John Baconthorp's doctrine the official teaching of the order met with little success.

Interest in the origins of the Carmelites produced an abundant historical literature, not always of a critical nature. Juan Bautista de *Lezana wrote the official history of the order, *Annales* (4 v. Rome 1645–56). Daniel of the Virgin Mary edited early texts in his *Speculum Carmelitanum* (4 v. Antwerp 1680). The appearance of the *Acta Sanctorum,* which called into question the Carmelite claim that the prophet Elias had founded the order, was the signal for a violent debate with the *Bollandists. In 1698 Innocent XII imposed silence on both parties.

Carmelite devotion to Mary found expression in

Fig. 2. Aerial view of Aylesford Monastery, Kent, England.

numerous works by authors, such as Lezana, Matthias of St. John, Daniel of the Virgin Mary, and Andrea Mastelloni. It was principally through popular devotional works and sermons that the order spread devotion to the Blessed Virgin. The brown scapular of Our Lady of Mount Carmel became one of the most widespread Marian devotions in the Church. In Michael of St. Augustine and the Carmelite tertiary *Mary of St. Theresa Petijt, Marian devotion achieved mystical proportions.

In the period after Trent the missionary activity of the order took definite form. Although individual Carmelites labored in Spanish America (for example, Antonio *Vázquez de Espinosa), the organizing of work there was rendered impossible by the restrictions of Philip II and his successors. The province of Portugal founded a mission in Brazil (1580) from which the provinces of Bahia, Pernambuco, Rio de Janeiro, and Maranhão-Para developed. The province of Touraine founded a mission in the West Indies in 1646 that lasted until the French Revolution.

Destruction and Renewal. As in the case of other orders, the century between 1770 and 1870 was disastrous for the Carmelites. During the earlier part of this period absolutist governments suppressed convents and interfered in the internal government of the order. In 1766 the provinces of France were organized into a national order; in 1804 a similar arrangement was decreed in Spain. The French Revolution swept away the provinces in France and Belgium, while the Napoleonic hegemony led to suppression in Germany, Italy, and Spain. After 1815 absolutist and liberal governments alike continued the war on religious orders. The general chapter of the Carmelite order in 1788, on the eve of the French Revolution, was the last to be held for half a century. During the 19th century only four general chapters were convened, whereas these are normally held every 6 years.

With the relaxation of oppressive laws, the revival of the order became possible. In 1889 the province of Spain was erected. In Italy by 1909 the remnants of the order had been gathered into the provinces of Tuscany, Rome, Naples, and the commissariate of Sicily. In 1879 Straubing (Bavaria) was added to Boxmeer and Zenderen in Holland to make the province of Germany and the Netherlands. From Straubing in 1864 the present province of Chicago was founded. The province of Ireland had been reestablished as early as 1738 and in 1840 numbered seven houses. Ireland originated provinces in Australia (1881) and New York (1889). Spanish and Dutch friars helped revive the Brazilian provinces of Rio de Janeiro and Pernambuco early in this century. In 1900 the International College of St. Albert was opened in Rome. In 1904 the Prior General, Pius Mayer, issued new uniform constitutions, uniting the whole order under one observance. He also ordered the publication of a ritual (1903) and ceremonial (1906). In 1909 he inaugurated the journal for scientific studies, *Analecta Ordinis Carmelitarum.* His successor, Elias Magennis, published the present constitutions (1930).

Present Status. The order consists of 17 provinces and 5 commissariates situated in Italy, Spain, Portugal, Germany, Austria, Poland, Czechoslovakia, the Netherlands, England, Ireland, Australia, Brazil, and the U.S.

Fig. 3. Eremitical convent at Wölfnitz, Austria.

The Carmelites are also in charge of caring for the missionary dioceses of Malang (Indonesia) and Umtali (Rhodesia). Besides the prelatures of Paracatu (Brazil) and Sicuani and Chuquibamba (Peru), other developing areas are cared for in the Philippines, Puerto Rico, Venezuela, Colombia, Bolivia, Brazil, Argentina, Chile, and Peru. The order numbers about 3,000 members (1964).

It is governed by a prior general and his council, consisting of a procurator general and four assistants general. The general chapter, held every 6 years and attended by the priors provincial and their *socii,* elect the general and his council and enact general laws. Within each nation the order is divided into provinces, each governed by a prior provincial and four definitors. Individual houses or convents are governed by a local prior and his council. Priors and provincials are elected every 3 years at the provincial chapter for a maximum of two terms. The prior general and his council reside in Rome.

The *studium generale* of the order, the International College of St. Albert in Rome, affiliated with the Pontifical University of the Lateran, trains students from all the provinces for the priesthood. The Institute for Carmelite Studies, founded in 1951, publishes the review, *Carmelus,* as well as monographs on Carmelite spirituality, Mariology, and history. The eremitical convent of Wölfnitz, Austria, affords opportunity for a life of solitude, silence, and contemplation.

The Carmelite order proposes to its members the primary goal of a life of union with God through prayer. To this is added the work of the apostolate in preaching, teaching, and writing. The habit consists of a brown woolen tunic with leather belt, scapular, and hood. On certain occasions a white mantle is worn.

The Second and Third Orders. The female branches of the Carmelite second and third orders are treated elsewhere (*see* CARMELITES—SISTERS). In addition, men and women living in the world have adopted the Carmelite spiritual ideal by following the rule in accordance with their state in life. For the benefit of such persons the Carmelite Third Order was created by the bull *Dum attenta* of Sixtus IV (1476). The present rule was issued by the Prior General, Kilian Lynch, in 1948. The taking of vows by Carmelite tertiaries is optional. There is also a Carmelite *secular institute, The Leaven, which has its headquarters at Chislehurst, Kent, in England.

Bibliography: C. DE VILLIERS, *Bibliotheca carmelitana,* ed. G. WESSELS, 2 v. in 1 (Rome 1927). G. MESTERS, LexThK[2] 5:1366–72, esp. bibliog. FRANÇOIS DE SAINTE MARIE, *Les Plus vieux textes du Carmel* (2d ed. Paris 1961). A. STARING, *Der Karmelitengeneral Nicolaus Audet und die katholische Reform des 16. Jahrhunderts* (Diss. Rome 1959). P. R. MCCAFFREY, *The White Friars: An Outline of Carmelite History with Special Reference to the English-Speaking Provinces* (Dublin 1926). L. C. SHEPPARD, *The English Carmelites* (London 1943). P. W. JANSSEN, *Les Origines de la réforme des Carmes en France au XVII siècle* (La Haye 1963). G. MESTERS, *Die rheinische Karmeliterprovinz während der Gegenreformation (1600–1660)* (Speyer 1958). B. M. XIBERTA Y ROQUETA, *De scriptoribus scholasticis saeculi XIV ex ordine Carmelitarum* (Louvain 1931). T. BRANDSMA, *Carmelite Mysticism: Historical Sketches* (Englewood Cliffs, N.J. 1936). K. HEALY, *Methods of Prayer in the Carmelite Reform of Touraine* (Rome 1956). AnalOCarmD. AnalOCarmC. *Carmelus: Commentarii ab Instituto Carmelitano editi* (Rome 1954–). **Illustration credit:** Fig. 1, Photo Alinari.

[J. SMET]

CARMELITES—SISTERS

From the 13th century onward there are instances of women taking the habit and making vows according to the Carmelite Rule (*see* CARMELITES). The institution of Carmelite nuns, however, may be said to date from the bull *Cum nulla,* granted by Nicholas V, Oct. 7, 1452, during the generalate of (Bl.) John *Soreth. This bull, which gives permission to receive into the Carmelite Second Order devout women of celibate life, was obtained in connection with the founding of the monastery of Our Lady of the Angels in Florence, Italy, later rendered illustrious by St. Mary Magdalene de' *Pazzi. Carmelite nuns, who lead a strictly contemplative life, are now found in most parts of the world. Besides the cloistered nuns, at least 12 active sisterhoods, Third Order Carmelites, are affiliated with the order in the U.S., England, Italy, Spain, Portugal, Brazil, Venezuela, the West Indies, British Guiana, Puerto Rico, and the Dominican Republic.

[J. SMET]

Carmelite Nuns, Calced (OCarm). Under the title Carmelite Nuns of the Ancient Observance are included those cloistered religious who trace their origin to the middle of the 15th century, when Bl. John *Soreth organized the convents of the Carmelite Second Order, chiefly in the Low Countries. This work began on May 10, 1452, when he admitted into his order a group of *Beguines from Gelderland in the Netherlands. With the authorization provided by the bull of Nicholas V (1452), this foundation was confirmed, and other convents were established in the Low Countries and in Germany. In collaboration with Bl. *Frances d'Amboise, duchess of Brittany, Soreth introduced the nuns also into France. Other foundations were made in Italy and Spain.

From the convent established in Naples, Italy, in 1536, the calced Carmelite nuns came to the U.S. in 1930. In that year two nuns arrived in New York and founded their first convent in Allentown, Pa. Three other foundations followed in subsequent years: Wahpeton, N.Dak., in 1954; Asheville, N.C., in 1956; and Hudson, Wis., in 1963. Strictly cloistered and dedicated to the ideal of contemplation, the nuns make special supplication for priests and religious, and for all who are engaged in the work of saving souls. In order to support themselves, they make altar breads and vestments, and do needlecraft and artwork. In 1964 the four U.S. convents numbered about 40 professed nuns.

Throughout the world there were 58 convents, located in Italy, Spain, Portugal, Germany, Holland, England, Brazil, the Dominican Republic, the Philippine Islands, Indonesia, Kenya, and the U.S.

Bibliography: J. SMET et al., *Carmelus* 10 (1963) 1–312.

[P. H. OTTERSON]

Carmelite Nuns, Discalced (DC). Founded in Spain in the 16th century by St. *Teresa of Avila, the Discalced Carmelite nuns are probably the best-known of all cloistered orders of women. From the original foundation at Avila, this branch of the Carmelite reform movement spread throughout the world, and has numbered in its ranks many illustrious members.

Teresa of Avila entered the Carmelite convent of the Incarnation at Avila in 1533, but 20 years passed before she embarked on a completely generous program of spiritual living. As part of her own plan for a more dedicated life, she petitioned her superiors for permission to establish a single convent where a few nuns could follow the primitive Carmelite Rule and eliminate some of the abuses then existing at the Incarnation convent. There was much resistance and reluctance on the part of her own Carmelite superiors, the local ecclesiastical authorities, and the townspeople who feared that another convent would prove a financial burden to the area. But finally, on Aug. 24, 1562, Teresa and three other nuns occupied a small stucco building in Avila, which became known as the convent of St. Joseph. During her difficulties before, and following, the foundation at Avila, she was greatly aided by the Franciscan *Peter of Alcantara and the Dominican Pedro Ibáñez (d. 1565). Teresa originally intended to found only one convent, but her private revelations and the requests of bishops in Spain encouraged her to establish additional convents for cloistered Carmelite nuns. She spent the remainder of her life traveling through Spain organizing these convents, 15 of which she had founded by the time of her death in 1582. In 1600 there were 47 convents of Discalced Carmelite nuns.

*Anne of Jesus was the dominant personality among the nuns after Teresa's death, and it was she who established the first foundation in the Low Countries at Brussels. Bl. *Anne of St. Bartholomew is credited with having saved the city of Antwerp by her prayers during the siege of 1622. Barbe Acarie (1566–1618), a noblewoman and mother of six children, introduced the nuns into France in 1604. She herself entered one of the convents in 1614, after her husband's death. Adopting the name of Mary of the Incarnation, she died after only 4 years in the convent of Pontoise, and was beatified in 1791.

In the 18th century, the order was distinguished by Bl. Mary of the Angels, daughter of a noted Italian family, who died at the Carmel of Turin in 1717; St. *Teresa Margaret, who died at the age of 22 at the Carmel of Florence; and the 16 nuns from the Carmel of Compiègne who were guillotined during the French Revolution in 1794, and beatified by Pius X in 1906. The 19th-century Carmelite from the French province of Normandy, St. *Thérèse de Lisieux, added new luster to her order. Her memoirs, published after her death, became a best-seller in spiritual literature, and Pius XI called her the greatest saint of modern times. A contemporary of Thérèse, a young French nun from the Carmel of Dijon, Sister *Elizabeth of the Trinity, has also attracted considerable attention by her writings.

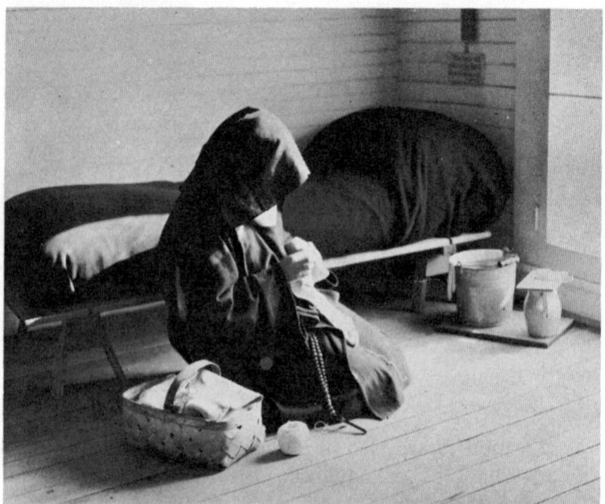

Discalced Carmelite nun at work in her cell.

The first Discalced Carmelite convent in the U.S. was founded at Port Tobacco, Md., in 1790, by a group of nuns from the Carmel of Antwerp. This was also the first foundation of female religious in the original 13 colonies. In 1830 the Port Tobacco community moved to permanent quarters in Baltimore, Md. By 1964 there were 64 convents in the U.S. The Discalced Carmelite nuns have foundations in every part of the world, and the 1961 census of the order registered 727 convents, with a total membership of more than 15,000 nuns.

The life and work of the Carmelite nun is exclusively one of prayer and penance. There is no active apostolate, since the nuns dedicate themselves to praying for the work of the Church and for the sanctification of priests. Perpetual abstinence is observed, as well as a yearly fast from September 14 until Easter. The Divine Office is recited in choir each day, and two hours are devoted daily to formal meditation. The nuns are cloistered; they speak to visitors only through a grillwork in the convent parlor. A nun remains all her life in the convent she first enters, except when she is sent to join a newly established convent.

Bibliography: W. NEVIN, *Heirs of St. Teresa of Avila* (Milwaukee 1959). ANDRÉ DE STE. MARIE, *The Order of Our Lady of Mt. Carmel* (Bruges 1913). **Illustration credit:** NCWC Picture Service.

[P. T. ROHRBACH]

Carmelite Sisters for the Aged and Infirm (OCarm). A congregation founded in 1929 by Mother M. Angeline Teresa to meet the need for modern methods of caring for the aged. The congregation, distinctively American in spirit, strives to preserve the dignity and independence of the individuals whom it serves. Mother Angeline Teresa, together with six companions who had gained experience in working with the indigent aged as Little Sisters of the Poor, began the community with the approval of Cardinal Patrick Hayes of New York. From 1929 to 1931 the sisters lived in the old rectory of St. Elizabeth's Church in New York City, where they prepared themselves spiritually and planned their new type of work. Toward the end of that period they accepted seven elderly guests and looked for larger quarters. The Catholic Charities of the Archdiocese of New York presented the religious with the down payment for the property located at 66 Van Cortlandt Park South,

Bronx, N.Y. Here the sisters maintained the motherhouse and novitiate until 1947 when they transferred the headquarters of the community to Avila-on-the-Hudson, Germantown, N.Y.

The first home, named St. Patrick's, became the prototype of the 29 that the sisters founded in subsequent years. The sisters plan each new home with a view to providing the best geriatric care for persons 65 years of age and over, without distinction as to race, color, or creed. In these establishments about 350 professed religious cared for more than 4,000 aged in 1964. Affiliated with the Carmelite Order, the sisters live a community life according to the Rule of St. Albert and their own constitutions, which received the initial approval at Rome, July 16, 1957.

[M. P. LA PORTE]

Carmelite Sisters of Charity (CaCh). A religious congregation with papal approval (1870, 1880), founded at Vich (Barcelona), Spain, in 1826 by St. Joaquina de *Vedruna, assisted by Esteban de Olot (1774–1854), a Capuchin priest. The scope of the institute, whose members assume simple perpetual vows, is education and the care of the sick. Governing the congregation is a superior general, who is elected by a general chapter and who resides in Rome, together with her council. Provincial and local superiors are appointed for 3-year terms by the superior general and council. By 1965 the congregation had spread from Spain to Italy, England, India, Argentina, Brazil, Chile, Peru, Venezuela, Cuba, Dominican Republic, Puerto Rico, and the U.S. (1955). Its 3,300 members were then working in 151 schools, 16 hospitals and 8 homes for the aged. In the U.S. there were 18 sisters teaching in two schools in the Archdiocese of San Francisco and the Diocese of Oakland.

[D. MC ELRATH]

Carmelite Sisters of Corpus Christi (OCarm). A congregation begun in 1908 when five English converts opened a school at the request of the Bishop of Leicester, England. The foundress was Clare Ellerker, later Mother Mary of the Blessed Sacrament. She remained the head and moving spirit of the community until her death in 1949.

In the beginning, Vincent *McNabb, who took an interest in their work, had formed them into Dominican Tertiaries. When the group grew to 50, they were invited to work in the British West Indies and in Duluth, Minn. (1920). They then petitioned the Holy See to become a religious congregation, but Rome refused because they were too few in number. Invited a few years later to become Carmelites, they accepted and became an active community in that order, to be known as Corpus Christi Carmelites. They have houses in North America, England, and the West Indies. In the U.S. their headquarters are at Middletown, N.Y., and the novitiate at Gloucester, Mass. The motherhouse of the congregation is in Port of Spain, Trinidad, W.I. The sisters, who numbered more than 200 in 1964, engage in varied work—homes for the aged and for children, Cana retreats, high schools and elementary schools, kindergartens, work with retarded children, and catechetical work. In 1958 the community received its final approval from Rome.

Bibliography: K. BURTON, *With God and Two Ducats* (Chicago 1958).

[K. BURTON]

Carmelite Sisters of St. Teresa. The first religious congregation for women among the Malabar Christians, founded at Koonammavoo, Kerala (India), in 1866. Cyriac Elias Chavara, priest and superior of the *Carmelites of Mary Immaculate, established the community with the collaboration of Father Leopold, OCD, an Italian missionary. Members take simple perpetual vows and wear either a brown or a white habit, scapular, and black veil. Their principal apostolate is education. The rule is modeled on that of the Italian Carmelite sisters of the third order regular, but in 1964 a new constitution was awaiting papal approval. In 1964 the original name, Carmelite Sisters of the Third Order (Syrian), was changed to the present one. The diocesan groups united in 1963 into a single papal congregation with one superior general. From the beginning the institute admitted candidates of both Latin and Malabar rites. Membership exceeded 50 by 1871. After Chavara's death (1871) Father Leopold directed the congregation until his transfer from India. The next few years were difficult until Louis Pazheparampil became director of the convents, and in 1896, vicar apostolic of Ernakulam. He strengthened the organization, provided it with a written constitution, and helped in the establishment of many convents. With the erection of the Malabar hierarchy, the congregation developed according to diocesan boundaries and made rapid progress under the native bishops. The congregation is divided into five quasi provinces (eventually to be called provinces). In 1964 the congregation had more than 3,000 sisters, 124 convents, 7 mission stations, 191 educational institutions, and 28 charitable institutions.

Bibliography: OrientCatt 755–756.

[A. M. MUNDADAN]

Carmelite Sisters of St. Thérèse of the Infant Jesus (CST). An American congregation begun in Bentley, Okla., in 1917. The founder, Agnes Cavanaugh, was born and educated in Schuylerville, N.Y. In its early years, the community worked in great poverty and hardship among the Choctaw Indians. Gradually, teaching became its most important work, and the congregation now staffs schools in Oklahoma and California. The sisters also conduct day nurseries, engage in catechetical work, and operate a home and school for mentally retarded children. In the early 1960s they entered the nursing field, and they have a foreign mission in San Carlos Sija, Guatemala. In 1964 membership was about 100 professed sisters.

[C. T. CARTER]

Carmelite Sisters of the Divine Heart of Jesus (DCJ). A pontifical congregation affiliated with the Order of Discalced Carmelites, founded in Berlin, Germany, in 1891 for the rescue of orphaned and abandoned children. The foundress, Mother Mary Teresa of St. Joseph (Anna Maria Tauscher van den Bosch), a convert from Lutheranism whose cause for beatification has been inaugurated, extended the work to Czechoslovakia, Hungary, Austria, Italy, Switzerland, and Holland. During her 8 years in the U.S. and Canada (1912–20), she established 18 St. Joseph Homes for the children of the poor and for the aged of the middle class.

In 1930 the foundress obtained final approbation from the Holy See for constitutions that correspond with the original Rule of Carmel and prescribe a life of contemplation and active reparative charity. Besides homes for children and the aged, the sisters conduct nurseries, kindergarten and day centers, and classes in religion and sewing. They also offer facilities for weekend retreats and days of recollection, and do house visiting.

In 1964 the congregation maintained 73 houses in Europe, the U.S., Canada, and Central America; the general motherhouse is in Sittard, Holland. Nine houses in Czechoslovakia and Hungary were confiscated. The sisters numbered 1,044, of whom 230 served in the U.S. in 19 establishments. There were three provincial motherhouses and novitiates located at La Mesa, Calif., and Milwaukee, Wis., for the U.S., and Erindale, Ontario, for Canada.

Bibliography: *The Servant of God, Mother Mary Teresa of St. Joseph,* tr. B. BITTLE (Pewaukee, Wis. 1953).

[M. A. ENCK]

Carmelite Sisters of the Third Order (OCDT). A congregation affiliated to the Order of Discalced Carmelites in 1920 and approved by the Holy See in 1949. The sisters are engaged in teaching, nursing, the care of the aged and orphans, conducting retreat houses, and working in missions. They were founded in Mexico in 1904 by Luisa Josefa de la Peña. During the persecution in Mexico, Mother Luisa Josefa fled to the U.S. (1927). After 1952 an American province was established in California with a novitiate for the training of sisters for work in the U.S. Their work includes conducting three grammar schools, two high schools, one general hospital, one boarding school, and one retreat house. Membership in 1964 was about 550 sisters, of whom 100 were in the U.S. The motherhouse is in Guadalajara, Mexico.

[M. I. COTA]

Congregation of Our Lady of Mt. Carmel (OCarm). A religious community of women devoted to teaching, nursing, and social service work, founded in 1825 in Tours, France, by Charles Boutelou and Mother St. Paul Bazire. Within a decade, because of persecution, the sisters were forced to disband in France. Mother Teresa Chevrel and Mother Augustine Clero, having volunteered for a foreign mission, had come to the U.S. in 1833. In 1839 Bp. Anthony *Blanc of New Orleans, La., invited them to teach in that city. Gradually other schools were established. By 1961 the sisters conducted nine schools and administered one hospital in the Archdiocese of New Orleans, and five schools in the Diocese of Lafayette, La. At the New Orleans motherhouse they also conduct Mt. Carmel Junior College for the education of their young religious. The congregation was aggregated to the Carmelite Order in 1930. In 1951 the sisters changed from the Rule of St. Augustine to that of St. Albert. They take simple perpetual vows. In 1957 the congregation became a pontifical institute, and in the following year its constitutions were revised accordingly. After 1960 applicants from the Philippine Islands were accepted, and in 1962 the first band of missionaries was assigned to the Philippines. There were nearly 200 professed religious constituting the community in 1964.

[M. E. ROMAGOSA]

CARMELITES (RITE)

Carmelites have their own rite in the sense that they celebrate the liturgy according to liturgical books that were edited on their own authority, with approval granted by the Holy See.

The Franco-Roman liturgy, brought to Jerusalem by the Crusaders (1099) and adapted to the particular needs of the Holy City, was probably imposed on the Carmelites by Albert, Patriarch of Jerusalem, when he wrote their rule (*c.* 1207). However, when the Carmelites moved to Europe and their order changed from an eremitical to a mendicant one, the new situation brought a need for uniform liturgical celebration. The Jerusalem rite was too local in character; it could hardly be followed outside the Holy City itself. In the beginning there was disagreement as to what adaptation should be made. The solution imposed by authority in 1281 and 1294 prescribed the rite of Jerusalem according to the old Ordinal, with exceptions only for whatever was universal practice. It seems that these exceptions were indicated by special rules for simplification. Very likely, the old Ordinal, together with these rules, was at the basis of the new Ordinal, which was composed by Sibertus de Beka in 1312 and was the official code for the Carmelite liturgy until 1580. A more radical solution, however, was proposed in another Ordinal, made probably in England. This Ordinal greatly reduced the local elements of the Jerusalem rite and presented a structure of the Divine Office that was both strictly canonical and clearer. Though not accepted by the order at first, except perhaps in England, this Ordinal was adopted in 1584 and has remained the basic form of the Carmelite liturgy ever since.

Sibert's Ordinal followed the Jerusalem rite rather closely but eliminated some of its characteristic elements, such as processions. While the Ordinary of the Mass was similar to that of the Dominicans, the Proper reproduced the Jerusalem rite. However, there was an important difference: from being a memorial to the Holy Land, the rite became an expression of Carmelite spirituality, especially its devotion to the Mother of God. Uniformity was difficult to maintain because of varying devotions and the influence of local customs. After several attempts to reintroduce uniformity, Carmelite service books after 1544 tended to follow the Roman rite more closely.

The General Chapter of 1580 finally decreed a radical reform, which Petrus ab Apostolis implemented by adopting the Ordinal elaborated in England in the 13th century. Historians have claimed that this Ordinal was taken over from the Dominicans. Although the Carmelite and Dominican rites are similar, there are too many differences to allow such a simple solution. Some saints proper to the Jerusalem rite, its commemoration of the Resurrection, and many of its liturgical texts have been retained in the Carmelite rite. The structure of the 1580 rite was completely different from that in Sibert's Ordinal. The 1580 reform resulted in a new and more logical Office: superfluous texts were eliminated, commemorations of the Resurrection were reduced, and a better correspondence between liturgical texts was worked out. Few changes were made in the Missal: the Italian text (unfortunately, not the best tradition) was adopted, the order of the Gospels after Trinity Sunday was changed, and the rubrics were further adapted to the Roman rite. But despite the alterations introduced, one can still speak of continuity with earlier Carmelite tradition. There was a constant endeavor on the part of the order's authorities to adopt the Roman rite as the Discalced Carmelites did, but the Congregation of Rites was opposed. Yet in 1648 the Order was obliged to observe all feasts introduced into the Roman Missal.

From the beginning of the 20th century the authority of the prior general over the liturgy of the order was recognized. Roman feasts were no longer automatically introduced. New service books were printed, one of which, the Ceremonial of 1906, eliminated all the changes made since 1580. The reform of Pius X gave the order the opportunity to return to its calendar of 1580 with but a few exceptions. Since 1956 the Carmelites have been preparing a reform in keeping with the spirit of the mid-20th-century liturgical renewal.

Bibliography: B. ZIMMERMAN, DACL 2.1:2166–74. A. A. KING, *Liturgies of the Religious Orders* (Milwaukee 1955) 235–324.

[H. SPIKKER]

CARMELITES, DISCALCED

The Order of Discalced Brothers of the Blessed Virgin Mary of Mount Carmel (OCD) sprang from the 16th-century reform inaugurated by St. *Teresa of Avila and St. *John of the Cross. The Discalced Carmelites, whose mode of life was a return to the observance of the primitive Carmelite rule, had their origin in Spain, but soon spread to Italy, the rest of Europe, and the missionary lands.

Reform Movement. Five years after Teresa of Avila had successfully launched the reform of the Carmelite nuns, she obtained permission, in 1567, from the prior general of the Carmelite friars, Giovanni Battista Rossi (1507–88), for the foundation of two monasteries of men who would follow the primitive rule. She acquired a small piece of property at Duruelo, a place equidistant between the Spanish towns of Salamanca and Avila, and there on Nov. 28, 1568, the first monastery was officially started. The original community comprised only three members: Joseph of Christ, a deacon; Anthony of Jesus, who had resigned as prior of the Carmelite monastery at Medina del Campo to become the new prior at Duruelo; and John of the Cross, then a young priest ordained only a year previously. Soon new members joined the reform in great numbers; some came from the Carmelite Order itself, while others were new recruits. Under the sponsorship of *Philip II, king of Spain, the Discalced Carmelites enjoyed an instant popularity and new monasteries were rapidly founded. By the time of Teresa's death (1582), there were 15 monasteries.

Teresa of Avila's purpose in sponsoring the reform of the Carmelite friars was to reestablish Carmelite objectives and disciplines that had become weakened over the 2 preceding centuries. The official mitigations in the rule allowed by Eugene IV in 1432, as well as the other unofficial mitigations of the pre-Tridentine era, were eliminated. Perpetual abstinence from meat and the yearly fast from September 14 to Easter were reinstated, and more time was given to the exercises of the spiritual life, particularly mental prayer. Members of the reform were originally called Contemplative Carmelites, but soon became known as Discalced Carmelites, because of their custom of wearing sandals. The older group hence came to be known, by way of contrast, as the Calced Carmelites.

Despite its rapid development, the reform movement was involved in severe difficulties at the outset. The initial permission for the reformed monasteries was granted by the prior general on the condition that the new monasteries be founded only in the province of Castile in Spain and that the whole reform movement remain within the original Carmelite Order. The discalced, however, began to found monasteries outside Castile, and there developed a desire to separate themselves from the original order. The difficulty between the calced and the discalced was based on the dual ecclesiastical jurisdiction that regulated the activities of the reform. Philip II, intensely interested in the regulation of the religious orders of Spain, had obtained from the Holy See apostolic visitators for the various orders. The visitators appointed for the Carmelites, Pedro Fernández de Recalde (d. 1580) and Francisco Vargas, both Dominicans, possessed more authority over the order than the general himself. The difficulty was compounded in 1573 when Vargas delegated his faculties to a young Discalced Carmelite priest, Jerome *Gratian. In 1574 Gratian received even wider faculties from the Apostolic Nuncio, Niccolò Ormaneto (d. 1577). In this peculiar jurisdictional arrangement, the discalced made new foundations with permission granted by Gratian. Primitive systems of communication and the uncertainty of both parties regarding the exact nature of Gratian's faculties produced a tense struggle.

At the general chapter conducted at Piacenza, Italy, in 1575, stern measures were adopted to curtail the activities of the discalced and limit them to a few monasteries in Castile. It was during the execution of these decrees that John of the Cross was apprehended by the calced friars in 1577 and imprisoned by them for 8 months in the monastery at Toledo. Ultimately, through the mediation of Philip II and the apostolic nuncio, the difficulties were settled, and the discalced were established as a separate province within the order in 1581. Finally, on Dec. 20, 1593, Clement VIII established the Discalced Carmelites as an independent religious order with their own superior general and administration.

Expansion and Subsequent History. In 1582 the discalced friars sent their first missionaries to the Congo, but the entire expedition was lost at sea. A second group suffered the same tragic consequences, but finally a third group reached the Congo successfully. The Spanish discalced, however, were not enthusiastic about the spread of the order beyond the confines of Spain. The worldwide expansion of the order thus fell to the Italian branch. Monasteries of the reform had already been founded in Genoa, Venice, and Rome, when Clement VIII in 1600 separated the three monasteries and their 30 priests from the Spanish Carmelites, thus creating two separate congregations within the reform, Spanish and Italian, a division that lasted until 1875. From the Italian group the reform spread throughout Europe in the early 17th century—to Belgium, France, Germany, Poland, Lithuania, and even to missions in England.

*Thomas of Jesus (Díaz Sánchez de Avila), whose work influenced the establishment of the Congregation for the *Propagation of the Faith, promoted missionary activity among the discalced. One of their more important mission endeavors was in Persia. In Sumatra two Discalced Carmelites, Bl. *Dionysius of the Nativity and Bl. Redemptus of the Cross, suffered martyrdom (1638). Prosper of the Holy Spirit led a small group to Palestine (1634) and reoccupied Mt. *Carmel, the ancient seat of the order, which had not been inhabited by Carmelites since their expulsion by the Saracens in 1291. The monastery newly reconstructed there was twice destroyed by the Turks in 1720 and 1821. The present monastery on Mt. Carmel, completed in 1853, houses the international school of philosophy for the order. The superior general who resides at Rome, is, according to the legislation of the order, the prior of the monastery on Mt. Carmel.

The European provinces of the order were largely destroyed during the revolutions and suppressions of the 18th and 19th centuries. The restoration of the provinces took place after the middle of the 19th century, and in 1875 Leo XIII united the Spanish and Italian congregations. A new missionary movement ultimately brought Discalced Carmelites to the Orient, South America, and the U.S. In 1907 there was founded in Rome the College of St. Teresa and St. John of the Cross, an international house of theology for members of the order; in 1957 the Institute of Spiritual Theology was established there. Three outstanding churchmen came from the ranks of the Discalced Carmelites during the 20th century: Cardinal Giuseppe Gotti, who served as prefect of the Congregation for the Propagation of the Faith under Pius X; Cardinal Raffaele C. Rossi, who was secretary of the Congregation of the Consistory; and Cardinal Adeodato Piazza, who later occupied the same post.

The first permanent foundation in the U.S. was made at Holy Hill, Wis., in 1906 by friars from the Bavarian province. In 1916 friars from the province of Catalonia founded a monastery in Washington, D.C. These two groups were united in 1940, and 7 years later the monasteries of this union were established canonically as the Province of the Immaculate Heart, which now has monasteries in the states of New York, Massachusetts, New Hampshire, Ohio, Wisconsin, and the District of Columbia. This province has missions also in the Philippine Islands, where it staffs the Diocese of Infanta on the island of Luzon. In 1915 Spanish friars exiled from Mexico established themselves in Oklahoma, and ultimately made additional foundations in Texas and Arkansas. These monasteries of the southwestern section of the U.S. were constituted as the Province of St. Therese (1947). Since 1925 friars from the Irish province have staffed four monasteries in California.

Carmelite Way of Life. The daily life of the Discalced Carmelite combines prayer and apostolic activity. The Divine Office is recited in common, and 2 hours are devoted to meditation each day, 1 in the morning and the other in the afternoon. Silence is maintained in the cloisters throughout the day, except for an hour of recreation in the afternoon and an extra hour in the evening during the summer. Perpetual abstinence is maintained, as well as the yearly 6-month fast. The friar lives in a cell, a small room containing only a simple desk and bed made of planks. Apostolic activities, such as, preaching, administration of the Sacraments, and spiritual direction, are undertaken insofar as they are considered comformable to the contemplative ideal of the order. Discalced Carmelites teach their own friars who are studying for the priesthood but do not conduct schools for lay people. The order has always considered itself the custodian of the writings and doctrine of St. John of the Cross and St. Teresa of Avila, and the 4 centuries of its existence have witnessed a large production of books and periodicals concerning spiritual theology.

One of the early institutions of the reform was the "desert," a monastery of complete eremitical life where the friars could retire for a year at a time to engage in a life of solitude and silence. The first desert was founded by Thomas of Jesus at Bolarque in Spain (1592). The deserts were destroyed during the revolutions, but a number have since been rebuilt. In 1964 there were four deserts in the order: at Roquebrune, near Nice in France; at La Reigada, in Navarre; at Las Batuecas, in Castile; and the most recent, near Florence, in Italy. Friars of any province may, with permission of the superior general, spend a year in one of these deserts. The census of the order of 1961 showed there were 361 monasteries grouped in 28 provinces. The total membership in 1964 was more than 4,000.

Bibliography: BRUNO DE JÉSUS-MARIE, *St. John of the Cross,* ed. B. ZIMMERMAN (New York 1957). E. A. PEERS, *Handbook to the Life and Times of St. Teresa and St. John of the Cross* (Westminster, Md. 1954). SILVERIO DE SANTA TERESA, *Historia del Carmen Descalzo en Espãna, Portugal y América,* 14 v. (Burgos 1935–49). JOACHIM DE L'IMMACULÉE CONCEPTION, *L'Ordre des Carmes* (Paris 1910). H. PELTIER, *Histoire du Carmel* (Paris 1958). AnalOCarmD. *Ephemerides Carmeliticae* (Rome 1947–).

[P. T. ROHRBACH]

CARMELITES OF MARY IMMACULATE,

a religious congregation (*Congregatio Fratrum Carmelitarum Beatissimae Virginis Mariae Immaculatae,* CMI) of priests and brothers of the Syro-Malabar rite, founded at Mannanam, Kerala (India), in 1831 by Thomas Palackal, Thomas Porukara, and Kuriackos Elias Chavara, three native diocesan priests. Palackal and Porukara soon died, and Chavara had to carry on the work alone. It was the first religious institute among the Malabar Catholics. Members, who are mostly clerics, take simple perpetual vows and follow a modified version of the Discalced Carmelites' rule. They wear a brown or white habit, scapular, and hood. For special functions a white mantle is worn.

The Holy See approved the first constitutions in 1885 and 1906, and a revision of them in 1958. Governing the congregation is a prior general, assisted by four councilors, all of whom are elected every 6 years. They reside at Ernakulam, India. Each provincial superior and his two councilors are chosen for 3-year terms. Father Kuriackos Elias *Chavara, who took his religious vows with 10 other priests when the institute was canonically erected (1855), ruled as superior until his death (1871). During his lifetime seven monasteries were established. The following 8 decades saw the Carmelites spread throughout Kerala. In the decade following the division (in 1953) of the congregation into three provinces in India, membership nearly doubled. In 1962 the congregation was entrusted with a mission territory in the Archdiocese of Nagpur in central India. In 1964 there were 54 houses with about 1,000 members, who directed 32 mission stations, 27 primary and secondary schools and 5 university colleges, 2 hospitals, 6 orphanages, and 17 catechetical centers. The congregation publishes three periodicals and one daily newspaper.

See also MALABAR RITE.

Bibliography: K. C. CHACKO, *Father Kuriackos Elias Chavara: Servant of God* (Mannanam, India 1959). *The Carmelite Congregation of Malabar, 1831–1931* (Trichinopoly 1931). *The Syrian Carmelite Congregation of Malabar* (Kottayam 1955). OrientCatt 609–611.

[A. M. MUNDADAN]

CARMINA BURANA, the most famous and extensive collection of medieval Latin songs and poems, in MS Clm 4660, which formerly belonged to the Benedictine Abbey of *Benediktbeuern (Raby). The MS has 112 parchment leaves (dated 13th century) containing 190 poems on many topics in Latin, Middle High German, and macaronic (i.e., mixed, Latin and Middle High German). Hilka and Schumann, editors of the critical text, distinguish two main sections in this collection: moralistic and satirical verses (Nos. 1–55) and love poetry (Nos. 56–186). The *Carmina burana* were not the earliest collection of this type. They were preceded by the Cambridge Songs (49 compositions), the love poems of the Manuscript of Ripoll, and poems found also in the British Museum MS Arundel 384 and Vatican Lat. 4389. Due to the special character, themes, and tenor of the poems, they were once ascribed to "wandering scholars" (*Vagantendichtung,* *Goliardic poetry), a romantic concept recently dispelled by Raby. He ascribes them to learned writers, some of whom lived a "rather careless life, dependent on the bounty of the great." The *Carmina burana* contain compositions of earlier date (12th century) by *Peter of Blois, *Walter of Châtillon, the *Arch-Poet, and *Philip the Chancellor of Paris. The anthology includes a few prose works and religious dramas, but consists mainly of erotic lyrics and drinking songs, as well as of satirical, political, and religious pieces. The tone varies: alongside deeply religious and moralistic poems clamoring for reforms in the Church and the Curia in Rome are some that are rather coarse and lascivious. A few among them refer to the earlier *Crusades. The German and macaronic songs are influenced by courtly love and themes of spring (*Minnesang,* troubadour lyric). They show, on the whole, highly developed poetic talent and a variety of metrical and rhythmical patterns. Classical learning, contemporary problems, and school training affected the character of many of these poems. Some of the *carmina* have been set to music by Carl Orff and Guido Turdini.

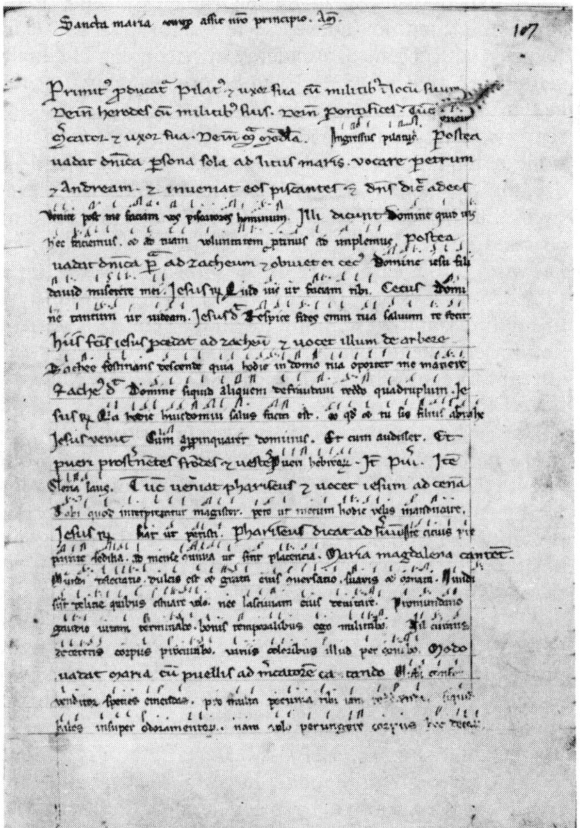

Page of the 13th-century MS of "Carmina burana," from the Abbey of Benediktbeuern (Clm 4660, fol. 107r).

Bibliography: *Carmina Burana: Lateinische und deutsche Lieder und Gedichte . . .,* ed. J. A. SCHMELLER (Stuttgart 1847), still indispensable. *Fragmenta Burana,* ed. W. MEYER (Berlin 1901). *Carmina Burana,* ed. A. HILKA and O. SCHUMANN (Heidelberg 1930–41), best critical ed. with commentaries. J. A. SYMMONDS, ed. and tr., *Wine, Woman and Song* (London 1925). H. J. WADDELL, *The Wandering Scholars* (6th ed. New York 1932; repr. Garden City, N.Y. 1955). Raby SecLP 2:256–279, 322–341. **Illustration credit:** Bayerische Staatsbibliothek, München.

[J. SZÖVÉRFFY]

CARMODY, MARTIN HENRY, attorney, Knights of Columbus executive, lecturer, and writer; b. Grand Rapids, Mich., Jan. 23, 1872; d. there, Dec. 9, 1950. He attended Valparaiso Normal College, Ind., and received degrees in philosophy and law at the University of Michigan, Ann Arbor. He was elected Deputy Supreme Knight (1909) and Supreme Knight (1927) of the *Knights of Columbus, a Catholic laymen's society of international membership. From 1927 until his death he served also as director of the Boy Activities department of the Knights. Carmody personally engaged in many of the Knights' activities, including the more than $40 million World War I Armed Forces welfare program, the extensive aid to victims of natural disasters at home and abroad, the liberal scholarship grants to Catholic schools, and the establishment of recreational facilities in Rome, Italy. Throughout his career, he lectured extensively on civic, humanitarian, and fraternal subjects, and he was a frequent contributor to the order's publication *Columbia.* He was the recipient of many honors; Pius XI made him a Knight of the Grand Cross of St. Gregory (1929) and his Secret Chamberlain (1931); France named him Chevalier, Legion of Honor, as well as Officer, French Order of Morocco (1920); and the decoration, Golden Rose of Tepeyac, was bestowed by the Mexican government (1931) for his interest in the cause of persecuted Mexican Catholics.

[J. W. SCULLY]

CARNESECCHI, PIETRO, b. Florence, Dec. 24, 1508; beheaded and burned as a heretic, Rome, Oct. 1, 1567. He was the son of a Florentine merchant and was well versed in the classics. He became the secretary of Clement VII, Cardinal Giulio de Medici. Between 1536 and 1540 he made the acquaintance of Juan de Valdés, Bernardino Ochino, and Peter Martyr Vermigli; in 1541 he was in the circle of Reginald Pole in Viterbo. The apostasy of Ochino and Vermigli in 1542 brought Carnesecchi under suspicion, but in 1546 he was acquitted of heresy for lack of evidence. He then was the guest of Catherine de Médici in France. In 1552 he was in Venice, where with D. Grimani he favored the Lutheran attitude toward the Reformation. He rejected Paul IV's demand that he appear in Rome, and was condemned for contumacy in 1558; but on the death of Paul IV, he secured an annulment of the condemnation. He remained under suspicion, however, and Pius V reopened the case. After a trial lasting a year he was condemned and executed.

Bibliography: G. K. BROWN, *Italy and the Reformation to 1550* (Oxford 1933). I. DANIELE, EncCatt 3:903. Mercati-Pelzer DE 1:524. J. LENZENWEGER, LexThK² 2:953. O. ORTOLANI, *Pietro Carnesecchi* (Florence 1963).

[E. A. CARRILLO]

CARNEY, ANDREW, merchant, philanthropist; b. Ballanagh, County Cavan, Ireland, May 12, 1794; d. Boston, Mass., April 3, 1864. He immigrated to the U.S. in 1816, and worked as a tailor in Boston. He subsequently organized the clothing firm of Carney and Sleeper, invested profitably in real estate, and became a director of the John Hancock Insurance Company. Carney devoted much of his time to Church affairs. He performed business services for Bp. John Fitzpatrick and supported the temperance work of Rev. Theobald Mathew. He also assisted John McElroy, SJ, in his efforts to found Boston College, which opened in 1864. In the field of philanthropy, Carney gave of his time as a trustee of St. Vincent's Orphan Asylum, and of his money as founder of the Carney Hospital in South Boston (1863). He donated $20,000 in matching funds to the Church of the Immaculate Conception, Boston, and came to the relief of unemployed textile workers in Lawrence, Mass. His will made provisions for several orders of sisters and for the House of the Guardian Angel, Boston.

Bibliography: J. B. CULLEN, ed. and comp., *The Story of the Irish in Boston* (Boston 1890). D. R. DUNIGAN, *A History of Boston College* (Milwaukee 1947).

[J. R. BETTS]

CARNOY, JEAN BAPTISTE, pioneer cytologist; b. Hainaut, Belgium, Jan. 22, 1836; d. Schuls, Switzerland, Sept. 6, 1899. His education included seminary training at nearby Tournai, where he was ordained. His deep interest in biology was fostered by a government postdoctoral travel fellowship and work under the masters of his time at universities in Bonn, Leipzig, Berlin, Vienna, and Rome. He returned to Belgium for pastoral work at Celles and Bauffe (1868–76), where, except for publication of one article on mushroom anatomy and physiology, he had little time for research. In 1876, however, he became permanently attached to Louvain, where he wrote *Manuel de microscopie* (1879), and established a school of cytology, perhaps the first in the world, using his own funds to equip it. Carnoy founded the periodical *La Cellule* (1884). In the same year he wrote the first (and only) segment of a projected series, *Traité de biologie cellulaire* (fasc. I, Lierre 1884). His interests and his research contributions continued in studies of the cell—the physical nature of protoplasm, types of nucleoli, cytokinesis and mitosis, giant chromosomes of Chironomus (50 years before *Drosophila*'s popularity), behavior of pronuclei, plasma membranes, and the techniques of cytopreparations (e.g., "Carnoy's fluid").

Bibliography: G. GILSON, *La Cellule* 17 (1900) i–xxiv.

[L. P. COONEN]

CARNUNTUM, ancient Celtic stronghold on the south bank of the Danube at the Pannonian (modern Austrian) border; it became a military and commercial center after the Roman conquest of Noricum (16–9 B.C.). Tiberius used it as his base of operations against Bohemia. Under Vespasian important military fortifications were constructed (A.D. 73) as part of a defense system that ran from Altenberg (Germany) to Petronell. Marcus Aurelius made Carnuntum the supply center for his campaign against the Marcomanni (172–175) and the base for his Danubian naval fleet. It was the headquarters of the XV, VII, VIII, and XIV Legions, the last being instrumental in elevating Septimius Severus as emperor in 193. Despite the efforts of Valentinian I (d. 375) it fell into decadence at the end of the 4th century. Christianity left ancient traces in monuments and archeological ruins, primarily a baptistery, and votive tablets, rings, terra-cotta lamps, and medallions with inscriptions such as *in Deo vivas.* A 4th-century bishop is attested by a bronze votive plaque (now in the Lateran Museum) found in Rome near the Sistine Bridge; the plaque bears an inscription recording gifts to a Roman church from the *gens Carnuntum* made by *Mandronius venerando nomine.* In the monogram of Christ, the style and paleography indicate its 4th-century origin. Modern excavations have revealed the site of the military camp, two amphitheaters, baths, and a civic center.

Bibliography: E. JOSI, EncCatt 3:907. H. LECLERCQ, DACL 13.1:1053. E. SWOBODA, *Carnuntum* (3d ed. Graz 1958). F. MILTNER, *Das zweite Amphitheater von Carnuntum* (3d ed. Vienna 1935). W. HEYDENDORFF, *Carnuntum: Geschichte und Probleme* (Vienna 1947).

[G. ORLANDI]

CARO, JOSEPH BEN EPHRAIM

Talmudic authority and codifier of Jewish law; b. Spain, 1488; d. Safed, Palestine, 1575. His family, after being exiled from Spain by the 1492 expulsion of the Jews, migrated to Turkey, where, for a time, Caro headed the Rabbinical Academy in Nicopolis. He finally settled in Safed in 1536. Even before his arrival at this center of Cabalistic activity (*see* CABALA), he was already strongly influenced by Jewish mystical speculation. A tendency to martyrdom and asceticism and his dreams in which his Maggid (spiritual mentor), believed by him to be the Mishnah personified, appeared and instructed him were major obsessions of his life. Although he was a strong supporter of the efforts of Jacob Berab (*c.* 1475–1546) to reinstitute the Semikhah (traditional ordination) and was among the first to enjoy its revival, he himself succumbed to the opposition created by this attempt to centralize Rabbinical authority after he conferred the honor on one disciple.

Caro's best-known work is his code of Jewish law, the *Shulḥan 'Arukh* (Prepared Table), published in 1564–65, an abridgement of an earlier massive undertaking, the *Beth Yoseph* (1550–59). While the former presents the simple statement of the law without exposition, the latter is a thorough analysis and critique of the Talmudic and post-Talmudic sources that serve to provide an authoritative basis for his conclusions. Intended to establish standards of legal interpretation and procedure in order to obviate the chaotic multiauthority method then prevalent, the *Beth Yoseph* was originally conceived as a commentary to the *Arba'ah Ṭurim* of Jacob ben Asher (*c.* 1270–*c.* 1343), retaining its outline but surpassing the model in comprehensiveness and decisiveness. Although he often tended to impose his own opinion in areas of dispute, he relied mainly on Alfasi (1013–1103), *Maimonides, and Asher ben

Yeḥiel (*c.* 1250–1327) as his standards, deciding the law in accordance with any two of the three in agreement. While these three were representative of the Ashkenazic (Franco-German-Polish) and Sephardic (Spanish-Near Eastern) currents in Jewish religious practice, the frequent agreement of Alfasi and Maimonides tended to favor the Sephardim. Much Ashkenazic opposition to Caro's code centered in the concern of the Askenazim for the priority of local custom, a matter ignored by him. But, unlike their rejection of Maimonides's *Mishneh Torah* for its failure to cite the sources of its decisions, his achievement gradually gained acceptance for its success in this regard. However, approval was assured only after the rules of the *Shulḥan 'Arukh* were interpolated with the comments of Rabbi Moses Isserles (*c.* 1525–72) of Poland, who vigorously upheld the authority of Ashkenazic practice.

Among Caro's other works are *Maggid Mesharim* (uncertainly ascribed to him), an account of his discussions with the personified Mishnah; *Keseph Mishnah,* a commentary on Maimonides's code defending the author's compilation; *Bedek ha-Bayit,* a supplement to the *Beth Yoseph* and a rejoinder to its critics; and *Kelale ha-Talmud,* a methodology of the *Talmud.

Bibliography: JewishEnc 3:583–588. S. GANZFRIED, *Code of Jewish Law (Kitzur Schulchan Aruch): A Compilation of Jewish Laws and Customs,* tr. H. E. GOLDIN (New York 1928), tr. of an abridgment of the *Shulhan 'Arukh.* H. L. GORDON, *The Maggid of Caro* (New York 1949). R. WERBLOWSKY, *Joseph Karo: Lawyer and Mystic* (New York 1962).

[R. KRINSKY]

CARO, MIGUEL ANTONIO, Colombian politician, jurist, orator, critic, philologist, and poet; b. Bogotá, 1843; d. there, 1909. He received his first education at home, then under the English humanist Samuel Bond and the Jesuits. He never attended a university, although he received honorary degrees from Chile and Mexico. He felt obliged to act in militant politics as an ideological agitator, legislator, magistrate, and party and government leader. He founded and edited *El Tradicionalista* and collaborated on various other periodicals. A convinced Catholic, he loved unity and order, and brilliantly and valiantly defended the rights of the Church, its doctrines, its practices, and its aspirations.

Miguel Antonio Caro.

With Rafael Núñez he undertook the social regeneration of Colombia, and he was the main author of the Constitution of 1886. As vice president, he governed from 1892 to 1896 because of the voluntary absence of President Núñez. He was the head of the Nationalist party, composed of moderate elements from the Liberal and Conservative parties. A man of high culture, he continued the humanistic tradition of Andrés *Bello, and he can be compared only to his friend Marcelino *Menéndez y Pelayo. He was a translator of Latin, English, French, and Italian poets and was the best translator of Vergil into Spanish. His own poetry, mystical and patriotic, was distinguished for its simplicity, beauty of form, and a certain serene melancholy. With the philologist Rufino José Cuervo he prepared an admirable Latin grammar. His best philological works were his *Tratado del Participio* and *Del uso en sus relaciones con el lenguaje.* As a speaker he excelled in dialectics, correctness of style, vigor of reasoning, and the devastating use of irony and sarcasm. He wrote philosophical and legal works and challenged utilitarianism in his *Estudio sobre el utilitarismo* and other essays. He refuted relativism in logic and ethics with arguments that were later developed by Husserl, Scheler, and Hartmann. In law he rejected pure formalism and defended the moral content of the law. If his work as a political leader has been criticized, his scholarly work has been neither disputed nor surpassed. His complete works have been published in many volumes in a number of official and private editions in Bogotá.

Bibliography: M. A. BONILLA, *Caro y su obra* (Bogotá 1947). L. LÓPEZ DE MESA, *Miguel Antonio Caro y Rufino José Cuervo* (Bogotá 1944).

[R. GÓMEZ HOYOS]

CARO RODRÍGUEZ, JOSÉ MARÍA

Cardinal, archbishop of Santiago de Chile, supporter of social reform and social action; b. San Antonio de Petrel, Province of Colchagua, 1866; d. Santiago, 1958. Born of poor but cultured parents, Caro Rodríguez was educated at home and in the public school. At 15 he entered the seminary of Santiago in the St. Peter Damian section for poor students. He was sent to Rome to study theology, and he received the doctorate and was ordained in 1890. There he contracted tuberculosis, from which he suffered throughout his life. From 1891 to 1911 he was professor of grammar, Greek, Hebrew, philosophy, and dogmatic theology at the seminary of Santiago. He was appointed apostolic vicar of Tarapacá in 1911 and titular bishop of Milas the next year.

Iquique, the city where the bishop resided, had an antireligious atmosphere, and he was attacked in the press and from the lecture platform. To teach and defend the faith he published a weekly news sheet, *La Luz,* which was distributed free of charge. To counteract the general atmosphere, he sponsored a series of public ceremonies: a celebration in honor of Constantine's Edict of Toleration, a Palm Sunday procession (during the course of which 300 men attacked the faithful, who defended themselves with blessed palms), and a Corpus Christi procession (for which he placed on trucks the altars he was not permitted to erect in the streets). His energetic spirit reassured the Catholics, and their numbers increased. On his pastoral visits he toured small towns in the high plateaus and deserts of the interior, traveling by truck, horse, or mule. In each town he walked about among the faithful and taught catechism to the children. He was welcomed here more cordially. He and his clergy were as poor as the people, and he defended the position of the workers in the disputes at the saltpeter works.

In 1925 he was transferred to La Serena. He continued his work as religious propagandist, catechist, and missionary. Again he was in an area indifferent to religion, and the Freemasons attacked him harshly; he replied with his polemical book, *Misterio*. The poverty of the prelate and the clergy was aggravated by a fire at the episcopal residence in which everything, including his library, was lost. One Catholic school had to close because of lack of funds. Caro Rodríguez continued his visitations of the interior and fostered piety by holding Eucharistic congresses. On his visitations his first stops were the hospitals and the jails; throughout his life he visited patients in the hospitals daily. In 1939 the Diocese of La Serena was elevated to an archbishopric, but that year he was transferred to Santiago as archbishop.

In Santiago he was faced with new problems in the needs of a growing urban population. He established 67 parishes, most of them within the city. To solve the problem of vocations, he fostered the recruitment of clerical students; built a new seminary in Apoquindo; sought the collaboration of male religious orders, who worked in the schools and parishes; and increased by 25 the number of religious congregations for women dedicated to teaching and charitable works. He continued the work of the Sacred Heart, Marian, and Eucharistic congresses, opened the votive shrine of Maipú (dedicated to the Virgin del Carmen), and presided at the first Chilean Provincial Council. His deep concern with social problems led him to originate or support Christian Social Aid, the Institute of Rural Education, the ASICH (an association of Catholic labor unions), Young Catholic Workers, and the USEC (Union of Catholic Employers). He was very interested in modern methods of communication applied to the apostleship and founded Radio Chilena and the newspaper *Luz y Amor*. He was made a cardinal in 1945.

Caro Rodríguez, a holy, humble, and simple man, was very popular, especially among the poor. He devoted his strong will and active intelligence to searching for, and carrying out personally, new methods for the apostleship. A prolific writer, he published 33 books and pamphlets of Catholic propaganda, instruction, and apologetics, written for the general reader. He produced a great deal for the newspaper and sent out a number of pastoral letters. His works were published in inexpensive editions so they could be given out generously. At his death about 400,000 copies of his works were in circulation.

Bibliography: J. VANHERK MORIS, *Monseñor José María Caro: Apóstol de Tarapacá* (Santiago de Chile 1963).

[W. HANISCH]

CAROCCI, HORACIO, Jesuit missionary and linguist; b. Florence, Italy, 1579; d. Tepotzotlán, Mexico, July 14, 1662. Having entered the Society of Jesus on Oct. 23, 1601, he was sent to Mexico in 1605. He was ordained in 1608 and after tertianship was sent to Tepotzotlán, where the society maintained a school for the natives who spoke only Mazahua (Mazagua), Nahuatl, or Otomí. Carocci became a specialist in Otomí. In 1625 a report sent by Diego de Torres to Jerónimo Díez, the provincial procurator appointed to Rome and Madrid, noted that the priests sent to Tepotzotlán to study Otomí learned only to hear confessions, poorly at that, for they did not wish to become proficient in the language for fear of being stationed permanently among the natives; only Carocci knew Otomí well. Torres requested that Carocci be allowed 100 pesos annually to pay the Indians who helped with the linguistic labors of preparing a grammar and vocabulary of Otomí. Carocci prepared also a grammar and vocabulary of Nahuatl, published in 1645, and he was familiar with Mazahua. He was rector of the major seminary from 1649 to 1653 and then rector of the school and novitiate in Tepotzotlán until his death. The Jesuit historian Francisco Javier *Alegre felt that Carocci's brilliant qualities, enhanced by humility and a zeal for souls, were stifled in the loneliness of an inhospitable village and sacrificed to his relations with the ungrateful Otomí.

Bibliography: F. J. ALEGRE, *Historia de la provincia de la Compañía de Jesús de Nueva España,* ed. E. J. BURRUS and F. ZUBILLAGA, 4 v. (new ed. Rome 1956–60). A. M. GARIBAY KINTANA, *Historia de la literatura náhuatl,* 2 v. (Mexico City 1953–54).

[F. ZUBILLAGA]

CAROL

There are almost as many definitions of the word as there are collections of carols or books about them: "a carol is a song of joy accompanying a dance" (Julian's *Dictionary*); "a hymn of praise, especially such as is sung at Christmas" (EncBrit); "songs with a religious impulse that are simple, hilarious, popular, and modern" (*Oxford Book of Carols*). It is a relief to find that from *c.* 1300 until the Reformation, at least, the word carol bore a definite and accepted meaning: in his now standard work, *The Early English Carols* (Oxford 1935), R. L. Greene defined it as a poem "intended, or at least suitable for singing, made up of uniform stanzas, and provided with a burden [that is, an external refrain], which begins the piece and is to be repeated after each stanza."

Essentially English Character. The carol, although associated with the medieval French *carole,* is essentially English, the English representative of a family of European poetic and musical *formes fixes,* such as the *rondeau, ballade,* and *virelai.* The closest analogy to the carol on the Continent is the 13th-century *lauda spirituale* of Italy (*see* JACOPONE DA TODI). Both carol and *lauda* manifest the homely didacticism and devotional fervor of vernacular religion, such as the Franciscans propagated; both are by origin popular songs for alternating chorus and solo singer, but they later undergo sophisticated musical treatment; both are probably to be associated with popular litanies and processions and give special honor to the Blessed Virgin, the Holy Family, and the saints of Christmas week. Whether the development of the carol owes most to this association (Sahlin derives "carol" ultimately from "kyrie eleison") or to the "godlification" of courtly or pagan round dances (Greene) is still a matter for scholarly dispute. About 500 English medieval carol texts survive, some of them in several versions; more than 100 of these have musical settings, ranging from simple melodies to elabo-

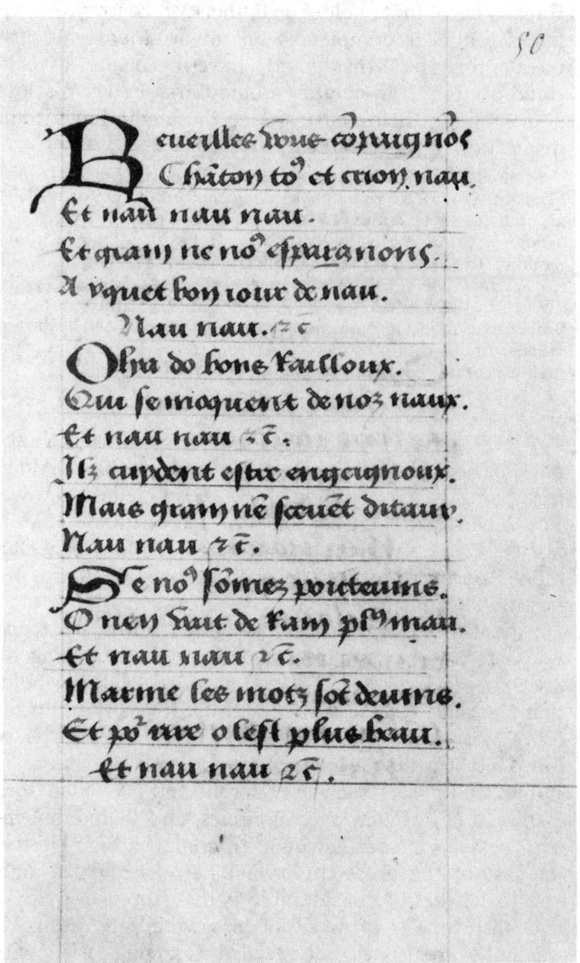

A portion of one of the oldest known French "carols" in a manuscript of c. 1483 (Bibl. de l'Arsenal MS 3653).

rate polyphonic settings in the late 15th and early 16th centuries.

There is little connection between the medieval carol and the folk ballad (the Corpus Christi carol is an exception), though a background of folk custom can often be sensed (the traditional strife between the Holly and the Ivy, for example). Nor, musically speaking, do medieval carol settings derive from folk song; their idiom is related to that of the *conductus,* one of the simpler styles of medieval art music. The carol tradition, in words and music, is a *written* one. Finally, despite the frequent occurrence of the word "nowell" as an exclamation of joy in the carol, the English medieval carol has no traceable links with the French *noël.* Although the *noël* is, like the carol, essentially a popular religious song drawing imaginative strength from the same world —apocryphal legend, the lives of the saints, the best-loved Latin hymns, the miracle and mystery plays—its vogue begins later, at the end of the 15th century, and continues for a long time after the Reformation. Most importantly, the *noël* was never a *forme fixe* as the English medieval carol was.

Disfavor during the Reformation. At the time of the Reformation the carol fell into disfavor, chiefly because it was associated with the "papist" and "superstitious" practices of "unreformed Catholicism." If the latest medieval carols were often processional songs sung in honor of the saints of Christmas, then the decline in the popularity of the carol is not surprising. Nor is it surprising to find that the nearest literary equivalents to the medieval carol survive in collections of Recusant poetry, where the spirit of the old faith is dominant (*see* RECUSANT LITERATURE). The carol lost much of its vitality with the gradual changes in religious temper and outlook. Nevertheless it continued to develop. Related to the elaborate polyphonic carols of the early Tudor period are William *Byrd's two consort songs in carol form, "Lullaby, my sweet little baby" and "An earthly tree." As a popular religious song the carol was replaced to some extent by the metrical psalm, especially in the version of Thomas Sternhold (d. 1549) and John Hopkins (d. 1570). But some Christmas themes found their way into the broadside ballads, cheaply printed and hawked about the streets to be sung to popular tunes of the day. The purely jovial and festive side, often present in the medieval carol (The Boar's Head carols; "Goday my lord, Sir Christemasse"; etc.), is now usually predominant ("drawe hogsheads drye / Let flagons flye / Make fires nose high"). But printed collections of the 17th century also contain crude, maudlin, and verbose carols of the saints (e.g., "A Carrol for St. Stephen's Day," to the tune of "Where is my true love"). These carols are in the familiar, jog-trot meters of the broadside ballad; the traditional form of burden and verse is seldom or never found.

During the 18th century the carol eked out a precarious existence as a broadside, possibly becoming more and more provincial and unfashionable, even as a type of popular song. As an art song it continued the lines established earlier by such songs as Henry Lawes's "'Tis Christmas now, 'tis Christmas now / When Cato's self would laugh" (in a tuneful contemporary style) and his pastoral verse anthem, "Hark, shepherd swains." Characteristic Augustan collections contain triumphal Christmas anthems (e.g., *A Collection of Psalms and Hymns for the Use of Bedford Chapel,* 1791) and elegant solo arias (e.g., J. F. Lampe's *Hymns on the Great Festivals,* 1746). Both these collections contain settings of Christmas hymns by the brothers Wesley (*see* WESLEY, CHARLES AND JOHN). This was appropriate and right, but it does not make these fine hymns into carols in the true sense of the word.

Revival in the 19th Century. The 19th century rediscovered the carol and its meaning. The modern habit of forming collections of carols seems to date from Davies Gilbert's *Some Antient Christmas Carols, with the Tunes to which They Were Formerly Sung in the West of England* (1822). He looked upon carol singing as a thing of the past and attempted, as a good antiquarian, to rescue the traditional songs from oblivion. Among his carols were "Whilst Shepherds Watched" (originally published in a supplement to Tate and Brady's psalms) and "The Lord at first did Adam make." Gilbert's work was supplemented by W. Sandys' *Christmas Carols, Ancient and Modern,* (1833): "Hark, the herald angels," "God rest you merry," "The first Nowell," etc. Not all early editors were in love with the traditional broadside carol. The editor of *Christmas Carols or Sacred Songs* (1833) intended his carols, "breathing proper sentiments of piety," to "supersede the rude strains which are current throughout the country"; in fact they breathed Gothic poeticisms and superseded nothing.

Christmas ca-
rolles newely Inprynted.

Inprynted at London in the Powl-
try by Rycharde Kele, dwellyng at the
longe shop vnder saynt Myldres
chyrche,

Title page of Richard Kele's "Christmas Carolles Newely Imprinted," a collection published in London (1550).

It was in stark reaction to this "sentimental" and pietistic view of the carol that Edmund Sedding published his *Collection of Antient Christmas Carols* (1860). For him carols were part of Catholic truth and Catholic worship, and in him we see the connection between the carol revival and the *Oxford Movement. One of his translators was J. M. Neale (1818–66), a great hymnwriter, translator, and a leading figure in the liturgical revival that followed the Oxford Movement. With a friend he had already produced two now famous carol collections: *Carols for Christmas-Tide, Set to Ancient Melodies by the Revd. T. Helmore . . . ; the Words, Principally in Imitation of the Original, by the Revd. J. M. Neale* (1853) and a similar *Carols for Easter-Tide.* In these books are summed up two great characteristics of the revival—the debt to the past and the rich Swedish collection of the late 16th century, *Piae Cantiones* (1582). It was to a Latin springtime carol from this book, "Tempus adest floridum," that Neale wrote the words of "Good King Wenceslas."

Folk songs and broadside balladry, Protestant piety, Gothic taste, doctrinal hymns and foreign carols, ancient Latin song, antiquarian scholarship, and the revival of catholic worship have all found a place in the revival of the carol that began about mid-19th century and is still vigorous. The paradox of it all is that the music of the English carol in its golden age, the 15th century, has remained almost completely unknown. Medieval carol poems, on the other hand, have been the favorite stand-by for 20th-century composers. Peter Warlock and Benjamin Britten are among those who have found inspiration in this rich field.

Bibliography: R. L. Greene, ed., *The Early English Carols* (Oxford 1935); *A Selection of English Carols* (Oxford 1962), an indispensable suppl. to the earlier book. J. Stevens, ed., *Medieval Carols* (Musica Britannica, 4; 1952), a "musical companion" to Greene's literary collections. M. R. Sahlin, *Étude sur la carole médiévale* (Uppsala 1940). P. Dearmer et al., eds., *The Oxford Book of Carols* (New York 1928), the most comprehensive modern collection, but not scholarly. **Illustration credits:** Fig. 1, Bibliothèque de l'Arsenal, Paris. Fig. 2, The Huntington Library, San Marino, Calif.

[J. E. STEVENS]

CAROLAN, TURLOUGH, Irish musician and poet; b. near Nobber, County Meath, *c.* 1670; d. Alderford, County Roscommon, 1738. His Gaelic name was Toirdhealbhach Ó Cearbhalláin. He became blind in his teens and, through the patronage of Mary MacDermott Roe of Alderford, learned to play the harp, the traditional and most respected instrument of the time. He spent the rest of his life traveling from one patron's house to another, singing, playing, and composing his own poems and music. A well-founded tradition holds that Carolan was acquainted with Dean Swift and often played for him in Dublin. Perhaps through visits of this kind, Carolan became familiar with the music of Italian composers such as *Corelli and *Vivaldi, then fashionable in Dublin social circles, and their influence is to be seen in some of his own compositions. He was the last of the great traditional harpers and the only one to leave any considerable body—about 200 songs and harp tunes—of music of his own composition. He was not a great poet, but excelled as a song writer with a great gift of melody. A collection of his works was printed (Dublin 1721), but only one imperfect copy is extant. His son published another collection in 1748, but all copies seem to have perished. Examples of Carolan's music are to be found in collections of Irish music published since 1726.

Bibliography: D. O'Sullivan, *Carolan: The Life, Times and Music of an Irish Harper,* 2 v. (London 1958) includes a full edition of the music. T. Carolan, *Amhráin Chearbhalláin: The Poems of Carolan,* ed. T. O Máille (Irish Text Society 17; London 1916); no translation of the poems is provided, but the introduction and notes are in English.

[G. S. MAC EOIN]

CAROLINE AND MARSHALL ISLANDS, a vicariate apostolic, erected July 4, 1946, embracing that part of Micronesia in *Oceania extending from about the international date line to 131° east longitude, and from the equator to 12° north latitude. It covers about 2 million square miles of ocean and has a land area of 516 square miles, consisting of about 2,000 small islands, of which 89 are inhabited. Politically, after having been under Spanish, German, and Japanese sovereignty successively, the islands are a trust territory under the United Nations. The U.S., as trustee, governs through the Department of the Interior with an appointive High Commissioner as executive officer. The people are of Malay origin, and have no elaborate or highly developed culture. There are six languages spoken, of considerable diversity, but all Malay-Indonesian basically.

In 1963 the total population was 74,715. Catholics numbered 30,370; Protestants (Congregationalists, Lutherans, Adventists), 39,128; pagans (animists), 5,215. Missionary work was confided to *Jesuits from the Buffalo, N.Y., province, with 25 Jesuit priests (3 being Spanish), and 10 brothers (4 being Spanish). One Jesuit priest is Micronesian. The first native secular priest was ordained in February 1964. There were also 2 congregations of sisters; 36 Mercedarian Missionaries of Berriz (16 Spanish, 20 Micronesian); and 13 Maryknoll sisters, working chiefly in elementary schools and catechetical centers. There were 16 elementary schools, with 3,339 pupils, and 1 high school for boys from all the districts on Truk with 96 students (1963).

After some abortive attempts by Spanish Jesuits in the 18th century, evangelization began with the arrival of Spanish Capuchins in the Carolines (1886), and of Missionaries of the Sacred Heart in the Marshalls (1892). At first there were two vicariates. The vicariate of the Carolines, erected Dec. 11, 1905, which was later extended to include all the Mariana Islands except Guam (March 1, 1911), and entrusted to the Capuchins. The vicariate of the Marshalls was erected Sept. 20, 1905, and was committed to the Missionaries of the Sacred Heart. After World War I, when Japan occupied all Micronesia except Guam, German missionaries were expelled. In 1921 Spanish Jesuits were admitted, and the vicariate of the Marianas, Carolines, and Marshalls was erected on May 4, 1923. After World War II, the Marianas were transferred to the vicariate apostolic of *Guam, and the vicariate of the Caroline and Marshall Islands was formed. Thomas J. Feeney, SJ, the first vicar apostolic, was consecrated bishop Sept. 8, 1951. He was succeeded by Vincent I. Kennally, SJ, who was consecrated bishop March 25, 1957. The episcopal residence is on Truk. (For map *see* OCEANIA.)

Bibliography: Latourette v.5. AnnPont (1964) 744.

[V. I. KENNALLY]

CAROLINE DIVINES

A term applied to a succession of theological writers, mostly of the 17th century, a good number of them under Charles I; they maintained that Catholicity, Biblical but non-Roman, rather than Puritan Protestantism was the chief feature of the Reformed Church of England in its organization and government (episcopal and not presbyterian), and in its ritual and theology, particularly on the Eucharist.

Such ideas as these emerged during the reign of James I and became prominent under Charles I. The pioneers were Richard *Hooker (1553–1600); Thomas Bilson (1547–1616), Bishop of Winchester, who declared that the Anglican disagreement with Rome on Holy Communion was not concerning the fact but only the manner of Christ's Presence; Lancelot *Andrewes (1555–1626); and John Overall (1560–1619), Bishop of Norwich, who pointed out that his church no longer spoke of the bread and wine as "creatures" after the consecration.

Principal Early Divines. Their terminology recalled the old traditional Catholic theology rather than the new Protestant theology. Chief among them were:

Christopher Sutton (1565–1629) of Westminster, author of the devotional works, *Dise Vivere* and *Godly Meditations upon the Most Holy Sacrament.*

William *Laud (1573–1645), Archbishop of Canterbury, most prominent of the divines.

Richard Montague (1577–1641), Bishop of Chichester, historian of Christian origins from which he tried to show that the Anglican position derived. He said his aim was "to stand in the gapp against puritanism and popery." He wrote on the Eucharistic Sacrifice.

Gregorio *Panzani, papal agent at the court of Charles I, reported to Rome that Montague admitted the authority of the Pope, and accepted the body of Catholic dogmas except transubstantiation. He suggested a conference in France to bring about reunion, which he thought would be easy.

Thomas Jackson (1579–1640), president of Corpus Christi College, Oxford, and Dean of Peterborough, moved from a Puritan to a Catholic position through his studies, which produced 12 books of *Commentaries on the Apostles' Creed.*

William Forbes (1585–1634), Bishop of Edinburgh whose writings on purgatory and the Eucharist were published posthumously in 1658 as *Considerationes Modestae et Pacificae.*

George Herbert (1593–1640), a typical country parson, was the poet of the Carolines who taught sacramental doctrine in verse (*The Temple: Sacred Poems*) and in prose (*The Priest to the Temple*).

Nicholas Ferrar (1592–1637), a deacon who founded, at the manor house of Little Gidding, Huntingdon, a family religious house where the piety of Caroline theology was put into practice with genuine fervor.

John Bramhall (1594–1663), Archbishop of Armagh, who upheld the Anglican doctrine of the real presence; repudiated the charge that the Church of England was in schism; and, in reply to the Catholic Bishop Richard Smith, published his *Replication* (1656), a prayer that he might live to see the reunion of Christendom.

John Cosin (1594–1672), Bishop of Durham; at Cambridge, and also at Durham, he introduced ornate altars with crucifix, candles, and vestments. He also put together a *Collection of Private Devotions,* in effect, the Catholic Breviary. For all of these he was charged by the Puritans with popery, but in fact he was anti-Roman and repudiated the doctrine of transubstantiation.

Herbert Thorndike (1598–1672), Canon of Lincoln and later of Westminster, wrote, among other similar works, the *Epilogue to the Tragedy of the Church of England,* a plea for return to the primitive Church, and the *Reformation of the Church of England better than that of the Council of Trent.* He stated that separation from Rome made a church schismatic before God (cf. Albion, 172.3).

Henry Hammond (1605–60), Archdeacon of Chichester, public orator at Oxford, Biblical critic and voluminous writer, tolerant rather than polemical, whose best-known work is the *Practical Catechism.*

Jeremy *Taylor (1613–67), Bishop of Down and Connor, perhaps the greatest Catholicizing influence among the Carolines because of the quality of writing in his *Worthy Communicant, Holy Living,* and *Holy Dying.* Yet he defended the *penal laws against papists and wrote a *Dissuasive from Popery.*

Later Divines. Among the later Caroline divines, so called because of the same school of thought, were:

Dr. Richard Sherlock (1612–89), "accounted by precise persons popishly affected," who wrote the *Principles of the Holy Catholick Religion* as well as a work entitled *The Practical Christian.*

Thomas Wilson (1663–1755), nephew of Sherlock and trained by him for the ministry. As Bishop of Sodor and Man, which was exempt from English law, he introduced "the ancient discipline of the Church." His *Instruction for the Lord's Supper* and *Sacra Privata* have remained popular devotional works.

Anthony Sparrow (1612–55), Bishop of Norwich; his *Rationale* of the Book of Common Prayer, illustrated from Catholic sources, was reprinted by John Henry *Newman in 1837.

Thomas Ken (1657–1711), Bishop of Bath and Wells, best known for his morning and evening hymns.

John Johnson (1662–1725), Vicar of Cranbrook, Kent, author of *The Propitiatory Oblation in the Holy Eucharist* and *The Unbloody Sacrifice,* aroused considerable opposition.

The aim of all these writers was to show the Church of England as reformed yet still Catholic, steering a middle course between Romanism and Presbyterianism and so providing support for the *via media* argument of the *Tractarianism and the *Oxford movement of the 19th century. All are pertinent to the ecumenical dialogue between Anglicans and Catholics in England following the Vatican Council II. (*See* ANGLICANISM.)

Bibliography: *The Library of Anglo-Catholic Theology,* 83 v. (Oxford 1841–63) republished the works of the divines mentioned. DNB lists their works in articles under their names. G. ALBION, *Charles I and the Court of Rome* (London 1935). D. CARTER RGG³ 1:1620–21.

[G. ALBION]

CAROLINGIAN ART

The art of the Carolingian period (later 8th and early 9th centuries) has a particular importance in that it reflects, for the first time, the Germanic North's critical interest in Latin culture and emotional concern over the interpretation of Scripture. The achievement of this era is known mostly through the illuminated book and the crafts of ivory carving and metal work. However, much building was done, especially of monasteries, under royal patronage. Carolingian art was an aristocratic expression, but it laid the foundation for the great popular expression of the later Middle Ages.

The impetus of the whole movement was *Charlemagne, who was impressed by the sumptuousness of Byzantium and even had diplomatic relations with the Moslems. However, he allied himself to the papal throne at the accession of Adrian I in 772. As a result of the iconoclastic struggle in the East (*see* ICONOCLASM), Charlemagne became concerned for the use of images in religious art and wrote to Adrian recommending pictures for their commemorative and decorative value. Aware of the mistakes that were being made in copying Scripture, he admonished the clergy to establish schools.

He himself founded the palace school at Aachen, with *Alcuin of York as its head. To this beginning must be attributed the later development of such scholars as *Rabanus Maurus, abbot of Fulda; Hincmar, Archbishop of Reims; and *John Scotus Erigena of Saint-Denis. Thus the influence of the schools was widely scattered, and distinctive styles developed in different localities.

Sculpture. The revival of the antique style is attested to by the casting of the great bronze doors at Aachen. Also of great interest is the bronze equestrian statuette, formerly in the Musée Carnavalet in Paris but now in the Louvre. While this object has no documentation prior to the 16th century, it is known that Charlemagne caused a mounted statue of Theodoric to be removed from Ravenna and set up in front of his palace at Aachen. The style of this small statue is certainly in keeping with work that Einhard, the director of the imperial workshops, might have accomplished.

Manuscript Illumination. The first book known to have been executed at the palace in Aachen is the Gospels of Godescalc (781–783). It is on purple vellum, and though somewhat crude, it originated an aristocratic style that was later developed under the Abbess Ada at Trèves and of which the Gospels of Saint-Médard-de-Soissons is the finest example. Both books are now in the Bibliothèque Nationale, Paris. Several works of this general type reveal a strong Syrian influence whether in the Hellenistic treatment of landscape, the theatrical backgrounds, or the portrait effigies recalling the consular diptychs.

The school of Tours is best exemplified by the Vivian Bible, or the First Bible of Charles the Bald (Bibliothèque Nationale). This is an extraordinary work of the middle of the 9th century; like other books from Tours, it uses subjects from the Old Testament which were popular in early Christian art. The dedication page is highly original, as is a page showing the dance of David, a Biblical figure to whom Charlemagne was likened. But the MSS done at Tours, where Alcuin had worked on the Vulgate, are most distinctive for their narrative scenes and the beauty of their script. It was this clear, minuscule lettering that inspired the Roman type of the 15th century.

Perhaps the most creative manuscript of the 9th century is the Utrecht psalter, which was written at Hautvillers, near Reims (*c.* 832). The text is in rustic capitals that derive from Western books of *c.* A.D. 400. The lively pen drawings were much admired; their influence can be detected not only in manuscript illumination, but in ivory book covers and silver work, done probably at Saint-Denis, and in the exquisite narrative scenes on the crystal of Lothair, which is now preserved in the British Museum.

Another work of great originality is the Sacramentary, now in Paris, executed before 855 for *Drogo, bishop of Metz; in it scenes taken mostly from the life of Christ are combined with richly foliated initial letters. In this work the beauty of the silhouette was fully achieved while maintaining a certain subservience to the classical tradition. Its ivory covers are in the same spirit and serve as important documents in the development of the liturgy. The taste for the silhouette combined with the flowing line undoubtedly derives from the linear animal style of the period of the racial migrations. Several examples exist that show creative adaptations of this style to the art of the Latinized West. Especially fine are the Gospels of Francis II and the Second Bible of Charles the Bald, both in the Bibliothèque Nationale. They come probably from the monastery of *Saint-Vaast at Arras.

Much uncertainty exists as to work that may have been executed either at *Corbie near Amiens or at Saint-Denis. The fact that Charles the Bald assumed the abbacy of Saint-Denis in 867 is not without significance, and much work is attributed to the monk Liuthard on stylistic grounds. At that time scenes of

Fig. 1. The presentation of the manuscript to Charles the Bald, dedication page of the Vivian Bible or First Bible of Charles the Bald, 846 (MS lat. 1, fol. 423r). Count Vivian stands at the right hand of the Emperor.

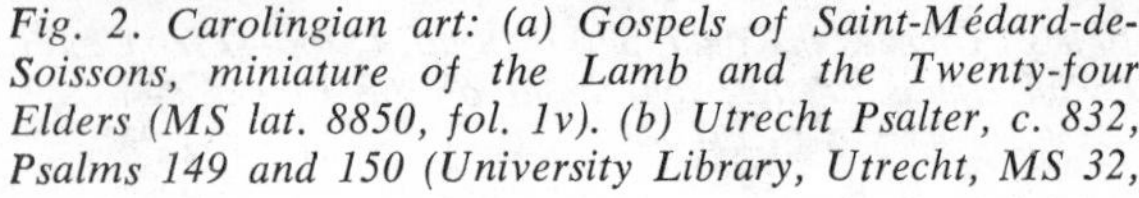

Fig. 2. Carolingian art: (a) Gospels of Saint-Médard-de-Soissons, miniature of the Lamb and the Twenty-four Elders (MS lat. 8850, fol. 1v). (b) Utrecht Psalter, c. 832, Psalms 149 and 150 (University Library, Utrecht, MS 32, fol. 83r). (c) Upper cover, the "Codex Aureus" of St. Emmeram (Munich, Bay. Staatsbibl. Clm. 14000), Reims or Saint-Denis, c. 870. (d) Upper cover, the Psalter of Emperor Charles the Bald (MS lat. 1152), c. 870.

Fig. 3. Carolingian art: (a) The "Lothair Crystal," engraved with scenes from the story of Susanna and the Elders, 9th century, diameter of crystal, 4½ inches. (b) Christ triumphant, carved ivory, 8th century, in the Musée Royal, Brussels. (c) Detail of the gold altar of S. Ambrogio, Milan. In the left roundel St. Ambrose blesses Bishop Angilbertus; in the right roundel, he blesses the goldsmith Volvinus, maker of the altar.

the Crucifixion appeared, probably as a result of the poem by Rabanus Maurus, *De laudibus Sanctae Crucis. See* CRUCIFIXION (IN ART). The Codex Aureus from St. Emmeram of Regensburg, now at Munich, is dated 870 and belongs to this northern school. Less original than some, it sums up the Carolingian tradition in magnificent fashion.

There can be no doubt but that France in the 9th century became the radiating center for the arts. Whether the golden altar of S. Ambrogio in Milan, which must date before 835, was executed in France or in Italy is uncertain, but in any case it reflects the spirit of Carolingian art, as does the Bible of St. Paul-Outside-the-Walls, Rome, which was executed in 880 for *Charles III, Frankish King and German Emperor, and the latter may be said to mark the termination of the tradition.

Architecture. In Carolingian architecture there are echoes of the two traditional styles, Roman and Byzantine, but fused as conditions dictated to form the basis of the great medieval development. The Palatine chapel at Aachen was begun in 792 and dedicated in 805. The plan is that of S. Vitale at Ravenna, from which monument Charlemagne plundered columns, but the construction was heavy Roman vaulting. *See* RAVENNA.

The church of Germigny des Prés near Saint-Benoît-sur-Loire was consecrated in 816 by Theodulf, a Goth from Spain. The quatrefoil plan with a center tower has many prototypes in the East, but the direct influences must have come from the Visigothic tradition. The apsidal mosaic is crude but reveals a desire to emulate the Byzantine style.

Of the Abbeys of S. Riquier near Abbeville and *Sankt Gallen in Switzerland there are no remains. The former, dedicated in 799, was basilican in plan with two great round towers reaching a height of almost 180 feet, one over the crossing, the other above an imposing façade. Other towers were composed with these, establishing a relationship that became traditional. The upper sections and spires were of wood. The entire length of the church (with atrium) measured some 340 feet. Something is known of Sankt Gallen from the famous plan of *c.* 820, preserved in the monastic library. Its most distinctive characteristic was an apse at either end, a feature that was used in an early Christian church in North Africa and was greatly developed in later German churches. Sankt Gallen, which had been founded in the 7th century by Irish monks, later came under Benedictine rule. There the stimulus from the great Western monastic centers of Carolingian culture had a final flowering.

See also MANUSCRIPT ILLUMINATION; CHURCH ARCHITECTURE, 4; ROMANESQUE ART.

Bibliography: General. C. R. MOREY, *Medieval Art* (New York 1942). R. P. HINKS, *Carolingian Art* (London 1935; repr. pa. Ann Arbor 1962). Laistner ThLett. P. LEPRIEUR et al., "L'Art de l'époque mérovingienne et carolingienne en occident," in A. MICHEL, *Histoire de l'art,* 8 v. in 17 (Paris 1905–29) 1.1:303–427. E. KITZINGER, *Early Medieval Art in the British Museum* (2d ed. London 1955). A. M. FRIEND, "Carolingian Art in the Abbey of Saint Denis," *Art Studies,* 8 v. in 9 (Princeton 1923–31) 1:67–75. J. M. K. CLARK, *The Abbey of Saint Gall as a Centre of Literature and Art* (Cambridge, Eng. 1926). M. BUCHNER, *Einhard als Künstler* (Strasbourg 1919). J. VON SCHLOSSER, *Schriftquellen zur Geschichte der Karolingischen Kunst* (Vienna 1896).

Architecture. A. K. PORTER, *Medieval Architecture: Its Origins and Development,* 2 v. (New York 1909) v.1. K. J. CONANT, *Carolingian and Romanesque Architecture, 800 to 1200* (PelHArt Z13; 1959). Decorative Arts. A. MASKELL, *Ivories* (London 1905). A. GOLDSCHMIDT, *Die Elfenbeinskulpturen,* 4 v. (Berlin 1914–26) v.1. G. H. LEHNERT et al., *Illustrierte Geschichte des Kunstgewerbes,* 2 v. (Berlin 1907–09) v.1. É. MOLINIER, "L'Évolution des arts mineurs du VIIIe au XIIe siècle," in A. MICHEL, *op. cit.* 1.2:815–881. O. K. WERCKMEISTER, *Der Deckel des Codex Aureus von St. Emmeram* (Strasbourg 1963).

Manuscripts. J. A. HERBERT, *Illuminated Manuscripts* (London 1911). A. C. L. BOINET, *La Miniature carolingienne* (Paris 1913). Plates only. A. GOLDSCHMIDT, *The Carolingian Period,* v.1 of his *German Illumination* (New York 1928). W. R. W. KÖHLER, *Die Karolingischen Miniaturen,* 3 v. in 4 (Berlin 1930–60). E. K. RAND, *A Survey of the Manuscripts of Tours,* 2 v. (Cambridge, Mass. 1929). F. F. LEITSCHUH, *Geschichte der Karolingischen Malerei* (Berlin 1894). J. EBERSOLT, *La Miniature byzantine* (Paris 1926); *Orient et occident,* 2 v. (2d ed. Paris 1954). E. T. DEWALD, *The Illustrations of the Utrecht Psalter* (Princeton 1932). E. H. ZIMMERMANN, *Die Fuldaer Buchmalerei in Karolingischer und Ottonischer Zeit* (Halle 1910). J. O. WESTWOOD, *The Bible of the Monastery of St. Paul near Rome* (Oxford, Eng. 1876). K. MENZEL et al., *Die Trierer Ada-Handschrift* (Leipzig 1889). **Illustration credits:** Figs. 1, 2*a, d,* Bibliothèque Nationale, Paris. Fig. 2*c,* Hirmer Fotoarchiv München. Fig. 3*a,* Courtesy of the Trustees of the British Museum. Fig. 3*b, c,* R. V. Schoder, SJ.

[W. R. HOVEY]

CAROLINGIAN DYNASTY

A dynasty in the medieval kingdom of the *Franks, which produced mayors of the palace (613–751), kings (751–987), and emperors (800–911); it is named for Charlemagne. The origin of this dynasty, which is variously called Arnulfings, Pippinids, or Carolingians, was in the marriage of *Begga, daughter of Pepin of Landen, the Austrasian mayor of the palace, to Ansegis, son of *Arnulf, later bishop of Metz. Pepin's son Grimoald attempted prematurely to replace the ineffectual but sacrosanct *Merovingian king with his own son but both were murdered in 661. Then Begga and Ansegis's son, Pepin II of Heristal (mayor 680–714), revived the family's prestige and Pepin governed the kingdom as mayor of the palace while carefully retaining the "do-nothing" kings. Only his illegitimate son *Charles Martel (714–741) survived him, but Charles succeeded in his 5-year struggle to win recognition as his father's heir. Charles's consolidation of the Frankish kingdom contributed to Carolingian greatness. He supported missionary efforts abroad as a means of unifying this extensive kingdom, although he secularized Church property at home to support his followers. His victory against the Moslems at Poitiers (Tours) in 732 checked their advance in the West. His sons, *Carloman and *Pepin III (741–768), continued to support the Church's missionary work and permitted St. *Boniface to reform the Church in Gaul itself. Carloman retired to a monastery in Italy (747) and Pepin seized his lands, uniting all under his rule. Deciding that the time was ripe to replace the effete Merovingian dynasty, Pepin gained the support of Pope *Zachary for his finally assuming the name of king (751) to match the regnal power he had long exercised. When Pope *Stephen II was at Pepin's court in 754, he anointed the King and gave him the title of *Patricius Romanorum. Pepin assisted Stephen against the *Lombards, "restoring" the Roman duchy and the Pentapolis to the Pope in 756, thereby establishing the basis of the *States of the Church (*see* DONATION OF CONSTANTINE). Pepin's sons Charles (768–814) and Carloman governed jointly until 771 when the latter died. Then Charles, or *Charlemagne, disregarding his brother's heirs, ruled alone.

Christ with the kings of the Carolingian dynasty, engraved cover of the "Golden Book of Prüm," made in the first half of the 12th century and preserved in the Staatsbibliothek at Trier, Germany.

Charlemagne's efforts to consolidate and expand his kingdom required almost incessant warfare; fortified border provinces were set up forming the east mark, the Spanish march, and Denmark. He finally conquered the Lombards (773–774) and, far from donating the conquered territory to the Pope, assumed the title King of Italy, to the dismay of Pope *Adrian I. He gradually conquered the pagan Frisians, but his struggle to subdue and convert the *Saxons required 20 campaigns (772–803) and was marred by his policy of forced conversions and harsh legislation, which *Alcuin and others criticized and finally caused Charles to modify (*see* CAROLINGIAN REFORM). His support of the calumniated Pope *Leo III was followed by his coronation as emperor of the Romans on Christmas Day, 800, certainly the high point in the fortunes of the Carolingian dynasty (*see* CAROLINGIAN RENAISSANCE; CAROLINGIAN ART). His administration through *missi dominici,* usually clerics, and his legislation, economic and ecclesial, through *capitularies were positive achievements. He was survived by only one son, *Louis I, the Pious (814–840), who seems to have glimpsed the advantages of undivided succession. Accordingly Louis made his eldest son, *Lothair I, emperor with some authority over both *Louis the German and *Charles II the Bald. Their furious resentment at these plans manifested itself even during Louis's lifetime and continued after his death in the civil wars that hastened the dismemberment of the Carolingian empire and caused its prostration before the Viking inroads. Six kingdoms were formed by the break-up of Charlemagne's empire: France, Germany, Lorraine, Italy, Burgundy, and Provence. All were ruled by Carolingian dynasties until the 10th century. The last Carolingian to rule in Germany was Louis the Child (d. 911); in France, Carolingians alternated with the Counts of Paris (Robertians, later *Capetians) until the accession of the latter family in the person of Hugh Capet in 987. Meanwhile the imperial title after the deposition of Charles the Fat (887) went begging among minor Carolingians until 911, becoming less and less meaningful (*see* HOLY ROMAN EMPIRE).

Bibliography: Sources. *Annales Fuldenses,* ed. F. KURZE (MGSrerGerm 7; 1891); *Annales regni Francorum,* ed. F. KURZE (MGSrerGerm 6; 1895). *Annales Mettenses primores,* ed. B. DE SIMSON (MGSrerGerm 10; 1905). J. F. BÖHMER, *Die Regesten des Kaiserreichs unter den Karolingern,* ed. E. MÜHLBACHER (Regesta imperii 1: 2d ed. Innsbruck 1908). Literature. G. SEELIGER, *Die Kapitularien der Karolinger* (Munich 1893). A. KLEINCLAUSZ, *L'Empire carolingien* (Paris 1902). G. MONOD, *Études critiques sur les sources de l'histoire carolingienne* (Paris 1898). C. H. DAWSON, *The Making of Europe* (New York 1932). H. ST. L. MOSS, *The Birth of the Middle Ages, 395–814* (Oxford 1935). Fliche-Martin 6. J. CALMETTE, *Charlemagne, sa vie et son oeuvre* (Paris 1945). L. HALPHEN, *Les Barbares* (Paris 1948); *Charlemagne et l'empire carolingien* (Paris 1947). C. ERDMANN, *Forschungen zur politischen Ideenwelt des Frühmittelalters,* ed. F. BAETHGEN (Berlin 1951). H. FICHTENAU, *The Carolingian Empire,* tr. P. MUNZ (Oxford 1957). **Illustration credit:** Marburg-Art Reference Bureau.

[C. M. AHERNE]

CAROLINGIAN REFORM

A century-long effort (*c.* 740–840) to revitalize spiritual life in the Frankish kingdom. The Carolingian reform was inspired initially by papal and Anglo-Saxon influences entering the Frankish realm in the first half of the 8th century and was successfully sustained by the powerful Carolingian rulers of this era. It was aimed at correcting conditions reigning in the Frankish church. Clerical corruption, ignorance, immorality, pagan survivals, extreme diversity in religious practice, and widespread seizure of *Church property were the most obvious signs of the low state of religious life prevailing in the Frankish kingdom.

Reform Beginning. The Frankish church, incapable of regeneration from within, found a model for reform in the missionary establishment created on the northern and eastern fringes of the kingdom by Anglo-Saxon missionaries working in close alliance with the papacy. The most influential missionary was St. *Boniface, who between 718 and 741 succeeded not only in winning numerous converts in Hesse, Thuringia, and Bavaria, but also in creating a solid ecclesiastical organization built around a series of newly established bishoprics. Supporting the new dioceses, e.g., Salzburg, Passau, Freising, Würzburg, and Erfurt, were several newly created monasteries (*see* FULDA, ABBEY OF), which served as missionary posts and as educational centers training a disciplined clergy to man the key positions in the emerging church organization. Boniface's pioneering work was carried on in close cooperation with the papacy. The reform movement began in the Frankish kingdom during the joint rule of *Pepin III and *Carloman, who turned to Boniface to direct an assault on the evils plaguing the Frankish church. The program was spelled out in a series of synods in the 740s, whose decisions the rulers promulgated as law. It was inspired by a dream of creating a Frankish church closely allied but subordinate to Rome, a possibility that did not receive strong support from the Frankish rulers or clergy. After Boniface returned to missionary work in 753, leadership in reform devolved on Pepin III, now king of the Franks, who made reform primarily a royal program.

Imperial Reform. *Charlemagne and *Louis I the Pious intensified the reform effort during their reigns. Both were convinced that their major responsibility consisted in the perfection of the spiritual life of their subjects and in building a more effective political regime through a strong Church. From their court issued a barrage of ecclesiastical legislation, contained in the *capitularies, especially the *Admonitio generalis* (789) and the capitulary of 802 (MGCap 1.22–33). Numerous episcopal synods, e.g., Frankfurt (794), sanctioned these measures. This legislation touched on a broad range of topics: the definition of episcopal powers, the revival of the collapsed metropolitan organization, the establishment of the canonical life for cathedral clergy, the unification of monastic life according to the Benedictine Rule (MGS 1:39), the protection of Church property and the assurance of its income, the regularization of liturgical practices, the correction of popular morals, and the improvement of church buildings. Enforcement of these laws was entrusted to the *missi dominici,* both lay officials and members of the upper clergy.

Nor were the rulers content merely to command reform by law alone. They endeavored to create an ambience that would afford an opportunity for a deeper spiritual life. Reforming clergymen, such as Alcuin, Paul the Deacon, and Benedict of Aniane, were given crucial positions in the royal court. Bishops and abbots were carefully selected and their conduct carefully supervised. Charlemagne patronized especially a revival of learning so as to mold a clergy well-

enough educated to grasp the spirit of reform (*see* CAROLINGIAN RENAISSANCE). Great effort was made to improve Biblical texts, based on the Latin version of Jerome [*see* BIBLE IV (TEXTS AND VERSIONS) 13], and to provide a theological literature oriented toward Scripture and the Fathers. Frequently the papacy was asked for guidance, particularly in matters of law (*see* CANON LAW, HISTORY OF, 2), thus maintaining the Roman connection established by St. Boniface.

Decline. After 840 the reforming spirit began to lose its effectiveness, not so much because the desire had died as because the Carolingian government grew increasingly weak amidst the difficulties that accompanied the collapse of the unified empire. Without a strong ruler, reform was impossible; the higher clergy could not sustain the work. The Frankish church drifted toward the chaos of the feudal age to await the *Gregorian reform of the 11th century.

Significance. In spite of ultimate failure, the Carolingian reform was of great historical significance. It did much to establish the norms upon which later reforms were built. The reforming zeal led to a recovery of the heritage of the early Church and its redefinition to fit the needs of a society influenced strongly by Germanic customs. The reform tied the Frankish church closely to Rome. It generated the significant idea of a uniform religious life for the West. The basic organizational pattern of the church was strongly fortified to assure the church a leading role in society even in the feudal age.

The chief shortcoming of the Carolingian reform was its failure to penetrate the mass of the population. As a movement confined primarily to an elite clergy and a small circle of royal officials, it hardly touched most of society except to alter somewhat the forms of external religious life. The great task of fully Christianizing Western European society remained for the future. The Carolingian reform, however, marked an important preliminary step toward that future.

Bibliography: Sources. *Capitularia regum Francorum,* ed. A. BORETIUS and V. KRAUSE, 2 v., MGL, Sectio 2 (Hanover 1883–97). *Concilia aevi karolini,* ed. A. WERMINGHOFF, MGConc 2 (Hanover-Leipzig 1906–08). Literature. H. VON SCHUBERT, *Geschichte der christlichen Kirche im Frühmittelalter: Ein Handbuch* (Tübingen 1921) 288–774, complete guide to sources. É. LESNE, *Histoire de la propriété ecclésiastique en France,* 6 v. (Lille 1910–43). Fliche-Martin 5:329–390; 6:71–106, 210–217, 255–266, 345–366. C. DE CLERCQ, *La Législation religieuse franque de Clovis à Charlemagne, 507–814* (Louvain 1936); *La Législation religieuse franque de Louis le Pieux à la fin du IXe siècle, 814–900* (Antwerp 1958). T. SCHIEFFER, *Winfrid-Bonifatius und die christliche Grundlegung Europas* (Freiburg 1954).

[R. E. SULLIVAN]

CAROLINGIAN RENAISSANCE

A revival of interest in classical learning in the Carolingian Empire (France, Germany, and Italy). Beginning under the patronage of *Charlemagne (768–814), it continued to the end of the 9th century. In its involvement with classical and patristic literature, the movement was similar to the Isidorian renaissance in 7th-century Spain, the *Ottonian renaissance of the

10th century, and the 12th-century renaissance in France and England. It differed from the Italian *Renaissance of the 14th and 15th century in its emphasis on clerical reform as originally inspired by St. *Boniface with the encouragement of *Pepin III (741–768) and as incorporated by Charlemagne into civil law (e.g., MGCap 1:22). The revived interest in learning is exemplified by Charlemagne's important "mandate" (not a capitulary; cf. L. Wallach), the *Epistola de litteris colendis* (tr. Laistner ThLett 152–153) written to Baugulf, Abbot of *Fulda between 794 and 796, urging him to promote education in the area around his abbey. The primary interest of the Carolingian revival, however, was not in the classics as such, but rather in their use as a means of studying the Latin language and culture—an attitude the Carolingian scholars inherited from the patristic period; it was the Fathers of the Church who were read for content. Yet a love of learning for its own sake was bred in such men as the Spanish-born *Theodulf of Orléans, who as a political prisoner wrote to his former colleague, Bp. Modoin of Autun, "Death is better than life without study, teaching, or worship." Carolingian poetry (MGPoetae v.1–4), more than other literary forms, demonstrates the influence of the Latin classics on the Carolingians; the prose compositions of the period, however, reflect the classical mood only incidentally (*see* MEDIEVAL LATIN LITERATURE).

Charlemagne and the Court Circle. Charles, King of the Franks (768–814), Emperor of the Romans from 800, was head and patron of the movement for education and reform that was the heart of the renaissance [*see* CAROLINGIAN REFORM; EDUCATION, I (HISTORY OF), 1, 2].

Alcuin. Charlemagne found in *Alcuin of York (*c.* 735–804) the man to organize and systematize his educational program, and it was as an administrator (781–796) that Alcuin made his mark, though he wrote a number of poems in the classical meters, some of considerable lyric power. He composed and edited texts for the education of clerics and authored textbooks on Latin grammar, rhetoric, dialectic, and orthography. He knew at first hand Vergil, Ovid, and Lucan. Alcuin, or "Horace," his nickname within the court circle, seems to have known Horace through quotations. Charlemagne initiated the *palace school—which lasted till the death of his grandson, Charles the Bald—when he attracted a galaxy of scholars to assist Alcuin: Paul the Deacon (in 782), Dungal (in 787), and Theodulf, the future bishop of Orléans (sometime after 787). *Paul the Deacon (730?–799?) came to Charles's attention when he wrote a plea in fine elegiac verses for the release of his brother, imprisoned for a political offense. He wrote also a poem in praise of Lake Como in epanaleptic verses and an abridgment of Festus' *De verborum significatione,* which was important for archaic Latin.

The Irishmen. *Dungal (d. after 827) was one of many wandering Irishmen who contributed greatly to the revival of learning on the Continent; Dungal knew the Fathers and was expert in astronomy (MGEp 4:570). *Clement of Ireland (d. after 828) succeeded Alcuin as master of the palace school (796), but was probably there earlier. He wrote an *Ars grammatica,* which he dedicated to Emperor *Lothair I (840–855). Another Irishman who contributed to the first generation of Carolingian scholarship is Colman (fl. early 9th century), who wrote a poem in fine Latin to a fellow countryman returning to Ireland. *Smaragdus of Saint-Mihiel was probably Irish; he wrote poetry (MGPoetae 1:602–619; 2:918–924) and taught Latin grammar, composing a commentary on *Donatus.

Theodulf of Orléans. The greatest scholar and author of the court circle was undoubtedly a Visigoth in the Isidorian tradition, Theodulf of Orléans (*c.* 770–821), whose writings (e.g., *Ad Carolum regem, Contra judices,* **Gloria, laus et honor*) show his classical training. His deep political insight reflects the Hispano-Roman sophistication that had been developed through the Councils of *Toledo. He tried in vain to persuade Charles not to divide his empire according to the Frankish principle of equal inheritance (MGPoetae 1:526). Emperor *Louis the Pious's attempt to maintain the primacy of his firstborn, Lothair I, over the two younger sons may have been an effect of Theodulf's hitherto unheeded advice. The results were disastrous in the 9th century, but ultimately (987) primogeniture became the rule in France. *Paulinus of Aquileia was another poet-member of the court circle (MGPoetae 1:123–128), while *Peter of Pisa, a grammarian, instructed Charles himself and illustrated his teaching—as was customary—with examples from ancient pagan and Christian authors. The only Frank to belong to the circle was *Angilbert, a disciple of Alcuin, who wrote *Ecloga ad Karolum regem.* Through an affair with Bertha, one of Charlemagne's daughters, he had two sons; one was the lay historian *Nithard. Angilbert later (between 796 and 802) became a monk and abbot of *Saint-Riquier, where he introduced the *laus perennis.*

The Second Generation. *Einhard (*c.* 770–*c.* 840) bridges two generations of the palace school. He was educated at Fulda and later at Aachen under Alcuin. His *Life of Charlemagne* is the best biography of the Middle Ages, and its strong classical orientation is evident in his use of *Suetonius as a model. Nithard continued the biographical tradition in his history of the sons of Louis the Pious (*Historiarum libri 4*). Some time earlier *Leidradus of Lyons (d. 814) had established an episcopal school in accord with Charlemagne's prescription, and there *Florus of Lyons (d. 860), who was possibly Spanish, continued to be the leading figure of the school.

Rabanus Maurus and His Circle. The royal monastery of *Fulda was an important educational and cultural center of the Carolingian renaissance, especially under its great abbot, *Rabanus Maurus (776–856). Sent to Tours in 802 to study under Alcuin, he returned to Fulda the following year to direct the monastic school. He was abbot from 822 until 842, when he became archbishop of Mainz. His *De arte grammatica* and *De rerum naturis* do not show great originality, but he unquestionably deserves his title of preceptor of Germany. His student *Walafrid Strabo (809–849), later abbot of *Reichenau, was the tutor of Emperor Charles the Bald (840–877). Although Strabo was acquainted with most of the Latin meters, he preferred the hexameter (MGPoetae 2:259–472). Another of Rabanus's students, *Lupus (*c.* 805–*c.* 862), later abbot of Ferrières, was sent to study at Fulda *c.* 828. His letters (MGS 6:1–26) and MS collection reveal his interests in the classics; for, of the 20 MSS that are certainly from his scriptorium at Ferrières, perhaps 10 are Lupus's own transcriptions. Another student, *Gottschalk of Orbais (*c.* 805–869), was dedicated as a child to the monastic life at Fulda by his parents but later wished to withdraw. His request was denied; he was transferred to Orbais, and finally, because of his views on predestination, he was imprisoned for the rest of his life in Hautvillers. He wrote a poetical *conflictus,* or debate, between the Old Testament as represented by Alethea, a shepherdess, and the New, represented by Pseustis. Further works included 17 original and very human poems and several excellent hymns. His rebellion against dedication as a child to monastic life was an important—though personally disastrous—step in the Church's insistence on absolute freedom in choosing the religious life. Wandelbert of Prüm, a member of the same circle of writers, wrote hymns in Sapphic meters.

Hincmar of Reims. In the zeal and uprightness that characterized his episcopate, *Hincmar of Reims (d. 882) might be considered the fruition of Charlemagne's reforming efforts. His verses and letters mark him as a product of the Carolingian renaissance. His political theory is expressed in his *De ordine palatii* and *De institutione regis;* his course of action regarding the divorce of *Lothair II confirms his position that the Emperor was subject to the Church *ratione peccati* (PL 125:623–772).

Two Irishmen also grace the second generation of the Carolingian renaissance: *Sedulius Scotus (fl. 848–858) and *John Scotus Erigena (*c.* 810–*c.* 877). The former was the leading figure among his compatriots at *Liège; the latter, at the court of Charles the Bald. Sedulius was an accomplished poet, a master of all types of classical verse, who was reluctant to depart from classical precedents in any of his 83 poems; he was also a grammarian who wrote commentaries on Eutyches and Priscian. He knew Cicero, Vegetius, Frontinus, Valerius Maximus, Macrobius, and Seneca.

The Court and Charles the Bald. *Charles II the Bald is often condemned—probably quite unjustly—for buying off the piratical *Normans. However, he appears in a much better light when one examines the patronage of learning at his court. The leading scholar in Charles's entourage was John Scotus Erigena, who wrote Greek verses and Latin poetry filled with Greek words and taught grammar and dialectic—rejecting absolute predestination on the basis of logic alone (*De predestinatione*). He was a commentator on Scripture and proved himself the first original philosopher of the Middle Ages (Gilson) in his *De divisione naturae,* which was based on the Greek and Latin sources of Platonism (*see* NEOPLATONISM). Milo of Saint-Amand, who also belonged to the same court circle, used patristic writers (e.g., Prudentius), as well as Macrobius. *Radbod of Utrecht (d. 917) was educated in Cologne and at Charles's court. As bishop of Utrecht he was forced to flee from the Northmen to Deventer, where he established an intellectual center. Radbod was the author of poems (MGPoetae 4:160–173), homilies, and historical works. *Hucbald of Saint-Amand (840–930), another member of Charles's circle (*Ecloga de calvis*), was a humanist who listed the books in his library (many of which are still preserved at Valenciennes). He wrote a work on chant, *De institutione harmonica,* in which he tried to bring Greek and Boethian musical theory to bear upon chant and to establish definite pitch. *Micon of Saint-Riquier (d. 865) compiled one of the better medieval *florilegia in which he arranged authors alphabetically. *Hagiography flourished in the time of Charles the Bald under Florus of Lyons, *Usuard, *Ado of Vienne, and others.

Medieval *libraries were small but were probably used exhaustively, given the monastic stipulation of meditative reading. At the beginning of the Carolingian period only a few places (Rome, Bobbio, York) had libraries, but in its course libraries were developed at *Corbie, *Luxeuil, *Lorsch, Fulda, *Fontenelle (Saint-Wandrille), *Saint-Amand-les-Eaux, and *Saint-Riquier. The Carolingian *scriptorium saw the full development of a distinctive half-uncial script now named Carolingian minuscule, the basis of the modern book and cursive hands (*see* PALEOGRAPHY, LATIN). As a result of Carolingian stimulation, cathedral schools flourished in *Utrecht, *Wurzburg, Magdeburg, *Laon, *Reims, Blois, *Orléans, *Chartres, *Bourges, and *Lyons.

The classical character of Carolingian art is evident in the revival of bronze-casting and the use of Roman and Byzantine elements in the small, octagonal royal chapel at *Aachen, based on San Vitale in *Ravenna from which its columns were taken. The church built by Theodulf at Germigny des Prés (near Orléans) has a quatrefoil plan; mosaics in the Byzantine tradition adorn the interior.

See also CAROLINGIAN DYNASTY; CAROLINGIAN ART; LIBRI CAROLINI.

Bibliography: MGPoetae aevi Carolini, 4 v. (1884–1923). Manitius v.1, 3. C. H. BEESON, *Lupus of Ferrières as Scribe and Text Critic: A Study of His Autograph Copy of Cicero's De oratore* (Cambridge, Mass. 1930). P. LEHMANN, "Die handschriftliche Überlieferung der römischen Literatur," *Philobiblion* 7 (1934) 209–238. Ghellinck, Litt. F. L. GANSHOF, "Charlemagne," *Speculum* 24 (1949) 520–528. M. HÉLIN, *A History of Medieval Literature,* tr. J. C. SNOW (rev. ed. New York 1949) 27–49. L. WALLACH, "Charlemagne's *De litteris colendis* and Alcuin," *Speculum* 26 (1951) 288–305. Laistner ThLett. H. LIEBESCHÜTZ, "Theodulf of Orleáns and the Problem of the Carolingian Renaissance," *Fritz Saxl Memorial Essays* (London 1957) 77–92. F. L. GANSHOF, LexThK² 5:1377–79. E. S. DUCKETT, *Carolingian Portraits* (Ann Arbor 1962). *Corbie, abbaye royale* (Lille 1963). R. P. HINKS, *Carolingian Art* (London 1935; repr. pa. Ann Arbor 1962). Szövérffy AnnLatHymn 1:167–312. D. T. RICE, ed., *The Dawn of European Civilization* (New York 1965) 197–218, 269–326.

[C. M. AHERNE]

CARON, REDMOND, Irish Franciscan theologian, the first to publish a systematic course on missiology; b. near Athlone, Westmeath, Ireland, *c.* 1605; d. Dublin, May 1666. He studied for the priesthood in Drogheda, Salzburg, and Louvain and then taught philosophy and theology in St. Anthony's College, Louvain. His mission (1649) as canonical visitor of the Irish Franciscan province was disastrous and his acts were annulled. Subsequently he served in Ghent and Antwerp (1651–52), in Paris (1652), in Flanders as chaplain to Spanish troops (1653–54), again in Paris (1655–61), in Britain (1661–65), and finally, in Dublin. Meanwhile he cared for refugee Irish Poor Clares (1655). He supported the Remonstrance (1661), a formal statement of grievances and allegiance to King Charles II written by Anglo-Irish laymen and championed by Peter *Walsh, and in its defense wrote his *Loyalty Asserted* and *Remonstrantia Hibernorum contra Lovanienses.* In 1653 he published a manual of apologetics and another of missiology for regular clergy and in 1659, a general work on missiology.

Bibliography: T. F. HENDERSON, DNB 3:1062. F. Ó BRIAIN, DHGE 11:1140–41. E. D'ALENCON, DTC 2.2:1799. B. MILLETT, *The Irish Franciscans 1651–1665* (Rome 1964), *passim.* M. O N. WALSH, "Irish Books Printed Abroad 1475–1700," *The Irish Book* 2 (1963) 9. *Archivium Hibernicum* 24 (1961), *passim;* 25 (1962), *passim;* 26 (1963), *passim.*

[B. MILLETT]

CARON, RENÉ ÉDOUARD, judge, lieutenant governor of Quebec, Canada; b. Sainte-Anne, Côte de Beaupré, Lower Canada, Oct. 11, 1800; d. Spencer Wood, Quebec, Dec. 13, 1876. He was the son of Augustin Caron, who served in the Legislative Assembly of Lower Canada. Educated at the Quebec Seminary and the College of St. Pierre, Rivière du Sud, he was called to the provincial bar in 1826 and served as mayor of Quebec City (1834–36, 1840–46). As a liberal he was elected (1834) to the Legislative Assembly for the upper town of Quebec, but he resigned in 1836 as a result of a disagreement with Speaker Louis Joseph *Papineau. He was appointed to the Legislative Council of Canada in 1841 and acted as speaker (1843–47, 1848–53). In 1853 he was appointed judge of the Superior Court of Lower Canada and was later promoted to the Queen's Bench. In 1873 he succeeded Sir N. F. Belleau as lieutenant governor of Quebec, an office he held until his death. In 1826 he married Joséphine de Blois. His *Correspondence* with W. H. Draper, L. H. Lafontaine, and A. N. Morin was published at Montreal in 1846.

Bibliography: L. P. TURCOTTE, *L'Honorable R. E. Caron* (Quebec 1873).

[J. T. FLYNN]

CAROSSA, HANS, German Catholic novelist and poet; b. Tölz, Dec. 15, 1878; d. Rittsteig bei Passau, Dec. 8, 1956. His great-grandfather from Piedmont and his father were physicians, and Hans received an M.D. degree at Leipzig. He practiced in Munich, Nuremberg, and Passau, and was a battalion physician in World War I. Toward the end of the 1930s he gave up medicine for writing. It is the common opinion of critics that Carossa of all modern writers is nearest to Goethe. This is based at least partly on similarities between his own biological interpretation of life and Goethe's approach to living. The first prose work, *Doktor Bürgers Ende* (1913), which seems to take *Werther* as its model, narrates the fate of a doctor who commits suicide after failing to save a tuberculous patient. In 1916 Carossa tempered this pessimistic ending in the poem *Die Flucht, Gedicht aus Dr. Bürgers Nachlass.* In the works that followed he did indeed observe destructive forces at work but, like Goethe, saw in decomposition the germs of a new life. In the description of his experiences as an army doctor in *Rumänisches Tagebuch* (1924), he went quietly about the work of reconstruction; because he objectively viewed the enemy as fighting men, he was denounced to the National Socialists as a pacifist. The healing of the scars of war is also the primary concern of *Der Arzt Gion* (1931).

Carossa treated the Nazi period in *Aufzeichnungen aus Italien* (1948) and *Ungleiche Welten* (1951). The second part of the latter work, *Ein Tag im Spätsommer 1947,* symbolically interprets the historical events narrated in the first section, *Lebensbericht.* All Carossa's works are autobiographical in nature. Volumes of the autobiography proper appeared under various titles between 1922 and 1956. A prominent characteristic of his style is the use of recurrent symbolic events. Personal experiences and a firm belief in the healing power of nature form the basis for much of his poetry, the definitive edition of which is *Gesammelte Gedichte* (1947).

Hans Carossa.

Bibliography: J. BITHELL, *Modern German Literature: 1880–1950* (London 1959). F. KLATT, *Hans Carossa: Seine geistige Haltung und sein Glaubensgut* (Wismar 1937). A. LANGEN, *Hans Carossa: Weltbild und Stil* (Berlin 1955). G. SCHAEDER, *Hans Carossa: Der heilkundige Dichter* (Hameln 1947). **Illustration credit:** German Information Center, New York City.

[J. E. BOURGEOIS]

CARPACCIO, VITTORE, Italian painter noted for the warm color and minute detail of his Venetian cityscapes; b. Venice, *c.* 1455; d. Venice, 1526. He was the pupil of Gentile *Bellini and, as the style of his earlier works demonstrates, also of Giovanni

Vittore Carpaccio, "The Dream of St. Ursula," oil on canvas, 69¾ by 68 inches, Academy of Fine Arts, Venice.

Bellini. He gained distinction by painting large narrative compositions commissioned by the confraternities, or *scuole.* The paintings illustrating the life of St. Ursula (1490–95) are filled with the local color of Venice. The cycle of scenes from the lives of SS. George, Jerome, and Trophimus (1502–07) for the Croatian *scuola* is still in place there. He also did cycles of the life of the Virgin (for the Albanian *scuola*) and St. Stephen (1511–20). Many of his altarpieces still remain in churches of cities on the Adriatic coasts of Italy and Yugoslavia. Outstanding individual paintings by Carpaccio include "The Courtesans" (Venice), "Lamentation over the Dead Christ" (Berlin), and the "Meditation on the Passion" (New York; *see* PASSION OF CHRIST, III). Though Carpaccio painted his contemporary Venice, he did not mechanically reproduce the city, but rather gave an imaginative and often slightly exotic rendering of the spirit of Venice.

Bibliography: J. LAUTS, *Carpaccio* (New York 1962), bibliog.
Illustration credit: Alinari-Art Reference Bureau.

[I. GALANTIC]

CARPANI, MELCHIORRE, Barnabite missionary to Burma; b. Lodi, Italy, 1726; d. there, July 8, 1797. When 18 years old he entered the *Barnabites, and in 1764 he departed for the missions of Ava and Pegù in Burma. There he was the first to study the characters of the Burmese alphabet, which he attempted to set in type for a printing press. In 1774, after an attempt upon his life, he was recalled to Rome. During his term as superior of the College of San Giovanni at Lodi (1775–85) he published the *Alphabetum Burmanum* (1776) and the *Memorie sopra la vita di Hyder Ali Kan* (1782). The latter biography of an Indian general is an important source for the modern history of India.

Bibliography: L. GALLO, *Storia del cristianesimo nell'Impero birmano,* 2 v. (Milan 1862), *passim.* G. BOFFITO, *Scrittori Barnabiti,* 4 v. (Florence 1933–37) 1:424–426.

[U. M. FASOLA]

CARPENTRAS (ELZÉAR GENÊT), Renaissance composer and priest; b. Carpentras (Vaucluse), France, 1475?; d. Avignon, June 14, 1548. Genêt was a singer in the papal choir under Julius II (1508), then was called (1508–13) to the court of Louis XII, where he learned to appreciate secular music. In 1518 he was appointed *maestro di cappella* under Leo X, and thus was brought under the influence of Leo's secretary, Cardinal *Bembo. In 1521 he left for Avignon, where he remained for the rest of his days except for a return to Rome (1524–26) under Clement VII. He is especially known for 5 four-part masses, named after French secular songs; a book of hymns (which is also a source for biographical details); Magnificats; three-voiced cantica; and the *Liber Lamentationum Hieremiae prophetae Carpentras* (Avignon 1532), which introduced the new Briard type, i.e., with oval noteheads. He made use of **falso bordone,* imitation, and melismas on Hebrew letters. His style strove for perfection not so much through complicated counterpoint as through simple musical methods.

See also MUSIC, SACRED, HISTORY OF, 4.

Bibliography: E. G. CARPENTRAS, *Liber hymnorum usus Romanae ecclesiae,* 3 v. (Avignon 1535). O. L. RIGSBY, *The Sacred Music of Elzéar Genet* (Doctoral diss. microfilm; U. of Michigan 1955). R. CAILLET and F. LESURE, MusGG 2:867–870. A. PIRRO, *Léon X et la musique* (Paris 1934). A. EINSTEIN, *The Italian Madrigal,* tr. A. H. KRAPPE et al., 3 v. (Princeton 1949). Reese MusR.

[F. J. SMITH]

CARPOCRATES, early 2d-century Gnostic teacher in Alexandria. Clement of Alexandria (*Strom.* 3.5–9) states that Carpocrates's son Epiphanes founded the sect of Carpocratians, wrote a work *On Justice,* and died at the age of 17, highly revered by his followers. Other sources mention only the name of Carpocrates (Irenaeus, *Adv. haer.* 1.25, and Hippolytus, *Philos.* 7.32). Origen (*C. Cels.* 5.62) speaks of a sect of Harpocratians, and many modern authorities deny the existence of a heresiarch Carpocrates and assume that the name originated in the adoption by the sect of the Egyptian god Horus-Harpocrates [see H. Kraft, "Gab es einen Gnostiker Karpokrates?" ThZ 8 (1952) 434–443]. A disciple, Marcellina, brought the sect to Rome in the reign of Anicetus. The Carpocratians taught the creation of the world by lower angels and successive reincarnations until the soul ascends to God. Strongly influenced by Hellenistic philosophy, the sect was noted for its magical practices and its antinomianism.

See also GNOSTICISM.

Bibliography: Texts. W. VÖLKER, ed., *Quellen zur Geschichte der christlichen Gnosis* (Tübingen 1932) 33–38. Studies. H. LIBORON, *Die karpokratianische Gnosis* (Leipzig 1938). G. BAREILLE, DTC 2.2:1800–03. G. SALMON, DCB 1:407–409.

[G. W. MAC RAE]

CARPZOV, an eminent Saxon family of orthodox Lutheran theologians and jurists of the 17th and 18th centuries.

Benedikt, b. Wittenberg, May 27, 1595; d. Leipzig, Aug. 30, 1666. He was a man of deep religious convictions. From 1620 on he was a member of the bench at Leipzig, serving as professor of law (1645), privy councilor at Dresden (1653), and again judge at Leipzig (1661). A judge for more than 40 years, he became the father of German penal law, and in *Jurisprudentia ecclesiastica* (1649) he systematized Lutheran episcopal polity and church law.

Johann Benedikt (I), brother of Benedikt; b. Rochlitz, June 22, 1607; d. Leipzig, Oct. 22, 1657. He was a pastor and professor of theology at Leipzig (1645), the author of *Isagoge in libros ecclesiarum luth. symbolicos* (1665), and a forerunner of the specialized study of symbolics. In the Syncretistic controversy he was a mediating influence, strictly Lutheran in principle, though respectful of the opinions of Georg *Calixtus.

Johann Benedikt (II), son of Johann Benedikt; b. Leipzig, April 24, 1639; d. Leipzig, March 23, 1699. He was a professor of ethics (1665) and of theology (1684), and a pastor of St. Thomas church (1679). He was a violent opponent of *Pietism; and against Philipp Jakob *Spener, August Hermann *Francke, and Christian *Thomasius he wrote *De jure decidendi controversias theologicas* (Leipzig 1696).

Samuel Benedikt, son of Johann Benedikt (I); b. Leipzig, Jan. 17, 1647; d. Dresden, Aug. 31, 1707. As a student at Wittenberg (1668), he became a friend of Abraham *Calov. He was court preacher at Dresden (1674), superintendent (1680), and successor of Philipp Spener as senior court preacher (1693). He wavered in his public attitude toward Pietism.

Johann Gottlob, son of Samuel Benedikt; b. Dresden, Sept. 26, 1679; d. Lübeck, April 7, 1767. He was the most learned of the family, an orthodox Lutheran OT scholar and an opponent of Pietists and Moravians (*see* PIETISM; MORAVIAN CHURCH). He served as professor of Hebrew at Leipzig (1713) and as superintendent at Lübeck (1730). His *Introductio ad libros canonicos bibliorum VT* (1714–21) vigorously defended the orthodox Lutheran view of verbal inspiration against the rising progressive Biblical criticism.

Johann Bendikt (III), grandson of Johann Benedikt (II); b. Leipzig, May 20, 1720; d. Königslutter, April 28, 1803. He was one of the last representatives of old Lutheran orthodoxy, an authority on the NT and patristics as well as on theology. Professor of philosophy at Leipzig (1747) and of Greek at Helmstedt (1748), he wrote *Liber doctrinalis theologiae purioris* (1767) to combat the rationalistic theology of W. A. Teller.

Bibliography: E. BEYREUTHER, RGG[3] 1:1623–24. F. SCHÜHLEIN et al., LexThK[2] 2:955–956. H. LEUBE, *Die Reformideen in der deutschen lutherischen Kirche zur Zeit der Orthodoxie* (Leipzig 1924).

[R. H. FISCHER]

CARR, HENRY, educator, superior general of the Basilian Fathers (1930–42), and founder of the *Pontifical Institute of Mediaeval Studies, Toronto, Canada; b. Oshawa, Canada, Jan. 8, 1880; d. Vancouver, Nov. 28, 1963. Carr graduated from the University of Toronto in honor classics in 1903, after interrupting his studies to enter the Basilian novitiate at Toronto in 1900. From the 1st year of his priesthood, 1905, Carr planned to make St. Michael's the Catholic college in the University of Toronto, and he fashioned a working partnership between a Catholic college and a state university that has since been widely copied in English-speaking Canada. From 1915 to 1925 he was superior of St. Michael's College. In 1929 Carr founded the Institute of Mediaeval Studies and served as its president until 1936. He later established St. Thomas More College at the University of Saskatchewan, Saskatoon, where he was principal from 1942 to 1948. At the age of 71 he organized St. Mark's College at the University of British Columbia, Vancouver; he remained at its head until his retirement in 1961. During these and other activities, his qualities of heart made him the center of an immense circle of friends. Carr held honorary degrees from every institution at which he had taught: the University of Toronto, 1912; the University of Saskatchewan, 1952; Assumption University of Windsor, 1955; and the University of British Columbia, 1956.

Bibliography: "Father Henry Carr: A Symposium," *Basilian Teacher* 8 (1963–64) 287–334. *Basilian Annals* 3 (Nov. 1964) 295–297.

[R. J. SCOLLARD]

CARR, THOMAS MATTHEW, founder of the Augustinian Order in the U.S.; b. Dublin, Ireland, 1755; d. Philadelphia, Pa., Sept. 29, 1820. As the son of Michael and Mary (McDaniel) Carr, he was baptized Matthew. He was professed in the Augustinian Order in Dublin, Nov. 6, 1772, taking the name Thomas. He attended the order's house of studies in Toulouse, France, and was ordained there on June 13, 1778. After holding several offices in Dublin, including that of prior (1795), he answered Abp. John Carroll's plea for priests in America. He arrived in Philadelphia early in 1796, and spent the rest of his life in two main endeavors: mission work in the Philadelphia area and founding an American province of the Augustinians.

Upon his arrival Carr set about establishing the parish of St. Augustine's. A tract of land was bought and construction began in September 1776. Despite financial help obtained from a state-approved lottery and from such prominent Philadelphia citizens as Pres. George Washington, various difficulties delayed the dedication of St. Augustine's until June 1801. In the meantime Archbishop Carroll made Carr vicar-general for all of Pennsylvania east of the Susquehanna River (1799). In this capacity he healed the trustee schism at Holy Trinity Church in Philadelphia. On Aug. 27, 1796, his superior general in Rome appointed him prior of the Philadelphia community and superior of the American Augustinian missions, with the title of vicar-general. He was empowered to found new houses and to establish a novitiate. Legal recognition was obtained in 1804 when Gov. Thomas McKean of Pennsylvania signed the act of incorporation of the Brothers of the Order of Hermits of St. Augustine. Carr then spent some time in retirement at Conewago, Pa., and St. Mary's Seminary, Baltimore, Md., but he returned to St. Augustine's and, in 1811, opened St. Augustine's Academy, a secondary school of classical and religious studies. In 1812 he published a devotional book, *The Spiritual Mirror*. Before his death Carr willed all properties held in his name to the Order of St. Augustine, thus guaranteeing the order's permanency in the U.S.

[A. J. ENNIS]

CARRACCI

A family of Bolognese painters who played a prominent role in the pictorial reforms of the late 16th century. *Ludovico* (b. Bologna, 1555; d. 1619) was the cousin of *Agostino* (b. Bologna, 1557; d. Rome, 1602)

Annibale Carracci and his school, "Polyphemus and Galatea," detail of frescoes, Farnese Palace, Florence.

and his brother *Annibale* (b. Bologna, 1560; d. Rome, 1609), the most famous of the three. They were a potent force in the overthrow of late mannerism and the re-establishment of a "great tradition" in painting based on intense study from life models combined with the time-honored method of learning from the supreme achievements of the past. The richness and authority of the new idiom created by Annibale inspired *Bernini, Domenichino, Pietro da *Cortona, *Rubens, *Poussin, and Claude, among others, who represent trends as diverse as classical idealism and the full-blooded exuberance of the high baroque.

Ludovico's artistic education was the most extensive. He first studied with Prospero Fontana (*c.* 1570–80), then was apprentice to Passignano, and probably also studied with Camillo Procaccini. He traveled to Florence, Parma, Mantua, and Venice to study the local traditions. It was he who introduced Annibale to painting. Agostino was apprenticed to a goldsmith; he then studied painting with Fontana and Passerotti before entering the shop of the engraver Domenico Tibaldi.

The Carracci began painting in a common studio; in 1582 they opened an academy (L'Accademia degli Incamminati, the prototype for later art schools), in which life drawing occupied the central place in the curriculum. They made trips to Venice and Parma; Correggio and the Venetians became fundamental sources for their early work. The most notable commissions on which the three collaborated were the frescoes of the Palazzi Fava (1583–84) and Magnani-Salem (1588–91), though gradually their roles and styles became distinct. Agostino, who worked principally as an engraver, was the most cultivated and served as spokesman for their theories. Ludovico, who was the most emotional, searched for a dramatic and passionate language in such works as the "Holy Family with St. Francis" (1591, Cento Museum). His colorism, stressing patterns of light and dark often independent of organic form, inspired the young painters Lanfranco and Guercino.

Annibale's Bolognese altarpieces, the "Baptism of Christ" (1583, S. Gregorio) and the "Virgin with John, Francis, and Matthew" (1588, Dresden Gallery), fuse Correggiesque grace and *sfumato,* warm Venetian hues, and a structural sense reminiscent of central Italy into a new 16th-century effect. In 1595 Annibale was called to Rome to decorate the Farnese Palace. The allegorical frescoes of the Camerino (1595–97) and the Gallery (1597–1604) were his greatest achievement. Agostino joined him in 1597 and left at the end of 1599 to decorate the Palazzo Giardino in Parma, a project interrupted by his death. The theme of the vault of the Farnese Gallery is an allegory of the power of earthly and celestial love. Scenes from Ovid's *Metamorphoses* are conceived as framed easel paintings. These are surrounded by an elaborate but harmonious system of simulated architectural mouldings with decorative herms and atlantes foreshortened for the spectator's viewpoint, all painted to look like flesh and blood, stucco, or bronze. The dynamically unified and illusionistic scheme seems to grow out of the real architecture of the walls.

Besides producing the tonic example of the Farnese Palace that rejuvenated official painting for more than a century, Annibale was a leader in other areas. His late paintings, such as "Domine, quo vadis" (1601–02, National Gallery, London), attempt a moving rhetoric of feeling and gesture akin to that of classical tragedy. He

Ludovico Carracci, "The Dream of St. Catherine of Alexandria," oil on canvas, 54⅝ by 43½ inches.

created a new poetic concept of pure landscape painting, incorporating naturalistic detail within a formally arranged panorama. Finally, Annibale was the inventor of modern caricature and, with Agostino, did much to stimulate the production of informal genre scenes observed from life.

See also BAROQUE ART.

Bibliography: Sources: G. MANCINI, *Considerazioni sulla pittura,* ed. A. MARRUCHI and L. SALERNO, 2 v. (Rome 1956–57). G. P. BELLORI, *Le vite de' pittori, scultori ed architetti moderni* (Rome 1672). C. C. MALVASIA, *Felsina Pittrice,* 2 v. (Bologna 1678; repr. 1841).

Literature. A. FORATTI, *I Carracci nella teoria e nella pratica* (Città di Castello 1913). H. VOSS, *Die Malerei des Barock in Rom* (Berlin 1925). H. BODMER, *Lodovico Carracci* (Burg b. Magdeburg 1939). D. MAHON, *Studies in Seicento Art and Theory* (London 1947); "Afterthoughts on the Carracci Exhibition," *Gazette des Beaux Arts,* 49 (1957) 193–207, 267–298. R. WITTKOWER, *The Drawings of the Carracci in the Collection of Her Majesty the Queen at Windsor Castle* (London 1952); *Art and Architecture in Italy, 1600–1750* (PelHart Z16; 1958). G. C. CAVALLI et al., eds., *Mostra dei Carracci: Catalogo critico* (Bologna 1956), has complete bibliog. to that date. Musée National du Louvre, *Dessins des Carrache,* ed. J. BOUCHOT-SAUPIQUE (Paris 1961). **Illustration credits:** Fig. 1, Alinari-Art Reference Bureau. Fig. 2, The National Gallery of Art, Samuel H. Kress Collection, Washington, D.C.

[R. M. ARB]

CARRANZA, BARTOLOMÉ DE, theologian; b. Miranda de Arga (Navarra), Spain, about 1503; d. Rome, May 2, 1576. Because of his place of birth he was called Fray Bartolomé de Miranda. He studied at Alcalá (1515–20) and entered the Dominican Order. He continued his studies at Valladolid, taught the liberal arts and theology in the same city (1530), and was promoted to master of theology at Rome (1539). He was present at the Council of Trent as the imperial theologian

(1545–47; 1551–52). He also served as a consultant during the Inquisition. He was named prior of Palencia (1549) and provincial of Castile (1550). He worked actively for the Catholic restoration in England (1554–57) and in Flanders. He was offered the bishoprics of Cusco, Peru (1542), and the Canary Islands (1549) but refused them both. Philip II, however, constrained him to accept the archbishropic of Toledo (1557). In his life and works he showed himself a zealous reformer; and he put his reforms into practice in his archdiocese, until in August of 1559 his apostolic activities were interrupted by his imprisonment by the Inquisition.

From prison he exercised great influence against a strong anti-Protestant reaction in Spain, the hatred and scheming of the Grand Inquisitor, Don Fernando de Valdes, and the theological formalism and passion of Melchior Cano. His trial began with the approval of Philip II, and under the authority of Paul IV; it continued during the reign of Pius IV, who succeeded in naming special legates. His refusal to accept the presence of the Grand Inquisitor was honored (1560), and he was defended by Martin de Azpilicueta, an eminent jurist. He was accused of teaching Lutheran doctrine in his books and sermons, and hundreds of propositions, allegedly heretical, were extracted from his works. Pius V ordered the prisoner to be brought to Rome (1566), but died as he was about to pronounce an acquittal (1572). Philip II and the Inquisition worked harder to obtain his condemnation. Gregory XIII made him retract 16 theological propositions as "vehemently suspicious of heresy" in April 1576. On his tomb in Santa Maria sopra Minerva, Gregory XIII ordered a laudatory inscription: "Viro genere, vita, doctrina, contione atque elemosinis claro."

His published works are: *De necessaria residentia episcoporum* (Venice 1547), *Summa Conciliorum . . . Quatuor Controversiae* (Venice 1546), and *Commentarios sobre el Catechismo Christiano* (Antwerp 1558). A great part of his theological, ascetical, Biblical, and pastoral works have not been edited. However, José I. Tellechea Idígoras was preparing an edition in 1964.

Bibliography: A. D'Amato, EncCatt 3:932. J. I. Tellechea Idígoras, LexThK[2] 2:957; *Fray Bartolomé Carranza: Documentos Históricos,* 2 v. (Archivo Documental Español 18.19; Madrid 1962–63); *Bartolomé Carranza, Arzobispo . . . de Toledo* (San Sebastián 1958); "Los prolegómenos jurídicos del proceso de Carranza," *Anthologica Annua* 7 (Rome 1959) 215–336; "Censura de Fray J. de la Peña sobre proposiciones de C.," *ibid.* 10 (1962) 399–449; "Melchor Cano y Bartolomé Carranza," *Hispania Sacra* 15 (1962) 5–93.

[J. I. TELLECHEA IDÍGORAS]

CARREL, ALEXIS

Surgeon, biologist, Nobel prize winner, and member of the Pontifical Academy of Science; b. Ste. Foy-lès-Lyon, France, June 28, 1873; d. Paris, Nov. 5, 1944. He studied at the universities of Dijon and Lyon, graduated from Lyon in 1890, and received his medical degree in 1900. For 2 years he remained at Lyon as prosector of the university, there initiating his own research. In 1905, Carrel went to the United States and continued his research at the Hull laboratory of the University of Chicago.

In 1906 he received a staff appointment to the Rockefeller Institute for Medical Research; he became a full member in 1912. That same year, he was awarded the Nobel prize in physiology and medicine for his discovery of new ways of suturing blood vessels and transplanting living organs. He also investigated the possibility of tissues living outside the body, suspecting that entire organs as well as tissue, if properly treated and fed, could live indefinitely. This hypothesis was confirmed when, in 1912, he removed, from a chicken embryo, heart tissue that remained alive until 1946. In addition to keeping it alive (*in vitro*), he discovered (1913) that its growth could be stimulated many times by adding certain substances from embryonic animal tissue. He continued to conduct major experiments at the Rockefeller Institute until 1939, during which time, in collaboration with Charles Lindbergh, in 1935, he developed the beginnings of the artificial heart (heart pump).

In 1914 Carrel returned to Compiègne, France, where through the Rockefeller Foundation he established a laboratory and military hospital, and with *Lecomte du Noüy and others examined the healing of wounds. There too, he and H. D. Dakin, the noted English chemist, devised from easily obtainable ingredients an antiseptic that did no damage to living cells, was able to retain its strength in blood serum, and aided in the separation of dead from living cells for treating wounds. This Carrel-Dakin solution (Dakin's fluid) saved countless lives and prevented amputations during World War I. In 1919 Carrel returned to the U.S. to resume medical experimentation.

In 1936 he published *Man the Unknown,* which was translated into 18 languages. In France again in 1939, after retirement from the Rockefeller Institute, he tried in vain to establish a research center to study the effects of malnutrition in children. He sought financial assistance in Spain and the U.S., and in 1941 he finally received Marshal Henri Petain's authorization to establish the French Foundation for the Study of Human Problems, in Paris. This was closed shortly before his death. Carrel's other published works are *Culture of Organs,* with C. A. Lindbergh (1939); *Prayer* (tr. D. Wright, London 1947; New York 1948); *Voyage to Lourdes* (tr. V. Peterson, New York 1950); and *Reflections on Life,* (tr. A. White, London 1952; New York 1953). Carrel had always maintained a Christian attitude, and his scientific study of the miracles at Lourdes intensified this. He had not been a practicing Catholic during most of his life, but he was reconciled with the Church a few weeks before his death.

Bibliography: R. Soupault, *Alexis Carrel, 1873–1944* (Paris 1951).

[W. C. MANION]

CARREÑO, ALBERTO MARÍA, Mexican scholar; b. Tacubaya, Mexico, Aug. 7, 1875; d. Mexico City, Sept. 5, 1962. He was permanent secretary of the Mexican Academy of Linguistics; director of the Mexican Academy of History; professor and lecturer; and a prolific writer on scientific, economic, sociological, literary, historical, and philological subjects. As secretary of Joaquín D. Casasús, Mexican agent in the arbitration of the Chamizal affair, Carreño was well informed on this question. From 1927 to 1929 he held a professorship at Fordham University, New York. His serious and conscientious research work in the archives of Mexico and the United States resulted in two voluminous documented books: *Méjico y los Estados Unidos de*

América, on the territorial gains of the U.S. at the expense of Mexico from the colonial times to the 20th century, written in 1913 and published in 1922, and *La diplomacia extraordinaria entre Méjico y Estados Unidos, 1789 to 1947,* 2 v. (Mexico City 1951). As private secretary of the Archbishop of Mexico, Pascual Díaz, he had to mediate in many hazardous affairs during the religious persecution by Calles (1926–29). He preserved, even in old age, his intellectual and physical vigor, a powerful and clear voice, and indefatigable energy. Among his numerous works, all of them showing sound scholarship, are: *El Chamizal y el Presidente Woodrow Wilson* (1913), *Jefes del ejército mejicano en 1847* (1914), *La fuerza como base del derecho natural y como génesis del derecho artificial* (1919), *Federico Alejandro, Barón de Humboldt* (1919), *La guerra actual y la dictadura económica del estado* (1919), *Fray Domingo de Betanzos* (1934), *Problemas indígenas* (1936), *Semblanzas,* 3 v. (1936–38–39), *Temas económicos* (1938), *Lugares, hombres y cosas* (1938), *El Padre Miguel Agustín Pro* (1938), *Historia de la Academia Mejicana correspondiente de la Española* (1945), *Hernán Cortés y el descubrimiento de sus restos* (1947), *Don Fray Juan de Zumárraga, teólogo y editor, humanista e inquisidor* (1950), and *La Real y Pontificia Universidad de México, 1536–1865* (1962).

[A. JUNCO]

CARRIÈRE, JOSEPH, Sulpician moral theologian; b. Panouze-de-Cernon, near Rodez, France, Feb. 19, 1795; d. Lyons, April 23, 1864. He attended the Sulpician seminary at Issy, where he taught theology even before ordination. Immediately after ordination in 1817 he was assigned to teach the postgraduate course in moral theology at the seminary in Paris. Here he composed a remarkable course, *Praelectiones theologicae majores in seminario Sancti Sulpitii habitae* (1837–47), of which he published three sections: *De matrimonio* (2 v. Paris 1837); *De justitia et jure* (3 v. Paris 1839); and *De contractibus* (3. v. Paris 1844–47). These treatises went through several editions and won him great acclaim. He was the first writer of note to treat of theology in its relations to the Napoleonic Code, and his expositions of French law were accepted as authoritative by the jurists of his time, who admired him greatly for his knowledge, clarity, fairness, and decisiveness of judgment and his simplicity and modesty of character. Extant correspondence with bishops, priests, and laymen show how highly his advice was esteemed. As official visitator of the Sulpician houses in the U.S. in 1829 he attended the First Council of Baltimore. In 1850 he became the 13th superior general of the Society of Saint Sulpice.

Bibliography: E. LEVESQUE, DHGE 11:1131–32; DTC 2.2: 1804–05. L. BERTRAND, *Bibliothèque sulpicienne,* 3 v. (Paris 1900) 2:272–281. P. H. LAMAZOU, *M. Carrière, supérieur de Saint Sulpice* (Paris 1864). Hurter Nomencl 5.1:1389.

[M. J. BARRY]

CARROLL, CHARLES

Statesman, signer of the Declaration of Independence; b. Annapolis, Md., Sept. 19, 1737; d. Baltimore, Md., Nov. 14, 1832. The only son of Charles and Elizabeth (Brooke) Carroll, he used "of Carrollton," the name of one of his estates, to distinguish himself from his father, "of Annapolis," and his grandfather, "the Attorney General." The first Charles Carroll had emigrated to Lord Baltimore's tolerant palatinate because of English religious discriminations; these extended to Maryland after 1688 and he lost his attorney general's commission. Disbarred from political life, he concentrated on amassing wealth so that his grandson, Charles Carroll of Carrollton, was born to the greatest fortune in the American colonies.

Charles Carroll of Carrollton, watercolor by T. Sully, 1829.

Early Life. Bohemia Manor Academy, secretly conducted by the Society of Jesus in defiance of Maryland law, prepared Charles Carroll and his cousin John, afterward Archbishop *Carroll, for the English Jesuit college of St. Omer, in French Flanders. Following his studies there, Carroll attended the Collège Louis-le-Grand in Paris. Although religious disability would prevent his practising in Maryland, he studied law in Bourges, Paris, and London. After 16 years of European education, he returned to Annapolis June 5, 1768, and married Mary Darnall. All but three of their seven children died young.

The Stamp Act had had violent repercussions in Maryland, and Carroll's father was one of those who, on the passage of the Townshend Acts, set up manufactories. However, a provincial matter was responsible for Carroll's entry into public life. Under Gov. Robert Eden, the assembly and council of 1770 were bitterly opposed on the question of regulating officers' fees and stipends of the clergy of the Established Church. On Jan. 7, 1773, a dialogue in the *Maryland Gazette,* unsigned but generally believed to be the work of Secretary Daniel Dulany, received wide attention. It presented a "First Citizen" whose arguments against the official position were demolished by a "Second Citizen's" replies, at least for the time being.

"Second Citizen," however, did not have the last word. In the *Gazette* of Feb. 4, 1773, "First Citizen" was victor in another dialogue, written obviously by another author. Dulany, replying, signed "Antilon"; Carroll, replying in turn, signed "First Citizen"; and so the exchange continued until midsummer. Resorting finally to sneers at Carroll as a disfranchised Catholic, Dulany's weapon boomeranged as feeling in favor of the discriminated-against "First Citizen" mounted. The controversy established Carroll's preeminence in Maryland, where citizens publicly thanked him for defending their liberties. *See* CHURCH AND STATE IN THE U.S. (LEGAL HISTORY), 1.

Public Career. Carroll became a member of the Committee of Correspondence for Annapolis in 1774 and was active in the "Peggy Stewart" affair. Suspecting that anti-Catholic sentiment engendered by the recent Quebec Act would mar his usefulness, he declined as delegate to the first Continental Congress but accompanied the Maryland delegation as unofficial consultant. Although his religion was unpopular, his Catholicism was the chief reason for his appointment to the first American diplomatic mission to try to ingratiate the French Canadians. His fellow members were Benjamin Franklin and Samuel Chase, and his cousin John Carroll, SJ, was asked to accompany them. The mission was sent too late to be successful, but it established Carroll as a national figure. On July 4, 1776, he was elected to Congress from Maryland. He took his seat July 18, and on August 2 signed his customary "Charles Carroll of Carrollton" to the Declaration of Independence, which his efforts had influenced Maryland to support.

Carroll was placed on the Board of War, which during the Conway Cabal "investigated" George Washington at Valley Forge. He resigned from Congress in 1778, after the consummation of the French alliance; he also refused to accept reelection later in the year, and did not return to national politics until 1789, when he became a U.S. senator under the new constitution. He had refused, moreover, during a Maryland political emergency, to go as a delegate to the Constitutional Convention in Philadelphia, but he worked for ratification, becoming strongly and permanently identified with the new Federalist party. His Senate service ended in 1792 when Congress passed a law forbidding state legislators to serve in Congress. Carroll's service in the Maryland body was continued until 1800, the year of the Federalist overthrow. He viewed with alarm the election of Thomas Jefferson and opposed most Republican measures. He later reprobated the War of 1812.

Carroll spent his old age in studious pursuits, one of his extensive projects being a comparative study of religions. He also interested himself in charitable and educational movements and served as president of the American Colonization Society, which founded Liberia. He was identified with companies promoting westward expansion and, as a director, laid the cornerstone of the Baltimore and Ohio's new railroad July 4, 1828. This was his last appearance in public. He lived 4 years longer, dying at the age of 95, the last surviving signer of the Declaration of Independence.

Bibliography: E. H. SMITH, *Charles Carroll of Carrollton* (Cambridge, Mass. 1942). **Illustration credit:** Courtesy of the Walters Art Gallery, Baltimore.

[E. H. SMITH]

CARROLL, DANIEL, American patriot, delegate to the Continental Congress and Constitutional Convention, signer of the U.S. Constitution; b. Upper Marlborough, Md., July 22, 1730; d. Rock Creek, Md., May 7, 1796. He was the son of Daniel and Eleanor (Darnall) Carroll and brother of John, the future archbishop of Baltimore. The family was related to the Darnalls, Digges, Lees, and Horseys of Maryland, and

Daniel Carroll.

to the Carters and Brents of Virginia. Daniel Carroll II, who also married an Eleanor Darnall, daughter of Ann Rozier Darnall of England, was a first cousin by marriage to Charles Carroll of Carrollton. With his successful ventures into the business of merchant, plantation owner, and tobacco farmer, and with the large inheritance from both his father and wife, Daniel Carroll II early became a prosperous aristocrat of great wealth.

He entered political life in 1777, at a time when Maryland, of all the colonies, was most opposed to independence. Despite the stern opposition of the proprietary government, Carroll realized the need for more democratic legislation if unity was to be assured in the colony. For 18 years, in both state and national affairs, he fought the prevailing conservative, political, and religious views of his day: in the Maryland Senate and Council (1777–80); in the Continental Congress (1780–84); in the Constitutional Convention (1787–88); as member of the U.S. House of Representatives (1780–91); and as a commissioner for planning the capital in Washington (1791–95).

Carroll believed that a strong, centralized Federal government was necessary for the preservation of the nation. He favored Federal control of western lands and believed that the growing radicalism in state governments should be checked and religious toleration practiced in all states. In his view, reserved powers should be given to the people if not delegated to the central government. Despite divided opinion on the issue in his own state, he strongly urged Maryland's ratification of the Constitution, of which he was one of the two Catholic signers.

Though frequently overshadowed by his more famous cousin, Charles Carroll of Carrollton, eclipsed by his brother John, first archbishop of Baltimore, and confused with his distant relative, Daniel Carroll of Duddington, Daniel Carroll II of Upper Marlborough made a lasting contribution in his emphasis on the value of strong, centralized government and the recognition of the dignity of man and his need for religious liberty.

Bibliography: M. V. GEIGER, *Daniel Carroll* (Washington 1943); "Daniel Carroll," *Catholic World* 163 (May 1946) 163–166. **Illustration credit:** From the Collections of the Maryland Historical Society.

[M. V. GEIGER]

CARROLL, HOWARD JOSEPH, bishop, administrator; b. Pittsburgh, Pa., Aug. 5, 1902; d. Washington, D.C., March 21, 1960. He was educated at Duquesne University, Pittsburgh; St. Vincent's College, Latrobe, Pa.; and the University of Fribourg, Switzerland, from which he earned a doctorate in sacred theology. Carroll, ordained on April 2, 1927, was a curate at Sacred Heart Church, Pittsburgh, from 1928 to 1938, and also taught philosophy at Mt. Mercy College, Pittsburgh, during that period. During World War II he held high offices in the National Catholic Community Service, and he was an original member of the board of directors of the United Service Organizations (USO). He also served as Chairman of the Overseas Committee of the USO. From 1944 to 1957 he was the general secretary of the National Catholic Welfare Conference (NCWC). In this office he assisted in the organization of the NCWC Catholic Relief Services, Departments of Youth and Immigration, Office for United Nations Affairs, Catholic Resettlement Committee, Foreign Visitors Office, Bureau of Health and Hospitals, National Council of Catholic Nurses, and Bureau of Information. He also helped establish *Noticias Catolicas,* the Spanish and Portuguese translations of the National Catholic News Service. In 1955 he became the U.S. representative of the Supreme Council for Emigration of the Consistorial Congregation, and 2 years later he was consecrated as the first bishop of Altoona-Johnstown, Pa. As bishop he undertook an ambitious building program that included a new cathedral in Altoona. Carroll was honored as a papal chamberlain (1942), a chevalier of the French Legion of Honor (1949), and a recipient of the LL.D. from St. Vincent's College (1958).

Howard Joseph Carroll.

[P. F. TANNER]

CARROLL, JOHN

First Catholic bishop of the U.S., Archbishop of Baltimore; b. Upper Marlborough, Md., Jan. 8, 1735; d. Baltimore, Dec. 3, 1815. The third of seven children of Daniel and Eleanor (Darnall) Carroll was born of a distinguished family. Through his father he descended from Keane Carroll of Ireland, the elder brother of Charles Carroll who migrated to Maryland and served there as attorney general. Through his mother he was related to the Darnalls, whose American branch was founded by Col. Henry Darnall, brother-in-law of Lord Baltimore.

Early Years. Carroll's education began at home with his mother, who had been educated in France; later he attended Bohemia Manor, a short-lived Jesuit school in northern Maryland. In 1748, with his cousin Charles, a signer of the Declaration of Independence, he went to St. Omer, conducted by English Jesuits in French Flanders. He entered the Jesuit novitiate at Watten in 1753 under Father Henry Corbie and in 1755 became a Jesuit scholastic. Completing the scholasticate at Liège, he taught philosophy there, made his profession in 1771, and then taught at the Jesuit college in Bruges. The exact dates of his ordination and renouncing of his father's legacy cannot be documented, but the former probably took place in 1769 and the latter between 1764 and 1771.

After teaching a few months at Bruges, with his superior's consent he toured the Continent as tutor to Charles Philippe, son of the English Lord Stourton. His journal of the tour (1771–73) offers interesting comment on the central and southern Europe of that time. In the summer of 1773, he became prefect of the sodality at Bruges, where he received news of the dissolution of the Society of Jesus by papal action on July 21, 1773. In October, Austrian officials invaded the college and he was arrested. On the intervention of the English Lord Arundell of Wardour Castle, he was released and went to Wardour as family chaplain until the spring of 1774.

Return to America. Carroll returned in 1774 to live with his mother at Rock Creek, Md. In 1776, the Continental Congress persuaded him to accompany Charles Carroll, Samuel Chase, and Benjamin Franklin to Canada in an effort to win the province to the side of the Colonies in their revolt against England. Arriving in Montreal in April, he was shown no courtesies on the order of Bp. Joseph *Briand and had to offer Mass privately in the house of Father Pierre Floquet, a former Jesuit. After the commission's failure, he went to Philadelphia with the ailing Franklin, earning his gratitude for his "friendly assistance and tender care."

After his return to Rock Creek, his zealous ministry soon necessitated the building of St. John's Chapel at Forest Glen on the property of his brother Daniel, one of the framers of the Constitution; he also had to travel 60-mile journeys to reach a Virginia congregation.

Desiring to protect former Jesuit properties in the new nation and to organize the clergy for a more effective ministry, in 1782 he devised a plan that was in substance adopted in 1784, creating a "Form of Government, Rules for the Select Body of Clergy, and Regulations for the Management of Plantations." The American clergy petitioned Rome to name Father John Lewis their superior; but when a vicar-general was appointed, Carroll, on Franklin's recommendation, was made "head of the missions in the provinces . . . of the United States" on June 9, 1784. During the next 6 years he visited his territory, reported to Rome on conditions (March 1, 1785), and publicly defended the beliefs and rights of Catholics in the new Republic.

In 1784, he published the *Address to the Roman Catholics of the United States of America,* defending the Faith against the attacks of the apostate Jesuit Charles Wharton, whose *Letter to the Roman Catholics of Worcester* had appeared in Philadelphia earlier that year. In the Philadelphia *Columbian* of December 1787, he answered attacks on religious liberty made in its pages, saying: "Freedom and independence acquired by the united efforts, and cemented with the mingled blood of Protestants and Catholic fellow-citizens, should be equally enjoyed by all." In the *United States Gazette,* June 10, 1789, under the name "Pacificus," he reiterated the principle that the Republic had been created by the "generous exertion of all her citizens to redress their wrongs, to assert their rights, and to lay its foundations on the soundest principles of justice and equal liberty." In December 1789, he composed an "Address of the Roman Catholics" to President Washington, congratulating him on his office and reasserting that Catholics had a well-founded title to justice and equal rights in return for their exertions in the nation's defense.

First U.S. Bishop. In 1788 Rome had decided to create the first diocese in the U.S., and on Sept. 17, 1789, Pius VI ordered the bull prepared naming Carroll bishop of *Baltimore, thereby confirming the choice of the American clergy. *See* BALTIMORE, ARCHDIOCESE OF. His consecration took place Aug. 15, 1790, in Lulworth Chapel on the estate of Thomas Weld in Dorset, England, with Bp. Charles Walmesley presiding and Father Charles Plowden preaching the sermon.

As first Catholic bishop, Carroll set a precedent for cordial relations between the government and the hierarchy. In 1791 at his first synod, he initiated the custom of public prayers for the president and the government. He influenced Washington to ask Congress for an appropriation to support the work of two priests among the Indians of the Northwest Territory. Carroll also visited Washington in retirement at Mount Vernon and preached the first president's eulogy at St. Peter's Church in Baltimore on Feb. 22, 1800.

His relations with Jefferson were equally cordial, and when the Louisiana Territory was purchased in 1803, he secured Jefferson's protection for the Ursuline nuns and their properties. In return, he appointed to Louisiana priests devoted to American principles, eliciting Jefferson's comment that he had perfect confidence in Carroll's "patriotism and purity of views." Although opposed to the War of 1812, he defended Madison for his religious principles and his endeavors to preserve peace. In tribute to his patriotism, Carroll was invited to speak at the laying of the cornerstone of the Washington Monument in Baltimore but had to decline because of illness.

Interest in Education. Carroll was also a promoter of culture. From its founding until his death, he was president of the Baltimore Library Company and instituted its printed catalog. Under his auspices Catholic colleges for men were founded in Maryland at Georgetown (1788), Baltimore (St. Mary's, 1799), and at Emmitsburg (Mt. St. Mary's, 1808). Academies for girls were begun at Georgetown (Visitation, 1799), Emmitsburg (St. Joseph's, 1809), and Bardstown, Ky. (Nazareth, 1814).

Although primarily concerned with religious education, he had so deep a conviction that education must flourish in the Republic that he became famous in Maryland as a patron of secular schools as well. In 1784 he became a member of the board of directors of the newly chartered St. John's College at Annapolis and was elected president of the board 4 years later. In 1785 at the second annual commencement of Washington College, Chestertown, Md., honorary degrees were conferred on both George Washington and Carroll. The next year he presided at the public meeting held to initiate a boys' academy for Baltimore. In 1801 he began serving as director on the board of the nonsectarian Female Humane Association Charity School. Two years later he was elected president of the board of trustees for the newly founded Baltimore College open to all denominations. When the University of Maryland was rechartered in 1812 he was elected provost, but had to decline because of ecclesiastical burdens. A monument to Carroll's cultural influence is the old Cathedral of the Assumption in Baltimore, whose cornerstone he laid on July 7, 1806, and whose design he influenced by collaborating with the architect, Benjamin Latrobe.

Portrait of Abp. John Carroll, on view at Georgetown University; painted from life by U.S. artist Gilbert Stuart.

Ecclesiastical Administration. Carroll possessed a genius for organization. To him are due the formulation of the principles and the foundations that made possible the later expansion and status of the Church in the U.S. As first bishop, and later first archbishop of Baltimore, he deserves full credit for the vitality of the faith in the early years of the Republic.

After his consecration, faced with the task of coordinating the work of his clergy he called the first national synod in 1791. Under his guidance, rules were drawn up governing the administration of the Sacraments of Baptism, Holy Eucharist, Penance, and Matrimony for a country where the Catholic minority were scattered, often far from priests, and frequently parties to mixed marriages. The problem of his successor was also discussed and the synod recommended to Rome that the diocese be divided, with a second bishop at Philadelphia, or that a coadjutor with the right of succession be appointed. When Rome adopted the second alternative, he was given a coadjutor in 1794, but it was not until December 1800 that the first coadjutor bishop, Leonard * Neale, was consecrated.

In 1802 Carroll again suggested a division of his diocese and received Rome's permission to recommend boundaries, episcopal cities, and candidates for the new dioceses. He then recommended four sees: Boston, comprising the five New England states of that time; New York, with jurisdiction over that state and eastern New Jersey; Philadelphia, controlling the rest of New Jersey, Pennsylvania, and Delaware; and Bardstown, Ky., embracing Kentucky and Tennessee. For bishop of Boston, he recommended Jean * Cheverus; for Philadelphia, Michael * Egan; for Bardstown, Benedict * Flaget; for New York, however, he made no recommendation, believing that no worthy candidate could be found in that city. When, on April 8, 1808, Pius VII created the sees, Carroll's candidates were appointed and Richard Concanen was named bishop of New York. Carroll continued his jurisdiction over Maryland and the South; and because Concanen, who was in Italy when he was consecrated, could not find transportation to New York, Carroll made Anthony Kohlmann vicar-general until the bishop should arrive. He consecrated the other new bishops in Baltimore in 1810. The hierarchy then drew up an agreement for the uniformity of Catholic discipline throughout the country. Together with the regulation of the Synod of 1791, this agreement constitutes the earliest codification of Canon Law for the church in the U.S. Carroll and his suffragans also drafted, on Nov. 15, 1810, a solemn protest against Napoleon's captivity of Pius VII and sent it with their first joint encyclical to the hierarchy of Ireland.

Carroll received the *pallium brought by the British minister, Augustus Foster, on Aug. 18, 1811. By this time he believed that Louisiana and Florida warranted another diocese and recommended the president of St. Mary's College in Baltimore, Louis Dubourg, who went to New Orleans in 1812 as apostolic administrator of the diocese and was consecrated bishop in 1815.

Religious Foundations. Deeply concerned for the spiritual and educational needs of the laity, he encouraged foundations of religious orders for women: the Carmelites, who settled at Port Tobacco, Md., in 1790; the Poor Clares, who first settled at Frederick, Md.; the Sisters of Loretto at the Foot of the Cross, founded in 1812 at Hardin's Creek, Ky.; and the Sisters of Charity of Nazareth, also founded in Kentucky in 1812.

The foundation of the first distinctly American community of religious women, the Sisters of Charity of St. Joseph, was due to his encouragement of their founder, Bl. Elizabeth * Seton. He had first heard of Mrs. Seton through the Filicchi brothers of Leghorn, Italy; the younger, Antonio, interested him in her conversion in 1804. Carroll confirmed her in New York on May 25, 1806. Two years later he encouraged her to start a school for Catholic girls in Baltimore. In March 1809, he permitted her to take vows, insisting, however, that she accept a dispensation from complete poverty so that she might provide for her five children. During her first difficult years as superior of the small community in Emmitsburg, Carroll was her support and mentor. When on Jan. 17, 1812, he confirmed the rules for her community, although they were substantially those of the French Daughters of St. Vincent de Paul, he saw to it that modifications allowed for conditions in the United States and for Mother Seton's peculiar situation as religious superior and mother of five children.

Carroll encouraged religious orders of men as well. An Augustinian monastery was established in Philadelphia in 1796 under Thomas Matthew *Carr, with George Washington among the contributors to the building fund for St. Augustine's Church. The Dominicans, arriving in 1804, hoped to start a monastery under Edward *Fenwick in Maryland, but were persuaded to go to Kentucky where Carroll saw greater need for them. By 1807 they had opened St. Thomas School for boys there.

Having been himself a Jesuit, Carroll hoped to see the Society restored in the U.S. Moreover, rather than see the Jesuits divested of any part of their original strength, he opposed in 1800 the affiliation of the former Jesuits of the U.S. with a pseudo-Jesuit society calling themselves the *Paccanarists. On March 7, 1801, when a pontifical brief granted canonical existence to the Society in Russia, he sought means of aggregating the American group to the Russian; and on June 21, 1805, he named Robert *Molyneux to head the qualified restoration. On Dec. 7, 1814, he had the pleasure of receiving a copy of the bull that restored the Society throughout the world. He was too old to rejoin, but cherished "the greatest sensation of joy and thanksgiving" that the Society of Jesus would flourish in the U.S.

To foster the increase of a secular clergy, he supported the establishment of St. Mary's Seminary. While still in England for his consecration in 1790, he had begun negotiations with the French Society of Saint Sulpice to found a seminary in Baltimore, which opened the following year; and in 1802 he vigorously opposed the recall of the Sulpicians to France.

Dissension and Controversy. Thirty priests were trained at St. Mary's between May 25, 1793, when Carroll ordained Stephen * Badin, the first graduate, and Carroll's own death in 1815. The growth of a native clergy was slow, however, and he had to rely increasingly upon priests from Ireland, France, and Germany—clergy whose temperaments and nationalistic leanings created problems. Germans in Philadelphia and Westmoreland County, Pa., disputed his jurisdiction in 1798; in the former case causing his arrest, and in the latter taking him to court, where Judge Alexander Addison vindicated him, declaring him "the sole episcopal authority . . . of the United States." The next year in Baltimore, a German priest and congregation at St. John's Church began open opposition that resulted in 4 years of controversy and another court action in which he was again vindicated.

In Norfolk, Va., Charlestown, S.C., and Augusta, Ga., Irish priests allied themselves with trustees to resist his authority. Although the majority of the French clergy proved invaluable, three of their number becoming his suffragan bishops, a few caused scandal and a few returned to France when the position of the Church there improved after 1802. And while Carroll appreciated the ideals and labors of the priests in religious orders, he nevertheless suffered opposition from some of their superiors, among them Charles Neale and John Grassi of the Jesuits.

Significance. Carroll's leadership and administration of the Church in the U.S. fixed traditions that later enhanced its prestige. His devotion to religious freedom and his delineation of the relations of the Church with Rome in spiritual matters defined and gave proof of the compatibility of Catholicism and democracy. His charity was endless. In these difficult years he measured each crisis by the ultimate and common good not only of the Church but also of the nation. He lived to see independence declared, won, and again preserved in the War of 1812; the Catholic population quadrupled and the clergy doubled. As Cardinal Gibbons expressed it: "His aim was that the clergy and people should be . . . identified with the land. . . . From this mutual accord of Church and State there could but follow beneficent effects for both." Enfeebled by age and illness, Carroll received the last Sacraments on November 23 and died on Dec. 3, 1815. He was buried in the chapel of St. Mary's Seminary, but in 1824 his body was removed to the Cathedral (later Basilica) of the Assumption.

Bibliography: D. BRENT, *Biographical Sketch of the Most Rev. John Carroll,* ed. J. C. Brent (Baltimore 1843). P. GUILDAY, *The Life and Times of John Carroll, Archbishop of Baltimore, 1735–1815* (Westminster, Md. 1954). J. D. SHEA, *Life and Times of the Most Rev. John Carroll, Bishop and First Archbishop of Baltimore* (New York 1888). A. M. MELVILLE, *John Carroll of Baltimore* (New York 1955). **Illustration credit:** Georgetown University News Service.

[A. M. MELVILLE]

CARROLL, JOHN LEE, lawyer, governor; b. Baltimore, Md., Sept. 30, 1830; d. Ellicott City, Md., Feb. 27, 1911. His great-grandfather was Charles Carroll, the last surviving signer of the Declaration of Independence. His parents were Charles and Mary Digges (Lee) Carroll. He was educated at Mt. St. Mary's College, Emmitsburg, Md., Georgetown College (now University), Washington, D.C., St. Mary's College, Baltimore, and Harvard Law School. Admitted to the Maryland bar in 1851, he ran for election to the state legislature in 1855 but lost to a Know-Nothing opponent. The next year he married Anita Phelps of New York; after her death in 1873, he married Mary Carter Thompson of Virginia in 1877. After holding a minor post in New York State (1858–61), he returned to Maryland and was elected (1867) to the state senate. In 1874 he became president of the senate and the following year was nominated for governor on the Democratic ticket. He carried the state by more than 10,000 votes. His administration followed constructive policies, but was marred by the Baltimore and Ohio Railroad strike of 1877. Before it could be settled, raging mobs destroyed railroad property from Baltimore to Pittsburgh, and scores of men were killed or injured. When local regiments showed signs of sympathizing with the strikers, Carroll incurred labor enmity by calling for Federal troops to help preserve order. He left office in 1880 and thereafter devoted himself to the management of his personal affairs.

Bibliography: M. W. WILLIAMS, DAB (1957) 2.1:528.

[H. W. KIRWIN]

CARROLL, JOHN PATRICK, bishop; b. Dubuque, Iowa, Feb. 22, 1864; d. Fribourg, Switzerland, Nov. 4, 1925. He was the son of Martin and Catherine (O'Farrell) Carroll. After completing his primary education at St. Raphael's School, Dubuque, he entered the secondary department of St. Joseph's College (later Loras) in the same city. He attended the Grand Seminary, Montreal, Canada, for philosophical and theological studies and was ordained in 1889. He served as

John Patrick Carroll.

professor of philosophy at St. Joseph's until 1894, when he was appointed president of the college. In 1904, Carroll succeeded John B. Brondel, first bishop of Helena, Mont. His first concerns as bishop were the erection of a larger cathedral and the establishment of a diocesan college. He laid the cornerstone of the new cathedral in 1908, formally dedicated it in 1914, and arranged its formal consecration in 1924. Construction of Mount St. Charles College in Helena (later named Carroll College in his honor) was begun in 1909.

In 1908, Carroll was proposed as successor of Bp. Denis J. O'Connell as rector of The Catholic University of America, Washington, D.C., but the Holy See did not make the appointment. Carroll served in 1910 and 1912 as national chaplain of the Ancient Order of Hibernians. He was nationally known as an orator, and he delivered the principal address at the Washington Celebration in Portland, Ore.; preached at the dedication of the cathedrals in Cheyenne, Wyo., and Seattle, Wash.; delivered the oration of the Catholic Day at the Alaska-Yukon Pacific Exposition; and addressed the national convention of the American Federation of Labor at Seattle in 1913. In 1925, during the crisis aroused by the Oregon School Case, he opposed an Oregon statute, which was ultimately declared unconstitutional, requiring public school attendance of all children between 8 and 16. Carroll died while en route to Rome for his ad limina visit.

Illustration credit: Ackad, Washington, D.C.

[T. A. CLINCH]

CARROLL, WALTER SHARP, papal diplomat; b. Pittsburgh, Pa., June 18, 1908; d. Washington, D.C., Feb. 24, 1950. He received his B.A. (1930) from Duquesne University, Pittsburgh, and his Ph.D. (1933) from the University of Fribourg, Switzerland, before being ordained on Dec. 8, 1935. He subsequently attended the Universities of Tours, France, and of Florence, Italy, and obtained his S.T.L. (1936) from the Gregorian University and his J.C.D. (1939) from the Pontifical University of the Lateran in Rome. Following a brief assignment as curate at St. Basil's Church, Pittsburgh, in 1940, he served from 1944 to 1950 as attaché in the Vatican Secretariate of State and as U.S. military vicar delegate. In 1943–44 he was sent to North Africa to facilitate its communications with the Holy See and to assist war prisoners. He performed a similar mission in Austria and Germany during 1944–45. When Rome was captured by the Allies in June 1944, he improvised a Vatican press office and instituted press conferences to inform the world of Vatican events. He was also instrumental in arranging audiences with Pius XII for Americans in military service. After the war, he represented the Holy See at the 1947 meeting of the International Refugee Organization in Geneva, Switzerland. His wartime efforts were honored by his appointment as papal chamberlain (1943) and domestic prelate (1944).

[P. F. TANNER]

CARROLL COLLEGE

A 4-year liberal arts college in Helena, Mont., Carroll College was founded under the auspices of the diocese of Helena in 1909. The Most Reverend John P. *Carroll, second Bishop of Helena, broke ground for the institution on June 16, and the cornerstone was laid by President William Taft on September 27 of the same year. As early as 1884, Bp. John Baptist *Brondel sought to establish a college in Helena. Initial steps were taken in 1887, but the project was abandoned when a financial campaign failed to raise sufficient funds. The immediate predecessor of Carroll College was St. Aloysius' Institute, opened as a grammar school and high school for boys in 1906. Its rapid growth called for a larger institution that Carroll, a former college president, planned as a college and junior seminary combined.

The new College opened in September 1910 and admitted its first students the following year. At first known as "Capitol Hill College" since it was built on a site once selected for the State Capitol, it was officially named Mt. St. Charles College. In 1917 a gymnasium wing was added to the original structure, and a dormitory wing in 1924. The school's first graduate, Patrick McVeigh, of Butte, Mont., later became the first native priest of the diocese. In 1932 the name of the College was changed to Carroll College to honor its founder, Bishop Carroll, and in 1936 the high school department was discontinued. During World War II the College was a training ground for over 1,200 Navy V-5 and V-12 trainees. In 1946 it became coeducational.

Carroll College was incorporated under the laws of Montana in 1916. Degrees granted by the college have been registered and approved by the Board of Regents of the University of the State of New York since 1924. It was accredited by the North Central Association of Colleges and Secondary Schools from 1932 to 1949. Since 1949 it has been accredited by the Northwest Association of Secondary and Higher Schools. It became a member of the Association of American Colleges in 1932, and was affiliated with The Catholic University of America in 1940. Certificates to teach in elementary and secondary schools are granted to qualified graduates by the State Board of Educational Examiners.

Carroll's board of trustees consists of three ex officio members and two appointed members, with the bishop of Helena as chairman. The board selects the president of the College, approves faculty appointments recommended by the president, approves the college budget, assists in fund raising, and approves new buildings and general planning. Administrative officers include the president, academic vice president; vice president in charge of financial affairs, dean of studies, and dean of admissions. Borromeo Hall, the diocesan seminary on campus, has a rector and a spiritual director. An administrative council serves in an advisory capacity to the president. In 1964 there were 70 members on the College faculty, including 25 diocesan priests, 5 sisters, and 40 laymen. They held 12 doctorates, 3 professional degrees, and 34 master's degrees. The institution is financed through student fees, gifts, and an endowment fund valued at $2,500,000. A diocesan fund campaign in 1955 financed a seminary building and a science-library building costing $1,750,000. A cafeteria-student union and a women's dormitory were built in 1961 with the aid of Federal Housing Administration (FHA) loans.

Twenty-three departments of study are grouped in eight divisions: philosophy and theology, education, literature and communications, languages, natural sciences and mathematics, social sciences, health and physical education, and medical arts. A school of nursing is affiliated with the College. Lecture and laboratory are the chief methods used, with seminars and independent study for honor students. The College grants the B.A. degree and the B.S. degree in medical technology and in medical records library science. Preprofessional curricula are offered in the fields of dentistry, law, medicine, and veterinary medicine. A double-degree engineering program has been inaugurated in cooperation with *Notre Dame University (Indiana), Montana State College, and *Gonzaga University (Spokane, Wash.).

In 1964 the library housed 35,000 volumes and received 300 periodicals. College enrollment numbered 853 full-time students and an additional 300 in the summer session. Sixty-two students, half of whom were from the Helena Diocese, attended the diocesan preparatory seminary at Borromeo Hall. Eighty-seven priests of the Helena Diocese and more than 30 priests from other dioceses or religious orders completed their philosophy courses at Carroll. A development program begun in 1963 provides for an enrollment of 1,200 to 1,500 students.

Bibliography: *The Register,* Western Montana ed., Centenary ed., Aug. 27, 1941; Double Anniversary Suppl., April 19, 1959. L. B. PALLADINO, *Indian and White in the Northwest: A History of Catholicity in Montana* (2d ed. rev. and enl. Philadelphia 1922). W. P. SCHOENBERG, *Gonzaga University, Seventy-five Years, 1887–1962* (Spokane 1963).

[J. R. WHITE]

CARTAGENA, ARCHDIOCESE OF (CARTHAGINENSIS), created a diocese April 24, 1534; raised to an archdiocese June 20, 1900. It is located in the department of Bolívar, Colombia, and the see city is the capital of the department. In 1964 it had three suffragan sees: Barranquilla (1932), Montería (1954), and Santa Marta (1534).

The city of Cartagena was founded in 1533 by the Spanish conquistador Pedro de Heredia and was one of the most active ports during the Spanish period. As a result it was ringed with fortifications. The city was the seat of court of the Inquisition. St. Luis *Beltrán lived there, as did St. Peter *Claver. In the 19th century Cartagena suffered a period of decline, but it is beginning to revive in the 20th. It has become an industrial center and a busy port. The first bishop was the Dominican Tomás Toro (1534–36). The organization

The church of St. Peter Claver in Cartagena, Colombia.

of the diocese was done by Jerónimo de *Loaysa (1537–41), who was then transferred to Lima. Dionisio de *Sanctis was another 16th-century bishop. Controversy arose during the episcopate of Miguel de Benavides y Piédrola (1681–1713). He deprived the Franciscans of jurisdiction over the convent in Santa Clara and threw the city into a serious conflict. Cartagena was placed under interdict. The bishop was twice arrested by order of the *audiencia* of Santafé and of the Inquisition of Cartagena. From Madrid and Rome came orders to free him and punish those responsible for the imprisonment. In 1691 the bishop went to Europe to ask more severe punishment for his adversaries. Instead the Holy See took from him the administration of the diocese and refused to allow him to return to it. During the independence movement Bps. Custodio Díaz de Merino (1809–15) and Gregorio Rodríguez Carrillo (1816–20) were both expelled for refusing to support the movement for separation from Spain. The diocese remained vacant until 1834, when the Colombian Juan Fernández de Sotomayor (1834–49) became bishop. The middle of the 19th century saw the exile of another bishop, Bernardino Medina y Moreno (1856–77), because he refused to obey the antireligious laws of Gen. Tomás C. de Mosquera. In 1963 the archdiocese had 51 parishes, 51 secular priests, and 30 religious priests. Its population of about 669,000 was almost all Catholic.

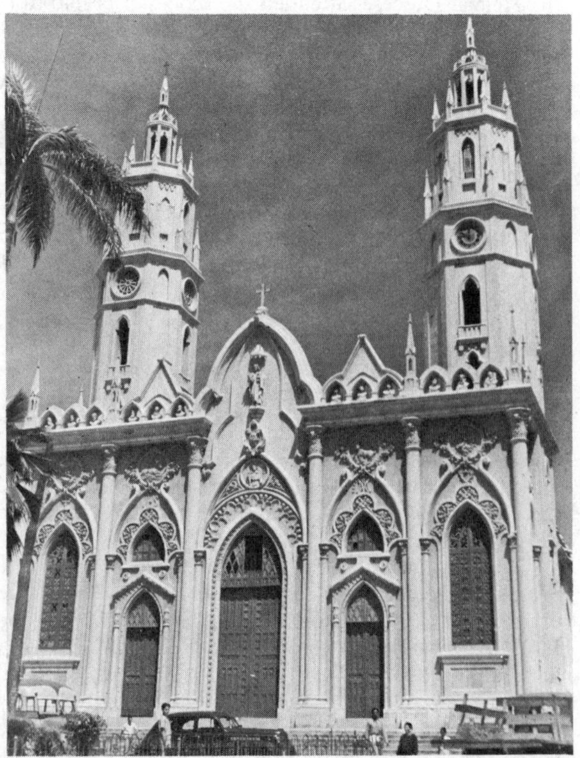

The cathedral of Barranquilla, Colombia, in the Archdiocese of Cartagena.

See also COLOMBIA.

Bibliography: G. PORRAS TROCONIS, *Cartagena hispánica* (Bogotá 1954). G. URIBE VILLEGAS, *Los arzobispos y obispos colombianos . . .* (Bogotá 1918). J. RESTREPO POSADA, "Cronología de los obispos de Cartagena de Indias," *Boletín de historia y antigüedades* 42 (1955) 302–320. J. M. PACHECO, "Los primeros obispos de Cartagena," *Ecclesiastica xaveriana* 6 (1956) 357–392. **Illustration credits:** Fig. 1, Pan American Union, Washington, D.C. Fig. 2, Pan American Airways.

[J. M. PACHECO]

CARTER, JAMES, education reformer; b. Leominster, Mass., Sept. 7, 1795; d. Chicago, Ill., July 21, 1849. He received his early instruction at Groton Academy, Conn., before entering Harvard College, Cambridge, Mass., in 1816. At Harvard, Carter distinguished himself as a scholar, and received many academic honors. Upon graduation in 1820, he became a teacher at a private school at Cohasset, and then at a preparatory school in Lancaster, Mass. At both institutions he showed Pestalozzian influence in the teaching of mathematics and strongly championed the inductive method of learning to replace memorization. In collaboration with William H. Brooks, he published illustrated geographies of the Massachusetts counties of Essex, Middlesex, and Worcester, in 1830, and a geography of New Hampshire in 1831.

Educational reform was always a driving influence in Carter's career. As early as 1821, he published a series of articles in the *Boston Transcript,* agitating for state control of education and greater local supervision of educational practices. In 1824 these articles appeared in the pamphlet, *Letters to the Honorable William Prescott on the Free Schools of New England with Remarks on the Principles of Instruction.* Detailed proposals, which followed in the *Boston Patriot* under the pen name "Franklin," appeared in 1826 in the pamphlet, *Essays Upon Popular Education Containing a Particular Examination of Massachusetts and an Outline of an Institution for the Education of Teachers.*

A bill containing Carter's ideas on normal schools, presented to the state Legislature in 1827 by William B. Calhoun, was defeated by a single vote. In 1835, Carter was elected to the Legislature and named chairman of the committee on education. He championed several education bills through the Legislature, notably, "Better Education for those Employed in Manufacturing," and "Revenue for Training Common School

Teachers." His greatest triumph was a bill stipulating the creation of a board of education and the establishment of a state secretary of public schools in 1837. This bill provided the setting for Horace *Mann as the first secretary of public schools for Massachusetts.

Bibliography: D. WILDER, *The History of Leominster* (Fitchburg, Mass. 1853). A. P. MARVIN, *History of the Town of Lancaster, Massachusetts* (Lancaster, Mass. 1879). Monroe Cyclop Ed 1:542. H. BARNARD, ed., *Educational Biography: Memoirs of Teachers, Educators, and Promoters and Benefactors of Education, Literature, and Science* (New York 1859).

[A. M. FLYNN]

CARTER, WILLIAM, VEN., English printer and martyr; b. place and date unknown; d. Tyburn, Jan. 11, 1584. In 1563 he was apprenticed to John Cawood, Queen's printer, and later he became amanuensis to Nicholas Harpsfield in Fleet prison. He married and had children. Carter was imprisoned "divers times" for printing "lewd [i.e., anti-Protestant] pamphlets," and was put on surety for good behavior. He was finally detained in the Tower (July 1582), tortured, and brought to trial for printing Gregory Martin's *Treatise of Schisme* (issued 1578 with a false imprint), an action that he had earlier confessed. The prosecution alleged that the book contained a passage concerning Judith and Holofernes that urged the killing of Queen Elizabeth. He was condemned at the Old Bailey on Jan. 10, 1584, and executed the next day.

Bibliography: E. H. BURTON and J. H. POLLEN, eds., *Lives of the English Martyrs,* ser. 2, v.1 (London 1914), no further v. pub. A. F. ALLISON and D. M. ROGERS, *A Catalogue of Catholic Books in English . . . 1558–1640,* 2 v. (London 1956).

[D. M. ROGERS]

CARTESIANISM

A philosophical doctrine initiated by René *Descartes and subsequently developed by a number of his disciples and later philosophers. Although the term is used in a general way to designate the fundamental tenets of *rationalism, it is more properly applied to the movement that was closely associated with Descartes and consciously sought to propagate his thought. In this article, such terminological usage is first explained and then a survey given of the development of the movement, in its stricter sense, as this took place in Holland, France, and England.

Terminological Usage. The specialists who were collaborators on the classic *Vocabulaire technique et critique de la philosophie* (ed. A. Lalande, Paris 1st ed. 1926, 8th ed. 1960) refused to authorize an article setting out the theses of Cartesianism because, in their view, the editorial committee could not agree on the thinkers, or the characteristics of the doctrine, that could be properly called Cartesian. This incident illustrates the change of climate in the historical exegesis of authors since the time when E. Caird (1835–1908) wrote the article "Cartesianism" for the 11th edition of the *Encyclopaedia Britannica* (1910–11) and gave simply a masterly exposition of Descartes, N. *Malebranche, G. W. *Leibniz and B. *Spinoza.

If by the term Cartesian is meant a thinker who accepts the fundamental theses of Descartes himself, then it must be objected that the extent to which Leibniz and Spinoza withdrew from the principles radically weakens their affiliations with him. Despite the important formative influence Descartes exercised upon their thought, it is only by a traditional "historical" usage that they can be called Cartesians, a usage that presents many opportunities for misunderstanding. It is true that Leibniz insisted that Spinoza's philosophy was an exaggerated Cartesianism, but he equally denied that he himself was a Cartesian. In some ways, the fourth book of Locke's *Essay* has more claim to be called Cartesian than any work of Leibniz or Spinoza. Malebranche alone, of the important thinkers, both in his expressed intentions and in much of his doctrine, would perhaps qualify as a disciple.

Possibly owing to the influence of G. W. F. *Hegel, in his *Lectures on the History of Philosophy,* it has become customary to divide the 17th century into two schools—the rationalist, of which Descartes was the founder, and the empiricist, with John *Locke as its progenitor. Moreover, it has been widely accepted that the French *philosophes* of the 18th century (Voltaire, Diderot, etc.) based their theories on the empiricist doctrines of Locke and Newton and brought about the downfall of the rationalist doctrines of Cartesianism. As has been suggested, rationalism is as an essential element of Locke's theories, as it is of Descartes's. The conventional linkage between Newtonianism and French materialism, accepted by F. Bouillier (1813–99) in his *Histoire de la philosophie cartésienne* (Paris 1854), can no longer be regarded as acceptable in view of recent scholarship. It is therefore more accurate to restrict the term Cartesian to those thinkers, mostly minor figures, who claimed the title for themselves and attempted to be, in varying degrees, disciples of Descartes.

Holland. It is natural that the first Cartesians were to be found in Holland, where Descartes was living and where most of his works were first published. Their activities were centered at the Universities of Utrecht and Leyden.

Utrecht. At the University of Utrecht, Henri Reneri (1593–1638), professor of philosophy, was one of the first to defend publicly the new doctrine, as did his successor, Regius (Henri de Roy, 1598–1679), who was in frequent communication with Descartes and read through the manuscript of the *Meditations.* Voëtius (Gijsbert Voët, 1589–1676), professor of theology at the same university, was a bitter opponent of the new theories, which were forbidden by a university decree. Descartes himself feared that Regius might become "the first martyr of his philosophy." When Regius published his own *Fundamenta Physices* in 1646, there was a break in the close friendship. The fundamental criticism that Descartes made of Regius's views was that he reversed the order of his philosophy, putting his metaphysics after, and not before, his physics. The *Notae in programma quoddam,* published by Descartes in 1647, are a refutation of certain theses elaborated by Regius as an attack on the nature of soul as this is expounded in the *Meditations.*

Leyden. At the University of Leyden, as early as 1647 there were bitter attacks on the doctrine of Descartes, mainly on the use of methodological doubt and the guarantee of human veracity based on the proof of the existence of God. The chief exponents of these attacks were Revius (Jacques de Rèves, d. 1658), who was the regent of the theological faculty and a pastor, and Triglandius (Jacobus Trigland, d. 1654), professor of theology. The first publicly accused Descartes of Pelagianism; the second damned him as an atheist.

There were a number who replied on behalf of Descartes. Among them was J. Clauberg (1622–65), who was professor in several German universities and wrote *Defensio Cartesiana adversus Jacobum Revium* (1652), as well as several commentaries on the major works of Descartes. In his latter works, he gave his attention especially to the problem of the relations of body and soul and denied that there could be any real interaction between the two: the interaction he described as "procatarctic," after a theory akin to occasionalism. Other defenders were Andriaan Heereboord (1614–61); C. Wittich (1625–87), who later attacked Spinoza in terms of orthodox Cartesian doctrine; and Heidanus (A. van der Heiden, 1597–1678), who protested so strongly that he lost his professorial chair.

Arnold *Geulincx was professor at the University of Louvain, but he went to Leyden in 1658 and there became a Protestant. His most important work is his *Ethica,* which was not published in complete form till after his death. Starting from the dualistic division of matter and mind, he argued that a material thing cannot be a true cause, since it cannot know that it acts. It follows then that the soul does not really produce the effects on bodies that it thinks it does. Descartes, it may be noted, had denied action in the sense of causing the existence of a change or movement, but he admitted that action could determine the character a change could assume or the direction of a motion. Regius and Clauberg follow their master in allowing the second sense of action: Geulincx, and later Malebranche, deny action in both senses. The denial of interaction, even in the second sense, leads Geulincx to the theory of *occasionalism. When one perceives a certain change occurring in his body and wills a certain action designed, for instance, to ensure its alteration, and then performs the action willed, the occurrence of the perception and the occurrence of the bodily behavior are both effects of divine intervention. A person's act of will is due wholly to himself; the perception is caused by God. The self-caused volition is the occasion on which God caused the bodily behavior (Malebranche differs here in attributing both volitional and bodily states to God). The volitional act itself is accordingly an occasional cause. The analogy of the two clocks, synchronized by God to keep perfect time, is found to be the most apt illustration. For Geulincx, then, only two substances manifest their essential nature in real causal activity, that is, finite selves and God.

France. The reaction to Descartes's philosophy in France, if not so openly violent, was equally mixed. A typical composite of opinions is to be found in the *Objections* published as an appendix to the *Meditations,* the manuscript having been circulated to various individuals and groups by Father Marin *Mersenne, of the Order of Minims, who was aptly called "the great businessman of letters" of the 17th century. Descartes published a series of replies to each set of objections.

The third set of objections is by Thomas *Hobbes, but they merely serve to show that the English philosopher, rather characteristically, was rooted in his own radical *empiricism and understood little of the text he was criticizing.

The fourth set are due to Antoine *Arnauld, who was to prove himself one of the most ardent defenders of the Cartesian doctrine, and one of the authors, together with Pierre *Nicole, of the textbook known as the *Logic of Port Royal,* an attempt to formulate a logic according to Descartes's principles (*see* LOGIC, HISTORY OF). Even when official opposition to the new doctrine was widespread, especially after Descartes's works had been placed on the Index *donec corrigantur* in 1663, he continued his polemic in their favor and was forced to flee to Holland later before the threat of civil intervention. Despite his general acceptance of the main doctrine, Arnauld was the only critic to call attention to the confusion caused by Descartes's theory of representative ideas and to note the essential difference between his view and the scholastic doctrine of *species.

Pierre *Gassendi, the author of the fifth set of objections, was a canon of Dijon and later professor of mathematics at Paris. Although he was himself opposed to Aristotelian scholasticism, he nevertheless was a bitter opponent of Descartes. His own doctrine was a revival of *atomism, akin to that of Epicurus, but essentially empirical in outlook. He rejected entirely the dualistic distinction of body and soul. Locke was very sympathetic to his views.

Jesuit Reaction. The seventh set of objections, published only in the second edition of the *Meditations,* were made by a Jesuit professor, Pierre Bourdin (1595–1653). The objections in themselves were not notably pertinent, but they illustrate the effort Descartes made to stay on good terms with his previous teachers at La Flèche. Father Jacques Dinet (1580–1653), who had taught Descartes, was instrumental in keeping good relations with the philosopher. At the college of La Flèche, where Descartes had been a pupil, he found two fervent advocates in Fathers Antoine Vatier (1591–1659) and Pierre Mesland (1596–1639); but this was exceptional and, on the whole, the Society of Jesus showed reserve, if not open hostility, to him. A general congregation of 1682 forbade the teaching of any Cartesian doctrines. Other religious orders had adepts of the Cartesian philosophy in their midst, notably, of course, the Oratorians with Malebranche. In the famous Benedictine monastery of St. Maur was the erudite Jean *Mabillon, who recommended the study of Descartes in his treatise on monastic studies.

Other Views. At the University of Paris were other exponents of Cartesian doctrine. Jacques Rohault (1620–75), a professor of physics, was one of the most successful. His weekly lectures were attended by all the leading personalities of the time, and his *Traité de Physique* (Paris 1671) became the textbook of most European universities. He also published *Entretiens de philosophie* (Paris 1671), a philosophical work of almost literal Cartesian orthodoxy. His pupil, Pierre Sylvain *Régis, first taught in Montpellier and Toulouse but came to Paris in 1680, where he continued to expound his views, published in his *Système de Philosophie* (Paris 1690). He differed from Descartes in maintaining that the existence of bodies is as evident as the existence of selves, and that ideas arise from the union of body and soul and are not innate. Mention should also be made of Claude Clerselier (1614–84), who edited the letters of Descartes, as well as the posthumous works of Rohault, a pious Catholic whose main anxiety was to defend the doctrines of Descartes against accusations of atheism and libertinism.

In the 1660s, two works appeared that had a short-lived but widespread influence in France. The first was the *Traité de l'esprit de l'homme* . . . (Paris 1661) by Louis de la Forge; the second, by Géraud de Cordemoy (1620–84), was *Le discernement du corps et de l'âme* (Paris 1666). Cordemoy, a lawyer by profession, had been chosen by J. *Bossuet as tutor to the elder son of Louis XIV. He was thoroughly convinced of the dualistic distinction between soul and body, although he introduced atomic divisions into the definition of matter; in attempting to solve the problems thereby raised, he arrived at a theory of interaction that presupposes the instrumentality of God as its efficient cause, a form of occasionalism akin to that developed later by Malebranche. For De la Forge, a doctor who had edited Descartes's posthumous *Traité de l'homme,* Cartesian dualism was a vital innovation and most important discovery, although he insisted that it was in principle identical with the doctrine of St. *Augustine. He defended also the doctrine of representative ideas, and placed the cause of the substantial union of body and soul in the will of God, arriving then at a theory of psychophysical parallelism. According to De la Forge the difference between the philosophy of Descartes and that of his spiritual forebears was that Descartes alone had given an adequate definition of matter. (*See* MIND-BODY PROBLEM; SOUL-BODY RELATIONSHIP.)

England. The works of Descartes were translated rapidly into English. Cambridge was slightly sympathetic toward the new doctrine. Henry More, a fellow of Christ's College and a correspondent of Descartes, professed himself an ardent disciple but later publicly renounced his adhesion. Ralph Cudworth, professor of Hebrew and master of Christ's College, while making a distinction between the conscious object and unconscious tendency of Descartes's doctrine, denounced it as a mechanistic atheism. Although these and other *Cambridge Platonists read Descartes's works, it cannot be asserted that their views are colored, except negatively, by his philosophical principles.

At Oxford, Anthony Legrand (d. 1699) published an *Institutio Philosophiae* (London 1672), but he was violently opposed by Samuel Parker (1640–88), Bishop of Oxford, who confounded Descartes and Hobbes in the same imprecation. Despite this condemnation, the works of Descartes were widely read in the university, and Locke began to study them immediately after his graduation; the extent of his debt can be measured by the great number of references in his notebooks and journals.

Growth and Decline. The doctrine of Descartes spread among the society of Paris, as well as among the Cartesians of Port Royal, in the midst of whom Blaise *Pascal was an outstanding exception. De la Forge noted the names of four Cartesian "salons," later to be satirized by Molière in *"Les Femmes Savantes."* Descartes's funeral in 1667, at the church of Saint-Étienne-du-Mont, became a kind of manifestation on behalf of the new doctrine. But official opposition grew, especially after the publication of the decree of 1663 placing his works on the Index; in 1669, candidates to doctorates were obliged to defend anti-Cartesian theses at the Sorbonne; in 1671, the archbishop of Paris forbade the teaching of Descartes's opinions, and a further decree of the Parlement of Paris was stopped only by a clever satire of N. *Boileau-Despréaux. Pierre Daniel *Huet, Bishop of Avranches, who had himself professed Cartesian views, made an elaborate attack in his famous *Censura* (Paris 1689), and Father Gabriel *Daniel, in his *Voyage du monde de Descartes* (Paris 1690), presented a semiserious novel deriding the philosophy and science of Descartes.

The heyday of the new doctrine can be placed between 1660 and 1690. Afterward there was a steady decline of Descartes's influence, which became almost—at least directly and openly—a dead letter in the 18th century. It is noteworthy that no work of Descartes was printed in France between 1724 and 1824, when Victor *Cousin once more drew attention to the greatest of French philosophers.

See also PHILOSOPHY, HISTORY OF; DESCARTES, RENÉ; DUALISM; INNATISM; SUBJECTIVISM.

Bibliography: C. L. THIJSSEN-SCHOUTE, *Nederlands Cartesianisme* (Amsterdam 1954). A. G. A. BALZ, *Cartesian Studies* (New York 1951). E. J. DIJKSTERHUIS et al., *Descartes et le cartésianisme Hollandais* (Paris 1950). G. COHEN, *Écrivains français en Hollande* (Paris 1920). W. H. BARBER, *Leibniz in France* (Oxford 1955). R. PINTARD, *Le Libertinage érudit,* 2 v. in 1 (Paris 1943). G. SORTAIS, *La Philosophie moderne,* 2 v. (Paris 1920–22). J. B. BORDAS-DEMOULIN, *Le Cartésianisme,* 2 v. (Paris 1843). R. LENOBLE, *Mersenne* (Paris 1943). M. MERSENNE, *Correspondence,* ed. C. DE WAARD, 4 v. (Paris 1945–55).

[L. J. BECK]

CARTHAGE

Town of 5,000 on the Gulf of Tunis; 12 miles northeast of Tunis, capital of *Tunisia. Carthage, founded by *Tyre *c.* 841 B.C., long dominated the western Mediterranean, which it contested with Rome. Destroyed (146 B.C.) and rebuilt (29 B.C.) by Rome, it came under the *Vandals (439), Byzantium (533), and the Arabs (698); it was held by Spain (1535–74) but yielded to the Ottoman Turks and then became part of the French protectorate (1881), which gained its independence (1956).

Christianity was introduced into Carthage by A.D. 150, from both Rome and the East it seems, and flourished quickly (more than 20 known basilicas); but it suffered repeatedly from persecution and heresy. The acts of the 12 Scillitan martyrs (d. July 17, 180) is the oldest document of Christian North Africa. Christian Latin letters in the area were distinguished by *Tertullian (who was inclined to *Montanism), *Minucius Felix, *Arnobius the Elder, *Lactantius, the poet Commodian (probably 3d century), *Marius Victorinus, *Dracontius, *Fulgentius of Ruspe, *Ferrandus, and, above all, *Augustine. Carthage's first known bishop, Agrippinus, presided over 70 bishops in a council (*c.* 220) that declared baptisms administered by heretics invalid. Carthage's greatest bishop, the martyr St. *Cyprian, from whose episcopacy (248–258) dates Carthage's ecclesiastical primacy in Africa, condemned *Novatian but disputed with Rome about rebaptism; a council of 87 bishops under him defended the traditional African practice of rebaptism (256), which was not abandoned until the Council of Arles (314). Donatists, with their bishops, afflicted Carthage from 311 until after the time of St. Augustine, who studied in Carthage and became there an advocate of *Manichaeism. *Donatism was occasioned by the *dissimulation of Bp. Mensurius of Carthage in the persecution of Diocletian (303), by the unorthodox reconciliation of *lapsi, and by the ever available dispute over rebaptism.

Pelagianism (*see* PELAGIUS AND PELAGIANISM) appeared in Carthage in 411, the year a council of 286

Catholic and 275 Donatist bishops broke the strength of Donatism. Pelagianism was condemned in a council of more than 200 bishops held in 418 under Bishop Aurelius (391–429), who had a codex of canons of the African Church compiled; the council's canons on original sin, grace, and the necessity of prayer show the influence of Augustine, Aurelius's close friend and collaborator. After the death of Aurelius, heterodox elements rose and sided with the Arian Vandals, who took Carthage (439), sacked Rome (455), and all but ended Carthage's ecclesiastical primacy in a persecution that had but few respites. *Victor of Vita describes the Vandal persecution. From 439 to 454 the see was vacant, Genseric installing an Arian bishop who was patriarch of the Vandal Church; as in other barbarian Arian Churches, neither the bishop nor his clergy had any influence in affairs of state. The Vandals used their vernacular in their liturgy, as opposed to the orthodox liturgy of Carthage, which was almost identical with that of Rome. Bishop Deogratias (454–457), known for his charity to captives from the sack of Rome, was succeeded after 24 years by Eugene, a saintly bishop also known for charity. Eugene was condemned to hard labor by the Vandals (484–487) and then exiled to *Albi in France (496), where he died (505). There was no successor until 523.

Although Justinian rebuilt churches and protected orthodoxy and although Carthage became a Byzantine exarchate along with *Ravenna, the city declined under Byzantine rule. Bishop Reparatus, because of his defense of the *Three Chapters, was exiled to Asia Minor and died there (563). After Justinian's death (565) weak bishops could not prevent abuses by imperial officials; and Catholics turned to Rome, which intervened even in administrative affairs. Christian refugees from the Arab conquest of Syria and Egypt brought *Monophysitism and *Monothelitism to Carthage *c.* 640. A council of 646 condemning Monothelitism is the last known event of the Church in Carthage before the Arab conquest (698). *See also* NORTH AFRICA, EARLY CHURCH IN.

The Church survived after 698, though its status was inferior. A monk from the monastery of St. Sabas in Jerusalem found the Church of "Africa" suffering from the attacks of "tyrants" *c.* 850, and he continued to Spain in search of stipends for his monastery. In 990 Carthage sent its elected bishop to Rome for consecration, and Popes wrote to bishops and the Church of Carthage (1053, 1073, and 1076), as well as to local rulers of North Africa concerning Christians there. *Constantine the African was born in Carthage (1010–20). After the Norman conquest of Sicily (1061–91) and the Almohad conquest of North Africa (1160), Christianity almost disappeared in Carthage. From the 13th century Europe sought to regain Christian North Africa. St. *Louis IX of France died besieging Tunis (1270), which had replaced Carthage in importance. Christian merchants and mercenary troops in the region required chaplains. Trinitarians and Mercedarians ransomed Christian slaves. Franciscans and Dominicans carried on missionary work. Raymond *Lull's school for Arabic studies was in Tunis.

The Congregation for the *Propagation of the Faith sent Capuchins (1624) and Vincentians (1645) to Carthaginian Africa. The Vincentians, chaplains of French consuls, were regarded as vicars by the Holy See, as if the See of Carthage still existed. Jean *Le Vacher, vicar apostolic (1650–66), was succeeded by Italian Capuchins (who cared for French, Italians, and Maltese) as provicars under the Vincentian Vicariate of *Algeria and Tunisia (in *Algiers). In 1741 Carthage was made a vicariate apostolic. A chapel of St. Louis in Carthage (1839), French sisters (1840) who expanded beyond Carthage, and Brothers of the Christian Schools (1855) were followed by White Fathers (1875), who carried the apostolate to the Moslems. Under the French protectorate, Carthage was restored as a metropolitanate without suffragans (1884) and primate of Africa (1893) under Cardinal Charles M. A. *Lavigerie. The Church was governed by a concordat between France and the Holy See (1894–1964) until the see was suppressed, made titular, and replaced by a prelacy *nullius* of Tunis comprising the same jurisdiction (Tunisia). The lack of local recruits for the clergy and Italo-French friction hurt religious life in the archdiocese, but a eucharistic congress was held in Carthage in 1930.

Bibliography: P. MONCEAUX, *Histoire littéraire de l'Afrique chrétienne,* 7 v. (Paris 1901–23; repr. Brussels 1963). H. LECLERCQ, *L'Afrique chrétienne* (2d ed. Paris 1904); DACL 2.2: 2190–2330. G. LAPEYRE, *L'Ancienne église de Carthage,* 2 v. (Paris 1933). C. COURTOIS, "Histoire de l'Afrique du Nord des origines à la fin du Moyen-Âge," RevHist 198 (1947) 228–249; *Les Vandales et l'Afrique* (Paris 1955). G. LAPEYRE and A. PELLEGRIN, *Carthage latine et chrétienne* (Paris 1950). P. HUBAC, *Carthage* (Paris 1952). J. FERRON and G. LAPEYRE, DHGE 11: 1149–1233. P. ROMANELLI et al., EncCatt 3:942–956. P. KAWERAU, RGG[3] 3:1160–61. A. STUIBER et al., LexThK[2] 6:1-4. G. BARDY and E. JARRY, *Catholicisme* 2:602–607. Pauly-Wiss RE, suppl. 10:957–992.

[E. P. COLBERT]

CARTHAGE, COUNCILS OF

Many councils were held in *Carthage (3d to 6th centuries). Under Agrippinus 70 bishops in 225 considered the validity of Baptism by heretics. Donatus called a council in 235. Of many councils called by *Cyprian, Bishop of Carthage (*c.* 249–258), those of 251, 252, 253, 255, and 256 dealt with the **lapsi,* Christians defecting in the fearful Decian persecution. Unwilling to absolve them through the Sacrament of Penance, the Church granted forgiveness if a confessor awaiting martyrdom interceded for them with the bishop. Cyprian decided to permit the *lapsi* sacramental absolution, a practice ultimately universal. In 252, 253, and 256 the councils also reexamined the validity of Baptism by heretics. Under Gratus (349) and Genethlius (390), disciplinary measures were enacted for clergy and bishops. A canon of Scripture (397) included a prohibition against all other reading in the churches (Denz 186). Aurelius, Bishop of Carthage (391–429), held councils frequently and dealt with problems of *Donatism and Pelagianism (*see* PELAGIUS AND PELAGIANISM). In 411 a confrontation of Donatist and Catholic bishops (June 1, 3, 8) resulted in complete defeat for the Donatists—imperial legislation strengthening the orthodox position.

The most important councils in Carthage dealt with Pelagius, a Celtic monk denying the necessity of grace, whose tergiversations successfully deceived the Council of Diospolis (Palestine), where he was exonerated after his African condemnation. A meeting of 67 bishops in Carthage and 18 at Milevis in Numidia (416) sent letters (*Augustine, *Epist.* 175; PL 33:758–762) to Innocent I begging him to secure a disavowal from Pelagius himself. Innocent I wrote in reply (Augustine, *Epist.* 181–183; PL 33:779–788), insisting on man's daily need of grace, but willing—even eager—to pardon a repentant Pelagius (Jan. 27, 417). He wrote again to Carthage, where another council sat (417), emphasizing his own primacy (CSEL 44:715–723; Jaffé K 321). Zosimus, his successor (417–418), wrote a similar letter (Jaffé K 342) the following year (CSEL 35:115–117). Meantime Pelagius and his disciple Celestius convinced the Pope of their innocence, the former being reinstated and Celestius tentatively approved. Zosimus ordered Carthage to reexamine its position. Put on the defensive, Augustine spent the most painful year of his episcopate. Celestius, however, behaving disgracefully, came under the censure of Emperor Honorius and fled. Nine articles (Denz 222–230) on grace and original sin were formulated by 214 African bishops in council (May 1, 418). [Canon 3, condemning unbaptized infants to hell on the principle "Whoever is not on the right hand is doubtless on the left," does not appear in Mansi (4:326–334) or in Roman collections.] Zosimus finally condemned Celestius and excommunicated Pelagius. From May 25 to 30, 419, 217 bishops met; canons of previous councils were read before papal representatives; thus they received a quasi-ecumenical validity.

The Arian *Vandals invaded North Africa (429), persecuting the Church and setting up rival bishops. Thus 466 bishops met in Carthage (Feb. 1, 484) before Huneric, the Vandal king. The Catholic bishops were exiled. Justinian's African conquest (534) made possible a Carthaginian council in that year, dealing with policies regarding converted Arians, cleric and lay.

See also GRACE, CONTROVERSIES ON; SALUTARY ACTS; GRACE, ARTICLES ON.

Bibliography: CYPRIAN, *Epistolae* 44, 45, 48, 57, 59, 61, 64, 70, 71, 72. Mansi 1:840–851, 863–866, 868–872, 881–882, 897–900, 900–902, 923–926, 951–992; 3:143–158, 671–678; 7:1056–59, 1171–74. A. STUIBER, LexThK² 6:1–2. P. FRANSEN, *ibid.* 3–4. A. AUDOLLENT, DHGE 1:747–750, 811–822, lists all councils of Carthage. G. BARDY, *Catholicisme* 2:606–607. Hefele-Leclercq 1.1:165–176; 1.2:837–841, 1101, 1105–06, 1107–18; 2.1:76–78; 2.2:1136–39. L. DUCHESNE, *The Early History of the Christian Church,* 3 v. (New York 1909–24) 1:282–313. H. LECLERCQ, *L'Afrique chrétienne,* 2 v. (2d ed. Paris 1904).

[C. M. AHERNE]

CARTHUSIAN SPIRITUALITY

The pattern of the Carthusians' semieremitical life has remained substantially unchanged for the more than 800 years since its inception in 1084. The chief purpose of this way of life is to lead men to union with God in contemplation, through liturgical celebrations in choir and spiritual exercises in the silence and solitude of the hermitages.

In one sense there is no Carthusian spirituality—no particular type of spirituality, e.g., Biblical, patristic, monastic, Ignatian, is imposed on the Carthusian hermit, nor is he pressed to take up Thomism, Scotism, Molinism, or to associate himself with any other theological school. He lives alone with God and is free to follow the inclinations of his mind and heart within the limits of Catholic faith and morals, the rules of his order, and the dictates of prudence.

On the other hand, the Carthusian has become a hermit precisely in order to learn to be attentive to the guidance of the Holy Spirit and to follow it faithfully. Superiors and directors help him to distinguish between

Interior of a Carthusian cell. The mode of construction illustrates the semieremitical nature of Carthusian life.

what may be the will of God and what is really illusion, and to decide whether his aims are compatible with the essential Carthusian observances: external and interior silence and solitude. The preference for all that is consonant with these two preferred conditions for achieving mystical union with God may be called characteristic of Carthusian spirituality.

Main Contributions. The chief and permanent contribution of the order to Catholic spirituality has been the establishment and continuation in the Church of a type of life eminently suited to aid men who are seeking to achieve union with God in prayer. Its major contribution to spiritual literature is its rule, first codified in the *Consuetudines* (customs) of *Guigo I. Adherence to the rule has preserved the Carthusians from the need of reform, and has inspired numberless reforms in other monastic institutes. The "golden" *Epistle to the Carthusians of Mont-Dieu* written by *William of Saint-Thierry (PL 184:307–354; English ed. London 1930) testifies to the enthusiasm the Carthusian example inspired among other monks, and the **Ancrene Riwle* is evidence that Guigo's *Consuetudines* influenced strictly eremitical environments also. (Cf. B. du Moustier, *Carthusian Inspiration in the Ancren Riwle,* Pax, Prinknash Abbey, England, May 1935.) To the last edition of the Carthusian Statutes Pius XI added by way of preface the apostolic constitution *Umbratilem,* which is regarded as the Magna Carta of the contemplative monastic life (ActApS 18, 1926).

Apostolic Activities. Although Carthusian solitude rules out the possibility of engaging in most forms of the active ministry, still the monks are not forbidden apostolic activities compatible with their special form of contemplative life. At Cologne *Lanspergius and at Paris Richard Beaucousin (d. 1610) became famous directors of souls. Lanspergius influenced some early followers of St. Ignatius, and Beaucousin influenced Pierre de *Bérulle, François du Tremblay (the *Eminence grise*), and Benedict Canfield (d. 1611). In the course of time, however, spiritual direction was severely limited because it endangered Carthusian silence and solitude.

The *Consuetudines* of Guigo made it a duty for the hermits to "preach" by copying books. It was appropriate, therefore, that with the invention of printing they should become printers. St. Barbara's, Cologne, was engaged in printing in 1465; the Strasbourg charterhouse in 1474; the Parma monastery in 1477; and the charterhouse of Gripsholm, Sweden, in 1498. They edited and published the works not only of Carthusian mystics, such as *Hugh of Balma, *Denis the Carthusian, Lanspergius, but also of St. Gertrude, *Tauler, *Henry Suso, *Ruysbroeck, and many others.

Carthusian Writers. In order to "preach with their hands," the Carthusians not only copied, printed, and edited books, but they also composed a great many of them. In the *Dictionnaire de spiritualité ascétique et mystique* Dom Yves Gourdel filled 16 columns with his list of Carthusian authors (art. *Chartreux*). Guigo I wrote one of the most original books of the 12th century. The "four rungs" of the "ladder" by which the soul ascends to mystical union were described by *Guigo II. Hugh of Balma insisted on the practice of anagogic movements. Denis of Ryckel and *Guigo de Ponte introduced the soul into the secrets of the Pseudo-Dionysian *via negativa.*

Translators, compilers, and editors of mystical writings abounded among Carthusians of the 16th to 18th centuries (e.g., Lanspergius, *Surius). A voluminous cycle of patristic literature on the life of Christ was compiled by *Ludolph of Saxony, and Surius did the same for the lives of the saints. The writings of others, such as *Dominic of Prussia, *Dorland, and Lanspergius played an important part in developing and popularizing the Rosary and devotion to the Sacred Heart. In about 1700, in opposition to both Jansenism and quietism, Innocent *Le Masson compiled and composed several books noteworthy for their sound ascetical doctrine.

The writings of François de Sales *Pollien were an important contribution to the renewal of Catholic spirituality in the first quarter of the 20th century. The works of Dom Augustine Guillerand (published in French by the *Benedittine di Priscilla,* Rome) enjoyed popularity in the mid-century, and Dom Pablo M. (Thomas) Verner Moore applied the findings of modern psychology to the spiritual life. The tradition of the former Cologne Carthusians was resumed by a recent French translation of the Flemish mystic *Hadewijch d'Anvers* (ed. Du Seuil, Paris, n.d.).

Bibliography: Y. GOURDEL, DictSpirAscMyst 2.1:705–776. T. MERTON, *The Silent Life* (New York 1957). GUIGO II, *The Scale of the Cloister,* tr. B. S. JAMES (London 1937). ADAM OF DRYBURGH, *Eden's Fourfold River,* ed. and tr. a monk of Parkminster (London 1927). BONAVENTURE, *A Mirror of the Blessed Life of Jesu Christ,* tr. NICHOLAS LOVE, ed. a monk of Parkminster (London 1926), passages from the *Meditationes vitae Christi* ascribed to St. Bonaventure, tr. with additions by NICHOLAS LOVE. I. LE MASSON, *Spiritual Reading for Every Day,* tr. K. D. BESTE (London 1897); *A Treatise on Interior Prayer,* tr. B. WALLIS (London 1951); *A Treatise on the Religious Life* (London 1953). C. M. BOUTRAIS, *Mary the Mirror,* tr. a monk of Parkminster (London 1963); ed., *Ancient Devotions to the Sacred Heart of Jesus, by Carthusian Monks of the 14th–17th Centuries* (4th ed. London 1953). A Carthusian, *They Speak by Silences,* tr. a monk of Parkminster (London 1955); *The Prayer of Love and Silence,* tr. a monk of Parkminster (London 1962). A. GUILLERAND, *Where Silence is Praise,* tr. a monk of Parkminster (London 1960). H. C. MANN, *A Cloistered Company* (London 1935). T. V. MOORE, *The Life of Man with God* (New York 1956); *Heroic Sanctity and Insanity* (New York 1959); *The Home and Its Inner Spiritual Life* (Westminster, Md. 1952).

[B. DU MOUSTIER]

CARTHUSIANS

The Carthusian Order is a purely contemplative monastic order that was founded in 1084 by St. Bruno (*see* BRUNO THE CARTHUSIAN, ST.). The name Carthusian is derived from *cartusia,* the Latin word for the French *chartreuse.* The English word "charterhouse" is a corruption of this French term.

Origin. In 1084 Bruno and six companions, under the guidance of St. *Hugh of Grenoble, arrived in the Chartreuse mountains, a section of the French Alps about 30 miles from Grenoble. The solitary and austere site, together with the severe climate, profoundly influenced the life and growth of the young community. When Urban II (1088–99) called Bruno to Rome in 1090, the new order passed through a severe crisis and the Carthusian foundation was temporarily abandoned. After a short time, the community reformed under Landuin the new prior (d. 1100) and resumed its solitary life. At the papal court Bruno still longed for the solitary life, and after some months the Pope permitted him to withdraw to Calabria in southern Italy, where he founded a second Carthusian monastery similar to the one in France. While returning from a visit to Bruno in Calabria, Landuin fell into the hands of the forces of the antipope Clement III (1084–1100) and perished in prison because of his allegiance to the true Pope; he was thus the first of many Carthusian martyrs.

Rule. Since Bruno did not intend to found a new monastic order, he wrote no rule. The example of his life entirely "hidden in the Face of God" served, however, as the source of inspiration for all the succeeding generations of Carthusians. As the community of La Grande Chartreuse flourished and its reputation for austerity and sanctity became known, other groups of hermits desired to adopt the Carthusian way of life. It was for these new communities that Guigo, the fifth prior, at the request of Hugh of Grenoble, compiled in 1127 the *Consuetudines* (customs) according to which the Carthusians lived. This primitive legislation was supplemented by ordinances of the general chapters. On several occasions the ordinances were gathered together in a single edition, such as that of 1581, when the *Nova Collectio* was published. The latest revision (1924) brought the statutes into conformity with the Code of Canon Law and was approved *in forma specifica* by Pius XI in the apostolic constitution *Umbratilem* (July 8, 1924).

The supreme authority of the order is vested in the general chapter, which meets every 2 years at the Grande Chartreuse and is composed of the priors of all the monasteries and the professed members of the community of the Grande Chartreuse. The business of the chapter, however, is transacted by a definitory elected for each session. The prior of the Grande Chartreuse, elected only by the community and not by the other priors, is the superior general of the order. His authority is supreme between the sessions of the general chapter. Although each monastery is *sui juris* and its prior a major superior according to Canon Law, the government of the order is nonetheless highly centralized.

History. Under Guigo, the fifth prior (1109–36), seven more charterhouses were founded. In the following years still other groups of hermits requested copies of the *Consuetudines* in order to become affiliated to the sons of St. Bruno. In all, 38 charterhouses, including 2 for nuns, were opened during the 12th century and extended as far as Denmark. In 1178 the first charterhouse in England was opened at Witham in Somerset. As the result of a vow made after the murder of Thomas Becket, King Henry II invited the Carthusians to establish a foundation and promised them large grants of land in Selwood Forest. Henry, however, failed to provide for the people who were already living off the donated land, and the foundation almost ended in tragedy. The ability of Hugh, the prior of Witham, in dealing with Henry saved the foundation and the Carthusians became firmly established in England. Hugh later became the celebrated bishop of Lincoln and because of his firmness in defending the rights of the Church became known as "The Hammer of Kings" (*see* HUGH OF LINCOLN, ST.).

In the beginning the new foundations remained under the jurisdiction of the local bishop; but as the order expanded, the need of a central governing body became evident and a general chapter of all the priors was held in 1140 at the Grande Chartreuse under the leadership of St. *Anthelm of Chignin. The priors, released from the authority of their bishops, promised obedience to the general chapter. The exemption from episcopal jurisdiction was approved by Rome. The expansion of the order continued throughout the 13th century, when 34 monasteries were founded, including a brief experiment in Ireland between 1280 and 1321. The Carthusian foundation in Ireland has never been renewed.

Growth and Vicissitudes. The 14th century marked an extensive development of the order with 107 new foundations. Charterhouses were opened for the first time in Germany and Prussia. In the same century, however, the order also suffered severe reverses. In 1349, during the ravages of the Black Death, more than 400 Carthusians perished. In one house, Montrieux, all but the prior were victims of the plague. After the plague the order regained its vigor; in 1371 there were 150 monasteries spread throughout Europe. It is interesting that during these first 4 centuries of the order's history there were no less than 26 pontifical bulls exempting the Carthusians from the payment of all tithes because of their poverty. Toward the end of the century the *Western Schism divided the order in two; the houses of Italy and Germany adhered to the Pope of Rome, Urban VI, while the monasteries of Spain and France gave their allegiance to Clement VII at Avignon. The division gave rise to the election of two generals, both claiming the rights of the prior of the Grande Chartreuse. Although many attempts were made at unification during the schism, it was only after the election of Alexander V (1409) that a reunion was effected through the resignation of the two contending priors general. Despite the difficulties experienced throughout the Church in the 15th and early 16th centuries, the Carthusian Order continued to grow; 43 foundations were made in the 15th century, and an additional 13 in the 16th. By 1521 the order numbered 195 houses; never before or since have the Carthusians been so flourishing.

A serious decline set in during the Reformation, when 39 houses were suppressed and more than 50 Carthusians gave their lives for the faith. Notable among these martyrs were the 18 English monks who were tortured and killed in the period from 1535 to 1540 (*see* MARTYRS OF ENGLAND AND WALES). Carthusian blood flowed also in Yugoslavia and Austria at the hands of the heretics and of the Turks; in Holland and France the Reformers destroyed charterhouses and massacred the monks. In 1562 the Grande Chartreuse itself was completely destroyed by the Huguenots. In spite of wars and persecutions, however, the Carthusians continued to attract numerous vocations; during one period of 13 years in the 16th century the book of profession at the Grande Chartreuse registered the vows of 115 novices. In the first half of the following century, 21 foundations were made, and these were the last new charterhouses to be founded before the French Revolution. Carthusians were once more put to death by the Huguenots in France and by the Turks in Yugoslavia.

17th and 18th Centuries. In 1676 the order numbered 173 charterhouses with 2,300 choir monks, 1,500 lay brothers, and 170 nuns. In that same year the Grande Chartreuse, destroyed by fire for the eighth time, was completely reconstructed by Innocent *Le Masson, one of the most outstanding generals of the order (d. 1703). In addition to the traditional eremitical and conventual buildings, spacious pavilions were provided to receive the priors coming to the general chapter. The proponents of *Jansenism, prevalent during this period, tried to infiltrate into the order under the appearances of a higher spirituality. Because of the traditional simplicity of solitaries, the Jansenists expected no obstacle in spreading their doctrines. The vigorous action of Le Masson in banning Jansenist books from all charterhouses and in writing a dogmatic treatise on the questions under dispute did much to save the Carthusians from the contamination of this heresy. In 1710 the general chapter required all the monks to sign the formulary of Alexander VII (1656) and decreed that no one would be admitted to profession who had not done so. In only one of the seven Carthusian provinces of France was the submission incomplete. After a prolonged and patient procedure, 31 monks were excommunicated and separated from the order. They took refuge in Holland, where, with the exception of a few who repented and returned to the order, they remained until their deaths in the most miserable circumstances, both spiritual and material. These religious represented less than 1 per cent of the entire order, which maintained a remarkable fidelity to orthodoxy.

The 18th century was characterized by a nationalist spirit according to which many of the Catholic rulers desired to exercise complete control over the Church within their realms. Upon the insistence of the royal power, the two Carthusian provinces of Spain were erected as an autonomous congregation by Pius VI in 1784. Shortly afterward the court of Naples published a decree uniting all the Neapolitan houses as a separate body. The Republic of Venice and the Emperor Joseph II of Austria suppressed all the charterhouses in their states under the pretext of need of monastic property for public education. In Tuscany the Grand Duke closed the two houses in his territory. At the beginning of the French Revolution the general chapter had authority over only 126 houses, 75 of which were in France. The decrees of the revolutionary government confiscated all the French houses, and these were subsequently thoroughly pillaged by the army. During the bloody days of the Revolution many Carthusians were imprisoned; some died in prison, and others were put to death or exiled. During the Napoleonic era all but five of the houses of the order were suppressed.

Recent History. The restoration of the former monarchies favored the religious orders. Without returning their property, King Louis XVIII of France permitted the monks to live at the Grande Chartreuse (1816). The order immediately attracted large numbers of pos-

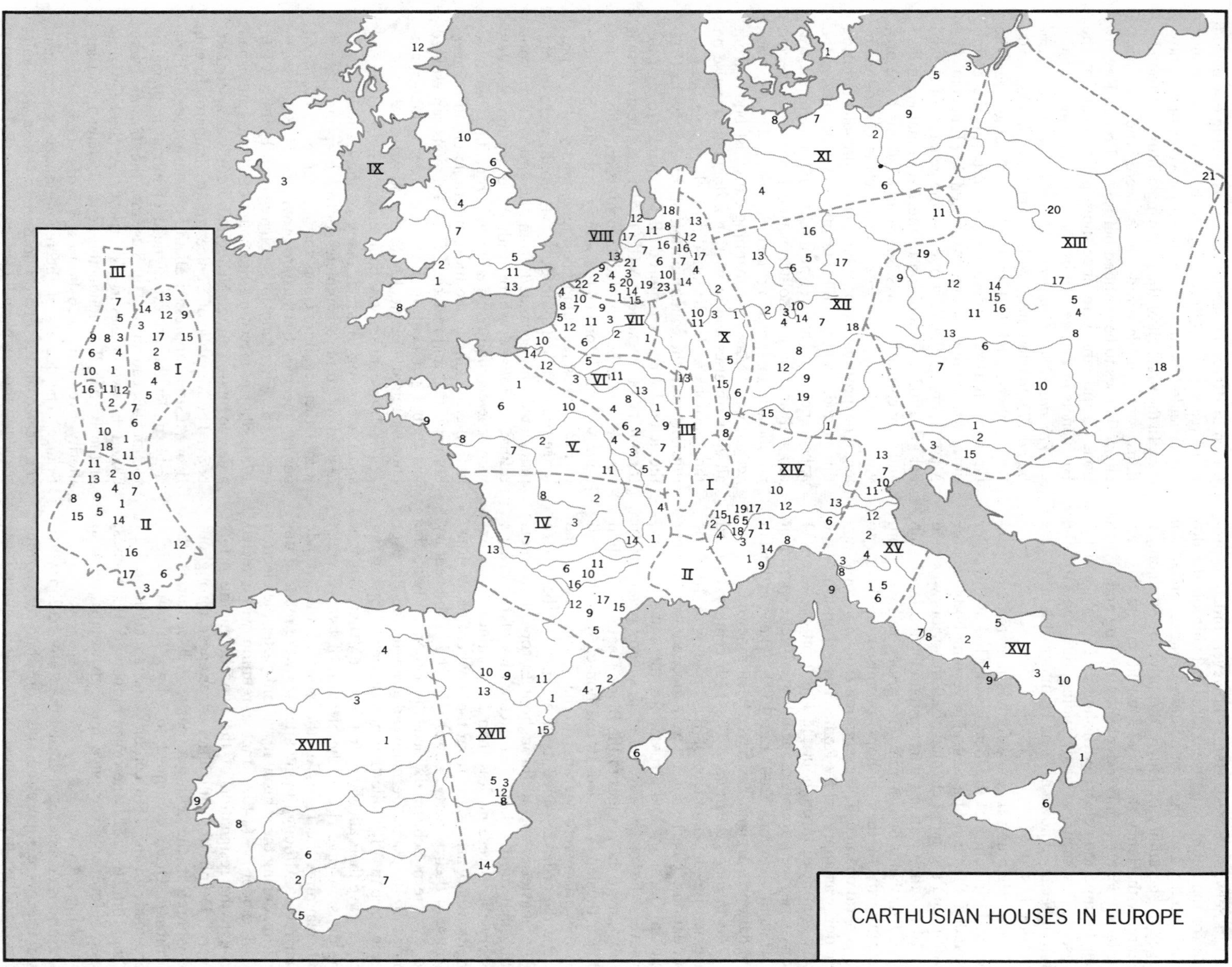

Fig. 1. Carthusian houses in Europe, with list of dates of foundation and suppression.

Carthusian Houses in Europe with Dates of Foundation and Suppression

WOMEN'S CONVENTS IN CAPITALS

I Province of Chartreuse, 1301

1 Grande Chartreuse 1084
2 Vallon 1136-1544
3 Oujon 1146-1536
4 Reposoir 1151-1901
5 Pomiers 1170-1793
6 St-Hugon 1173-1793
7 Aillon 1178-1793
8 MELAN 1282-1793
9 Valsainte 1294
10 Currière 1296-1790
11 Chalais 1303-1793
12 La Part-Dieu 1306-1848
13 La Lance 1317-1538
14 Val de Paix 1327-1333
15 Geronde 1330-1349
16 Lyons 1584-1793
17 Ripaille 1623-1793
18 BEAUREGARD 1822

II Province of Provence, 1301

1 Durbon 1116-1791
2 Les Ecouges 1116-1422
3 Montrieux 1117
4 Val Ste-Marie 1144-1791
5 ST-ANDRÉ DE RAMIERES 1145-1228 (moved to II, 9)
6 La Verne 1170-1792
7 BERTAUD 1188-1446 (moved near II, 1, 1446-1610)
8 Valbonne 1203-1901
9 PRÉBAYON 1228-1336
10 PRÉMOL 1234-1791
11 PARMÉNIE 1257-1407
12 CELLE-ROUBAUD 1260-1420
13 EYMEU 1300-1310
14 Bonpas 1318-1791
15 Villeneuve 1356-1792
16 Aix 1625-1791
17 Marseilles 1633-1791

III Province of Burgundy, 1301

1 Portes 1115
2 Sylve Benite 1116-1792
3 Meyriat 1116-1792
4 Arvières 1132-1791
5 Vaucluse 1139-1791
6 Seillon 1168-1792
7 Bonlieu 1171-1789
8 Sélignac 1202
9 Montmerle 1210-1790
10 POLETEINS 1230-1605
11 SALETTES 1299-1792
12 Pierre-Châtel 1383-1790
13 Bosserville (Nancy) 1632-1901

IV Province of Aquitaine, 1369

1 Bonnefoy 1156-1791
2 Port Ste-Marie 1219-1791
3 Glandier 1219-1901
4 Sainte Croix en Jarez 1280-1791
5 La Louvetière 1320-1427
6 Cahors 1328-1792
7 Vauclaire 1330-1901
8 Mortemer 1335-1413
9 Castres 1361-1791
10 Villefranche 1450-1791
11 Rodez 1511-1791
12 Toulouse 1602-1791
13 Bordeaux 1605-1791
14 Le Puy 1628-1791
15 Mougères 1825
16 MONTAUBAN 1852-1903 (moved to XIV, 18)
17 NONENQUE 1929

V Province of the Loire, 1701

1 Val Dieu 1170-1790
2 Liget 1178-1790
3 Apponay 1185-1790
4 Bellary 1209-1791
5 Val d'Espérance 1222-?
6 Le Parc 1236-1790
7 Oyron 1396-1443
8 Nantes 1446-1790
9 Auray 1480-1791
10 Orléans 1621-1791
11 Moulins 1627-1790

VI Province of the Seine, 1701

1 Lugny 1170-1791
2 Val St-Georges 1234-1792
3 Vauvert (Paris) 1257-1792
4 Valprofonde 1301-1790
5 Bourgfontaine 1325-1790
6 Basseville 1328-1790
7 Fontenay (Beaune) 1328-1790
8 Troyes 1329-1620 (moved to VI, 13)
9 Dijon 1383-1790
10 Rouen (Rose Notre-Dame) 1384-1667 (moved to VI, 14)
11 Maillard 1503-1520
12 Bourbon-lez-Gaillon 1571-1790
13 Largentière (Troyes) 1620-1790
14 Rouen (St-Julien) 1667-1791

VII Province of Picardy, 1332

1 Mont Dieu 1134-1791
2 Val St-Pierre 1140-1791
3 Valenciennes 1288-1790
4 St-Omer 1298-1792
5 Abbeville 1300-1791
6 Noyon 1308-1790
7 Gosnay 1320-1791
GOSNAY 1329-1791
8 Montreuil 1324-1901
9 Tournai 1377-1783
10 La Boutillerie 1618-1791
11 Douai 1662-1791
12 LE GARD 1871-1906 (moved to VIII, 23)

VIII Province of Teutonia, 1474 (part of Picardy to 1474)

1 Herne (La Chapelle) 1314-1783
2 Brugge 1318-1783
BRUGGE 1348-1783
3 Kiel (Antwerp) 1323-1542 (moved to VIII, 20)
4 Gent 1328-1783
5 Geeraardsbergen 1328-1783
6 Diest 1328-1794
7 Geertruidenberg 1336-1573
8 Arnhem 1342-1585
9 Cadsant 1346-1385
10 Liège 1357-1794
11 Utrecht 1392-1580
12 Amsterdam 1393-1577
13 Zierikzee 1434-1572
14 Scheut 1455-1578 (moved to VIII, 16)
15 Brussels 1592-1783
16 s'-Hertogenbosch 1466-1576 (moved to VIII, 21)
17 Delft 1470-1572
18 Campen 1484-1580
19 Louvain 1491-1783
20 Lier 1544-1783
21 Antwerp 1624-1794
22 Nieuwpoort 1626-1783
23 BURDINNE 1906-1929 (moved to IV, 17)

IX Province of England, 1369

1 Witham 1178-1539
2 Henton 1227-1539
3 Kinaleghin (Ireland) 1252-1321
4 Beauval 1343-1539
5 London 1370-1537
6 Hull 1378-1539
7 Coventry 1381-1539
8 Totnes 1383-1386
9 Axholm 1396-1538
10 Mount Grace 1398-1539
11 Shene 1417-1559
12 Perth 1429-1535
13 Parkminster 1875

X Province of the Rhine, 1400

1 Mainz 1320-1781
2 Koblenz 1331-1802
3 Trier 1331-1794
4 Cologne 1334-1794
5 Strasbourg 1335-1591 (moved to X, 15)
6 Freiburg 1346-1782
7 Roermond 1376-1783
8 Bern 1397-1528
9 Basel 1401-1564
10 Sierck 1415-1431 (moved to X, 11)
11 Rettel 1431-1790
12 Wesel 1418-1590 (moved to X, 16)
13 Dülmen 1476-1803
14 Vogelsang (Jülich) 1478-1802
15 Molsheim 1600-1791
16 Xanten 1628-1802
17 Hain 1869-1964 (moved to XIII, 1)

XI Province of Saxony, 1412

1 Lund (Sweden) 1162-1181
2 Stettin 1360-1524
3 Danzig 1381-1826
4 Hildesheim 1388-1777
5 Rügenwalde 1394-1534
6 Frankfurt am Oder 1396-1568
7 Rostock 1396-1532
8 Arensbök 1398-1564
9 Schievelbein 1442-1552
10 Gribsholm (Sweden) 1494-1527 (not shown)

XII Province of Lower Germany, 1355

1 Schnals 1326-1782
2 Grünau 1328-1803
3 Würzburg 1348-1803
4 Tückelhausen 1351-1803
5 Erfurt 1372-1803
6 Eisenach 1380-1525
7 Nürnberg 1380-1525
8 Nördlingen 1384-1648
9 Buxheim 1402-1803
10 Astheim 1408-1803
11 Liegnitz 1423-1540
12 Güterstein 1439-1534
13 Eppenberg (Vogelsberg) 1442-1532
14 Ilmbach 1453-1803
15 Ittingen (Switzerland) 1461-1848
16 Conradsburg 1477-1525
17 Crimmitschau 1477-1527
18 Prüll (Regensburg) 1484-1803
19 Marienau (Leutkirch) 1962

XIII Province of Upper Germany, 1355

1 Seitz 1160-1782
2 Geirach 1169-1591
3 Freidnitz 1255-1782
4 Letenkow 1300-1563
5 Lechnitz 1300-1563
6 Mauerbach 1313-1782
7 Gaming 1330-1782
8 Tarkan 1330-1552
9 Prague 1342-1419
10 Lewel 1350-1551
11 Brünn 1370-1782
12 Leitomischl 1376-1394 (moved to XIII, 14)
13 Aggsbach 1380-1782
14 Dolan (Olomouc) 1394-1437 (moved to XIII, 16)
15 Pleterje 1403-1595, 1899
16 Olomouc 1437-1782
17 Kraków 1479-1480
18 Grosswardein 1494-1498
19 Walditz 1627-1782
20 Gidle 1641-1832
21 Bereza 1650-1831

XIV Province of Lombardy, 1301

1 Casotta 1171-1802
2 Losa 1171-1200 (moved to XIV, 4)
3 Valle di pesio 1173-1802
4 Monte Benedetto 1200-1498, 1630-42 (moved to XIV, 15, 1498-1630; moved to XIV, 17)
5 BUONLUOGO 1237-1304
6 Parma 1285-1769
7 Mombracco 1286-1642
8 Genoa 1297-1798
9 Albenga 1315-1799
10 Milan 1349-1779
11 Asti 1387-1801
12 Pavia 1396-1947
13 Mantua 1408-1782
14 Savona 1492-1802
15 Banda 1498-1598 (moved to XIV, 16)
16 Avigliana 1598-1630 (moved to XIV, 4)
17 Collegno (Turin) 1642-1855
18 PINEROLO 1903
19 GIAVENO 1904

XV Province of Tuscany, 1414

1 Maggiano 1314-1782
2 Bologna 1334-1797
3 Farneta (Lucca) 1338
4 Florence 1342-1957
5 Pontiniani 1311-1785
6 Belguardo (Siena) 1345-1636
7 Montello (Treviso) 1349-1810
8 Calci (Pisa) 1366
9 Gorgona 1373-1424
10 Venice 1422-1810
11 Padua 1449-1769
12 Ferrara 1452-1801
13 Vedana 1455

XVI Province of SS. Stephen and Bruno (part of Lombardy to 1369)

1 Serra San Bruno 1090
2 Trisulti 1204-1947
3 Padula 1306-1866
4 Naples 1337-1929
5 Giulianova 1338-1420
6 Catania 1360-1381
7 Rome (S. Croce) 1370-1561 (moved to XVI, 8)
8 Rome (delle Angeli) 1561-1884
9 Capri 1370-1808
10 Clermont 1394-1806

XVII Province of Catalonia, 1396

1 Escala de Dios (Scala Dei) 1163-1835
2 S. Pablo del Mar 1269-1415
3 Puerta del Cielo (Porta Coeli) 1272
4 S. Jaime de Valle Paraiso 1345-1415
5 Valle de Cristo (Vallis Christi) 1385-1835
6 Valldemosa (Majorca) 1399-1835
7 Montalegre 1415
8 La Anunciata 1442-1445
9 Las Fuentes 1507-1835
10 Casa de Dios (Aula Dei) 1563
11 Altar del Cielo (Ara Coeli) 1569-1596
12 Altar de Cristo (Ara Christi) 1585-1835
13 La Concepcion 1633-1835
14 Camino del Cielo (Via Coeli) 1640-1681
15 BENIFACA (Tortosa) 1960

XVIII Province of Castile, 1442

1 El Paular 1390-1835
2 Seville 1400-1835
3 Aniago 1440-1835
4 Miraflores 1441
5 Jerez de la Frontera 1476
6 Cazalla 1490-1835
7 Granada 1515-1835
8 Évora (Portugal) 1588
9 Lisbon (Portugal) 1593-1834

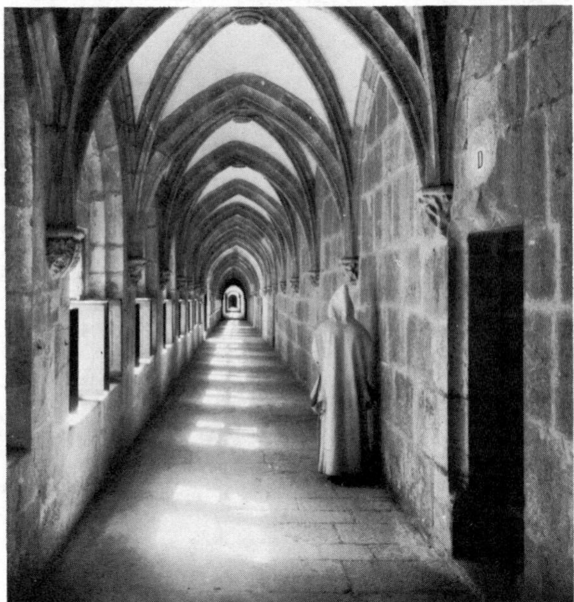

Fig. 2. The 14th-century Gothic "Great Cloister" at the monastery of La Grande Chartreuse.

tulants, who after their formation were sent to other charterhouses that were repurchased as the number of subjects increased. Gradually, monasteries were also reacquired in Italy and Savoy. While the Carthusians were experiencing a rebirth in France and in Italy, the revolution of 1834 in Portugal suppressed all the charterhouses in that kingdom. The following year the Spanish government dispersed the Carthusian congregation and seized its property. The houses of the order in Switzerland were likewise suppressed. In the last quarter of the 19th century, as the antireligious spirit subsided, the Grande Chartreuse repurchased monasteries in Germany, Italy, Switzerland, Spain, and England, as well as in France. Several of these houses were for Carthusian nuns. At the end of the century the order, divided into 3 provinces, numbered about 700 monks and brothers, and 100 nuns.

Because of the anticlerical laws of the early 20th century, the Carthusians once more were exiled from France and 10 charterhouses were confiscated. The community of the Grande Chartreuse, together with the prior general, was established at Farneta in Italy. The monks remained in exile until 1929, when the first French house, Montrieux, was reopened. It was only in 1940, during the confusion of the war, that they were able to reoccupy the Grande Chartreuse.

Carthusian Life. The Carthusian family is comprised of choir monks, brothers, and nuns.

Monks. The choir monks, all of whom must become priests, are bound to the sung, canonical Office in choir. In addition, each monk says the Office of Our Lady in his cell. The monk lives in a hermitage consisting of a covered ambulatory, private garden, and workshop on the ground floor; above is the *cubiculum,* or living room, where he prays, studies, eats, and sleeps. Here he passes the greater part of his life. The cells, entirely separated from one another, open on the main cloister, which connects with the church and other conventual buildings. Toward midnight, the monk rises to go to the church to sing Matins and Lauds, after which he returns to his cell for a second period of sleep of about 3 hours. In early morning he leaves his cell for conventual and private Masses, and again in the afternoon for Vespers. The remainder of the day, spent in solitude, is given to the

Fig. 3. Exterior view of the main monastery buildings of La Grande Chartreuse, Isere, France.

recitation of the Office, mental prayer, spiritual reading, study, and manual labor. In winter one meal is taken at noon, and a collation of bread and beverage is taken in the evening; in summer there are two meals. There is no breakfast, and meat is never allowed, even in cases of sickness. A black fast on bread and water is kept once a week. Within the monastery silence is strictly observed. Once a week the monks take a brisk walk of 3 or 4 hours in the surrounding countryside, during which they converse freely in a spirit of fraternal charity.

Lay Brothers. Brothers were among St. Bruno's first companions and have always formed an integral part of the Carthusian family. They are religious contemplatives like the choir monks but are called to a solitude less exacting, and enjoy a well-balanced life in which prayer and spiritual reading alternate with periods of work. They attend the night Office of the fathers and recite their own Office of *Paters* and *Aves* silently. Their day begins with Mass and Communion, and there are two short visits to the Blessed Sacrament during the day. Each brother has his own simple cell where he says his Office, reads, sleeps, and takes his meals, except on Sundays and certain feasts when meals are taken in the refectory. Devoted to the service of the fathers, who by their rule may not leave their cells to work, the brothers care for the material needs of the monastery. When possible they work alone; when obliged to work with others, they observe silence so far as practicable. Thus, whether in their cells or at work, they live as solitary contemplatives. They benefit, moreover, from the atmosphere of peace and tranquillity created by the more secluded life of the choir monks, who provide them with daily Mass as well as the liturgical life and spiritual guidance needed to help them attain their ideal.

Nuns. Female religious have been affiliated to the order since the 12th century. They follow a rule similar to the fathers, but their life is less solitary. After profession of solemn vows they receive the consecration of virgins and possess the unique privilege of the ancient blessing of *deaconesses. Lay sisters lead a life of humble service similar to the brothers and like them aspire to a life of contemplative union with God.

Current Status. Vocations to Carthusian solitude are relatively rare. In 1964 the order had 5 houses in Spain, 4 in France, and 4 in Italy. There were charterhouses also in Portugal, Yugoslavia, Germany, Switzerland, and England. There were 4 houses of nuns, 2 in France and 2 in Italy. A foundation exists in the U.S. at Arlington, Vt., but until regular life can be established, candidates are sent to Europe for their novitiate and studies. In addition to 75 novices, the order's professed members numbered 315 choir monks, 245 lay brothers, 82 choir nuns, and 61 lay sisters. The Carthusian emblem is a globe surmounted by a cross and seven stars with the motto "While the world changes, the cross stands firm."

Bibliography: Y. Gourdel, DictSpirAscMyst 2.1:705–776. H. Sommer, LexThK² 5:1381–84. Heimbucher 1:376–391. S. Autore, DTC 2.2:2274–2318. R. Webster, CE 3:388–392. B. Tromby, *Storia critico-cronologica diplomatica del patriarca S. Brunone e del suo ordine cartusiano,* 10 v. (Naples 1773–79). C. Le Couteulx, *Annales ordinis cartusiensis (1084–1429),* 8 v. (Montreuil 1887–91). A. P. F. Lefebvre, *St. Bruno et l'ordre des Chartreux,* 2 v. (Paris 1883). C. M. Boutrais, *La Grande Chartreuse* (Grenoble 1881; rev. 1964), Eng., *The History of the Great Chartreuse,* tr. E. Hassid (London 1934). T. Merton, *The Silent Life* (New York 1957). Knowles MOE. Knowles ROE. E. M. Thompson, *The Carthusian Order in England* (New York 1930). Adam, Chaplain of St. Hugh, *Magna vita Sancti Hugonis: The Life of St. Hugh of Lincoln,* ed. D. L. Douie and H. Farmer, 2 v. (London 1961–62), Latin and Eng. **Illustration credits:** Fig. 2, SPADEM, Paris, by French Reproduction Rights, Inc. Fig. 3, Archives Photographiques, Paris.

[A MONK OF THE GRANDE CHARTREUSE]

CARTHUSIANS (RITE)

The Carthusians have a manner of celebrating the liturgy proper to their Order. This article traces the origins and history of the rite and its specialties in Mass and Office.

Origins and History. It seems certain that the predominant and exclusive influence in the formation of the Carthusian liturgy was the rite of the primatial See of Lyons, of which Grenoble was a suffragan. This is true of the Mass and very largely of the Office, though for the latter the order of psalmody (which governs the form of the Hours) laid down by the Rule of St. Benedict was adopted; for the other variable parts of the Office, the Antiphonary of Lyons was drawn upon.

There is considerable evidence for these assertions. One of the earliest Carthusian liturgical manuscripts (MS 33 at St. Hugh's Charterhouse, Parkminster, England) shows that the octave day of Pentecost was celebrated with the Mass of the feast, so that the series of Masses for the Sundays after Pentecost are one behind the corresponding series in the Roman rite; the last of the series is *Si iniquitates* instead of *Dicit Dominus.* This, the versicle *Pone, Domine, custodiam ori meo,* said before the Confiteor at Mass, and the prayer at the mixing of the wine and water (*De latere,* etc.) are all features common to the early Carthusian liturgy and to that of Lyons. Similar influences may be seen in the Antiphonary. Guigo I, the fifth prior of Chartreuse, who compiled both books, followed the principle advocated by Agobard, Archbishop of Lyons (d. 840), that only Scripture and sermons from the Fathers could be used at Office or Mass. As a consequence "ecclesiastical compositions" were excluded from the rite: Mass for the dead had as Introit *Respice* instead of *Requiem,* and many well-known pieces found no place. Although at a later date some nonscriptural matter found its way into the Missal and Office, the Carthusians have always been conservative in this matter; there are no "historical" second nocturn lessons in the Carthusian Office. Hymns were allowed in the Office though at Lyons there were none until a late date. Guigo's work is to be found in the *Consuetudines Cartusiae;* his successors coordinated successive enactments of general chapters in a collection known as *Statuta Antiqua* (*c.* 1222), which remained in force until 1582 when a reform of the rite produced the *Ordinarium.* However, little real change was effected in the rite. Even today the Carthusian liturgy is largely as it was codified by Guigo.

Mass. The celebrant of a high Mass is attended by a deacon (there is no subdeacon). Mass begins below the step at the Gospel side where the celebrant sings the versicle *Pone, Domine,* etc., to which the choir answers, and the Confiteor follows (a short form). Introit, Kyrie, and Gloria are recited by the celebrant while they are sung by the choir; after the Collect he goes to his seat at the Epistle side and listens to the Epistle sung by a monk from the choir; meanwhile the deacon prepares the offerings. Immediately after the Gospel (or Credo) the celebrant washes his hands and receives the paten and chalice from the deacon. As the drop of water is poured into the chalice, the celebrant says *De latere Domini nostri Jesu Christi exivit sanguis et aqua, in nomine Patris,* etc. Paten and chalice are offered simultaneously with the prayer *In spiritu humilitatis.* The priest then washes his hands again. Meanwhile the deacon incenses the altar, walking around it, swinging the thurible at the full length of its chains. During the Canon the celebrant holds out his arms in the form of a cross, unless some manual act is necessary. The pax is given with an instrument. The deacon communicates with the priest on Sundays and certain feasts. Having drunk the ablutions the celebrant leaves the chalice for the deacon to purify and goes to the Epistle corner to sing the *Complendae* (Postcommunions). There is no blessing or *Placeat.* The blessing of candles, ashes, and palms takes place after the preparatory prayers at the foot of the altar, but the Carthusians have no liturgical processions.

Office. The Carthusian Office follows the general pattern of the monastic Breviary, but the lessons at Matins are very long by modern standards (e.g., two or three chapters of a book of Scripture make up the three lessons of a ferial night). All the day Hours conclude with long ferial preces before the Collect. The Carthusian Breviary, used only by those unable to go to choir, contains short lessons on the pattern of the modern Roman Breviary. Simplicity and sobriety are the chief characteristics of the Carthusian liturgy.

Bibliography: A. DEGAND, DACL 3.2:1045–71. A. A. KING, *Liturgies of the Religious Orders* (Milwaukee 1955). L. C. SHEPPARD, *The Mass in the West* (New York 1962); "How the Carthusians Pray," *Thought* 4 (1929) 294–311.

[L. C. SHEPPARD]

CARTIER, SIR GEORGE ÉTIENNE, statesman and father of the Canadian Confederation; b. St. Antoine, Quebec, Canada, Sept. 6, 1814; d. London, England, May 30, 1873. He was the son of Lt. Col. Jacques and Margaret (Paradis) Cartier, and probably a descendant of a collateral branch of the family of the explorer Jacques *Cartier. In 1835, following studies at Montreal College, Quebec, he was admitted to the bar of Lower Canada. In the rebellion of 1837 he fought with the patriots and was forced to become an exile in the U.S. He returned to the country (1838) and was elected to the Canadian Legislative Assembly (1848); he remained a member until his death. He became provincial secretary (1855) and attorney general (1856) of Lower Canada, and later the leader of the Lower Canadian branch of the Macdonald-Cartier administration (1857–62). Again in the capacity of attorney general (1864–67), he played an important part in the movement advocating a Canadian Confederation and served as minister of the militia in the first Canadian government. He married (1846) Hortense Fabre, and they had two daughters. As a man of great energy and executive ability, he was the undisputed leader of the French Canadians (1858–73). He was created a baronet of the United Kingdom (1868) and was the author of a popular song, *O Canada! mons pays, mes amours.*

Sir George Étienne Cartier.

Bibliography: J. BOYD, *Sir George Étienne Cartier* (Toronto 1914). R. RUMILLY, *Georges-Étienne Cartier,* v.1 of *Histoire de la province de Québec* (Montreal 1940–). **Illustration credit:** Château de Ramezay Museum, Montreal.

[G. CARRIÈRE]

CARTIER, JACQUES

Explorer; b. Saint-Malo, France, probably Dec. 31, 1491; d. there, Sept. 1, 1557. He was the son of Jamet and Geseline (Jansart) Cartier; little else is known of his early life. In 1519 he held the rank of master pilot of the King of France, and he married Marie Katherine des Granches, daughter of the high constable of Saint-Malo; the marriage was childless. Cartier's office suggests that the discoverer of interior Canada had frequently crossed the Atlantic prior to 1519, especially since his port town of Saint-Malo was a departure point for the fishermen of the Newfoundland Grand Banks. He may have been employed by the Portuguese to visit Brazil about 1527, for in the accounts of his first and second recorded voyages to Canada (1534, 1535) he compared the agriculture of Canada and Brazil, and in 1543 he was chosen royal interpreter of Portuguese. On the first of his recorded voyages to Canada, the ships arrived at Newfoundland on May 10, 1534, and spent 10 days preparing for further exploration, during which Cartier passed through the strait of Belle Isle and crossed to the coast of Gaspé, where he first came into contact with the Indians. He penetrated the Gulf of St. Lawrence and reached Anticosti Island, returning to Saint-Malo on Sept. 5, 1534. Cartier mistrusted or feared the Indians and returned their motions of friendship with cannon fire. Despite this the French did some trading with the Indians and came to the conclusion that they could easily be converted to Catholicism.

Having received immediate favor from King Francis I for his first voyage, Cartier was commissioned on Oct. 30, 1534, to engage at the King's expense three ships, equipped for 15 months, so that he could spend at least a year in actual exploration. On May 19, 1535, he set sail with 112 persons, including two Indians who had been brought from Gaspé in the preceding voyage and who were to return as guides and interpreters. On this famous voyage the explorer ascended the St. Lawrence River as far as the island of Montreal. After wintering in the area of present-day Quebec City, he set sail for Saint-Malo on May 6, 1536, arriving on July 6.

Again Cartier brought back Indians from Canada; the Indians learned the French language, spoke with Francis I, and on March 25, 1538 or 1539, three of them were baptized in Saint-Malo. In 1541 Cartier made a third voyage to Canada; he revisited Montreal and again spent the winter in Canada, awaiting the arrival of the new viceroy of New France, Sieur de Roberval. In the spring of 1542, as Cartier was returning to France, he passed Roberval at St. John's, Newfoundland. Cartier probably spent the remainder of his life in Saint-Malo and at a country residence at Limoilou. In certain records of Saint-Malo in 1549, Cartier is referred to as the Sieur de Limoilou. This may indicate an elevation in rank awarded him by the King or may have been merely a sort of courtesy title often given to the proprietors of small landed estates.

Bibliography: *The Voyages of Jacques Cartier,* ed. and tr. H. P. Biggar (Ottawa 1924). H. P. Biggar, comp., *Collection of Documents Relating to J. Cartier* (Ottawa 1930). G. Vattier, *Jacques Cartier et la découverte du Canada* (Paris 1937). H. B. Stephens, *Jacques Cartier: His Four Voyages to Canada* (Montreal 1890). S. B. Leacock, *The Mariner of St. Malo: A Chronicle of the Voyages of Jacques Cartier* (Toronto 1920). For bibliographical data on Cartier's narratives, see H. Harrisse, *Notes pour servir à l'histoire de la Nouvelle France* (Paris 1872).

[F. BOLAND]

CARTOGRAPHY

The science of making maps is an ancient one, for human beings knew how to make maps before they knew how to write. Its beginnings are almost impossible to ascertain. Primitive peoples have a talent for making maps. Eskimos have constructed maps of their coasts, and Marshall Islanders have made charts indicating their location by means of palm leaves and sea shells.

Ancient Period. The oldest map known today is a small red stone tablet showing the location of a man's estate in Mesopotamia, dating from before 3000 B.C. The map was discovered during excavation of the ruined city of Ga sur, about 200 miles north of Babylon. The Babylonian contribution to cartography, besides the stone map, included the division of the circle into 360 degrees.

The early Egyptians also made maps. For the practical purposes of taxation, they carefully measured the registered land and marked boundaries. They used a geometrical method for measuring the land on the delta of the Nile. Ancient China, too, excelled in regional descriptions. The Chinese prepared gazetteers known as *Fang Chih,* which included tens of thousands of volumes and were accompanied by maps. The earliest-known cartographer was Pei Hsiu (3d century A.D.). He laid down such principles of cartography as scale, direction, distance, and relief. Apparently Chinese mapmaking had reached a high accuracy, but Chinese cartography was totally different from that of the West. Pei Hsiu anticipated Western cartographers, but his network is not comparable to the modern meridians and parallels, for the Chinese conceived the earth as a flat surface with China in the middle. Pei Hsiu's influence dominated Chinese cartography for more than 1,200 years—until Matteo *Ricci introduced his world map to China in the 16th century.

The foundation of modern scientific cartography was largely laid down by the ancient Greeks. They recognized the spherical shape of the earth, measured its size, and defined the poles, the equator, and the tropics. They designed the parallel-meridian system, divided into degrees, the system as it is used today. One important cartographer was Eratosthenes of Cyrene (276–196 B.C.). He measured the earth and also made a map of the habitable world with seven parallels and seven meridians. The map was lost, but it has been described in sufficient detail so that its restoration can be attempted. It gives rich geographic information gathered by Alexander the Great and his successors.

Fig. 1. Pictographic land record tablet of red stone, dated before 3000 B.C.

The culmination of Greek cartography was reached in the work of Claudius *Ptolemy of Alexandria. Primarily an astronomer and mathematician, he produced his famous *Geographia* in eight volumes. The most important is the eighth volume, which deals with the principles of cartography, mathematical geography, projections, and methods of astronomical observation. The text of Ptolemy's *Geographia* was accompanied by the map of the world and 26 detailed maps. He made two projections, both modifications of the conic projection. Ptolemy's maps had an enormous influence on cartography in the ancient world.

The cartography of the Romans was totally different from that of the Greeks. For the Romans, a map had to be a practical aid to the journey of their officials and the campaigns of their legions. They were not interested in the mathematical approach to the earth's latitude and longitude, its astronomical measurements and its projections. Rather, they were concerned with the actual problems of the maps as efficient guides to the use of roads by their military and administrative officials. The Romans designed the famous disk-shaped map, the "Orbis Terrarum," or "Survey of the World." The map was no doubt based on the Roman road systems. In the development of cartography it is not difficult to differentiate between the practical approach of the Romans and the scientific approach of the Greeks.

Middle Ages. Toward the end of the 13th century, the development of cartography centered on the evolution of sea charts, which represented a great advance beyond earlier products of medieval cartography. In their essentials these charts marked a complete break with tradition; the fundamental difference was that the sea charts were based on direct observations made by means of new instruments. On them the coast of the Black Sea, the coast of the Mediterranean, and southwest Europe were laid down with considerable accuracy. For the first time Europeans included the continent of Asia in their world picture. These charts are frequently referred to as portolan charts; they were divided into sections and sometimes were supplemented by a calendar, a world map, or astronomical data. The best-known is the *Great Catalan Atlas,* produced in 1375, which embodied the results of the efforts of 14th-century cartographers.

Renaissance. Never in history did man's conception of the earth change more rapidly than in the years *c.* 1500. Accordingly, the technique of mapmakers pushed ahead. One of the notable steps toward improvement in cartography was the invention of the method of representing relief. In this age, three major events contributed to the renaissance of cartography.

The first of these was the rediscovery of Ptolemy's *Geographia,* which was translated into Latin *c.* 1400. Starting with the portolan charts, cartography came to full bloom in the 16th century. A new interest in the outside world replaced the inward-looking attitude of medieval man.

The second event that stimulated the progress of cartography was the invention of printing and engraving. Thitherto all maps had to be drawn by hand, laboriously and expensively. Now thousands of copies could be obtained from a single plate, and the price of maps dropped.

The third and perhaps most far-reaching event leading to a renaissance of cartography was the work of the great discoverers—the navigators of many nations, Italian, Portuguese, Spanish, French, Dutch, and English—who in little more than a century opened up the oceans of the world. Maps and charts were needed to present the land of the Americas and the routes to the Indies. The result was an outburst of cartographical activity unparalleled until very recent times.

The best maps of the late 16th and the 17th century came from the Netherlands. Many great cartographers produced maps characterized by beauty and a high quality of the engraving. The central position of the Netherlands, the industrial and artistic ability of the people, and their interest in distant lands made the Dutch first-class mapmakers.

The father of Dutch cartography was Gerardus *Mercator. The chief merit of Mercator's work was the liberation of cartography from the influence of Ptolemy. He compiled his material from all available sources, examined critically the older maps and read the records of sailors and travelers, and traveled widely himself. Mercator is best known for the Mercator projection, which, since the lines of compass directions appear straight, is well adapted for use in navigation. Mercator designed this projection in 1560 for his large chart of the world.

In the course of his long life Mercator acquired a profound knowledge of cosmography and was recognized as the most learned geographer of his day. His achievements were his globe (1541); his celebrated world projection (1569); his large map of Europe (1554); his edition of Ptolemy (1578); and his atlas, published by his son in 1595.

Mercator encouraged his friend Abraham Ortelius to prepare an atlas, and the *Theatrum Orbis Terrarum* was published in 1570. It is regarded as the first modern atlas of the world. The distinguishing features of Ortelius's *Theatrum* were critical selection from the best maps available, to give a comprehensive coverage of the world; uniform size and style of the maps; and the citing of the authorities on whose work each map was based. Ortelius's list of authorities, which includes the names of 87 cartographers, is an invaluable source for the history of cartography. The general characteristic of the Dutch Renaissance maps is their decorative quality. The title, scale, and descriptive material are usually collected into decorative frames called cartouches, often adorned by pictures of animals and of the products of the country.

The end of the 17th century was called the era of the reformation of cartography. It began with longitudal measurements made by the French Academy. The 18th-century maps are far less decorative but much more accurate than their 17th-century Dutch predecessors. Their cartographic motive was scientific reputation. The greatest achievement of this age was the triangulation and topographic mapping done in France. This set the pattern for the national surveys of the 19th century. Large-scale topographic maps and charts of a nation can be produced only by a large organization, and the tasks of the independent cartographers were narrowed mostly to small-scale maps.

In the 17th century the desire to test new hypotheses concerning the physical universe stimulated attempts to determine accurately the dimensions and figures of the earth. Also more precise instruments were invented, which made the necessary observations possible. These instruments, which included the telescope and the clock

Fig. 2. Gerardus Mercator, engraving in the "Biblioteca Chalcographica," published in 1650.

Fig. 3. Map of the world in two hemispheres on a double cordiform projection, published at Louvain in 1538. This is the first map of the world compiled by Mercator and the second map he is known to have produced. It is the first map to make a distinction between and to name North and South America. One of two known surviving copies of the map was found pasted into Mercator's personal copy of his 1578 edition of Ptolemy's "Geographica."

pendulum, as well as the compiling of tables of logarithms, led to the successful measurement of an arc on the earth's surface. All this contributed eventually to the improvement of mapping and the advance of cartography.

Modern Cartography. At the end of the 19th century a new type of atlas came into fashion, the national atlas, a large volume containing all available information about a single nation. Climate, soil, and economic, health, and social conditions were shown in maps, cartograms, and diagrams. These atlases form a valuable basis for geographic study of the individual nations. Finland, Sweden, Scotland, France, and Czechoslovakia have produced outstanding atlases of this sort.

The Royal Scottish Geographical Society's atlas of Scotland, published in 1895, is an early example of this type. The atlas of Finland (1st ed. 1899, 3d ed. 1925) is an extremely comprehensive and well-produced work. In addition to physical geography and geology, the second edition covers also hydrology, flora, archeology, and demography. Less extensive in scope and understandably emphasizing economic factors is the atlas of Canada (1st ed. 1906, 2d ed. 1915); more elaborate were those prepared in Czechoslovakia and Germany. One of the most comprehensive was the "Atlas de France" printed by the Service Geographique de L'Armee. Of much wider interest than is suggested by its title is the "Atlas of American Agriculture," prepared by O. E. Baker and published in 1936.

The two-volume *Great Soviet Atlas of the World* is a combination of a general and a national atlas. Volume 1 (1937) deals with the world and the Soviet Union in general; volume 2 (1939) deals in greater detail with the political and administrative units, the topography, and the economic geography of the U.S.S.R.

Although the concept of a national atlas of the U.S. had been discussed since early 20th century, no definite plan for such a publication was prepared until after World War II. The first manuscript prototype was completed in 1952 by the American Geographical Society. Between 1955 and 1961 about 80 sheets of maps were published by several agencies of the Federal government. In 1961, however, a committee of the National Academy of Sciences recommended its own termination and transfer of responsibility for the national atlas to the Geological Survey, U.S. Department of the Interior. Congress appropriated funds to enable the Survey to begin work on the atlas in fiscal year 1963. Publication of the atlas was planned for 1968.

At the beginning of the 20th century cartography received a new stimulus from the introduction of aerial photography. This is the most important event in the history of cartography since the "great discoveries" of the 15th and 16th centuries. Aerial photography makes it possible to map even the most inaccessible areas of the world with great speed and accuracy.

Bibliography: L. Bagrow, *History of Cartography,* rev. and enl. R. A. Skelton, tr. D. L. Paisey (Cambridge, Mass. 1964). L. A. Brown, *The Story of Maps* (Boston 1949). E. J. Raisz, *General Cartography* (2d ed. New York 1948). R. V. Tooley, *Maps and Map Makers* (New York 1949). G. R. Crone, *Maps and Their Makers* (New York 1953). **Illustration credits:** Fig. 1, The Walters Art Gallery. Fig. 3, American Geographical Society.

[C. M. HSIEH]

CARTWRIGHT, PETER, Methodist preacher; b. Amherst County, Va., Sept. 1, 1785; d. Pleasant Plains, Ill., Sept. 25, 1872. His family migrated to Logan County, Ky., where the Great Revival began in 1800. Cartwright was converted at a camp meeting and commissioned (1802) to create a new circuit in western Kentucky and Tennessee. He was ordained a deacon in 1806 and an elder in 1808. A lifelong foe of slavery, he moved in 1824 to Sangamon County, Ill., where he was elected (1828) to the state legislature and reelected (1832) over Abraham Lincoln. Cartwright helped develop Illinois public schools and was a founder of Illinois Wesleyan University, Bloomington. He remained active as a preacher in Kentucky, Illinois, and Indiana.

Bibliography: P. CARTWRIGHT, *Autobiography*, ed. C. L. WALLIS (Nashville 1956) with bibliog. W. W. SWEET, *Methodism in American History* (Nashville 1954). E. S. BATES, DAB 3:546–548.

[R. K. MAC MASTER]

CARTWRIGHT, THOMAS, *Puritan controversialist; b. Herts, 1535; d. Warwick, Dec. 27, 1603. Thomas, son of a yeoman, studied at Clare and St. John's Colleges, Cambridge (1547–53), where he absorbed Reformation ideas. At Mary's accession he left the university to read law. Between 1558 and 1570, except for 2 years in Ireland, he held fellowships at St. John's and Trinity Colleges, becoming Lady Margaret Professor in 1569. He used this chair primarily to promote the Puritan cause, to which he had committed himself in the Vestiarian Controversy of 1566. He became identified more closely with nonconformity by actively preaching reform of the constitution and ecclesiastical polity of the Established Church along Presbyterian lines, proposing that the bishops and the crown governing the church be replaced by ministers and elders. Although these views deprived him of his professorship and enforced, over the next 15 years, periodic exile in Geneva, Antwerp, and Middelburg, he remained the most articulate spokesman for the Puritans in the Admonition Controversy against Abp. J. *Whitgift. Cartwright urged, especially in his three *Replies* to Whitgift's *Answere* and *Defense of the Aunswere* [sic], the restoration of the Established Church to the simplicity of doctrine and practice of Apostolic Christian times; he advocated sweeping Calvinist reforms of religious ceremonies extending to many ceremonies prescribed in the Book of *Common Prayer. Contemporaries regarded him as the leading 16th-century Puritan. He authored the Millenary Petition (1603) but died before the Hampton Court Conference.

Bibliography: A. F. S. PEARSON, *Thomas Cartwright and Elizabethan Puritanism, 1535–1603* (Cambridge, Eng. 1925). D. J. MCGINN, *The Admonition Controversy* (New Brunswick, N.J. 1949). C. H. and T. COOPER, comps., *Athenae cantabrigienses*, 3 v. (Cambridge, Eng. 1858–1913) 2:360–366. J. B. MULLINGER, DNB 3:1135–39.

[M. J. HAVRAN]

CARVAJAL

Juan de, cardinal bishop and papal legate; b. Trujillo, Estremadura, Spain, *c.* 1400; d. Rome, Dec. 6, 1469. An auditor of the Rota and governor of Rome in 1440, he was sent to persuade the Emperor Frederick III and the German princes to abandon the neutrality they had assumed in the struggle between Eugene IV and the Council of Basel, and he appeared before the Diet of Mainz in 1441 and the Diet of Frankfort in 1442. In the later Diet of Frankfort in 1446 he was associated with Tommaso Parentucelli (later Pope Nicholas V); their work culminated when the Emperor and the princes went into opposition to the Council of Basel. Later in 1446 Carvajal and Parentucelli were both made cardinals. In the same year Carvajal was named bishop of Plasencia in Spain. In 1448 he negotiated the Concordat of Vienna regulating German relations with the papacy. He served also as legate to Bohemia, where the Hussite problem continued, and on missions to Hungary (1455–61) and Venice (1466–67) he sought to stiffen resistance against the Turks. In Hungary he was accompanied by *John Capistran, and while he was there, John *Hunyadi defeated the Turks at Belgrade. Carvajal became bishop of Porto in 1461 and chamberlain of the College of Cardinals in 1469.

Bernardino Lopez de, cardinal bishop, member of the uncanonical council of Pisa-Milan, nephew of Juan; b. Plasencia, Estremadura, 1456; d. Rome, Dec. 16, 1523. He became bishop of Astorga in 1488, of Badajoz in 1489, of Cartagena in 1493, and of Sigüenza 1495 to 1519. He was made a cardinal in 1493 and sent as legate to Germany in 1496. As one of the Spanish cardinals favored by Alexander VI, he did not get on well with Julius II. In 1504 he was entrusted with the custody of Cesare Borgia, whom he allowed to escape. Following the negotiation of peace between Venice and the papacy, the withdrawal of the Pope from the League of Cambrai, and the dispatch of a papal army against Ferrara (whose duke was supported by the French), Carvajal and other dissident cardinals assembled at Pisa and proclaimed a council, summoning Julius II to appear. They were excommunicated, and Julius convoked the Fifth Lateran Council. When Leo X became pope, Carvajal recognized the Fifth Lateran Council and, having pledged obedience, was absolved and restored to his honors. In 1521 he became bishop of Ostia.

Bibliography: T. MINGUELLA Y ARNEDO, *Historia de la diócesis de Sigüenza y de sus obispos*, 3 v. (Madrid 1910–13). P. PASCHINI, *Roma nel Rinascimento* (Bologna 1940). L. GÓMEZ CANEDO, *Un español al servicio de la S. Sede: don J. da C.* (Madrid 1947). P. ALONSO and M. ALAMO, DHGE 11:1239–42. N. DEL RE, EncCatt 3:962–963. J. WODKA, LexThK[2] 2:959–960.

[D. R. CAMPBELL]

CARVAJAL, GASPAR DE, Dominican explorer and missionary; b. Trujillo, Estremadura, Spain, *c.* 1504; d. Lima, Peru, 1584. According to his own testimony he came from Spain with Bp. Vicente *Valverde to establish the Order of St. Dominic in Peru. He arrived there in 1538 and in November of that year, while established in a convent in Lima, he had to defend the rights of his community. In 1539 he was in Cuzco where he became the legal guardian of two of the sons of Atahualpa, Francisco Ninancuro and Diego de Ilaquita. Early in 1541, as vicar-general appointed by Bishop Valverde, he went to Quito where, as a chaplain, he joined the expedition organized by Gonzálo Pizarro to explore the province of Canela. Once in the eastern forests, he joined Francisco Orellana in the discovery and the navigation of the Amazon River. He was the chronicler of that expedition, on which he lost an eye. When he arrived in Cubagua and heard of the deaths of Valverde and Francisco Pizarro, he returned to Lima at once. His personal prestige enabled him to mediate first in the dispute between the *oidores* and Viceroy

Núñez Vela, then in the actions of La Gasca in Cuzco, and finally in the disagreements between Viceroy Andrés Hurtado de Mendoza and Bravo de Saravia. He was prior of Lima and of Cuzco, and in 1557 was elected provincial of the Dominicans in Peru. His jurisdiction then included Quito, Lima, Cuzco, Guamanga, and Chile. In his late years he wrote his eyewitness account of the discovery of the Amazon River to correct some of the reports of that discovery that had already appeared.

Bibliography: G. DE CARVAJAL, *Descubrimiento del río de las Amazonas,* ed. J. T. MEDINA (Seville 1894; reprint Cáceres 1953).

[J. M. VARGAS]

CARVAJAL, LUISA DE, Spanish ascetic who ministered to persecuted English Catholics; b. Jaraicejo (Cáceres), Spain, Jan. 2, 1568; d. London, Jan. 2, 1614. Luisa, of noble birth, was orphaned at the age of 6, and raised by her aunt and uncle at Pampeluna (Pamplona), where she showed early evidence of sanctity. She refused either to marry or to become a nun; instead, after the death of her aunt and uncle, she vowed herself to poverty and prayer with a group of women from her uncle's household. After 12 years she was permitted by her Jesuit confessor to fulfill a long-cherished desire to minister personally to persecuted English Catholics. Upon reaching London (1606) she gathered helpers, who lived in poverty and visited sufferers in their homes and in prison. She feasted the prisoners John *Roberts and Thomas Somers the night before their martyrdom (1610). The government, complaining that she did more to convert Protestants than 20 priests, twice imprisoned her. She was released only at the request of the Spanish ambassador, who probably could not have prevented her eventual deportation, had she not died in his residence on her 46th birthday. Her body was taken back to Spain. Among her numerous charities were funds to found the English Jesuit novitiate in Flanders.

Bibliography: G. FULLERTON, *Life of Louisa de Carvajal* (London 1873), based on a full-length contemporary biog. by L. Muñoz (Madrid 1632).

[D. M. ROGERS]

CARVALLO Y GOYENECHE, VICENTE, Chilean historian and soldier; b. Valdivia, 1742; d. Buenos Aires, April 17, 1816. He took up a military career and in 1774 was a cavalry captain. For many years he served under the commanding officer of the frontier, Ambrosio O'Higgins, with whom he quarreled when O'Higgins became governor of Chile. In 1790 he was granted permission to go to Santiago to collect material for a historical work, *Descripción histórico-geográfica del reino de Chile.* The following year, despite O'Higgins's opposition, the Spanish government granted him permission to go to Madrid to complete his book. He left his country in ecclesiastical disguise. He returned to America in 1800 and lived in Montevideo, Buenos Aires, and Córdoba. The independent Argentine government promoted him to the rank of lieutenant colonel, and shortly afterward he retired. Medina refers to his *Descripción histórico-geográfica del reino de Chile* as "the most complete work about our history of any written during the colonial period." It was published by Miguel Luis Amunátegui in volumes 8 to 10 of the *Colección de historiadores de Chile y documentos relativos a la historia nacional* (Santiago 1875).

Bibliography: J. T. MEDINA, *Historia de la literatura colonial de Chile* 3 v. (Santiago 1878) 2:489–508. G. GUARDA, "¿Carvallo Goyeneche o Goyonete?" *Revista de Estudios Históricos* 11 (1963) 5–26.

[A. M. ESCUDERO]

CARVE, THOMAS, historian of the Thirty Years' War; b. Mobernan, County Tipperary, Ireland, 1590; d. Vienna, Austria, 1672?. Carve's real name was Carew; he was a member of the prominent Carew family that had played an important role in the affairs of Munster. Carve's patrons, the Butlers of Ormonde, were responsible for his early education. He was ordained for the diocese of Leighlin sometime before 1620, and he left Ireland for Germany shortly after the beginning of the Thirty Years' War. Carve served as chaplain to Walter Butler (d. 1634), the colonel of an Irish regiment serving in the Imperial army of Ferdinand II. After several trips back and forth from Germany to Ireland, Carve served as chaplain to Walter Devereux, Butler's successor as colonel of the Irish troops. During these years, Carve compiled the materials for his *Itinerarium R.D. Thomae Carve . . .* (parts 1 and 2 published in Mainz 1639–41 and part 3, Spires 1646). This personal account of the Thirty Years' War is an important contemporary source for these years. Since Butler and Devereux were active in the conspiracy that resulted in the assassination of *Wallenstein (1634), Carve's account is practically an eyewitness report. At the conclusion of the war, Carve devoted himself chiefly to writing and to his positions as prothonotary apostolic and choral vicar of St. Stephen's Cathedral in Vienna, posts he had received in 1643. His last published work, *Responsio veridica* (Sulzbach 1672), is generally cited to determine the year of his death. The *Itinerary,* issued in several limited editions, is his major work. Its many details of European and English life have made it an important historical source that must be used with care and prudence.

Bibliography: T. COOPER, DNB 3 (1949) 1143–44. E. O'DONNELL, *The Irish Abroad* (New York 1915). J. WARE, *The History and Antiquities of Ireland . . . with the History of the Writers of Ireland,* tr. W. HARRIS, 2 v. in 1 (Dublin 1764).

[P. S. MC GARRY]

CARVILLE, EDWARD PETER, governor, U.S. senator; b. Mound Valley, Nev., May 14, 1885; d. Reno, Nev., June 27, 1956. "Ted" Carville was the son of Edward F. and Emily (Porcher) Carville. He received his early schooling in Mound Valley and at Elko, Nev., high school, and attended the University of Notre Dame, Ind., receiving his law degree in 1909. He married Irma Callahan of South Bend, Ind., in 1910. Carville was Elko's district attorney from 1912 to 1918 and its district judge from 1926 to 1934, when Pres. Franklin D. Roosevelt appointed him U.S. attorney for Nevada. He was elected Nevada's 18th governor in 1938 and reelected in 1942, establishing a reputation for economy and conservative government. After resigning in 1945 to fill a vacancy in the U.S. Senate, he suffered his only political defeat in the Democratic primary contest in 1946. After this unsuccessful attempt he returned to his private law practice in Reno.

[M. L. WELSH]

CARY, JOYCE, English novelist; b. Londonderry, North Ireland, Dec. 7, 1888; d. Oxford, England, March 29, 1957. He was born of a Protestant family originally from Devon, England, and though he spent his childhood summers in Ireland, he regarded England as his

Joyce Cary.

home. In 1905 he went to Paris and studied art for several months. He was at the Art School of the University of Edinburgh (1905–08), and then attended Oxford University. Cary took part in the Balkan War (1912–13), with both a Montenegrin battalion and the British Red Cross. He went to Nigeria in 1913 and remained in Africa for 6 years, serving in the Cameroons campaign (1915–16) and later acting as a district officer at the lonely outpost of Borgu. Cary married Gertrude Ogilvie (who bore him four sons) in 1916 and settled in Oxford in 1920, after having been invalided out of the Nigerian service. He led a retiring life, interrupted by infrequent trips or lecture tours abroad, and published his first novel in 1932. His wife died in 1949, and in 1955 he began to suffer from progressive muscular dystrophy. But like his own hero Gulley Jimson he "kept on keeping on" with his work. He wrote right up to the time of his death, and his last novel was published posthumously.

Cary's varied experiences are reflected in his novels, all published between 1932 and 1959. Four deal with Nigeria: *Aissa Saved* (1932), *An American Visitor* (1933), *The African Witch* (1936), and *Mister Johnson* (1939). Two are about childhood: *Charley Is My Darling* (1940) and *A House of Children* (1941). British history from Victorian to modern times is chronicled in *Castle Corner* (1938), *The Moonlight* (1946), and *A Fearful Joy* (1949). Art and the English soul are examined in the first trilogy, *Herself Surprised* (1941), *To Be a Pilgrim* (1942), and *The Horse's Mouth* (1944); while the second trilogy, *Prisoner of Grace* (1952), *Except the Lord* (1953), and *Not Honour More* (1955), deals with politics. *The Captive and the Free*, Cary's posthumous novel (1959), treats religion and the press. His other writings include a book of short stories and two long narrative poems. *Art and Reality* (1958) sets forth his aesthetic doctrine, while *Power in Men* (1939) presents his political theories.

Cary's basic insights are embodied consistently in his novels. Men are gloriously free and brimfull of creative imagination, and this leads them continuously to reshape the world. Life is full of evil, injustice, and insecurity, yet the world contains much good and thus reveals God to man. Politics—the difficult management of free human agents—permeates all human activity, which is essentially moral because it demands free choice. Finally, art, which presents ideas suffused with feeling, keeps men in contact with the "real" reality.

Bibliography: W. E. ALLEN, *Joyce Cary* (London 1953), a good short study. A. H. WRIGHT, *Joyce Cary: A Preface to His Novels* (New York 1958), excellent and with fuller coverage. M. M. MAHOOD, *Joyce Cary's Africa* (Boston 1965). **Illustration credit:** Photo by Mark Gerson.

[J. TEELING]

CASA, GIOVANNI DELLA, Italian priest and poet; b. Mugello (Florence), June 28, 1503; d. Montepulciano, Nov. 14, 1556. Della Casa had a good classical education at Florence and Bologna. After taking minor orders—he delayed final ordination for some years—he entered the clerical bureaucracy at Rome, meanwhile leading the rather dissipated life reflected in the verses he wrote at that time. In 1544 he was named archbishop of Benevento, but he never resided in that see. Instead Paul III appointed him apostolic nuncio to Venice, the chief duties imposed on him being to ward off the influence of Charles V over that city and to repress any nascent Protestantism. He prosecuted both tasks with skill and resolution. His indictment of Vergerio, Bishop of Capodistria, for heresy caused the bishop to flee from Italy. Vergerio composed a scathing denunciation, on moral grounds, of Della Casa, a document that may have helped to impede the archbishop's ecclesiastical advancement. His nunciature ceasing upon the death of Paul III (1549), Della Casa retired to the country and to his books. In 1555 Paul IV recalled him to Rome and made him secretary of state, but not, to Della Casa's disappointment, a cardinal. Yet it was the failure of his worldly ambitions that in fact brought out his best capacities as a poet. The whole theme of his last and finest sonnets—poems that place him high among the Italian masters of this form—is bitter reflection on the vanity of human wishes and the need for humble conversion to God.

Galateo (1551–54), his elegant treatise on good manners, was a compliment to Galeazzo Florimonte, Bishop of Sessa, who had suggested its composition. While stressing external civilities, the work also insinuates the claims of conscience; and it is perhaps this discreet edge of moral teaching, along with the polished style, that has kept the work alive. But it is on his small output of Italian poems, mostly sonnets, that Della Casa's reputation ultimately rests. He is a minor poet, but a very remarkable one, and this for reasons both of content and of style. Della Casa's chief theme was the old Augustinian and Petrarchan one: the desperate need of the soul for the peace to be found in God alone. The poet treated his material with a certain adult gravity; his stress on the insufficiency of the "world" rather than the "flesh" struck a distinctly new note in 16th-century Italian poetry. To this relative novelty of theme Della Casa brought a distinctive style, at once weighty and musical, involved and delicate. His last poems mark a saturation point; here the Italian sonnet has received all it can from classical influences without losing its native grace.

Bibliography: Works. *Opere*, ed. G. PREZZOLINI (Milan 1937). *Lirici del Cinquecento*, ed. L. BALDACCI (Florence 1957). Studies. B. CROCE, *Poesia popolare e poesia d'arte* (Bari 1933) 375–384. L. BALDACCI, *Il petrarchismo italiano nel Cinquecento* (Milan 1957) 181–268.

[K. FOSTER]

CASALE, GIACINTO DA, Capuchin preacher and diplomat; b. Casale dai conti Natta, Jan. 21, 1575; d. there, Jan. 18, 1627. He was by birth the Count of Alfiano, influential figure of the Catholic reformation. After studying letters at Padua and law at Bologna, he was employed at the Count of Mantua. He entered the Order of Friars Minor Capuchin at Venice in 1601. After his ordination he preached popular missions in Italy. In 1606 he went to Prague, where he preached with great effect and succeeded in reconciling Emperor Rudolph II with his brother and heir, Matthias. Thereafter he was active as a diplomat at almost every court in Europe. Pope Gregory XV chose him to accompany Cardinal Carlo Gaudenzio *Madruzzo to the Diet of Regensberg in 1613. There, his eloquence and diplomatic skill were employed successfully in inducing Emperor Ferdinand II to confer the palatinate on Duke Maximilian of Bavaria, thus assuring the Catholic League a majority of the votes among the Imperial electors. He refused the cardinal's hat offered to him soon after. Among his published writings are ten volumes of sermons and three ascetical works, one of which, *Tractatus de paupertate religiosi* (Mantua 1622), was issued in French and Italian translations.

Bibliography: FATHER CUTHBERT, *The Capuchins,* 2 v. (London 1928) 2:297–305. G. DA CITTADELLA, *Giacinto da Casale . . . nella sua predicazione* (Verona 1948); EncCatt 6:308. V. DA LAGOSANTO, *Apostolo e diplomatico: Il P. Giacinto da Casale* (Milan 1886). *Lexicon Capuccinum* (Rome 1951) 777–778.

[C. J. LYNCH]

CASANATE, GIROLAMO, cardinal, founder of Casanatense Library; b. Naples, Feb. 13, 1620; d. Rome, March 3, 1700. After law studies at the University of Naples, he began, under Innocent X, a long career in various ecclesiastical offices. From 1648 to 1658, he governed Sabina, Fabriano, Ancona, and Camerino; then he was inquisitor at Malta and after 1666 a consultor to several of the Congregations, including the Propagation of the Faith. He was assigned to the Supreme Tribunal of the Apostolic Signature and later was assessor of the Holy Office as well as secretary to the Congregation of Bishops and Religious, as it was then known.

In 1673 Casanate received the title of cardinal deacon and after his ordination in 1686, cardinal priest. Innocent XII bestowed on him the title Librarian of the Holy Church in 1693. Casanate is an example of the profound learning of his century. In dealing through his official capacities with the controversial issues of his day (including quietism, Gallican liberties, and foreign missions), he displayed remarkable knowledge. His library was renowned. By augmenting the private library inherited from his father with purchases, in some cases of whole library collections from major European countries, and with his own scholarly papers, he left at his death a collection estimated at more than 25,000 volumes. The library was endowed and placed under the direction of the Dominicans at Santa Maria sopra Minerva. At that time it ranked second to the Vatican Library in size and value of manuscripts and volumes. It was one of the first libraries opened for general public use (1701). Its collection contained examples of both contemporary scholarship and early Latin and Greek works on the Church. A special papal dispensation allowed heretical works to be kept there for consultation by a theological faculty of six Dominicans chosen from England, France, Germany, Italy, Poland, and Spain, who were commissioned by the Casanate endowment to teach and to defend the faith with the writings of Thomas Aquinas. The library holdings were increased and catalogued in the 18th century. In the 19th century it was taken over by the state and today remains as state property.

Bibliography: M. D'ANGELO, *Il Cardinale Girolamo Casante, 1620–1700* (Rome 1923). A. SALIMEI, EncCatt 3:968–969.

[P. D. SMITH]

CASANI, PIETRO, VEN., companion of the founder of the Pious Schools; b. Lucca, Sept. 8, 1570; d. Rome, Oct. 17, 1647. Of noble birth, he entered the Congregation of the Mother of God in Lucca at 23. He was a student of St. Robert *Bellarmine in Rome and was ordained in 1600. In the union of the Luccan congregation with the Pious Schools of St. *Joseph Calasanctius in 1614, Casani became secretary-general and rector of St. Pantaleon in Rome. When the union dissolved in 1617, he remained a Piarist. He was novice master, rector of five foundations, assistant general, provincial of Genoa and Naples, and visitor of schools. He adapted a Latin grammar for the Pious Schools and wrote on theology and exorcisms. In Germany he converted many by preaching and charity. He received Emperor Ferdinand III at Nicolsburg. When Ladislas IV invited the Piarists to Poland, Casani visited proposed school-sites. He was in Rome from 1641 to 1647. His body is in the church of St. Pantaleon. The loss of important documents interrupted the process of beatification, introduced in 1922.

Bibliography: *Epistolario di Calsanzio,* ed. L. PICANYOL, 9 v. (Rome 1950–56). G. SÁNTHA, *San José de Calasanz, su obra . . .,* tr. C. AGUILERA and J. CENTELLES (Madrid 1956). *Memorie storiche . . . P. Casani* by an anon. Piarist (Rome 1904).

[M. O'CALLAGHAN]

CASAS MARTÍNEZ, FELIPE DE JESÚS, ST., Mexican protomartyr of Japan; b. Mexico City, May 1, 1572; d. Nagasaki, Japan, Feb. 5, 1597. His Spanish parents, Alonso de las Casas, a rich merchant, and Antonia Martínez, went to Mexico in 1571. Felipe entered the Franciscans in Puebla in 1589, but did not persevere. He decided instead to become a merchant and went to the Philippines. In Manila he took the habit once more in May 1593 and made his profession the next year. He embarked for Mexico July 12, 1596. A storm damaged the ship and took it to the shores of Japan Oct. 18, 1596. Felipe received lodgings at the Franciscan convent of Miyaco, Kyoto. On Dec. 11, 1596, the order to imprison and crucify the Christian missionaries of the district of Miyaco was given. Felipe was not included on the list, but by his vehement desire for martyrdom he managed to become one of the group. The 26 missionaries were taken from Miyaco to Nagasaki, where they were martyred. Each cross had five iron rings for the neck, hands, and feet, and a pedestal. Raised on the cross, Felipe could not rest his feet because the pedestal was low; the neck ring choked him. He cried out three times "Jesus." His body was pierced by three lances, and in this manner he who was the last to arrive was the first to die. He was beatified Sept. 14, 1627, and declared patron of Mexico Feb.

5, 1629, in ceremonies that his mother witnessed. Felipe was canonized June 8, 1862.

Bibliography: J. A. PICHARDO, *Vida y martirio del protomártir mexicano san Felipe de Jesús las Casas* (Guadalajara, Mex. 1934). E. E. RIOS, *Felipe de Jesús: El santo criollo* (Mexico City 1954).

[E. GÓMEZ TAGLE]

CASAUBON, ISAAC, one of the greatest of French classical scholars; b. Geneva, Feb. 18, 1559; d. London, July 1, 1614. Until his 18th year he was taught exclusively by his father, a Huguenot pastor; he then attended the Academy of Geneva and was appointed professor of Greek there in 1581. He had already acquired a profound knowledge of Greek, was well versed in Hebrew, and was the master of an excellent Latin style. After teaching at Montpellier and Lyons, he went to Paris. His religion barred him from appointment to a professorship at the University, but he was made royal librarian. Following the assassination of Henry IV in 1610, he went to England, where he spent the last 4 years of his life. A man of great learning and piety, he was cultivated and helped by distinguished Catholic as well as Protestant officials and scholars. Calvinists were severely critical of the position he took in the Conference of Fontainebleau in 1500 (*see* DUPERRON, JACQUES DAVY), but there is no evidence that he ever planned to join the Catholic Church. Among his numerous scholarly works, special mention must be made of his edition of Athenaeus and that of the *Characters* of Theophrastus. At the urging of Thomas Morton, Bishop of Durham, and other Anglican friends, he was engaged in writing an elaborate refutation of the *Annals* of Baronius at the time of his death. He was buried in Westminster Abbey.

Bibliography: J. H. OVERTON, DNB 3:1166–70. Sandys 2:204–210. M. PATTISON, *Isaac Casaubon,* ed. H. NETTLESHIP (2d ed. Oxford 1892). L. J. NAZELLE, *Isaac Casaubon* (Paris 1897).

[M. R. P. MC GUIRE]

CASAVANT, JOSEPH, Canadian organ manufacturer; b. 1807; d. St. Hyacinthe, Canada, March 9, 1874. He was the descendant of a 17th-century Canadian soldier trumpeter. He began building organs in his own workshop; and by 1866, when he retired, he had completed the construction of 16, among them the organs for the Roman Catholic cathedrals at Ottawa and Kingston, Canada. At this time organs were considered a definite social amenity; although Casavant's specialty was church organs, he was a small part of a very large industry that had an annual turnover value of more than $250,000 (1869). His sons Joseph Claver and Samuel founded Casavant Frères to carry on his work, which, because of its high quality, attracted orders from all parts of North America. In time organs from the Casavant Frères Limitée were placed in churches and concert halls all over the world.

Bibliography: F. ÉLIE, *La famille Casavant* (Montréal 1914). G. MORISSET, *Coup d'oeil sur les arts en Nouvelle-France* (Quebec 1941). H. KALLMANN, *History of Music in Canada: 1534–1914* (Toronto 1960).

[C. W. WESTFALL]

CASCIOLINI, CLAUDIO, baroque church composer in the Roman "conservative" tradition; b. Rome, *c.* 1670; date and place of death unknown. Casciolini was choirmaster at San Lorenzo in Damaso in Rome. Although none of his compositions were published during his lifetime, they were apparently in the regular repertory of various Roman churches. When F. X. *Haberl was in Rome (1867–70) he heard several performances of Casciolini's two Requiems, one of them in the Sistine Chapel. His works are found in various MSS, notably in the Santini collection of church music now in the university library at Münster, Westphalia. Of his works available in modern editions, most are for three or four unaccompanied voices in homophonic style, with only occasional sections in a more contrapuntal texture. The text is clearly and sensitively expressed, and his use of chromatic progressions in melody and harmony contributes to the emotional effect of his musical language, at times bringing it close to sentimentality. Among his more complex works is *Angelus Domini descendit,* an Easter motet for two 4-voiced choirs, which contains brilliant antiphonal effects.

Opening page of the autograph MS of Claudio Casciolini's Easter motet "Angelus Domini descendit," preserved in the Santini Collection of Church Music, Münster.

Bibliography: J. KILLING, *Kirchenmusikalische Schätze der Bibliothek des Abbate Fortunato Santini* (Düsseldorf 1910). Eitner QuellLex 2:354–355.

[R. STEINER]

CASEL, ODO, liturgy scholar; b. Koblenz-Lützel, Sept. 27, 1886; d. Herstelle-Weser, March 28, 1948. He became a Benedictine monk in 1905; studied at Maria Laach, Rome, and Bonn; and earned doctoral degrees in both theology and philology. He was spiritual director for the Benedictine sisters at Herstelle from 1922 until his death during the Easter Vigil, 1948.

Casel attained prominence as a liturgical scholar through his editorship of the *Jahrbuch für Liturgiewissenschaft.* His special achievement, however, was to bring out the meaning of liturgy as a celebration of the mysteries of Christ and His Church: the ritual and sacramental deed of the Church makes present Christ's act of salvation.

Casel obtained his first insights from the liturgy and the Fathers of the Church, whose traditional teachings

Odo Casel.

he wished merely to hand on faithfully. But he took formal elements also from the history of religions, which, especially the Hellenistic mystery cults, were a sort of preparation for Christ. Although he in no way intended to dispute the uniqueness of Christian cult he encountered opposition. In the course of the ensuing controversy Casel perfected his conception of the liturgy, especially through the inclusion of scriptural teaching and a more positive evaluation of Old Testament worship. After Casel's death, his rich insights were further developed. Thus his doctrine, with light nuances and corrections, became one of the most valuable elements of contemporary theology on the liturgy, the Sacraments, and the Church. (*See* MYSTERY THEOLOGY.)

His principal works are: *Das Gedächtnis des Herrn in der altchristlichen Liturgie* (Freiburg 1918), *Die Liturgie als Mysterienfeier* (Freiburg 1922), *The Mystery of Christian Worship* (Westminster, Md. 1962), *Faites-ceci en mémoire de moi* (Paris 1962), *La Fête de Pâques dans l'Eglise des Pères* (Paris 1963), *Das Mysterium des Kommenden* (Paderborn 1952), *Das Mysterium des Kreuzes* (Paderborn 1954), *Mysterium der Ekklesia* (Mainz 1961). He also published numerous original contributions in the *Jahrbuch für Liturgiewissenschaft* (Münster 1921–41).

Bibliography: T. FILTHAUT, *Die Kontroverse über die Mysterienlehre* (Warendorf 1947). *Maison-Dieu* 14 (1948) 1–106. *Das Paschamysterium. P. Odo Casel zum Gedächtnis,* Liturgie und Mönchtum 3 (1949). A. MAYER et al., eds., *Vom christlichen Mysterium* (Düsseldorf 1951), containing a complete bibliography. T. KAMPMANN, *Gelebter Glaube* (Warendorf 1957) 105–115. B. NEUNHEUSER, LexThK[2] 2:966.

[B. NEUNHEUSER]

CASGRAIN, HENRI RAYMOND, French-Canadian historian; b. Rivière-Ouelle, Province of Quebec, Dec. 16, 1831; d. Quebec City, Feb. 11, 1904. While at the college of Sainte-Anne-de-la-Pocatière, where he completed his classical studies in 1852, he became a great admirer of Chateaubriand and Lamartine; their influence was strong throughout his life. In the same period he was deeply impressed by the patriotic fervor of F. X. Garneau's *Histoire du Canada* and the poems of Octave *Crémazie. Casgrain, ordained in 1856, was assigned to the cathedral parish, Quebec, in 1860, and the following year appointed chaplain to the Convent of the Good Shepherd there, a post he was forced to relinquish in 1870 because of a severe eye malady.

Casgrain played a major role in a group of intellectuals later known as the École de Québec. He was one of the founders of *Les Soirées canadiennes* (1861) and *Le Foyer canadien* (1863), two important literary periodicals. By his counsel, encouragement, and example, he inspired Canadian writers of the time with a sense of mission. His own chief interest was history, a field he approached rather circuitously. Heeding the counsel of the French writer Charles Nodier that popular lore was an important key to the proper understanding of a nation's history, Casgrain published his *Légendes canadiennes* (1860–61), narratives on the life and customs of French-Canadian pioneers. From these romanticized sketches, he passed to historical monographs; the most notable were *Histoire de la Mère Marie de l'Incarnation* (1864), *Histoire de l'Hôtel-Dieu de Québec* (1878), and *Montcalm et Lévis* (1891), his masterwork. He also rendered yeoman service to historians by editing the 12-volume *Collection des manuscrits du Maréchal de Lévis* (1889–95). Unfortunately, Casgrain's avowedly patriotic purpose often impaired the objectivity of his historical accounts, and his enthusiastic imagination impelled him to project his personality into his work. Nevertheless, the influence he exerted upon French-Canadian intellectuals of the 1860s, and the devotion he brought to historical research, justify the attention his works have received from students of Canadian literature.

Bibliography: S. BAILLARGEON, *Littérature canadienne-française* (3d ed. Montreal 1962). C. ROY, *Historiens de chez nous* (Montreal 1935). G. TOUGAS, *Histoire de la littérature canadienne-française* (2d ed. Paris 1964).

[J. M. CARRIÈRE]

CASHEL AND EMLY, ARCHDIOCESE OF (CASSILIENSIS ET IMOLACENSIS), metropolitan see since 1152, in south central Ireland. In 1963 it had 118 secular and 74 religious priests, 171 men in 13 religious houses, 467 women in 20 convents, and 83,900 Catholics; it is 1,193 square miles in area. Its six suffragans, which had 931 secular and 477 religious priests, 3,947 sisters, and 739,950 Catholics, were: Cloyne, Cork and Ross (united in 1954), Kerry, Killaloe, Limerick, and Waterford and Lismore (united in 1363). Catholics did not recognize the union of the Sees of Cashel and Emly decreed by the English Parliament (1568), but Cashel has been apostolic administrator of Emly since 1718. In 1965 Bishop Comerford moved the episcopal residence to Thurles, where it remains. Bishop James Butler II (1774–91) was the author of a widely used catechism.

St. *Patrick *c.* 450 evangelized Cashel, seat of the kings of Munster, at least four of whom later were ecclesiastics. St. Ailbe, patron of the archdiocese, is regarded as the founder of a monastery (with a famous school) and the first bishop of Emly (the leading see in Munster to the 10th century). From 1101, when the King gave Cashel to the Church, Emly yielded leadership to Cashel. The Synod of Rathbreasail (1111), which es-

The ruins of the 13th-century Gothic cathedral on the Rock of Cashel, Archdiocese of Cashel and Emly.

tablished canonical territorial dioceses in Ireland, fixed the borders of Emly, which became a suffragan of Cashel at the Synod of Kells (1152). This synod also raised *Armagh, *Dublin, and *Tuam to metropolitan status. Henry II received the submission of the princes and bishops of Munster at Cashel (1172) and convoked a reform council. Cashel and Emly were thereafter troubled by intervention of the kings of England in episcopal appointments. Emly, whose chapter as a rule elected its prelates in the 13th and 14th centuries, had a number of Cistercian and Franciscan prelates. Both Cashel and Emly suffered from the administration of the Anglican Bp. Miler MacGrath of the "united" sees in the late 16th century. Dermot *O'Hurley, Bishop of Cashel (1581–84), died a martyr, and Terence Albert *O'Brien, Bishop of Emly (1647–51), was hanged in Cromwell's time. Archbishop Thomas *Croke (1857–1902) was transferred to the archdiocese from Auckland.

The Celto-Romanesque "Cormac's Chapel" (consecrated in 1134) and the Gothic cathedral of the late 13th century on the Rock of Cashel have fallen to ruin since the 16th century. The Abbeys of *Holy Cross, Kilcooley (Cistercian), and Athassel (Augustinian) are also in ruin. Archbishop Patrick Leahy (1857–75) built the Romanesque cathedral in Thurles and helped establish the Catholic university in Ireland. Thurles seminary (1837) has sent many priests to all parts of the world.

The archdiocese had (1963) 16,240 pupils in 189 primary schools and 3,630 pupils in 23 secondary schools.

Bibliography: F. O'Briain, DHGE 11:1277–82. C. Mooney, DHGE 15:414–422. *Irish Catholic Directory,* annual. AnnPont (1964) 96. **Illustration credit:** Bord Failte Photo.

[W. G. SKEHAN]

CASIMIR, ST., patron saint of Poland and Lithuania; b. Cracow, Poland, Oct. 5, 1458; d. Grodno, Belorussia, March 4, 1484 (feast, March 4). He was the third son of King Casimir IV of *Poland and Elizabeth, an Austrian princess. For his teacher he had the learned historian Jan *Długosz. At the age of 13, Casimir was asked to accept the throne of *Hungary from a faction opposed to King *Matthias Corvinus, but the plan never materialized. After his brother Władysław became ruler of Bohemia, Casimir became heir apparent to the Polish crown. While his father was in *Lithuania on affairs of state from 1481 to 1483, Prince Casimir governed Poland in his stead with conspicuous prudence and justice. Not wishing to renounce his celibacy, he rejected his father's plans for him to wed the daughter of Emperor Frederick III of Germany. He died while on a trip in Lithuania, of which he was also Grand Duke, and was buried in the cathedral at *Vilna. Casimir was noted for his deep piety, chastity, and a spirit of prayer with special devotion to the Blessed Virgin. The number of attributed miracles caused him to be

St. Casimir, Lithuanian woodcut of the 16th century.

venerated as a saint, and he was canonized in 1521. Pope *Paul V extended his feast to the entire Church.

Bibliography: ActSS March 1:334–355. F. JAROSZEWICZ, *Matka Świetych Polska* (Craçow 1767; repr. in 4 pts. Poznań 1893) 1:209–216. F. PAPÉE, *Święty Kazimierz królewicz polski* (Lemberg 1902); *Studya i szkice z czasów Kazimierza Jagiellończyka* (Warsaw 1907). J. DUBOIS, *Catholicisme* 2:614. B. STASIEWSKI, LexThK² 6:12. **Illustration credit:** Warburg Institute, London.

[L. SIEKANIEC]

CASONI, FILIPPO, cardinal, papal secretary of state; b. Sarzana (La Spezia), Italy, March 6, 1733; d. Rome, Oct. 9, 1811. After completing his studies in Rome at the *Sapienza,* where he became *doctor utriusque juris* (1767), he was governor of Narni and Loreto, in the States of the Church, and the papal vice-legate to *Avignon. In this city and in the County of *Venaissin, Casoni at first appeased (March 1789), by free distribution of grain, the popular movements provoked by the food shortage after the poor harvest of 1788. In vain, however, did he attempt to calm those who were enthused by the *French Revolution and the propaganda of local patriots and wanted to attach Avignon and Venaissin to France. He instituted a national guard and established new municipalities that greatly reduced the authority of the pope and the vice-legate; but Pius VI disavowed these concessions, and the local revolutionaries remained dissatisfied. Far from remedying the situation, which the Pope ascribed to Casoni's weakness, the dispatching of an apostolic commissioner charged with restoring the former state of affairs and reestablishing order met with failure. So agitated did matters become that Casoni had to leave Avignon (June 1790), and he retired first to Carpentras and then to Chambéry. After being vice-legate to Nice he became titular archbishop of Perge and went as nuncio to Madrid (1794–1800), where he clashed with the regalism of the Spanish government. Conflict became acute when Urquijo, the prime minister, profited from Pius VI's death by publishing a decree that attributed to bishops the plenitude of faculties, and reserved to the crown whatever concerned episcopal consecration and to the Spanish Rota what pertained to the Roman tribunals. With the support of Manuel Godoy, who aspired to power, Casoni obtained from King Charles IV the recall of the decree, the publication of the apostolic constitution **Auctorem fidei,* and on Dec. 13, 1800, the dismissal of Urquijo. Casoni was created cardinal (Feb. 23, 1801) and succeeded *Consalvi as secretary of state (June 1806–February 1808). Charles Alquier, the French ambassador to Rome, appreciated his moderation, but Casoni played an unobtrusive role, since *Pius VII assumed responsibility for papal policy concerning *Napoleon I. Old and ill, he retired in 1808 and died 3 years later.

Bibliography: J. BECKER, *Relaciones diplomáticas entre España y la Santa Sede durante el Siglo XIX* (Madrid 1909). A. MATHIEZ, *Rome et le clergé français sous la Constituante* (Paris 1911). L. SIERRA, "La Caída del Primo Ministro Urquijo en 1800," *Hispania* 23 (1963) 556–580; "La Reacción del Episcopado español ante los decretos de matrimonio del ministro Urquijo de 1799–1813," *Estudios de Deusto* 11 (1963); 12 (1964). Schmidlin v.1. S. FURLANI, EncCatt 3:987.

[J. LEFLON]

CASPAR, ERICH, eminent Protestant medievalist and historian of the papacy; b. Berlin, Nov. 14, 1879; d. Berlin, Jan. 22, 1935. Caspar's ancestors were Prussian landowners, and his father played an important role in German social legislation before World War I. Erich studied at Heidelberg, Bonn, and Berlin, where his teachers were, among others, Scheffer-Boichorst, the great diplomatist, Harnack, Brunner, and Gierke. He took his doctor's degree in 1902, with a dissertation on Roger I's foundation charters for Sicilian bishoprics. This was followed by his great book on Roger II and his role in the establishment of the Norman-Sicilian monarchy (1904), which is still the basis of research on this subject. In 1908 Caspar became *Privatdocent* at Berlin and published studies that clearly indicated his inclination toward ecclesiastical, and especially papal, history. As a collaborator of the *Italia Pontificia* and of the *Monumenta Germanae Historica,* he began to work on the papal Registers, publishing numerous articles and finally editing the Registers and Register fragments of Popes *John VIII, *Stephen V (VI), and *Gregory VII. His occupation with papal history led him to study the emergence of the Papal State (*see* STATES OF THE CHURCH), and this study (1914) is still basic to the understanding of the entangled history of the 8th century. Of particular interest are his works on the oldest list of Roman bishops, and on the historical development of papal *primacy, studies that betray a subtle grasp of complex historical factors. They are, with few exceptions, examples of exact, precise, and methodical investigation of the available but brittle material. The biographical essays on *Gregory I and on St. *Bernard in *Meister der Politik* are specimens of his literary skill and historical scholarship. Meanwhile he had received a call to Königsberg (1920), where he became rector of the university, migrating to Freiburg in 1929, only to receive a call to Berlin as ordinarius in the following year.

Caspar's main contribution to ecclesiastical history will always be his *Geschichte des Papsttums* (1930–33), which with only two volumes, remained a torso, reaching only the period of the mid-8th century. It is a masterpiece of mature historical writing that demonstrates the author's superb command of the sources, his critical detachment, and his masterly presentation. In both depth of analysis and breadth of synthesis the work achieves what few books concerned with so difficult a matter can hope to achieve. The papal personalities known only through their letters become, in Caspar's hands, living men who decisively shaped the historical process of medieval Europe and beyond.

Bibliography: P. Kehr, NeuesArch 50 (1933–35) 628–629. R. Holtzmann, HistZ 152 (1935) 218–219. E. Seeberg et al., ZKirchgesch 54 (1935) 105–131, list of works, *ibid.* 264–266. W. Holtzmann, NDB 3 (1957) 164–165.

[W. ULLMANN]

CASPICARA, Manuel Chili, nicknamed "Caspicara" (scar-faced); Ecuadorian sculptor and painter; dates of birth and death unknown. He was of Indian origin, but no indication of his ancestry has been found. His pure, refined taste, which tended toward beauty of detail, is characteristic of those reared in an environment of privilege and culture. His authenticated works date from the period 1790 to 1810. Caspicara's representations of the theological virtues, called *Sábana Santa,* have been preserved in Quito. The groups of the "Coronation of the Virgin" and of the "Assumption with the Twelve Apostles" are in the Monastery of San Francisco. Numerous scenes of the Nativity and the Calvary, removed from Ecuador, came from his workshop. All the images of Caspicara are characterized by impeccable anatomy, nicety of detail, and taste for polychrome. He was the last of the image makers of colonial times in Quito and the last representative of his race in Ecuadorian art. Of the Indians who learned painting in the Colegio de San Andrés before Caspicara, some, such as Andrés Sánchez Gallque y Pampite, showed what the Indian can accomplish when he is carefully educated and given the opportunity to fulfill himself. Caspicara's contemporary, Manuel Samaniego, wrote a treatise on painting in polychrome.

Caspicara's "Our Lady of Mount Carmel and Two Souls in Purgatory," in the church of San Francisco at Lima.

Bibliography: F. J. Santa Cruz y Espejo, *Escritos,* 3 v. (Quito 1912–23) 1:83. F. Gonzáles Suárez, *Historia general de la república del Ecuador,* 7 v. (Quito 1890–1903) v.7.

[J. M. VARGAS]

CASSANDER, GEORGE, humanist and liturgist; b. Pittem, Belgium, Aug. 15, 1513; d. Cologne, Feb. 3, 1566. His family name was Casant. At the Collège du Château in Louvain, he earned a master of arts in 1533. At Ghent and Bruges he taught literature. In 1544, after a tour of Italy, he enrolled in the theological faculty of Cologne and in 1549 undertook both the teaching of theology and the direction of the newly founded Academy of Duisberg. He bent his efforts to bring the Anabaptists back to the Catholic faith, and between 1561 and 1566 joined forces with the programs launched by the Emperors Ferdinand I and Maximilian II to reestablish unity in the Church. In his principal work, *De Officio Pii ac Publicae Tranquillitatis vere Amantis Viri in hoc Religionis Dissidio* (1561), he showed that abuses in the Church though real were insufficient grounds for leaving it. Later his *Consultatio de Articulis Religionis inter Catholicos et Protestantes Controversis* (posthumously published in 1577) tried to put a Catholic interpretation on Protestant tenets. These works met with strong opposition from both sides; he was accused of excessive tolerance, of being too ready for compromise. The fact is he realized that there were mistakes on the part of all concerned and refused to believe that the rupture within Christianity was definitive. While he defended the Church's stand regarding the rites of the Mass and the practice of infant Baptism [*De Baptismo Infantium* (1563)], he showed that the contemporary movement for return of the chalice to the laity also had a genuine tradition behind it [*De Sacra Communione Christiani Populi in utraque Panis et Vini Specie* (1564)]. His life and works (placed on the Index in 1617) have been a sign of contradiction for many. The strength of his convictions has often been called into question, without reason, however, for he died confessing to Novimula, the rector of Cologne, his truly Catholic sentiments.

Bibliography: J. Baudot, DACL 2.2:2333–40. R. Koper, LexThK[2] 2:968–969. R. Stupperich, RGG[3] 1:1625–26. R. Haass, NDB 3:166. H. de Vocht, *History of the Foundation and the Rise of the Collegium Trilingue Lovaniense, 1517–1550,* 3 v. (Louvain 1951–54) v.3 *The Full Growth* (University of Louvain, Recueil de travaux d'histoire et de philologie 4.5) 296–303. J. Lecler, *Toleration and the Reformation,* tr. T. L. Westow, 2 v. (New York 1960) 1:270–296.

[N. N. HUYGHEBAERT]

CASSANT, MARIE JOSEPH, Trappist Cistercian; b. Casseneuil-sur-Lot, France, March 6, 1879; d. Abbey of Notre Dame du Désert, June 17, 1903. Joseph desired intensely to become a priest, but was handicapped by an almost total lack of the necessary intellectual endowments. At the age of 15 he entered the Trappist Cistercian Abbey of Notre Dame du Désert (Dec. 5, 1894), where he received the habit of a choir religious, made his simple profession in 1897, and was solemnly professed on May 24, 1900. Weak in body, prone to discouragement, and unresponsive by nature to many aspects of monastic culture, this seemingly ungifted monk lived in a constant and vivid awareness of the essential Christian and monastic realities. Less articulate than Thérèse of Lisieux or Charles de Foucauld, Joseph nevertheless had the same thirst for the absolute, the same poverty of spirit, and the same intense charity. With the help of his spiritual father, André Malet (later abbot of the monastery), Joseph had the joy of being ordained on Oct. 12, 1902, and of living the last 8 months of his life as a priest. His cause for beatification was introduced at Rome, Feb. 19, 1956.

Bibliography: M. E. CHENEVIÈRE, *L'Âme cistercienne du Père Marie-Joseph Cassant d'après ses notes inédites* (Abbey of Sainte-Marie-du-Désert 1938); *L'Attente dans le silence: Le Père Marie-Joseph Cassant* (Bruges 1961), definitive biog.

[C. WADDELL]

CASSATT, MARY, American painter, pastelist, and printmaker; b. Allegheny City, Pa., May 22, 1845; d. Mesnil-Théribus (Oîse), June 19, 1926. After studying art in Philadelphia, Miss Cassatt settled permanently in France in 1866. She was acquainted with painters of the Impressionist circle, and her art was much influenced by their style, particularly in its bright, fresh colors and depiction of simple, intimate subjects. A great part of her work is based on the themes of mother and child or of women in their boudoirs. Her graphic art shows the influence of her enthusiasm for Japanese prints, an interest she shared with the Impressionists, and especially with her friend Edgar Degas. Miss Cassatt's work in this medium is perhaps more distinctive than her paintings. She never married; during the last years of her life she was blind.

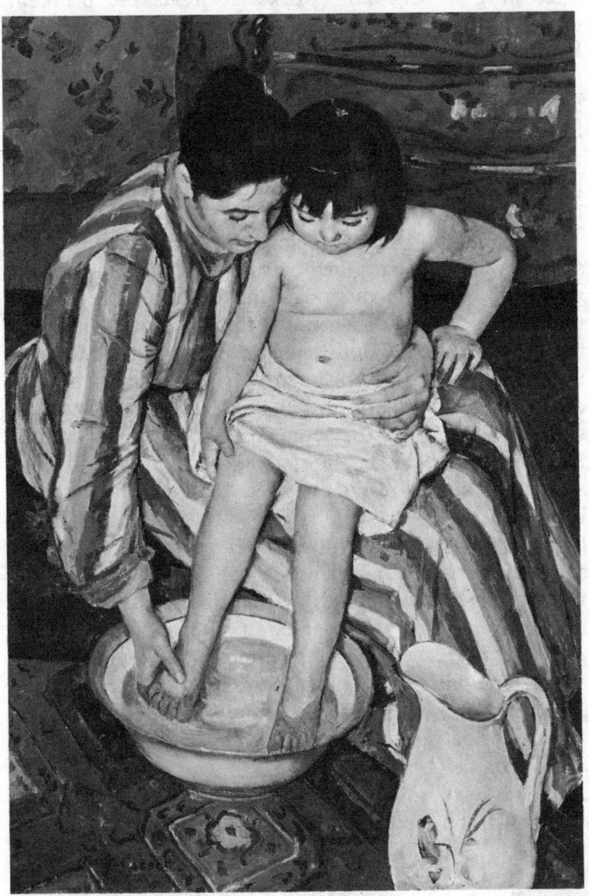

Mary Cassatt, "The Bath," 39 by 26 inches, c. 1892.

Bibliography: F. WATSON, *Mary Cassatt* (New York 1933), with bibliog. M. BREUNING, *Mary Cassatt,* ed. A. CRANEL (New York 1944). A. D. BREESKIN, *The Graphic Work of Mary Cassatt* (New York 1948). **Illustration credit:** Courtesy of The Art Institute of Chicago, Robert A. Waller Fund.

[D. DENNY]

CASSIAN OF NANTES, BL., Capuchin missionary and martyr; b. Nantes, France, Jan. 15, 1607; d. Condar, Ethiopia, Aug. 7, 1638 (feast, Aug. 7). He was born of a Portuguese merchant family. His early acquaintance with the Capuchins led him to enter their novitiate in 1623. In 1633 he was sent to the Cairo mission, where he joined his Capuchin confrere, Father Agathangelus. When their efforts to convert the dissidents were thwarted by the scandalous lives of Catholics living there, they left for Ethiopia (1637). To make entrance easier, they donned the habit of the dissident Coptic monks, but were discovered, taken prisoner, and hauled to Condar for trial. After a 3-day public ordeal, they were given the choice of accepting dissident doctrines or death by hanging. They chose the latter. Their untiring zeal for the reunion of the dissident Coptic Church with Rome led to their deaths. On Oct. 23, 1904, Pius X beatified them.

Bibliography: *Lexicon Capuccinum* (Rome 1951) 361. C. MALONEY, "Missionaries and Martyrs, Bl. Agathangelus and Cassian," *Round Table* 21 (1956) 136–145.

[J. SCHARDT]

CASSIAN, JOHN (JOHANNES CASSIANUS)

Monk and ascetical writer; b. Scythia Minor (modern Rumania), probably 360; d. Marseilles, between 432 and 435. While still a youth John was initiated into asceticism at a monastery in Bethlehem. Toward 386 with his friend Germanus he undertook a trip to Egypt, where they made contact with Egyptian monasticism; at the end of a 7-year period they returned to Palestine. A short while later they again went to the Nile regions and visited various monastic communities, perhaps going as far as the *Thebaid. It is difficult to determine the duration of this second sojourn, but certainly toward 399 or 400 the two friends were in Constantinople in contact with St. *John Chrysostom, by whom Cassian was ordained a deacon.

In 404 Germanus, then a priest, and Cassian arrived at Rome with a letter from the Constantinopolitan clergy in favor of their exiled bishop, John Chrysostom. In 414 or 415 on the occasion of the Schism of Antioch, a priest by the name of Cassian was invited to Rome from Alexandria; it is not certain that this was really John Cassian. In any case he was certainly a priest when, about this time, he went to Marseilles. There he founded two monasteries, one for men under the title of SS. Peter and Victor, and the other for women under the title of St. Savior. Nothing is known of the organization of these monasteries, but the type of ascetical life led there can be easily deduced from the works of their founder. After his death the cult of a saint was attributed to him in that region.

Works. All three of Cassian's works have been preserved. The *De Institutis coenobiorum et de octo principalium vitiorum remediis libri XII* was written in 417–418 at the solicitation of Bishop Castor. It is an integrated work divided in two parts as is indicated by the title. The first part (bks. 1–4) treats of the external institution of the monastery: the clothing of the monk (1), the nocturnal, canonical prayer (2), the daily monastic prayer (3), and the organization of the common life (4). The second part constitutes a description of the actual life, the spiritual doctrine of the battle to obtain *puritas cordis* (purity of heart) and the perfection of the cenobitic life. This is contained in the struggle against the principal vices (bks. 5–12): gluttony (5), luxury (6), avarice (7), wrath (8), sloth (9), *acedia* (discouragement) (10), vainglory (11), and pride (12).

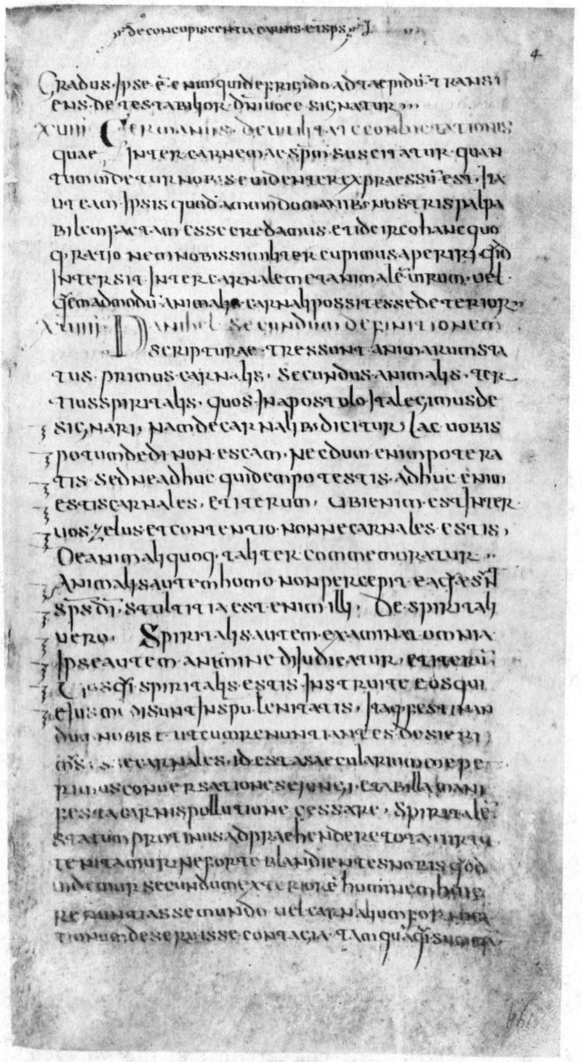

Collationes XXIV was written in three parts at the suggestion of Honoratus of Lérins, later bishop of Arles. The first part was published in 419–420; it is an organic treatise and contains a general idea of the problem of the spiritual life (nos. 1–10): the notion of Christian perfection (1); the fundamental disposition, discretion (2); vocation (3); obstacles, particularly concupiscence (4); vices (5); sin (6); the elimination of the obstacles—the spiritual battle (7); angels and demons (8); prayer and its forms (9–10). The second part (nos. 11–17), written before 426, treats of diverse arguments of spiritual theology distributed without apparent logical connection: charity (11); *apatheia* (12); the relation between grace and liberty, Cassian's *Semi-Pelagianism being most manifest there (13); spiritual science (14); charisms and miracles (15); friendship among the perfect (16); the essential and the accidental in the spiritual life (17). The third part was published between 426 and 429 and continues the method of the second by making a collection of ascetical problems: three kinds of monks (18); the cenobitic life and the anchoritic life (19); the purgative way (20); the liberty that comes from evangelical perfection (21); temptations against the flesh and their proper remedies (22); impeccability as not possible on this earth (23); and the advantages and demands of anchoritism (24).

De Incarnatione Domini contra Nestorium, libri VII, written perhaps originally in Greek at the request of a Roman archdeacon, later Pope *Leo I, is the least interesting of Cassian's works. It treats the problem of Nestorianism, affirming that this doctrine is derived from *Pelagianism. It defends the legitimacy of the title *Theotokos attributed to the Virgin Mary and concludes with expressions of recognition and veneration toward John Chrysostom. The documentation for this tract was sent to Cassian by Leo from Rome and included the letters of accusation against Nestorius from *Cyril of Alexandria.

Doctrine. On the theological plane the name of Cassian is connected with the doctrine of Semi-Pelagianism, which he explicitly defended and explained in various parts of his spiritual writings, though most clearly in the *Collatio XIII*. Semi-Pelagianism teaches that original sin is more a punishment than a true sin in the descendants of Adam and that man with original sin still has a capability of achieving his own justification, particularly at the beginning, and can desire it as a sick man can desire his own health. The grace of God is necessary for salvation but is rendered efficacious by concourse with the human will, so that in a certain sense grace is a recompense for the use of one's own will, which thus concludes by meriting salvation. There is thus no such thing as a predestination to glory (*ante praevisa merita*). This doctrinal notion was condemned at the Council of Orange (529), although the name of Cassian was not mentioned; however, in the Middle Ages the doctrine of Semi-Pelagianism was known under his name.

To understand how Cassian arrived at these conclusions in the theological field, although St. *Augustine attacked Pelagius and *Julian of Eclanum for their theories on grace, it is necessary to be aware that Augustine's term *gratia victrix* was considered by Cassian

Folio from an 8th-century manuscript (Cod. Vat. lat. 5766, fol. 4r) of John Cassian's "Collatio, IV."

as perilous for ascetical practice. He was concerned above all to safeguard the rights of liberty and of human responsibility even in the field of justification.

The spiritual works of Cassian have a double merit. From the point of historical interest, they constitute the most interesting documents for monasticism in the 5th century; from a doctrinal point of view they form the first *summa* of spiritual theology in the West; and what is even more remarkable, the statements of the problems of spiritual life as they are exposed by Cassian in his *Institutiones* and in his *Collationes* remained, with few variations, identical along the course of the history of Christian spirituality down to contemporary times.

The keystone of this structure of the spiritual life is exposed by Cassian in his *Collatio I*: the final end of monastic life consists in the acquisition of the reign of God; the immediate end is an entrance into the reign of God and a spiritual struggle that conducts to purity of heart.

Kingdom of God and Contemplation. By the kingdom of God Cassian understood, without doubt, heavenly recompense, that is, eternal life that is expected after death. But it is not necessary to await the end of earthly life to be incorporated into the kingdom of God. In some manner the achievement of the kingdom of God is possible even during earthly life if the monk orders his life in such fashion as to tend as far as possible toward unity with God. This union can be realized by contemplation. Man is placed between God's simplicity and the multiplicity of material things. With his knowledge he can penetrate the essence of known objects and can lose himself in the multiplicity of material; but he can also elevate himself to perfect simplicity by contemplating God alone. This attention directed to God progressively transforms man in God, until it reestablishes the image of God in the human spirit. The acquisition of the kingdom of God is thus attained by means of meditation. According to Cassian, this is perfectly realized in the life of the hermit.

Spiritual Combat and Purity of Heart. The state described as contemplation is the final plane to which Christian asceticism aspires. To arrive there, it is necessary to have a positive approach to life (*vita actualis*), which consists in the reordering of one's actions and the achievement of the perfect life. But this cannot be realized without combat, a battle against vices, sin, and the demons. This spiritual combat brings to the soul the virtues necessary for the perfect cenobitic life; and the result of a well-conducted campaign is purity of heart "which casts fear out" (*Coll. XI*). Whoever reaches the state of loving purity is on the borders of contemplation.

Among the explicit sources cited by Cassian, other than the Scriptures, which he quotes at least 1,800 times, are SS. Basil, Jerome, John Chrysostom, Athanasius, Palladius, Rufinus of Aquileia, and Evagrius Ponticus. Of the later writers who used or reflected Cassian's thought, SS. Benedict, Isidore of Seville, and Fructuosus of Braga indicate the wide diffusion of his writings in the 5th and 6th centuries; Alcuin, Rhabanus Maurus, Peter Damian, and St. Thomas Aquinas testify to his great influence on the Middle Ages; and the authors of the Devotio Moderna, as well as Ignatius of Loyola, Scupoli, Rodriguez, and Bernardino Rossignoli, assured his survival in modern times.

Bibliography: S. MARSILI, *Giovanni Cassiano e Evagrio Pontico* (StAnselm 5; 1936). L. CRISTIANI, *Jean Cassien,* 2 v. (Paris 1946). O. CHADWICK, *John Cassian: A Study in Primitive Monasticism* (Cambridge, Eng. 1950). M. OLPHE-GALLIARD, DictSpirAscMyst 2:214–276. P. T. CAMELOT, LexThK² 5:1016–17. P. GODET, DTC 2.2:1823–29. Altaner 537–540. **Illustration credit:** Biblioteca Apostolica Vaticana.

[F. CHIOVARO]

CASSIANO DA MACERATA, Capuchin priest, missionary, and scholar; b. Macerata, Italy, 1708; d. there, Feb. 4, 1791. Little is known about his early life. He received the religious habit in 1728. In 1738 he was sent to the Tibetan missions and on Jan. 6, 1741, arrived at Lassa, Tibet. Approximately 2 years later Cassiano left Tibet and entered Nepal in northern India. His missionary activities were beset with typical mission problems, i.e., the bad example of local Christians, misunderstandings, and persecution. The Holy See recalled him in 1756. He remained at Rome, where he devoted himself to writing accounts of his missionary activities. His work is used as a source by other authors, some drawing heavily from his unpublished works. Cassiano also spent time working on a Tibetan grammar, which was printed by the Holy See in 1773.

Bibliography: *Lexicon Capuccinum* (Rome 1951) 361. CLEMENTE DA TERZORIO, *Le Missioni dei Minori Cappuccini,* 10 v. (Rome 1913–38) 8:418; 9:600. AnalCap 50 (1934) 47–49.

[M. CRAIG]

CASSINI, GIOVANNI DOMENICO, Italian civil engineer and astronomer; b. Perinaldo (Nice, Italy), June 8, 1625; d. Paris, Sept. 14, 1712. He was educated at the Jesuit college in Genoa and in 1650 was appointed professor of astronomy at Bologna. He made observations of the comet of 1652 and the following year reconstructed the meridian of Egnazio Danti in the church of San Petronio at Bologna. He achieved fame with his measurement of the periodic rotations of Mars, Jupiter, and Venus between 1665 and 1667, and with the publication of his tables defining the motions of Jupiter's satellites. In 1669 Cassini accepted the invitation of Louis XIV to work at the new observatory at Paris and subsequently became a French citizen. He discovered four new satellites of Saturn (1671–84), observed the division of Saturn's ring by a cleavage named the "Cassini division" (1675), and determined that the ring consisted of an assemblage of smaller satellites. Cassini collaborated with Jean Richer in determining the parallax of Mars, from which the distance between Mars and the sun was estimated in 1673, and from which the flattening of the earth toward the poles was discovered. Cassini made the earliest sustained observations of zodiacal light, determined the obliquity of ecliptic and the eccentricity of the earth's orbit, and discovered the mathematical phenomenon called "the Cassinian oval."

Bibliography: J. D. CASSINI, *Mémoires pour servir à l'histoire des sciences et à celle de l'Observatoire Royal de Paris: Suivis se la vie de G. D. Cassini* (Paris 1810). A. MARUSSI, "Italian Pioneers in Geodosy," *Journal of World History* 7 (1963) 471–483. M. DAUMAS, ed., *Histoire de la science des origines au XXe siècle* (*Encyclopédie de la Pléiade* 5; Paris 1957). C. WOLF, *Histoire de l'Observatoire de Paris, de sa fondation à 1793* (Paris 1902) 61–156.

[S. A. BEDINI]

CASSIODORUS SENATOR, FLAVIUS MAGNUS AURELIUS

Sixth-century statesman, author, and scholar; b. Scyllacium, Calabria, *c.* 485; d. Vivarium, *c.* 580. Of a Calabrian family in the Ostrogothic civil service, Cassiodorus received an excellent classical education, entered the employment of the Ostrogothic kings, and became quaestor and secretary (507) to *Theodoric the Great (474–526), consul (514), and a little later master of offices, the equivalent of prime minister. In this position he worked for a reconciliation between the conquered Romans and the barbarians. In 533 he was made a praetorian prefect by Athalaric and under Vitiges received the title of patrician.

After the Byzantine invasions of northern Italy, the Ostrogothic kingdom crumbled and Cassiodorus attempted to found a school for theology in Rome under Pope Agapetus (535–536); failing, he retired to his villa at Vivarium in Calabria. There he founded a monastery whose monks devoted themselves to studying and copying books of both sacred and profane learning. Though not a monk himself, he followed the religious services as patron.

Writings. The writings of Cassiodorus reflect his interests as statesman and educator. His *De origine actibusque Getarum* is a history of the Gothic peoples compiled for Theodoric but completed under Athalaric. The text is lost, but the work is cited frequently by *Jordanis. Since the Goths were nomads without a written tradition, Cassiodorus collected the tribal legends and arbitrarily identified material found in the classic authors, which referred to the Scythians and Getes, with the Goths in order to compose 12 books in classic style.

His panegyric for Theodoric and other discourses are preserved only in fragments, but the *Chronicle* that he composed at the request of Eutharic (519) is a world history concentrating in later sections on the achievements of the Goths. Its purpose is apologetic.

About 537 Cassiodorus published his *Variae,* a collection in 12 books of official letters written while he was in service to the Ostrogothic kings. Composed as models of correspondence rather than as source material for historians, they frequently omit dates and personal names. Books 1 to 5 are from the reign of Theodoric; 6 to 8 contain chancellery formulas; 8 to 10 give the edicts published under Athalaric, Theodahat, and Vitiges; 11 and 12 contain letters Cassiodorus wrote as praetorian prefect and display his love of erudition, human interests, and observations on nature.

Of *Ordo generis Cassiodororum,* a family genealogy, only fragments remain. Finally, his *De anima* was written at the end of his public service and represents his leave-taking of the world. Influenced by Augustine and *Claudianus Mamertus, he discusses in it the problems connected with a knowledge of the soul from its origin to its immortal destiny.

Monastic Instructions. For the monks, Cassiodorus composed a series of instructions. His *Commentary on the Psalms* is a useful, mainly allegorical, explanation based on St. *Augustine but exhibiting personal opinions also. His *Expositio epistolae ad Romanos* is a corrected version of the originally heretical work composed by *Pelagius, in which Cassiodorus established the characteristic readings of the Vulgate text, apparently extending his revision to the whole Bible as is witnessed in the *Codex Amiatinus,* copied directly from a Cassiodoran manuscript. His *Complexiones in epistolis apostolorum* is a brief commentary on selected passages from the Gospels and Acts.

The *Institutiones divinarum et humanarum lectionum* is his most influential work. After deploring the lack of theological schools in the West (preface), the first book gives the monks an account of the theological treatises monks should have read in order to understand Scripture and appreciate the Church's teachings. It enumerates the older commentaries and the works of historians, and remarks that even monks who are educated enough to read or copy manuscripts should be made aware of the Christian heritage. The second book enumerates the secular (liberal) arts necessary for a comprehension of the Scriptures: grammar, rhetoric, dialectic, arithmetic, music, geometry, and astronomy. It lists also the authors dealing with these subjects. The Institutes is thus a catalogue of the books contained in the library at Vivarium.

Cassiodorus is responsible also for the compendium of the ecclesiastical histories written by Theodoret of Cyr, Socrates, and Sozomen, as translated and condensed by the monk Epiphanius and called the *Historia ecclesiastica tripartita.* Finally, in his 92d year he wrote a *De orthographia* at the request of monks seeking rules for copying manuscripts.

Intent on preserving the Church's culture, Cassiodorus performed an invaluable service in supervising translations from the Greek and in recopying all the books he had gathered in his long career. Unlike the monks of St. *Benedict at Monte Cassino, who combined physical labor with spiritual contemplation, he insisted on preserving the materials for the intellectual life of the Church. Thus he had an incalculable effect on the Middle Ages even though after his death the library at Vivarium was destroyed, most of its manuscripts finding their way to the papal library in the Lateran. He was not the author of the **Regula Magistri,* and the Benedictine rule was not observed at Vivarium. Only later did the Benedictines take over the intellectual interests cultivated by Cassiodorus.

Bibliography: *Opera Omnia,* 2 v. PL 69–70; *Chronica,* ed. T. MOMMSEN (MGAuctAnt 11; 1894) 109–161; *Variae,* ed. T. MOMMSEN and L. TRAUBE (*ibid.* 12; 1894); *Institutiones,* ed. R. A. B. MYNORS (Oxford 1937). E. K. RAND, "The New Cassiodorus," *Speculum* 13 (1938) 433–447. W. A. BAEHRENS, TU 42:186–199, Vivarium and its MSS. W. WEINBERGER, "Handschriften von Vivarium," *Miscellanea Francesco Ehrle,* 5 v. (StTest 37–41; 1924) 4:75–88. P. COURCELLE, "Le Site du monastère de Cassiodore," *Mélanges d'archéologie et d'histoire* 55 (1938) 258–307; *Les Lettres grecques en Occident: De Macrobe à Cassiodore* (rev. ed. Paris 1948) 313–388. G. BARDY, *Catholicisme* 2:618–621. D. M. CAPPUYNS, DHGE 11:1350–1408. R. HELM, ReallexAntChr 3:915–926. F. BLATT, "Remarques sur l'histoire des traductions latines," *Classica et Mediaevalia* 1 (1938) 217–242. L. SZYMANSKI, *The Translation Procedure of Epiphanius-Cassiodorus* (CUA StMedRen LatLangLit 24; 1963), with bibliog.

[F. X. MURPHY]

CASSIRER, ERNST

Neo-Kantian philosopher; b. Breslau, Poland, July 28, 1874; d. New York, April 13, 1945. At the age of 18 he entered the University of Berlin and in 1894 began studying I. *Kant under Georg Simmel (1858–1918). In 1896, now at the University of Marburg, he worked directly with Hermann Cohen (1842–1918), the guiding force of the neo-Kantian movement. Cassirer married in 1901 and established himself in Munich; later he moved to Berlin, where he became a *Privatdocent.* He accepted a full professorship in 1917 at the newly founded University of Hamburg, where he later became rector. By this time he had broken

Ernst Cassirer.

from Cohen's interpretation of Kant and had received the inspiration for his master work on symbolic forms. In 1933 he lectured at Oxford, and in 1935 he removed his family to Göteborg, Sweden. Cassirer went to Yale University as a visiting professor in 1941. In 1944 he left New Haven for Columbia University.

The philosophy of Ernst Cassirer has been characterized as idealistic naturalism, a characterization that perhaps accents best the line of advance Cassirer made beyond neo-Kantianism. His major work, *The Philosophy of Symbolic Forms* (tr. R. Manheim, 3 v., New Haven 1953–57), attempts to locate the exact place of mind in the framework of nature. Here he uses culture as the locus of mind in nature. The symbolic function is given as the ground of the possibility of a world. The sign relation in its office of organ of reality brings about, rather than indicates, the object. In this Cassirer's true debt to Kant can be seen. Somewhat in the manner that Kant assumed synthetic a priori judgments, Cassirer assumes the function of the symbolic relation, and proceeds to concern himself with the possibility of this alone. Cassirer felt that Kant's transcendental critique had not gone far enough. Its limitations could be found in the consideration of the theoretical sciences alone: the objectivity of Euclidian geometry and Newtonian physics had been reached, but not objectivity as such. For this a broader interpretation of knowledge was needed to include the intuition and expression of language, myth, religion, and art. From Kant's critique of reason the transition had to be made to a critique of culture.

Cassirer distinguishes three modal forms of the symbol function: the expressional, the intuitional, and the conceptual. The expressional function stems from emotive or affective experience and is found in such expressions of culture as art and myth. In this perspective there is a certain mingling of the sign and the signified. The intuitional function is on the level of volitional and teleological concerns. On this level there is a greater systemization of the sensuous, even though the data may be expressed in commonsense language. The final form is the conceptual function. Here theoretical interests have full play and the expression is that of science, the highest development of relational thinking. It may be questioned whether the formulation of the three modalities of symbolic representation is completely exhaustive of the varieties of experience. Cassirer offers no justification of these, merely presenting them as the actual situation of knowledge forms. Nor does he argue for the symbolic form concept; he cites empirical data from the evidence of the *Kulturwissenschaften* alone. The question of what reality is apart from the symbolic forms is considered irrelevant by Cassirer—there is no encountering of a world except in the mythical, artistic, perceptual, or scientific forms. These are the contexts of the object that is experienced and known. Space, time, cause, number, etc., constitute the objectivity of these symbol relations.

Among Cassirer's major works is his history of epistemology, *Das Erkenntnisproblem in der Philosophie und Wissenschaft der neueren Zeit,* 3 v. (Berlin 1906, 1907, 1920; Eng. *The Problem of Knowledge,* tr. W. H. Woglom and C. W. Hendel, New Haven 1950). Cassirer presented the directing lines of his philosophy of science in his early work (1910), *Substance and Function* (tr. W. C. Swabey and M. C. Swabey, Chicago 1923). Later works include *The Platonic Renaissance* in England (tr. J. P. Pettegrove, Austin, Texas 1953); *The Philosophy of the Enlightenment* (tr. J. P. Pettegrove and F. C. A. Koelln, Princeton 1951); an analysis of the most complicated problems of quantum theory in physics and knowledge, *Determinism and Indeterminism in Modern Physics* (tr. O. T. Benfey, New Haven 1956); and *Essay on Man* (New Haven 1944) and *Myth of the State* (New Haven 1946).

See also NEO-KANTIANISM.

Bibliography: A. PLEBE, EncFil 1:929–931. P. A. SCHILPP, ed., *The Philosophy of Ernst Cassirer* (Evanston, Ill. 1949). C. H. HAMBURG, *Symbol and Reality* (The Hague 1956). R. ALLERS, "The Philosophy of Ernst Cassirer," NewSchol 25 (1951) 184–192.

[M. J. M. REGAN]

CASSOCK, a close-fitting robe with long sleeves worn by clergy in ordinary life and by clergy and laymen as well when taking part in religious functions. This name was originally given to the dress of soldiers and horsemen but survives today in ecclesiastical use only.

The ordinary cassock varies in color and trim, as a signification of different degrees of ecclesiastical dignity: that of the pope is entirely white without trimmings of any color; that of cardinals is black trimmed with scarlet; that of archbishops and bishops is black trimmed with amaranth red, and that of pastors and curates is black without any trim.

The cassock reserved for choir and public ceremonies of the Church is more colorful but without contrasting trim. The pope wears white silk. Scarlet is worn by Cardinals at ordinary times, and purple in penitential season. Bishops wear purple, and pastors retain black. Laymen wear black when they are permitted to take the place of those in the minor orders of the clergy. The use of red for the cassock of laymen dates from the 19th century and should not be tolerated.

[M. MCCANCE]

CASTAGNO, ANDREA DEL, mural painter; b. Castagno, Italy, *c.* 1421; d. Florence, Aug. 19, 1457. His teacher is not known, but *Masaccio and *Donatello seem to have impressed him most profoundly and lastingly. His masterpieces, the frescoes of the Last Supper and the Passion in the refectory of S. Apollonia,

Andrea del Castagno, "The Last Supper," fresco, c. 1447, in the refectory of S. Apollonia, Florence, Italy.

Florence, were made in the late 1440s. About 1450 Andrea painted murals of the "uomini famosi" for a villa close to Florence. The statuesque figures of heroes from antiquity and from the Old and New Testaments, as well as those of heroes from Florence, depict the theme of deliverance in the religious, military, and artistic spheres. Andrea's powerful monumentality and austerity of figure-style, his ability to create an illusion of spatial recession, and his use of expressively accented light show his participation in early Renaissance aesthetics. But few of his generation were better able to find a compromise between the antinomies arising from the new Renaissance sense of reality and the continuation of transcendental Christian beliefs. Andrea's "Vision of the Trinity with St. Jerome" (SS. Annunziata, Florence) gives moving evidence of his ability to express the visionary and ecstatic in the Renaissance language of form. Other major works are the "Assumption of the Virgin," Berlin, and the mural of Niccolo da Tolentino, Florence cathedral.

Bibliography: M. Salmi, *Paolo Uccello, Andrea del Castagno, Domenico Veneziano* (Milan 1938); *Andrea del Castagno* (Novara 1961); EncWA 1:424–431. A. M. Fortuna, *Andrea del Castagno* (Florence 1957). **Illustration credit:** Anderson-Art Reference Bureau.

[C. SHELL]

CASTAÑEDA, CARLOS EDUARDO, educator, historian; b. Camargo, Mexico, Nov. 11, 1896; d. Austin, Tex., April 5, 1958. He arrived in the U.S. in 1908, and attended the University of Texas, Austin, where he earned his Ph.D. in 1932. He taught at a number of colleges and universities, including The Catholic University of America, Washington, D.C., and the University of Texas, where he was professor of history from 1946 until his death. Although he wrote numerous articles and pamphlets, Castañeda was best known for his larger works: *The Mexican Side of the Texan Revolution* (1928); the edited manuscript of *Juan Agustín Morfí's History of Texas, 1673–79* (2 v. 1935); and *Our Catholic Heritage in Texas, 1519–1950* (7 v. 1936–58), a monumental history that contains secular as well as religious data. His writings earned him the Serra Award of the Americas from the Academy of American Franciscan History in 1951, as well as honorary degrees from St. Edward's University, Austin (1941), and The Catholic University of America (1951). He was created knight of the Holy Sepulchre in 1941 and Knight Commander of the Order of Isabella the Catholic in 1950. Castañeda served as president of the American Catholic Historical Association (1939–40), and during World War II he was regional director of the Fair Employment Practices Committee in the Southwest.

Bibliography: *Americas* 8.4 (April 1952) 485–492, curriculum vitae and bibliog. of his writings. A. S. Perales, comp., *Are We Good Neighbors?* (San Antonio 1948).

[M. C. KIEMEN]

CASTAÑEDA, FRANCISCO DE PAULA, Franciscan journalist and defender of the Church in Argentina; b. Buenos Aires, 1776; d. Paraná, May 12, 1832. He was ordained in 1800 and, after teaching at the University of Córdoba, returned to Buenos Aires. In May 1815, when no one dared to speak patriotically because the revolution was thought to have failed, he did so and fought the disillusionment that was beginning to disturb the people. Chiefly during the government of Martín Rodríguez, when *Rivadavia initiated a religious persecution with the so-called reform of the clergy, Castañeda published simultaneously as many as six newspapers. Unfortunately, he found that he was forced to employ the same vulgar and even scurrilous language used by his enemies, who were also those of the Church. As a result of his publications, he was exiled six times. No one defended the religious orders as he did when Rivadavia took over the convents and the other possessions of the orders. Castañeda was vitally concerned with ending illiteracy and founded schools wherever he could, not only in Buenos Aires but also in Santa Fe and Entre Ríos. He established art classes everywhere, believing that there was nothing like drawing to refine a spirit and set it on the path of knowledge and virtue. The fact that Rivadavia did not commit greater excesses against the Church was due above all to Castañeda. His death was from natural causes, not, as his enemies wrote, from the bite of a rabid dog. The Italian José *Ingenieros wrote shockingly false pages about Castañeda, but another liberal writer, Arturo Capdevila, has written an enthusiastic and well-documented volume on his life and virtues.

Bibliography: A. CAPDEVILA, *La santa furia del padre Castañeda* (Madrid 1933). A. SALDÍAS, *Vida y escritos del P. Castañeda* (Buenos Aires 1907).

[G. FURLONG]

CASTE, INDIAN. In ancient India society was divided into four classes (*varṇa,* meaning literally "color"): Brahmins (priests), Kshatriyas (warriors), Vaiśyas (merchants and peasants), and Śūdras (servants). The caste system does not seem to have been derived from these classes, but rather to have been grafted upon them. It arose among the non-Aryan peoples of India and was the means by which different racial, religious, and social groups were assimilated within Hinduism. In the course of time the number of castes and subcastes has grown to over 2,000. The basic principle of caste is that no one may marry or entertain in his home a person of another caste. Thus, all the different castes are kept permanently separate, even though they may live together in the same village. Further, certain trades and habits of life were considered unclean, so that those who practiced them could not come within a certain distance of a member of another caste or drink of the same well. This prohibition is based on ritual purity and shows the fundamentally religious basis of caste. In modern times the extremes of "untouchability" have been legally abolished and many caste distinctions are breaking down, especially in the towns. But in the villages they remain in force, and it is still very rare for anyone to marry outside his caste. While caste has undoubtedly been responsible for much cruelty and inhumanity, it must be pointed out that it provides a system of social security for the villager, and no adequate substitute has yet been found.

See also INDIA; HINDUISM.

Bibliography: J. H. HUTTON, *Caste in India: Its Nature, Function and Origins* (Cambridge, Eng. 1952). B. RYAN, *Caste in Modern Ceylon* (New Brunswick, N.J. 1953). H. N. STEVENSON, *Encyc. Brit.* (1961) 4:972–982, with bibliog.

[B. GRIFFITHS]

CASTEL GANDOLFO, town of 3,000 population, 18 miles southeast of Rome on the west shore of Lake Albano; it is known for the villa used as an occasional papal residence since the 17th century. A large necropolis nearby indicates a population in prehistoric times. The ruins of a villa of the Emperor *Domitian can be seen in the garden of the present papal villa. A castle or villa *Gandulfi,* mentioned in 816, came into the possession of the Savelli family (1285), who, after losing it several times, ceded it to the Holy See for financial considerations (1596). The present villa, begun in 1629 by Urban VIII, who commissioned the work to Carlo *Maderno, served many popes as a late spring or fall residence and as a place for the reception of distinguished guests. Giovanni Lorenzo *Bernini built the cupola Church of St. Thomas of Villanova in a Greek cross (1661). Although the Law of *Guarantees (1871) granted the popes use of the villa, they did not visit it again until 1934. Under Pius IX two communities of nuns, deprived of their convents, were lodged at the villa. Giovanni Battista de *Rossi died and Cardinal Rafael *Merry del Val recuperated there. The *Lateran Pacts of 1929 accorded the Holy See extraterritorial rights over Castel Gandolfo and the nearby villas of Bernini and Cybò, all three of which are part of Italy; the villas cover about 100 acres. During World War II Castel Gandolfo sheltered 12,000 refugees, most of them from the fighting at Anzio. Pius XII died in Castel Gandolfo (1958).

Bibliography: E. BONOMELLI, EncCatt 3:1014–17. R. MOLS, DHGE 11:1417–18.

[A. RANDALL]

CASTEL SANT' ANGELO

Roman citadel, famed in the history of the city and the papacy. Its construction was begun in 130 by Emperor Hadrian (117–138) as a mausoleum for himself and family (*moles Hadriani*) and was completed by Antoninus Pius (138–161) in 139. Situated at the Tiber in the gardens of Domitian (81–96), it was composed of a square substructure (275 ft. wide and 164 ft. high) that supported a cylindrical tower (210 ft. in diameter) faced with marble. The tower was surmounted by a tumulus of earth, planted with cypresses surrounding a square altar and probably a bronze quadriga, guided by the sun-god, symbolic of the extent of imperial power. In the chambers of this tomb were sarcophagi that contained the ashes of Hadrian, his wife Sabina, and his sons, as well as other emperors to Septimus Severus (193–211). Aurelian (270–275) transformed it into a bastion at the head of a fortified bridge, and by the 5th century it had become important in the defense of

The Castel Sant' Angelo, Rome, as seen from the Tiber.

Rome. Its side facing the river was fortified with a wall, six towers, windows for archers, and battlements to mount catapults. It was used as a prison for the first time by Theodoric the Great (489–526).

According to legend Pope Gregory I, while crossing the Aelian bridge during the plague of 590 in a penitential procession, saw an angel on the summit of the citadel sheathing his sword as a sign that the plague was ended. From that time it was known by its present name. In the 10th century during the ascendancy of the House of Theophylact, Alberic and *Marozia made it their stronghold. Pope *John X (928) was imprisoned there and smothered by order of Marozia, who assumed the title, *Donna Senatrix;* *Benedict VI (974) was strangled in its dungeons by the faction of Crescentius and the deacon Boniface Franco (antipope Boniface VII); John XIV (984) after 4 months' imprisonment died either from starvation or poison administered by his successor, *Boniface VII. In 1277 a passageway (*passetto Vaticano*) was built by Nicholas III to connect the fortress with the papal palace. After the fateful election of Urban VI in 1378, it fell under the control of the French pope, Clement VII (*see* WESTERN SCHISM). The Romans stormed the castle, cut off the hands of the defenders, and stripped the marble from the walls. Restoration was begun by Boniface IX (1389–1404) and continued by Nicholas V (1447–55) according to plans drawn by the Florentine Bernardo Rosselino (1409–64). Alexander VI (1492–1503) entrusted the further work to the architect and military engineer, Antonio da Sangallo (1463–1534), who designed the octagonal dungeons at the corners. Julius II (1503–13) added a frontal loggia, and Leo X (1513–21) erected a chapel and extensive apartments for feasts and plays. When mutinous imperial troops sacked Rome (1527), *Clement VII (1523–34) sought its safety and remained there a virtual prisoner for 7 months. From the time of Urban VIII (1623–44) it was used primarily as a foundry and barracks, though its dungeons were still used. In the 18th century, the adventurer Alessandro Cagliostro (1743–95) was condemned by the Inquisition to life imprisonment within its walls. Here too Lorenzo *Ricci, general of the Society of Jesus at the time of its suppression, was confined during the 2 years before his death (Nov. 24, 1775). In 1752 the marble angel on the castle's summit, carved by Giacomo della Porta (1541–1604), was replaced by the bronze statue of St. Michael by the Flemish sculptor Pierre Verschaffelt (Pietro Fiammingo, 1710–93), which is there today. In 1886 excavations and restorations were performed under the direction of Mariano Borgatti. The Castel Sant' Angelo is now a national monument and military museum.

Bibliography: S. B. PLATNER, *A Topographical Dictionary of Ancient Rome,* cont. and rev. T. ASHBY (Oxford 1929). R. A. LANCIANI, *The Ruins and Excavations of Ancient Rome* (Boston 1897). P. PAGLIUCCHI, *I castellani del Castel S. Angelo di Roma* (Rome 1906–). M. BORGATTI, *Castel Sant'Angelo in Roma* (Rome 1931). E. GERLINI, EncCatt 3:1025–30. G. LUGLI, *Roma antica, il centro monumentale* (Rome 1946). **Illustration credit:** Foto-Enit-Roma.

[E. D. MCSHANE]

CASTELLANOS, JUAN DE, historian; b. Alanís, Spain, 1522; d. Tunja, Colombia, Nov. 27, 1607. He studied both in Alanís and in Seville under the tutelage of Bachiller Heredia. In 1539 he went to America and lived as a soldier in Puerto Rico, Santo Domingo, Curaçao, Aruba, and the islands of Cugagua and Margarita. From there, he proceeded to Cabo de la Vela, where he worked as a miner. He was ordained

Juan de Castellanos.

in 1544. He was a parish priest in Cartagena and a member of the cathedral chapter; also curate of Rio de la Hacha. In 1568 the King granted him the benefice of Tunja where he lived until his death. He took advantage of his long years of residence in Tunja to write *Elegías de varones ilustres de Indias* and the life of *San Diego de Alcalá,* now lost. The *Elegías* is divided into four sections. The first (Madrid 1586) concerns the discovery of America, with some material on the conquest of Mexico and the beginning of the conquest of Venezuela; the second is a continuation of the history of Venezuela, Cabo de la Vela, and Santa Marta; and the third, published with the first part in 1847, gives the history of the governorships of Cartagena, Popayán, Atioquia, and Chocó. The *Discurso del Capitán Drake,* in five cantos, is a continuation of the history of Cartagena and was first published in 1921; the fourth and last part, published in 1886, treats the history of the new kingdom of Granada. Castellanos, with Oviedo, is considered one of the most authoritative of the early historians of the New World. His work, written first in prose and later in verse, has been recognized as one of the most remarkable works in world literature. It is a rich source of information for the periods of the discovery and conquest. A careful observer, Castellanos described with skill the marvels of the American world in flora and fauna.

Bibliography: U. ROJAS, *Juan de Castellanos: Biografía* (Tunja 1958). I. J. PARDO, *Juan de Castellanos: Estudio de las Elegías de varones ilustres de Indias* (Caracas 1961). M. G. ROMERO, *Juan de Castellanos: Un examen de su vida y de su obra* (Bogatá 1964). **Illustration credit:** Library of Congress.

[M. G. ROMERO]

CASTELLI, BENEDETTO

Astronomer and physicist; b. Brescia, Italy, 1578; d. Rome, 1643. Baptized Antonio, he changed his name to Benedict when in 1595 he became a monk at Monte Cassino. While at Padua in 1604, he frequented the lectures and house of Galileo, developing among other things the technique for projecting the sun's image out of the telescope in order to be able to observe it conveniently (*see* GALILEI, GALILEO). An ardent disciple of the Copernican theory, he anticipated the phases of Venus while studying Galileo's *Sidereus Nuncius,* which phenomena the two soon verified by direct telescopic observation. In 1611 he moved to Florence, and with Galileo was a guest of Filippo Salviati. With them he observed the Medici planets and sun spots. In 1613 he was named reader in mathematics at the University of Pisa. He often went to Florence to lecture in physics and mathematics to Prince Lorenzo de Medici. Turning to hydraulics, he completed his celebrated treatise "On the Measurement of Running Waters" (*Della misura delle acque correnti*) dedicated to Pope Urban VIII; with this work Castelli raised the study of hydraulics to the dignity of science. Summoned to Rome by Urban VIII, he continued his interests, not only in hydraulics but in astronomy, mechanics, and physiology. From his school at Rome came his followers *Torricelli and Borelli. He received the highest honors of his order, was elected abbot in 1632, and invested with several abbeys.

Bibliography: G. GALILEI, *Le opere di Galileo Galilei,* ed. A. FAVRO, 20 v. (Florence 1929–39). *Dizionario letterario Bompiani degli autori,* 3 v. (Milan 1956). G. ABETTI, *Amici e nemici di Galileo* (Milan 1945).

[G. ABETTI]

CASTELLINO DA CASTELLI, Italian priest-apostle of religious instruction; b. Menaggio (Diocese of Como), *c.* 1476; d. Milan, Sept. 21, 1566. In 1536 he founded the first school in Milan for instructing children in Christian doctrine. Its name, *Compagnia della reformatione in carità,* aroused suspicion and was changed in 1546 to *Compagnia dei servi de' puttini in carità.* In the same year the Council of Trent approved the *Compagnia* and enriched its work with an indulgence of 7 years. At first Castellino had difficulty gaining the support of diocesan authority, but when Niccolò Ormaneto, vicar-general appointed by St. Charles Borromeo (the temporarily absent archbishop of Milan), arrived in 1564, he found 15 such schools; within 2 years their number doubled, and soon they were diffused throughout northern Italy. When Borromeo returned to Milan in 1566, he established in his diocese the *Confraternity of Christian Doctrine in order that children might be carefully and systematically instructed. His fame has eclipsed that of Castellino, who was his precursor in this work and therefore an important though little-known figure in the Counter Reformation.

Bibliography: G. DE MARCHI, EncCatt 3:1021. A. TAMBORINI, *La Compagnia e le scuole della dottrina cristiana* (Milan 1939).

[M. S. CONLAN]

CASTELLIO, SEBASTIAN (CHÂTEILLON), Protestant humanist and Biblical scholar; b. St.-Martin-du-Fresne (Department of Ain), Burgundy, France, 1515; d. Basel, Switzerland, Dec. 29, 1563. After his student days in Lyons, he became a Protestant and left for Strasbourg, where he made the acquaintance of John *Calvin (1540). The following year he was called by Calvin to Geneva, where he was made rector of the college. When he was denied ordination to the ministry because of his liberal exegesis, he moved to Basel (1545). Here, after several years of poverty, he was appointed professor of Greek at the university (1553). At Basel he had more controversies with Calvin and Theodore *Beza over exegetical matters and such theological questions as the Trinity and predestination. His opposition to the Calvinist execution of Michael *Servetus (1553) inspired his book *De haereticis, an sint persequendi?* (Basel 1554) and marked him as one of the few men of his age in favor of religious liberty.

Castellio, however, is best known as a Bible translator. A master of Latin, Greek, and Hebrew, he translated the whole Bible from the original languages into both Latin and French. Although his Latin version (Basel 1551) was done in elegant Ciceronian language, his French version, one of the most original of the 16th century, was written in the popular vernacular of his time and place.

Bibliography: P. CHIMINELLI, EncCatt 3:1021–22. J. HOMEYER, LexThK^2 2:973. H. LIEBING, RGG^3 1:1627. F. BUISSON, *Sébastien Castellion,* 2 v. (Paris 1892). S. L. GREENSLADE, ed., *The Cambridge History of the Bible* (Cambridge, Eng. 1963) 8–9, 71–72, 116.

[A. M. MALO]

CASTELLVÍ, MARCELINO DE, Capuchin linguist and anthropologist; b. Castellví de la Marca, Catalonia, Spain, Sept. 11, 1908; d. Bogotá, Colombia, June 25, 1951. His secular name was Juan Canyes Santacana and he belonged to a very religious family—four of his brothers joined the Capuchins. He entered the order on July 13, 1924, and pursued his ecclesiastical studies in the houses of the Catalan Province with brilliance. He completed his higher education at the Gregorian University in Rome, obtaining a licentiate in theology. After his ordination he was assigned to the apostolic mission of southern Colombia and went there on Nov. 2, 1931. He resided permanently in Sibundoy, except for periodic scientific trips. He was distinguished for his intelligence and exceptional memory, exemplary rectitude, and his affable, humble manner. In his work he showed himself intrepid and tireless. He knew a number of languages and devoted himself particularly to ethnologic and linguistic studies of Colombian Amazonia, and indeed of all Colombia, trying to find connections with other regions of America. He founded the Linguistic and Ethnological Research Center of Colombian Amazonia (CILEAC), with the support of his superiors and missionary companions. He organized a model card catalog, containing thousands of scientific references, which was used by various specialists, and brought together a library and a museum of anthropological sciences. He published the journal *Amazonia Colombiana,* the organ of the CILEAC, and several books, the outstanding ones being *Manual de investigaciones lingüísticas* (1934), *Propedeútica etnológica indoamericana* (1950), *Metodología de las encuestas folklóricas* (1941), and *Censo indolingüístico de Colombia* (published posthumously). Castellví carried on these scientific activities while performing his priestly duties diligently: preaching, serving as rector of the seminary for secular clergy, and teaching in schools and universities. After his death, the CILEAC materials were transferred to Bogotá, where greater use could be made of them.

[I. DE MONTCLAR]

CASTELO BRANCO, CAMILO, Portuguese novelist; b. Lisbon, March 16, 1825; d. S. Miguel de Seide, June 1, 1890. Though he is one of the two greatest Portuguese novelists, Castelo Branco is relatively unknown outside of Portugal. Part of his popularity in his native land sprang probably from his colorful life and violent personality, which fitted 19th-century notions about literary figures. An illegitimate child, he was at different times a theological student and recipient of minor orders, a seducer, a prisoner charged with adultery, a literary critic engaged in fierce controversies, and an unhappy father. Because of the early death of his parents, he was brought up by relatives in the remote province of Trás-os-Montes. There he married at 16, only to leave wife and child 2 years later to study in Lisbon and Oporto. In Oporto he entered into a permanent relation with Ana Plácido, whose husband obtained their imprisonment in 1860. Castelo Branco made good use of this year in prison to study the Portuguese classics, to translate, and to write. The death of Ana's husband provided them with a house in the province of Minho, but they did not marry until 1888, 2 years before he committed suicide.

There is a close connection between Castelo Branco's life and his writings. His favorite locales are Trás-os-Montes, Oporto, and Minho; his favorite personages, members of the Oporto bourgeoisie or peasants and landlords of Minho and Trás-os-Montes; his favorite themes, seductions, illegitimacy, adultery, and unhappy marriages. His need to support himself and his family (including an illegitimate daughter) explains his prolific output and his use of melodramatic plots that appealed to a public whose reading was confined to the *feuilleton* of the daily newspaper. Even his brilliant style shows the effect of episodes in his life: his studies during his 384 days in prison and his sojourn for many years among country people combined to endow him with a vast vocabulary that savored of both the country and the classics. For this reason, too, a reading of his novels gives a closer picture of 19th-century Portuguese life than any other source.

His works of fiction include novels of adventure and intrigue, à la Eugene Sue, an example of which is *Os mistérios de Lisboa* (1854); novels of passion, exemplified by his most famous though not his best book, *Amor de perdição* (1862); novels of satire and customs, such as *Coração, cabeça e estômago* (1862); and novels of rural life, such as the *Novelas do Minho* (1875–77), in which sensational plots cannot spoil the effect of sympathetically drawn characters and natural dialogue. His interest in moral and philosophical problems is shown in *Onde está a felicidade?* (1856) and his concern for social problems in *A queda de um anjo* (1866). Furthermore, his works of nonfiction and poetry should not be forgotten.

Bibliography: *Obra seleta,* ed. J. DO P. COELHO (Rio de Janeiro 1960–). J. DO P. COELHO, *Introdução ao estudo da novela camiliana* (Coimbra 1946). A. RIBEIRO, *O romance de Camilo* (Lisboa 1957).

[R. S. SAYERS]

CASTI CONNUBII

To warn the faithful of various errors and the prevalent corruption of morals with respect to marriage, and to expound more fully certain points of Catholic doctrine called for by the circumstances of his pontificate, Pius XI determined to reaffirm the doctrine of Leo XIII's *Arcanum Divinae Sapientiae* and speak "on the nature and dignity of Christian marriage, on the advantages and benefits which accrue from it to the family and human society itself, on the errors contrary to this most important point of the Gospel teaching, on the vices opposed to conjugal union and lastly on the principal remedies to be applied." The following is a summary of his encyclical, *Casti connubii,* issued Dec. 31, 1930.

While one may freely choose to marry or not, the choice of marriage implies a will to conform one's life to the laws laid down for it by its Divine Author. The failure to accept this responsibility wreaks havoc not only with family life directly, but indirectly it also disturbs the very foundations of society. Therefore it is incumbent upon the state to "restrict, prevent and punish base unions opposed to reason and nature."

The right to beget children imposes a corresponding duty to educate them for life here and hereafter, and thus clearly restricts the exercise of this right to the married state, wherein alone this duty can be adequately fulfilled. It is moreover a way of life in which husband and wife sanctify each other through that conjugal fidelity which deserved to be compared to the union between Christ and His Church which He loves "not for the sake of His own advantage, but seeking only the good of His spouse." By elevating marriage to the dignity of a Sacrament, Our Lord bestowed upon it the highest blessing possible, for the marriage contract itself became thereby an efficacious sign of sacramental grace. Consequently the spouses possess a "right to the actual assistance of grace whenever they need it for fulfilling the duties of their state."

This noble Christian concept of marriage stands opposed to evils that would debase so sacred an institution. The nuptial bond must never be subject to the whims of man or woman to allow them the unbridled liberty of those purely human unions, variously described as "temporary," "experimental," or "companionate." Nor may the obligations arising from the use of the marital right be avoided by the sins of contraception, direct sterilization, and abortion. Without prejudice to the dignity of woman but in support of it, Pius XI scored the errors of those who profess to free her from what they regard as the burdens of conjugal fidelity, obedience, and love. Abhorrent as these evils are, the greatest are those which undermine the sacramental nature of marriage by relegating it to the level of a merely civil institution, granting the state full authority to loose and even dissolve the marriage contract but denying the Church the right even to warn her children against the dangers of mixed marriages.

While we should not overlook the natural aids at our disposal to help us solve marital problems, the solution must be above all a spiritual one. The impressionable minds and tender hearts of the young must be fortified by strong Christian conviction and an indomitable fiber. Spiritual maturity is required of all Christians that they wisely obey the teaching of mother Church with regard to marriage. Lastly, society, which reaps the benefits of chaste Christian marriage, cannot stand idly by but must provide the economic climate wherein a sacred and solid family life can be more easily preserved.

Bibliography: PIUS XI, "Casti connubii" (encyclical, Dec. 31, 1930) ActApS 22 (1930) 539–592, Eng. *Catholic Mind* 29 (Jan. 1931) 21–64. J. L. THOMAS, *The Catholic Viewpoint on Marriage and the Family* (Garden City, N.Y. 1958). E. W. O'ROURKE, *Marriage and Family Life* (Champaign, Ill. 1956). J. E. KERNS, *The Theology of Marriage* (New York 1964).

[S. KARDOS]

CASTIGLIONE, BALDASSARE

Italian writer; b. Casatico, Mantua, Dec. 6, 1478; d. Toledo, Spain, Feb. 2, 1529. He was trained from early childhood in the amenities of courtly life, and studied Greek and Latin in Milan under George Merula and Demetrius Calcondila. In 1499 he entered the service of his lord and relative Francis Gonzaga, under whose leadership he fought against the Spaniards. In 1503 he moved to Urbino where he spent 11 important years enjoying the full confidence first of Duke Guidobaldo da Montefeltre and then of his successor, Francis della Rovere. During this period he carried out many important diplomatic missions for his patrons.

Diplomat and Nuncio. His activity spans the height of the Italian Renaissance during the papal reigns of Julius II, Leo X, and Clement VII. He was sent as ambassador from Urbino to Julius II and fought under this fiery pontiff at the siege of Mirandola in 1511. With both Julius II and Leo X he shared a passionate love for the fine arts, and he cultivated the friendship of artists, especially Raphael. Castiglione had an active interest in archeology. He was fond also of pageants and public spectacles. He was ambassador from Mantua to Leo X and to Clement VII, who, in 1524, made him prothonotary and sent him to Spain as his nuncio. As a convinced sympathizer of Charles V, Castiglione tried in vain to have the wavering Pope support the Emperor's cause in his struggle with Francis I. Since communications with the Curia had become strained and difficult, he could do nothing to prevent the sack of Rome (May 6, 1527), a failure for which Pope Clement sharply reproached him. Castiglione died without having witnessed the much-desired reconciliation between the Pope and Charles V. The Emperor, who esteemed Castiglione greatly, had obtained for him the bishopric of Avila.

Baldassare Castiglione, early 16th-century portrait by an unknown Italian master.

Castiglione's letters, written during the difficult mission to Spain, express a keen discernment of events and people, a dignified defense of his actions, and a serene confidence of having accomplished his duty. His habitual poise gives way to indignation only once: when he condemns the *Dialogue on the Sack of Rome*—itself a sharp attack on the corruption of the clergy, the veneration of false relics, and other abuses—a work written by the young secretary of Charles V, Alphonse of Valdes. The violence of the nuncio's reaction marks the last phase in the spiritual development of one of the foremost representatives of the Renaissance on the eve of the Counter Reformation.

Literary Activity. During most of his life Castiglione had devoted himself to secular and literary pursuits. He wrote Latin and Italian verses and, in honor of the Duchess and the court of Urbino, composed *Tirsi,* an eclogue in octaves, which was recited during the carnival of 1506. His long and intimate familiarity with the classics, his experience at several courts, especially the enlightened and orderly court of Urbino, his courage in battle and in loyalty to his lords, his respect for women, and his friendship with the most outstanding personalities of his time were among the influences that gave shape to his most famous work, *Il Libro del Cortegiano.* This book, considered by some of his contemporaries to be his autobiography, was conceived after the death of Duke Guidobaldo in 1508; the author intended it as a memorial to a great ruler and friend. It was written for the most part between 1513 and 1518, and published in Venice (1528) when Castiglione, then in Spain, decided to thwart its clandestine publication by others. The work was placed on the Index in 1590.

His Masterwork. In spite of the lack of a final revision and the many linguistic problems involved in publishing a modern critical edition, *Il Libro del Cortegiano* (*Book of the Courtier*) is a stylistic masterpiece. Castiglione's severest critics, who charge him with spiritual shallowness and insincerity, cannot deny the formal perfection of his work, in which the harmony of Ciceronian prose shines through the vernacular, the learned subject matter is fused with personal reminiscence, and a great variety of material is subtly blended into a graceful whole.

Taking the medieval knight as paradigm, Castiglione creates the 16th-century gentleman, in much the same manner as the architect Laurana transformed the medieval castle of Urbino into a Renaissance palace. Written with a characteristic *sprezzatura,* the *Book of the Courtier* is modeled on Cicero's *De oratore.* It takes the form of a conversation among real characters who contribute in turn their opinion on the main subject, the formation of a perfect courtier, a man of noble lineage, skilled in the use of weapons and in the laws of chivalry, carefully trained in letters and fine arts, graceful and polished in demeanor, accomplished and poised in conversation. Among the long digressions there is one on wit, which is based on the *De oratore* and illustrated with a collection of jokes, and another, by the lady of the court, on love. A fourth section, subsequently added to the original scheme, deals with the duties of the courtier as a mentor of princes, and with the rules of good government. The book closes with a Neoplatonic exaltation of spiritual over sensual love.

Castiglione's work had extraordinary influence, especially at the beginning of the Renaissance in England and Spain. In 1534, it was translated and published by Juan Boscan. Twelve more editions appeared in Spanish before the end of the 16th century. Its wide acceptance in Catholic Spain during this period shows that value was attributed to Castiglione's work in spite of his almost total lack of explicit reference to Christian teaching.

Bibliography: *Opere,* ed. C. CORDIÉ (Milan 1960); *Il cortegiano, con una scelta delle opere minori,* ed. B. MAIER (Turin 1955); *Il libro del cortegiano,* ed. V. CIAN (Florence 1894; 4th ed. 1947); *Lettere,* ed. P. SERASSI, 2 v. (Padua 1769–71); *Poesie volgari, e latine,* ed. P. SERASSI (Rome 1760); *The Book of the Courtier,* tr. T. HOBY (London 1928; ed. W. H. D. ROUSE, New York 1956). G. C. FERRERO, "Studi sul Castiglione," *Rivista di sintesi letteraria* 2 (1935) 473–480. V. CIAN, *Un illustre nunzio pontificio del Rinascimento: Baldassar Castiglione* (StTest 156; 1951); "Un episodio della storia della censura in Italia nel secolo XVI: La censura ecclesiastica del Cortegiano," *Archivio storico lombardo,* ser. 2, 14 (1887) 661–727. E. LOOS, *Baldassare Castigliones Libro del cortegiano: Studien zur Tugendauffassung des Cinquecento* (Frankfurt a. M. 1955). W. SCHRINNER, *Castiglione und die englische Renaissance* (Berlin 1939). M. MORREALE DE CASTRO, *Castiglione y Boscán: El ideal cortesano en el renacimiento español,* 2 v. (Madrid 1959). **Illustration credit:** National Gallery of Art, Washington, D.C., Widener Collection.

[M. MORREALE]

CASTIGLIONE, GIUSEPPE, Jesuit missionary in China, where he painted for the emperors at Peking and became a principal member of the Imperial Painting Bureau; b. Milan, July 19, 1688; d. Peking, China, July 16, 1766. After initial schooling in art, Castiglione was attracted to religious life and entered the Jesuit novitiate in Genoa (1707). He executed a number of paintings in Genoa and completed his novitiate in Portugal before he was finally sent by the superior general, M. *Tamburini, to Peking. He arrived in Peking on Dec. 22, 1715; there he became known as Lang Shihning and a favorite artist and architect in the imperial court. He was active under three emperors: the grand K'ang Hsi (d. 1722); his son Yung Cheng (d. 1735); and the nephew of K'ang Hsi, Ch'ien Lung (d. 1795). Ch'ien Lung was an atrocious persecutor of Christians, but his high esteem for Castiglione afforded opportunity to the painter to intercede for his fellow Christians.

Castiglione is of little importance in the history of Chinese painting but emerges as a symbol of Western influence in 18th-century China; apparently Chinese sophistication of the 18th century had an admiration for Europeanlike painting somewhat similar to Europe's interest at that time in Chinoiserie. Castiglione brought with him a competence in European painting ability and was able to please his imperial patrons with "realistic" portraits, narrative accounts of imperial conquests, and studies of nature (flowers, animals). He produced few paintings in a thoroughly Chinese style. His fusion of Western and Chinese elements may be seen in a wide handscroll, about 30 feet long, representing 100 horses (National Palace Museum, Formosa). In this work the mixture of light and shade with Chinese convention in composition and the more delicate Chinese brushwork produces a strong, almost surrealistic effect that is neither Chinese nor European in style.

Another scroll, "The Feast of Victory at the Purple Light Hall" (collection S. Kriger, Washington, D.C.), was painted to represent a victory feast (April 18, 1760) in celebration of the subjugation of the Eleuths. The painting, about 25 feet long, displays easy facility of delineation with a Western touch particularly marked in the rendering of the Emperor, which may very well be a true portrait likeness of Ch'ien Lung.

Castiglione served also as architect (in collaboration with the Jesuit M. Benoist) for the Emperor's Old Summer Palace (Yüan Ming Yüan), a European styled structure that gave the Emperor (Ch'ien Lung) his wish to have a Chinese equivalent of Versailles.

Castiglione is the only European painter recorded in the Chinese work *History of Painting,* composed in 72 chapters by P'eng Jün-ts'an about 1800. Other missionaries who were active artists in China during this period were Ignatius Sichelbarth (Ai Ch'i-meng, 1708–80) and Denis Attiret (Wang Chih-ch'eng, 1708–68).

[R. J. VEROSTKO]

Bibliography: Pfister 2:635–639. G. R. LOEHR, *Giuseppe Castiglione* (Rome 1940), with bibliog. and catalogue of paintings.

The Emperor Ch'ien Lung arriving for a victory feast at the Purple Light Hall, Peking, detail of a scroll painting, 1760, by the Jesuit artist Giuseppe Castiglione.

CASTILLO ANDRACA Y TAMAYO, FRANCISCO DEL, Peruvian poet; b. Lima, April 2, 1716; d. Lima, December 1770. In 1734 he entered the Order of Our Lady of Mercy as a lay brother, and because he had suffered since childhood from defective vision he became popularly known as "El Ciego de la Merced" or the "Blind Man of Mercy." From an early age he gave signs of a singular native intelligence and natural talent. When only 11 years old, he knew Latin well and could recite Latin poetry with ease, a remarkable feat considering that everything had to be read to him because of his poor vision. He had extraordinary powers of retention. Later, his talent for improvisation became proverbial—no public ceremony or feast took place without some display of his creative talent. The works that have been preserved, dramatic and poetic alike, are an indication of his fertile imagination. His romances and satires are especially famous. Among the theatrical works, aside from a number of prologues, interludes, and farces, the best extant works are a drama, *Mitrídates, rey del Ponto;* the comedies *El redentor no nacido: San Ramón, Todo el ingenio lo allana,* and *La conquista del Perú;* and a religious play, *Guerra es la vida del hombre.* His poetry, written in various meters, is on many subjects, the best being on religious themes. These express the piety and gentleness of the author, coupled with a fine lyric quality. His finest poems are a long composition on the passion and death of Christ according to the four Evangelists, a magnificent translation of the *Te Deum,* a dialogue of surprising philosophical and moral depth based on the *Epístolas familiares* of Antonio de Guevara, and a Spanish version of one of the best known of Horace's lyric poems, *Beatus illae.*

Bibliography: *Obras,* ed. R. VARGAS UGARTE (Clásicos peruanos 2; Lima 1948). G. LOHMANN VILLENA, *El arte dramático en Lima durante el virreinato* (Madrid 1945).

[G. LOHMANN VILLENA]

CASTILLO Y GUEVARA, FRANCISCA JOSEFA DEL, nun and author; b. Tunja, Colombia, 1671; d. there, 1742. She came from a distinguished Christian family and entered the convent of the Poor Clares of Tunja at 18. She held several positions as sexton, doorkeeper, and mistress of novices and was abbess in three different periods. Very spiritual, she was favored with visions and ecstasies, was able to foresee future events, and endured many mortifications. At the order of her confessors, she wrote several books: *Autobiografía* (Philadelphia 1817); *Sentimientos espirituales* (v.1, Bogotá 1843; v.2, Bogotá 1942). In her writings one can perceive the influence of her reading of the works of St. Teresa of Jesus. Her own work shows soundness of doctrine, a knowledge of the Bible, and an ardent love of God. She has been considered one of the best writers of the 18th century in Colombia. Even in the 20th century her exemplary life and her writings are a source of pride, since they depict an exceptionally high moral level in a period of the history of New Granada.

Bibliography: J. M. VERGARA Y VERGARA, *Historia de la literatura en Nueva Granada,* ed. A. GÓMEZ RESTREPO and G. OTERO MUÑOZ, 3 v. (Bogotá 1958). R. M. CARRASQUILLA, "Francisca Josefa del Castillo," *Obras completas,* ed. J. E. RICAURTE, 5 v. in 6 (Bogotá 1956–61) 2:257–277.

[J. RESTREPO POSADA]

CASTNER, GASPAR, missionary to China; b. Munich, Oct. 7, 1665; d. Peking, Nov. 9, 1709. He entered the Society of Jesus on Sept. 17, 1681, and, after distinguishing himself in his theological studies at Ingolstadt, he was named professor of philosophy at Regensburg in 1695. The following year he set out for China from Lisbon, arriving in Macao in 1697. For 5 years he preached in the neighborhood of Canton. He also directed the construction of a memorial church on the island of Sanchwan, where St. Francis Xavier had died in 1552. He was sent to Rome with Father Francis Noël in 1702 to represent the bishops of Nanking and Macao concerning the Chinese rites. Together with Noël he composed a memorial on the suitability of the Chinese words T'ien and ShangTi as the equivalent for God. Before returning to China in 1707 he convinced the Portuguese that ships sailing for China should strike out from the Cape of Good Hope directly for Timor, without passing through the Straits of Malacca, thereby cutting the journey to Macao to less than a year. After his return to China, Castner was ordered to Peking, where word of his skill in mathematics had already been received. The Emperor K'ang Hsi named him president of the bureau of mathematics and tutor to the imperial prince. He was also a noted cartographer and did excellent work mapping the Chinese empire.

Bibliography: Pfister 1:486–489. Koch JesLex 1:959–960. Sommervogel 2:853–854.

[J. H. CAMPANA]

CASTORENA Y URSÚA, JUAN IGNACIO DE, first Mexican journalist and bishop of Yucatán; b. Zacatecas, July 31, 1668; d. Mérida, Yucatán, July 13, 1733. He was a member of a noble, wealthy family, the son of Capt. Juan de Castorena Ursúa y Goyeneche and Teresa de Villarreal. He studied in Mexico City under the Jesuits and received a doctorate in law from the university and a doctorate in theology from the University of Ávila, Spain. For some time he lived in Madrid, where he was attached to the nunciature as a theologian. He was also an honorary chaplain and preacher at the court of Charles II. When he returned to Mexico, he received a royal appointment as canon of the cathedral of Mexico City. He served as censor of the Inquisition and as rector of the University of Mexico. In 1721 he founded a school for girls in Zacatecas, the Colegio de los Mil Angeles. He became bishop of Yucatán in 1729. Castorena y Ursúa is best known as the founder of *Gaceta de México.* Although news sheets had been published sporadically in Mexico since 1541 and gazettes since 1666, this was the first news periodical. It began on Jan. 1, 1720, and came out once a month. It contained religious, commercial, maritime, and social news and book reviews. On the occasion of the National Journalism Exposition in 1944, the Mexican government published a series of postage stamps honoring Castorena y Ursúa and a bio-bibliography on him.

Bibliography: M. OCHOA CAMPOS, *Juan Ignacio María de Castorena Ursúa y Goyeneche: Primer periodista mexicano* (Mexico City 1944). A. AGÜEROS DE LA PORTILLA, *El periodismo en México durante la dominación española* (Mexico City 1910). X. TAVERA ALFARO, ed., *El nacionalismo en la prensa mexicana del siglo XVIII* (Mexico City 1963).

[E. GÓMEZ TAGLE]

CASTRATION

Castration consists in the surgical removal or definitive ionizing of the male testicles or the female ovaries. The surgical ablation is known as orchiectomy in the male and oophorectomy in the female.

Castration of the male is referred to in Chinese medical history as early as 1100 B.C. and was at first imposed as a punishment for crime. Subsequently castration was sought voluntarily as a means of obtaining the lucrative and influential positions of eunuchs in the imperial court. The surgery seems to have included the amputation of the penis and scrotum as well as the testicles. There are likewise references to castration in pre-Christian times in other oriental kingdoms such as Egypt, Babylon, and Persia.

Some misguided early Christian sects practiced castration of the male for ascetical reasons and one such group existed in Russia in the late 19th century. Castration of young boys was popular, particularly in Italy, in the 16th and 17th centuries, for purposes of preserving the soprano voice for musical performances. These singers were called *evirati* or *castrati,* and were the supreme figures in Italian opera. Although St. Alphonsus Liguori records some conflicting opinions regarding the morality of this procedure for this purpose, the view that it was morally acceptable was never held by more than a few theologians (see Zalba 2:154); however, some historians have erroneously concluded that the practice had ecclesiastical approval because sometimes the *evirati* were allowed to sing in church choirs. Castration has sometimes been used for eugenic purposes, but this has always been condemned by the Church as immoral. Some theologians would defend castration as a punishment for certain crimes, if it were legally imposed (see Merkelbach, 76).

The removal or suppression of the testicles or ovaries not only results in infertility, but likewise seriously affects the general hormone balance of the body since these organs are not only the sources of the germ cells, but are likewise important endocrine glands. Hence more conservative approaches to the suppression of fertility are used today and castration is more likely to be done only in a clinical context and as a measure to correct some pathology that threatens the health of the individual. Such a procedure is properly called therapeutic castration and, provided it is free from contraceptive intent, is correctly evaluated in the moral context under the principle of *double effect.

Because of the inaccessibility of the ovaries, clinical castration of the female had to await the advent of abdominal surgery. The first oophorectomy was done in 1809 by a country doctor (Ephraim MacDowell) in a Kentucky cabin.

Irradiation and surgical castration are done today only as a therapeutic or prophylactic measure, and only in the presence of very serious medical indications, such as malignancy of the ovaries or testicles themselves or because the function of these organs as endocrine glands constitutes a threat to the patient's general welfare. Examples of the latter would be those cases of cancer of the prostate in the male, or cancer of the breast in the female, when the endocrine activity of the testicles or ovaries is judged to exert a deleterious effect. In these cases the gonads (testicles or ovaries), which are, in effect, both endocrine glands and reproductive organs, are properly removed as endocrine glands under the principle of *totality. The side effect is permissible under the principle of double effect.

Bibliography: PIUS XI, *Christian Marriage* (New York 1931). G. A. KELLY, *Medico-Moral Problems* (St. Louis 1958). T. J. O'DONNELL, *Morals in Medicine* (2d ed. Westminster, Md. 1959). A. CASTIGLIONI, *History of Medicine,* ed. and tr. E. B. KRUMBHAAR (2d ed. New York 1947). B. E. FINCH and H. GREEN, *Contraception through the Ages* (Springfield, Ill. 1963). T. S. NELSEN and L. R. DRAGSTEDT, "Adrenalectomy and Oophorectomy for Breast Cancer," *The Journal of the American Medical Association* 175 (1961) 379–383. M. M. COPELAND et al., "Bone Metastases and Their Treatment," *The Georgetown Medical Bulletin* 7 (1954) 76–85. M. ZALBA, *Theologiae moralis summa,* v.2 (BiblAutCrist 106; 2d ed. 1957) 154. B. H. MERKELBACH, *Quaestiones de embryologia et de sterilisatione* (Liège 1937) 76.

[T. J. O'DONNELL]

CASTRO, AGUSTÍN PABLO, Mexican Jesuit, scientist, and humanist; b. Córdoba, Mexico, Jan. 24, 1728; d. Bologna, Nov. 23, 1790. A brilliant student, he had such easy success in his studies in Puebla that he became somewhat conceited, so that he was criticized for indolence during his philosophy studies. His zeal did not wane again. He was ordained in Mexico City in October 1752 and from then on devoted himself to teaching and the ministry, finding time also to write humanistic studies and poetry. He served in Puebla, Veracruz, and Mexico City, always available to help in the confessional, to preach, and to assist the dying. From 1756 to 1763 he taught philosophy in Querétaro, was vice rector of San Ildefonso in Mexico City, worked in Guadalajara and Valladolid, and finally, taken ill, went to Tepotzotlán. During that period, somewhat influenced by the philosophical ideas of the Enlightenment, he devoted himself to philosophy and wrote his three-volume *Cursus philosophicus.* In May 1763 he went to Veracruz, where, as a result of coming in contact with business and commerce, he wrote some works in the field of economics. The next year he was assigned to the University of Mérida, Yucatán, where he taught moral theology, Canon Law, jurisprudence, and law, contributing effectively to the growth of the university. At the end of 1766 he went to Córdoba and then to Mexico City where he was stationed when the expulsion of the Jesuits was decreed on June 25, 1767. He and his companions went to Bologna. He resumed his literary activities, was named superior, went to Ferrara in 1773, and later returned to Bologna, again as superior. A great literary and scientific figure of his age, he was drawn into diverse fields by his intellectual curiosity. His writings show influence of the superficiality of the times.

Bibliography: M. VALLE PIMENTEL, *Agustín Pablo de Castro, 1728–1790* (Mexico City 1962). J. L. MANEIRO and M. FABRI, *Vidas de mexicanos ilustres del siglo XVIII,* ed. and tr. B. NAVARRO (Mexico City 1956).

[F. ZUBILLAGA]

CASTRO, IGNACIO DE, historian, scholar, educator; b. Tacna, Peru, July 31, 1732; d. Cuzco, 1792. He was a foundling, cared for by the priest Domingo de Castro. He studied at the Colegio de San Bernardo in Cuzco and received the doctorate at the Jesuit University of San Ignacio. He was a brilliant student and received both the licentiate and the doctorate in theology on Sept. 12, 1753. As pastor in Checa he gained the notice of Bp. Juan de Castañeda. In 1759–60 he was appointed synodal examinar and assigned to give the oration in honor of the new bishop of Cuzco, the

Panamanian Agustín de Gorrichátegui. The sermon was published in 1771, the same year his *Relación de méritos* appeared in Madrid. He failed to win the canonship of the cathedral of Cuzco in 1773, and again in 1781. However, on Dec. 4, 1778, Viceroy Manuel de Guirier named Castro rector of the Colegio de San Bernardo, a position he held the rest of his life. He was secretary to the Creole Bp. Juan Manuel de Moscoso y Peralta at the time of the rebellion of Túpac Amaru in 1780. His most important work, published posthumously in Madrid in 1795, was *Relación de la Fundación de la Real Audiencia del Cusco en 1787, y de las fiestas con que esta grande y fidelísima ciudad celebró este honor.* The original manuscript was lost until the middle of the 20th century, when it was found and newly edited by C. D. Valcárcel. It remains the best history of the imperial city. He wrote for the *Mercurio Peruano,* i.e., "Carta escrita" (from p. 2, 11.12 forward). He also wrote several pamphlets on the mystery of the Conception and devotional treatises.

Bibliography: C. D. VALCÁRCEL, *Ignacio de Castro, humanista tacneño y gran cusqueñista, 1732–1792* (Lima 1953).

[C. D. VALCÁRCEL]

CASTRO, MATEO DE, first Brahman bishop of the Latin rite; b. Divar, near Goa, India, *c.* 1594; d. Rome, 1668 or 1669. Castro, converted by the Theatines, studied under the Franciscans in Goa; then, convinced that his aspirations for the priesthood could not be realized under the Portuguese *padroado* (royal control of ecclesiastical appointments), he went to Rome, where he completed his theological studies under the Propaganda of the Faith. After ordination he was named missionary apostolic and entrusted with the evangelization of the Brahmans of India. He was already known as a critic of the Portuguese and of the Jesuits and other orders working in the *padroado,* and what was to be a long and bitter conflict between the *padroado* and the Propaganda began. Following a prolonged dispute with the bishop of Goa over the exercise of his faculties, Castro returned to Rome to present his case. In order to promote the more effective evangelization of peoples outside the patronage jurisdictions of Spain and Portugal, the Holy See was formulating its plan for erecting vicariates apostolic, and Castro was the first vicar apostolic so appointed. As titular bishop of Chrysopolis *in partibus infidelium* he was sent to Bidjapur in the native state of Idalkan, bordering directly on Portuguese Goa. There he established a seminary and consecrated a native Brahman clergy affiliated with the Oratory of St. Philip Neri. Although in accordance with the instructions of Propaganda, this move intensified the struggle between himself and the Portuguese, who resisted any encroachment upon their *padroado* rights. Charges of personal irregularities were levied against him in order to undermine his work; these difficulties led to Castro's making subsequent trips to Rome. Although aware that his conduct was at times intemperate and imprudent, Propaganda maintained its confidence in him. As a result of these storms, Castro spent his last years in Rome at the College of the Propaganda. His turbulent career highlights one of the tragic chapters in the history of the Church's missions. His zeal and sincerity are unimpugned, and the charges that he was plotting against the Portuguese political power have not been substantiated. Unfortunately, under the impact of opposition, he resorted to diatribe and imprudent conduct. His failure, and that of his two cousins, Custodio de Pinho and Thomas de Castro, who also became vicars apostolic, served to postpone efforts of the Holy See to foster a native episcopacy in mission lands until the policy was once more vigorously renewed by Pius XI, Pope of the Missions.

Bibliography: Delacroix HistMissCath 2:138, 194–197. T. GHESQUIÈRE, *Mathieu de Castro, Premier vicaire apostolique aux Indes* (Louvain 1937). A. HUONDER, *Der einheimische Klerus in den Heidenländern* (Freiburg 1909). A. JANN, *Die katholischen Missionen in Indien, China und Japan: Ihre Organisation und das portugiesische Patronat vom 15. bis 18. Jahrhundert* (Paderborn 1915). E. D. MACLAGAN, *The Jesuits and the Great Mogul* (London 1932). B. DE VAULX, *History of the Missions,* tr. R. F. TREVETT (New York 1961).

[A. M. CHRISTENSEN]

CASUISTRY

The term casuistry comes from the Latin *casus,* case. In general, casuistry denotes the method that applies the principles of a science to particular facts. Thus, there are casuistries proper to civil and canonical law (jurisprudence), to psychology (casework), to commerce (case system). In theology casuistry signifies that part of moral theology, or that method, that treats of the application of moral principles to singular cases. Hence, it is incorrect for some Protestant theologians to call the whole of Catholic moral theology by the name casuistry.

Basic Problem. The problem of casuistry is basically that of the unity of the singular reality conceived of through a multiplicity of general and abstract ideas. While the moral laws are known with sufficient certitude in their abstract formulation, the concrete act, unique and singular, to which one would apply them, remains difficult to analyze because of its complexity. Casuistry allows one to bridge the gap between the concrete action and the abstract norms. Thanks to it, conscience, which must base its judgments on an objective morality, can use the principles already particularized and more easily applicable to the singular. Nevertheless, despite their high degree of particularization, the enunciations of casuistry remain general, in the sense that they are of value, not just for a particular individual, but for every person placed in the same circumstances. They do not take into consideration, therefore, strictly personal factors that may be apposite in a case of conscience.

Necessity. Casuistry, essentially a science of application, is needed because of the imperfection itself of our knowledge. While casuistry does have limitations and dangers, it remains indispensable in our human condition subject to sin and error. "Anyone who perfectly knew the principles according to all their virtualities," says St. Thomas, "would not need any conclusions proposed to him separately. But, because those who know principles do not know them so as to consider everything that is found virtually contained in them, it is necessary for them that, in the sciences, the conclusions be deduced from principles" (ST 2a2ae, 44.2).

Function. Casuistry has a double function: to illustrate principles (case casuistry found in the manuals of cases of conscience) and to study moral problems of concrete life (practical casuistry found in the various treatises on special moral theology).

Case Casuistry. Through means of typical examples, real or fictitious, future confessors and counselors are taught the correct way to handle moral principles. They are initiated into the prudent and judicious solution of cases of conscience. This scholastic exercise is necessary for the formation of future priests.

Practical Casuistry. By the very logic of its development, moral theology should be perfected by its casuistic rules that bring it closer to the singular reality. Since it is a normative science, it demands not only a clarification of Christian principles, but also their application to contemporary life. It ought to "make real" the Christian ideal in the various spheres of individual, family, social, and professional life. Since it is the purpose and end of moral investigation, practical casuistry performs a "realizing" function in moral theology. It, therefore, presupposes in the moralist, perspicacity, a decisive mind, and sure judgment.

Limitations. Casuistry does not replace either conscience or prudence. It does not free conscience from its responsibilities by giving it ready-made answers that could be applied without personal reflection. Its role is to clarify conscience by showing why a particular solution is obligatory or better. It aids conscience to decide for itself. It cannot foresee all possible cases. There will always be more or less extended zones not subject to the perfect control of casuistry between the analyses, the most searching practical conclusions of casuistry, and the ultimate decision of conscience. Here, prudence must complete the work of casuistry. Especially when absolutely obligatory norms are not involved, prudence aids in weighing with care all the circumstances of the case.

Casuistry and the Moral Minimum. We should distinguish between the casuistry as applied to an action already done and as applied to an action not yet performed. The first, known as the merciful casuistry of the confessional, is adapted to the judgment of a past action. It can easily content itself, as a result, with the formulation of a moral minimum. Taking its inspiration from the words of Jesus to the adulterous woman, "Neither will I condemn thee" (Jn 8.11), it is designed especially for the confessor who must make an objective yet merciful judgment of his penitent, and even hold him innocent, if possible, in doubtful cases. Casuistry even in its application to the future, in order to avoid rigorism, must also indicate the lower limits of the love of God set forth in the commandments, i.e., the precise point where sin begins. By doing this, it inculcates respect and fidelity toward the law. Once the minimum is indicated, it should also speak about the opportunity, the utility, and even the comparative perfection of particular acts. If it seeks to help man resolve his cases of conscience in a Christian way, something of counsel and a certain evangelical plenitude must find a place in it.

History. Beginning with the Gospel, the morality of the New Testament focused on concrete life. It therefore is the beginning of Christian casuistry (Lk 20.20–26; 6.7; Mk 2.23–28). Applying the Christian ideal to a pagan surrounding quickly posed cases of conscience that had to be resolved. St. Paul solved several of them (eating sacrificial food, work, virginity).

Patristic Age. Casuistic elements are also found in the Fathers, particularly in Origen, Clement of Alexandria, and St. Augustine. These concerned, for example, military service, persecutions, lying, the Sabbath, and dress. It is therefore inaccurate to claim that casuistry invaded Christianity through the influence of Stoicism or the Jewish law. At the end of the patristic age, from the 6th to the 11th century, a casuistry of sin was formed, which was connected with the development of auricular confession. It is contained in the *Penitentials.

The Middle Ages (13th–16th Century). The Fourth Lateran Council (1215) made annual confession and Communion obligatory. This accentuated the practical character of clerical studies and gave a new importance to casuistry. Clerics were initiated into cases of conscience by the *Summae confessorum,* which replaced the Penitentials. These works contained a résumé of morality from the practical and limited point of view of the confessor. They coexisted with the great commentaries on the *Liber Sententiarum* of P. Lombard.

16th–17th Century. The significant contribution of this period was the *Institutiones Theologiae Moralis.* In the 16th century, a particular circumstance, the creation of a course in cases of conscience, gave a new spirit to casuistry and made it more scientific. Tridentine legislation insisted on the pastoral formation of clerics and on the obligation of the penitent to accuse himself of sins according to number and species. As a result there was instituted, along with the course in scholastic theology (destined for those who wished to obtain the title of doctor), a course in cases of conscience (destined first for those who took only 2 years of theology, then made obligatory for all clerics). As a manual for this course, the *Institutiones Theologiae Moralis* (Azor, Laymann) were created, as a sort of a compromise between the *Summae Confessorum,* which were henceforth considered to be insufficient, and the great commentaries (*Summae*), which omitted the practical and pastoral aspect. These works, oriented especially toward practical morality, besides assuring all clerics a better pastoral preparation, enriched moral theology by giving it clarity, precision, and a high degree of accuracy in analysis.

This was the golden age of casuistry. Progress was interrupted in the middle of the 17th century by the quarrels concerning Jansenism and probabilism. Absorbed by these polemics, moralists neglected the deepening of principles so much that moral theology was reduced practically to the knowledge required of a confessor and was oriented toward a minimalist casuistry. It was forgotten that casuistry could not be perfectly autonomous and that it must rest on a solid moral system. It was sometimes cultivated for itself, like a mental puzzle, on the level of pure dialectic without any relation to concrete life. The most improbable hypotheses were imagined and discussed. By splitting hairs about how far one could go and where one must stop, certain authors fell into laxism. Casuistry, as a result, had to submit to the attacks of Pascal. Henceforth it had a bad name, which it never completely lost.

18th–19th Century. If one excepts the beginning of reform at Tübingen, Germany, about the middle of the 18th century, one may say that at the beginning of the 18th century moral theology was contained almost exclusively in predominantly casuistic manuals. The *Medulla* of Busenbaum (d. 1668), commented upon by Lacroix (d. 1714) and St. Alphonsus (d. 1787), left a profound mark upon moral theology and, through St. Alphonsus and J. P. Gury (d. 1866), exercised its influence up to the beginning of the 20th century.

20th Century. Today, the adversaries of casuistry no longer, as they did in Pascal's day, accuse it of laxism but reproach it rather for turning toward rigorism. Thus, certain partisans of situational morality would like to free moral theology from the subtleties and sophisms of the casuistic method. According to them the proper field of casuistry is law. When it is brought into morality, it brings with it an atmosphere that is too juridical. In short, the very legitimacy of this method for morality is called into question by these authors.

Conclusion. The renewal that moral theology has experienced since World War II has brought casuistry back to its just place by emphasizing its value and utility, and by indicating its dangers and its limitations. When it is well used, casuistry remains indispensable; it is an art that demands flexibility and awareness of the concrete. But, while keeping to its method and its proper purposes, it must remain connected to the more elevated parts of moral theology. Conscious of its own limitations, it must allow itself to be complemented by prudence, not forgetting the other aids at the disposal of a Christian for finding the correct solution of his doubts of conscience, prayer, and docility to the inspirations of the Holy Spirit.

Bibliography: E. Hamel, "Valeur et limites de la casuistique," *Sciences ecclésiastiques* 11 (1959) 147–173. M. Pribilla, "Klugheit und Kasuistik," StimZeit 133 (1938) 205–216. J. Vialatoux, "Réflexions sur les idées de casuistique et de loi morale," *Mémorial J. Chaine,* ed. Faculté Catholique de Théologie (Lyon 1950). R. Egenter, "Kasuistik als christliche Situationsethik," MünchThZ 1 (1950) 54–65. M. Reding, "Situationsethik, Kasuistik und Ethos der Nachfolge," *Gloria Dei* 6 (1951) 290–292. Y. Congar, "Die Kasuistik des heiligen Paulus," *Verkündigung und Glaube: Festgabe für Franz X. Arnold,* ed. T. Filthaut and J. A. Jungmann (Freiburg 1958). R. M. Wenley, Hastings ERE 3:239–247. K. Goldammer et al., RGG³ 3:1166–71. R. Brouillard, *Catholicisme* 2:630–637. I. Tarocchi, EncCatt 3:981–983. F. Böckle, LexThK² 6:18–20.

[E. HAMEL]

CATACOMBS

Ancient Christian subterranean cemeteries found in Naples, Syracuse, Malta, Tunisia, and various parts of the Roman Empire, but particularly in the environs of Rome. The name comes from the accidental location of the cemetery of Callistus on the Via Appia near the circus of Maximus and the basilica of St. Sebastian in a depression (κατὰ κύμβας, near the low place) between two hills. The term was used to locate the cemetery of Callistus in the 3d century. As this was the only underground cemetery known during the Middle Ages, upon the rediscovery of the early Christian cemeteries in the 16th century the word catacomb was applied generally to all such subterranean burial places.

Christian Cemeteries. The primitive Christians interred their dead in the pagan burial places. Gradually, however, they obtained control of sections of these burial sites that they called cemeteries (κοιμητήρια, place of rest) as an indication of their belief in a final resurrection. Roman law forbade burial within populated areas; hence cemeteries were located outside the city walls, particularly alongside the main or consular roads. Roman families constructed mausoleums and funeral monuments in rows on the large thoroughfares, where they could be seen by passersby and could be used for memorial services and banquets. The ashes of infants, slaves, freedmen, clients, and relatives of a family were buried in these usually commodious structures; the poorer classes, particularly when inhumation became more general (during the 1st century A.D.), used obscure parts of the terrain for simple graves in the cemetery areas, and there were also various types of funeral monuments placed at ground level.

Christian Burial. Since the Christians were opposed to cremation, under the influence of Jewish practice and in imitation of the burial of Christ, they apparently used the simplest types of ground burial at first. Information revealed by the excavations of the tomb of St. Peter in the *Vatican and details regarding the care for the remains of the martyr *Polycarp of Smyrna (d. *c.* 156) indicate that during the 2d and early 3d centuries special attention was paid to preserving the identity of Christian martyr graves, and memorial ceremonies were held on occasion in the cemeteries in keeping with the customs of Roman society. During this period likewise, Christians were buried in the large vaults of the nobler families to which they were attached by relationship or service.

The earliest catacombs as such date from the 3d century; they appear to be extensions of the family-type mausoleum that could no longer accommodate new burials, although they were continually in process of reuse from generation to generation. Despite the fact that the Christian religion was not officially tolerated in the Roman Empire, the family ownership of burial sites was not generally challenged, and cemeteries were protected by law as *loca religiosa,* or religious places. Evidently a number of Christian family-owned sites were joined together, and as space on the ground level became inadequate, caves were dug out beneath the soil after the fashion of the Etruscan burial sites. These were linked together eventually by networks of passages, a yard or so wide, and about 6 feet in height; and graves (called *loculi*) were dug in the tufa walls, between 1½ and 2 feet high and 4 to 5 feet in length, one on top of the other. Some were wide enough to hold two or three bodies (*locus bisomus, trisomus*). These individual graves were closed with rectangular slabs of slate, marble, chalk, or earthenware. The name of the defunct person was chiseled or scratched on this cover, frequently with the age, date of death, and a symbol or blessing formula. Sometimes a representation of the deceased in a gold glass, coin, ivory, or metal figure was affixed. Often small vessels with perfume or oil lamps were found in or near these graves, but the majority lack identification and appear to be the burial places of the unknown or of abandoned children.

The nature of the soil in the Roman countryside made this type of cemetery possible, since the low hills are composed of tufa, a soft clay that on drying becomes hard as stone. The digging was done by *fossores,* a corporation of grave diggers who apparently plotted the direction of their excavations and dug 2, 3, or 4 levels, going further into the earth for expansion, but respected the property rights of surrounding owners and understood basic geological principles for safety. In the 3d century Christian places of burial came under the ownership of the local community. The cemetery of Callistus on the Via Appia had been confided to the charge of the Deacon Callistus (later pope) by Pope *Zephyrinus (199–217); and under Pope *Fabian (236–250) the seven (regionary) deacons had control of the cemeteries attached to the churches of their regions. In the 4th century, they came under the charge of the

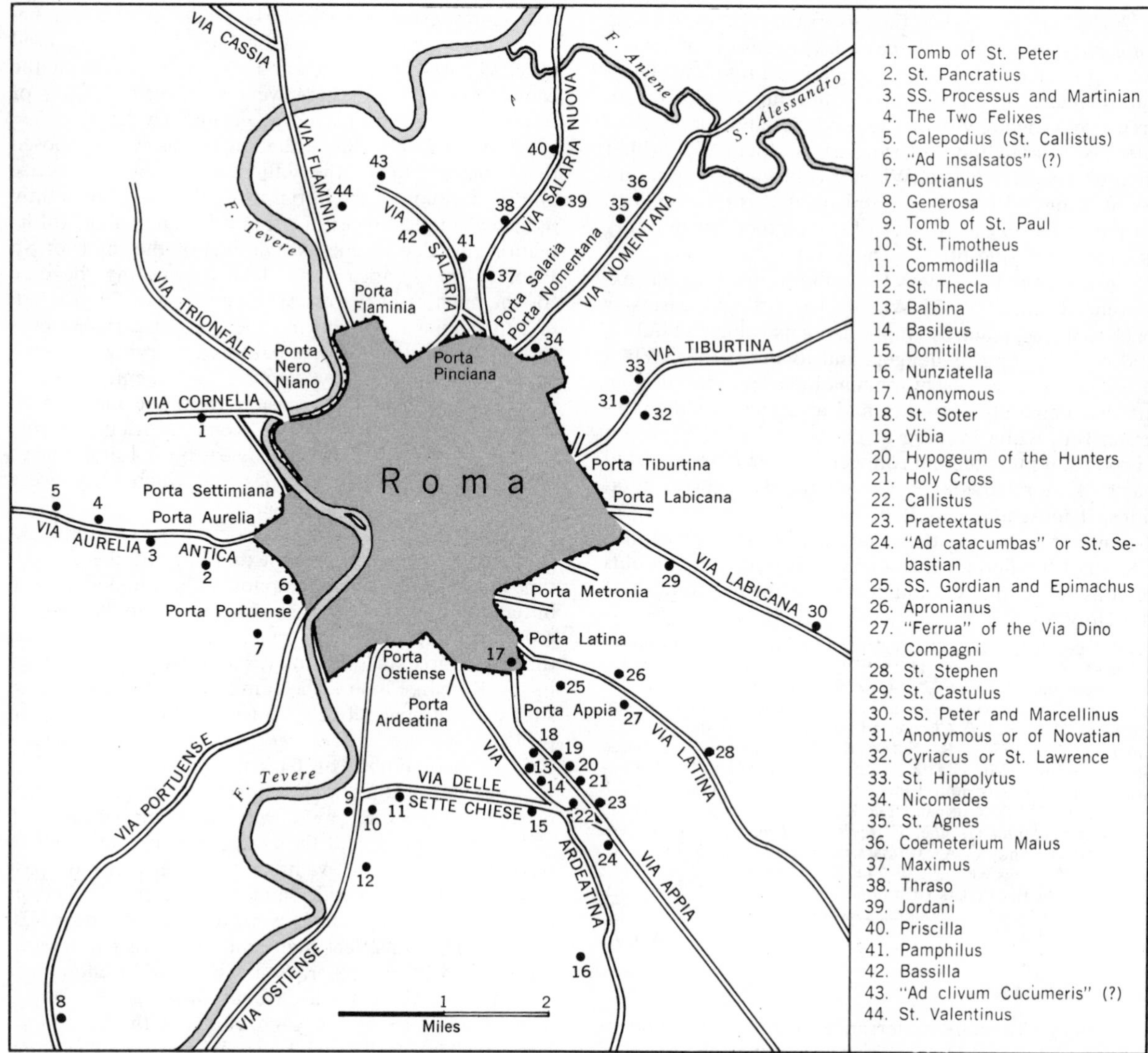

Fig. 1. Principal Christian cemeteries in Rome.

priests attached to the title churches, each of which had its own cemetery along the nearest consular road outside the city.

There is no evidence for the construction or use of the catacombs as refuges during the periods of persecution. It was only in the 4th century, when the cult of martyrs became general, that they were used for memorial services. Within the complex of the net of corridors constituting the catacombs, rectangular or round rooms were also constructed and used for burial; bodies were buried in the walls, or in sarcophagi, sometimes placed in a recess or niche with an arched top called an *arcosolium*. The walls of these rooms, called *triclia,* as in the cemetery beneath the basilica of St. *Sebastian, were decorated at first with figured motifs similar to pagan ornamentation, then gradually with specifically Christian symbols. Only toward the middle of the 3d century is there evidence of the introduction of definitely Christian scenes. The figures used are borrowed from contemporary art.

In the 4th century both on the walls of the catacombs and on the sides of the sarcophagi, representations of the Good Shepherd, the Orans, the Zodiac, Daniel, Noe, Jona, catechetical and baptismal scenes appear (*see* SYMBOLISM, EARLY CHRISTIAN). Scenes from the Old and New Testaments, particularly the Eucharistic banquet, become somewhat common; and after the 4th century and the construction of the basilicas, Christ is depicted among the Apostles and the Christian faithful (*see* ART, EARLY CHRISTIAN).

In estimating the place and extent of use of the catacombs by the early Christians, it must be remembered that, as they disappeared from sight from the 9th to the 16th century, and despite the removal of many of the remains authorized by the 9th-century popes, they were preserved almost intact, while the ground and open air level cemeteries were destroyed by the ravages of time. It would seem that before the Constantinian Peace of the Church (313) the catacombs were considered an integral part of the Christian cemetery. They were confiscated during the Valerian (258) and Diocletian (303) persecutions, but they were later restored to Christian control (specifically, in 260 and 311, respectively).

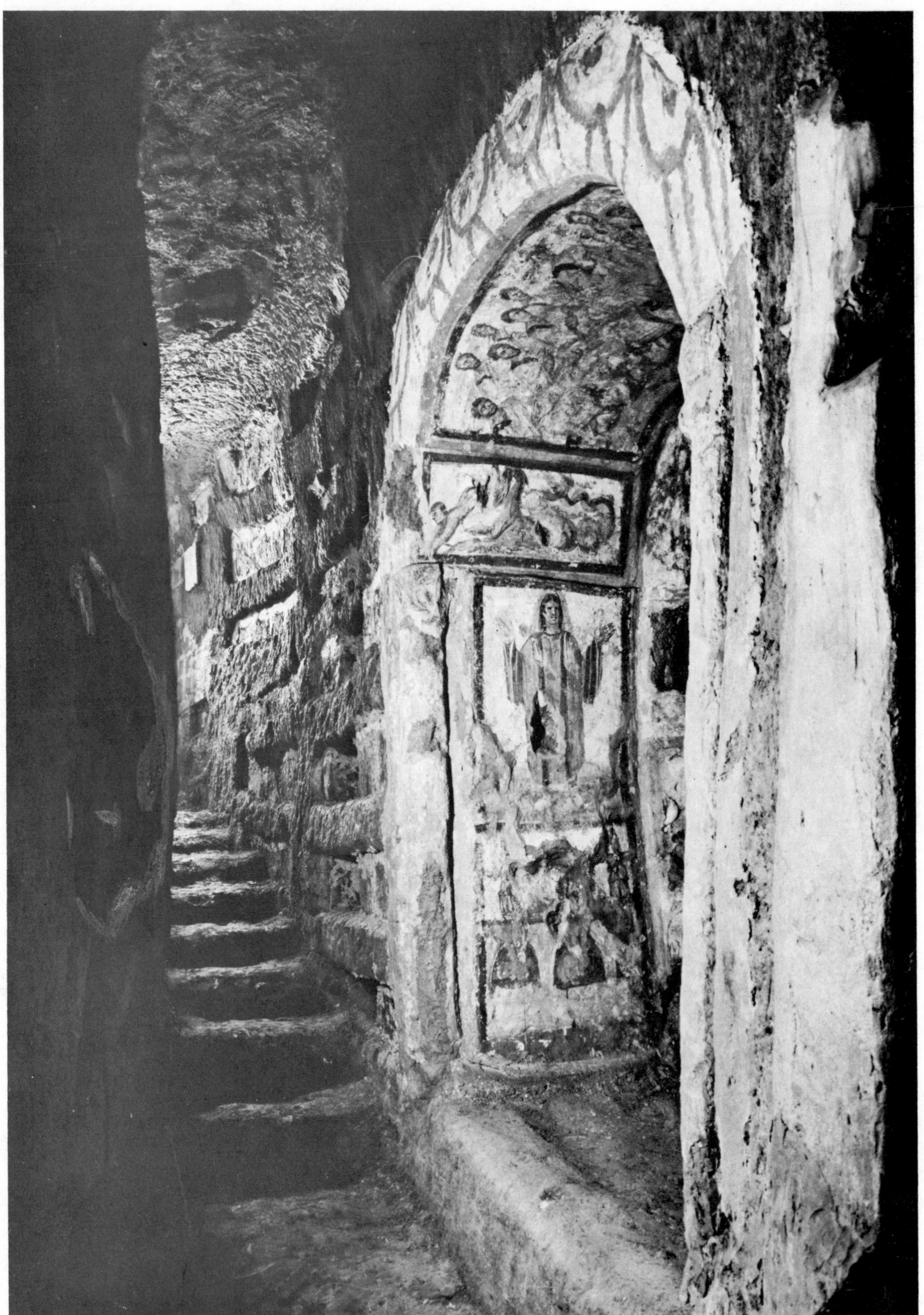

Fig. 2. Catacomb of the Giordani, Rome. The arcosolium tomb on the right is decorated with late 3d- and early 4th-century paintings of Christ and the Apostles, Jona, an orans figure, and the three youths in the furnace.

Fig. 3. Catacombs: (a) Arcosolium tomb in the catacomb of the Giordani, with paintings of the Raising of Lazarus and the Good Shepherd. (b) Entrances to two tombs in the "ad catacumbas" under the basilica of St. Sebastian. (c) Crypt of the Popes in the catacomb of St. Callistus. The memorial inscription dates from the 4th century.

Rediscovery. The catacombs were rediscovered in the 16th century by Renaissance humanists whose primary aim was a search for ancient inscriptions and artifacts. Antonio Bosio described his findings in his *Roma sotterranea.* His immediate successors pillaged the catacombs for works of art and the relics of the martyrs, frequently using false criteria in their attempts to utilize their discoveries for apologetic purposes.

In the 19th century the Jesuit G. *Marchi (1795–1860) and G. B. de *Rossi (1822–94) undertook a scientific study of the Roman catacombs, using for guidance evidence furnished by the calendars, martyrologies, legends, liturgical texts, and patristic writings, as well as the *itineraries of pilgrims from the Byzantine and Carolingian ages and sylloges or collections of inscriptions. Thus they were able to identify and give chronological and cultic placement to the main factors of early Christian life to which the catacombs witness. This work of discovery and identification is still being pursued.

The Principal Roman Catacombs. The excavations beneath St. Peter's Basilica in the Vatican revealed a number of burial sites, mainly rows of mausoleums along the roads that bifurcated the original hill. These had been originally pagan monuments that were gradually utilized by the Christians; and from the 3d century, Christian symbols and decorations appear in some of the tombs. Peter had apparently been buried in a simple grave in a clear space that had other, mainly primitive-type, graves; and in the late 2d century a small monument was erected in a wall that passed over the Petrine grave. The 2d- and early 3d-century popes seem to have been buried in the vicinity of Peter's grave. There is no indication of catacomb construction in this area; but the information supplied by these discoveries proved most useful in interpreting findings in other Christian cemeteries and catacombs.

On the Via Appia there were three cemeteries, each with its catacombs: Callistus, with its crypt of 3d-century popes and St. Cecilia; Praetextatus, near the Roman Jewish catacombs and the syncretist hypogeums; and the *Ad Catacumbas* under the basilica of St. Sebastian. On the Via Ostiensis were the tombs of St. Paul and St. Timothy; and the cemeteries of Commodilla and of St. Thecla. The cemetery *Ad Duas Lauras* on the Via Labicana has preserved some of the better 3d- and 4th-century Christian art, including agape banquet scenes and depictions of New Testament incidents from the Constantinian age.

On the Via Tiburtina were the cemetery of Cyriacus, where St. *Lawrence had been buried; the cemetery of *Hippolytus; and an anonymous cemetery, discovered in 1927 almost intact, with the tomb of the martyr Novatian. The Via Nomentana had the cemetery of SS. Alexander, Eventius, and Theodulus at the 10th milestone. It contained a *memoria* over which was built a basilica honoring these martyrs. It was the site likewise of the cemetery and basilica of St. *Agnes, of the cemetery of St. Nicomedes, of the *Coemeterium maius* with the picture of four saints, and an *arcosolium* in which a cathedra and benches had been carved out of tufa.

On the Via Salaria were the catacombs of Priscilla and of the Giordani; of Maximus and Felicitas; and of Traso or St. Saturninus. The Via Aurelia contained the cemeteries of St. Pancratius, SS. Processus and Martinian, and Calepodius, where St. Callistus was buried. The last was discovered in 1960 and contains paintings that represent the martyrdom of the saint. A similar new discovery was made at the conjunction of the Via Salaria with the modern Via Dino Compagni. Its contents were explored by A. Ferrua.

The cemetery of Pamphilus was discovered on the Via Salaria Vetus in 1920. One of the oldest catacombs is that of Domitilla on the Via Ardeatina, with its reminiscences of the ancient Roman family of the Flavii. The names given these catacombs reflect the earliest owners of the property, the title churches or locations in which they were found, or the names of martyrs actually or allegedly buried in them.

See also ARCHEOLOGY, III (CHRISTIAN); ART, EARLY CHRISTIAN.

Bibliography: P. TESTINI, *Archeologia cristiana* (Rome 1958). A. BOSIO, *Roma sotterranea,* ed. G. SEVERANO (Rome 1632). G. MARCHI, *Monumenti delle arti cristiane primitive . . .,* v.1 *Architettura cimiteriale* (Rome 1844–47). N. MAURICE-DENIS and R. BOULET, *Catholicisme* 2:637–643. H. LECLERCQ, DACL 2:2376–2512. P. STYGER, *Die römischen Katakomben* (Berlin 1933). J. KOLLWITZ, ReallexAntChr 1:645–646. L. HERTLING and E. KIRSCHBAUM, *The Roman Catacombs and Their Martyrs,* tr. M. J. COSTELLOE (2d ed. London 1960). A. FERRUA, *Le pitture della nuova catacomba di Via Latina* (Rome 1960). U. FASOLA, LexThK[2] 6:20–24. F. DEVISSCHER, "Le Régime juridique des plus anciens cimetières chrétiens à Rome," AnalBoll 69 (1951) 39–54. **Illustration credits:** Fig. 2, Leonard Von Matt. Fig. 3*a* and 3*c*, Pontificia Commissione di Archeologia Sacra. Fig. 3*b*, Alinari-Art Reference Bureau.

[F. X. MURPHY]

CATAFALQUE (from the Italian *catafalco,* derivation of which is uncertain), a wooden or steel structure used particularly for the absolution after *Requiem Masses. It designates (1) a framework supporting the coffin at funerals when the corpse is physically present; (2) more currently, the structure used to simu-

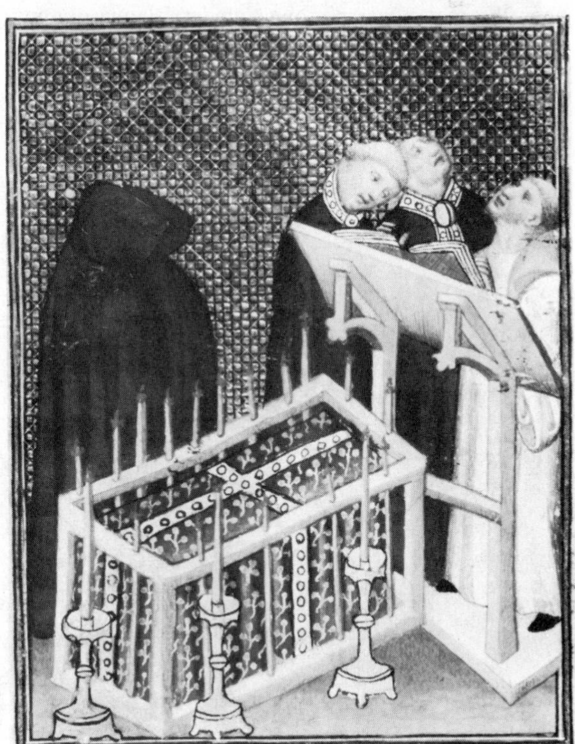

Catafalque in illumination, Book of Hours, Paris, c. 1410.

late the presence of a corpse; a practice of questionable meaningfulness. Originally the catafalque was nothing but the bier or support for the corpse. The use of a catafalque to represent an absent body seems to have originated later with the introduction of absolutions for the dead. Gradually the structure was increased in size, and frequently it was covered with a baldachin so that it came to assume monumental proportions when used for persons of high rank. In some countries the size of the catafalque is still a symbol of rank and wealth. The place for the catafalque is before the altar outside the sanctuary. It is covered with a black cloth or pall (except for little children for whom white is used), and surrounded by candles. A black cloth may take the place of the catafalque.

Bibliography: F. Oppenheim, EncCatt 3:1061–62. P. Bayant, "Le Mobilier d'Église," *Liturgia,* ed. R. Aigrain (Paris 1930) 256–257. J. B. O'Connell, *Church Building and Furnishing* (Notre Dame, Ind. 1955) 239–242. G. Malherbe, "Le Castrum Doloris ou catafalque des services funèbres" *Paroisse et Liturgie* 33 (1951) 116–121. J. B. O'Connell, *The Celebration of Mass* (new ed. Milwaukee 1956) 634–636. **Illustration credit:** Courtesy of the Walters Art Gallery, Baltimore, Md.

[A. CORNIDES]

CATALAN ART

Catalonia, the region of Spain northeast of the Ebro, produced a wealth of Romanesque fresco painting that has escaped destruction through the centuries. At the beginning of the 20th century Catalan scholars discovered many of the frescoes in isolated churches and chapels in valleys of the Pyrenees and in the mountainous and hilly regions of the provinces of Gerona, Lérida, and Barcelona. Many were carefully transferred and installed in the Museum of Catalan Art in Barcelona (also in museums of Vich and Solsona), where they have been available for study since 1934. These frescoes were executed in the 11th, 12th, and 13th centuries when the region was no longer under Islamic domination. Romanesque monuments of other areas of Europe suffered more from changes of taste and destruction through historical events and time, while those of the outlying areas of Catalonia were fortunately preserved.

The Catalan Romanesque frescoes reflect a style and a tradition that is neither primitive nor wholly indigenous; the sources of this tradition are not clearly established, although it seems certain that a pre-Romanesque local tradition of wall painting and book illumination served in its formation. Italian immigrants, perhaps Lombard masters, and certainly Mozarabic art were contributing factors. The churches that contained the murals, with the exception of a few larger structures, were single nave, basilica-type structures with one or two aisles without a transept and terminating with either one or three semicircular apses. They were built of blocks of rough stone that might be slightly hewn to achieve a more even surface.

The rapidity with which architecture, sculpture, and painting spread throughout western Europe is explained partly by the growth of monasticism during the Romanesque period. The monastic life provided the means for illumination, which enhanced the transcription of numerous manuscripts. These illuminations not only reflected architectural principles, such as the column and arch, but also had designs that, in turn, later inspired architecture. A notable example was the *Commentary on the Book of Revelation* written by the monk from the monastery of Valcavado in Léon, *Beatus of Liébana, in the latter part of the 8th century; illuminated copies such as the one for Abbot Gregory of Saint-Sever (Bibl. Nat. lat. 8878) influenced Romanesque sculptors in France and probably had a similar influence in Spain.

The copying of the Beatus manuscripts continued in the 10th and 11th centuries along with other Spanish illumination, such as the Bibles of 920 (cathedral, Léon) and of 960 (the church of San Isidoro, Léon). Such artistic work had its influence on the structure and

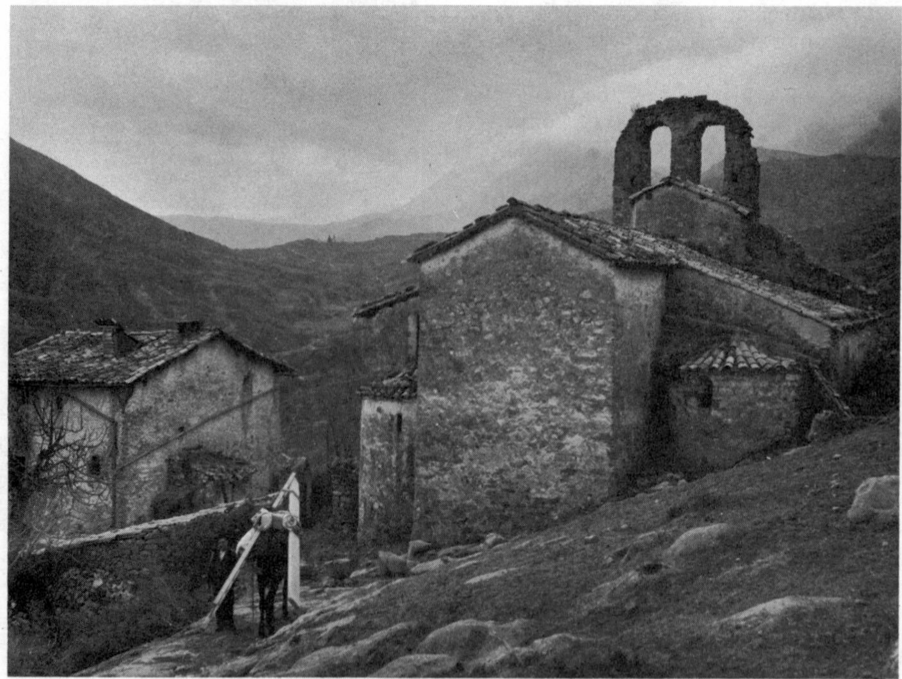

Fig. 1. The church of San Quirce de Pedret, Catalonia, Spain, built in the 10th century.

Fig. 2. Catalan art: (a) Lion of St. Mark and an angel, detail of the fresco from the apse of San Clemente de Tahull, 1123. (b) Altar frontal of Christ and the Twelve Apostles, from La Seo de Urgel, 12th century.

Fig. 3. The frescoes from the apse of Santa María de Tahull, as reconstructed in the Museum of Catalan Art.

themes of church murals and altar frontals. Cupolas, apses, walls, and sometimes columns were covered with scenes and figures, at first according to Byzantine rule, then under influences from northern Italy, and later with varying degrees of individual expression.

The mural art of Catalonia, even in the simplest examples, was monumental, severe, and grandiose in form, aesthetic and religious in idea. Sacred character is stressed through position on the walls. The principal place, center of the main apse, was reserved for Christ the Pantocrator, or Judge (referred to also as Christ in Majesty), whose severe image appears seated on an arc of a great mandorla, with feet resting on the sphere of the world, holding the Sacred Book in one hand and raising the other hand in the sign of blessing. The principal apse figure was sometimes the Theotokos, God-bearer, or Mother of God. In both cases the central figure is surrounded by the symbols of the four Evangelists. Below the concha, on the cylindrical walls, appear complementary iconographic elements such as the Virgin, Apostles, saints, and various New Testament scenes, constituting a rather fixed range of subjects.
San Quirce de Pedret, perhaps its oldest church, is Mozarabic. San Quirce was built in the 10th century and twice renovated. The representation of the Wise and the Foolish Virgins, as well as the theme of the Four Horsemen of the Apocalypse, is unusual iconography not followed in subsequent Catalan murals.

In both Santa María de Tahull and Santa María de Esterri de Aneu the apse contains the Virgin and Christ Child, surrounded by the Magi bringing gifts. In the latter church there is also much variation in the representation on the cylindrical wall: the Old Testament theme from Isaia, wheels of fire, seraphim holding live coals with tongs and purifying the lips of Isaia.

One of the most impressive of Spanish Romanesque paintings is the mural in San Clemente de Tahull (1123). Here the commanding gaze of the Pantocrator is portrayed with vitality and severity; still this solemn rigidity and absolute frontality are enhanced with ornamental line work, wholly Byzantine in style. Within the apse are two angels, symbolizing Matthew and John; below them are two corresponding pairs of circular discs with each couplet containing the bust of an angel in one disc holding on to its corresponding symbol in the other; thus in rather unusual manner are Mark and Luke portrayed. All four Evangelist figures have more moving attitudes than the Judge. In the cylindrical wall the Virgin and five Apostles stand motionless like the severe Judge. The concept of the heavenly New Jerusalem resting on the Apostles with the Virgin is dominant. There is no attempt at a plastic articulation of figures; a superb unity is achieved through planar drawing that exhibits extraordinary understanding of the conventions then followed. The frescoes gather force in the remarkable vibrant quality of coloring that was employed symbolically.

In Santa María at Tarrasa, near Barcelona, the theme of the fresco is that of the martyrdom of St. Thomas Becket (1170). Lafuente-Ferrari notes that the narrative character of the painting is comparable to that of manuscripts of the 10th century.

Fig. 4. "The Adoration of the Lamb," full-page miniature in a manuscript of Beatus of Liébana, A.D. 926 (Morgan MS 644, fol. 87r), the oldest dated manuscript of the 30 or so extant illuminated manuscripts of the work.

Fig. 5. Christ Pantocrator, detail of the frescoes from the apse of the church of San Clemente de Tahull, 1123.

The Spanish frontal (panel painting and stucco relief on front and ends of altar table) affords an opportunity for further study of Catalan art. After liturgical custom required the priest to be in front of the altar, the retable was instituted and the frontal fell into disuse. Since many of these Spanish frontals have been preserved, it can be noted that the iconography of the apse was usually duplicated on the frontal. One example is that of La Seo de Urgel, which shows the traditional iconography of Christ with the 12 Apostles; it has a quality of enamel, which is rarely found in Spanish frontals.

In later work, the art of both apse and frontal became more realistic with less stylization of faces. With the introduction of the retable, conflicts arose between the retable painters and the old fresco workers. Iconography changed, themes multiplied, and simplicity was lost. A new surge of Italo-Byzantine influence resulted in the loss of that monumental quality which had been so prevalent in the Catalan mural.

See also ROMANESQUE ART; MANUSCRIPT ILLUMINATION.

Bibliography: W. W. S. COOK and J. GUDIOL RICART, *Ars Hispaniae,* v.6 (Madrid 1950) 21–105, 187–246. A. GRABAR and C. NORDENFALK, *Early Medieval Painting* (New York 1957) 161–175; *Romanesque Painting* (New York 1958) 66–85. O. F. L. HAGEN, *Patterns and Principles of Spanish Art* (Madison 1943) 85–130. F. JIMÉNEZ PLACER, *Historia del arte español,* 2 v. (Barcelona 1955) 1:189–220. E. LAFUENTE FERRARI, *Breve historia de la pintura española* (4th ed. Madrid 1953) 33–60. **Illustration credits:** Fig. 1, MAS, Barcelona. Figs. 2, 3, and 5, Museo de Arte Cataluña, Barcelona. Fig. 4, The Pierpont Morgan Library, New York City.

[A. L. MARTIN]

CATALAN LITERATURE

Catalan, a Romance language, is spoken by or familiar to approximately 6 million inhabitants in the areas that include the ancient principality of Catalonia, the Balearic Islands, the ancient kingdom of Valencia, the principality of Andorra, Roussillon and other districts in France, and the city of Alghero in the Island of Sardinia. Catalan originated between the 6th and 9th centuries, a period when late Latin was becoming fragmented into the Romance languages. It was oriented toward the language of southern Gaul, which decisively influenced its internal structure. Catalan is a bridge-language between the Ibero-Romantic and the Gallo-Romantic; most of its components, however, are of Gallo-Romantic form. It is therefore not strange that during the 11th, 12th, and 13th centuries elegant Catalan poetry was associated with the art of the *troubadours. However, during the 13th to the 15th centuries, when Catalonia achieved a role of prime importance in medieval Mediterranean culture, a complete national literature arose that extended beyond the frontiers of Catalonia.

Raymond *Lull is greatly representative of this period of Catalan literature and is one of the most important figures in medieval Christian culture. He alone created a whole literature, from works of mysticism, such as *Llibre de contemplació* (1282), to the novel *Blanquerna* (*c.* 1295), which contains the 365 lyric verses of the famous *Llibre d'Amic i Amat.* Contemporaneous with Lull there was a rich flowering of historiography, eminently exemplified by four great chronicles: those of Jaume I, Bernat Desclot, Ramon Muntaner, and Pere III el Cerimoniós. In addition to their extraordinary historical importance, these works constitute a decisive stage between the *Chansons de geste* (whose subjects the chronicles put into prose and supplemented) and the narrative prose of novelistic and chivalric character. At any rate, the folk epic was the immediate antecedent for the first three chronicles, at least in some of their parts. The autobiographical chronicle of Jaume I was probably redacted in two stages, in 1244 and 1274. Desclot's work refers principally to the reign of Pere II el Gran; it is objective and contains much firsthand information as recorded by a courtier; it ends about 1288. Muntaner, redactor of the third chronicle, is a clearly identified historical personality; he wrote a *llibre,* as he called it, of memories in which he emphasizes the account of a Catalan expedition to the Orient in which he played a leading role. The fourth chronicle is also autobiographical, but it belongs to a mature period of Catalan letters; it is parallel to the work of Lull and coeval with the first works in Renaissance style and with numerous versions of classical Latin authors.

Bernat Metge, court secretary, incarnates this new spirit (e.g., in *Lo Somni,* 1396), which introduced the golden age in Catalan literature. The center of this literary production shifted from Barcelona (although Lull was from Majorca) to Valencia with such poets as Jordi de Sant Jordi (*c.* 1395–*c.* 1440), Joan Roís de Corella (1430–1500), and especially Ausiàs March (1397–1459); there was also an abundant narrative production. Of significance are the work of the satirist Jaume Roig (*c.* 1405–*c.* 1478), the novel *Curial e*

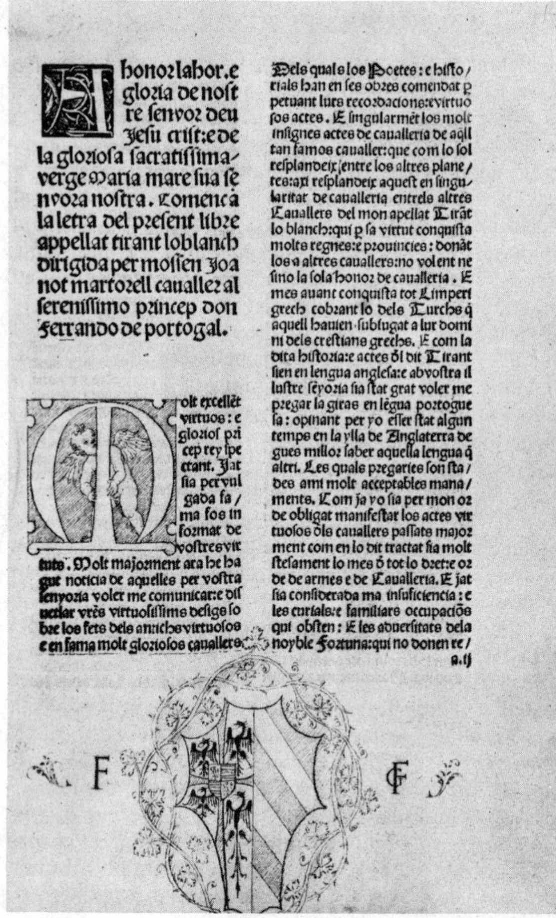

A honor labor. e
gloria de nost
re senyor deu
Jesu crist: e de
la gloriosa sacratissima
verge Maria mare sua se
nyora nostra. Comença
la letra del present libre
appellat tirant lo blanch
dirigida per mossen Joa
not martorell caualler al
serenissimo princep don
Ferrando de portogal.

Molt excellent
virtuos: e
glorios pri
cep rey spe
ctant. Jat
sia per vul
gada fa
ma fos in
format de
vostres vir
tuts. Molt majorment ara he ha
gut noticia de aquelles per vostra
senyoria voler me comunicar: e dis
uetlar vres virtuosissims desigs so
bre los fets dels antichs virtuosos
e en fama molt gloriosos cauallers.

Dels quals los Poetes: e histo
rials han en ses obres comendat p
petuant lurs recordacions: e virtuo
sos actes. E singularmet los molt
insignes actes de cauallería de aqll
tan famos caualler: que com lo sol
resplandeix entre los altres plane
tes: axi resplandeix aquest en singu
laritat de cauallería entre los altres
Cauallers del mon apellat Tirat
lo blanch: qui p sa virtut conquista
molts regnes: e prouincies: donat
los a altres cauallers: no volent ne
sino la sola honor de cauallería. E
mes auant conquista tot L'imperi
grech cobrant lo dels Turchs q
aquell hauien sublugat a lur domi
ni dels crestians grechs. E com la
dita historia: e actes d'l dit Tirant
sien en lengua anglesa: e a vostra il
lustre senyoria sia stat grat voler me
pregar la giras en legua portogue
sa: opinant per yo esser stat algun
temps en la ylla de Anglaterra de
gues millor saber aquella lengua q
altri. Les quals pregaries son sta
des a mi molt acceptables mana
ments. Com ja yo sia per mon or
de obligat manifestar los actes vir
tuosos d'ls cauallers passats major
ment com en lo dit tractat sia molt
stesament lo mes d' tot lo dret: e or
de de armes e de Cauallería. E jat
sia considerada ma insuficiencia: e
les curials: e familiars occupacios
qui obsten: E les aduersitats de la
noyble Fortuna: qui no donen re
a.ij

F F

The opening text page of Joanot Martorell's Catalan novel "Tirant lo Blanch" (1st ed., Valencia 1490).

Güelfa; and the great novel of Joanot Martorell, *Tirant lo Blanch* (1490), a courtly adventure.

But a rude interruption occurred with Catalonia's loss of political autonomy (1714). The break was so complete that no figure comparable to the earlier writers appeared until the 19th century, when, with the diffusion of liberal and Romantic ideas and the political decline of Spain, interest in Catalan was revived, the medieval festival of the Jocs Florals (popular literary contests) was restored, and a political movement established an autonomous Catalonia (1931–39), which was again suppressed after the Spanish Civil War. This movement toward independence, called the Renaixença, began with the poet Jacint Verdaguer (1845–1902), author of *L'Atlàntida y Canigó,* and with the dramatist Angel Guimerà (1845–1924) and reached an apex in the work of Joan Maragall (1860–1911), poet, essayist, and cofounder of the Institut d'Estudis Catalans. This scientific body, together with the work of Pompeu Fabra (1868–1948), Carles Riba (1893–1959), and other leading writers, has fixed the norms of the current literary language. In spite of restrictions (since 1939) that make the normal use of Catalan in public life impossible, there is nonetheless a literature that is renewed, diverse, and vigorous.

Bibliography: A. M. BADIA MARGARIT, *Llengua i cultura als Països Catalans* (Barcelona 1954). J. MOLAS, *Literatura catalana antiga* (Barcelona 1961–) v.3 *El segle XV* (1963). J. RUBIÓ BALAGUER, *La cultura catalana del Renaixement a la Decadència* (Barcelona 1964). M. DE RIQUER, *Història de la literatura catalana* (Barcelona 1964–), 5 v. planned, the modern period ed. A. COMAS. R. TASIS I MARCA and J. TRIADÚ, eds. *La poesia catalana,* 2 v. (Barcelona 1949–51). J. TRIADÚ, comp., *Anthology of Catalan Lyric Poetry,* ed. J. GILI (Berkeley 1953), contains a fine survey of the literature.

The works of Jaume I, Desclot, Muntaner, Bernat Metge, Ausiàs March, and Fabra are pub. by Barcino in Barcelona; those of Martorell, Verdaguer, and Guimerà, by Biblioteca Selecta, Barcelona; the *Obres* of Maragall, by Edimar, Barcelona; and the poetry of Jordi de Sant Jordi, by the Universidad de Granada.
Illustration credit: Library of the Hispanic Society of America, New York.

[J. TRIADÚ]

CATALDINO, JOSÉ, Jesuit missionary; b. Fabriano, Italy, April 1571; d. Reduction of San Ignacio Miní, Paraguay, June 10, 1653. He was already a priest when he entered the Society of Jesus on March 1, 1602. On April 30, 1604, he left Spain for Peru in the expedition of Father Diego de Torres; they arrived in Lima on Nov. 22, 1604. Cataldino was immediately appointed to the mission of Tucumán and Paraguay, arriving in Asunción for the first time on Dec. 13, 1605. In 1609, he and Father Mascetta, also an Italian, began their evangelical work in the large area of Guairá. Cataldino's years among these tribes were long and painful. After he founded the Reductions of San Ignacio Miní and Loreto, Cataldino was named superior of all the Paraguayan missions. This appointment induced him to work harder, and he created the new Reductions of San Pablo, San José, and Encarnación. After 11 years in this position, he was in charge of the Indians at Villarica, and subsequently worked for the conversion of the natives of Uruguay. (*See* REDUCTIONS OF PARAGUAY.)

Bibliography: F. XARQUE, *Vida apostólica del ven. p. Josef Cataldino* (Zaragoza 1664). P. PASTELLS, ed., *Historia de la Compañia de Jesús en la provincia del Paraguay,* v.1–2 (Madrid 1912–15).

[H. STORNI]

CATALDO, JOSEPH MARY, missionary; b. Terracina, Italy, March 17, 1837; d. Pendleton, Ore., April 9, 1928. He was the son of Antonio and Sebastiana (Borusso) Cataldo. He became a Jesuit novice on

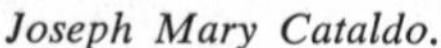

Joseph Mary Cataldo.

Dec. 23, 1852, and was ordained on Sept. 8, 1862, in Liège, Belgium. Two days later he departed for the U.S., where he studied and taught at Santa Clara College, Calif., until 1865. From 1865 to 1877 he worked among

Old Catholic mission church near Cataldo, Idaho, built in 1851 and served for many years by Fr. Joseph Maria Cataldo. It is the oldest mission in the Northwest.

the Nez Percé, Coeur d'Alène, and Spokane Indians, whose languages he mastered. Before his death he had learned eight Indian tongues and two Alaskan languages in addition to French and English.

Appointed superior of the Jesuit Rocky Mountain Mission in 1877, Cataldo sent missionaries to the Gros Ventres, Crow, Blackfoot, Assiniboine, and Arapaho tribes in Montana; to the Cheyenne in Wyoming; the Okanogan in Washington; the Umatilla in Oregon; and the Alaskan Eskimos. He founded Gonzaga College, Spokane, Wash. (1883), and approved the establishment of Immaculate Conception College, Seattle, Wash. (1892). After he was replaced as superior in 1893, he worked with the Indians of Montana, Idaho, Oregon, and Alaska and with the settlers in the Pacific Northwest. His greatest attachment was to the Nez Percé Indians at St. Joseph's Mission, Culdesac, Idaho, for whom he wrote a prayerbook and a life of Christ in the Nez Percé language.

Bibliography: W. N. BISCHOFF, *The Jesuits in Old Oregon* (Caldwell, Idaho 1945). **Illustration credit:** Fig. 1, Montana Historical Society. Fig. 2, Idaho Historical Society.

[W. N. BISCHOFF]

CATALDUS OF RACHAU, ST., bishop and patron of Taranto; b. Ireland, early 7th century; d. Taranto, Italy, *c.* 671 (feast, May 10). Everything known concerning him is based on legends dating from the 12th century. He was born close to the monastery of *Lismore, became a monk there, and then later became bishop of Rachau. On the return from a pilgrimage to the Holy Land he was shipwrecked off the Gulf of Taranto. Supposedly he then became bishop of Taranto, where he was considered a great reformer and builder of churches. He is venerated as a miracle worker in Italy, especially at his see city, where his body was buried in the cathedral, and also at Sens and Auxerre in France.

Bibliography: ActSS May 2 (1863) 568–577. F. UGHELLI, *Italia sacra,* ed. N. COLETI, 10 v. in 9 (2d ed. Venice 1717–22) 9:121. B. MORONE, *Vita e miracoli di S. Cataldo . . .,* 2 pts. (Naples 1779). C. STORNAJOLO, "Crocetta aurea opistografa della cattedrale di Taranto," *Nuovo bollettino di archeologia cristiana* 21 (1915) 83–93. G. BLANDAMURA, *Un cimelio del s. VII esistente nel duomo di Taranto* (Lecce 1917). Kenney 1: 185. F. LANZONI, *Le diocesi d'Italia dalle origini al principio de sec. VII (an. 604),* 2 v. (Faenza 1927) 1:79. A. M. TOMMASINI, *Irish Saints in Italy,* tr. J. F. SCANLAN (London 1937) 401–432. Baudot-Chaussin 5:196. MartRom 183. H. HOHENLEUTNER, Lex ThK[2] 2:978. BHL 1652–55. F. O'BRIAIN, DHGE 11:1490–91. C. TESTORE, EncCatt 3:1064.

[R. E. GEIGER]

CATANIA, ARCHDIOCESE OF (CATANENSIS), archbishopric immediately subject to the Holy See since 1844, in east central *Sicily. In 1963 it had 298 secular and 227 religious priests, 492 men in 30 religious houses, 1,279 women in 108 convents, and 561,000 Catholics; it is 514 square miles in area. The city of Catania, at the foot of Mt. Etna, is the main seaport for east Sicily. It was founded by Greeks *c.* 750 B.C. and taken by Rome in 263 B.C. Under Byzantium from *c.* 550 and raided by Saracens (from 853), to whom it fell in 974, it was taken by Normans (1061), went to Aragon (1282), and followed the fortunes of the kingdom of *Naples.

Early Christian martyrs were SS. *Agatha (probably under Decius), patroness of Catania, and Euplius (under Diocletian). In the 8th-century iconoclast controversy (*see* ICONOCLASM) Catania became a Greek archbishopric under the Patriarchate of *Constantinople. The Saracen conquest destroyed ecclesiastical organization and made most of the population Moslem. Normans restored the diocese (1092), which was put under the Abbey of St. Agatha; in 1183 the see became suffragan to *Monreale. Until 1578 the cathedral chapter was composed of Benedictines. Pope Hormisdas sent St. Fortunatus, Catania's first known bishop, to Constantinople (515); Euthemius sided with *Photius (850); Walter (1207–32) was tutor of *Frederick II and chancellor of the kingdom; Gerard Odone was a theologian, patriarch of Antioch (1342–48), and minister general of the Franciscans. The 11th- to 12th-century cathedral was restored, with most of Catania, after the disastrous earthquake of 1696. The Benedictine Abbey of S. Niccolò, of great influence in Sicily's history, was founded in 1328, moved into the city in 1577, and was suppressed in 1860. The university, modeled after that of Bologna, was founded in 1444.

Bibliography: O. VIOLA, *Saggio di bibliografia storica catanese* (Catania 1902). C. NASELLI, "Saggio di bibliografia benedettina catanese," *Archivio Storico per la Sicilia Orientale* 25 (1929) 324–349. R. PIRRI, *Sicilia sacra,* ed. A. MONGITORE, 2 v. (3d ed. Palermo 1733) 1:513–597. F. LANZONI, *Le diocesi d'Italia,* 2 v. (Faenza 1927) 1:624–629. Gams 944–945. L. T. WHITE, *Latin Monasticism in Norman Sicily* (Cambridge, Mass. 1938). S. LO PRESTI, *Memorie storiche di Catania* (Catania 1961). M. SCADUTO, EncCatt 3:1080–85. R. VAN DOREN, DHGE 11:1492–95. AnnPont (1965) 98, 1415. *Seminaria ecclesiae catholicae* (Vatican City 1963) 797–798.

[F. RAFFAELE]

CATANZARO, ARCHDIOCESE OF (CATACENSIS), metropolitan see since 1927, without suffragans, in south Italy on the Gulf of Squillace. Catanzaro was a Byzantine fortress to which Pope

Calixtus II transferred the See of Tres Tabernae (1121). It was suffragan to *Reggio-Calabria (1121–1927). The regional seminary established in 1914 has, since 1953, served upper Calabria. A college founded under the French by Joachim Murat in 1811 absorbed the private schools run by ecclesiastics and monasteries. The cathedral of the Blessed Virgin and SS. Peter and Paul was rebuilt in neoclassical style in 1665 after an earthquake. The church of St. Dominic has noteworthy paintings (15th–18th century). St. Dominic Church in nearby Taverna is rich in tapestries by Mattia Preti, a native of Taverna. Calixtus II gave Catanzaro the relics of its patron St. Vitalian. In 1962 Catanzaro, occupying 371 square miles, had 47 parishes, 62 secular and 22 religious priests, 24 men in 4 religious houses, 177 women in 26 convents, and 110,800 Catholics.

Bibliography: Gams. Eubel HierCath. G. ISNARDI et al., EncIt 9:430–433. F. RUSSO, EncCatt 3:1085–86. R. VAN DOREN, DHGE 11:1495–97, with list of bishops. AnnPont (1964) 98, 1412.

[G. A. PAPA]

CATECHESIS, I (EARLY CHRISTIAN)

Catechesis, or oral teaching, in the primitive Church signified usually a moral instruction. The word κατηχεῖν is used to signify teaching or instruction in the law of God (Acts 18.25; Rom 2.18; Gal 6.6). It differs from the *kerygma, or announcement of the kingdom of God, and from the *didascalia,* or doctrinal teaching of the homily for the baptized. The practice of catechesis is referred to by the author of the Epistle to the Hebrews (5.12–14; cf. 1 Cor 3.1–3) as feeding children with milk rather than the solid food of justice.

The primitive catechesis as revealed in the Epistles of Paul, Peter, and James in particular seems to have developed in two forms. The first, addressed to converts from Judaism, was based on the Holiness Code of Leviticus (17–19) and followed the lines of the Jerusalem apostolic decree that had prescribed Baptism and abstention from uncleanliness and idolatry (Acts 15.19–21) as essential for entrance into the Church of Christ. This early catechesis emphasized adherence to the Word of God as truth in contrast with idolatry and stressed the requirements of fraternal charity. It contained an instruction on worship and was completed with an exhortation that, as children of light (Lk 16.8), Christians should excel in virtue. There are numerous indications in the NT of the use of catechetical formulas based on Christ's Sermon on the Mount and of lists of vices and virtues (Mt 5.3–11; Lk 6.20–23) that seem to have been formed into groups of texts for teaching. This catechesis was used in preparation for Baptism and was accompanied by exorcisms and the scrutiny of sponsors as well as fasting.

With the expansion of the Church to Syria, Asia Minor, and Greece, a different emphasis appeared, directed toward the Hellenistic proselytes and converts from paganism. While the basic abstentions were inculcated, further moral instruction based on Jewish teaching in the Psalms and Proverbs was introduced along with catalogues of virtues that were common to both the Hellenistic (Aristotle, *Eth. Nic.* 2.7) and Jewish ethical codes (Deuteronomy ch. 30). Both the *Didache and the Letter of *Barnabas supply examples of the primitive catechesis in the guise of the two ways, of life and of death (Did.), or of light and darkness (Bar.), and were based on Jewish synagogue practice. The Didache proclaimed the law of the love of God and of neighbor taken by Christ from the Old Testament (Dt 6.5; Lv 19.18) and the golden rule (Did. 1.2). It described the virtues (1.3–4.14) and vices (5–6.3) that characterize respectively life and death by way of preparation for Baptism (7), and described participation in the Eucharist (9.1–5).

The Letter of Barnabas inculcated the virtues of wisdom, prudence, understanding, and knowledge (2.1–5), and described the two ways (18–20) on an eschatological background (4.1–14), insisting on the imitation of Christ in His Passion (5, 6). It explained the significance of Baptism in connection with the cross (9.1–11), and exhorted to familial and social virtue (19.4–12), encouraging its hearers by a reminder of the Resurrection and final retribution (21.1).

On *Polycarp's letter to the Philippians, *Irenaeus remarked (*Adv. haer.* 3.3, 4) that "those seeking salvation can apprehend the nature of the faith and the teaching of the truth." On a background of hope in the Resurrection and of Our Lord's commands (2.1–3), Polycarp stressed the imitation of Christ in His patience (8.2, 9.1) and inculcated the virtues that lead to holiness (9.1–12). Christians must flee avarice (2.1, 11.2–3); husbands, wives (2.2), widows (2.3), deacons (5.2), young men, virgins (5.3), and priests (6.1–3) are to practice kindness, forgiveness of injuries, and moderation toward the culpable (6.2), praying for all, particularly civil rulers (12.3).

The *apologists of the 2d century combined the kerygma and the catechesis in the enunciation of the *Christian way of life (*Justin, *Athenagoras, *Theophilus of Antioch). With the rise of the *catechetical schools toward the end of the century, the bishops prepared the candidates for Baptism (*catechumenoi*) by a series of moral instructions accompanied by exorcisms and fasting. This took place in the house churches (*see* DURA-EUROPOS) and followed a pattern leading to the handing over of the *creed (*traditio*). With the emancipation of the Church (313), these instructions assumed a more formal character as is exemplified in the *Catechetical Lectures* of *Cyril of Jerusalem, *Ambrose's *De Sacramentis* and *De Mysteriis,* and the *Catecheses* of *Theodore of Mopsuestia. *Augustine discussed the method in his *De catechizandis rudibus,* linking it with salvation history, which leads the catechumen from faith to hope and from hope to charity. With the spread of infant Baptism, the catechesis was generally replaced by home instruction of the children and by liturgical homilies in church. During the Carolingian reform and the 12th century, a partial revival of the catechesis took place because of the need of basic instruction for Christians. Today, great attention is being paid to the primitive catechesis as a means of renewing modern catechetical methods.

Bibliography: P. CARRINGTON, *The Primitive Christian Catechism* (Cambridge, Eng. 1940). G. SCHILLE, NTSt 4 (1958) 101–114; ZNTWiss 51 (1960) 112–131, Baptism; 49 (1958) 31–52, Barnabas. E. G. SELWYN, ed., *The First Epistle of St. Peter* (London 1946). L. W. BARNARD, AnglThRev 41 (1959) 177–190. G. SLOYAN, ed., *Shaping the Christian Message* (New York 1958) 3–37. F. X. MURPHY, *Studia moralia,* v.1 (Rome 1963) 54–72. L. BOPP, LexThK² 6:27–29. C. H. DODD, *The Apostolic Preaching and Its Developments* (London 1936; repr. 1963); *Gospel and Law* (New York 1951).

[F. X. MURPHY]

CATECHESIS, II (MEDIEVAL AND MODERN)

For the first 5 centuries of Christianity, catechesis was primarily a prebaptismal instruction given to adults. From the 6th century on, the catechumenate began to decline, and Baptism of adults became the exception rather than the rule.

A new concept of catechesis emerged as Germanic tribes were brought into the Church, or became at least nominally Catholic. With these mass conversions, entire tribes were baptized after a preparation of only a few weeks, or with little or no instruction. From this time the Church had to take into account the problem of educating in the faith large groups of rude, unlettered people.

The usages of the ancient catechumenate were incorporated in the rite of Baptism, now regularly administered to infants. There is no trace of a formal, ecclesiastical postbaptismal catechesis for children. It was assumed that the task of their education in the faith was the normal responsibility of their parents and godparents. From the 8th century, synods decreed that parents and godparents were obliged to know by heart the Our Father and the Creed, and to teach these to their children. These two formulas were considered the basic statements of the essentials of Christian doctrine.

There are no written accounts of instructions given to the barbarians, or treatises on catechesis from this period. To gain an idea of the content and flavor of the oral catechesis in the period from the 5th to the 11th centuries, one must study the pastoral treatises written by bishops and missionary monks. These works reflect the characteristics of an oral method and aim at practical education in Christianity, not at speculation. The history of liturgy, the development of religious art, and records of local councils also reveal something of catechetical practice. Medieval penitentials are another written source shedding light on methods of teaching Christian morality to peoples of tribal culture.

Gregory the Great. Pope Gregory I (d. 604) stands out as the most important single influence in the history of catechetics of his era. He saw an inner relationship between missiology, liturgy, and catechesis and proposed a form of catechesis wonderfully adapted to his times. His *Libri dialogorum* illustrates one typical approach in handing on the faith. This collection of tales of the marvelous and miraculous became a major source of the Christian cult of the saints. For centuries it was to their local saints that Europeans looked for a vivid illustration of the Christian life and for a bond with the next world.

Complementing the *Libri dialogorum* was the *Liber regulae pastoralis,* a pastoral manual for bishops. Widely distributed even during Gregory's lifetime, the work firmly established in Europe the ideal of the bishop as teacher and father of his flock. If the *Liber regulae pastoralis* is not important for catechetical content, it is nonetheless most significant for its concept of the bishop's teaching office. Gregory's *Homilies* give a picture of his own idea of the essence of the Christian message. A major theme is the Person of Christ, Mediator between God and men, who in His holy Church pours out on the world the gift of the Holy Spirit.

In a letter to a monk who was going to join St. Augustine of Canterbury, Gregory outlined important principles of missionary catechesis. He wrote that the temples of the idols should be converted to places of Christian worship, "that the nation, seeing their temples are not destroyed, may remove error from their hearts, and knowing and adoring the true God, may the more familiarly resort to the places to which they have been accustomed" (St. Bede, *Hist. Eccl.* 1.30). Gregory followed the same principle with regard to pagan festivals, directing that Christian feasts be gradually substituted for the pagan celebrations.

A letter of A.D. 624 from Boniface V to Edwin, King of Northumbria, gave a program of fundamental catechesis. The pagans were to be taught the emptiness of idols, and the importance of belief in a Creator God, who sent His Son to redeem the human race. As a consequence, they were called to embrace the Gospel and to be reborn as children of God by Baptism (PL 80:438). Throughout this period of evangelization among the barbarians, Christ was seen especially as an opponent of their heathen gods. He was the true God to whom they had vowed their loyalty, and it was their duty to live out that loyalty according to the pattern set down for them by the ministers of His Church.

7th to 11th Centuries. A discourse of St. Gall (d. 627) contained a catechesis faithful to the tradition established by St. Augustine of Hippo in his *De catechizandis rudibus*. Gall's discourse gave a résumé of the religious history of the world from the Fall to the Redemption and treated the mission of the Apostles, the vocation of the gentiles, and the divine constitution of the Church (PL 87:13–26).

A work attributed to St. Eligius (d. 658) shows him insisting on parental responsibility in handing on the truths of faith. "Know by memory the Symbol and the Lord's Prayer, and teach them to your children. Instruct and admonish the children, whom you have received as newborn from the baptismal fount, to live ever in the fear of God. Know that you have taken an oath on their behalf before God" (PL 87, 527).

St. Boniface. St. Boniface (d. 754) provided a link between the Romano–Anglo-Saxon religious tradition and the religious culture that flowered in the next century under the early Carolingians. Boniface's missionary efforts were characterized by fidelity to Rome, a spirit of adaptation to local customs where this could be harmonized with the Christian life, and an understanding of the need to establish permanent monastic centers for the preservation and diffusion of Christianity. The correspondence of St. Boniface shows that he always looked to Holy Scripture for the substance of his teaching.

A letter from Gregory II in 719 approved his method. "You are to teach [the pagans] the service of the kingdom of God by persuading them to accept the truth in the name of Christ, the Lord our God. You will instill into their minds the teaching of the Old and New Testaments, doing this in a spirit of love and moderation, and with arguments suited to their understanding. Finally, we command you that in admitting within the Church those who have some kind of belief in God you will insist upon using the sacramental discipline prescribed in the official ritual formulary of the Holy Apostolic See" [C. H. Talbot, tr. and ed., *The Anglo-Saxon Missionaries in Germany* (New York 1954) 68].

In 735 St. Boniface wrote to the Abbess Eadburga in England, "I beg you to continue the good work you have begun by copying out for me in letters of gold the epistles of my lord, St. Peter, that a reverence and love of the Holy Scriptures may be impressed on the minds of the heathens to whom I preach, and that I may ever have before my gaze the words of him who guided me along this path" (*ibid.* 91).

Fifteen sermons traditionally attributed to St. Boniface, but whose authorship is now questioned, are important as indicating a medieval catechesis that is faithful to the Christocentric synthesis handed down from the age of the Fathers. The moral teaching of these sermons is noteworthy for its consistent development of the law of charity (PL 89:843–872).

Other Works. A 9th-century work, *Disputatio puerorum per interrogationes et responsiones,* illustrates a more formal, systematic catechesis in a somewhat stilted, dialogue form. The work shows clearly an analytical approach to the teaching of Christian doctrine that was later to become a dominant method for many centuries. In its 9th-century context, however, it can hardly be taken as typical of popular catechesis, which was not yet generally directed to children or centered in schools (PL 101:1097–1144).

Indicative of the prevailing pattern in Germany is the work of one of Alcuin's disciples, Rabanus Maurus (d. 856). His treatise *De disciplina ecclesiastica* (PL 112:1193–1262) aimed to show a method of instructing pagans who asked for Baptism. The work is divided into three short books, of which the third is an amplification of the teaching of the two ways of the *Didache.*

A work of a contemporary, *De institutione laicali,* by Bishop Jonas of Orleans, is in the same tradition and emphasizes the responsibility of parents and godparents in the training of their children (PL 106:121–278). From the same period is a fragment attributed to a Christian woman, Dodena, entitled *Liber manualis.* The treatise illustrates the way a home catechesis might have been carried on at its best (PL 106:109–118).

Legislation. Ecclesiastical legislation of this early period makes it clear that the minimum aimed for, sometimes evidently in circumstances of great difficulty, was the universal memorization of the Creed and the Our Father, together with a basic understanding of Christian morality. It was consistently held that around these two formulas could be developed a fuller understanding of the Christian life. The Council of Clovesho in 747 instructed bishops to visit the outlying districts of their dioceses annually, to teach the people who rarely heard the word of God to avoid pagan practices. Boys were to be chosen for the study of Holy Scripture. Above all it was necessary to teach the essentials of the Faith: the doctrine of the Trinity and the Creed, and to see that godparents knew these truths (Mansi 12:396–398). The Council of Frankfort (794) decreed that all Christians should be taught the Creed and the Our Father (Mansi 13:908). The Council of Arles (813) insisted on the duty of parents to instruct their children (Mansi 14:62).

Liturgy. Since it was in a liturgical context that the Christians of this era were instructed, there is no doubt that the language of divine worship was a significant factor in catechesis. Latin, as the language of a higher culture and the instrument of unity during this period of cultural amalgam which lasted many centuries, was recognized as indispensable and carefully cultivated and transmitted to the literate minority. Nevertheless, because of the unintelligibility of Latin to most of the people, popular participation in public worship diminished considerably from what it had been in the days of primitive Christianity. This situation was detrimental to catechesis.

A letter from St. Bede (*c.* 672–735) to Egbert, Archbishop of York, recommended that those, priests included, who understood only their native tongue, be taught the Creed and the Our Father in the language they understood, though Bede also insisted that Latin was to be preferred for those who could manage it (PL 94:659). A similar policy was advocated by King Alfred the Great in the 9th century. The single instance during this period of a policy of complete adaptation to the vernacular was the effort of SS. Cyril and Methodius among the Slavs.

The liturgical celebration of greatest catechetical significance was the Easter Vigil service in which the faithful participated sacramentally in the mystery of Christ's redemptive act. The fact that certain didactic elements of the liturgy developed into miracle, mystery, and morality plays is an indication of the strength of social and cultural elements in handing on the Christian tradition. Throughout the medieval period, innumerable religious customs and works of religious art created an atmosphere that supported a vital Christian society.

Defects. A number of abuses resulted when certain elements of medieval cultural catechesis were carried to a logical extreme. Memorization and analysis of the Creed and the Our Father was sometimes overemphasized to the exclusion or neglect of the Biblical narrative method, which had been so favored by the Fathers. The medieval fascination for numbers, coupled with a recognition of the need for memory aids, fostered another abuse in the ordering of the truths of the Faith according to artificial and arbitrary classifications. Thus, the number seven was used as a teaching aid: seven Sacraments, seven works of mercy, seven petitions of the Lord's Prayer, seven capital sins. Such a methodology easily distorted the inner logic, coherence, and symmetry of the Christian mystery.

12th to 15th Centuries. From about mid-11th century, the revival of commerce, with its accompanying growth of town life and urban institutions, affected the religious orientation of European civilization and the traditional modes of catechesis. The function of community custom in religious education was recognized as inadequate. Local councils in the 13th century imposed on parish priests the obligation of explaining to the people on Sundays the articles of faith in simple and clear fashion. The Council of Lambeth (1281) provided a brief summary of the instructions priests were to give their people (Mansi 24:410–413).

Mendicant Orders. In the rise of the new orders, especially the Dominicans and Franciscans, can be seen a remarkable effort to adapt catechetical methods to the needs of urban society. The mendicants brought about a revival of popular preaching, but they were not exempt from the intellectual influences that had affected the traditional structure of the Christian message. The history of catechesis here followed closely the development of philosophy and theology. The recovery of the Aristotelian corpus and the development of systematic theology in the high Middle Ages had a profound influence on catechetical methodology, though this influence was not fully realized until the discovery of printing made it widespread. A key difference between the catechesis of the early Middle Ages, as exemplified by St. Gregory in the late 6th century, or Rabanus Maurus in the 9th, and that of the period marked by the rise of the universities was in the change from a historico-narrative to a logical organization of the content of the catechesis. Popular catechesis still emanated chiefly from the pulpit, but as the analytic method of the universities tended to carry over into the methods of the preacher, the purposes of theology and catechesis were not always clearly distinguished. That there was a significant difference between the two was clear to St. Thomas Aquinas (d. 1274), as a study of his catechetical sermons reveals [see *St. Thomas Aquinas, The Catechetical Instructions,* tr. J. B. Collins (New York 1939)]. Even in these sermons, however, St. Thomas reveals how controlling were the intellectual and social influences of his age. The traditional framework of salvation history had all but disappeared in the writings of the 13th century.

Jean Gerson. Among the most active of 14th-century catechists was Jean *Gerson (1363–1429), chancellor of the University of Paris. Gerson, who devoted his later life to laboring for the instruction of children in Lyons, is credited with having compiled the first catechism specifically for children. In his work, *Tractatus de parvulis trahendis ad Christum,* he emphasized the need of teaching in terms a child could understand. He tried to persuade university theologians to produce simple treatises of the essentials of religion for common folk, and proposed that the treatises be made in the form of posters to be displayed in public places where people could gather to read and ponder them. Gerson is thus a significant transition figure to the next period of catechesis, which became characterized by an important innovation, the printed catechism manual.

Influence of Social Changes. The Middle Ages had produced a culture that rested largely on the strength of Christian family and community life as the channel for transmitting the truths of the faith to the laity. As social values became more secularized, this kind of catechesis became increasingly insufficient. By the later Middle Ages there was in Europe a gradual but perceptible change in the religious spirit and practice that showed itself in an overemphasis on the external elements of religion. More subtle were the effects of the widespread disintegration of a catechetical synthesis, and abuses in liturgical and sacramental practice. Records of local councils show grave concern over abuses in the matter of indulgences, pilgrimages, and in the use of relics. In some areas popular devotion to the Holy Eucharist had degenerated to a kind of superstitious confidence in the Blessed Sacrament as a kind of wonderworking element, and many people lost sight of the centrality of the Mass in Christian life and worship.

Renaissance and Reformation Period. In the Renaissance there was a new surge of interest in educational theory and in the rise of schools for the upper classes. Among the prominent 16th-century educators, men like Juan Vives, Erasmus, and John Colet were mindful of the place of religious formation in the humanistic education they proposed.

On the popular level, the 15th and 16th centuries saw a proliferation of devotional works, many containing a kind of catechesis. A 16th-century Austrian work, *Road to Heaven,* exhorted the head of the family to attend the sermon and recall it after dinner with his family. He was also supposed to question them on the Ten Commandments, the seven deadly sins, the Our Father, and the Creed. Finally, he should have a little drink brought in for the group and lead them in singing a hymn referring to God, Our Lady, or the Saints [P. Janelle, *The Catholic Reformation* (Milwaukee 1949) 23].

A decree of the Fifth Lateran Council (1514) recognized a general need for better religious instruction. Schoolmasters were to teach religious truths: the divine precepts, the articles of faith, sacred hymns and psalms, and the lives of the saints (Mansi 32:881).

Luther. Preaching and formal catechesis were not enough to stem the abuses that prepared the way for the Lutheran movement. Luther's teachings captured the popular mind in large areas of Germany through the medium of a highly effective catechesis. Luther's catechism first appeared in 1528 in the old medieval form of *tabulae,* or wall charts. This was followed within a year by a printed version. The arrangement of Luther's 1529 catechism—commandments first, then the Creed, followed by prayer and the Sacraments—threw the doctrine of grace out of context, thereby destroying the vital synthesis of the divine message of salvation. The organization of the work revealed Luther's own religious and spiritual problems, and marked the beginning of a long history of catechisms that used the threefold division of creed, code, and cult, with a major emphasis on code. This arrangement was logical in the light of Lutheran theology, but it ill suited a Catholic catechesis.

It was only with Luther that the term catechism came to refer to a book, both to the manual used by the catechist and to the simpler text placed in the hands of a child. Until this time, the term catechism referred only to the content of the catechesis. The period of the Reformation coincided, therefore, with the significant transition to that period in which the catechism manual began to play a dominant part in forming both the theory and practice of catechesis. Luther left detailed directions for the use of his catechisms, insisting on rote memorization of the exact text as a means of preserving his teaching intact. Memorization was to precede an analysis of the material.

Catholic Reaction. Of necessity, in the face of heresy, Catholic catechesis reacted to Protestantism by becoming greatly concerned with theological accuracy, as this was necessary to keep clear the essential differences in doctrine that separated the Church from the new sects. The Catholics in their reaction to the propagation of Lutheranism did not immediately recognize the implications and consequences of Luther's innovations in catechesis. Catholic catechisms countered by an imitation of Luther's short question and answer method, satisfied for the most part that so long as orthodoxy was guaranteed a satisfactory solution to the problem posed by Luther's catechism had been found.

The first Catholic catechism written as a reaction to Luther's was published in Augsburg in 1530, and was followed by a series in German and Latin. The first efforts were not very successful because they lacked clarity and conciseness. Many were too long and learned for popular use. They differed in wording of essential matters, a decided weakness in the face of the lucid and uniform presentation provided by Luther's rapidly spreading catechism.

St. Peter Canisius. St. Peter *Canisius (1521–97) produced three catechisms that remedied many of the weaknesses of the earlier Catholic efforts. In 1555 his large catechism, *Summa doctrinae christianae* appeared. He had been asked to gloss it with references to Holy Scripture, the Fathers and Doctors, and Canon Law, as an aid to preachers and school masters. Realizing the impossibility of satisfying the needs of theologians, parish priests, and youthful students with a single work, Canisius published the *Catechismus minimus* (1556), which first appeared as the appendix to a Latin grammar. This small work contains only 59 questions divided into 6 short chapters, treating in order: (1) faith and the Creed, (2) hope and the Lord's Prayer, (3) charity and the decalogue, (4) the Sacraments, (5) the avoidance of sin, (6) good works. A few months later a German version of the little catechism appeared. Canisius added to this book a series of prayers for all occasions: morning and evening, before and after meals, and a daily prayer for all the needs of Christendom. Almost 40 years later he prepared an edition of the *Catechismus minimus* with the words divided into syllables to make mastery of the text easier for small children.

The third catechism of Canisius, the *Parvus catechismus catholicorum* (1558), was intended for youths of about 14 years. This book set the tone of catechesis in Germany for the next 200 years. By 1597, 134 editions of the work had been published. It underwent many revisions and additions at the hands of the author himself, who enriched it with prayers and meditations on the life of Christ. Some of the editions were richly illustrated.

The catechisms of Canisius were written to defend the faith against heresy, and therefore they necessarily had a strong intellectual quality. They were admirably devoid of polemics, however, and although they are written in question and answer form, they retained much of the spirit and even the language of Scripture and the Fathers.

Other Efforts. In France, Edmund Auger, SJ, produced catechisms in 1563 and 1568, similar in approach to the works of Canisius. During the same period, Gaspar Astete and Martínez de Ripalda, Jesuits, wrote catechisms which were still in use in the 20th century in Spain. In England, Dr. Laurence Vaux's *A Catechisme of Christian Doctrine necessarie for children and ignorante people* (1562) also showed the influence of Canisius.

The Roman Catechism. During the Council of Trent there was an effort to provide for the drafting of two catechisms: one in Latin for the learned, and one to be translated into vernaculars for the unlettered and children. Only the first was attempted and completed by a postconciliar commission in 1566. Using the catechetical works of Canisius as a model, the *Catechismus ex decretis Concilii Tridentini ad Parochos,* or *Catechismus Romanus,* was intended as a reference book for pastors and a norm on which subsequent texts were to be based.

The preface of the work notes that catechesis is not the same as theology, but treats only those things "that belong peculiarly to the pastoral office and are accommodated to the capacity of the faithful." The pastor is urged to keep before his mind the general plan of the catechesis that is summed up in three points: (1) all Christian knowledge and eternal life is to know Jesus Christ; (2) but to know Christ is to keep His Commandments; (3) and charity is the end of the Commandments and the fulfillment of the law. The pastor is also reminded of the importance of the manner of imparting the truths of faith. He should adapt his instruction to the age, capacity, and condition of those being instructed. Further, since all the doctrines of Christianity are derived from the word of God, the pastor should devote himself to the study of the font of catechesis. Pastors are expected to correlate their instructions with the homily on the Sunday Gospel, and for this purpose the catechism provides a supplement giving references to the sections in the catechism which could be related to the Gospel for each Sunday of the liturgical year.

The *Roman Catechism* was approved by Pius V in 1566, and by Gregory XIII in 1583. It has since enjoyed continual recommendation. Leo XIII, Pius X, and Pius XI recommended its use by the clergy in more recent times.

The *Catechismus Romanus* was translated immediately into Italian by order of Pius V, and within the next 3 years into German, French, and Polish. A Spanish translation was resisted by some influential Spaniards who were opposed to the publication of religious books in the vernacular, and also because some theologians objected to the catechism's interpretation of a passage in St. Matthew regarding Baptism (Mt 28.18–19).

The Council of Trent also promoted the progress of catechesis by decreeing that the people, and especially the children, be carefully instructed. "The bishops shall also see to it that at least on Sundays and other festival days, the children in every parish be carefully taught the rudiments of the faith and obedience toward God and their parents by those whose duty it is, and who shall be compelled thereto, if need be, even by ecclesiastical censures" [H. J. Schroeder, *Canons and Decrees of the Council of Trent* (St. Louis 1941) 196].

Local Legislation. Diocesan statutes further specified the Tridentine decrees. The Synod of Besançon (1571) directed that the prayers that every Christian should know were to be recited at the Sunday sermon. In rural areas the pastors were obliged to gather the children one day a week in order to have them recite their prayers in Latin and in French (DTC 2:2.1919).

This same period saw a council in Lima, Peru, approve a catechism authorized by Philip II of Spain. This catechism was translated into Quechua and Aymara for use among the Indians. The Council of Mexico in 1585 called for a short and simple catechism containing the Lord's Prayer, the Hail Mary, Apostles' Creed, Salve Regina, 12 articles of the faith, the Ten Commandments of God and five precepts of the Church, the seven Sacraments, and the seven capital sins. A translation was to be made for the Indians of each diocese, and the text was to be explained on the Sundays of Advent and during Lent. Before receiving Baptism, Indian adults were to know the Our Father, the

Creed, and the Ten Commandments in their language.

Efforts at Implementation. The Confraternity of Christian Doctrine, approved by Pius V in 1571, was a significant agency of catechesis. A cooperative work of clergy and laity from the beginning, the confraternity, founded in Milan and fostered by St. Charles Borromeo, was especially widespread in Italy and spread to France and Germany. Members of the confraternity undertook the responsibility of furthering the work of religious instruction among the members of their own families.

St. Robert Bellarmine's catechisms, written at the order of Clement VIII for use in the Papal States, were the most influential of the catechisms written shortly after the Council of Trent. The *Dottrina cristiana breve* is a short summary of Christian doctrine for pupils (1597). The following year Bellarmine produced a teacher's manual in catechetics, *Dichiarazione piu copiosa della dottrina cristiana* (1598). These books do not present so synthesized a catechesis as do those of Peter Canisius, but they are of great doctrinal clarity and rich in psychological insights. In the short catechism the questions avoid abstractions and are placed in a context a child can understand. In the larger catechism the usual question and answer pattern is reversed and the questions are put in the mouth of the pupil, while it is the teacher who answers. Here, Bellarmine had in view a method of helping the inexperienced catechist anticipate his pupil's questions, and a guide for clear, complete, and adequate explanations. The catechesis was to be built around the theological virtues: faith centered in the Creed, hope expressed in the Our Father, and charity in the Commandments of God and of the Church. The Sacraments are treated as sources and means of the Christian life.

In a brief of 1598 Clement VIII exhorted bishops throughout the world to "use their utmost endeavors to have this catechism, written at Our command, adopted and followed in their respective churches, dioceses, and parishes" [J. Brodrick, *The Life and Work of Blessed Robert Bellarmine* (New York 1928) 395]. The catechism was translated eventually into more than 60 different tongues and dialects, including editions in Arabic, Hindustani, Chinese, Congolese, Ethiopian, Hebrew, and Peruvian. It was the only catechism St. Francis de Sales allowed in his diocese. Urban VIII in 1633 recommended its use in the missions; a century later Benedict XIV, in a special constitution to all the bishops of the Church, advised its adoption as the official manual of every diocese. When at Vatican Council I a uniform and universal catechism was proposed, it was Bellarmine's catechism that was recommended as a model.

The catechisms engendered as part of the Catholic reformation provided excellent summaries of doctrine in relatively simple language. Thus, they satisfied a critical need, and were a major factor in checking the spread of heresy and preserving the purity of doctrine. Today, writers active in the catechetical renewal hold that these catechisms also had the less desirable effect of fostering a catechesis that ran counter to the inherent dynamism of the Biblical narrative approach in teaching Christian doctrine. According to these writers, in the post-Reformation catechisms the relation between the parts of Christian doctrine was not established, and thus the message was not presented as an integrated whole, the good news of salvation centered in Christ (see Hofinger, Jungmann, Sloyan).

Important advances were made in school catechesis, though this remained subordinate to the teaching of religion in the Church and in the home. Charles Borromeo's work in fostering schools was imitated by other dioceses throughout Italy. Besides the Jesuits, other religious congregations that made notable contributions to the theory and practice of school catechesis were the Ursulines, Somaschi, Barnabites, and the Clerks Regular of the Christian Schools.

Post-Reformation Period. Diocesan catechisms, special children's catechisms, and treatises on catechetics multiplied during the 17th century. Francis de Sales personally instructed children of his diocese. In 1602 in Toulouse, a 14th-century work of Jean Gerson was reprinted as part of a teacher's manual. Adrien Bourdoise opened a school in Paris in 1622 especially for the purpose of bringing religious influence into families through teaching young children. He also produced an original book on catechetical pedagogy, *Les rudiments de la foi en faveur des simples fidèles.* Among the contributions of Bourdoise was the division of the pupils into age groups, with particular adaptations for each group. This practice became customary in the large cities of Europe, where lay catechists sometimes assisted as instructors. It was widely taken for granted that catechesis meant an explanation of the text of a catechism followed by recitation of questions and answers.

St. Vincent de Paul (1581–1660) incorporated a catechesis as an integral part of the missions preached by his priests in rural areas. During their missions his priests were to teach catechism twice a day. In the afternoon they were to catechize the children for an hour in a simple manner. In the evening the same material was to be taught to adults. The catechesis was never to be replaced by a sermon. Guided by Vincent de Paul, St. Louise de Marillac provided a special manual for teaching catechism to the poor in their homes.

The Sulpician Method. In the Sulpician method, inaugurated by Jean Jacques Olier (1608–57), seminarians were the principal catechists. Distinctive features included the care to adjust the catechesis to the age level of the child, and a concern for helping children live in accord with the doctrine taught. In promulgating the method, great emphasis was given to the qualifications of teachers, who were supposed to reflect a strong love of God and of children. Sulpician techniques did not shun an appeal to a spirit of competition. Teachers made use of a point system for correct answers, gave places of honor in class, and awarded prizes for outstanding recitations. Hymn singing in the course of a catechism lesson was intended to keep a happy atmosphere. There was a conscious effort to supplement the analytical approach, though there was still much stress on memorization. Children were to memorize the Sunday Gospel as preparation for the catechism lesson. The class, regularly held on Sunday afternoon, included a homily on the Gospel by the catechist and an attempt to make an application of the day's lesson to the everyday life of the child. Much of the catechetical practice since the 17th century bears the mark of the influence of the Sulpician method.

St. John Baptist de la Salle. The method of St. John Baptist de la Salle (1651–1719) brought a renewed appreciation of the use of narrative in catechesis, although one of his chief catechetical works, *Duties of a Christian,* makes little or no advance over the customary arrangement of the text, which proceeded from Creed to Commandments, Sacraments, and prayer. De la Salle's method was unusual at his time in holding that memorization should follow the explanation of the text, not precede it. Formulas were to be memorized as summaries only after a careful development of the lesson. Though a Biblical-liturgical approach was lacking, the method did emphasize the value of teaching the life of Christ and the lives of the saints. Passages from Scripture were used, but chiefly as illustrations of a point of dogma.

Other Influences. Among the other figures who contributed significantly to the theory and practice of catechesis in the 17th century were St. John *Eudes, *Bossuet, Charles Thuet, and Claude Fleury. Thuet produced a manual showing three distinct methods for effectively using the *Roman Catechism:* in sermons, dialogues, and meditations. Claude *Fleury published a catechism containing an abridgement of sacred history, one of a growing number of catechisms seeking to make a closer correlation between Holy Scripture and the question and answer treatment of dogma by this time considered standard.

All the methodological weaknesses of the 16th and 17th centuries were countered by the fact that catechesis was still given in a Christian environment. Formal catechesis was enforced and supported by the religious orientation of family and society well into the 18th century. It was only then that secular values began to set the tone of European culture.

18th and 19th Centuries. The 18th century was generally a somewhat sterile period in the history of catechesis. The rationalistic spirit of the Enlightenment had the effect of making catechesis increasingly speculative. In 1761 Clement XIII wrote against errors arising from rationalism in current pedagogy. Jansenism and Gallicanism also affected the content of catechesis, and in France a number of catechisms were placed on the Index. There was an attempt to provide an official uniform catechism in many dioceses, especially in France, but these efforts met with only a limited success. The effort to reintegrate Bible history with the teaching of Catholic dogma continued, notably in Germany, but without any large-scale achievements. For the most part catechetical instruction in Europe, at least as far as it is revealed by the catechisms of the period, continued to proceed from definition to analysis. An English catechism which follows this pattern, *An Abridgement of Christian Doctrine,* is attributed to Bp. Richard *Challoner (1691–1781). This book, which has the merit of simple, direct language, formed the basis of the later English "penny catechism."

A most significant change in the 18th century was brought about by the altered relationship between the family and the school in the education of the child. In the course of the century, as civil authorities began to make universal school attendance compulsory, the Sunday catechesis moved to the classroom. This had the advantage of giving catechesis a definite place in the curriculum, making it possible to give a fuller instruction in the truths of faith. Since the formative religious influence of the community was considerably weakened by this time, there is no doubt that the more fully developed catechesis made possible by classroom teaching was indispensable. Nevertheless, there was a concomitant danger in the substitution of the classroom for the church as the place of catechetical instruction. In such a setting it became increasingly difficult to establish the intrinsic relationship between the liturgical and instructional elements of total Christian formation.

Among the important figures in the 18th and 19th centuries were Bernard *Overberg, who emphasized the value for children of presenting matter in the form of a narrative, J. B. *Hirscher, who held that Christian doctrine should be presented as far as possible in historical form rather than by definitions, and Augustin Gruber, who went back to the *De catechizandis rudibus* for the principles of his pedagogy. However, it was the catechism of Joseph *Deharbe, SJ, published in Germany in 1847, which exerted the greatest influence for the next half-century. Deharbe's catechism was along the line traditional since the Council of Trent, following the logical arrangement of creed, code, and cult. Though the book came to be used as a text for children, it was not intended for them. Its outstanding virtues were its completeness, correctness, and clarity of expression.

At Vatican Council I (1869–70) many bishops favored a proposal for a universal catechism, but the arguments against the plan prevented its realization. Regional uniformity in catechism texts continued as a goal in many countries.

The 20th Century. By the end of the 19th century, catechetical theory, especially in Germany and Austria, was being influenced by new psychological and pedagogical theories. Catechetical reviews, societies, and courses contributed to the growth of a movement that led to the first Catechetical Congress in Vienna in 1912. It was at this congress that the "Munich Method" received its formulation as a text-developing rather than a text-explanatory method (*see* MUNICH METHOD IN CATECHETICS). At the second congress, in 1928, it was evident there had been growth in the understanding of the intrinsic relationship between liturgy and catechesis. It was this catechetical movement, initiated at the beginning of the 20th century, that motivated continual efforts to improve not only the method, but the content of catechesis. Interest in method led to an awareness that the content of the catechesis must appear as a synthesis and be appreciated as a message, the joyful news of salvation.

Catechesis today centers around the idea of the kerygma, or good news of salvation. The Christian mystery is presented as event rather than idea. God's plan of salvation, centered in Christ, is presented as evoking a return response of love from the human family called to union with God through Christ in His Church. Thus, creed, code, and cult are integrated in a catechesis which is Christocentric, sacramental, and Biblicohistorical.

Although much of the work of 20th-century catechesis has been centered on a catechesis for children, other currents in the life of the Church have affected catechetical theory and practice. Notable among these influences have been the liturgical movement, advances in Biblical scholarship and in theology, and the impetus given to a deeper Christian life and worship by such encyclicals as *Mystici Corporis* (1943), *Divino afflante Spiritu*

(1943), and *Mediator Dei* (1947). Earlier in the century, the reforms of Pius X presaged these developments. In his encyclical *Acerbo nimis* (1905), the Pope cited ignorance of divine things as the principal cause of the intellectual debility and decay of religion that marked the era, and ordered the establishment of the Confraternity of Christian Doctrine in each diocese. He went on to describe the sublimity of the work of the catechist and directed that where there was an insufficient number of priests, pastors could secure lay help in the teaching of catechism.

There has been, as one outcome of these influences, a return to a broader concept of catechesis as including the instruction of adults. Modern missiology is another force that has thrown much light on the problems of transmitting Christianity in non-European cultures, and contemporary catechesis now takes into consideration the need for special approaches in pre-evangelization before actual catechesis can be realistically undertaken.

Catechesis in the U.S. Catechesis in the U.S., as in Canada, from the beginning depended on Europe for texts. The works of James Butler and Joseph Deharbe were widely used. A distinctive feature of catechesis in the U.S., especially in the 19th century, was the problem of providing for the needs of national minority groups. German-English catechisms were commonly used in many areas.

An effort toward a uniform textbook of Christian doctrine, begun as early as 1829, culminated in 1885 in the *Catechism of the Third Council of Baltimore,* which was approved by Archbishop Gibbons and became the most widely used English text. A thorough revision, the collaborative effort of many theologians and teachers, was completed in 1941.

In the U.S. the growth of the parochial school system tended to bring about an identification of catechesis with classroom instruction. Since 1930, however, the work of the Confraternity of Christian Doctrine among Catholics in non-Catholic schools has grown rapidly also.

Meanwhile, the German catechetical movement had at first its imitators, then its counterpart in the U.S., producing a large number of new texts as well as works on catechetical content and method (see G. S. Sloyan, "The Good News and the Catechetical Scene in the United States," in Jungmann, *The Good News Yesterday and Today*).

See also CATECHESIS, I (EARLY CHRISTIAN); CATECHESIS, MISSIONARY; CATECHETICS; CATECHISM.

Bibliography: J. A. JUNGMANN, *Handing on the Faith,* tr. and rev. A. N. FUERST (New York 1959); *The Good News Yesterday and Today,* ed. and tr. W. HUESMAN, with essays in appraisal of its contribution ed. J. HOFINGER (New York 1962). G. SLOYAN, ed., *Shaping the Christian Message* (New York 1958). G. DELCUVE and A. GODIN, *Readings in European Catechetics* (Brussel 1962). G. E. CARTER, *The Modern Challenge to Religious Education,* ed. W. J. REEDY (New York 1961). J. HOFINGER, ed., *Teaching All Nations,* tr. C. HOWELL (New York 1961). L. BOPP, LexThK[2] 6:27–31. G. BOVINI, EncCatt 3:1094–1116. G. BAREILLE and E. MANGENOT, DTC 2.2:1877–1968. H. LECLERCQ, DACL 2.2:2530–79. P. GÖBL, *Geschichte de Katechese im Abendlande vom Verfalle des Katechumenates bis zum Ende des Mittelalters* (Kempten 1880). C. HEZARD, *Histoire du catéchisme depuis la naissance de l'église jusqu'à nos jours* (Paris 1900). A. E. CRUZ, *Historia de la Catequesis* (Santiago de Chile 1962). Journals. *Lumen Vitae* (1946–). *The Living Light* (1964–).

[M. E. JEGEN]

CATECHESIS, MISSIONARY

Missionary catechesis, taken in the widest sense, includes the whole sequence of instruction and guidance offered to the adult non-Christian (pagan) from his first contact with the Catholic religion until he is baptized. The specific missionary problem in this whole process is the transmission of faith: how to guide and dispose a man so that he may come to believe.

Faith is the answer to the proclamation of the Christian message. But is a man prepared and disposed to accept it, or even to listen to and understand it? The parable of the sower (Lk 8.5–15) illustrates what is the daily experience of the missioner. He recognizes it as his task to prepare the ground (first step, pre-evangelization), to sow the seed of God's word (second step, evangelization), and to endeavor to develop the incipient faith to a fuller understanding of God's revelation and introduce the catechumen to the practice of a Christian life in preparation for Baptism (third step, catechesis proper). These three steps, characterized and distinguished by their specific goals, which in turn are the prerequisite for the next step, should be observed in any missionary catechesis, as the Study Week on Missionary Catechesis of Bangkok (1962) showed and the Pan-African Study Week of Katigondo, Uganda (1964), confirmed.

Pre-Evangelization. In a new mission area the missioner generally finds that most of the people have heard little or nothing of the Catholic religion. The information about it that some may have is likely to be fragmentary, at best, and distorted in such a way as to disincline them to give a favorable hearing to the missioner's message. He is apt to find himself regarded by the people as propagator of a new religion that is probably identified in their minds with Western culture. The more their own indigenous religion is interwoven with the fabric of their culture and daily lives, the more reluctant will they be to think of changing to another. Conversion can appear to them a defection from their inherited culture and a denial of its values; it may involve formidable social consequences and arouse their fear of bringing down upon themselves the indignation of their repudiated gods. Other influences often contribute to prejudice even where no strong religious loyalties stand in the way of conversion—for example, materialism, rationalism, agnosticism, indifferentism, superstition, and low standards of morality. In consequence of these and other factors the missioner commonly finds the people indifferent, if not actually antagonistic, to his teaching. He may find nothing to encourage him except perhaps the natural courtesy of the people. It may seem difficult to him to propose Christianity as something needed, particularly since it is presented in Western forms and terms and based on many religious suppositions, known and familiar to those of a Christian culture but strange, if not unintelligible, to the mission people. As a result there is in most cases no readiness to accept or even to listen to the Christian message. This condition necessitates a special preparation before the missioner can proclaim the gospel and hope for its acceptance. First, he has to find human contact, understanding, and confidence and must arouse a personal interest in religious questions; he has to shake man loose from his false security and thus dispose him for the reception of God's message. This stage, preliminary to the proclamation of the gospel, is called pre-evangelization.

Various circumstances may help the missioner to pursue the aim of pre-evangelization. When priests and sisters come to a new area, the people are likely to be curious about them. Questions are put to the missioners, and these should be answered in such a way as to stimulate further curiosity and so lead the questioners to greater interest and willingness to give attention to the talks, the showing of pictures, or other activities designed for the purpose of the pre-evangelization. Care for the indigent and afflicted may attract the notice of others, for the evidence of unselfish charity can be most impressive to people accustomed to exploitation. The opening of schools, the offering of special courses, exhibitions, and public celebration also help to gain attention. Radio, television, and the distribution of printed material are other useful means, provided, however, there is discussion of questions and problems that appeal to non-Christians (or a particular group of them) and stimulate their interest in religion. Evidence that the missioner shares in the personal joy or sorrow of those living in his district (e.g., on the occasion of birth, marriage, death) will not pass unnoticed. The dignified celebration of Catholic feasts is likely to impress those who witness them. Of special missionary value are the celebrations of such occasions as marriages and funerals that bring together large numbers of non-Catholic friends. But there is no other more effective means of gaining favorable attention than the testimony of a good Christian life itself. If people can observe in the life of Christians the value of being Christian, they will be interested. The apostolic importance of a truly Christian life can hardly be overemphasized (cf. Mt 5.16; 1 Pt 2.12). But whenever possible the missioner himself should take the initiative, show an interest in the questions and problems of the people, and manifest appreciation and respect for their cultural and religious values. This will not only earn him the confidence of his people but will also give him an acquaintance with their customs and a familiarity with their character that is invaluable for his missionary task. Such contacts will also provide him with opportunities to discuss or answer religious questions that come up quite spontaneously. All this can stimulate interest in, and prepare for a better understanding of, the Christian religion.

The missioner will also try to establish a favorable public image of the Catholic religion, for this will contribute greatly to the success of his work, particularly in gaining inquirers and converts. In this the missioner will find much that is useful in the research and advice of psychologists, sociologists, and anthropologists, who can also be of valuable assistance in the matter of adaptation, which is essential for a true "incarnation" of the Christian revelation in a new culture.

When some initial contact is made it must be used prudently to develop or to deepen interest in the Catholic religion. The topics and problems discussed should be both of interest to the listeners and of religious significance: for example, the purpose of life; what is known about God (this not so much to prove God's existence, which in its purely philosophical approach is a question likely to be more harmful than helpful to many listeners, but rather to show God's power, wisdom, etc., which implicitly contain the proof for God's existence); the immortality of the soul; conscience; good, evil, sin; life hereafter; reward and punishment; death; labor and the hardships of life; and Catholic social teaching. The purpose of treating these questions is not to give a comprehensive explanation or a compelling proof of the Catholic position but to show that Catholicism interests itself in these universal human problems, and that it gives a fuller and clearer answer to them than do other religions. A prolonged discussion of such philosophical-apologetical questions as these, although they were part of, and preparation for, the missioner's own theological training, will not generally prove helpful. They could, indeed, raise new and unnecessary problems and might end by confirming the listener in his attachment to his old religion rather than drawing him toward Christ.

As the discussion of various topics proceeds, now or at a later stage, Christ's teaching will appear as a challenge to the indigenous religion. Pagans also know God's law (Rom 2.15). "Similarities" are therefore to be expected. The listeners will note them and make comparisons with the teachings of their own sages. Such comparisons should not be left to the spontaneous perception of the listeners. If the missioner refrains from taking notice of indigenous beliefs and customs, the omission could be attributed to ignorance or to contempt for the local religious culture. Moreover, the listeners will not accept Christ's teaching before His superiority is recognized. Comparison is therefore useful and necessary, but it should not be restricted to points of similarity. The listener should be led to see that along with some obscure light and certain elements of good, the non-Christian religion contains much darkness, doubt, and even error, while Christ's message is filled with light, and His teaching clear and certain. Furthermore they should be brought to realize that Christ not only taught ethical principles but also gives the strength to live by them.

If these assertions can be demonstrated by the moral standards of the Christian community, especially by the practice of charity, the missioner's work will be greatly facilitated, and it will lead to a more ready acceptance of Christ's divinity and the authenticity of His Church. Observations of this kind, as well as other experiences sent by God's providence, may arouse the spontaneous interest of pagans in the Catholic religion so that they seek out a priest or seem to be waiting for him, already appearing disposed to receive without delay the Christian message that is given in the evangelization stage. On such occasions it becomes evident that in the work of pre-evangelization, which aims at creating interest in and arousing esteem and desire for the Catholic religion, Christian lay people by the testimony of their lives frequently have a greater missionary opportunity and effectiveness than the priest.

When a spiritual unrest has been aroused in a man, and he shows personal interest in the Christian religion and manifests the desire to hear more about Christ, he is disposed for the evangelization.

Evangelization. The purpose of this second stage in the missionary catechesis is to make known to disposed listeners the good news of our salvation in Christ and to solicit the answer of faith. This is to be done by means of a brief but dynamic and challenging presentation of the Christian message (kerygma). This message should not be given as a set of intellectual truths drawn from God's revelation, but God's own revelation should be retold and His plan of salvation announced with all the striking, challenging, and moving power that lies in its very content.

It is the message of God's love for men who are sinners, and of God who wants men to be His children (1 Jn 3.1). His love is so great that He gave His own Son for human souls (Jn 3.16) so that they might share in His divine life (Jn 10.10; 2 Pt 1.4), and He is ready to give all that is needed (Rom 8.32) for their entrance into the kingdom prepared for His children from the foundation of the world (Mt 25.34). The way to the kingdom is Christ (Jn 14.6). And it is in the name of Him who was sent by the Father (Jn 20.21) that the missioner appeals: "now is the day of salvation" (2 Cor 5.20–6.2), "repent and be converted" (Acts 3.19). Whoever accepts Christ and believes will be saved (Jn 6.47; Mk 16.16).

Thus Christ stands in the center of the whole message. Generally it will be better to unfold God's plan of salvation not by beginning with a detailed account of Genesis (which might too easily sidetrack the interest, create nonessential and time-consuming difficulties without answering to the listener's real interest) but by going straight to Christ, in whom the grace of God has appeared to all men (Ti 2.11). From Christ man hears of God's invitation, of the happiness awaiting him, and of the way that leads to heaven. From Christ he hears how God embraces him with love and care. Christ tells him how to answer God in faith and love, in praise, thanksgiving, and confident prayer; how to become and to live as a child of God and to gain salvation.

More extensive apologetical arguments may be saved for a later stage of instruction and Christian formation. At this time the interest of man is held by the "unfathomable riches of Christ" that the missioner is "to announce among the Gentiles" (Eph 3.8). Thus the pagan hears of Christ and the "gift of God" (Jn 4.10) before he is led to rational arguments.

At this stage of instruction the transcendent superiority of Christ must be made apparent to the listener. As the conclusion of such comparisons as were mentioned above, which will spontaneously occur to any adult listener, he should come to understand that Christ's wisdom could not come "from below" (i.e., from the natural human milieu in which He lived) as did that of other religious leaders; but that His teaching, since it reached an essentially higher level, must come "from above." When the adult perceives this, he finds himself confronted with the inevitable question: "Who do you say that I am?" (Mt 16.15). If the heart has been won for Christ, the answer, prompted by grace, will be an act of faith.

Thus faith in Christ's divinity marks the culmination of the missionary catechesis and permits the beginning of the third stage, catechesis properly so-called. It should not be started before a man shows clear "signs" of faith and conversion. Since the conversion is not merely an intellectual process but a surrender that affects the whole man and his whole life, some authors (as did also the Study Week of Bangkok) speak of a "shock" that accompanies conversion and define it as "the internal change in a man whereby he accepts Christ as the Lord." Other signs are: a break with a sinful past, the desire to find Christ, intensive personal prayer, and the desire and effort to live a life that is truly Christian.

Catechesis Proper. By faith man becomes a "catechumen" (in the proper sense) and enters the last stage of preparation for Baptism, the "catechumenate." As distinct from this third stage the two preceding stages combined are frequently called "precatechumenate." However, a more systematic (course-like) presentation links the second and third stage, while the first stage of pre-evangelization does not need and generally does not involve a very methodically planned instruction.

Catechesis systematically develops a fuller understanding of the Catholic faith and at the same time introduces a person into the practice of Christian life to the extent that this is possible before Baptism. Because this is the purpose of the catechesis, it is evident that faith in Christ's divinity must be its starting point and base. Only for the believer are Christ's words divine revelation, the Church a divine institution, and Christ's teachings divine commands. Moreover, since the Christian religion is no longer to be seen as the development of a human and natural culture but as having a divine origin and coming therefore from Him who is the author of the universe and of all the values reflected in the various cultures, Christ's teaching will not mean the disfigurement or suppression of any true culture but will rather be its divine fulfillment: "I have not come to destroy, but to fulfill" (Mt 5.17). This reflection will refute the prejudice that considers conversion to Christianity as a defection from one's inherited culture.

Care must be taken that the "systematic" presentation of the teachings of our faith does not cause the essential structure of God's revelation to be lost or distorted. Since the catechesis has to serve the purpose of the divine message, it has to go beyond the aim of mere intellectual understanding and retention by memory. Catechesis is never mere information; it is essentially invitation. To assure this the structure of the Christian kerygma must be preserved, and all the details of Christian teaching must be seen in their organic coherence with the central message of God's design for man's salvation.

This third stage of missionary catechesis must also provide initiation to the Christian way of living, and during it the catechumens should "learn by doing." Instructions should aim at developing attitudes that dispose for justification (Denz 1526). Particular stress should be laid upon prayer; and as soon as the instruction has progressed sufficiently, participation in the Mass and the practice of Christian virtues, especially of charity, should be encouraged.

Postbaptismal Guidance. Although the catechumenate formally ends with Baptism, the newly baptized will need special guidance until they have become more deeply habituated to Christian ways of thought and living. The importance of this, a fourth, stage in the process of Christianization was emphasized by the Pan-African Study Week, Katigondo, Uganda (1964). The Christian community ought to protect the newly baptized, because of their pagan environment, and help them to grow in strength. In many places it is an established practice to provide this kind of help by assigning "patrons" from the time someone shows active interest in the Catholic religion at least until the end of the catechumenate. Postbaptismal instruction should stress the spirit of gratitude (2 Thess 2.13) and the apostolate (1 Pt 2.12); fittingly, too, it may touch on apologetical points that the new Christians need to know.

Methods and Adaptation. Missionary catechesis has much to gain by way of inspiration and help from the modern developments of catechetics in Christian countries. The suggestion of ways to accommodate particular pedagogical procedures to the special situation existing in a mission land should be among the tasks of regional catechetical centers. The exchange of experience and ideas among the various catechetical centers is most valuable. Significant in this respect was the international study week on mission catechetics held in Eichstätt, Germany (1960), which had a follow-up for East Asia in Bangkok (1962) and for Africa in Katigondo (1964).

There is a growing conviction that a thorough adaptation is needed, not only for a more effective missionary catechesis, but also out of respect for the indigenous cultures of the mission people. There must first be a pedagogical adaptation. The missioner must seek to meet the people on their own level. He must search out ways of making his message meaningful to them in terms of the ideas, beliefs, and practices with which they are already familiar; and upon this basis he must build with a constructive mind and a desire to save whatever is noble and good in their inherited culture. What is defective he will try to eliminate, but rather by fostering the good than by "fighting" what is wrong. Ultimately the whole missionary effort aims at the incorporative adaptation that is effected in the "incarnation" of Christianity in a new culture. The explicit introduction and formulation of the pre-evangelization is the practical fruit of the need and desire for adaptation (*see* ADAPTATION, MISSIONARY).

Duration of Instruction. The length and intensity of instruction needed for conversion cannot be decided beforehand; faith is the free gift of God. Also, the length of the catechumenate will depend on many factors (age, character, education, God's grace, and man's response) that have to be judged by the pastoral experience of the missioner. Perhaps the most important factor in determining the time for Baptism will be the generosity and perseverance with which the catechumen applies himself to the practice of a Christian life. Certain norms are generally established by local ordinaries. Practice varies in different areas. Most frequently the catechumenate lasts for about 1 year; in some places a period as long as 4 years of contact, acquaintance, instruction, and practice of Christian life is required.

Bibliography: J. HOFINGER, ed., *Teaching All Nations,* tr. C. HOWELL (New York 1961), *International Study Week on Missionary Catechetics* with program for the catechetical apostolate: basic principles, practical directions for catechists, and rules for drawing up textbooks of religious education; list of catechetical centers in the world; list of catechetical reviews. T. OHM, *Das Katechumenat in den katholischen Missionen* (Münster 1959); *Asia Looks at Western Christianity,* tr. I. MARINOFF (Freiburg 1959); *Machet zu Jüngern alle Völker* (Freiburg 1962). A. V. SEUMOIS, *Introduction à la missiologie* (Beckenried, Switz. 1952). M. RAMSAUER, *The Qualities and Achievement of a Good Mission Catechism* (Hong Kong 1960); "The Catechetical Task of Disposing the Pagans for the Faith," LumV 16 (1961) 591–606; "Die Hinführung des Menschen zum Glauben," *Einübung des Glaubens,* ed. G. STACHEL and A. ZENNER (Würzburg 1964). J. HOFINGER, *The Art of Teaching Christian Doctrine* (Notre Dame, Ind. 1957). J. A. MCCOY, *Advice from the Field* (Baltimore 1962). L. J. LUZBETAK, *The Church and Cultures: An Applied Anthropology for the Religious Worker* (Techny, Ill. 1963). J. J. SPAE, *Precatechetics for Japan* (Tokyo 1964). A. M. NEBREDA, *Kerygma in Crisis?* (Chicago 1965); "The Theological Problem of Transmission," in *Apostolic Renewal in the Seminary* (New York 1965) 123–138.

[M. RAMSAUER]

CATECHETICAL CENTERS

Catechetics is a branch of the Church's pastoral mission that has undergone extensive renewal in modern times. Much of the creative thinking in catechetics has been occasioned by two developments in Western Europe during the 19th and the beginning of the 20th centuries: first, the psychological research that profoundly affected all education, secular as well as religious; and second, the dechristianization of wide areas of Western Europe. Finding themselves faced with mass indifference to the Christian message, Catholic educators looked to new psychological methods for a more effective religious formation of Christians, young and old.

By definition catechesis is the transmission of the Christian message. Proponents of the new approaches to catechetics cautioned against what had become an all too common practice of cold indoctrination, and favored a more psychologically oriented approach. Instead of being satisfied with imparting knowledge alone, religious educators of the catechetical renewal aimed at inspiring their students to live their faith in a vital, dynamic way. Departures from stereotyped presentations of content and from formalistic method necessitated the rise of research centers to develop fresh methods and above all to reshape the essential content of the Christian message into its most attractive patterns.

Germany. Through pioneers in the 19th century, such as Johann Michael *Sailer and Johann *Hirscher, the Germans were among the first to give impetus to the new movement. The Munich Catechetical Congress at the beginning of the 20th century marked an early fruition of German initiative, which in more recent years has culminated in the famous German Catechism. The catechetical center in Munich, Deutscher Katechetenverein, and the catechetical programs at the University of Munich have figured prominently in this German renewal of modern times.

The Low Countries. The revival in Germany stirred interest within the Low Countries. Two centers in particular spearheaded serious catechetical reform, the International Center for Studies in Religious Education at Brussels, Belgium, widely known as Lumen Vitae, and the Canisius Institute at Nijmegen, Holland. Both centers have thrived and by their research and teacher formation programs have made significant contributions to the pastoral work of the Church.

Lumen Vitae is the accomplishment of a group of Jesuit priests who in the early 1940s founded a small catechetical research center at Brussels. Inspired by the theologian, Emil Mersch, SJ, they labored to reshape the content of catechesis along the lines of a Christocentric synthesis, and were alive as well to the new psychological methods. These pioneers of the Belgian renewal attacked the problem of dechristianization of their own land, but never limited their apostolic vision to its borders. On the contrary, the distinctive feature of the Lumen Vitae center that they eventually founded is precisely its international dimension. Under the direction of Georges Delcuve, SJ, the International Center has achieved a worldwide influence through its quarterly review, *Lumen Vitae,* and beginning in 1957, through its 1-year program of higher catechetical studies, "Année Catéchétique Internationale."

The Canisius Institute at Nijmegen, Holland, is the national catechetical center that serves the Dutch episcopate. Under the direction of the Society of Jesus, the center originated as a catechetical library in Maastricht, Holland, but in the 1950s it expanded its activities and moved to more spacious quarters in Nijmegen. William Bless, SJ, the director of the institute, and an excellent staff of religious educators, serve the Dutch dioceses with research and pre-service and in-service training of teachers. The Institute's catechetical review, *Verbum,* has helped significantly to form the priests of the country catechetically, while its other review, *School and Religion,* has done much to assist Holland's many lay catechists. Although the immediate aim of the Canisius Institute has been its own national needs, its cooperation with other centers, most notably Lumen Vitae, has extended its catechetical influence to the rest of the Catholic world.

France. The years following World War II ushered in an active period in French catechetical circles. France had not been without her great catechists up to that time, but perhaps a shocking experience was necessary to accelerate a national effort in the catechetical field. The shock was delivered in a provocative book by the Abbé Godin, *France, Mission Country?,* which took a hard look at the mass dechristianization of Catholic France.

The bishops of France responded with vigor by founding the Institut Supérieure Catéchétique at Paris in 1951. Under the direction of two Sulpicians, Fathers Joseph Colomb and François Coudreau, a 2-year program in higher catechetical studies was initiated in 1957. The roster of the faculty has been impressive, and achievements in research and teacher formation have put France among the world's leaders in serious catechetical renewal.

Another important foundation in France is the catechetical center at Strasbourg. The diocese of Strasbourg has an impressive history of catechetical endeavor, chiefly owing to the labors of Bp. Arthur Elchinger of Strasbourg, who even in the years preceding his elevation to the episcopate played an important role in the French catechetical renewal, especially through the publication of *Vérité et Vie,* a periodical emanating from Strasbourg's Centre de Pédagogie Chrétienne. In the early 1960s at Strasbourg Joseph Colomb began a 1-year program of catechetical studies adapted to the needs of secondary schools.

The United Kingdom. A National Catechetical Center for England and Wales was established by the English hierarchy in 1959 and placed under the direction of Francis Somerville, SJ; Bishop Beck, representing the English hierarchy, was the chairman (1964) of the Catholic Education Council, which is charged with the ultimate supervision of the center.

East Asia. Under the direction of Johannes Hofinger, SJ, the East Asian Pastoral Institute in Manila, Philippine Islands, has been preeminent for research in mission catechetics. Two periodicals emanate from this center, *Teaching All Nations* and *Good Tidings.* The former is a more scientific type of review for mission catechetics, while the latter is a popular practical guide for all catechists, whether within or outside of the mission apostolate.

The U.S. The catechetical renewal in the U.S. has begun to be deeply rooted in the last half of the 20th century. The national center of the Confraternity of Christian Doctrine had exerted a notable influence through parish Confraternity catechetical programs. In the 1960s it began the publication of a catechetical review, *The Living Light.* Some religious communities have made their colleges centers of catechetical activity, for example, the Sisters of Charity of the Blessed Virgin Mary at Mundelein College, Chicago, and the Sisters, Servants of the Immaculate Heart of Mary at Marygrove, Monroe, Mich. But in addition to these and the increasing number of summer institutes in catechetics, a most promising sign of maturity in catechetical renewal in the U.S. was the seriousness of purpose evidenced at universities. Several Catholic universities have launched solid graduate programs in religious education. Upon such research and continuing scholarship depends the catechetical movement in the Church of America.

[V. M. NOVAK]

CATECHETICAL SCHOOL, the organization for the religious instruction of adults in preparation for baptism in the early Church. The expression is actually a misnomer due to the misreading on the part of 16th- and 17th-century patrologists of evidence supplied by *Eusebius (*Hist. Eccl.* 3.3; 5.10; 6.15–19; 7.32), since the only evidence for the existence of such a school is connected with the Church of Alexandria in the last decades of the 2d century.

Paul mentioned instruction (*catechein*) in the elements of the faith (Rom 2.18; 1 Cor 14.19; Gal 6.6), and the so-called second letter of Clement (17.1) connects this instruction with baptism, as did Tertullian, who described the *catechumenate in his *De baptismo.* However, this instruction was given in connection with liturgical gatherings, exemplified in the Didache, as well as in the 4th-century catechetical homilies of *Cyril of Jerusalem, *Theodore of Mopsuestia, Hilary of Poitier, Ambrose of Milan, and John Chrysostom.

At Alexandria, *Origen had been charged by Bishop Demetrius (*c.* 202) with instructing prospective converts, and he passed on this duty to Heraclas for the less cultivated (Eusebius, *Hist. Eccl.* 6.1–6). In actual fact, Origen, and evidently Pantaenus and *Clement of Alexandria, who were named as his predecessors, conducted their philosophical lectures on Christian doctrines after the fashion of the philosophical schools of the day (Orig., *Contra Cels.* 3.57–58; 6.10). *Justin Martyr, and evidently *Tatian also, had conducted this type of school earlier in Rome. Clement's *Stromateis* gives an indication of the missionary and pastoral function behind such a school, which dealt with cultural and doctrinal interests of the learned listeners as an introduction to the doctrines and ethical teachings of Christianity. Evidently under Heraclas, Bishop of Alexandria (*c.* 232), an official character was given to this type of school; and similar organizations existed at Caesarea in Palestine and at Jerusalem.

In the 5th century, Augustine's *De catechezandis rudibus* outlined methods and material for instructing the ordinary convert; but his approach might be called today the background and method of religious education for the preacher or teacher assigned to the function of instructing prospective converts. There is no evidence for a school devoted simply to giving religious or catechetical instruction in the early Church. The procedure had a liturgical function as foundation and was known as the catechumenate. When infant baptism became common, the parents were charged with the religious instruction of their children (Aug., *In Ioh.* 51.13). In the monasteries and later in connection with diocesan centers, religious instruction was given to the monks and candidates for the clerical life. But little is known about procedures or methods in this type of school during the first centuries of the Christian era (*see* ALEXANDRIA, SCHOOL OF).

Bibliography: A. KNAUBER, TrierThZ 60 (1951) 243–266; Lex ThK[2] 6:34–35. K. RAHNER, *ibid.* 1:323. G. SLOYAN, ed., *Shaping the Christian Message* (New York 1958, pa. 1963) 3–37. G. BARDY, RechScRel 27 (1937) 65–90.

[F. X. MURPHY]

CATECHETICS

Term of 19th-century origin describing that branch of pastoral theology devoted to ordering the principles of religious pedagogy as they apply to extraliturgical formation in Christ through initiation into the mysteries of faith. It is allied to homiletics and pastoral liturgy, the theological disciplines that govern the formation of Christians within a context of formal worship. Like them, it is concerned with the engagement of the whole person in all his faculties, cognitive, conative, and emotive, although it has a special concern with knowledge as the way to love.

Those Formed by Catechetics. Whereas the celebration of the liturgy presumes faith in those who assemble to worship, those who are catechized may lack faith (inquirers) or be weak in faith although Christians in name and hence require "pre-evangelization." When neither is the case, catechetics nonetheless has to do with an engagement in faith by those capable of growing in this virture—not yet perfect in it, therefore—under the guidance of fully committed believers. This is especially true of the young, who, although radically *fideles* in virtue of their Baptism, i.e., members of faith communities (Church, family, parish), are at this time in their lives being inducted into a state of conscious faith adherence. This means that all catechetical attempts must keep in mind the primacy of the progress of those catechized from a noncommitted state to a committed. Faith is always a conscious and free act under the influx of grace; it is never automatic or necessitated by environment.

Influence of Culture. The effect of a totally Christian (or non-Christian) culture on the young may be assumed, but its power to beget genuine faith (or to stifle it) is something that never works apart from the mystery of God's action and the equally mysterious efforts of Christians in concert with that action. Certain cultural periods and milieux work against the possibility of faith in the young more than others. It can be said without exaggeration or alarm that the present age seems particularly inimical to belief; hence a special delicacy is required in inducing the beginnings of faith in the young. They should not be instructed (i.e., informed) about divine persons or the "truths of faith" as if they were already believers and simply required knowledge. No catechesis from a past age that went on such an assumption, e.g., one prepared for adults or for adult seekers after religious perfection, will be valid for them.

The world of faith and the world of fantasy will always need to be distinguished for the young child. In contemporary culture even fancy recedes in face of the claims made on the child's attention by the immediate and the empirical. Little can be assumed about the existence of a nonfanciful, unseen world. Often the adult who takes on the formal catechetical task must look to the whole structure of faith in the child's life. Knowledge is essential to faith; faith is personal commitment to God by way of knowledge. Faith speaks of God as known and adhered to in hope and love through Jesus Christ, in the power of his Spirit. Charity is the matrix and condition of faith from earliest youth. There is no legitimate expectation that Catholic faith will flourish apart from the meaningful celebration in love of the signs of faith, the holy Sacraments, or that learning will go ahead in a catechetical situation (home, parish, or school) where love is absent.

Finally, because the venture of faith and hence of catechetics is supernatural in its entirety, the supposition that progress in faith-knowledge is possible is valid only when the laws of human psychology and physical and emotional maturation are fully taken into account. The order of grace is the order of nature brought to perfection, not disregarded or set at nought. Hence catechetics attempts to discover how children and adults learn, how they make progress in moral formation, how they respond to frustrations; and it builds on this knowledge. Only when the creature man is taken into account in all his various stages of development can he be confronted with Christ and the gospel.

Confrontation with God. Similarly, only when God confronts man as He chooses to reveal Himself in Christ can it be said that the work of Christian formation is being attempted. Catechetics, therefore, assumes the full reality of man in his life situation and the full reality of God's self-disclosure to man with the will to save him. It cannot hope to succeed as theory or practice if any element in the delicate divine-human interplay is neglected.

HISTORY

There is no evidence that the special needs of childhood were attended to for almost the first 1,000 years of Christianity. St. Clement of Rome's first letter (PG 1:257) speaks of the formation (παιδεία) in Christ that parents should give children, while Tertullian in his treatise *De baptismo* (18) proposes deferring baptism beyond infancy for the children of adult converts, in the interests of a longer and sounder formation, although he advised otherwise for the children of Catholics (*De anima* 39, 40). The assumption was that parents would attend to the catechetical needs of their children, a task subsequently shared with sponsors (*fideiussores, compares*) who originally served adults [cf. M. Dujarier, *Le parrainage des adultes aux trois premiers siècles de l'Église,* Paris 1962; C. Brusselmans, *The Functions of Sponsorship at Infant Baptism in the First Centuries of the Church (100–500),* unpub. diss. CUA Washington 1964].

The Adult Catechumenate. The adult catechetical scheme featured inquiry into the lives of candidates with regard to their practice of charity and their setting aside pagan ways (in the case of 1st-century Jewish candidates, their renunciation of the power of the Law to save). The earliest moral instruction was in the "two ways," one leading to life, the other to death. A more complex paraenesis based on the virtues and vices was used subsequently. Certain sapiential books of Scripture, selectively employed, also contributed to the ethical ideal held out to inquirers before their Baptism. Second-century works such as the letter of Pseudo-Barnabas and *Shepherd of Hermas* testify to the allegorical use made of the OT in attempts to show how it is fulfilled in the NT. A "rule of faith" that summarized the principal points of doctrine emerged in some quarters; in others, elaboration of the threefold interrogation made at the triple immersion of Baptism led to the formation of various local creeds. The exposition of the two baptismal prayers, *Credo* (once it was formulated), and *Pater,* comprised the core of much early catechizing. Homilies were the normal form taken by such prepaschal instruction; the same was true of the postpaschal formation of the baptized. St. Justin tells something of the initiation of new Christians in his mid-2d-century *1 Apologia* (61). His indication by his reference to "instruction, fasting, and prayers" that candidates were being prepared in groups is the earliest evidence of that procedure. The Αποστολικὴ παράδοσις (20) of Hippolytus (*c.* 215) is the second clear reference to the Roman institution known as the catechumenate. Little, in fact, is sure about the way it was organized beyond that it was held over a 3-year period in Rome and a 2-year period in Africa. Its Oriental (i.e., Syrian) counterpart is an uncertain matter. The catechumenate culminated in a voluntary signing of *accedentes* who went forward for a succession of *scrutinia* (exorcisms accompanying inquiry into their perseverence in good conduct) spread out over periods varying from 3 to 6 and 8 weeks. The latter observances set the tone for Lent, which is basically a celebration of baptismal renewal. (Cf. Thierry Maertens, *Histoire et pastoral du rituel du catéchuménat et du baptême,* Bruges 1962.) Those who signed up for Baptism went from the status of catechumens, or hearers, to that of those to be "enlightened" (i.e., baptized; in Rome, *electi*). The Επίδειξις [Proof (Demonstration) of the Apostolic Preaching] of St. Irenaeus is an example of the typological catechesis—the latter a late 2d-century term, like the treatise itself—which disclosed Christ as Savior through an examination of selections from the OT narrative.

Augustine's early 5th-century *De catechizandis rudibus,* like Gregory of Nyssa's Λόγος κατηχήτικος, testifies to the practice of an introductory summary of the story of salvation to help inquirers know whether they wished to persevere. The various 4th- and 5th-century catechetical lectures that are extant (Cyril of Jerusalem, Theodore of Mopsuestia, Ambrose, the pilgrim Aetheria, Nicetas of Remesiana) indicate that the normal progression was from sin and the need for repentance—often in the context of a Biblical *narratio*—to Baptism as the effective sign of new life, then to a phrase-by-phrase explanation of the creed and, by analogy, the Lord's Prayer. Doctrine and Christian life were harmoniously intertwined. The threefold sacramental initiation (*illuminatio, consignatio, coena Domini*) was the death and burial of the Christian in sign, the fuller anointing of his whole being as he rose to new life, and his eating of the Lord's Body as the food of everlasting life.

To illustrate these sacramental realities the symbolic riches of both testaments of Scripture were brought to bear. That is why it is correct to say that the catechesis of the patristic period at its high point was entirely in a context of the liturgy. There were, to be sure, certain other theological genres at a popular or catechetical level, notably apologetic writings, commentaries on individual books of Scripture, and expositions of particular doctrines. The basic catechetical pattern, however, concerned itself with the need for repentance, the steps to probity of life and what it consisted in, God's saving action in Christ through the Holy Spirit, and the *bona redemptionis* (Church, fellowship of Sacraments, remission of sins, everlasting life in the body). On the occasion of the one rite of initiation, usually administered on Easter eve, an explanation of the meaning of these holy signs was begun, to be continued through a postpaschal period that varied in length depending on the place. The "catechetical schools" of Rome (Justin), Alexandria (Pantaenus, Origen), and Edessa (Tatian) were actually academies for theologians and exegetes in which philosophy and rhetoric were brought under tribute to the gospel.

Adaptation to Changing Circumstances. When the catechumenate ceased to be a practical possibility, brought to an end by the increasing numbers born into the Church after the political settlement of Constantine and the problem of catechizing the invading Germanic (and other) tribes, men such as SS. Columbanus, Gall, Boniface, and Januarius created a new type of missionary preaching. It was almost exclusively post- rather than prebaptismal. Not much literature on it exists. It is assumed that they framed oral catecheses in the various vernacular tongues on the basis of remembered knowledge from their monastic or other training. This catechetical formation was largely concerned, however, with the extirpation of pagan customs. It engaged in various attempts to demolish superstition. (See *Vita S. Eligii;* PL 87:524–550; and the Council of Leptines's *Indiculus superstitionum et paganiarum;* PL 89:810–824.) A letter of St. Boniface to King Edwin stressed the folly of idol worship; the goodness of God, the Creator, who had sent His Son to save us; and the need to accept the gospel and be reborn in Baptism (PL 80: 438–440).

A sermon of St. Gall tells the story of God's plan from the fall of Adam down to the work of redemption in Christ, the mission of the Apostles and call of the gentiles, and the works of the Church, which is the ark of salvation (PL 87:13–26). It is sacred history in the Augustinian manner, as are a variety of long and generally bad poems from the Carolingian era (Eligius, Fulcoius).

By the 8th century, however, a variety of synods was telling the clergy to "instruct the faithful in doing penance for their sins and going to confession" and to "exhort them to pray and have a care for the salvation of their souls" (Synod of Riesbach, 799; Mansi 13: 1026). Concern for didactic preaching on Sundays and feasts of obligation was constant in these years, and always on "those matters which lead to eternal life": the Holy Trinity [deriving from Augustine's version in *De doctrina christiana* (5), which ultimately achieved the form of the Athanasian creed]; the Incarnation after the formulation by the Council of Chalcedon; the Redemption in terms of a purchase of mankind back from Satan at the price of Christ's blood; the sins to avoid; the meaning of faith, hope, charity, chastity, continence, and the works of mercy.

It is impossible to find fault with this doctrinal and moral summary. The history of heresy had given it its shape and the barbarian invasions had separated the faith of Christians from the Biblical books and the living liturgy in which it was meant to find its chief expression. The separation was not only linguistic; it was theological (in the broader sense) as well. Thus, the importance of David was no longer his role as "the Lord's anointed" in the brief history of the undivided monarchy. Rather, his comeliness and his friendship with Jonathan were featured in that edifying tale; his sin with Bathsheba and repentance; and his immediate typological relation to Christ. History in any modern sense did not exist for this age. The "truth of faith" or the sacred proposition (e.g., creedal article) stood free of history, both the human history of Jesus, to whom it happened, and the life story of the Frankish peasant, who had to accept it as a condition of his Baptism. The latter doubtless supposed the event had taken place in some distant time past, but it was for him much more an ahistorical *mýthos* true in a transcendent "religious" sense than true with the truth of history, which for the Christian is always the locus of God's saving action.

Medieval Catechetics. The Manichaean strain of Augustine's writings was never absent from the moral catechesis of the West. Genuine NT eschatological thought yielded to a concern *de novissimis;* in these "last things," the central importance of a risen life in this body had yielded to hope for a Platonic, heavenly existence in the spirit after one had successfully got past the hurdle of Christ, the *iudex supremus.* In a word, Christianity in medieval catechetics consisted of a world of archetypes. One memorized them so as to be somehow conformed to them. In this scheme the great archetype for humanity, Christ raised up in the flesh by the power of the Spirit, played very little part. As the symbols of the liturgy, including the Bible correctly understood, came to mean less and less to medieval man, he devised symbols that meant more to him. Wayside shrines of the Crucified, of Jesus' Mother, of the Apostles were ubiquitous. Patron saints for every need and calling were multiplied. Feast days, which were holidays from back-breaking labor, increased in number and with them a meaningful "liturgy" of procession, image, and mime.

The Friars Minor developed devotion to the infancy of Christ; and after the experience of the Crusades to the holy places, to His Passion and Way of the Cross. The Capuchins later popularized this devotion. Early sets of "stations" varied from seven "falls" to 43 distinct happenings; but that of 14, ending in his entombment, prevailed. Thomas of Celano spoke for a whole age in his mournful, all but hopeless *Dies Irae.* Apocalyptic preachers multiplied. Witch-burning flourished. Life, being short and in itself unimportant, was cheap. Consolation came from looking on the Sacred Host, gazing at the wall-high paintings of St. Christopher and the Child to ensure safety, allying oneself firmly with SS. Barbara, Becket, George, or the 14 holy martyrs—whoever was in charge of one's special interests. The images of the saints went richly vested. Not a figure in the Nativity scene was without its moving parts. Heaven was indeed on earth, if in a considerably improved economic condition. This incarnational catechesis was immensely effective. Its affinity with, and its chasm from, the word of salvation joined to the true sacramental signs of life in Christ were both the strength and the weakness of medieval catechetics.

Emphasis on faith through hearing was by no means an absentee in these years. This stress was the whole meaning of the phenomenon of the mendicant friars. SS. Vincent Ferrer, Bernardine of Siena, and Peter of Alcántara happened to be prisoners of their time in their pleas for the defense of God's honor against the Jew and the Moor, but their intent was to preach God's love and human repentance. The warm sermons of St. Francis's "little brothers" and the affirmation by the confreres of St. Dominic of the goodness of food and drink and sex stood off the pessimism and the dualism to which the age might otherwise have fallen victim. Neither tradition felt that stress on the gospel meant the repudiation of the Sacraments; neither viewed the charism of the word as inimical to bishopric or to papacy, only to unworthy holders of those offices.

The special contributions of medieval catechetics were the engagement of the hearer in his whole person, since an incomprehensible liturgy no longer accomplished this. Visual aids, sacred verse, and song counted for much in this age, e.g., the mnemonic device on the four senses of Scripture in the version of Nicholas of Lyra, *c.* 1330, familiar in its prose form at the beginning of Aquinas's *Summa theologiae* (1a, 1.10) and in *Quodl.* 7 (446): "Littera gesta docet, quid credas allegoria,/Moralis quid agas, quo tendas anagogia." [Cf. H. de Lubac, *Exégèse médiévale* (Paris 1959) 1:23.] The woodcut accompanied by a rhymed couplet was standard in catechetical usage. (Cf. J. Geffcken, *Der bilder Katechismus des 15. Jahrhunderts und die katechetischen Hauptstücke bis auf Luther,* Leipzig 1855.) So, too, was the question-and-answer technique (cf. Catechism of Bruno of Würzburg; PL 142:557–568) and the division of materials for memorization into groups of seven [cf. St. Edmund of Canterbury, *Speculum Ecclesiae,* in *Maxima Bibliotheca Veterum et Antiguorum Scriptorum Ecclesiasticorum,* ed. Dela Bigne (Lyons 1677) 25:316–327; old French text in Harry W. Robbins, *Le Merure de Seint Eglise* (Lewisburg, Pa. 1924)]. Advent and Lent were the favored times for preparing the young, at the age of 7, for confession and Communion. (Medieval thinkers conceived human life in successive cycles of 7 years.) They would receive instruction from parish priests or parents in the articles of the Creed, the Commandments, and the sins contained in "mirrors of perfection" that were catalogued according to duties of state. In general, the chief concern of the times was with explicit belief in the principal mysteries of faith and implicit adherence to all that the Church taught, accompanied by the practice of good works. Preachers were exhorted to speak simply to people, using many examples and the Biblical accounts to unfold the sacred doctrine contained in the Scriptures and the facts of Christian life (cf. Guibert de Nogent, *Liber in quo ordine sermo fieri debeat;* PL 156:21–32).

Moral teaching was stressed more than doctrinal, both because the people were assumed to have the virtue of faith already and because the allegorical use of Scripture by the Fathers, often directed to Jews or pagans, was thought to be beyond them. The medieval adult or child was dealt with in terms of the axiom that "preaching is the public proclamation of the word of God which enjoins what is right and forbids what is wrong." One has every reason to suppose that, as they mastered prayers (including acts of faith, hope, and love, which were basically theological definitions of these virtues), doctrinal facts, and lists of obligations, the Augustinian axiom of Rabanus Maurus that "the work of catechizing is to be accomplished *narratione, exhortatione, atque* in *hilaritate*" had long since lapsed into desuetude (*De disciplina ecclesiastica,* 1; PL 112: 1193).

Humanism. The late medieval concern with humanism in a sense of the term traceable to A. S. Pringle-Pattison (*Man's Place in the Cosmos,* 1897), i.e., the revived interest in the classical rhetoricians, poets, and artists as opposed to philosophers, is generally conceded to have flourished in two streams, one religious and the other nonreligious. The latter was marked by an all but exclusive anthropocentric concern, the former by attempts at synthesizing this-worldly interests with a religious orientation formerly so transcendent as to correspond little to actual human needs. Names associated with this Christian renaissance (term popularized in this sense by J. Burckhart, *The Renaissance in Italy,* 1885) begin with Dante and Tasso and include Nicholas of Cusa, Vittorino de Feltre, Pico della Mirandola, and Erasmus. In his adult catechism of 1533 Erasmus employed the classical forms of rhetoric *prótasis,* man before the Fall; *epítasis,* the cross; and *katástrophē,* the change in man's fortune that came with the Resurrection [*Opera Omnia* (Leyden 1706) 5.1133–96]. The numerical influence of this stream on catechetics was minimal. Like Origen's "catechetical school" at Alexandria, however, its seminal value for subsequent Christian education, synthesizing sacred and profane elements so-called, is incalculable. The 15th- and 16th-century humanists tended to oppose scholasticism bitterly as obscuring the gospel and were convinced that critical texts (of the kind possible in those times) of the Bible and the Fathers would serve the Church's theological needs sufficiently. Catechetically their position tends to be vindicated after the many intervening centuries, when an approach that is not less but rather more theological, concentrating on the sources of faith, begins to be favored.

Vittorino is known for his *Casa giocosa,* a peaceful setting for the child's harmonious development. Erasmus is no less interested in the youth's progress, but more specifically in piety by way of conscious faith, reliance on the Scriptures, love of God as a Father, and a patient attempt to do good to all and harm none [cf. *Colloquium "Pietas puerilis"* (Lyons 1533) 53–65]. He considers moral conduct to be faith in practice and is much more concerned with motive and intention than with the analysis of individual acts. Prayer for Erasmus centered on the *Pater* and stressed the advance of the kingdom; like a sovereign, God would know how to reward the good *miles Christi* in his own way. The Lord's Prayer was the epitome of common prayer; yet Erasmus strongly favored participation of the faithful in the sacred rites as well.

Reformation Period. Luther thought Erasmus subtle and satanic in his catechetics (despite having hailed his Greek NT joyfully in his theological lectures in Wittenberg in 1516). Bellarmine and Canisius both opposed him, and the charge of heresy (as early as 1523) resulted in his works being placed on the Index under Paul IV and Sixtus V. Their limited diffusion had unfortunate consequences for catechetics. An influence on the *Roman Catechism* is claimed for them, but except for the order employed this influence is hard to sustain as to particulars. His poetic catechism *Christiani hominis institutum,* written at Colet's request about 1514, is full of conceits (cf. *Opera Omnia* 5.1357–60), but the fresh spirit of his prose works could have done much in a post-Reformation period that otherwise went unchanged.

Catechetical Schools. The catechizing of children, left mainly to parents except for instruction of the few preparing for clericate or priesthood in cathedral and monastic schools, became a matter of specific concern from the end of the 15th century onward. The large numbers of orphans left after the "black death" were one cause; another was the general interest in learning that the Crusades spurred; but most influential of all was the catechetical thrust of the Anabaptist, Lutheran, and Calvinist reformers and the need felt by Catholics to neutralize it. The first catechetical schools are claimed for Milan (F. Grassi, "Preti di Santa Corona," 1473; A. Bellarati, "Scuola d'Albertino," 1481; Bl. Angelo Porro, "Scuola del Paradiso," 1491). Venice had an all-day school for orphans (St. Girolamo Miani, 1530), but the beginnings of the modern Sunday school or Confraternity of Christian Doctrine effort were the work of *Castellino da Castelli at Milan, 1536. Three years later he founded a company for this apostolate of regular instruction on Sunday and feastday afternoons (cf. A. Tamborini, *Le Compagnie e le scuole della dottrina cristiana,* Milan 1939). Trent required weekly catechizing of the young (25th sess., Nov. 11, 1562). St. Charles Borromeo, Archbishop of Milan, set up a school of Christian doctrine of five classes in each parish of his diocese in 1577, approving at the same time a company of priests and laymen for the task. Its rule was finally approved in 1585, a year after his death, but it had apparently been in force since 1579 [cf. L. Csonka, *Educare* (Zurich 1964) 3:112–116]. Rome, meanwhile, in 1560 had set up a confraternity to teach Christian doctrine, which Pius V approved in 1571 and Paul V erected as an archconfraternity in 1607. The Reformers' efforts went on concurrently, beginning with Luther's *Kleiner Katechismus oder christliche Zucht* (1529), assembled from earlier writings after his eye-opening visitation of the peasantry, and the theological, less down-to-earth efforts of the Zwinglian Bucer (1534) and John Calvin (1535).

Methods. Methods of catechetical instruction did not undergo notable change until the period of the German Enlightenment, when the "Socratic" inquiries of J. Spendu, A. V. Winter, and J. M. Leonhard, an early attempt at a psychology of learning, began to be employed by J. I. von *Felbiger and J. Grueber first, then by B. Galura and J. *Hirscher. The derivation of the truths of faith from sacred history was the major methodological advance, although intermittently throughout a century it was supposed that the step ahead consisted in engaging the child's attention with the Biblical narrative, more concrete than the abstract truth, which latter ultimately had to be identified to him for acceptance as the Church's faith.

Grueber examined the maieutic method that Galura had devised in an effort to come to terms with the

Aufklärung's inquiring spirit but rejected it in favor of the notion of the catechist as a messenger of God and primarily a communicator. The four Augustinian steps in catechizing are identified as *narratio, explicatio, interrogatio* (to check on understanding), and *exhortatio* (cf. *De cat. rud.* 3–7; *De doctr. Christ.* 4.4; 6; 13). This reached late 18th-century classrooms in the form *propositio* (for memorization), *explicatio* (analysis, including questions), *applicatio* (to the students' lives), and *exercitatio* (recapitulation of the whole, "fixing in"). It was the virtue of Socratic method that it sought understanding through persistent inquiry; its drawback for Christians was the supposition that the young already possessed the content of faith, which skillful midwifery could bring forth. This approach, however, never seriously threatened the four-step method immediately above (or more commonly the first three). The "theological clarity" of J. *Deharbe's *explicatio* (1847), with its imposition of the threefold obligation to believe all God has revealed, keep His Commandments, and use the means of grace, reigned supreme. It was never dislodged by the principle enunciated by the pastoral theologian J. M. Sailer that said, "The catechist first approaches the heart, then the understanding, and then goes back to the heart."

About 1900 the *Münchener Katechetenverein* (founded by A. Seidl, 1887, organized under G. Götzel in 1921 as the German Catechetical Association, reorganized 1945) began to evolve the "Munich method," namely, that of lesson-synthesis. Instead of the prevailing analysis of text material (way of deduction), the attempt was made, on sound psychological principles, to have teacher and pupil arrive at the truth of faith inductively. J. F. Herbart had proposed as the three steps in learning: "observe, think, act." O. Willmann, a student of Herbart's student T. Ziller, popularized the technique in Catholic circles (*Didaktik als Bildungslehre,* 1882–89) using these steps: presentation, explanation, application (from the child's point of view: perception, assimilation, response). Subsequently a first and fifth steps were added, preparation and recapitulation. The scheme, basically Ciceronian, had already emerged in the catechetical treatises of C. J. Vidmar (Vienna 1895), Skočdopole (Vienna 1897), and S. Katschner (Graz 1899), but not as formal "steps."

20th Century

Catechetical congresses were held all through these years (Vienna 1905, 1912; Munich 1905, 1911, 1912; Piacenza 1899; Milan 1907; Rome 1908). France was kept from moving nationally by "secularization laws" (1901, 1905) and made its first advance with a pastoral letter by Bp. A. Landrieux of Dijon (1922) that called for a return to "the method of the gospel" as the most efficacious of all. During the first 4 decades of this century the chief stress was on: the catechist as a witness and emissary of Christ, learning by doing, incidental learning, and the building of a lesson that would have as its purpose bringing home a single point through engaging the child in all his faculties. Adolescent pedagogy was not a matter of practical concern because the Sacrament of Confirmation (about age 12–14) comprised a "Church-leaving certificate" in most Catholic cultures; religious education, like formal, was terminal then except for a *catéchisme de persévérance* among the very few. No serious adult catechetical effort was undertaken on a national basis. Attempts were made to relate catechetics to liturgy, but this necessarily meant an explanation of ceremonies owing to the condition of public worship. Eucharistic devotion stressed the grace of "receiving," there being little current theology of a fuller Eucharistic participation. Such as there was received great impetus, as did the catechetical effort generally, by the decrees of Pius X on frequent (1905) and early (1910) Communion, and his encyclical letter of April 15, 1905, *Acerbo nimis,* on religious formation.

In the U.S. In the U.S. the Religious Education Association was founded at the University of Chicago (1903), the president of which, W. R. Harper, served as first chairman of the board. The early membership, all Protestant, included J. Dewey, N. M. Butler, G. A. Coe, H. Van Dyke, S. P. Cadman, and B. T. Washington. With it, the U.S. "religious education movement" was launched, to promote "a new methodology, new materials, a new philosophy, and a new understanding." Msgr. T. J. Shahan gave an early paper (1905) as did Rabbis M. J. Gries (1908) and E. G. Hirsch (1909). At first Protestant in membership, the association early became interconfessional on a token basis but in substantial numbers only in the late 1940s.

The National Catholic Educational Association (all-day schools) was founded in 1904, and the department of education at The Catholic University of America (C.U.A.), in 1905. Consistent critics of parrot-style religion in those years included T. E. Shields of the latter department (*The Catholic Education Series,* 1909–18), P. C. Yorke (San Francisco), Joseph Newman (Louisville), R. MacEachen (*The Teaching of Religion,* 1921). At the college level Msgr. J. M. Cooper (C.U.A. 1909–49) founded that university's department of religious education (1936) and wrote *Religious Outlines for Colleges* (1924–30, 2d rev. ed. 1935–46) as a challenge to the 19th-century-type theology manuals in use, e.g., Wilmers, Sheehan, and Doyle-Chetwood-Herzog. J. J. Baierl of Rochester, N.Y., adapted in English the catechisms of F. Stieglitz of Munich (1915, 1916). The Grueber-M. Gatterer *Katechesen* were translated by G. Dennerle as *Leading the Little Ones to Christ* (1932), and the Innsbruck lectures of Gatterer were given English dress by A. N. Fuerst as *The Systematic Teaching of Religion* (2 v. New York 1938–43). Widely used children's aidbooks in the Munich spirit included those of J. Brownson, M. Bolton, A. Heeg, E. Horan, A. Schorsch, and V. Michel–J. M. Murray.

Catechetical Renewal. The catechetical movement suffered severe setbacks early in the 20th century, as did all sacred science, through the swift and often uncomprehending repression of *Modernismus.* Not only was a false theory of evolution in faith and dogma reprobated but also the true developmental and adaptive principle at work in the Church, even in the formation of the Gospels written in a spirit of faith in the meaning and message of Jesus. A "nonhistorical orthodoxy," as it has been called, prevailed. The holding back of scholarly progress in the sources of Christianity for 50 years necessarily impeded the catechetical renewal, which is so dependent on the Bible, the liturgy, and theology rightly conceived. In 1936 J. A. Jungmann challenged seminary theology, though in fact he identified all scholastic theology with it, as incapable of bringing the gospel in all its simplicity and directness (*Die Frohbotschaft und unsere Glaubensverkündigung*, Regensburg). He held that theology had as its formal object the "true" (e.g., *Deus sub ratione deitatis*), whereas pastoral care or catechetics centered on the "good" (e.g., *Verbum caro factum propter nostram salutem*). He called, in effect, for a second, "kerygmatic" theology to nourish faith as distinct from a speculative, defensive, and polemical one. In the ensuing debate, interrupted by World War II, Jungmann's demand was rejected, but only because the community of Catholic theologians came to see that all theology had to be kerygmatic (i.e., evangelical) and that the more speculative it was, the greater the necessity. Jungmann's catechetical revolution brought the center of gravity from method to message, or rather affirmed that these inseparable two were related in this way: the message and its mode of coming to us, both in history and in mystery, always determine the basic method of its presentation. The catechetical renewal in this stage has had several centers of influence: Innsbruck, where Jungmann teaches; Lumen Vitae Centre, first at Louvain, then Brussels (G. Delcuve, M. Van Caster); Tübingen (F. X. Arnold); Washington, department of religious education, C.U.A.; Munich (Fischer, J. Schreibmayr, Tilmann); Paris (Coudreau, Brien, Liégé, Babin); Strasbourg (Elchinger, Colomb). No list of 20th-century catechetical effort would be complete that omitted mention of F. H. Drinkwater of Birmingham, England (The "Sower" Scheme, 1920; *Educational Essays*, London 1951; *Telling the Good News*, 1960).

U.S. catechetical progress between 1930 and 1950 is associated chiefly with the names R. G. Bandas, J. B. Collins, Sr. M. Rosalia Walsh, M. I. Schumacher, W. H. Russell, W. Farrell, and Abp. E. V. O'Hara of Kansas City, Mo. (protagonist of the Confraternity of Christian Doctrine and religious vacation school movement). More recent influential figures have been J. Hofinger (*The Art of Teaching Christian Doctrine*, 2d ed. Notre Dame 1962), Sister Maria de la Cruz (*On Our Way* series, 1959–), T. C. Stone (ed. *Pastoral Catechetics*, with J. Hofinger, 1964), B. Cooke, G. Diekmann, M. P. Ryan, W. J. Reedy.

The chief modern landmarks in the catechetical renewal have been international meetings in Rome (1950), Antwerp (1956), and Eichstätt (1960), the latter devoted to missionary catechetics especially, as also an earlier one in Léopoldville (1955) had been, and later ones in Bandung (1962) and Katigondo (1964). Antwerp yielded the scheme of *les trois grandes lignes* in catechizing: Scripture, liturgy, and formal doctrinal instruction. To this was added at Eichstätt the witness of a Christian life. Subsequent analysis has tended to disfavor this scheme since the "ways" are disparate and give the appearance of being four entities in the same order.

Characteristics of Modern Catechetics. Probably the chief characteristic of modern catechetics is its return to the conception of Christian education as basically formative, a progressive initiation into new life. Supreme value is put on the witness to Christ provided by the community or by individual parents, clergy, and catechists. This is the chief exterior motivation to Christian living, the interior Teacher, the Holy Spirit, being the other indispensable figure. A word of God is addressed in the Church to the person catechized. It is testified to by the Scriptures, which receive their best proclamation (and exposition) in a living liturgy. Formal instruction helps the learner know what things to listen for in that optimum situation ("summit" and "source" of all Christian activity) and in all his life circumstances since this word comes to him in various ways. He is helped to see his place in the centuries-long story of salvation, the working out in time of God's design to save all men in his Son through the power of the Spirit.

If the characteristics of modern catechetics were to be listed they would include: concreteness, immediacy, relevance to life, knowledge in depth of the God who saves through the signs that save, a sense of mission to the entire human family, and the supreme claim made on those whom God calls to love Him, and all men, in Christ Jesus, the Lord.

Bibliography: L. BOPP et al., LexThK² 6:35–55. K. B. CULLY, ed., *The Westminster Dictionary of Christian Education* (Philadelphia 1963). J. A. JUNGMANN, *The Good News Yesterday and Today*, ed. and tr. W. HUESMAN, with essays in appraisal of its contribution, ed. J. HOFINGER (New York 1962); *Handing on the Faith*, tr. and rev. A. N. FUERST (New York 1959). L. CSONKA et al., *Educare: Sommario di scienze pedagogiche*, 3 v. (3d ed. Zurich 1964) 3:195–554. Bureau International Catholique de l'Enfance, *Dix années de travail catéchétique* (Paris 1960). H. W. OFFELE, *Geschichte und Grundanliegen der sogenannten Münchener katechetischen Methode* (Munich 1961). J. HOFINGER, ed., *Teaching All Nations*, tr. C. HOWELL (New York 1961).

[G. S. SLOYAN]

CATECHISM

From the Greek κατηχεῖν (to speak so as to be heard, hence to instruct orally; cf. Lk 1.4; Act 18.25; Rom 2.18; Gal 6.6). A catechism according to an English-speaking and German usage is a manual of Christian doctrine, often in question and answer form (German, *Katechismus*). In Romance languages, the term also signifies the act of catechizing, the work of presenting Christian doctrine or an individual lesson, especially to the young (French, *catéchisme;* Italian, *catechismo*).

Patristic and Early Medieval Periods. Catechisms (*catecheses*) in the patristic era were traditionally prebaptismal and adult in orientation (e.g., Cyril of Jerusalem, Κατηχήσεις; John Chrysostom, Ὁμιλίαι κατηχητικαί; Augustine, at end of *Catech. Rud.*, *Sermones* 212–215; Rufinus of Aquileia, *Commentarius in symbolum apostolorum*). At times these lectures and homilies dealt with the immediately postbaptismal doctrinal needs of new Christians, in which case they were called "mystagogic" or simply "paschal" (e.g., Cyril of Jerusalem, Κατηχήσεις μυσταγωγικαί; Augustine, *Selected Easter Sermons*, ed. P. Weller, St. Louis 1959). The oral method of instructing apparently first gave its name to the student's handbook as a book title in the work of the Protestant Andreas Althamer (*Catechismus in Frag und Antwort*, Nuremberg 1528). Throughout the Carolingian and early and high medieval periods, numerous handbooks were produced that had the Christian formation of clergy and laity as their aim. Among these might be named the *Disputatio puerorum per interrogationes et responsiones* attributed doubtfully to Alcuin (d. 804; PL 101:1097–1144), the 9th-century *Catechesis Weissenburgensis* by a monk of that monastery (ed. G. Eckhard, Hanover 1713), the 12th-century *Elucidarium* attributed to Honorius of Autun (PL

172:1109–76; cf. Y. Lefèvre, *L'Elucidarium et les lucidaires,* Paris 1954), and the ingenious compendium of Hugh of Saint-Victor in that same century, *De quinque septenis seu septenariis* (PL 175:406–414). These treatises might be called the second layer of adult catechetical formation, suitable for those who could read Latin.

More basic were the catechisms proposed by bishops, emperors, and Church synods to be spoken orally to the unlettered faithful by those who had the *cura animarum.* Among these, which invariably assumed phrase-by-phrase expositions by the clergy of the two baptismal prayers, Apostles' Creed and Our Father, and a list of vices to be avoided, might be mentioned the *Capitularia* of Charlemagne (A.D. 802; PL 97:247) and his letter (15) to Garibaldus (PL 98:917–918); the synods of Leipzig (A.D. 743; PL 89:822, c.25), Clovesho (A.D. 747; Mansi 12:398, c.10), Frankfurt (A.D. 794; Mansi 13:908, c.33), Aachen (A.D. 802; PL 97:247, c.14), Arles (A.D. 813; Mansi 14:62, c.19), Mainz (A.D. 813; Mansi 14:74, c.45, 47), and Trier (A.D. 1227; Mansi 23:31, c.8). The synod of Albi (A.D. 1254; Mansi 23:836, c.17, 18) required pastors to explain the articles of the creed simply each Sunday, and children to be brought to Mass from the age of 7 onward, and at the same time to have the *Pater, Ave,* and *Credo* explained to them. The Council of Lambeth demanded that this instruction be given by pastors four times a year on feast days, "without any fantastic weaving of subtle adornment," and that it include "the fourteen articles of faith [i.e., the Creed], the Ten Commandments of the Decalogue, the precepts of the gospel, namely the two concerned with charity, the seven works of mercy, the seven capital sins and their progeny, the seven principal virtues, and the seven Sacraments of grace" (A.D. 1281; Mansi 24:410). The acts of a similar council in Lavaur, France, provided a more complete catechism (A.D. 1368; Mansi 26:486). A good summary of the necessity of faith comes first; next, a severe charge to the clergy on its obligations to catechize; third, the 14 articles and seven Sacraments, "on which the whole Christian religion is based." Seven virtues and their opposing vices come after these "truths to be believed." These, together with the seven gifts of the Spirit and the beatitudes that correspond to them, are the "things that are to be loved," and the seven petitions of the Our Father describe the "things to be hoped for." In the 14 articles of the Creed, seven are said to pertain to the Deity proper, seven others to the humanity of Christ.

Influence of St. Augustine. The scheme of multiples of seven seems to have originated with Augustine's treatise on the Sermon on the Mount (PL 34:1229–1308), in which he reduces the beatitudes to seven by identifying the last one in Matthew's Gospel with the first, then compares them with the seven gifts of the Spirit from the Vulgate version of Is 11 in reverse order. This mnemonic device, probably Augustine's least helpful contribution to catechetical theory, emerged as supreme in medieval practice via popularizers such as Isidore of Seville and Rabanus Maurus.

A second insight of Augustine was his threefold division of all doctrine in his *Faith, Hope, and Charity* (*c.* A.D. 422; known as *Enchiridion;* ed. J. Krabinger, Tübingen 1861). In it the "confession of faith is briefly summed up in the Creed. . . . But of all those matters which are to be believed in the true spirit of faith, only those pertain to hope which are contained in the Lord's Prayer" (114), while "all the divine commandments hark back to charity . . .. Of course the charity meant here is the love of our neighbor" (121). Although Augustine does not divide the creedal articles into two sevens, his extended treatment of them (9–113) is in the speculative vein, not the immediately Biblical vein, that became so familiar to later generations. The petitions of the Lord's Prayer (114–116) are seven in number, "three of which request eternal goods, the remaining four, temporal goods necessary for the attainment of the eternal." In dealing with charity (117–122) he entirely subordinates the Decalogue to the Gospels. The Ten Commandments are not listed, hence the familiar division into three and seven does not appear. The Holy Spirit, it is pointed out, "diffuses charity in our hearts" (121). This balancing off of the three theological virtues with the two prayers and the divine law was Augustine's second most influential contribution (his numerological wordplay that yielded the "sevens" being the first).

Paradoxically, Augustine's best insight survived least well, namely, the *narratio* of the story of salvation in six epochs (*aetates*), of which the seventh was eternity, the Day of the Lord. This idea is developed in two sample introductory catecheses at the end of *De catechizandis rudibus.* The landmark figures of the six ages are Adam, Noe, Abraham, David, the Babylonian captivity, and Christ, "from [whose] coming the sixth age is dated" (39). Augustine was still in a millenarian phase at this writing (*c.* 405), but the important matter was his presentation of the Church's faith in a historical framework. He was the first to deal with the life of the Church (the sixth *aetas*) as sacred history in the same sense as the events described in Scripture. It is sometimes claimed for this "first catechetical instruction" that it was not simply Augustine's best but also his chief contribution to the field. The facts belie the claim. It is true that the pedagogic insights of this treatise periodically emerge over the centuries from a welter of "sevens" or treatments of the "Creed, Lord's Prayer, and Commandments" over the years, but the lineal descendants of his narrative technique are all too easily named: C. Fleury, F. A. Pouget, J. J. Gruber, then the Innsbruck-Louvain-Paris resurgence beginning in 1936.

Augustine also pioneered in presenting the Decalogue as a framework for Christian morality (*Catech. Rud.* 35.41). This had tragic consequences. The convenient 10 headings prevailed, and indeed in a Mosaic spirit of observance, while Augustine's stress on the Holy Spirit as the finger of God who wrote on the stone tablets and again at Pentecost was largely forgotten (cf. P. Rentschka, *Die Dekalogkatechese des hl. Augustinus, Kempten* 1905).

Augustine's greatness as a catechist resided in his musings on the relation between symbol and reality, word and truth, speech and thought. The psychological optimum for the reception of an idea figured largely in his catechetical theory. Lesser teachers, unable to handle his poetic diction or his psychology, gravitated to his reasoned reflections on the mysteries. The result was a rationalized Christianity cut off from its Biblical sources despite the massive use of the Bible made by Augustine (42,816 citations from both Testaments, according to P. de Lagarde). The catechisms derived from his writings set the tone of Christianity in the West for 1,000 years. In departing from his Biblical and liturgical concerns and concentrating on his rationale of the mysteries, they created a vacuum of evangelical preaching and catechizing that the Reformers filled.

Augustine's influence added the Decalogue to the two baptismal prayers as matter for catechizing. The Hail Mary and the Sacraments (as distinct from the *communio sanctorum*—and they are *sancta*—in the Creed) came in the 13th century. Lists of sins and virtues were added last as part of confessional practice. Absolution was withheld if penitents did not pass the annual scrutiny that accompanied the paschal confession. This technique helped to proliferate lists (*libelli*) compiled for memorization.

Middle Ages. Treatises on Christian life, such as Alcuin's *De virtutibus et vitiis* on perfection for the soldier (PL 101:613–638), continued into the Middle Ages as a genre on the art of living and dying. Among these were *L'Art de mourir* attributed to Matthew of Cracow, Bishop of Worms (1478), *Tafel der kerstlygken Levens* (1475), and various shepherd's almanacs filled with secular and sacred information, such as the *Compost ou Kalendrier des bergiers* (Paris 1492). From the invention of printing onward, and even before, woodcut illustrations were used both in books and as wall charts (*tabulae*).

Gerson. Jean *Gerson, forcibly retired as chancellor of Paris in his last years (1409–12), taught catechism in Lyons. He is best known for *L'ABC des simples gens* (MS 1067 Mazarin Library), for a personal apologia for his engagement in the work of catechizing entitled *Tractatus de parvulis trahendis ad Christum* [*Opera Omnia,* (Antwerp 1706) 3.278–291], and an *Opus tripertitum* (*ibid.* 1.426–450) on the Commandments, confession, and dying well. In the last-named work the attention given to moral precepts is so considerable that the writer's initial concern with the mysteries of faith has shrunk to a kind of prologue. It may be true, as Hugh of Saint-Victor says, that "all divine Scripture is related to the *finis* of moral formation" (*Didascal.* 5.6; PL 176:794C), but this *correctio morum* and *forma vivendi* (741C) are not meant to dislodge the mystery of God's action, to which they are basically a response.

St. Thomas Aquinas. St. Thomas in his various adult catechetical treatises had not been guilty of an imbalanced concern with Christian behavior. These works were chiefly his *Compendium theologiae,* done on Augustine's pattern of faith, hope, and charity (1272–73, broken off when he was only 10 chapters into hope and the petition "thy kingdom come") and the *reportatum* in Latin of 57 of his Italian sermons delivered at Naples during Lent 1273 on the Creed (15), the Lord's Prayer (10), and the law, i.e., charity and the Decalogue (32), to which should be added his earlier conferences on the Hail Mary and a treatise on the Church's Sacraments done for the archbishop of Palermo in 1261. In these lectures, fully scholastic in tone though they were, there was at least a healthy concern for the revealed mysteries.

Pre-Reformation. The lectures survived in medieval pulpit preaching until Trent, but the strain represented by Gerson's writing continued much stronger. Thus, Dietrich Kolde's influential *Christenspiegel* of 1480 (ed. C. Drees, Werl 1954) was extremely moralistic, as was Johannes Herolt's *Liber discipuli de eruditione Christi fidelium* (Strasbourg 1490). The latter devotes 6 pages to the Creed, 3 to the Our Father, and 101 to morality under the headings Commandments, deadly sins, and various moral precepts [cf. P. Bahlmann, *Deutschlands katholische Katechismen bis zum Ende des 16 Jahrhunderts* (Münster 1894) 12; also P. Göbl, *Geschichte der Katechese im Abendland vom Verfall des Katechumenates bis zum Ende des Mittelalters* (Kempten 1880)].

From the close of the patristic period (i.e., from the 9th or 10th century) through the whole Tridentine era, little was done to relate beatitudes, works of mercy, evangelical counsels, fruits of the Holy Spirit, prayer, and almsgiving to the story of salvation as it culminated in the redemptive deed of Christ. They are lumped together with *effectus divinitatis* or *bona redemptionis,* i.e., related in a most general way to the works of the Spirit that conclude the Apostles' Creed. Rudolf Padberg (*Erasmus als Katechet,* Freiburg 1956) is quite right in describing the entire medieval period as a catechetical vacuum. Jungmann's studies (*Pastoral Liturgy,* New York 1962) show the conservative force of medieval culture on folk piety, but Padberg's judgment leveled against sermons and catechisms is irrefutable.

Humanism. The late medieval humanists tried another tack but unsuccessfully. Among their attempts were the brief *Cathecyzon* (*c.* 1510) by John Colet, Dean of St. Paul's and founder of its school, and Erasmus' adult catechism of 1533 [*Dilucida et pia explanatio symboli . . . decalogi praeceptorum, et dominicae praecationis; Opera Omnia* (Leyden 1706) 5.1133–96]. By the onset of the Reformation the Catholic catechisms in commonest use included books of piety such as the *Liber Jesu Christi pro simplicibus* (1505) and the catechisms of J. Dietenberger (Cologne 1530) and G. Witzel or Vicelius (Leipzig 1535).

Luther. Martin Luther's *Kleiner Katechismus,* which appeared first in 1529, was influenced by those of the Waldensians and Bohemian Brethren. His *Grosser* followed the next year. Some of Luther's sermons and tracts are marvelously evangelical in a way that his catechism (popularly called *Enchiridion*) is not. Rather, it is a medieval handbook that stresses duties of state. Luther required verbatim memorization of its contents by the peasantry, like any medieval bishop. The *Grosser* is distinguished chiefly by its insight into the daily life of the peasant, its concern with the "existential" character of the gospel, and its reliance on God's action rather than man's as ultimately effective in the work of salvation.

St. Peter Canisius. Canisius, the apostle of Catholic Germany in the Reformation period, produced three handbooks of Catholic faith: a *maior catechismus* (Vienna 1555), a *minimus* bound in with a Latin grammar, as Colet's had been (Ingolstadt 1556), and a *parvus* or *minor* (Cologne 1558). All three were done in Latin first, then in German (*S. Petri Canisii Cat. Lat. et Germ.,* ed. F. Streicher, Munich 1933–36). The intermediate one, entitled *Capita doctrinae christianae compendio tradita . . .,* became normative in many countries. It was composed of 124 questions and two appendices, one of Scripture texts against heretics and the other a quotation from Augustine on steadfastness in faith. There were five parts, three on the theological virtues and the matching prayers (or law), a fourth on the Sacraments, and a fifth on "duties of Christian holiness" (the smallest catechism had featured sins and the opposing goods in this fifth place). The first four doctrinal sections taught *sapientia;* the last, *justitia.* Canisius claimed authorship of the books only in 1566, although publishers had attributed it to him as early as 1559. He thought that the supposition of multiple authorship would recommend them better.

St. Robert Bellarmine. Bellarmine produced his *Dottrina cristiana breve* in 1597 [*Opera omnia* (Paris 1874) 12:261–282], a brief handbook deriving from his instruction of Jesuit brother cooperators at Rome. It began with the sign of the cross, then went on to Creed, Our Father, Hail Mary, Ten Commandments, precepts of the Church, counsels, Sacraments, virtues, gifts, works of mercy, gifts of the Spirit, four last things, and mysteries of the rosary.

A year later (1598), motivated by the demands of office in his brief archbishopric of Capua, Bellarmine produced what might be called a teacher's manual of doctrine, *Dichiarazione più copiosa della d.c.* (*ibid.,* 283–332). The student is the questioner here, and the teacher, the respondent at length. Bellarmine follows Augustine's three virtues as the way to know what things are *credenda, speranda,* and *amanda.* The Sacraments that follow the threefold listings of obligations (cf. above) are those means "by which the grace of God is acquired." All the matters that come after "the four principal parts of doctrine," i.e., from the theological and moral virtues onward, "help greatly in living in conformity with the will of God."

Other Efforts. The Jesuits Edmond *Auger writing in France (Lyons 1563) and Juan Martinez de *Ripalda, in Spain (Saragossa 1616) produced handbooks similar to the above two. Canisius' work is fittingly coupled with Bellarmine's as to framework and outlook, but it was more like Luther's in the warmth of its diction and popular appeal; this derived in the case of Canisius from much reliance on Scripture. In 1569 a fellow Hollander named P. de Buys (*see* BUSAEUS, PETRUS) produced with Canisius' help a work that supplied more than 4,000 references to Scripture and the Fathers for the *Catechismus maior* (4 v. Cologne 1569–70); this work is generally known as *Opus catechisticum,* a title given it in its revision by J. Hase (Cologne 1577).

In general, these late medieval handbooks had as their framework a theology based on an analysis of terms (cf., e.g., Isidore of Seville, *Etymologiae;* Pseudo-Dionysius, *De nominibus divinis*). This analytical theology, while it was meant as a paraphrase and exposition of the revealed message, in fact departed notably from the Biblical testimony to the way God revealed Himself to men. The Creed rightly understood is a Christ-kerygma, which at the same time shows the progress of the Trinitarian revelation and the invitation of men to divine life through Church and Sacraments by way of Spirit-filled likeness to the risen Lord. The Pater and the Ave (in its shorter medieval form) are NT prayers, the twofold commandment is Jesus' teaching on the fulfillment of the whole law. Despite the possibility of framing a Biblical catechism from these prayer sources, it did not happen so. The form imposed on the message remained extrinsic to it. Quite simply, categories foreign to the Biblical deliverance were imposed on it. Among the reasons that account for this were: the preoccupation with God as He is in Himself that replaced the NT presentation of Him exclusively as He is in relation to us; the suppression of the NT portrait of Christ as an intercessor in our behalf in favor of a God in human form who saves from the cross (fruit of the anti-Arian reaction); the transition from grace as the self-donation of Father and Son through the Spirit to the qualitative difference effected in man by Their dwelling in him; the gradual deterioration of the idea of Redemption to that of a commercial settlement in the realm of justice (not uninfluenced by Germanic tribal law); and an overall retrogression from gospel to law, a threat from which the Church is never free.

The inexorable *quaestio* of the logicians and rhetoricians with its tendency to distinguish and define to the last degree was taken over from trivium and quadrivium and applied to the divine mysteries. Theretofore, the monastic approach to the sacred page had been a reading followed by prayerful *contemplatio.* Chiefly, however, the catechetical picture was marked by a departure from the Bible or a use of it only as an arsenal of saving "facts" in a spirit quite foreign to its meaning as development. Between 1100 and 1300, when scholastic theology made the important step of a return to the Scriptures as source, starting with the work of Peter Lombard after the arid logic of the prescholastics, catechizing and preaching remained absolutely static. Nothing could improve matters, not even the Biblically fragmented catecheses of Aquinas (for the Middle Ages lacked any genuine sense of history), until the 15th-century humanists began to rediscover the Bible for the kind of book it was. Despite Luther's overt rejection of humanism, his Biblical lectures that began at Wittenberg's university were possible only in terms of the recovery of Greek and Hebrew by humanist circles, and something of the mode of Biblical thought. There can be no doubt that the static condition of faith in theology, pulpit, and catechism could be relieved only by a return to the gospel in its sources. This, in fact, is what happened.

Council of Trent. Trent adjourned in 1563, and the catechism its Fathers asked for was ready in Latin (having been composed in Italian) by 1566. A trio of Dominicans led by a certain Foreiro wrote it; a secular priest humanist named Poggianus was the polisher of its phrasing. This manual for parish priests, running to more than 400 pages, is popularly known as *Catechismus Romanus,* though its full title in its first edition (Rome 1566) was *Catechismus ex Decreto Concilii Tridentini ad parochos Pii V Pontificis Maximi iussu editus.* Its fourfold division is: (1) faith and the Creed, (2) the Sacraments, (3) the Decalogue and the laws of God, (4) prayer and its necessity, chiefly the Lord's Prayer. The restoration of the Sacraments to an integral place in the plan of Redemption rather than as aids to observing the precepts is important; so is the book's heavy reliance on Scripture and the Fathers in place of a metaphysically tinged vocabulary. The general tenor of doctrinal exposition is Augustinian, for the West was, even after Trent's debates, still firmly on the plateau where he had lodged it. The avoidance of scholastic terms brought the Roman Church back only to the 5th century, in other words, not to the 4th or more importantly the lst.

Attempts such as that of Trent in a humanist vein had been made by Cardinal Stanislaus Hozjusz (Hosius),

Confessio catholicae fidei christianae vel potius explicatio quaedam confessionis (Vienna 1561), and by Bp. Friedrich Nausea, *In catholicum catechismum libri sex* (Cologne 1543); but all three were fated to lose out in popular exposition to the medieval lists or "truths." Canisius genuinely admired Trent's catechism but his neater summaries and classifications prevailed. Bellarmine said it was his model, but it is doubtful that he understood the attempt it represented. In fact, the lip service paid to it and the little use (more accurately, the highly selective use) made of it by catechism authors since 1566 is perhaps the most notable feature about it. There is reason to think this handbook was quite influential in the pulpit over the years, but again, in proportion to the capacities of the priests who used it. It is quite unmarked by a polemical tone once it has mentioned "pernicious errors" in the introduction. The same introduction gives high promise of a throughgoing evangelical or kerygmatic theology that is never realized. The times were simply incapable of it, the more especially as a genuine evangelical release was overtaking the Church in tandem with unmistakably heretical positions.

After Trent. Post-Tridentine catechisms were in the mold of those by Bellarmine, Canisius, Auger, and Ripalda in the four chief language groups or in translations from one of the first two.

English and American. Laurence Vaux translated and adapted Canisius in 1567 as *A Catechisme of Christian doctrine necessarie for Children and ignorante people* (Louvain 1567; repr. Manchester 1885), deriving additional help from Pedro de *Soto's *Methodus confessionis . . . seu epitome* (Dillingen 1567). What came to be known as the Doway Catechism was produced by Henry Turberville, a professor at the English College there, sometime before 1649, the date of a third edition (*An Abridgment of the Christian Doctrine: with Proofs of Scripture on Points Controverted*). The order is Bellarmine's, but the treatment is Turberville's own. Its tenor is Bible-quoting, polemical, allegorical, adult. Two other British efforts were those of Richard *Challoner of London (*The Catholic Christian Instructed,* 1737) and George Hay of Edinburgh (*The Sincere Christian,* 1781; *The Devout Christian,* 1783). John *Lingard wrote *Catechistical Instruction on the Doctrines and Worship of the Catholic Church* in 1836 (London 1840). All the above-mentioned were being published in the U.S. until well into the 19th century. Abp. John *Carroll abridged Hay's larger works (1772) in a form that contributed verbally to the Baltimore catechism. Meanwhile, in Ireland Abp. James Butler of Cashel produced a catechism (1775) that was revised by order of a Synod of Maynooth (1875) and in that form (1882) recommended itself to substantial borrowings in the U.S. Archbishop John McHale oversaw a bilingual *The Christian Doctrine* (1865) for his Irish-speaking Diocese of Tuam. Among those in the U.S. who produced catechisms in the 19th century, all of them European-derived, were J. H. *McCaffrey (Baltimore before 1865) and J. P. A. *Verot (Augusta 1864). The English-language efforts described above were all lineal descendants in the tradition of the "four principal parts of doctrine." When they halted to make a brief explanation, it was generally in the spirit of a work such as Rufinus of Aquileia's *Commentarius in symbolum* or a similar Augustine-derived source.

French. Attempts were made in France in the Enlightenment period to follow through on Augustine's two Biblical catecheses in *De catechizandis rudibus.* They included Claude *Fleury's *Catéchisme historique* (Paris 1683), which is prefaced by a claim of the superiority of the Bible's method of storytelling and a fairly mild disquisition against the usefulness of theology's method in catechetics. Methodologically Fleury presented material in expository lesson form with prayers from the liturgy interspersed and questions at the end.

François *Pouget, an Oratorian, produced a similar Bible-oriented catechism, *Instructions générales en forme de catéchisme où l'on explique en abrégé, par ecriture sainte et par la tradition, l'histoire et les dogmes . . . la morales . . . les sacraments, les prières . . .* (Paris 1702). Fleury subsequently went on the Index as a Gallican; Pouget, too, because his patron Bp. Colbert of Montpellier was a Jansenist. Both catechisms were unexceptionable.

Jacques Benigne Bossuet, Bishop of Meaux, produced the Biblical *Le second catéchisme* before his formal doctrinal one [*Oeuvres complètes* (Bar-le-Duc 1687) 10].

Italian. Italy broke away from the Bellarmine mold somewhat with the *Compendio della dottrina cristiana* by Bp. Casati of Mondovì (1765). It was in the spirit of the catechisms of Montpellier and Meaux and was probably the work of Canon G. M. Giaccone.

German. Similar forerunners of modern Biblical catechisms appeared in Germany in the 19th century, beginning with the *Biblische Geschichte des Alten und Neuen Testaments* by Bernard von *Overberg (Münster 1804). J. I. von *Felbiger (1785), C. von *Schmid (1801), I. Schuster (1845), G. *Mey (1871), and F. J. Knecht (1880) all produced "Bible histories" in which virtuous conduct was excerpted from the Scriptures to illustrate and augment the catechism lesson. Overberg had the larger vision, seeing the Bible as the "history of God's gratuitous concern for man's salvation." The same idea was found in the *Biblische Geschichte der Welterlöserung durch Jesum der Sohn Gottes* (Augsburg 1806) by B. Galura, Bishop of Brixen. Overberg was the reformer of the schools of Westphalia and a friend of Goethe; he rightly deserves to be named with educators such as Pestalozzi and Herbart. Galura studied at the University of Vienna for a year before his ordination—uncommon enough—and tried to come to terms with the spirit of the *Aufklärung* in his *Grundsätze der sokratischer Katechisier-methode* (1793). In a six-volume reform of the plan of theology, *Neueste Theologie de Christentums* (Augsburg 1800–04), he identified as the *Grundidee* of the Bible the kingdom of God or the kingdom of heaven. Other important figures were Augustin Gruber, Archbishop of Salzburg (1823–35), who gave lectures to his priests on the Augustinian technique of the sacred *narratio* and the necessity of inductive explanation before any memory is required (*Katechetische Vorlesungen,* 1830–34); Johann Baptist *Hirscher, who tried to bridge the gap between sacred history and doctrinal formation in his theoretical essay *Katechetik* (Tübingen 1831) and his larger and smaller Catholic catechisms (Freiburg 1842, 1845); and another professor of the new discipline pastoral theology, J. M. *Sailer, whose lectures on that subject (Munich 1788) demanded instruction based on the Bible for pedagogic reasons of concreteness and immediacy, so as to "form man in the divine life rather than instruct him intellectually." It is evident that in German-speaking lands the demands of child nature were being heard for perhaps the first time. France had known something similar through the efforts of the clergy at the parish of Saint-Sulpice, Paris, and of Bp. Dupanloup of Orléans (cf. J. Colomb, "The Catechetical Method of St. Sulpice" in *Shaping the Christian Message,* ed. G. Sloyan, New York 1958); but the pedagogic efforts of the Germans, Austrians, and Swiss were much more realistic in their developmentalist theories on the nature of the child.

Universal and National Catechisms. A number of 19th-century catechisms tried to depart from subject matter orientation and to center on the individual's natural concern for himself with questions like "Why did God make you?" The only clear result was an anthropocentricism in a pejorative sense. Very shortly the authors were back at the business of a summary of doctrine in theological form with a largely apologetic concern. The great figure in Germany who updated Canisius, but without his Biblical or patristic unction, was Josef *Deharbe, SJ, whose catechism, or *Lehrbegriff* (1847), based on the theological manual of G. Perrone, had a vigorous history (in German-speaking America, among other places). His work was subsequently revised by Josef Linden, SJ (1900), and T. Mönnichs, SJ (1925), the latter the so-called German *Einheitscatechismus.*

In the U.S., a similar attempt at unity was achieved through the *Catechism of the Third Plenary Council of Baltimore* (1885), the fruit of the labors of J. de Concilio, priest of Newark, and J. L. *Spalding, Bishop of Peoria, Ill. It had 421 questions in 37 chapters and more than 72 pages. There are no "parts"; the order is Creed, Sacraments (gifts, fruits, and beatitudes after Confirmation), prayer, Commandments, and last things. A revision of 1941 by the bishops' committee of the Confraternity of Christian Doctrine, with which the name of F. J. Connell, CSSR, is most closely associated, returned to the order Creed, Commandments, Sacraments, prayer. Both are theological summaries (the latter testifying to little of the theological progress of the intervening 55 years). Neither professes any pedagogical concern.

The same was true of the 19th-century efforts at a "universal catechism." Pius IX proposed to Vatican Council I that he himself should prepare one modeled on Bellarmine's. In the Council Bishops Sola of Nice and Vérot of Savannah pressed for it, and Dupanloup led the opposition. The vote in mid-May 1870 was 491 *pro,* 56 *contra,* and 44 *secundum modum.* With the adjournment of the Council, the decree was not promulgated and the project was never heard of again.

There were brief, abortive efforts in the same direction by Pope Pius X in favor of his own *Compendio della dottrina cristiana* (1905) and likewise by Cardinal Gasparri with his three-level *Catechismus catholicus,* which Pope Pius XI praised faintly. In a similar vein, France produced a national catechism in 1938 that was much criticized for its length and technical vocabulary. A national commission for its revision was set up in 1941, and in 1947 under the authorship of Canons Camille Quinet and André Boyer a much-improved catechism in the form of a pupil text was produced. It is composed of lessons and has a general Biblical-liturgical orientation, though "doctrines of faith" provide the *Leitmotiv.* Belgium received a revised national catechism unmarked by distinctive features in 1947. The German national *Katholischer Katechismus* appeared in 1955 (Freiburg) after having been begun in 1938 and interrupted by World War II. It is intended for children of the upper elementary years and is in four parts, following the schema of the Creed in 12 articles. Almost half the lessons fall under the heading "The Forgiveness of Sins," including temptation, sin, the Sacraments, and grace. A multivolume teacher's manual, at present incomplete, accompanies it. The initial claims in its favor that it fulfilled all the hopes of the kerygmatic renewal have been tempered somewhat by closer examination, but it is unquestionably a modern watershed. It was translated into 22 languages within 5 years of its appearance. Although the catechism is anonymous, the men most closely connected with its production included G. Fischer, H. Fischer, F. Schreibmayr, and K. Tilmann. Austria produced a national catechism conceived along similar lines in 1960, guided by Vienna's director of religious education, L. Lentner. England's bishops have one in preparation.

In 1963 and 1964 the Australian bishops published a *Catholic Catechism* for the upper four elementary grades in two volumes with matching teacher's manuals (Sydney). J. Kelly of the Archdiocese of Melbourne is its chief architect. The trend begun in the German catechism is brought to a relative perfection in the two pupil's books of the Australian product. So much is this so that national hierarchies now have to face the question of the merit of expressing the Church's faith in a single, fixed form for school children in these sensitive years. Modern universal literacy is a major consideration. The "official" catechism took its rise in a period of near illiteracy, and its commitment to memory was largely predicated on that fact. Ecclesiologically, the position that saw in the fixed formularies of the catechism a faithful reflection of the *fontes revelationis,* to be coupled, after the Scriptures, with liturgies, creeds, and councils, prevailed for 15 centuries.

The vehicles of living teaching have lately become so numerous and various, however, that this single-sourced witness to faith in pulpit and classroom is coming to enjoy less and less favor. Moreover, since the Church's problem in every age is the explicitation of Biblical faith, and since the derivation of her doctrine from that source as it is proclaimed in the liturgy is the Church's chief catechetical problem, she begins anew to be wary of whatever comprises a threat to the genesis of Biblical faith. Catechisms have a long history in the latter role, although the intent in devising them was quite the opposite. In any case, a variety of catechetical aid books deriving from the Bible itself and from a living liturgy is being looked to much more than the proliferation of national catechisms. The latter are testimonials to a mode of transmitting the faith that was resorted to when people no longer had the Scriptures in their vernacular languages or celebrated the sacramental rites meaningfully. (Witness the Eastern Churches, which are largely without catechism except under Western influence.) With the slow restoration of the Biblical and sacramental heritages in the West, the problem is altered notably.

Catechisms and Religious Formation. The question at issue is the relation of the catechism to the total work of religious formation. For centuries it was assumed that a verbal mastery of the Church's faith, even under simple, summary headings, stood for a conceptual grasp of it, and was in fact proof of the minimum understanding (*intellectus*) that faith required. It cannot be argued that memorization of verbal responses impeded understanding or, again, that it actively contributed to it. What is clear is that living faith came from other sources (parental teaching and example, religious observances, pastoral care) and that catechism answers fit into that matrix as a help or hindrance to faith, depending on the psychological wisdom that attended their use.

The psychological wisdom of such a technique is, of course, the first problem to raise. The case for the necessity of speaking to children and adolescents in the accents of those periods of development has successfully been made in the pedagogy of the last 200 years. Since the Church never speaks directly to children in her doctrinal pronouncements and since noncatechist theologians do not do so either, there is a painful ambiguity in the supposition that sound doctrine can be conveyed only in such language. The misconception is passing, but it is contributed to by the appearance of any catechism that originated in a milieu other than that of childhood (adolescence, nontheological adulthood).

The nation that is pastorally and catechetically active will produce numerous aids to sound religious formation—clear, accurate, and profound—at all levels, whereas a country or region where these arts are static will barely be able to bring a single such product into being. A quasi-national effort at a catechism can be a healthy sign of growth if it is put out as the first contribution in a new direction. When an official character is claimed for it, it immediately becomes the mixed blessing that monopolies generally are. Any attempt at casting thought in a single mold is a matter of major concern in the modern world, so little is it in tune with the pursuit of truth or understanding in any other field. It is unwise and unfair to claim a sanction higher than human for any human attempt to speak of divine truth. The catechisms of the future are likely to be what in concept they always were, namely, paraphrases of the divinely inspired Scriptures and the holy mysteries designed to lead to the hearing of that word and celebration of that deed. Books of explicit doctrinal and moral formation will always have a place in the Church, and they will always be subordinated to the work of active initiation into the Christian mysteries in liturgy and in life.

Bibliography: E. MANGENOT, DTC 2.2:1895–1968. J. A. JUNGMANN, LexThK² 6:27–54. L. CSONKA, "Storia della catechesi," *Educare III* (3d ed. Zurich 1964) 61–190. T. FILTHAUT, *Das Reich Gottes in der katechetischen Unterweisung* (Freiburg 1958). J. HOFINGER, "The Right Ordering of Catechetical Material," LumV 2 (1947) 718–746; *The Art of Teaching Christian Doctrine* (2d ed. Notre Dame, Ind. 1962). J. A. JUNGMANN, *Die Frohbotschaft und unsere Glaubensverkündigung* (Regensburg 1936); *Glaubensverkündigung im Lichte der Frohbotschaft* (Innsbruck 1962). E. KAPPLER, *Die Verkündigungstheologie* (Freiburg 1949). H. KREUTZWALD, *Zur Geschichte des Biblischen Unterrichts* (Freiburg 1957). L. LENTNER et al., eds., *Katechetisches Wörterbuch* (Freiburg 1961). R. PADBERG, *Erasmus als Katechet* (Freiburg 1956). G. S. SLOYAN, ed., *Shaping the Christian Message* (New York 1958); *Modern Catechetics* (New York 1963). G. WEBER, *Religionsunterricht als Verkündigung* (Braunsschweig 1964).

[G. S. SLOYAN]

CATECHISM, IMPERIAL. Name given to the *Catéchisme à l'usage de toutes les Églises de l'Empire français*, published by order of Emperor *Napoleon I (May 1, 1806). When the *Concordat of 1801 was promulgated, the French government promised in the *Organic Articles (art. 39) attached to it a single liturgy and a single catechism for all dioceses in the country. Unification had previously been urged in the *cahiers* of the clergy in 1789, and its need became more evident with the Concordat's new division of dioceses. Pre-Revolutionary sees were accustomed to their own catechisms. New dioceses often comprised portions of three or four former ones, with the result that there were instances of several different catechisms in use within a single diocese. The task of composing a uniform catechism was confided to the Director of Cults *Portalis, and to the worthy Abbés d'Astros and Jauffret, who drew inspiration from the catechism composed for the Diocese of Meaux by Bossuet.

Between the completion of the draft copy (1803) and the published version (1806), Napoleon proclaimed the French Empire. To gain a populace submissive to such innovations as military conscription and the novel taxes suggested by his ambitious policies, and to heighten his authority, he sought more and more to utilize the Church. At his insistence the chapter in the new catechism on the Fourth Commandment contained audacious statements concerning the respect and affection due to authority, and specifically to Napoleon's person and dynasty. When Pius VII refused to grant needed ecclesiastical approval, Napoleon turned to the compliant *Caprara, papal legate to Paris, and pretended that his approbation was that of the Holy See.

This catechism's deviation from traditional Catholic teachings on submission to authority, and its endeavor to remove from bishops liberty to establish the text of the catechism caused lively emotion among French Catholics, and in Rome. Despite the Emperor's injunctions, episcopal submission was merely nominal. On one pretext or another bishops avoided use of the catechism. In Belgium, opposition was open; in France, it kept increasing with Napoleon's persecution of Pius VII. In 1814, with Napoleon in defeat, King *Louis XVIII hastened to suppress the Imperial Catechism, and to restore to each bishop the power to provide a catechism for his own diocese.

Bibliography: A. LATREILLE, *Le Catéchisme impérial de 1806* (Paris 1935).

[A. LATREILLE]

CATECHISM OF THE COUNCIL OF TRENT, also called the Roman Catechism, projected as early in the Council as 1546, was completed only after the Council, in 1564, and published in Latin in 1566. As its full title indicates—Catechism of the Council of Trent for Parish Priests Issued by Order of Pope Pius V—it is not a manual for the faithful but for priests, "a book issued by the authority of the Holy Synod from which pastors and others who hold the office of teaching could seek sure doctrine and then set it forth for the building up of the faithful" (preface). The Catechism is divided into four parts concerned with the Creed, the Sacraments, the Commandments, and the Lord's Prayer. More than current *catechisms, it incorporates, besides revealed doctrines, theological teaching; in this latter it leans heavily on St. Thomas Aquinas. The presentation of doctrine is marked by clarity and a genuinely kerygmatic approach. Though issued at the height of the Counter Reformation, controversy is kept to a minimum. Its doctrinal importance lies in (1) its content, the complete doctrine of salvation, and (2) the universality of its use in the Church. It is thus a norm of orthodoxy. It has been translated into the principal European languages.

See also TRENT, COUNCIL OF; CONCILIAR CATECHISMS; CATECHISMS, CRITERION OF REVELATION.

Bibliography: E. MANGENOT, DTC 2.2:1917–18. J. HOFINGER, LexThK[2] 2:977–978. J. A. MCHUGH and C. J. CALLAN, *Catechism of the Council of Trent* . . . (New York 1923; repr. 1947).

[P. DE LETTER]

CATECHISMS, CRITERION OF REVELATION. Whether conciliar or diocesan (interdiocesan) or private (with ecclesiastical approval), *catechisms are summaries of Christian doctrine written for the Christian instruction of youth or converts. More developed than baptismal creeds or symbols of faith, they seek to connect the articles of the faith or truths of revelation in a rational and systematic manner. In doing so, they include not only revealed truths but also theological teaching, namely, such conclusions from, or presuppositions to, revealed doctrine as are necessary or helpful in proposing the revelation.

Insofar as expressive of the Church's ordinary and universal magisterium, or of what the college of bishops in communion with the pope teaches the world over as pertaining to revelation, they are a valid criterion of revelation in all matters that they definitely propose as teachings of the gospel. This may be clear either because they say so or from the object, e.g., mysteries. What catechisms teach the world over presumably pertains to revelation; caution, however, is warranted as there may be a doctrine generally accepted but not certainly revealed, e.g., the existence of limbo. Where catechisms differ they propose theological, not doctrinal, teaching.

See also TEACHING AUTHORITY OF THE CHURCH (MAGISTERIUM); CONCILIAR CATECHISMS; CATECHISM OF THE COUNCIL OF TRENT.

Bibliography: E. MANGENOT, DTC 2.2:1895–1968. J. HOFINGER, LexThK[2] 6:45–50. J. A. JUNGMANN, *Handing on the Faith,* tr. and rev. A. N. FUERST (New York 1959).

[P. DE LETTER]

CATECHISMS IN COLONIAL SPANISH AMERICA

To the Anglo-Saxon reader the word catechism conjures up the picture of a small, poorly printed book in question-and-answer form, dedicated to teaching children the essential truths of the Catholic faith. To the Spaniard and to the Spanish American during the colonial period, a catechism meant a treatise intended to teach neophytes the Catholic philosophy of life, as well as the essential truths of the faith as a whole. The essence of a Spanish American catechism of that period was the *doctrina cristiana,* and hence catechisms were frequently known by this title (*see* ENCOMIENDA-DOCTRINA SYSTEM).

Primitive Catechisms. The need for a catechism was felt from the very beginning in the evangelization of the Indians of the New World. Father Ramón Pane, the first missionary to the Indians in Española (*c.* 1495), described the failure of his efforts. He had not used any form of catechism, but apparently relied only on teaching the Indians the Our Father and other customary prayers. There is no mention of systematic instruction. With the conquest of Mexico, the first formal catechisms appeared. The earliest-known catechisms were written in the picture language of the Aztecs. A fragment of one of them was probably among the Mexican manuscripts collected by Lorenzo *Boturini Benaduci. Rediscovered in Mexico (1806) by Alexander von Humboldt and presented to the Royal Library at Berlin, it has since been lost. Another example is the complete catechism of Pedro de *Gante, still preserved in the Biblioteca National of Madrid. Other early catechisms date from the decade after the conquest of Peru. These are generally written in Spanish. One feature of these primitive catechisms is their diversity. The first Archbishop of Lima, Jerónimo de *Loaysa, declared that almost every missionary in the diocese had written his own catechism, a situation to which the archbishop objected highly. These catechisms did not merely confine themselves to eternal truths, but also touched on many aspects of earthly existence. They included advice on the need and methods of personal cleanliness for the Indians, especially if they were going to confession or Communion; instructions on how to bring in running water and how to take care of bridges; discussions on the obligation of the Indians to keep roads in repair; and so on.

As the conquest of America was consolidated, pressure mounted for the complete destruction of the old catechisms. There was too much diversity in their doctrinal teaching, and as order was established, counsels governing the personal and civic life of the Indians were gradually taken care of by the civil government. As a result, few of the primitive catechisms are extant. The work of their radical revision was facilitated by the Council of Trent, which issued the Roman catechism. This was used by the Council of Lima (1583), the Council of Mexico (1585), and by Luis *Zapata de Cárdenas, Archbishop of Bogotá, as the basis for new catechisms for Spanish America.

Printing. Because of the need for dictionaries of the native languages and for catechisms, the Church was responsible for the introduction of the printing press in the New World. Of the 223 titles of works printed in 16th-century Mexico, more than 85 per cent were connected with the Church's proselytizing work. In 1544 the *Doctrina breve* was published. Written in Spanish, it contained the elements common to all catechisms of the era: the Ten Commandments, the Creed, the Sacraments, the laws of the Church, the capital sins, works of mercy, and prayers. The first catechism in an Indian language was that of Alonso de Molina, printed in 1546. Both he and the chronicler-explorer Bernardino de *Sahagún wrote in Nahuatl; other works were printed in the Tarasco, Otomi, Pirinda, Mixteco, and Zapoteca dialects. In Peru the *Doctrina christiana y catecismo para instrucción de los indios,* written in Spanish, Quechua, and Aymara, was printed in 1584

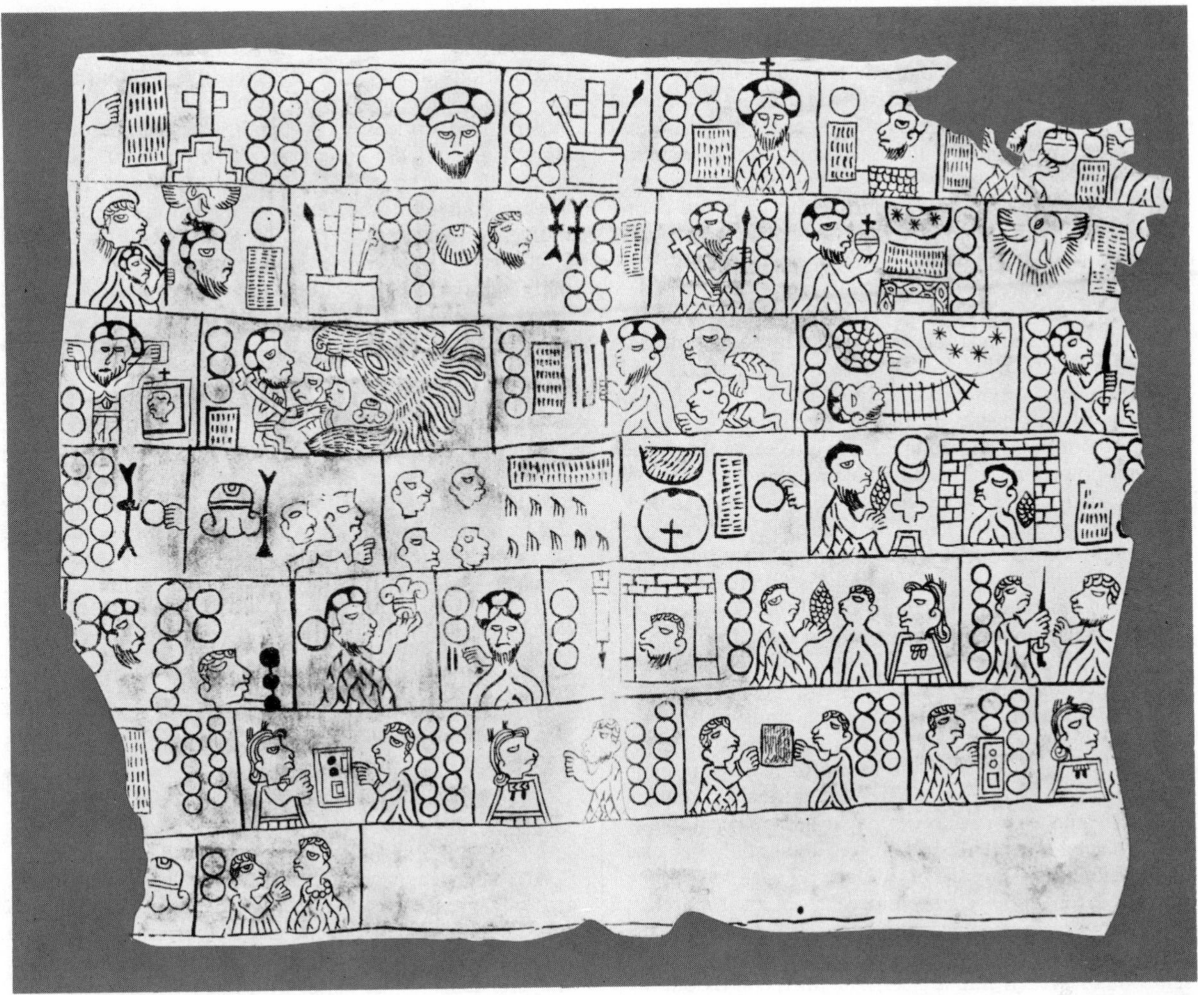

Fragment of a catechism in Mexican picture writing, black ink drawings on agave paper, 35 cm long by 45 cm wide, probably dating from the first half of the 16th century. The pictures read alternately from left to right and right to left. The first picture in the top row is the beginning of an exposition of the Fourteen Articles of Faith; the last picture in row 4 is the beginning of an explanation of the Ten Commandments.

by Antonio Ricardo on the first type brought to Mexico. That same type was later passed on to the Jesuits, who took it to the Paraguayan Reductions and were using it there in the 18th century.

Attitudes Shown in Catechisms. In presenting dogmas, such as the Trinity and Incarnation, in the native languages, there was the danger that using Indian terms would cause the pagan meaning to linger. Therefore, if paraphrasing of the concept was impossible, some European words were introduced. The Dominican Martín de León used a combination of Indian and Spanish to signify God, saying "Teotl Dios." Others retained the entire Spanish word, such as "Dios" or "Cristo." Bishop Zumárraga urged that the Scriptures be translated into the native languages, disagreeing with those who feared putting the Sacred Books in the hands of the newly converted Indians. The catechisms reveal that the Spaniards regarded the Indian as having a child's mentality. Zumárraga continually advised his priests to use simple language and concepts. The Peruvian catechism of sermons of 1585 warned the missionaries not to preach as if they were in a court or a university, for to do so would overwhelm and confuse the Indians. Priests adapted some native customs to the Christian faith. Pedro de Gante, upon seeing how the Indians sang in praise of their pagan gods, composed songs about God, Christ, and the Virgin Mary. Father Lucerno placed great drawings of the Last Judgment in public places to arouse the curiosity of the people and cause them to seek explanations.

The Church was conscious of the danger that mass conversions could result in a superficial knowledge of the Catholic faith. Zumárraga warned in the *Doctrina christiana* of 1546 that some Indians were Christians in name and appearance only, but were not well versed enough in their religion to explain it when questioned by nonbelievers. He often stressed the need of real understanding, rather than ceremony and memorization.

Methods and Problems of Teaching. The catechisms were not in a question-and-answer form, but arranged according to themes that were then explained. Applications were made to daily situations. The Seventh Commandment was explained as prohibiting the use of false weights, mixing bad products with good in order to deceive the buyer, and wrapping tamales in many leaves so as to make them appear larger. Zumárraga presented as violators of the Fourth Commandment those parents who neglected their children, kings who passed unjust laws, and Church officials who cared more for the temporal than the spiritual. Masters who treated their servants badly or who did not pay them fairly were breaking the Seventh Commandment. The Dominican catechism of 1548 explained that because woman was made from man, she should not be regarded as a slave, but rather loved and respected. The concept of the Trinity was explained in Indian terms with the comparison being made to the rugs they made. The rug could be folded three, four, five times; it was still the same rug. So it was with the Trinity.

Idolatry. The two main obstacles in the initial conversion of the Indians were idolatry and polygamy. To combat idolatry, the friars utilized reason, fear, and love. Sahagún offered the natives the argument that the pagan gods were unable to free them from the Spaniards because the conquerors were servants of the true, all-powerful God who had helped them. Legendary heroes, such as Quetzalcóatl, were false deities, now dead and burning in hell. The God of the Christians was one of kindness who did not want human sacrifices, wishing instead the reverence and love of the Indians. The Peruvian catechism demonstrated that upon rejecting their false gods, the natives could love, rather than fear, the grandeur of nature. They should not worship the sun because, as human beings with souls, each one of them was better than the sun, who could not speak, sense, or know about God.

To avoid the danger of the return of paganism, each catechism stressed the difference between honoring Christian images and adoring pagan idols. The Indians were warned that drink endangered their souls because it occasioned memories of idolatry. Pedro de Gante separated the upper-class children from their parents, so that living in the boarding school, they would forget their pagan ways. The educated youths were then sent out to preach Sunday sermons in the surrounding towns.

Polygamy. In the Aztec culture women, besides being wives, were also servants. Consequently, the limitation to one partner in the Christian religion was an economic hardship. This was an impediment in the conversion of the upper class. The promiscuous example of the Spaniards also gave the Indians the opportunity to counter the missionaries' reprimand with the observation that many conquerors did not obey the Christian precept.

When an Indian did renounce polygamy, was converted, and prepared to receive the Sacrament of Matrimony, the problem arose concerning which woman should be his wife: the present partner, his first mate, or his favorite woman. In 1537 it was decided that the legal wife would be the first partner or else the woman at the time of conversion. As time progressed and the Indians were educated in the faith from early childhood, the difficulties in connection with idolatry and polygamy decreased.

Confession. The catechisms dealt extensively with confession. In the pagan religion there had been a form of confession which dealt with corporal transgressions and carried a judicial pardon. The act of telling sins to the Catholic priest, therefore, was not too different, but the concept of its supernatural character was new. In addition to corporal sins, the friars had to emphasize in their catechisms the sins of thought. Sins committed while intoxicated could no longer be blamed on the liquor rather than on the responsibility of the individual. Most of the books had a formal series of questions that the priest asked the penitent so as to make confession easier and more orderly. Some Indians experienced difficulty concerning the number of their sins. They did not intend to lie, but because of confusion or fear were not accurate. Martín de León advised confessors to be very patient and not pressure the natives for exact numbers. Motolinía, one of the original Franciscan priests in Mexico, read a list of sins, and the penitent would signify the number by putting aside a seed or pebble for each transgression. God's mercy and His desire that the sinner change his life were stressed. Generally confession was received once a year in Lent, and Communion, once during the Easter season.

The early catechisms presented the Church in the image of the fatherhood of God. This gave equality to all people in the eyes of God, no matter what their condition on earth. Those who were patient in their sufferings, no matter how conquered or humiliated, would be rewarded with the eternal joys of heaven.

Bibliography: R. Ricard, *La conquista espiritual de México,* tr. A. M. Garibay Kintana (Mexico City 1947). M. Cuevas, *Historia de la Iglesia en México,* 5 v. (5th ed. Mexico City 1946–47) v.1, 2. H. R. Wagner, *Nueva bibliografía mexicana del siglo XVI supplemento a las bibliografías de don Joaquín García Icazbalceta, don José Toribio Medina y don Nicolás León,* tr. J. García Pimental and F. Gómez de Orozco (Mexico City 1946). **Illustration credit:** Reproduced from *Bureau of American Ethnology Bulletin* 28 (1904) plate XXI.

[D. E. TANCK]

CATECHIST

One who teaches doctrine; in the Christian context, one who proclaims the mystery of Christ to those who are *catechumens and deepens the commitment to Christ after the initiation of Baptism. The Apostles were the first catechists in this sense, with the mandate from their Master: "Go, therefore, and make disciples of all nations . . . teaching them to observe all that I have commanded you" (Mt 28.19). The discourses of St. Peter, notably that of Pentecost (Acts 2.14–36), and St. Paul's preaching of the *kerygma to the Gentiles became the paradigm for future catechists.

In the first few centuries of the Church, when formal catechesis was directed mainly to adult catechumens, the bishops were the primary catechists, and it was left to Christian parents to instruct their children in religion. With the rise of heresies and schisms, the catechist became more of an apologist than an exponent of the kerygma, and catechists came to have the duty not only of expounding the faith but of defending it as well.

In recent times there has been a renewal in *catechetics motivated largely by the necessity for a personal encounter with Christ. With this latest development in the evolution of catechetics, the role of the catechist has changed back again from apologist to witness, with the realization of a need for a deep personal, religious formation. Whereas formerly there seemed to be no special requirements for the catechist other than practical faith, availability, and willingness, the neccessity of a careful doctrinal and pedagogical preparation, as well as a strong personal commitment came to be recognized.

A strong revival in pastoral catechetics and liturgy occurred in Europe in the 1930s, and special centers for training catechists, both lay and clerical, were instituted. (*See* CATECHETICAL CENTERS.) After some years' delay the revival spread to certain parts of the U.S. By the mid-1960s a widespread teacher-training program in doctrine, liturgy, and Scripture had been established under the direction of the *Confraternity of Christian Doctrine (CCD), which recognized the importance of its role more vividly because of the shortage of parochial schools. In urban areas a large number of laymen from all walks of life enrolled in the CCD courses for formation as catechists. Yearly regional CCD institutes have been held for catechists in the U.S., and many excellent publications and audio-visual aids became available. Statistics for 1965 indicated that more than 4,500,000 Catholic children outside parochial schools in the U.S. were receiving instruction in religion from an estimated 325,000 CCD lay and religious catechists.

See also CATECHESIS, MISSIONARY; RELIGION, TEACHER OF.

Bibliography: M. VAN CASTER, *The Structure of Catechetics,* tr. E. J. DIRKSWAGEN et al. (New York 1965). R. MARIVOET, "A Program for the Formation of Catechists," LumV 14 (1959) 423–448, with bibliog. SISTER MARIA DA GRAÇA, "Catechists," *ibid.* 395–402. G. S. SLOYAN, ed., *Shaping the Christian Message* (New York 1958); *Modern Catechetics* (New York 1963). F. H. DRINKWATER, *Telling the Good News* (New York 1960). J. HOFINGER, *The Art of Teaching Christian Doctrine* (2d ed. Notre Dame, Ind. 1962). J. A. JUNGMANN, *Handing on the Faith,* tr. and rev. A. N. FUERST (New York 1959); *The Good News Yesterday and Today,* ed. and tr. W. HUESMAN (pa. New York 1962). SISTER MICHAEL, *Communicating the Mystery* (pa. Huntington, Ind. 1963).

[C. CLARKSON]

CATECHIST, MISSIONARY

The institution of catechists in mission countries, which is neither general nor homogeneous, belongs to the modern missionary period. Missionary catechists are indigenous lay people, mostly fathers of families, taken into the service as salaried employees and dependent on missionary priests, in order to help in catechetical work as well as in the other functions of the ministry for which Holy Orders are not necessary. The catechist in mission countries is thus a kind of lay assistant pastor, collaborating as a subordinate helper in priestly missionary work.

Function. One cannot generalize readily about catechists in the missions, because of the variety of situations prevailing in the different missionary regions and because of the difference in the organizational development reached by different regional churches. The functions of the "classic" catechist, however, vary in the three following situations.

The Itinerant Catechist. He has the task of penetrating into the non-Christian milieu already, in most cases, familiar to him, in order to prepare for the missionary's arrival, to make some preliminary announcement of the Christian message, and to stir up interest among prospective converts. He may also be called upon to visit and foster the growth of Christian cells already established. In this he functions as an intermediary between them and the priest.

Catechists in Charge of Out-Stations. They have more stability. Not uncommonly, a principal mission station may have as many as 30 widely scattered out-stations dependent on it. These out-stations are entrusted to catechists, whose duty it is: to direct the Sunday assembly, at which they may be expected to give some religious instruction; be in charge of the instruction of children and catechumens; perform emergency baptisms; make premarriage enquiries; visit the sick; assist the dying; conduct para-liturgical funerals; watch over the interests of the missions; keep registers; and see that the missionary is kept informed. Often they are expected to manage small bush schools where children are taught the catechism in addition to reading and writing.

Catechists in the Central Stations. These are generally in charge of a number of catechumens and may give religious instruction in the school or busy themselves with tasks as parish helpers. Among the catechists in the central stations, especially in the Asian missions, women are included, who generally belong to religious or quasi-religious institutes, and are thus closely connected with the native structures of the young Church.

Usefulness. The role of the male missionary catechist answers a particular need of the missions, and his utility is especially apparent in the initial period of missionary penetration. If the missionary priest has reliable catechists, he can multiply his apostolic efforts. The catechists can make up in some measure for the insufficiency of foreign personnel. They also have the advantage of familiarity with the local dialect and are able to move freely in circles where a foreigner might not be acceptable. They are not shocked or upset by the conditions or way of life that they encounter. Their knowledge of the language and habits of thought of their listeners frequently enables them to expound Christian doctrine in a popular and intelligible way and to foresee and overcome difficulties more easily than the missionary himself.

The Holy See has recognized the institution of catechists, while insisting upon the necessity of providing for their adequate religious formation. [See Collectanea S.C. de Propaganda Fide (Rome 1907), 1.557.342 (1782); 2.1606–10.192–193 (1883); Pius XI, "Rerum Ecclesiae," ActApS (1926) 78; Pius XII, "IIe Congres Mondial Apostolat des laics," ActApS (1957) 937; John XXIII, "Princeps Pastorum," ActApS (1959) 855.] Their importance, however, is not such that all the work

Missionary catechists often must lead devotions in the absence of a priest. Here, a catechist in the province of Huchuetenango, Guatemala, leads the recitation of the rosary at a graveside.

of Christian training should be entrusted to them, nor should the more important role of the missionary priest be minimized [Benedict XV, "Maximum illud," ActApS (1919) 449]. The slogan sometimes heard—"A missionary at the head of an army of catechists"—is not beyond reproach. The priest cannot dispense himself from personal and humble contact with his people. Moreover, a personnel of salaried employees is not perfectly conformed to the evangelical model for apostolic workers. It is a necessary but still a provisional and transitory arrangement that ought to yield, as soon as the indigenous Christianity permits, to better staffed organizations for religious instruction [Pius XII, ActApS (1957) 937] and to become integrated with apostolic and catechetical initiatives of the lay apostolate under the direction of the local bishop [Pius XII, "Evangelii praecones," ActApS (1951) 514; John XXIII, "Princeps Pastorum," ActApS (1959) 854–857].

History. Missionaries have always had the duty of setting up as quickly as possible the framework for the future regional church by the establishment of a clergy and an indigenous lay elite, who in the beginning would necessarily be associated as helpers with the apostolic and pastoral work of the foreign missionaries. The missionary staff of St. Paul included presbyter-bishops and lay persons, men and women (e.g., Priscilla and Aquila). The lay missionary was concerned, above all, with a direct apostolate, hence with *kerygma and *catechesis. As they were established, Christian communities were provided with an autochthonous clergy, who, with the help of local people, could provide the necessary pastoral catechetics. But the institution of catechists who were neither clerics nor lay missionaries, but a substitute who represented a kind of intermediary "apostolate of sacristans" between those two categories, is characteristic of modern missions and dates from the regime of the **patronato real*. The Spanish Franciscans in Mexico in 1523 made an early appeal for the collaboration of certain Indian lay persons, called *fiscales*. These were ordinarily between 50 and 60 years of age. Their duties were to get the people together for religious instruction and for worship, to perform the work of sacristans, to keep the missionaries informed of what was going on in the villages, especially births, deaths, marriage plans, and the return to pagan practices that came to their attention. They were expected also to keep registers, to baptize in danger of death, to conduct burials, and to teach catechism. The other missionary orders in Mexico adopted this practice, and it spread to other regions of Spanish America, especially to Peru (Specker J., SMB, "Die Missionsmethode in Spanisch-Amerika im 16. Jahrhundert," "NZMissw Supplementa," n. 4, Schöneck-Beckenried 1953, 232–235).

India. In 1543, seeing that expected reinforcements of missionaries were not arriving, St. Francis Xavier organized an institution of catechists, called *canacapillai*, to take charge of the small, scattered Christian communities. He also made use of catechists as interpreters during his trips. For them, he wrote an *Instructio pro catechistis* in 1545 (A. Brou, SJ, *S. François Xavier. Conditions et methodes de son apostolat,* Museum Lessianum, Louvain 1925, 56–57).

China. At Macao about 1580 Giovanni Battista da Pesaro, OFM, founded a school for catechists for China, Japan, and Indochina; they would sow the first seeds of the Gospel while awaiting the arrival of missionaries. Doubtless it was from this school that the first Christian preachers of Vietnam came.

Japan. The first Jesuits of Japan surrounded themselves with catechists (*dogiku*) who contributed much to the remarkable success of their beginnings in that country where there were 300,000 Christians in 1614. Alessandro Valignano, SJ, visitator to Japan (1592–1606), wanted to recruit an indigenous clergy, then nonexistent, from the ranks of the catechists.

Vietnam. Alexandre de Rhodes, SJ, founded in Tonkin in 1627 and in Cochin China in 1642 a kind of religious institute for catechists, who bound themselves by the three vows and were totally dedicated to the evangelization of their compatriots and to the care for Christian groups. They numbered more than 100 in 1653, in a population of more than 300,000 faithful. This institution, known as the "House of God" (Nha Chua), marked for the mission catechists a conspicuous evolution toward a more normal status, by being integrated, according to a formula of totally dedicated mission-laity, in the autochthonous structure of the young Church. Furthermore it provided for native priestly vocations. (The first two native priests were ordained in 1668.)

A parallel institute for women, but more closely bound to the common life, was founded in Annam in 1670 by Bishop Lambert de la Motte; its members were known as "Lovers of the Cross" and numbered 2,700 in 1923. This marked the beginning of the feminine missionary catechetical apostolate. As with the men, the trend toward normalization in the indigenous structures of the young Church deserves to be pointed out. The forms of monastic life were avoided, although the idea of a "secular institute" was then nonexistent and unthinkable. A feminine institute was founded in China on the model of that established by Bishop de la Motte, and another in Japan.

Africa. The pioneers in the evangelization of sub-Saharan Africa in the 19th century made wide use of male catechists, under the strategic direction of F. Libermann, Superior General of the Holy Ghost Fathers, and Cardinal Lavigerie; but in the beginning there was opposition on the part of certain missionaries who doubted the capacity of natives to assume the task of catechetical instruction. The ancient and "under-developed" formula, as used earlier in Mexico or in India at the beginning, was adopted, and soon became a kind of "classic" formula for Africa. Nevertheless, the success of missionary penetration in sub-Saharan Africa is due in great part to the humble and generous work of these catechists.

Present Situation. A certain evolution of the institution of catechists has taken place in missions everywhere, and there are those who think the existing situation is critical. The same is true of the Protestant missions (see B. Sundker, *The Christian Ministry in Africa*, Swedish Institute of Missionary Research, Uppsala 1960, 154–159). The number and the efficiency of catechists has diminished in recent years, although it is impossible to document this fact with satisfactory statistics. In an estimate made with regard to the territories dependent upon the Congregation for the Propagation of the Faith, the number of catechists in Asia was set at 22,000, and those in Africa at 18,000 (Fides News Service, Sept. 26, 1959, 702–703). The figures were probably overestimated, especially so far as Asia is concerned. [On the present problem, see J. Hofinger, SJ, "Developing our Lay Catechists," *Mission Bulletin* (Hong Kong 1959), 556–563; J. de Reeper, "Streamlining the Catechist," *Worldmission* (1954) 163–171.]

Formation. One of the problems requiring more immediate solution is that of the formation of catechists and their training in the best of contemporary catechetical methods. Schools for catechists are therefore of great importance, for there should be a rebirth in catechetics as well as a readjustment of the institution of catechists. Among the centers or schools of particular interest are the following: in Asia, the Catechist Training Center of Nagoya (Japan), the Catechetical Center of Poona and the Catechist Training Center of Tindivanam (India), the Catechetical Center of Singapore (Malaysia), and the Catechetical Center "Source de Vie" of Taipei (Taiwan); in Africa, the Catechist Training Center of Mwanza (Tanganyika), the Catechetical Documentary Center of Mayidi and the Catechist Center of Windhoek (South-West Africa); and in Latin America, the Centro Nacional Catequético of Botafogo (Brazil), the Hogar Catequistico of the Catholic University of Santiago (Chile), the Comisión Central de Instrucción Religiosa de la Acción Católica (Mexico), and the Secretariado de Catequesis of Lima (Peru).

Bibliography: A. V. SEUMOIS, "Problems of the Missionary Catechist," *Euntes Docete* 15 (1962) 198–213. J. A. MCCOY, *Advice From the Field* (Baltimore 1962). FATHER DUBOIS et al., "Le Congrès Missionnaire de Lisieux: Le rôle des catéchistes en pays de missions . . .," *Missions Catholiques* 61 (1929) 508–536. For other bibliography, *see* CATECHETICS; CATECHESIS, MISSIONARY. **Illustration credit:** Maryknoll Fathers.

[A. SEUMOIS]

CATECHUMEN

The term catechumen is often used in a broad sense. In a strict sense, however, one would define catechumen as a person (1) who has attained the use of reason—the Roman Ritual has a separate rite for infants; (2) who definitely desires Baptism—this implies conversion, hence, *justification (Denz 1918, 1933, 1943, 1520–83); it also excludes non-Catholics already validly baptized and nominal catechumens who defer Baptism indefinitely (e.g., as did many in the 4th and 5th centuries); these latter became catechumens in the strict sense only when they enrolled among the *competentes,* or *electi,* in the Lenten preparation for Baptism; (3) who enrolls in the catechumenal preparation for Baptism. Since this last institution began *c.* 190, disappeared in the Middle Ages (*c.* 6th century on), and was restored only in 1962 [ActApS 54 (1962) 310–338], this condition has not been realized often.

Sacred Scripture. Though the *catechumenate is a later development, one gathers some understanding of the catechumen from New Testament writings. John the Baptist's call for confession of sins, interior conversion, as a condition for baptism (Mt 3.1–6; Mk 1.4–5), was reechoed in Peter's early preaching (Acts 2.38). But catechetic instructions generally followed Baptism till the 2d century; kerygmatic preaching sufficed as preparation in the first years (Maertens, 63). The conversions of St. Paul (Acts ch. 9) and of Cornelius (ch. 10, 11) give more detailed insight into practice regarding the first catechumens. The community was concerned about who belonged to the Church and was represented by an early equivalent of a godparent (Acts 9.10–19, 27; ch. 10 and 11); the Church wanted assurance of the candidate's good dispositions (9.13–16, 26). The question, "What must I do?" (cf. 2.37; 9.6; 22.10; 16.30) reflects the convert's openness. The mention of 3 days (9.9; 10.30) possibly refers to the paschal triduum context of baptismal preparation (cf. Lk 24.7; Os 6.2–3).

Positive Theology of the Catechumen. Magisterial teaching offers little source material. However, one finds the mind of the Church reflected in the catechumenate institution and its liturgical rites. A theological understanding of the catechumen is really a study of conversion, but here one considers conversion in the context of the catechumenate. In this institution one sees how the Church has fostered and developed the call to *faith. Though this institution is changeable and even disappeared for centuries, there are certain constant factors in the Church's dealings with the catechumen that throw light on its understanding of him.

First, there is attention to the individuality of the catechumen enrolling in the catechumenate. Each enrolls with a significant prehistory to his conversion; he is not a *tabula rasa:* he reacts to the Church in a way in keeping with his background. That is why the Church first assures itself of his good dispositions. The precatechumenate period includes a period of *preevangelization for arousing his curiosity and a period of kerygmatic evangelization leading to conversion (see Hofinger).

The Church, represented by the priest, godparents, and the community, plays an important role in forming the catechumen for his place in the Church. His vocation to Baptism and its development comes from the Church. Godparents should be guides to converts throughout this period of preparation, but too often their role is merely nominal. It is through the Church and her spouse, Christ, present in the liturgical rites, that the new member of the Church is conceived.

The dialogue of God's word to the catechumen and his response to it continues throughout the catechumenate. God's word comes in the form of instructions, especially on the Creed, the Our Father, and the Gospels. These give him a new outlook on life, a new set of values. His life in Christ grows and deepens as he responds by assimilating God's word and turning away from sin. As exorcisms, prayer, and fasting have their effect, the catechumen makes difficult, often heroic, decisions for Christ. A new exodus from sin takes place; the liberating work of Christ's Redemption becomes visible in the catechumen's development.

Time for development is a fundamental law of divine action. This new paschal journey once again (since 1962) has its stages of development. The length of time may vary according to the individual's dispositions, but ordinarily the convert's formation suffers if the period of maturation is too short.

Liturgical rites introduce the convert to Christ's prayer and grace; they sanctify and consecrate the stages of the catechumen's development. When these rites are given all at once (e.g., in the adult rite of Baptism), there is great danger of empty ritualism; it is very difficult to assimilate them, especially the repetitive rites.

Membership in the Church. Though the catechumen is not yet sacramentally united to Christ through Baptism, he can be called a member of the Church by intention (*in voto; see* VOTUM). "Catechumens who, moved by the Holy Spirit, seek with explicit intention to be incorporated into the Church are by that very intention joined with her; with love and care Mother Church already embraces them as her own" [*Dogmatic Constitution on the Church* 14; ActApS 57 (1965) 19]. The catechumenate's first stage with its imposition of hands and signing officially makes them Christians. Church Fathers have described them as conceived in the Church, but not yet born, living members but in a period of gestation [M. Dujarier, *Maison-Dieu* 71 (1962) 78–93]. Although not subject to ecclesiastical laws (CIC c.12), they share in some of the benefits of full members: ecclesiastical burial (c.1239.2); various blessings (c.1149); exorcisms (c.1152); reception of blessed ashes, palms, and candles [ActApS 14 (1922) 271; 16 (1924) 102].

See also BAPTISM (THEOLOGY OF); CONVERSION, I (IN THE BIBLE); CONVERSION, III (THEOLOGY OF); METANOIA; PREEVANGELIZATION.

Bibliography: DTC, Tables générales 16:553. R. NAZ, DDC 2:1435–36. M. DUJARIER, *Le Parrainage des adultes aux trois premiers siècles de l'église* (Paris 1962). T. MAERTENS, *Histoire et pastorale du rituel du catéchuménat et du baptême* (Bruges 1962). J. HOFINGER, "Stages Leading to Faith and Their Role in the Catechesis of the Faithful," in *Pastoral Catechetics,* ed. J. HOFINGER and T. C. STONE (New York 1964) 144–159. W. SEUMOIS, "The Catechumenate: A Paschal Journey," LumV 15 (1960) 667–685. *Maison-Dieu* 71 (1962), the whole issue.

[R. X. REDMOND]

CATECHUMENATE

An institution in which adult candidates are prepared for Baptism according to a strict method. Some kind of instruction has always been necessary for those who wanted to be baptized and received into the Church. Such instruction, given orally, is called catechesis.

Beginnings. Mention of the catechumen is found already in St. Paul, when he reminds the catechumen of his duty to provide for the needs of his instructor (Gal 6.6). The Didache's teaching on the "Two Ways" (1–6; AncChrWr 6:15–19) shows that definite forms of instruction had already been developed before the end of the 1st century. Even so, this kind of instruction cannot really be called a catechumenate until the end of the 2d century. Justin Martyr (d. *c.* 165) reports (1 *Apologia* 61.2; Quasten MonE 14) that it was customary to combine fasting and prayer with instruction and that the faithful prayed and fasted with the candidates. Tertullian (d. *c.* 220) used the Latin word *catechumini* and reproached the heretics for not making a distinction between the faithful and the catechumens (*De praescriptionibus adversus haereticos* 41; PL 2:56). In fact, Tertullian himself seems to have been a catechist in Carthage. According to Eusebius (*Hist. Eccl.* 6.3; PG 20:527), the Alexandrian Bishop Demetrius conferred the office of catechist on the young Origen in 204 because other catechists had fled during the persecution. Moreover, the need for an adequate doctrinal preparation of candidates for Baptism must have been increasingly felt in the course of the 2d century, especially in view of the rise of the Gnostic sects, which were sources of confusion for the faithful.

3d Century. A full-blown catechumenate was in operation by 215; the *Apostolic Tradition* of Hippolytus, which appeared at that time, describes a complete arrangement of the institution (15–19; Botte LQF 32–40). If one wished to enter the Church, he had to be presented to the leaders of the Church by other Christians, who were catechumenate witnesses (later known as godparents). There followed an examination to ascertain the motives of the candidate for seeking Baptism and to obtain information on his state in life: whether he was free or slave, married or single, and if married, whether his manner of living corresponded to the Christian concept of marriage. Some professions had to be given up; others completely barred entrance into the Church. It was precisely such strictness that enhanced the Church's image and power to attract.

Ordinarily the catechumenate lasted for 3 years; this time was intended primarily as a test of the catechumens' moral improvement. It is evident from Tertullian (*De baptismo* 20; PL 1:1222) that the catechumens were exhorted to frequent prayer, fasting, and other penitential exercises. During the catechumenate the candidates were to hear the word of God from their teacher, who was to pray with them after each lesson and—even if he was a layman—to impose his hands on them as a blessing. The catechumens were permitted to attend the Service of the Word, or *Mass of the Catechumens, but not the Eucharistic service, or Mass of the Faithful.

Instruction consisted in the teacher's taking the catechumens through those books of Sacred Scripture in which the principles of the Christian life are presented. Origen cited the books of Esther, Judith, Tobias, and the Sapiential Books as the first spiritual nourishment of the Christian (*In Numeros hom.* 27.1; PG 12:780). Athanasius offered a similar list (*Epist. festalis* 39; PG 26:1457), which included the Didache and the *Shepherd of Hermas.* At the end of the 3 years (which could be shortened with industry and application) there was an examination that was concerned not so much with the knowledge of the catechumens as with "whether they lived devoutly, whether they honored widows, visited the sick, and practiced every good work" (*Apostolic Tradition* 20; Botte LQF 42). If this examination was favorable, there followed a more thoroughgoing preparation for Baptism, which took place on Easter.

Hippolytus underlined this transition with the words "Then they are to hear the Gospel." Probably "hearing the Gospel" meant receiving a well-planned instruction on the mysteries of the faith according to the New Testament and Christian salvation history. The Apostles' Creed provided the synthesis of Christian doctrine—the catechism, so to speak, of those times. During this stage of training the catechumens received a daily imposition of hands and exorcism, later given by the bishop himself. Two distinct stages, then, must be differentiated in the catechumenate: the actual catechumenate and candidacy for Baptism. In the East candidates were subsequently called those given light φωτιζόμενοι, for Baptism is an enlightenment (Heb 6.4; 10.32); and in the West, *competentes* or (in Rome) *electi.* Besides these, another preparatory step can possibly be distinguished, that of hearer. The Foremass was open to all who were interested in Christianity. The Church, however, assumed no responsibility for them whatsoever; they were admitted only as guests. The *Apostolic Constitutions* of the 4th century (8.6.2; Funk DidConst 1:478) named them as a distinct group. After the scriptural readings, they were simply asked to leave without being given a blessing.

4th and 5th Centuries. With the persecutions over, there came a new phase in the history of the catechumenate. When conversion of the masses then began, it proved altogether impossible to retain the old system, for many were satisfied merely to enter the catechumenate in order to become "Christians"; catechumens were regarded as Christians even though they did not yet belong to the faithful (Augustine, *In Ioh.* 44.2; PL 35:1714). Indeed, it was common during the 4th and 5th centuries, even in Christian families, for a person to receive Baptism as an adult. For example, Basil (d. 379) was baptized at 26, Augustine (d. 430) at 32, and John Chrysostom (d. 407) and Gregory of Nazianzus (d. 389) at comparable ages. The almost unbearable stringency of the penitential discipline of that time for those who had relapsed into serious sin after Baptism may have contributed to this practice. Under these conditions it was necessary to include an adequate preliminary instruction at the time of reception into the catechumenate, for the catechumenate itself was by then of an undetermined length and had only a loose affiliation with the Church. The catechumens, however, belonged to the hearers, those addressed by the Fathers in their sermons. Hence the frequent pause during these sermons to clarify for the benefit of the catechumens ("*Norunt fideles* . . .," e.g., in Augustine, *Sermo* 4.28, 31 and 5.7; PL 38:48, 58) secret doctrines, knowledge of which had not yet been permitted the catechumens. For this reason, too, as Easter approached there were increasingly more frequent exhortations to the catechumens finally to present themselves for Baptism: "Easter is coming; register for Baptism" (Augustine, *Sermo* 132.1; PL 38:735).

Because of these new conditions the heathen who wanted to become a Christian first received an introductory catechesis. There is a classic example of this in St. Augustine's *De catechizandis rudibus* (PL 40: 309–348), which develops the principles for this kind of catechetics and presents two model catecheses. The catechist, a deacon or priest, was to choose the form of *narratio;* when he was convinced of the candidate's motives, he was to present the divine plan of redemption by telling the story of salvation from the creation of the world and man's fall to the work of Christ and the last judgment. His task was to lead the candidate to a faithful acceptance of doctrine; but he had to lead him beyond that from faith to hope, and from hope to love. He was to see to it that in his catechesis a basic tenor of *hilaritas* was maintained. In the East there was a similar plan in the *Oratio catechetica* of Gregory of Nyssa (PG 45:10–106). This is a work of 40 chapters that, although it is aimed at beginners, already comes close to being a systematic theology.

After this preliminary instruction one could be received into the catechumenate. For this, also, a rich ceremony was by then developed. From ancient times, in East and West, this included the signing of the candidate's forehead with the Cross and usually an imposition of hands. Constantine was received with prayer and the laying on of hands (*see* Eusebius of Caesarea, *Vita Constantini* 4.61; PG 20:1213). This marked the candidate as belonging to Christ. In the West there followed the *sacramentum salis,* the giving of salt, of which St. Augustine often speaks (*Catech. rud.* 26.50; *PL* 40:344–345). This symbolized, especially if salted bread was used [F. J. Dölger, *Der Exorzismus im altchristlichen Taufritual* (Paderborn 1909) 89, 92], that the catechumen was receiving a preliminary holy meal that prefigured the Eucharist. Hence Augustine reminds his hearers that "although it is not the body of Christ, still it is sacred" (*Pecc. merit.* 2.26.42; PL 44:176). The Eastern custom of breathing on the candidate was adopted by the West. The meaning was twofold: as an exsufflation, in the sense of a gesture of contempt towards Satan who was to be "blown away," and as an insufflation, in the sense of a first infusion of the Holy Spirit. These rites were later combined to form the *ordo ad catechumenum faciendum.*

If the catechumen finally reported for Baptism, he was enrolled in the ranks of the *competentes.* By this time the enrollment took place at the beginning of Lent, which was a period of serious penance and intensive learning. The most important document containing these last instructions is the 18 *Catechetical Lectures* of Cyril of Jerusalem, given in about 348. They first deal with sin and Baptism and then provide a detailed explanation of the Creed.

A short time later, in her diary, Etheria related similar forms of catechesis, also from Jerusalem [46; ed. H. Pétré, *Éthérie, Journal de voyage* (Paris 1948) 256–261]. To this same category belong the explanations of the creed by Nicetas of Remesiana (d. *c.* 414; PL 52:865–874) and St. Augustine (*Sermo* 212–215; PL 38:1058–76). At Rome, according to Leo the Great (*Epist.* 16.6; PL 54:702), the candidates for Baptism were prepared by means of doctrinal talks (*frequentibus praedicationibus*), which took place outside the regular services, apparently in a special room. Here, too, the summary of these talks was the Creed, which was taught to the catechumen in a special celebration called *traditio symboli.* At this period other celebrations were added for the teaching of the Lord's Prayer and an explanation of the four Gospels. The 3d, 4th, and 5th Sundays of Lent were appointed for this. These three celebrations took the same form that was used in the 6th century, as reported in the *Roman Ordinal 11* (Andrieu OR 2:417–447) and in the Gelasian Sacramentary [1.34–36; ed. Mohlberg, 46–53; cf. A. Chavasse, *Le sacramentaire gélasien* (Tournai 1958) 160–161]. These documents indicate that on the above-mentioned Sundays the godparents were given special prominence: their names were mentioned at the *Memento* of the living, in which only the baptized could be named (*qui tibi offerunt*). The names of the *electi* were read at the *Hanc igitur,* in which the intention or persons prayed for could be named. These three sessions were called scrutinies—not that a special examination of knowledge took place, but because of the exorcisms connected with them.

Near the end of this last period of preparation there was, according to ancient tradition, the recital of the creed (*redditio symboli*). The *apertio aurium,* or the *Ephpheta* (the opening of the ears, from the example of Our Lord; Mk 7.33), preceded this *redditio* in olden times.

In a wider sense one can also speak here of an extension of the catechumenate beyond Baptism. In the 4th and 5th centuries, when the discipline of secrecy (*see* SECRET, DISCIPLINE OF THE) was in full vigor, one did not discuss the particulars of the Sacraments of the Church with those who were not yet baptized. This material was the subject of special catecheses after Baptism. In connection with this type of catechesis, there came from Jerusalem another series of five *Mystagogical Catecheses,* attributed to Cyril of Jerusalem. In these, the Sacraments (Baptism, Confirmation, and the Eucharist) that the newly baptized had just received were explained. Similar catecheses by Theodore of Mopsuestia have been preserved, in which the author also treats briefly of the Sacrament of Penance. St. Ambrose's *De sacramentis* records the oral catechesis he used in Milan.

Middle Ages. After the 6th century, because adult Baptism had become a rarity, the traditional rites of the catechumenate were used for infants with only superficial adjustment. The scrutinies, now transferred to weekdays, served as a substitute for catechesis, which was no longer possible; and they were increased to seven, which included the Holy Saturday morning preliminary rites to Baptism (*Ordo Rom.* 11; Andrieu OR 2:417–447). However, already in Carolingian times, these scrutinies were compressed into one complicated and meaningless rite with only the baptismal act itself left as a separate rite.

There was no longer a catechumenate even for adults in the Middle Ages. The traditional forms were no longer used either upon the conversion of the Germans, or when the Slavs embraced the Church. Although Gregory the Great still demanded a preparation of 40 days, the Apostle of the Suevians, Martin of Braga (*Capitula c.* 49; Mansi 9:855.2), insisted on only 20 days; however, even this policy was often not followed in the case of mass Baptism.

Modern Times. Mass Baptisms preceded by very little instruction have not been unknown in the missions of America and the East Indies. However, provincial councils of Mexico and Peru demanded a 40-day instruction period; in other places, e.g., the East Indies, a minimum of 20 days was the rule. The directives of the Congregation for the Propagation of the Faith were not consistent, although they did encourage attempts at greater strictness, along the lines of the ancient catechumenate. The early Christian catechumenate experienced a widespread renewal in the African missions through the efforts of Cardinal Lavigerie and his community, the White Fathers. A 4-year preparation for Baptism was again broken down into the stages of *postulantes, catechumeni,* and *electi,* and the training period closed with retreat exercises. Having proved extremely fruitful, this procedure had a favorable influence on other missions. Thus in Africa, a 2-year catechumenate has become the general rule.

However, in general, a modern catechumenate cannot be spoken of except in the broad sense that catechumens are present who are being prepared in an ordered fashion. Modern methods are very different from those of Christian antiquity. The chief element in modern practice came to be the explanation and memorization of a *catechism, whether it was a special one created for missionary situations or one taken from Europe. Catechism instruction was associated more and more with the school, first with schools of purely religious instruction, later with general elementary schools.

Since the time of A. de Rhodes, SJ (d. 1660), institutes for catechists have played an ever-growing role in religious instruction in the missions, and the formation of catechists and their training with regard to content and method have become one of the most important tasks of mission work. Concerning the details in the organization and duration of the catechumenate, the greatest diversity existed at mid-20th century.

But at the same time, a return to the ancient catechumenate was in process. On the one hand, the catechetical movement had made religious educators conscious of the excessive intellectual emphasis in catechisms. On the other hand, liturgical studies had awakened interest in the baptismal rite contained in the *Rituale Romanum,* which for the most part consists of ceremonies stemming from the early Christian catechumenate, and which placed religious instruction in a liturgical framework. On April 16, 1962, the Congregation of Rites took the first step toward a revitalization of the baptismal ritual by publishing a new ordinal [*Ordo baptismi per gradus catechumenatus dispositus;* ActApS 54 (1962) 310–338] that allowed the various parts of the ceremony to be spread over a rather long process of catechetical preparation. Since much more must be done to make the liturgy of Baptism a truly functional part of the training of candidates, Vatican Council II, on Dec. 4, 1963, ordered a complete reform of the baptismal rites (*Constitution on the Sacred Liturgy,* 1:64–70).

See also CATECHESIS, I (EARLY CHRISTIAN); CATECHESIS, II (MEDIEVAL AND MODERN); CATECHESIS, MISSIONARY; CATECHIST, MISSIONARY.

Bibliography: H. LECLERCQ and P. DE PUNIET, DACL 2.2: 2530–2621. Eisenhofer HdbL 2:244–256. A. DONDEYNE, "La Discipline des scrutins dans l'église latine avant Charlemagne," RHE 28 (1932) 5–33, 751–787. L. KILGER, "Zur Entwicklung der Katechumenatspraxis vom 5. bis 18. Jahrhundert," ZMiss Relw 15 (1925) 166–182. T. OHM, *Das Katechumenat in den katholischen Missionen* (Münster 1959). J. BECKMANN and W. BÜHLMANN, "Missionen," *Katechetisches Wörterbuch,* ed. L. LENTNER (Freiburg 1961) 506–532. A. STENZEL, *Die Taufe* (Innsbruck 1958). *St. Cyril of Jerusalem's Lectures on the Christian Sacraments,* ed. F. L. CROSS (London 1951). F. R. MCMANUS, "The Restored Liturgical Catechumenate," *Worship* 36 (1962) 536–549. A. STENZEL, "Zum neuen Ordo der Erwachsenen-Taufe," LiturgJB 13 (1963) 87–91.

[J. A. JUNGMANN]

CATEGORICAL IMPERATIVE

The Kantian categorical imperative follows from a conception of rational morality that is valid and binding for all rational minds. Just as Kant, in his *Critique of Pure Reason,* considered rational science as knowledge valid and binding for all rational minds, so in his *Critique of Practical Reason,* he considered morality as comparable to science in the sense of being true necessarily and universally without qualification. The categorical imperative is categorical not because of a divine command, nor because of a conformity with nature, nor because of any consensus, however large; rather it has the category of an a priori. Once rational knowledge and rational morality are agreed to, according to Kant's reasoning, their universality and validity give evidence of their a priori character.

Explanation. The principle of Kantian rational morality is that an act is moral if and only if the principle in the act is capable of universalization without an internal contradiction. Even more fundamental for Kant, however, is the deontological primary principle that "there is nothing in the world or even out of it that can be called good without qualification except a good will." The principle on which the good will wills its acts must not contain any implication of circumstances or pragmatic consequences, because these would introduce contingencies that Kant wished to avoid. The right act is determined, for him, by a principle that is the same for every individual regardless of circumstances. To admit contingent circumstances would destroy the purely rational and categorical nature of the imperative.

First Formulation. Such reasoning led Kant to the first formulation of his categorical imperative: "Act only on that maxim which you can at the same time will to become a universal law." This categorical imperative is present in every moral act that is obligatory in itself without reference to any other end. In this way the categorical imperative is distinguished from the hypothetical, which represents the practical necessity of a possible act as a means to something else that is willed or might be willed. An act that is good only as a means to something else is commanded by a hypothetical "ought" or imperative, but an act that is conceived to be good in itself without any ordination to a further end is commanded by a categorical "ought" or imperative. The hypothetical imperative asserts only that an act is good for some purpose, actual or possible. The categorical imperative declares an act to be binding and exacting in itself, without reference to any purpose or end beyond itself.

If nothing can be called good without qualification except a good will, the good will is good in itself and not because of what it accomplishes or the uses to which it is put. Even if a good will achieves nothing, for Kant it is comparable to a jewel that would shine by its own light as something with intrinsic value. This good will operates solely from the motive of duty, not because God commands the act, but because it is good in itself. This deontological strain in Kant leads him to consider the good will as the will to do what ought to be done on the presupposition that man is free. Freedom and duty are reciprocal terms for Kant, although he admits that morality requires man only to be able to think freedom without self-contradiction, not to understand it. Freedom is postulated by the moral law, but human intelligence will never fully uncover how freedom is possible.

Other Formulations. Kant stated the categorical imperative in two other forms in addition to the one enunciated above. The second form was "Treat every rational being including yourself always as an end, and never as a mere means." The third form asserted that "a principle of moral conduct is morally binding on me if and only if I can regard it as a law which I impose on myself." The latter form stresses the autonomous morality of Kant, which denies that the moral law is something imposed upon man *ab extra.*

Critique. All three formulations of the Kantian categorical imperative have been criticized on the grounds of their *ethical formalism, which would in application lead to conclusions opposed to established moral judgments. Refusing to repay borrowed money, for example, does not seem to involve a contradiction that is purely logical or formal, but it is dependent upon social and economic conditions in which people would not lend money if there were no assurance of repayment. A good will seems to require definition in terms of content as well as form. Again, a formal principle or categorical imperative to obey laws that are universal and necessary leaves out of the moral sphere the performance of unique acts in particular existential circumstances. It implies a consistency and uniformity in good acts that is not borne out in practice, where moral life is rich in diversity.

Kantian formulations of the categorical imperative are to be criticized as much on grounds that they cannot be validly applied as on grounds of their formalism. In addition there is a rigidity, an inflexibility, and a harshness in the application of these principles. They restrict morally good acts to those done out of respect for the moral law; and yet it is good to help others from motives of compassion and love when duty and obligation are not clearly present. These motives have independent moral value according to most moralists, but Kant seems to consider all inclinations other than that to duty as morally irrelevant. He also confuses the goodness of an act with the merit one receives in performing it.

For the philosopher with theistic presuppositions there is a further criticism of the autonomous, rather than the heteronomous, nature of Kantian morality. The human reason does not create morality; it merely articulates morality in practical prudential judgments of conscience, which may be termed the "prismatic analysis" through which the law of God is transmitted. Obligation is not self-imposed; it is heteronomously imposed through the mediation of law in the individual conscience of man. Circumstances and motives are required for the existential consideration of the moral act, and the moral act is good if motivated by charity as well as by duty.

Kant's dissatisfaction with a theistic ethics arose both from his own moral philosophy and his epistemology. For him a theistic ethics would imply a theological voluntarism, because the divine perfection in such an ethics would be God's will considered as independent of His goodness and wisdom. However one may criticize theological voluntarism, even Kant would not conclude that in such an ethic *every* moral law would depend exclusively on God's will alone. Kant's fundamental objection to a theistic ethics arose from his epistemological position that God is accessible neither to intuition nor to demonstrative knowledge. Thus any critique of the Kantian categorical imperative is reductively a critique of Kant's philosophical position on the possibility of man's speculative knowledge of God and of the nature of the moral "ought."

See also DEONTOLOGISM; ETHICS, HISTORY OF.

Bibliography: I. KANT, *The Moral Law; or, Kant's Groundwork of the Metaphysic of Morals,* tr. and ed. H. J. PATON (New York 1948). W. T. JONES, *Morality and Freedom in the Philosophy of Immanuel Kant* (London 1940). J. D. COLLINS, *A History of Modern European Philosophy* (Milwaukee 1954).

[T. A. WASSMER]

CATEGORIES OF BEING

The categories of being are defined variously as the most general predicates expressive of real *being or as pure conceptions of the understanding. The most important and influential doctrines on the categories are those of *Aristotle and *Kant. Since that of Aristotle is prior to Kant's and may well have been the first elaboration of a doctrine of categories (see Plato, *Soph.* 254B, for a possible adumbration of it, however), it is granted priority of exposition here.

The Greek term κατηγορίαι, meaning predicates, links the doctrine of categories with the *proposition. This simple fact has been the cause of a number of different views on the origin and nature of the doctrine of categories in Aristotle. Some have maintained that the doctrine arose from a consideration of grammar; others that it is a logical doctrine that came to have ontological import; others that, originally an ontological doctrine, it came to be expressed in logical terminology. Since there was no developed grammar in the relevant sense for Aristotle to rely on, and since the doctrine of categories makes distinctions where grammar would not and does not honor possible grammatical distinctions, the first view is implausible. The other views involve a problem that, as applied to Aristotle, often smacks of anachronism. For when it is asked whether the doctrine of categories is logical or metaphysical, it is not always clear whether the question turns on the meaning these adjectives might have had for Aristotle or on the meaning they have today. Yet, even when restricted to the Aristotelian perspective, one cannot always grasp the precise import of a given statement about the categories. If the categories are predicates and genera, it is not the case that every predicate falls within a category. Indeed, Aristotle broaches the problems of metaphysics by way of the categories, thereby indicating that the categories are not a list of just any uses of being, but are rather the highest genera predicable of real being as opposed to accidental being. Therefore, if the categories, since they are genera, are logical, they are logical relations that attach to real being. In short, they are not classifications derived from *language simply, but classifications found in language expressive of real being.

Aristotle's Treatise on Categories. Although its authenticity has been questioned, most scholars now accept the *Categories* as the work of Aristotle. This treatise prefaces the actual listing of the supreme genera with a number of distinctions that indicate what the author intends to do. First it notes that some verbal expressions are complex while others are incomplex. A complex verbal expression is one that admits of truth or falsity; e.g., "The man runs." Incomplex expressions are neither true nor false and can be components of complex expressions. Examples of incomplex expressions are "man" and "runs." The categories themselves are incomplex expressions.

Aristotle then distinguishes being predicable of a subject and being present in a subject. To be present in a subject means to pertain to the subject accidentally and not essentially; thus what is present in a subject in this sense is not part of the subject's *quiddity. The author adds that what is present in a subject is incapable of existence apart from a subject. What is predicable of a subject, on the other hand, means whatever can be said of a subject whether essentially or accidentally. Predicability involves universality and, on this assumption, Aristotle divides things themselves as follows: (1) Some things are predicable of a subject but are never present in a subject; the author has in mind universal expressions of what a thing is, such as "man." (2) Some things are present in a subject but are never predicable of a subject; such are singular accidents, e.g., a particular whiteness. (3) Some things are both predicable of a subject and present in a subject; these are accidents considered universally, e.g., whiteness. (4) Finally, some things are neither present in a subject nor predicable of a subject; e.g., the individual man or the individual horse.

Substances are precisely things of this fourth kind. Such singular entities Aristotle calls first substances; second substances are all predicates that can be affirmed essentially of first substances, i.e., things falling in the first class. Examples of second substance, accordingly, are: man, horse, animal, living organism, and, finally, substance itself.

If man can be predicated of Socrates and animal can be predicated of man, then animal can be predicated of Socrates. This observation indicates that a hierarchy of predicates can be found that will end ultimately with such terms as substance.

Aristotle then lists his categories: "Incomplex expressions signify either substance, quantity, quality, relation, place, time, situation, condition, action or passion" (*Cat.* 1b 25–27). Aristotle offers the following examples of things of which these are predicated as supreme genera: of substance, man or horse; of quantity, two inches long; of quality, white and grammatical; of relation, double, half, and greater; of place, in the market, in school; of time, last year and yesterday; of situation, lying and sitting; of condition, shod and armed; of action, to lance, to cauterize; of passion, to be lanced, to be cauterized. Such expressions are neither true nor false, although true or false expressions are composed from them.

Categories and Real Being. Aristotle's intention in enumerating these ten highest predicates or supreme genera is not made explicit in the *Categories,* as it is elsewhere. That he was not merely classifying all possible predicates is evident enough from the *Metaphysics* (1017a 7–1017b 9). Acutely aware of the variety of uses and meanings of "is" and "being," Aristotle emphasizes that not every use of these terms is relevant to the science of being as being. Some uses do not purport to assert that what is said "to be" exists independently of human knowledge. Yet even when interest is confined to real being, "being" and "is" do not have a unique sense. "On the other hand, the varieties of essential being are indicated by the categories; for in as many ways as there are categories may things be said to be. Since predication asserts sometimes what a thing is, sometimes of what sort, sometimes how much, sometimes in what relation, sometimes in what process of doing or undergoing, sometimes where, sometimes when, it follows that these are all the ways of being" (1017a 22–27; tr. Hope).

In an effort to understand the things that are, man arrives at knowledge that expresses itself in such propositions as "Socrates is man," "Socrates is seated," "Socrates is five feet tall." Predicates attributed to such entities as Socrates are not all of a piece, however, though some (e.g., "man," "animal," and "living thing") are related as more and less general. To say of Socrates that he is seated is not an expression of what Socrates is essentially, but of something "present in him." Since for a thing to be is for it to be something or other, and what it is said to be relates to it, either essentially or accidentally, the categories are the logical arrangement of predicates expressive of modes of real being.

Logic vs. Ontology. Is Aristotle's teaching on the categories a logical or metaphysical doctrine? To be a *substance or an *accident is a mode of real being; the names

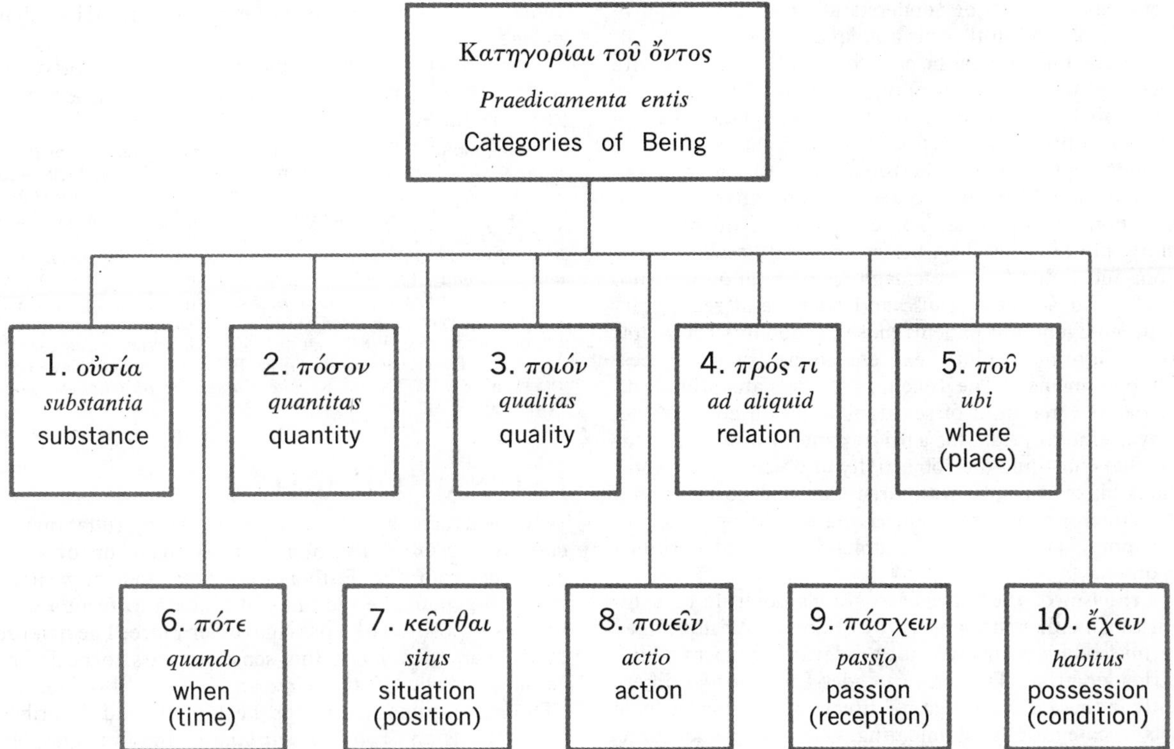

Aristotle's categories of being. Names are given in Greek and Latin, with approximate English equivalents.

of the supreme genera, like the names of subordinate genera and of the ultimate species, are not logical terms. Moreover, Aristotle speaks of the categories of *being.* On the other hand, to be a predicate is no more an ontological characteristic than to be a *genus, *species, or difference, and yet these terms figure prominently in the elaboration of the doctrine (*see* PREDICABLES).

Such considerations have led a significant number of scholars to say of the doctrine of categories that it lies in the shadowy region between logic and ontology. Perhaps it is more accurate to say that what is categorized is real being, but that to be categorized, to be a genus or species, is to take on a logical relation. If it is generally true that logical relations attach to real things because of our way of knowing them, the apparently anomalous character of the categories also furnishes a general view of the nature of the logical. There is nothing merely logical about being a substance, but to say of substance that it is a supreme genus is to relate the content of one concept to the meanings of a number of predicates subordinate to it and, like it, expressive of the natures of things like Socrates and Alcibiades. To say of substance that it is a category, then, is like saying of horse that it is a species; in both cases one is asserting of something real a kind of predicability that is consequent upon man's abstractive manner of knowing real things (*see* ABSTRACTION).

The reluctance to call the doctrine of categories logical is based on the recognition that substance, quantity, quality, etc., signify modes of real being; the reluctance to call the doctrine ontological is based on the recognition that the ascending series of predicates, man-animal-living substance, does not answer to any real division in the thing of which all these terms are predicated. Moreover, it would be fallacious to argue as follows: Substance is a supreme genus; man is a substance; therefore, man is a supreme genus. For real being to fall into the schema of the categories, it must be universal, but universality and predicability are not ontological characteristics. Therefore the correct conclusion is this: only real being falls under the categories; but, in order to be in a category, real being must be considered as the subject of such logical relations as predicability, genus, and so forth.

Kantian Categories. Kant arrives at his categories, which are principles of pure or a priori synthesis on the part of the understanding, by a consideration of classes of judgment (*Kritik der reinen Vernunft*). These classes are more reminiscent of Aristotle's *On Interpretation* than of his *Categories,* for they involve the comparison of propositions with respect to their quantity and quality and modality, together with the notion of simple and complex propositions. Kant suggests that, if one abstracts from the content of judgments and concentrates on their form alone, he finds that the function of thought in a judgment can be brought under four headings: quantity, quality, relation, and modality. Each heading comprises three "moments." With respect to quantity, judgments are universal, particular, or singular; with respect to quality, they are affirmative, negative, or infinite; with respect to relation, they are categorical, hypothetical, or disjunctive; with respect to modality, they are problematical, assertorical, or apodictical. Kant gives at this point a hint as to why he has called these trichotomies moments. Speaking of modalities of judgment, Kant says that problematical judgments are those in which an affirmation is accepted as merely possible; in assertorical judgments the affirmation is regarded as true; in the apodictical it is regarded as necessary. In a note he suggests that it is as if thought were in the first instance a function of *understanding, in the second of *judgment, and in the third of *reasoning.

Kant connects what he chooses to call categories with these divisions of the form of judgments: by a category he means a pure conception of the understanding applicable a priori to objects of *intuition. Since the table of judgments exhausts the function of the understanding, one should be able to arrive at an exhaustive enumeration of categories. The categories of quantity are unity, plurality, totality; those of quality, reality, negation, and limitation; the categories of relation are substance and accident, cause and effect, and reciprocity between agent and patient; those of modality the pairs: possibility-impossibility, existence-nonexistence, necessity-contingency. The function of the categories is to render the manifold of sensuous intuition conceivable; they are, so to speak, the a priori patterns of understanding that constitute the *objectivity of objects. Kant compares his own results with Aristotle's and observes that the Greek philosopher, not having a guiding principle, hit upon his categories in a haphazard and adventitious manner.

Criticism of the Categories. Kant's doctrine of categories is neither the same sort of thing as Aristotle's, as he misleadingly suggests, nor a relevant criticism of the earlier doctrine. The term category functions so differently in these authors that no direct comparison of their lists of categories is illuminating. One must rather go to the most general presuppositions of Aristotelian and Kantian philosophy. Depending on which basic option he prefers, he will regard one of these doctrines on categories as hopelessly wrongheaded; in more sanguine moments, he will doubtless find some remote glimmer of plausibility in the other view, though he will not think it a doctrine of categories.

Difficulties of much the same kind arise when one turns to contemporary discussions of categories that are influenced by the theory of types (*see* ANTINOMY). Such discussions often suggest that Aristotle intended to formulate a general theory of types of predicate and find, of course, that the Aristotelian categories are woefully inadequate. Here, too, the initial impression that wholly opposed views are being juxtaposed soon gives way to the thought that the views may after all be complementary. Such an irenic moment is achieved, however, at the expense of any genuinely common meaning of the term category, since agreements are not reached under the aegis of what either side would be willing to call categories.

The main complaint of J. S. *Mill against the Aristotelian categories was that they left out of account such realities as man's feelings. One is tempted to see as akin to Mill's more recent suggestions that, since the categories are classifications of things and man is not a *thing, "existentials," or categories of human being, must be devised.

The fate of the Aristotelian doctrine of categories depends on one's ability to resist the anachronistic impulse to see what adumbrations of familiar procedures can be discovered in Aristotle, and to regain the more basic kind of thinking underlying science and logic that permeates Aristotelian philosophy. From a variety of quarters, notably from *phenomenology, philosophers are being urged to recognize the continuing and fundamental validity of a knowledge that requires taking the knower into account. Perhaps it is only by heeding these hints that one can grasp the nature of the Aristotelian categories.

See also SUBSTANCE; ACCIDENT; QUANTITY; QUALITY; RELATION; PLACE; SITUATION (SITUS); ACTION AND PASSION; TIME.

Bibliography: L. M. DE RIJK, *The Place of Categories of Being in Aristotle's Philosophy* (Assen, Netherlands 1952). M. SCHEU, *The Categories of Being in Aristotle and St. Thomas* (CUA Philos. Stud. 88; Washington 1944). R. J. BLACKWELL, "The Methodological Function of Categories in Aristotle," NewSchol 31 (1957) 526–537. J. A. OESTERLE, *Logic, the Art of Defining and Reasoning* (2d ed., Englewood Cliffs, N.J. 1963). L. DE RAEYMAEKER, *The Philosophy of Being,* tr. E. H. ZIEGELMEYER (St. Louis 1954). R. E. MCCALL, *The Reality of Substance* (CUA Philos. Stud. 168; Washington 1956). G. RYLE, "Categories," *Logic and Language,* ed. A. G. N. FLEW (2d series; New York 1953) 65–81. E. FREEMAN, *The Categories of Charles Peirce* (Chicago 1934).

[R. M. MC INERNY]

CATENAE, BIBLICAL

Biblical catenae (from *catena,* chain; fuller name, *catenae patrum*) are commentaries made up of short excerpts from the Fathers or other ancient writers, strung together like the links of a chain to form a continuous exposition of a passage of Scripture. The first use of the name *catena* in this sense appears to be in the *editio princeps* of the *Catena Aurea* (1484) of St. *Thomas Aquinas, although he himself had described this work as an *expositio continua* of the four Gospels. Among earlier names were exegetical eclogues, collected explanations, and simply interpretations. Some catenae are drawn from one Father exclusively; others from two or three, with an evident attempt to give equal place to the Antiochene and Alexandrian schools of exegesis; still others are based on as many as 80 or more sources. In the better catenae each excerpt is introduced by the name of the commentator or by an identifying abbreviation. Where this is not the case, some excerpts can only be tentatively ascribed to a given Father or be left as of unknown authorship. As this suggests, much research remains to be done in this field. In typical appearance the manuscript has either only relatively few words of text in large letters in the center of the page surrounded by abundant commentary, or the text is immediately followed by the commentary written in parallel columns. There are Greek, Latin, and Eastern (mostly Syriac) catenae.

Greek Catenae. These are valuable to both the exegete and the textual critic. For the former, they possess a unique importance in that they offer him a vast storehouse of otherwise unknown patristic exegesis. It is estimated that over half of the commentaries of the Fathers have been preserved through catenae, including passages from heretical writers otherwise doomed to possible oblivion. To the textual critic, as so far studied, catenae reveal many variant readings of the Hexapla text [*see* BIBLE, IV (TEXTS AND VERSIONS), 9]. In both these respects Latin catenae are far less important than Greek ones, since they present the Biblical text and much of the commentary only in translation.

Greek catenae first appeared as the golden age of patristic exegesis came to a close at the end of the 5th century. Original, creative commentators gave way to compilers of exposition culled from their predecessors. At the same time the very mass of accumulated commentary created the need for some sort of analysis and methodical classification, if it was to be made generally

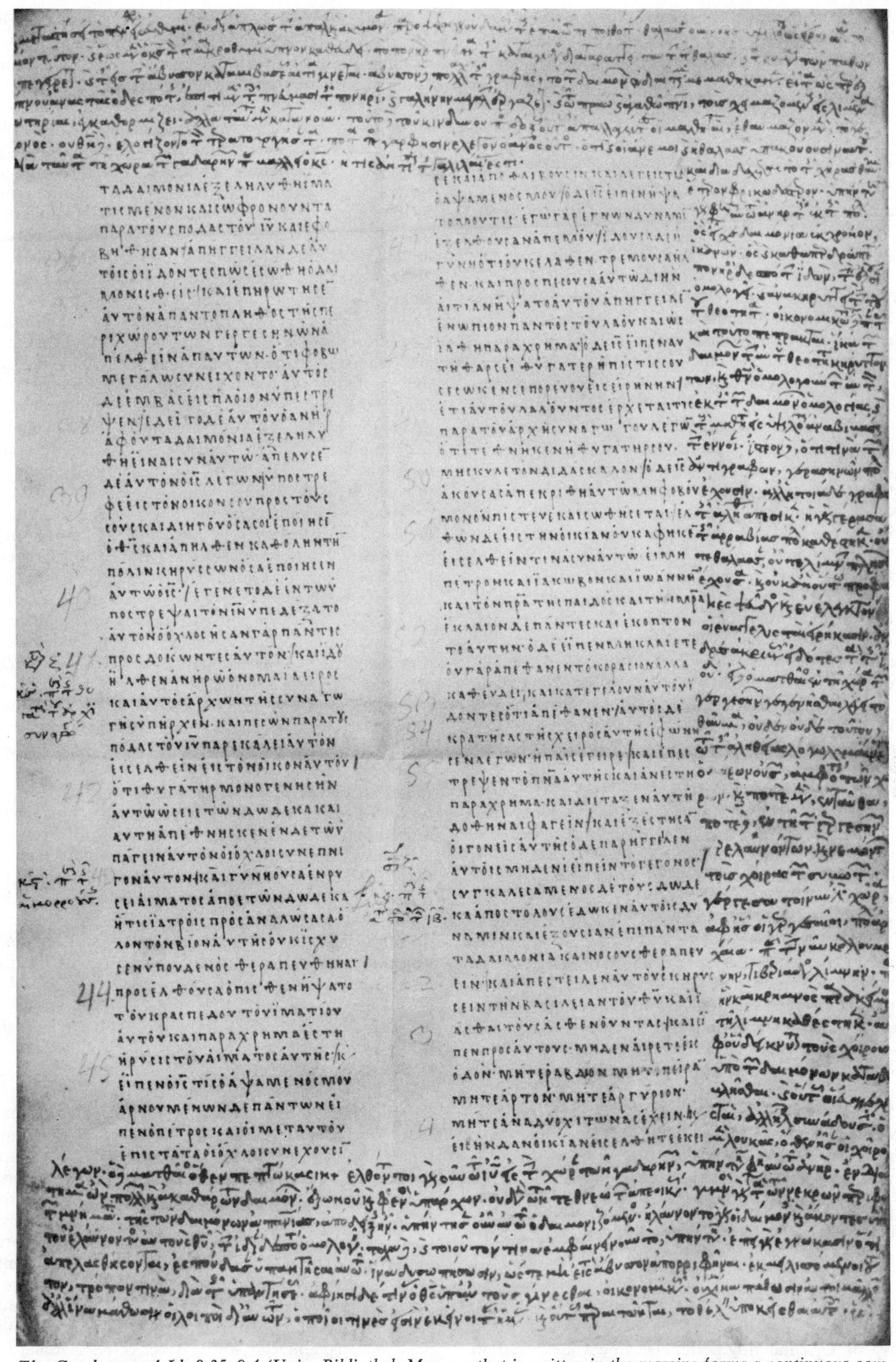

The Greek text of Lk 8.35–9.4 (Univ. Bibliothek Munich, 2 Cod. MS 30, fol. 72r). The cursive Greek text that is written in the margins forms a continuous commentary called the "catena."

available. The earliest known Greek to compile extensive catenae is *Procopius of Gaza (d. 538), who edited a commentary on the Octateuch (the Pentateuch plus Josue, Judges, and Ruth) drawn from the writings of *Cyril of Alexandria, *Basil the Great, and *Gregory of Nyssa. He compiled catenae also on 1 and 2 Samuel, 1 and 2 Kings, 1 and 2 Chronicles, Isaia, and Canticle of Canticles. Among other Greek catenists are Olympiodorus of Alexandria (6th century), John Drungarios (7th century), Andreas the Presbyter (7th century), and Nicetas of Heraclea (11th century).

Latin Catenae. With roots going back to *Bede's commentaries, Latin catenae came to flower during the 11th century as part of the *Carolingian Renaissance. This medieval revival of learning gave a place of preeminence to the Bible and its patristic exegesis. The compilation of catenae was encouraged, and by the end of the 9th century virtually every book of the Bible had its commentary pieced together from the Fathers. Outstanding among early catenists were *Alcuin (d. 805), *Claudius of Turin (d. 827), *Rabanus Maurus (d. 865), and *Walafrid Strabo (d. 849). For 2 centuries following their first appearance, Latin catenae went through a period of deterioration. Compilers were unlearned, their work careless and uncritical, and their exegesis often inconsistent if not in contradiction with itself. Spurred on perhaps by the reform in theological *florilegia (e.g., Peter *Abelard's *Sic et non*), scripturists undertook to remedy this confused state of affairs. Thus, by degrees, out of the chaos of the 11th century just described and as a by-product of scholasticism, came improvement culminating in the *expositio continua* of St. Thomas on the four Gospels, later known as the *Catena Aurea,* a model for all future labors. Its excerpts, drawn from over 80 sources, are gracefully interlocked to produce pleasant as well as instructive reading (repr. Turin 1938; Eng. tr. 4 v., Oxford 1841–45).

Among modern works akin to the medieval catenae are: J. M. Péronne, *La Chaine d'or sur les psaumes,* 3 v. (Paris 1879); J. M. Neale and R. F. Littledale, *Commentary on the Psalms from Primitive and Medieval Writers . . .,* 4 v. (London 1860–74); and G. Bellino, *Gesù Cristo nelle S. Scritture e nei SS. Padri e Dottori,* 9 v. (Turin 1911–15).

Syriac Catenae. Of Eastern catenae may be mentioned the following Syriac ones of: (1) an anonymous compiler known as *Garden of Delights* (7th century), (2) Severus, an Antiochene monk (9th century), (3) Bp. Dionysius bar Ṣalībī (12th century), and (4) *Bar-Hebraeus, a commentary on both the OT and the NT entitled *Storehouse of Mysteries.*

For the publication of the various catenae, see bibliography below.

See also BIBLE, VI (EXEGESIS), 2.

Bibliography: R. DEVREESSE, DBSuppl 1:1084–1233. K. STAAB, LexThK[2] 6:56–57. A. VACCARI, EncCatt 3:1132–36. W. ELTESTER, RGG[3] 1:1627–28. G. BARDY, *Catholicisme* 2:860–862. **Illustration credit:** Universitäts Bibliothek, München.

[C. O'C. SLOANE]

CATHARI

Members of a medieval sect adhering to a dualistic heresy of Oriental origin that became widespread in Western Christendom after 1150 (*see* HERESY, HISTORY OF, 2). The present study covers its origins, history, organizations, and disappearance.

Origins. Beginning with the 11th century, religious life in western Europe had difficulty maintaining its equilibrium, despite the *Gregorian reform movement and the new monastic trends (e.g., *see* CLUNIAC REFORM; CISTERCIANS). Some sought to satisfy their aspirations by a return to evangelical poverty (*see* POVERTY MOVEMENT) and simplicity, from which it was easy to fall into heresy. This was the origin of many sporadic movements superficially labeled Manichaean by contemporaries, but of which little is actually known (*see* PETER OF BRUYS; HENRY OF LUSANNE; ARNOLD OF BRESCIA). It was Bogomilism that provided these indistinct currents with the doctrinal framework they lacked. Bogomilism itself traced its origin to those Paulician colonies settled in Thrace by the Emperor Nicephorus I (802–811), through which a dualistic and iconoclastic heresy, originally of Armenia, took root in the Balkans. It penetrated into Bulgaria and during the reign of Czar Peter (927–969) inspired the preaching of the priest Bogomil, who taught contempt for the official Church, held the Sacraments to be useless, rejected the Old Testament, and retained but one prayer, the Our Father. The world, which was the creation and domain of the devil, was evil. But the dualism of the *Bogomils was not radical, inasmuch as the devil was a rebellious and fallen angel inferior to the principle of Good. This heresy is known principally through the *Treatise* of Cosmas the Priest, written in 972. In the early 11th century, the Bogomils in Constantinople developed a more radical doctrine that admitted complete equality between the principle of Good, i.e., the creator of the invisible world, and the principal of Evil, the creator of the material world. This doctrine was characteristic of the Church of Dragovitsa.

History in Europe. This Eastern Heresy was not found in the West until the middle of the 12th century when its adherents are called Cathari from καθαροί, a traditional name for Manichaeans. Transferred from the Balkan Peninsula principally by knights returning from the Second *Crusade, the heresy spread rapidly in northern France, through the Rhine countries where Cathari were mentioned in 1163, to southern France (the *Boni homines* of Lombers in 1165). They spread also into Italy, especially Milan where, *c.* 1176, many heretics resided. However, there could not have been a Catharist bishop in Italy before 1170.

At first all Cathari in Italy were subject to Bishop Mark, who professed the moderate dualism of the Catharist church of Bulgaria. The arrival in Italy soon after 1174 of Nicetas, Catharist bishop of Constantinople, an absolute dualist, led Mark to transfer to the order of Dragovitsa, which Nicetas represented. Under Mark's successor, John the Jew, the Cathari divided into separate groups. The first was composed of the partisans of absolute dualism, called Albanenses, organizing themselves in the church of Desenzano south of Lake Garda. They were particularly numerous in Verona. Those who remained faithful to the moderate Bulgarian dualism, the Garatenses, constituted the church of Concorezzo, near Milan. Moderate dualists came together also around the church of Bagnolo, near Mantua, adhering to the order of Esclavonia. Like these, the Catharist churches of Vicenza, Florence, and Spoleto rejected absolute dualism.

In northern France, Catharism was practically limited to *Charité-sur-Loire, but heresy made extraordinary strides in the south. Through contact with the Albanenses absolute dualism was quickly accepted. Soon all heretics in the Midi, both Cathari and *Waldenses, came to be known as *Albigenses. By the end of the 12th century there were four Albigensian bishops, with sees at Carcassonne, *Toulouse, *Albi, and *Agen. Around 1225, a church of Razès in the Limoux region was added. The capture of Montségur (1244) precipitated the rapid decline of Catharism within France.

Organization. There was no real unity of doctrine among the Cathari, excepting their agreement on the principle that the visible world was evil. They rejected the Sacraments of the Church, particularly Baptism of water and Matrimony. Although absolute dualists recognized a portion of the Old Testament, the great majority of Cathari accepted only the New Testament, which they read in its Catholic version.

Absolute dualists held that Good and Evil constituted two distinct spheres; one the kingdom of the good god who was spiritual and suprasensible; and the other, the kingdom of the evil god, creator of the material world. For the moderate dualists, or monarchists, the supreme god had created the invisible heaven, the heavenly spirits who inhabited it, and the four elements, whereas the devil was merely the organizer of the sensible world. The Cathari explained the creation of man by myths: the evil god, or Satan, had imprisoned spirits in material bodies. The only salutary way to escape this evil world, was by the reception of the *consolamentum,* the Cathari's unique sacrament administered by the imposition of hands. Christ had come to reveal to men the means of salvation. His earthly life had been simply an appearance.

The Catharistic church considered as its members only the Perfect, who had received the *consolamentum.* They were subject to strict poverty and a rigorous asceticism, their diet being completely vegetarian except for fish. They observed three lents each year. The Perfect, who for the most part were poor peasants or artisans, were accorded great veneration. In the hierarchy of the Perfect, deacons were above the ordinary Perfect, and at the head was the bishop who was assisted by a "major son" and a "minor son." The major son succeeded the bishop.

The ordinary Cathari, the Believers, lived according to their beliefs, without fixed rules of morality. It was sufficient for them to believe that the *consolamentum* assured their salvation. During the ceremony of the *melioramentum* the Believers "worshipped" the Perfect and listened to their preaching; their chief concern was the reception of the *consolamentum* when in danger of death. Catharism was well received by the lesser nobility, who were poor and turbulent, by peasants and artisans, and above all by the burghers of the cities who profited from *usury that the Cathari had legalized.

Catharism has long been known only by the refutations found in the works of Catholic authors, e.g., *Alan of Lille's *Summa,* prior to 1200, the compilations attributed to Bonacursus and Prepositinus of Cremona, and the *Summa* of Rainier of Sacconi, 1250. The *Liber de duobus principiis,* written by an Italian dualist *c.* 1230 [ed. A. Dondaine, *Un Traité néomanichéen . . .* (Rome 1939)], is now available as well as the anonymous Catharist treatise ed. by C. Thouzellier, *Un Traité cathàre inédit . . .* (Louvain 1961).

Disappearance of the Cathari. Long before 1250, the church of the Cathari in France was fragmented, and before 1260 the Catharistic bishops of Toulouse sought refuge in Italy. There, the entire hierarchy disappeared before the end of the 13th century. In the Midi, the last strongholds of the heresy, which were in the upper valley of Ariège and in the Carcassonne region, disappeared before 1330; in Italy Catharism died out quietly toward the end of the 14th century. In addition to the inherent weakness of the Catharist principle of passivity the most vital factor in its disappearance was the example of the *mendicant orders. The *Dominicans and *Franciscans had presented an effective alternative to Catharism, and this rather than the *Inquisition was probably most responsible for its disappearance.

Bibliography: C. G. A. SCHMIDT, *Histoire et doctrine de la secte des Cathares ou Albigeois,* 2 v. (Paris 1849). A. BORST, *Die Katharer* (Stuttgart 1953). J. GUIRAUD, *Histoire de l'Inquisition au moyen âge,* 2 v. (Paris 1935–38) v.1. E. G. A. HOLMES, *The Albigensian or Catharist Heresy* (London 1925). S. RUNCIMAN, *The Medieval Manichee* (Cambridge, Eng. 1947; repr. 1955). COSMAS LE PRÊTRE, *Le Traité contre les Bogomiles,* ed. and tr. H. C. PUECH and A. VAILLANT (Paris 1945). D. OBOLENSKY, *The Bogomils: A Study in Balkan Neo-Manichaeism* (Cambridge, Eng. 1948). A. DONDAINE, "La Hiérarchie cathare en Italie," ArchFrPraed 19 (1949) 280–312; 20 (1950) 234–324. T. KAEPPELI, "Une Somme contre les hérétiques de S. Pierre Martyr (?)," *ibid.* 17 (1947) 295–335. *The Summa contra haereticos: Ascribed to Praepositinus of Cremona,* ed. J. N. GARVIN and J. A. CORBETT (Notre Dame, Ind. 1958). ILARINO DA MILANO, "Il *Liber supra stella* del piacentino Salvo Burci contro i Catari e altre correnti ereticali," *Aevum* 16 (1942) 272–319; 17 (1943) 90–146; 19 (1945) 281–341.

[Y. DOSSAT]

CATHEDRAL

The principal church of a diocese in which the bishop has his throne and where he preaches, teaches, and conducts religious services. The term is derived from the Greek καθέδρα, which passed into Latin as *cathedra,* the word for the bishop's seat or throne. In the early Christian era the *cathedra* was a symbol of authority (*see* CHAIR OF PETER), and the expression *ex cathedra* signifies the solemn teaching authority of the pope as the successor of St. Peter (see Denz 3074). Although the bishop may set up a temporary throne in any church within his diocese, one particular edifice, usually in the city in which he resides, is designated for the establishment of a permanent *cathedra* and is called the diocesan cathedral. The original position of the bishop's chair was in the apse at the east end of the building, so that he looked westward across the high altar, at the congregation, but it is now customary to place it at the north (Gospel) side of the sanctuary. The usual throne is raised on three steps and surmounted by a canopy representative of the dignity of the episcopal office. Only a residential bishop may establish a cathedral; titular bishops who never take actual possession of their sees are not authorized one. In the East the term cathedral is not used, and the building in which a prelate has his *cathedra* is simply referred to as a church.

The cathedral is not necessarily the largest or most splendid religious edifice in the diocese, for at Rome St. John *Lateran is the cathedral proper of the pope as bishop of Rome, rather than the more magnificent *St. Peter's Basilica. Many of the cathedrals throughout the world, however, represent the very best architectural developments of the periods in which they were constructed (*see* CHURCH ARCHITECTURE). The highly developed iconographical cycles in many of the medieval cathedrals served both a didactic and a decorative purpose, and they have been justly termed "the Bibles of the illiterate." Often the *baptistery was a separate building, and there was also a bishop's palace, bell tower, and accommodations for the monks, or for the canons serving in the chapter. The cathedral complex found at *Pisa is representative of this development.

The juridical character of a cathedral does not depend on its form, dimensions, or decoration. Without undergoing any physical change beyond the erection of a *cathedra,* a parish or mission church may become a cathedral, as is often the case when a new diocese is formed. What properly constitutes a cathedral is its assignment by proper authority—the Holy See in most cases—as the residence of a bishop in his hierarchial capacity. Such official designation is known as canonical erection and is usually included in the Apostolic Letters by which a diocese is formed, although the Third Council of *Baltimore authorized bishops in the U.S. to select the location themselves.

The cathedral may be transferred from one location to another within a city or from one city to another within a diocese, but there is usually only one cathedral, just as there is only one residential bishop. In exceptional circumstances, when two dioceses are united *aeque principaliter,* such as in the ancient See of *Bath and Wells, each will retain its right to maintain a permanent throne for the bishop in separate cathedrals, known as co-cathedrals. By special indult of the Holy See, when a new cathedral was built in the Archdiocese of *Baltimore, the old cathedral and the new cathedral were given the status of co-cathedrals. The seat of an *abbot nullius or a *prelate nullius who exercises episcopal functions also takes on the character of a cathedral, and such foundations are known as quasi cathedrals. A procathedral is one temporarily used by a bishop until a more suitable structure can be built. No differentiation is made between the cathedrals of patriarchal, primatial, metropolitan, and episcopal sees. Cathedrals rank immediately after the four major Roman *basilicas (St. John Lateran, St. Peter's, St. Paul-Outside-the-Walls, and St. Mary Major), and the cathedral clergy take precedence over the clergy of all other churches in the diocese, even the clergy of a minor basilica. When the cathedral itself is not a minor basilica, the clergy of the minor basilicas are not permitted to carry the paraphernalia indicative of their dignity, such as the standard, when in procession with the cathedral clergy.

The actual construction of a cathedral is governed by those statutes of *Canon Law that apply to churches (cc.1161–87); in addition, the Code declares that cathedral churches should be dedicated by a solemn consecration (c.1165). The feasts of the dedication and of the titular patron are first class feasts and are celebrated in all churches of the diocese. Canon Law requires also that the major feasts of the Church calendar be celebrated in the cathedral and that it be the usual location for ordinations (c.1009) and for the diocesan synod, required every 10 years (cc.356–357). A bishop takes possession of his cathedral by a solemn entrance and enthronement, and the liturgical functions performed by him or in his presence follow the Roman *Pontifical [*see* BISHOP (CANON LAW)]. The Code also allows a bishop to be buried in his cathedral church.

European cathedrals are often served by a chapter of canons (*see* CATHEDRAL CHAPTER) who celebrate the Divine Office and assist the bishop in pontifical ceremonies. They also give counsel to their ordinary and assist in the administration of the diocese. The Third Council of Baltimore decided that chapters should not be introduced into the dioceses of the U.S. at that time, and the administrative functions usually assigned to canons elsewhere are carried out by clerical consultors in the U.S. (cc.423–444). A cathedral may serve also as a parish church for those residing in the immediate vicinity, and in such cases a curate is appointed to administrate to their needs. The **cathedraticum,* payed by all the churches subject to the episcopal jurisdiction, along with the revenues from the cathedral's property and investments, is applied to the maintenance of the bishop and the cathedral structure. In U.S. sees, voluntary offerings of the faithful are often the major source of revenue.

Bibliography: M. A. FRANCES DE URRUTIGOYTI, *Tractatus de ecclesiis cathedralibus earumque privilegiis et praerogativis* (Venice 1698). A. D. SERTILLANGES, *La Cathédrale: Sa Mission spirituelle, son esthétique, son décor, sa vie* (Paris 1922). C. A. BACHOFEN (C. Augustine), *Rights and Duties of Ordinaries according to the Code and Apostolic Faculties* (St. Louis 1924). L. SYLVESTRE, *Le Cathédratique* (Quebec 1946). P. AHEARNE and M. LANE, *Pontifical Ceremonies* (London 1947). N. DIDIER, *Les Églises de Sisteron et de Forcalquier du XI*[e] *siècle à la Révolution: Le Problème de la "concathédralité"* (Paris 1954). R. NAZ, DDC 5:228–233. C. CECCHELLI, EncCatt 3:1166–72. Cross ODCC 248–249.

[B. J. COMASKEY]

CATHEDRAL AND EPISCOPAL SCHOOLS

Medieval institutions usually connected with the cathedral church. The cathedral school arose from the bishop's desire to prepare men for the priesthood, and it admitted both laymen and clerics; the episcopal school, which was chiefly for clerics, was generally conducted by the bishop himself.

Origin of the School. In the first 3 centuries the Church prescribed no training for men who desired to be clerics. Christians received their elementary and literary education in pagan schools. A youth wishing to become a cleric was usually apprenticed to a bishop who taught by action the functions of a church's minister, imparted a minimum of sacred doctrine, and guided the youth's moral formation. After the Christians gained legal rights in 313 (Edict of Milan), the Church experienced a wave of conversions that created the need for more clerics. Eusebius of Vercelli in 354 and Augustine of Hippo in 394 introduced formal courses in Scripture and theology into the training of clerical candidates. Until the suppression of the pagan schools under Justinian I in 529, however, no change occurred in the elementary or literary education of clerical aspirants.

With the suppression of the pagan schools and the general political and social turmoil of the 6th century, bishops could no longer presume that candidates had received preliminary elementary and literary training. Thus, from the 6th century the cathedral schools assumed the role of teaching grammar and literature. The school thereafter offered all levels of instruction from reading and writing to formal theology and courses in Sacred Scripture.

Curriculum of the School. Before 313 there was very little formal schooling. The young men received an apprenticeship training in performing the sacred functions and in governing the Church; the bishop gave some informal instruction in reading, understanding, and explaining the Scriptures. After 313, however, more formal education, especially in Scripture and theology, was possible.

When the cathedral schools assumed the task of elementary education, they accepted the regular courses offered in the schools of the late Roman Empire, a combination of the trivium and quadrivium, or liberal arts (*see* LIBERAL ARTS, 2). From the trivium came grammar, how to read and write Latin correctly, and some reading in pagan and Christian classics; and rhetoric, some principles of correct speaking and preaching. From the quadrivium came arithmetic, how to count and compute dates, especially that of Easter; and music, how to sing the Psalms and the liturgy. The cathedral schools, however, offered also higher education, a training in Sacred Scripture, apologetics, and some dogmatic theology.

Teachers in the School. Until 313 usually the only teacher in the cathedral school was the bishop, who shared his knowledge and experience with the young candidates. With the new freedom after 313, however, the bishop could travel more extensively in his diocese, and to compensate for his absence, generally appointed a cleric called *scholasticus* to preside over the six or seven men apprenticed to the Church.

In time, others came forward to aid and, later, to supplant the bishop's direct work in the school. *Chrodegang, Bishop of Metz from 742 to 746, wrought the most radical change throughout Europe by introducing canonical life into episcopal sees. Henceforth, a group of priests dedicated to performing the liturgy at the cathedral lived with the bishop. Since they followed a community life based on a rule or canon, they were called "canons." In addition to performing the liturgy, the canons were also responsible for educating the young men living with the bishop. The priest governing the canons was called the dean or archdeacon; the canon in charge of the grammar school was the *scholasticus* or headmaster; the music school was ruled by the *precentor*. Most European dioceses adopted this mode of cathedral life. It was generally from these cathedral schools and from the ruling canons that the universities and their officials developed in the 12th century.

Famous Cathedral Schools. In Rome in 190, Pope Eleutherius appointed Victor, the Archdeacon, to conduct a school; by 220 the school had grown into a formal organization. After 313 the school moved into the Lateran palace where it established a famous library. In 394, Augustine, Bishop of Hippo, organized a formal school with a schedule similar to that of the monasteries of the East. This organization of the cathedral and its school served as Chrodegang's model in 742.

In 598 Augustine, the apostle of England, founded King's School as an integral part of Christ Church Cathedral at Canterbury. The school, which had a section for grammar and another for song or chant, served as a model for England. The school at York educated *Alcuin, and in 767 named him chancellor or *scholasticus*. Alcuin followed the organization of York's school in his educational reform of Charlemagne's kingdom in 781 (*see* PALACE SCHOOLS).

Lubin, consecrated bishop of Chartres in 544, first taught in his own school but later appointed Caletric to conduct it. This school gained its title to fame under a series of gifted scholars and teachers such as John of Salisbury and Bernard of Chartres who led a classical renaissance in the early 12th century. The cathedral school of Norte Dame in Paris, which dates from the 11th century, was the nucleus of the University of *Paris.

Bibliography: Laistner ThLett. E. S. DUCKETT, *Carolingian Portraits: A Study in the Ninth Century* (Ann Arbor 1962). H. I. MARROU, *A History of Education in Antiquity*, tr. G. LAMB (New York 1956). H. RASHDALL, *The Universities of Europe in the Middle Ages*, ed. F. POWICKE and A. B. EMDEN, 3 v. (new ed. Oxford 1936) v.1. P. RICHÉ, *Education et culture dans l'Occident barbare, VIe–VIIIe siècles* (Paris 1962).

[E. G. RYAN]

CATHEDRAL CHAPTER

A corporation of clerics, instituted to celebrate more solemnly the Divine Office, to assist the bishop as his senate and council, and to govern the diocese during a vacancy of the episcopal see (CIC c.391). Other canons determine the method of establishing chapters (392), providing for their livelihood (393–396), the appointment of certain officials (398–401), and of canons (403), their rights (405), of honorary canons (407), the rights of precedence (408), the drawing up of statutes (410), the times of meeting (411), and the duties of the chapter as a body (411–415) and as individuals (416–422). Despite its canonical status, the chapter is no longer an essential feature of episcopal administration—e.g., there are none in the United States—and in the traditional European countries the cathedral chapter exists in a very much modified form from that which it had in the Middle Ages (*see* CANONS, CHAPTER OF).

Yet the cathedral chapter of the Code of 1917 bears the marks of its former medieval status, i.e., as a spiritual body (duties at divine service), an advisory body (to the bishop), and a governing body *sede vacante* (when the see is vacant). Its position today is the outcome of 1500 years of development, during which it began as subordinate to the bishop, by the 13th century became independent, and finally was itself eclipsed by papal authority.

Development to the 13th Century. In the early Church all priests belonged to the bishop's *familia* and served the cathedral church. They lived a *common life with the bishop. But by the 4th century rural and cathedral clergy were being distinguished. The latter gradually acquired an existence separate from the bishop, and the common life disappeared. By the 9th and 10th centuries episcopal and chapter properties were often separately administered. However, the frequent attempts of reformers to revive the common life gave rise to various canonical rules. The most famous and successful was that of Bishop *Chrodegang of Metz, *c.* 755, which became the basis of later rules. But the common life always met with resistance. The cathedral clerics acquired personal property and separate houses and prebends. Hence the term "secular canons." The *Gregorian reform of the 11th century sought again to impose stricter obligations, e.g., the common life, choir duty, and residence, but did not meet with much success. A special attempt was made to solve the problem in England by introducing religious canons who were

Benedictine monks at Canterbury, Durham, Ely, Norwich, Rochester, Worcester, Winchester, Bath, and Coventry. There were thus nine regular and nine secular chapters as well as a chapter of *Canons Regular of St. Augustine at Carlyle. On the continent the Austin canons were introduced for the same reason. But conflict was not thereby avoided. The monks tried to maintain their electoral rights and at the same time, like the secular chapters, tried to extend their jurisdiction at the expense of the bishop, their titular abbot.

During the period from the 11th to the 14th century conflict with the bishop arose with the development of the cathedral chapter as a corporate body with rights and status in Canon Law. Powerful officials emerged, and secular chapters divided into residential and nonresidential canons. General chapters were held for all canons, but most of the work and voting rights belonged to the residential canons. The main officials were the dean (the prior in a regular chapter), precentor, treasurer, and chancellor. In the 12th century the office of canon theologian and later that of canon penitentiary came into vogue. The position of canon was often a source of wealth and influence.

Later Development. The dispute between the bishop and cathedral chapter centered on what degree of control the bishop should have over the chapter. This was complicated by the fact that by the 12th century the bishop often owed his election to the chapter. The reformed papacy, in order to offset lay influence in the church, had encouraged chapter election of bishops. Eventually the Fourth *Lateran Council (1215) recognized the chapter as having the sole right to elect the bishop. But papal approval of elections had always been understood as necessary. And political influence was never completely eliminated. Papal reservations were introduced in the 13th century. Subsequently, *Clement V in 1305 reserved to himself appointments to vacant bishoprics in the Diocese of Rome, and his successors extended this system of *provision throughout the Church. Of course, until the Code of 1917 election by the cathedral chapter was still in theory the principal element in the making of a bishop; but with the possible exception of the 13th century—and even then there were many exceptions—in no period did the chapter enjoy full and complete control.

Parallel with the power of election was the power to administer the see during a vacancy, which the chapter developed gradually, and then kept from the later 13th to the 16th century. Then the Council of *Trent ordered that within a week of the bishop's death the chapter must appoint a vicar capitular to administer the see. Under these new conditions the bishop retained control of appointment to the cathedral clergy, but generally lost the right to sit in chapter or to determine statutes.

By the time of the *Reformation the cathedral chapter had acquired a political and formal character. During the Reformation chapters were either abolished in the reformed churches or maintained in modified form in the Anglican Church. In Catholic countries they continued, but often with a low degree of spiritual life. Finally, the Code of 1917 strictly regulated the whole system, but at the same time recognized (CIC cc.423–428) the alternative system of diocesan *consultors, which had been set up in the United States in 1835 at Mobile, Ala., and which gradually expanded.

Today the establishment, restoration, and suppression of cathedral chapters belong to the Holy See. The same authority controls the appointment of certain dignitaries, namely, those whose rank once betokened jurisdiction. The number of canons varies from place to place depending on the arrangement. Income, mainly in the form of *benefices, must be adequate. The first official must be a Doctor of Theology or Canon Law or hold a degree in Sacred Scripture. The provost does the external business and the dean, the internal. The dignitaries summon and preside over the chapter and represent the bishop, if absent, on high feast days, or assist him when present. The priest canons are appointed by the bishop with advice of the chapter. There may be nonresidential canons and honorary canons who have only the right to the insignia of a canon and to a choir stall.

Despite its great loss of power since the Middle Ages, the cathedral chapter as a collegiate body has certain definite spiritual and temporal rights and duties, and it is autonomous in its own sphere, provided Canon Law is followed. It has rights and precedence over other collegiate bodies and over the ordinary clergy. It has certain advisory functions, but its rights *sede vacante* are limited to the election of a vicar within 8 days of the notification of the vacancy. The duties include choir service. Individual canons have the right to choir place, a place and voice in the chapter, and a share in the income. A canon enjoys precedence and may wear certain distinguishing dress within the diocese, but not outside unless he is accompanying the ordinary or acting as his representative. The chapter makes statutes, but these must be approved by the bishop. Appointee canons, before installation, must make a profession of faith and take the oath against *Modernism.

The foregoing makes it clear that the cathedral chapter today is but a shadow of its medieval self. Its period of greatness was from the 12th to the 14th century, a time when the great complex of a cathedral, with its wealth and corporate life, its business and religious interests that could take its members far afield, provided satisfying careers for those who constituted the body of canons.

Bibliography: P. J. KLEKOTKA, *Diocesan Consultors* (Gettysburg 1920). H. NOTTARP, "Ehrenkanoniker und Honorarkapitel," ZSavRGKan 45 (1925) 174–335. P. HOFMEISTER, *Bischof und Domkapitel nach altem und nach neuem Recht* (Württemberg 1931). G. BARRACLOUGH, "The Making of a Bishop in the Middle Ages," CathHistRev 19 (1933–34) 275–319. C. R. CHENEY, *English Bishops' Chanceries, 1100–1250* (Manchester, Eng. 1950). É. FOURNIER, *Nouvelles recherches sur les curies, chapitres et universités de l'ancienne Église de France* (Paris 1942). K. EDWARDS, *The English Secular Cathedrals in the Middle Ages* (Manchester, Eng. 1949). Abbo 1:391–422. G. H. COOK, *English Collegiate Churches of the Middle Ages* (New York 1960). S. L. GREENSLADE, "*Sede vacante* Procedure in the Early Church," JThSt 12 (1961) 210–226. F. LOT and R. FAWTIER, eds., *Histoire des institutions françaises au moyen âge*, 3 v. (Paris 1957–62). R. I. BURNS, "The Organization of a Mediaeval Cathedral Community: The Chapter of Valencia (1238–1280)," ChHist 31 (1962) 14–23. M. BIERBAUM, LexThK[2] 3:496–500.

[J. GILCHRIST]

CATHEDRATICUM, a term employed to signify a moderate tax that is paid annually to the bishop of a diocese as a token of subjection to him by all churches and benefices subject to his jurisdiction as well as by all lay confraternities (CIC c.1504). The amount of this tax, unless it has been determined by a long standing custom, is established on a provincial basis and approved by the Holy See, so that all churches, benefices, and lay confraternities within a province pay the same amount, regardless of the size of their income or membership (CIC cc.1504, 1507.1). The cathedraticum is not paid to the vicar capitular or the apostolic administrator when the diocese is without a bishop.

This notion of the cathedraticum dates back before enactment of the Code of Canon Law. In the U.S., however, since the second Plenary Council of Baltimore of 1866 (n. 100), the term cathedraticum has been extended to refer to a tax given for the support of the diocese by each church, and this tax is proportionate to the income of that church. This arrangement was approved by the Congregation of the Propagation of the Faith and continued after the U.S. became subject to the Consistorial Congregation (1908) and even after the Code of Canon Law went into effect in 1918.

Bibliography: M. N. KREMER, *Church Support in the United States* (CUA CLS 61; Washington 1930). Vermeersch-Creusen EpitCanIur. "Cases and Studies: Fees and Stipends," *Jurist* 1 (1941) 340–341.

[J. W. GOEKE]

CATHER, WILLA SIBERT

American novelist; b. Winchester, Va., Dec. 7, 1873; d. New York City, April 24, 1947. She spent her early childhood in northern Virginia, where she formed enduring impressions of a gracious way of life, to be recorded later in *Sapphira and the Slave Girl.* When she was 9, her family moved first to a Nebraska ranch, and shortly afterward to the frontier town of Red Cloud, Nebr., where Willa grew up, joyously, among pioneer immigrants, many of German, Bohemian, Polish, and Irish stock. Although a very active tomboy in her earlier years, she was secretly and profoundly in love with literary classics, particularly Vergil, and with native and European music. She seemed early to sense, as one critic wrote, that epics slept in the dreams of the pioneers "waiting for the kiss of art to awaken them." By the time she entered the University of Nebraska she was already half aware of her destiny to be both the epicist and elegist of pioneer experience. At the University Cather was active in dramatics, music, and journalism while she worked diligently at her humanist studies. Upon graduation (1895) she became a reporter on the *Pittsburgh Daily Leader* and wrote for other journals. Because newspaper work allowed little time for creative writing, she became a high school teacher of Latin and English. In her spare time and during vacations she wrote poetry, *April Twilights* (1903), and short stories, *The Troll Garden* (1905). A vigilant editor, S. S. McClure, found her work so promising that he invited her to join the staff of his popular, crusading *McClure's Magazine.* After an active 6 years as writer and editor for *McClure's* she retired to devote herself to creative writing.

Willa Sibert Cather.

Although in fact Cather struggled from book to book to achieve, clarify, and express her vision, in retrospect her career seems to be as direct, purposeful, and beautiful as the flight of a well-aimed arrow. Her themes, for example, are all interrelated. Her tragic stories for the most part show that we are defeated by our own inner weaknesses. Thus in *Alexander's Bridge* (1912) the hero's vain ambition, symbolized by the destruction of his bridge, leads to disaster. "Paul's Case," which appeared in *Youth and the Bright Medusa* (1920), points to the fatal flaw in a bright creative spirit. In *A Lost Lady* (1923) Marian Forrester's disgrace is due less to the abrasive crudities of frontier life than to her own ineluctable narcissism. That each human being (however well endowed by fortune and gifted in grace) is his own nemesis is most clearly revealed in *My Mortal Enemy* (1926).

Contrariwise, Cather's stories of triumph all celebrate what she called "disciplined endeavor," desire, devotion to an appointed destiny, a serene fidelity to duty however great the austerities that duty requires. Thus, in *O Pioneers* (1913) Alexandra Bergson represents the eternal vitality of the valiant woman; in *The Song of the Lark* (1915) Thea Kronborg portrays the victory of the dedicated artist; in *My Ántonia* (1918) Antonia Shimerda manifests the triumph of humble acceptance; in *One of Ours* (1922) Claude Wheeler exemplifies the idealism that overcomes death; in *Death Comes for the Archbishop* (1927) Archbishop Latour and Father Vaillant reenact the salvific role of their master Christ. Sometimes, as in *Shadows on the Rock* (1931) and *Sapphira and the Slave Girl* (1940), Cather's characters are less vivid as personalities than they are as illustrative types and thus they fade, like figures in a legend, into the larger, timeless story of man's movement toward his full humanity.

Cather has long puzzled those readers who, attracted by the Whitmanian exuberance of *O Pioneers* and the triumphalism of *The Song of the Lark,* could not understand why her later novels seemed to communicate disgust for the tone of the time. For Cather, American civilization seemed to come apart after World War I. She bitterly criticized materialism in *One of Ours.* In the language of *A Lost Lady* the brave pioneer was supplanted by "the shrewd young man trained to petty economics. . . . That which was great has passed away." Similarly, the imaginative scholar was supplanted by the pedant, the missionary saint by the competent manager. Increasingly she seemed to feel, in the language of Godfrey St. Peter in *The Professor's House* (1925), that "the only happiness lies in the memory of the past" and that the future belongs to sophists, shopkeepers, and small-minded men. One may argue, however, that Cather's apparent rejection of contemporary values was not, as Maxwell Geismar has suggested, the result of "infantile malice." Rather it is more probably the dark side of a love that venerated the vocations of the saint, the artist, the scholar, and the pioneer, indeed of all those who are loyal to their visions of truth and beauty.

Bibliography: M. R. BENNETT, *The World of Willa Cather* (New York 1951). E. K. BROWN and L. EDEL, *Willa Cather, a Critical Biography* (New York 1953). F. X. CONNOLLY, "Willa Cather: Memory as Muse," *Fifty Years of the American Novel,* ed. H. C. GARDINER (New York 1951) 69–87. D. DAICHES, *Willa Cather: A Critical Introduction* (New York 1950). M. D. GEISMAR, *Last of the Provincials* (Boston 1947). F. J. HOFFMANN, *The Modern Novel in America* (Chicago 1956). P. M. HUTCHINSON, "The Writings of Willa Cather: A List of Works by and about Her," *Bulletin of the New York Public Library* 60 (1956) 267–288, 338–356, 378–400. A. KAZIN, *On Native Grounds* (New York 1942). E. LEWIS, *Willa Cather Living* (New York 1953). E. S. SERGEANT, *Fire Under the Andes* (New York 1927). E. C. WAGENKNECHT, *Cavalcade of the American Novel* (New York 1952). **Illustration credit:** Photograph by Steichen.

[F. X. CONNOLLY]

CATHERINE II (THE GREAT), EMPRESS OF RUSSIA

Reign 1762 to Nov. 17, 1796; b. Stettin, Prussia, May 2, 1729; d. St. Petersburg. Sophia Augusta Frederica was the daughter of Christian Augustus, Prince of Anhalt-Zerbst, and his wife, Johanna Elizabeth of Holstein-Gottorp. When selected by the Empress Elizabeth Petrovna to be the bride of the future Peter III, Princess Sophia abandoned Lutheranism to embrace the Orthodox religion and took the name Catherine Alexeyevna. Her marriage to Grand Duke Peter on Sept. 1, 1745, was unsuccessful from the start; his talents and interests were childish and contrasted with Catherine's ambitions, self-will, and intelligence. During her 17 years as Grand-duchess, she was estranged from her husband and took several lovers, although a son, the future Tsar Paul I (reign 1796–1801) was born on Oct. 2, 1754. At the death of Empress Elizabeth on Jan. 5, 1762, the Grand-duke ascended the throne as Peter III, but because of his imprudent pro-Prussian policies and his threat to divorce Catherine, he aroused opposition. Gregory Orlov and his three brothers swore allegiance to Catherine on July 9, 1762, and with the help of the regiments of the guard, seized Peter, obtained his abdication, and imprisoned him in the Castle of Ropsha, where he and Ivan VI, son of Anna Petrovna, died violently shortly after.

Catherine II (The Great), Empress of Russia, miniature by Augustin Ritt (1765–90) after a portrait by D. G. Levitsky.

Uprisings and National Reforms. Catherine corresponded with *Diderot, *Voltaire, and the *Encyclopedists, and in the beginning of her reign she inclined to their "enlightened absolutism." In 1767 she published her famous *Nakaz* (instruction) for law reform in which she urged the equality of all before the law and the freedom of all under the law, whose function is to protect, not oppress. Her demand that punishment should never be torture and that death sentences should be rare was acclaimed throughout Europe. However, the deputies assembled to codify the laws were inept. In fact even Catherine's equality before the law did not apply to serfs and peasants, who were openly bought, sold, and exploited as sheep and cattle. In the 1760s, at least 40 uprisings occurred; they culminated in the Ural Cossack Uprising or Peasant Rebellion (1773–75), led by Yemilyan Pugachev, who pretended to be Peter III. Pugachev was executed, but this uprising, added to the French and American Revolutions, blunted the desire for enlightened reform. Catherine's *Nakaz* became a dead letter. She now turned to a stricter control of her domestic administration. She created 80 provinces (*guberniya*) in which she allowed a limited measure of democracy and permitted the local gentry to elect the councilors of the district (*uyezd*) director. But as Catherine enlarged and ensured the privileges of the gentry, she paved the way for a more permanent and oppressive serfdom. To her a privileged gentry meant a closer supervision of the popular mood and a tighter control over incipient unrest. Little came of her attempts to democratize the cities, since the poor quality of urban education did not prepare the people for civic responsibility.

Foreign Policy. Catherine's activity in foreign affairs led to the successful pursuit of the war against the Turks to secure better trade routes on the Black Sea. She also strengthened Russia's strategic position in the West. The Lithuanian-Polish state, she felt, must be either brought under the influence of, or conquered by Russia. Through manipulation of the "liberum veto," Poland became so weak that Russia, Austria, and Prussia were able to partition this state in 1772, 1792, and 1795. Catherine thus extended the Russian border further west. She also encouraged the colonization of Alaska. The two Turkish wars (1764–74, 1781–91) ensured safe trade routes and fertile farm lands and secured the southern borders against the Turks and Crimean Tatars. These wars called attention to the genius of her generals, P. A. Rumyantsev, A. V. Surorov, A. Galitsin, P. Panin, and G. A. Potyomkin, whose military ability was mediocre but whose talent for organization and colonization of these areas was more noteworthy.

Catherine's personal life was lonely. She did not marry a second time, and her son Paul lived apart from the court. History seems to have forgotten the daughter born to her in 1758. While she cultivated leaders of European thought, she assiduously made favoritism a quasi-official institution. During her reign of 34 years she had more than 10 favorites, who were handsomely rewarded, and some (G. Orlov, G. A. Potyomkin, P. L. Zubov, and S. Poniatowski) were of importance to Russian and Polish history.

Catherine and the Jesuits. As Emperor Peter I before her, Catherine saw the need for education in Russia. She founded the Academy of Fine Arts, the Academy of Sciences, the Moscow and Smolny Institutes for Young Ladies, and facilities for the study of medicine. This interest also ensured the continuity of the Society of Jesus in the Catholic Church. At the first partition of Poland (1772), four Jesuit colleges and two residences —201 Jesuits—passed under Russian rule. Because she was pleased with the Jesuit methods of teaching youth, she refused to allow Pope *Clement XIV's Brief of Suppression of the Society of Jesus (July 21, 1773) to be promulgated in Russia. Pius VI granted permission to the Jesuits in White Russia to receive into the society former confreres living in other countries. At Catherine's urging, the Latin bishop of White Russia ordained 20 Jesuit scholastics in 1777, and 2 years later he authorized a novitiate in Polotsk. When Gabriel Gruber, later general of the Jesuits, came to St. Petersburg in 1785, he found 10,000 Catholics in the capital. It was at the request of Paul I that Pope Pius VII restored the Society of Jesus on March 7, 1801.

Although the Jesuits found protection with Catherine, the Uniates were persecuted. After the first partition of Poland, she sent missionaries, accompanied by soldiers, to restore the "renegades" to Orthodoxy. She did agree to the nomination of a new bishop for the Uniate diocese at Polotsk, but later, after the second partition of Poland and despite her promise to protect Catholics of both rites, Catherine suppressed all other Uniate dioceses, forcibly united over 1.5 million Uniates to Orthodoxy, and dispersed the Order of Basilians.

Her Importance. Catherine left a Russia whose boundaries were the Neman River, the Dniester River and the Black Sea. She is significant in the history of the Catholic Church for her protection of the Society of Jesus. Intellectual circles and the courts of Europe admired her brilliance and grandiose political projects. She wrote much: memoirs, comedies, comic operas, and fairy tales for her grandchildren. Catherine was the real successor to Peter the Great. Yet by her stratification of classes in Russia, she perhaps did more to prepare the coming of the 1917 revolution than any other single Russian monarch.

Bibliography: CATHERINE II, *Memoirs of Catherine the Great*, tr. K. ANTHONY (New York 1927). G. S. THOMSON, *Catherine the Great and the Expansion of Russia* (London 1947). F. D. DAVID and M. L. KENT, *Rome and Russia: A Tragedy of Errors* (Westminster, Md. 1954). B. VON BILBASSOFF, *Katharina II, Kaiserin von Russland im Urteile der Weltliteratur* (Berlin 1897). G. P. GOOCH, *Catherine the Great and Other Studies* (New York 1954). M. E. VON ALMEDINGEN, *Catherine, Empress of Russia* (New York 1961). O. HÖTZSCH, "Catherine II," CModH 6:657–701. **Illustration credit:** Courtesy of the Walters Art Gallery, Baltimore, Md., from the A. J. Fink Collection.

[W. C. JASKIEVICZ]

CATHERINE OF ALEXANDRIA, ST., martyr (feast, Nov. 25). Data of her life derive from two works without historical value. A *Conversio* recounts her royal birth and her mystical espousal with Christ in a vision just after her baptism. A *Passio* reports her discourses at Alexandria before the Emperor with pagan philosophers whom she converted. When she persuaded the Empress to become a Christian, Catherine was tortured on the wheel and decapitated (Nov. 24 or 25, 305). The *Passio* ends with angels translating her relics to Mt. Sinai, where, however, nothing seems to have been known of her *c.* 820. The earliest evidence of her cult, apparently introduced by Eastern monks who had fled from *iconoclasm, appears in a painting of the early 8th century in Rome. After the 10th century her cult became very popular, especially in Italy. She is one of the *Fourteen Holy Helpers; is the patroness of some 30 groups, including philosophers and maidens; and is portrayed with a book (knowledge), a crown (royal birth), and a wheel.

St. Catherine of Alexandria, devotional painting by Pietro Lorenzetti (d. 1348) of the school of Siena.

Bibliography: A. P. FRUTAZ, EncCatt 3:1137–39; LexThK[2] 6:60–61. D. BALBONI, BiblSanct 3:954–965. **Illustration credit:** National Gallery of Art, Washington, D.C., Samuel H. Kress Collection.

[M. J. COSTELLOE]

CATHERINE OF ARAGON

Queen of England, daughter of Ferdinand of Aragon and Isabella of Castile; b. Alcalá, Spain, Dec. 1485; d. Kimbolton, England, Jan. 7, 1536. In October 1501, she arrived in England for her marriage to Arthur, Prince of Wales, the eldest son of Henry VII. The marriage took place in November 1501, at St. Paul's Cathedral, London. Unfortunately, Arthur died in April 1502, but in 1503 Catherine was betrothed to Prince Henry, Henry's sole surviving son. Because of consanguinity a papal dispensation was obtained for the proposed union. Catherine was for years a mere pawn in a shabby diplomatic game played between her own father and Henry VII, and she suffered accordingly; but soon after Henry *VIII's accession in 1509 he married Catherine, and her life was for some time a comparatively happy one. The King was a devoted husband; Catherine bore him 4 children; the court was brilliant.

Catherine of Aragon, contemporary portrait by an unknown artist.

Catherine was an able regent while Henry was at war in France in 1513, and she took every possible means of maintaining the Anglo-Spanish alliance. But the capture of the French King, *Francis I, by *Charles V (1525) upset the balance of power in Europe, and early in 1527 England offered her support to France against Spain.

Meanwhile, probably in the latter part of 1526 or the beginning of 1527, Henry began to feel an attraction for Anne Boleyn, one of Catherine's ladies-in-waiting, and in the spring, 1527, he professed doubts about the validity of his marriage. He commenced to think of its dissolution by the Pope. In May, Cardinal *Wolsey and William Warham, Archbishop of Canterbury, arranged a collusive suit, and Henry was cited to answer a charge of having lived for 18 years in incestuous relationship with his brother Arthur's widow.

The international situation complicated English affairs. The armies of Charles V sacked Rome in May 1527, and made Pope *Clement VII their prisoner. Eventually a commission was issued to the papal legates, Wolsey and Cardinal *Campeggio, to hear the divorce suit in open court in England and to pronounce a decision, if necessary. This legatine court first met in May 1529. Catherine appeared before it in June, refused to recognize its jurisdiction, and appealed to the Pope. On July 23, 1529, Campeggio adjourned the court until October. It never met again. In 1530, Thomas *Cranmer appealed to the European universities about the validity of the marriage. The Pope in November 1532 warned Henry not to divorce Catherine or to remarry. But in January 1533, he married Anne Boleyn secretly, and in May, Cranmer, as the new Archbishop of Canterbury, pronounced sentence of divorce. At length (in March 1534) the Pope declared Catherine's marriage to Henry to be valid. Catherine, after her final separation from the King in July 1531, was subjected to increasingly harsh treatment, until she died at Kimbolton, having previously been imprisoned at a number of other places. *See* REFORMATION, PROTESTANT (IN THE BRITISH ISLES).

Bibliography: G. CAVENDISH, *The Life and Death of Cardinal Wolsey,* ed. R. S. SYLVESTER (1st ed. pub. 1641; EEngTSoc 243; London 1959). G. MATTINGLY, *Catherine of Aragon* (Boston 1941). Hughes RE[5]. J. E. PAUL, *Catherine of Aragon and Her Friends* (London 1965). **Illustration credit:** National Portrait Gallery, London.

[J. E. PAUL]

CATHERINE OF BOLOGNA, ST., Poor Clare, mystic, writer, and artist; b. Bologna, Sept. 8, 1413; d. there, March 9, 1463. She was the daughter of John de Vigri and Benvenuta Mammolini. As companion to Margaret d'Este she was educated at the ducal court until Margaret's marriage. Catherine, then 14, joined a group of Franciscan tertiaries in Ferrara who later adopted the Rule of St. Clare. She served first as convent baker and portress, then as mistress of novices. During this time she wrote an important treatise on what she called the seven spiritual weapons; the treatise reflects the mystical quality of her interior life. It was also during this period, according to her own statement, that she was visited one Christmas Eve by Our Lady, who placed the newborn Christ in her arms. In 1456 Catherine was made abbess of a new convent of Clares in Bologna, and she remained in that office almost without interruption until her death. Clement XI canonized her May 22, 1712. Her body, seated and richly garbed, is incorrupt but blackened by age and dampness. Usually represented as a Poor Clare holding the Infant, she is also honored as patron of artists. Paintings and miniatures of hers, notably her illuminated Breviary, are extant. Writings include *Le sette arme necessarie alla battaglia spirituale,* in many editions and translations, from 1475 (Bologna) to 1922 (Florence); *Sermones ad sacras virgines* (Bologna 1522, 1635); *Rosarium metricum de mysteriis Passionis Christi Domini et de Vita BVM;* and minor works in verse and prose.

Bibliography: G. GRASSETTI, *Vita della beata Caterina da Bologna* (Bologna 1724). F. VAN ORTROY and R. LECHAT, "Une Vie italienne de Sainte Catherine de Bologne," AnalBoll 41 (1923) 386–416. J. STIÉNON DU PRÉ, *Sainte Catherine de Bologne* (Bruges 1949). J. HEERINCKX, DictSpirAscMyst 2.1:288–290. A. VAN DEN WYNGAERT, DHGE 11:1505–06. M. MUCCIOLI, *Santa Caterina da Bologna: Mistica del Quattrocento* (Bologna 1963).

[F. LAUGHLIN]

CATHERINE OF GENOA, ST.

Widow, mystic, heroic servant of the poor and sick in her native city, hospital administrator; b. Genoa, toward the close of 1447; d. probably Sept. 15, 1510; canonized May 18, 1737 (feast, Sept. 15).

Life. Catherine was the youngest of five children in the Fieschi family, then the most powerful of the Guelph families of Genoa. She was a descendant of Robert, brother of Innocent IV. Her father was Viceroy of Naples; her mother, Francesca di Negro, belonged to an ancient, noble family of Genoa. They had three sons, then two daughters: Limbania, who became a nun, and Caterinetta. Reliable details of Catherine's early years are scarce. At 13 (1460) she attempted unsuccessfully to enter religious life. Late in 1461 her father died, and in the ensuing political realignments Catherine became an unhappy family pawn in the union of the Guelph Fieschi with the Ghibelline Adorni. On Jan. 13, 1463, at only age 16, she was married to

Giuliano Adorno, a wayward, self-indulgent man. Neglected by her husband, the lively, sensitive Catherine spent 10 dreary years, the first 5 in utter loneliness and the rest in futile, if innocent, worldly gaieties, while her inner depression deepened to desperation. On March 20, 1473, while attempting to make her confession to a priest, she felt herself suddenly overwhelmed by the immense love of God, lifted above her miseries, enlightened by grace, and radically changed. The experience lasted for some time and was followed at home shortly after by a first (and last) vision of the Crucified. She made a general confession on March 24 and entered a new life. Almost simultaneously Giuliano's affairs had moved toward bankruptcy. This misfortune, together with Catherine's prayers, brought about his conversion. He agreed to a life of perpetual continence and became a Franciscan tertiary, although Catherine, in spite of her devotion to the Franciscan mystic Jacopone da Todi, did not. Giuliano disposed of valuable properties and together with Catherine lived in a small house near the hospital of the Pammatone to serve the sick and help the poor of the district. In this humble work they persevered until Giuliano's death, Jan. 10, 1497.

From 1479 on, they occupied two small rooms within the hospital, serving without pay and at their own expense. From 1479 to 1490 Catherine worked as an ordinary nurse. From 1490 to 1496 she was administrative head (*rettora*) of the hospital. During the epidemic of deadly fever of 1493, which is said to have carried off as much as 80 per cent of the population, her heroism and efficiency intensified. Her remarkable friendship with Ettore Vernazza, a young Genoese lawyer, began that same year. Much of the authentic information known about Catherine is due to this intimate friend and associate.

For almost 25 years up to 1479 Catherine's life, so interiorly rich, so externally fruitful in charitable works, developed solely under the impulse of grace without human help. It was marked by frequent ecstatic absorptions and by long, mysterious fasts, during which she was unable to take food—apparently an operation of God in which (as she said) her will had no part and to which she attached no great significance. With the death of Giuliano, this middle period came to a close and with it her fasts and spiritual isolation. Shortly after, she came under the spiritual direction of a priest, Cattaneo Marabotto, to whose firsthand knowledge of her spirit, doctrine, and interior life, history is much indebted. Catherine appreciated Marabotto's presence and help, his capacity to understand and not interfere with the work of God's grace in her soul. She continued her hospital work, managed the detailed finances of Giuliano's estate, and extended her influence in conversations with disciples. Becoming more expansive and communicative, she opened up to share with them her intense love and mystical insight. From 1506 until her death in 1510, gathering infirmities took their toll, and she was incapacitated for increasing periods of time, but she continued at her work almost to the end.

Cult and Relics. A popular cult began 18 months after her death when her body was exhumed to be placed in a marble sepulcher and was found almost perfectly preserved. In response to popular demand, her remains were exposed for 8 days. Cures attributed to her intercession began to occur, and popular veneration continued. Official efforts to have her canonized began in 1630, but her canonization did not take place until May 18, 1737, when she received that honor together with Vincent de Paul, Francis Regis, and Giuliana Falconieri. Her portrait without nimbus found in the sacristy of the hospital church may be the picture mentioned in the hospital accounts less than 2 years after her death and approved by Marabotto.

St. Catherine of Genoa, portrait in the hospital of the Pammatone, Genoa.

Writings. The works commonly attributed to Catherine present a problem. There is no solid evidence that Catherine ever wrote down her thoughts and sayings. All extant biographies, editions, and translations of her works go back to the *Vita e Dottrina,* published in Genoa by Jacobo Genuti in 1551. It is the joint production of Catherine's confessor, Marabotto, and her spiritual son Ettore Vernazza, both of whom faithfully recorded her sayings, but with interspersed interpretations of their own. Thus the luminous, fascinating, spontaneous utterances of Catherine, obviously born of intense experience and insight, rest in a matrix of dull comment.

The *Treatise on Purgatory* ascribed to her is a collection of her sayings first written down (as part of the *Vita*) by Vernazza, but later enlarged by theological additions that convey little of Catherine's fresh and lively spirit. The *Spiritual Dialogues* depend on the *Vita* but chiefly convey Battista Vernazza's version of Catherine's spirit, learned at second hand. They make a solid, intelligent, and well-organized treatise, but one that contains little of Catherine's rich spontaneity. Nevertheless, the words of Catherine scattered through these works constitute a precious record of her spiritual doctrine and mystical insight.

Doctrine. Although Catherine's authentic teaching drew its nourishment from the pre-Reformation Church, it has nevertheless a remarkably contemporary, or perhaps timeless, ring and resonance. In spirit it is open, positive, joyous, trustful of the all-embracing goodness of God. It shows the unstudied spontaneity of a saintly soul's personal experience; there is a soaring and yet sober quality in it, a refinement at once of holy liberty and of docility to the Holy Spirit. It is a rich mystical realization of the immense, tireless love of God, always expressed in new turns, applications, and rediscoveries. Lift sin, she said, from a man's shoulders, then allow the good God to act. God seems to have nothing else to do but to unite Himself to men. Everything she said is a variation on this theme.

Theologians and spiritual writers have singled out her thoughts on purgatory for special notice, but these with other eschatological texts are part of the larger intuition of God's loving way with souls. The historical emphasis on her *Treatise on Purgatory* (originally but a chapter in the *Vita*) derived in part from the Lutheran controversy shortly after her death. There are indications that early editors conventionalized some of her phrases. But the central thought comes through: purgatory is the projection beyond of that mystical purgation which also takes place in this world in souls open to God's action. Frederick William Faber approved her concept of purgatory; Cardinal H. E. Manning wrote a preface to an English translation; Cardinal J. H. Newman enshrined it in his *Dream of Gerontius;* Aubrey de Vere wrote a poetic paraphrase of it.

According to Catherine, the imperfect soul at death plunges willingly into its purgation with joy and pain. The same law of purification is at work Here-and-Now and Beyond—there is essential continuity of the interior life; the difference is rather in extent and intensity. The fundamental and universal experiences of the soul Here also have their place There. Hence her eschatology focuses on those features that she can forecast on the basis of her experience. She speaks of the holy soul, still in the flesh, placed in the purgatory of God's burning love so that it might, at the time of death, go straight to God. In this way one is to understand how it is with the souls in purgatory, abiding content in the fire of divine love.

Initial Experience and Act. In passing out of this life the soul to be purged perceives its sinful self as cause of its purgatory just once, never to dwell on the fact again, since it would be a self-centered thought. Then, wholly centered on God, it plunges eagerly into the ocean of purifying fire. The motive force is impetuosity of the "love which exists between God and the soul and tends to conform the soul to God." The soul seems to find God's great compassion in being allowed to remove the impediment within.

Subsequent Process. This involves the dispositions, joys, and sufferings of the soul during its purgation, and finally comes the conclusion of the process. It is the story of Catherine's own mystical experience of purgation and her interpretation of that experience. The souls in purgatory simply accept the consequence of their epoch-making choice to deliver themselves to purgation. They do not dwell on their past sins; they do not compare themselves with others. They see themselves in God only; otherwise they would be letting self come in. Though the pain of purgatory is "horrible as hell," yet these souls are content, cannot find the pain to be pain. There is no joy comparable to that of a soul in purgatory, except the joy of the blessed in paradise. Because the soul has an instinct for God and its own perfection, an extreme fire springs up within it. As it approaches its original purity and innocence, that instinct of God releases increasing happiness, "for every little glimpse that can be gained of God exceeds every pain and every joy that man can conceive without it." The joy of the soul in purgatory continually increases because of the inflowing of God into it as the impediments diminish. The soul becomes progressively impassible. The fire burning within it without opposition is like the fire of life eternal. The soul purified remains in the fire, and the fire remains what it was, God. Thus, the pain of purgatory arises from the discord of spirit with Spirit and ends when they are in complete concord.

Bibliography: C. Marabotto, *Vita della serafica s. Caterina da Genova* (Genoa 1737). F. von Hügel, *The Mystical Element of Religion,* 2 v. (2d ed. London 1923). *Life and Doctrine of Saint Catherine of Genoa* (New York 1874). P. Garvin, ed. and tr., *The Life and Sayings of Saint Catherine of Genoa* (New York 1964). M. Viller and U. da Genova, DictSpirAscMyst 2:290–325. P. Pourrat, *Catholicisme* 2:691–693. P. Debongnie, DHGE 11:1506–15.

[P. L. HUG]

CATHERINE DE MÉDICIS

Queen of France, wife of Henry II (1547–59), daughter of Lorenzo de' Medici, Duke of Urbino, and of Madeleine de la Tour d'Auvergne, Countess of Boulogne; b. Florence, April 13, 1519; d. Blois, Jan. 5, 1589. In 1533 Catherine married Henry (then Duke of Orléans), second son of Francis I of France; she later became Queen of France on her husband's acces-

Catherine de Médicis, portrait by an unknown 16th-century artist of the French school, Musée du Louvre.

sion to the throne in 1547. Three of her four sons became kings of France. She was kept out of politics during the reigns of Henry II and Francis II (her eldest son), but after being declared regent during the minority of Charles IX, her second son, she remained in virtual control to the end of his reign (1574).

Political Policy. Her chief traits were her "possessive maternalism" and her devotion to politics. Her outlook was essentially political: even in promoting the careers of her children she found an outlet for political machinations. An admirer of Machiavelli, she worked toward the goal of national unity. Deeply involved as she was in the problems of the Huguenots, the warring religious factions, and the ambitions of the nobility, she showed ability in retaining power and defending the crown. The only principle to which she adhered in her religious policy was *Gallicanism: she considered matters of faith to be under royal prerogative. She was not a fanatic, but was notoriously unscrupulous in her actions—her weapons included intrigue, duplicity, violence, and perjury. Antidoctrinaire, she pursued a piecemeal, pragmatic policy in the form of a series of expedient moves, and she thought in terms of "a temporary policy leading to a permanent solution" (J. E. Neale), an expedient with disastrous consequences. Her vision as a ruler was limited; she was often erratic and inconsistent, and consequently she never rose to the stature of a statesman.

Religious Controversy. Catherine began with designs for partial toleration toward the Huguenots and advocated coexistence of the two religions. Indifferent to dogmas, she professed a liberty of doctrine that was unacceptable to contemporary theologians, and she was inclined to regard religious rifts mainly as court intrigues amenable to personal conciliation. In July 1561, together with Louis I de Guise, Cardinal de Lorraine, she launched the Colloquy of Poissy, which she hoped to turn into a National Council of the Gallican Church to foster reconciliation between the Huguenots and Catholics. Her inability to grasp the importance of doctrinal matters caused the failure of this meeting. She found an abyss separated Cardinal de Lorraine and Theodore de Bèze (or *Beza), the Huguenot theologian, and the debate at Poissy aroused religious feelings and widened the gap between the two groups, thus preparing a way for armed conflict. Tension was further increased when the Edict of January 1562, designed to grant the Huguenots civic status and abolish the death penalty for heresy, came up for registration before the Paris high court of justice (*parlement*). Finally, the Massacre of Vassy (March 1, 1562) began the religious wars. Catherine's policy of expediency proved ineffective. Trying to keep in check the Catholic Triumvirate (Duke Francis de Guise, Constable Anne de *Montmorency, and Marshal de Saint-André) and forestall its armed uprising, she encouraged the strengthening of the Huguenot party and completion of the Huguenot military organization. Catherine, captured with the King by the Triumvirs on March 27, entered the war on their side. She curtailed the liberties of the Huguenots and, while negotiating with their chiefs, sought external allies—the Pope, Spain, and Savoy. The Huguenots were aided by Elizabeth of England, to whom Louis I *Condé ceded Le Havre. Catherine besieged Rouen (September). The war freed her from the Triumvirs' control: Guise was assassinated at Orléans and Saint-André at Dreux; and Montmorency was captured. Catherine had Condé and Montmorency (each a prisoner of the other side) conduct negotiations leading to the Pacification of Amboise (March 19, 1563). Liberty of conscience was achieved, but serious restrictions were imposed on freedom of worship. Catherine recaptured Le Havre from the English (July 28) and on signing the Treaty of Troyes (April 12, 1564) regained Calais, lost by the Treaty of Cateau-Cambrésis (March 1559).

She then undertook a long tour of France lasting until May 1566. At Bayonne she met her daughter Elizabeth (married to Philip II) and some members of the Spanish court, including the Duke of Alva, to discuss a possible league between France, Spain, and the Emperor. The suspicions of the Huguenots were soon aroused by Alva's rule of terror in the Netherlands; they feared concerted action, led by Catherine, against the Protestants. New hostilities broke out in September 1567 with an abortive attempt by the Huguenots to seize the King. The second religious war ended officially with the Treaty of Longjumeau (March 23, 1568), but sporadic hostilities and atrocities continued. Catherine's policy toward the Huguenots became aggressive: already in 1567 she had dismissed Chancellor Michel de l'Hôpital (who had previously guided her policy of moderation) and then planned to seize the Huguenot leaders Louis I Condé and Gaspard de *Coligny. Coligny rose in defense in August 1568, and the third religious war began. Catherine took offensive action against the Huguenots grouped in Poitou. Her army, commanded by Tavannes, defeated Coligny at Jarnac (May 13, 1569), where Condé was killed, and at Moncontour (October 3). She outlawed Coligny in September 1569, and on Aug. 8, 1570, she signed a peace treaty at Saint-Germain. Influenced by the moderately inclined *politiques,* she tried to establish a balance between the parties. She decided to marry her daughter Margaret to Henry de Navarre, the titular head of the Huguenot party, and made unsuccessful plans for the marriage of her son, Henry, the Duke of Anjou, to Elizabeth I of England. At court, the Huguenots replaced the Guises as the influential party. A project was born for a united Huguenot-Catholic force to challenge Spain in the Netherlands; Coligny was to cooperate with William of Orange, the leader of the Dutch uprising. Dreading the might of Spain and resentful of Coligny's unprecedented influence over Charles IX in the planning of the campaign, Catherine stopped the expedition. When Coligny's attitude became threatening, she ordered Maurevel to assassinate him. Coligny was wounded in Paris on Aug. 22, 1572. Fearing revenge, Catherine obtained from the King permission to massacre the Huguenots who were assembled in Paris for the wedding of Henry de Navarre.

Her subsequent moves were ineffectual. For the Massacre of St. Bartholomew's Day she never found a plausible excuse. She resorted to a short-lived expedient of legal toleration, which involved bribing Huguenot nobles with titles and sinecures. But her grip over national affairs was lost: she was never able to impress Henry III with her counsels.

Appreciation. Catherine was a woman of superior intelligence and prodigious energy and was well read and eloquent; she had a fine taste for the arts and constructed, among others, the palace of Tuilleries and the castles of Monceaux and Chenonceaux. Despite the short-sightedness of her political plans, as Neale put it, "she was a woman of great qualities, if not a great woman."

Bibliography: J. Héritier, *Catherine de Médicis* (Paris 1959), Eng., tr. C. Haldane (New York 1963). J. E. Neale, *The Age of Catherine de Medici* (London 1943; new ed. London 1957). P. Van Dyke, *Catherine de Médicis,* 2 v. (New York 1923). L. Romier, *Le Royaume de Catherine de Médicis,* 2 v. (Paris 1922). J. H. Mariéjol, *Catherine de Médicis* (Paris 1920). L. M. Tocci, EncCatt 3:1144. R. Roeder, *Catherine de Medici and the Lost Revolution* (New York 1937). **Illustration credit:** Archives Photographiques, Paris.

[W. J. STANKIEWICZ]

CATHERINE OF RACCONIGI, BL., mystic; b. Racconigi, province of Cuneo, Piedmont, Italy, June 24?, 1486; d. Caramagna, Piedmont, Sept. 4, 1547 (feast, Sept. 4). Catherine was the youngest of seven children of a blacksmith. She worked as a weaver and distributed her wages to the poor. She loved solitude and contemplation and was vowed to virginity; she is known to have been favored with many mystical graces and prophecies as well as being privileged with the stigmata. From her Dominican confessor she received the habit of a tertiary on Dec. 22, 1513. Although she was esteemed and consulted by illustrious personages, she was also persecuted by the envious. When forced to take refuge in Caramagna, Catherine offered herself as a victim for sinners and for the maintenance of peace. Pius VII authorized her Mass and Office on April 9, 1808. She is commemorated in the Order of Preachers and in the dioceses of Turin and Mondovì, and is particularly venerated in Racconigi, where her house was made into an oratory and chapel in the Dominican church, in Caramagna, and in Garessio (Cuneo), where there is a chapel in her honor.

Bibliography: G. F. Pico della Mirandola and P. M. Morelli, *Compendio delle cose mirabili della beata Caterina da Racconigi* (Chieri-Turin 1858). G. Bonetti, *Vita. . . .* (Turin 1876). A. Ferraris, *Beata Caterina Mattei da Racconigi* (Alba 1947). A. Guarienti, *La Beata Caterina da Racconigi* (Alba 1964).

[I. VENCHI]

CATHERINE DE' RICCI, ST., Dominican contemplative of the Counter Reformation; b. Florence, Italy, April 23, 1522; d. Prato, Feb. 2, 1590 (feast, Feb. 13). She was a child of patrician lineage, and spiritually formed by her aunt, a Benedictine abbess, but she entered the Dominican convent of San Vincenzio, Prato, founded 1503 in the spirit of *Savonarola's reform. At 14 she was professed, taking her deceased mother's name. From the first she endured physical afflictions and spiritual raptures that her sisters doubted until won over by her humility and holiness. During Holy Week of 1542 her ecstasies began; thereafter for 12 years from Thursday noon to Friday at 4 P.M. she relived Christ's Passion. Among her other supernatural gifts were mystical visits with St. Philip Neri and St. Mary Magdalen de' Pazzi, neither of whom she had met. She led an uncommonly effective life, advising bishops, cardinals, generals of orders, and three future popes; directing disciples in person and in letters of great charm; looking after the poor and distressed; and, as prioress (1560–90), administering the convent with wisdom and energy. Her spirituality was that of Savonarola, softened by her optimism and compassion; she promoted frequent confession and Communion, and a spirit of joy, peace, and energetic action (*gagliardo combattimento*). She composed a *lauda* in honor of Savonarola and a Bible-based canticle of the Passion, *Amici mei,* used in the Dominican Liturgy of Good Friday. The *promotor fidei* in the process of her beatification was Cardinal Prospero Lambertini (later Benedict XIV), who afterward made frequent reference to her in his classic *De servorum Dei beatificatione.* Her iconography includes a death mask made by her brother, a portrait probably by Naldini (*c.* 1570), and an unfinished sketch of her miraculous crucifix by H. Besson, OP.

St. Catherine De' Ricci, portrait probably by Naldini in the Museo Civico at Montepulciano, Italy.

Bibliography: *Le lettere di S. Caterina de' Ricci,* ed. A. Gherardi (Florence 1890). *Lettere inedite di S. Caterina de' Ricci,* ed. S. Pardi (Florence 1912). *Compendio della vita della beata Caterina de' Ricci: Estratto da' processi fatti per la sua beatificazione* (Florence 1733). S. Razzi, *La vita della reverenda serva di Dio, la Madre Suor Caterina de' Ricci* (Lucca 1594). F. M. Capes, *St. Catherine de' Ricci* (London 1905). Butler Th Attw 1:328–331. G. Di Agresti, *S. Caterina de' Ricci: Fonti* (Florence 1963). **Illustration credit:** Alinari-Art Reference Bureau.

[M. E. EVANS]

CATHERINE OF SIENA, ST.

Dominican tertiary and mystic; b. Siena, probably in 1347; d. Rome, April 29, 1380 (feast, April 30).

Life. Catherine was the 23d child (a twin) of Jacopo Benincasa, a dyer, and his wife, Lapa Piagenti. Jacopo was a good Christian and was to prove a true father to Catherine in her struggle for freedom to follow her unusual vocation. Lapa was an average Italian housewife; she was hardworking, maternally affectionate, but spiritually rather obtuse. Catherine grew up intelligent, cheerful, and intensely religious. It is reported that at the age of 7, following a vision of Christ in glory, she vowed her virginity to Him. Later on, her mother repeatedly urged her to care more for her appearance with a view to marriage. Catherine at first yielded a little but then proved intractable, and to show her resolution cut off her hair. This led to a persecution from her family, which was ended when Jacopo ordered that Catherine be left in peace and allowed her a room of her own for prayer and meditation. Catherine was already being guided in her spiritual life by the Dominicans, and she greatly desired to become a tertiary of the order. This was accomplished, after some difficulty, in 1364 or 1365. The next 3 years she spent in seclusion from the world, devoting herself to prayer and the practice of severe austerities. It proved to be a preparation for the active apostolate that was to follow, and it ended, probably in the spring of 1368, with a vision that convinced Catherine that Christ had accepted her as his "bride." She received His command to carry her love for Him out into the world and so give full scope to the charity within her.

Catherine's life from that time until her death fell into three somewhat clearly marked periods: from 1368 to the summer of 1374; from this date to November 1378; and then the year and a half until her death in 1380. The first period was spent entirely in Siena and is marked by four important developments. First, there gathered around her the nucleus of the group of friends and disciples with which her name is associated: men and women; priests both secular and religious, among whom Dominicans naturally predominated; and layfolk; most of them her seniors, but all in some measure her spiritual pupils, and all accustomed to calling her "mother." The formation of this "family" led in turn to the beginning, not later than 1370, of the great series of Catherine's letters. Probably she could already read, and later would learn to write, but she dictated nearly all her letters to secretaries chosen from her "family." At first simply vehicles for spiritual instruction and encouragement, the letters soon began to touch on public affairs. The first public issue to receive her attention was a projected Crusade against the Turks. Meanwhile, in the little world of Siena, it was inevitable that her personality and influence should arouse some opposition and even slander. She was a saint who mixed fearlessly in the world and spoke with the candor and authority of one completely committed to Christ. At the same time she was a woman, young and with no social position. She was accused of hypocrisy and presumption. At this critical point it was her Dominican affiliation that saved her. Summoned to Florence to give an account of herself to the general chapter of the order held there in May and June of 1374, she satisfied the rigorous judges, and her work was given official Dominican protection. The chapter appointed Bl. *Raymond of Capua (1330–99) as director of Catherine and her followers; from then on he was very closely associated with her activities.

The next 4 years saw Catherine's influence on public affairs at its greatest. Two issues in particular led her into Church politics: the Crusade already mentioned and the war between Florence and her Italian allies against the papacy (1376–78). Catherine's political achievements should not, however, be overestimated. She had no interest in secular politics as such and often

St. Catherine of Siena, contemporary portrait by Andrea Vanni, in the church of St. Dominic at Siena.

showed herself naïve and ingenuous when involved in them. Such influence as she had was due to her manifest holiness, to her Dominican connection, and to the impression she made on Gregory XI and, to a lesser degree, on his successor, Urban VI. She first saw Gregory at Avignon in June 1376. She had gone there at the request of the Florentines, hoping to make peace between them and the Pope. This effort was in vain, but she did have much to do with Gregory's decision to bring the Curia back to Rome in that same year. She had persisted also in her efforts for the Crusade, the project that so often recurs in her letters and that had brought her to Pisa in 1375. This visit is worth recording because it was during an ecstasy in a church in that city that Catherine received the stigmata, though the wounds were visible only to herself. By January 1377 Catherine was back in Siena. During the next 2 years she continued her tireless apostolate in that city and in the Tuscan countryside and, with less success, her efforts for peace in Florence. Gregory had died in March of 1378, and his successor was the well-meaning but often harsh and tactless Urban VI. In the autumn the Great Schism began.

This disaster overshadowed and saddened the last phase of Catherine's life. From November 1378 until her death she was in Rome, occupied chiefly with her prayers and pleading on behalf of Urban VI and the unity of the Church, and with the composition of her book, the *Dialogue,* written in four treatises, which she intended as her spiritual testament to the world. Early in 1380 her agony over the state of the Church, for which she had offered herself as a victim to God, brought on a seizure, the prelude to her death. She died, surrounded by her "children," and was buried in the church of the Minerva at Rome. Her head is at S. Domenico in Siena.

Spirituality. Spiritually, Catherine ranks high among Catholic mystics and spiritual writers. Her spirituality is markedly Christocentric: gifted by nature with a fine intelligence and intense vitality, she surrendered herself to the incarnate Word. The basic theme of her teaching is God's creative and recreative (redemptive) love, expressed and symbolized in the Precious Blood. Her stress on the importance in Christian living of clear, exact knowledge shows her Dominican training, but her teaching derives at least as much from SS. Augustine and Bernard as (indirectly in any case) from St. Thomas. Venerated in her lifetime as a saint, she was canonized by Pius II in 1461. In 1939 Pius XII declared her and St. Francis of Assisi the chief patron saints of Italy.

Bibliography: Works. The standard complete edition of Catharine's letters is *Le lettere di s. Caterina da Siena,* ed. N. TOMMASÈO, 4 v. (Florence 1860), rev. ed. P. MISCIATTELLI, 6 v. (Siena 1913–21; repr. Florence 1939–40). Of the critical ed. by E. DUPRÉ-THESEIDER, *Epistolario da Santa Caterina da Siena,* v.1 has appeared (Rome 1940). *Saint Catherine of Siena as Seen in Her Letters,* tr. V. D. SCUDDER (New York 1905), a selection. *Dialogue* or *Libro della divina dottrina,* ed. M. FIORILLI (2d ed. Bari 1912), rev. S. CARAMELLA (1928), Eng. tr. A. L. THOROLD (London 1896).

Literature. *Fontes vitae s. Catharinae Senensis historici,* ed. M. H. LAURENT et al. (Siena 1936–). The most authoritative early life is RAYMUND OF CAPUA'S *Leggenda Major,* Eng. tr. G. LAMB, *The Life of St. Catherine of Siena* (New York 1960). Of recent biographies and critical studies the following are esp. noteworthy: A. LEVASTI, *My Servant Catherine,* tr. D. M. WHITE (Westminster, Md. 1954). A. GRION, *Santa Caterina da Siena: Dottrina e fonti* (Brescia 1953). A. CURTAYNE, *Saint Catherine of Siena* (New York 1935). R. FAWTIER, *Sainte Catherine de Sienne et la critique des sources,* 2 v. (Paris 1921–30), v.1 *Sources hagiographiques,* v.2 *Les Oeuvres de s. C. de S.* R. FAWTIER and L. CANET, *La Double expérience de Catherine Benincasa* (Paris 1948). Fawtier's radical criticism of the sources was examined by E. JORDAN in AnalBoll 40 (1922) 365–411. E. DUPRÉ-THESEIDER, "La Duplice esperienza di S. C. da S.," in *Rivista storica italiana* 62 (1950) 533–574. **Illustration credit:** Alinari-Art Reference Bureau.

[K. FOSTER]

CATHERINE OF SWEDEN, ST., Bridgettine; b. 1331 or 1332; d. Vadstena, March 24, 1381 (feast, March 24). She was the daughter of St. *Bridget of Sweden. In early youth she married the nobleman Eggard von Kürnen, with whom she lived in continency. In 1350 she joined her mother in Rome, sharing as daughter and companion Bridget's life of prayer, pilgrimage, and charitable works. After her husband's death (1351), Catherine refused many offers of marriage. Having accompanied her mother's remains to Sweden (1375), she devoted herself to the interests of the community founded by Bridget at Vadstena, becoming its first superior. From 1375 to 1380 she was in Rome to further her mother's canonization and the approbation of the *Bridgettine rule. At this time she became the friend of *Catherine of Siena. Though not formally canonized, she is listed in the Roman martyrology. A chapel in the Piazza Farnese is dedicated to her. Her devotional writings, including *The Consolation of the Soul,* have not survived.

Bibliography: Mercati-Pelzer DE 1:548. Butler Th Attw 1: 669–671. H. JÄGERSTAD, LexThK^2 6:62–63. A. L. SIBILIA, Bibl Sanct 3:994–996.

[M. J. FINNEGAN]

CATHERINE THOMAS, ST., Canoness Regular of Saint Augustine; b. Valdemuzza, Majorca, 1533; d. Palma, Majorca, 1574 (feast, April 5). Catherine, orphaned at the age of 7, already showed signs of great piety and gifts of prayer. She went to work as shepherdess for an uncle, who beat and starved her. In spite of this treatment she made great strides in the spiritual life. At the age of 16 she was accepted at the convent of St. Mary Magdalen in Palma, at her confessor's insistence, for she had no dowry. Here she tried to hide her spiritual gifts under a cloak of stupidity. Strange phenomena soon made her the center of controversy. She apparently had the gift of prophecy and also conversed with angels. She was said to have been attacked by devils who filled the cloisters with fearful shrieks and who once tossed her into a cistern full of muddy water. Distinguished visitors came continually to see her. She foretold the day of her own death at the age of 41. She was beatified in 1792 and canonized in 1930.

Bibliography: Butler Th Attw 2:6–7. Baudot-Chaussin 4:135–136. N. DEL RE, EncCatt 3:1160–61.

[M. J. DORCY]

CATHERINE SPALDING COLLEGE

A liberal arts college for women located in downtown Louisville, Ky., Catherine Spalding College was founded as Nazareth College in 1920 by the Sisters of *Charity of Nazareth. The first liberal arts college for women in Kentucky, it is empowered to confer degrees by a state charter granted in 1829. Since 1925 the College has been recognized by the State Department of Education. In 1938 it was accredited by the Southern Association of Colleges and in 1963, by the National League for Nursing. The College is affiliated with The Catholic University of America.

Nazareth College was formerly a two-campus college, a second campus being located at Nazareth, Ky. In 1961, however, the College became two separate units, and in 1963 the Louisville college changed its name to Catherine Spalding College in memory of the foundress of the Sisters of Charity of Nazareth (*see* SPALDING, CATHERINE, MOTHER).

The College is governed under the direction of the board of trustees at Nazareth. Administrative officers include the president, academic dean, chairmen of departments, registrar, business manager, librarian, and the director of student affairs. Administration is assisted by the board of counselors, a body of laymen and a priest. Faculty members in 1964 included 1 priest, 34 sisters, and 33 laymen, who held 13 doctoral and 55 master's degrees. Faculty-student ratio was 1 to 12; full-time

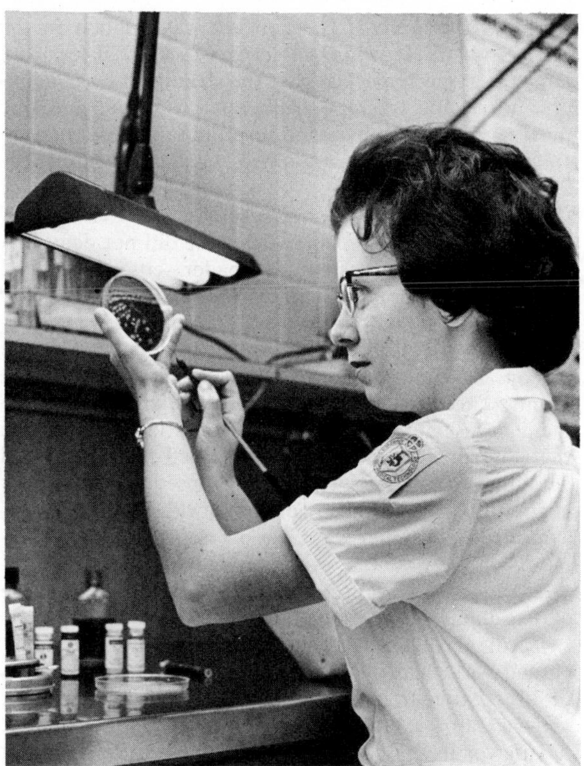

Student at Catherine Spalding College, in the laboratory.

students numbered 535; part-time students, 850. A library housed 51,787 volumes and received 520 periodicals. A science building and a college center were added to the 2-block, 6-acre campus, and construction was begun on a new library.

The College is supported largely by tuition and fees and by the contributed services of the religious administrators and faculty. Other income includes an annuity from the board of trustees, a grant from the Ford Foundation, and gifts from patrons.

Catherine Spalding College provides the traditional liberal arts program leading to the B.A. degree with majors in English, history, Latin, mathematics, natural and social sciences, modern languages, philosophy, and psychology. The College offers professional programs leading to the B.S. degree in elementary education, home economics, medical technology, and nursing. These professional programs incorporate a generic core of liberal arts with the professional, state, and national curriculum requirements. There are advanced-placement programs in mathematics, foreign languages, logic, and chemistry. The College offers a junior-year-abroad program.

Since 1952 the institution has offered a graduate program leading to the master's degree in theology, library science, and education, with special courses leading to certification in principalship, supervision, librarianship, and counseling and guidance.

Regular classes are conducted by a combination lecture and discussion plan, with laboratory and clinical experience provided where applicable. Many upper-division courses follow the seminar plan, and in several fields independent study projects are arranged. Men are admitted to graduate classes and to undergraduate classes in the part-time program.

The College sponsors its own cultural program and engages with other local colleges in the book-a-semester plan and similar extracurricular activities. An extensive guidance program is conducted through the College's psychological center, which serves the city and county as a testing bureau, and is patronized by local school boards.

[L. M. FREIBERT]

CATHOLIC

The word catholic means general or universal (from the Greek καθολικός). Originally applied to the universal care and providence of God (by Tertullian), to the general resurrection (by Theophilus of Antioch), it is still used of those Epistles addressed to the Church at large and not to particular communities.

But today the term is more often applied to the Church founded by Christ, which is of its nature intended for all races and all times. The Prophets of the Old Law announced the universal reign of the Messiah, and this was established by Christ, who spoke of the kingdom as being destined for all men and who sent out His disciples to teach all nations. The reception of Cornelius marked an important step in the realization of this ideal; St. Paul in his day could already speak of the faith as being known throughout the whole world (Rom 1.8). Early Church documents (Didache, St. Polycarp) speak of universality as one of the characteristics of Christianity, and St. Ignatius of Antioch (*Smyrn.* 8.2) was the first to use the expression the Catholic Church. The growth of the Church in the first 2 centuries is often taken as a sign of its divine origin, since up to the time of Constantine there were very few material advantages to be obtained by a profession of Christianity; yet persecution increased rather than diminished the spread of the Church [*see* MIRACLE, MORAL (THE CHURCH)]. The struggle with the Donatists helped to clarify catholicity as a *mark of the Church. The claim of the Donatists to be the one true church of Christ was seen to be inadmissible, since they were but a sect in a small corner of the globe. Optatus of Mileve and St. Augustine particularly insisted on this aspect of the Church of Christ spread throughout the world. Throughout history, as new lands and peoples have been discovered, the one and same Church has been extended to all parts of the world.

The word Catholic is also applied to the teaching and the faith of the Church of Christ, and in this sense it means what is believed by the whole Church. Thus Catholic teaching becomes a test of orthodoxy. It is sound doctrine as opposed to heresy, or, as Vincent of Lérins said, "that which has been believed everywhere, always, and by all. This is what is truly and properly Catholic" (*Common.* 1.2; EnchPatr 2168). What is believed by the universal Church must be true, otherwise there would be a total defection from the teaching of Christ.

Finally the word Catholic is used of individual Christians insofar as they belong to the Catholic Church and are orthodox in their belief.

See also CATHOLICISM; CATHOLICITY; ROMAN CATHOLIC; CHURCH, ARTICLES ON.

Bibliography: K. RAHNER and F. MUSSNER, LexThK[2] 6:88–90. G. W. H. LAMPE, ed., *A Patristic Greek Lexicon* (Oxford 1961–). "Catholicus" in TLL 3:614.53–618.35. Y. M. J. CON-

GAR, *Divided Christendom,* tr. M. A. BOUSFIELD (London 1939) 93–144. H. DE LUBAC, *Catholicism,* tr. L. C. SHEPPARD (New York 1958); *The Splendour of the Church,* tr. M. MASON (New York 1956). G. THILS, *Les Notes de l'église dans l'apologétique catholique depuis la réforme* (Gembloux 1937) 214–254.

[M. E. WILLIAMS]

CATHOLIC ACTION

A term used to designate both a concept and an organization of laity, and having a variety of meanings depending upon the decade and the region to which reference is made. This article treats (1) the definition of the term, (2) its origins and development, (3) organizational forms of Catholic Action, and (4) its theological significance.

Definition. At one extreme Catholic Action has been used to refer to any external action of a Catholic layman inspired by his faith. This is Catholic Action only in a loose or accommodated sense. At the other extreme, Catholic Action refers only to such actions of lay groups as have been so defined, and mandated by the local ordinary. In this sense, the term denotes a tightly structured organization that serves as an arm of the hierarchy in lay life. The mandate is essential. Between these extremes are the multiple types of organization which may or may not be classified as Catholic Action depending upon the concept prevailing in a particular country at a particular time.

This ambiguity of concept became apparent during the pontificate of Pius XII. As late as 1957 he acknowledged "a regrettable and rather widespread uneasiness which arises from the use of the term 'Catholic Action.' " The Pope proposed "to restore to the term 'Catholic Action' its generic sense and to apply it simply to all organized movements of the lay apostolate recognized as such, nationally or internationally, either by the bishops on a national level or by the Holy See for movements desiring an international status. It would then be sufficient for each movement to be designated by its name and characterized by its specific form, and not by a common term." Further, he suggested an organizational reform: "All groups would belong to Catholic Action and would preserve their own autonomy, but together they would form, as Catholic Action, a federated unit. Every bishop would remain free to accept or reject a movement, to entrust it or not entrust it with a mandate, but he could not refuse it recognition on the ground that it does not belong to Catholic Action by its nature" [*Six ans se sont,* ActApS 49 (1957) 929–930].

This juridic and hierarchical concept of Catholic Action underwent further refinement after the death of Pius XII. However, John XXIII showed little concern for the tight legal categories of his predecessors. Meanwhile, during the 1950s, the term *lay apostolate received wide usage. It offered a practical way of avoiding the problem of definition. It was generic. It could be used to refer to all Catholic lay activity, whether organized or unorganized, episcopally mandated or simply of Christian inspiration, without danger of quibbles over terms or ecclesiastical jurisdiction.

Origins and Development. The term Catholic Action is a literal translation from the Italian, "Azione Cattolica," a specific national organization or movement. St. Pius X seems to have been the first pope to use the term, stressing its importance in several encyclicals. Pius XI, however, gave to it its classical definition as "the participation of the laity in the apostolate of the Church's hierarchy." The concept was implicit in the encyclical *Ubi Arcano Dei* [ActApS 14 (1922) 695] and later the Pope remarked that the definition was "delivered after due thought, deliberately, indeed, and one may say not without divine inspiration" (Discourse to Italian Catholic Young Women, OssRom, March 21–22, 1927). Through his voluminous writings and addresses, Pius XI gave Catholic Action a charter, a spirit, and an apocalyptic urgency. While he did not deny that the term could be used in a broader sense, he tended throughout his pontificate to restrict it to (1) action or work of the laity, which was (2) organized, (3) apostolic, and (4) done under a special mandate of the bishop. A spate of manuals developed each of these points. Theorists tended to be juridical and pedantic in their discussions, while the priests and laity engaged in the work of Catholic Action developed their organized activities with less rigidity as a consequence of their encounter with the needs of the world. The most outstanding practitioner was Canon Joseph Cardijn of Belgium, whose work Pius XI regarded as a model of Catholic Action and whom Paul VI elevated to the College of Cardinals in 1965.

Cardinal Saliége, Archbishop of Toulouse, less concerned with theory than with contemporary conditions of life that many found unworthy of human beings, viewed Catholic Action in terms of institutional change, having for its task "to modify social pressure, to direct it, to make it favorable to the spread of the Christian life, to let the Christian life create a climate, an atmosphere in which men can develop their human qualities, can lead a really human life, an atmosphere in which the Christian can breathe easily and stay a Christian." It would, he said, "lift up the mass, not a couple of individuals; the mass, prompted and set in motion by a natural leader chosen from the mass and remaining part of the mass" [*Documentation catholique* 42 (1945) 266].

Organization. Each country gave to Catholic Action specific and varied forms. Italian Catholic Action and Belgian *Jocism are probably the polar types. The former, which had its origins in movements beginning as early as 1863, was intended to overcome open hostility to the Church. Six divisions were organized, for men, women, young men, young women, male students at universities, and female students. It was viewed at times by the Italian government as a political threat and was defended by Pius XI in a concordat and an encyclical, *Non abbiamo bisogno* (1931). Its main concerns were to establish better relations between the Church and the government and to revive Catholic practice among the negligent. Jocism, on the other hand, was concerned with changing or Christianizing economic and social institutions through a technique expressed in the formula, "see, judge, act," applied in small groups in a specialized or like-to-like apostolate.

Between the extremes of the monolithic Italian structure and the specialized forms there developed many movements directed to specific tasks such as the teaching of religion or the amelioration of conditions in a single area, e.g., motion pictures, literature, or the labor movement. In the U.S. there are, on the one hand, the highly centralized National Councils of Catholic Men and Women and the Confraternity of Christian Doctrine that are professedly the arm of the bishop in each diocese. On the other are activities of such diverse groups as the Christian Family Movement, the Sodality, Serra International, Labor Guilds, Catholic Interracial Councils, and study clubs that, while usually not mandated by the local bishop, nevertheless exist with his approval. This variety of organizations, methods, and objectives has compounded the confusion of those struggling with the concept of Catholic Action.

Theological Significance. Pius XI claimed that Catholic Action had its origins in the New Testament. St. Paul, for example, referred to his lay helpers who "have toiled with me in the gospel" (Phil 4.3). Although social conditions in an industrial society call for different approaches to the world and new forms of collaboration between clergy and laity, Pius XI saw the layman essentially as an extension of the priest. He wrote that, "especially in our times, when the integrity of the faith and of morals is daily approaching a more dangerous crisis, and when we lament such a scarcity of priests that they seem to have proven unequal to caring for the necessities of souls, more reliance must be placed on Catholic Action" [*Quae Nobis,* ActApS 20 (1928) 384–385]. It was his genius to see that the layman's life in the world must be related in a dynamic way to the mission of the Church. Catholic Action, he insisted, "is also social action, because it promotes the supreme good of society, the Kingdom of Jesus Christ. It is not unmindful of the great problems which vex society and which are reflected in the religious and moral order, but under the guidance of the hierarchy, it studies them and proposes to solve them according to the principles of justice and Christian charity" [*Con singular complacencia,* ActApS 34 (1942) 256]. The "Pope of Catholic Action" also developed the theology of the priesthood through his many references to the priest as "the soul of Catholic Action."

The concept that a hierarchical mandate is necessary for Catholic Action has been questioned anew by the developing theology of the laity. In the militant language of Catholic Action, in the sense of Pius XI, the layman may be said to receive his commission from his bishop. If his role is to act as a soldier whose chief virtue is obedience rather than initiative, there is no difficulty. If, on the contrary, the mark of the authentic layman is a spirit of discovery and autonomy in lay life, issuing from competence based upon the development of his natural talents, it is difficult to see how his ministry can be conceived as an extension of the clerical or hierarchical Church.

Bibliography: J. NEWMAN, *What Is Catholic Action?* (Dublin 1958). L. MATHIAS, *Catholic Action, Theory and Practice* (Madras 1952). J. FITZSIMONS and P. MCGUIRE, eds., *Restoring All Things: A Guide to Catholic Action* (New York 1938). W. FERREE, *Introduction to Catholic Action* (Washington 1942). T. M. HESBURGH, *The Theology of Catholic Action* (Notre Dame, Ind. 1946).

[D. J. GEANEY]

CATHOLIC ANTHROPOLOGICAL ASSOCIATION, founded in 1926 as the Catholic Anthropological Conference according to a plan discussed previously by John M. *Cooper and Leopold Tibesar, MM, to advance anthropological science through promotion of anthropological research and publication by missionaries and professional anthropologists and of anthropological training of candidates for mission work. To fulfill the first aim, the quarterly *Primitive Man* was inaugurated in 1928. A series of publications of the conference was inaugurated also, in which 15 technical ethnological monographs written by missionaries were issued between 1929 and 1941. The series was financed largely by Cooper, who was the editor and also secretary of the conference until his death in 1949. Notable in the series are several monographs on the Isneg and Mayawyaw, pagan tribes of the Philippines, by Francis Lambrecht, CICM, and by Morice Vanoverbergh, CICM. The contribution of research materials by missionaries dropped sharply when communications were disrupted during World War II, and the series was terminated. The periodical has continued, however, although with a higher proportion of articles by professional anthropologists. In 1953 the title was changed to *Anthropological Quarterly,* and editorial responsibility was transferred to the department of anthropology of The Catholic University of America. Subsequently the name of the conference was changed to the Catholic Anthropological Association.

[R. F. HERZFELD]

CATHOLIC APOSTOLIC CHURCH, originated when a group of Christians in England in the early 19th century concluded that the Second Coming of Jesus Christ (*see* PAROUSIA) would be preceded by a restoration of the original college of 12 Apostles. They belonged to a prayer circle that, beginning in 1826, met once a year at the country estate of Henry Drummond, a devout and wealthy London banker. The rationalism of the age and the spiritual lethargy of the established church led them to pray for a revival of the gifts of the apostolic church. These Christians came under the influence of Edward *Irving (1792–1834), pastor of a Presbyterian church in London, who had joined the Drummond group. Because of Irving's leading role in the movement the members of the Catholic Apostolic Church were often called "Irvingites." Irving became convinced that Christ would return in 1864, in preparation for which there should be a revival of the offices of the early Church—apostles, prophets, evangelists, pastors, and teachers, to which angels (bishops) and deacons were added later. He himself was removed from his pastorate by the Church of Scotland in 1832 because he encouraged speaking in tongues in his congregation. The first apostle of the Catholic Apostolic Church was appointed in 1832 and the second in 1833. Before his early death, Irving was made an angel, or bishop, but not an apostle. The organization of the new church was completed in 1835, when the other apostles were selected and held their first council in London. These 12 men spent a year in prayer and then left England for their missionary assignments around the world. In general their evangelistic labors were fruitless, but they did win some followers in Germany; a Catholic Apostolic Church was opened in Berlin in 1848. A schism in North Germany in 1863 led to the formation of the *New Apostolic Church.

As the church drew away from Protestantism and closer to Roman Catholicism, its liturgy developed along Catholic lines and emphasized the sacrificial character of the eucharist. Its priests wore vestments, and soon veneration of the Mother of God, anointing of the sick, and the use of a tabernacle, sanctuary lamp, and holy water were introduced. Its doctrine was based on the *Nicene, Apostles, and *Athanasian creeds (*see* CREED). For some years the 12 apostles directed the church, but when they began to die off, no successors were chosen. The last apostle died in 1901, and the church suspended all ordinations and confirmations. Since then the Catholic Apostolic Church has disintegrated and declined in members; only a few elderly priests survive. Some of the congregations affiliated with Protestant bodies. By 1964 there were about 60,000 members of the sect, half of whom lived in Germany. There were never more than a handful of adherents in the U.S.

Bibliography: P. E. SHAW, *The Catholic Apostolic Church* (New York 1946).

[W. J. WHALEN]

CATHOLIC ASSOCIATION FOR INTERNATIONAL PEACE (CAIP)

An organization of U.S. Catholics that seeks to educate "all men of good will about their obligations" to attain world peace through justice and charity. Members include not only experts in the application of Catholic teachings on international order, but also others who are interested in learning and promoting these principles. Headquarters are in the National Catholic Welfare Conference Department of Social Action.

The CAIP was established and held its first meeting at The Catholic University of America during Easter Week, 1927. There had been two previous discussions by clerical and lay leaders. The first was attended by 50 participants in the Eucharistic Congress held at Chicago in 1926. Meeting at Loyola University, they elected Patrick Henry *Callahan of Louisville, Ky., as chairman of an organizing committee, and decided on a second session in Cleveland on October 6 of the same year. Bishop Peter J. *Muldoon of Rockford, Ill., chairman of the NCWC Department of Social Action, had initiated these meetings, having told its director, Msgr. John A. *Ryan, and assistant director, Father Raymond *McGowan, that he thought the department was not doing enough to educate Catholics on world affairs.

At the first meeting of the new organization, Bp. Thomas J. *Shahan, Rector of The Catholic University of America, was named honorary president, and Judge Martin T. Manton of New York City was elected president. A statement on international ethics, prepared by an ethics committee, was the first of many such statements, each prepared by a study committee and approved for publication by the executive committee. Pamphlet publications of the CAIP include longer statements of study committees, proceedings of annual conferences, and papers on special topics prepared by individual authors. In its first decade or two, the CAIP maintained close contact with international relations clubs at Catholic colleges and universities. In 1952, an annual award was established to recognize noteworthy contributions to world peace. It conferred the first award posthumously on Sen. Brien *McMahon for his attention to the problems posed by nuclear energy.

It is noteworthy that the CAIP pioneered in proposing many policies that eventually gained favor. Among these were proposals for technical assistance, a federated Europe, a world police force, and a world bill of rights. It warned against the world threat of Soviet Communism as early as 1931, pointed out the necessity of halting Japanese aggression when the Japanese imperialists first attacked China in Manchuria in 1932, warned against the consequences of the Munich Pact in 1938, and called upon the U.S. to take a positive stand against Nazism when Adolf Hitler became a world threat in the early 1930s. Since World War II, the CAIP has taken stands against the admission of Communist China to the United Nations, for the elimination of the veto in the UN, and for the Alliance for Progress and foreign aid. Annual conferences have been devoted to these and similar subjects.

[H. W. FLANNERY]

CATHOLIC BOARD FOR MISSION WORK AMONG THE COLORED PEOPLE, founded in the U.S. in 1906, at the request of Pius X to the American hierarchy, and incorporated under the laws of the state of Tennessee in May 1907. This episcopal agency for raising funds for the education of Negroes in the southern part of the U.S. is composed of seven bishops, a board of directors, one priest as director general, and whatever help he can recruit. Funds are solicited by mail or by visitation tours to the clergy and hierarchy. In 1964 two priests directed the work from headquarters in New York City, where three sisters of the Franciscan Handmaids of Mary helped in a secretarial capacity.

[B. M. HORTON]

CATHOLIC CENTRAL UNION

In 1855 the societies of German Catholics in the U.S. formed Der Deutsche Romisch-Katholische Central-Verein von Nord-Amerika, the German Roman Catholic Central Union (Verein) of North America; "of North America" was dropped in 1907 and Verein was later replaced by its translation, Union. In 1916 the auxiliary societies of German women were formally added to the Verein and continued their special works of charity along with the men's organization. Later a youth section was added, with the three divisions meeting in annual convention. A Central Bureau in St. Louis, Mo., established in 1908, had Frederick P. Kenkel as its founder and director until his death in 1952; its official organ is the monthly *Social Justice Review*. As occasion arises, the bureau issues pamphlets, leaflets, and brochures on questions of the day. It also promotes educational projects, supports many charitable works, maintains St. Elizabeth's Settlement in St. Louis, and is the archdiocesan agency charged with aiding refugees and immigrants.

Origin and Development. In April 1855 the numerous German Catholic parish societies then flourishing in the U.S. were invited to send delegates to a national meeting. It was held in Baltimore, Md., because its sponsors were advised by their bishop, John Timon, CM, to hold the convention elsewhere than Buffalo, N.Y., which was then suffering an outbreak of *trusteeism. With a view to increasing the proposed organization's effectiveness among the people generally, he also suggested that it be overtly the work of laymen only. Nearly the entire membership of these societies had been reared in Germany and were familiar with the Piusvereine and other semicivic societies there, whose declared objective was to bring Catholic morality into politics and to counteract the amorality and immorality of the various creeds from liberalism to communism. The societies formed by the German Catholics of the U.S. not only shared this objective but also attempted to provide primitive insurance arrangements for members. The founders of the Verein, therefore, envisioned a union that would strengthen these benevolent societies and more closely unite the members according to the spirit and laws of the Church, promote their temporal and spiritual interests, increase their zeal, and multiply their works of charity. Once established, the federation was maintained with scrupulous respect for the autonomy of constituent societies. In the beginning, when the usual constituent society was a benevolent one, each member carried a card showing the amount and terms of benefit to which he was entitled; this was honored by cooperating societies wherever he happened to be residing when need arose. However, with the advent of more efficient insurance companies, this feature disappeared.

In 1870 an improved constitution was adopted stating the aim of the Central Union to be "mutual assistance in sickness and need among the different fraternal benevolent German Roman Catholic societies," and in 1878, by agreement with the Irish Catholic Benevolent Union, the benefits were extended to each organization's members by the other. Another declared aim, secondary in 1870 but later of greater importance, was to "champion Catholic interests according to the mind of the Catholic Church." To this end the annual conventions were elaborate, well advertised, and programed with nationally known figures voicing the mind of the Church on current social problems. Practices of their German homeland, e.g., Catholic Days (*Katholikentage*), were adopted, affording opportunity for more intensive study of these questions. The Central Union was incorporated under the laws of Missouri in 1883; Henry J. Spaunhorst served as president from 1873 to 1891. Under him a widows' and orphans' fund was established (1881) and was continued until 1906 when, because of the small number of participants and disproportionate cost, it was separated from the Union and separately incorporated under the laws of another state. To operate more effectively in the states where social legislation existed, the Union's constituent societies reorganized whenever possible along state lines, and these state unions kept a vigilant eye on state legislation.

Accomplishments. Soon after the Union established its Central Bureau near St. Louis University, Mo., a library was added and housed in a building adjacent to the bureau headquarters. Under Kenkel's direction the library acquired a priceless collection of German-Americana, as well as many English volumes in the social science field. The official organ of the Central Union was founded in 1908 as *Central-Blatt,* published entirely in German; a year later 20 per cent of its material was in English and the title was changed to *Central-Blatt and Social Justice*. By 1941 *Social Justice Review* had a 10 per cent German content, and in 1946 use of German was dropped. Meanwhile it had become a monthly magazine of wide Catholic interest, publishing contributions from a variety of sources. In 1963 the magazine was probably the most effective and far-reaching of the works of the Central Union.

During its more than 100 years of existence, the Union's member societies increased from 17 in 1855 to 55 in 1865; 328 in 1880; 455 in 1890; 903 in 1905; and 1,108 in 1910. In 1914 the members of constituent societies totaled 121,374. World War I, with its Germanophobia, accounted for the decrease in members to 113,400 and in societies to 1,100. In 1960 there were 78,400 members in 570 societies in the Central Union. The fraternal societies then affiliated with the Central Union included such organizations as the Western Catholic Union, Catholic Knights of St. George, Catholic Knights of St. John, Catholic Family Life of Wisconsin, and Catholic Life Insurance Union of Texas; membership lists showed more than a sprinkling of non-German names. When the member organizations were still benevolent societies, funds were collected for charitable purposes and expended in various ways to aid German immigrants. Provisions were made for meeting travelers and aiding them to reach their destinations safely. The Leo House in New York City was originally designed as a hospice for German immigrants. The Central Bureau in St. Louis served as a Catholic immigration center for victims of the Nazi persecution, displaced persons, and war victims. Several thousands of these, about two-thirds of them non-German, were aided by the bureau in its capacity as the archdiocesan agency for such work. The Central Bureau played a significant role also in the development of Catholic Action in the U.S. The social teaching of the Church was consistently emphasized and every effort made to spread it by lectures, Catholic days, and publications. Virtually every Catholic German newspaper and magazine in the U.S. received financial assistance from the Union and later from the Central Bureau. Moreover, for many years the Josephinum Papal College at Worthington, Ohio, and the Holy Family Teachers' College near Milwaukee, Wis., were aided by the Union. As an antidote to socialism, the Union advocated workingmen's organizations and social legislation; and it sponsored courses of instruction in the rights, duties, and responsibilities of workers. For both workingman and farmer, agencies for self-help and mutual help, such as credit unions and cooperatives, were promoted.

Frederick Philip Kenkel.

An endowment fund for the maintenance of the Central Bureau was begun in 1920. However, the establishment of the National Catholic Welfare Conference absorbed many of the purposes to which the Central Union had devoted its efforts. Hoping to expand its social action program, the Union added social action members, individuals whose larger dues were designed to replace continually dwindling organization members.

Bibliography: M. L. BROPHY, *The Social Thought of the German Roman Catholic Central Verein* (Washington 1941). C. J. BARRY, *The Catholic Church and German Americans* (Milwaukee 1953). Central Bureau Publications, *The Central Verein: History, Aim, and Scope* (St. Louis 1946), pamphlet. J. P. GLEASON, *The Central Verein, 1900–1917: A Chapter in the History of German American Catholics* (Doctoral diss. microfilm; U. of Notre Dame 1960).

[M. L. BROPHY]

CATHOLIC CHURCH EXTENSION SOCIETY, established Oct. 18, 1905, to serve the needs of the home missions—those areas of the U.S. where the work of the Church is seriously handicapped by lack of personnel, organization, finances, etc. The society was organized under the direction of the board of governors—the American cardinals and archbishops, and 12 bishops, priests, and laymen. The first president was Rev. (later Bp.) Francis Clement *Kelley. In 1910 Pius X raised the society to pontifical status. To publicize the missionary needs of the southern and western states especially, but also of Alaska, Hawaii, Puerto Rico, and the Philippines, *Extension Magazine* was initiated as a national Catholic monthly. Throughout these areas the society has helped to build more than 7,000 small churches. In addition, regular support of needy clergy and seminarians, as well as missionary help of all kinds, has been provided through the years. The society also recruits, trains, and assigns lay mission workers in its Extension lay volunteer program, developed under Abp. William D. O'Brien, president of Extension for nearly 40 years.

Bibliography: F. C. KELLEY, *The First American Catholic Missionary Congress* (Chicago 1909); *The Second American Catholic Missionary Congress* (Chicago 1913); *The Story of Extension* (Chicago 1922); *The Bishop Jots It Down* (New York 1939). F. P. LEIPZIG, *Extension in Oregon* (pa. St. Benedict, Ore. 1956).

[J. L. MAY]

CATHOLIC COMMISSION ON INTELLECTUAL AND CULTURAL AFFAIRS, an association founded on June 23, 1946, to encourage the interchange of ideas and a consciousness of solidarity among Catholic thinkers in the U.S.; to focus attention on problems of intellectual and cultural life especially as they present themselves to Catholics; and to promote Catholic international intellectual and cultural cooperation. Invitations to membership are extended to persons recognized for productive scholarship, creative contributions to letters or the arts, or leadership exercised through the expression of ideas. Membership numbered about 300 persons from all parts of the U.S. in 1965. The Commission holds annual meetings devoted to such themes as "The Catholic Scholar in a Secularist World," "American Catholics and the Intellectual Life," "The Influence of Modern Government on Intellectual and Cultural Life," and "The Intellectual and Cultural Dimensions of Contemporary International Relations." Proceedings of two early meetings were printed under the titles *Catholic Participation in the Intellectual Movements of Today* (1951) and *UNESCO and Catholic Collaboration* (1953). The Commission also sponsors regional meetings of members, undertakes cooperative studies of problems of concern, and maintains a register of American Catholic scholars. One of its special activities is the conduct of William Joseph Kerby Seminars for younger scholars to further interdisciplinary and interinstitutional communication and the relation of the scholars' specialities to the tradition of Christian wisdom. The first chairman of the Commission was David A. McCabe, professor of economics at Princeton University. The first executive director was Edward V. Stanford, OSA; he was succeeded in 1954 by Rev. William J. Rooney.

[C. J. NUESSE]

CATHOLIC COMMITTEE OF THE SOUTH, an organization that developed from the efforts of five of the Southern participants in the second National Catholic Social Action Congress, held in Cleveland, Ohio, in June 1939. Foremost among them was Bp. Gerald P. O'Hara, then of Savannah-Atlanta, and Paul D. Williams of Richmond, Va. This small group succeeded in having panels on agriculture and industry in the South incorporated into the Congress program. The conviction that the South was not only "the nation's number one economic problem," as Pres. Franklin D. Roosevelt had described it, but also "the Church's number one opportunity" and "the nation's promise" was expressed in a statement of principle and led to the establishment of the Catholic Conference of the South at a 2-day regional meeting of bishops, clergy, and laity at Atlanta, Ga., in 1940. Rt. Rev. Msgr. T. James McNamara of the founding group was elected first general chairman. Subsequently, meeting in Birmingham, Ala., the bishops of the region accepted the suggestions of the general secretary of the National Catholic Welfare Conference that the name be changed to the Catholic Committee of the South. The Committee first sought to implement its objectives through five departments for education, labor relations, race, rural life, and youth. A department on the lay apostolate was added to stress the apostolic character of each department. Counterparts of the regional departments were sought in each diocese. The impact of the Committee was registered through annual conventions, through annual awards to individuals—among them George Washington Carver—for contributions to the progress of the southern region, and through its summer school. It is significant that the Committee received national publicity for the advocacy of racial integration of schools as early as its 1949 convention in Covington, Ky. The Committee has been dormant for some years, however, having held its last convention in Columbia, S.C., in 1951.

Bibliography: Catholic Conferences of the South, *Reports of the Proceedings and Addresses of the Annual Meeting* (Richmond, Va. 1941–46). T. J. HARTE, *Catholic Organizations Promoting Negro-White Race Relations in the United States* (CUA Stud. in Sociol.; Washington 1947) 145–154.

[T. J. MC NAMARA]

CATHOLIC CONFERENCE ON INDUSTRIAL PROBLEMS, an association "to discuss and promote the study and understanding of industrial problems" founded upon the initiative of the then recently established Department of Social Action of the *National Catholic Welfare Conference. At the organizational meeting held at Loyola University, Chicago, Ill., on Dec. 29, 1922, David A. McCabe, professor of economics at Princeton University, was elected the first president, and Rev. Raymond A. *McGowan of the Social Action Department, secretary-treasurer. The first meeting was held in Milwaukee, Wis., June 27–28, 1923. Such meetings, devoted to discussion but not to voting "on any question of industrial policy," were the principal activity of the Conference. Attendance was drawn principally from representatives of labor, education, and social work; fewer employers participated, although some, such as Patrick Henry *Callahan, one of the first vice presidents, assumed an active role. The Conference was an important medium for the dissemination of the teachings of **Rerum novarum* and of the Bishops' Program of Social Reconstruction of 1919. Its interests were too restricted to assimilate the widening types of Catholic *social action, however, and in 1957 it gave way to a successor organization of broader scope, the *National Catholic Social Action Conference, for which the NCWC Department of Social Action continues to provide a secretariat.

See also SOCIAL MOVEMENTS, CATHOLIC, 8.

Bibliography: A. I. ABELL, *American Catholicism and Social Action: A Search for Social Justice, 1865–1950* (Garden City, N.Y. 1960) 214–216.

[C. J. NUESSE]

CATHOLIC COUNCIL ON CIVIL LIBERTIES, a group founded by laymen in the Archdiocese of Omaha, Nebr., in 1958, to reassert "the tradition of Natural Law as it applies to civil and religious liberty . . . along with the original American consensus." The founders decried a general lack of Catholic participation in the defense of *civil liberties guaranteed by the Constitution of the U.S. Encouragement was given by the then Sen. John F. *Kennedy and by John Courtney Murray, SJ, who supplied a motto—"The love of the common good is an obligatory virtue." The membership has included bishops, both diocesan and religious clergy, and several hundred laymen. Board and advisory committee members have included several law school deans, a state attorney general, journalists, educators, and theologians. The council has filed *amicus* briefs before the U.S. Supreme Court in desegregation and birth control cases. Its members cite the words of John XXIII in *Pacem in terris*, "The common good is chiefly guaranteed when personal rights and duties are maintained" (45).

[R. W. GIBBONS]

CATHOLIC DAUGHTERS OF AMERICA, a charitable organization of women founded by the Knights of Columbus in Utica, N.Y., June 18, 1903,

Emblem of the Catholic Daughters of America.

for "the propagation and preservation of the Faith, the intensification of patriotism, the spiritual and intellectual development of Catholic womanhood and the promotion of Catholic charitable projects." Its motto is "Unity and Charity." From the original 60 members the organization had increased by 1963 to 215,000, of whom more than 550 members were in religious communities, 2,000 were serving as lay missionaries, and 10,000 were converts. The units, known as courts, were organized in 44 states, the District of Columbia, Puerto Rico, Cuba, and the Canal Zone.

Its plan of organization includes the supreme directorate, consisting of five officers and nine members elected by the membership at the biennial conventions; national committees for civil defense and highway safety, education, extension, leadership institutes, legislation, public relations, relief for peace, religious vocations, rural life, share the faith, social welfare, veterans' hospitals, women for decency, and world missions; and a junior commission. The Junior Catholic Daughters, organized on Feb. 22, 1926, and later part of the Youth Department of the National Catholic Welfare Conference, had a membership of 310 junior courts in 1963 with an extensive program of service in home, school, church, and community, and an accompanying system of honors and awards.

In its 60 years of organization the Catholic Daughters have given more than $33 million to religious and charitable causes including $250,000 to the National Shrine of the Immaculate Conception in Washington, D.C., for five apsidal altars, and $50,000 to the *Missionary Society of St. James the Apostle for the Church's program in Latin American countries. They have erected chapels and churches for the Extension Society, built a chapel in Uganda and a memorial in North Carolina. Substantial donations in the field of education include scholarships for sisters to study the teaching of braille and the teaching of handicapped children, as well as scholarships to the Catholic Press Association for students in journalism. A drive among their members for funds for the Vatican Radio Station was designed to help increase the power of its transmission to the strength needed to offset jamming beyond the Iron Curtain.

The Catholic Daughters work with mentally retarded and physically handicapped children; serve in city and veterans' hospitals, homes for the aged, and orphanages; and help with migrants, immigrants, and foreign visitors. Overseas, they participate in the Madonna Plan and Feed-a-Family program; they are the only Catholic organization in the U.S. that adopts the untainted children of leper parents in Korea.

[P. K. KERWIN]

CATHOLIC ECONOMIC ASSOCIATION, founded in 1942 by a group of economists from Catholic universities to whom Thomas F. Divine, SJ, had proposed the idea. Its purpose is to promote discussion of economic problems in terms of both economic science and Christian social philosophy. Other objectives are to evaluate in the light of Christian moral principles the assumptions, methods, and objectives of economic science; and to assist in the formulation of practical programs for the application of Christian social principles. To achieve these objectives the CEA encourages research and publication (particularly in its journal), and holds meetings at regular intervals. National meetings are scheduled annually in conjunction with the conventions of the American Economic Association and allied social science groups. Regional meetings are held in many areas. The official journal of the CEA is the *Review of Social Economy*. Membership is open to all interested in applying the social teaching of the Church to problems of economic policy.

Bibliography: T. F. DIVINE, "The Origin of the Catholic Economic Association," *Review of Social Economy* 2 (Jan. 1944) 102–103.

[T. F. DIVINE]

CATHOLIC EPISTLES, collective term used for seven short NT Epistles—James; 1 and 2 Peter; 1, 2, and 3 John; and Jude—to distinguish them from the 14 Pauline Epistles (including Hebrews). Both groups of Epistles form the 21 "Apostolic Letters" (the *Apostolicum* collection of the ancient canons and MSS). In the present canon and Bible they follow the Pauline Epistles; but in some ancient canons and codices they preceded the Pauline collection, and the seven were sometimes in different sequence.

The origin and meaning of the term catholic (i.e., universal) in this connection, in which it was employed as early as the 2d century (*Muratorian Canon, 68–69), are uncertain. Eusebius, who speaks of James as "the first of the Catholic Epistles" (*Hist. Eccl.* 2.23.25; 6.14.1), understands the term to mean canonical, i.e., received universally (*ibid.* 3.3.2). But actually the canonicity of some of the seven Epistles was disputed in the Church for several centuries, even after the time of Eusebius. According to the common modern opinion the term means universal in the sense that these letters were addressed to the universal Church or to many Christian communities, as distinct from the Pauline letters, which were sent to individual churches or persons. Yet this is true only of 2 Peter (to all Christians), 1 John (no address), James ("to the twelve tribes that are in the Dispersion"), and 1 Peter ("to the sojourners of the Dispersion in Pontus, Cappadocia, Asia and Bithynia"); 2 John is addressed to an unspecified church ("the Elect Lady"), and 3 John to an individual ("to Gaius"). Perhaps because the term could thus be applied to most of the seven letters, it was extended to all of them.

For details and bibliographies on the individual Catholic Epistles, *see* JAMES, EPISTLE OF ST.; PETER, EPISTLES OF ST.; JOHN, EPISTLES OF ST.; JUDE, EPISTLE OF ST.

Bibliography: P. DE AMBROGGI, EncCatt 3:1177–78. F. W. MAIER, LexThK[2] 1:740–741. E. FASCHER and W. WERBECK, RGG[3] 3:1198–99. EncDictBibl 329.

[L. F. HARTMAN]

CATHOLIC EVIDENCE GUILD. The purpose of the Catholic Evidence Guild (CEG) is to teach the Catholic religion at street corners to all who will stop and listen. It was founded in London shortly after the end of World War I by Vernon Redwood, a New Zealander, with the approval of Cardinal Bourne, then archbishop of Westminster. This first guild operated only in the Archdiocese of Westminster, but subsequent guilds were established in other English dioceses, and in the U.S. and Australia. These guilds were and are independent of one another. Early in the existence of the first guild a training scheme was devised, providing elementary and more advanced classes in theology, scholastic philosophy, and Scripture. In addition, technical training is given on how to handle open-air meetings. Examinations for speakers are conducted by the director of studies and other examining chaplains appointed by the bishop of the diocese, together with a lay "devil's advocate" who represents the crowd. Speakers take a separate examination for every doctrine they teach outdoors. J. P. Arendzen was director of studies of the Westminster Guild for many years, and later a prominent part in the training was taken by Father Charles Davis. Among the distinguished lay members of the guild are Frank Sheed, Maisie Ward, and Cecily Hastings. Popular speakers' pitches include Hyde Park in London, Wall Street and Times Square in New York, and the Domain in Sydney. Over the years the CEG has learned to replace controversy by exposition; its teaching has become more scriptural; it has moved toward ecumenism. This process of reform continues in the guild, as in the Church. The guild's textbook is *Catholic Evidence Training Outlines,* compiled by Frank Sheed and Maisie Ward. It was first published in 1925, was revised in 1948, and is in the process of being rewritten.

Bibliography: M. WARD, *Unfinished Business* (New York 1964) 78–95, a brief hist. of the Guild. E. A. SIDERMAN, *A Saint in Hyde Park* (Westminster, Md. 1950), recollections by a Jewish heckler of one of the most colorful guild speakers, the Dominican V. McNabb.

[E. FALLAUX]

CATHOLIC HOSPITAL ASSOCIATION

An organization founded in 1915 in Milwaukee, Wis., "for the promotion and realization of progressively higher ideals in the religious, moral, medical, nursing, educational, social, and all other phases of hospital and nursing endeavor and other consistent purposes especially relating to the Catholic hospitals and schools of nursing in the United States and Canada." Because the national health system of Canada differs from that of the U.S., Canadian Catholic hospitals in 1945 formed their own hospital council that, in 1954, became the Catholic Hospital Association of Canada.

Early Years. By 1914, the American College of Surgeons was establishing minimum standards for the practice of surgery in hospitals and the American Medical Association was beginning to insist that only hospitals with adequate facilities should be entrusted with internships and residencies. Aware of these developments, Charles B. Moulinier, SJ, Regent of the Marquette University Medical School (Wis.), took the occasion of a retreat that he had given to the Sisters of St. Joseph of Carondelet in St. Paul, Minn., to discuss with the hospital sisters of that order how Catholic hospitals should best meet these new standards. They agreed that an effective means would be the formation of an association of Catholic hospitals.

With the encouragement of Sebastian G. Messmer, Archbishop of Milwaukee, Moulinier took the initiative for forming such an association and prepared a constitution for it. The Association's first convention, held in Milwaukee in 1915, adopted the constitution and elected Moulinier president, a position he held until 1928. Moulinier worked assiduously at the CHA's immediate objective—preparing Catholic hospitals for standardization. The existence of the CHA and its cooperation with the American College of Surgeons contributed significantly to the success of his efforts. In May 1920, the CHA began publication of *Hospital Progress,* a professional periodical, which proved to be an effective means for keeping the Association's members abreast of developments in hospital sciences.

Affiliation with NCWC. In 1928, Alphonse M. Schwitalla, SJ, Dean of the St. Louis University Medical School, became president of the CHA and held that office until 1947. Since 1915 Archbishop Messmer, as honorary president of the CHA, had provided an informal liaison between the Association and the hierarchy. During Schwitalla's presidency, however, the need for a closer relationship became apparent, and in 1933 the CHA became affiliated with the Social Action Department of the *National Catholic Welfare Conference. Thereafter the officers of the NCWC worked closely with the CHA, particularly in the field of Federal legislation.

The cooperation between the American hierarchy and the CHA became even closer after 1939. In that year, the American bishops formed an organization known as the Conference of Bishops' Representatives. In 1942 the executive committee of this conference and the existing executive board of the CHA joined to form an administrative board for the CHA. The first chairman of the new board was Karl J. Alter, at the time bishop of Toledo and later archbishop of Cincinnati. The administrative board advises Catholic hospitals in matters of public policy and proposed legislation that affects them.

Following the Depression and World War II, Federal outlays for public health substantially increased; and Federal legislation was being proposed that seemed to favor the public over the private hospital and thus to endanger the traditional American health system. The CHA and other voluntary hospital associations formed a committee to assure that Federal legislation would accord proper recognition to the private hospital. Their efforts were in part responsible for the passage of the Hill-Burton Act for hospital construction in 1946.

From 1915 until 1947, continuity in the CHA's administration had been preserved by reelecting the president. Father Moulinier served as president from 1915 to 1928; Father Schwitalla was president from 1928 to 1947. In 1947 the CHA amended its constitution to limit the term of the president to 1 year. At the same time, it assured continuity in administration through a new office of executive director. The Association entered into a contract with the Missouri province of the Society of Jesus that provided that St. Louis University should appoint an executive director for the CHA who would serve for an indefinite period. The University appointed John J. Flanagan, SJ, to this position in 1947. During the same year Msgr. Maurice F. Griffin of Cleveland, Ohio, was elected president of the Association. He determined that the central office should be strengthened with a view to providing better and more regular services for the membership. Mr. M. R. Kneifl, who had served as executive secretary under Fathers Moulinier and Schwitalla, was selected to carry out this project, and the central office was permanently located in St. Louis, Mo. Professionally trained personnel were hired for the central office staff, enabling it to become a ready source of information for its members and to undertake educational programs in the form of institutes, workshops, and seminars.

Expanded Activities. Recognizing the organizational problems peculiar to Catholic hospitals, the CHA in 1953 and 1958 sponsored regional conferences for religious superiors to inform them about hospital problems and needs. In 1956 the CHA began another series of regional conferences for discussion of medico-moral questions arising from Canon or civil law. A major contribution to medical literature was made in 1957 when the CHA published *Medico-Moral Problems* by Gerald Kelly, SJ. In addition to publishing its official journal, the CHA makes periodic contributions to the literature of the hospital and paramedical fields. The staff of the central office has also cooperated closely with St. Louis University's graduate program in hospital administration.

In 1957 CHA, aided by a grant from the Kellogg Foundation, began a program of continuing education. Now self-supporting, this program provides yearly basic and refresher courses for hospital administrators, anesthetists, dietitians, engineers, nursing supervisors, personnel administrators, purchasing agents, and other hospital personnel. In 1961 another Kellogg Foundation grant helped to establish correspondence extension courses in purchasing, engineering, and personnel administration—with courses in other subjects to be added later.

By 1963, 840 member hospitals of the CHA had 142,363 hospital beds and were caring for 5,253,000 patients each year. Approximately 12,000 members of 241 religious orders and congregations cooperate with 302,460 lay personnel in this important work of the Church's apostolate.

[R. T. SHANAHAN]

CATHOLIC INTERRACIAL COUNCILS

The first Catholic Interracial Council in the U.S. came into being in New York on Pentecost Sunday 1934, at an interracial mass meeting convened by the Catholic Laymen's Union, a group of Negro professional and business men founded in 1927 by John *La Farge, SJ. An organizing committee was selected from the 600 persons in attendance; episcopal approval was obtained from Cardinal Patrick Hayes; and a headquarters was established. More than 60 such councils were inaugurated in all parts of the country during the next 30 years.

The New York council's first president was James J. Hoey, in whose memory there was later established a national award given annually to a Negro and a white layman outstanding for the promotion of interracial goodwill in their communities. The first executive secretary, George K. Hunton, and the chaplain, Father La Farge, continued in office until 1962. The headquarters became a major center of Catholic interracial leadership, publishing the monthly *Interracial Review* (founded originally by the *Federated Colored Catholics of the U.S.), providing a clearinghouse of information, distributing interracial materials, rendering consultative services to other councils, and federating with them in 1960 in the *National Catholic Conference for Interracial Justice.

Aims. All councils seek to bring the influence of Catholic teaching to bear upon society so as to secure just and charitable relations between racial or ethnic groups. Precisely how this is to be accomplished is a matter of local initiative and enterprise, for each locality is confronted with its own special problems. Each council is autonomous, responsible only to the bishop of the diocese in which it is located.

The primary activity of the councils is educational: to teach and publicize moral, scientific, and democratic principles concerning race, i.e., the dignity and equality of all men as children of God; the brotherhood of all members of the human family; the accidental nature of skin pigmentation; the right of all people, regardless of race, to share fully in the rights, privileges, and responsibilities of citizenship.

The second major effort of the councils has been to strive to eliminate all vestiges of racial discrimination in Catholic churches, schools, hospitals, and other institutions and societies of all kinds. The first 30 years of unremitting effort yielded a rich harvest of racial understanding, although not all Catholics became convinced that racial justice is a moral issue or ceased to practice racial discrimination in their daily lives.

Third, the councils offer collaboration with existing interracial, social action, and community organizations. Interracial justice is no longer regarded as merely an enlarged phase of the Church's work for a particular group, but as a contribution to the welfare of the community as a whole—including the religious community of the Church and the civil community in which the Church functions in the U.S.

Methods. The councils have long sought to achieve better housing; better job opportunities; and better cultural, educational, and health facilities for minority groups so as to make it possible for them to enter the mainstream of American life. In order to accomplish these goals more effectively, the councils have attempted to move from an amateur, volunteer basis to professional operations with permanent staffs and headquarters.

Amid the racial tensions of the early 1960s, the councils began to devote more time and attention to direct action methods as well as to a wide range of person-to-person activities. Priests were arrested while protesting racial segregation in Baltimore, and nuns picketed against racial discrimination in Chicago. Seminarians took part in an interfaith vigil at the Lincoln Memorial in Washington, D.C., in support of national civil rights legislation. Interracial home visits became increasingly popular, and members of various councils offered their services to tutor underprivileged children in their school work, to provide them with wholesome recreation, and to help young people to become better acquainted with their own communities.

Not least among the councils' accomplishments is the help and guidance given to many institutions and organizations to undertake and to persevere in interracial activities. Similarly, the councils have been a principal means of bringing about better understanding among people of different religious preferences who work together to achieve a better society for people of every race and creed.

Bibliography: J. LA FARGE, *The Race Question and the Negro: A Study of the Catholic Doctrine on Interracial Justice* (New York 1943); *No Postponement: U.S. Moral Leadership and the Problem of Racial Minorities* (New York 1950). T. J. HARTE, *Catholic Organizations Promoting Negro-White Race Relations in the United States* (CUA Stud. in Sociol.; Washington 1947) ch. 1–2.

[J. J. O'CONNOR]

CATHOLIC KNIGHTS OF AMERICA, a fraternal organization founded at Nashville, Tenn., in 1877. James J. McLoughlin promoted this first Catholic fraternal insurance society in the U.S. at a meeting held at Emmett Hall, Nashville, on April 23, 1877. The society, at first called the Order of United Catholics, adopted its present title on June 19, 1877, at the suggestion of the Bishop of Nashville, Patrick A. Feehan (1865–80), and placed itself under the patronage of St. Joseph. Its government is organized under a national council that rules over state councils made up of local branches. On May 29, 1877, the state of Tennessee granted the first operating charter to the branch in Nashville, of which McLoughlin was president. The object of the society is to engage in Catholic fraternal activities by offering insurance plans, organizing spiritual and cultural activities, supporting foreign missions, and promoting religious vocations. Membership has increased greatly in recent years and by 1963 there were approximately 20,000 members throughout the U.S. Financially, it was one of the strongest organizations of its kind, having by Dec. 31, 1962, a margin of safety of 111.71 per cent to meet its insurance claims in the adult department and 126.28 per cent in the juvenile department. The national headquarters of the Catholic Knights of America is in St. Louis, Mo.

[V. L. NAES]

CATHOLIC LAWYERS' GUILDS. Guilds for Catholic lawyers or organizations created for similar purposes exist in many of the Christian countries throughout the world. The French equivalent of the Catholic lawyers' guild was organized in 1945, although a Catholic Group of Law Courts in Lille had been founded just before World War II. In 1949 the Unione Gieuresti Catholica Italiana was organized in Rome. In England several groups are flourishing. Among the more prominent of these are the Newman Association, the Edmund Plower Society, the Thomas More Society, and the Langhorne Society. In Scotland the Thomas More Society is active. The idea of the guild of Catholic lawyers in America was conceived by Monsignor L. J. Evers, pastor of the Church of St. Andrew in New York City, and brought to fruition by his successor, the New York guild's founder and first spiritual moderator, Monsignor W. E. Cashin. In the U.S. there is no national federation of Catholic lawyers. The creation of one has frequently been talked about, but to organize one would entail serious if not insurmountable difficulties.

The purposes of all Catholic law guilds and similarly designed organizations is to aid their members in knowing, understanding, and applying the precepts of Catholicism in the daily practice of the law. A secondary aim is to aid in the spiritual development of the lawyer himself.

Although Catholic guilds such as the above are all designed to accomplish the same ultimate purpose, they individually apply many and diverse means of accomplishing their mission. Some guilds devote time and study to the matter of juvenile delinquency. During World War II the New York guild arranged for the handling of legal problems for the men in the armed services without charge.

The guilds sometimes enter as participants in areas of legal controversy that directly affect the community or society in general. Others present panel discussions to assemblies or discussions that are occasionally broadcasted. Guilds have entered cases and filed briefs as *amici curiae,* for example, in the **Everson v. Board of Education* (330 U.S. 1, 1947) upholding the constitutionality of a New Jersey statute that provided public transportation for school children attending parochial schools.

Most of the Catholic law guilds in America annually sponsor a *Red Mass for the spiritual and mental enlightenment of the members. The first Red Mass was celebrated in 1928 and was sponsored by the New York guild. The custom of having Red Masses, which began early in England, has become traditional among American Catholic law guilds.

Bibliography: R. E. McCormick et al., "The Guild of Catholic Lawyers of New York—A History of 27 Years," *The Catholic Lawyer* 1 (1955) 101–112. A. J. Faidherbe, "The French Federation of Catholic Groups in the Law Courts," *ibid.* 2 (1956) 56–60.

[R. H. NOLAN]

CATHOLIC LAY MISSION CORPS, an apostolate of *lay missionaries devoted to education as a means of total Christian human development and directed particularly to underprivileged peoples in neglected areas. It was founded in 1958 as the Volunteer Teacher Service by the Holy Cross Fathers Fred Underwood and Joseph Haley, and renamed in 1962 to stress the missionary and lay character of the organization. The Corps works in Catholic schools, the field of catechetics, and in youth, vocational, and community development—particularly among the needy of Texas and Latin America. Formation and spirituality of its members are based on liturgical and apostolic living and working in the Church and in the secular community. Special orientation and continuing in-service training are provided. A group of permanent members seeks vocational fulfillment and effectiveness in work toward the formation of volunteers and in the exercise of the apostolate. Members include both married couples and single men and women engaged as teachers, administrators, catechetical and community workers. The age limit is generally 21 to 35 years. Provision is made for living expenses, hospitalization, and social security. A lay director and board are assisted by a full-time chaplain and other volunteer priests. Support through prayer, money, and services is received from Missio, a home auxiliary. With its center in Austin, Tex., the Corps has the approval of the ordinary and is a member of the Committee of International Lay Associations affiliated with the Mission Secretariat and the Latin America Bureau of the National Catholic Welfare Conference.

[J. E. HALEY]

CATHOLIC LIBRARY ASSOCIATION

Professional organization founded to promote the growth and improvement of Catholic libraries and to advance librarianship. In 1964 the association had over 4,000 members in the U.S., Canada, and 17 other countries. Headquarters are in Haverford, Pa.

Cooperation among Catholic librarians was first promoted by Paul J. *Foik, CSC, who introduced a library section into the *National Catholic Educational Association (NCEA) in 1921. The library section met in annual convention with the educational group for 10 years, but in 1931 formed an independent association under the leadership of William Stinson, SJ.

As an independent organization, the Catholic Library Association (CLA) broadened its program to include the production of Catholic bibliographical tools; the stimulation of good writing, publishing, and reading; the development of Catholic library schools; cooperation with standardizing agencies; representation of the interests of libraries before governmental organizations; and assistance in the establishment and development of libraries in foreign countries. The expansion of Catholic educational institutions in the U.S., especially on the secondary and college levels, moved the association to emphasize the training of librarians and to encourage the planning of functional library facilities.

The association is organized into sections, each representing a type of library (school, college, seminary, hospital, parish) or a kind of activity (cataloguing, classification, library education). It is governed by an executive board of 10 elected members and carries on its activities under the supervision of an executive director assisted by a staff of 7. Forty-one local units bring the work of the association to almost every section of the country through regional meetings, workshops, and bibliographical projects. An advisory council serves as the official means of communication between the membership and the executive board, and 23 committees assist in implementing directives. The CLA also maintains representation on liaison committees of 18 national organizations.

The association established the Regina Medal award in 1959 to emphasize its standards for the writing of good literature for children. Recipients include Eleanor Farjeon, Anne Carroll Moore, Padraic Colum, Frederic Melcher, Ann Nolan Clark, May Hill Arbuthnot, and Ruth Sawyer. It gives an annual scholarship (since 1960) for graduate library science study. Other projects include the compilation of bibliographies in specific Catholic fields and the development of standards for selection applicable to Catholic elementary, secondary, college, seminary, and hospital libraries.

The association publishes an official journal, the *Catholic Library World*; a quarterly *Catholic Periodical Index*; and an annual *Guide to Catholic Literature* and *Catholic Booklist*. It has also sponsored publication of *An Alternative Classification for Catholic Books, Catholic Subject Headings, Catholic Bookman's Guide, Books for Catholic Colleges*, and the *Catholic Supplement* to the *Standard Catalog for High School Libraries*.

Although a unit of the CLA was established in Ontario in 1959, Canada has also an Association Canadienne des Bibliothécaires de Langue Française, founded in 1943 in the Province of Quebec for the purpose of aiding libraries in French Canada. The secretariate in Montreal serves a membership of 600 and uses French as its official language. Since it received its 1960 charter from the federal government in Ottawa, the association is not formally a Catholic organization, but all members are Catholic and most of the member libraries are located in Catholic institutions.

Bibliography: Catholic Library Association, *Handbook and Membership Directory, 1963–1964* (Haverford, Pa., 1963).

[M. C. CARLEN]

CATHOLIC NEAR EAST WELFARE ASSOCIATION, the pope's mission aid for the Near and Middle East and principal support of the Oriental Congregation, founded March 11, 1926. Pius XI had decreed that all American organizations working for Russia and the East be consolidated and that the funds collected be placed at the disposal of the papacy for the Church in the Near and Middle East. The organizations consolidated were: The Pontifical Mission for Russia, headed by Edmund A. Walsh, SJ; the Catholic Near East Welfare Association, established in Philadelphia by

Msgr. Richard Barry-Doyle in 1924; and the American branch of The Catholic Union, an organization founded in Germany. Approving this consolidation, the American Bishops resolved on Sept. 15, 1926, that "The Catholic Near East Welfare Association shall be the sole instrumentality authorized to solicit funds for Catholic interests in these regions and shall be so recommended to the entire Catholic population in the United States . . .." On Aug. 20, 1931, Pius XI specified that the funds collected should be used in mission territories confided to the Oriental Congregation and ordered that the Association should receive 9 per cent of the annual Mission Sunday collection gathered throughout the U.S. The Catholic Near East Welfare Association thus took its place side by side with the Society for the Propagation of the Faith and other pontifical mission aids. In addition to providing material support for the Oriental Congregation, the Association attempts—by means of a weekly column in the Catholic press, publications, and lectures—to spread information about the Eastern rites. Cardinal Patrick Hayes became president of the Association in 1931, and was succeeded in 1939 by Cardinal Francis Spellman. The following have served as national secretary: Rt. Rev. James B. O'Reilly (1931–41), Rt. Rev. Bryan J. McEntegart (1941–43), Rt. Rev. Thomas J. McMahon (1943–55), Rt. Rev. Peter P. Tuohy (1955–60), and Rt. Rev. Joseph T. Ryan (1960–).

[J. T. RYAN]

CATHOLIC ORDER OF FORESTERS

A fraternal beneficiary society, founded on May 24, 1883, by 42 men of Holy Family parish in Chicago, Ill. On that date the society obtained a charter from the state under the title of the Illinois Catholic Order of Foresters. The goal was to acquire a membership of 1,000, with the plan that when a member died, each of the others would contribute $1 toward a $1,000 benefit for the widow. Men of all ages were admitted on an equal assessment basis. The movement spread rapidly; and after a unit was established in Wisconsin in 1888 (the same year in which extension into Canada made the society international), the corporate name was changed to Catholic Order of Foresters. Membership was extended in 1928 to boys from birth to age 16, and since 1953, to women and girls, thus creating a complete Catholic family society with father, mother, and children associating for religious, athletic, social, cultural, and other fraternal activities. The admission age for all is from birth to 65 years.

Participation in the charitable purpose of providing life insurance protection for men whose economic circumstances denied them such protection with the insurance companies of the late 19th century was the original object. This, along with the ideal of practicing Catholic life, continues to be the membership requirement. Units, known as subordinate courts, are generally located in a parish and perform direct fraternal and charitable services for the parish and community, and for persons in need, in accordance with Forester principles of Friendship, Unity, and Christian Charity, ideals developed from the virtues of faith, hope, and charity inscribed on the emblem of the order. The courts operate on majority rule, under a representative form of government. A quadrennial convention of representatives is the supreme authority and elects a high court of five executive officers and ten trustees to govern, direct policy, and operate routine business between conventions from the main offices in Chicago. Each court has a spiritual director. The following have been the spiritual directors of the high court: Abps. Patrick A. Feehan and James E. Quigley; and Cardinals George Mundelein, Samuel Stritch, and Albert Meyer, all of the Chicago archdiocese.

The original flat assessment system was wisely recognized as financially inadequate and was gradually eliminated through a graded system of assessment insurance in 1895; a national fraternal congress table of rates in 1913; and a scientifically established, actuarially correct, American experience table of rates and reserves in 1922. Subsequently, rates were consistently reduced to conform to advancing longevity. In 1963 the Commissioners 1958 Standard Ordinary 2½ per cent Mortality Table was adopted. As of Dec. 31, 1962, death claims paid totaled $112,910,000. Donations for church, charity, education, and relief were $16,500,000. Assets of $79,562,639 included $61,445,249 segregated as insurance reserves. Nearly $100,000 is expended annually on an active juvenile program for the religious, physical, mental, and moral development of young members. Licensed in 30 states, the District of Columbia, and 6 Canadian provinces, the society in 1962 operated through 1,315 adult courts and 1,137 juvenile courts with a total of 187,457 members holding $252,092,131 of insurance protection.

[R. T. TOBIN]

CATHOLIC PRESS, ARTICLES ON. The Catholic press is covered by a generic article, CATHOLIC PRESS, that specifies the ideals and goals of that press, and by an extensive historical survey of the rise and development of the Catholic press, by country and region, entitled CATHOLIC PRESS, WORLD SURVEY. As in the surveys of national literatures, prominent individuals in the history of the Catholic press are marked with an asterisk (*) in the surveys, indicating treatment in separate articles. The histories of prominent Catholic publishing houses fall in this area. Related topics, such as the history of publishing and paperbacks, fall into their schematic place under LITERATURE, ARTICLES ON.

See also JOURNALISM, CATHOLIC; PRESS ASSOCIATIONS AND SERVICES, CATHOLIC; UNIVERSITY PRESSES, CATHOLIC.

[H. C. GARDINER]

CATHOLIC PRESS

The press in the Western world had its beginnings in printing and publishing, since there was then no real distinction between the two functions. This survey, accordingly, covers the origin of printing and publishing (1) from the beginning to approximately 1520; (2) its development from 1520 to the late 18th century, when the modern Catholic press generally began to emerge. This modern history is traced, country by country and area by area, in the composite article CATHOLIC PRESS, WORLD SURVEY.

The transition from manuscripts to printed book in the 15th and early 16th centuries is covered in the article *Incunabula. (*See* BOOK, THE MEDIEVAL; BOOK, THE PRINTED.) Up to the Reformation, all this printing and publishing was Catholic, in the sense that many of the products were Bibles, theological and devotional works, or that the printers were frequently commissioned by the Holy See itself or by other ecclesiastical authorities.

Catholic Press to 1520

Printing was technologically the first major mass-production industry; culturally, it revolutionized communication through provision of identical, correct copies of all forms of writing; it gave printed documents dominance over oral and MS transmission and permitted an indefinite geographical and chronological spread of information.

Forms Prior to Printing. The invention of printing in the 15th century developed from earlier forms of communication. Handwritten books in roll and codex form were common among the Egyptians, Hebrews, Greeks, and Romans. Early in the Christian period the codex form of folded-leaf signatures of papyrus, parchment, or vellum was adopted, especially, at first, in the production of Biblical MSS in the 14th century. Throughout the Middle Ages the monastic *scriptorium was the source of the bulk of codices until, with the rise of universities and the emergence of commercial and political needs, a class of secular scribes came into being. By mid-15th century there were several thousand known secular copyists.

By the early 15th century, paper prints from wood blocks, called xylographica, were produced in quantity to meet popular needs. At first these woodcuts were printed on a single sheet, as seen in the 1423 St. Christopher print; later, block books of many sheets developed. Many of the block prints and books appeared in Germany and the Netherlands, often being produced by the *Brethren of the Common Life, who have been credited with 25 per cent of all 15th-century book production. Because of the number of xylographica, it was once assumed that printing from metal type evolved directly from this form. It is now recognized that technical aspects of printing from wood and metal differ radically and should be considered as separate forms answering a common need. Both woodblocks and metal type used existing MS styles as models. By 1480, block books began to disappear; the bilingual Spanish-Tagalog *Doctrina Christiana* (Manila 1593) is a late example, probably undertaken in xylographic form because of lack of suitable type or the desire to reproduce over many years large quantities of a standard work for which the blocks could be preserved.

Development after Printing. The European invention of printing from movable metal type began in Germany (*c.* 1440–50), in what might broadly be termed a "Catholic climate," with the consent and, at times, the active encouragement of the hierarchy. However, it was primarily an enterprise in the hands of laymen who had the intellectual and economic incentives and who supplied the necessary personnel and capital. Printing succeeded because of the various religious, cultural, social, and technical developments of the preceding 3 centuries. Chief among these at first were the establishment of Catholicism in western Europe (within which monasticism was a major institution), the tradition of Roman and Canon Law, and the international use of Latin. From the 12th to the 15th centuries, the rise of universities, the expansion of urban life, the spread of commerce (which gave rise to a class of merchant princes and lawyers), the origin of vernacular languages, and the growth of national parliaments, as well as of international church councils, all developed a need for more available and more accurate forms of written communication. The growing class of lay readers provided the intellectual and financial base for success.

On the technical side, paper manufacture had begun in Spain in the 12th century and had reached Italy by 1270 and Germany by 1320; a viscous ink needed for metal type was a by-product of oil painting in the early 15th century; the press was already employed in the olive and grape industries; and knowledge of metallurgical processes as used by goldsmiths and bell casters was well advanced. The calligraphic work of scribes in monasteries and universities had established styles of letter formation and decoration that were emulated by the protoprinters. Thus, the inventor of printing was able to adapt from the work of his predecessors and, above all, to provide a major communication breakthrough in meeting the needs of his time and future ages.

Printing has been described as "the rendering of existing forms and conventions [of the MS period] in a new medium." The essence of the invention consisted in providing a tool, a casting-box, to hold the brass matrices from which individual pieces of type could be accurately cast in large quantities. Early experiments probably reproduced short works, such as a German apocalyptic poem, a calendar, various issues of Donatus's Latin grammar, and papal letters of indulgence. The major experiment was the Constance Missal. The so-called Gutenburg Bible, bibliographically described as the 42-line Bible (from the average number of lines in a column), was apparently completed somewhat prior to Aug. 24, 1456, the date inscribed by the hand rubricator in the Mazarin Bible. Because by that date Johann *Gutenberg had lost his plant and equipment to Johann Fust, this famous Bible is really the product of the firm of Fust and Peter *Schöffer, who had begun printing in 1455. Gutenberg, with some equipment remaining after his bankruptcy, may subsequently have printed a 36-line Bible. In 1457 Fust and Schöffer produced a Psalter, the first dated and signed printed book, with which, technically, the invention of printing was completed, as it achieved the prime objective of two-color (red and black) printing required for liturgical books. Schöffer's displays at the Frankfort fairs contributed to the widespread dissemination of printing and led to the establishment of hundreds of firms during the 16th century, which became known as the incunabula period.

The rapid increase in the number of printing presses in operation had an important cultural effect by making available to the reading public a growing number of books and pamphlets in vernacular languages. The early printers were generally not idealists or artists but businessmen who worked for profit. Each printer was his own publisher, in competition with his rivals, and attempted to discover new markets for his products. By 1500 nearly all the Greek and Roman classics, as well as many of the scholar's Latin books, were made available to laymen in translation by enterprising printers. The Bible was printed in nearly every European language. In England, printed translations of the Bible were proscribed by the state as a result of the Lollard heresy; yet even there William *Caxton incorporated

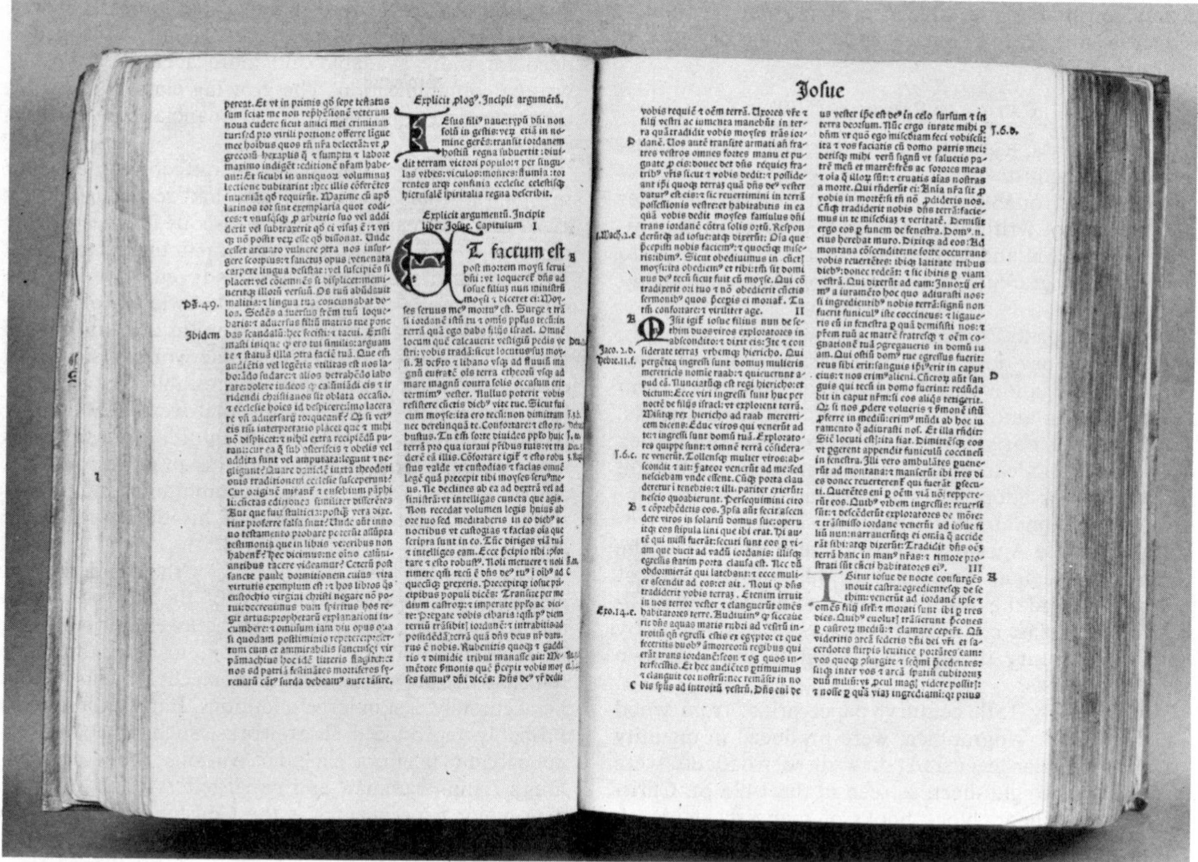

Fig. 1. Bible printed in Basel by Johann Froben, 1491. It was the first edition of the Bible in the octavo size.

sections of the Bible into his translation of *James of Voragine's *Legenda aurea* (*Golden Legend,* 1483).

Printing spread throughout Europe with incredible speed. More than 40,000 titles were printed by 1500. At a moderate estimate there were 200 copies in the average edition, meaning that between 1450 and 1500 some 8 million books were printed, more than were produced by hand during the preceding millennium.

In 1905, before European national boundaries had been altered by two world wars, an estimate of the number and location of printing presses existing in 1500 showed the following distribution.

Country and date of first press	No. of cities	No. of presses
Germany (1447)	54	213
Italy (1465)	79	532
Switzerland (1466)	9	29
Holland (1469)	14	37
France (1470)	43	163
Belgium (1473)	7	30
Austria-Hungary (1473)	10	20
Spain (1473)	27	72
England (1476)	2	13
Denmark (1482)	2	2
Sweden (1483)	3	5
Portugal (1487)	5	7
Montenegro (1493)	1	1
Turkey (1494)	1	1
Totals	257	1,125

[E. P. WILLGING]

FROM 1520 TO LATE 18TH CENTURY

Printing in the 16th century witnessed the rise of a succession of famous printing families in various European centers: Aldus Manutius in Venice, Froben in Basel, Badius and the Estiennes in Paris, and the Plantins in Antwerp. They realized the importance of good type design and illustration and directed their activities to satisfy the widespread Renaissance desire for learning in all fields. Since Latin was the language of scholarship, every printer's work was international in scope.

Italy. The greatest Venetian printer was Aldus *Manutius. His reputation rests on his octavo series of Greek and Latin authors based upon exact scholarship. Inexpensive small books also were an innovation that marked the beginning of the contemporary book and of modern publishing techniques. Moreover, in these small books Manutius produced a new type face known as chancery, italic, or Aldine, modeled on the calligraphy used for Vatican briefs. The new design began a vogue and was especially popular for octavo books printed between 1502 and 1540.

Another variety of the italic derived from the more formal Vatican chancery hand was cut for Ludovico degli Arrighi and based on his own script. From 1524 to 1527 Arrighi used two different fonts; the second font had great influence on subsequent typography, as seen in the work of the Roman printer Antonio Blado (1490–1567), who devoted most of his career to the printing of books at the Vatican. Over 430 books, largely bulls and official Church documents, issued from his press. His output of Greek texts was considerable, and Pope Paul III chose him (1539) to print Greek MSS for the Vatican Library.

Although the Venetian Council gave Aldus exclusive rights to his new italic type face, the privilege was of no help outside of Venice and he had to compete with pirated editions issued in other countries, some bearing the name of Aldus. The Aldus Greek type face also was frequently imitated, but it was his fine roman letters, cut by his skilled craftsman Francesco Griffi, that were later copied in France by Garamond and Colines. Although ignored in the 18th and 19th centuries, the Aldine Roman is today the basis for the finest typography on two continents.

Counterfeiting and Papal Privilege. A serious problem for printers was counterfeiting, which was a common practice in the absence of copyright. As a protection, printers applied for an exclusive license ("privilege") to print and sell specified works. It was granted for a limited period—2 to 10 years. Venetian authorities often granted a patent that carried the exclusive right to print in Venice for a specified duration, exacting a promise that the printer would not leave Venice before the term expired. Manutius was granted a privilege for Greek works, for Latin translations from the Greek, and for the use of his Greek and italic type faces. Penalties for counterfeiting usually included the confiscation of counterfeit copies and a monetary fine.

Papal privileges also were granted for important works printed not only in Rome and the Papal States, but at many other places in Italy and outside the pope's secular jurisdiction abroad, such as at Basel. Any infringement carried the threat of excommunication, a fine, and the confiscation of the offending books. The earliest known example of papal privilege was that granted to Manutius for a 10-year period with a warning to all Italian printers against the reprinting of his Greek and Latin classics in his types or any similar imitation. Leo X made many such grants.

The Holy See and Printing. The need of a printing press close to the Holy See was considered as early as 1539 when Paul Manutius, the son of Aldus, suggested that some unprinted Greek texts in the Palatina (as the Vatican Library was then called) be published. Apparently the project had already been assigned to Blado, but he had to wait until 1549 before receiving the title of Printer to the Apostolic Camera. The most important of his undertakings was Eustathius's commentary on the *Iliad,* the first volume appearing in 1542 and the third in 1549; a volume of indexes appeared later.

A serious problem for the Church in the 16th century was the deluge of printed heretical books that swept across the Continent from Germany, Switzerland, England, and the Netherlands. Prior to the invention of printing, the small number of MSS had not posed this problem. The Council of Trent was opened in 1545 to deal, among other matters, with Protestant publications. One result was the printing of a catalog of restricted books (*Index Auctorum et Librorum*) in 1559 at Rome (see INDEX OF FORBIDDEN BOOKS). Among other planned Tridentine projects that required additional printers in Rome was the publication of disciplinary decrees, a Catechism, and a revised Latin Bible. Paul Manutius left for Rome in 1561 to become a second official printer to the Holy See, but his productions were limited to theology and scholarship. His first printed book was a work by Cardinal Reginald *Pole. He also issued the *Catechismus ex decreto Concilii Tridendini ad parochos* in 1566. While Manutius did produce some contemporary theological books, the main concern of the Holy See was with disciplinary decrees. This left little time for scholarly projects, and Paul suspended his operations at Rome in 1570 and returned to the family press in Venice.

An interest in cultural activities led Ferdinando de' Medici (1549–1609), a son of Cosimo, to sponsor some typographical projects for the Holy See in the creation of the Medicean Press, specializing in Oriental books. The noted French type designer Robert Granjon, who had done considerable work for Plantin at Antwerp, was invited to engrave punches for Arabic and several other Oriental languages. A magnificent Arabic folio edition of the four Gospels (*Evangelia Arabice,* 1590), with 150 wood engravings, is a masterpiece of type design. The press also produced a *Missale Chaldaicum* in 1596, and then was transferred to Florence. Its successor, the press of Jacobus Luna, was apparently connected with the Maronite College in Rome and printed only books required by this Eastern Church. Its first book was the *Liber ministri Missae* (1596). Evidently the press operated privately, as did that which the Jesuits set up in their Collegio Romano in the same year.

The Vatican Press. The Vatican Press was originally established by Sixtus V in 1587 when Domenico Basa was made its first director to print the Vulgate edition

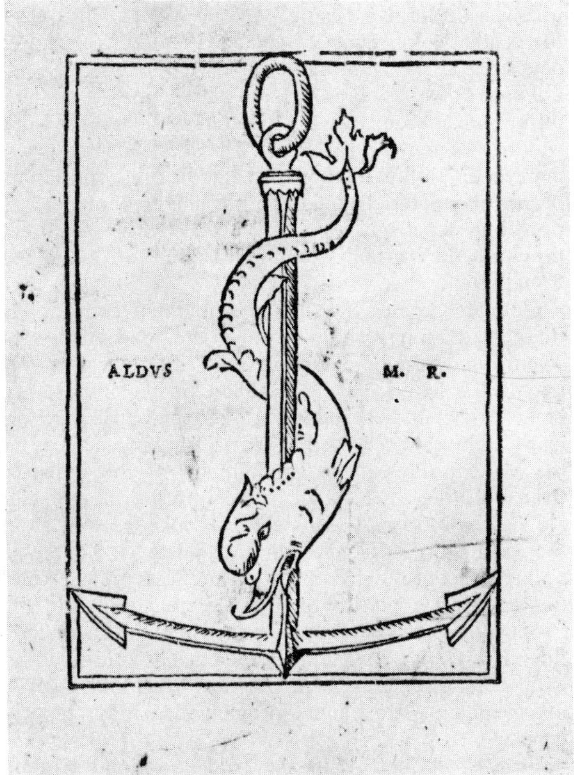

Fig. 2. The famed dolphin and anchor printer's device of the Venetian printer Aldus Manutius.

of the Bible. This printing, commonly known as the Sistine Bible, appeared in 1590, but with a new scheme of paragraphing and the elimination of the system of cutting up the text into verses that Robert Estienne had invented. Because of typographical shortcomings, all available copies were taken out of circulation. A revised edition under the editorship of Robert *Bellarmine was printed in 1592. The press expanded with the publication of a number of patristic works. A quarto Vulgate was issued in 1593, followed 5 years later by an octavo Bible.

When Andrea Brogiotti became head of the Vatican Press in 1626, the Church was increasing her activities in foreign missionary fields. This required an extensive collection of matrices and type fonts to provide official documents. These were assembled in the publication of *Indice de Caratteri* (1628), which comprises Greek, Latin, Oriental, and music type faces. A second official press was established at the Vatican in 1626 to assist the Congregation for the Propagation of the Faith. The printing program was limited exclusively to the needs of the foreign missions, such as catechetical, grammatical, and liturgical books in Eastern languages. Linguistic scholarship was also a necessity and occasioned *Prodromus Coptus* (1628), by Athanasius *Kircher, SJ, a work that marked the first use of Coptic type and also initiated the study of Egyptian hieroglyphics.

The early decades of the 19th century were unfortunate for printing presses of the Vatican. The impact of *Napoleon I on the Papal States was disastrous: the Treaty of Bologna (1796) required Pope *Pius VI to surrender some 500 MSS. Much Arabic and Greek typographical material was expropriated for the use of the armed forces in Egypt and for the installation of a press on the Ionian Islands. After a series of transfers, the Vatican collection of matrices and punches was deposited at the Imprimerie de la République.

Peace between *Pius VII and Napoleon was of short duration, for Rome was occupied in 1808 and the Pope was a prisoner 1 year later. The Vatican Press suspended operations; in spite of Napoleon's confiscation of printing materials, the Pope was able to compose and print one papal bull, that of June 10, 1809, which announced the formal excommunication of Napoleon Bonaparte.

Vatican Council I in 1870 stimulated printing, in that the attending bishops had to be provided with extensive printed data on Church matters. But it was largely Leo XIII's letter (Aug. 18, 1883) on the importance of historical studies, following the opening of the Vatican Archives (1881), that led to growing activity at the Vatican Press. The appointment of the dynamic Franz *Ehrle, SJ, resulted in the printing of new catalogues of MSS and 15th-century books, as well as in the issuance of facsimile editions and texts.

Pius X consolidated the Vatican Press (1909) and the printing activities of the Congregation for the Propagation of the Faith under one roof with the official title Tipografia Polyglotta Vaticana. It continued to issue official documents in practically all languages—liturgical texts, missionary propaganda, and scholarly works.

France. Around 1530 the French scholar-printers assumed international leadership with a unique typographical style, and Paris became the European center in the book arts. The first in quality printing was Jodocus Badius Ascensius (1462–1535?), who employed roman type faces that, although heavy, were regarded as clearer and more legible than the prevailing gothic fonts. Nearly 400 editions, most of them in folios, came from the press of Ascensius.

The Estiennes. The Estienne family played a dominant role in printing for 150 years. The founder of the house, Henri Estienne (d. 1520), was well known for the accuracy of his texts and for his woodcut-borders in Renaissance style. Within 8 years he printed more than 100 editions of the classics in the Aldine tradition. Upon his death, his foreman Simon de Colines (fl. 1520–46) administered the press until Henri's son Robert was of age to assume control. Colines then embarked on an independent career and produced 734 books.

Robert Estienne (1503–59) had a reputation as a Latin scholar when he succeeded to his father's business with the intention of promoting the study of Latin. He was the compiler and printer of a Latin dictionary (*Thesaurus linguae Latinae,* 1538) that became a standard work and was still being reprinted as late as 1734. His greatest achievement was a Latin edition of the New Testament (1523), which, however, introduced readings that were far from the accepted ones and brought him into conflict with the theological faculty of the University of Sorbonne. Bible publications made him widely known, for he printed 11 editions of the whole Bible, 8 of them in Latin, 2 in Hebrew, and 1 in French, and 12 editions of the NT, of which 5 were in Greek, 5 in Latin, and 2 in French. Francis I appointed him printer to the King for Hebrew and Latin in 1539, and a year later, the King's printer for Greek. This resulted in Estienne's commissioning of Guillaume Lebe to engrave Hebrew characters and in Claude Garamond's producing of Greek, roman, and italic type faces of great beauty.

The accession of Henry II (1547) left Robert without a patron; his brother Charles came into control, and Robert moved (1551) to the more congenial climate of Geneva, where he set up a publication outlet for the theological writings of John Calvin. The original firm in Paris remained Catholic; its chief contribution was the beauty of its printing of standard classical texts.

Claude Garamond. One of the most artistic typeface designers, Claude Garamond (d. 1561), cut the three different sizes known as *Grecs du Roi* and demonstrated that the Aldine cursive could be adapted to a design of unusual grace. All sizes appear in Estienne's folio NT, one of the most striking books of the century. Most of the present typefaces known by the name Garamond, however, are actually derived from the less skillful hand of Jean Jannon. Apparently Jannon worked with Garamond's alphabet as his model and transmitted the spirit of the original in a type known as "Caracters de l'Université."

Geofroy Tory. Among the most gifted of French Renaissance book designers was Geofroy Tory (1480?–1533) of Bourges, scholar and printer. A prolonged stay in Italy inspired his book decorations. At the beginning of his printing career he was associated with Simon de Colines, but later he established his own firm as an engraver, printer, and bookseller. In contrast to the heavy style of German gothic type designs, Tory's were lighter and blended harmoniously with the roman

Fig. 3. Printers operating a 16th-century press, woodcut from the title page of a book printed in Paris by Michel Vascosan in 1536.

type faces of Colines and Garamond. His genius is reflected in the floral evolutions that he put into exquisite use in borders, decorations, and title pages. Several sets of ornamental initial letters were cut by Tory to harmonize both with the typeface and the headpiece. As a publisher he often utilized the services of colleagues with similar high standards. Jodocus Badius was contracted to print for him an elegant series of the classics translated into French. Lovers of fine printing prize his numerous *Books of Hours,* which improved on the Estienne typeface in their delicacy of execution. Tory was also a writer; his best-known work, *Champfleury* (1529), concerns in part the form of alphabet letters and helped to popularize in France his own enthusiasm for roman type.

The early printers at Lyons gained notoriety by pirating Aldine and other model editions of the classics. But the craftsmanship of Sebastian Gryphius (*c.* 1524–56) brought the city a reputation for attractive italic types used in his numerous convenient pocket editions of the classics. Guillaume Roville, also of Lyons, adopted the same popular format in his series of Latin and Greek classics. The two series of Hans *Holbein's (1497–1543) woodcuts, the Dance of Death and the Old Testament illustrations, were printed at Lyons by John Frellon. These are remarkable for their simplicity of line. In the fifth edition (1549), English inscriptions were substituted for Latin ones, with a view to sale among the reading public in England. The city of Lyons became a center for a group of skilled engravers, of whom the most outstanding was Bernard Salmon, or Le Petit Bernard, who appears to have done all of his superb woodcuts and other decorations for Jean de Tournes.

Jean de Tournes. The finest Lyonese printer was Jean de Tournes (1504–64), who had begun as a foreman for Gryphius, although he was more influenced by the Paris press. His interest in history led him to employ roman types cut probably by Robert Granjon and used for the folio books of Comines, Froissart, Claude and Guillaume Paradin, and Jean de Maire. He obtained a beautiful italic type face to print exquisite editions of French poets, such as Pernette du Guillet, François Habert, Louis Labbe, Margaret of Navarre, and Pontus de Tyard.

Robert Granjon. The attractive series of italics employed by Tournes were designed by Robert Granjon (fl. 1550–1600). His type faces were acclaimed and used at Lyons, Frankfurt, Nuremberg, Basel, Florence, Rome, London, and Antwerp. Plantin bought his italic type face. After settling at Lyons, Granjon printed some 20 books in an unusual rendition, "Civilité," based on cursive gothic French handwriting and so called because *La Civilité puérile* by Erasmus was one of the first books printed in such a type. Granjon spent his last years in Rome on special assignments for the Vatican Press, working particularly on Oriental type faces.

One of the greatest printing ventures in France was the publication, beginning in 1632, of the **Jesuit Relations,* annual reports from the missionaries in North America. This quickly became a best-seller and had incalculable influence on European attitudes toward the "noble savage."

Spain. Printing in Spain began in such cities as Alcalá de Henares, Barcelona, Burgos, Medina, Salamanca, Saragossa, Seville, Toledo, Valencia, and Valladolid. Seville became the capital in 1560 and had its first printing establishment in 1568. The total number of books from all the Spanish presses during the 16th century is estimated at 10,000; yet the total production of books at Lyons alone for the same period was some 13,000.

A striking Spanish printing project was the scholarly Polygot Bible, edited by Stunica under the sponsorship of Francisco *Ximénez de Cisneros and printed at Alcalá (1514–17). It is commonly known as the Complutensian Bible, after *Complutum,* the Latin name for Alcalá. This vast undertaking took some 10 years. Its six folio volumes contain, in parallel columns, the Hebrew and Greek versions of the OT, and the Greek and Latin of the NT, with critical notes and a Hebrew dictionary.

Holland and Belgium. The great competitor of the Estiennes was the Frenchman Christophe *Plantin, who settled in Antwerp when it was the intellectual capital of the Netherlands, and next to Paris the most important European book center. Although Plantin does not rank with Aldus, the Estiennes, or Froben as an editor or in the quality of his productions, he was a courageous publisher destined to become the greatest in northern Europe. His Antwerp office had branches in Paris, Leyden, and Salamanca. At one time Plantin operated 22 presses.

Plantin was granted valuable exclusive patents to print all liturgical works in the Spanish Netherlands, and from his presses poured forth a mass of educational, musical, and theological literature. These profitable privileges enabled him in 1559 to embark upon a costly project to surpass the Ximénes Polyglot Bible. His eight-volume work was completed in 5 years and printed in an edition of 1,200 copies; the text is in Hebrew, Latin, Greek, and Chaldaic. This was his most important work, but it proved a financial disaster.

The Plantin press was officially Catholic, but on one occasion during his absence it issued a heretical pamphlet, and some unsigned heretical books without imprint were clandestinely printed without Plantin's knowledge. Plantin was succeeded in his business by a son-in-law, John Moretus, and Moretus in turn by his son Balthasar. The firm continued under the direction of Plantin's descendants, but with a decline in printing.

Prior to Plantin's establishment in Antwerp, several smaller printing firms had been making significant contributions. Jean Loe printed many philosophical and theological dissertations for the University of Louvain, and a Catholic Flemish Bible translated by Nicolaus Van Winghe was printed for the University in 1546 by Bartholomaeus Gravius. It became recognized as the standard Vulgate until replaced by the Vatican Bible (1590).

A later significant development was the beginning of the work of the *Bollandists, whose corporate scholarship on the *Acta sanctorum* (1643) set a superb standard of historical research that they have since maintained.

Germany. The Reformation occasioned from both Catholics and Reformers a flood of books and pamphlets, not only in Latin but also in German, later in English, and finally, but to a lesser degree, in French. Within the first century of printing the press became a potent instrument of argument, persuasion, public appeal, and propaganda addressed to the general public. The Protestant movement itself was in part an appeal to history. The arguments were often historical, and historical criticism became a chief weapon for both parties. On the Protestant side it found expression in a book commonly called the *Magdeburg Centuries* (*Historia Ecclesiae Christi,* or *Centuriae Magdeburgenses,* Basel 1559–74), the first comprehensive history of Christianity to A.D. 1400, written from the ultra-Protestant view. It was edited by Matthias Flacius (1520–75), who began the project at Magdeburg in 1552 (*see* CENTURIATORS OF MAGDEBURG). In reply, the Vatican librarian Caesar *Baronius published *Annales Ecclesiastici* (1588–1607), telling the story as he saw it, century by century up to 1198.

German printing during the Reformation was engaged mainly in producing controversial tracts. Besides the active presses mentioned earlier, there was a vigorous press at Wittenberg, the home of Luther and a focal point for Protestant pamphlets. Presses were established in two German-speaking Swiss cities, Basel and Zurich. Finally, Frankfort arose as a center in the latter half of the 16th century.

Johann *Froben of Basel was one of the leading printers of his day, producing 256 titles in Latin and French. His publications were on the side of Catholicism; Erasmus joined him in 1514 as an author, editor, and proofreader. In 1516 Froben published Erasmus's edition of the first Greek text of the NT. Hans Holbein the Younger joined Froben and Erasmus in 1515 and, until his departure for England 11 years later, contributed decorative initials, title borders, headpieces, and Biblical illustrations to Froben's books. Johannes *Amerbach was the first Basel printer to use a roman type face. His major contribution was a scholarly printing of St. Jerome's works. Three of his sons became scholars in Latin, Greek, and Hebrew and joined their father in the production of this costly and laborious project.

Denmark. The outstanding printer of Catholic publications in Denmark during the Reformation period was Canon Poul Raeff. He printed mostly ritual books and Catholic propagandist literature. At the suggestion of Abp. Erik Valkendorf of Trondheim he published a *Missale Nidrosiense* for the Trondheim Diocese in 1519. His last publication appeared in 1533.

Sweden. Swedish printing of the 16th century was inaugurated with the establishment of a press in Uppsala in 1510 by Paul Grijs; a *Psalterium* for the diocese was his first publication. In 1523 Bp. Hans *Brask established a small press at Söderkoping to produce liturgical books for his diocese. Later, propagandist Catholic literature was added to their output. Other names associated with Catholic publishing in Sweden are Bartholomaeus Fabri and Jurgen Richolff the Younger; the latter became especially important in the history of Swedish printing.

Iceland. In an effort to further the education of his priests, the Catholic Bishop of Iceland, Jon Arason (1484?–1550), invited (*c.* 1530) a Swedish printer, Jon Matthiasson, to establish a press in the episcopal residence at Holar. In 1534 he published *Breviarium Holense,* the only book known to have been printed in Iceland prior to the Reformation.

England. The development of Catholic printing in England was handicapped through a series of governmental restrictions that was to influence all book production and distribution for 150 years from the middle of the 16th century. To limit the spread of heresy, a system of book licensing was begun. The Stationers' Company was issued a charter in 1557 whereby only members of the Company were permitted to print anything for sale, and every member was required to enter into the Company's register the title of any book to be printed. The register entry was the only method of copyright recognized at the time, and such limitation of the craft of printing to a known circle made it easier to control publications of the secret presses.

An injunction issued by Elizabeth in 1559 required the approval of any book in advance through the issuance of a license and also permitted books already in print to be banned. The regulations were indifferently observed, and a Star Chamber decree of 1586 codified all prior enactments and gave the authorities a tighter hold on the press: first, printing was restricted to London and its suburbs, and to one press each at Oxford and Cambridge; second, the number of printers, apprentices, and presses was limited; third, all publications issued without a proper license were banned; finally, the wardens of the Stationers' Company were authorized to search for unlicensed "wildcat" presses and publications. Apparently the suppression of heretical books continued to be a problem, as many were printed abroad and imported surreptitiously. The activity of secret presses in England suggests that the regulations were not strictly enforced. (*See* RECUSANTS; RECUSANT LITERATURE.)

The decree of 1586 continued in force until superseded by the harsher legislation of 1637 and 1643, which led to greater persecution and hindrances to the progress of typography. It was against the severity of these decrees that John Milton wrote his pamphlet in favor of liberty of the press, called *Areopagitica* (November 1644). Yet even Milton excluded Catholicism from freedom of the press.

Dangers to Catholic Printers. The danger to Catholics employed in the book trades throughout this period is therefore quite evident. Though many of them were imprisoned and at least one, William Carter, was put to death (1584), Catholic printing was not entirely suppressed. In the early 1600s John Heigham was instrumental in smuggling a number of Catholic books into England and was particularly active during the time when King James' preoccupation with Spanish and French affairs caused a slackening of the persecution of Catholics in England. One of the most active English Catholic publishers was Richard *Verstegan, who in 1582 produced an account of *Campion's martyrdom and was forced to flee to France. He settled in Antwerp, where he labored as publisher, translator, and writer. His most successful venture was the printing of a Primer or Office of the Blessed Virgin. A number of printers emigrated, particularly to Antwerp and Louvain. Some 18 Catholic writers published works between 1564–67, and about 45 books were issued. It is estimated that approximately 20,000 copies of Catholic books were smuggled into England.

At the close of the 17th century an increasing number of Catholic printers appeared in London and the provinces. In the Stationer's Company register for 1669, Nathaniel Thompson admitted his religion, although he had been in trouble before. Thomas Meighan became established as a London Catholic printer by 1717 and produced an edition of Verstegan's Primer in the same year; it included a catalog of his other publications. Among his other works is a supplement to Dugdale's *Monasticon,* the continuation of the *Philosophical Transactions,* and a number of Bp. R. *Challoner's writings. After 1760 the *Laity's Catholic Directory* was issued, and the day for secret presses and the smuggling of devotional literature from the Continent had passed.

Versions of the Bible. Although the Catholic Bible, as such, did not appear in English translation until the 1582 printing of the NT, parts had been issued much earlier, e.g., Caxton's translation of *Voragine's *Legenda aurea,* of which certain portions are little more than disguised versions of the Bible, containing practically all of the Pentateuch and large sections of the Gospels. The earliest formal translation of any part of the Bible was St. John *Fisher's version of the Penitential Psalms (*The Fruytfull Sayings of Davide,* 1508; six other editions were printed up to 1555, and a later edition in 1714). Paraphrases of the Psalms were printed as follows: in two editions of a Primer (St. Omer's 1617, 1631); by J[ohn] H[awkins] in 1635; in a *Manual of Prayers* (Antwerp 1650); in a Primer (Antwerp 1658); in *The Key to Paradise* (St. Omer's 1675); and in the *Ascent of the Soul,* by Henry Hare (1681). And Thomas Caryll's anonymous printing of the Psalms appeared in 1700 and 1704.

The Apocalypse was popular in penal times, nine editions of Charles Walmesley's *Exposition of the Apocalypse* appearing between 1771 and 1821 under the pseudonym of "Sig. Pastorini." A. *Geddes published a new translation of the OT from Genesis to Ruth in London between 1792 and 1797. English inscriptions accompanied Hans Holbein's famous woodcuts of *Images of the Old Testament,* printed at Lyons (France) in 1549.

For the Rheims and Douay Versions, *see* BIBLE IV, 22.

The accompanying table presents a chronological list of English versions of the Catholic Bible from 1483 to 1950.

ENGLISH CATHOLIC VERSIONS

Date	OT	NT	Psalms	Portion	Whole Bible
1483–99				9	
1500–24			5		
1525–49			2		
1550–74			2		
1575–99		2			
1600–24	1	4	1		
1625–49	1	3	2		
1650–74			2		
1675–99			2		
1700–24		2	3		
1725–49		5			
1750–99	1	8		1	4
1800–49		58	1	4	48
1850–99		33	1	8	35
1900–50	1	33	7	11	15

The Western Hemisphere. Printing did not come to North America until 1638, but it began in Latin America a full century earlier. These beginnings in the Spanish colonies have long been shrouded in obscurity, and at many points the evidence is highly conjectural and open to varying interpretations. For complementary material in the whole area of Latin America, *see* LATIN AMERICA (COLONIAL), DEVELOPMENT AND INFLUENCE OF PRINTING IN.

Mexico. Certain documents seem to imply that one Estéban Martín (fl. 1539) was printing in Mexico in 1533–34, but no specimen of his work has ever been identified, and many authorities reject the tradition. The first certain evidence is a document of June 12, 1539. It shows that Juan Cromberger (d. 1540) of Seville, the foremost printer of Spain, had obtained from the crown the privilege of printing in the new colony. The document is a contract between Cromberger and Juan Pablos (Giovanni Paoli, d. 1561?), an Italian of Brescia, who was to go to Mexico and act as Cromberger's agent. Three months later Pablos arrived in Mexico City and settled at the House of Bells (*Casa de las Campañas*), opposite the residence of the Franciscan Bp. Juan de *Zumárraga. Zumárraga needed some religious books and underwrote the cost of printing most of the earliest works.

The first book printed by Cromberger was *Breve y más compendiosa doctrina christiana en lengua mexicana y castellana* (1539). This was followed by a complementary work, *Manual de Adultos* (1540), of which only a fragment of three pages is extant. The *Doctrina breve* appeared in a new edition on June 14, 1544; it is the earliest surviving book printed on the American continent. In all, 37 books were printed by him, largely in the field of religion. No less than 16 are missionary texts for use among the Indians, 4 are handbooks of an ecclesiastical nature, 2 are texts for students' use in the new university, 2 are of a governmental character, and 1, a pamphlet of public interest, contains an account of an earthquake in Guatemala.

Except for the missionary tracts with certain texts in the native languages, the imprint known as *Speculum conjugiorum* (April 15, 1556) is probably the most important for scholarship, as it provides firsthand material for both the historian and the anthropologist. In Mexico, as elsewhere, one of the major problems of the colonists was to reconcile the social customs of the natives with the standards of European civilization, and in this regard the matter of marriage was one of the most difficult.

Pablos enjoyed a monopoly on all printing in Mexico until 1559, when one of his assistants, Antonio Espinosa, received permission to set up a rival firm, and in 1561 he printed the folio volume of 330 pages known as *Missale Romanum ordinarium.* This service book is considered the most beautiful work of colonial days in the New World. By 1600, 234 imprints had appeared in Mexico and nine presses were in operation, turning out books in Spanish, Mexican, Tarascan, Zapotecan, Mixtecan, and Mayan. The needs of the missionaries encouraged the establishment of private presses. The Franciscans had their press in the Santiago monastery of Tlatelolco (1567–1604), and the Augustinians established a press in the St. Augustine monastery in Mexico City, where Juan Ruiz printed (1626) a history of the Augustinians in America. The Jesuits operated two presses in Mexico City: one at their scholasticate, and another at the College of St. Ildefonse (1577–79) under the supervision of Antonio Ricardo of Turin. His productions were mainly textbooks and some liturgical books. Later the government held that no liturgical books could be printed in Mexico, since such works infringed on the monopoly of the El Escorial monastery in Spain.

At the beginning of the 17th century the Mexican press ceased copying European models. It introduced native ideas and produced an impressive annual list. The number of volumes became notable after 1645 and reached its peak in 1680, averaging from 20 to 28 publications a year until 1700. From 1601 to 1700, Mexican presses produced 1,288 volumes, which reflected the social and educational developments of colonial Mexico.

Over 3,000 books were issued in Mexico from 1701 to 1800. Mexico City remained the printing center for more than 300 years. Printers apparently enjoyed great liberty during this period; restrictive monopolies were established in 1588, and printers were free to establish themselves in any place. The contents of books, however, were subject to a rigorous examination on religious orthodoxy. A catechism in the Michoacán language by Mathurin Gilberti, printed in 1588 by Juan Pablos in Mexico City, was condemned. Censorship in Mexico, however, was abolished in 1811. By Spanish law all printers employed on missionary presses were laymen.

Argentina. As early as 1748 Ladislas Orosz, SJ, had proposed the creation of a printing press. Permission from Spanish officials was obtained in 1764. Father Orosz established the first press in the College of Montserrat at Córdoba, where a lay brother, Pablo

Fig. 4. "Sanctus" woodcut from the "Missale Romanum" printed in Mexico City by Antonio de Espinosa in 1561.

Karer, printed the first work in 1766, a Latin quarto of 90 pages on the beginnings of the college. This was followed in the same year by a pastoral letter in Spanish, of 130 pages in octavo. Printing continued until the Jesuits were expelled in 1767. In 1779 the government purchased their press for 1,000 pesos and transferred it to the orphan asylum in Buenos Aires in 1780. For the next 27 years this former Jesuit printing press was the only one in operation in the whole colony. In 1780 it issued the first newspaper of Argentina, the *Gazeta de Buenos Aires*. For further history of the press in Buenos Aires, *see* LATIN AMERICA (COLONIAL), DEVELOPMENT AND INFLUENCE OF PRINTING IN.

Bolivia. The Jesuits operated a press (1610–12) at their college on Titicaca Lake in the Province of La Paz. Four books with the imprint date of 1612 were issued: a grammar of the Aymara language (*Arte de la lengua Aymara*), a vocabulary of the Aymara tongue, a life of Christ printed both in Aymaran and Spanish, and a similar *confesionario*. All were written by Ludovico *Bertonio, SJ, and were rather large publications of 372, 873, 570, and 350 pages.

Brazil. A secular printer, Antonio de Fonseca, set up a press *c.* 1747, but as soon as the first books were issued, officials in Portugal ordered the press's closure. The Portuguese government was not as receptive to the creation of a press as was the Spanish. The Jesuits nevertheless managed to publish booklets until 1767. All larger works were required to be printed in Portugal.

Colombia. About 1738 the Jesuits set up a printing press in the College of Santafe at Bogotá, formerly called New Granada. In 1739 a lay brother, Francisco de Peña, printed a Latin work on the privileges granted to missionaries. Only a limited number of their publications are extant, and the press ceased operation in 1767.

Ecuador. The present country was part of Colombia until 1830. The Jesuits established a printing press at their house at Hambato (Ambato) *c.* 1750, issuing prayer books, catechisms, leaflets, and a large *Pontificale Romanum*. A German lay brother, Adam Schwarz, was the printer for 9 years. The press was transferred in 1759 to their College of Sain Luis in Quito and continued under Schwarz until 1767. Nine works were issued.

Guatemala. When the missionaries arrived in Guatemala they found natives with an advanced pagan culture; the spread of Christianity was assisted by the use of books printed in Mexico. Francisco *Marroquín's catechism in the Quitché language was printed in Mexico in 1556; other books followed. In 1660 printing began in the city of Guatemala, and up to 1800, 160 books were issued. A complete description of these works appears in J. T. Medina and J. D'Oryan.

Paraguay. For a discussion of printing in the Jesuit missions in Paraguay, *see* LATIN AMERICA (COLONIAL), DEVELOPMENT AND INFLUENCE OF PRINTING IN.

Peru. Antonio Ricardo of Turin had first printed books in Mexico City and established his own press in 1577 adjacent to the Jesuit College, where for 2 years he produced at least one book every 3 months. When the Jesuits set up their own press, Ricardo moved his to Lima, "the city of Kings," and there founded the first printing establishment in South America. Much of his work was done in connection with the University of San Marcos. Because he was a foreigner, complications delayed his getting a license for 4 years. When the license was finally approved, the Jesuits in Lima were searching for a printer for their recently completed catechism, *Tercero catecismo y exposición de la doctrina Christiana.* The text is in the Quechua and Aymara languages, with the Spanish shown above in italics. Ricardo had no competition and hence received permission from the Royal Audiencia to print the book. His work on the catechism was soon interrupted by another commission from the authorities to print a pamphlet, *Pragmática sobre los diez días del año* (1582), announcing a new style calendar made by Pope Gregory XIII. Only one copy of this work survives and is probably the first South American imprint. A larger catechism in Spanish and Quechua, together with a vocabulary of the same languages, was issued in 1586. Ricardo appears to have produced other books on the Jesuit press, and in 1598 he printed in his own name a catechism and the creed. In 1606 the Spaniard Francisco del Canto established his press in Lima, and in the following year he issued a great Quechua grammar; 9 years later he produced the Aymara grammar of Diego de Torres, SJ.

Up to 1820, records show 12,412 books printed in Mexico and 3,948 in Lima. One difficulty faced during the first 3 centuries of printing in Latin America was that presses had to rely on European sources for paper.

For the early days of printing in such areas as China, Japan, the Philippines, and Thailand, *see* CATHOLIC PRESS, WORLD SURVEY, 8.

The U.S. The statutes of the early American colonies were dotted with restrictions on the Catholic religion, and the printing of Catholic books was generally forbidden, even in Maryland, where toleration prevailed. Catholics had to depend on books printed on the Continent by English refugees or in Dublin or London on clandestine presses. The Challoner Bible of 1763–64, printed probably in Dublin, had Americans on its list of subscribers. Evidence shows that missionaries had to transcribe service books by hand.

The earliest attempt at publishing was Challoner's *Garden of the Soul* (1773) by Joseph Crukshank. A *Manual of Catholic Prayers* (Baltimore 1774) was printed by Robert Bell. The sponsor of both books was probably the missionary Robert Molyneux, SJ. Prior to 1776, eight titles by Catholics were printed in the Colonies, including works by Fénelon, Thomas à Kempis, and St. Thomas More. The first known Catholic publisher in the U.S. was Christopher Talbot, who issued Joseph Reeve's *New History of the Old and New Testament* (Philadelphia 1784).

See also CATHOLIC PRESS, WORLD SURVEY, 27; CATHOLIC PRESS, ARTICLES ON.

Bibliography: H. G. ALDIS, *The Printed Book* (3d ed. Cambridge, Eng. 1951). A. F. ALLISON and D. M. ROGERS, *A Catalogue of Catholic Books in English Printed Abroad or Secretly in England, 1558–1640,* 2 v. (London 1956). H. S. BENNETT, *English Books and Readers* (Cambridge, Eng. 1952). T. H. CLANCY, *Papist Pamphleteers . . .* (Chicago 1964). C. J. H. DAVENPORT, *The Book, Its History and Development* (New York 1908; facs. repr. Gloucester, Mass. 1930). H. GENTRY and D. GREENHOOD, *Chronology of Books and Printing* (rev. ed. New York 1936). R. GORMAN, *Catholic Apologetic Literature in the United States, 1784–1858* (CUA StAmChHist 28; Washington 1939). L. I. GUINEY and G. BLISS, eds., *Recusant Poets* (New York 1939). A. HUONDER, *Verdienste der katholische Heidenmission um die Buchdruckerkunst in überseeischen Ländern vom 16.–18. Jahrhundert* (Aachen 1923). D. C. MCMURTRIE, *The Book: The Story of Printing and Bookmaking* (3d ed. New York

1943). S. MORISON, *Four Centuries of Fine Printing* (New York 1944; new. ed. 1960), 272 examples of the work of presses established between 1465 and 1924; *The Typographic Arts* (Cambridge, Mass. 1950). J. C. OSWALD, *A History of Printing* (New York 1928). W. PARSONS, *Early Catholic Americana: A List of Books and Other Works by Catholic Authors in the United States, 1729–1830* (New York 1939). H. POPE, *English Versions of the Bible,* rev. S. BULLOUGH (St. Louis 1952). A. C. SOUTHERN, *Elizabethan Recusant Prose, 1559–1582* (London 1950). S. H. STEINBERG, *Five Hundred Years of Printing* (2d ed. Penguin Bks; Baltimore 1962). D. B. UPDIKE, *Printing Types: Their History, Forms, and Use,* 2 v. (Cambridge, Mass. 1922). L. C. WORTH, ed., *A History of the Printed Book* (New York 1938). V. DE P. ANDRADE, *Ensayo bibliográfico mexicano del siglo XVII* (2d ed. Mexico City 1899). N. LEÓN, *Bibliografía mexicana del siglo XVIII,* 6 v. (Mexico City 1902–08), somewhat incomplete. J. T. MEDINA, *Historia de la imprenta en los antiguos dominios españoles de América y Oceanía,* 2 v. (Santiago de Chile 1958). J. E. O'RYAN, *Bibliografía de la imprenta Guatemala en los siglos XVII y XVIII* (Santiago de Chile 1897). **Illustration credits:** Fig. 1, The Walters Art Gallery, Baltimore. Fig. 2, Library of Congress.

[R. A. BURKE]

CATHOLIC PRESS, WORLD SURVEY

The following survey of the Catholic press around the world reviews the history, the achievements and failures, and the status in the mid-1960s of Catholic newspapers, magazines, and journals of general interest. Specialized publications are treated in separate articles (*see* THEOLOGICAL JOURNALS, SCHOLARLY; LITERARY PERIODICALS, CATHOLIC; BIBLICAL PERIODICALS) and in articles devoted to special disciplines. It is to be noted that in some areas of the world, especially in Africa and Asia, the status of the Church in the mid-1960s was one of crisis and that consequently the Catholic press was subject to sudden and unpredictable changes. All information given in these areas was applicable to the end of 1965.

1. AFRICA

The history and the present status of the Church and of the Catholic press is quite different in the three areas into which the African continent is generally divided: northern, sub-Saharan, and southern Africa.

North African Press. In North Africa, with the exception of the United Arab Republic, Christianity remains a religion of Europeans. The Catholic press, therefore, has been mainly directed toward the European faithful and has been a local supplement to the Catholic publications of France, Italy, and Spain, which constitute the main religious reading of North African Christians. Large-scale immigration to Europe drastically reduced this number when independence came to Morocco, Algeria, and Tunisia, and the local Catholic press suffered greatly. Morocco, however, has a monthly, *Ensemble* (1947), addressed particularly to the clergy and religious, and the Sudan has two biweeklies, *As-Salan* in Arabic and the *Messenger.* Almost every diocese has its weekly or monthly bulletin, along the lines of the traditional French Semaine Religieuse. These publications provide news of the diocese and a means for the bishop to communicate with his priests and people. Several specialized sociological and cultural publications continue to exist, such as the monographs published by the Secretariat Social of Algiers and *Ibla* (1937), a quarterly issued by the *White Fathers in Tunisia.

Below the Sahara. The situation is strikingly different south of the Sahara. The Catholic press there grew out of the needs of a dynamically developing missionary Church and reflects its vitality; in many countries it plays an important role in national life.

The earliest Catholic printing was done on rudimentary presses or even on mimeograph machines scattered in the larger mission centers. It consisted of vernacular catechisms and religious tracts and books adapted to the mentality and culture of the few literate Christians. The development of the press in each country followed the tempo of the general evolution of the people. When secular papers began to appear in a country, the local Catholic bulletins, especially after World War II, were transformed into general newspapers to keep pace with the growing desire of readers to be better and more widely informed.

Early Developments. The first Catholic printing establishment in sub-Saharan Africa was set up (1849) at Ngasobil, Senegal, by the *Holy Ghost Fathers. The first Catholic newspapers for Africans made their appearance at the other end of the continent when the *Mariannhill missionaries in Natal, South Africa, began two papers, one religious and one secular (1888), a venture that lasted only 2 years. The first attempt to publish a monthly in West Africa was made at Saint-Louis, Senegal (1906), by Daniel Brottier, CSSp, but the journal died when he returned to France (1911). The oldest continuously published Catholic paper in Africa in *Munno,* begun (1911) by the White Fathers at Kisubi, Uganda, and published (1965) daily.

Catholic press development in Africa owes much to the *Sodality of St. Peter Claver, which has printed innumerable books in Europe and America since 1920. They are catechisms and pamphlets, principally in African languages, to be used by missionaries. In 1955 the society extended its publishing efforts to Africa, where it began the Marianum Press at Kisubi, Uganda, and other plants at Lusaka, Zambia, and Ibadan, Nigeria. All these efforts encountered special difficulties, many of which still obtain. Since practically the entire Catholic press was initiated and developed by missionary priests, it has had a decidedly clerical outlook and tone. Again, in the absence of native African journalism, the papers and magazines were at first imitations of the press of the colonial powers; only in the mid-1960s did they begin to develop an originality in closer harmony with the African mentality.

Personnel and Financial Problems. Such development requires trained African personnel. The coming of independence attracted many capable men from the Catholic press into government service, thus compounding the problem. For the most part, on-the-job training has been the only possible preparation; a few fortunate men were able to continue this training in Europe or America. The first school of journalism in middle Africa was started by the White Fathers in Mwanza, Tanzania, in 1963.

African papers face many financial problems: all newsprint must be imported from Europe, and printing costs run high; outside of the urban center where a paper is published, practically all papers must be distributed by air, and some even serve several countries. Circulation remains low because the percentage of literate people all over Africa is small, and even for the literate a newspaper is a luxury item. Moreover, individual sales vary greatly from month to month, rising sharply during harvest time and thereafter dras-

Fig. 1. Publications of the Catholic press in Africa, in English, French, Arabic, and other African languages.

tically declining. Readership per paper, however, is high: it is estimated that each weekly has an average of 10 readers. Many are read aloud in a village or posted on bulletin boards; they are rarely thrown away—they wear out. Every Catholic paper is concerned with formation as much as or more than with information, particularly since in Africa radio is now the principal medium of information. The Catholic press does not limit itself to religious formation but is concerned with the social, economic, political, and cultural development of its readers. Its pages are filled with interpretative articles on problems of the day, feature articles, texts of speeches, and reports of meetings. Women's and youth pages and readers' forums are very popular.

West and East Africa. West Africa's leading weekly newspaper is *Afrique Nouvelle* (1947), founded by the White Fathers at Dakar and now completely staffed by African laymen; its 17,000 readers are found all over French-speaking West Africa. The other important papers of this area are *Présence Chrétienne* of Lomé, Togo (biweekly, 4,000); *La Croix au Dahomey* of Cotonou, Dahomey (biweekly, 5,000); *L'Effort Camerounais* of Yaoundé, Cameroon (weekly, 6,000); and *La Semaine Africaine* of Brazzaville, Congo (weekly, 12,000). The last named serves also Gabon, Congo, the Central African Republic, and Chad.

Ghana has a national Catholic biweekly, the *Standard* (6,000), published at Cape Coast. Nigeria has two weeklies, the *Independent* of Ibadan (13,000), published in English for the western region of the Federation, and the *Leader* of Owerri (35,000) for the eastern region. Nigeria also possesses a good monthly magazine, *Catholic Life* (Calabar), with 40,000 circulation, the largest of any Catholic periodical in Africa. A thriving press in the Congo (Leopoldville) was deeply affected by the postindependence disorders. *Le Courrier d'Afrique* has emerged as Leopoldville's leading daily (15,000), and its editor Gabriel Makoso was awarded the Gold Pen (1963) by the International Press Association for his defense of the freedom of the press. The weekly *Afrique Chrétienne* (1961) is the Congo's largest Catholic paper, with a constantly rising circulation (20,000 in 1965). Other weeklies or biweeklies are in French and in the Congo's major African languages. Both Burundi and Rwanda have a national Catholic publication in the vernacular. *Temps Nouveaux* of Bujumbura (formerly Usumbura) was one of Africa's major papers (1952–62) until increasing government pressure caused its demise.

In East Africa the accent in the press is on the vernacular. Only one newspaper and two magazines are published in English, whereas there are 20 in the vernaculars. The major papers are *Kiongozi* of Tabora, Tanzania (biweekly, 26,000), and *Munno* of Kisubi, Uganda (daily, 15,000). To the south, Malawi has a four-lingual biweekly newspaper, the *African* of Lilongwe (9,000). Zambia has a monthly magazine, *Kacema* of Ndola (5,000), and a weekly, *Northern Star*.

Southern Africa. The dichotomy between the white and African populations is reflected in the press of this area. Rhodesia has two monthlies: *Moto* of Gwelo (21,000) is trilingual and directed toward African Christians, while the *Shield* of Salisbury (1,000) caters to the white population. No vernacular press exists in the Portuguese territories of Angola and Mozambique because of rigid government restrictions. Angola has a semiweekly, *O Apostolado,* of Luanda (4,000) and a monthly from Nova Lisboa, *O Peregrino de Fátima* (10,000). There are two Catholic papers in Mozambique, *Diário* (Lourenco-Marques) and *Diário de Mocambique* (Beira, 5,000), read by Europeans and *assimilados.*

The Catholic press in the Republic of South Africa is vigorous and varied. The first Catholic periodical in the country was the *Colonist* (Grahamstown, 1850–59). The *Catholic Magazine* (1891–1924) exercised great influence under its editors, Msgr. Frederick *Kolbe and Father Sidney *Welch. The *Southern Cross,* the semiofficial organ of the South African hierarchy, was founded in 1920 and has a circulation of 17,000. It is complemented by two monthlies in Afrikaans, *Die Brug* (4,000) and *Die Katolieke Wereld* (2,000), and two African vernacular weeklies, *Umafrica* from Mariannhill (20,000), published in Zulu, and *Moeletsi oa Basotho* from Mazenod, Basutoland (14,600), published in Sesotho. Several diocesan monthlies exist, as well as specialized magazines for youth, teachers, and the educated African elite.

The island of Madagascar has a flourishing press in the Malgache language, the weeklies *Lakroan'i Madagasikara* (1926, 6,000) and *Fanilo* (1939, 4,500), and one weekly in French, *Lumière,* published at Fianarantsoa (4,500). Some 12 monthlies are devoted to religious formation and the promotion of various movements. The island of Mauritius has one of the most widely circulated papers in *La Vie Catholique* (1930, 12,000); *Legionnaires,* the organ of the Legion of Mary, reaches 3,500 readers every 3d week.

In general, the papers of French-speaking Africa carry more world news, both secular and Catholic, than those of the English-speaking areas. They are serviced by Agence France Presse and rely heavily on the International Fides Service and other European Catholic news agencies. Local Catholic press services exist in the Congo (Leopoldville), Uganda, Tanzania, and Nigeria. Several specialized periodicals are worthy of note. *Revue du Clergé Africain* [1946, Mayidi, Congo (Leopoldville)] is a bimonthly review for the clergy. Its contributors are almost exclusively from the Congo, but it is read in other French-speaking countries. Its English counterpart, *African Ecclesiastical Review* (1959, Katigondo, Uganda), draws contributors from all over Africa. *Afrique Documents* (1962, Dakar) is a general sociological review of small circulation but high quality.

Look to the Future. The future of the Catholic press in Africa is quite unpredictable. Many independent papers had by the mid-1960s felt the heavy hand of government pressure—censorship, seizure of issues, and expulsion or imprisonment of editors. Even the most prosperous Catholic weeklies may run into serious trouble, in which event they may either go under or be obliged to curtail their Christian witness. If this happens, it will be possible to exercise Catholic journalism only within the framework of the secular press. In any event, the general pastoral tendency in all of Africa is away from specifically Catholic undertakings and in favor of full participation in national and interdenominational projects. There will always be need, however, for modest publications geared to the intensive formation of a truly apostolic laity. The influence on society will be indirect; it will come not from what these papers contain nor from wide circulation but from the action that their well-formed readers will be inspired to carry out.

Bibliography: "La Press catholique en Afrique noire," *Vivante Afrique* 232 (May–June 1964), special issue. Streit-Dindinger 23:1460, 2044, 2547, e.g., indicate studies of the Catholic press in mission countries; the latest, however, is dated 1952.

[J. A. BELL]

2. Asia

The Catholic press in China, Taiwan, Hong Kong, and India are treated separately (*see* CATHOLIC PRESS, WORLD SURVEY, 8, 13). This section covers the rest of Asia.

Burma. In December 1912, Father Eugene Luce, pastor of St. Mary's Cathedral, Rangoon, converted the cathedral's parish bulletin into an English monthly, the *Voice.* He died in 1915, but the journal continued until the Japanese invasion (March 1942). From 1925, the *Sower,* a monthly, had been published in Burmese at Thonze in the Rangoon Diocese, but it also succumbed to the invasion. It resumed as a Burmese fortnightly in 1946 and, beginning with February 1947, included a short English supplement. In April 1949 the *Sower* was divided into an English edition (fortnightly circulation 2,000) and a Burmese edition (monthly circulation 3,500). There are also three small monthly magazines: one in a Karen dialect published in central Burma by the Pontifical Society for the Foreign Missions; one in Tamil (Rangoon); and one in Kachin, published by the Columban Fathers in north Burma.

[J. F. MURPHY]

Cambodia. The Catholic press has not yet made much headway in Cambodia. Catholics of Vietnamese and Chinese stock avail themselves of doctrinal and devotional reading matter from elsewhere. The Catholic weekly *Neak Nom Sar* (Messenger) was founded in Phnompenh in 1962 by a group of social-minded laymen. Of its eight pages, seven were in Khmer (Cambodian) and one was in French. A journal of Catholic "information and formation," it quickly gained prestige, but pressure from hostile papers caused it to suspend publication.

Ceylon. Two Catholic weeklies were founded in the 1860s. *Gnanartha Pradipaya* in Singhalese, with the larger circulation (18,000), dates from 1866; the English-language *Messenger* (12,000), from 1869. The monthly *Messenger of the Sacred Heart* was founded in 1904. It has a Singhalese counterpart, *Divya Hurdaye Duthaya.* The monthly *Novena News* promotes devotion to Our Mother of Perpetual Help. The *Messenger* and *Novena News* are read by many non-Catholics. All are published in Colombo.

About 35 Catholic books and 25 booklets are published annually in Ceylon, all by Catholic institutions or agencies and mostly in Singhalese. A high percentage are translations.

Indonesia. In 1965 Indonesia had four Catholic papers—a recently founded daily, the lay-edited *Kompas* (Compass), published in Djakarta, and three weeklies. The chief weekly, *Hidup Katolik* (Catholic Life), published by the Jesuits in Djakarta, was founded in 1946. *Penabur* (The Sower), conducted by the Franciscans in the same city, also was founded in 1946 and ranks second in circulation. Six Catholic monthly magazines are published, one of which, *Patuh,* is exclusively for members of the armed forces and is financed by the government. *Utusan* (The Messenger) is devotional, *Basis* (Foundation) caters to the better-educated class, non-Catholic and Catholic, *Semangat* (The Spirit) is for Catholic youth, and *Intisari* (The Nucleus), lay-edited, is a general human-interest magazine of Catholic inspiration, directed to the public at large. Some of these periodicals are published in Jogjakarta. Catholic publishing is done in Djakarta and Jogjakarta, in Semarang in Java and in Enden (Flores), where the Divine Word Fathers have a press. Between 140 and 150 Catholic books, nearly all in Indonesian, are in the catalogues. Liturgy, hagiography, dogma, and catechetics lead in numbers. Before World War II, Indonesia had a Catholic daily, *De Koerier; Hidup* (Life), another daily, was published during the revolutionary period immediately after the war.

[P. O'CONNOR]

Japan. In 1595 the Jesuits and the Franciscans published a Latin-Portuguese-Japanese dictionary, and during the 16th and 17th centuries they issued a Japanese catechism and books on the rosary, meditation, and confession. After the long decades of persecution (1613–1858), Bishop Petijean published *Seikyo Shoku Yori* (1868; Fundamentals of Christian Doctrine) and *Seikyo Nikka* (1868; Daily Prayers of a Christian); in 1875 he gave the first *imprimatur* for a new Japanese catechism prepared in the Chinese style. In a more scholarly vein, the Paris Foreign Missionary Society published (1904–10) *Mélanges Japonaise,* a review of Japanology. Emile Raguet, PME, completed a translation of the New Testament from the Latin Vulgate into classical Japanese; a new version into colloquial Japanese was made by A. Magriaria, SDB, and Father Bunkyo Totsuka in 1930.

In 1935 Rupert Enderle came to Japan to start a Catholic encyclopedia in Japanese and to establish an agency of the Herder Publishing Co. Two years later Paul Marcellino, SP, established another printing firm, Shikosha. About the same time, the Jesuits of Tokyo's Sophia University started publishing the *Monumenta Nipponica;* it continued until 1943, was suspended during the war, and resumed in 1951.

An amalgamation of Catholic publishers in the Tokyo Archdiocese, the Chuo Shuppan Sha, was set up in 1943 to unify effort; its first venture was to reprint the New Testament. In 1945 it began the publication of a monthly Catholic newspaper at the request of the hierarchy. Chuo Shuppan became an independent publishing house of the St. Paul Society in 1949, and the editorial responsibility for the paper was transferred to the society, which also supplies Catholic Japan with catechisms, prayer books, New Testaments, and a wide variety of religious books. A Catholic broadcasting company, Bunka Hoso, also is connected with the work of the society. At this time, Heinrich Dumolin, SJ, began publication of *Seiki,* a scholarly monthly Catholic review. Several popular Catholic monthlies compete in popularity with nonreligious publications.

[A. R. O'HARA]

Korea. Almost all of the early Catholics were from the upper class, so that literature from China was widely read. Between 1784 and 1801, the faith began to spread, and Korean liturgical and other instructional texts, often freely adapted from the Chinese, began to appear. One of the earliest was the two-volume *The Principal Articles of the Catholic Religion,* by catechist Augustin Tjung, who began but did not finish a *Complete Treatise on Religion.* John Choi translated *A Direct Explanation of the Bible* from Chinese and did much work in copying and distributing Bibles.

From 1802 to 1866 persecutions and wars prevented almost all publication. Bishop L. Imbert (martyred 1839) had issued a prayerbook (1838), the basis of a manual still in use; and by 1854 a book of Gospel homilies, several lives of the saints, and four books of the *Imitation of Christ* had been translated. In 1859 a Catholic printing press with wooden type was set up; it branched out into publications on Korean culture, history, etc., only to be suppressed by another persecution. One of the greatest achievements of this venture was to popularize the Korean *hangul* alphabet of 10 vowels and 14 consonants, devised by King Seijong in the mid-15th century but scorned by the learned. In order to reach people unfamiliar with Chinese characters, most Catholic books were printed in *hangul;* this had the secondary result of helping Koreans rediscover their own language and culture.

In 1906 *Kyeong Hyang Shimmun,* a weekly with a four-page religious supplement, was begun under Catholic auspices. The paper was suppressed by the Japanese in 1910, and sold by the Archbishop in the 1950s to avoid the suspicion of any political involvement. The supplement continued to appear as *Kyeong Hyang Magazine;* it is still the official Catholic publication. There is also a weekly, *Catholic Shibo.* There was some increase of Catholic publishing after 1948 (mainly of books by some seven firms), but most of it consisted of translations.

[A. CHOÍ]

Laos. In 1965 the Catholic press could hardly be said to exist in Laos. The Gospels, a simple catechism, and a prayer book, printed by photo-offset in Paris, had been published for Lao-speaking Catholics. In the late 1950s, Yves Bertrais, OMI, working with a U.S. Protestant missionary, romanized the language of the Meo mountain tribesmen and compiled the first Meo dictionary (1961). He issued, from typescript and a duplicating machine, Meo texts of the Gospels, a life of Christ, a history of the Church, a catechism, the Sunday Masses, parts of the Old Testament, a simple geography, etc. Catholic books from Vietnam and Thailand are used in Laos. No Catholic newspaper or review had been launched as of 1965.

[P. O'CONNOR]

Macao. Most of Macao's 10,000 Catholics get whatever they need in the way of Catholic publications from Hong Kong. There is, however, one weekly, *O Clarim* (Clarion), published in Portuguese by the diocese.

[A. R. O'HARA]

Malaysia. The first Catholic newspaper in the territories that now form Malaysia was the English-language *Malaya Catholic Leader* (1935), now called the *Malaysian Catholic News,* a fortnightly. The historic Portuguese Mission publishes a magazine, the *Rally.* The Central Catholic Bureau of Singapore, under the direction of the apostolic visitor for the overseas Chinese, publishes the illustrated fortnightly *Hai Sing Pao* (1955; Star of the Sea), which circulates mainly in Southeast Asia but also in Africa, America, Europe, and Oceania. The *Lo Feng Pao* (Joyful Vanguard) for youth is published, under the auspices of the Catholic Bureau, in Chinese, Thai, and English, in Hong Kong, Bangkok, and Singapore.

[P. O'CONNOR]

Pakistan. In East Pakistan, at Dacca, a religious weekly in Bengali, the *Pratibeshi,* is published almost exclusively for the Catholic community; it has a circulation of 2,000. The *Christian Voice* (Karachi, West Pakistan, 1951), formerly the *Standard* and the *Catholic Chronicle,* is published by an editorial board that includes three priests; it covers local and foreign news and items of Catholic interest. Its high quality and the fact that it is the largest Catholic paper in the country (2,000 circulation) give it a marked influence. *Achcha Charwaha* (The Good Shepherd, Rawalpindi, West Pakistan, 1936) is a monthly in Urdu, founded as a means of contact with dispersed Catholics and those leaving school to start work; its circulation is quite small, but it is widely read in school libraries. The *Catholic Nagib* is a monthly in Urdu published by the Diocese of Lahore, West Pakistan.

[J. CORDEIRO]

The Philippines. The history of the Catholic press in the Philippines developed in three stages: beginnings under Spain, the American transition, and the period of Philippine autonomy.

Beginnings under Spain. The first presses were established by missionaries who turned out books and pamphlets for doctrinal purposes. Two editions of *Doctrina Christiana,* one in Tagalog and Spanish, the other in Chinese, bear the earliest Philippine imprint: 1593. By 1800 religious presses had published some 500 titles embracing works on devotion, morals, and linguistics. These included the first Philippine book set in movable type (1602), Tomás Pinpín's Spanish grammar for Tagalogs (1610), and the first printed books in five other Philippine dialects. Until the 19th century, when Spanish had become the language of culture, publications by Catholic presses constituted the major portion of the Filipino's intellectual diet. In 1862, Rev. Pedro Pelaez founded the first religious newspaper, *El Católico Filipino,* and introduced to its columns the writings of the priest-patriot José Burgos. Four other Catholic newspapers of varying life-spans were published during the Spanish regime.

The American Transition. After the islands were ceded by Spain to the U.S. (1898), Catholic journalism in the Philippines acquired two characteristics; it became polemical—a feature it has never altogether lost—and it began to use English. A few newspapers began publishing in Spanish: *Libertas* (1899–1918), founded by Archbishop Nozaleda of Manila to counteract the liberalist-humanist *La Democracia; La Vida Filipina* (1906–10), designed to combat the Aglipayan "national church" heresy; and *La Defensa* (1920–35), founded by the Philippine hierarchy. Spanish readership, however, was shrinking; and even the prestigious monthly magazine *Cultura Sociál* (1913–41) could not be revived after World War II. *La Defensa* emerged again (1937) as the *Philippines Commonweal,* a financially feeble but otherwise vigorous newspaper that reached a peak circulation of 20,000. *Filipinas,* a Tagalog magazine with a more modest audience, appeared in 1927 and continued publishing Catholic miscellanea until 1958.

The Period of Philippine Autonomy. After World War II, the *Philippines Commonweal* became the *Sentinel.* Its circulation rose to over 30,000, and it helped establish local periodicals in many provinces. It addresses itself to the whole nation, although an encouraging postwar development is the increasing appearance of archdiocesan and diocesan periodicals. Of these, the more important are the new *Filipinas* (Manila), *Veritas* (Jaro), the *Lungsuranon* (Cebu), the *Mindanao Cross* (Cotabato), and the *Sulu Star* (Jolo). While many periodicals have columns in the vernacular, English remains the principal language of these papers, and the *Cultura Sociál* has been replaced by a counterpart in English, *Philippine Studies.*

Devotional and doctrinal books continue to be published by the Catholic Trade School press of the Divine Word fathers, and by the Daughters of St. Paul.

Bibliography: J. T. MEDINA, *La imprenta en Manila desde sus origenes hasta 1810* (Santiago de Chile 1896). W. E. RETANA Y GAMBOA, *El periodismo filipino* (Madrid 1895). J. Z. VALENZUELA, *History of Journalism in the Philippine Islands* (Manila 1933). G. F. ZAIDE, *Catholicism in the Philippines* (Manila 1937). *Sentinel* 4 (1952), the issue for Nov. 1 is devoted to the growth of Catholic journalism.

[A. P. G. MANUUD]

Thailand. The first Catholic printing press in Thailand was founded by the Paris Foreign Missionaries in 1795. Early in the 18th century a royal decree had forbidden the writing of Christian books in Thai or Pali. Hence the first Catholic books were printed in phonetic romanized spelling. By the end of the 19th century, however, the Catholic press in Bangkok was printing in both Thai and roman letters. Bishop Jean Baptiste Pallegoix (d. 1862) published his *Kham Son Phrd,* a catechism, in 1848, a book of apologetics in 1850, and dictionaries, Latin-Thai (1850), English-Thai (1851), and Thai-Latin-French-English (1854).

About half a dozen Catholic periodicals are published in Thailand, all in the capital, Bangkok, and all except one in Thai. *Udomphan* (1936; Fruitful Seed) is a 16-page illustrated journal of news and feature articles published three times monthly by the Salesians. The Paris missionaries publish *Sarasat* (Announcement). A weekly magazine for youth, *Viratham* (Voice of Heroes), founded in 1956 by the Brothers of St. Gabriel, is the most widely read periodical of its kind in Thailand. Informed by a Catholic spirit, it appeals to non-Christians and Christians alike. *Au Pays des Pagodes* is a monthly review in French primarily for the missionaries. The Jesuits publish two small reviews for university circles.

Bibliography: *Catholic Directory of Thailand* (Bangkok 1963). A. LAUNAY, *Mémorial de la Société des missions étrangères, 1658–1913,* 2 v. (Paris 1920).

Vietnam. The first Catholic Vietnamese book was the catechism of Alexandre de Rhodes, SJ, in Latin and romanized Vietnamese, printed (1651) in Rome. The use, now universal, of the roman alphabet, with accents, for the six-toned monosyllabic Vietnamese language originated with De Rhodes and his Italian and Portuguese colleagues. Catholic literature was produced in manuscript and print during the next 230 years amid the difficulties resulting from intermittent persecutions in an East Asian land. It included a versified life of Our Lord and other basic instructive and devotional compositions. The printing was done in India, Thailand, and Hong Kong, as well as Vietnam.

While priests, Vietnamese and foreign, used the romanized form, books for catechists and other layfolk were printed in the traditional modified Chinese characters (Chu Nom). A Catholic educator and official, Tru'o'ng vinh Ky, better known as Petrus Ky (1837–98), initiated the general use of the missionaries' romanization. In 1865 he established the official *Gia Dinh*

Bao, the first Vietnamese journal in the roman alphabet. Catholic missionaries led in producing books for inter-language study. De Rhodes published a Vietnamese-Portuguese-Latin dictionary (Rome 1651), and versatile Bp. Pierre Joseph Georges Pigneaux de Behaine (d. 1799) began two dictionaries, Vietnamese-Latin-Chinese and Latin-Vietnamese. These were finished by Bp. Jean Baptiste Taberd (d. 1840) and published in Calcutta. Bishop Joseph Theurel (d. 1868) published a dictionary in north Vietnam.

Presses. A Catholic printing press, already long established by the Paris missionaries in Tonkin (north Vietnam), had produced at least 14 books, printed in Chu Nom from wooden plates, when it was destroyed (1854) by fire. It was quickly restored, and a priest who had learned printing in Paris added type for romanized Vietnamese. Again destroyed during persecutions, this press was replaced in 1864 by Father (later Bishop) Paul Puginier. Within 2 years it had issued nine books of devotion and doctrine, including translations of standard European spiritual works. This press was the forerunner of the Imprimerie Ste. Thérèse of Hanoi, taken over by the Communist regime after 1954. A Catholic press in Vinh, southern Tonkin, was printing religious books in Chu Nom in the second half of the 19th century. After the south had become the French colony of Cochin-China in 1862 and the center and north had become the French protectorate of Annam and Tonkin in 1883, the French language was widely taught and read. Thenceforward a number of Catholic books were printed in French for Vietnamese, especially for school use. In 1864 a French missionary in Saigon founded the Imprimerie de la Mission, which a century later was still producing Catholic books. Another notable press was founded by Father (later Bishop) Martial Jannin (d. 1940) in Kontum for the Bahnar mountain tribe. It prints books in Bahnar and other mountain tribe languages, romanized by the Paris missionaries, and a monthly Bahnar periodical that is edited by a Bahnar priest.

In general, the Vietnamese Catholic press came to bloom in the 1930s, a time of literary flowering in the country. World War II (when Vietnam was occupied by Japanese forces) and its aftermath (a Communist regime and a longer war) caused important publications to disappear. In the feverish days of the early 1960s, Catholic papers appeared again, showing traces of the temperature of the country's crises. Monthly magazines and reviews have had a more even history through the decades.

Newspapers. The first newspaper in the north, the French-language *L'Avenir du Tonkin* (Hanoi 1884), while not professedly Catholic, was animated by a Catholic spirit. It became a daily, and once a week it included a Catholic religious page. Edited by a French layman, it was closely linked with the missionaries; it ceased publication in 1941. Revived under the title of *Action* by a Vietnamese layman, it lasted until March, 1945. In 1943 the same layman bought the Hanoi Vietnamese-language daily *Tin Moi* (News), the most widely read newspaper in the north, and gave it a definitely Catholic tone. Under the Viet Minh (Communist) regime of 1945–46 it was crippled and died. Another Catholic-oriented daily, *Y-Dan* (People's Opinion), founded during the Viet Minh regime, was shut down after 6 months.

The first professedly Catholic newspaper (Hanoi 1924) in the Vietnamese language was the *Trung Hoa Nhat Bao* (Moderation Daily), a triweekly that ceased in 1943. In midsummer 1962 the first Vietnamese Catholic papers to appear in nearly 20 years were launched in Saigon. They were weeklies: *Thang Tien* (Advance), a development from the cathedral bulletin, and *Song Dao* (Live the Faith), edited by laymen with emphasis on social questions. Another Catholic weekly, *Nguoi Moi* (New People), lay edited, was founded in 1964. The chief Catholic paper is the militant daily *Xay Du'ng* (Construct), founded in January 1964. It is published with the permission of ecclesiastical authorities, is edited by a priest, but is not an official Catholic organ. The entry of an aggressive Buddhist faction into the political field and the possible implications for Catholics obliged the Catholic press of the mid-1960s to be often disputatious.

Magazines and Reviews. The first Vietnamese Catholic magazine was the Saigon *Nam Ky Dia Phan* (Southern Diocese), a weekly patterned on the *Semaine Religieuse* of France. It was published from 1908 to 1942. Next came the monthly *Loi-Tham* (Message) of Qui Nhon. Thereafter reviews and magazines were launched in various dioceses. Among the more noteworthy, prior to 1945, were the thoughtful *Vi Chua* (For the Lord), a weekly, later monthly, published in Hue, and the Jociste-inspired *Thanh Nien* (Youth), a weekly founded in textile-manufacturing Nam Dinh by Father André Vacquier, a Paris missionary killed by the Communists in 1945. A review for priests, *Sacerdos* (1926), is the oldest surviving Catholic periodical.

In 1965 there were about 10 Catholic magazines and reviews, mostly devotional and informative, popular in style. The Redemptorists' *Duc Me Hanh Cu'u Giup* (Mother of Perpetual Help) and *Trai Tim Duc Me* (1948, Heart of the Blessed Mother), now published by the all-Vietnamese Congregation of the Blessed Mother Co-Redemptrix, are the best known. Most of the 11 dioceses in South Vietnam have their own bulletins.

The technical quality of Catholic newspapers and periodicals is equal to that of secular publications. Most of the Catholic books published in Vietnam are small devotional works. Seven Catholic publishing institutions are listed in Saigon. No general publishing firm issues Catholic books. The better-educated Catholics read French; their reading needs are met by Catholic books imported from France.

No Catholic newspaper or periodical is published in the Communist-ruled "Democratic Republic" in north Vietnam.

Bibliography: A. DE RHODES, *Catechismus: Pro iis qui suscipere Baptismun in octo dies divisus* (Rome 1651); new ed. A. MARILLIER (Saigon 1961), biog. by C. LARRE and PHAM DINH KHIEM. *Viet-Nam Cong Giao Niem-Giam* (1964), Vietnam Catholic Yearbook, in Vietnamese and French. Streit-Dindinger v. 23; entries 1460, 2044, 2547, e.g., list studies on the Catholic press in mission countries, but the latest is dated 1952.

[P. O'CONNOR]

3. AUSTRALIA

The history of the Catholic press in Australia resembles in many ways that of its U.S. counterpart; its founders were mostly Irish, its difficult beginnings occurred in the eastern cities, and it gradually expanded throughout the continent as the population grew and new towns and states were created. The first Australian Catholic newspaper, the *Australasian Chronicle* (Sydney 1839), was edited by a Scottish convert, William Augustine Duncan, known as Australia's first Catholic scholar. A stormy character, he frequently clashed with the leading citizens and the clergy, and the paper closed in 1848. Archdeacon John McEncroe, an Irishman educated in the U.S., founded the *Freeman's Journal* (Sydney 1850), the country's major Catholic paper for generations. These early Catholic newspapers reflected the problems of a minority group, mainly Irish, in the pioneering days of a harsh country. To Catholics their press was a vital part of their existence, ready to inform them on key issues, defend their interests, and campaign against exploitation and reaction. The press played a major role in the Church's campaign against the abolition of State assistance to private schools in the 1880s—a campaign still to be won.

The six major metropolitan sees of Australia each have weekly newspapers, and some of the country dioceses conduct journals, some fortnightly, others monthly. The largest Catholic publication—indeed the largest religious newspaper—is the Sydney *Catholic Weekly*. This was founded (1942) with the merger of the *Freeman's Journal* and the *Catholic Press* (1895), and in 1964 had a circulation of well over 60,000. Melbourne supports two weeklies, the *Advocate* (1868) and the *Tribune* (1900). Other weeklies are the *Catholic Leader* (Brisbane, Queensland), the *Southern Cross* (Adelaide, South Australia), the *Record* (Perth, Western Australia), and the *Standard* (Hobart, Tasmania).

There are no national Catholic magazines. This field is covered mainly by monthly and quarterly publications of religious orders; the largest are the *Messenger of the Sacred Heart* (Jesuit), *Harvest* (Marist), and the *Annals* (Missionaries of the Sacred Heart). The Jesuits publish also the *Twentieth Century,* a high-quality quarterly review. The *Catholic Worker,* a lay-controlled radical Melbourne monthly, is aimed mainly at intellectuals, as is the quarterly *Prospect*. There are a number of foreign-language publications, including *La Fiamma* (Italian, Capuchin Fathers), *Het Kompas* (Dutch), *Tygodnik Katolicki* (Polish), and the *Maltese Messenger*.

Distribution to a comparatively small population scattered across a vast continent has been the chief obstacle to the development of Catholic publishing in Australia.

There is a Catholic Press Association of Australia and New Zealand.

[K. HILFERTY]

4. Austria

The Catholic press in Austria has a relatively short history. It was not until the Revolution of 1848 that the press in general emerged as a factor in the molding of political opinion, and the beginnings of the Catholic press likewise date from that period. But the Catholic press had little influence during practically the whole second half of the 19th century; it was overshadowed by the great liberal and secular Austrian, especially Viennese, press. A change occurred when, following a resolution of the Austrian Catholic Conference in 1892, the *Reichspost* was founded in Vienna as a Catholic daily newspaper; Friedrich *Funder became its editor in 1896. For the financial support of the Catholic press (a series of small local papers had been founded by Catholic press associations in the Austrian provinces) the Pius Association was created, which, until its dissolution in 1919, numbered more than 150,000 members.

First Austrian Republic. In the first Austrian republic (1918–38), the Catholic press was almost exclusively a party press, i.e., it represented the policies and interests of the contemporary Christian Social party, although it was not under party control. This state of affairs at that time reflected the position of the Church, which was likewise closely identified with this one party. In 1928 the *Reichspost,* which had never achieved a high circulation (20,000–30,000), was joined by another paper, *Das kleine Volksblatt,* founded in the interests of the whole Catholic populace. Daily papers, edited by the Catholic press associations, likewise made their appearance in the principal cities of all Austrian provinces. There was, besides, a regular ecclesiastical press consisting of episcopal news-sheets.

Nazi Occupation and After. The occupation in 1938 of Austria by Germany brought an end to the Catholic press in Austria. All Catholic newspapers were suppressed or forced into conformity. After the restoration of Austria in 1945, the Catholic press only partially revived. Allied occupational forces allowed, in the beginning, only party papers. As a result, the numerous old Catholic newspapers of the period before 1938 appeared no longer as independent Catholic publications, but as organs of a party, i.e., the Austrian *Volkspartei* (Popular party). In 1946 Funder, who, like other Catholic journalists, had spent many years in Nazi concentration camps, founded the Catholic weekly *Die Furche*. An attempt to revive the independent daily *Reichspost* failed. *Die Furche* has remained the leading Catholic weekly paper, in fact the leading Catholic publication of any kind, in Austria. Besides *Die Furche,* a second Catholic weekly, *Der Volksbote,* is published at Innsbruck.

Press Associations. In the years following the war, it was possible to restore the Catholic press associations, which had been expropriated by the Nazis. Most of these press associations, which are ecclesiastical property, control modern presses and publish daily and weekly papers. At present the following press associations exist in Austria:

1. Herold (Vienna), under the direction of the archbishop of Vienna. Herold possesses a large publishing house (originally the possession of the *Reichspost*) and a large press. It publishes *Die Furche,* (its own publication), as well as the Jesuit journal *Der grosse Entschluss*. Herold controls, besides, an extensive book production, particularly in the religious sphere.
2. Styria (Graz), association of the Diocese of Graz-Seckau. Styria publishes a daily paper, *Kleine Zeitung* (circulation more than 100,000), which appears under the title *Kleine Zeitung Klagenfurt*. It has also a large book production, including the German editions of French religious and theological literature.
3. Press Association of St. Pölten, one of the most modern presses in Austria. St. Pölten publishes more than a dozen local weeklies and owns Austria's only Catholic book club, "Welt und Heimat."

4. Oberösterreichischer Landes verlag, the press association of the Diocese of Linz. It publishes the daily *Linzer Volksblatt* and four local weeklies.
5. Tyrolia (Innsbruck), publisher of the weekly paper *Der Volksbote*, as well as significant books in the fields of belles-lettres, religion, and theology.

The great Catholic publishing house of *Herder also has an Austrian publishing company, Herder Wien, which, besides its extensive publication of Catholic books, puts out the two leading Catholic monthlies of the German-speaking world, *Wort und Wahrheit* and *Orbis Catholicus*. There are smaller press associations in Salzburg and Klagenfurt.

Diocesan and Parish Papers; Publishers' Association. The ecclesiastical press as such is relatively strong in Austria. Each of the eight dioceses has its own episcopal paper, with a total circulation of over 50,000. Most important are the Church papers of Vienna and St. Pölten. Besides these, there exist a great number of parish publications. Each large parish, especially in the cities, has its own paper; they are generally monthlies.

An important function in the Catholic press life of Austria is exercised by the Catholic news agency Kathpress, whose sponsor is an association to which the above-mentioned press associations and the Austrian Bishops' Conference belong. The president of the association is the bishop currently in charge of press affairs.

There are few Catholic daily newspapers in Austria (*Kleine Zeitung Graz-Klagenfurt, Linzer Volksblatt*), but Catholic journalists are represented on nearly all newspapers. They are incorporated into the Union of Catholic Journalists of Austria; in Vienna alone the union has 80 members. With the union, there also exists an organization of journalists and publishers, the Association of Catholic Publishers of Austria. Despite its various allegiances, nearly the whole Austrian press is open-minded on matters of religion and Church. The public utterances of the Archbishop of Vienna, Cardinal König, for example, were given generous coverage in the Austrian press, and reports on Vatican Council II were likewise strong and sympathetic.

[R. BARTA]

5. Belgium

In 1620, with official consent (*Met gratie ende privilegie*), Abraham Verhoeven founded in Antwerp a periodical news bulletin, the first illustrated newspaper in Europe. Like other periodicals published a short time later in Antwerp, Ghent, Bruges, and Brussels, Verhoeven's was censored by ecclesiastical authorities, carrying in every issue the initials of the censor and some phrase such as *imprimi potest.* For a time after the revolution of 1830 all political groups forgot their ideological conflicts and collaborated for the free socioeconomic reconstruction of the country, and a new free press reflected this harmony. After 1845, liberal opposition gave rise to the Liberal Party, followed some years later by the Catholic and Socialist parties. With the exception of *Le Soir* (1887), a politically independent newspaper, the Belgian press engaged in the struggles of the major ideological tendencies of the country: Catholic, socialist, communist, and "neutral."

The six Liberal newspapers, *La Dernière Heure* (171,000 circulation), *La Nouvelle Gazette* (70,000), *Le Matin* (25,000), *La Flandre Libérale* (9,750), *Het Laatste Nieuws* (315,000), and *De Nieuwe Gazet* (25,-

Tijdinghe wt
Weenen ende Praghe/
met den Nombre van de principaelste Heeren/ die in den Slach ghebleuen zijn/van d'een zijde ende d'ander/ende hoe dat elck sijn quartier hadde om den Vyant aen te tasten.
Eerst Ghedruckt den 16. December 1620.

Chronographicum.
freDerICVS Den VIIf Den
Is VerIaeght.

Het Casteel de Sterre * daer den Slach was.

T'Hantwerpen/ By Abraham Verhoeuen/ op de Lombaerde Veste/inde gulde Sonne.
Met Gratie ende Privilegie. P p.

Fig. 2. Front page of Abraham Verhoeven's "Tidings from the Battlefront" (Antwerp Dec. 16, 1620), Europe's first illustrated paper.

000), sell nearly 620,000 copies daily, about 21 per cent of all Belgian newspapers. The eight Socialist newspapers, *Le Peuple* (80,360), *La Wallonie* (59,000), *Le Travail* (10,000), *Indépendance* (38,200), *Journal de Charleroi* (46,000), *Volksgazet* (104,800), *Vooruit* (41,415), and *Le Monde du Travail* (32,000), produce 411,000 copies, some 14 per cent. The five "neutral" or politically independent papers, *Le Soir* (301,285), *La Meuse* (204,500), *La Lanterne* (60,000), *Le Jour* (22,-000), and *Lloyd Anversois* (10,000), attain a daily circulation of 597,000 copies, about 21 per cent. The only Communist newspaper, *Le Drapeau Rouge,* has a circulation of 25,000, or .87 per cent (1962 figures).

The Catholic press, by far the most powerful, has 23 of the total of 45 daily newspapers and in 1962 sold 1,194,000 copies a day (nearly 42 per cent). Many practicing Catholics also read a Liberal, a neutral, or, exceptionally, a Socialist newspaper. One reason is that many neutral and Liberal newspapers have shown during recent years increased respect for religious convictions.

Catholic Dailies. The most important Catholic dailies in Flemish are *De Standaard* and *Het Nieuwsblad,* which, with four local editions, sell 250,000 copies, *De Gazet van Antwerpen* (155,000), and *Het Volk* (220,-000). In French there are: *La Libre Belgique* (170,000),

La Cité (65,000), *Gazette de Liège* (35,000), *Le Courrier* (10,000), *Vers l'Avenir* (36,000), and *Le Rappel* (75,000).

Some Belgian Catholic newspapers are titled "Catholic journal" or "Christian journal"; others mention their Catholic political party. One paper, *La Métropole,* calls itself "a conservative daily." These different expressions illustrate the many senses in which the word "Catholic" is used in the Belgian Press. A Catholic newspaper may be published by the Catholic hierarchy as an instrument of the apostolate and of Catholic action. No Belgian daily is identified simply as "Catholic," but some powerful weeklies, such as *Kerkelijk Leven,* edited by an interdiocesan bureau in Antwerp (600,000 copies), and *Dimanche,* published in Mons (500,000), fully realize that ideal.

Catholic Weeklies and Journals. The weeklies edited by Catholic organizations, such as the Union of Christian Laborers (*De Volksmacht,* 502,000), or the Union of Catholic Woman-Workers (*Vrouwenbeweging,* 244,000), express the spirit of their movement and are, moreover, supervised by the chaplains and religious directors of those organizations. Catholic newspapers differ from these by economic, social, and even ideological independence from ecclesiastical authorities.

The Catholic publishing groups, for the most part set up as limited liability companies, are closely controlled by a small number of Catholic families and organizations. Some papers, for example *Het Volk* and *La Cité,* belong to the powerful Union of Christian Laborers, others (like *De Nieuwe Gids*) to the Catholic Party. The directors, appointed by the assembly of shareholders, choose the journalists and other collaborators according to their Catholic attitudes. No ecclesiastical censors' initials, however, nor any imprimatur from the diocesan authorities appear in these papers.

Catholic newspapers, differing from the Liberal, Socialist, or humanistic point of view of non-Catholic newspapers, reflect a unity of religious belief, but such unity does not create an identity of social and political opinions. Belgian Catholic newspapers may follow, according to political or social preference, a socially conservative or progressive line. They express nuances of public opinion and reflect the views of different social and linguistic groups. Hierarchical authorities remain on good terms with the directors of the Catholic newspapers and exercise some influence on the editorial staffs.

Many Catholic centers of higher education and scientific institutions, especially the University of Louvain, publish a large number of specialized periodicals in such fields as theology, history, philosophy, sociology, economy, and medicine. Catholic social organizations publish monthlies, which, although devoted to the special problems of labor unions, agriculture, the middle-classes, etc., reflect interest in scientific and cultural subjects. Because of this large output, Catholic reviews and periodicals of general interest are not numerous. The Flemish monthly *Kultuurleven* (1933) specializes in the study of the relationships between Catholicism and the modern world. It is edited at Louvain by the Dominicans in collaboration with a group of Catholic intellectuals. The monthly *Streven* (1933), edited by a group of Belgian Jesuits, reflects a wider interest in the arts, the sciences, and education.

An organ not under clerical supervision, *De Maand* (1958), deals with cultural subjects, social action, and politics. The best-known Catholic review of general interest in French is the monthly *La Revue Nouvelle,* edited in Brussels by a group of Catholic intellectuals. Exact circulation figures of these journals are not available; it is probable that 5,000 is a maximum. Taking into account the two languages of the country, this figure may be considered a satisfactory manifestation of Catholic influence on the cultural life of the country.

The Interdiocesan Bureau of the Press works to educate Catholic readers to recognize the errors of anti-Catholic papers and to communicate better with Catholic journalists. The University of Louvain, starting in 1946 with a school of journalism, has developed a school of mass media and a center for communication research.

Bibliography: A. Warzee, *Essai historique et critique sur les journaux belges* (Ghent 1845). *Officieel Jaarboek van Belgische Pers,* ed. Algemene Belgische Persbond (Brussels 1955, 1962). M. Deforge, "Présent et avenir de la presse Belge de Province," *La Presse* (Jan. 1954). P. U. de Volder, "Situation and Charakteristik der Tagespresse in Belgien," *Publizistik,* heft 6 (Bremen 1956). *Indicateur Publicitaire—Reklamegids* (Brussels 1963).

[P. U. DE VOLDER]

6. Brazil

Newspapers were prohibited in colonial Brazil until Sept. 10, 1808. By 1830, an average of 100 were published and in some years more than 300. However, they were short lived, small, and technically poor. They asserted themselves through the personality and popularity of their founders and the opportuneness of their topics, e.g., the *Aurora Fluminense* (1827–39) of Evaristo da Veiga, and *Sete de Abril* (1833–39) of Bernardo Vasconcelos, both politicians; journalists in general during this period wrote as politicians rather than as Catholics. The Catholic press arose in 1830 but remained on the sidelines of public life until 1866. *O Apóstolo* (1866–1901), by the fact that it treated the "Religious Question" (1872–76), which was a religious-political problem of national interest, equaled the great secular newspapers of the period.

The great modern Brazilian press emerged in 1900, and a notable vitality energized the Catholic press as well. Antonio Felício dos Santos, doctor, member of parliament, and the "grandfather of Catholic journalists," established the *Hebdomedário Católico* (1907) and *União* (1905–31, temporarily a daily); the latter, although faced with financial difficulties, had a marked influence in its time. It followed the editorial policy of the **Osservatore Romano*. Great efforts to improve the Catholic press were made in this period, notably by Pedro *Sinzig, OFM, through the Centro da Boa Imprensa; but it is now acknowledged that the vastness of the country makes national dailies impossible, while there is a need for superior regional ones.

The press department of the Brazilian Religious Conference (CRB) compiled the following statistics for 1962: There are 20 journalistic publishers. Twenty-five organs, daily, weekly, and biweekly have a total circulation of 779,300 copies; 114 monthlies, bi- and trimonthlies, and semiannuals distribute 1,039,400 copies; 7 annuals circulate 1,233,000 copies. Of these organs, 93 have a circulation of 10,000; 2, a circulation greater than 100,000. The total of 146 organs of the Catholic press accounts for 2,053,290 copies. The Catholic press in the interior is superior to the secular press both in circulation and technical excellence. In the large capitals, the opposite is true, with the exception of *O Jornal do Dia* (1946, Porto Alegre) and *O Diário* (1934, Belo Horizonte).

Progress in Catholic publishing other than that of journalism has been more noteworthy. The largest publishing house, Editôra Vozes (1901), of the Franciscans in southern Brazil, reaches even foreign readers through its many translations. Other publishing houses are conducted by the Franciscans in the north (Mensageiro da Fé); by the Pia Sociedade de S. Paulo (Edicões Paulinas); by the Sociedade de Verbo Divino (Lar Católico); by the Congregacão de N. Senhora do Santíssimo Sacramento (O Lutador); by the Salesians (Leituras Católicas and Livraria da Doutrina Cristã); by the Claretians (Ave Maria), and others. Some publishing houses just beginning in the 1960s, e.g., Edições Loyola of the Jesuits of Belo Horizonte, show great promise.

[A. STULZER]

7. CANADA

A great variety of periodicals published in English, French, and several other languages, including native Eskimo, serves Canada's 8½ million Catholics. The history of the Catholic press in Canada goes back to 1806, when *Le Canadien* appeared in Quebec. Because all French-speaking Canadians were then Catholics, it was considered a Catholic publication.

Diocesan Weeklies and Monthlies in English. The first English Catholic diocesan weekly was founded in 1826 by Bp. Alexander Macdonell who brought it to his See of Kingston (1830) and gave it the title of the *Catholic*. The *Casket* (circulation 13,000), founded in Nova Scotia (1852) as a commercial newspaper, became a religious newspaper by 1885, retaining a commercial section. The *New Freeman* (1900) is the official weekly of the Diocese of St. John, New Brunswick. The *Canadian Register* (79,700), Canada's only chain of diocesan papers, is published jointly by the archbishops of Ontario. It was founded in 1941 through the amalgamation of five diocesan weeklies: the *Canadian Freeman* (Kingston), the *Catholic Register and the Canadian Extension* (Toronto), the *Northern Catholic* (Sault Ste. Marie), the *Crusader* (Pembroke), and the *Beacon* (Montreal). The *Canadian Register* now has a national edition and separate editions for the Dioceses of Kingston, Toronto, Hamilton, Fort William, Pembroke, Peterborough, and Alexandria. In May 1963 the Diocese of Sault Ste. Marie began the *Northern Ontario Record,* to replace its edition of the *Canadian Register*. In 1948 the *Canadian Register* and London's *Catholic Record* (1878), as well as Winnipeg's *North-West Review* (1885), merged into a national Catholic weekly the *Ensign*. In 1949 the *Canadian Register* resumed publication for the Dioceses of Kingston, Toronto, Hamilton, and London. In December 1956 the *Ensign* ceased publication. The *North-West Review* was published in Winnipeg, Manitoba, from 1885 to 1948 until its merger with the *Ensign*. In 1956 the first diocesan edition of *Our Sunday Visitor* in Canada was founded under the title of *Western Sunday Visitor* to serve the Latin-rite Catholics of Manitoba. It was succeeded in 1961 by the *Sunday Herald* (7,600). Saskatchewan is served by the *Prairie Messenger* (1923; 11,700); the *Western Catholic* (1921; 10,500) serves the province of Alberta; the *British Columbia Catholic* (1911; 9,100) is the official organ of the Archdiocese of Vancouver. The *Prospector* (4,000) was begun in Nelson, British Columbia, in 1937. The lay-edited *Western Catholic Reporter* was launched in September 1965 in Edmonton, Alberta; it is explicitly devoted to fostering the ecumenical spirit.

There are three diocesan monthlies: the *Monitor* (1933; 8,000), for the province of Newfoundland; the *Torch* (1940; 2,100), published in Victoria, British Columbia, and the *Challenge,* founded in Montreal in 1963. (A Canadian edition of *Our Sunday Visitor,* 1958, has a circulation of 51,500 across Canada.)

Catholic periodicals in English include the official organs of the Pontifical Societies, of the Catholic Women's League (*Canadian League,* 1921; 50,100); *Canadian Messenger* (1891; 27,900); *Oratory* (19,000); the *Annals of St. Anne* (88,000); *Annals of Our Lady of the Cape* (14,500); *Companion of St. Francis,* Toronto (13,500); *Our Family,* Battleford, Saskatchewan (5,900); *Young Missionary,* St. Catherine's, Ontario (165,000); *Scarboro Missions* (70,000); *Indian Record* (for Catholic Indians, 1938; 3,000); *Restoration,* Combermere, Ontario (4,500); and the *Eskimo,* Churchill, Manitoba (1946; 4,000).

French Dailies and Weeklies. The 5½ million French-speaking Catholics of Canada read large-circulation dailies such as Quebec's *L'Action* (47,000) and *Le Soleil* (151,000), Three Rivers' *Le Nouvelliste* (38,000), Montreal's *La Presse* (262,000) and *Le Devoir* (37,000), Granby's *Voix de L'Est* (12,000), Sherbrooke's *La Tribune* (42,000), Ottawa's *Le Droit* (35,000), Moncton's (New Brunswick) *L'Evangeline* (10,000), and many others that are essentially Catholic in editorial and news content.

Two dioceses publish their own weeklies: Sherbrooke, *Le Messager de St. Michel* (5,000); and Sault Ste. Marie, *L'Information.* The Archdioceses of Quebec and Montreal publish a *Semaine Religieuse;* and Catholic weeklies include *La Liberté et Le Patriote,* Winnipeg (1913, 8,000), and *La Survivance,* Edmonton (1928, 2,100). A monthly, *Cloches de St. Boniface,* is published at St. Boniface, Manitoba (1901; 400). These are not diocesan weeklies in the strict sense of the term but are recognized by the hierarchy as serving the same purpose.

European-language Catholic Weeklies. *Glos Polski-Gazeta Polska* (1907; 6,000), in Polish, merged with Toronto's *Glos Polski* in 1948. *Teviskes Ziburiai* (Lights of Homeland, 5,200) is a Lithuanian weekly published in Toronto. To serve Byzantine-rite Catholics, two diocesan weeklies are published in Ukrainian: *Ukrainski-Visti,* (the Ukrainian News, 9,430), in Edmonton, where it has a monthly English edition, the *Ukrainian Record,* 1961; and the bilingual *Postup-Progress,* 6,900 (Ukrainian and English), founded in Winnipeg in 1959.

Magazines in French and Other Languages. There are about 100 Catholic magazines published in the province of Quebec; these are the organs of the national shrines, religious orders, Catholic institutions and associations, universities and colleges. Several of these magazines have a particular field, e.g., the family, education, art, literature, clerical life and theology, or history. The most influential are *Relations* (1940; 13,000), and *Actualités* (1909; 95,000—it was called *Ma Paroisse* until 1960), both edited by the Jesuits; and *Maintenant* (1962; 12,000), a continuation of *La Revue Dominicaine* (1915).

Periodicals in other languages include *La Famiglia* (Italian), Montreal (6,850); *Maria* (Slovak), Hamilton, Ontario (4,000); The Ukrainian *Redeemer's Voice* (1928; 4,000); *Magyar Elet* (Hungarian), Toronto (1948; 4,900); *Ahbarijiet Ta Malta* (Maltese), Windsor, Ontario (1954; 1,600); *Katonik Anashinabe Enakamigak* (the Catholic Indian News; 1956; 500, Spanish, Ontario); and *Nana* (Eskimo), Inuvik, Mackenzie Territory (1960; 500).

The Catholic hierarchy of Canada created a national French news service in 1953 and an English service in 1955 to supply news to all newspapers in the nation. The English-language Catholic press is linked with that of the United States through membership in the Catholic Press Association, New York; all diocesan weeklies subscribe to the U.S. National Catholic Welfare Conference news service of Washington, D.C. The English Catholic press in Canada holds national Catholic conventions every second year, alternating with regional conventions held in both Eastern and Western Canada.

[G. LAVIOLETTE]

8. China, Taiwan, and Hong Kong

After the first solid penetration of China by the Jesuits in the 16th century, their numerous publications on religion, science, and culture soon appeared.

China. Not much later, the Bible, Missal, Breviary, and the *Summa theologiae* were translated, the last being the monumental though uncompleted work of L. Buglio, SJ. In the latter half of the 19th century, when missionary work opened up again after the long period of persecution, great publishing centers for catechetical, apologetic, and devotional works were started by the Lazarists in Peking, the Jesuits in Sienhsien, Hopeh, and Shanghai, the Society of the Divine Word in Yenchowfu and Shantung, and the Franciscans in Hupeh and Shantung. Of major importance was the establishment (1912) of the first Catholic weekly, the *Kuang I Lu* (Public Benefit Record), and (1916) of a large Catholic daily, *I Shih Pao* (People's Welfare Daily), by Father Vincent *Lebbe for Tientsin, Peking, and Shanghai.

The Society of the Divine Word opened presses in Yenchowfu, Peking, and Tsingtao. By 1948 St. Paul's Press in Yenchowfu had published 243 books and pamphlets in 18 different categories. The Peking press published the scholarly review of Fu Jen University, and its weekly Catholic paper, *Pai Hua Pao* (Common Language News), started in 1914 and was very popular until it was suppressed in 1950.

The Jesuit Tu-Se-Wei Press at Zikawei, Shanghai, started in the 1890s and had published more than 900 books and pamphlets in Chinese by 1950. The Jesuits also published in Chinese such monthlies as the *Catholic Review, Sacred Heart Messenger, Eucharistic Crusade,* and *Sodality Review*. Scholarly reviews of the Aurora University, the Heude Museum, and the Zikawei Observatory also came from this press.

The Franciscans successively opened presses in Hankow (1910), Ichang (1912), and Wuchang (1930) for the Hupeh province. They also began presses in Tsinanfu (1920) and Chefoo (1924) for Shantung. Each province had a Catholic weekly called *Kwang Hwa Pao* (Splendid News), and there was a Latin-Chinese monthly for the clergy called the *Apostolicum*.

The Jesuit press at Sienhsien, Hopeh, started in 1863, and produced the necessary Chinese books for the missionaries, but it was noted especially for the sinological works of Father L. Wieger, studies of the Chinese language by S. Couvreur, archeological works by P. Licent, and translations of the New Testament (more than 100,000 copies) and spiritual books by Father Hsiao Ch'ing-shan, SJ. In 1947 all Catholic publishers met for the first time at the Catholic Central Bureau in Shanghai and set up a Catholic press bureau.

As the Bamboo Curtain descended on the China mainland, the *Annuaire de l'Église catholique en Chine* for 1950 reported that in China, Taiwan, Hong Kong, and Macao there were 33 publishing houses, 4 Chinese Catholic weeklies, 24 periodicals (monthlies, bimonthlies, and quarterlies), and 18 European-language and 2 bilingual periodicals. Of a dozen reviews of a scholarly nature all but 5 had been suppressed by the Communists. The Catholic News Bureau was transferred from Shanghai to Taiwan (Formosa), Free China, where it continued to function.

Taiwan. From 1859 to 1945 the necessary Catholic books for Taiwan's 8,000 Catholics were provided by importations from abroad and by local reprinting by the Spanish Dominicans. By 1949 the influx of expelled Catholic missionaries and the surprising increase of Catholics (more than 250,000 in 1964) required a local press. The Salesians started the Hwa Ming Press under the Catholic Press Bureau, which had moved from Shanghai. This work was taken over by the Scheut Fathers in 1955 and became a Scheut enterprise in 1960. The press averages one new work a month, largely translations from European books, and its printings for Taiwan alone average about 40,000. It publishes a Chinese monthly, *Review for Catechists*, and directs a correspondence course on religion, the Bible, and marriage.

In 1954, J. Goyoaga, SJ, opened the Kwang Chi Press in Taichung with a reprint of Father Ch'ing-shan's translation of the New Testament. Two-thirds of the press's publications are original compositions or translations from other languages and one-third are reprints from the China mainland. Kwang Chi averages from 3 to 5 new books a month; it publishes many books of literary rather than religious value in order to win acceptance for its books in all bookshops. More than 600 titles are distributed in Taiwan, Hong Kong, and in the diaspora.

Since 1949 a Chinese Catholic weekly, *Shan Tao Pao* (The Good Leader Newspaper), sponsored by the Vincentians, has risen in circulation to more than 6,000. Another weekly, *Chiao-Yu Sheng Huo* (The Catholic's Life), of the Taipei Archdiocese, has grown from a small sheet to four full-size pages with a circulation of more than 5,000. They both supply international, national, and diocesan news. Monthly reviews in Chinese, such as *To Sheng* (Voice of the Clergy), *Heng-Yi* (Constant and Resolute), for adults, and *Shih Yin* (Voice of the Times), have an established circulation of 500 to 1,000. The *Sacred Heart Messenger* and the *Eucharistic Crusader,* both in Chinese, and *Hsien Tai Hsueh Yuan* (Collectanea of Modern Learning) all fall within the range of 500 copies.

Hong Kong. Before 1933, Catholic press work in Hong Kong was carried on by the Foreign Mission Society of Paris and by the Salesians. Both presses supplied the missionaries with religious books necessary for their work. The Nazareth Press of the Missions-Étrangères de Paris, the earlier of the two, published in a variety of languages—Latin, French, Annamite, Chu-nom, Japanese, Thai, Lolo, Miao-nung, Cambodian, Laotian, Bahnar, Malayan, Tibetan, Chamorro, Palau, and Canaque. The Nazareth Press closed in 1953. The Salesian Press in Aberdeen, Hong Kong, began by reprinting Catholic works in Chinese and continued the same policy.

In 1933 N. Maestrini, PIME, started the now famous Catholic Truth Society, whose purpose is the publication and distribution of Chinese Catholic literature. One of its first and most successful efforts was *My Sunday Missal* by Father Stedman, translated by John C. H. Wu. In 1939, the society published a general catalog of Chinese Catholic publications of all China, every title being briefly annotated in Chinese, English, French, and Latin. By 1949, the society's distribution throughout China had passed the 500,000 mark. More recent major publications are the *Chinese Daily Missal,* Butler's *Lives of the Saints,* and American and German catechetical series in Chinese. In the 30 years of its existence, the Catholic Truth Society has published more than 600 titles and distributed more than 3 million pamphlets. By 1950 the society's efforts had turned to overseas Chinese.

Of major importance is a new scholarly translation of the Old and New Testaments of the Bible, prepared and published by the Studium Biblicum of the Franciscans. It is printed in separate volumes with copious notes. The Chinese Catholic weekly *Kung Kao Pao* (Catholic News) started in 1928 and by 1964 had reached a circulation of 8,000. Its counterpart in English, the *Sunday Examiner,* had a circulation of 7,800. Both papers exerted a strong influence on both Catholics and non-Catholics by their editorials and news reports, and were frequently quoted by the secular press.

Bibliography: Streit-Dindinger 23:1460, 2044, 2547, e.g., list studies on the Catholic press in mission countries; the latest, however, is dated 1952. *Annuaire de l'Église catholique en Chine, 1950* (Shanghai 1950). *Annuelle des oeuvres du Vicariat Apostolique de Shanghai, 1945–46* (Taichung 1964), list of publications.

[A. R. O'HARA]

9. England

At the beginning of the 19th century, efforts to publish a Catholic periodical were made in London by such publishers as Marmaduke, Keating, and Brown, who had already issued directories for the laity. They had also launched the earliest Catholic journal, the *Catholic Messenger* (1790), which lasted some 4 years. The *Catholic Magazine and Reflector* (1801) survived for only six numbers, and the *Catholic Magazine and Review* (1810, 1813) proved abortive. The *Conciliator* was projected in 1813 with an ambitious range of topics, but it is not clear that it even saw the light. In the same year, a pioneer, William Eusebius Andrews (1773–1837), issued the *Orthodox Journal and Catholic Monthly Intelligencer,* though his main efforts were devoted to the *Norfolk Chronicle.* Andrews also began (1820) the first Catholic weekly newspaper, the *Catholic Advocate of Civil and Religious Liberty,* whose crusade for full emancipation lasted only a year. He ran another series of the *Orthodox Journal* for 18 months and then changed its name to the *Weekly Orthodox Journal of Entertaining Christian Knowledge,* generally known as "Andrews's Penny Orthodox Journal." It became *Andrews's Weekly Journal* (1834) and then, in the following year, the *London and Dublin Orthodox Journal of Useful Knowledge;* this ran until 1845.

The *Publicist or Christian Philosopher* lasted for 6 months in 1815 and the *Catholicon or Christian Philosopher* for about as long in 1818. The song publishers Keating and Brown attempted (1823) the *Catholic Spectator, Selector & Monitor or Catholicon,* which appeared irregularly until 1826. Sylvester Palmer inaugurated the *Catholic Gentleman's Magazine* (1818), which was edited for its 1-year life by a distinguished chancery lawyer, Charles *Butler, who had played a leading role in the campaign against the laws then preventing Catholics from exercising full civic liberty.

Another unsuccessful venture of Andrews, the *Catholic Miscellany,* appeared in 1822, and Keating and Brown's *Christian Tablet* came out occasionally after 1832. The monthly *Edinburgh Catholic Magazine* (1832), edited by the convert James *Smith (1790?–1866), appeared for three numbers; it began a new series in 1837 and ran for a year and a half. Charles Dolman's *Catholic Magazine* survived from 1838 to 1842, lapsed for a time, and died in 1844. E. W. B. Lee, a convert, began (1836) the *Mediator and British Catholic Advocate,* which soon expired.

The present *Catholic Directory* began (1838) as a rival to the *Laity's Directory* of the previous century. The penny *Catholic Magazine* (1839) managed to live for a year. In 1840, the year of the foundation of the *Tablet,* the convert George Duncombe Cox launched in Edinburgh a literary and scientific journal, the *Phoenix;* when the *Tablet* refused to amalgamate with it, Cox abandoned his venture, which had lasted only 9 months.

The 1840s saw almost as many attempts at Catholic publishing as the 1830s had witnessed; nearly all of them shared the same fate, expiring after two or three numbers. They all suffered from the heavy stamp tax on newspapers and periodicals; this, together with the lack of a sufficiently large public, explains the shortness of their lives.

Enduring Foundations. The Catholic emancipation (1829) opened the way for the real establishment of the Catholic press in England. The first national Catholic publication was named the *Dublin Review,* and fittingly so, because the emancipation was the achievement of the Irish, led by Daniel *O'Connell, and because its founder was Nicholas (later Cardinal) *Wiseman, of an Irish family from Cork. The name was chosen also to present an antithesis to the famous *Edinburgh Review,* Whig and Protestant, then at the height of its influence. Since the *Dublin Review* was launched only 3 years after the beginning of the *Oxford Movement, many Anglican clergymen read it, among them John Henry *Newman, who later recorded that an article by Wiseman on the 4th-century Donatists had shown him how closely parallel the Anglican position was to that of the unorthodox Donatists (*see* DONATISM).

The *Tablet* was founded in London in 1840 as a weekly journal for the educated laity by Frederick *Lucas, a convert from Quakerism. Lucas, an Englishman, championed the Irish in their agitation for the repeal of the Union and was returned to the House of Commons from an Irish constituency. He died young, in 1855, shortly after returning from Rome, where he had gone to defend the interests of the Irish; he was frustrated in this, but he did not die without the satisfaction of knowing that the *Tablet* was firmly established as the leading Catholic weekly. Another convert, John Wallis, acquired the journal in 1855 and edited it until 1868. The journal's importance was shown by the efforts of the new archbishop of Westminster, Henry Edward *Manning, to gain control of it before *Vatican Council I convened on Dec. 8, 1869. He persuaded a young priest, Herbert *Vaughan (later his successor as cardinal), to buy the *Tablet* and to edit it as Manning desired. In 1884 Vaughan appointed as editor his cousin, John George *Snead-Cox, who held this post under Vaughan's general direction, and then under that of the next archbishop of Westminster, Francis *Bourne, for 36 years.

Vaughan died in 1903, having bequeathed the *Tablet* to the Archdiocese of Westminster with a stipulation that a third of the profits should go to his foundation, the *Mill Hill Missionaries. Under Vaughan and Bourne the *Tablet* was strongly conservative and became essentially the mouthpiece of the old Catholic families, whose social movements it recorded. It waged ceaseless war against the Anglicans; in fact, Snead-Cox's successor, Ernest *Oldmeadow, was chosen by Bourne because, as a convert from Methodism, he was experienced in conducting controversy. His style, however, did not appeal to the old Catholic families. The *Tablet* declined, and Bourne's successor, Cardinal Arthur *Hinsley, sold the paper to a group of laymen (1936). Douglas Woodruff became editor and was able, by broadening the paper's range of interest, to reestablish its fortunes.

The *Tablet* and the *Dublin Review* are the only survivors of the Catholic press of the 1840s and 1850s. The *Weekly Register,* edited (1854–63) by an Oxford Movement convert, Henry *Wilberforce, son of William *Wilberforce, the emancipator of the slaves, was bought at the time of Vatican Council I by Manning and later edited as he desired by Wilfrid Meynell. But it closed before the end of the century. The *Rambler,* founded by another convert, J. M. Capes, was even more short-lived. It began to make a great name in the 1850s, when editorial control was assumed by the convert clergyman Richard Simpson (1820–76) and the young Sir John Dalberg (later Lord) *Acton. Simpson thought he could bring into the Catholic Church the free and spacious habits of the Church of England, including open criticism of ecclesiastical authority; Acton set out to show non-Catholic England that true scholarship and a scientific attitude not only could flourish inside the Church, but were also native and congenial to it. They had the friendship and support of Newman at the Birmingham Oratory, but they soon caused disquiet among the newly established hierarchy, whose head, Cardinal Wiseman, thought that no Catholic paper should publish what might divide the small and struggling Catholic body. An article by Newman, "On Consulting the Faithful on Matters of Doctrine," offended readers at Rome and some of the English bishops, and Newman withdrew. Profoundly discouraged, Acton changed the *Rambler* to the quarterly *Home and Foreign Review,* but in 1864, the year of the *Syllabus of Errors, he abandoned his attempts at scholarly Catholic journalism.

Through these years, Acton had been opposed by the editor of the *Dublin Review,* W. G. *Ward, one of the first of the Oxford converts. The high reputation he won for the review was maintained by his son Wilfrid, editor from 1890 to his death in 1916 (*see* WARD, WILFRID). It became evident after World War I, however, that the era of the great quarterlies was over. Most of them have ceased publication, and, since Ireland has become an independent republic, the *Dublin Review* changed its name to the *Wiseman Review;* it remained the property of the archbishop of Westminster and in 1964 was edited by Norman St. John Stevas (1929–), who renamed it the *Dublin Review.* One of the most notable Catholic journalists, the convert Wilfrid *Meynell, founded the monthly *Merry England* (1883–95), in which the poems of Francis *Thompson first appeared. His wife, Alice *Meynell, though best remembered as a poet, made notable contributions to Catholic journalism, and she and her husband greatly advanced Catholic publishing when he became head of Burns and Oates.

Intellectual journalism was reinforced when the Jesuits founded the London *Month* in 1864; a succession of scholarly editors, beginning with Henry *Coleridge, and erudite Jesuit writers, with Herbert *Thurston prominent among them, maintained a tradition of quality. John Moffat (1964) somewhat modified the more exclusively literary approach of his predecessor, Philip Caraman. For 40 years the Dominicans have maintained their monthly *Blackfriars* to reflect the order's open-minded response to new ideas and artistic forms. The Benedictines at *Downside Abbey publish the *Downside Review,* an admirable example of the Benedictine intellectual tradition.

Popular Press. The Catholic body had no popular press until Irish immigration, caused by the famine of 1847, changed the face of English Catholicism. The *Catholic Times* (1859) and the *Universe* (1860) were founded by Irishmen with the full support, almost at the request, of the hierarchy. Both papers were in constant financial difficulties, and as late as World War I the *Universe* was saved from collapse by Sir Martin *Melvin, who sent a young editor to the U.S. to study the techniques of Catholic journalism there. The paper's circulation was raised from 20,000 to more than 300,000 (1962), when it absorbed the *Catholic Times* and became the most widely circulated religious paper in the country. Before this merger, the *Catholic Times* had prospered under the direction of Henry Vaughan and later (1934–59) under the proprietorship and editorship of James Walsh.

In 1894 Charles *Diamond established the *London Catholic Herald,* which had originally been the *Weekly Herald* (founded 1888). He built up circulation by a large number of local editions in the dominantly Catholic towns of Lancashire. Vernon Miles (1902–) acquired the *Herald* after Diamond's death and raised its character to make it appeal to the growing number of Catholic students at the provincial universities. Michael de la Bedoyère (1900–), who became editor in 1934, struck a balance between the *Tablet* and the *Universe;* together with its subsidiary, the *Glasgow Observer,* the *Herald* reached a six-figure circulation. Upon Bedoyère's retirement (1962), Desmond Fisher (1920–), previously the London representative of the Irish daily press, became editor and continued the paper's forward-looking tradition.

Short-lived ventures included a magazine for juveniles, the *Catholic Junior* (1910–14), and *Heritage* (1952–60), a monthly devoted to graphic depictions of Catholic churches, colleges, and buildings of historical interest. Intellectual reviews, such as the *Coliseum* (1934–37), edited by Bernard Wall (1908–), and the *Wind and the Rain,* begun by M. Allmand (1940), and in 1941 and thereafter edited by Neville Braybrooke (1929–), gave great promise but did not take lasting root.

The Knights of Columba published a flourishing monthly, *Columba* (1923), and the Jesuits issued the devotional *Stella Maris* (1901). The *Catholic Fireside* (1879), another devotional magazine, met the continuing demand for homely, edifying tales. The *Catholic Pictorial,* under lay ownership, appeared in Liverpool with archiepiscopal support in the late 1950s.

[D. WOODRUFF]

Wales. There is no organized Catholic press in Wales, where the scattered Catholics have no opportunity to nurture collective opinion. Most press activity has sprung from the zeal of parish priests. In the past, some of their work was of permanent merit, e.g., *Cennad Catholig Cymru* (Little Messenger of Catholic Cambria), a trilingual (Welsh-Breton-English) paper issued by Father Trebaol of the Breton mission (1910–14). *See* WALES.

St. Peter's Magazine (Cardiff 1921–29), which was edited by John Cronin, IC, was outstanding for much original research. A small quarterly publication, *Llais Cyfeillion Cymru,* issued at Liverpool by Winifred Loughlin for the past 25 years, contains Welsh historical information in order to maintain interest among world-wide prayer circles that financially assist struggling parishes in Wales. A quarterly magazine-type *Menevia Record* in English is published at Wrexham. It is popular in its appeal and supplies the non-Welsh Catholic with the historical and apostolic background to his life in Wales.

Efrydiau Catholig (1946–55, Catholic Studies), edited by Saunders Lewis, published annually by Y Cylch Catholig, produced articles in Welsh of the highest scholarly and literary merit; it was superseded by *Ysgrifau Catholig* (Catholic Essays). Y Cylch also publishes the quarterly *Cylch Translations,* edited by J. P. Brown, a collection of excerpts concerning Catholicism, drawn from the numerous weekly and monthly Welsh Church and Nonconformist publications.

For 40 years the *Catholic Times* ran as a supplement the *Welsh Catholic Times,* published at Cardiff to report Church life in Wales. This ceased in 1962 upon amalgamation with the London *Universe.* Regular Catholic press activity is carried on by the Welsh Catholic minority in the many Welsh denominational non-Catholic papers that are ecumenically disposed and publish articles on Catholic doctrine and exegesis.

See also CATHOLIC PRESS, WORLD SURVEY, 14, 24.

[C. DANIEL]

10. France

The Catholic press has played, and still plays, an important role in the religious and cultural life of France. It has had a long and stormy history, the storms arising not only from within the Church but from adversaries outside it.

Beginnings to the 20th Century. In 1701 *Le Journal de Trévoux* was founded by the Jesuits. In 1728 the first issue of *Nouvelles Ecclésiastiques,* a Jansenist paper, appeared; and in 1734 the first edition of *Le Supplément des Nouvelles Ecclésiastiques* was launched in turn by the Jesuits (*see* JANSENISM). *Les Annales de la Religion,* the official publication of the constitutional clergy (supporters of the *Civil Constitution of the Clergy), appeared on May 2, 1795. In 1796 *Les Annales Religieuses, Politiques et Littéraires* was begun by the clergy who did not support that constitution; it became *L'Ami de la Religion et du Roi* in 1814. Under the first restoration the struggles between the ultramontanists and the Gallicans arose (*see* ULTRAMONTANISM); *Le Mémorial Catholique* was started by H. *Lamennais (1824), and *Les Tablettes du Clergé* made its debut in the same year. During the second restoration, *Le Correspondant* (1829) appeared as the organ of the association for the defense of the Catholic religion. It was revived in 1843 by *Ozanam, *Montalambert, and *Lacordaire. *L'Avenir* was launched by Lamennais at the beginning of this second epoch on Oct. 16, 1830. He sought to unite the cause of liberty with that of religion, but was condemned by the encyclical *Mirari vos* of Gregory XVI (Aug. 15, 1832). The newspapers founded by P. Buchez appeared next—*L'Européen* (1832–35) and *L'Atelier* (1840), the first paper established by workers. *L'Univers* was founded (1833) by Abbé Ming, and Louis *Veuillot joined it in 1840. It defended religion in a conservative fashion. The Christian Democrats founded *L'Ere Nouvelle* in 1848; it was purchased by the conservatives in 1849. *Les Semaines Religieuses,* the official organ of the bishops, appeared in 1850. Newspapers for young people, which had begun in 1828 (e.g., *L'Abeille Française*) were followed by *Le Jeune Ouvrier* (1856). In 1860 *Le Monde* made its appearance (destined to replace *L'Univers*), and later the liberal *Le Français* (1868) entered the scene.

After 1870 the democrats opposed the conservatives. *Le Peuple* of Abbé Garnier was founded in 1893; *La Justice Sociale* of Abbé Naudet was begun in the same year at Bordeaux. Abbé Sixte began *La Démocratie Chrétienne* at Lille in 1894. The principal rightist papers were *Libre Parole* (1892), *L'Action Française* (1908), and *L'Univers,* which absorbed *La Vérité.* (*See* ACTION FRANÇAISE.)

Large Publishing Houses. At this juncture, the character of the press was dominated by the creation of specializing publishing houses; the publications of the various movements of Catholic Action likewise shifted to this system. La Maison de la Bonne Presse was founded by the Assumptionists in 1873. Around *Le Pèlerin,* an offshoot of the first pilgrimages to La Salette and Lourdes, and *La Croix,* a daily newspaper, there sprang up all the various publications required to fill the needs of the Church. Les Editions du Cerf appeared in 1919 when Father Vincent *Bernadot issued the first edition of *La Vie Spirituelle;* in 1928 he began *La Vie Intellectuelle.* Many reviews and magazines published by religious or lay groups in support of his work followed. In 1928 L'Union des Oeuvres, at the urging of Father G. Courtois, bought two magazines, *Patronage* and *La Vie au Patronage,* in which Courtois endeavored to satisfy the reading needs of young people and to provide a pastoral type magazine for parishes.

The house of Bloud and Gay published the first *Vie Catholique* in 1924, partly to give the Church an image different from that presented by *L'Action Française. La France Catholique* was founded in 1925 by the National Catholic Federation. *L'Echo des Françaises* appeared in 1903. In 1935 a missionary magazine, *Missi,* was founded. Along with these productions of Catholic Action, magazines were started by the group inspired by the Jesuits and known as *Action Populaire, which concerned itself with social questions. In general, the French Catholic press is much more concerned with forming public opinion and advancing the apostolate than with disseminating news.

National Press of General Interest. There were few Christian dailies that fall within the usual definition of "the press." The one incontestable exception is *La Croix,* whose press run reaches 150,000 copies if its subsidiary edition, *La Croix du Nord,* is included.

Weeklies. These are numerous. The most important are *Le Pèlerin,* published by La Maison de la Bonne Presse (1877), with a circulation of 600,000, and *La Vie Catholique Illustrée* (1945, 500,000). These are illustrated weeklies of general interest. They cover current questions both religious and secular. Much of their space is given over to family life and leisure activities, but they try to bring to their readers an awareness of the supernatural and to instruct them in the current thought of the Church. A concern for temporal matters is more evident in *La Vie Catholique Illustrée* than in *Le Pèlerin.* Among the large Catholic weeklies, *Télérama* (120,000 circulation) has a special place; it is a cultural weekly that publishes radio, TV, and movie programs and prints reviews of them with an eye to general cultural and spiritual education and not solely to their moral aspects. There are also such public opinion weeklies as *Témoignage Chrétien* (1941, 50,000), liberally oriented and outspoken on a number of current events, or *La France Catholique* (1925, 70,000), with a more traditional viewpoint than *Témoignage.*

Monthlies and Bimonthlies. The religious information bimonthlies are *La Documentation Catholique* (1919) and *Informations Catholiques Internationales* (1955, after the disappearance of *Actualité Religieuse dans le Monde,* founded 1953). While the first of these reproduces texts and documents already published and is, in general, of an official nature, the second gives extensive religious reports designed to demonstrate the varied activities of the Church. Since 1963 it has had a Spanish edition in Mexico.

There are, in addition, some illustrated monthlies that present materials of interest to a more advanced readership, such as *Panorama Chrétien* (1957, 150,000). *Croissance des Jeunes Nations* (1961, 15,000) is devoted to the problems of the development of the newly emerging nations. *Fêtes et Saisons* (100,000) presents each month an illustrated series on one subject: religious, such as Baptism, or social, such as the single woman.

A number of general interest monthlies follow the old typographical format of presenting text without illustrations. Some of these have a glorious history in the struggle for the defense and propagation of the faith. One such is *Études* (1856, 20,000), published by the Jesuits. *Signes du Temps* (1959, Editions du Cerf), issued jointly with the publications of *La Vie Catholique Illustrée,* has a circulation of 10,000 and draws its inspiration from the encyclical *Pacem in terris* of John XXIII. *Esprit* (1933, 10,000) publishes many special editions. One of its characteristics is the impartial collaboration in its content of believers and unbelievers alike. *Economie et Humanisme* appears every other month and seeks to promote a more humane world. Its counterpart is *Civilisation et Développement,* a quarterly that deals with the problems of the underdeveloped nations.

Fig. 3. Publications of the Catholic press in France.

Among the monthlies, mention should be made of those published by the various groups of Catholic Action, either alone or in conjunction with the publishing houses. The general men's group of Catholic Action issues *France Monde Catholique;* that of the women publishes *L'Echo des Françaises,* an eight-page monthly with a circulation of 1 million. The Rural Family Group publishes a weekly, *Foyer Rural,* and a monthly, *Clair Foyer. Masses Ouvrières* is a monthly dealing with the problems of the apostolate among workers.

Agricultural and student Catholic youth groups publish, in conjunction with La Maison de la Bonne Presse, an illustrated monthly for young people between the ages of 14 and 18, *Le Rallye Jeunesse* (300,000). The student group issues, in conjunction with *La Vie Catholique Illustrée,* a monthly, *Le Cri* (30,000), devoted to the social and cultural problems of collegians.

Children's Papers. L'Union des Oeuvres publishes *Fripounet et Marisette* (8 to 11 years, 225,000), *J. 2 Jeunes* (boys 11 to 14, 100,000), and *J. 2 Magazine* (girls 11 to 14, 100,000). La Maison de la Bonne Presse published *Nade* for girls (8 to 14, 70,000) and *Record* for boys of the same age (100,000).

Parochial Bulletins. The editions of these run to several million copies, usually monthly. Certain of these contain a general section that permits the insertion of religious material among the current-event discussions. These general sections, called "Matters in Common," are frequently furnished to the parishes by the large publishing houses, which send them to the priest editors of the parish bulletins. The principal publishing houses are L'Office Technique de la Presses Paroissiale, which publishes *Nos Quartiers* and *Présences* (Lille); Les Publications de La Vie Catholique Illustrée, which issues *Images de Mois* (Paris); and *Le Journal Paroissal de Limoges,* which specializes in the needs of rural parishes and is edited differently for each parish according to the degree to which it has become dechristianized.

The regional Catholic press includes 20 weeklies published to serve 60 dioceses, with a circulation of some 1 million copies. These editions, usually weekly, are of size to cover either a single diocese or several. Their object is to combat the effect of the secular dailies that are widely read, even in regions staunchly Catholic, as well as to provide news of the life of the Church and of the organizations of Catholic Action.

The most important regional newspapers are *Le Courrier Français* (Bordeaux), with 22 editions serving 14 dioceses in the southwest, west, and central areas; *La Croix du Midi* (Toulouse), with 9 editions for 7 dioceses; and *Semailles* (Marseilles), with 6 editions for 4 dioceses. *La Croix du Dimanche,* published by La Maison de la Bonne Presse, serves some 10 dioceses.

La Vie Catholique Illustrée has its own delivery system, independent of the commercial network that distributes the secular press. Workers undertake its sale at church doors or even from door to door in residential areas. There workers are organized into parochial press committees (6,000) and diocesan committees (600). Certain chaplains in the Information Service are charged with maintaining liaison between the Catholic Action groups, the press committees, and the individual workers. The French hierarchy maintains an Information Bureau.

The directors of the Catholic Press are organized into two main bodies, Le Centre National de la Presse Catholique and L'Association Nationale des Périodiques Catholiques de Province, which jointly consider their common problems and discuss them with the hierarchy.

Bibliography: G. HOURDIN, *La Presse Catholique* (Paris 1957).

[G. HOURDIN]

11. GERMANY

The situation of the press at mid-20th century, especially in multidenominational countries like the Federal Republic of Germany (West Germany), inclines one to designate as "Catholic" all newspapers and journals that agree with Catholic faith and morals and actively support the Church's undertakings, spread her teaching, defend her interests, and provide a forum for the voice of the Catholic portion of the population in the pluralistic society of their country. Even if they are not intended to serve an exclusively Catholic reading public, such publications are in reality Catholic, as long as they are entirely or predominantly managed by Catholic publishers and editors. Any more restricted definition of the Catholic press, e.g., as simply those publications belonging to a bishop, a religious order, or a section of Catholic Action, would not do justice to the very complex current situation. A further pertinent consideration is the fact that after World War II many Catholic journalists transferred their services to the nondenominational press and have remained in its service. This shift was prompted partly by the licensing policy practiced by the occupation forces after the war and partly by the decision of the journalists themselves.

Prior to 1933 the Zentrums-Partei (Center party), Catholic in practice if not in theory, represented the political home for zealous practicing Catholics; after 1945 this political home came to be the biconfessional Christian Democrat party(CDU). The result has been a decline in the Catholic dailies in favor of Christian—biconfessional—ones (which, however, still have a pronounced Catholic character in predominantly Catholic areas); there has been a concurrent increase in the importance of the Catholic weeklies, diocesan papers, Sunday bulletins, and monthlies, all of which take stronger stands on topical questions than they had formerly done. Radio and television have contributed greatly to this evolution. The demand for up-to-the-minute information is being satisfied to a great extent by these electronic media. The weekly, with its strong theoretical and political commitment, its main stress on commentary with only secondary attention given to factual reporting, tends to devote itself to a classification and evaluation of the plethora of news taken from radio, television, and the local newspapers (which for the most part have no pronounced theoretical slant). This state of affairs has led to a considerable enhancement of the role of the diocesan papers, depending on their circulation and influence. Catholicism in West Germany as in other countries has also provided itself with special organs of information, such as the *Herder Correspondence* (Freiburg 1946; circulation 15,000), to give a thorough documentation, with some commentary, on the life of the Church and on the general domestic and foreign questions of importance to the religious activity and political involvement of the Church and that of other religious denominations (*see* HERDER). An important innovation was the founding of the Catholic News Agency (KNA; see below).

Development to 1945. Johann Joseph von *Görres, active in Strasbourg and later in Munich after the *Rheinischer Merkur* period (1814–16), ranks as the first great pioneer of modern German Catholic journalism. But even before him there had been such press organs as the *Augsburger Post-Zeitung* (1689) and the *Relationes extraordinariae* (Cologne 1675), which had looked after the interests of Catholics. The freedom of the press and assembly granted in 1848 brought in its train, together with a growth in the Catholic movement for political, ecclesiastical, and social freedom, the birth of the modern Catholic press. Often press unions were themselves the founders or at least the promoters of new newspapers. The conservative tone of the early Catholic dailies gave way during the *Kulturkampf (after 1870) to a forthright support of the program and policy of the Center party. During this period the Catholic press became the mouthpiece, weapon, and rallying point of the Catholic population and developed the local paper, often small and always with a quite spirited tone, as its typical manifestation. The development can be seen from the following statistics: in 1848 there were 6 Catholic dailies; these grew to 20 in 1865, 120 in 1873, 271 in 1878, 325 in 1903, 445 in 1912, 451 in 1925, dropping to 434 in 1931–32. The total circulation of about 3 million in 1931–32 means that the Catholic press then accounted for one-eighth of the total circulation of the German daily press. But no single Catholic newspaper had a circulation in excess of 70,000.

Besides these dailies, the German Catholics had at their disposal in 1933 about 420 journals, church magazines, weekly bulletins, etc., with a total circulation of 9.5 million; this circulation rose in the first years of the National Socialist regime to 11.5 million in 1935; of these periodicals, 29 had a circulation of more than 100,000. In 1939, the Catholic press was completely suppressed by the National Socialists: only church bulletins could appear and even these were under state censorship, which forbade discussion of many topics and even barred publication of certain texts. During the war paper shortage was used as a pretext for closing these publications altogether.

Development since 1945. Prior to the currency reform (1948), every journalistic activity needed a license. Denominational and political party dailies were not permitted by the military government. The only exception (*Deutsche Tagespost*) came into being only because Johann Wilhelm Naumann (1897–1956) gave up his rights as coowner of the large *Schwäbische Landeszeitung* in Augsburg in the autumn of 1948 and exchanged them for a license to found a small Catholic paper. This restriction on Catholic dailies made its consequences felt for a long time. But the fact that there was in West Germany in 1965 no large, widely influential supraregional Catholic daily was in line with the general development since 1945, which has seen a decline in periodicals with a clearly defined philosophical or political outlook in favor of "independent" papers. The eight Catholic dailies published in 1965 totaled only about 1 per cent of the combined circulation of German dailies (more than 20 million). They are all regional except the *Deutsche Tagespost* (Würzburg; circulation 20,000 to 25,000). Of the total circulation of German newspapers, 10.2 per cent rank as Christian dailies closely associated with the Christian political parties.

Weeklies in Germany are a post-World War II novelty. There are today under Catholic management the *Allgemeine Sonntagszeitung* (Würzburg; circulation 20,000), *Der christliche Sonntag* (Freiburg im Breisgau; 20,000), the *Rheinischer Merkur* (Cologne; 30,000), the *Echo der Zeit* (Recklinghausen; 30,000), and *Das Wort* (Hildesheim; 12,000). These politico-cultural weeklies are supraregional in circulation and exercise a strong influence in molding public opinion. Related to them in political stance are two large Catholic labor-union monthly publications: *Kettelerwacht* (Cologne; 150,000), the organ of the Catholic Worker Movement; and *Mann in der Zeit* (Augsburg; 700,000), organ of the Arbeitsgemeinschaft der katholischen Männerwerke. Catholic magazines occupy a considerable place in the total magazine output. There were in 1965 more than 420 Catholic magazines, with a total circulation of more than 15 million. This includes missionary magazines; diocesan bulletins; Sunday and family bulletins; women's magazines; and educational, professional, and youth magazines.

The total circulation of Catholic "cultural journals," however, is a modest 30,000 or slightly more; but the circulation of the journals that are most important for the prestige and dissemination of Catholic thought is considerably higher than it was prior to World War II. Such journals are *Wort und Wahrheit* (Vienna and Freiburg 1945), *Hochland* (Munich 1903), and *Stimmen der Zeit* (founded Munich and Freiburg 1871 as *Stimmen aus Maria Laach*). These journals undoubtedly exercise a greater influence than formerly on non-Catholic intellectuals.

Isolated Catholic picture magazines are the *Feuerreiter,* founded by Hans Struth (Cologne 1925; 250,000), the monthly *Erdkreis* (Würzburg 1951; 9,700), with its penchant for art photography, and *Kontraste* (Freiburg im Breisgau, 30,000). The *Katholischer Digest* (Aschaffenburg 1947; 100,000) is patterned on its U.S. namesake (*see* DIGEST MAGAZINES, CATHOLIC). The experiment of a weekly "Catholic boulevard newspaper" called *Neue Bildpost* (Bödefeld 1952; 400,000) is still very controversial.

In contrast to this opportunity for a free and rich development of the Catholic press in West Germany stands the almost total suppression in the Soviet zone. Only two small Church bulletins are permitted by the authorities: *St. Hedwigsblatt* (Berlin, weekly) and *Tag des Herrn* (Leipzig, fortnightly). Their circulation and scope are prescribed by the Communist regime. Even quantitatively they cannot begin to satisfy the demand of the Catholics there—and they cannot speak freely. The so-called "Christian-Democratic Union" of the Soviet zone is ideologically and organizationally dependent on the Communist Unity party; its press (central organ, *Neue Zeit*) can in no sense be called Christian; indeed, it distinguishes itself occasionally by its campaign against religion and church.

The Katholische Nachrichtenagentur. Prominent among the innovations since 1945 because of its great importance for German Catholicism and Catholic journalism is the Katholische Nachrichtenagentur (KNA: Catholic News Agency). It was found in 1953, and is supported by the German diocese, the diocesan bulletins, and the Christian dailies; it represents the fulfillment of a measure repeatedly called for during the 19th century.

The KNA publishes a daily press service bulletin containing current news and reports on events in ecclesiastical, cultural, and social life, domestic and foreign. Editorial boards, associations, government offices and private individuals can subscribe to this bulletin. Important announcements are transmitted by teletype. KNA also publishes an information service bulletin (weekly), the "Catholic Correspondence" for the diocesan press (weekly), a special service covering Vatican Council II (published weekly, daily during sessions, with very wide circulation), and six regional service bulletins. In collaboration with KNA are published "The Socio-Political Information Service Bulletin" (fortnightly), "The Christian Family" (monthly), and correspondence on school, radio and film questions (each fortnightly). KNA also has an efficient news picture service (KNA-Pressebild). The dispatches and articles of the KNA are utilized not only by Catholic newspapers and periodicals; they also have been widely incorporated into the non-Catholic press and into radio broadcasts. The KNA is, in the mid-1960s, one of the most important instruments of Catholic journalism.

Organizational Questions. The Augustinus-Verein zur Pflege der katholischen Presse (Augustine Union for Promotion of the Catholic Press), founded in 1878, was suppressed by the National Socialist regime. At the first postwar Catholic Day in Mainz (Sept. 2, 1948) the Gesellschaft katholischer Publizisten Deutschlands (Society of Catholic Journalists of Germany) was founded to include not only newspapermen but also Catholic journalists in all communications media. It had 321 members as of 1965, and has set itself the aims of "a closer union of the Catholic journalists, in order to cope with their professional concerns and, should the occasion arise, to take a common stand on the great questions of the German press," promotion of the recruitment and training of young journalists, and the resumption of contact with the Catholic press abroad. It is a member of the Paris Union Internationale de la Presse Catholique (*see* PRESS ASSOCIATIONS AND SERVICES, CATHOLIC).

Practically all Catholic journalists were formerly employed by the numerous Catholic newspapers and periodicals; today the majority of them work in the denominationally heterogeneous environment of the various media. Thus special priority is given to strengthening personal contact and solidarity and to providing opportunities for specialized pastoral work (retreats and days of recollection for Catholic journalists). An information bulletin provides advice on professional matters and affords professional and social assistance. Regular contacts are maintained with the Catholic journalists and publishers of the neighboring countries, especially France, Austria, and Switzerland.

Aside from this general organization of the Catholic journalists of Germany, there has been in existence since 1949 the Arbeitsgemeinschaft kirchliche Presse, comprising some 70 publishing houses with about 140 media. The German hierarchy has formed a Journalism Commission of three bishops, one of whom devotes himself principally to work with the press. The press workshop of the Central Committee of German Catholics was put on a permanent basis in 1958; it meets for consultations in the main at Catholic Days and working sessions of the Central Committee; its reports and resolutions are published in the minute books of the Central Committee.

Summing Up. Social conditions and the general state of communications media must be taken into account in any proper judgment on the function and significance of the Catholic press in the German Federal Republic. The Catholics are no longer oppressed as in the days of the Kulturkampf; they are no longer on the defensive, as they were under the Kaisers; they, like other Germans, have found in politics and cultural endeavor the opportunity for free development. They are also active in the communications media, although not yet to a degree proportionate to their percentage of the total population. Yet Suffragan Bishop Walther Kampe could state in Münster in 1964: "It must be gratefully acknowledged that there are Catholic journalists active on many editorial boards of non-aligned or non-Catholic Christian dailies, in radio stations and publishing houses, who are definitely not hiding the light of our faith under a bushel basket. The Church has today acquired a journalistic influence over the public which she did not have prior to 1933. National Socialism unintentionally forced us out of the ghetto of Catholic journalism; and even though we did have to pay a bitter price for it (above all, the loss of valuable Catholic dailies of worldwide renown and of important regional newspapers as well), it cannot be denied that the general public is today far more extensively informed on things Catholic than ever before." Vatican Council II has been of special importance in promoting this development.

Bibliography: K. BACHEM, *Josef Bachem und die Entwicklung der katholischen Presse in Deutschland,* 2 v. (Cologne 1912). K. LÖFFLER, *Geschichte der katholischen Presse Deutschlands* (München-Gladbach 1924). W. KISKY, *Der Augustinus-Verein zur Pflege der katholischen Presse von 1878 bis 1928* (Düsseldorf 1928). J. H. KRUMBACH, *Vorfragen einer Soziologie der katholischen Presse* (Munich 1932). O. B. ROEGELE, "Zum Problem der katholischen Presse in Deutschland," *Hochland* 44.1 (1951–52) 24–34; "Katholischer Journalismus in der heutigen Zeit," *Südtirol in Not und Bewährung: Festschrift Michael Gamper,* ed. T. EBNER (Innsbruck 1955). *Leitfaden für Presse und Werbung,* ed. W. STAMM (Essen 1947–), annual reference work for circulation statistics. *Adressbuch für das katholische Deutschland* (Cologne 1965), includes publishers. O. B. ROEGELE and H. AUHOFER, StL 4:888–899.

[O. B. ROEGELE]

12. HUNGARY

In the late 1930s, 3 Catholic dailies, 3 weeklies, and several monthlies were published in Budapest alone; in the provinces there were 19 Catholic dailies and a proportionate number of weeklies and monthlies. Six large Catholic publishing houses supplied the country's needs for literature and textbooks. The volume of publishing fell substantially during the war, and many newspapers were forced to suspend publication. In 1945, nevertheless, the country had 2 Catholic dailies, 18 weeklies, 25 monthlies, 3 quarterlies, and about 20 other periodicals. The total output reached 1½ million copies monthly, not counting textbooks and books on purely religious subjects.

When the Soviet armies occupied Hungary, a decree of early 1945 imposed the obligation of special authorization for any publication and severely controlled newsprint allocations. An immediate result was the suppression of the old Budapest Catholic paper *Nemzeti Ujság* (National Journal). In April 1945, the Inter-Allied Commission authorized a weekly, *A Szív* (The Heart), as a purely religious publication. The following month permission was given for *Új Ember* (New Man), to treat social and political problems. It later became the official organ of Catholic Action and its subscriber list grew to 150,000, but by 1949 its newsprint allocation was cut to 50,000. A literary review, *Vigilia,* was authorized in 1947. That was the entire extent of an authentic Catholic press. Even these publications were rigidly supervised; no criticism of the regime was possible.

In the late 1940s, the government took various steps to infiltrate the Catholic publishing field. A number of publishing houses were nationalized and textbooks were rewritten to conform to Marxist philosophy. An index of books to be withdrawn from circulation was compiled, and books and files of magazines in both public and monastic libraries were destroyed. Prepublication censorship was extended not only to printed matter but to every work produced in several copies, even typed carbons. An organization with communist sympathies, headed by an excommunicated priest, Istvan Balogh, and former Cistercian, Richard Horvath, called itself the Peace Committee of Catholic Priests and started a pseudo-Catholic periodical, *A Kereszt* ("The Cross"), in 1950. The situation eased somewhat after Stalin's death in 1953, but without any basic change in the attitude of the regime to the Catholic press. In June 1955, Rome condemned *A Kereszt* and the *Hun-*

garian Catholic Bulletin, published by the government in several languages for distribution mainly outside the country for the purpose of proving that religious freedom existed in Hungary. A new Catholic publication, *Katolikus Szó* (Catholic Word), appeared in 1956 with Church approval. In the same year, the Society of St. Stephen was authorized to publish a catechism. Horvath was excommunicated in February 1957, but a few months later 36 members of the "peace movement" in which Horvath was active submitted themselves to their bishops and pledged fidelity to the Holy See. Horvath thereupon asked and received absolution from the sentence of excommunication.

Pressure on the Catholic press continued nevertheless, especially after the revolt of October 1956 had been crushed. By 1959, distribution of Catholic papers and journals was greatly curtailed and the copy was rigidly censored. In the field of books, only bibles and religious manuals were permitted to be printed, and no Catholic books could be imported. By the early 1960s, the regime obviously thought that the Catholic press had ceased to be influential and could be given more freedom under an unwritten understanding that it would avoid all controversy. In 1963, the Catholic press consisted of a bulletin or news service called *Magyar Kurir* (Hungarian Courier) and the three publications *Új Ember*, *Katolikus Szó*, and *Vigilia*.

Bibliography: A. GALTER, *The Red Book of the Persecuted Church* (Westminster, Md. 1957). G. MACEOIN, *The Communist War on Religion* (New York 1951). *Bilan du Monde* (1964).

[G. MAC EOIN]

13. INDIA

Catholics in India number less than 7 million in a population that exceeds 400 million. This small community employs about 50 languages. A survey of the Catholic press in India is, accordingly, a catalogue of regional and multilingual efforts.

Native-Language Publications. About two-thirds of the Catholic community is concentrated in southern India—particularly in the states of Kerala, Madras, Mysore, and the Union territory of Goa. In Kerala, where the language is Malayalam, an exceptional feature is the existence of four Catholic dailies, of which *Deepika* (Light), published by the Congregation of Mary Immaculate, is the largest, with a circulation of 25,000 (*see* CHAVARA, KURIACKOS ELIAS). The others are *Kerala Times* (published at Ernakulam), *Malabar Mail* (Ernakulam), and *Thozilali* (Worker, Trichur).

In Madras State most Catholic publications are in Tamil, and the majority are devotional monthlies. *Poyya Vilakku* (Infallible Light, published at Dindigul), a monthly intended for non-Catholics, has a circulation of 12,500. The monthly *Narkarunai Veeran* (Knights of the Blessed Sacrament, Dindigul) is noteworthy for being adapted in other vernaculars to reach a total circulation of 140,000 (Tamil circulation 18,000). Another sizeable group of Catholic publications with distribution chiefly in Mysore State and on the southwest coast has Konkani for its medium—most are monthlies published at Mangalore. The Mangalore weekly *Rakno* (Guardian) has a rising circulation

Fig. 4. The Catholic press in India publishes in many languages. The mastheads shown here are from newspapers printed in Hindi, Bengali, Marathi, Portuguese, Malayalam, Tamil, and English.

(7,000 in 1964). The chief Catholic publications in Goa (three dailies, four weeklies) have been printed in Portuguese and Konkani but are in a transition period.

The Hindi *Sanjivan,* founded at Patna, Bihar (1950), as a 4-page weekly, moved to Delhi in 1963, and became a 10-page issue with a circulation of 7,000. Other leading Hindi publications are the Sodality monthly *Nishkalanka* (Immaculate, Ranchi, Bihar 1921), and *Sandesh* (Patna 1949), a Messenger of the Sacred Heart.

English Publications. Since English is still the language of prestige, the most influential Catholic publications are three national English weeklies—the *Examiner* at Bombay (*see* HULL, ERNEST REGINALD), the *Herald* (Calcutta), and the *New Leader* (Madras). Weekly circulation ranges from 5,000 to 8,000.

The attempt to exert influence outside Catholic circles through English periodicals has had negligible success. The *Light of the East* (Calcutta), an apologetic monthly founded in 1922, suspended publication in 1946 (*see* DANDOY, GEORGE). In the sociocultural field the *New Review* (Calcutta) survived from 1935 to 1950. In 1951, *Social Action,* monthly organ of the Jesuit Institute of Social Order, commenced publication at Poona; it has since shifted to New Delhi and has a circulation not above 2,000. The Catholic Truth Society (CTS) of India (Tiruchirappalli, South India), modeled on the CTS of England, has rendered long service. It has published a monthly and religious tract since April 1, 1919, and has averaged an annual distribution of 220,000 tracts throughout India, Burma, Ceylon, and Pakistan. Also published in English are the organs, usually monthly, of specialized groups, e.g., the Sodality (*Ave,* Kurseong, W. Bengal; *Morning Star,* Bombay); university students (*King's Rally,* Madras); Nurses' Guild (*Lotus and the Lamp,* New Delhi); and Hospital Association (*Medical Service,* New Delhi). *The Clergy Monthly,* published by the Jesuits (Kurseong 1938), has a circulation of 4,000.

The Catholic News Service of India (New Delhi), a professional news agency for all of India, was launched in 1962, has 40 correspondents, and began sending dispatches to foreign papers in June 1963. The special needs of the Catholic Press in India are advanced techniques for prompt coverage of national Catholic news and mature comment on current events.

Bibliography: Streit-Dindinger 23:1460, 2044, 2547, e.g., list studies on the Catholic Press in mission countries; the latest, however, is dated 1952.

[H. ROZARIO]

14. IRELAND

More than 94 per cent of the population of the Irish Republic is Catholic. It is remarkable, therefore, that before the beginning of the 20th century there was no Irish newspaper Catholic in outlook and nationwide in circulation.

Newspapers. Such a press in Ireland dates only from January 1905, when the Dublin *Irish Independent* was founded by William Martin *Murphy. It rapidly established itself as the national newspaper, the daily circulation rising from an initial 20,000 to 71,000 in 1912 and 174,000 in 1962. Its closest competitor is the *Irish Press* (Dublin 1930), the organ of the Fianna Fáil (Republican) party, which sells 116,000 copies daily. Evening counterparts of these papers—the *Evening Herald* (1907) and the *Evening Press* (1954)—divide about equally a circulation of 244,000. Daily papers with a Catholic viewpoint are published also in Belfast (*Irish News,* 1855, 48,000) and Cork (*Examiner,* 1841, 50,000; and *Echo,* 1892, 34,000). Practically every home in Ireland is reached by the *Sunday Independent* (1907) and the *Sunday Press* (1950), which respectively sold 316,000 and 355,000 copies weekly in 1962.

These are secular papers, but all are Catholic in outlook, observing Catholic moral and social principles in their presentation and analysis of news. All give full publicity to public statements by prominent churchmen; to the work, tribulations, and achievements of the Church; and to its views on current social and political matters. The independence of their reports and opinions is accepted where bias might be suspected of similar statements in a religious paper. The same is true of two-thirds of the 96 provincial weekly papers that are Catholic in outlook.

Only two Catholic religious newspapers are published in Ireland—the weeklies, *Irish Catholic* (1888) and *Standard* (1927), which sell 66,000 and 42,000 copies, respectively. Their news, features, and articles are purely religious in character. About 100,000 copies of English Catholic papers, notably the *Universe* and the *Catholic Herald,* circulate weekly in Ireland. Ample coverage is given in these papers to matters of Irish concern.

Magazines. The lack of religious newspapers is compensated for by the high quality and general appeal of many magazines published in Ireland by religious orders and Catholic action groups.

The *Irish Messenger of the Sacred Heart* (1888), organ of the Apostleship of Prayer, reaches one Irish home in three (circulation 238,000) and circulates in a score of countries. It is published by the Society of Jesus, which also produces the *Pioneer* (1947), a popular family monthly promoting temperance (53,000). Superb illustrations and attractive articles on persons and places sell 90,000 copies of the Divine Word Society's monthly, the *Word* (1953), in Ireland, and more than 100,000 copies in the U.S., Britain, and the Commonwealth. The journal with greatest influence among Irish intelligentsia, despite a limited circulation of 1,600, is *Studies,* a Jesuit publication founded in 1912 (contemporaneously with the establishment of Dublin's National University) by a group of professors and graduates. Originally confining itself to philosophical, scientific, and literary subjects, *Studies* now reaches out to wider interests. It anticipated by many years such developments as European unity and the Ecumenical Council. *Hibernia* (1936, 24,000) is a trenchant monthly appealing to adult students.

The *Irish Ecclesiastical Record,* official journal of the Irish clergy, was founded in 1864 by Cardinal Paul *Cullen. A professional journal for priests (4,300 circulation), it avoids being so specialist as to deter lay readers, feeling that what concerns the priest is the concern of all Catholics.

Practically every religious order with a foundation in Ireland publishes a magazine providing light reading leavened with devotional articles, and promoting vocations, especially by publicizing the missionary activities of the order. Most popular are the *Cross* (1909, Passionist), *Assisi* (1932, Franciscan), and *Good Counsel* (1933, Augustinian).

Catholic books of general interest have made the names of Irish publishers, such as Gill, Clonmore and Reynolds, and Mercier Press, known in every English-speaking land.

[S. O' HANLON]

15. Iron Curtain Countries

Communist expansion during and after World War II brought more than 60 million Catholics behind the Iron Curtain. Monopoly of communications media is basic to the Communist program, and so destruction of a free press received high priority in every country seized. Where there were many Catholics, and Communist control was insecure, indirect pressures were first applied: newsprint allocations were cut on the plea of paper shortage; distribution arrangements were disrupted; editorial processes were upset by arbitrary and constantly changing censorship procedures; staff members were arrested on trumped-up charges and puppets named to policy posts. The result was that by the late 1950s the Catholic press was almost wholly liquidated in all but two Eastern European satellites. Because of the strength of Catholic resistance, the situation was different in Poland and Hungary (see 12. HUNGARY; 21. POLAND).

Albania. Catholics had three important publishing houses in 1944: the Jesuit press, established secretly in 1870 when Albania was part of the Turkish Empire; the Franciscan press, established in 1916; and the Scanderberg printery. The Communist regime consolidated its rule rapidly and in a single stroke wiped out the entire social and cultural organization of the tiny Catholic minority (7 per cent of population). The three publishing firms were expropriated. The Catholic periodical press, consisting of two cultural revues, *Ayllii Drites* and *Leka;* two devotional monthlies, *Zani* and *Majoritari;* and the weekly, *Kumbona,* were simply suppressed.

Baltic States. Estonia, Latvia, and Lithuania were under Czarist Russia from the end of the 18th century until they became independent in 1918. The Russian Orthodox Church was the state religion, and activities of both Catholics and Protestants were severely curtailed. They both, however, began immediately in 1918 to develop vigorous social and cultural institutions and the Catholic press blossomed rapidly. Even Estonia, with only about 2,000 Catholics among a million, had two Catholic newspapers by 1940, and a Catholic version of the New Testament was being printed in Estonian.

Latvia's half-million Catholics (33 per cent of population) made an important contribution in every phase of national life. Catholics started a printing and publishing house in 1921, and by 1940 there were two Catholic weeklies and five monthlies, the most important being *Katolu Dzeive* (12,000 circulation) and *Latgolas Vords* (10,000).

Lithuania, over 90 per cent Catholic, had proportionately more Catholic publishing. Circulation of Catholic Action's weekly was 70,000. The country's largest daily, *Dvideshimtas Amzkius* (36,000), was Catholic. There were in all 3 Catholic dailies, 17 weeklies, and 7 monthlies. Five Catholic publishing houses issued 300 to 800 books yearly. The St. Casimir Press Society alone issued millions of copies of pamphlets, books, and magazines each year.

In all three countries Catholic publishing was wiped out when the Soviets took over in 1940. The Nazi occupation brought no improvement, and Soviet reoccupation in 1944 sealed the fate of Catholic publishing.

Bulgaria. Between 1945 and 1948 the Communists constantly accused the 1 per cent of Bulgarians belonging to the Catholic Church of being in league with Bulgaria's enemies, and expelled many foreign-born priests and sisters. The only Catholic periodical was the weekly *Istina.* Seeking to use it to influence the Catholic community, the Communists offered the editors a weekly article, at the same time arresting one of the regular contributors as a kind of blackmail. The bishops, however, rather than surrender control of editorial content, suspended publication. The two editors, both laymen, were then sentenced to 12 years imprisonment after a staged trial in which their codefendants were a bishop, 26 priests, and 2 nuns. The charges ranged from espionage to illegal possession of arms and anti-Communist propaganda. Thus ended the Catholic press in Bulgaria.

Czechoslovakia. Immediately after World War II a transition government with Communists in key positions was imposed by the Russians. The Church in overwhelmingly Catholic Slovakia was particularly vulnerable, because during the war the Slovaks had set up a separate regime with approval of the occupying Nazis. In May 1945 the Communists dissolved Catholic Action youth associations and confiscated their property, including libraries. All religious books were withdrawn from public libraries. Progressive restrictions on the press forced the Catholic reviews, *Kultura* and *Obroda,* to suspend publication, and printing presses of three major Catholic publishing houses were seized.

Pressures from both inside and outside the country caused some restrictions to be lifted before the 1946 elections, and several Catholic publications reappeared. By 1948, however, the regime had suppressed most of the Catholic newspapers in all Czechoslovakia, including the three weeklies, *Rozsevac* (220,000), *Nedele* (120,000), and *Katolik* (30,000). The Slovak weekly, *Katolike Noviny,* was spared, but only because the Communists planned to make it the organ of a schismatic movement.

Early in 1949 a further Government decree purported "to end the capitalist exploitation and anarchy prevalent in the book publishing business." It established a monopoly of all publishing other than periodicals, and by failing to include the Catholic Church among bodies entitled to own a publishing business, it ended in one move all Catholic book and pamphlet publishing. In addition it transferred to the State all church libraries. Retail sale of books of all kinds was permitted only in state-owned stores, which ceased to stock religious and devotional books, prayer books, papal documents, and theology. Thus all Catholic publishing and distribution of literature was wiped out by late 1949, more than 50 newspapers and periodicals having been eliminated.

East Germany. The strong sentiment for reunion of the partitioned country, which in 1953 flared into open revolt, is a constant reminder of the narrow base on which the Communist regime in East Germany rests. Nevertheless the Communists continued Hitler's policy of discrimination and censorship, and have pursued a consistent policy of control of the press, including Catholic publications. In December 1949 Cardinal Conrad von Preysing of Berlin protested that the Catholic press was not free. The following April he formally asked permission to publish Church journals and to bring religious periodicals into the Communist zone without censorship or police interference. The reason was that distribution of *Petrusblatt,* Berlin's diocesan official weekly, produced in the American sector, had been banned by Soviet authorities on the ground that "there was no demand for it."

The Communists replied with increased harassment. In November 1950 the owner of the last-known Catholic bookstore in the Soviet sector of Berlin was arrested for distributing "illegal" religious literature. Shortly afterward, Morlus Verlag, last remaining Catholic publisher in the Soviet zone, announced that all efforts to get permission to distribute Catholic books and periodicals had failed. Some token Catholic publishing was, however, still permitted, though under strict controls. In 1953 the *Tag des Herrn,* sole Church periodical in East Germany, was forced by newsprint rationing to cut circulation from 100,000 to 50,000. In 1956 the Church bulletin of East Berlin, *St. Hedwigsblatt,* was seized for publishing the collective pastoral of the German bishops condemning dialectical materialism.

Rumania. About two-thirds of Rumania's 3 million Catholics belonged to the Rumanian Uniat Church. The 1923 Constitution gave them an official status second only to that of the dominant National Orthodox Church. They played a decisive part in developing Rumanian culture and in the national reawakening, both political and social, of the 19th and 20th centuries. Twenty weeklies and monthlies had a combined circulation of over 250,000 copies per issue, and five printeries published many important religious books and pamphlets.

Latin-rite Catholics, mostly of Hungarian and German ethnic origin and language, maintained a daily newspaper in Hungarian with a 35,000 circulation, and 23 periodicals in German and Hungarian with a combined circulation of 338,000. A rigged convention staged at Cluj in 1948 decreed the liquidation of the Uniat Church. Some churches were transferred to the Orthodox, but most assets were seized by the Communists, who immediately suppressed all newspapers and other publications. Next came the turn of the Latin-rite Catholics. When a schismatic organization failed to win any mass backing, the entire Catholic press was suppressed.

Ukraine. Catholic Ruthenians have been found since the 18th century principally in the Hapsburg empire, in Galicia, Subcarpathian Ruthenia, Transylvania, and Bucovina. Between 1919 and 1939 they numbered about 5 million among Poland (Galicia), Rumania (Transylvania and Bucovina), and Czechoslovakia (Subcarpathian Ruthenia), and were served by a substantial press and book publishing industry. The monthly *Misionar,* founded in 1897, had a circulation of 80,000. Weeklies included *Nova Zorva, Pravda, Dobry Pastyr,* and *Blahovistnyk.* Major publishing houses of the Basilian Fathers at Zhovkva and Uzhorod turned out great numbers of books, mostly on religious subjects. Galicia in 1938 had 27 Ukrainian Catholic book and newspaper publishers, with 21 regular periodicals. Much of this publishing was destroyed by the Nazis during World War II. Some publications were revived in 1945, but when the territories were forcibly incorporated into the Soviet Union, the Communists quickly completed the work begun by the Nazis. All distinctive social and religious activities, including publications, were eliminated, making this in the most literal sense a part of the Church of Silence.

Yugoslavia. During World War II, while Yugoslavia was occupied by the Nazis, it was also rent by bitter internal conflict. The Western allies finally abandoned popular partisan groups in favor of the Soviet-supported Communist leader, Tito. The already widespread campaign to destroy the Catholic press was made official when the Tito regime was firmly established. The Catholic press was almost completely wiped out by a decree requiring government approval of all publications. In Croatia, for example, Catholic periodicals in 1939 had a combined monthly circulation of 700,000 copies; but in 1945 this was reduced to a few pamphlets, all strictly censored. Before the war Yugoslavia had 152 Catholic periodicals, counting daily and weekly newspapers and monthly magazines. Most of these were published by 24 major publishing houses, each with its own printing plant. All physical assets and equipment that had survived the war were seized by the state. For a short time three weeklies, *Verski List, Oznanilo,* and *Gore Scra,* and one monthly, *Blagovest,* were allowed to publish limited editions. The pressures were eased somewhat in 1949 when Tito broke with his fellow dictator, Stalin. The respite, however, was short-lived. By 1955 all independent Catholic publishing had been eliminated. What remained were four periodicals issued by the regime or by a group of Communist-sympathizing priests.

The many political maneuvers of Tito in the early 1960s brought about an easing of pressure on Catholics. *Druzina* continued to be published as a bimonthly in Slovenian. It had at times to include articles favorable to the regime but was generally religious in content. *Vjestnik* appeared monthly in Croatian and a monthly called *Blagovest* was issued in Serbian. The other magazines had either disappeared or had ceased to be regarded as part of the religious press.

Bibliography: A. Galter, *The Red Book of the Persecuted Church* (Westminster, Md. 1957). G. MacEoin, *The Communist War on Religion* (New York 1951). *Bilan du Monde,* 2 v. (2d ed. Tournai 1964).

[G. MAC EOIN]

16. Italy

The Catholic press in Italy has two characteristics: a large number of titles and a rather limited circulation. Even general dailies and weeklies do not have a circulation comparable to that in other countries; it is estimated that the 80 Italian dailies have a joint press run of not more than 6 million copies. The circulation of the Catholic press is limited for another reason: an expressly anti-Catholic or anticlerical press has largely disappeared since 1945. Many Catholics, accordingly, are satisfied to support a general press that usually respects Christian thought and values. The explicitly Catholic press, therefore, appeals almost exclusively to the more dedicated Catholic.

Dailies. Daily newspapers were founded in the different states of the Italian peninsula in 1847–48 when freedom of the press was granted by the various governments after the social and political agitations that had shaken Europe in that year.

The first Catholic daily, *L'armonia (della religione con la civiltà)*, began at Turin (capital of the Kingdom of Piedmont) in July 1848 under the direction of Father Giacomo *Margotti; the paper made a name for itself

Fig. 5. Giacomo Margotti.

by its vigorous defense of the rights of the Holy See and the Catholic Church during the events that led up to the unification of Italy under the House of Savoy (1870). Those events had given an anticlerical and even anti-Catholic orientation to the Italian **risorgimento,* and in 1857 the newspaper issued a call to Catholics not to participate in political elections until free elections were guaranteed; the counsel to be "neither elected, nor electors" was heeded by increasing numbers of Catholics. On Sept. 10, 1874, the Holy See made this position binding on all Italian Catholics, declaring that their participation in legislation was not expedient (*non expedit*).

Margotti left *L'armonia* in 1863 and founded *L'unità cattolica* (at Turin and then Florence), another daily of single-minded character, which from 1870 to 1898 appeared with its first page bordered in black as a symbol of mourning for the end of the *temporal power of the pope. *L'armonia* ceased publication in 1870, and *L'unità cattolica* ceased in 1929 after the Vatican pacts had ended the *Roman question and established relations between the Kingdom of Italy and the Holy See.

Other Catholic dailies had meanwhile been born and died: in 1893 there were no less than 26, almost all of minor importance. Worth remembering are *L'osservatore cattolico* (Milan 1864–1907), which, under the leadership of Father Davide *Albertario, conducted a lively campaign against Catholics inclined to collaborate with the state; *Il cittadino* (Brescia 1878–1928), which won wide acclaim under the direction of Giorgio Montini (the father of Paul VI), a lawyer and deputy to Parliament, who effectively maintained that Catholics should prepare themselves for immediate participation in political life whenever the Holy See should lift its ban, as it did on Nov. 11, 1919; *La difesa* (Venice 1882–1917), the favorite newspaper of Pius X; and the entire group of dailies linked with the Catholic Action of that day—*L'Italia* (Milan 1912), *L'avvenire d'Italia* (Bologna 1896), *Il corriere d'Italia* (Rome 1903–30), *Il Momento* (Turin 1903–29); *Il cittadino* (Genoa 1873–1928), *Il messagero toscano* (Pisa), and *L'eco di Bergamo* (Bergamo 1880). These papers, which attained the largest circulation, were the voice of the group of progressive Catholics, among whom young Father Angelo Roncalli (later Pope John XXIII) received his early training in the social apostolate. Because they supported collaboration with the state, the Holy See ruled their orientation not consonant with papal directives and in December 1912, prohibited Catholics from reading them. The prohibition was lifted by Benedict XV in 1914.

The Catholic dailies again found themselves in serious trouble after 1922 during the period of Fascist rule. Like the press of the whole peninsula, they were obliged to adhere to the political line of the regime in order to continue publication, but they did maintain the defense of their religious positions. During World War II, almost all stopped publishing either because of war damage or in order to evade the demands of the occupying Nazis. They resumed publication after the rebirth of the democratic regime in 1944–45, and in 1964 there were seven Church dailies, all but one in northern Italy: *L'avvenire d'Italia* (Bologna), *L'Italia* (Milan), *L'eco di Bergamo* (Bergamo), *Il nuovo cittadino* (Genoa), *L'Adige* (Trent), *L'ordine* (Como), and *Il quotidiano* (Rome). The last closed down on May 1, 1964, because of small circulation. Since 1947 the editors of these papers have been associated in a conference aimed at ideological, journalistic, and economic cooperation. The Roman Service of Catholic Dispatches, also established in 1947, publishes the journalistic aspects of the conference.

These dailies, insofar as they are official Church publications, are not, strictly speaking, political organs, even though they naturally concern themselves with political topics. Catholic Italians engaged in political activity have their own daily, *Il popolo,* the organ of *Christian Democracy. It was founded in April 1943, during the underground anti-Fascist struggle, by Alcide De *Gasperi, who adopted for it the title of the daily founded by Don Luigi *Sturzo (Rome 1923–25) as the organ of the Popular Italian Party (the first political party of Italian Catholics). *Il popolo* is nationwide in scope. Three minor local dailies also promote Christian Democracy: *Il giornale del mattino* (Florence), *Il corriere del giorno* (Taranto), and *Voce adriatica* (Ancona).

Periodicals. Among Italian Catholic magazines the only one with a reputation outside Catholic circles is the biweekly *La civiltà cattolica,* founded in 1850 at Naples by Carlo Curci, SJ. It has always been edited by a staff of Jesuit writers. Its earlier editors included Antonio Bresciani, Luigi Taparelli d'Azeglio, Matteo *Liberatore, G. B. Pianciani, and Francesco Pellico. Pius IX gave approval to the journal, which proposed always and in all matters to reflect the thinking of the Holy See. Since it maintained, in keeping with Christian principles, that any form of government could be good as long as it did not disavow these principles, the journal was obliged by the absolutist regime of the Bourbons to leave Naples in 1850; it has been published in Rome since then. During the pontificate of Pius X it played an important role in the struggle against *Modernism. Its opinions are always regarded with close attention in both religious and political circles.

Notable among the cultural magazines are: *Rivista di filsofia neoscolastica* (Milan 1909), which promoted neothomism in Italy; *Vita e pensiero* (founded at Milan by Agostino *Gemelli, OFM, in 1914), which contributed importantly to the establishment of the University of the Sacred Heart; *Humanitas* (Brescià 1946);

Studi cattolici (Rome 1957), journal of applied theology edited by *Opus Dei; and a group of periodicals devoted to sociological studies—*Aggiornamenti sociali* (Milan 1950), edited by a group of Jesuits, *Orientamenti sociali* of the Catholic Institute for Social Action, and *Rivista internazionale di scienze sociali* (Milan 1894), which paced the Catholic social movement in Italy. Besides the official periodicals of the major religious orders, there are numerous publications on theology, Biblical study, patristics, liturgy, and sociology. In the group of magazines specifically directed to the clergy two should be noted: *Rivista del clero italiano,* part of the series published by the University of the Sacred Heart (Milan) and *L'amico del clero,* organ of the Federation of Italian Clerical Associations. The Catholic University of Milan also issues various publications of a scientific nature.

Italian Catholic Action publishes many periodicals; every type of national organization has one or more periodicals devoted to matters of interest to members of Italian Catholic Action. The general presidency has its own biweekly, *Iniziativa.*

Among the rotogravure weeklies (which in Italy have wider circulation than the dailies), two Catholic weeklies deserve mention: *Orizzonti* (Rome 1948), edited by the Pious Society of Saint Paul; and *Alba* (Milan 1922), for women. In the group of missionary magazines, *Le missioni cattoliche* (Milan 1872), monthly of the Pontifical Institute of Foreign Missions, is noteworthy because it dedicates studies of a general nature to mission countries and to ecumenical problems. In the various dioceses, aside from bulletins, numerous weeklies for laymen are published; some, like *Famiglia cristiana* (Alba 1930), have many editions, but their circulation is not impressive. Catholic Action provides them with a weekly release of news and articles (S.I.S., *Servizio informazioni settimanali*) to assist the priest-editors.

For Catholics engaged in politics, Christian Democracy publishes several magazines with significant circulation: *La discussione* (a weekly founded by Alcide De Gasperi in 1953); *Civitas* (Rome 1919), a review of political studies; and various other weeklies and monthlies inspired by the different elements in the Christian Democratic Party.

Publishing Houses and Journalism Schools. There are about 50 publishers in the Union of Italian Catholic Publishers. Notable are Belardetti, Coletti, Storia e letteratura, and Cinque Lune (works on Christian Democracy); the Società editrice internazionale of the Salesians of Don Bosco at Turin, specializing in scholarly work; Marietti, also at Turin for publications of a devotional nature; Morcelliana, at Brescia, for philosophical and historical publications. There is no news service in Italy for the Catholic-oriented press. There are, however, two schools of journalism inspired by Catholic principles: one founded in 1947 by Felix A. Morlion, OP, as a Higher Institute for the Sciences of Public Opinion of the International University for Social Studies *Pro Deo,* and the other, founded in 1961 by the University of the Sacred Heart at Bergamo, restricted to pre- and postdoctoral students.

[E. LUCATELLO]

17. Latin America

The history of the Catholic press in Latin America begins with the history of printing (*see* CATHOLIC PRESS). The Franciscans and Jesuits introduced printing onto the continent (the first press, for instance, was set up in Mexico City in the 1530s) and published books and pamphlets to spread the faith among the native population. The Catholic journalistic press, however, originated only after the 20 Latin American republics had won their independence. *El Catolicismo* (1846), the archdiocesan weekly of Bogotá, Colombia, a pioneer, is still published. Another weekly, *El Mensajero* of Montevideo, Uruguay, existed for some time before the first diocese in that country was established (1856).

These early publications had a dual objective: to serve as a bond between ecclesiastical authority and the clergy at a time when distance was an obstacle to permanent direct communication, and to be a medium for the diffusion of doctrine and religious practice. This type of Catholic press continues to function.

Early Social Orientation. Another kind of publication began to develop during the late 19th century; it was inspired by social purpose, and its aim was to infuse civic spirit with Christian principles. Its general themes are marriage and divorce, the organization of the family, religious teaching in the schools, working conditions, and the promotion and defense of the city of man organized on the order of the city of God.

Daily and weekly papers and reviews devoted to this objective spread throughout Latin America: *La Religión* of Caracas, Venezuela (1900), *El Pueblo* of Buenos Aires, Argentina (1899–1960), and *El Bien Público* of Montevideo, Uruguay (1878), are representative. The last suspended publication temporarily in 1962; it returned in February 1965 as *B. P. Color.* All three participate in debate on social issues and represent the Church as spokesman for the almost unanimous feeling of the people. Any effort by non-Catholic minorities to suggest that the Church and the people do not always see eye to eye was offensive to militant Catholics and frequently led to lamentable dispute.

Change in Social Attitude. This rather touchy attitude, however, has been changing, at a different rate in each country, from the mid-19th century, though it still obtains in some countries. In others, where pluralism is already clearly evident, such attitudes are seen to be outmoded, and this realization has brought to a crisis the decline of a Catholic journalism that had enjoyed years of great brilliance under such leaders as Padre Federico Grotte, founder of *El Pueblo,* Juan Zorrilla of San Martín, founder of *El Bien Público,* and Msgr. José M. Pellin, director of *La Religión,* the papers mentioned above. Though it frequently exercised good influence, this type of journalism sometimes led to unpleasant confusions; the *Diario Ilustrado* of Santiago de Chile, for example, had been founded to assert the Christian presence in the temporal order but was converted into the mouthpiece of a specific political party.

In recent times this older type of journalism has been complemented by weekly publications and reviews that envision different goals. La Pia Sociedad publishes in Bogotá and Buenos Aires a chain of reviews with the uniform title *Familia;* these are directed chiefly at women as the center of the Christian family, and they seek to satisfy the spiritual and material needs of the household. *Criterio* (1929) of Buenos Aires and *Mensaje* (1945) of Santiago de Chile are reviews of high intellectual character directed toward the analysis of social problems and toward philosophical, theological, and pastoral discussion; they exercise wide ecumenical influence. *El Mensajero,* published by the Jesuits in Argentina, Uruguay, and Chile; *Alborada,* published in Medellin, Colombia; and *Reina y Madre* of Buenos Aires correspond approximately to the digest magazine type. There are also comic-strip magazines, such as *Avanzada* in Lima, Peru; magazines for adolescents, such as *Anhelos* of Buenos Aires; trade periodicals, such as *Brujula* in Montevideo; and those to serve the special interests of the clergy, such as *Psallite* of Buenos Aires.

Needs for the Future. Despite this variety of interests, however, some areas await more attention. Information on the Church and its life and on the current international scene is not adequate to the needs. Some weeklies, such as *Esquiú* (1960) in Buenos Aires, provide comprehensive information, but the Catholic dailies (more than 12) do not match this brilliant exception.

Perhaps these gaps and the relative excess of doctrinal and polemic periodicals correspond to the Latin temperament—more inclined to emphasize principles and less attentive to practical consequences. But social structures in Latin America are changing rapidly, chiefly because the large urban masses are changing in culture, and simple formulas no longer suffice to define attitudes and ways of life. There is great need in the Catholic press for a pastoral point of view; the objective of succoring man in his daily business in the world requires full and timely information.

But before such informational gaps can be filled, more primary needs must be met. A modern, efficient system of communication for the exchange of information is not available, mainly because of different legislation, authorities, and governments, lack of an organized transportation system, and the scarcity of suitably coordinated radio and cable facilities.

It is true that *Noticias Católicas NC,* the Spanish-language service of the U.S. *National Catholic Welfare Conference, in operation for more than 20 years, makes an important contribution and offers hope for the future. It provides varied and trustworthy information, distributed biweekly by plane to the most distant cities of Latin America, but the time-lag robs the information of its freshness, especially for the dailies. The NC will become the news service that the Catholic press in Latin America needs to the extent that it achieves effective coordination of local agencies. These exist in some countries, but not in all; moreover, they have no common bond of interest because they serve principally the local needs and thus lack continental focus.

Training in journalism is being extensively given. Caracas, Bogotá, Lima, Santiago de Chile, and Buenos Aires have schools of journalism in Catholic universities or institutes. Every year hundreds of graduates provide enough trained journalists to staff the Catholic press. Existing problems must be attributed mainly to material limitations; their solution is still not within the compass of the countless efforts, still isolated from each other, spread throughout Latin America.

A means of solving this isolation appeared to be the Unión Latino Americana de la Prensa Católica (1959), founded by journalists of 17 countries in order to encourage and coordinate the activities on the entire continent.

Leading Publications. The chief Catholic publications in Latin America (excluding Mexico and Brazil) are given in the following paragraph lists; the ascertainable dates of foundation are given in parentheses.

Daily newspapers: *La Unión* (1928), Catamarca, *La Verdad,* Junin, *Los Principios,* Córdoba—Argentina; *Presencia* (1952), La Paz—Bolivia; *El Heraldo* (1958), Ambato, *La Verdad* (1944), Ibarra—Ecuador; *El Bien Público* (1878–1962; *B. P. Color,* 1965), Montevideo—Uruguay; *Diario Católico* (1924), San Cristobal, *El Vigilante,* Merida, *La Columna* (1924), Maracaibo, *La Religión* (1900), Caracas—Venezuela.

Weeklies and periodicals: *Esquiú* (1960), Buenos Aires—Argentina; *La Voz* (1956), Santiago—Chile; *El Campesino* (1958; the Catholic periodical with the greatest Latin American circulation, 120,000 copies, in 1962), Bogotá, *El Catolicismo* (1846), Bogotá, *El Obrero Católico* (1924), Medellin—Colombia; *El Eco Católico* (1931), San José—Costa Rica; *Fides* (1962), Santo Domingo—Dominican Republic; *Catolicismo* (1926), Guayaquil and Quito—Ecuador; *Catolicismo*—Guatemala; *Fides,* Tegucigalpa—Honduras; *Novedades,* Managua—Nicaragua; *Comunidad* (1952), Asunción—Paraguay; *Actualidad* (1961), Lima—Peru; *El Debate* (1961), San Juan—Puerto Rico; *Orientación*—San Salvador; *El Diario* (1916), Paysandú, *La Idea Nueva* (1910), Trinidad, *Los Principios,* San José—Uruguay.

Doctrinal reviews: *Criterio* (1929), Buenos Aires—Argentina; *Mensaje* (1945), Santiago—Chile; *Revista Javeriana* (1933), Bogotá—Colombia; *Sic* (1938), Caracas—Venezuela.

Illustrated reviews: *El Mensajero,* Buenos Aires, *Reflector,* Buenos Aires, *Reina y Madre* (1914), Buenos Aires—Argentina; *Familia,* Buenos Aires—Argentina (1942) and Bogotá—Colombia (1953); *Presencia* (1950), Bogotá—Colombia; *El Faro* (1931), Panama—Republic of Panama.

Bibliography: E. Gabel, "La presse catholique en Amerique Latine," *Informations Catholiques Internationales* (August 15, 1959) 21. C. L. Aguiar, "O que é a Uniao Latino-Americana de imprensa católica," *Vozes de Petrópolis* 55 (1961) 389–391; "Struggles for Christ and Life," *Catholic Press Annual* 3 (1962) 9–11.

[C. L. AGUIAR]

18. Mexico

The Catholic press in Mexico dates back to the 16th century. The first bishop and archbishop of Mexico City, Fray Juan de *Zumárraga, introduced between 1534 and 1536 the New World's first printing press into what was then New Spain. Its output in the 16th century reached 118 volumes—bilingual and native-language catechisms; grammars and dictionaries of various Indian tongues for missionary use; and textbooks of philosophy, theology, Canon Law, medicine, etc.—invaluable for their content and as incunabula. Similar in content but much more extensive was the output (1,228 volumes) of the 17th century. The 18th century accounts for 3,300 volumes (see bibliography for works dealing with an analysis of the publications of these 3 centuries). In 1728 Father J. F. Sahagún de Arévalo founded New Spain's first newspaper, the *Gazeta de Mexico.* Similar to this was the *Diario Literario* founded by Father J. A. Alzate in 1768. During the Mexican struggle for independence, the newspapers published by the revolutionaries were also Catholic.

After Independence. Once Mexico had attained its independence in 1821, a few anti-Catholic newspapers made their appearance. Catholic newspapers as such, then labeled "conservative," did not appear until the struggle between the liberals and the conservatives reached greater proportions. The first of these were *El Tiempo* (1846) and *El Universal* (1848–55). The offices of the latter were sacked and burned during the successful revolution of Ayutla. Their immediate successors were the doctrinaire magazine *La Cruz* (1855–58); the *Diario de Avisos* (1856–60), whose fiery editor, D. Vicente Segura Argüelles, was assassinated for imprudently baiting his adversaries; and the *Pájaro Verde* (1861, 1863–77), whose offices were burned by a mob in 1861. It was later reorganized and during its 14-year history served for 2 years (1863–65) as the official organ of the second empire. Although all of these were published in Mexico City, they had many counterparts, usually short-lived, in other parts of the country. In Guadalajara the Catholic press was represented by *La Illustración, La Tarántula,* and *La Religión y la Sociedad;* in Morelia by *La Lealtad, La Discusión,* and *La Tempestad.*

Under Dictatorships. During the dictatorships of Juárez, Lerdo, and Díaz (1867–1911), anti-Catholic newspapers flourished, but their effect was largely counterbalanced by excellent Catholic papers published in Mexico City: *La Voz de México* (1870–1909) of Rafael Gómez, *El Tiempo* (1883–1912) of Victoriano Agüeros, and *El País* (1899–1912) of Trinidad Sánchez Santos. *El País,* outstanding for articles on Mexican politics, had a circulation of 250,000, the largest at that time. In other parts of the country the Catholic press was represented by *El Amigo del Pueblo* in León, *El Pensamiento Católico* and *El Derecho Cristiano* of Benigno Ugarte in Morelia, *La Linterna de Diógenes* of Atilano Zavala and *El Regional* (1904–14) in Guadalajara, and *El Amigo de la Verdad* (1870–1914) in Puebla. With the successful revolution of Madero in 1911, a Catholic political party was founded and undertook the publication of several newspapers, notably *La Nación* (1912–14) in Mexico City, and *El Heraldo* (1912–14) in Morelia. The revolution of 1914 outlawed all Catholic newspapers then in existence.

Restrictions and Renewal. Since 1917 the Mexican government has placed heavy restrictions on the press in general and on the Catholic press in particular. In the face of this limitation, Catholic writers have continued their work in the leading dailies of Mexico City, *El Universal* (1916), *Excelsior* (1917), and *Novedades* (1935). Some of the more significant contributions were from writers like José Elguero (1885–1939), a scintillating editorialist for *Excelsior* who was exiled from 1927 to 1928; D. Alfonso Junco, who contributed incisive and fearless articles to *El Universal* and later to *Novedades;* Father Antonio Brambila, Chestertonian writer for *El Universal;* Father Gabriel and Alfonso Méndez Plancarte, both with wide humanist and cultural backgrounds; and the outspoken Fernando Diez de Urdanivia and Pedro Vázquez Cisneros.

Catholic magazines and reviews underwent a decline between 1914 and 1920. Yet a few new reviews were published during the period; e.g., *La Epoca* (1917) in Guadalajara which, under the direction of Pedro Vázquez Cisneros, launched a memorable journalistic campaign in defense of Catholicism. A whole new series of magazines appeared in 1921 headed by Francisco Elgueró's creditable *América Española,* a literary, historical, and scientific publication with an excellent editorial staff. In the following decade publications began to multiply. Among those founded in the 1930s and still widely read are *Christus* (1935), a review for the clergy published by Buena Prensa; *Abside* (1936), a magazine founded by Gabriel and Alfonso Méndez Plancarte and similar in content and editorial policy to *América Española;* and *Schola Cantorum* (Morelia 1939), dedicated to sacred music. Among the weeklies currently enjoying wide popularity are *Unión* (1935), published by Buena Prensa, *Señal* (1954), by the Missionaries of the Holy Spirit, and *Mundo Mejor* (1955), by the Carmelites.

Fig. 6. José A. Romero.

After Mid-Century. Every diocese has its own official newspaper; in a few cases, several dioceses collaborate in a joint publication. Various parishes, popular shrines, diocesan seminaries, schools, and Catholic clubs publish their own magazines. In 1964 there were more than 200 Catholic publications, 21 publishing houses, and some 100 writers. More noteworthy among the publishers were Buena Prensa (1937), Jus (1941), and Ediciones Paulinas (1947). One of the leading figures in the Mexican Catholic Press was José A. Romero, SJ (1888–1961), who founded several magazines, including *Unión* and *Christus,* and organized Buena Prensa and the Asociación Nacional de Prensa, Editores, Libreros, y Escritores Católicos.

Bibliography: V. DE P. ANDRADE, *Ensayo bibliografico mexicano del siglo XVII* (2d ed. Mexico City 1899). J. BRAVO UGARTE, *Historia de México,* 3 v. (Mexico City 1941–44). J. GARCÍA ICAZBALCETA, *Bibliografía mexicana del siglo XVI,* ed. A. MILLARES CARLO (Mexico City 1886; new ed. 1954). N. LÉON, *Bibliografía mexicana del siglo XVIII,* 6 v. (Mexico City 1902–08). Asociación Nacional de Prensa, Editores, Libreros, y Escritores Católicos, *Directorio ANPELEC* (Mexico City 1961).

[W. GUINEA]

19. THE NETHERLANDS

In the early 1820s the Catholics of the Netherlands made their first journalistic efforts to rectify the disabilities under which they had labored for generations in a predominantly Protestant environment. In 1822 at The Hague, the blind scholar, Le Sage ten Broek (1775–1847), a convert and apostle of Catholic emancipation, founded the first Catholic newspaper, *Roomsch Catholyke Courant.* It was forced in 1823 to change its title to *Noord-Nederlandsche Courant.* The timidity of Catholics to support it in the face of prejudice doomed it to die in 1824. Undaunted, Broek began *Godsdienstvriend* (Friend of Religion), the first Catholic periodical to be viable. For these and similar enterprises, Broek has been called the Father of the Catholic Press in the Netherlands.

In 1829 another effort was made in the North Brabant capital, s'Hertogenbosch (Bois-le-duc), with *De Noord Brabander,* which survived for several decades as a poor, small newspaper with little support either from advertisers or the clergy. Other weekly papers, nevertheless, soon followed: *De Gelderlander* (Nijmegen 1848), now the largest regional Catholic daily in the Netherlands, the *Limburger Koerier* (1847) and *Het Centrum* (1884). *De Tijd* (Amsterdam 1845) was the first newspaper to become a daily.

Social and Cultural Background. The Catholic press in the Netherlands began in a period of stress and poverty. Catholicism was barely tolerated; its adherents themselves were often backward, even illiterate, and this early Catholic journalism, which espoused Catholic emancipation, met in its own house an apathy conditioned by centuries of suppression. Catholics were loath to claim their rights as citizens and even resented or were suspicious of those fellow Catholics who openly questioned the denial of those rights. Even the clergy feared reprisals and dared not support the efforts of the nascent press; Catholic businessmen were afraid to advertise in it. It is no exaggeration to say that the Catholic press of the Netherlands was born in the financial sacrifices of journalists whose apostolic zeal alone slowly laid the foundations of the thriving modern press.

N°. 1. Dingsdag, 17 Junij. 's Hertogenbosch. Eerste Jaar. 1845.

DE TIJD.

GODSDIENSTIG-STAATKUNDIG DAGBLAD.

Fig. 7. First issue of "De Tijd" (1845), the first Catholic newspaper in The Netherlands to become a daily.

20th-century Expansion. Its major expansion, however, came only in the 20th century. This history of growth is almost an index of the progress of Catholic emancipation in the Netherlands.

The Catholic press consists of 23 dailies, of which 2 are national; they are *De Tijd de Maasbode* and *De Volkskrant* (both Amsterdam), the first more prestigious, the second more popular. There are 2 weeklies, and about 400 periodicals, which range from important scientific journals to publications about bee-culture. Many of these periodicals (weeklies, monthlies, bimonthlies) are of a religious nature. The diocesan press limits itself to information concerning local church services and activities, and to articles about religious topics in general. The diocesan press is further differentiated by the fact that its editorial staffs are responsible to the local bishop, and the journals are the official or semiofficial voices of the bishops. In the "free" Catholic press neither of these conditions exists.

To secure official ecclesiastical approval as a "Catholic" paper, a priest-moderator must be associated with the staff, and he may be consulted on matters dealing directly with faith and morals. On the whole, laymen control, operate, edit, and write for the Catholic press, although priests of acknowledged competence in secular fields are occasionally employed. Editors in the diocesan press, however, are priests, as are the editor and staff of the liberal weekly, *De Bazuin* (Trumpet), published by the Dominican Fathers. In 1963 the Jesuit weekly *De Linie* (Line) changed its name to *De Nieuwe Linie* and came under lay-journalist editorship. Several diocesan weeklies were transferred in the mid-1960s to lay or mixed lay-clerical direction.

Press Agencies and Associations. The Catholic daily press seeks extensive coverage of the news; it receives reports from its own staff of correspondents all over the world; from all the major international news agencies, such as AP, UPI, and Reuters, and from the national press agencies, including the Catholic Netherlands press agency in the Hague (KNP). This agency is the successor to the *Catholic World Post,* whose struggle against both Communism and Nazism ended with its dissolution by the German occupational forces in World War II. Many of its editorial staff died in concentration camps.

The Catholic dailies, with the cooperation of Catholic Action, organized KNP in February 1947. Its mission is news gathering; its specialty, the assembling of information on topics relevant to Catholic life generally. Its editorial board consists of the managers of the Catholic dailies, and its staff is lay.

There are two national associations of Catholic Press editors and managers: the Association of the Catholic Press, and the Association of Catholic Newspapers. The Catholic Journalists Union is the representative organization for the journalists and writers themselves. All of these independent organizations work closely with their neutral and Protestant counterparts.

[N. J. ADEMA]

20. New Zealand

The Catholic press in New Zealand originated in the need of Catholics for a medium in which to urge recognition of their civil claims and to expound their principles against widespread prejudice. Catholic journalism began with the campaign for public aid for Catholic schools by Patrick Francis Moran (1823–95), first bishop of Dunedin. Denied a voice in the local press, Bishop Moran, with a board of lay directors, founded the *New Zealand Tablet;* and, as its first editor, vigorously proposed the Catholic case in its columns. Since the first issue (May 3, 1873), the journal has appeared weekly. Editors to serve longest have been Rev. James Kelly (1917–32), A. B. Carter (1937–52), and Rev. F. D. O'Dea (1952–). Its circulation in 1963 was 14,000.

A former editor of the *Tablet,* Rev. H. W. Cleary, became bishop of Auckland in 1910. He found the largest diocese in the land without a Catholic paper, and bigotry making a last-ditch stand against public toleration of the Church. In July 1918, he founded the *Month,* originally a 20-page magazine costing a penny a copy. Bishop Cleary's forthright journalism did much to clear the air and to improve the Catholic image in the eyes of New Zealanders. His successor, Bishop (later archbishop) J. M. Liston, edited the *Month* for some years, then in 1934 replaced it with *Zealandia,* a fortnightly newspaper, edited first by Rev. P. B. McKeefry (later archbishop of Wellington) and from 1947 to 1962 by Rev. O. N. Snedden (later auxiliary bishop of Wellington). In 1937, *Zealandia* became a weekly, and in 1942, adopted tabloid size and format. Its circulation in 1963 was 27,000.

The *Tablet* and *Zealandia* remain the sole Catholic weekly papers in New Zealand. The *Marist Messenger* (circulation 4,000), a devotional monthly and the official organ of the Marist Missions, was established in 1930 by K. I. McGrath, SM, who was still editor in 1963. The Marist Maori Missioners produce a small

WHITTOME'S PICKLES JUST PERFECT Manufactured and Packed in NEW ZEALAND

Zealandia

THE CATHOLIC FORTNIGHTLY

BE HEALTHY! BE HAPPY! Eat and Enjoy KRAVMORS

VOL. I.—No. 1. AUCKLAND, MAY 10, 1934. PRICE—THREEPENCE.

"Blessed Apostle of Youth"

Don Bosco Canonised

Inspiring Scenes at St. Peter's

UNTIMELY DEATH

Delegate to Holy Land

CARFIN CURE

Doctors Investigating

PRIEST WHO ABJURED FAITH

Now Returns to Church

IRISH PILGRIMAGE TO ROME

Boy Scouts' Holy Year Visit

THE CHURCH IN RUSSIA

Only 30 Priests at Liberty

THE CATHOLIC WORLD

Missionaries for the South Seas

BI·SAL

INSTANT RELIEF FOR INDIGESTION

DYSPEPSIA · ACIDITY · WIND · FLATULENCE · HEARTBURN

Fig. 8. Front page, first issue of "Zealandia," May 10, 1934.

magazine, *Whiti Ora,* partly in English and partly in Maori. The *Catholic Citizen,* founded (1935) at Wellington by the St. Vincent de Paul Society, was superseded in 1954 by the Society's *Quarterly Bulletin.* Catholic journals are issued to both primary and secondary schools. The *Primary Schools Journal* (1932) is now published three times yearly (circulation 35,000). The *Secondary Schools Journal* (1938) also appears three times a year (circulation 4,500).

Various other Catholic publications have had a brief life, such as the *Catholic Times,* established in 1889 at Wellington. The most noteworthy of these was the *Catholic Review,* a scholarly monthly, which ran from 1945 to 1949. British and Australian Catholic papers circulate widely in New Zealand.

[J. C. REID]

21. Poland

Independent Poland after 1918 quickly developed a strong Catholic press including four dailies. The German and Russian occupations from 1939 to 1945 wiped out all Catholic publishing. Censorship and newsprint controls after World War II restricted any revival to a few Catholic weeklies. The most important were the Cracow *Tygodnik Powszechny* (Universal Weekly), allowed paper for 50,000 copies when demand approached 100,000, and *Tygodnik Warszawski* (Warsaw Weekly), both intended for Catholic intellectuals. These publications and the monthly *Znak* (Sign) were controlled by lay Catholics who enjoyed the confidence of the bishops. Soon two state-encouraged publishing ventures emerged that avoided open conflict with the Church though they were either Communist or ambiguous in sympathy. "Veritas," connected with Pax Publishing, was given a near-monopoly on catechisms, Missals, and prayer books in the late 1940s. "Ars Christiana," started by one Frankowski, was absorbed for a time by Pax but restored to Frankowski's control in the mid-1950s. The main fellow-traveler publications before 1950 were the weekly *Dzis i Jutro* (Today and Tomorrow), "organ of progressive Catholics," and the popular daily *Slowo Powszechne* (Universal Word), a name selected to suggest association with the Cracow weekly.

Between 1945 and 1950 Catholic publications grew to about 32, one-tenth the number before World War II. They included seven major weeklies and nine major monthlies, for example, *Rycerz Niepokalanej* (Knight of the Immaculate), with nearly a million circulation. State pressure began to mount, however, in 1949. A joint episcopal pastoral in July protested suspension of two Catholic weeklies and nationalization of the country's 15 Catholic printing and publishing establishments. Although the government promised in April 1950 that Catholic publications would "enjoy in common with other sections of the press the rights defined by the relevant laws and legal provisions of the authorities," the bishops within 6 months protested the outrageous violations, including "severe restrictions imposed by the political censorship on Catholic newspapers and other publications with a view to their total extinction." *Tygodnik Warszawski* had already been suppressed.

Survivals after 1951. Only 12 publications survived in 1951, their circulations reduced to some thousands or even hundreds by newsprint control. All newsprint for independent Catholic publications was denied in

March 1953. *Znak* ceased publication in February 1953; *Tygodnik Powszechny* went into eclipse on March 9, 1953, but it reappeared in July under different management and in collaboration with Pax. It was placed on the Index by Rome in 1955, as was *Dzis i Jutro,* and the two were amalgamated in 1956 under the name *Kierunki* (Orientations). This left only the daily *Slowo Powszechne,* also part of the Pax group. In March 1957 a weekly illustrated magazine following a similar line as "organ of militants of social Christian action," *Za i Przeciw* (For and Against), was begun under Frankowski's management. After the Gomulka regime seized power in 1957, the Znak group re-formed as a nonprofit corporation under the same lay Catholic who had controlled it 10 years earlier. It publishes the monthly *Znak* (7,000 circulation) and weekly *Tygodnik Powezechny* (40,000—far below the demand), as well as 8 or 10 Catholic books a year. Like all Catholic publishing it is strictly and arbitrarily supervised by the Ministry of Cults, which exercises prepublication censorship.

Specialized Publications. Since 1958 Warsaw has had an additional intellectual monthly, *Wiez* (The Ties), connected with clubs of Catholic intellectuals. Specialized publications for the clergy are *Homo Dei* and *Collectanea Theologica* (Warsaw) and *Ateneum Kaplańskie* (Wloclawek). *Ruch Biblijny i Liturgiczny* (Biblical and Liturgical Movement) is also important. Two diocesan weeklies, of the three or four existing before 1953, resumed publication in 1958, *Przewodnik Katolicki* (Catholic Guide)—formerly *Glos Katolicki* (Catholic Voice)—Poznan, and *Gosc Niedzielny* (Sunday Visitor) of Katowice. Circulation, while short of the demand, runs from 60,000 to 80,000. Surviving Catholic publishing houses are Albertinum (Poznan); Znak; St. Jacinthe (Katowice); Catholic University of Lublin; and Pallottinum.

The regime gave a particularly brutal reminder of the precarious nature of the *modus vivendi* in October 1963. As a tribute to Cardinal Wyszynski the World Union of Catholic Women's Organizations had printed a collection of his sermons and lectures and sent him 60,000 copies. All were seized on reaching Warsaw and reported burned, although no part of the contents had previously been censored or challenged.

See also CATHOLIC PRESS, WORLD SURVEY, 15. For bibliography, *see* CATHOLIC PRESS, WORLD SURVEY, 12.

[G. MAC EOIN]

22. Portugal

Though the first periodical was issued in Portugal in 1641, there were few regular newspapers until toward the end of the 18th century, and it was not until 1853 that the first Catholic weekly appeared; it was *Domingo* (1855–57), edited by Father José de Sousa Amado. This was succeeded by the *Bem Publico,* which was published until 1877 when an anti-Catholic campaign inspired largely by grand orient *freemasonry was at its height.

Dailies. The Portuguese hierarchy founded the *Correio Nacional* in 1893. It continued for 13 years, first under the editorship of Ferreira Lobo and then of Fernando de *Sousa, who continued with its successor *Portugal,* to which he gave a clearly militant character. This paper closed down with the revolution of 1910 when the monarchy was overthrown and the republic was established.

A Ordem (1916) was first under the direction of Camossa Saldanha and then of Fernando de Sousa; it was suppressed by the government in 1919 after a minor monarchist uprising. The following year *A Epoca* was founded by Father José Alves Terças, and once again Fernando de Sousa, who is regarded as the precursor of the modern Catholic press in Portugal, was called in as editor. Disagreements with the hierarchy made De Sousa suspend this paper and start *A Voz* in 1927; this has since then been the leading independent Catholic daily, and is edited and staffed by laymen under the editorship (1964) of Pedro Correio Marques.

In December 1923 *Novidades* reappeared as a Catholic daily under the control of the hierarchy. Since then it has always had clerical editors, though it is autonomous, being owned and published by the União Grafica of Lisbon. The Livraria Morais (Lisbon) is a prominent Catholic publishing house. The Catholic daily in Oporto, *A Palavra* (1870), was succeeded by several short-lived periodicals. In Braga, a Catholic daily, the *Diario do Minho* (1919), is, like *Novidades,* under the control of the bishops.

Weeklies. The most important weeklies are *A Guarda,* which defended the Catholic point of view during the years of strife after the revolution of 1910 and was still vigorous in 1964; *A Ordem,* under lay editorship in Oporto; and *Flama* (1943), a popular illustrated weekly with lay staff and editorship.

Monthlies. *Broteria,* founded by Manuel Fernandes Santana, SJ, in 1902 as a scientific journal, has since been enlarged to cover theological, literary, and historical subjects. *O Tempo e o Modo* (1963) gives a platform to the young Catholic liberal intellectuals. *Lumen* is published for the clergy. There are about 125 small Catholic publications under the aegis of various organizations, such as Catholic Action.

In general, the Catholic press carries little weight and finds survival difficult. Although 95 per cent of the Portuguese declared themselves Catholic at the last census, the circulation of the two Catholic dailies in Lisbon is very small. Catholic news is well covered in the secular newspapers. Censorship is not strict, and few complain of it.

There is a lively and well-run Catholic broadcasting station, Radio Renasçenca, under a clerical director, but there are no Catholic news services or schools of journalism in Portugal.

Bibliography: P. CORREIA MARQUES, "La prensa católica e as suas responsibilidades," in *Rumo* (Aug. 18, 1958).

[S. LOWNDES]

23. Scandinavian Countries

Although there had been some form of periodical literature in Scandinavia from the 18th century, the beginnings of the Catholic press there date from the mid-19th century.

Denmark. The religious freedom guaranteed by Denmark's constitution of June 5, 1849, made possible the founding on Sept. 23, 1853, of the Ansgariusforening (St. Ansgar League) for the furtherance of the Catholic press and literature. On October 2, this group issued the first number of the weekly *Skandinavisk Kirketidende for Katholske Kristne,* which became, after 1885, the *Nordisk Ugeblad for Katholske Kristne,* and after 1939, the *Katolsk Ugeblad.* It appeared first in quarto, after 1856 in octavo, and since 1939 again in quarto, with an average of 18 pages per issue. Subscriptions have increased from an initial 200 to about 3,000 (in 1964). It is intended as a Church publication, although different editors have interpreted that role differently.

The early editor Johannes von Euch (1860–64), who later became vicar apostolic, was succeeded by Jörgen L. V. Hansen (1864–83), a former Lutheran minister, who favored a strongly theologico-historical approach. Father Andreas Johansen (1883–1905), and another former Lutheran minister, Niels Hansen (1909–20), preferred to concentrate on the practical life of the Church. Niels Hansen brought form and order to the material; the General Index, added in 1917, provided a good view of all Danish Catholic life. Father Bernhard Jensen (1921–30) succeeded Hansen. Increased canvassing activities under Gustave Scherz, CSSR (1932–39), and others, led to the publication of various extra issues (two, for example, about Niels *Stensen) and a press issue in connection with the International Catholic Press Congress in Rome in 1936.

At the Scandinavian Catholic Press Congress in Oslo (1936), the *Nordisk Katolsk Presseforbund* (Scandinavian Catholic Press Organization) was founded. The *Katolsk Ugeblad,* published after 1939 under the editorship of two laymen, Helge D. T. Kiaerulff and Jörgen Berg, attempted to win a wider public by adopting more modern journalistic techniques, an effort continued from 1959 to 1963 by Rev. G. M. Nielsen and then by Martin Drouzy, OP. In its development the publication had many eminent collaborators, both religious and lay, and was strengthened by various parallel publications. For instance, from 1898 to 1902, it enjoyed the support of a supplement, the *Katholiken,* edited by the convert writer Johannes *Jørgensen. His clear pronouncements on art and literature, as well as on religious and social questions, contributed greatly to the prestige of Catholic thought in a country predominantly Protestant.

From 1903 to 1913, there appeared, under Oskar V. Andersen as publisher and editor, the excellent literary and intellectual Catholic monthly (later biweekly) *Varden.* After some lesser attempts, the biweekly *Katholsk Ungdom* for Catholic youth took its place in 1919 alongside *Nordisk Ugeblad.* It was published by the Danmarks Katholske Ungdomsforbund (Danish Catholic Youth Organization) and edited until 1927 by Joseph Koch, SJ, then by Fr. Cay Benzon; it had 1,000 subscribers when its last editor, Helge D. T. Kiaerulff, merged it with the *Nordisk Ugeblad* in 1939. Beginning in 1943, the quarterly *Catholica* (circulation about 800) appeared under the editorship of Lars B. Fabricius, Tove Rasmusson, and Heinrich Roos, SJ. Its purpose was to represent Danish Catholicism in the world of culture, art, and ideas. With it, there has appeared three times a year since 1957 the 64-page theological publication *Lumen,* edited by the Dominicans and circulating to 550 readers in 1963. Since 1962, the Katolsk Pressetjeneste (Catholic Press Service) has been sending current news three times a month from Copenhagen to about 200 newspapers and journalists in Norway and Denmark.

Norway. Shortly after his appointment (1892) as vicar apostolic, Johannes B. C. Fallize launched the weekly *St. Olav* in Norway; he soon changed it to a biweekly. For years in his native land, Msgr. Fallize had been editor of the *Luxemburger Volksblatt* and he had established there the great St. Paul's Press. In addition to edifying, apologetic, and entertaining articles, *St. Olav* for many years ran a political survey that analyzed doubtful or false political outlooks. The first issues vividly presented many of the difficulties the Catholic Church once had faced in Norway; later controversies have been milder. Since 1949, the journal, under the editorship of Msgr. I. Hansteen Knudsen, has had the subtitle "Catholic Periodical for Religion and Culture." It has become more and more a theologico-cultural journal, especially since 1959 under the editorship of Hallvard Rieber-Mohn, OP, and Erik Gunnes, OP. The contributions of Sigrid *Undset, among others, added to its prestige. The journal had a circulation of 2,200 in 1963, with a yearly gain of about 160 subscribers, among them many Protestants. It is frequently quoted in the great newspapers of the land.

Sweden. The *Katolsk Kyrkotidning* was founded in 1926 under the title *Hemmet och Helgedomen* and is edited by a group of priests and laymen. It appears in Stockholm 22 times a year, and it had a circulation of 2,800 (in 1963). Under Msgr. Berndt D. Assarson the periodical *Credo,* founded in 1921, became a monthly journal concerned with cultural and intellectual interests. Since 1939, under the editorship of Joseph Gerlach, SJ, the 48-page *Credo* has been published in Uppsala, five times a year. It had a circulation (1964) of about 1,000, and has been widely recognized for its scholarship. The *Sankt Michael* (Stockholm 1954), a journal for Catholic youth, appears 10 times a year with 12 pages per issue. It had 700 subscribers in 1964.

Finland and Iceland. In Finland, the monthly *Uskon Sanomat* (Messenger of Faith, 1925) had a circulation (1964) of 500, and *Kellojen Kutsu* (1937), 1,200 in 1964. The *Documenta* (circulation in 1963 of 300) was founded by the Dominicans in Helsinki (1955) as a Catholic cultural journal. In Iceland, a quarterly, the *Merki Krossius* (The Sign of the Cross), was started in 1926 by priests of the Catholic mission.

[G. SCHERZ]

24. Scotland

The Catholic periodical press in Scotland developed slowly in comparison with the modern expansion of Catholicity in that country. Before World War I, the Catholic community was too small and poor to support such publications in competition with the heavily financed publications of Dublin and London. The earliest periodical was the *Catholic Directory for the Clergy and Laity in Scotland* (1828), edited by John *Macpherson. It still appears annually, but in 1903 the liturgical section began to be published separately as the *Ordo Divini Officii Recitandi juxta Kalendaria Propria Scotiae,* and since 1961, the *Directory's* annual chronicle of events has been published separately as the *Saint Andrew Annual.* The ecclesiastical Province of Glasgow has its own yearbook, the *Western Catholic Calendar,* founded in 1894.

Monthlies. The earliest monthly, the *Edinburgh Catholic Magazine,* edited by James *Smith, appeared intermittently from 1832 to 1842. Other short-lived monthlies were the *British and Irish Catholic Magazine,* published for a few months in 1837 by Denis Kennedy, a Glasgow bookseller; the *Labourer and North British Catholic Herald* (Edinburgh 1865), which had a maximum circulation of 360 and did not outlive that year; and the *Scottish Catholic Monthly,* edited by Goldie Wilson, which appeared from October 1893 to December 1896. The French Premonstratensian Canons, established at Whithorn in 1889, published the *Liberator* at irregular intervals. The Benedictines of Fort Augustus Abbey published the organ of the League of St. Andrew, the *Saint Andrew's Cross;* it was first a quarterly in 1902 and 1903, then a monthly until it was discontinued in 1905. *Round the World,* founded in January 1946 by Colm Brogan, discontinued in January 1950, when the editor moved to London; and the monthly, the *Mercat Cross,* published by the Jesuits of Edinburgh (1951–62), ceased publication for lack of support. To serve the Gaelic-speaking northwest of Scotland, a quarterly, *Guth na Bliadhna* (Voice of the Year), was founded (1904) by Ruairi Erskine of Mar and edited by him until 1925, when publication ceased. The first specialized journal produced by Scottish Catholics is the *Innes Review* (1950), a biannual review devoted to Scottish ecclesiastical history; it has achieved an influential position among Scottish historians, Protestant as well as Catholic.

Weeklies. From early in the 19th century, the politically minded Irish immigrants to Scotland had discussed the possibility of a Catholic weekly newspaper. The *Catholic Vindicator,* published in Glasgow by William Eusebius Andrews (December 1818–December 1819), first attempted the task. Similar attempts were the *Phoenix: A Political, Literary and Scientific Journal,* published for a few months (1840) in Edinburgh, and somewhat later, the *Greenock Mirror.* The first really influential weekly was the *Glasgow Free Press* (1851–68); the anticlericism of its editor, Augustus Henry *Keane, brought about its condemnation by ecclesiastical authority. The *Irish Banner* continued the policy of the *Free Press,* but survived for only 5 months. A weekly, the *Exile,* ran for 18 months in 1884 and 1885. Finally, an effective weekly newspaper was started—the *Glasgow Observer* (1885). Charles *Diamond took it over in 1894, published subsidiary editions in several districts and, in 1908, acquired a rival paper, the *Star,* launched in 1895. The *Glasgow Observer* is the only Catholic weekly printed and published in Scotland: it serves the Catholic population of southwest Scotland and appears as the *Scottish Catholic Herald* in the eastern and northern areas. Irish and English Catholic weeklies publish Scottish editions: the *Irish Weekly* from 1892, and the *London Catholic Times* and the *Universe* from 1936. In June 1963, the *Scottish Universe* incorporated the *Scottish Catholic Times* and appears as the *Scottish Universe and Catholic Times.*

Bibliography: J. E. HANDLEY, *The Irish in Modern Scotland* (Cork 1947).

[D. MC ROBERTS]

25. SPAIN

There are well over 100 morning and evening papers in Spain for a population of 30 million. It is impossible to draw a clear line between the Catholic and the secular press (all papers carry religious news and papal and episcopal pronouncements in full), but about 25 per cent may be classified as definitely Catholic. The Spanish periodical press may be dated from the end of the 18th century, a decisive time in the history of the country. Widespread anticlericalism followed the Cortes of Cadiz in 1812, and Catholic polemical journalism rose to counter it. Writings of this nature were those of Fray Raimundo Strauch, a Franciscan who contributed to the *Diario de Mallorca* and other publications. *Roca y Cornet came somewhat later, contributing articles on Church problems to the *Diario de Barcelona* (1792). In 1837 he founded *La Religión,* thus becoming the creator of the Spanish Catholic press. Another influential figure, Father Jaime *Balmes, founded, together with Roca, the fortnightly *La Civilización* in 1842, and *La Sociedad* (Barcelona) and *El Pensamiento de la Nación* in 1843. *Aparisi y Guijarro succeeded Balmes as the leading figure in Catholic journalism; he founded *La Restauración* (1843) and *El Pensiamiento de Valencia* (1855). In 1847 St. Anthony Mary *Claret started the *Librería Religiosa* in Barcelona that in his lifetime issued nearly 8 million books. After the revolution of 1869 several short-lived periodicals appeared, but under the liberal monarchy there was a period of relative inactivity. *El Siglo Futuro,* founded by Cándido Nocedal in 1875, was extremely right wing and ceased publication only at the time of the Civil War of 1936. The daily *A.B.C.,* founded (1905) in Madrid by Torcuato Luca de Tena, has the largest circulation (about 350,000) and has always been stanchly royalist and orthodox, though not specifically Catholic.

Certain papers, such as the weekly *Ecclesia,* are under direct ecclesiastical direction, but the majority are owned and run by laymen. They are preoccupied with sociological affairs; agriculture, basic to the Spanish economy, is widely treated, particularly in *Pueblo* of Madrid, an evening paper with a Catholic trend and an organ of the National Central Syndicate. There is little comment on internal affairs, though these, like foreign affairs, are reported.

Dailies. Two dailies, *El Correo Catalán* (Barcelona 1876) and *El Correo Callego* (Santiago de Compostela 1878), were still being published in the 1960s. *El Correo Catalán* is the oldest Spanish daily under ecclesiastical censorship among the 34 daily newspapers that, as of 1964, were subject to governmental and Church control. The most famous and influential of the Catholic dailies is *Ya* of Madrid, which the present (1964) bishop of Malaga, Angel Herrera Oria, edited for 20 years as a layman. He was a brilliant journalist and started *El Debate* in 1911. This paper, which became *Ya* in 1935, was the first really modern one in Spain. It was suppressed by the Popular Front Government during the Civil War but resumed publication at the war's end. The domestic and foreign news coverage is comprehensive, and the fact that it is a Catholic paper is not immediately evident to the casual reader. It is published under a lay editor by the Editorial Católica, which also runs an independent news agency, Logos, and a school of journalism in Madrid. In addition, Editorial Católica founded 3 large provincial dailies, *Ideal* (Granada 1932), *La Verdade* (Murcia), and *Hoy* (Badajoz, both 1933), as well as a weekly of general interest, *Digame. El Ideal Gallego,* a daily started by José Toubes Pego in 1917, came under Editorial Católica's control in 1932. This publishing house, one of the best in Spain, has issued an extensive series of Catholic books under the general title of *Biblioteca das Autores Cristianos.*

Every provincial town has one or more morning or evening papers. Bilbao has two Catholic dailies, *La*

Gaceta del Norte (1901), an independent morning paper, and *El Correo Español,* started in 1910 as *El Pueblo Vasco. El Diario Vasco* (San Sebastian 1934) was often suspended during the Civil War. *El Correo de Andalusía* (Seville 1899) has many subscribers all over the world. Valencia possesses one of the oldest dailies in Spain, *Las Provincias* (1866), which has always been strongly Catholic. It was suppressed during the Civil War, as was *El Noticiero* (Zaragoza 1901).

Weeklies. *Ecclesia* is the most influential. It started in Madrid (1940) as the organ of Catholic Action and is read by most of the clergy. It is (1964) edited by Msgr. Jesus Iribarren, and has the distinction of being the only publication in the country that, by agreement under the Concordat with the Holy See, is not submitted to government censorship. *Vida Nueva* (Madrid) gives information of general Catholic interest. *Signo* (Madrid 1936) is the Catholic Action youth paper; it deals with current affairs and is quite outspoken on matters of Church and State. *Nuestro Tiempo* (Madrid 1954) is a notable intellectual review founded by Antonio Fontán.

Monthlies. The illustrated *Mundo Cristiano* (1961) enjoys the largest circulation (100,000 in 1964). The widely read *Juventud obrera,* the organ of the Young Christian Workers, is lively and frank in political discussion. The Jesuit periodical *Abside* (Burgos 1956) is distinguished, but, like most of the secular intellectual reviews, attracts relatively few readers. Important reviews include *El Ciervo* (Barcelona 1964), *Hechos y Dichos* (Zaragoza 1943), *Nuestro Tiempo Orbis Catholicus* (Barcelona 1958), and *Razón y Fe* (Madrid 1940). Two journals dealing with social questions, *Fomento Social* (Madrid 1945), a semestral publication, and *Mundo Social* (Zaragoza 1962), are particularly significant.

The Catholic press in Spain has an impressive vitality and a wide range. Government censorship is concerned mainly with political commentary, a concern not new in Spain: censorship existed under the Republic. There are two institutes of journalism in Madrid and one conducted by the *Opus Dei at the University of Navarre in Pamplona. Catholic Press Congresses are held from time to time, and there is a Catholic press association, the Junta Nacionál de Prensa Católica.

Bibliography: *La Prensa de la Iglesia en España* (Madrid 1957).

[S. LOWNDES]

26. Switzerland

The Catholic press in Switzerland comprises 29 dailies (22 in German, 5 in French, 2 in Italian), 44 bi- or triweeklies (36 in German, 4 in Italian, 3 in French, and 1 in Romansh), and the reviews *Nova et Vetera* (Fribourg), *Orientierung* (Zurich), *Schweizer Rundschau* (Solothurn), *Civitas* (Lucerne), and *Die Familie* (Zurich). The most important papers are *Vaterland* (Lucerne, 30,000 circulation), *La Liberté* (Fribourg, 20,000), and *Giornale del Popolo* (Lugano, 13,000). The fourfold linguistic division of the country has thus far made the Catholic press more or less provincial, but the inauguration of a nationwide publication with regional editions, the *Neue Zuercher Nachrichten* (Zurich, 16,000) presages an important development.

The earliest Catholic papers, e.g., the *Schweizer Kirchenzeitung* (Lucerne 1832), were concerned mainly with the defense of the Church against the concerted anti-Catholicism that took shape in 1830. After the new constitution of 1848, Catholic journalistic emphasis shifted to dissemination of Catholic social ideas; a leader in this field was Joseph Beck (1858–1943). Many of the leading Catholic journalists were prominent in politics as well: in Lucerne, P. A. von Segesser (1817–88); in St. Galen, G. J. Baumgartner (1797–1869), Josef Gmuer (1821–82), and Franz Furger (1839–66); in Basel, E. Feigenwinter (1853–1919); and in Zurich, G. Baumberger (1855–1931).

Catholic press organizations are the Association Catholique des Journalistes Suisses (Geneva), Schweizer Katholischer Pressverein (Zug), Vereinigung Katholischer Publizisten (Lucerne), and Arbeitsgemeinschaft Katholischer Zeitungsverleger (Fribourg). Courses in journalism are given at the Catholic University of Fribourg.

Bibliography: E. MÜLLER, "Das Katholische Zeitungswesen," in *Katholisches Handbuch der Schweiz* (Lucerne 1943). *Jahresberichte des Schweizer Katholischen Pressvereins.*

[E. MÜLLER-BÜCHI]

27. United States

The following survey covers: (a) 19th-century English-language periodicals, (b) 19th-century foreign-language newspapers and periodicals, (c) 19th-century English newspapers, (d) 18th- through 20th-century books and pamphlets, (e) 20th-century newspapers, (f) 20th-century periodicals.

a. 19th-Century English-Language Periodicals. The history of U.S. Catholic magazines began with the *Metropolitan,* or *Catholic Monthly Magazine* (Baltimore, Jan. to Dec. 1830), published and edited by Rev. Charles Constantine *Pise, a pioneer in Catholic literature. Three months later the first Catholic juvenile, the *Expostulator,* or *Young Catholic's Guide* (March 31, 1830–March 23, 1831), a weekly founded and edited by Bp. Benedict Joseph *Fenwick of Boston, appeared, with the aim of explaining "the principles of the Catholic Church." In 1813–14 Anthony *Kohlmann, SJ, and Fenwick had plans for a learned monthly in New York, but the project fell through. Pise and Rev. Félix *Varela founded another monthly with the unlikely name of *Protestant's Abridger and Expositor* (New York 1830), but it had less success than Pise's first venture. The two priests made a third attempt with the *Catholic Expositor* (New York 1841–44). The brief existences of these four magazines were typical of those originating prior to the end of the Civil War. Not one survived, mainly because the editors, frequently able and prominent, were engaged in other duties as well and had little financial support. Further, the more urgent need in this period was for weekly news journals that would also explain Catholic doctrines and answer the rising tide of charges against Catholicism.

After the Civil War, magazines increased in quantity and quality. From 1885 to 1900 Catholic journals numbered "more than a hundred at any time" (F. L. Mott, 4:297). Some weekly news journals are included in Mott's figure, but 19th-century Catholic periodicals are too numerous to name here. J. T. Ellis's *Guide to American Catholic History* (Milwaukee 1959) cites the import of 19th-century Catholic magazines. He lists 26 as helpful to students; 12 of them originated in the 19th century, and 6 of the 12 were current in

DIOCESES OF THE UNITED STATES
WHICH PUBLISH WEEKLY NEWSPAPERS
(SEE LIST BELOW).
● Independent
Local Editions of National Papers
○ Register
■ Our Sunday Visitor
Seattle
Spokane
Yakima
Portland
Great Falls
Helena
Baker
Boise
Santa Rosa
Sacramento
Reno
Stockton
Oakland
San Francisco
Salt Lake City
Monterey-Fresno
Los Angeles
San Diego
Tucson
Cheyenne
Denver
Pueblo
Sante Fe
El Paso
Bismarck
Fargo
Crookston
Duluth
St. Cloud
Superior
Marquette
Sioux Falls
St. Paul
Green Bay
La Crosse
Winona
Milwaukee
Madison
Saginaw
Grand Rapids
Detroit
Sioux City
Dubuque
Davenport
Rockford
Chicago
Gary
Joliet
Toledo
Omaha
Grand Island
Lincoln
Des Moines
Lafayette
Fort Wayne-South Bend
Peoria
Springfield
Belleville
Indianapolis
Covington
Cincinnati
Columbus
Steubenville
Wheeling
Salina
Kansas City
Dodge City
Wichita
Kansas City-St. Joseph
St. Louis
Jefferson City
Evansville
Louisville
Springfield-Cape Girdeau
Nashville
Oklahoma City
Little Rock
Dallas-Ft. Worth
San Angelo
Austin
San Antonio
Corpus Christi
Galveston-Houston
Alexandria
Natchez-Jackson
Baton Rouge
Lafayette
New Orleans
Mobile-Birmingham
Atlanta
Savannah
Charleston
St. Augustine
Miami
Raleigh
Richmond
Washington
Greensburg
Pittsburgh
Youngstown
Harrisburg
Erie
Cleveland
Buffalo
Rochester
Scranton
Ogdensburg
Syracuse
Albany
Burlington
Hartford
Portland
Springfield
Boston
Worcester
Fall River
Providence
Norwich
Bridgeport
Rockville Centre
Brooklyn
New York
Paterson
Newark
Trenton
Allentown
Camden
Philadelphia
Wilmington
Altoona-Johnstown
Baltimore
Albany, N.Y.: The Evangelist
Alexandria, La.: The North Central Louisiana Register
Allentown, Pa.: The Catholic Standard and Times
Altoona-Johnstown, Pa.: The Catholic Register
Atlanta, Ga.: The Georgia Bulletin
Austin, Tex.: The Lone Star Register
Baker, Ore.: The Catholic Sentinel
Baltimore, Md.: The Catholic Review
Baton Rouge, La.: The Catholic Commentator
Belleville, Ill.: The Belleville Messenger
Bismarck, N. Dak.: The Dakota Catholic Action
Boise, Idaho: The Idaho Register
Boston, Mass.: The Pilot
Bridgeport, Conn.: The Catholic Transcript
Brooklyn, N.Y.: The Tablet
Buffalo, N.Y.: The Catholic Union and Echo
Burlington, Vt.: The Vermont Catholic Tribune
Camden, N.J.: The Catholic Star Herald
Charleston, S.C.: The Catholic Banner
Cheyenne, Wyo.: The Wyoming Catholic Register
Chicago Ill.: The New World
Cincinnati, Ohio: The Catholic Telegram
Cleveland, Ohio: The Catholic Universe Bulletin
Columbus, Ohio: The Catholic Times
Corpus Christi, Tex.: The Texas Gulf Coast Register
Covington, Ky.: The Covington Messenger
Crookston, Minn.: Our Northland Diocese
Dallas-Ft. Worth, Tex.: The Texas Catholic
Davenport, Iowa: The Davenport Messenger
Denver, Colo.: The Denver Catholic Register
Des Moines, Iowa: The Des Moines Messenger
Detroit, Mich.: The Michigan Catholic
Dodge City, Kans.: The Southwest Kansas Register
Dubuque, Iowa: The Dubuque Witness
Duluth, Minn.: The Duluth Register
El Paso, Tex.: The Southwest Catholic Register
Erie, Pa.: The Lake Shore Visitor
Evansville, Ind.: The Southwestern Indiana Register
Fall River, Mass.: The Anchor
Fargo, N. Dak.: The Catholic Action News
Fort Wayne-South Bend, Ind.: Our Sunday Visitor
Galveston-Houston, Tex.: The Texas Catholic Herald
Gary, Ind.: Our Sunday Visitor
Grand Island, Nebr.: The Nebraska Register
Grand Rapids, Mich.: The Western Michigan Catholic
Great Falls, Mont.: The Montana Catholic Register
Green Bay, Wisc.: The Green Bay Register
Greensburg, Pa.: The Catholic Accent
Harrisburg, Pa.: The Catholic Witness
Hartford, Conn.: The Catholic Transcript
Helena, Mont.: The Western Montana Catholic Register
Indianapolis, Ind.: The Indianapolis Criterion
Jefferson City, Mo.: The Catholic Missourian
Joliet, Ill.: The Catholic News Register
Kansas City, Kans.: The Eastern Kansas Register
Kansas City-St. Joseph, Mo.: The Catholic Reporter
La Crosse, Wisc.: The Times-Review
Lafayette, Ind.: Our Sunday Visitor
Lafayette, La.: The Southwest Louisiana Register
Lincoln, Nebr.: The Southern Nebraska Register
Little Rock, Ark.: The Guardian
Los Angeles, Calif.: The Tidings
Louisville, Ky.: The Louisville Record
Madison, Wisc.: The Catholic Herald Citizen
Marquette, Mich.: Our Sunday Visitor
Miami, Fla.: The Voice
Milwaukee, Wisc.: The Catholic Herald Citizen
Mobile-Birmingham, Ala.: The Catholic Week
Monterey-Fresno, Calif.: The Central California Register
Nashville, Tenn.: The Tennessee Register
Natchez-Jackson, Miss.: The Mississippi Register
Newark, N.J.: The Advocate
New Orleans, La.: The Clarion Herald
New York, N.Y.: The Catholic News
Norwich, Conn.: The Catholic Transcript
Oakland, Calif.: The Catholic Voice
Ogdensburg, N.Y.: The North Country Catholic
Oklahoma City, Okla.: The Oklahoma Courier
Omaha, Nebr.: The True Voice
Paterson, N.J.: The Advocate
Peoria, Ill.: The Peoria Register
Philadelphia, Pa.: The Catholic Standard and Times
Pittsburgh, Pa.: The Pittsburgh Catholic
Pittsburgh (Archeparchy): The Byzantine Catholic World
Portland, Maine: The Church World
Portland, Ore.: The Catholic Sentinel
Providence, R.I.: The Providence Visitor
Pueblo, Colo.: The Southern Colorado Register
Raleigh, N.C.: The North Carolina Catholic
Reno, Nev.: The Nevada Register
Richmond, Va.: The Catholic Virginian
Rochester, N.Y.: The Courier Journal
Rockford, Ill.: The Observer
Rockville Centre, N.Y.: The Long Island Catholic
Sacramento, Calif.: The Catholic Herald
Saginaw, Mich.: The Catholic Weekly
St. Augustine, Fla.: The Florida Catholic
St. Cloud, Minn.: The St. Cloud Visitor
St. Louis, Mo.: The St. Louis Review
St. Paul, Minn.: The Catholic Bulletin
Salina, Kans.: The Northwestern Kansas Register
Salt Lake City, Utah: The Intermountain Catholic Register
San Angelo, Tex.: The Texas Concho Register
San Antonio, Tex.: The Alamo Messenger, La Voz (Spanish Language)
San Diego, Calif.: The Southern Cross
San Francisco, Calif.: The Monitor
Sante Fe, N.M.: The New Mexico Register
Santa Rosa, Calif.: The Monitor
Savannah, Ga.: The Southern Cross
Scranton, Pa.: The Catholic Light
Seattle, Wash.: The Northwest Progress
Sioux City, Iowa: The Globe
Sioux Falls, S. Dak.: The Bishop's Bulletin
Spokane, Wash.: The Inland Catholic Register
Springfield-Cape Girardeau, Mo.: The St. Louis Review
Springfield, Ill.: The Western Catholic Sunday Visitor
Springfield, Mass.: The Catholic Observer
Steubenville, Ohio: The Steubenville Register
Stockton, Calif.: The Monitor
Superior, Wisc.: The Catholic Herald Citizen
Syracuse, N.Y.: The Catholic Sun
Toledo, Ohio: The Catholic Chronicle
Trenton, N.J.: The Monitor
Tucson, Ariz.: The Arizona Register
Washington, D.C.: The Catholic Standard
Wheeling, W. Va.: The West Virginia Register
Wichita, Kans.: The Advance Register
Wilmington, Del.: The Delmarva Dialog
Winona, Minn.: The Courier
Worcester, Mass.: The Catholic Free Press
Yakima, Wash.: Our Times
Youngstown, Ohio: The Catholic Exponent

Fig. 9. U.S. dioceses which publish weekly newspapers, with a listing of titles of the publications.

1965. This section is limited to the more important English-language magazines, adult and juvenile. With few exceptions the weeklies have been considered news journals or newspapers. The organs of benevolent and fraternal societies, unless noteworthy on some other score, have been omitted.

Magazines to 1865. The need for weekly news journals rather than for literary monthlies is illustrated by the next two magazines that appeared. The *St. Joseph's College Minerva* (Bardstown, Ky. 1834–36), the first Catholic periodical in Kentucky, was founded and edited by Rev. Martin John *Spalding and published by the faculty of St. Joseph's College. Devoted to national and foreign literature, the monthly was more literary than religious in content, but it was soon discovered that the times called for a news journal. It was accordingly succeeded by the weekly *Catholic Advocate* (1836–58) with Spalding as editor and Benedict J. *Webb, a journalist, as proprietor. The monthly *Religious Cabinet* (Baltimore 1842–49), the project of Rev. Charles Ignatius *White and Rev. James Dolan, had sound prospects of enduring success. White was a leading editor and author, and as editor of the *Annual Catholic Almanac and Directory* for the years 1834 to 1857 had contact with the hierarchy and prominent Catholics. Like Pise and Spalding, he was American-born with roots in the traditions of Maryland Catholicism and an understanding of the country's history. This monthly provided domestic and foreign religious news and comment, literary articles, and notices. After a year it was renamed *United States Catholic Magazine* and continued to fare well. However, with the Jan. 6, 1849, issue it became a weekly and the official organ of the Baltimore archdiocese; the next year it appeared as the *Catholic Mirror* (1850–1908), with White as editor (1850–55). Baltimore soon had, with the aid of White, another magazine, the *Metropolitan* (1853–59), a monthly devoted to religion, education, literature, and general information. Though both magazines were failures, Baltimore for a time gave U.S. Catholics a monthly that compared well with others.

St. Louis had a monthly for a few years, the *Catholic Cabinet* (1843–45), founded and edited by Bp. Peter Richard *Kenrick, who had had editorial experience on the weekly *Catholic Herald* of Philadelphia. Besides being the first Catholic monthly of Missouri, it was "the first literary magazine west of the Mississippi River" [J. E. Rothensteiner, *History of the Archdiocese of St. Louis* (St. Louis 1928) 2:165]. It was literary and historical in content, a chronicle of religious intelligence with original and reprinted or abridged articles from the better contemporary magazines, such as *Blackwood's* the *Dublin Review,* the London *Tablet,* and the *Edinburgh Review*. Lack of financial support compelled its suspension, and Kenrick turned, without much success, to weekly journals. Yet his monthly fared better than the one started by his brother, Abp. Francis Patrick of Philadelphia, the *National Catholic Register*. It did not survive the first issue (Jan. 1844). This was the month, too, when Orestes *Brownson revived his quarterly, the most important Catholic magazine of the period.

After allowing his first quarterly, the *Boston Quarterly Review* (1838–42), to merge with the *Democratic Review,* Brownson recognized that he needed his own journal; shortly before his conversion to the Catholic faith (Oct. 1844), he started the *Brownson Quarterly Review* (Boston; New York 1844–75, with one suspension). Catholics urged him to continue it as a Catholic magazine. This review of religion, philosophy, and general literature was uniquely Brownson's: he seldom relied on contributors but gave Catholic literature personal journalism at its best.

Catholic magazines declined during the 1850s and had practically disappeared by the end of the Civil War. A few short-lived juvenile magazines were started. Fenwick's weekly was followed by *Children's Catholic Magazine,* later *Young Catholic's Magazine* (New York 1838–41), a monthly edited by Rev. Félix Varela and considered by the Boston *Pilot* (Oct. 12, 1839) as an "interesting little work" that deserved a larger circulation. The *Young Catholic's Friend* (Boston 1840), edited by the convert Henry B. C. Greene, was abandoned after a year. *Boys' and Girls' Weekly Catholic Magazine* (Philadelphia 1846–56), later called the *Catholic Weekly Instructor,* had the longest run of Catholic juveniles in this period. But the *Catholic Youth's Magazine* (Baltimore 1857–61), a monthly published by John Murphy and Co. and edited by Martin J. Kerney, was the best and the most promising (*see* MURPHY, JOHN JOSEPH). The author of many school books and the editor of the *Metropolitan* (1857–59), Kerney gave his young readers an illustrated magazine of 40 pages of entertaining knowledge. The death of Kerney and the outbreak of the Civil War brought the publication to an end with the August 1861 edition. Finally, there was the *Wreath* (York, Pa. 1861–62), a monthly of instruction and entertainment.

When the *Metropolitan* was suspended in 1859, Brownson's quarterly was the only adult Catholic magazine available. The nadir came when Brownson, his loyalty to the faith wrongly suspected, and grief-stricken by the loss of two sons in the war, suspended the review with the October 1864 issue.

From 1865 to 1900. Catholic magazines quickly revived after the war. One, in fact, appeared before the conflict ended: the *Monthly* (Chicago 1865). It was founded by Rev. John McMullen, president of St. Mary of the Lake University, edited by Peter Foote, a member of the faculty, and published by the University. The first issue was dated January and the last December. Its suspension was soon followed by the closing of the University. In the next decade the faculty of St. Francis Seminary, Milwaukee, published the *Salesianum* (1873–78), a monthly edited by Rev. Thomas Fagan, a professor of English who gave variety and scholarship to its contents and published documents valuable to historians [P. J. Johnson, *Halcyon Days: the Story of St. Francis Seminary, Milwaukee 1856–1956* (Milwaukee 1956) 372–373]. However, with the exception of student publications, Catholic colleges and seminaries did not contribute much to the 19th-century Catholic magazines. The principal sources of successful magazines were religious orders or congregations. They entered the field in 1865 and within a year had established three magazines: the *Catholic World* (April 1865), the *Ave Maria* (May 1, 1865), and the *Messenger of the Sacred Heart* (April 1866).

The *Catholic World,* a monthly of general literature and science, was published in New York by the Paulists and edited by Rev. Isaac Thomas *Hecker, CSP, assisted by Rev. Augustine Francis *Hewit, who succeeded him (1889–97). The *Ave Maria,* a weekly magazine, and the *Messenger,* a monthly, discovered the formula for a popular Catholic journal in the 19th century—the promotion of a Catholic devotion combined with a family magazine. The *Ave Maria,* published at Notre Dame, Ind., by the Congregation of the Holy Cross, grew in prestige and circulation under the long (1875–1929) editorial guidance of Rev. Daniel Eldred *Hudson, CSC.

The *Messenger of the Sacred Heart* (Georgetown, D.C.; later New York), the major publication of the U.S. Jesuits in the 19th century, offered devotional literature, learned articles, fiction, poetry, literary criticism, and editorials. By 1897 it had developed into a journal of 100 pages with a circulation of 20,000. Rev. John Joseph *Wynne, who became editor in 1892, divided the monthly into two magazines (1907), the one with the original title remaining primarily devotional and the other, called simply the *Messenger,* becoming a journal of general literature. This latter monthly was suspended when Wynne started *America* (April 17, 1909), a national Catholic weekly review that soon became a highly respected journal of Catholic opinion.

Another of Hecker's press projects was the Catholic Publication Society, which the hierarchy praised in its pastoral letter in 1866. The society published the *Illustrated Catholic Family Almanac,* later changed to *Annual* (New York 1869–97), which gave its readers, in addition to information generally found in almanacs, biographical sketches of prominent Catholics and historical and literary articles by contributors such as John Gilmary *Shea, Maurice Francis *Egan, and George Parsons Lathrop. Benziger Brothers entered this field with the *Catholic Home Almanac,* later changed to *Annual* (1884–1924), introducing in the late 1890s a new format and improved contents. These two annuals are minor sources of information on U.S. Catholic life in the second half of the century.

The 1866 Plenary Council of Baltimore observed that "the power of the press is one of the most striking features of modern society." New features of Catholic journalism appeared, although frequently they were the work of individuals without organized support and met with little success; a few women became editors and publishers; there was an interest in the problems of the farmers, in the literary bent of young men, and in art.

Patrick *Donahoe, publisher of the Boston *Pilot,* was the first to revive the juveniles with *Spare Hours* (1866), an illustrated monthly that lasted a year. Another Boston juvenile monthly, *Young Crusader* (1869–76), edited by Rev. William *Byrne, had a longer life. The *Guardian Angel* (Philadelphia 1867–1909), originally a monthly, became a weekly when its publisher merged it with his other weekly juvenile, *Vesper Bells* (Camden, N.J. 1884–88). The *Young Catholic's Guide* (Chicago 1867–71) was combined with another monthly, the *Sunday School Messenger* (Chicago 1869–1920). *Young Catholic,* later the *Leader* (New York 1870–1923), was a Paulist publication planned by Father Hecker. This monthly and the *Guardian Angel* were rated among the best Catholic juveniles of the 19th century. One other noteworthy juvenile originated in the 1870s, the *Catholic Young People's Friend* (Chicago 1877–), a weekly that is now published monthly and that appeared also for years in a German edition as *Katholischer Jugendfreund* (1877–1952).

Rev. Abram Joseph *Ryan, poet-chaplain of the Confederacy, edited the weekly *Banner of the South* (Augusta, Ga. 1868–72?), a religious and political magazine that "exerted no small influence on the thought of the state," and in which some of his best poems originally appeared [F. V. W. Painter, *Poets of the South* (New York 1903) 109, 235–37]. The monthly *Our Own* (Philadelphia 1869) was a bold adventure; it was a home magazine for women edited by Mrs. Fanny Warner, but the response was poor and it ceased publication after a few months. The *Central Magazine* (St. Louis 1872–75) was a bolder experiment, inspired more by the feminist movement than by the pastoral letter of 1866; this monthly was published, edited, printed, and mailed entirely by women under the guidance of its publisher and editor, Mary Nolan, who set out to prove there was a place for women in Catholic journalism (see Mott, 3:95). The *Star of Bethlehem* (Milwaukee 1869–71) is noteworthy because it was the first English-language Catholic periodical in Wisconsin; it was concerned primarily with the farmer and the working man. This monthly merged with the weekly *Catholic Vindicator* (Monroe, Wis.; Milwaukee 1870–78), which also stressed agrarian topics.

The *De la Salle Monthly,* later *Manhattan Monthly* (New York 1869–77), described itself as a Catholic magazine for young men and carried biographies, articles, tales, editorials, poetry, book reviews, and scientific notes. The *New York Tablet,* edited by Brownson, found it an "excellent little magazine" (Oct. 1, 1870). However, it abandoned its original purpose and became a popular magazine of general literature. Another monthly, the *Milwaukee Catholic Magazine* (1875), was devoted to discussion of ethics, literature, and art. It was planned and edited by Bernard Isaac Durward, painter, poet, and convert, but it survived only for a year. *McGee's Illustrated Weekly* (New York 1876–82), a journal of Catholic art, literature, and education, fared somewhat better.

The four superior achievements of the 1870s were the *Woodstock Letters* (1872–), the revival of the *Brownson Quarterly Review* (New York 1873–75), the *American Catholic Quarterly Review* (Philadelphia 1876–1924), and *Donahoe's Magazine* (Boston 1879–1908). The *Woodstock Letters,* a quarterly that records the activities of U.S. Jesuits in their educational institutions, parishes, and missions, is published at Woodstock College, Md. Although privately circulated, it is a primary source for one segment of American Church history. Brownson was in his 70th year when he revived his quarterly (Jan. 1873), with the hope of removing suspicions in his loyalty "for the sake of the Catholic cause." The response, a circulation better than in its best previous years, greatly encouraged him, but his declining strength forced him to accept the help of others (see Oct. 1874 issue, 571), and he wrote his valedictory in the October 1875 issue. Another quarterly, however, had been planned by Charles A. Hardy and D. H. Mahony of Philadelphia to fill the void. They entered journalism with the *Catholic Record* (Philadelphia 1871–78), a monthly miscellany of Catholic knowledge and general literature. Brownson thought the first issue promised "well for the future," but it never gave serious competition to the *Catholic World.* The ACQR staff was directed by Rev. James Andrew *Corcoran, who retained the post until his death (1889) and was succeeded by Abp. Patrick John *Ryan (1890–1911). The review carried numerous articles on American and European history (John Gilmary Shea contributed 50 articles) and on all aspects of education and government, as well as on religion. It lacked the spark and controversial tone of Brownson's review, but it was more representative of U.S. Catholic thought and scholarship while under the direction of Corcoran and Ryan.

Patrick Donahoe offered readers an illustrated monthly of light fiction, articles, biographical sketches, book notices, and editorials in his *Donahoe's Magazine.* Irish-oriented at the start, it became the most popular Catholic monthly in the 1890s (42,755 circulation in 1897); it declined, however, after Donahoe relinquished control, and in 1908 the *Catholic World* acquired it. Four other monthlies originating in the Middle West had brief lives: *La Salle Journal* (St. Louis 1872–74), the *Toledo Review* (Toledo, Ohio 1873–76), *Iowa Catholic Advocate* (Davenport 1874), and *Catholic School Record* (Milwaukee 1875–80).

More than 50 Catholic magazines began in the 1880s, most of them organs of fraternal, temperance, and philanthropic societies. For adults new kinds appeared—reviews for the clergy, parish journals, and historical publications that were inspired mainly by the work of Martin Ignatius Joseph *Griffin and John Gilmary Shea. The *Pastor: A Monthly Journal for Priests* (New York 1882–89), the first venture in pastoral theology, was published by *Pustet and edited by Willian J. Wiseman, who stressed the practical rather than the speculative in theological and liturgical articles, documentation, and book reviews. No issues appeared between November 1888 and June 1889, and during this period Pustet started another monthly, the *American Ecclesiastical Review* (Jan. 1889), edited by Rev. Herman Joseph *Heuser, whose long tenure (1889–1914, 1919–27) insured his continuity and high quality. Heuser planned a scholarly journal attractive to clergy and educated laity alike, but it had little appeal to the laity. He therefore began the *Dolphin* (1901–05), a monthly better adapted to the layman. John Baptist *Singenberger (1849–1924), editor of the German-language monthly *Caecilia* (Dayton, Ohio, etc. 1874–), the oldest music journal in the U.S., persuaded Pustet to publish an English-language Church music monthly; but there was little response to *Echo* (New York 1882–85). *Caecilia* became bilingual in 1906, and with the January 1925 issue, an English-language magazine.

American Catholic Historical Researches (Philadelphia 1884–1912), the pioneer Catholic historical journal, first appeared as *Historical Researches in Western Pennsylvania,* edited by Rev. Andrew Arnold *Lambing of Pittsburgh. Griffin acquired it, changed its name, and until his death edited this quarterly of disorganized but valuable material on American Catholic history. It was then merged with *Records* (1887–), the publication of the American Catholic Historical Society of Philadelphia (1884), which appeared irregularly until 1893, when it became a quarterly. These two quarterlies and the society aroused interest in the preservation of sources of Catholic history. The U.S. Catholic Historical Society (1884) limited its publications at first to its *Proceedings* (1885–87) and then published a quarterly, *United States Catholic Historical Magazine* (New York 1887–92), but it did not survive the death of its editor, John Gilmary Shea. The society resumed publication in 1899 with the annual *Historical Records and Studies.*

Parish journals, a sound index of interest in journalism, became popular in the 1880s. In Massachusetts alone, Quincy had its monthly *Monitor* (1886–98), Marlboro its fortnightly *Star* (1887–93), Chelsea its weekly *Catholic Citizen* (1888–1937), Lawrence its Sunday *Register* (1892–1913), and Haverhill its monthly *Index* (1895–1907). Unique among these parish journals was the weekly *Sacred Heart Review* (1888–1918), established and edited by Rev. John O'Brien of East Cambridge, assisted by Susan L. Emory, a convert author familiar with journalism. It soon became a family magazine with a wide circulation (40,000 in 1894), an attractive variety of departments, and foreign correspondents. Journals to promote the interest of the Negroes and Indians also appeared. *St. Joseph's Advocate* (Baltimore 1884–95) was an illustrated quarterly published by the Josephite Fathers to promote their work among the Negroes. This was followed by their monthly *Colored Harvest* (1888–), currently known as the *Josephite Harvest. The Indian Advocate* (Sacred Heart Mission, Okla. 1889–1910), a quarterly (later a monthly) and the only Catholic publication of the 19th century in the Territory, was the work of the Benedictines. Its files contain interesting material on the American Indians of the West.

The more successful juveniles of the 1880s were weeklies: the illustrated *Chimes* (Baltimore 1880–1907?); *Catholic Youth* (Brooklyn 1881–97), which was published also in a monthly edition; *Little Crusader* (Columbus, Ohio; Chicago 1882–1900); *Angelus* (Detroit 1882–1919); and *Young Folks' Catholic Weekly* (Philadelphia 1889–1916). The sole survivor, however, is the *Young Catholic Messenger* (Dayton 1885–), which started as a monthly but is now a widely circulated weekly (860,258 in 1964). As the new century began there were only six worthwhile Catholic juveniles, two of them published in Philadelphia, and the others in New York, Chicago, Detroit, and Dayton. The few originating in the 1890s had at best a modicum of success, like the monthly *Catholic Religious Youth* (Chicago 1895–1907) and the biweekly *Our Young People* (Milwaukee 1892–1961). Benziger started an illustrated monthly, *Our Boys and Girls Own,* but in April 1900 it was converted into a family magazine, *Benziger's Magazine* (New York 1898–1921).

Catholic magazines continued to expand in the 1890s, although quality, not quantity, was an obvious need. On the score of continuity the new family magazines, published by religious orders, were the most successful, but there were noteworthy efforts in the field of education, social work, Catholic doctrine, and devotions, and two examples of personal journalism in the tradition of Brownson. Three family monthlies, the *Rosary Magazine* (1891–) by the Dominicans, *St. Anthony's Messenger* (1893–) by the Franciscans, and *St. Joseph's Magazine* (1897–) by the Benedictines, have had continual publication. The *Carmelite Review* (Falls View, Ontario; Chicago 1893–1906), after moving to Chicago and under a new editor, became concerned with contemporary political, economic, and social problems. But in the 1890s *Rosary* was the most important; its vigorous editorial policy offered strong competition to the *Catholic World* and *Donahoe's Magazine*.

Three monthlies and a quarterly promoted interest in education. The *Teacher and Organist* (Cincinnati; St. Francis, Wis. 1890–1910) was bilingual, English and German. The *Catholic School and Home Magazine* (Worcester 1892–97), a pioneer in Catholic education, was suspended when its editor, Rev. Thomas James *Conaty, was appointed rector of The Catholic University of America. The *Catholic Reading Review* (Youngstown, Ohio 1891–1903) was the organ of the Catholic Reading Circle and the Catholic Summer School. Under the editorship of Warren E. Mosher, it was called *Mosher's Magazine* (1898–1903) and then *Champlain Educator* and, as one of the better Catholic journals, was a stimulus to educational and intellectual activities. The *Catholic University Bulletin* (Washington 1895–1928), a quarterly, was planned as a competitor of the *ACQR* and the *Catholic World,* but became a review by and for university professors whose articles reflected the views and trends of American Catholic intellectual circles.

In social work there was the *Saint Vincent de Paul Quarterly* (New York 1895–1916); it was superseded by the monthly *Catholic Charities Review* (Washington 1916–), the organ of both the Society and the National Conference of Catholic Charities. Two devotional monthlies also survived: *Emmanuel* (New York 1895–), published by the Fathers of the Blessed Sacrament for the Priests Eucharistic League; they also published the *Sentinel of the Blessed Sacrament* (New York 1898) for the laity, now *Eucharist* (1962–), a journal of modern spirituality. Two other monthlies provided a better understanding of Catholic doctrine and practices. *Missionary* (Washington; New York 1896), published by the Paulists, promoted their work among non-Catholics. When its objective was modified it was renamed *Information* (1946) and later became the *Catholic Layman. Truth* (Raleigh, N.C. 1897–1932) developed, under Rev. Thomas Frederick *Price, into a nationally known journal; when he became cofounder of the Maryknoll Society, he ceded the title to the International Catholic Truth Society of Brooklyn (1911).

Two editors enlivened Catholic journalism in the 1890s, giving their readers the views of able minds, freely and even bluntly expressed. William Henry Thorne founded and edited the *Globe* (Philadelphia; New York 1889–1904), a quarterly review of world literature, society, religion, and politics. Thorne had become a Catholic in 1892 after religious experiences similar to Brownson's; his blunt criticism of other Catholic editors and of the views of Abp. John *Ireland irked some readers. Though his statements were bold, honest, and original, the objection that there was "too much Thorne" in the quarterly was valid.

Arthur *Preuss, son of the convert Edward Preuss (who edited the successful German Catholic *Amerika*), founded and edited the *Fortnightly Review* (Chicago; St. Louis 1894–1935), which started as the monthly *Chicago Review* and soon became the weekly *Review*. Ably presenting the views of the Catholic German-Americans during a controversial decade, the review broke the communication barrier between the English- and German-speaking groups. Independent to the point of refusing advertisements, Preuss did not spare Catholic editors and the views of some bishops, but his comments on the issues of the day were lucid and competent. This kind of magazine died with its editor, but Thorne and Preuss improved the standards of 19th-century Catholic magazines, the best of which were the *Brownson Quarterly Review,* the *Catholic World, Ave Maria,* the *Messenger of the Sacred Heart,* the *American Catholic Quarterly Review,* the *American Ecclesiastical Review,* the *American Catholic Historical Researches,* the *Sacred Heart Review,* the *Rosary Magazine,* the *Catholic Reading Circle,* and the *Catholic University Bulletin.*

Bibliography: F. L. MOTT, *A History of American Magazines,* 4 v. (New York 1930–38; repr. Cambridge, Mass. 1957) esp. v.3–4. F. MEEHAN, "The First Catholic Monthly Magazines," HistRecStud 31 (1940) 137–144. W. L. LUCEY, *An Introduction to American Catholic Magazines* (Philadelphia 1952).

[W. L. LUCEY]

b. 19th-Century Foreign-Language Newspapers and Periodicals. Olszyk's statement of the purpose of the Polish press applies to all foreign-language serials of the 19th and 20th centuries: "First, to answer the desire and need of unity and understanding among the immigrants cast on a new land; secondly, to inform them of the duties and advantages of their citizenship; thirdly, to keep them informed of the activities of their fellow Poles in Europe and all over the world." These points apply equally to the Irish-American publications.

Franco-American and French. Quantitatively first were the Franco-American and French titles. For the 19th century the Willging-Hatzfeld list (see bibliog. after section c. 19th-Century English Newspapers) has 151 titles designated as "Franco-American" and 13 entirely in French. In New England, political aspects dominated. A. Belisle has recorded many more but without adequate definition of their Catholic scope. The heaviest concentrations were in New England, especially Massachusetts, and in Louisiana.

German. While the Germans (and other foreigners) imported most of their books, a native newspaper-periodical press developed rapidly, especially with the heavy immigrant influx in the late 1840s. The Willging-Hatzfeld list records 120 titles in the 19th century, beginning with *Der Wahrheitsfreund* (Cincinnati 1837–1907). There soon followed the *Katholische Kirchenzeitung* (Baltimore, etc. 1846–82), *Der Herold des Glaubens* (St. Louis 1850–1924), *Der Seebote* (Milwaukee 1852–1924), the *Täglicher Pittsburger Republikaner* (1854–79), *Der Wanderer* (St. Paul 1867; now in English), *Pastoralblatt* (St. Louis 1866–1925), and the very significant daily *Amerika* (St. Louis 1872–1924), to mention only a few of the 113 titles in the 19th and 20th centuries cited by Timpe, of which 9 were dailies. In 1936 there were still 23 German Catholic periodicals in existence; by 1964 all had expired or changed, like the *Wanderer,* into English-language titles. Wittke has written that "prior to World War I the German press in the U.S. still led all other foreign-language publications, and in many cases was superior in quality as well."

Polish. From the 1880s Polish immigration expanded, reaching a total of 865,361 in the 1901–10 decade with a resultant development of serial literature. More than 140 Polish papers and periodicals were begun after 1863. Grzybowska has noted that "the outstanding feature of Polish publishing activities in the 19th century was their dependence on the Catholic Church." The Willging-Hatzfeld survey recorded 63 titles founded in the 19th century alone, of which there were 44 newspapers, including 8 dailies, 16 magazines, and the balance miscellaneous. Many others (see Olszyk) began in the 20th century; by 1940 there were 10 Polish-language dailies in existence. Of these, *Dziennik Chicagoski* (*Polish Daily News*), founded in 1890, still existed in 1965 with a circulation of more than 13,000. Samsel has noted that "in the main it was the newspaper publishers that served as agencies for the publication (and distribution) of Polish books" in the U.S. The same applied to other foreign-language imprints.

Bohemian (Czech). By 1905 there were approximately 500,000 Bohemians in the U.S., with the greatest concentrations in Chicago, Cleveland, New York, and St. Louis. There were many fraternal and benevolent organizations, which naturally had their own publications. The first major serial was *Hlas* (The Voice), founded in St. Louis in 1874 by Msgr. Joseph Hessoun. Cited as the best periodical (CE 2:621) was *Katolik,* founded in 1892. Also well known was the daily *Narod;* the major publisher was the Bohemian Benedictine Press of Chicago. Willging-Hatzfeld records 19 Bohemian titles in the 19th century.

Portuguese. Of the 19 Portuguese 19th-century Catholic serials, 13 were published in California. The first and most popular, with a circulation of 1,650, was *A Voz Portuguesa* (1880–88). Massachusetts also had several significant Portuguese titles.

Others. In the early 19th century the Spanish-Cuban press was led by the Rev. Felix Varela (1788–1853), who founded *El Habanero* (as well as five English-language publications) in Philadelphia in 1824; it died in New York City in 1826. Willging-Hatzfeld lists 11 Spanish-Cuban 19th-century serials. According to their survey there were the following other foreign-language serials in the 19th century: Italian, 9; Lithuanian, 9; Slovak-Slovenian, 6; Dutch-Flemish, 3; (American) Indian, 3; Ukrainian, 2; Basque, 1; Hungarian, 1; Ruthenian, 1; and Syriac-Arabic, 1.

Bibliography: Franco-American and French. A. BELISLE, *Histoire de la presse franco-américaine* (Worcester, Mass. 1911). M. TÉTRAULT, *Le Rôle de la presse dans l'évolution du peuple franco-américain de la Nouvelle Angleterre* (Marseille 1935). A. L. HOULE, *A Preliminary Checklist of Franco-American Imprints in New England, 1780–1925* (Master's diss. unpub. CUA 1955).

German. K. J. ARNDT and M. E. OLSON, *German-American Newspapers and Periodicals 1732–1955: History and Bibliography* (Heidelberg 1961). G. TIMPE, "Hundert Jahre Katholischer deutscher Presse," in *Katholisches Deutschtum in den Vereinigten Staaten von Amerika: Ein Querschnitt,* ed. G. TIMPE (Freiburg 1937) 4–33. C. F. WITTKE, *The German-Language Press in America* (Lexingon, Ky. 1957). Further state-by-state detail in Willging-Hatzfeld.

Polish. E. G. OLSZYK, *The Polish Press in America* (Milwaukee 1940). M. A. SAMSEL, *Polish Catholic Book Publishing in the U.S. and Its Distribution during the Period 1871–1900* (Master's diss. unpub. CUA 1957). E. P. WILLGING and H. HATZFELD, "Nineteenth-Century Polish Publications in the U.S.," *Polish American Studies* 12 (July–Dec. 1955) 84–100; 13 (Jan.–June, July–Dec. 1956) 19–35, 89–101.

Bohemian (Czech). J. ŠINKMAJER, "Bohemians of the U.S.," CE 2:620–622. J. CADA, *Czech-American Catholics, 1850–1920* (Lisle, Ill. 1964).

Portuguese. C. SOARES, *California and the Portuguese* (Lisbon 1939).

Others. Master's diss. unpub. CUA: O. A. TABORSKY, *The Hungarian Press in America* (1955). D. D. TAUTVILAS, *The Lithuanian Press in America* (1961). G. L. YASHUR, *A Preliminary History of the Slovak Press in America* (1950).

[E. P. WILLGING]

c. 19th-Century English Newspapers. This section supplements the survey above (see section 27*a*) of 19th-century English-language periodicals.

After several abortive attempts, such as the *Michigan Essay* of the Rev. Gabriel *Richard, Irish-born Bp. John *England of Charleston, S.C., founded the *U.S. Catholic Miscellany* (1822–61) primarily for the apologetic reasons that motivated most of its contemporaries, such as the *Truth Teller* (New York 1825–55). Despite several title changes, the Boston *Pilot* (1829–), which developed from *The Jesuit, or Catholic Sentinel* (1829), is considered the oldest of the Catholic newspapers. Long the property of Patrick *Donahoe, under whom it became the most significant medium of Irish communication, it passed from lay to archdiocesan hands in 1908. In Cincinnati, Bp. Edward D. *Fenwick founded the *Catholic Telegraph* in October 1831; it also is still current. It was under lay management from 1898 to 1937, when it was acquired by the archdiocese and joined with the *Register* chain. In 1844 the *Pittsburgh Catholic,* also current, was founded by Bp. Michael *O'Connor, to whom the idea had been suggested by a non-Catholic printer, A. Anderson; it was lay published until 1954. In New York the *Freeman's Journal* (1840–1918) began as a diocesan organ, but was soon sold by Bp. John *Hughes to James A. *McMaster, probably the most vigorous lay editor of the 19th century. The *Catholic News* (New York 1886–) was founded by Herman Ridder, who was of a famous German publishing family. On the West Coast an early, still-current paper was the lay-initiated San Francisco *Monitor* (1858–); it had the unique distinction in 1945 of typesetting the UN Charter in Russian. The *Catholic Sentinel* of Portland, Ore., began Feb. 5, 1870; it changed to diocesan ownership in 1928. Humphrey J. Desmond of Milwaukee was noted for purchasing financially weak papers and developing a chain, which at one time included the Milwaukee *Catholic Citizen,* the St. Paul *Northwestern Chronicle,* the Washington (D.C.) *New Century,* the Memphis *Catholic Journal,* and the Sioux City *Iowa Catholic Citizen.* The current Philadelphia *Catholic Standard and Times* had its origin in the *Catholic Standard* of 1866. The Baltimore *Catholic Mirror,* predecessor of the present *Catholic Review,* originated in 1849. Kentucky's first major paper was the *Catholic Advocate,* founded in 1835 by Benjamin J. Webb, printer and publisher; later it became the *Catholic Guardian.* The current Louisville *Catholic Record* began in 1878. The *Michigan Catholic* started in 1872 and the Chicago *New World* in 1892. Fuller data on these and hundreds of short-lived papers are given in the Willging-Hatzfeld survey, a state-by-state record.

The ideal of a Catholic daily paper was constantly in the mind of planners. The first in English was the *American Citizen* (New York 1835–41), followed by the *Catholic Telegraph* (*Daily Telegraph,* also New York), which began and died in 1875. Shortly after the turn of the century, in 1902, the Chicago *New World* also made an unsuccessful attempt at daily publication.

These three English-language trials were in sharp contrast with the 35 fairly successful foreign-language dailies of the 19th century, two of which, *Draugas* (Lithuanian, Chicago) and *Dziennik Chicagoski* (Polish Daily News, Chicago) were still current in 1965.

The most significant segment of the English-language newspaper press was that of the Irish contribution, through persons such as Bp. John England (*U.S. Catholic Miscellany*), Patrick Donahoe and John Boyle *O'Reilly (Boston *Pilot*), James Alphonsus McMaster (New York *Freeman's Journal*), and Patrick *Ford (*Irish World* of New York). In addition, many Irish journalists worked on leading secular papers; Wittke has written that a list of all would be "almost encyclopedic in nature, for many Irishmen had special gifts for the newspaper field." The Willging-Hatzfeld survey designates 75 titles as being Irish-American in the 19th century alone.

Since Catholic press directories are a 20th-century product, it is to be noted that annual lists usually appeared in the various national Catholic clergy and diocesan directories, as well as in such general trade media as Alden's *American Newspaper Catalogue* (1875–92), Ayer's *American Newspaper Annual* (1880–), Dauchy's *Newspaper Catalogue* (1890–1914), Rowell's *American Newspaper Directory* (1868–1908), and other publications of a specialized regional and subject nature.

While a complete tabulation of 19th-century newspapers must await the completion in 1966 of the Willging-Hatzfeld survey, it appears likely that about 50 per cent of the approximately 1,200 Catholic serials of the 19th century were newspapers.

Bibliography: E. P. WILLGING and H. HATZFELD, *Catholic Serials of the 19th Century in the U.S.: A Descriptive Bibliography and Union List,* 2d ser. (Washington 1959–), a state-by-state survey. For complete list and publication record, which also covers the 1st ser. pub. in RecAmCHSPhila, see pt. 10: *Massachusetts* (1965). States for which the record has not been pub. as of April 1965 are Kentucky, Louisiana, Maryland, Mississippi, New York, Ohio, Texas, and the District of Columbia; publication of these is scheduled for late 1965 and 1966. *Catholic Press Annual* (New York 1960–). M. S. CONNAUGHTON, *The Editorial Opinion of the Catholic Telegraph of Cincinnati on Contemporary Affairs and Politics 1871–1921* (Washington 1943). J. G. DEEDY, "The Catholic Press," in *The Religious Press in America,* ed. M. E. MARTY (New York 1963). P. J. FOIK, *Pioneer Catholic Journalism* (HistRecStud; 1930). M. A. FRAWLEY, *Patrick Donahoe* (Washington 1946). P. K. GUILDAY, *The Life and Times of John England, First Bishop of Charleston, 1786–1842,* 2 v. (New York 1927). M. A. KWITCHEN, *James Alphonsus McMaster* (Washington 1949). T. F. MEEHAN, "Periodical Literature, Catholic," CE 11:692–696; "The Catholic Press," in *Catholic Builders of the Nation,* ed. W. S. BENSON et al., 5 v. (Boston 1923) 4:219–234. C. WITTKE, "Irish-American Journalism," in *The Irish in America* (Baton Rouge 1956) 202–215. E. BOULARAND, "Les Débuts d'Arius," *Bulletin de littérature ecclésiastique* 75 (1964) 175–203.

[E. P. WILLGING]

d. 18th- through 20th-century Books and Pamphlets. The father of U.S. Catholic publishing was Mathew *Carey, whose 1790 Bible was the beginning of a list of 26 titles. His immediate successor in Philadelphia was Eugene Cummiskey (d. 1860), whose 62 imprints included a long series of Bibles, John *Lingard's *History of England,* and *The Catholic Family Library.* In common with later practice he also issued a newspaper, *The Catholic Herald and Visitor.*

Origins. As the premier see, Baltimore became a major publishing center, at first through the activity of Fielding *Lucas, Jr., who had collaborated with Carey and acquired plates of many of his publications. As with Carey, his general line of atlases and maps provided a financial base to support the religious titles. Of particular significance was his establishment of the *Metropolitan Catholic Almanac and Laity's Directory* (1833–57). Lucas's 204 publications rank him in 10th position among 19th-century Catholic firms. A younger contemporary, Irish-born John *Murphy, was also a noted publisher of general as well as Catholic titles; of his 1,458 editions of 817 titles, 673 were Catholic, ranking him fourth. His edition of Gibbons's *Faith of Our Fathers* sold more than 2 million copies; as publisher of 64 texts he helped provide for the needs of the expanding school system. Murphy was also prominent as a periodical publisher. When his successors dissolved the firm in 1943, and the assets were taken over by P. J. *Kenedy in New York, Baltimore's century of publishing prominence was over.

In Boston Patrick *Donahoe, best known as publisher of the *Pilot,* ranked fifth with 386 pulications. Most of his titles dealt with Irish literature, history, and biography; as a bookseller he carried a stock of some 900 titles.

New York City's present dominance began with John and Patrick Kenedy; though in the 19th century they produced only 101 titles, Kenedy has ranked consistently among the 20th-century leaders. In the beginning the firm was noted for catechisms, prayerbooks, and Bibles; later it expanded into trade books; their *Official Catholic Directory* (1913–), with its subsidiary mailing lists, has provided an invaluable basis for direct-mail promotion. The firms of *Benziger and *Sadlier ranked second and third in the 19th century; both had their own printing establishments. Sadlier continued Lucas's example through an annual *Catholic Directory* (1864–96); in 1965 it was exclusively a textbook firm.

Ranked first among the 19th-century Catholic publishers with 988 titles was the Catholic Publication Society (CPS), founded in 1866 by Paulist Isaac *Hecker, whose press apostolate marked a major new era. The CPS was directed by Irish-born Lawrence Kehoe (1832–90); as a firm it was the first to separate from church-goods sales. After Kehoe's death and until World War I there was a gap in Paulist activity. Under Joseph Menendez it concentrated on pamphlets priced from 5 to 25 cents and achieved annual sales of over 6 million copies. In the 1960s it acquired the Newman Press, expanded into the book field, and now ranks among the top 10 Catholic publishers in the U.S., with a significant record also as a distributor.

The following table lists the major publishers of Catholic books in English from 1831 to 1900; the figures are derived from the 11 dissertations cited in the bibliography:

Publisher	Titles
Catholic Publication Society, New York	988
Benziger, New York	937
D. & J. Sadlier, New York	684
John Murphy, Baltimore	673
Patrick Donahoe, Boston	386
Patrick O'Shea, New York	309
Edward Dunigan, New York	248
Kelly, Hedian & O'Brien; Kelly & Piet, John B. Piet, Baltimore	230
F. Pustet, New York, etc.	211
Fielding Lucas, Jr., Baltimore	204
H. & C. McGrath, Philadelphia	186
B. Herder, St. Louis	163
D. Appleton, New York	149
Peter Dunningham, Philadelphia	138
P. J. Kenedy, New York	101
Total:	5,607

Total 19th-century production (1831–1900), as so far recorded in the 11 dissertations cited, was 9,122.

Catholic Books from General Firms. The first trend of the "general" (non-Catholic) firms toward publishing Catholic authors began with Appleton's edition of Newman's *Essay on Development of Christian Doctrine* (1845) and his later *Apologia* (1865). From 1890 to 1930, as recorded by Lonergan, the general firms of Longmans, Macmillan, Dodd Mead, Doubleday, and Harper published the leading foreign Catholic authors, such as Baring, Belloc, Chesterton, Gilson, Greene, Maritain, Undset, and Waugh. With the advent of Bruce, Newman, and Sheed & Ward's U.S. branch in the early 1930s, a new, vigorous group of strictly Catholic firms began, later supplemented by Fides, Helicon, Daughters of St. Paul, Franciscan Herald, and Herder and Herder. About the same time, in the 1950s and 60s, some of the general firms, notably Doubleday, Hawthorn (then a Prentice-Hall subsidiary), Regnery, McGraw-Hill, Farrar, Straus and Cudahy (now F. S. and Giroux), and World, either developed new Catholic lines or expanded dormant ones. About the same time the *university presses, such as those of The Catholic University of America, Fordham, Loyola, and Notre Dame, enlarged their lists.

In order to provide a systematic record, as well as to assist libraries, The Catholic University of America Library began (1935) its "Weekly List of New Catholic Books," describing annually over 1,200 titles of more than 200 publishers; an annual classified list now appears in the *National Catholic Almanac.*

Paperback Books. As part of the general trend toward *paperback books, Doubleday began its Image Books series (1954), which now comprises almost 200 titles. Other general and Catholic firms expanded their output so that by 1965 more than 2,300 titles were recorded in the annual *Catalog of Catholic Paperback Books.*

Pamphlets. At first the success of paperbacks resulted in a sharp decline in pamphlet production, but in the late 1950s and early 1960s there was a revival, and now about 250 titles appear annually from America Press, Ave Maria, Daughters of St. Paul, Divine Word Publications, Guild Press, Liguorian–Queen's Work Pamphlets, Liturgical Press, National Catholic Welfare Conference, Paulist Press, George Pflaum, St. Anthony's Guild, St. Paul Publications, and the Spiritual Life Press. The history of the pamphlet, usually defined as a paper-covered publication of less than 100 pages, begins with the origin of printing. It has always been significant in political and religious controversies; when Newman and his associates launched the Oxford (Tractarian) Movement, the 90 *Tracts for the Times* were the major media. In 1884 James Britten launched the Catholic Truth Society (CTS) in London, which pioneered in developing a rack for parish church use and a Boxtenders' Association with more than 2,500 members. Annual CTS sales are in excess of 3 million copies.

In the U.S. various Catholic tract societies, such as one begun by Bp. John Hughes in Philadelphia in 1827, began to answer the attacks of "the Protestant crusaders." The Rev. Isaac Hecker, CSP, and Lawrence Kehoe established the Catholic Publication Society, which published its first four-page tract in May 1866; by 1871 it had produced 45 titles and had printed 2,250,000 copies, chiefly distributed gratis. The Paulists have continued this pamphlet apostolate for a full century. *The Index to (American) Catholic Pamphlets* (v.3, 1942–46) estimated annual sales of 25 million copies, a low figure since products of many religious societies were not recorded. By 1952 probably 5,000 different titles were in print in the catalogues of 44 publishers.

A major development occurred in 1947 with the establishment of the Knights of Columbus Religious Information Bureau in St. Louis, Mo. It has sent millions of apologetic titles in response to inquiries received from their advertising campaign in national magazines. At present, according to records of Catholic book and pamphlet production issued annually by The Catholic University of America Library, 59 publishers are issuing almost 300 different titles each year. With advances in cost of printing and distribution, the margin is closing between the inexpensive pamphlet and the paperbacks in book size, of which 2,500 were recorded in the 1964–65 *Catalog of Catholic Paperback Books.* The great weakness in pamphlet publishing has been in distribution; the expanded program of the Paulist Press (Glen Rock, N.J.) now provides the long-needed national center.

Textbooks, Bibles. Textbook publishing, especially of catechisms and Church histories, for the ever-expanding parochial school market was initially in the hands of the church-goods firms, such as Benziger, Herder, and Pustet; but the need for better distribution in the 20th century brought a shift to more specialized firms, such as Bruce, Catholic Book Publishing Co., and Sadlier among the Catholic firms, and Ginn, Heath, Scott-Foresman, and others among the general firms.

The publishing of "subscription" books has received inadequate historical treatment; it might be noted that Peter F. *Collier had a strong Catholic and secular list, which branched into periodicals, reference sets, and paperbacks in the mid-20th century. Subscription salesmen were most influential in bringing "parlor" Bibles and large sets, such as the *Catholic Encyclopedia,* Butler's *Lives of the Saints,* Lingard's *History of England,* and Montor's *Lives and Times of the Popes,* into many rectories, convents, schools, and homes.

Bible publishing, from the time of Carey's 1790 Douay version, has played a major role with all firms; the development of stereotyping in 1812 and electrotyping in 1841 made possible cheap and regular Bible production, so that such firms as Carey, Cummiskey, Dunigan, Lucas, Murphy, Sadlier, Bruce, Kenedy, Catholic Book Publishing Co., and others usually offered 10 or more different editions in their catalogues. From the time of World War II the Confraternity of the Precious Blood has been noted for its large line of inexpensive scriptural, liturgical, and meditation titles.

Various religious orders have often maintained their own presses, sometimes for their own exclusive use, such as that of the Jesuits at Woodstock, Md., which issued 190 titles between 1869 and 1955. Others, notably the Benedictines through the Liturgical Press, The Grail, the Paulists, Divine Word Fathers, Redemptorists (Liguorian Press), Daughters of St. Paul, and the Society of St. Paul, have specialized in popular titles, often pamphlets, to reach a market not served fully by the general and Catholic book publishers.

Foreign-language Titles. Every immigrant group developed forms of printed communication; they usually preferred newspapers and periodicals, relying heavily upon imports for major book titles. German immigration was already strong by the 1830s and expanded rapidly during the late 1840s. As a result, the Benziger family established a New York branch in 1853, which became noted for devotional, liturgical, and popular works, as well as for texts. In Dayton, Ohio, Joseph Fischer began a music-publishing firm. Pustet's New York branch opened in 1865, and B. Herder's St. Louis office began in 1873. The Grothe study recorded almost 300 German Catholic books and pamphlets from 16 major firms between 1865 and 1880; probably an even higher rate of publication occurred prior to 1914. Timpe has noted that the German publishers, especially when issuing periodicals or newspapers (as most did), developed series of almanacs or calendars that often sold 50,000 or more annually. Foreign-language book publication was often of the type that could be used as premiums for subscriptions or as school prizes and could not be highly rated as literature. Book distribution was, as a rule, very closely linked with church-goods sales.

Houle has recorded 309 Franco-American imprints in New England between 1780 and 1925. When the survey of Louisiana is completed, probably a similar number of French imprints from the South will be noted. Over 400 Polish titles between 1871 and 1900 were recorded by Samsel. Yashur has given attention to Slovak works; Taborsky, to Hungarian; and Tautvilas, to Lithuanian. There is also a fair amount of Spanish and Italian publication still unrecorded.

Finally, it should be noted that book publishing is a most overlooked field for Catholic lay action; e.g., the energetic manager of the Paulists' Catholic Publication Society was Lawrence Kehoe. This trend continued into the 20th century even when newspaper publishing was shifting to diocesan control and periodicals were developing under auspices of religious communities.

Bibliography: Book and pamphlet publishing. P. J. FULLAM, "The Catholic Publication Society and Its Successors 1866–1916," HistRecStud 47 (1959) 12–77. DictEngCath. R. GORMAN, *Catholic Apologetical Literature in the U.S., 1784–1858* (Washington 1939). R. C. HEALEY, *A Catholic Book Chronicle: The Story of P. J. Kenedy & Sons, 1826–1951* (New York 1951). M. T. HILLS, *The English Bible in America: A Bibliography . . .* (New York 1961). H. LEHMANN-HAUPT, *The Book in America* (2d ed. New York 1951). D. MARTIN, *American Catholic Convert Authors: A Bio-bibliography* (Detroit 1944). W. PARSONS, *Early Catholic Americana . . . 1729–1830* (New York 1939), sup. by F. B. BOWE, "Some Additions and Corrections . . .," CathHistRev 28 (1942) 229–247. H. POPE, *English Versions of the Bible,* rev. S. BULLOUGH (St. Louis 1952). *Guide to Catholic Literature 1888–* (Detroit-Haverford, Pa. 1940–). *A Survey of Catholic Book Publishing in the U.S., 1831–1900* (11 Master's diss. on 1 microfilm reel; CUA 1960). E. P. WILLGING, *The Index to American Catholic Pamphlets,* 6 v. (St. Paul, Minn.-Washington 1937–53), kept up to date through the card service in the "Weekly List of New Catholic Books" (CUA; Washington). R. A. BILLINGTON, *The Protestant Crusade, 1800–1860* (New York 1938; repr. Chicago 1964).

Foreign-language book publishing. J. GROTHE, *German Catholic Publishing and Book Distribution within the U.S. from 1865 to 1880* (Master's diss. unpub. CUA 1950). A. L. HOULE, *A Preliminary Checklist of Franco-American Imprints in New England, 1780–1925* (Master's diss. unpub. CUA 1955). A. SAMSEL, *Polish Catholic Book Publishing in the U.S. and Its Distribution during the Period 1871–1900* (Master's diss. unpub. CUA 1957).

[E. P. WILLGING]

e. 20th-Century Newspapers. Before World War I, most U.S. Catholic newspapers were chiefly concerned with the apologetic aspects of religion. The Catholic press was considered to be a sort of "answer sheet" for objections to and threats against the Church. It looked upon itself as a crusader against injustice to immigrant groups (usually to the Irish; to a lesser extent toward the Germans and Italians).

Changing Character. National and international news came increasingly to the fore during the post-World War II era. Such news had previously followed the general plan of answering attacks and publicizing news of nationalistic interest (e.g., Irish freedom). Thus, in answer to a questionnaire submitted to all U.S. Catholic papers as a preparation for this survey, the Boston *Pilot* categorized Catholic news coverage as: in 1900, Irish; in 1920, Catholic; in 1940, Catholic; and in 1960, ecumenical. In the 1960s the *St. Louis Review* (1941) characterized its shift in editorial policy as one that places greater emphasis on meaningful local stories that "teach"; gives much less attention to parish events, weddings, and social news in general; and is marked by a focus on current moral, theological, and social areas (e.g., *Vatican Council II, the liturgy, the human rights issue).

At the beginning of the 20th century, the Catholic press included 63 weekly newspapers, 102 magazines, and 145 foreign-language publications in 16 languages. Circulation and subscriptions rates can best be illustrated by these examples. In 1908 the *Tablet* of Brooklyn, N.Y., had a circulation of 13,000 at $2 per year; in 1964 its circulation was 138,871 at $5. The Baltimore *Catholic Review* charged its 15,000 subscribers $1 in 1913; 50 years later its 44,496 readers paid $4.50. Total similar statistics for the early part of the century are not available.

John Mark Gannon, then bishop of Erie, Pa., and later episcopal chairman of the Catholic Press Association, outlined in 1939 a rather drastic plan to get the diocesan newspaper into every Catholic home. Parish lists were to be submitted by pastors to the chancery office. The last Sunday of February (Catholic Press Month) and the first Sunday of October were designated as Catholic Press Sundays. On these days a special collection envelope would be distributed for subscription fees and the pastor billed twice a year by the chancery for each name on his parish list. Under this plan, the diocese would be responsible for collection from the pastors and act as guarantor to the publisher. A modification of this plan is used in some dioceses where school children take on the duty of collecting subscriptions. The Archdiocese of St. Louis amended the statutes of its synod to provide for the circulation of the archdiocesan newspaper, deciding that each pastor, beginning in 1951, would attach a list of his parishioners due to receive the paper to the annual report of the parish, which is submitted to the chancery office in January. That office thereupon forwards the lists to the archdiocesan newspaper.

Shifts in Ownership. In 1900 ownership of the diocesan Catholic press was still generally vested in the founding laymen or their families. Of the major papers of the diocesan press, the *Catholic News* of New York City, owned by the Ridder family, is one of the few still remaining (*see* RIDDER, CHARLES). The Brooklyn *Tablet's* early career, before it became the property of the diocese, reflected the usual struggles and trials of a Catholic newspaper. Its founder, James P. Lawlor, offered the diocese half interest but was advised to start the enterprise and await development. A year later, in 1909, for $5,000, the diocese became sole owner.

When, in the early 1900s, ownership of Catholic newspapers shifted from lay hands to diocesan control, many of them added the subtitle "official organ of the diocese." Nevertheless, though the diocesan press was to be the "voice" of the local ordinary, its views were not necessarily his. Pope Pius XII clarified this point in 1957 in a radio address to the 47th Annual Convention of the Catholic Press Association. He stated: "In regard to questions in which the divinely appointed teachers have not pronounced judgment—and the field is vast and varied, saving that of faith and morals—free discussion will be altogether legitimate, and each one may hold and defend his own opinion" [*The Pope Speaks* (Autumn 1957) 212]. The Indianapolis *Criterion,* for example, states on its editorial page: "The opinions expressed in these editorial columns represent a Catholic viewpoint—not necessarily THE Catholic viewpoint. They are efforts of the editors to serve public opinion within the Church and within the Nation."

Charitable Purposes. Many of the early newspapers were founded to raise money for charities. The Louisville *Record,* to name but one, stated on its masthead until 1946 that it was "published for the benefit of the Orphans and Seminary." During the years preceding the Depression, the *Record* turned over to the orphans of the diocese $80,000 in 10 years. But the Depression years handed the *Record* a financial setback, and it abandoned this purpose. Diocesan charities in Boston have likewise benefited from the *Pilot's* espousal, and stories of missionaries' sacrifices and appeals for aid have long been a familiar part of its coverage.

Emergence of Chains. During the early part of the century, two Catholic newspaper chains came into existence. In 1905 Thomas Jefferson Casey started a branch publication in Denver, the *Catholic Register.* In 1906 this paper gave notice of the establishment of the Colorado Springs *Catholic Register* and the Pueblo *Catholic Register,* but these were not yet separate editions. In June 1929, under the direction of Msgr. Matthew J. W. Smith, the *Register* published its first diocesan paper outside of Denver. By 1938 the system had grown to 19 editions with a circulation of 400,000, including a national edition begun in 1924. Circulation figures for 1964 indicated 33 editions and 778,196 subscribers.

Our Sunday Visitor (OSV) was founded (1912) by Father (later Abp.) John Francis *Noll of Fort Wayne, Ind., as an instruction paper to bring the truth about the Catholic Church to Catholics and non-Catholics, many of whom were being deceived by anti-Catholic and prosocialist papers, such as the *Menace* and the *Appeal to Reason.* In 1937 OSV published the first diocesan edition other than that for the Diocese of Fort Wayne. Figures for 1964 showed OSV circulation at 892,148 with 11 diocesan editions, a Canadian national edition, and a national news edition. Other chains included the Catholic Quality Newspapers of Northern Ohio with editions in Cleveland, Toledo, and Youngstown. Circulation in 1964 was 201,840. The *Catholic Herald Citizen,* with a total circulation of 172,313 in 1964, published editions for Milwaukee, Madison, and Superior, Wis.

Corporate Activities. In 1905 Catholic journalists formed the Catholic Associated Press for the purpose of "supplying the Catholic Press with short articles, discussing social, economic, educational, and other subjects." This organization was more a news service, but it led to the establishment of the American Catholic Press Association in 1908. The association's purpose was "to promote the educational, literary, news, and business interest of the papers concerned, and to establish a closer fraternity among Catholic editors." Members drew up plans for an exchange of news and the formation of an advertising bureau.

At a meeting in Columbus, Ohio, in 1911, the Catholic Press Association (CPA) was formed from the 1908 organization to "assist members in publishing effective periodicals according to the demands of technical standards, and the truths of human reason and the Catholic Faith." Founders of the CPA included Simon A. Baldus of *Extension,* Richard *Reid of the *Catholic News* (New York), Vincent de Paul Fitzpatrick of the *Catholic Review* (Baltimore), Patrick F. Scanlan of the Brooklyn *Tablet,* Msgr. Peter M. H. Wynhoven of *Catholic Action of the South* (New Orleans), Alexander J. Wey of the *Catholic Universe Bulletin* (Cleveland), and Humphrey E. Desmond of the *Catholic Herald Citizen* (Milwaukee).

This period saw, too, the founding of the National Catholic Welfare Conference News Service (1920), which enabled publications to receive worldwide Catholic news (*see* PRESS ASSOCIATIONS AND SERVICES, CATHOLIC). The Religious News Service (RNS), an affiliated but independently managed agency of the National Conference of Christians and Jews, began service in 1934. Worldwide coverage of non-Catholic as well as Catholic news is provided by RNS.

Ventures in Daily Papers. In 1920 Nicholas E. Gonner began in Dubuque, Iowa, publication of the daily *Tribune.* The outgrowth of a weekly venture, it was the first major English-language Catholic daily in the U.S. Gonner considered every editor to be a missionary for the faith and ran his daily accordingly.

In September 1922 Gonner took the *Tribune* to Milwaukee and embarked on a subscription campaign. The *Tribune* and the Milwaukee *Catholic Herald* were to be sold through a club subscription offer. After Gonner's death the *Tribune* was purchased by William George *Bruce and other prominent Milwaukee men. Publication ceased on June 6, 1942. A second attempt at a Catholic daily was begun in October 1950 in Kansas City, Mo., by a group of Catholic laymen. The *Sun Herald,* under Robert Hoyt, was a tabloid of eight pages, "heavily analytical, concerned less to record events than to discover their meaning." The paper began with about 2,500 circulation and reached 8,000 in February 1951. An appeal for subscriptions brought circulation to 10,000 by April 5; but this did not cover costs, and publication was suspended and later abandoned. In 1964 the *National Catholic Reporter* (Kansas City, Mo.) was launched under lay editorship. Its fresh and even daring approach to news interpretation made it controversial but stimulating.

Deepening of Ecumenical Spirit. In 1949 the Institute of the Catholic Press was established under David Host as a research division of the Marquette University College of Journalism (*see* JOURNALISM, CATHOLIC SCHOOLS OF). The institute's aims are to study the techniques of journalism; to gather all available significant knowledge about the periodicals that comprise the Catholic press in the U.S.; to investigate the particular and common practices and problems of U.S. Catholic newspapers and magazines; and to make known the results of its own and other studies among Catholic publishers, journalists, and teachers.

At the beginning of Vatican Council II in 1962, Ralph Wiltgen, SVD, established the Divine Word News Service. The DNS served 103 countries in 11 languages; it was most beneficial during the first session of the council, when restrictions made news gathering difficult.

The spirit of the ecumenical era can be illustrated by the goals of the Baltimore *Catholic Review:*

> If we had to summarize the commanding concern of this paper, its galvanizing policy, we might describe it as the desire to help knit together whatever belongs together and has been separated by lack of love or lack of knowledge.
>
> We want closer bonds between clergy and laity, nearer involvement of the laity with liturgy, of God's Word with God's People. We want deeper commitment of 20th-century Catholics to 20th-century problems. We want warmer fraternal bonds between Catholics and other Christians, between the Catholic conscience and every sincere, rightfully free conscience. We want to help bind up the wounds of a nation which is still dangerously sick from racial injustice.
>
> Representative of this unifying policy of ours, our tabloid section has been devoted to one of the master hopes of this Ecumenical century: that religious men everywhere draw closer together to solve the critical moral and social problems of the thermonuclear age.

Leading Papers. In terms of circulation, apart from the chain publications mentioned above, the leading papers were (1965)—100,000 and over: *Long Island Catholic* (Rockville Center, N.Y.), *Clarion Herald* (New Orleans, La.), *New World* (Chicago, Ill.), *Catholic Herald Citizen* (Milwaukee, Wis.), *Tablet* (Brooklyn, N.Y.), *Advocate* (Newark, N.J.), *Michigan Catholic* (Detroit, Mich.), *St. Louis Review* (St. Louis, Mo.), *Tidings* (Los Angeles, Calif.), *Pilot* (Boston, Mass.), and *Universe Bulletin* (Cleveland, Ohio); 80,000 to 100,000: *Catholic Standard and Times* (Philadelphia, Pa.), *Pittsburgh Catholic* (Pittsburgh, Pa.), *Catholic News* (New York, N.Y.), *Catholic Transcript* (Hartford, Conn.), *Monitor* (Trenton, N.J.), and *Texas Catholic Herald* (Houston, Tex.); 60,000 to 80,000: *Catholic Telegraph* (Cincinnati, Ohio), *Voice* (Miami, Fla.), and *Courier Journal* (Rochester, N.Y.). All figures are from the *Catholic Press Directory,* 1964–65.

Foreign-Language Newspapers. The Chicago *Polish Daily News* (*Dziennik Chicagoski*), founded in 1890 by the Resurrection Fathers, continues to report all activities of Polish-Americans on local, state, national, and international levels. *La Voce del Popolo* (Detroit 1910), a national Italian-American weekly, is published by the Pious Society of St. Paul. *Il Crociato* (Brooklyn, N.Y. 1933) is an Italian weekly of the diocese. The official newspaper of the First Catholic Slovak Union, *Jednota,* was founded in Middletown, Pa., in 1891. *La Voz* (San Antonio, Tex. 1935) was the official Spanish newspaper of the archdiocese.

[B. L. BARNES]

f. 20th-Century Periodicals. Among the earliest U.S. 20th-century Catholic periodicals were those whose purpose was to stimulate interest in and support of the foreign missions. Some had this as an exclusive goal; others mingled this purpose with general consumer interest.

Mission Magazines. An early missionary or semi-consumer publication was the *St. Anthony Messenger* (Cincinnati, Ohio 1893), the organ of the Third Order of St. Francis; it soon became a popular family magazine dedicated to spreading devotion to St. Anthony. It grew from a circulation of 2,000 in 1900 to 330,000 in 1960. *Extension* (Chicago, Ill. 1906) was begun as a quarterly bulletin whose purpose was to make known the work of the *Catholic Church Extension Society. Beginning with a circulation of 50,000 (distributed on a voluntary donation basis), it was soon enlarged to a monthly, and by 1963 it reached 400,000 readers. The *Field Afar* (Maryknoll, N.Y. 1906) was the first magazine devoted exclusively to promoting the foreign missions; it later changed its title to *Maryknoll* and in 1964 had a circulation of more than 300,000. These earlier mission magazines were followed by the *Far East* (the Columban fathers; St. Columbans, Nebr. 1918; 150,-000); *Mission,* the organ of the Propagation of the Faith (New York, N.Y.; 1.7 million); the *Divine Word Missionaries* (Techny, Ill.; 152,000); *Jesuit Missions* (New York, N.Y. 1926; 170,000); *Worldmission* (New York, N.Y.); and many more that publicize the missionary work of various religious orders and congregations.

General Interest Magazines. The monthly *Catholic World* (New York, N.Y.; 19,900) and the weekly *Ave Maria* (Notre Dame, Ind.; 49,900), both established in 1865, are the oldest U.S. Catholic journals. The purpose of the *Catholic World,* as outlined by its founder, Isaac *Hecker, CSP, was the conversion of America. He saw "in the union of Catholic faith and American civilization a new birth and future for the Church brighter than any past." *Ave Maria* was dedicated to the Christianization of family life. These pioneer journals were followed by such periodicals as the *Messenger of the Sacred Heart* (New York, N.Y. 1866; 148,000), the *Liguorian* (Liguori, Mo. 1913; 330,000), and the *Sign* (Union City, N.J. 1921; 324,000), which is published by the Passionist fathers and is designed to blend Catholic teaching, reports and comments on affairs of the world of particular interest to Catholics, and entertaining features. *Columbia* (New Haven, Conn. 1893), the official organ of the *Knights of Columbus, had a circulation in 1964 of 1.2 million. A magazine of devotional and general interest is *The Lamp* (Peekskill, N.Y. 1903; 160,000), founded by the Franciscan fathers.

The weekly *America* (New York, N.Y. 1909) was intended by its founder, John J. *Wynne, SJ, to fill a role in the U.S. somewhat similar to that of the London *Tablet* (*see* CATHOLIC PRESS, WORLD SURVEY, 9). Its contents include criticism of the life and literature of the day and discussions of vital problems from a Catholic viewpoint. The integrity of its position and its wide circulation (100,000 in 1965, the largest in the U.S. of any weekly journal of opinion) have won it wide ecumenical respect at home and abroad. In 1924 Michael *Williams established the *Commonweal* (New York, N.Y.), a lay-edited weekly journal of opinion designed to be a periodical that would "apply the conserving and regenerative forces of the fountainhead of Christian tradition, experience, and culture to the problems that today all men of good will are seeking to solve." Its circulation in 1964 was 35,000, but its influence far outran that figure. The *U.S. Catholic* (Chicago, Ill.; 60,000) was formerly the *Voice of St. Jude* (1934).

Newer periodicals are *Integrity* (New York, N.Y. 1946), whose ideological roots were in the *Catholic

Worker movement, but which succumbed to financial difficulties in 1956; *Jubilee* (New York, N.Y. 1953; 44,500), which very successfully employs the picture-text technique to illustrate the life of the modern Church; *Cross Currents* (New York, N.Y.), which reprints essays and studies by the world's leading thinkers; and *Ramparts* (Menlo Park, Calif. 1964; 4,900), a crusading journal that does not always avoid brashness in its attempt to galvanize readers to Catholic action. The *Catholic Mind* (New York, N.Y. 1902; 17,900), one of the oldest U.S. reprint magazines, offers articles, speeches, etc., by leading figures and is especially valuable for its documentation of papal allocutions, statements of the hierarchy, etc. Papal documents are thoroughly reissued in the *Pope Speaks Magazine* (Washington, D.C. 1953; 12,000). A very influential monthly is the *Interracial Review* (New York, N.Y.), the organ of the *Catholic Interracial Conference. Several journals of greater specialization deserve mention in this survey, such as *Thought* (1926; 1,640), the scholarly quarterly issued by Fordham University, New York; *Liturgical Arts* (New York, N.Y.); and the *Benedictine Review* (Atchison, Kans. 1946; 900). (For Catholic literary journals, *see* LITERARY PERIODICALS, CATHOLIC.)

Several journals have been established to serve the interests of Catholic youth. Two of these, *Catholic Boy* (1932; 72,000) and *Catholic Miss* (1942; 95,200), are published at Notre Dame, Ind. Another, *Catholic Youth* (Salvatorian Center, Wis. 1914), has a circulation of 44,200.

Most Catholic periodicals encourage non-Catholic readership; the *Catholic Digest* (1936) had a circulation of 650,000 in 1964 and claimed a pass-along readership of seven for each copy (*see* DIGEST MAGAZINES, CATHOLIC). Catholic periodicals increasingly welcome contributions from non-Catholic authorities.

Foreign-Language Periodicals. In 1900 there were approximately 145 foreign-language publications, newspapers and magazines, in the U.S. Among them were publications in German, French, Polish, Bohemian, Slovak, Italian, Spanish, Portuguese, Gaelic, Syrian-Arabic, Indian, Ukrainian, Luxemburgian, Lithuanian, Hungarian, Dutch, and Flemish. (See section above for a more detailed discussion of the newspapers.) In 1964 there were 13 foreign-language newspapers, with a combined circulation of 195,434, and 24 magazines, with a combined circulation of 228,988. Among the magazines are *Amerikanski Slovenec* (Cleveland, Ohio), a weekly with 17,230 circulation; *Celle Qui Pleure* (Attleboro, Mass.), a monthly, 19,700; *Katolicky Sokol* (Passaic, N.J.), a Slovak weekly, 18,200; *Miesiecznik Franciszkanski* (Pulaski, Wis.), a Polish monthly, 24,670; and *L'Union* (Woonsocket, R.I.), a bimonthly, 45,000 (figures are for 1964).

Overall U.S. Catholic Press Figures. In 1925 the Catholic press in the U.S. had a total circulation of 6.4 million; in 1932, 7.3 million; and in 1944, 10.6 million. This includes magazines and newspapers accepting and not accepting advertising. In 1964 there were 121 weekly newspapers, with a circulation of 4,569,230; 53 diocesan directories, with 377,303; 59 consumer magazines, with 7,042,996; 50 business and professional magazines, with 455,931; and 241 magazines not accepting advertising, with 12,934,017 circulation. The total circulation, including the foreign publication mentioned above, was 25,504,277.

For specialized journals, *see* BIBLICAL PERIODICALS; THEOLOGICAL JOURNALS, SCHOLARLY; LITURGIOLOGY; SCHOLASTICISM, 3.

Bibliography: For details of individual periodicals and papers, see *Catholic Press Annual* (New York 1960–). J. G. DEEDY, "The Catholic Press," in *The Religious Press in America,* by M. E. MARTY et al. (New York 1963).

[B. L. BARNES]

28. OTHERS

This concluding section of the world survey covers the Caribbean area, the Middle East, the Pacific Islands, Malta, and Luxembourg.

Caribbean Area. The Catholic press is well represented in this vast section, though it has not yet been established in some regions (e.g., the Bahamas and the Barbados).

British Guiana (Georgetown). The *Catholic Standard* (1905 as a magazine; later a fortnightly; 1962 as a weekly newspaper) has a circulation of 4,500 and reaches into the remote interior, where the secular press does not penetrate. There is a magazine of the same name.

Cuba. In the colonial era (prior to 1889) the fortnightly *La Verdad Católica* (1858–66) was the only paper of general interest, though its main purpose was to stimulate devotion to the Immaculate Conception. In 1866 the Bishop of Havana, Jacinto Martínez, founded the *Boletín oficial eclesiástico;* suppressed in 1869, it reappeared from 1880 to 1960. In the republican period the Catholic University Association (1931) published the scientific journal *Lumen* (1944), and the Catholic University of Santo Tomás de Villaneuva issued *Noverim* (1946) for its faculty and *Insula* (1957) for its alumni. During the same period the Franciscans issued the widely read fortnightly review *La Quincena.* The two great colleges of Havana, La Sale (Brothers of the Christian Schools) and Belén (Jesuits), published well-edited journals for their alumni. A notable contribution to Catholic journalism, though not officially a Catholic paper, was *El Diario de la Marina* (1836), the oldest newspaper in Latin America; it consistently defended Catholic principles and interests. After the consolidation of power in the hands of Fidel Castro (1959), all Catholic publications were suppressed. The Church nevertheless inaugurated (1964) *Prisma Conciliar,* which gave news of Vatican Council II, and published the monthly bulletin *Entérate* and the catechetical publication *El K-T-Kista* (since the Castro regime has confined the work of the Church strictly within the churches, this catechetical work has assumed great importance in Cuba). It is to be noted that the director of *El Diario de la Marina* at the time of its suppression, José I. Rivero, carries on the work of this paper from his exile in Miami, Fla., with the review *Foto-Impresiones.* A total of 92 Catholic publications of all types appeared prior to 1955.

Dominica (Roseau). The *Dominica Chronicle* (1909, 1,200) circulates in the West Indies Islands; its reader ratio is high for a poor, largely illiterate area.

Guadeloupe. In this overseas department of France, *Clartés* (1945, 10,000) is a weekly newspaper serving the Leeward Islands.

Jamaica. The *Catholic Opinion,* under the direction of the Jesuits, was first a monthly (1896), then a weekly (1942). It exerts great influence, with a circulation of 7,000, through its liberal, articulate policy on matters both religious and secular. It won two awards in the 1955 competition sponsored by the U.S. Catholic Press Association.

Martinique (Windward Islands). There are two weeklies, *La Paix* (1912, 3,500) and *Aujourd'hui Dimanche* (1962, 11,000). The first is a journal of general information; the second is geared more to religious instruction.

Netherland Antilles (Curaçao). The *Amigoe de Curaçao* (1884, 8,000), published in Dutch, has the largest circulation of any daily paper in the Dutch West Indies. There are also two weekly papers, *La Cruz* (1900, 6,000) and *La Union* (1922, 3,000).

Puerto Rico. The earliest Catholic publication was *El Boletín Eclesíastico* (1859). The weekly *El Ideal Católico* was published in Ponce (1899–1915) until it was succeeded by a number of parish bulletins. *El Debate* (1961, 35,000) is a weekly that serves the Archdiocese of San Juan and the Dioceses of Ponce, Arecibo, and Caguas, having absorbed *Luz y Verdad* (1952). *El Debate* was suspended in 1965 for lack of funds. *El Apostol* (1910), the monthly organ of the Confraternity of Christian Doctrine, reaches 12,000 subscribers. The weekly *El Piloto* (1924, 2,500) exercises considerable influence among the intellectuals. The Holy Ghost fathers publish *El Mensajero* (1957, 15,000). *La Milagrosa* (1923) is the oldest review in Puerto Rico.

St. Lucia (Windward Islands). The *Saint Lucia Catholic* magazine (1930) expired during the early days of World War II; the present *Castries Catholic Chronicle* (1957), a fortnightly, has a total circulation of about 1,500.

Trinidad. The *Catholic News* (1891, 18,000) appears weekly. It is frequently quoted on the radio and in the local secular papers.

[J. F. BRENNAN]

Middle East. Considering the small percentage of Catholics in the area, the Catholic press is remarkably vital.

Egypt. One weekly, *Le Messager* (1958, 3,000), deals with the general life of the Church. An Arabic monthly, *Haqlona* (1949, 3,000), is the organ of Catholic Action and of the Egyptian Catholic Youth movement. A second Arabic monthly, *In Salah,* is a scientific and religious review of the Catholic Coptic patriarchate; it circulates mainly among the clergy and religious. *Le Lien* is a religious review published every 3d week for Greek Catholics; and *La Voce del Nilo* (1942) is published in Italian by the Franciscans. *Rayon d'Egypte,* a semiofficial and well-informed newspaper, was suppressed (1957) by the government; and in general, restrictions on the Catholic press became increasingly heavy after the nationalization of the secular press in 1960.

[J. A. BELL]

Lebanon. There are two monthly reviews, *Al-Maçarra,* the organ of the Greek-Melchite patriarchate, and *As-Sanabil,* the Maronite organ (their importance nationally is not strong). The influential trimonthly *Travaux et Jours* (1961), under the direction of the Jesuits of Université Saint-Joseph at Beirut, has a circulation of 2,000.

[H. JALABERT]

Israel. The Arabic monthly *Ar-Râbita* (1944, 4,000) is the organ of the Greek Catholic (Melchite) hierarchy. Another Arabic monthly, *As-Salaam Wal-l Kheir* (1950, 2,000), is published by the Franciscans at Nazareth. Two annuals, *Message de Galilee* (1953, 4,000) and *Message of Galilee* (1964, 3,000), are edited by Abp. G. Hakim at Nazareth.

[G. HAKIM]

Jordan. Le Moniteur Diocésain de Patriarcat Latin de Jérusalem (1934) was suspended in April 1948 because of the Arab-Israel war but reappeared in January 1950 as a bimonthly with widened scope. The official monthly journal of the Franciscan Custody of the Holy Land has appeared since 1924 in three languages: Italian (*La Terra Santa,* 5,000), French (*Le Terre Sainte,* 3,800), and Spanish (*Tierra Santa,* 8,400); since 1940 an Arabic edition, *Al-Ard Al-Muqaddasah,* reaches about 800 subscribers. *Proche-Orient Chrétien* (1950, 900), edited by the White fathers at the Greek-Catholic seminary of Sainte-Anne in Jerusalem, is a trimonthly devoted to religious, social, and literary matters. The Arabic monthly *Al-Hayat Al-Masihiyat* (10,000), published by the Latin Patriarchate of Jerusalem, is concerned with religious, moral, and liturgical formation.

[J. BELTRITTI]

Pacific Islands. Except for Hawaii, which is now part of the U.S. Catholic press, there is not much Catholic publication in this vast area.

Cook Islands. The monthly *Torea Katorika* (1914) was established when the mission was under the vicar apostolic of Tahiti; it has a circulation of 600.

[F. DE LEEUW]

Gilbert Islands. The monthly *Itoi Ni Kiribati* (1952), with a circulation of 1,200, is a continuation of *Nutibeba* (1940).

[P. GUICHET]

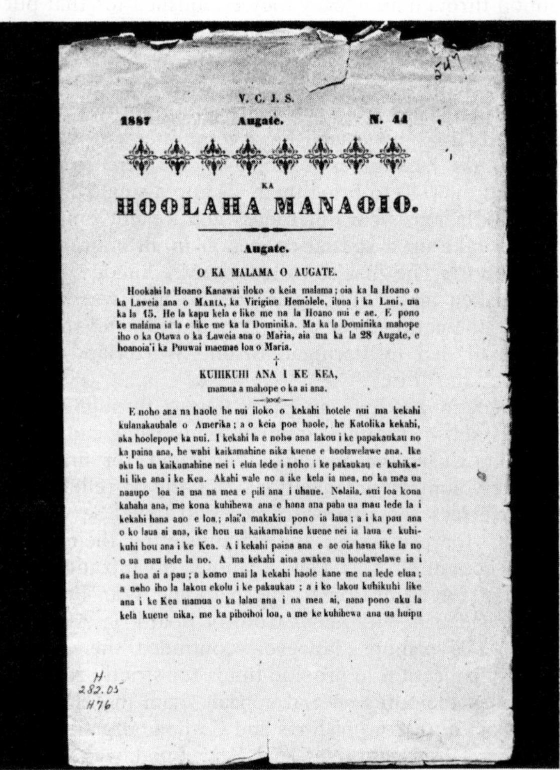

V. C. J. S.

1887 Augate. N. 44

KA

HOOLAHA MANAOIO.

Augate.

O KA MALAMA O AUGATE.

Hookahi la Hoano Kanawai iloko o keia malama; oia ka la Hoano o ka Laweia ana o MARIA, ka Virigine Hemolele, iluna i ka Lani, ma ka la 15. He la kapu kela e like me na la Hoano nui e ae. E pono ke malama ia la e like me ka la Dominika. Ma ka la Dominika mahope iho o ka Otawa o ka Laweia ana o Maria, aia ma ka la 28 Augate, e hoanoia'i ka Puuwai maemae loa o Maria.

†

KUHIKUHI ANA I KE KEA,
mamua a mahope o ka ai ana.

E noho ana na haole he nui iloko o kekahi hotele nui ma kekahi kulanakauhale o Amerika; a o keia poe haole, he Katolika kekahi, aka hoolepope ka nui. I kekahi la e noho ana lakou i ke papakaukau no ka paina ana, he wahi kaikamahine nika kuene e hoolawelawe ana. Ike aku la ua kaikamahine nei i elua lede i noho i ke pakaukau e kuhikuhi like ana i ke Kea. Akahi wale no a ike kela ia mea, no ka mea ua naaupo loa ia ma na mea e pili ana i uhane. Nolaila, nui loa kona kahaha ana, me kona kuhihewa ana e hana ana paha ua mau lede la i kekahi hana ano e loa; alai'a makakiu pono ia laua; a i ka pau ana o ko laua ai ana, ike hou ua kaikamahine kuene nei ia laua e kuhikuhi hou ana i ke Kea. A i kekahi paina ana e ae oia hana like la no o ua mau lede la no. A ma kekahi aina awakea ua hoolawelawe ia i na hoa ai a pau; a komo mai la kekahi haole kane me na lede elua; a noho iho la lakou ekolu i ke pakaukau; a i ko lakou kuhikuhi like ana i ke Kea mamua o ka lalau ana i na mea ai, nana pono aku la kela kuene nika, me ka pihoihoi loa, a me ke kuhihewa ana ua huipu

Fig. 10. "Hoolaha Manaoio" (August 1887), the longest lived Catholic publication in the Hawaiian language. This rare copy is preserved in the first printing house of the Hawaiian Mission Children's Society, Honolulu.

Hawaii. The periodical press in this U.S. state began tentatively in 1860 with the semimonthly *Hae Kiritiano;* this became a monthly in 1871 under the title *Hae Katolica,* but soon ceased publication. The last and longest lived periodical in the native language was *Hoolaha Manaoio* (1883–1929). After the annexation of the islands by the U.S. (1898), English quickly became the language of journalism, and after several abortive efforts *Church Bells* (1926) became the first official Catholic journal. It lapsed in 1933 with the death of its editor, but two parish journals somewhat filled the gap until the weekly *Catholic Herald* (14,000) appeared in 1936. It changed its name to the *Hawaii Catholic Herald* in 1947 and in 1964 was the third largest of all newspapers in the state.

[R. SCHOOFS]

Various. There is one weekly, *Lehen Is-Sewa,* in the Island of Malta. Luxembourg has one bilingual daily, *Luxemburger Post,* which reaches 68,000 subscribers in a population of 315,000; there is also one weekly, *Luxemburger Sonntagsblatt.*

Illustration credit: Fig. 10, Raymond Sato.

[H. C. GARDINER]

CATHOLIC RELIEF SERVICES—NCWC

The overseas aid agency of the Catholic bishops and people of the U.S., originally called War Relief Services—NCWC. Since its establishment in 1943, the agency has engaged in a broad program of relief, rehabilitation, and resettlement activities.

Early History. Before the outbreak of World War II, the bishops of the U.S., at the request of the German hierarchy, had been aiding refugees from Nazi persecution through an agency they established for that purpose, the Catholic Committee for Refugees and Refugee Children. After the outbreak of the war, the bishops attempted to meet the rapidly increasing and urgent appeals for help from ecclesiastical authorities in war-afflicted areas by establishing committees of national groups. As the number of such agencies increased it was decided in 1940 to bring them all into a single committee, the Bishops' War Emergency and Relief Committee, and to take up a special collection in all churches for its support. The first so-called Laetare Sunday Collection, taken up in 1941, was used to help war victims among the nationals of some 15 countries, and refugees who had fled to Portugal, Spain, Switzerland, Italy, France, and Iran.

When, in 1942, Community Chests throughout the U.S. established a single, annual fund-raising campaign, later known as the National War Fund, for financing private voluntary organizations carrying on relief activities overseas, the bishops formed War Relief Services—NCWC for promoting and administering their direct relief activities. This new Catholic organization was certified for admission to the National War Fund by the President's War Relief Control Board on April 28, 1943. The bishops, however, continued the Laetare Sunday collection to provide funds for strictly religious purposes, including special appeals from the Holy See and from numerous bishops and Catholic organizations overseas. When the National War Fund was discontinued in 1947, the bishops broadened their annual fund-raising appeal to provide continued support for the wide program of overseas relief, rehabilitation, and resettlement that War Relief Services—NCWC had been administering.

Activities of War Relief Services. In establishing War Relief Services (WRS), the American hierarchy hoped: (1) to bring aid and comfort to refugees, prisoners, and other victims of war; (2) to strengthen and reestablish local Catholic welfare agencies and institutions that had been weakened or damaged or destroyed by the ravages of war. During the war years, the efforts and resources of War Relief Services were directed chiefly toward aiding four categories of war victims: (1) religious and political persecutees from Germany and the Axis countries; (2) Polish refugees dispersed in 23 countries; (3) stateless persons in Spain and Portugal; and (4) needy persons in unoccupied Allied countries. In addition, WRS provided welfare and religious services and supplies for merchant seamen and for prisoners of war in Prisoner-of-War camps in the U.S., Canada, and other countries. The agency also cooperated with groups providing help for students whose educational pursuits had been disrupted by the war.

As countries were successively liberated from Axis control, even before the cessation of hostilities, War Relief Services extended prompt assistance to the inhabitants of the war-torn lands, establishing relief programs in France, Belgium, Holland, Poland, the Philippines and Czechoslovakia. Urgently needed supplies of food, clothing, and medicine were sent to Greece, India, Luxembourg, Madagascar, the Dutch East Indies, Yugoslavia, Rumania, and Korea. Soon after the war ended, extensive relief programs were launched in former enemy countries, such as Germany, Italy, Austria, Hungary, and Japan. Where governmental and nongovernmental agencies, such as the United Nations Relief and Rehabilitation Administration, assumed responsibility for basic maintenance of the peoples in the war-devastated countries, War Relief Services, in cooperation with other American voluntary agencies, supplemented government programs by caring for the most hopeless of the victims of war—undernourished children, orphans, the sick, the aged, and the infirm. As Soviet control spread and tightened over Eastern Europe, the assistance programs of War Relief Services were suppressed in Poland, Hungary, Czechoslovakia, Rumania, and Yugoslavia.

Catholic Relief Services. In 1955, when it became clear that War Relief Services—NCWC, which had been set up on an emergency and temporary basis, was permanently needed, its name was changed to Catholic Relief Services—NCWC. Because of its facilities through indigenous agencies and its expanding network of aid programs, Catholic Relief Services—NCWC was able to take full advantage of U.S. surplus foods that first became available for overseas relief operations in the 1950s. In addition to these foodstuffs supplied by the U.S. government, to clothing donated by Catholics in the annual Thanksgiving Clothing Collection, and to funds realized from the Bishops' Relief Fund Appeal, Catholic Relief Services—NCWC received financial support for its aid programs from a variety of sources including the United States Escapee Program, The Intergovernmental Committee for European Migration, The United Nations High Commissioner for Refugees, local governments, and private groups.

By the end of 1963, Catholic Relief Services—NCWC had shipped overseas and distributed to needy persons food, clothing, medicines, and other relief supplies having a gross weight of 5,600,000 tons and a total value of $1.25 billion. Since 1945, Catholic Relief Services—NCWC has helped more than 400,000 refugees to resettle in the U.S. and other countries of asylum. An important byproduct of the programs carried on by Catholic Relief Services—NCWC has been the impetus they gave to the hierarchies of other countries to establish Catholic charities organizations on a diocesan and parish level as well as organizations comparable to the National Catholic Welfare Conference of the American bishops. This has been effectively done in nearly all the countries of Asia and the Far East, and notably in Latin America.

In recent years, Catholic Relief Services—NCWC has been expanding its programs in the newly independent, emergent nations of Africa and in the underdeveloped countries of Asia and Latin America. Increasing emphasis has been placed on technical assistance and self-help projects designed to eliminate social injustice, economic deprivation, disease, and ignorance. Operating in more than 70 countries, Catholic Relief Services—NCWC is the nation's largest private voluntary overseas aid agency. All supplies are allocated and assistance rendered to those in need without regard to race, religion, or color. The sole criterion is need.

The initial activities of Catholic Relief Services—NCWC were, of a necessity, confined to rendering emergency, on-the-spot aid to victims of war. However, the long-range policy of the agency is aimed toward improving and eventually eradicating the shocking social and economic conditions that constitute the root cause of much of the tragic hunger, destitution, disease, and unrest that afflict and degrade more than one-third of mankind.

Bibliography: E. E. SWANSTROM, *Pilgrims of the Night: A Study of Expelled Peoples* (New York 1950). *National Catholic Welfare Conference: An Agency . . . to Organize, Unify and Coordinate Catholic Activities* . . . (Washington 1961) pamphlet.

[E. E. SWANSTROM]

CATHOLIC SOCIAL GUILD, an organization, founded in 1909 with headquarters at Oxford, England, that seeks to promote the social teaching of the Catholic Church. Its inception and early development owed much to Charles *Plater, SJ. It early became an adult-education movement, providing material for workingmen's study groups. Its first materials were pamphlets, then larger yearbooks, and later still a regular monthly, the *Christian Democrat,* which reached its maximum circulation in the 1950s under the vigorous editorship of Paul Crane, SJ. By 1921 the Guild was also organizing annual summer schools on the pattern of the French *Semaines Sociales de France.

At Oxford the Guild maintains the Catholic Workers College (also known as Plater Hall), which provides residential 1- or 2-year courses in social studies for adults. Together with its secular counterpart, Ruskin College (maintained by supporters of the Labour Party and the trade unions), it enjoys a privileged status in its relations with the University of Oxford and the Ministry of Education. Its students are allowed to use university facilities and to sit for a university diploma (but not for a degree), and the government makes a grant toward expenses. Also, since the Education Act of 1944, some students have secured grants from local education authorities to defray their fees, and this has helped to expand enrollment. In 1921 there were 3 students and the number never rose to more than 14 before World War II, but by 1964 the College was accommodating more than 40, several from overseas. From 1921 to 1953 the principal was Leo O'Hea, SJ, who during most of that time also was secretary of the Guild; he was succeeded in the latter post by A. Gordon, SJ. In 1958 a layman, R. P. Walsh, was appointed secretary, and 4 years later another layman, J. R. Kirwan, became principal of the College.

The Guild's purpose necessitates close ties with the bishops, who themselves revised its statutes in 1961. The four archbishops of England and Wales have been trustees of the College since 1925, and a bishop acts as president of the Guild. There is also a priest director to represent the bishops at Guild headquarters and one in each diocese to stimulate interest in the Guild and to make sure that its apostolic activities are duly subject to the ordinary.

In spite of these measures, by 1964 membership had fallen to less than half of the postwar maximum of more than 4,000. Although more people were prepared to admit the importance of the Guild's aims, study circles had gone out of fashion and changed social conditions were calling for revision of traditional techniques.

Bibliography: J. M. CLEARY, *Catholic Social Action in Britain 1909–1959: A History of the Catholic Social Guild* (Oxford 1961).

[H. O. WATERHOUSE]

CATHOLIC STUDENTS MISSION CRUSADE, a national federation of mission societies; founded in 1918. The primary aim of this federation is to acquaint Catholic students with the problems and goals of the missionary Church in the U.S. and in foreign countries. Publications of the Catholic Students Mission Crusade include *The Shield;* the *CSMC Yearbook;* and texts or research reports such as *Latin America, Program for the Sixties,* and *The Church at Work in the World.* Membership in 1965 was estimated at 1,000,000 students from 3,100 educational institutions. The national center for the Crusade is in Cincinnati, Ohio.

[M. MC DONNELL]

CATHOLIC THEATER MOVEMENT

As an attempt on the part of Catholics in the first half of the 20th century to infuse spiritual values into the drama, the Catholic theater movement was most significant on the North American continent, though there were scattered traces of it in South America and western Europe. Three factors seem to have been responsible for its rise: the secular little theater movement of the 1920s, which crusaded for artistic as against commercial values (*see* AMERICAN LITERATURE, 2); the Catholic *literary revival; and the practice of using drama as a parish social activity and fund-raising device. Without the first two impulses, the third would have come to nothing; but because of the third, the first two were for some time inhibited in their effect.

Henri *Ghéon, a French playwright who drew his inspiration from the medieval mystery plays (*see* DRAMA, MEDIEVAL, 1), was the representative of the Catholic literary revival who had the most important single influence on drama. In 1913 some of his short plays (including *The Poor Man under the Stairs*) were presented by the eminent producer, Jacques Copeau, himself a Catholic, and in time translations of these plays were staged in America and Canada. Ghéon's work was filled with the same sort of genial faith he found in his models and exuded both a religious and a comic spirit.

Negative Beginning in the U.S. American attention to the drama was negative before it became positive. In 1912 the Catholic Theater Movement, organized in New York under the sponsorship of Cardinal John *Farley, published a "white list" of Broadway plays "not offensive to Catholics" in a quarterly bulletin that also contained "suggestions in regard to parish dramatics, and to sisters in academies and colleges who conduct courses on the drama." The white list was far shorter than the implied black list, and by 1932 only two inoffensive plays could be found. The slogan of the movement was "to oppose the wrong with the right kind of propaganda," and this state of mind encouraged parish groups to present plays of Biblical content, such as *Veronica's Veil* and *The Upper Room.*

Parish Activities. The first effort to link together existing parish groups was made by the Rev. Matthias Helfen, who organized the Catholic Dramatic Movement in Milwaukee, Wis., in 1923. For more than 25 years he produced, wrote, and published plays and tried to enlist others in his crusade; but his work is more an essay in persistence than a chapter in dramatic art.

Peaks of eminence in production were achieved in the 1930s by the Loyola Community Theater, the Blackfriars' Guild, and by Les Compagnons de St-Laurent. Rev. George F. Dinneen, SJ, and Charles Costello were the prime movers at Loyola, which began as a parish activity in Chicago and expanded into a citywide group. The Blackfriars' Guild was founded in St. Dominic's parish in Washington by Rev. Urban *Nagle, OP, and Rev. Thomas Carey, OP, who envisioned a network of Catholic theaters and were able by 1940 to boast chapters in 16 cities. The Montreal group, under Father Emile Legault, was distinguished for skillful productions of both religious and secular plays in French, especially the plays of Ghéon.

These disparate efforts were brought together in answer to an article in *America* magazine in 1937 by playwright Emmet Lavery, whose call for unity resulted in the formation of the (later National) Catholic Theater Conference. Its purpose was defined as "the dissemination of Catholic Theater in harmony with Catholic spirit and philosophy," though its early years were marked by lengthy disputes over the precise relation of the words "Catholic" and "play." By February 1938 it had enlisted 235 individuals and 128 groups in its membership. By means of a monthly bulletin, an annual survey, and periodic conventions, it strove by an exchange of information to propose ideals and to elevate the standards of production. In 1958 it published a *Blue Book of Recommended Plays,* a positive move in marked contrast to the white list.

Shift to Colleges and Universities. Partly as a result of the conference and partly as a result of a Blackfriars Summer Institute of Dramatic Art, The Catholic University of America installed a department of speech and drama in 1937. Under the leadership of Rev. Gilbert V. Hartke, OP, Walter Kerr, Josephine McGarry Callan, and Ralph Brown, this department achieved a national reputation. Soon formal instruction in drama was offered by many Catholic schools, notably Fordham (New York City), Boston College, Loyola in Chicago, St. Louis University, Marywood in Scranton, Clarke College in Dubuque, and Immaculate Heart in Los Angeles. This was in concert with an increased emphasis on theatrical study in secular schools, stemming from G. P. Baker's pioneer work at Harvard and Yale.

The significant element in this shift to the Catholic campus was a change in point of view: in the 1920s the drama was conceived as a tool of propaganda, and fervor was thought to be the chief element necessary; by the 1950s study and experience had enthralled its devotees to drama as an art. The National Catholic Theater Conference (which by 1964 represented 14,000 individuals) reflected this altered view with the publication in 1958 of *Drama Critique,* a thrice-yearly scholarly periodical. The Blackfriars' Guild, giving up its dream of a chain of theaters, established itself in New York City in 1940 and can lay claim to being the first of the off-Broadway theaters.

In the sphere of aesthetics, such books as *Christ and Apollo* (1960), by Rev. William Lynch, SJ, and *The Decline of Pleasure* (1962), by Walter Kerr, demonstrate the advance of the movement from the days of the white list. The story of the Catholic theater movement records an alteration of attitude: from the censorial and the amateurish in the beginning to the positive and fully artistic at maturity. As it developed, the Catholic theater movement sought not so much to create a Catholic theater as to stimulate contributions by Catholics to the art of the drama.

Bibliography: U. NAGLE, *Behind the Masque* (New York 1951). *History of the N.C.T.C.* (rev. ed. Washington 1964). *Theatre for Tomorrow: Damien, Savonarola, Campion; Three Plays by Emmet Lavery, Grace Murphy, Urban Nagle, Richard Breen, and Harry Schnibbe, with a Survey of the Catholic Tradition in Drama* (New York 1940).

[L. BRADY]

CATHOLIC THEOLOGICAL SOCIETY OF AMERICA, a professional and learned society, was founded in 1946 "to promote an exchange of views among Catholic theologians, . . . to further studies and research in sacred theology," and "to relate theological science to current problems." The first president was Francis J. Connell, CSSR. It was incorporated by an absolute charter granted by the Regents of the University of the State of New York in 1961. The Society has an active membership open to all who are professionally competent in sacred theology and who are or who have been actively engaged in the promotion of studies and research in theology. In general, the purposes of the Society are accomplished by furthering the education of the members, most of whom teach theology in seminaries and colleges. In particular, these aims are achieved by the annual national convention, the publication of its *Proceedings,* and the convocation of regional meetings. Meetings have been held also with theologians of other faiths and scholars from other disciplines. Each year, the society confers the Cardinal Spellman award, endowed in perpetuity by His Eminence, on a theologian who has made a distinct contribution to the science. The Society had about 925 active and associate members listed in its *Directory of American Catholic Theologians* published in 1963.

See also BIBLICAL SOCIETIES.

[C. L. SALM]

CATHOLIC TOTAL ABSTINENCE UNION OF AMERICA, founded in Baltimore in 1872 by delegates of 207 societies from 11 states; it remained an effective force until the era of federal prohibition. At the height of its power, around 1896, the Union represented about 100,000 total abstainers. Although its platform emphasized moral suasion, many member societies supported local prohibition, and later a few of the leaders supported it on a national level. Constituting an area where Catholic and Protestant leaders could and sometimes did cooperate effectively, the movement helped to improve interfaith relations. In the effort to find wholesome substitutes for social drinking, member societies provided libraries, bands, and other recreational opportunities. While Abp. John Ireland of St. Paul provided leadership for the Union and most bishops of Irish blood supported it, those of German background generally regarded it as fanatical. Since World War II several priests have tried to revitalize the organization, which has never ceased to hold conventions.

Bibliography: J. BLAND, *Hibernian Crusade* (Washington 1951).

[J. BLAND]

CATHOLIC TRUTH SOCIETIES

The first Catholic Truth Society came into being in England in 1869, when Herbert Vaughan (later cardinal), seeing the need for an organization to make good and inexpensive Catholic literature available to the public, established a group that issued a number of penny books and leaflets. This group, however, was disbanded in 1872 when Vaughan was appointed bishop of Salford.

Twelve years later, in October 1884, a layman and convert to Catholicism, James Britten, alarmed by the abundance and viciousness of anti-Catholic tracts in circulation in bookstalls and shops, determined to take steps to publish well-informed rebuttals. Raising funds by soliciting a pound from each of 12 friends, Britten had printed a number of prayer cards and meditations on the Sacraments. This work attracted the attention of Bishop Vaughan, who was still interested in the project he had been forced to abandon. A meeting of those to whom Britten had appealed and who had shown a willingness to help was held Nov. 5, 1884, at the home of Lady Herbert of Lea. Bishop Vaughan acted as chairman at this meeting and suggested that the new organization be formed under the name he had chosen for his earlier group, the Catholic Truth Society. The society was formally established, and the second period of its existence began under the presidency of Bishop Vaughan and the chairmanship of T. E. Bridgett, CSSR, with W. H. Cologan and James Britten serving as honorable secretaries.

The aims of the Catholic Truth Society are: (1) to spread among Catholics small devotional works, (2) to assist the uneducated poor to a better knowledge of their religion, (3) to spread among Protestants information regarding Catholic faith and practice, and (4) to promote the circulation of good and cheap Catholic literature.

Its engagement at various times in the public discussion of matters of current interest—for example, the Maria Monk issue (1886), the question of the validity of Anglican orders (1896), sociopolitical ideologies in the 1920s and 1930s, and more recently the birth control problem—has caused the society to be regarded as controversial. Its chief aim, however, has been neither attack nor counterattack, but rather the instruction of Catholics by bringing to them much needed educational and suitable devotional material at small cost. For example, *The Simple Prayer Book,* first compiled by Cologan in 1887 in the hope of distributing 100 copies, has reached a total printing of about 10 million copies. Historical works, studies in comparative religion, essays by C. C. Martindale, H. Thurston, H. Belloc, A. Fortescue, and many others, books and leaflets for children, novels, critiques, and missals have all been brought to the Catholic reader at slight expense to himself.

The growth of the Catholic Truth Society in England must be attributed to the zeal of its leaders and workers. The founder of the society, James Britten, labored in a truly dedicated way for nearly 40 years until his death on Oct. 8, 1924. George Elliot Anstruther aided Britten in many ways and himself served as organizing secretary from 1909 until 1920. Another layman prominent in the society was the American William Reed-Lewis, who contributed his executive abilities and library skills and was greatly responsible for the expansion program of 1921–22, when the headquarters of the society was moved and enlarged to include Bexhill Library, a Catholic free library formerly owned and operated by Reed-Lewis himself. Administrative secretaries have included Stephen Harding, Frank Sheed, Oswald Heath, John P. Boland (Mrs. Boland founded the Box-Tender's Association by means of which the more than 2,000 public distribution boxes for publications are kept stocked and supervised), and T. H. Rittner.

The Catholic Truth Society in 1888 began the Annual Catholic Conferences, gatherings attended by representative clergy and laity, which were occasions for discussion of the work and welfare of the Church in England. Their success paved the way for a development by which, from 1910, the society's conference has been merged in the National Catholic Conference. These gatherings resulted also in the formation of other societies for the welfare of Catholics in England, notably the Catholic Seamen's Guild (now the Apostleship of the Sea), the Catholic Needlework Guild, the Catholic Social Guild, the Catholic Guardian's Guild, and also a Braille library for the blind.

Branches of the Catholic Truth Society were established throughout England, as well as in Scotland, Ireland, Australia, India, Hong Kong, and the U.S.

The International Catholic Truth Society (ICTS) was founded in Brooklyn, N.Y., by Bp. William F. McGinnis, March 22, 1899. It was first entitled the Metropolitan Truth Society, but upon its incorporation under the laws of the State of New York (April 24, 1900), the present title was adopted as more in accord with its purpose. The society was established to defend Catholicism against misrepresentation and to propagate the faith through the spoken and written word. The ICTS produces pamphlets on all phases of Catholic thought, history, and action; it also purchases and distributes foreign pamphlets and those of other domestic publishers. Lectures to non-Catholic groups have long been a part of the society's work. The ICTS is supported by membership fees and voluntary contributions; its headquarters are located in Brooklyn, N.Y.

Bibliography: J. BRITTEN and T. F. MEEHAN, CE 15:77–79. C. COLLINGWOOD, "Catholic Truth Society," ClergyRev 37 (1952) 641–658.

[M. MCDONNELL]

CATHOLIC UNIVERSITIES, INTERNATIONAL FEDERATION OF

The Federation originated in 1924, when 18 rectors of Catholic universities, under the initiative of Agostino Gemelli, OFM, and of Msgr. Joseph Schrijnen, rectors of the Catholic universities of Milan, Italy, and Nijmegen, Netherlands, met for the first time in Louvain, Belgium. Their purpose was to discuss the problems concerning their universities, to evaluate their own experiences, and to devise the best means of promoting the progress of science in the light of faith. During further meetings they planned the establishment of a solid organization to foster union and collaboration among Catholic universities; World War II, however, delayed the project. On July 27, 1949, Pius XII, convinced of the necessity of greater international cooperation, issued the apostolic letter *Catholicas Studiorum Universitates* (ActApS 42:385), which established the Federation of the Catholic Universities under Canon Law. The Congregation of Seminaries and Universities approved the statutes on Jan. 11, 1951.

The constitutions of the Federation give as its aim the promotion of close union and collaboration with universities in the examination and solution of problems concerning their existence and development, and in research and diffusion of the truth. Membership in the Federation is open to any Catholic university that has at least three academic faculties, including one of nonecclesiastical studies. It is administered by a board of directors composed of a president, two vice presidents, a general secretary, and three counselors who are elected by the general assembly of rectors, chosen from present or past incumbents. The headquarters of the Federation is in Vatican City; the center of administration is in the general secretariat.

To promote knowledge of Catholic universities and Catholic institutions of higher learning, an indispensable requirement for unity and collaboration, the Federation has published the *Annuarium Foederationis Universitatum Catholicarum* (Rome 1954), the *Catalogus Catholicorum Institutorum de Studiis Superioribus* (Rome 1957), and the *Supplementa* (Rome 1960).

General assemblies of rectors of Catholic universities took place in Rome (1949), in Quebec, Canada (1952), in Louvain, (1955 and 1958), in Rio de Janeiro, Brazil (1960), and in Washington, D.C. (1963). At these meetings, rectors who represented about 40 nations in America, Europe, Asia, and Africa discussed the most pressing university problems, especially those concerning the intellectual formation of their students, as well as questions of scientific, religious, social, and international import. In recent years the Federation has actively collaborated with other international Catholic organizations, especially the Conférence des Organisations Internationales (Fribourg, Switzerland) and with secular international organisations of a cultural and scientific character, such as the United Nations Educational, Scientific and Cultural Organization, and the Association des Instituts d'Études Européenes. The Federation is an associated member of the Association Internationale des Universités, which has its headquarters near UNESCO in Paris. In keeping with the directives of the Holy See it has engaged in various fields of activity in the service of the Church. At the invitation of John XXIII, expressed in the audience granted to the Federation on April 1, 1960, the Federation and its members actively collaborated in preparing the second Vatican Council (*Acta et Documenta Concilio Oecumenico Vaticano II apparando, Series Antepraeparatoria,* v.4).

In the Americas, membership in the Federation includes 12 universities in the U.S., 4 in Canada, and 14 in South America.

[P. DEZZA]

CATHOLIC UNIVERSITY OF AMERICA, THE

Incorporated in 1887 under the laws of the District of Columbia and canonically erected with pontifical status by Leo XIII in 1889, The Catholic University of America, Washington, D.C., was the first institution of its kind to be established in the U.S. It is governed by the bishops of the U.S., exercising their authority through a board of trustees composed *de jure* of the cardinals and other archbishops who rule dioceses of metropolitan rank, the chancellor (the archbishop of Washington), the rector, and a number of elected bishops, priests, and laymen.

The University has schools of Sacred Theology, Canon Law, and Philosophy; a Graduate School of Arts and Sciences; a College of Arts and Sciences; and schools of Social Work, Engineering and Architecture, Law, and Nursing. The largest is the Graduate School of Arts and Sciences with 22 departments or divisions. The School of Engineering and Architecture has six departments and two areas of special research. The School of Education, approved in 1964, opened in 1965.

In 1964 the University had a total enrollment of 5,805 students and had granted 1,341 degrees during the preceding academic year. A charter member (1900) of the Association of American Universities, the University also holds membership in the Middle States Association of Colleges and Secondary Schools. In 1942 a chapter of the national honor society, Phi Beta Kappa, was installed at the University. In 1963 there were 56 houses of study for male religious and 31 houses for religious communities of women established near the University. Throughout the U.S. more than 700 Catholic institutions have affiliated with the University: these include 176 colleges, 89 junior colleges, 415 secondary schools, and 22 major seminaries. The *Catholic Sisters College, founded in 1911, was discontinued as an academic unit in 1950 but has continued to serve as a sisters' residence for students at the University.

History. Action for the establishment of a national Catholic university was successfully initiated in 1884 at the Third Plenary Council of Baltimore by the efforts of Bp. John L. *Spalding of Peoria. His proposal gained force when the council learned that Mary Gwendolyn *Caldwell had offered $300,000 as a founding endowment.

The need for a university had been mentioned as early as 1819 by an Irish-born Augustinian missionary to the U.S., Robert Browne. In succeeding years the idea had interested such men as Abp. Martin J. *Spalding of Baltimore, Bp. Thomas A. *Becker of Wilmington, and Isaac T. *Hecker. There was persistent opposition to the plan from some of the hierarchy, including Bp. Bernard J. *McQuaid of Rochester and Abp. Michael A. *Corrigan of New York, as well as from certain representatives of the German Catholics, some members of the Society of Jesus, and a segment of the Catholic press.

Despite these opposing forces, the bishops meeting during the Third Plenary Council of Baltimore in 1884 authorized their Apostolic Delegate, Abp. James * Gibbons, to appoint a committee to initiate the project. During the next few years plans were formulated at committee meetings. The Catholic University of America was decided upon as the name and Washington, D.C. selected as the site. At the meeting of October 1886, Bp. John J. *Keane of Richmond was chosen as the first rector after Bishop Spalding of Peoria had declined the post.

In 1885 Pope *Leo XIII had sent his private approval of the project and in 1887 gave his endorsement in a letter to Gibbons and his fellow bishops. On April 19, 1887, the University was incorporated by Congress under the laws of the District of Columbia. On March 7, 1889, in the apostolic letter *Magni Nobis Gaudii* the Pope formally approved the statutes and accorded the institution pontifical status, at a time when there were only nine other institutions outside the city of Rome with that rank.

The University was formally opened on Nov. 13, 1889, with Pres. Benjamin Harrison among the many guests who attended the ceremony, which was the final event in the centennial celebration of the U.S. hierarchy.

Besides Keane as rector and Philip J. Garrigan as vice rector, the faculty numbered 10. Of these, two were Sulpicians, John B. Hogan, the librarian, and Alexis Orban, the spiritual director. Two were Paulists, Augustine F. *Hewit, lecturer in church history, and George M. *Searle, lecturer in science. The only layman, Charles W. Stoddard, was lecturer in English. Five of the faculty were European-born: Henri *Hyvernat, professor of Scripture; Joseph *Pohle, philosophy; Joseph *Schroeder, dogmatic theology; Thomas J. *Bouquillon, moral theology; and Joseph Graf, music.

Of the 46 students, 36 were drawn from 21 dioceses, with Baltimore in the lead with 4. One student was a Sulpician and nine were from the Paulist house of studies.

Early in 1889 Cardinal Gibbons had been asked by Hewit, Superior General of the Paulists, if his community might establish a house of studies near the University. Gibbons replied on February 19 that the trustees would permit and would also invite communities to establish such houses. The Paulists were thus the first of many orders to found houses of study in the neighborhood.

At the time of its founding, the University was the only Catholic institution in the U.S. professing to offer graduate studies exclusively. There were, however, 125 Catholic institutions called colleges, besides the 30 theological seminaries for the secular and religious priesthoods that had a combined total of 1,631 students. The estimated Catholic population of the country was then 8,300,000. Despite these figures, it is not surprising that so few priests came to the University for graduate work—graduate study had been only recently introduced into the U.S. Hitherto, those desirous of university training had studied abroad.

Although the University had opened as a graduate school of theology for the clergy only, it was not long before the need was felt for additional academic disciplines as well as for the increased revenue that would accrue from an enlarged student body. In October 1895 the School of Philosophy and the School of Social Sciences were opened to all qualified male applicants.

The new students included three Negroes, of whom Bishop Keane said, "They stand on exactly the same footing as other students of equal calibre and acquirements." When the newspapers reported, however, that women would also be enrolled and some began to apply, the University announced that it regarded the matter as too important for hasty decision and therefore "it has not yet been considered by the Board of Directors, and nothing will be done except as they decide . . .." Although later years saw a certain variation in policy regarding the admission of both groups, properly qualified women have been admitted since 1928 and Negroes since 1937.

Academic procession forming against background of the University's McMahon Hall, named for Msgr. James McMahon, an early benefactor of the University, and dedicated by Cardinal Gibbons in 1895.

Finances and Growth. In its early years the University depended entirely on student fees, gifts, and a meager investment income. The total was too small to permit the University to fulfill its purpose as an institution of graduate instruction.

Finances proved still to be the chief problem facing the third rector, Denis J. * O'Connell, who assumed office in March 1903. At O'Connell's suggestion, strongly supported by Cardinal Gibbons as chancellor, Pius X in September of that year gave public authorization for an annual collection to be taken up throughout the dioceses of the U.S. The first year's collection of $105,051 was insufficient to cover the initial loss of $876,168 suffered as a result of the bankruptcy of the University's treasurer in the summer of 1904. The debt was eventually reduced to a little more than $500,000. In the emergency Cardinal Gibbons appealed to the hierarchy to contribute to a special collection to aid the University. Despite his personal efforts and the "Cardinal's Fund" established by him, donations came to only $136,229 during the next 6 years. In 1910 the collected money was merged with a new fund for the construction of Gibbons Memorial Hall. Small as it was, the Cardinal's

Fund, added to the continuing annual collection, enabled the University to cover its losses.

Another change hastened by the financial crisis was the introduction of undergraduate lay students in the fall of 1905. The step was taken both to increase income and to bring the University's facilities to more students. The first 15 years had proved there were too few students either prepared for or interested in graduate instruction to warrant continuing on that level alone.

During the administrations of the nine rectors of the University in its first 74 years, other schools and departments were added and a few were suppressed, but at no time did it lose its predominantly graduate character. At the commencement of 1962, for example, 61 per cent of the 1,203 degrees conferred were masters, licentiates, and doctorates, while another 10 per cent were professional baccalaureates.

Through the early decades, enrollment was often far below the number that could be accommodated. After World War II enrollment was no longer a serious problem and at times the University was strained to provide for the number of applicants. By 1964 there were 2,600 male lay students, 1,755 laywomen, 1,283 priests, brothers, and seminarians, and 406 sisters. Of these, 4,115 were full-time students and 1,935 were part-time. The faculty at the same time numbered 437 full-time members, as well as 128 lecturers and 106 graduate assistants.

Resources and Activities. In 1911 a summer session was inaugurated in Washington; branches were later established at San Rafael, Calif. (1932); Dubuque, Iowa (1934); San Antonio, Tex. (1935); and Toledo, Ohio (1958). The summer enrollment in 1963 included 4,696 on the home campus and a total of more than 485 at the branches. Besides the summer session, a series of workshops in various phases of education have been held between the close of the regular academic year and the opening of the summer session.

In 1938 the Commission on American Citizenship was established at the University to further education in the social ideals recommended by Pius XI. The Commission issues the *Faith and Freedom* series of textbooks for Catholic elementary schools. In addition, the Child Center has been in operation since 1916 to treat the emotional problems of children. The Marriage Counseling Center since 1952 and the Speech Clinic since 1953 have likewise provided valuable services to clients and served as training centers for students.

The Speech and Drama Department, besides offering graduate and undergraduate programs of instruction, has become well known in Washington and throughout the U.S. in dramatic circles for the quality and originality of its productions.

The University's Mullen Library has 614,636 catalogued holdings. Among its special collections are: the Clementine Library of books, pamphlets, and periodicals that once formed a large part of the library of Pope Clement XI (1700–21); the special library of the Institute of Christian Oriental Research which is unusually rich in periodicals and collections of texts; and the Lima Library which has specialized holdings for research in Brazilian, Portugese, Spanish, and other Latin American cultures.

Publications. Scholarly publications produced under the auspices of the University, or edited by its faculty members, include many studies and series: the *Corpus Scriptorum Christianorum Orientalium, Studies in Psychology and Psychiatry, Publications of the Catholic Anthropological Conference, Educational Research Monographs, The Catholic University of America Patristic Studies, Ancient Christian Writers, the Fathers of the Church* series, *The Catholic University of America Studies in Medieval and Renaissance Latin Language and Literature, Studies in American Church History, Studies in Library Science, Philosophical Studies, Studies in Sacred Theology, Studies in Canon Law, Studies in Christian Antiquity, Biological Series and Studies, Anthropological Series, Studies in Medieval History, Studies in Romance Language and Literature, Studies in Politics, Government and International Law, Studies in Social Work, Studies in Sociology, Studies in Economics, Studies in Nursing Education,* and *Studies from the Bureau of Social Research.*

Periodicals sponsored by the University or edited by members of its faculty include the *American Ecclesiastical Review, Anthropological Quarterly, Catholic Biblical Quarterly, Catholic Historical Review, Catholic University Law Review, Jurist, Coleopterist's Bulletin,* and the *Catholic Educational Review.*

The University has expanded constantly throughout the years, adding new buildings and extending older halls and residences. In November 1956, at their annual meeting, the bishops of the U.S. pledged $3,600,000 for these purposes, in addition to the regular annual collection. With the increased income, facilities, and faculty, the University has been able to reach an ever-widening audience for whom it endeavors to fulfill the aims defined in its statutes: "To search out truth scientifically, to safeguard it, and to apply it to the moulding and shaping of both private and public life."

In 1964 the Joint Graduate Consortium was formed to enable the five participating D.C. universities—American, Catholic, George Washington, Georgetown, and Howard—to coordinate their respective graduate faculties. This arrangement, with certain restrictions, enables graduate students enrolled in an approved degree program to supplement their own university's curriculum with those of the other four.

Bibliography: P. H. AHERN, *The Catholic University of America, 1887–1896: The Rectorship of John J. Keane* (Washington 1949). C. J. BARRY, *The Catholic University of America, 1903–1909: The Rectorship of Denis J. O'Connell* (Washington 1949). R. J. DEFERRARI, *Memoirs of the Catholic University of America, 1918–1960* (Boston 1962). J. T. ELLIS, *The Formative Years of the Catholic University of America* (Washington 1946); *The Life of James Cardinal Gibbons,* 2 v. (Milwaukee 1952) 1:389–438, 2:141–203. P. E. HOGAN, *The Catholic University of America, 1896–1903: The Rectorship of Thomas J. Conaty* (Washington 1949). F. A. KUNTZ, *Undergraduate Days, 1904–1908: The Catholic University of America* (Washington 1958).

[J. T. ELLIS]

CATHOLIC UNIVERSITY OF PUERTO RICO

A coeducational institution founded in the city of Ponce in 1948 by the bishops of Puerto Rico, to foster Catholic education on the Island. The University received its charter in the same year. Authority is vested in a board of trustees, among whom are the bishops of Puerto Rico and the Virgin Islands. The chancellor is the executive officer. Other officers are the president, vice president for academic affairs, vice president for financial affairs, and the deans of the colleges and divisions. The University is financed by gifts, student tuition, and the contributed services of teachers who are members of the clergy and/or religious communities. Among the faculty are 6 diocesan priests, 22 priests of religious communities, 3 brothers, 48 nuns, and 71 lay teachers. In 1964, the staff held 30 doctoral, 10 professional and 81 master's degrees.

The law school was founded Aug. 23, 1961. In 1963 it had 134 students in the first 2 years of studies leading to the L.L.B. degree. A college of education established in 1952 confers the B.A. degree in elementary education and the B.S. degree in secondary education. In the division of business administration, inaugurated in 1961, bachelor degrees are granted in business administration and in secretarial science. Both the college of education and the business division offer associate degrees.

The college of arts and sciences was founded in 1952. It offers B.A. degrees in the humanities; Spanish; and natural, political, and social sciences. Preprofessional training is provided in medicine, dentistry, and social work. B.S. degrees are conferred in mathematics, biology, and chemistry. Within the College is a department of nursing education, founded in 1955, which also confers the B.S. degree.

There are evening sessions in business administration, which enrolled 138 students in 1964. The Saturday session, with 235 students in 1964, is conducted for teachers who desire to complete their college work or obtain a certificate in teaching. The summer sessions registered 1,905 in the June session and 1,217 in the July session. Extension programs of the University, leading to associate degrees in arts, business administration, and education, are conducted in the cities of Aguadilla, Caguas, Arecibo, Bayamón, Guayama, and Mayagüez in Puerto Rico. Total enrollment in extension classes in 1964 was 3,118 students. In August 1964, enrollment in the regular session of the University in Ponce was 2,206, of which 1,064 were men and 1,142, women.

Distinctive programs of the University include the Institute of Intercultural Relations to train personnel for dealing with Latin-American problems, and the English Institute offering intensive training in the English language and in the teaching of English as a second language.

In 1964 the University library housed 77,562 volumes and received 859 periodicals. Student publications include the yearbook, *Senda,* and *La Nao,* which describes student activities. Literary works of the faculty appear in *Horizontes.*

The University is chartered by the Board of Regents of the State of New York. It is accredited by the Council of Higher Education of Puerto Rico and by the Middle States Association of Colleges and Secondary Schools. It is affiliated with The Catholic University of America.

Bibliography: *Catholic Life Annual,* ed. E. P. WILLGING, 2 v. (Milwaukee 1958–59) 2:58–66. Catholic University of Puerto Rico, *Self-Evaluation Report* (Dec. 1962 Ponce, P.R.), limited circulation.

[M. MC CABE]

CATHOLIC UNIVERSITY OF THE SACRED HEART (MILAN, ITALY)

A Catholic university canonically erected by the Congregation of Seminaries and Universities in the decree of Dec. 25, 1920. On Oct. 2, 1924, the Italian government recognized the University and authorized it to confer degrees.

Catholic University of the Sacred Heart, Milan.

Origin and Development. Attempts to establish the University began immediately after World War I with the efforts of G. Toniolo, Professor of Economics at the University of Pisa. After Toniolo's death Agostino *Gemelli, OFM, a convert to Catholicism from socialism who entered the Franciscan order after taking his degree in medicine and surgery, actually founded the University.

Gemelli, with his two Milanese friends, Lodovico Necchi and Francesco Oligiati, had already instituted two periodicals for the spread of Catholic thought. Armida Barelli, a devout client of the Sacred Heart, accepted the task of fund raising for the University to be named in honor of the Sacred Heart. Industrialist Ernest Lombardo gave the first million lire with which an ancient palace in the Via Sant' Agnese in Milan was purchased to house the University. The generosity of large corporations and private citizens provided money to adapt the building to the needs of an institution of higher learning. Gemelli drew up the statutes, the governing and teaching order of the University; he served as its president until his death in 1959.

On Dec. 7, 1921, the University of the Sacred Heart opened its doors with two Faculties, Philosophy and Social Science, 22 professors, and 92 students. Cardinal Achille Ratti (2 months later Pius XI) greeted the new University with the words: *vivat, crescat, floreat.* It was Ratti who advised financing the University by an annual collection in all parishes of Italy, which, when he became Pope, he decreed should be made every Passion Sunday. Through the cooperation of the clergy and young Catholic Action groups, especially the Young Catholic Women, collections on University Day 1923 totaled more than 1 million lire. From that day on financial aid grew in proportion to the growth of the University. Offerings came from intellectuals, peasants, shepherds, fishermen, workingmen, soldiers, small industrialists, and employees.

Under the direction of Gemelli and his associates, who had won the confidence of the nation, the institution expanded rapidly. In 1923 the Faculty of Letters was added; and in succession the Faculties of Education, 1928; Economics and Commerce, 1933; Political Science (joined to that of Social Sciences), 1936; Agriculture, 1953; and Medicine and Surgery, 1961. This development was accompanied by an adequate physical expansion. In 1926 by order of Pius XI the Apostolic Institute of the Sacred Heart opened at Castelnuovo Fogliano in Piacenza to enable religious women of all congregations to continue their studies and obtain the certificates necessary to teach in secondary schools.

In 1932 the University transferred to larger facilities in a former Cistercian monastery designed by Donato Bramante in the 15th century. In 1946, for the first time in Italy, the Faculty of Economics and Commerce inaugurated night courses, which developed into another Faculty. In 1953, by opening, with government authorization, the Faculty of Agriculture in Piacenza, the University of the Sacred Heart set the example of a Faculty established at a distance but still administered by the central university. Six years later the University established the Faculty of Medicine in Rome. In 1954 the University founded the Center Mary Immaculate for summer courses at Passo della Mendola (Trent), and in 1962, the School of Journalism and Audio-visual Mediums at Bergamo.

Administration and Organization. The University is governed by the council of administration composed of a rector, who acts as council president; a member elected by the professors; six members named by the Giuseppe Toniolo Institute; representatives of the Holy See, the government (named by the board of education), and Catholic Action. These members hold office for 3 years and may be reelected. The rector is chosen from among the professors by the council of administration after a hearing in the academic senate. It is customary to consult student organizations and associations when preparing programs of University activity.

In 1963 the University of the Sacred Heart comprised seven Faculties: Law; Political Science; Economics and Commerce; Letters and Philosophy, including education and mathematics; Higher Education, including liberal arts; Agriculture, including forestry and viticulture; and Medicine and Surgery. Each Faculty has a dean named by the rector on advice of the faculty council, which is composed of the regular professors. The deans form the academic senate. The University operates 11 postgraduate departments.

Each Faculty at the end of 4 years, and the Faculty of Medicine after 6 years, confers its respective doctoral degree. Each Faculty has annexed to it a normal school, which grants a diploma after 2 years. Scientific study and research is conducted in numerous laboratory facilities. There are institutes for jurisprudence and seminars for philosophy, philology, and history.

In 1964 the library housed 800,000 volumes and received 4,000 periodicals; the student body numbered 15,143, 145 priests and religious, 11,102 men, and 3,896 women; and the teaching staff totaled nearly 600. Italian students enrolled must be Roman Catholics and present a baptismal certificate and a diploma from a secondary school. There is no religious requirement for foreign students; they must, however, present a certificate of study from a secondary school that corresponds to an Italian equivalent. Students from all countries and all races are admitted. There are refresher courses for graduate students; a series of public lectures; University colleges; scholarships and other financial aid to students unable to pay tuition; medical assistance; and graduate associations. Since the early 1960s large university residences for men and women as well as for ecclesiastics have grown up around the University; free accommodation for students in need and low rates for paying residents are available.

The University has its own publishing house, located in the central building of the campus. Publications include: *Orbis Romanus* (collection of medieval texts); *Pubblicazioni dell' Università del S. Cuore,* divided into two sections, *Contributi* (in 14 series) and *Saggi e ricerche* (scientific works of young graduate students). Scientific reviews are: *Aevum* (summary of the sciences of history, linguistics, and philology); *Aegyptus* (a periodical of Egyptology); *Annali della Facoltà di agraria; Archivio di psicologia, neurologia e psichiatria; Jus* (a review of jurisprudence); *Rivista di filosofia neoscolastica; Rivista Internazionale di Scienze Sociali; Bibliografia italiana delle Scienze sociali; Studi di sociologia; Bollettino della Società italiana di fonetica;* and *Acta Medica Romana.* Periodicals include: *Alma Mater,* bulletin of the Necchi Association among the graduates of the Catholic University; *Cronache dell'Università,* periodical of academic activities; *Dialoghi,* a student review; *Itinerarium cordis,* a student news sheet; *Rivista degli Amici dell'Università Cattolica; Rivista del Clero italiano;* and *Vita e Pensiero,* a cultural review.

Biological institute, Catholic University of the Sacred Heart.

Bibliography: A. GEMELLI and J. SCHRYNIN, *Annuaire général des universités catholiques* (Nijmegen 1927). P. BONDIOLI, *L'Università cattolica in Italia dalle origini al 1929* (Milan 1929). M. STICCO, *Vita universitaria* (Milan 1939). F. OLGIATI, *L'Università Cattolica del Sacro Cuore* (Milan 1955). G. DALLA TORRE, *La grande meta: L'Università Cattolica del S. Cuore nei voti e nell' opera dei Cattolici Italiana* (Rome 1945). M. E. VIORA, *Padre Gemelli e l'università cattolica* (Milan 1960).

[M. STICCO]

CATHOLIC UNIVERSITY OF THE WEST (ANGERS)

A coeducational institution of higher learning founded in France in 1875. As early as 1010, there existed at Angers an internationally known cathedral school, later to become a university that numbered among its outstanding students: St. *Bruno the Carthusian; Bl. *Robert of Arbrissel, founder of the Order of Fontevrault; Ulger Roger de Beaufort and his brother, Pierre, later *Gregory XI, who attended the University in 1350. The Faculty of Theology numbered among its alumni Bl. Noel *Pinot, Jean Robert Queneau, and Turpin de Cormier, martyred for the faith in 1794 during the French Revolution.

The University, suppressed during this time, was reestablished in 1875 by Charles Émile *Freppel, Bishop of Angers. Freppel had already established the nucleus of a Faculty of Letters in the École Saint-Aubin, but it was the Faculty of Law that was the first to be officially recognized, Oct. 1, 1875, and solemnly inaugurated in November. One of the Faculty of Law's first professors was the jurist François Hervé-Bazin, who had as his pupil the future novelist René Bazin, later professor of criminal law at Angers. The Faculty of Letters was opened in 1876, and in 1877, the Faculty of Science that counted on its roster the Abbé Hy, one of the foremost botanists in France. The Faculty of Theology opened in 1879 with Louis *Billot, SJ, as professor of dogma. Called to the Gregorian University in Rome by Leo XIII, he was later named cardinal-deacon.

The principal aim of this foundation was, originally, to assure the education and formation of professors to staff the seminaries and colleges of the 13 dioceses of western France where private education was favored. However, the bishops soon realized the necessity of providing training for specialists in various fields of economic life and, therefore, added several schools and colleges to the four original Faculties.

The governing body of the University is the council of bishops of the dioceses of the region. They are represented at the University by the rector, the vice-rector and the secretary general. In civil matters the University is subject to the jurisdiction of the Ministry of Education. In 1964 the academic staff numbered 77 full-time and 131 part-time professors; student enrollment totaled 1,703 French and 72 foreign students. The Lamoricière library housed 100,000 volumes.

The University is composed of four Faculties: Theology, Law and Economics, Letters and Human Sciences, and Science; the Institutes of Philosophy and of Sacred Music; Schools of Social Work, Domestic Science, and Teacher Training (handicapped and kindergarten); and Centers of Agriculture and Viticulture, Commerce, Social Work, Rural Studies and Domestic Science, Industrial Chemistry, Electrical Engineering, Chemical Research, Botanical Research, French Language and Literature, Zoological Research, and the Psycho-Pedagogical Center.

Since, under French law, Catholic institutions may not grant university degrees and diplomas, the students prepare for state degrees and diplomas. The Faculty of Theology, however, awards the baccalaureate, licentiate, and doctorate.

In addition to a numismatic museum, the University operates museums of ornithology, palaeontology, geology, and botany. It publishes a quarterly, *Revue des Facultés Catholiques de l'Ouest.*

Bibliography: R. Aigrain, *Les Universités catholiques* (Paris 1935). *International Handbook of Universities,* ed. H. M. R. Keyes (2d ed. Paris 1962).

[E. BRICARD]

CATHOLIC WAR VETERANS

An organization of American Catholic men and women, who have been wartime members of any branch of the U.S. Army, Navy, Marine Corps, Coast Guard, or Air Force; and who hold honorary discharges from military duty. They must have served at least 90 days in a U.S. war, including those wars, rebellions, insurrections, and campaigns recognized by the U.S. Veterans Administration (VA). Also eligible for membership are those who have served less than 90 days, have been honorably discharged because of a disability incurred in the line of duty, and are entitled to receive war-service benefits from the Veterans Administration.

Catholic War Veterans (CWV) was founded and chartered in the state of New York in 1935; Msgr. Edward J. Higgins established the first post at Astoria, N.Y. From this foundation developed the national body, which in 1963 had a membership of 120,000 in nearly 40 states. The CWV is recognized as a bona fide veterans' organization by the VA, which gives official accreditation to its service officers. National headquarters are located at Washington, D.C. The organization is governed by a national commander and a board of 18 other officers, all of whom are elected at a national convention. This executive board has its counterpart in each state and local area where the CWV is organized. There is a national chaplain, as well as chaplains for each state and local organization. A ladies' auxiliary to the Catholic War Veterans (CWVA) has analogous organization and activities on national, state, and local levels.

The purposes of the CWV are stated in the constitution and bylaws under three general headings: For God—to promote through aggressive organized Catholic Action a greater love, honor, and service to God; an understanding and application of the teachings of Christ in everyday life, recognizing the wisdom of the Church in all matters of faith and morals. For Country—through a more vivid understanding of the U.S. Constitution and through active participation in the promotion of the ideals of life, liberty, and the pursuit of happiness, to develop a more zealous citizenship; to encourage morality in government, labor, management, economic, social, fraternal, and all other phases of American life; to combat aggressively the forces that tend to impair the efficiency and permanency of free institutions. For Home—to promote realization of the fact that the family is the basic unit of society; to aid in the development of an enlightened patriotic American youth; to assist with an active service program all veterans, and widows, and dependents of deceased veterans.

In accordance with the purposes stated, the CWV follows on all levels of its organization a 5-point program covering Americanism, Catholic activity, leadership, membership, and veterans affairs. The group has a long record of participation in efforts to combat communism and extremist ideologies in the U.S. The fostering of Catholic action and American ideals is sought by annual essay and oratorical contests. Other services to youth include an extensive camping campaign for needy children and the sponsoring of four college scholarships a year. The CWV is one of the leading organizations involved in campaigns for the promotion and circulation of decent literature. The unsegregated membership of the body is engaged in the civil rights movement and has many other commitments in the affairs of local communities. The Veterans Administration Hospital Volunteer Service program maintained by the CWV and the Auxiliary has been commended by VA officials as the outstanding one of its kind. Members of the CWV and CWVA give voluntary service to patients in VA hospitals throughout the U.S. Charitable and missionary aid projects include the raising of funds and the collection of clothing and religious articles for use in the propagation of the faith. The CWV gives cooperative aid to the Christophers, the Catholic Information Society of New York, the Chaplains Aid Association, and to various community agencies, which operate on the local level.

The organization's two principal honorary awards are the Honor et Veritas and Celtic Cross bronze plaques; the former was presented to Gen. Douglas MacArthur, and the latter, to the seven original American astronauts. A newspaper, the *Catholic War Veteran,* is published bimonthly.

[A. J. SCHWIND]

CATHOLIC WORKER, THE

Monthly newspaper and social movement, founded in 1933 in New York City. Dorothy Day, a free-lance writer from Chicago, was inspired to start the paper by Peter *Maurin, a native of France, who was a Christian agrarian and proponent of *distributism. She had been too recently converted from communism, with its preoccupation with the industrial world, to accept all at once a mission to reverse the modern movement from the land to the factory. The first issue of the paper, on May Day, 1933, declared its intention "to popularize and make known the encyclicals of the Popes in regard to social justice." It had stories about strikes and unions, the fight for new social legislation in Washington, and the plight of the Negro. Peter Maurin said that "everybody's paper is nobody's paper" and withdrew his name from the masthead. He was unwilling to compromise with the wage system and wanted to "fire the boss."

One plank of his platform was adopted almost immediately, however, and it became the most popular and appealing activity of the Catholic Worker movement. This was his call for the practice of the works of mercy and the establishment of Houses of Hospitality. The first was in an empty barbershop beneath Dorothy Day's apartment on East 15th Street. There the Worker's daily breadline for unemployed, homeless men was started. More space was soon found in a tenement house on Mott Street, where the Catholic Worker had its national headquarters for 14 years. More than a score of such Houses of Hospitality were founded all over the country by dedicated apostles, to feed the hungry, clothe the naked, and shelter the shelterless.

The *Catholic Worker* had an immediate impact on American Catholics, many of whom were deeply troubled about the economic breakdown of the 1930s and the widespread suffering of the poor. Circulation rose to more than 150,000 within a few years. Priests and laymen who were interested in every aspect of social reform—trade unions, interracial justice, cooperatives, credit unions, the back-to-the-land movement, the liturgical movement—flocked to "round-table discussions," where more often than not Peter Maurin held the floor declaiming in "easy essays" about "cult, culture, and cultivation." Before World War II the paper came out more and more strongly for pacifism and a policy of unilateral disarmament and nonresistance. It was a voice for Catholic conscientious objectors during the war. This alienated some readers, whereas others were gained after the wholesale destruction resulting from the war and the invention of the atom bomb. There was also an advocacy of "Christian anarchism" that irritated some; its most famous exponent was Ammon Hennacy, a convert to the Catholic Worker and Catholicism.

In the early days the Catholic Worker movement appealed strongly to those who were not content simply to talk or read about social reform. Young men and women left their jobs and went to the Catholic Worker to work for nothing but bed and board. They marched on picket lines, ran soup kitchens for striking seamen, and went out to the country to prove, usually unsuccessfully, that men could find work, food, and shelter on the land. They went from the *Catholic Worker* to join the editorial staffs of journals such as *Commonweal, Ave Maria, Jubilee, Today, Work,* and a growing number of diocesan papers. They founded or joined Catholic labor and interracial groups; it was at the Catholic Worker house that the *Association of Catholic Trade Unionists was founded. Dorothy Day herself moved thousands to a better life by her articles and books, but particularly by her saintly example of love for the least of Christ's brethren. Although Catholic social action in America has for the most part repudiated the agrarianism and anarchism of the Catholic Worker, no one can deny the compelling power of the latter in the sphere of Christian example.

Bibliography: D. DAY, *From Union Square to Rome* (Silver Spring, Md. 1938); *House of Hospitality* (New York 1939); *On Pilgrimage* (New York 1948); *The Long Loneliness* (New York 1952); *Loaves and Fishes* (New York 1963). A. SHEEHAN, *Peter Maurin: Gay Believer* (Garden City, N.Y. 1959). A. HENNACY, *Autobiography of a Catholic Anarchist* (New York 1954).

[J. C. CORT]

CATHOLICISM

Since Christ intended His Church to be universal, all those who claim to be members of that Church must profess catholicism at least implicitly. However, the word catholicism is more often used by those Christians who claim to be neither Orthodox nor Protestant but to be in possession of a continuous historical tradition of faith and practice that goes back beyond the Reformation and the East-West schism. In particular the word Catholicism is applied to that Christianity that owes allegiance to the pope. This usage has led to a certain amount of misunderstanding. No one who professes to be a Christian can very well deny that he is catholic, and only the extreme reformers omitted the word catholic from the creed's reference to the Church.

But this association of the word Catholic with those Christians in union with Rome has meant that it has become simply a useful term to designate a particular group of Christians. For many it has a sectarian connotation that is quite at variance with its original meaning. However, those who do owe allegiance to the pope often see in this designation Catholic an implicit admission that they alone are the true Church of Christ. They do not realize that the term is often used merely as a convenient label and no deep signification or recognition of the papal claims is intended.

There is need to see catholicism in a less polemical light. The experience of ecumenism has taught that separated Christians can and do share in many of the characteristics of Christ's Church, and one cannot deny that those not in union with Rome do possess *catholicity to the extent to which they are united with Christ. Catholicism implies *unity in multiplicity and the catholicism of the Church derives from the catholicism of its head. Christ was constituted head of the human race, and in Him dwells the plenitude of grace that is to bring about the renewal of all things (Eph 1.22–23; 3.19; Col 2.9). All the potentialities of a regenerated human nature find their source in Him, the one mediator. Through His one Church, the *Mystical Body, these potentialities are actualized in time through faith and the Sacraments. Catholicism is this capacity that the Church has of saving all mankind by bringing it into unity through Christ. It is a dynamic force within the Church due to the abiding presence of the Holy Spirit. The Church looks to man in all his variety and complexity both as an individual and as a member of society, and while preserving this diversity the Church strives to unite and harmonize it in the formation of the new *people of God. This task will be completed only at the *Parousia; and so catholicism is not only something actual, the measure of what has already been achieved, it is also something that has yet to be perfected. The Church in its missionary activity is striving toward this ultimate goal. Today this activity has taken the form of an awareness of the need to speak to the world by making contact with human values in order to transform them by the gospel. The summoning of the Second Vatican Council and the new impetus given to the *ecumenical movement are an attempt to manifest more fully to the whole world the unity of Christ's teaching.

See also CATHOLIC; MARKS OF THE CHURCH (PROPERTIES); MEMBERSHIP IN THE CHURCH; ROMAN CATHOLIC; UNICITY OF THE CHURCH; CHURCH, ARTICLES ON.

Bibliography: Y. M. J. CONGAR, *Catholicisme* 2:722–725; *Divided Christendom,* tr. M. A. BOUSFIELD (London 1939). DTC, Tables générales 1:605. W. VON LOEWENICH and W. SUCKER, RGG³ 3:1206–26. Holböck-Sartory. H. DE LUBAC, *Catholicism,* tr. L. C. SHEPPARD (New York 1950; 1958); *The Splendour of the Church,* tr. M. MASON (New York 1956). A. RÉTIF, *The Catholic Spirit* (New York 1959).

[M. E. WILLIAMS]

CATHOLICITY

Alhough the idea of universality was highly developed in the Bible, catholic (καθολικός) is not a scriptural word. The term appears for the first time in St. Ignatius of Antioch (*Smyrn.* 8.2).

History. In the first 2 centuries, two ideas of catholicity were predominant: first, geographical universality (with all its consequences, including universality of people, of conditions of life, etc.); then, in a subsidiary way, universality of truth and orthodoxy. See A. Göpfert, *Die Katholizität der Kirche* (Würzburg 1876) and R. Söder, *Der Begriff der Katholizität der Kirche und des Glaubens nach seiner geschichtlichen Entwicklung* (Würzburg 1881). St. Augustine, particularly, in opposing the Donatist schism, developed the notion of geographical catholicity. See P. Batiffol, *Le Catholicisme de saint Augustin* (5th ed. Paris 1929). In St. Augustine also—and sometimes in St. Optatus of Milevis—one finds the word *catholica* as a noun; it denotes the Church, the *magna catholica,* and not the *fides* or the *religio.* See O. Rottmanner, "Catholica," RevBén 17 (1900) 1–9. However, the Fathers gladly explain catholicity by all the aspects of the Church capable of being universal: it is spread over all the earth; it brings the true religion to all men; it speaks to people of all conditions; it heals all kinds of sin; it offers men the most varied spiritual gifts. Thus, for example, St. Cyril of Jerusalem (*Catech.* 18.23; PG 33:1044) explains it.

The Middle Ages were to gather and synthesize all that the Fathers had written; hence the long lists of aspects of catholicity that one finds especially in the commentaries on the ninth article of the Creed, *et unam, sanctam, catholicam et apostolicam ecclesiam.* See, for example, James of Viterbo, *De regimine christiano* (1301–02), in *Le Plus ancien traité de l'église,* ed. H. Arquillière (Paris 1926), or Juan de Torquemada (d. 1468), *Summa de ecclesia* (Venice 1561). An unpublished text characteristic of the abundance of the aspects of the idea of catholicity is one by John of Ragusa, *Tractatus de ecclesia* (Basel, University Library, MS A I 29, fol. 302v–431r). The Church is catholic, he says; it extends to all places, over all times, from Abel to the end of the world; it has spread among all peoples (Ap 7.9); it propounds all the universal precepts, and not the particularist obligations of Judaism; it possesses every sacramental remedy, for every ill and every fault; it teaches a complete doctrine, which gives to all men all that is necessary for salvation; it is the means of universal salvation, for outside the Church there is no salvation; it is catholic in virtue of its worship, which is set forth in every way and at all times; finally, it embraces all men, the good and the wicked (*Tractatus de ecclesia* 2.11–12).

In modern times, the development of controversial theology gave some vitality to the question of the notes of the Church, but they were understood in a very apologetic sense. The Church is catholic, it was said, because it extends over all the earth; this diffusion, without being absolute, is greater than that of the other Christian communions and progressively tends toward absolute universality. The catholicity of time—uninterrupted continuance since antiquity—is of secondary importance. Finally, a universality of doctrine appeared, particularly in Suárez in his controversy with James I. For 3 centuries quantitative catholicity was emphasized for an apologetic purpose; see G. Thils, "La Notion de catholicité de l'église à l'époque moderne," Ephem ThLov 13 (1936) 5–73.

At the end of the 19th century, attention was given to a notion of qualitative catholicity. In the beginning there was reference to the transcendence of the Church in comparison with all the particularisms of nation, language, race, etc.; see A. de Poulpiquet, "La Notion de catholicité," RevScPhilTh 3 (1909) 17–36. Later was stressed the fundamental capacity of the Church to touch and to transfigure all things in restoring them to unity in Christ; see Y. M. J. Congar, *Christianity Divided, tr. M. Bousfield* (Philadelphia 1939) 93–114. At present, there is insistence on diversity in unity, catholicity being the opposite of uniformity; see G. Thils, *Histoire doctrinale du mouvement oecuménique* (2d ed. Louvain 1963) 262–275.

Theology. A historical survey shows sufficiently how complex is the catholicity of the Church. By catholicity one understands the Church itself insofar as it is constituted in the plenitude of Christ and is capable of expanding totally and universally in all its elements and according to all its dimensions.

One may distinguish, first of all, catholicity as note, as a distinctive sign permitting the discernment of the true Church—the universal extension of the Church, its transcendence in comparison with all that is particularized, and its multiform incarnation in all reality. There is also catholicity as property, which is an essential constitutive element of the Church.

Catholicity, like the Church itself, involves an interior and divine aspect, and an exterior, visible and social aspect. As for the invisible aspect, God the Father has made His Son the Christ, the one in whom dwells and is incorporated all the plenitude of the divinity (cf. Col 2.9). And Christ has sent the Spirit, who pours into men's hearts a varied abundance of gifts. Thus engendered by the Holy Trinity, the Church is "the Body of Christ, the fullness of Him who fulfills Himself in and by all things" (Eph 1.22); it ought to attain the whole new universe, recreated in embryo in the Resurrection of the Lord. But there is also a visible and social aspect. The extension of the Church, the active presence of the Lord to all the world, the universal epiphany of the gifts of the Spirit are sensible and visible both in the Church—the institution of salvation—and in men and the effects achieved by its spiritual work.

Catholicity may also be considered as a gift and as a mission: *Gabe und Aufgabe.* A gift, since it is one of the constitutive dimensions of the Church itself, which is a gift of God, instituted by Christ, engendered by the power of the Spirit. But also a mission. The grace of the Lord ought to be applied to all men of all times "in order that they may enter into all the plenitude of God" (Eph 3.19). Thus is achieved the fullness of the total Christ, the Church, which visibly manifests this spiritual plenitude in a world itself in a state of perpetual becoming. The mission is the very expression of this catholicity.

The Church is thus a mystery of unity and of diversity. As for diversity, it should realize concretely in its structure and in its daily life all legitimate diversity and variety out of regard for the Holy Spirit and the multitude of His gifts: diversity in spirituality and in rites; in languages and institutions; in doctrinal categories and philosophical systems. But this marvelous diversity would be only chaos without the cement of the essential unity of the Spirit, of dogma, and of structure. It is important to recall this aspect of diversity in unity at a time when the Church is confronted with other Christian communions and non-Christian religions.

In regard to ecumenism, it should be noted that other Christian communions also lay claim to catholicity, even if some have hesitated to use the name. For Anglicanism, see G. H. Tavard, *The Quest for Catholicity: A Study in Anglicanism* (New York 1964). For Lutheranism, see H. Asmussen and W. Stählin, *Die Katholizität der Kirche* (Stuttgart 1957). For the Reformed Churches, see H. Berkhof, *De Katholiciteit der Kerk* (Nijkerk, Netherlands 1962). For the Orthodox, *see* SOBORNOST. For the World Council of Churches, see the various speeches delivered at Montreal in 1963 [*Ecumenical Review* 16 (1964) 24–42].

See also MARKS OF THE CHURCH (PROPERTIES); MYSTICAL BODY OF CHRIST; RESURRECTION OF CHRIST, 2; CHURCH, ARTICLES ON.

Bibliography: J. SALAVERRI, LexThK² 6:90–92. Y. M. J. CONGAR, *Catholicisme* 2:722–725. J. L. WITTE, "Die Katholizität der Kirche," Greg 42 (1961) 193–241.

[G. THILS]

CATHOLICOS, title of the heads of the Armenian, Georgian, and Nestorian Churches. Catholicos in its first usage signified the head of a church who was dependent on a patriarch but also acted as his vicar. Later, the titles of patriarch and catholicos had the same denotation. The leader of the Armenian Church at Etshmiadzin bears the title supreme patriarch and catholicos of all the Armenians. The Church of Georgia, formerly under the Armenian catholicos, separated in 609 and later became autocephalous. Its primate also is called catholicos. The patriarch of the Catholic Armenians and catholicos of Cilicia is the head of the Armenians united with Rome.

The title of catholicos was given the bishops of Seleucia during the 4th century. After becoming the Nestorian Church, they added the title of patriarch. The patriarch-catholicos of Babylon is the head of the Chaldeans (the name given to the Nestorians who returned to Rome).

Bibliography: H. LECLERCQ, DACL 8.1:686–689. D. ATTWATER, *The Christian Churches of the East,* 2 v. (rev. ed. Milwaukee 1961–62).

[S. J. BEGGIANI]

CATHREIN, VIKTOR, Jesuit moral philosopher and spiritual writer; b. Brig, Switzerland, May 8, 1845; d. Aachen, Germany, Sept. 10, 1931. He entered the Jesuits in 1863 and became a professor in the scholasticate of the German province. Cathrein was a leading

Viktor Cathrein.

neo-Thomist and was distinguished for his vigorous attack upon positivism in ethics and jurisprudence and for his opposition to the idea that morality can be separated from religion. His criticism of socialism was influential in shaping Catholic thought upon the subject. His *Der Sozialismus* (Freiburg 1890) went through 23 editions up to 1923 and was translated into the principal modern languages. Among his other philosophical works were: *Moralphilosophie* (2 v. Freiburg 1890–91; 20th ed. 1955); *Grundbegriffe des Strafrechts* (Freiburg 1905); *Die Einheit des sittlichen Bewusstseins* (3 v. Freiburg 1914); *Die Grundlage des Völkerrechts* (Freiburg 1918). Cathrein also took an interest in spirituality, and some of his last writings are in this field: *Die Verheissungen des göttlichen Herzens Jesu* (Freiburg 1919); *Die Christliche Demut* (Freiburg 1919); *Eucharistische Konvertitenbilder* (Leipzig 1923); *Die lässliche Sünde* (Freiburg 1926); *Lust und Freude, ihr Wesen, ihr sittlicher Charakter* (Innsbruck 1931).

Bibliography: Koch JesLex 307. W. SCHÖLLGEN, LexThK² 2:980. E. RAITZ VON FRENTZ, DictSpirAscMyst 2:352.

[L. B. O'NEIL]

CATRIK, JOHN, bishop, royal envoy; b. Catterick, Yorkshire; d. Florence, Dec. 28, 1419. He graduated bachelor of Canon and Civil Law and licentiate of Canon Law at Oxford by 1406. After having held many benefices, mostly in the Diocese of Lincoln, he was papally provided to the bishopric of *Saint David's, April

27, 1414. He was translated to *Coventry and Lichfield by papal bull on Feb. 1, 1415, and then to *Exeter, Nov. 20, 1419. He was chancellor to Cardinal Henry *Beaufort, and later served Kings Henry IV and Henry V as a diplomat in France and Burgundy from 1405 to 1411 and in 1416. On May 22, 1414, he was appointed the king's proctor at Rome. In October 1414 he was an envoy to the Council of *Constance, and headed the English delegation there from April to May 1415, and again from Sept. 24, 1416, to the end of the Council. He left Constance with *Martin V and remained at the Curia until his death.

Bibliography: C. L. KINGSFORD, DNB 11:78–79. Emden 1: 371–372.

[G. WILLIAMS]

CATROU, FRANÇOIS, Jesuit historian, littérateur, and preacher; b. Paris, Dec. 28, 1659; d. there, Oct. 18, 1737. He was admitted to the Jesuit novitiate, Oct. 28, 1678, and during his studies he showed a marked ability for eloquence and literary expression. He preached with success at Rouen, Bourges, Tours, Orléans, Paris, and elsewhere for 7 years. In 1701 he gave up this career to become the first editor of the *Mémoires de Trévoux pour servir à l'histoire des sciences et des beaux-artes* (often shortened to *Journal de Trévoux*); he remained in this office for 12 years. The *Mémoires* continued in the hands of the Jesuits until their suppression in France (1762), by which time 265 volumes had been published. Articles by Joseph René Tournemine (1661–1739), Pierre François de Charlevoix (1682–1731), Guillaume François *Berthier, Charles Merlin (1678–1747), Étienne Souciet (1671–1744), Jean *Hardouin, Édouard Vitry (1666–1730), and others made it a powerful voice against Jansenists, Protestants, and the *Encyclopedists (*see* FRENCH LITERATURE, 4). In 1768 it was continued as the *Journal des beaux-arts et des sciences,* ed. Abbé Aubert (32 v. 1768–75) and brothers Castilhon (18 v. 1776–78), and as the *Journal de littérature, sciences et arts,* ed. J. B. Grosier (6 v. 1779–82).

During these years Catrou began the research that prepared him for his three major historical works: *Histoire général de l'Empire du Mogul depuis sa fondation* (2 v. Paris 1705; Eng. tr. 1826); *Histoire du fanatisme dans la religion protestante* (2 v. Paris 1733), a study of several Anabaptist sects (parts published separately as *Histoire des anabaptistes,* Paris 1705) and Quakers; and *Histoire romaine* (21 v. Paris 1725–37). This last work, though criticized often as more pompous than precise, had much influence. It was reedited by Pierre Rouillé, SJ (1737), with extensive notes and translated into English by R. Bundy (6 v. London 1728–37). It also became the basis for Nathaniel Hooke's (d. 1764) *The Roman History from the Building of Rome to the Ruin of the Empire* (4 v. London 1757–71). Catrou's translation of Vergil, *Les oeuvres de Vergile, traduction nouvelle . . .* (Paris 1716), in spite of inaccuracies, was in wide use.

Bibliography: Sommervogel 2:882–889; 8:227–229; 9:11–12. H. CHÉROT, DTC 2.2:2012–13. M. PREVOST, DictBiogFranc 7: 1428. For the *Mémoires de Trévoux,* see G. DUMAS, *Histoire du Journal de Trévoux depuis 1701 jusquén 1762* (Paris 1936). P. C. SOMMERVOGEL, *Table méthodique des Mémoires de Trévoux 1701–1775,* 3 v. (Paris 1864–65). J. P. GRAUSEM, DTC 15.1: 1510–16.

[E. D. MC SHANE]

CATTANEO, LAZZARO, Jesuit missionary to China; b. Sarzana, near Genoa, 1560; d. China, Jan. 19, 1640. He entered the Society of Jesus at Rome in 1581. After being ordained he sailed from Lisbon in 1588 for Goa. The next year he was made superior of the mission for the Malabar coast. In 1593 he went to Macao, and from there into China. He studied Chinese at Chaoking with Matteo *Ricci, and in 1598 he joined Ricci in a journey to Peking. After labors in Nanking and Macao, he became the first missionary to Shanghai, arriving there in 1608 at the invitation of a famous and influential Chinese convert, Siù Kwang-ki. Cattaneo's work took him also to Hangchow in 1611, and later to Loshan (Kiangsu province), where he founded a new mission. In 1622 he retired to Hangchow and spent his remaining years writing spiritual treatises in Chinese and working in linguistics.

Bibliography: Pfister 1:51–56. P. M. D'ELIA, "Arrivo del Cattaneo," in *Fonti Ricciane,* ed. M. RICCI, 3 v. (Rome 1942–49) 1: 331–334. E. LAMALLE, EncCatt 3:1164–65.

[J. C. WILLKE]

CAUCHIE, ALFRED HENRI JOSEPH, Belgian historian; b. Haulchin (Hainaut), Oct. 26, 1860; d. Rome, Feb. 22, 1922. His thesis, *La Querelle des investitures dans les diocèses de Liège et de Cambrai* (Louvain 1890), secured for him the chair of church history at *Louvain, which he retained until his death. Here Canon Cauchie modernized instruction, instituted a history seminar, established with P. *Ladeuze, later rector of the university, the *Revue d'histoire ecclésiastique* (1900), gave new impulse to the *Recueil des travaux* published by the faculty (46 volumes at his death), and organized the project to draw up inventories of foreign documents relative to Belgian history. He was one of the founders of L'Institut Historique Belge in Rome, which he directed from 1919 to 1922. His works on the *investiture struggle, *Jansenism, the *assemblies of the French clergy, and the religious history of Belgium are found chiefly in the *Bulletins de la Commission royale d'histoire* and the *Analectes pour servir à l'histoire ecclésiastique de Belgique.* His influence on American Catholic church history was felt, in particular, through his student, Peter *Guilday.

Bibliography: L. VAN DER ESSEN, RHE 18 (1922) 213–239. U. BERLIÈRE in *Annuaire de l'Académie royale de Belgique* 91 (1925) 199–252. L. MOHLBERG, LexThK[2] 2:981.

[J. DAOUST]

CAUCHY, AUGUSTIN LOUIS, mathematician and physicist; b. Paris, France, Aug. 21, 1789; d. Sceaux, May 23, 1857.

Cauchy's home background was thoroughly Catholic and scholarly. At 13 Cauchy captured all the prizes in classics and humanities at the Central School of the Pantheon. His parents, discovering his genius for mathematics, sent him to the École Polytechnique.

In 1810, like many other mathematicians of the day whom Napoleon used to accomplish his own grandiose ambitions, Cauchy was commissioned as a military engineer at Cherbourg. The contents of his bag at the time is indicative of his career: Laplace's *Celestial Mechanics,* Lagrange's *Analytic Functions,* a Kempis's *The Imitation of Christ,* and Vergil's *Aeneid.*

At 22, a series of his memoirs attracted Pierre Simon de *Laplace and Joseph Louis *Lagrange and won him a chair at the École Polytechnique. One of these early writings helped establish the wave theory of light. When Cauchy was 27, only Gauss surpassed him in mathematical stature. He was then author of 26 volumes, which he had completed in spite of his teaching duties not only at the Polytechnique but also at the Collège de France and the Sorbonne.

In 1818 Cauchy married Aloise de Buie with whom he spent 40 happy years. There were two daughters.

At 40 he gave up his many positions and followed Charles X into exile. He was appointed professor of mathematical physics at the University of Turin by the King of Sardinia and became the reluctant tutor of the royal heir, the 13-year-old Duke of Bordeaux. Cauchy's family rejoined him at Prague, where he began writing some 500 papers in every branch of mathematics, physics, and astronomy.

For 100 years after his death, mathematics bore the impress of Cauchy's genius through his introduction of rigor into the foundations of analysis and his pioneer work in the theory of groups.

Cauchy's work as a scholar, teacher, mathematician, author, and public servant can be summarized in his last words addressed to the archbishop of Paris: "Men pass away but their deeds abide."

Bibliography: *Oeuvres complètes,* 1st ser. 12 v.; 2d ser. 10 v. (Paris 1882–1903). M. M. MARIE, *Histoire des sciences mathématiques et physiques* (Paris 1883–88). C. A. VALSON, *La Vie et les travaux du Baron Cauchy,* 2 v. (Paris 1868). D. E. SMITH, *History of Mathematics,* 2 v. (New York 1958).

[M. S. REGES]

CAULET, FRANÇOIS ÉTIENNE, bishop of Pamiers, staunch opponent to the *régale* of Louis XIV; b. Toulouse, May 19, 1610; d. Pamiers, Aug. 7, 1680. He was the Jesuit-educated son of a well-to-do parliamentary family. Caulet first came into prominence as director of the seminary of Saint-Sulpice in Paris in 1642. Having been appointed bishop of the small and heavily Protestant Diocese of Pamiers in 1644, he attracted wide attention by his sweeping program of reform and the austerity of his life. In 1655 he was one of five French bishops who refused to sign the formulary condemning Jansenism, but this was probably as much a matter of principle as it was a sign of adherence to Jansenist doctrines. A decade later, he became the central figure in the opposition to the King's efforts to extend the *régale* into hitherto exempt dioceses. His appeal to Innocent XI for assistance was answered with alacrity, but for 3 years the diocese was in a state of siege, with Caulet, deprived of his temporalities, holding out the best he could against the combined forces of king, parliament, intendant, and even his own metropolitan. He maintained this stubborn resistance until his death at the age of 70.

Bibliography: L. BASSETTE, *Jean de Caulet* (Grenoble 1946). M. DUBRUEL, *Innocent XI et l'extension de la Régale* (Paris 1907). J. CARREYRE, DHGE 12:7–10. G. GRAGLIA, EncCatt 3:1182–83.

[L. L. BERNARD]

CAULITES, extinct French monastic order, named after the motherhouse, Val-des-Choux (Vallis Caulium), founded in 1193 in a remote wilderness by Ven. Viard (Guy), a Carthusian lay brother of Lugny. Land for the foundation was granted by the Duke of Burgundy. The order's life and discipline were based on the Rule of St. Benedict as interpreted by Cîteaux, but the monks wore the habit of the Carthusians. They lived a rigid community life, and observed strict silence and perpetual abstinence. Their source of livelihood was agricultural labor, but the Caulites never accepted or cultivated land beyond the immediate neighborhood of the monastery. The prosperous organization spread quickly and incorporated about 30 houses in France, Scotland, Spain, and Portugal during the 13th century. The head of the order was the grand prior of Val-des-Choux; priors governed the subordinate houses and convened each year for a general chapter. The first constitution was approved by Innocent III in 1205, but it was moderated in 1226 by order of Honorius III. In the 16th century wars and the commendatory system weakened the order to such an extent that by the 18th century only a few depopulated houses remained. After vain efforts at reform, the Grand Prior, Chevenet, with the approval of Dorothée Jalloutz, the abbot of *Sept-Fons, merged with the flourishing community of reformed Cistercians of that monastery. In 1761 the union was sanctioned by Clement XIII. The Cistercians rebuilt and repopulated Val-des-Choux, renamed it Val-Saint-Lieux, but in 1791 it was suppressed, as were all monastic establishments, by the Revolution. During the 19th century the monastic buildings housed various industrial projects while the church was left in ruins.

Bibliography: BEAUNIER, *Abbayes et prieurés de l'ancienne France,* ed. J. M. L. BESSE, 12 v. (Paris 1905–41). P. VERMEER, "Cîteaux: Val-des-Choux," CollOCistR 15 (1954) 35–44. H. WOLTER, LexThK[2] 6:95.

[L. J. LEKAI]

CAUNTON, RICHARD, papal chaplain, English royal servant; b. Pembrokeshire, Wales; d. June or July, 1465. He became principal of Haberdash Hall, Oxford, in 1428, and by 1450 was a doctor of canon and civil law. He held a number of livings, mostly in southwest Wales, and was archdeacon of Salisbury 1446 to 1465, and of Saint Davids 1459 to 1465. Richard was king's clerk under *Henry VI in 1437 and was probably appointed king's proctor at Rome in 1441, a position he held for many years. He was also employed on a number of royal embassies to France (1439), to Denmark (1449), and to Poland, Denmark, Prussia, and the Hanse towns in 1464. He became a clerk of the Apostolic *Camera in 1443 and was a papal chaplain by 1453. Between 1442 and 1446 he was proctor at Rome for a number of English bishops, and in December 1445 acted as the envoy of *Eugene IV to King Henry.

Bibliography: Emden 1:373–374. C. L. SCOFIELD, *The Life and Reign of Edward the Fourth,* 2 v. (New York 1923) v.1. E. YARDLEY, *Menevia Sacra,* ed. F. GREEN (London 1927).

[G. WILLIAMS]

CAUSALITY

In a general sense causality designates anything that has the character of a cause; more specifically it describes the relationship between cause and effect. Sometimes it is distinguished from causation, which is taken to mean any type of causative action (*see* ACTION AND PASSION). Cause (Gr. *αἰτια, αἴτιον;* Lat. *causa*) is itself defined by scholastics as that from which something else proceeds with a dependence in being. It is related to *principle, which is that from which something proceeds in any way whatsoever; to *condition, which is a prerequisite factor needed to make causal action effective; and to *occasion, which is an opportunity that may induce a free agent to act.

This article first exposes Greek and scholastic teaching on causality, furnishing a brief historical survey of its development to medieval times, together with an analysis of the nature of causality and the corollaries it entails. It then recounts and criticizes views on causality held by some of the principal philosophers of the modern and contemporary periods.

GREEK AND SCHOLASTIC TEACHING

The origins of causality in Greek thought are summarized in various works of *Aristotle (esp. *Meta.* 983a 25–984b 20). Aristotle notes that while none of the previous philosophers had furnished a systematic exposition of causality, their separate and sometimes confused treatments give evidence of four different types of causes.

Classification and History. The four causes enumerated by Aristotle are "the matter, the form, the mover, and 'that for the sake of which'" (*Phys.* 198a 20–25). These have become known as the material, formal, efficient, and final causes.

Basic Definitions. By *matter or material cause Aristotle means "that out of which a thing comes to be and which persists." Examples would be the cloth out of which a suit is made, and the tobacco of a cigar. By *form or formal cause he refers to "the form or archetype, i.e., the statement of the essence." In art, the shape of a bowl would constitute its formal cause; in nature, the soul of a living thing would be its formal cause. By mover, *agent, or efficient cause Aristotle understands the "primary source of the change or coming to rest" (*see* EFFICIENT CAUSALITY). Thus a carpenter is the efficient cause of a house's being built, or wind is the cause of the motion of waves on water. By final cause, he means that "in the sense of end or that for the sake of which a thing is done" (*see* FINAL CAUSALITY; TELEOLOGY). For example, one studies in order to become learned, or the natural camouflage of animals is for the sake of protecting them from their enemies. Final cause may also refer to the object of desire or the desire of the object. (Cf. *Phys.* 194b 20–35.)

Pre-Socratics. The earliest of the causes, sought by the pre-Socratics although not formally recognized as such, was the material cause. All the Ionians searched for one or more types of matter composing the cosmos, some opting for water (Thales), others for air (Anaximenes) or an indeterminate *apeiron* (Anaximander). Later philosophers enquired into the material and the efficient causes of things. *Empedocles, for example, posited friendship and strife as the forces uniting or dissolving the combination of the elements, thus accounting for order and chaos respectively. Such forces can be interpreted along the lines of efficient causality. *Anaxagoras also apparently hinted at efficient causality in his doctrine of Nous, although, as Aristotle observed, this offered more promise that it gave. (*See* GREEK PHILOSOPHY.)

Socrates and Plato. *Socrates may be said to have searched for the final causes of human conduct in his quest for the virtuous life. The Pythagoreans, and especially *Plato, made further advance into the quest for causes by investigating formal causality. For Plato, these forms or archetypes in the world of ideas are the patterns participated and imitated by sensible reality. Analogously, as a shadow has its meager reality from the tree that casts it and the sun that makes this possible, so the sensory world has its reality by virtue of the ideas (forms) it imitates and the One above the ideas. This theme of *participation runs throughout many of Plato's middle and later works. Plato also makes use of efficient causality when he speaks of the demiurge (cf. his *Timaeus*) as forming the world below.

Aristotelian and Other Usage. Aristotle not only presented a thorough enumeration and description of the various causes, but went on to employ them extensively in his works. He viewed all *science (*scientia*) as a search for causes, for only causal knowledge is scientific knowledge. His theory of proof or *demonstration (cf. his *Posterior Analytics*) is rooted in this doctrine of causes. The connecting link between a subject (*S*-term) and its attribute (*P*-term) is a cause (*M*-term). Thus the cause (*M*-term) always tells why *P* belongs to *S* or how one knows that *P* belongs to *S*. Hence, all science is "a search for the middle term." Both in the *Physics* and in the *Metaphysics,* Aristotle concludes to the existence of an Unmoved Mover or an Uncaused Cause. The Uncaused Cause is commonly viewed as an object of desire and thus as a final cause, while the Unmoved Mover is often interpreted as an efficient cause. To sum up the importance of Aristotle's contribution on the subject of causality, this lay in his showing to others what to look for when seeking scientific knowledge and how to proceed in such investigation. His systematic treatment and delineation of the causes changed the search for truth from a random groping to a systematic enquiry.

Later Greek Thought. After Aristotle, there was comparatively little stress on formal recognition and use of causes. Skeptics rejected them, and the Stoics were primarily interested in the ethical life of virtue amidst a pantheistic setting. The latter did, however, stress the immanent causality of the *logos* in the world, and of "seeds" in things as active forms from which reality emerges. The Epicureans accepted *atomism with its consequent denial of teleology or final causality. Neoplatonists were principally noted for their attempt to merge Aristotelian and Platonic teachings on causality. They gave further impetus to recognition of a fifth cause, the exemplary cause (*see* EXEMPLARY CAUSALITY).

Scholastic Development. Although Aristotle laid the essential groundwork for the doctrine of causality, it was mainly the scholastics who further clarified, refined, and applied his doctrine. Nearly all employed the Aristotelian terms, but many offered various interpretations and applications of the doctrine.

Since the most notable Aristotelian in the medieval Latin West was St. *Thomas Aquinas, his views will be summarized here. St. Thomas defines cause in a number of ways, but two of his definitions contain the essential elements. A cause is "that upon which something else follows of necessity" (*In 5 meta.* 1.749). Again, a cause is that which "brings some influence on the being of the thing caused" (*ibid.* 751.) The key to understanding causality, for Aquinas, is to see that it always involves a positive principle exerting some influence on a perfection or thing that is coming to be, i.e., an influx into being. His definitions are necessarily obscure, for the notion of causality is fundamentally analogical, and no analogical term admits of a strict *definition (*see* ANALOGY). One error of present-day thinkers in appraising causality is to ignore this analogical character of the causes and attempt to reduce all causality to some type of efficient cause. This preoccupation leads automatically to *mechanism.

Justification of Causality. Virtually no philosopher has denied the practical utility and necessity of the concept of causality, although frequent efforts have been directed toward showing that, in the real order, this concept is speculatively unverifiable. Yet man can and does regularly verify the extramental existence of causal influences. His starting point, most evident in experience, is the fact of *change. He observes change in nature and experiences himself as capable of producing it. Explanation of the obvious fact of change and *motion thus leads to explicit knowledge of the doctrine of causes.

In the most commonplace examples of change, e.g., the sculpting of a statue, an agent (efficient cause) does something to a marble subject (material cause). As a result of the agent's activity, the marble comes to possess actually a new shape or determination (formal cause). What prompted this action on the part of the agent was the fact that he sought to produce something: he had some goal at which he aimed (final cause). Briefly, then, in changes produced by *art, one observes that there must be a substratum (material cause), a determination (formal cause) that comes to be actually present in the substratum through the activity of an agent (efficient cause), for some purpose (final cause).

Making an analogous transition from art to the order of *nature, one sees that the material cause accounts for the continuity that is evident in all changes in the universe; the formal cause is the principle of novelty, without which no change would be manifest; the efficient cause initiates and makes this novelty to come about actually; and the final cause accounts for the action's tending to a determinate effect. The principles involved in this explanation apply then, not merely to art, but to nature and to physical change as such. Consequently, and in analogous fashion, one can understand that such causes are also required for any change in the physical world, whether these be substantial or accidental.

St. Thomas summarizes this line of reasoning as follows:

> There must of necessity be four causes: because when a cause exists, upon which the being of another thing follows, the being of that which has the cause may be considered in two ways. First, absolutely; and in this way the cause of being is a form by which something is a being-in-act. . . . It follows of necessity that there are two other causes, namely the matter and the agent that reduces the matter from potency to act. But the action of an agent tends to something determinate, just as it proceeds from some determinate principle, for every agent does what is in conformity with its nature. That to which the action of the agent tends is called the final cause. Thus, there are necessarily four causes. [*In 2 phys.* 10.15.]

Since change is an objective occurrence in the real order, the principles without which it would be unintelligible are clearly objective as well; hence the foregoing explanation is not to be construed as psychological, but as ontological in character. It requires, moreover, an intellectual insight into the nature of real beings and their operations. Hence, nominalists and empiricists, denying the intellect's ability to grasp natures, also reject this explanation. The exposition above is predicated on the indemonstrable first principle that being is intelligible and accordingly, that man can know (in the sense of understand) reality itself (*see* FIRST PRINCIPLES).

Analysis of Causality. Because the rejection of scholastic views on causality by modern philosophers is based largely on a misunderstanding of what is meant by causality and how it occurs, some refinements of the explanation already given are now attempted.

One or More Effects. In a certain sense, the effect of the various causes is but one effect of all four—each contributing to this effect in its own special manner. Yet the following distinctions obtain. Material and formal causes may be regarded as intrinsic, for they enter into the composition of the thing. Efficient and final causes are said to be extrinsic. The material cause influences the being of the effect through its role as subject, recipient, and passive principle, thereby limiting the act that it receives. The formal cause has for its effect the determination or specification of the being of the effect, thereby making it to be this kind of thing rather than that. The efficient cause has for its effect the coming-to-be of the new determination (form) in the subject. Lastly, the final cause has for its effect the perfection itself that has come to be, formally considered as a term of the intention of the agent. It should be noted that this intention need not be conscious or cognitive in the agent; it can be simply a tendency of the agent.

Reciprocity of Causes. Reciprocity is often evident between causes. The final cause explains why the agent causes, while the agent makes the final cause or end come to be. When the final cause is considered in the order of intention, it is what moves the agent to act. When it is considered in the order of execution, it is what the agent has produced. Thus, as Aristotle observes, health is the final cause of walking, but walking in turn produces or contributes to health. Hence, the final cause may be termed first in the order of intention and last in the order of execution. It is also termed the highest of the causes for without it none of the other causes could actually cause.

Nature of Causal Action. No agent loses anything in causing. To cause is itself a perfection; for an agent to necessarily lose in causing would be for it to become increasingly less perfect, and this implies a contradiction. It must be noted, therefore, that there is no transfer in causing as such—a position St. Thomas calls *ridiculum* (*C. gent.* 3.69)—as though the agent causes by "giving up" its own form or perfection, thereby entailing its loss. Leibniz apparently misunderstood the scholastic doctrine in this manner.

Instead, causing by finite beings involves an eduction of the form from the potency of the matter (*see* MATTER AND FORM). Strictly, the form does not come from the agent. Rather, by means of the action of the agent, the form that was already potentially in the matter comes to be present there actually. Thus water in becoming warm does not literally receive heat from the fire. It is because the flame is actually hot that water, which is potentially hot, comes to be actually so.

It is nonetheless true to say that finite causes lose in causing, although this is not because they are causing as such. Their loss is due to the presence of other causes acting reciprocally upon them. Since in the physical order every action involves a reaction, it is impossible to separate physically the activity of an agent from its being acted upon by a reciprocal agent. A physical agent, when acting, is always a patient with respect to something else. What is required to understand causality, therefore, is an intellectual abstraction whereby one considers separately two distinct but inseparable elements as these occur in the physical order.

Priority of Nature. The priority of the cause to the effect, considering both in the order of act, is not a priority of time but one of nature. The effect flows from the cause, and not conversely. Although parents, as human beings, exist temporally before their offspring, they do not do so strictly qua parents. They become parents only at the moment of conception. In the order of act, therefore, a cause and its proper effect are simultaneous. For this reason the effect continues to be only so long as its cause(s) continue to act. It is important to distinguish, therefore, the proper effect of a cause from its general effect. One can say that a tailor is the cause of the suit, as his general effect, but not that the suit is the proper effect of the tailor, for obviously the suit can continue to be when the tailor has died. Rather the proper effect of the tailor is the suit in its coming-to-be. Thus, the suit begins to become, continues becoming, and ceases to become only so long as the tailor begins, continues, and stops working on it. The suit continues to be, therefore, not because of the tailor—who no longer exerts causal influence with respect to it—but because its material and formal causes effect this conjointly.

Action and Passion. With respect to efficient causality, there is only one motion or action, but this gives rise to two *categories of being: passion, from the viewpoint of the patient; and action, from the viewpoint of the agent. There is then but one actuation, and the change as such is in the patient, not in the agent. This can be more easily stated by saying that the effect is a prolongation of the act of the agent in the patient. There are not two separate acts that somehow must be connected by a third, essentially the mistaken view of Hume; there is but a single act.

Causes of Being and Becoming. The distinction between a cause in the order of becoming (*in fieri*) and a cause in the order of being (*in esse*) must also be noted. A creature's causality is limited to the order of becoming, while only God can cause in the order of being. The limitation of a creature's causality is shown by the fact that *existence (*esse*) proceeds from the form, and no creature is a total cause of any form. Rather, creatures are causes of a form's eduction from the potentiality of matter. If creatures do not cause the form as such, much less are they causes of the *esse* resulting from the form. God's unique causality in the order of being is also clear from the fact that only what is *esse* can cause it. Since creatures merely have *esse,* they cannot cause it in the strict sense.

From these notions a number of corollaries follow. One is that nothing can escape the universal causality of God. Since becoming proceeds from being as its principle and tends toward being as its term, becoming always presupposes causality in the order of being. Another corollary is that the causality of any creature presupposes the concurrent causality of God (*see* CONCURRENCE, DIVINE). This should not be viewed as prohibiting genuine secondary causality by creatures, as proposed by occasionalism. Rather it is the very thing that makes creatures capable of exercising their own causality. (*See* CAUSALITY, DIVINE.)

Subdivisions of Causes. Among the many distinctions that can be employed to render causality intelligible are those that subdivide the various causes. Thus, material cause may refer to primary matter or secondary matter in physical things, depending on whether one is concerned with substantial or accidental change. Formal cause may be subdivided into substantial formal cause, e.g., the soul of an animate being, or accidental formal cause, e.g., quantity or various qualities. Efficient cause may be divided in many ways. The most important of these would be the divisions into primary and secondary; principal and instrumental; necessary and free; ultimate, intermediate, and proximate; and total and partial. The final cause may be viewed as either the object of desire or the desire of the object, the end of generation or the end of the generated thing, etc. A fifth cause, of which Aquinas makes fruitful use, is the exemplary formal cause. Briefly, it is "a form, in imitation of which something comes into being from the intention of an agent that determines its end for itself" (*De ver.* 3.1). This is like a blueprint in the mind of an artificer, according to which some artifact is fashioned.

CAUSALITY IN MODERN THOUGHT

Entering the era of modern philosophy, one experiences a consensus that is definitely antithetic to the traditional doctrine of causality. In what follows, the principal teachings of philosophers who have been most influential in this area, viz, empiricists, rationalists, and positivists, will be sketched.

Bacon and Descartes. Francis *Bacon is representative of this movement in its early stages. He appears to be interested primarily in formal causes, although these for him often serve as nothing more than laws of nature. However, at times his formal causes bear a resemblance to efficient causes. Final causality he removes from the realm of natural philosophy and bequeathes it to metaphysics. For all practical purposes, he seems to have regarded final causes as an anthropomorphism that had best be purged from the field of science.

René *Descartes added further impetus to this general opposition to traditional causes. In making matter inert and in reducing all motion to local motion, he prepared the way for mechanism. The Cartesian view does not admit that things have intelligibility or necessity in their own right, because, as J. Maritain has rightly observed, Descartes made things depend for their intelligibility upon a divine will and not upon divine ideas. Hence, for him, final causes lead to a fruitless search and can be dismissed from human enquiry.

Locke and Hume. John *Locke and David *Hume were both empiricists and nominalists, Hume being the more consistent of the two. Their rejection of causality could easily have been anticipated. However, in Locke's case, rather than reject causality outright, he preferred to relegate it, as he did substance, to the realm of the unknowable. For both Locke and Hume, all that man can know are successive phenomena.

It is primarily by Hume that the major attack is launched upon efficient causality. According to Hume, man knows only his ideas and images directly, and not the world of reality. Mind is, for him, simply a state of successive phenomenal impressions, and judgment is replaced by association. In asking whether causality can be justified, Hume requests that one show how its most important characteristic, necessary nexus, is grounded in experience. Not finding it rooted there, he concludes that the necessary connection between cause and effect is psychological, having its ground in custom and the association of ideas. Cause thereupon becomes a relationship among ideas, and no longer an influence of one thing upon the other in the real world. However, Hume never berated the practical utility of the notion of cause; he simply maintained its speculative unverifiability. Again, for Hume, instinct is more to be trusted than reason.

The principal shortcoming of Hume's view stems from his *empiricism and *nominalism. He attempted to have the senses detect, in a formal way, causality and necessity per se—something that those powers are incapable of doing. Aquinas had himself observed that not even substance is sensible per se, but only *per accidens*. Since he did not admit abstraction of an intellectual nature, Hume was consistent within his own system in rejecting causality and substance. And, unable to justify causality ontologically, he did the next best thing in justifying it psychologically. Yet Thomas *Reid, of the "Common Sense" school of philosophy, disagreed violently with Hume's conclusions and reacted by making causality a first principle of knowledge.

Kant's Critique. Immanuel Kant, awakened by Hume from the "dogmatic slumber" of Wolffian rationalism, saw Hume's problem but was not content to accept his solution. For Kant, Hume's was no solution, and so he himself faced the thorny problem of justifying causality. Kant's faith in Newtonian physics and mathematics required him to find an answer that would preserve the status of those disciplines. He felt no such concern for metaphysics, however.

Briefly, Kant's position is this. Man knows but the order of appearance or *phenomena, not the order of things-in-themselves or *noumena. Now, to know means to change the datum by locating it within a spatio-temporal relationship, which structure is supplied by the knower through the a priori forms of sensibility. Next man must impose upon this spatio-temporal datum certain other categories that are also rooted in the knower a priori. These are the categories of the understanding (*Verstand*): Quantity, Quality, Relation, and Modality. Causality is contained as a subdivision of Relation. Together with the forms of space and time, these categories are constitutive of experience, as opposed to the ideas of reason (*Vernunft*), which can only be regulative of experience. Previous philosophy erred in confusing the regulative function of ideas with the constitutive functions of the categories. The categories (including causality) are valid when applied to the phenomenal order, but not valid when applied beyond this to the noumenal order. To attempt the latter is to court transcendental illusion (or metaphysics, as Kant understood it). Nevertheless, such a tendency is natural to man, and he must always be wary lest he give in to it.

Since Kant allowed a valid but restricted use of causality and other categories within the phenomenal order, he felt that he had preserved the legitimate character of the positive sciences. But maintaining the inapplicability of such categories to the noumenal order led Kant to conclude that metaphysics was impossible as a science. For Kant, then, man does not discover causality in the order of things; rather, he prescribes it and imposes it upon the phenomena in order to render them intelligible (*Prolegomena to Any Future Metaphysics,* a. 36). Interestingly enough, Kant himself refers causality to the noumenal order, an error he specifically warns against (cf. *Prolegomena,* a. 13, Remark 2, and *Critique of Pure Reason,* Introduction, 1). While Kant's general position is understandable in the light of his conceptualism, it is not amenable to a philosophy of moderate realism.

Hegel renders Kantian thought more idealistic, accounting for causality by an unfolding of Absolute Mind, although the process is somewhat obscure. To a considerable extent, the Cartesian demand for clear and distinct ideas and for certitude is at the root of the denial or misunderstanding of causality in modern philosophy. It is true that causality is fundamentally a mystery, and therefore lacks the clarity one might desire as an optimum. But opaque though it may be, its certitude is guaranteed by man's direct insight into the real. That this insight is limited can readily be granted.

Positivism and Modern Science. In the main, contemporary philosophy follows the pattern set by its predecessors. *Positivism accepts causality only as invariable sequence, and this is really to deny its acceptance. *Pragmatism, while granting the usefulness of the concept of cause, remains close to positivism. Current scientific empiricism generally regards causality as a convention. Representative of both positivism and scientific empiricism, Moritz Schlick of the Vienna Circle says, "The sentence: 'A follows necessarily from B,' so far as content is concerned, is completely identical with the sentence: '*In every case* where the state A occurs, the state B follows,' and says nothing more whatsoever" (*Philosophy of Nature,* tr. A. Van Zeppelin, New York 1949, 89). Charles Sanders *Peirce reduced efficient cause to its effect, and its effect to an irreducible fact. Thus, for him, there are only facts. "The existence of a fact is equivalent to the existence of its consequence. Thus if the consequences of a supposed fact exist, then, so does the supposed fact for the pragmatist" (*Values in a Universe of Chance,* ed. P. Wiener, Garden City, N.Y. 1958, 129). Rudolf Carnap and Phillip Frank look upon cause as a convention; A. S. Eddington, L. Boltzmann, and E. Mach see nature as acausal.

With the increasing mathematization of the sciences, causality is rapidly losing all dynamical significance and becoming more statistical. Contributing to this view is the current tendency among modern scientists to investigate logical constructs, instead of the world of reality itself. Yet there are indications of a resurgence of interest in causality among philosophers of science such as Mario Bunge, and perhaps the future will see a reinstatement of traditional notions.

Conclusion. The principle of causality must be seen and grasped in the sensory order, but by an intellectual rather than by a sensory act (*see* CAUSALITY, PRINCIPLE OF). Consequently, nominalism and empiricism, in denying such an ability to man, are logically forced to deny causality as having no more than psychological value. Conceptualism is itself little more than a refined *associationism, a position whose depths were adequately plumbed by Hume. Hence, unless one grants the epistemological position of moderate *realism, he will be led to reject causality as metaphysically and scientifically unverifiable. Yet the doctrine of causes is of greatest importance, not only for philosophy and theology, but for the sciences as well. Causality is precisely what enables these disciplines to discern connections and acquire *certitude, instead of merely accumulating facts. The manipulation of nature does not require such a doctrine, but an understanding of nature does. For without causality, man necessarily becomes limited to the order of *opinion, and thereby hopelessly frustrated in his quest for knowledge.

See also METAPHYSICS; METAPHYSICS, VALIDITY OF; INSTRUMENTAL CAUSALITY.

Bibliography: G. B. KLUBERTANZ and M. R. HOLLOWAY, *Being and God* (New York 1963). J. F. ANDERSON, *The Cause of Being* (St. Louis 1952). F. X. MEEHAN, *Efficient Causality in Aristotle and St. Thomas* (Washington 1940). M. A. BUNGE, *Causality* (Cambridge, Mass. 1959). V. F. LENZEN, *Causality in Natural Science* (Springfield, Ill. 1954). E. NAGEL, *The Structure of Science* (New York 1961). A. GUZZO and F. BARONE, EncFil 1:957–975. A. E. MICHOTTE, *La Perception de la causalité* (2d. ed. Louvain 1954).

[G. F. KREYCHE]

CAUSALITY, DIVINE

God, however conceived by those who speak of Him, is generally thought of as in some way the cause of the world. His *causality has in fact been expressed in terms of all four causes, pantheists seeing God as immanent and identical with the world, others seeing Him as an extrinsic source affecting the universe through *efficient causality and *final causality. This article restricts itself to God's influence as the *agent, or efficient cause, of the existence and activity of His creation and the relationship of secondary causes to His primary causality.

Antiquity. Historically it is quite evident that until God was known through Christian revelation as the Creator, the divine causality was only partially and hesitatingly grasped. Early Greek philosophers simply assumed the existence of the world and attempted to explain it through material principles. Only with *Anaxagoras was a type of divine causality introduced to explain the universe. This philosopher's concept of the Nous, the intelligent source of the *order in things, was a giant step beyond the theories of his materialist predecessors. While recognizing in such an Intelligence the source and continuator of order, however, Anaxagoras still thought in terms of a causal contact that was somehow physical and local; his Nous was a kind of *world soul, a demiurge. The concept of the demiurge is to be found too in *Socrates, for whom God is the organizer of the cosmos and the provident cause of ordered finality.

The concept of God advanced by *Plato has been variously evaluated by historians. The demiurge seems to perdure in his explanation of the actual causality of the sensible world. This is the supreme efficient cause of the world of appearances, but it is subordinated to its exemplar in the world of Ideas and to the Idea of the Good as to a final cause. The kind of efficient causality conceived is imperfect; it seems to include a localized contact with effects, making God again a world soul and dependent on higher causes. In his perception of the exemplarity of Ideas, however, and in the notion of efficient causality producing participations in the world of Ideas, Plato provided themes that were later to be fruitfully developed.

*Aristotle had an exalted concept of God, but one conditioned by (and perhaps derived from) his conception of the eternity of the heavenly bodies. Because such bodies are perfect and eternal, they require a First Mover who is the source of such perfection and thus is *Pure Act. The life of this First Mover is described as the activity of subsistent intelligence contemplating itself (*Meta.* 1074b 15–1075a 11). But the relations of such an intelligence to the material world are very remote. His causality is primarily final, since all tendency in nature is toward God as end. Simply because of the divine perfection, providence is so impersonal as to be nonexistent; there is no contact with the world, and the finalism averred is fatalistic. God is efficient cause of the movement of the first heaven; from its movement the rest of the universe revolves, obeying in its processes the rigid laws of finality. Both Plato and Aristotle were seen by St. Thomas Aquinas, however, as having conceived the problem of the universe in terms of the causality of its very existence (ST la, 44.1–2).

The Stoics assumed much of the terminology of their predecessors but used it in a basically materialist sense (*see* STOICISM). Their God was a Logos whose fundamental attribute is providence; but they described Him literally as the soul of the corporeal world, entering into composition with its effects. Providence is the inexorable and immutable unfolding of the necessary laws of being of the Logos. Opposed to their view was the teaching of *Epicurus, who posited the clinamen or principle of deviation within the atomic realm. For him, motion in the cosmos is an effect of pure chance, stable enough for practical living, but prevented by the clinamen from being a rigid destiny oppressing men.

These influences were synthesized and refined by the Romans, who were largely eclectic in their philosophizing but who favored Stoic doctrines, particularly in the fatalistic aspects of their philosophies (*see* FATE AND FATALISM).

The final significant phase of ancient thought on God's causality was *Neoplatonism. The presuppositions of this movement were avowedly theological, since it considered the visible world only in its relationship to God. Neoplatonist thinkers regarded God as utterly transcendent, and thus it became necessary for them to posit intermediaries to allow for some type of contact with the cosmos. *Philo Judaeus was a precursor, naming the angels of the Old Testament as such intermediaries. With *Plotinus, however, the doctrine of *emanationism characteristic of Neoplatonism came to be fully articulated. God is the One, from which Intelligence emanates as a kind of necessary creation; then Soul proceeds in its turn, and finally matter. It is from Intelligence that the world emanates, corresponding to Intelligence's contemplation of the Platonic Ideas. The entire explanation, being based on a necessary emanation from the perfection of the One, leaves the system open to the charge of *pantheism. Nor does Plontius explain the kind of causality exercised on the world except as an inevitable consequence of the perfection of the One and as an influence of Intelligence, its immediate cause.

Thus the Greco-Roman world, in various ways, recognized a causal relationship between God and the universe. The primary emphasis was not so much on the concept of source or origin as it was on providence. Nor was the causality explained in very precise terms, and this for want of knowledge of the manner of origin of things from God the Creator.

Patristic Era. In the Christian Era the creative causality of God was explained by St. *Justin Martyr, among others; he used but corrected Platonic concepts. He maintained the idea of *creation *ex nihilo* and avoided so exaggerating the divine *transcendence as to cut God off from His creatures. Like Justin, St. *Irenaeus opposed *Gnosticism, with its Neoplatonic emanationism and its hierarchy of eternal intermediaries or aeons that went to form the pleroma. By the doctrine of creation Irenaeus excluded both pantheism and the conception of God as cause of the continued existence of creation. *Clement of Alexandria, while employing Platonic elements in his writings, defended the doctrine of creation. *Origen rejected the eternity of matter, but his maintaining the eternal creation of spirits gave occasion for error. *Tertullian, also denying the eternity of matter, was a strong defender of the creation of the world in time.

In St. *Augustine is to be found the fullest explanation of the divine causality by any Father of the Church. Augustine saw all being, unity, truth, goodness, and beauty as participations of the Subsistent Word. These participations are not Neoplatonic, necessary emanations, but a true creation as taught by Scripture, *ex nihilo* and beginning at a definite point in time. Time itself is a part, a mode, of this creation. No change in God is implied, for God is above time and is its cause, planning through all eternity for creation to take place and for time to begin. Augustine saw divine *conservation as the continuation of creation, with all things continuing in existence as dependent reflections of Uncreated Truth. Typical of Augustine is the *exemplarism he taught as part of the divine causality. The Ideas of Subsistent Truth are the exemplars of all beings in the universe. They are not the separated Ideas of Plato, consulted by the demiurge; they are the content of the divine mind itself. They are at once exemplary and efficient, since God puts them into existence in His creatures. Augustine also defended divine providence as the conscious source of the order and goodness of all things; God wills their perfection and His will is effective. Vexed by the problem of *evil, he formulated his basic principle for addressing the problem: "The cause of evil is not efficient but deficient, for evil is a defect, not an effect" (*Civ.* 12.7). *See* PATRISTIC PHILOSOPHY.

Early Scholasticism. In the centuries before the zenith of *scholasticism, there were reflections both of Neoplatonism and of Aristotle. *John Scotus Erigena represents the Neoplatonic line. Creation is the evolving of the being of God (*natura increata creans*), first in Intelligence (*natura creata creans*), then in the visible world (*natura creata non creans*). God, as it were, creates Himself in the world by these necessary emanations, and the world, in its turn, returns inevitably to Him (*natura nec creata nec creans*). The Arab philosophers were important for their interpretation of Aristotle. In *Avicenna there was a reassertion of the Neoplatonic hierarchy, but now expressed in terms of the Aristotelian heavenly spheres. The Avicennian concept of providence is fatalistic. *Averroës reaffirmed the necessary eternity of the universe, holding that the heavenly spheres and matter are coeternal with God, who is the cause of their movement as final cause exclusively. God has no knowledge of anything outside Himself, and the laws of the universe are expressions of a deterministic finality. (*See* ARABIAN PHILOSOPHY.)

Among the scholastics, it was primarily Augustinian teaching that served to express the theology of God's causality. St. *Anselm of Canterbury restated the doctrine of creation and conservation as found in Augustine. St. *Bonaventure significantly developed Augustine's concept of exemplarity. But it was in the grand synthesis of St. *Thomas Aquinas that the fullest and most satisfying analysis of divine causality was finally achieved.

Thomistic Analysis. God's causality as efficient, or productive, is required by Aquinas on three counts: the initial production of the universe, the conservation of all things in their existence, and the actual exercise of causality by all agent causes.

Production and Conservation. As to the initial production, St. Thomas deals first with the procession of all beings from God (ST la, 44) and then with creation itself (la, 45). God is the efficient cause of all, including matter; He is the exemplar above whom there is no further model; and He is the final cause of all. There is here an obvious echo of positions adopted throughout history, an echo that is particularly pronounced in the treatment of efficient causality. The argument Aquinas uses, found in various forms in Plato, Aristotle, and Augustine, is briefly this. All being apart from God must come from Him, for God is Subsistent *Esse; esse* is uniquely an effect of God, and therefore all other beings must participate in *esse* from Him. While invoking both Plato and Aristotle in support of this argument, Aquinas is more profound—if only because of his knowledge of the revealed truth of creation. From this truth comes his insight into the meaning of God as Subsistent *Esse* and the implications of this concept for an understanding of divine causality.

*Creation is the production of the total being of the universe from nothingness, i.e., from no subject that exists anteriorly. This total production is not a necessary emanation; rather it is a free act accomplished by the divine fiat. It is not eternal but takes place in time. The implications of this for clarifying what is meant by God's own perfection and causality are clear. The very being of things is conferred on them from God as from a primal source; whereas there formerly was God and nothing else, other beings suddenly began to exist. God as the source is the fullness of being—His own an unreceived, limitless being; the being of all else an effect that He produces. Thus what the divine causality explains is the very fact of *existence. This means that God alone is the first and proper cause of *esse*. It means that the divine causality does not work physically on a preexistent matter, that God's causality does not require His physical contact or His *immanence in creation. Rather this causality is a pure communication; the First *Cause is perfective of its effects without being itself perfected or changed in any way. On the other hand, the creature is totally dependent on such divine causality; this dependence makes all the difference between its existing and its not existing.

Through his concept of creation Aquinas was able to clarify the nature of creatural dependence on God. The pagan philosophers, it is true, were able to discern the relationship between limited being and a primary unlimited source, but they did not appreciate its significance or the precise dependence it implied. Once the revealed fact of the absolute emergence of all existents from God was understood, on the other hand, the concept of God as Subsistent *Esse,* with all its implications, became clear. God alone is His being; He created other existents from nothingness. This revealed truth thus guided the Christian interpretation of the meaning of God's subsistence. If any other being exists apart from God, it can only be a participated being and must receive its *esse* from the One who is being without limitation. When God causes, His initial causality must be a bestowal of existence as such. There is no other source, nor can anything be presupposed to the divine causality.

The knowledge of creation thus led to a formulation that applies to the whole range of divine causality, viz, "*esse* is the proper effect of God." That God did produce the universe from nothingness makes clear the basis of the statement that God is His own *esse,* that "to be" is, as it were, the very nature of God. Therefore *esse,* wherever it is found outside of God, is an effect—an effect that God alone can produce. Every existent, as a consequence, actually and continually depends on God. Thus could Aquinas adopt and explain in his own way Augustine's teaching that conservation is the continuation of creation. Any effect that is dependent on its cause not only for its coming-to-be but also for its actual being is continually dependent on such a cause. All creatures, because they exist and for as long as they exist, actually and continually receive their existence from God (ST la, 104.1).

Exercise of Causality. The teaching that *esse* is the proper effect of God need not entail a rejection of creatural causality. St. Thomas was at pains to preserve the reality of both divine and created causality, rejecting an error of his own times that would eliminate either type and even refuting a position later to be adopted by *Durandus of Saint-Pourçain (*De pot.* 3.7; ST 1a, 105.5). The production of creatures, for Aquinas, means the communication of being in various and limited ways. Since God willed to create, His creatures must be limited and cannot themselves be Subsistent Being. Their limitation is in their essence, which is made to be actualized by *esse;* in this way God is the cause of the entire being of His creatures. But the perfection of the divine causality precisely as communicative embraces the production of certain creatures that are more perfect than others in that the former can contribute actively to the development of creatures, whereas the latter cannot. Stated somewhat differently, God makes at least some things to be efficient causes (ST 1a, 103.6).

Aquinas explains, moreover, how God's causality does not eliminate the causality of secondary causes but rather causes them to be themselves causes actually causing. Efficient causality is always the active communication of existence to an effect. Because *esse* is the proper effect of God, every other agent in causing must participate in the influence of divine causality. Not only does it do this in view of its essence and its power to operate, received initially from God, but also in actual subordination to God's influx in the very exercise of its causality. The power actually to share in God's proper causality is communicated as a passing force, one that can be received only transiently and subordinately to God. But it is this power that is the ultimate completion of every created cause and renders it capable of actually causing. Only through this power can it impress its proper likeness on its effect, thus functioning on its own level of causality. The completion of its power to cause enables it to make its effect exist, since it communicates *esse,* the ultimate actuality of all perfections. The particular kind of existence is made actual by *esse,* and the power received from God to enter into this communication makes the secondary cause actually the cause of its own effect. Because this ultimate power derives from its subordination to God, both God and the secondary cause are total causes of the entire reality of the effect—God as primary, the created agent as secondary, cause.

Aquinas explains the subordination of secondary causes to God by teaching also that God "applies" the power of the secondary cause to its exercise. This point became the occasion for acrid controversy between Thomists and Molinists in the 16th and 17th centuries (*see* CONGREGATIO DE AUXILIIS; BÁÑEZ AND BAÑEZIANISM; MOLINISM; PREMOTION, PHYSICAL; CONCURRENCE, DIVINE). St. Thomas maintains simply that God applies all causes to their actual operation because they are moved movers and He is the First Mover. Yet even this is but another facet of the dependence of the creature, as composed of essence and existence, on the unique Subsistent *Esse.* It is because, in their ontological structure as substances, created causes are so composed that they cannot be identical with their own operation (ST la, 54.1–2). Their exercise of operation is the acquisition of a new accidental *esse* to which, as created, they are merely in potency. This potentiality cannot be actualized unless through the intervention of God, who is First Mover and Pure Act precisely because He is Subsistent *Esse.* The communication of *motion by God is not the bestowal of a reality distinct from the transient power by which the created agent participates in the production of *esse.* It is simply another facet of the dependence of creatural causality on God's causality.

The causality of God, particularly with regard to conservation and concurrence with secondary agents, is considered by Aquinas an effect of God's government (ST la, 103). This, in turn, is simply the execution of divine providence (ST la, 22). God acts intelligently, and His causality follows a plan. In defending the rightness and goodness of this causality as it extends to every single entity and to every mode of being, Aquinas treats also the problem of evil. He does so by invoking and elaborating upon the teaching of Augustine noted above (ST la, 49; 1a2ae, 79). Arguing that the whole of creation and the causality of God is an act of His intelligence and free will, he further rejects all types of fatalism and *determinism from God's causal influence on creatures.

Later Scholasticism. Apart from those who continued and explored the insights of Aquinas (*see* THOMISM), several notable figures in the era before the age of modern philosophy contributed to thought on the divine causality. *Duns Scotus, in his critical assaults on Thomistic teaching, claimed that St. Thomas's insight to the effect that God is the sole proper cause of *esse* is indefensible; he likewise rejected the notions of the ubiquity of the divine causality and the action of God on all created causes. He did not, however, offer any positive rational substitute for the Thomistic positions on these subjects (*see* SCOTISM). *William of Ockham also introduced a skeptical theme concerning reason's power to know God and His action on His creation (*see* OCKHAMISM). F. *Suárez, while professing to comment on Aquinas, actually sought a middle way between Thomism and Scotism; in his eclecticism, however, he rejected the key notion, the real distinction between essence and existence. His theories of divine causality are built rather on what may be called the factual or contingent aspect of the creature and on the grandeur of the universe, leading him to accent the notion of divine providence (*see* SUAREZIANISM).

Modern Thought. Two features regulate the conceptions of the divine causality in modern philosophy. One is that the object of thought is the *idea; the other, that the content of knowledge matches only sensible *phenomena, which are usually explained mechanistically. These assumptions, in various combinations and applications, run throughout modern philosophical systems and so qualify them that in fact they are not concerned with problems of the real but with problems of thought. This general concern conditions and often characterizes what is said about divine causality.

Rationalism, Empiricism, and Idealism. The God of R. *Descartes is one of his clear and distinct ideas, postulated a priori by the very existence of the thinking self. God is involved in the creation of movement—the local movement typical of Descartes's concept of the corporeal universe. This movement is initiated when created by God in a constant and determined degree; through it the corporeal world develops according to mechanical laws, which guarantee the conservation of this constant energy.

In the spirit of Descartes, N. *Malebranche developed his *occasionalism, according to which God alone is a true cause. This basic concept follows from the clear idea of God as infinite, since in Malebranche's view the finite is utterly dependent on the infinite. Further, for him all corporeal creation is contained in the idea of *extension, which is pure passivity. God acts where His creatures are present; they do not truly act, and thus they are not causes.

For B. *Spinoza, God is the sole substance. Spinoza explains the world as a series of emanations from the divine attributes, which proceed from God by natural necessity and are coeternal with Him. There is no efficient causality; creatures are formal effects of a fatalistic evolution. G. W. *Leibniz, on the other hand, stays within the world of ideas. His *monad is the primordial substance of all being. From the order of possibles in the divine mind, God chooses the best possible world; this is the only sufficient reason for His action (*see* SUFFICIENT REASON, PRINCIPLE OF).

The phenomenalistic strain is particularly stressed by T. *Hobbes, who is agnostic with regard to God and thus puts any knowledge of Him beyond the reach of mind. Hobbes is content simply to call God the omnipotent source of all the mechanistic movement by which the world of impressions is explained. Caught up also in an examination and classification of ideas, J. *Locke presents an argument for God's creative power, but the very notion of causality is so invalidated by his system that the argument reduces to mere assertion. I. *Kant has in fact nothing positive to say about the divine causality; rather his critique renders any such affirmation impossible (*see* AGNOSTICISM).

For G. W. F. *Hegel, the extreme idealist, everything real is rational. The world is but the evolution—through a dialectic of thesis, antithesis, and synthesis—of the Infinite Idea. The world is distinguished from this Idea only as a step in its evolution. Since the evolution is conceived as rigidly deductive through the process of dialectic, Hegel's system is one of determinism. God is in truth measured by the necessity of the laws of Hegelian logic.

Positivism, Evolutionism, and Subjectivism. On the positivist level, the influence of F. *Bacon is important because of the mentality his scientific method engendered. The sound procedures of experiment, hypothesis, and verification he proposed, when extended to the investigation of metaphysical problems by later thinkers, led to agnosticism. So too did the success of I. *Newton in applying the laws of mathematics to nature; from this arose the conviction that scientific knowledge is alone valid knowledge. These positivist beginnings matured into the materialism and naturalism of the Deists, both French and English, of the 17th and 18th centuries (*see* DEISM). God was acknowledged only as a blind impersonal force behind a purely mechanistic universe (*see* GOD AND MODERN SCIENCE). *Positivism itself has its foremost spokesman in Auguste *Comte, whose system, if not atheistic, is at best a materialistic pantheism—although later positivists preferred to classify themselves as agnostic.

With C. R. *Darwin and his theory, *evolutionism came into ascendancy as a monistic explanation of the universe through the development of matter. Herbert *Spencer, its outstanding spokesman, explained everything by the law of evolution; for him an Absolute exists and is the object of religion, but it is for the human mind completely unknowable. Another evolutionary thinker whose view of divine causality is noteworthy is the French Jesuit Pierre *Teilhard de Chardin. Although professing orthodoxy in matters of faith, Teilhard seems to limit God's causality to that of the "Omega Point"—a type of final cause that terminates the evolutionary process [*The Phenomenon of Man,* tr. B. Wall (New York 1959) 271]. He speaks of the universe as "a mysterious product of completion and fulfillment for the Absolute Being Himself" [see C. Tresmontant, *Pierre Teilhard de Chardin—His Thought* (Baltimore 1959) 93]. Again, his attitude toward evil is somewhat unorthodox, for he sees this as physically inevitable in the world, arising through a type of statistical necessity (*ibid.* 94).

An attempt to escape the positivist and the materialist spirit of modern science characterized the Modernist movement of the 19th century. *Modernism avers an absolute agnosticism with respect to intellectual efforts to reach God but asserts an immediate experience of divinity immanent within the soul. Such experience is regarded as the source of all philosophy and theology. Affirmations about God have no absolute value; their value is their meaningfulness to the person. Another philosophical system that relies heavily on subjective elements is that of H. *Bergson. For Bergson, the real is pure becoming; in such becoming, *intuition discovers the explanation of all things. God is the Creator by a loving energy that must express itself and must produce creatures, especially men, who are able to love. Like the thought of Teilhard de Chardin, which it undoubtedly inspired, that of Bergson seems to favor a form of pantheistic evolution.

Conclusion. From the foregoing survey of the concept of divine causality, it becomes clear that the full grasp of the concept depends on two factors. First, only with the revelation of the fact of creation can the tentative insights, even the most profound metaphysical discoveries, of philosophers receive their full understanding and application. It was the concept of creation that enabled Aquinas to see the full import of God's being the unique Subsistent *Esse,* and thus to appreciate the subordination of all creation to Him in being and action. Second, modern philosophers cut themselves off from the real problem and from a genuine metaphysical insight simply by so distorting the power of intelligence as to turn it away from being and concentrate it on itself. Certainly, to evaluate the dependence of the world on God pertains to the highest reaches of human wisdom; it needs not only the assistance of God's revelation but also every resource to be found in the soundness of human reason.

See also GOD, 1–4, 9, 10; CREATION; PROVIDENCE OF GOD (THEOLOGY OF).

Bibliography: R. GARRIGOU-LAGRANGE, *God: His Existence and His Nature,* tr. B. ROSE, 2 v. (St. Louis 1934–36); *The Trinity and God the Creator,* tr. F. C. ECKHOFF (St. Louis 1952). J. D. COLLINS, *God in Modern Philosophy* (Chicago 1959). J. F. ANDERSON, *The Cause of Being: The Philosophy of Creation in St. Thomas* (St. Louis 1952). L. R. WARD, *God and World Order* (St. Louis 1961). N. DEL PRADO, *De veritate fundamentali philosophia christianae* (Fribourg 1911).

[T. C. O'BRIEN]

CAUSALITY, PRINCIPLE OF

The principle of *causality has been variously stated in the history of philosophy. Among such formulations are the following: Every effect has a cause. Every contingent being has a cause. Whatever is reduced from potency to act is reduced by something already in act. Whatever comes to be has a cause. What is, has sufficient reason for its existing (*see* SUFFICIENT REASON, PRINCIPLE OF).

Different Evaluations. With the exception of empiricists, nominalists, and skeptics, the vast majority of philosophers have all agreed on the validity of the principle of causality. However, dispute has taken place with respect to the limits of its valid use. For example, I. *Kant accepted the proposition as synthetic a priori, hence as capable of extending man's knowledge, as well as being universal and necessary. Nonetheless, he restricted its employment to the order of *phenomena, refusing to permit it a legitimate role in the interpretation of *noumena. Others have argued as to whether the law of causality is a self-evident principle, or a demonstrable conclusion. Still others have viewed the proposition as analytic or synthetic or both.

All agree that the causal proposition is not established by the presentation of evidence that this effect was produced by that cause—an individual fact easily verified empirically. Rather, the proposition is one that asserts necessity and claims universality. Usually, however, it is not viewed as applicable to being as such, but only to created or finite being.

Many positivist philosophers, as well as a number of linguistic analysts, admit the universality of the causal proposition, but only because they view it as a tautology. From the viewpoint of the formulation, "Every effect demands a cause," if effect and cause be taken as correlatives, the proposition does seem to differ in no way from the statement, "*A* is *A*." Such thinkers claim the proposition is certain only because of the syntax of language. Accordingly, for them, its certainty can be guaranteed only at the expense of sacrificing content.

Initially, perhaps the most basic question that can be asked about the causal proposition is this: Is it necessary that when something comes to be, it does so under the influence of another? This question should be understood as applying to the coming to be of any *act, substantial or accidental; to any *change; and even to *creation. Those maintaining the validity of the causal proposition answer this question in the affirmative. Immediately, the subsequent problems arise. Why is such a necessity demanded, and how does one know this? The necessity cannot be simply a psychological necessity, i.e., one on the part of the knower, as proposed by David *Hume; rather, it must be an ontological necessity.

Some seek this necessity through an analysis of the concept of cause, as though a conceptual analysis of contingent being could reveal its relation to a cause. Yet neither the concept of being nor its contraction to that of finite being implies dependence upon a cause. The reason is quite clear. As St. *Thomas Aquinas puts it, "Relation to its cause is not part of the definition of a thing caused" (ST 1a, 44.1 ad 1). Causality is thoroughly existential, and since existence is not contained in the concept—which pertains to the essential order—no amount of conceptual analysis can reveal the exercise of causality. Hume's rejection of causality as real may well be explained by his having searched for it where it could not be found, i.e., in the order of conceptual analysis.

Justification of the Principle. To justify the causal proposition, then, one must show that the being of a finite thing is from another and that this is necessarily so. This truth is comprehended in the real order through judgment and reasoning, not through mere logical analysis. Thus St. Thomas continues: "still it [the relation to the cause] follows as a result of what belongs to its nature. For from the fact that a thing is a being by participation, it follows that it is caused. Hence, such a being cannot be without being caused, just as man cannot be without having the faculty of laughing" (*ibid.*). But how does one know that a creature is a "being by participation"? This follows from the fact that its essence and existence are really distinct principles. In short, whatever a finite being possesses, it has from its essence or what results from its essence (as a property), or from something nonessential and extrinsic to it. Since creatures are many, since there is in each a composition of potency and act, and since no creature has its existential necessity from itself, its existence must be from another. Its being therefore is *ab alio.* (*See* ESSENCE AND EXISTENCE; PARTICIPATION.)

When it has been established that the being of a creature comes necessarily from without, the causal proposition is itself established. "Whatever participates in something, receives what it participates from that from which it participates; and to this extent that from which it participates is its cause" (*De subs. sep.* 3; see also *C. gent.* 2.15). Because only God has existence in virtue of His essence, whatever else has existence has it through the action of another, i.e., God. This consequent then is the causal proposition stated on the highest metaphysical plane. To put it differently, the moment one sees that the essence of creatures manifests an indifference to existence, at that moment he can grasp that any creatural act demands influx from another. This again is to state the causal principle, not merely as applying in a particular case, but as having universal validity for the realm of finite being.

Although the validity of the causal proposition is seen in concrete experience, *induction and *abstraction are required to render its formulation universal. Summing up the views of J. Owens (see bibliography), one can state that the causal proposition is not analytic with respect to a consideration of the mere concept of contingent being; however, it is analytic with respect to a judgment wherein one comes to grips with the existential order. Thus the nominalist, in refusing to accept an intellectual insight into the real, is consistent in denying real meaning to the universal validity of the causal proposition. For the causal principle is no more sensible per se than is *substance.

In light of the causal proposition one sees that all things, either ultimately or proximately, bear some relationship to each other; that there is an existential bond in the order of *being; and that the sciences, and especially metaphysics, possess validity.

See also METAPHYSICS, VALIDITY OF; FIRST PRINCIPLES.

Bibliography: Syntopicon 1:155–178. L. DE RAEYMAEKER, *The Philosophy of Being,* tr. E. H. ZIEGELMEYER (St. Louis 1954). B. GERRITY, *Nature, Knowledge and God* (Milwaukee 1947). J. OWENS, "The Causal Proposition—Principle or Conclusion?" ModSchoolm 32 (1954–55) 159–171, 257–270, 323–339.

[G. F. KREYCHE]

CAUSE, FIRST

The concept of first cause, by which, in the absolute sense, God is understood, is derived from the metaphysical demonstration of the necessity of an ultimate efficient per se (direct) cause of the existence of multiple and diverse finite realities (St. Thomas, ST 1a, 2.3). The first cause is the ultimate uncaused cause, the one cause of all other reality. In the relative sense, the first cause may be the cause that is first in any order of created causes.

Finite reality, in which essence and existence are distinct, requires an efficient proper cause of its being, for its nature is not sufficient reason for its finite existence. A proper effect demands the actual operation of the cause of which it is the effect and ceases with the cessation of that cause (ST 1a, 104.1). Whatever demands a cause of its becoming (*in fieri*), demands also a cause of its existence (*in esse*), since the first of all effects is being, which is presupposed to all other effects, and does not presuppose any other effect (*C. gent.* 2.21). Continued existence, therefore, is a present effect that must be due to the operation of the present cause of that existence.

The argument proceeds from the premise, an obvious fact of sensory and intellectual experience, that realities, both substance and accidents, come into existence through the action of a series of essentially subordinated efficient causes. But it is a contradiction in terms that such a series should proceed to infinity. The existence of a first cause, itself uncaused and self-subsistent, must be admitted necessarily.

The same conclusion follows an argument proceeding from the consideration of contingent realities (that may either exist or not exist). It is evident that such realities are not the reason for their own existence, otherwise they would be self-existent. Their existence, therefore, must be the effect of the proper efficient first cause of existence. The existence of all being, therefore, is the direct proper effect of the per se causality of the first uncaused cause.

All causes, other than the first cause, whether they be properly principal or instrumental, are secondary causes whose very existence as causes, as well as whose operations as causes, is an effect of their proper direct cause, God Himself.

The concept of first cause, therefore, signifies not only the primary causality of all causal activity in the created universe, but the primary causality of the very being of all causes. Moreover, the conservation of all created reality in existence is the proper effect of the first cause, whether the reality be of the material or spiritual order, or the composite of the two. Whatever is, or can be, is an effect of the first, efficient, causality of the first cause.

See also EXEMPLARISM; EXEMPLARITY OF GOD; GOD, 7, 8; GOD, PROOFS FOR THE EXISTENCE OF; GOOD, THE SUPREME.

Bibliography: DTC, Tables générales 1:557–560. J. DE VRIES et al., LexThK[2] 6:96–100. I. M. DALMAU, SacTheolSumma BAC 2.1:1–36.

[M. R. E. MASTERMAN]

CAUSSADE, JEAN PIERRE DE

Jesuit spiritual writer; b. Cahors, capital of Quercy, March 7, 1675; d. Toulouse, Dec. 8, 1751. He studied at the Jesuit university in Cahors, where Fénelon had also been a student. On April 16, 1693, he entered the novitiate of the Society of Jesus at Toulouse. For more than 20 years he taught the classics, philosophy, and the sciences in the various colleges in his province. He was ordained in 1704 and added to his responsibilities as a teacher those of confessor and preacher, besides acting as spiritual director for his confreres. He gave up teaching in 1724 to become a member of a team of preachers working in "urban missions." In 1729 or 1730 he was sent to Lorraine and became acquainted with the Visitation nuns at Nancy. He was publicly denounced, probably by a Jansenistic pastor, for imprudence of language in one of his sermons, and was sent back to his province where he spent 2 years in semidisgrace in the seminary at Albi. His spiritual correspondence with the Visitation nuns at Nancy, which extended over a period of about 10 years, is the major evidence of his spiritual guidance. From Albi, Caussade was recalled to Nancy, where he divided his time between retreats given at the house of St. Ignatius and the spiritual direction of sisters, especially those of the Visitation and the Good Shepherd. Already deeply influenced by Fénelon's spirituality, Caussade then became familiar with the writings of Bossuet and studied especially the *Instruction sur les états d'oraison.* He wrote a work in the form of dialogues in which he treated of the teaching of the two prelates whose controversy had divided the Church in France at the end of the 17th century. This book was published in 1741 at Perpignan when Caussade was rector of the college in that city. He had left Nancy in 1739 and later was rector of the College at Albi. In 1746 he returned to Toulouse.

The work printed at Perpignan in 1741 was titled: *Instructions Spirituelles en forme de Dialogues sur les divers états d'oraison, suivant la doctrine de M. Bossuet, évêsque de Meaux* (Spiritual Instructions in the Form of Dialogues on the Various States of Prayer according to the Doctrine of Bishop Bossuet of Meaux). Since the author was not named, the work was attributed to Paul Gabriel *Antoine, a theologian of repute, whose name appeared in connection with the imprimatur. It would seem that the work caused no stir when it appeared. The *Journal de Trévoux,* edited by Jesuits, referred to it in moderate terms in 1745. In 1752, a short time after his death, Caussade was attacked by the *Nouvelles Ecclésiastiques,* a Jansenistic publication.

Caussade is known especially for a work called *Abandon à la Providence divine,* for which he was not directly responsible. Henri Ramière, SJ, who published it in 1861, tells how the Visitation nuns had kept the letters received from their spiritual director. One of them, Mother Sophie de Rottembourg, had made a kind of treatise of them by grouping into 11 chapters certain passages from his correspondence and from notes taken at his conferences. Ramière learned of this manuscript from the Religious of Nazareth, who had a copy of it. He reworked the text and arranged it according to what seemed to him the dominant theme. He divided it into two parts, the first dealing with the virtue and the second with the state of abandonment. It was printed in Le Puy and enjoyed a considerable success. The treatise was completed in later editions, by the addition of a series of letters gathered from collections preserved at the Visitation convent of Nancy.

Caussade's doctrine is dominated by the idea of peace. A disciple of St. Francis de Sales and of Fénelon, he remained faithful to Ignatian spirituality as interpreted by Louis *Lallemant. He relates all spirituality to interior peace, obtained by fidelity to the order of God, by faith in the universal and ever actual working of the Creator, by accepting one's cross, and by a confidence in God's fatherly goodness. This is the Salesian ideal of evangelical simplicity and of absolute docility to the will and pleasure of God.

Bibliography: H. Bremond, *Apologie pour Fénelon* (Paris 1910). M. Olphe-Galliard, DictSpirAscMyst 2.1:354–370; "Le Père de Caussade, directeur d'âmes," RevAscMyst 19 (1938) 394–417; 20 (1939) 50–82; "L'Abandon à la Providence divine et la tradition salésienne," *ibid.* 38 (1962) 324–353.

[M. OLPHE-GALLIARD]

CAUSSIN, NICHOLAS, preacher, confessor of Louis XIII, and spiritual writer; b. Troyes, France, 1583; d. Paris, 1651. He entered the Jesuits in 1607 and began his career as a preacher in 1620. He became the confessor of Louis XIII in 1637 and played an important part in the reconciliation of Louis and his wife Anne of Austria. Cardinal Richelieu later exiled Caussin to Quimper for political reasons. After the deaths of Louis XIII and Richelieu in 1643 Caussin returned to Paris, where he became confessor to the Prince of Condé and spiritual director of a number of leading noblemen. Among his numerous writings on the spiritual life, the most important is *Cour Sainte,* 5 v. (Paris 1624).

Bibliography: C. de Rochemonteix, *Nicolas Caussin, confesseur de Louis XIII et le cardinal de Richelieu* (Paris 1911). H. Fouqueray, *Histoire de la Compagnie de Jésus en France des origines à la suppression, 1528–1762,* 5 v. (Paris 1910–25) 5:85–106. B. Duhr, *Jesuiten-Fabeln* (Freiburg im Br. 1904). Sommervogel 2:902–927. H. Chérot, DTC 2.1:2043–44. M. Olphe-Galliard, DictSpirAscMyst 2:371–373.

[J. M. HAYDEN]

CAVALCANTI, GUIDO

Italian poet; b. Florence, *c.* 1259; d. there, August 1300. He was prominent in the political conflicts between factions of the *Guelfs and died of a fever contracted in political exile. Dante called him "the first of my friends" and dedicated the *Vita Nuova* to him. Guido's name appears several times in the *Divina Commedia* as the poet who had stolen the glory of G. Guinizelli's style, and Guido's poems are praised in Dante's *De vulgari eloquentia* as "most subtle and smooth." These references led to the conclusion that Cavalcanti's poetry sprang from the same conceptual and poetic sources, the same atmosphere, from which the *Vita Nuova* arose, and that he manifests the qualities generally judged characteristic of the *dolce stil nuovo*—mainly the idea that poetry is inspired by love and that the mystic conception of beauty is the source of nobility and perfection and a ladder to God. There is indeed considerable insistence in Cavalcanti's poetry on the destructive force of love and on the fear and torment caused by the approach of the beloved; these aspects were considered personal quirks of his pessimistic and melancholy mind.

It is clear now, however, that these views have to be abandoned. There can be no doubt that when Dante speaks of himself and of the *dolce stil nuovo* in the famous lines "I mi son un che quando Amore spira noto . . .," he does not speak of love that inspires, but of the spirits, the movements of love that he and his friends are able to detect and describe. In fact, the most important of Guinizelli's and Cavalcanti's poems are a kind of scientific analysis of love, with no reference to personal sentiment. Considered without reference to background, these poems seem inspired by Christian *mysticism, but Guinizelli's key thought clearly derives from Avicenna's pagan conception of beauty as an emanation from a higher Intelligence and as a ladder to perfection. Cavalcanti speaks of love in conformity with Averroes' thought; he explains it as a passion of the sensitive appetite and holds that "from its power death often originates," because it prevents rational activity, the true life of man. Caval-

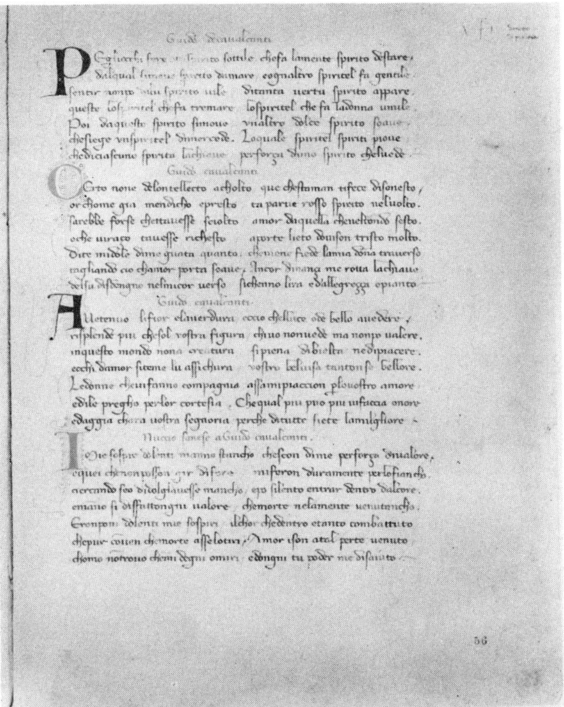

Folio from a 14th-century manuscript of poems by Guido Cavalcanti (Cod. Chigiano 1. VIII. 305, fol. 56r).

canti's conception of love as something that alienates the soul from the "supreme good" and brings death to man is to be found in the Averroist treatise *De summa felicitate* by G. da Pistoia, which is significantly dedicated "to Guido, most beloved friend." Cavalcanti's *canzone* "Donna mi prega" clearly expresses the repudiation of love by a philosopher who praises contemplation of the truth above all and rejects the fears and mutability of lovers.

It must be added that Cavalcanti is not simply a rigorous Averroistic philosopher. He is a poet first of all; he strove to create pure intellectual poetry, excluding every hint of sentiment or personal experience. His is a stern, sententious language, obscure, aphoristic, making no concession to common speech. It was a necessary cloak to hide his atheism, but it sprang primarily from the disdain of the philosopher (clearly expressed in a polemic against Guido Orlandi) for all ordinary people unable to understand his "scientific demonstration." Further, Cavalcanti conceived of poetry as something difficult and subtle. He was a versatile poet, however, and wrote in the *dolce stil nuovo* some pieces not inferior to Dante for grace and limpidity, and also some delicate, fresh pastorals. His *ballata* "Perch'io non spero," written during his exile from Florence in 1300, expresses with deep sincerity and moving tenderness his sorrow and nostalgia.

If at times Cavalcanti reverts to the themes and modes of Guinizelli, it is clear that he is not speaking of a real woman whom he adores, but of philosophy, his true lady. It is of her that he spoke in a sonnet to Guido Orlandi, opposing her to the Blessed Virgin and praising her for her power to heal and other miracles. Dante implies that Cavalcanti was excluded from the way to God because he had been a follower of Aristotelian naturalism and had disdained the help of Vergil, the poet of the divine mission of Rome. Cavalcanti mirrors the last years of the secularism of the 13th century. With him the religious superficiality of the *troubadours turns into a pronounced repudiation of religion. He was dedicated to poetry, philosophical rigor, and a treatment of love on a purely psychological level, to the complete exclusion of moral and religious values.

Bibliography: G. CAVALCANTI, *Le rime,* ed. G. FAVATI (Milan 1957). M. CASELLA, "La Canzone d'amore di Guido Cavalcanti," *Studi di filologia italiana* 7 (1944) 95–160. O. BIRD, ed., "The Canzone d'amore of Cavalcanti according to the Commentary of Dino del Garbo," MedSt 2 (1940) 150–203; 3 (1941) 117–160. B. NARDI, "L'averroismio del *primo amico* di Dante," *Studi danteschi* 25 (1940) 43–79; "Noterella polemica sull'averroismio di G. Cavalcanti," *Rassegna di filosofia* 3 (1954) 47–71. J. E. SHAW, *Guido Cavalcanti's Theory of Love* (Toronto 1949). G. FAVATI, "La Canzone d'amore del Cavalcanti," *Letterature moderne* 3 (1952) 422–453. P. O. KRISTELLER, "A Philosophical Treatise from Bologna Dedicated to G. Cavalcanti and His *Questio de Felicitate,*" in *Medioevo e Rinascimento: Studi in onore di Bruno Nardi,* 2 v. (Florence 1955) 1:425–463. R. MONTANO, *Storia della poesia di Dante,* v.1 (Naples 1962). **Illustration credit:** Biblioteca Apostolica Vaticana.

[R. MONTANO]

CAVALIER POETS

The mid-17th-century English poets, Herrick, Carew, Suckling, and Lovelace share qualities that allow them to be loosely grouped in literary history. They, and others such as Edmund Waller (1606–87) and Sir William Davenant (1605–68) share not only mutual acquaintance and allegiance to king and established church, but the whole tenor of thought, feeling, and expression prevailing at the end of the Stuart period.

Background. In style and feeling Cavalier poetry somewhat resembles that of Ben *Jonson. His poetry, however, rooted in a deeper vision of reality and a higher conception of the art, is far richer and stronger than theirs. Some critics see an influence of John *Donne on Cavalier poetry. The deeper origins of Cavalier poetry lie in the thought and feeling of the times. The shocks of the Civil War and the decadent brilliance of the court of Queen Henrietta Maria (1625–49) gave a distinct tone to Cavalier poetry, but of profounder influence was that pessimism and fragmentation of vision of which *Hobbes (1588–1679) was a characteristic example. Under his influence and that of the whole scientific movement, Englishmen were redefining their attitudes toward human nature. The net result was an alienation of reason from both faith and imagination, a restriction of knowledge to the measurable, and a consequent retreat from traditional efforts to approach the central mysteries of experience.

Range of Interest. Cavalier poetry is narrow in range. Love is the almost exclusive subject matter, and it is a love shorn of emotional, intellectual, and social significance. Cavalier love is an artificial game that may be amusing or pretty or sensuously intense, but that no man and no poet should take seriously. The result of this attitude is an artificial poetry with little relevance to human experience.

The Cavalier poets are remembered chiefly for their lyrics, which are more conversational and intellectual than the Elizabethan, but achieve neither the full sense of the human person of Donne's lyrics, nor the direct veracity of Jonson's. Cavalier poetry deliberately avoids high thoughts or deep feelings, preferring wit and refined, if uncomplicated, sentiment. When the Cavaliers achieve clarity of definition, it is reductive rather than illuminating clarity. Critical appreciation of these poets has depended largely upon tastes for lyric grace and technical virtuosity.

Poets. Robert Herrick (1591–1674), after early years in London when Ben Jonson reigned at the Sun, the Dog, and the Triple Tunne, became vicar of Dean Prior in Devonshire in 1629. There he remained, except for the interlude when he was expelled by the Puritans. Herrick's description of his secular poems as his "unbaptized rimes" is accurate. The landscape of "A Country Life" is nearer that of Horace than that Edenlike state described in Jonson's "To Penshurst." In his love lyrics, for which he is best known, Herrick usually confines himself to pretty compliments to imaginary ladies and delicate evocations of the "Gather ye rosebuds while ye may" theme. His "Nuptial Song to Sir Clipseby Crew" focuses with artful and suggestive intensity upon sexual desire, sharply reducing the religious and social significance so prominent in epithalamiums by Edmund Spenser, Jonson, or Catullus. His few religious poems (in *Noble Numbers,* 1647) are simple and pious but lack a dimension of mystery and a sense of personal intimacy with God that are present in George Herbert (1593–1633), whom Herrick admired. In religion Herrick belonged to the new common sense school, which attempted to avoid both Puritan enthusiasm and Catholic speculation.

Thomas Carew (1594 or 95–1640) was a favorite of Charles I and contributed notoriously to the dissipation of the court. Most of his lyrics are amatory, portraying

Sir John Suckling, portrait by T. Russel after Van Dyck.

well a courtly world where sophisticated ladies and gentlemen play the trivial but pleasant game of love. Carew's technique is appropriately refined and elegant. His famous elegy on Donne defines poetic greatness mainly in terms of style and wit (meaning mental dexterity) and is thus a symptom of the critical trend of the day.

Sir John Suckling (1609–42), one of the most notorious rakes of the time, cultivated in poetry an attitude of amateur carelessness and ease that is often regarded as characteristic of Cavalier poetry. His good-natured satire, "A Session of the Poets," ridiculed the studied artfulness of Carew and all who take poetry seriously. The love lyrics are fashionably anti-Platonic, but Suckling possessed some of the forthright humor of Thomas Wyatt (1503?–42), which allowed him to reveal the perennial follies of lovers.

Richard Lovelace (1618–57), widely regarded both by contemporaries and by some later critics as the last of the Renaissance gentlemen, was scholar, courtier, poet, and soldier. His best poetry, a handful of lyrics in *Lucasta* (1649), deals with love and chivalry. These poems have been praised for their sweet gravity and idealism. The "honor," however, which he makes the basis for his love of king, country, and mistress, is not the great Christian ideal that had once informed *chivalry.

Bibliography: Editions. R. HERRICK, *Poetical Works,* ed. L. C. MARTIN (Oxford 1956). T. CAREW, *Poems,* ed. R. DUNLAP (Oxford 1949). J. SUCKLING, *Works,* ed. A. H. THOMPSON (New York 1910). R. LOVELACE, *Poems,* ed. C. H. WILKINSON (Oxford 1930). R. SKELTON, *Cavalier Poets* (London 1960). D. BUSH, *English Literature in The Earlier Seventeenth Century* (OxHist EngLit 5; 2d ed. rev. Oxford 1962). C. H. HARTMANN, *The Cavalier Spirit and Its Influence on the Life and Work of Richard Lovelace* (London 1925). E. SELIG, *The Flourishing Wreath: A Study of Thomas Carew's Poetry* (New Haven 1958).
Illustration Credit: National Portrait Gallery, London.

[D. B. QUINN]

CAVALIERI, FRANCESCO BONAVENTURA, mathematician; b. Milan, 1598; d. Bologna, 1647. He entered the Hieronymites (*Jesuati) at a very early age. In 1616, he attended the Studium of Pisa as a student of *Castelli who introduced him to *Galileo with whom he then regularly corresponded about his scientific work. In 1629 he was named professor of mathematics at the University of Bologna, a post he retained until his death. His principal and most important work, one of the most ingenious mathematical treatises of the 17th century, is that on the "geometry of indivisibles" (*Geometria indivisibilibus continuorum nova quadam ratione promota*). It represents the beginning of differential and integral calculus. As a complement to his theory of indivisibles, Cavalieri wrote the "Esercitazioni geometriche," an integral part of his *Geometria.* He received ecclesiastical permission to include a discussion of the Copernican system in his lectures at Bologna. Cavalieri immediately perceived the significance of J. Napier's discovery of logarithms and introduced them into Italy, preparing practical tables for their application. Galileo thought so highly of Cavalieri and his contribution to the field of mathematics that he dubbed him *alter Archimedes.*

Bibliography: P. FRISI, *Elogi di Galileo Galilei e di Bonaventura Cavalieri* [*da Paolo Frisi*] (Milan 1778). C. B. BOYER, "Cavalieri, Limits and Discarded Infinitesimals," *Scripta Mathematica* 8 (1941) 79–91. G. GALILEI, *Le opere di Galileo Galilei,* 20 v. (Florence 1929–39). *Dizionario letterario Bompiani degli autori,* 3 v. (Milan 1956). G. ABETTI, *Amici e nemici de Galileo* (Milan 1945).

[G. ABETTI]

CAVALLERA, FERDINAND, Jesuit scholar and patrologist; b. Le Puy, France, Nov. 26, 1875; d. Toulouse, March 10, 1954. He entered the Society of Jesus on Nov. 11, 1892, and studied at Vitoria, Toulouse, Uclès, Vals, Jersey, and Enghien (Louvain), having served meanwhile as professor of literature at the Jesuit juvenate. He was ordained Aug. 26, 1906, and was named ordinary professor of positive theology at the Institut Catholique of Toulouse as successor to E. Portalié; he added courses on the social thought of the Church (1926) and patrology (1932). He served as librarian of the Institut (1911–31) and gave lectures on Italian literature from 1917 to 1924. He was a founder and director of the *Bulletin de littérature ecclésiastique, Revue d'Ascétique et de Mystique,* and the *Dictionnaire de spiritualité ascétique et mystique.*

His doctoral dissertation on *Le Schisme d'Antioche* (1905) was well received, and he produced in succession *Saint Athanase* (1908), *Index de la Patrologie grecque* (1912), *Thesaurus doctrinae catholicae ex documentis magisterii ecclesiae* (1920), and *Précis de la doctrine sociale de l'Église* (1931), besides writing innumerable articles and reviews in collaboration with learned and influential periodicals and weeklies such as *France Catholique.* His two-volume *Saint Jérôme* (Paris 1922) is the best monograph yet to appear on the life and character of that great but difficult saint and Scripture scholar. Cavallera, a scholar of the old school, kept himself completely up to date in mentality, method, and knowledge of affairs.

Bibliography: *Mélanges . . . R. P. Ferdinand Cavallera* (Toulouse 1948). R. BROUILLARD, *Catholicisme* 2:740. DTC, Tables générales 1:560–561.

[F. X. MURPHY]

CAVALLI, FRANCESCO, baroque opera and church composer (original name, Pier Francesco Caletto-Bruno); b. Crema (Lombardy), Italy, Feb. 14, 1602; d. Venice, Jan. 17, 1676. He received musical training under his father, G. B. Caletto, an organist, and in March 1616 undertook studies with *Monteverdi in Venice, adopting the surname of Federigo Cavalli, the patrician who made his education possible. He spent his life in Venice, serving at San Marco as singer, organist, or *maestro di cappella.* While he was the leading exponent of early Venetian opera, he composed also a number of Masses and motets in various forms, from solo monodies to two-choir works, all in the *stile moderno.* These works, though dramatic, are not operatic, and it is clear that Cavalli distinguished between church and stage music. In the smaller ones there are devices common to less pretentious *concertato* music, and in the polychoral works there is the fullness of sound characteristic of Venetian religious music of that time. Like almost all his sacred music, his unpublished Requiem, reputedly a work of great solemnity, is still unavailable in a modern edition.

Bibliography: A. A. Abert, MusGG 2:926–932. E. J. Wellesz, Grove DMM 2:128–132. W. S. Newman, *The Sonata in the Baroque Era* (Chapel Hill, N.C. 1959). Láng MusWC. Buk MusB. Grout HistOp.

[T. CULLEY]

CAVALLINI, PIETRO, Roman painter and mosaicist who transformed Romanesque style into a more humanistic idiom; b. Rome, *c.* 1250; d. *c.* 1334. Cavallini's known activity dates from about 1270, when he began the paintings (no longer extant) for the interior of St. Paul-Outside-the-Walls. His signed mosaics in the apse of S. Maria in Trastevere (1291) already show an expansion of setting and more plastic rendering of the drapery despite the use of Byzantinizing models for the iconography. The reliance on antique inspiration and early Christian sources is apparent in his "Last Judgment" fresco (*c.* 1293, S. Cecilia in Trastevere), where the large figures of Christ as Judge and the Apostles show the modeling of faces with green underpainting according to classical technique and garments rendered in a painterly fashion by means of highlights. Cavallini's figures are imbued with a new spirit of humanity and immediacy. In 1308 he was at the court of Charles II in Naples and was working on frescoes for S. Maria Donnaregina, Naples, from 1316 to 1320. Although a large portion of the work was relegated to assistants, Cavallini's supervision is apparent in the greater humanization of the figures. Because his late works, e.g., the paintings for the façade of St. Paul-Outside-the-Walls (1316–34), have been destroyed, it is difficult to assess his relationship to the slightly younger *Giotto, but some degree of influence is probable.

Pietro Cavallini, "Apostles," detail of the fresco of the "Last Judgment" in S. Cecilia in Trastevere, Rome.

Bibliography: E. Lavagnino, *Pietro Cavallini* (Rome 1953). P. Toesca, *Pietro Cavallini,* tr. E. Andrews (New York 1961).
Illustration credit: Alinari-Art Reference Bureau.

[M. M. SCHAEFER]

CAVAZZONI, GIROLAMO, Renaissance organist and polyphonist; b. Urbino, Italy, *c.* 1520; d. Venice, 1560. He was a son of Marco Antonio *Cavazzoni, godson of Cardinal *Bembo, and pupil of *Willaert. His fame rests today on his extensive volume of keyboard music, *Intavolatura cioè Ricercari, Canzoni, Hinni, Magnificati* (Venice 1542), comprising 4 *ricercari,* 2 *canzone,* 12 hymns, and settings of the odd-numbered verses of the Magnificat in tones I, IV, VI, and VIII. This was followed in 1543 by a similar work containing three organ Masses: *Missa Apostolorum, Missa Dominicalis,* and *Missa de Beata Virgine.* His collections contain many marks of originality. The *ricercari* received the first polyphonic treatment of this form, and his two *canzoni* initiated a new distinct *canzona* literature for keyboard. In the *Gloria* and *Credo* settings of his Masses, the alternation plan is clearly regular; e.g., "Gloria" (celebrant), "Et in terra" (organ), "Laudamus Te" (choir), "Benedicimus Te" (organ), "Adoramus Te" (choir).

See also MUSIC, SACRED, HISTORY OF, 4; ORGAN MUSIC.

Bibliography: Modern eds. of selections from the *Intavolatura* in L. Torchi, ed., *L'arte musicale in Italia,* 7 v. (Milan 1897–1908) v.2–3. G. Benvenuti, ed., *I classici della musica Italiana,* v.6 (Milan 1919). G. Tagliapietra, ed., *Antologia di musica antica e moderna per pianoforte,* 14 v. (Milan 1931–32) v.1. I. Fuser, ed., *Classici italiani dell'organo* (Padua 1955). A. Schering, ed., *Geschichte der Musik in Beispielen* (Leipzig 1931) 103. Davison-Apel HAM 1:121–127, general. H. Klotz, MusGG 2:934–937. J. A. Fuller-Maitland, Grove DMM 2:132.

[M. T. HYTREK]

CAVAZZONI, MARCO ANTONIO, baroque organist and composer (also da Bologna or d'Urbino); b. Urbino, Italy, *c.* 1490; de Venice(?), *c.* 1570. His career included service to the Venice patrician Francesco Cornaro, Pope Leo X, and Cardinal Pietro Bembo at Padua. From 1536 to 1537 he was organist at the Choggia cathedral, and from 1545 to 1559, a singer at St. Mark's in Venice under *Willaert. His one known

Title page of Marco Antonio Cavazzoni's "Recerchari, Motetti, Canzoni" in the first edition of 1523.

collection, *Recerchari, Motetti, Canzoni, Libro I* (Venice 1523), is, after the *Frottole* of Andreo Antico (fl. after 1510), the earliest printed organ music (copies in British Museum and Newberry Library, Chicago), and it marks a significant step toward emancipation of organ literature from the prevalent vocal style and the establishment of a true keyboard style. The volume contains two *ricercari,* two motets (*Salve Virgo* and *O Stella Maris*), and four *canzoni francesi.* His keyboard style shows the influence both of lute technique, with its free use of chordal and scale passages, and of the Venetian organ tradition, characterized by improvisation.

Bibliography: M. A. CAVAZZONI, *Ricercari, Mottetti, Canzoni,* ed. G. BENVENUTI (I classici musicali italiani 1; Milan 1941). I. FUSER, ed., *Classici italiani dell'organo* (Padua 1955). T. DART, "Cavazzoni and Cabezón," MusLett 36 (1955) 2–6. K. JEPPESEN, "Cavazzoni - Cabezón," JAmMusSoc 8 (1955) 81–85, a rebuttal of Dart's article; ed., *Die italienische Orgelmusik am Anfang des Cinquecento* (2d ed. Copenhagen 1960). Reese MusR. **Illustration credit:** Courtesy of the Newberry Library, Chicago, Ill.

[M. T. HYTREK]

CAVE, WILLIAM, Anglican scholar, b. Pickwell, Leicestershire, England, Dec. 30, 1637; d. Windsor, England, Aug. 4, 1713. Educated at Cambridge (1653–60), where he received his master's degree, he was vicar at Islington (1662–79), All Hallows the Great (1679–89), and Isleworth (1690–1713). In 1674 he published *Tabulae ecclesiasticae,* a catalogue of church authors in the tradition of Jerome's *De viris illustribus* and Bellarmine's *De scriptoribus ecclesiasticis.* Expanded into an ecclesiastical archive in 1685, Cave's *Tabulae* served as a basis for his monumental *Scriptorum ecclesiasticorum historia literaria* (1688–99), which dealt by epochs with the whole of church literature to Luther. Cave also published a series of historical monographs: *Primitive Christianity* (1672); the *Apostolici* (1677), covering the chief figures of the first 3 centuries; and the *Ecclesiastici* (1683), on the Fathers of the 4th century. In 1685 he published a tract on church government in which he attacked the Roman primacy. Although logical and erudite, he lacked a critical sense and was censured by continental Protestants as well as by Catholics for his attempt to identify the Anglican Church with the primitive Christian Church. All of Cave's works were placed on the Index of Forbidden Books in 1693.

Bibliography: J. OVERTON, DNB 3:1250–52. C. CONSTANTIN, DTC 2.2:2044–45.

[F. X. MURPHY]

CAVIEDES, JUAN DEL VALLE, Peruvian poet; b. Porcuna, Jaén, Andalusia, 1651(?); d. probably Lima, 1697(?). The birth date is pure conjecture. The first specific date for Caviedes is that of his marriage in Lima, March 15, 1671. When he was very young, he went to America, where his uncle was a member of the *audiencia* of Lima. Caviedes worked in the mines for most of his life; he was very poor and never had a patron for his poetry, contrary to the report of a fictional biography that appeared about the middle of the 19th century, which has no basis in fact. He had five children and apparently was never able to support them very well. He was seriously ill in the 1680s, and it was after 1683 that he wrote most of his poetry and certainly the satiric writing for which he is best known. About 180 poems are credited to him. Some were written to commemorate important events, particularly catastrophes such as the earthquake of 1687. Most circulated in manuscript form in two collections: *Poesías diversas,* or *Poesías varias y jocosas,* and *Diente del Parnaso,* almost all satires on the medical profession. His writing was widely known: Sor Juana Inés de la Cruz evidently requested copies of his poems, for his reply is extant though her letter is not. There is a tradition that he went insane a year or so before his death.

Bibliography: *Obras,* ed. R. VARGAS UGARTE (Lima 1947). G. L. KOLB, *Juan del Valle y Caviedes* (New London, Conn. 1959).

[J. HERRICK]

CAVO, ANDRÉS, Mexican historian; b. Guadalajara, Jan. 21, 1739; d. Rome sometime after 1794, although some biographers give 1800. He entered the Society of Jesus at the age of 20 and a few years later was sent to the missions in the northwest, where he performed excellent service as a catechist until the expulsion of the Jesuits (1767) compelled him to leave Mexico. Cavo went to Veracruz to take passage, and there he formed a close friendship with Father José Julián Parreño, a distinguished citizen of Havana, former rector of the College of San Ildefonso in Mexico City, and one of the highest authorities in the Province of Mexico. Both established their residence in Rome. Since expatriation became unbearable to both Cavo and Parreño, they decided to be secularized; therefore, their names do not appear in the catalogues made up at that time of the Mexican Jesuits resident in Italy. Cavo wrote *De vita Josephi Juliani Parreni, Havanensis* (Rome 1792), a tract written in good Latin that contains some details of the calamities suffered by the expelled Jesuits on their voyage to Rome, and *Historia civil y política de Méjico,* left in manuscript form and dedicated to the municipal government of Mexico City. The only evidence of the existence of the latter work was the brief mention of it by Beristaín in his *Biblioteca,* until Carlos María Bustamante found a copy in the library of the bishop of Tenagra and published it in Mexico in 1836, under the title *Los tres siglos de Méjico durante el gobierno español.* It covers the period from the conquest of Mexico by Cortés in 1521 to the end of the Viceroyalty of the Marquis of Cruillas, who preceded Croix, in 1766. It is written in an easy simple style, without pretension or presumption. Cavo appears to have been a person of a gentle and peaceful nature, sincerely pious, studious, modest, faithful, and constant in his friendships.

[M. DELA PAZ PANI CARRAL]

CAVOUR, CAMILLO BENSO DI

Italian statesman, leader in the **Risorgimento;* b. Turin, Aug. 10, 1810; d. there, June 6, 1861. Camillo, Count of Cavour, was the son of Michele, a marquis and Turin's police chief, and of Adele (de Sellon) Cavour, a devout convert from Calvinism. During his youth Cavour developed a rationalistic attitude toward religion, influenced by visits to his mother's family and perhaps by his travels in England and France. Cavour was educated for a military career but resigned his commission in 1831 and then occupied himself for several years in the successful management of his family's properties. The July Revolution of 1830 in France greatly influenced Cavour's political outlook and led him to hope that a constitutional monarchy could be established also in Piedmont. In 1847 he founded in Turin the newspaper *Il Risorgimento* to represent the moderate liberal party and wrote for it chiefly on economic and financial questions. He was elected to the legislature in 1848. In the cabinet of Massimo d'*Azeglio he served as minister of agriculture, industry, and commerce, and later as minister of finance. He broke with d'Azeglio in 1852 and traveled in France and England for several months. As premier of Piedmont (1852–59, 1860–61) Cavour distinguished himself for his financial and economic reforms and diplomatic maneuvers against Austria to promote the power of Piedmont and then to unite Italy politically.

Camillo Benso di Cavour.

Ecclesiastical Policies in Piedmont. Cavour was secular in mentality and believed that in Church-State conflicts the interests of the latter must prevail. In 1850 he joined the radical deputies in support of the Siccardi laws, which were contrary to the concordat of 1841 between the Holy See and Piedmont, and sought to abolish clerical immunities in civil courts, to suppress certain feast days of obligation (which were also civil holidays), to restrict the property rights of religious congregations, and to introduce civil marriage. As premier he defended the Rattazzi bill of 1855 to suppress all religious communities except those dedicated to preaching, teaching, or care of the sick. The bill proposed also to utilize the revenue derived from the sale of confiscated religious properties to increase the stipend for the lower clergy. Cavour claimed that religious orders might have been useful during the Middle Ages but had no utility in his day. As proof he contrasted the progress of England, France, and Prussia with the stagnation of Naples and Spain where religious were numerous. To defeat the Rattazzi bill, the bishops offered to contribute money to increase the stipend of the lower clergy. Cavour resigned as premier because of his cabinet's hesitancy, but he soon returned to office, and the Rattazzi bill was enacted. Cavour was excommunicated for his promotion of the legislation.

Italian Unification. As Cavour's ambitions widened, he sought to unify all Italy under *Victor Emmanuel II. To gain help against Austria he allied Piedmont with France. At Plombières, France, *Napoleon III and Cavour agreed to wage a joint military campaign in Lombardy against Austria. Cavour resigned as premier in 1859 when France withdrew from the war, but he continued, through the Italian National Society, to encourage the revolutionaries in the central duchies and the Romagna district of the *States of the Church to seek annexation to Piedmont. When Cavour returned to the premiership in 1860, he annexed Romagna and the duchies after plebiscites. The action against Romagna caused Cavour to be excommunicated anew. To prevent an advance on Rome by *Garibaldi, Cavour dispatched Piedmontese troops into the Marches and Umbria. After the papal forces were defeated at Castelfidardo, these papal lands were also annexed.

In 1861 the new Kingdom of *Italy was officially proclaimed, with Victor Emmanuel II as king, Cavour as premier, and Rome as capital. *Pius IX, however, still retained the government of Rome and the surrounding territories under the protection of a French garrison. Cavour sought to win this prize through diplomatic negotiation. His representatives, Diomede Pantaleoni and Carlo Passaglia, offered the Pope complete freedom of spiritual jurisdiction, the right to maintain diplomatic relations, possession of the Roman basilicas, an annual income, and protection. Pius IX refused to abdicate his temporal power, and Cavour's previous attitudes toward the Church and his extension of the Rattazzi laws to all the Italian states created suspicion concerning his future actions. Negotiations abruptly broke off. In June Cavour died, and the *Roman Question remained a major problem until 1929.

Mystery continues to surround Cavour's deathbed religious sentiments. It was stated officially that he received the last rites of the Church. Father Giacomo da Poirino was summoned from the local parish church shortly before Cavour's death. Later Pius IX questioned the priest, but the latter did not explain the details of his ministrations, nor did he reveal whether Cavour was conscious and went to confession, or merely received conditional absolution while unconscious.

Cavour never shared the extreme anticlericalism of the leftists and seemed often to be motivated by political expediency in his ecclesiastical policies. He was fond of justifying his actions by quoting the phrase, "a free Church in a free State"; but he interpreted this motto to justify unilateral despoliations of Church rights guaranteed by concordats. Cavour was the outstanding figure in the *Risorgimento.*

Bibliography: A. C. Jemolo, *Church and State in Italy, 1850–1950,* tr. D. Moore (Philadelphia 1960). D. Mack Smith, *Ca-*

vour and Garibaldi, 1860: A Study in Political Conflict (Cambridge, Eng. 1954); *Italy: A Modern History* (Ann Arbor 1959). E. PASSERIN D'ENTRÈVES, *L'ultima battaglia politica di Cavour: I problemi dell'unificazione italiana* (Turin 1956). R. AUBERT, *Le Pontificat de Pie IX* (Fliche-Martin 21; 2d ed. 1964). R. GREW, *A Sterner Plan for Italian Unity: The Italian National Society in the Risorgimento* (Princeton 1963). M. MAZZIOTTI, *Il conte di Cavour e il suo confessore* (Bologna 1915). P. PIRRI, EncCatt 3:1213–21. **Illustration credit:** Italian Information Center, New York.

[M. L. SHAY]

CAXTON, WILLIAM

Merchant, man of letters and first typographer of England; b. Weald of Kent?, *c.* 1422; d. Westminster, 1491. The evidence for his birthplace is sparse. He was apprenticed in 1438 to a London mercer who died in 1441. Caxton then went to Bruges, seat of the Burgundian Court and center of the European wool trade. There he flourished and became governor of the English Nation of Merchant Adventurers in the Low Countries in 1463. In 1470 he accepted a court appointment to Margaret, Duchess of Burgundy, sister of Edward IV, King of England; she employed Caxton also as a commercial agent. During these years of business he maintained his early interest in books and literature. Thus in 1468 he began a translation of what became the *Recuyell of the Historyes of Troye;* the French original of this chivalric romance was written by Raoul le Fevre, chaplain of Philip, Duke of Burgundy. Caxton, persuaded by the Duchess to complete the translation, did so while in Cologne from 1471.

Caxton presenting a copy of his book to Margaret of York; woodcut frontispiece in "Recuyell of the Historyes of Troye," printed in Bruges, 1475.

Caxton's own statement to this effect led historians to assume that the book was also printed in Cologne. As a corollary it was believed that Colard Mansion was the first printer at Bruges and that Caxton was his pupil. It has recently been convincingly argued by L. A. Sheppard, of the British Museum, that Caxton learned and practised the art in Cologne, not in Bruges; that Mansion was Caxton's pupil; and that the first Bruges press was set up by Caxton when he began printing the *Recuyell.* The output of Caxton's press in Bruges is known to comprise six works. It is possible that Caxton so mastered the art in Cologne as to print there a *Bartholomeus Anglicus,* as Wynkyn de Worde (Caxton's successor in London) says.

Toward the end of 1476, Caxton returned to England with a plan to establish a press to print works of general interest to English readers. He quickly found rich patrons. His first dated book *Dictes and Sayengis of the Philosophres* appeared on Nov. 8, 1477. It is a translation by the Earl of Rivers, who commissioned its printing. Among the 100-odd books from Caxton's press, 24 are translations by himself. He printed all the major works of English literature then available to him, including Chaucer's *Canterbury Tales* (*c.* 1478), Gower's *Confessio Amantis* (1483), and Malory's *Le Morte Darthur* (1485).

Caxton's numerous liturgical productions include the *Ordinale seu Pica Sarum* (1477); for its sales promotion he printed a handbill, famous as the first known advertisement. He also printed a *Psalterium* and a *Horae,* both in 1480. The volume of output of his press; the character of his chosen texts; and the extent of his personal authorship, conscientiousness of editorial and translation labors (from French, Flemish, and Latin), and supervision, were so considerable as to effect markedly the stabilization of a tongue in transition from the vernacular into a printed literary medium, and to give him credit as one of the makers of the English language.

Bibliography: W. CAXTON, *The Prologues and Epilogues of William Caxton,* ed. W. J. B. CROTCH (EEngTSoc 176; London 1928). The editor's introduction contains the fullest biographical account. W. BLADES, *The Life and Typography of William Caxton, England's First Printer,* 2 v. (London 1861–63), the basic work. S. DE RICCI, *A Census of Caxton* (Oxford 1909). E. G. DUFF, *William Caxton* (Chicago 1905); *Fifteenth Century English Books* (London 1917). N. S. AURNER, *Caxton: Mirrour of Fifteenth-Century Letters; A Study of Literature of the First English Press* (London 1926), best available study of his literary and linguistic influence. L. A. SHEPPARD, "A New Light on Caxton and Colard Mansion," *Signature* (NS 15; 1952) 28–39. **Illustration credit:** The Huntington Library, San Marino, Calif.

[S. MORISON]

CAYET, PIERRE VICTOR, theologian; b. Montrichard, France, 1525; d. Paris, either March 10 or July 22, 1610. He studied arts and law at Paris under P. Ramus and followed him into Calvinism. He left Paris for Geneva and devoted himself to the study of theology. After a tour of German universities he was named pastor of the Calvinist church at Montreuil-Bonnin near Poitiers. Having been created an official of the court of Henry of Navarre, Cayet followed that king to Paris, where he came into contact with Cardinal Du Perron. Accusations of practicing sorcery and magic caused him to lose favor with the Calvinists. On Nov. 9, 1595, he abjured Protestantism, returned to the religion of his birth, and, in a letter, told of the reasons for his return. This document was violently attacked by the Calvinists, and their provocations occasioned Cayet's vigorous defense of Catholicism in a fusillade of works published between 1596 and 1599. In 1598 he was named rector of the University of Paris, a post he never accepted, since he was not a doctor of theology. After his ordination in 1600, he continued to publish works of an apologetic nature. His *Chronologie septennaire* (Paris 1605) was placed on the Index for its denial of the authority of the pope over bishops. He defended this work, and at his death his religious loyalties were suspect.

Bibliography: E. Mangenot, DTC 2.2:2046–48. V. Zollini, EncCatt 3:1222–23. Hurter Nomencl³ 3:412–414.

[C. R. MEYER]

CEBU, ARCHDIOCESE OF (NOMINIS IESU OR CAEBUANUS), metropolitan see since 1934, in the Visayan Islands, central *Philippines. In 1963 it had 129 secular and 143 religious priests, 124 men in 13 religious houses, 207 women in 19 convents,

Juan B. Gorordo, first Filipino bishop of Cebu (1910–31).

and 1,310,000 Catholics in a population of 1,337,500; it is 1,880 square miles in area. Its 5 suffragan sees, which had 298 secular and 86 religious priests, 160 sisters, and 3,285,000 Catholics in a population of 3,528,000, were: Borongan (created in 1960), Calbayog (1910), Dumaguete (1955), Palo (1936), and Tagbilaran (1941); the Vicariate Apostolic of Palawan (1955), with 9 secular and 18 religious priests, 41 sisters, and 116,500 Catholics in a population of 163,000, also was suffragan to Cebu.

Ferdinand *Magellan set up a wooden cross in Cebu before he was slain on Mactan Island opposite Cebu's excellent port (1521). Miguel López de Legazpi and the Augustinian Andrés de *Urdaneta founded a settlement in Cebu (1565), which was the Spanish capital of the Philippines until removal to *Manila took place (1571). The city of Cebu (251,000 population), second in size and importance in the Philippines, is the capital of Cebu Island, which has the largest single copper mine (open pit) in East Asia and produces more than half the coal in the Philippines. In 1942 the Japanese almost completely destroyed Cebu in reprisal for guerrilla operations. The Catholic University of *San Carlos is one of several colleges and universities in the city.

The Diocese of Cebu (or of the Name of Jesus) was created as a suffragan of Manila (1595–1934). The first bishop was Pedro de Agurto. Augustinian and Jesuit (1595) missionaries devoted much of their labor to the defense of Visayans against Moslem Moros. The original diocese has been diminished by the detaching of other jurisdictions: *Jaro (1865), the Mariana and *Caroline Islands (1907), *Zamboanga and Calbayog (1910), and Tagbilaran (1941).

Bibliography: *Catholic Directory of the Philippines* (Manila), annual. AnnPont (1965) 99. D. Abella, "The Succession of Bishops of Cebu," *in Philippine Studies* 8 (1960) 535–543.

[D. ABELLA]

CECILIA, ST., virgin and martyr (feast, Nov. 22). Though she is one of the most celebrated Roman martyrs, there is no trace of a cult of Cecilia in early times. She is not mentioned by the *Chronographer of 354 or by Ambrose, Damasus, Jerome, or Prudentius; nor is she represented in any of the early Christian decorated "gold glasses" (*see* GLASS). A fragmentary inscription dated by G. B. de *Rossi between 379 and 464 refers to a church (*titulus*) named after her. On Nov. 22, 545, her feast was celebrated in the basilica of St. Cecilia in Trastevere. According to a legend of the 5th or 6th century, Cecilia was a young Christian of high rank betrothed to the noble Valerian, whom she converted to Christianity, and who was executed, together with his brother Tiburtius, by the Roman prefect, Turcius Almachius.

Cecilia, though ordered to be suffocated in a hot bath, escaped unharmed. After being struck three times on the neck with a sword, she lived for 3 days and asked Pope Urban to convert her house into a church. These events are connected with a persecution under either Marcus Aurelius or Diocletian. Cecilia was buried in a crypt next to that of the popes in the Catacomb of Calixtus. It is possible that a pious Christian woman of the old Caecilian family, but not a martyr, obtained this site for Cecilia's burial. In April 821 her body was removed from the crypt by Pope *Paschal I and placed under the altar of the basilica of St. Cecilia, though the Liber pontificalis states that the body was found in the Catacomb of Praetextatus. In 1599 this tomb was reopened, and Maderna carved the statue of the saint that is now seen beneath the altar. From the time of the Renaissance, St. Cecilia is usually portrayed with a small organ or viola.

Bibliography: V. L. Kennedy, *The Saints of the Canon of the Mass* (Rome 1938). E. Josi, BiblSanct 3:1226–29. C. Cecchelli, EncCatt 3:1226–29. **Illustration credit:** R. V. Schoder, SJ.

[M. J. COSTELLOE]

Ninth-century mosaic, Church of S. Cecilia in Trastevere, Rome. Depicted are Pope Paschal I; SS. Agatha and Paul; Christ; SS. Peter, Valerian, and Cecilia.

CECILIA OF THE NATIVITY (CECILIA MORILLAS), Discalced Carmelite, spiritual writer, and poet; b. Valladolid, Spain, 1570; d. Valladolid, April 7, 1646. Under the personal teaching of her mother, she learned letters and rhetoric, philosophy, Sacred Scripture, and painting. When she was 19 years old, she took the Discalced Carmelite habit in her native city (1589), making her profession the following year. After being novice mistress at Valladolid, she was sent by her superiors to the newly founded convent of Calahorra (Logroño). In the following year the community elected her prioress (Jan. 29, 1605), and they reelected her in 1608. She was instrumental in bringing the Discalced Carmelite friars to the city. After completing her term of office she returned to her original convent of Valladolid in 1612. Her chief writings, which remained unpublished until the 20th century, are *Transformación del Alma en Dios* and *Tratado del Alma en Dios.*

Bibliography: EMETRIO DE JESÚS MARIA, "Vida y escritos poéticos de la Madre Cecilia del Nacimiento, 1570–1646," *El Monte Carmelo* 47 (1946) 107–304. E. A. PEERS, *Studies of the Spanish Mystics,* 3 v. (London 1960). SILVERIO DE S. TERESA, *Historia del Carmen Descalzo en España, Portugal y América,* 15 v. (Burgos 1935–).

[O. RODRIGUEZ]

CECILIA ROMANA, BL., Dominican nun; b. Rome, *c.* 1200; d. Bologna, 1290 (feast, June 9). Cecilia began her religious life in the monastery of S. Maria in Tempulo, Rome. In 1221 she moved with her community to S. Sisto, a reformed monastery founded in that year by St. *Dominic, from whom the group received the Dominican habit and in whose hands they renewed their vows. In 1225 Cecilia and three other S. Sisto nuns were sent to Bologna to the monastery of S. Agnese, newly founded by (Bl.) *Jordan of Saxony and (Bl.) Diana d'Andalo, in order to establish the Dominican life there. Cecilia was prioress of S. Agnese in 1237. Her reminiscences of Dominic, embodying much information about the foundation of S. Sisto, and including the only eyewitness description of Dominic's features, were preserved in writing by another nun *c.* 1280.

Bibliography: A. M. WALZ, ed., "Die *Miracula Beati Dominici* der Schwester Cäcilia," in *Miscellanea Pio Paschini, Studi di storia ecclesiastica,* 2 v. (Rome 1948–49) 1:293–326. H. M. CORMIER, *La Bienheureuse Diane d'Andalò et les bienheureuses Cécile et Aimée* (Rome 1892). H. WILMS, *Geschichte der deutschen Dominikanerinnen* (Dülmen 1920) 25–28. G. GIERATHS, LexThK² 2:868.

[J. A. DOSHNER]

CEDD (CEDDA), ST., Northumbrian monk, missionary bishop; d. Oct. 26, 664 (feast, Oct. 26; among the English *Benedictines, March 2). He was the brother of St. *Chad and a disciple of *Aidan of Lindisfarne. He was sent from Northumbria to assist King Peada of Mercia in the evangelization of his kingdom (653). He was then sent to help the recently converted King Sigebert of Essex to Christianize his people and was consecrated bishop of the East Saxons (654) by *Finan of Lindisfarne. He founded two monasteries among the East Saxons, one at Bradwell-on-Sea, where a contemporary church still survives and the other at Tilbury. He founded also a monastery at Lastingham, Yorkshire (658). *Bede describes the elaborate ritual, the fasting and prayers that Cedd and Chad used in consecrating this site. In 664 Cedd attended the Council of *Whitby to act as interpreter for the Irish party though he accepted the council's "Roman" decision. Shortly afterward he died of plague and was buried in the churchyard at Lastingham; his remains were later translated to the stone church there. Bede is the main authority for his life.

Bibliography: T. F. TOUT, DNB 3:1322–23. BEDE, *Eccl. Hist.* 3.21–26; 4.3.

[B. COLGRAVE]

CEDRON (KIDRON), 3-mile-long valley that begins about a mile north of ancient Jerusalem, cuts a 100-foot gorge between the eastern wall of the city and the *Mount of Olives, and joins the Valley of Ben-Hinnom (*see* GEHENNA) below the southeastern corner of the city, to form the modern Wâdī en-Nār that descends southeastward to the Dead Sea. The Cedron (Heb. *qidrôn,* black, turbid), called a *naḥal* in Hebrew (2 Sm 15.23; 3 Kgs 15.13) and *χείμαρρος* in Greek (Jn 18.1), both words equivalent to Arabic *wâdī,* carries water only during and shortly after heavy rains. It is the natural eastern border of Jerusalem, and at times it is referred to simply as *hannaḥal,* "the wadi" (2 Chr 33.14; Neh 2.15). The idolatrous altars, images, and *aseras (asherahs) were burned in the Cedron by the reforming Kings Asa (3 Kgs 15.13), Ezechia (2 Chr 29.16; 30.14), and Josia (4 Kgs 23.4, 6, 12). David, in his eastward flight from Jerusalem at the time of Absalom's revolt, crossed over the Cedron (2 Sm 15.23). In the NT the Cedron is mentioned only once—when Jesus, after the Last Supper, crossed it to enter the Garden of *Gethsemani (Jn 18.1).

Bibliography: EncDictBibl 333. A. LEGENDRE, DB 2.1:380–386.

[W. F. CUMMINGS]

CEFALÙ, CATHEDRAL OF, an edifice that combines a *Romanesque exterior with the oldest Byzantine mosaics in Sicily. The cathedral was founded in 1131 as a political gesture against *Innocent II. The Norman King Roger II originally intended it as his sepulcher but soon lost interest. Although sporadically continued by Roger's son, the cathedral was not finally consecrated until 1267. Baroque-type decorations contrast with intersecting arcades on the apse's exterior and with the Saracenic arches of the nave and its classicizing capitals. Heavy buttresses support the rib vaults of the choir, but the nave and north transept have only an open woodwork roof.

Despite this diversity the processional axis is undisturbed and culminates magnificently in the Pantocrator. The apse mosaics suggest the adaptation to basilican form of middle Byzantine decoration. They are justly celebrated as Greek works on Sicilian soil, the model for other 12th-century schemes at the Palatine Chapel (Palermo) and *Monreale. Nevertheless it is obvious that the formal Byzantine program is here radically redistributed. The conch (apse) figure is displaced from its traditional position in the cupola. The Virgin, customarily between the Apostles, here stands between the Archangels and above the Evangelists. Cherubim and Seraphim in the choir continue the hierarchy, which ends with the Prophets, warrior saints, and deacons on the side walls.

Notwithstanding the misfortune of thorough 19th-century restorations, the total effect is of a visual litany

The cathedral at Cefalù, 12th-century mosaic of Christ Pantocrator in the apse.

for the defense of King and Church. Roger's theme was Byzantine but set, not altogether incongruously in the last analysis, within the framework of a Western basilica.

See also PALERMO, ARCHDIOCESE OF.

Bibliography: O. DEMUS, *The Mosaics of Norman Sicily* (London 1950). F. DI PIETRO, *I musaici siciliani dell'età normanna* (Palermo 1946). H. M. SCHWARZ, "Die Baukunst Kalabriens und Siziliens im Zeitalter der Normannen," *Römisches Jahrbuch für Kunstgeschichte* 6 (1946) 1–112. G. SAMONÀ, *Il duomo di Cefalù* (*I Monumenti italiani* fasc. 16; Rome 1939). V. LASAREFF, "The Mosaics of Cefalù," ArtBul 17 (1935) 184–232. **Illustration credit:** Alinari-Art Reference Bureau.

[A. CUTLER]

CEILLIER, REMI, patristic scholar, b. Bar-le-Duc, France, May 14, 1688; d. Flavigny, France, May 26, 1761. He entered the Benedictine monastery of Moyen-Moutier in the Vosges in 1704, where he was ordained in 1710 and taught theology until 1716. In 1718 he became prior of St. Jacques de Neufchâteau and in 1733 of Flavigny-sur-Moselle, where he is buried. His first work was the *Apologie de la morale des Pères* (1718), a defense of the moral doctrine of the Fathers from Athenagoras to Augustine against the strictures of Jean Barbeyrac of Lausanne. The *Nouvelle bibliothèque des auteurs ecclésiastiques,* published by Louis Dupin in 1686, inspired Ceillier to begin a collection of sacred writers. In 1729 the first volume of his annotated *Histoire générale des auteurs sacrés et ecclésiastiques* appeared. Aided by his confreres he completed 23 volumes in the next 34 years. The series begins with the Old Testament and extends to the middle of the 13th century. Supplied with a 2-volume index in 1782, the work was re-edited by Armand Caillau, and republished in 17 volumes by L. M. Bauzon (1858–69). Although suspected of Jansenistic tendencies, even in passages quoting or explaining the Fathers on grace and free will, Ceillier was highly regarded by Benedict XIV.

Bibliography: A. BEUGNET, *Étude biographique et critique sur Dom Remi Ceillier* (Mémoires de la Société des Lettres, Sciences et Arts de Bar-le-Duc 2.10; Bar-le-Duc 1891); DTC 2.2:2049–51. M. JUGIE, EncCatt 3:1251.

[F. X. MURPHY]

CELEBRATIONS IN CATECHETICS

A catechetical, or paraliturgical, celebration is a pedagogical and active technique used for the Biblical and liturgical initiation of children and adult catechumens and for deepening Biblical and liturgical knowledge and experience of the Christian community. It consists in a solemn proclamation of the word of God within an ecclesial milieu in a ceremony similar to the liturgy of the word of the Mass. It aims at evoking a Biblical event in the Old or New Testament in order that its inherent mystery may be lived again by the participants. Through active participation in the celebration and effective contemplation of the word of God, conversion of the heart and lifelong commitment are aroused and facilitated both for the individual in particular and for the community as a whole (Vatican Council II, *Constitution on the Sacred Liturgy,* 7; 24; 31.1; 35.4; 56).

It is important that the place of the catechetical celebration should allow for an atmosphere appropriate to a liturgical assembly. Therefore, the most suitable place is a church or chapel. However, a classroom may also be adapted to this purpose by the introduction of a few objects that will create a liturgical atmosphere (pulpit or table where the Bible, candlesticks, crucifix, etc., can be placed). Certain persons are designated for particular functions. The presence of the celebrant is almost indispensable, for he presides over the ceremony, gives the homily, and directs the prayer. The reader should be chosen from among the children or adults present and should wear a liturgical garment in order to proclaim God's word with becoming dignity. The leader is usually the catechist, who directs the ceremony by means of precise and discreet orders that introduce the readings, songs, prayers, and liturgical actions. He also intones and directs the singing. Other minor liturgical functions may be performed by additional children or adults suitably vested. The most important participant of the celebration is the community, which takes part by listening, answering, and adhering to the mystery proclaimed and celebrated throughout the ceremony.

A catechetical celebration is normally made up of the following elements: (1) the entrance procession, hymn, or Psalm; (2) the enthronement of the Bible; (3) orientation of the theme; (4) solemn proclamation of the word of God; (5) meditation Psalm or acclamation to the word of God; (6) a short homily; (7) the prayer; (8) additional liturgical actions that are possible when the celebration is centered on a specific liturgical sign or Sacrament, such as the paschal candle, baptismal font, altar, Bible; (9) recessional hymn or Psalm.

Bibliography: F. COUDREAU, "Celebration in Catechism and Catechesis" in *Readings in European Catechetics,* ed. G. DEL-

CUVE and A. GODIN (Brussels 1962) 139–151. F. DERKENNE, *La Vie et la joie au catéchisme* (Lyons 1943). C. BRUSSELMANS, "The Relationship between Teaching and Celebrating," ProcLitWk 25 (St. Louis 1964) 210–220. M. JOHNICE and M. ELIZABETH, *The Lord Jesus* (Bible, Life, and Worship Series 1; Boston 1964) 5; *Come Lord Jesus* (*ibid.* 2; 1965) 6. J. M. RENFRO, *Teacher's Guide* (Going to God our Father; New York 1965) 5. M. V. PFEIFFER, *Teacher's Guide* (Our Life with God 1; New York 1965).

[C. BRUSSELMANS]

CELEBRET, the popular name for the document called a "commendatory letter," obtaining for a priest admission to the celebration of Mass in a church other than the one to which he is attached. By means of these letters the competent superior bears witness to the bearer's legitimate ordination to the priesthood, his good moral standing in his own diocese or religious group, his freedom from any ecclesiastical penalty that excludes the celebration of Mass, his freedom from any irregularity, and his consequent commendable status in general. Since the beginning of the Church, clerics traveling for one purpose or another were furnished with such introductory letters. These ensured their hospitable reception in other places and enabled them to exercise their respective orders. For a priest this involved, as time progressed, the offering of Mass. Various names have been used for these documents: "letters," "canonical letters," and "testimonial letters"; but the most commonly used term was "commendatory letters." The term celebret, a Latin word meaning "let him celebrate," has been commonly used since the latter part of the 19th century. The exact origin of this term is not determinable. It may have been taken from the primary purpose of commendatory letters, namely, the admission of the bearer to the celebration of Mass. The earliest legislation concerning commendatory letters appeared in the 4th century, implying that they were used to some extent before that time. The present Church law concerning the celebret is found in CIC c.804.

Bibliography: É. JOMBART, DDC 3:126–131. G. SCHORR, *The Law of the Celebret* (CUA CLS 332; Washington 1952).

[G. F. SCHORR]

CELESTINE I, POPE, ST.

Pontificate, Sept. 10, 422, to July 27, 432 (feast, April 6). Celestine, from the Roman campagna, was the son of Priscus and had been archdeacon of the Roman Church. What is known of his reign is recorded in his extant correspondence and relates mainly to the Nestorian controversy. Here his vigorous assertion of the authority of his see was in marked contrast to the passivity of Pope *Sylvester I when confronted by the Arian heresy a century earlier.

Nestorianism. Celestine had approved the choice of *Nestorius as bishop of Constantinople (428), but he soon manifested misgivings as a result of Nestorius's friendly reception of the Pelagian *Julian of Eclanum, and his letters and sermons in which he criticized the term *Theotokos, or Mother of God, a doctrine traditional in Rome. Informed of the controversy brewing in Constantinople, Celestine commissioned *Cyril of Alexandria to investigate the orthodoxy of Nestorius. In August 430, on the basis of Cyril's findings and evidence gathered by the deacon Leo, Nestorius was solemnly condemned for his "innovations" by a Roman synod over which the Pope presided. Nestorius was to be informed that he must retract his errors within 10 days, and Cyril was entrusted with the responsibility of attending to the execution of the sentence.

The traditional rivalry between Alexandria and Constantinople made Cyril eager to take on this responsibility; and in an Egyptian synod in November he drew up a list of 12 anathemas by which the doctrine of Nestorius was to be tested. This was a gratuitous gesture, unauthorized by Celestine and made worse because the propositions used the terminology of the Alexandrian school, which was not acceptable to the Antiochenes.

Before Cyril's summons had expired, the Byzantine Emperor Theodosius II convoked an ecumenical council to meet at *Ephesus in 431. As legates the Pope sent Bishops Arcadius and Projectus and the priest Philip, instructing them "to execute what has already been decided by us" and to work closely with Cyril. The Emperor had intended *John of Antioch to preside. Unfortunately, both John and the legates were delayed in arriving.

Council of Ephesus. Armed with authority from Celestine, Cyril opened the Council and proceeded to condemn Nestorius, relying on the support of the more than 50 Egyptian bishops who accompanied him, together with Memnon of Ephesus and Juvenal of Jerusalem (June 22, 431).

In spite of these irregularities, when the legates arrived (July 10), they approved what had been done by Cyril and confirmed the deposition of Nestorius. It was on this occasion that the legate Philip uttered his famous words: "There is no doubt, and in fact it has been known in all ages, that the holy and most blessed Peter, prince and head of the Apostles, pillar of the faith and foundation of the Catholic Church, received the keys of the kingdom from our Lord Jesus Christ, the Savior and Redeemer of the human race, and that to him was given the power of loosing and binding sins: who, even to this time and for ever, lives and judges in his successors." There is no recorded objection to this assertion of the Roman primacy.

The Council ended with an exchange of excommunications between Cyril and John of Antioch, since John had refused to join the assembly dominated by the Egyptian "Pharaoh." On being informed of this impasse, Theodosius II ordered the arrest of Nestorius and Cyril. Nestorius was banished to Antioch and later to Egypt; but Cyril was able, after considerable intrigue and the expenditure of bribes, to return eventually to his See of Alexandria.

Pope Celestine hailed the outcome of the council, though the acts were not submitted to him for approval. However, he took exception to the excommunication of John of Antioch and sent an emissary to win John's acceptance of the deposition of Nestorius, thus healing the breach between *Antioch and *Alexandria. Finally, he approved the election of Maximian, well-known in Rome, as the Bishop of Constantinople in place of Nestorius.

African Church. Celestine repeated the mistake of Pope *Zosimus and lent too ready an ear to the complaints of the African priest Apiarius, who again appealed to Rome when he was convicted of misdeeds at Tabraca. Apiarius was sent back to Africa with the same legate, Faustinus, who had irritated the African bishops earlier. After 3 days of hearings at a plenary council in Carthage, Apiarius suddenly confessed all his misdeeds, and the legate was obliged to disavow him.

Meanwhile, it had been determined that the canons to which Celestine's predecessor, Zosimus, had appealed in dealing with African affairs were not those of Nicaea but of the Council of *Sardica, which were unknown and hence not recognized in Africa. In their dignified but forthright reply to Celestine, the bishops took the occasion to read the Pope a lecture on the autonomous rights of the African Church. They criticized the Pope for lending an ear to complainers and for receiving into communion those who had been excommunicated by their own bishops, a practice forbidden by the Council of *Nicaea I, which reserved such appeals to provincial councils (c.5), "because this right has not been taken away from the African church by any definition of the fathers." They further asked that the Pope should send them no more legates *a latere,* "since we have not found this to be ordered in any synod of the fathers." They expressed the hope that so far as "our brother Faustinus" was concerned, "Africa would not have to suffer any more from him."

Another case of an appeal from Africa was somewhat similar but concerned a bishop, Anthony of Fussala, whom (St.) *Augustine had ill-advisedly raised to the episcopate and then had to remove when he was convicted of shearing his sheep rather than looking after their souls. Through weakness on the part of the primate of Numidia, Anthony was allowed to refer his case to Pope *Boniface I. Without hearing his accusers, Celestine listened to the appeal, absolved him "if he has truthfully told us the facts," and sent him back to his see, to the distress of Augustine, who threatened to resign if Anthony were restored to Fussala.

Augustine and Pelagianism. Celestine had great respect for Augustine, however, and sent *Prosper of Aquitaine a letter commending the bishop of Hippo's orthodoxy after his death (430). Prosper was the champion of Augustinian theology against *Pelagianism in Gaul and Britain, where the heresy had gained a foothold in the mitigated form of Semi-Pelagianism.

Influenced by the deacon Palladius, Celestine sent a mission, headed by Germain of Auxerre and Lupus of Troyes, to deal with Pelagianism in Britain. Palladius himself was sent to Ireland and began the conversion of that island (431), a work carried on by St. *Patrick.

The so-called Chapters of Celestine, summarizing the decisions of the Apostolic See in the matter of grace, that are found in the MSS as an annex to Celestine's letter to the bishops of Gaul were not written by the Pope; they were probably compiled by Prosper of Aquitaine a few years after Celestine's death.

Celestine repaired the church of S. Maria in Trastevere, damaged by fire when the city was sacked by Alaric many years before, and the priest Peter began the construction of S. *Sabina on the Aventine. Celestine was buried in the basilica of Sylvester in the cemetery of Priscilla on the Via Salaria. He is not commemorated in the **Martyrology of St. Jerome;* his feast in the *Synaxarium Constantinopolitanum* is kept on April 8.

Bibliography: PL 50:417–553; PL Suppl. 3:18–21, editions. Dekkers CPL 1650–54. Duchesne LP 1:230–231; 3:84–85. Caspar 1:381–416, 609. G. BARDY, Fliche-Martin 4:256–258; DHGE 12:56–58. H. LECLERCQ, DACL 13.1:1203–04. I. DANIELE, EncCatt 3:1255–56. R. U. MONTINI, *Le tombe dei Papi* (Rome 1957) 99–100. R. VIELLIARD, *Recherches sur les origines de la Rome chrétienne* (Mâcon 1941; repr. Rome 1959) 87–88. T. G. JALLAND, *The Church and the Papacy* (SPCK; 1944) 295–300.

[J. CHAPIN]

Pope Celestine III and Henry VI, miniature in a 12th-century manuscript of the verse chronicle of Petrus de Ebulo in the Municipal Library at Bern, Switzerland (Cod. 120, fol. 105r). In the first register Henry rides into Rome; in the second he is received by the Pope; the third shows the anointing of the Emperor and the transmittal of the sword; the last register shows the transmittal of the scepter, the ring, and the miter.

CELESTINE II, POPE, Sept. 26, 1143, to March 8, 1144; b. Guido de Castellis, presumably at Macerata in the March of Ancona. An admirer and former student of *Abelard and a learned scholar himself, he was also a friend of *Peter the Venerable of Cluny. Under *Callistus II, he was brought to Rome, and he was named cardinal deacon in 1127 and cardinal priest in 1134. As legate and vigorous supporter of *Innocent II during the schism with Anacletus (*see* PIERLEONI), he was present with *Bernard of Clairvaux in his championship of the Pope's claims before *Roger II of Sicily. His election without controversy 2 days after the death of Innocent II was widely acclaimed. Celestine, already an old man, was destined to govern the Church only 6 months. As cardinal he had opposed Innocent's concessions to Roger of Sicily made in the Treaty of Mignano (1139), but was apparently seeking new negotiations at the time of his death. Following

*Louis VII's abandonment of opposition to the incumbency of Pierre de la Châtre in the See of *Bourges, he removed the interdict placed by his predecessor on certain French lands because of Louis VII's attempt to depose the archbishop of Bourges.

Bibliography: PL 179:761–820. *Pontificum romanorum . . . vitae,* ed. J. M. WATTERICH, 2 v. (Leipzig 1862) 2:276–278. Duchesne LP 2:385, 449. Jaffé L 2:1–7. Mann 9:102–112. P. BREZZI, *Roma e l'Impero medioevale 774–1252* (Bologna 1947). Seppelt v.3.

[M. W. BALDWIN]

CELESTINE III, POPE, March 30?, 1191, to Jan. 8, 1198; b. Giacinto Bobo, Rome, *c.* 1106. Giacinto, of noble Roman ancestry, served the papal court as cardinal deacon for 47 years (1144–91). He had been a student of *Abelard at Paris and had defended his master unsuccessfully at the Council of Sens (1140). His diplomatic skill proved useful in two legations to Spain (1154–56 and 1172–74) and one to the Emperor (1158) and in numerous missions in the service of the exiled *Alexander III. At his election to the papacy, Celestine was 85 years of age; his vigor and independence were gone. *Henry VI and the Romans both threatened opposition; Celestine purchased peace by crowning Henry emperor and by allowing the Romans to destroy their archrival, Tusculum. Henry's invasions of Sicily caught Rome in a vise that threatened the independence of the papacy; Celestine merely broke off relations with the imperial court. Henry also escaped the consequence of the murder of the bishop of Liège and the imprisonment of *Richard I of England, who as a returning crusader was under the protection of the pope. In his relations with the other countries of Europe, Celestine usually displayed the same temporizing attitude. In 1197 Celestine, then gravely ill, proposed that the cardinals accept his designate, John of S. Prisca, as his successor; he even offered to resign if they would consent to this revolutionary step. The cardinals refused, and the Pope died shortly afterward.

Bibliography: Jaffé L 2:577–644. PL. 206:863–1280. R. MOLS, DHGE 12:62–77. Mann 10:383–441. Haller 3:273–299. L. SPÄTLING, EncCatt 3:1256–58. P. ZERBI, LexThK² 2:1254–55. **Illustration credit:** Leonard Von Matt.

[J. R. SOMMERFELDT]

CELESTINE IV, POPE, Oct. 25, 1241, to Nov. 10, 1241; b. Goffredo Castiglioni. A Milanese, he was the nephew of *Urban III. For a time archpriest and chancellor of Milan, he entered the *Cistercians of *Hautecombe in 1187. In 1227 he became cardinal priest of S. Marco; in 1239, cardinal bishop of Sabina. When *Gregory IX died (August 1241), the Roman Senator Matteo Rosso *Orsini, in order to forestall *Frederick II's influence and secure a quick papal election, at once enclosed in the Septizonium, a run-down palace, the 10 cardinals then in Rome, including, however, John *Colonna, Frederick's ally. On Oct. 25, 1241, this divided "first *conclave" finally elected Colonna's candidate, the aged, infirm Goffredo, as Celestine IV. He died within the month, possibly before he was crowned.

Bibliography: Potthast Reg 1:940–941. Mann 13:440–450. K. WENCK, "Das erste Konklave der Papstgeschichte, Rom, August bis Oktober 1241," QuellForschItalArchBibl 18 (1926) 101–170. E. KANTOROWICZ, *Frederick the Second, 1194–1250,* tr. E. O. LORIMER (New York 1957). R. MOLS, DHGE 12:77–79. Seppelt 3:449–451, 616. G. SCHWAIGER, LexThK² 2:1255.

[W. H. PRINCIPE]

CELESTINE V, POPE, ST., July 5 to Dec. 13, 1294; b. Peter of Morrone, Isernia, 1215; d. Castello di Fumone, May 19, 1296 (feast, May 19). He joined the Benedictines at Faifoli (Benevento), but inclining to a life of solitude, he lived as a hermit on Monte Palleno, Monte Morrone, and Monte Maiella, where he influenced the founding of the *Celestines. In the conclave, following the death of *Nicholas IV (April 4, 1292) the rivalry between the *Orsini and *Colonna made the election of a successor immediately impossible. After more than 2 years, influenced by Charles II of *Anjou, the cardinals elected the unaffected Peter of Morrone. He was consecrated Aug. 27, 1294, and crowned 2 days later.

Celestine's reign was marked by an unfortunate subservience to Charles II and by administrative incompetence. He appointed seven French and five Italian cardinals, all suggested by Charles. The son of Charles, Louis of Toulouse, he appointed Archbishop of Lyons. The Pope's naïveté was reflected in the multiplicity of contradictory and arbitrary favors he dispensed. The disorder from these concessions was such that *Boniface VIII, possibly at the request of Celestine himself, later revoked all privileges granted by him and ordered all bulls given by Celestine to be sent to Rome for reexamination.

Realizing his incompetence, Celestine issued a constitution (December 10) declaring a pope's right to resign, and on December 13 freely resigned. In the succeeding conclave Boniface VIII was elected. His contemporaries openly discussed the validity and propriety of Celestine's resignation. Treatises in favor of its validity were writ-

Celestine V dictating his life to Cardinal Stefaneschi (MS Vat. lat. 4932, fol. 1ʳ, 14th century).

ten by *Peter John Olivi, *Godfrey of Fontaines, *Peter of Auvergne, and *Giles of Rome. The principal opposition to the resignation was urged by the two Colonna cardinals who received confirmation of their opinions from the University of Paris. In the literary area, *Petrarch had the highest admiration for the Pope, whereas there are two lines in *Dante (Inferno 3:59–60) that have been interpreted as placing Celestine in hell.

Fearing that the guileless Celestine might become the center of schismatic intrigue, Boniface decided to keep him in custody in the castle of Monte Fumone. It was commonly agreed by contemporary historians that Celestine was treated with consideration. He was canonized by *Clement V, May 5, 1313.

Bibliography: ActSS May 4:418–537. G. CELIDONIO, *Vita di s. Pietro del Morrone* (Sulmona 1896). J. LECLERCQ, "La Renonciation de Célestin V et l'opinion théologique en France du vivant de Boniface VIII," RevHistÉglFranc 25 (1939) 183–192. Mann v.17. R. MOLS, DHGE 12:79–101. F. X. SEPPELT, ed., *Monumenta coelestiniana* (Quellen und forschungen aus dem gebiete der geschichte 19; Paderborn 1921). L. OLIGER, EncCatt 3:1258–61. Haller 5:91–97. A. DIECKMANN, LexThK² 2:1255–56. **Illustration credit:** Biblioteca Apostolica Vaticana.

[J. J. SMITH]

CELESTINES, a branch of the *Benedictines, called also Hermits of St. Damian or Hermits of Morrone. They were founded by the hermit Peter of Morrone, later Pope *Celestine V. Peter became a Benedictine monk at Faifoli (Benevento diocese) in 1235 and spent the next years in seclusion on Monte Morrone. His asceticism attracted several companions; and though originally the group followed no set religious practice after their approval by Urban IV in 1264, they adopted the *Benedictine Rule. The Hermits, who were noted for the severity of their way of life (e.g., perpetual abstinence), were approved again by Gregory X in 1274 and by Peter, once he became pope. From 1240 to 1243 Peter and his companions were temporarily at Monte Maiella, but after a short period they returned to their original site. All Celestine priories were subject to visitation by the abbot of the monastery of the Holy Ghost on Monte Morrone at Sulmona, Italy. The abbot general was elected for a 3-year term by the annual general chapter. As pope, Peter ordered that lay brothers be admitted into the congregation. The Celestines, who numbered 150 monasteries on the Continent at their height in the early 15th century, weathered the Reformation and the Wars of Religion, but became extinct in the late 18th century because of a decline in membership and a general hostility on the part of society toward monasticism. The choir dress was black, and the working habit was a white tunic with black scapular and hood. The lay brothers wore a brown habit. The symbol of the order was a cross entwined with the letter "S" sewn on the scapular.

The name Celestines was given also to some of the radical Franciscan *Spirituals. This group derived their name from the fact that Celestine V placed them under his special protection, but they were distinct from the Benedictine Celestines. In 1294 Pietro da Macerata and several companions approached the Pope and asked permission to live as monks under the rule of St. Francis, but directly under papal authority rather than under the superior of the Franciscans. This new group was called the Poor Hermits of the Lord Celestine and, after papal jurisdiction, were subject to their leader, Macerata, who changed his name to Liberato. Their official protector was Cardinal Nicholas Orsini, and their houses were obtained from the Benedictine Celestines. When Celestine resigned in 1294, his successor, Boniface VIII, revoked the privileges of these Franciscan Celestines. His action caused several of them to move to the island of Trixoma in the Gulf of Corinth and later to Thessaly. In 1303 they returned to Rome in an unsuccessful attempt to have their rights restored. The remaining members gathered at Narbonne (the Franciscans of Narbonne) in 1308 to live a strict, cloistered life.

Bibliography: J. HOLLNSTEINER, "Die Autobiographie Cöleston V," RömQuartalsch 31 (1923) 29–40. Heimbucher 1:212–214. L. OLIGER, EncCatt 3:1254–55. P. SCHMITZ, DHGE 12:102–104. For additional bibliography, *see* CELESTINE V.

[C. L. HOHL, JR.]

CELIBACY, CANON LAW OF

Celibacy is the canonical state of abstinence from marriage freely undertaken for the purpose of dedicating one's life totally to God's service in the clerical state. The Church has always considered supernaturally motivated celibacy an efficacious incentive to practical charity toward all men, especially for shepherds of souls, as the unanimous tradition of both the Latin and the Oriental Churches testify (ClerSanc c.68). The legislation of the Church in regard to celibacy has traditionally centered on two questions: the marriage of clerics after ordination to sacred orders and the reception of sacred orders by married men. Furthermore, the approach of the Latin Church to these questions differs considerably from that of the Oriental Churches.

Latin Church. In the ancient Church married men were accepted into the clergy as long as they were married only once (I Tm 3.2; Ti 1.7). But many of the early clergy practiced celibacy by choice, after the example of Christ and most of the Apostles. By the 4th century the unwritten law of custom prohibited married clerics in major orders the use of their marital rights and excluded unmarried clerics from marrying after their ordination to sacred orders. This was first written into law by the Council of Elvira (306), which forbade bishops, priests, deacons, and other ministers of the altar to have wives. The Council of Carthage (419) explicitly included subdeacons. Other local councils followed suit, some of them even imposing a vow of chastity in the ceremony of sacred ordination to effectuate the observance of continence.

But these early statutes were not universal, nor did they clearly declare null the marriages of major clerics who defied these prohibitions. The First Lateran Council (1123) extended the obligation of celibacy to all major clerics of the Latin Church. Local councils of the early 12th century seem already to have assumed marriages of clerics in sacred orders to be null: such unions, they held, were not marriage but fornication. The Second Lateran Council (1139) seems to have enacted the first written law making sacred orders a diriment impediment to marriage for the universal Church. This legislation was endorsed by the Council of Trent's dogmatic decree in 1563 (sess. 24, *De Sacr. Matr.* c.9) against Martin Luther and the reformers who opted for a married clergy and against some German princes who hoped to effect religious peace by abrogation of the rule of celibacy. In 1920 Benedict

XV, condemning a Bohemian association that agitated for abolition of clerical celibacy, declared that the Church would never abrogate or mitigate the law of priestly celibacy.

Fundamental Obligation. Clerics, once ordained to the subdiaconate, are excluded from marriage and are obliged to observe chastity to the extent that any sin of lust on their part is, besides a violation of the virtue of chastity, also a sin of sacrilege, involving as it does a violation of the virtue of religion (CIC c.132.1). Thus the celibacy of major clerics involves more than a negative legal obligation to refrain from marriage. It entails also a positive obligation to a life of perfect perpetual chastity, which forbids as sacrilegious not only exterior acts but, in common interpretation, even merely interior sins against chastity. Celibacy to this degree is more exactly designated celibate chastity.

There is some dispute as to the source of this obligation. The more commonly held opinion, the vow theory, is that the candidate for subdiaconate makes implicitly and tacitly a public solemn vow of perpetual chastity in his reception of this first major order. The legal obligation of celibacy is thus implemented by the personal bond of the vow of perfect chastity, which is a positive aid to the cleric's total devotion to God; and sins against this vow, even internal sins, have the double species of lustful and sacrilegious guilt. The current law does not mention this vow, and there is no explicit formulation of it in the ordination ceremony, because time-honored custom in the Church has considered this vow to be implied in the total consecration of the major cleric to God. A second opinion, the law theory, finds the source of the obligation exclusively in the Church's law: the major cleric is bound to a life of unmarried chastity not by virtue of a vow implicit in his ordination but solely because the Church's law imposes this obligation on him. Sins against chastity are sacrilegious for him because he is a sacred person, consecrated to God by his ordination, not by any personal vow. Both theories are tenable and in fact come to the same practical conclusion: celibate chastity forbids both external and internal sins of lust under the additional species of sacrilege. And if, in the vow theory, a cleric positively excludes this vow by a contrary intention elicited at the time of his ordination as a subdeacon, he remains bound by celibacy, not in virtue of a vow but in virtue of positive ecclesiastical law (Roman Rota, Jan. 13, 1928).

The obligation of celibacy is validly assumed only if the cleric knowingly and freely receives the sacred orders to which it is attached by law and accepts the challenge of celibate chastity without the constraint of grave fear. If he were ordained to sacred orders invalidly because of the compulsion of force or extreme fear that precluded his consent, he would not be bound to celibacy. And even if he received these orders voluntarily and validly, but without full freedom because of grave fear exerted on him, he would escape the obligation of celibacy, despite the validity of his ordination. The law gives a remedy for this cleric: he may make a plea to have declared null his duty of celibacy and to be reduced to the lay state by judicial sentence of the Church court; but he must prove that he received major orders under constraint of grave fear and that he never ratified his ordination later when the source of this fear was removed, not even tacitly by exercising his orders and thereby intending to submit himself to the duty of celibacy (CIC cc.214.2, 1994.2).

The Church tries to render easier the lifetime observance of celibate chastity by warning clerics not to house or associate with suspect women (CIC c.133) and by recommending that clerics live together in a common house or rectory whenever feasible (CIC c.134).

By contrast, clerics who are only tonsured or in minor orders are not bound by any obligation of celibate chastity, neither by law nor implicit vow. They are free to marry, and they are not guilty of sacrilege in acts of unchasteness, although they do become liable to punishment for external sins against the Sixth Commandment (CIC c.2358) and should consider habitual unchasteness a sign of lack of a vocation to the priesthood (Congregation of Religious, Jan. 23, 1961).

Diriment Impediment to Marriage. Clerics in sacred orders who attempt marriage do so illicitly (CIC c.132.1) and invalidly (CIC c.1072). It is entirely due to the will of the Church that sacred orders invalidate marriage—whether the source of the diriment impediment be considered a public solemn vow of chastity (for it is only by positive ecclesiastical law that a solemn vow invalidates marriage) or simply the Church's legislator who opts to declare the impediment an incapacitation for marriage. But a cleric is subject to this impediment only under three conditions. First, he must have received a sacred order validly, otherwise the basis for the impediment is missing. If he pleads nullity of his sacred orders, he must adduce proof acceptable in the external forum before he will be declared free to marry in the Church as a layman. Second, he must know celibacy is legally attached to the sacred order and receive the order aware of the incapacitation for future marriage. Ignorance of this is practically impossible today in a candidate for the subdiaconate: seminarians are carefully investigated and instructed, and they must sign an explicit declaration before ordination to major orders that they are clearly aware of what the law of celibacy entails (Congregation of Sacraments, Dec. 27, 1930, and Dec. 27, 1955; Congregation of Religious, Dec. 1, 1931, and Feb. 2, 1961). Third, he must receive the sacred order of his own free will, without the compulsion of force or the duress of grave fear, as explained above.

It is within the Church's power to dispense from this impediment, since it is of merely ecclesiastical origin. Priests have been dispensed in the past, under Mary Tudor in England to ease the reform schism and in France after the Revolution; but these were general dispensations, given for the common good, to allow unfortunate priests to regularize civil unions. To date there is no public record of a dispensation that has permitted a priest to marry for his own private good, or even to validate an invalid marriage in danger of death (Sacred Penitentiary, April 18, 1936). The Holy See will dispense deacons and subdeacons more easily today than formerly, even for private reasons of a serious nature; with the dispensation they are, of course, laicized. Below the Holy See, local ordinaries can dispense to allow a deacon or subdeacon to marry when he is in danger of death (CIC c.1043) and in the emergency of an already prepared marriage (c.1045); and pastors, confessors, and priests assisting at marriages celebrated under the extraordinary form of c.1098 enjoy the same powers when the local ordinary is unavailable (cc.1044–45). But local ordinaries cannot dispense from this impediment, even for a deacon or subdeacon, in the urgency envisaged by c.81 (Code Commission Jan. 26, 1949).

The obligation of celibacy is not automatically removed should a major cleric be returned to the lay state (CIC c.213.2) through the punishment of degradation or through a decree of laicization, unless the decree dismissing him from the clerical state expressly dispenses from celibacy. If a religious who has received sacred orders obtains a dispensation from his religious vows (CIC c.640.1n2) or an indult of qualified exclaustration from the religious cloister (Congregation of Religious, 1955) or is dismissed from his religious institute (CIC cc.648, 670), he remains bound by the celibacy attached to his sacred orders unless, in the case of a deacon or subdeacon, the indult expressly dispenses from this obligation.

A cleric in sacred orders and his female accomplice who defy this impediment and presume to contract marriage, even only civilly, automatically incur excommunication reserved simply to the Holy See (CIC c.2388.1). If it is a priest who does this, as long as he is unable to separate from his woman partner he cannot be absolved from this excommunication outside danger of death except by the Sacred Penitentiary; in danger of death he can be absolved by any priest, but recourse must be made later to the Penitentiary in the event of his recovery (Sacred Penitentiary, April 18, 1936, and May 4, 1937). If the priest has already separated from the woman as a result of her death, civil divorce, or desertion, he can be absolved from this excommunication under the usual rules (CIC cc.2253–54). In all cases, however, his rehabilitation, release from the irregularity, and readmission into the active priesthood must follow the normal papal procedure. Moreover, any major cleric who has attempted marriage and who, after being warned to cease cohabitation, fails to do so within the time determined by the ordinary, is to be degraded (CIC c.2388.1). He also loses automatically any ecclesiastical office he possessed (CIC c.188n5) and becomes irregular because of delictual unworthiness (CIC c.985n3). And if he is a religious, he is *ipso facto* dismissed from his religious institute (CIC c.646.1n3), incurs general suspension until he has been absolved by the Holy See (CIC c.671n1), and is permanently deprived of the right to wear ecclesiastical dress (CIC c.670).

Clerics in tonsure and minor orders, by comparison, can marry both validly and licitly—they are under no impediment; but they are automatically reduced to the lay state at the time of their marriage, with loss of the clerical privileges, unless force or extreme fear exerted on the cleric render the marriage invalid (CIC c.132.2) and this can be proved to the satisfaction of an ecclesiastical tribunal.

Marriage as an Impediment to Holy Orders. A married man who wants to go on for the priesthood while his wife is still alive is under a simple impediment to orders; he must be dispensed from this impediment by the Holy See before he can receive tonsure or any orders licitly (CIC c.987n2). He is also under an invalidating (CIC c.542n1) and a simply prohibitive (CIC c.542n2) impediment to the novitiate if he wants to enter the priesthood in a religious institute; these impediments must be dispensed by the Holy See before he receives the religious habit. If a married man whose wife is living receives sacred orders without dispensation from the Holy See, even in good faith, he is forbidden to exercise these orders (CIC c.132.2) until his case has been resolved by Rome. And if he culpably breaches this prohibition, he incurs an irregularity resulting from his delict (CIC c.985n7).

The Church does not dispense too easily in these cases, because of the man's prior obligation of common life with his wife, from whom he must separate permanently if he is to live a chastely celibate life as a priest in the Latin Church. The Church will dispense, however, to allow a married man to receive orders if his wife gives free consent and encouragement and offers adequate assurance that she will not later demand resumption of married life or interfere in the exercise of his priestly duties. She need not make a private vow of perpetual chastity in the world or request dispensation so she can enter a convent, although this is usually considered the best assurance that she will not later renege on her agreement.

Exceptions in this discipline have been made recently in Europe in favor of non-Catholic ministers converted after their marriage: the Holy See has dispensed from this impediment in certain cases to allow them to be ordained Catholic priests while continuing to live with their wives. And Vatican Council II (*Constitution on the Church,* Nov. 21, 1964, n.29), in restoring the permanent diaconate as a terminal rank in the hierarchy, indicates that the practice of the Church is to approve the promotion of married men of more mature age to this terminal diaconate. Unmarried men also may be ordained as permanent deacons, in which case the law of celibacy will remain their way of life and will constitute a diriment impediment to marriage unless the Holy See provides to the contrary.

Oriental Churches. Historically the discipline of clerical celibacy in the Eastern rites differed from the Latin mainly in the admission of married men to sacred orders. From the early centuries the Orientals permitted married men to be promoted to the subdiaconate and major orders—not to the episcopacy, however, without special dispensation—and to cohabit with their wives, although several days of abstinence from sexual relations were usually expected as a preparation for their celebration of the liturgy. Unmarried men, however, who were ordained to subdiaconate or higher orders were prohibited from marrying afterward, and they courted deposition if they dared to disobey (Council of Trullo, 692, c.6). This prohibition came to be interpreted commonly as a diriment impediment, even among the dissident Orientals, but it would be rash to propose this as certain for all the Eastern rites. Benedict XIV in the 18th century evidenced some doubt about the invalidating effect of this impediment: when a married priest from a dissident Eastern rite was converted, Benedict's policy was to grant a precautionary dispensation from this impediment but not to require renewal of consent by the priest husband and his wife. The impediment was clearer in certain individual rites: among the Rumanians and Italo-Greeks subdiaconate and major orders constituted an incapacitation for marriage; among the Maronites subdeacons and among the Ruthenians even deacons were not excluded from marrying validly. But married priests who became widowed were never permitted to remarry. This was the rule even in the dissident Oriental rites.

Current legislation of the Oriental Code corresponds basically with the law of the Latin Church, but there are some expected differences. In regard to the admission of men already married to the subdiaconate or major orders the new law makes no innovations (Cler Sanc c.71); each Eastern rite follows its own discipline. Some rites leave married men absolutely free to be ordained to any order except the episcopacy, for which only celibates or men lawfully released from the bond of a previous marriage are eligible throughout the whole Oriental Church. Other rites have an impediment barring married men from orders, but the patriarch or the local ordinary (the vicar-general excluded) can dispense. Still others exclude married men entirely from holy orders unless the Holy See dispenses; and in these rites, just as in the Latin Church, minor clerics below the subdiaconate who get married automatically retire from the clerical state unless the marriage was invalid, and married men who are ordained subdeacons or major clerics without dispensation from the Holy See, even in good faith, are disbarred from exercising these orders (ClerSanc c.72). But celibate priests are preferred for certain missions outside their patriarchate, even in rites that admit married men to the priesthood. Thus Oriental priests coming to the U.S., Canada, or Australia to minister to the faithful of their rites must be celibates or widowers who have no children living in the locale of their ministry (Bousc-O'Connor 1:10, 20, 33). By exception some married Oriental priests with families, refugees from Europe as a result of World War II, were permitted the priestly ministry in these countries. But new candidates for the clergy in these missions must be celibates.

The diriment impediment to marriage for all Oriental rites binds not only clerics in major orders but also subdeacons, even though the subdiaconate is not considered a sacred order in any Eastern rite except the Armenian (CrebAllat c.62; ClerSanc c.70). Hence the marriages of all Eastern-rite clerics attempted after ordination to the subdiaconate are invalid. All Oriental clerics, even married ones, are expected to be eminent for their chastity and are made liable for punishment for sins against chastity (ClerSanc c.73). But the Oriental Code is silent about the sacrilegious character of such sins, seemingly because celibacy among the Eastern clergy was not considered to be based on an implicit vow of chastity.

Bibliography: W. Bertrams, *The Celibacy of the Priest,* tr. P. Byrne (Westminster, Md. 1963). O. M. Cloran, *Previews and Practical Cases on Marriage* (Milwaukee 1960–) v.1, *Preliminaries and Impediments.* BouscEllis. Pospishil LawMarr. Pospishil PersOr. E. Jombart and É. Herman, DDC 3:132–156.

[J. W. REHAGE]

CELIBACY, HISTORY OF

The practice of celibacy in the Church, or the renunciation of marriage undertaken implicitly or explicitly for the purpose of practicing perfect chastity, is an almost uniquely Christian institution whose history reflects the idealism and, at times, the contradictions of Christian asceticism.

Antiquity and the Old Testament. Among ancient peoples celibacy, especially female celibacy or *virginity, was given a sacral value but was not considered to be a way of life. Temporary continence was often imposed as a form of corporal purification (*lustratio*), but only in relation to worship. Virgins, moreover, were consecrated to a female deity—the six Roman Vestals for 30 years— but perpetual celibacy was ordinarily not practiced. In Sparta, the unmarried lost civic rights (ἀτιμία) and were given menial tasks. After the time of Camillus (402 B.C.), Roman bachelors had to pay special taxes (*aes uxorium*); during the imperial period, they were deprived of parental inheritance (*caducariae leges*).

In the OT, sexual acts, even when not sinful, were considered defiling (Lv 15). Virginity in the bride was the object of high praise (Dt 22.14–29), and, in practice, a girl who had been violated was unable to find a husband (2 Sm 13.20). But the state of virginity was not to be permanent; to be unmarried and childless was to be the object of shame (Gn 30.23; Is 4.1; 54.4; Jgs 11.37–40). Marriage was considered honorable and compulsory for all, and to have many children was viewed a sign of divine favor (Gn 22.17). Thus, in OT times, virginity as a state of life consecrated to God was unknown, except in the period of the *Essenes.

The New Testament. In the New Dispensation, on the contrary, especially in discussion of the higher aspects of morality, the NT emphasizes the value of virginity as a means of worshiping God. This is apparent in the example of Christ, Mary, John the Baptist, as well as in the teaching of the Lord. Virginity is presented as a state of eschatological beatitude. In heaven men will not marry because they will not die; in this respect they will be like the angels (Lk 20.36; also Mt 22.30 and Mk 12.25, texts that are still more significant for the traditional comparison of angelic life with that of the unmarried). Prior to beatitude, however, celibacy is the way of consecrating oneself to God, if it is accepted freely for the sake of the kingdom of heaven (Mt 19.12, 19). Nevertheless, it is a special grace and vocation; "not all can accept this teaching" (Mt 19.11–12).

Paul did not underestimate *marriage, nor, with the Gnostics, did he consider it useless in view of the world's imminent destruction. He was generous in his advice to married Christians, helping them in their special vocation (Col 3.18; 4.1; Eph 5.22; 6.9; 1 Tm 4.3; 5.14). In any event, he stated that "it is better to marry than to burn" (1 Cor 7.2–6, 9, 27–28, 36); but for him, marriage, like all created things, is secondary if compared to the life in Christ (1 Cor 7.29–31). With this in mind, Paul praised celibacy and virginity as a more perfect state, since it is the condition for a more fervent consecration to God, avoids earthly concerns, and prepares for the possession of eschatological goods (1 Cor 7.26–35). The unmarried are able to concentrate only on God, while married persons must think on each other. Paul's teaching, however, is not a universal law. He presented it as a counsel, as a grace or as an individual charism, as a special vocation (1 Cor 7.6–7, 25). This charism, however, does not seem to have been granted to all the leaders of the Pauline churches. Besides, it is difficult to find a peremptory argument in favor of a universal law in view of 1 Cor 9.5 and of the matrimonial status of Peter, of the other Apostles, and of the brethren of Christ there cited. The question is controversial, but the pastoral Epistles give clear evidence that the Pauline churches were ruled by married *episcopoi, presbyteroi,* and *diakonoi.* Ministers of the NT were not obliged to celibacy, but only to what would traditionally be called *boni mores.* Duties in this regard were presented in stereotype form (1 Tm 3.2–13; Ti 1.6–9), with emphasis on three points: the bishop should be married but once; he should rule well his own household, keeping his children under control and perfectly respectful; for, as Paul asked, if a man cannot rule his own household, how is he to take care of the Church of God?

The Patristic Age. During the first 3 or 4 centuries, no law was promulgated prohibiting clerical marriage. Celibacy was thus a matter of choice for bishops, priests, and deacons. Under certain conditions, as shall be evident below, they were permitted to contract marriage and live as married men.

Clerical Marriage Permitted. *Clement of Alexandria (*c.* 150–*c.* 215), commenting on the Pauline texts, stated that marriage, if used properly, is a way of salvation for all: priests, deacons, and laymen (*Stromata* 1.3.12; PG 8:1189). The Synod of Gangra (*c.* 345) condemned manifestations of false asceticism, among others the refusal to attend divine worship celebrated by married priests (c.4; Mansi 2:1101). The **Apostolic Constitutions* (*c.* 400) excommunicated a priest or bishop who left his wife "under pretence of piety" (Mansi 1:51). Socrates (*Hist. eccl.* 1.1.11; PG 67:101), Sozomen (*ibid.* 1.1.23; PG 67:925), and Gelasius of Cyzicus (*Hist. concilii Nicaeni* 1.2.32; Mansi 2:906) stated that new tendencies at the beginning of the 4th century had tried to prohibit clerical marriage, but until that time individual choice had been the rule. They reveal that when Bp. *Hosius (Ossius) of Córdoba sought to have the First Council of *Nicaea (325) pass a decree requiring celibacy, the Egyptian Bishop *Paphnutius, himself unmarried, protested that such a rule would be difficult and imprudent. He further emphasized that celibacy should be a matter of vocation and personal choice. The Council accepted this point of view and took measures to prohibit clandestine marriages with consecrated virgins (*agapete;* see John Chrysostom, *Fem. reg.,* PG 47:513–532; *Subintr.,* PG 47:495–514). Gregory the Elder of Nazianzus (*c.* 274–374) was bishop of that city when his son and successor, *Gregory of Nazianzus the Younger, was born (*c.* 330). *Gregory of Nyssa lived with his wife after his consecration (372), and the succession of *Gregory the Illuminator (*c.* 240–332), the first Catholicos of Armenia, remained in his family for four generations, passing from father to son.

However, there is evidence to show that a great number of clerics in the early Church were unmarried or else left the married state after ordination. The testimony of *Tertullian (*De exhortatione castitatis* ch. 13; PL 2:390) and *Origen (*In Levit. hom.* 6.6; PG 12:474) may be suspect in that both authors were sympathetic to the sect of the Encratites (it may be noted that Origen castrated himself); but many other authors, cited by Eusebius (*Demonstratio evangelica* 1.9; PG 22:81) and Jerome (*Adversus Vigilantium* ch. 2; PL 23:341), testify to clerical renunciation of marriage. During the 4th century most of the bishops in Thessaly, Greece, Macedonia, Egypt, Italy, and western Europe were unmarried or left their wives after consecration. But for priests and deacons clerical marriage continued to be in vogue. A famous letter of *Synesius of Cyrene (d. *c.* 414) is evidence both for the respecting of personal decision in the matter and for contemporary appreciation of celibacy. Elected bishop of Ptolemais, he noted that many Egyptian bishops were unmarried. For himself, Synesius declared that he would refuse consecration if it meant abandoning his wife and the prospect of rearing many children. He was permitted to retain his status (*Epist.* 105; PG 66:1485).

Conditions of Clerical Marriage. Legislation concerning the marriage of bishops, priests, and deacons is a valuable source of information for these practices in the early Church. First, it was declared that marriage could precede but not follow ordination. This general rule was applied according to circumstances of age and person. If a married candidate for major orders had been baptized as an adult (as was the case with many bishops of the period), he might keep his wife; unmarried candidates were free to marry before consecration or to remain unmarried. Other candidates, however, were baptized as children. Ordinarily, they became clerics while yet quite young, and upon ordination as lector or cantor they were permitted to choose between marriage and continence. Thus, the Council of Hippo in 393 (Mansi 3:922) declared that lectors might function until the age of puberty; "thereafter, however, unless they had married while enjoying a good reputation, or unless they vowed continence, they are not permitted to read." The condition of "good reputation" (*custodita pudicitia*) was understood to mean chaste; if the young man committed a sin against chastity, he could not be accepted into the clerical state without renouncing his right to marry; for, according to *Innocent I (PL 20:477), "any baptized, but defiled [*corruptus*] person wishing to become a cleric, must promise that he will never marry." The canonical reason for this decision was that the marriage of a *corruptus* would not have been officially blessed by the Church and would therefore become the object of popular derision. Monks, however, if they became clerics, were not permitted to marry even if they were *incorrupti* (Siricius, *Epist.* 1; PL 13:1137). Accordingly, the practice may be summed up as follows: generally speaking, marriage was permitted before the diaconate. One exception, however, must be mentioned. In 314 the Council of *Ancyra (c.10; Mansi 2:517) permitted deacons to marry after ordination if they had previously declared their intention to marry.

Secondly, the marriage must be monogamic, in accord with the words of St. Paul, that a bishop be *unius uxoris vir.* Even though variously interpreted, these words were given at least one universal application: if a married cleric should lose his wife, he was not permitted to marry again. The *Apostolic Constitutions* (Mansi 1:462), for example, declared that after ordination bishops, priests, and deacons were not permitted to contract marriage if they had no wife, nor to cohabit with another if they had one; they were to be satisfied with the wife they had had at ordination. The attitude of the early Church, which looked with disfavor upon second marriages, was a sufficient reason for this law. If second marriages were considered inexcusable even for allaying the passions of youth, for a cleric they would have been scandalous. More lenient interpretations of this Pauline text, e.g., that of *Theodoret of Cyr (PG 82:805), stated that since St. Paul was aware of the polygamy practiced by both Jews and Gentiles, he was merely reminding clerics of the general law of monogamous Christian marriage. Consequently he forbade only simultaneous polygamy. Ordinarily, however, this interpretation was not accepted and monogamy was understood to exclude successive polygamy as well. Second marriages were considered contemptible and without blessing, and a man who had twice been married could not be accepted into the clergy. Later casuistry led many authors to distinguish between marriages contracted before and after baptism. Thus *Jerome (*Epist. 69, ad Oceanum;* PL 22:654) stated that several bishops and priests had been ordained after a second marriage, if the first had been performed before baptism. This distinction was no longer admitted after *Innocent I and *Leo I, when any man twice married was refused ordination. By extension, the same popes refused ordination to a man who had been married but once, whose wife, however, had lived with another man either legitimately or illegitimately.

The Eastern Church. During the 4th century, as a result of the diversity of practice, the Church felt the need for legislation in this field of clerical activity. The growth of monastic influence, moreover, promoted the cause of virginity and celibacy, as is evident in the letters and sermons of *Ambrose and Jerome. When the opposition of Jovinian and Vigilantius brought on a reaction to the monastic spirit, the Church was forced to take cognizance and to act decisively. Neoplatonic ideas also were at work. Laws passed in the East and in the West generally followed regional custom. Eastern practice and law were usually more liberal than those of Rome, Gaul, or Africa, and were codified by *Theodosius II and *Justinian I, both Christian Emperors enjoying great authority in the Church. Urging national custom, both codes forbade bishops to marry; the Justinian code even denied episcopal consecration to the father of a family; if the married man were without children, he might be consecrated provided he separated from his wife. In all cases, unmarried men were preferred for episcopal consecration (CorpIurCivCod 1.3.47; *ibid.* Nov 6.1; 123.1).

Priests, deacons, and other clerics, however, were permitted to live in marriage contracted before ordination but were forbidden to take another wife if the first should die. If they did so, they were to be degraded; the second marriage was judged invalid, and the children were considered illegitimate and even incestuous (CorpIurCivCod 1.3.44). The Trullan Synod in 692 (*see* QUINISEXT) passed similar laws. Bishops were to observe absolute continence; if the bishop-elect was married, his wife had to live in a remote monastery (at her husband's expense). She was permitted to become a deaconess.

For all other clerics, however, the Synod permitted marriage before ordination and the use of marriage rights afterward; it further condemned all forms of bigamy. The Synod, by indirection, criticized Latin marriage legislation: if anyone should attempt to deprive a married priest, deacon, or subdeacon of his marriage rights, or if one of the aforesaid should renounce his wife "on the pretense of piety," he was to be condemned and deposed. Several concessions, however, were made to Latin usage: sexual relations were prohibited prior to the celebration of the liturgies (in practice, on Saturday); a Greek priest was not to have relations with his wife while traveling in barbarian (Latin) countries (cc.3, 13). No further legislation on celibacy and clerical marriage was issued by the *Eastern Church throughout its history.

From these laws varying usages grew, both before and after the *Eastern Schism, as well as after partial reunions with Rome. In the Byzantine and Russian Church, bishops had usually been monks; if an unmarried priest was elected bishop, he ordinarily took vows similar to those of the monk, before consecration. Many priests, moreover, who were immediate assistants of the bishop, were unmarried. On the other hand, a priest attached to a country parish was required to marry. If his wife died, he was compelled to renounce his office and retire to a monastery. The *Coptic Church followed canon 10 of the Council of Ancyra, allowing all deacons to marry except those who explicitly promised to live as celibates. Among the Ethiopians and Chaldeans, priests were permitted to marry after ordination.

The Uniate Churches, in theory, follow the legislation of 692, which has been approved by several popes (Clement III, Innocent III, and Benedict XIV); in practice, however, Latin influence has altered the situation. Priests and deacons of the Syro-*Malabar rite must remain unmarried; the same is true for the Uniate Abyssinians, except that the bishop might dispense in the matter. The Syrians (1888) and the Copts (1899) demand celibacy, except for a convert from Orthodoxy. Melkite, Maronite, and Armenian priests and deacons, however, may be married before ordination. Many priests stationed in towns remain unmarried after seminary training. Lacking priests for rural parishes, bishops have often ordained pious married laymen without benefit of full clerical studies. Among the Ruthenians and the Romanians priests are generally married, even in city parishes.

Legislation and Practice in the West. Celibacy became a canonical obligation for the clergy in the West through the combined efforts of popes and regional councils. It is the earliest example of general legislation based on the papal authority of decretals and the collaboration between Rome and the bishops acting collectively. About 300, a Spanish council at *Elvira (near Granada) required absolute continence for all its clergy under pain of deposition (c.33): "We decree that all bishops, priests, deacons, and all clerics engaged in the ministry are forbidden entirely to live with their wives and to beget children: whoever shall do so will be deposed from the clerical dignity" (Mansi 2:11). One of the Spanish bishops, Hosius of Córdoba, who had been present at Elvira, tried in vain for the same decision at the First Council of Nicaea. This legislation, however, did not enter the Western Church until the second half of the 4th century and was effected through the decretals of various popes: *Damasus I (*Ad Gallos episcopos,* 366–384); *Siricius (*Ad Himerium Tarraconensem,* 385; *Ad episcopos Africae,* 386); Innocent I (*Ad Vitricium Rothomagensem,* 404; *Ad Exuperium Tolosanum,* 405; *Ad Maximum et Severum,* 401–417); Leo I (*Ad Anastasium Thessalonicum,* 446?; *Ad Rusticum Narbonensem,* 458). Councils issued the same decrees for Africa (Carthage, 390, 401–419; cf. cc.3–4 of 419), France (Orange, 441; Tours, 461), and Italy (Turin, 398). No longer could priests, deacons, and (after Leo I) subdeacons be married.

The first letter of Damasus I (wrongly ascribed to Siricius in PL 13:1181–96; cf. *Clavis patrum* No. 1632) gave the classic arguments of the period urging celibacy. How can a cleric advise perfect continence to widows and virgins if he does not observe celibacy? Ministers of Christ must obey the Scriptures, which authoritatively require them to live in celibacy (cf. Rom 8.9; 1 Cor 7.29; Rom 13.14; 1 Cor 7.7). Marital acts were repugnant to the sacred ministry; pagan and Jewish priests were aware of the necessity of refraining from sexual relations. St. Paul counseled abstinence even for laymen, whose duty it was to bear children (1 Cor 7.5). The statement of Damasus, "that since intercourse is a defilement, surely the priest must undertake his duties with heavenly aid," may appear to favor Encratism; but it seems that the Pope, in alluding to St. Paul and to the OT, understood defilement (*pollutio*) to mean a legal impurity and not a sin.

In practice, before ordination the candidate was required to take a vow of chastity (*professio conversionis*). This *conversio* legally placed him in the state of public penitents who were forbidden the use of marriage. Thus, married candidates were required to promise continence in the legislation of the Councils of Orange (441, c.22), Arles (*c.* 450, c.2; 524, c.2), and Orléans (537, c.6). *Gregory I (PL 77:506) made this profession the general rule for the subdiaconate, and the Fourth Council of Toledo (663), presided over by *Isidore of Seville, decreed this profession for priests and deacons assigned to parishes. Before the subdiaconate, moreover, the candidate had to declare under oath that he had not committed the four major sins of sodomy, bestiality, adultery, or the violation of consecrated virgins (*Ordo Romanus* 34; Andrieu OR 3:549, 607).

Custom and legislation provided for the status of clerical wives. On the day of the husband's ordination, the wife received a special blessing. Such wives, known as *presbyterissae* (*presbyterae*) and *diaconissae* (*diaconae*), wore a distinctive garb and were not permitted to remarry, even after the death of their husbands (Orléans, *c.* 573, c.22; Andrieu OR 4:140–141). At the time of Leo I, clerics were not obliged to dismiss their wives, but could live with them in celibacy. Writing to Bp. Rusticus of Narbonne, Leo stated that married clerics should not give up their wives but should live together in wedded love, without the acts of love, so that a spiritual marriage might replace a carnal one (PL 54:1204). Later, however, such cohabitation appeared to be overly difficult and suspicious, and canonical legislation proceeded more cautiously. A bishop was required to provide another household for his wife. Each day she might come to the bishop's house and carefully look after its needs; but she was not to bring her servants, and, as a safeguard, the bishop was always to be attended by clerics. A priest, on the other hand, was permitted to keep his wife in his home (probably for reasons of economy), but they were not to share a common room (Orléans, 541, c.17). The archpriest was always to be attended, especially at night, by his clerics (*canonici clerici*), and one of them, or if necessary a layman, was to sleep in his room. Other priests and deacons slept alone, but were expected to provide a female servant who should sleep in the wife's room to warrant her virtue. Married clerics who disregarded these precautions were branded with the heresy of Nicolaitism (Tours 557, c.20). Priests were forbidden to have other women in their household, and **Virgines subintroductae* were especially suspect (Bordeaux, 663, c.3). In the cities, common sleeping quarters were to be provided for priests and for lesser clerics (Tours, 567, c.15).

The Gregorian Reform. The period following the decline of the Carolingian Empire was a time of crisis for clerical celibacy. The disorganization of society and the concomitant destruction of churches and monasteries by the Northmen and other invaders of the Empire, and the progressive secularization of Church lands led to the demoralization of the clergy. Councils in the 10th and 11th centuries regularly protested against the two chief vices of the clergy; simony and clerical marriage (Nicolaitism) [see H. Maisonneuve, *La morale chrétienne d'après les conciles des Xe et XIe siècles* (Namur 1950–)]. Thus, e.g., the Council of Trosly (Soissons, 909) stated that in the monasteries enclosure had been abandoned and many priests were married. The Synod of Augsburg (952) and the Councils of Anse (994) and Poitiers (1000) all decreed the law of celibacy. *Burchard of Worms in his *Decretum* (*c.* 1110) recalled the ancient law prohibiting the marriage of priests (PL 140:645–646). About 1018 *Benedict VIII protested against the current subversion of celibacy and strengthened the legislation of the Church, especially by imposing penalties for offenders. Priests, deacons, and subdeacons were forbidden to marry or to cohabit with a woman. Their children were declared to be forever serfs of the Church and could not be freed or granted rights of property and inheritance. The purpose of these canons (similar to that, perhaps, of the Justinian *Corpus*) was to prevent the secularization of ecclesiastical property by the families of priests.

Disorder existed not only in the practice of the period but even in the field of doctrine. Arguments circulated against celibacy were answered by *Peter Damian in his *Liber Gomorrhianus* and in *De coelibatu sacerdotum ad Nicolaum II* (PL 145:159–190, 379–388). He in turn was answered by Ulric, Bishop of Imola (*c.* 1060), in his *Rescriptum seu epistola de continentia clericorum* (MGLibLit 1), a pamphlet once attributed to St. *Ulric of Augsburg and condemned by *Gregory VII (1079). Ulric appealed to the texts of St. Paul and to the freer practices of the first several centuries, forgetting the power of the Church to initiate new laws. These errors were renewed in the *Tractatus pro clericorum connubio,* the enlarged Norman edition of Ulric's work, and by the *An liceat sacerdotibus inire matrimonium* (MGLibLit 3). These writings claimed that celibacy was a personal vocation, not a canonical state, and that marriage in itself was not evil. In the next century the Goliards appealed to the natural law as an argument for greater freedom.

Against these conditions, many popes in the 11th century proceeded with vigor. *Leo IX (1049) assigned the wives and concubines of priests to servitude as *ancillae* to the Lateran palace. *Nicholas II (1059) deprived married priests, even in the external forum, of the right to perform liturgical acts of worship, and they were forbidden to live in the *presbyterium* of the churches. They were also denied all further rights to ecclesiastical prebends. To further his effort, the Pope tried to enlist the support of the laity by prohibiting them to attend Mass offered by a married priest or by one who lived in concubinage. Many laymen, indeed, were gravely scandalized by clerical immorality and supported the program of papal reform. Some of these, however, belonging to the sect of the *Patarines, fell under the influence of *Manichaeism and became *Cathari.

*Gregory VII issued no new decretals on the subject, but energetically applied existing law through the action of his legates and by extensive correspondence with bishops. Writing to Otto of Constance, the Pope summarized his actions and intentions: "Those who are guilty of the crime of fornication are forbidden to celebrate Mass or to serve the altar if they are in minor orders. We prescribe, moreover, that if they persist in despising our laws, which are, in fact, the laws of the Holy Fathers, the people shall no longer be served by them. For if they will not correct their lives out of love for God and the dignity of their office, they must be brought to their senses by the world's contempt and the reproach of their people" (PL 148:646; Jaffé L 4932). By his courage and zeal, Gregory must be credited with being the true restorer of sacerdotal celibacy in those disturbed times.

The last stage in the struggle against clerical marriage, until that time considered only illicit in the Western Church, was to declare such marriages invalid. This action was taken at the First and Second *Lateran Councils of 1123 and 1139. In the latter (cc.6–7; Con OecDecr 174), the impediment of orders was definitively declared to be a diriment impediment. In explaining this decision, canonists commonly state that the candidate for ordination to the subdiaconate tacitly takes the vow of celibacy; thus *Boniface VIII (Corp IurCan VI° 3.15). This theory recalls similar vows taken in the Merovingian period and in the Russian Church. Other explanations are based on the power of the Church to annul marriages contracted contrary to her laws, or on arguments that clerical marriage is contrary to the divine law (e.g., Sanchez, *De sancto matrimonii sacramento* 7.27). This latter explanation came up for further discussion at the Council of *Trent.

The Age of the *Reformation. By the end of the Middle Ages the Church again experienced a period of decline in clerical morality, occasioned by the *Black Death, the Hundred Years' War, the *Western Schism, and the pagan spirit of the *Renaissance. Most historians of this period point to clerical marriage as a common practice and to the sons of priests who were legitimated, and, as in the case of *Erasmus, even ordained to the priesthood with a dispensation from the Roman Curia (at the cost of 12 gros tournois). In his *Commentary on the Galatians* (4.30; 1535), *Luther stated that his movement would have made little headway against the papacy if clerical celibacy had then been observed as it was in the time of Jerome, Ambrose, and Augustine; that "celibacy was something remarkable in the eyes of the world, a thing that makes a man angelic."

At the time of his break with the Church (1517), Luther did not promote sacerdotal marriage, and, in a letter of Jan. 17, 1522, refused to encourage it. But by the end of that year he condemned celibacy in his *De votis monasticis,* and in April 1523 he officiated and preached at the wedding of Wenzeslaus Link, the late vicar general of the *Augustinians. Finally, Luther himself was married on the evening of June 13, 1525, to the scandal of many of his friends and the applause of many married priests of his day. Luther then attempted a doctrinal justification based on the authority of the Pauline texts, denial of the Church's authority to issue new laws (he burned the books of Canon Law in 1530 as the work of the devil), denial of the Sacrament of Holy Orders, the futility of good works, and the necessity of marriage for fallen nature (cf. Luther, *Werke* 6:442, 550; 8:654; 10.2:276). *Calvin was perhaps less radical than Luther; for, while requiring marriage as the general rule, he admitted (commenting on Mt 19.12 and 1 Corinthians ch. 7) that celibacy may be an acceptable means of serving God. But Calvin claimed that celibacy as a personal vocation cannot be judged of greater value than the common way of life. The Geneva reformer protested against the despising of marriage, found in the writing of St. Jerome and, in his opinion, in the average treatise on theology (cf. Calvin, *Commentaires sur le Nouveau Testament* 1561; Matthew ch. 19 and 1 Tm 4.3).

The Council of Trent. Opposition to the Protestant position, by popes, bishops, priests, and kings, failed to agree on the methods to be used or on the nature of true reformation within the Church. Several of the princes, e.g., Emperor *Ferdinand I, thought it opportune to grant Germany a married priesthood as well as Communion under both species. Duke Albert V of Bavaria suggested that only married men be ordained and that the Church be indulgent to priests who sinned. According to L. von Pastor, *Pius IV did not altogether refuse to examine the matter, but distinguished the possibility of practical and individual grants of dispensation (such as were given later in the case of the *Utraquists) from the general problem, which was submitted to the Council of Trent.

In its 24th session, the Council studied these questions together with others related to marriage. On Feb. 2, 1563, the cardinal of Mantua presented the theologians with a list of Protestant theses for their examination. Here were found (Hefele-Leclercq 10:507; Conc Trid 9:376) the statements equating virginity and marriage (No. 5), and the legitimacy of marriage for priests in the Latin Church and for everyone who has not received the grace of perfect chastity; otherwise marriage would be degraded (No. 6). Discussion of No. 5 was neither difficult nor protracted. Theologians brought arguments to bear from Matthew ch. 19 and 1 Corinthians ch. 7, from the Fathers and the example of the Blessed Virgin, leading to the definition of the superiority—objectively speaking—of virginity dedicated to God (sess. 24; c.10; ConOecDecr 731). From the psychological point of view, however, for those who are not called to celibacy, a vow is neither proposed nor advised as something better. Many opponents of the Council's definition, both then and now, forget this distinction. To understand Tridentine thinking, reference must be made to 1 Corinthians ch. 7: the Council did not go beyond the words of St. Paul.

Discussions on sacerdotal celibacy, however, were longer and of greater moment. In general, theologians and canonists expressed opinions that were more severe than canon 9, which was finally voted by the Fathers of the Council. Concerning the suitability of celibacy to the sacerdotal vocation, the Council cited texts from Scripture (1 Cor 7.5, 33), the Fathers (e.g., Jerome), and various papal decretals. In the first place, it was argued, celibacy is the condition of God's service in the apostolate. A married minister of religion is too preoccupied with his wife and family to give such service. Secondly, the priesthood, even in the OT, requires a form of sanctity that implies the curbing of carnal desires. In the OT, priests were obliged only to a limited time of worship; but now they were totally consecrated to God. These arguments were presented by Jean Peletier, Jean de Lobera, Claude de Sainctes, and Miguel de Medina. Regarding the nature of the obligation and the possibility of general or individual dispensation, two opposing views were introduced. The more rigid view, expressed by De Sainctes and De Lobera, claimed that marriage and the priesthood were incompatible. While good in itself, marriage nevertheless rendered one unfit for the ministry. Consequently, celibacy for the priest was a duty based on divine law. Since Holy Orders obliged the candidate to celibacy as Baptism did to the Christian life, a vow was unnecessary.

Such views were difficult to reconcile with historical evidence, and De Sainctes was content to gloss over such evidence. For him, the early Church had always required celibacy—only the Trullan Synod had permitted marriage for incontinent Greek priests, and Rome had tolerated its decision to avoid greater evil. But this was not a true dispensation, for none could be given by the pope.

Fortunately, other theologians were historically better informed and proposed more realistic views. The majority claimed that clerical celibacy was required by ecclesiastical law (Jean Peletier, Antonius Solisius, Richard du Pre, Lazarus Broychot, Francisco Foriero, Ferdinand Tritius, John de Ludegna, and Sanctes Cinthius). In their opinion, a priest was unable to contract marriage either by the will of the Church or by reason of an implicit vow involved in ordination to the subdiaconate. Despite the suitability of celibacy to the sacerdotal state, the pope might fundamentally dispense from the law, or, as some thought, at least dispense from the vow. At length, the debate was resolved into the question of whether it was opportune to dispense priests at that time. The Portuguese Dominican, Francisco Foriero, argued in the affirmative, stating that the Church might allow clerical marriage for such grave reasons as combating schism or heresy in a particular country. Three other Dominicans, John Valdina, Cinthius, and De Ludegna, and the Franciscan Lucius Angusiola, agreed with this opinion. Others, however, such as Broychot and Tritius, denied the utility and prudence of such a dispensation.

In voting to accept canon 9 (Denz 1809), the Council rejected the opinion that celibacy was of divine law. It taught, first, that the Church had the right to prohibit and invalidate sacerdotal marriage by reason of ecclesiastical law or of vow. If the Church should change its legislation or not require the vow, priests would not be obliged to celibacy. Thus, the canon did not distinguish between the Eastern and the Western Church; for both, the fundamental law was the same. Secondly, the Church taught that in holding sacerdotal celibacy in such high regard, it wished in no wise to minimize its regard for marriage. Both vocations were distinct and each had its distinctive obligations. Thirdly, the Council rejected the claim of those priests who held that celibacy was impossible. Since priests had accepted celibacy by vow, they should implore the grace of God, which would be sufficient to reinforce them in their resolve. Implicitly, therefore, the Church refused to grant a dispensation for the clergy of Germany.

Current Position. The common opinion today may be summed up as follows: clerical celibacy is considered most proper to the sacerdotal ministry; it is in no sense a depreciation of marriage, but is the condition for greater freedom in the service of God. The law of celibacy is of ecclesiastical origin and may therefore be abrogated by the Church. In the early Church and in the East the marriage of bishops, priests, and deacons was permitted for good reason. In recent times, Pius XII, John XXIII, and Paul VI have found similarly good reason to dispense from celibacy in the case of married Protestant pastors who converted and desired ordination. *Vatican Council II, at the request of the bishops from many countries, has permitted a married diaconate, admitting married men of mature years.

Bibliography: E. VACANDARD, DTC 2.2:2068–88; "Les Origines du célibat ecclésiastique," in *Études de critique et d'histoire religieuse,* 4 v. (Paris 1909–23) v.1. H. C. LEA, *History of Sacerdotal Celibacy in the Christian Church,* 2 v. (3d ed. London 1907), uncritical in details. H. LECLERCQ, DACL 2.2:2802–32. G. LE BRAS, DTC 9.2:2123–2317. A. FLICHE, *La Réforme grégorienne,* 3 v. (Louvain 1924–37). E. JOMBART and É. HERMAN, DDC 3:132–156. C. SPICQ, *Les Épîtres pastorales de Saint Paul* (Paris 1947). P. RENARD, DB 2.1:394–396. M. SCADUTO, EncCatt 3:1261–65. P. DELHAYE, "Le Dossier anti-matrimonial de l'*Adversus Jovinianum* et son influence sur quelques écrits latins du XIIe siècle," MedSt 13 (1951) 65–86. F. SPADAFORA, *Temi di esegesi (1 Cor 7.32–38) e el celibato ecclesiastico* (Rovigo 1953). P. VAN IMSCHOOT, *Théologie de l'Ancien Testament,* 2 v. (Tournai 1954–56). JOHN CHRYSOSTOM, *Les Cohabitations suspectes,* ed. and tr. J. DUMORTIER (Paris 1955). A. BIELER, *L'Homme et la femme dans la morale calviniste* (Geneva 1963), often erroneous. EncDictBibl 2548–49. P. H. LAFONTAINE, *Les Conditions positives de l'accession aux ordres dans la première législation ecclésiastique, 300–492* (Ottawa 1963).

[P. DELHAYE]

CELL DIVISION

Cell division is a process of reproduction undertaken by the unit of living matter called the cell. In lower plants and animals, the purpose is to produce offspring; in higher organisms, it is a phase of growth.

Cell division is either mitotic, meiotic, or amitotic. Mitosis, the normal form of cell division that occurs in somatic cells, produces two genetically equivalent "daughter" nuclei. Meiosis is a sequence of two divisions resulting in the production of haploid gametes or spores from diploid somatic cells. Amitosis is generally defined as a nuclear division in which the visible manifestations of mitosis are not observed. Since the term mitosis may evolve to mean any division that shows a regular distribution of genetic material, there is some controversy over the use of the term amitosis. It is perhaps best used to characterize unorganized divisions that occur only in pathological conditions or in nuclei with a limited genetic future.

Cell division is in all cases initiated and controlled by the division of the nucleus, which division is followed by the division of the cytoplasm. The nucleus directs and controls the activities of the cytoplasm, and its sphere of influence is limited to a definite volume of cytoplasm. Increase in this volume is generally the stimulus for the cell to divide.

Mitosis. There are two intervals associated with mitosis: the preparation for division and the division itself. When the interphase or resting embryonic cell has reached optimum size, a number of essential events take place prior to division.

The following interphase events are necessary for mitosis: (1) In animal cells, centrosomes consisting of centrioles and astral rays are reproduced; centrosomes function in the polarization of the fibers of the nuclear spindle. In plant cells, this function is generally ascribed to the "polar cap"—a differentiated area of cytoplasm occupying a position similar to that of the centrosomes of animal cells. (2) In late interphase the essential components of the chromosomes, the *nucleic acids, deoxyribonucleic acid (DNA) and ribonucleic acid (RNA), as well as the chromosomal proteins, both of the histone and nonhistone types, are synthesized. This results in a duplication of the chromosomes. This duplication is a necessary condition for cell division; cells that do not increase their DNA-histone content do not divide. (3) Besides the chromosomes, such structures as the spindles, asters, and centrioles required for cell division are produced. (4) Since dividing cells are in a state of reduced metabolic activity, an energy reservoir must be filled.

In the second interval, the events present a dynamic picture. The names—prophase, metaphase, anaphase, and telophase—are assigned to stages for descriptive purposes, but mitosis is a continuous process. In prophase the chromosomes, which were not visible during interphase because of the hydration and the uncoiled nature of the chromonemata (threadlike units of chromosomes), become visible as a result of the imposition of several orders of coiling on the chromonemata. Matrix material, probably proteinaceous, is deposited between the coiled chromonemata, and with this deposition the nucleolus disintegrates, indicating that a function of the nucleolus may be the synthesis and the storage of nuclear proteins as well as of RNA. When coiling and matrix deposition are completed, prophase chromosomes are visibly double, consisting of two longitudinally oriented chromatids, each with two chromonemata held together only at the centromere (kinetochore or spindle fiber attachment region). See Figs. 1 and 2.

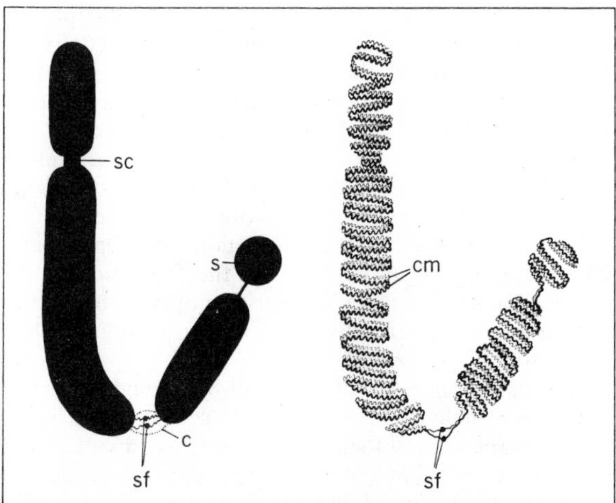

Fig. 1. Diagram of a chromosome in mitotic anaphase.

Prophase merges into metaphase with the disintegration of the nuclear membrane and the movement of the chromosomes to the equatorial plate of the cell, midway between the two poles. Continuous fibers extending from pole to pole confine the chromosomes within the nuclear spindle, and discontinuous chromosomal fibers connect the centromeric regions of the chromatids of each chromosome to the nearest pole. With the division of the centromere at anaphase, the chromatids, now the new daughter chromosomes, move poleward. During telophase the mitotic apparatus is dissociated, and the cell's structure begins to return to the interphase state, reversing the prophase sequence. The chromosomes are despiralized to randomly extended threads; the nucleoli and the nuclear membranes are reformed.

The division of the cytoplasm occurs in telophase; in the plant cell, with the formation of the cell plate at the equatorial region; in the animal cell, with the furrowing of the cell membrane at a point midway between the poles. Thus two daughter cells are formed, each with the same number of chromosomes as the parent cell. Because of the exact replication of the DNA molecules of the parental chromosomes in premitotic interphase, the daughter nuclei are genetically equivalent to the parental nucleus. The fundamental importance of mitosis is that it is a mechanism that insures that all daughter cells receive a set of chromosomes identical not only in number but in gene (i.e., DNA) content to that of the parent cell.

Since multicellular organisms result from successive mitotic cell divisions every cell of the organism will contain equivalent chromosomes, and genetic continuity will be maintained. The somatic cells of sexually reproducing organisms usually have nuclei with the diploid number of chromosomes, each chromosome having an identical partner or homologue, which corresponds in size and shape and in the genes it carries. The gametes, however, have the haploid number, and the halving of the diploid number is brought about by meiosis.

Meiosis. Meiosis is a sequence that comprises a single chromosomal duplication in premeiotic interphase followed by two successive nuclear divisions. The chromosome number of the species is kept constant since the doubling of the chromosome number in the fusion of the gametes (fertilization) to produce the zygote is compensated for by the reduction of the chromosome number of the diploid gamete or spore-producing cell in meiosis.

Meiosis differs from mitosis in the duration of prophase I and the events characteristic of this phase. Although a continuous process, prophase I is divided for convenience of description into the following phases: leptonema, zygonema, pachynema, diplonema, and diakinesis. See Fig. 3.

The onset of the meiotic process is marked by an increase in nuclear volume, the chromosomes become condensed by coiling, the chromomeres being differentiated as areas where the gyres are closer together. The larger chromomeres are constant in size, position and number. The double nature of the leptotene chromosome, coupled with the fact that the synthesis of DNA and histone occurs before zygonema, suggests that the chromosomes come into the synaptic association of zygonema in a divided condition, each consisting of two chromatids. Homologous chromosomes are brought

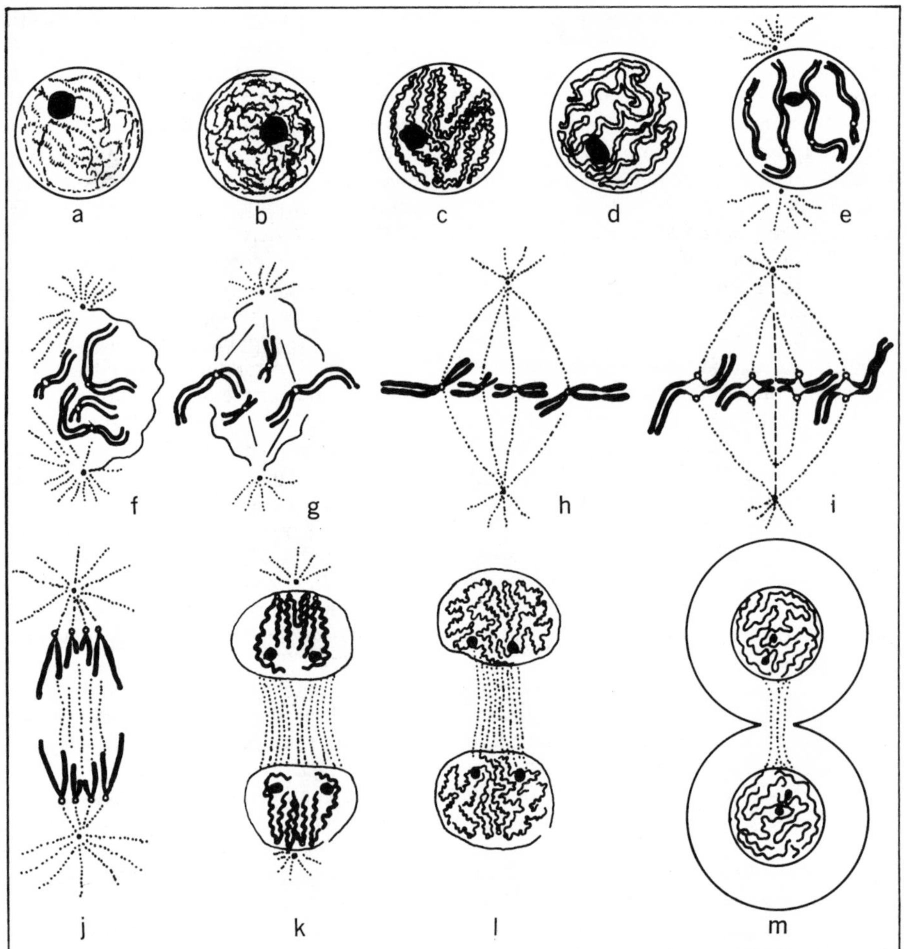

Fig. 2. Diagram of the different stages of mitosis. (a) Interphase. (b), (c), (d), (e) Prophase, in which there is progressive contraction and condensation of the chromosomes (each one composed of two chromatids). (f), (g) Prometaphase; the spindle is beginning to form and the nuclear membrane is disappearing. (h), (i) Metaphase. (j) Anaphase. (k), (l), (m) Telophase. The centromere is indicated by a celar circle in each chromosome.

into apposition at one or several points, and after initial contact is effected, pairing is continued in a zipperlike fashion along the chromosomes. In pachynema, the chromosomes become thicker and shorter with a progressive increase in the diameter of their gyres; the two closely apposed chromosome homologues are relationally coiled forming bivalents. This coiling has been held to play an important role in chiasmata formation and crossing over, which take place during this stage.

Diplonema is characterized by repulsion of the intimately paired homologues of pachynema, a repulsion so strong that each bivalent would dissociate completely to form univalents except for the presence of one or more chiasmata, which bind them together. As the kinetochores of the paired homologues move to opposite poles of the cell, the chiasmata (places where interchanges occur between the chromatids) become visible. Only two of the four chromatids of each bivalent are involved at each point of exchange. There is good evidence that observed chiasmata correspond to points where genetic crossing over has taken place. The position and number of the chiasmata determine the configuration of the bivalents at diplonema. From diplonema to diakinesis, the chromosomes become shorter by an approximation of their gyres to form contracted, deep-staining bodies. Nucleoli have disappeared, and the bivalents migrate to widely separated areas on the periphery of the nucleus. In late diakinesis, the nuclear membrane breaks down, the spindle is formed, and chiasmata move to the ends of the chromosomes. The bivalents move into the spindle and congress at the metaphase plate with the two kinetochore regions of each bivalent oriented in the longitudinal axis of the spindle and equidistant from the plate. This orientation of kinetochores is in contrast to that of mitotic metaphase, in which the kinetochores of all chromosomes are aligned on the equitorial plate. Chromosomal fibers connect kinetochores to the poles and control the anaphase separation of each tetrad into two dyads. As the kinetochore regions move poleward, chiasmata slip to and finally off the free ends of the chromosomes. Thus dyads consisting of two chromatids are formed, their arms diverging as if mutually repelling each other.

Normally, once the dyads reach the spindle poles, a telophasic nucleus is formed. A short interphase is followed by the second meiotic division. No duplication of chromosomes occurs at this interphase, the dyads of anaphase reappear unchanged at second prophase. In many plants, cytoplasmic division occurs at the end of the first nuclear division, but in other organisms cyto-

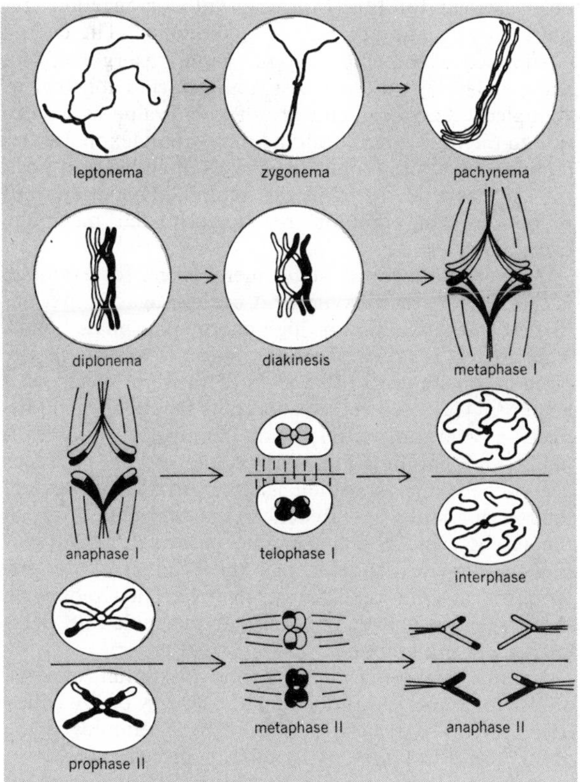

Fig. 3. Diagram of the principal stages of meiosis.

kinesis is deferred until the end of both meiotic divisions. The events of the phases of the second meiotic division are identical with those of mitosis since it involves the separation in anaphase II of the two chromatids forming each dyad of anaphase I.

Fertilization and meiosis are compensating events of tremendous evolutionary importance whereby the chromosome number and the genetic continuity of the species is maintained. Meiosis also provides for individual variation within species since the orientation of each bivalent consisting of two chromatids of paternal origin and two chromatids of maternal origin is at random at metaphase I. Thus in human gamete production where the diploid chromosome number is 46, the chance that a gamete would have all maternal or all paternal chromosomes would be 1 in 2^{23}. Another basis for variation is crossing over, which results in exchanges between paternal and maternal chromatids. Cross-fertilization and the recombination of genes that is possible as a result of the meiotic process has a very high adaptive value in the evolution of the species.

See also CYTOLOGY; CELL PHYSIOLOGY; NUCLEIC ACIDS.

Bibliography: C. P. SWANSON, *Cytology and Cytogenetics* (Englewood Cliffs, N.J. 1957). A. HUGHES, *The Mitotic Cycle* (New York 1952). D. MAZIA, "Mitosis and the Physiology of Cell Division," *The Cell,* ed. J. BRACHET and A. E. MIRSKY, 6 v. (New York 1961) 3:77–412; "The Central Problems of the Biochemistry of Cell Division," *Biological Structure and Function,* ed. T. W. GOODWIN and O. LINDBERG, 2 v. (New York 1961) 2:476–496; "Biochemistry of the Dividing Cell," *Annual Review of Biochemistry* 30 (1961) 669–688. M. M. RHOADES, "Meiosis," *The Cell,* ed. J. BRACHET and A. E. MIRSKY, 6 v. (New York 1961) 3:1–76. H. J. TAYLOR, "Physiology of Mitosis and Meiosis," *Annual Review of Plant Physiology* 12 (1961) 327–344.
Illustration credits: Figs. 1 and 2 from De Robertis, Nowinski, and Saez, *General Cytology* (ed. 3, Philadelphia, W. B. Saunders Company, 1960). Fig. 3, from M. M. Rhoades, "Meiosis in Maize," *Journal of Heredity,* 41 (1950) 59–67.

[J. J. CALLAGHAN]

CELL PHYSIOLOGY

The study of the fundamental activities of living cells. The activities include: nutrition, metabolism, irritability, motility, maintenance of a specific cell organization (*see* CYTOLOGY), cell division and reproduction (*see* CELL DIVISION; GENES; CHROMOSOME), growth and differentiation (*see* CELL DIVISION; CELL THEORY OF LIFE), and maintenance of internal colloidal activities (*see* PROTOPLASM). Only the first four topics listed are discussed here.

Nutrition. The cell environment must contain the nutrients necessary to build cell protoplasm and to furnish the energy for cell work. These nutrients are effective only over narrow ranges of temperature, acidity or alkalinity, and oxygen concentration; the exact range varies with the specific type of cell. Most cells function best between 50 and 110°F, but certain types grow best at temperatures near 180°F, while others prefer temperatures only slightly above 32°F. Atmospheric oxygen is necessary for the many cells called aerobes, while such anaerobes as the tetanus bacilli grow better in the total absence of oxygen. Many cells are facultative and grow in either the absence or presence of oxygen. Acid-base balance must be closely adjusted for most cells. For example, human blood plasma and interstitial fluids maintain a slightly alkaline range, but other cell types require an acid medium.

Water, in which various solutes are dissolved, surrounds most cells. In man and many animals intercellular fluid and blood plasma are aqueous solutions of relatively constant solute concentration, but elsewhere the cell environment may vary in solute concentrations from the very dilute (pond water) to the highly concentrated (sea water). Solutes include both inorganic and organic substances, as well as dissolved gases. Common inorganic materials include salts of the metals potassium, sodium, calcium, and magnesium, together with those of the nonmetals phosphorus, chlorine, sulfur, and nitrogen. Organic nutrients in blood plasma include glucose, lipids, vitamins, enzymes, and over 100 other substances. Most natural fluids contain buffers that maintain the delicate acid-base balance necessary for cell life.

The entrance of nutrients into cells depends on forces in the environment, plus forces originating within the cell itself. A selectively permeable membrane bounds living cells. This membrane is usually, but not in all cases, permeable to water, oxygen, and carbon dioxide, as well as to many fat-soluble molecules. Substances that penetrate the membrane slowly or not at all include electrolytes, sucrose, the higher carbohydrates, and many proteins. Environmental factors influencing entrance of materials include their concentration; temperature; acid-base balance; ionization of nutrients, which retards penetration; and lipid solubility, which accelerates it.

The major force leading to entrance of materials is that of diffusion along a concentration gradient. Substances tend to diffuse from places of higher concentration to places of lower concentration, until general concentration is equalized. In this manner, relatively high concentrations of oxygen and water outside the cell may produce diffusion into the cell, while carbon dioxide, accumulating from cell metabolism inside the cell, will diffuse outward. In the case of water, diffusion is expressed as osmosis, or modifications of osmotic process. Since the constituents of cell structure do not vary directly with their concentrations in the environment, the cells must be regulating the entrance of individual nutrients. Potassium concentration is often much higher inside cells than outside, while sodium concentration is frequently lower inside cells. This ability of cells to select certain substances and reject others is a basic characteristic of cells while living. Several substances move in or out of cells against the concentration gradient, toward areas of their greater concentration. This "uphill" movement is not simple diffusion but requires energy from cell metabolism. This movement is called active transport, and includes the movement of glucose from the intestines and of wastes and glucose in the kidneys.

Pinocytosis has been considered as an explanation of the known entrance into cells of various macromolecules, such as proteins and some enzymes. Pinocytosis refers to the formation of cuplike invaginations in the cell membrane, in response to such inductors as amino acids, electrolytes, and proteins. These membrane invaginations enclose a sample of environmental solution, then close to form pinosomes that sink into the cytoplasm.

Metabolism. This means the complex but orderly series of chemical changes inside the cell by which the energy of entering molecules is transferred either into high-energy phosphate bonds for storage or into the work of the cell. A major product of cell metabolism is synthesis of new molecules, including the enzymes needed to accelerate these chemical reactions. The enzymes are often localized in small organelles: ribosomes, lysozomes, mitochondria, plastids, vacuoles, the Golgi apparatus, and the cell nucleus. Physically, many of these appear connected through the endoplasmic reticulum, a network of submicroscopic tubes and saccules throughout the cell. Ribosomes contain ribonucleic acid (RNA), and therefore govern protein synthesis. Lysozomes, slightly larger than ribosomes, contain hydrolytic enzymes. Mitochondria contain all the enzymes necessary for oxidation of glucose aerobically to carbon dioxide and water. Since this oxidation supplies the usable energy of the cell, mitochondria are often called the "powerhouse" of the cell. Plastids include such materials as chloroplasts of green plants, the starch containing leucoplasts, and many forms of chromoplasts. Vacuoles may contain water, salts, waste products, or various enzymes. The nucleus functions in heredity and cell organization.

Energy is transferred from entering molecules through metabolic cycles that intersect to provide an orderly sequence of chemical reactions. In a step-by-step fashion the energy is transferred either into storage reservoirs or into pathways concerned with biosynthesis and work of the cell. The storage reservoirs consist of high-energy phosphate bonds in substances such as adenosine triphosphate or adenosine diphosphate (ATP or ADP).

Biosynthetic reactions in these cycles produce the very structure of the cell, the enzymes, and the molecules needed for life. Most biosynthetic reactions require energy, and are called "endergonic." The energy is supplied by other energy-releasing, "exergonic," reactions. These two types of reactions occur together as "coupled" reactions: and are of great value as a solution to the problem of building more complex molecules from simpler compounds. Again, as in active transport, the cell has a device for going "uphill." Oxidations and reductions are common reactions in the metabolic cycles.

A major pathway of sugar metabolism, for example, is the Krebs tricarboxylic acid cycle. Sugar is first activated by the addition of high-energy phosphate bonds. This process is called phosphorylation. The high-energy bond is transferred to the sugar from ATP, which then becomes ADP. A series of anaerobic reactions then produces a 3-carbon pyruvic acid. Removal of carbon dioxide and combination with coenzyme A produces acetyl-coenzyme A, which is a crossroads for several intersecting pathways. Reactions may continue through the Krebs cycle or may go into pathways of fat synthesis. Likewise, fragments of the product of fat metabolism can enter the Krebs cycle here. The Krebs cycle itself transfers energy of the sugar molecule into high-energy phosphate bonds.

Irritability. Living cells respond to stimuli, and the ability to do this is a fundamental property of life called irritability. The response induced by a stimulus is the observable indication of irritability in cells. The term excitability is often used instead of irritability when precise measurements are made.

L. V. Heilbrunn defined stimulus as "any change in the immediate environment of a living system." Specific stimuli include:

1. Mechanical forces—impacts from objects, sudden pressure changes, gravity, and even very loud noises.
2. Physical and chemical changes. Pathological changes of blood potassium and sodium can lead to convulsions. Osmotic changes due to loss of salt may stimulate nerve cells. J. Loeb used osmotic changes of sea water as stimuli to induce cleavage of unfertilized eggs. Chemical stimuli may result also from changes in oxygen content of the atmosphere or hydrogen-ion concentrations of surrounding fluids, from glandular secretions, or from such nerve stimulus mediators as epinephrine and acetylcholine. Stimulation of embryonic growth and development is induced by various organizers within the embryo, and cellular metabolism is stimulated by a very small amount of thyroxine. Growth response is stimulated by a hormone from the pituitary gland. The maintenance of cells in the body is dependent on chemical stimuli from many sources, both immediate environment and distant glands.
3. Radiations, including visible and ultraviolet light. Visible light stimulates growth in plants, often discernible as a directional growth of stems toward light and roots away from it. Such predictable responses are called **tropisms* and include responses to gravity (geotropism), to light (phototropism), to chemicals (chemotropism), or to electric current (galvanotropism).
4. Electrical stimuli are frequently used in research

on cell irritability, since the stimuli can be precisely controlled, and make possible a quantitative study of irritability.

5. Temperature changes.

Responses to stimuli are manifested as (1) growth and development; (2) cell membrane phenomena; and (3) motility, either of cell contents or of the cell as a whole. Cell growth as a response includes cell division of one-celled organisms; membrane phenomena refers to such changes as the loss of electrical polarity at the membrane, following a stimulus. Cell membrane phenomena due to stimuli are variations in the potassium-sodium exchange between cell and environment. As the cell dies simple diffusion occurs until concentrations are alike inside and outside the cell. Stimuli and injury produce changes in the same direction—potassium tends to leave cells, sodium tends to enter them more rapidly than usual.

Motility. This is expressed in living cells in two ways: (1) by internal movements, and (2) by movements of the cell in relation to the environment. Internal movements occur in all living cells. Chromosomes move extensively during cell divisions and meiosis. Protoplasmic streaming, cyclosis, is a constant movement of the protoplasm, usually around the center of the cell. Higher temperatures favor the streaming, while flashes of light or electrical impulses inhibit it. Amoeboid movement results from evaginations of the cell borders called pseudopodia. Changes in viscosity of the cell cytoplasm are often offered as an explanation for the formation of pseudopodia. Ciliary movement refers to motility of the entire cell, resulting from fine hairlike appendages. The beating of cilia in vertebrate respiratory tract cells and elsewhere keep surface fluids circulating.

Muscle cells are specialized to change their shape as a response to stimuli. The use of energy for muscle contraction is not fully understood, though most of the information regarding cell metabolism has come from research on muscle cells. Three proteins are known in muscle: myosin, actin, and tropomyosin. Adenosine triphosphate is bound to the myosin, and it is generally accepted that the change from ATP to ADP, with transfer of high-energy phosphate bonds, is in some way connected with the phenomena of muscle contractions and ciliary movement.

Response and stimuli are necessarily interrelated, and both are related to irritability of the cells. However, the single, observable response is seldom due to a single, simple stimulus; rather, it is the result of many influences acting simultaneously. In a similar manner, all the topics considered under cell physiology are interrelated and interdependent. The problem of regulation of these many interrelated factors is the topic of current research.

Bibliography: C. P. Swanson, *The Cell* (pa. Englewood Cliffs, N.J. 1060). W. D. McElroy, *Cellular Physiology and Biochemistry* (pa. Englewood Cliffs, N.J. 1961). P. M. Ray, *The Living Plant* (pa. New York 1963). A. G. Loewy and P. Siekevitz, *Cell Structure and Function* (pa. New York 1963). J. Brachet, "The Living Cell," *Scientific American* 205 (Sept. 1961) 50–61. A. C. Giese, *Cell Physiology* (2d ed. Philadelphia 1962). L. V. Heilbrunn, *An Outline of General Physiology* (3d ed. Philadelphia 1952). R. W. Gerard, *Unresting Cells* (Torchbook; New York 1961). J. Brachet and A. E. Mirsky, eds., *The Cell,* 5 v. (New York 1959–61). T. C. Ruch and J. F. Fulton, eds., *Medical Physiology and Biophysics* (18th ed. Philadelphia 1960). E. H. Starling et al., *Principles of Human Physiology,* ed. H. Davson and M. G. Eggleton (13th ed. Philadelphia 1962). E. B. Wilson, *The Cell in Development and Heredity* (3d ed. New York 1928), the classical statement of the early knowledge of the cell. C. de Duve, "The Lysosome," *Scientific American* 208 (May 1963). H. Holter, "Pinocytosis," *International Review of Cytology* 8 (1959) 481–504.

[B. H. CARLETON]

CELL THEORY OF LIFE

The essence of the cell theory is that the basic and universal structural element of life is the cell. Generally, the German physiologist Theodor *Schwann (1810–82) and the German botanist Matthias Jakob Schleiden (1804–81) are credited with the formulation of this theory. However, numerous investigators expressed its major tenets somewhat earlier and played a significant role in providing the groundwork essential for its formulation. Additionally, the development and refinement of the light microscope was an absolute necessity for the gathering of data essential to the cell theory.

The theory of cell lineage, the essence of which lies in H. Virchow's 1858 statement that cells arise only from preexisting cells ("Omnis cellula e cellula"), coupled with the cell theory to provide a dynamic or "modern" cell theory. This along with the theory of evolution are the cornerstones of modern biology.

Once developed, the cell theory had a catalytic effect upon the scientific climate—an effect that is still very much felt. Interest in cellular studies rose meteorically, resulting in findings that not only corrected and extended earlier interpretations of the cell theory, but which provided insights into numerous basic biological problems. The evolution of the cell theory has had a significant impact outside of the biological sciences as well, playing a major role in the revision of concepts in such areas as theology, philosophy, and sociology.

The Microscope. The origin and development of the miscroscope was intimately associated with spectacle making and the formation of optical science. Optical properties of curved surfaces were known to Euclid (300 B.C.) and described by Ptolemy (A.D. 127–151) and Alhazan (965–1039). Armati invented spectacles in Italy around 1285. However, it was Leonardo da Vinci and Maurolyco in the 16th century who first advocated the utilization of lenses for small object study. It is interesting to note that Roger Bacon (1214–94) considered the possible value of lenses as an aid to vision, but his works lay unknown until their discovery in 1733. The Janssen brothers, Zachary and Francis, were the first to combine two convex lenses within a tube in 1590 and thus construct the direct forerunner of the compound microscope.

The art and techniques of polishing short focus lenses developed rapidly, and A. Leeuwenhook (1632–1723) obtained adequate lens systems in 1674 for simple scientific observations. *Galileo (1564–1642) is credited with the construction of the first microscope in 1610. The term microscope was coined by Faber of Bamberg, physician to Pope Urban VII, around 1590.

The first systematic utilization of the microscope in the study of disease is credited to Athanasius *Kircher in the 17th century. Mechanical improvements of the microscope occurred rapidly and included such refinements as a third lens between the ocular and objective, which eliminated chromatic aberration (Monconys and Campani, 1655). Such improvements rendered many new scientific observations possible. These findings served as the groundwork for and led directly to the formulation of the cell theory.

Development of the Cell Theory. Robert *Hooke (1635–1703) published his *Micrographia* in 1665. In this collection of essays, Hooke, a noted physicist, turned his attention to biological matters and described in detail his observations of the microscopic structure of a thin slice of cork sectioned with a penknife. He reported a porous network of rectangular holes, which he termed "cells." Although Hooke, in reality, observed and described the dead remnants of what in life is a fluid-filled vesicle, the name was retained in biology and has become as universal in that discipline as has the "atom" of *Democritus in physics and chemistry.

M. *Malpighi continued and extended Hooke's findings to other plant tissues and carried out extensive investigations concerning the anatomy and embryology of both plants and animals. In 1661 he published his studies on the existence of capillaries (the existence of these structures had been predicted some 30 years earlier by W. *Harvey). N. Grew (1672) published an extensive account of detailed plant cellular structure. Both Malpighi and Grew reported the presence of "utricles or vesicles" present within the homogeneous mass of tissue, which were, of course, the "cells" of Hooke. The actual nature of the cell, however, still remained to be observed.

Several important technical advances were made in the 18th century, which included J. Hill's introduction of tissue-preserving fluids and staining substances such as carmine. The microtome (a device for cutting very thin tissue sections) was developed around 1780. But in general, knowledge concerning the true nature of the cell advanced little from the time of Hooke's formulations until the start of the 19th century, for until that time only the cellulose membrane of plants (the cell of Hooke or utricle of Grew and Malpighi) had been described.

Ostensibly, the cell theory states that all organisms, plant and animal, are composed of cells. Schleiden (1838) and Schwann (1839) often are credited with the formulation of this theory, and they indeed played a major role in its articulation. However, the list of cosponsors is quite long and should include C. Mirbel, who in 1808–09 suggested a membranous cellular tissue structure for plants. J. B. *Lamarck (1809) correlated "life" with a cellular tissue structure. H. Dutrochet (1824), P. Turpin (1826), and H. von Mohl (1831) clearly stated the essential aspects of the cell theory in their writings.

The earliest definitive expression of the cell theory was that of Schleiden on plant tissues and extended to animal tissue by Schwann, who utilized the expression "cell theory" for the first time. Perhaps Schwann's greatest contribution, however, was his genius in considering the physiological significance of the cell. He considered cellular phenomena as falling into two groups: "plastic phenomena" (or morphological ones) and "physiologic phenomena" (which he designated also as metabolic phenomena). However, the overwhelming morphogenetic climate of the 19th century led to an almost complete concentration on what Schwann termed plastic or morphological phenomena of the cell and an almost complete disregard of the physiological.

Extension of the Cell Theory. The cell theory was now firmly established, and the balance of the 19th century saw it developed and extended. Robert Remak (1841) and Karl Nageli (1844) accurately described cell division and in so doing corrected the misinterpretation of Schleiden, which had been passively accepted by Schwann. C. von Siebold (1845) concluded that the protozoa were in fact single-cell animals. Sperms and eggs were recognized as cells by A. Kolliker in 1841 and 1844, respectively, and the cell theory was extended to the field of pathology by Virchow in 1858, when he demonstrated that cells were the sites of pathological processes.

The scientists of the 17th and 18th centuries investigated primarily the plant cell membrane. The 19th century saw, however, a marked trend toward consideration of the contents of the cell, which was first described by various investigators as being a gelatinous-like juice. The Scottish botanist Robert Brown (1773–1858) was the first to describe the presence of the nucleus (Latin, "little nut") in the "cellular juice" of orchid cells in 1831.

F. Dujardin detailed the nature of the living cellular contents in 1835, which he termed the "sarcode." This later received the name of "protoplasm" from Purkinje and Von Mohl. The basic similarity of plant and animal protoplasm was established by Max Schultze in 1861, when he established the groundwork for the formulation of the "protoplasm theory," as it was to be called by O. Hertwig (1892). Essentially this theory states that a cell contains a living substance(s) termed the protoplasm, a nucleus, and a cell membrane. Numerous exceptions to this, such as the bacteria and plasmodia where the cellular structure is not nearly so well defined, are now known. Modification of the protoplasm theory was thus necessary and Hanstein's (1880) "protoplast" (consideration of the cell as a delimited mass of protoplasm in which a nucleus is contained) is more nearly correct.

The development of the cell theory, theory of cell lineage, and protoplasm theory led to an acceleration of investigations and discoveries of a histological nature. Cell and nuclear division was detailed in plant materials by Edvard Strasburger and published in 1875. Similar studies of animal mitosis were developed by Walther Flemming, his reports appearing in 1879, 1882, and during the next decade. It was Flemming who introduced such terms as mitosis, prophase, metaphase, anaphase, telophase, and chromatin in describing the behavior of structures (termed chromosomes by W. Waldeyer in 1888), which appeared only during the division stages of the cell. Hertwig's discoveries of the ovum and fusion of the pronuclei in 1875 were also of major importance. By this time, various cytoplasmic components such as the chondriome (mitochondria) and Golgi bodies had been discovered. Structural and functional qualities of the cell were now considered as an integrated entity established most notably by Hertwig's monograph "The Cell and the Tissues" published in 1892. That the root of basic biological problems lay at the cellular level was here firmly established and marked the formal birth of the discipline of cytology.

The 20th century has seen still further acceleration of advances in knowledge of the cell. This has been made possible primarily through rapid technical develop-

"The Adoration of the Lamb in Heaven," full-page miniature in a manuscript of Beatus of Liébana's *Commentary on the Apocalypse,* written and illustrated in Spain, A.D. 926 (New York, Pierpont Morgan Library, MS 644, fol. 174v). This manuscript, the earliest dated copy of this popular medieval work, is noted for its graphic, intensely colored miniatures.

ments. Important among these was the ability to maintain and grow cells outside of the living body in cell or tissue cultures. This technique was pioneered and developed in 1907 by Ross Harrison and significantly advanced by Alexis *Carrell and Charles Lindberg. The phase-contrast microscope developed in 1941 rendered possible the detailed observation and study of living cells, and the invention and perfection of the electron microscope enabled the investigation in fixed tissue of the submicroscopic (ultra) structure of the cell. Interest in the chemistry of the cell (cytochemistry) has paralleled the rapid developments in *biochemistry. Continued technological advances in the physical sciences and their incorporation and application to biological studies are ever more commonplace and expected.

Problems and Exceptions. In some respects various groups of organisms do not easily conform to the tenets of the cell theory. The lack of formed nuclei in the *bacteria apparently caused serious concern. However, the presence of nuclear material has been clearly established in this group, and recent studies strongly suggest a nuclear organization reminiscent of higher forms.

Viruses, particles that are much smaller than cells and regarded by virtually all biologists as living, exhibit some but not all qualities of cells. Most notably different is that they do not possess the mechanism for their own replication, but need to utilize that of a host cell. The simplest reconciliation of the position of the viral particle is to consider it a highly specialized form of life that has replaced its less efficient form of reproduction with a much more efficient replicative process. Such a replacement is a ubiquitously evidenced aspect of organic evolution. An additional exception to the definition of a cell as a delimited mass of protoplasm in which a nucleus is contained can be found from studies of molds where certain species form coenocytes or structures in which nuclei are found suspended in a "nonpartitioned" cytoplasm. Other such "exceptions" also are known. Nevertheless, the overwhelming majority of plant and animal cells do manifest separateness and conformance to the cell theory.

Perhaps the most difficult question raised by the cell theory is whether it is the cell or the organism as a whole that is the unit of life in multicellular forms. Most generally, the relationship of the organism as a whole is considered the criterion of life.

Bibliography: I. ASIMOV, *Biographical Encyclopedia of Science and Technology* (Garden City, N.Y. 1964). E. D. P. DEROBERTIS, et al., *General Cytology* (3d ed. Philadelphia, Pa. 1960). M. L. GABRIEL and S. FOGEL, eds., *Great Experiments in Biology* (Englewood Cliffs, N.J. 1955). E. J. GARDNER, *History of Biology* (2d ed. Minneapolis, Minn. 1965). G. SARTON, *A History of Science*, 2 v. (Cambridge, Mass. 1952–59). *Scientific American* 205 (Sept. 1961), 10 excellent articles. G. G. SIMPSON et al., *Life: An Introduction to Biology* (2d ed. New York 1965). C. P. SWANSON, *Cytology and Cytogenetics* (Englewood Cliffs, N.J. 1957). G. B. WILSON and J. H. MORRISON, *Cytology* (New York 1961).

[H. A. BENDER]

CELLES-SUR-BELLE, MONASTERY OF, former Augustinian foundation near the village of Melle, France, Diocese of Poitiers. It was founded early in the 11th century, on property originally given to the *Benedictines of *Saint-Maixent by William of Aquitaine, as a priory of *Canons Regular of St. Augustine dependent on the Abbey of Saint-Pierre de Lesterp. It was created an *abbey by Bp. William II Adelelme of Poitiers in 1140 with Jean de Uzon as the first abbot, and had its independence from Lesterp ratified under Bp. *Gilbert de la Porrée in 1148 through a bull of *Eugene III. The abbey was dedicated to Our Lady, and the fame of the miracles attributed to her intercession at Celles made it a pilgrimage center from *c.* 1095, although the great annual pilgrimage, the *Septembresch,* or the Feast of the Nativity of the Virgin Mary, is first mentioned only in 1395. The pilgrimage flourished into the 15th century, reaching its apogee in the reign of *Louis XI, who visited the abbey about 10 times, left lavish gifts, and had the 12th-century monastery church reconstructed during the years 1470 to 1477. The pilgrimage was restored in 1899, and Bishop Durfort of Poitiers solemnly crowned the venerated statue of Notre-Dame de Celles on Sept. 26, 1926. The practice of *commendation was introduced in 1515 with the nomination of Geoffroy d'Estissac, later abbot-bishop of Maillezais. The monastery was pillaged by the *Huguenots and abandoned by the monks in 1568. It was besieged again in 1569 by Admiral *Coligny, but defended by the Barbeziére family, on whom King Charles IX of France (d. 1574) subsequently bestowed its income. Following attempts by Cardinal F. de *La Rochefoucauld and Henri-Louis II de La Rochefoucauld to wrest the control from the Barbezières, the abbey was finally united to the Congregation of France (*see* BENEDICTINES) in 1651. The church was rebuilt in 1669, and new cloisters were constructed in 1682. Its income in 1787 was estimated at 14,000 livres, and it had several priories, 12 parishes, and some chapels dependent on it. The last titular abbot was C. *Talleyrand-Périgord. The monks were expelled in 1791, and the property served as a prison for the Vendée rebels. Today the church serves parish needs and is administered by the *Montfort Fathers, who in 1921 established a novitiate in the former cloisters of the abbey.

Bibliography: Cottineau 1:649. P. CALENDINI, DHGE 12:116–118. R. GAZEAU, *Catholicisme* 2:773. A. LARGEAULT, *Notre-Dame de Celles, son abbaye, son pèlerinage* (Parthenay 1900).

[G. E. GINGRAS]

CELLINI, BENVENUTO, goldsmith, sculptor, and writer; b. Florence, Italy, Nov. 3, 1500; d. there, Feb. 13, 1571. In 1519, after several years as an apprentice to a Florentine goldsmith, he went to Rome. He worked at his craft there until 1540, with intervals in Florence and Mantua. He took part in the defense of Rome against Charles V (1527), and received from Clement VII the title of master of the press of the pontifical mint (1529). He fell into disfavor with Paul III and was imprisoned in Castel Sant'Angelo (1538), but was freed the following year through the influence of Cardinal Ippolito d'Este. At the court of Francis I of France (1540–45), he worked as goldsmith (creating the famous salt-cellar) and as architect and sculptor (designing the gate at Fontainebleau and decorating it with statues and bas-reliefs). Having returned to Florence, he gained the favor of Grand Duke Cosimo I de'Medici who commissioned him (1549) to do, among other pieces, the bronze Perseus in the gallery of the Lanzi. The envy of rival artists and the loss of the Grand Duke's patronage embittered the last years of a turbulent and not too edifying life—he was a quarreler and a dueler, and, though he had received minor orders (1558), managed to marry in 1565.

Cellini began his autobiography (*La Vita de B.C. scritta da lui medesimo*) in 1558. It is not only an exciting and impassioned (and substantially accurate) account, varied and rich in events, in encounters and clashes, in human and artistic experiences, but also a vindication of Cellini himself. Despite the fact that it seems to echo the thematic and stylistic conventions of Renaissance biographical and autobiographical literature, Cellini's account stands out as an idealized self-portrait. Its central qualities are its strongly distorted and partial viewpoint, from which Benvenuto always dominates people and events, and its emphasis on his struggle with the world and his own fate. It is thus a kind of Renaissance contrast between *virtú* and Fortuna, emotional and informal, yet rising at times to epic and dramatic heights. He wrote also technical treatises (*Trattato dell' oreficeria,* and *Trattato della scultura*), and a certain number of *Rime,* but his autobiography is unique in Italian literature.

Bibliography: *La vita,* ed. O. Bacci (Florence 1901), rev. B. Maier (new ed. Florence 1961); *La vita . . .: Con l'aggiunta di tratto dell'oreficeria, tratto della scultura, discorsi sopra l'arte, lettere e suppliche, poesie,* ed. G. Cattaneo (Milan 1958). B. Croce, *Poeti e scrittori del pieno e del tardo rinascimento,* 3 v. (Bari 1952–58). B. Maier, *Umanità e stile di Benvenuto Cellini* (Milan 1952); "Benvenuto Cellini," *Letteratura Italiana: I minori,* 4 v. (Milan 1961) 2:1133–55.

[B. MAIER]

CELSUS, Greek philosopher, author of the *True Discourse* (Ἀληθὴς Λόγος), the most important pagan intellectual opponent of Christianity before Porphyry; fl. 2d half of 2d century A.D. No details on his life and place of his activities are extant. The original text of the *True Discourse* (*c.* A.D. 178) is lost, but about nine-tenths of the treatise can be reconstructed with practical certainty from the extracts and arguments found in *Origen's elaborate refutation, *Against Celsus* (Κατὰ Κέλσου) in eight books, composed nearly 70 years later (A.D. 246). Celsus was an adherent of Middle Platonism, but was, above all, a champion of Hellenic culture in all its aspects. In his polemic he showed a marked familiarity with the Old and the New Testaments and Christian teachings in general. However, he was not always aware of the precise differences between Judaism and Christianity, nor of those between Christian orthodoxy, heresy, and Gnosticism. While showing some appreciation for the Christian concept of the Logos and for Christian ethics, he rejected the Christian concept of God as the absolute Creator, and branded the teachings on the Incarnation and Crucifixion as absurd. He ridiculed likewise many of the Biblical narratives and miracles. On the political side, he accused the Christians of being unpatriotic because of their attitude toward the religious policy of the state. Celsus was not so much a philosopher as an ardent champion of Hellenism as expressed in a long and venerable tradition. On the twin pillars of *logos* and *nomos,* to which antiquity had given authority, he erected a philosophy of history. Christianity was rejected as being new and outside the Hellenic tradition, indeed even a repudiation of it. This argument against Christianity was resumed by Porphyry and the Emperor Julian.

Bibliography: Cross ODCC 256. H. Huhn, LexThK[2] 6:108–109. C. Andresen, RGG[3] 1:1630–31; *Logos und Nomos: Die Polemik des Celsus wider das Christentum* (Berlin 1955). Quasten Patr 2:52–57, with good bibliography. P. C. de Labriolle, *La Réaction païenne* (6th ed., Paris 1942) 109–169.

[M. R. P. MC GUIRE]

CELTIC ART

The expansion of the Celts from their Alpine homelands led them to many regions, among them Greece and Italy, where they broke Etruscan power and occupied Rome briefly in 390 B.C. Greco-Etruscan bronze wine vessels, red-figured pottery, and other luxury goods have been found in the Alpine region in Celtic graves of *c.* 450 B.C. The second Celtic style (called La Tène), which was brought to Britain by Celtic invaders in the 4th century B.C., was based on an assimilation of certain classical naturalistic figural and foliate themes and their transformation into an abstract, conventional style. Ornament was built up of S-shapes, spirals, and flowing curves, set out in a strict symmetry of pattern. The Celts also developed a sculptural art both of animals and of human figures, in relief and in the round, that was simplified and powerful in its stylization. A considerable body of Gaulish sculpture, chiefly figures of deities, is extant. Later, from perhaps the 2d century A.D., there survives a dramatic repertoire of figural art, with scenes of gods, warriors, animals, and human sacrifice, on the great silver cauldron from Gundestrup (National Museum, Copenhagen). In Britain, La Tène art had a distinctive and vigorous development. It appears on weapons (swords, scabbards, shields, helmets, and spearheads); on horse harness, mirrors, pottery, ritual objects, votive or personal collars, ornaments, and coinage. It is known also from wooden vessels, in vestiges of stone and wood sculpture, and even in giant figures cut on the chalk downs, such as the White Horse at Uffington, Berkshire. There is an evolution from the early delicate running scrolls of the Irish-found Lisnacroghera scabbard, or the Northumberland sword (private collection), or the Witham shield (British Museum), in which the foliate basis of the scroll and palmette are still visible, to the more purely abstract engraved and embossed curvilinear pattern of the Battersea shield, the Snettisham gold torc, or Desborough mirror (all British Museum). The fine period of Celtic art in Britain belongs to the 2 centuries from *c.* 150 B.C. to A.D. 50. Degeneration and loss of impetus followed contact with mass-produced Roman industrial art after the Claudian conquest of A.D. 63. Celtic art virtually died out in the British Isles after A.D. 200 (*see* IRISH ART). Certain clichés and the knowledge of enameling must have survived somewhere in the Celtic-inhabited areas of Britain through the period of the Saxon settlement of England. In the revival, under fresh stimuli and the new patronage of the Church, the fully mature style, though incorporating new themes of interlacing, animal patterns, and geometric rectilinear designs, was Celtic not only in being art of the Celtic-inhabited areas, but also in its exploitation of scrolls, spirals, and champlevé enamel technique, and especially in its fluidity and essential dynamic quality.

Bibliography: P. Jacobsthal, *Early Celtic Art,* 2 v. (Oxford 1944). E. T. Leeds, *Celtic Ornament in the British Isles down to A.D. 700* (Oxford 1933). T. G. E. Powell, *The Celts* (New York 1958). R. Lantier, EncWA 3:175–186. **Illustration credits:** Figs. 1*a,* 1*b,* 1*c,* 1*d,* Bibliothèque Nationale, Paris. Fig. 1*e,* Giraudon.

[R. L. S. BRUCE-MITFORD]

Celtic art: (a) Obverse and (b) reverse of the Stater of the Parisii, 1st century B.C., *diameter, 1 inch. (c) Obverse and (d) reverse of the Stater of the Bellovaci, 1st century* B.C., *diameter,* $^{11}/_{16}$ *inch. (e) Helmet, copper, iron, and gold, c. mid-4th century B.C., excavated at Amfreville, Eure, France (Musée du Louvre).*

CELTIC RELIGION

The ancient Celtic-speaking peoples were distributed over a wide area from Ireland to Asia Minor, and their religious ideas and practices reflect in part borrowings from other early or contemporary cultures. Greek and Roman writers supply valuable information on Celtic religion from the 3d century B.C., but they tend to be superficial and to be satisfied with rough identifications of Celtic divinities with their own gods and goddesses. Much information is furnished also by a critical sifting of the pagan traditions preserved in medieval Latin, Irish, and Welsh sources. A fairly rich mythology can be reconstructed especially out of the Irish literature in Latin and in Old and Middle Irish.

The gods in the historical period were largely anthropomorphic, and several of them corresponded to Mars, Mercury, and Apollo. However, many of the gods were local or tribal or, at least, given different names in different areas. Celtic personal and place names frequently reflect divine associations. Thus, Lugdunum (modern Lyons) was "the town of Lug," a divinity found on the Continent and in Ireland. Mother goddesses, the *Matronae* or *Matres,* were worshiped, especially in the region of the Rhine, by both Celts and Germans, and the cult of a horse goddess Epona was widespread and popular. Sacred plants (especially the mistletoe), trees, hills, mountains, rivers, springs, and remote open places, played a special role in Celtic religion. Major or minor divinities were associated with such sacred objects or places. In Ireland the belief in the *Sid*-folk or fairies, originally divine beings affecting various aspects of human life, is very old. They were thought to dwell chiefly under hills. Animals also were assigned divine attributes, especially bulls, horses, boars, and bears. Magic, magical formulae, spells, and curses are frequently mentioned and their effects described. Old Irish literary remains, with their emphasis on *geis* (taboo), reflect the important place of taboos in pagan Celtic religious and social life. The pagan Celts are thought to have had a vivid belief in a life beyond the grave and even a belief in transmigration of souls, but on this point there are no certain details.

Altar to the Matronae Aufaniae at Bonn, A.D. *164.*

On the Continent, in Britain, and in Ireland, the priestly class, the druids, played a major part in religion, law, education, and the determination of public policy. They were of royal blood and had to undergo a long period of training. There seem to have been divisions or grades among the druids, but the evidence is in part vague and conflicting. They were specialists in divination and were regarded as having prophetic powers. They performed certain religious rites and presided at sacrifices. In the historical period at least, there were sacrifices of animals and offerings of various kinds. Although there are references to human sacrifice in Gaul and Britain, it must have been rare. At any event, there is no evidence that this practice was approved or conducted by the druids.

Like the Roman *pontifices,* the druids had charge of the calendar, which, as all early calendars, was religious in character and indicated the days on which ordinary business could be carried out and those on which all or some actions were forbidden. As champions of Celtic traditions in all phases of life, the druids were deprived of their authority in Gaul by the Romans from the time of Claudius. However, they continued to flourish in Ireland until the triumph of Christianity. In Irish tradition much stress is placed on their wondrous powers as diviners and magicians. The brehons and bards of Christian Ireland became the heirs of the druids and, like them, were the tenacious preservers and champions of national cultural traditions.

Bibliography: F. N. ROBINSON, OxClDict 758–759. J. A. MACCULLOCH, Hastings ERE 3:277–304. J. RYAN, König Christus 2:245–265. R. HERTZ, RGG³ 3:1238–41. T. G. E. POWELL, *The Celts* (New York 1958). J. ZWICKER, *Fontes historiae religionis Celticae* (*Fontes historiae religionum,* ed. C. CLEMEN, 5.1–3; Bonn 1934–36). R. LANTIER, "Keltische Mythologie," *Wörterbuch der Mythologie,* ed. H. W. HAUSSIG (Stuttgart 1961–) Abt. 1.2.1, fasc. 5, 100–162. J. VENDRYÈS et al., *Les Religions des Celtes, des Germains, et des anciens Slaves* ("Mana" ser. 2.3; Paris 1948) 235–320. J. DE VRIES, *Keltische Religion* (Die Religionen der Menschheit 18; Stuttgart 1961). **Illustration credit:** Rheinisches Landesmuseum, Bonn.

[M. R. P. MC GUIRE]

CELTIC RITE

Lack of evidence about liturgical practice in the localities in which the Celtic rite is said to have existed precludes arriving at a clear picture. There has never been a distinct Celtic rite in the strict sense of the term "rite" as we apply it to the Mozarabic or Milanese rites.

Origins. The Celtic monks, tireless missionaries who traveled widely, did not intend to draw up a new liturgy. They seem to have chosen elements from different rites and combined them. The Celtic rites, therefore, were an eclectic composition of foreign customs, Roman and Gallican. We know indeed that in Scotland, Ireland, Wales, Cornwall, and Brittany—the regions to which the

Saxon invasion had confined the remains of Celtic culture and Christianity—there were certain disciplinary differences from Roman customs and those introduced by St. *Augustine of Canterbury, who landed in Kent in the summer of 597. These differences applied principally to the form of the *tonsure, the date of Easter, and the general form of ecclesiastical organization, heavily influenced by the monastic element. After the abortive synod to which the Celtic Christians were summoned by St. Augustine in 603, the Synod of Whitby (664) witnessed their complete submission. Yet traces of an independent liturgy lingered on for about 500 years in parts of Ireland and Scotland until the Synod of Cashel (1172) when the Anglo-Roman liturgy was introduced into Ireland. Brittany probably lost its distinctive rites at the time of *Louis I, the Pious (817), and Scotland lost its rites in the 11th century through the efforts of Queen Margaret (d. 1093, canonized 1250).

Sources. The principal sources are to be found in three liturgical books—the Bangor Antiphonary, the Bobbio Missal, and the Stowe Missal, all of monastic origin. As its name implies, the Bangor Antiphonary is a collection of antiphons, versicles, hymns, canticles, etc., and was compiled probably for the use of the abbot of the famous monastery of Bangor in Ireland. The book dates from the end of the 7th century (between 680 and 690); it is now in the Ambrosian Library at Milan. The Bobbio Missal, a 7th-century manuscript discovered by J. Mabillon at Bobbio, Italy, is one of the earliest witnesses for the history of the Roman Canon; it represents a local liturgy influenced by Rome and includes certain borrowings from Rome, despite a different Mass order. Lastly, the Stowe Missal, a manuscript of the late 8th or 9th century, was composed probably for the abbey of Tallaght near Dublin. It contains, in addition to part of the Gospel of St. John (with which it is bound), the Ordinary of the Mass, three Mass Propers, and the rites of Baptism, Anointing, and Communion of the Sick. In addition there are various liturgical fragments to be found in several manuscripts of Irish origin. From the slender evidence at our disposal, the most that can be asserted is that the Gallican rite was the principal formative factor of the Celtic liturgy, which in course of time became increasingly Romanized.

Characteristics. The preparation of the oblations took place before the celebrant's entrance, as in the *Gallican rites. The introductory prayers include a confession of sins and examples of lengthy apologies, as well as a litany of Irish saints. The first part of the Mass, in its later form in the Stowe Missal, follows the Roman form: Gloria, one or more Collects, Epistle, Gradual, and Alleluia. At this point was said a litany, borrowed from the East, the *Deprecatio Sancti Martini* (which occurs also in the Milanese rite). After two prayers and the partial unveiling of the offerings with a threefold invocation over them, the Gospel was sung, followed by the Credo (including the *Filioque). At the Offertory, after the complete unveiling of the offerings, the chalice, and sometimes the paten, were elevated. There followed a commemoration of the dead and reading of the *diptychs. The Preface with the usual preliminary dialogue and followed by the Sanctus came next with, usually, a post-Sanctus. Though the Canon in the Stowe Missal is headed *Canon dominicus papae Gilasii,* it is in fact the Gregorian Canon with several Irish saints named in it. It is evidence of the use of the Roman Canon in the Celtic Church at the beginning of the 9th century. After the Memento of the living occurs a list of more than 100 holy people (Old Testament and Irish saints among them). Various chants were designated for Communion, including (in the Bangor Antiphonary) the beautiful hymn *Sancti venite.*

Great latitude appears to have been allowed to individual monasteries in the arrangement of the Divine Office, and details of it are to be found in the various monastic rules. The Celtic monks exerted their greatest influence in the evolution of the Sacrament of Penance, for it was largely through them that the practice of private (as opposed to public) satisfaction for sin became popular.

Bibliography: L. GOUGAUD, DACL 2.2:2969–3032 treats the subject exhaustively with full bibliographical references. A. A. KING, *Liturgies of the Past* (Milwaukee 1959) 186–275 has full bibliography and list of sources, including those of liturgical fragments in various MSS. *Bobbio Missal,* ed. A. WILMART, et al. (HBradshSoc 61; 1924). *Antiphonary of Bangor,* ed. F. E. WARREN (HBradshSoc 4, Pt. 1, 1893; 10, Pt. 2, 1895). *Stowe Missal,* ed. G. F. WARNER, (HBradshSoc 32; 1915). F. E. WARREN, *Liturgy and Ritual of the Celtic Church* (Oxford 1881).

[L. C. SHEPPARD]

CELTIS, CONRAD

The first German poet laureate and organizer of Renaissance humanist sodalities; b. Wipfeld, Feb. 1, 1459; d. Vienna, Feb. 4, 1508. He studied at Cologne, Heidelberg, Rostock, and Leipzig. In 1487 he toured Italy, traveled to Cracow to study mathematics and natural philosophy, and moved from there to Nuremberg and to Ingolstadt, where he was appointed professor of rhetoric. In 1497 on Maximilian's invitation he transferred to the University of Vienna, where he founded the College of Poets and Mathematicians, and taught poetry and rhetoric until his untimely death. Celtis, the best lyric poet among the German humanists, was crowned the poet laureate of the empire by Frederick III in Nuremberg on April 18, 1487. He was a genial personality given to a carefree, irresponsible way of life, who celebrated in his book of *Amores* (1502) his four loves symbolizing the four parts of Germany. In his *Odes,* done in the manner of Horace, he rose to high levels in writing of life, love, and learning. His book of *Epigrams* was clever and cutting. He wrote two known dramas after the pattern of Terence, the *Ludus Dianae* and the *Rhapsodia.* He contributed to the rising tide of romantic cultural nationalism, publishing a textbook edition of Tacitus's *Germania,* and the plays of the 10th-century nun Roswitha, which he had discovered in a monastery and which illustrated the existence of a literary culture in the Ottonian period. He also discovered the *Ligurinus,* a medieval epic poem praising the deeds of Emperor Frederick Barbarossa.

Celtis organized Rhenish and Danubian sodalities, loose associations of humanists, to undertake scholarly publication, encourage creative writing, and provide mutual encouragement. These sodalities, together with other local groups, were to contribute collectively to a large historicogeographical compilation entitled *Germania illustrata,* to which Celtis's own poetic *Germania generalis* and his descriptive masterpiece, the *Norimberga,* were intended to serve as an introduction and model. To Celtis, philosophy in the broadest sense of the word meant all humanist learning. In a narrower

Conrad Celtis, woodcut portrait by Hans Burgkmair, commissioned by the sitter to commemorate his impending death.

sense his philosophy was antique-naturalistic, strongly influenced by Neoplatonism. He was opposed to scholasticism on cultural grounds, although he planned a work, the *Parnassus biceps,* that was to effect harmony between the poets and the theologians. In bitter anticlericalism, he criticized the moral abuses in the Church, including in his attacks even such Renaissance popes as Innocent VIII. Despite his estrangement from orthodoxy and his radical departures in spiritual and moral philosophy, he retained a certain piety and respect for traditional Christianity. He was buried in St. Stephen's Cathedral.

Bibliography: C. CELTIS, *Selections,* ed. and tr. L. FORSTER (Cambridge, Eng. 1948). L. W. SPITZ, *Conrad Celtis, the German Arch-Humanist* (Cambridge, Mass. 1957). ALBERT WERMINGHOFF, *Conrad Celtis und sein Buch über Nürnberg* (Freiburg 1921). H. RUPPRICH, ed., *Der Briefwechsel des Konrad Celtis* (Munich 1934). A. FINGERLE, LexThK² 2:991. **Illustration credit:** Austrian National Library, Vienna.

[L. W. SPITZ]

CEMETERIES, CANON LAW OF

From the beginning the Church has followed the practice of burying its dead. It urges that each parish have its own cemetery, or, if more feasible, the local ordinary may permit several parishes to use an interparochial cemetery (CIC c.1208.1). Congregations and communities of religious men and woman, and even lay organizations and private families, may have their own cemeteries (CIC c.1208.2,3).

Blessings of Cemeteries. The Church requires that the cemeteries it owns be blessed (CIC c.1205.1). The blessings may be solemn or simple, but the solemn blessing is preferred.

The rite of solemn blessing (sometimes referred to as consecration) is found in the *Pontificale Romanum* under the title "De Coemeterii Benedictione." (*See* PONTIFICAL, ROMAN.) The minister of solemn blessing is the bishop of the place or another in episcopal orders. Should a priest be authorized by the local ordinary (or by the religious ordinary if the cemetery is owned by a religious community), he must use the rite of the *Pontificale,* disregarding only those rubrics which evidently refer exclusively to bishops.

The simple blessing is a rite found in the *Rituale Romanum* tit. 8, c.29. (*See* RITUAL, ROMAN.) The ordinary minister is a priest delegated by the local or religious ordinary.

In cases where the Church *cannot* (e.g., because all cemeteries are government owned) or *does not* (e.g., because of religious prejudice, bigotry, the poverty of the people) own its cemeteries, the law makes special provisions. Consistent with the Church's desire that every Catholic be buried in blessed ground, the law provides: (1) when Catholics are permitted to have the exclusive use of a separate section of the community or municipal cemetery, this special Catholic section is to be blessed; (2) when Catholics cannot have their own section and must be buried indiscriminately with non-Catholics in a community cemetery, the whole cemetery is to be blessed, provided the burials are predominantly Catholic (CIC c.1206.2); (3) when Catholics cannot have their own section and non-Catholic burials exceed Catholic burials, each individual grave is to be blessed before the body of the deceased is lowered into it (CIC c.1206.3). The rite for blessing a single grave can be found in the *Rituale Romanum* tit. 6, c.3n12.

Although the law makes no mention of the type of blessing that a cemetery or section not owned by the Church should receive, it would seem, from a study of the parallel legislation on the blessing of churches (CIC c.1165), that the rite should be that taken from the *Rituale,* a simple blessing.

Loss of blessing can occur in two ways: (1) utter destruction of the cemetery, e.g., through a severe earthquake, flood, aerial bombing; or (2) conversion of the cemetery to profane purposes by decree of the local ordinary (CIC c.1170). A cemetery that has lost its blessing can regain it only through a reblessing.

Violated and Interdicted Cemeteries. A blessed cemetery, like a blessed church, can be violated or placed under interdict (CIC c.1207). Neither involves a loss of blessing.

Violation is a temporary curtailment of some of the effects of the blessing. Until the moral defilement is removed by the rite of reconciliation (found both in the *Pontificale* and *Rituale Romanum*), the cemetery is legally unfit for Christian burial. Violation follows such acts occurring in a cemetery as criminal homicide, sinful and copious shedding of blood, putting a cemetery to impious and sordid uses, or interment of those legally denied Christian burial.

Ordinarily a bishop reconciles a solemnly blessed cemetery; a priest, a simply blessed one. In a grave and urgent emergency, a priest may conduct the rite of reconciliation of a solemnly blessed cemetery.

An interdicted cemetery differs from a violated cemetery in that, in the case of the former, burial itself is not prohibited, but none of the liturgical rites of burial are permitted. In effect, the deceased may receive all of the customary funeral rites at the church, including a funeral Mass and the absolution, and even burial in blessed ground, but the liturgical service at graveside is denied during the period of the interdict (*see* INTERDICT).

The Holy See or the local bishop imposes a cemetery interdict with respect to certain specified persons or to a whole community, over a designated period, for some gravely sinful act. The interdict remains until the time has elapsed or until the penalty is lifted.

Special Sections. In its blessed cemeteries the Church prefers to have priests and clerics buried in a section set apart from the laity (CIC c.1209.2). It likewise considers it fitting that infants be interred in a special plot reserved for them (CIC c.1209.3).

The Church also provides in the law (CIC c.1212) for the burial of those who, through some gravely sinful personal acts unrepented at death, have disqualified themselves for ecclesiastical burial (CIC c.1240). They are to be buried in an unblessed section of the cemetery.

Care and Control. The care and control of blessed cemeteries are the responsibilities of the local or religious ordinary or his delegate. There will generally be a full- or part-time caretaker. For security and privacy cemeteries are usually enclosed by a fence or wall (CIC c.1210).

The bishop or religious superior will see to it that the epitaphs, memorial tablets, and monuments reflect the Church's belief that not only the souls but also the bodies of the faithful departed are destined for immortality.

Permission of the ordinary of the place or of the major religious superior is required for the exhumation of bodies which have received ecclesiastical burial. This is true whether the body is in a Church-owned cemetery or not. The ordinary will not permit exhumation at all if the body to be disinterred cannot be distinguished from the remains of others.

Bibliography: H. LECLERCQ, DACL 3:1626–65. J. GULEZYNSKI, *The Desecration and Violation of Churches* (CUA CLS 159; Washington 1942). S. MANY, *Praelectiones de locis sacris* (Paris 1904). F. J. MOULART, *De sepultura et coemeteriis* (Louvain 1862). C. M. POWER, *The Blessing of Cemeteries* (CUA CLS 185; Washington 1943). A. C. RUSH, *Death and Burial in Christian Antiquity* (CUA, Studies in Christian Antiquity 1; Washington 1941).

[C. M. POWER]

CEMETERIES, U.S. LAW OF

Discussion of the civil law of cemeteries will follow this general outline: establishment of cemeteries; rights and duties of cemetery owners, plot-purchasers, and others; and the position of religion in the law.

Establishment. Property may be set aside for the burial of the dead by private persons, by municipalities, and by profitmaking or charitable organizations. No particular form of "dedication" is required, though it is commonplace for the property owner to execute a written deed. There must be public acceptance of the dedication; but this may be implied from the acts of the grantor in marking the property, or from its actual use for burials. Local statutes usually regulate the establishment of cemeteries to prevent them from becoming public nuisances or health hazards. Once dedicated, cemetery land cannot be used for other purposes.

Rights and Duties. The owner of land that is set aside for sepulture retains the fee-simple title. Although the grantor cannot later revoke the dedication, he may sell the property so long as he does not attempt to extinguish its use as a cemetery. If cemetery land ever ceases to be used for burials and there is no indication that bodies remain interred there, the cemetery is considered abandoned. Absolute title then reverts to the original fee-simple owner or his heirs.

If the cemetery is operated by a corporation, it is usually regulated by the state's general corporation laws. The validity of state or local regulations for cemeteries depends on whether the regulations are reasonable exercises of the state's "police power."

A cemetery association may set up its own rules and regulations, which will be given effect unless unreasonable. Restrictions on the use of the cemetery must be included in the plot-purchase contract or in the charter of the association.

The purchaser of a cemetery lot does not acquire fee title, but only an easement or license to inter there. This right may be restricted by the cemetery association or by the state, may pass by will or intestacy, and may be sold (subject to the regulations of the cemetery). The purchaser has a right to tend and visit the plot.

The purchaser of a lot in a cemetery operated by a religious organization takes title subject to the rules of that organization. Generally, Catholic restrictions are enforced, even against the purchaser himself, and even if the regulation is imposed after the purchase. This is based on the theory that the purchaser gave the Church exclusive jurisdiction, and any decision is appealable only to Rome.

The purchaser, or the relatives of the deceased, may sue for damages or an injunction for any trespass or desecration of the grave.

A mortgagee of the cemetery land may sue to foreclose the mortgage, but he cannot disturb the status of the premises or the rights of the lot owners. Persons injured by a cemetery's operation may sue to abate the nuisance, but strangers, including the cemetery owner, may not interfere with the purchaser's right to use the cemetery lot. In many states desecration of grave or tombstone is a criminal offense.

Religion in the Law. Courts generally enforce purchase contracts according to their terms, but they also enforce religious restrictions on cemetery use if these do not conflict with established law or state policy. Thus when the tenets of a particular faith prohibit burial of certain persons, courts enforce such rules.

For example, the courts have ruled that an archbishop could compel the disinterment of a woman married outside the Church who had been mistakenly buried in consecrated ground; a Catholic cemetery could refuse to bury a lot owner who had given up the faith, or one who had died by suicide.

But the courts are reluctant to refuse burial rights where there has been no ecclesiastical hearing or where there is only circumstantial evidence of suicide. Where a person died after reportedly attending a meeting conducted by atheists, the court ruled that this alone was insufficient proof of a renunciation of faith and allowed the deceased to be interred in the religious cemetery.

Moreover, a church may not be compelled to sell cemetery space to a nonmember who claims the same faith and who has relatives buried in the cemetery. Any religious cemetery can restrict interment to those who die in communion with that faith.

Bibliography: R. L. BRENNAN, *Cemetery Rules and Regulations* (Los Angeles 1951). "Cemeteries," *Corpus Juris Secundum* 14:1–37, 25, 31, 36b. "Cemeteries," *American Jurisprudence* 1–40. "Right to Exclude from Privilege of Burial in Cemetery," *American Law Reports* 110 (1937) 388–393. "The Cemetery Lot: Rights and Restrictions," *Univ. Penna. Law Review* 109 (1960) 378–400.

[R. J. ROHNER]

CENACLE

Traditional site of the room in which Jesus had His *Last Supper with His Apostles. The term comes from the Latin *coenaculum* (dining room), which is used in the Vulgate as the translation of two different Greek words. The first of these, ἀνάγαιον (upper room), used in Mk 14.15 and Lk 22.12, refers to the large furnished upper room chosen by our Lord for the celebration of His Last Supper and the institution of the Holy Eucharist. The average ancient-Palestinian home was one storied and flat roofed. The homes of the wealthy, however, often included a guest room, penthouse-fashion, on the second or upper floor, having an outer staircase often leading up to it. The other word, ὑπερῷον, also meaning upper room, was applied by St. Luke in Acts 1.13 to the place where Mary and the Apostles stayed in prayer after the Ascension of Jesus into heaven, presumably until Pentecost day. Since both Greek words are practically synonymous, as shown by the single term *coenaculum* of the Latin Vulgate for both and by their use in the Septuagint, where the two words are employed interchangeably, it seems probable that Luke wished to identify the "upper room" of the first Christian Pentecost with that of the Last Supper.

Today, southwest of the present walls of the Old City of Jerusalem, in the State of Israel, the memory of the Cenacle is attached to a large (45 by 29½ feet) Gothic room of the 14th century, on the second floor of an ancient building. This is a reconstruction of an older chapel that had been left in a dilapidated condition at the departure of the Crusaders (A.D. 1187). A cenotaph of David is venerated on the ground floor and has become, since 1948, a favorite pilgrimage spot for the Israeli.

The history of this site, according to St. Epiphanius (d. 403), goes back to the 1st Christian century. According to him, a small church that had been built here in apostolic times survived the destructions inflicted by Titus and Hadrian. About A.D. 350 this old church was given needed restoration, and in 390 a great basilica, known as Holy Sion, was erected near it. The basilica is clearly represented on the famous 6th-century mosaic map of *Medaba and was lovingly referred to by the Byzantines as "The Mother of All Churches." As early as the 4th century, and more generally in the 6th, this church was clearly identified as the site of the Last Supper. The Crusaders, when they captured Jerusalem in 1099, found both churches in ruins. They restored the basilica in Romanesque style, but of this construction nothing was left after the destruction ordered by the Sultan of Damascus in 1219.

The title of Holy Sion contributed to an erroneous identification of the hill of the Cenacle with the Davidical Sion, which actually was on the opposite hill to the east, Mt. Ophel, beyond the Tyropeon Valley. A tomb of David, therefore, made its appearance here in the 12th century and prompted the Moslems' desire to possess the site. In 1342 the Franciscans received from Pope Clement VI the care of the Cenacle in perpetuity. It was then that they built the small Gothic chapel described above. In 1523 the Moslems transformed the chapel into a mosque and finally, in 1551, expelled the Franciscans from the site.

Today's Cenacle building cannot evidently be anything but a commemoration and an approximate localization, yet it clearly deserves reverence and respect. The same, however, cannot be said for the later precarious detailed identification of the different rooms in it, e.g., where St. John said Mass. Surrounding the modern tomb of David are various chambers consecrated symbolically to certain important events of Judaism in the past and in modern times. Mention may be made, among other things, of the Chamber of the Harp, a sort of Psalms museum; and the Chamber of the Scrolls of the Law, containing ancient Bible manuscripts. The Franciscans were able to return to a new monastery *ad coenaculum* (near the cenacle) on March 26, 1936, but were obliged to evacuate during the troubles in 1948. In 1960 they were allowed to reoccupy their monastery and chapel, which had been badly damaged by mortar fire.

See also PALESTINE, 9.

Bibliography: C. KOPP, *The Holy Places of Gospels,* tr. R. WALLS (New York 1963) 321–334; LexThK² 3:30–31. L. H. VINCENT and F. M. ABEL, *Jérusalem Nouvelle,* 2 v. (Paris 1922) 1:421–481. E. POWER, DBSuppl 1:1064–84. D. BALDI, *Enchiridion locorum sanctorum* (2d ed. Jerusalem 1955) 597–675. F. H. DALMAIS, "La Sainte Sion, mère de toutes les églises," *Bible et Terre Sainte* 11 (May 1958) 3–5. EncDictBibl 334. A. KLEINHANS, EncCatt 3:1287–89.

[E. LUSSIER]

CENACLE, RELIGIOUS OF THE (RC), congregation of women religious with papal approbation, founded in 1826 at Lalouvesc, France, by (Bl.) Marie Victoire Thérèse *Couderc. The official title is Congregation of Our Lady of the Retreat in the Cenacle. The constitutions of the community are based on the Rule of St. Ignatius of Loyola, whose *Spiritual Exercises,* together with the spiritual heritage of the foundress, constitute the bases for the formation and training of the religious.

The apostolate of the Cenacle is both contemplative and active, employing spiritual retreats and instructions in Christian doctrine as means of educating people in the interior life. The word Cenacle comes from the Latin *coenaculum* (supper room) and designates the place of retreat, the upper room, in Jerusalem, where Our Lady, the Apostles, and the followers of Our Lord met in prayer in the days preceding the first Pentecost. Modeling their life and work on that first spiritual retreat of early Christian times, the Religious of the Cenacle find in it the inspiration for the interior life and spirit of their congregation and their particular apostolate. On the contemplative side, prayer occupies the first place in the life of the sisters and includes the following elements: exposition and perpetual adoration of the Blessed Sacrament, maintained in all their houses; recitation of the Divine Office in choir according to the Roman Breviary; an hour of private meditation; and other spiritual exercises that total almost 5 hours daily. The active apostolate stemming from this life of prayer takes the form of private and preached retreats, catechetical instruction of adults and children, guilds, study clubs, and the training of lay catechists, all of which aim to increase the development of the supernatural life of those who directly and indirectly come within the orbit of the spiritual influence of Cenacle retreat houses. The Cenacle seeks to put to work in the civic community the fruits of contemplation.

By 1964 membership in the congregation had grown to about 1,500 sisters, who conduct 71 retreat houses for women throughout the world. There were 19 houses in the U.S.; 18 in France; 13 in Italy; 4 each in England and Brazil; 3 each in Africa and New Zealand; 2 each in Belgium and Canada; and 1 each in Switzerland, Ireland, and Holland. There were 420 professed members in the U.S.

Bibliography: H. M. LYNCH, *In the Shadow of Our Lady of the Cenacle* (New York 1941).

[T. HALL]

CENCI, an ancient Roman family famous chiefly for the story of Francesco Cenci (b. 1549; d. 1598) and his daughter Beatrice (b. Feb. 6, 1577; d. Sept. 11, 1599). The Cenci, whose palace stood near the Roman Ghetto and the church of S. Tommaso dei Cenci, became notorious in the second half of the 16th century. Francesco Cenci married Ersilia Santa Croce, who bore him 12 children. In 1593, 9 years after Ersilia's death, Francesco married Lucrezia Petroni, a widow with three daughters. In 1594 Francesco, a brutal and dissolute man, was prosecuted for sodomy, and fined 100,000 scudi. He left Rome in 1597 to live in the kingdom of Naples at Rocca Petrella near Avezzano; he took with him two of his sons, Paolo and Bernardo. His daughter Beatrice and his wife had been in residence there since 1595. Giacomo, the eldest son, who had been disinherited for marrying against his father's wishes, remained in Rome, as did the other living sons. In the autumn of 1598 Paolo and Bernardo escaped from Rocca Petrella, aided by their castellan, Olimpio Calvetti. Francesco became angry upon learning of his daughter Beatrice's infatuation with Calvetti, a married man. She was punished and confined to the castle with her stepmother. Beatrice continued her relations with Calvetti and with him and her brother Giacomo planned the murder of her father. This was accomplished on Sept. 9, 1598, at Rocca Petrella by Calvetti and another, and with Lucrezia's consent. Lucrezia, Beatrice, Giacomo, and Bernardo Cenci were arrested, imprisoned, and tortured. From the proceedings of the trial it is clear that Beatrice and Giacomo were the instigators of the affair. They were condemned to death. Bernardo's punishment was commuted to the galleys, but the others were executed on Sept. 11, 1599, at the place of execution near the Ponte S. Angelo; Lucrezia and Beatrice were beheaded; Giacomo was killed with a mace, then drawn and quartered. The death of Beatrice aroused the compassion of the Roman crowd, who followed her body to its burial in S. Pietro in Montorio. The facts of the case had been kept secret and the crowd, unaware of them, acclaimed Beatrice as a martyr. This image has been continued by a painting of her, attributed to Guido Reni, in the Galleria Barberini. The confiscation of the family property by Clement VIII, which followed the condemnation and was quite normal in cases of this kind, has been criticized as having no other purpose than the enrichment of the Aldobrandini. The story of the Cenci has been much embroidered by later writers, usually to show the depravity of the papal court. The light of more sober scholarship has shown these stories to be untrue.

Presumed portrait of Beatrice Cenci, attributed to Guido Reni, now in the Galleria Barberini, Rome.

Bibliography: Pastor 24:420–426. H. LUTZ, LexThK[2] 2:991–992. A. BERTOLOTTI, *Francesco Cenci e la sua famiglia* (2d ed. Florence 1879). **Illustration credit:** Alinari-Art Reference Bureau.

[R. L. FOLEY]

CENOBITES, religious who, by contrast with hermits or anchorites, live their life in common. In precise usage, however, cenobites (Gr. κοινός, common, and βίος, life) is not applied to all religious, though all religious, according to Canon Law, have a "stable form of common life" (CIC c.487); rather it is limited to members of monastic communities whose lives are spent primarily in the monastic *cenobium* and not in apostolic work of a kind that leads the religious outside. Thus among contemporary religious, the Benedictines, Cistercians, and Oriental monks are properly termed cenobites; and religious of orders such as the Carthusians, Camaldolese, and Valambrosians, may be called cenobites because their life consists of a blend of the eremitic and cenobitic lives. Though the early hermits of the East occasionally convened for common worship, the religious life in common actually had its origin at the beginning of the 4th century with the monasteries of St. Pachomius, where the essential features of cenobitism were established: life together according to a rule under the supervision of a recognized religious superior. In the East, the Pachomian type of monasticism gave way in the course of the 5th century to that of St. Basil, who replaced the militarism of Pachomius with a more domestic spirit and corrected the overemphasis on manual labor by carefully subordinating work to prayer. In the West, after a century and a half of experiment (400–550) based on various Eastern precedents, the Rule of St. Benedict appeared and, in the course of the next 2 centuries, replaced virtually every vestige of earlier forms of monasticism. Whereas the cenobitic rules of the period of experiment had often emulated the most striking and excessive elements of Eastern asceticism, the cenobitism of St. Benedict developed the discretionary spirit of St. Basil, strengthening it with a wisdom derived from Roman governmental experience. St. Benedict contributed to the cenobitic institution especially by his emphasis on stability, the vow and virtue that binds the monk to one particular community, and in his development of St. Basil's ideal of the monastery as a family under the abbot as a father and representative of Christ. The Rule of St. Benedict outlines a form of cenobitism that has proved remarkably durable. Among the monks of the West, it has never been replaced, while all the newer institutions, which for the most part have been directed to some kind of specific apostolic work, have not strayed far from the spirit of St. Benedict in those aspects of their lives that have remained cenobitic.

Bibliography: H. Leclercq, DACL 2.2:3047–3248. J. Olphe-Galliard, DictSpirAscMyst 2:404–416.

[A. DONAHUE]

CENOBITISM

An early form of monastic organization. Although the monastic ideal began primarily as a flight from the world in search of inwardness, recollection, and a life hidden in God, the dangers of solitude and its temptations quickly became apparent. The gathering of hermits into loosely knit groups with a free and personal relationship to a spiritual father, the abbot, did not eliminate these dangers. Gradually a tendency toward communal institutions became manifest since these provided a material and spiritual support for the interior life.

St. Pachomius. The earliest communal monastic foundation was located in the Thebaid (northern Egypt), where St. *Pachomius organized large communities with heads and deputy heads. They were federated into a congregation whose superior had authority over all the houses and whose members met in two annual chapters. Well-organized and financially remunerative work was combined with silence to frame and support prayer; and this was regulated partly as a common exercise and partly house by house; spiritual instructions followed a similar plan. The asceticism was reasonable; and though the discipline of the individual will was its essential goal, nevertheless the system left scope for personal initiative. The charismatic gifts of the founder were not stabilized in juridical structure, and after his death tendencies to disintegration manifested themselves; some of his imitators, such as Shenoute, had to resort to outright violence to maintain order. But the first rules created remarkably balanced formula that exercised a profound influence, especially in the West. In the East, *Basilian monasticism is an independent initiative; in it the common life is based on sociological and ecclesiastical considerations.

Lower Egypt. The ideal of solitude indulged by hermits in lower Egypt was tempered by the proximity of other cells, the meeting every Sunday for the Office, and the moral authority of the elders. It is here that the term *coenobium* and the classification of the monks into different kinds are encountered. These distinctions must not be absolutized or made into antithetical categories. They existed side by side, and the same monk passed from one category into another.

In 5th-century Palestine the laura was a synthesis; it had an organized center where the young monks were trained and isolated cells for the full-fledged monks who maintained regular relations with the community. These institutions did not prevent the monks, among whom there were saints, from passing from one community to another with a freedom that may surprise the legal-minded men in the West.

A return to the strict Basilian conception, actualized on the scale of large communities, can be seen in the Studite reform of the late 8th century. But this was never an absolute ideal in the East, where order did not eliminate *charism. Colonies of hermits and lauras (not to be identified with the Palestinian lauras) remained licit. The price of this liberty was *idiorythmia,* or a type of monastic independence that tolerated the retention of some private property and called only for limited obedience; it became an abuse in the 14th century, beginning at Mt. *Athos. It gradually spread and was finally legitimized.

In the West, the strict cenobitic rule instituted by St. *Benedict became the norm, and the reformers always saw in it the touchstone of observance. There is nothing contradictory in recognizing that this has been combined through the centuries with an aspiration to solitude, for inwardness and sociability complement each other. In modern religious congregations, cenobitism has been assimilated into centralized juridical structures that render pointless the notion of stability, understood as a bond to a certain definite house.

See also CENOBITES; HERMITS.

Bibliography: H. Leclercq, DACL 2.2:3047–3248. J. Olphe-Galliard, DictSpirAscMyst 2:404–416. C. Lialine and P. Doyère, *ibid.* 4:936–982, s.v. érémitisme. A. Plé, ed., *Communal Life* (The Religious Life 8; Westminster, Md. 1957).

[J. GRIBOMONT]

CENSER

A vessel for holding glowing coals on which *incense is strewn for the sake of producing a fragrant smoke. It is known also as a thurible, from the Latin word for censer, *thuribulum.*

In the Bible. The censer that was used in Israelite worship and is spoken of in the OT (Ex 27.3; 38.3) is not to be identified with the modern censer that is held and swung with a chain. In the Bible the word censer (*maḥtâ*) refers to a shallow cup or bowl used for carrying glowing embers to the altar of holocausts (*see* ALTAR, 2). Probably it was provided with a wooden or ceramic handle. In the Mosaic sanctuary the "fire pans" were made of bronze and kept on the altar with the other utensils of the altar when the Israelites broke camp and traveled (Nm 4.14). They were also made of bronze at the time the Babylonians plundered the Temple (4 Kgs 25.15; Jer 52.19), but they were of "most pure gold" in the original temple of Solomon (3 Kgs 7.50; 2 Chr 4.22). The same word (*maḥtâ*) also designates the "trays" or small receptacles for the burned-out wicks used with the lampstands in the sanctuary (Ex 25.38; 37.23).

Besides being burned on the altar of incense, either as a separate offering or along with a sacrificial victim, incense could be burned also in fire pans. The incense was thrown into the fire or embers in these pans and this resulted in a cloud of smoke being offered up (Lv 10.1; 16.12) or covering the propitiatory on the ark of the covenant in the Mosaic sanctuary (Nm 16.16–24, 35; 17.1–15). The fire pan then became a censer. The only mention of a censer in the NT is in Ap 8.3, 5, where the angel is described as holding a golden censer (λιβανωτός), which was in the form of a fire pan.

In Christian Worship. When incense was introduced into the Christian liturgy in the 4th century, the censer was of the same form as that commonly used in pagan worship, i.e., a small metal pot hanging from three relatively short chains, which were joined at the top in a metal ring. This type of censer without a cover is represented in several mosaics and paintings from the 5th and later centuries and is the kind still used by the Copts. However, in the early Middle Ages a perforated metal cover was often placed over the pot to prevent the coals from falling out when the censer was swung. A fourth chain was then added to facilitate the raising of the cover when incense was put on the coals. All the chains could then be made longer. This soon became the prevalent form throughout Christendom.

Both the pot and its cover were often plated with gold or silver and adorned with symbolic figures or with elaborate architectural designs representing small castles, churches, arcades, etc.

The auxiliary cup (with a flat base or a foot) for holding the incense to be used in the censer was originally of hemispherical form and called in Latin by such words as *pyxis, busta, capsella,* and *acerra.* From the 12th century on this was often made in an oblong or boatlike shape and therefore is known in Latin as *navis* or *navicula;* hence the English word "boat" for the incense holder.

Bibliography: EncDictBibl 335. A. WECKWERTH, LexThK[2] 8:1012–13. R. AVERNINI, EncCatt 12:639–641. H. LECLERCQ, DACL 5.1:21–33. R. LESAGE, *Catholicisme* 4:109. P. MORRISROE, CE 3:519.

[J. J. MC GARRAGHY]

CENSORSHIP

The action by which public authority controls, limits, or suppresses the expression of various thoughts, attitudes, and philosophies in the different media of social communication. This exercise of authority is deemed necessary generally on either political or moral grounds; i.e., the opinions, attitudes, or philosophies are thought to pose a threat either to the stability or well-being of the body politic or to public morals. An essential element in the concept of censorship, properly so-called, is that control is exercised by an authority that has legitimate power to enforce the restrictions that may be imposed. This element springs from the very nature of the positive human law, which has as its primary purpose and goal the regulation of the external human acts of the members of society so as to achieve the common good of society (generally summarized as peace and prosperity).

Law and the Common Good. Law serves the common good in two ways. First, it positively advances the common good (as in establishing minimum wages, for example); second, it can forbid what would injure the common good. To perform this second task effectively, the public authority must have power to penalize those who violate the common good. Legitimate authority in other words, has punitive power, which it has not only the right but also the duty to exercise when necessary for the common good. Censorship is generally exercised after the material in question has been published (books and other printed matter) or publicly displayed (motion pictures, etc.) and challenged as being detrimental to public morals. Courts are then called upon to decide the issue, and the material may be suppressed if the charge against it is sustained. This is called repressive censorship. Another type, less frequently employed, is called prior censorship; i.e., prior to publication or display the work is denied access to the public. This type faces the more serious objection, because it most radically restricts freedom of expression. It may be noted, however, that even this type of censorship is not inherently undemocratic or unreasonable. Felix Frankfurter, while a member of the U.S. Supreme Court, for example, stated that "just as *Near v. Minnesota,* one of the landmark opinions in shaping the constitutional protection of freedom of speech and of the press, left no doubts that 'liberty of speech, and of the press, is . . . not an absolute right' . . . it likewise made clear that 'the protection even as to previous restraint is not absolutely unlimited.' " (cited in Gardiner, 77). In either type of censorship the justifying norm is the same: the protection of the common good through the coercive power of authority.

Justice as the Goal of Law. This brief sketch of the nature of human law (*see* LAW; LAW, PHILOSOPHY OF) is in practice, if not in theory, repudiated by those who hold that the essential purpose of law is the enlargement of the horizons of liberty. The classic definition of the ultimate goal of law, however, is still *finis legis justitia.* Justice is what the law envisions; and justice may demand, under one set of circumstances, wider freedom, and, under other circumstances, reasonable restriction. Whatever the circumstances, the common good of society is the norm for the quest for justice. It is true that restrictive aspects of the law are never justifiable unless they are imposed in view of a greater ultimate freedom, and not merely for the sake of restriction, but the principle holds that limitations of freedom are at times as essential for the attainment of the common good as are extensions of freedom.

Criticism vs. Censorship. It is from this concept of law that the justification of censorship, strictly so-called, arises. Since the actual requirements of the common good in a given society are determined by the governing authority, individuals or subordinate groups have no right to exercise strict censorship and, practically speaking, they cannot do so. Picket lines, boycotts, and the like are frequently thought of as manifestations of censorship, but they are in reality means of persuasion; they cannot enforce the restrictions they advocate. Agencies in the U.S. such as the National Legion of Decency, which issues moral classification of motion pictures, and the *National Office for Decent Literature, which lists reading material deemed not suitable for young people, in reality offer guidance to those who wish to use their services; they engage in forming public opinion, but they cannot enforce either nonattendance at the films or nonreading of the offending reading material. It is undoubtedly a fact that the activity of such noncensorship agencies often has, to some extent, the same result that would arise from strict censorship by authority—a motion picture might fail at the box office because millions would heed the adverse rating given by the Legion, and the failure might be as complete as if the government had closed the theater. This, however, would be a byproduct of the Legion's work, whereas it would be a necessary consequence of strict censorship. In other words, criticism, even if highly organized, in a free society is never to be confused with strict censorship. *See* NATIONAL CATHOLIC OFFICE FOR MOTION PICTURES.

Conditions for Sane Censorship. This statement of the principle that underlies the exercise of censorship seems to be clear. The problems arise, especially in a pluralistic society, when the principle is applied in individual cases, any of which may give rise to the possibility that this particular control of expression is tyrannical, unnecessary, or fruitless. Two conditions would go far to assure a just exercise of censorship. First, authority will have recourse to strict censorship as a last resort, not as a first step. Motion-picture producers, for instance, can be educated to the fact that they have civic responsibilities not to debauch public morals and that they should set up a code for their own self-censorship. If such education fails over the long run, public authority may have to step in to regulate them. Second, censorship should be exercised to a minimum extent, that is, as little as is necessary for the protection of the common good being threatened. This principle was admirably stated by the Catholic hierarchy of the U.S. in their statement of 1957 on censorship:

> Although civil authority has the right and the duty to exercise such control over the various media of communication as is necessary to safeguard public morals, yet civil law, especially in those areas which are constitutionally protected, will define as narrowly as possible the limitations placed on freedom. The one purpose which will guide legislators in establishing necessary restraints to freedom is the securing of the general welfare through the prevention of grave and harmful abuse. Our juridical system has been dedicated from the beginning to the principle of minimal restraint. Those who may become impatient with the reluctance of the state through its laws to curb and curtail human freedom should bear in mind that this is a principle that serves to safeguard all our vital freedoms—to curb less rather than more; to hold for liberty rather than for restraint. (quoted in Gardiner, Appendix E, 188).

St. Thomas Aquinas sums up this aspect of the extent to which the coercive elements of law are justly operative when he states: "Human laws do not forbid all vices, from which the virtuous abstain, but only the more grievous vices, from which it is possible for the majority to abstain; and chiefly those that are injurious to others, without the prohibition of which human society could not be maintained" (ST 1a2ae, 96.2).

If one does not agree that the principle of censorship is valid, one is logically forced to hold that freedom of speech is an absolute right. Such a view is philosophically and politically untenable and practically repudiated in all civilized societies—every stable modern state, for instance, has laws against obscenity in the printed word. Censorship in practice is one of the most difficult problems in modern society, for it is a most sensitive area in the whole field of the proper balance between authority and freedom. It is practically impossible to formulate one simple, effective rule that will safeguard both freedom and authority in each individual case; but if the principle of the right and duty of authority to censor is not respected, the logical result is an unbridled license of expression that of its very nature would be a menace to the common good of society.

See also FREEDOM OF SPEECH; FREEDOM OF SPEECH AND PRESS, U.S. LAW OF; AUTHORITY; AUTHORITY, CIVIL; CENSORSHIP OF BOOKS (CANON LAW); BOYCOTT; OBSCENITY, U.S. LAW OF.

Bibliography: H. C. GARDINER, *Catholic Viewpoint on Censorship* (New York 1958; rev. ed. Image Bks. 1961). N. ST. JOHN-STEVAS, *Obscenity and the Law* (London 1956), esp. valuable for summaries of materials deemed subject to censorship in various countries. T. J. MURPHY, *Censorship: Government and Obscenity* (Baltimore 1963). M. L. ERNST, *The First Freedom* (New York 1946), Ernst has been one of the leading advocates of "no censorship at all" and, logically, of freedom of speech as an absolute right. W. KERR, *Criticism and Censorship* (Milwaukee 1954).

[H. C. GARDINER]

CENSORSHIP OF BOOKS (CANON LAW)

The censorship of books is the control of literature that is exercised by the Church for the salvation of souls. It is a judgment made by ecclesiastical authority whether a book adheres to Catholic teaching on faith and morals. This control is deemed censorship in its strict sense when it is exercised prior to the publication of a literary work.

History. Ecclesiastical censorship began with St. Paul at Ephesus and the burning of pagan books (Acts 19.19). The early Church acknowledged as morally and doctrinally sound some works contained in the Muratorian Fragment (2d century), the *Constitutiones Apostolorum* (4th or 5th century), the *Decretum Gelasianum* (5th century), and the writings of St. Jerome (d. 420). There also existed antecedent disapproval of anonymous and/or apocryphal works.

Some of the early Fathers voluntarily practiced individual censorship. St. Ambrose (d. 397) and St. Augustine (d. 430) are two who submitted their works to others for prior censorship. Baronius (1538–1607) held that censorship was customary as early as the 5th century. Two later instances of censorship, the letter of Pope Nicholas I (867) and the citation of Abelard (1079–1142) before the Council of Soissons (1121), indicate that censorship had become obligatory through custom.

The Franciscan Order first legislated concerning censorship under the influence of St. Bonaventure (d. 1274) in the *Constitutiones Narbonnenses* (1260). The medieval universities enacted similar laws in the same century, and by the 15th century diocesan synods had passed laws of censorship also.

The invention of the printing press in 1453 hastened the need of legislation for the entire Church; such legislation first appeared in the 1487 bull *Inter multiplices* of Pope Innocent VIII (1482–92). This bull was reissued in 1501 by Pope Alexander VI (1492–1503) and was included in the Fifth Lateran Council (1512–17). The Council of Trent (1543–63) dealt with the censorship of books, and Pope Pius IV (1559–65) published the constitution *Dominici gregis* in 1564, reaffirming the need of censorship. Although many popes had issued subsequent legislation concerning the censorship of books, it was not until the reign of Pope Leo XIII (1878–1903) that this entire field of law was reorganized in the constitution *Officiorum ac munerum* (Jan. 25, 1897). Many of the provisions of this constitution appeared in the Code of 1918. Pope Pius X (1903–14) strengthened the regulations of censorship in the encyclical *Pascendi dominici gregis* (Dec. 8, 1907). He did this in order to halt the spread of Modernism.

Legal Foundation. In general, the law of the Church favors freedom over censorship inasmuch as any law that restricts the free exercise of rights must be strictly interpreted (CIC c.19). On the other hand, freedom is not without its limits, and the Church may draw up legislation restricting this freedom for two reasons.

First, the Church has the right of censorship of books by virtue of the natural law. By the natural law a father has the right to protect his children from bad companions; by the natural law the state has the right to protect its citizens against the danger of water or air pollution or to regulate the sale of liquor, poisons, and narcotics. In the same way the competent ecclesiastical authorities in matters of religion have the right to protect their membership from any danger to faith or morals or both. The Church enjoys the right to protect itself from these dangers and to use the means within its competence (censorship) to prevent the exposure to the faithful of reading matter that may be injurious.

Second, the Church enjoys the right of censorship by virtue of its supernatural mission. The Church was founded by Christ Himself as the effective instrument for the salvation of the human race. Christ entrusted the Church with the duty of teaching, interpreting and safeguarding the deposit of revelation as He committed it to the Church. The Church enjoys the exclusive right, therefore, of interpreting and teaching in the name of Christ in matters pertaining to faith or morals or both, and of preserving the deposit of revelation from erroneous doctrines and evil or superstitious practices. This right is also a duty that is imposed upon the Church, for "Our Lord Jesus Christ entrusted the deposit of faith to the Church, that under the constant guidance and assistance of the Holy Spirit, she might sacredly guard and faithfully explain this divine revelation. The Church has therefore the right and the duty, independently of any civil power, to teach all nations the full evangelical doctrine" (CIC c.1322.1). The Church exercises this right and duty in part through the censorship of books.

Substance of the Law of Censorship. Censorship is that right of the Church, exercised in behalf of the salvation of souls, whereby books written by baptized Catholics are subject to ecclesiastical approval before publication. The process includes the examination of the material to be published, an official judgment by the competent ecclesiastical authority concerning the conformity of the book with the doctrine and practice of the Church, and, in the event of an affirmative decision, permission to publish the book (CIC c.1385.1). A negative decision prohibits the publication of the book (CIC c.1384.1).

A book is generally considered to be a publication that by its size, unity of subject matter, external appearance, and means of printing is generally accepted as a book. The law also (CIC c.1384.2) includes daily publications, periodicals, and any other edited writings under the term book unless the contrary is evident from the context of the law. A reply of the Pontifical Commission for the Interpretation of the Code of Canon Law of June 7, 1932 (ActApS 24:241) implied the extension of the term books in CIC c.1385.1n1 to include periodicals.

The CIC subjects the following categories of books to ecclesiastical censorship: books of Sacred Scripture and their annotations and commentaries (CIC c.1385. 1n1); books pertaining to Sacred Scripture, to sacred theology, to Canon Law, to Church history, to natural theology (theodicy) and ethics, and books pertaining to religious and moral branches of knowledge. Also subject to ecclesiastical censorship are books and booklets of prayers, devotion, religious, moral, ascetical, and mystical doctrine and instruction, and the like, as well as writings, even profane, that contain something of special interest to religion or morals (CIC c.1385.1n2).

Sacred images, however they are printed and whether they have prayers adjoined to them or not, also require ecclesiastical censorship (CIC c.1385.1n3). Either the local ordinary of the author of such above-mentioned writings and sacred images or the local ordinary of the place where the writings or images are published or the local ordinary of the place where they are printed may grant the permission required by law. The law mentions, however, that if any one of these local ordinaries has denied permission to publish a writing or a sacred image, the author cannot obtain the permission from another local ordinary without informing him of the prior denial by another local ordinary (CIC c.1385.2). Religious, moreover, need the permission also of their major superior before the publication of a writing or a sacred image (CIC c.1385.3).

Certain works require special permission of the Holy See before they may be published. Among those works are the collections and decrees of the several Roman Congregations, which cannot be republished without permission from the prefects of the individual Congregations. Implicit in the grant of permission to publish again the decrees is the fulfillment of whatever conditions are prescribed in the granting of the permission (CIC c.1389). The publication of whatever pertains in any way to causes of the beatification and canonization of the faithful requires the antecedent permission of the Congregation of Rites. Express permission of the Holy See is also required for the publication in any language of authentic collections of prayers and pious works to which the Holy See has attached indulgences; it is needed also for the publication of a handbook of indulgences granted by the Holy See, for the publication of a summary of indulgences, whether already collected but never approved or recently collected from different sources (CIC c.1382.2). Similar permission is required, moreover, for the publication of translations of the Sacred Scriptures into the vernacular tongue without accompanying annotations taken from the Fathers of the Church or from learned Catholic Biblical scholars (CIC c.1391).

The permission of the local ordinary is needed for the publication of some materials. The permission of the local ordinary is demanded by law (CIC c.1388.1) for the publication of all books containing indulgences and for all booklets, summaries of indulgences, and prayer cards in which concessions of indulgences are contained. Before the publication of liturgical books or parts thereof and of litanies approved by the Holy See, the local ordinary must attest to the conformity of the texts to be published with approved editions of the same (CIC c.1390). Similar permission is required, furthermore, for the publication of translations of the Sacred Scriptures into the vernacular if these translations include annotations taken from the Fathers of the Church and of learned Catholic Biblical scholars, and if these translations are published under the supervision of the local ordinary (CIC c.1391).

The permission of the local ordinary is also required for secular clerics to publish books treating even of nonreligious subjects and to contribute to or edit papers, magazines, or reviews (CIC c.1386.1). Religious clerics also need the permission of the local ordinary. Even Catholic laymen must not contribute anything to newspapers, magazines, and reviews that habitually attack the Catholic religion or good morals, unless there is a just and reasonable cause, approved by the local ordinary, for doing so (CIC c.1386.2).

Procedure. In every diocesan curia there are diocesan censors ex officio to examine works that are to be published (CIC c.1393.1). Censors are obliged to make the profession of faith (CIC c.1406.1.7); they should be learned in theology and perform their function seriously (Holy Office, March 29, 1941, ActApS 33:121). Censors should be chosen from the secular and religious clergy; religious should be chosen upon the recommendation of their major religious superiors. In any event they should be men of mature age, erudition, and prudence in approving or disapproving doctrine (CIC c.1393.3).

In performing their function censors must lay aside all respect of persons, having before their eyes only the doctrines of the Church and the common teaching of the Church as it is found in the decrees of the general councils, or in the constitution and prescriptions of the Apostolic See and in the common opinion of approved authors (CIC c.1393.2). The diocesan censor must give his judgment in writing. If the judgment is favorable, the ordinary may give permission for publication of the work, prefixing to it the judgment and the name of the censor. Only rarely and in extraordinary circumstances, in the prudent judgment of the ordinary, may the name of the censor be omitted (CIC c.1393.4). The name of the censor must never be divulged to the authors until the ordinary has given a favorable judgment (CIC c.1393.5). If the permission to publish is denied, the reasons for the denial should be indicated to the author at his request, unless there is a grave reason to the contrary (CIC c.1394.2). Finally, the permission that the ordinary grants for the publication of the works is to be made in writing and must be printed at the beginning or end of the books, paper, or picture, giving the name of the person granting the permission and also the date and place of the grant of permission (CIC c.1394.1).

See also CENSORSHIP; LITERATURE, NATURE AND FUNCTION OF; EROTIC LITERATURE; FREEDOM OF SPEECH AND PRESS, U.S. LAW OF; ART, 4; INDEX OF FORBIDDEN BOOKS.

Bibliography: D. H. WIESK, *The Precensorship of Books* (CUA CLS 329; 1954). H. C. GARDINER, *Catholic Viewpoint on Censorship* (New York 1958; rev. ed. Image Bks. 1961). J. A. GOODWINE, "Problems Respecting the Censorship of Books," *Jurist* 10 (1950) 152–183.

[J. C. CALHOUN]

CENSURE, THEOLOGICAL, a pejorative judgment that indicates that a proposition is in some way opposed or harmful to faith or morals. Theological censures were already used in the Middle Ages by John XXII against the errors of the *Fraticelli, and by the Council of Constance against the errors of Wycliff and Hus. One of the most extensive lists of such censures was put forth by Clement XI in his condemnation of many propositions of *Quesnel (Denz 2502). All these censures seem reducible to three general categories: heretical, erroneous, and rash. A proposition is censured as heretical if it contradicts a truth of divine and Catholic faith; as erroneous in Catholic doctrine or in theology if it contradicts a truth that is Catholic doctrine or theologically certain; as rash if it contradicts a proposition that is not a strict theological conclusion but is well grounded and commonly held by theologians.

See also NOTES, THEOLOGICAL.

Bibliography: SacTheolSumma BAC 1.3:884–913.

[E. J. FORTMAN]

CENSURES, ECCLESIASTICAL

A penalty in ecclesiastical law is the privation, in consequence of the commission of a crime, or delict, of some good to which a person would be otherwise entitled. The delict, or crime, must be an external and morally imputable violation of a law or precept to which a canonical sanction, or penalty, is attached (CIC c.2195).

A censure in Canon Law is a penalty that deprives a baptized person who is delinquent and contumacious of spiritual goods, or temporal goods connected with spiritual goods, until such time as, receding from his contumacy, he is absolved from the censure (CIC c.2241.1). The canonical sanction of censure looks primarily to the correction of an offender, or delinquent, whereas a vindicative penalty is concerned primarily with the punishment of a crime. Censures are therefore called medicinal penalties.

Kinds and Conditions. Censures are either *latae sententiae* or *ferendae sententiae*. The former are incurred *ipso facto,* that is, in the very violation of a penal law or precept, so that the violator is sentenced to the observance of the censure by the law or precept itself. The latter must be inflicted by proper ecclesiastical authority after the fact of violation. Subsequent to infliction, *ferendae sententiae* censures are called *ab homine* censures because their infliction comes directly and proximately, not from the law or precept, but from the act of a man, that is, from an ecclesiastical superior.

Contumacy is really the distinguishing note of the penalty of censure. It involves deliberate insistence in the commission of the crime or persistence in impenitence after commission. Only a crime that is external, grave, consummated, and conjoined with contumacy merits the punishment of censure (CIC c.2242.1).

In relation to the infliction of a *ferendae sententiae* censure, a person is contumacious only if, after proper warnings, he does not desist from delinquency or declines appropriate repentance for a crime already committed, together with reparation of damages and scandal. A *latae sententiae* censure is not incurred unless the delinquent is contumacious in the very commission of his crime. The transgression of a law or precept sanctioned with a *latae sententiae* censure may or may not be indicative of contumacy. Contumacy is indicated by the transgression itself unless some extenuating factor recognized by ecclesiastical law excuses the delinquent from incurring the censure (CIC c.2242.2). Such factors, or excusing causes, are many (CIC cc.2229–31). Simple ignorance, for instance, of the fact that a censure is attached to a law or precept excuses a delinquent from incurring a *latae sententiae* censure.

The goods of which a censure deprives the delinquent are various. In general they are: a share in the public prayers of the Church; the reception or administration of the Sacraments; the right to assist at divine services; the right to perform certain ecclesiastical functions and acts of orders or jurisdiction; the holding of ecclesiastical offices, benefices, and dignities, and the revenues attached to them.

Appeal of Censures. *Ferendae sententiae* censures are inflicted either by judicial sentence or by precept of a competent superior in an administrative decree. The delinquent has the right of appeal or recourse from the sentence or decree, but only in such a way that the decision concerning the justice of the infliction devolves upon the higher authority to whom appeal is made or recourse is had. The appeal or recourse does not have the effect of suspending the observance of the censure while appeal or recourse is pending.

Latae sententiae censures do not admit of either suspensive or devolutive appeal or recourse if the law or precept comes from jurisdictional authority of the pope. *Latae sententiae* censures of inferior ecclesiastical authorities, however, do admit of appeal or recourse with devolutive effect to higher authority. Moreover, against a sentence or decree declaring a *latae sententiae* censure to have been incurred, appeal or recourse may be interposed to suspend the juridical effects of the sentence or decree, but not the censure itself. Finally, against a sentence or a precept that threatens a censure, either *ferendae* or *latae sententiae,* appeal or recourse is possible with suspensive effect in ordinary matters, but only with devolutive effect in extraordinary matters in which the canons clearly exclude suspensive appeal or recourse (CIC c.2243).

Multiplication of Censures. A person may be under censure on several charges. The same censure as well as different censures may be multiplied in the same subject. There may be as many *ab homine* censures as there are sentences or precepts, or distinct parts thereof, inflicting a censure. Multiplication of *latae sententiae* censures is effected by the commission of different delicts, by distinct repetition of the same delict, or by the commission of one delict that is virtually plural because it violates several laws to which a censure is attached. Also, multiplication is possible if the same delict is punished by different superiors with different *latae sententiae* censures (CIC c.2244).

Reservation of Censures. Reservation is the restriction of power to absolve from censures; such restriction is made by a competent ecclesiastical superior who has the jurisdiction to enact censures. Thus censures are either reserved or nonreserved. The absolution of an *ab homine* censure is reserved to the person responsible for its infliction, to his superior or successor, or to one delegated to absolve. The absolution of a *latae sententiae* censure is not restricted unless its reservation is clearly stated in the law or precept to which it is attached (CIC c.2245). Some censures attached *latae sententiae* to general laws of the Church are of the nonreserved kind; others are reserved to ordinaries or to the Holy See. Censures are reserved to the Holy See either simply (*simpliciter*), in a special manner (*speciali modo*), or in a most special manner (*specialissimo modo*).

There is a connection between reservation of a censure and reservation of sin only in the case of excommunication and personal interdict. A reserved excommunication or personal interdict implies reservation of the sin committed in violation of the law or precept to which the censure was attached. Thus, a confessor who cannot absolve from a reserved excommunication or personal interdict cannot absolve from the sin. A suspension, on the other hand, does not forbid the reception of the Sacraments, even the Sacrament of Penance. Hence the reservation of a suspension does not carry with it reservation of sin.

Once a reserved censure is remitted by absolution, given even in the external forum, the sin that was reserved by reason of the censure is no longer reserved and can be absolved by any confessor. Moreover, if contumacy is absent, so that a reserved *latae sententiae* censure was not actually incurred, the sin committed in the violation of a penal law of precept is not reserved (CIC c.2246.3).

The reservation of a *latae sententiae* censure of particular territorial law ceases outside the limits of the territory, even if the one under censure leaves the territory for the purpose of obtaining absolution. An *ab homine* censure retains its reservation everywhere (CIC c.2247.2).

Absolution of Censures. Censures, once contracted, are taken away by lawful absolution. Recession from contumacy is a prerequisite for absolution. When a delinquent repents of his delict and makes satisfaction, or at least gives a serious promise of satisfaction, for any harm or scandal caused so that contumacy is absent, he has a right to absolution (CIC cc.2242.2, 2248.1, 2).

Absolution from censures is imparted in the sacramental forum of Penance by the confessor immediately before absolution from sin. Confessors may absolve from all nonreserved censures and from reserved censures for which they have received requisite jurisdiction from some source. Remission of censures outside the tribunal of penance is imparted by a proper ecclesiastical superior who has the requisite jurisdiction by reason of his office or by delegation, or by another who is duly delegated (CIC c.2253).

Special provision is made in Canon Law for absolving penitents in danger of death. Such penitents may be absolved by any priest from all censures, no matter how reserved. Recourse to proper authority after recovery is enjoined by law under penalty of reincurring the censure, but only in cases of *ab homine* censures and censures reserved in a most special manner to the Holy See (CIC c.2252).

Likewise, Canon Law makes provision for absolution in certain more urgent cases of reserved *latae sententiae* censures for which a confessor would not otherwise have jurisdiction. The confessor so absolving enjoins submission of the case, under penalty of reincurring the censure, to the Sacred Penitentiary or to someone having power to absolve (CIC c.2254).

Types of Censures. Censures are either excommunications, suspensions, or interdicts. An excommunication is always a censure; a suspension or interdict may be either a censure or a vindicative penalty. Interdicts are personal or local.

Excommunication excludes a person from the community of the faithful and deprives him of certain spiritual benefits, especially the reception of the Sacraments. The effects of a personal interdict are practically the same as those of an excommunication, with the exception of exclusion from communion with the Church. Local interdicts affect places directly, forbidding the celebration of certain divine offices and sacred rites. Although there are various kinds and degrees, a suspension in general forbids a cleric the exercise of the powers of orders and jurisdiction, the administration of ecclesiastical offices, and the revenues of ecclesiastical benefices.

See also EXCOMMUNICATION, CANONICAL; INTERDICT; RESERVED SINS; SUSPENSION (CANON LAW).

Bibliography: Wernz-Vidal 7:241–361. F. CAPPELLO, *Tractatus canonico-moralis de censuris* (4th ed. Rome 1950). O. M. CLORAN, *Previews and Practical Cases: Code of Canon Law, Book Five, Delicts and Penalties, Canons 2195–2414* (Milwaukee 1951). Bousc-Ellis. Abbo 2:2241–85.

[C. L. PARRES]

CENSUS (IN THE BIBLE)

In the OT the practice of taking a census, though in opposition to the older Israelite amphictyonic traditions, arose with the monarchy in connection with the centralization of military organization; in postexilic times the priestly editors incorporated the census lists into their writings according to certain then-prevalent notions and thus, at times, outside the original historical context of the particular census; in the NT St. Luke mentions two distinct Roman censuses, the first in dating the birth of Christ, the other in alluding to a temporary rebellion led by Judas, the Galilean.

Censuses in the Old Testament. The census lists of the OT represent genuine sources, though colored and interpreted by later redactors according to the latter's understanding and aims. In its historical origin the census served the purpose of ascertaining the military strength of the tribes. When the monarchy began its program of centralizing the nation's military organization by a census, there was religious and political opposition, since the census was understood to be an impingement upon Yahweh's kingship, as well as upon the autonomous liberty of the tribe. The documents, uncovered at Mari, attest the widespread Semitic antipathy to the census (see E. A. Speiser, 24–25). The power of the people was in the hands of its god; hence, taking a census implied lack of confidence in the nation's god and incurred guilt. In the light of census-incurred guilt, the law of Ex 30.11–16 is to be understood: each person registered in the census had to pay a half shekel to be used for cultic atonement made to Yahweh. The law shows postexilic redaction in that the sanctuary shekel referred to (Ex 30.13) is of postexilic terminology; also, this law, claiming Mosaic institution, gave additional authority to the Temple tax that was necessary in postexilic times to support the Temple (Mt 17.24). Besides its military motive, the OT census served also as a basis for taxation and the state-imposed corvée (2 Sm 20.24; 3 Kgs 5.13; 9.15; 2 Chr 8.8; 10.18).

Censuses in the Book of Numbers. The Pentateuchal *priestly writers used two census lists in the Book of Numbers (Nm 1.1–46; 26.1–51) to underline the sacerdotal functions of the tribe of Levi (1.47–54) and to preface the allotment of the Promised Land to the individual tribes; "Among these groups the land shall be divided as their heritage in keeping with the number of individuals in each group" (Nm 26.52). The lists follow the tribes (Numbers ch. 1) and clans (ch. 26) of Genesis ch. 46 with some slight discrepancies, e.g., Becher, son of Benjamin (Gn 46.21) is said to be the son of Ephraim (Nm 26.35). The only ones alive for both censuses, the one at Sinai and the one on the Plains of Moab 40 years later, are said to be Moses. Josue, and Caleb (Nm 26.63–65). In both censuses the number for half the tribes is more than 50,000. The changes in the numbers of each tribe between the two censuses probably indicates their changing relative importance. The main problem raised by both these censuses is the sum total of more than 600,000 fighting men in each census, which implies a total population well over 2 million. When one considers that the Israelites subsisted for 40 years in a barren desert, marched as a group (with 25 abreast and a yard apart, as stated, the column would be 44 miles long), could all be summoned by the sound of two trumpets, and could gather at one Tent of Meeting (Nm 10.2), it is evident that the figure is grossly exaggerated. According to G. E. Mendenhall, the census lists of Numbers are anachronistic in their present context; historically they represent traditions from the time of the amphictyony that record the military units (*'ălāpîm*) of each tribe ready for war in case the common welfare of the tribes is threatened. The original, premonarchical *'elep* was the technical term of a subsection of a tribe that the later priestly editor, in his redaction of pre-existing sources, interpreted in the light of the later military *'elep* of the monarchy that comprised about 1,000 men. Thus the extravagant census figures of Numbers would lie in a postexilic misunderstanding of earlier terminology. W. F. Albright suggests that figures in Numbers may be based on actual figures found in the Davidic census that the priestly writers adapted for their purpose; if the 603,550 of Nm 1.46 and the 601,730 of Nm 26.50 represent the total population and not just the warriors, these figures would not be incredible for the time of David. A possible, but unlikely, solution, suggested by A. Bentzen, is that the figures are arrived at by gematria, giving a numerical equivalent to the Hebrew letters for "Sons of Israel."

Census in the Book of Samuel. The figure of 1,300,000 warriors given for the census of David in 2 Sm 24.9 is also incredibly high, while the figure of the Chronicler for the same census, reckoned over less territory, is even higher (1 Chr 21.5). These figures can only be due to the exaggeration or misunderstanding of a later age; it would give the semibarren land of Israel a population density twice that of any modern European country. The horror engendered by David's census and the punishment that follows seem to indicate not only the usual Semitic antipathy to a census but also an antipathy for the centralizing policies that came with the monarchy. Previously, Yahweh was king (1 Sm 8.7); great numbers did not matter, since He had led the people in the holy war (Judges ch. 7); but now, under the monarchy, what had been cultic and religious was being arrogated by the civil and military authority. By putting trust in numbers as other kings did (Prv 14.28), David showed a lack of faith in Yahweh. Moreover, the census, administered by a central authority, violated the tribal freedom formerly enjoyed under the amphictyony (see G. E. Mendenhall, 56). The people were reluctant to surrender tribal freedom that David was encroaching upon little by little. A census would also lead to more taxes (1 Sm 8.10–18) and forced labor, of which an official was already in charge (2 Sm 20.24). The Chronicler, in his account of the census (1 Chronicles ch. 21), is interested primarily in glorifying the piety of the king and emphasizing the high price paid for the Temple site. A later theology is reflected in that it is Satan and no longer Yahweh who incites David to take the census (2 Sm 24.1; 1 Chr 21.1).

Postexilic Census Lists. The census lists found in Ezr 2.1–67 and Neh 7.6–69 are almost identical. The one in Nehemia; used for underscoring the importance of having pure Jewish ancestry, seems to be original and apparently shows the actual population at the time of *Nehemia (2d half of the 5th century B.C.). As reused in Ezra, it has for its purpose to make it appear that vast numbers returned immediately after the edict of Cyrus. Neither here nor in the apocryphal 3 Esdras do the figures add up to the given total of 42,360 (Neh 7.66; Ezr 2.64). The list contains, not only personal names, but also names of clans and cities, and in some cases it is difficult to say which is which.

Censuses in the New Testament. St. Luke mentions two Roman censuses: the first in connection with the birth of Christ, which took place when *Cyrinius (Quirinius) was governor of Syria (Lk 2.2), the other as occasioning the short-lived rebellion led by Judas the Galilean (Acts 5.37). Josephus (*Bell. Jud.* 2.8.1; 7.8.1) makes explicit mention of Judas's rebellion against Rome, when the Romans, upon reducing Judea to the status of a province in A.D. 6, took a census. Also, according to the chronological date of Josephus (*Ant.* 18.1.1, 2.1; 17.13.2), Cyrinius was governor of Syria in A.D. 6, and seemingly for the first time.

The difficulty caused by the reference to the census of Cyrinius in Luke's Gospel lies in the fact that in profane sources there is no explicit record corroborating his statement that Cyrinius was legate in Syria when a census was taken in Judea before the death of Herod the Great (4 B.C.). According to Josephus, Cyrinius held power as a legate, with authority over Judea, *c.* A.D. 6–7. Yet, the nativity narratives place Christ's birth in the reign of Herod the Great. A possible solution may lie in the fact that Cyrinius was in Syria with special powers waging the Homonadensian War also between 12 B.C. and 9–8 B.C. at the time when Saturninus was the legate there (see Tacitus 3.48; Strabo 12.6.5). Tertullian (*Adv. Marc.* 4.19) dates the birth of Christ by a census that he says took place under Saturninus (see W. Ramsay, *The Bearing of Recent Discovery . . .,* 243–245). Thus, Cyrinius, in Syria with Saturninus at this time, could very well be credited with carrying out or at least initiating a census at the earlier date (perhaps completed only in A.D. 6 when he became legate). This would be compatible with the thought of most scholars that Christ was born *c.* 8–7 B.C. A frequent objection that Rome would not take a census in Herod's territory is not compelling when it is remembered that Herod, though a *rex socius,* held his authority and its exercise at the discretion of the emperor. Although no extra-Biblical record mentions this census (if it is completely distinct from that of A.D. 6), there is evidence of periodic Roman census-taking in Egypt and Gaul during the 1st Christian century (see W. Ramsay, *Was Christ Born at Bethlehem?,* 131–148). The "census of the whole world" does not mean that it was accomplished in all parts of the empire simultaneously. Although a return to the place of family origin is unknown in other Roman censuses, it is a fact that the Romans respected the customs of subjugated peoples, and to the Jews, one's tribe and place of origin had great importance. Despite these concurrences, Luke's citation still raises questions. He calls it the first under Cyrinius and feels that it is so well known, that he can date the birth of Christ by it. Yet, there is no notice of it in Josephus, who is rather detailed for the reign of Herod. Josephus calls the census of A.D. 6 "the first." The attempt to solve the discrepancy by giving the adjective πρώτη a comparative force and translating: "This census took place earlier than that which occurred when Cyrinius was governor of Syria" is not supported by any similar use of πρώτη in Luke (see A. N. Sherwin-White, 171). Other possible solutions are that Josephus had gotten his facts wrong, or that Luke, knowing the early Christian tradition that the Davidic origin of Christ had been established by an official census, took it for granted that the census was at the time of his birth, when actually it was the same census of A.D. 6, which he already shows himself familiar with in Acts.

On the difficulty in Acts 5.36–37, where the revolt of Theodas is placed before that of "Judas the Galilean in the days of the census," *see* THEODAS.

Bibliography: InterDictBibl 1:547. EncDictBibl 335–338. De Vaux AncIsr 65–67. E. A. SPEISER, "Census and Ritual Expiation in Mari and Israel," BullAmSchOrRes 149 (1958) 17–25. G. E. MENDENHALL, "The Census Lists of Numbers 1 and 26," JBiblLit 77 (1958) 52–66. W. F. ALBRIGHT, "The Administrative Divisions of Israel and Judah," JPalesOrSoc 5 (1925) 20–25. A. BENTZEN, *Introduction to the O.T.,* 2 v. (2d ed. Copenhagen 1952) 2:34. W. M. RAMSAY, *Was Christ Born at Bethlehem?* (3d ed. London 1905); *The Bearing of Recent Discovery on the Trustworthiness of the N.T.* (4th ed. London 1920). M. J. LAGRANGE, "Où en est la question du recensement de Quirinius?" RevBibl 18 (1911) 60–84. A. DEISSMANN, *Light from the Ancient East,* tr. L. R. M. STRACHAN (rev. ed. New York 1927) 270–271. T. CORBISHLEY, "Quirinius and the Census," *Klio* 29 (1936) 81–95; "The Date of Our Lord's Birth," *Scripture* 1 (1946) 77–80. A. N. SHERWIN-WHITE, *Roman Society and Roman Law in the N.T.* (Oxford 1963) 162–171. H. U. INSTINSKY, *Das Jahr der Geburt Christi* (Munich 1957).

[S. C. DOYLE]

CENTER PARTY

The Center was one of the leading parties in the Reichstag in *Germany between 1871 and 1933. Its achievements in uniting Catholics of widely different social backgrounds, defending Catholic interests, and promoting social reform had a marked influence on Catholic parties elsewhere in Europe.

Definition. The Centrist leaders always insisted that it was a nonconfessional party open to non-Catholics; its founders made serious efforts to attract Protestant members in the early 1870s. But the substantial failure of the initial attempt, the ability of the party to play an important political role on a Catholic basis, and extensive Catholic opposition to the Center's conversion into a real interconfessional party made the leadership cool to anything but a formal definition of nonconfessionalism in its later history. The party name described its favorite position in the Reichstag—between the conservative parties (chiefly Prussian and representative of authoritarian monarchical traditions, Prussian hegemony, and state control over the churches) and the democratic parties (desirous of a secular and centralized democratic state). The pre-1918 Center regarded constitutional monarchy and a federal-state system as necessary safeguards against a possible democratic majority that would separate Church and State, secularize education, and tend toward socialism. The party placed itself on a factual basis after the overthrow of monarchical institutions in November 1918 and collaborated with the liberal and democratic parties in trying to create a viable republic. Its leaders justified their change of course on the grounds that the Weimar Republic liberated the Church, provided support for the clergy and ecclesiastical institutions, and ensured Catholics of complete civic equality. In the later 1920s and early 1930s the party's basic concern with Catholic cultural objectives and its social structure drove it toward the right and to a consideration of the advisability of supporting constitutional changes along semi-authoritarian lines.

Origins and Early History. Neither the party name nor its basic position from 1871 to 1918 were new, since three of its first leaders, Peter *Reichensperger, his brother August, and Herman *Mallinckrodt, had helped to found in 1852 the Catholic fraction in *Prussia, later renamed the Center fraction, after the Protestant monarchy withdrew some of the Church's constitutional liberties. However, the party foundered in 1862–63 when many Catholic voters, especially in the liberal Rhineland, chose to back the liberal parties in their conflict with the Bismarck ministry over expansion of the Prussian army rather than the Center, which sought to preserve the constitutional status quo in the contest. A more basic cause of its failure was the absence of any deep Catholic concern about the Church in a state in which it still enjoyed considerable freedom and in which the monarchy and liberal majority seemed to be hopelessly at odds with each other.

The action by representative personalities throughout Catholic Germany to create new Center parties in the Reichstag and Prussian Landtag sprang essentially from their fear of an anti-Catholic alliance between the hegemonic Prussian government and the liberal parties after the unification of Germany (1870–71). Catholics in Prussia and southern Germany alike had not concealed their dismay over Prussia's replacement of Catholic Austria as the leading state in Germany; their acceptance of the definition of papal infallibility by *Vatican Council I led secular and nationalistic liberals to believe that Catholics could not be loyal Germans while under papal authority. The appearance of 57 Catholic Centrists in the first Reichstag session indicates that many Catholics shared the fears of the party's founders regarding the freedom and rights of the Church. The prime factor, however, in the party's growth from a respectable 57 members in 1871 to 100 in 1881 was Bismarck's major error in associating his person and the Prussian state with the liberal parties in a massive legislative and administrative assault on the Catholic Church, which he believed to be the source of the Center's strength and a part of a general Catholic alliance trying to weaken the Protestant empire.

The Center met its severest test not in the *Kulturkampf but in the 1880s when Bismarck became fully conscious of its legislative power following the disintegration of the National Liberal party. By negotiating a settlement with the Vatican and appealing to the monarchical sentiments of the Center's aristocratic-conservative wing, the chancellor hoped to split the party in two. *Windthorst, the Center's leader since 1874, was deeply discouraged by his exclusion from the negotiations between Bismarck and the Vatican that ended the Kulturkampf, but he was able to preserve his party's unity. His colleagues and followers substantially backed him when he twice refused papal requests that the Center support the chancellor in his military legislation (1887). After the 1890 elections, even Bismarck recognized that the government would have to work with the Center party unless it was willing to abolish universal and equal suffrage.

The Center from 1890 to 1918. After Bismarck's forced retirement (1890), the Centrist leadership envisioned considerable domestic influence. Bismarck's successors rejected all suggestions of a *coup d'état* against the constitution and sought a working relationship with the Center. But Windthorst's sudden death (March 1891) deprived the Center of the one personality able to draw the Catholic electorate into the new course without serious difficulty. The task was all the greater because the government sought the Center's support for heavy military expenditures and for legislation favorable to labor, industry, and commerce in a time of deep agricultural depression. Ernst Lieber, Windthorst's successor, was too uncertain about his own position and too worried about party unity in the face of serious agrarian disaffection to support wholeheartedly the government's policies before the later 1890s. Deep concern lest reactionary advisers convince Emperor William II that the monarchy could not govern with a Reichstag under Centrist leadership led Lieber to move his party steadily in the government's direction after 1895. Before his premature death (1902), Lieber received credit for the passage of the new national civic code, two major naval bills, and legislation supporting Germany's colonial program.

Insurgency by younger Centrists who opposed the colonial administration's treatment of natives and of Catholic missions disrupted the party's relationship with the government (1906). It was restored in 1909 because the Conservative party found it more comfortable to collaborate with the Center than with democratic liberals who wanted political reforms in Prussia, the Conservative stronghold.

Before 1918. The gradual improvement of the position of German Catholics after 1895 justified the Center's course. All religious orders, except the Jesuits, regained corporative rights. The Church regained some supervisory influence over Prussian confessional schools. Some concessions were made toward parity for Catholics in the Prussian and imperial civil service. But Catholic support of the party declined from 85 per cent during the Kulturkampf to 55 per cent in the 1912 elections. Much of the defection occurred in the working classes. The Center had not been late in its awareness of the humane and political necessity of social action. It had supported Bismarck's insurance legislation for the aged, injured, and ill in the 1880s and assisted in the introduction of the 6-day week, labor courts, better working conditions, and pensions for widows and orphans. It had cooperated in the formation of Catholic unions and, later, of interconfessional ones. The Center had also helped to establish and to direct the People's League for Catholic Germany, which promoted Christian social reform among middle-class German Catholics and educated Catholic labor leaders. These efforts did much to keep large numbers of Catholic workers loyal to the party and to the Church. But the predominant influence of urban and rural propertied elements in the Center, its conservative policy on taxation and tariffs, its silent opposition to democratic suffrage in Prussia, and its initial inability to win general ecclesiastical approval for interconfessional unions alienated all but devoutly Catholic workers.

World War I. During this war of total mobilization, the question of workers' rights in Prussia and of Catholic labor's place in the Center assumed new significance. Throughout most of the war, the Centrist leadership, concerned about the future of Church-State relations and confessional education in Prussia, and under heavy pressure from Catholic business and agrarian groups, refused to sponsor Prussian electoral reform. Catholic labor leaders, in heavy competition with the Social Democratic unions for the allegiance of Catholic workers, insisted on labor suffrage in Prussia. Even the major representatives of Catholic labor followed Matthias Erzberger without enthusiasm when he argued convincingly in 1917 that the war was at best a stalemate and that the Center should join with the democratic parties in an effort to secure a compromise peace. Early in 1918, when Germany's war prospects had brightened, the old leaders isolated Erzberger by pledging support of electoral reform in Prussia. But they had to follow Erzberger's lead when Ludendorff informed the government (September 1918) that the war was lost and that the Emperor should appoint a democratic cabinet to negotiate peace with the U.S. and its allies. All the Centrist leaders were taken unawares by the November revolution that they considered unnecessary in view of recent constitutional changes. Nevertheless, they accepted the revolution and aided the early convocation of a democratically elected constitutional assembly that would restore parliamentary government and the rule of law.

The Center in the Weimar Republic (1919–33). In postwar Germany the Center party achieved influence and assumed responsibilities beyond anything it had known in its earlier history. Despite heavy criticism from Catholic rightists and conservatives, it collaborated with the Social Democrats and Democrats in providing Germany with a moderate constitution and a responsible government in this critical period. Under Erzberger's direction the party insisted that Germany must accept the Versailles Treaty. Later it supported Stresemann's policy of reconciliation with the other Western powers, though concern for its conservative supporters made the party do so cautiously. But the Center's responsible conduct and the frequency with which prominent Centrists held the chancellor's office did not satisfy the party's Bavarian wing, which had broken away in 1920, and other Catholic critics of the Center's course prior to the later 1920s. Internally, the party was increasingly wracked by disagreements among agrarians, laborites, and civil servants over economic policy. The German bishops were disturbed over the Center's inability to win the support of its democratic allies for a national confessional school law, placing confessional schools on the same legal plane as the interconfessional schools of the Weimar constitution. The election of a priest, Ludwig *Kaas, as party chairman (1928) reflected the belief of many members that only a clergyman could restore party unity. The concern with unity, the desire for a school law, and the essential weakness of the party's democratic elements were important factors in the Center's steady movement toward political alliance with the non-Nazi right. Kaas's efforts in this direction were thwarted by the intransigence of the conservative Nationalist leader, Alfred Hugenberg, and by President Hindenburg's replacement of Chancellor Heinrich Brüning, a moderate conservative Centrist, by the Catholic reactionary Franz von Papen (June 1932).

Dissolution of the Center. Both anger against Von Papen and fear of his intentions led the Center's leaders to seek a coalition with *national socialism, which they underestimated as a threat to parliamentary government. They were bitterly disappointed when *Hitler was appointed chancellor by Hindenburg in January 1933 after the failure of Von Papen's successor, General von Schleicher, and did not invite the Center to join his coalition cabinet. Two months later the party voted for the Enabling Act, which gave legal sanction to Hitler's dictatorship. The party leadership had decided that it was hopeless to resist Hitler and hoped that their action would cause him to preserve the Reichstag, respect the rights of the Church, and permit Catholic civil servants to continue in office. Most scholars believe there was a connection between the Center's approval of the Enabling Act and Kaas's interest in a German concordat with Rome. It is also the preponderant opinion that the sudden dissolution of the party in early July 1933 stood in direct relationship to the concordat negotiations then reaching their high point in Rome. But Hitler's possession of total power and the flight of members from the party between March and July would in any case have made it virtually impossible to avoid dissolution. The Nazi dictator was wise enough to focus his attack on the party and not on the Church as Bismarck had done.

See also PIUS XII.

Bibliography: C. BACHEM, *Vorgeschichte, Geschichte, und Politik der deutschen Zentrumspartei,* 9 v. (Cologne 1927–32). K. EPSTEIN, *Matthias Erzberger and the Dilemma of German Democracy* (Princeton 1959). R. MORSEY, StL 8:966–970. J. ROVAN, *Le Catholicisme politique en Allemagne* (Histoire de la démocratie chrétienne 2; Paris 1956). E. ALEXANDER, "Church and Society in Germany," *Church and Society,* ed. J. N. MOODY (New York 1953).

[J. K. ZEENDER]

CENTRAL AFRICAN REPUBLIC, an inland country in central *Africa, independent since 1960. It is a plateau about 2,500 feet in elevation and 238,224 square miles in area. The capital, *Bangui, is in the south on the Ubangi River. The forests of the south thin out to a savanna in the north. As the Territory of Ubangi-Chari, the region formed part of French Equatorial Africa with *Chad, *Gabon, and the *Congo Republic (Brazzaville), which border it, as do *Cameroon and the *Congo Republic (Léopoldville). The dominantly pagan population of 1.2 million in 1963 included 55,000 Moslems, 115,000 Protestants, and 165,000 Catholics (16 secular and 124 religious priests, 186 sisters).

From the Vicariate of the French Congo (1886) was detached the Vicariate of the French Upper Congo (1890), called Upper Congo and Ubangi (1894), now *Brazzaville. From this vast vicariate were detached the Prefecture of Ubangi-Chari (1909), made a vicariate (1937), called Bangui (1940); and the Prefecture of Berbérati (1940), made a vicariate (1952). From Berbérati were detached the Prefectures of Fort Lamy (1947) and Moundou (1951) in Chad; from Bangui

was detached Bangassou (1954). In 1955 Bangui became a metropolitan see with Berbérati as a suffragan; Bangassou and Bossangoa (a prefecture detached from Berbérati in 1959) became suffragan sees in 1964.

The country was occupied by pygmies, it seems, before the 19th century, when the slave trade forced tribes into the area from Chad, the Congo, *Somalia, and the lakes region. France began to explore and occupy the area (1890–1908), incorporating it in French Equatorial Africa in 1910. The mission founded with great difficulty by Prosper Augouard at Saint-Paul-des-Rapids near Bangui in 1894 was a precarious one, amid a hostile population given to cannibalism. When the three missions became a prefecture (1909), the government instituted forced labor for the rubber enterprise, causing an exodus of natives. Lack of personnel hurt the missions during World War I, after which they expanded beyond the rivers into the interior. In 1938, when the first African priest was ordained, French Capuchins driven from Ethiopia began to labor in Berbérati. After World War II they were joined by Italian Capuchins, also driven from Ethiopia. Dutch Holy Ghost Fathers received Bangassou in 1954. The minor seminary for Bangui and Bangassou in Sibut and that for Berbérati and Bossangoa in Berbérati had 87 seminarians in 1964. There are many primary and secondary mission schools. Protestant missions, mainly American, began in 1920 and are strongest in Bangassou and Bossangoa.

Bibliography: *Bilan du Monde* 2:206–210. AnnPont has annual data on all dioceses and vicariates.

[J. LE GALL]

CENTRAL SENSE

In scholastic psychology, the central sense (*sensus communis*) is an internal organic power for acquiring sense knowledge, distinct from the external and other internal *senses. Its function is to grasp all the stimuli known through the external senses, to compare them, unifying or distinguishing among them, and to know the very activity of the external senses, i.e., to be conscious of sensation. Its organ is to be found in the sensory and psychosensory zones of the cerebral cortex, in the associative cortical zones, and in the long and short associative fibers that link these zones.

Necessity. At the close of his study on the external senses, Aristotle concluded that there was need for a superior function of sense knowledge to explain certain activities closely associated with external sensation, but not themselves reducible to the operations of the external senses. These activities are (1) consciousness of the operation of the external senses and (2) knowledge of the similarities and differences between the objects of the various external senses. Each sense knows only the *sensibles that are proper to it. Sight is aware of color but not of sound, just as hearing is aware of sound but not of color. Again, sight is not audible and therefore is unknowable through hearing. Hearing is not colored and cannot be grasped by sight. No direct exchange is then possible between the external senses, either at the level of their proper object or of their specific activity. Moreover, no external sense can know its own sensation. In fact, not being colored, sight is not visible. The same is true of the other senses. For to know its own sensation, the sense would have to double itself in such a way that the sensory organ would become detached from itself as knowing subject to consider itself as object of its knowledge—an impossible dissociation at the level of organic operative powers. Therefore these two kinds of operations—discerning among the sensible objects of the various senses and being conscious of sensation—require an organic cognitive power superior to the external senses, common to all, and central as regards their specific operation. This is the central sense.

Operation and Functions. The roles of the central sense in elaborating sense knowledge can best be discussed in terms of its various functions in sensation, in perception, and in consciousness.

Sensation. *Sensation here is understood as knowledge of the action exerted upon sensory receptors by a specific stimulus, whatever be the nature of the object causing the stimulation. According to St. *Thomas Aquinas (*In lib. de sensu* 19.282–296) the central sense, as a superior power, uses the external senses as instruments to know sensible things. For it is from the central sense, as from a common source, that the power to sense (*vis sentiendi*) diffuses itself into the external senses. This explains why the stimulations of all the senses converge and terminate at the central sense (*In 3 de anim.* 3.599–613). Therefore no expressed species is needed in the *sensus communis* (*see* SPECIES, INTENTIONAL). The central sense collects the data of the various external senses in a global way. From this comes its aptitude for comparing the stimulations of the various senses, for grouping and synthesizing these, as well as for distinguishing and dissociating them.

To explain how the central sense operates in the distinction and synthesis of sensation, St. Thomas takes a rather obscure Aristotelian comparison and likens the central sense to a point toward which various lines converge (*In 3 de anim.* 3.599–613, 12.773). Just as the point can be considered indivisible in itself, or as multiple as the terminus of various lines, so it is with the central sense. To the extent that it integrates explicitly and actually the activity of each of the external senses, giving it special attention, the central sense can discern the likenesses and differences among sensations and among objects of the various external senses. To the extent that it operates at its own level, which surpasses that of the external senses (*De ver.* 15.1 ad 3; ST 1a, 57.2), it can synthesize the objects of the various senses and reconstitute the unity of the stimuli affecting the knowing subject.

Perception. *Perception designates the identification by the knowing subject of the object that is the source of the stimulus affecting the sensory receptors to bring on sensation. The identification takes place with dependence upon the global cognitive and affective context of the subject, within which it acquires a specific meaning. It presupposes a holistic organization of all qualitative and quantitative data supplied by sensation. Perception thus implies the discovery of values in the object that the external senses cannot recognize, and permits the establishing of a functional contact between the object and the knowing subject. Given this unifying and discriminating function, the central sense plays an important role in elaborating the knowledge that makes perception possible. Some scholastics attribute this elaboration entirely to the central sense. It seems that St. Thomas makes it the task rather of all the internal senses (without excluding *intellect), while recognizing the preponderant role of the *cogitative power (particularly in the elaboration of the *experimentum,* with the concurrence of *memory). For the cogitative power alone perceives the individual existing in its ineffable singularity and detects in it values that escape the external senses and the central sense (*In 2 de anim.* 13.396–398). Thanks to its organizing activity the central sense prepares the sensory matter through which the superior powers (cogitative, then intellect) better perceive the object's profound reality. Since the sensory data centralized by the *sensus communis* in some way already reveal, as impressions produced by the accidents of the object, the nature of that object, there can be no doubt of the importance of this first organization of knowledge effected by the central sense.

Consciousness. The central sense initiates the conscious awareness of the whole object and begins perceiving the distinction existing between subject and object. This awareness, however, remains as frail and as limited as the sensation upon which it is based. In fact, the central sense grasps in sensible objects only the forms of energy (qualities affected with a certain quantity) that stimulate the sensory receptors, without perceiving the singular existent being as such, for this is the proper object of the cogitative power. It follows that the distinction recognized by the central sense between sensations and their specific content is again found at the accidental level, qualitatively and quantitatively, without reaching the level of the concrete substance, which is perceived only by the cogitative power. This occurs whether the substantial reality of the object or that of the subject, the ego, is concerned. The contribution of the central sense to the total consciousness of the subject is thus constituted by the perception of the distinction between, on the one hand, the continuing flux of sensations (as activities following each other, without implying the grasping of an underlying, subsisting subject) and, on the other, sensory impressions relating to the accidental properties of the objects affecting the senses. But without this first distinction it would be impossible for the subject to arrive at a total consciousness of himself as a subsistent being distinct from every other existing being. This consciousness is deepened at the cogitative level (with which memory is associated) and at the level of intelligence. (*See* CONSCIOUSNESS.)

Unconscious Knowledge. Although a partial function of consciousness, the central sense is an organic power subject to the limitations and imperfections inherent in every organic faculty. Thus a stimulation may remain below the threshold required to transmit sufficient disturbance to the organ of the central sense to make it aware of the stimulation. The stimulation will, however, have excited the external sense in which it leaves its trace to the point where a subsequent stimulation, even subliminal, may reactivate it, and, by summation, finally arrive at the threshold needed to awaken the central sense. On the other hand, the energy available for sensory perception, as for every vital operation, is necessarily limited; thus an increased expenditure of this energy on a given perception proportionately reduces the energy available for other purposes that play only a secondary role in consciousness (cf. *De ver.* 13.3). For example, while concentrating its attention on the work of a given sensation, the central sense is not able to give equal attention to another sensation. The latter escapes its vigilance, even though it is perceived confusedly. It may, in its turn, emerge at the level of consciousness if it becomes the object of special attention. Consequently, even though in principle the central sense can perceive all sensations, the beam of its clear and distinct attention cannot be simultaneously applied with equal effectiveness to all sensations. A goodly number thus remain at the edge of conscious perception. Further research on the organic structure of the central sense is needed before the phenomenon of unconscious sensations can be more fully explained. (*See* SUBLIMINAL PERCEPTION.)

Role in Sleep. To the degree that it implies a loss of consciousness, sleep requires a corresponding inhibition of the central sense and of all the senses whose thresholds increase as a result. If a sensory stimulation is strong enough, it can go beyond the threshold of sensation without reaching consciousness as a sensation, because the central sense is bound in sleep and does not perform its proper functions. Such a stimulation is eventually integrated in disguised fashion within some oneiric content of the imagination. Reducing the inhibition of sensitiveness can bring a corresponding freedom to the central sense. This allows the subject a certain discrimination between dream images and sensations brought on by stimuli coming from extrasubjective reality. However, as long as some inhibition persists, perception from the central sense remains proportionately handicapped. The subject still confuses dreams and reality, not clearly distinguishing between reality and its representation in the *imagination (ST 1a, 84.8 ad 2).

See also SLEEP; SENSE KNOWLEDGE; KNOWLEDGE, PROCESS OF.

Bibliography: M. STOCK, "Sense Consciousness according to St. Thomas," *Thomist* 21 (1958) 415–486. B. J. MULLER-THYM, "Common Sense, Perfection of the Order of Pure Sensibility," *ibid.* 2 (1940) 315–343. E. J. RYAN, *The Role of the "Sensus Communis" in the Psychology of St. Thomas* (Carthagena, Ohio 1951). M. DE CORTE, "Notes exégétiques sur la théorie aristotélicienne du 'Sensus communis'," NewSchol 6 (1932) 187–214. E. BARBADO, "La conciencia sensitiva según S. Tomàs," *Ciencia tomista* 30 (1924) 169–203.

[A. M. PERREAULT]

CENTURIATORS OF MAGDEBURG

The *Centuries,* 16th-century Lutheran account of Church history, were conceived by Matthias *Flacius Illyricus, a devout and strict follower of Martin Luther. The work was begun in 1559 and completed in 1574. It was originally published under the title *Ecclesiastica historia . . .,* but the third edition printed at Nürnberg in 1757 entitled the work *Centuriae Magdeburgenses,* and it has been known by that title ever since. Flacius was aided by a number of prominent Protestants, among whom were Aleman, Wigand, Judex, and Copus. This group conceived their project to be a treatment of Church history that would prove the veracity of the Lutheran Church and disprove the theological claims of Rome. As a result the *Centuries* are passionate Lutheran polemics. The work consists of 13 volumes, each representing a century of ecclesiastical history. Flacius rejected the humanistic view of history as an all encompassing study of the phenomena of man and concentrated upon Church affairs. In the Augustinian manner, the *Centuries* view history as the eternal struggle between the forces of good and evil, of God and the devil. History is consequently the story of God's will.

A central theme runs throughout the work: the pure, pristine doctrines of Apostolic Christianity have been perverted by the Romanists, while the Lutherans have rediscovered the true doctrines of God. Many critical and uncomplimentary anecdotes are used to undermine Catholic doctrine and worship. As an example, the legend of Pope Joan is accepted as historically accurate. The papacy consistently appears as the anti-Christ, which has diverted God's teachings.

DE TRANSLATIONE IMPERII ROMANI AD GERMANOS.

Item DE ELECTIONE EPISCOPORUM, quòd æquè ad plebem pertineat.

MATTHIA FLACCIO ILLYRICO AVTORE

XXVII-A-49

BASILEAE 1566.

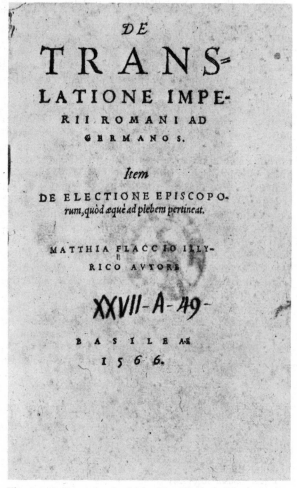

The frontispiece of v.9 of Matthias Flacius's "Ecclesiastica historia . . ." printed at Basel in 1566.

The role of the *Centuries* in historiography in general, and in Reformation historiography in particular, is most important. The *Centuries,* with their obvious Lutheran tone, passed into the stream of ecclesiastical literature many legends that persist to the present day. The uncritical use of spurious sources beclouded the true sources of Church history. Many miracles, at least those that proved Flacius's thesis, were presented as historically verified. Historical writing became a tool that could be utilized for partisan causes and for a prolonged mechanical and chronological study of facts. However, the very purpose of the work was indirectly to aid the cause of sound ecclesiastical scholarship. Flacius's attack upon the sources and documents of the Catholic Church forced her to return to the very same sources and documents to verify her position. The Catholic historians were required to use profane history in their own defense. Thus ecclesiastical history became historically minded. Research, always the most valuable method in any intellectual confrontation, assumed new proportions and importance.

Each century was assigned a volume divided into 16 basic titles and subjects under such headings as rites, Church doctrine, schisms, heresies, and political changes—all of which had taken place within that century. Thirteen volumes were printed by 1574; the three remaining volumes appeared in MS but were never published. The most effective Catholic response to the Centuriators was written by Cardinal Caesar *Baronius in his famous *Annales Ecclesiastici* (1588–1607).

Bibliography: W. PREGER, *Matthias Flacius Illyricus und seine Zeit,* 2 v. (Erlangen 1859–61). C. CRIVELLI, EncCatt, 3:1305–06. R. BÄUMER, LexThK² 6:1274. **Illustration credit:** Biblioteca Apostolica Vaticana.

[C. L. HOHL, JR.]

CENTURION, Roman military officer in command of a "century," nominally 100 foot soldiers; 10 centuries constituted a cohort; and 60, a legion. The centurion's duties consisted in training, inspecting, and disciplining the troops in his charge (cf. Mt 8.9) and leading them in battle. At times he was the highest-ranking official in a particular area, especially in the provinces. The NT mentions five centurions. Three remain unnamed: one at Capharnaum (Mt 8.5–13; Lk 7.2–10), one in charge of Jesus' execution (Mt 27.54; Mk 15.39, 45; Lk 23.47), and another in Jerusalem at the time of Paul's arrest (Acts 22.25–26; 23.17, 23). The names of the other two are *Cornelius, whom Peter received into the Church (Acts 10.1), and Julius, who brought Paul safely to Rome (Acts 27.1, 11, 43).

Bibliography: EncDictBibl 338–339. F. D. GEALY, InterDict Bibl 1:547–548. Hastings DB 1:366–367.

[R. MERCURIO]

CEOLFRID OF WEARMOUTH, ST., Benedictine abbot; b. *c.* 642; d. Langres, France, Sept. 25, 716 (feast, Sept. 25). Born of a noble family, he entered the monastery of Gilling at the age of 18 but in 664 moved to *Ripon where the Benedictine Rule had

Dedication stone of the church of St. Paul at Jarrow. The Latin inscription reads: "The dedication of the church of St. Paul on 23 April in the 15th year of King Ecgfrith and the 4th year of Ceolfrid abbot and, under God's guidance, founder of this same church."

been introduced under *Wilfrid of York. *Benedict Biscop brought him to *Wearmouth as prior in 674, and together they traveled to Rome (678–680) to obtain books, pictures, architects, stonemasons, and glassmakers for England. They also brought John, Archchanter of St. Peter's, from Rome to teach and write music at Wearmouth. When Benedict founded the abbey at *Jarrow in 681, Ceolfrid, together with Easterwine (d. 686), was made deputy abbot under the founder. The dedication stone from this monastery, dating from 685, is the oldest written record in Northumbria. The twin foundation of Wearmouth-Jarrow was very rich and had one of the best schools and libraries in England. The *Codex Amiatinus,* the oldest and best Vulgate Bible extant, may have been made at Wearmouth-Jarrow *c.* 700, and Ceolfrid, taking it to Rome as a gift, died on his journey through France. His relics were translated to Wearmouth-Jarrow and later to *Glastonbury. Ceolfrid's influence was especially important in the Romanization of the Celtic Church and in the cultural renaissance of Europe in the 8th century. The two chief vitae of the saint are an anonymous *Vita abbatum* (tr. Douglas S. Boutflower, Sunderland 1912) and the *Vita beatorum abbatum* of *Bede.

Bibliography: ActSS Sept. 7:113–126. BEDE, *Hist. Eccl.* 2:79–103, 325–361, 375–389. W. HUNT, DNB 3:1333–35. P. H. BLAIR, *An Introduction to Anglo-Saxon England* (Cambridge, Eng. 1959). BiblSanct 3:1126–27. A. M. ZIMMERMANN, LexThK[2] 2:993. Butler Th Attw 3:635–637. **Illustration credit:** Joseph Connacher, Jarrow.

[H. E. AIKINS]

CEPEDA, FRANCISCO, Dominican missionary and grammarian; b. Spain, 1532; d. Guatemala, 1602. He entered the Dominicans in the Convent of Santo Domingo de Murcia of the province of Andalucía. He went to America and to Chiapas, Guatemala, before 1560 and worked as a missionary. He became prior of the Zacapula convent and was a definitor at the provincial chapters of 1580, 1587, 1591, and 1602. He also served as commissary of the Holy Office. On May 16, 1593, he was elected provincial. He is best known as a grammarian. From the writings of his Dominican comissionaries he composed a uniform simplified grammar of various Indian languages in the area, *Artes de las lenguas de Chiapa, Zoques, Cendales (Celdales), y Cinacantecas.*

Bibliography: A. DE REMESAL, *Historia general de las Indias occidentales y particular de la gobernación de Chiapa y Guatemala,* 2 v. (2d ed. Guatemala City 1932). F. XIMÉNEZ, *Historia de la provincia de San Vicente de Chiapa y Guatemala de la Orden de predicadores,* 3 v. (Guatemala City 1929–31).

[A. B. NIESER]

CEPEDA ÁLVAREZ, FÉLIX ALEJANDRO, Chilean Claretian scholar; b. La Serena, Chile, 1854; d. Madrid, 1930. As a student at the diocesan seminary of La Serena, he had a brilliant career, graduating as a lawyer at 18. After 4 years of teaching he was ordained in 1876. He was appointed pastor of the parish of Calera (1882–87), but despite his success there, Cepeda entered the religious life. On March 19, 1888, he took his vows in the Congregation of Claretian Missionaries in Santiago. That same year he was sent to Spain. His holiness and learning made him an obvious choice for positions of responsibility. In 1895 he was appointed provincial superior of Catalonia; he held this post until 1902 when he was transferred to Mexico where he directed the vice province until 1918. Cepeda was responsible for important foundations there and in the United States. He was recalled to Madrid to take up residence at the general curia as general consultor of the Congregation. Despite all the administrative work and responsibility, Cepeda always found time to continue his work in the confessional and pulpit. His writings include some 20 volumes noted for their theological, literary, and historical value.

[P. HILL]

CERAMICS

A family of art products whose common denominator is that they are made of nonmetallic earthen materials that are fashioned when cold and hardened into permanent form by firing. The form may vary from household pottery and dishes to figurines, reliefs, and tiles. Technically, three kinds of ceramic work are distingished according to the methods of firing and the porousness of the result. (1) Terracotta, or baked clay, is the most primitive technique. It involves the firing of nonglazed clay to produce a porous vessel that may be made waterproof by painting or pseudoglazes, such as those perfected by the Greeks. (2) Glazed ware goes a step beyond terracotta by adding an alkaline slip that vitrifies in the firing and fuses with the clay in a hard, nonporous, highly finished surface. The addition of various metallic oxides to the glaze or to subsequent luster glazes provides the artist with a wide palette of brilliant colors. Glazing techniques were known in the 6th century B.C. in the Near East, whence knowledge of the techniques spread as far as China. Faience and majolica are the best-known European varieties of glazed ware. (3) Stoneware and porcelain are made of a clay to which fluxes have been added that in firing cause the clay to lose its porousness and transform it into a compact, opaque body. Porcelain, with its fine, white, translucent quality, was discovered by the Chinese in the T'ang period (618–906); it was not discovered in Europe, however, until the 18th century.

Fig. 1. Terracotta lamp from the catacombs of Rome, 3d century; the top bears an image of the "Good Shepherd."

Early History of Ceramics. Though there are scattered finds of prehistoric pottery from Italy to Scandinavia, the European tradition in ceramics really begins with Greek pottery. The Greek potters not only achieved a technical mastery of complex and elegant ceramic forms, but also provided the first instance of pictorial painting on vases beyond simple decorative schemes. In this they foreshadowed the distinctive European taste in ceramics that continually turns to narrative interest in ceramic decoration, as opposed to Oriental preferences for pure colors and simple forms. The "black-figure" wares of the 6th century B.C. and the later "red-figure" wares of the 5th represent the climax of Greek vase painting with exquisite scenes of the epic age as well as vignettes of everyday life. Roman times saw the advent of standardized moulds and factory methods of reproducing ornament; this, plus the ever wider use of metals, led to the rapid decline of the ceramic art.

The first appearance of Christian motifs in ceramics comes on terracotta lamps of the 3d and 4th centuries A.D. in Italy and North Africa. These common household objects bore the symbolic subjects usual in early Christian iconography—the monogram of Christ, the chalice, the peacock, etc. The ampullae carried by pilgrims to the shrines in Palestine were similarly decorated, or had figures of the saints. But these are of more interest for their iconography than for their workmanship. In Byzantine art, too, ceramics played a very minor role except for the manufacture of mosaic tesserae. By far the bulk of their pottery was imported from their Islamic neighbors, among whom a continuous tradition of very advanced ceramic work was maintained throughout the Middle Ages, while the art remained at a fairly primitive level in Europe. In emulation of Chinese ware, which was imported to Samarra as early as the 9th century, Islamic potters developed a wide variety of glazes—iridescent, metallic lusters, the Hispano-Moresque luster of golden brown hue, and eventually blue and white glazes. Tiles, too, became very important in the decoration of mosques. Trees, animals, and birds figured in their decorations; and tile mosaics of Chinese blue and white were used to adorn the Great Mosque of Damascus in the 15th century.

In the Middle Ages. In the Middle Ages Europe did preserve her own tradition of tile manufacture, though the tiles were generally relegated to floor decorations (e.g., the floor of St. Denis was decorated in tile mosaic *c.* 1260). Yet it was from Moorish Spain that renewed interest in ceramic art drew its inspiration. Workshops in Málaga and Granada, and later in Valencia and Barcelona, exported to the rest of Europe pottery of blue and cream color that was known as majolica, probably after Majorca, an intermediate port in their shipping. It was the aim of the majolica potters to create a perfectly white ground on which to draw their decorations; this they achieved first through a *bianchetto* slip clay and later through a tin-enamel glaze that became standard in the 15th century. In Florence and Faenza potters were soon vying with Renaissance painters in the new art. Not satisfied with decorative motifs, the Faenza potters began employing the humanist themes of Renaissance art in a style called *istoriato,* or narrative. Portraits, sacred subjects, and historical scenes were all executed in brilliant polychromy on white ground. The pure white of the tin-enamel glaze soon attracted the attention of the Florentine sculptor Luca *della Robbia, who saw in it an economical substitute for marble. Della Robbia composed simple sculptural relief figures in white set off against a plain blue

Fig. 2. Majolica plate from Urbino, painted by Francesco Xanto, c. 1528. The decoration is a scene from the "Metamorphoses," (bk. 4) of Ovid.

Fig. 3. "The Immaculate Virgin," Schrezheim faience statuette by Johan Martin Mutschele, Bamberg 1771.

background in a style that immediately proved very popular. His work, continued by his nephew Andrea and his sons, eventually provided the ceramic industry, particularly at Faenza, with a new interest in figure and relief sculpture. This city became so well known for its ceramics that it gave its name, faience, to the kind of pottery it produced; eventually, however, the name came to be used more exclusively to designate white glazed French, German, and Dutch potteries of the 17th and 18th centuries made in imitation of Oriental porcelain.

Modern Developments. In the baroque era the town of Delft in Holland assumed primary importance in the production of ceramics. The importation of Chinese ware at this time inspired wide imitation of Oriental styles. Chinese porcelain had been known in Europe since the 13th century as a luxury item, and repeated attempts were made to reproduce it in local kilns. The credit of the European discovery of porcelain technique belongs to Johann Friedrich Böttger, who established a center for its manufacture at Meissen in 1710. Though the secret was jealously guarded, within a decade it had leaked out to rival firms in Vienna. Porcelain suddenly became the vogue all over Europe, and countless details of household decoration were executed in this medium. Meissen, Vienna, and Berlin led the ceramic world in their production of delicate *rococo figurines.

Late in the 18th century, Josiah Wedgwood forced a break with rococo style by producing in mass quantities ceramics of neoclassic design. He perfected techniques of producing hard earthenware, called creamware, with designs impressed by copper plates. Produced in England, the ware sold widely in Europe and America and was a major force in the shift to neoclassical taste. At the same time it presaged the advent in the 19th century of the industrial manufacture of pottery that was to eclipse the art of ceramics down to the beginning of the 20th century.

In the 20th century, especially in France, a strong "studio" movement has grown up in opposition to manufactured ceramics. The collaboration of prominent painters gave special impetus to the movement. The potter André Metthey set up a studio in 1903, to which Ambroise Vollard sent many of the symbolist and *Fauves painters with whom he dealt. The attractive results were exhibited at the Salon d'Automne and the Salon des Indépendants. Later *Braque, Chagall, and Picasso took up ceramics in earnest. Also well known for their wall ceramics are Fernand *Léger, Alfred Manessier, and Henri *Matisse. The wall ceramics at the Dominican convent at Vence are Matisse's last work in this medium. (*See* WAY OF THE CROSS, illus. by Matisse.)

Bibliography: G. M. A. RICHTER, *The Craft of Athenian Pottery* (New Haven 1923). W. B. HONEY, *The Art of the Potter* (New York 1950); *European Ceramic Art: From the End of the Middle Ages to About 1815*, 2 v. (London 1949–52). G. LIVERANI et al., EncWA 3:186–325. **Illustration credits:** Fig. 1, Pontificia Commissione di Archeologia Sacra. Fig. 2, Walters Art Gallery, Baltimore, Md. Fig. 3, Museum of Fine Arts, Boston, Mass.

[T. F. MATHEWS]

CERBONIUS, ST., bishop of Populonia; d. island of Elba, late 6th century (feast, Oct. 10). When in the 6th century the Vandals drove the bishops out of Africa, Cerbonius went with St. Regulus (d. 542) to Tuscany and was made bishop of Populonia, where he lived a communal life with his clergy. Totila (d. 552), King of the Ostrogoths, ordered Cerbonius exposed to a bear in punishment for sheltering Roman soldiers, but when the bear did not attack, the bishop was freed. Because of this legend he is often pictured in art with a bear. The Lombards exiled him on Elba, where he died 30 years later. His body was buried at Populonia; He is the patron of Massa Marittima, the diocese into which his see was later incorporated. A later and even more legendary life asserts that he was denounced and summoned by Pope *Vigilius for celebrating Mass too early on Sunday, but the marvels attending his trip to Rome moved the Pope to meet him on the road and send him back to Populonia with honor.

Bibliography: ActSS Oct. 5:87–102. A. BIGELMAIR, LexThK^2 2:994. Butler Th Attw 4:80. GREGORY I (the Great), *Dialogus* 3.11.

[B. CAVANAUGH]

CEREAL OFFERING, a special kind of sacrifice in ancient Israel called in Hebrew *minḥâ.* Originally the term signified, in secular life, gift (Gn 32.14) or tribute (2 Sm 8.6), and in religious life, any offering made to God (Gn 4.3–5; 1 Sm 2.17; etc.). In the

Pentateuchal *priestly writers, however, the term *minḥâ* designates a specific kind of offering best expressed in English as cereal offering.

Detailed legislation is given in Leviticus ch. 2 on the cereal offering. Ordinarily it consisted of a choice grade of flour called *sōlet* (probably bolted meal, as distinct from common flour, *gemaḥ,* containing bran). This as such could be offered to the Lord with prescribed ceremony (Lv 2.1–3); or it could be made into salted unleavened dough, which was then baked, grilled, or fried (2.4–7, 13). Also, *first fruits of grain could be brought to the Lord as a cereal offering in the form of roasted gifts (2.14). All forms of cereal offerings had to have olive oil and frankincense poured on them (2.1, 15). Part of every cereal offering was burned as a "token" to the Lord, the rest was eaten by the priests (2.3, 8–10, 16).

The cereal offering could be offered alone or together with various other sacrifices. It formed an independent sacrifice as the daily offering of a priest (Lv 6.14–15), as the *sin offering of a poor man (Lv 5.11–13), and as the "jealousy offering" of a wife suspected of adultery (Nm 5.15). Usually, however, the cereal offering was merely an adjunct to other sacrifices. Thus, it formed part of the sacrifice on the Sabbath, the New-Moon Feast, the Passover, Pentecost, and the Day of Atonement (Nm 28.9–29, 39). The cereal offering formed part also of the morning and evening sacrifice (Ex 29.41; Ez 46.14; 4 Kgs 16.15), and with an unblemished animal it constituted a *peace offering (Lv 7.11–14). It was part also of the sin offering (Nm 15.22–23), the *Nazarite dedication ceremony (Nm 6.13–20), and the ordination (*see* ORDINATION TO OLD TESTAMENT PRIESTHOOD) of priests (Lv 8.26–28; 9.4). The *showbread (Lv 24.5–9) was really a special kind of cereal offering.

See also SACRIFICE, III (IN ISRAEL).

Bibliography: EncDictBibl 339. F. NÖTSCHER, *Biblische Altertumskunde* (Bonn 1940) 322. De Vaux AncIsr 421–422.

[J. S. HOMLISH]

CEREMONIES, CONGREGATION OF

The Congregation of Ceremonies is the commission of cardinals within the Roman Curia that is charged with the direction of the liturgical and diplomatic ceremonial of the papal court.

History. The existence of this Congregation dates back at least to the early years of the 17th century. Concerning its history prior to that time, there is some disagreement. Most authors hold that the Congregation had its origin in the Sacred Congregation of Rites and Ceremonies founded by Sixtus V in his constitution *Immensa dei* of 1588. Subsequently, either by another decree of Sixtus V or through a gradual evolution, the Congregation of Ceremonies broke off from the parent Congregation and assumed a separate existence. Another theory places the beginnings of the Congregation in a cardinalatial commission formed by Gregory XIII in 1572 to reform the ceremonies of the papal chapel. This commission was absorbed by the new Congregation of Rites and Ceremonies established by Sixtus V, and then later once again resumed its independent status.

The reorganization of the Curia effected by Pius X in 1908 left the Congregation of Ceremonies relatively untouched. The reform constitution, *Sapienti consilio,* merely reaffirmed the traditional prerogatives of the Congregation and gave a brief outline of its competency. This legislation was repeated by the Code of Canon Law in 1918.

Competency. It is the responsibility of the Congregation of Ceremonies to take care of "the regulation of the ceremonies to be observed in the papal chapel and court, and of the sacred functions performed by cardinals outside the pontifical chapel; also the same Congregation handles questions of precedence of cardinals and of diplomatic representatives sent by the various nations to the Holy See" (CIC c.254; ClerSanc 201).

The competency of the Congregation in matters of liturgical or religious ritual extends primarily to the ceremonies of the papal chapel. In addition, because of the close relationship of the cardinals with the pope, the Ceremonial Congregation is entrusted with the regulation of the ceremonies performed by cardinals even when they are outside the pontifical chapel. It is also from this Congregation that instructions are issued for the ceremonial to be observed when a papal representative (ablegate) and a member of the Noble Guard carry to any newly created cardinal outside Rome the news of his promotion, together with the cardinal's zucchetto and biretta. This procedure is followed in certain traditionally Catholic countries where the head of state has by custom the privilege of bestowing the red biretta on new cardinals. This Congregation is competent also in all matters concerning the dress and insignia of cardinals, bishops, prelates, and members of the papal household.

In the difficult area of diplomatic ceremonial, it is this Congregation that handles the many details of ceremony, etiquette, and precedence affecting the papal court. Its activity in this field is similar to that of the protocol staff of the U.S. Department of State. Chief among its diplomatic duties is the organization and direction of the solemn reception by the pope of heads of state, prime ministers, and ambassadors. The secretary of the Congregation plays a prominent role in these formal receptions.

Any questions of precedence involving cardinals, diplomats accredited to the Holy See, and others attached to the papal court are decided by the Congregation of Ceremonies. The pope also acts through this Congregation to grant—by way of privilege—special positions of honor or precedence in the "papal chapel." (The papal chapel is the group of personages that attends the pope in certain solemn religious functions.)

Organization. The cardinal prefect and several other cardinals constitute the membership of the Congregation. The dean of the College of Cardinals usually holds the position of prefect since his experience and seniority should enable him to handle effectively any delicate questions of protocol or precedence. In addition to the cardinals, there are three officers of the Congregation: the secretary, subsecretary, and archivist. There is also attached to the Congregation a small group of consultors among whom the papal masters of ceremonies are included by law.

Bibliography: M. LALMANT, DDC 3:258–60. N. DEL RE, *La Curia Romana* (2d ed. Rome 1952). P. C. VAN LIERDE, *The Holy See at Work,* tr. J. TUCEK (New York 1962). Abbo 1:254.

[R. J. BANKS]

CERIOLI, COSTANZA, BL., religious foundress; b. Soncino (Cremona), Italy, Jan. 28, 1816; d. Comonte di Seriate (Bergamo), Dec. 24, 1865 (feast, Dec. 24). She was the daughter of the wealthy Count Francesco Cerioli. After attending the school run by the Visitandines in Bergamo (1826–32), she married the sexagenarian Gaetano Buzzechi Tassis, a noble and wealthy widower (1835). The disparity in age and spiritual outlook between wife and husband, the latter's ill health, and the premature deaths of their three children, only one of whom reached adolescence, were trials that Costanza bore patiently. After Gaetano's death (1854), his widow dedicated her wealth and energies to works of charity. She began caring for rural orphan girls in her home and kept increasing the number of persons who supervised their formation as the number of children grew. In 1857 she founded the Sisters of the Holy Family of Bergamo to carry on this work and took Paola Elisabetta as her name in religion. By 1962 this institute had 400 members in 61 houses. To care for orphaned boys she founded, with the help of Giovanni Capponi, the Brothers of the Holy Family. Costanza wrote the rules for both congregations, which were approved by the Holy See. She was beatified March 19, 1950.

Bibliography: E. FEDERICI, *Suor Paola Elisabetta Cerioli, Vedova Buzecchi-Tassis* (Comonte di Seriate 1948). Butler Th Attw 4:606–607.

[V. A. LAPOMARDA]

CERONE, DOMENICO PIETRO, Renaissance music theorist and singer; b. Bergamo, Italy, 1566; d. Naples, 1625. In 1592 this priest and gifted cantor went to Spain, where he sang in the chapel of Philip II and later of Philip III. In 1608 he became singer in the chapel of the Spanish viceroy of Naples. There he published his lengthy treatise in Spanish entitled *El melopeo y maestro, Tractado de música teórica y práctica* (1613), dedicated to Philip III, a valuable detailed exposition of 16th-century counterpoint and musical practice. Of special interest are his chapters on the composition of motets, Masses, psalms, and other settings; on formulas of vocal ornamentation; and on instruments and their tuning. Cerone looked backward to classic contrapuntal style. He did not understand *Marenzio's innovations, nor did he mention *Monteverdi. Within his limitations his taste was good and his teaching sound.

Bibliography: D. P. CERONE, *El melopeo y maestro,* bk. 12, tr. in Strunk SourceR 262–273. R. HANNAS, "Cerone: Philosopher and Teacher," MusQ 21 (1935) 408–422; "Cerone's Approach to the Teaching of Counterpoint," *American Musicological Association: Papers* (1937) 75–80. H. ANGLÈS, MusGG 2:969–973. G. GROVE, Grove DMM 2:141.

[I. POPE]

CERQUEIRA, LUÍS DE

Bishop of Japan; b. Vila de Alvito, Portugal, 1551 or 1552; d. Nagasaki, Feb. 16, 1614. On July 14, 1566, he entered the Jesuit novitiate in Evora, where he studied philosophy and theology. About the end of 1575 he was attached to the secretariate of the Jesuit general curia in Rome. There he worked until early 1577. From 1585 to 1586 he was professor of theology in Coimbra; from 1586 to 1589, socius of the Portuguese provincial; and thereafter, again professor of theology. While teaching theology in Evora, he learned, in January 1592, of his appointment as coadjutor to the bishop of Japan. The papal bulls did not arrive until early 1594, and in the meantime he took his doctorate in theology at Evora (November 1593). Finally, on March 30, 1594, he set out for Asia. On Sept. 22, 1594, he arrived in Goa, whence he proceeded on April 21, 1595, to Macao, arriving Aug. 7. He became bishop of Japan in February 1598 upon the death of Bp. Pedro Martins just before the latter reached Malacca on a journey from Macao to India. Despite the threatening situation in Japan, Cerqueira risked sailing for Japan, July 16, 1598, in company with the visitator Alessandro *Valignano; they landed on Aug. 5, 1598. On that same day Toyotomi Hideyoshi, the military dictator of Japan who issued an edict against Jesuits, was stricken with a fatal illness and died in September. Cerqueira remained in Japan, mainly in Nagasaki, until his death.

Cerqueira was a gentle and zealous pastor whose practical capacities had been sharpened by his work in the Jesuit general curia and as socius of the provincial. He was prudent and energetic and managed to maintain a dignified independence even vis-à-vis such a commanding personality as his fellow worker and visitator Valignano. Cerqueira's impressive conscientiousness made him insist energetically on the observance of the directives in papal communications, even in cases in which the effort was made (e.g., by the Franciscans from the Philippines) to present him with a *fait accompli.* He also gave proof of remarkable diplomatic talent in his dealings with the Japanese princes. A deeply religious man, he sought zealously to intensify religious life in Japan.

At the very beginning of his reign, he created, at a meeting in October 1598, the legislative basis for his activity. He opened the first seminary for Japanese candidates for the secular priesthood and installed the first Japanese pastors in Nagasaki. Cerqueira undertook a series of apostolic journeys; in 1606 he paid an unofficial visit to the former Shōgun, Tokugawa Iyeyasu, in Fushimi (near Kyōto); at this time he became personally acquainted with the Christian communities in central Japan. Cerqueira's term coincides with the flowering of the early Japanese Church; there were many conversions, including those of influential feudal lords. There were also local persecutions (Ōmura, 1606; Arima, 1612). In 1612 there began the great persecution that was to lead to the decline and fall of the Japanese Church. Cerqueira was dead before the definitive expulsion of the missionaries (November 1614).

Cerqueira as professor wrote various treatises (*De legibus, De gratia,* preserved in manuscript), and as bishop he wrote extensive reports on the state of the Japanese Church, memoranda and apologia for Pope and King, a report on the martyrs of Higo (1603). In 1605 there appeared in Nagasaki his work *Manuale ad Sacramenta Ecclesiae ministranda,* with a Japanese appendix.

Bibliography: H. CIESLIK, "Zur Geschichte der kirchlichen Hierarchie in der alten Japanmission," NZMissw 18 (1962) 42–58, 81–107, 177–195. J. F. SCHÜTTE, "A história inédita dos 'Bispos da Igreja do Japão' do P[e]. João Rodriguez Tçuzu, S.J.," *Congresso Internacional de História dos Descobrimentos, Actas* 5.1 (Lisbon 1961) 297–327. Sommervogel 2:1000–02; 9:23. E. LAMALLE, EncCatt 3:1324–25. A. FRANCO, *Imagem da virtude* (*Noviciado de Evora*) (Lisbon 1714) 461–477.

[J. F. SCHÜTTE]

CERTITUDE

The term certitude derives from the Latin, *cernere* (Gr. *κρίνειν*), which means to resolve, decide after seeing the evidence. St. Thomas Aquinas defines certitude as "the firmness of the adherence of a knowing power to the thing known" (*In 3 sent.* 26.2.4). Primarily a quality of the *judgment, certitude can be considered positively to indicate the firmness of the mind in its assent, and negatively, the exclusion of all prudent fear of *error. It is distinguished from other states of mind such as *doubt, which is an inability either to affirm or deny; and *opinion, which is the acceptance of a judgment as probable. Since the *intellect is made for knowing *truth, and its perfect actuation is had only when the truth is known with *evidence, formal certitude is had when what is known presents itself as objectively evident.

Historical Development. Among the early Greek philosophers the question of certitude was not formally considered, although the reasonings of the early cosmologists implied the view that ordinary certitudes were not reliable. With the rise of the *Sophists there developed an explicit questioning of the ability of the human mind to arrive at true and certain knowledge. For some, such as *Heraclitus, Protagoras, and Gorgias, reality was in such flux that it could never be known as it is.

Classical Greeks and Medievals. Against these, *Socrates and *Plato contended for the possibility of the human mind's arriving at true certitudes. While Plato fostered a skepticism relative to sense perception, he claimed certitude to be attainable in the intelligible sphere, where knowledge is had of Ideas or ideal Forms. These are the ultimate realities and the only objects of knowledge in the strict sense. For *Aristotle first principles are self-evidently certain and hence indemonstrable. He held that sensible beings can be known by virtue of the *form (the inner principle of determination), and that all the materials of intellectual knowledge are somehow derived from and through the senses.

After Aristotle, speculative philosophy made little progress. For the Epicureans the one thing necessary was pleasure, in the sense of a lack of perturbation (*ἀταραξία*); and truth, virtue, and all else are of value only in so far as they promote this. The Stoics implied that (subjective) certitude is attainable, especially in the knowledge of what constitutes an ethically good and wise life. Against the alleged certitude of this position the Skeptics reacted, and for about five hundred years (*c.* 300 B.C.–A.D. 200) *skepticism exercised great influence in Greek and Roman thought.

St. Augustine's *Contra academicos* is a refutation of the skeptical positions of the New Academy; and in general the Church Fathers and the scholastics through the Middle Ages discouraged skepticism and affirmed the ability of the mind to know with certitude. They distinguished between what the mind knows by the natural light of reason and what it accepts on testimony, and between intrinsic and extrinsic evidence; the latter being important for Divine Revelation (cf. St. Augustine, *C. acad.* 2.7; St. Thomas, *In 3 sent.* 26.2.4; ST 2a2ae, 2.1.) In the *nominalism of *William of Ockham, however, skepticism did find some expression.

Modern philosophers. From its beginning, modern philosophy was characterized by the firm conviction that if the true object of the mind is philosophically determined, or if its proper limits are faithfully respected, man is capable of certitude. One may be asked to admit that the object of reliable knowledge is the unique divine substance (*Spinoza), or the Absolute Spirit in itself and in its self-manifestations (*Hegel); true knowledge may be limited to ideas and their interrelation (British *empiricism), or to sense presentations as informed by the categories of the understanding (*Kant); but with these qualifications settled, the outstanding thinkers are convinced that truth and certitude are attainable.

Thus, *Descartes, facing the anti-intellectualism of the Renaissance, and the atheism and skepticism of his day, sought to find a new and firm foundation for certitude in metaphysics. Beginning with the self and using the technique of doubt, he was convinced that his reflections finally overcame doubt, gave him true knowledge of his own existence, of God, and of the external world. *Rationalism glorified the power of the mind to know and to build systems, but it has been accused of vastly exaggerating man's capacity for certain knowledge. While the empiricists limited the immediate objects of human knowledge to ideas or impressions, they (apart from David *Hume) were convinced that in this narrow area certitude was to be had. Kant, impressed by the success of the physical sciences, decided that only scientific truth and certitude were reliable; hence metaphysics, which deals with "questions such as cannot be answered by any empirical employment of reason, or by principles thence derived," is not available with the certitude of evidence (*Critique of Pure Reason,* Introd. A3; B6). So questions on the nature of the soul, of the world, and of God lead only to illusion.

Scholastic and Contemporary Thought. As a result of the works of modern philosophies, scholastic philosophers have devoted much time to questions of truth and certitude. In the 19th century many of them, influenced by the thought of J. *Balmes, held that man naturally possesses some absolutely certain truths that need no justification whatsoever. Later, Cardinal Désiré *Mercier and others taught that man's many spontaneous certitudes need further philosophical reflection in order to establish the human capacity for truth and to arrive at reflex certitudes. Others admit some naturally known certitudes, and since these are known implicitly in each judgment, one needs merely to become explicitly aware of them.

Leaving *scholasticism aside, one can say that the contemporary philosophical scene is very complex, but that one of its outstanding features is an antimetaphysical attitude that becomes an outright skepticism for many. This is due in no small measure to the skepticism of Hume, who paved the way for most of contemporary empirical philosophy, and for the antimetaphysical views of *positivism, *phenomenalism, and *pragmatism. Developments in scientific method and studies in the nature of language and logic have contributed much to the skeptical mood of *logical positivism and *linguistic analysis. When there is admission of truth, it is often with a relativistic twist, in terms of scientific *verification, utility (personal or public), or adaptation to an evolving environment.

Kinds of Certitude. That there may be intellectual convictions or firm assents of the mind of various kinds can be seen by brief reflection. One may be certain that

Julius Caesar was stabbed to death; that the human soul is immortal; that another person loves him; that God exists; and that he himself exists. In all these areas certitude may be claimed, and yet it is obvious how different are the assents, for example, to one's own existence and to Caesar's murder. Moreover, whether because of prejudice or training, men do at times assent to a false doctrine or position with a dedication worthy only of the truth. Hence it has become usual and necessary to distinguish various kinds of certitude.

Subjective vs. Objective. Since certitude is primarily a characteristic of human assent, it can be said that all certitude is subjective. However, it is called purely subjective when evidence is lacking, or is not known to be present, for the firm assent then given is in reality only an affective disposition of the subject, who believes without doubt and without proper motivation that he possesses the truth. Objective certitude means a firm assent of the mind to a known truth, an assent motivated by the evidence, and wherein the known motive for assent excludes all prudent fear of error.

Absolute vs. Conditional. This division, common in scholastic manuals, is made in view of the foundation on which the certitude rests. The former is said to rest on the natures or essences of things; the latter on the connection between finite natures and their operations. Absolute (or metaphysical) certitude is had in the knowledge of self-evident truths, such as the proposition that a thing cannot simultaneously be and not be; of demonstrated conclusions, such as the spirituality of the soul; or even of the contingent fact of one's own existence. When any given truth is known with metaphysical certitude, this means that the denial of that truth would be a denial of the very nature of what is known; hence its opposite is excluded as utterly impossible. However, in the operations of finite beings, it is possible that the nature, while remaining essentially unchanged, may be impeded in the production of its natural operation or effect, and thereby a note of the conditional or hypothetical enters in. Since finite agents are divided into the two classes of (1) free—man in his deliberate acts—and (2) determined—all other material beings and even man in his nonfree operations such as growth—conditional certitude is of two kinds, physical and moral.

Physical Certitude. This certitude characterizes assent to concrete applications of *physical laws. Such laws come to be known through *induction, and they tell how nonfree natures operate. Presupposing the accuracy of observation and the correct use of induction, such laws are themselves metaphysically certain, since they reveal the natures of things. In simple examples, it is of the nature of fire to burn, of unsupported heavy bodies to fall, of hydrogen and oxygen to unite to form water. However, when it comes to the operation of these laws in concrete instances, some defect of matter or agent may impede such operation from taking place. The law is still certain conditionally, however, on condition that such defects do not occur.

Scholastic manuals usually insist here that divine cooperation also is necessary, and that God can (for some special reason) suspend a physical effect without at all changing the nature of the agent (*see* MIRACLES). Hence, although absolute certitude is not to be had, one can and does give a firm assent without prudent fear of error in given instances. One can be certain that this food will nourish him, that this fire will burn this dry log. This assent is motivated by the knowledge of how the given nature operates, and, granting no indication of divine intervention, it provides a certitude that is called physical.

Moral Certitude. This is said to be had in some concrete applications of moral laws. The laws are arrived at by induction, and they enunciate truths about how human beings freely operate. Traditional examples have to do with maternal love, the natural veracity of men, and the reliability of historical testimony. Since exceptions to such "laws" can be had by the abuse of free will, it is clear that the necessity found in this area is far less rigorous than in the working of the laws of nature; so certitude here is not easily had, and when had, is of a very different kind. However, presupposing knowledge of the apposite law of human conduct, and knowing from the circumstances that there need be no fear of an exception, one can have moral certitude about his friend's loyalty, his wife's fidelity, or a particular person's veracity.

Some philosophers have been willing to call only metaphysical certitude true certitude; and they speak of physical, and especially of moral certitude as only very high probabilities. However, for others this places too stringent limitations on the nature of certitude and fails to recognize that scientific progress presupposes physical certitude, and that human life and communication presuppose the reliability of moral certitude.

Speculative vs. Practical. Certitude is divided also into speculative and practical. The former is taken to refer either to what is theoretically valid or to the sphere of being in general. The latter means either a high degree of probability that is sufficient for the ordinary activity of daily living, or refers to particular judgments applying law to a specific case, to what actually ought to be done (*see* PRUDENCE).

Necessary vs. Free. Considering the role of the will in assents, one can speak of necessary and free certitude. The former is had in response to truths so immediately evident that the intellect, having once adverted to them, cannot refuse its assent. Here the will merely directs attention to the proper consideration. Examples are: one's own existence, one's immediate experience, the principle of contradiction. However, most truths are not so immediately evident, and the will usually has a more important role in the exercise of judgments. Truths such as the existence of God, of the spirituality of the soul, and those deriving from human testimony may indeed be assented to firmly and securely; but they can be, and have been, doubted, and they do not force the mind's assent. These are free certitudes.

Natural, Reflex, and Supernatural. Natural certitude is sometimes taken to mean the spontaneous, pre-reflective convictions of men relative to such truths as one's own existence, the existence of other beings, or the need of living a morally good life; in this sense it is distinguished from reflex certitude, which is known to be based on objective evidence, and which presupposes awareness of the powers and limits of the human mind. However, from the point of view of the means whereby truth is acquired, natural certitude refers to truths that are legitimately acquired by the natural powers of the human mind in the light of objective evidence; and is thus distinguished from supernatural certitude, which is had in truths that are accepted on the authority of God revealing.

Objective Natural Certitude. Of special importance for philosophy are firm assents that are acquired by the natural operations of the human mind (hence not in virtue of revelation), and are based on the self-manifestation of what is known. Whenever this sort of certitude is had, no matter what the process through which the being that is known manifests itself in one or other intelligible aspect, it is always characterized by the note of *necessity. In this sense what is assented to with this sort of certitude must present itself as infallibly and necessarily true. Only in this way can the intellect be perfectly actuated in its natural drive for truth, and find that satisfaction and joy that results only from the secure possession of its proper good, which is the truth.

First Principles. This sort of certitude can be had by the intellect in either its immediate or mediate assents. In the knowledge of *first principles one is dealing with truths that can be recognized and affirmed by a sort of natural instinct or *intuition, once the meaning of the subject and predicate has been grasped. Thus, if a person knows the meaning of "whole" and of "part," he can immediately affirm the relation between them. As St. Thomas says, first principles "are not acquired by reasoning, but from the sole fact that their terms are known" (*In 4 meta.* 6.599). This holds for such truths as the principles of *contradiction, of *identity, of *finality, etc. In these cases there is a recognition of truths that are infallibly, necessarily, and evidently true; whose evidence, in fact, is self-manifesting; and whose truth is so totally and so evidently present that there can be no room for doubt, hesitation, or any sort of incertitude.

While these principles are grasped with supreme evidence and certitude, it must be admitted that they are vague in content and come far from satisfying man's desire for truth. St. Thomas looks on them as a sort of seedbed (*De ver.* 18.4.) wherein truths are contained in an imperfect manner, and which must be brought to flower in the actual and certain knowledge of what is virtually contained in the principles. By this is meant the vast area of mediately known truths that are acquired by *demonstration.

Certitude of Demonstration. Demonstrated truths are all conclusions of science and philosophy derived from premises that are certain and evident, so that the new truths themselves are, by the process of demonstration and through the mediating function of some middle term between subject and predicate, rendered evident and certain. Unlike the evidence and certitude of first principles, the evidence and certitude of conclusions are themselves mediate and derived. Yet, even in these truths, it is the object known that thus mediately manifests itself to the mind and specifies the intellectual act. It does reveal itself as necessarily and infallibly true, and it can be justified in the light of first principles; hence this sort of scientific certitude also results in the perfect satisfaction of the mind in its quest for truth.

As St. Thomas points out, the certainty of the conclusions rests ultimately on the evidence and certitude of first principles; hence the function of demonstration is to render the evidence of the conclusion present to the intellect by showing its connection with first principles. "The whole certainty of scientific knowledge arises from the certainty of principles. For conclusions are known with certainty when they are reduced to principles. Therefore, that something is known with certainty is due to the light of reason divinely implanted within us . . ." (*De ver.* 11.1 ad 13).

Church Teaching on Certitude. In this matter the Catholic Church has consistently and officially taken a clear stand. Its expressed views are: (1) The human mind is capable of arriving at truth. (2) Of itself it is incapable of arriving at knowledge of supernatural truths concerning God and man. (3) Even with regard to some truths about God that can be naturally known, it is not easy for man to arrive at them, and so it is fitting that God should come to man's aid by revealing them to him.

Human Certitude. While these themes can be illustrated from the whole history of Church teachings, a few brief references to the documents will suffice. On the ability of the human mind to know truth and to know it with certitude: "The reasoning process can prove with certitude the existence of God, the spirituality of the soul, and the freedom of man" (Denz 2812; cf. 3004, 3026). Pope Pius XII presents the abiding views of the Church in this matter when he says: "It is well known how highly the Church esteems human reason for its function to demonstrate with certainty the existence of God, personal and one; to prove beyond doubt from divine signs the foundations of the Christian faith itself; to express properly the law which the Creator has imprinted in the hearts of men; and finally to attain to some understanding, indeed a very fruitful one, of mysteries" (Denz 3892). Speaking of *scholastic philosophy he continues: "This philosophy, acknowledged and accepted by the Church, safeguards the genuine validity of human knowledge, the unshaken metaphysical principles of sufficient reason, causality, and finality; in a word, the possibility of attaining certain and unchangeable truth" (*ibid.*).

Supernatural Truths. However, the Church has been fully aware also of the fact that what man can learn by his own natural powers is quite limited. These limitations are found in two areas, the natural and the supernatural. With an eye to constant Church teaching, Vatican Council I clearly points out that there is an order of knowledge entirely beyond the natural powers of man, a supernatural order, wherein revelation is required if man is to learn anything at all about it: The Church has always held and holds "that there are two orders of knowledge, distinct not only in origin but also in object. They are distinct in origin, because in one we know by means of natural reason; in the other, by means of divine faith. And they are distinct in object, because in addition to what natural reason can attain, we have proposed to us as objects of belief mysteries that are hidden in God and which, unless divinely revealed, can never be known" (Denz 3015). This position is reinforced by a corresponding canon (Denz 3041).

Divine Revelation. Even in those matters pertaining to God that the human mind can learn by the natural light of reason, the same Council explicitly states that such truths have also been revealed by God so that they may "easily be known by all men with solid certitude and with no trace of error" (Denz 3005).

Relative to the acceptance of the fact of revelation, the Council teaches that God provides all the means necessary for (moral) certitude in this matter. To ensure the reasonableness of our assent, "God has willed that external proofs of His revelation, namely divine acts and especially miracles and prophecies, should be added to the internal aids given by the Holy Spirit" (Denz 3009). This position is reaffirmed in the corresponding canons, and the possibility of knowing miracles with certitude is restated in the words: "If anyone says . . . that miracles can never be recognized with certainty . . . let him be anathema" (Denz 3034).

While the certitude respecting the fact of revelation is normally moral, the certitude had in the supernatural act of faith itself, made by divine *grace, and having the authority of God Himself as its motive, is of a higher quality than any natural certitude.

Certitude and Faith. Supernatural certitude, having as its motive not the evidence of what is assented to, but the authority of God revealing, and being informed by grace, has special pertinence in the matter of the virtues of faith and hope. Revelation, by providing the believer with the opportunity for a secure assent to new truths, is a source of new certitudes and of renewed security in assents to some naturally knowable truths about God's existence and nature.

In the process of passing from unbelief to belief, we can distinguish various steps and indicate briefly the role of certitude in each. The initial steps, which help to turn the person towards the acceptance of faith, concern things that are naturally known, and for which natural certitude can be had. As initial steps towards faith, these natural acts are motivated by divine grace. In the process one must come to know and admit the credibility of God as witness to truth; and as this rests on the demonstrated existence and veracity of God, it is known in an evident and certain judgment. There must then follow the knowledge that God has actually revealed some particular truth; and the acceptance of this, in order to be reasonable, must rest on such proofs as will render it evident and certain to the human mind. Finally, in making the act of faith itself, one assents firmly, and with certainty, to what God has revealed, motivated only by the knowledge that He has so revealed. In this assent the mind does not see or understand what it believes—the object of faith, for example, the Holy Trinity—but it recognizes with certitude that it should assent for motives that are now evident. In making the full act of assent, the will has an important role to play, since the object is not evident and therefore cannot determine the intellect.

Certitude and Hope. The supernatural virtue of *hope is a habit whereby man confidently expects eternal happiness as well as the means necessary to arrive at it. Thus the acts of this virtue have as their object the possession and enjoyment of God by vision and love, as well as the supernatural help to attain this end; they have as their motive God's fidelity, power, and mercy. In addition to this divine side, there is the human side, man's cooperation with grace and his fidelity to the will of God. Insofar as hope rests on the firm foundation of God's fidelity to His promises, it is characterized by complete certitude, since God will most certainly fulfill His promises. However, insofar as hope includes the human element of man's cooperation with, and fidelity to, grace and his final perseverance—and of these one cannot be so sure—it is always colored by some uncertainty. As St. Paul says, "work out your salvation with fear and trembling" (*Phil* 2.12), and this must be because we may fail and not because God can fail us. St. Thomas points out that "filial fear is not opposed to the virtue of hope, for thereby we do not fear that what we hope to obtain through God's help will fail us, but rather we fear that we may withdraw ourselves from that help" (ST 2a2ae, 19.9 ad 1). So hope, as an act of the will elicited under divine grace, does not have the same sort of certitude as an act of faith.

Rejection of Certitude. Only a radical skepticism positively rejects all certitude and gives up in despair when faced with the problems of human knowledge. Still, very many schools of philosophy do, at least implicitly, reject the possibility of certitude in one area or another. Such schools have flourished not only in the ancient, but also in the modern world, and are treated in detail elsewhere in the *Encyclopedia* (*see* SKEPTICISM; KNOWLEDGE, THEORIES OF).

Summarily it can be said that in many contemporary philosophies there is either a skepticism about *sense knowledge and a consequent rejection of the noetic role of *sensation, or a skepticism about intellectual *knowledge and a consequent limitation of valid knowledge to the empirically verifiable. Concretely what is needed is an analysis of both knowledge and certitude that recognizes the complexity of the knowledge process. In the attainment of knowledge one finds aspects of singularity and universality, of necessity and contingency, of materiality and spirituality, and of identity and diversity between knower and known. These elements are not easily harmonized in any theoretical exposition of the nature of knowledge. However, an adequate explanation must preserve all the experienced elements, even those difficult to reconcile. Because knowledge is of the universal and necessary, one cannot reject the singular and contingent. Knowledge means an identity between knower and known; still, the diversity between them cannot be denied.

Since man is a composite unity of body and soul, of mind and matter, his cognitional situation reflects this; he is limited neither to pure sense perception nor to a purely intellectual vision entirely divorced from the senses. The human contact with experienced being occurs at various levels. One has sense knowledge of sensible beings; one also has intellectual knowledge of these same beings according to one or another aspect of their intelligible structure. With these as a foundation, one can go on to a deeper intellectual knowledge of material things and their operations, of one's own mental and volitional activities as spiritual, and finally of God.

The problem of human certitude is identical with the general problem of human knowledge, with the study of its proper object and of its nature. The doubt that characterizes skepticism is self-defeating, whether as a general theory or as limited to some area of inquiry, and results in despair and the abandonment of inquiry rather than a fruitful investigation and evaluation of the facts.

See also EPISTEMOLOGY; KNOWLEDGE; TRUTH; EVIDENCE.

Bibliography: THOMAS AQUINAS, *Truth,* tr. R. W. MULLIGAN et al., 3 v. (Chicago 1952–54). R. F. O'NEILL, *Theories of Knowledge* (Englewood Cliffs, N.J. 1960). L. M. RÉGIS, *Epistemology,* tr. I. C. BYRNE (New York 1959). I. TRETHOWAN, *Certainty, Philosophical and Theological* (Westminster, Md. 1948). W. A. WALLACE, *The Role of Demonstration in Moral Theology* (Washington 1962). R. HOUDE and J. MULLALY, eds., *Philosophy of Knowledge* (Philadelphia 1960). J. OWENS, *An Elementary Christian Metaphysics* (Milwaukee 1963). F. A. CUNNINGHAM, "*Certitudo* in St. Thomas Aquinas," ModSchoolm 30 (1952–53) 297–324. S. HARENT, DTC 6.1:201–215.

[R. F. O'NEILL]

CERTITUDE, JUDICIAL (CANON LAW)

Judicial certitude is the degree of persuasion that is required of the judge regarding the matter to be decided by the sentence or decision of a tribunal. It must derive from the evidence laid down before the court and hinges on the valuation of proofs adduced by the litigants.

History of the Valuation of Proof. Historically, there are two well-known systems of valuation of proofs leading to two different conceptions of a judicial verdict: the system of formal or legal proof based on Germanic law, and the system of rational or free-valued proof proper to Roman law (CorpJurCivDig 22.5.3.2). In the first the weighing of evidence is not left to the judge's free conscience, but it is determined by legal rules (e.g., recourse to ordeals, use of decisory oaths, necessity of a certain number of witnesses or of a certain quality in witnesses), which go as far as obliging a judge to reject a petition even when he is convinced that it is well founded. In the second the valuation of the proofs is left to the subjective free conscience of the court, although Roman law, under the jurisconsults and the emperors, limited this liberty to a certain extent.

Canon Law has always remained substantially faithful to the principle of Roman procedure, even if it did introduce some elements of Germanic procedural law. In fact, the Canon Law of the later Middle Ages developed an elaborate, arithmetic-like system for the weighing of testimony "in terms of the number of witnesses and of a legally fixed credibility of one unexceptionable witness," as Roscoe Pound describes it (*Jurisprudence,* 5:575). Two unexceptionable (*omni exceptione maiores*) witnesses constituted a full proof while other witnesses accounted only for fractions of such a proof. The English common law rejected this system, adopting a procedure by which a 12-man jury rendered a verdict.

Rule of the Code of Canon Law. The CIC, reverting more closely to the old Roman principle, lays down as its primary rule that "the judge must have in his mind moral certainty about the matter to be defined by the sentence" (CIC c.1869.1; SollNostr c.393.1) and "must weigh proofs according to his conscience, unless the law itself explicitly determines the effect of some proof" (CIC c.1869.3; SollNostr c.393.3). Therefore, in the Code, moral certitude arising from the free weighing of proofs is the rule, and any legal proofs whose valuation is determined by law are to be considered as exceptions (*nisi lex aliud expresse statuat*) and interpreted strictly (CIC c.20). Among the legal proofs still recognized by the Code, some are equated to a full proof, e.g., certain judicial confessions (CIC c.1751; SollNostr c.273), refusal to write constituting an admission of authenticity (CIC c.1800.4; SollNostr c.323.4), the testimony of two or three unexceptionable witnesses (CIC c.1791.2; Soll Nostr c.314.2), public documents (CIC c.1816; SollNostr c.339), *juris et de jure* presumptions (CIC c.1826; SollNostr c.349), decisory oaths and the refusal, under certain circumstances, to take a decisory oath (CIC c.1836.2,4; SollNostr c.360.2,4), notorious facts (CIC c.1747nl; SollNostr c.269nl); some do not go beyond an incomplete (*semiplena*) proof, e.g., a supplementary oath (CIC c.1829; SollNostr c.352), simple presumptions of law (CIC c.1827; SollNostr c.350), testimony of one witness (CIC c.1791.1; SollNostr c.314.1), *septimae manus* witnesses (CIC c.1975.2; SollNostr c.482.3).

Moral Certitude. The term "moral certitude" expresses a concept borrowed from scholastic philosophy. It is a certitude, therefore a state of mind that implies a firm and unwavering assent, without fear of error, to a judgment regarding persons or things. It is moral, therefore differing from both metaphysical and physical certitude.

Metaphysical certitude supposes the unwavering assent of the mind to what things are in their essence and nature; they cannot be otherwise. The axiom that a totality is always greater than any one of its component parts is always true because it excludes even the possibility of the contrary. Physical certitude means the unwavering assent of the mind to what is necessary according to the physical laws of nature. But this kind of certitude admits the possibility of the contrary: death brings the decomposition of the body unless the laws of the physical world are suspended by a miracle. Moral certitude is likewise a firm assent of the mind, but to propositions accepted upon evidence taken from the normal mode of action in human conduct. A fact vouched for by credible witnesses is to be considered as certain, because honest men normally tell the truth. Evidently the possibility of the contrary is not excluded.

Morally certain judgments are neither absolutely certain nor universally true. In a matter of this order there is certainty in the sense that the mind gives full assent to a given proposition, although the judgment is not true without exceptions and the intellect is aware of their existence. It remains morally certain to say that mothers love their children, even if a few perverted mothers do not love them. It is not only possible but it does happen that several witnesses perjure themselves, that an allegedly authentic document is spurious, that experts err in their judgment; notwithstanding a few derogations to the general rule, however, it remains certain that in most cases such a derogation does not occur. St. Thomas states this point very clearly. "According to the Philosopher we must not look for an equal certitude in every matter. In human acts, on which judgments are passed and evidence is required, it is impossible to have demonstrative certitude (i.e., metaphysical), because they are contingent and variable things. Hence the certitude of probability suffices, one that reaches the truth in the greater number of cases (*quae ut in pluribus veritatem attingat*), although it does fail in a small minority (*ut in paucioribus*) of cases. Now it is probable (*i.e., morally certain*) that the assertion of several witnesses contains the truth rather than the assertion of one; and since the accused is the only one who denies, while several witnesses affirm the same as the actor, it has been reasonable, established by divine and human law, that the assertion of several witnesses should be upheld" (2a2ae, 70.2.c).

Pope Pius XII in his allocution of Oct. 1, 1942, to the Rota [ActApS (1942) 339] taught the same doctrine when he declared that moral certitude stands between the two extremes of absolute (metaphysical) certitude and simple probability; the first one excluding the possibility of the contrary, the other admitting a well-founded doubt in favor of the contrary. Moral certitude therefore differs from common probability for the simple reason that it implies necessarily the exclusion of a well-founded or reasonable doubt; it differs from absolute certainty because moral certitude does admit the possibility of the contrary.

The exclusion of fear of error is a condition of moral certitude as it is an essential element of any certitude. Whenever an objective reason remains in favor of the contrary, the fear of error subsists and there is no certainty; but the fear of error is eliminated and subjectively to be discarded when it is morally impossible for the contrary to be true. A certain and vague uneasiness may persist in the mind; this is explained by the fact that the intellect has not fully attained its connatural end: intrinsic truth excluding absolutely the possibility of the contrary. Intrinsic evidence is impossible in a realm of truth that depends not on the essence of things but on the constancy of moral human actions. In moral certainty a real objective fear of error is unreasonable whenever no sólid argument can be brought forward to justify it.

Moral certitude admits of various degrees, as Pius XII declares explicitly in the 1942 allocution. Evidently a fact is always morally certain when it excludes all reasonable doubts to the contrary, and it must not be forgotten that slight discrepancies are to be disregarded. But, within these limits, one can undoubtedly find degrees in moral certitude: when a fact is established by a score of highly credible witnesses, corroborated by undisputably authentic documents, by all the circumstances surrounding the case, confirmed by presumptions of law and fact, surely the certainty attained is greater and more satisfying for the mind than when something is proved only by three witnesses, however trustworthy they may be.

Canon Law. The principle adopted by the code of Canon Law is clear: The judge must have moral certitude in order to pronounce judgment. He cannot be satisfied with less but cannot demand more than ordinary moral certitude, i.e., an objective moral certainty excluding all possible doubt, and he cannot require a higher degree or a special degree of certitude except where he orders more complete proofs in view of the importance of the case (CIC c.1791.2; SollNostr c.314.2) or where the law makes provision for an especially valued legal proof (CIC c.1869.3; SollNostr c.393.3). Some of the legal proofs recognized by the CIC are of positive nature and force the judge to accept them as sufficient to pronounce sentence (CIC cc.1159.1, 1593, 1758, 2020, 2033; SollNostr cc.70; 280); some others are of a negative nature and forbid the judge to consider them as sufficient (CIC c.1791.1,2; Soll Nostr c.314.1,2).

Regarding the cases of importance that require a greater degree of certitude, it must be admitted that they are not clearly defined in the Code and cannot be easily ascertained. Under the previous law, canonists tried to determine some of them by specifying several cases that required more than two witnesses. This was true especially in criminal indictments concerning a person of high dignity or standing, such as a cardinal or a bishop, and would be equally true today. Under the present rule it is left to the judge to decide if more complete proofs are necessary.

A question of practical importance arises here. Are marriage cases to be considered as matters of graver importance requiring more complete proofs? Despite the opinion of several authors and certain expressions of the CIC that seem to postulate clear evidence (CIC cc.1515, 1814; SollNostr c.337) in order to destroy the queen of all presumptions—as the presumption of law in favor of the validity of the matrimonial bond is sometimes called—and despite some rather strong if not always unquestionable statements of the Roman Rota [SRR 21 (1929) 509; 34 (1942) 126], it appears exaggerated to claim that cases of nullity of marriage are to be classified among the matters that because of their very special gravity require more complete proofs or more than ordinary moral certitude. Nothing in the present law or in the 1936 instruction of the Congregation of the *Sacraments for the handling of marriage cases (ActApS 28:313n1) justifies such a contention. In particular, art. 136.1 of the instruction simply confirms the general rule of CIC c.1791.1 (SollNostr c.314.1) stating that the testimony of two or three unexceptionable witnesses constitutes a sufficient proof.

Finally it should not be forgotten that "the judge must obtain his certainty from the acts and proofs of the case" (CIC c.1869.2; SollNostr c.393.2). Anything that has not been brought before the court as part of the evidence and has not been consigned to the acts can have no bearing on the judicial sentence according to the old axiom *quod non est in actis non est in mundo* (What is not in the record does not exist). Hence arises the canonical problem facing a judge who knows, from private knowledge, that a decision based exclusively on the acts will be unjust. Canonists and theologians have not always agreed regarding the solution to be given to this thorny problem. It was generally taught that a judge could accept the evidence introduced in the acts and free an accused person even though he knew that person to be guilty, but on the contrary if he knew through private knowledge a defendant to be innocent while the acts indicated guilt, he was to abstain from pronouncing sentence, leave the bench, and ask to be replaced.

See also EVIDENCE (CANON LAW); EXPERTS (CANON LAW); JUDGES (CANON LAW); WITNESSES (CANON LAW).

Bibliography: R. POUND, *Jurisprudence,* 5 v. (St. Paul 1959). A. REIFFENSTUEL, *Jus canonicum universum,* 7 v. (Paris 1864–70). F. SCHMALZGRUEBER, *Jus ecclesiasticum universum,* 5 v. in 12 (Rome 1843–45). M. LEGA and V. BARTOCETTI, *Commentarius in iudicia ecclesiastica juxta codicem iuris canonici,* 3 v. (Rome 1950) 2:628–632. H. FLATTEN, "Qua libertate index ecclesiasticus probationes appretiare possit et debeat," *Apollinaris* 33 (1960) 185–210. V. SCIALOJA, *La procedura civile Romana* (Rome 1936) 124. J. NOVAL, *Commentarium codicis iuris canonici* (Rome 1920), *De Processibus* 4.1:408–412.

[A. CARON]

CERTITUDE OF FAITH. Unlike the motives for *certitude that characterize the natural and philosophical sciences, the certitude of faith is based on the fact that a truth is revealed by God, who can neither be deceived nor deceive. Such certitude is not based on *evidence that is internal to the truth in question but rather on the omniscience and veracity of God, who has revealed. It is of the nature of moral-historical certitude in that it depends upon testimony, but is elevated above this type of certitude since the Person testifying is God. The certitude of faith does not depend upon the certitude surrounding the *preambles of faith. Regardless of the rigor of the reasoning employed in arriving at the judgment of credibility or even of credendity regarding the *deposit of faith, the act of faith itself transcends such reasoning and remains entirely free, since an act of supernatural faith cannot be made on the basis of natural reason alone. Faith is a mutual and free gift that is exchanged between God and the believer. The act of faith is congenial to the truths of natural reason that are used in explanation or amplification of it but does in no way depend upon them.

Apart from scattered remarks in several of the Fathers, dealing with God's fidelity, the question of the certitude of faith did not receive serious theological consideration until the early Middle Ages. With the scholastics, and especially the commentators on St. Thomas Aquinas, the doctrine of the formal object of faith began to develop until it achieved final form in the definition of Vatican Council I. According to Vatican I, the certitude of faith depends upon two facts: that God has revealed and that He can neither deceive nor be deceived. Once the fact of revelation is recognized (Denz 428, 3004, 3420–26), and the fact that God cannot be deceived nor deceive (Denz 3008), there results in the believer a freedom from the fear of error that forms the basis for a loving *commitment to the content of revelation. The fact that this commitment is free, however, means that it is not compelling in the way that conclusion compels assent once the premises are known. A number of intellectual, nonintellectual, or even unconscious influences may interfere with man on his way to the certitude of faith (Denz 3876) or in his possession of it. Faith depends on the action of grace both for its inception and for the certitude that follows from it (Denz 3004, 3015).

See also FAITH; FAITH, BEGINNING OF; MYSTERY (IN THEOLOGY).

Bibliography: A. CHOLLET, DTC 2.2:2155–68. M. C. D'ARCY, *The Nature of Belief* (New York 1931; new ed. 1958). R. AUBERT, *Le Problème de l'acte de foi* (3d ed. Louvain 1958). A. GARDEIL, *La Crédibilité et l'apologetique* (Paris 1908). J. PIEPER, *Belief and Faith,* tr. R. and C. WINSTON (New York 1963).

[J. P. WHALEN]

CERTON, PIERRE, Renaissance polyphonist of the Franco-Flemish school; b. Melun?, France, *c.* 1510; d. Paris, Feb. 22, 1572. He was assigned to Notre Dame in Paris from 1529 before his appointment in 1532 to Sainte-Chapelle, where he remained as master of the choirboys (from *c.* 1542) and perpetual chaplain (from 1548 until his death). He held a canon's prebend from 1560 at Melun (possibly his birthplace). His compositions include 8 Masses, individual Mass movements, about 70 motets, 50 French psalms (dedicated to Diane de Poitiers), and about 300 chansons. More prolific but less varied or cosmopolitan in style than Sandrin or *Sermisy, Certon nevertheless exhibits in his best works a pleasant and direct quality. His humorous imitative chansons aptly depict their unsophisticated literary texts. He is also significant in the development of the *voix-de-ville* type of chanson.

Bibliography: H. EXPERT, ed., *Monuments de la musique française au temps de la Renaissance,* 4 v. (Paris 1925) v.2. S. J. VAN SOLKEMA, *The Liturgical Music of Pierre Certon* (Doctoral diss. unpub. U. of Mich. 1963). P. PIDOUX, "Les Psaumes . . . de Pierre Certon . . .," *Annales Musicologiques* 5 (1957) 179–198. F. LESURE, MusGG 2:976–981. Roland-Manuel v.1. Reese MusR.

[I. CAZEAUX]

CERVANTES SAAVEDRA, MIGUEL DE

Spanish novelist, dramatist, poet; b. Alcalá de Henares, 1547; d. Madrid, April 23, 1616. His family was of modest financial and social standing and while he received ordinary early schooling, he had no university training; he undoubtedly owed his literary knowledge to his reading. He left Madrid for Italy in 1569 and returned to Spain only in 1580, settling in Madrid.

His stay in Italy left a deep impression upon his spiritual life (see *El licenciado Vidriera* and *La fuerza de la sangre*), but this was primarily his heroic period: he was wounded in the Battle of Lepanto (1571), held in captivity in Algiers (1575–80), and ransomed by the Trinitarian friars. On his return to Spain he obtained only modest positions, among others that of tax collector for the Armada. He traveled throughout Andalusia, and he was imprisoned for debt. We know very little of his later life, save that his financial worries were never eased, although he found some patronage. The two great periods of his life were his heroic phase and the period of literary creation.

Cervantes published *La Galatea* (1585), *Don Quixote* (1605), *Novelas ejemplares* (1613), *Don Quixote* (second part, 1615), and *Los trabajos de Persiles y Sigismunda* (issued posthumously in 1617). In addition to these four novels and the collection of short tales, he published the *Viaje del Parnaso* (a poem) in 1614, and in 1615 *Ocho comedias y ocho entremeses,* plays that had not been accepted for staging. Although the copious poetic production of Cervantes is not to be ignored, the author himself knew that he was not attaining the high level reached by the great Spanish poets of the 16th century and their successors of the 17th—*Góngora, *Quevedo, and Lope de *Vega. This lack of distinction in verse was an obstacle to Cervantes' dramatic creation at a time when Lope was transforming dramatic art and giving it the poetic power that marked the baroque theater (*see* BAROQUE, THE).

Nevertheless, Cervantes' theater is forceful. His

Miguel de Cervantes Saavedra, antique engraving after the portrait done in 1615.

dramatic art is worthy of consideration not only in itself but also by virtue of its ranking among the best work of the pre-Lopean epoch; the *Numancia*, for example, is dramatically powerful. Moreover, some aspects of Cervantes' personal experiences—religion and captivity—find their best expression in his drama; there, too, his way of looking at and feeling the world attains its most complete form (see *El rufián dichoso* and *Pedro de Urdemalas*). His one-act farces are among the best of that genre in Spanish literature.

Achievements in Prose. The glory of Cervantes is the novel; the instrument that he played to perfection is prose. He is distinguished as the creator of the modern European novel and the first writer of short novels in Spain. The publication dates of his five volumes are indicative of the process of his creative progress, the problems involved, and the solutions found. When he arrived in Spain in 1580, two types of fiction were in vogue, books of chivalry and pastorals. The first type was the older and more popular—cultured and uncultured folk alike enjoyed them. The pastoral novels, however, were aimed at a select audience; the subject and the mode of its treatment could attract only a limited circle. Cervantes resorted to this genre in *La Galatea*, but soon realized that the idealized Renaissance world was not his, nor was it of his time (*see* ARCADIANISM).

Break with the Renaissance. In the prologue to the *Quixote* of 1605 Cervantes called attention to the 20 years that had elapsed since *La Galatea*. Those decades had brought profound changes to Spanish literature: Lope had created the new theater, Góngora the new lyric poetry. During that period of silence Cervantes had been thinking about the novel, the new world he bore within himself and the form he was to give it. Unlike Lope and Góngora, Cervantes was not alone in his creation; Mateo Alemán (1547– after 1613) had preceded him. They agreed in considering the Renaissance form unsatisfactory and on the need for a more complex form. This new form contained three elements: adventures of the protagonist, interpolated episodes, and digressions, of a moral nature (as they had been in Alemán's *Guzmán de Alfarache*), or of a literary nature (as in *Don Quixote*). Alemán had felt himself wholly alien to the world of the Renaissance, with its partial vision of man, and in creating the picaresque genre he wanted to grasp the world, society, and man, in totality. And he did it, staying within the medieval Christian tradition, as all the baroque writers in Spain had done. Man and sinner are synonymous; men are not to be trusted.

Perhaps no one read *Guzmán* more carefully than Cervantes, who was making ready to use its threefold narrative channel. Yet he separated himself completely from the picaresque view, which he considered as unilateral as that of the Renaissance, with the difference that the pastoral did not pretend to include man and society in their totality, while the picaresque did.

Basic Religious Attitude. It is clear that Cervantes considered man a sinner, but he placed emphasis on salvation, and on the hope of attaining it. Life is sin, sadness, death; but also grace, repentance, and redemption.

Hope is Cervantes' dominant motif. If he eschews sarcasm and if his sometimes grotesque irony is full of kindness, it is because of his hope that man will save himself, that he will attain happiness. Grief is temporary; Cervantes knows and believes that God is ready to help the sinner, to grant him His mercy. If the sinner does not have the hellish pride of a Lucifer, he may be only an ignorant man, more deserving of compassion than of anathema. This hope is the light that brightens all Cervantes' work. Accordingly, he has no desire to write of the past; he does not look back on life as it has been, but sees it as it is, under the promise always of a better future. He creates characters—Rinconete, Cortadillo, Carriazo—expressly to present them from their youth, with a desire for regeneration, with a secure future.

Reality of Hope. While Cervantes' world is based on hope, the experiences he embodies in his work are grounded on the reality of man's historical being. Thus he created Don Quixote, Knight of La Mancha, who was launched upon the world with the lofty ideal of protecting virtue and helping bring about justice, but he made him real in a form related to the past and at odds with the present. Cervantes does not despise the past, but sees it as something irretrievable, gone. Ideas are changeless and eternal; each epoch, however, incarnates them in a different form. Through the chivalric theme (adventures) Cervantes presented the contrast between the past and present in a comic manner; not to see the form that the present demands and imposes was to him very grotesque. He treats the love theme (episodes) dramatically—as life itself, with its ceaseless action and decision, is dramatic. Instead of engaging in the more or less academic study of amorous and moral feeling characteristic of the Renaissance, he treats love and morality as ways of life that, through numerous sufferings, do not lead to death, but to the social and spiritual fulfillment of matrimony.

In order to portray this new world, Cervantes felt it necessary to avail himself of a third theme, the literary one—an exposition of the pretensions of the novel and a presentation of his personal idea of the novel. Paralleling the action runs the constant comparison of the attitudes of other times with those of the present. Cervantes has described in the words of Don Quixote the baroque artist's method of composing—employing comparison and contrast—and the ruling principle of baroque composition, disordered order. Disorder is implicit in the world's confusion, but Cervantes sees a prevailing divine order, which the Church teaches, and which the poet reveals. Hence, side by side with the temporal comparison and contrast throughout *Don Quixote,* stands the timeless ideal, expressed in an "invented" realism with no relationship to the realism and naturalism of the 19th century, which themselves are the fruits of observation.

Don Quixote. If *La Galatea* won Cervantes prestige among men of letters in Spain, the *Don Quixote* of 1605 made him famous inside Spain and far beyond its borders. It is true that the stage treated the love theme constantly, but it had been unable to present in perspective the human dilemma, the necessity to strive for the ideal under the concrete circumstances of human frailty. Cervantes' attitude toward this dilemma was to give rise to the frequently misunderstood word "quixotism." This is not a tag for false idealism or the pursuit of an unattainable ideal, but designates an attempt to achieve a noble ideal without, however, having the adequate means for doing so.

EL INGENIOSO HIDALGO DON QVIXOTE DE LA MANCHA,

Compueſto por Miguel de Ceruantes Saauedra.

DIRIGIDO AL DVQVE DE BEIAR, Marques de Gibraleon, Conde de Benalcaçar, y Bañares, Vizconde de la Puebla de Alcozer, Señor de las villas de Capilla, Curiel, y Burguillos.

Año, 1605.

CON PRIVILEGIO, EN MADRID, Por Iuan de la Cueſta.

Vendeſe en caſa de Franciſco de Robles, librero del Rey nro ſeñor.

Title-page of the first edition of the first part of Cervantes' "Don Quixote" printed at Madrid, 1605.

This singular vision of Cervantes immediately took possession of the imagination of his contemporaries, so that they were able to project it into society, politics, economics, morality, or the treatment of the sentiment of love. From *Garcilaso de la Vega to Jorge de Montemayor (*c.* 1520–59), the Renaissance had seized upon particular situations, states, and accidents in the moral and emotional life of man. Like Alemán and Lope, Cervantes dramatized man's ultimate destiny. In the picaresque genre there is an anguished lament; the theater of Lope captured destiny as grace, enchantment, elegance, with a movement full of joy and sometimes of melancholy. The picaresque is a marsh, the theater of Lope a stream; *Don Quixote* is a labyrinth, with an inexhaustible and intricate richness of perspective.

The Novelas Ejemplares. The editions of the novel multiplied, but Cervantes did not issue the sequel until 10 years later—the *Don Quixote* of 1615. During this relatively brief time there was intense creative activity in Spain; in the novel there was, thanks to Cervantes, a profound change. It would be well to recall here that the *Novelas ejemplares* preceded the *Don Quixote* of 1615 by 2 years. Cervantes was wise in publishing this collection; not only did it have as much success as the *Don Quixote* of 1605, but it put him on the same level as Lope and Góngora. Góngora unquestionably held first place in lyric poetry; Lope was recognized as the leading dramatist. From 1613 on, all agreed that Cervantes, the master romancer, took the first rank in prose. In this collection he offers 12 stories in the effort to divert (transport to a pure plane) and illuminate (reveal to him the destiny of man and the sense of life) the reader; in them he compares and contrasts the higher world of ideals with the lower world of ignorance, error, egoism, and cynicism.

The crux of this contrast is the relation of liberty to virtue and the effects of original sin on the intellect and will. In all the novels he insists upon matrimony as an expression of love. He contrasts the sufferings of the lover, as portrayed in the code of love that the medieval world had inherited from Ovid, with the new pains of man's fulfillment as a religious and social being in matrimony.

Don Quixote of 1615. It appeared to Cervantes that it would obscure the beauty and meaning of his exemplary stories to insert them into a longer narrative framework. His publication of them as short novels, however, is chiefly owing to the fact that at that time he conceived the long novel (as Alemán had not done) as a unity of action and character. Cervantes had decided that instead of the threefold narrative channel (see above), he was going to handle a continuous action in both the *Don Quixote* of 1615 and the *Persiles y Sigismunda.* He would suppress the literary theme and closely interweave the episodic material with the adventures of the protagonists. The work of 1615 is therefore different from that of 1605. The subject matter of the latter is grouped into 4 books, each of a varying number of chapters—8, 6, 13, 25; the baroque balance of interwoven subject matter takes the place of Renaissance symmetry, which consisted in adding units. In the first book Cervantes presented the chivalric theme, let a long pause intervene, and in the second book took up the love theme; in the third book he united the two themes, moving rapidly to the fourth, the epilogue. The third is balanced with the first two books, as the 25 chapters of the epilogue are balanced with the 27 preceding chapters. The literary theme runs throughout the novel, but it is concentrated in the first and last books.

The form of the *Don Quixote* of 1615 is completely different. Division into books is abandoned; the continuous action is grouped into chapters and is concentrated in the central ones, where the events in the house of the Duke and Duchess are recounted. Instead of three themes, he offers a new composition on the basis of motifs. The five basic ones are palace and home, money, counsel, animals, and dramatic representations. The novel leaves the road (life) and the roadside inns (the world) for houses and cities (society). The only one of the characters, other than Don Quixote and Sancho, who reappears, is Ginés de Pasamonte. The housekeeper and the niece, who had brief but significant roles in 1605, are of almost no importance in 1615. The priest and the barber are replaced by a new character, the *bachiller* Sansón Carrasco.

In addition to being centered in the ducal house, the story's action is outlined by the *bachiller,* who carries out the two roles played by the priest and the barber in 1605, that of directing the literary theme—making Don Quixote return to his village, which itself remains nameless, but acquires great topographical, economic, and social reality. The wife and daughter of Sancho also have more weight. Don Quixote casts his eyes on Dulcinea; Sancho is appointed governor of an island. The knight dies at last, having regained his reason; the lawyer Vidriera also recovers his reason, which he had lost by eating the fruit poisoned by sensuality. In 1605 it is not said how he dies; the burial is referred to in order to burlesque, through epitaphs, the subject matter of funereal and elegiac poetry. The meaning of the two works is also different. We have neither the historic-metaphysic experience (past-present, seeming-being) of the *Don Quixote* of 1605, nor the contrasting balance of the *Novelas Ejemplares.*

The *Don Quixote* of 1615 is an inquiry into the relationships of ideas, society, and art. Idea is deformed and humbled upon being incarnated in social form (Dulcinea enchanted, Sancho on the island), and art, by reflecting society, restores to the idea its original, pristine state. Taking this knowledge as his point of departure, Cervantes can explore society, of which his concept is not satiric. He conceives society as consisting of birth, marriage, and death, and thus displays for the reader the total social structure; starting from matrimony he arrives at death through a world of interests and passions rather than of vices and virtues. He emphasizes man's natural inclinations and the elements that make up the family and the group. He conceives of mankind—from the gang of robbers to the state—as maintained by discipline and the principle of authority. The individual must be sacrificed to the group; this sacrifice cannot be sweetened by anarchical freedom of conscience, but only by the piety and compassion of the other individuals of the society and, above all, by the piety and compassion of authority.

Cervantes' Deeper Significance. Mateo Alemán created a literary genre, the picaresque novel. Cervantes created the modern short novel, and his prose had great influence. His true influence, however, goes beyond the purely literary. It is through the concept of man in *Don Quixote,* and especially through his realization of the conscious function of the novel-writer that Cervantes has not only given novelists a sense of the significance of their art, but has become one of the guides of modern occidental culture.

The two books of *Don Quixote* and some of the exemplary stories transcend the epoch in which they were written. The beauty of the *Persiles y Sigismunda,* on the other hand, is strictly of the 17th century. This posthumous novel offers the same kind of beauty as the music and plastic arts of the epoch. Along with its dazzling style, composition, and invention, it presents Cervantes' Catholic-baroque concept of the history of humanity, a pilgrimage that began with the state of original sin and ended in 17th-century papal Rome, successor to, and fulfillment of, ancient Rome. The human couple in the story, supported by the *Credo,* is not moving in the direction of death, but toward the Church, the depository of virtue and wisdom. *Persiles y Sigismunda* deals also with the unity and diversity manifested in the Church and in the theater of Cervantes. In his dramas we see man's diversity in his different states and on the multiple roads of life. In the Church we find unity; with a true desire for salvation, man accompanies his repentance with words of thanksgiving.

See also NOVEL; CHIVALRY.

Bibliography: *Obras completas,* ed. R. SCHEVILL Y ADOLFO BONILLA, 18 v. (Madrid 1914–41). L. RÍUS Y DE LLOSELLOS, *Bibliografía crítica de las obras de Miguel de Cervantes Saavedra,* 3 v. (Madrid 1895–1905). R. L. GRISMER, *Cervantes: A Bibliography,* 2 v. (New York-Minneapolis, 1946–63). L. ASTRANA MARÍN, *Vida ejemplar y heroica de Miguel de Cervantes Saavedra,* 7 v. (Madrid 1948–58). C. DE LOLLIS, *Cervantes reazionario* (Rome 1924). A. CASTRO, *El pensamiento de Cervantes* (Madrid 1925); *Cervantes* (Paris 1931). J. ORTEGA Y GASSET, *Meditaciones del Quijote* (Buenos Aires 1942). H. HATZFELD, *Don Quijote als Wortkunstwerk* (Leipzig 1927); Span. ed., *El "Quijote" como obra de arte del lenguaje* (Madrid 1949). L. SPITZER, "Linguistic Perspectivism in Don Quijote," in *Linguistics and Literary History* (Princeton 1948). A. FLORES and M. J. BERNARDETE, eds., *Cervantes across the Centuries* (New York 1947). A. F. C. BELL, *Cervantes* (Norman, Okla. 1947).

Illustration credit: Courtesy, the Hispanic Society of America.

[J. CASALDUERO]

CESALPINO, ANDREA, Italian biologist; b. Arezzo, Tuscany, June 6, 1519; d. Rome, Feb. 23, 1603. He studied anatomy under M. Colombo at Pisa and Padua, and medical botany under Ghini at Pisa. After completing his medical studies (1549) he became professor of pharmacology at Pisa; later at Bologna he directed the botanic garden and founded the herbarium. He spent his last years in Rome as physician to Clement VIII.

He taught and wrote successfully in botany and physiology, both traditional disciplines in the medical curriculum. He was best in floral anatomy, wherein he uncovered ideas that eventually made botany independent of medicine. Although he wrote an herbal, *De Plantis* (1583), much in the spirit of the Renaissance, he devoted 30 pages of Book 1 to a significant departure—a new philosophy of classification. Thereby he did more for taxonomy than all the German herbalists had done in their thousands of pages. Cesalpino introduced the anatomy of fruits, seeds, and reproductive organs, with their concomitant variations, as indices of basic differences between plant groups. *Linnaeus acknowledged this and built his taxonomy upon it. Over a 30-year period (1571–1602) of teaching and writing on medical physiology he attacked the problem of blood dynamics and nearly discovered systemic circulation. He clearly described pulmonary circulation (*Questionum medicarum,* 1593), noted the centripetal movement of venous blood (*ibid.*), and stated the main function of arteries and veins (*Questionum peripateticarum,* 1571). Yet his writings of 1602–03 confuse the direction of blood flow.

Although Cesalpino never attained complete comprehension of plant sexuality or blood circulation, he made stimulating and pioneering efforts in both sectors. His works are only of historical interest today.

Bibliography: U. VIVIANI, *Vita e opere di Andrea Cesalpino* (Arezzo 1922). E. NORDENSKIÖLD, *The History of Biology* (New York 1935).

[L. P. COONEN]

CESARINI, impoverished noble family of Rome that achieved importance and wealth after 1400. When the family became extinct in 1686, four members had been cardinals and for nearly 200 years it had had hereditary right to the office of gonfalonier, flagbearer of the people. *Giuliano,* cardinal 1426 (d. Nov. 10, 1444), taught at the University of Padua (where he knew *Nicholas of Cusa and Domenico *Capranica) and was nuncio in France and England before being created cardinal. Legate to the Council of *Basel, he served as its president until the extremists became radically antipapal (1437). At the Council of *Florence his work and exemplary character impressed his contemporaries. His successful mission in Hungary (1442), activated Pope *Eugene IV's crusade against the Turks. King Ladislaus III of Poland and John *Hunyadi defeated the Turks in 1443 but were then overwhelmed by them at Varna (1444), where Ladislaus and Cardinal Cesarini were killed. For years historians believed the cardinal guilty of making Ladislaus break his oath to the Turks by renewing the war, but recent research has disproved this charge. *Giuliano,* cardinal 1493 (d. 1510), set an example by opening his collection of antiquities to the public. *Alessandro,* cardinal 1517 (d. Feb. 13, 1542), served under Pope *Paul III as legate to Emperor *Charles V, as legate to France, and as member of the commission preparing for the Council of *Trent.

Bibliography: VESPASIANO DA BISTICCI, *Vite di uomini illustri del secolo XV,* ed. P. d'ANCONA and E. AESCHLIMANN (Milan 1951). P. LITTA et al., *Famiglie celebri italiane,* 14 v. (Milan 1819–1923) v.5. Pastor 1:282–328; 4; 5. R. A. LANCIANI, *The Golden Days of the Renaissance in Rome* (Boston 1906). O. HALECKI, *The Crusade of Varna* (New York 1943). T. V. TULEJA, "Eugenius IV and the Crusade of Varna," CathHistRev 35 (1949–50) 257–275. R. O. AUSENDA and M. PETROCCHI, Enc Catt 3:1351–52. Cross ODCC 258. R. MOLS, DHGE 12:216–250.

[M. L. SHAY]

CESLAUS OF SILESIA, BL., Dominican missionary priest; b. Kamien, Poland, *c.* 1184; d. Wrocław, Poland, July 15, 1242 (feast, July 17; July 20 in Wrocław). He was probably of the noble Polish family of Odrowaź, a relative of St. *Hyacinth and the famous Bishop Iwo Odrowąź of Cracow. Hyacinth and Ceslaus, both canons of the cathedral of *Cracow, joined the *Dominicans in Rome *c.* 1218. Ceslaus established the first house of his order in Prague, Bohemia, and preached throughout the neighboring countries. The center of his activity was in Poland, where about 1224 he founded the Dominican priory at Wrocław and became its prior. He also served as spiritual director of St. *Hedwig. Through his prayers, Ceslaus is credited with saving Wrocław from the siege of the Tartars (*c.* 1240–41). His long-standing cult was confirmed by Pope *Clement XI in 1713.

Bibliography: ActSS July 4:182–199. B. ALTANER, *Die Dominikanermissionen des 13. Jhs.* (Habelschwerdt 1924) 212–218. A. ZAHORSKA, *Illustrowane Żywoty Świętych Polskich* (Potulice, Pol. 1937) 143–151. M. NIWIŃSKI, in *Polski Słownik biograficzny* (Cracow 1938) 4.4:357. P. DAVID, DHGE 12:252–253. J. KŁOCZOWSKI, *Dominikanie polscy na Śląsku w XIII–XIV wieku* (Lublin 1956) 147– . J. GOTTSCHALK, LexThK² 2:997–998.

[L. SIEKANIEC]

CEUPPENS, FRANCIS, Biblical scholar; b. Tirlemont, Belgium, Sept. 14, 1888; d. Brussels, Feb. 28, 1957. He entered the Dominican order in 1907 and was ordained in 1912. He taught Sacred Scripture at the Studium Theologicum of his Dominican province in Louvain from 1914 to 1927, and at the Studium Philosophicum in Ghent from 1921 to 1927. From 1927 to 1954, with a few short interruptions, he was professor of Scripture at the Pontifical Institute Angelicum in Rome. He received the licentiate in Semitic languages at Louvain in 1926, and in the same year the licentiate in Sacred Scripture from the Pontifical Biblical Commission. In 1932 he received the degree of master of sacred theology, and in 1952 an honorary doctorate from Laval University, Quebec. Besides several Latin articles on Biblical subjects, mostly published in the periodical *Angelicum,* he wrote brief commentaries in Flemish on several books of the Bible, and a few articles in French. His principal works, however, were written in Latin and published in Rome. Among these are *De Prophetiis Messianicis in V.T.* (1935); *Quaestiones Selectae ex Historia Primaeva* (1953³); *Quaestiones Selectae ex Epistulis S. Pauli* (1952); and, most important of all, his works on Biblical theology in five volumes: *De Deo Uno* (1949²), *De Sanctissima Trinitate* (1950²), *De Incarnatione* (1951²), *De Mariologia Biblica* (1952²), and *De Sacramentis* (1959). These works are not intended for specialists, but for students, who will find in them solid, up-to-date Catholic doctrine and true Biblical significance of the Scripture texts on which fundamental, dogmatic, and moral theology is based.

[P. G. DUNCKER]

CEYLON

Island country of the Indian Ocean, located southeast of the tip of the Indian subcontinent, 25,332 square miles in area. Ceylon is inhabited mainly by Singhalese and Tamils who migrated from India; the island was discovered by the Portuguese in 1505. The Dutch captured Ceylon in the 17th century, and in 1796 it was occupied by the British and became a Crown colony (1802). In 1948 it was granted independence as a member state of the British Commonwealth. The population (1963) was estimated at 10,625,000, of which about 69 per cent was Singhalese and 23 per cent Tamil (equally divided between Ceylon Tamils and Indian Tamils). There were also about 600,000 Ceylon and Indian Moors, more than 50,000 Burghers (Eurasian descendents of Portuguese and Dutch colonists), 25,000 Malays, and 6,500 Europeans. Buddhism is the religion of 61 per cent of the people (mostly Singhalese), Hinduism of 22 per cent (mostly Tamils), Christianity of 9 per cent (7 per cent Catholic), and Islamism of 7 per cent.

Catholic History. Ceylon was first evangelized by Portuguese Franciscans, but the mission was not systematically organized before 1543. Although most attention was given to the west coast, a mission was established in the north at Mannar, where 600 Christians are said to have been massacred by the King of Jaffna (1544). St. Francis *Xavier sent a missionary to Ceylon in 1544, but never visited there himself. The Franciscans had exclusive charge of the Ceylon missions until the arrival of the Jesuits in 1602, and of the Dominicans and Augustinians soon after. By the middle of the 17th century there were 170 churches and 120 missionaries. The Dutch occupation led to serious difficulties for the Ceylonese Church. Priests were expelled (1658), and the Dutch Reformed Church was the only recognized form of Christianity. No priest worked in Ceylon until Joseph *Vaz, a member of the Oratory of Goa arrived secretly (1687) to begin reorganizing the Church. Of the other *Oratorians who followed him, the most outstanding was J. Gonçalvez (d .1742), who was a pioneer in the development of Christian literature in Singhalese and Tamil. By the end of the Dutch period (1796), Catholicism, though still officially prohibited, was tolerated in practice, and Catholics outnumbered Protestants.

Under British rule the anti-Catholic laws were abolished (1806), and Gov. Thomas Maitland officially proclaimed freedom of conscience and worship. In 1809 there were 83,595 Catholics in Ceylon. As the Church continued to grow, the Vicariate of Ceylon, with headquarters at Colombo, was separated from the Diocese of Cochin in 1836. The Oratorians, unable to supply priests

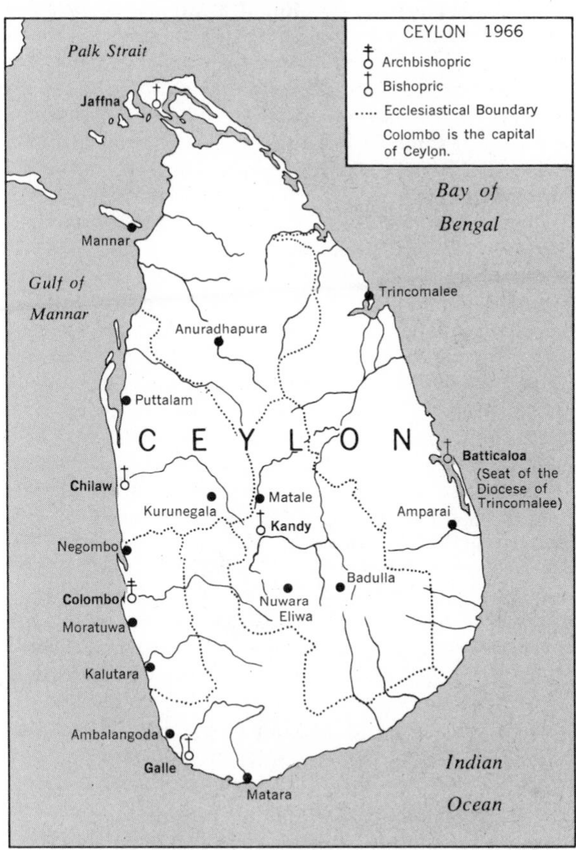

for the growing mission, were obliged to ask for European missionaries. In 1848 the vicariate was divided, and the Silvestrine Benedictines were entrusted with the Vicariate of Jaffna. The Benedictines confined their activity to the Vicariate of Kandy after 1857, while the Oblates of Mary Immaculate assumed responsibility for Jaffna (1857) and Colombo (1883). The hierarchy was established in 1886 with *Colombo as the metropolitan see and Jaffna and Kandy as suffragan sees. Dioceses were erected at Galle and Trincomalee (1893) and entrusted to the Jesuits, who at the same time founded a pontifical seminary at Kandy to serve both India and Ceylon. In 1939 the Diocese of Chilaw was erected and entrusted to secular clergy under the first Ceylonese bishop. The great organizer of the Ceylonese Church in the 19th century was C. E. Bonjean, the Oblate bishop of Colombo (1883–92). He established a network of parochial missions and Catholic schools, encouraged native vocations, and recognized the value of a Catholic press. His aim was more a revival of faith among Catholics than an attempt at mass conversions.

Mid-20th Century. After Ceylon's independence, the Church's position was threatened by nationalism, a Buddhist revival, and leftist governments. In 1961 Catholic schools, with few exceptions (e.g., the Catholic University College of Colombo), were nationalized. Sisters were required to leave the hospitals (1963). Foreign missionaries were not allowed to enter the country, or, if they were in the country, were required to renew annually their residence permits. The Ceylonese Church was fortunate in possessing a high percentage of native clergy. In 1962 there were 385 Ceylonese priests and 140 priests of foreign birth. Even within religious communities of European origin the ratio of native membership was high; 260 of the 344 Oblates were Ceylonese, as were 684 of the 741 Sisters of the Holy Family of Bordeaux. The Archbishop of Colombo, Cardinal Thomas Cooray, is Ceylonese, as are his auxiliary and the bishops of Chilaw, Jaffna, and Kandy. In 1964 there were 737,300 Catholics with 517 priests, 126 major seminarians, 364 religious men, and 2,234 sisters. There is one indigenous contemplative community of men, the Rosarians, founded by P. T. Thomas, OMI, in 1928; there were 84 members in 1960. The Rosarian nuns were founded in 1950 and had 22 members in 1960. The *Young Christian Workers and the *Legion of Mary are active in the towns. A Catholic weekly, *The Ceylon Catholic Messenger,* publishes in Singhalese and Tamil as well as in English.

Bibliography: F. DE QUEYROZ, *The Temporal and Spiritual Conquest of Ceylon,* tr. S. G. PERERA, 3 v. (Colombo 1930). S. G. PERERA, *The Jesuits in Ceylon in the XVI and XVII Centuries* (Madura, Ind. 1941). R. BOUDENS, *The Catholic Church in Ceylon under Dutch Rule* (Rome 1957). J. ROMMERSKIRCHEN, *Die Oblatenmissionen auf der Insel Ceylon* (Hünfeld, Ger. 1931). W. L. A. PETER, *Studies in Ceylon Church History* (Colombo 1963). H. HAAS, "Zur gegenwärtigen Lage der katholischen Kirche auf Ceylon," NZMissw 19.4 (1963) 300–311. *Bilan du Monde* 2:210–215.

[R. BOUDENS]

CÉZANNE, PAUL, most important painter of the Postimpressionists; b. Aix-en-Provence, France, Jan. 19, 1839; d. Aix-en-Provence, Oct. 22, 1906. He was the son of Philippe Auguste Cézanne, a banker, and was educated at the Pensionat-St. Joseph and Collège Bourbon, where he became a friend of Émile Zola. His formative years at school and his patriarchal family in a conservative Catholic town rooted in him the humanist values of classical and French culture. Abandoning law for art, he studied at the École des Beaux Arts in Aix and the Académie Suisse in Paris. In his youthful romanticist period (*c.* 1864–*c.* 1873) he produced emotionally charged pictures, e.g., "The Orgy" (*c.* 1864–68) and "The Temptation of St. Anthony" (*c.* 1873–77), painted with a heavy color impasto, at once clumsy

Paul Cézanne, "Self-portrait at Easel," c. 1900, lithograph.

and expressive. But such pictures as the "Black Clock" (*c.* 1869) and the "Railway Cut" (1870–71) show a breakthrough to a more objectively viewed reality in simplified, monumental shapes.

Paul Cézanne, "The Bathers," 1898–1906, 6 *feet* 8⅞ *inches by* 8 *feet* 2 *inches.*

In the middle period (*c.* 1873–*c.* 1881) he called himself an "Impressionist painter"; he exhibited with the group and absorbed their theories of light and color. Even in this period, however, there is a predilection for already organized shapes in nature, and a use of color to express the form of objects and not merely their surface.

In his mature, "classical" phase (*c.* 1882 to his death) there is a growing emphasis on color as a means of modeling. "When color has its greatest richness, then form has its plentitude," he claimed. Most of his paintings were executed in his native Provence and register the intensity of southern light by their heightened contrasts in purple and orange, red, and green. They constantly strive for a balance between deep space and picture plane, and between geometric patterns underlying the visible world and the surface physiognomy of nature. In his series of "Bathers" undertaken from the 1870s on, he aimed at a unification of the figurative idyll with landscape painting.

His is the most comprehensive synthesis of painting in the 19th century. In his extensive work there is a slow and laborious, but in the end grandly achieved synthesis of Impressionist chromatic painting with an art of classical organization, eliminating the accidental and ephemeral. His influence on Cubism, Expressionism, and 20th-century painting in general has been profound.

Bibliography: P. Cézanne, *Letters,* ed. J. Rewald, tr. M. Kay (3d ed. Oxford, Eng. 1946). J. Rewald, *Paul Cézanne: A Biography,* tr. M. H. Liebman (New York 1948). L. Venturi, *Cézanne: Son Art, son oeuvre,* 2 v. (Paris 1936), catalog and bibliog; EncWA 3:339–356. H. Perruchot, *Cézanne,* tr. H. Hare (New York 1963). M. Schapiro, ed., *Cézanne* (New York 1952). C. Badt, *Die Kunst Cézannes* (Munich 1956). A. Neumeyer, ed., *Drawings* (New York 1958). **Illustration credits:** Fig. 1, Library of Congress. Fig. 2, Philadelphia Museum of Art.

[A. NEUMEYER]

CHABHAM, THOMAS, English canonist; educated about 1190 at Paris, where he studied under Peter the Chanter. He spent a period in the service of the bishop of London before becoming, on Oct. 15, 1206, perpetual vicar of Sturminster Marshal, Dorset, in the diocese of Salisbury. Shortly afterward he became subdean of Salisbury, an office he filled until at least 1239. He is the author of a *Summa de arte predicandi* and of many sermons, still unpublished, but is chiefly known for a *Summa* for confessors that was written about 1222, possibly as a pendant to the synodal statutes of his diocesan, Richard Poore. This *Summa* is extant in some 85 manuscripts, and has been printed twice, at Cologne and Louvain in 1485. It was so celebrated that it was often ascribed to writers such as Rabanus Maurus, John of Salisbury, Innocent IV, or Thomas Aquinas. Chabham, breaking away in the *Summa* from the cut-and-dried schemata of the traditional penitential literature and from a too juridical approach to the confessional, gives valuable advice to priests on their lives as pastors, telling them what they should know and do, and what virtues they should inculcate in their penitents. Hence, while professing to be nothing more than a *Summa de poenitentia,* Chabham's *Summa* is in effect a manual of the pastoral care in general, the first of a new style of pastoral manual.

Bibliography: H. F. Rubel, "Chabham's Penitential and Its Influence in the 13th Century," PMLA 40 (1925) 225–239. J. C. Russell, *Dictionary of Writers of Thirteenth Century England* (New York 1936) 159. C. R. Cheney, *English Synodalia of the 13th Century* (Oxford 1941) 49, 54. T. Kaeppeli, "Un Recueil de sermons prêchés à Paris et en Angleterre," ArchFrPraed 26 (1956) 161–191. P. Michaud-Quantin, *Sommes des casuistique et manuels de confession au Moyen Age* (Louvain 1962).

[L. E. BOYLE]

CHABOT, JEAN BAPTISTE, Orientalist; b. Vouvray, France, Feb. 16, 1860; d. Paris, Jan. 7, 1948. He was ordained May 30, 1885, and studied at the École des Hautes Études and at Louvain, where he obtained his doctorate of theology in 1892 with a brilliant thesis on the 7th-century ascetic Isaac of Ninive. He continued Syriac studies at the Collège de France under R. Duval, whom he succeeded. With H. *Hyvernat and J. Forget in 1903 he founded the *Corpus scriptorum christianorum orientalium,* a collection of texts and Latin translations of the works of Syriac, Coptic, Arab, and Armenian Fathers. He was the sole director of this enterprise for 10 years and continued until shortly before his death as chief editor and general manager after the Catholic universities of Louvain and Washington assumed financial and administrative responsibility of the *Corpus.* In and apart from the *Corpus* he published many texts, translations, and studies of early Syrian theology and history: Denis Tell-Mahre, Elias of Nisibis, Michael the Syrian, the *Synodicum orientale,* *Theodore of Mopsuestia, *Cyril of Alexandria, James of Edessa, the Hexaemeron, etc. He became a member of the Académie des Inscriptions et Belles Lettres in 1917 and edited Phoenician and Aramaean inscriptions for the Institute's *Corpus inscriptionum Semiticarum.* He published works of a more popular nature on inscriptions of Palmyra (1922) and the history of Syriac literature (1934). His valuable library and personal papers were left to the University of Louvain.

Bibliography: G. Ryckmans, "Jean-Baptiste Chabot," *Muséon* 61 (1948) 141–152. G. Bardy, *Catholicisme* 2:855.

[T. PETERSEN]

CHAD, also called Tchad, tropical, semi-arid inland country in north central *Africa, south of Libya, 495,652 square miles in area. This former territory of French Equatorial Africa became in 1960 an independent republic as a member state of the French Community. The 1961 census recorded 2,675,000 inhabi-

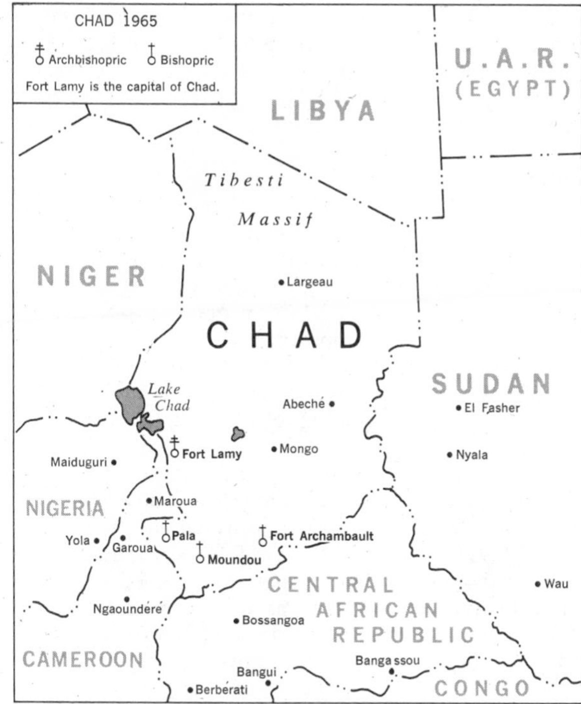

tants, including fewer than 5,000 Europeans. Paganism, the religion of about half the populace, predominated among the Negroid agricultural dwellers in the south. Another 45 per cent, mostly among the racially mixed, nomadic tribes of the north, were Moslems. Christianity had about 150,000 followers, concentrated in the south. Approximately one-third of them were Protestants.

Catholic evangelization began in 1929 when some Holy Ghost Fathers arrived in southern Chad. In 1938 two Capuchins, expelled from Ethiopia, took charge of the mission. Not until the arrival of Jesuits and Oblates of Mary Immaculate in 1946, however, did organized mission activity start. The Prefecture Apostolic of Fort-Lamy, embracing all but the southernmost part of the country, was created in 1947 and was confided to the Jesuits. Oblates were entrusted with the section in the southwest that became in 1956 the Prefecture Apostolic of Pala. French Capuchins worked to the east of Pala in the area that became in 1951 the Prefecture Apostolic and in 1959 the Diocese of Moundou. *Fort-Lamy became a diocese in 1955 and an archdiocese in 1961, when Fort-Archambault was created as a diocese from its southernmost territory and confided to the Jesuits. As metropolitan see for Chad since 1961, Fort-Lamy had as suffragans in 1964 the Dioceses of Moundou, Fort-Archambault, and Pala. There were then about 100,000 Catholics, 120 priests, 20 brothers, 96 sisters, and 1,800 catechists. Three-fourths of the Catholics were found in the Moundou diocese.

Bibliography: *Bilan du Monde* 2:833–836. AnnPont (1965) 154, 155, 288, 322. For additional bibliography, *see* AFRICA.

[J. BOUCHAUD]

CHAD (CEADDA), ST., Northumbrian monk, bishop of Lichfield; d. 672 (feast, March 2). Chad was a disciple of St. *Aidan and one of four brothers who were priests. Although a native of Northumbria, he studied later on in Ireland. When his brother *Cedd died in 664, he succeeded him as abbot of Lastingham, Yorkshire. While Bp. *Wilfrid of York was in Gaul, King Oswiu of Northumbria had Chad uncanonically consecrated bishop and placed him over all or part of Wilfrid's Diocese of *York. When Abp. *Theodore of Canterbury made his first *visitation in 669, he reconsecrated Chad and restored Wilfrid to York. Chad was soon made bishop of Mercia with his see at Lichfield, but he died 3 years afterward of the plague. *Bede, the main authority for his life, vividly describes his last days. Many miracles reportedly took place at his tomb. His relics are said to be in St. Chad Cathedral, Birmingham.

Bibliography: BEDE, *Eccl. hist.* 3.23, 28; 4.3. W. R. W. STEPHENS, DNB 3:1300–02.

[B. COLGRAVE]

CHAIN OF CAUSATION, Sanskrit, *Pratītyā-samutpāda,* or the doctrine of Dependent Origin, a basic tenet of Early and all Hīnayāna Buddhism. It is contained essentially in the Buddha's Second and Third Noble Truths, which explain the cause of suffering and point the way to the cessation of suffering, respectively. There are 12 links in the Chain of Causation, or 12 spokes in the Wheel of Dependent Origin, representing three consecutive existences. The first two, ignorance of the way to salvation (*avidyā*) and the karma-forming forces that determine the form of the next existence (*saṃskāra*), refer to the former life. Three to ten, namely, the initial consciousness of the embryo (*vijñāna*), the psychophysical organization comprised in the five elements of existence (*nāma-rūpa*), the six senses including the mind (*saḍāyatana*), the contact of the senses with the world, beginning at birth (*sparśa*), sense experience (*vedanā*), thirst for things of the world (*tṛṣṇā*), clinging to the world of sense (*upādāna*), and becoming or the will to be born (*bhava*)—refer to the present life. Eleven and twelve, new birth (*jāti*), and old age and death (*jarāmarana*), refer to future life. The Chain of Causation can be destroyed only when ignorance, its initial and fundamental cause, is destroyed, and this can be accomplished only through the knowledge that gives liberation. The cause of suffering is ignorance, and the cessation of suffering is found by entering into *nirvāṇa.*

See also BUDDHISM; ELEMENTS OF EXISTENCE; NIRVĀṆA.

Bibliography: C. SHARMA, *Indian Philosophy: A Critical Survey* (pa. New York 1962) 60–63. H. L. FRIES, *Non-Christian Religions* (pa. New York 1963) 34–38. C. REGAMEY, König Christus 3:229–303, esp. 271–274.

[M. R. P. MC GUIRE]

CHAINE, JOSEPH, exegete; b. Lyons, France, Dec. 24, 1888; d. there, March 24, 1948. He studied at Lyons, where he was ordained in 1913. After serving for a while as assistant priest in Villefranche, he commenced his Biblical studies at Jerusalem (1919–20) under the direction of M. J. *Lagrange. From 1927 to 1948 he was professor of Sacred Scripture at the Institut Catholique of Lyons. In order to propagate the method and principles of the Jerusalem School of Biblical Studies, he published the *Oeuvre exégétique du P. Lagrange* (Paris 1935). His critical studies led also to the publication of the following: *L'Épître de S. Jacques* (Paris 1927), *Les Épîtres Catholiques* (Paris 1939),

Une introduction à la lecture des prophètes (Paris 1932), and *Le Livre de la Genèse* (Paris 1948). For several years he was editor of the Biblical reviews in the periodical *L'Ami du Clergé*. He acted also as chaplain to the university students of Lyons and collaborated in the works of the *Chronique Sociale de Lyon* and the *Semaines Sociales*. He courageously asserted his position on the Jewish question by publishing in collaboration with Fathers H. de Lubac, J. *Bonsirven, and L. Richard a booklet on *Israel et la Foi chrétienne*. Until his death he collaborated also on the encyclopedia *Catholicisme*.

Bibliography: H. CAZELLES, *Catholicisme* 2:858–859. J. DUPLACY, LexThK[2] 2:1001.

[M. G. BULTEAU]

CHAIR OF PETER, as a theological expression, signifies the authority, especially the teaching authority, of the pope. The chair in which a bishop presides over his people was from early times regarded with respect as symbolizing his authority, since it was from his official chair (in which he sat, facing his people) that he gave the homilies by which he instructed his flock in the word of God. Hence the Feast of St. Peter's Chair, whether at Antioch or Rome, commemorated his authority there. Since the teaching power of the pope is not merely that of a bishop but that of the successor of St. Peter, the chair of Peter indicates the authoritative doctrinal power of the pope as the successor of St. Peter. This is the origin of the expression *ex cathedra* definition; such a papal pronouncement (very rarely made) is one in which the pope infallibly defines a doctrine that is irrevocably binding on all the faithful.

[B. FORSHAW]

CHAIR OF UNITY OCTAVE

An 8-day period of prayer, January 18 to 25, for the cause of Christian unity. It began in 1908 under the inspiration and leadership of Paul James Francis *Wattson, SA (1863–1940), of Graymoor, near Garrison, N.Y. At the time Wattson was an Anglican clergyman who had founded the Society of the Atonement at Graymoor (*see* ATONEMENT, SOCIETY OF THE). The organization included both friars and sisters, the latter being also founded by Mother Lurana Mary Francis White, SA (*see* FRANCISCAN SISTERS OF THE ATONEMENT).

Wattson had preached often about the need of reunion with Rome for all Protestant bodies; he had written frequently on the matter since the inception of the monthly magazine, *Lamp,* in 1903, of which he was the editor. He began the Octave, which he first called "a Church Unity Octave," as a kind of experiment and wrote to both Catholics and Anglicans to join with him in prayer. Archbishop (later Cardinal) William O'Connell of Boston and many Catholic priests and religious observed the Octave, and, almost as tangible proof of the efficacy of this exercise of prayer, the Society of the Atonement entered the Church on Oct. 30, 1909.

Official Approval. On Dec. 27, 1909 Pope St. Piux X blessed Wattson, the Society of the Atonement, and the Unity Octave—the first papal blessing upon the work. Pope Benedict XV extended the Octave to the universal Church and accorded it indulgences through the apostolic letter *Romanorum pontificum,* of Feb. 25, 1916. In part, the document reads: "In every age the Roman Pontiffs, our predecessors, have had much at heart and it is our own very particular concern that Christians who have separated themselves from the Catholic religion should return to the Church as to a mother whom they have abandoned. For it is especially in unity of faith that the truth of the Church shines forth; and the Apostle Paul to exhort the Ephesians to keep unity in the bond of peace tells them there is only 'one Lord, one faith, one baptism' " [ActApS 9 (1917) 61]. In 1921 the hierarchy of the U.S. agreed to adopt the Octave in each diocese. Pope Pius XI often offered Mass during the Octave for its development and success. Pope Pius XII renewed and increased the indulgences (Dec. 10, 1946) and wrote a letter to commemorate the 50th anniversary of the beginning of the Octave (Nov. 1, 1957).

Pope John XXIII wrote a letter to the father general of the Atonement Friars to commend the observance of the Octave ever more widely throughout the world (Oct. 28, 1959). "Prayer," Pope John XXIII said, ". . . is the first and principal means to be used to bring about this yearned-for unity, as your beloved Founder, Father Paul Wattson, so clearly saw; and he therefore promoted the Chair of Unity Octave, during which fervent supplications should be raised to the Almighty for the return of all to the one true Faith." Pope John also urged the Friars of the Atonement to "ever more strenuous efforts in the propagation of the Chair of Unity Octave."

Development. The founder had promoted the Octave assiduously until his death in 1940. It may be said that, whatever form is used, every observance each Jan. 18 to 25 goes back directly or indirectly to his inspiration. In his later years he hoped to have the Octave observance made of obligation throughout the Catholic world by papal decree, but, despite his great efforts, his hope did not materialize. Abroad, the Abbé Paul Couturier of Lyons, France (d. 1953), also promoted the Octave. He preferred to call it the Week of Prayer for Unity and to use intentions different from those established by Wattson.

Wattson appealed to all people of good will to join in this prayer and placed this work for unity under the patronage of Our Lady of the Atonement. In 1920 the *Faith and Order movement, an antecedent of the *World Council of Churches, first called for a week of prayer during Pentecost. In 1940 it commended the January observance so as to coincide with the Catholic time of prayer. Since the formation of the World Council at Amsterdam in 1948, this period of prayer for unity has been sponsored by its Faith and Order Commission. Since 1935 various Orthodox groups, chiefly Russian congregations in France, have been interested in the Unity Octave. It has gradually spread among them in various lands. Anglicans are the most interested among non-Catholic groups. Spencer Jones of Moreton-on-Marsh, England, an Anglican clergyman, helped Wattson considerably, especially in the early years. As a development of the Unity Octave, the Graymoor Friars promote the League of Prayer for Unity under the patronage of Our Lady of the Atonement. In 1964 it had 250,000 members in most countries of the world.

The name Chair of Unity Octave was chosen by the Graymoor Friars in 1949 after the original title, Church Unity Octave, had led to some confusion and ambiguity. The Chair of Unity title, referring to the *Chair of Peter, now occupied by his successor, the Pope, was originally proposed by Mother Lurana Mary Francis in 1926, and it was used as an alternate title until its formal adoption as preferred by the Atonement Friars and Sisters. Today it is often called simply the Unity Octave.

See also ECUMENICAL MOVEMENT; UNITY OF THE CHURCH.

Bibliography: G. K. A. BELL, ed., *Documents on Christian Unity, 1920–24* (London 1924); 2d ser. (1930); 3d ser. 1930–48 (New York 1948); 4th ser. 1948–57 (New York 1958). Y. M. J. CONGAR, *Divided Christendom,* tr. M. A. BOUSFIELD (London 1939). T. F. CRANNY, *Father Paul and Christian Unity* (Peekskill, N.Y. 1963); *Father Paul: Apostle of Unity* (Peekskill, N.Y. 1965). D. GANNON, *Father Paul of Graymoor* (New York 1951). E. F. HANAHOE and T. F. CRANNY, eds., *One Fold* (Peekskill, N.Y. 1959). R. ROUSE and S. NEILL, eds., *A History of the Ecumenical Movement 1517–1948* (SPCK; 1954). M. VILLAIN, *L'Abbé Paul Couturier* (Paris 1957). *Lamp* (Peekskill, N.Y. 1903–).

[T. F. CRANNY]

CHAISE-DIEU, ABBEY OF, former *Benedictine abbey, Haute-Loire Department, France, in the Diocese of Le Puy, but formerly in the Diocese of Clermont. Founded in 1046 by Robert of Chaise-Dieu, the abbey was endowed by Popes *Gregory VII, *Paschal II, and *Eugene III. After a first "century of saints," it reached the height of its influence during the second half of the 13th century, when it was second in power and prestige only to *Cluny as the head of a highly centralized congregation of more than 300 abbeys and priories in France, Spain, and Italy. The congregation began to decline in the 14th century, but this was a period of seigneurial expansion and of reconstruction for the abbey. A new church was built there by Pope *Clement VI, a former monk of Chaise-Dieu. The *Gothic structure with three naves of equal height was completed in 1352 and still survives as a parish church.

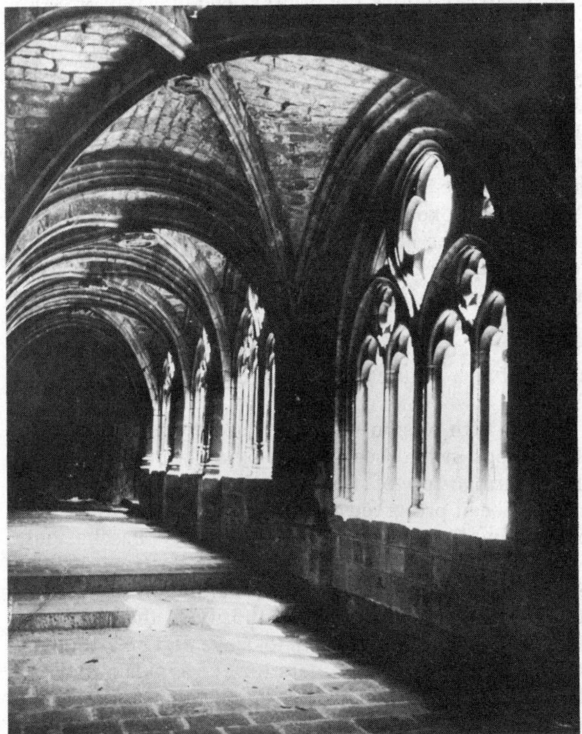

Gothic cloister of the Abbey of Chaise-Dieu, Haute-Loire.

In 1640 Chaise-Dieu was affiliated with the *Maurists through the influence of *Richelieu, who held the abbey in *commendation. Plundered during the *Wars of Religion, it was suppressed during the *French Revolution. The church still contains magnificent sculptured choir stalls, a 15th-century *danse macabre,* and a collection of early 16th-century tapestries. A notable part of the archives is preserved at Le Puy.

Bibliography: Cottineau 1:667–669. R. VAN DOREN, DHGE 12:264–266. P. DESCHAMPS and J. LECLERQ, *La Chaise-Dieu* (Paris 1946). U. ROUCHON et al., *La Chaise-Dieu, commemoration du IXe centenaire* (Le Puy 1952). H. GLASER, LexThK^2 2: 1001. P. R. GAUSSIN, *L'Abbaye de la Chaise-Dieu 1043–1518* (Paris 1962). **Illustration credit:** French Embassy Press and Information Division, New York City.

[A. H. TEGELS]

CHALCEDON, city founded *c.* 678 B.C. by the city of Megara in Bithynia across the Bosporus from Byzantium on the site of a former Phoenician trading post. It shared the fate of Byzantium, passing under the domination of Athenians, Persians, and Romans. It seems to have had a Christian bishop at the end of the 2d century, and Constantine considered establishing his capital there. The scene of the Fourth Ecumenical Council, it was made a metropolitan see without suffragans by Marcian and Pulcheria in 451. After being destroyed by the Persians in A.D. 616, it fell in 1350 to the Turks, who changed its name to Kadiköy.

Its most famous church was the basilica of St. *Euphemia, where the Council of *Chalcedon was held, and the city proper boasted of its St. George and Holy Redeemer churches as well as of six monasteries. Along the coast toward the East in Hiereia (modern Phanaraki) were the church of the Virgin, the chapel of St. Elias, and the Eutropius monastery; still farther out were the settlement of the Oak (Drys, modern Djadi-Bostan), famous for the church of the Apostles SS. Peter and Paul, where St. *John Chrysostom was condemned in 403, and three monasteries, including that of St. Satyrus. During the Middle Ages the nearby hills were settled by monks dependent on the monastery of St. Auxentius, which is surrounded by the ruins of Christian monasteries.

In 1958 the modern city had about 10,000 Christians, among whom were 200 Catholics. In 1925 the Assumptionists had to close their Oriental seminary there, and in 1937 the Institute for Byzantine Studies was transferred to Rumania. It is the seat of a Greek Orthodox Metropolitan and a Latin titular archbishopric.

Bibliography: Pauly-Wiss RE 10.2:1552–59. H. LECLERCQ, DACL 3.1:90–130. R. JANIN, DHGE 12:270–277; LexThK^2 2: 1005–06. A. M. SCHNEIDER, Grill-Bacht Konz 1:291–302.

[P. T. CAMELOT]

CHALCEDON, COUNCIL OF

The Fourth Ecumenical Council, held at Chalcedon Oct. 8 to 31, 451. Considered here are its historical antecedents, history, dogmatic decisions and canons, historical and doctrinal significance.

Historical Antecedents. The Council of Chalcedon marks a final episode in the quarrels over doctrine and policy that followed the Council of *Ephesus (431) and the *Latrocinium,* or Robber Council of *Ephesus (449). The Robber Synod resulted in the triumph of *Dioscorus of Alexandria and *Eutyches and the defeat of those who (e.g. *Flavian of Constantinople and

*Theodoret of Cyr) were labeled Nestorians because they acknowledged two natures in Christ.

Leo I was informed of the errors of Eutyches by letters from Flavian, Eusebius of Doryleum, and Theodoret of Cyr and through communication with his deacon Hilary. Leo protested strongly to Emperor *Theodosius II and his sister Pulcheria, requesting (Oct. 13, 449) the convocation of a general council in Italy. No reply was made to his letters or to those Leo wrote on December 24. The intervention of the Western Emperor *Valentinian III (February 450) likewise had no effect. Theodosius abided by the decisions taken at the Robber Synod and brushed aside any intervention by the Roman Pontiff in Eastern affairs. Later (July 16, 450) in writing to the Emperor concerning the election of *Anatolius to the See of Constantinople, Leo maintained his position as arbiter of the faith: Anatolius should make a profession of the Catholic faith as it had been set forth in Leo's *Tome* to Flavian.

The sudden death of Theodosius (July 28, 450) brought about a reversal of the situation. *Pulcheria came to power and immediately married the senator Marcian, who thereupon became emperor (Aug. 24, 450). The all-powerful eunuch Chrysaphius, the godchild of Eutyches, was put to death, and Eutyches was exiled and interned. Writing to the Pope to announce his accession to the throne, Marcian suggested calling a council, which a short while later (September 22) he decided should be held in the East. But Leo temporized in his reply of April 451, and in another letter (June 9) he asserted that the peril of invasion by the Huns appeared to make a convention of the bishops inopportune. Leo preferred a council in Italy rather than in the East, where there would be political intrigues and influences. But on May 23 Marcian convoked a council to meet on Sept. 1, 451, at Nicaea in Bithynia.

The definition of Chalcedon in a 15th-century MS (Codex Vat. gr. 831, fol. 169 v.).

On the conciliar agenda was an important doctrinal problem. It now seemed necessary to complete the work of the Council of Ephesus by settling the question as to the one or two natures in Christ; only thus could an end be made to the error of Eutyches and of those who restricted and deformed the thought of St. *Cyril of Alexandria. Leo believed that his *Tome* should suffice without a council, which would risk a renewal of the disorders caused by the Robber Synod. Marcian, on the other hand, though adhering firmly to the orthodox position, desired a council in the East, where the imperial authority could adjudge the doctrinal question. Beyond the theological problem, there was a problem of a possible quarrel between the Pope and the Emperor.

History. On receiving the news of the convocation, Leo replied that he would not oppose the decision of the Emperor and would send legates to preside in his place. It was necessary, however, to maintain the faith as defined at Ephesus and as set forth in his *Tome* to Flavian. The bishops summoned to the council first met at Nicaea, but were soon transferred to Chalcedon so that Marcian could more easily supervise the debates. They actually numbered 350 or 360, although later tradition mentions 600 or 630. These bishops were almost all from the East. The West was represented by three Roman legates and two African bishops.

The Council commenced on Oct. 8, 451, in the basilica of St. *Euphemia in the presence of 19 imperial commissioners under the effective presidency of the Roman legates (Bps. Paschasinus of Lilybeum and Lucentius of Ascoli, and Boniface the priest). The first four sessions (Oct. 8–17) constituted a trial of the instigators of the Robber Synod of Ephesus, and from the outset Paschasinus demanded the condemnation of Dioscorus, who in fact was deposed at the third session (Oct. 13). The two synodical letters of St. Cyril were solemnly approved but no mention was made of the 12 anathemas. Likewise, Leo's *Tome* was accepted with the cry, "Peter has spoken through Leo."

Although the bishops were reluctant to add anything to what had been set forth at the Councils of Nicaea I and Ephesus, Marcian wanted a doctrinal definition that would abolish the controversy, the more so when he discovered that there were some who hesitated to speak of two natures in Christ in the same manner as Leo.

At the fifth session (Oct. 22) a text was presented to the bishops; it had been edited by a commission under the chairmanship of Bp. Anatolius of Constantinople and has been preserved in the conciliar acts. It was approved by the bishops but opposed by Paschasinus, who did not think it did justice to the doctrine of Leo. Since this matter dealt with two natures in Christ and touched immediately on the authority of the Apostolic See, Paschasinus threatened to leave if Leo's thought was not given proper consideration. To avoid an impasse the imperial commissioners proposed that a new commission of six bishops produce a new version and gave the bishops a choice of siding with either Leo or Dios-

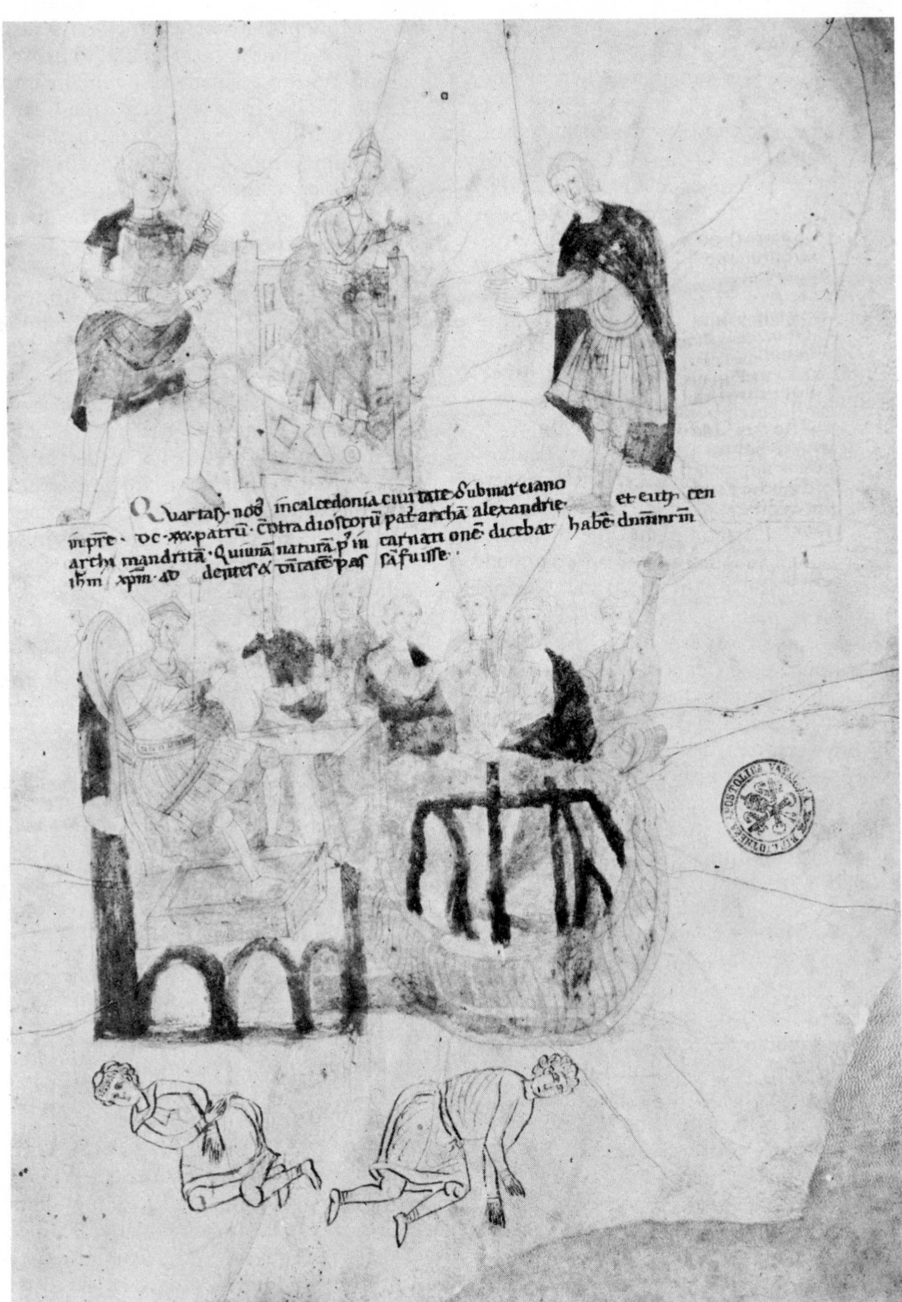

Events at the Council of Chalcedon, illumination in a 11th-century "Collectio canonum" (Cod. Vat. lat. 1339, fol. 9r).

corus. The commission developed a new formula of faith, which conformed to Leo's thought by explicitly defining the two natures in Christ. This statement was accepted by the bishops and was solemnly approved on October 25 in the presence of Marcian and Pulcheria. The Emperor confirmed all that had been done by the Council.

In the 10 (or 11) remaining sessions (Oct. 26–31) the cases of *Theodoret of Cyr, Ibas of Edessa, and *Domnus of Antioch were considered, and a number of disciplinary canons were promulgated. After dispatching a long letter to the Pope explaining their actions and asking his confirmation of the Council's decrees, the bishops departed.

Dogma and Canons. The formula of faith is based expressly on Scripture, the definitions of Nicaea and Constantinople I, and on the teachings of the Holy Fathers, and takes particular note of the synodical letters of St. Cyril and the *Tome* of Leo. It is opposed to those who would destroy the mystery of the Incarnation by partitioning Christ and refusing to call Mary *Theotokos (the Nestorians), to those who claim that divine nature is capable of suffering, and to those who confuse or amalgamate the two natures and speak of only one nature after the union (Eutyches). The Council defined one Christ, perfect God and man, consubstantial with the Father and consubstantial with man, one sole being in two natures, without division or separation and without confusion or change. The union does not suppress the difference in natures; however, their properties remain untouched, and they are joined together in one Person, or *hypostasis*.

This definition was elaborated from formulas of Cyril, Leo I, John of Antioch, Flavian of Constantinople, and Theodoret of Cyr in remarkable balance, and it put an end to the Christological uncertainties of the 4th and 5th centuries. It excluded the "one nature of the Incarnate Word," which was an Apollinarian formula that St. Cyril had employed in a sense that could be accepted, but to which Eutyches had given a clearly heterodox meaning. It distinguished between nature and person. It stated that in Christ there were two distinct natures whose individual properties had not been destroyed in the union. They subsisted in the unity of one Person, or *hypostasis*. This precision of vocabulary gave the word *prosopon* (person) a much stronger significance than it had in the thought of Theodore of Mopsuestia or Nestorius. It completed the theology of Cyril with that of Leo and definitively proclaimed the unique Person of Christ son of God and son of Mary, true God and true man.

On October 25 the Council, in response to the invitation of Marcian, promulgated 27 canons devoted to ecclesiastical discipline and to the direction and moral conduct of the clergy and monks. It defined the individual rights of bishops and metropolitans: priests were to be under the authority of the bishop; monks were to reside in their monasteries and were to be under the jurisdiction of the bishop; they were both to observe celibacy under pain of excommunication. All these regulations were justified by events preceding the Council.

On October 29, however, another canon gave to the See of Constantinople privileges equal to those of ancient Rome and granted its bishop jurisdiction over the Metropolitans of Pontus, Asia, and Thrace. This primacy in the Orient was based on the political position of the "new Rome," in which the Emperor and senate now resided. The following day the Roman delegates protested vigorously in the name of the Pope and called attention to the canons of Nicaea that had determined the hierarchical order of the patriarchal sees.

Leo put off his reply to the letter of the Council that requested him to confirm its decrees. Letters from Marcian and Anatolius also went unanswered. Then on May 22, 452, the Pope annulled everything that had been done in disregard of the canons of Nicaea. It was not until March 21, 453, that Leo confirmed the decrees of the Council, and then only regarding matters of faith. This incident was a significant episode in the opposition that was to increase between Rome and Constantinople in the following centuries.

Significance. The Council of Chalcedon represented a culmination in the history of the dogma of the Incarnation. Beyond dealing with the diverse theological tendencies that confronted each other, it stated the Catholic doctrine that preserved indissolubly the two facets of the mystery: the unity of person in the Incarnate Word and the perfect integrity of His two natures. The theology of St. Cyril and that of Leo, as inheritor of St. Augustine and Tertullian, are merged in these formulas; and they do justice also to what was of value in the Antiochene theology. Nevertheless the Cyrillan partisans remained absolutely opposed to two natures, in which they were determined to see a form of Nestorianism. *Monophysitism, even though frequently only verbal, was about to be born and to provoke many quarrels and schisms, which still remain unresolved.

From another point of view, the Council of Chalcedon marked an important step in the development of the Roman primacy. The authority of Celestine had been affirmed at Ephesus; that of Leo was imposed with still greater vigor at Chalcedon. The doctrine of the primacy of the Apostolic See, as opposed to a "Church of the Empire" held by the emperors of Constantinople, was affirmed. Even though this primacy was unanimously recognized at Chalcedon, it still ran the risk of being questioned, and the unity of the Church was compromised by the dangerous political principle that was invoked to justify the primacy of Constantinople in the East. On this problem further disputes and schisms were in the offing; all was not settled in 451.

The Acts of Chalcedon are preserved in several ancient collections. In Greek there are three compilations of letters and a record of the minutes in which the order of the second and third sessions is reversed. In Latin, documents are contained in the *Collectio Novariensis de re Eutychis* (before 458) and *Coll. Vaticana* (*c.* 520). There are three recensions of translations of the Acts from Greek (6th century) and several collections of the letters of Leo. All these documents are published (Mansi 6). There is a more recent edition by E. Schwartz (ActConcOec 2.2–5).

Bibliography: Altaner 291–293. *Gesta de nomine Acaci,* ed. O. GUENTHER (CSEL 35.1; 1895) 440–453. EVAGRIUS, *Hist. eccl.* PG 86.2:2415–2886. LIBERATUS OF CARTHAGE, *Breviarium causae Nestorianorum et Eutychianorum* (ActConcOec 2.5; 1936) 98–141. Grill-Bacht Konz v.1–3. PIUS XII, "Sempiternus Rex" (Encyclical, Sept. 8, 1951) ActApS 43 (1951) 625–644. R. V. SELLERS, *The Council of Chalcedon* (London 1953). F. X. MURPHY, *Peter Speaks through Leo* (Washington 1952). H. M. DIEPEN, *Douze dialogues de christologie ancienne* (Rome 1960); *Les Trois chapitres au Concile de Chalcédoine* (Oosterhout, Neth. 1953). A. GRILLMEIER, LexThK[2] 2:1006–09; *Christ in Christian Tradition,* tr. J. S. BOWDEN (New York 1965) 480–495. P. T. CAMELOT, *Éphèse et Chalcédoine,* v.2 of *Histoire des Conciles Oecuméniques* (Paris 1962). **Illustration credit:** Biblioteca Apostolica Vaticana.

[P. T. CAMELOT]

CHALCONDYLES, DEMETRIUS, Byzantine humanist in the West; b. Athens, 1423; d. Milan, 1511. One of the most influential Byzantine humanist émigrés to appear in Italy during the later 15th century, he was a teacher, translator, and grammarian who contributed much to the revival of Greek letters in western Europe.

Leaving Greece *c.* 1447, Chalcondyles went first to Rome, where he became a member of Cardinal *Bessarion's humanist circle, which emphasized Greek studies. After teaching at Perugia (1450–63) he moved to Padua, where he became the first occupant of the chair of Greek studies at that university (1463). His appointment there was apparently arranged by Cardinal Bessarion and through the efforts of Gaza, *Filelfo, and Palla *Strozzi. This chair was to have an illustrious history and make Padua one of the most important centers of Greek learning in all Europe. In 1475 Chalcondyles was summoned to Florence by Lorenzo de' *Medici to fill the post of professor of Greek vacated by the Byzantine humanist John *Argyropoulos. Chalcondyles's fame spread through Italy, and Ludovico *Sforza later invited him to Milan (1492). He spent his last years in that city, carrying on his activities as editor of Greek texts and teacher of Greek.

Demetrius Chalcondyles, detail of a 15th-century fresco by Domenico Ghirlandaio, S. Maria Novella, Florence.

In his influence on the revival of Greek letters in the West, Demetrius Chalcondyles ranks with such leading Greek humanists as Bessarion and Argyropoulos. Chalcondyles's Greek grammar became a standard text for the teaching of Greek; and his editions of Homer, Isocrates, and the *Suidas (Suda) lexicon were important contributions to *Renaissance Greek studies. Chalcondyles's most basic contribution to Western Hellenism, however, may well have been his activity as teacher of Greek; for some of the foremost humanists of the age were among his students, including the Italian *Poliziano, the German *Reuchlin, and the English *Linacre, all of whom stimulated Greek learning in their respective countries.

Bibliography: E. L. J. Legrand, *Bibliographie hellénique,* 4 v. (Paris 1885–1906; repr. Brussels 1963) 1:xciv–ci; 2:304–311, still useful. G. Cammelli, *Demetrio Calcondila,* v.3 (1954) of *I dotti bizantini e le origini dell' umanesimo* (Florence 1941–). D. J. Geanakoplos, *Greek Scholars in Venice: Studies in the Dissemination of Greek Learning from Byzantium to Western Europe* (Cambridge, Mass. 1962), for Greek studies during the Renaissance. **Illustration credit:** Alinari-Art Reference Bureau.

[D. J. GEANAKOPLOS]

CHALDEAN RITE

One of the 18 canonical *rites recognized by the Holy See, the Chaldean rite is composed of the faithful residing in Iraq, Iran, Syria, Lebanon, and Turkey who are subject to the Chaldean patriarch of Babylon. They are descendants of the East Syrian and Persian Christians who once accepted the heresy of Nestorianism and are now in union with Rome.

History

For the early history of these Christians, *see* EASTERN CHURCHES. For the 6th- and 7th-century reaction against the Christology of *Nestorius among the Christians of the Sassonid Persian Empire, *see* NESTORIANISM. The history of the *Nestorian Church is also found under that title. The contacts with the Holy See that resulted in a permanent Catholic Chaldean community began with the period of the Crusades.

Early Attempts at Union. The first Nestorian patriarch known to have made contact with Rome was Sabrishō'ibn-al-Masīḥī (1226–57). Latin missionaries commended him to Innocent IV, and the Pope in turn addressed a letter of good wishes and encouragement to the patriarch. In 1247 Rabban Ara, the Patriarchal Vicar, acknowledged receipt of the Pope's letter and thanked him in terms indicative of respect for the papal authority. Rabban Ara's letter was accompanied by two others, one brought from China by Rabban Ara himself, and the other containing the profession of faith of Ishō'yab bar Maldon, Metropolitan of Nisibis, two other metropolitans, and three bishops. It seems that a collective union was being sought. The letter that Ya-balāhā III (1281–1317) addressed to Pope Benedict XI on May 18, 1304, contained his profession of Catholic faith and the expression of his obedience and loyalty, in union with his metropolitans and bishops.

Circumstances of time, place, and persons played a controlling part in the instability of the union. In Cyprus, dispositions made by the Holy See impelled lay Nestorians to resist union for 120 years and to oppose and repudiate members of their clergy who favored it. For example the bull of Honorius III of Feb. 12, 1222, had commanded the Latin patriarch of Jerusalem, the Latin archbishop of Caesarea, and the bishop of Bethlehem to bring the dissidents to obedience to the Latin archbishop of Nicosia; and the bull of John XXII of Oct. 1, 1326 had ordered the patriarch of Jerusalem to extirpate heresies by whatever means he chose. A brief union was effected in 1340 by Elias, Nestorian Bishop of Cyprus. Several of those converted during the union achieved in 1445 by Timothy, Bishop of Cyprus, returned to Nestorianism 5 years later. A rigid policy of Latinization was applied by the Doge of Venice, who succeeded the Lusignans as ruler of the island in 1489.

Union with Rome. The definitive union that brought forth the Chaldean Catholic Church took place in the 16th century. Simon III Basidi (1480–93) and his successors introduced a hereditary succession to the patriarchate, from uncle to nephew or cousin. Since the Nestorian Church reserved to metropolitans the right to consecrate the patriarch, the Basidis, known as the "Abuna" (patriarchal) family, sought to create metropolitans only from among their own number, as a precaution. This reduced the number of metropolitans until under Simeon V bar Māmā there was only one, his 8-year-old nephew. The practice brought ignorant and unworthy minors to patriarchal rank, for which they were unprepared, and imposed celibacy on them. The conscience of the hierarchy was aroused; they sought a radical remedy in union with Rome.

The movement was led by the three bishops of Irbīl, Salamas, and Azerbaijan. They met at Mosul with the clergy, the monks, and three or four lay delegates from each of ten regions to elect a patriarch. Their choice was Sulāqā, a religious priest since 1540 and superior of the Convent of Rabban-Hormizd, near Alkosh, approximately 25 miles from Mosul. He refused, even after a second ballot. After a third ballot, in which he still led, the assembly decreed that force be used, if necessary, to oblige the candidate to present himself. Sulāqā was haled before the assembly, and his election was proclaimed amid cries of joy and applause. The bishops among the electors seem to have excluded themselves to avoid any suspicion of self-interest.

Armed with the proper documents and accompanied by three notables, Adam, Thomas, and Khalaph, Sulāqā left Mosul for Rome, with an escort of 70 as far as Jerusalem. On Nov. 15, 1552, he arrived in Rome, accompanied only by Khalaph. One companion had died on the way, and another had been detained by illness. On the basis of a report by Cardinal Maffei, Pope Julius III promulgated his bull of Feb. 20, 1553, proclaiming Sulāqā patriarch of Mosul. This was the official birthday of the Chaldean Catholic Church.

Sulāqā was consecrated a bishop on April 9, 1553, by Pope Julius III in the Basilica of St. Peter and received the pallium from the hands of the Pope at a secret consistory held at the Vatican on April 28. At Sulāqā's request for help in his ministry, the Pope appointed the Dominican Ambrose Buttigeg as representative of the Holy See to the Chaldeans of Mosul. In July Sulāqā left Rome, accompanied by A. Buttigeg; Antoninus Zahara, a Dominican from Malta; and a certain Matthew; as well as by his first companion Khalaph. He arrived in Diarbekir, his patriarchal residence, on Nov. 12, 1553, where he was received triumphally by clergy and people, as evidenced by his letter to Julius III (one of two letters remaining of his correspondence). On Nov. 19, 7 days after his return, he consecrated Bp. Ḥabīb Elias Asmar. In December he obtained in Aleppo from the Sultan documents that acknowledged him head of the Chaldean nation, "after the example of all the Patriarchs." In 1554 he consecrated Metropolitan 'Abdīshō' of Jezireh. Elias Asmar later identified five bishops and metropolitans consecrated by Sulāqā.

With the help of a hierarchy of eight bishops, assisted by Ambrose and Antoninus, and armed with documents from the Sultan, Sulāqā initiated the expected reform. As was quite natural, opposition to his efforts soon made itself felt. In fact, the Nestorian Patriarch Simeon Denḥā, now Sulāqā's rival and bitter enemy, prevailed upon the Pasha of Amadya to invite Sulāqā there under the pretext that his presence in that region could contribute to the union of the Nestorians. Once in Amadya, Sulāqā was imprisoned and subjected to every sort of torture for 4 months. Finally, by order of the Pasha, he was put into a sack and thrown into a lake to drown, about Jan. 12, 1555.

Three Centuries of Conflict. Mar 'Abdīshō' of Jezireh succeeded Sulāqā. He was not able to leave for Rome until 1561; he was confirmed there on April 17, 1562, and received the pallium on May 4. In haste to return to his threatened flock, he did not attend the Council of Trent. In 1578 'Abdishô died in the Convent of St. James the Recluse, where he had established his residence. The electoral synod was prevented by great difficulties from meeting until 1579, when it elected as patriarch the aged Mar Yabalāhā IV, Bishop of Jezireh and administrator of the vacant patriarchate. The new patriarch died in 1580, before he could send his profession of faith to Rome.

His successor was Simeon IX, Bishop of Gelu, Seert, and Salamas. He and all his flock had recently been converted through the zeal of Elias Asmar, Metropolitan of Diarbekir. The electoral synod commanded Elias Asmar to go to Rome to seek confirmation and the pallium. Simeon IX made the mistake of residing in the Convent of St. John, near Salamas, where he was the butt of vigorous attacks by the Nestorians. The mountainous terrain and the conflict between Turks and Persians made communication difficult, thereby inhibiting contacts between this patriarch and Rome. Leonard Abel, Archbishop of Sidon and envoy of Pope Gregory XIII since January 1584, unable to reach the patriarch at his residence, sent him the profession of faith, which he signed once again in 1585. Simon IX died in 1600.

As a result of the continuing difficulties, the electoral synod was unable to meet, and the election of Simeon X took place in accordance with hereditary law. The profession of faith that the new patriarch sent to Rome by Thomas, Metropolitan of Diarbekir, was not deemed satisfactory. The Franciscan Thomas Obicini brought the patriarch another formula to sign. He received a most cordial welcome, and the formula was signed on July 28, 1619.

Professions of faith were sent to Rome by Simeon XI in 1653, Simeon XII in 1658, and Simeon XIII in 1670. The last-named besought Pope Clement X to leave the ancient rites intact. The pressure of serious local difficulties made frequent contacts with Rome impossible. Simeon XIII finally felt obliged to return to Nestorianism. He established himself at Kotchannes, where, ensconced among impenetrable mountains, he became the first of a new series of Nestorian patriarchs that has continued until the present.

The Chaldean Catholic community of Diarbekir was thus left without a shepherd; and a Nestorian bishop, dependent on Rabban-Hormizd, resided in Diarbekir. Yet the Catholic community remained favorable to union, as it had been since 1552. It was supported in its loyalty by the work of the Capuchin John Baptist of St. Aignan. Conversions continued, the most famous being that of Joseph, the Nestorian Bishop of Diarbekir. Opposed, cruelly persecuted, and several times imprisoned at the instigation of the Nestorian Patriarch Elias X, Bishop Joseph received a brief of felicitations from Pope Clement X, dated Jan. 25, 1677. Soon afterward the Sultan acknowledged his right to the title of patriarch of Diarbekir, Mardin, and other places. Joseph besought Rome for confirmation of this title and also for the pallium. At first Rome hesitated, but it granted them to him on Jan. 8, 1681, under the title *Patriarchatus nationis chaldaeorum patriarchae regiminis destitutus.* Rome did not grant him the title of patriarch of the Oriental Assyrians, reserved out of diplomacy for the Nestorian patriarchs, successors of Sulāqā, who resided at Kotchannes, or the title of patriarch of Babylon, reserved for the Nestorian patriarchs of the Abūna-Basidi family, who resided at Rabban-Hormizd.

The Chaldeans thus had their own patriarch in the person of Joseph I, the first of the *ad interim* series of patriarchs of Diarbekir. In 1691 Joseph I, having grown old and wanting to assure the patriarchal succession and thus avoid all possible intrigue after his death, dared to consecrate his coadjutor, Joseph Ṣlībā, as patriarch, even before he himself resigned. Because of this irregular procedure, the Holy See did not recognize Joseph II

Slībā until June 18, 1696. Discouraged by persecutions and difficulties of all sorts, Joseph II asked to retire to Rome. However, stricken with the plague, he died in 1713 before he could leave for the Eternal City.

Timothy Mār Eugene, Bishop of Mardīn since 1691, succeeded him under the name of Joseph III. His patriarchate was marked by great progress. On the occasion of his official visit to Mosul, 3,000 Nestorians were converted, and 3,000 others followed later. The fury of the Nestorians knew no bounds, and they had the patriarch imprisoned several times. To make things worse, a decree by the Sultan had just granted Mosul and Aleppo to the Nestorians, giving the Catholics Diarbekir and Mardīn. This made the situation of the Catholics in Mosul and Aleppo very critical.

When Joseph III arrived in Rome on Jan. 1, 1732, he offered his resignation, but it was not accepted. The war between the Turks and the Persians obliged him to remain in Rome until the end of 1741, when he returned to his anxious flock. He died on Jan. 23, 1757.

His successor was Lazarus Hindi, Joseph IV. Rome first recognized him by the title of archbishop of Amīd, then as patriarch of the united Chaldeans on March 24, 1759. His resignation, presented on Aug. 21, 1780, was not accepted until Dec. 7, 1781. But not finding anyone to take his place, Rome turned again to Joseph IV and named him patriarchal administrator *ad interim*. On March 21, 1791, Joseph was called to Rome, and John Hormizd, the neoconvert bishop of Mosul, of the Abūna family, was designated apostolic administrator. Joseph and the clergy of Diarbekir forsaw serious danger for Catholicism in the naming of this neoconvert. In 1792 Joseph went to Rome, and on Feb. 3, 1793, he succeeded in annulling the nomination of John Hormizd and reestablishing himself as Patriarchal administrator of Amīd, with Joseph Attar as his vicar-general. Joseph IV died in 1796.

The 19th and 20th Centuries. In 1802 the priest Augustine Hindi was named administrator of the Patriarchate of Diarbekir. On Sept. 8, 1804, he was consecrated bishop at Mardīn. Following the suspension of John Hormizd (1812), Augustine Hindi was named apostolic delegate for the Chaldeans, a post he held for 15 years. Rome did not want to name him patriarch, for there was hope of one day winning over one of the two Nestorian patriarchs of Kotchannes or Rabban-Hormizd, who had been in correspondence with Rome since 1770–71. The aim was to unite the Chaldeans under a single patriarchate. Meanwhile, Rome rewarded Hindi by granting him the pallium, which it sent to him on Nov. 2, 1818. Seeing in this act his recognition as patriarch, Augustine declared himself Patriarch Joseph V. Rome corrected his error by pointing out to him that the pallium signified nothing more than the rank of archbishop. Augustine died in Diarbekir on April 3, 1827, putting an end to the series of patriarchs of Diarbekir, begun 147 years earlier.

Immediately after Hindi's death, Rome was ready to grant the pallium and patriarchal authority to John Hormizd, the 74-year-old metropolitan of Mosul. The party opposed to John, then represented in Rome by Gabriel Dambo, founder of the Catholic Chaldean Monastic Institute of Rabban-Hormizd, was able to delay the execution of this plan until July 5, 1830. From that date on, John Hormizd, the last of the Abūna family, was the sole representative of the Chaldean Catholics, under the name of John IX Hormizd, Chaldean Patriarch of Babylon. He continued the succession that had originated with Addai and Mari in subapostolic times and from which Sulāqā had separated in 1553 to form a union with Rome. To the Nestorians there remained only the Patriarchate of Kotchannes, which continued the succession of Sulāqā that had reverted to Nestorianism.

John died on Aug. 16, 1838, after a long and checkered life. His successor was Nicholas Zaya, formerly bishop of Salamas, and coadjutor of John Hormizd, with the right of succession. Nicholas was confirmed on April 27, 1840. The Chaldean bishops were displeased with this choice, which deprived them of their right to a free election. Zaya resigned in 1847 and retired to his former diocese, where he died in 1855.

Joseph Audo, administrator of the patriarchate, was elected patriarch in 1847 and confirmed on Sept. 11, 1848. His long pontificate was marked by many conversions and also by great dissension with Rome, which began in 1860, on questions of jurisdiction, especially over the *Malabar rite. The national synod that he held June 7 to 21, 1858, at the Convent of Rabban-Hormizd, was never approved by Rome. Joseph Audo died on March 14, 1878. Speaking of him at the consistory of Feb. 28, 1879, Leo XIII said, ". . . Quem eximius pietatis et religionis sensus ornabat."

His successor, Elias Peter Abūlyonan, Bishop of Jezireh, was confirmed on Feb. 28, 1879, and died of typhoid fever on June 27, 1894. Elias Peter was succeeded by Abdisho V Khayyāth, who was elected on Oct. 28, 1894, and confirmed on March 28, 1895, and who died in Baghdad on Nov. 6, 1899. Joseph Emmanuel II Thomas, who was unanimously elected on July 9, 1900, and confirmed on Dec. 17, 1900(?), died on July 21, 1947, at age 97; in a decree of July 3, 1902, the Holy See named him apostolic delegate for the Nestorians. He was a member of the Iraqi Senate for 25 years, and his long pontificate was marked by a return of several Nestorian villages to Catholicism, with two bishops and many members of the clergy. It also saw the massacres of 1918 (World War I), when four bishops, many priests, and 70,000 faithful died. His successor was Joseph VII Ghanima, who was confirmed June 21, 1948, and who died in Baghdad on July 7, 1957. Paul II Cheikho was elected Dec. 13, 1958, and confirmed March 13, 1959.

Organization and Status

The spiritual leader of all the Chaldeans in the world is the Chaldean patriarch of Babylon, who exercises a strictly personal jurisdiction over hierarchy, clergy, and people, according to the sacred canons (ClerSanc c.241). The patriarch is assisted: (1) by the Chaldean hierarchy, in the administration of the eparchies, (2) by the patriarchal synods of the entire hierarchy, convoked every 20 years, and also whenever the patriarch deems it opportune or necessary, e.g., to provide for vacant eparchies or to erect or divide an eparchy, (3) by the permanent synod, which is part of the patriarchal curia and which the patriarch must constitute according to the norms of the sacred canons (ClerSanc cc.288–289) and convoke at least three times a year (ClerSanc c.295) to deal with the most important questions regarding the patriarchate—the synod consists of four bishops, with the patriarch as president, and it may be replaced by a patriarchal council of two bishops presided over by the patriarch—and (4) by the remainder of the patriarchal curia.

Hierarchy. The patriarch is elected by the Chaldean hierarchy and enthroned even before he is confirmed by Rome. Canonical election confers on the patriarch the right to the patriarchal office, and papal confirmation grants him the exercise of this office. The bishops are elected by the Chaldean hierarchy, assembled in an electoral synod presided over by the patriarch or consulted individually by mail, and voting in absentia. The election must receive papal confirmation before the nominee may be consecrated.

Residential Sees and Membership. In 1963 there were 12 residential sees: 1 patriarchal see, Baghdad (Iraq); 3 metropolitan sees, Kirkuk (Iraq), Urmia, and Sena (Iran); 1 archiepiscopal see, Basra (Iraq); 7 episcopal sees, Amadya, Zakho, Akra, Mosul, Alkosh (Iraq), Aleppo (Syria), and Beirut (Lebanon). These 12 eparchies, with the two patriarchal vicariates of Turkey and Rau, plus the other countries of the Near East, form the canonical territory of the patriarchate. Two titular bishops—the coadjutor of Beirut, with right of succession, and the patriarchal auxiliary of Baghdad—brought the total of the hierarchy in 1965 to 14.

It is unfortunate that a rite with so glorious a past, once so flourishing and widespread, should be reduced to a membership of some 200,000 Catholics and 75,000 Nestorians.

Secular Clergy. The priestly education of the Chaldean clergy is provided: (1) by the intereparchial Chaldean patriarchal seminary of St. Peter, founded in Mosul in 1866 by Rev. Raphael Masadji and until 1960 directed by the Chaldean clergy; this seminary has been transferred to Baghdad and entrusted to the Chaldeo-Malabarian Carmelites, and is soon to pass to the direction of the Jesuit fathers; (2) by the Syro-Chaldean seminary of St. John, founded in Mosul in 1877; it is under the supervision of the apostolic delegate, but is directed by the French Dominican fathers; Chaldean and Syrian students are accepted each year, and two priests (a Chaldean and a Syrian) provide services for the seminarians of the two rites; (3) by the intereparchial minor seminary of St. Joseph, founded in Teheran in 1950 by Mar Joseph Cheikho, Metropolitan of Sena, Iran; (4) by the eparchial minor seminary erected in Kirkuk, Iraq, in 1963 by Mar Raphael Rabban, Metropolitan of Kirkuk, and directed by the diocesan clergy; and (5) by the Chaldean preseminary of Urmia, which was originally the major seminary founded at Salamas, Iran, in 1846 by the Vincentians, closed in 1934, and reopened in 1951. Clerics of special ability go on to seek appropriate degrees in Rome, Paris, Constantinople, or Beirut. Although the secular clergy is not canonically bound by the law of celibacy, it has great esteem for it. There are very few married priests, and most of these are converts from Nestorianism.

Religious Orders and Congregations. The Chaldean monastic institution has been reduced to a single religious order for men and a single religious congregation for women. The Antonine Order of St. Hormizdas was founded on March 29, 1808, in the Convent of Rabban-Hormizd by Gabriel Dambro of Mardīn. Its constitutions were approved by Rome on March 29, 1830. The order has been a source of holiness for the Chaldeans and has given them many missionary priests who have contributed to the return of thousands of Nestorians. Several members of the hierarchy, including the famous Patriarch Joseph V Audo, belonged to this order. It had 3 religious houses with 51 religious and 12 novices in 1963. The novitiate is now in Baghad. The Chaldean congregation of the Daughters of Mary Immaculate, of patriarchal right, was founded on Aug. 7, 1922, by Chorbishops Antūn Zebūni, with the encouragement and support of Joseph Emmanuel II Thomas, then patriarch. It provides religious instruction to youth by means of schools and charitable institutions such as orphanages.

In addition to this Chaldean congregation, there is the interritual Chaldeo-Syro-Armenian congregation of the Dominican Sisters of St. Catherine of Siena of the Third Order Regular of St. Dominic, founded in Mosul in 1894, affiliated with the Dominican Order in 1927, and approved by the Holy See in 1935.

Legislation. Since the Chaldean Catholic rite has not had its own approved synod, it derives most of its legislation from the common law of the Church. In addition to this law, there are instructions and decrees relating to the Chaldean rite, promulgated by the Congregation for the Propagation of the Faith and contained in the last edition of the bullarium of this congregation: R. de Martinis, *Ius Pontificium de Propaganda Fide,* v.6, pts. 1–2 (Rome, 1894–95) and *Decreta* (Rome 1909). The publications *Crebrae allatae* (Feb. 22, 1949) on marriage, *Sollicitudinem Nostram* (Jan. 6, 1950) on judicial law, *Postquam Apostolicis* (Feb. 9, 1952) on religious and ecclesiastical property, and *Cleri sanctitati* (June 2, 1957) on persons, annul all preceding decisions in these fields.

Bibliography: S. GIAMIL, *Genuinae relationes inter Sedem Apostolicam et Assyrorum Orientalium seu Chaldaeorum Ecclesiam* (Rome 1902). J. M. VOSTÉ, "Mar Iohannan Soulaqa: Premier Patriarche des Chaldéens," *Angelicum* 8 (1931) 187–234. G. BELTRAMI, *La chiesa caldea nel secolo dell'unione* (Orientalia Christiana 83; 1933). E. TISSÉRANT, "Nestorienne (l'Église)," DTC 11.1:218–247. R. RABBAN, *Shahīd al-Ittiḥad* (Martyr of Union; Mosul 1955), a biography of Sham'un Yoḥannan Sulāqā. ABDOULAHAD, ABP. of AMID, "Vie de Mar Youssef Ier: Patriarche des Chaldéens," ed. and tr. J. B. CHABOT, *Revue de l'Orient Chrétien* 1.2 (1896) 66–90. S. BELLO, *La Congrégation de S. Hormisdas et l'Église chaldéene dans la première moitié siècle* (OrChrAnal 122; 1939). D. ATTWATER, *The Christian Churches of the East,* 2 v. (rev. ed. Milwaukee 1961–62) v.1. OrientCatt 359–377, 516–519, 606–608, 753–754, bibliog. 366–367. J. DAUVILLIER, DDC 3:292–388, with bibliog.

[R. RABBAN]

CHALDEAN RITE, LITURGY OF

That form of Christian worship which takes its name from the ancient region that the West called Mesopotamia. It is also known as the East Syrian rite, indicating its similarity to and origin from the primitive Jerusalem-Antioch Liturgy and distinguishing it from the rite of Syrian Catholics and Jacobites. It is sometimes known as the Nestorian rite, indicating its use by those Christians who rejected the teachings of the Council of Ephesus (*see* NESTORIAN CHURCH). This article treats the churches using this rite, the history of this rite, its characteristics, churches, vessels, and vestments, and liturgical books.

Churches Using this Rite. The rite is still used by members of the Catholic Patriarchate of Babylon of the Chaldeans. These are principally in Iraq, Iran, and

Syria although they are found also in Western countries. Several thousand Chaldean-rite Catholics live in the U.S. The rite is observed also by those Christians of the Middle East and elsewhere who are known as Nestorians or Assyrians. All these use the Syriac language in the Liturgy, although Arabic is used for many prayers and readings in the preanaphora; in the U.S., English is used more and more frequently. The Chaldean rite is the mother rite of the Malabar Church of India, which was evangelized by Nestorian missionaries (*see* MALABAR RITE, LITURGY OF).

History. The lack of documents prior to the 5th century makes it difficult to determine the rite's precise origin, although there is no doubt that its primitive form was Antiochene. Most probably it originated in Edessa in the early 2d century. The Synod of Seleucia (410) reformed this Edessan Liturgy to correspond more with "the Western fathers," i.e., those of Syria. The chief sources of its 5th-century formulary are the homilies of *Theodore of Mopsuestia and Narsai of Nisibis. In the 7th century, the Katholikos Iso'jahb III (647–657) instituted a number of important ritual reforms. He regulated the preanaphora prayers, prescribed the use of only three Anaphoras (excluding all others), abbreviated the ordination rite, and removed the exorcisms from the baptismal rite. Apart from occasional additions of liturgical poetry, the rite has remained substantially unchanged since the 7th century. In the periods of union with the Catholic Church (16th and 18th centuries) few changes were necessary and no obvious Latinization took place. Some Western customs were adopted (e.g., genuflections at the Consecration and the use of the corporal) in imitation of the Latins.

Characteristics. Although it shares language and hymns with the West Syrian Liturgies, its prayers, gestures, and calendar mark it as independent and as a proper rite. The simplicity of the prayers with many repetitions, the lack of a rich Scripture lectionary, and the few saints commemorated give evidence of its primitive form.

Mass. The Eucharistic Liturgy is always chanted, sometimes to the accompaniment of cymbals and triangles. There are three Anaphoras. The Liturgy of the Apostles Addai and Mari is used on most Sundays, feasts, and ferias of the year. The Liturgy of St. Theodore of Mopsuestia and the Liturgy of St. Nestorius (called by Catholics "the Second" and "the Third") are used less frequently.

The prayer Lakhumara (to Thee, Lord) and the general incensation of the entire church are characteristics of its preparatory rite. Catholics add to this the preparation of the oblata. The instruction part of the Liturgy opens with the Trisagion, and normally four lessons are read, each with its proper diaconal announcement and prayer.

The dismissal of the catechumens and the penitents is formal and (at least among the Nestorians) seems to require noncommunicants to leave. The Nicene Creed (with some variant phrases) is sung; into it Catholics have inserted the *Filioque clause.

The Liturgy of the Apostles is distinctive among Christian liturgies in that much of it is addressed to the Second Person of the Trinity, not to the Father, and —a fact that has long puzzled liturgists—in that the Words of Institution are missing from all the Nestorian formularies. The Catholics inserted the formula from the Maronite Anaphora (A. Raes, "Le récit").

Long commemorations and intercessions before the Epiclesis are likewise characteristic of the Chaldean Liturgy. Before the Fraction the hands of the celebrant are incensed. Catholics receive Communion under the species of bread only; the Nestorians when all have received of the bread, drink of the chalice. Both use fermented bread.

Rite of Initiation. The structure of the Baptism-Confirmation rite is analogous to that of the Eucharistic Liturgy. Oil is carried to the altar at the Offertory, covered with a veil and following the Sanctus it is consecrated with an Epiclesis. The baptismal water is blessed after the Lord's Prayer. The infant's body is immersed in the water three times. In the church, the newly baptized is then anointed and signed on the forehead. The ancient rite of the newly baptized receiving Communion has not been preserved.

Penance and Anointing of the Sick. The Nestorians seem to have known of auricular Confession only for the reconciliation of apostates and heretics (see J. M. Vosté). The Catholics use the translation of the Latin form of absolution. The same is true for the Sacrament of the Sick.

Marriage. The form of this Sacrament seems to occur at the blessing of the ring. The bride's ring together with blessed water and a small cross are placed in a chalice of wine. This is blessed and then both spouses drink from the chalice after which they are crowned by the priest.

Holy Orders. The Chaldean rite preserves the ancient simple structure. The kneeling ordinand covers his eyes with his hands while the bishop recites a prayer of imposition. Catholics have two minor orders (lector and subdeacon) to which the Nestorians add a third (awakener). A new Chaldean Pontifical with 12 ordination ceremonies was published in 1957 at Rome.

Church Building, Vessels, and Vestments. The traditional form of the Chaldean church is a simple rectangular hall with the sanctuary enclosed at its East end by a stone wall. A single door covered by a curtain gives access from the sanctuary to the nave. Benches are rare; clergy and laity alike sit on the rug-covered floor.

Latin style chalice and paten are used on a stone altar with wooden mensa. Catholics have adopted the use of the corporal while the Nestorians use a piece of the hide of an ass (recalling the entry of the Lord into Jerusalem).

Liturgical vestments appear to be a mixture of Eastern and Western types. Generally a cope is worn over the stole and alb by the celebrant. Catholic priests wear the cuffs and Catholic bishops have adopted the miter, crozier, ring, and pectoral cross of the West. They retain the hand cross with the pendant veil for blessing.

Liturgical Books. There are some 16 distinct liturgical books. The most important is the *Takhsa,* which contains the three Anaphoras and the prayers for the Sacraments. The others include Lectionaries, marriage and funeral Rituals, Hymnals, and Ordinals. Editions of these have been printed in Rome and Mosul.

Bibliography: A. A. KING, *The Rites of Eastern Christendom* (2 v. London 1950) v.2. D. ATTWATER, *The Christian Churches of the East,* 2 v. (rev. ed. Milwaukee 1961–62); *Eastern Catholic*

Worship (New York 1945). A. RAES, *Introductio in liturgiam orientalem* (Rome 1947); "Le Récit de l'institution eucharistique dans l'anaphore chaldéenne et malabare des Apôtres," OrChrPer 10 (1944) 216–226; "Les Ordinations dans le pontifical chaldéen," *L'Orient Syrien* 5 (1960) 63–80. J. M. VOSTÉ, "La Confession chez les Nestoriens," *Angelicum* 7 (1930) 17–26.

[C. K. VON EUW]

CHALDEANS, properly the designation for the inhabitants of Babylonia in the first millennium B.C., but commonly employed by Greek and Roman writers, following the death of Alexander, to signify astrologers or diviners. The astrology of Babylonia spread to Egypt and throughout the cities of the Greek and Roman world. Its practitioners ranged from learned men, well versed in mathematics—hence the name "Mathematicians" (Greek, μαθηματικοί; Latin *mathematici*) for astrologers—to mere charlatans. Under the Roman Empire, many of the leading writers and thinkers in East and West were profoundly influenced by the Chaldean astrology and were convinced that it could ascertain the will of the gods and man's destiny. The Chaldeans were repeatedly attacked and refuted in the writings of the Church Fathers.

See also ASTROLOGY; DIVINATION.

Bibliography: W. J. W. KASTEN, ReallexAntChr 2:1006–21.

[T. A. BRADY]

CHALDEANS (IN THE BIBLE), an Aramaic-speaking people called in Akkadian *kaldu* (the Babylonian form of a presumed original *kašdu*), in Hebrew *kaśdîm,* in Aramaic *kaśdāi,* and in Greek Χαλδαῖοι. The Chaldeans made their first appearance in history around the end of the 2d and the beginning of the 1st millennium B.C. as raiders (cf. Jb 1.17) and later settlers in the semi-swampy regions at the head of the Persian Gulf. Apparently they had come from the western coast of the Persian Gulf, where they seem to have been in contact with people using a form of South Arabic script [see W. F. Albright, BullAmSchOrRes 128 (1952) 39–45]. In periods when Assyrian control of southern Mesopotamia was weak, the Chaldeans were able to establish small independent kingdoms, of which the most important was Beth-Yakin. In the 8th century B.C. even the city of Babylon was held for short periods by Chaldean princes, e.g., by Mukîn-Zêri (731–728) and *Merodach-Baladan (722–710, 703) of Beth-Yakin, who, around the time of his revolt against *Sennacherib of Assyria in 703, sent an embassy to King *Ezechia of Juda (4 Kgs 20.12–19; Is 39.1–8; 2 Chr 32.31). The speedy decline of Assyria after the reign of Assurbanipal (668–627) allowed the Chaldean Nabopolassar to make himself independent king of Babylon (626–604). In 612 the allied forces of the Medes and the Chaldeans captured Ninive and destroyed the Assyrian Empire. Nabopolassor's son *Nabuchodonosor (Nebuchadrezzar; 604–561) continued the work of his father in conquering all of northern Mesopotamia and then proceeded to incorporate into the Chaldean Neo-Babylonian Empire all of Syria and Palestine. However, with the capture of Babylon by the Persian King Cyrus the Great (539) from *Nabu-na'id (Nabonidus) the Chaldean Empire came to an end. (On the history of Babylonia during this period, *see* MESOPOTAMIA, ANCIENT, 2.)

In the Bible the terms Chaldeans and the land of the Chaldeans (Chaldea) become synonymous with Babylonians and Babylonia from the 7th century B.C. on (4 Kgs 25.4, 13, 24–26; Is 13.19; 23.13; 43.14; Jer 21.4; 22.25; 24.5; 25.12; Ez 1.1–3; 11.24; 16.29; Hab 1.6). In the pseudohistorical stories of the Book of *Daniel the word Chaldeans means sometimes Babylonians (Dn 1.4; 2.5; 5.30; 9.1) and sometimes magicians, soothsayers (2.5, 10; 4.4; 5.7, 11); on the use of the term in the latter sense, see the preceding article. According to Gn 11.28, 31; 15.7 (see also Neh 9.7; Jdt 5.6; Acts 7.4), *Abraham came originally from "Ur of the Chaldeans"; since the Chaldeans could hardly have been in the ancient Sumerian city of *Ur as early as the time of Abraham, the phrase "of the Chaldeans" must apparently be taken as an anachronism.

Bibliography: Pauly-Wiss RE 3:2045–62. A. DUPONT-SOMMER, *Les Araméens* (Paris 1949). K. F. KRÄMER, LexThK[2] 2:1002–04. G. BOSON, EncCatt 3:332–333. EncDictBibl 341–342.

[J. B. WHEATON]

CHALICE, PATEN, AND VEIL

The chalice and paten are vessels used in the Eucharistic liturgy; the veil, a covering for them. This article treats of their development and use.

The most essential of all the liturgical vessels is the chalice in which the wine at Mass is consecrated. It is the only vessel mentioned in all four scriptural accounts of the institution of the Eucharist. Early chalices were akin to the drinking vessels normally in use and were distinguished from these only by ornamentation. They were made from any metal, and chalices of glass, wood, or horn were not unknown; since the 9th century, however, only precious metals have been used. Besides the chalice there have existed at various times in history the *calix ministerialis,* a cup without a base and with two handles, used for giving communion to the faithful; and also the *calix offertorialis,* which was a larger form of the same shape, into which the faithful poured their contributions of wine at the Offertory procession. By the 9th century these chalices for the faithful had fallen into disuse; there remained only the priest's chalice, to which a base was added. The bowl became hemispherical; next a stem was introduced between bowl and base; then a node (knob) was made in the middle of the stem. During the Middle Ages the base became large, the bowl smaller, egg-shaped, and (later) conical. Under baroque influence the base was made larger still, the node pear-shaped, the cup shaped like a lily. Decorations of engraved patterns on early chalices gradually became more complicated by the 8th century and sometimes included texts on the base or around the bowl. Later decorations became even more lavish, often incorporating inlaid precious stones, pearls, and enameled medallions. The modern chalice, under the influence of functional design, concentrates on gracefulness of line, balance of proportion, and excellence of material rather than applied ornament, and its shape is inspired chiefly by forms in vogue during the 1st millennium. It is prescribed that the cup be of gold, of silver, or even of tin, but gold-plated within; its neck should be designed in a way that does not impede handling by the priest, and its base, wide enough to ensure relative stability.

Before use a chalice must be consecrated by a bishop or abbot (CIC cc.294, 323, 1147). Until the Middle Ages it was customary for each church to have but one chalice; since Masses have become more numerous, most churches have several chalices, and a great many priests possess their own.

(a)

(b)

(c)

(d)

Fig. 1. Chalices: (a) Syrian?, glass with engraved decoration, early 6th century, height 5½ in. (b) Early Christian, the so-called "Great Chalice of Antioch," silver, partially gilt, 4th or 5th century, 7½ in. (c) Byzantine, silver, 6th century, 6⅝ in. (d) Merovingian, copper alloy, gilted, 8th century, 6 in.

Fig. 2. Early 13th-century Eucharistic set from the Abbey of St. Trudpert, near Freiburg, Germany, silver, partially gilt, with niello and jewels. Only two or three complete sets of chalice, paten, and Eucharistic straws of medieval workmanship are known to survive. One other set is in the Kunsthistorisches Museum, Vienna.

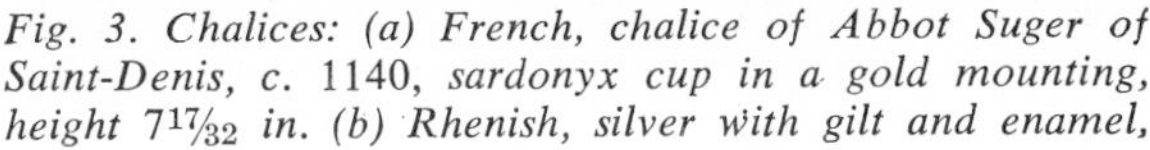
Fig. 3. Chalices: (a) French, chalice of Abbot Suger of Saint-Denis, c. 1140, *sardonyx cup in a gold mounting, height* $7\frac{17}{32}$ *in. (b) Rhenish, silver with gilt and enamel, c.* 1320. *(c) Spanish, silver with gilt,* 16*th century. (d) Contemporary, sterling silver covered with white enamel, by the goldsmith Meinrad Burch of Zurich.*

Fig. 4. Chalice and paten used by James Haddock, early missionary priest in Maryland. The chalice, 8⅜ inches high, is called a "saddle chalice," as it is made in three pieces for easy packing into a saddlebag on missionary journeys. It is believed to have been made in England in 1674 *and brought to America shortly thereafter. This silver chalice and paten are now on display at St. Francis Xavier church, Newton, Maryland, where Father Haddock served in* 1699.

Fig. 5. Chalice, partially covered by the folded veil, illuminated initial in the 13th-century Missal of St. Corneille de Compiègne in the Bibliothèque Nationale at Paris (MS lat. 17318, folio 173r, detail).

The paten is a shallow plate on which the large host rests at times both before and after consecration. It may be of gold or silver, gilt on the concave surface. Like the chalice, it requires consecration before use. Originally, a paten was a very large dish, sometimes of metal but often of wood, from which the Eucharist was distributed to the faithful in the days when unleavened bread was in use. By the 9th century, when Communion of the faithful had become infrequent, the paten was reduced in size and in time assumed its present form. (For further consideration of the art of the chalice and paten, *see* LITURGICAL ART, 6).

The veil covering the chalice and paten as they are carried to the altar is, at least in the Latin rite, of comparatively recent origin. Not until 1570 was it prescribed. It must be the same color as the Mass vestments.

Bibliography: J. BRAUN, *Das christliche Altargerät in seiner geschichtlichen Entwicklung* (Munich 1932). H. LECLERCQ, DACL 2.2:1595–1645. J. BAUDOT, *ibid.* 1646–51. V. H. ELBERN, *Der eucharistiche Kelch im frühen Mittelalter* (Düsseldorf 1961). Righetti 1:461–71. **Illustration credits:** Fig. 1*a* and *d*, Courtesy of the Dumbarton Oaks Collection. Fig. 1*b*, Metropolitan Museum of Art, The Cloisters Collection, Purchase, 1950. Figs. 1*c* and 3*b*, Courtesy of the Walters Art Gallery. Fig. 2, The Metropolitan Museum of Art, The Cloisters Collection Purchase, 1947. Fig. 3*a*, National Gallery of Art, Washington, D.C., Widener Collection. Fig. 3*c*, Courtesy of the Hispanic Society of America. Fig. 3*d*, Carl Erhardt. Fig. 4, Neal, Baltimore.

[C. W. HOWELL]

CHALLONER, RICHARD

Bishop, vicar apostolic of the London district, author; b. Lewes, Sussex, Sept. 29, 1691; d. London, Jan. 12, 1781. Challoner, the resolute leader of English Catholics during the 18th century, combined a firm administration with spiritual prudence necessitated by the times. His pastoral leadership, devotional writings, and exemplary life of prayer and mortification have made him one of the most venerated vicars apostolic of England. Challoner was converted from Presbyterianism to Catholicism in his youth while living at Lady Anastasia Holman's Warkworth Manor, where his widowed mother was housekeeper. He was tutored by the Holman's chaplain, John Gother, famed apologist and missionary, who arranged for Challoner's admittance to the English College at Douai (1705). He spent 25 years at Douai displaying ability and exceptional industry as student, teacher, and administrator. He completed the 12-year course in 8 years. After entering the seminary, he taught poetry, rhetoric, and philosophy; he was ordained (1716) and received his bachelor of divinity degree (1719), whereupon college officials appointed him vice president, professor of theology, and prefect of studies. He later earned a doctorate in divinity (1727).

Receiving a long-awaited missionary assignment, Challoner returned to England (1730). Although the penal laws were not as rigorously enforced as in former times, he was nevertheless compelled to live under layman's disguise, celebrate Mass secretly, and conduct religious meetings in obscure inns. Success as missionary priest and "controversial writer" led to his appointment as vicar-general. Controversy over a pamphlet by Challoner, in part refuting an attack on Catholicism by Dr. Conyers Middleton, a prominent Anglican divine, forced him to return to Douai (1738). Anticipated papal appointment of Challoner to the Douai College presidency prompted vigorous intervention by Bp. Benjamin Petre, vicar apostolic of the London district, who pleaded to Rome that Challoner be made his coadjutor bishop. After difficulties and delay, Challoner returned to England and was consecrated titular bishop of Debra and nominated coadjutor with right of succession to Petre (1741). He assumed much of the work of the aging Petre and succeeded him in 1758. For the next 23 years he successfully administered the London district, which included 10 counties, the Channel islands, and British North America.

Challoner's pastoral achievements are especially noteworthy when it is recalled that, due to existing laws, he spent his life in clandestine service. A zealous preacher particularly devoted to the poorer classes, he made numerous conversions in the London slums; he founded

Richard Challoner, from an engraving of 1781.

the "Benevolent Society for the Relief of the Aged and Infirmed Poor" and established three schools. Although Jacobite in sympathy, Challoner eventually recognized George III as *de jure* sovereign. He unsuccessfully sought practical solutions for Catholics forced by law to marry under Anglican rite. He defended episcopal authority over regular clergy and instituted conferences that increased clerical unity during a period of threatened imprisonment for "exercising the functions of a popish priest." In general, Challoner's episcopacy was marked by efforts to infuse into the ancient faith a spirit of resistance to the anti-Catholic forces so prevalent in the 18th century. He labored to save Catholicism in England from extinction; his writings and preachings served to strengthen the faith of the Catholic minority and to condition them to the possibility of a permanently hostile society. Challoner lived to see official signs of Catholic toleration, however, in the Catholic Relief Act (1778). During the Gordon Riots he fled London temporarily; he died several months later.

Challoner wrote numerous books and pamphlets. His major literary efforts were *Think Well On't* (1728), a book of meditations; *The Garden of the Soul* (1740), the most popular of his devotional writings, although subsequent editors radically altered the original; *Memoirs of the Missionary Priest* (2 v. 1741–42); *Britannia Sancta* (1745), a treatise depicting lives of English, Scottish, and Irish saints; *Meditations for Every Day in the Year* (1753); and *British Martyrology* (1761). Moreover, he revised the English Catechism, made several translations, e.g., *The Imitation of Christ* and St. Augustine's *Confessions,* and provided English Catholics with a more readable Bible by revising the Douay-Rheims. Although unsuccessful in making English Catholics steady readers of Scripture, Challoner's Bible (1749–52) was the standard Catholic version until recent times.

Bibliography: E. H. BURTON, *The Life and Times of Bishop Challoner, 1691–1781,* 2 v. (London 1909). M. TRAPPES-LOMAX, *Bishop Challoner* (New York 1936). T. COOPER, DNB 3:1349–52. D. MATHEW, *Catholicism in England* (2d ed. New York 1950). E. I. WATKIN, *Roman Catholicism in England* (New York 1957). J. CARTMELL, "Richard Challoner," Clergy Rev 44 (1959) 577–587.

[J. T. COVERT]

CHALMERS, THOMAS, Scottish Presbyterian theologian; b. Anstruther, Fifeshire, Scotland, March 17, 1780; d. Edinburgh, May 30, 1847. After studying at the University of St. Andrews, he taught mathematics and was ordained a minister. In 1810 he experienced a conversion and adhered to the evangelical party of the Church of *Scotland. His preaching was highly praised by William Wilberforce and others of the Clapham Sect. His *Astronomical Discourses* (1817), a series of lectures on the relations between astronomy and Christian revelation, gained wide popularity. Chalmers won a respected reputation also as a political economist and philosopher. In 1815 he was appointed to the Tron Church, one of the leading churches in Glasgow, but he transferred to the largest and poorest parish in the city, St. John's Church, where his success was remarkable. He became professor of moral philosophy at St. Andrews (1823) and professor of theology at Edinburgh (1828). After his election to the General Assembly of the Church of Scotland (1832), he supported the "veto act" of 1833, restricting the rights of laymen to nominate candidates for ecclesiastical positions. Together with the evangelical party, Chalmers advocated that ministers be selected by the congregations. The civil courts declared this procedure illegal (1838–39). When Parliament did not take action on the matter, Chalmers led nearly a third of the clergy and laity of the Church of Scotland into a schism known

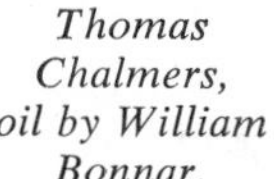

Thomas Chalmers, oil by William Bonnar.

as "the Disruption" (May 1843), which lasted until 1929. Chalmers was chosen first moderator of the Free Protesting Church of Scotland (later the Free Church of Scotland) and was responsible for establishing it on a solid financial basis. He acted also as professor of divinity in the Free Church's New College at Edinburgh. Chalmers also published numerous works, which have been collected in 34 volumes.

Bibliography: W. HANNA, *The Life and Writings of Thomas Chalmers,* 4 v. (Edinburgh 1849–52). H. WATT, *Thomas Chalmers and the Disruption* (Edinburgh 1943). W. G. BLAIKIE, DNB 3:1358–63. **Illustration credit:** National Galleries of Scotland.

[T. P. JOYCE]

CHALMERS, WILLIAM (CAMERARIUS), theologian; b. Aberdeen, Scotland, date unknown; d. Paris in 1678. After training for the priesthood at the Scots' College in Rome, he became a Jesuit. In 1625, following a brief sojourn in England, he left the Jesuits and became an Oratorian. At Paris in 1630 he published his *Selectae disputationes philosophicae.* He edited several opuscula of Augustine, Anselm and Fulgentius in 1634. A work on moral theology, *Disputationes theologicae de discrimine peccati venialis et mortalis* (Fastemburg), appeared in 1639. He published a short ecclesiastical history of Scotland, *Scotianae ecclesiae infantia, virilis aetas, senectus* (Paris 1643). He is, however, known mostly for his spirited rejection of *Molinism and vigorous defense of physical premotion in his *Antiquitatis de novitate victoria* (Fastemburg 1634) and his *Dissertatio theologica de electione angelorum et hominum ad gloriam* (Rennes 1641).

Bibliography: A. INGOLD, DTC 2.2:2211. V. ZOLLINI, EncCatt 3:1375.

[C. R. MEYER]

CHALON-SUR-SAÔNE, COUNCILS OF, various national (Merovingian), provincial, and diocesan councils held at the former diocesan seat of Chalon-sur-Saône (Latin, *Cabillonum*) in the Province of Lyons. In 579 Guntram, King of Orléans, convoked there a national council that deposed the bishops of Embrun and Gap for armed violence. In 603 another national council, held at the instigation of Queen *Brunhilde of Austrasia and Abp. Aridius of Lyons, deposed Bp. *Desiderius of Vienne. Another national council, held sometime between 643 and 652, promulgated 20 disciplinary canons, prescribing fidelity to the Nicene Creed and the ancient canons and making provision for the election and authority of bishops, the administration of Church property, the government of monasteries, and Christian morals. It prohibited abbots and monks from going to the king without episcopal permission; it forbade simony, selling slaves outside the realm, and farm labor on Sunday; and it recommended private sacramental confession with imposed penances. In 813 *Charlemagne ordered reform councils to be held throughout his Empire, at Mainz, Reims, Tours, Arles, and Chalon-sur-Saône. The 66 bishops and abbots of the Lyonnais who met at Chalon urged *cathedral schools for future clerics; forbade simony; recommended the *Benedictine Rule for monasteries, the restoration of public penance, private confession to God and a priest and the imposition of canonical penance; forbade masters to dissolve slaves' marriages; required Communion by all on Holy Thursday; and prescribed for monasteries of women. The canons appeared in the second *capitulary of the Diet of Aachen (813); Gratian's *Decretum* also contains some of them. Other provincial councils were held at Chalon in 873, 894, and 1056. In 1064 a provincial council under *Peter Damian who had been sent by Pope Alexander II at the request of *Hugh of Cluny, ended the claims of the Bp. Drogo of Mâcon by confirming Cluny's exemption from diocesan authority. In 1072 Alexander II's legate held a council there to oppose simony, with prelates from the Provinces of Vienne and Besançon in attendance.

Bibliography: C. PERRY, *Histoire civile et ecclésiastique . . . de Chalon-sur-Saône* (Chalon-sur-Saône 1659). Hefele-Leclercq 3:201, 246–247, 282, 1143; 4:104, 636, 687, 697, 733, 1122, 1231, 1283. P. GRAS, DHGE 12:294. DTC Tables générales 704.

[A. CONDIT]

CHÂLONS-SUR-MARNE, French city and diocese, suffragan of Reims, located in northeastern France about 100 miles east of Paris, and about 25 miles southeast of Reims. L. Duchesne dates the founding of the see in the 4th century. Amandinus, who attended the Council of Tours in 461, was the ninth bishop of the see. In the 10th and following centuries, Châlons attained great prosperity under its bishops, who were ecclesiastical peers of France. In the 16th century the town sided with Henry IV, King of France, who transferred the parliament of Paris to Châlons (1589) and shortly afterward burned the bulls of Gregory XIV and Clement VIII.

The cathedral of St-Étienne dates from the 12th century, and was consecrated by Pope *Eugene III, who was assisted by 18 cardinals and St. *Bernard of Clairvaux. Its stained glass windows in the north transept were fashioned in the 13th century. The church of Notre Dame of the 12th and 13th centuries is noted for its four Romanesque towers, two flanking the apse, and two flanking the main façade. The Diocese of Châlons contains four celebrated abbeys: that of St. Memmius (5th century), Toussaints (11th century), Montier-en-Der (7th century), and St. Pierre au Mont (7th century).

Interior of the cathedral of St-Étienne at Châlons.

In 1802 Châlons was united with the Diocese of Meaux, and in 1821, with that of Reims. The Diocese of Châlons was reestablished in 1822 and since then, it has been suffragan to Reims. In 1964 the diocese had 477 parishes or quasi parishes, 260 diocesan priests, 29 seminarians, 11 religious priests, 1 newly ordained priest; 6 houses for its 65 men religious, 50 houses for its 436 women religious, 35 institutes of learning (6,210), and a Catholic population of 230,000 out of a total population of 235,894.

Bibliography: É. DE BARTHÉLEMY, *Diocèse ancien de Châlons-sur-Marne,* 2 v. (Paris 1861). J. RATH, LexThK² 2:1011. Duchesne FÉ 3:92–99. C. LAPLATTE, DHGE 12:302–329. E. JARRY, *Catholicisme* 2:873–877. **Illustration credit:** Archives Photographiques, Paris.

[D. KELLEHER]

CHAMBERS, SIR WILLIAM, with Robert Adam, dominated the English architectural scene from about 1760 to 1790; b. Sweden, 1723; d. London, 1796. After traveling extensively in the Orient with the Swedish East India Company from 1743 to 1749, Chambers studied architecture in France and Italy from 1749 to 1755. In England he became architectural tutor to the Prince of Wales and architect to the Princess Dowager, for whom he laid out the gardens at Kew Palace, Surrey (1757–1762), with Oriental and classical pavilions and temples. With this work and two publications—*Designs of Chinese Buildings, Furniture, Dresses, etc.* (1757), based on sketches made during his travels, and *Treatise on Civil Architecture* (1759)—Chambers helped to set two contrary trends that continued in England for several decades, i.e., *chinoiserie* and Neopalladianism. In 1760 Chambers and Robert

Adam were appointed royal "Architects of the Works." Chamber's fame spread by means of his many public and private buildings, and he was elected to the Swedish Academy of Sciences, the French Academy of Architecture, and the Royal Society. In 1768 Chambers became one of the founding members of the Royal Academy, which he dominated with Sir Joshua *Reynolds for nearly 30 years.

Sir William Chambers, by Joshua Reynolds.

Bibliography: H. M. COLVIN, *A Biographical Dictionary of English Architects: 1660–1840* (London 1954). J. N. SUMMERSON, *Architecture in Britain, 1530–1830* (4th ed. PelHArt Z3; 1963). **Illustration credit:** National Portrait Gallery, London.

[R. O. SWAIN]

CHAMBÉRY, ARCHDIOCESE OF (CHAMBERIENSIS), metropolitan see since 1817, corresponding to Chambéry *arrondissement* in Savoie Department, southeast France, 649 square miles in area. In 1963 it had 178 parishes, 230 secular and (in 1957) 120 religious priests, 117 men in 9 religious houses, 610 women in 65 convents, and 143,000 Catholics. Its three suffragans, which had 493 parishes, 895 priests, 1,370 sisters, and 426,506 Catholics, were: (1) *Annecy (created in 1822), which has the relics of SS. *Francis de Sales and Jane Frances de *Chantal and is the residence of the bishops and chapter of Geneva (since 1535); (2) Saint-Jean-de-Maurienne (*c.* 580, suppressed 1796–1825), which began as a shrine with relics (three fingers) of St. John the Baptist; and (3) Tarentaise (*c.* 450), a metropolitan from the 8th century until suppressed (1801) and restored as bishopric (1825). Chambéry, once part of the Diocese of *Grenoble, was long under the House of Savoy, who sought to make it a see (1474, 1515). It was created in 1779 and suppressed in the Revolution (1793) but restored by the *Concordat of 1801, with the departments of Mont-Blanc and Léman, as a suffragan of *Lyons. When Savoy went to the kingdom of Sardinia (1817), Chambéry became an archbishopric with Aosta as suffragan. In 1819 Swiss parishes went to Geneva-Lausanne; in 1822 French parishes went to Belley, and Annecy was restored; in 1825 Maurienne and Tarentaise were restored and, with Annecy and Aosta, made suffragan to Chambéry. Annexation by France (1860) removed Aosta as a suffragan. Once the capital of the Duke of Savoy, Chambéry possessed the Holy *Shroud (1502–78) before it went to *Turin; the dukes built the Sainte-Chapelle for it. Noteworthy are the pilgrimages to Our Lady in Myans (13th century), Rumilly, and Bellevaux, as well as the chapel dedicated to the Carthusian St. *Anthelm (d. 1178) and the Abbeys of *Hautecombe and Tamié.

Interior of the church of the Abbey of Hautecombe in the Archdiocese of Chambéry, France.

Bibliography: E. JARRY, *Catholicisme* 2:879–882. M. A. DIMIER, DHGE 12:331–339. AnnPont (1965) 101. **Illustration credit:** French Embassy, Press and Information Division, New York City.

[E. JARRY]

CHAMINADE, GUILLAUME JOSEPH, founder of the *Marianists and the *Marianist Sisters; B. Périgueux (Dordogne), France, April 8, 1761; d. Bordeaux, Jan. 22, 1850. After ecclesiastical studies in Périgueux, Bordeaux, and Paris, he was ordained (1784) and earned a doctorate in theology (1785). He then joined his two brothers as a teacher in the seminary of Mussidan. During the *French Revolution he refused to take the oath in support of the *Civil Constitution of the Clergy. As a nonjuring priest he exercised his ministry in disguise at Bordeaux until forced into exile in Spain (1797–1800). At the shrine of Our Lady of the Pillar in *Saragossa he was inspired to found sodalities and religious societies. Upon his return to France he centered his activities in Bordeaux for the remainder of his life. He acted as administrator of the Diocese of Bazas (1800–02) before his appointment as canon of the Bordeaux cathedral (1803). Chaminade was responsible for the return of many of the constitutional clergy and for the reestablishment of various religious societies. In 1816 he founded the Marianist Sisters; and in 1817, the Marianists. The origins of almost all pious works and benevolent institutions in Bordeaux during the first half of the 19th century have been traced to Chaminade's efforts. The *Manuel du Serviteur de Marie*

(Bordeaux 1801) was Chaminade's sole published work, but his numerous writings extant in MS form, together with the notes taken by those attending his conferences, supply a complete picture of his spirituality.

Guillaume Joseph Chaminade.

The decree introducing his cause for beatification was issued in 1918.

Bibliography: H. ROUSSEAU, *William Joseph Chaminade* (Dayton 1914). G. GOYAU, *Chaminade, fondateur des Marianistes, son action religieuse et scolaire* (Paris 1914). H. LEBON, Dict SpirAscMyst 2:454–459. K. BURTON, *Chaminade: Apostle of Mary* (Milwaukee 1949).

[G. J. RUPPEL]

CHAMINADE COLLEGE OF HONOLULU, a 4-year, coeducational liberal arts college, founded in Honolulu in 1955 by the Society of Mary, Chaminade operates as an institution of the Marianist Province of the Pacific. The board of trustees of the College is composed of administrators of the province; the advisory board, of laymen. Administrative officers include a president, an executive vice president, academic dean, dean of students, business administrator, and development director. These officers, and a faculty representative, comprise the administrative council, which is the highest policy-making body on the operational level. Chaminade is financed by a combination of tuition and fees, gifts, and a subsidy from the Society of Mary.

The faculty, averaging 32 members, is composed of Marianist priests and brothers and lay teachers. The religious-lay ratio is about equal. In 1964 faculty degrees included 9 doctorates, 1 licentiate, and 19 master's degrees. The 1963–64 enrollment was 300 students, including those from Hawaii and the U.S., South Pacific islands, and Asia.

Henry Hall on Chaminade College of Honolulu campus.

The College offers courses leading to the B.A. degree with majors in accounting, chemistry, business, liberal arts, and mathematics. Chaminade also offers elementary and secondary education programs that meet the requirements of the Hawaii Department of Education.

Campus facilities include a library containing approximately 15,000 volumes and subscribing to over 100 periodicals. The library houses a small collection of Hawaiiana. There are language and science laboratories. Some student-faculty work has been instituted in basic cancer research under a grant from the Hawaii Chapter of the American Cancer Society.

Chaminade graduated its first class in 1960. In April 1962 the College announced a long-range physical expansion program to include enrollment projection. Long-range academic planning has been inaugurated.

In 1959 the College was affiliated with The Catholic University of America, and in 1960 became the first private college in Hawaii to be accredited by the Western Association of Schools and Colleges. It is accredited by the State Department of Public Instruction, and is affiliated with the National Catholic Educational Association. It holds membership in the Council for the Advancement of Small Colleges, the American Association of Collegiate Registrars and Admissions Officers, and various other educational associations.

[T. J. MULLIGAN]

CHAMOS, national god of the Moabites (3 Kgs 11.7, 33; 4 Kgs 23.13; Jer 48.7, 13), who were "the people of Chamos" (Nm 21.29). Solomon built a temple for him on the Mount of Olives (3 Kgs 11.7, 33), which Josia destroyed (4 Kgs 23.13). He is mentioned several times in the *Mesha Inscription (Pritchard ANET 320–321): "Chamos was angry with his land" and therefore allowed the Israelites to oppress Moab many years. It was probably in these dire straits that King Mesha sacrificed his eldest son as burnt offering (4 Kgs 3.27). Appeased, the god ordered Mesha to drive out the Israelites, whom Mesha then slew at Ataroth and Nebo. The fact that children were offered to Chamos and his identification or confusion with the Ammonite god *Moloch or *Melchom in Jgs 11.24 (if not a scribal error) supports the conclusion that Chamos and Moloch were the same god. This is confirmed by the consideration that the terms Chamos, Moloch, and Melchom are merely other names for *Nergal, the Mesopotamian god of the underworld. *Astarte, who is mentioned as Chamos's consort in the Mesha Inscription, would then be equivalent to Eresh-kigal, the wife of Nergal.

Bibliography: EncDictBibl 343.

[H. MUELLER]

CHAMPAGNAT, MARCELLIN JOSEPH BENÔIT, BL., founder of the *Marist Brothers; b. Le Rosey (Loire), France, May 20, 1789; d. Notre-Dame de l'Hermitage (Loire), France, June 6, 1840 (feast, June 6). He was the second youngest of 10 children of a miller. At the major seminary in Lyons his fellow seminarians included St. Jean Baptiste *Vianney (the Curé of Ars), St. Peter *Chanel, and Ven. Jean Claude *Colin. Champagnat was one of the original group of seminarians who discussed with Colin the foundation of the *Marist Fathers. Champagnat envisioned teaching brothers as well as priests in this future congregation, and he was entrusted with carrying to

Marcellin Champagnat.

fulfillment this part of the project. After ordination (1816) Champagnat was assigned as a curate in La Valla (Loire). An encounter there with a dying boy who was totally ignorant of Catholic teachings expedited the foundation of the Marist Brothers (Jan. 2, 1817). In 1824 he was relieved of parish duties to devote himself to organizing and directing his institute, which had 240 members by 1840, but it remained separate from the Marist Fathers. Champagnat continued meanwhile to work toward the creation of the Marist Fathers. He pronounced his vows as a member in 1836 when Rome approved the congregation. In 1853 Champagnat published his pedagogical ideas in *Guide des Écoles,* a work that has been reprinted many times and that serves as a norm for the Marist Brothers. Champagnat was beatified May 29, 1955.

Bibliography: BROTHER JEAN BAPTISTE, *Life and Spirit of J. B. M. Champagnat* (Paris 1947). G. CHASTEL, *Marcellin Champagnat* (Paris 1939). BROTHER IGNACE, *Le Bx. Marcellin Champagnat* (Paris 1955). J. VIGNON, *Le Père Champagnat* (Paris 1952). J. ÉMILE, DictSpirAscMyst 2:459–461. J. COSTE and G. LESSARD, eds., *Origines maristes,* 4 v. (Rome 1960–66).

[L. A. VOEGTLE]

CHAMPAIGNE, PHILIPPE DE (CHAMPAGNE), one of the original members of the Academy of Painting and Sculpture, later (1655) professor and then rector of that institution; b. Brussels, Belgium, May 26, 1602; d. Paris, Aug. 12, 1674. Trained in Brussels, chiefly by Jacques Fouquières (Fouquière), as a landscape artist, Philippe moved to Paris (1621), where he entered the atelier of Georges Lallemand. At about the same time he collaborated with Poussin on the decoration of the Luxembourg palace. In 1628 he was appointed painter to the Queen Mother, Marie de' Medici. He gained the favors also of Louis XIII and Cardinal Richelieu, for whom he executed both easel paintings and mural decorations. Philippe is remembered principally, however, for his masterfully objective portraiture in a baroque style reminiscent of *Rubens and *Van Dyck (e.g., "Cardinal Richelieu," 1635–40, National Gallery, London; *see* RICHELIEU, ARMAND JEAN DU PLESSIS DE). After 1643, when he began to work for the Jansenists of Port Royal, his style became increasingly austere and more strictly naturalistic. The masterpiece of this period, unsurpassed for its simplicity and religious feeling, is the "Two Nuns of Port Royal" (1662, Louvre; *see* ARNAULD).

Bibliography: H. STEIN, *Philippe de Champaigne et ses relations avec Port-Royal* (Paris 1891). A. GAZIER, *Philippe et J.-B. de C.* (Paris 1893). S. MEUNIER, *P. de C.* (Paris 1924). H. S. EDE, "The Drawings of P. de C.," *Art in America* 12 (1924) 253–268. W. WEISBACH, *P. de C. und Port-Royal* (Berlin 1929). A. MABILLE DE PONCHEVILLE, *P. de C.* (Paris 1938). B. DORIVAL, *P. de C.* (Paris 1952); "P. de C. et Robert Arnauld d'Andilly," *Revue des Arts* 8 (1958) 128–136. J. VERGNET-RUIZ, "Les Peintures de l'Ordre du Saint-Esprit," *Revue du Louvre* 12 (1962) 160–162. **Illustration credit.** National Gallery of Art, Washington, D.C., Samuel H. Kress Collection.

[L. A. LEITE]

CHAMPLAIN, SAMUEL DE

Explorer and colonizer; b. Brouage, Saintonge, France, *c.* 1567; d. Quebec, Canada, Dec. 25, 1635. He was the son of Antoine and Marguerite (LeRoy) Champlain. In the capacity of King's geographer, he visited the West Indies and Mexico, and in 1603 he

Philippe de Champaigne, "Omer Talon," oil on canvas, 88½ by 63⅝ inches.

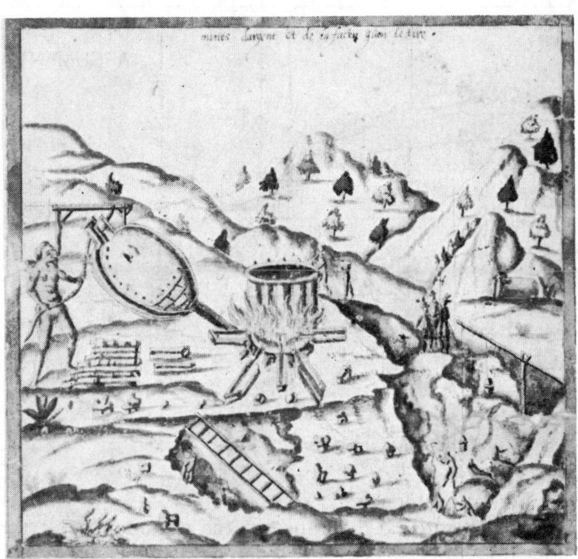

Drawing showing the workings of a silver mine, from an autograph manuscript of Samuel de Champlain's "Narrative of a Voyage to the Spanish Indies" (c. 1602).

went to Canada, visiting the St. Lawrence River and exploring the Saguenay gorge and the Richelieu River. The following year he first became associated with the fur trading expedition of Sieur de Monts, who unsuccessfully attempted to form a settlement on St. Croix Island in Acadia (Nova Scotia); Champlain then crossed the Bay of Fundy to make a second unsuccessful attempt at Port Royal. Despite the failures, Champlain was not particularly discouraged, and between 1604 and 1607 he explored the coastline southward to Martha's Vineyard. For France the potential value of the newly discovered region (the present day Provinces of the Maritimes and Quebec) lay in the fur trade, and in 1607 Champlain was selected as the leader of another fur trading company to found a trading post further in the interior of the continent. In 1608 he founded Quebec City, which, with its tremendous natural fortification on the St. Lawrence River, became the center of a French colony and of continental exploring operations that eventually reached the Western prairies, the Gulf of Mexico, and the frozen north. Within 150 years after Champlain's foundation, the vast colony of New France extended from New Orleans to Hudson Bay and from Quebec to the Rockies.

To secure the fur-bearing animals the assistance of the Indians was essential, and in 1613 Champlain ascended the Ottawa River and reached Georgian Bay, where he made an alliance with the Huron Indians. Unfortunately a subsequent French-Huron attack on the Iroquois Indians in northern New York had disastrous and far-reaching effects on the French—for the next 50 years Quebec and later Montreal were subject to almost constant forays by the savage Iroquois. By 1648, through the efforts of Franciscan and Jesuit missionaries who accompanied Champlain on his voyages, a large part of the Huron tribe had been civilized and Christianized. Champlain was first named commandant (1612) and later became governor (1627) of New France under A. J. Richelieu's Company of One Hundred Associates, formed to correct abuses and further France's interests in the New World. However, the fur traders had little interest in permanent colonization; and the cold climate as well as the menace of Indians, the hardships of primitive conditions, and the presence of the hostile English to the south in New England were further deterrents to the establishment of a flourishing New France. Consequently the colony progressed very slowly. In 1629 the English under Louis Kirks forced the surrender of Quebec, and Champlain returned to Europe, where he spent 3 years negotiating for the return of Quebec. After this was accomplished by the Treaty of St. Germain-en-Laye (1632), he returned to his post, landing May 1633 at Quebec, where he died 2 years later.

Champlain's works describing his explorations include *Des sauvages* (1604), *Les voyages du Sieur de Champlain* (1613), *Voyages et découvertes faites en la Nouvelle-France* (1619), *Les voyages du Sr. de Champlain* (1620), *Les voyages de la Nouvelle France occidentale* (1632). His works were reprinted, translated, and annotated under the general editorship of H. P. Biggar (Toronto 1922–36).

Bibliography: M. G. Bishop, *Champlain: The Life of Fortitude* (New York 1948; pa. Toronto 1963); *White Men came to the St. Lawrence: The French and the Land They Found* (Montreal 1961). C. W. Colby, *The Founder of New France* (Toronto 1920). N. E. Dionne, *Samuel Champlain, fondateur de Quebec,* 2 v. (Quebec 1891–1906). G. Gravier, *La Vie de Samuel Champlain* (Paris 1899). F. Parkman, *The Pioneers of France in the New World* (Boston 1865). **Illustration credit:** John Carter Brown Library, Brown University, Providence, R.I.

[F. BOLAND]

CHAMPOLLION, JEAN FRANÇOIS, founder of *Egyptology; b. Figeac, Lot, France, Dec. 23, 1790; d. Paris, March 4, 1832. After his early education received at home from his older brother Jacques Joseph, he studied Oriental languages at Paris (1807–09) and at the Lycée de Grenoble, where he was later appointed professor of history (1816). This post, however, he soon had to relinquish because of his liberal views. Thereafter, having mastered Coptic before he was 16, he devoted much time to the study of Egyptian monuments and in 1814 published his two-volume *L'Égypte sous les Pharaons.* The bilingual inscription on the *Rosetta Stone served him as the means for deciphering the Egyptian hieroglyphic and demotic scripts. The results of this study were presented to the Académie des Inscriptions et Belles Lettres in his *Lettre à M. Dacier relative à l'alphabet des hiéroglyphes phonétiques* on Sept. 29, 1822, and in his *Précis du system hiéroglyphique* in 1824. In 1824 he left for Italy to study Egyptian manuscripts and monuments in the museums of Turin, Leghorn, Rome, and Naples. In 1828–29 he led a joint expedition, with Ippolito Rosellini, to Egypt and Nubia. In 1831 he became professor of Egyptian archeology at the College de France. His Egyptian grammar and dictionary, as well as the epigraphical material from his archeological expeditions, were published posthumously by his older brother.

Bibliography: H. Hartleben, *Champollion: Sein Leben und sein Werk,* 2 v. (Berlin 1906). G. Castellino, EncCatt 3: 1380–81.

[B. MARCZUK]

CHANCA ÁLVAREZ, DIEGO, Spanish physician of the 15th century, first European scientist who observed and described nature in America; b. Seville, date unknown; place and date of death unknown. In 1491 he was at the court and served as physician to Princess Juana. In May 1493 he received a royal command to sail with Christopher Columbus on his second voyage to America, and was given the title of scribe of the Indies. Accordingly, at the close of January 1494 he wrote a *Carta relación* addressed to the city of Seville, in which he told of his voyage and described customs and elements of nature observed on the island of Santo Domingo. He later returned to Spain, and in 1506 published in Seville the study *Para curar el dolor de costado.* In 1514 he printed, at the print shop of Cromberger in the same city, *Commentum novum in parabolis divi Arnaldi de Vilanova.* The *Carta relación* was not published until Martín Fernández de Navarrete published it in 1825 in *Colección de los viajes y discubrimientos que hicieron por mar los españoles,* taking it from a 16th century copy that is still preserved in the Academy of History of Madrid. Sometimes his names appear in reverse order as Diego Álvarez Chanca.

[G. SOMOLINOS]

CHANCE

The term chance (Lat. *casus*) is used in a variety of ways. In some contexts it is considered as that which is entirely without cause; this was the view of *Democritus and *Lucretius. Other writers count chance as a cause, but differ as to the kind of causality it exercises. Thus some modern scientists, such as Max Born, maintain that chance is the cause of all things; A. *Einstein, on the other hand, protested against this thesis by saying that God does not play dice. Others call chance a cause but insist that it is indeterminate, either because it is the result of a basic *indeterminism in *nature or because the human intellect cannot encompass the various lines of causality that exist. What these various notions have in common can be clarified by a proper definition of chance, and this is the burden of the present article.

Aristotle's Analysis. *Aristotle attempted such a clarification in bk. 2 of the *Physics* (195b 30–198a 13), where he made use of several distinctions in his search for a definition of chance. Of things that come to be, some come to be always in the same way, whereas others do not. Of the latter, some come to be often, whereas others come to be seldom. Chance is found among those things that happen seldom; however, since not everything that happens seldom is by chance, other divisions are necessary to manifest the definition. A further division considers events that happen for a purpose and those that do not. Of the former, some are the result of an intention—whether this be the intention of an intelligent agent or simply what is intended by nature—whereas others are not.

Apart from these distinctions, Aristotle proposes also a division based on causes, since most thinkers agree that chance is in some way a cause. Thus he holds that just as beings are either *per se* or *per accidens,* so also are causes. For example, assuming that a white, musical builder constructs a house, the builder is the *per se* cause of the house, whereas white and musical are its *per accidens* causes. Among *per accidens* causes, some are such by reason of something accidentally associated with the cause, as in the example mentioned, and others are such by reason of something accidentally associated with the effect—for example, an argument that might arise over the house already built. The difference is shown in the accompanying diagram. Chance itself is a kind of *per accidens* cause that results from something

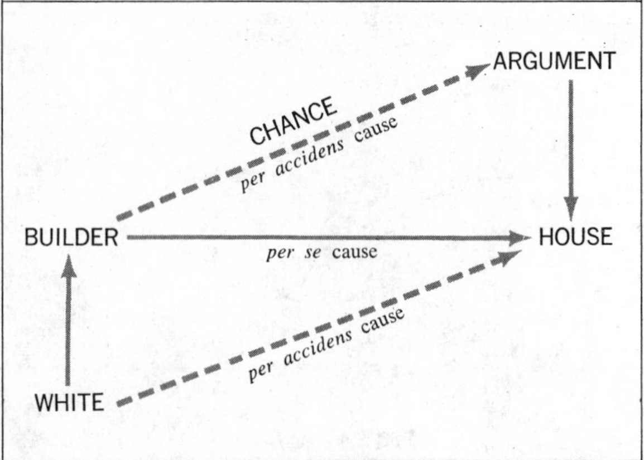

Accidental causality of chance.

accidentally associated with an effect, as the builder just chances to be the cause of the argument over the house. (Notice that in this case one *per se* cause is also a *per accidens* cause; in the case of a *per accidens* cause that is such by reason of something accidentally associated with a *per se* cause, the latter cause is itself composite, namely, the white builder.)

Utilizing these divisions, Aristotle defines chance as a *per accidens* cause in things that are for an end and that happen seldom. As something happening seldom, the effect in chance is something neither intended nor expected by the agent. Aristotle's example is a man who collects money by going to market for some purpose other than collecting money. If such a man always or usually collected money by going to market, this event would not be by chance.

A further clarification of the notion of chance is achieved by Aristotle's contrasting the chance with the vain. An action is vain when that which was intended does not happen. Aristotle shows that actions can be (1) vain and chance, (2) vain and not chance, (3) chance and not vain, and (4) neither vain nor chance. Suppose that Socrates goes to market to buy cabbage. It might happen that the store is out of cabbage but that Socrates does meet his friend who owed him a debt: vain and chance. Again, he might neither get the cabbage nor meet his friend: vain and not chance. Yet again, he might get the cabbage and meet his friend: chance and not vain. Finally, he might get the cabbage and not meet his friend: neither vain nor chance.

The failure to distinguish between the chance and the vain has led some to hold that chance happens only when the intended end is not achieved. However, as has been seen, there can be chance whether the intended end is achieved or not. What is necessary is that some end be intended. If an agent who acts by intelligence and will attains the unintended end, this is usually called *fortune. Among Aristotelians, the term chance is reserved for agents who act by nature.

Causal Intersections. From this definition of chance it is possible to explain the various positions held concerning it. In the first place, philosophers who hold that all things happen of necessity deny that chance exists. Even among philosophers who admit the existence of chance, there are those who hold that chance causes nothing since it is a *per accidens* cause. It is certainly true that there is an accidental unity in whatever results from chance. It is true also that two or more *per se* causes will be found to have been acting in the production of such an event. St. *Thomas Aquinas thus says that ". . . a cause which hinders the action of a cause so ordered to its effect as to produce it in the majority of cases, clashes sometimes with this cause by accident: and the clashing of these two causes, inasmuch as it is accidental, has no cause. Consequently what results from this clashing of causes is not to be reduced to a further pre-existing cause, from which it follows of necessity" (ST la, 115.6). The last statement, that the *per accidens* intersection of two lines of causality is not to be reduced to a further preexisting cause, must be understood of a cause preexisting in nature. Aquinas notes in another place: "Let us suppose that a man is prompted to dig a grave by the influence of a celestial body, working through his emotions, as was said. Now the grave and the location of the treasure are united only accidentally, for they have no intrinsic relation to each other. Thus the power of the celestial body cannot directly give an inclination to this entire result, namely, that this man should dig this grave and that it should be done at the place where the treasure is. But an agent working by intellect can be the cause of an inclination to this entire result, for it is proper for an intelligent being to order many things toward one" (*C. gent.* 3.92). Aquinas further observes that man's intellect can cause an event that in nature would be by chance. He continues, ". . . fortuitous events of this kind, when referred to their divine cause, lose their fortuitous aspect; but when referred to a celestial cause, they do not" (*ibid.*). Thus chance remains even when the combined effect might be caused by the ordering of a higher cause. The reason is that nature, in this case the celestial body as a natural cause, produces effects that are *per se* one. It cannot have, as a proper effect, something that is only accidentally one. Of such it can be only the *per accidens* cause. This shows also that chance is more than mere ignorance of the concatenation of causes and that chance results from the inability of the lower cause to control causal intersections.

Accidental Causality. The notion that chance is the cause of all things results from a different kind of confusion over the *per accidens*. In the *Metaphysics* (1013b 34–1014a 20) Aristotle again discusses the causes and their division into *per se* and *per accidens*. St. Thomas's commentary on this point is illuminating (*In 5 meta.* 3.789). He states that the *per se* cause can become a *per accidens* cause by reason of something happening to the effect in one of three ways. (1) It may come about in such a way that what is added to the *per se* effect has a necessary order to it, as happens when the primary effect removes an obstacle to the secondary effect. This may happen when a contrary is removed, as when food is spoiled by removing it from a refrigerator, not because heat itself spoils the food, but because the refrigerator's cold opposed the growth of bacteria that is a cause of the food's spoiling. There can also be a necessary connection of effects when there is no contrariety, as when an arch falls because a pillar is removed. When the secondary effect follows the primary in this way, the *per accidens* cause is not called chance, since such added effects follow always or often. (2) Again, the secondary effect can follow the primary effect, not as something necessary or often, but as happening seldom, as the argument over the house or the finding of a treasure by one digging a grave. The *per accidens* cause of such a secondary effect is called chance or fortune. (3) Finally, the connection between two events may be only in the mind, as one might imagine that his opening a door was the cause of an earthquake, because a tremor occurred just as he was opening the door.

Chance and Luck. Thus not every intersection of lines of causality is to be attributed to chance. If a person decides to cross a muddy street, he should not attribute the soiling of his shoes to chance merely because he did not intend this effect. Such would be chance only if it happened seldom to one who crossed a muddy street. In spite of this, many use the term chance in such indiscriminate fashion. They speak of taking a chance on the horses or of luck in a dice game. Chance in a strict sense is not found in such actions. Suppose, for example, a person bets on a horse and loses. This is not chance but vain. Similarly, if he bets on a horse and wins, to call this chance is to overlook the fact that the winning was what was intended, whereas chance is something that is not intended but is accidentally associated with a primary effect. There is justification for the use of the term chance in such instances, however, because the mind, seeing the general rule, counts what departs from this only slightly as something that has already happened. For example, a person calls the lost wager bad luck because he has carefully considered the factors and come to the firm belief that the possibility of this horse's losing the race is so small that it can be ignored. In other words, he considers the connection of primary and secondary effects to be that of (1) above. The winning is attributed to chance in a similar way. The person bets on the horse, keenly aware that he wins seldom; considering this, he in effect forgets or ignores the fact that he actually intends to win. When he does win, it is something that happens seldom and is, in a way, unintended.

Randomness and Probability. Chance is used improperly in another way when applied to *randomness or *probability. For example, it might be said that an even distribution of sand and cement comes about by chance since it is the result of a random mixing. Again, the killing of a bird by one or two of the many shot pellets fired is said to be accounted for by the laws of chance. This overlooks the fact that the end was intended and, more important in this example, is something probable, whereas chance is what happens seldom. Yet nature is also said to use chance in this way to accomplish her ends. In her production of great numbers of seeds and of many individuals of each species, she intends the preservation of such species. In the circumstances, this seems to be the most economical means of achieving her ends.

That such a use of the term chance is that of Democritus, of Lucretius, and of many modern scientists seems further evidenced by the latters' reference to the laws of chance as laws of probability. Even the term law, when used here, indicates a regularity that is foreign to the proper definition of chance. On the other hand, Einstein's maintaining that God does not play dice is well founded. If God is throwing dice to achieve His effects, He does not do so as a casual player awaiting a fortunate turn of a seven or eleven. Rather, He is more like the scientist investigating probabilities, who throws the dice countless times with the firm assurance that these numbers will occur with a definite frequency.

This last consideration seems to be the basis of the denial of chance by such thinkers as B. *Spinoza, and G. W. *Leibniz. They hold that chance results only from the fact that man's intellect cannot encompass the causes at work in any event. Thus, for a greater intellect, chance would not exist. However, although it is true that for a greater intellect there are fewer effects owed to chance and that for the divine intellect nothing is by chance, chance is nonetheless a reality. In effect, these last thinkers are denying indeterminism in nature. Such a solution ignores the fact that something ordained with certainty by a higher cause can still be contingent when considered in its relation to lower causes.

See also FATE AND FATALISM; CONTINGENCY; DETERMINISM, PHYSICAL; NECESSITY.

Bibliography: H. J. FREEMAN, *The Problem of Chance* (Doctoral diss. unpub. River Forest, Ill. 1963). M. BORN, *Natural Philosophy of Cause and Chance* (Oxford 1949). C. DE KONINCK, "Abstraction from Matter, III," *Laval Théologique et Philosophique* 16 (1960) 169–188. A. ALIOTTA, EncFil 1:921–927. Eisler 3:667–670. Syntopicon 1:179–192.

[R. A. KOCOUREK]

CHANCELLOR, DIOCESAN (EPARCHIAL)

The chancellor of a diocese is a priest whose principal work is to care for the archives of the diocese. The word "chancellor" comes from the Latin *cancellarius.* In ancient Rome the *cancellarius* was the doorkeeper who stood at the latticework or chancel, which separated the magistrate in the law courts from the people, and admitted petitioners. He gradually assumed the work of a kind of secretary or notary with judicial powers. The term chancellor was later given to the civil notaries whom the bishops were empowered to appoint by the legislation of Charlemagne.

As the curias of the bishops began to develop, the need grew for repeated use of authentic documents and written testimony drawn up by a public person of ecclesiastical authority. The Fourth Council of the Lateran (1215) ordered bishops to have a public person or two other competent men for the work of drawing up both judicial and extrajudicial acts (CorpIurCan X 2.19.11; cf. Mansi, 23.154). These officials came to be termed variously: chancellors, notaries, actuaries, and *tabelliones.*

The Third Provincial Council of Milan (1573), besides designating the chancellor as notary, also made him custodian of the archives. One of its decrees ordered the curial documents to be preserved in the episcopal archives under the care of the chancellor, who was to keep the key to them. This and other local legislation and custom gradually produced the general law setting up the office of chancellor with his double function of public notary in the curia and custodian of the diocesan archives.

Under present law (CIC c.372), the chancellor is the authorized official whose chief functions are to preserve in the archives the acts of the curia, to arrange them in chronological order, and to compile an index of them. By reason of his office the chancellor is also a notary (CIC c.373).

As to qualifications, he must be a priest of good reputation and of undisputed reliability. Though the Code does not say so, it is obvious that he must be proficient in Canon Law.

His appointment, as well as its revocation, depends entirely on the will of the bishop (CIC c.152). It cannot be revoked by the vicar capitular (or diocesan administrator) without the consent of the cathedral chapter (or the assembled diocesan consultors). If necessary, the chancellor may be given an assistant with the name of vice-chancellor. The chancellor performs his duties in subordination to the bishop and the vicar-general.

In many dioceses, particularly in the U.S., the chancellor enjoys many of the powers of the bishop. These are not given to him, however, by the general law, which defines his duties merely as those of archivist-notary. In such instances he receives delegated jurisdiction, in whole or in part, from his bishop (CIC c.199.1), and not by virtue of his office (CIC c.198).

See also CURIA, DIOCESAN (EPARCHIAL).

Bibliography: Abbo 1:372. Woywod-Smith 277. L. MATHIAS, *The Diocesan Curia* (Madras 1947) 35-39. J. E. PRINCE, *The Diocesan Chancellor* (CUA CLS 167; Washington 1942). Wernz-Vidal 2:644–645.

[E. A. FORBES]

CHANCERY, APOSTOLIC

The Apostolic Chancery is that office of the Roman *Curia charged with sending the more important apostolic letters, or bulls.

History. Its origin goes back to the early ages of the Church when notaries were first appointed to draw up papal documents. Under Constantine it assumed a more definite form, presumably modeled after the Roman chancery. Under Gregory the Great the notaries were organized as a group or "college," headed by the chief notary, the *primicerius notariorum.* Other functions besides the recording of documents came to be associated with these officials, some of whom under the name of *scrinarii* had charge of the papal archives. The *primicerius* had also judicial functions and, as head of the *iudices palatini,* was for a time the most influential official in the papal administration. Toward the end of the 8th century the functions of the *primicerius* passed to the *bibliothecarius* (librarian). Under Pope Gelasius II (1118–19) this official was a cardinal; the office was later suppressed, giving place to that of the cardinal *cancellarius,* or chancellor, true successor of the *primicerius.* The office was afterward held by clerics not of cardinalitial rank, with the title of vice-chancellor, a designation that was retained even when (under John XXII, 1316–34) the office was definitely assigned to a cardinal.

Pius X restored the title of chancellor. The second in command under the chancellor is called the regent, an office that originated in this way. When Gregory XI, persuaded by St. Catherine of Siena, left Avignon for Rome in 1377, the Cardinal Vice-Chancellor, Pierre de Montéruc, refused to follow him and remained in France; whereupon the Pope named Bartolomeo Prignano to take his place with the title of regent. When this same Bartolomeo was elected pope (Urban VI) a new regent was appointed, and this practice continued even after the vice-chancellor again resided regularly in Rome. The successors of the ancient notaries are, since the 14th century, called protonotaries. As the work of the Chancery grew, a host of minor offices were created: *abbreviatores, correctores, scriptores, plumbatores.* The college of *abbreviatores* consisted of no fewer than 72 members, divided into three groups: *de parco maiori*

(12), *de parco minori* (22), and *de prima visione* (38). These officials had also some judicial functions and enjoyed special privileges by grant of various popes.

From the 15th century the competence of the Chancery was much reduced by the introduction of the new form of apostolic letters called briefs, and later by the creation of the Secretariate of Briefs (Innocent XI, 1678). The so-called *Regulae Cancellariae,* first developed by tradition and later reduced to writing (under John XXII), were 72 norms governing the practice of the Chancery. They were supplanted by the Code in 1918.

Present Organization and Practice. The Apostolic Chancery consists of the cardinal chancellor, a regent, seven protonotaries apostolic *de numero participantium,* and seven subordinate officials. The constitution *Sapienti consilio* provided that the cardinal in charge should thenceforth be called chancellor, not vice-chancellor, and that the sole function of the Chancery should be the sending of bulls for the provision of consistorial benefices, the establishment of new dioceses and chapters, and other important matters upon order of the Consistorial Congregation or the Pope. The *abbreviatores* are suppressed, and their function restored to the protonotaries.

Of the four former methods of sending the letters, the three less formal ones, viz, *per viam secretam, de Camera* and *de Curia* are suppressed; all must thenceforth be sent *per viam Cancellariae,* that is, observing the traditional formalities of the Chancery. These provisions passed into the Code of Canon Law in canon 260. The document called a bull, more solemn and important than a brief, was formerly distinguished by a hanging seal (*bulla*) of lead (*sub plumbo*). Leo XIII substituted, for all but the more momentous ones, a red seal with the images of SS. Peter and Paul and the name of the reigning pontiff. A decree of the Consistorial Congregation, issued in 1910 by special mandate of Pius X requiring that bulls be signed by both the cardinal chancellor and the cardinal prefect of the Congregation that is competent in the matter at hand, is still observed. Upon the death of a pope, the office of the chancellor does not expire, but his power to issue bulls is suspended and the seal of the Chancery is broken.

Bibliography: N. HILLING, *Procedure at the Roman Curia* (New York 1907). M. MARTIN, *The Roman Curia as It Now Exists* (New York 1913). E. HESTON, *The Holy See at Work* (Milwaukee 1950). B. OJETTI, *De Romana Curia: Commentarium in constitutionem apostolicam "Sapienti consilio"* (Rome 1910). Wernz-Vidal 2.

[T. L. BOUSCAREN]

CHANDLER, JOSEPH RIPLEY, journalist; b. Kingston, Mass., Aug. 25, 1792; d. Philadelphia, Pa., July 10, 1880. He was the son of Joseph and Saba (Ripley) Chandler. Although largely self-educated, he conducted a girls' seminary in Philadelphia from 1818 until 1826, when with a small group of associates he purchased the newspaper *Gazette of the United States.* He eventually became sole proprietor and made the *Gazette* one of the most influential Whig journals until 1847, when he sold it to the *North American.* In 1848 he became an editor of *Graham's American Monthly Magazine of Literature.*

Chandler was a member of Philadelphia's common council (1832–48) and a delegate to the state constitutional convention of 1837; he was also president of the first board of trustees of Girard College, Philadelphia, and grand master of the Pennsylvania Freemasons. He had married a Catholic in 1833 and in 1849 was received into the Church. Elected to Congress in 1848 as a Clay Whig, he was twice reelected. His speech "The Temporal Power of the Pope," delivered in the House in 1855, answered Rep. Nathaniel Banks's charge that Catholicism was incompatible with political liberty. In 1858 Chandler was appointed U.S. minister to the Kingdom of the Two Sicilies, where he served until 1861. Returning to Philadelphia, he renewed an earlier interest in penology. A member of the board of inspectors of the county prison (1861–80), he represented the Philadelphia Society for Alleviating the Miseries of Public Prisons at an international congress in London in 1872.

Several of Chandler's orations were published in pamphlet form, but the elegant and highly moral fugitive pieces upon which his literary reputation rested have never been collected. His other works include *A Grammar of the English Language* (1821, rev. ed., 1848), a text widely used in public schools, and *The Beverly Family or the Home Influence of Religion* (1875), a didactic novel preaching religious tolerance.

Bibliography: M. SHAVER, DAB (1928) 3:614–615.

[F. GERRITY]

CHANDLER, THEOPHILUS PARSONS, American architect; b. Boston, 1845; d. Delaware County, Pa., 1928. After attending Harvard University he studied architecture both in the U.S. and in Paris. On his return he opened an office in Boston, but in 1870 he moved to Philadelphia. Chandler is best known for his church designs. Two of these in Philadelphia were the Swedenborgian Church on Chestnut Street, and the

Theophilus Parsons Chandler, St. Thomas Episcopal Church, Washington, D.C., c. 1900.

Bethlehem Presbyterian Church. He planned the neo-Gothic First Presbyterian Church in Pittsburgh in 1905 as well as St. Thomas Church in Washington, D.C. Other Chandler buildings in Philadelphia were a residence for John Wanamaker, and the Liverpool, London, and Globe Insurance Building. He was an eclectic designer, not following consistently any particular period. His Grace Memorial Church in Darlington, Md., was simple Gothic revival. However, some of the residences that he planned show details from a variety of styles, as was fashionable in the late 19th century. Chandler helped organize the University of Pennsylvania School of Architecture and was its first director. He also helped to found the Philadelphia chapter of the American Institute of Architects and later was made a fellow of the institute.

Bibliography: Pennsylvania Writers' Project, *Pennsylvania: A Guide to the Keystone State* (New York 1940). *American Architecture and Building News* 4 (Aug. 10, Aug. 17, Oct. 5, 1878); 5 (June 14, 1879); 12 (Dec. 2, 1882); 21 (March 5, 1887); 26 (Oct. 5, 1889). H. F. and E. R. WITHEY, *Biographical Dictionary of American Architects* (Los Angeles 1956).

[M. E. STITES]

CHANEL, PETER, ST., missionary; b. Cuet (Ain), France, July 12, 1803; d. Futuna Island, Oceania, April 28, 1841 (feast, April 28). After ordination he joined the recently founded *Marist Fathers (1831) and sailed (1836) with Bishop *Pompallier as provicar and superior of the seven Marists to whom was entrusted the vicariate of Western Oceania, established that year. When still 1,500 miles from his eventual headquarters in New Zealand, the Bishop left Pierre *Bataillon and one brother on Wallis Island, and Chanel and Brother Nizier on neighboring Futuna (1837). Pompallier proposed to return in 6 months, but circumstances delayed him for 5 years. In his isolation Chanel struggled with an unknown language and was wholly dependent on inconstant chiefs for material needs, but he made the difficult adjustment to a world of whalers, traders, and warring tribes of savages. His serene, gentle character endured with profound faith, patience, and fortitude the frustrations of apparent failure, severe privations, and finally, active persecution by the principal chief. A few had been baptized, a few more were being instructed, when Chanel was surrounded in his hut and clubbed to death, becoming thereby Oceania's first martyr. In 1843 the whole island became Catholic and has remained so. Chanel was beatified Nov. 17, 1889, and canonized June 12, 1954.

St. Peter Chanel.

See also WALLIS AND FUTUNA ISLANDS.

Bibliography: C. ROZIER, *Écrits du Père Pierre Chanel,* (Paris 1960), with full bibliog. W. SYMES, *Life of St. Peter Chanel* (Bolton, Eng. 1963).

[J. E. BELL]

CHANGANACHERI, ARCHDIOCESE OF (CHANGANACHERRENSIS), a *Malabar-rite metropolitan see since 1956, in Kerala state, south *India. In 1963 there were 134 parishes, 261 secular and 105 religious priests, 129 men in 22 religious houses, 1,416 women in 85 convents, and 361,713 Catholics in a population of 5 million. A surge in religious life, conversions, and missionary activity has almost doubled Catholic statistics (1959–64). Its suffragans, Kottayam (created in 1923) and Palai (1950), had 475 priests, 1,823 sisters, and about 1 million Catholics. From the vicariate established in 1896 to care for Malabar Catholics was detached the vicariate of Kottayam (1911), comprising parishes of Southists (descended from 4th-century Syrian immigrants). Northists descend from native Malabar castes. In 1923 Changanacheri became a diocese, suffragan to *Ernakulam. There are 4 university colleges, 171 primary and secondary schools, one daily newspaper, and 5 monthly periodicals.

Bibliography: E. TISSERANT, *Eastern Christianity in India,* tr. E. R. HAMBYE (Westminster, Md. 1957). OrientCatt 379–392. *The Catholic Directory of India, 1962* (Allahabad, India 1962). AnnPont (1965) 101.

[E. R. HAMBYE]

CHANGE. Greek philosophy had its origin in curiosity over the change that takes place in nature. The fact of change is evident and neither can, nor needs to be proved. *Heraclitus and his followers saw change as the essential characteristic of all things, to the exclusion of any permanent being. *Parmenides, by emphasizing the permanence of being, denied the reality of change. *Aristotle, at the beginning of his *Physics,* had to defend the possibility of change by assigning principles that make change intelligible. In speaking of change in general (μεταβολή) he sometimes uses in an equivalent sense the terms κίνησις, motion, and γένεσις, becoming. Usually the two latter are given as species of μεταβολή.

The pre-Socratics had not distinguished types of change, but attempted to explain all changes in terms of the most obvious kind, local motion. Aristotle, by distinguishing the types of being, was able to assign corresponding types of change. For him, changes are substantial when a new nature comes into existence. Such changes are called generation or *becoming of the new substance and corruption or passing away of the old (*see* GENERATION-CORRUPTION). *Substantial changes are instantaneous. Continuous changes are called *motion. These include local motion; alteration, or change in quality; and growth and decline, or change in quantity.

Christian theology added the concepts of *creation, a kind of production that is not strictly a change, because there is no subject that undergoes change; and of *transubstantiation, or the change of the whole substance, which takes place in the consecration of the Eucharist. Modern biology speaks of evolution and of mutations. The nature, principles, causes, and laws of change enter into the subject matter of psychology, history, and political science and into every human endeavor. Change, or process, is seen by modern thinkers such as Henri *Bergson and A. N. *Whitehead as the very essence of reality.

See also PHILOSOPHY OF NATURE.

[M. A. GLUTZ]

CHANGSHA, ARCHDIOCESE OF (CIAMSCIAVENSIS), metropolitan see since 1946, in central *China. The city of Changsha (Ch'ang-sha) is the capital of Hu-nan province. Statistics of 1950, the latest available, showed the see, 8,811 square miles in area, to have 11 parishes, 6 secular and 27 religious priests, 36 women in 4 convents, and 9,000 Catholics in a population of 5 million. Its three suffragans, all created in 1946, Ch'ang-te, Heng-yang, and Yüan-ling, had 69 priests, 45 sisters, and 22,000 Catholics in a population of 11 million.

The area of Changsha, evangelized *c.* 1650, was part of the Diocese of *Macao, administered by François *Pallu (1659), and then part of the Diocese of *Nanking (1690) before becoming in 1696 the Vicariate of Hukwang (Hu-nan and Hu-pei provinces). Despite the lack of a resident vicar apostolic in the 18th century, and despite persecutions (1752–53, 1816), the Church survived, thanks especially to Jesuit missionaries. The Vicariate of Hukwang, restored in 1838, was divided into the Vicariates of Hu-nan and Hu-pei in 1856. Hunan was divided into north and south vicariates (1879), the latter being called Changsha in 1924. From the Changsha Vicariate (1924–46) were carved the Vicariate of Heng-yang (1930) and the Prefectures of Lingling or Yung-chow (1925) and Hsian-yang (1937). Changsha's Christian history is parallel to that of *Hankow.

Bibliography: *Annuaire de l'Église catholique en Chine* (Shanghai 1950). MissCattol 366–371. G. TRAGELLA, EncCatt 3:1381–82.

[J. KRAHL]

CHANNING, WILLIAM ELLERY, Unitarian clergyman and author; b. Newport, R.I., April 7, 1780; d. Bennington, Vt., Oct. 2, 1842. He belonged to a prominent New England family. Five years after his graduation (1798) from Harvard, he was ordained a minister in the Congregational Church. Shortly afterward he became pastor of Federal Street Church in Boston, Mass., where he remained until his death. In 1814 he married his cousin Ruth Gibbs. Channing's sermon at Jared Spark's ordination (1819) in Baltimore, Md., earned him the title "apostle of Unitarianism." He soon became involved in the controversy that divided the Congregationalists of New England into the so-called orthodox Calvinists and the opposition group, or Unitarians. In 1820 he organized a conference of liberal Congregational ministers, and 5 years later he formed the American Unitarian Association (*see* UNITARIAN UNIVERSALIST ASSOCIATION). Channing's form of religious liberalism emphasized humanitarianism and toleration rather than doctrinal novelties. His sermons and writings exercised considerable influence over American authors such as R. W. Emerson, W. C. Bryant, H. W. Longfellow, J. R. Lowell, and O. W. Holmes. For Channing, all questions were moral questions. He was ahead of his time in his views on temperance, labor problems, and public and adult education. He considered slavery an evil to be wiped out at the earliest possible opportunity. A pacifist, Channing organized the Massachussetts Peace Society to destroy the romantic glamour of war.

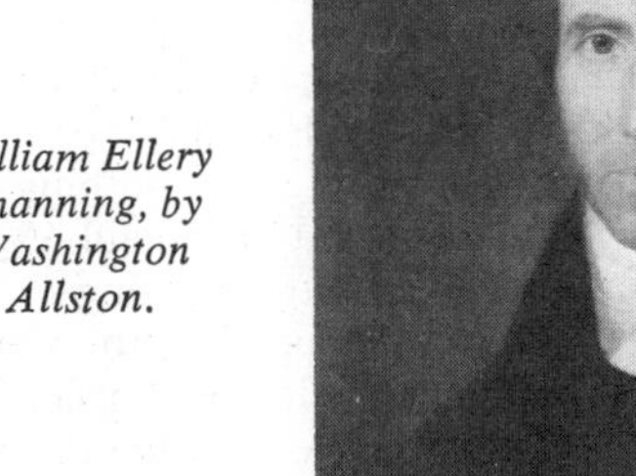

William Ellery Channing, by Washington Allston.

Bibliography: D. P. EDGELL, *William Ellery Channing: An Intellectual Portrait* (Boston 1955). **Illustration credit:** Courtesy, Museum of Fine Arts, Boston.

[J. Q. FELLER]

CHANT BOOKS, PRINTED EDITIONS OF

The first Catholic liturgical book was the Bible, from which the Lessons were read and the Psalms chanted, at least until the 4th century, when the codifying of Catholic ritual and ritual music began. Only printed collections of Gregorian chant used in the Latin Mass and Divine Office will be discussed in this article.

The books necessary for the chants of Mass are the Missal and Graduale, and, for the Office, the Antiphonale and Responsoriale. The Missal contains only the chants of the celebrant and the responses of the choir and congregation. Chants for the Mass Propers and Ordinarys are found in the Graduale. Chants for the Divine Office are found in the Liber Antiphonalis, which contains the music for Lauds, the minor hours, Vespers and Compline, and in the Liber Responsoriales, which contains the *responsories and chants of Matins (*see* DIVINE OFFICE, ROMAN, CHANTS OF). Other chant books, arranged for popular use and greater convenience, are the Liber Usualis (Solesmes 1896; revised 1903 and 1934), which combines chants from both the Graduale and Antiphonale and contains the Ordinary and Proper of the Mass, Lauds, minor hours, Vespers, Compline, the Requiem Mass and Office; Liber Brevior (Solesmes 1954), containing the Mass chants of the Liber Usualis, but omitting the chants of the Divine Office with the exception of Vespers; Kyriale Vaticanum, containing the Ordinary of the Mass, the Requiem Mass, the common tones of the Mass, and other useful chants; Variae Preces (Solesmes 1893), containing hymns, antiphons, Sequences, and other chants not included in the standard books (*see* HYMNS AND HYMNALS; ANTIPHON; SEQUENCE).

Medicean Edition. The first important printed edition of *Gregorian chant, the Medicean, published by the Medici press at Rome in 1614–15, has been incorrectly associated with *Palestrina. In 1577 he and *Zoilo had been commissioned by Gregory XIII to systematize the chants contained in the Missals and Breviaries newly revised in conformity to the decrees of the Council of Trent. Zoilo had corrected the sanctoral cycle of Masses and Palestrina the Sunday Masses, but both of their MSS were lost after the death of Palestrina in 1594, and never published. The Roman printer Giovanni Battista Raimondi had contracted with Palestrina to complete the work, but after Palestrina's death and the deceitful intrigues of his son Iginio, nothing was done until 1608. On May 31 of that year Paul V gave Raimondi permission to undertake the printing of new chant books. Six editors were appointed to prepare the MSS: G. B. Nanino, C. Mancini, F. Soriano, R. Giovanelli, P. Felini, and F. *Anerio; and the resulting Medicean edition appeared only in 1614–15, after the death of Raimondi. This edition contains a mutilated and truncated melody. The editors considered it barbaric to allow many notes on syllables not containing the tonic accent of the Latin word, nor would they allow long notes over the grammatically short syllables, or vice versa. Moreover, they eliminated many of the melismatic passages in the Graduals and Alleluias.

Ratisbon Edition. The most important editions printed in the 19th century were those of Ratisbon and Solesmes. The Ratisbon work was edited by Msgr.

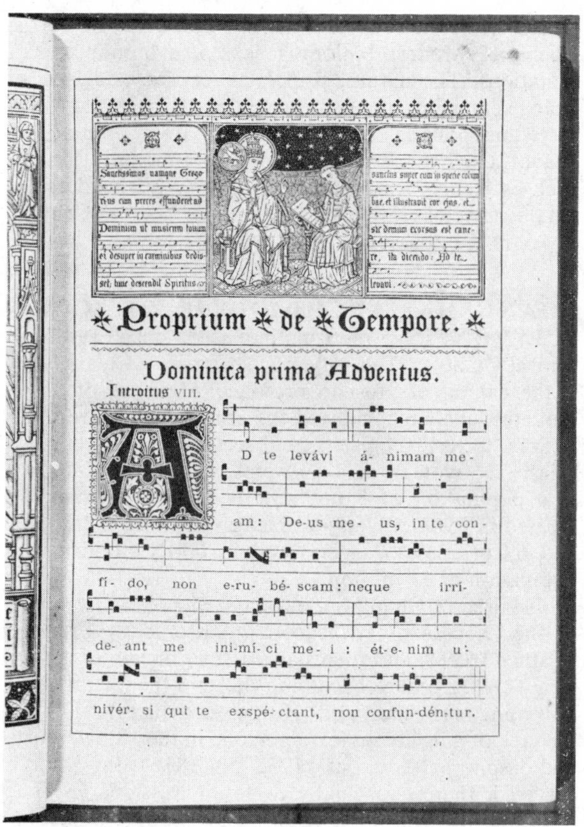
Proprium de Tempore.

Dominica prima Adventus.

Introitus VIII.

Ad te levávi ánimam meam: Deus meus, in te confído, non erubéscam: neque irrídeant me inimíci mei: étenim univérsi qui te exspéctant, non confundéntur.

Opening page of the 1883 Liber Gradualis, showing beginning of the Introit for the First Sunday of Advent.

Liber Gradualis

a S. Gregorio Magno olim ordinatus postea Summorum Pontificum auctoritate recognitus ac plurimum auctus cum notis musicis ad majorum tramites et codicum fidem figuratis ac restitutis in usum Congregationis Benedictinae Galliarum praesidis ejusdem jussu editus

Tornaci Nerviorum, Typis Societatis Sancti Joannis Evang. Desclée, Lefebvre et Sociorum.

m.dccc.lxxxiii. Jus proprietatis vindicabitur.

Title page of Liber Gradualis published at Solesmes in 1883, first of the chant books of the Vatican edition.

F. X. *Haberl and published in 1869 by F. *Pustet of Ratisbon (Regensburg), Germany. Haberl had found a copy of the Medicean edition in the seminary library at Freising and was convinced that it was based on the MS that Palestrina had prepared for Gregory XIII. Subsequent researches of R. Molitor, C. Respighi, and R. C. Casimiri proved that Haberl's claim was unfounded. In 1868 Pustet received permission for the exclusive printing of chant books for 30 years. This was followed by a long series of decrees and approbations by Pius IX and Leo XIII, which in effect gave an "official" character to this edition. Thus Haberl's work prolonged the errors of the Medicean edition.

Vatican Edition. The Vatican edition was based on paleographic researches by the monks of Saint-Pierre de *Solesmes, Solesmes-sur-Sarthe, France. It was initiated under Abbot *Guéranger and carried out by Dom *Pothier, and Dom *Mocquereau; the Liber Gradualis of 1883 and 1895 was the work of Pothier, and the Liber Usualis of 1903 that of Mocquereau. In 1904 Pope St. Pius X appointed a commission under the presidency of Pothier to prepare an official edition of the chant books. Since the commission decided to base the new edition on the Pothier works of 1883 and 1895, and not that of 1903 by Mocquereau, the Solesmes monks withdrew from the work. The books of the Vatican edition appeared as follows: Kyriale, Aug. 14, 1905; Cantus Missae, June 8, 1907; Graduale Vaticanum, Aug. 7, 1907; Officiorum Defunctorum, May 12, 1909; Cantorinus, April 3, 1911; Antiphonale Diurnum Romanum, Dec. 8, 1912. Even though the Solesmes monks did not officially participate in this edition, Pothier incorporated more than 2,000 improvements in the 1907 Graduale Vaticanum that he had taken from the Liber Usualis prepared by Solesmes in 1903. Since 1913 all Propers for new feasts and new saints have been entrusted to the monks of Solesmes.

The Vatican edition chants are available with or without the Solesmes rhythmical signs, which represent devices and letters found in some 10th-century MSS (they appear in the Desclée editions of Tournai Belgium). At first the Solesmes monks attached them to the notes and even altered the shape of certain notes in order to reproduce them. Many musicians did not accept the Solesmes interpretation, and a decree of the Congregation of Sacred Rites, dated Feb. 14, 1906, has directed that all reproductions of the Vatican edition must reproduce the notes exactly; if any rhythmical signs are added they must be separate from the neums and not alter their shape in any manner. The present rhythmical signs of Solesmes have followed this decree and are separate from the notes themselves. In the Sept. 3, 1958, *Instruction on Sacred Music and Sacred Liturgy* it is stated that rhythmical signs may be admitted, provided that the nature and arrangement of the notes as given in the Vatican editions of chant be preserved intact.

Bibliography: A. GASTOUÉ, *Musique et liturgie: Le Gradual et l'Antiphonaire romains: Histoire et description* (Lyon 1913). F. X. HABERL, *Giovanni Pierluigi da Palestrina und das Graduale Romanum Officiale der Editio Medicaea von 1614* (New York 1894). A. MARCHESAN, "L'Opera di Pio X nella restauratione della musica sacra," *Bollettino Ceciliano* 5 (1910) 209–224. R. MOLITOR, *Die Nach-Tridentinische Choral-Reform zu Rom,* 2 v. (Leipzig 1901–02). A. PONS, *Droit ecclésiastique et Musique sacrée,* 4 v. (St. Maurice 1958–61). C. RESPIGHI, *Giovanni Pier Luigi da Palestrina e l'Emdazione del Graduale Romano* (Rome 1899). F. ROMITA, *Jus musicae liturgicae* (Turin 1936); *La preformazione del Motu Proprio di S. Pio X sulla musica sacra* (Rome 1961). A. FORTESCUE, CE 9.1:296–304. R. HAYBURN, *St. Pius X and the Vatican Edition of the Chant Books* (Los Angeles 1964). For further bibliog., *see* SANTI, ANGELO DE. **Illustration credits:** Photo Abbaye de Solesmes.

[R. F. HAYBURN]

CHANTAL, JANE FRANCES DE, ST.

Foundress of the Order of the Visitation of Holy Mary; b. Dijon, France, Jan. 23, 1572; d. Moulins, Dec. 13, 1641 (feast, Aug. 21).

When Jane was 18 months old, her mother, Marguerite de Berbisey, died. Her father, Bénigne Frémyot, councilor and afterward president of the parliament at Dijon, became the main influence in her formation. She was educated at home by visiting tutors in reading, writing, dancing, and playing musical instruments—the usual subjects for girls of her station. She developed into a woman of beauty and quality, with good judgment and a lively, gay temperament.

At the age of 21 she married Baron Christophe de Rabutin-Chantal. At their residence, the castle of Bourbilly, near Semur-en-Auxois, she reestablished the custom of daily Mass, introduced other communal practices of piety, and engaged in works of charity. Of the couple's six children, two died at an early age; a boy and three girls survived. After 7 years of marriage her husband was killed in a hunting accident.

She returned to her father's home, where, desiring to make progress in the spiritual life, she sought priestly guidance. Her director encouraged her in a piety that was already excessive and austere.

Under threat of disinheriting her children her father-in-law required her to return in autumn 1602 to live with him at Monthelon. There she spent 7½ years exercising the virtues of patience and humility, and working on the education of her children.

St. Jane de Chantal.

In 1604 on a visit to her father she met Francis de Sales and wished to place herself under his direction. After some hesitation he consented and began her spiritual formation according to his principles. She made a double vow—to remain unmarried and to obey him. The fulfillment of her wish to enter the religious life was deferred and she was counseled to have patience. In 1607 he disclosed to her his plan for founding a group of women who would especially imitate the virtues exemplified in Mary's visit to Elizabeth and secondarily engage in works of mercy toward the poor and sick. On June 6, 1610, she and two companions assisted at Mass, which he celebrated in his chapel, received their rule from him, and afterward retired to their convent, known as the Gallery House. First vows were pronounced a year later.

Both the name and the constitutions of the institute underwent various changes. The official title became the Visitation of Holy Mary. A second revision of the rule in 1613 established its general plan, which was further modified when the external works of charity were eliminated and the cloister adopted under the influence of the bishop of Lyons, Denis Simon de Marquemont. On April 23, 1618, Paul V elevated the institute to the dignity of a religious order.

After the foundation of the Visitation, Jane de Chantal was concerned both with perfecting herself and her followers in its spirit and with establishing new monasteries. By the time of her death there were 80 houses. Benedict XIV beatified her on Aug. 21, 1751; canonization took place under Clement XIII on July 16, 1767.

See also FRANCIS DE SALES, ST.

Bibliography: *Sa Vie et Ses Oeuvres,* 7 v. (Paris 1874–79). É. BOUGAUD, *St. Chantal and the Foundation of the Visitation,* tr. A. Visitandine, 2 v. (New York 1895–1902). E. K. SANDERS, *Saint Chantal* (New York 1928). E. STOPP, *Madame de Chantal* (Westminster, Md. 1963), with bibliography. **Illustration credit:** Visitation Convent, Turin, Italy.

[E. J. CARNEY]

CHAOS (BIBLICAL), word (χάος) used by the ancient Greeks to designate the amorphous state of primeval matter prior to creation. This notion of a murky and watery primitive world-mass, found also in Egypt and Mesopotamia, is reflected in the Biblical *creation account, where the earth is described as formless and void (*tōhû wābōhû*), and entirely submerged beneath dark waters (Gn 1.2–3). The word *tōhû* occurs several times in the Bible: in its most concrete usage it designates barren wasteland (Dt 32.10; Jb 6.18); but it often signifies emptiness, vanity, nothingness in general (Is 40.17, 23; 41.29; etc.). The word *bōhû* appears only three times in the OT (Gn 1.2; Is 34.11; Jer 4.23), in each instance strengthening the idea of desolation already present in *tōhû*. The controversial passage concerning a *rûaḥ 'ĕlōhîm* that hovered or soared above the abyss is to be rendered by some as "the spirit of God hovering above the waters"; by others as "a tremendous wind was stirring over the waters." The main point of theological interest here is whether or not the priestly writer affirms that this dark, watery, and unproductive mass was created by God. This problem cannot be solved by purely grammatical considerations. The theology of the priestly writer is to be considered. It is improbable that, with his concept of creation through God's word (Gn 1.3, 6, 9, etc.), he could, under any circumstance, conceive of a first creation resulting in disorderly chaos. In the first verse, the creation of heaven and earth already implies an orderly creation. Thus, the second verse, speaking of the earth as *tōhû wābōhû,* although borrowing this image from Semitic creation myths, intends to indicate in creation the presence of a negative element actively opposing God's will (cf. Jer 4.23). The author contrasts God's creation, not with a neutral nothingness, but with an element, represented in the *tōhû wābōhû,* that is ever ready to pull God's creation toward disorder and chaos.

Bibliography: H. GUNKEL, *Schöpfung und Chaos in Urzeit und Endzeit* (2d ed. Göttingen 1921). B. S. CHILDS, *Myth and Reality in the O. T.* (Naperville, Ill. 1960) 30–42. R. DUSSAUD, "Les Trois premiers versets de la Genèse," RevHistRel 99 (1929) 123–141. M. GRUENTHANER, "The Scriptural Doctrine on First Creation," CathBiblQuart 9 (1947) 48–58, 206–219, 307–320. W. H. MCCLELLAN, "The Meaning of *rûaḥ 'ĕlōhîm* in Gen. 1.2," *Biblica* 15 (1934) 517–527. K. GALLING, "Der Charakter der Chaosschilderung in Gen. 1.2," ZTheolKirche 47 (1950) 147–157.

[L. F. HARTMAN]

CHAPEAUVILLE, JEAN, Belgian theologian and historian; b. Liège, Jan. 5, 1551; d. Liège, May 11, 1617. Chapeauville was a young teacher in Liège when the plague broke out in that city in 1581, and was exemplary in his solicitude for the sick. He rose to a prominent position in the Church of Liège and was made inquisitor, canon of the cathedral, grand penitentiary, archdeacon, and vicar-general of the prince bishop, Ernest of Bavaria. When appointed to examine the case of the subprior of Stavelot Abbey, Jean Delvaux, who was accused of witchcraft, Chapeauville supported the decision condemning Delvaux. As an influential cleric in his diocese, Chapeauville attempted to enforce the Tridentine reforms in Liège, especially regarding the establishment of a clerical seminary and the *concursus* for the nomination of parish priests. He is the author of numerous works in theology, which were widespread in his day, if forgotten now. However, his main contribution to learning is his collection of original documents pertaining to the history of Liège and his history of the bishops of Liège, *Qui gesta pontificum Tungrensium, Trajectensium, et Leodiensium scripserunt auctores praecipiri . . . de primi Tungrorum seu Leodiensium episcopi historica disputatio itemque chronologia posteriorum* (3 v. Liège 1612–16).

Bibliography: A short biog., "Anonymi periocha vitae Chapeauvilli, fideliter post ipsius obitum contracta," is prefixed to certain copies of v.1 of *Qui gesta pontificum, op. cit.* A. G. DE BECDELIÈVRE-HAMAL, *Biographie liègeoise,* 2 v. (Liège 1836–37). X. DE THEUX DE MONTJARDIN, *Biographie liègeoise* (2d ed. Bruges 1885). H. HELBIG in *Biographie nationale de Belgique* v.3 (Brussels 1872) 428–432. A. VAN HOVE, CE 3:574.

[C. HOLMES]

CHAPEL

A miniature church, established originally as a place of prayer or *oratorium,* in royal or episcopal residences. With the extension of Christianity to the rural areas, the establishment of an oratory as a place of worship for a local population gave the chapel a public function. In some sections the *martyrium* or *memoria,* a shrine erected to house the relics of a saint or to honor the place of his martyrdom, became a center for religious services. In the 5th century the councils gave these private centers of worship an official character by bringing them under the jurisdiction of the local bishop. The chapel remained, however, the possession of the founder and his heirs. Clerics attached to a private church often became subject to the will of the owner rather than to the jurisdiction of the bishop, and the clergy of the king's chapel played a major role in the management of the realm.

Charlemagne's Palatine chapel at Aachen, now the cathedral, built between 796 and 814, with later additions.

The etymology of the word "chapel" is based upon the *capella* of St. *Martin of Tours, which the Merovingian kings kept in the oratory of their palace. This precious relic was the legendary cape Martin divided with a beggar and later beheld in a vision as worn by Christ Himself. The *capella* was carried into battle as a pledge of victory and used as a surety for the verification of oaths. Confusion between the *oratorium,* where the oath was administered, and the *capella,* upon which it was sworn, caused the oratory of the palace to become known as the *Capella s. Martini,* the chapel of St. Martin. The priest in charge of the royal oratory came to be called the *chaplain from his office as *capellanus,* guardian of the cape. Under *Charlemagne this office gained important status and was sometimes exercised by a bishop.

At the same time the famous church of *Aachen was built as the royal chapel, setting the model for a type of ecclesiastical institution whose office and influence far exceeded the meaning of its name. The great architectural developments of the medieval centuries found original and characteristic expression in chapels independently constructed or integrally attached to a cathedral or monastic church. Notable examples may be found in the abbey church of *Saint-Denis and the Sainte-Chapelle of *Louis IX. In modern times the word is applied to a variety of ecclesiastical buildings, smaller than churches and attached to universities, colleges, and hospitals. The papal chapel (*capella pontificia*), originally the site of liturgical service within the *Lateran or the Vatican (see SISTINE CHAPEL), is today the assembly of the sacred college of cardinals and of other dignitaries, both clerical and lay, meeting with the pope in solemn liturgical ceremonies.

See also ORATORIES, CANON LAW OF.

Bibliography: Sources. MGCap v.2. HINCMAR, *De ordine palatii,* ch. 15 in MGCap 2.3:523. EINHARD, *The Life of Charlemagne,* tr. S. E. TURNER (Ann Arbor 1960). *Vita Betharii,* MGSrerMer 3:615. SUGER, *Abbot Suger on the Abbey Church of St. Denis and Its Art Treasures,* ed. and tr. E. PANOFSKY (Princeton 1946). Literature. H. LECLERCQ, DACL 3.1:406–428; 10.2: 2512–23. A. VILLIEN and H. LECLERCQ, ibid. 3.1:390–399. W. HENRY, *ibid.* 1.1:1039–42. G. SPINELLI and M. ZOCCA, EncCatt 9:194–199. G. JACQUEMET et al., *Catholicisme* 2:933–939. E. H. SWIFT, *Roman Sources of Christian Art* (New York 1951). H. SAALMAN, *Medieval Architecture* (New York 1962). O. VON SIMSON, *The Gothic Cathedral* (2d ed. New York 1962). Cross ODCC 263. **Illustration credit:** German Information Center, New York City.

[P. J. MULLINS]

CHAPELLE, PLACIDE LOUIS, diplomat, archbishop; b. Runes, France, Aug. 28, 1842; d. New Orleans, La., Aug. 9, 1905. He was educated at Mende, department of Lozère, and at Enghien, Belgium. At 17 he immigrated to the U.S. and entered St. Mary's Seminary, Baltimore, Md. Before his ordination in June 1865, he taught at St. Charles College, Catonsville, Md. His first years as a priest were spent as assistant at St. John's Church, then pastor of St. Joseph's, both in Baltimore; in 1882, he became pastor of St. Matthew's, Washington, D.C. In November 1891, he was consecrated titular bishop of Arabissus and coadjutor with right of succession to Abp. J. B. Salpointe of *Santa Fe, N.Mex. When Salpointe resigned, Chapelle became archbishop in 1894 and ruled Santa Fe until 1897.

On Dec. 1, 1897, shortly before the outbreak of the Spanish-American War, Chapelle was transferred to the Archdiocese of *New Orleans as its sixth archbishop. In 1898 he was appointed apostolic delegate to Puerto Rico and Cuba and chargé d'affaires of the Philippine Islands. Early in 1899, he visited the Caribbean area, returning to his see in April to receive the pallium from Bp. Edward Fitzgerald of Little Rock, Ark. Later that year, he went to the Philippines and while in Manila secured the release of priests and religious taken prisoner by Aguinaldo. He later helped in solving the many problems pertaining to Church properties and parochial rights of the Spanish clergy in the islands. Leo XIII, in a pontifical brief, praised the archbishop's work; he was named an assistant to the pontifical throne and count of the Roman Court. Although Chapelle asked to be relieved of diplomatic duties in order to devote his energies to New Orleans, he continued temporarily as apostolic delegate to Cuba and Puerto Rico, directing the redistribution of dioceses and parishes there.

Despite frequent and lengthy absences from New Orleans, Chapelle founded 12 parishes and missions, brought the Dominican fathers to the archdiocese, and opened the St. Louis theological seminary in Faubourg Bouligny. One of his main concerns throughout his tenure in New Orleans was the reduction of the diocesan debt that had burdened three of his predecessors. He succeeded in liquidating the debt but not without alienating some of his priests, who claimed that the tax imposed by the archbishop, in addition to the normal assessments, was excessive. Another cause of complaint was the number and length of his absences from the archdiocese on diplomatic missions. As if to answer his critics, the archbishop scheduled a series of parish visitations in 1905, reaching the farthermost parish, Lake Charles, in July. There he learned that an epidemic of yellow fever had broken out in New Orleans. He hastened back to the city, but a few days later he died, a victim of the disease.

Bibliography: F. J. TSCHAN, DAB 4:11–12.

[H. C. BEZOU]

CHAPLAINS

A chaplain is a priest appointed to exercise the sacred ministry for a particular institution or group of people. This article is restricted to chaplains of religious communities, confraternities, hospitals, and prisons. *See also* MILITARY ORDINARIATE (U.S.).

Chaplains of Religious Communities. Since nonexempt lay religious are under the care of the local pastor, it is not always necessary to appoint a separate chaplain. However, when the ordinary deems it advisable, he may withdraw the community from the care of the local pastor and confide it to a chaplain (CIC c.464.2). In the case of exempt lay religious institutes, the regular superior appoints the chaplain who exercises the pastoral care of the community. In nonexempt communities that have been removed from the care of the pastor, the chaplain administers the last rites (CIC c.514.3) and conducts the funeral services (CIC c.1230.5). The latter function is also the duty of the chaplain of exempt institutes, although it is the confessor in these communities who administers the last sacraments. However, funeral services may also be delegated to the confessor (CIC c.514.2). Confessors are designated separately from the chaplains, but chaplains may be appointed as confessors. In order to preach to the community, the chaplain must have faculties from the diocese (CIC c.1338.3).

Chaplains of Confraternities. Confraternities are sodalities formally erected for the promotion of public worship (CIC c.707.2). The chaplain of a confraternity is charged with the performance of sacred functions under the supervision of the moderator, and during his term of office the chaplain is authorized to bless the habit worn by the members, as well as the insignia, scapulars, and the like. He also possesses the authority to invest the candidates in them (CIC c.698.2). If a confraternity has been erected in a church not its own, which is the usual case in the U.S., it may conduct nonparochial functions in a chapel or at an altar assigned to it. This is with the provision that the parochial ministry of the local parish does not suffer detriment (CIC c.717). If this same condition is fulfilled, confraternities may conduct nonparochial functions in their own churches (owned by them) independently of the pastor of the local parish. The chaplain is not empowered to preach by virtue of his office and therefore he is bound by the canons dealing with preaching, canons 1337–42.

Chaplains of Hospitals and Prisons. The duties of these chaplains are not mentioned in the Code of Canon Law. In general, however, they coincide with the duties of those who are charged with the care of souls. Although the functions of these chaplains can be surmised from the consideration of the nature of the place, these functions are not then created as an office by the common law. The priest does not receive his powers through the medium of the chaplaincy, but through the ordinary's direct commission.

By reason of the common law, hospitals and prisons come under the pastor of the territory where they are located. In the case of a Catholic hospital, the ordinary can remove the institution from the care of the pastor and place it under a chaplain (CIC c.464.2). Since secular hospitals and prisons are not "pious houses," they cannot be withdrawn from the local parish in virtue of canon 464.2. However, the ordinary can assign a curate in the local parish to care for the patients or prisoners, or he can appoint a priest as the chaplain and confer on him the necessary faculties.

The chief obligations of these chaplains are usually to administer Holy Communion, hear confessions, and administer the last rites. Where the ordinary has granted permission for an oratory, the chaplain offers Mass there and cares for the oratory. Obviously, the chaplain may administer private Baptism when there is danger of death. If the oratory does not enjoy the permission to have a baptismal font, special permission would be required to confer solemn Baptism (CIC c.776). The hospital or prison chaplain as such has no jurisdiction to assist at marriages. He may, however, receive general delegation for marriages by being appointed an assistant in the parish where the hospital is located.

In the motu proprio *Pastorale munus* of Nov. 30, 1963, Pope Paul VI conceded to the local ordinary the faculty to grant to chaplains of hospitals, maternity homes, and prisons the faculty to administer Confirmation to the faithful who are in danger of death if the parish priest is not present.

Bibliography: Abbo 1:524, 698. T. SCHÄFER, *De religiosis ad normam codex iuris canonici* (4th ed. Rome 1947). W. M. DRUMM, *Hospital Chaplains* (CUA CLS 178; Washington 1943).

[R. J. MURPHY]

CHAPLEAU, SIR JOSEPH ADOLPHE, Canadian statesman; b. Sainte Thérèse de Blainville, Lower Canada, Nov. 9, 1840; d. Montreal, Canada, June 13, 1898. He was educated at Manon College and the Sainte Hyacinthe seminary, and was called to the bar of Lower Canada in 1861 (queen's counsel, 1873). As Conservative member for Terrebonne in the provincial Legislative Assembly (1876–82), he served as solicitor general (1873–74), provincial secretary (1876–78), and premier (1879–82). During his tenure as premier, the division within the provincial Conservative party, between the ultraclerical *Castors* and the secular School of Cortier, was accentuated. Chapleau attempted to suppress the *Castors* by a coalition with the moderate Liberals. He joined John Macdonald's government (1882) as secretary of state and, except for 10 days in June 1891, held this portfolio until 1892. From January to December 1892, he served the Abbott government as minister of customs. He was appointed lieutenant governor of Quebec on Dec. 7, 1892, holding this office until his resignation 6 months before his death. He was created a Knight Commander of St. Michael and St. George, in 1896. He wrote a pamphlet, *Leon XIII, homme d'état* (Montreal 1888), and a number of political pamphlets.

Bibliography: A. DE BONNETERRE, *L'Honorable J. A. Chapleau: sa Biographie, suivie de ses principaux Discours* (Montreal 1887). *Encyclopedia Canadiana,* 10 v. (Ottawa 1957–58) v.2.

[J. T. FLYNN]

CHAPMAN, JOHN, Benedictine historian and exegete; b. Ashfield, England, April 25, 1865; d. Downside, Nov. 7, 1933. He was educated at Christ Church, Oxford, and took Anglican orders in 1889 but joined the Catholic Church in 1890. In 1892 he became a Benedictine at *Maredsous, and he was ordained in 1895. He was master of novices and prior at *Erdington (1895–1912), superior at *Caldey (1913–14), and a chaplain in England, France, and Switzerland during World War I. After the war he worked on the commission for the Vulgate in Rome (1919–22), and became prior (1922) and then abbot (1929 to his death) of *Downside, to which he had transferred his residence in 1919. He contributed numerous articles on patrology and Church history for the *Revue Bénédictine,* the *Dublin Review,* the *Catholic Encyclopedia,* and the *Encyclopedia of Religion and Ethics.* The most important of his early works are *Notes on the Early History of the Vulgate Gospels* (Oxford 1908) and *John the Presbyter and the Fourth Gospel* (Oxford 1911). He wrote several treatises on problems of the spiritual life and on mysticism. After his death his *Spiritual Letters* (London 1935) and *Matthew, Mark and Luke* (London 1937) were published; the latter argues that the Greek text of Matthew is earlier than that of Mark.

Bibliography: Cross ODCC 264. A. METZINGER, EncCatt 3:1388. G. R. HUDLESTON, DictSpirAscMyst 2:488–492. R. GAZEAU, *Catholicisme* 2:946–947.

[F. X. MURPHY]

CHAPPOTIN DE NEUVILLE, HÉLÈNE DE, foundress of the *Franciscan Missionaries of Mary; b. Nantes, France, May 21, 1839; d. San Remo, Italy, Nov. 15, 1904. Hélène, the daughter of Sophie Caroline (du Fort) and Paul Charles Chappotin, early displayed interest in the missions. She entered the Society of *Mary Reparatrix in 1864 and took the name Mother

Mary of the Passion. From 1865 to 1876 she labored in the Madura missions of India, and was appointed provincial superior there at the age of 29. In 1877 Pope Pius IX authorized her to found the Institute of Missionaries of Mary. The foundress had been interested in the Franciscan mode of life since her brief association with the *Poor Clares in 1860. She was received into the *third order of Franciscans in 1882, when her own institute became permanently affiliated with the *Franciscans and took the name Franciscan Missionaries of Mary. Mother Mary of the Passion received final approbation of her constitutions from the Holy See (May 11, 1896). Her *Meditations liturgiques et franciscaines* (5 v. Paris 1896–98) constitutes a legacy of spiritual writings for her missionary sisters. Her cause for beatification was introduced in 1923.

Hélène de Chappotin de Neuville.

Bibliography: T. F. CULLEN, *Mother Mary of the Passion* (abr. ed. North Providence, R.I. 1942). G. GOYAU, *Valiant Women: Mother Mary of the Passion . . .*, tr. from French by G. TELFORD (London 1936).

[M. F. CONDON]

CHAPPUIS, MARIA SALESIA, VEN., Visitation nun; b. Soyhières, France, June 16, 1793; d. Troyes (Aube), France, Oct. 7, 1875. Soyhières was a town in the Jura Mountains that has since become part of Switzerland. Maria was the sixth of ten children of Catherine (Fleury) and Pierre Chappuis, a judge. After attending a school (1805–08) run by the *Visitation Nuns at Fribourg, Switzerland, Marie entered this order in 1811 but soon left. She returned in 1814 and pronounced her first vows in 1816. Soon after this she was assigned to Metz to start a new Visitation convent, but ill health compelled her return to Fribourg. At Troyes she was chosen superior in 1826 and held this office for 11 terms. From 1838 to 1844 she was superior in Paris. In both Troyes and Paris she served also as mistress of novices. At Troyes she was associated with Louis *Brisson and collaborated with him in the foundation of the *Oblate Sisters of St. Francis de Sales (1866) and the *Oblates of St. Francis de Sales (*c.* 1871). Her cause for beatification was introduced in 1897. Questions have since been raised concerning her spiritual doctrines, which did not, however, profess to inaugurate a new school.

Bibliography: L. BRISSON, *Vie de la vénérée Mère de Sales Chappuis* (Paris 1891). P. DUFOUR, DictSpirAscMyst 2:496–498.

[E. J. CARNEY]

CHAPT DE RASTIGNAC, ARMAND, BL., theologian; b. the Périgord, Oct. 2, 1729; d. Paris between Sept. 3 and 5, 1792 (feast, Sept. 2). He received his doctorate at the Sorbonne, was appointed pastor at Saint-Mesmin d'Orléans, and eventually took the post of vicar-general of the Diocese of Arles. He was a deputy at the assembly of the French clergy in 1755 and 1760. He participated in the meetings of the Estates General in 1789 and tried to forestall action against ecclesiastical property. Because of the weakness of his voice, he wrote out and published two of his most important statements: *Question sur la propriété des biens ecclésiastiques* (Paris 1789) and *Accord de la révélation contre le divorce* (Paris 1791). In addition he translated and published with notes the famous synodal letter of Patriarch Nicholas III (d. 1111) of Constantinople to the Emperor Alexius I Comnenus (d. 1118) regarding the authority of emperors with relation to the erection of ecclesiastical sees, *Lettre synodale de Nicolas* (Paris 1790). He signed protests against the arbitrary anticlerical laws of the Constituent Assembly. He fell sick and was bedridden for many months; when finally arrested for his views, he could scarcely walk. After a short imprisonment, he was killed in the September massacres. His beatification took place on Oct. 17, 1926.

Bibliography: C. TOUSSAINT, DTC 2.2:2215–16. G. JACQUEMET, *Catholicisme* 2:949. V. ZOLLINI, EncCatt 3:1389. Hurter Nomencl[3] 5:306.

[C. MEYER]

CHAPTAL, JEAN ANTOINE, French chemist, famous as industrialist, administrator, and author; b. Nojaret, June 4, 1756; d. Paris, July 30, 1832. He was the fourth child of a rich landowner; his uncle Claude was a famous physician. He became a doctor of medicine in 1776 at University of Montpellier and, after further studies, took over the newly created chair in chemistry there. In 1793, the National Convention called him to design a powder plant. He then extended his industrial activities to textiles and dyeing. He became minister of the interior in 1801 and organized the defense of Lyons against the Coalition in 1814. Louis XVI raised him to the nobility, Napoleon named him Comte de Chanteloup; later, after returning from Elba, he made him director of commerce and manufactures. During the restoration Chaptal became a peer of France. He wrote, "I believe I was the first in France who applied chemical knowledge in its full extent to the manufacturing arts." His *Traité de Chimie* (4 v., 1807) was widely translated. He also wrote a *Chimie appliquée à l'Agriculture* (1823, 2d ed. 1829) and articles about the distillation of wine, sugar beets, dyeing, and ancient painting.

Bibliography: J. PIGEIRE, *La Vie et l'oeuvre de Chaptal* (Paris 1931).

[E. FARBER]

CHAPTER OF FAULTS, a meeting of the members of a religious community, held at an appointed time and place (usually the chapter house or room), at which those members guilty of some transgression of the rule publicly confess their faults. The custom serves, on the one hand, to guard the religious discipline of the house, and on the other hand, to exercise the members in humility and mutual understanding. From its beginnings in the 3d century, monasticism has included in its daily or weekly schedule some kind of public confession. Precepts in St. Basil's *Rules,* observed by contemporary Eastern monks, provide for a confession comparable to the modern Western form of the chapter; and from the 4th to the 9th century, both in the East and the West, customs similar to the modern chapter were practiced wherever monasticism was found. But the *Rule of St. Benedict,* though it provided for public acknowledgment of faults, did not specifically provide for a chapter. The chapter in its contemporary form did not appear until the time of the customaries of the 8th and 9th centuries. In customaries, such as those of Cluny and Hirschau, the modern chapter is prescribed in detail; even the verbal formulas are still in use: the monks were to confess their faults in turn before the community and receive their penances from the abbot. The *clamatio* or *proclamatio,* the accusation of one monk by another in chapter, was generally included as an essential part of the chapter. This custom was more or less uniform and universal throughout the later Middle Ages. The monastic reforms and new institutions of each generation incorporated it into their constitutions. Notable among them in the 12th century were the Cistercians and the new orders of friars—the Dominicans, Carmelites, and Franciscans. It was preserved also by the new institutions of the Counter Reformation, with the exception of the Society of Jesus, which substituted other forms of discipline. The influence of Jansenism in ascetical theology helped to ensure the preservation of this custom into the 20th century; but with the widespread modern reaction against Jansenist tendencies, the chapter of faults (along with other ascetical practices misunderstood by the Jansenists) has tended to play a less serious role in monasticism than that envisioned by the early medieval constitutions. In most—though by no means in all—religious congregations the *proclamatio* has fallen into disuse.

Bibliography: P. SCHMITZ, DictSpirAscMyst 2:483–488.

[A. DONAHUE]

CHAPTERS, RELIGIOUS

The canonical religious chapter may be defined as a collective moral person, composed of the religious who have the right of suffrage according to the proper constitutional law and constituted as an independent authority in the government of the institute.

The word "chapter" is derived from the Latin *capitulum* through the French *chapitre. Capitulum* is a diminutive of *caput,* meaning "head."

The use of the word to designate an assembly of religious can be traced to the monastic practice of assembling daily for the reading of a chapter of the rule. The place where this assembly was held came to be known as the chapterhouse and the assembly was called the chapter. At these daily meetings the superior proposed any business for which he needed the advice or consent of the brethren, and to this practice is due the legal character that the religious chapter now possesses.

Types. By reason of the moral personality that they represent, chapters are called: general, representing the whole religious institute; provincial, representing a province of the institute; local, representing an individual religious house. *See* PROVINCE, ECCLESIASTICAL. By reason of the purpose for which they are convoked, chapters are called: business chapters, to treat of business of various kinds within the competence of the chapter; electoral chapters, to elect the superiors of the institute; and mixed chapters, for conducting both types of business mentioned above.

By reason of the time or occasion when they are convoked, chapters are called: ordinary, or convoked at the times or for the causes prescribed by the constitutions; or extraordinary, that is, called at a time or for a cause not prescribed by the constitutions. However, these terms are not understood in this sense by all. Some understand the term ordinary chapter to mean one that is celebrated after a definite term of years determined by the constitutions; any other chapter is extraordinary.

The chapter of faults is not a canonical chapter but an ascetical practice during which each religious accuses himself of external faults against the rules and constitutions. It probably owes its designation as a chapter to the fact that this exercise took place in the chapterhouse on the occasion of the daily assembly to hear the reading of the rule.

Divisions. The formal divisions of a chapter are convocation, celebration, and confirmation. Convocation is the authoritative announcement to all who have the right of suffrage to assemble in a definite place at a definite time to decide a matter within the competence of the chapter. Convocation is ordinarily a necessary part of the chapter, since it is of the essence of collective moral action that the decision be reached by voting in assembly, and convocation is the ordinary means of bringing the assembly together.

Celebration is the series of actions prescribed by common and particular law so that the decisions of the chapter will be valid. The primary source of norms specifying and governing these actions is the prescriptions of the rules and constitutions of each particular religious institute. When such prescriptions of particular law are lacking, the norms are taken from the common law: for collective action in general, CIC c.101; ClerSanc c.29; and for elections and postulation in particular, CIC cc.160–182, 506–507; ClerSanc cc.102–120, 121–124.

Confirmation is the act by which a competent superior approves the acts of the chapter and by this approval renders them binding. Ordinarily the acts of moral persons are concluded by the votes of those who have the right of suffrage. Confirmation, therefore, is not required for the acts of religious chapters unless it is expressly prescribed by general or particular law.

Competence. The competence of any religious chapter is determined solely by the particular law of the institute, but a guiding principle is set down in Canon Law. It is established there that superiors and chapters, according to the norm of the constitutions and the CIC, have dominative power over subjects and that in clerical exempt institutes they have ecclesiastical jurisdiction for both internal and external forum (CIC c.501.1; PostApost c.26.1).

Canonical writers make the general statement that chapters ordinarily have greater authority than individual superiors. Usually this authority of chapters embraces the right to legislate, to elect superiors, and to administer the more important business of the institute. The ultimate decisive norm for determining whether and to what extent a specific religious chapter can exercise any of these functions will always be the rules and constitutions of the particular religious institute, for nowhere in the CIC is any particular act definitely and positively committed to any specific religious chapter.

Bibliography: L. R. MISSEREY, DDC 3:595–610. G. LEWIS, *Chapters in Religious Institutes* (CUA CLS 181; Washington

1943). A. C. ELLIS, "The General Chapter of Elections in a Religious Congregation," *Review for Religious* 1 (1942) 146–156; "The Chapter of Affairs in a Religious Congregation," *ibid.* 253–258.

[G. LEWIS]

CHARACTER

A term derived from the Greek χαρακτήρ, meaning engraving. Since the engraving on an object originally showed the worth of the thing, moralists use the term character to designate the moral worth or value of a human *person. In a wider sense, character has come to mean any distinctive sign; psychologists use the term in this sense to designate particular dispositions of an individual or of a group that account for their distinctive modes of behavior. This article treats of both meanings under the headings of character in moral science and character in psychology respectively.

CHARACTER IN MORAL SCIENCE

In a broad sense, character signifies a strong adherence to principles that can be morally good or bad. Taken in this meaning, a strong character enables a person to do what he wants and to dominate over his environment and other individuals; in this understanding, a person with a strong character can be morally objectionable. More properly, however, character signifies the good moral values manifested in a person's deliberate actions. An individual has a strong character if his responsible actions are in accord with objectively good moral principles. A man of character consistently lives up to moral norms as he knows them. His subjective knowledge of what is morally acceptable concurs with objective norms given by nature and God's revelation. The remainder of the discussion is concerned with character in this more proper meaning.

Role of Will. In character, the *will plays a leading role. Although the will is a spiritual faculty of the soul, it is nevertheless indirectly influenced by an individual's physical *disposition and *temperament. Native physical endowments of temperament affect the acquisition of a good character. Moreover, the environment of family and other social relationships, by affording favorable opportunities, provides wholesome influences in the formation of character. Although *heredity and environment can give a suitable background, the formation of a good character develops from personal efforts required in doing what is known to be right. Undoubtedly an individual can surmount the unfavorable moral circumstances of family and environment and acquire a strong moral character.

The will is the faculty of *choice. In its act of choosing, the will prefers one course of action from the several motives proposed by the *intellect (*see* MOTIVE). When the choice of the will is expressed externally, the character of the person is manifested. If the choices are consistently bad morally, the character is noted as bad; if the choices are good, the character is likewise good. If a choice is a departure from the usual pattern of morality, it can be said that the act is not characteristic of the individual.

Frequently the will is presented with several possible courses of action of which some may be morally bad. It is the will that must choose either to follow an easier but morally wrong course or to adhere to principles that assure good moral conduct. This dilemma of the will takes place under *temptation when there are alternatives either of pursuing the advantage of the moment when to do so is not morally good or of choosing what *conscience dictates as morally right. Although actual grace from God gives supernatural assistance in such a choice, the inherent strength of will provides the natural dispositions for God's grace. The choice that the will makes remains the responsibility of the individual. A strong moral character enables the person to cooperate more easily with the helping grace of God.

Character Formation. Because the will is the most important factor in the formation of a good moral character, the will must be made strong. Strength of will is acquired through the practice of virtues, while natural virtues result from repeated and consistently good actions. It is the purpose of a *virtue to give an added power and inclination to a faculty. The will is given this power when it has become qualified by the four cardinal virtues of prudence, justice, fortitude, and temperance. Growth in these virtues is essential for building a strong and good character. Catholic theology rightly asserts that the cardinal virtues are infused and remain with sanctifying grace; however, promptness and facility in the use of these virtues comes only from putting them into practice.

*Prudence is a virtue of the practical intellect that inclines one to choose the most suitable means to effect a good result. However, prudence has a definite effect also on the choices of the will. It trains one to think before making decisions, and it inclines him to be firm in carrying out what has been sufficiently deliberated. Prudence is the director for the other cardinal virtues. This direction makes a person's choices reasonable, so that they escape the pitfalls of both foolish excess and regrettable deficiency. A good moral character must have the balance afforded by prudence.

*Justice plays an important part in character, for it directly inclines the will to respect the rights of other persons. The man of character is truthful and honest because others have the right to be dealt with truthfully and honestly. He is habituated to act justly: this course of action is his mark or characteristic. Temperance brings to the will an added impetus to control the concupiscible emotions that pull toward isolated sense pleasures that sometimes are contrary to the total moral good of the person (*see* TEMPERANCE, VIRTUE OF). Although the desires and aversions of the senses tend to what is good, their goals are limited goods that must be reconciled with the entire pattern of life. A man of character is strong enough to resist the advantage of the moment. Fortitude, or *courage, when it has been acquired through practice, enables the will to use the strong irascible emotions rather than take the line of least resistance (*see* FORTITUDE, VIRTUE OF). This virtue urges a person to pursue a good course of action despite the difficulties encountered.

See also WILL POWER; HABIT.

Bibliography: THOMAS AQUINAS, ST 1a2ae, 49–89. R. ALLERS, *Psychology of Character,* tr. E. B. STRAUSS (New York 1939). G. W. ALLPORT, *Pattern and Growth in Personality* (New York 1961). E. B. BARRETT, *Strength of Will* (New York 1915).

[J. A. BURROUGHS]

CHARACTER IN PSYCHOLOGY

Descriptions of character in modern psychology can be reduced to three, following these orientations: psychopedagogical, psychomedical, psychophilosophical.

Psychopedagogical Orientation. Character is here reduced to one or more qualities, generally empirical, that can be utilized in education. In this orientation the ethical dimension of character most frequently dominates. A. *Bain attempts to reduce the qualities to a psychical energy that is channeled through three distinct activities, giving place to three types of character, viz, mental, motor, and vital. A. Roback reduces character to a capacity of inhibition that is distinct in each individual and is in agreement with moral principles. Other authors are atomistic. F. Paulhan establishes character according to the predominance of the rules of association, inhibition, quality, and dominance of tendencies; this allows for balanced types, unified types, reflexive types, etc. A. Shand admits one basic law: each sentiment tends to form a particular character; but from this he deduces 144 laws that differentiate character. A. Burloud uses an analysis of tendencies as his basis for character.

The most famous classification in the psychopedagogical orientation is that of G. Heymans, which is based on an analysis of biographies. Heymans notes three fundamental properties: emotivity (*E*), activity (*A*), and permanence, which is of two types—primary (*P*) does not last beyond the present, whereas secondary (*S*) does. Combining these properties he obtained the following character types (*n* means "not"):

nE, nA, P: Amorphous	*E, nA, P:* Nervous
nE, nA, S: Apathic	*E, nA, S:* Sentimental
nE, A, P: Sanguine	*E, A, P:* Choleric
nE, A, S: Phlegmatic	*E, A, S:* Passionate

R. *Le Senne makes use of basically the same principles as Heymans.

Psychomedical Orientation. Character is here determined by deep-seated impulses about which the mental representations and interests of the individual are said to be concentrated. Orthodox *psychoanalysis bases character on the predominance of one of the phases of the evolution of the libido and of love toward an object. C. G. *Jung reduces the types of character to two principal groups: extroverts and introverts. H. Rorschach bases character on the type of perception shown in response to ink blots; in his view responses are motivated by movement (introverted), by color (extroverted), by form (constrained), or by color and movement (ambivalent). E. *Jaensch distinguishes character by the degree of subject-object coherence and man-world relationships. In the disintegrated type intrapsychical tensions predominate, viz, between the psyche and body and between the subject and the outside world. In the integrated type the psychosomatic and the psychosocial are interwoven. This psychotypology is related to temperaments that are associated with various biotypes (*see* TYPOLOGY; TEMPERAMENT).

Psychophilosophical Orientation. Character is here identified with *personality, which is related more or less to the philosophical concept of the individual. L. *Klages conceives character as the vital unity of the self-conscious *ego. Instead of relying on abstractive self-reflection, however, he holds that a person's character can be ascertained from his similarity with others and from personal information about him. Character manifests itself at different layers in faculties, talents, aptitudes, etc. At the deeper levels are tendencies that belong "to the nature of personality"; also present are interests that elaborate a general tendency and particular desires of a person.

For E. Spranger internal experience supplies forces that elaborate the subjective spirit and a pattern of life. His classification of character is based on the predominance of a series of personal values that yields either theoretical man, economic man, aesthetic man, social man, political man, or religious man. Each one of these types subdivides itself into others according to a further determination of the particular spirit.

P. Lersch adopts a layer theory (*Schichtentheorie*) to explain character. The individual manifestation acquires a self-unity emerging from the profound layers of nature and going toward awareness (*Bewusstheit*). The dispositions integrated in character are in constant interrelation. These interrelations of integration constitute the structure of character, in which is realized the special mode of being of the individual personality.

E. Mounier holds that the basis for the empirical concept of character is a personality beyond the data. He denies the possibility of a science of character. Psychological types never project a complete description of the living person. Pure types do not exist, are not fixed forever, and, being statistical concepts, are valid only for the mean of the group. It is only in metapsychology (i.e., metaphysics) that one can clarify character structures (*see* PERSONALISM).

See also GRAPHOLOGY; PERSONALITY; SELF, THE.

Bibliography: A. BAIN, *On the Study of Character* (London 1861). A. A. ROBACK, *The Psychology of Character* (New York 1927). F. PAULHAN, *Les Caractères* (Paris 1894). A. F. S. SHAND, *The Foundations of Character* (London 1914). A. BURLOUD, *Le Caractère* (Paris 1942). G. HEYMANS, "Über einige psychische Korrelationen," *Zeitschrift für angewandte Psychologie und psychol. Sammelforschung* 1 (1908) 313–383. R. LE SENNE, *Traité de caractérologie* (Paris 1949). C. G. JUNG, *Psychologische Typen* (Zürich 1921). H. RORSCHACH, *Psychodiagnostik* (Bern 1921). E. R. JAENSCH, *Eidetic Imagery and Typological Methods of Investigation,* tr. O. OESER (London 1930). L. KLAGES, *Die Grundlagen der Charakterkunde* (Leipzig 1936). E. SPRANGER, *Lebensformen* (repr. of 5th rev. ed. Heidelberg 1950). P. LERSCH, *Aufbau der Person* (6th ed. Munich 1954). E. MOUNIER, *Traité du caractère* (rev. ed. Paris 1946). W. REICH, *Character-analysis,* tr. T. P. WOLFE (3d ed. New York 1949). Character and Personality Series, Duke U. (Durham, N.C.)

[E. MARTÍNEZ]

CHARBONNEAU, JOSEPH, archbishop; b. Lefaivre, Ontario, Canada, July 31, 1892; d. Victoria, British Columbia, Canada, Nov. 19, 1959. He studied at the Sulpician College and at the Grand Seminary, Montreal, where he was ordained June 24, 1916. He continued his studies at The Catholic University of America, Washington, D.C., and later at the Canadian College, Rome, receiving the degrees of D.D.C., Th.D., and Ph.D. He was appointed superior of the major seminary at Ottawa, Ontario, and served as vicar-general of the Ottawa diocese. He was consecrated first bishop of Hearst, Ontario (Aug. 15, 1939), and named titular archbishop of Amorio and coadjutor with the right of succession to Abp. Georges Gauthier of Montreal (May 18, 1940); he succeeded to the see (Aug. 31, 1940). As archbishop of Montreal he was renowned for his work in welfare, education, and immigration. He came into conflict with the provincial government, the Union Nationale, headed by Premier Maurice *Duplessis, especially in 1949 when the archbishop opposed the labor legislation on the grounds that it was deficient in social justice. In the same year he threw his support to the laboring class in the famous strike at Asbestos. On Feb. 9, 1950, he resigned his see "for reasons of health," was appointed titular archbishop of Bosphorus by Pius

XII, and retired to the convent of the Sisters of St. Anne, Victoria, British Columbia, where he died.

[J. T. FLYNN]

CHARBONNEL, ARMAND FRANÇOIS MARIE DE, missionary, educator; b. Monistrol-sur-Loire, France, Dec. 1, 1802; d. Crest, Drome, France, March 29, 1891. Educated at the Basilian College, Annonay, he joined the Society of the Priests of Saint Sulpice in Paris and in 1825 was ordained. He volunteered for missionary work and was sent to Montreal, Canada, where he served from 1840 to 1847. After refusing several bishoprics in France, Canada, and the U.S., he was consecrated bishop of Toronto on May 26, 1850. There he founded St. Michael's College (1852) and led a successful struggle for tax-supported Catholic schools. In 1856 he brought about the division of his jurisdiction by the erection of dioceses at Hamilton and London. He resigned from his see on April 29, 1860, and entered the Capuchin Order at Rieti, Italy. He was named titular bishop of Sozopolis in 1869, and made titular archbishop in 1881. The last years of his life were spent in France preaching on behalf of the Society for the Propagation of the Faith.

Bibliography: C. CAUSSE, *Vie de Monseigneur de Charbonnel: Évêque de Torento* (Paris 1931).

[R. J. SCOLLARD]

CHARCOT, JEAN MARTIN, French neurologist, psychiatrist, and teacher of great influence; b. Paris, Nov. 29, 1825; d. Morvan (Nièvre), Aug. 16, 1893. He received his M.D. at Paris (1853), and in 1860 became professor of pathological anatomy in the medical faculty of Paris. In 1862 he began his association with the Salpêtrière, where he established his famous neurological clinic. Around 1880, having carried out extensive work on muscular atrophy and sclerosis, Charcot turned his attention to the neuroses. He attempted a clinical description of hysteria and reestablished the validity of *hypnosis, which had been in ill repute since Mesmer's time. Charcot provided the impetus for the study of psychological phenomena at a time when psychiatrists conceived of a psychiatry without psychology. He had a decisive influence on the careers of three of his pupils, Alfred *Binet, Pierre *Janet, and Sigmund *Freud. His works include *Lectures on the Diseases of the Nervous System* (Philadelphia 1879), *Lectures on the Pathological Anatomy of the Nervous System* (Cincinnati 1881), and *Lectures on the Localization of Cerebral and Spinal Diseases* (London 1883).

Bibliography: I. S. WECHSLER, "Jean Martin Charcot 1825–1893," *The Founders of Neurology,* ed. W. HAYMAKER (Springfield, Ill. 1953) 266–269. P. PICHOT, *Contemporary European Psychiatry,* ed. L. BELLAK (New York 1961) 3–29.

[J. BROŽEK]

CHARDIN, JEAN BAPTISTE SIMÉON, French painter of still-lifes and intimate scenes of bourgeois life; b. Paris, Nov. 2, 1699; d. Paris, Dec. 6, 1779. Having inherited high standards of craftsmanship from his father, a cabinetmaker, he perfected his art under N. N. Coypel, from whom he learned the correct placing and lighting of objects by painting directly from nature. Chardin rarely drew except to record a passing notion. "The Ray" and "The Buffet" (both in the Louvre), shown at the Exposition de la Jeunesse (1728), won him immediate recognition and membership in the Royal Academy as "painter of animals and fruit." His work exhibits a craftsmanship and perfection attained by creamy impasted techniques with subdued light and color; the result is a straightforward representation of fact elevated to the realm of poetry. During his last 8 years he turned from still-life and genre scenes to pastel portraiture. His "Lady Sealing a Letter" (Potsdam) shows a quiet interior setting, which, in an age of opulence, provoked a nostalgia for a simpler way of life; the picture breathes a spiritual solitude that results from the artist's fusion of the classical norms of beauty with the naturalism of everyday life.

Jean Baptiste Siméon Chardin, "The Kitchen Maid," canvas, 18⅛ by 14¾ inches, 1738.

Bibliography: G. WILDENSTEIN, *Chardin, l'oeuvre complet* (Paris 1933). E. and J. DE GONCOURT, *French XVIII Century Painters* (New York 1948) 107–153. **Illustration credit:** National Gallery of Art, Washington, D.C., Samuel H. Kress Collection.

[R. P. WUNDER]

CHARDON, LOUIS, Dominican mystical theologian and spiritual director; b. Clermont (Oise), March 12, 1595; d. Paris, Aug. 17, 1651. As a member of a well-to-do family, he pursued his higher studies at Paris, where, attracted by the order's intellectual apostolate, he became a Dominican in the Annunciation Priory, taking the habit and the name Louis in May 1618. In 1632 he went to Toulouse as "ordinary preacher," but in 1645 returned to Paris where he devoted his remaining years to writing and spiritual direction. All his works were written during the last 4 years of his life. His French translations of the *Dialogue of St. Catherine of Siena* (1648) and the *Institutiones divinae* of John Tauler (1650) were followed by his most popular work, *Meditations on the Passion of Our Lord Jesus Christ;* another treatise on the art of meditation is extant. His principal work, *The Cross of Jesus* (1647), is a precise theology of Christian suffering, especially of fervent souls; its main theme is the spiritual progress of the Christian through the cross. It is both a speculative and practical work, a perfect blend of the theologian's knowledge and the mystic's experience. Though some consider his spirituality Carmelite, owing to his emphasis on the way of negation, his doctrine is in complete harmony with the teachings of Dominican spiritual theology (unity of the spiritual life, the mystical state as a development of the life of grace and virtue) especially of the German Dominican school with its doctrine of purification, all of which Chardon explains by means of the Thomistic doctrine concerning the nature and function of sanctifying grace.

Bibliography: H. BRÉMOND, *Histoire littéraire du sentiment religieux en France,* 11 v. (Paris 1916–33) v.8. L. CHARDON, *The Cross of Jesus,* tr. R. T. MURPHY and J. THORNTON, 2 v. (St. Louis 1957–59). F. FLORAND, DictSpirAscMyst 2.1:498–503.

[C. HAHN]

CHARDON, MATHIAS CHARLES, theologian; b. Yvois-Carignan (Ardennes), Sept. 22, 1695; d. Abbey of St. Arnoul, Metz, Oct. 20, 1771. He was a Benedictine of the Abbey of St. Vannes, Verdun, where he served as novice master and later taught philosophy and theology until he was deposed by the general chapter of the Congregation of St. Vannes in 1730 for refusing to submit to the constitution *Unigenitus.* His great work, which still has value, is a history of the celebration and administration of the Sacraments from apostolic times to his own day, *Histoire des sacrements* (6 v. Paris 1745). It is to be found in Migne's *Cursus Theologiae completus* (v.30).

Bibliography: B. HEURTEBIZE, DTC 2.2:2216.

[A. ROCK]

CHARISM

The word charism or charisma (from Gr. χάρισμα) denotes a gift freely and graciously given, a favor bestowed, a grace. Charism as understood in the Bible is first treated, then its relation to the individual possessing it, and finally its meaning for the corporate Church.

IN THE BIBLE

Except for two variants in the Greek Version of Sirach (Sir 7.33; 38.30) and Theodotion's translation of Ps 30(31).22, the use of the word charism in the Bible is confined to the NT, in which it occurs 17 times, principally in Romans and 1 Corinthians. The usage, however, is not uniform, varying between a general meaning equivalent to grace (χάρις) and the technical meaning, which is treated here.

Technical Usage. In its technical meaning, a charism is a spiritual gift or talent granted by God to the recipient not primarily for his own sake but for the benefit of others "in order to perfect the saints for a work of ministry, for building up the body of Christ," i.e., the Church (Eph 4.12; see also 1 Cor 14.26). St. Paul gives it a quasi definition in 1 Cor 12.7 as a "manifestation of the Spirit for profit," i.e., for the profit of others.

Some eight lists of charisms occur more or less clearly in the NT: (1) Rom 12.6–8; (2) 1 Cor 12.4–10; (3) 1 Cor 12.28–31; (4) 1 Pt 4.10, and, without mention of the term, (5) 1 Cor 14.6, 13; (6) 1 Cor 14.26 and (7) Eph 4.11 as well as (8) Mk 16.17–18. Although these lists are neither uniform nor complete, it is possible to group the charisms contained in them according to similarity of function and to arrive at their probable meaning, as follows.

Various Kinds of Charisms. Teaching charisms comprise those of *apostles (ἀπόστολοι) or itinerant missionaries (Didache 11.3–6), evangelists (εὐαγγελίσται; *see* EVANGELIST) or preachers of the gospel, prophets (προφῆται) who spoke in God's name under the inspiration of the Holy Spirit, and teachers (διδάσκαλοι) who instructed the Christians and *catechumens. To the teaching charisms one may also conjoin those of exhorting (παρακαλεῖν), speaking (λαλεῖν), and hymnody (ψάλλεην), as well as the more important, yet more indefinable, utterances of knowledge and wisdom (λόγος γνώσεως and λόγος σοφίας), i.e., of different grades of supernatural understanding.

Service charisms include gifts for governing and guiding as well as serving, since administration is interchangeable with ministration among Christ's followers, e.g., presiding (προστασία), governing (κυβέρνησις), ministering (διακονία) giving (μετάδοσις), mercy (ἔλεος), and services of help (ἀντιλήμψεις). The exercise of Holy Orders might possibly be included here as well.

Extraordinary or miraculous charisms embrace the gifts of healing (ἴαμα), miracles (δυνάμεις), faith (πίστις), such as would "move mountains," exorcism (ἐξόρκωσις), and immunity from harm arising from deadly things such as serpents or poison. Among miraculous charisms of the intellectual order would be included *prophecy (προφητεία), in as far as it involved revelation (ἀποκάλυψις), reading of hearts, or prediction of future events, and the gift called *discernment of spirits (διάκρισιτ πνευμάτων), i.e., the supernatural ability to distinguish between true and false spiritual phenomena. Finally, the popular *gift of tongues or glossolalia (γένη γλωσσῶν), and the related interpretation, or possibly translation, of tongues (ἑρμηνεία γλωσσῶν) complete the lists.

Value. Although the phenomenon, if not the name, of charismatic gifts was evident in the OT (e.g., in Moses, the Prophets), the full outpouring of the Spirit was reserved for messianic times [Ps 67(68).19; Eph 4.7–13]. This was particularly true of the Church's early years, when it needed special helps for its consolidation, survival, and expansion. Human pride, however, tended to overemphasize the spectacular gifts such as tongues, and it became necessary for the Church's leaders, e.g., in 1 Corinthians ch. 12–14, to remind Christians of (1) the common source of all gifts, the Holy Spirit; (2) the comparative value of the charisms, e.g., prophecy far surpassing tongues; (3) the superiority of love (ἀγάπη) over all charisms; and (4) what should be the orderly interaction of hierarchical and charismatic functions in the Church.

Bibliography: EncDictBibl 350–351. A. LEMONNYER, DBSuppl 1:1233–44. É. OSTY, *Les Épîtres de St. Paul aux Corinthiens* (BJ 37; 1949) 52–60. G. RICCIOTTI, *Paul the Apostle,* tr. A. ZIZZAMIA (Milwaukee 1953) 171–179. J. BONSIRVEN, *Theology of the New Testament,* tr. S. F. L. TYE (Westminster, Md. 1963) 324–331. F. PRAT, *The Theology of St. Paul,* tr. J. STODDARD, 2 v. (London 1926) 1:127–133, 423–428.

[W. F. DICHARRY]

GIVEN TO INDIVIDUAL

In accordance with the technical meaning of the word charism as found in the NT and particularly in St. Paul, theology defines charism as a gratuitous gift from God, *supernatural, transitory, given to the individual for the good of others, for the benefit of the

ē qui diligit me · Qui autem diligit
me · diligetur a patre meo · Et ego dili
gam eum · & manifestabo ei me ipsū ·

Pentecost, miniature in a pericope book from Salzburg, mid-11th century (Bayerische Staatsbibliothek, Munich Clm. 15713, fol. 37 v). This first outpouring of the Holy Spirit (indicated by the tongues of flame radiating from the center of the concentric circles) upon the Apostles was a charismatic visitation (Acts ch. 2).

*Church. This section discusses: (1) the nature of this gift, namely, what it consists of and what it implies in the individual receiving it; and (2) the different types of charisms as theology views them.

Nature. The early Fathers and ecclesiastical writers used the word loosely in the sense of *grace or gift. St. Thomas Aquinas stated that it is a grace given by God not for the personal *justification or sanctification of the individual, but for the spiritual welfare of others. It differs essentially from the type of grace that renders the individual pleasing to God or holy in His sight (*gratia gratum faciens*). All grace, as the very name implies, is gratuitously given (*gratis data*) by God; yet, since charism lacks the added perfection of rendering the individual holy, it retains for its name the merely generic term of gratuitously given grace (*gratia gratis data;* see ST 1a2ae, 111.1 ad 3). In this sense charisms differ from sanctifying or actual grace, from *virtues, gifts of the Holy Spirit (*see* HOLY SPIRIT, GIFTS OF), and from graces of state of life. All these graces are entitative or operative *habits or dispositions that inhere in the subject and have as their primary purpose the subject's perfection.

Charisms on the other hand may be given to the individual in a purely instrumental manner to accomplish some salutary effect in others. Thus a charismatic person might not necessarily be a holy person, although ordinarily God will use as His instrument one who is close to Him. As a matter of fact at times there might exist a correlation between certain gifts of the Holy Spirit and certain charisms, for instance, between the gifts of wisdom and counsel on the one hand, and the charisms of supernatural understanding and discernment of spirits on the other. In these cases the individual is instrumentally empowered with extraordinary ability to communicate to others that which he had received permanently through a gift.

The superiority and permanency of those graces that render the individual holy do not detract from the ontological and supernatural perfection of charisms. Charisms are the product of special intervention of God in man's faculties and operation. Metaphysically speaking, they may be reduced to the category of accidents, of transitory qualities or instrumental operative powers by which man's faculties are elevated to behavior beyond their natural capacity. They consist in different types of intellectual illuminations, in facility of communication with others, in ability to perform miraculous deeds, etc.

In the strictest sense charisms stand only for extraordinary gifts such as prophecy, glossolalia, etc. Yet, gifts such as ecclesiastical jurisdiction, exercise of Sacred Orders, and infallibility also fulfill the definition, for all these are supernatural, freely given gifts ordained for the benefit of the Church. These latter gifts, however, are more permanent in nature.

Types. Arrangements or classifications made by theologians are somewhat arbitrary. St. Thomas, visualizing the role of these gifts in the Church precisely in a doctrinal and apologetic function, states that "they are ordained for the manifestation of faith and spiritual doctrine" (ST 3a, 7.7). With this criterion in mind he divides charisms into three categories (ST 1a2ae, 111.4). First, there are those charisms that empower the apostle with extraordinary knowledge of divine things. This is done by special faith, by word of wisdom (cognition of divine things, λόγος σοφίας), and word of knowledge (cognition of human affairs, λόγος γνώσεως). Second, he numbers those charisms by which one may efficaciously confirm in the eyes of his audience the divine origin of his teachings. Through these he instrumentally performs deeds that are proper to God—prophesies, discerns spirits, heals, and works miracles. Finally he considers those charisms concerned with the actual deliverance of the gospel, by which the minister of it is enabled to present efficiently the divine doctrine to his audience. To this realm of charisms belong glossolalia and the related interpretation.

See also PROPHECY (THEOLOGY OF).

Bibliography: DTC, Tables générales 1:582–583. J. GEWIESS and K. RAHNER, LexThK[2] 2:1025–30. H. LECLERCQ, DACL 3: 579–598. X. DUCROS, DictSpirAscMyst 2.1:503–507. C. BOYER, EncCatt 3:793–795. C. PESCH, *De gratia,* v.5 of *Praelectiones dogmaticae,* 9 v. (Freiburg 1910–22), app., "De gratiis gratis datis."

[R. J. TAPIA]

FOR THE CHURCH

It is to the Church on earth, to the messianic community of *salvation, that the Spirit has been sent—to dwell in the Church, to animate it, to pour out upon it His gifts and graces. Those gifts and graces that are of a manifest nature and given to the individual for the Church, gifts that are created, supernatural and gratuitous, are called charisms. This section deals with the role of charism in the Church, its various forms, and the relation of charism to the ministry of the Church.

A Sign. The *Holy Spirit dwells actively in the Church (*see* SOUL OF THE CHURCH); this makes the Church essentially a charismatic Church. Charism is the living sign both to Christians and to the world that Christ has been victorious over death, that the messianic age of the Spirit has come, that God has saved His people. For Christians charism is for their consolation, encouragement, and edification. For the world the charism of the Church's unity and universality, apostolicity, holiness, and fecundity in good works makes the Church itself the greatest motive of credibility (Denz 3013). It is through charism that mankind finds Christ in His Church.

This is not to say that charism cannot exist outside the Church. But charism is "connatural" to the Church, leads to the Church, and outside the Church will never be so intense as to be a sign of the truth of another way to God.

Analogous Concept. The notion of charism in the Church is an analogous one. The ministry of the Church is itself a charismatic ministry. It is given to the individual not for his own sake but for the service of the Church. The powers of Orders, magisterium, and jurisdiction are ordered to the building up of the *Mystical Body of Christ. Moreover ecclesiastical office brings to its recipient not only sacramental grace, character, and the special grace of state but also the "supernatural gifts of knowledge, understanding and wisdom" to make the ministry effective (Pius XII MysCorp 49), and this to such extent that the official ministry of the Church is indefectible and infallible (*see* OFFICE, ECCLESIASTICAL).

Structural. Because the office of the *hierarchy has been established by Christ as part of the Church's structure and the coordination of the action of the Spirit with that of the ministry has been guaranteed by Christ, the charism of office may be called "structural" charism.

Nonstructural. The action of a free and autonomous Spirit dwelling in the Church, however, cannot be limited to structural forms. The activity of the Spirit for the Church in free, noncovenanted ways may be called "nonstructural" charism. Ever new and diverse, its precise form cannot be anticipated. Still, in some form such charism belongs to the Church of the messianic era (*ibid.* 17) and historically speaking has been characteristic of the Church in every age, although more strikingly so in the period of foundation.

Nonstructural charism, given to members of the hierarchy or the laity, may be a motion of the Spirit (and thus not a habit usable at will by the individual), a *gratia gratis data,* beyond the powers of man and miraculous in the strict sense (St. Thomas, ST 1a2ae, 111). *Miracles, gifts of tongues, private revelations, ecstasies, visions, and prophecy are all gifts of the Spirit not due to the merit of the individual nor directly for his sanctification, but for the good of the Church.

The urgings, promptings, motions, and impulses of the Spirit that come to the Church in this way form a channel of direction from the Spirit that is nonstructural. In every age the Spirit has raised up saints, founders of orders or movements, popes, bishops, or laymen—men who spoke to their own age, who had a message for the Church of their age. This is a gift to the individual for the Church, a charism (Pius XII MysCorp 38; ST 2a2ae, 174.6 ad 3).

Nonstructural charism may also be in a form that does sanctify the individual but is directed also to the good of the Church. Every grace of constant, lifelong fidelity to the living of the Christian life in one's state in the Church, despite trials and difficulties of every type, is a grace not for the sanctification of the individual alone; it is a social grace, it leads the recipient to the total service of Christ *in the Church,* to the cooperation with Christ in the work of the Church for men. The grace given a hospital sister sanctifies her, but it also draws her to the lifelong service of Christ's sick members; it is a grace given her for the Church. Her loving care is a sign to the world of the love of Christ. The same may be said of the lives of bishops, priests, teaching sisters, mothers, fathers, Christian workers, and for every state of life in the Church, including the contemplative (Pius XII MysCorp 17, 78, 97, 98).

Such graces of the Spirit have led innumerable Christians to martyrdom, have brought thousands to the religious life and the priesthood, have sent missionaries to every part of the globe, have built charitable works of every variety (*ibid.* 65). These sanctifying graces are seen in their effects, the faithful service of the Church according to each one's vocation.

One Spirit. Since the Spirit acts freely on the laity as well as on the hierarchy, the question of the relation between structural and nonstructural charism must arise. As far back as *Montanism and as recently as R. *Sohm and E. Brunner there has been a tendency to oppose charism and a sacramental ecclesiastical office. This has led to a certain depreciation of charism among Catholic theologians.

With the same Spirit acting in both, there can be no true opposition between office and charism. There may indeed be a certain tension, but this tension is not undesirable. It ensures the truth of the charism against illusion and deception. It preserves hierarchy from becoming an absolute type of authoritarianism in which all initiative must come from above.

The hierarchy must judge the truth of the charism, using the criteria for the discernment of spirits, neither hastily seeing it where it is not, nor demanding excessive proof so as to stifle the Spirit [Vatican II, *Dogmatic Constitution on the Church* 12; ActApS 57 (1965) 16–17].

The laity must see their gifts as ordered to charity and must use them with courage for the good of the Church.

The theology of charism in the life of the Church must be further studied and a history of it written. Appreciation of charism leads to a vital ecclesiology in which the Spirit is seen as the source of all activity among the *people of God.

See also FREEDOM, INTELLECTUAL; FREEDOM OF SPEECH; TEACHING AUTHORITY OF THE CHURCH; LAITY, THEOLOGY OF.

Bibliography: K. RAHNER, "The Charismatic Element in the Church," in *The Dynamic Element in the Church,* tr. W. J. O'HARA (Questiones Disputatae 12; New York 1964); *Visions and Prophecies,* tr. C. HENKEY and R. STRACHAN (*ibid.* 10; 1963); *Free Speech in the Church* (New York 1959); "The Individual in the Church," *Nature and Grace,* tr. D. WHARTON (New York 1964). Y. M. J. CONGAR, *The Mystery of the Church,* tr. A. LITTLEDALE (Baltimore 1960) 147–186. J. RATZINGER, "Free Expression and Obedience in the Church," *Church: Readings in Theology* (New York 1963) 194–215. L. VOLKEN, *Visions, Revelations and the Church,* tr. E. GALLAGHER (New York 1963). B. MARÉCHAUX, *Les Charismes du Saint-Esprit* (Paris 1921). T. WOTHERSPOON, *The Ministry in the Church in Relation to Prophecy and Spiritual Gifts (Charismata)* (London 1916). J. B. A. ENGLMANN, *Von den Charismen im Allgemeinen und von dem Sprachen-Charisma im besonderen* (Ratisbon 1848). M. SCHMAUS, *Katholische Dogmatik,* 5 v. in 8 (5th ed. Munich 1953–59) 3.1:362–366. E. BRUNNER, *The Misunderstanding of the Church,* tr. H. KNIGHT (Philadelphia 1953). R. SOHM, *Kirchenrecht,* 2 v. (Leipzig 1923) v.1. **Illustration credit:** Hirmer Verlag München.

[J. F. GALLAGHER]

CHARITÉ-SUR-LOIRE, ABBEY OF, the former Benedictine priory of *B. Maria de Caritate ad Ligerim,* near Nevers, France, Diocese of Nevers. The basilican monastery founded in 706 was devastated in 771. At the request of Bp. Geoffrey of Auxerre and Count William of Nevers, it was restored (1056) by the monks of *Cluny under the direction of St. *Hugh of Cluny. As one of the five "daughter" monasteries immediately dependent on Cluny, it in turn governed 52 monasteries. Pope *Pascal II consecrated the church in 1107. By 1343 it numbered 80 monks, but this number had dropped to 18 in 1436. Jean de Bourbon, Abbot of Cluny (1456–85), tried to reform the monastery but he could not stem the monastic and economic decline. Having been progressively ruined by the rule of commendatory abbots imposed in 1538, it was united to the Cluniac Congregation of Strict Observance March 13, 1634. It was suppressed in 1790. Most of the buildings of the cloister are still standing. The church, despite later changes, remains a model of Roman Burgundian architecture.

Bibliography: Cottineau 1:705–706. R. VAN DOREN, DHGE 12:419–421. H. H. HILBERRY, "La Charité-sur-Loire Priory Church," *Speculum* 30 (1955) 1–14.

[R. GRÉGOIRE]

CHARITIES, TORT LIABILITY OF (U.S.)

The doctrine that a charitable institution is immune from liability for torts committed by its employees had a questionable origin and has had a history of growing exceptions. The doctrine originated in decisions by Massachusetts and Maryland in the last part of the 19th century that relied upon English precedents by then already repudiated in England.

Opposing Arguments. The original justification for immunity was that awarding damages diverts trust funds from the objectives of the charitable donor to the completely different purpose of paying damages to persons injured by tortious conduct of employees of the charity. A second basis for immunity is that *respondeat superior* —the rule that the master must answer for the acts of his servant—should not apply to a charity because a charity gets no profit from the enterprise in which it employs its servants. A third thesis is that the beneficiaries of a charity, by accepting its largesse, impliedly waive any claim for compensation for torts or assume the risk of torts being committed upon them. A fourth theory is the general one that sound public policy demands immunity. This theory assumes that charitable institutions will be so hampered by tort damages that they will be unable to discharge their public purposes properly and donors will be discouraged from making donations, since such donations may be used to pay damages rather than for direct charitable purposes.

All these theories have been repudiated in many decisions; the most celebrated of these is *President and Directors of Georgetown College v. Hughes,* 130 F. 2d 810 (D.C. Cir. 1942). Decisions opposed to immunity frequently state that, if immunity was ever needed to foster development of charitable institutions, that need has long since passed. It is often asserted that the charities of today must and do operate on sound business principles and will not be crippled by having to purchase liability insurance against tort liability any more than they are crippled by payment of other administrative expenses, including insurance against fire damage to their buildings. It is further argued that a charitable enterprise is in a better position to provide insurance protection than is the individual victim—often the impecunious beneficiary of the charity—who is hurt by the misdeed of the charity's employee. The opponents of immunity also point out that there is no evidence that the operations of charities have been hampered in the many jurisdictions that deny charitable immunity, or that charitable donations have been discouraged in those jurisdictions. Basically, the advocates of full liability for charities assert that, under long-established principles, liability for tortious conduct is the general rule and that no sufficient cause appears why charities should be specially exempt from the general rule.

Courts are accepting more and more the arguments in favor of liability for charities. In such a fluid field it is difficult to make an accurate count of the jurisdictions. The opinions of the courts of some states are not clear on the subject and, in others, older decisions, recognizing full or partial immunity, are subject to imminent legislative or judicial overturning. It is certain that more states reject immunity than grant it fully. But many remain part way between these two positions.

Erosion of Immunity. In jurisdictions where partial immunity is in force, the decisions run the gamut from nearly complete liability to nearly complete immunity. A frequent exception to the immunity rule, in the partial-immunity states, is that a charity is liable for injury by one of its employees to another employee. Another holding that is often seen is that a charity is liable for injury to a "stranger" to the charity. This concept has lead to difficulty in distinguishing between a "stranger" and one who is a "beneficiary" of the charity. A person purchasing religious articles has been held to be a beneficiary. The status of one attending a church social has been said to be a question of fact that, presumably, is resolvable either way, depending upon the evidence in a particular case. Spectators at a football game have been considered strangers. So have visitors to hospital patients, although not uniformly so.

In some partial-immunity states, charities have been held liable for the tort of nuisance or for injuries resulting from the violation of specific statutes but not for negligence. Other cases have decided that the immunity does not apply where the activities are noncharitable, such as the operation of income-producing property for investment purposes. A number of jurisdictions allow recovery where the charity has negligently selected for employment or negligently retained in employment the servant who commits the wrong. This has sometimes been characterized as "corporate negligence." "Corporate negligence" creative of liability has also been found where the misconduct was that of managerial officials of the charity in adopting rules and regulations or in selecting or supplying equipment. Still other opinions have declared that the immunity rule protects only property that is part of the charitable trust, and that recovery may be had out of assets, such as the proceeds of a liability insurance policy that are found not to be part of the charitable trust. Other courts have decided that the existence of insurance is not material and cannot create liability where it would otherwise not exist.

The typical historical development is an initial holding of full immunity followed by ever broadening exceptions and culminating in complete abandonment of immunity. Some courts have declined to take the final step of abandonment on the ground that such a decision is within the legislative province, but this is not the usual attitude. It is likely that the future will see a complete elimination of the immunity.

Bibliography: F. V. Harper and F. James, *The Law of Torts,* 3 v. (Boston 1956) v.2. W. L. Prosser, *Handbook of the Law of Torts* (2d ed. St. Paul 1955). L. W. Feezer, "Tort Liability of Charities," *University of Pennsylvania Law Review* 77 (1928) 191–212. J. J. Simeone, "The Doctrine of Charitable Immunity," *St. Louis University Law Journal* 5 (1959) 357–373. A. Joachim, "The Policymakers: Courts or Legislatures?" *Boston University Law Review* 39 (1959) 349–364. E. H. Schopler, "Immunity of Non-governmental Charity from Liability for Damages in Tort," *American Law Reports Annotated* 25 (1952) 29–200.

[H. F. MC NIECE]

CHARITY

Charity (from Old French *charité,* Latin *caritas*) stands in general for the state of being in and responding to God's love and favor, more specifically for our wholehearted love of God, who reveals Himself in the Scriptures, and for the love of our neighbor as ourselves there inculcated, and most specifically for the third and greatest of the theological virtues. These senses are kept in the vocabulary of English-speaking Catholicism, although there, and even more elsewhere, the word has gone down in the world and is applied to an active benevolence toward those in need and sometimes to a dutiful or even a patronizing regard for those one finds socially and psychologically taxing. This decayed usage, however, will be neglected in this article, which summarizes the teaching of (1) the Scriptures; (2) the Fathers; and (3) St. Thomas Aquinas, whose theological formulation is at once more systematic than that of his predecessors and less confined by the concept of obligation than that of most of his successors. There is need to avoid the two extremes: making charity an ineffable impulse, defying description, and isolating it as a technical way of loving God or of treating one's neighbor with supernatural kindliness.

Sacred Scripture. Words from the Hebrew root verb *'āhēb* are rendered to mean, first, God's love for men; second, men's love for God; and third, the love between men in this religious setting. Such love involving a special choice, as in the Latin *dilectio,* is called ἀγάπη, a word adopted by the NT and later Church writers to signify the love of God for Christ (Jn 17.36) and for men (Rom 5.8), of Christ for men (Rom 8.35), of men for God (Jn 2.5) and for one another (Jn 12.35); there is no clear instance of its employment in a non-Christian context. Ἔρως, a sexual love, is not referred to in the NT, which speaks of ἐπιθυμία, i.e., *concupiscentia;* there also φιλία means ordinary friendship or natural affection.

Agape was translated by the Vulgate as *caritas,* possibly because *amor* had impure associations and *dilectio* and *amicitia* were too secular. Charity is the word consistently used by the Reims and Douay versions, and often by the Authorized and Confraternity Versions; and it never occurs in Revised Version, though the Revised Standard Version adopts it for Acts 9.36; it seems less ambiguous than "love" and will not go flat while kept close to the etymology *carus,* French *cher,* and to the idea of holding dear and cherishing.

The dominant theme is that God first loves us (1 Jn 4.9) and commends His charity toward us in the death of His Son (Rom 5.8–10). Our love in return springs from the new man who is now dead to sin and born afresh to life in Christ (Jn 3.3; Rom 6.6; 2 Cor 5.17; Col 3.10; 1 Pt 1.23). We are now members of God's family, like little children (Mt 8.2), receiving the spirit of adoption whereby we cry "Abba! Father!" (Rom 8.15; Gal 4.6). The Trinity dwells in us (Jn 14.23); we are members of the same body of Christ (1 Cor 12.27), branches of the same vine (Jn 15.4); and Christ lives in us (Gal 2.20). We form one body and one spirit in the hope of our calling (Eph 4.4), to become partakers of the divine nature (2 Pt 1.4).

To live in this way goes with loving God with our whole heart and soul and mind and loving our neighbor as ourselves; such is the fulfillment of the law, the summing up of all the Commandments and prophecies (Mt 22.36–40; Rom 13.9–10). This is charity, that we walk according to God's Commandments (2 John ch. 6); and the thought was related by St. John to the key ideas of God as light (Jn 1.4; 8.12; 1 Jn 1.5; 2.8), and life (Jn 1.4; 5.26; 14.19), and Father (Jn 4.14; 14.21–23; 15.10; 2 Jn 4), and to the revelation of God as charity itself (1 Jn 4.16). To St. Paul it was the bond of union (Rom 12.10; Eph 4.15; Col 1.4; 3.14) and the most excellent and lasting activity of immortal life (1 Cor 13.1–13). St. Peter preached the same message of charity born from incorruptible life and receiving salvation in the final issue (1 Pt 1.8–9; 22.23; 3.8; 4.8).

The Fathers. The early writers of the Church devoted no set treatise to the virtue of charity. For them, it was the way of Christian life; and their teaching, which appeared in their comments and homilies on the Scriptures, was directed to maintaining the unity of the faithful, realized in the Eucharistic communion, and to fostering their practical love for one another. Thus SS. Ignatius of Antioch, Clement of Alexandria, and Polycarp. Clement of Alexandria was more speculative; charity is bound up with the gnosis, or knowledge of God freeing us from the material world. SS. Basil, Gregory of Nazianzus, and John Chrysostom brought out what it means to love one's neighbor as oneself. It was not until St. Augustine, named the *Doctor Caritatis,* that one sees the first sketches, somewhat darkly edged by the contrasts between the laws of nature and grace, of a systematic treatment. Charity is the perfect justice that obeys the sovereign law of love; the essence of sin is to go against it. The *De diligendo Deo,* though wrongly attributed to him, represents his doctrine; the classical synopsis of it is St. Thomas's three questions on the gospel law (ST 1a2ae, 106–108). Gregory the Great wrote as a pastoral theologian; and the topic of charity, although elaborated in terms of literature and spiritual direction by the great monastic writers, notably St. Bernard, and interpreted according to the Platonist mystical tradition, notably by the Victorines, received no strictly theological development until the 13th century, when the great scholastics, having girded up the loins of their understanding (1 Pt 1.13), set about analyzing the concepts in the Christian mind.

St. Thomas. Here St. Thomas offers the best theological centerpiece, for apart from the fact that he has been declared an authentic exponent of what the Church thinks, his treatment, which is profoundly scriptural, draws together the strands of many different traditions—Platonist, Aristotelean, Stoic, patristic, and even romantic—into the best pattern of reference for later discussions and disagreements. The *ex professo* treatise of the *Summa theologiae* on charity (2a2ae, 23–46), which is followed here, should be complemented (1) by the questions on the nature of love (1a2ae, 26–28), on the gospel law already referred to, which introduced the treatise on grace, on the life of perfection (2a2ae, 184); and (2) by the debates *De caritate.*

Friendship. Charity itself (2a2ae, 23) is introduced as the kind of love called friendship (23.1), in agreement with Our Lord's words, "No longer do I call you servants, but friends" (Jn 15.15). It goes beyond the love of what is good for us, as in the theological virtue of hope, and the disinterested love for another (*benevolentia*) and the doing of good to another, to a condition of mutual loving between persons who are sharers. This sharing (*communicatio, participatio*) is God's granting to us His own happiness, *beatitudo.* The teaching of *Nicomachean Ethics* bk 8 on the association implied in all friendship is equably assumed into the apostolic preaching; our citizenship is in heaven in fellowship with God's Son (1 Cor 1.9; Phil 3.20) and is invested with the NT κοινωνία. This is the basis that makes charity different from other forms of friendship and the friendliness that is part of social justice (2a2ae,

114); indeed all friendship that has this glow from within imparted by God's own joy is charity, and any religious account that excludes it may be talking about some sort of love of God, but not about charity (*see* FRIENDSHIP).

This relationship between persons means that the charity of God poured forth in our hearts by the Holy Spirit, who has been given to us (Rom 5.5), is still our own act of loving (23.2). We are not, as it were, swamped, for the first cause maintains secondary causes as principals (cf. 1a, 105.5); and were we to be merely God's instruments, then our active friendship with God would lack the spontaneity, ease, and delight to be expected of godlike operations. The argument against the singular opinion of Peter Lombard that charity is the Holy Spirit in us was confirmed at Trent (Denz 1529). It is wholly the effect of God's power, giving us a power, or *virtus,* of activity by which we pass from what we were to what we want to be. It is not one of the moral virtues enabling us to live according to right reason but a theological virtue, conjoining us, as St. Augustine says, to God Himself (22.3). His goodness lies beyond the immediate objectives of all the other virtues; and consequently charity, through which we reach it, is a special virtue, although not in the limited sense that other virtues are, since its objective, which is not one among many particular kinds of good, embraces them all while holding them distinct and subordinate (23.4). Moreover, charity is a single virtue, for despite its manifold activities its end and basis remain always the same, namely, God's sharing His goodness in everlasting happiness (23.5). It rests on God for Himself, not for what He gives to us, and therefore it is the greatest of all the virtues (23.6; cf. 1 Cor 12.8, 13).

St. Augustine spoke of virtue as the ordering of love; and although we may be well ordered with respect to particular and limited ends, we are not fully virtuous unless our charity bears us to the ultimate end of the whole of life (23.7); "if I distribute all my goods to feed the poor, and if I deliver my body to be burned, yet do not have charity, it profits me nothing" (1 Cor 13.3). From this principle is developed the theology of charity as the "form" of all the virtues (23.8). The term is used teleologically rather than typologically, for it is not that charity gives to each virtue its own specific interest, which is largely abstract, but that in the concrete it makes each virtue serve the final blessedness of being in love with God and His friends—hence St. Paul's injunction, "Let all that you do be done in charity" (1 Cor 16.14). Here again, it is not that behavior has to become stilted or interrupted by an extrinsic ordination, as seems suggested by spiritual writers who have not grasped the theology of God's universal causality, but that it should well up unaffectedly from our friendship with God. "For his workmanship we are, created in Christ Jesus in good works" (Eph 2.10). There is a distinction between intention and attention; God can be actually, though implicitly, loved without being thought of, and He is virtually loved in all the activities, except sin, of those who continue to set their heart on Him. "For the rest, brethren, whatever things are true, whatever honorable, whatever just, whatever holy, whatever lovable, whatever of good repute, if there be any virtue, if anything worthy of praise, think upon these things" (Phil 4.8).

Charity in Relation to Us. Charity is an immortal love (2a2ae, 24), and therefore its seat is the will (*appetitus intellectivus*), not the emotional powers (*appetitus sensitivus*). It ranges beyond our present environment and breaks through the obscurities of faith to reach the mystery of God; "so that, being rooted and grounded in love, you may be able to comprehend with all the saints what is the breadth and length and height and depth, and to know Christ's love which surpasses knowledge in order that you may be filled unto all the fullness of God" (Eph 3.18–19). This Pauline concept of being filled runs throughout this part of the theological study. For as charity is not limited by the knowledge furnished by the mind, so it lies more deeply in the will than at the level of its choices (24.1) and comes to us not through our own efforts but by God's gift, or "infusion" (24.2). And like his other supernatural gifts, "these are the work of one and the same Spirit, who allots to everyone according as he will" (1 Cor 12.11). And charity is not measured by natural capacity (24.3), nor is it because of temperament or force of circumstances that some become better lovers of God than others, but "according to the measure of Christ's bestowal" (Eph 4.7).

That charity can grow was declared at Trent (sess. 6, ch. 10), and theology draws analogies between bodily and spiritual increase through nourishment and exercise. The preoccupation of later scholastic writers with the amount (*quantitas*) of charity and the effects on it of acts that are below strength (*actus remissi*) may appear quaint to the modern reader, but the theory that it grows, not by addition, but by intensification, a deepening participation or possession (*per majorem radicationem in subjecto*), accords with the psychology of disposition or "habits" (1a2ae, 52–53) and the thought of St. Paul (Eph 3.17). To this growth no term can be fixed in this present life, because the love it shares, namely, the Holy Spirit, is infinite and so is the power of God who causes it; and man's questing heart can always love more than it does (24.4–7). On the other hand, venial sin does not reach deep enough directly to effect or cause a weakening of charity, although it may dispose to its being lost (24.10) through grave sin, for according to the teaching of the Church charity in fact does not make a man impeccable (24.11–12).

Charity, then, is an analogical idea in that a single meaning may exist at different strengths, and charity allows for a difference of degrees (*secundum magis et minus*). This raises the question in spiritual theology whether and when charity in this life can be called perfect (24.8); and the discussion, which may be regarded as an extension of St. Thomas's fourth proof for the existence of God, proceeds according to the traditional Platonist terms of participation and of drawing closer to God. If love matches the beloved, then God alone can love Himself as much as He can be loved, and no creature can ever hope to attain such perfection. If love is in proportion to the lover, then different degrees are possible. God may be wholeheartedly and actually loved always, but this is the condition of charity as it is in heaven (*caritas patriae*); until we see Him in vision and so long as we hold Him by faith, He does not always engage our attention and expressed affection. As for our love in the present life (*caritas viae*), it is possible for us to set aside all other things,

"Charity," marble relief by Pisan sculptor Giovanni di Balduccio (active 1317–49), 17¾ by 13⅞ in.

except insofar as the necessities of life require them, and devote ourselves to divine things. Yet such perfection is rare; what is common to all who are in God's friendship is that their whole heart is steadily (*habitualiter*) given to God in such sort that they neither harbor nor will anything contrary to His love. This is sane and generous doctrine, and it avoids the division, of which the classical theologians of the Church have always been suspicious, between a mystical elite and plain Christians who are well content if they can keep the Commandments. The precepts of charity are first and foremost, not of the Decalogue (cf. 1a2ae, 100, 107; 2a2ae, 44); and it should be remembered that the "state" of perfection constituted by vows and the episcopal order is directly a category of Canon Law, not of spiritual theology (cf. 2a2ae, 184).

The progress possible in this life is stated according to three stages—beginners (*incipientes*), those who are advancing (*proficientes*), and those who are well advanced (*perfecti*)—which may be taken as corresponding approximately to the purgative, illuminative, and unitive ways (24.9). The distinction should be taken to represent not three different compartments but rather three emphases in principal occupations. At first we strive to keep alive our friendship with God, afterward seek to deepen it, and finally may come so to cling as to "desire to depart and to be with Christ" (Phil 1.23). The process is continuous; the end is in the beginning, the first grace of Baptism is the seed of glory, and holiness in this life is never so secure as not to be fearful of a fall; "work out your salvation with fear and trembling" (Phil 2.13).

The Objects of Charity. An esoteric treatment of such a high virtue is forestalled by the scriptural and patristic insistence on its social force: "if anyone says that he loves God, and hates his brother, he is a liar. For how can he who does not love his brother, whom he sees, love God, whom he does not see? And this commandment we have from Him, that he who loves God should love his brother also" (1 Jn 4.20–21).

God is loved, first of all, not merely as integrating our human experience but as revealing Himself and pledging the communication of His joy. That He is loved for His own sake was taken quite simply, until with the refinement of abstractions in theology and their isolation as representing concrete situations, coupled with a spiritual theory of abnegation and practice of introspection to bring about the purification of motives, men began to ask themselves whether the pure and disinterested love of God was compatible with thoughts of self or indeed with images of His Incarnation and Sacraments. The question, which came to a head in the troubles between Fénelon and Bossuet, is summed up by R. A. Knox [*Enthusiasm* (Oxford 1957) 249]: "When I meditate about God I seldom lose sight of what *he is for me,* whereas when I use the prayer of contemplation my mind is more easily directed to the thought of what God is *in himself.* The contrast should not be overstressed; if it had not been, Quietism would probably have ended with Molinos, and the Church in France would have been spared a long and painful controversy." Knox also draws attention to a certain Platonism separating pure forms from the rich complex of God's loving action in us. Moreover the theological sense of symbolism seems to have been lost (cf. 3a, 8.3 ad 3; 23.3) in an attempt to strip love down to one element. Certainly there was a movement against the pregnant words of Scripture: "if thou didst know the gift of God, and who it is who says to thee, Give me to drink, thou, perhaps, wouldst have asked of him, and he would have given thee living water" (Jn 4.10). God gives Christ to us, and has given us to Christ (Jn 17.6). "How can he fail to grant us also all things with him?" (Rom 8.32). The ordinary teaching authority of the Church was quick to keep charity related to the ordinary works of virtue and quite properly expecting its reward not, as it were, by a quasi-juridical grant of a prize, but by the demand of love that it should find what it seeks (cf. 1a2ae, 114.4); "If anyone love me he will keep my word, and my Father will love him, and we will come to him and make our abode with him" (Jn 14.23).

The same movement of God goes to God and to all who are or can be His friends; it is not, as sometimes suggested, that we love God and because of this by a further and imperated act love our neighbor, as if one were our end and the other our means. Our love is elicited from charity (25.1), other persons being taken in God and as companions in His happiness; underlying this is the theology that creatures are true principal agents, though secondary, and true ends, though nonultimate. Notice also that we are bidden to do to our neighbor as we do to ourselves, and how unforced, and in a sense "undutiful," that is. It is to love our neighbor as a sharer in happiness, and this charity itself, not to make too fine a point, is itself lovable; for like happiness itself, it is not so much a virtue itself as a total condition (25.2).

And who is my neighbor? As in the story of the good Samaritan, charity is not restricted to a circle formed by one's customs, tastes, prejudices, or religious or cultural training; but as an impulse it knows no limits: all creatures of mind and heart who can share in the fellowship of eternal life are the proper objects of its love, and other things too can be cherished as existing for divine honor and human benefit; so by charity does God love them (25.3). Strictly speaking we cannot be friends with ourselves. Yet as belonging to God, who is our friend, we should love ourselves, and also our bodies; an unearthly love that disdains the material world as evil is rejected (25.4–5). It will be noticed how sound Catholic tradition has excluded from this love in Christ neither the self nor the whole of creation that will be restored in Christ, "the firstborn of every creature, things visible and things invisible, and in him all things hold together, and through him he should reconcile all things, whether on earth or in the heavens" (Col 1.15–20), "who will refashion the body of our lowliness, conforming it to the body of his glory, by the power by which he is able to subject all things to himself" (Phil 3.21).

"I say to you, love your enemies" (Mt 5.44). It would be perverse to force oneself to cherish an enemy as such. One may hate the sin, but not the sinner (25.7). As contained potentially at least in the divine goodness that charity loves, an enemy must be regarded with fundamental good will by a Christian and may not be denied a place among those whom one wishes well. Moreover, one must be prepared to love his neighbor effectively should the occasion arise and to do him the good of which he is in need. "If your enemy be hungry, give him food to eat, if he be thirsty, give him to drink"

(Prv 25.21). The more we love God, however, the less we shall wait for this need or be blocked by any enmity (25.8–9); "If you salute your brethren only, what are you doing more than others? You therefore are to be perfect, even as your heavenly Father is perfect" (Mt 5.47, 48).

Priorities in Charity. Charity is not an attitude of generalized affection but has its predilections and special occasions (2a2ae, 26), according to two principles: (1) what is better (*melior*), and therefore more like to God, and (2) what is nearer to us (*conjunctior*); for as we have seen, such polarization is essential to charity as it is to friendship. God's love comes above all, for even in natural love the part loves the whole even more than itself; much more in charity, then, is He loved as the fount of all that shares His happiness (26.1–3). The only break with this rule comes from that kind of self-love called sin. For the rest, after God we should first love ourselves, not in any self-regarding sense, but with a sober recognition that unless we are friends with God we cannot be in charity with others, even though we set their eternal welfare above our temporal good (26.4–5).

Charity also responds to the varieties in companionship (*consociatio*). It would be unreasonable to expect us to bear an equal affection for all; some do not enter into our life, and of those who do, some are better and therefore more lovable in themselves. Yet charity goes past esteem, and to others we warm because we are closer, and therefore love them with more intensity (26.6–12); there is no reason to suppose that any good reason for loving will be taken away in heaven (26.13).

Main Act of Charity. This is called *dilectio* (2a2ae, 27). "Dilection" is now a pallid translation, and there is no single equivalent term in English for this committed love that picks out its beloved. It seeks rather to love than to be loved; yet when it is mutual, all is well (27.1). It is not simple benevolence, although this is comprehended; but according to the dialectic of the deepest loving, often referred to in the *Summa,* this love, unlike knowing, transforms itself into the condition of its object—the beloved is treated as the self, and the practical axiom of morality, that we should do to others as we would be done by, takes on a new dimension in the friendship of charity (27.2).

The loving is on account of (*propter*) God, and nothing else. If one takes "on account of" in terms of final, formal, and efficient causality, then He is the ultimately, wholly, and underivatively lovable good; if it is taken in terms of material or dispositive causality, then rightly He is loved on account of other things, the blessings that draw us to Him gratefully, and even the penalties that make us fearful of losing Him (27.3). Moreover this love takes over where our knowledge leaves off, for faith is only a mediate and partial possession; whereas charity cleaves immediately "to God Himself and to other things only as being in Him," there is nothing in God that cannot be loved and nothing we can love that cannot be for Him (27.4–5). Finally, there is no limit to be set to this loving, and no excess is possible as there is in the moral virtues (27.6).

It may be observed parenthetically that although the terms of causality have been applied to charity and, by implication, to grace, both are constituted by the special presence of God as an object of knowledge and love, not by the general presence of His power (cf. 1a, 8.3). If we have to use the Aristotelean categories, it is to *relation* that we should look, and treat the life of divine grace and friendship within us as the coming forth into us of the life of the Blessed Trinity (cf. 1a, 43.3).

Corollaries. There is an abandon about charity—more congenially in the sense of being unconstrained than surrendered to outside control—and its interior effects are joy, peace, and mercy (2a2ae, 28–30). "These things I have spoken to you that my joy may be in you, and that your joy may be made full" (Jn 15.11); and again, "Peace I leave with you, my peace I give to you" (Jn 14.27). Both are the consequences of virtue, rather than virtues in themselves, and are considered among the beatitudes and the fruits of the Spirit (cf. 1a2ae, 69.70). "Rejoice with those who rejoice, weep with those who weep" (Rom 12.15); *misericordia* seems to be a special virtue, although it is wider in meaning than the English "mercy," but includes all gracious, familiar, compassionate loving-kindness [cf. E. Hill, *Blackfriars,* 46 (1965), 411–417].

External Acts. External acts of charity are benefaction, almsgiving (*see* ALMS AND ALMSGIVING), and fraternal correction (2a2ae, 31–35). "Therefore while we have time let us do good to all men" (Gal 6.10), beginning with those who are nearest to us. "He who has the goods of this world and sees his brother in need and closes his heart to him, how does the love of God abide in him?" (1 Jn 3.17); the giving we are charged with is conveniently summarized under the headings of the corporal and spiritual works of mercy. "Do not regard him as an enemy, but admonish him as a brother" (2 Thes 3.15); such a benefaction of charity is perhaps the most difficult to perform.

Sins against Charity. The sin against the principal act of charity is hate (2a2ae, 34). The sins against joy are *acedia and *envy (2a2ae, 35, 36). The first, well diagnosed by Cassian, is commonly translated sloth, but it means rather a boredom with divine things, no more to be confused with the spiritual dryness described by the spiritual writers than the steady choice of charity is to be confused with sensible devotion (*see* ARIDITY, SPIRITUAL). Envy, too, is not desire, but sadness about another's good. The sins against peace are discord in the heart, contentiousness in speech, and schism, strife, and rebellion in deed (2a2ae, 37–42). Most of the sins against the external acts of charity are forms of injustice, but *scandal in a special manner is a sin against the loving-kindness we should show to one another (2a2ae, 43); it does not mean shocking another, but providing the occasion for his spiritual ruin.

Precepts. There are two great commandments of charity, that we should love God with our whole heart and our neighbor as ourself (2a2ae, 44). All other precepts are subordinate to these; Christian perfection consists mainly in their observance and not in the counsels (2a2ae, 184.3). Such is the law of love, but it is not an ordinance in the juridical sense, for it is not directed to the well-being of a group, but only to the happy intercommunication of persons in friendship [cf. T. Gilby, *Between Community and Society* (London and New York 1953) 194–202].

Gifts. The classical theological teaching culminates in the consideration of the gift of the Holy Spirit called *wisdom (2a2ae, 45). There the great mystical writers see how our knowledge shaped by love can rise to an experience of God that has gone beyond all concepts: "we speak a wisdom of God, mysterious, hidden which God foreordained before the world to our glory . . . to us God has revealed them through his Spirit. For the Spirit searches all things, even the deep things of God . . .. The spiritual man judges all things, and he himself is judged by no man. For who has known the mind of the Lord that he might instruct him? But we have the mind of Christ" (1 Cor 2.7–16). It is noteworthy that St. Thomas, revising a previous judgment that made of this gift a sort of gnosis, took it also into the practical business of intelligent living (45.3) and related it especially to the seventh beatitude (45.6), "Blessed are the peacemakers, for they shall be called the children of God" (Mt 5.9).

Bibliography: F. PRAT et al., DictSpirAscMyst 2:507–691. C. SPICQ, *Agape in the New Testament,* tr. M. A. MCNAMARA and M. H. RICHTER (St. Louis 1963). J. E. VAN ROEY, *De virtute caritatis quaestiones selectae* (Mechlin 1929). G. GILLEMAN, *The Primacy of Charity in Moral Theology,* tr. W. F. RYAN and A. VACHON (Westminster, Md. 1959). B. HÄRING, *The Law of Christ,* tr. E. G. KAISER (Westminster, Md. 1961–). **Illustration credit:** National Gallery of Art, Washington, D.C., Samuel H. Kress Collection.

[T. GILBY]

CHARITY, BROTHERS OF, a religious congregation of brothers (*Fratres a Caritate,* FC) with papal approval (1888, 1899), founded at Ghent, Belgium, in 1807 by Canon Peter Joseph *Triest. Vows are simple, temporary for 5 years, and then perpetual. Governing the congregation is a superior general, elected every 12 years and aided by four assistants and a procurator chosen by a general chapter. The general council, composed of the superior general and his assistants, appoints provincial and local superiors. After Triest assigned the first members to a hostel for elderly men, his congregation received local episcopal approval in 1809 "for works of charity, service of the poor and destitute." The institute spread to Canada (1865), the U.S. (1874), England (1881), Ireland (1883), and the Netherlands (1894). Missions were established in the Congo (1911), Transvaal (1928), Rwanda and Indonesia (1929), India (1936), Cuba (1950), and Peru (1962). The apostolate encompasses the care of aged men and of the mentally ill; the education of retarded, deaf, mute, blind, and disabled children; and teaching in primary, secondary, and technical schools. The congregation, whose motherhouse is in Ghent, has five provinces (Belgium, Netherlands-Indonesia, England-Ireland, Africa, and Canada-Peru) and one district in the U.S. In 1964 there were 1,537 professed members in 90 houses, working in 124 institutions (13 in the missions) with 28,413 students and 12,440 patients. In the U.S. there were 10 brothers located at the novitiate in Philadelphia.

Bibliography: C. REICHGELT, *Les Frères de la Charité,* v.1 (Ghent 1957), covers 1807–76.

[L. C. DE BEUCKELAER]

CHARITY, DAUGHTERS OF

Includes various groups of sisters in Europe and the U.S.

Daughters of Charity of Canossa. A religious congregation with papal approval (1829), popularly known as Canossian Sisters (FdCC), founded at Verona in 1808 by Bl. Gabriella *Canossa, to run schools, provide religious instruction, and visit hospitals. Members take simple perpetual vows. Governing the congregation is a superior general residing in Rome. Provincials are elected; local superiors are appointed. The sisters dress in a maroon habit, black shawl, and cap and veil, and wear a medallion of Our Lady of Sorrows. In mission territories the garb is white. The first school opened in Verona in 1805 to educate girls of the middle and lower classes. During the lifetime of the foundress four more schools were started, in Venice, Trent, and Bergamo. Later the congregation spread to England, Portugal, Spain, China, India, Malaysia, and Indonesia. Since World War II the Canossians have opened 12 houses in South America, 6 in Australia, 5 in Japan, 4 in Africa, and 3 in the Philippines. Since 1961 the sisters have been located at a school in Albuquerque, N.Mex. In 1964 there were about 5,000 sisters in 371 convents, who directed 302 charitable institutions, including 11 hospitals and 3 leper clincs. They operated also 456 schools, including a university college, and 1,002 centers of religious instruction.

Bibliography: I. GIORDANI, *Ho visto la Chiesa nascente* (Rome 1960).

[A. MENATO]

Daughters of Charity of St. Vincent de Paul. Founded in France (1633) by St. *Vincent de Paul and St. *Louise de Marillac, they have devoted themselves to works of mercy in all the countries of the world except Russia and Sweden. Bl. Elizabeth Bayley *Seton introduced the community into the U.S. by founding a branch in Emmitsburg, Md., in 1809. Its members are often known as Sisters of Charity; but their official title, Daughters of Charity of St. Vincent de Paul (DC), distinguishes them from sisters of other religious communities bearing a similar title and performing similar work.

Foundation. The establishment of the community by Vincent de Paul and Louise de Marillac was a work that developed gradually from the needs of poverty-ridden and war-torn France of the 17th century. Vincent, whose career as parish priest in country districts and chaplain to the galley slaves of the French navy rendered him particularly sensitive to the plight of the unfortunate, founded a Confraternity of Charity among women of rank and fortune who wished to help the poor. In nearly every country place where he gave missions, "charities," as he called the local confraternities, were established. Before long the work spread to the larger cities and by 1635 found zealous workers among even the ladies of the court. When practical difficulties prevented the women from continuing their work, Vincent persuaded some country girls who were interested in devoting themselves to the poor to come to Paris and work with the Ladies of Charity. The first of these girls, Marguerite Naseau, later known as the first Daughter of Charity, died in 1633, a victim of an illness contracted while nursing a woman afflicted during a plague. After 3 or 4 years, Vincent, still desirous only of assisting the poor and with no thought of founding a religious community, entrusted the care of the girls to Louise de Marillac (known as Mademoiselle Le Gras), a widow he had been directing for 10 years. Since the death of her husband in 1625, she had devoted herself to the underprivileged while awaiting the permission of her director to embark on some

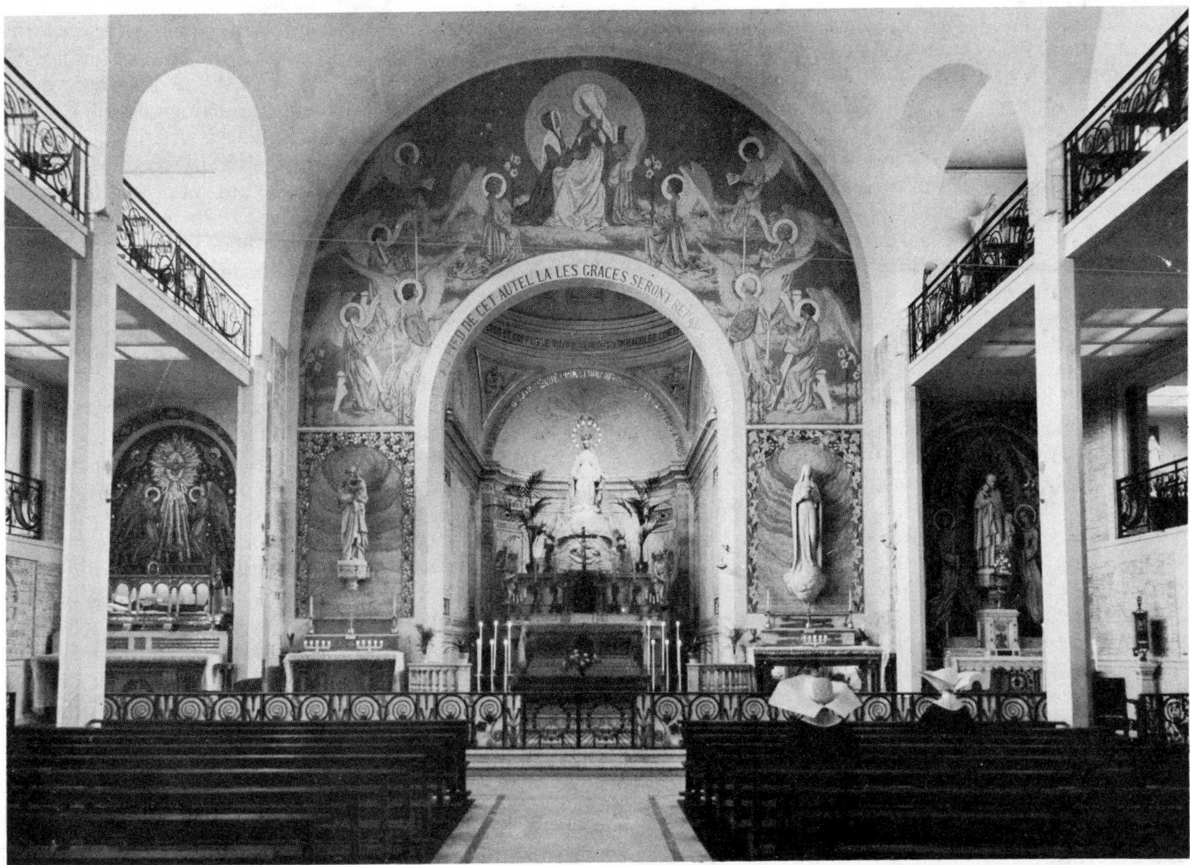

Chapel of the Miraculous Medal, motherhouse of the Daughters of Charity of St. Vincent de Paul, Paris.

definite work in their behalf. In 1633 Louise received four or five country girls into her own home in Paris to train them for their mission of spiritual and corporal assistance to the poor. This was the beginning of the Daughters of Charity.

Louise was the first superior of the community, although Vincent was responsible for the initiation of its work. In words destined to become famous, he directed his daughters to have "for a monastery the house of the sick, for a cell a hired room, for a chapel the parish church, for a cloister the streets of the city or the wards of the hospital, for a grate the fear of God, and for a veil holy modesty." The costume the sisters adopted was that of the peasant women of the Isle de France, a gray-blue dress, white collar, and tight fitting linen cap. They added the cornette later.

Development. By 17th-century standards, consecrated women belonged within the confines of a cloister. Vincent's enterprise was, for those times, an innovation truly revolutionary. The idea that nuns must be cloistered was so much a part of the thinking of the day that St. Francis de Sales, who had planned to engage his Visitation nuns in visiting the sick, was forced to relinquish the idea. Vincent, wishing to prove the practicality of his plan before applying for ecclesiastical approval, allowed the work to develop gradually. In 1646, after the sisters had lived a form of religious life and worked among the poor for 13 years, he sought the approbation of the archbishop of Paris. Permission was granted in 1655, and in 1668 Clement IX issued a pontifical decree to the same effect. The original work of the Daughters of Charity was not limited to the care of the indigent sick in their homes. Within 3 years of the community's foundation, the sisters undertook to instruct poor children in religion and in the elementary branches of secular knowledge. Soon afterward they began to care for foundlings, and in 1640 the sisters assumed complete charge of a hospital in Angers.

Poland was the first country after France to receive the Daughters of Charity. Queen Marie Louise requested their services, and in 1656 the sisters appeared for the first time on the battlefield. Their services during various wars in many countries have won for them the title Angels of the Battlefield. In 1640, in his capacity as chaplain general of the galleys of France, Vincent sent sisters to serve the galley slaves, who lived in intolerable conditions and frequently died without physical or spiritual assistance. During Vincent's lifetime, the sisters expanded their work to take care of foundlings, the aged, and the insane. In 1660, when both Vincent and Louise died, there were more than 40 houses of the Daughters of Charity in France alone. Eventually the community spread to Switzerland (1750), to Italy (1778), and to Spain (1790). By 1963 there were 2,900 houses in Europe, 52 in Asia, 79 in Africa, 920 in North and South America, 42 in Oceania, and 216 in countries under Communist domination.

Outstanding Members. When the Reign of Terror began in France, the sisters were ordered to leave the motherhouse in Paris, and at the end of 1793 the community was officially disbanded. Sister Antoinette Duleau, then superior, tried to keep the community intact, but four members, Sisters Marie Fontaine, Jeanne Gerard, Marie Lanel, and Madeleine Fantou met death by guillotine (June 26, 1794) for their refusal to take the constitutional oath. By 1797 the sisters could again assemble as a religious body, and on Dec. 12, 1800, the government accorded them legal recognition. Six years later the community had made such progress that there were 283 establishments in France alone. In the cholera epidemics of 1832 and 1849 the sisters offered their services to the public authorities, and 52 of them fell victims of this disease. Several years later the community answered the call to provide nurses for the wounded in the Crimean War.

Perhaps the best-known Daughter of Charity is St. Catherine *Labouré, to whom the Blessed Virgin appeared in the chapel of the motherhouse at rue du Bac, Paris. Although the Mother of God offered advice to Catherine for the benefit of the community just emerging from the storms of the French Revolution, one of the chief reasons for her visit was to entrust to this Daughter of Charity the mission of disseminating the medal that has come to be called "miraculous." During the course of the apparitions the Blessed Virgin also instructed Catherine that when another community should seek to join the Daughters of Charity, it was to be received. This message was interpreted later as applying to the Sisters of Charity of St. Joseph's at Emmitsburg, Md.

Heavenly visions were also granted to Sister Appoline Andriveau, who in 1846, while praying in the chapel of the House of Charity at Troyes, France, saw Our Lord bearing in his hands a scarlet scapular. Pius IX granted afterward a rescript authorizing the Scapular of the Passion of Our Lord and of the Sacred Hearts of Jesus and Mary, popularly known as the red scapular. Six years earlier, in 1840, Sister Justine Bisqueyburu had received a similar mission from the Blessed Virgin, that of propagating the badge of her Immaculate Heart. This badge has come to be known as the green scapular, and the wearing of it is credited with bringing about numerous favors. Another Daughter of Charity worthy of special note is Sister Rosalie Rendu, who entered the community in France in 1802. For years after her death, because of her great love for the poor, her name was legendary in Paris. The people of the San Marceau district named one of their streets after her. Hers was the special gift of inspiring the rich to provide assistance for their less fortunate brethren. At the beginning of his career of charity, Antoine Frédéric *Ozanam worked under the guidance of Sister Rosalie; her cause of canonization is under consideration (1965). Ten sisters gave their lives as martyrs of charity in the Republic of China, where they began their labors in 1862. Although their devotedness to the unfortunate won for them the love and confidence of many of the people, others spread false rumors and calumnies concerning them. On June 21, 1870, a band of brigands broke into the convent in Tientsin, murdered the sisters, and burned their home.

U.S. Foundations. The Emmitsburg community, founded by Mother Seton with the assistance of Bp. John Carroll of Baltimore, Md., and other eminent clergymen of the day was known as the Sisters of Charity of St. Joseph's. Many joined her, among them Sisters Cecilia Conway, Marie Murphy, Mary Ann Butler, Susan Closkey, and Rose White. The records kept in the community archives at Emmitsburg indicate that it was Mother Seton's desire that her young community be affiliated with the Daughters of Charity in France. As early as 1810 she requested that a group of the French sisters bring their rules to the U.S., but Napoleon prevented the departure of the sisters from France. However, Bp. Benedict J. Flaget, while visiting Paris, negotiated the affair for the sisters, obtained the rules, and brought them to Emmitsburg. In 1849 a formal petition was sent to the superior general of the Congregation of the Mission (Vincentians) in Paris, assuring him that a union was desired by the majority of the sisters in Maryland. In 1850 affiliation with the French community was finally achieved, and the sisters, who had formerly worn a black dress and widow's bonnet, assumed the grey-blue habit and white cornette and adopted the Rule of St. Vincent de Paul.

Sixty years after the affiliation with France, difficulties in transportation and the large number of sisters led to the erection of a western province, with headquarters at Normandy, Mo. By 1963 the Daughters of Charity in the U.S. numbered about 3,000 members, out of a total world membership of more than 45,500. Best known as teachers and nurses (they distinguished themselves on the battlefields of the Civil and Spanish American Wars), the sisters in the U.S. devote themselves to many different works of mercy. They staff two colleges (*St. Joseph's in Emmitsburg and Marillac in Normandy) and numerous elementary and secondary schools, conduct hospitals for the physically and mentally ill, and direct child-care institutions and social centers. Notable among their works in the U.S. is the National Leprosarium at Carville, La., and the U.S. Soldiers' Home Hospital in Washington, D.C. American Daughters of Charity served in China until 1952, when they were expelled by the Communists. They care for the unfortunate in Japan, Taiwan, and Bolivia.

Government and Rule. The Daughters of Charity make simple vows that they renew annually on March 25, the Feast of the Annunciation. Although their exterior works are subject to the bishop of the diocese in which they reside, the sisters owe obedience in all

The campus of St. Joseph's College, Emmitsburg, Md.

that regards their community life and the observance of their rules to the superior general of the Congregation of the Mission, whose headquarters are in Paris. He is considered the direct successor of St. Vincent, and the priests of his community are responsible for the spiritual direction of the sisters. Each house is governed by a superior who is called the "sister servant," because St. Vincent wished those in charge of the sisters to look on themselves as servants. The rules and constitutions regulating the lives of the sisters have remained virtually unchanged since the time of the founders. Under Pius XII, the Congregation of Religious examined these rules and constitutions, which were then approved without notable change. Vincent's choice of the three virtues of humility, simplicity, and charity as fundamental for the sisters seems as relevant to the 20th-century Daughter of Charity working in the slums of London, Berlin, or Chicago as it was for the first country girls who visited the poor in the villages of France.

The sisters follow a simple order of the day, allowing ample provision for service. Meditation, vocal prayer, and the Mass follow their 5 A.M. rising. They make a particular examination of conscience at noon, followed by spiritual reading and another meditation later in the afternoon. In the evening the community enjoys recreation in common, followed by night prayers and retiring at 9:30. The sisters do not recite the Divine Office, but they recite the rosary during the course of the day. The rest of their time belongs to the duties that make up each sister's service to the poor.

Upon their entrance into the community, the aspirants spend 6 months as postulants; they are initiated into the work of their vocation and continue their education. At the end of this period they enter the seminary or novitiate, where their spiritual formation continues in a more intense form for a year. Then the novice is clothed in the habit and continues her studies and professional preparation, after which her superiors assign her to a duty in one of the houses of the province to which she belongs. At the end of 5 years, dating from entrance to the seminary, she pronounces her first vows of poverty, chastity, obedience, and service to the poor.

Bibliography: P. COSTE et al., *Les Filles de la Charité* (Paris 1933). A. BUGNINI, EncCatt 5:1262–64. *Sisters of Charity, Emmitsburg, Maryland 1809–1959* (Emmitsburg, Md. 1959). P. L. JOHNSON, *Daughters of Charity in Milwaukee* (Milwaukee 1946).

[M. M. CONSIDINE]

CHARITY, SISTERS OF

Under this title are included numerous congregations of sisters, many of whom follow a rule based on that of St. Vincent de Paul, but modified according to the constitutions of each institute. Several of the congregations are branches of the community founded by Mother Elizabeth Bayley *Seton at Emmitsburg, Md., in 1809.

Irish Sisters of Charity. Popular name for the Pious Congregation of the Religious Sisters of Charity (*Societas Sororum Caritatis in Hibernia,* SSC), a religious congregation with papal approval (1834) founded in Dublin (1815) by Mary *Aikenhead in cooperation with Abp. Daniel *Murray. The rule was modeled on that of the Jesuits. Members take simple vows, temporary for 3 years, and then perpetual. In addition to the usual three vows of religion, there is a fourth vow to serve the poor. Governing the congregation is a superior general, who is elected for a 6-year term and who can be reelected; she resides at the motherhouse, Mount St. Anne's, Milltown, Dublin. The superior general appoints all local superiors for 3-year terms, which can be renewed once.

The original apostolate was to the poor and sick. Mary Aikenhead opened St. Vincent's Hospital, Dublin, and thereby pioneered in the staffing and managing of hospitals by religious women trained in nursing. Later the congregation established convalescent homes, institutions for blind, deaf, crippled, and aged persons, maternity welfare centers, homes for widows, Magdalen homes, recreational centers, and hostels; it undertook also teaching in primary and secondary schools and in vocational colleges. From Ireland the institute spread to England, Scotland, U.S., Zambia, and Nigeria. The sisters went to Australia in 1838, and were the first religious women to take vows there; but they have since developed in Australia a separate congregation, the Daughters of Mary Aikenhead. In 1965 there were 811 professed sisters, 61 novices, and 9 postulants in 66 houses. Their primary and secondary schools enrolled 30,960 pupils. Since 1953 the congregation has labored in the Archdiocese of Los Angeles, Calif., where in 1965 its 47 members staffed a convalescent home, and four elementary schools and a secondary school with 4,100 students.

[T. A. HESKIN]

Sisters of Charity and Christian Instruction of Nevers. A religious congregation with papal approval (1852) founded in France in 1680 by the Benedictine Jean Baptiste de Laveyne to engage in Christian instruction and care of the sick. After 2 years as novices, members take simple vows, temporary for 6 years, then perpetual. By 1789 the congregation had in France 120 foundations that were closed by the French Revolution. In 1961 there were 1,269 members in 145 houses in France, Italy, Switzerland, Spain, England, Iceland, Tunisia, Japan, and Ivory Coast. The sisters engage in teaching and in hospital and social work. A contemplative branch was started in 1958. St. Bernadette *Soubirous is the best-known member. Since 1685 the motherhouse has been in Nevers, France.

Bibliography: Heimbucher 2:498–499.

[T. F. CASEY]

Sisters of Charity of Cincinnati (SC). A congregation that was founded in 1852 and traces its origin to Mother Elizabeth *Seton of Emmitsburg, Md. In 1869 the motherhouse and novitiate were transferred outside Cincinnati to a site at Mount St. Joseph, Ohio. Cincinnati was without sisters in 1829, when four from Mother Seton's foundation in Emmitsburg arrived to care for orphan girls and open a free school. When the Emmitsburg foundation became affiliated with the Daughters of Charity whose central house is in France, seven of the Cincinnati group formed a separate community in 1852, and Sister Margaret Cecilia George became the first mother superior. The new foundation grew rapidly; within a year its work expanded to include the care of orphan boys and the administration of the city's first Catholic hospital, St. John's. In 1861 Mother Josephine Harvey, second superior of the congregation, placed a larger St. John's Hospital at the disposal of wounded Civil War soldiers; she also supplied 38 sister-nurses who, under the leadership of Sister Anthony *O'Connell, served in army hospitals in Ohio, Kentucky, Tennessee, Maryland, and Virginia. The Cincinnati community was called upon also to assist in forming two other congregations: the Sisters of Charity of Convent Station, N.J.; and the Greensburg, Pa., Sisters of Charity.

The principal work of the congregation is education; hospital service comes second on the basis of the number of sisters involved, and the care of dependent children ranks third. Other establishments staffed by the sisters include a social service center, a day nursery, and a retreat house for women. The congregation conducts the College of *Mt. St. Joseph on the Ohio, and the sisters teach in 24 high and 75 elementary schools located in 13 dioceses and archdioceses of the U.S. In Cincinnati they staff an archdiocesan school for the deaf that has both elementary and high school programs. Besides the collegiate program conducted at Mt. St. Joseph for the education of nurses, there are separate training programs in seven of the nine hospitals operated by the congregation. Affiliated with one of the hospitals is a home for unmarried mothers and their infants; this institution was established in 1873 under the direction of Sister Anthony O'Connell and was the first of its kind in the Cincinnati area.

By 1961 the congregation had three missions. One was in Rome, Italy, where the sisters taught at Villa Nazareth, a school for gifted boys belonging to poor families. The other two were schools in Peru—the school in Lima served a colony of 10,000 Chinese refugees, while the other was a catechetical center for Indians at Huancane, near Lake Titicaca. The first Asiatic venture of the congregation was in Wuchang, China, in 1928. When Communists seized their property in 1949 the sisters had to leave China and abandon a hospital, orphanage, school, and novitiate. The Sisters of Charity of Cincinnati became a pontifical congregation in 1939 when their constitution received definitive approval from Pius XI.

Bibliography: Archives, Sisters of Charity, Mount St. Joseph, Ohio. M. A. McCann, *History of Mother Seton's Daughters,* 3 v. (New York 1923).

[L. C. FEIERTAG]

Sisters of Charity of Convent Station (SC). Founded by Mother Mary Xavier *Mehegan in Newark, N.J., at the request of James Roosevelt Bayley, first bishop of Newark and Mother Elizabeth *Seton's nephew. Under his direction Mother Mary Xavier organized an independent diocesan community, the Sisters of Charity of St. Elizabeth, Convent Station, N.J., to serve the newly created diocese. The New Jersey community separated from the New York motherhouse of the Sisters of Charity in September 1859.

Earlier, at Bayley's request, the New York sisters had opened missions in New Jersey at Paterson and Newark, establishing a small orphan asylum and a school for the children of the cathedral parish. Soon, however, the bishop decided to expand the educational facilities of his diocese and appealed to the sisters at Mt. St. Vincent in New York for help in founding a diocesan community. Unsuccessful in this attempt and in subsequent efforts to enlist the aid of other religious communities, Bayley applied to the Sisters of Charity of Cincinnati, Ohio, another offshoot of the original Emmitsburg foundation, whose superior at that time was Mother Margaret Cecilia George, friend and former companion of Mother Seton. She agreed to receive any candidates recommended by the bishop and to send them back, after a year of training in her own novitiate, under the care of two professed sisters. These latter were to remain in Newark until the new community was well established. Accordingly, five young women went to Cedar Grove, Cincinnati, to undergo the canonical period of training before taking up their work as pioneers in the projected community. When it was time for them to return, however, no professed sisters were available to go with them. Bayley again laid his case before the superiors of Mt. St. Vincent, who this time agreed to send Sisters Mary Xavier Mehegan and Mary Catherine Nevin to take charge of his novices and help to establish his new foundation. After 3 years they were to have the option of returning to New York or remaining with the new community. Together with five novices they formed the nucleus of the New Jersey Sisters of Charity.

On Sept. 29, 1859, the little group formally took up residence in Newark and opened a school for girls. In less than a year it became necessary to provide more adequate quarters for the 21 who then made up the growing community. The Seton Hall property in Madison, N.J., vacated by the seminary and college for more commodious quarters in South Orange, was offered to Mother Xavier for $25,000. On July 2 the new motherhouse, St. Elizabeth, was opened in Madison, later known as Convent Station. The work of the New Jersey community expanded from the opening (1860) of the select school for girls to the opening (1899) of *St. Elizabeth's, the first college for women in the state of New Jersey. The sisters staffed private and parochial schools on both the elementary and secondary levels, and a juniorate for the higher education of their young professed sisters. They also established orphanages, a home for foundlings, a residence for working girls, a home for the aged and indigent, hospitals, and schools of nursing.

In 1924, in addition to their work in New Jersey, New York, Massachusetts, Connecticut, and Florida, the sisters undertook missionary ventures outside the U.S. Of the hospital and schools in China and the schools in Puerto Rico and the Virgin Islands, only the last-named mission remained under their care in 1963. By that date, the eighth successor of Mother Xavier directed the work of nearly 1,800 sisters in almost 120 institutions at home and abroad. The Sisters of Charity of St. Elizabeth now enjoy pontifical status. Their novitiate of a year follows a year's postulancy, after which the sisters pronounce temporary vows for another year. The vows are renewed for 1 year and then for a period of 2 years before the sisters pronounce perpetual vows.

Bibliography: M. A. Sharkey, *The New Jersey Sisters of Charity,* 3 v. (New York 1933). B. M. McEniry, *Woman of Decision: The Life of Mother Mary Xavier Mehegan* (New York 1953).

[B. M. MC ENIRY]

Sisters of Charity of Greensburg (SC). This congregation is the youngest of Mother Elizabeth Seton's communities. It dates from Aug. 7, 1870, when, at the request of Rt. Rev. Michael Domenec, five Sisters of Charity of Mt. St. Joseph's, Cincinnati, Ohio, arrived at Altoona, Pa., to open St. John's school and to begin an independent foundation. Soon the superior, Mother Aloysia Lowe, realizing the need for a new motherhouse in a country environment but within easy reach of the city of Pittsburgh, purchased the Jennings Farm near Greensburg, Pa. The property was later named Seton Hill, and in August 1882 the motherhouse and novitiate were moved from Altoona to Greensburg. Three years later the new foundation was incorporated under the laws of the Commonwealth of Pennsylvania with the title Sisters of Charity of Greensburg, Pa.

By 1965 the community had acquired the status of a pontifical institute and numbered more than 800 professed members. They follow the rule of St. Vincent de Paul, with modifications in accord with the regulations of Canon Law for religious, issued in 1919. Since the foundation of *Seton Hill College in 1914, the educational development of the congregation has been centered there, and the college has provided the sisters with early academic and professional training. The educational work of the community, beginning with St. John's parochial school, Altoona, St. Mary's Preparatory School for boys (1880), and St. Joseph Academy for girls (1883) at Seton Hill, gradually expanded to other dioceses in Pennsylvania, Maryland, Arizona, and California. The community also established a number of institutions in Pennsylvania to care for the sick, the poor, and the orphaned: the Roselia Foundling Asylum and Maternity Hospital in Pittsburgh (1892); the Charity Hospital, later known as the Pittsburgh Hospital (1897); the De Paul Institute for the Deaf and Blind, Pittsburgh (1908); Providence Hospital, Beaver Falls (1909); the House of Mary, a social center for Negroes, Pittsburgh (1942); the McGuire Convalescent Home, New Brighton (1953); and Jeannette Memorial Hospital (1959). In September 1960 four sisters opened a house in the Vicariate of Kwangju, Korea.

[M. T. GEARY]

Sisters of Charity of Halifax. The Congregation of Sisters of Charity of St. Vincent de Paul, Halifax, Nova Scotia (SCH), was founded in 1849, when, at the request of Bishop (later Archbishop) William Walsh, four sisters arrived from the motherhouse at Mt. St. Vincent, New York City. The superior of the group, Mother Basilia McCann, had been associated with Mother Elizabeth Seton at St. Joseph's, Emmitsburg, Md. With the rapid growth of the new foundation, an independent community was formed (1855), and on Feb. 17, 1856, Pius IX conferred on it all the privileges and indulgences that had been granted to the motherhouse in New York. The habit and constitutions of the New York Sisters of Charity were retained, and when the sisters built a new motherhouse at Rockingham in the suburbs of Halifax (1873), it also was named Mt. St. Vincent.

From the earliest years the congregation conducted institutions for the care of orphans and the aged, residences for young women, and hospitals; but its principal work has been in the field of education. In 1960 more than 1,600 members worked in 4 archdioceses and 7 dioceses of Canada and in the vicariate of Bermuda; in the U.S. the sisters served in 3 archdioceses and 6 dioceses, staffing elementary and high schools, orphanages, homes for the aged, and hospitals. Mt. St. Vincent College, Halifax, was chartered in 1925; fully accredited, it receives annual grants from the federal and provincial governments. The sisters teach in the public (government controlled) schools in Nova Scotia, New Brunswick, Quebec, and Alberta, with the same rights and privileges as teachers trained in the provincial teachers' colleges. They also staff parochial schools in those areas in Canada where Catholics are in a minority.

The constitutions of the congregation received temporary approbation from Pius X; on July 24, 1913, the Holy See granted final approval. In 1921 the sisters adopted a headdress consisting of a white cap and black veil but otherwise retained the habit as worn by Mother Seton. General administration is conducted from the motherhouse at Halifax, by a superior general and four assistants, a secretary general, and a bursar general. There are 5 provinces: 2 in Nova Scotia, 1 in Western Canada, 1 in Boston, Mass., and 1 in New York, N.Y.

[F. D'A. MC CARTHY]

Sisters of Charity of Jesus and Mary (Ghent). A religious congregation (SCJM) with papal approval (1816), founded at Lovendegem, near Ghent, Belgium, in 1803 by Peter *Triest. The congregation, whose members take simple perpetual vows and wear a white habit with black scapular, has as its scope education and nursing. It is governed by a superior general, elected for a 6-year term. She is aided by four assistants, who also are elected by the general chapter. In 1805 the bishop and the civil authorities called the sisters to Ghent. After establishing many houses throughout Belgium, the congregation spread to England (1888), the Belgian Congo (1892), India (1896), Netherlands (1908), Ireland (1946), and Australia (1962). Besides teaching in primary and secondary schools, the sisters care for persons who are blind, mute, and physically or mentally handicapped; they engage also in nursing. In 1964 the congregation had 2,123 professed members in 89 communities distributed over 9 countries on 3 continents. Its schools had 35,000 students. The sisters had charge of 7,600 mental or physical defectives and 26,000 sick and aged persons. The motherhouse is in Ghent.

[L. C. DE BEUCKELAER]

Sisters of Charity of Leavenworth (SCL). Founded in 1858 by a group of Sisters of Charity of Nashville, Tenn., who had previously branched off from the community in Nazareth, Ky. At the invitation of John Miège, SJ, Vicar Apostolic of the Indian Territory, Kans., 16 sisters arrived in Leavenworth on Nov. 11, 1858, when Kansas, not yet a state, was the scene of rioting, border warfare, illegal elections, and insecure titles to property. Despite these circumstances, the sisters began to teach regular classes and to nurse the sick in private homes until they open the first civilian hospital in Kansas (1863).

During the sisters' 1st decade in Kansas, membership in the community increased; they established a novitiate, orphanage, hospital, two academies, and three day schools, in Leavenworth and Lawrence, Kans. In 1869 five sisters went by rail and stagecoach to Helena, Mont., to open an academy, the first in that territory. Riding horseback through the mountains, two sisters collected sufficient funds to pay for this school and, within a year, to erect a frame hospital with a separate building for a psychiatric ward. In time their consistent service built up a reservoir of good will in the public mind. Under such leaders as Mother Xavier Ross, the foundress, and Sisters Joanna Bruner, Julia Voorvoart, and Josephine Cantwell, they established schools, hospitals, orphanages, and infant homes, in Kansas, Colorado, Montana, and New Mexico.

During the 20th century the sisters extended their work into Missouri, Illinois, Wyoming, California, Oklahoma, and Nebraska. They taught religion to the inmates of penitentiaries and reformatories, to the Indians at Haskell Institute, and to children in weekday and vacation schools; they nursed in homes and public institutions during epidemics, conducted rehabilitation centers for crippled children, and provided a cerebral palsy and development clinic, with separate schools for the mentally retarded and emotionally disturbed. On the same campus as the motherhouse at Xavier, Kans., the sisters staff *St. Mary College, with a graduate division offering a Master of Science degree in various fields of education. They teach also at Carroll College, Helena, Mont. In addition, members of the community staff 14 hospitals, 3 schools for nurses, 10 secondary and 62 elementary schools, 3 homes for children, and 1 home for the aged. A papal institute since 1915, the congregation had, by 1963, more than 1,000 professed members.

[J. GILMORE]

Sisters of Charity of Lovere. Commonly known as Sisters of the Infant Mary (*Maria Bambina*), a religious congregation founded Nov. 21, 1832, at Lovere (Lombardy), Italy, when the two foundresses SS. Bartolomea *Capitanio and Vincenza *Gerosa dedicated themselves to works of charity. Pope Gregory XVI approved the institute, June 9, 1840. The constitutions, which are substantially the same as those given by St. *Vincent De Paul to the Daughters of *Charity, were approved by Leo XIII, Sept. 30, 1896. The sisters take simple vows; temporary profession comes after a 2-year novitiate; perpetual profession, 5 years later. At the head of the congregation is a superior general, whose 6-year term of office can be extended to 12. She is aided by an assistant and by at least four counselors, whose 6-year terms also can be extended. Provincial superiors may remain in office in the same province for three terms of 3 years. Each community is headed by a local superior whose term may not exceed two 3-year periods. The superior general, her assistant, the counselors, and the procurator are elected by the general chapter, which meets every 6 years. The motherhouse is in Milan.

The sisters engage in all forms of charitable works; they conduct hospitals, homes for aged, mental institutions, sanatoriums, out-patient centers; homes for foundlings, orphans, abandoned children, the blind, and penitents; elementary and secondary schools, colleges for girls, and residences for students and clerks. On the missions (since 1860) they have operated leprosaria, hospitals, dispensaries, laboratories, catechism schools, and primary and secondary schools. In 1964 the 8,925 members were distributed in 19 provinces (12 in Italy, 2 in North and South America, 5 in Asia) and 641 houses. Of these houses, 535 were in Italy, mostly in Lombardy and Venezia; the others were in England, Spain, the Western Hemisphere, Africa, India, Pakistan, Burma, and Japan.

Bibliography: L. MAZZA, *Della vita e dell'Istituto di Bartolomea Capitanio,* 2 v. (Modena 1905). A. PREVEDELLO, *Istituto delle Suore della Carità fondato in Lovere,* 5 v. (Venice 1933).

[M. C. BIANCHI]

Sisters of Charity of Nazareth, Ky. (SCN). Founded at St. Thomas farm near Bardstown, Ky., December 1812, at the request of Bp. Benedict J. *Flaget, under the direction of Rev. (later bishop) John Baptist *David. Teresa Carrico, Elizabeth Wells, and Catherine Spalding were the first to receive from David their provisional rules, assignment of duties, and horarium. Within a few months the arrival of three new postulants justified the holding of an election that resulted in the choice of Mother Catherine *Spalding as first superior. Intermittently, until her death in 1858, Mother Catherine directed the congregation and laid the foundation for its many future works.

Nazareth Academy, opened in 1814, inaugurated one of the principal activities of the congregation, that of teaching in elementary and secondary schools, colleges, and schools of nursing. Mother Catherine also directed the establishment of St. Vincent Academy in Union County (1820) and Presentation Academy (1831), St. Vincent Orphanage (1832), and St. Joseph Infirmary (1836) in Louisville, Ky. Eight years after the beginning at St. Thomas, when the sisters found they could not establish a clear title to the land on which they had built, Mother Catherine acquired from a Presbyterian minister nearly 1,000 acres on a main highway, 38 miles from Louisville. The Kentucky Legislature ensured legal status when it incorporated Nazareth Literary and Benevolent Institution in 1829.

Nazareth Academy, operating continuously since 1814 and under charter since 1829, has served many generations of students, particularly from the Southern states and, in more recent years, from nearly every state in the Union as well as from Latin America and the Orient. In 1825 the statesman Henry Clay presented the first diploma of the academy to Margaret Carroll. Later, as Sister Columba Carroll, she served as directress of the academy for many years before being elected to the office of mother superior of the congregation. The sisters, in their pioneering days, gave dedicated service to the students of St. Thomas Seminary, to cholera and yellow fever victims during epidemic years, to soldiers of the Confederate and Union armies during the Civil War, and to influenza victims at Camp Zachary Taylor during World War I.

In 1824 a little colony of sisters opened the first Catholic school in Indiana at Vincennes. Nashville, Tenn., was the location of a school and a hospital in 1842. In 1858 a group of six Sisters of Charity stationed in Nashville separated from Nazareth to form a diocesan community. Later they answered the call of Bp. John Miège and, under the guidance of Mother Xavier Ross, became the nucleus of the Sisters of Charity of Leavenworth, Kans. As the number of vocations increased in the Nazareth community, new foundations were opened throughout the South and Southeast and in the North, in Massachusetts. Following the Civil War, schools for Negroes were opened in a number of southern cities, and Holy Family Hospital, Ensley, Ala., was established. The congregation opened its first over-

Fig. 1. Mt. St. Vincent, New York City, first motherhouse of the Sisters of Charity of New York.

seas mission in Patna District, India, in 1947; in 1963 a hospital and adjoining leper clinic, a school for nurses, and a novitiate were in operation at Mokameh Junction, India, while nearby Gaya had an academy and a school for aspirants.

In their sesquicentennial year (1962) the Sisters of Charity of Nazareth numbered 1,600 members, who staffed 105 grade schools, 31 high schools, 2 colleges, 12 hospitals, 3 orphanages, 1 convalescent home, 1 home for infants, and 2 summer camps, located in 11 states—Alabama, Arkansas, Kentucky, Louisiana, Maryland, Massachusetts, Mississippi, North Carolina, Ohio, Tennessee, Virginia—as well as the District of Columbia and India.

Bibliography: Archives at Nazareth Motherhouse. M. C. Fox, *The Life of the Right Reverend John Baptist Mary David* (New York 1925). A. B. McGill, *The Sisters of Charity of Nazareth, Kentucky* (New York 1917).

[A. G. MC GANN]

Sisters of Charity of New York (SC). A branch of the community founded by Mother Elizabeth Seton at Emmitsburg, Md. (1809). The Sisters of Charity of St. Vincent de Paul of New York became independent in 1846 at the urging of Bp. John Hughes of New York. The motherhouse, originally at McGown's Pass, now a section of Central Park, New York City, was transferred in 1859 to Mt. St. Vincent-on-the-Hudson, former estate of Edwin Forrest, the Shakespearean actor. Mother Elizabeth Boyle, assistant and intimate associate of Mother Seton in Emmitsburg, was the first mother general of the New York congregation, which for nearly 40 years was guided by superiors who had received their religious training in the Emmitsburg novitiate.

From 1817 to 1841 the Sisters of Charity pioneered in every phase of educational and social work in New York, creating precedents, developing techniques in new fields, and offering hospitality and assistance to incoming religious communities. A foundation made in Halifax, Nova Scotia, in 1849, evolved in 1855 into the independent congregation of Sisters of Charity of Halifax. Similarly, missions established from New York in Jersey City, Newark, and Paterson, N.J., became in 1859 the nucleus of the community of Sisters of Charity of Convent Station.

Following the trend of population, the New York Sisters of Charity opened parochial schools and academies throughout greater New York, in Westchester County, and in the Hudson River Valley. By 1875 they had schools in Pennsylvania, Rhode Island, and Connecticut, and in 1889 they began work in the Bahama Islands. St. Vincent's Hospital of New York was founded in 1849 and became a recognized medical and teaching center. During the 1860s the sisters staffed a military hospital in their former motherhouse in Central Park, developed a program of industrial training in the girls' department of the Catholic Protectory, and undertook the care of abandoned infants in the New York Foundling Hospital, opened by Sister Mary Irene *Fitzgibbon in 1869.

In 1963 the community conducted 126 schools and institutions in the Archdiocese of New York and in the Dioceses of Brooklyn and Rockville Centre, N.Y.; Harrisburg, Pa.; and Nassau, Bahama Islands. Major works included 2 colleges, 80 elementary and 12 sec-

Fig. 2. Mt. St. Vincent-on-the-Hudson; right, Elizabeth Seton Library; left, the administration building.

ondary schools, 2 high school departments, a secretarial and home economics school, 5 schools of nursing, 1 psychiatric and 3 general hospitals, and 3 child-care institutions. The community numbered more than 1,400 members.

Bibliography: M. DE L. WALSH, *The Sisters of Charity of New York, 1809–1959,* 3 v. (New York 1960). **Illustration credit:** Fig. 1, Courtesy, New York Historical Society.

[M. DE L. WALSH]

Sisters of Charity of Our Lady Mother of Mercy (SCMM). A congregation with papal approval founded in 1832 at Tilburg, Holland, by Rev. John Zwijsen to minister to the sick poor and the aged. As the community grew, the sisters established houses in many parts of the world and expanded their work to include educational institutions and hospitals. In 1874 the first foundation was made in the U.S., where an American province developed with headquarters at Baltic, Conn. The total membership of the congregation in 1964 was about 4,000; of these, approximately 150 served in the U.S., staffing 6 elementary and 3 secondary schools, a college, a hospital, and 3 homes for the aged.

[T. M. BILOTTA]

Sisters of Charity of Our Lady of Mercy (OLM). A diocesan congregation founded in 1829 at Charleston, S.C., by Bp. John *England. The original group included Sister Mary Joseph O'Gorman, the first superior, and three companions. The congregation, known first as the Sisters of Our Lady of Mercy, adopted a rule based upon that of St. Vincent de Paul. When the constitutions were revised in 1949 the title was changed to Sisters of Charity of Our Lady of Mercy. The sisters opened their first school in 1830, and 2 years later began to care for orphans. In 1838, during a yellow fever epidemic, they opened a temporary hospital. The first permanent hospital, St. Francis Xavier, was opened in Charleston in 1882, and a school of nursing was inaugurated in 1900. A branch house, opened in Savannah, Ga., in 1845, joined the Sisters of Mercy after Savannah became the seat of a new diocese in 1850. Similarly, a house opened at Wilmington, N.C. (1869), later became a separate community. During the Civil War six sisters staffed the Confederate army hospital at White Sulphur Springs, Va. The sisters' kindly treatment of Union soldiers imprisoned at Charleston was later rewarded when the U.S. Congress voted a generous grant to restore their orphanage destroyed in the war. The congregation became interdiocesan in 1949 when schools were accepted in Trenton and Camden, N.J. In 1963 more than 85 sisters staffed 2 high schools, 8 elementary schools, 2 hospitals, 1 school of nursing, 1 orphange, 1 social service center, and 3 vacation camps.

[R. C. MADDEN]

Sisters of Charity of St. Joan Antida (SCSJA). Although the first vows were pronounced by Joan Antida *Thouret, the foundress, and her companions on Oct. 15, 1800, the community observes April 11, 1799, the opening of their first free school in Besançon, France, as their foundation date. The Sisters of Charity of St. Joan Antida spread rapidly in France, and after 10 years accepted an invitation to open a house in Naples, Italy. In 1819 Joan Antida received the approbation of Rome for her community and the rules that she had

Fig. 3. St. Joan Antida Thouret, a portrait after a drawing done at her deathbed.

written. However, Abp. G. D. de Pressigny of Besançon refused to recognize the independence of the Italian foundations and the foundress was forced to relinquish the convent at Besançon. The two branches remained separated until 1957 when the superior general of the Besançon group made her submission to the mother general in Rome, thus reuniting the two groups.

While no work of charity is foreign to the community, the sisters generally serve in hospitals, homes for the aged, schools, day nurseries, and foundling homes, as well as in various social centers and foreign missions. In September 1932 the first members arrived in the U.S. and settled in Milwaukee, Wis. In 1963 this community, numbering about 65, conducted day nurseries and kindergartens, parochial and high schools, and a convalescent home, and directed the domestic department of St. Camillus Hospital for men. Since 1934 the community has served also in the Far East and in Central and Southern Africa. By 1963 world membership included about 10,000 professed sisters. The general motherhouse is in Rome.

[M. TARANTOLA]

Sisters of Charity of St. Louis (SCSL). A congregation founded in 1803 in Vannes, France, by Countess Louise Elizabeth Mole de Champlatreux, for the education of young girls made homeless by the Revolution. The congregation was known as the Sisters of Charity of St. Louis after its patron, St. Louis of France. The foundress, whose husband was guillotined in April 1794 and who was herself imprisoned for months, wished her followers to devote their lives principally to contemplation and reparation. In 1840 the rules received final approbation from Rome. Since then, the congregation has kept much of its original contemplative spirit, but it has also extended its charitable works to include the maintenance of elementary and secondary schools and colleges; private home economics and secretarial schools; hospitals, clinics, and convalescent homes; and retreat houses. These institutions are located in France, England, Canada, the U.S. (including a novitiate in Cheshire, Conn.), Haiti, and Madagascar. The generalate is in Rome, Italy. In 1963 there were more than 1,300 members, including about 55 in the U.S. The cause for the beatification of Madame Mole was introduced in 1962.

[M. B. ROYAL]

Sisters of Charity of the Blessed Virgin Mary. A congregation with papal approbation devoted to the apostolate of education. It was founded in Philadelphia, Pa., on Nov. 1, 1833, by Mary Frances *Clarke and four companions, Margaret Mann, Rose O'Toole, Catherine Byrne, and Eliza Kelly, under the spiritual direction of Fr. Terence James Donaghoe of Philadelphia.

The five young women were drawn together originally in Dublin, Ireland, by their efforts in behalf of the victims of the cholera epidemic of 1831. They continued their association after the epidemic had subsided by opening a school for poor children in Dublin on March 19, 1832. Despite the success of their venture, the young women emigrated to the U.S. the following year in response to a plea for aid in the education of the immigrant poor of Philadelphia. There they taught in a parochial school founded by Donaghoe, who, recognizing the possibility of forming a religious congregation, undertook the spiritual direction of the group. With Mary Frances Clarke as their appointed superior and Donaghoe as their spiritual director, they drew up a constitution based on the Rule of St. Ignatius and compiled a book of customs. Their work in Philadelphia continued for 10 years. The school prospered, a novitiate was opened, and membership steadily increased.

In 1843, at the request of Bp. Matthias Loras of Dubuque, Iowa, the entire community moved to Dubuque, where the permanent motherhouse was established. At Lora's request, no schools were opened outside of his territorial jurisdiction until 1867 when the sisters accepted the first schools in Chicago, Ill. As the community grew and membership increased, the scope of educational work widened, and schools were opened in 20 states from New York to Hawaii and from Montana to Mississippi. Missionary sisters were sent to Latin America. Between 1950 and 1960 membership was maintained at 2,200. The sisters staffed 2 novitiates, 2 liberal arts colleges, 45 high schools, and 146 elementary schools. In 1963 more than 90,000 students were enrolled in their schools while an additional 20,000 received religious education either in catechetical centers or in vacation schools.

The institute received recognition from the Holy See in 1845 when Gregory XVI granted a special blessing to the work of the sisters, as did Pius IX in 1847, and Leo XIII in 1883. After the death of Donaghoe in 1869, Mother Clarke assumed complete direction of the institute of which she had been successively appointed superior since 1833. She immediately incorporated the congregation under the laws of the state of Iowa for religious and educational purposes and set about the work of having the constitutions approved by Rome. On Feb. 21, 1878, the laudatory brief was signed in Rome, followed 6 months later by the decree of temporary approbation. In the first triennial elections, held in 1878, Mother Clarke was unanimously elected to the office of superior general. Final approbation of the constitutions was granted by Leo XIII on April 25, 1885, and in June of that year the Holy See authorized Bp. John J. Hennessey of Dubuque to confirm Mother Clarke as superior general for life at the unanimous request of the professed sisters.

Mother Clarke died on Dec. 4, 1887, and was succeeded by Mother Mary Gertrude Regan (1888–94; 1900–06); Mother Mary Cecilia Dougherty (1894–1900; 1906–12; 1915–19); Mother Mary Ascension Lilly (1912–15); Mother Mary Isabella Kane (1919–31); Mother Mary Gervase Tuffy (1931–43); Mother Mary Josita Baschnagel (1943–55); and Mother Mary Consolatrice Wright (1955–61; 1961–). Three of the original five members preceded Mother Clarke in death; Sister Mary Rose O'Toole, last of the five, died on March 10, 1890, in the 57th year of her religious life.

A revision of the constitutions was authorized in 1915 and received definitive approbation in 1927. Further modifications were approved in 1958. The congregation is divided into four provinces and is governed by the superior general and her curia—four councilors assisted by a secretary general and treasurer general. All sisters bound by perpetual vows have both active and passive voice in the choice of delegates to the general chapter, which is held regularly every 6 years. Provinces are governed by provincial superiors appointed by the superior general; mission houses are directed by a local superior appointed in like manner.

[M. D. CLIFFORD]

Sisters of Charity of the Immaculate Conception of Ivrea (SCIC). Popularly known as the Sisters of Ivrea, they form a religious congregation with papal approval (1904) founded in Piedmont, Italy, in 1828 by Antonia Maria Verna (1773–1838) to engage in education and in other social and religious works. Members take simple vows, temporary at first and then perpetual. Governing the congregation in Rome is a general council composed of a superior general (elected by the general chapter), four councilors, a secretary, and a treasurer. Local superiors are appointed by the general council.

Fig. 4. First motherhouse of the Sisters of Charity of the Blessed Virgin Mary, near Dubuque, Iowa.

In 1964 the congregation, divided into seven provinces (all in Italy), one vice province, and two delegations, was active in Italy, Turkey, Lebanon, Jordan, Libya, Tanganyika, Argentina, Switzerland, England, and the U.S. (the last three being dependent directly on the general council). Besides teaching in elementary and secondary schools, the sisters also engage in hospital work, direct homes for the aged, and devote themselves to other charitable works. The 2,388 members in 1964 were located in 316 houses and enrolled 15,370 students. Since 1961 the sisters have been in the U.S., where they labor in the New York archdiocese and the Greensburg diocese. A special treasure of the institute is "The Immaculate of Miracles," a painting with reputed miraculous properties, which was received in 1860 as a gift from some Protestants who had previously sought to destroy it. The picture is kept in Ivrea (Torino), Italy, in a chapel built to house it. The congregation publishes a monthly periodical, called *Il Piccolo Messaggero dell' Immacolata.*

Bibliography: P. A. Pierotti, *La vita e l'opera della Serva di Dio Madre Antonia Maria Verna* (Florence 1938). R. Bazzano, *Un'eroina del Canavese* (Florence 1952).

[V. L. LA FRATTA]

Sisters of Charity of Zams, Austria. A diocesan congregation whose full title is Sisters of Charity of St. Vincent de Paul (CSVP), begun in Austria in 1821 by Rev. Nikolaus Tolentin Schuler (d. 1831) and Mother Josepha Nicolina (Katharina) Zins. The sisters, who adopted the rule of St. Vincent de Paul, are engaged in the education of youth and care of the sick and the aged. The congregation spread throughout Austria and Hungary, and in 1927 the sisters established a foundation in the U.S. at Kirkwood, Mo. A province was later created with the motherhouse at Watertown, Wis. (founded in 1946). In 1963 there were 33 professed members in the U.S. They staffed 2 homes for the aged and the domestic department of 2 major seminaries. Their houses were located in the Archdioceses of Milwaukee, Wis., and St. Louis, Mo., and in the Diocese of Madison, Wis.

Bibliography: Heimbucher 2:466–467.

[A. J. ENNIS]

CHARITY, WORKS OF

The word charity derives from the Latin *caritas,* which meant family affection, friendship, patriotism. It was used by Cicero to express love for humankind, an important tenet of Stoic doctrine (*see* STOICISM). But the Christians used *caritas* to translate the Greek *agape—impregnating the Latin word with all the meaning of the Greek term in Holy Scripture and in particular in the teaching of Jesus—love of God and love of men with all the duties that this rich concept implies [see H. Petré, *Caritas. Étude sur le vocabulaire latin de la Charité chretienne* (Louvain 1948) 96–]. Works of charity are the practical embodiment of those duties of love for one's neighbor. They will be considered historically in this survey as they existed in Christian antiquity and in the Middle Ages, and as they continue in modern times.

In Christian Antiquity

The dynamic concept of charity that was to flower in works of charity was implanted in His Church by Jesus Christ.

The Teaching of Jesus. In the mind of our Lord, the precept of loving God is inseparable from that of loving our neighbor: they are two aspects of the same virtue. Christ places these two precepts of love at the center of His teaching. Loving God means striving to become like Him—reproducing His universal goodness to men who, as a consequence, have a right to our love and, if necessary, to our pardon (Mt 5.43–48). Christ calls his teaching on charity a "new commandment" (Jn 13.34). Under the Mosaic Law one's neighbor was a Hebrew and the love of others was primarily negative; it consisted in seeking to avoid all that could provoke reprisals according to the terms of the laws of retaliation. Even when the law of love was translated into positive acts, the precept always remained self-interested, inspired by self-love. Even the most humane of the Hebrew moralists, Hillel, understood this when he said: "Do not to your neighbor what you do not want done to you."

Christ denounced this narrow interpretation of the Scribes (Mt 5.43), thereby defining the law of charity as a law of social relations. It is not enough to love one's friends; one must do good to one's enemies (Mt 5.46–48; Lk 10.25–37). The new commandment obliges one, as well, to love the neighbor as Christ has loved him—to the point of giving one's life for him (1 Jn 3.16). Love of neighbor in Christ's teaching (Jn 15.17) is not something optional, but a categorical imperative that all disciples must obey in order to belong to the Master. Jesus calls it "my commandment"; it is not just one of the precepts of His code but His favorite one—the mark of those who believe in Him (Jn 13.35). The command (at the same time a privilege) will make charity in the sight of heaven the touchstone for discerning Christ's own (Mt 25.34–45). Protestations of love for God will not be acceptable to God if they are not translated into acts beneficial to the neighbor in the form of assistance, material aid, etc. The two precepts are in fact one. Jesus is not content with declaring the second similar to the first. He wished to bestow on it a high dignity and stress its serious importance. He even gives it precedence over public worship: "To love one's neighbor as oneself is more precious than all holocausts and sacrifices" (Mk 12.33).

The transition from the love for man to love for God, besides revealing the originality of Christ's teaching, is the secret of all Christian works of charity and makes them transcend even the most impressive secular humanitarian achievements. The message of Christ, rooted in the universal fatherhood of God, has swept away national and religious differences, attacked racial and caste discrimination (Gal 3.28), and inspired heroic dedication.

The Apostolic Tradition. Christ's message of brotherly love constantly leavened the preaching and teaching of the Apostles and the first believers. St. John, the apostle of charity, never tired of recommending it and delighted in insisting (1 Jn 4.20–21) on the fusion of the two precepts into one. St. Paul synthesizes the essence of Christianity into charity (Gal 5.14; 6.2; Rom 13.8); reiterates the equality of the master and slave (Philemon ch. 16) and the obligation of the rich to supply the wants of the poor (2 Cor 8.12); and points out the free character of charity in the example of Christ (2 Corinthians ch. 7–8). St. James proclaims: "Religion pure and undefiled before God the Father is this: to give aid to orphans and widows in their tribulation, and to keep oneself unspotted from this world" (Jas 1.27).

This teaching was immediately translated into action. The author of the Acts thus pictures the first Church of Jerusalem:

> Now the multitude of the believers were of one heart and one soul, and not one of them said that anything he possessed was his own, but they had all things in common. And with great power the apostles gave testimony to the resurrection of Jesus Christ our Lord; and great grace was in them all. Nor was there anyone among them in want. For those who owned lands or houses would sell them and bring the price of what they sold and lay it at the feet of the apostles, and distribution was made to each, according as any one had need. [Acts 4.32–34; also 2.44.]

A concrete example of this practice is seen in the Cypriote Barnabas (Acts 4.35). It is true that community ownership of goods was unique to the Church in Jerusalem, and even there it tended to disappear as circumstances were modified.

This thirst for an enthusiastic sharing was not strange in the state of endemic misery that the Mother Church was enduring, tried by hunger, persecution, and political agitation. Moreover, it was necessary to beg constantly in Antioch (Acts 11.29), in Galatia (1 Cor 16.1), and in Macedonia (2 Cor 8.1–15; Rom 15.26), for the faithful in Jerusalem.

As the Christian community grew the first difficulties arose. The author of the Acts tells of the discontent among the Greek-speaking Jews because they felt that the widows of their group were being neglected in the daily ministrations (Acts 6.1–6). The problem sprang from a lack of personnel; the Apostles accordingly ordered the election of seven men to whom they confided the work of helping the poor. Until that time it had been done by the Apostles themselves. The very fact of the election of these deacons (as they were later called by St. Irenaeus) shows the supreme importance the Apostles attached to charitable works.

The special task of the deacons was to assist at the common meal or agape, originally connected with the Eucharistic celebration. According to the tradition, which persisted even later on, the poor had to receive food and drink since a common table, to which all contributed according to their means, united rich and poor alike. However, even here difficulties arose and were denounced by St. Paul (1 Cor 11.18–22). The agape very soon lost its importance.

To aid the poor was not simply a public duty assigned to deacons. They were assisted by widows possessing special qualities precisely outlined by St. Paul: "Let a widow who is selected be not less than 60 years old, having been married but once, with a reputation for good works in bringing up children, in practicing hospitality, in washing the saints' feet, in helping those in trouble, in carefully pursuing every good work" (1 Tim 5.9–10). Private charity thus stood side by side with public charity and Paul frequently emphasized the obligation of each Christian to practice it (Gal 6.10). He held out the example of Tabitha (Dorcas) at Joppa (modern Jaffa) who had "devoted herself to good works and acts of charity" (Acts 9.36). When she died the Christians sent for Peter, who was in nearby Lydda, and on his arrival, "all the widows stood about him weeping and showing him the tunics and cloaks which Dorcas used to make for them" (*ibid.*).

Charity in the Persecuted Church. Thus the gospel was transformed into a social message that stimulated it and gave it a special character harmonizing with the growth of the new faith in time and space.

There are reliable proofs from both Christian and pagan sources, of the increasing charity of the generations of Christians that followed the Apostolic age. Lucian writes: "Their law-giver has taught them that they are all brothers; as soon as something happens which touches their common interests nothing is too difficult for them and they are capable of incredible activity" (*Peregr.* 10). Tertullian says: "Our care for the derelict and our active love have become our distinctive sign before the enemy. . . . See, they say, how they love one another and how ready they are to die for each other" (*Apol.* 39). Justin in his *Apologia* to the Emperor affirms: "We, who loved above all else the ways of acquiring riches and possessions, now hand over to a community fund what we possess and share it with every needy person; we, who hated and killed one another, now, after the coming of Christ, live in community and pray for our enemies" (*Apol.* 1.14). Already in the year 96, Pope Clement, sketching the ideal picture of a Christian community, as Corinth was before it was torn by internal strife, stressed the spirit of charity: "Who, living among you, has not heralded abroad your reputation for unbounded hospitality? You were all happier to give than to receive . . ., day and night you kept up your efforts on behalf of the whole brotherhood" (1 Clem 1.2). Christian practice was seen against a transcendent background as in the following passage from the *Letter to Diognetus* (ch. 10): "Any man can be an imitator of God, if he takes on his own shoulders the burden of his neighbors, if he chooses to use his advantage to help another who is underprivileged, if he takes what he has received from God and gives to those who are in need—for such a man becomes God to those who are helped. Then, even though you are on earth, you will see that God rules in heaven."

Prescriptions for the Practice of Charity. Almsgiving, in particular, was considered spiritual ransom, as Clement stated in his second letter to the Corinthians: "Almsgiving is good as a penance for sin; fasting is better than prayer, but almsgiving is better than both, and charity covers a multitude of sins" (2 Clem 16). For this reason the exercise of charity was intimately connected with worship; every Sunday in fact (2 Cor 16.2), or every month, or whenever they wished (Tertullian, *Apol.* 39), the believers brought their gifts (in money or kind) during the celebration of the Mass and presented them to the bishop (Justin, *Apol.* 1.67) who placed them on the altar table, as offerings to the Lord. Thus the needy received them from the hand of the Lord. "The grace and kindness of the Lord supported all the poor," writes Pope Cornelius (Eusebius, *Hist. eccl.* 6.43). The task of distributing the offerings belonged to the deacons who at the end of the divine service divided them among those present. A part of the offerings was reserved for the needy who were not at the service and later was brought to their homes; the remainder was used for the agape feast. The Deaconesses (*Const. Apost.* 2.17) continued helping them. However, the entire work of assistance was directed by the bishops (*Const. Apost.* 1.1; 2.25, 26, 27) who "have made their ministry a perpetual refuge for the needy and widows" (*Shepherd of Hermas*); in the Didache they were considered as fathers of the poor (ch. 1, 3, 4) and by St. Ignatius of Antioch as "guardians of widows" (*Ad Polycarp* 4).

The *Apostolic Constitutions* are filled with detailed prescriptions for the practice of charity in the first centuries—prescriptions for the ministers and the beneficiaries, and details about the means, the abuses, and the value of sacrifice (see ch. 1, 2, 4, 8). Origen has handed down valuable principles to guide the Church in aiding the poor (*Comm. Ser. 16 in Mt.*).

> Let us be prudent, so that we may come to the aid of every man according to his dignity, recalling the words: "Blessed is he who is wise in dealing with the needy and the poor." We must not give away too easily the goods of the Church, caring only not to destroy or steal them. Rather we must make distinctions regarding the causes of poverty, the dignity of each indigent person, his education and the degree of his need. . . . Therefore, we must not treat equally one, who from his infancy, has led a hard and straitened life and one, who accustomed to ease and wealth, has fallen into poverty. Nor must we give the same things to men and women, to the aged and the young, to the sick who can provide nothing for themselves and those who can help themselves in some small way. It is important also to inquire about the needs of large families, especially those who are industrious but still cannot make ends meet. In short, he who wishes to use the goods of the Church well must be very wise.

The same writer, in accord with St. Paul (1 Cor 9.14), vindicating the right of the clergy to live on the revenues of the Church, states: "Our food must be simple and our clothing plain so that we do not keep for ourselves more than we give the naked and thirsty or those who suffer a lack of material things."

It was this prudent spirit of wise administration and a fear of abuses that led the deacons to keep lists and records of the names and conditions of those they assisted. Accordingly, it is known that in the year 250 the Roman Christian community had about 100 ecclesiastics and 1,500 poor; the result was a heavy demand on the common treasury. The funds kept in this treasury were not only the regular offerings of the faithful made during the sacred liturgy, but also periodic contributions, gifts of money or valuables given on special occasions such as Baptism or death, tithes (*Const. Apost.* 5.20), alms collected in time of emergencies (Cyprian, *Epist.* 60; PL 4:359), and almsgiving united to fasting to make this good work valuable for salvation (*Shepherd of Hermas* 5.3; Origen, *Hom 10 in Lev;* Chrysostom, *Sermo de ieunio;* Augustine, *Sermo 208 in quadrag.*, etc.).

Widows and Orphans. These "deposits of piety" as Tertullian (*Apol.* 39) called them, were distributed according to a scale—the first places being reserved, as we see from ancient church sources, for widows and orphans. The reason for this was the real poverty of these two groups in ancient times, as well as the esteem widows enjoyed in the primitive community (1 Tim 5.16). St. Polycarp called them "altars of God" (*Ad Philipp.* 4). They formed a category apart, performed special tasks, and were enrolled in a separate register [see J. Danielou, *Le Ministère des femmes dans l'Eglise Ancienne,* in *Maison Dieu* 61 (1960) 70–96].

Prisoners and Captives. In a period when Christians paid for their faith in Christ by prison and forced labor, the Church could not be indifferent to the lot of her children. Prisoners were the special objects of both public and private charity (Tertullian, *Ad Mart.* 1). It was a duty to visit and care for a prisoner and to work for his liberation—this duty was repeatedly inculcated by the *Apostolic Constitutions* (7.1, 3) and by St. Cyprian (*Epist.* 37; PL 4:326). St. Ignatius wrote to those in Smyrna: "When the Christians become aware that one of their number is a prisoner or suffering for the name of Christ, they take upon themselves all his needs and, if possible, they free him" (*Ad Smyr.* 6). It is said of Origen that "he was with the holy martyrs not only while they were in prison, and not only while they were being examined up to the last sentence, but also after this when they were led away to death, displaying great boldness and coming into close contact with danger" (Eusebius, *Hist. eccl.* 6.3–4).

Although it was one of the duties assigned to the deacons, the visiting of prisoners was done also by private individuals as a duty of charity, and no one hesitated to bribe the jailor to that end (Lucian, *Peregr.* 12; Eusebius, *Hist. eccl.* 6.61). The example of the deacons Tertius and Pomponius in Africa, and the charity shown to the martyrs Perpetua and Felicity is well known [see O. Gebhardt, *Acta martyrum selecta* (Berlin 1902) 66]. The writings of early Christians are filled with histories of this kind and they indicate the double aim of the visits—to console and to sustain the prisoners and to be consoled by their blessing.

Christian charity also reached the brethren condemned to forced labor in the mines. The Christian community tried to keep in touch with them and obtain their liberty. Examples of this type of charity are recorded about the Roman community at the time of Pope Soter (Eusebius, *Hist. eccl.* 6.23; Hippolytus, *Philos.* 9.12) and the Egyptian community during the persecution of Diocletian (Eusebius *De mart. palest.* 10.1; 11.5).

Besides alleviating the sufferings of prisoners, the Christians sought to ransom them. Episodes of this kind were probably not rare, even though today it is difficult for the historian to say in individual cases whether it was a question of freeing prisoners or ransoming slaves. It would seem, though, that the initiative fell to some courageous individuals rather than to the community. There were numerous occasions of real heroism. "We know that many among ourselves have given themselves up to chains in order to redeem others; many have surrendered themselves to slavery and provided food for others with the price they received for themselves," notes St. Clement of Rome (*Ad Cor.* 1.2). When, in 253, Numidian brigands seized a number of Christians, the community of Carthage quickly collected 100,000 sesterces for ransom, declaring that they were ready to raise more if necessary. In 255 the Christians of Rome contributed money when the Goths captured some members of the Christian community in Cappadocia (Basil, *Epist. 70 Ad Damasum,* PG 32.435–436). Such liberation of prisoners by ransom is often mentioned in 4th- and 5th-century Gallic epitaphs.

Slaves. Particular care was taken of slaves and Christianity had a decided influence in ameliorating their condition. Converted slaves were accepted as brothers and in the face of this reality their social condition took second place (*Iren.* 4.21.3; Tertullian, *De Corona* 13). "Nor is there any other reason," wrote Lactantius, "why we take for ourselves the name of brothers one to another, unless it is that we believe that we are equal; for since we measure all human things, not by the body, but by the spirit, and although the condition of the bodies may be diversified, there are not slaves among us, but we regard them and speak of them as brothers in spirit and as fellow slaves in religion." Slaves participated fully as members of the community and could become clerics and even bishops. As persons, in the moral sense, they enjoyed the same esteem as free men. The honesty and chastity of slaves could not be violated. Since they were expected to practice the same virtues as free men, their virtues were likewise recognized and extolled. The *Acts of the Martyrs* offer ample proof of this in their frequent praise of the heroism of Christian slaves.

Such presuppositions underlie the recommendations to masters to treat their slaves kindly and not to forget that they are brothers. On their part slaves—conforming to the Pauline teaching prevalent in the ancient Church—were to endure their slavery for the glory of God and obtain true liberty, which is that of the spirit (1 Cor 7.21–24). This did not prevent Christian masters from freeing their slaves and in some instances community funds were used to purchase their freedom, but those so released were not to regard their liberty as a right (Ignatius, *Ad Polyc.* 4.3). The Synod of Elvira in 300 denounced ill treatment of slaves (c.5.41; also Origen, *Comm. in Rom.* 3.4).

The Sick and the Dead. The community assisted the sick, especially the incurable, with the consolation of their prayers, their visits, and material help (Tertullian, *Ad Uxor* 2.4). But Christian charity was not limited to the living; according to Emperor Julian one of the factors that favored the growth of Christianity was the great care the faithful took to bury the dead (Sozomen, *Hist. eccl.* 5.15). This pious task was performed willingly even by individuals (Aristides, *Apol.* 15); but usually the Church as a community took charge and entrusted the work to the deacons (*Const. Apost.* 3.7) and expenses for the burial of the poor were paid by the community (Tertullian, *Apol.* 39). The Christians did not limit their burial duties to members of their own faith; Lactantius writes: "We will not therefore allow the image and workmanship of God to lie as prey for beasts and birds, but we shall return it to the earth, whence it sprang; although we will fulfill this duty of kinsmen on an unknown man, humaneness will take over and fill the place of kinsmen who are lacking" (*Instit.* 6.12). Their concern for the dead led the Christians to pray and make offerings for the repose of their souls. This ancient custom had important repercussions on the living, bringing them comfort and strengthening the cause of Christianity.

These pious duties became very impressive in the event of public disasters. During the plague that devastated Alexandria in 259 Bishop Dionysius bore witness to the conduct of the faithful:

> Most of our brethren, in their surpassing charity and brotherly love did not spare themselves and clinging to one another fearlessly visited the sick and ministered to them. Many, after having nursed and consoled the sick, contracted their illness and cheerfully departed this life. The best of our brethren died in this way, some priests and deacons, and some of the laity. The conduct of the pagans was just the opposite; they would drive away those beginning to fall sick and people fled from their dear ones; they threw the dying into the street and bodies were left unburied. [Eusebius, *Hist. eccl.* 7.22.9–10.]

St. Cyprian recorded much the same regarding the plague in Carthage in 252 (*De Mortalitate* 14; PL 4: 591–593); while others fled, he gathered his own congregation and reminded them of their duty, setting them the example (*Vita Cypriani,* PL 3:1489). During the plague that raged in the reign of Maximinus "all the pagans were aware of the zeal and piety of the Christians. They alone, in such evil surroundings, showed their compassion and love for all men by actual deeds. Some dedicated themselves to caring for the sick and burying the dead. Others gathered together crowds of hungry people and fed them. These glorified the God of the Christians and confessed that only the Christians were pious and religious" (Eusebius, *Hist. eccl.* 9.8.14–15).

Travelers. Outside their own community the Christians sought to provide for strangers, especially for their brothers in the faith. This assistance was not left to the good will of individuals; although hospitality was widely practiced by Christians as a duty (Rom 12.13; 1 Pt 4.9; Didache 12; *Hermas* 8.10; Tertullian, *Ad Uxor* 2.4; Cyprian, *Epist.* 7, etc.), it also had a community character. In his first letter to the Corinthians, Clement stresses, among the other virtues that had signalized the Church, the splendid and noble custom of hospitality (1 Cor 1.2). The example of the Roman community is particularly worthy of note. In a letter written during the time of Marcus Aurelius, Dionysius, Bishop of Corinth, mentions the ancient custom of receiving any of the brothers who passed through Rome: "You keep up the ancestral custom of the Romans, a custom which your blessed bishop Soter has not only maintained but even increased, providing abundant help to the saints and, with blessed words, encouraging the brethren who come to Rome as a loving father his own children" (Eusebius, *Hist. eccl.* 4.23.10). The great regard in which the Roman community was held did not depend so much on its being the center of apostolic activity in the West, as on its charity. In a period when Christianity existed in scattered communities, the infrequent trips of some of the brethren were the only contact between them. For this reason hospitality was of vast importance and was the subject of a treatise (now lost)—*Peri filoxenias*—by an oriental writer, Melito, Bishop of Sardis (Eusebius, *Hist. eccl.* 4.26). Clement never tired of extolling hospitality (1 Cor 10.7; 11.1; 12.1).

This spirit of welcome occasioned some abuses: heretics, tricksters, and vagabonds could infiltrate and jeopardize the community. However, measures were taken to forestall this: the new arrival had to prove that he was a Christian; if he possessed the gift of prophecy his works had to correspond to his words. Hospitality was limited to 2 or 3 days, after which the guest had either to leave or earn his own living (Didache 11, 12). Later, a traveling Christian had to present a kind of passport issued by the community he was leaving (Council of Elvira, c.25).

Beginning of Union among Scattered Church Communities. The care lavished on a wayfaring brother in the faith formed a bridge, as has been stated, between the scattered communities. What the guest had to tell of the sufferings or the good fortune of his own church was of common interest. The ancient churches felt a strong bond between them and reacted according to the Pauline rule: "If one member suffers anything, all the members suffer with it, or if one member glories, all the members rejoice with it. Now you are the body of Christ, member for member" (1 Cor 12.26–27). Such a spirit made brotherly love dynamic and the most distant people neighbors. "They know each other and love each other by invisible signs even before they meet," exclaims the pagan Cecilius (Minutius Felix, *Octav*. 9.3).

The knowledge of belonging to a holy society very early took deep roots in the minds of individuals and it was linked with a sense of responsibility toward the whole company, even toward all mankind. "Pray for all the saints," Polycarp counseled, following St. Paul (1 Cor 59.2), "pray for the emperors, and authorities and rulers, for those who persecute and hate you, and for the enemies of the cross" (*Ad Phillip.* 12.3). The bishops worked to put this concept of charity into action, intervening in particular circumstances to eliminate the motives for dispute and to create a climate of common understanding. But charity shone with a special light in extraordinary cases when one community would make its own the suffering of another community.

St. Paul had worked from the beginning of his missionary life among the pagans to foster these bonds of charity, promoting the idea of helping the Church in Jerusalem. A generation later, the persecutions began, and those who lived in relative tranquillity worried about those who were threatened or stricken. Dionysius, Bishop of Corinth, affirmed this, writing to the Romans about the year 170: "It has been your custom from the beginning to do good in various ways to all the brethren, sending help to the Christians in the mines" (Eusebius, *Hist. eccl.* 4.23.10). A hundred years later, another Dionysius, Bishop of Alexandria, in a letter to Pope Stephen mentioned, almost in passing, the assistance given by the Pope to the Churches in Syria and Arabia (*ibid.* 7.5.2). Basil of Caesarea narrated that at the time of Pope Dionysius (259–269) the Church of Rome sent money to Cappadocia to liberate the Christians who had fallen into the hands of the barbarians. This fact was remembered with gratitude in that country as late as the 4th century (*Epist.* 70 *Ad Damasum* PG 32.435–436). Eusebius recalled also that the Roman Church kept alive the custom of helping suffering communities even during the last persecution of Diocletian (Eusebius, *op. cit.,* 4.22.9).

From the satire on Peregrinus (*Peregr.* 13) by Lucian, we learn how lively and active the interest and preoccupation of all the communities were for their distant sister-communities during the persecution under Marcus Aurelius. The letters of Ignatius to the various Churches are also an eloquent commentary. From this source we learn of the sincere interest of the communities of Asia Minor and Rome in the fate of a bishop they had never seen and the care they took of his Church at Antioch, left without a shepherd. Monetary aid took second place to the personal interest that led whole communities, bishops and faithful alike, to console and encourage one another and bear each other's sufferings.

From the Edict of Constantine to Gregory the Great. The conversion of some of Roman society to Christianity was not immediately followed by a flowering of evangelical ideals. However, from the 4th century Christianity introduced new notions even into secular civilization; one of these is the concept of charity in the social sense of the word, of the fellowship and responsibility of man toward his brothers, the disinherited, the poor, the homeless, the vagabonds, the sick, and the mentally ill. There is no text of Roman law that is inspired by *caritas*. This concept remained foreign to the juridical order of the classical Roman age. But once *caritas* became a fundamental Christian virtue, it inspired juridical texts of the postclassical age and texts inserted by the Justinians [E. Albertario, " 'Caritas' nei testi giuridici romani" in the *Rendiconti dell'Istituto Lombardo di scienze e lettere* 64 (1931) 375–392]. Respect for the human person, founded on the religious conviction that he is an object of the merciful love of God, was unknown to the pagan world. The liberality of the master toward his slaves was a very different thing, as were the benefits—bread and circuses—which the people received from the government: dividends of the spoils of conquests.

Liberty of worship, the juridical right to own property, and the restoration of the wealth confiscated by Diocletian (Lactantius, *De morte persecutorum* 48) allowed the Church a more liberal and substantial organization of charity. And it was a providential coincidence that as the end of persecution brought an influx of conversions to the Church so it also brought an increased number of needy converts who had to be assisted. The Church was able to raise money from the large fortunes of converts from aristocratic families. In 367 the consul Lampadius, on taking office, made large donations for the needy (Ammianus Marcellinus 27.3.5) and the prefect Nebridius, at Constantinople, did the same from his annual income (Jerome, *Epist.* 85). Placilla, the wife of Theodosius (Theodoret, *Hist. eccl.* 5.18), engaged in works of charity and many noble Roman women followed her example, e.g., Pauline, daughter of Paula; Fabiola; and Melania. St. Jerome bore witness to this in his writings (*Epist.* 77, 108; PL 22:690, 878), as did St. Paulinus of Nola (*Epist. 29 ad Severum;* PL 61:315). At the death of his wife Paulina in 396, the senator Pammachius gave a banquet in the Vatican basilica for all the poor of Rome. St. Jerome noted: "The precious stones which once adorned her neck now serve to feed the poor" (*Epist.* 66; PL 22:641). The name of Pammachius was connected with a hospice he founded at the port of Rome, near Ostia; and the name of Fabiola was linked to a hospital in the city where she gave personal service as well as financial aid to the poor. Paulinus of Nola, who knew all these instances well, summed up the complete change in social values when he called the beggars "patrons of our souls" (*Epist. 13 ad Severum;* PL 61:313). It was now the rich who appeared in the place of servants.

But the principal source of charitable endeavors was the possessions of the Church, which had come to her through imperial favor and which, besides covering the expenses of the clergy, were used to carry on charitable works. "The possessions of the Church are the patrimony of the poor," said St. Ambrose (*Epist.* 18.16; PL 16:1018). The bishops, as usual, assumed the leadership. From the time of Constantine the emperors gave them authority to administer the provision of food for orphans and widows, and later for prisoners (Theodoret, *Hist. eccl.* 1.10). The councils reminded them of their obligation to care for the needy. From their ranks came some of the most representative apostles of charity both in the East and the West.

The Rise of Church-sponsored Charitable Institutions. In Caesarea of Cappadocia, St. Basil, not content with having provided food for an entire year (368) to a region devastated by famine, began to construct (372) on the edge of the city a group of buildings (church, monastery, school of arts and trades, hospices, and hospital) destined to receive wayfarers, sick persons, and especially lepers, and staffed them with qualified personnel (Sozomen *Hist. eccl.* 6.34; Allard, *St. Basil* 109–111). Such "homes for the poor" (*ptochotrophia*) were not isolated phenomena. During the same period many others could be found, for example, at Amasya in Pontus and elsewhere. The Church of Alexandria had a group of nurses (*parabolani*) under the protection of the bishop; their number in the period from 416 to 418 exceeded 500. Another organizer of charitable works in Constantinople was St. John Chrysostom, who was aided by some generous souls of the aristocracy [C. Baur, *Johannes Chrisostomus und seine Zeit,* 1 (Munich 1929) 130, 303; 2 (Munich 1930) 55, 73]. Such was his ardor in condemning the avarice of the wealthy that in many texts he seemed to doubt the right of individuals to own private property. He did not, however, sanction the right of the poor to revolt against the rich. Rather he intended to incite the rich to the practice of charity.

In the West it is sufficient to name such bishops as Ambrose of Milan, Epiphanius of Pavia, Maximus of Turin, Paulinus of Nola, Martin of Tours, Nicetius of Lyons, and Sidonius Apollinarius. Ambrose was interested in everyone without distinction of rank; anyone could approach him, wrote St. Augustine (*Conf.* 6.3), unless the crowds of needy formed an impenetrable barrier around him. As soon as he was consecrated bishop, he gave all the gold and silver he possessed to the Church and to the poor; later on he bequeathed all he owned to the church in Milan (*Vita Ambr.* 38; PL 14.42). In the second book of his *De Officiis,* he insisted on the duties of charity, good works, and hospitality, and when in 378, after the defeat of Adrianople, many Christian soldiers fell into the hands of the Goths, Ambrose ordered all the vessels that had not yet been used for the sacred rites to be melted down and used as ransom. To justify his action he said: "It is better to conserve the living chalices of souls than those of metal! How beautiful is the sight of a procession of prisoners of whom it can be said: Christ has ransomed them. Here is useful gold, the gold of Christ that frees from death, the gold that ransoms modesty and saves chastity" (*De Off.* 2.28.136–143; PL 16.148).

It can be affirmed without a doubt that many of the bishops were very much aware of the urgent need for charity in all areas: from providing food and clothing to protecting the poor against the avidity of tax collectors and defending debtors from the mercilessness of usurers; from combating the rigors of the law to the guardianship of the rights of the poor of whom the bishops were, by their office, the defenders. In tragic times, such as those of the 5th century, when, according to St. Jerome, on account of the incessant wars "satis dives est, qui pane non indiget, nimium potens, qui servire non cogitur" (he is rich enough who does not lack bread; he is strong enough who is not compelled to be a slave; *Epist.120 ad Rusticum;* PL 22.1085), the preoccupations of a bishop could not differ from those of Peter Chrysologus: "Where are the barns . . . kept for the hunger of the poor?" (*Sermo* 122; PL 52). By this time the organized charity of the bishops had passed beyond the simple stage of a private duty and assumed a public character. The continual increase of the needy and the growing lack of those who could care for them conferred on the bishops a kind of investiture, which the events of the time made quite natural.

Development of Charitable Institutions under Church Administration. The bishops' work assumed a particular importance in regard to hospitality; the numerous hospices and hospitals erected during this period, although administered autonomously, were the property of the Church and as such headed by the bishops. The laws of the Later Empire recognized their position and entrusted the control to them, leaving to the heirs of the benefactors and their executors the tasks of administration. In the time of Justinian the juridical picture of hospital administration under the vigilance of the bishop was traced in its essential lines. These, it may be noted, were institutions that are today in the hands of the laity and have become an essential characteristic of every civilized state. But the historian of civilization must stress the fact that they are derived from a Christian inspiration and developed for many years under the protection of the Church. Herein lies the value and importance of the first 2 centuries of the free Church. Instead of being amazed at the length of time it took for the Christian ideal to penetrate human society, the historian must recognize the Christianization of social institutions that later expanded into the medieval city. In fact Emperor Julian the Apostate testified to the influence of Christian charity on society when he wrote in 362 to the priest Arsacius: "Why do we not turn our eyes towards those institutions to which the impious religion of the Christians owes its growth, towards the help it gives to aliens? Build many xenodochia in every city. It is a shame for us that the inhuman Galileans sustain not only their poor but ours as well" (Sozomen, *Hist. eccl.* 5.16).

Active assistance was already considered a fundamental element of monastic life as early as the 4th century, the heroic era of the Fathers of the desert. There is, in the technical language of the Egyptian monks, evidence that the strong disciplinary organization of the cenobite community tended to centralize the gathering and distribution of alms to the needy in a specialized service that was called diaconia. Cassian was the first to explain the meaning of this word, which was the name given to the almshouse of the Egyptian monastery of Diolco, supplied by the faithful and headed by a monk with the title of *diaconetès* [H. I. Marrou, *L'origine orientale des diaconies romaines, in Mélanges d'Archéologie et d'histoire* 57 (1940) 95–142]. Cassian's text brings us back to the middle of the 4th century. Little by little as they developed, the monastic diaconias tended toward autonomy. Almsgiving was made possible more by the contributions of the faithful than by the work of the monks. When larger offerings, such as lands, possessions, etc., were added to the fruits of the earth brought by the peasants, the diaconia became a proprietor, and had to receive juridical recognition. This autonomy was the first step toward independence, which probably was realized at Aphroditus from 573 to 574. Favored by the imperial government, the diaconias soon spread widely in Egypt, in Palestine (Marrou, *op. cit.* 9), in the Greek East (*ibid.* 10–11), and after the Justinian reconquest, in the Italian peninsula and even in Rome (*ibid.* 11–14).

Papal Patronage. At Rome, for that matter, thanks to the solicitous vigilance of the popes, the practice of charity always held first place. Reference has already been made to Pope Cornelius's interest in the poor. The pope as "Father of the Poor" meets us in the persons of Leo the Great and Gelasius. Symmachus founded three homes for the poor. Pelagius I was anxious that the patrimony of the Church should always be sufficient to care for the needy (*Lib. pont.* 1.263). But the service of the poor reached its peak under Gregory the Great.

Gregory had scarcely ascended the pontifical throne when he made his first concern the assuring of provisions for the city. He therefore warmly recommended to Peter, administrator of the patrimony of Sicily, that he not permit the consignments of grain to decrease. In the absence of civil authority and even contrary to it, Gregory felt it his imperative duty to protect the interests of the needy. "We have no wealth of our own, but the care and administration of the goods of the poor have been confided to us" (*Registrum Epistolarum* 13.23). This was his aim in the wise administration of the wealth of the Church and he stressed it to his administrators: "Have the Judge before your eyes for He will come; and remember you gather the best treasure for me, not when you acquire new riches but when you bring me the blessings of Heaven through your service to the poor" (*ibid.* 13.37).

The term "goods of the poor" is often used to indicate the patrimony of the Church, which by that time had developed to a notable degree. Gregory took charge of this patrimony energetically and made it a masterpiece of administration as well as an important organ of ecclesiastical government. The saint did not distribute alms at random; a special register listed the names of the persons aided and the date and amount of the alms donated (Giovanni Diacona, *Vita Gregorii* 2.30), but when there was a famine he opened the granaries of the Church to the poor. His charity was clothed with delicacy and is sometimes quite touching. Wracked with pain on his deathbed, he remembered a bishop who suffered from the cold and sent him a cloak, insisting that the messenger go at once because of the rigor of the season (*Epist. Reg.* 14.15). According to the well-known saying of John the Deacon, Gregory was "the father of the family of Christ" [H. Grisar, *San Gregorio Magno* 65 (Rome 1928) 324].

The Middle Ages

By the Middle Ages the Church had spread throughout the Western world and its charitable works and institutions flourished under the influence of Rome.

Charity in the Western Church. Many churches in the West were inspired by the Roman example that "charity resides in the bishop." This was especially true of the Frankish Church, which for all of the 5th and part of the 6th centuries was one of the most glorious of the ecclesiastical provinces, known both for its men of virtue and its fervor in good works. The bishops led exemplary lives and were distinguished for their doctrine and piety. Many of the bishops carried out the ideal of charity, first realized by Martin of Tours, the great anticipator, whose glory increased as his example encouraged. The Church, in fact, continued that tradition and felt honored to dedicate her strength to all kinds of poverty and need. Lists of the needy were kept and the *matricularii* formed a kind of association of the poor of Christ who had the privilege of begging from door to door, of receiving regular subsidies and of living in "a house of the poor." The bishop was the official protector of both the poor and the oppressed, and defended them in the courts.

An analogous situation existed in the British Isles at the time of Gregory the Great, but we do not know how far the results fulfilled the wishes of the Pontiff (*Epist.* 12.21). It would seem that the ancient rivalry between Britons and Anglo-Saxons injured discipline as well as charitable efforts. It was only later, at the time of Pope Vitalian, that the monk Theodore of Tarsus skillfully succeeded in bringing about peace. A new spirit then appeared in the field of charity. Bishops and abbots took great interest in the lower classes whom they protected against the power of the wealthy. Sometimes they acted as a curb, sometimes as a spur through penitential discipline, encouraging good works and pious foundations, liberating slaves, improving roads, aiding the peasants who were reduced to hunger by wars, and reconstructing destroyed dwellings.

In the Iberian Peninsula charity suffered as a result of the political and religious activities of the Arian government, which harassed the Church and confiscated its possessions. Only after the conversion of the Visigoths did Spain slowly accept the discipline and institutions already in use in other Western churches. St. Leander of Seville made his influence felt in the reorganization of charity under the protection of the bishops. According to the prescriptions given by the Council of Chalcedon, the bishops were obliged to appoint an *econome* to administer the goods of the Church [*Conc. Hisp.* (*c.* 590) c.6]. From the end of the 6th century, through the urging of wise and saintly men such as the above-mentioned St. Leander, and Isidore of Seville, Masona of Emerita, John of Gerona, and Fulgentius of Astigi, the bishops were established as fathers of the poor and defenders of the goods of the Church, which were considered as the patrimony of the poor [*Conc. Tolet.* (*c.* 589) c.3, 5, 6; (*c.* 638) c.15].

The Influence of the Councils. The most prominent bishops of the time did not limit their work to their own dioceses. By encouraging regional councils they gave greater influence to the tenets of the Church and established uniformity in practice throughout an entire kingdom. This was true in Merovingian France, where from 511 to 614 more than 30 national synods were held. During these synods the issue of church discipline was discussed and questions regarding the practice of charity periodically recurred.

The documents of the time recall the dignity of the poor to whom a quarter of the tithes belonged, according to the Roman custom mentioned by Gregory the Great (*Epist.* 11.64). The synods recommended assistance for those unable to work and the infirm [*Conc. Aurel.* (*c.* 511) c.16]; for wayfarers and pilgrims; for abandoned children and lepers. This latter category of unfortunates attracted the particular attention of all the saints of the period, e.g., Romain of Luxeuil (d. 653), Aregus, Bishop of Gap (d. 604), Radegunde, Odile, etc. The West did not possess, as did the East, different types of institutions to aid various classes of needy. In the East, from the 4th century, rich and populous cities could boast of hospitals and other institutions adapted to the types of unfortunates who needed help. In the 9th century the *xenodochium* or hospice, principally for pilgrims and the poor, appeared, and sometimes, like the one in Lyons founded by King Childebert and mentioned in the Council of Orléans [(*c.* 549) c.15], accepted also the aged and infirm.

The Status of Slaves. The synods definitely brought about the penetration of Christian ideals into legislation and morals. The problem of slaves is an example. Among the pagans during the early Middle Ages, the condition of slaves was no better than it had been in ancient times. The Church did not remain insensible to their fate and acted in various ways to alleviate it, for example, by encouraging emancipation, as happened in England through the work of those monasteries that received slaves in order to free them. This practice influenced the conduct of private citizens. Adopting a solution offered by German law, which recognized servitude as an intermediate condition between liberty and slavery, the Church transferred a number of slaves into this category, prescribing at the same time that the "servants of the family of God, through motives of justice and mercy, should be obliged to work less than the servants of private individuals" [*Conc. of Eauze* (*c.* 551) c.6; *ibid.* 114]. The synod of Agde (*c.* 506) obliged the bishops to give these servants wages, in money or in kind. Many laws of the councils took pains to make the condition of servants as humane as possible, forbidding labor on feast days, upholding the right of slaves to indissoluble matrimony and—in some cases—even recognizing their right to receive Holy Orders. Finally, codifying a Roman law on the right of asylum, the Council of Orléans (*c.* 511) offered slaves recourse to a privilege that saved them from torture and unjust condemnation to death (cc.1–3; *ibid.* 2).

The Status of Women and Children. Another important step in the progress of charity was the slow transformation of the position of women. The Council of Mâcon (585) assured to widows and orphans the assistance of the bishop in judgment (*Monumenta Germaniae Historica,* c.12, *Concilia aevi merovingici,* 169). Particular protection was given to those widows who intended to live in a state of religious consecration [*Conc. Paris.* (*c.* 556–573) c.6; *ibid.* 144]. The Church also ruled against the German custom of repudiating a wife, and the synod of Orléans (533) forbade the breaking of the marriage contract for reasons of illness (c.11; *ibid.* 63). The actions of queens, such as St. Radegunde and St. Bathilde, contributed to mitigating the violence of the period, and the example of consecrated virgins, such as St. Genevieve and St. Odile, who delighted in serving the poor and infirm, "precious members of the Lord," was of great influence.

Greater protection was assured also to abandoned children. Roman legislation, amended in the 5th century under Honorius and Theodosius II, had given ample powers to the Church in this matter. This law protected the Church in her actions even after the new peoples in France, England, and Spain had come under its influence [*Monumenta Germaniae historica Leges Visigothorum,* ed. Zeumer, 193; *Formulae merovingici et Karolini aevi,* ed. Zeumer, n. 49, 21; n. 11, 241].

The Status of Prisoners. Another Roman law inspired prescriptions in favor of prisoners. The Council of Orléans (*c.* 549) decreed that the archdeacons should pay a weekly visit to prisoners to provide for their needs and console them (*Conc. aevi merovingici,* c. 20, 107). The Church frequently paid the prisoners' expenses and bishops ransomed prisoners of war. The public was particularly influenced by these works of mercy.

Decentralization. After Gregory the Great the religious and political scene of the Christian world changed rapidly. Byzantium lost its hold on the West; Africa and Spain became Moslem camps, and Christianity turned to the Germanic peoples. The affairs of the Church were more and more discussed in national diets and councils, where the decisive word was often left to the secular power.

The very organization of charity among the new peoples mirrored social and economic conditions very different from those of the preceding epoch. In the ancient Church, most of the poor were urban and all charitable works stemmed from the bishop; but the Germanic people were rural. To adapt to this situation, a process of administrative decentralization slowly developed through the erection of rural churches (parishes) served by resident clergy to whom were confided those charitable works that had been the concern of the bishops [see G. Forchielli, *La pieve Rurale* (Bologna 1938)].

The evolution is especially clear in Merovingian France of the 6th century. With the increase of conversions in the country and the expansion of dioceses, the relations between the rural community and the bishop became more and more difficult. A need for churches that would be religiously and economically independent, though still under the authority of the bishop, consequently arose. A step toward decentralization of administration was occasioned by the prohibition to transfer ecclesiastical possessions [*Conc. Epaon.* (*c.* 517) c.12 in *Conc. aevi merovingici* 22]. The rapid growth of the bishops' patrimonies made efficient administration impossible, and distribution of assistance to the poor declined. A solution was found in the free transfer or rent of small properties to poor laymen (the *precaris*) or ecclesiastics. When the Council of Orleáns (*c.* 538) forbade the bishops to take back the grants already made to ecclesiastics (c.20; *ibid.* 79) the foundations of the regime of *benefices was laid. The Council of Carpentras (*c.* 527) went further and authorized rural churches to accept legacies (*ibid.* 41). As a consequence canonical legislation regarding the role of bishops in patrimonial matters was extended to the parish priests. The decentralization of the administration of Church funds was accompanied by the decentralization of charitable work as well. This took place toward the middle of the 6th century and was sanctioned by the synod of Tours in 567, which imposed on each ecclesiastical community or parish the obligation of taking care of its own poor: "Each city shall nourish its poor and needy with suitable food—according to its means" (c.5 *ibid.* 123). This new approach to charity was authorized in all the states of the Carolingian Empire and even beyond: in Spain, England, and even in Rome during the time of Adrian I (772–795).

Before Charlemagne, the practice of charity involved the Church in great difficulties under the last of the Merovingian kings. Clovis claimed and obtained the right to name the higher clergy (*Conc. Aurel.* c.4 in *Conc. aevi merovingici,* 4). As a result, the dioceses were soon occupied by men from the court who used the goods of the poor for their personal needs. The golden age of charity was only a memory.

Decadence reached its peak under Charles Martel, who handed over Church property to his own vassals. Their misuse of it brought on the impoverishment and demoralization of the clergy. The strenuous efforts of St. *Boniface, the apostle of Germany, succeeded in obtaining the recognition of Church property and the promised payment of an annual rent by the new beneficaries [Synod of Lestinnes (*c.* 743) *Monumenta Germaniae historica, Conc. Aevi Karolini,* 1.7, iii]; but with Pepin the Short secularization of Church revenues returned.

The Work of Charlemagne and Feudal Decadence. A renewal took place under Charlemagne, who, although holding firmly to the idea that the sovereign had a right to dispose of Church property, was faithful to his program of becoming the refuge of the needy [*Monum. Germ. Hist. Capitulare Missorum* (*c.* 802) in *Capitularia Regum Francorum* 1.93]. He sought to stop abuses and both supported and encouraged ecclesiastical benefices; decisions in this matter can be found in the *capitularia* of Charlemagne. They contain norms for providing shelters [*Cap. Franc.* (*c.* 783)], assistance to widows and orphans [*Cap. Saxon.* (*c.* 797)], and hospitality to strangers [*Cap. Missorum* (*c.* 802)]. At the Chapter of Nimwegen (806), which regulated the practice of begging and the repression of vagabondage, the duties of the nobles toward the poor of their domains was also fixed as well as the obligation of running the *xenodochia* according to the intentions of the founders. The *missi dominici,* charged with controlling the administration of the nobles, had to watch over and respect the rights of the poor and the correct use of revenues and resources destined for them.

Under Louis the Pious another strong impulse toward charitable action on the part of the clergy was attempted in the synod of Aachen (*Aquisgranum, c.* 817). In the spirit of the canonical reform introduced by Chrodegang of Metz, some decisions of the synod referred to the organization of charity: each bishop was obliged to maintain a hospice for the needy, and the clergy was obliged to contribute to its support by paying a tax on their income. The direction of the hospice was to be in the hands of a canon. Monks were obliged to erect a hospital outside the cloister, but within the monastery, and were required to shelter widows and destitute women in a suitable house.

The influence of the Carolingian legislation was felt in England where, as in the imperial dominions, the economic basis for charity was the payment of tithes [*Canones Aelfrici* (*c.* 960) in D. Wilkins, *Concilia Magnae Britanniae et Hiberniae* (London 1737) 1.253] imposed on the nobles of the kingdom as well as on the clergy [*Constit. Regis Aethelstani* (*c.* 928); *Canones sub Edgaro Rege,* (*c.* 960); Wilkins, 1.205, 238]. Even after the decadence caused by the Lombards in Italy, the Carolingian influence was felt. Old hospices were restored to their original use after the secularization of Charles Martel [*C. Mantuanum* (*c.* 782) c.12; *Pippini capitulare italicum* (*c.* 801–810) in *Capitularia Regum Francorum* 1.195.3; 210.9]. Others arose in the course of the next century. The foundation by the archpriest Datheus in Milan of a hospice for abandoned children was characteristic (Muratori, *Antiquitates Italicae* 3.587). In Rome the charitable activity of the popes was noteworthy: Paul I, a worthy emulator of Gregory the Great (*Lib. pont.* 1.463); Adrian I, (772–795); Leo III (795–816); and Pascal I (817–824). The *Liber pontificalis* stressed the interest and charity of Pascal I toward distant communities like those in Spain, to which he sent help for the ransom of prisoners (*Lib. pont.* 2.60).

The principal means the popes employed in Rome to administer "alms to our brethren in Christ—the poor" (*Liber diurnus,* form. 95) were the diaconias, which from the end of the 7th century to the 9th kept their specific character of public institutions for charitable aid. Popes, clergy, and laity contributed to their upkeep [A. P. Frutaz, "Diaconia" in EncCatt; and G. Ferrari, OSB, *Early Roman Monasteries* (Rome 1957) 355–361].

Decline of Charitable Institutions. After Charlemagne, notwithstanding the precautions sanctioned by Louis the Pious, charitable organizations underwent another decline. In fact, the general historical situation did not leave much room for charity. Europe was again in conflict and countries were devastated; on the north by the Normans and Danes; on the east by the Magyars; on the southwest by the Saracens. The struggle between the successors of Charles increased the feudal anarchy, and the insecurity of the country and the difficulties of transport greatly reduced agriculture and trade.

The Church in councils frequently raised its voice on behalf of the oppressed: first through the "*Peace of God," which obliged belligerants to respect the rights of the innocent; then through the "Truce of God," which attempted to limit wars by making the belligerents respect Sunday as a holy day; later, the truce extended from Wednesday to the following Monday.

Effect of Feudalism on Charity. The exercise of charity was impeded also by the complex structure of feudal society. In principle, the Church maintained the supervision of public assistance but the spiritual power was limited by a network of privileges annexed to the land of a parish or a diocese; the clergy themselves were divided by diverse obediences. Besides, the feudal lord was obliged to assist the poor who lived on his lands and depended on him. In addition, trade associations, confraternities, and similar groups carried on works of charity. Hence, the exercise of charity was no longer the exclusive task of the Church. A common characteristic, however, signalized the most diverse initiatives, namely, the religious inspiration that was faithful to the teaching of the Church and a lively faith that put its resources at the service of the poor and suffering.

The breakdown of the practice of charity continued during the feudal period. In fact, except for England, the care of the poor by the Church does not reappear even in the 11th century when a new spirit of religious reform began that was to establish itself strongly in the following century. The absence of the Church's voice from the *Decretals* of Gratian is symptomatic. The task of caring for the poor was left for individual institutions—the monasteries, hospital orders, and secular associations.

The Monasteries. The charitable preoccupation of Eastern monasticism permeates the rule of St. Benedict and the customs of the great medieval abbeys. Almsgiving was traditionally one of the fruits of monastic labor. St. Basil, Cassian, the *Regula Magistri*—principal sources of St. Benedict's rule—taught that the monk should not only support himself but also give the fruit of his labor to the poor. St. Benedict lists comforting the poor (*pauperes recreare*) as an example of good works, and he confides this task to the particular attention of the *cellerarius,* stating that "in them we minister to Christ." Following his example the medieval abbeys practiced great charity toward the poor, often devoting a large part of the monastery's income to that purpose. In 1 year, for example, the monastery of Cluny provided for 17,000 needy persons, and that of Saint-Riquier daily supplied the needs of 300 destitute persons, 150 widows, and 60 members of the clergy.

The reception of guests in the Middle Ages was an indirect form of giving alms to anyone who had need of a bed or a meal or was infirm or unable to work. St. Benedict dedicated a chapter of his rule to hospitality (*Regula* ch. 53). The guest house (*hospitale hospitum*), designed to receive travelers, pilgrims, clerics, monks, and nobles both secular and ecclesiastic, was separated from the hospice for the poor (*xenodochium*), which received beggars, invalids, the aged, and the infirm. After the reform of Charlemagne, *Cluny encouraged hospitality in all its forms and exemplified it throughout Europe. The Council of Mainz (1261) explicitly mentions that such hospices are usually annexed to every monastery [P. Schmitz, OSB, *Histoire de l'Ordre de Saint Benoit* 2 (Maredsous 1942) 34–50].

In the 12th century the Cistercians, wishing to live the Benedictine Rule in its original purity, gave a new impulse to charity. Outstanding among the members of this order was St. Bernard of *Clairvaux whose abbey practiced almsgiving in all its forms. During a famine in Burgundy (1125) 2,000 poor were cared for by the saint. Every Cisterian abbey had a guest house where pilgrims, travelers, and the infirm received lodging and care. The abbot himself waited on them after having welcomed them by prostrating himself at their feet [E. Vacandard, *Vie de Saint Bernard* v. 1 (Paris 1910) 454)]. The monastery of *Heisterbach in 1197 distributed food daily to 1,500 poor people.

Canons Regular and Secular Associations. If the exercise of charity and, in particular, of hospitality was considered in the Benedictine monasteries as a function subordinated to the contemplative ideal, the inherent value of this service was stressed by the *Canons Regular who, in the renewed religious climate of the 12th and 13th centuries, were responsible for the renewal of *hospitalitas* in its widest social implication, viz, assistance to pilgrims and travelers, permanent and occasional care of the sick, the poor, expectant mothers, the aged, and abandoned children. Bound to cathedral chapters during the time of the Gregorian reform, they were genuine religious orders. The laity cooperated in providing hospices. The geographical location of these foundations—at a river crossing, in the heart of a forest, or an alpine pass—symbolized this intention to aid traveelers and pilgrims. Together with the monks of Cluny, the Canons Regular played an important part in the organization of pilgrimages to the shrine of St. James in Compostella. The vogue of the legend of St. Julian the Hospitaler illustrates this movement in which the laity played an important part (C. Dereine in *Dictionnaire d'histoire et geographie eccl.* 12.385–386).

Augustinian hospital work flourished from the beginning of the 12th century, when many communities, all living under the rule of St. Augustine, devoted themselves to the care of the sick. Among the first were the Hospitalers of St. John of Jerusalem whose motto was: "Defense of the Faith and Service to the Poor." In the rule, written by Raymund of Puis, the sick man is defined as "quasi dominus" of the house [L. Le Grand, "Les maisons-Dieu," *Revue des questions historiques* 16 (1896) 134)].

The *Teutonic Knights added the obligation of serving the sick and pilgrims to military service. The Antonines directed the hospital of Mota (Vienne) and became the largest order of hospitalers in Europe. The order of the Holy Spirit was founded between 1170 and 1180 at Montpellier; to its founder, Innocent III confided the direction of the Roman hospital of S. Spirito in Sassia built in 1204.

The possession of hospitals by secular associations began in the 12th century when the Canons ceased to live a common life. Hospitals belonging to them were little by little taken over by groups other than religious orders. Thus, the Hôtel Dieu of Paris, which had been the hospital of the Chapter of Notre Dame, was confided (1217) to a corporation of 4 priests, 30 lay brothers, and 25 lay sisters. Although not bound by religious vows, this and similar autonomous communities of hospitalers lived a common life under the direction of a prior or prioress, and obeyed a rule of life based on that of a religious order, usually the rule of St. *Augustine. The latter was adapted to the particular circumstances and was completed by special statutes. Associations of this kind prospered everywhere: the Brothers of Penance in Brussels, the Beghards, the Alexians, the Hospitalers of Aubrac, Rodez, etc. Some joined an already existing order of hospitalers: for example, the Brothers of the Holy Spirit became associated with the order of the same name [M. Heimbucher, *Die Orden und Kongregationen der Katholischen Kirche* (3d ed. Paderborn 1933–34) 1:611–620].

Under the impulse of both the hospital orders and the autonomous associations, the network of new foundations spread rapidly in the 13th and 14th centuries. At first, these, too, were under the director of the bishops, but the movement for emancipation of the cities, which tended to centralize public works in the hands of the city government, brought about the exclusion of the bishops from charitable institutions. The intervention of city magistrates did not limit itself to controlling the financial direction of the institutions but extended even to the choice of hospital personnel. Charity became the business of the state. The aim of this intrusion was not to remove pious works from religious influence but to avoid the guardianship of the bishops. This movement was felt particularly in Italy where bishops and abbots found themselves involved as temporal princes in a bloody rivalry between citizens and feudal authority. Nothing damaged charity so much as the quest for wealth and power. Because the Church was so intimately bound to the structure of medieval society it did not escape this pitfall, especially when peace brought wealth and well-being to the West. The luxury and worldly spirit displayed by many bishops and prelates provoked protests, one of the strongest being that of St. Bernard, who contrasted the hunger and nakedness of the poor with the pomp of bishops (*De moribus et officio episcoporum* 2 in PL 182.810) and even with the luxury displayed by monks in their churches: "The

Church shines with walls, but is lacking in care for the poor" [*Apologia* 12.28 in *S. Bernardi Opera III* (Rome 1963) 105].

The Influence of the Mendicants. It is not surprising that when heretical movements arose in revolt against this neglect of the poor (*Waldenses, *Brothers and Sisters of the Free Spirit, *Albigenses) St. *Francis of Assisi's call to poverty and penance served as an exorcism (1182–1226). He does not belong to the heroes of charity for any external acts: he was not an innovator in works of charity; he did not found any charitable institutions. But the influence of the Poverello was extraordinary; his mysticism of poverty gave a new character to the exercise of charity. Medieval mysticism saw Christ in the poor; Franciscan spirituality gave this mysticism an intimate, fraternal spirit.

St. Francis has been perpetuated not only in the order he founded but also in the *Third Orders and the Confraternities that incorporate his spirit. The same may be said of St. *Dominic. The Third Orders Regular for women prepared the way for the modern congregations of charity. They still exist in great numbers under Franciscan and Dominican titles. The Beguines also participated in this religious renewal and led many women to the practice of charity. (*See* BEGUINES AND BEGHARDS.) Living a religious life in small communities, although not bound by vows, these women dedicated themselves to pious works and the care of the sick both in hospitals and in their own homes. The movement had notable success in the Rhine Valley and the Low Countries. *See* SPIRITUALITY, RHENISH; SPIRITUALITY IN THE LOW COUNTRIES.

The increasing numbers of lay people of both sexes serving in health and welfare institutions can be explained by the growth of cities in which poor hygienic conditions contributed to illness, and inadequate sources of food supply created hunger. Preachers did not fail to encourage the alleviation of these conditions. Best known was the Franciscan Berthold von Reichensberg (d. 1272) who in his missions throughout Europe constantly extolled works of mercy as a true service of God. The response of the people is evident in the number of legacies to pious works and charitable foundations. In 1244 Pier Luca Borsi, head porter of a wool guild in Florence, founded the Company of Mercy with money he collected by taxing his colleagues for swearing. The Company of Bigallo (1256) in the same city developed into a powerful charitable institution. Symbols of the age's pious emulation are the hospitals in Chartres, Florence, Cologne, Lübeck, Milan, and Rome. But their grandiose exteriors were more impressive than their interior development and the services offered. In this respect the West had nothing to compare with contemporary Byzantine hospitals. The monastery of Pantocrator of Constantinople, which made such an impression on Anselm of Havelberg (1134–36), had annexed to it a series of charitable-social institutions. Beside the hospital itself, there was a home for the aged, a section for special diseases (the mentally ill and epileptics), a pharmacy run by laymen, and a school of medicine that carried on the tradition of *Aesculapius. A century later James of Vitry called attention to the hospitals of St. Anthony and St. Sanson, worthy to be numbered among the principal hospitals of Christianity [G. Schreiber, *Gemeinschaften des Mittelalters* (Regensberg, Münster 1948) 3–80].

Special Charitable Activities. In the West, although hospitals admitted those suffering from almost every kind of sickness, for sanitary reasons they did not accept those with diseases considered contagious, such as leprosy. Hospitals for lepers (*leprosaria*) were organized outside the cities and were financed by legacies and donations. They were staffed by communities of lay brothers and sisters, such as the Franciscans and the Knights of St. Lazarus. The latter group founded a large number of *leprosaria,* possibly 3,000, throughout Europe.

From the time of St. Louis IX hospitals for the blind had been established in Paris (L'Hôpital des Quinze-Vingts), Hanover (1256), Tournai (1351), and Padua (14th century). Toward the end of the Middle Ages conditions for the care of the mentally ill, who until then had been treated as prisoners or worse, were greatly improved and hospitals were erected in Hamburg (1375) and Mirandola (1400). Special hospices for orphans and foundlings increased in number, especially in Italy as early as the 15th century. One of the most famous was the Hospital of the Innocents founded in Florence in the 15th century.

Special concern was shown for prostitutes. Their number had multiplied after the Crusades through the dissoluteness of the soldiers and the development of the towns. Innocent III in 1198 called attention to this social calamity. A house of refuge, the first nucleus of a religious congregation, was founded in Paris in 1204 by Folcus of Neuilly. His example soon found imitators in Marseilles, Bologna, Rome, and Messina. In Germany the Congregation of the Penitents of St. Mary Magdalen was founded. Its inspiration grew out of the Council of Mainz (1225) and the congregation was constituted an order for penitents by Gregory IX as a result of their favorable influence in various cities. In the 13th century there were 50 houses of the order.

Special hospices for the assistance of travelers greatly increased. From the 11th century hospices were established near mountains, forests, and rivers—special hazards for the traveler. Hence arose the mountain refuges (Roncesvalles, Grand-Saint-Bernard, Aubrac, Vallombrose, etc.); the work of the "Fratres Pontifices" (Bridge Builders) in Provence and Spain, who constructed bridges and roads, and the Congregation of Altopascio, in Italy, whose members transported travelers across the marshes of Lucca; and the forest refuges in the North (Flône, Affligem, Vicogne, etc). Associations for the maintenance of roads and bridges were protected by kings and lords and favored with indulgences by the bishops.

Another work prompted by charity was the ransoming of prisoners captured in the long struggle against the Moors in Spain. The first to dedicate himself to this work was St. *John of Matha. The *Trinitarians, founded by St. John and approved (1198) by Innocent III, ransomed prisoners and labored to alleviate the condition of those who remained in slavery. The Order of Mercy, founded by St. *Peter Nolasco, was also dedicated to this work. It began as a military order but soon became a mendicant order.

Toward the end of the Middle Ages the shortcomings of the charitable institutions became many and evident. The cause of the poor suffered from the consequences of the Great Western Schism, the worldly spirit of many spiritual leaders, and the piling up of benefices and the system of giving *in commendam* that converted so many charitable institutions into sources of easy gain for those who held them. Added to this was the misery of the age: destitution caused by wars and the endless calamities that accompanied them. Charity, it is true, still had at its disposal resources and an organization: confraternities increased in number; the instinct for charitable giving, as is shown by the number of legacies and bequests, remained alive in individuals. But charity lost its luster because it was no longer in intimate touch with the misery of the poor; it took on bourgeois attitudes and its very instruments became fossilized. In the 16th century the revival of the Church in its better representatives moved toward a revival of charity. Meanwhile, the Church had to meet the new era under unfavorable conditions, giving ground in some regions to the attacks of the Protestant *Reformation and surrendering a large part of its position to the civil power.

Modern Times

The secularization of charity, which began during the period of the communes, spread considerably at the beginning of the 16th century and achieved a complete separation from the Church because of the Reformation. The process was closely related to contemporary socioeconomic developments and to the new spiritual movements inherent in humanism. The object of charitable assistance was no longer the poor man as a brother in Christ but the citizen as such. Charity was divested of its transcendent quality. Currents of the new orientation were strong in the Flemish cities, in the Rhineland, in other sectors of the Empire, and in Italy.

It was not that the Church relegated, even temporarily, her charitable action to convents and religious sodalities. The intervention of the Church continued to leave its mark on social institutions; e.g., the measures it took against the abuses of usurers, and in particular the erection of public pawnbroker establishments, **Montes Pietatis,* protected by the Franciscans. These developed especially in Italy in the 15th century through the initiative of Barnabas of Terni, St. James of the Marches, Louis of Verona, St. John Capistran and, above all, by Bl. Bernadine of Feltre [M. Weber, *Les Origines des Monts-de-Piété* (Rixheim 1920)]. In countries not yet touched by heresy there was beneficial collaboration between civil and religious authorities. Thus in Italy, Pius II in 1458 issued a bull recognizing the statutes of hospitals founded by the state in Milanese territory. In Portugal the popes were always disposed to collaborate with secular authority for the expansion of charitable institutions: e.g., Alexander VI, who (1499) authorized the king Don Manuel to incorporate small hospitals in Coimbra, Evora, and Santarem into the larger hospitals of the same locality, and finally extended the permission to other places; Leo X, who at the request of the King (1516) provided benefices for All Saints' Hospital in Lisbon. Since most charitable institutions were of ecclesiastical origin, jurisdiction over many of them was given to the clergy [F. de Almeida, *Historia da Igreja em Portugal,* v. 1 (Coimbra 1915) 2:467–470].

Where the secular power violently attacked the rights and works of the Church, as in Protestant countries, there were grave results. "Under the Popes," *Luther admitted, "there was a strong drive to give alms to the poor, but now everyone has become cold and insensible" [H. Grisar, *Martin Luthers Leben und sein Werk* (Freiburg 1926) 497]. It was really Luther himself who contributed to this situation by his doctrine on the inefficacy of good works for salvation, at a time when there was a fresh outbreak of poverty largely as a result of the confiscation by secular authority of monasteries and other sources of Catholic charity.

The Work of the Council of Trent. The Council of *Trent contributed greatly to improving the spirit of charity. The earnest entreaties of that synod had antecedents that cannot be ignored. Such, for example, was the initiative of the bishop of Verona Gian Matteo Giberti (1495–1543). Assisted by Louis di Canossa, Bishop of Bayeux, Giberti founded (1528) a large Xenodochium Misericordiae for orphans and infirm; the following year he founded a society of charity; he reopened many *Montes Pietatis* and provided for the rehabilitation of prostitutes; he named visitors for each parish to make a census of the poor in order to assist them with public funds. At his death he left 6,000 gold florins for charitable works. Many of his recommendations to the clergy were included in the canons of the Council of Trent.

At the same time, numerous charitable associations were carrying on important works: the Company of St. Jerome and the Company of Divine Love, founded respectively at the end of the 15th century and the beginning of the 16th, did much to revivify charitable endeavors. From the Company of Divine Love sprang a new institution to assist those afflicted with syphilis, for which there was then no cure. Syphilitics were always refused by hospitals for fear of contagion. Thanks to the generosity of Ettore Vernazza, the first hospital for such incurables was erected in Genoa (1499); Rome, Naples, and other cities followed suit [P. Cassiano da Langasco, *Gli ospedali degli incurabli* (Genoa 1938)].

New Charitable Orders. Charity was revived with the rise of new religious orders that either made charity a primary end or gave it an important place. Among the first group were the Congregation of Clerks Regular of Somascha founded about 1530 by St. Jerome *Emiliani for the care of orphans; the Brothers of St. John of God, and the Ministers of the Sick of St. Camillus for the care of the sick and for hospital service. The second group included the Barnabites, Capuchins, Jesuits, Clerks Regular of the Religious Schools, and the Theatines.

Through the Council of Trent the Church not only reaffirmed the validity and the indispensability of good works for salvation but even promulgated a juridical order for the development of this position, proclaiming indirectly, by numerous works of mercy, the primacy of charity.

The Influence of the Bishops. Both the means approved by the council for the administration of pious works and the powers of control confided to the bishops influenced more or less extensively the bishops' actions. There was almost no activity in the countries won over to Protestantism; episcopal action was fettered in France, where civil authority was dominant, but functioned freely in Spain and Italy, where the authority of the bishops was recognized. A noble example was St. Charles *Borromeo in Milan who devoted himself to put the spirit of Trent into practice. He lived so much like the poor that in his funeral oration it was said: "Charles had of his wealth what the dog had of the wealth of his master; a little water and a little straw." The 11 diocesan synods and the six provincial synods over which he presided regulated the care of the needy with a real sense of pastoral responsibility. He approved the new society of Ursulines in Brescia, founded to educate the children of the poor, and he aided in every possible way the development of numerous houses already existing in Milan for the rehabilitation of wayward girls. To the Oblates of St. Ambrose, which he founded in 1578, he assigned the care of souls in charitable institutions. During a plague in 1576, he replaced the governor who had fled and went about among the stricken, consoling and assisting them. He exhorted his clergy to aid the victims of the plague even to the point of sacrificing their lives [*Delle cure della peste. Istruttione di s. Carlo card. di Santa Praesede ed arciv. di Milano* (Venice 1630)].

Charity in Mission Lands. The missionary work of religious orders opened new fields for Christian charity and enlarged others already initiated by the hierarchy. After the conquest of New Spain, institutions for the relief of the natives had been established under the direction and with the cooperation of the Church. Vasco de *Quiroga, Bishop of Michoacán (1537–65), was one of the pioneers of charity. While still a layman and a member of the second tribunal of Mexico he learned of the extreme misery of the Indians and with his own money built a hospital, Santa Fé, which he later completed by adding a home for abandoned children. In 1533 he was sent on a mission to the Province of Michoacán and built another Santa Fé on the banks of Lake Pátzcuaro near Vayámeo. When he returned to Michoacán in 1538 as bishop, he began, with the favor of the crown, the organization of work in common, the equal division of the fruits of labor, civil and religious education, and the eradication of begging and vagabondage. Before Quiroga, others had begun similar institutions such as the hospital of Jesus Nazareno, founded (*c.* 1521) by Fernando Cortés. Later, in 1534, Bishop *Zumárraga founded an institution of charity in Mexico, called Amor de Dios, which grew through revenues from Charles V. Toward the middle of the 16th century, the hospital of St. Joseph was founded for the Indians. In 1564 Dr. Pedro Ortiz founded the hospital of St. Lazarus for lepers. This was followed by another, Nuestra Señora de Los Desamparados, for Negroes, mulattoes, and poor children. The *Franciscans and *Augustinians were energetic hospital builders in New Spain, especially in Michoacán, where charitable institutions developed rapidly. This work was especially necessary because of the severe epidemics. In 1555 the provincial synod of Messino decreed that there should be a hospital next to the church in every village. This decree bore fruit in the following decade.

Charitable works had other promoters as well—among them viceroys, governors, confraternities, and private citizens. They met the most diverse needs and populated the southern provinces with hospitals, hospices for the poor and penitents, maternity homes, and homes for abandoned children. *Montes Pietatis* were established at Darien and Bogota in Colombia (1555); Lima (1538), Cuczo (1538), Huamanga (1555), and Juli (1570) in Peru; Santa Cruz de la Sierra (1612) and La Paz (1617) in Bolivia; Quito (1565) in Eucador; Santiago (1540) and La Imperial (1570) in Chile. The work developed from Mexico to Argentina and from the Antilles to the Philippines.

In the Portuguese colonies overseas, the practice of charity flowed naturally from the tradition of the mother country. In addition to the usual relief given to beggars by the secular and religious clergy particular help was given during epidemics or other public calamities. Such, for instance, were the famine (1564–76) in Braga; the plague (1569, 1579, 1598) in Lisbon, in Braga (1569) in Evora (1580), and at other times in Algarve, Santarem, and Coimbra. In these crises the generosity and heroism of priests and religious and particularly of Bps. Bartolomeo dos Mártyres and Theotonio de Braganza were exemplary. Among works begun by the clergy were the hospital of St. Mark in Braga, the orphanages of Our Lady of Grace and Our Lady of Hope in Oporto, the Pietà hospital and orphanage in Evora, the retreats of St. Mary Magdalen in Castillo Branco and Coimbra, the orphanage of Jesus and the retreats of Our Lady of the Incarnation and Our Lady of the Angels in Lisbon [F. De Almeida *Historia de Igreja en Portugal,* v.3 (Coimbra 1915) 2:467–488].

During the Middle Ages many religious associations of the laity in Portugal were dedicated to charitable practices, e.g., Espíritu Santo, Nossa Senhora de Rocamador, Nossa Senhora de Piedade, Penitêncîa, and Santissima Trinidade. Queen *Isabella greatly influenced these organizations and in her will she mentioned "Santa Misericordia de Rocamador." The name "Misericordia" is especially connected with two persons: Queen Eleanor, wife of John II, and Fra Miguel Contreras, a Spanish Trinitarian. On the advice of the latter, the Queen founded (1498) the Confraternity of Misericordia in Lisbon, which spread rapidly throughout Portugal and across the ocean. The statutes (*compromisso*) of this pious association (issued 1516) bound the 100 members, half of whom belonged to the nobility and half to the working class, to the practice of the 14 works of mercy. Members went in pairs to visit the sick, prisoners, and poor people in their homes to discover their needs and supply them with food, money, dwellings, beds, etc. The many privileges that King Manuel granted to the association occasioned its rapid spread. At the death of Queen Eleanor (1525), 61 branches of the Misericordia had taken solid root in metropolitan territory [see V. Ribeiro, *A santa casa da Misericordia de Lisboa* (Lisbon 1902)].

From the 17th to the 19th centuries the Misericordia spread to Portuguese dominions overseas. In Asia there were more than 25, some of which still exist (Goa, Ormuz, Diu, Damâo, Chaul Cannanore, Cochin, Quilon, Nagatapam, Colombo, Mannar). The Misericordia at Goa, the first (1519) and most important branch, added to the general charitable program outlined by the *compromisso* of Lisbon the establishment of the Hospital del Rei (1542) and the Hospital dos pobres (1568) for Christian natives and the care of needy young girls, especially orphans. Another social and religious problem arose—that of the prostitutes whom the confraternity sought to help by founding homes for penitents, such as Nossa Senhora da Serra (1605) and Santa Maria Magdalena (1609). Furthermore, in the East the Misericordia took on the functions of a bank and became the guardian of legacies and inheritances which, after the death of the owners, were transferred to their heirs in the mother country.

Pietro della Valle summed up the work of the Misericordia in Goa: "... almost all the works of mercy which elsewhere are performed by diverse institutions and societies are carried on here by the Misericordia, which keeps deposits, handles letters of credit, helps the poor, the sick, hospitals and prisoners, protects children, arranges marriages, looks after converted prostitutes, redeems slaves; in short, does all the works of mercy of which a city or country has need. Surely it is a holy thing and of infinite service to the public ..." [J. Wicki, SJ, "Die Bruderschaft der 'Misericordia' in Portugiesisch-Indien," *Das Laienapostolat in den Missionem* (Beckenried 1961) 79–97].

In the 16th century offsprings of the Portuguese Misericordia were found even in Japan (Nagasaki, Sakai). But the activity of the famous institution did not cover all charitable work in the Far East when missionaries entered the scene. The Jesuits in Japan began a hospital at Oita (Kyushu) with the help of a Portuguese doctor, Luis d'Almeida (*c.* 1555); foundations of the same kind for men, women, and lepers multiplied in the following decade at Nagasaki, Sakai, and Urakmi. Through the work of the Franciscans, who had erected St. Anne's Hospital in Manila (1580–81), two others were built (1594–97) at Miyako [D. Schilling, OFM, *Hospitäler der Franziskaner in Miyako* (Beckenried 1950)]. The Jesuits also founded hospitals in India for the natives at Margão (Salsete) and especially in the Pescadores and Mannar, where there were seven by 1571 (*Mon. Hist. S.J., Documenta Indica* 8:32–33).

In Brazil, the Misericordia worked in Baía, Maranhão, Santos, and Rio de Janeiro, and missionaries ran hospitals in all the great centers. The Jesuits were especially active [S. Leite, *Historia da Companhia de Jesus no Brazil* (Lisbon 1938) 2.570]. The college at Rio had a hospital annexed to it and provided two large rooms where slaves and their families were cared for. The colleges in general were centers of charitable work. In every college there was a priest who was "procurator of the poor." The work of assistance included another beneficial social function: the workmen were the first to benefit from the harvest on the estates connected with the missions.

Mention must be made of those who tried to limit the effects of the commercial organization of slavery after the conquest of South America. If, notwithstanding the abominable crimes of which they were victims, the slaves embraced the religion of their oppressors, it was because of the charity of its missionaries. Peter *Claver (1580–1654), "the slave of the Negro slaves," is a symbol; for 40 years he was the incarnation of heroic charity. Other protectors of the natives and slaves were Bartolomé de *Las Casas (1474–1566) and Antonio Vieira (1608–97), who dared to condemn the iniquity of government officials and slave traders.

The Problem of Begging and St. Vincent de Paul. Economic and political factors at the beginning of modern times brought about an almost permanent state of pauperism for large segments of the population and led to the consequent problem of begging. The Spanish humanist Juan Luis *Vives had studied the problem in *De subventione pauperum, sive de humanis necessitatibus* (Bruges 1526). The Benedictine Juan de *Medina published *De la orden que en algunos pueblos de España se ha puesto en la limosína para remedio de los verdaderos pobres* (Salamanca 1545). Both books advocated the suppression of begging and the gathering of the genuinely poor into public institutions. Practical application of these principles was attempted in Flanders and the Spanish countries, but protests arose, e.g., D. de Soto's authoritative *Deliberacion en la causa de los pobres* (Salamanca 1545). [On this question see A. Muller, *La querelle des fondations charitables en Belgique* (Brussels 1909).] The secular power intervened to repress begging, first by general prohibitions and then by threats of corporal punishment, including death (as in England, the Low Countries, and Flanders).

The prohibitions were useless; the necessity of offering asylum to the homeless, the sick, and the unemployed remained. Attempts to solve the problem were made by housing beggars in buildings destined for this purpose and providing work for them. Hospices of this kind appeared everywhere. Sixtus V founded one in Rome; it soon closed for lack of funds, but was reopened by Innocent XII and Clement XI. In Spain shelters (*albergues*), extolled by Christoval Perez de Herrera in *Discursos del amparo de los legitimos pobres y redutión de los fingidos . . .* (Madrid 1598), multiplied but without significant results. In England workhouses developed around the end of the 17th century. Fruitless attempts to cope with the problem were made in France, where in Paris alone there were about 40,000 beggars.

St. *Vincent de Paul came on the scene at this juncture. He is considered the most characteristic representative of Catholic charity in modern times, justly called "Le ministre de la charité nationale, le grand aumônier de la France." The confraternity of charity that he organized (1617) among his parishioners of Chatillon-les-Dombes to visit the sick poor in their homes was the seed from which a remarkable number of charitable institutions grew. He brought women into charitable works more completely and more independently than ever before. For members of the nobility he founded the Ladies of Charity, who soon spread to all the provinces of France. Since they were unable to cope with all the needs of the poor, the saint, with the aid of St. *Louise de Marillac, founded (1633) the Daughters of *Charity, a religious congregation devoted entirely to the service of the poor. Similar institutions were founded under the influence of the Daughters of Charity: the Daughters of St. Géneviève, founded by Françoise de Blosset; the Daughters of the Holy Family, by Maria Miramion; the Daughters of Providence, etc. Pauperism was reduced in France by the untiring work of these institutions. In 1653 the hospital of the Holy Name of Jesus was founded in Paris (the modern Hospital of the Incurables) to take care of the aged. In 1656 the General Hospital was founded to care for and give work to beggars. Louis XIV donated a number of buildings for this purpose, thus enabling the hospital to receive as many as 10,000 needy persons and foundlings. With the help of the clergy, especially the Jesuits, other general hospitals were founded in the provinces. Père Chaurand alone founded about 123 and Père Guevarre, who succeeded him after his death, continued the work in various parts of France and in Piedmont [C. Joret, *Le*

P. Guevarre et la fondation des bureaux de charité du XVII siècle (Toulouse 1899)].

Specialized Assistance. Failing in their aim to eliminate begging, the general hospitals took up their original role of helping the really poor, the infirm, orphans, and destitute women. In France the Hôtels-Dieu, open to all types of unfortunates, spread throughout the country, though often the help they gave was more generous than wise. Every year 25,000 persons passed through the *Hôtel-Dieu in Paris. The same was true of Rome's hospital of St. James in Augusta. But certain categories of needy were taken care of in specialized houses. Hospitals for strangers in Rome have been mentioned: there were 22 of these, 7 of which were founded after the 15th century [Piazza, *Opere pie di Roma* (Rome 1697)]. Through the initiative of St. Philip *Neri, the hospital of the Trinity for pilgrims was founded in Rome; another of the same type was started in Naples. Orphans found asylum with the *Somaschi (an order founded by St. Jerome Emiliani *c.* 1528 for the care of orphans), while other institutions provided for the moral preservation of young girls; 17 in Rome, 22 in Naples, etc. Refuges for the rehabilitation of prostitutes were numerous in Palermo, Naples, Florence, etc.

The Mentally Ill. Vives in his *De subventione pauperum* had given wise counsel for the treatment of these unfortunates, but his contemporaries continued to consider the mentally ill as possessed or sorcerers. They were interned in common prisons, not with a view to cure but to assure public safety. They were treated like animals until the end of the 18th century, and very few asylums were provided for them in any country before the 19th century. In Spain there were asylums at Valencia, the Association of the Innocents (1409) founded by a member of the Order of Mercy; at Saragossa, the hospital of Our Lady of Grace (1425) founded by Alfonso of Aragon; and other institutions at Seville (1436), Valladolid (1489), and Toledo (1483). In Italy the care of the insane was confided to the Roman confraternity of S. Maria della Pietà, which rose under Pius IV (1561) and which in the 18th century came under the direction of the Hospital of the Holy Spirit. In England, an ancient priory in London (Bedlam) was transformed into a mental hospital at the time of Henry VIII. In the 18th century, similar asylums rose in York, Nottingham, Manchester, Norwich, and Liverpool. At the same period, there were houses for the insane in Frankfurt, Amsterdam, and Ghent. Coercive methods used with the violent were often nothing less than torture; and patients were chained, not only during their violent seizures, but permanently. It was only at the end of the 17th century that courageous doctors in France began using the straight jacket.

Deaf Mutes. As early as the 16th century serious efforts had been made to rehabilitate deaf mutes. This problem greatly interested the former Jesuit L. Hervás y Panduro toward the end of the 18th century [see his *Escuela española de sordomudos,* 2v. (Madrid 1795) 1.8]. Spain was the first country to provide educators for these unfortunates: the Benedictine Pedro Ponce de León (d. 1584) taught speaking, writing, arithmetic, and religion to deaf mutes (Hervás y Panduro, *op. cit.,* 1:297–305). His example bore fruit and in 1620 Juan Pablo Bonet of Aragon suggested in *Reducción de las letras y arte para enseñar a hablar los mudos* grammatical instruction according to the inductive method. Attempts of this kind multiplied everywhere: in England, by an Oxford professor, John Wallis (1660–61); in Holland, at Amsterdam, by a Swiss doctor Johan Konrad Amman (*Surdus et mutus loquens,* 1692); in Italy, by Fabrizio d'Acquapendente at Padua and by the Jesuit F. Lana-Terzi at Brescia; in France, by the Spanish Jew Jacob Rodriguez Pereira. But it was Abbé Charles-Michel de l'Épée (*c.* 1712–89) who opened institutions for these unfortunates, teaching them by a method of imitation. Abbé Tommaso Silvestri, who opened a similar school in Rome in 1784; Abbé Stork, who perfected the one already existing in Vienna; and Henri Daniel Guyot, who in 1790 started a like institution in Groningen, Holland, all studied and used the method of Charles-Michel. Religious and priests were pioneers in this difficult field of education.

Prisoners and Captives. Christian charity placed special emphasis on aid to the incarcerated. Prison conditions were atrocious and cruelty was commonplace. But protesting voices offered concrete suggestions: in Spain, Cristóforo Pérez de Herrera (1598) called for prison inspection to correct negligence and limit the absolute power of those in authority; in Italy, G. Battista Scanaroli of Modena (1655) published a work rich in interesting proposals, and in France D. Mabillon (1695), referring to the imprisonment of religious, proposed an excellent program that seemed to be a forerunner of the penal reform of the 19th century [Thuiller, *Ouvrages posthumes de D. Mabillon* (Paris 1724) 2:321–335]. But public attention was especially awakened in the 18th century when an Englishman, John Howard, revealed the condition of European prisons after firsthand inquiry in different countries.

In the meantime the Church supplied these deficiencies as best she could. Hundreds of confraternities with this specific aim developed. A few examples will suffice: in Rome, the Archconfraternity of Charity founded in 1519 by Cardinal Giulio de Medici (later Pope Clement VII); in Milan (where work for the imprisoned was quite ancient and greatly influenced by Charles Borromeo), the confraternities of Pietà and Our Lady of Loreto, which constituted, according to the judgment of G. Toniolo "a reform school for penal law and prisons much older and more efficacious than the writings of Beccaria" [*L'Histoire de la Charité en Italie* in *Congrès scientif. des Catholiques* (Brussels 1895)]. There were numerous confraternities of this kind in France: at Aix, the White Penitents (1517) and the Sisters of the Dominican Third Order who took care of female prisoners; at Marseilles, the Work of Prisons (1674); at Lyons the Confraternity of Mercy (1636). In France the intervention of St. Vincent de Paul on behalf of those condemned to the galleys was particularly effective.

This latter group of unfortunates calls to mind another great social problem. After the defeat of the Moors in Spain, piracy became organized. Pirate ships from the Mediterranean ports of North Africa sacked the coasts of Spain, France, and Italy, and carried men, women, and children into slavery. Their sufferings awakened heroic dedication all over the West. Trinitarians and *Mercedarians continued their mission, although the difficulties of the time obliged them to modify their primitive rule. The Trinitarians organized confraternities to gather funds for the ransom of captive Christians. Other societies performed the same tasks, e.g., the Roman confraternity of the Gonfalone. The Lazarists in Tunis and Algiers sacrificed themselves for the material and spiritual comfort of Christian slaves. Lack of documentation makes it difficult to determine the number of persons ransomed. In the 18th century the Trinitarians and Mercedarians united their efforts and special missions went abroad every 3 or 4 years. In 1720 about 1,000 prisoners were liberated.

Charity after the French Revolution. Works of charity in the second half of the 18th century dried up at the source in many European countries after the suppression of *mortmain and the secularization of public help. States confiscated the property of pious foundations and used it for other purposes. In France this confiscation was carried out on a large scale by the Revolution of 1789; the goods of the clergy were seized (Nov. 2, 1790) and religious congregations suppressed (Aug. 18, 1792). Hospital funds were declared national property (1794) and all assistance centralized in the state. The repercussions in the field of charity were disastrous. On the eve of the Revolution the poor and sick found help from 35,000 religious, in 2,000 hospitals, capable of receiving 100,000 unfortunates and spending annually 30 million lire (R. Herrman, *La Charité de l'Église,* 149). When private charity was abolished by the Revolution as being humiliating, the poor fell into the most complete destitution.

Resurgence of Religious Institutions. But the state had to retreat. By 1796 it became necessary for the French government to give back to charitable institutions all property that had not been sold or given away; an effort was made in the towns to organize offices of assistance and committees for the poor; nursing sisters had to be called upon to staff hospitals while awaiting Napoleon's decree of 1804, which reestablished religious teaching congregations. Charitable congregations of women were then aided by the state.

In the 19th century the resurgence of charity was so great that it is impossible to measure its achievements. The growth of charitable institutions already in existence was significant (the Daughters of Charity in less than 50 years increased from 1,500 members to 8,000). A great number of new institutions, especially those for women, made the service of the poor the principal aim of their vocation. They spread rapidly in countries like Germany, where after the secularization of relief and the near disappearance of local hospitals, a rebirth of religious congregations was evident. The Daughters of Charity, the Franciscan Sisters of the Poor, and the Sisters of St. Charles may be instanced. Even important personages in the political and cultural fields wrote their names in the annals of charity: Antonio *Rosmini-Serbati (1797–1855), for example, was the founder of the Institute of Charity (1828) and the Sisters of Providence (1833).

Needs of the Period Met by New Foundations. Works of charity proliferated to such an extent as to pose a problem of wise administration. In Turin, for example, the Little House of Divine Providence, founded by St. Giuseppe *Cottolengo (1786–1842), formed a city within a city with its 8,000 unfortunates of all classes (aged, sick, insane, retarded) who were cared for by hundreds of nuns and priests [P. Gastaldi, *I prodigi della carità cristiana* (Turin 1910)]. St. John *Bosco (1815–88) assured the continuity of his institutions for needy youth by founding the Salesian Fathers (1859) and the Daughters of Mary Help of Christians (Salesian Sisters, 1874).

There was no type of misery that did not find a vocation to succor it: in France a young servant girl, Jeanne Jugan, founded the *Little Sisters of the Poor and Aged (1840) to provide homes for the aged; Anna M. Jahouvey founded the Sisters of St. Joseph of Cluny in 1807 (*see* ST. JOSEPH SISTERS) to care for infants; Father Ludovico da Casoria in Naples founded the Grey Brothers and the Sisters of St. Elizabeth for the care of the blind and deaf mutes; St. M. Euphrasia *Pelletier founded the Sisters of the *Good Shepherd (1835) to aid women with criminal records or who had fallen into vice; and the Marchesa Giulia Falletti Barolo founded the Daughters of Anne of Providence. Don L. *Orione (1872–1940), who with Don Bosco and Cottolengo, forms the Italian triumvirate of great apostles of charity, founded the Daughters of Divine Providence and the Little Missionary Sisters of Charity. "Convinced that the world would be conquered by love," he created in Italy and beyond an immense network of foundations.

The Introduction of the Catholic Laity. In the first half of the 19th century a new phenomenon arose in the history of charity—the organized participation of Catholic laymen. In 1801 in Paris, under the direction of the former Jesuit Delpuits and through the initiative of some medical and law students, the Congregation of Maria Auxilium Christianorum was founded; it is recognized as the source of modern French charity [G. de Grandmaison *La Congregation* (Paris 1902)]. It was destroyed by the revolution of 1830, but 3 years later it was replaced by another group of lay apostles, the nucleus of the Conference of Charity, called, after 1836, the Conference of St. Vincent de Paul. This group was composed of six university students in Paris led by A. Frédéric *Ozanam (1813–53) who, envisioning a vast association of charity for the relief of the lower classes in every country, saw his work spread rapidly through the whole Christian world. In the mid-1960s the membership numbered more than 210,000, divided into more than 15,000 working groups in 80 nations aiding all types of unfortunates with no distinction of religion and employing no humiliating investigations [Ozanam, *Le Livre du Centenaire* (Paris 1913)]. The work has female branches, such as the Society of St. Elizabeth in Germany and the Female Society of St. Vincent de Paul founded in 1856 by Celestine Scarabelli in Italy.

The plan of Ozanam was to put a group of selected Catholics at the service of the poor and thus establish bonds of brotherhood among those separated by rank and fortune. Using different means, others aimed at the same end: in Italy there were those who listened to the voices of Bruno Lanteri and Rosmini; in England a great number were mobilized by H. E. *Manning, the cardinal of the poor, in his war against misery. The very birth of Catholic socialism is associated with this movement of charity. In Germany, A. *Kolping and W. von *Ketteler, before being social reformers, were men of charity for the essence of charity is the desire to raise one's neighbor from his misery. One of the admirable features of the St. Vincent de Paul Society is that it avoids bureaucracy by direct and personal contact with the needy.

With the industrial revolution and the consequent accumulation of wealth by the few and the misery of the many, it became evident that the old idea of pure charity could not offer an adequate solution unless it were associated with the goals of "social justice." A few isolated attempts were made to infuse charity with the concepts of social justice. Such were, for example, Ozanam's advocacy (1840) of a "natural wage" that would assure the workingman and his family enough money to live and be educated; the beginnings of Christian socialism promoted by Père J. B. *Lacordaire, Abbé H. L. C. *Maret, and Ozanam in 1848; the "Union of Fribourg" (1886), which gathered a nucleus of interested Catholics from various countries in order to find a just solution for social problems. Some prelates, such as Ketteler, the bishop of Mainz in Germany, and Cardinal Manning in England, addressed themselves to the problem. But it was Pope Leo XIII, who wrote the Magna Carta of Christian social activity in the encyclical **Rerum novarum* (1891). Pius XI's encyclical **Quadragesimo anno* (1931) reaffirmed and updated Leo's teaching.

One essential point emerges from these solemn pontifical documents: the coexistence of two leading principles, social justice and social charity. Social justice must erect "a juridical and social order which can penetrate all economic life"; social charity "must be the soul of this order and public authority must work to protect it" (*Quadragesimo anno*).

When social questions are discussed, temporal society and its common well-being are directly concerned. In this field the charity of the Church cannot indefinitely operate alone. Its role is sometimes temporary, until public authority takes necessary measures; at other times the Church assumes a complementary role, helping those who, for one reason or another, are not protected by laws that must be generalized and are sometimes too slow to meet cases of immediate need.

National Associations of Charity. The scope for charity and relief is, nevertheless, still quite vast. It includes efforts to secure decent living conditions for all (the aim of the Company of Emmaus), protection of the young, assistance to workers in foreign countries, physical and psychological rehabilitation of minors, prevention and cure of diseases (tuberculosis, polio, etc.). Given the enormity of the task, collaboration on a national level becomes necessary. An example is the Deutsche Caritasverband, which was established in Germany in 1897 through the initiative of the prelate L. Wethmann, with the aim of coordinating and orientating the charitable activity of German Catholics. In 1915 the German episcopacy, assembled at Fulda, conferred an official character on the institution. By 1931 it numbered 600,000 members, with an administrative center at Fribourg including a specialized library of 40,000 volumes and numerous periodicals. This organization undertook the study of all current trends regarding the well-being of the neighbor, the publication of books and periodicals, the drawing up of work programs common to similar organizations. Rendered inactive by the Nazi regime, Caritas was reorganized after the war and is now developing rapidly [see statistics in *Vom Werden und Wirken des deutschen Caritasverbandes* (Fribourg 1957) 292–298]. Similar institutions arose in Austria (the Federation of Charitable Organizations, 1903) and Switzerland (Caritaszentral, 1920). In France, after Aumônerie Générale des Prisonniers de Guerre, organized by Abbé Rodhain during World War II, Secours Catholique and Caritas Alsace, the Commission des Oeuvres sociales et charitables, presided over by Cardinal Richaud, and the Union Nationale des Congrégations hospitalièrs et d'aide sociale all came into being.

The intensification and acceleration of communication have enlarged the horizons of charity beyond political boundaries and ethnic differences. The Church has set the example of this worldwide extension of charity. Benedict XV and Pius XII intervened to halt or at least mitigate the horrors of the last two wars. The Pontifical Office of Relief (originally called the Pontifical Relief Commission by Pius XII) spent between 1944 and 1947 a total of 9,285,986,396 lire for papal soup kitchens, refugee camps, sanitary assistance, aid to foreigners, social work, etc. Its field of action was soon extended to all parts of Italy and even beyond the country. The assistance originally given to refugees became, with the return to more normal conditions after the war, relief to those who had returned to their own homes and work. In time, this assistance became more specialized, for example: for youth (summer colonies, homes for children, student recreational centers and mess halls, hostels for university students, institutions for the physical and psychological care of minor children); for shepherds, fishermen, laborers, appointees of the Reform Corporations (through the Pious Unions, then members of the Laborers' Community); for emigrants; for food supplies through the papal soup kitchens, which developed into organized relief in the event of disasters; for the distribution of American aid; for social rehabilitation by helping prisoners and their families; for health care in unhealthy zones; for professional training made available in the institutions of a related corporation; for the formation of centers of human relations, which in turn developed into the Central Italian Institute of Human Relations (CIRU) [F. Ricci, SJ, *Origini e sviluppo della Pont. Opera de Assistenza,* in *Atti del primo Congresso Nazionale della P.C.A. 1956* (Rome 1957) 11–26].

The Caritas Internationalis. In September of the Holy Year, 1950, after a study week held in Rome, it was decided through the initiative of the secretary of state of the Holy See to create the Caritas Internationalis. This crowned former efforts at international collaboration that had taken the form of periodical meetings at Amsterdam (1924), Lucerne (1926), and Basel (1928 and 1930). Today the Caritas Internationalis exists in 73 countries. Its aim is the spread of Christian charity throughout the world and, in particular, the promotion of collaboration and the coordination of national charitable activities with a view to improving them for the solution of international problems, regarding relief and charity in their religious, moral, social, juridical, and economic aspects; the representation of Catholic charitable organizations on an international level; the creation, with approval of the hierarchy, of a national charitable organization in every country that does not already have one; the coordination of Catholic charitable activities in places where particular circumstances require it and especially for the urgent relief necessary in disaster areas where adequate organization is lacking. Permanent delegations reside in New York and Geneva in order to collaborate with the United Nations and its specialized institutions.

Because an analogy exists between the proletariat of the 19th century and the present conditions in underdeveloped countries, the concern of the Church extends to the latter and she has not failed officially and repeatedly to appeal to wealthy nations to provide for those less favored.

According to statistics of 1954, the institutions supported by Catholic charity in the world numbered 30,649 with a total of 9,913,776 people aided [*Guia de la Iglesia en España* (1954) 136]. To this must be added the thousands of religious men and women and lay personnel engaged in this work.

Thus, notwithstanding the periodic disorders of history and the appearance of social theories that deny the excellence of charity, works of charity continue to flourish in the Church. As Pius XI said (*Quadragesimo anno*), "even if someone should obtain all that is his due, a wide field will nevertheless remain open for charity. Justice alone, even though most faithfully observed, can remove the cause of the social strife but can never bring about a union of hearts and minds.. . . Then only will it be possible to unite all in harmonious striving for the common good, when all victims of society have the intimate conviction that they are members of a single family and children of the same Heavenly Father."

See also CHILD WELFARE; NURSING, HISTORY OF; PONTIFICAL MISSION FOR PALESTINE; REFUGEES AND DISPLACED PERSONS; REHABILITATION; WELFARE AND WELFARE SERVICES; NATIONAL CONFERENCE OF CATHOLIC CHARITIES; NATIONAL CONFERENCE OF RELIGIOUS ON CATHOLIC CHARITIES; CATHOLIC NEAR EAST WELFARE ASSOCIATION; CATHOLIC RELIEF SERVICES, N.C.W.C.; LATIN AMERICA (COLONIAL), HOSPITALS IN; HOSPITALS, HISTORY OF; MERCY, WORKS OF.

Bibliography: E. T. DEVINE, *Practice of Charity* (New York 1901). G. NEYRON, *Histoire de la charité* (Paris 1927). Union des oeuvres catholiques de France, 65th, 1950, *L'Église, éducatrice de la charité* (Paris 1951). F. ZOEPFL, *Mittelalter Caritas im Spiegel der Legende* (Frieburg 1929). A. BAUDRILLART, *La Charité aux premiers siècles du christianisme* (Paris 1903). G. SUHR, *Volksnot und Kirche* (Gütersloh 1948). M. W. JERNEGAH, *Laboring and Dependent Classes in Colonial America, 1607–1783* (Chicago 1931). C. R. HENDERSON, *Modern Methods of Charity* (New York 1904). F. D. WATSON, *The Charity Organization Movement in the U.S.: A Study in American Philanthropy* (New York 1922). R. GUARDINI, *Der Dienst am Nächsten in Gefahr* (Würzburg 1956). International Labor Office, *Approaches to Social Security* (Montreal 1942). F. R. SALTER, ed., *Some Early Tracts on Poor Relief* (London 1926). G. UHLHORN, *Christian Charity in the Ancient Church* (New York 1883). K. WOODROOFE, *From Charity to Social Work in England and the United States* (Toronto 1962). W. J. MARX, *Development of Charity in Medieval Louvain* (New York 1936). H. F. WESTLAKE, *Parish Gilds of Medieval England* (New York 1919). H. BRANDENBURG, *Caritas und Wohlfahrtspflege* (Freiburg 1959). H. WOLFRAM, *Vom Armenwesen zum heutigen Fürsorgewesen* (Greifswald 1930). K. DE SCHWEINITZ, *England's Road to Social Security* (New York 1961). F. M. EDEN, *The State of the Poor* (London 1928). W. K. JORDAN, *Philanthropy in England, 1480–1660* (New York 1959). H. BOLKESTEIN, *Wohltätigkeit und Armenpflege im vorchristlichen Altertum* (Utrecht 1939). E. L. CHASTEL, *Charity of the Primitive Churches* (Philadelphia 1857). L. LALLEMAND, *Histoire de la charité*, 4 v. in 5 (Paris 1902–12). W. LIESE, *Geschichte der Caritas*, 2 v. (Freiburg 1922). A. C. MARTS, *Man's Concern for His Fellow Man* (Geneva, N.Y. 1961). E. ABBOTT, ed., *Some American Pioneers in Social Welfare* (Chicago 1937). V. D. BORNET, *Welfare in America* (Norman, Okla. 1960). N. E. COHEN, *Social Work in the American Tradition* (New York 1958). A. DE GRAZIA, *American Welfare* (New York 1961). W. A. FRIEDLANDER, *Introduction to Social Welfare* (New York 1955). F. E. LANE, *American Charities and the Child of the Immigrant* (Washington 1941).

[M. SCADUTO]

CHARLEMAGNE

Charles the Great (Carolus Magnus, Karl der Grosse), King of the Franks from 768 to 814 and after 800 Emperor in the West; b. 742; d. Aachen, Jan. 28, 814. He is buried in the imperial church he had built there. Little is known of Charles's youth. He received thorough religious training from his mother, Bertrada, and from Abbot Fulrad of Saint-Denis, a confidant of his father, King *Pepin III. Charles learned to read Latin at the palace school but never to write. He first appears in historical records in 753, when he played a part in receiving Pope *Stephen II at the Frankish court. In 754, along with his father, mother, and brother *Carloman, he received a special papal anointment. During the remaining years of Pepin's reign, Charles took part in military campaigns and in administrative affairs, thereby mastering the skills needed to rule the kingdom. In 768 Pepin III died leaving a well-organized kingdom to be shared by Charles and Carloman, who ruled jointly until Carloman's death in 771.

King of the Franks. As sole ruler Charles launched into an extraordinarily active career. During the first 30 years of his reign Charles's major preoccupation was with military affairs. Some of his campaigns were directed against peoples already under Frankish rule but anxious for autonomy, especially the *Bavarians and the Aquitanians, who were compelled to accept Frankish overlordship. Charles's chief military concern was with independent neighbors. Of these the *Saxons were most threatening. More than 30 years of warfare, accompanied by extreme brutality and enforced deportation of rebellious Saxons, were needed to annex Saxony. Saxon resistance was nourished by Charles's effort to compel the Saxons to accept Christianity as a sign of political submission. In the course of the long Saxon war, the neighboring Frisians became involved and were conquered. In Italy Charles crushed the *Lombards in 774 and assumed the title of king of the Lombards. This campaign was a logical conclusion to the obligations Pepin III had assumed to protect the papacy. No more fortunate than the Saxons and the Lombards was the huge Avar Empire facing the Franks in the southeast. In campaigns in 791, 795, and 796 the empire of the *Avars was destroyed and a large bloc of territory was annexed to the Frankish kingdom. As a consequence of these conquests Charles greatly enlarged the Frankish kingdom and established his fame as a warrior to be feared by all.

Expansion created a long frontier to defend, a problem that Charles met by military and diplomatic means. On the east and north the Franks faced numerous small Slavic principalities and the internally disturbed Danish kingdom. Against any who showed hostility Charles promptly directed punitive raids that usually ended with the exaction of tribute. Those who preferred peace were permitted to become Frankish vassals. These tactics kept this frontier relatively quiet. The most ominous development was the beginning of Viking sea raids on Frankish territory, a threat that Charles tried to face, though he had no great success (*see* NORMANS).

On the southern frontier the foes were more formidable. In *Spain were the Moslems, who as late as 732 had threatened the very existence of the Frankish kingdom until checked by Charles's grandfather, *Charles Martel. By the time of Charles's reign the Moslem state in Spain was breaking into numerous principalities. He sought to capitalize on this situation by annexing territory south of the Pyrenees. His first effort ended in the defeat at Roncevalles in 778, an episode immortalized in the *Song of Roland* (*see* FRENCH LITERATURE, 1). However, the Basques, not the Moslems, were the cause of this defeat. Charles persisted in his effort, and in subsequent years established an important enclave,

Charlemagne (a) 9th-century bronze statuette in the Louvre, Paris. The horse is a restoration of the 16th century. A detail of the head of Charlemagne (b) shows the same features appearing on other contemporary portraits.

called the Spanish March, south of the Pyrenees. In seeking to weaken the Spanish Moslems, Charles established diplomatic ties with the Abbasid caliph in Baghdad, Harun-al-Rashid, who was likewise hostile toward the Moslems in Spain. This connection also provided Charles with the means to bring diplomatic pressure on the Byzantine Empire. The conquest of the Lombards and the Avars brought about a direct confrontation of the Franks and the Byzantine Empire. A complex series of diplomatic negotiations, punctuated by occasional military clashes in Italy and along the Dalmatian coast followed. In general, Charles strengthened his position vis à vis the Greeks from these encounters. His successes in the Mediterranean area not only assured the security of the Frankish frontier but elevated Charles's kingdom to the rank of a major power.

Government. Military and diplomatic concerns did not detract Charles from the governance of his realm. He was not a political innovator, being content to use the political institutions and techniques he inherited from his predecessors. His aim was to improve these institutions. Inspiring this effort was a more sophisticated concept of the nature of government than had guided his predecessors. Charles saw the state as more than the king's private property. He was strongly influenced by the ideas of St. Augustine and the Old Testament and felt a responsibility to create an ordered, harmonious society in which all men could work toward eternal salvation. To achieve Christian concord he labored to discover the causes of disorder and injustice. He issued a flood of laws, called *capitularies, to correct abuses and to prevent their recurrence. He imposed on his local agents, the counts, the responsibility to enact these laws and to do justice to all who had complaints. Repeatedly he sent his loyal agents, the *missi dominici,* across his realm to check on the state of local affairs and to correct abuses. This activity did much to bring order and justice out of the political chaos that had plagued the Frankish state in an earlier age.

The greatest obstacle to the restoration of public order was the King's lack of material and human resources. There was no effective tax system to supply money to hire soldiers and civil servants; even the royal household was supported from the produce of royal estates. To overcome this difficulty Charles relied heavily on a system of personal ties. He encouraged many powerful men to swear oaths that they would become his vassals and give him their loyalty and service. To these vassals he granted benefices in the form of land, the income from which each vassal used to support himself on military campaigns and in performing political duties. Charles's successful exploitation of these primitive feudal institutions was the key to his political success. It created a special circle of men, bound to the King personally and enjoying special wealth, who had an interest in sound government. As long as the King was able to keep this group loyal to himself and his program, its members aided immensely in establishing peace and concord.

The Church. Given his concept of government, it was natural that Charles would take a serious interest in religion. His reign saw the religious reform begun in the reign of his father reach its greatest intensity. Charles, seeing no difference between political and religious affairs, intervened in every aspect of religious life to encourage reform. A large portion of his legislation was devoted to such ends as strengthening the ecclesiastical organization, protecting church property and assuring church income, improving the quality and the conduct of the clergy, regularizing and standardizing liturgical practices, and purifying and deepening popular piety. Schools were established, books were collected, and churches were built anew or repaired in order to permit the more perfect practice of Christianity. Charles even plunged into doctrinal disputes in order to safeguard orthodoxy (*see* LIBRI CAROLINI). Throughout his reign he was an avid promoter of missionary work; his efforts resulted in the conversion of the Saxons and the Avars. Most of the higher clergy of his realm supported this effort and lent their advice to help their king purify religious life. By controlling the appointments of bishops and abbots Charles improved the quality of the higher clergy considerably (*see* CAROLINGIAN REFORM).

Charles's aggressive secular domination of religious affairs did not alienate him from the popes of his reign, *Adrian I and *Leo III. Both were fully aware of the extent to which the safety of the Papal State depended on Charles's protection. The King himself was moved by the deepest respect for the spiritual head of Christendom. He was especially bound to Adrian by personal friendship. On numerous occasions he sought papal advice and sanction for his religious program. Fairly often the popes complained of his political intrusions in the Papal State and on occasion even refused to sanction his religious decisions, as did Adrian when Charles undertook to define the position of the Western Church on *iconoclasm. These disagreements were always settled amicably, and the pope remained in Charles's eyes the head of the Church.

Not the least of Charles's accomplishments was his patronage of the *Carolingian "renaissance." Believing that the success of his politico-religious program depended on learned men, he gathered around his court scholars from England, Italy, Ireland, and Spain. Led by the Anglo-Saxon *Alcuin, this circle improved education, collected and copied nearly forgotten manuscripts from the classical Roman and patristic ages, and began to produce theological tracts, scriptural commentaries, poetry, and histories bearing some marks of originality. Charles encouraged the arts through his building program (*see* CAROLINGIAN ART). The churches and palaces constructed at *Aachen and Ingelheim represented notable departures in architecture and decoration. Cultural influences spread from the court to *monastic and cathedral schools (*see* CATHEDRAL AND EPISCOPAL SCHOOLS) to produce a rich harvest of literary and artistic works after Charles's death. His initiative was chiefly responsible for western Europe's first cultural revival.

Imperial Coronation. These accomplishments set the stage for the most momentous event of Charles's reign, his coronation as emperor by Pope Leo III on Christmas Day, 800. Historians have long debated the responsibility for and significance of this event. His biographer and confidant, *Einhard, avowed that Charles knew nothing of this event and would not have been present at St. Peter's church for Christmas services had he known what would occur. This places the responsibility for the coronation on Leo III. Such a position is untenable. Both Charles and Leo gained advantages from the coronation and surely had agreed on it in advance.

In many ways the more exalted title suited Charles. His conquest of diverse people made the title "king" inadequate. His mounting prestige among his subjects suggested something more exalted than a title held by numerous less eminent princes. The increasing knowledge in the court circle of classical history suggested interesting comparisons with the great Roman emperors. Charles's politico-religious ideas pointed toward the institution of a new community of Christians who adhered to the true faith of Rome, of a "Christian Roman Empire" comparable to that of *Constantine the Great. The situation in the Byzantine Empire, where after 797 a woman, *Irene, ruled, pointed up what Charles had long believed—that the Greek emperors were not fit to wear the imperial crown and to mete out haughty treatment to princes who were more able, more Christian, and more reputable but who held inferior titles (*see* ROMAN EMPIRE; HOLY ROMAN EMPIRE).

The situation in Rome translated these ideas into a program. In 799 Leo III was brutally attacked by conspirators and forced to flee to Charles. To settle the conspiracy Charles journeyed to the Holy City. Leo cleared himself of charges of grave misconduct in a public oath of purgation. To close the whole affair and to safeguard against recurrence there was need to constitute an authority with sovereign powers over the city of Rome. Only an emperor could by ancient tradition claim such legal authority. Certainly the woman ruling in Constantinople could not be summoned to act as sovereign of Rome. The logical conclusion was to elevate Charles to the imperial office.

What Charles and Leo believed they had accomplished is an enigma. They certainly made no claim to remove the imperial office from Constantinople and to transfer it to Rome, for they continued to recognize the legitimacy of the Byzantine emperors. Nor were they merely resurrecting an ancient title long vacant. Perhaps they felt that they had constituted a new Christian empire embracing the lands ruled by Charles and inhabited by those united by common adherence to the true faith taught at Rome. The new Emperor inherited the powers of the old Roman emperors, but these were to be applied to a new political entity built around Christian ideals.

The last years of Charles's reign provide little to clarify what the imperial coronation meant. In his program of government, church reform, and cultural patronage the aging Emperor pursued a course similar to that prior to his coronation, suggesting that the imperial title meant little new in terms of the internal administration of the kingdom. Occasionally a royal action seemed to contradict the entire idea of empire. For example, in 806 Charles provided for his own succession by ordering that his empire be divided among his three living sons, a move that clearly compromised the idea of imperial unity. In 813, after two of his sons had died, he personally crowned *Louis (the Pious) as his successor, thereby excluding the papacy from any part in the selection or installation of the emperor. In other ways, Charles acted as if the imperial title were crucial to his power. He maintained a close and somewhat onerous supervision over affairs in Rome. He conducted a skillful diplomatic program aimed at forcing the Byzantine emperors to recognize his imperial title, an end that he achieved in 812. However, this apparent wavering in no sense diminished Charles's fame. Until his death he remained a hero to his subjects and a respected figure among the other princes of the era.

The Man. In outlining Charles's many accomplishments and activities one is likely to overlook his personal qualities. This must be avoided, for his powerful personality was a vital force in a society in which institutions were weak and in which personal relationships were necessary to maintain order. Although he gained the admiration of an elite circle of nobles and clergymen for his interest in learning, his new political concepts, and his progressive religious ideas, to most of his subjects Charles was preeminently an ideal Germanic warlord and family head. He was a giant man blessed with extraordinary energy and vitality. He loved the active life—military campaigning, hunting, and swimming. And he was no less at home at the banquet table, where quantities of food and drink created an atmosphere of joviality. He was naturally gregarious and loquacious, so that he made friends easily. Never far from his mind was the interest of his large family. In the course of his life, Charles was married five times and enjoyed the favors of several mistresses. These marriages produced a numerous brood of children. The royal sons began early to learn the arts of being king. Charles kept his daughters with him to adorn his court, refusing to allow them to marry. Two of them bore illegitimate children as a consequence of liaisons with court officials, but Charles's love for them blinded him to their faults. One of the tragic episodes in his life was the death within a 2-year span (810–812) of four of these children, all in the full flower of adulthood. In spite of the low moral standards of his conduct toward women, Charles was a model of piety in the eyes of his subjects. He attended Mass daily, prayed frequently, gave generously to support the Church, and acted frequently in the interests of the poor. These qualities and traits made him a figure capable of commanding the respect, loyalty, and affection of his subjects; upon these feelings rested much of his power.

Charles's reign represented an important stage in western European history. His empire did not survive for long after his death, but his memory did. He emerged as the ideal prince of the Middle Ages. The ideals he pursued—orderly government, religious reform, cultural regeneration, Christian expansion—inspired the programs of most later medieval kings. What he actually achieved during his reign laid a firm basis upon which an orderly, civilized, Christian society was later built in western Europe. For these reasons, he justly deserved to be called "the Great."

Bibliography: Sources. *Die Urkunden der Karolinger,* ed. E. MÜHLBACHER, MGD Karolinorum 1:77–484. *Capitularia regum Francorum,* ed. A. BORETIUS, MGCap 1:44–259. *Concilia aevi Karolini,* ed. A. WERMINGHOFF, MGConc 2.1:74–306. *Epistolae Karolini aevi,* ed. E. DÜMMLER et al., MGEp 3:558–657; 4:494–567; 5.1:1–84. ALCUIN, *Epistolae,* ed., E. DÜMMLER, MGEp 4:1–493. EINHARD, *The Life of Charlemagne,* tr. S. E. TURNER (Ann Arbor, Mich. 1960); Latin edition, *Einhardi Vita Karoli Magni,* ed. O. HOLDER-EGGER, MGSrerGerm v.24. Monk of St. Gall, *Deeds of Charlemagne* in EINHARD, *Early Lives of Charlemagne,* ed. and tr. A. J. GRANT (London 1922); Latin edition, Notker Balbulus, *Gesta Karoli,* ed. H. F. HAEFELE, MGSrerGerm NS 12 (Berlin 1959). *Poetae latini aevi Carolini,* ed. E. DÜMMLER, MGPoetae v.1. *Annales regni Francorum,* ed. F. KURZE, MGSrerGerm 6:26–141. *Karl der Grosse: Werk and Wirkung* (Aachen 1965), exhibition catalogue, ed. W. BRAUNFELS.

Literature. J. F. BÖHMER, *Die Regesten des Kaiserreichs unter den Karolinger,* ed. E. MÜHLBACHER, v.1 of *Regesta Imperii* (2d ed. Innsbruck 1908). B. GEBHARDT, *Handbuch der deutschen Geschichte,* ed. H. GRUNDMANN, 2 v. (8th ed. Stuttgart 1954–55) 1:132–144, for excellent bibliog. L. HALPHEN, *Charlemagne et l'empire carolingien* (Paris 1947) 57–223. J. L. A. CALMETTE, *Charlemagne: Sa vie et son oeuvre* (Paris 1945). A. J. KLEINCLAUSZ, *Charlemagne* (Paris 1934). S. ABEL and B. VON SIMSON, *Jahrbücher des fränkischen Reiches unter Karl dem Grossen,* 2 v. (v.1 2d ed. Leipzig 1883–88). Fliche-Martin 6:7–200. Laistner ThLett. E. PATZELT, *Die karolingische Renaissance: Beiträge zur Geschichte der Kultur des frühen Mittelalters* (Vienna 1924). C. ERDMANN, *Forschungen zur politischen Ideenwelt des Frühmittelalters,* ed. F. BAETHGEN (Berlin 1951). P. MUNZ, *The Origin of the Carolingian Empire* (Dunedin, N.Z. 1960). F. L. GANSHOF, *The Imperial Coronation of Charlemagne: Theories and Facts* (Glasgow 1949). H. FICHTENAU, *Das karolingische Imperium: Soziale und geistige Problematik eines Grossreiches* (Zurich 1949). W. OHNSORGE, *Das Zweikaiserproblem im früheren Mittelalter* (Hildesheim 1947). P. E. SCHRAMM, "Die Anerkennung Karls des Grossen als Kaiser," HistZ 172 (1951) 449–515. H. BEUMANN, "Nomen imperatoris: Studien zur Kaiseridee Karls d. Gr.," *ibid.* 185 (1958) 515–549. E. S. DUCKETT, *Alcuin, Friend of Charlemagne: His World and his Work* (New York 1951). R. FOLZ, *Le Souvenir et la légende de Charlemagne dans l'empire germanique médiéval* (Paris 1950).
Illustration credit: Archives Photographiques.

[R. E. SULLIVAN]

CHARLES II, KING OF ENGLAND

Reigned 1660 to 1685, second son of Charles I, of the royal house of Stuart, and Henrietta Maria; b. London, May 29, 1630; d. London, Feb. 6, 1685. The education of the young Prince was cut short by the outbreak of the English Civil War in 1642. Young Charles took an active role in the struggle and witnessed a number of battles during the war. When his father's cause collapsed he fled the country and found a refuge on the Continent.

Following the execution of his father, Charles was proclaimed King in Scotland in February 1649. After extensive negotiations Charles accepted the condition of the Scots that he become a Presbyterian, and landed in that country in June 1650; he was finally crowned King at Scone on Jan. 1, 1651. The defeat of the Presbyterian forces by Oliver *Cromwell allowed Charles to assume command of the army, and he invaded England. Defeated at Worcester in September 1651 by Cromwell, Charles was forced to flee for his life. After some 40 days of wandering, he arrived safely in France. Often destitute, the King spent the next few years moving about the Continent seeking support. The death of Cromwell paved the way for his restoration. Charles landed at Dover in May 1660 to resume his throne. In May of the following year Charles married Catherine of Braganza, the daughter of the King of Portugal. They had no children; and although Charles showed the Queen respect, he became notorious for the large number of mistresses he maintained.

It is doubtful whether Charles was ever deeply touched by any belief, but he was virtually a Catholic by the time he returned to England. In order to grant relief to the Catholics in England and to win the support of the Dissenters, Charles issued two Declarations of Indulgence in 1662 and 1672. Both of these met intense opposition in Parliament and resulted in the passage in 1673 of the Test Act, which was intended to bar Catholics from all governmental offices. The Popish Plot, a supposed conspiracy of Catholics to kill the King and other officials, was set off in 1678 by Titus Oates and other informers (*see* OATES PLOT). The news that the King's brother and heir-apparent, the Duke of York, later *James II, had become a Catholic led to an attempt in Parliament to exclude him from the throne.

Charles II, King of England, portrait by J. M. Wright.

The exclusion failed, but the Whig and Tory political parties were born out of the struggle.

Charles triumphed over his opponents when public opinion switched to support the King and his brother with the discovery of the Rye House Plot, a Whig effort to assassinate the royal pair. John *Huddleston, OSB, Queen Catherine's chaplain, received Charles into the Roman Catholic Church on his deathbed.

Bibliography: A. W. WARD, DNB 4:84–108. D. OGG, *England in the Reign of Charles II,* 2 v. (Oxford 1934). J. R. TANNER, *English Constitutional Conflicts of the Seventeenth Century* (Cambridge, Eng. 1928). G. DAVIES, *The Restoration of Charles II, 1658–1660* (San Marino, Calif. 1955). A. BRYANT, *King Charles II* (rev. ed. London 1955). G. N. CLARK, *The Later Stuarts, 1660–1714* (2d ed. Oxford 1955). G. M. TREVELYAN, *England under the Stuarts* (New York 1949). H. W. CHAPMAN, *The Tragedy of Charles II* (Boston 1964). J. A. WILLIAMS, "English Catholics under Charles II: The Legal Position," *Recusant History* 7 (1963–64) 123–143. **Illustration credit:** National Portrait Gallery, London.

[A. M. SCHLEICH]

CHARLES VII, KING OF FRANCE, 1422 to July 22, 1461, fifth of the Valois dynasty and victor in the Hundred Years' War; b. Paris, Feb. 22, 1403; d. Mehun-sur-Yèvre. Charles VII, a son of the insane Charles VI, inherited a divided *France whose northern half, thanks to the Treaty of Troyes (1420), was ruled in the name of the infant Henry VI by an Anglo-Burgundian coalition. Against it his successes were few until *Joan of Arc appeared to raise the siege of Orléans (May 8, 1429) and to have "her Dauphin" crowned in Reims cathedral (July 18). Inactivity followed Joan's capture (May 13, 1430), but in 1435 Philip the Good, Duke of Burgundy, changed sides, an event that made French victory inevitable. Paris was taken the next year; Normandy in 1449–50; and Guienne in 1453, thus ending the war. The rehabilitation trial of St. Joan soon followed (1455–56).

Though personally weak, Charles helped create French absolutism by centralizing administration, introducing permanent and arbitrary taxation, and creating a standing army. He showed sympathy for *conciliarism and accepted many decrees of the Council of *Basel when he asserted the liberties of the Gallican Church (*see* GALLICANISM) in his *Pragmatic Sanction of Bourges (1438). Yet he refused to recognize the election of the antipope Felix V at Basel and worked hard for both his resignation and the reconciliation of the council with Rome.

Bibliography: G. L. E. DU FRESNE DE BEAUCOURT, *Histoire de Charles VII,* 6 v. (Paris 1881–91). R. WITTRAM, *Die Französische Politik auf dem Basler Konzil* (Riga 1927). L. A. CALMETTE, *Chute et relèvement de la France sous Charles VI et Charles VII* (Paris 1945). É. PERROY, *The Hundred Years War,* tr. W. B. WELLS (New York 1951).

[C. T. WOOD]

CHARLES VIII, KING OF FRANCE, 1483 to April 7, 1498, seventh of the Valois dynasty, whose invasion of Italy is taken as the start of the French *Renaissance; b. Amboise, June 30, 1470; d. Amboise. Having succeeded his father *Louis XI at the age of 13, Charles was under the tutelage of his sister Anne de Beaujeau for 8 years. Revolts against her were ended in 1488 when their leader, the future *Louis XII, was imprisoned. Control of Brittany was ensured in 1491 by Charles's marriage to its heiress. The Italian expedition of 1494 arose from French claims to the Kingdom of Naples and was encouraged by Ludovico *Sforza of Milan. While initially triumphant, Charles incurred the wrath of Pope *Alexander VI who allied the papacy with most of Italy, Spain, and Germany in the Holy League. Faced with this danger, the French abandoned Naples and fled Italy (July 1495). Although Charles dreamed of another expedition to be followed by a crusade, he died before his plans could be realized.

See also MAXIMILIAN I, HOLY ROMAN EMPEROR; FERDINAND V, KING OF CASTILE; SAVONAROLA, GIROLAMO.

Bibliography: C. J. DE CHERRIER, *Histoire de Charles VIII, roi de France,* 2 v. (2d ed. Paris 1870). F. ERCOLE, *Da Carlo VIII a Carlo V: La crisi della libertà italiana* (Florence 1932). R. DOUCET, CModH[2] 1:292–315.

[C. T. WOOD]

CHARLES X, KING OF FRANCE, 1824 to 1830; b. Versailles, Oct. 9, 1757; d. Goritz, Austria (now Gorizia, Italy), Nov. 6, 1836. Charles Philippe, Count of Artois, was the fourth son of the Dauphin Louis, and grandson of Louis XV. As a young man at the court of Versailles he lived as a light-hearted playboy. In 1789 he opposed the *French Revolution and fled France until 1814. After the abdication of *Napoleon I, he received an enthusiastic welcome in Paris. During the reign of his brother *Louis XVIII, Monsieur, as he was called, was a figurehead buoying the hopes of the ultraroyalist party, opposed to the government's moderate policies. When he came to the throne (Sept. 16, 1824), Charles X, though 67, still cut a smart figure and remained kind and gracious. Since the death (1805) of his last mistress, Louise de Polastron, his conduct in this respect had been unimpeachable; and his manifestations of piety caused him to be lampooned as the tool of the clergy. His rule was reactionary, impervious to the aspirations of the new French society, but favorable to the Church. Bishops gained seats in the Chamber of Peers. Education at all levels came under clerical control. Women's religious societies won legal status (1825). A law defining as felony, and punishing accordingly, sacrileges against sacred objects or the Blessed Sacrament, was passed (April 20, 1825) despite the commotion roused in the Chamber and among the populace. The strong liberal, anticlerical reaction that set in compelled Charles X to sign (June 1828) ordinances prohibiting educational work by the Jesuits and limiting to 20,000 the enrollment in minor seminaries. The King fought this trend, named Prince Jules de Polignac to head a conservative ministry, and dissolved the uncooperative Chamber of Deputies (March 1830). Even after the opposition victory at the polls, he issued four ordinances (July 25) that nullified the elections, changed the electoral regulations, and imposed censorship. A Parisian uprising forced him to abdicate and flee the country. After a sojourn in England, he accepted asylum from the Austrian Emperor, passing his final years at Prague.

Bibliography: J. VIVENT, *Charles X* (Paris 1958). J. LUCAS-DUBRETON, *Le Comte d'Artois, Charles X* (2d ed. Paris 1962). G. DE BERTIER DE SAUVIGNY, *La Restauration* (rev. ed. Paris 1963). C. LEFEBVRE, DHGE 12:476–483.

[G. DE BERTIER DE SAUVIGNY]

CHARLES II THE BALD, GERMAN EMPEROR, 840 to Oct. 6, 877; b. Frankfurt am Main, June 13, 823; d. Avrieux, in the Alps. He was the son of *Louis the Pious and his second wife Judith and received the western portion of the Empire at the death of his father, thus becoming the first ruler of France proper. He and his mother had been the excuses for two revolts of his elder half-brothers, but by the time of his accession he was in league with *Louis the German against the other brother, *Lothair I. This alliance occasioned the Oaths of Strasbourg in 842, which recorded the first use of French as a written language. The Treaty of Verdun (843) confirmed the three-way division of the Empire. From 844 to 852, Charles struggled successfully with his nephew, Pepin II, for the control of Aquitaine. Later, in 870, by the Treaty of Mersen, he and Louis the German divided between them the lands of another nephew, *Lothair II. Charles tried constantly to stem the tide of Norse invasion, usually by paying tribute. His own children often revolted against him and frequently his magnates were insubordinate. He intervened in Italy to aid the Pope against the Saracens, for which he was crowned emperor by Pope *John VIII on Christmas 875, his nephew, Emperor *Louis II having already died. Charles confirmed the donations of the Carolingians to the Roman Church and gave the overlordship of Benevento and Spoleto to the Pope. Charles married twice, to Ermentrude and to Richilde. He was succeeded by his son, Louis the Stammerer.

Charles II the Bald, miniature from his psalter, illuminated between the years 842 and 869 and preserved in the Bibliothèque Nationale, Paris (MS lat. 1152, fol. 3 v.).

Charles's court resembled that of his grandfather, *Charlemagne, in that it welcomed scholars such as the influential Archbishop *Hincmar of Reims, the classical scholar *Lupus of Ferrières, *Walafrid Strabo, and the famed Irishman *John Scotus Erigena.

Bibliography: F. LOT and L. HALPHEN, *Le Règne de C. le Chauve* (Paris 1909–) v.1. H. LECLERCQ, DACL 3.1:825–866. CMedH 3. G. TESSIER, *Recueil des Actes de C. le Chauve,* 3 v. (Paris 1943–56). A. DUMAS, DHGE 12:441–445. G. BÖING, LexThK[2] 5:1356–57. E. S. DUCKETT, *Carolingian Portraits* (Ann Arbor 1962).

[A. CABANISS]

CHARLES III, FRANKISH KING AND GERMAN EMPEROR; b. Bavaria(?), 839; d. Neidingen, on the Danube, Jan. 13, 888. His surname "the Fat" is historically insignificant and can be traced back only to the 12th century. He was buried in the monastery at *Reichenau. The youngest of the three sons of *Louis the German and *Hemma, he married Richardis in 862. In the division of the East Frankish Kingdom, after the death of his father in 876, he received Swabia. His sickly brother Carloman (d. 880) had already ceded to him the rule of Italy (879), and Pope *John VIII crowned him emperor in February 881. Thereby Italy and the imperial dignity were joined with the East Frankish line, whose political tendencies were later to be reassumed by German kings. At the death of his brother Louis the Younger in 882, Charles became king of the entire East Frankish Realm, which thereafter remained united and eventually developed into the German Empire. When the West Frankish kings Louis III (882) and Carloman (884) also had died, Charles III fell heir to the entire kingdom of *Charlemagne. Although the usurper, Boso, who had set up a special kingdom in Burgundy in 879, died, too, in early 887, Charles III's rule was only a short-term personal union, because the political self-consciousness of the single kingdoms had already become too strong and the Emperor quickly lost his authority. Plagued by serious illness, Charles failed in the difficult tasks that confronted him. The popes hoped in vain for help from him against the Saracens. Neither in the Netherlands in 882 nor near Paris in 886 did he dare confront the Norsemen, to whom he paid tribute each time. The East Frankish revolt, led by his nephew, the future Emperor *Arnulf of Carinthia, resulted in his downfall and deposition by the German magnates at Tribur or Frankfort in November 887. The collapse of his regime meant the final dissolution of the

Carolingian Empire and the separation of Germany and France into distinct nations.

Bibliography: Sources. J. F. BÖHMER, *Die Regesten des Kaiserreichs unter den Karolingern,* ed. E. MÜHLBACHER, v.1 of *Regesta imperii* (2d ed. Innsbruck 1908). *Die Urkunden Karls III.,* ed. P. KEHR, MGD 2.1:3–325. Literature. E. DÜMMLER, *Geschichte des ostfränkischen Reiches,* v.3 (2d ed. Leipzig 1888; repr. 1960). H. LÖWE, "Das Zeitalter der Karolinger," Gebhardt-Grundmann 1:118–159, esp. 153–155. T. SCHIEFFER, LexThK[2] 5:1357. A. DUMAS, DHGE 12:445–446.

[T. SCHIEFFER]

CHARLES IV, HOLY ROMAN EMPEROR

German king, 1346; king of Bohemia, 1346; king of the Lombards, 1355; Holy Roman Emperor, April 5, 1355, to Nov. 29, 1378; b. Prague, May 14, 1316; d. Prague. He was the son of John of Luxembourg, King of Bohemia, and Elizabeth, sister of the former King Wenceslaus III of Hungary and Bohemia. In 1324 Charles married Blanche, sister of King Philip VI of France. The name "Charles" was added to his original name (Wenceslaus) while he was at the court of his uncle King Charles IV of France from 1323 until 1330. He then went to live in Italy, where he directed affairs for his father (1331–33). In 1333 he was made margrave of Moravia. In 1336 he held the Tirol for his brother John Henry against the Wittelsbachs. On July 11, 1346, Charles, with the help of Pope Clement VI, was elected German King, i.e., King of the Romans, despite Emperor *Louis IV. He fought in the battle of Crécy (August 1346), where his father was killed. Thus he succeeded as king of Bohemia in 1346 and was crowned at Bonn November 26 of that same year. The Wittelsbachs, age-old enemy of Charles's family, nominated as successor to Emperor Louis (d. 1347) Günther of Schwarzburg; but Charles easily defeated him.

Charles's administration centered in Prague, where he created an archbishopric (1344), founded *Charles University (1348), constructed a bridge over the Vltava, and finished building the cathedral church. There he entertained *Petrarch, who was recommended to him by *Cola di Rienzo. It was Charles, however, who had earlier imprisoned Rienzo and handed him over to Pope Clement VI at Avignon in 1351. Charles was crowned king of the Lombards at Milan (Jan. 6, 1355) and was crowned Holy Roman Emperor at Rome (April 5) by Cardinal Peter of Ostia. In 1356 Charles promulgated the *Golden Bull. Under his rule the territories of the Bohemian crown grew enormously. He acquired the Upper Palatinate in 1355; annexed Lusatia in 1367; inherited the Mark of Brandenburg for his son, *Wenceslaus IV (1373). His third wife, the Polish Princess Anne (d. 1362), brought him the principalities of Jawor and Swidnica in Silesia, to add to the other principalities of Silesia, which the Bohemian crown then dominated. One year before his death he partitioned the Bohemian domains among his three sons, Wenceslaus, *Sigismund, and John Henry, and among his nephews, Prokop and Jobst of Moravia. His friendship with the *Avignon papacy, especially with Pope *Urban V, facilitated his becoming king of Burgundy in 1365 and securing the German throne for his eldest son and successor, Wenceslaus, in 1376. Despite his superstitious bent, Charles proved to be a clever, intellectually acute, and strong ruler. He was a man of great diplomatic ability and a strong supporter of the Church.

Emperor Charles IV, obverse of his gold seal on the document of his investiture, dated April 5, 1355.

Bibliography: *Karoli IV imp. Rom. vita ab eo conscripta,* ed. K. PFISTERER and W. BULST (Heidelberg 1950). *Die St. Wenzellegende Kaiser Karls IV,* ed. A. BLASCHKA (Prague 1934). J. F. BÖHMER and A. HUBER, eds., *Die Regesten des Kaiserreichs unter Kaiser Karl IV* (Innsbruck 1877; Additions 1889). E. WERUNSKY, *Geschichte Kaiser Karl IV, und . . . seiner Zeit,* 3 v. (Vienna 1880–96). Gebhardt-Grundmann 1:451–455, 458–480. F. DVORNIK, *The Slavs in European History and Civilization* (New Brunswick, N.J. 1962). **Illustration credit:** Archivio Segreto Vaticano.

[B. B. SZCZESNIAK]

CHARLES V, HOLY ROMAN EMPEROR

Reigned 1519 to 1558; b. Ghent, Flanders, Feb. 24, 1500; d. San Jerónimo de Yuste, Province of Estremadura, Spain, Sept. 21, 1558. As the son of Philip the Handsome, Duke of Burgundy, and Joanna, third child of Ferdinand of Aragon and Isabella of Castile, he was heir presumptive to an empire vaster than Charlemagne's, and over which the "sun never set." It included the Netherlands and claims to the Burgundian circle, which came to him at the death of his father (Sept. 25, 1506); it included Castile, Aragon, the conquered kingdoms of Navarre and Granada, Naples, Sicily, Sardinia, the conquests of the New World, and possessions in North Africa, all of which after the death of Ferdinand (Jan. 23, 1516) he ruled jointly with his mad mother; and it included the Hapsburg duchies of Austria with rights over Hungary and Bohemia, inherited from his paternal grandfather, Emperor Maximilian I (Jan. 12, 1519).

Education in Flanders. Charles, 6 years old at the death of his father, was placed in the guardianship of his aunt, Archduchess Margaret of Austria, who, as regent of the Netherlands, proved a shrewd ruler and a firm but devoted foster-mother to Charles and his sisters Eleanor, Isabella, and Mary; his brother Ferdinand and his sister Catherine were reared in Spain. Among his tutors at Mechlin (Malines) were Robert of Ghent, Adrian Wiele, Juan de Anchiata, and Charles de Poupet, but it was Adrian of Utrecht (Pope *Adrian VI, 1522–23) who taught him piety and also won his

Charles V, Holy Roman Emperor, etching, 1521, by the German artist Hieronymus Hapfer (active 1520–50).

lifelong affection. The ways of the court he learned from the experienced politician Guillaume de Croy, Lord of Chièvres, appointed his governor by Maximilian in 1509. Mercurino Arborio di *Gattinara, Margaret's jurisconsult and an admirer of Dante's ideals of universal monarchy, instructed him to transcend dynastic nationalism for the universalism connected with the imperial office to which he was destined. On Jan. 5, 1515, Charles was declared of age by the Estates at Brussels. The next year he succeeded Ferdinand, and as Charles I of Castile and Aragon he traveled to Spain to accept this new power from the 80-year-old viceroy, Cardinal *Ximénez de Cisneros, who died of fever at Roa on his way to meet the King. At Tordesillas Charles visited his insane mother, whom he had never known, and met his brother Ferdinand (age 15), whom he had never seen. In the first months of his reign Charles, through his ministers, arbitrated the grievances of the grandees and the demands of the *Cortes* and appointed Gattinara his grand chancellor to succeed the unpopular Jean de Sauvage, who died June 7, 1518. These first steps in government were accelerated by the news of the death of Maximilian; Charles was now Archduke of Austria and a candidate for the vacant imperial throne.

Imperial Election. Though his choice was opposed by Pope Leo X, who feared the union of the imperial and Neopolitan crowns on the head of the same sovereign, and by Francis I, Henry VIII, and Frederick the Wise of Saxony, his rivals for the title, Charles won the votes of the 7 electors, partly through intrigue and liberal bribery (it cost the Hapsburgs 850,000 gulden, borrowed from the banking house of the Fuggers). Scarcely 20 years old, Charles swore to the exacting terms of the coronation oath before the electoral college, and on Jan. 23, 1520, he was crowned in Charlemagne's cathedral at Aachen. The empire that came to Charles was held together by a net of dynastic marriages; hence the dictum,

> *Bella gerant alii, tu felix Austria nube,*
> *Namque Mars aliis, dat tibi regna Venus.*

> Let others make wars, you happy Austria make marriages;
> While Mars gives kingdoms to others, Venus gives them to you.

The first objective of his reign was not new conquest but the protection and consolidation of his inheritance. To this end he arranged strategic matrimonial alliances: Isabella was married to Christian II of Denmark (1514); Ferdinand to Anne, daughter of Ladislaus of Hungary and Bohemia (1521); Mary to Louis II of Hungary (1522); Catherine to John III of Portugal (1524); Eleanor, widow of Emmanuel of Portugal, was betrothed to Francis I, King of France (1530); Charles himself, after numerous engagements, married Isabella of Portugal (1526). His aunt, *Catherine of Aragon, was already the wife of *Henry VIII of England, and his son Philip was later joined in a hapless marriage to *Mary Tudor (1554). His niece Christina of Denmark was wed to Duke Francesco Sforza II of Milan; his sister-in-law Beatrice of Portugal, to the Duke of Savoy; other relatives were married into the families of the Medici, Farnese, and Gonzaga.

Opposition and War. The maintenance of his wide power brought him into conflict from the inception of his reign.

Spain. Charles, with his French speech, Flemish background, and Burgundian councilors, was looked upon as a foreigner in Spain, and he had to face attempts to seize or limit his royal right. These he thwarted by defeating the *comuneros* in the Battle of Villalar (April 23, 1521) and executing their leader, Juan de Padilla; the next year he captured Vicente Pirez, captain general of the *Germanía;* in 1525 he put down the Valencian *Moriscos.*

France. Charles's relations with the King of France narrowed into a contest for the control of the Italian peninsula and the hegemony of Burgundy. He challenged *Francis I's rights to Milan, which had been reconquered by the French King at the Battle of Marignano (1515), as well as his dynastic claims to Naples. Four wars followed, interrupted by inconclusive and violated truces. On Feb. 24, 1525, the imperial army, commanded by the *condottiere,* Fernando Pescara, captured Francis at Pavia. By the terms of the Treaty of Madrid (Jan. 14, 1526), Francis relinquished his titles to Italy and his suzerainty over Artois and Flanders, ceded Burgundy, and surrendered his two sons to Charles as hostages. The French King upon liberation repudiated the treaty and entered the Holy League of Cognac (May 22, 1526) with *Clement VII, Venice, Florence, and the deposed Duke of Milan, Francesco Sforza II; he was also allied with Henry VIII of England. The next year imperial troops under the command of Constable Charles de Bourbon sacked Rome (May 7, 1527) and besieged Clement VII in the *Castel Sant' Angelo. Charles made peace with the

Pope (Treaty of Barcelona, June 29, 1529) and with Francis (Peace of Cambrai, Aug. 2, 1529), winning favorable terms and a ransom of 2 million gold crowns for Francis' sons. At Bologna, on Feb. 23, 1530, Charles was crowned King of Lombardy and Holy Roman Emperor by Clement VII. He was the last Holy Roman Emperor to be crowned by a pope. When Sforza, who had been reinstated as Duke of Milan, died childless in 1535, the contest was reopened. Francis invaded Savoy and Piedmont in his third attempt to capture Milan, but his early successes were checked by Charles's invasion of Provence (1536). This war terminated with the Treaty of Nice (June 18, 1538), which reaffirmed the conditions of the Treaty of Cambrai, but left Francis in occupation of two-thirds of Piedmont. In 1542 Francis tried again, this time with the aid of *Süleyman I, Ottoman Emperor. His victory at Ceresole (1544) was again nullified when Charles invaded the valley of the Marne and marched on Paris. By the Treaty of Crépy (Sept. 18, 1544), Francis abandoned claims on Italy, Flanders, and Artois, and Charles renounced Burgundy. In secret clauses of the treaty Francis promised to help the Emperor fight *Protestantism, regain Calvinist Geneva for the Duke of Savoy, and further the Council of *Trent.

German Estates. The element of universalism in Charles's political conception met its strongest test from the German Estates. When he outlawed Martin *Luther at the Diet of Worms (1521), he believed he was removing not only an innovator in doctrine, but an opponent to authority, his own and *Leo X's. In effect he established the reformer as a mustering-point for anti-Romanists and for German princes who sought territorial independence and chafed under the annoyance of heavy imperial taxation. While Charles proceeded to the French Wars, his brother Ferdinand, whom he appointed president of the *Reichsregiment* (council of regency), faced the problems of religious and political unrest. The Knights' Revolt (1522–23), in which Franz von *Sickingen and Ulrich von *Hutten led troops against the ecclesiastical princes, was followed by the *Peasants' War (1524–25). In 1526 princes sympathetic to the reformers formed the League of Torgau and at the second Diet of Speyer (1529) they protested against its strict reaffirmation of the terms of the Diet of Worms. Thus when Charles returned to Germany after his coronation to preside in splendor at the Diet of Augsburg (1530), he confronted an assembly factionally divided. Conciliatory religious formulas failed (*see* INTERIMS), and on Feb. 27, 1531, the Protestant princes and representatives of the free cities met in the town hall of Schmalkalden to form the league that provoked the Schmalkaldic Wars (1546–47). The Emperor's victory at Mühlberg (April 24, 1547) and the capture of John Frederick of Saxony and Philip of Hesse were high points of power, but they later faded in the French capture of Metz, Toul, and Verdun, and in the great triumph of territorialism, effected by the Peace of *Augsburg (Sept. 25, 1555), which gave recognition to Lutherans (but not Calvinists) within the Empire, provided they followed the religion of their prince (*cujus regio, ejus religio*).

Ottoman Empire. From his Spanish and Austrian forebears Charles inherited a traditional hostility toward Islam. The reconquest of lands taken by the Turks in Hungary and along the Mediterranean became a chivalric ideal. Under Süleyman I, Belgrade (1521) and Rhodes (1522) fell, and King Louis of Hungary was defeated in the Battle of Mohács (1526), which led to a disputed dynastic succession and the siege of Vienna (1529) by a Turkish army. In 1532 Charles was able to organize resistance, and although the small fortress of Güns in western Hungary withstood assault (Aug. 7–28), and German troops overcame the Turkish rear guard in Styria, little was achieved beyond moving the locale of the war to the Mediterranean. In North Africa, Khair ed-Din (Barbarossa), corsair and since 1533 admiral of the Ottoman fleet, had seized the Peñon (1516) and Algiers (1518), making the Barbary States a strong garrison for Mediterranean piracy. When diplomacy failed to win Khair ed-Din away from allegiance to the Sultan, Charles risked a maritime expedition. Commanded by the Genoese admiral, Andrea *Doria, it drove the Turks from La Goletta (1535) in an engagement that cost Khair ed-Din 75 sail. Tunis was taken on July 31, and 20,000 Christian slaves were liberated. In 1538 Charles entered a Holy League with *Paul III and Venice, but it was ineffective; the Venetian fleet was defeated at Prevesa, and Ferdinand was forced to a truce with Süleyman, after the latter's successes in Hungary in 1547.

Abdication. By 1555 Charles saw how far his policies had fallen from their mark. His vision of a united Germany was permanently blurred by the terms of the Peace of Augsburg; his proposal of the succession of his son Philip to the imperial title was rejected at the Diet of Augsburg (1550–51); Henry II of France continued to harass Italy (the 10-year conflict between Spain and France was not settled until the Treaty of Cateau-Cambrésis in 1559); Gian Pietro Carafa, strong opponent to Spanish interests, was elected *Paul IV (1555–59); Turkish power was undiminished; and the imperial treasury was drained through continuous warfare. Fatigue, frustration, and long suffering from gout led Charles to surrender the weight of office. On Oct. 25, 1555, in the great Hall of the Golden Fleece at Brussels, he gave the government of the Netherlands to Philip; the next year Spain and Sicily. To Ferdinand he relinquished the Hapsburg Empire (1556), but not the title of Emperor, which he retained until 1558. In September 1557, old beyond his years, he retired to a house that edged the Hieronymite monastery of San Yuste, where he lived until his death, not as a recluse, but quietly giving advice, receiving dispatches, and performing pious acts.

Sobriety, reserve, humorlessness, and self-conscious plainness placed him in contrast to contemporary Renaissance monarchs. Charles, well named the "last of the medieval emperors" (P. Rassow), was loyal to the interests of the Church, but he was also convinced that Rome had scant comprehension of his problems in ruling an Empire that contained a body of subjects stubbornly adhering to popular heresy. Thus he was initially cool to the idea of a general council at Trent, since he feared that it would end his attempts at conciliation with organized Lutheran churches, sheltered by princes whose support he needed for his warfare. This explains his disregard for Rome in his promulgation of the Augsburg Interim, when he presented the document to the papal legate, Francesco Sfondrati, to be sent to the Pope not for opinion or approval, but as a simple announcement of its contents. When criticized, he replied that he was not acting beyond his competence as a Catholic prince. Charles was faithful to his wife during her lifetime. His natural daughter Margaret of Austria was born of a liaison with Johanna van der Gheynst 5 years before his marriage; his natural son Don Juan, who led the Christian fleet to victory at *Lepanto (Oct. 7, 1571), was born to him and Barbara Blomberg in 1545, 6 years after his wife's death.

While Charles's regime in Europe was reduced to a policy of uneasy containment, he was the true parent of a new empire in America. He encouraged Spain's *conquista,* thereby securing the economic and fiscal advantages of exploration: Ferdinand Magellan, the Portuguese navigator, was commissioned to chart a western route to the Spice Islands (1519); Hernando Cortés entered Mexico City (1519); Juan Ponce de León made his second expedition to Florida (1521); Pedro de Alvarado conquered Guatemala and Salvador (1523); Sebastian Cabot, the Emperor's pilot, explored the Rio de la Plata (1526–30), on whose estuary Santa María de Buenos Aires was founded by Pedro de Mendoza (1536); Francisco Pizzaro founded Lima, the capital of Peru (1535), after seizing large quantities of gold at Cuzco; Hernando de Soto crossed the Mississippi River (1539); and Francisco Vásquez de Coronado explored the California coast (1540). During his reign, 2 viceroyalties, 29 governorships, 4 archbishoprics, and 24 bishoprics were formed; universities were founded at Santo Domingo (1536), Mexico (1551), and Peru (1551); and at Seville the *Casa de contratación* (bureau of trade) and the *Consejo de Indias* (council of the Indies) were set up for the central administration of the growing colonies. Merchant cargoes and—most important for the subsidy of Charles's wars—silver bullion from the mines of Zacatecas (Mexico) and Cerro Rico de Potosí (Bolivia) reached the ports of Spain. The wealth of the New World and the complication of its colonial government became the heritage of *Philip II (*see* PATRONATO REAL).

Bibliography: W. BRADFORD, ed., *Correspondence of the Emperor Charles V . . .* (London 1850), also contains his itinerary from 1519 to 1551. K. LANZ, ed., *Correspondenz des Kaisers Karl V,* 3 v. (Leipzig 1844–46); *Staatspapiere zur Geschichte des Kaisers Karls V* (Stuttgart 1845). L. GROSS, ed., *Die Reichsregisterbücher Kaiser Karls V* (Vienna-Leipzig 1930). A. DE SANTA CRUZ, *Crónica del Emperador Carlos V,* 5 v. (Madrid 1920–25). P. MEXÍA, *Historia del Emperador Carlos V,* ed. J. DE MATA CARRIAZO (Madrid 1945). G. DE LEVA, *Storia documentata di Carlo V in correlazione all'Italia,* 5 v. (Venice 1863–94). H. BAUMGARTEN, *Geschichte Karls V,* 3 v. (Stuttgart 1885–92); *Karl V und die deutsche Reformation* (Halle 1889). W. ROBERTSON, *The History of the Reign of the Emperor Charles V,* 3 v. (Philadelphia 1902), with his life after abdication by W. H. PRESCOTT. P. RASSOW, *Die Kaiser-Idee Karls V* (Berlin 1932); *Die politische Welt Karls V* (Munich 1942); *Karl V, der letzte Kaiser des Mittelalters* (Göttingen 1957). A. HENNE, *Histoire du règne de Charles-Quint en Belgique,* 10 v. (Brussels 1858–60). F. CHABOD, *Lo stato di Milano nell'impero di Carlo V* (Rome 1934); *Per la storia religiosa dello stato di Milano durante il dominio di Carlo V* (Bologna 1938), heavily documented study of Counter Reformation in Milan. G. CONIGLIO, *Il regno di Napoli al tempo di Carlo V: Amministratione e vita economico-sociale* (Naples 1951). C. HARE, *A Great Emperor, Charles V, 1519–58* (New York 1917). Jedin Trent 1 and 2. R. B. MERRIMAN, *The Rise of the Spanish Empire in the Old World and the New,* 4 v. (New York 1918–34) v.3. M. SALOMIES, *Die Pläne Kaiser Karls V für eine Reichsreform mit Hilfe eines allgemeinen Bundes* (Helsinki 1953). H. HOLBORN, *A History of Modern Germany: The Reformation* (New York 1959). W. FRIEDENSBURG, *Kaiser Karl V und Papst Paul III* (Leipzig 1932). R. TYLER, *The Emperor Charles V* (Fair Lawn, N.J. 1956). P. RASSOW and F. SCHALK, eds., *Karl V: Der Kaiser und seine Zeit* (Cologne 1960), essays for the quadricentennial of his death. K. BRANDI, *The Emperor Charles V: The Growth and Destiny of a Man and a World-Empire,* tr. C. V. WEDGEWOOD (New York 1939). **Illustration credit:** National Gallery of Art, Washington, D.C., Rosenwald Collection.

[E. D. MC SHANE]

CHARLES OF THE ASSUMPTION (CHARLES DE BRYAS), theologian; b. Saint-Ghislain, Belgium, 1625; d. Douai, France, Feb. 23, 1686. He entered upon a military career, was captured in a battle against the French near Lens, France, and was taken as a prisoner to Paris. After his release he was inspired, perhaps by the death of his uncle, to join the discalced Carmelites at Douai (1653). After his ordination in 1659, he requested permission to become a missionary in Persia, but he was assigned to teach theology at Douai instead. He became prior of this community and served two terms as provincial superior of the Carmelites in Belgium and France. His first works, published under the pseudonym Germanus Philalethes Eupistinus, placed him in the middle of the fray over predestination and grace. His first book, *Auctoritas contra praedeterminationem physicam pro scientia media* (Douai 1669), defended the *scientia media,* that is, the doctrine that teaches that God sees not merely all possible and actual situations in the universe He created, but also what a person would do if placed in various circumstances with different graces; He then predestines by merely actualizing one of these orders. Charles's second work, *Scientia media ad examen revocata* (Douai 1670), manifests some of his doubts about the *scientia media.* Charles, attacked by the Dominican Jerome Henneguier for his defense of *Molinism, reversed his position in his third book, *Thomistarum Triumphus* (2 v. Douai 1670–73), and defended the idea of the *praedeterminatio physica,* that is, God predestines not by means of the *scientia media* but through a modality of grace that infallibly brings the subject to whom it is given to cooperate freely with it. Having been confronted with an attack by the Jesuit Fourmestraux, he published two new works, *Thomistarum Triumphus in perpetuum firmatus* (Douai 1674) and *Funiculus triplex* (Cambrai 1675), indicating his firm adhesion to the Bañezian doctrine of *praedeterminatio physica* (*see* BÁÑEZ AND BAÑEZIANISM). In 1678, as provincial, he published, without the permission of higher superiors, his famous *Pentalogus diaphoricus* in which he declared that a penitent who confesses the same mortal sins week after week ought to be absolved without any hesitation by the confessor. (*See* RECIDIVISM.) This book was publicly burned by the superior general of the Carmelites, Emmanuel of Jesus, and in 1684 it was placed on the Index until it should be corrected. The reason for the condemnation was brought out by the theologians who attacked it. Among these was the Bishop of Tournai, Gilbert de *Choiseul du Plessis Praslin. He stated that sufficient emphasis was not placed on the idea that a penitent must sincerely intend to avoid sin and take what measures he can to carry out this purpose of amendment. In an exchange of publications with Gilbert, Charles, with permission of the general, published a further explanation of his doctrine, *Éclaircissement* (Lille 1682). This attracted the attention of the famous Jansenist Anthony *Arnauld and elicited from him a sharp response. In his final works, seeking approval for his doctrine, Charles made appeals to the bishop of Arras and the King of France.

Bibliography: E. Mangenot, DTC 2.2:2272–74. Hurter Nomencl 4:325–327. A. di S. Teresa, EncCatt 3:837–838.

[C. MEYER]

CHARLES OF BLOIS, BL., claimant of the Duchy of Brittany, Franciscan tertiary; b. *c.* 1319; d. Auray, Sept. 29, 1364 (feasts, Blois, June 20; Vannes, Oct. 14). He was the son of Guy of Châtillon, Count of Blois, and Margaret of Valois, Philip VI's sister. Charles married Joan of Penthièvre, and they had five children. Supported by France, he was engaged from 1341 in constant war for his wife's and his own succession to Brittany against the De Montforts aided by *Edward III of England. From 1347 to 1356 he was an English captive; when he was killed in 1364, his wife surrendered her claim to John IV de Montfort in 1365. Charles supported vigorously the cause of St. *Ivo of Brittany, canonized 1347. His contemporaries respected him as a saint and wonder-worker. After his death an extraordinary cult developed, propagated by the Franciscan Order; but in 1368, at Duke John de Montfort's urging, it was condemned by Urban V as premature and uncanonical. Investigations of his cause were interrupted by the Great Schism; the cult was authorized only in 1904. Charles is buried at Graces near Guicamp.

Bibliography: L. Maître, "Répertorium analytique des actes du règne de Charles de Blois" in *Bulletin de la Société archéologique de Nantes* (1904). F. Plaine, ed., *Monuments du procès de canonisation du bienheureux Charles de Blois* (Saint-Brieuc 1921). B. A. Pocquet du Haut-Jussé, "La *Sainteté* de Charles de Blois," RevQuestHist 105 (1926) 108–114. E. Déprez, *La "Querelle de Bretagne" de la captivité de Charles de Blois à la majorité de Jean IV de Montfort, 1347–1362* (Rennes 1926). F. Baix, DHGE 9:223–228.

[V. I. J. FLINT]

CHARLES MARTEL, mayor of the palace (714–741) and actual ruler of the Merovingian Frankish kingdom; b. *c.* 688; d. Quierzy, Oct. 22, 741. Of the three sons of Pepin of Heristal (d. 714), only Charles, a natural son, survived his father. Until 719 he fought to establish an uncontested title. Through victories over the Frisians, *Saxons, *Alamanni, Bavarians, and Aquitanians he rebuilt the crumbling Frankish state, retaining Merovingian "do-nothing" kings until 737. At the death of Theuderich IV in that year, Charles did not appoint a successor. He checked the Moslem advance in the West by his victory won between Poitiers and Tours (October 732), where the Franks stood "like a wall of ice" and the Moslem leader, Abd-ar-Rahman, was killed. The significance of the battle (for which Charles in the 9th century received the name *Martellus,* the Hammer) has been variously estimated: Western historians since Gibbon have considered it a turning point; Moslem historians feel that the Arab-Berber wave had already spent itself (Hitti, 501), although the Moslems were not finally dislodged from Septimania until the time of *Pepin III (759). Because the Lombard King Liutprand had aided him against the Moslems, Charles turned a deaf ear to Pope *Gregory III's request for aid against Lombard aggression in the vicinity of Rome. Charles's activity in regard to the Church was dictated by a policy of expediency: at home he employed the *secularization of church property to support his followers; abroad he protected the great missionaries *Willibrord in Frisia and *Firmin and *Boniface in Germany to consolidate his more remote conquests. He secularized monastic lands, e.g., *Fontenelle, which lost a third of its possessions to laymen; or he intruded laymen into sees and abbeys. Charles's own nephew Hugh, already bishop of Rouen, became abbot of Fontenelle in 723 and was later appointed bishop of Paris and of Bayeux, as well as abbot of Jumièges. Ecclesiastical discipline declined, and Charles would not permit reforming councils in Gaul. Although Boniface appreciated Martel's indispensable protection of his missions, he complained of him to Pope Zachary and later assured his son Pepin that his father was certainly in hell. At his death Charles divided the kingdom between *Carloman and Pepin. He laid the foundation for the greatness of the *Carolingian dynasty. He is buried in Saint-Denis.

Bibliography: Fliche-Martin 5:357–363. Gebhardt-Grundmann 1:121–124. T. Schieffer, *Winfrid-Bonifatius und die christliche Grundlegung Europas* (Freiburg 1954) 127–133. M. G. Lecointre, "La Bataille de Poitiers . . .," *Bulletin de la Société des Antiquaires de l'Ouest* 6 (1924) 632–642. P. K. Hitti, *History of the Arabs* (7th ed. New York 1960).

[C. M. AHERNE]

CHARLES OF SEZZE, ST., Franciscan lay brother and ascetical writer; b. Sezze, Italy, Oct. 19, 1613; d. Rome, Italy, Jan. 6, 1670 (feast, Jan. 7). Raised by devout parents, Gian Carlo Marchionne had only a few years' schooling, followed by farmwork, before joining the Reformed Franciscan province in Rome in 1635. In 10 years of extreme asceticism and intense interior life at small friaries in Latium, he advanced through acquired and infused contemplation into the prayer of ecstatic union. During a Mass in 1648 he received the mystical grace of the Wound of Love: a dart of light from the consecrated Host pierced his heart. From 1646 until his death he resided at San Francesco a Ripa or San Pietro in Montorio, Rome. Under obedience he wrote five long treatises on the spiritual life in a relatively simple and clear style. His major published works were: *Trattato delle tre vie della meditazione* (Rome 1654, 1664, 1742); *Camino interno dell'anima* (Rome 1664); and *Settenari sacri* (Rome 1666). From 1661 to 1665, when his soul had attained the transforming union, he wrote an autobiography, *Le grandezze delle misericordie di Dio,* which has been compared favorably with that of St. Teresa of Avila for its masterful analyses of the successive phases of mystical union. His eminently Franciscan ascetical and mystical theology have been judged sound, substantial, and practical. Innocent X, Alexander VII, and Clement IX valued his company and counsel. A hard nail-shaped growth of flesh was observed under his left breast after his death and was eventually accepted as one of the two miracles required for his beatification (1882). He was canonized by John XXIII on April 12, 1959.

Bibliography: *Opere complete,* ed. R. Sbardella, v.1–2 *Le grandezze delle misericordie di Dio* (Rome 1963–65), with important introd., biog., and extensive bibliog; *Autobiography* (abr.), tr. L. Perotti (Chicago 1963). V. Venditti, *S. Carlo da Sezze* (Turin 1959). R. Brown, *The Wounded Heart: St. Charles of Sezze* (Chicago 1960).

[R. BROWN]

CHARLES OF VILLERS, BL., abbot; b. Cologne, Germany; d. Hocht near Maastricht, Netherlands, *c.* 1215 (feast, Jan. 29). He entered the *Cistercian Abbey of *Himmerod in 1184 or 1185 and visited the monastery of Stromberg in 1188, and in

1191 he was at the Abbey of *Heisterbach, where he served as prior. The Abbey of *Villers enjoyed its golden age from 1197 to 1209 under Charles, although he is not responsible for the construction of the great abbey church there. He resigned his office as abbot in 1209 and returned to Himmerod, but he was soon summoned from retirement to make the foundation at Hocht, where he is buried.

Bibliography: MGS 25:220–226. É. DE MOREAU, *L'Abbaye de Villers-en-Brabant* (Brussels 1909) 40–50. Zimmermann KalBen 1:141–143. K. SPAHR, LexThK² 5:1362.

[B. D. HILL]

CHARLES, JACQUES ALEXANDRE CÉSAR, physicist and discoverer of the law that bears his name; b. Beaugency, Nov. 12, 1746; d. Paris, April 7, 1823. Charles was professor of physics at the Conservatoire des Arts et Métiers in Paris and is best known for his improvements in the design of balloons. After the two brothers Robert had prepared for him a balloon of taffeta coated with caoutchouc 12 feet in diameter, he filled it with hydrogen, generated from iron and sulfuric acid, and released it on Aug. 27, 1783. On December 1 he and one of the Roberts ascended in the gondola attached to the balloon from a basin on the Tuileries grounds and landed safely after 100 minutes—the first flight with a hydrogen-filled balloon. Louis XVI rewarded Charles with a pension and accommodations in the Tuileries where he could live and experiment. When the palace was invaded on Aug. 10, 1792, during the revolution, Charles saved himself and his brother, a priest, who was hiding with him, by reminding the invaders of his great deed that had brought honor to France.

Charles extended Benjamin Franklin's discoveries on electricity and gave well-attended lectures on physics. His work on the heat-expansion of oxygen, nitrogen, hydrogen, and carbon dioxide was used by Gay-Lussac (1787), who gave him full credit for what was called Charles's law. He improved W. J. Gravesande's (1688–1742) heliostat, invented a "megascope," a projector for pictures, and published work on differential equations.

Bibliography: J. B. J. FOURIER, "Éloge historique de M. Charles," *Académie des Sciences Mémoires* 8 (1825) 73–76. Représentation du Globe aerostatique, *Journal de Paris* (Dec. 13/14, 1783), with 2 color plates. (The first of these is reproduced here in black-and-white.) **Illustration credit:** Library of Congress.

[E. FARBER]

Contemporary engraving of Charles and Robert ascending in their balloon; Dec. 1, 1783.

CHARLES UNIVERSITY OF PRAGUE

A state institution of higher learning in Czechoslovakia, founded in 1348 by Charles IV, and therefore called the Charles, or Caroline University.

History. A *studium particulare,* which belonged to St. Vitus cathedral, flourished in Prague from the 11th century. King Wenceslas II (Václav 1283–1305) attempted to raise the *studium particulare* to the status of a university but was thwarted by the nobility, who feared that this would strengthen the power of the Church, on whose support the King relied in his dispute with the aristocracy. Charles, as a young prince, became acquainted with the organization of the University of *Paris, where he had spent 8 years with his uncle, King Charles of France. His teacher was Peter de Rosiers, later Clement VI. When Charles I (1346–78), who reigned over the Holy Roman Empire as Charles IV, requested permission to establish a *studium generale,* Clement VI issued a bull on Jan. 26, 1347, giving his assent to the founding of the University. The teachers and the students (*legentes et studentes*) received all customary freedoms, rights, and privileges. The bull provided that degrees be awarded with the consent of the archbishop of Prague. The future masters and doctors were granted the right to lecture at all other universities without limitations. The foundation of the University was solemnly proclaimed by a charter issued by Charles and sealed with the Golden Bull on April 7. By a special decree of Jan. 14, 1349, Charles, as German king, conferred on the University of Prague all the rights that Roman emperors or kings had granted to other universities. Ernest of Pardubice, Archbishop of Prague, former student at the Universities of *Bologna and *Padua, became the first chancellor of the University. The revenues of the University were derived partly from the Archdiocese and partly from public revenues. The first graduation ceremonies took place in 1349.

Early Organization and Administration. The University, composed of four Faculties, Arts, Theology, Medicine, and Law, was divided into four nations: Bohemian, Bavarian, Saxon, and Polish. The rector was elected for 1 year. Each Faculty had its elected dean as head; professors elected their provost. Professors lived in celibacy, and they also adhered to the rules followed by the orders of friars.

In 1372 the Faculty of Law formed an independent unit, and soon after the question of the nations became a thorny problem. This was resolved by the *Kutná Hora* decree of 1409, which allowed the Czech nation three votes and other nations only one. John Hus became nrst rector. The result of this decision was the emigration of the German professors and students to the newly founded University of *Leipzig and the consequent loss of the University of Prague's international character. During the period of 1417 to 1430, when the University was involved in Hussite and Utraquist affairs, no degrees were granted; and in 1419 the Faculties of Theology and Law ceased to exist. Three factors helped the University to recover from its national isolation: (1) the Council of Basel (1431–49), (2) the influx of students from the University of *Vienna in 1443, and (3) the bull issued by Nicholas V in 1447 to confirm the University's old privileges.

The University has been the center of many world scholars: Tadeas Hajek, Czech mathematician and astronomer; the Slovak Ján Jesenský, rector, who performed the first dissection in 1600 and was executed on June 21, 1621; the astronomers Tycho *Brahe and Johann *Kepler; the Slovak Lawrence Benedict of Nedožiery, author of a Czech grammar; Marcus Marci of Kronland; the mathematicians J. Stephig, and B. *Bolzano; the physiologist J. E. Purkingje (1787–1869); the physicists E. *Mach and A. *Einstein; and the Nobelist (1959) J. Heyrovský, founder of polarographic research.

Jesuit Control. The University underwent a great change in character when Ferdinand I invited the Jesuits to Prague in 1556. They opened the academy near St. Clement's Church that became known as the Clementinum in contrast to the older institution, the Carolinum. A radical change followed the Battle of White Mountain (1620) with partisans of the Counter Reformation.

By an imperial decree of September 1622, the University was reorganized and fused with the Jesuit academy, whose rector became rector of the University, then called the Carolo-Ferdinandea. In protest, the archbishop of Prague founded his own major seminary. In 1644 the University was reunited under the chancellorship of the archbishop of Prague with imperial supervision, while the Jesuits retained control of the Philosophy and Theology Faculties until 1757.

State Control. Catholic supervision lost its momentum with the reforms of the Austrian University at Vienna (1752–54). The rectors, deans of Faculties as well as professors, became state appointees. With the suppression of the Jesuits in 1773 secular priests and laymen filled the University posts. The Academia Metalurgica, affiliated with the University, was transferred to Slovakia in 1780. In 1784 the Institution became a state-controlled University with German replacing Latin as the official language until 1848. With the awakening of Nationalism, the reform of Oct. 1, 1850, restored the autonomy of the University. Because of the constant German-Czech tension in 1882, the University was divided into two completely independent institutions, both called Charles or Carolinum and both having access to the library. On Feb. 19, 1920, parliament repealed the 1882 act, declared the Czech University the successor of the old Caroline University, abolished the title Charles-Ferdinand University, and later stipulated that the German institution should be known as the German University of Prague.

However, the Munich Pact of 1938 and the proclamation of the Protectorate of Bohemia and Moravia (March 15, 1939) changed the status of the University in favor of the Germans. On Nov. 4, 1939, the German University, under the name of the German Charles University, was incorporated in the German Reich. The Czech University was closed Nov. 17, 1939, because of student demonstrations against German occupation. In May 1945 the Caroline University resumed its activities and the German University was abolished. The Czech Faculty of Theology was separated from the University and transferred to Leitmeritz in 1949.

The importance of the Faculty of Marxist Philosophy is reflected in the number of foreign students from the Middle East, Africa, India, Indonesia, and China. This department is chief propagator of new methods of scientific work. In 1959 the Egyptological Institute of Caroline University was founded in Cairo. With the opening of the new universities of Olomouc and Kŏsice, the number of students was stabilized at 11,000.

Contemporary Development. The University is under the jurisdiction of the Ministry of Education and Culture. The governing body is the University council.

In 1965 the University was composed of Faculties of Mathematics and Physics; Natural Sciences; Law; Philosophy; and five Faculties of Medicine, including general medicine, pediatrics, and hygiene; the Institutes of sports and gymnastics; culture and journalism; mathematics and physics; psychology, history of music, Egyptology; and an institute for correspondence courses. The teaching staff numbered approximately 1,995 and student enrollment, 12,259. The library housed about 1,600,000 volumes.

Bibliography: F. KAVKA, *The Caroline University of Prague* (Prague 1962). O. ODLOŽILÍK, *The Caroline University 1348–1948* (Prague 1948). V. CHALOUPECKÝ, *The Caroline University: Its Foundation, Character and Development in the Fourteenth Century,* tr. V. FRIED and W. R. LEE (Prague 1948). V. V. TOMEK, *Geschichte der Prager Universität* (Prague 1849). *Die Karl-Ferdinands Universität in Prag* (Prague 1899). H. RASHDALL, *The Universities of Europe in the Middle Ages,* ed. F. M. POWICKE and A. B. EMDEN, 3 v. (new ed. Oxford 1936). K. ZEUMER, ed., *Die Goldene Bulle Kaiser Karl IV,* 2 v. (*Quellen und Studien zur Verfassungsgeschichte des Deutschen Reiches* 2; Weimar 1908). L. KLIEMAN et al., eds., *Monumenta Vaticana res gestas bohemicas illustrantia* (Prague 1903–) v.1. E. WERUNSKI, *Excerpta ex registris Clementis VI. et Innocentii VI. historiam S. R. Imperii sub regimini Karoli IV. Illustrantia* (Innsbruck 1885). A. K. HUBER, LexThK[2] 8:679. W. WEIZSÄCKER, RGG[3] 5:499–502.

[J. PAPIN]

CHARLESTON, DIOCESE OF (CAROLOPOLITANA)

Suffragan of the metropolitan See of Atlanta, embracing the state of South Carolina, an area of 30,989 square miles with a total population (1963) of 2,383,549, of whom 36,796 were Catholics. It was established by Pius VII on July 11, 1820, at the request of Abp. Ambrose Maréchal of Baltimore and remained part of that province until 1962 when it was transferred to the Province of Atlanta.

John Carroll, from his first appointment as prefect apostolic, showed an awareness of the need for a priest at Charleston. The first priest, Matthew Ryan, in the fall of 1788 gathered about 200 Catholics into a congregation. His successor, Thomas Keating, purchased the

Bishop John England of Charleston, S.C.

property that was being used as a church and had the congregation incorporated by the state on Feb. 17, 1791. Simon Felix *Gallagher succeeded to the parish in 1793. He was an able man, but he permitted authority to be taken over by the vestry and precipitated the Charleston schism (*see* TRUSTEEISM).

From 1820 to 1883. As constituted in 1820, the Diocese of Charleston consisted of North and South Carolina, and Georgia. John *England, consecrated Sept. 21, 1820, in Ireland, was named the first bishop. His 22-year episcopate set the diocese on a firm footing. There were 2 churches in 1820; at his death in 1842 there were 14, and a total of 47 centers of Catholicism. He introduced two communities of women religious: the Ursulines and the Sisters of Charity of Our Lady of Mercy (*see* CHARITY, SISTERS OF), a diocesan community that he founded in 1829 to operate schools and an orphanage. He established the *United States Catholic Miscellany,* the first Catholic newspaper of the nation. His seminary, St. John the Baptist, was firmly established and had trained 20 priests for his successor.

The second bishop, Ignatius Aloysius Reynolds, was consecrated in Cincinnati on March 19, 1844. During his episcopate (1844–55), Reynolds published his predecessor's writings in a five-volume collection. He constructed an outstanding cathedral. At his request the state of Georgia was separated and erected as the Diocese of Savannah in 1850. Charleston's third bishop, Patrick N. *Lynch, had served as administrator of the diocese before his consecration on March 14, 1858. The Civil War brought many losses: the cathedral was burned; the diocesan newspaper was bankrupted; and the bishop had to beg the rest of his life to pay the debts of the diocese. In 1868 the vicariate of North Carolina was formed, leaving the Diocese of Charleston coterminous with the state of South Carolina. By 1882 when Lynch died, parochial schools had been established at Columbia and Charleston and a special mission program for Negroes inaugurated under the care of secular priests and religious congregations.

From 1883 On. Henry P. Northrop, born in Charleston in 1842, had been vicar apostolic of North Carolina when he was appointed Charleston's fourth bishop on Jan. 27, 1883. Under his direction the first hospital was opened by the Sisters of Charity of our Lady of Mercy. The Bishop England High School, the first Catholic secondary school in the diocese, was founded in 1916. The present Cathedral of St. John the Baptist was consecrated April 14, 1907. The 10-year administration of William T. *Russell, fifth bishop of Charleston, was inaugurated with his consecration on March 15, 1917. He provided St. Francis Xavier Infirmary and Bishop England High School with fireproof buildings. New parishes were opened and the work among Negroes was strengthened by the introduction of the *Oblate Sisters of Providence into the diocese.

Emmet M. Walsh, born in Beaufort, S.C., in 1892 was consecrated sixth bishop of Charleston on Sept. 8, 1927. Under his direction four Catholic hospitals were added. Many new parishes for the care of Negroes were opened and several religious communities, of both men and women, opened houses in the diocese. Walsh gave particular attention to Catholic education, encouraging more parochial schools and establishing summer vaca-

United States
CATHOLIC MISCELLANY.

Congress shall make no law respecting an establishment of religion, or prohibiting the free exercise thereof.—Art. I. Amend. Con. United States.

VOL. I.] CHARLESTON, WEDNESDAY, JUNE 26, 1822. [No. 4.

Page from the U.S. Catholic Miscellany, *first Catholic newspaper of the nation, established (1822) by Bishop England.*

tion school camps for children who could not attend Catholic schools. His 22-year administration included the years of World War II and its aftermath of increased population and renewed spirit of religion. A diocesan council of the *National Council of Catholic Women was established. The Oratory of St. Philip Neri, the first in the U.S., was founded in 1934 at Rockhill. The Abbey of Our Lady of Mepkin, a monastery of Trappists, was founded in 1949. Walsh was transferred in September 1949 to become bishop of Youngstown.

John J. Russell, nephew of William T. Russell, was named to the see on Jan. 31, 1950. During his administration, which lasted until 1958 when he was transferred to Richmond, he founded the diocesan newspaper, the *Catholic Banner*. These years were marked by a growth in lay organizations: the diocesan Council of Catholic Women was strengthened, the diocesan Council of Catholic Men organized, and the youth council reorganized. Considerable emphasis was placed upon the *Confraternity of Christian Doctrine. In 1955 the Monastery of St. Clare, the first order of contemplative nuns in the diocese, was dedicated at Greenville. Russell was transferred to the See of Richmond July 9, 1958. Paul J. Hallinan was named to the see in September 1958. He was consecrated in Cleveland on Oct. 28, 1958, and installed in Charleston on Nov. 25, 1958, where his brief rule was terminated in 1962 when he was made archbishop of the newly erected Atlanta archdiocese. His successor, Francis F. Reh of St. Joseph's Seminary, Yonkers, N.Y., was consecrated on June 29, 1962, as the ninth ordinary of the diocese. In August 1964 Bishop Reh was appointed rector of the North American College in Rome and was succeeded (Dec. 16, 1964) by Ernest L. Unterkoefler, former auxiliary bishop of Richmond.

Illustration credits: Buckler Studios of Charleston.

[R. C. MADDEN]

CHARLEVOIX, PIERRE FRANÇOIS XAVIER DE, French educator and historian; b. Saint-Quentin, France, Oct. 24, 1682; d. La Flèche, France, Feb. 1, 1761. The son of François de Charlevoix, deputy attorney general, and Antoinette (Forestier) de Charlevoix, he entered the Society of Jesus in Paris in 1698. He was sent to Canada, where he taught in the Jesuit college at Quebec from 1705 to 1709. After returning to France in 1709, he was assigned to the College of Louis-le-Grand, Paris. In 1720 he was commissioned by the French government to return to New France to seek a new route to the Western sea. In the pursuit of this goal, he journeyed through the Great Lakes and down the Mississippi River, reaching New Orleans early in 1722. He returned to France the following year to report his lack of success, but expressed his readiness to continue the mission, an offer that was not accepted. He resumed his teaching career for a time and then served as editor (1733–55) of *Mémoires de Trévoux,* a monthly journal published by the Jesuits from 1701 to 1762.

Charlevoix's published works include *Histoire de l'éstablissement, des progrès et de la décadence du christianisme dans l'empire du Japon* (Paris 1715), revised as *Histoire et description générale du Japon* (Paris 1736); *La vie de la Mère Marie de l'Incarnation* (Paris 1724); *Histoire de l'Isle Espagnole ou de Saint Domingue* (Paris 1730); *Histoire et description générale de la Nouvelle France* (Paris 1744); and *Histoire du Paraguay* (Paris 1756). His *Histoire de la Nouvelle France,* the first general history of Canada to be published, was translated into English by J. G. Shea

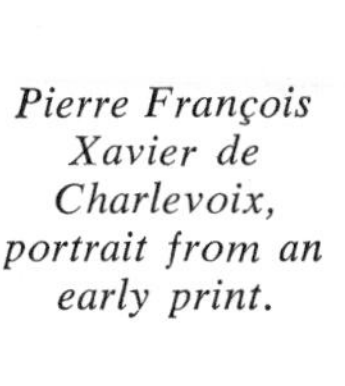

Pierre François Xavier de Charlevoix, portrait from an early print.

(6 v. New York 1866–72; new ed. New York 1900). The appendix of the original contained the journal of his American voyage in the form of a series of letters to the Duchess de Lesdiguières, compiled to describe the country through which he journeyed and Indian and Canadian life and customs. It had a separate title, *Journal historique* (1744); it was first translated into English and published in London (1761), and later edited by Louise P. Kellogg (Chicago 1923).

Bibliography: J. E. ROY, "Essai sur Charlevoix," *Transactions of the Royal Society of Canada,* ser. 3, v.1 (1907). Sommervogel 2:1075–80. **Illustration credit:** Château de Ramezay Museum, Montreal.

[R. N. HAMILTON]

CHARNEL HOUSE, in the Middle Ages, a structure (called *carnarium, oss*[*u*]*arium*) attached to a church, to the churchyard wall, or free standing, used for depositing bones, especially painted or inscribed skulls, that might be thrown up when new graves were being opened. The use of charnel houses was obligatory in certain parts of Germany (synods of Münster, 1279 and Cologne, 1280), and customary throughout Christian Europe. Very early, chantry chapels were attached to the charnel houses, sometimes as an upper story, where Masses for the dead were read and a sanctuary light was kept burning. The walls were usually painted with scenes representing purgatory, the Last Judgment, and similar subjects. The chapels were usually tended by members of pious societies or brotherhoods. There were several architectural forms for charnel houses: chapels, niches, and crypts. Many of them were destroyed during the Reformation, and then rebuilt in the 17th and 18th centuries, but during the Enlightenment they fell into desuetude. In popular belief, charnel houses were the meeting place of the poor souls who were supposedly freed from purgatory from Saturday night until Monday morning and during Embertide.

See also BURIAL, CANON LAW OF; CEMETERIES, CANON LAW OF.

Bibliography: H. BÄCHTOLD-STÄUBLI, ed., *Handwörterbuch des deutschen Aberglaubens,* 10 v. (Leipzig 1927–42) 5:1427.

Reallexikon zur deutschen Kunstgeschichte, ed. O. SCHMITT (Stuttgart 1937–) v.2. W. PESSLER, *Handbuch der deutschen Volkskunde,* 3 v. (Potsdam 1938). A. L. VEIT and L. LENHART, *Kirche und Volksfrömmigkeit im Zeitalter des Barock* (Freiburg 1956) 138. H. SCHAUERTE, LexThK² 2:133–134.

[M. F. LAUGHLIN]

CHARONTON, ENGUERRAND, painter, active in Provence; b. Laon, *c.* 1410; d. Provence?, *c.* 1466. He was said to have created a new style of Provençal painting influenced by both Flemish and Italian sources. Charonton's authenticated works represent a Mariology unusual in its intensity even in his day. The "Madonna of Mercy" in the Musée Condé, Chantilly, done in collaboration with Pierre Villate, was commissioned by Pierre Cadart in 1452; this work and the "Coronation of the Virgin" in the Hospice of Villeneuve-lès-Avignon, commissioned by Jean de Montagnac in 1453, represent the undisputed core of his oeuvre. However, attempts have been made to assign to him several anonymous panels in the severely monumental Provençal style, notably the "Avignon Pietà." Many questions concerning style, attribution, and the relative importance of Villate are yet unresolved; nevertheless, the quality of documented works established his reputation.

See also AVIGNON, SCHOOL OF.

Bibliography: M. MARIGNANE, *Enguerrand Charonton* (Paris 1938). A. CHÂTELET and J. THUILLIER, *French Painting from Fouquet to Poussin,* tr. S. GILBERT (Cleveland 1963) 61–67, *passim.* C. STERLING, *Le Couronnement de la Vierge* (Paris 1939). H. VOLLMER, Thieme-Becker 6:403–405. **Illustration credit:** Archives Photographiques, Paris.

[O. A. RAND]

CHARPENTIER, MARC ANTOINE, baroque composer noted for his oratorios; b. Paris, *c.* 1634; d. Paris, Feb. 24, 1704. He was a versatile and artistic man who had intended to become a painter, but he studied music in Italy with *Carissimi and became the leader of the Italian camp in the war between French and Italian tastes. His career included posts with the Princesse de Guise and the Duc d'Orléans (later regent), then at the Jesuit College, and finally, in 1698, at Sainte-Chapelle.

A fecund composer, Charpentier produced both sacred and secular forms, including Masses, motets, *Leçons de ténèbres,* a Magnificat, a *Te Deum,* cantatas, many theater works (an opera, *Medée,* was produced in Paris in 1693), songs, and occasional pieces, in addition to the two dozen oratorios (*Histoires sacrées*), of which *La Reniement de St. Pierre* (The Denial of St. Peter) is best known. Although the grand motet was to become the great form of the "spiritual concerts" of the next century, the motets of *Lalande, *Mondonville, and others owe much to Charpentier's oratorios, works of rare delineation and power.

Enguerrand Charonton, "Coronation of the Virgin," 1453, in the Hospice of Villeneuve-lès-Avignon, France.

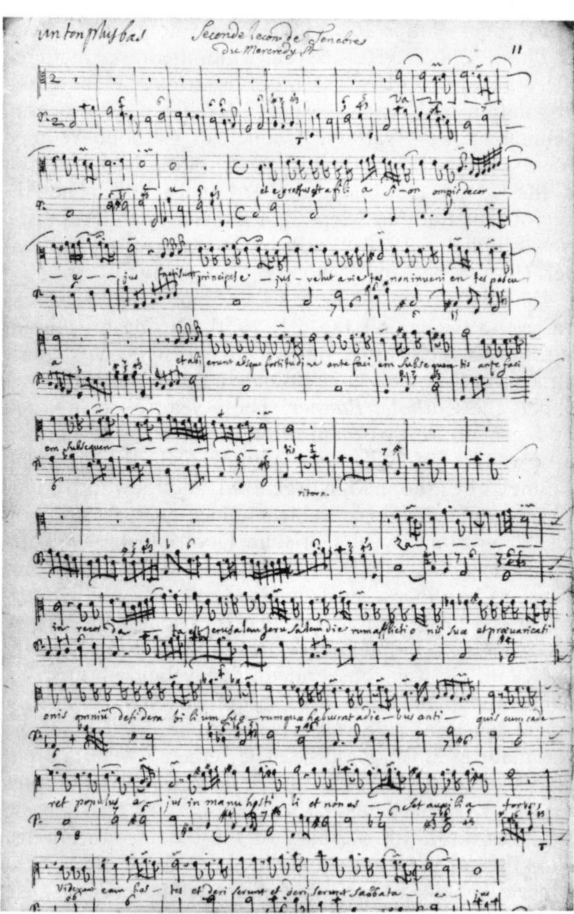

A page from the holograph MS of Marc Antoine Charpentier's "Second Lesson of Tenebrae for Holy Wednesday."

See also MUSIC, SACRED, HISTORY OF, 5; ORATORIO; JESUIT DRAMA.

Bibliography: P. PINEAU, ed., *Musique d'Église des XVIIe et XVIIIe siècles,* ser. A. of *Repertoire de musique religieuse et spirituelle,* ed. H. EXPERT (Paris 1913). C. CRUSSARD, *Un Musicien français oublié, Marc-Antoine Charpentier* (Paris 1945). R. W. LOWE, *L'Oeuvre dramatique de Marc-Antoine Charpentier* (Paris 1964). H. W. HITCHCOCK, *The Latin Oratorios of Marc Antoine Charpentier* (Doctoral diss. microfilm; U. of Michigan 1954); "The Latin Oratorios," MusQ 41 (1955) 41–65. Roland-Manuel v.1. C. STAINER et al., Grove DMM 2:187–189. **Illustration credit:** Bibliothèque Nationale, Paris.

[E. BORROFF]

CHARRON, PIERRE, philosopher and theologian, whose writings are important in the development of modern philosophical skepticism; b. Paris, 1541; d. Paris, Nov. 16, 1603. He was one of 25 children. He studied at Paris, Orléans, Bourges, and Montpellier, receiving a law degree in 1571. Earlier he had become a priest; he was renowned as a preacher and theologian, serving Queen Marguerite of Navarre as preacher-in-ordinary, as theological adviser in several dioceses, and as canon in Bordeaux. In 1589 he tried to retire to a monastic life, but was refused because of his age. He met M. E. de *Montaigne in the 1580s, and became his close friend and disciple.

Charron's major writings are *Les trois vérités* (1593), *Discours Chrétiens* (1600), and *De la Sagesse* (1601). The first is primarily an attack on Calvinism, arguing against atheists, non-Christians, and non-Catholics. Charron contended that man cannot have rational knowledge of God because of man's limitations and God's immensity. Hence, he asserted, He can be known only by faith. Atheists, non-Christians and non-Catholics all presume, he claimed, to possess actually unattainable rational knowledge. The *Discours Chrétiens* consists of pious discussions of theological and religious questions. *De la Sagesse,* his most famous work, presents Montaigne's skepticism about knowledge in didactic form. Wisdom, Charron argued, leads to complete doubt, and prepares man to receive revelation by freeing him from all prejudices and wrong opinions. The highest wisdom, prior to receiving revelation, is doubting all rational claims, and living according to nature, like the "noble savage." *De la Sagesse* was extremely popular in the 17th century, and greatly influenced modern philosophical thought by its critique of knowledge, its "method of doubt," and its presentation of a natural morality.

See also SKEPTICISM.

Bibliography: *Oeuvres* (Paris 1635). R. H. POPKIN, *History of Scepticism from Erasmus to Descartes* (Assen 1960). J. B. SABRIÉ, *De l'humanisme au rationalisme: Pierre Charron* (Paris 1913).

[R. H. POPKIN]

CHARTER OF LIBERTIES AND PRIVILEGES

The Charter of Liberties and Privileges of 1683 was the result of 18 years of agitation by the people of New York Colony for a popular assembly to enact laws and taxes. Between 1665 and 1683 the colony, a feudal proprietary of the Duke of York, was ruled by a governor and council of not more than 10 select men according to the "Duke's Laws," a group of statutes derived from New England precedents.

After repeated warnings from Governor Edmund Andros, the Duke sent to the colony Thomas Dongan, who convoked the first legislative body in the history of New York (Oct. 17, 1683). Nine communities stretching from Schenectady to Pemaquid were represented. The Charter of Liberties and Privileges, the first enactment of the assembly, was passed on Oct. 30, 1683. Under this charter the assembly was established according to English custom, composed of freemen representing both town and population. The assembly had the power to call and adjourn itself and to judge its own qualifications for membership. All legislation was subject to the Duke's approval. All taxes in the colony were to be levied through the assembly. Freemen were granted the privilege of civil rights and ownership of property within the province. Judicial procedure was established entailing indictment by grand jury, right of trial by jury, and release upon surety of bail. Liberty of conscience for Christians, never interfered with by the Duke of York, was given legislative sanction:

> Thatt no person or persons, which
> proffesse ffaith in God by
> Jesus Christ, shall, at any time,
> be any wayes molested, punished
> disquieted, or called in question
> for any difference in opinion or
> matter of religious concernment.

The charter was approved by the Duke before it was returned to New York. King Charles II died, and the Duke of York became King James II. Now New York was a royal colony subject to king and parliament. The Lords of Trade, a committee of the privy council, reviewed the charter, found it in conflict with the legislative supremacy of Parliament, and in May 1686 disallowed it. New York was brought under the jurisdiction of The Dominion of New England in April 1688. These circumstances created a distrust among the people of New York for James II that found expression in the uprising led by Jacob Leisler in 1689.

See also CHURCH AND STATE IN THE U.S. (LEGAL HISTORY), 1.

Bibliography: C. M. ANDREWS, *The Colonial Period of American History,* 4 v. (New Haven 1934–38) 3:70–137. J. MUNSELL, *The Annals of Albany,* 10 v. (Albany 1850–59) v.4.

[R. A. RYAN]

CHARTRES

Town of 27,000 population on the Eure River, 48 miles southwest of Paris; capital of Eure-et-Loire Department, which comprises the Diocese of Chartres (*Carnutensis*). The state of the Carnutes, which included Orléans (*Genabum*) and Chartres (*Autricum*), was reorganized before 400 to form the *civitas Aurelianorum* (*Orléans), while Chartres came under *Sens, to which the see was suffragan until 1622; thereafter it was suffragan to *Paris.

History. Chartres was sacked by Burgundy (600), by Aquitaine (743), by Normans (858), and, after sustaining a Norman attack in 911, by the Duke of Normandy in 963. Its counts, in the 10th century, ruled Blois and Champagne. As an intellectual center in the 11th and 12th centuries, Chartres was united to the crown of France (1286) and given a town charter. The English held Chartres from 1417 to 1432. It was made a duchy in 1528, survived a Huguenot siege in 1568, and then lost its particular history with the accession of the Bourbons; Henry IV was consecrated king in Chartres (1594). Although the French Revolution was not violent in Chartres, documents were systematically destroyed; the library was destroyed in World War II.

The Church was organized in Chartres probably with the peace of Constantine (311–313), but paganism was still a problem at the time of the first known bishop, Valentinus (*c.* 400). St. Solemnis has been associated with the conversion of *Clovis; St. *Leobin (*c.* 550) was the first to fix the borders of the diocese, and Pappolus thwarted an attempt to detach Chateaudun as a separate see (573). The Merovingians founded a number of monasteries in the diocese, which by 1272 had 921 parish churches. Blois was detached as a see in 1697. In the Diocese of Chartres, 810 parishes had been formed by 1789.

It was a rich town in Carolingian days, and counts of Chartres shared lordship of the town with its famous bishops and the powerful cathedral chapter. The chapter, which benefited from pilgrimages and fairs, contested authority with the bishops (1300–1700). The number of religious houses increased through the Middle Ages, and religious practice in Chartres seems to have been active at the time of the Reformation. Protestantism, which appeared in 1523, was strong enough to warrant a church in Chartres (1559). Reorganization of Huguenots after the Edict of *Nantes (1598) was countered by the establishment of more religious houses and a seminary (1659). By 1789 materialism and the lack of pastoral care had weakened religious life; 82 per cent of the clergy accepted the *Civil Constitution of the Clergy. The Concordat of 1801 assigned Chartres to Versailles, but the see was restored in 1821.

The schools of Chartres may have been well known at the time of St. Betharius (*c.* 600), whose 9th-century vita lacks credibility. An episcopal school dating from the 10th century became famous under Bishops *Fulbert (d. 1028) and *Ivo (d. 1116). It had for its chancellors *Bernard, *Gilbert, de la Porrée, and *Thierry, and educated students such as *Berengarius, *William of Conches, *Bernard Silvestris, and *Clarenbaud of Arras. By the late 12th century Chartres was in the shadow of the University of *Paris but through its *magistri* retained its importance; *John of Salisbury and *Peter of Celle were bishops of Chartres. Humanism based on the study of classical authors and the philosophy of *Plato, *Boethius, and *Macrobius characterized Chartres, which inclined to *realism in the *universals controversy; *Aristotle's logic also was studied. With *translations by *Constantine the African and Herman of Dalmatia available, medicine and natural science, too, were studied. Secular studies in general were pursued to confirm the harmony between faith and reason, between Biblical revelation and Platonic cosmology. Holy Scripture and the Fathers were read also.

According to a legend based on a chronicle of 1389 and works of 1609 and 1664, Druids in Chartres had a statue on an altar in a grotto dedicated to a *Virgo paritura c.* 100 B.C. They were evangelized by martyrs *c.* A.D. 44, and sent an embassy to the Blessed Virgin, who, in a letter written in Hebrew, was said to have accepted coronation as their queen. A 1389 statue of her, burned in 1793, was replaced in 1855. Chartres also has possessed a "tunic" of the Blessed Virgin, which, according to 12th-century tradition, was given to the cathedral by Charles the Bald in 876 and enclosed in a casket in the 11th century. The relic was cut up and dispersed in 1793, but part of it has been recovered. Pilgrimages, at a peak in the 12th and 13th centuries, came to an end with the Revolution. The crypt was restored in 1860, and the pilgrimages, especially among students, have revived. A miraculous well in Chartres, reputedly the resting place of martyrs in the 1st century and victims of the Normans in 858, had a hospital associated with it from the 11th century, where sisters cared for pilgrims and the sick until the Revolution.

Bibliography: U. TURCK and L. OTT, LexThK[2] 2:1034–35. T. DELAPORTE, DHGE 12:544–574. A. CLERVAL, *Les Écoles de Chartres au moyen-âge* (Chartres 1895). Manitius 3:196–220. E. JARRY et al., *Catholicisme* 2:999–1006.

[E. P. COLBERT]

Cathedral. Nôtre-Dame de Chartres, one of the supreme monuments of Gothic architecture, embodies in its different sections a history of this style from the 12th through the 16th century, with outstanding examples of architecture, sculpture, and stained glass, for the most part well preserved.

Erected above a grotto associated with the legend of the Druidic shrine of a *Virgo paritura,* the cathedral is the successor of several early Christian structures. It occupies the highest elevation in the town and dominates the countryside of Beauce; the contrasting 12th- and 16th-century towers of its west façade are visible for miles around the town.

Although the main body of the structure, including nave, transept, and chevet, dates from the 13th century, the west façade remains from a 12th-century church destroyed by fire in 1194. It retains the extraordinary sculptural ensemble of the Royal Portal, dominated by solemn, elongated figures representing Old Testament figures of Kings and Queens of Juda, royal ancestors of Christ. Above the three doorways of the portal are three stained glass windows (*c.* 1150), whose subject matter echoes the main themes of the sculpture, the royal genealogy and life of Christ and the Virgin Mary. These windows, depicting the Tree of Jesse, the Life of Our Lord, and the Passion, constitute, with the rose window above (*c.* 1200), the finest group of early Gothic windows in existence.

The interior, 428 feet by 105 feet (150 feet at the transepts), and 120 feet high, creates an overwhelming impression. No other cathedral possesses a comparable ensemble of 12th- and 13th-century stained glass. The subdued light, rich with the reds and blues of the windows, creates a mystical atmosphere consonant with the faith and its liturgical forms. Notable among the 176 windows are the rose of France of the north transept, donated by *Blanche of Castille, and the rose of the south transept (the Triumph of Christ), a gift of the Count of Dreux, both dating from the early 13th century. The "Nôtre-Dame de la Belle Verrière," a window saved from the 12th-century church, is now in the south ambulatory.

The sculpture of the portals of the north and south transepts, with figures drawn from the Old and New

The famed Gothic cathedral of Nôtre-Dame de Chartres.

The early 16th-century choir screen in Chartres cathedral.

Testaments and from the *Golden Legend* (1300–35), marks a tendency in Gothic art toward greater naturalism in proportion and bodily movement, without forsaking strong idealism. Completing the encyclopedic range of sculpture in the cathedral are numerous scenes from the life of Christ and the Virgin on the choir screen between the sanctuary and the ambulatory, examples of the *détente* style which was popular in the early 16th century.

North of the chevet is the old episcopal palace (17th century), now a museum of art and history. The nearby church of St. Pierre (12th–13th centuries) contains good examples of 14th-century stained glass (*see* STAINED GLASS).

Bibliography: H. ADAMS, *Mont Saint Michel and Chartres* (Washington 1904). Y. DELAPORTE and E. HOUVET, *Les Vitraux de la cathédrale de Chartres,* 4 v. (Chartres 1926). L. GRODECKI, *Chartres,* tr. K. DELAVENAY (New York 1963). A. E. KATZENELLENBOGEN, *The Sculptural Program of Chartres Cathedral* (Baltimore 1959). **Illustration credits:** French Embassy Press and Information Division, New York City.

[J. R. JOHNSON]

CHARTULARY

A medieval manuscript register or volume containing the muniments of the owner, i.e., copies of original title deeds and other documents relating to the foundation, property, privileges, and legal rights of ecclesiastical establishments, municipal and other corporations, colleges, universities, or private parties (also cartulary, Lat. *cartularium, pancarta, codex diplomaticus*). The great majority of such documents are in the diplomatic form of the charter (*carta*), hence the name chartulary for such a collection. The typical chartulary is a businesslike manuscript, written in an ordinary charter hand similar to that of the original documents and containing few or no illustrations, rubrications, or decorated initial letters. However, some chartularies (often later ones that are copies of earlier chartularies rather than immediate copies of original documents) are written in fine book hands and provided with elegant illuminated decorations and illustrations.

There are several types of chartularies. General chartularies were intended to contain all of the archives of the owner, often arranged chronologically but sometimes according to the places to which documents refer, or else according to subject matter or to the grantors of the charters. Most frequently some combination of these factors governs the internal arrangement. Because general chartularies, especially those of ecclesiastical houses, tended to be unmanageably large—extending to several volumes or being contained in a single volume of enormous dimensions—they were often replaced or supplemented by special chartularies. These contain documents of one particular nature, sometimes corresponding with a specific chest or receptacle employed for storage of the originals. Thus a special chartulary might be reserved for all papal, episcopal, royal, or other privileges, or for all documents relating to a single place or endowment. Other special chartularies contain records (plus memoranda) pertaining to recurring administrative problems or legal disputes. Their contents vary according to the nature of their purpose: *privileges, title deeds, compositions, ordinations, material relating to tithes, pensions, rents, surveys and extents, extracts from plea rolls, other records of legal proceedings, etc. Another type is the combination chronicle-chartulary, in which the documents serve to illustrate a running account of the foundation and subsequent growth of the house. In some sections (usually the earlier parts) the narrative will be little more than some brief notes between the charters, in others the narrative almost supersedes the records.

Some form of chartulary may have existed as early as the 6th century (*Gregory of Tours refers to *chartarum tomi*), but the oldest surviving chartularies date from the 11th or, in a very few cases, from the 9th and 10th centuries. The great majority of extant manuscripts are of the 13th century and later.

Chartularies by their very nature are extremely rich historical sources; nevertheless, they must be used with caution. Forgeries, which often sought to bolster immemorial rights, were frequent. As copies of original documents, chartularies were subject to error through carelessness, or through the well-intentioned efforts of copyists to correct MSS that they did not understand.

Bibliography: H. BRESSLAU, *Handbuch der Urkundenlehre für Deutschland und Italien,* 2 v. (2d ed. Leipzig 1912–31). A. GIRY, *Manuel de diplomatique* (new ed. Paris 1925) v.1. G. R. C. DAVIS, *Medieval Cartularies of Great Britain* (New York 1958) xi–xvi. F. ZOEPFL, LexThK[1] 10:444–447.

[R. S. HOYT]

CHASTITY

Translating the Latin *castitas,* chastity is the moral virtue that moderates and regulates the sexual appetite in man.

The Natural Virtue of Chastity. Man is by nature a sexual being, endowed with specifically sexual desires or drives. Some regulation of his sexual appetite is required by the nature of human life, both personal and social. When self-moderation and self-regulation in sexual life are apprehended and practiced by man as inherently right or good they assume a moral character and become the natural virtue of chastity. The forms of sexual self-moderation that are concretely apprehended as good or morally necessary have varied greatly in history and still vary among men. They are to a large extent determined by sociological patterns. The principle of sexual self-moderation is, however, an absolute of human morality. It is the foundation of natural law and natural virtue in the sexual sphere. Ideally, a rational analysis of human sexuality in terms of this basic principle should lead to the apprehension of the truth of all that Christian ethics places under the heading of natural chastity. In practice this conclusion is rarely reached on rational grounds alone. Christian ethics tacitly benefits by the higher light of revelation in positing the natural conjugal act as the only good fulfillment, in the moral sense, of the genital impulse in man.

Anatomically, physiologically, and emotionally sexuality is profoundly rooted in human nature and in the human person. This is a fact of general human experience that has been scientifically pursued and analyzed in modern sexological studies. The moderating virtue of chastity thus involves a rectification and harmonization of the whole man at the different levels of sexual experience, physical, emotional, and mental. Mere conscious rejection or unconscious repression of sexuality is not chastity, for neither constitutes a moral moderation of sexuality but only warps and frustrates it.

The modern psychological distinction between sexual fulfillment in a broad, or generic, sense and genital (or, in scholastic terminology, venereal) fulfillment in the strict organic sense clarifies the moral issue at this point. The conjugal act is the moral act of genital fulfillment, but sexuality in the general sense can be and is fulfilled in a well-ordered personal and social life. This is verified in conjugal life, where general sexual fulfillment in everyday relationships is at least as important for husband and wife as genital fulfillment. A satisfactory single life fulfills sexuality in another way. Basic personal energies, including basic sexual energy (i.e., the basic masculine energy of a man, the basic feminine energy of a woman), are channeled into the pursuit of life-enhancing goals. The urge toward genital fulfillment is transcended in the self-realization achieved through general personal and social fulfillment. Chastity, whether practiced in forms appropriate to conjugal life or in those required by single life, always maintains its character as virtue. It is the positive moral moderation and regulation of sexuality.

Modern anthropological research establishes another dimension of sexuality and chastity. Over and above its strictly moral function in human society chastity has a religious or sacred function. There is a divine design of sexuality, and observance of it by man is a prerequisite for his communion with the Divine. Cult forms of chastity differ historically as do its particular moral forms, but the cult significance of sexual "consecration" emerges everywhere in the history and anthropology of religions.

Chastity in Scripture and the Fathers. The Yahwistic creation narrative sets sexuality within the divine design of creation; sacred and purposeful, the sexual differentiation of mankind leads to monogamous sexual union (Gn 2.18–24). This highly religious and moral vision of sexuality underlies the Judeo-Christian theology of chastity, though in practice it was greatly blurred in the OT by the tolerance of polygamy and divorce (Mt 19.8; *see* MARRIAGE). Moral chastity in married life is praised in the later wisdom literature (Sir 26.14–18; Wis 3.13; 4.1–2), and there are outstanding individual examples of chastity—Joseph (Gn 39.9), Susanna (Dn 13.22–23), and Sarah and Tobias (Tb 3.14–18; 8.4–9).

In the NT the full sacredness and the full moral ideal of chastity are repeatedly stressed. Chastity (ἐγκράτεια in the sexual sphere) and purity (ἁγνεία) denote the general integration of sexuality with the life of the spirit. Chastity resides above all in the heart and spirit (Mk 7.14–23; Mt 15.10–20) but embraces also the sphere of conduct (Phil 4.8: "whatever is pure," ἁγνά). It is a God-given adornment of man, a fruit of the presence and action of the Spirit (Gal 5.23; 1 Thes 4.3–8).

Patristic teaching on chastity—except when given an antisexual slant by Neoplatonic and Stoic ideas—develops the Biblical theology of chastity as the sanctification of sexuality. The Eastern Fathers emphasize its mystical and transcendent character; the Western, its practical aspects. Chastity is a radiance of the divine beauty (Gregory of Nyssa), makes men akin to God (John Climacus), is divinely fertile (Origen). It belongs to the order of love (Augustine, *Civ.* 15.22) and requires purification from all sensuality (Cassian, *Collationes* 12.7). With Ambrose the three forms of chastity—conjugal, widowed, and virginal—become an established schema in Western theology.

St. Thomas's Theology of Chastity. St. Thomas Aquinas, accepting sexuality as a normal constituent of human nature, makes its moderating virtue, chastity, a subjective part of the cardinal virtue of temperance (ST 2a2ae, 141.4). Its subject is the sense appetite and involves both body and soul, or in other words the whole man. Thus chastity involves more than the strengthening of the spirit against the assaults of passion: this is the imperfect virtue of continence (*ibid.* 155.1). Chastity moderates and tranquilizes the genital impulse itself. Its highest form is *virginity, which demands complete immunity from coital pleasure (*ibid.* 152.3 ad 5).

There is also a spiritual or metaphorical chastity that consists in the due regulation of experiences of pleasure in the mind (*mens*) of man. To delight in God is an act of chastity in this spiritual sense (*ibid* 151.2).

St. Thomas did not distinguish a form of chastity that is not metaphorical but truly sexual and is yet not genital. Modern psychological findings require a supplementation of his theology of chastity on this point. There is a chastity of the emotions that regulates and sanctifies sexuality in the general sense even where the exercise of genital, or venereal, chastity is not called for. Feminine possessiveness, for instance, can enter deeply into mother-love, especially toward a son. Genital chastity is not in question here; but there is a definite want of sexual moderation and therefore of chastity at the emotional level. St. Thomas is not concerned with emotional chastity. Following St. Augustine, he relates sexuality to the genital act (*commixtio venerea*) in firmly biological terms. Sex belongs to man's animal life, whereas his life in society belongs to the rational and strictly human aspect of being (ST 1a2ae, 94.2). But chastity in moderating genital sexuality moderates and sanctifies the human person, and in marriage the human couple.

The Asceticism of Chastity. Chastity is both a gift of the Holy Spirit and a task of self-discipline. The asceticism of chastity forms an important theme of Christian spirituality in all ages (*see* LUST). In practice the subject has often been befogged by the predominance of fear of sexuality in the manner of treating it (*see* MODESTY). In modern times the training of youth in chastity has become more positive and realistic (*see* SEX EDUCATION).

Chastity in Modern Catholic Theology. The trend of modern Catholic theology has been toward a closer integration of sexuality with the distinctively personal life of man. Sexuality in the general sense is a form, sign, and expression of the human personality itself. Man is man and woman is woman at every level of personal life from the humblest to the most exalted. In this sense—and it is a very far-reaching one—sexuality affects the entire individual, social, and religious life of mankind. It derives its morality (chastity in the generic sense) from the positive and constructive function it should exercise in personal and social life as a whole, in accordance with each one's calling in life. Genital sexuality on the other hand—the specific sexuality proper to married life—is the specific form, sign, and expression of conjugal love. It derives its morality and chastity from its authentic love function in married life, to which it belongs exclusively. The procreative function of genital sexuality is in no way overlooked in this synthesis but assigned its rightful and necessary place within it. At the supernatural level sexuality is integrated with charity. Conjugal genital union stands as specific form, sign, and expression of conjugal charity, which is also procreative charity.

There is no difficulty in admitting and welcoming this development of the theology of chastity at the personal and existential level; but the traditional theology requires that the biological finality of the conjugal act—and of each and every conjugal act—in marriage be maintained in the new synthesis. Artificial defertilization of the conjugal act is always unchaste, and no considerations of conjugal love can justify it. The absoluteness of traditional theology on this point has lately been called in question by some. The problem of adjusting and reconciling the two aspects of genital union in married life—genital union as *opus naturae* and as *opus personae*—constitutes a point of controversy in the theology of chastity at the time of this writing.

Bibliography: L. M. WEBER, LexThK[2] 6:133–136. W. E. MÜHLMANN and F. BLOEMHOF, RGG[3] 3:1257–61. A. WILLWOLL, DictSpirAscMyst 2:787–809. A. AUER, Fries HbThGrdbgr 1: 498–506. J. FUCHS, *De castitate et ordine sexuali* (Rome 1959), standard modern textbook with good bibliog.; *Die Sexualethik des heiligen Thomas von Aquin* (Cologne 1949), analyzes St. Thomas's concept of sexual order. P. LAFÉTEUR, "Temperance," *The Virtues and States of Life*, ed. A. M. HENRY, tr. R. J. OLSEN and G. T. LENNON (*Theology Library* 4; Chicago 1957) 533–613, on St. Thomas's theology of chastity. Modern expositions of personalized chastity. É. MERSCH, *Love, Marriage and Chastity*, tr. from Fr. (New York 1939). D. VON HILDEBRAND, *In Defense of Purity* (New York 1931; repr. Baltimore 1962). H. DOMS, *Der Einbau der Sexualität in die menschliche Persönlichkeit* (Cologne 1959). P. RICOEUR et al., *Esprit* 28 (1960) 1665–1964, on different aspects of sexuality. J. CAZENEUVE, *Les Rites et la condition humaine d'après des documents ethnographiques* (Paris 1958), on sexual ethnology. On the psychology of chastity. L. C. SHEPPARD, tr., *Chastity* (Westminster, Md. 1955). VIIe Congrès international de psychologie religieuse, *Mystique et continence* (Bruges 1952). A. PLÉ, *Vie affective et chasteté* (Paris 1964). A. AUER, "Eheliche Hingabe und Zeugung," ThPraktQ 112 (1964) 121–132, on current theories on the subordination of *opus naturae* to *opus personae* in conjugal chastity. For additional bibliog. *see* VIRGINITY; MARRIAGE; LUST; MODESTY; SEX EDUCATION.

[S. O'RIORDAN]

CHASUBLE

The outermost vestment worn by the priest celebrant of Mass. The original chasuble, a genuine everyday garment of Greco-Roman times, was conical in shape, reaching close to the feet on all sides. Its use was not at first restricted to priests or to the celebration of Mass. The restriction came about with the gradual introduction of an investiture ceremony as part of the rite for ordination. The first clear evidence of the chasuble's presentation to the newly ordained priest appeared in the 9th-century Roman Ordinal 35 (27.31; Andrieu OR 4:38–39).

Reverence for the garment explains the existence of ornate chasubles from early times. This very ornamentation was responsible for the first alteration of the original vestment's appearance. The orphreys on the chasuble were at first bands of material used to hide and strengthen the seams. Often a vertical orphrey was applied to the front and back. In the medieval period oblique side bands were joined to the central vertical orphrey to form a Y. Orphreys became more elaborate with the use of embroidered figures of the Lord and the saints. Since medieval Christians placed greater emphasis on the sacrificial rather than on the meal aspect of the Mass, it is not surprising that the customary image was that of the crucified Lord, causing the Y to be squared off to form a Latin cross.

The second alteration in the form of the chasuble came about as a result of the use of brocades. Medieval and Renaissance love of color prompted vestment makers to employ what were considered at the time the very best weaves. Unfortunately many of the great brocades were heavy and unwieldy. This led to a reduction of the material falling over the arms. Eventually only the front and back panels remained, the back one being decorated with a large cross. By the end of the 18th century particular models of the abbreviated vestments were favored in different countries and were known as the French, Italian, and Spanish chasubles. The last, which broadened toward the bottom, was the most imperfect of all.

The 19th-century renewal of interest in the Middle Ages led to an attempt to restore a more ample style vesture to liturgical functions. Unfortunately, the Gothic revivalists did not offer a restoration of the original chasuble at all, but a garment quite different and imperfect in form, which they called "Gothic." Its use gradually spread despite the opposition of the Congregation of Rites (1863, 1925). Later (1957) the Congregation decided to leave the matter to the judgment of ordinaries. In the last instance the Holy See's reaction was considerably tempered by the fact that it was concerned with the use of a conical chasuble form more faithful to the dignity of the original Greco-Roman garment.

Bibliography: E. J. SUTFIN, "The Chasuble in the Roman Rite," *Liturgical Arts* 24 (1956) 76–104; "How to Make a Chasuble," *ibid.* 25 (1957) 66–86. For additional bibliog. *see* LITURGICAL VESTMENTS. **Illustration credits:** Fig. 1, Landesamt für Denkmalpflege, Munich. Fig. 2, National Gallery of Art, Washington, D.C., Widener Collection. Fig. 3, Courtesy of the Hispanic Society of America. Fig. 4, Courtesy of St. Mark's Episcopal Church, Philadelphia, Pa. Fig. 5, Peter Ammon, Lucerne.

[M. MC CANCE]

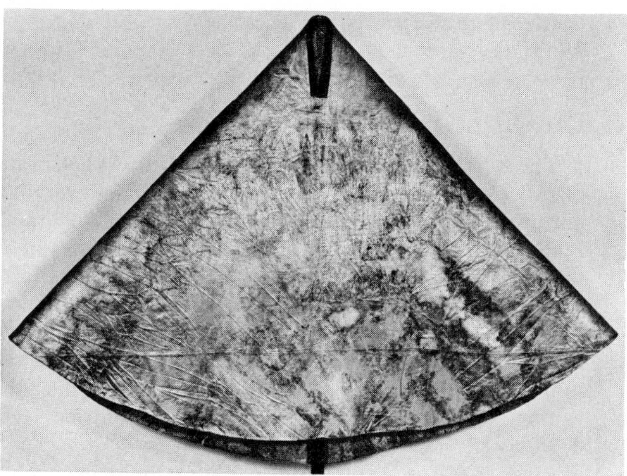

Fig. 1. Conical, yellow silk damask, c. 1047, from the tomb of Pope Clement II, in the Bamberg cathedral.

Fig. 2. Detail of an altarpiece, c. 1500, showing a bishop-saint clothed in the chasuble of the period.

CHASUBLE

Fig. 3. Spanish, 15th-century fabric and embroidery, probably cut into its present shape in the 17th century.

Fig. 4. "Gothic Revival," white silk with gold and silk embroidery, English, 1890 to 1900.

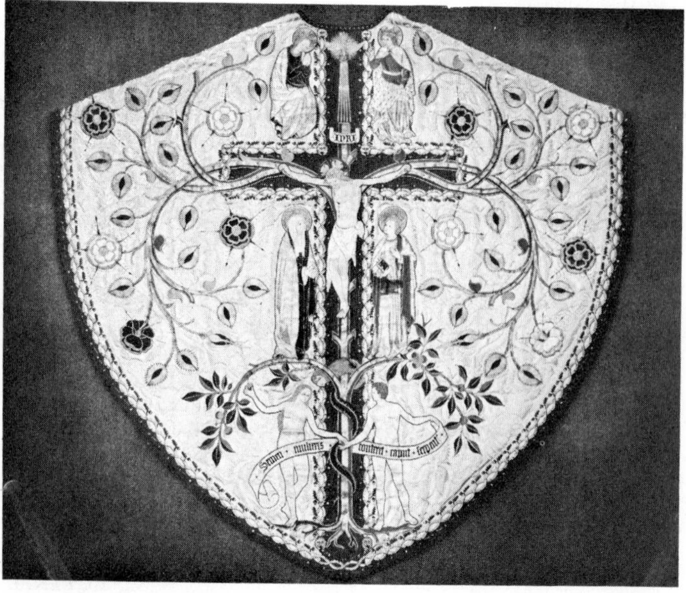

Fig. 5. Conical, by the Paramentenwerkstätte St. Klara, Stans, Switzerland.

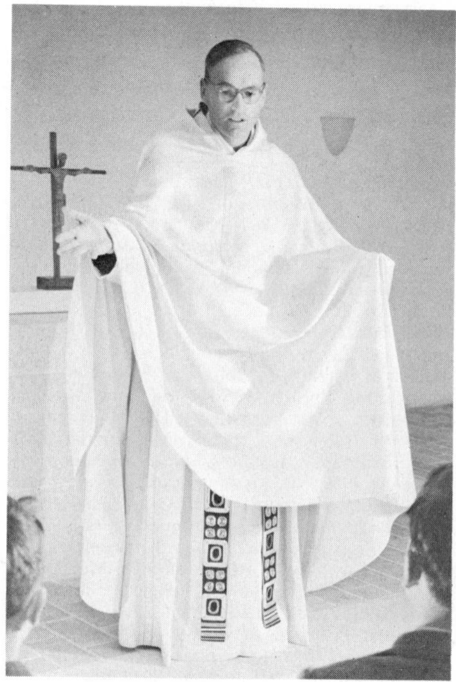

CHATARD, FRANCIS SILAS, fifth bishop of Vincennes (now *Indianapolis), Ind.; b. Baltimore, Md., Dec. 13, 1834; d. Indianapolis, Sept. 7, 1918. Both his father, Ferdinand, and his paternal grandfather, Pierre, an emigrant from Santo Domingo, West Indies, were physicians in Baltimore; his mother was Eliza Anne Marean of Massachusetts. Chatard attended St. Francis Xavier Institute, Baltimore, and Mt. St. Mary's College, Emmitsburg, Md., from which he graduated in 1853. He received his degree in medicine from the University of Maryland, College Park, in 1856, and served for a year as resident physician in the Baltimore Alms House, which later became the City Hospital.

Chatard abandoned medicine to enter the Urban College of Propaganda Fide, Rome, Nov. 5, 1857, as a student of the Archdiocese of Baltimore. He was ordained in Rome by Cardinal Constantine Patrizi June 14, 1862; he received his doctorate in theology in 1863 and was appointed vice rector of the North American College, Rome, assisting William McCloskey. In 1868 Chatard became prorector of the college and in 1871 was officially named rector. Pius IX appointed him papal chamberlain in 1875. Although Chatard was a capable college administrator, he encountered financial difficulties under the new Italian regime, and made a visit to the U.S. in 1877 to appeal for support. The following year Leo XIII named him to the Diocese of Vincennes, and he was consecrated in the North American College chapel on May 12, 1878. Extensive reorganization marked his episcopal administration. He summoned synods in 1878, 1880, 1886, and 1891; raised the status of the clergy; improved the schools; encouraged the founding of hospitals and religious institutions; and established 47 new parishes and missions. After the title of his see had been changed to Indianapolis (1898), he built SS. Peter and Paul Cathedral, in the crypt of which he is buried.

In the ecclesiastical controversies of the day, among which the question of secret societies was of particular concern to him, Chatard was classed among the conservatives. He represented the Province of Cincinnati in the Roman meetings preliminary to the Third Plenary Council of Baltimore, and also wrote numerous articles for American magazines, chiefly the Paulist periodical, *Catholic World*. Some of his formal lectures were published as *Occasional Essays* (1881) and *Christian Truths* (1881), and he translated Abbé G. Chardon's *Memoirs of a Seraph* (2 v. 1888).

Bibliography: H. J. ALERDING, *A History of the Catholic Church in the Diocese of Vincennes* (Indianapolis 1883). C. BLANCHARD, ed., *History of the Catholic Church in Indiana,* 2 v. (Logansport, Ind. 1898). R. F. MCNAMARA, *The American College in Rome: 1855–1955* (Rochester 1956).

[R. GORMAN]

CHATEAUBRIAND, FRANÇOIS RENÉ DE

French writer and politician; b. Saint-Malo, Sept. 4, 1768; d. Paris, July 4, 1848. His isolated tomb is on a tiny island off Saint-Malo, le Grand Bé. He was the last of an old Breton family—his eldest brother, who inherited the title of count of Chateaubriand, having died on the scaffold during the Revolution. One of his sisters, Lucile, a woman of fine but morbid sensitivity, wielded a strong influence on his poetic imagination. He grew up first at Saint-Malo, then at his father's château of Combourg, then in various Breton schools (Dol, 1778–80; Rennes, 1781–82; and Dinan, 1784–86). Destined first to a career as a seaman, for which he studied briefly and unsuccessfully at Brest (1783), he received in 1786 a lieutenancy in the regiments of Navarre and spent several years in garrisons (Cambrai, Dieppe). He passed his vacations with his sisters at Fougères, and led a dissipated existence in Paris among men of letters and philosophers such as Évariste Désiré de Parny, Ponce Écouchard Lebrun, Sébastien de Chamfort, and Pierre Ginguené. After watching the first bloody days of the Revolution he left for the U.S. on April 8, 1791.

François René de Chateaubriand, portrait by A. L. Girodet-Trioson, 1809, in the museum at St. Malo, France.

His account of this journey, published in 1827 as *Voyage en Amérique,* has aroused well-founded doubts (especially concerning his intention of discovering a Polar Sea, his unlikely itinerary, and the account of a visit to George Washington) and critics have looked into accounts of various missionaries, naturalists, and historians for its sources. Whatever the case, after arriving in Baltimore on July 10, 1791, he left suddenly on December 10 and arrived at Le Havre on Jan. 2, 1792. He married Celeste Buisson de Lavigne at Saint-Malo on March 19, 1792, then, after a stay with old friends, men of letters at Paris, he joined a company of émigrés and finally went to England (May 17, 1793). He knew the miseries of emigration, in spite of meager resources augmented by his compatriot J. Peltier and by the French lessons he gave during 1795. He did not give up his literary ambitions, however, but worked on *Les Natchez,* translated English poetry (Milton's and Gray's), and published the *Essai sur les Revolutions,* his first book (1797).

Genesis of Génie du Christianisme. This essay on revolutions, edited by Deboffe at London, proposes an ingenious parallel between the revolutions of antiquity and the French Revolution. It reveals a troubled 30-year-old Chateaubriand torn between the irreligious skepticism of the 18th century and the need for faith. In confidential notes, scribbled a little later in the margins of this work, the author stresses more boldly his doubts and denials. In a new edition (1826), he inserted severe notations on his unbelieving youth, while emphasizing the religious torment that had then begun.

He soon recovered his faith, however, moved particularly by the death of his mother and of one of his sisters, Mme. de Farcy. Under the urging of his friend Louis de Fontanes, he began the preparation of an apology of Christianity. Whatever doubts have been raised about the account he gave of the genesis of this work, and of the circumstances of his conversion, he appeared, on his return to France (May 1800), as the most brilliant member of the group of social and religious reformers whose organ was the *Mercure de France.* His reputation grew further by his refutation of Mme. de Staël's *De la Littérature,* and by the publication (1801) of *Atala,* an episode of his *Génie du Christianisme. Atala* is an "American" nouvelle in the genre of the exotic tales so popular in the 18th century; its defense of the "noble savage," echoing the thought of *Rousseau, ends with an idyllic sketch of the primitive world. Christianity and its benefits, however, are represented in it by an old missionary, Father Aubry. A year later (April 1802), *Atala* appeared in its proper place in *Génie du Christianisme.*

This work is divided into four sections, *Dogmes et Doctrines, Poétique du Christianisme, Beaux Arts et Littérature,* and *Culte.* The first part examines the mysteries and the Sacraments, the virtues and the moral law founded on the Decalogue; it affirms the superiority of the Mosaic tradition over all the other cosmogonies; finally, following many apologists of the 18th century, it searches among the wonders of nature for proofs of the existence of God. The second and third parts are given over to the poetry of Christianity and to the philosophical theories it evoked: the epics, the dramatic characters, the portrayal of the passions (and here one chapter is devoted to the "evil of the century" under the title *Vague des passions*), the Christian feeling for nature ("The mythology of the Ancients," says Chateaubriand, "depreciates nature"), the music, especially of Gregorian chant, the architecture, particularly of the Gothic churches—all are called forth as witnesses. In addition, the thinking of Pascal, the eloquence of Bossuet, the "harmonies" of art and nature, which Chateaubriand understood as Bernardin de Saint-Pierre had understood them, all are pressed into service. The last part recalls the beauty of the liturgy, the song of the bells, the solemnities of the Church, Christian festivals; the spectacle of the tomb, sad but at the same time comforting; the role of the clergy and the work of the missions; the humanitarian generosities that manifest themselves in hospitals, schools, legislation, and civilization.

Two novels of love and sin, *Atala* and *René,* appear in this religious apologetic, to show the harmonies a religious soul may establish between the beauties of nature and the human heart, and the remedy Christianity proposes to the *vague des passions. René* is autobiographical in large part and concludes with a thought put into the mouth of a missionary priest (but surely Chateaubriand's own): "Solitude is bad for him who does not live with God."

Political Embroilments. The *Génie du Christianisme* corresponded with Bonaparte's views in that year of the Concordat (1802), and Chateaubriand was sent to Rome as secretary to the French ambassador. His discovery of Italy and the Roman countryside is recounted in *Voyage en Italie* (1826). On his return to Paris in 1804, he was preparing himself for a new diplomatic post as minister of France in the Valais, when he learned of the execution of the Duke of Enghien; he then resigned. Two years later he went to Greece, the Orient, Africa, and Spain. This trip provided him with the elements for a novel begun in 1802 or 1804, *Les Martyrs de Dioclétien,* which became the prose poem *Les Martyrs* (March 1809). In its picture of Roman decadence, *Les Martyrs* is partly Chateaubriand's own confession and partly an attack on Napoleon. But its general design, the clash between dying paganism and nascent Christianity, is an illustration of the thesis of the *Génie du Christianisme.*

Napoleon recognized the polemic intent that had been directed against him. To be sure, Chateaubriand admired the great man; but even though he admitted this, it pleased him to be defiant, to "feel his claws." He had served the political aims of the First Consul in his work toward social restoration; but the aristocratic connections of the author of the *Martyrs* turned him against the Emperor who had attacked the very life of the old France in the person of a prince of the blood, the Duke of Enghien, that is, the last of the line of Condé. And Napoleon, who had cherished the idea of turning to his own ends the genius of Chateaubriand, sensed in him the daily growth of a rebellious and rival force. Chateaubriand had clearly aimed at Napoleon, under the names of Neron and Sylla in an article in the *Mercure* (July 1807). Nevertheless the Emperor nominated him to the French Academy (1811), but the rebellious genius wanted to make his reception speech a new weapon against the Emperor, and therefore the talk was never given.

In 1811 the *Itinéraire de Paris à Jérusalem* recounted Chateaubriand's pilgrimage from April 23, 1806, to March 19, 1807, during which he became a knight of the Holy Sepulchre. Only 3 days out of 332 had been spent in Jerusalem, and such haste, the borrowings from numerous books, and the contradictions between the *Itinéraire* and the journal edited by Chateaubriand's servant, Julien, published in 1904, have cast doubt on the authenticity of Chateaubriand's work. But a *Journal de Jérusalem* by Chateaubriand, found and published in 1950, but probably contemporaneous with the journey, restores confidence in the account.

When the Empire fell, Chateaubriand zealously championed the restoration of the Bourbons with *De Buonaparte et des Bourbons* (1814) and *Reflexions politiques* (1814). With the return of Napoleon during the Hundred Days, he followed Louis XVIII to Ghent and acted as minister of state for political affairs. But when the King again ascended the throne, Chateaubriand judged himself to have been poorly rewarded for his services in spite of his elevation to the title of peer of France (Aug. 17, 1815). He fought against the ministry in *De la Monarchie selon la Charte* (1816), was active in the campaign of the ultraroyalists in *Le Conservateur*

(1818–20), and shared their triumph following the assassination of the Duke of Berry (Feb. 13, 1820). He was in turn minister to Berlin (January–July 1821) and ambassador to London (January–September 1822), and he was sent to Congress of Verona and entered the ministry with a portfolio of foreign affairs (Dec. 28, 1822–June 6, 1824). He pushed for French intervention in Spain (1823) and had a part in its success. But the animosity of the head of the ministry, Joseph de Villèle, and of Louis XVIII, threw him into opposition. His implacable war against the government was sustained in the *Journal des Débats*. After the fall of Villèle (1827) he became ambassador of France to Rome (June 2, 1828) and tried to play a role in the conclave that elected Pope Pius VIII (1829). During the same period, he undertook the edition of his *Oeuvres complètes* (28 v., 1826–31), in which appeared a few new works: *Les Aventures du dernier Abencérage* (1826), a Spanish novella on the 16th century; *Les Natchez* (1826), both an exotic novel and a prose epic; and the *Voyage en Amérique* (1827).

The politics of Charles X and the formation of the Polignac ministry caused Chateaubriand to resign his ambassadorship (Aug. 30, 1829). He reaffirmed, however, his loyalty to the King, who had fled from France in the revolution of July 1830, and his opposition to the new regime of Louis Philippe, against whom he entered the service of the monarchy exiled in Prague, and the Duchess of Berry, daughter-in-law of Charles X. Chateaubriand was on trial twice in 1832; the first time charges were dismissed and the second time he was acquitted.

His last works are *Études historiques* (1831), a large, though incomplete and uneven fresco, in which he describes the advent of the modern world and in which his philosophy of history, always faithful to a Christian perspective, and aware of the action of Providence, shows his faith in human progress; the *Essai sur la littérature anglaise* (1836), in which he sums up his opinion of a literature that profoundly influenced him; *Le Congrès de Vérone* (1838), an apology of his political activity from 1822 to 1823; and the *Vie de Rancé* (1844), a biography of the great Trappist reformer Armand *Rancé.

Mémoires d'Outre-tombe. Above all he devoted the rest of his life to altering a great work, the *Mémoires d'Outre-tombe* (begun 1803, published posthumously). These *Mémoires* passed through various stages in the course of 45 years. From 1833 an initiated public heard it read in Mme. Récamier's salon at the Abbaye-aux-bois. Chateaubriand wanted it to be the poem of his life and his time; he made it above all the poem of his friendships, of his loves (Mme. de Beaumont, Mme. de Custine, Mme. de Noailles, Hortense Allart, and especially Mme. Récamier), and of his hates (Fouché, Talleyrand, Decazes, Thiers, and others). Published in series form in *La Presse* (Oct. 21, 1848–July 5, 1850), and collected in 12 volumes from January 1849 to October 1850, these *Mémoires* are his most lively work, the one that contributed most powerfully to perpetuate his influence on French poetic expression, imagination, and sensitivity from Flaubert and Renan to Maurice Barrès and Marcel Proust. This influence survived French Romanticism, of which, more than any other work, it had revived themes and style, enriched horizons, and shaped thought in several general areas—religious, poetic, and aesthetic.

Bibliography: *Oeuvres complètes,* 14 v. (Paris 1864–73); *Les Martyrs de Dioclétien,* ed. B. D'ANDLAU (Paris 1951); *Itinéraire de Paris à Jérusalem,* ed. E. MALAKIS, 2 v. (Baltimore 1946); *Journal de Jérusalem,* ed. G. MOULINIER and A. OUTREY (Paris 1950); *Les Aventures du dernier Abencérage,* ed. P. HAZARD and M. J. DURRY (Paris 1926); *Les Natchez,* ed. G. CHINARD (Baltimore 1932); *Mémoires d'outre-tombe,* ed. M. LEVAILLANT, 4 v. (Paris 1948). Various editions of correspondence, notably the *Lettres de Chateaubriand à Madame Récamier,* ed. E. BEAU DE LOMÉNIE (Paris 1929). C. A. SAINTE-BEUVE, *Chateaubriand et son groupe littéraire sous l'Empire,* 2 v. (Paris 1861). A. CASSAGNE, *La Vie politique de François de Chateaubriand* (Paris 1911). G. CHINARD, *L'Exotisme américain dans l'oeuvre de Chateaubriand* (Paris 1918). V. GIRAUD, *Le Christianisme de Chateaubriand,* 2 v. (Paris 1928). M. J. DURRY, *La Vieillesse de Chateaubriand, 1830–1848,* 2 v. (Paris 1933). P. MOREAU, *La Conversion de Chateaubriand* (Paris 1933); *Chateaubriand: L'Homme et l'oeuvre* (Paris 1956). M. LEVAILLANT, *Chateaubriand: Prince des songes* (Paris 1960). P. CHRISTOPHOROV, *Sur les Pas de Chateaubriand en exil* (Paris 1961). **Illustration credit:** Archives Photographiques, Paris.

[P. MOREAU]

CHATEL, FERDINAND TOUSSAINT,

French priest, founder of the *Église catholique française;* b. Gannat (Allier), Jan. 9, 1795; d. Paris, Feb. 13, 1857. Chatel, who came from a poor family, was ordained (1818) after seminary training under the Sulpicians. He served 3 years in parish work and then acted as a military chaplain until 1830. In that year he was reprimanded by the archbishop of Paris for unorthodox opinions expressed in periodical articles. In 1831 in Paris Chatel started his own sect, l'Église catholique française (French Catholic Church), which gained a limited following for a few years. It was redolent of *deism and *rationalism and abolished auricular confession, fasting, and clerical celibacy and substituted the vernacular for Latin in the liturgy. Chatel assumed the title "primate of the Gauls" after going through a ceremony of episcopal consecration performed by Bernard Fabré-Palaprat, who falsely claimed to be a bishop. Before long Abbé Auzou, one of the members, parted company with Chatel and took most of the members of the cult with him. Later differences led to further splinterings. The group's political radicalism caused the police to close the temple in Paris (1842). Chatel was imprisoned for a time and then fled to Belgium, but by 1843 he was back in Paris, where he agitated for the emancipation of women, divorce, and socialism. By the time of his death, unreconciled with the Church, Chatel was impoverished and almost alone.

Bibliography: E. MANGENOT, DTC 2.2:2339–50. R. LIMOUZIN-LAMOTHE, DictBiogFranc 8:784–785.

[L. P. MAHONEY]

CHAUCER, GEOFFREY

Greatest English poet of the Middle Ages; b. London, *c.* 1340–45; d. there, Oct. 25, 1400. From surviving official records, Chaucer would appear to have been a moderately successful public servant. He was bourgeois by birth, the descendant of a prosperous family long associated with London and the wine trade. The first records (1357) place him as a member of the household of Elizabeth, Countess of Ulster and wife of Lionel, third son of the reigning king, Edward III. Chaucer's father, John Chaucer, had already made a beginning in service to the crown, and the presence in a noble household of the son of a well-to-do bourgeois was not unusual during that period.

Life. The exact nature of Chaucer's early schooling is uncertain, but another form of his education is not. He accompanied the expedition to France in 1359, probably as a member of the company of Lionel, and was captured and ransomed. He probably rejoined the army and was present at the Peace of Brétigny (1360). The timing of Chaucer's military service is important, because the campaign of 1359 marked the turning point in English arms for his century. After the stunning defeats of Crécy (1346) and Poitiers (1356), French military policy consisted almost solely in refusal to give battle. The result was a devastated French countryside and a devastated English army. Little in what Chaucer had seen of war inclined him toward the profession of arms.

From 1360, when Chaucer is recorded as still in the service of Ulster, to 1366, when he received a safe-conduct for travel in Navarre—a document difficult to dissociate from the Black Prince's campaign of the following year—Chaucer's life is a blank. With the *Book of the Duchess,* however, Chaucer emerges as an accomplished and confident poet, well read in the polite French literature of the day. Since the most persuasive evidence one has from this period is precisely this poetic ability, the rather slightly founded theory that Chaucer was a favorite of Alice Perrers is not without some probability. Patronesses were not sparing in their demands for poetic tribute, and the court of Edward would have afforded the kind of reading with which Chaucer shows himself familiar. The composition of the numerous amatory lays he dimly remembers in the *Retraction* could most easily be assigned to this period. In addition there is the important evidence of the annuity of 20 marks granted Chaucer in 1367, by Edward III. Since the annuity specifically connects him with the household of Edward, rather than with that of Lionel, the theory of pragmatic poetical devotion to the highly pragmatic Alice seems not impossible.

Marriage. An advantageous marriage seems to have been one of the perquisites of an esquire attached to the court, and Chaucer's career in this respect parallels that of other esquires of the court. In 1366 or before, Chaucer married Philippa Roet, daughter of Sir Payne Roet, who had come to England with her younger sister Katherine in the entourage of Philippa of Hainault at the time of the latter's marriage to Edward III. If Chaucer's marriage is to be regarded as one of love, it conformed to the adage: it was not smooth. Chaucer's bride Philippa retained her position of attendant (*domicella*) upon Queen Philippa, just as her sister Katherine, who had from a very early age been attached to Blanche of Lancaster, retained her position in the Lancastrian household after her marriage to the short-lived Sir Hugh Swynford. In 1372, some 3 years after the death of the Queen (1369), Philippa joined her sister Katherine in the Lancastrian household, where Katherine's position was undoubtedly strengthened by the death, in the same year, of the Duchess Blanche, wife of John of Gaunt. It is certain that after the death of Blanche, Katherine Swynford was the acknowledged mistress of John of Gaunt, but at what point she became his mistress is uncertain. In any case, Philippa's attachment was to the Lancastrian household and Chaucer's to the King's. Because of this mutual and conflicting complex of loyalties and duties, it is likely that it was not until 1374, with Chaucer's appointment as Comptroller of Customs that Philippa and Geoffrey were able to set up something approaching a normal household. Even so connubial life must have been difficult, for Philippa did not abandon her connections with Lancaster, and Chaucer's diplomatic services were becoming increasingly in demand. Hence, perhaps, a certain absence of domesticity in Chaucer's self-portraits.

Italy and Humanism. The date of outstanding importance in Chaucer's intellectual life is 1372. Although it is possible that Chaucer could have gotten to Italy as early as 1368 or 1370, it is unquestionable that in 1372 he was appointed to a commission to treat with the Genoese regarding the establishment of a commercial center in an English port. Chaucer not only reached Genoa, but spent some time in Florence, almost certainly as negotiator for a much-needed loan to England. The mission is important in showing the trust that Chaucer enjoyed, but its real significance lies in the fact that from this journey dates Chaucer's knowledge of *Dante, *Boccaccio, and *Petrarch, and of Italian humanism in general. A second mission in 1378 must have deepened their impression on him.

The Public Servant. With rare exceptions, the remaining records reveal the vicissitudes of a public servant who wished to be a poet. In 1372 Philippa received a life pension of £10 from John of Gaunt, and in 1374 Chaucer received a like pension, but in terms indicating that it was Philippa's services, rather than his own, for which he was being rewarded. Chaucer's financial situation further improved in 1374, when he obtained the positions of Comptroller of Customs on wool and of the Petty Customs on wine, and on other merchandise in the Port of London. The difficulty was, however, that the duties of the Comptroller involved an independent audit of the Collectors' accounts, and therefore had to be kept in Chaucer's own hand. The position was lucrative, but hardly a sinecure. In addition, Chaucer was engaged in two diplomatic missions in 1377–78: the first probably concerning a projected French marriage for Richard II; the second, in regard to an attempt to gain military aid in Italy. However beneficial these activities may have been to Chaucer the man of affairs, they left little time for Chaucer the poet. In 1385 he successfully petitioned for leave to exercise his office through a permanent deputy. To what extent political factors affected his decision is uncertain. Henceforth, he resided in Kent.

One would wish that this well-timed withdrawal had led to a prolonged period of literary productivity, but absolute detachment from the world of affairs did not come easily to Chaucer. From 1385–89 he was a Justice of the Peace in Kent, and in 1386, Member of Parliament for Kent. In 1387, Philippa died, with the consequent loss to Chaucer of her royal and Lancastrian annuities. The extent to which Chaucer's finances were actually affected by this event is problematical, but it is clear that during this period he was involved in numerous law suits, mostly for debt, and that in 1388 he assigned both his exchequer annuities, probably for a cash sum. Public office seems again to have become a necessity. In 1389, he was appointed Clerk of the Works, a position he held until 1391. Possibly he resigned this demanding and hazardous task in favor of a less demanding one as subforester of the King's Park in North Petherton, Somersetshire, but the date of this latter appointment is highly uncertain. Further favors were forthcoming from Richard, but the poet seems nevertheless to have remained in difficult financial circumstances. The deposition of Richard II in 1399 could have been disastrous, entailing as it would the loss of these favors, but Richard's successor was Henry IV, son of John of Gaunt, who had both family and personal reasons for assisting Chaucer. Henry's actions were generous, and in 1399 Chaucer was able to take a lease on a house in the garden of St. Mary's Chapel, Westminster Abbey. The action seems singularly appropriate: Chaucer's withdrawal from the world shows an awareness of mortality characteristically medieval, while the length of the lease (53 years) suggests a characteristically Chaucerian optimism. Whatever kind of work he intended to write in his last years, the uninterrupted time to create, which throughout his life he had so earnestly sought, had finally come. Some 10 months later, he died.

Works. At the center of any consideration of Chaucer's works is the date 1372. Previous to his first Italian journey, Chaucer's sources had been French. After his return, it is obvious that he became an avid reader of Italian literature, especially of Boccaccio. Hence, he has in the past been said to have had a French, an Italian, and curiously enough, from the point of view of sources, an English (*Canterbury Tales*) period. More recently, influences have remained the basis for establishing Chaucer's periods of composition, but judgments as to maturity or lack of maturity of a poem have been allowed a greater scope. However, it is questionable whether the term "influence" is with Chaucer not more confusing than useful. For example, Chaucer may be said to have devoured Boccaccio's romances and meditated upon the philosophy of Boethius. In the *Knight's Tale,* the latter is imposed upon the former. Both are influences, but hardly of the same sort. Thus it has seemed preferable to abandon the conception of "influence" as an organizing principle and to consider the various periods of Chaucer's works in terms of those activities or attitudes that were sufficiently dominant during the various periods of his life to make division meaningful.

Court Poems (*1361?–80*). As noted above, Chaucer's earliest works were probably court poems of a rather simple variety. Although the invariable principles of court poetry were well established, what is interesting about Chaucer is a certain artistic waywardness. It was acceptable, if not obligatory, to translate the conventionalized process of enamorment in the first part of the *Roman de la Rose,* but the sexual naturalism of the second part, no matter how Christian and philosophic, was not acceptable to the court for which Chaucer wrote. It is known from the "Prologue" to the *Legend of Good Women* that Chaucer translated the objectionable second part, but of the acceptable first part no mention is here made. So well known were the allegorical personages of the Garden of Love in the *Roman de la Rose* that Chaucer could not have avoided making their acquaintance; yet he could, and did, avoid taking them seriously. The most one can say is that a part of a Middle English translation may be attributed to him (cf. *Roman de la Rose* with Chaucer's "Romaunt of the Rose" in *Works*).

When the Black Death of 1369 took from England one of its most beloved women, the Duchess Blanche of Lancaster, Chaucer seems to have been urged or commissioned to write an elegy, presumably as a consolation directed to her husband, John of Gaunt. This elegy, *The Book of the Duchess,* is a literary masterpiece, the finest of all his early poems. Blanche stands out as if alive in all her native beauty, goodness, and intelligence. Yet the poem bestowed upon its creator no immediate rewards—probably because its success depended upon the highly daring and unconventional device of introducing humor into an elegy. It is Chaucer's first-known use of the "persona," or mask, and in the *Book of the Duchess* its function is central; for it is the bemused stupidity of the persona-Chaucer that evokes from the Black Knight the lyrical praise of his departed lady, Blanche. But the stupidity of the oaf is humorous, and unconventional in an elegy. Almost as unconventional is the failure to present a vision of the subject of the elegy among the joys of heaven. In a complex way, which accepted the convention of the mistress as well as that of the wife, John of Gaunt was highly conventional, and Chaucer must have known it. Yet he refused to sacrifice his own personal vision of the earthly Blanche to a conventionally pious one.

The same is true of the incomplete *House of Fame.* It seems inescapable that the court poet was expected to prepare a romantic poem culminating in the announcement of a forthcoming wedding of no small consequence. But the poem prepared is pure parody—parody of Dante; parody of a second persona-Chaucer, the overfed and underrewarded servant of Venus; parody even of the set beginning of the metrical romance. Yet in the wildness and unevenness of the parody, as in the portrait of Geoffrey seeking to overcome the fatigue of the day in order to read yet another book, one senses not so much comedy, as a strongly implied appeal for relief from his customs duties, and for the opportunity to acquire the learning he considers necessary to the kind of poetry he wishes to write.

Philosophic Period (*1380–85*). Throughout his life Chaucer was never without an interest in ideas. In this brief period, however, one would judge that much of the reading he had been seeking to do had in fact been accomplished. The *Parlement of Foules* is an occasional poem (perhaps for St. Valentine's Day), cast in the familiar form of the love-debate. However, its questioning of the function of love in the universe, and its debating of the values of the various forms of love by a wide range of social classes, seem to indicate a philosophical interest both in an abstract concept and in its operation throughout society. Chaucer's most explicit philosophical venture, however, is his Herculean struggle to translate Boethius's *De consolatione philosophiae.* It must be kept in mind that the nonexistence of a philosophical vocabulary in English inevitably forced Chaucer into a heavily circumlocutional style, but, with the aid of a massive use of explanatory phrases, Chaucer, who left so much unfinished, indomitably struggled through. One may presume that the labor could not have been as painful as it would appear, for it is the Boethian view of the world that dominates *Troilus and Criseyde,* the most ambitious poem Chaucer ever completed. This story of a noble Trojan prince who finds his goddess in the beautiful and gentle Criseyde, who loves her with a love in which sheer adoration exceeds passion, yet is betrayed by her and gives his life for the loss of his love, has a magnitude and artistic perfection Chaucer never attained before or after. Yet it has a fault. It has to be read by human beings. The human being likes to believe in love, himself falls in love with the exquisite Criseyde, forgets the opening statement that flatly states Criseyde's ultimate falseness, and himself experiences the anguish of Troilus over an event he, as reader, has foreknown since the poem began. Nor can he, like Matthew Arnold in "Dover Beach," take refuge from the treacherous world in human love. It is precisely because Criseyde's love is human that it fails. Only God's love will betray no one.

At the end of the poem, Chaucer calls *Troilus and Criseyde* his "tragedye" (ed. Robinson, V, 1786). It is a ruthlessly logical working-out of the Boethian-Christian view of the nature of the world, and of the nature of the human soul. Chaucer has expressed the view with a completeness that leaves very little further to be said: its precision is almost too absolute. When Chaucer begs of God strength to create an undefined "comedye" (V, 1788), there is more than a suggestion that a kindlier, more complex, more expansive treatment of the phenomenon of human nature is forthcoming.

Canterbury Tales. "Chaucer," says Dryden, "must have been a man of a most wonderful comprehensive nature, because, as it has been truly observed of him, he has taken in the compass of his *Canterbury Tales* . . . the whole English nation, in his age. Not a single character has escaped him. All his Pilgrims are severally distinguished from each other" (Spurgeon, 1.278). Dryden's statement is important not only because it emphasizes the comprehensiveness of Chaucer's art, but because, by the phrase "severally distinguished," he points to Chaucer's method of imparting particularity to generality, a literary method perhaps drawn from the *substance and *accident of medieval philosophy. Thus the Miller and Reeve share the common acquisitive instincts of their class, but their physical and temperamental attributes are exact opposites. The comprehensiveness of class coverage was not an idea entirely new with Chaucer, but the matching of tale to teller, apparent as early as the first two tales of the Pilgrimage, was new, and remains sufficiently new to cause difficulties even for present-day readers.

The question inevitably arises: Why should a respected author like Chaucer include such "low" tales as those of the Reeve and the Miller? The answer would appear to be relatively simple. If Chaucer was to achieve the comprehensiveness for which he has been consistently praised, he had to include uncultured as well as cultured classes, and with them, the tales they might naturally be expected to tell. The Miller, drunk before the pilgrimage even begins, is not a likely narrator for a saint's legend. Furthermore, it cannot be overemphasized that in including such tales, Chaucer, dependent upon court favor, is activated by no profit motive. On the contrary, he knows the risk he is running, as is apparent from his remarks preceding these tales [I(A) 725; 3170]. For the court poet, profit lay in the forms of literature known to be in favor at court—romances, chronicles, moralities—certainly not the "vileinie" of the classes living close to the land. Characteristically, Chaucer took the chance of court disapproval, and in the high comedy of his so-called "low" tales, he demonstrates an artistic skill and, more important, an artistic conscience unequalled in his time.

Artistic Devices. Numerous devices are used in the *Canterbury Tales.* Two have already been mentioned—the breadth of class and attitude included, and the imposing of individual characteristics and attitudes upon those of the class. The latter technique at its best creates the illusion of immediate experience; the former—together with Chaucer's almost complete suppression of references to the events of his age—tends to remove the pilgrims from time and to make of them universal figures. A further device, related to both of the above, is that of the "persona" or mask. Behind his chosen mask—in the *Canterbury Tales* that of the ingenuous bourgeois—Chaucer withdraws from the stage and leaves it open for the dramatic interplay of the Pilgrims. It is one of the major contributions of modern criticism to have made a sharp distinction between this Pilgrim Chaucer, as much an artistic creation as any of his characters, and Chaucer, man and poet. The most extensive opportunity for failure to observe this distinction is offered by the *Prioress's Tale.* Even so reputable a historian as Cecil Roth believes that anti-Semitism had penetrated the soul of "gentle Geoffrey Chaucer," apparently because the *Prioress's Tale,* which he considers simply an imitation of the Hugh of Lincoln legend, is included in the *Canterbury Tales* [*History of the Jews in England* (3d ed. Oxford 1964) 57, 89].

However, it is not Chaucer, nor even the fictive Pilgrim Chaucer, who tells the tale. It is the Prioress. Like Browning's monk in the *Soliloquy in a Spanish Cloister*—with whose attitudes Browning himself seems customarily not to have been identified—the Prioress is an artistic creation, and it is her own attitudes and her own personality she is exposing. It is essential to observe that the Prioress's personality is plastic; she conveys no sense of the energy and vocation of the otherwise colorless Second Nun. It may be presumed that the Prioress was the younger daughter of a well-to-do bourgeois family, where one imitated both the manners and the customs of the nobility. One of the latter was to attempt the provision of adequate land and dower for elder children, and positions of distinction in the Church for younger. The Prioress has dutifully imitated polite manners, and this imitation she has brought with her into the cloister; but once inside the cloister, she has adopted the ideal of the cloister—the ideal of virginity, and its conception of virginity as involving participation in the Incarnation. Thus, she thinks of Christ as the infant Christ, and of Mary as mother [VII(B^2) 467]. In her tale, the principal figure is a "litel clergeon" who goes to a "litel scole" where he reads a "litel boke" (453, 495, 516). Furthermore, the "cursednesse" of the Jews when finally defined is that of Herod—the attempted murderer of Christ, and the actual murderer of the Holy Innocents, with which latter the "litel clergeon" is, in the Prioress's mind, associated (574, 566). It is important to realize that the Prioress has never seen a Jew—they were expelled from England in 1290—and that the death of "yonge" Hugh of Lincoln, mentioned as a recent outrage (686), happened about a century and a half earlier.

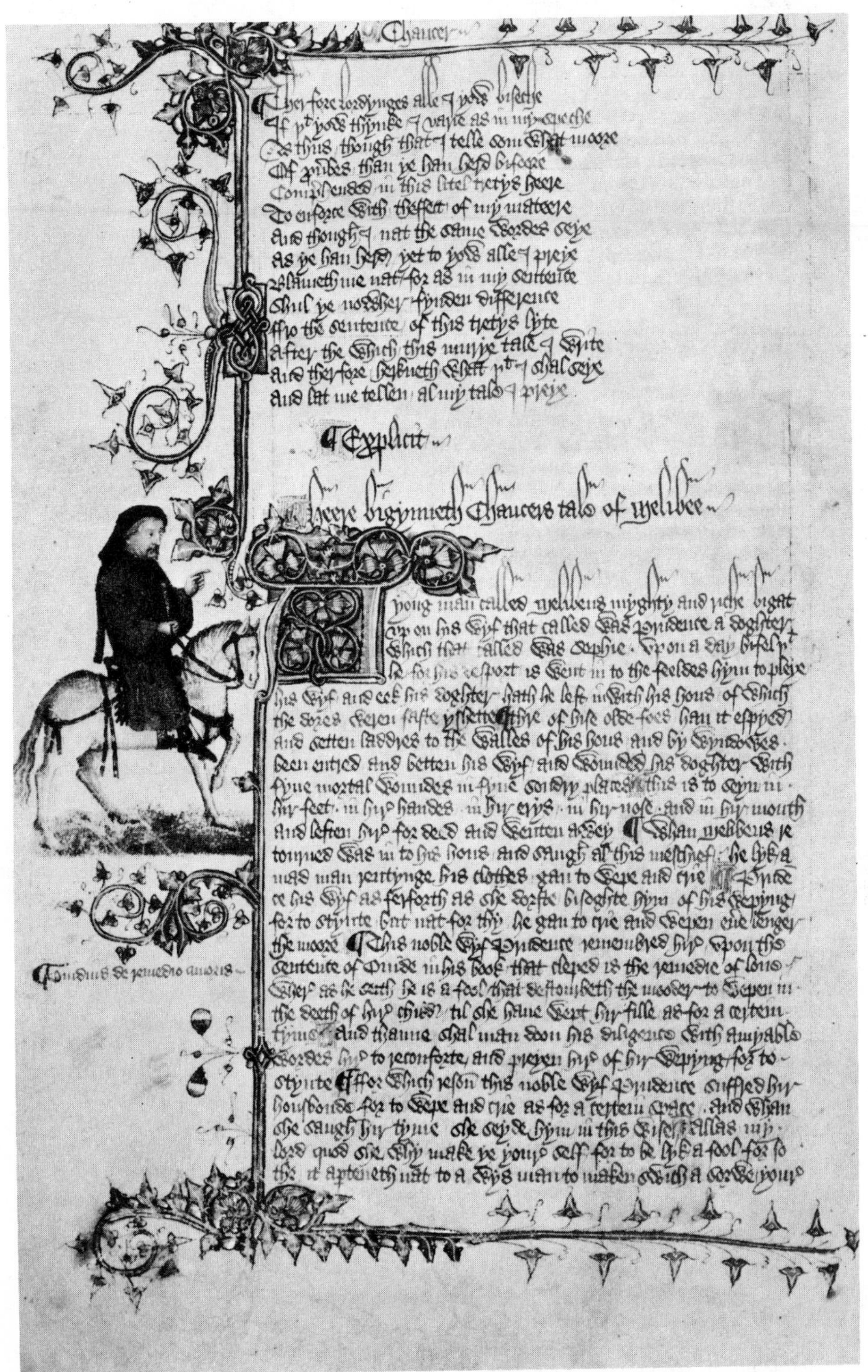

Fig. 1. Geoffrey Chaucer as a mounted pilgrim, miniature in a margin of the "Ellesmere Chaucer," a manuscript written in England c. 1400 (MS El.26.c.9).

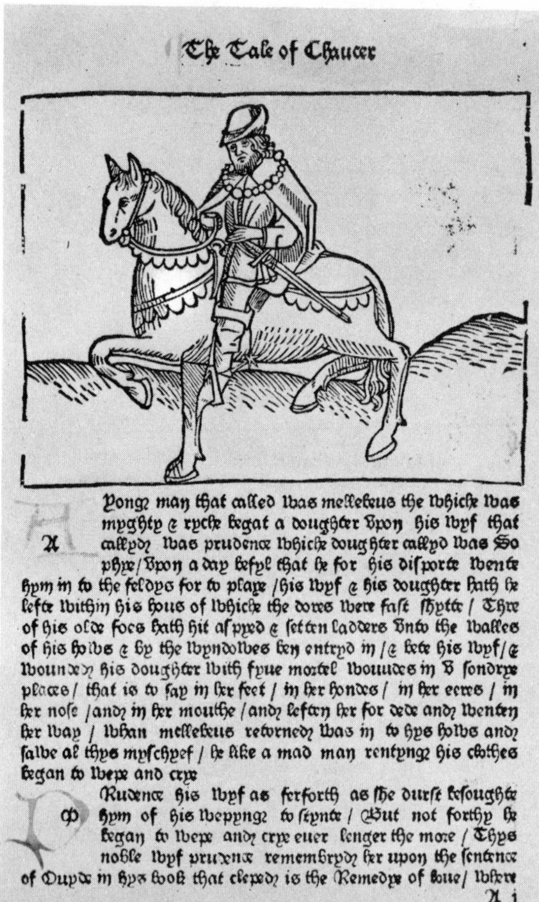

The Tale of Chaucer

A Yonge man that called was mellebeus the whiche was myghty & ryche begat a doughter vpon his wyf that callyd was prudence whiche doughter callyd was So phye/ Vpon a day befyl that he for his disporte wente hym in to the feldys for to playe /his wyf & his doughter hath he lefte within his hous of whiche the dores were fast shytte / Thre of his olde foes hath hit aspyed & setten ladders vnto the walles of his hows & by the wyndowes ben entryd in /& bete his wyf/& wounded his doughter with fyue mortel woundes in v sondrye places/ that is to say in her feet / in her hondes / in her eeres / in her nose /and in her mouthe /and leften her for dede and wenten her way / whan mellebeus retorned was in to hys hows and sawe al thys myschyef / he lyke a mad man rentyng his clothes began to wepe and crye

P Rudence his wyf as ferforth as she durst besoughte hym of his wepyng to stynte / But not forthy he began to wepe and crye euer lenger the more / Thys noble wyf prudence remembryd her vpon the sentence of Ouyde in hys book that cleped is the Remedye of loue/ where

A j

Fig. 2. Page from the first illustrated edition of Chaucer's "Canterbury Tales," published by William Caxton at Westminster in 1484.

Nevertheless, the Prioress is persuaded that the Jews are bad people and should therefore be executed like other bad people. Her description of the execution of the Jews, horrible though it is, actually contains only the rudest elemental basics—which anyone could have heard or read—of the fine and much appreciated art of execution. It is just as unlikely that the Prioress ever saw an actual execution as that she ever saw a Jew. One has no real basis for assuming that she would have felt less pain over the tearing apart of a human being than over the sufferings of a mouse. She simply loves what, in her position, it is conventional to love, and hates what it is conventional to hate—without any knowledge of either. What is really important is that her hate as well as her love are deferentially accepted by the Pilgrims. The *Prioress's Tale* is prophetic, in that it deals with an aspect of the problem of evil that mankind has met again and again, and is still far from solving. Chaucer, who broke his self-imposed silence on contemporary happenings to permit the Nun's Priest's satirical allusion to the mass murder of the Flemings [VII(B^2) 3397], is not a likely supporter of genocide, no matter how conventional.

Philosophy of the Tales. The preceding section has dealt with some of Chaucer's literary techniques and some of the misunderstandings to which they have given rise. At least one major question concerning the *Canterbury Tales* remains: Did Chaucer in his "comedye" have in mind any philosophical conception such as that which informed his "tragedye," *Troilus and Criseyde?* Or was he content simply to present a great panorama of human personalities and attitudes? The answer to this question is made difficult by the simple fact that Chaucer, at the time of his death, left the *Canterbury Tales* in a very incomplete state, so incomplete that even the order of the tales has furnished material for extensive controversy. Thus it has become customary, as in the present article, to cite the order of the generally authoritative Ellesmere Manuscript as I, II, III, etc; to include parenthetically (A, B^1, B^2, etc.) the order long ago created by the Chaucer Society to render consistent the geographical references in the *Tales;* and to return to the Ellesmere MS for line references. However neither order is devoid of objections, and much recent work has been devoted to establishing a definitive order (see Manly, Dempster, Pratt).

The *General Prologue,* however, is highly finished and might be expected to give some indication of the presence or absence of some unifying conception. At first glance, the pilgrims of the Prologue appear to be a highly world-oriented group—prosperous, concerned with the pleasures and profits of life. Furthermore, the company is dominated by the Host of the Tabard, Harry Bailly, whose plan, accepted by the pilgrims, would place the emphasis of the pilgrimage on the pleasure of exchanging stories and would make the climactic event not the arrival at Canterbury, but the return to London and the festive dinner at the Tabard. Yet among the worldly pilgrims there is a distinctly different group: the Knight, the Plowman, and the Parson. Rather interestingly, they represent the old feudal economy—the Knight, who protects Church and people; the Plowman, who provides material food; the Parson, who provides spiritual food. These three are old also in a deeper sense. None of them is materially motivated; each performs his feudal duty as a duty owed in a universe of which God is the author. It is evident that Chaucer intends to give this group positions of the highest dignity in the order of Tales. Although the *Plowman's Tale* is never told, the first of the tales is the Knight's, and the last, which is explicitly stated as knitting up the whole matter of the pilgrimage, is the Parson's.

Paradoxically, it is equally evident that the old are presented as pale and shadowy, while the new are burgeoning with color and energy. It is here that the extraordinary aptness of the pilgrimage fiction becomes evident. In its origin, the pilgrimage had been an act of piety carried out under great hardship and danger; by Chaucer's day, it had become generally, though not necessarily, more pleasurable than devotional. These two attitudes toward the pilgrimage correspond very closely with the attitudes of the worldly and unworldly pilgrims toward life. The central problem posed by Chaucer in the *Canterbury Tales* may possibly be stated thus: Is life in fact the traditional Christian pilgrimage through trial and temptation toward a future eternal city (Heb 11.13; 13.14); or is it a forward movement toward a new and better earthly city, a simple historical change in which an old set of values inevitably yields to a new? Or finally—an idea dear to the 14th-century humanist—are the temporal and eternal worlds not really antithetical, but in fact complementary, the logical movement from a lesser good to a greater good?

The "Marriage Group." If this problem is ever argued out, it is in the so-called "Marriage Group," comprising fragments III(D), IV(E), and V(F). The device of argumentation used in the Group is, of course, not new. It is a dramatic device used constantly; but only in the Marriage Group is the argument so carefully structured and the subject so consistently adhered to. The first speaker is Alice of Bath, Chaucer's greatest, because most lovingly wrought, personality. As she reveals herself, the Alice of the *General Prologue,* with her well-rewarded profession of wool weaving in a prosperous wool country, disappears: Alice is first and foremost a professional wife, the respectability of whose profession has been called into question. Alice's career has embraced five husbands, and she is seeking to continue that career with a sixth. However, someone has recently intimated to her that, according to authoritative scriptural (Jn 2.1) interpretation, her profession of multiple wifehood could be construed as a considerably less respectable one—and a sixth husband (Jn 4.18) as particularly compromising (*Sources and Analogues* 209).

Alice's counterarguments are revealing. To "auctorite," or "gloss," as she prefers to call it [III(D) 26, 119], Alice opposes the "express word" of Scripture (27, 61). Alice finds the gentle text "increase and multiply" (Gn 1.28) literally comprehensible, and she intimates that a careful literal reading of Christ's remarks about the Samaritan woman's five husbands would remove any opprobrium from her own career (19–20).

Fig. 3. Page from an illuminated manuscript of Chaucer's "Troilus and Criseyde," written in England in the first decade of the 15th century (Morgan MS 817, fol. 1).

Alice thus purports to discard the ancient allegorical in favor of the modern literal. However, she is more than slightly self-contradictory. She not only comically misreads on the literal level—as, for instance, that St. Paul (1 Cor 7.4) explicitly confers upon her the power to govern her husbands—but her completely perverted interpretation of 1 Cor 7.7 indicates that she not only does not reject the old allegorical and authoritarian, but seeks to place it on her own side in a fashion so ruthless as again to be comic. In accord with her position as practicing wife of Bath, her Prologue is a tale of the practical values of dominating husbands; but the tale itself is not one of experience. It is Arthurian, drawn, one is led to suppose, from the Arthurian lore surrounding Bath, where Arthur won perhaps his most famous victory.

The tale Alice tells is strikingly different from the *Prologue* in several respects. For one, although the tale accords superficially with Alice's customary theme of practicality and female dominance, there is none of the preoccupation with sex made so explicit in the *Prologue,* and the Hag, whose transformation into youth and beauty is the central event of Alice's story, lives happily ever after with a single husband. Finally, the Hag's discourse shows an awareness of the conflict of grace and sin (1173–76) that is quite surprising—until one recalls that, in her Prologue, Alice's lyrical praise of past sexual delight is accompanied by her outcry: "Alas! Alas! that evere love was sinne!" (614). Alice, like Bath, is an uneasy compound of new and old, and perhaps this is why Chaucer becomes progressively more deeply interested in her.

Though Alice has, almost unconsciously, revealed a sort of indefeasible Christian heritage, every pronouncement she has made concerning the inevitability of female dominance is heresy. The reader expects these pronouncements to be answered, but instead is carried away by two masterpieces of invective, the tales of the Friar and Summoner, in which each reveals the corrupt practices of the other. By the time the Clerk of Oxford has been called upon, the reader has rather forgotten Alice, but it is clear that the Clerk of Oxford has not. What the story of the Clerk does is to set up against the husband-crushing Alice the portrait of the humble, patient, loving Griselda, the medieval ideal of womanhood, whose perfection is reflected in her horror at remaining anything but a "widwe clene" (836). Before Alice can retort, the tale of the Merchant and the incomplete tale of the Squire intervene, widening the subject of the debate from marriage to love—the first questioning whether love is not in fact simply lust, and the second questioning (though fragmentarily presented) whether the ideal relationship is not *courtly love. The *Franklin's Tale,* which concludes the Group, seems at first glance a model of balance among the positions presented. It is old in that it insists on the basic rightness of the marriage relationship. It is new in that love, which marital constraint can never drive from Griselda, the Clerk's medieval ideal, is presented as something that vanishes at constraint—a "thing as any spirit free." Love within marriage is indeed dependent upon the virtue of patience, as the Clerk has maintained, but it is neither the patience demanded by Alice of her husbands, nor that demanded by the Clerk of the ideal wife—it is a mutual patience demanded as much of the husband as of the wife. The husband is to retain his realm of sovereignty in the world of affairs, but to the woman is accorded sovereignty in the realm of love.

Old and new seem neatly balanced in the *Prologue,* but what upsets the balance is the view of the nature of man expressed in the *Tale.* Medieval theology regarded human nature as corrupted by the Fall, and the manifestation of its flawed state as a certain likeness to him whose lies caused the Fall (Jn 7.44). Truth is an attribute of God; lying, a characteristic of man (Rom 3.4). In grace lay the only means to truth. Yet in the *Franklin's Tale* every man keeps to truth, and woman also—though the scene is pagan Brittany to which grace has yet to come. As in traditional Christian symbolism, woman (Emotion) needs the control of man (Reason), but in the *Tale* both man and woman are essentially good. If mankind is essentially good, then the ideal of the Knight and the raw energy of Alice of Bath have something in common. They are not really antithetical, but complementary. As humanity and its ideals progress, a progressively better world becomes possible. This is the highest point of Chaucer's humanism.

Religious Contrition (1399–1400). Chaucer's last works, the *Parson's Prologue and Tale* and the *Retraction,* are probably best understood in terms of the medieval attitude toward the activities proper to the ages of men. Traditionally, as the early years of one's life were devoted to action, the later and final were devoted to meditation and prayer. This was not only a theory but a practice. For those whose life had been letters itself, declining years posed a particular problem. Why had they not applied their talent to glorifying God, rather than to attracting the praises of men? Both Boccaccio and Petrarch had religious experiences that profoundly affected the nature of their last works. In England, the strictures of St. Paul on any form of writing not conducive to moral instruction had great currency, especially as stated in the opening of Rom 15.4: "All that is written is written for our instruction." One may find this passage cited in any number of explicitly devotional works, or even attached to works of doubtful moral content, such as Caxton's pious prologue to the *Morte Darthur.* The prevalence of Rom 15.4 is apparent also in the *Canterbury Tales.* When the Nun's Priest suddenly senses that pure comedy does not befit his calling and urges his listeners to seize the miniscule morality of his great satire, it is this same admonition of St. Paul that he quotes [VII(B²) 3441].

Chaucer too knew the passage and its meaning. In his *Retraction,* he states that his intention is in accord with St. Paul: "Al that is writen is writen for our doctrine" [X(I) 1083]. The grand comedy of his life is past, and he is eager to have his readers note his moral works but is unable to enumerate as many as he would wish. He therefore strives to add to the list of devotional works he has already composed or translated a relatively new type of religious work that was becoming very popular at the end of the 14th century. This was a kind of handbook containing an exposition at greater or lesser length of various matters of doctrine. Originally, these manuscripts had been written in Latin and were designed for use by the parish priest. Later they began to be written in English or translated into English, in part to aid the parish priest's Latin, but principally to meet the demand for works of piety and meditation that was rising within a society that was becoming increasingly literate.

Although Chaucer's *Parson's Tale* was almost certainly translated from Latin tractates designed for use within the Church, there can be little doubt that Chaucer intended it for the same audience as that of the rest of the *Tales.* He earnestly wished it to circulate with the other *Canterbury Tales* and to offset the effects he feared of some tales, as Boccaccio feared the effects of the *Decameron.* The *Parson's Tale* itself represents an apparently hasty and awkward attempt to incorporate an extensive treatise on the Seven Deadly Sins into a rather small one on penitence. However artistically inept it may be, the *Parson's Tale* does communicate, and what it communicates is Chaucer's uncompromising acceptance of medieval Christian doctrine. Heaven is worth striving for, as Chaucer is striving to complete the number of works he believes his calling as poet demands of him. Human nature is worth very little striving for. It is "roten and corrupt" (461). Salvation is not to be found in faith in humanity, any more than in poetic excellence. Art in and for itself has no standing. It is a talent in the scriptural sense (Mt 25.14), and Chaucer at the end of his life is much concerned with the use he has made of it.

Character and Accomplishment. Chaucer has traversed the whole span of human experience, and he ends as human as he began. One meets him first in the *Book of the Duchess* as a rebel against conventional religiosity; next as the philosopher-artist, inquiring in the *Parlement,* positive in *Troilus,* tentative again in the great debate of the *Canterbury Tales,* but strongly inclined toward a humanistic view of man and his relation to eternity; finally, like Petrarch and Boccaccio, ending his life very unsure of man and the world he inhabits, and very sure of the traditional religious beliefs of his age and the ages before him. Chaucer's powers of observation have never failed to be observed, nor the artistic mastery that transformed observation into character, and character into drama. However, it is perhaps not simply the great art he strove for and attained, but the passion for ideas—the ceaseless striving for a comprehension of the relationship of man to man and man to God—that enabled him to endow his characters and particularly the Canterbury pilgrims with so great a range of attitude that they seem humanity itself. It is true that humanity never changes, but neither does the search for ideas. Perhaps it is in this sense that one may understand Blake's marvelously simple statement: "Every age is a Canterbury Pilgrimage."

Bibliography: Editions. *Complete Works,* ed. W. W. SKEAT, 6 v. and suppl. (Oxford 1894–1900); ed. F. N. ROBINSON (2d ed. Boston 1957); *Poetry,* ed. E. T. DONALDSON (New York 1957); *Major Poetry,* ed. A. C. BAUGH (New York 1963); *Text of the Canterbury Tales,* ed. J. M. MANLY and E. RICKERT, 8 v. (Chicago 1940); *Canterbury Tales,* ed. R. D. FRENCH (New York 1948); *Book of Troilus and Criseyde,* ed. R. K. ROOT (Princeton 1926).

Criticism. G. L. KITTREDGE, *Chaucer and His Poetry* (Cambridge, Mass. 1915). N. COGHILL, *The Poet Chaucer* (New York 1949). J. S. TATLOCK, *Mind and Art of Chaucer* (Syracuse 1950). D. BETHURUM, ed., *Critical Approaches to Medieval Literature* (New York 1960). R. SCHOECK and J. TAYLOR, eds., *Chaucer Criticism,* 2 v. (Notre Dame 1960–61). W. W. LAWRENCE, *Chaucer and the Canterbury Tales* (New York 1950). E. T. DONALDSON, essays in D. BETHURUM and R. SCHOECK, *op. cit.* W. F. BRYAN and G. DEMPSTER, eds., *Sources and Analogues of Chaucer's Canterbury Tales* (Chicago 1941). G. DEMPSTER, "Manly's Conception of the Early History of the *Canterbury Tales,*"

PMLA 61 (1946) 379–415. R. A. PRATT, "Order of the *Canterbury Tales*," PMLA 66 (1951) 1147–67. R. K. GORDON, *Story of Troilus* (London 1934). A. DENOMY, "Two Moralities of Chaucer's *Troilus and Criseyde*," *Transactions of the Royal Society of Canada,* ser. 3, v.44.2 (1950) 35–46. R. A. PRATT, "Note on Chaucer's Lollius," *Modern Language Notes* 65 (1950) 183–187.

Literary and other relationships. C. S. LEWIS, *The Allegory of Love: A Study in Medieval Tradition* (Oxford 1936). W. A. PANTIN, *The English Church in the Fourteenth Century* (Cambridge, Eng. 1955). W. FARNHAM, *Medieval Heritage of Elizabethan Tragedy* (Berkeley 1936; repr. Oxford 1956). C. F. SPURGEON, *Five Hundred Years of Criticism and Allusion,* 3 v. (Cambridge, Eng. 1925). C. MUSCATINE, *Chaucer and the French Tradition* (Berkeley 1957). R. D. FRENCH, *Chaucer Handbook* (2d ed. New York 1947). R. S. LOOMIS, *A Mirror of Chaucer's World* (Princeton 1965). M. M. CROW and C. C. OLSON, *Chaucer: Life-Records* (Oxford 1966). **Illustration credits:** Fig. 1, The Huntington Library, San Marino, California. Figs. 2 and 3, The Pierpont Morgan Library, New York.

[A. L. KELLOGG]

CHAUMONT, HENRI, ascetical theologian and spiritual director; b. Paris, Dec. 11, 1838; d. Paris, May 15, 1896. While attending the seminary of Saint-Sulpice in Paris, Chaumont studied constantly the works of St. *Francis de Sales and after his ordination in 1864 made the teaching and spirit of the bishop of Geneva the basis of his preaching and direction. His major work, *Directions spirituelles de Saint François de Sales,* (Paris 1870–79), a series of small treatises, proved tremendously successful, and Chaumont was soon in constant demand as a preacher and spiritual director. He founded three societies dedicated to St. Francis de Sales, which had as their chief objective the sanctification of their members within the framework of their particular ways of life. The women's organization, founded in 1872 with the co-operation of Mme. Carré de Malberg, grew rapidly and soon included many of the highest social class. The society of priests, begun in 1876, to which that of the laymen was soon amalgamated, spread more slowly; but it proved very effective in instilling in the diocesan clergy the spirit of Francis de Sales, and within a few years it numbered in its ranks the elite of the French clergy. For all three groups Chaumont provided spiritual direction by a priest of the society; a carefully worked-out method of probation during which a regular plan of meditations, readings, and religious exercises was followed; and spiritual reading lists, monthly meetings, and the study of the works of Francis de Sales, which helped to maintain a high level of spirituality. The diocesan groups are autonomous, but a director general and a general council elected by the total membership preserve unity within the organization.

Bibliography: H. DEBOUT, DictSpirAscMyst 2:813–818; *Le Chanoine Henri Chaumont et la sanctification du prêtre* (Paris 1930). A. LAVEILLE, *L'Abbé Henri Chaumont, fondateur des trois sociétés salésiennes* (Tours 1919). S. HECQUET, *Catholicisme* 2:1029–30.

[M. J. BARRY]

CHAUNDLER, THOMAS, Oxford scholar, early English humanist; b. Wells, Somerset, England, *c.* 1417; d. Nov. 2, 1490. He was educated at William of *Wykeham's two foundations, being admitted to *Winchester in 1431 and going on to New College, *Oxford, in 1435. He was ordained in 1444 and became a doctor of theology in 1455. In 1450 he left Oxford on being appointed warden of Winchester, but he returned in 1454 on his election as warden of New College. He was chancellor of Oxford from 1457 to 1461 and from 1472 to 1479. From 1450 he enjoyed the patronage of several bishops, notably Thomas *Bekynton of Bath and Wells. Chaundler resigned the wardenship in 1479, probably when he entered royal service. Shortly after his presentation to the deanery of the cathedral of *Hereford by Edward IV in 1482, Chaundler described himself as a councilor of the King and dean of the chapel in the royal household. Chaundler had an important part in the introduction of *humanism into England. His own attempts to write like a humanist are deplorable; his style shows Ciceronian influence but the themes of his few surviving writings are typically medieval. Hitherto, however, appreciation of the literary revolution in Italy had been confined to a small number of clerics whose employment by the government gave them Italian contacts; but Chaundler, as a prominent figure in the university, helped to bring an interest in polite letters into scholastic circles.

Bibliography: M. R. JAMES, ed., *The Chaundler MSS* (London 1916). R. WEISS, *Humanism in England during the 15th Century* (2d ed. Oxford 1957). Emden 1:398–399.

[R. L. STOREY]

CHAUTARD, JEAN BAPTISTE, reformed Cistercian abbot, ascetical theologian, and writer; b. Briançon, March 12, 1858; d. Sept-Fons, near Moulins, Sept. 29, 1935. Chautard entered the Trappist monastery at Aiguebelle, near Valence, at the age of 19. In 1897 he was elected abbot of Chambarand, near Grenoble, and 2 years later abbot of Sept-Fons, a position that he held until his death. In addition to the heavy spiritual and temporal responsibilities of his own monastery, Chautard had the direction and control of several other monasteries of the order. In 1903 he pleaded so well before the senate and G. Clemenceau the cause of the Trappist communities threatened with dissolution that the government reversed its decision and the order was allowed to continue in France. A man of action with little time for writing, Chautard exercised his great influence within the monastery by his daily conferences to his monks and outside by his tremendous correspondence. Among his various writings he is noted particularly for *L'Âme de tout apostolat* (1910, numerous editions and translations). This book, written without regard for style, but filled with the fire of Chautard's spirit, became immensely popular at once. Its great success in spite of its austere tone proved the value of Chautard's central theme that to be fruitful in the ministry of souls one must lead a truly interior life and keep close contact with God. Chautard based his teaching on the Rule of St. Benedict and the writings of St. Bernard. The means that he recommended for a fruitful apostolate are those of these two great masters of the spiritual life: personal prayer, full liturgical life, and self-renunciation.

Bibliography: Abbaye de Sept-Fons, *Dom-Jean-Baptiste Chautard, Abbé de Sept-Fons* (Paris 1937). E. MAIRE, *Images de dom Chautard, abbé de Sept-Fons* (Paris 1938). M. GODEFROY, Dict SpirAscMyst 2:818–820. M. B. BRARD, *Catholicisme* 2:1030.

[M. J. BARRY]

CHAUTAUQUA MOVEMENT

An educational program in the U.S. that influenced American religion and popular culture. In August 1874 Rev. John Heyl Vincent, a Methodist Sunday school superintendent and pastor in Illinois, summoned the first Chautauqua Assembly as a summer training school for Sunday school teachers at Fair Point on Lake Chautauqua, N.Y. During the first assembly, a call was issued for the first conference of the Women's Christian Temperance Union (WCTU), thereafter closely linked with Chautauqua. The assembly was projected as an annual event thereafter; and in 1876, in addition to the training course for Sunday school teachers, a scientific conference, a temperance conference, varied lectures, a music festival, and concerts were added to the summer program. In 1878 Vincent and his associates devised the Chautauqua Literary and Scientific Circle to provide a reading course equivalent to a college education to any interested person. Kate Fisher Kimball directed the program from 1878 to 1917. Members read J. R. Green's *Short History of the English People,* J. P. Mahaffy's *Old Greek Life,* and general works on English literature, astronomy, and psychology. Under the plan, local circles were formed for discussion, and eventually a 4-year reading course was set up. By 1887 the circle boasted 80,000 enrolled members, and the enrollment increased to more than 100,000 by 1891.

Soon after establishing the assembly at Chautauqua Lake, Vincent developed similar assemblies at Lakeside, Ohio; Lake Bluff, Ill. (1877); and Round Lake, N.Y. (1878). Numerous others followed the Chautauqua pattern, notably the Bay View Assembly on Lake Michigan with a similar reading circle, begun by John M. Hall (1876), and the Kansas Chautauqua Assembly, begun (1878) by Jesse L. Hurlbut and Rev. J. E. Gilbert. There was a Chautauqua at Pacific Grove, Calif., by 1879, but the influence of the daughter assemblies never equaled that of the parent assembly. In 1879 the Chautauqua Normal School of Languages was established. After 1880 regular debates between national figures became a feature of the assemblies, and readings by well-known authors were common. In 1885 the institution was chartered by the State of New York as Chautauqua University and added a School of Journalism (1890), School of Fine Arts (1896), and a School of Sacred Literature (1897). A year later the charter lapsed, but the educational work continued. The *Chautauquan Magazine,* founded in 1880, reached an enormous circulation; and the extension programs and adult education efforts were developed at the University of Chicago, Ill., by William R. Harper, a member (since 1883) of the staff of the Fair Point university.

Although formal educational efforts declined, the summer assembly, addressed by statesmen and educators, and the reading circle grew in popularity and were more widely imitated. The Epworth League, an outgrowth of Vincent's youth organization at Fair Point, multiplied Chautauquas after 1890; and individuals developed others, both separately and as chains. The problem of bringing eminent lecturers to so many assemblies was solved by the formation of lecture circuits, such as the Western Federation of Chautauquas (1897) and the International Chautauqua Alliance (1899). A further development was the Chautauqua week program, which brought a varied program of informative lecturers and entertainment to small towns across the U.S. This innovation, introduced (1904) by Keith Vawter of the Redpath Lyceum Bureau, was taken up by other firms. With World War I the circuit Chautauqua began to decline and practically disappeared in the postwar years.

Bibliography: J. E. Gould, *The Chautauqua Movement* (New York 1961). H. P. Harrison, *Culture under Canvas* (New York 1958). L. H. Vincent, *John Heyl Vincent* (New York 1925). T. W. Goodspeed, *William Rainey Harper* (Chicago 1928). J. H. Vincent, *The Chautauqua Movement* (Boston 1886). J. L. Hurlbut, *The Story of Chautauqua* (New York 1921). H. A. Orchard, *Fifty Years of Chautauquas* (Cedar Rapids 1923). L. J. Wells, *History of the Music Festival at Chautauqua Institution from 1874 to 1957* (Washington 1958).

[R. K. MAC MASTER]

CHAUVEAU, PIERRE JOSEPH OLIVIER, Canadian author and public official; b. Quebec City, Canada, May 30, 1820; d. there, April 4, 1890. He was the son of Charles and Marie Louise (Roy) Chauveau. After education at the Quebec Seminary, he was called to the bar of Lower Canada in 1841 (queen's counsel 1853). He represented Quebec County in the Legislative Assembly of Canada (1844–55) and in the Canadian House of Commons and the Legislative Assembly of Quebec (1867–73). In the Hincks-Morin administration, he served as solicitor general for Lower Canada (1851–53) and provincial secretary (1853–55), resigning in 1855 to become superintendent of public instruction in Lower Canada. During his tenure he founded the *Journal of Public Instruction,* published in French and English (1857–79). Normal schools were established and separate schools created in Lower Canada (1863). In 1865 he traveled abroad to study the European public school system. In 1867 he became the first premier of Quebec, holding the additional portfolios of education and provincial secretary, which offices he resigned on his appointment to the Senate in 1873. A year later he married Marie Louise Flore Massé; they had two sons and six daughters. In 1878 he was appointed professor of Roman law at Laval University, Quebec, where he later served as dean. Chauveau was prominent also as an orator and author. He was honored with an LL.D. from McGill University and a D.C.L. from Laval. He was at various times president of the Quebec Literary and Historical Society, the Royal Society of Canada, the Institut Canadien of Quebec, and the Institut Canadien Français of Montreal. His writings include poems, novels, and essays on politics and education. His poetry was collected in *Le Répertoire National* (4 v. 1848–50). His outstanding novel was *Charles Guérin, roman de moeurs canadiennes* (Montreal 1852). He published also a study of education in Lower Canada (1876), a life of François Xavier Garneau (1883), and *Souvenirs et Légendes* (1877). His history of the Universities of Laval, McGill, and Toronto appeared serially in his *Journal of Public Instruction.*

Bibliography: L. O. David, *Biographies et Portraits* (Montreal 1876); *Mes Contemporains* (Montreal 1894).

[J. T. FLYNN]

CHAVARA, KURIACKOS ELIAS, founder and first superior general of the Syro-Malabar Carmelites and a pioneer figure in the Catholic Press in India; b. Kainakary, Kerala State, India, 1805; d. Coonemmavu, Kerala State, Jan. 3, 1871. Ordained in 1829, he founded an institute, which was canonically erected as a Carmelite congregation in 1855, when he was confirmed as its superior. He was appointed vicar-general of the Vicariate Apostolic of Verapoly in 1861. Two printing presses set up by early Portuguese missionaries to Kerala in South India had disappeared, and in 1844 Chavara determined to reactivate this apostolate. Designing his own press and using type made by a local blacksmith, he was able in a few years to send to the Congregation of the Propagation of the Faith in Rome copies of 10 published books mainly devotional and catechetical. He also edited the liturgical books of the Syro-Malabar rite. In 1887 the press he founded first issued *Deepika,* now the oldest daily paper in Malayalam, and in 1902 the *Flower of Carmel,* the most widely circulated Catholic magazine in Kerala. In 1963 the Church in Kerala maintained some 20 publishing establishments issuing 4 Catholic dailies, 12 weeklies or monthlies, and a great volume of other Catholic literature. The diocesan process for Chavara's beatification was inaugurated by the archbishop of Changanacherry on Jan. 3, 1958.

See also CATHOLIC PRESS WORLD SURVEY, 13.

[F. MAURILIUS]

CHAVES DE LA ROSA, PEDRO JOSÉ, Spanish bishop and reformer; b. Cádiz, Spain, June 27, 1740; d. there, Oct. 26, 1821. He went to Peru as bishop-elect of Arequipa and was consecrated in Lima on Jan. 23, 1788. When he took over the diocese, it was in a state of neglect and decadence, but he was prompt in launching a major reform, which, although it caused him serious difficulty, was one of the most successful in the history of Peru. He had the special virtue of carrying out his duties with a clear vision of the future at a crucial moment for Latin America. The buildings, discipline, and curriculum of his seminary he restored in accordance with the latest standards of the time; there he prepared a generation of men whom he infused with the desire for reform. These men played an outstanding role in politics, education, and religion during the first years of the republic. Chaves de la Rosa's progressive and firm determination was not well understood by those who should have been his closest collaborators. Vexed at encountering opposition from his own chapter, the clergy, and some religious orders, he sent his resignation to the pope, who accepted it on Aug. 9, 1805. Upon his return to Spain in 1809, he participated in some sessions of the cortes of Cádiz, which honored him with various titles. In 1813 he was appointed Patriarch of the Indies, but 2 years later he resigned this honor also. Just before he died he donated his library to the seminary of Arequipa and the rest of his possessions to the orphan asylum he founded in his episcopal city, which still exists as the Instituto Chaves de la Rosa.

Bibliography: M. DE MENDIBURU, *Diccionario histórico-biográfico del Perú,* 11 v. (2d ed. Lima 1931–34) 4:344–346. R. VARGAS UGARTE, *Historia de la Iglesia en el Perú,* 4 v. (Lima 1953–62).

[E. T. BARTRA]

CHÁVEZ, DENNIS, U.S. Senator; b. Los Chávez, N.Mex., April 8, 1888; d. Washington, D.C., Nov. 18, 1962. He had to discontinue grammar school because of family need, but by reading and night-school work, he earned an engineering degree for employment with the city of Albuquerque. After his marriage in 1911, he was employed as a senatorial clerk, took up the study of law, and received his degree (1920) from Georgetown University, Washington, D.C. He then served a term in the New Mexico Legislature, where he sponsored the first bill for free school textbooks. Elected in 1930 and 1932 to the U.S. House of Representatives, he became chairman of the Indian Affairs Committee. In 1935 he was appointed to fill out the term of U.S. Senator Cutting. Reelected for four consecutive terms, he became the third-ranking member of the powerful Appropriations Committee and chairman or member of several of its important subcommittees, through which he consistently upheld national defense and the development of national resources. The rights of all minorities, in particular the welfare and full citizenship of Indians, were his prime concern, as were also the rights of veterans. He fought hard for every labor bill and all measures benefiting small farmers and civil service employees. While not rabidly anticommunistic, he helped to prevent the lifting of an arms embargo during the Spanish Civil War, and years later he opposed aid to Yugoslavia while it was being withheld from Spain. He helped formulate the Good Neighbor policy, secured legislation for completion of the inter-American highway, and in many other ways created goodwill with the Latin American countries, later receiving the highest decorations from the Panamanian and Mexican governments. In 1963 he was awarded, posthumously, the Reserve Officers Association's citation for one "who had contributed most to national security in our times." Among the national figures attending the funeral Mass in Albuquerque was his close friend, Lyndon B. Johnson, then U.S. Vice President, who gave the graveside eulogy. The 1963 Legislature selected him to represent New Mexico in National Statuary Hall.

[A. CHAVEZ]

CHEATING, here understood to mean the use of fraud or deceit, or the violation of the rules of honesty, as, for example, in competitive games and examinations.

In amateur sports of a competitive type there is a tacit agreement on the part of the competitors to observe the rules of the game. Otherwise the whole purpose of the game is defeated, except in that kind of play in which the attempt to circumvent the rules is considered a part of the fun. Normally, therefore, cheating involves what fault there is in the violation of an agreement of this kind. The agreement would rarely be considered to involve a serious commitment on the part of the competitors, and consequently its violation would not be gravely sinful. This is not to say, however, that it is a matter of little consequence, for attitudes and tendencies can be developed by resort to petty dishonesty that can lead to graver offenses.

In professional sports there are frequently explicit standards of behavior required of the competitors. Because of the advantages to be gained by success, there is also an unexpressed agreement to follow the rules. It would be dishonest to break the rules, to resort to unfair practices, or to make an unjust attempt to control the score, especially when money is wagered on the outcome. A violation of rules if aimed at or seen as resulting in monetary loss to another would seem to be an offense against commutative justice.

The acceptance of admission to an educational institution includes a tacit promise to abide by the rules of the school. One can assume that there is a rule against cheating in examinations and in performing assignments, even if it is not explicitly mentioned. Cheating not only interferes with the proper operation of the grading system, which is considered essential to the educational process, but also with competition, which is a normal motivational device used by educators. Cheating also puts the honest student at an unfair disadvantage.

In some types of examination there is also a specific monetary advantage involved for those who succeed with special distinction, e.g., a civil service examination, examinations for scholarships, etc. In such situations an element of commutative justice is involved, and one who succeeds by unfair means deprives another of a valuable consideration. Cheating in these circumstances is not only a grave sin but could also involve an obligation to make restitution to the party or parties injured by the dishonesty.

Some educational institutions dispense with procedures of policing examinations and put the students on their honor not to cheat. The honor system as such does not add to the moral obligation of following the rules of the school, unless the students in accepting the system are understood to bind themselves by a special, though implicit, promise to abstain from cheating.

[J. D. FEARON]

CHECA Y BARBA, JOSÉ IGNACIO, archbishop of Quito; b. Quito, Aug. 4, 1829; d. there, March 30, 1877. The son of Col. Feliciano Checa, one of the founders of Ecuadorean independence, he studied in Quito and in Rome. He was ordained in 1855, and he was named auxiliary bishop of Cuenca in 1861, bishop of Ibarra in 1866, and archbishop of Quito in 1868. Of a quiet and studious nature, Checa y Barba labored throughout his life to raise the spiritual and intellectual level of his clergy. He convoked the second and third councils of Quito, as well as two diocesan synods. His pastorals were noted for their calm charitable tone. He brought the Daughters of Charity and the Vincentians to Ecuador. On March 25, 1874, he led the official consecration of Ecuador to the Sacred Heart, even though his relations with Pres. *García Moreno were not particularly warm.

The manner of his death has made Checa y Barba memorable. García Moreno had been assassinated on Aug. 6, 1875. His immediate successor was Borrero, a Catholic liberal. He in turn was overthrown on Sept. 8, 1876, by Gen. Ignacio Veintemilla, a liberal who got firm support from *El Comercio,* a Guayaguil newspaper. In February 1877 the bishop of Riobamba, José Ignacio Ordoñez, censured this paper for its heretical attacks on the Church. Checa y Barba stood with his suffragan when the government objected. On March 1, 1877, Father Gago, a Franciscan, preached to a large gathering in the church of San Francisco on the Syllabus of Errors of Pius IX and on Liberalism. Spies carried the news to Veintemilla, who inspired the police to try to arrest the friar. When Gago protested against the attempt, stating that he was just practicing some of the freedom of thought so highly praised by the Liberals, the bungling, puzzled police captain withdrew to consult his superiors. By the time they arrived, the rumor that the friars were to be expelled had brought about 6,000 people to the church, so that soldiers were called to save the police. The Liberals cried that the clergy had stirred up the people and took occasion from the police stupidity to subject all sermons to complete censorship. On March 7, Checa y Barba, who in the past had tended to remain aloof from all quarrels with the government, protested against this measure as unjust and uncalled for. The protest was rejected. On March 10 the archbishop issued a pastoral warning the faithful against heretical publications. This time the government protested (March 12). Checa y Barba answered in a note of March 17, in which he refused to give to Caesar what did not belong to Caesar. A visit from Veintemilla on March 24 failed to change the archbishop's mind. On Good Friday (March 30) after consuming the Host during the Mass of the Presanctified, the archbishop took some wine to purify the chalice. At the time he remarked to the deacon on the bitter taste. He completed the services but died amid horrible convulsions a short while after. The autopsy revealed that he had been poisoned by strychnine. No one was ever punished for the crime.

José Ignacio Checa y Barba.

Bibliography: J. TOBAR DONOSO, *El Ilmo. Sr. Dr. José Ignacio Checa* (Quito 1937).

[W. LOOR]

CHEFFONTAINES, CHRISTOPHE DE, theologian; b. near Saint-Pol-de-Léon, Brittany, 1512; d. Rome, May 26, 1595. He was born to the noble Breton family Penfentenyou, joined the Franciscan Observants in 1532 at Cuburien, near Morlaix, and studied in Paris. In both preaching and writing he quickly became a powerful adversary of the Huguenots. After having been guardian at Cuburien and provincial of Brittany in 1565, he was elected minister general of his order (1571–79). This was a critical period in the history of the Franciscan Observants, for the triumph of Protestantism in northern Europe had inspired a move toward independence among religious of weakened fervor. In accordance with Pius V's (d. 1572) program of reform, Cheffontaines dedicated his 8 years as general to visiting the houses of his order with the hope of leading his confreres back to a better observance of the religious spirit. Upon the expiration of his term of office as minister general in 1579, he was named auxiliary bishop of Sens. His theological activity was considerable. So vigorous was his opposition to the errors of the day, that he fell into error himself or at least came close to it. The novelty of some of his opinions caused him to be denounced at Rome. Three of his works were put on the Index, while the rest were prohibited until corrected. His principal work, *Deffence de la foi de nos ancêtres* (Paris 1570), concerned the Eucharistic Presence.

Bibliography: E. D'ALENÇON, DTC 2.2:2352–53. É. LONGPRÉ, *Catholicisme* 2:1032–33. A. PIOLANTI, EncCatt 3:1404–05.

[J. CAMBELL]

CHELIDONIA, ST., virgin and recluse; d. Subiaco, Oct. 13, 1152 (feast, Oct. 13). All information on Chelidonia (the forms of the name as Cledonia or Cledona are incorrect) is based on the vita composed by Guglielmo Capisacchi, a monk of *Subiaco who was professed in 1525 and who completed the chronicle of Subiaco to the year 1573. He claims that he used an early anonymous vita, but he is the sole authority for its existence. According to his vita, Chelidonia was a virgin and anchoress. She received the veil in the Church of St. Scholastica, and became an abbess in a convent near Subiaco. She returned, however, to her life as a recluse. She was distinguished for her virtues, prophecies, and miracles. In 1578 her remains were deposited in a shrine under the altar of the Blessed Virgin in the abbey church of Subiaco.

Bibliography: ActSS Oct. 6:362–377. Zimmermann KalBen 3:177. J. BAUR, LexThK² 2:1042.

[M. R. P. MC GUIRE]

CHELLES, CONVENT OF, former royal Benedictine abbey, in the canton of Lagny, arrondissement of Meaux (Seine-et-Marne), France; in the old Diocese of Paris, modern Meaux (Latin, *Calae*). It was founded in 656 by Queen *Bathildis; its first abbess was *Bertilla, who came with nuns from *Jouarre-en-Brie (658–659), a foundation following the rule of St. *Columban. Chelles was a double *monastery and represented a step in the progress of Columbian monasticism into Burgundy. The abbey early attracted many young women from England; its scriptorium was notable. Having become Benedictine, it was often ruled by Carolingian princesses; after being plundered by the *Normans, it was restored. St. Elizabeth Rose (d. 1130) was professed a religious there. Reforms in the 12th and 14th centuries culminated in the reform of *Fontevrault (1498–1500), which Chelles, with its 90 nuns, had in large part propagated. In 1543, however, its abbesses began once again to be appointed for life. Chelles was suppressed in 1792; only vestiges of the cloister, some tombstones, and several buildings bought by private individuals remain.

Bibliography: Cottineau 1:753–755. R. VAN DOREN, DHGE 12:604–605. R. GAZEAU, *Catholicisme* 2:1033–35. Lowe CodLat Antiq 6:xxi–xxii. B. BISCHOFF, "Die Kölner Nonnenhandschriften und . . . Chelles," *Karolingische und Ottonische Kunst*, v.3 of *Forschungen zur Kunstgeschichte und christlichen Archäologie* (Baden-Baden 1952–) 395–411.

[H. TARDIF]

CHEMICAL BINDING

In N. Bohr's original (1913) paper on the hydrogen atom there is a now-forgotten discussion of chemical binding. This attempt to understand the combination of atoms to form molecules in terms of the basic postulates of the Bohr theory was singularly unsuccessful. It was recognized very early that chemical binding depends on the electrons in the outermost shell of the atom, and that neither the *nucleus nor the filled inner shells are of much importance for understanding how atoms combine to form molecules. The full understanding of chemical binding, however, could come only after the development of *quantum mechanics.

There are several different kinds of chemical binding, and between the different kinds all possible intermediate stages occur. For purposes of classification, however, the decisive criterion is whether a molecule in dissociating splits up into neutral atoms, or into ions, i.e., into atoms which have gained or lost electrons and hence are negatively or positively charged.

Ionic Binding. Here the molecule breaks up into charged ions on dissociating. The extreme case of this is when the atoms are charged even in the molecule. Thus in sodium chloride, NaCl, the atoms occur as Na^+ and Cl^-, and it is the electrostatic attraction between these charged ions that holds the molecule together. This type of binding can be understood on the basis of the classical physics of the 19th century combined with the insights of the Bohr theory into the electronic configuration of atoms. The sodium atom has one electron outside the closed-shell neon structure, while the chlorine atom has one electron missing from a closed-shell argon structure. Since closed-shell structures are particularly stable and hence of lower energy, the sodium atom loses one electron to the chlorine atom and the resulting $Na^+ Cl^-$ molecule has a lower energy than the two separated atoms. Hence a stable molecule held together by an ionic or electrostatic bond is formed.

Atomic Binding. Here the molecule dissociates into neutral atoms. Classical electrostatics cannot explain this type of binding, and quantum mechanics is needed. Several subclasses may be distinguished.

The Covalent or Homopolar Bond. This is the type of bond which holds together homonuclear diatomic molecules like H_2, O_2, and N_2, in which the binding is obviously not electrostatic. The first successful description of this type of bond came in 1927 in a paper by W. Heitler (1904–) and F. London (1900–54) on the H_2 molecule. They showed that the homopolar bond depends on the fact that electrons are indistinguishable one from the other. Thus in the hydrogen molecule there is one electron on each atom, but if the two atoms are close enough together it becomes impossible to know which electron is associated with which nucleus, for according to Heisenberg's *uncertainty principle the electrons cannot be located too precisely in space without imparting to them sufficient energy to knock them completely out of the molecule. As a result the equations describing the hydrogen molecule allow each electron to spend part of its time on one nucleus, part on the other. This "exchange" process leads to a lowering of the energy of the combined atoms relative to the isolated atoms and hence to a stable molecule. G. N. Lewis (1875–1946) pointed out in 1923 that homopolar binding is often associated with the existence of an electron pair, and quantum mechanics has confirmed the fact that two electrons with spins paired off (one up, one down) give rise to a stable structure similar to that resulting from closed shells in atoms. For this reason the molecule He_2 does not exist in nature, for the two electrons in each helium atom already are in closed shells with their spins paired off. Hence the two isolated atoms are very stable and do not combine to form a molecule. This is true of all rare gas atoms. The pairing off of electron spins is characteristic of the homopolar bond, and it is for this reason that molecules with an odd number of electrons are a great rarity in nature.

The Metallic Bond. The existence of metals cannot be explained by the types of binding dealt with thus far. Metals are composed of a solid symmetric lattice of positive ions with a large number of electrons free to move through the crystal. These electrons stabilize

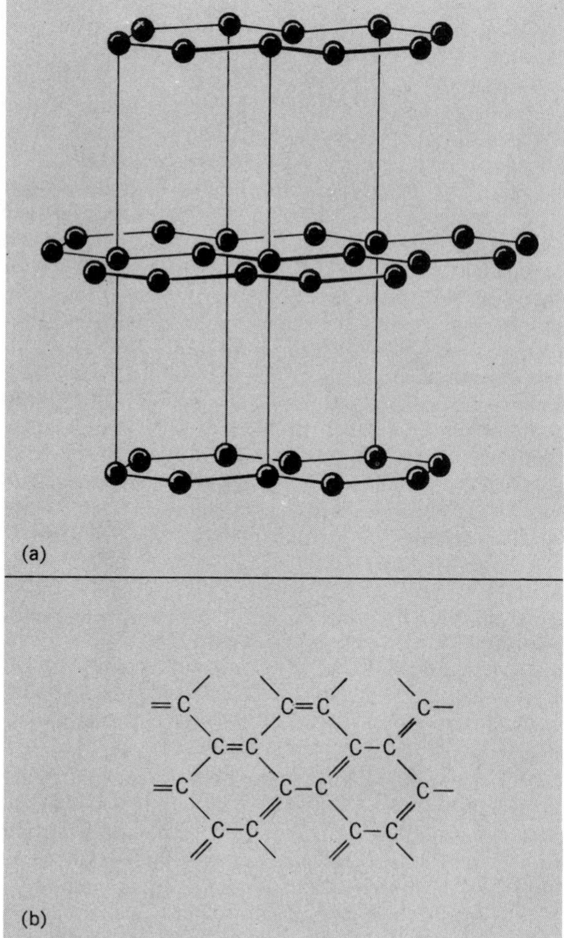

(a) The arrangement of carbon atoms in a graphite crystal. The crystal consists of hexagonal layers of molecules separated by so large a distance (3.40A) that there can be no covalent bonds between them; each layer is a giant molecule and adjacent layers are held together by weak Van der Waals forces. (b) Binding in a graphite layer.

the structure by lowering its energy, and are the carriers responsible for the large electrical and thermal conductivities exhibited by metals.

Other Types of Atomic Binding. The binding in unsaturated hydrocarbons, the hydrogen bond, and Van der Waal's forces leading to long-range, weak bindings, all of somewhat less importance, are well understood at least qualitatively in terms of quantum mechanics.

Present-day theories of the binding of atoms in molecules are able to predict not merely whether a molecule will exist in nature, but what its approximate size and shape will be. A consideration of the electronic structure of the atoms involved (more exactly, of the quantum mechanical wave functions describing the electrons) leads to a basic understanding of the reason why, for example, H_2O is triangular in shape, while NH_3 assumes the form of a pyramid. Since the molecular symmetry can be precisely determined by infrared, Raman, and microwave spectroscopy, this affords a critical test of theories of chemical binding. Comparison of theory and experiment shows the essential correctness of the present-day theories of the structure of molecules, but also indicates that most molecules are too complicated to allow precise quantitative calculation of their basic properties.

The chemical and physical properties of atoms and molecules are determined principally by the outer-shell electrons. Atoms like the rare gases with completely filled outer shells are ordinarily chemically inert, and are affected by neither electric nor magnetic fields. Recent work (1962) by Bartlett showed, however, that xenon would form a compound with platinum hexafluoride. Intensive work in the Argonne Laboratory has confirmed this finding with the production of xenon fluorides. The nature of the bonding involving rare gases is under study. The alkali atoms that make up the first column of the *periodic table, on the other hand, have one electron outside closed shells. This electron easily forms bonds with other elements and hence the alkalis are chemically very active. In addition the alkalis form molecules in which the electron is displaced with respect to the center of nuclear charge, and this leads to strongly polar bonds and to large electric dipole moments. The fact that the spin of the outermost electron in the alkalis is unpaired with any opposite spin leads also to a magnetic dipole moment for the isolated atom. Much the same can be said about the halogen atoms, but here the properties are a result of a "hole," or electron deficiency, in the outermost shell, instead of the presence of one electron outside closed shells.

In this way it is possible to go through the periodic table and predict many of the chemical, electrical, magnetic, and spectroscopic properties of atoms and molecules solely on the basis of their electronic structures. The valence of an atom, for example, is directly related to the number of electrons (or holes) which it has in its outer electron shell, for this indicates the number of electron-pair bonds it can form. There are exceptions, of course, but even the exceptions can also be understood in the light of refinements of the theory. Thus the fact that the oxygen molecule is paramagnetic (i.e., has a net positive magnetic moment) was not understood for many years. It is now known that the paramagnetism is due to the way the electrons on the two oxygen atoms pair off in forming the molecule. They do it in such a way that the two outermost electrons have unpaired or parallel spins, and the molecule is hence paramagnetic.

The Structure of Solids. Large assemblages of atoms and molecules can exist in either the gaseous, the liquid, or the solid state, depending on the pressure and temperature of the system. Thus at atmospheric pressure nitrogen is a gas at ordinary temperatures, but liquifies below −195.8°C, and solidifies below −209.9°C. The properties of gases are determined by the structure of the individual molecules involved and by the statistical behavior of the very large number of molecules involved. This is well understood in terms of the *kinetic theory of gases and *statistical physics (*see* MATTER, STRUCTURE OF). Liquids are much less well understood than either gases or solids, for liquids lack both the simplicity of the gas phase and the high symmetry of the solid phase, which make theoretical calculations practical.

The physics of the solid state is in a very active state of development at the present time. Solids can be divided into three classes depending on their electrical conductivity. Metals have extremely large electrical conductivities; insulators have extremely small conductivities; and semiconductors have intermediate values of the conductivity. If the binding of the crystal is metallic, then there are free electrons capable of moving through the crystal lattice and carrying an electric current. This is the case with silver, copper, gold, and the other good conductors. If all electrons are tightly fixed in bonds between atoms, then there are no electrons free to carry the electrical current through the lattice. This results in insulators such as sulfur and diamond, which latter substance is composed entirely of carbon atoms in a particular lattice arrangement. Insulators are therefore analogous to rare-gas atoms and to molecules in which all the valencies are saturated, whereas metals are similar to atoms with incomplete shells and to unsaturated molecules.

Semiconductors are solids with electrical conductivities in the range between those of metals and of good insulators. The concentration of electrons free to carry electric current increases with temperature in semiconductors, but the number of free electrons always remains small compared to the number in metals. In intrinsic semiconductors the free electrons (or holes) are created by temperature excitation; in impurity semiconductors the presence of impurities in the lattice provides the electrons (or holes) to carry the electric current.

The behavior of semiconducting materials can be understood in terms of the so-called band theory of solids. In solids the interactions between the atoms broaden the energy levels of the individual atoms into bands. In metals the two highest energy bands, usually called the valence and the conduction band, overlap, and hence are both partially empty. As a result electrons can easily change their energy states in the conduction band, which means that they can move freely through the crystal. In insulators, on the other hand, there is a large gap between the valence and the conduction band, and the valence band is completely filled (i.e., the valencies are completely saturated), the conduction band completely empty. Hence it takes a great deal of energy to excite an electron to the conduction band where it can conduct current. In intrinsic semiconductors the band gap is quite small and electrons can be excited from the valence band to the conduction band by heating the crystal. This produces free electrons in the conduction band, and holes in the valence band. These holes behave like positive charges, and conduction in intrinsic semiconductors is due both to electrons and to holes. In impurity semiconductors foreign atoms that replace some of the lattice atoms are responsible for the conductivity. Thus the silicon crystal is formed from atoms in the fourth column of the periodic table, and the four valence electrons of each silicon atom combine with four electrons from the four neighboring silicons in electron-pair bonds. Hence the silicon valencies are all completely saturated. If phosphorus atoms are introduced as impurities into the silicon lattice, the fifth of the five phosphorus valence electrons is free to move through the crystal and electrical conductivity results. Semiconductors doped with electron-excess impurities are called *n* type, and the phosphorus atoms are called donors, since they give up electrons to the lattice. Atoms from the third column of the periodic table (gallium, indium), when introduced into the silicon lattice, produce electron-holes in the lattice and these conduct the current. These are called *p*-type semiconductors, and the impurity atoms are called acceptors.

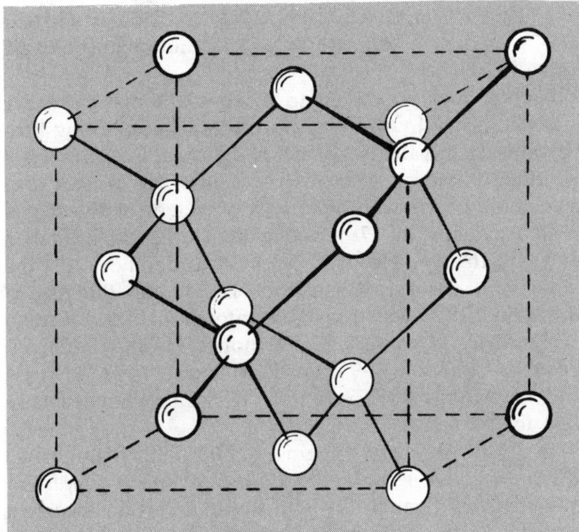

The arrangement of the carbon atoms in a diamond crystal. Each atom has four near neighbors, which are arranged about it at the corners of a regular tetrahedron.

The most important semiconductors are the two group-four elements, silicon and germanium, and a great deal of effort has gone into obtaining these crystals with extremely high purities (less than 1 part in 10^{10} of impurities) and then doping them with impurities for the particular application desired.

Bibliography: G. N. LEWIS, *Valence and the Structure of Atoms and Molecules* (New York 1923). L. PAULING, *The Nature of the Chemical Bond, and the Structure of Molecules and Crystals* (3d ed. New York 1960). F. SEITZ, *The Modern Theory of Solids* (New York 1940); *The Physics of Metals* (New York 1943). J. C. SLATER, *Quantum Theory of Atomic Structure,* 2 v. (New York 1960); *Electronic Structure of Molecules,* v.1 of *Quantum Theory of Molecules and Solids* (New York 1963–).

[J. F. MULLIGAN]

CHEMISTRY

The science which deals with the composition of substances and the transformations they undergo. Chemistry developed into a true science only in modern times, but its origins lie much earlier in the pseudo-science of *alchemy. The present article begins with (1) the history of chemistry, and reviews the present state of three of its branches: (2) inorganic, (3) organic, and (4) physical chemistry.

1. HISTORY OF CHEMISTRY

By 1700 chemistry had made considerable progress toward evolving as a science. It had been enriched by a great amount of practical working knowledge of metals and alkalis, natural products, and gases and liquids of many kinds. Moreover, serious attempts had been made to reduce this mass of miscellaneous information to some kind of system. Though the principles underlying this systematization were not always correct, they were at least rational and a long way removed from the alchemical blind alleys that were often followed during earlier centuries.

Pioneers. The emergence of chemistry as a modern science owed much to the clearsightedness of Robert *Boyle, who has been rightly called the father of modern chemistry. Boyle was the first to formulate our modern concept of elements (or "principles" as he called them) as simple bodies of which compounds are composed and into which these compounds can ultimately be resolved.

As a result of the writings of Boyle and his contemporaries, it became obvious that the old hypotheses as to the nature of matter were inaccurate. An example is the phlogiston theory, which assumed that matter contained a combustible principle. When a substance was burned, it "lost" the combustible principle or phlogiston. An early proponent of this theory was Johann Joachim Becher (1635–82), whose theories were expanded by George Ernest Stahl (1660–1734). In effect, Stahl inverted the true theory of combustion and calcination, for adding phlogiston was really removing oxygen, and removing phlogiston was adding oxygen.

Prominent during the phlogiston phase of chemistry was the Swedish scientist Carl Wilhelm Scheele (1742–86). He was the first to isolate the element chlorine and was an independent discoverer of oxygen, ammonia, and hydrochloric acid, as well as a variety of organic acids and other compounds. Joseph Black (1728–99), of Dublin and later of Edinburgh, who discovered "fixed air," or carbon dioxide, and Henry Cavendish (1731–1810), an Englishman, who discovered "inflammable air," or hydrogen, were important pioneers in the evolution of modern chemistry. Joseph *Priestley, who was born in England and died in America, collected and prepared oxygen gas for the first time. He called it "dephlogisticated air" in line with the prevailing concept of combustion.

It was the French scientist Antoine Laurent *Lavoisier who finally took the experimental facts of his predecessors and exploded the false notion of phlogiston. In a classical series of experiments he proved that burning was in fact oxidation, or a combination of a metal with a *principle oxigine* (oxygen) from the air.

Fig. 1. Carl Wilhelm Scheele.

From this he developed the concept that all mineral acid anhydrides consist of different bases united with oxygen. Lavoisier was responsible also for the important discovery that respiration (the oxygen and carbon dioxide exchange in the body) was a chemical reaction similar to combustion.

Lavoisier's many chemical experiments using exact weights gradually brought about a recognition that com-

Fig. 2. Joseph Louis Gay-Lussac.

bining ratios were constant; for example, that specific but dissimilar *weights* of hydrogen and oxygen were involved in combining these gases to form water. However, when Cavendish sparked hydrogen and oxygen to produce water in 1783, he had noted that the *volumes* of the two gases involved were always identical.

Lavoisier, working with other French chemists, introduced a new nomenclature (1787); his textbook, *Traité Élémentaire de Chimie* (1789), systematizing the new theory was rapidly adopted. Lavoisier's work on the analysis of organic substances by combustion in oxygen laid the foundations of quantitative organic analysis. His death on the guillotine in 1794 ended a brilliant career, still full of promise.

Though much of the credit for introducing the quantitative method into chemistry belongs to Lavoisier, the experiments of Black, Cavendish, T. Bergman (1735–84), C. F. Wenzel (1740–93), J. B. Richter (1762–1807), and R. Kirwan (1733–1812) must not be overlooked.

Richter had attempted to bring mathematical order into chemistry by drawing up tables of combining proportions (equivalents) of acids and bases. Another set of quantitative experiences on combining proportions was made by Kirwan, who was president of the Royal Irish Academy in 1799 and a man of great brilliance and originality. He was at first a defender of the phlogiston theory. When his "Essay on Phlogiston" (London 1787) was translated into French and refuted in detail by Lavoisier, C. Berthollet (1748–1822), A. Fourcroy (1755–1809), G. de Morveau (1737–1816), and G. Monge (1746–1818), Kirwan became a convert to the newer ideas.

In 1789 William Higgins (1763–1825) published *A Comparative View of the Phlogistic and Antiphlogistic Theories.* Though this still favored certain incorrect aspects of the phlogiston hypothesis, it put forward some interesting speculations on the way in which chemical combinations of "particles" occur. John *Dalton took this reasoning considerably further in his atomic theory in 1808. Dalton was the first to understand that chemical elements are composed of very minute particles or atoms. These basic particles of a particular element are identical to each other in every way including weight. Different elements have atoms of different weights. Each element is characterized by the weight of its individual atom. The weight ratios in which atoms combined were therefore constant.

While Dalton's theory did much to explain equivalent weights (the specific and actual weight ratios involved in the combining of particles of different elements), it still left unanswered the question of the straight one-to-one ratios in which certain gases combined. The French chemist J. L. Gay-Lussac (1778–1850) suggested that the reason was that all gases occupied the same volume, no matter what the weights of their individual atoms. With the aid of the German scientist A. von Humboldt (1769–1859), Gay-Lussac developed volume ratios for a whole series of chemical compounds, including ammonia, hydrochloric acid, nitrous and nitric oxides, and sulfur dioxide. The ratios were always simple and often implied equal volumes for different atoms.

There were some flaws in this reasoning, as Dalton pointed out. When one volume of nitrogen combined with one volume of oxygen, two volumes of nitric oxide resulted. In other words, here was a gas that apparently occupied twice the volume of the other gases.

However, A. *Avogadro of Turin in 1811 (and *Ampère independently in 1814) overcame the difficulty by supposing that the atoms of some (but not all) gases went about in pairs. In other words, there might be "molecules" of elements as well as of compounds.

The next milestone in chemical history was the verification by Humphry *Davy of Lavoisier's prediction of the existence of the alkali metals. In 1807 Davy announced the decomposition of potash by electricity to yield potassium and of caustic soda to yield sodium. He soon obtained electrolytically the alkaline earth metals magnesium, calcium, strontium, and barium.

Fig. 3. Humphry Davy, portrait after Thomas Lawrence.

Fig. 4. Friedrich Wöhler.

Davy's researches laid the foundation of electrochemistry and of the association of chemical affinity with electrical charges. Even more important, Davy redressed the balance of Lavoisier's overestimate of the central position of oxygen by showing that the essential element in an acid is hydrogen and not oxygen.

Then, as chemistry attracted more attention and new facts came to light at a fast pace, J. J. *Berzelius, one of the greatest figures in the science, came on the scene. In a few short years, almost singlehandedly and with exceptional skill and accuracy, he determined the atomic weight of every known element and the composition of many compounds. He established Dalton's atomic theory on a sound footing and substituted for Dalton's hieroglyphic symbols the letters still used for the elements.

The Development of Organic Chemistry. While the chemistry of the metals and basic elements, such as sulfur, phosphorus, and nitrogen, was well established by the early 19th century, the chemistry of carbon compounds (organic chemistry) was still poorly understood at that time.

Carbon chemistry in 1800 was usually thought of as vegetable chemistry (sugar, acids, gum, indigo, sap, and plant extracts) or animal chemistry (gelatin, albumin, fibrin, urea, body fluids). While it was known that all these materials contained carbon and hydrogen (and sometimes oxygen, nitrogen, and sulfur), few definite chemical substances had been isolated or identified from either plant or animal materials. However, the French chemists A. Fourcroy and L. *Vauquelin had examined several so-called "proximate principles" of animal and vegetable matter (sugar, gum, and camphor, which can be extracted by solvents or other simple methods) and had discovered such new substances as pectin (1790) and daphnin (1812). These organic materials could not usually be crystallized; consequently purification and accurate analysis of them were very difficult in comparison with inorganic materials, which could be analyzed more easily.

As late as 1835 Friedrich Wöhler (1800–82) wrote to Berzelius that "organic chemistry appears to me like a primeval forest of the tropics." However, by that date, the work of Berzelius and others had already established

Fig. 5. Justus von Liebig.

that the laws of chemical combination applied in the organic area as well as in that of inorganic metals and salts.

M. E. Chevreul investigated the makeup of oils and fats and of vegetable colors. Through improved methods of analysis, he showed clearly that the formation of soaps from fats and alkali (saponification) was chemically akin to the formation of inorganic salts from mineral acids and alkalis.

Justus von Liebig (1803–73), one of the giants of organic chemistry, clearly established through his extensive researches on a wide variety of organic substances that organic compounds were often constructed of building blocks (called radicals) where certain elements were always present in the same proportions. Probably the best known such building block is the ethyl radical (C_2H_5), which Liebig recognized in 1834 as a component of alcohol, ether, and muriatic ether. Von Liebig, though German-born, studied in Gay-Lussac's laboratory in Paris before becoming professor in Giessen in 1824. The Giessen school became world famous during his 28-year tenure there and was one of the first in the world where practical instruction in chemistry was systematically given.

Von Liebig contributed extensive experimental work and made accurate analyses of many organic compounds. Besides his analytical inventions, he rendered valuable service to agriculture by introducing mineral fertilizers and also did important work in physiological chemistry by analyzing fats and body fluids. He was also the founder of *Annalen der Pharmacie,* which later became *Annalen der Chemie,* one of the world's greatest scientific journals.

A close associate of Liebig was Wöhler, who was professor at Göttingen from 1836 to 1882. Among his notable experiments was one in which he synthesized urea in the laboratory. Urea, previously considered as a natural product, was prepared by him from ammonium cyanate, an inorganic salt.

Von Liebig's radical theory of organic structure was supported by the classical research of R. W. *Bunsen, Wöhler's successor at Göttingen, and remembered today primarily in the laboratory heating device that is known as the Bunsen burner.

It is not possible to give in detail here the subsequent theoretical advances in organic chemistry, including the development of the theory of substitution and of the nucleus and type theories. Some mention should be made, however, of A. W. von Hofmann (1818–92), who did valuable work on organic nitrogen compounds and was an eminent teacher in both London (1845) and Berlin (1865). Notable also was S. *Cannizzaro, professor in various Italian universities, who explained how the atomic weight of an element may be found by applying Avogadro's hypothesis supplemented by the law of atomic heats. Organic chemists know him best for his production of derivatives from benzaldehyde by treatment with potash (the Cannizzaro reaction).

Modern organic chemistry owes much, too, to August Kekulé (1829–96), professor in Ghent and later in Bonn, who discovered that each atom had a definite combining power and that certain organic chemicals contained closed-ring structures, so that the carbon atoms are linked together to form a whole array of compounds.

Kekulé's theory of atomic linkage gave chemists an almost limitless number of possible arrangements of carbon atoms in straight or branched chains or in rings with intermediate links that could also form part of closed-ring structures. These possibilities chemists explored without delay in two ways. First, they tried to build up new complex molecules in the laboratory. Second, they tried to break down complex natural chemicals to find their structure and then reassemble them in the laboratory.

Among the great, almost accidental discoveries of chemistry was that of the coal-tar dyes by William Henry Perkin (1838–1907) in 1856 at the Royal College in London. Perkin, trying to synthesize quinine (useful in the treatment of malaria), was cleaning a brown mess from a reaction vessel with alcohol when he noticed a purple solution that yielded dark crystals. The material was aniline blue, the first synthetic dye, which eventually became highly popular in Paris under the name of mauve or mauveine. From this accidental discovery the modern dye industry had its beginning.

Toward the end of this fascinating era of organic chemistry it was recognized simultaneously by J. *van't Hoff and A. Le Bel (1847–1930) that account would have to be taken of atoms arranged in three-dimensional structures. Kekulé had recognized this, but he had thought that physics, not chemistry, would reveal the actual structure of these large molecules.

*Pasteur in 1845 had already shown from the rotation of the plane of polarized light passing through tartaric acid solutions that either left-handed or right-handed molecules were possible. Van't Hoff and Le Bel showed that this was due to the presence of carbon atoms combined with four different groups that could be arranged spatially in right- or left-handed forms. Besides, the arrangement of the atoms in space could account for a number of unexplained properties. Since that time stereochemistry, or the arrangement of atoms in space, has been an important branch of organic chemistry.

Atomic Weights. In 1815 and 1816 William Prout (1785–1850), a London physician, had suggested that atomic weights of all elements were exact multiples of

Fig. 6. Sir William Henry Perkin, by A. S. Cope, 1906.

that of hydrogen and that hydrogen was the primary substance, or first matter.

However, later work on the accurate determination of atomic weights by E. Turner (1796–1837), J. B. *Dumas, J. Marignac (1817–94), and especially J. S. Stas (1813–91) indicated that these were not always whole numbers. Chlorine, for instance, gave a figure of 35.46. This seemed to give the lie to Prout's hypothesis.

As the volume of chemical facts continued to grow with the isolation of new elements and of such complicated materials as the phosphoric acids with their acid salts and hydrates, existing structural theories were proving far from adequate. Scientists sought for some clear scheme or pattern of the elemental organization that would systematize existing knowledge.

In 1817 and 1829 J. W. Döbereiner (1780–1849), professor in Jena and the chemistry teacher of Goethe, had noted that in certain groups of three elements (e.g., calcium, strontium, and barium) the atomic weight of the middle element was approximately the mean of the first and third.

A little later, J. A. Newlands, a London industrial chemist, drew up a table of the elements arranged in order of atomic weights and noted that "the eighth element, starting from a given one, is a kind of repetition of the first, like the eighth note in an octave of music." He called this the law of octaves.

Almost simultaneously in 1869 J. L. Meyer (1830–95) in Germany and D. I. *Mendeleev in Russia put forward the periodic law stating "the properties of the elements are in periodic dependence upon their atomic weights" (*see* PERIODIC TABLE).

The periodic law made clear some previously unsuspected analogies among the elements and stimulated the study of inorganic chemistry. Notable work was done in the inorganic field by H. Roscoe (1833–1915) in Manchester, B. Brauner (1855–1935) in Prague, and H. Moissan (1852–1907) in Paris (who first synthesized diamonds in the electric furnace). Knowledge of inorganic chemistry was extended also by the work of William Crookes (1832–1919), who discovered thallium (one of the rare earths), and William Ramsay (1852–1916), who collaborated with Lord *Rayleigh in the discovery of argon in 1894. Although the atmosphere had been analyzed by many chemists, it had not been recognized that it contained over 1 per cent of an inert component. This was later identified as containing several other unsuspected elements.

The 12 atomic weights Stas had established in the 1860s were considered the last word in accuracy until almost the end of the century. But in 1894 Theodore William Richards (1868–1928), a notable American chemist who had been offered but had turned down a chair at Göttingen to remain at Harvard, noticed an apparent error in Stas's chlorine figure.

Richards found that the chloride and bromide of metals were more suitable than the oxides for atomic weight determinations. Over a 20-year period he and his students determined and corrected the atomic weights of 28 different elements. For this work he received the Nobel prize in 1914, the first American chemist so honored.

Industrial Chemistry. The change in production of industrial chemicals from 1800 to 1900 was striking. Whereas they had been prepared by hand in laboratory quantities in 1800, most of the widely used heavy chemicals were major tonnage items of high purity and at low prices by 1900. Typical of the growth of the chemical industry in that period was the alkali industry. In the late 18th century the difference between the two fixed alkalis, sodium and potassium carbonates, was known. The sodium salt, termed barilla, was made chiefly from ashes of seaweed, whereas the potassium salt, potash, was made from ashes of land plants. At the time potash dominated the alkali picture, for it was cheaper and more readily available than barilla. However, the demand for alkali for making soap and glass was constantly rising, and the burning of wood promised only a limited supply of potash, so chemists turned their attention to common salt, present in almost inexhaustable amounts, to yield in some way large quantities of soda ash.

The French government in 1775 offered a prize of 2,400 livres for the making of artificial soda from common salt. The offer stimulated research not only in France but also in England and other countries. Jean Claude de la Métherie (1743–1817) proposed to ignite sodium sulfate with coal and extract carbonate from the product.

La Métherie's impractical process suggested to Nicholas Leblanc (1742–1806), about 1787, the real solution of the problem, and a plant was built at Saint-Denis in France under the patronage of the Duke of Orléans. In Leblanc's process salt is treated with sulfuric acid to produce sodium sulfate, which is roasted with calcium carbonate and coal to produce "black ash" from which soda ash is washed out with water. Leblanc's plant did well until 1793, when the Duke of Orléans was guillotined in the Revolution and the plant confiscated and its materials sold piecemeal by public auction. The revolutionaries were shortsighted in this action, for the wars with other countries that followed cut off potash supplies and curtailed the industries that depended on alkali. An appeal was made to French chemists to utilize all materials native to France, so as "to render abortive the efforts and hatreds of despots." The revolutionary regime apparently came to realize the value of Leblanc's process, for they proceeded to annul his patent and compelled him to make public his method of making soda.

Following the publication of Leblanc's process, other alkali works were opened in Paris, Dieuse, Chauny, Marseilles, and other French cities. These works prospered, and while the war lasted the secret was held in France.

During the uneasy Peace of Amiens in 1802, W. S. Losh, an Englishman, visited France and learned the details of the Leblanc process. In 1814 he used the process to make small quantities of soda in England. C. Tennant, another Englishman, followed with another plant in 1818. However, expansion was greatly hampered by the high revenue tax of £30 charged on every ton of common salt used.

That England became a world leader in the soda industry was due in no small measure to the abolition of this penal tax a few years later. Without the tax, industrial chemists were free to expand on the basis of the Leblanc process. Many English plants were built, principally in the areas of Lancashire and Tyneside, within easy reach of raw materials, including coal and salt. Germany followed soon afterward with the first Leblanc factory at Schönebeck, near Magdeburg, making 200 tons in 1843, and another small plant built near Cassel soon afterward. Numerous alkali plants were later erected in other parts of Germany, while in Austria, by 1865, three big plants were operating in Moravia, Silesia, and Aussig.

In many Leblanc plants sulfuric acid was also made, generally from iron pyrites and Chile saltpeter by the chamber process. In the largest Leblanc plants pig iron and metallic copper from the burnt pyrites were additional products. In this way, the making of many heavy chemicals had a start with the Leblanc plants.

The Leblanc process has now almost entirely disappeared. It did not make pure products except by expensive recrystallization, and by-product waste disposal also was a problem. For these reasons the Leblanc process was supplanted entirely by the simpler and more economical ammonia-soda process, which was perfected by E. Solvay (1838–1922), who built a works at Couillet, Belgium, in 1863 and began producing soda soon afterward. In the Solvay process ammonia and carbon dioxide are passed into a saturated sodium chloride solution, and sodium bicarbonate precipitates. The bicarbonate is converted to the carbonate by heating.

There followed a period of continuous alterations, mishaps, and improvements, which would have discouraged many other pioneers, but Solvay held to his process in the full belief of its value. By 1869 Solvay's difficulties were over, and the plant had been doubled and production trebled.

Additional plants were built in Belgium, France, Germany, Austria, Russia, Italy, and the U.S. The success of the process in the period under review is illustrated by the jump in production from 300 tons in 1864–68 to 1,616,000 tons in 1902.

In 1850 the whole chemical industry of the heavy type naturally centered about the Leblanc process. For instance, the first major outlet for sulfuric acid in Europe was in the Leblanc plants, where it was used in the first reaction stage in forming salt cake and hydrochloric acid from common salt. The next important expansion in the use of sulfuric acid in Europe resulted from the invention of superphosphate fertilizer by Lawes in 1842 and the commercial production of nitroglycerine explosive by A. Nobel in 1863.

Except for certain metals, chlorine is one of the few industrial chemicals of tonnage importance that is shipped as the element. From its discovery in 1774 by Scheele through the first patent on its use as a bleaching agent in 1799, and on through the first half of the 19th century, it had little industrial importance. Not until the end of the 19th century, when the development of direct-current generating equipment made electrolytic production commercially feasible, did chlorine in elemental form attain industrial significance.

It is not possible here to mention the many 19th-century advances in the making of a variety of other assorted salts and chemicals. However, it can generally be assumed that such manufactures were in association with, or in close proximity to, the larger developments of the soda ash and mineral acid plants. The progress from theoretical reasoning through laboratory scale preparation to pilot plant and finally large tonnage units followed lines similar to those described earlier. In general, a number of independent investigators were responsible for the original scientific work, and very often the majority of these worked in France. However, industrial development usually followed either in Great Britain or on the European mainland with British aid and encouragement. Later in the century there was often a swing to Germany and to Austria, and these two countries tended to be among the top producers as the century came to an end.

Conclusion. Chemistry, up to this point in history, has contributed much to satisfy the intellectual curiosity of man about the structure of everyday materials. In addition, in a very practical way, chemistry has through specially tailored synthetics added greatly to the material welfare of man. The rate of progress, virtually nonexistent until 2 centuries ago, remains rapid today. The chemists of the 19th and 20th centuries built a sound theoretical base on which modern chemistry now flourishes.

Chemistry has become highly specialized and has been broken down into many subdivisions. Yet the contemporary chemist, despite a healthy and inquisitive skepticism about possible flaws in earlier hpotheses, has a deep respect and a solid appreciation of the sound base on which Lavoisier and his successors founded the science.

Bibliography: J. H. White, *The History of the Phlogiston Theory* (London 1932). W. A. Tilden, *Famous Chemists* (London 1921). W. Ramsay, *The Life and Letters of Joseph Black* (London 1918); *The Gases of the Atmosphere: The History of Their Discovery* (4th ed. London 1915). A. J. Berry, *Henry Cavendish, His Life and Scientific Work* (London 1960). A. Holt, *A Life of Joseph Priestley* (New York 1931). J. R. Partington, "Chemistry Through the 18th Century," *Philosophical Magazine, Commemoration Number* (July 1948) 47–66; *A Short History of Chemistry* (3d ed. New York 1957; repr. pa. 1960); *Origin and Development of Applied Chemistry* (New York 1935). L. K. Nash, *The Atomic-Molecular Theory* (Cambridge, Mass. 1950). E. Blanc and L. Delhoume, *La Vie émouvante* *et noble de Gay-Lussac* (Paris 1950). *Perkin Centenary London: 100 Years of Synthetic Dyestuffs* (New York 1958). B. JAFFE, *Crucibles: The Lives and Achievements of Great Chemists* (New York 1934). A. J. IHDE, *The Development of Modern Chemistry* (New York 1964). H. T. PLEDGE, *Science Since 1500* (pa. New York 1959). F. S. TAYLOR, *A History of Industrial Chemistry* (New York 1957). E. FARBER, *Great Chemists* (New York 1961); *The Evolution of Chemistry* (New York 1952). C. J. S. WARRINGTON and R. V. V. NICHOLLS, comp., *A History of Chemistry in Canada* (New York 1949). F. P. VENABLE, *History of Chemistry* (Boston 1922). J. M. STILLMAN, *The Story of Early Chemistry* (New York 1924), repr. as *The Story of Alchemy and Early Chemistry* (New York 1960). H. M. LEICESTER, *The Historical Background of Chemistry* (New York 1956). On American chemistry see C. A. BROWNE, "History of Chemistry in America," *Journal of Chemical Education* 19 (1942) 379–381. **Illustration credits:** Fig. 1, Swedish Information Service, New York. Fig. 2, French Embassy, Press and Information Division, New York. Figs. 3 and 6, National Portrait Gallery, London. Figs. 4 and 5, German Information Center, New York.

[D. M. C. REILLY]

2. INORGANIC CHEMISTRY

Inorganic chemistry is the science that treats of the chemical *elements, their *compounds and mixtures with each other, and the natural laws that govern their chemical and physical behavior. For convenience most of the vast number of known carbon compounds—which are mainly of commercial interest—are now classified separately under the title of organic chemistry. Furthermore, such subjects as physical and colloid chemistry, molecular and nuclear physics, chemical *thermodynamics, and spectroscopy have split off from inorganic chemistry to become separate objects of study and research. The present-day inorganic chemist is apt to be a mixture of chemist, physicist, and mathematician.

Altogether there are more than 40,000 different inorganic compounds whose compositions and chemical and physical properties have been determined. In current handbooks they are listed alphabetically according to the most positive element contained in them. Thus potassium perchlorate, $KClO_4$, is listed under potassium and not under chlorine or oxygen; similarly sulfur hexafluoride, SF_6, and iodine chloride, ICl, are listed under sulfur and iodine, respectively. Classifications based on fundamental principles would be advantageous, but chemistry is not yet an exact science, and therefore firsthand knowledge and memory of chemical and physical properties of the elements and their compounds play an important role in the study and understanding of chemistry.

Acids, Bases, and Salts. A considerable number of inorganic compounds can be classified under the heading of acids, bases, and salts. All acids contain in their molecules one or more hydrogen atoms, which in aqueous solutions are capable of ionizing to form hydrogen ions H^+. Thus for hydrochloric and sulphuric acids one writes, respectively:

$$HCl + \text{water} = H^+ + Cl^-, \text{ in solution}$$
$$H_2SO_4 + \text{water} = 2H^+ + SO_4^{--}, \text{ in solution}$$

As a rule acids have a sour or tart taste. Some acids do not ionize freely, and therefore their solutions have only a faint sour taste. This is the case with carbonic acid, H_2CO_3, which is formed by dissolving carbon dioxide in water: $CO_2 + H_2O = H_2CO_3$. Acids have the property of neutralizing bases to form salts.

All bases, when dissolved in water, furnish hydroxyl ions, OH^-. If a solution of a base is rubbed between the fingers it feels slippery, much as soap does. Common bases are sodium and postassium hydroxides, NaOH and KOH, and ammonium hydroxide NH_4OH (aqueous solution of ammonia, NH_3). Sodium and potassium hydroxide ionize freely (strong bases) in aqueous solution to form $Na^+ + OH^-$ and $K^+ + OH^-$, but ammonium hyroxide is a weak base since only a small fraction of the NH_4OH molecules ionize into $NH_4^+ + OH^-$. Bases have the property of neutralizing acids to form salts, thus:

$$Na^+ + OH^- + H^+ + Cl^- = Na^+ + Cl^- + H_2O$$

the OH^- and H^+ combine to form the neutral water, H_2O. On evaporating this solution one obtains NaCl, common salt.

A weak base, say NH_4OH, will also combine with a weak acid, say H_2CO_3, to form an ionizing salt, NH_4HCO_3. This particular reaction is the basis of an important industrial process (Solvay's process). If ammonia, NH_3, and carbon dioxide, CO_2, are dissolved in water, the soluable salt ammonium bicarbonate, NH_4HCO_3, is formed, which will be present as NH_4^+ and HCO_3^- ions. If, however, ammonia and carbon dioxide are dissolved in a moderately concentrated sodium chloride (NaCl) solution, the ions Na^+, Cl^-, NH_4^+, and HCO_3^- will be present. Since sodium bicarbonate is much less soluable than NaCl and NH_4HCO_3, it precipitates as a solid, $NaHCO_3$, leaving mainly NH_4^+ and Cl^- in solution. The solid after filtering and washing is the familiar bicarbonate of soda. The filtrate contains ammonium chloride, and this on treatment with slaked lime, $Ca(OH)_2$, leads to the economical recovery of the ammonia. Written as chemical reaction equations the process is

$$Na^+ + Cl^- + NH_3 + CO_2 + H_2O = NaHCO_3 + NH_4^+ + Cl^-$$
$$2NH_4^+ + 2Cl^- + Ca^{++} + 2OH^+ = Ca^{++} + 2Cl^- + 2NH_4OH = Ca^{++} + 2Cl^- + 2H_2O + 2NH_3$$

The ammonia, being a gas at ordinary temperatures, can be freed from the calcium chloride solution by heating.

Water is not the only ionizing solvent for inorganic substances. Liquid ammonia also dissolves a variety of salts, and the solutions are conductors of electricity, showing that ions are present. In liquid ammonia the definitions of acids and bases have to be changed; a typical base in liquid ammonia is KNH_2, and a typical acid is NH_4Cl, the neutralization reaction being

$$K^+ + NH_2^- + NH_4^+ + Cl^- = K^+ + Cl^- + 2NH_3$$

A number of other inorganic solvents are known in which interesting chemical reactions take place. Among these are liquid HF, HCN, BrF_3, NO_2, N_2H_4, $SeOCl_2$, and HN_3. The last, HN_3, is a sensitive and dangerous explosive and must therefore be handled with great care.

Solids, Liquids, and Gases. A second classification of inorganic elements and compounds is that into solids, liquids, and gases. Present-day theories of solids and liquids are quite complicated and not easy to explain in detail. The forces holding the atoms or molecules together in even an ideal or perfect crystal are undoubtedly of an electrical nature arising from the outer electrons of the atoms, but the calculation of all the chemical and physical properties of the crystal on this basis is practically impossible. In liquids the forces are of the same general nature as in crystals, but the atoms or molecules are not arranged in a regular order as in crystals. Accordingly, detailed theories of the liquid state are more difficult to deal with than those of the crystalline (solid) state. On the other hand in a gas at moderate or low pressures, the forces between the atoms or molecules of which it is composed are quite small—except during a molecular collision—and can therefore be neglected. This means that the behavior of a gas can be considered as depending on the properties of its individual particles (atoms or molecules), which are moving rapidly about in a random manner. Statistical mechanics plus spectroscopic determinations of the nature and energy states of individual molecules make possible the calculation (i.e., prediction) of both the thermodynamic properties of a given gas as well as its kinetic behavior when mixed with another given gas. Thus when the gases NO and O_2 are mixed, at moderate pressures, the chemical reaction

$$2NO + O_2 = 2NO_2$$

takes place. An experimentally determined knowledge of the properties of the molecules NO, O_2, and NO_2 permits of an accurate calculation of the extent to which the reaction goes, as well as an approximate evaluation of the rate at which the reaction is proceeding at any given time after the gases NO and O_2 have been mixed.

Many other gases exist that are of interest or importance. Thus N_2, O_2, CO_2, and water vapor are important constituents of the earth's atmosphere. At high altitudes oxygen absorbs extreme ultraviolet radiation to form ozone, O_3, and the high-altitude blanket of ozone thus formed absorbs ordinary ultraviolet radiation and protects the earth and its plants, creatures, and man from the damaging radiation from the sun. Nitric oxide, NO, is also formed during the burning of gasoline and oil; with the oxygen in the air, NO_2 is formed, and this in turn absorbs light to give indirectly some ozone. The ozone is believed to be directly and indirectly responsible for the bad effects of "smog."

Other important gases are SO_2, H_2S, SF_6, SeF_6, TeF_6, BF_3, CH_4, SiH_4, GeH_4, B_2H_6, PH_3, AsH_3, NF_3, and $Ni(CO)_4$. Metallic elements are less apt to form gaseous compounds at ordinary temperature than are nonmetallic elements.

As a final class of important inorganic compounds, the so-called complex or coordination compounds will be discussed briefly. When iron fillings, potash (K_2CO_3), and leather or horn are fused together and the cooled mixture then extracted with water, the yellow compound $K_4Fe(CN)_6$, potassium ferrocyanide, can be recovered from the extract. When $K_4Fe(CN)_6$ is dissolved in water, one finds that the ions K^+ and $Fe(CN)_6^{4-}$ are present in the solution. Furthermore, a number of salts containing the $Fe(CN)_6^{4-}$ radical can be prepared with ease without in any way changing its composition; in other words $Fe(CN)_6^{4-}$ presents a composition of considerable stability and is called a complex ion. As another example, if a solution of cobaltous chloride, $CoCl_2$, is treated with ammonia, charcoal, and oxygen or hydrogen peroxide, H_2O_2, the stable golden-brown-colored compound $Co(NH_3)_6Cl_3$ is formed, which in aqueous solution furnishes the stable ions $Co(NH_3)_6^{3+}$ and Cl^-; it is to be emphasized that the complex ion $Co(NH_3)_6^{3+}$ is quite stable and is not easily decomposed. The CN^- in $K_4Fe(CN)_6$ and the NH_3 in $Co(NH_3)_6$ are called addenda in these complex compounds.

These two simple examples illustrate a large number of known complex or coordination compounds. Additional examples are $K_2[PtCl_6]$, $K_2[PtCl_4]$, $[Pt(NH_3)_2Cl_2]$, $[Cu(NH_3)_4]SO_4$, $[Co(NH_3)_4(NO_2)_2]Cl$, $K_3[Co(NO_2)_6]$. After extensive investigations the Swiss chemist, Alfred Werner (1866–1919) came to the conclusion that the addenda in complex compounds are arranged in a fixed symmetrical way about the central atom. Thus in $[Co(NH_3)_6]^{3+}$ the six ammonias are located at the six corners of a regular octahedron, the cobalt being at the center; in $K_2[PtCl_4]$ the four chlorine atoms are at the corners of a (plane) square, the center of the square being occupied by a platinum atom. The four addenda in the nonionizing compound $[Pt(NH_3)_2Cl_2]$ are also located at the corners of a (near) square; but it will be noted that there are two ways in which this is possible, viz,

```
       NH3                    Cl
        |                      |
   Cl—Pt—Cl      and      Cl—Pt—NH3
        |                      |
       NH3                    NH3
```

This suggests that $[Pt(NH_3)_2Cl_2]$ may exist in two isomeric forms; experiments have confirmed that there are two distinct compounds (isomers) having the formula $[Pt(NH_3)_2Cl_2]$. There are also two distinct compounds (of different color) having the formula $[Co(NH_3)_4(NO_2)_2]Cl$, and the geometry of a regular octahedron is such that only two compounds are possible. X-ray studies of crystal structure have verified Werner's hypothesis, and there is little doubt left now about the structural nature of complex (coordination) compounds.

The number of addenda attached to a central atom is called the coordination number of the central atom. For a given element in a given valence state the coordination number tends strongly to be the same regardless of the nature of the addenda. Thus in $[Co(NH_3)_6]Cl_3$ and $K_3[Co(NO_2)_6]$ the coordination number of the trivalent cobalt atom is 6 for both compounds. There are, however, cobalt complexes containing only three ethylenediamine molecules, H_2NH_2C—CH_2NH_2, hereafter en, or only three oxalate ions $(O_2C—CO_2)^{--}$, hereafter Ox^{--}, and so at first sight the coordination number of cobalt in $[Coen_3]Cl_3$ and the green $K_3[CoOx_3]$ would appear to be three. But Werner pointed out that one en or one Ox^{--}, being rather long addenda, could each occupy or bridge two adjacent corners of an octahedron (or two adjacent corners of a square) thus leaving the coordination number of cobalt equal to six. This supposition implies, however, that $[Coen_3]Cl_3$ and $K_3[Co(Ox)_3]$ can each exist in two optically active forms and hence would be capable of rotating the plane of polarization of light passing through solutions of the active forms of the compounds. One of the finest accomplishments in inorganic chemistry came when it was found that a compound such as $K_3[Co(Ox)_3]$ could actually be separated into two optically active isomers.

See also PERIODIC TABLE; ISOTOPES.

Bibliography: J. R. PARTINGTON, *A Short History of Chemistry* (3d ed. New York 1957). F. J. MOORE, *A History of Chemistry* (3d ed. New York 1939). G. AGRICOLA, *De re metallica,* tr. H. C. and L. H. HOOVER (London 1912; reprint New York 1950). D. I.

MENDELÉEV, *The Principles of Chemistry,* tr. G. KAMENSKY (New York 1897). M. SIEGBAHN, *The Spectroscopy of X-Rays,* tr. G. A. LINDSAY (London 1925). F. A. COTTON and G. WILKINSON, *Advanced Inorganic Chemistry* (New York 1962). W. G. PALMER, *Experimental Inorganic Chemistry* (Cambridge, Eng. 1954). H. J. EMELÉUS and J. S. ANDERSON, *Modern Aspects of Inorganic Chemistry* (2d ed. New York 1952).

[N. SCHEEL]

3. ORGANIC CHEMISTRY

Organic chemistry may be defined as the study of chemical compounds containing carbon and hydrogen in combination with other elements, such as oxygen, nitrogen, sulfur, phosphorus, the halogens, and various metals. This broad definition distinguishes organic chemistry from other related physical sciences, such as biochemistry, inorganic, physical, and analytical chemistry, although the organic chemist often uses the information and techniques of these fields in his own specialized interest. Organic chemistry deals with the study of the structure, properties, reactions, and synthesis of organic substances.

Scope. Well over 1 million organic compounds exist. Generalizations about the physical and chemical properties of such a vast number of materials are of little value; however, certain properties, such as relatively low melting point, solubility in nonpolar solvents, and relatively high volatility, are characteristic features of organic compounds. Inorganic compounds, on the other hand, are generally high melting, soluble in polar solvents, and usually nonvolatile. These differences between organic and inorganic compounds are ultimately based upon the type of chemical bond found in each class. Organic materials that contain carbon and hydrogen are often combustible and in burning yield carbon dioxide and water. Inorganic salts normally do not burn.

The scope of organic chemistry is extremely broad. Since all living materials contain carbon, the investigation of life on the molecular level and in terms of chemical phenomena are among the important areas of concern to the organic chemist. Building blocks of organisms such as coenzymes, enzymes, and nucleoproteins are ultimately constructed from simple organic molecules. Such varied biochemical processes as metabolism, the transmission of nerve impulses, muscle contraction, and sight are basically chemical reactions. Although these processes are inherently complex and involve very complicated molecules, they are fundamentally related to familiar organic reactions carried out in the laboratory. The production of drugs, synthetic hormones, vitamins, and chemotherapeutic agents involves organic compounds and reactions.

Apart from living systems, the production of synthetic fibers, plastics, fuels, perfumes, dyes, explosives, and insecticides depends upon organic chemistry. Organic compounds enter into every phase of our existence, and the constant progress of knowledge and technology in this field has greatly influenced our present culture and society.

Early History. The study of organic materials dates back to ancient times. Reference to the preparation of beer as early as 7000 B.C. in the Tigris and Euphrates area has been found. Dyes obtained from plant and animal sources, such as Tyrian purple dye, were used in 1500 B.C. Centuries before Christ, the use of organic compounds as drugs and remedies was widely practiced. Distillation was known and described in considerable detail and used as an important method for the isolation of volatile organic materials. Organic chemistry, as a separate discipline, began with the recognition that certain substances possessed properties that were quite different from those of mineral substances. These "organic substances" were derived largely from animal and vegetable sources, hence, the name organic, introduced by J. J. *Berzelius (1779–1848) in 1808 to indicate their origin from organized nature. Unfortunately, this division led to the belief that organic compounds possessed a "vital force" or mysterious property that set them apart from inorganic or mineral substances. Furthermore, in this period the foundations of quantitative chemistry were being developed. While inorganic materials composed of two elements, such as sodium and chlorine, represented one compound, it was soon found that carbon and hydrogen could combine to yield a large number of different compounds. This problem was explained in terms of the vital force; that is, if organic compounds possessed a vitalistic spirit, they need not obey the laws of simple and multiple proportions of J. *Dalton, which had been proved valid for mineral materials.

The vitalistic theory was seriously challenged in 1828 by Friedrich Wöhler (1800–82), who found by accident that the organic compound urea could be prepared by evaporating a solution of the purely inorganic substance ammonium cyanate. Publication of this result led to a good deal of skepticism and suspicion, particularly since it opposed the beliefs of Berzelius, the most influential chemist of the period. In communicating his results to his former teacher, Wöhler wrote Berzelius, "I must tell you that I can prepare urea without need of a kidney of an animal, either dog or man."

Organic chemistry, unshackled from the restrictions of vitalistic mystery, emerged as a branch of science fundamentally similar to other sciences and based upon rational physical laws. In addition to the activity in the synthetic area, parallel progress in the isolation of pure organic compounds from animal and plant sources was also under way. The isolation of sterols, such as cholesterol from animal fat, and terpenes and alkaloids from plant sources, marked the beginning of the organic chemistry of natural products.

Organic Formula. With the advent of analytical methods, it became possible to determine the percentage of carbon, hydrogen, and nitrogen in organic compounds. From a knowledge of atomic and molecular weights, the molecular formulas of various substances could be derived. Thus, methane, CH_4; ethane, C_2H_6; and methanol, CH_3OH, were shown to possess the indicated C, H, O ratios. But the organic formula seeks to depict the number, kind, and arrangement of atoms within a molecule. The formulation of the theory of valence by E. Frankland (1825–99) made the next step possible. Hydrogen was assigned a valence or combining ability of 1, while carbon was assigned a valence of 4. Carbon and hydrogen were bound by a dash indicating a bond joining the two atoms. Methane, CH_4, was, and is today, depicted as:

```
    H
    |
H—C—H
    |
    H
```

A. Kekulé (1829–96) and A. Couper (1831–92) extended the theory of Frankland to include structures in which carbon was bound to carbon. Thus, propane is represented as:

```
    H  H  H
    |  |  |
H—C—C—C—H
    |  |  |
    H  H  H
```

with each tetravalent carbon atom joined to four other atoms. Similarly, carbon bound to divalent atoms, such as oxygen in carbon dioxide, and trivalent atoms, such as nitrogen in hydrogen cyanide, is depicted by double and triple bonds respectively:

O=C=O	H—C≡N
Carbon dioxide	Hydrogen cyanide

As early as 1822, it was realized that two substances could possess the same percentage composition of elements and yet be entirely different materials. This phenomenon was explained in terms of the existence of two different structural formulas for the same group of atoms, for example for butane, C_4H_{10}, one finds:

```
    H  H  H  H
    |  |  |  |
H—C—C—C—C—H
    |  |  |  |
    H  H  H  H
```

n-butane, boiling point (bp) – 0.5°C, and

```
      H
      |
  H—C
      | \       H
      H  \      |
           C—C—H
      H  / |    |
      | /  H    H
  H—C
      |
      H
```

isobutane, bp – 10°C.

Berzelius named such compounds isomers. The phenomenon of isomerism refers to substances of the same molecular formula that exhibit different chemical properties. Ethane, CH_3CH_3, and propane, $CH_3CH_2CH_3$, may exist only in the linear form as drawn; butane, however, may exist in a linear form and in a branched form as indicated above. As the number of carbon and hydrogen atoms increases through the homologous series of hydrocarbons, the number of possible structural isomers also increases. For decane, $C_{10}H_{22}$, 75 isomers exist; while dodecane, $C_{12}H_{26}$, may exist in 375 different structural variations. Another type of isomerism is found among olefinic compounds. Olefins are hydrocarbons that have a carbon-carbon double bond. The presence of a double bond causes the two carbon atoms and the four groups bound to them to lie in one plane. As a result, disubstituted olefin such as 2-butene (the number 2 refers to the position of the double bond, i.e., $C_1–C_2=C_3–C_4$) may exist in two separate forms. These two forms are called the *cis* and *trans* forms from the Latin prepositions meaning "on this side" and "across." This type of isomerism is called geometric isomerism:

```
H       CH3        CH3      CH3
  \    /              \    /
   C=C                 C=C
  /    \              /    \
CH3      H           H      H
```

trans 2-Butene   *cis* 2-Butene

The structural formula enabled the organic chemist to visualize the molecules with which he experimented and to categorize them in terms of structure and properties. Furthermore, valid predictions could be made about the properties and chemical behavior of unknown molecules based upon proposed structures.

Chemical Bond. The chemical bond may be defined as the force holding two atoms or groups of atoms in an aggregate of sufficient stability to allow the chemist to consider it as a unique molecular unit.

Several different kinds of chemical bonds exist. The ionic bond is the type that joins oppositely charged ions. Sodium chloride is composed of positively charged sodium ions and negatively charged chloride ions joined together in a crystalline lattice. The ions result from a transfer and acceptance of electrons. The ionic bond is the type of chemical bond found most often among inorganic compounds, such as salts, minerals, and metallic oxides. The relatively high melting point of such materials reflects the strength of the forces binding the ions within the crystalline aggregate.

The covalent bond is the bond type of most interest to the organic chemist because it is the one that normally joins carbon to carbon. The concept of the covalent bond was introduced in 1916 by G. N. Lewis and is of central importance in the study of organic chemistry. Although the attraction of positive for negative ions in the ionic bond is quite apparent, the covalent bond is somewhat less easily explained. The latter is formed by the mutual sharing of electron pairs between two atoms. The covalent bond is weaker than the ionic bond. The electron pair is designated by a straight line joining the two atoms just as in the Kekulé structures.

The single, double, and triple bonds are formed by different hybridization of the valence electrons of the carbon atoms. In the methane molecule, CH_4, the central carbon atom is said to be sp^3 hybridized. The carbon-hydrogen bonds are called sigma bonds, σ. In the ethylene molecule, the carbon atoms are sp^2 hybridized. They are connected by a σ bond and a π bond. These three bonds are shown below:

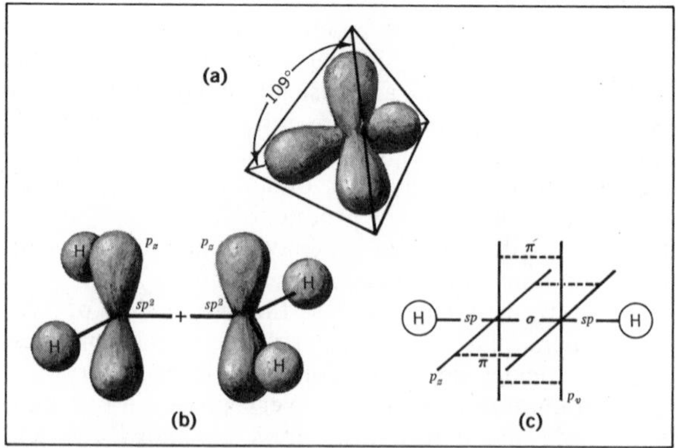

sp^3 Carbon atom sp^2 Ethylenic bond sp Acetylenic bond

(*See* CHEMICAL BINDING.)

Stereochemistry. Stereochemistry may be defined as the study of the spatial arrangement of atoms or groups of atoms within a molecule or ion. The proposal of J. A. Le Bel (1847–1930) and J. H. van't Hoff (1852–1911) of a tetrahedral structure for carbon was put forth in 1873 to explain the property of optical activity, that is, the ability of certain substances to rotate the plane of plane-polarized light. Le Bel and Van't Hoff realized independently that this ability was possessed by those molecules in which a central carbon atom was surrounded by four different groups, $CR_1R_2R_3R_4$. They proposed that the optical rotatory power was due to asymmetry in the optically active molecule. In order for the arrangement of atoms R_1, R_2, R_3, and R_4 about the central carbon atom to produce an asymmetric molecule, a tetrahedral structure must exist. Thus lactic acid, $CH_3CHOH–COOH$, occurs in an optically active form in which $R_1 = CH_3$, $R_2 = OH$, $R_3 = H$ and $R_4 = COOH$. Two possible tetrahedral arrangements may be drawn:

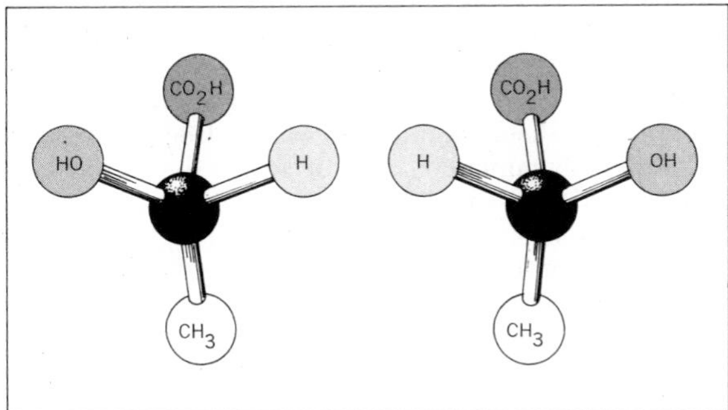

The two structures are mirror images of each other and correspond to a different sequence of groups counting in either a clockwise or counterclockwise direction, that is, H, CH_3, OH compared to H, OH, CH_3. These two optical isomers stand in the same relationship as the left and right hand. Each isomer rotates plane-polarized light, but one form will rotate the light to the left, and the other will rotate it to the right. The magnitude of the rotatory power, either dextrorotatory (D) or levorotatory (L), is equal but opposite in sign for the D and L isomer of a compound possessing one asymmetric center.

From a historical point of view, it is interesting to note the reluctance with which the views of Van't Hoff and Le Bel were received. One of the most outstanding chemists of the period, H. Kolbe (1818–84), disparaged the theory as "fanciful nonsense" and "supernatural explanations" by two "unknown" chemists. On the weight of rapidly accumulated evidence, however, the theories of Van't Hoff and Le Bel were accepted and conclusively proven.

Many organic compounds exist in a ring form. For example, saturated (nonolefinic) paraffin conforming to the general formula C_nH_{2n} belong to the cycloparaffin class. Cyclopropane, C_3H_6; cyclobutane, C_4H_8; cyclopentane, C_5H_{10}; and cyclohexane, C_6H_{12}, are the first four members of a homologous series of cyclic hydrocarbons. Another feature of these compounds is the existence of *cis* and *trans* isomers. For example, in 1,2-dichlorocyclohexane, the two chlorine atoms may be on the same side of the average plane of the ring or on opposite sides. In a planar representation the chlorine atoms are bound by solid or dotted lines as shown.

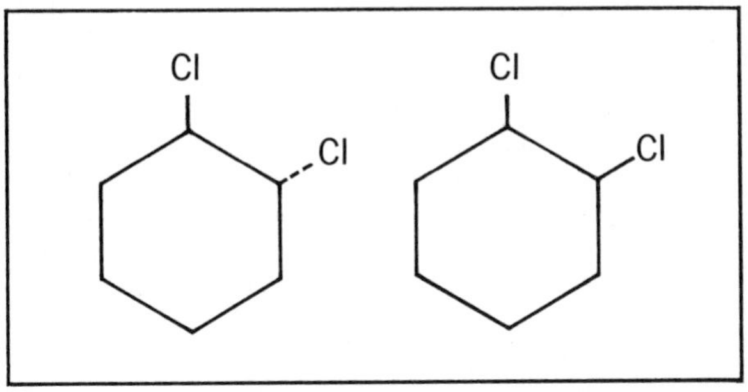

Aromatic Compounds. The connotation of the word "aromatic" has undergone considerable change during the development of organic chemistry. Originally it was applied to compounds possessing a distinctively fragrant odor such as vanilla or wintergreen. In the current context of organic chemistry, aromatic implies stability and special reactivity. Aromatic compounds are thermochemically more stable than related nonaromatic ones. Furthermore, they display a distinct type of reactivity; characteristically they undergo substitution rather than addition reactions, thus retaining their aromatic structure. In 1865, Kekulé suggested the cyclic structure of three double bonds for the benzene molecule. This proposal was not based upon chemical analogy, since benzene does not behave as a typically unsaturated material. However, the accumulated evidence at Kekulé's disposal, such as the orientation of groups in substituted benzenes led him to his famous formulation. Several facts about the behavior of benzene, however, could not be rationalized in terms of the Kekulé structure. For example, the lack of reactivity of the double bonds and the existence of only one 1,2-disubstituted derivative instead of two, i.e.:

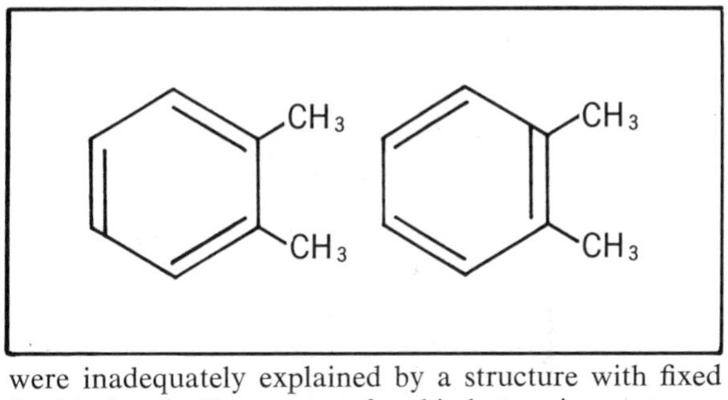

were inadequately explained by a structure with fixed double bonds. To account for this latter circumstance, Kekulé suggested a very rapid oscillation between the two forms. Apparently, he believed that if the rate of interconversion between the two forms were sufficiently rapid, neither would be isolable. A more correct concept of the structure of benzene was later developed and is based upon the resonance theory.

Benzene is the prototype of aromatic compounds from which many of the terms such as "aromaticity" and "aromatic" character owe their origin. The enhanced thermochemical stability of benzene compared to a suitable model may be demonstrated by a comparison of heats of hydrogenation. An approximately suitable value for the heat of hydrogenation of benzene would be 85.8 kcal/mole if it possessed three double bonds of the type found in cyclohexene. Actually, the experimentally determined value for benzene is 49.8 kcal/mole. The difference, 36 kcal/mole, is a measure of the enhanced stability of benzene. The stabilization is termed the resonance energy. Similarly, resonance energy may be determined from heats of combustion data, and also from theoretical considerations using quantum-mechanical calculations. The key question that must be answered is why benzene possesses unusual stability. Resonance theory provides the explanation in the following way. For a molecule such as benzene, two equivalent electronic structures may be drawn:

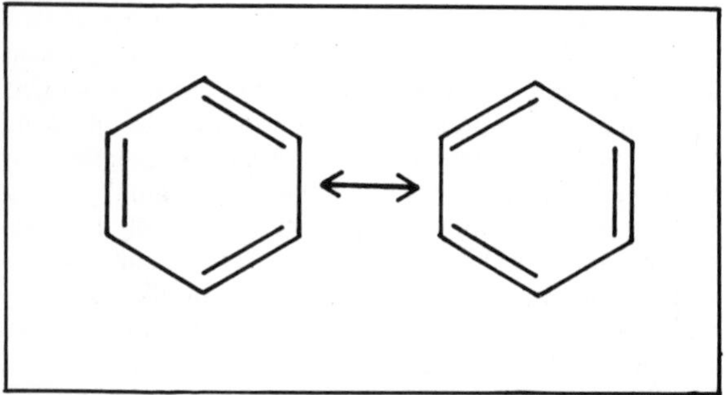

The true structure of benzene is not accurately described by either alone. The total energy of the molecules is lower than either structure would indicate.

The actual benzene molecule is an intermediate between the two forms shown above. Benzene is often spoken of as a resonance hybrid of the two structures. This is not meant to imply that the benzene molecule rapidly alternates between the two structures, since this would be contrary to physical evidence. The structure is perhaps better referred to as mesomeric (between the forms) since this makes clear the intermediate structure of the molecule.

See also BIOCHEMISTRY; CHEMICAL BINDING.

Bibliography: History. E. FARBER, *The Evolution of Chemistry* (New York 1952). F. J. MOORE, *A History of Chemistry* (3d ed. New York 1939) 175–246. General Texts. L. F. and M. FIESER, *Advanced Organic Chemistry* (New York 1961). D. J. CRAM and G. S. HAMMOND, *Organic Chemistry* (New York 1959). Theory. E. S. GOULD, *Mechanism and Structure in Organic Chemistry* (New York 1959). M. S. NEWMAN, ed., *Steric Effects in Organic Chemistry* (New York 1956). J. S. HINE, *Physical Organic Chemistry* (2d ed. New York 1962).

[R. M. MORIARTY]

4. PHYSICAL CHEMISTRY

Physical chemistry came to conscious development, in the decade 1880–90, through the activities of W. Ostwald (1853–1932), J. *van't Hoff, and S. *Arrhenius. The Leipzig school of Ostwald was the focus of an effort that emphasized the contributions to chemical science that could stem from the application of physical measurements to chemical systems. Chemistry had just passed through a very productive period. C. Guldberg (1836–1902) and P. Waage (1833–1900) had finally formulated the hazily understood law of mass action (1864–67), which placed chemical equilibrium on a firm theoretical basis. W. *Gibbs had supplied (1875–78) the general equations governing equilibria in gaseous, liquid, and solid phases in systems of many components (the phase rule). W. Hittorf (1824–1914) had revealed that the positive and negative carriers of the electric current in solution did not carry equal amounts of current (1859). Each carrier transmitted a particular fraction of the total and had a characteristic transport number. The refined conductance measurements of electrolytic solutions of F. Kohlrausch (1840–1910) in 1879, the fundamental studies of F. Raoult (1830–1901) on the molecular weight of dissolved substances as revealed by freezing point lowering and boiling point elevation, and W. Pfeffer's (1845–1920) researches (1877) on osmotic pressures with synthetic semipermeable membranes such as copper ferrocyanide—all these served as the bases on which the new science of physical chemistry could be built.

L. Wilhelmy's (1812–64) pioneer investigations on chemical *kinetics and his data on the velocity of inversion of cane sugar were reinterpreted in terms of the catalytic activity of the hydrogen and hydroxyl ions that Arrhenius postulated as the essential characteristic constituents of acids and bases. Ostwald applied the Law of Mass Action successfully to the ionic equilibria of weakly dissociated acids and bases, using the postulate of Arrhenius, of ionization measured by conductance, as the measure of H^+ and OH^- on acids and bases respectively. Strong electrolytes, typified by the salts of strong acids and bases, did not obey Ostwald's dilution law. Valiant efforts were made to discover the reasons for the anomaly; these were not successful until P. Debye (1884–) revealed that the ionic *activity* rather than the concentration was a true measure of the thermodynamic behavior of an ion in aqueous and other solutions. The necessity for activity rather than concentration is most readily glimpsed by considering the equilibrium existing in a two-phase system, e.g., ether-water, in which an organic acid such as benzoic acid is distributed. Most of the acid is concentrated in the ether phase. Its activity in the two phases in equilibrium must be equal. It is the extent of solute-solvent interaction that is dominant in such cases. G. N. Lewis (1875–1946) and his coworkers in Berkeley, Calif., provided much of the basic quantitative data on the activities of salts dissolved in aqueous media.

The final decade of the 19th century was one of intensive development of the principles of equilibrium and of reaction velocity and their application to industrial chemistry. M. Bodenstein (1871–1942) began a 40-year effort on the velocities of gas reactions, hydrogen iodide synthesis and decomposition being the first reactions studied. Catalysis achieved major importance in industry with the use of platinum catalysts for the conversion of sulfur dioxide and oxygen to sulfur trioxide to make sulfuric acid. P. Sabatier (1854–1941) solved a century-old problem by showing that hydrogen gas combined readily with unsaturated oils and fats in the presence of finely divided nickel catalysts. Finally, on the eve of World War I, the German chemical industry brought to technical fruition the basic equilibrium and catalytic studies of F. Haber (1868–1934) on the synthesis of ammonia from its elements. This development filled a worldwide need for nitrogen and ushered in an era of high-pressure techniques in industry.

The fundamental bases upon which the science of catalysis rests were formulated by I. Langmuir (1881–1957) in researches on the reactions of gases at the surfaces of a tungsten filament. His studies, beginning before World War I, led to a definition of the short range of chemical forces and the discovery of the existence of chemisorption in monolayers at such surfaces. These ideas prompted the Langmuir formulation of velocity of chemical reactions in monolayers at surfaces and contributed to the concept of orientation in monolayer films of insoluble oils at water surfaces. The areas of these oil films revealed the length and cross-sectional areas of long-chain molecules having a nonpolar, normally hydrocarbon, body insoluble in water and a polar head soluble in water. Such measurements confirmed the data newly revealed by X-ray studies and by induction from valency considerations concerning tetravalent carbon and the carbon-hydrogen and carbon-carbon bond distances. The technique of monolayer formation contributed significantly to knowledge concerning the geometry and structure of complex molecules.

Quantum Chemistry. A new chapter in physical chemistry began with the development of *quantum theory. M. *Planck's quanta of radiant energy, proposed in 1901 to account for the experimental observations of energy distribution in black-body radiation, were generalized by *Einstein, in 1905, for all types of radiant energy, from infrared to extremely hard X rays and gamma rays. In 1907, Einstein extended the concept of quanta to the vibrations of the atomic constituents of solid substances and accounted for the variation in the heat capacity of elements at constant volume from zero at 0°K to the limiting value, given by the Dulong and Petit law, of approximately 6 calories per mole per degree at high temperature. Heat-capacity measurements by W. Nernst (1864–1941) and his school over the range from liquid hydrogen temperatures to room temperature abundantly confirmed this idea, which was refined by Debye. It followed from these latter considerations that, in the neighborhood of the absolute zero, the heat capacity of a solid was proportional to the cube of the absolute temperature.

The photoelectric effect, investigated by P. Lenard (1862–1947) in 1902, found a ready interpretation in terms of light quanta and the associated energy, $E = nh\nu$, where ν is the light frequency, h is Planck's constant, and n is an integer. This development preceded the formulation of line spectra of atomic systems in emission by N. *Bohr, in 1913, and his interpretation of earlier empirical series relationships, e.g., the Balmer series of hydrogen lines. Sufficiently energetic light energy in the region of continuous absorption by an atomic vapor was shown to result in ionization of the species. The line-emission spectra were indicative of excited, energy-rich atoms.

Molecular spectra were more complex, with absorption or emission bands in place of lines, since the molecule could receive energy in rotational, vibrational, and electronic levels as well as in the three degrees of freedom of translational motion. The significance of these developments for physical chemistry was manifold. Quantum theory provided a rational basis for photo- and radiation chemistry. It provided not only a theory of specific heat of solids but also of gases, illuminating the variation of specific heat of gases with temperature in terms of translational, rotational, and vibrational energies, each contributing to the heat capacities at temperatures determined by the size of the quantum involved.

X-ray and Electron Diffraction. Other physical tools broadened the physical chemist's horizon. The X-ray analysis of crystals, developed by W. H. and W. L. Bragg, not only elucidated the elements of crystallography in solid crystals, but went on to reveal the structures of organic molecules including fibers, plastics, and biological systems. Electron diffraction made possible the exploration of gases as well as solids and liquids. Basic data on bond distances and, hence, on atomic structure of gaseous molecules became available. These data were supplemented by measurements of dipole moments and dielectric constants of gaseous systems, not only giving checks on the atomic distances but also revealing the polarity of the molecule. This latter in its turn was indicative of structure. Thus, carbon dioxide is nonpolar and a linear array: O = C = O. The polarity of sulfur dioxide, SO_2, indicates that it is nonlinear. With more complex molecules—for example, pentatomic AB_4—the absence of polarity in a variety of compounds is indicative of the accepted tetrahedral structure. *Trans*-methylene chloride

```
H     Cl
 \   /
   C
 /   \
Cl     H
```

has a dipole moment. It cannot, therefore, be a plane molecule.

The wave theory of matter, proposed in 1924 by L. de Broglie (1892–), was the basis on which electron diffraction could be used to supplement the findings of X-ray scattering. It led also to the construction of the electron microscope and the consequent increases in resolving power, permitting, finally, the examination of particles containing only a small number of atoms, and providing inorganic and colloid chemistry with a powerful new tool.

The main impact of the wave mechanics on physical chemistry lay (1) in its rationalization of much that had resulted empirically from the exploration of the internal energies of molecules, especially rotational and vibrational energies; (2) in its indication of two forms of homonuclear molecules, notably the spin isomers *ortho-* and *para*-hydrogen; (3) in its formulation of the concept of both coulombic and exchange energies as determining the binding of atoms in molecules, leading to a rationalization of the Lewis covalent bond of two electrons. W. Heitler (1904–) and F. London (1900–54) showed that application of the Pauli exclusion principle required that the spins of the shared pair of electrons must be opposed or antiparallel. The foundation of a coherent valence theory was thereby secured. The theory, in the case of polyatomic molecules, provided for the idea of directed valence so necessary for structure theory of organic chemistry. It led also to the concept of nonlocalized orbitals resulting in extra binding energy, now known as resonance energy. The best-known example is benzene, the alternate double and single carbon bonds in the ring structure now being replaced by six mobile electrons, completely delocalized, giving a resulting resonance energy of 40 kcal per mole, thus accounting for the remarkable stability of the benzene ring. Extension of the Heitler-London theory to a system of three or more atoms led directly to the formulation of rate processes in terms of potential energy barriers. In the hands of H. Eyring (1901–), this led to the absolute rate theory, applicable not only to chemical reactions but to all physical processes involving the dimension of time, such as viscosity, diffusion, and transport phenomena generally.

Eyring demonstrated how the statistical-partition function approach to the definition of stable molecular systems, so fruitful in the solution of thermodynamical problems, could also be used to define the properties of an activated complex, the transition state from reactants to products in rate processes. In defining the transport properties of liquids, Eyring made use of a concept of free volume, or holes, increasing with increase of temperature and determining the flow properties in their temperature variation.

After the scientific developments associated with World War II, a number of new tools and techniques became available for the prosecution of physicochemical objectives. Microwave spectroscopy, using wavelengths in the range 0.1 to 1.0 cm, advanced rapidly as a result of radar research. Monochromatic waves that can be rapidly varied (frequency modulated), generated by an electronically controlled oscillator, are passed through the substance under study, the emergent beam being picked up, suitably amplified, and recorded. High resolution is attainable. One spectacular result of such studies is the recording of the vibration associated with the passage of the nitrogen atom in an ammonia molecule, through the triangular plane of three hydrogen atoms, to its extreme positions as the apex of a pyramid either above or below the plane. The resolution is such as to give the rotational fine structure of both light nitrogen ($N^{14}H_3$) and the heavier isotope $N^{15}H_3$. The spectra of both normal molecules and those in an electric field can be studied. From the latter data, dipole moments can be determined.

Field-emission microscopy was developed in 1936 by E. W. Müller. The emission of electrons from the sharp tip of a heated wire, principally tungsten, can be revealed on a fluorescent screen adjacent to a spherical metal anode. The bright and dark regions on the screen are indicative of the plane faces of the single crystal forming the tip, the emission of electrons from a given plane being dependent on the work function of the plane—this, in its turn, being dependent on the atom spacing in the plane. The position of molecules adsorbed on the plane faces can be revealed, as well as their behavior during adsorption. More recently, the technique has been reversed to produce a field ion microscope. A positively charged tip causes the emission of positive adsorbed ions or cations of the metal tip. The larger masses emitted permit higher resolution.

Nuclear Magnetic Resonance. Nuclear magnetic resonance was discovered in 1946 by Felix Bloch and E. M. Purcell independently. As a physicochemical tool, it is especially applicable to the location of protons in chemical molecules. This is very advantageous, since hydrogen atoms are not located by X-ray and electron microscopy. It is applicable also to the nuclei C^{13}, F^{19}, P^{31}, B^{11}, N^{14}, O^{17}, and Si^{29}. Nuclei having neither spin nor magnetic moment cannot be detected, for example, C^{12} and O^{16}, which thus become transparent in the location of the protons, as in organic molecules. Two lines of experiment are underway, known respectively as broad-line and high-resolution studies. Each has proved invaluable in the determination of structural formulas, in problems of hindered rotation, tautomerism, motion in molecular crystals, and the related mechanical properties of such solids, as, for example, in solid polymeric materials and protein solutions. Fluorine resonance permits examination of fluorine compounds, including the fluo-polymers. Even C^{13}, present in its natural low abundance in ordinary carbon, is in sufficient concentration for application to organic chemical problems. Organic phosphorus chemistry and silicon chemistry can likewise be served. Nuclear magnetic resonance has also been applied to studies of multilayers of adsorbed water, alcohols, and hydrocarbons on adsorbing surfaces. In a similar manner electron-spin resonance can be used as a parallel tool of investigation.

One of the newest techniques employed in physical chemistry is the use of shock waves. During the 1920s, qualitative investigations began, with detonations and the initiation of these processes as the focus of interest. Quantitative studies began only in the 1950s, one of the earliest being a study of the kinetics of dissociation of nitrogen tetroxide, N_2O_4, by Carrington and Davidson in 1953. This dissociation is a very fast reaction, and it is in this area that shock waves can be particularly useful, since the compression, occurring adiabatically, raises the temperature of the gas suddenly to a calculable value, determined by the compression ratio. The recent publications in this field are very numerous and may be classified as measurements of (1) equilibria between molecules and their dissociation products over an extended range of temperature, (2) spectra of gases at high temperatures, and (3) measurement of the velocities with which equilibria are established in very fast reactions.

Bibliography: G. W. CASTELLAN, *Physical Chemistry* (Reading, Mass. 1964). E. HUTCHINSON and P. VAN RYSSELBERGHE, eds., *Physical Chemistry,* 12 v. (New York 1952–63). H. S. TAYLOR and S. GLASSTONE, eds., *Treatise on Physical Chemistry,* 2 v. (3d ed. New York v.1, 1942, v.2, 1951). E. R. ANDREW, *Nuclear Magnetic Resonance* (Cambridge, Eng. 1955).

[H. S. TAYLOR]

CHEMNITZ, MARTIN, Lutheran theologian; b. Treuenbreitzen, Nov. 9, 1522; d. Braunschweig, April 8, 1586. Educated despite his lack of financial resources, at Magdeburg (1539–42), Frankfurt (1543), Wittenberg (1545), Königsberg (M.A. 1547), Chemnitz was librarian to Albert of Prussia, Königsberg (1550). Returning to Wittenberg (April 1553), he entered the

Portrait of Martin Chemnitz that appears in the "Bibliotheca Chalcographica," 1650.

ministry in December 1553 as pastor of St. Aegidi and assistant to Superintendent Mörlin in Braunschweig. Chemnitz, a fellow student of Melanchthon, replied to the attack on Lutheranism by young Jesuits of Cologne in his *Theologiae Jesuitarum praecipua capita* (1562). In answer to attacks by the Portuguese Jesuit Andradius, Chemnitz worked 8 years on his *Examen concilii Tridentini* (1565–73). His four-volume, scholarly analysis of Trent's decisions, based on Scripture, the Fathers, and the history of Catholic dogma, enhanced his reputation far beyond Germany and elicited Jesuit respect for a formidable opponent and scholar. Chemnitz was then in demand as a consultant in doctrinal disputes.

In 1567, upon the request of Duke Albert, Chemnitz accompanied Superintendent Mörlin to Prussia to reorganize the church after the Osiander confusion. Chemnitz's role in drafting the *Corpus doctrinae Prutenicum* (1567) and a similar church ordinance for Braunschweig-Wolfenbüttel, the *Corpus doctrinae Julium* (1569), secured his reputation as a church organizer. Although defending Melanchthon against Flacius in earlier vain attempts to straighten out the *Adiaphora Streit,* Chemnitz maintained his more conservative orthodox Lutheran position. He contributed significantly to the final draft (1580) and later defense of the *Konkordienformel,* and was particularly effective in clarifying the doctrines on the Person of Christ and His place in the Lord's Supper. Chemnitz's *De duabus naturis in Christo, de hypostatica earum unione, de communicatione idiomatum,* etc. (1570) laid the foundation for article 8 in the Formula of Concord (1580). His "Postilla" likewise exemplified clear and excellent Biblical exposition. Chemnitz was by nature a reflective if eclectic theologian, a profound scholar, and an accomplished linguist, but withal a practical churchman. His goal was to set forth in simple, concise form what the Word of God taught. Doubtless, Chemnitz's inclination toward the reduction of his beliefs to a *corpus doctrinae* tended to crystallize and formalize the *Grundsätze* of the Reformers. Also his insistence in creating a definite church polity with the accompanying purist forms, such as black attire without ornamentation for women at communion, tended to standardize church customs.

Bibliography: T. PRESSEL, *Martin Chemnitz (Leben und ausgewählte Schriften der Väter und Begründer der Lutherischen Kirche,* ed. J. HARTMANN, v.8; Elberfeld (1862). P. J. RECHTMEYER, *Der berühmten Stadt Braunschweig Kirchenhistorie,* v.3 (Braunschweig 1710) 273–536, best source of his life. E. W. ZEEDEN, LexThK[2] 2:1043–44. F. LAU, RGG[3] 1:1647–48. G. NOTH, *Grundlinien der Theologie des M. Chemnitz* (n.p. 1930). E. WOLF, NDB 3:201–202.

[E. G. SCHWIEBERT]

CHENOBOSKION, GNOSTIC TEXTS OF

A collection of 13 Coptic manuscripts of the 3d and 4th centuries A.D., also commonly called the Nag Hammâdi manuscripts. These documents have major significance, for they bring to light for the first time since antiquity a considerable body of original Gnostic literature, much of it completely new to us.

Discovery. They were found by Egyptian peasants around 1945 in a cemetery at the foot of Jebel el-Tarif, near the modern village of Nag Hammâdi and the site of ancient Shenesit-Chenoboskion where *Pachomius founded his first monasteries in the 4th century, approximately 60 miles down the Nile from Luxor. The fellahin unearthed a jar containing 13 papyrus codices, many in excellent condition, which they sold to antiquarian dealers. About 2 years later one codex came into the possession of the Coptic Museum of Old Cairo, another (the Jung Codex), after a few changes of ownership, came into that of the C. G. Jung-Institut in Zurich, and the remainder were sold first to private owners in Cairo and later to the Coptic Museum in that city. Political upheavals in Egypt and subsequent international complications delayed the publication of most of the documents, but the project was placed eventually in the hands of an international committee of specialists in the Coptic language and in Gnosticism.

View of Jebel el-Tarif, near the site of the ancient village of Shenesit-Chenoboskion, where the 3d- and 4th-century Gnostic manuscripts were discovered in 1945.

Contents. Nine of the books are more or less complete; some are still in their original bindings. The collection comprises in all about 1,130 pages and 15 fragments. With the sole exception of the Jung Codex, which is longer and narrower, the codices measure on the average about 10 by 5½ inches and vary in thickness. For the most part these Gnostic texts are written in Sahidic Coptic (*see* COPTIC LANGUAGE AND LITERATURE) with some evidence of early stages of the dialect. The Jung Codex is in the Subakhmimic dialect (from the city of Akhmim, or Panopolis, in Upper Egypt). On paleographic grounds, they are thought to range in date through the 3d and 4th centuries. The handwriting sometimes differs even in the same codex, and the calligraphy is often rather unusual. The works appear to be translations from Greek, and some were composed much earlier than the time of translation. There are 51 works, a few of them in two or more versions. The only two works previously known (the first and fourth of Codex III) were found in the Berlin Codex, described by C. L. Schmidt in 1896 and published by W. Till in 1955 (*Die gnostischen Schriften des koptischen Papyrus Berolinensis 8502,* TU 60). The 13 books, comprising treatises, letters, dialogues, discourses, apocalypses, apocryphal "gospels" and acts, and the like, coming from originally different branches of Gnosticism, constituted the library or part of the library of an Egyptian Gnostic sect living near Chenoboskion. The sect probably came to an end with the rise of monasticism in the region. While it would be premature to attempt a detailed evaluation of the Chenoboskion MSS until all have been published and studied, some of them at least can be singled out for brief discussion.

Codices I, II, III. The first piece in Codex III (to adopt the numbering of P. Labib) is a theogonic and cosmogonic treatise called the *Apocryphon* (*Secret*

Book) of John. There are three copies of the work in this collection, and it is found also in Berlin Papyrus 8502. The treatise stems from obscure myth-centered Barbelo-Gnostic or Sethian circles and was used as a source by Irenaeus (*Adv. Haer* 1.29–30) in his description of these. Codex I is the Jung Codex, unique in its size and in the dialect in which it is written, and especially significant because the five works contained in it represent Valentinian rather than Sethian Gnosticism. One, the *Gospel of Truth,* is attributed with very high probability to *Valentinus (2d century A.D.) himself; another, the *Letter to Rheginus on the Resurrection,* to Valentinus or to an Oriental disciple of his; and a third to *Heracleon, the Western disciple of Valentinus, which is provisionally entitled the *Treatise on the Three Natures.* In Codex II, which is beautifully written, the most important work is the controversial *Gospel of Thomas* but not to be identified with the apocryphal infancy gospel of that name. It is a collection of 114 sayings of Jesus, some of them the same as the celebrated Oxyrhynchus *Logoi* [see J. A. Fitzmyer, SJ, "The Oxyrhynchus *Logoi* of Jesus and the Coptic Gospel according to Thomas," ThSt 20 (1959) 505–560]. The sayings are in part similar to the sayings of Jesus in the canonical Gospels, especially the Synoptics; some are Agrapha or sayings attributed to Jesus in early Christian tradition, already known from other sources; and some are sayings previously unknown. They do not all reflect typical Gnostic ideas, and it is debated whether the document had a "pre-Gnostic" history, and whether it depends on independent Gospel traditions or makes rather perverse use of the canonical Synoptics.

Codices VI, VIII, XI. Several works in the collection, such as the *Supreme Allogenes* (Stranger) and the *Revelation of Messos* from Codex XI, and the *Discourse on Truth of Zostrian* from Codex VIII, appear to be writings mentioned by Porphyry (*Vita Plotini* 16) as having been refuted by Plotinus. Codex VI also possesses a unique feature: in addition to two Gnostic works, the *Acts of Peter,* and a Sethian revelation, it contains many Hermetic treatises, one of which is identical with the *Asclepius,* ch. 21 to 29. Some of these writings contain ideas and terms common in the great Gnostic systems but hitherto not found in the *Hermetica.* (*See* HERMETIC LITERATURE.)

Importance of the Chenoboskion Discoveries. Except for a few extant documents such as the Berlin Codex, the Bruce Codex, and the Codex Askewianus, scholars hitherto depended for their knowledge of Gnosticism upon the refutations of the great ancient writers on heresy, especially Irenaeus. The Chenoboskion documents provide firsthand evidence of this widespread religious movement and serve as a confirmation of patristic accounts of Gnosticism that, from the first impressions of the manuscripts, do not appear to have been exaggerated. The manuscripts reveal, for the most part, a popular form of Gnosticism, the Sethian, and were probably the property of a Sethian community. The presence among them of Valentinian and Hermetic works raises questions about the interrelation of Gnostic sects and of the relationship of these to the kindred but entirely pagan phenomenon of Hermeticism. They should enable scholars to make much further progress in the investigation of the origins and formative influences of Gnosticism, its inner developments through the centuries, its own conception of gnosis, and its relation to Manichaeism. The Chenoboskion documents must rank among the most significant literary discoveries of the 20th century.

See also GNOSTICISM; MANICHAEISM.

Bibliography: Texts and translations. P. LABIB, *Coptic Gnostic Papyri in the Coptic Museum at Old Cairo,* v.1 (Cairo 1956). M. MALININE et al., *Evangelium veritatis* (Zurich 1956); *Suppl.* (1961); *De resurrectione (Epistula ad Rheginum)* (Zurich 1963). A. GUILLAUMONT et al., *The Gospel according to Thomas* (New York 1959). W. C. TILL, ed., *Das Evangelium nach Philippos* (Patristische Texte und Studien 2; Berlin 1963). M. KRAUSE and P. LABIB, eds., *Die drei Versionen des Apokryphon des Johannes im Koptischen Museum zu Alt-Kairo* (Wiesbaden 1962). A. BÖHLIG and P. LABIB, eds., *Die koptisch-gnostische Schrift ohne Title aus Codex II von Nag Hammadi* (Berlin 1962); *Koptisch-gnostische Apokalypsen aus Codex V von Nag Hammadi* (Halle 1963). General studies. H. C. PUECH, "Découverte d'une bibliothèque gnostique en Haute-Égypte," *Encyclopédie française* 19.42 (1957) 4–13. F. L. CROSS, ed., *The Jung Codex* (New York 1955). J. DORESSE, *The Secret Books of the Egyptian Gnostics,* tr. P. MAIRET (New York 1960). H. JONAS, *The Gnostic Religion* (2d ed. Boston 1963) 290–319. M. KRAUSE, "Der koptische Handschriftenfund bei Nag Hammadi: Umfang und Inhalt," *Mitteilungen des Deutschen Archäologischen Instituts, Abteilung Kairo* 18 (1962) 121–132. Particular studies and commentaries. K. GROBEL, *The Gospel of Truth: A Valentinian Meditation on the Gospel* (New York 1960). J. E. MÉNARD, *L'Évangile de Vérité: Rétroversion grecque et commentaire* (Paris 1962). R. M. GRANT and D. N. FREEDMAN, *The Secret Sayings of Jesus* (Garden City, N.Y. 1960). R. M. WILSON, *Studies in the Gospel of Thomas* (London 1960); ed. and tr., *The Gospel of Philip* (New York 1963). **Illustration credit:** Pontifical Biblical Institute, Rome.

[G. W. MAC RAE]

CHERUBIM

An order of angelic spirits usually ranked after the *seraphim. Although the Hebrew word k^e*rûbîm* (plural of k^e*rûb*) may be connected with the Akkadian verb *karābu,* "to bless, to praise," there is no evidence that the Israelites ever considered cherubim as intercessors or

Cherub, ivory fragment from a piece of household furniture, c. 1350–1150 B.C.; *from Samaria in Palestine. The human face and animal body are typical of these chimerical guardians of palaces, temples, or as here, households.*

praisers of Yahweh. Nor were cherubim thought to be angels, i.e., God's messengers. Cherubim were closely linked with God's glory. As representations in gilded wood and in relief carvings (3 Kgs 6.23–29; 2 Chr 3.7, 10–13), in gold and woven into cloth trappings of the *Tent of Meeting and the veil of the *Holy of Holies (Ex 25.18–20; 26.1, 31; 2 Chr 3.14), they were prominent figures where God's glory was believed to dwell [*see* GLORY (IN THE BIBLE)]. They were manlike in aspect but double-winged and were apparently reminders and guardians of Yahweh's glory.

Yahweh enthroned upon cherubim became a common concept in Israelite cultic lore [1 Sm 4.4; 2 Sm 6.2; 4 Kgs 19.15; 1 Chr 13.6; Is 37.16; Ps 79(80).2; 98(99).1]. Once they were assigned "to guard the way to the tree of life" in God's garden (Gn 3.24). Perhaps a guarding function was normal for them, but there is no other explicit evidence. In 2 Sm 22.11 [Ps 17(18).11] a cherub was Yahweh's flying steed that He mounted to come swiftly to the psalmist's rescue and may have been symbolical of God's ubiquity and agility.

Ezechiel described God's chariot as supported and moved by "figures resembling four living creatures" (Ez 1.4–28) and in 10.20 recognized them as cherubim. He saw them as human in form but four-winged and four-faced. Their wings were outstretched and supported the firmament above which God was enthroned in splendor. When they moved, their wings clapped like thunder, and they sounded like an army shouting a battle cry. They symbolized, then, God's power and mobility.

The part man and part animal mythical creatures of the ancient Middle East may have been the source of the much modified Israelite conception of cherubim. In Phoenician culture a *krb* had the function of ushering worshipers to the deity and representations of *krb* guarding an enthroned King have been found. In the more ancient Akkadian culture a *kāribu* was an adviser to the gods and an advocate for devotees. In Israelite religion they had no direct role concerning the faithful, nor were they God's advisers. Their attendance on God's glory, their terrifying superhuman mobility, and in general the development of *angelology in the postexilic period led to their identification with God's heavenly courtiers.

In the NT they are alluded to as celestial attendants in ch. 4 to 6 of the Apocalypse, where the author used imagery derived from Ezechiel. Catholic tradition describes them as angels who have an intimate knowledge of God and continually praise Him. This seems to be a theological development stemming from the four living beings of the Apocalypse.

Bibliography: EncDictBibl 353–356. De Vaux AncIsr 319. J. FINEGAN, *Light from the Ancient Past* (2d ed. Princeton 1959). M. J. STEVE, *The Living World of the Bible,* tr. D. WOODWARD (New York 1961). **Illustration credit:** Palestine Archaeological Museum, Jerusalem, Jordan.

[T. L. FALLON]

CHERUBIN OF AVIGLIANA, BL., Augustinian friar; b. Avigliana (in Piedmont), 1451; d. Avigliana, Sept. 17, 1479 (feast, Feb. 20). Of the noble Testa family, Cherubin entered the Augustinian monastery at Avigliana in his youth and from the beginning gave evidence of great holiness. He had ardent piety (which expressed itself particularly in devotion to the crucified Savior), a deep spirit of obedience, and a purity that impressed itself sensibly on those with whom he dealt. The usual *mirabilia,* reported in medieval hagiography, contributed to the development of his cult: at the time of his death, it is said, the church bells rang unaided by human hands; his body continued to give off a sweet odor long after he died. Perini identifies a sermon printed *c.* 1477 as probably his. He was beatified in 1865.

Bibliography: J. LANTERI, *Postrema saecula sex religionis Augustinianae,* 3 v. (Tolentino-Rome 1858–60) 2:58–59. G. B. IMPEROR, *Cuor-Giglio ossia il beato Cherubino da Avigliana* (Turin 1880). D. A. PERINI, *Bibliographia Augustiniana,* 4 v. (Florence 1929–38) 1:71.

[J. E. BRESNAHAN]

CHERUBINI, LUIGI, composer of classical church music and opera; b. Florence, Italy, Sept. 14, 1760 (baptized Maria Luigi Carlo Zenobio Salvatore); d. Paris, March 15, 1842. Cherubini's catalogue is headed by a Mass in F which he composed at 13, after study from the age of 6 with his father and later with B. Felici and his son. In 1778, through the Grand Duke of Tuscany (later Emperor Leopold III), he began studies under Giuseppe Sarti at Milan and then Bologna, which resulted in 20 Palestrina-styled motets. From 1780 to 1806 he concentrated on opera, and in his eight serious Paris operas (he had settled there in 1788) extended the reforms initiated by *Gluck. In 1795 he was appointed professor of counterpoint at the newly founded Paris Conservatory, and became director in 1822. Meanwhile, since Napoleon disliked his music, he moved in 1805 to Vienna, where he met *Beethoven (who regarded him as preeminent among living composers) and F. J. *Haydn, and was warmly received by the public; but he returned to Paris after the outbreak of war between Austria and France. Ill and depressed, he ceased composing altogether, until, while he was recuperating at the chateau of the Prince of Chimay, the local music society pleaded with him to compose a Mass for their church; thus began the great series of church music he produced between 1808 and 1836. Outstanding are the two orchestral Requiems, in C-minor and in D-minor (composed for his own funeral).

Luigi Cherubini, portrait by J. A. D. Ingres.

In a memorable phrase about the C-minor's *Agnus Dei,* Cardinal J. H. Newman spoke of "the lovely note C. which keeps recurring as the *Requiem* approaches eternity." In both operatic and sacred forms he combined classic severity of style (tempered by modern harmonic resources and colorful orchestration), great contrapuntal skill, and dramatic power.

See also MUSIC, SACRED, HISTORY OF, 7.

Bibliography: E. BELLASIS, *Cherubini* (enl. ed. Birmingham, Eng. 1912). E. BLOM, "Cherubini in Church," *Stepchildren of Music* (London 1925). G. CONFALONIERI, *Prigiona di un artista: Il romanzo di Luigi Cherubini,* 2 v. (Milan 1948). M. QUATRELLES L'EPINE, *Cherubini, 1760–1842: Notes et documents inédits* (Lille 1913). A. LOEWENBERG, Grove DMM 2:198–201. Baker 282–283. **Illustration credit:** The Cincinnati Art Museum.

[A. ROBERTSON]

CHESTER, ANCIENT SEE OF. The city of Chester in Cheshire, northwest England, south of Liverpool, may have been, at times, the seat of those bishops of the Anglo-Saxon kingdom of Mercia who are usually associated with Lichfield (*see* COVENTRY AND LICHFIELD, ANCIENT SEE OF). Medieval Chester became important when it was fortified in 907 by Queen Ethelfleda, becoming the site of a royal palace and the scene (973) of the submission of the kings of Britain to King *Edgar the Peaceful. There were two collegiate churches at Chester by the 10th century: St. Werburgh, which was first attested in a document of King Edgar dated 958, and St. John the Baptist. These collegiate churches were restored by Leofric of Mercia *c.* 1057, and are both mentioned as having considerable endowments in the *Domesday survey. This same survey indicates that the bishops of Lichfield had retained a strong position in Chester until the time of the Conquest. Then in 1075 the Council of London, under the primacy of Abp. *Lanfranc of Canterbury, decreed the removal of the See of Lichfield to Chester. Bishop Peter of Lichfield moved there accordingly, and the collegiate church of St. John the Baptist became the cathedral. In 1102, however, the second bishop of Chester, Roger de Limesey (1086–1117), transferred his see to St. Mary's, Coventry, perhaps because of the hostility of the Welsh. The Abbey of St. Werburgh, refounded with Benedictine monks from *Bec by Earl Hugh of Chester (1092), remained important, and it seems that Chester still gave the bishop his title, although no bishop seems to have lived there until the founding of the new see under *Henry VIII in 1541. At that date the abbey church of St. Werburgh became the cathedral.

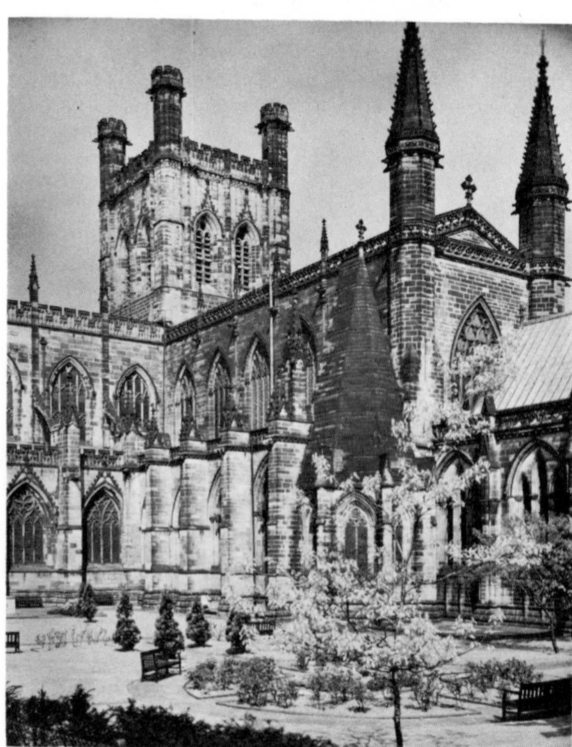

The cathedral at Chester, formerly the abbey church of St. Werburgh.

Bibliography: C. HIATT, *The Cathedral Church of Chester* (London 1897). J. TAIT, ed., *The Domesday Survey of Cheshire* (Edinburgh 1916). D. JONES, *The Church in Chester, 1300–1540* (Manchester 1957) 4–5. Cross ODCC 270. **Illustration credit:** Courtesy of the British Travel Association, New York.

[V. I. J. FLINT]

CHESTERTON, GILBERT KEITH

Writer, journalist, apologist, illustrator; b. London, May 29, 1874; d. Beaconsfield, June 14, 1936. The Chestertons were of the middle class, "liberal" in politics and religion, and reasonably well to do. From their father, Edward, who "knew all his English literature backwards" and who "never made a vulgar success of all the thousand things he did so successfully," Gilbert and his brother Cecil (1879–1918) learned a love of literature. The Chestertons, in the noblest and most literal sense, were amateurs. From St. Paul's School, where he had been chairman of the junior debating club, and edited its journal (called, significantly, the *Debater*), Chesterton went (1891) to the London Slade School of Art, and, somewhat later, to lectures in English literature at University College, London.

First Three Periods. Chesterton's career falls into four periods. Before 1900 his work was sporadic, intuitive, and romantic. Swayed by idealism, he rebelled against decadent *fin de siècle* pessimism by adopting a Whitmanian optimism. He had not yet learned to distinguish rationalism (which he continued to abhor) from reason (which he came to rely upon in all judgments less than *de fide*); he had not become, as he labeled himself in his *St. Thomas,* a "moderate realist." Realizing that his work of these years was often unbalanced and antirational, Chesterton destroyed many early MSS and left "an absolute command" that his solipsistic juvenilia never be published.

In 1900 Chesterton emerged from obscurity. His periodical essays, collections of verse, and fantasies transformed him from publisher's reader to a Fleet Street legend. He had published his first poem in 1891, but it was not until 1901, the year of his marriage to Frances Blogg, that he settled in "the Street" for good and began his 12-year long weekly column in the *Daily News.* The first of his 1,500-odd essays in the *Illustrated London News* appeared in 1905. The Chesterton of these years—a huge man, equipped with a sombrero, a swordstick, a cape, and attended by an ever-waiting hansom cab—remained the public's image of "G. K. C."

The forerunner of Chesterton's third period (1908–21) was *Heretics* (1905). A critic's challenge led to Chesterton's rebuttal, and his career as a Christian, but not yet Catholic, apologist opened in 1908 with *Ortho-*

Gilbert Keith Chesterton, posthumous portrait painted by the English artist Edwin Swan.

doxy. These were the years when the two Chestertons, Hilaire *Belloc, H. G. *Wells, and G. B. *Shaw were influencing each other and England. The debate leading up to and following World War I hit Chesterton hard: the Marconi scandal of 1912–13 (*see* MARCONI, GUGLIELMO), a nearly fatal physical and emotional breakdown in 1914, and the death of his brother Cecil in 1918 were the crises he faced.

The Final Period. Chesterton entered his final period by being received into the Catholic Church in 1922. His conversion, at 48, had been gradual, carefully reasoned, and deeply felt. His work in these last years was less gay and more polemic, perhaps less imaginative, but more serious and lasting than much of his earlier writing. Although his illustrations and prefaces became less numerous in the 1920s and 1930s, his contributions to journals were virtually innumerable. As one of the most prolific writers in modern times (especially in this last period), he wrote more than 3,000 prose and verse pieces for *G. K.'s Weekly* alone—sometimes as many as 10,000 words a week. His social, economic, and political propaganda became more searching, and in order to find an even wider audience for "orthodoxy," he turned to weekly broadcasts over the BBC. It was partly his lifelong success in finding new audiences that led Pius XI to bestow upon him (1936) the title of Defender of the Catholic Faith.

His Unique Achievement. Chesterton was neither conventional nor reactionary. He was, to put it bluntly, a rebel. His very reliance upon tradition was original and creative. Almost alone in the midst of the pessimists, agnostics, materialists, and aesthetes of the earliest years of the 20th century, Chesterton "came home." He rediscovered England, Rome—and the Occident. The Thomism latent in his early writings became manifest. (*See* THOMISM, 1.) He taught the primacy of idea and a teleology of limits, and his religious teaching attacked doubt with commitment. He sought to undermine secularism with an apologia that took religion as the guide and goal of all thought and action. The core of Chesterton's moral thought was the vow; of his social thought, the family. The enemies were eleutheromania and slavery. He fought capitalism and socialism with distributed ownership (*see* DISTRIBUTISM); industrialism and the "servile state" (the phrase is Belloc's) with the concept of the craftsman; imperialism and cosmopolitanism with nationalism; the expert and the misanthrope with the Common Man. He found sanity and creativity in a God-centered, not man-centered, universe; in an informed heart, not in rationalism or irrationalism.

Chesterton's aesthetics stressed art as a rational craft, as meaning. His literary theory was intellectual and antiromantic: literature is secondary—and never "autotelic." Chesterton might be called a metaphysical-moral critic: art is inseparable from creation and from morality. His styles followed his dogmas as conclusions follow premises.

In later life Chesterton's judgments became firmer. He attacked unreason and irrationalism with a style of topsyturvy that was wholly conscious and wholly controlled. His was not an intuitive but an individuating-synthesizing mind. The essence of Chesterton and his thought is balance, a balance seen in his dynamic syntheses of reason and faith, the real and the ideal, optimism and pessimism, the urgent and the absurd, the prose and the poetry of life. Because he related the ephemeral to the eternal, issue to principle, few of his writings will date. Not a few thinkers, among them C. S. *Lewis and Ronald *Knox, have acknowledged their intellectual and spiritual debt to this man, whom Étienne Gilson has called "one of the deepest thinkers who ever existed."

A selection of Chesterton's most significant works would include: poetry—*The Wild Knight* (1900), *The Ballad of the White Horse* (1911), *The Queen of the Seven Swords* (1926), *Collected Poems* (1927); novels and fantasies—*The Napoleon of Notting Hill* (1904), *The Man Who Was Thursday* (1908), *Manalive* (1912), *The Flying Inn* (1912); essays—*The Defendant* (1901), *Twelve Types* (1902), *Heretics* (1905), *Tremendous Trifles* (1909), *What's Wrong with the World* (1910), *Fancies versus Fads* (1923), *The Thing* (1929), *The Well and the Shallows* (1935); criticism and biography—*Robert Browning* (1903), *Charles Dickens* (1906), *George Bernard Shaw* (1909), *William Blake* (1910), *The Victorian Age in Literature* (1913), *William Cobbett* (1925), *Robert Louis Stevenson* (1927), *Chaucer* (1932); Christian apologetics and religious biography—*Orthodoxy* (1908), *St. Francis of Assisi* (1923), *The Everlasting Man* (1925), *The Catholic Church and Conversion* (1926), *St. Thomas Aquinas* (1933); plays—*Magic* (1913), *The Judgement of Dr. Johnson* (1927), *The Surprise* (1952); shorter fiction—*The Father Brown Stories* (omnibus ed. 1929), *The Poet and the Lunatics* (1929); travel, memoirs—*The New Jerusalem* (1921), *What I Saw in America* (1922), *The Resurrection of Rome* (1930), *Autobiography* (1936).

Bibliography: J. SULLIVAN, *G. K. Chesterton: A Bibliography* (London 1958). M. WARD, *Gilbert Keith Chesterton* (London 1944). C. E. CHESTERTON, *G. K. Chesterton: A Criticism* (London 1908). R. AROCENA, *El sembrado de Chesterton* (Montevideo 1934). E. CAMMAERTS, *The Laughing Prophet: The Seven Virtues* *and G. K. Chesterton* (London 1937). H. Belloc, *On the Place of Gilbert Chesterton in English Letters* (New York 1940). R. A. Knox, *Captive Flames* (New York 1941). V. J. McNabb, *The Father McNabb Reader* (New York 1954) 82–93. G. Wills, *Chesterton: Man and Mask* (New York 1961). *G. K. Chesterton: The Man Who Was Orthodox*, ed. A. L. Maycock (London 1963). **Illustration credit:** Library, John Carroll University, Cleveland, Ohio.

[A. HERBOLD]

CHESTNUT HILL COLLEGE

A 4-year liberal arts Catholic college for women, the College is situated in suburban Philadelphia, Pa., with easy access to one of America's oldest centers of culture. It was established as an academy in 1858 by the Sisters of St. Joseph, a branch of the French religious community founded in 1650 primarily for the education of women. In 1871 the school received from the city of Philadelphia a charter to grant degrees, but it continued as an academy until 1924, when the college opened. Sister Maria Kostka Logue was first dean, and later president. The first freshman class numbered 15; the first faculty, 12. When 28 sisters of St. Joseph began Saturday and summer classes that same year, they presaged what was to become one of the main concerns of the College—the education of the sister-teachers of the community. By the fall of 1928, the administration building was completed and named Fournier Hall in honor of the foundress of the Philadelphia Sisters, Mother St. John *Fournier, a scholar and educator. In 1938, after several years' deliberation, the original name of the college, Mt. St. Joseph, was changed to Chestnut Hill College, in order to avoid confusion with the many academies and colleges of that name.

As early as 1932, the College introduced a departmental honors program to enable superior students to pursue independent study through seminars, tutoring, and advanced research. The curriculum, rooted in the tradition of the liberal arts, and leading to a B.A. or a B.S. degree, offers preparation for secondary teaching, for law, medical, or graduate schools, and for other careers open to women. With religion and philosophy as required courses, the student can specialize in the humanities, and in the social or natural sciences. Despite the range of major fields, however, the liberal arts background remains a requisite for a degree from Chestnut Hill.

In 1941 the administration established an alumnae office to be directed by an executive secretary-treasurer. The alumnae won national recognition for its support when it received the 1960 U.S. Steel competitive award from the American Alumni Council. In 1960 the College launched an expansion program to provide new quarters for faculty and alumnae, and new laboratories and classrooms for students. Two buildings completed in 1961, Memorial Library and Fontbonne Hall, brought the total to 6 on the 50-acre campus.

When the rise in college enrollments became almost a national emergency, Chestnut Hill was forced to define its role. In 1958 the 10-member board of trustees decided that rather than jeopardize its standards of excellence, the College would continue to limit enrollment (600 in 1960), in order to maintain a faculty-student ratio of 1 to 10. They confirmed their intention to resist pressures for technical or vocational education by adhering to the original ideal of a small liberal arts college.

In 1964 the administration and teaching faculty included 5 priests, 34 sisters, and 29 laymen, who held 19 doctorate and 38 master's degrees. There were 622 students enrolled full time and 515 sisters during the 1962 summer session. The library housed 56,400 volumes and received 318 periodicals.

Chestnut Hill is accredited by the Middle States Association of Colleges and Secondary Schools and by the State Department of Public Instruction. It holds membership in the American Association of University Women, the National Catholic Educational Association, the American Council on Education, and the Institute of International Education. [A. E. BENNIS]

CHEVALIER, JULES, religious founder; b. Richelieu (Indre-et-Loire), France, March 15, 1824; d. Issoudun (Indre), Oct. 21, 1907. Because of his family's poverty he was apprenticed early to a shoemaker, but in 1841 he entered the preparatory seminary at Saint-Gauthier. After studies in the major seminary in Bourges he was ordained (1851) and spent the remainder of his life working in that archdiocese. He served in several parishes until in 1854 he became a curate in Issoudun. From 1872 until his death he was pastor and archpriest in Issoudun. With the encouragement of Father Maugenest, who had been a fellow seminarian, he founded the *Sacred Heart Missionaries (1854) and acted as their superior general until 1901.

Jules Chevalier.

In 1882 he collaborated with Marie Hartzer to found the Daughters of *Our Lady of the Sacred Heart. Devotion to the *Sacred Heart, around which his spirituality centered, formed the subject of all his writings. His two principal works, reprinted several times, are: *Notre-Dame du Sacré-Coeur de Jésus* (1895) and *Le Sacré-Coeur de Jésus* (1900). Chevalier was one of the leading promoters of devotion to the Sacred Heart in the 19th century.

Bibliography: C. Piperon, *Le Très Révérend Père Jules Chevalier* (Lille 1924). K. Schneider, *Wege Gottes R. P. J. Chevalier* (Schwann 1928). H. Vermin, *Le Père Jules Chevalier* (Rome 1957). R. Limouzin-Lamothe, DictBiogFranc 8:1064–65. A. Bondervoet, DHGE 12:647–648. L. Despresse, DictSpirAscMyst 2:829–831.

[L. F. PETIT]

CHEVALIER, ULYSSE, French bibliographer and historian; b. Cyr Ulysse Joseph Chevalier, at Rambouillet, Seine-et-Oise, France, Feb. 24, 1841; d. Romans, Drôme, France, Oct. 27, 1923. Chevalier was ordained in 1867, and was later named professor of archeology at the major seminary at Romans (1881) and then of Church history at the Institut catholique of Lyons (1887). He was the recipient of academic honors and a member of many learned societies, including the Académie des inscriptions et belles-lettres. Guided by the great Léopold *Delisle, Chevalier followed a life of scholarship, and by 1912 his publications totaled 512. Among the most important are: *Répertoire des sources historiques du moyen âge:* pt. 1 *Bio-bibliographie* (2d ed. 1905–07) and pt. 2 *Topo-bibliographie* (1894–1903; repr. New York 1962); *Gallia christiana novissima* in seven volumes (begun by J. H. Albanès but published with additions by Chevalier, 1899–1920); and *Repertorium hymnologicum* in six volumes, a catalogue of more than 30,000 hymns and chants used in the Roman rite (1892–1921). He wrote also numerous works on the history of Dauphiné. His name is associated with famous controversies over the authenticity (which he denied) of the Holy *Shroud of Turin (1900) and the Holy House of *Loreto (1907). Chevalier's works are somewhat uneven in performance and some of them have become outdated. However, they have rendered appreciable service in the past and remain useful today, especially for the medievalist.

Bibliography: *M. le Chanoine Ulysse Chevalier, correspondant de l'Institut: Son oeuvre scientifique, sa bio-bibliographie* (new ed. Valence 1912). H. Leclercq, DACL 9:1743–44. P. Thomé de Maisonneufve, *L'Oeuvre scientifique du chanoine U. Chevalier* (Grenoble 1933). G. Bardy, *Catholicisme* 10:1048–49. R. Limouzin-Lamothe, DictBiogFranc 8:1071–72.

[M. I. J. ROUSSEAU]

CHEVERUS, JEAN LOUIS LEFEBVRE DE

First bishop of *Boston, Mass., bishop of Montauban, France, and cardinal archbishop of Bordeaux; b. Mayenne, France, Jan. 28, 1768; d. Bordeaux, July 19, 1836. He was the eldest of six children of Jean Vincent and Anne Charlotte (Lemarchand) Lefebvre de Cheverus. Educated first at the local *collège* of Mayenne, he was awarded a scholarship in 1781 for Louis-le-Grand in Paris. He subsequently entered Saint-Magloire Seminary and was ordained in Paris on Dec. 18, 1790, just as the French Revolution was gathering momentum. Returning to Mayenne he became (1791) an assistant to his uncle Louis René de Cheverus, pastor of Notre Dame de Mayenne. He refused to take the oath required by the Civil Constitution of the Clergy and fled to England in 1792. He first taught French and mathematics in a Protestant school in Wallingford and offered Mass at Overy until he learned enough English to serve a congregation. In 1794 he founded Tottenham Chapel, one of three *émigré* foundations in the London suburbs that endured.

In 1796 he went to Boston at the invitation of Francis A. Matignon, pastor of Holy Cross Church. Submitting to the authority of Bp. John Carroll, he was first destined for the Detroit mission, but Matignon's protests retained him for the Boston area. In Maine he did yeoman service among the scattered white Catholics and the Passamaquoddy and Penobscot Indians, receiving for his mis-

Jean Louis Lefebvre de Cheverus, portrait by Gilbert Stuart.

sionary efforts among the latter an annual stipend from the state of Massachusetts. Owing to the prejudice against Catholic clergy in New England he was brought to court in 1800–01 in both civil and criminal actions for having officiated at the marriage of a Maine couple, but was exonerated in both suits. His labors in Boston won the affection of Protestants and Catholics alike, particularly after his fearless and charitable efforts during the yellow fever epidemic of 1798. He was instrumental in the conversion of Elizabeth Bayley Seton, of New York; Dr. Stephen C. Blyth, of Salem; Thomas Walley, of Boston; Calvin White, of Connecticut; and Daniel Barber, of Vermont. His defense of the Church against an attack by John Lowell in the *Monthly Anthology and Boston Review* in 1807 earned him the respect and lifelong friendship of Anthology Club members Harrison Gray Otis, Josiah Quincy, John Kirkland, and Theodore Lyman. To the club's Athenaeum Library he left his personal library on leaving Boston.

When Boston was created a diocese in 1808 he was named first bishop and was consecrated in Baltimore on Nov. 1, 1810. During his American episcopate (1810–23) he traveled ceaselessly, "more priest than bishop," in the pastoral care of a diocese that included all of New England. A fine preacher, he graced the pulpits of New York, Philadelphia, and Baltimore on his wider travels. In 1815 he dedicated old St. Patrick's Cathedral in New York. In Boston he founded an Ursuline convent (1817) and a second Catholic church, St. Augustine's (1819). His greatest contribution was fostering genuinely friendly relations between the Catholic minority and the non-Catholic majority. Protestant ministers, notably William Ellery Channing, Edward Everett, and

Thaddeus M. Harris, remained his warm friends for life. When in 1823 Louis XVIII summoned Cheverus back to France, 226 Protestants framed a petition to the King pleading that Cheverus be left in Boston, saying, "We hold him to be a blessing and a treasure in our social community which we cannot part with." Among the signers were Elbridge Gerry, Daniel Webster, Josiah Quincy, and John Lowell.

Returning to France he became bishop of Montauban, a strong Protestant city, rebuilding from 1824 to 1826 a diocese that had suffered the ravages of the Revolution and the Napoleonic era. In 1826 he was made archbishop of Bordeaux and peer of France, serving in the upper chamber of the French legislature from 1827 to 1830. In 1828 Charles X made him councilor of state and in 1830 conferred the office of Commander of the Order of the Holy Spirit. In 1829 Cheverus instituted the first retirement plan for the clergy in the Diocese of Bordeaux. Although devoted to the Bourbon monarchy, he nevertheless became a supporter of the Orleanist regime after the July Revolution of 1830. On the recommendation of Louis Philippe he was named cardinal in the consistory of Feb. 1, 1836, with the King himself conferring the red hat in the Tuileries Chapel on March 9, 1836. One of his last pastoral acts was the creation of an association for the care of 167 children left fatherless by a fishing disaster at the Teste in April 1836.

Bibliography: A. J. HAMON, *Life of the Cardinal Cheverus, Archbishop of Bordeaux,* tr. R. M. WALSH (Philadelphia 1839). A. M. MELVILLE, *Jean Lefebvre de Cheverus, 1768–1836* (Milwaukee 1958). W. M. WHITEHILL, *A Memorial to Bishop Cheverus* (Boston 1951). **Illustration Credit:** Courtesy of the Museum of Fine Arts, Boston.

[A. M. MELVILLE]

The altar of the Oriental-style church of the Monastery of Chevetogne, near Rochefort, Belgium.

CHEVETOGNE, MONASTERY OF, Benedictine foundation outside Rochefort, Diocese of Namur, southeast Belgium; dedicated to the Exaltation of the Holy Cross. Founded in 1925 at Amay-sur-Meuse (Diocese of Liège) by Lambert *Beauduin in response to Pius XI's *Equidem verba* (1924) inviting Benedictines to work for Christian unity, it became a priory (1928) and moved to Chevetogne (1939). It seeks to establish a *rapprochement* between Rome and other Christian groups, especially Russian and other Orthodox Churches, working for corporate reconciliation rather than for individual conversions. The community of 45 members (13 nationalities) celebrates divine services in the Latin and Byzantine (Greek and Slavonic) rites and pursues studies in the history, theology, and spirituality of non-Catholic groups. The "irenic" method has been presented in the review *Irénikon* since 1926. Works on history, ecclesiology, the liturgy, and comparative theology and spirituality appear in *Editions de Chevetogne.* Byzantine and Russian religious art are reproduced. Annual conferences have been held since 1942. The monastery, which has directed the Pontifical Greek College in Rome since 1956, depends on the Congregation for the Oriental Church. The monastery church (1957) is in Oriental style. A center for ecumenical training was established in 1964.

Bibliography: *Le Monastère de Chevetogne: Notice historique* (Chevetogne 1962). L. BOUYER, *Dom Lambert Beauduin, un homme d'Église* (Paris 1964). G. CURTIS, *Paul Couturier and Unity in Christ* (Westminster, Md. 1964). R. GAZEAU, *Catholicisme* 1:406–407. N. EGENDER, LexThK² 1:421. Kapsner Ben Bibl 2:196–197. **Illustration credit:** Official Belgian Tourist Bureau, New York City.

[N. EGENDER]

CHEVREUL, MICHEL EUGÈNE, French chemist, whose work on fats and colors was fundamental for theory and practice; b. Angers, Aug. 31, 1786; d. Paris, April 9, 1889. His father was a leading physician. Chevreul studied in Paris under L. *Vauquelin in 1803 and succeeded him as professor at the Natural History Museum in 1830. From 1824 to 1885 he was director of dyeing at the Manufacture Royale des Gobelins. He presented 12 years' work on animal fats in a book (1823) in which he described and named several fatty acids and explained the process of soapmaking. In 1839 he wrote about the law of contrasts of colors, in 1846 about the optical effects of dyed fabrics, and in 1861 about systematic definition of colors. In 1879 he resigned from the Museum (Jardin des Plantes) directorship, which he had held for 15 years, but kept his professorship. He remained active to the age of 102.

Bibliography: G. BOUCHARD, *Chevreul* (Paris 1932). A. B. COSTA, *Michel Eugène Chevreul* (Madison, Wis. 1962).

[E. FARBER]

CHEYENNE, DIOCESE OF (CHEYENNENSIS), suffragan of the metropolitan See of Denver, Colo., erected Aug. 2, 1887. It is coterminous with the state of Wyoming and has an area of 97,548 square miles, not including Yellowstone National Park, which also lies within its boundaries. In 1963 Catholics numbered more than 49,200 in a total population of about 330,000. Early explorers of the region included a number of French-Canadian Catholics, two brothers of whom, François and Louis de la Vérendrye, were probably the first white men in the state. Entering the area

St. Lawrence O'Toole Church, Laramie, Wyo.

St. Mary's Cathedral, Cheyenne, Wyo.

from Montana, they are thought to have reached a spur of the Big Horn Mountains, Jan. 12, 1743. Among the missionary pioneers, Pierre J. *De Smet, SJ, offered the first Mass in the state at the trappers' station on the Green River, July 5, 1840, with Snake and Flathead Indians as well as traders and trappers in his congregation. One of the earliest Catholic churches is St. Lawrence O'Toole Church, built in 1872.

The diocese, erected 3 years before Wyoming became the 44th state of the Union (July 10, 1890), had been part of the Vicariate of Nebraska from 1857 to 1885, when it was included in the newly established Diocese (later Archdiocese) of *Omaha. Maurice Burke, a priest of Chicago, was consecrated first bishop on Oct. 28, 1887, and ruled until his transfer to the See of St. Joseph, Mo. (later Kansas City–St. Joseph), June 19, 1893. His successors in Cheyenne included Thomas M. Lenihan (1897–1901), James J. Keane (1902–11), Patrick A. McGovern (1912–51), and Hubert M. Newell, who was appointed coadjutor with right of succession, Aug. 2, 1947, and became Cheyenne's fifth bishop, Nov. 8, 1951. Because of the lack of industry in the state the growth of the population has been slow. Hence the development of the Church has followed the missionary pattern, with principal emphasis on the extension of parishes and missions to meet the needs of the faithful in the widely scattered and sparsely settled areas of the diocese. In 1963 there were 38 parishes, 38 missions, and 9 stations, or places without chapels, in which Mass was regularly offered. Of the several Indian tribes that once roamed Wyoming, only two maintained numerical strength. One of these, the Arapaho tribe, had a large percentage of Catholics, and was cared for by the Jesuit fathers and Franciscan sisters who staff St. Stephen's Mission on the Wind River Reservation. Other religious serving in the diocese included priests of the Third Order Regular of St. Francis, Sisters of Charity, and Benedictine and Dominican sisters.

Among the outstanding achievements of the Church in Wyoming was the expansion of Catholic educational facilities, which in 1963 included 2 high schools, 9 elementary schools, several catechetical centers, and a vigorous Confraternity of Christian Doctrine program for the education of children and young people in those areas in which parish schools were not possible. St. Joseph's Orphanage, Torrington, was directed by Franciscans, and De Paul Hospital, Cheyenne, by Sisters of Charity.

Bibliography: P. A. McGovern, *History of the Diocese of Cheyenne* (Privately printed; Cheyenne 1941). V. Linford, *Wyoming, Frontier State* (Denver 1947). **Illustration credit:** Fig. 1, Wyoming State Archives and Historical Department.

[H. M. NEWELL]

CHEZAL-BENOÎT, ABBEY OF, Saint-Pierre de Chezal-Benoît (known also as Chazeau-Benoist; Latin, *Casale Malanum, Casale Benedictum*), a Benedictine abbey, located in the Diocese of Bourges, parish and township of Chezal-Benoît, department of Cher, France. The abbey was founded in 1093 by Andrew of Vallombrosa (d. 1112) in a deserted spot. Nothing certain is known of the abbey's history before 1479, when Peter of Mas, the prior of Castres in the Diocese of Albi, became abbot and introduced the reform of the Congregation of St. Justina (Padua). *See* BENEDICTINES. He abolished the long offices, fasts, and severe punishments, and established a 3-year term for the abbots who were elected by a general chapter. The reform, ratified by the Holy See in 1491, was adopted by the following abbeys: Saint-Sulpice of Bourges in 1499, Saint-Allyre of Clermont in 1500, and Saint-Vincent of Mans in 1502. The religious of Chezal-Benoît were formed into a congregation in 1505. There was a continuous line of abbots regularly elected from 1515 to 1763. The following abbeys were attached to Chezal-Benoît: Saint-Martin of Sées in 1511, *Saint-Germain-des-Prés in 1514, Brantôme in 1541, Sainte-Colombe of Sens in 1580, and *Jumièges in 1515 and 1580. Several monks were outstanding for their virtue or for their contributions as historians or men of letters: Charles Fernand, Guido Jouvenaux, Jehmann Bondonnet, and Jacques du Breul, who contributed to the *Maurist tradition of learning and industry. When the congregation fell into decline, it was absorbed by Saint-Maur (May 2, 1636). The name of Chezal-Benoît was given to the Maurist houses (numbering about 25) in the region between the Loire and the Dordogne. The abbey was abolished in February 1790, but the abbey church remains.

Bibliography: Sources. Archives Nationales, Paris, LL.1328–32. Bibliothèque Nationale, Paris, MS Lat. 12787. Bibl. Bourges MSS 184, 187, 191. GallChrist 2:162–168. L. V. DELISLE, ed., *Rouleaux des morts du IXe au XVe siècle* (Paris 1866) 168–171. U. BERLIÈRE, "La Congrégation de Chezal-Benoît," *Mélanges d'histoire bénédictine*, 4 v. (Maredsous 1897–1902) 3:97–198. F. DESHOULIÈRES, "L'Église abbatiale de Chezal-Benoît," *Bulletin monumental* 71 (1907) 287–306; "L'Abbaye de Chezal-Benoît," *Mém. soc. antiq. centre* 32 (1909) 149–229. J. LAPORTE, "Aperçu des déclarations de la congrégation de Chezal-Benoît sur la Règle," *Revue Mabillon* 29 (1939) 143–157. Cottineau 1:766–767.

[J. LAPORTE]

CHÉZARD DE MATEL, JEANNE MARIE, foundress of Sisters of the Incarnate Word and the Blessed Sacrament; b. Matel, France, November 1596; d. Paris, 1670. She was a mystic and writer, known for her elevated states of prayer and her infused knowledge of Latin. Although she was an almost illiterate person, she wrote letters and a spiritual journal that have caused her to be compared with Saint Gertrude the Great. Because her devotional writings were framed in technical theological terms, doubts of her authorship were aroused in the mind of Cardinal Alphonse Richelieu. He removed all of her references and then commanded her to write her autobiography and spiritual history. She produced a work of lofty style, replete to an astonishing degree with mystical speculations and liturgical texts. Her institute was authorized in 1633 but not formally begun until 1639 at Matel; it was finally approved in 1644. Her second monastery was erected at Grenoble, and the third, at Paris. Here, on her deathbed, she received the habit of the institute she had founded and made her profession of vows. American branches of her foundation are in Galveston, Tex., and in Mexico.

Bibliography: L. CRISTIANI, DictSpirAscMyst 2:837–840. H. WAACH, LexThK² 2:1049. Heimbucher 2:427–428. ST. PIERRE OF JESUS, *Life of the Reverend Mother Jeanne Chézard de Matel*, tr. H. C. SEMPLE (5th ed. San Antonio 1922).

[M. J. DORCY]

CHIBCHA RELIGION. The Chibcha, a group of South American Indians, occupied the high valleys surrounding the modern cities of Bogotá and Tunja in Colombia before the Spanish conquest. The Chibcha religion was of both state and individual concern. Each political division had its own set of priests. Apparently some kind of hierarchy was recognized and the priests were a professional hereditary class. Priests, who were clearly distinguished from shamans, had as their functions the intercession at public ceremonies for the public good, the dispensing of oracles, and consultation with

Chibcha figurines of gold, cast in the lost-wax process, discovered in Colombian Chibcha burial places.

private individuals. Shamans served the individual more than the state and cured illnesses, interpreted dreams, and foretold the future. The Chibchas had an elaborate pantheon of gods headed by Chiminigagua, the supreme god and creator. In addition to the state temples and idols, many natural habitats were considered to be holy places. Ceremonial practices included offerings, public rites, pilgrimages, and human sacrifice. Human sacrifice was said to be fairly common and was made primarily to the sun.

Bibliography: A. L. KROEBER, "The Chibcha," *Handbook of South American Indians*, ed. J. H. STEWARD, 2 v. (Bureau of American Ethnology, Bulletin 143; Washington 1946) 2:905–909. J. PÉREZ DE BARRADAS, *Los Muiscas antes de la conquista*, 2 v. (Madrid 1950–51) 2:435–511. **Illustration credit:** Courtesy, the Cleveland Museum of Art.

[J. RUBIN]

CHICAGO, ARCHDIOCESE OF (CHICAGIENSIS)

Metropolitan see comprising Cook and Lake counties, Ill., an area of 1,411 square miles, with a population (1963) of 5,566,000, of whom 2,293,900 (41 per cent) were Catholics; diocese erected Nov. 28, 1843; archdiocese, Sept. 10, 1880. The suffragan dioceses of Belleville, Joliet, Peoria, Rockford, and Springfield constituted, with Chicago, the territory of the original see.

Since 1673, when Jacques Marquette, SJ, and Louis Jolliet (Joliet) passed through what is now Chicago on their return after exploring the Mississippi River, the area has had Catholic associations. A year later, fulfilling a promise he had made to the Kaskaskia Indians, Marquette left Green Bay, Wis., with two French *voyageurs* and reached the south branch of the Chicago River, where severe weather and serious illness forced him to remain several months. During their stay he offered Mass daily. Subsequently the area was visited by other missionaries and *voyageurs* including, in 1696, François Pinet, SJ, first resident priest and founder of the Mission of the Guardian Angel, which for unknown reasons closed in 1700. Originally part of the Quebec diocese, Chicago was transferred in 1784 to the prefecture apostolic of the U.S., which became the Baltimore diocese in 1789; in 1808 it passed under the jurisdiction of the new Diocese of Bardstown, Ky. Thereafter Chicago was visited by Gabriel Richard, SS, who arrived from Detroit in September 1821 to offer Mass and preach to the garrison at Ft. Dearborn, and Stephen Badin, the first priest ordained within the U.S., who came in October 1830 from his Potawatomi mission near Niles, Mich. In 1834, when the Diocese of Vincennes was erected, eastern Illinois was included in its territory. When Chicago was incorporated as a town in 1833, its 130 Catholic inhabitants, under the impression that they belonged to the St. Louis diocese, petitioned Bp. Joseph Rosati for a resident pastor. To the distant mission was sent the newly ordained John Mary Irenaeus St. Cyr, who built the first Catholic Church, St. Mary's, on the southwest corner of Lake and State Streets. (It was later moved to Madison Street and Wabash Avenue.)

DIOCESE

At the request of the Fifth Provincial Council of Baltimore (1843), Gregory XVI on Nov. 28, 1843, created the new Diocese of Chicago, embracing the entire state of Illinois.

Quarter. The first bishop of Chicago was William *Quarter, pastor of St. Mary's Church, New York City, who was consecrated by Bp. John Hughes in New York on March 10, 1844. The new bishop, with his brother, Father Walter Quarter, arrived in Chicago on May 5 where he soon learned that all but 8 of the 24 priests who had been serving throughout the state had been recalled to their respective dioceses by the bishops of St. Louis and Vincennes. Undaunted by the shortage of clergy and the poverty of the settlers, Quarter first opened the College of St. Mary's as a boys' school and seminary and then petitioned the Illinois Legislature, which passed an act on Dec. 19, 1844, incorporating The University of St. Mary of the Lake. In New York the following April, he begged funds to provide this first institution of higher learning in Chicago with a suitable university building; this was dedicated July 4, 1846. At his invitation, the Sisters of Mercy established St. Xavier's Academy for girls in September 1846.

St. Mary's was Chicago's only church when Quarter arrived. In 1846 St. Patrick's was built for the West-side Irish; St. Peter's, for the South-side Germans; and St. Joseph's, for the North-side Germans; while English-speaking Catholics on the North side used Holy Name, the university chapel. By the end of his 4-year episcopate he had built 30 churches; ordained 29 priests; traveled extensively throughout the diocese preaching and administering the Sacraments; convened the first diocesan synod in April 1847, preceding it by a 3-day retreat for all priests; successfully petitioned the state legislature to enact a law (1845) constituting the Catholic bishop of Chicago and his successors a corporation sole to hold property in trust for religious purposes; and arranged what was reputed to be the first theological conference held in the U.S., which assembled Nov. 12, 1847 in the university chapel. On Passion Sunday, April 9, 1848, the bishop preached with his usual vigor at the cathedral, but died the following morning. All his property was willed to St. Mary of the Lake University.

Van de Velde. To succeed Quarter, Pius IX appointed the Belgian James Oliver van de Velde who had entered the Society of Jesus when he immigrated to the U.S. in 1817 at the age of 22. After completing his studies he

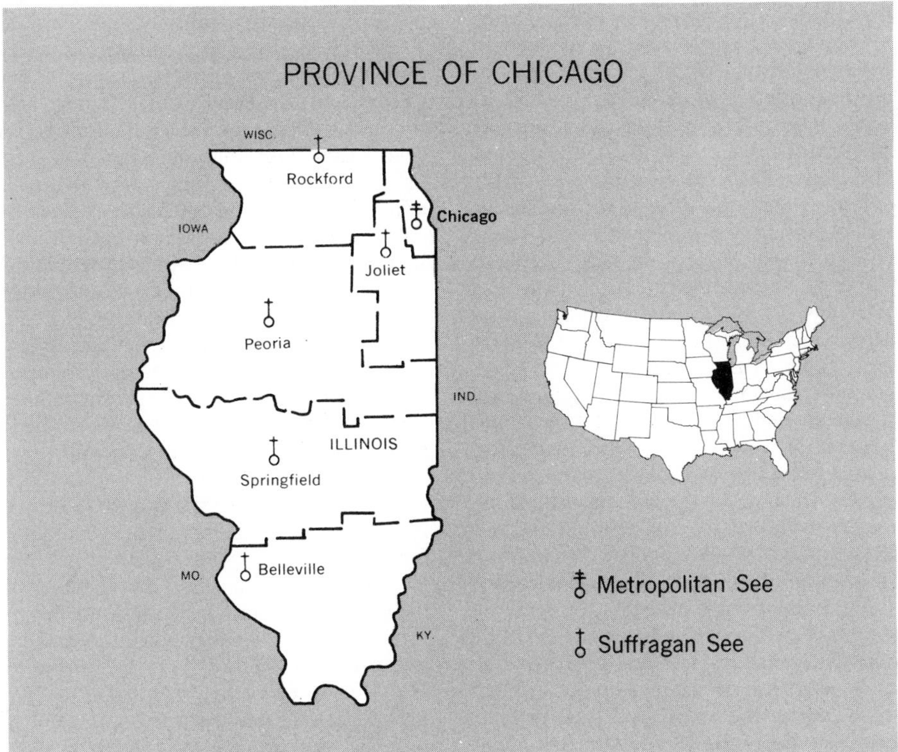

Fig. 1. Province of Chicago, comprising the Archdiocese of Chicago, known as the metropolitan see, and five dioceses, known as suffragan sees. The archbishop has metropolitan jurisdiction over the province.

Fig. 2. St. Mary of the Lake, 1844. Watercolor by Justin Herriott, American School, about 1902.

had served at St. Louis University, where he was in turn professor, vice president, and president. Despite his efforts to decline the episcopal honor, he was released from his vows and persuaded by Abp. Peter Kenrick of St. Louis and a board of three theologians to receive consecration on Feb. 11, 1849, in St. Louis. On his way to Chicago for installation on Palm Sunday, April 1, 1849, the new bishop visited many parishes of his diocese. Upon learning that his predecessor's will left property, including the episcopal residence, to the University of St. Mary of the Lake, Van de Velde ordered that it be completely restored to him. A serious disagreement resulted when the university faculty failed to accede to all his demands, insisting that the property had been purchased with the personal funds of the two Quarter brothers. This disagreement plus his desire to become a Jesuit again, the rigors of the northern Illinois climate, and his declining health led Van de Velde in 1852 to tender his resignation as bishop. A year later he was restored to the Society of Jesus, and Pius IX transferred him to the see at Natchez, Miss., at the same time dividing Chicago by creating Quincy a diocese for the southern half of Illinois. At his departure, Nov. 4, 1853, there were 119 churches in the state, 70 of them having been commenced by him. Of these, 53 were in places where no church had previously existed. The first Catholic hospital, the first orphanage, and 10 new parochial schools likewise owe their origin to this prelate.

O'Regan. The third bishop, Anthony O'Regan, of County Mayo, Ireland, had been educated at St. Patrick's College, Maynooth, Kildare, Ireland, and then made professor and later president of St. Jarlath College, Tuam, Galway, Ireland. At the invitation of Kenrick of St. Louis, O'Regan became first president of the new theological seminary at Carondelet, Mo., from which post he was called to head the Chicago diocese. Consecrated in St. Louis on July 25, 1854, he was installed in his see city the following September. Within 5 months misunderstandings concerning finances led him to dismiss the four diocesan priests who constituted the faculty of St. Mary of the Lake. The four priests, whose withdrawal was lamented by the students, subsequently rendered distinguished service in the dioceses of Trenton and New York. After O'Regan's unsuccessful efforts to induce the Jesuits to assume direction of the university, the building was rented to Father Edward Sorin, founder of Notre Dame University, Ind., for a high school.

The success of a series of parochial missions conducted by the Jesuit Arnold Damen in 1856 in Chicago led to the establishment of Holy Family Church, which later developed into a large parish with St. Ignatius College and High School on its property. To provide for the French-speaking people of Illinois, Van de Velde had admitted into the diocese Charles *Chiniquy, a Canadian priest in trouble with his bishop. In 1856 O'Regan was forced to suspend and excommunicate the priest for his unorthodox sermons and strange conduct. The prelate's difficulties with the university faculty and with Chiniquy prompted him to resign. In 1858 he went to Rome, was appointed titular bishop of Dora, and retired to Brompton, London, England, where he died Nov. 13, 1866. Meanwhile in 1857 the Alton diocese (later Springfield) was erected, and Quincy, established in 1853 but never occupied, was joined to it, thus separating central and southern Illinois from Chicago's jurisdiction.

Duggan. Chicago's fourth bishop was well-acquainted with the diocese. Born in Maynooth, County Kildare, James Duggan had left Ireland at 17 to study philosophy and theology at St. Vincent's, Cape Girardeau, Mo.; was ordained by special dispensation at 22; and 6 years later was made administrator of Chicago following Van de Velde's departure in 1853. Only 10 years after he was ordained, he was consecrated bishop of Antigone and coadjutor to Kenrick of St. Louis. Upon O'Regan's resignation he again became administrator of Chicago, succeeding to the see on Jan. 21, 1859.

Chicago's growth was temporarily interrupted during the first 2 years of the Civil War, but thereafter parishes began to multiply; 16 were founded during Duggan's tenure. His negotiations with Sorin for the return of the university property culminated in July 1861 when the Holy Cross Fathers left Chicago, and the institution reopened under Father John McMullen. Two years later the seminary department was established under Rector James McGovern. The university, affiliated in 1863 with Rush Medical College and the City Law School, flourished until January 1866, when it was closed abruptly and turned into an orphanage. Duggan, whose inconstancy of purpose and action began to indicate incipient insanity, closed the seminary in August 1868 and ordered the faculty to leave the diocese. By spring 1869 his mental collapse was complete and he was confined to an asylum conducted by the Sisters of Charity near St. Louis, where he lived until 1899 without showing any improvement.

Foley. For the difficult position of administrator, Rome chose Thomas Foley, long-term rector of Baltimore's (old) Cathedral of the Assumption and, at different times, chancellor, vicar-general, and administrator of the Baltimore archdiocese. Appointed titular bishop of Pergamus and coadjutor bishop and administrator of Chicago with right of succession, he was consecrated Feb. 27, 1870, in Baltimore and installed in Holy Name procathedral the following month. During his first year 15 new parishes, a hospital, and several new schools were founded. When Chicago's great fire of Oct. 9, 1871, gutted the whole center of the city, seven churches and adjoining rectories and schools were destroyed at a loss of $1 million. In the work of restoration, more substantial and modern structures were built; the cathedral was moved to Holy Name parish, where the new structure was dedicated on Nov. 21, 1875. To help care for the immigrants streaming into Chicago during these years, Foley welcomed many religious orders, including the Franciscans, Lazarists, Servites, Viatorians, and Resurrectionists. At his suggestions, the Peoria Diocese was established in 1877.

Archdiocese

When Foley died on Feb. 19, 1879, it was evident that the ailing Duggan would not recover, so Rome rectified the situation by creating Chicago an archdiocese, with Bp. Patrick A. *Feehan of Nashville, Tenn., as first archbishop.

Feehan. After being educated at St. Patrick's College, Maynooth, Ireland, and the seminary at Carondolet, Mo., Feehan was ordained in 1852. Being a man of unusual administrative ability for which he was subsequently noted, he was an obvious choice for Chicago. He was named on Sept. 10, 1880, and installed in Holy Name Cathedral on November 28. During the next 20 years he worked to provide clergy, churches, and schools for the waves of Catholic immigrants descending upon Chicago. Under him Chicago's churches increased to 298; the number of priests to 538; grammar schools to 166, with 62,723 pupils; and the Catholic population, to 800,000.

The first archdiocesan synod was held on Dec. 13, 1887, when the decrees of the Third Council of Baltimore were promulgated and the first diocesan consultors and permanent rectors appointed. When Feehan's advanced age and increasing burdens made an assistant necessary, Alexander J. McGavick, pastor of St. John's Church, was appointed titular bishop of Narcopolis and auxiliary bishop of Chicago. Soon after his consecration on May 1, 1899, he became incapacitated and was replaced by Peter J. Muldoon, pastor of St. Charles Borromeo, who was appointed titular bishop of Tamassus and consecrated by the apostolic delegate, Cardinal Sebastian Martinelli, on July 25, 1901. Some Irish-born Chicago clergy resented the choice of Muldoon, a native-born American who had been Feehan's chancellor for many years. One of the malcontents, Jeremiah J. Crowley, pastor of St. Mary's Church, Oregon, Ill., was excommunicated for his stubborn opposition, and this situation clouded the last year of Feehan's life. He died suddenly on July 12, 1902, from an apoplectic stroke.

Quigley. On Jan. 8, 1903, Pope Leo XIII transferred James Edward Quigley, Bishop of Buffalo, to Chicago where he was installed on March 10. Born in Canada, he had moved as a youth to Buffalo; and had studied at the seminary in Niagara, N.Y., at Innsbruck, Austria, and at the Propaganda College in Rome, where he was ordained April 12, 1879, and received a doctorate in theology. Upon his return to the U.S. he was pastor of St. Vincent's, Attica, N.Y., for 5 years, rector of the cathedral for 12 years, and pastor of St. Bridget's for a few months. On Feb. 24, 1897, he was consecrated bishop of Buffalo, where he won recognition for his administrative ability and for his part in settling the Buffalo dock strike of 1899.

Soon after his installation as Chicago's second archbishop on March 10, 1903, Quigley realized the need for increased facilities for training the clergy and, in

Fig. 3. St. James Chapel of Quigley Preparatory Seminary North. This example of early French Gothic, modeled after the Sainte-Chapelle of Paris, was completed in 1918.

October 1905, he opened Cathedral College of the Sacred Heart as a preparatory seminary. During his episcopate the second archdiocesan synod was held on Dec. 14, 1905; a missionary congress met in Chicago Nov. 16–18, 1908; Paul P. Rhode, the first priest of Polish lineage to be elevated to the U.S. hierarchy, was consecrated on July 29, 1908, as one of Quigley's auxiliary bishops; and Rockford was established as a diocese Sept. 23, 1908, with Bishop Muldoon as first ordinary. With the assistance of the archbishop, the Catholic Church Extension Society for home missions was founded in 1905 in Chicago by Francis C. *Kelley, pastor of Immaculate Conception Church at Lapeer, Mich. When he died on July 10, 1915, Quigley's administration had restored peace to the archdiocese where, in 12 years, parish churches had increased to 326 and clergy to 790, despite the loss of 55 parishes and 74 priests to the new Rockford diocese in 1908.

Mundelein. Rome again looked to New York in selecting George William *Mundelein, auxiliary bishop of Brooklyn, to be Chicago's third archbishop. He was installed Feb. 9, 1916, by the apostolic delegate, Abp. (Cardinal) John Bonzano. Finding the facilities of Cathedral College inadequate, the archbishop initiated Quigley Preparatory Seminary in May 1916, and made plans for the erection of a theological seminary on the shores of Lake Eara in Lake County near Area, Ill. Under the charter for the University of St. Mary of the Lake, which had been closed since 1866, Mundelein had 14 separate buildings of uniform Georgian style erected there from 1920 to 1934 to constitute St. Mary of the Lake Seminary. After Mundelein was made a cardinal by Pius XI on March 24, 1924, the town of Area changed its name to Mundelein and, with Chicago,

Fig. 4. Cardinal Pacelli, later Pope Pius XII, visiting St. Mary of the Lake Seminary with Cardinal Mundelein in 1936.

was host to the 28th International Eucharistic Congress (June 20–24, 1926).

Catholic Charities was founded in January 1918 to organize the welfare work of the archdiocese. From World War I to the Depression of the 1930s, churches, schools, convents, rectories, and hospitals multiplied rapidly. In 1930 Mundelein directed his auxiliary, Bp. Bernard J. Sheil, to establish the Catholic Youth Organization for the spiritual, mental, and physical development of Catholic youth. Despite the Depression, the finances of the archdiocese were so carefully managed that Bishop of Chicago bonds remained at par during these years. Under Mundelein's vigorous administration, Chicago also attained international recognition. In 1929 the archdiocese contributed $1.5 million toward the new Propaganda College in Rome; and in 1934 for his silver episcopal jubilee, the cardinal acquired the Collegio S. Maria del Lago, a residence for postgraduate students in Rome. When Mundelein died suddenly on Oct. 2, 1939, 82 new parishes had been established and the clergy in the archdiocese had increased to 1,779.

Stritch. On Dec. 27, 1939, Rome announced the transfer of Samuel Alphonsus *Stritch, archbishop of Milwaukee, to Chicago where he was installed on March 7, 1940, by the apostolic delegate, Abp. (Cardinal) Amleto Cicognani. A firm believer in the Catholic press, Stritch promoted the diocesan paper, the *New World,* which increased its circulation from 10,000 in 1940 to 210,000 in 1958. In 1941 he established the Confraternity of Christian Doctrine for teaching released-time programs, parish high schools of religion, lay teacher training courses, parish information classes, and home study courses. He reorganized the Archdiocesan Council of Catholic Women in 1942 and affiliated it with the National Council of Catholic Women; added to Catholic Charities specialized services for the deaf and blind, a guidance center for children, and a house for alcoholics; opened the Catholic Action Federations Office to coordinate the Young Christian Students (YCS), the Young Christian Workers (YCW), and the Christian Family Movement (CFM); set up the Catholic Council on Working Life in 1943; formally recognized the Cana movement, begun in Chicago in 1944, by the appointment of a full-time chaplain in 1946; opened Cardinal Stritch Retreat House for diocesan priests on St. Mary of the Lake Seminary grounds in 1951; appointed an archdiocesan commission on sacred music in 1953; and 4 years later set up an archdiocesan office for radio and television.

The post-World War II years witnessed the phenomenal growth of the Negro population in Chicago and the movement to the suburbs. Stritch founded a Catholic Interracial Council in 1945; he insisted upon racial integration and kept all parishes functioning in Negro neighborhoods. A group of parish priests formed the Cardinal's Conservation Council to meet the problem of changing neighborhoods. To keep pace with the population explosion on the city's periphery and in the suburbs, 77 new parishes were founded and the Diocese of Joliet was established on Dec. 11, 1948, leaving Chicago with only two counties, Cook and Lake.

Elevated to the College of Cardinals by Pius XII on Feb. 18, 1946, Stritch was appointed pro-prefect of the Congregation for the Propagation of the Faith in 1958. Shortly after his arrival in Rome, he suffered a stroke and died there on May 27, 1958. He was buried on June 3 in Mt. Carmel Cemetery, Hillside, Ill.

Meyer. Chicago's fifth archbishop, Albert Gregory *Meyer, was born in Milwaukee, Wis., March 9, 1903; he attended St. Mary's Parochial School, Marquette High School, and St. Francis Preparatory Seminary in Milwaukee, and the North American College in Rome, where he was ordained by Cardinal Basilio Pompilj on July 11, 1926. After receiving the licentiate in Sacred Scripture from the Roman Pontifical Biblical Institute,

Fig. 5. Cathedral Square, Chicago, with the Cathedral of the Holy Name on the right.

he returned to the U.S. where he was curate for a year, then professor, and later rector of St. Francis Seminary until he was named bishop of Superior, Wis., on Feb. 18, 1946. He was consecrated in Milwaukee by Abp. Moses E. Kiley on April 11, 1946, and enthroned in Superior the following month. Seven years later he was summoned back to be archbishop of Milwaukee and installed on Sept. 24, 1953. His transfer to Chicago came on Sept. 19, 1958, and he was enthroned there by the apostolic delegate Cicognani, on Nov. 16. John XXIII created him cardinal in the consistory of Dec. 14, 1959.

Shortly after Meyer's arrival in Chicago, a fire in Our Lady of the Angels School, Dec. 1, 1958, resulted in the death of 92 children and 3 Sisters of the Blessed Virgin Mary. He immediately initiated a campaign for greater school safety that involved the expenditure of millions of dollars for fire-protection devices. His high school expansion plan provided for a continuous building program over a 10-year period. The inadequacies of Quigley Preparatory Seminary led to the opening in September 1961 of Quigley South at 79th Street and Western Avenue for a 4-year preparatory course, and of St. Mary of the Lake Seminary, Junior College Division, in the completely remodeled St. Hedwig's Orphanage in Niles.

To keep the church abreast of urban renewal, he appointed a full-time priest director to the Archdiocesan Conservation Council, established under Stritch. At a clergy conference on Sept. 20, 1960, Meyer exhorted all his priests to assume leadership roles in integrating the Negro into Chicago's parishes, schools, hospitals, and other institutions. He endeavored to care for the expanding suburbs by founding 14 new parishes, thus bringing the total for the archdiocese (1963) to 447 parishes and 13 missions with 1,316 diocesan priests and 1,539 religious priests. Its school system then included 6 Catholic higher institutions: De Paul and Loyola universities and Barat, Mundelein, Rosary, and St. Xavier colleges; 88 Catholic secondary schools; and 435 Catholic elementary schools. These 529 schools and colleges had a total of 11,972 teachers and 379,072 students.

Cardinal Meyer was one of the 12 presidents of Vatican Council II; by the end of the third session he had addressed the Council more often than any other American bishop and had become the intellectual leader of the U.S. hierarchy. His untimely death on April 9, 1965, following brain surgery, was a misfortune for the Universal Church, as well as for the archdiocese. On June 16, 1965, Abp. John P. Cody of New Orleans, La., was transferred to Chicago as its sixth archbishop.

Bibliography: C. J. Kirkfleet, *The Life of Patrick Augustine Feehan* (Chicago 1922). B. L. Pierce, *A History of Chicago* (New York, v.1–3, 1937–57; v.4 in progress). J. E. McGirr, *The Life of the Rt. Rev. Wm. Quarter, DD* (Des Plaines, Ill. 1920). M. M. Quaife, *Checagou: From Indian Wigwam to Modern City, 1673–1835* (Chicago 1933). G. J. Garraghan, *The Catholic Church in Chicago, 1673–1871* (Chicago 1921). J. T. Ellis, *The Life of James Cardinal Gibbons,* 2 v. (Milwaukee 1952). J. J. Thompson, *The Archdiocese of Chicago: Antecedents and Development* (Des Plaines, Ill. 1920). **Illustration credit:** Fig. 2, Chicago Historical Society.

[H. C. KOENIG]

CHICAGO, EPARCHY OF (UKRAINIAN RITE), suffragan of the metropolitan Byzantine Ukrainian Archeparchy of *Philadelphia, Pa., comprising all the U.S. west of the western borders of Ohio, Kentucky, Tennessee, and Mississippi. Although it was established Aug. 14, 1961, its origins go back to the early part of the century when the Holy See authorized an exarchate (apostolic vicariate in the Latin rite canonical terminology) for the Ukrainian immigrants in the U.S. Prompted by the uniqueness of their Byzantine rite, traditions, culture, language, and increasing numbers, Pius X established the exarchate May 28, 1913, naming Philadelphia the episcopal city. On Aug. 8, 1956, the Holy See created the new Exarchate of Stamford, Conn., consisting of the New York and New England States, which were separated from the Philadelphia exarchate. Two years later Pius XII gave permanence to the hierarchical structure of the Ukrainian Church by raising the Exarchates of Philadelphia and Stamford to Archeparchy (Archdiocese) and Eparchy (Diocese), respectively, forming the Ukrainian Catholic Province of Philadelphia, Byzantine rite.

St. Nicholas Ukrainian Catholic Cathedral, Chicago, Ill.

In 1961, when the territory of the Philadelphia archeparchy was further reduced by the establishment of a third diocese in the province with Chicago as see city, Jaroslav̌ Gabro was named first ordinary of the new see and canonically installed in Chicago by the Apostolic Delegate to the U.S., Abp. Egidio Vagnozzi, on Dec. 12, 1961. Within the limits of the designated territory, his jurisdiction extended to all Catholics of the Byzantine rite who immigrated to the U.S. from Galicia, Bucovina, and other Ukrainian provinces; to their descendants; and all who have transferred or been converted to the rite.

In 1963 the Chicago eparchy numbered 20,604 Catholics, organized in 29 parishes and 4 missions and served by 39 priests, including 8 religious of the Order of St. Basil the Great. The educational institutions included one high school and four elementary schools, staffed by the Sisters of the Order of St. Basil the Great, the Sisters Servants of Mary Immaculate, and lay teachers.

Bibliography: H. J. Heuser, "The Appointment of a Greek Catholic Bishop in the U.S.," AmEcclRev 37 (1907) 457–467. L. Sembratovich, *Strangers within Our Gates* (Detroit 1936).

I. SOCHOCKY, "The Ukrainian Catholic Church of the Byzantine Rite in the U.S.A.," *Ukrainian Catholic Metropolitan See, Byzantine Rite USA,* (Nov. 1 1958) 199–287, available through the Byzantine Rite Archeparchy of Philadelphia. I. NAHAYEWSKY, *History of Ukraine* (Philadelphia 1962).

[I. SOCHOCKY]

CHICAGO SCHOOL (ARCHITECTURE), a commercial style of architecture developed in Chicago during the latter half of the 19th century; marked by the use of the rectilinear skeletal steel frame encased in masonry as the chief means of architectonic expression. A number of unprecedented factors emerged at about the same time and led to this style: the invention of the elevator by Otis (1853); the need for adequate fireproofing following the Chicago fire (1871); and the demand for high-rise city structures because of the desirability of housing great numbers in centrally located commercial establishments. The definitive solution was reached in W. Jenny's Home Insurance Building, (1883–85), where the masonry-clad metal frame solved the problems of both fireproofing and the height restrictions imposed by heavy masonry construction. Despite its excellent use of wide glass areas that allowed for maximum natural lighting, this building suffered aesthetically because of the exterior detailing derived from Victorian historicisms. The direct handling of glass and stone in H. H. *Richardson's Marshall Field Warehouse (1885–87) greatly aided the Chicago architects toward a skeletal frame determination of the exterior façade. This was partly achieved in Jenny's Second Leiter Building (1889) and the Fair Building (1891), although both contained slight classicizing details, and Burnham and Roots' raw unadorned masonry Monadnock Building (1889–91). The Chicago Style achieved maturity in the Reliance Building by Burnham (1894); delicately clad in white tile, infilled with the wide unencumbered glass areas (the "Chicago window"), the skeletal frame finally became an adequate means for architectural expression. Louis *Sullivan, the master of the movement, extended the school's influence eastward with the Wainwright Building (1890–91, St. Louis) and the Guarantee Trust, (1894–95, Buffalo). Sullivan's Carson, Pirie, and Scott Store, (1899) was the last outstanding work of the Chicago Style; his superb handling of horizontals and verticals manifested the visual equilibrium inherent in skeletal construction. Further development of the Chicago School was stifled by the abrupt termination of Chicago's commercial growth and by the World's Fair of 1893, which effectively promoted a popular eastern *beaux-arts* classicism. The turn of the century saw the end of the movement. However, the unaffected structural vernacular and the boldness and purity of steel construction passed into the best of American architectural thinking. The Larkin Building, Buffalo (1904), and the Unity Temple, Chicago (1906), by F. L. *Wright, were late witnesses to the direct exterior wall treatments advocated by Sullivan and the Chicago School.

Bibliography: C. W. CONDIT, *The Chicago School of Architecture* (Chicago 1964), best available analysis and bibliog.

[D. WALL]

CHICHELE, HENRY, Archbishop of Canterbury; b. Higham Ferrers, Northants, *c.* 1361; d. Canterbury, April 12, 1443. Educated at Oxford, he became doctor of laws, 1396. At this time he was ordained and had already held a number of minor ecclesiastical benefices. In 1404 he became chancellor of the Diocese of Salisbury. Henry IV employed him on several diplomatic missions. It was while Chichele was at the Curia of *Gregory XII, that he was appointed Bishop of St. David's (Wales). The Pope consecrated him June 17, 1408, though he was not enthroned until May 11, 1411. In the meantime he was a member of the English embassy (together with Bp. Robert *Hallum) to the Council of *Pisa. When Abp. Thomas *Arundel died, Henry V proposed Chichele for the archbishopric of Canterbury, where he was duly elected March 4, 1414. He governed the province for nearly 40 years. The edited archiepiscopal registers prove Chichele a first-class administrator, lawyer and lawgiver. In his judicial functions he was greatly assisted by the canonist, William *Lyndwood, whom he appointed his vicar-general. Chichele was anxious to raise the standard of both the clergy and the laity. He took effective steps to prevent the spread of the *Lollards.

Chichele was permanently estranged from the papacy when *Martin V made the Bishop of Winchester, Henry *Beaufort, a cardinal in 1426. Domestically, Chichele sided with Beaufort's opponents, notably Duke Henry of Gloucester, who was instrumental in bringing a charge of *praemunire against Beaufort. When Abp. John *Kemp (Kempe) of York was appointed a cardinal in 1439 and by reason of this appointment claimed public precedence over the archbishop of Canterbury, Chichele took the matter before *Eugene IV, who upheld Kempe. Chichele's career is not considered outstanding. His generosity to Oxford, especially All Souls College, is noteworthy.

Bibliography: A DUCK, *The Life of H. Chichele, Archbishop of Canterbury* (London 1699). W. F. HOOK, *Lives of the Archbishops of Canterbury,* 12 v. (London 1860–84) v.5. E. F. JACOB, "Two Lives of Archbishop Chichele," BullJRylLibr 16 (1932) 428–481. Cross ODCC 271. Emden 1:410–412. *The Register of Henry Chichele: Archbishop of Canterbury, 1414–1443,* ed. E. F. JACOB and H. C. JOHNSON, 4 v. (Oxford 1937–47). W. ULLMANN, "Eugenius IV, Cardinal Kemp, and Archbishop Chichele," *Medieval Studies Presented to Aubrey Gwynn, S.J.* (Dublin 1961) 359–383.

[W. ULLMANN]

CHICHESTER, ANCIENT SEE OF, medieval diocese of England, coterminous with the County of Sussex, suffragan of *Canterbury. Neither *Ethelbert of Canterbury's missionary success in Kent nor *Birinus's in Wessex had any effect on the neighboring South Saxons, and their conversion to Christianity came much later, under *Wilfrid of York, who successfully preached the gospel to them while exiled from *York (*c.* 681–686). He founded the first diocese there, with its see at Selsey. However, when he returned to York, Cadwalla, King of Wessex, who had conquered the South Saxons in 685, attached Selsey to his See of *Winchester, and Selsey regained its autonomy only in 709. In accord with the decrees of the Council of London (1075) that all sees must be in towns, not villages, the bishop's seat was transferred from Selsey to Chichester in 1082 with no changes in the diocesan boundaries. There the energetic Norman Bishop Ralph de Luffa (1091–1123) reorganized the diocese and began the Norman cathedral, while Bishop Seffrid II (1180–1204) introduced Early English elements into the structure. Chichester's best known medieval bishop was *Richard of Chichester (1245–54), friend and chancel-

"The Raising of Lazarus," Saxon relief, c. 1130–40, from the cathedral at Selsey, now in the cathedral at Chichester, England.

Section of the retrochoir in the cathedral at Chichester, England, showing elements of transitional design.

lor of St. *Edmund of Abingdon and *Boniface of Savoy, both archbishops of Canterbury. In the 14th and 15th centuries the bishops of Chichester were often men of substance but were primarily involved with non-diocesan projects; e.g., John Langton (1305–37) and *Robert of Stratford (1337–62) were both chancellors of England. However, the scholar-bishop *William Rede (1369–85), who collected the early records of the see, helped revive the diocese, which had been hard hit by the *Black Death. The Dominican Bishop Robert Rede (1397–1415) compiled the earliest extant episcopal register, and the controversial Reginald *Pecock, bishop from 1450 to 1456, was succeeded by John *Arundel (1459–78). Bishop Edward Storey (1478–1503) spiritually revitalized the diocese. Robert Sherborn (1508–36) protested against King *Henry VIII, but in the end he resigned his see to the King's man, Richard Sampson (1536–43), under whom the diocese became Anglican. George Day (1543–47) was instituted by Henry VIII, but he was subsequently imprisoned on account of his resistance to the King. He regained his see under Queen *Mary. John Christopherson (1557–59) was the last Roman Catholic bishop, and today Chichester is a see of the Church of England. *Battle Abbey and *Lewes Priory were the chief monasteries in the diocese.

Bibliography: F. G. Bennett et al., *Statutes and Constitutions of the Cathedral Church of Chichester* (Chichester 1904). *The Victoria History of the County of Sussex*, ed. W. Page et al. (London 1905–) v.2, L. F. Salzmann; v.3, W. H. Godfrey and J. W. Bloc. H. C. Corlette, *Catholic Church of Chichester* (London 1911). A. S. Duncan-Jones, *Story of Chichester Cathedral* (London 1933). W. D. Peckham, ed., *Chartulary of the High Church of Chichester* (Sussex Record Society 46; 1946). K. Edwards, *The English Secular Cathedrals in the Middle Ages* (Manchester, Eng. 1949). J. Warrilow, DHGE 12:665–674. Cross ODCC 271. **Illustration credit:** Leo Herbert Felton.

[M. J. HAMILTON]

CHIDWICK, JOHN PATRICK, chaplain, educator; b. New York City, Oct. 23, 1862; d. New York City, Jan. 13, 1935. He was ordained at Troy, N.Y., Dec. 17, 1887. Chidwick gained fame as chaplain of the U.S. battleship "Maine" when it was blown up in Havana harbor, Cuba, in 1898. His heroism on that occasion was praised in a dispatch from Captain Charles Sigsbee, the "Maine's" commander, to John Long, Secretary of the Navy. Chidwick was interested in young people, and his youth organizations were most successful. He filled also various offices in the Archdiocese of New York, serving as police chaplain, pastor, founder of a high school, and president of the College of New Rochelle in Westchester County, N.Y. From 1909 to 1922 he was rector of St. Joseph's Seminary, Dunwoodie, Yonkers, N.Y., where he exercised a lasting influence on the students confided to his care. He was appointed a papal chamberlain and served as pastor of St. Agnes parish, New York City, until his death.

[J. P. MONAGHAN]

CHIEF PRIESTS, a specific group of temple priests, administrators of the temple's liturgy, buildings, and finances. The Greek plural ἀρχιερεῖς (chief priests), occurring 62 times in the NT books and often in Josephus, refers to this important priestly group; whereas the singular ἀρχιερεύς (high priest, chief priest), appearing 38 times in the Gospels and Acts, refers to the *high priest, president of the *Sanhedrin.

The chief priests are sometimes mentioned alone as acting for the whole Sanhedrin (Mt 26.14; Mk 15.3;

One of the chief priests arguing with Pilate over the inscription for the cross of Jesus, enlarged detail of the walrus-ivory cross executed for Abbot Samson de Tottingham of Bury-St.-Edmunds Abbey, late 12th century.

Lk 23.4; Jn 18.35; Acts 9.14—the Sanhedrin) or with "the whole Sanhedrin" (Mt 26.59), the *scribes (Mt 2.4; Lk 20.19), the *elders (Mt 21.23; Acts 4.23), the scribes and elders (Mt 16.21; 28.41; Mt 15.1; Lk 22.66), the captains or overseers (Lk 22.4), the rulers (Lk 23.13), or the *Pharisees (Mt 27.62; Jn 7.45; 11.47; 18.3). From these passages it is clear that the chief priests were prominent and influential members of the Sanhedrin. According to some scholars (E. Schürer, 2.1:204–206) the chief priests comprised the ruling high priest, former acting but deposed high priests, and leading members of the families from which the high priests were selected. But according to others (J. Jeremias, 38; G. Schrenk, 271) it appears more probable that this group was composed of administrators of the Temple, its buildings, and its treasures, e.g., in descending rank, the Temple governor or captain (στρατηγὸς τοῦ ἱεροῦ), who was next in dignity after the high priest (Acts 4.1; 5.24, 36, Schrenk, 271); the heads of the 24 priestly classes conducting the weekly services (cf. Lk 1.9); the leaders of those conducting the daily services; the overseers (Heb. *'ămark^e lîn;* Gr. στρατηγοί; Lk 22.4, 52), the treasurers (Heb. *qizbārîm*).

Bibliography: G. Schrenk, Kittel ThW 3:270–272. E. Schürer, *A History of the Jewish People in the Time of Christ,* division 2, v.1, tr. S. Taylor and P. Christie (Edinburgh 1898) 203–206. J. Jeremias, *Jerusalem zur Zeit Jesu* (Göttingen 1958).
Illustration credit: The Metropolitan Museum of Art, The Cloisters Collection, Purchase, 1963.

[J. E. STEINMUELLER]

CHIEREGATI, FRANCESCO, papal nuncio and bishop of Teramo; b. Vicenza, 1478; d. Bologna, Dec. 6, 1539. Chieregati (Chieregato) studied law at Padua, Bologna, and Siena, where he received the degree of *doctor utriusque juris.* During his early career he held various positions dealing with the secretarial and diplomatic work of the Church. In 1516 he was sent as papal nuncio to England to notify Henry VIII that the Concordat of Bologna between the Papacy and Francis I of France had been concluded. Subsequently, he represented the Papacy at the courts of Spain and Portugal. While in Spain, he became acquainted with Cardinal Adrian Florensz, Bishop of Tortosa, later Pope Adrian VI, the Dutch teacher of Charles V. Adrian VI created Chieregati bishop of Teramo in the kingdom of Naples. As an indication of the Pope's esteem for his virtue, learning, and diplomatic skill, Chieregati was sent as papal nuncio to represent the Pope at the Diet of Nuremberg in the fall of 1522. He was entrusted with the task of obtaining obedience to and enforcement of the bull *Exsurge* and the Edict of Worms against Luther, as well as of persuading the German princes to take a stronger stand against the Turks in Hungary. The reaction of the Diet was not favorable. After three unsuccessful exhortations, Chieregati, on Jan. 3, 1523, took the step of reading publicly a papal brief issued on Nov. 25, 1522, to the members of the Diet. At the same time, he read instructions prepared for him at least in substance by the Pope himself and bearing the same date as the brief. The brief was an appeal to the Diet to suppress religious sedition and to force Luther and his followers to stop their disruptive activities. In essence, Chieregati's instructions constituted a public confession by the Pope that the shortcomings of the Curia and the clergy were in a large part responsible for the religious problems of the day. The document also set forth the Pope's determination to effect reforms. This public confession was without precedent and both a German and a Latin version were printed for further dissemination in 1523, but did not provoke a sympathetic response. Individual reaction at the Diet was skeptical about the Pope's ability to implement his promises, and on February 5 the Diet demanded that the Pope, with the approval of the Emperor, call a council to meet in a German border city, a council that would operate independently of the Pope. It also prepared a list of financial grievances for submission to the Pope. Chieregati failed to soften the Diet's position and left Nuremberg in February 1523. With the death of Pope Adrian VI, he lost his diplomatic standing and he spent the rest of his life in relative obscurity.

Bibliography: Jedin Trent 1:210–213. Pastor 9:127–141. B. Morsolin, *Francesco Chieregati* (Vicenza 1873). *Deutsche Reichstagsakten unter Kaiser Karl V,* 7 v. (Gotha 1893–1935) v.3. L. Van Meerbeeck, DHGE 12:676–678.

[V. H. PONKO, JR.]

CHIETI, ARCHDIOCESE OF (THEATINUS), metropolitan see since 1526, without suffragans, in central Italy near the Adriatic. Originally founded by Greeks from Magna Graecia, the city was destroyed by Visigoths (410) and by Franks (810); in the 10th century it had its own dynastic counts; taken by the Normans (1078) and by the kingdom of Sicily (1140), it was autonomous under the Hohenstaufen and flourished under the Aragonese. The first known bishop of Chieti, Theodoric, dates from 879. When the three suffragan sees that Clement VII designated for Chieti refused submission (1526), Pius V created the suffragan See of Ortona (1570), which passed to the jurisdiction of *Lanciano (1818). In 1853 Pius IX created the See of Vasto, investing its title and perpetual administration in the bishop of Chieti. The Cathedral of SS. Thomas and Justin (11th century) has a campanile from 1335. The diocese has had noteworthy monasteries: S. Angelo in Bareggio (founded 725), S. Liberatore de Maiella (before 800), S. Stefano (9th century), S. Salvatore de Maiella (before 1000), S. Martino del Valle (1044), S. Pietro de Vallebona (before 1149), Rabona (1209), and S. Maria de Canneto. In 1963 Chieti had 312,000 Catholics in 138 parishes; 186 secular and 91 religious priests, 120 men in 28 religious houses, and 545 women in 89 convents; it is 946 square miles in area.

Bibliography: Gams. Eubel HierCath. S. Prete, EncCatt 3: 1528–29. M. H. Laurent, DHGE 12:682–684, with list of bishops. AnnPont (1964) 106, 1412.

[G. A. PAPA]

CHIGI

An important family of Siena, Italy, mentioned in sources since the 13th century; ennobled in 1377. About that time it was distinguished by two and perhaps three members who were beatified in the era of *Fabio* Chigi, who became Pope *Alexander VII.

Bl. Giovanni da Lecceto, b. Maciareto, near Siena, 1300. He entered the order of the *Augustinians of Lecceto as a lay brother and lived an exemplary life, first in Vallaspra, then in Siena, and Pavia, and again in Siena, where he died Oct. 28, 1363.

Bl. Angela, niece of Giovanni da Lecceto, also belonged to a congregation of hermits of St. Augustine. She lived in Siena where she died a holy death in 1400.

She was never officially beatified. (See the *Vitae synopsis,* supplements to the Roman editions of Hoyerus, cited below.)

Bl. Giuliana was recently affiliated (rightly or wrongly) with the Chigi family. After being widowed four times, she spent her remaining years as a tertiary of St. Augustine, and died in Siena in 1400 (Mercati-Pelzer DE 1:609).

The head of the family is said to have been *Agostino,* known as the Elder, from whom the various branches of the family descended: the Chigi-Albani; the Chigi Camollia, later the Chigi-Saracini; the Chiga *di citta,* or of Siena, extinct in 1758; the Chigi of Rome, extinct in 1573; the Chigi of Viterbo, later the Chigi-Montoro and the Montoro-Patrizi; and the Chigi Zondadari. *Mariano* (1439–1504) was the most prominent of Agostino's sons. He was a prosperous banker in Siena, the founder of a banking house, and on occasion an ambassador of Siena to the court of Pope *Alexander VI and to the Republic of *Venice. He became a humanist and patron of the arts.

Agostino the Magnificent (1464–1520) was the most outstanding among Mariano's sons. As the representative of his father's banking house, he established himself in Rome and embarked on a successful career. Having won the confidence of three successive popes (Alexander VI; *Julius II, who adopted him into his family; and *Leo X, who honored him with his visits), he obtained several monoplies (on grain, salt, alum, and right of entry), and carried on an international trade, using the Porto d'Ercole, obtained from the Republic of *Siena. As a patron of the arts, he showed favor to men of letters, such as P. *Bembo, Giovio, and P. *Aretino; and to architects, especially Baltasar Peruzzi who built his superb palace, the Farnesina; as well as to the painters *Raphael, Perino del Vaga, Julius Romano, and J. A. Bazzi, who decorated the Farnesina and the chapel of the Chigi in Santa Maria del Popolo. Agostino founded a printing establishment and a library. At his death in 1520, his enterprises were liquidated; his lineage became extinct in 1575.

Monument of Sigismondo Chigi, executed after a design by Raphael, in the church of Santa Maria del Popolo, Rome.

The Chigi of Siena returned to Rome through the descendants of *Sigismondo* (1479–1525), second son of Mariano, prosperous banker. His great grandson, *Fabio,* a young ecclesiastic, came to Rome, where he made his career. When he became Pope Alexander VII (1655), he practiced nepotism, giving his family every sort of advantage. His nephew *Agostino,* the founder of the Chigi-Albani family, obtained for himself and his family the title of marshal of the Church and guardian of the Conclave. His niece *Agnes* married Ansano Zondadari, and founded the Chigi-Zondadari family. Beginning with the pontificate of Alexander VII, the Chigi were cardinals. First, there were his three nephews: *Flavio* (1631–93), legate, librarian; *Sigismondo* (1649–78) of the Order of Malta, legate; and *Antonio* Bichi (1614–90), son of one of the Pope's half-sisters, internuncio at Brussels, and Bishop of Osimo. Later there were also the following cardinals: *Flavio the Younger* (1711–71), prefect of the Congregation of Rites; *Flavio* Chigi-Albani (1801–73), nuncio in Bavaria and France; and two members of the Chigi-Zondadari family, *Antonio Felice the Elder* (1665–1737), nuncio in Spain, and *Antonio Felice the Younger* (1740–1823), internuncio at Brussels and Archbishop of Siena.

The Chigi Library was one of the glories of the Chigi family. Fabio Chigi began the collection in his palace in Rome and took advantage of his pontificate to enlarge it. The Chigi cardinals, especially *Flavio the Elder,* continued its growth. It now contains about 3,000 MSS (86 with miniatures, 56 Greek, 190 Latin, and many volumes of archival materials). Purchased by the Italian Government in 1918 and ceded to the Vatican in 1923, it has been integrated into the *Vatican Library. Besides the Greek MSS, described by Pio Franchi de Cavalieri (Rome 1927), the other MSS also have been well catalogued.

Bibliography: M. HOYERUS, *Vita b. Joannis Chisii* (Antwerp 1641; Rome 1655–75). ActSS Oct. 12:724–735. A. MASSERON, *Les "Exemples" d'un ermite siennois* (Paris 1924). G. CUGNONI, "Agostino Chigi il magnifico," *Archivio della società romana di storia patria,* 2–4 (1879–81), 6 (1883). U. FRITTELLI, *Albero genealogico della nobile famiglia Chigi* (Siena 1922). P. PASCHINI, *I Chigi* (Le grandi famiglie romane 3; Rome 1946). G. I. DELLA ROCCHETTA, EncCatt 3:1529–34. M. H. LAURENT, DHGE 12:684–685. **Illustration credit:** Alinari-Art Reference Bureau.

[L. CEYSSENS]

CHIHUAHUA, ARCHDIOCESE OF (CHIHUAHUENSIS), Mexican ecclesiastical province, created a diocese 1891; raised to an archdiocese Nov. 22, 1958. In 1964 it included the suffragan Diocese of Ciudad Juárez (1957), and the Vicariate Apostolic of Tarahumara (1958). Chihuahua had 41 parishes, with 79 secular priests and 25 religious priests, for a Catholic population of about 673,000. The first religious to establish themselves in the city of Chihuahua were Franciscans. For this reason, in 1717 St. Francis of Assisi was declared the patron of the city with the approval of

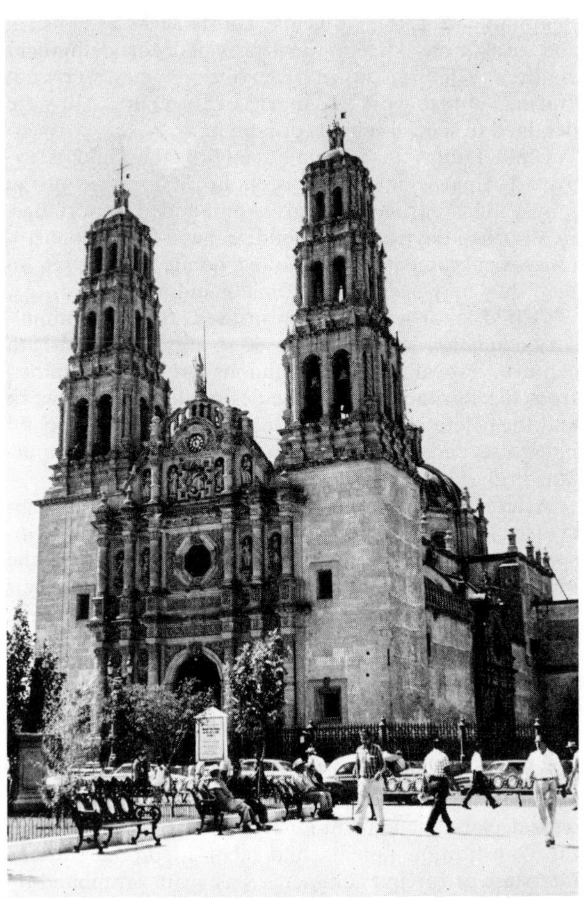

The cathedral of the Archdiocese of Chihuahua, Mexico.

the bishops and of the governor of Nueva Vizcaya, and his feast (October 4) became the most important date in the civic and religious calendar. So influential was this date in the life of Chihuahua that it was chosen for the installation of the first popularly elected officials of the province in the 1820s. At the end of 1817 the bishop of Durango Marqués de Castañiza instituted a general vicariate with José Mateo Sánchez Álvarez as chaplain. His jurisdiction extended over the parishes of Chihuahua, Aquiles Serdán, Cusihuiriachi, San Buenaventura, and all the missions of Upper and Lower Tarahumara. The vicariate was suppressed in 1824. When Leo XIII created the Diocese of Chihuahua, the first bishop, José de Jesús Ortíz, took possession of his see Oct. 10, 1893. He was succeeded by Nicolás Pérez Gavilán, and then by Antonio Guizar y Valencia, who became the first archbishop. The Vicariate Apostolic of Tarahumara is cared for by the Society of Jesus.

[I. GALLEGOS]

CHILD

Childhood, the period from infancy to adult status, is marked not only by physical development but also by acquisition of a way of life. This article is concerned principally with the effects of major social trends upon the child's status in society.

The Child's Role. The child, the link between generations, receives his orientation toward group behavior in the *family. As he learns what is expected of him, he begins to fill social roles. Before the age of 2, he learns that he has a subordinate role, and he acquires an appreciation of the necessity for *obedience. By school age, in Western societies, the concept of obedience is practically universal.

As the child matures, his role expands. He learns to recognize the social expectations of the family and of the neighborhood; he is expected to conform to moral and religious precepts; he assumes the responsibilities of school life. During adolescence, he prepares for adult roles. In American society, part-time work may be obtained and earnings spent with varying degrees of parental guidance; *dating begins; considerable time is given to choice of a "state of life"; and more independence is allowed in work, use of earnings, and social life. Emancipation from parental control occurs when the adolescent leaves home, for example, when he contracts a valid marriage, reaches his majority (usually at age 21), or enters the armed forces. One who is financially self-supporting but remains at home is under parental control; a physically or mentally incapacitated child who remains at home may never be emancipated.

Rights of the Child. Concomitant with the duties of obedience and filial piety, the child has basic rights. Most essential is his right to life. According to Catholic teaching, the primary end of marriage is the child. The child has a right to spiritual direction, for he is destined to be a citizen of the kingdom of God. Religion is an integrating principle, helping the child to develop a sense of God, a sense of direction, a sense of responsibility, and a sense of mission in this life (*see* PIETY, FAMILIAL).

A Declaration of the Rights of the Child, proclaimed by the UN General Assembly, states that every child has a right to opportunities to develop physically, mentally, morally, spiritually, and socially; to a name and nationality; to health and social security; to love and understanding under the care of parents; and to education. A handicapped child has a right to special treatment, education, and care. Every child has a right to protection against neglect, cruelty, exploitation, and discrimination in every form.

In the U.S., parents have a legal right to custody and control of their child; they also have the corresponding duty to support the child: to provide him with food, clothing, shelter, education, religious instruction, medical care, and any other necessity. Parenthood also carries with it the right to discipline a child and to delegate this authority to someone else (*see* PARENT AND CHILD, U.S. LAW OF).

Variations in Patterns of Child-Rearing. In all cultures child-rearing is primarily a parental responsibility; however, it follows a variety of patterns. Among surviving primitive peoples, young children are usually cherished. Permissiveness does not preclude respect. When parents believe children old enough to understand, the necessity of obedience is strongly impressed upon them.

The mother plays an important role in child-rearing in all cultures. She is often the principal influence in forming the child's personality, due to the great amount of time the child spends in her care. In patriarchal-type families, however, the father has a strong voice in all family matters. Among the Chinese and other Eastern peoples, the patriarch's authority may extend to choosing mates for his offspring, and sons may be expected to bring their wives to live in the parental compound.

In contemporary Western culture, patterns of child-rearing vary according to *social class. In the upper classes, children are usually highly valued. They learn that they come from a distinguished lineage, and they are expected to take advantage of educational and other opportunities. Since sons carry on the family name, and often the family enterprises as well, they are given special importance. Children of the middle classes, too, are essential to realization of family goals. Parents generally hope to prepare them for future positions with a little more prestige than those which they themselves occupy. The expectation that a child will go to college is one of the indexes of middle class status. In the lower classes the norms of behavior are often at variance with those of the middle and upper classes, despite the tendency of the state, church, and school to apply middle class norms to them. Lower class parents may experience great insecurity and loss of hope in social mobility; therefore, it is difficult for them to expect their children to defer immediate satisfaction for the attainment of future goals.

Responsibility for Offenses. Regardless of class origins, the child's *conscience, which is an activity of judgment, becomes clearly evident by the age of 3: he has abstracted a certain sense of "right" and "wrong" actions on the basis of what he knows to be approved or disapproved by his elders. By the time he is 4 or 5 years of age he is able to differentiate clearly right and wrong; however, the concept of good is not expressed by the average child, even at the age of 7, and his ideals of truth, honesty, and courage, which begin to be evident at the age of 5, do not demand that he take the initiative in reporting on himself by the time he is 7. He does have a very clear concept of the rights of ownership long before he is interested in others as fellow companions.

A child who is considered personally and morally responsible for a violation of norms is liable to punishment. Although the age of 7 is usually referred to as the age of *reason—the age when a child has acquired the concept of guilt and is judged to be capable of committing sin—no specific age can arbitrarily be so defined. Many 7-year-olds have not yet reached this stage whereas some precocious children may reach it earlier.

Historically, the concept of punishable offenses has varied. Sixteenth-century English children between the ages of 5 and 14 who were "idle" or found begging were bound into agricultural or industrial service by local officials. In the U.S., such children were "farmed out" to contractors with a special wage agreement. Later, a plan was evolved whereby industries operated their own plants within institutions. In 1825, New York City established the first institution for delinquents, a house of refuge that was empowered to bind children out as apprentices or servants, presumably to prepare them for trades and to reform them. Seventy such institutions, later known as "reform schools," were established in the U.S. between 1824 and 1900.

Gradually, the courts began to distinguish between offenses committed by children (acts of *juvenile delinquency), and those by adults. Although state laws vary, the majority of them indicate that a child may be judged delinquent if he is habitually truant, incorrigible, growing up in idleness or crime, willfully associating with immoral persons and engaging in immoral conduct, absenting himself from home without consent and just cause, and beyond the control of parent or guardian. Beginning in 1899, *juvenile courts were established and probation officers were provided for delinquent children. Children taken from their homes were not "farmed out" to work as a means of correction, but were detained in special schools or homes.

Child Labor. In agrarian societies, the child is expected to participate in the economic enterprises of the family. This participation gives him added importance. In an urban environment, children have fewer opportunities to participate in family economic enterprises; in fact, they may even be economic liabilities.

*Child labor was common in the U.S. until compulsory education laws were passed in about the mid-19th century. Prevailing early opinions probably stemmed from the Puritan belief in the desirability of hard work and the deleterious effects of idleness; and, in fact, child indenture and apprenticeship were considered important in the development of the nation's economy.

After the Civil War, employment of children increased rapidly because of the failure to provide inspectors to enforce compulsory education laws, the unwillingness of parents to relinquish earnings of their children, and insufficient educational opportunities. In 1900, the census showed that approximately 18 per cent of all children in the U.S. were gainfully employed, an increase of nearly 1 million between 1870 and 1900.

Shortly after the turn of the 20th century the Children's Bureau was established by Congress in the Department of Commerce and Labor, and one of its first considerations was child labor. After two Federal laws were declared unconstitutional and an attempt to amend the Constitution failed, child labor in production for interstate or foreign commerce was again prohibited by the Fair Labor Standards Act which was passed in 1938, and upheld by the courts. Amendments to the act in 1949 extended its provisions to children under 18 employed by their parents in hazardous occupations, and to children who were formerly allowed by local authorities to work in agriculture during school hours.

Education. *Education, the process of transmitting *culture to a new generation, is universal, but formal education, especially apart from the family, is not (*see* EDUCATION, PRIMITIVE). Formal education can be traced back to ancient times, and found to show variations in emphasis, from the wisdom of Confucius to the physical training of the Spartans. In Western society, formal learning was not stressed during the Middle Ages. Weaned children were allowed to mix freely with adults in work and in play. But after the 17th century more concern was shown for education.

In colonial New England, where Calvinistic ideals of religion and education prevailed, the initiative in establishing schools was taken by the towns themselves, beginning as early as 1625. In the South, education was normally looked upon as the private concern of those parents who were capable of providing it. The wealthy attended private schools or had tutors. In the Middle Colonies there was a combination of both private and public control over education.

The concept of free, coeducational, compulsory schooling in the U.S. gained acceptance during the 19th century, on the theory that a democratic society requires a universal system of public education. Public schools became a means of accelerating the assimilation of the immigrants. Massachusetts passed the first compulsory attendance legislation in 1852 and, except in the South, most of the other states followed precedent by 1900, with variations in the age limit and the length of the school term.

In the early American schools, the European tradition of discipline prevailed. Since children were held to be infected with original sin and naturally inclined toward evil, the educational system relied strongly upon instilling fear, demanding obedience, and resorting to strict physical and mental discipline. The ridicule associated with the use of the dunce's cap and stool was considered a good means of discipline.

During the late 19th century attitudes toward discipline began to change. John *Dewey held that repression weakened intellectual curiosity and initiative. He saw the child's nature as inherently good. The *progressive movement in the 20th century placed more emphasis on involving the individual in group activities than on the teacher's authority. Conservatives criticized the progressive schools for their lack of discipline and failure to impart fundamental information and skills. The curriculum began to be shaped also by the needs of society.

Social Services. The *United Nations Children's Fund (UNICEF) offers services to children throughout the world, especially in underdeveloped areas. Although it was originally established as an emergency fund to provide for children left homeless by World War II, it became permanent because of the continuing need. Milk distribution, disease control, and establishment of child welfare centers are some of its activities.

In the present boundaries of the U.S., *child welfare was one of the first fields of social service to be developed. Institutional care of children began prior to 1800 in private orphanages for homeless children, and expanded with the establishment of quasi-private institutions for the deaf, the blind, the mentally retarded, and delinquents. Special attention is now given to all types of exceptional children. The Child Welfare League of America, which is national in scope, was incorporated in 1920; it promotes better understanding of child welfare problems, formulates standards and improves methods in all forms of services to children, provides information on sound child welfare practice, and develops interagency cooperation.

Changing Patterns of Family Life. In most primitive societies, as well as in some contemporary ethnic families such as the Chinese and the Mexican, the family is large, extending beyond the nuclear unit to relatives on both the husband's and wife's sides of the family. Only in deviant cases is the nuclear family cut off or isolated from other kinsfolk. After a child is weaned, a number of relatives assist the mother with its care.

The American family today is predominantly a nuclear, urban one, consisting of parents and children, living in a single-family dwelling. In this small conjugal unit the child depends almost entirely upon its parents. Since the nuclear family is usually isolated from relatives, the caring for the children falls to the mother, for there are no surrogates—grandmothers, aunts, or older cousins—available to give the child affection and care.

In the small, conjugal family unit children have an importance in family affairs that contrasts sharply with their role in a rural society or in an extended family system, especially a patriarchal one. Some observers of the American family note that a cult has developed around the child. He lives in a world of his own, sheltered from the harsh realities of adult life, but voicing his preferences, which very often take precedence over those of parents or others.

See also ADOLESCENT PSYCHOLOGY; CHILD PSYCHOLOGY.

Bibliography: O. W. RITCHIE and M. R. KOLLER, *Sociology of Childhood* (New York 1964). J. H. S. BOSSARD and E. S. BOLL, *The Sociology of Child Development* (3d ed. New York 1960). F. J. WOODS, *The American Family System* (New York 1959). P. ARIES, *Centuries of Childhood,* tr. R. BALDICK (New York 1962). D. ZIETZ, *Child Welfare* (New York 1959). National Catholic Welfare Conference, *The Child: Citizen of Two Worlds* (Washington 1950). M. C. MCGRATH and M. M. HUGHES, *The Moral and Religious Development of the Preschool Child* (Baltimore 1936). R. F. BUTTS, *A Cultural History of Western Education* (2d ed. New York 1955).

[F. J. WOODS]

CHILD LABOR

In common usage the term child labor refers to an economic practice and an attendant social evil. Yet the term cannot be given precise definition since the meanings attributed to both "child" and "labor" are relative to a given culture and social milieu. In the present context childhood signifies the period after infancy during which the individual develops to physical maturity and acquires the knowledge, skills, and habits needed for adult participation in the community; while "labor" denotes either employment in some gainful occupation or work that contributes to the income of the family. The connotation of social evil derives both from the possible moral and physical dangers associated with some types of employment and from the deprivation of needed education and training.

The tragic history of child labor after the advent of the industrial revolution can be understood only in terms of its wider cultural setting. The conception of childhood as a special period required for growth and formal training was late to develop in the Western world. Up to the 17th century the majority of children received little formal education and after reaching the age of 7 or 8 were apprenticed out by their parents to learn some trade, skill, or service through practical experience. By introducing machines and harnessing natural power, industrialization created new employment opportunities at all levels of skill. Since the working classes at the time were regarded as a natural resource and consequently as expendable, men, women, and children were employed more or less indiscriminately.

In early industrialization the numerous orphans and workhouse or pauper children were the first to be employed, and business men offering them work were regarded as public benefactors on the convenient assumption that they relieved the community of a burden while teaching the children good work habits early. Soon, however, because working conditions, hours, and wages were unregulated, children between the ages of 7 and 16 became preferred employees because they were cheap, easily exploitable workers; and many parents, impelled either by poverty, avarice, or indifference, freely cooperated with management in this regard. Hence the evil practice enjoyed widespread support until organized labor, developments in industry, and growing public awareness of the need for formal education led to its elimination in most industries.

In the United States the Fair Labor Standards Act of 1938, representing roughly a half century of organized effort, is the major Federal law regulating child labor. Employers in interstate or foreign commerce may hire no child under age 16 for general work or for farmwork during school hours; age 18 is minimum for certain hazardous occupations; and age 14, for a few office- and sales-type jobs outside of school hours. In addition there are various state laws that regulate the employment of children, while compulsory school attendance laws are an important aid to enforcement. Nevertheless, the regulation of child labor in agriculture, particularly during nonschool periods, remains inadequate; and there is some support for amendments to the child-labor statutes that would permit the full-time employment of children of 14 or 15 years who are delinquent or who present serious disciplinary problems at school.

Bibliography: P. L. J. MANTOUX, *The Industrial Revolution in the 18th Century,* tr. M. VERNON (New York 1928). E. GINZBERG and D. BRAY, *The Uneducated* (New York 1953).

[J. L. THOMAS]

CHILD PSYCHOLOGY

Child psychology is the scientific study of the child with reference to his intellectual, emotional, social, and ethical development from birth to adolescence. Its field of investigation includes many topics traditionally treated in its parent science, *psychology, while it contributes to, and is influenced by, such diverse disciplines as pediatrics and basic medical sciences, *psychiatry and *psychoanalysis, cultural *anthropology and *sociology, and *education. Child psychology also finds practical application in institutions such as child guidance clinics, adoption agencies, and schools for gifted, retarded, and handicapped children. This article first discusses its historical origins and methods, and then surveys its general conclusions regarding the various stages of child development, with some comments of special relevance to Catholics.

HISTORY AND METHODS

While childhood has been a subject of serious concern throughout recorded history in all societies, early views were based more on folklore or on philosophical speculation than on observation of the child himself. In Western society the *child has been alternately viewed as an adult in miniature or as raw material to be fashioned into the yeoman, soldier, or citizen. Some saw him as innately depraved until civilized; and others, as innately good until corrupted by a depraved civilization. Such ideas were expressed in Biblical maxims on child rearing, in the educational theories proposed in Plato's *Republic* and Aristotle's *Politics,* in medieval syntheses, and in the writings of such moderns as J. J. *Rousseau. *See* EDUCATION II (PHILOSOPHY OF).

Development as a Science. It was not until the 19th century, however, and largely through the influence of the doctrine of evolution, that scientists began to observe and record systematically the development of young children, often their own offspring. The early baby biographies included Charles Darwin's diary of his infant son (1870) and Wilhelm Preyer's *Mind of the Child* (1882). These were rich in factual information but methodologically weak, using as they did a longitudinal approach rather than a cross-sectional one. *See* METHODOLOGY (PSYCHOLOGY). As a result they could offer no conclusions about individual differences or the great variety of environmental determinants of development; moreover, the interpretations they gave their observations were often subjective. Nevertheless, their naturalistic method—with some refinements—has continued as a major research tool in child study.

Hall's Work. G. Stanley *Hall, who was active in founding societies and periodicals devoted to child study, introduced the questionnaire method in 1894. He enlisted teachers and parents to administer 102 questionnaires to their children on topics ranging from lying, anger, and fear, to attitudes toward religious experiences and prayer. The approach was suitable only for children old enough to comprehend the questions and provide answers. Self-report inventories on values, interests, and sociometric patterns commonly used today follow in this tradition.

Binet and Terman. In the first quarter of the 20th century Alfred *Binet in France and J. B. *Watson in the U.S. gave further impetus to child psychology. Binet published the first of the intelligence tests that bear his name in 1905, thereby providing a scale of age norms, later called mental ages, by which a child's test performance could be compared with that of age peers. In 1911 William Stern proposed that the mental age of the child be divided by his chronological age to yield a mental quotient, or constant index of relative brightness. Lewis Terman renamed this ratio the intelligence quotient (or IQ) when he issued the Stanford revision of the Binet scale in 1916 (*see* INTELLIGENCE; PSYCHOLOGICAL TESTING). An important application of the IQ test was Terman's "Genetic Studies of Genius," a longitudinal study of a large group of gifted children made in the 1920s. Follow-up studies of this group over the past 30 years have effectively demolished the notion that mental superiority is associated with emotional instability and physical frailty.

Behaviorism. Whereas Binet's work lent itself initially to an uncritical support of nature over nurture, Watson's experiments had the opposite effect. In 1920 Watson, the founder of *behaviorism, demonstrated that a fear reaction could be experimentally induced in a young child by conditioning principles. Experimental psychologists following his school prefer to focus on observable environmental stimuli and equally observable contingent responses by children. Their work shifts the burden of explanation away from such concepts as instinct or maturation to observable interactions between the child and specifiable events in the environment.

Psychoanalysis. Although Sigmund *Freud never studied children himself, his writings have prompted intensive study of *personality development in children. He wrote on stages of child development that were simultaneously biological and psychological, on the genesis in early childhood of adult neurotic disorders, on rivalries and alliances within the family circle, and on sexual manifestations in childhood. Freud's theories may be said to have stimulated—or provoked, depending on one's point of view—considerable research in such areas as feeding and habit training, patterns of parent-child relationship, dreams, and child play and imitation. Through his influence, the psychiatric interview with adults was modified to become the play-therapy interview with emotionally disturbed children; techniques designed to elicit fantasy via inkblots, thematic cards, figure drawings, and completing sentences came into extensive use.

Gesell and Maturation. Arnold Gesell of Yale University amassed carefully controlled cross-sectional observations of children from birth through adolescence. He stressed maturation over learning in the unfolding of behavior, and emphasized regularity of maturational sequences and differences between age levels rather than differences between children at a given age level. Gesell's developmental norms for children—subdivided under such headings as motor coordination, language ability, adaptive or problem-solving behavior, and personal-social maturity—have been extensively employed in the evaluation of mentally retarded and handicapped children; implicitly they are used by pediatricians, parents, and teachers throughout the U.S.

Factors Influencing Method. There are no research methods peculiar to child psychology. The methods of observation, interview, behavior ratings, self-report, tests, and experimental control are modified by the requirements of particular cases and the special characteristics of children as objects of study.

Nonverbal Techniques. Children are less verbal than adults, especially in the preschool years, and thus unable to engage in complicated verbal communication. In working with children, for example, one is not always certain that they have fully understood verbal instructions. An equivalent problem is that of interpreting a child's verbal responses, since children may not share with adults the frame of reference implied by some terms. Moreover, many children remain nonverbal throughout childhood, e.g., deaf and aphasic children, speech-handicapped children, mentally retarded persons, and some who are emotionally disturbed. Nonverbal techniques of communication and instruction are necessary for working with these children.

Lack of Control. A second problem arises from the inability to control the environment of children over any reasonable length of time. For example, if some children are given special training over an extended period while others are not, the resulting superiority of the former may be attributed to the special training, or possibly to the interim behavior of parents pleased by the knowledge that their children are participating in a scientific experiment. A special drawback is that children are not free agents and their participation in a scientific study is contingent upon the permission and cooperation of parents or teachers. Certain types of inquiry are less likely to elicit this cooperation than others. Some classes of adults are reluctant to grant permission for any type of psychological research, with the result that children used in a given study may be a special sample by virtue of their cooperative parents; conclusions from such a sample of children may not be applicable to the children of parents who would not grant permission.

Observer Influence. A third difficulty is created by the fact that the act of observation or measurement may influence the phenomenon under study. A teacher attempting to assess student attitudes toward schoolwork by questionnaire or interview is likely to obtain different answers when the pupils' attitudes are tapped by some other method, e.g., an anonymous questionnaire or disguised projective techniques. This difficulty applies to research with both adults and children; with the former, elaborate techniques have been developed to obviate it or compensate for it. With children one is on less secure grounds, since it is commonly assumed that they are more open than adults, less sophisticated, and less guarded about self-revelation. This assumption appears reasonable enough, but it is not clear at what age, with what type of child or problem, it becomes false; and erroneous implications may be drawn.

Child Development

Child development may be summarized longitudinally, in terms of separate mental or physical abilities and their waxing and waning with time; or cross-sectionally, viewing the entire spectrum of behavioral accomplishments in the child at different ages. The latter is favored in popular texts on child behavior, and has the special virtue of depicting the interrelationships of abilities in the formation of personality traits, levels of aspiration, and patterns of interest.

Prenatal Period. This phase of life has been exhaustively studied by basic medical sciences because of the potentially serious consequences to the newborn of such factors as poor nutritional status of the mother, her physical and mental health during pregnancy, the precise timing of any disease contracted by the mother and the point in the gestation cycle when it occurs, injuries sustained by the child at birth, iatrogenic diseases such as retrolental fibroplasia caused by excessive hospital use of oxygen with premature births. Recent advances in this area include the early identification of inborn errors of metabolism that customarily retarded mental development, and the introduction of corrective measures to prevent mental retardation.

Infancy. Fundamental homeostatic processes (e.g., respiration and digestion) are well established during the first year of life. During this period there is a transition from a neonate status of helplessness, total response to internal needs, and obliviousness to external demands, to that of the 1-year-old who is emotionally responsive, has a rudimentary awareness of external reality, and has perfected some skills in his varied encounters with things. It seems that if the child is reasonably well handled and nurtured during this period, he will develop trust, security, and interest in others; in the absence of adequate mothering he becomes insecure and mistrustful. In a more general way, studies show that the need for stimulation and varied experiences is primary for the refinement and coordination of basic perceptual and cognitive abilities; without experiential aliment, the child is malnourished.

Toddlerhood. During the 2d and 3d years the child becomes aware of himself as a person among persons and wants to do things for himself. He vacillates between dependence and independence and often displays negativism and willfulness in learning to accept some restraints upon his newly won freedom and newly acquired skills. He has acquired proficiency in locomotion and initial language skills and is expected to internalize some degree of control over his actions and reactions.

Intelligence test items at this age level are predominantly nonverbal; they consist of tests of color and form perception, manual dexterity, sequence learning, etc. When the IQ scores obtained are compared with those of the same children 4 years later, the correlation coefficients are quite low; shifts up or down of 20 IQ points are not uncommon. Lack of constancy of the IQ is not surprising here, since there is no reason to assume that above or below average performance on one type of item at age 2 is tantamount to comparable performance on another type at age 6. It should be noted, however, that the extremely low IQ scores of severely retarded children do remain constant over many years.

Preschool. During the 4th and 5th years the child learns to cooperate with others, to lead as well as to follow in increasingly complex play activities, and to utilize his imagination to test and establish guidelines for reality. Child's play is a serious business. It is his way of finding out what he and his world are like, of mastering concrete materials, of perfecting social and linguistic skills and conventions, and of learning the intricacies of subtle sex differences (e.g., boys play with guns; and girls, with dolls).

This period has been investigated more than any other because of the child's spontaneity on the one hand and his verbal proficiency on the other. Some of the classical studies on the child's language and thought, concept of causality, number, space, notions of morality and justice were published by Jean Piaget, a Swiss scholar of international renown.

Until recently it has been assumed that children must have attained a mental age of 6 before they are ready to assimilate elementary instruction in reading and writing. Recent tests and reviews have asserted, however, that the quantity and quality of preschool experience are far more crucial in the promotion of cognitive development than was previously assumed. The right kind of experience can lay the foundation for special instructional methods that will teach major academic skills at a far younger age than by traditional methods. J. M. Hunt has argued that early cognitive stimulation and the enhancement of curiosity may significantly alter the time table described by Gesell's developmental norms, not merely for the bright child, but for the entire spectrum of mental ability. A portent of major changes in educational practice may be seen in O. K. Moore's teaching children to read proficiently at an early age and in the resurgence of interest in the Montessori method. This method, used for the instruction of retarded children by an Italian physician, Maria *Montessori, involves orderly play and the manipulation of concrete materials to teach abstract concepts and cognitive operations.

Middle Childhood. From age 6 to adolescence the child in Western society learns academic, physical, and social skills and acquires thereby a sense of competence and self-respect vis-à-vis his peers in age and his parents. He lives, more or less comfortably, within a special subculture of children and is party to its traditions, games, values, loyalties, privileges, and prohibitions. He constantly assimilates adult policies and practices, but does this according to his own whims, espousing the romantic and adventurous aspects and rejecting some of the mundane and practical features. During this span of years there is marked physical and intellectual growth, increasing differentiation of sexual role and greater knowledgeability about sex, and emancipation from blind adherence to parental wisdom.

Age 6 has been suggested as a transition point so far as the complex relationship of *language and thought is concerned. Prior to this time speech has more of a signaling function both for intra- and interpersonal communication; after age 6 it comes to assume a mediational and conceptional function. Parallel to the conceptual maturity attained during middle childhood, language becomes more adept in facilitating and representing complex cognitive operations. Words are a most convenient way to communicate symbols, and the concepts for which they stand, to children who acquire and share common referents for these symbols. Piaget has developed a highly elaborate and formal theory to account for cognitive development during this time span and distinguishes between concrete operations at the beginning, and logical operations at the end, of this developmental period. Another researcher, J. R. Suchman, has proposed an "inquiry method" to foster a logical approach toward causal relations in comprehending scientific phenomena. By methods of this type children receive training in desired cognitive operations, and then are tested for grasp of the conceptual principle by exposure to different problems that can be solved by application of this principle. (*See* PSYCHOLINGUISTICS.)

Children's Concepts of Morality. Piaget's flexible interview method with children has yielded some of the following conclusions about their concepts of justice and morality. There is evidence of a shift from obeying moral prescriptions because of fear of external consequences to following one course of action and rejecting another because of internalized moral rules of right and wrong. A 6-year-old tends to disregard the internal motives for an act and to focus more on the external acts themselves. For the child of 6 or younger, an act is regarded as more or less immoral depending on the seriousness of the objective consequences, e.g., breaking 15 cups by accident is judged worse than breaking 1 cup in a fit of anger. Similarly, younger children regard a lie as culpable in the degree that it deviates from the truth, regardless of the intent of the teller. For Piaget these immature conceptions of morality correspond to the equally immature forms of logical thinking in the child; he considers that with age and experience, greater maturity is achieved in both domains. Piaget has suggested that logic is the morality of thought just as morality is the logic of action, implying an intrinsic connection between the two. From this view it follows that efforts to inculcate moral teachings must take into consideration the child's logical capabilities and the false reasoning to which he may be prone. The perfect recital from memory of moral doctrine is no guarantee that the reciter understands what he is saying or, if he does, that he lives by it.

Catholic Institutions. Scientific study of the child has influenced the conduct of Catholic child institutions to some extent. In Scotland Sister Marie Hilda *Marley founded the Notre Dame Child Guidance Clinic (1931). In the U.S., Father T. V. Moore opened a psychological clinic at Providence Hospital, Washington, D.C. (1916), and moved it in 1937 to the campus of the Catholic University, where it continues as the Child Center. Child guidance clinics of this type serve not merely to provide psychotherapy for disturbed children and counseling for their parents, but also to train specialists in mental health for service in other Catholic agencies. Finally, their existence and functioning has successfully dispelled the initially hostile reaction among some Catholic leaders to the practice of *clinical psychology with children.

Techniques for evaluating and training the mentally retarded have been incorporated into the standard procedures of the many residential and day schools for mentally retarded children that are conducted under Catholic auspices. Through the continuing support of Joseph Kennedy and his family, several institutes have been founded in the U.S. to investigate, diagnose, and treat the various manifestations of mental retardation.

Nor is the interest of Catholic institutions restricted to the mentally retarded alone. All types of exceptional children—blind, deaf, physically handicapped, and emotionally disturbed—are receiving evaluation and instruction based on current views of clinical psychology as applied to children.

Considerable research effort in child psychology has been stimulated by the urgent need to evaluate and treat the various kinds of maladjustment mentioned above. This emphasis on studying maladjustment has been supported by church and society on the premise that better understanding of the factors that contribute to undesirable behavior can lead to its prevention or amelioration. In general, this faith has been upheld. More recently the view has begun to prevail that the proper subject of child psychology is the acquisition of behavior and personal characteristics that promote human welfare. As P. H. Mussen has suggested, child psychology has the potential, at least in theory, for discovering the kinds of social learning experiences that lead to the development of positive characteristics, such as personal happiness, emotional maturity, creativity, social tolerance, humanitarian values, and motivation to contribute to the general welfare.

See also ADOLESCENT PSYCHOLOGY; DEVELOPMENTAL PSYCHOLOGY; EXPERIMENTAL PSYCHOLOGY; PSYCHOLOGY, HISTORY OF.

Bibliography: L. CARMICHAEL, ed. *Manual of Child Psychology* (New York 1954). P. H. MUSSEN, ed., *Handbook of Research Methods in Child Development* (New York 1960). L. J. STONE and J. CHURCH, *Childhood and Adolescence* (New York 1957). B. R. MCCANDLESS, *Children and Adolescents: Behavior and Development* (New York 1960). J. M. HUNT, *Intelligence and Experience* (New York 1961). J. H. FLAVELL, The *Developmental Psychology of Jean Piaget* (New York 1963).

[N. A. MILGRAM]

CHILD WELFARE

Child welfare, as the term is used in social work, encompasses all services designed to promote the well-being of children. It includes services provided directly to children in their own homes and to children in foster care and institutions. It is concerned also with the preservation and strengthening of family and community life as environmental influences conducive to wholesome child development.

In colonial U.S., homeless children were cared for either in almshouses or through apprenticeship to families. The apprenticeship system was generally preferable to placement in almshouses, since children were often exposed to depraved or diseased adults in the latter. As the need for religious training and education was recognized, separate institutions for child care were established. One of the earliest of these (for girls) was founded by the Ursuline Sisters in New Orleans in 1729. Toward the end of the 18th century the first public institutions for child care were established, and by 1850 there were at least 116 such institutions in the U.S.

The Children's Aid Society of New York City (1853) is credited with having been the first agency to place children outside institutions. In the early 19th century provisions for the care and training of handicapped children, the blind, the deaf, and the mentally deficient, were being organized (*see* BLIND AND VISUALLY HANDICAPPED, EDUCATION OF; DEAF, EDUCATION OF; MENTALLY RETARDED, EDUCATION OF); and in the mid-19th century, institutions for juvenile offenders and homes for unmarried mothers were established.

In the 20th century the White House Conferences and the establishment of the Children's Bureau (1912) are of major significance in the history of child welfare. The first White House Conference (1909) emphasized the desirability of keeping children in their own homes, and, where this was not feasible, initiated the trend toward foster care in preference to institutional care. For more detailed historical background, including organization and financing, *see* WELFARE AND WELFARE SERVICES.

Services to Children in Their Own Homes. In the contemporary U.S. many factors have contributed to the need for expansion and development of services to children: increase in size of families; in the rate of desertion, divorce, and separation of parents; in the number of working and unmarried mothers; in juvenile delinquency; and in problems of maladjustment and emotional disturbance.

Where many homes, unaided, cannot adequately meet a child's needs, the provision of services to supplement and reinforce family resources helps to keep the family together. If the child derives emotional satisfaction and security from his family relationships, his health, nutritional, and other physical needs can be met by the educating of the parents in budgeting, food values, hygiene, etc., and by financial assistance. Even where disturbed family relationships exist, improvement can often be achieved through casework or counseling and therapy in child guidance centers where parents and child are jointly treated. If these resources fail, then consideration of placement outside the home may be indicated. However, emphasis is placed on preventive rather than remedial services.

Financial Assistance. Under the Social Security Act, Aid to Dependent Children grants, administered by the local Public Welfare agency, afford financial help for the child in his own home. Allowances for children are included also in Old Age and General Assistance budgets, permanent disability grants, and survivors' insurance.

Protective Services. These are directed toward parents who have been brought to the attention of the authorities for abuse or neglect of their children. Formerly such children were removed from the home to an institution or foster care, but at present every effort is made to protect the children in their homes by helping the parents to cope with their problems. Cases of abuse and neglect are less often intentional than the result of stress; and with the relief of pressures, whether environmental or emotional, a basically sound family relationship can often be salvaged.

Correctional Services. Help is given in the direct dealing with the juvenile offender who has come to the attention of the juvenile court. Prior to the court hearing, a presentence report is prepared identifying the influences contributing to delinquency. Depending upon the findings, the court decides whether the child may remain in his own home or should be placed in a foster home, under the supervision of a probation officer. Generally, commitment to an institution is made only after repeated offenses or the failure of efforts to rehabilitate the child in the community.

Homemaker Service. A short-term service is sometimes provided that enables a family to remain together during the absence or temporary incapacity of the mother, without loss of time on the job for the father. A homemaker, employed, trained, and paid by a welfare agency, assumes the housekeeping duties and care of the children. Generally, she works on an 8-hour basis, but may occasionally live in if the situation requires it. A fee, based on income, is paid to the agency by the family. The homemaker is placed with the family only after it is determined that neither relatives nor friends are available to take over in the emergency.

Special Services in Schools. The interrelationship of poor learning and poor emotional adjustment has gained a slow and somewhat reluctant recognition. The educational experience is affected by the individual's ability, interests, cultural background, and degree of maturity. Accordingly, the careful individualization of the child is of utmost importance if he is to profit fully from the school program.

Poor academic performance may be attributable to emotional and behavioral disturbances; need for remedial reading, speech therapy, or placement in a special class; illness; or inadequate nutrition or clothing. The school social worker investigates and refers the child or his family to the appropriate resource for help, whether within the school system or the community. Her knowledge of community resources affords more effective use of these agencies than is possible to those outside the profession. She may serve as a consultant to help the teacher to an understanding of the dynamics of a particular child's behavior, provide information about community resources to parents and school personnel, interpret the need for new programs and services within the school system, make recommendations to policy-making groups, and participate in in-service training programs and parent-teacher meetings.

Allied services for children within the school include: guidance and counseling programs, psychological testing services, visiting teacher service for convalescent or disabled children in their own homes, remedial reading and speech therapy programs, medical and dental services, free lunch programs, and transportation, especially for handicapped children. Related facilities and services in the community include: child guidance clinics for evaluation and therapy, outpatient medical and dental care in Public Health clinics and private hospitals, visiting nurse service, recreational facilities, and special schools for handicapped and retarded children. The Kennedy Institutes in various cities are examples of education for the retarded child that endeavor to develop the child's capacities to their highest level.

Services to Children outside Their Homes. These include temporary substitutes for parental care in foster homes or institutions and permanent placement in adoption.

Foster Care. The primary consideration in placing a child with a foster family is the capacity of the foster parents to provide the love, understanding, care, and guidance essential to the child's security and the development of his own potentialities for adequate social functioning.

Foster home placement is made on the basis of careful study of both child and foster parents. An investigation is made of the child's physical condition and health history, mental capacity, temperament, family background and experience, relationships with parents and siblings, attitudes, habits, and behavior. As to the foster parents, inquiry is made of their financial status, housing and housekeeping standards, composition of family group, background, intelligence, interests, expectations for the foster child, and willingness to share with the agency the responsibility and care of the child. Both foster family and child have a right to expect mutual satisfactions and fulfillment. Despite careful study, however, placements often prove unsuccessful or unsatisfactory, and a child may be tried in several foster homes before a reasonable adjustment is effected.

Many agencies use a temporary placement as a transitional experience with which the child can more easily cope. The temporary home makes fewer demands of the child than a permanent home, and the child, threatened with the loss of his own family and the accompanying sense of rejection, needs to work through his feelings before he is able to establish new and satisfying relationships. Generally, rebellion, hostility, resistance, and even delinquency are manifestations of a child's fear, his need to belong, and his need for security engendered by proper discipline; and the temporary foster home provides the opportunity for him to test himself and others while it imparts some stability by demanding that the child meet the ordinary requirements of home life.

Following placement of a child in a foster home, the agency maintains contact periodically, offering consultation to the foster family for the understanding of and proper dealing with the child, suggesting resources where needed, and arranging visits between the child and his natural parents. Eventually, whether the child's own home becomes ready to receive him, or he comes of age to assume responsibility for himself, the agency cooperates in making necessary plans.

Institutional Care. It should be emphasized that institutional care is not a last resort in child placement. The decision between foster home and institutional placement, aside from availability of resources, involves consideration of the needs of the individual child and the type of setting best adapted to meeting them. Some children benefit more from a group living experience, while others adjust more readily in a family situation. The child whose emotional experience in his own home has been traumatic cannot immediately take on new intimate relationships.

The initial reaction against institutional care, precipitated by the White House Conference, has been modified as institutional care has been reassessed and restructured. From an essentially self-contained unit, the institution has become primarily residential, with arrangements for children under care to attend public and parochial schools in the community and to participate in recreational and other community activities. This arrangement affords a realistic and normal kind of social experience. Many of the newer child-caring institutions have adopted the cottage plan in preference to the congregate unit, each cottage being supervised by house parents or counselors. Qualified case and group workers have been added to the staff of such institutions. The caseworker's function includes admission and postdischarge planning and direct help to the child with any difficulties he may experience in everyday living and in relationships with administration, house parents, school personnel, friends, and family during his stay in the institution. It is essential that the caseworker's role be nondisciplinary, nonauthoritative, and nonadministrative.

Another type of institutional care is afforded by the treatment-centered institution for emotionally disturbed children. The entire staff must be oriented to the problems of the disturbed child, and the program designed to afford maximum opportunity for study and treatment. In addition to the administrative and social work personnel, a resident or consulting psychiatrist and psychologist are essential. Convalescent homes for children and residential schools for the handicapped and retarded represent other aspects of institutional care.

Other institutional programs include group homes, which combine the principles of foster and institutional living and day nursery care for children of working mothers. A concomitant of day nursery care is foster day care in selected foster homes.

Adoption. The process of adoption will be covered briefly in this article; for the legal aspects of adoption and the problem of illegitimacy, including discussion of services to unmarried mothers and fathers, *see* ILLEGITIMACY; ADOPTION (U.S. LAW OF).

Child welfare services requiring adjudication must be handled cooperatively by the courts and social agencies, public and private. The court is the sole authority in the limiting or terminating of parental rights, in the awarding of legal custody of a child to a designated individual or agency, appointing a guardian for a child, and granting adoptions.

Many of the children placed for adoption are born out of wedlock, but children born to a married woman of a man other than her husband, orphans, and children otherwise deprived of their parents are adoptable also. Some are adopted by relatives; others are placed with families seeking children through agencies.

In any adoption there are three basic considerations: the needs of the child (of primary importance), the needs of the natural parent, and the needs of the adoptive parents. The natural mother, if she decides to give up her baby for adoption, signs a notarized release, which terminates her contact with and knowledge of the child. The agency compiles as complete a history of the child as possible, including the nationality of both parents, their intelligence, education, occupation, medical history, physical characteristics, and social status.

An exhaustive study of the prospective adoptive parents also is made, covering their motivation for adopting a child, their attitudes, interests, relationships with their respective families and each other, stability, level of intelligence, expectations for themselves and a child, standard of living, health, age, and cultural and religious background. The prospective parents are interviewed individually and together, and periodic visits to the home are made to enable the caseworker, through observation and conversation, to understand them and to evaluate, in relation to the child to be placed, their ability to provide a normal, healthy, and emotionally satisfying life. This is further reinforced by an interview with the parish priest or minister and several friends (suggested by the couple) who know them well. Generally a child is placed with adoptive parents of the same religious affiliation as the natural mother (though the trend is away from this policy except in Catholic agencies) and the same nationality as that of the natural parents.

Following the placement of a child with adoptive parents, there is a probationary period of 6 months to a year (according to state law) during which the caseworker visits the home periodically to help with difficulties that may arise. The caseworker's contact ends when the adoption becomes legally final.

Correctional Institutions. Commitment is not a punitive measure but rather a protective one aimed at rehabilitation. The institution should afford the child security and stability, a sense of belonging and acceptance, and an opportunity for growth and learning. He should be assured of help in retaining his identity, of a return to the community, and of the preservation of family ties. Most institutions offer a regular program of vocational training and psychiatric, psychological, and casework services. The juvenile is prepared for his return to the community and upon discharge is assigned to a parole officer who will help him in effecting a favorable adjustment.

Broad Services for the General Welfare of Children. These programs, administered primarily by governmental agencies, conduct research projects and studies in matters pertaining to the welfare of children; are responsible for standards of service and licensing of child-care agencies; and serve as consultants and provide information in the child welfare field.

The Children's Bureau, established on the recommendation of the first White House Conference (1909), is charged with the responsibility of investigating and reporting on all matters pertaining to the welfare of children and administers grants-in-aid for child welfare services—Aid to Dependent Children (under the Social Security Act) and programs for crippled children and maternal and child health programs.

The U.S. Public Health Service administers prenatal, well-baby, pediatric, and mental health clinics. The U.S. Department of Health, Education, and Welfare has responsibility for a wide range of services in the child welfare field.

The Child Welfare League of America, established in 1920, is responsible for the development of standards of service for child protection and care in agencies, institutions, day care centers, and the community. Cooperative programs between government departments of child welfare are encouraged by the League, which also issues publications, provides exchange of information, record forms, case records, and field consultation, sponsors regional conferences, and maintains loan libraries.

The White House Conferences, initiated in 1909 under Theodore Roosevelt and held every 10 years thereafter, have dealt with such topics as child welfare standards, child health and protection, and children in a democracy. A special White House Conference was convened in 1955 to discuss the subject of education. The first conference was responsible for the establishment of the Children's Bureau and the initiation of the policy of maintaining children in their own homes by provision of necessary services. The third conference (1930) was responsible for the Children's Charter, which included in its provisions the right of every child to a secure home, to health care, to education, and to the "guarding of his personality as his most precious right."

Catholic agencies and Catholic leaders in the child welfare field have participated actively in the White House Conferences and hold membership in national and international organizations, governmental departments, etc., concerned with child welfare.

Bibliography: E. A. FERGUSON, *Social Work: An Introduction* (New York 1963). M. O. HUNT, "Child Welfare," *Social Work Year Book*, ed. R. H. KURTZ (New York 1960). R. J. GALLAGHER, "Catholic Social Service," *ibid.* A. E. FINK et al., *The Field of Social Work* (4th ed. New York 1963). R. E. PUMPHREY, ed., *The Heritage of American Social Work* (New York 1961).

[A. B. MC PADDEN]

CHILDERIC III, KING OF THE FRANKS,

743 to 751, last monarch of the Merovingian dynasty. *Carloman and *Pepin, sons of *Charles Martel, were faced with insurrections upon their accession as "mayors of the palace" (October 741) and therefore raised Childeric (743) to the throne, which had been vacant since Theuderic IV died (737). Although even the name of Childeric's father is unknown and narrative sources overlook his elevation, *Einhard colorfully described his powerless reign and those of his immediate predecessors. When Pepin became king (751), Childeric was deposed without difficulty (November 751). He was tonsured and relegated to the monastery of Sithiu (*Saint-Bertin), and his son, to *Fontenelle (Saint-Wandrille).

Bibliography: EINHARD, *Vita Karoli magni*, ed. O. HOLDER-EGGER, MGSrerGerm 24, tr. S. E. TURNER (Ann Arbor 1960). H. HAHN, *Jahrbücher des fränkischen Reichs, 741–752* (Berlin 1863) 40–43, 144–148, 164–165. MGSrerMer 7:507–512. J. M. WALLACE-HADRILL, *The Long-Haired Kings and Other Studies in Frankish History* (New York 1962) 239–248.

[W. GOFFART]

CHILDREN'S LITERATURE

Children's literature encompasses more than material composed specifically for young people. From its roots in folklore not meant for children at all, it developed through epochs in which writers concerned themselves more with the young readers' spiritual and educational welfare than with their pleasurable emotions. It began to burgeon in the second half of the 19th century, and by the 20th century distinguished writers, brilliant artists, and experts in all fields were producing books for children through the agency of forward-looking publishers and editors.

TRADITIONAL LITERATURE TO THE PRINTED BOOK

The rhymes, myths, legends, and magical tales of ancient peoples were transmitted orally for centuries before they were committed to writing. The oldest stories come from the Mediterranean lands and from the Orient. Greek myths and heroic adventures found permanent form in Homer's *Iliad* and *Odyssey*, and in the works of Hesiod and other poets. It is certain that by the 4th century B.C. southern European children were enjoying the fables attributed to Aesop, little knowing or caring that many of them were familiar to children of the Orient as the *Jataka* tales.

Middle Ages. During the so-called Dark Ages (*c.* A.D. 400 to 800) the monks wrote down Biblical material, stories of the saints, Oriental tales of wonder, fables and—in Ireland at least—native legends and hero tales. Thus it was that the wealth of Christian and pagan lore was available for the few who cared to learn to read and for the many adults and children who listened to what had been read by the few. By the 6th century, schools were established in Western Europe, and it became necessary to write textbooks and general information books for pupils. Aldhelm of Malmsbury (639?–709), Bede (673?–735), Alcuin (735–804), and Aelfric (955?–1020?) stand out for their contributions.

As the Middle Ages advanced, musicians and storytellers sang songs and composed heroic stories in courts and castles, and built on the sagas and epics that had been taking form in different countries over the years. Thus it was that children heard of Cuchulain, of Beowulf, of Siegfried, and later of Arthur's Round Table and Charlemagne's paladins, and even of Oriental Rustum and Rama. For this was a period of travel—on pilgrimage or crusade or foray—and where the knights went, the minstrels went too (*see* TRAVEL LITERATURE).

No discussion of this period would be complete without mention of the **Gesta Romanorum*, that amazing compendium of homilies and tales—some of the latter rather broad—collected for the edification of church congregations. This supposedly "Roman" book proved a rich plot source for such later writers as Chaucer and Shakespeare. Writers picked up also the stories in the *Vulgaria*, a collection of popular tales of Robin Hood, Guy of Warwick, Reynard the Fox, Patient Grisel.

Courtesy Books. A side effect of the Norman Conquest was the blending of Norman-French with the more earthy Anglo-Saxon to produce the English language. With the merging of the races came an increased consciousness of good manners and minor moralities, and so it was that a new type of book was directed to children. Many of these "courtesy" books were in Latin. Some appeared originally in French or Italian; others were composed in England. Typical were *Stans Puer ad Mensam*, which gives hints for pages serving in noble households, and *How the Good Wife Taught Her Daughter*, which proves that the girls were not neglected.

THE COMING OF THE PRINTED BOOK

In 1476 William *Caxton brought the first printing press to England. He had the imagination to foresee the types of books readers would enjoy; and when he could not find what he wanted in English-language manuscripts, he translated from French, Dutch, German, or Latin. He put some of the children's courtesy books into print; but their recipients soon discovered the more enticing books intended for their elders. Among the publications children took over were Aesop's *Fables*, which Caxton translated from a French edition; *Reynard the Fox*, which he took from a Dutch version instead of directly from the French; and the stories of King Arthur that Sir Thomas *Malory had written down in 1470. These great stories had already had a long history. Malory's versions were drastically pruned by Caxton, and as the centuries passed they were to be edited and illustrated and reworked by authors, poets, artists, musicians, and dramatists.

Godly Children. Serious-minded adults of the Puritan ascendancy in 17th-century England recognized the importance of books to the spiritual welfare of children. Typical of the treatises prepared at this time was *A Token for Children* (1676) by James Janeway, subtitled "An exact account of the conversion, holy and

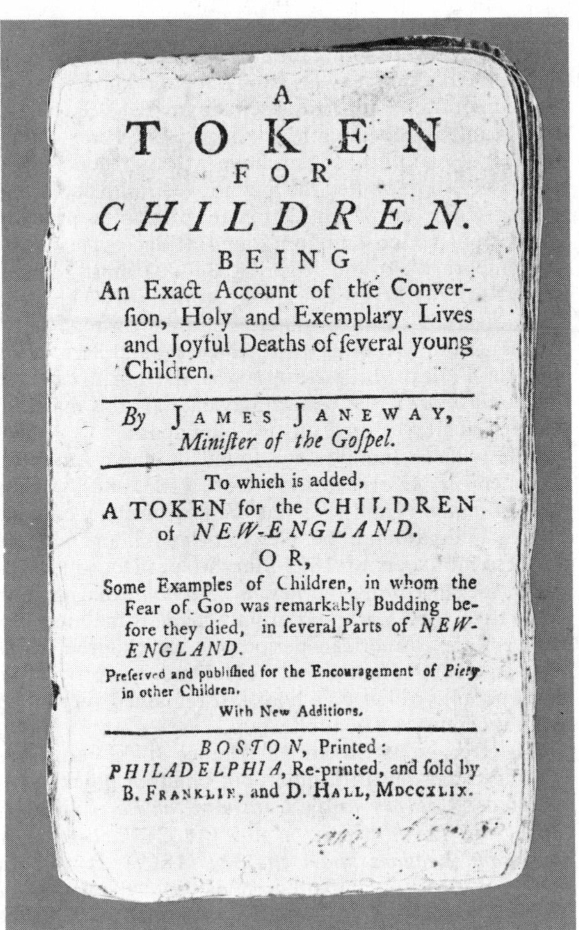

A
TOKEN
FOR
CHILDREN.
BEING
An Exact Account of the Converſion, Holy and Exemplary Lives and Joyful Deaths of ſeveral young Children.

By JAMES JANEWAY, *Miniſter of the Goſpel.*

To which is added,
A TOKEN for the CHILDREN of *NEW-ENGLAND.*
OR,
Some Examples of Children, in whom the Fear of GOD was remarkably Budding before they died, in ſeveral Parts of *NEW-ENGLAND.*
Preſerved and publiſhed for the Encouragement of *Piety* in other Children.
With New Additions.

BOSTON, Printed:
PHILADELPHIA, Re-printed, and ſold by B. FRANKLIN, and D. HALL, MDCCXLIX.

Fig. 1. The title page of Janeway's "A Token for Children," printed by Benjamin Franklin and D. Hall (1749).

exemplary lives and joyful deaths of several young children." Cotton Mather wrote a similar *Token* for New England children in 1700. Characteristically, children were turning to adult literature to satisfy their imaginations. In his own lifetime *Cervantes found that children were laughing over the obvious fun in *Don Quixote* (1605; 1615). In 1678 *Bunyan published *Pilgrim's Progress;* and before long the children had appropriated this tremendous allegory for its adventure and drama. Children have cherished Daniel Defoe's *Robinson Crusoe* since its first appearance in 1719. (It has given rise to an international genre of robinsonnades, of which *The Swiss Family Robinson* by Johann Rudolf Wyss, published originally in German between 1812 and 1827, is perhaps the most famous example.) Generations of young readers have immersed themselves in *Gulliver's Travels* (1726), unaware or in disregard of the savage satire that lies beneath *Swift's story line.

Side by side with the pabulum and the great adult books read by children in the 17th and 18th centuries stood cheap pamphlets hawked by chapmen or peddlers. These chapbooks were badly printed and had blurred woodcut illustrations; the style was slipshod and the contents sometimes obscene. Yet children who paid their pennies for them discovered Jack the Giant-Killer, Robin Hood, and many other traditional characters who had been banished from God-fearing nurseries.

John Newbery. In 1744 the English printer *Newbery set out to provide children with books that would be entertaining as well as instructive. *A Little Pretty Pocket Book* (1744) was a charming miscellany of information and entertainment. The most famous Newbery publication was *Mother Goose's Melody* (*c.* 1760), a compilation of old English nursery rhymes that had survived in oral tradition. Newbery's choice of a title for these rhymes has caused confusion through the years, for either by accident or design he appropriated the term from the fairy-tale collection published in 1697 by Charles *Perrault under the title *Histoires ou Contes du Temps Passé,* with the inscription *Contes de ma Mère l'Oye* printed beneath the frontispiece. Within a very few years of Newbery's book, Perrault's enchanting French stories had been translated into English—fortunately indeed, for all imaginative literature was soon to be declared anathema.

Didactic Period. The theories on child training promulgated in Jean Jacques Rousseau's *Émile* (1762), taken together with John Locke's *Some Thoughts Concerning Education* (1693), fostered an entire school of writing: the moral and didactic tale. The all-knowing adult, the questioning child, reward for virtue, and punishment (often terrible) for naughtiness—all were ingredients. *L'Ami des Enfants* (1782–83) by Armand Berquin, a typical French example, was quickly translated into English. *Sandford and Merton* (1783) by the eccentric Thomas Day, *The Fairchild Family* (1818–47) by Mary M. B. Sherwood, and *Moral Tales* (1800) and other collections by Maria *Edgeworth wielded enormous influence in English nurseries through the Victorian era.

The essayist Charles Lamb and his sister Mary did their part to offset this dreary literature. *Tales from Shakespeare* (1806), a classic prose retelling of the most appropriate plays, stood alone in its field until in 1956 the American writer Marchette Chute published *Stories from Shakespeare.* Lamb also retold the Homeric *Adventures of Ulysses* (1808).

Folklore Again—and Fantasy. Despite the efforts of the Lambs and a few others, the didactic school dominated the field for some time. But a quixotic fate was at work. Two philologists while journeying through their native Germany collected examples of primitive oral literature. The result was that the brothers Jakob and Wilhelm Grimm gave the children of the world *Hansel and Gretel, Snow White,* and many other marvelous tales published in three volumes between 1812 and 1822. A little later, the scholarly Norwegian friends Peter Asbjörnsen and Jörgen Moe collected old tales from the peasants and published the first volume as *Norwegian Popular Tales* (1842).

In England Joseph Jacobs (1854–1916) and Andrew Lang (1844–1912) were noted collectors and editors who wrote directly for children. Seumas MacManus (1869–1960) became known on both sides of the Atlantic for his story programs based on the Irish tales he had heard in boyhood and had written down with flavor and wit in *Donegal Fairy Stories* (1900) and other volumes. Much the same was done for the folklore of various other Old World countries.

In the U.S. from 1837 to 1853 Nathaniel *Hawthorne produced a series of books retelling the myths and hero tales of antiquity for boys and girls. The series included *A Wonder Book* (1852) and *Tanglewood*

Fig. 2. Drawing of Alice and the Caterpillar, by Sir John Tenniel in the first English edition of "Alice's Adventures in Wonderland" (London 1865), by Lewis Carroll.

Tales (1853). In the 1850s the ethnologist Henry R. Schoolcraft pioneered in recording American Indian folklore. Joel Chandler Harris (1848–1908) gave children the Brer Rabbit tales that the American Negro had inherited from his ancestors. Various writers published those most typical of all American stories, tall tales of Paul Bunyan, Joe Magerac, and other folk heroes of the New World.

Parallel with these investigations into folklore was the rise of fantasy. Hans Christian *Andersen introduced *The Ugly Duckling, The Tin Soldier,* and the rest of his characters and personifications. In 1846 the English artist Edward Lear published *A Book of Nonsense,* the first of several collections of verses. The rhythmic humor of *The Owl and the Pussycat* and the absurdity of limericks such as "There was an old man with a beard . . ." set a standard for the generations to come.

Under the pseudonym Lewis Carroll, Charles Lutwidge Dodgson (1832–98), a mathematician at Oxford University, introduced a gallery of unique characters in *Alice's Adventures in Wonderland* (1865) and its sequel, *Through the Looking-Glass* (1871). New fantasy linked itself with old magic in these momentous stories —with satire, humor, wit, puns, and crazy logic tossed in. The illustrations by Sir John Tenniel set a crown of perfection on the stories.

Developments in the U.S.

The establishment of the American Tract Society in 1825 stimulated material directed to the children of the Protestant ascendancy. This "Sunday school" literature was dreary in the extreme until stories, well spiced with morals, were added to the basic informational fare. Samuel Goodrich (1793–1860), better known to his contemporaries under his pseudonym Peter Parley, is significant as the author of the prolific *Peter Parley* travelogues and other instructive works. Jacob Abbott (1803–79) contributed the much-loved *Rollo* books and other stories in which Christian principles predominated, but action and fun found a place. Their near contemporary Horatio Alger (1834–99) must be mentioned for his "rags to riches" stories in which poor boys invariably gained material success through faithfulness to the virtues of thrift, courtesy, and hard work. Martha Finley (1828–1909) was the creator of the *Elsie Dinsmore* series. Amazingly enough, this mawkish heroine achieved fame on two continents.

The realistic family story found its finest American exponent in Louisa May Alcott (1832–88), whose *Little Women* (1868–69) was the first of many credible stories built around the New England home life she knew so intimately. In 1873 Mary Mapes Dodge (1831–1905) began editing the new *St. Nicholas* magazine in her native New York and rapidly made it the most distinguished of American periodicals for children. *Hans Brinker* (1865), a story set in Holland, has proved the most popular of her own books. It remained very much alive a century after publication.

The Deepening Stream. In France Jules Verne was writing ostensibly for adults, but children quickly discovered *A Journey to the Centre of the Earth* (1864), *From the Earth to the Moon* (1865), and *Twenty Thousand Leagues under the Sea* (1869). It was not long before these and other books by "the father of modern science fiction" were available in English. Some

Fig. 3. Joel Chandler Harris's character Brer Rabbit, from an original drawing by A. B. Frost (1896).

Fig. 4. Recto (a) and verso (b) of a watercolor by Beatrix Potter, dated 1894. On the recto is a note (not shown), "Turn over," written by the artist. These are prototypes of the drawings in "The Tale of Peter Rabbit" (1903).

parents deplored their children's reading *The Adventures of Tom Sawyer* (1876) and *The Adventures of Huckleberry Finn* (1885) by Mark Twain; in the next century, long after both books had won immortality as children's classics, some still regretted them. Johanna Spyri (1827–1901) interpreted life in a Protestant region of the Swiss Alps to generations of children who read her most beloved story *Heidi* (1880) in the original German and in translations. About this same year Carlo Lorenzini as "C. Collodi" (1826–90) gave the world the irrepressible Italian marionette, *Pinocchio.* In 1883 Robert Louis Stevenson published *Treasure Island,* which is considered the most magnificent desert-island adventure story ever written. Its fame has increased as each succeeding generation has fallen under its spell.

The distinguished American artist-author Howard Pyle (1853–1911) put future generations in his debt through his adaptations of English hero stories. *The Merry Adventures of Robin Hood* appeared in 1883; four volumes of Arthurian stories, between 1903 and 1910. Among Pyle's other works are the excellent stories *Otto of the Silver Hand* (1888) and *Men of Iron* (1891), which show sensitivity to the spirit of the Catholic Middle Ages. Rudyard Kipling brought romantic India to the children of the world with *The Jungle Book* (1894), and published the absurdly humorous *Just-So Stories* (1902) for younger children.

Catholic Writers of the 19th Century. It is obvious that those Continental European Catholics whose works have lived on into the 20th century wrote for children in general rather than for a specific Catholic market. But in both the British Isles and the U.S., Catholic authors were writing with a more special purpose. The Church was fighting, and the children had to take their places on the battlefield. Thus it was that Catholic boys and girls were subjected to the Sunday-school type of story, to religious tracts sometimes thinly coated with a story film, to insipid lives of the saints. Yet many adults remember their "parish library" books with pleasure, quite likely because Catholic writers tended to dwell on God's love, on the blessedness of doing right rather than on dire punishment for doing wrong. Anna Hanson Dorsey (1815–96) and Anna T. Sadlier (1854–1932) were writing novels that proved popular with children as well as adults. *Nan Nobody* (1901) is representative of the stories that endeared Mary T. Waggaman (1846–1931) to girls. *Tom Playfair* (1892), *Percy Wynn* (1891), and numerous other stories of Catholic boarding school life made the name of Father *Finn loved in the British Isles as well as in the U.S. Father *Tabb made a very definite contribution with his exquisite short poems, some of which he collected under the title *Child Verse* (1899). Inextricably connected with the authors mentioned above are the venerable Catholic publishing houses—Kenedy, Benziger, Murphy, Sadlier, and others—and the far-seeing general houses such as Longmans, which did so much to put books in the hands of Catholic boys and girls.

Illustration Moves Ahead. In the late 19th century certain English illustrators of children's books, notably Randolph Caldecott (1846–86), Kate Greenaway (1846–1901), and Leslie Brooke (1862–1940), developed their individual styles, heralding the advances of the 20th century when new techniques in printing enabled the artist to give his imagination full rein and to undertake experiments in different media. (American librarians have given Caldecott's name to their annual award for a distinguished picture book and their British compeers have named their similar medal in honor of Kate Greenaway.) Beatrix Potter (1866–1943) gave the children of the world the first of many picture-book classics with *The Tale of Peter Rabbit* (1903).

Foremost among artists of the 20th century are the American Wanda Gāg (1893–1946), whose picture books have folk tale elements in illustrations and text; Ludwig Bemelmans, the Austrian-American author-illustrator of the classic *Madeline* (1939); the American "Dr. Seuss" (Theodore Geisel) who invents zany contortions with line, color, and words; Leo Politi, an Italian-American whose deep-toned pictures enrich his simple stories of Catholic minority groups in the United States; and Fritz Eichenberg, whose Germanic genius achieved fulfillment in America.

20th-Century Trends

After World War I, stories of foreign lands flooded the American market. Most of them flaunted their formula so openly that they met swift oblivion. Outstanding among survivals remains *The Trumpeter of*

Krakow (1928) by Eric P. Kelly, a story about medieval Catholic Poland. As the century advanced, authors faced realism in different types of fiction. Doris Gates's *Blue Willow* (1940), which describes a girl's life in a migrant-worker family environment, is representative of the regional-sociological type. *Bright April* (1946) by Marguerite de Angeli, and *And Now Miguel . . .* (1953) by Joseph Krumgold, show, respectively, how a little American Negro girl and a Spanish-American boy adjust to life. Eleanor Estes introduces children to the affectionate and lighthearted relationships within a poor New England family in *The Moffats* (1941) and its sequels, set in the first quarter of the 20th century.

Nonni and Manni (1953) and other delightful stories written in German by Jesuit Jon Svensson, and translated into many languages, reconstruct Iceland of a century ago. The English authors Rosemary Sutcliff and Cynthia Harnett have, in their different ways, brought Roman, medieval, and Tudor Britain to life, with sympathetic understanding of Catholic historical roots. In the *Little House* series of true-to-life stories, Laura Ingalls Wilder (1867–1957) bases the action on her own childhood in the pioneer settlements of the Middle West in the 1870s and 1880s. Mary O'Hara's horse story, *My Friend Flicka* (1941), has set the standard for modern realistic animal stories. Humorous stories, such as *Mr. Popper's Penguins* (1938) by Richard and Florence Atwater, *Ben and Me* (1939) by Robert Lawson, and *Homer Price* (1943) by Robert McCloskey, have become beloved classics.

After World War II. World War II and its aftermath inspired children's writers in different countries. Many stories were grimly realistic—a far cry from the tailored stories that sprang from World War I. Others stressed the innate brotherhood of the world's children. A poignant and humorous example of the latter group is *Twenty and Ten* (1952) by Claire H. Bishop, which relates how French children protected refugee Jewish children from the Nazis.

Modern stories of fantasy hold astonishing appeal for children of the atomic age. Ever since Kenneth Grahame published his classic account of the adventures of Rat, Mole, and the other little creatures in his *The Wind in the Willows* (1908), British authors have been eminent in this field. In 1934 Pamela Travers gave children the first magical achievements of the salty-tongued *Mary Poppins.* Shortly afterward J. J. R. Tolkien published *The Hobbit* (1937), weaving mythology and wit into the activities of some extraordinary little creatures. These little people are not to be confused with *The Borrowers* (1953) and its sequels, in which Mary Norton delineates the problems of quite a different diminutive race. C. S. *Lewis gave children a series of significant fantasy-adventure-allegorical stories—based firmly on Christian idealism—in *The Lion, the Witch and the Wardrobe* (1950), and other chronicles of the imaginary land Narnia. Meriol Trevor has impregnated her science-fiction fantasy *The Other Side of the Moon* (1957) with Catholic philosophy. In 1955 the notable Catholic convert Eleanor Farjeon gathered some of her finest imaginative tales into *The Little Bookroom.* In the U.S., E. B. White gave children a bittersweet classic centering around the heroic spider in *Charlotte's Web* (1952); and in 1954 Edward Eager published *Half Magic,* which has remained the most popular of his stories of modern boys and girls enmeshed in magical adventure. New hands are working on old magic. Early in the century Padraic Colum retold the Homeric epics and the Norse myths in his singing prose. Since then Barbara L. Picard, Olivia Coolidge, and other distinguished writers have retold similar material.

Popularity of Poetry. A respectable body of poetry is available to 20th-century children. *Belloc's *A Bad Child's Book of Beasts* (1896) has been reprinted in whole and in part for humor-loving moderns. In the 1920s A. A. Milne published his *When We Were Very Young* and *Now We Are Six.* Some sensitive American poets have written especially for children—notably Rachel Field and Aileen Fisher. Carl Sandburg and Robert Frost edited compilations of their own work particularly for young readers. New editions of Walter de la Mare's and Eleanor Farjeon's fine poems have been published for U.S. as well as British children, and Phyllis McGinley and John Ciardi have written near masterpieces for young audiences. Careful and imaginative editors have produced anthologies suitable for every age and all tastes.

Books of Information. Scarcely a subject is now considered outside a child's interest. Books on areas of science from atomic energy to microbiology are produced by authorities to suit all age levels. Much of the science material is materialistic in outlook, but rarely does a writer overtly set out to disturb the readers' sensibilities. History and the social sciences are approached with realistic competence; writers of biography avoid the didactic approach, choose a wide range of subjects, and usually endeavor to paint an objective picture.

Trends in Publishing. Early in the 20th century some of the great publishing houses established juvenile departments under brilliant and dedicated editors. The librarian Anne Carroll Moore (1871–1961) did much to encourage the critical evaluation of children's books with her pioneer reviewing in the twenties. The public libraries in the United States began developing the new profession of children's librarian at the end of the 19th century, and now the British Isles and other countries have trained children's librarians at work in their public and school libraries.

Children's books have become big business. One result is keen competition among publishers to produce better books. Another is the proliferation of books in series, with gradations from the series in which authoritative writers treat individual episodes and personalities of history, to series of boys' and girls' stories produced by the assembly-line method. Concern with reading difficulties has occasioned books with "controlled vocabulary." Most are for young children; others are for older retarded readers. Many inferior picture books are sold in supermarkets or drug stores, and paperback editions of the classics and popular ephemeral books are making an appeal to young people. Great novels are abridged or adapted for slow or reluctant readers, a practice that engenders controversy among parents, teachers, librarians, and publishers. The so-called "comics" are as worrisome to parents as dime novels were in the 19th century; but as surely happened with the dime novels, the comics are a temporary craze with most children. Adults who distrusted television during its early years have on the whole concluded that this medium has furthered rather than hindered reading, and that their own energies should be directed toward improving the quality of programs.

Catholic publishing took a long step forward during the second quarter of the 20th century. New companies competed with the familiar old houses. There are still many mediocre and pietistic books published for Catholic children, but the trend is toward realism, and more and more distinguished authors are turning to the Catholic juvenile field. In biography the plaster saint stereotype is giving place slowly to the objective, well-authenticated biographies of heroic men and women. Fiction on the whole still has a long way to go.

Many Catholics are writing as authors who "happen to be" Catholics, while many non-Catholics are impregnating their books with Catholic spirit. It may well be that writing for children of the next half-century will become increasingly Catholic in tone and decreasingly apologetic in style.

See also FOLKLORE; LITERATURE, ORAL TRANSMISSION OF; SAGA; EPIC; LEGENDS, MEDIEVAL.

Bibliography: B. P. ADAMS, *About Books and Children: Historical Survey of Children's Literature* (New York 1953), includes exhaustive bibliographies. F. J. H. DARTON, *Children's Books in England: Five Centuries of Social Life* (2d ed. London 1960). A. M. JORDAN, *From Rollo to Tom Sawyer* (Boston 1948), an American survey. P. HAZARD, *Books, Children and Men,* tr. M. MITCHELL (4th ed. Boston 1960), a French savant's brilliant criticism and evaluation of the development of children's literature in different lands. L. H. SMITH, *The Unreluctant Years: A Critical Approach to Children's Literature* (Chicago 1953). A. DUFF, *Bequest of Wings: A Family's Pleasures With Books* (New York 1944), enticing recommendations and general suggestions for parents. N. LARRICK, *A Parent's Guide to Children's Reading* (New York 1958), covers all fields and includes annotated lists of children's books. I. SMITH, *A History of The Newberry and Caldecott Medals,* (New York 1957). C. MEIGS et al., *A Critical History of Children's Literature* (New York 1953). **Illustration credits:** Figs. 1–4, from original in the Rare Book Department of The Free Library of Philadelphia.

[E. SHEEHAN]

CHILE

The territory of Chile, without Antarctica, extends over an area of 286,397 square miles and occupies the southwestern part of the continent (between 17° 30′ and 56° S.) bounded on the east by the Andes and on the west by the Pacific Ocean. The Spaniards were not able to conquer the southern region because of the resistance of the Araucanians and of the geographic and climatic difficulties. Colonization limited itself to the area between parallels 27° and 37° W. and to Valdivia and Chiloé. There the principal cities were founded: Santiago (1541), La Serena (1544), and Concepción (1550). After independence, colonization extended to Magallanes (1843), Llanquihue (1848), and Araucania (1884), while in the north the Provinces of Tarapacá and Antofagasta were added after the War of the Pacific (1879–84) against Peru and Bolivia. During the 17th and 18th centuries the basic wealth was in agriculture; later, mining predominated, especially that of saltpeter (19th century) and of copper (20th century). Lately, industrialization has been encouraged. The population in 1960 was 7,367,856, rigidly stratified, although with a numerous and increasing middle class. The racial composition is basically Spanish and Indian. In 1620 the colonized area was 10 per cent white and mestizo white, 86 per cent Indians and mestizo Indians, and 4 per cent Negro and mulatto. In 1813 the proportion was: 64 per cent white and mestizo white, 32 per cent Indian and mestizo Indian, and 4 per cent Negro and mulatto in the process of being absorbed and eliminated.

Evangelization. The conquest of America by Spain entailed the obligation to evangelize the Indians. But in the case of Chile, grave obstacles were encountered:

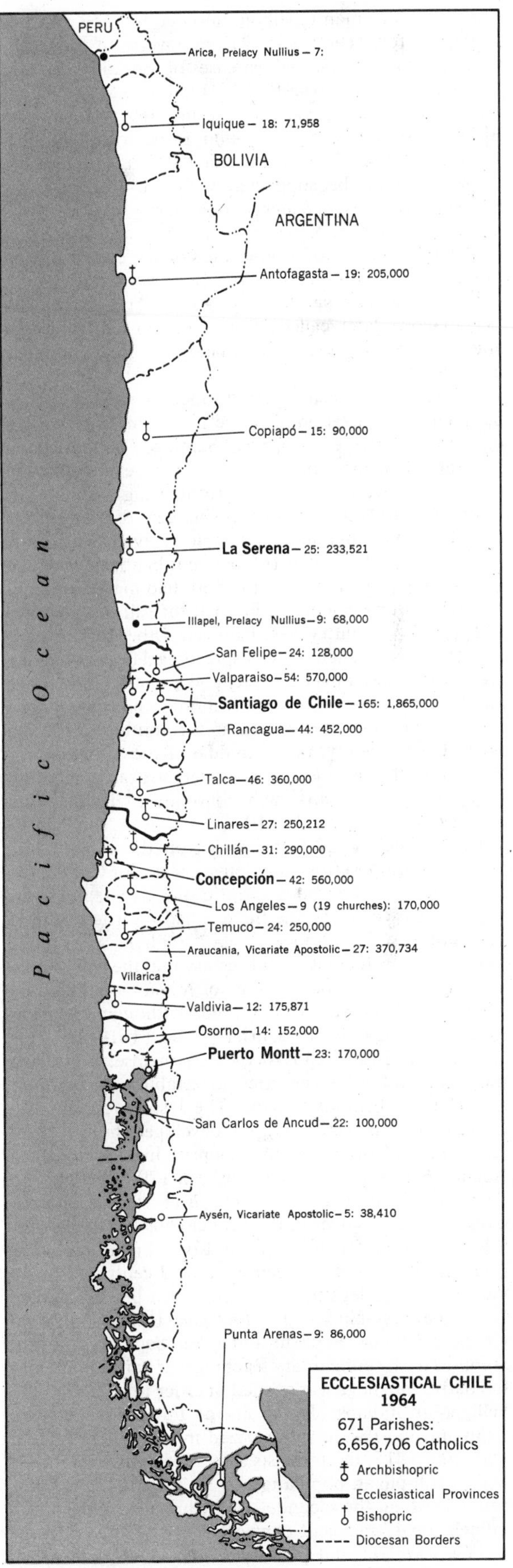

Chile, showing points of ecclesiastical interest.

(1) the Araucanian rebellion, initiated in 1553 and not controlled for 3 centuries; (2) the poverty of the country in relation to material expenses of the missions; and (3) the shortage of priests. The situation was somewhat remedied by the arrival in Chile in 1569 and 1576 of Bishops San Miguel and Medellín, respectively, who organized the Church. It was decided at that time that the *doctrina* would be supported with the Indians' own money; that one *doctrinero* would serve several towns at the same time; and, finally, that a Spaniard or mestizo would take charge of simple missionary duties during the absence of the *doctrinero*. (*See* ENCOMIENDA DOCTRINA SYSTEM IN SPANISH AMERICA.) These were the "sayapayos," later called "fiscales," who had a certain amount of importance in Santiago and great influence in Chiloé.

After the 17th century, a distinction must be made between evangelization of peaceful Indians and warlike ones, the first in the bishopric of Santiago and the second in that of Concepción. In Santiago, evangelization seemed to have rapid success. Comparing a sample of five towns in 1579, when only 36 per cent of the families were Christian, and another sample of five towns in the same zone in 1621, with 100 per cent baptized, one can say that the propagation of the faith had made apparent progress. It was calculated in 1650 that all the peaceful Indians in the country were baptized. Other factors contributed to this, such as widespread racial mixture, the creation of new convents in city and country, and, above all, the concentration of colonization in the central zone of Chile because of the loss of the southern cities in 1600. Consequently, in the middle of the 17th century the *doctrinas* disappeared and were transformed into parishes, a system that was consolidated in the 18th century and lasted until 1810.

In the Diocese of Concepción, on the other hand, there were more serious problems; except for Chiloé, the region between the Maule and Bío Bío Rivers, and some regions near the forts, the Indians had returned to their pagan state. The Jesuit Luis de *Valdivia maintained that to convert them it was necessary that the war should be suspended and the entrance of missionaries without military aid should be permitted. Although his ideas were accepted only for a brief period (1610–15), the Jesuits and Franciscans dedicated themselves during the 17th and 18th centuries to establishing missions among the rebellious Indians. The Jesuits founded the Colegio de Castro (Chiloé) and developed the system of circulating missions in both bishoprics in order to reach isolated places. They created also, in 1700, the Colegio de Naturales de Chillán, which, after various alternatives, was turned over to the Franciscans in 1786. After the expulsion of the Jesuits in 1767, the Franciscans took all the work upon themselves and centralized it in the Mission College in Chillán, founded in 1756. From there they established 16 *doctrinas* from Chillán to Chiloé; in them, Baptism and other Sacraments were administered, rudimentary teaching was carried out, and the native language was studied in order to preach to the belligerent Indians. The fruits of this labor between 1756 and 1817 were summarized in two reports, dated 1807 and 1815; the first lists a total of 7,469 Christians with a still-pagan population of 10,761, that is, 41 per cent Christian; the second, 9,644 Christians and 10,707 infidels, or 47 per cent converted.

The wars for independence created a momentary stagnation. But after 1830, when the republic was definitively organized, the once suspended activity assumed greater proportions, especially since the Chilean government reincorporated the regions lost by the Spaniards in 1600 and made itself effective in the extreme south. While during the 19th century the central zone was considered totally Catholic, in the southern regions the propagation of the faith was advanced through the importation of Salesians and Capuchins, among others. The missionary reports say that in 1892 the prefecture of the old Colegio de Chillán was in Collipulli and had six *doctrinas;* that the prefecture of the Colegio de Jesús was in Angol with another six; and that the Capuchin fathers had 15 more in the Provinces of Cautín, Valdivia, and Llanquihue. The six missions of the Colegio de Jesús, in the heart of the Araucanian territory, where no missionary work had been done since the 16th century, had a Christian population of 19,000 (29 per cent) in 1892. The Salesians founded four missions in the Austral zone, and were aided by the Daughters of Mary who had centers in Punta Arenas, Dawson Island, and Tierra del Fuego. The Apostolic Prefecture of Araucania, created in 1848, became an apostolic vicariate in 1928. It included part of the Provinces of Malleco, Cautín, and Valdivia, and the evangelization was carried on in the 1960s by Capuchins in 12 parishes. Also in the same zone are the Carmelite Sisters of Charity, Dominican Sisters of the Holy Family Congregation, Franciscan Sisters of the Sacred Heart, Missionary Catechists of the Sacred Heart of Jesus, School Sisters of the Holy Cross, and Maryknoll Sisters. The Dioceses of Valdivia and Osorno are in the care of Capuchins, who have four missions. Magallanes continues to be attended by Salesians, Sisters of Charity, and Daughters of Mary, the latter two established in Punta Arenas, Porvenir, and Puerto Natales.

A serious falling away from the Church has become apparent especially in urban centers. Among the various means used to remedy it has been the General Mission, preached in Santiago and other cities since 1963. Missions are entrusted to the laity and based on modern media of communication. In rural zones, isolated from parishes, annual missions bring together for some days the inhabitants of one or more agricultural estates.

Diocesan Organization. Churchmen arrived in Chile with the conquistadores. One of them, Rodrigo González de Marmolejo, founded the first parish in 1547 on receiving the title of pastor and foreign vicar sent to him by the bishop of Cuzco. In 1561 the bishopric of Santiago was created, and the same González became its governor. Nevertheless, because of the death of this man and of his successor, the Chilean church was organized only in the last third of the 16th century through the work of Bishops Diego de Medellín in Santiago and Antonio de San Miguel in the Diocese of La Imperial (created in 1563). Both attended the Third Council in Lima in 1581 and collaborated so that the decrees of the council on Sacraments, doctrine, catechism for natives, and reform and discipline of the clergy would have rapid application in Chile. Following the destruction of the southern cities between 1599 and 1602, the bishop of La Imperial moved his see to Concepción. During the 17th century the Church prepared its consolidation. In spite of clashes with civil powers and conflicts between religious orders, the prelates were able to give a solid base to the clergy and to construct churches, cathedrals, and

Chile: (a) The "Christ of the Andes," on the mountain border between Chile and Argentina. (b) The church of San Francisco, Santiago, the only intact colonial church in the city. (c) General view of the city of Santiago.

seminaries; but the buildings were frequently destroyed by earthquakes and by invasions of rebellious Indians. In the 18th century the Church in Chile was strengthened. The synods, especially those of Bishop Carracso in 1688, Bishop Alday in 1763 (both in Santiago), and Bishop Azúa in Concepión in 1744, dealt with such problems as the conduct of priests, parochial schools, observance of holidays, catechisms, and teaching of the lower classes. Their canons served well into the 20th century.

With the struggles for emancipation (1810–18), the Church suffered a grave recession. The bishop of Santiago, José Santiago Rodríguez, was exiled because of his royalist sympathy, and the Colegio de Misiones de Chillán was disbanded for similar reasons. The clergy was divided, and these evils reached a high point between 1824 and 1830. The *Muzi mission sent by the Pope to settle ecclesiastical matters in Chile was unsuccessful and returned to Rome. The government decreed the sequestration of the property of the regular clergy (1824). Religious services decreased, and numerous parishes had no one to serve them; the orders were disorganized, and many priests were secularized during the stay of Vicar Muzi. This sad situation changed when order was restored in Chile, and its institutions were established, after 1830. The sequestered properties were returned, and normal relations were resumed between the government and Rome. This produced the erection of the archbishopric of Santiago, to which Manuel *Vicuña Larraín was named, and the erection of the Dioceses of La Serena and Ancud (1840). In 1845 the See of Santiago was occupied by Rafael Valentín *Valdivieso Zañartu, and in 1854, that of Concepción by José Hipólito Salas Toro, who, both, like their forerunners of the 16th century, carried out far-reaching reforms. The work of Valdivieso in matters relative to offices of the Curia, religious orders, restoration of the seminary, parish schools, etc., gave the Church in Chile a very solid base for the modern period. At the end of the century, with the effective occupation of Antofagasta and Tarapacá, corresponding apostolic vicariates were created. At the beginning of the 20th century, the Church increased its hard-earned prestige under the administration of Crescente *Errázuriz y Valdivieso in the archdiocese of Santiago. In 1946 Abp. Jóse María *Caro Rodríguez was elevated to the dignity of cardinal, a rank held also by his successor, Raul Silva Henríquez (1962). In 1964 there were four archbishoprics in Chile: La Serena, Santiago, Concepción, and Puerto Montt; 15 bishoprics, the *nullius* prelatures of Arica and Illapel; the Apostolic Vicariates of Aysén and Araucania, and a General Military Vicariate created by Pius X in 1910 for the religious service of the Chilean armed forces.

Composition of the Clergy. During the colonial period the racial factor limited vocations. In 1565, 17 per cent of the priests in Chile were mestizos or quadroons, but an order from Philip II prohibited their ordination thereafter. During the colonial period, undoubtedly, people with one-quarter or less Indian blood could be ordained, but the general order prevailed until independence; an exception was made when four natives were ordained in 1794 in the Colegio de Naturales de Chillán. After 1810 the new spirit and the greater racial homogeneity produced by a long-standing mixture caused the prohibition against such ordinations to disappear.

Clerical Shortage. A greater problem to the Church has been the chronic shortage of priests in the country. The table below shows that only in the 17th and 18th centuries was there an increase in the number of priests in proportion to the number of inhabitants:

Year	Clergy			Population	Inhabitants per priest
	Reg.	Sec.	Total		
1567	56	24	80	650,000	8,125
1600	191	50?	241	638,000	2,647
1700	400	250	650	590,000	923
1800	615	310	925	660,000	713
1907	825	705	1,530	3,231,022	2,111
1960	1,561	820	2,381	7,367,856	3,094

But this was not through a real increase in vocations; it was rather on account of the reduction in the congregation by the defection of the rebellious Araucanians and a concentration of the population in the central zone between 1600 and 1800. When the colonized territory increased again after 1840, it was again necessary to increase the number of foreign priests. The religious orders that in colonial centuries had no more than 20 per cent non-Chileans, averaged 63 per cent in foreigners in 1964. It can be assumed, therefore, that aside from real and sincere vocations, entrance into the orders increased in the past by such factors as the security provided by the cloisters, the poverty of many old families that could not establish all their offspring, and the freedom from an entrance payment in the male communities. This chronic ailment in Chile, long kept hidden, reappeared after independence. The arrival of new congregations, without an increase in vocations, had made the problem more obvious.

Religious Orders. These held a preferred position in colonial society and attracted the majority of the vocations. They arrived early: the Mercedarians in 1550, the Franciscans in 1553, the Dominicans in 1557, the Jesuits in 1593, the Augustinians in 1595, and Hospitallers of St. John of God in 1617. Similarly, convents of nuns were established, such as Limpia Concepción in Santiago (1574), as well as the lay order of Isabelas de Osorno. In the 17th century there were four convents of nuns in Santiago, all cloistered, and in the 18th, seven appeared in addition to that of the Trinitarians in Concepción. The religious had great influence during the colonial period, not so much for their wealth, which was always relatively modest in Chile, but for their prestige. The Jesuits were the guides of a large segment of society before their expulsion. The popularity of the orders was limited after 1810 because of the disorganization produced by independence and the measures taken by Chilean governments before 1830. Afterward the traditional orders did not regain their former place; nevertheless the number of congregations has increased notably since 1840. In 1964 there were in Chile 56 male religious orders and institutes with 297 establishments, and 19 institutes of cloistered nuns and 104 of active nuns with 441 establishments.

Social and Educational Institutions. To the primitive hospital of St. John of God, founded in Santiago in 1541, were added new establishments of this kind in the following centuries: in 1810 there were in the country eight hospitals, all in the care of the Hospitallers of St. John of God. Besides this, charitable works were carried out on the basis of private initiative and the assistance given by the convents. Since Chile won independence, this work has been organized and coordinated. In 1964 the Church not only maintained its own hospitals or collaborated with the state in others but it had more than 36 social agencies, among which were Hogar de Cristo, Mi Casa, Caritas-Chile, Hogar Catequístico, Instituto de Educación Rural, Hermandad de Dolores, Instituto de Viviendas Caritas, and the Society of St. Vincent de Paul.

Teaching holds the first place in ecclesiastical activities. During colonial times, education was exclusively in the hands of the Church and was distinguished at the beginning of the 17th century by the establishment of the Colegios de San Miguel and Santo Tomás with the rank of universities, operated by Jesuits and Dominicans, respectively. Convents and parishes created schools closely connected with them. Of equal importance were the Convictorios de San Francisco Javier in Santiago and San José in Concepción, both run by the Jesuits. After independence, the teaching work of the Church was revived, especially with the arrival of new religious orders, and it began to compete with the state in the field of education. In 1888 the Catholic University of Chile was created, approved by Pope Leo XIII on July 28, 1889, and erected canonically by Pius XI, Feb. 11, 1930. Afterward came the Catholic University of Valparaiso (1928) and the Catholic University of the North, in Antofagasta; the last recognized by the state in 1963. In 1964 the male religious orders had 172 establishments for primary, secondary, special, or technical education, while nuns maintained another 309 schools of every kind. In addition, there were many parochial schools throughout Chile.

Relations between Church and State. The Church was organized in Chile after the 16th century under royal patronage exercised by the Spanish sovereigns, who had, or took for themselves, the right to present prelates, the right to make rules in religious matters, power before tribunals, the *placet* or permission to receive bulls and pontifical documents, etc. The republic, without Rome's accepting it, made use of these same prerogatives. Such situations created a crisis during the second half of the 19th century, and only in 1925 was an agreement reached thanks to the intervention of President Arturo Alessandri and Archbishop Crescente Errázuriz of Santiago. As a result, the constitutional reform of that year established total religious liberty, the separation of Church and State, and, in consequence, the definitive disappearance of patronage. This was the situation in Chile in 1964.

Protestant Activity. Non-Catholic Christians appeared in Chile after the country had gained its independence. Its first proponents, such as James Thompson in 1821, were agents of the British and Foreign Bible Society and carried out their mission by traveling through the country on foot. The first Anglican church was built in Valparaiso and was inaugurated in 1858. In the south of the country, among German immigrants, there was already a Lutheran group. However, these churches made no great progress because of the limited number of Germans or Englishmen living in Chile. The Methodist Church had greater importance; it grew in Chile from the preaching of the Spaniard Juan Bautista Canut de Bon at the end of the 19th century, for which reason they are called "canutos." In 1909 part of the Methodists adopted the Pentecostal doctrine and began to develop their cult among the lower classes. After the constitutional reform of 1925, the Protestants, particularly the Methodists, Pentecostals, and Baptists, increased noticeably to the point of having almost 10 per cent of the population in 1964. The reasons for this growth are usually stated as follows: (1) the eminently missionary character of these churches; (2) desire for faith and religious spirit in the lower classes; (3) ignorance of Catholic doctrine among the lower classes; (4) popular character of Protestant liturgy and authority; and (5) organization adapted to the spirit and preference of modest Chilean classes.

Year	Population	Protestants	Per cent
1920	3,753,799	54,165	1.4
1930	4,287,445	62,267	1.4
1940	5,023,539	119,092	2.3
1952	5,932,995	240,856	4.06
1960	7,367,856	620,000	8.4

Bibliography: R. Poblete, *La Iglesia en Chile* (Madrid 1961); "La situación religiosa en Chile," *Teología y vida* 3 (1962) 229–235. I. Vergara, *El protestantismo en Chile* (2d ed. Santiago de Chile 1962). L. Galdames, *A History of Chile,* ed. and tr. I. J. Cox (New York 1964). **Illustration credits:** Fig. 2*a, b, c,* Pan American Airways.

[J. A. DE RAMÓN]

CHILE, CATHOLIC UNIVERSITY OF

A private institution of higher learning founded in Santiago on June 21, 1888, by decree of Archbishop Marianno Casanova. The University began classes April 1, 1889, in the Faculties of Law and Mathematics under the direction of the rector, Bishop J. Larrain. Through the leadership of Msgr. C. Casanueva, who served as rector from 1920 until 1953, the institution developed into a modern university. Under the laws of 1929 and 1931 Casanueva obtained government recognition of the University's rights and academic privileges. During his tenure the University added four Faculties to the curricula and was canonically erected as a pontifical university.

Expansion of the University coincided with the post-World War II economic and social development of Latin America, under the tenure (1953–) of Msgr. Alfredo S. Santiago. During the 1950s the University continued its growth by adding five departments and increasing the number of scientific research centers. By 1963 enrollment totaled 4,532 men and women; the academic staff, both full- and part-time, numbered 775 professors and 447 assistants. Enrollment in summer sessions averaged 2,000 students. The University maintains (1965) a central library and 21 specialized libraries housing 85,614 volumes and 1,400 magazine titles.

Officers of administration comprise the rector, prorector, secretary general, and two vice rectors. A council, headed by the rector and consisting of the administrative officers, deans, and six counselors, determines the general policy of the University. Leaders of the student body are elected through the Student Federation. The University derives most of its income from endowed properties, gifts and bequests, an annual state subsidy, and student fees. It spends approximately 65 per cent of income in teaching, and somewhat more than 15 per cent in research.

The academic year is divided into three trimestral periods; March to May, June to August, September to December. The basic unit of research and teaching is the Faculty, which grants professional titles and academic degrees. There are related departments within the Faculty in which courses generally follow fixed programs compulsory to all students on semester or yearly terms. The programs for professional studies usually last 5 years. The University grants the professional titles of industrial, agricultural, and civil engineer, civil building constructor, teacher, and electrical technician; the licentiate in chemistry; master in law, surgery, and architecture; and doctor in theology.

In the early 1960s the University comprised 9 Faculties and 19 departments. These included the Faculty of Physical Sciences and Mathematics, with engineering and physics departments; Architecture and Arts; Agriculture; Economics and Social Science, including departments of economics and sociology; Law, Political, and Social Sciences, with departments of law and social service; Philosophy and Education, including departments of teaching, letters, languages, philosophy, psychology, and journalism; Theology; Medicine and Biology; with the departments of medicine, biological sciences, and nursing; and Technology, including departments of civil construction, electrical engineering, and chemistry.

The University maintains Schools of Civil Engineering, Journalism, Psychology, Teacher Training, Social Work, Nursing, Sociology, and Chemistry and the School of Rural Studies for Women. It conducts Institutes of Physics and Astronomy, Anthropology, German Culture and Language (the Albertus Magnus Institute), a film institute, an institute for girls, and an institute of religious culture. It operates the Agricultural and Rural Center, and the department of scientific and technological research.

Scientific research is developed in institutes and centers with permanent staffs. A central scientific committee coordinates all research plans of the 29 research centers covering nearly all sciences. Through its Cultural Extension Programs the University promotes general cultural interest among students and community. Cooperating in these programs are the Film Institute, a television station, an experimental theater, and a department of music.

University publications include *Anales de la Academia Chilena de Ciencias Naturales, Historia, Anales Juridico-Sociales, Anales de la Facultad de Teología, Finis Terrae,* and *Teología y Vida.*

Bibliography: *Memoria de la Universidad Católica de Chile* (Santiago de Chile 1932). *Anuario de la Universidad Católica de Chile* (Santiago de Chile 1938). P. LIRA, *Don Carlos* (Santiago de Chile 1962). "Vida de la Universidad Católica de Chile," *Finis Terrae* (1954–).

[A. RAMIREZ]

CHILEAN LITERATURE

Like the literature of most Latin American countries, Chilean literature had its origins in the classical tradition of the Spanish and Italian Renaissance. At first, it was written by Spaniards for Spaniards. The American setting appeared only as an exotic world to captivate the fancy of Europeans. As some of the writers began to settle permanently in America, a sense of attachment and loyalty to the New World developed in their work. For the understanding of the evolution of Chilean literature, three periods should be distinguished, each marked by an event of historical significance: the period of conquest and colonization, from the 16th to the 18th century; the period of independence, from 1810 to 1850 approximately; and the period of nationalism, from the second half of the 19th century to the middle of the 20th century.

Period of Conquest and Colonization. Two literary genres rose to eminence during this epoch: epic poetry and the *crónicas,* a form of history in which the autobiographical element plays an important role.

Among the epic poets Alonso de Ercilla (1533–94) is the most famous. In *La Araucana* (1569, 1578, and 1589), a poem based on the wars between the Indians of southern Chile and the *Conquistadores, Ercilla sings the birth of a nation, portraying the Indian as the classical symbol of man's struggle for freedom. Ercilla's idealized image of the Araucanians had a strong influence on the philosophical and social thought of European writers of his time. In America he had many imitators but only one is still worthy of mention: Pedro de Oña (1570–1643), the author of *El Arauco domado* (1596).

As fearless and determined as the Conquistador, and no less significant in the history of Spanish American letters was the missionary. Spanish priests of different religious orders wrote poetry, history, and didactic essays that revealed the American Indian to Western civilization. In Chile the missionaries distinguished themselves particularly in history and natural science.

Alonso de *Ovalle, SJ, was the first historian of Chile. His *Histórica relación del Reino de Chile* (1646) is more than a mere narrative of events related to the conquest and the wars against the Araucanians; it is also a nostalgic, poetic description (written in Rome) of the majestic beauty of Chilean nature. Diego de Rosales, SJ (1603–77), was the author of several historical works, among which the best known is the *Historia general del Reino de Chile,* published in 1877. His views were deeply influenced by his compassion for the Indians. Miguel de Olivares, SJ (1672–1768?), distinguished himself as the historian of the early period of colonization. In his *Breve noticia de la Compañía de Jesús en Chile* (1864), and *Historia militar, civil y sagrada del Reino de Chile* (1864), he attempted a characterization of the Chilean people, and offered valuable information on their customs, legends, and ideas. The great theologian of this period was Manuel *Lacunza, SJ, whose *La venida del Mesías en gloria y majestad* (1816), a book of minute analysis of Biblical texts, engendered a heated controversy in Rome and Spain; it is considered the most erudite work written during colonial times in Chile. Juan Ignacio *Molina, SJ, wrote much of his valuable work on natural sciences in Italian and translated it himself into Spanish. His *Compendio de la historia geográfica, natural y civil del Reino de Chile* (1776) is one of the first anthropological studies attempted in Spanish America. Other *cronistas* worthy of mention are Felipe Gómez Vidaurre, SJ (1748–1818), Francisco Núñez de Pineda y Bascuñán (1607–80), and Juan de Barrenechea y Albis (second half of the 17th century).

Period of Independence. The French *Encyclopedists left a deep impression on Chilean letters during the period of national independence. In the first half of the

19th century, Chile experienced a far-reaching cultural revolution out of which a national literary expression was born. Historians identify this movement as the work of the "Generation of 1842," whose leaders were

Domingo Sarmiento.

Andrés *Bello, a Venezuelan scholar who settled in Chile, and Domingo *Sarmiento, the Argentine educator who later became president of his country. Bello, a philosopher, linguist, jurist, and historian, took an eclectic position in regard to the values of classicism and romanticism. Sarmiento, on the other hand, proclaimed the need to bury what he considered the dead tradition of Spanish classicism. In spite of their differences of opinion and attitude, both of them contributed jointly to the foundation of a national literature that never cut its ties with Spain, as Sarmiento suggested, and which borrowed from French romanticism and realism. The most important poets of the romantic school in Chile were Eusebio Lillo (1826–1910), author of the Chilean national anthem; Guillermo Blest Gana (1829–1905); Guillermo Matta (1829–99); Eduardo de la Barra (1839–1900), and José A. Soffia (1843–86).

Period of Nationalism. Toward the end of the 19th century, the Nicaraguan poet Rubén *Darío, while working as a journalist in Chile, published a little book of poetry and prose, *Azul* (1888), which was eventually to bring about a major revolution in the literature of both Spanish America and Spain. Darío had a number of followers in Chile, among them Pedro A. González (1863–1905), Samuel Lillo (1870–1958), Antonio Bórquez Solar (1874–1938), Diego Dublé Urrutia (1877–), Manuel Magallanes Moure (1878–1924), and Carlos Pezoa Véliz (1879–1908), who is recognized by critics as the most important Chilean modernist and whose works have been compiled by Armando Donoso in *Poesías y prosas completas* (1927). Pezoa marks the beginning of a new era in Chilean poetry, away from Darío's *préciosité* and closer to the roots of an American tradition.

An interesting phenomenon in Chilean letters during the 19th century was the prominence gained by a school of historians who produced massive narratives dealing especially with the struggle for independence and the first years of the new republic. The most distinguished of these historians were Miguel L. Amunátegui (1828–88) and his brother Gregorio (1830–99); Diego Barros Arana (1830–1907), whose *Historia general de Chile* (16 v., 1884–1902) is a classic in its field; Benjamín Vicuña Mackenna (1831–86); and José Toribio *Medina, the greatest bibliographer of Chile, author of the *Historia de la literatura colonial de Chile* (1878) and *Colección de historiadores de Chile y documentos relativos a la historia nacional* (1861–1919).

New Movement in the Novel. While Darío was leading Chilean poets along a path obviously directed by parnassian and symbolist influences, novelists and short-story writers were striving to create a form of regionalism with a strong nationalistic background (*see* PARNASSIANISM; SYMBOLISM, LITERARY). The leading figure in this movement was Alberto Blest Gana (1830–1920), some of whose novels—such as *Martín Rivas* (1863), *Durante la Reconquista* (1896), and *Los transplantados* (1904)—are still popular with Chilean readers. The tradition of realism and social consciousness initiated by Blest Gana was continued by a brilliant generation of storytellers: Luis Orrego Luco (1866–1948), Baldomero Lillo (1867–1923), Augusto D'Halmar (1880–1950), Eduardo Barrios (1884–1963), and Joaquín Edwards Bello (1886–). Some of these novelists, and others living in the same period, drew away from the excesses of realism and searched for new themes and forms in psychology, philosophy, and religious thought. Barrios, for instance, wrote an admirable story of mystical experience in *El hermano asno* (1922). Pedro Prado (1886–1952) adapted the myth of Icarus to a Chilean situation in *Alsino* (1920), a novel of exceptional poetic beauty. Regionalistic writers (*criollistas*) emphasized the mysterious forces of nature and became obsessed with the importance of detail. Mariano Latorre (1886–1955) was perhaps the most talented and industrious among them. Other eminent *criollistas* were Fernando Santiván (1886–), Rafael Maluenda (1885–1963), and Luis Durand (1895–1954).

Toward 1930 a new trend appeared in the Chilean novel, based on the search for understanding man's anguished condition in the modern world. Characters were studied with reference to universal problems. Style became poetic in tone and philosophical in its implications. The initiator of this trend was Manuel Rojas (1896–), author of numerous short stories and a trilogy of novels: *Hijo de ladrón* (1951), *Mejor que el vino* (1957), and *Sombras contra el muro* (1964). Other important fiction writers of this period are Salvador Reyes (1899–), Juan Marín (1900–62), González Vera (1896–), Marta Brunet (1901–), María Flora Yáñez (1901–), Lautaro Yankas (1901–), Benjamín Subercaseaux (1902–), Luis E. Délano (1907–), Gonzalo Drago (1906–), Francisco Coloane (1910–), and Reinaldo Lomboy (1910–).

Twentieth-Century Poetry. Chilean poetry reached a high point of development during the first half of the 20th century. Several Chilean poets traveled to France and Spain and played a significant role in the literary revolution that followed World War I. Vicente Huidobro (1893–1948), one of the founders of creationism, published books in Spanish and French; one of them, *Altazor* (1931), is considered one of the finest examples of Spanish abstract poetry. Pablo Neruda (1904–) adopted *surrealism early in his career (as in *Residencia en la tierra,* 1934, 1935, 1939), but proceeded to develop a style that is unanimously considered the highest expression of neobaroque poetry in modern Spanish literature. Neruda has also written much political poetry, the best of which can be found in *Canto general* (1950).

Gabriela *Mistral made a place for herself in Chilean letters without being identified with any literary school. In *Desolación* (1922–23) she overcame despair by identifying the image of her dead beloved with the image of Christ. A second book, *Tala* (1938), plunged even more deeply into the transmutation of human passion into religious love. *Lagar* (1954) gathered most of her poetry written in praise of Spanish America. She was awarded the Nobel prize for literature in 1945. Several other Chilean poets have gained international reputations during the 20th century; for instance, Pablo de Rokha (1895–), Angel Cruchaga (1893–), Juan Guzmán (1896–), Rosamel del Valle (1901–), Humberto Díaz Casanueva (1905–), Juvencio Valle (1905–), and Julio Barrenechea (1910–).

New Ideologies. During the second half of the 20th century a generation of Chilean writers has already left its mark: their ideas are influenced by the social upheavals of the time. Some of them lean toward an existentialist view of life, others toward a Marxist ideology (*see* EXISTENTIALISM IN LITERATURE; MARX, KARL). Together they strive to place Chilean literature beyond the limitations of artificial regionalism, without losing sight of their personal identity. Influential writers of this generation are Oscar Castro (1910–47), María Luisa Bombal (1910–), Gonzalo Rojas (1917–), Braulio Arenas (1913–), Nicanor Parra (1914–), Nicomedes Guzmán (1914–), Volodia Teitelboin (1917–), Antonio Campaña (1922–), Fernando González U. (1922–), Eliana Navarro (1923–), José Donoso (1925–), Miguel Arteche (1926–), Claudio Giaconi (1927–), Enrique Lafourcade (1927–), José M. Vergara (1929–), Enrique Lihn (1929–), and Efraín Barquero (1931–).

Theater, Criticism. Chilean theater was unimportant during the 19th century. In the second half of the 20th century it has gone through a revision of themes and techniques, and has definitely come of age. This has been due largely to the work of two university theaters: the University of Chile's Teatro Experimental, and the Catholic University's Teatro de Ensayo. The leader of this movement has been Pedro de la Barra (1914–), a director and author. Outstanding Chilean playwrights of the 20th century are Victor D. Silva (1882–1960), Antonio Acevedo Hernández (1887–1962), Armando Moock (1894–1942), Santiago del Campo (1916–61), Isidora Aguirre (1919–), Fernando Debessa (1921–), Fernando Josseau (1924–), Egon Wolf (1926–), Sergio Vodanovic (1927–), and Luis A. Heiremans (1928–).

Chile has had many essayists and critics. In philosophy and social studies the leading figures are Valentín Letelier (1852–1919), Enrique Molina (1871–1964), Alejandro Venegas (1871–1924), Francisco Encina (1874–), Jaime Eyzaguirre (1908–), Hernán Ramírez (1917–), Jorge Millas (1918–), and Luis Oyarzún (1920–). Among literary critics the most influential have been Emilio Vaisse (1860–1935), Armando Donoso (1888–1946), Domingo Melfi (1890–1946), Hernán Díaz Arrieta (1891–), E. Solar Correa (1891–1935), A. Torres-Ríoseco (1897–), Ricardo Latcham (1903–65), Raúl Silva Castro (1903–), Juan Uribe Echevarría (1908–), Mario Osses (1915–), and Cedomil Goic (1928–).

See also SPANISH LITERATURE 2, 3, 4, 5; ARGENTINE LITERATURE; MEXICAN LITERATURE; LATIN AMERICAN LITERATURE.

Bibliography: E. ANDERSON-IMBERT, *Spanish American Literature: A History* (Detroit 1963). R. SILVA CASTRO, *Panorama literario de Chile* (Santiago 1961). A. TORRES-RÍOSECO, *Breve historia de la literatura chilena* (Mexico 1956). H. DÍAZ ARRIETA, *Historia personal de la literatura chilena* (2d ed. Santiago 1962). H. MONTES BRUNET, *Historia de la literatura chilena* (Santiago 1957). H. CASTILLO y RÁUL SILVA CASTRO, *Historia bibliográfica de la novela chilena* (Charlottesville 1961). F. ALEGRÍA, *La poesía chilena, orígenes y desarrollo del siglo XVI al XIX* (Berkeley, 1954). J. DURÁN CERDA, *Panorama del teatro chileno, 1842–1959* (Santiago 1959). **Illustration credit:** Library of Congress.

[F. ALEGRIA]

CHILIASM, from Greek χιλιάς (1,000) or *millenarianism, from Latin *mille* (1,000) teaches the visible personal rule of Christ on earth for a millennium before the *end of the world. Its most ancient form, based on a literal interpretation of Apocalypse 20, speaks of the resurrection of the just and that of the damned. The first will be followed immediately by the millennium; the second will precede the last judgment. The Holy Office censured a recent revival of the idea: "A system of mitigated millenarianism cannot safely be taught" (Denz 3839).

Bibliography: J. MICHL and G. ENGLHARDT, LexThK[2] 2:1058–62. G. GILLEMAN, "Condamnation du millénarisme mitigé," NouvRevTh 67 (1945) 239–241.

[G. J. DYER]

CHILLENDEN, THOMAS, prior of Christ Church, *Canterbury; d. Aug. 15, 1411. He was professed a Benedictine at Christ Church in 1365 and was a scholar at Canterbury College, the cathedral priory's college in Oxford, becoming bachelor of Canon Law by 1378 and doctor by 1383. He also studied Canon Law at the Roman Curia in 1378–79. He wrote a number of canonical studies, one of which, the *Sexti libri decretalium reportorium,* presumably had some reputation, since five copies still exist. Chillenden was an outstanding administrator. He became treasurer of Christ Church in 1377 and retained the office after his election as prior in 1391. He abandoned the policy of direct exploitation of the conventual estates and leased them all, a program being forced on every great landowner as a result of the decline in population following the *Black Death. He secured good terms for these leases and thereby greatly increased the revenues of the house. In consequence he was able to undertake an extensive rebuilding program for Canterbury; he employed the great mason Henry Yevele to rebuild the cathedral nave, which, together with the choir screen and chapter house, justifies Leland's tribute of Chillenden as "the greatest Builder of a Prior that ever was in Christes Chirche." Other building projects were carried out on conventual properties and at Canterbury College. Chillenden declined his election to the See of Rochester in 1400. In 1409 he attended the Council of *Pisa as a delegate of the province of Canterbury.

Bibliography: Knowles ROE 2:189–190. Emden 1:415–416.

[R. L. STOREY]

CHIMALPÁIN, DOMINGO, Indian historian; b. Amecameca, Mexico, 1579; d. Mexico City, 1660. He was a descendant of the kings of Chalco. His Indian name was Chimalpáin Cuauhtlehuanitl; his full Spanish name, Domingo Francisco de San Antón Muñón Chimalpáin. He lived most of his life in Mexico City in the service of the church of San Antonio Abad though he was neither a cleric nor a religious. He wrote many works, cited in bibliographies like that of *Beristáin, which were not published and have been lost. Among them are *Crónica de México desde 1068 hasta 1597 de la era vulgar* and *Apuntamientos de sucesos desde 1064 hasta 1521,* both in Nahuatl, and *Historia mexicana antigua que comprende los sucesos y sucesión de reyes hasta 1526,* in Spanish. Under the title of *Historia de las conquistas de Hernando Cortés* he translated into Nahuatl part of the *Historia general de las Indias* of Francisco López de *Gómara; this was later retranslated into Spanish and printed in Mexico in 1826. His *Ocho relaciones históricas* in Nahuatl was published in a facsimile edition by Ernest Magin (Copenhagen 1949–52); the *Memorial breve acerca de la fundación de la ciudad de Culhuacán,* also in Nahuatl, by Walter Lehmann and Gerdt Kutscher (Stuttgart 1958).

Bibliography: G. KUTSCHER, "Le *Memorial breve* de Chimalpáin: Un Manuscrit mexicain inédit de la Bibliothèque National à Paris," *Actes du XXVIII*[e] *Congrès international des américanistes* (Paris 1948) 407–418. G. ZIMMERMANN, *Das Geschichtswerk des Domingo de Muñón Chimalpáhin Quauhtlehuanitzin* (Hamburg 1960).

[E. GÓMEZ TAGLE]

CHINA

This article treats the origins and historical development of the Catholic Church in China and includes a brief survey of the current status of other religions. Including Manchuria, Sinkiang, *Taiwan, and other islands, China has an area of 3,876,956 square miles, the third largest country in the world. It borders on the *Union of Soviet Socialist Republics, *Mongolia, *Korea, *Vietnam, *Laos, *Burma, *India, *Bhutan, *Nepal, and *Afghanistan. *Tibet was absorbed into China in 1959. China is the most populous country in the world, with 591 million inhabitants recorded in the 1951 census and an estimated 785 million in 1965. Since 1949 sovereignty has been claimed by two governments. The People's Republic of China, under Communist rule, has controlled the mainland from the capital in Peking. Taiwan and other offshore islands have been governed as the Republic of China (Nationalist China) with the capital in Taipei.

CATHOLIC DEVELOPMENT TO 1949

The old legend that St. Thomas the Apostle preached in China has no solid foundation.

Nestorianism. China's first known contact with Christianity was in 635, during the T'ang Dynasty, when Alopen (Olopen), a Nestorian monk from Syria or Palestine settled at Ch'ang-an, near modern Sian, Shensi province, then the capital of the Middle Kingdom. This event is recorded on the famous monument of Sianfu, a very important source for Chinese religious history, which was discovered in 1625 and brought to the attention of Jesuit missionaries who had only recently reintroduced Christianity into China. The monument, a marble slab 7 feet 9 inches high, 2 feet 9 inches wide, and 10 inches thick, bears the heading: "Monument commemorating the introduction and propagation of the noble law of Ta Ts'in in the Middle Kingdom." In 1,878 characters, the inscription gives the main points of Christian doctrine, the development of the *Nestorian Church in China from 635 until 781 (when the monument was erected), and the names and titles of about 70 Western missionaries.

Received with great respect by the court, the Nestorian missionaries undertook the task of translating into Chinese some of the 530 Christian books they brought with them. Soon they built monasteries in various parts of the empire and spread Christianity from those centers. The imperial decree of 845, which ordered the destruction of Buddhist monasteries, also dealt a serious blow to Nestorianism.

Nestorianism flourished again from the 11th through the 13th centuries. Nestorian monks from central Asia were successful in converting to Christianity some non-Chinese tribes, such as the Keraits, the Uighur and Ongut Turks, and the Naimans. Christian Keraits numbered 200,000, and several Christian princesses of this tribe were married to Mongol khans. The Nestorians spread southward also. Between 1275 and 1292 the Italian traveler *Marco Polo found them in northern, central, and southern China. Nestorian relics of that period, unearthed recently in Mongolia and China, include medals, crosses, and Christian tombs and sarcophagi with Christian names and Syriac inscriptions. Nestorianism flourished in China until the end of the Mongol Dynasty (1368), when it was swept away by the new Chinese Ming Dynasty.

Franciscan Mission (1294–1368). To avert the threatened invasion of the *Mongols into Europe, Pope Innocent IV sent a Franciscan, *John da Pian del Carpine, as legate to the Great Khan of the Mongols (1245). The first to travel to the Far East by the overland route, Carpine returned with much information, although the mission itself was a failure. St. *Louis IX, King of France, while on a crusade to recover the Holy Land, sent *Andrew of Longjumeau, OP, in 1249 and *William of Ruisbroek, OFM, in 1253 as ambassadors to the Mongol khans in order to win them as allies against the Moslems. These missions had meager results, and none of the friars remained in the East.

When the Italian travelers Maffeo and Nicolò Polo returned from the East in 1269 with letters from Kublai Khan asking for 100 missionaries, Western interest in the Mongol Empire revived. After an unsuccessful attempt by friars to reach China and the sensation caused by the Nestorian monk Rabban Sauma, who came from Khanbaliq (Peking) to visit Europe, Pope Nicholas IV sent *John of Monte Corvino, OFM, to the Mongol Khan. After traveling through India, John disembarked at Zaytun [Ch'üan-chou in Fukien (Fu-chien), South China] and arrived at Khanbaliq ("City of the Great Khan") during the first months of 1294, shortly after the death of Kublai. Soon after his arrival he built a church and converted Prince George, ruler of the Ongut Turks, and many of his people from Nestorianism to Catholicism. During the next 12 years John administered more than 6,000 baptisms, erected 3 churches in Khanbaliq, and trained a group of boys in the Latin chant and liturgy, probably with a view toward the priesthood. He translated the New Testament into

Fig. 1. China, showing points of ecclesiastical interest

Fig. 2. Vatican Museum cast of the Nestorian monument discovered at Sian, China, in 1625. The inscription, in Chinese and Syriac, states that it was erected in 781 in honor of the Nestorian Bishop Wang She-Cheng. It also gives a narrative of Creation and Christian doctrine.

Uighur and copied the Psalms, Breviary, and liturgical hymns for the Onguts.

When, in 1307, Clement V first learned about John of Monte Corvino's success in Cathay and his request for missionaries, he ordered six Franciscans to be consecrated bishops and sent to the East. He also named Monte Corvino as archbishop of Khanbaliq and patriarch of the East. Three of the bishops arrived at their destination to consecrate John bishop; he in turn founded the bishopric of Zaytun and sent Franciscan friars to establish houses at Hangchow (Hang-chou) and Yangchow (Yang-chou).

Between 1325 and 1328 the Franciscan Bl. *Odoric of Pordenone stayed at Khanbaliq. Returning to Europe, he recruited 50 Franciscan missionaries for China. Their leader, the papal legate, John Marignolli, arrived in Khanbaliq in 1342 and stayed 3 or 4 years. On his return, he recommended the mission to Innocent VI, who was unable to send more bishops and missionaries because the *Black Death had decimated the ranks of the clergy. Thereafter missionary zeal declined, and, in any event, missionaries were not available. Although the popes continued for some time to name titulars to the See of Khanbaliq, there were no more missionary expeditions to China under the Mongols. When the Mongol (Yüan) Dynasty was replaced by the Chinese Ming Dynasty in 1368, the Franciscan mission disappeared without trace.

Most historians conclude from the existing evidence that very few, if any, native Chinese were converted by the Franciscans or the Nestorians. Catholics in China in the 14th century may have numbered as many as 30,000, but they were probably aliens. Established with the toleration and protection of the Mongol emperors, these Christian communities shared the fate of the Mongols when a national reaction set in and swept away the foreign dynasty and all those allied with it.

Jesuit Mission. The valiant effort of the Franciscans in Cathay was forgotten. China and the road leading there had to be rediscovered. This was done by Portuguese navigators in the 16th century. St. Francis *Xavier, one of the first members of the newly founded Society of Jesus and its greatest missionary, soon became interested in China. During his stay in *Japan (1549–51), he discovered the importance of China, and he decided to enter the empire. His plan of accompanying a Portuguese embassy to the Emperor failed. Destitute of hope and help, he died (Dec. 3, 1552) on the island of Sanchwan, a few miles from the Chinese mainland. Xavier's tragic death brought the importance of China to the attention of the West. During the 30 years that followed, *Jesuits, *Franciscans, *Augustinians, and *Dominicans tried in vain to win a foothold in China. Its doors were closed to foreigners and traders could stay only at the port of Canton for short periods and under strict supervision.

The man who planned an effective method of penetrating China was the Jesuit official visitor of the missions in the East, Alessandro *Valignano. As the key to success he advocated a thorough preparation that included learning the language and adapting oneself to the culture, customs, and mentality of the Chinese. He summoned a Jesuit from India, Michele Ruggieri, and later Matteo *Ricci, both Italians who learned Chinese and succeeded in establishing themselves permanently at Shiuhing (Chao-ch'ing) on Sept. 10, 1583. Dressing first as bonzes and later, when they discovered that the most respected class in China were the learned men, as scholars, the two Jesuits displayed scientific instruments from the West and engaged in conversation and discussion with the literati and gained their respect. To strengthen their foothold, they sought to establish themselves in the capital of the empire, *Peking. While Ruggieri returned to Europe in an unsuccessful effort

Fig. 3. Astronomical instruments in Peking, used by the 17th-century missionary Matteo Ricci.

to solicit an embassy from the Pope, Ricci went north and settled in Peking (1601), 18 years after entering China. With indefatigable zeal, he exercised a fruitful apostolate, both by the spoken word and by numerous writings. When he died (1610), the 2,500 Catholics in China included many from the educated class. Nine of the 18 Jesuits were Chinese. Ricci could rightly tell his confreres: "I leave you before an open door . . .."

Two years after Ricci's death a Belgian Jesuit, Nicolas *Trigault, was sent to Europe on a multiple mission. Besides recruiting missionaries and obtaining financial help and books, he requested the Holy See to allow priests in China to wear a headpiece (*chi-chin*) during liturgical functions and to use the vernacular (Chinese) in the celebration of Mass, the administration of the Sacraments, and the recitation of the Breviary. The unusual request was granted by Paul V in two documents, the second a brief, *Romanae Ecclesiae Antistes* (June 27, 1615). The privilege could not be used at once since no Chinese translation of the sacred texts and of the Bible was available. Later requests for its use were refused by the Congregation for the *Propagation of the Faith (Propaganda). The Jesuits hoped that the substitution of Chinese for Latin as the liturgical language would help the recruitment of vocations, especially among the mature and highly respected literati, who were unable to learn enough Latin to be ordained.

One achievement responsible for the success of the Jesuit mission was the reform of the imperial calendar, which had accumulated many serious errors in the course of centuries. Deprived of scientific instruments and methods, the Chinese astronomers were unable to rectify these errors. When Ricci was urged to make the corrections, he felt unprepared for the complicated task. In reply to his request for trained astronomers, the Italian Giacomo *Rho, the Swiss Johann Schreck (Terrentius), and the German Johann Adam *Schall von Bell sailed from Europe to China. Since persecution forced these three Jesuit priests to take refuge either in hiding or in Macao, they were not officially entrusted with the reform of the calendar until 1629, when they proved their competence by accurate predictions of eclipses. After the premature death of the brilliant Schreck, the work was done by Rho and Schall with the help of the Christian scholars Hsü Kuang-ch'i and Li Chih-tsao. When the corrected calendar was presented to the Emperor (Feb. 28, 1634), it greatly increased the prestige of the missionaries throughout the empire.

Franciscan and Dominican Mission (1632–33). In response to a request by the Portuguese King and to ensure a uniform missionary method in the early stage of evangelization, Pope Gregory XIII gave (1585) the Society of Jesus the exclusive right to preach in Japan and China. Moreover, all missionaries had to embark at Lisbon. Paul V and Urban VIII gradually lifted the restriction. In 1632 and 1633 the Franciscan Antonio *Caballero a S. Maria and the Dominicans Angelo Cocchi da Fiesole and Juan B. Morales arrived. Coming from the Philippines through Formosa, they settled in the province of Fukien (Fu-chien), where they were soon joined by other confreres in a zealous apostolate. The first Augustinians arrived in 1680, and the first members of the newly founded *Paris Foreign Mission Society (MEP), in 1684. The Dominicans retained Fukien as their main area of activity; the Franciscans, Kiangsi (Kiang-hsi), Shantung (Shan-tung), Shansi (Shan-hsi), and Shensi (Shen-hsi); the Augustinians, the southern provinces; and the MEP, Szechwan (Szu-chüan) and other southern and southwestern territories.

Under the Manchu Dynasty. The progress of Christianity in China was temporarily halted by the change of dynasties in 1643. The last of the Mings were weak monarchs unable to control rebellion. The vigorous Manchus, attacking from the north, easily took Peking and gradually the whole empire by chasing the Mings southward. By then the gospel was being preached in all provinces of the empire with the possible exception of Yünnan and Kweichow (Kuei-chou). By 1636 there were 140 Catholics among the princes, 40 among the court, and 70 to 80 among the ladies in attendance. Anna, the wife of Prince Yung-ming (Kuei), last pretender to the throne, Constantine, his son, Mary, his mother, Helena, the empress dowager, and others later received baptism. These converts sent the Polish Jesuit Michael Boym to Rome to request prayers and missionaries from the Pope and the Jesuit superior general.

Unfortunately, the great hopes attached to the conversion of the last Mings dwindled because of the disorder caused by the change in dynasty. Several missionaries, including seven Jesuits and the Dominican Bl. Francis de *Capillas (d. 1648), protomartyr of the Church in China, lost their lives. The flourishing mission of Fukien was devastated. The missionaries were divided between the two dynasties. Some Jesuits followed the Mings in their retreat to the south. Schall, who first helped the unfortunate Ch'ung Chên emperor to resist the Manchus to the extent of casting cannons for him, remained in Peking after the takeover and soon found favor with the new rulers. The first Manchu emperor was still a boy, and the regent, respecting the scientific abilities of Schall, reinstated him in his former position as imperial astronomer. Schall exercised great influence over the young Shun Chih emperor, and for a while there was hope that the Emperor, who was on familiar terms with the Jesuits, might embrace the Christian faith. He embarrassed Schall by forcing on him the high dignity of mandarin of the first class.

After the untimely death of the Shun Chih emperor, an anti-Christian reaction set in. Schall, the second founder of the mission, was by then old and sick; yet he was condemned to death. The sentence, however, was never carried out. Other missionaries were imprisoned or deported. When the young Emperor K'ang Hsi took over the government from the regents, he rehabilitated Schall (d. 1666) and later proved to be a great protector of the mission. The Belgian Jesuit Ferdinand *Verbiest, successor to Schall as president of the board of astronomy, found special favor with the Emperor, who showed much interest in Western thought and science. During the K'ang Hsi reign, a French Jesuit mission was established in Peking (1687). Its members served the Emperor as astronomers, linguists, and artists, as did other Jesuits. Tomás *Pereira, SJ, a Portuguese, and Jean François *Gerbillon, SJ, a Frenchman, had important roles in the conclusion of the Treaty of Nerchinsk (1689), which determined the border between China and Russia. In gratitude for their services, K'ang Hsi published an edict of religious freedom (1692) permitting the Christian religion to be preached freely in Peking and the provinces. Aided by the prestige acquired by the Jesuits at the imperial court, the Church reached its greatest numerical extension in 1700, when there were 300,000 Catholics.

Jurisdictional Problems. For some time the whole of China had been under the jurisdiction of the See of Macao (erected in 1575), and missionary activities were regulated by the right of *padroado* (*see* PATRONATO REAL), given to the Portuguese kings by the Holy See. In an effort to create more ecclesiastical divisions and to overcome the influence of the *padroado,* which was considered harmful to the missions, the Holy See established vicariates apostolic with bishops *in partibus infidelium* directly dependent on the Holy See and independent of the crown of Portugal. The first three vicars apostolic were the cofounders of the MEP: François *Pallu, Pierre Lambert de la Motte, and Ignace Cotolendi. They were sent to the Far East in 1659 to administer the whole of China, in addition to Cochin China, Tonkin, and Laos. In 1674 the Chinese Dominican Lo Wen-tsao (Gregory Lopez) was appointed vicar apostolic of Nanking (Nan-ching) and became the first Chinese bishop when he was consecrated (1685). In 1680 Pallu was appointed vicar apostolic of Fukien and administrator of the whole of China.

The creation of the vicariates provoked a violent reaction from Portugal. The ensuing conflict between the Holy See and Portugal concerning the *padroado* created for the missionaries in China painful problems of conscience and divided their allegiance. Under strong pressure from Portugal, Rome was forced to compromise. In 1690 Alexander VIII created the two bishoprics of Peking and Nanking and made them suffragans of the metropolitan See of *Goa, as Macao was already. The Pope conceded to the King of Portugal the right of the *padroado* over the new sees and even let him determine the boundaries of the new dioceses. This settlement left no room for the vicariates in China. As a result of complaints from Propaganda, however, the Pope

Fig. 4. The Virgin and Child, executed by a Chinese artist, Ming Dynasty, c. 1600.

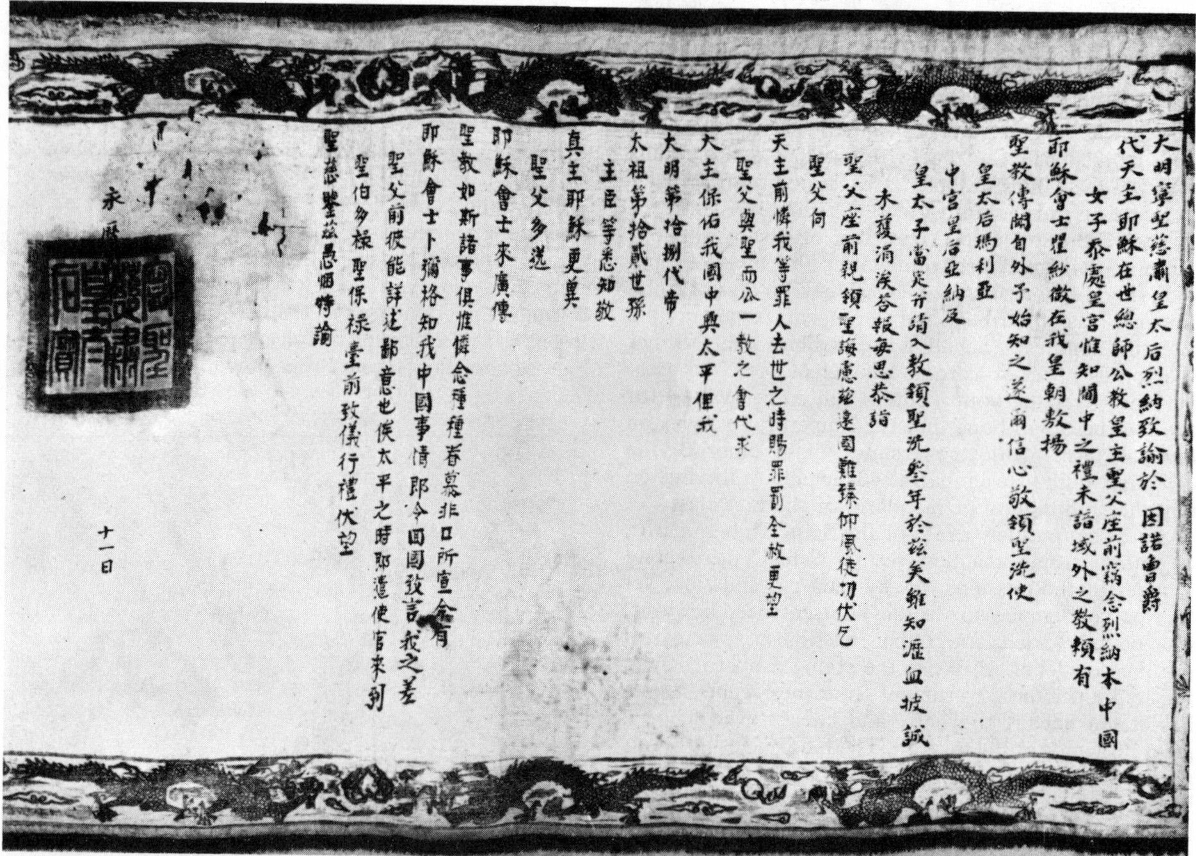
大明寧聖慈肅皇太后烈納致諭於 因諾曾爵
代天主耶穌在世總師公教皇主聖父座前竊念烈納本中國
女子忝處皇宮惟知閫中之禮未諳域外之教賴有
耶穌會士瞿紗微在我皇朝敷揚
聖教傳聞自外予始知之遂爾信心敬領聖洗使
皇太后瑪利亞
中宮皇后亞納及
皇太子當定并請入教領聖洗三年於茲矣雖知瀝血披誠
未獲涓埃答報每思恭詣
聖父座前親領聖誨慮茲遠國難臻仰風徒切伏乞
聖父向
天主前憐我等罪人去世之時賜罪罰全赦更望
聖父與聖而公一教之會代求
天主保佑我國中興太平俾我
大明第拾捌代帝
太祖第拾貳世孫
主臣等悉知敬
真主耶穌更冀
聖父多遣
耶穌會士來廣傳
聖教如斯諸事俱惟憐念種種眷慕非口所宣今有
耶穌會士卜彌格知我中國事情即令回國致言我之差
聖父前彼能詳述鄙意也俟太平之時即遣使官來到
聖伯多祿聖保祿臺前致儀行禮伏望
聖慈鑒茲愚悃特諭
永曆
十一日

Fig. 5. Letter written on silk, sent to Pope Innocent X by a 17th-century dowager empress of China. The empress, who had been baptized and had taken the name Helena, asks that more Jesuit missionaries be sent to China.

in 1696 limited the jurisdiction of the three new dioceses to one or two provinces each and also created eight vicariates in the remaining territories: Fukien, Chekiang, Kiangsi, Szechwan, Yünnan, Hukwang, Kweichow, and Shansi-Shensi. The new organization was meant to be temporary, but it remained until the middle of the 19th century.

Chinese Rites Controversy. Soon after the arrival of the first Franciscans and Dominicans, the *Chinese rites controversy broke out; it continued throughout the 17th century. In 1645 Propaganda issued the first condemnation of the rites, but in 1656, following a report by the Jesuit Martino *Martini, it permitted their practice. Later, unwilling to pass final judgment on the facts of the case, it left both decisions standing. At the discussions held during their forced detention at Canton (1665–68), all the missionaries of all the orders agreed that it was imperative to practice adaptation in the matter of the rites. However, the controversy was reopened by Bp. Charles Maigrot, Vicar Apostolic of Fukien, who induced the Holy See to reexamine the question in order to have the practices condemned. After protracted discussion by a commission of cardinals, the Holy Office condemned the rites in a decree of 1704. A papal legate, Charles Maillard de *Tournon, Patriarch of Antioch, was sent to China to communicate the decision. By his prejudices and lack of tact and diplomatic skill, De Tournon aroused the suspicion, and even the hostility of Emperor K'ang Hsi, who had been favorably disposed to the Church. After being expelled from Peking, De Tournon published the decree of the Holy Office at Nanking on his way to Macao. On his part K'ang Hsi ordered all missionaries to accept a *p'iao* (certificate of imperial approval) as a condition for continuing their ministry. This was given only to those who promised to respect the rites and customs of the nation.

In 1715 the apostolic constitution *Ex illa die* of Clement XI sanctioned the decree of 1704. To make some accommodations and to save the mission from mass apostasy and persecution, Rome sent another legate, Carlo *Mezzabarba, Patriarch of Alexandria. He gave eight permissions, which mitigated somewhat the rigor of the previous prohibitions. However, missionaries could not agree on a uniform attitude in the matter of rites. Benedict XIV issued the final judgment in his apostolic constitution *Ex quo singulari* (July 11, 1742), which revoked the permissions of Mezzabarba and reiterated the earlier condemnations.

Persecution. It is a singular tragedy that Emperor K'ang Hsi, who first issued an edict of freedom for Christianity, later became its persecutor. An imperial decree of 1717 prohibited the preaching of Christianity and ordered the deportation of missionaries from the empire with the exception of those working at the court. The decree was not fully carried out, but under his successor, Yung Chêng (1724–36), persecution became severe, and most missionaries were deported to Macao. The long reign of Ch'ien Lung (1736–96) began with a decree proclaiming the death penalty for preaching and embracing Christianity. While Jesuits, such as Giuseppe *Castiglione, and other missionaries in the service of the Emperor at Peking enjoyed his favor, missionaries in the provinces could work only in secret and under the greatest hardships. Periodically persecution flared up and sometimes enflamed the whole of China. Five Dominicans (Bl. Pedro Sanz and companions) were martyred in Fukien (1747–48), and two Jesuits (Antonio Henriquez and Tristano d'Attimis) in Kiangnan (1748). Numerous Christians suffered death in the persecution of 1784–85. After this, few missionaries remained in the country (*see* CHINA, MARTYRS OF).

A great loss for the missions was occasioned by the imprisonment and deportation of missionaries from Macao (1762) and by the suppression of the Society of Jesus by Clement XIV (1773). Propaganda tried to fill the gap, but most of the missionaries who were then sent to China fell victims to the persecution of 1784. The *French Revolution and the Napoleonic War diverted European interest from the missions. A few heroic bishops, such as Eugenio Piloti, OFM, of Shansi-Shensi; Gottfried X. von Laimbeckhoven, of Nanking and Peking, a former Jesuit; and François Pottier, MEP, of Szechwan; together with a small number of dedicated priests, worked under the greatest trials to save the Chinese Christians for better times. The severe persecution during the Chia Ch'ing reign (1796–1820) brought martyrdom to Bl. Gabriel Taurin Dufresse and companions in Szechwan, and to Bl. Jean Pierre Néel in Kweichow. Even the few remaining foreigners in Peking, French and Portuguese Vincentians, were expelled. Some churches were confiscated, and others were razed.

19th Century. During the first half of the 19th century the missions in China were in a deplorable situation. Intermittent persecutions reduced the number of European missionaries (Franciscans, Dominicans, *Vincentians, and MEP) to less than 40. The number of Chinese priests did not exceed this total. Between 1800 and 1840 the number of Catholics was between 200,000 and 250,000.

A change occurred when China was forced to conclude international treaties with the Western powers: the U.S., England, and France. In the Treaty of Nanking (1842), which terminated the Opium War, China agreed to open five ports to commerce. In a supplementary treaty (1844), the U.S. and England were allowed to construct churches and hospitals in the five ports. France obtained the same rights in the Treaty of Whampoa (1844). At the insistence of the French plenipotentiary Théodore Lagrené, an imperial decree was issued (1846) permitting the Chinese to profess the Catholic faith and authorizing preaching and construction of churches. It also ordered the restitution of confiscated church property and the punishment of local officials who persecuted Catholics. This decree was never published in proper form and remained largely ineffective. In the Treaty of Tientsin (1858) religious liberty was extended to the interior of China and efficacious protection was guaranteed to missionaries traveling to the interior, provided they carried valid passports. All anti-Christian legislation was revoked. As the sole Catholic power among the signatories, France assumed the protection of all missionaries of whatever nationality. The Peking Convention (1860) gave missionaries the right to buy property for religious purposes. This matter was further regulated by the Berthemy Convention (1865). With the tacit consent of the Holy See, France effectively exercised her exclusive protection over all missionaries between 1860 and 1880. In 1882 Germany claimed the right to protect German missionaries, and in 1888 Italy did the same for her own nationals.

In spite of imperial decrees guaranteeing religious freedom, anti-Christian sentiment persisted. Occasionally it erupted into violence as in the T'ai P'ing Rebellion (1850–64); the martyrdom of Bl. Auguste Chapdelaine (1856); the massacre at Tientsin of the French consul, 2 priests, 10 Sisters of Charity, and 8 lay persons; and the slaying of two German missionaries in Shantung (1897). Most serious of all was the Boxer uprising (1900). Some of these incidents were utilized by Western powers as justifications for launching military action against China and forcing her to grant concessions.

After 1842 the number of missionaries increased. In that year, French Jesuits began their apostolate in the provinces of Kiangnan (modern Kiangsu and Anhwei) and Chihli. In 1858 the first members of the newly founded Foreign Mission Institute of Milan arrived in Hongkong. In 1865 the Belgian Congregation of the *Immaculate Heart of Mary (Scheut Fathers) came to take charge of the evangelization of Mongolia. The Augustinians returned in 1879, the year the Society of the *Divine Word arrived. A Trappist monastery was founded at Yangkiaping, Hopeh (1883). The opening of hospitals, orphanages, and, above all, schools supplied great opportunities for an apostolate by women religious. The first to arrive were the Daughters of Charity of St. Vincent de Paul, who came to Macao in 1847. Sisters of St. Paul of Chartres came in 1848; Daughters of Charity of Canossa, in 1860; Helpers of the Holy Souls, in 1867; Franciscan Missionaries of Mary, in 1886; and Dominican Sisters, in 1889. Many other congregations of women followed.

1900 to 1949. The 20th century brought tremendous changes to China. The older order and traditional institutions disappeared as wars, revolutions, and national disasters followed one another in almost uninterrupted succession.

In 1900 the Catholic missions in northern China suffered persecution from the Boxers. About 30,000 Christians, including several bishops and priests, fell victim to their hatred. Beatifications have since then honored 29 who were martyred in Taiyüan and 56 who were put to death in the Vicariate Apostolic of Southeastern Chihli. In Peking 3,500 Christians heroically withstood the siege of the Boxers at the Pei-t'ang (Northern Church) for 2 months before they were rescued by allied troops.

In 1911 the monarchy collapsed, and a republic was proclaimed. Since there was no strong central authority to unify the country, factions and warlords created much disorder, during which many missions suffered seriously. When unity was finally restored, the Sino-Japanese War and World War II threw the nation back into turmoil.

In spite of all these disturbances, mission work progressed as the number of foreign missionaries increased.

In 1900 there were 886 male missionaries belonging to 10 institutes; by 1949 the total was 4,415 in 47 institutes. Congregations of sisters multiplied also. From 10 in 1900, they increased by 1949 to 58 (not counting 63 native Chinese congregations), and their membership grew from 59 to 6,927 during the same period. Catholics totaled 742,000 in 1900, 1 million in 1907, 2 million in 1921, and 3 million in 1938.

Catholic educational and charitable institutions were organized at a rapid rate. In addition to numerous primary and secondary schools, three Catholic universities were founded. Aurora University of Shanghai was opened by the Jesuits in 1903. The Catholic University of Peking, established by the Benedictines in 1925, was taken over by the Society of the Divine Word in 1933. Tsinku University of Tientsin was founded by the Jesuits in 1922 as the Industrial and Commercial College and was raised to university status in 1947. Despite all these educational efforts, the Catholic missions remained predominantly rural.

The increased number of Catholics made it necessary to reorganize the ecclesiastical divisions. In 1856 the two bishoprics of Peking and Nanking, nominally still under the Portuguese *padroado,* were suppressed, and their territory was divided into vicariates apostolic. The 22 vicariates in 1865 increased to 41 by 1900. In 1924 the first plenary council was held at Shanghai and established greater uniformity in ecclesiastical organization and in the missionary apostolate. The hierarchy was established in 1946.

For a time the protection of all foreign missionary interests was undertaken by the French government. When this practice began to have unfavorable repercussions, the Holy See, although opposed by France (1881, 1885, 1918), made several attempts to establish diplomatic relations with China and thus assure the safety of missionaries without foreign political intervention. In 1922 an apostolic delegation was established at Peking but without diplomatic character. In 1943 China sent an ambassador to the Vatican. In 1946 France renounced all her rights and privileges emanating from the treaties of the 19th century. In the same year the Vatican sent an internuncio to China.

During the 20th century the Chinese clergy played an increasingly important role. As early as 1591, when China had only 80 Catholics, Ricci admitted into the Society of Jesus the first two Chinese candidates for the priesthood. The first Chinese priest, Lo Wen-tsao, OP, was ordained only in 1656. Jesuits and Vincentians had many Chinese members during the 18th and 19th centuries, and the MEP trained a large number of Chinese priests in their major seminary in Ayuthia, Thailand, which was transferred later to Penang, Malaysia. Another institution for training Chinese priests was the Holy Family College in Naples, Italy, founded by Matteo Ripa. The number of Chinese priests reached 400 in 1900 and 1,369 in 1929. Pius XI made a historic gesture of consecrating personally six Chinese bishops (1926). Thomas Tien Ken-sin became in 1946 the first Chinese Cardinal.

Another important decision of the Holy See that greatly facilitated mission work was the instruction of Propaganda declaring the veneration of Confucius, ceremonies in honor of deceased ancestors, and other national customs to be purely civil in character and therefore permissible to Catholics.

Fig. 6. Thomas Tien Ken-sin, first Chinese cardinal.

Catholics in Communist China

With the removal of so many former obstacles and the development of a well-trained Chinese clergy and sound institutions, the Church confidently looked forward to a bright future after World War II. These hopes were tragically shattered by the Communist takeover.

Persecution. At the end of World War II, Communist armies controlled large areas of northern China, and Catholics in that area suffered severe persecution. In August 1945, monks of the Trappist monastery at Yangkiaping were massacred. During the "Bloody Winter" (1947–48) almost 100 priests, brothers, and sisters plus many lay persons were murdered. In face of the advancing Communist armies the papal internuncio Abp. Antonio Riberi ordered all missionaries, with the exception of the young in training, the sick, and the old, to stay at their posts. Convinced of their imminent victory the Communists changed to a tactic of toleration in the summer of 1948 in order to win popular support. Priests were freed from prison, confiscated church buildings were given back, and freedom of conscience was proclaimed. By the end of 1949 the whole of mainland China was under Communist control, and the People's Republic was proclaimed. Soon harassment was renewed. Through "professors of politics," an insidious atheistic propaganda campaign was waged in all schools, which passed progressively under government control. Two of the principal targets of attack by the government were the sodalities and the *Legion of Mary. Although freedom of religion was still proclaimed, it was more and more restricted, especially in the countryside. Zealous priests were confined to their houses, condemned to inaction, or imprisoned.

The government tried to realize its objectives in three phases. It sought (1) to have all foreign missionaries expelled, if possible at the request of Chinese Catholics; (2) to institute a reformed national Church, i.e., one separated from Rome; and (3) to destroy all influential persons who refused to collaborate with the government's anti-Catholic program. As a result, the 5,496 foreign missionaries in 1947 declined to 723 in 1952, 86 in 1954, and 23 in 1957. After taking similar action against the Protestants, the government launched the Triple Autonomy Movement (December 1950), which sought to force Catholics to create a schismatic national Church by insisting on their independence in matters concerning authority, finances, and propagation of doctrine. With the help of the police, Committees of Reform were organized and seized control of churches. They also provoked public accusations against the clergy and religious. Thus the committees made monstrous accusations against Catholic orphanages and sisters and solicited petitions for the expulsion of the internuncio and foreign missionaries.

Seeing the total failure of the Triple Autonomy Movement among Catholics and irritated by their resistance, the government proceeded to arrest all influential persons unwilling to yield. Numerous arrests occurred in Peking (1951, 1954), Shanghai (1953, 1955), and in many other places. In Shanghai alone (September 1955) Bp. Ignatius Kung, 50 priests, and several thousand lay Catholics were imprisoned. Meanwhile several bishops and priests had died in prison of privation and bad treatment.

Under government pressure, a Patriotic Congress of Catholics assembled in Peking (July 1957). In opposition to the desires of most of the delegates, it published a declaration attacking the Pope. After renewed violence and prolonged indoctrination, the government forced the Catholic Patriotic Associations to elect bishops in a "democratic way." At least 51 men were elected bishops in this illicit fashion (1957–60), and 36 of them accepted episcopal consecration. In 1964 the number of these illicit bishops was 46.

Five Chinese bishops died in prison, and nine more were still in prison in 1964; they have been replaced by illicit ones. Of the 1,300 Chinese priests presumably alive at that date, no information was available concerning their whereabouts, whether in prison or free and active. Only 13 foreign missionaries were then in China. Bp. James Walsh, a Maryknoll Missioner from the U.S., was in prison. One priest and 11 sisters, Franciscan Missionaries of Mary, were serving Catholics and their children in the foreign embassies in Peking.

On several occasions Pius XII and John XXIII asked for prayers for the Catholics of China and praised these Catholics for their heroic faith. Pius XII condemned the Triple Autonomy Movement in the encyclical *Evangelii praecones* (1951) and in the document *Ad Sinarum gentes* (1954). Pius XII also solemnly condemned the so-called Catholic Patriotic Association and declared the elections of bishops invalid and the consecrations illicit (June 29, 1958). He further recalled the excommunications that both the consecrating and illegitimate bishops incurred. Pope John XXIII issued similar condemnations.

Catholic Organization and Life. Since the creation of the hierarchy in 1946, China has been divided into 21 ecclesiastical provinces. The following 20 archdioceses form the metropolitan sees in the People's Republic: Anking, Canton, Changsha, Chungking, Foochow, Hangchow, Hankow, Kaifeng, Kunming, Kweiyang, Lanchow, Mukden, Nanchang, Nanking, Nanning, Peking, Sian, Suiyüan, Taiyüan, and Tsinan. (Individual articles on each list their suffragans; a total of 93 dioceses in 1965.) There were also 29 prefectures apostolic, 1 apostolic administration (Harbin), 1 apostolic exarchate for Russians of the Byzantine rite (Harbin). In 1952 *Taipei was made an archdiocese and metropolitan see for the island of Taiwan; it had 6 suffragan sees.

In 1950 the Chinese secular clergy controlled 20 of the above sees including those on Taiwan, and 7 of the prefectures apostolic. Two sees were entrusted to Chinese Vincentians and one to Chinese Franciscans. The other sees and prefectures were confided to various religious orders and congregations.

The latest reliable religious statistics are those of 1949. At that time China, with Taiwan, had 96 bishops, 5,700 priests (2,820 Chinese), 978 brothers (589 Chinese), 874 major seminarians (including religious), and 2,689 minor seminarians; 94 priests were ordained. Priests were trained in 15 regional seminaries.

There were 47 religious institutes of men with 4,415 members, divided as follows, with totals of native Chinese in parentheses: 85 bishops (10 Chinese), 3,474 priests (484), 856 brothers (532). The following groups had the largest representation. The Franciscans (OFM), whose first mission to China was in 1294 and whose later settlement came in 1632, had 757 members in China, including 20 bishops (1 Chinese), 592 priests (110), and 95 brothers (55); they had charge of 27 sees. The Jesuits, who came in 1583, included 9 bishops (2), 588 priests (92), and 291 brothers (175) for a total of 888; they were entrusted with 9 dioceses, 2 universities, and schools in 5 cities. The Dominicans, who have been in China since 1633, had 3 bishops, 122 priests (5), and 49 brothers (18) and were in charge of 4 dioceses. The MEP, in China since 1684, had 12 bishops and 280 priests and were entrusted with 14 dioceses. The Vincentians, in China since 1780, had 13 bishops (5), 366 priests (180), and 21 brothers (20), and were entrusted with 11 sees. The *Maryknoll Missioners, in China since 1917, had 3 bishops, 119 priests, and 5 brothers and had charge of 5 sees. There were also 160 Salesians, 195 Scheut Fathers, and 431 members of the Society of the Divine Word.

There were 6,927 women religious (4,832 Chinese) in 58 congregations of foreign origin and 63 (mostly diocesan) of Chinese origin. The largest of the native congregations were the Presentandines, founded in 1855, with 389 sisters, and the Sisters of St. Joseph, founded in 1872, with 266 members. The largest foreign congregation was that of the Franciscan Missionaries of Mary, with 789 (333) members.

There were 3,295,000 Catholics and 147,000 catechumens in 1949 when the total population was about 461 million.

There were 3 Catholic universities with 4,638 students in 1950. The Catholic University of Peking (Fujen) opened in 1925 and was run by the Society of the Divine Word. Its 2,324 students included 407 Catholics. Tsinku University, founded in 1923 as Hautes Études industrielles et commerciales, had 86 Catholic and 800 non-Catholic students under Jesuit directions.

Fig. 7. "The Last Supper," detail of a painting by the 20th-century artist Wang Su Ta, in the Lateran Museum.

Jesuits controlled also Aurora University, founded in 1903. Its student body of 414 Catholics and 1,058 non-Catholics included the students in the Aurora College for Women, directed by the Religious of the Sacred Heart. The 202 Catholic secondary schools had 53,306 students and the 1,849 primary schools, 183,233 pupils.

Catholics directed 257 orphanages with 15,000 orphans and aided 107,000 patients in 194 hospitals and hospices. The 864 dispensaries treated 11,620,000 persons. There were 6 Catholic leprosaria.

The 42 Catholic publications included 4 weekly newspapers and 24 periodicals in Chinese and 18 periodicals in English, French, Spanish, or Portuguese (*see* CATHOLIC PRESS, WORLD SURVEY, 8).

In 1949 there were 29,453 adult converts baptized and another 28,359 adults baptized when in danger of death. Of the 249,574 Baptisms of children, 67,786 were from Christian families and 123,976 from non-Christian ones. Confirmations totaled 32,253, annual confessions 892,700, annual Communions 882,700, and Anointing of the Sick 20,240. There were 13,094 marriages among Catholics and 4,526 mixed marriages.

Other Religions. Protestants and Orthodox exist in China in relatively small numbers. The disciples of Islam are much more numerous. The mass of the Chinese adhere traditionally to Confucianism, Taoism, or Buddhism, often to all three simultaneously.

Protestantism. Protestant missionary activity in China was inaugurated in 1807 by Robert Morrison (d. 1834) of the London Missionary Society, but important centers developed only after the International Treaties (1842). Missionaries from the U.S. have been very prominent in this development. In 1914 the number of adherents was 235,000. In 1922 several Protestant denominations, accounting for half the Chinese Protestants, united into the Church of Christ in China. Other important Protestant bodies in China were Methodists, members of the Church of True Jesus, Anglicans, Lutherans, Baptists, and the nondenominational China Inland Mission established (1866) by Hudson Taylor. In 1938 there were 123 separate missionary organizations at work in China. Protestants ran 13 universities, some of them enjoying high reputation. Their secondary schools were also numerous, and before the Sino-Japanese War they had 322 hospitals. For the most part, Protestant missions and institutions were centered in the cities, whereas Catholics were found more often in rural areas. In 1949 Protestant bodies counted 1,401,-000 members. Protestant Churches in China made great efforts to be independent and self-sufficient. Communist persecution severely crippled Protestant communities. The Triple Autonomy Movement apparently had greater success among them than among Catholics (*see* MISSIONS, PROTESTANT).

Russian Orthodox. The Russian Orthodox Church had a mission in China from 1727. After the Russian revolution in 1917 the main activity of this mission was among the 200,000 emigrants living in China. The East Asian Exarchate of the Patriarcate of Moscow existed until 1957, when it became autonomous with a Chinese titular. In 1950 the Orthodox had one archbishop, five bishops, and 150 parishes. The departure en masse of the Russian-born clergy after the Communist takeover in 1949 created an acute shortage of priests. Chinese Turkestan counted 80,000 Orthodox Christians (*see* MISSIONS, ORTHODOX).

Islam. Arab merchants introduced *Islam into China in the time of the Sung Dynasty (960–1280). During the Mongol (Yuan) Dynasty (1280–1368) many non-Chinese tribes were converted to Islam. Estimates of the number of Moslems in China vary between 10 and 50 million. The majority of them live in the northwestern provinces of Ninghsia, Kansu, and Chinghai.

Traditional Religions. The three traditional religions of China are Confucianism, Taoism, and Buddhism. The philosophy of *Confucius (551–549 B.C.) was elaborated by subsequent generations of scholars to provide a moral basis for the social and political structure of China and to embrace the traditional forms of *ancestor worship. At present Confucianism is more an ethical code than a religion or a school of philosophy.

*Taoism derives from Lao-Tsu, who in the 6th century B.C. taught a quietistic religion of living the way (*tao*) of nature. Superstitious practices, mixed with magic, were added later to Taoism in its popular form.

Mahayana *Buddhism (Great Vehicle) was brought to China in the 1st century A.D. and soon mingled with Confucianism and Taoism. Before 1940 there were about 5 million Buddhist monks and nuns in China. The Communists confiscated the monasteries, dispersed the monks, and forced the nuns to marry. *Lamaism is the Westernized name of Buddhism of the Tibetan and Mongolian peoples. It is estimated that there were some 2,000 lamaseries with 100,000 lamas in Tibet, Sinkiang, and Chinghai before March 1959, when the Chinese Communist government began drastic persecution of the lamas in Tibet.

Exact membership figures for each of these religions are unascertainable because many Chinese follow all three religions. The number of Buddhists is estimated roughly at 100 million.

Bibliography: Complete bibliography in Streit-Dindinger v.4, 5, 7, supplemented by J. ROMMERSKIRCHEN and J. DINDINGER, *Bibliografia missionaria* (Rome 1936–), annual. J. BECKMANN, "Neuerscheinungen zur Chinesischen Missionsgeschichte, 1945–1955," *Monumenta Serica* 15 (Tokyo 1956) 378–462.

General works. C. CARY-ELWES, *China and the Cross: A Survey of Missionary History* (New York 1957). H. BERNARD-MAITRE, DHGE 12:693–741. Delacroix HistMissCath. Mulders. Latourette v.1, 2, 3, 6, 7. Latourette Christ19th-20thCent v.3, 5. K. S. LATOURETTE, *A History of Christian Missions in China* (New York 1929); *The Chinese: Their History and Culture,* 2 v. in 1 (4th ed. rev. New York 1964). J. G. LUTZ, ed., *Christian Missions in China* (pa. New York 1965).

Special studies. H. LECLERCQ, DACL 3.1:1353–85. C. DAWSON, ed., *The Mongol Mission* (New York 1955). Y. SAEKI, *The Nestorian Documents and Relics in China* (2d ed. Tokyo 1951). G. H. DUNNE, *Generation of Giants* (Notre Dame, Ind. 1962). Pfister. J. DE LA SERVIÈRE, *Les Anciennes missions de la Compagnie de Jésus en Chine, 1552–1814* (Shanghai 1924); *La Nouvelle mission du Kiangnan, 1840–1922* (Shanghai 1925). J. NEEDHAM, *Science and Civilization in China,* 3 v. (Cambridge, Mass. 1954–59). O. MAAS, *Die Wiedereröffnung der Franziskanermission in China in der Neuzeit* (Münster 1926). J. M. GONZALES, *Misiones dominicanas en China, 1700–1750* (Madrid 1950). *Sinica Franciscana,* ed. A. VAN DEN WYNGAERT, 5 v. (Rome 1929–54). J. VAN DEN BRANDT, *Les Lazaristes en Chine* (Peking 1936). A. LAUNAY, *Histoire des missions de la Chine: Mission de Kouang-si* (Paris 1903). N. GUBBLES, *Trois siècles d'apostolat: Histoire du Catholicisme au Hu-Kwang, depuis les origines, 1587 jusqu'à 1780* (Wu-chang 1934). P. A. COHEN, *China and Christianity: The Missionary Movement and the Growth of Chinese Antiforeignism, 1860–70* (Cambridge, Mass. 1963). J. P. RYAN, "American Contribution to the Catholic Missionary Effort in China in the 20th Century," CathHistRev 31 (July 1945) 171–180. P. M. D'ELIA, *Catholic Native Episcopacy in China: Being an Outline of the Formation and Growth of the Chinese Catholic Clergy, 1800–1926* (Shanghai 1927). T. BAUER,

The Systematic Destruction of the Catholic Church in China (New York 1954). F. DUFAY and D. HYDE, *Red Star versus the Cross: The Pattern of Persecution* (London 1954). A. FREITAG et al., *The Twentieth Century Atlas of the Christian World* (New York 1964), tr. from French. H. EMMERICH, ed., *Atlas missionum* (Vatican City 1958), to be used with L. SCHORER'S *Data statistica* (Vatican City 1959). MissCattol 288–395. *Bilan du Monde* 2:223–245. *Annuaire de l'Église catholique en Chine* (Shanghai 1950), for latest statistics. Ann Pont (1965). **Illustration credits:** Fig. 2, Art Reference Bureau. Fig. 3, Jesuit Missions. Fig. 4, Courtesy of Chicago Natural History Museum. Fig. 5, Archivio Segreto Vaticano. Fig. 7, Leonard Von Matt.

[J. KRAHL]

CHINA, MARTYRS OF

This term refers to a group of 119 martyrs beatified between 1889 and 1956. Among them were 5 European bishops [3 Franciscans (OFM), 1 Dominican (OP) and 1 member of the Paris Foreign Mission Society (MEP)], 1 Dominican bishop-elect, 25 European priests [9 Franciscans, 6 Dominicans, 4 Jesuits (SJ), 3 members of the MEP, 2 Vincentians, 1 member of the Milan Foreign Mission Society], 4 Chinese secular priests, 1 European Franciscan lay brother, 7 Chinese seminarians, 7 Sisters of the Congregation of the Franciscan Missionaries of Mary, and 8 Chinese catechists. The rest were Chinese lay persons, 8 of whom were youths under 20 years of age.

Early Persecution. Catholic missions to *China since the Middle Ages have seldom been free from persecution. When the Franciscans went to the medieval Mongol Empire, Nestorians harassed them and their converts. After the fall of the Mongol dynasty, Christianity was obliterated in China and Central Asia. Since the 16th century hostility has been distilled by deeply rooted dislike for foreigners, by fear lest Confucianism and the traditional ancestor cult be undermined, and by special interest groups such as the Moslem astronomers at Peking. Repeated persecutions occurred during the 17th century after the Manchus expelled from Peking the Ming court, at which the Jesuits had enjoyed influence.

Francisco de *Capillas, OP (b. 1607), a Spaniard, became the protomartyr of the Church in China when he was beheaded in Fukien Jan. 15, 1648. He was beatified May 2, 1909 (feast, January 15). After the Jesuits regained influence at the Manchu court, Emperor K'ang Hsi granted religious toleration (1692). Partly as a result of the *Chinese Rites controversy, persecution was renewed in 1717 and became especially severe under Emperors Yung Chêng (1724–36) and Ch'ien Lung (1736–96). On May 26, 1747, in the Province of Tunkien, Bp. Pedro Sanz (b. 1680), Vicar Apostolic of Tunkien, was beheaded at Fukien. Bishop-elect Francisco Serrano (b. 1695), Juan Alcober (b. 1694), Francisco Diaz (b. 1713), and Joaquin Royo (b. 1691) were strangled in Fukien Oct. 28, 1748. All five of these Spanish Dominicans were beatified on May 14, 1893 (feast, June 5).

19th Century. Persecution continued into the 19th century. Bishop Gabriel Dufresse, MEP (b. 1774), Vicar Apostolic of Szechwan, was beheaded at Chengtu, Szechwan Province, Sept. 14, 1815. Beatified with him May 27, 1900, were the priests of Szechwan, Augustine Chao Sung (d. 1815), Joseph Yüan Tsai-te (d. 1817), Paul Liu Han-tso (d. 1818), and Thaddaeus Liu (d. 1823); the catechists Peter Wu (d. 1814) and Peter Liu Wen-yüan (d. 1834); and Ho Kai-che (d. 1839), Lawrence Pai Man (d. 1856), and Agnes Tsao Kuo (d. 1856). Their feast is November 27. Giovanni da Triora *Lantrua (b. 1760), an Italian Franciscan, was strangled at Changsha, Hunan, Feb. 7, 1816, and was beatified on May 7, 1900 (feast, February 13). The French Vincentian priest François Clet (b. 1748), who died at Wuchangfu Feb. 17, 1820, was beatified May 27, 1900 (feast, February 17). Another French Vincentian priest, Jean Gabriel *Perboyre (b. 1802), suffered martyrdom also at Wuchangfu Sept. 11, 1840. He was the first of the Chinese martyrs to be beatified, Nov. 10, 1889 (feast, November 7).

After the Treaty of Nanking (1842) European governments forced a diminution of the persecution against all Christians. In 1846 the French obtained from the Emperor a decree permitting Chinese to become Christians. The Treaty of Tientsin (1858) guaranteed religious liberty and revoked anti-Christian legislation. Religious antipathies persisted, however, and Catholic missionaries and native Christians continued occasionally to be put to death. Auguste Chapdelaine, MEP (b. 1814), was slain at Silin, Kwangai, Feb. 26 or 27, 1856. He was beatified May 27, 1900 (feast, November 27). Another priest of the MEP, Jean Pierre Néel (b. 1832), was beheaded in Kweichow Feb. 18, 1862. Beatified with him May 2, 1909, were the catechists Joseph Chang Ta-peng (d. 1815), Jerome Lu Ting-mei (d. 1858), Lawrence Wang Ping (d. 1858), and Martin Wu Hsüeh-chang (d. 1862); the seminarians Joseph Chang Yüeh-yang and Paul Chen Chang-ping (d. 1861); Agatha Lin Chao (d. 1858); John Baptist Lo and Martha Wang (d. 1861); John Chang, John Chen, and Lucy I (d. 1862). Their feast is February 18.

Boxer Rebellion. After 1898, under Emperor Ts'eu-hi, a reaction set in against the reforms pressed upon China by the Western powers. Xenophobia was especially strong among the I Ho Ch'üan or Boxers, organized bands who attacked foreigners and Christians in 1900. This persecution lasted only about 2 months, but it is believed that nearly 30,000 Catholics were massacred. At Hengchow the Italian priest Cesidio Giacomantonio, OFM (b. 1873), was slain July 4, 1900. Three days later his Franciscan colleagues, Bp. Antonio Fantosati (b. 1842), Vicar Apostolic of Southern Hunan, and Guiseppe Gambaro, a priest (b. 1869), went to their deaths. Also on July 7 the French priest Théodoric Balat, OFM (b. 1858), was put to death at Taiyüan. In the same place on July 9 were killed Bp. Gregorio *Grassi (b. 1833), Vicar Apostolic of Northern Shansi, his coadjutor, Francesco Fogolla (b. 1839), the priest Elia Facchini, and the Alsatian lay brother André Bauer (b. 1866), all Franciscans. Seven Franciscan Missionaries of Mary suffered martyrdom on the same occasion: Sisters Marie Hermine de Jésus (b. Irma Grivot, 1866), Maria della Pace (b. Marianna Giuliani, 1875), Maria Chiara (b. Clelia Nanetti, 1872), Marie de Ste. Nathalie (b. Jeanne Marie Kerguin, 1864), Marie de St. Just (b. Anne Françoise Moreau, 1866), Marie Adolphine (b. Anne Catherine Dierkx, 1866), and Marie Amandine (b. Pauline Jeuris, 1872). They were joined by the Chinese seminarians John Chang, Patrick Tung, John Wang, Philip Chiang, and John Chiang; and by the Chinese servants Thomas Sen, Simon Tseng, Peter Wu An-pan, Francis Chang Yüan, Matthias Fun Te, James

Yen Ku-tung, Peter Chang Pan-niu, James Chao Ch'üan-hsin, and Peter Wang Erh-man. They were all beatified Nov. 24, 1946 (feast, July 4). Alberico Crescitelli (b. 1863) of the Milan Foreign Mission Society, who died July 21, 1900, at Yentsepian, Shensi, was beatified on Feb. 18, 1951 (feast, July 24).

In the Vicariate Apostolic of Southeastern Chihli, Hopeh Province, about 5,000 Catholics were victims of the Boxers from June to August 1900. After examining 2,072 of these cases, Pius XII beatified 56 (April 17, 1956). Four were French Jesuit priests, and 52 were Chinese. Their feast is July 20. León Ignace Mangin, SJ (b. 1857), and Paul Denn, SJ (b. 1847), died at Chukiaho July 20, 1900. At Wuyi the same day Remi Isoré, SJ (b. 1852), was martyred, while Modeste Andlauer, SJ (b. 1847), preceded him on July 19. The following Chinese were martyred. They are listed in alphabetical order with their ages noted in parentheses when known: Anna An Chiao-shih (26), Anna An Hsin-shih (72), Mary An Kuo-shih (64), Mary An Ling-hua (25), the catechumen Chang Huai-lu (57), Thérèse Chang Ho-shih (36), Mary Chao Kuo-shih (60), Mary Chao Kuo-shih (17), Rose Chao Kuo-shih (22), Peter Chao Ming-chen (62), John Baptist Chao Ming-hsi (56), Rose Ch'en Ai-chieh (25), Teresa Ch'en Chin-chieh (25), Mary Cheng Hsü (11), the catechumen Chi'i Chu-tzu (18), Mark Chi T'ien-hsiang, Mary Ch'i Yü (15), Simon Chin Ch'un-fu (14), Elizabeth Chin Pien-shih (54), Peter Chou Jih-hsin, John Baptist Chu Wu-jui (17), Mary Chu Wu-shih (40), Mary Fu (37), Mary Fu Fan-k'un (16), Paul Ko T'ing-chu (61), Mary Kuo Li-shih (65), the catechumen Lang Yang-shih (29), Paul Lang Fu (7), Peter Li Ch'üan-chen (63), Raymond Li Ch'üan-hui (59), Paul Liu Chin-te (79), Peter Liu Tzu-yü (57), Joseph Ma Tai-shun (60), Barbara Ts'ui Lien-shih (51), Mary Tu Chao-shih (51), Magdalen Tu Feng-chü (19), Mary Tu T'ien-shih (42), Anna Wang (14), Lucy Wang Ch'eng (18), Rose Wang Hui (45), Joseph Wang K'uei-chü (37), John Wang K'uei-hsin (23), Mary Wang Li-shih (49), Andrew Wang T'ien-ching (9), Peter Wang Tso-lung (58), Lucy Wang Wang-shih, Joseph Wang Yü-mei, Paul Wu Chü-an (62), John Baptist Wu Man-t'ang (17), Paul Wu Wan-shu (16), John Wu Wen-yin, and Joseph Yüan Keng-yin (47).

During the succeeding decades of the 20th century Catholic missionaries have been targets for attack. A militantly atheistic Communist regime gained control of China in 1949, and began systematically to eradicate Christianity. In the process many Catholics have been put to death.

Racial and political reasons account for some Christian deaths; but it has been established beyond doubt that those who have been beatified died for their faith.

Bibliography: ActApS 1 (1909) 171–173, 452–458. A. M. BIANCONI, *Vita del B. F. de Capillas* (Rome 1909). ActSSed 26 (1893–94) 79–85. M. J. SAVIGNOL, *Les Martyrs dominicains de la Chine au XVIIIe siècle* (Paris 1893). H. I. IWEINS, *Le Bx Pierre Sanz et ses quatre compagnons* (Ostende 1893). J. M. GONZÁLEZ, *Misiones dominicanas en China, 1700–1750* (Madrid 1952). A. LAUNAY, *Les Bx martyrs des Missions étrangères* (Paris 1929). J. TOUSSAINT, *Un Martyr normand: Le Bx Auguste Chapdelaine* (Coutances 1955). J. ESCOT, *Le Bx Jean-Pierre Néel et ses compagnons, martyrs* (Lyons 1951). G. DE MONTGESTY, *Soldat du Christ: Le Bx François-Régis Clet, martyrisé en Chine, 1748–1820* (Paris 1906). ActSSed 22 (1889–90) 405–410. A. CHATELET, *J.-G. Perboyre . . ., martyr* (Meudon 1943). ActApS 39 (1947) 213–221, 307–311. *Les Vingt-neuf martyrs de Chine, massacrés en 1900, béatifiés par Sa Sainteté Pie XII, le 24 novembre, 1946* (Rome 1946). M. T. DE BLARER, *Les Bse Marie Hermine de Jésus et ses compagnes, franciscaines missionnaires de Marie, massacrées le 9 juillet 1900 à Tai-Yuan-Fou, Chine* (Paris 1947). L. M. BALCONI, *Le Martiri di Taiyuen* (Milan 1945). ActApS 47 (1955) 381–388. P. X. MERTENS, *Du sang chrétien sur le fleuve jaune. Actes de martyrs dans la Chine contemporaine* (Paris 1937). J. SIMON, *Sous le sabre des Boxers* (Lille 1955). C. TESTORE, *Sangue e palme sul fiume giallo. I beati martiri cinesi nella persecuzione della Boxe Celi Sud-Est, 1900* (Rome 1955). L. M. BALCONI, *Vita del b. A. Crescitelli* (Milan 1950). G. MENCAGLIA, *Il servo di Dio Alberico Crescitelli, martire della Cina* (Milan 1930). ActApS 43 (1951) 159–163, 165–168. Butler Th Attw 1:98–99, 361–365; 2:402; 3:59–62. Baudot-Chaussin 1:317; 2:402–403, 603–607; 4:464–465; 7:215–223; 9:289–293; 10:954–957; 13:198–205.

[J. KRAHL]

CHINESE LITERATURE

The prevailing influence on Chinese literature through the ages has almost invariably been Confucianism (*see* CONFUCIUS AND CONFUCIANISM). The classics that make up the canon of the Confucian school fall into the categories of divination, documents, annals, rituals, and songs.

Chou Dynasty. The only work of this period that has unmistakable literary value is the *Book of Songs,* religious odes and hymns composed by the nobles of the Chou dynasty (1122–265 B.C.); it existed as a book before Confucius (551–479 B.C.). Some other classics provide literature of a sort, but it is the existence of the canon as a whole that is of historical and literary importance. This stems from the fact that even these very early works are written in classical Chinese—a written language based on the Chinese ideograms, each of which is a unique representation of an idea. It is an elegant language, accurate and concise, far removed from the wordiness that the profusion of homonyms imposed on the spoken or colloquial language, and was used by writers almost exclusively until 1920. Toward the second half of the Chou dynasty, a number of philosophers flourished whose able writings, though not primarily literary in intention, nevertheless influenced the writers of later generations. Outstanding among such works are the *Lun yü* (Analects) of Confucius, the *Meng tzu* (Book of Mencius), and especially the beautifully written and vividly imaginative *Book of Chuang tzu.*

At the beginning of the 4th century B.C., there appeared in the state of Ch'u (Hunan and Hupeh provinces) poems attributed to Ch'u Yüan and his followers; they were later collected into an anthology known as *Ch'u tzu.* Unlike the *Book of Songs,* which is an anthology of realistic poetic descriptions of peasant life in northern China, the *Ch'u tzu* presents the literature of the south, and gives great importance to priests and priestesses in its accounts of imaginary shamanistic deities.

Han Dynasty. The Han dynasty (206 B.C.–A.D. 220) saw the development of a new form of poetry known as *fu,* derived from the *Ch'u tzu* but distinguished by its elegance and hyperbole. The *fu* neglects thought and in quest of elegance uses an extraordinarily elaborate vocabulary. Another Han poetic form, the *yüeh-fu,* had its sources in aristocratic ceremonies, contemporary folk songs, and songs of foreign origin. The *yüeh-fu* that derive from contemporary folk songs are worth special consideration; they embrace a vast variety of subjects and in simple, graceful language reflect the minds of the common people.

Poetry was commonly written in four-word lines until the middle of the Han period. After that, whole poems in five- or seven-word lines began to appear. Among the best poets of this period were Ts'ao Ts'ao (A.D. 155–220), founder of the Wei dynasty, and his two sons, the younger of whom, Ts'ao Chih (192–232), still ranks as one of the greatest of Chinese poets, and T'ao Ch'ien (365–427), a superb nature poet.

The outstanding prose works of this period are the *Shih-chi* (Historical Records) of Ssu-ma Ch'ien (145–90? B.C.), and the *Han shu* (History of the "Early Han" Dynasty) of Pan Ku (A.D. 32–92). The literary merit of all these is seldom challenged.

From A.D. 300 to 600, called roughly the "period of the Six Dynasties," the *fu* style prevailed in poetry, and prose tended to the parallel style, i.e., four- and six-word parallel phrases. This style had charm and grace, euphony and balance, often accompanied by a balance of ideas; but since it was artificial, it was a poor medium for thought or narration and tended to impersonality. Throughout this period, China was in a chaotic state. Nearly the whole of the north was occupied by frontier peoples, and dynasty followed dynasty as successive warlords seized power. Insecurity, especially among the intelligentsia, gave rise to a neo-Taoist philosophy that taught resignation to the decree of heaven and neglected the moral code. Indulgence in license became so common among scholars that it ultimately characterized the literature of the time and influenced literary practice for centuries to come.

The Six Dynasties saw also the introduction of highly influential Buddhist literature into China. Hsieh Ling-yün (385–433), Liu Hsieh (6th century), and Wu-ti (464–549), founder of the Liang dynasty, were devout believers, and Buddhist thought and terminology were common in learned writings from that time on. The seizure of North China by the frontier peoples also influenced Chinese literature. The martial spirit, the simplicity and frankness of the nomads' folk songs, were a welcome change from the emotionalism and sentimentality that had pervaded southern literature. Some Chinese poets incorporated these new qualities into their songs and produced stirring ballads.

Two great books belong to this period. Prince Hsiao T'ung (501–531) of the Liang dynasty compiled *Wen hsüan* (The Anthology of Literature), material gathered from pre-T'ang poets and prose writers; the book, which is a conspectus of literature from the Han to the Six Dynasties, is still highly esteemed. *Wen-hsin tiao-lung*, by Liu Hsieh (6th century), a systematic technical discussion of literature, divided into 50 short essays in beautiful parallel prose, is a monument of the history of Chinese literary criticism.

Golden Age of Poetry. Under the T'ang dynasty (618–907), one of the greatest periods in China's history, China was again unified, North and South being reunited after more than 2½ centuries of separation. The amalgamation of peoples and the presence of different religions helped to evoke a new literary vitality. The expansion of the empire and its good communications with the world of that time made the capital, Chang-an, a cosmopolitan center. Several emperors were accomplished litterateurs and their example and patronage greatly encouraged scholars. In early T'ang days, both style and thought still conformed to the models of the Six Dynasties period, but development came quickly.

The T'ang period is generally recognized as the golden age of Chinese poetry. Two new verse forms won recognition. One was the *lü-shih* (regulated verse), which consisted of five- or seven-word lines in eight-line stanzas with a fixed scheme of rhyme, verbal parallelism, and tonal sequence. The other, the *chüeh-chü* (broken-off lines), is similar except that each poem consists of four lines. Originally both forms, the *chüeh-chü* especially, could be put to music and song. Such forms were suitable only for lyric poems—as a matter of fact, long poems make little appeal in China and epics are almost unknown.

The poet Li Po, by Liang K'ai, hanging scroll, 13th-century Chinese.

Li Po and Tu Fu. T'ang poetry reached its zenith in the reign of the emperor Yüan-tsung (685–762), when Li Po (699–762) and Tu Fu (712–770), for example, set a standard that later centuries have not approached. Li Po, a genius deeply imbued with Taoist ideas, used material from his own turbulent career as the stuff of his poetry. Tu Fu, on the other hand, was a realist, a Confucian, and a patriot, writing at a time when revolts had temporarily disrupted the T'ang peace; he was able to sympathize with hardships that he himself had experienced. His poems describe the sufferings of the poor with a power and sincerity that have won him enduring fame.

Buddhist Poets. Other poets were devout Buddhists whose writings came from and evoked profound peace of mind. Of these Wang Wei (699–750) and Po Chu-i (772–846) were outstanding. Like Tu Fu, Po Chu-i wrote many poems concerned with social themes; unlike Tu Fu, however, he was a strong advocate of reform. The parallel prose style derived from the Six Dynasties prevailed during the first 2 centuries of the T'ang period. Many who regarded this style as too elaborate and artificial for proper clarity wished to return to pre-Han models. This movement was not new; similar efforts had been made, unsuccessfully, in the mid-6th century and later. Now, however, Han Yü (768–824), a scholar of practical bent, found the parallel prose style intolerable, and under his leadership the ancient prose began to gain ground.

Han Yü held that since literature was didactic it could not be artificial. Assuming the role of a Confucian teacher, he waged war on Taoism and Buddhism, treating them as unorthodox despite their great influence in contemporary intellectual circles. His success came largely from a natural reaction against the long domination of the parallel prose and a resurgence of Confucianism in the intellectual world.

New Prose Style. The triumph of the ancient prose style gave rise to a new form of fiction known in the T'ang dynasty as *ch'uan-ch'i.* This was quite different from the fiction of the Six Dynasties, which consisted of formless strings of Buddhism-impregnated anecdotes. T'ang fiction was a more natural literary form, cultivated by scholars who wished both to create and to amuse. The themes of the tales ranged from pure fantasy to complicated social narratives and love stories.

Sung and Yüan Dynasties. Though the Sung dynasty (976–1279) was one of the weakest politically, it played a superb role in literature. Prose had returned after the T'ang dynasty to artificial elaborate parallelism, but great efforts were made to repeat Han Yü's reform, and ultimately Ou-yang Hsiu (1007–71) and other great scholars established the ancient prose style as the only one acceptable. Its literary hegemony remained fixed until the parallel prose style reemerged in the early 18th century to challenge but not to upset this supremacy.

New Poetic Flexibility. The poetry of the Sung period, though inferior to that of the T'ang era, is still great poetry—philosophic in tendency, impatient of T'ang rigidity in meter and rhyme, natural and quiet in expression, extensive in poetic vocabulary, and often even tolerant of colloquialisms. The Sung poets excelled all others in the composition of *tz'u,* poems consisting of lines of unequal length modeled after certain patterns (each of which bears the name of a musical air) with rigidly prescribed rhyme and tonal sequences. The origin of the *tz'u* is disputed, but the form was certainly well developed by the end of the T'ang period. The *Hua-chien chi* is a good representative anthology of pre-Sung *tz'u,* but the form did not develop fully until the Sung period, when several emperors and many poets composed excellent *tz'u.* The early *tz'u* were closely associated with music, but many later *tz'u* composers, themselves not musicians, gave the form a purely literary character.

Growth of Short Story. Another Sung development was the short story in colloquial Chinese. In T'ang days the Buddhists had attempted to propagate their beliefs in a simplified form of the classical language known as *pien-wen,* sometimes employed also in popular stories. Short stories in the Sung period, however, were written in true colloquial Chinese, a practice that had originated in popular storytelling. The numerous storytellers of Hangchou, the southern Sung capital (1127–79), usually kept rough manuscript outlines of their stories. Many of these highly colloquial drafts were later polished by scholars and published in book form. The *Ch'ing-ping-shan-t'ang hua-pen* and the *Ching-pen t'ung-shu hsiao-shuo* contain such Sung stories.

Drama in the Yüan Period. Drama developed rather late in China. There are traces of it in the T'ang period or even earlier, but as an art it dates from the Yüan dynasty (1271–1368). Scholars dispute why drama flourished under the Yüan. The common opinion is that the foreign conquest of China broke the old tradition of regarding the classical language as the sole medium for writing. Furthermore, the nomad Mongols, though puzzled by the ancient culture, had no difficulty in enjoying drama in colloquial language. It is true that under the Sung, drama had already developed in the south (*nan-hsi,* southern drama), but it was eclipsed by northern drama (*pei-ch'ü*). Seemingly the southern music did not appeal to the northerners, and since Ta-tu (Peking) was the capital, northern drama prevailed. The Yüan drama is natural and simple. Few dramatists were litterateurs, and since they wrote solely to amuse, they were not tempted to insincerity or artificiality. Their plots ranged from history and legend to popular stories of daily life. Most of the great Yüan playwrights were natives of Peking; among the best known were Kuan Han-ching and Wang Shih-fu.

Ming Dynasty. The Ming period (1368–1644) saw the revival of the southern drama and a diminution of northern influence. The rigidity of Yüan drama may have hindered its development; southern drama was more flexible.

Emergence of Southern Drama. The *P'i-pa chi,* by Kao Ming (1310–80), a southern drama written in early Ming days, won great popularity, but dramatic writing soon became a scholarly recreation tending to an elaborate classical style, sometimes to the detriment of the music. After the *P'i-pa chi,* the best-known Ming play is probably *Mu-tan t'ing,* by T'ang Hsien-tsu (1550–

"Orchid," painting and poem by Chêng Ssŭ-hsiao (1239–1316). The small characters on the left are translated "On the 15th day of the first month of the year Ting Wu, I made this scroll"; this dates the work Jan. 29, 1306.

1667). From the Wan-li period (1573–1619) onward, the theater was dominated by the *K'un-ch'ü* plays, which originated in K'un-shan, Kiangsu province, and have beautiful and graceful melodies; they tend to be long, however, often running to 50 or 60 acts. The predominance of *k'un-ch'ü* plays was to last until the middle of the Ch'ing dynasty (1644–1911).

Buddhist Novels. Vernacular novels, short or long, attained their perfection under the Ming. It is significant that many late Ming scholars, abandoning the traditional Confucian contempt of storywriting, held that novels can influence the people even more than the classics. In reading Ming novels, however, one must bear in mind that the late Ming period was a time of flourishing Buddhism, and that society was in a chaotic state. The novels of the period are therefore full of Buddhist ideas of cause and effect and of vivid social comment.

Among the best-known long novels were *San-kuo-chih yen-i,* a semihistorical novel; *Shui-hu chuan,* also partly historical; *Hsi-yu-chi,* pure fiction; and *Chin-p'ing mei,* a novel of the society of the time (though set in the Sung dynasty). *Chin-p'ing mei* is considered pornographic, though this element appears in only a small portion of the work.

The prose and poetry of the Ming period followed the ancient models fairly closely. Toward the end of the dynasty, however, a new movement led by the *Kung-an* and *Ching-ling* schools vehemently attacked slavish imitation of old writers and advocated a freer expression that would catch the spirit of the ancient writers rather than merely follow their form. This movement failed because of the opposition of eminent scholars; its supporters, moreover, overindulged their imaginations and their work tended to be obscure.

Influence of Missionaries. The coming of the Jesuit missionaries to China in the 16th century marked a new epoch not only in the history of the Church in China, but in the culture of the country as well. Matteo *Ricci and his fellow religious wrote books on apologetics and asceticism that showed profound knowledge of traditional Chinese writing. Several of these books were incorporated into the *Ssu-k'u ch'üan-shu,* an encyclopedic series collected in 1782. There was a great project among the missionaries to translate into Chinese the 7,000 European volumes brought as a gift to the emperor Ch'ien-lung from Pope Paul V by Father Nicolas *Trigault.

The sudden end of the Ming dynasty undercut the plan. Li Chih-tsao (?–1629), an official and a scholar converted by Ricci, compiled the *T'ien-hsüeh ch'u han,* a collection of books written by the missionaries on the Catholic faith and on scientific subjects. This compilation, very popular at the end of the Ming dynasty, still ranks as a major Catholic contribution to the literature on China. The fact that Li Chih-tsao called it "first series" (*ch'u-han*) implies that he intended to continue it, but he died the following year.

Ch'ing Dynasty. Under the Ch'ing dynasty (1644–1911), there were no new literary developments in China, though scholarly enthusiasm for the traditional classics bore much fruit in many branches of learning. The Manchu rulers, foreigners who owed all to conquest, were careful to prevent discussion of nationalism and often used literary censorship to suppress criticism. The study of history, especially of recent history, was sternly discouraged and the scholars concentrated upon pure literature and other studies approved by the government.

The scholars' attitude toward study became notably more serious and objective, partly, no doubt, in reaction to the philosophy of the many-branched Wang Shou-jen (1472–1528) school, which widely disseminated a form of idealism, and partly as a result of the early Catholic missionaries' introduction of scientific methods of study, which consciously or unconsciously influenced Chinese scholars.

Poetry. Ch'ing poetry followed either T'ang or Sung trends. Among the most eminent poetic schools, the one led by Wang Shih-chen (1634–1711) advocated a theory of mysterious spiritual harmony, i.e., that the appeal of poetry is to imagination and feeling rather than to reason. The greatest painter of this period, *Wu Li, was also an oustanding Christian poet. The school under Yüan Mei (1716–98) held that the purpose of poetry is to delight, and that great verse depends primarily not on adherence to fixed form but on the poet's scope and individuality. Certain scholars in the last years of the Manchu decline, moved by government corruption, the interference of foreign powers, and the influence of their literature, discerned the need for a renewal of spirit and sought to break away from the imitation of ancient schools. "Let my hand write what I speak," wrote Huang Tsun-hsien (1848–1905), perhaps the most successful poet of this group, and he succeeded in breathing a new spirit into the old forms. The Ch'ing poets' greatest achievements were their *tz-u,* which in meter, melody, and diction surpassed the Ming *tz-u.* Na-lan Hsing-te (1655–85), a Manchu, was indisputably the greatest *tz'u* poet of the entire post-Sung period.

Drama and Prose. Ch'ing drama was less successful: the early Ch'ing scholars were more interested in poetry and later in textual criticism; moreover, enthusiasm for music had declined. Nevertheless, two dramatic masterpieces belong to this period: the *T'ao-hua shan* (The Peach Blossom Fan) by K'ung Shang-jen (1648–1708?) and the *Ch'ang-sheng-tien* (The Palace of Long Life) by Hung Sheng (1650?–1704).

Prose in the parallel style revived and flourished in Ch'ien-lung's reign, a time of great peace and prosperity, but it never displaced the ancient prose style maintained by the *T'ung-ch'eng* school, so called from the name of a place in Anhui province. This school stressed thought, diction, and research as the essentials of prose. Very few of these writers reached greatness, but the school retained its importance throughout the period.

Fiction developed notably. Even at the zenith of classical studies, the novel was never neglected. The *Liao-chai chih-i* (Strange Stories), by P'u Sung-ling (1640–1715), is a collection of 431 short stories written in beautiful classical language of the *ch'uan-ch'i* style. The *Hung-lou meng* (The Dream of the Red Chamber), a romantic yet realistic and partly autobiographical novel of 120 chapters begun by Ts'ao Chan (?–1763) and completed by Kao E (*c.* 1795), is one of the masterpieces of Chinese literature. At about the same time another great novel appeared, the *Ju-lin wai-shih* (Unofficial History of Officialdom), by Wu Ching-tzu

(1701–54). This work was a satirical picture of the bureaucratic society of the day, written in a limpid, colloquial style that has been a model for later writers.

Influx of European Novels. Toward the end of the dynasty, European novels were introduced into China and gradually prepared the way for a new epoch in Chinese literature. Lin Shu (1852–1924), a scholar of the T'ung-ch'eng school, relied upon interpreters to translate more than 100 novels from various languages, not one of which was known to him.

Impact of the 1911 Revolution. The success of the political revolution in 1911 led many scholars to think that Chinese literature was in need of a change. The ancient literature was, they thought, the preserve of a minority and, worse still, belonged to the past; literature must be living and must belong to the common people; therefore it must be in colloquial language (*pai-hua*). Hu Shih and Ch'en Tu-hsiu were the two leading figures in this movement, which was obviously inspired largely by European literature. May 4, 1919, is still its commemorative day, marking the first demonstration by the students of Peking, soon to be supported by students throughout the country. Eagerly discarding old traditions, they devoured literature from abroad. Philosophical books and political writings of all schools were translated and published, and the chief result was intellectual confusion.

Unfortunately, few writers in those days had a real grasp of the Western literature they were imitating. Many had to rely on translations, usually from Japanese. Translated Russian authors were especially favored and thus had great influence among the intellectuals, especially among students. The lack of understanding of the spirit of Western literature resulted in superficial and at times childish imitation. There was nevertheless a real determination to create a new literature in colloquial Chinese. The work of scholars such as *Ma Liang was here influential. In 1920 the Education Department issued an instruction for the Republic that the Peking dialect was to be the national language (*kuo-yü*) and was to be taught in all primary schools—a great triumph for the advocates of the colloquial language as the written medium.

One new school advocated "art for life's sake": the purpose of art is not amusement but the depiction of man's life in society. Another school held to "art for art's sake": literature creates the beautiful and its creation must be independent of politics and the moral law. Through the long years of civil war and foreign aggression, however, literature became progressively didactic. Its advocacy of chauvinism, reform of society, unity of the people, etc., rendered merely adjunctive any serious treatment of aesthetics. Writers gathered into societies and cliques; and political parties, the Communists above all, were quick to employ them as instruments of propaganda.

The Japanese invasion in July 1937 helped to unify the people in opposition to foreign aggression. The literature (especially short stories and drama) produced at this period was dominated by the theme of patriotic resistance, and few genuine literary works appeared.

Communist Takeover. The Communists seized power and set up a government in Peking in 1949. Earlier, in two speeches on art and literature given in Yenan (1942), Mao Tse Tung had laid down the basic Communist principles for artists and men of letters. Political content rather than artistic form determines literary worth. "The more reactionary a piece of literature is," Mao declared, "the more artistic it appears; and the more it poisons the people, the more reason is there to eliminate it." He decreed that since art and literature exist for the workers, peasants, and soldiers, they should be about the workers, peasants, and soldiers. Even illiterate workers and peasants were and are encouraged to write; the result is that many present-day novels can hardly be taken seriously, though they are assertions of intense feelings. Lao She, chairman of the Peking Federation of Writers and Artists and a prominent writer in prewar days, was forced to admit in 1959 that "for some years all writers have been striving to write, but what has been written has been lacking in grandeur." Perhaps this can be explained by the words of another comrade, Mao Tun, Minister of Culture and a veteran author who has been acclaimed in the Communist press as China's leading novelist. He remarked in 1960 that the monotony of so much of the literature of Communist China springs from the endless repetition of a formula. (*See* SOCIALIST REALISM.)

Literature in Taiwan. Education has become universal in Taiwan under the Nationalist government. This has produced a keen desire for a more highly developed literature; but there are difficulties. In the past, few of the native Taiwanese had a thorough education in Chinese culture, and Chinese immigrants from the mainland since 1948 have found themselves in a strange atmosphere that, to some extent, has deprived them of inspiration. Earnest attempts have been made, however, to create truly literary work. In general, writers of the older generation have adhered more or less closely to the *pai-hua* style, enriched with classical expressions, whereas the younger generation has been influenced by the West. Traditional Chinese prose and poetry have been popular among litterateurs of the old school but the young have preferred blank verse. In 1963 the World Book Company in Taipei brought out a series of literary works, the *Wen-Hsing ts'ung-k'an,* which contained a good selection of literary writings, most of them original, a few in translation. The series was a heartening glimpse of literary stirrings that were becoming noticeable among the free Chinese.

Bibliography: J. R. HIGHTOWER, *Topics in Chinese Literature* (Cambridge, Mass. 1953), contains comprehensive bibliographies in Chinese and other languages. CH'EN SHOU-YI, *Chinese Literature: A Historical Introduction* (New York 1961). H. A. GILES, *A History of Chinese Literature* (New York 1927; reprint 1958). LIU TA-CHIEH, *Chung-kuo wen-hsüeh fa-chan shih,* 2 v. (Shanghai 1942–49). CHENG CHEN-TO, *Ch'a-tu-pen Chung-kuo wen-hsueh-shih,* 4 v. (Peking 1957). KUO SHAO-YÜ, *Chung-kuo wen-hsüeh p'i-p'ing shih,* 2 v. (Shanghai 1934). CH'EN CHU, *Chung-kuo san-wen shih* (Shanghai 1937). SAWADA FUSAKYO, *Chung-kuo yün-wen shih,* tr. WANG HO-I, 2 v. (Shanghai 1936). LIU LIN-SHENG, *Chung-kuo p'ien-wen shih* (Shanghai 1937). LU K'AN-JU and FENG YÜAN-CHÜN, *Chung-kuo shih shih,* 3 v. (Shanghai 1935–39). WANG YI, *Tz'u ch'ü shih,* 2 v. (Taipei 1960). CHOU SHU-JÈN, (LU HSUN), *Chung-kuo hsiao-shuo-shih lüeh* (Hong Kong 1958). KUO CHIEN-I, *Chung-kuo hsiao-shuo-shih,* 2 v. (Changsha 1939). T'AN CHENG-PI, *Chung-kuo hsiao-shuo fa-ta shih* (Shanghai 1935). K. E. PRIESTLEY, ed., *China's Men of Letters: Yesterday and Today* (Hong Kong 1962). LAI MING, *A History of Chinese Literature* (New York 1964). **Illustration credits:** Fig. 1, Tokyo National Museum. Fig. 2, Courtesy of the Smithsonian Institution, Freer Gallery of Art, Washington, D.C.

[A. CHAN]

CHINESE PHILOSOPHY

Philosophical discussion in China has always been humanistic—focused on the moral, the socioeconomic, and the political. The Chinese are not notable for philosophical achievement in cosmology, ontology, or psychology, although these fields were not completely neglected by their scholars. Their main contributions can be surveyed generally in three chronological divisions, viz, the ancient, middle, and modern periods.

Ancient Period

The earliest written documents in China are the five books known as Canons or Ch'ing, composed by numerous unknown writers over a long period of time. Confucius compiled all of these ancient documents and edited them in the present form of five books. In the Ch'ing, one can find the teachings of the ancient sage kings, considered by Confucius and all other philosophers (except Lao Tzŭ) as God-sent infallible teachers of morality. They were King Yao, King Sun, King Yu, King T'ang, King Wen, King Wu, and the great Duke of Chou, all of whom lived between 2400 and 1000 B.C. These men believed in a unique, all perfect, invisible, intelligent, personal God, distinct from the world, whom they called Shang Ti (the Emperor on High) or T'ien (Heaven). He was acknowledged to be the Creator and Supreme Ruler of the Universe. The Emperor of China, on the other hand, was only human, and ruled over the people by the mandate of God or Heaven; for this reason he was often called the "Son of Heaven." God might punish him, banish him, or even kill him if he committed crimes in disobedience to God's laws.

Such traditional orthodox teachings of the ancient sage kings, based as they were on natural theology, led the Chinese people to follow a natural religion, the only religion in China until the introduction of Buddhism.

Confucianism. *Confucius (551–479 B.C.) claimed that he did not invent any new doctrine, but labored only to restore the teachings of the ancient sage kings, which, to his regret, were neglected by the people of his time. He nevertheless developed a great many practical moral axioms while in discussion with his thousands of disciples and some occasional inquirers. The following is a summary statement of his moral doctrine: "What is ordered by Heaven is called nature [natural law]; to follow nature is the way to virtue; to practice virtue is an aid to education" (*Book of the Mean,* ch. 1). Confucius believed that human nature per se is good.

*Mencius (371–289 B.C.) later had to defend this Confucian doctrine against those who believed that human nature is evil or essentially indifferent. The former group noted that it seems to be easier to do evil, and that man must make efforts to do good. The principal argument of Mencius was negative. He observed that if man's nature were evil, then to do good would be to act against nature, which is absurd. However, he still had difficulty explaining the origin of evil and the seemingly natural inclination of man to follow his concupiscence. Catholics believe that this cannot be fully understood unless one accepts the fact of the *original sin and its consequences, which pertains to the realm of faith.

Moism and the Egoism of Yang Tzŭ. Mencius described the great influences of these two schools at his time: "The words of Yang Tzŭ and Mo Ti fill the country. If you listen to the discourses of the people throughout the land, you will find that they adopted the views either of Yang or of Mo" (*Works of Mencius,* 6.1). He also summarized their teachings: "The principle of philosopher Yang was 'each for himself.' Though he might have benefited the whole country by plucking out a single hair, he would not have done it. The principle of philosopher Mo was 'to love all universally.' If he could benefit the country by a slow painful death, he would not have hesitated to accept it" (*ibid.* 7.1). Mencius's only criticism of Moism was that by loving all equally, one might regard a total

"Painting of 'To Please my Parent' Hall . . ." by Wang Meng (d. 1385), Yuan dynasty. The inscriptions that follow the painting, and describe its subject matter, allude largely to the writings of Mencius. They illustrate the subtle blending of philosophy and art that is common in Chinese culture.

stranger on the street or even a malefactor as equally deserving of his love as his own father. This would cause disorder in the well-established five human relations of Confucian teaching.

Yang Tzŭ's philosophy was that of individualistic socialism; his views, like those of Mo, were considered by Mencius to be extreme and therefore erroneous. Yang Tzŭ left no written works, and his teachings are known through references in books by others. *Mo Tzŭ left a voluminous treatise of 71 chapters, of which only 53 now exist. In fairness to the latter, it must be said that his teachings were not as extreme as Mencius described them. Mo Tzŭ claimed to restore once again the teachings of the ancient sage kings, which, according to him, had been distorted by the disciples of Confucius, once these became agnostic and did not sincerely believe in God. The existence of a personal and all-knowing God he claimed to be most important, because the ultimate standard of morality is the "Will of God," who as common Father of all mankind wishes all men to love and help each other for mutual benefit.

Taoism and Legalism. Although Taoists claimed *Lao Tzŭ as their founder, it is certain that the formation of the Taoist school came later even than the time of *Chuang Tzŭ. Because *Taoism and legalism gained public attention after the time of Mencius, they were free from his criticism, even though, as the most zealous defender of Confucianism, he strongly attacked Yang Tzŭ and Mo Tzŭ. But Taoism and legalism represented two extreme views also. The former preached a kind of naturalistic individual liberalism, whereas the latter urged the practice of strict utilitarian socialism enforced by law.

Tao was said to be the ultimate but immanent principle of the universe; all human beings became self-developing parts of this eternal Tao. To be moral or virtuous is to live close to nature and to avoid all social complications, the sources of disorder and unhappiness. Happiness is based on the satisfaction of desires. If one knows how to be satisfied with very little, one will be always happy. A happy person is *ipso facto* a virtuous person.

The legalists, on the other hand, worked for social progress and material prosperity. Under the leadership of Han Fei Tzu (d. 233 B.C.) they believed that human nature is inclined to do evil unless it can be corrected by law enforcement. The individual exists for society and not vice versa. The ruler must establish a set of ironclad but just laws to govern the people effectively in order to promote security and prosperity for all.

MIDDLE PERIOD

When the Han dynasty (206 B.C.–A.D. 221) was established, Confucianism regained its scholastic supremacy and all dissenting doctrines were regarded as heretical. However, in the absence of serious opposition, Confucianism soon lost its vitality and became a routine formality. This condition perdured until the influence of Buddhism threatened to overthrow Confucianism's supremacy.

Buddhism as a Philosophy. The introduction of *Buddhism into China caused a great sensation, for scholars considered it to be some kind of occult art, while common people accepted it as a religion promising salvation to the poor and the unfortunate. When the Buddhists' sacred books were translated into Chinese, philosophers also showed interest in it as furnishing a new basis for thought. They eventually formed a kind of Buddhist philosophy that combined views of several different Chinese schools of thought, but was mainly Taoist in inspiration. They even preferred using Taoist terms to adopting the Indian terms introduced by Buddhism.

Since each group of scholars had its own preferred view, many Chinese schools of Buddhism developed, some idealistic, others realistic or practical. The former concentrated on metaphysical meditations with a view to purifying man's mind from materialistic desires; the latter, accepting the necessities of material life, occupied themselves in doing good and performing charitable deeds to help the poor and unfortunate. One can see Taoism in the former and Moism in the latter groups. The Zen school developed an idealistic Chinese Buddhist philosophy that, in the 20th century, seems to be reflourishing in Japan and even in some parts of the U.S. All these Chinese Buddhist philosophers were somewhat pantheistic, whereas Buddhism as a popular religion in China was more or less polytheistic, varying with different groups.

Neo-Confucianism. As Buddhism became stronger as a religion and a philosophy, the reaction of Confucian scholars led to the birth of a so-called neo-Confucianism. Its adherents exploited the *Book of Changes,* adopting the principles of Ying and Yang as ultimate constituents of the universe. Yang is the principle of positive action, power, light, density or solidity, and virility. Ying is the principle of passive potency, shade, rarefication or softness, and femininity. However, they believed that Ying and Yang are really two aspects of one and the same ultimate element of the universe, which some of them called Tao, in Taoist fashion. Others preferred the name Ch'i (air); this, according to their minute explanations, was a kind of energy. By the combination of its two opposing forces, Ying and Yang, Ch'i produced all the things that existed in the universe.

Chu Hsi (*c.* 1130–1200 A.D.) used the term Li (reason or rationale) to indicate such an energetic ultimate principle and thus became even more idealistic. According to him, Li is immaterial, it is above (or without) any shape, Hsing Shang, and therefore invisible. Whatsoever is visible or sensible is below (or within) shape, Hsing Hsia, and such entities are called Wu (matter or things). From that time on, the technical Chinese term for metaphysics is Hsing Shang Shuo (the doctrine of beings above shape).

In natural theology, Neo-Confucianists seemed to follow *pantheism, in spite of the fact that they were supposedly fighting the pantheism of Chinese schools within Buddhism. Their moral doctrine emphasized that the way to perfection is to cultivate the principle of Ch'i, Yang Chi, or to understand fully the principle of Li, Ming Li, since Ch'i or Li is in one's mind, heart, and soul. Thus, they made the standard of morality more or less subjective, and the whole aspect of their philosophy idealistic. While these Neo-Confucianists made Confucianism less Confucian and more Taoistic, Taoism itself began to die out as a school of philosophy because its followers permitted it to become a superstitious popular religion.

Modern Period

The first contact between Western philosophy and that of China was made by Jesuit missionaries under the leadership of Father Matteo *Ricci who translated some current textbooks of scholastic philosophy into Chinese with the help of his first converts among Chinese scholars. Unfortunately subsequent persecutions against the Catholic Church rendered these books suspect and unsuitable for public acceptance. However, a few scholars who had the chance to read them were impressed by the logical force of scholastic philosophy, its clear presentation of problems, and its accurate solutions, particularly in ontology and in ethics. In accepting scholastic philosophy, they also became converts to the Catholic faith.

American Influence. After the Boxer Rebellion (1900), China was forced to open its doors; the Chinese realized that Westerners had a stronger (if not better) civilization from which they could learn. The U.S. proposed that the Chinese government should send students to America and Europe, using the Boxer damage payments to Western nations to finance their studies. Under this proposal, thousands of Chinese students went abroad; the great majority enrolled in secular universities, and there learned modern materialism or idealism. When they returned to China, they imported *naturalism, *utilitarianism, *evolutionism, *socialism, *pragmatism, and even *Marxism. The influence of Marxism was obviously quite strong with the result that China was soon lost to communism, a change that was undoubtedly advanced by the other materialisms mentioned. *See* COMMUNISM, INTERNATIONAL, II.

The most influential of the imported "isms," one that still dominates much of the thought of Free China, was the pragmatism of John *Dewey. Hu Shih (1891–1963), who led a literary revolution to overthrow traditional Chinese philosophy, was one of the early Chinese students at Columbia University. He looked upon traditional philosophy as a useless and ancient relic. John Dewey and Bertrand *Russell were invited to lecture in the University of Peking and other places (1919–20). Naturalism and evolutionism were also forced upon children in all public schools. Since that time, the Ministry of Education has been controlled by a pragmatic philosophy. Religion classes are outlawed not only in public schools, but also in private schools, which must have their curriculum approved by the Ministry of Education. As a consequence, most modern Chinese scholars are materialists, some are idealists, and only a very few accept scholastic philosophy and the Catholic faith.

Critique and Evaluation. Ancient Chinese philosophy, as described and explained by Confucius and Mencius, is compatible with scholastic philosophy and with Christian morals. While most pagan nations became polytheistic and idolatrous, China remained monotheistic in the strict sense until the introduction of Buddhism. Taoism as a philosophy was similar to Neoplatonism on many points; yet its influence was limited and almost negligible. The Moism of ancient China, on the other hand, was the philosophy closest to Christianity, except for the fact that Mo Tzŭ was so practical minded as to sound utilitarian at times. The political views of most Chinese philosophers through the ages have favored a democratic government with the king as head of the nation; that is, they have urged that the king use able and virtuous persons to govern the common people with justice and benevolence. The basic rights of the individual have been recognized by almost all scholars. The family was held sacred, considered to be a God-given institution and the natural foundation of the nation. Divorce was never approved. Although polygamy was permitted, it was practiced only by a few.

Thus traditional Confucianism prepared the Chinese to accept Christian faith and morality. Taoism and Buddhism are no longer accepted by the scholars, although they still influence the common people. On the other hand, the newly imported materialism of the West constitutes a serious obstacle to the propagation of the faith among Chinese intellectuals.

Bibliography: FUNG, YU-LAN, *A Short History of Chinese Philosophy,* tr. D. BODDE (New York 1960). F. O'NEILL, *The Quest for God in China* (New York 1925). W. S. A. POTT, *Chinese Political Philosophy* (New York 1925). K. S. LATOURETTE, *The Chinese: Their History and Culture* (New York 1934). A. A. TSEU, *The Moral Philosophy of Mo-Tze* (Taipei, Taiwan 1965). **Illustration credit:** Courtesy of the Smithsonian Institution, Freer Gallery of Art, Washington, D.C.

[A. A. TSEU]

CHINESE RELIGION

The use of the singular is justified because the religion of the Chinese is a syncretism of many elements and beliefs that has taken place over more than 3 millenniums. Confucianism and Taoism are not new religions in any strict sense, but developments of the older and contemporary Chinese religion. Mahāyāna Buddhism was introduced into China from India, but it assumed definite Chinese characteristics and was completely assimilated into the religious beliefs and practices of its new environment. The annual cycle of religious feasts exhibits a fusion of all religious elements, and there is a peaceful and friendly participation on the part of adherents of Confucianism, Taoism, and Buddhism.

Primitive Chinese religion was a form of *Animism. The numerous forces of nature were worshiped. The highest power was T'ien (Heaven) or Shang-Ti (Supreme Ruler). Whether this power was already regarded as a personal being in the early period is a disputed question. A code of duties prescribed by Heaven was already in force at the end of the 3d millennium B.C. Beside and under Heaven, Chinese religion exhibits a large number of provincial and local divinities, and numerous river, mountain, and other kinds of spirits. It was a religion of the land, reflecting the interests and life of an agricultural society. The higher powers were worshiped by an elaborate ritual, including sacrifices, music, and dancing, conducted by the civil and military authorities rather than by a professional priesthood. From prehistoric times divination and superstition in general have had a major role in Chinese public and private life, and religion and magic are often inseparably combined. In the cycle of feasts, the most important is New Year, which falls between January 21 and February 19.

Ancestor worship has been one of the most important features of Chinese religion from the earliest times. The souls of ancestors were honored as guardian spirits of the family. According to traditional belief, man has two souls, a spiritual soul and a corporeal soul. At death, the first goes to the realm of the Lord of heaven, but the second at first remains with the corpse and is sustained by offerings. This second soul eventually becomes an ancestor, who is replaced in turn by a new ancestor from the next generation. A knowledge of early Chinese religious beliefs and practices, ancestor worship, and elaborate ritual, is indispensable for understanding the environment in which Confucius lived and developed his teachings.

The Communist regime in China, not only by its antireligious policy, but also by its agricultural program, has undermined the whole traditional religious structure of China. What will survive cannot be determined at this time (1965).

See also CONFUCIUS AND CONFUCIANISM; TAOISM; BUDDHISM; ANCESTOR WORSHIP.

Bibliography: K. S. LATOURETTE, *The Chinese: Their History and Culture,* 2 v. in 1 (2d ed. rev. New York 1946) 2:120–132. M. EDER, "China," König RelwissWbh 146–150; "Die Religion der Chinesen," König Christus 3:319–373, esp. 325–333. R. DES ROTOURS, "La Religion dans la Chine antique," in *Histoire des religions,* ed. M. BRILLANT and R. AIGRAIN, v.2 (Paris 1954) 7–83, esp. 7–41.

[M. R. P. MC GUIRE]

CHINESE RITES CONTROVERSY

In the long history of Christian ideas the struggle over the nature of the Chinese rites was among the most momentous. A number of exceptional factors made it such: (1) the high standard of the intellectual and moral forces drawn up in opposing alignments; (2) the passionate ardor with which the respective theses were combated or defended throughout Christendom, and the floodtide of polemical literature that resulted; (3) the pressure exerted on one side or the other by university faculties, princes, powerful churchmen, and national episcopates; (4) the exhaustive search for the truth pursued for a century by the Holy See and marked by a succession of pontifical acts, including two extraordinary legations to the Sino-Manchu Empire; (5) the Holy See's decision and its tragic aftermath for the young Church of the Orient; (6) finally, after 2 centuries, the partial reversal of the decision by a more positive approach to ethnico-cultural integration. In this vast socio-religious drama, the transition from the historic past to the contemporary fluid age of change provides a convenient division of time-periods that this exposition adopts. Major emphasis, however, is given to the second period, the 20th century, because of its greater significance in the modern Church's world view. Moreover, in accordance with the Clementine prohibition of 1710, still in force, this treatment severely excludes all critical discussion of the opinions and arguments in conflict, as well as of the personal, corporate, and nationalistic antagonisms that both envenomed the quarrel and gave it universal dimensions.

THE AGE OF CONTROVERSY (17TH AND 18TH CENTURIES)

Since this long-agitated history profoundly affected the missiology of the Orient for the better part of 2 centuries, no adequate account is possible within the limits of a brief condensation. Instead, a bare synthesis is proposed here, leaving to the available bibliographical sources the detailed outlines of events, the assessment of leading personages, briefs, and other rulings. This summation accordingly centers on the two pivotal elements: (1) definition of the rites and the fundamental tension in the dispute; (2) confrontation between the Jesuit *thesis* and the *antithesis* proclaimed by the Holy See.

Definition and Essence of the Rites Problem. Considered technically in the present context, the expression "Chinese rites" is not coextensive with the aggregate of indigenous ritual practices, but is restricted in substance to three specific, self-defined cases, differentiated from the general religious amalgam: First, certain periodic ceremonies in honor of Confucius, performed by the scholar class in temples or halls dedicated to the apotheosized national philosopher (this raised the question: could Confucian ethics be an adjunct to Christian apologetics?). Second, the cult of the familial dead, a cult embedded in the social structure from top to bottom and universally manifested by such forms of piety as prostrations (the *kotow*), incense burning, serving of food, etc., before the corpse, grave, or commemorative tablet (this posed the problem of "ancestor worship"). These two usages constitute the rites in their organic character as social acts of the individual or group. To them is attached a third case, not one of human action but of semantics: a missionary catechetical vocabulary culled from the old Chinese canonical texts, notably the terms *Tien* (heaven) and *Shangti* (Supreme Lord or Ruler Above), deemed sufficiently meaningful to convey the Christian concept of God and hence destined to win acceptance for the faith in intellectual circles (this brought into question the monotheism of the ancient Chinese). The special problem it created, distinct from the ritual ceremonies, is called the "Term Question."

This summary should consequently make clear the important fact that the rites under controversy were on an entirely different level from various popular practices that survived from a primitive animism or later developed from Taoist and Buddhist mythology. Patently repugnant to the Christian conscience, these modes of pagan cult were banned outright by the total missionary consensus. Under scrupulous examination, on the contrary, because much more subtle and intangible, were the psychological implications of the two acts defined above and the religious thought and behavior patterns governing the ethnic community at large.

The Chinese, as a whole, possessed a pervasive sense of the preternatural and expressed their myriad rapports with the spirit world in symbolic externals. To the missionary from Europe this deep-rooted ethos presented a challenging alternative. Is the average Chinese, in his official cult of Confucius and the ritualistic reverence he pays his deceased forebears, so compulsively motivated by pagan instincts that these everyday social acts are actually no less than illicit spirit worship? Or do these aspects of a high ancient culture spring instinctively from some inborn virtue of the race and hence, in themselves, have only a civil and familial function, even though an individual might observe them for obviously superstitious reasons? More simply, are the several particular acts here analyzed objectively separable from the total complex of religious habits and beliefs that condition the Oriental mind? Here precisely lies the heart of the crisis over the rites. Overlooking or misunderstanding it, writers have arbitrarily lumped the disputed ceremonies with the entire gamut of condemnable native practices, even those overtly idolatrous. From this generalization they then conclude that Chinese Catholicism risked being drawn ineluctably into the vortex of an amorphous, Christo-pagan syncretism, caricatured in the "Confucius-Christ" image the Jansenists denounced. Both the premise and the assumption from it are in point of fact untenable historically, and do violence to the Holy See's express ruling on the subject.

Confrontation: Thesis and Antithesis on the Rites. Matteo *Ricci (in China 1582–1610), the founder of the modern Chinese Church, initiated the preponderance of Jesuit influence and evangelization that marked the 17th century as the society's "Golden Age." Ricci's genius and the secret of his extraordinary apostolate consisted, humanly speaking, in bridging the chasm between the cultures of the West and of the Middle Kingdom—until then ignorant of each other "like two separate planets" (Leibniz). Ricci thus opened channels along which the Gospel could penetrate Chinese intellectual life. Within areas ethically irreproachable, this large concept inspired the utmost adaptation to the life and civilization of the Chinese as a necessary means of evangelization. (*See* ADAPTATION, MISSIONARY.) It was to help reach this high objective that the rites first entered Christian history. Since throughout the century that followed at least four-fifths of China's Christian communities were founded and shepherded by the Jesuit missionaries, observance of the rites became a characteristic of practically the entire Church in China; nonconformity marked a relatively small minority group.

The Decision of 1603. Ricci's studies and vast experience in China had matured for 20 years when as mission superior he issued his history-making directive on the rites (December 1603), following its authorization by the Jesuit general's field representative (visitator), Alessandro *Valignano. Although no longer extant, it is known to have prescribed, as a licit and even indispensable aid in the Christian apostolate, observance of the two ritual customs defined above: traditional honors to Confucius (appraised as definitely academic and outside religious philosophy) and the essential ancestor ceremonies, which, because of their suggestive externalization, Ricci later in his public memoirs thought prudent to qualify simply as "perhaps" (*forse*) nonsuperstitious, even while setting forth in their favor reasons that would seem to admit a positive certainty. The subject of a Chinese theological terminology did not arise in this directive, but such terms passed into current usage from Ricci's published apologetics, and after his death occasioned a division among Jesuits for 2 decades. The debate centered on the legitimacy of the classical terms *Tien* and *Shangti,* which Ricci had recommended for the deity.

Foundations of the Jesuit Thesis. It was Ricci who developed the principle, basic to the directive, that the rites were morally admissible because they were *isolated* in their individual entity from the surrounding superstitions. To document this viewpoint, his writings offer three main lines of argument, drawn, respectively, from the ancient Confucian texts as he interpreted them (the sinological argument), the contemporary intellectual agnosticism (the philosophical), and the indecisive popular sentiment (the psychological). (1) Primitively, the Confucian rites had originated as social virtues in a climate of relatively pure monotheism, and only in the course of time were they overlaid with illicit accretions; by stripping these away and reeducating the people themselves in the sources of their ritual customs, the primeval core could be exposed anew in its original simplicity and meaning. (2) The Sung neo-Confucian naturalism of the office-holding scholar caste, dominant in the state bureaucracy of the day, not only made the cult of Confucius a philosophical exercise in disbelief, but also acted as a counterpoise to the superstitious pietism of the masses. (3) Exploratory probing of individual minds by Ricci and his associates frequently revealed that there was no conclusive evidence that the rites were conceived superstitiously, and indeed much evidence that excluded such conception. Cumulatively, then, this evidence removed the ceremonies in question from any category of actions clearly forbidden to the well-instructed Christian neophyte, whatever superstitious intention pagans individually might attribute to them. Moreover, retention of the usages was in the practical order the absolute condition for any large-scale conversion of Chinese society.

The ordinances of the rites directive were quickly put into practice and governed to the end of the era the generally uniform operation of the Jesuit personnel, in which they were joined in the second half of the century by a respectable number of missionaries of the other three major religious orders in China. Consultations continued for years, wherever possible, however, among neighboring groups of Jesuit field workers preoccupied with the nature of a multitude of rites peripheral or unrelated to Ricci's minimal directives. Such a rite was, e.g., the "Christianized" mandarinal cult of *Ch'eng Huang Lao Yeh* (Spiritual Magistrate of the City Walls), which was strictly prohibited after some local beginnings. In his abstract to the Holy Office at midcentury, Martino *Martini summarized the thesis handed down by Ricci and argued for pontifical recognition of it. Thus Alexander VII's favorable decision of March 23, 1656, meant endowing the rites *prout exposita* (as explained) with a juridical status that for another 50 years rendered their Christian adaptation more normal and authoritative.

The Antithesis of the Church. When Charles Maigrot, Vicar Apostolic of Fukien, on March 26, 1693, launched an indictment of the rites, the Holy See became involved in a judicial process of extraordinary complexity. What it now proposed to do, over and above giving a theoretical ruling about moral principles as hitherto (*quaestio juris*), was to fathom the spirit of a race untouched by European mentality and to determine some of its innermost spiritual resonances (*veritas facti*). For the larger part of 7 years (1697–1704), first Innocent XII, then Clement XI, and a special commission of cardinals pursued this resolve with painstaking thoroughness in the examination of the witnesses and argumentative briefs presented by the two parties to the debate. When Clement signed the resultant decree in the congregation of Nov. 20, 1704, he felt that both the opponents and the protagonists of the rites would have reason to be satisfied, the first because the ceremonies they assailed were in the main proscribed, the second because of the conciliatory middle-course nuancing of ideas that tempered the papal sentence. Besides a first confirmation on Sept. 25, 1710, which rejected appeals against the Nanking *Regula* of Patriarch Maillard de *Tournon, Clement's plenipotentiary to China, two subsequent apostolic constitutions solemnly reiterated the 1704 decree, criticized recalcitrants and their delaying tactics, and reinforced its provision with sanctions, including an obligatory oath of observance: *Ex illa die,* Clement XI, March

Imperatoris Decretum

Quae in hoc scripto continentur optime scripta sunt, planeque concordant cum* Magna Doctrina. Caelo, Dominis, parentibus, magistris ac pravis debita obsequia praestare, ista universo orbi communis lex est. Ea quae in hoc scripto continentur, sunt verissima, neque egent ulla prorsus emendatione.

* Sinae Doctrinam Confucii magnam doctrinam appellant.

Anno Cam-hi 39° die 20ª decimae lunae, hoc est anno domini 1700° die 30ª novembris.

Nos infra scripti quibus praesentibus intimatum est authenticum Imperatoris Decretum, in horum fidem testamur die 2ª decembris ejusdem anni. omnes e Soc[te] Jesu Sacerdotes, et Jurati testes

Philippus Grimaldi Col. Rector, et substitutus V. Provlis Italus
Antonius Thomas Superior domus Orientalis Belga.
Thomas Pereyra
Joannes Franciscus Gerbillon Superior domus Borealis Gallus

Joachimus Bouvet gallus.

Authenticated copy of Emperor K'ang Hsi's decree of Nov. 30, 1700, approving as "very true" the Jesuit interpretation that certain rites honoring Confucius and the dead were national customs without religious significance and that the terms "Tien" and "Shangti" were monotheistic in concept. The decree was signed by the five Peking priests who had presented the exposition (Filippo Grimaldi, Anton Thomas, Jean François Gerbillon, Thomas Pereyra, and Joachim Bouvet), and the entire act was enclosed in an expository letter to the Pope dated Dec. 2, 1700.

19, 1715, and *Ex quo singulari,* Benedict XIV, July 11, 1742. This last, most trenchant of all, definitively closed the age of controversy. From then on Rome's intervention was confined to replies, always in the sense of strictest application, to individual *dubia* or petitions from the China field, itself sealed off in part by government persecution.

The real meaning of the rites problem, therefore, as understood and authentically interpreted by the Church, must be sought in the decree formulated in 1704. Its analysis reveals three salient features. (1) Condemnation: Out of Maigrot's seven *quaesita,* the terms *Tien* and *Shangti* for God are prohibited (1–2), as are both the solemn equinoctial and the frequent ordinary honors to Confucius, and the various ritual services to the dead as these are described in the bill of arraignment (4), although a simplified commemorative name tablet may be tolerated in the home (5). On the other hand, the judges refuse to consider the accusation, nub of the whole antirites offensive at this period, that Martini had deceived the Holy See by an exposition of the facts "false in many things" (3); and in answer to the prosecutor's criticism leveled at Confucian moral and spiritual literature—one of the props of the Jesuit intellectual apostolate—Pope and tribunal confess inadequate knowledge of the situation to form a judgment and charge Legate De Tournon to study the case firsthand (6–7). (2) Tenor: In drafting these decisions, the commission, presided over by the Pope, juxtaposes the irreconcilable terms used in an exclusive sense respectively by the contestants, partisan and adversary, and abstains from any commitment on the validity of one or the other: "in halls of Confucius or temples of idols," *in aedibus Confucii seu miao;* "in [true] sacrifices or offerings," *in sacrificiis seu oblationibus;* etc. By this equilibrating of fundamental opposites, the practice itself of the rites is condemned but without any qualifying statement as to what these rites are in their essence as social human actions, e.g., their constitution and purpose in antiquity, the religious or purely cultural character of the buildings employed in their exercise, the personality of Confucius and the ancestors to whom the ceremonies are directed. The Pope prescinds from these institutional elements of the case and concentrates on a sole capital point, i.e., the source of the supposed compatibility of the rites with the Christian way of life. (3) Motive: Consequently, in handing down its adverse judgment and invoking the motive that dictated it, the Holy See affirms as its mature conclusion that, contrary to the century-old rites thesis, separation of the current practice from the superstition enveloping it is proved to be a practical impossibility in the religious-minded Chinese society then existing: *praedicta omnia . . . ita peragi comperta sunt, ut a superstitione separari nequeant.* Here in truth was the underlying issue over which the historic confrontation took place, not the alleged "Chinese idolatries," nor even superstition as necessarily inherent in the nature of the rites.

It must be emphasized that the condemnation of the rites was not merely a disciplinary measure aimed at bringing about uniformity of pastoral action on the mission, but was relevant to Catholic doctrine itself: *non ad disciplinam, sed ad doctrinam pertinere* (instruction of the Holy Office to Anthony M. Anderledy, General

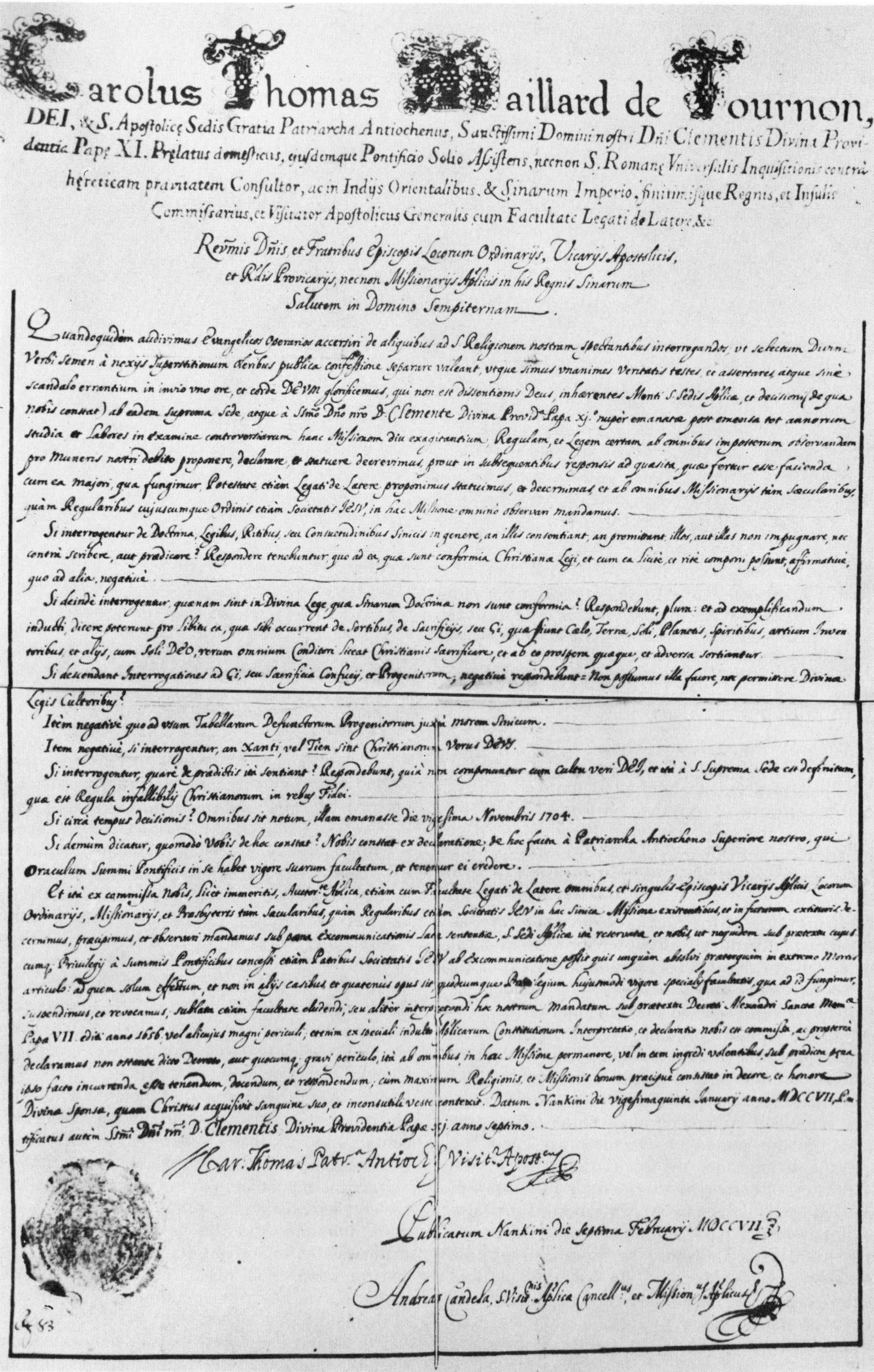

Carolus Thomas Maillard de Tournon,
DEI, & S. Apostolicę Sedis Gratia Patriarcha Antiochenus, Sanctissimi Domini nostri Dni Clementis Divina Providentia Papę XI. Prælatus domesticus, ejusdemque Pontificio Solio Assistens, necnon S. Romanę Universalis Inquisitionis contra hęreticam pravitatem Consultor, ac in Indijs Orientalibus, & Sinarum Imperio, finitimisque Regnis, et Insulis Commissarius, et Visitator Apostolicus Generalis cum Facultate Legati de Latere &c.

Revmis Dnis et Fratribus Episcopis Locorum Ordinarijs, Vicarijs Apostolicis,
et Rdis Provicarijs, necnon Missionarijs Aplicis in his Regnis Sinarum
Salutem in Domino Sempiternam.

Quandoquidem audivimus Evangelicos Operarios accersiri de aliquibus ad S. Religionem nostram spectantibus interrogandos, ut selectum Divini Verbi semen à nexijs Superstitionum sentibus publica confessione separare valeant, utque simus unanimes Veritatis testes, et assertores, atque sine scandalo errantium in invio uno ore, et corde DEUM glorificemus, qui non est dissentionis Deus, inhærentes Menti S. Sedis Aplicæ, et decisioni (de qua nobis constat) ab eadem suprema Sede, atque à Smo Dno nro D. Clemente Divina Provid.a Papa XI.o nuper emanatæ post emensa tot annorum studia, et Labores in examine controversiarum hanc Missionem diu exagitantium, Regulam, et Legem certam ab omnibus imposterum observandam pro Muneris nostri debito proponere, declarare, et statuere decrevimus, prout in subsequentibus responsis ad quæsita, quæ fieri contingat esse facienda, cum ea majori, qua fungimur, Potestate etiam Legati de Latere proponimus statuimus, et decernimus, et ab omnibus Missionarijs tam Sæcularibus, quam Regularibus cujuscumque Ordinis etiam Societatis IESU, in hac Missione omnino observari mandamus.

Si interrogentur de Doctrina, Legibus, Ritibus, seu Consuetudinibus Sinicis in genere, an illis consentiant, an promittant illos, aut illas non impugnare, nec contra scribere, aut prædicare? Respondere tenebuntur, quo ad ea, quæ sunt conformia Christianæ Legi, et cum ea licitè, et ritè componi possunt, affirmativè, quo ad alia, negativè.

Si deindè interrogentur, quænam sint in Divina Lege, quæ Sinarum Doctrinæ non sunt conformia? Respondebunt, plura: et ad exemplificandum induci, dicere poterunt pro libitu ea, quæ sibi occurrent de Sortibus, de Sacrificijs, seu Ci, quæ fiunt Cælo, Terræ, Soli, Planetis, Spiritibus, artium Inventoribus, et alijs, cum Soli DEO, rerum omnium Conditori liceat Christianis sacrificare, et ab eo prospera quæque, et adversa sortiantur.

Si descendant Interrogationes ad Ci, seu Sacrificia Confucij, et Progenitorum, negativè respondebunt: Non possumus illa facere, nec permittere Divinæ Legis Cultoribus.

Item negativè quo ad usum Tabellarum Defunctorum Progenitorum juxta morem Sinicum.

Item negativè, si interrogentur, an Xanti, vel Tien sint Christianorum Verus DEUS.

Si interrogentur, quarè de prædictis ita sentiant? Respondebunt, quia non componuntur cum cultu veri DEI, et ita à S. Suprema Sede est definitum, quæ est Regula infallibilis Christianorum in rebus Fidei.

Si circa tempus decisionis? Omnibus sit notum, illam emanasse die vigesima Novembris 1704.

Si demum dicatur, quomodò Vobis de hoc constat? Nobis constat ex declaratione, de hoc facta à Patriarcha Antiocheno Superiore nostro, qui Oraculum Summi Pontificis in se habet vigore suarum facultatum, et tenemur ei credere.

Et ita ex commissa Nobis, licet immeritis, Auctor.te Aplica, etiam cum Facultate Legati de Latere omnibus, et singulis Episcopis Vicarijs Aplicis Locorum Ordinarijs, Missionarijs, et Presbyteris tam Sæcularibus, quam Regularibus etiam Societatis IESU in hac Sinica Missione existentibus, et in futurum extituris decernimus, præcipimus, et observari mandamus sub pœna Excommunicationis latæ sententiæ, S. Sedi Aplicæ ita reservatæ, et nobis, ut nequidem sub prætextu cujuscumq. Privilegij à Summis Pontificibus concessi etiam Patribus Societatis IESU ab Excommunicatione possit quis unquam absolvi præterquam in extremo Mortis articulo: ad quem solum effectum, et non in alijs casibus et quatenus opus sit, quodcumque Privilegium hujusmodi vigore specialis facultatis, qua ad id fungimur, suspendimus, et revocamus, sublata etiam facultate eludendi, seu aliter interpretandi hoc nostrum Mandatum sub prætextu Decreti Alexandri Sanctæ Mem.æ Papæ VII. editi anno 1656, vel alicujus magni periculi; etenim ex speciali indulto Aplicarum Constitutionum Interpretatio, et declaratio nobis est commissa, ac propterea declaramus non obstante dicto Decreto, aut quocumq. gravi periculo, ita ab omnibus in hac Missione permanere, vel in eam ingredi volentibus, sub prædicta pœna ipso facto incurrenda esse tenendum, docendum, et respondendum; cum maximum Religionis, et Missionis bonum præcipuè consistat in decore, et honore Divinæ Sponsæ, quam Christus acquisivit sanguine suo, et inconsutili veste contexit. Datum Nankini die vigesimaquinta Januarij anno MDCCVII, Pontificatus autem Smi Dni nri D. Clementis Divina Providentia Papæ XI. anno septimo.

Car. Thomas Patr.a Antioch. Visit.r Apost.cus

Publicatum Nankini die septima Februarij MDCCVII.

Andreas Candela, S. Visit.nis Aplicæ Cancell.us, et Mission.us Aplicus

483

The original of the condemnatory decree ("Regula") drawn up by Charles Thomas Maillard de Tournon, Patriarch of Antioch and Visitator Apostolic, and promulgated by him at Nanking on Feb. 7, 1707. Under pain of excommunication, the decree bound the missionaries, when interrogated by the imperial authorities, to repudiate the Chinese rites as gravely illicit.

of the Society of Jesus, and by him communicated to the whole society by circular letter of Oct. 10, 1891).

The Epoch of Ethnico-Cultural Integration (20th Century)

From the first half of the 20th century dates what some have termed the "era of enfranchisement" in regard to the rites that the Church had outlawed for more than 200 years under stringent sanctions.

Basis for a Revisionist Policy. Five discernible currents brought about a revisionist policy by the Holy See: (1) the development of historical studies, through which modern problems of ethnic adaptation were reevaluated in the light of similar situations facing Christianity in the Greco-Roman world; in this field the historians L. Bréhier and P. Batiffol are conspicuous; (2) a more ecumenical doctrine of grace and other spiritual forces latent in non-Christian peoples (the *infideles*), such as those of the ancient religions of the East, as against the rigid Augustinian "theology of damnation" that colored much of the old anti-Confucian militancy; (3) the rise of nationalisms in the East and their induction into the mainstream of international politics, paralleled in the West by a "deeper appreciative insight" (Pius XII) into the historical cultural treasures of these races; (4) transformation of the Oriental mind owing in major part to the impact of Western ideas in the spheres of the natural sciences, education, philosophy, jurisprudence, etc., and leading progressively to a secularizing of thought patterns that from immemorial ages had been cast in a stereotyped religious mold; (5) formal declarations by high government representatives that, in line with freedom-of-worship clauses embodied in national constitutions (e.g., Republic of China 1914), state-prescribed acts of reverence, whatever their primitive origin and meaning, express today nothing of religious cult but only the natural virtues of good citizenship and urbane social graces.

The factor of social evolution, namely, the process by which ancient superstitious acts were in the course of time emptied of their spiritual content, *mutatis saeculorum fluxu moribus et animis,* was brought into sharp relief by the Holy See's formulation of the basic principles of its new legislation. Further, the non-Christian civil power, both interpreter and guide of the national spirit, exercised the role of witness to the objective "laicization" that had taken place in age-old spiritual ideas and habits, thus laying the groundwork for Catholic motivation. In the expository justification of changes, then, these two factors complemented one another. Hence the Holy See's acceptance of the rites, if viewed in historical perspective, in no way spells a repudiation of its former deterrent action. From the very start of the controversy the contested ceremonies had been proscribed, not because they were judged as evil in themselves (*intrinsece malae*), but solely on the grounds that the human factor of social custom could transfuse into speech and gestures otherwise indifferent (*per se indifferentes*) an infecting superstition or at least the suggestion of superstition (*species superstitionis*). Given the mass psychology prevailing at the time, these acts had become so enmeshed into the national cast of mind that the separation envisioned by the missionaries as a probably attainable reality was judged by the ecclesiastical tribunal to be unattainable in the circumstances (*separari nequeunt*). Only a radical change in social thinking would be able to disassociate the interrelated components, and this was brought about in large measure, as is now evident, by the slow erosion of time.

All that the present-day congregation does, therefore, is to take cognizance of a proved phenomenon in a segment of human society and apply the Church's moral code to the emergence of a new concrete situation at the opposite pole of the determinant hitherto governing the case. Before the end of a decade Rome had crystallized her pastoral approach along these lines and through a succession of memorable "instructions" clarified the principles sustaining it. The following are the main sequences of this development.

Program of Toleration for Manchukuo (1935). In the 20th century the challenge of the rites first thrust itself forcibly into the open in the wake of armed conquest and the creation in February 1932, under the tutelage of Japan's expansionist authorities, of the short-lived state of Manchukuo (Manchuria). By its attempt to promote civic unity through the *Wang Tao* (Royal Way), the new government made the cult of Confucius obligatory on all citizens, thus forcing a serious crisis of conscience on the native Catholics. Faced with this dilemma, the Congregation for the *Propagation of the Faith (SCPF) asked the bishops in the area to study the problem and to supply Rome with the elements of a directive solution. As a first step Bp. Auguste Gaspais, Vicar Apostolic resident at the Manchukuo capital of Hsinking (Changchun), sounded out the Ministry of Worship on whether the prescribed ceremonies were conceived of as religious in character, or deemed a "purely civil homage to a distinguished man and philosopher" (Feb. 27, 1935). In replying a week later, the ministry categorically excluded any sectarian implication and affirmed that the sole purpose of the rites in question was to extol Confucius' teachings as the fountainhead of civic morality and good government.

With this official pronouncement to guide them, the bishops deliberated in a meeting at Hsinking and on March 12, 1935, dispatched to Rome a list of situations and practices concretely involved in the new social order, each assessed respectively as unlawful (*illicitum*) or as now permissible, though under a cautious formula (*tolerari potest*). Because of its extraordinary gravity, the case was referred to the Pope (May 14). Polarizing his decision on the Manchukuo government's liberal interpretation of March 5 as the basis for positive solutions, Pius XI set forth three terse imperatives, each beginning with *oportet:* The responsible ecclesiastical authorities must with due prudence publicize the official declaration, thus forestalling any possible scandal. They must conform their own practical viewpoint to it when dictating to the faithful relevant norms of action. Priests on their part must give unquestioning adherence to the instructions laid down by their superiors. Following the Pope's summary resolution of the issue, SCPF approved on May 28, 1935, as "sound and well thought out" the provisory measures adopted at Hsinking [*Sylloge* (1939) 479–482].

A year later Pius XI, the Pope of the Missions, gave further emphasis to the movement of harmonizing Oriental traditions with Catholic culture when, through a SCPF decree in favor of the Church of Japan (May 18–26, 1936), a far-reaching program of permissions was promulgated with respect to certain ceremonial usages in imperial Shintoism (the *Jinja* shrines), as well as matrimonial, funeral, and other social customs, all hitherto under the Christian ban (ActApS 28 (1936) 406–409). By this time the principle of wider latitude of adaptation had become settled policy. It is found applied, and in the same emphatic terms, to a particular case of funeral rites in the Belgian Congo (July 14, 1938; SCPF, *Sylloge* 576–578).

The "Liberating Decree" for China (1939). On ascending the papal throne, Pope Pius XII paid high tribute to the breadth of vision and apostolic spirit that inspired these "generous decisions" and announced that he intended to follow unhesitatingly in his predecessor's footsteps (ActApS 31 (1939) 548–549, Eng. text). In one of its major objectives this promise was fulfilled almost immediately. Adopted on Dec. 4, 1939, endorsed by the Holy Father 3 days later, and officially published on December 8, the *Instructio circa quasdam caeremonias super ritibus sinensibus* ranks among the more noteworthy documents emanating from SCPF in the 20th century. Where the Hsinking pioneers had to grope warily along uncertain terrain, Rome's 1939 *Instructio* stands out for its masterly articulation of principles and the resultant precepts that would henceforth affect Chinese Catholic life.

The preamble restates the significant lesson, previously brought out in the decree for Japan, that certain ceremonies, though in antiquity linked to heathen rites, at present retain no more than a civic sense of piety toward the ancestors or of love for the fatherland or of courteous relations with the neighbor: *pietatis in antenatos vel amoris in patriam vel urbanitatis in proximos.* Four statutes make up the pastoral legislation: (1) Lawful for Catholics are public honors paid to Confucius before his portrait or honorific scroll in Confucian edifices (*monumentis*) or schools. To give force to this innovation the Holy See invoked the oft-repeated denial of the Chinese government, made explicitly or implicitly, that any intention of religious cult is nowadays implied in these community exercises; their sole purpose is to foster and express honor to an illustrious person and the reverence due to the sacred heritage of the fathers, *in virum clarissimum dignus honor et in traditiones patrum debitus cultus*—a concise formula for the rites in their modern setting. (2) The image or name-tablet of Confucius may be placed in Catholic schools, especially if the public authorities so require, and saluted by a head bow. Where risk of scandal is feared, a statement of right Catholic intention should be made. (3) If Catholic magistrates and students are obliged to assist at public functions that present an aura of superstition, they may take part (*tolerandum*) as long as they maintain a passive attitude and proffer only those signs of respect that can justly be appraised as purely civil. If the need arises, they should make public their real sentiment to dispel erroneous interpretations of their acts. (4) The fourth statute regards the veneration of the dead, the nerve center of the rites controversy. Several years earlier the Manchukuo bishops had discussed the delicate problem of private funerals, specifically of inclinations before the corpse, but because of the rigidity of the older prohibition—*olim Christianis rigorose interdicta*—they dared not go on record one way or the other. They did, however, give a pointed recommendation for the future. The contemporary Oriental mind (*actualis mentalitas*), they informed SCPF, tends to regard this ceremonial as no more than an expression of civil respect for the dead, just as the Occidental does, thus clearing the way for an eventual Christian acceptance of the rite, *tempore futuro hanc salutationem tolerandi* (SCPF, *Sylloge* 482).

Rome went far beyond the Manchukuo bishops' discreet hint. In the nature and extent of pastoral application, in fact, this provision is the most positive of the four contained in the Instruction. Bowing the head, the decree teaches the Chinese faithful, and other manifestations of civil observance before defunct persons or their portraits, and even before the tablet of a deceased inscribed simply with his name, are to be held licit and good, *ut licitae et honestae habendae sunt.* The funeral rites designated here, therefore, are not only morally admissible (*licitae*), but possess a commendable righteousness (*honestae*).

A corollary to the decree abolishes the now superfluous antirites oath, prescribed by Benedict XIV in 1742, but keeps effective the interdict on contentious public discussion of the controversy (ActApS 32 (1940) 24–26).

Climactic Supplement to Rites Integration (1941). Reaction to this pastoral legislation was similar to the uncertainty that, in the early China Church, perplexed the Jesuit mission body for several decades after Ricci drafted his code on observance of the rites. In neither case were the key specifics called into question; but endless consultations took place on what to make of the numerous ramifications, the local and regional "peripheral rites," in some way connected with but not expressly covered in the several main permissible rites of code or instruction. Fortunately, SCPF intervened promptly to cut short all narrow casuistry on the subject. By a *Mens nostra* dispatch of Feb. 28, 1941, directed to Abp. Mario Zanin, Apostolic Delegate to China, SCPF laid down three meticulous prescripts: (1) Composition of a catalogue of permitted and forbidden ceremonies [like the Hsinking list of 1935] is absolutely to be avoided (*absolute evitanda*). (2) Where necessary, the bishops themselves can give rules and define general standards of behavior, but in view of the fact that this age is a period of transition, they must not descend to details. (3) Even priests and good Christian laymen should in particular cases be left to direct themselves according to their own lights, *se dirigere secundum suam conscientiam.* In sum, the door must be kept as wide open as possible to the emerging exigencies of accommodation [*Collectanea commissionis synodalis in Sinis* 14 (Peking 1941) 562].

More perhaps than the formal *acta* themselves, these supplementary injunctions reveal the climactic orientation of the Holy See's present attitude, in contrast to the old, where the rites are concerned, namely, broad comprehension and the spirit of liberty in action wherever the inconsistency of traditional ethnic customs with Christian faith and morality is not overwhelmingly evident. Far-reaching in application, this principle is formulated in apodictic terms in the two relevant decisions indicated above, those for Japan (1936) and the Congo (1938). What makes it more significant is that not only the principle but the very terms translating it are phrased textually from a remarkable *Monitum,* or Manual of Mission Apostolate, that SCPF had issued to its first vicars apostolic as long ago as 1659, but which had later become obscured by the passions engendered in the rites controversy. SCPF exhorted missionaries to make no attempt to change these customs, nor for any reason to persuade people to change their customs as long as they are not obviously contrary to religion or moral conduct: "Nullum studium ponite, nullaque ratione suadete illis populis ut ritus suos, consuetudines et mores mutent, *modo non sint apertissime religioni et bonis moribus contraria*" (clause thus italicized in the Congo text of 1938). More impressive still, this pastoral law is central to those pages of two of his encyclicals wherein Pius XII affirmed the Church's appreciation of and concern for the cultural and spiritual riches conserved in non-Christian races [*Summi pontificatus,* Oct. 20, 1939: Act ApS 31 (1939) 429, 549, Eng. text; *Evangelii praecones,* June 2, 1951: ActApS 43 (1951) 521–524].

By contrast with the understanding tolerance of the present, the 18th-century papacy excluded, with inflexible severity as particular doubts of interpretation arose, even the shadow of superstition (*species superstitionis*) from observance by the Chinese Christian community, e.g., the Holy Office's universal condemnation of the *kotow* in 1777. To judge this rigorism equitably, it must be situated against the background of a historic missionary force just then advancing toward world encounter. The agonizing concern of the Church in the crisis that followed was to preserve inviolable the integrity of a faith that was submerged amid ethnic populations of massive numbers, lying far beyond the bounds of Christianity, spiritually and intellectually alien to the Western heritage. A stress of this unprecedented magnitude left little margin for receptive attitudes in the matter of indigenous traditions not evidently (*apertissime*) devoid of indications of superstition.

On the contrary, in the highly unified structure of modern society, problems of the apostolate and cult in non-Christian lands, like political and social matters in general, arise and are settled in a climate incomparably more favorable than that of even the recent past. Understood in its ultimate reality, then, the history of the Chinese rites controversy is a convincing demonstration of how through the centuries the Church penetrates the complex universe of men and wisely conforms the mode of transmission of her basically changeless teaching to the evolving standards of human thought and action.

Bibliography: For the relevant decrees, see the indices of *Iuris Pont. de Prop. Fide,* par. la, II (1888) and III (1890), and *Collectanea S. Cong. de Prop. Fide,* 2 v. (Rome 1907) v.1. Recent "Instructions" up to 1938 are in *Sylloge: praecipuorum recentium Summorum Pontificum et S. Congregationis de Propaganda Fide, necnon aliarum SS. Congregationum Romanorum ad usum missionariorum* (Rome 1939). Streit-Dindinger 5 (1929), 17th century; 7 (1931), 18th century; 12 (1958), 1800–84; 13 (1950), 1885–1909; 14 (1961), 1910–50. *Sinica franciscana,* v.5, ed. G. MENSAERT and A. VAN DEN WYNGAERT (Quaracchi-Florence 1954); v.6, ed. G. MENSAERT (Rome 1961), cover the acute period 1684–1726. No objective history drawn from the enormous archival deposit has been attempted. Published studies include: A. S. Rosso, *Apostolic Legations to China of the 18th Century* (South Pasadena 1948) 63–146, opposed to the rites. D. FERNÁNDEZ NAVARRETE, *The Travels and Controversies of Friar Domingo Navarrete, 1618–1686,* ed. J. S. CUMMINS, 2 v. (Cambridge, Eng. 1962) 1:xxxviii–lxxii, opposed to the rites. O. MAAS, *Die Wiedereröffnung der Franziskanermission in China in der Neuzeit* (Münster 1926). B. M. BIERMANN, *Die Anfänge der neueren Dominikanermission in China* (Münster 1927). J. BRUCKER, DTC 2.2:2364–91, still the standard exposition of the controversy. Pastor 33:393–484. Two lesser works, often mentioned but unreliable for the history of the global controversy: A. THOMAS, *Histoire de la Mission de Pékin,* 2 v. (Paris 1923–25) v.1, excessively critical of the Jesuits; M. V. HAY, *Failure in the Far East* (Philadelphia 1957), poorly researched defense of the Jesuits. H. BERNARD-MAITRE, DHGE 12:731–741. J. BECKMANN, Lex ThK[2] 8:1322–24. F. A. ROULEAU, "Maillard de Tournon, Papal Legate at the Court of Peking," ArchHistSocJesu 31 (1962) 264–323. G. H. DUNNE, *Generation of Giants* (Notre Dame, Ind. 1962) 282–302. J. KRAHL, *China Missions in Crisis* (Rome 1964) 159–189, for Rome's strictures after 1742. P. D'ELIA, "La recente istruzione della S. C. di Propaganda Fide sui riti cinesi," CivCatt 91 (1940) 123–137, 191–202, origin and significance of SCPF's modern policy.

[F. A. ROULEAU]

CHINIQUY, CHARLES PASCAL, author, renegade; b. Kamouraska, Quebec, Canada, July 30, 1809; d. Montreal, Canada, Jan. 16, 1899. He was the son of Charles, a sailor, and Marie (Reine) Chiniquy and was orphaned in 1821. After study at the seminary of Nicolet, Quebec, he was ordained Sept. 21, 1833, and then served as curate at Saint-Charles de Bellechasse (1833), officiating minister at Charlesbourg (1834), curate at Saint-Roch of Quebec (1834–38), and chaplain of the naval hospital. He offered his services to Bp. Norbert Provencher for the Northwest missions and was refused. In 1838 he became pastor of the important parish of Beauport. Two years later he began preaching on temperance, founding a temperance society (1840) and becoming known as "Father Mathew of Lower Canada" (*see* MATHEW, THEOBALD). He was transferred to the parish at Kamouraska (1842), where he scandalized the population by his conduct and was obliged to leave the Diocese of Quebec (1846). He joined the Oblates of Mary Immaculate but was dismissed and took up temperance preaching in the Diocese of Montreal. Bishop Ignace Bourget of Montreal revoked Chiniquy's powers (1851), giving him his exeat to the Diocese of Chicago, Ill. As a schismatic after 1852, he attracted a number of French-speaking faithful and even attempted to attract a group of initiates from Canada to Illinois. Denounced by Bps. J. O. Vandervelde, A. O'Regan, and J. Duggan of Chicago, he was placed under interdict in August 1856 and excommunicated in September of the same year. He then founded the Christian Catholic Church and joined the Presbyterian Church in Chicago, from which he was later expelled. Accepted by the Presbyterian synod of Canada, he became an official preacher in Canada and moved to Montreal with his family in 1875.

Chiniquy made many trips abroad. He published several anti-Catholic works that enjoyed great success and were translated into many languages. Among these were his autobiography *Cinquante ans dans l'Eglise de Rome* (1885) and *Quarante ans dans l'Eglise du Christ,* for the period from 1859 to 1899, which was published posthumously; and *La Femme, le prêtre, et le Confessional* (1878). *Mes Combats, Autobiographie de Charles Chiniquy, Apôtre de la Tempérance* was published in Montreal (1946). In 1844, while still a Catholic, Chiniquy published a short work, *Manuel ou Règlement de la Société de Tempérance.* Six days before his death he published in the Montreal *Gazette* his religious testament, replete with blasphemy against the Catholic Church.

[G. CARRIÈRE]

CHISHOLM, CAROLINE (JONES), philanthropist, assisted migration to and settlement in eastern Australia; b. at or near Northampton, England, 1808; d. Fulham, England, March 25, 1877. She was the daughter of William Jones, a yeoman farmer, and she grew up with a strong evangelical sense of duty in social service. In 1830 she married Capt. Archibald Chisholm of the East India Company and became a Catholic. Catholic fervor thereafter reinforced her humanitarian zeal. The couple spent some years in India before settling in Sydney (1838). At that time arrangements for the reception and dispersal of free immigrants in eastern Australia were unsatisfactory. Mrs. Chisholm became concerned for the moral welfare of young unmarried women in a population composed partly of convicts and former convicts, and in 1841 she established a hostel where they could stay until they found employment. From this beginning grew her later social work. She recognized that New South Wales was deficient in "God's police"—women and children. She therefore strove, in several trips through the country in the 1840s, through the Family Colonization Loan Society, which she established in London (1849), and through her pamphlets on colonization, to facilitate the immigration of the better sort of working-class people, especially single women, family groups, and the wives and children of emancipists. Approximately 5,000 people seem to have settled in Australia as a result of her efforts. Her headstone at Northampton is fittingly inscribed "The Emigrant's Friend."

Caroline Chisholm.

Bibliography: M. KIDDLE, *Caroline Chisholm* (Melbourne 1950).

[L. GARDINER]

CHIVALRY

Term that "denotes the ideals and practices considered suitable for a noble." Deriving its origins from the long military tradition of the Germanic peoples, chivalry reached fruition during the 12th century. The typical noble of that epoch was a knight or mounted warrior, usually bound by feudal ties to his lord and vassals. As knights became increasingly self-conscious, they thought of themselves as forming a clearly defined class, the order of chivalry, with its distinctive ceremony of admission, known as dubbing, and with its appropriate rules of conduct. The true knight was expected to be courageous in battle, loyal to his lord, honest and generous toward his fellow knights and subordinates. Such ideals found their characteristic expression in the *chansons de geste* (*see* FRENCH LITERATURE, 1), but they were ideals that were not always attained in contemporary society.

Christian Influence. Although Christian influence on the origins of chivalry was slight, the Church always sought to inculcate right standards of morality among the nobility and to ameliorate the worst aspects of feudal behavior. For this reason churchmen emphasized the solemn and sacred character of the contract between lord and vassal, with their reciprocal rights and duties. Church councils (e.g., Valence, 855) condemned the judicial duel, a defective means of settling litigation—though churchmen sometimes were involved in them—and the tournament, or mock battle [Second Lateran (1139), c.14; ConOecDecr, 176], a favorite pastime of knights when they were not engaged in serious combat.

Peace and Truce of God. From the late 10th century the Church proclaimed the *Peace of God as a means of checking the excesses of private warfare (Councils of Charroux, 989; Narbonne, 990; etc.). Through the Truce of God (Council of Elne, 1027) knights were asked to pledge themselves not to attack the weak and defenseless, such as widows, orphans, merchants, and unarmed clergy, and to refrain from the use of arms on holydays and during sacred seasons of the year such as Lent and Advent.

Crusades. The Church's concern for the pacification of western Europe and the improvement of morality received new meaning when in 1095 Pope *Urban II summoned the nobles to liberate the Holy Land (*see* CRUSADES). Let those, he said, who hitherto have lived as brigands and mercenaries become true knights by devoting themselves to a cause that is just and promises an eternal reward. In making his plea the Pope was pointing to a spiritual ideal that he considered especially suitable to those who professed to be knights. In so doing he was imparting a religious significance to the code of chivalry.

Initiation Ceremony. The spiritualization of chivalry is reflected in the liturgy devised by the Church for the ceremony of initiation into the order of knighthood. In the late 12th and 13th century the vigil of arms, the ritual bath, and the blessing of the sword were common practices, though not essential to the making of a knight. While watching his arms reposing upon the altar, the future knight was expected to meditate upon the honor that he was to receive and the obligations that it entailed. The bath symbolized his purification and was likened to a second baptism. Various liturgical manuscripts, such as the late 13th-century pontifical of William *Duranti the Elder, contain blessings for the sword with which the initiate girded himself. The blessing reminded him that he should use his weapon for the defense of the Church and the protection of the weak. By surrounding the rite of initiation with religious symbolism and endowing it with a quasi-sacramental character, the Church fostered the idea that the knight was a man consecrated to the fulfillment of God's work on earth.

Contemporary Theories. The fullest exposition of the nature and functions of Christian knighthood is found in the writings of 12th- and 13th-century thinkers. In his *Liber de vita christiana,* written in the late 11th century, *Bonizo of Sutri stressed the knight's duty to keep faith with his lord, to abstain from pillage, to protect the poor and the weak, and to champion

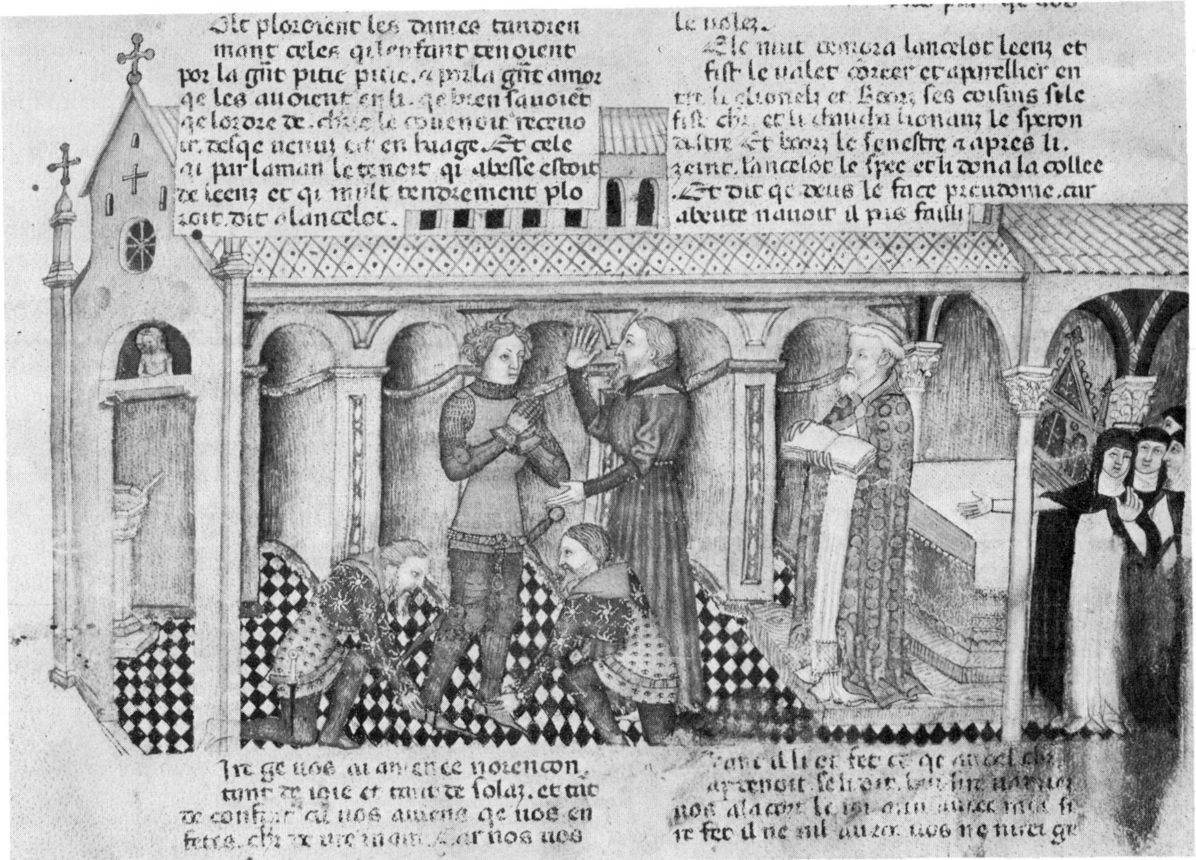

The dubbing ceremony, miniature in a 14th-century French manuscript (Paris, B. N. Fr. 343, fol. 1v).

orthodoxy against heresy and schism. To these obligations Urban II added that of defending the Christian people against the infidels.

Early in the 12th century *Bernard of Clairvaux wrote his *Liber de laude novae militiae* in justification of the newly formed Order of the Temple, whose members tried to combine the ideals of monasticism and chivalry. Bernard sharply contrasted the life of the *Templars (the *militia Christi*) with that of contemporary lay knights (the *militia saecularis . . . non militia, sed malitia*). Condemning the latter for their "insane appetite for glory and insatiable greed for land," the abbot of Clairvaux leaves one with the impression that only the Templars could be considered true knights.

Later in the century *John of Salisbury in his *Policraticus* expressed the view that knights constituted an order instituted by God for the service of both the Church and the State. The knight should be the guardian of justice, obedient to God, Church, and prince. The contemporary Stephen of Fougères set forth similar ideas in his *Livre des manières*.

At the close of the 13th century, in his *Libre del orde de cauayleria*, Raymond *Lull propounded a conception of chivalry drawn from both secular and religious sources. He believed that the knight should embody the virtues most admired by soldiers as well as those exalted by the Church. Lull described in some detail the religious ceremonies that ought to attend admission to knighthood, and he explained the symbolism of knightly accoutrements.

Effects. The Church made unceasing efforts to permeate the code of chivalry with Christian principles both by conciliar legislation and by instruction. By upholding the idea that the true knight must wield his sword only in the cause of right and justice, the Church appealed to the highest sentiments of western European nobility. The crusading movement and the *military orders were manifestations of this ideal. On the other hand the pages of medieval chronicles reveal that knights frequently were motivated by worldly rather than religious ends. Yet by giving a spiritual meaning to the institution of chivalry the Church tempered much of the brutality, frivolity, and artificiality of feudal and courtly society.

Bibliography: L. Gautier, *La Chevalerie* (Paris 1884). S. Painter, *French Chivalry* (Baltimore 1940). M. Bloch, *Feudal Society*, tr. L. A. Manyon (Chicago 1961). G. Cohen, *Histoire de la chevalerie en France au moyen âge* (Paris 1949). **Illustration credit:** Bibliothèque Nationale, Paris.

[J. F. O'CALLAGHAN]

CHLODULF (CLOUD) OF METZ, ST., bishop; d. May 8, *c.* 663 or 696 (feast, June 8). Chlodulf, son of *Arnulf of Metz and brother-in-law of (St.) *Begga, became bishop of *Metz in 652 or 656. There he trained *Trudo of Brabant. The discrepancy in his death dates results from the attempt to give him the 40-year episcopate that a 9th- or 10th-century catalogue attributed to him. But although a passage from the *Miracles* of St. *Gertrude of Nivelles says that he was alive at her death, March 16, 659, and his name is among those who witnessed a document of Numerius of Trier *c.* 663, it was Chlodulf's successor at Metz who signed the charter of Drausius of Soissons for the monastery of Sainte-Marie, June 25, 667. Chlodulf's vita (ActSS June 2:127–132) is 9th-century and unhistorical. The celebration of his feast on June 8 may stem from a mistake in months in the Roman Martyrology. His bones are in the former Benedictine church, Lay-Saint-Christophe, near Nancy, and in St. Arnuf's, Metz.

Bibliography: MGS 2:264, 267, 269. BHL 1:1735. J. DEPOIN, "Grandes figures monacales des temps mérovingiens," *Revue Mabillon* 11 (1921) 245–258; 12 (1922) 13–25, 105–118. R. VAN DOREN, DHGE 13:22. H. LECLERCQ, DACL 11.1:828. Baudot-Chaussin 6:147–148. Butler Th Attw 2:503. R. AIGRAIN, *Catholicisme* 2:1262–63.

[G. J. DONNELLY]

CHOICE

The act of the *will that is concerned with means to an *end; as such, it is distinct from the act of deliberation that precedes it and from the act of execution that follows it. (For a discussion of the interrelationships between these acts, *see* HUMAN ACT.) This article discusses the teachings of various philosophers concerning choice and is divided into two parts: the first is devoted to ancient and medieval thought on the subject, the second to modern and contemporary views.

Ancient and Medieval Thought. According to *Aristotle, when one wishes an end, which he sees as his *good, his choice must necessarily be concerned with the means to that end, i.e., with the actions that will attain it, insofar as these lie in his power. "Wish relates to the end, choice [προαίρεσις, meaning preference] to the means; for instance, we wish to be healthy, but we choose the acts which will make us healthy . . . ; for, in general, choice seems to relate to the things that are in our own power" (*Eth. Nic.* 1111b 27–29). From this he deduces that choice in man must be voluntary: "The end, then, being what we wish for, the means what we deliberate about and choose, actions concerning means must be according to choice and voluntary" (*ibid.* 1113b 3–5).

St. *Augustine, reflecting on the concept of choice within the context of Christian revelation, sees it as being vitiated by sin; in his view, it was a perfection of man before original sin, a perfection that can be restored only by the gift of divine grace. "From the bad use of free will, there originated the whole train of evil, which, with its concatenation of miseries, convoys the human race from its depraved origin, as from a corrupt root, on to the destruction of the second death, which has no end, those only being excepted who are freed by the grace of God" (*Civ.* 13.14).

According to the doctrine of St. *Thomas Aquinas, "choice is substantially not an act of the reason but of the will; for choice is accomplished in a certain movement of the soul toward the good which is chosen. Consequently, it is evidently an act of the appetitive power" (ST 1a2ae, 13.1). Aquinas follows Aristotle's teaching on choice's being concerned with means to an end: "Just as intention regards the end, so choice regards the means" (*ibid.* 13.4). He likewise sees in man's faculty of choice the proper explanation of his freedom, or *free will: "Man does not choose of necessity. . . . Now the reason why it is possible not to choose or to choose, may be gathered from a twofold power in man. For man can will and not will, act and not act; and again he can will this or that, and do this or that. . . . Man chooses, not of necessity, but freely" (*ibid.* 13.6). Most scholastics are in basic agreement with this teaching. The Franciscan school generally accords more autonomy and primacy to the will, and thus sees free choice more as the will's prerogative than something it obtains from its dependency on the intellect (see *Duns Scotus, *Opus Oxon.* 1.1.4.16). Jesuit writers generally follow Thomistic doctrine, although they dispute over the precise relationship that obtains between choice and the last practical judgment (see St. Robert *Bellarmine, *De gratia et libero arbitrio* 3.8; G. *Vázquez, *In ST 1a2ae,* 44.3).

Modern and Contemporary Thought. R. *Descartes makes the important point that liberty of choice is not to be confused with indifference toward various alternatives, which he sees more as a defect of knowledge than as a perfection of the will: "In order that I should be free it is not necessary that I should be indifferent as to the choice of one or the other of two contraries; but contrariwise the more I lean to the one . . . the more freely do I choose and embrace it" (*Meditat.* 4.5). G. W. *Leibniz associates choice with the will's being induced to act by the element of goodness in what it chooses. "The will is never prompted to action save by the representation of the good, which prevails over the opposite representations. . . . For that very reason the choice is free and independent of necessity, because it is made between several possibles, and the will is determined only by the preponderating goodness of the object" (*Theodicy, Essays on the Justice of God . . .* 1.45).

Thinkers in the British empiricist tradition locate liberty or freedom in man's ability to choose, which they regard as being without external constraint or coercion. This is stated quite clearly by D. *Hume: "By liberty . . . we can only mean a power of acting or not acting, according to the determination of the will; that is, if we choose to remain at rest, we may; if we choose to move, we also may" (*An Enquiry Concerning Human Understanding* 8.73). J. *Locke further discusses the case of choice with respect to an end. "Liberty, it is plain, consists in the power to do, or not to do; to do, or forbear doing, as we will. . . . In most cases, a man is not at liberty to forbear the act of volition . . .. Yet there is a case wherein a man is at liberty in respect of willing; and that is the choosing of a *remote* good as an end to be pursued. Here a man may suspend the act of his choice from being determined for or against the thing proposed, till he has examined whether it be really of a nature, in itself and consequences, to make him happy or not" (*An Essay Concerning Human Understanding* 2.21.57).

For I. *Kant and the German idealist tradition that followed him, freedom of choice is derived from the exigencies of the practical reason and from moral law; thus choice is nothing more than man's autonomy in legislating for himself. In Kant's view, freedom does not consist in being able to choose one alternative or the other, but in the will's not being passively determined; will is a law unto itself independent of any quality in the object presented to it. "The principle of autonomy then is: 'Always so to choose that the same volition shall comprehend the maxims of our choice as a universal law' " (*Fundamental Principles of the Metaphysic of Morals* 2).

William *James accepts free choice as a pragmatic option, although he argues that man has an immediate awareness of his ability to choose. For those who have scruples about introspective aspects of consciousness he writes: "Let there be no such consciousness; let all our thoughts of movements be of sensational constitution; still in the emphasizing, choosing, and espousing of one of them rather than another, in the saying to it, 'be thou the reality to me,' there is ample scope for our inward initiative to be shown. Here, it seems to me, the true line between the passive materials and the activity of the spirit should be drawn" (*Principles of Psychology* ch. 26).

It is among the existentialist thinkers, however, that choice has received the greatest emphasis as a philosophical concept. For S. A. *Kierkegaard, choice is so fundamental that without it there can be no such thing as good or evil. "My either/or does not in the first instance denote the choice between good and evil, it denotes the choice whereby one chooses good *and* evil/ or excludes them. . . . It is, therefore, not so much a question of choosing between willing the good *or* the evil, as of choosing to *will*, but by this in turn the good and the evil are posited" [*Either/Or*, ed. R. Bretall, *A Kierkegaard Anthology* (New York 1946) 107]. M. Heidegger is even more emphatic; in his view, both the present state and the ultimate potentiality of Dasein (i.e., of human existence) are rooted in the attitude toward choice. "Dasein makes no choices, . . . and thus snares itself in inauthenticity. This process can be reversed only if Dasein specifically brings itself back to itself from its lostness in the 'they.' . . . This must be accomplished by making up for not choosing. But 'making up' for not choosing signifies choosing to make this choice—deciding for a potentiality-for-Being, and making this decision from one's own Self. In choosing to make this choice, Dasein makes possible, first and foremost, its authentic potentiality-for-Being" [*Being and Time*, tr. J. Macquarrie and E. Robinson (London 1962) 312–313]. *See* EXISTENTIALISM.

See also FREE WILL; FREEDOM; VOLUNTARITY; VOLUNTARISM; VALUE, PHILOSOPHY OF.

Bibliography: Syntopicon 2:1071–1101, 1309. G. PEDRAZZINI and G. MASI, EncFil 4:333–337. W. H. ROBERTS, *The Problem of Choice* (New York 1948). J. GRENIER, *La Choix* (Paris 1941). R. Z. LAUER, "St. Thomas's Theory of Intellectual Causality in Election," NewSchol 28 (1954) 299–319. H. RENARD, "The Functions of Intellect and Will in the Act of Free Choice," Mod Schoolm 24 (1947) 85–92.

[W. A. WALLACE]

CHOIR

Although the most common meaning of choir is a group of singers performing during a liturgical function, the term has come to mean also the place in the church from which they sing. The choir in this second sense was located, if the singers were clerics, directly behind or to the side of the altar, or between the altar and the nave if the architecture demanded it. Sometimes it was hidden from view by elaborately ornamented screens. Later, a balcony in the rear of the church served as the choir loft, especially for choirs of lay men and women. A trend toward returning the choir to the apse or nave began after promulgation of the *Constitution on the Liturgy* by Vatican Council II (1963).

Middle Ages. The earliest records of Christian worship show that the community, men and women, sang as a body in response to the ministers. The practice of having male cantors act as soloists undoubtedly was one taken over from the synagogues. There is evidence that even as late as St. Ambrose's time women alternated with the men in psalm-singing, but the general movement toward prohibiting women from singing in liturgical services seems to have reached a peak in the 6th century. This prohibition destroyed the unity of the congregation and led to the use of a select group of clerical singers (*see* SCHOLA CANTORUM).

The history of the choir in the Middle Ages revolves around the great monasteries and, later, the cathedral schools. The growth and development of polyphony increasingly demanded trained singers and tightly organized choir structure. Accurate information about the performance of early polyphony is scarce, but there is reason to believe that it was solo-polyphony rather than choir-polyphony. The medieval structure of the choir was maintained: the precentor, or leader; the succentor, or assistant; the first cantors, or rulers, who intoned and guided the chant and often sang the solo passages at the lectern; and the men and boys who formed the body of singers.

Origin of the Renaissance Choir. Before the 15th century one cannot speak of a choir in the generally accepted sense. The monastic choir was really a congregation of monks with a few specialists; the cathedral choir also was a group of relatively unskilled canons and a few soloists. The rise of private chapels (e.g., those of the Dukes of Burgundy, Berry, Orléans, and Savoy in France, and of St. George's at Windsor, St. Stephen's at Westminster, and the Royal Household), but especially the rivalry among college chapels (such as at Queen's College, Oxford; Eton College; and King's College, Cambridge, in England), brought a new professionalism into church music. For the first time small groups of trained singers were performing the polyphonic repertoire. At the turn of the 15th century and for the first part of the 16th, the average choir consisted of 15 to 20 members. Even in 1586 the papal choir had only 21 members, made up chiefly of young boys. As late as the 17th century, when clarity of tone was the chief aim, the choir was still generally small in size. Women often appear in contemporary illustrations of 17th-century choral groups, but these groups, also small in size, did not perform at church services.

The polyphony of the Renaissance is not easily performed by modern choirs, which generally lack the high male countertenor voices to sing alto parts. Another characteristic of the polyphonic choir was the *castrati* voice. From the 16th to the 18th century in Italy the practice of castration to preserve the boyish character of the voice was common. The *castrati,* highly paid and much in demand, had great range and power, combining the special timbre that came from the adult male lungs and chest with the soprano voice. The most famous choirs were the *Sistine choir in Rome and the Venetian choir at St. Marks. The Sistine choir established the *a cappella* tradition; the Venetian choir developed the use of opposing sonorities and instrumental accompaniment (*cori spezzati*).

Subsequent History of the Choir. The history of the choir during the baroque and later periods of music is largely a reflection of the history of music in general. The Roman tradition continued to dominate, but it was affected by the colossal (e.g., the multiple choirs of *Benevoli). During the late baroque, however, there was a growth in small parish choirs, as well as in a special repertory for them. These choirs were always accompanied by organ (or instruments) and sang only the Ordinary of the Mass. Major cathedrals, on the other hand, possessed well-trained choirs of some size that performed on Sundays and special occasions. Members of cathedral choirs were often the singers and instrumentalists who formed the local opera company; their repertory consisted mostly of the newly composed baroque and classical Masses. Under the influence of the *Caecilian movement, there was a return to the **a cappella* style, and interest was renewed in the 16th-century repertory. A whole new repertory of compositions for small parish choirs was written by the post-Caecilians; these works imitated in an academic fashion the 16th-century style but retained organ accompaniment. Large choirs continued to flourish at the major churches, especially in Austria and Germany; and the concerted Masses of the neoclassical period continued to be the standard repertory.

The 20th Century. With the motu proprio on sacred music of 1903, a search began for trained choral groups to perform the difficult Gregorian chants and polyphonic works. The establishment of boys' choirs, inspired by such examples as *Montserrat in Spain, led to cathedral and parish church choral organizations, which in some instances became very capable. The lack of real solfeggio instruction, however, opened the way for a repertory tailored to rote learning, making little or no demand on reading ability or ear training. The resulting paucity of art in choir loft and sanctuary was generally made worse by a dearth of male voices and inadequate rehearsal. Capable, well-trained choir directors were scarce, as was money to pay them adequately. The amateurish approach quickly proved destructive of good church music.

In the mid-20th century choirs were again receiving the benefit of skilled directors and organists, and the repertory of choir music began to show the influence of professional work. At the same time, the change from Latin to the vernacular in the liturgy created new problems for the church choir; for not only are there repertory difficulties, but choirs, far from being obviated, have been restored in an important role. The choir has today been given new settings for the Proper of the Mass, and it shares with the congregation the singing of the hymns, canticles, psalms, and the Ordinary of the Mass. Future years may see the choir restored to a place near the altar, either the front pews or one end of the transepts; choir robes may give way to conventional dress; and women may once again be admitted to full participation.

See also CHOIR MUSIC; GREGORIAN CHANT.

Bibliography: EncBrit v.5, s.v. Choir. A. JACOBS, ed., *Choral Music* (Baltimore 1963). Fellerer CathChMus.

[C. A. PELOQUIN; R. G. WEAKLAND]

CHOIR MUSIC

The repertory of music written for liturgical worship is staggering in volume. This article presents a brief panoramic view of that music which was designated to be sung for a specialized group or choir in Christian worship and which is part of the heritage of the Church (*see* MUSIC, SACRED, HISTORY OF). The *Constitution on the Liturgy* (1963) of Vatican Council II makes clear that this heritage is to be preserved: "The treasure of sacred music is to be preserved and fostered with great care" (114).

Middle Ages and Renaissance. *Gregorian chant is the first body of Christian music that has been preserved in the West. Although it may have had its origins in a practice that involved for the most part the alternation between soloists and congregation, the extant repertory is music that belongs to the choir. This is especially the case with the Introits, Graduals, Alleluias, Tracts, Offertories, Communions, and grêat Responsories. Although this repertory is in unison, it should rightly be sung by choirs and soloists. "The Church acknowledges Gregorian chant as specially suited to the Roman liturgy: therefore, other things being equal, it should be given pride of place in liturgical services" (*Constitution on the Liturgy* (116). The current chant repertory could be increased by including the numerous pieces that remain unedited.

Of the early polyphonic works, some of the pieces by *Léonin and *Pérotin are not beyond the abilities of the average choir. The famous *Messe de Notre-Dame* by *Machaut still sounds striking to the modern ear. Editions of the works of the Renaissance masters from Dufay to Monteverdi, adapted to modern performance, are available in ever-increasing quantity. Although the works of *Palestrina have been performed frequently since the *Caecilian movement of the 19th century, there is increased interest in the work of other composers as well, especially that of Josquin *Desprez, Orlando di *Lasso, and *Victoria. While the melodic lines of these composers are not difficult to sing, the subtle rhythmic problems and the clarity and independence of parts makes performance difficult for an untrained choir. Many of the compositions by Lutheran composers of the 16th century, from Johann Walther (1496–1570) through Hans Leo Hassler (1564–1612)

Page of a choir piece by Josquin Desprez in a 15th century manuscript in the Biblioteca Nazionale Centrale, Florence (MS. II.I.232, fol. 176v).

to Heinrich Schütz (1585–1672), could well be performed as motets during liturgical services. The works of the English school, especially those of William Byrd (1543–1623), have an interest for the contemporary composer, since they represent the first attempts at English settings of service texts by first-rate composers.

From the Baroque to the 19th Century. Many of the masterpieces of the baroque, classical, and romantic periods require large choruses or the use of instrumental ensembles, which make their rendition difficult except under unusual circumstances. There is, nevertheless, a large quantity of superior music that is not outside the range of the average choir and is being published in modern performing editions: e.g., the works of L. *Viadana (1564–1645) from the early baroque, and A. *Lotti (*c.* 1667–1740) from a later period. The French school of the 17th century is again receiving due interest from both organists and choir directors; J. B. *Lully (1632–87), M. A. *Charpentier (1634–1704), and M. Delalande (1668–1733) are among the most frequently edited today. Many works of J. S. *Bach also are available for Church use. From the romantic period few compositions are recommended for the liturgical services, although many other religious works are available for concert use.

The 20th Century. In the 20th century there has been a revival of interest among composers both in works of a religious nature and in music written especially for the liturgy, particularly the Roman rite. The more prominent composers and their works (including concert pieces) are: Gustave Holst, *The Hymn of Jesus;* Claude Debussy, the *Martyrdom of St. Sebastian;* Sir Edward Elgar, *The Dream of Gerontius* (based on Cardinal Newman's poem); Ralph Vaughan Williams, Mass in G Minor; Leoš Janáček, *Glagolitic Mass;* Bohuslav Martinu, *Songs of Mary* (for women's chorus); Arnold Schoenberg, *Kol Nidre, Prelude to "Genesis," Out of the Depths* (Hebrew text), and the unfinished opera *Moses and Aaron;* and Igor Stravinsky (b. 1882), *Pater Noster, Ave Maria,* the popular *Symphony of Psalms, Canticum Sacrum* (dedicated to the city of Venice), and a Mass for men's and boy's voices and wind instruments, which employs Machaut-like sonorities. Other composers in the modern group are: Charles Koechlin, *L'Abbaye;* William Walton, *Belshazzar's Feast;* Arthur Honegger, *King David, Joan of Arc at the Stake,* and *Dance of Death,* the latter two with text by Paul Claudel; Edmund Rubbra, *Five Motets* and *Missa Cantuariensis;* Paul Hindemith (1895–1964), a Mass for *a cappella* choir, which deserves serious attention; Francis Poulenc, a Mass in G Major (for unaccompanied voices), *Litanies of the Black Virgin of Rocamadour,* a *Stabat Mater,* and a Gloria (the latter two with orchestra); Albert Roussel, a setting for Psalm 80; Florent Schmitt, a setting for Psalm 47 (46 in the Vulgate); and particularly Benjamin Britten, *Ceremony of Carols* (for women's voices and harp), *Hymn to St. Cecilia, Festival Te Deum, Rejoice in the Lamb,* the cantata *Saint Nicholas,* and the monumental *A War Requiem,* using the text of the Latin requiem Mass and poems by Wilfred Owen.

The following composers also are significant for their contributions to sacred choral music: Ernst Bloch, *Sacred Service;* Zoltan Kodaly, *Te Deum* and *Missa Brevis;* Frank Martin, *The Mystery of the Nativity;* Goffredo Petrassi, *Psalm 9* and *Magnificat;* Virgil Thomson, *Missa Brevis, Requiem,* and *Scenes from the Holy Infancy;* Alan Hovhaness, *Magnificat;* Randall Thompson, *Alleluia;* Charles Ives, *Sixty-seventh Psalm;* Heitor Villa-Lobos, *Mass in Honor of St. Sebastian;* Russell Woollen, Mass No. 2; C. Alexander Peloquin, *Te Deum* and *Missa Domini;* Herman Schroeder, *Missa Coloniensis;* Flor Peeters, *Missa Festiva;* and Jean Langlais, *Messe Solennelle.*

First page of the holograph copy of the score of the American composer Charles Ives's "Sixty-seventh Psalm."

Bibliography: A. Colling, *Histoire de la musique chrétienne* (Paris 1956). Fellerer CathChMus. C. H. Dawson, *Progress and Religion* (Garden City, N.Y. 1960). J. Gélineau, *Voices and Instruments in Christian Worship,* tr. C. Howell (Collegeville, Minn. 1964). A. Jacobs, ed., *Choral Music* (Pelican Bks. Baltimore 1963). A. Machabey, ed., *La Musique religieuse française* (La Revue musicale 222; Paris 1953). C. G. Parrish, ed., *A Treasury of Early Music* (New York 1958). A. Richard, ed., *La Musique sacrée* (La Revue musicale 239–240; Paris 1957). A. Robertson, *Christian Music* (New York 1961). Roland-Manuel. P. A. Scholes, *The Oxford Companion to Music* (8th ed. New York 1950). **Illustration credits:** Fig. 1, Photo by Sansoni. Fig. 2, Yale University Library.

[C. A. PELOQUIN; R. G. WEAKLAND]

CHOISEUL, ÉTIENNE FRANÇOIS DE

French statesman; b. Lorraine, June 28, 1719; d. Paris, May 8, 1785. As the Comte de Choiseul-Stainville, he served as a talented army officer, and at 31, on Dec. 22, 1750, married the 15-year-old Louise Honorine Crozat du Châtel. She was of a titled family and granddaughter of the receiver-general of the finances of Bordeaux and founder of the Louisiana Company, who made an immense fortune from his American possessions. Through intrigue Choiseul eventually gained favor at the court of Louis XV, and in 1754 at the behest of Madame de Pompadour, was made ambassador to

Étienne François de Choiseul, portrait by Carle Van Loo, in the Musée de Tours.

Rome, a position he retained until January 1757. Some historians believe that it was during this tenure that Choiseul resolved to abolish the Society of Jesus. His letters from Rome, however, do not mention the society, although they contain sketches of individual Jesuits.

Choiseul next became ambassador to Vienna and served successively as minister of foreign affairs (1758), as minister of war, and as minister of the Navy. He achieved a brilliant record through his enormous reduction of expenditures and his reorganization of the artillery and military engineering corps. He was known also for his political adroitness, especially for his role in bringing about the alliance of all the Bourbons, "the Family Compact" (1761). France was torn by religious difficulties resulting from the teaching of Gallicans, Jansenists, and *philosophes.* Choiseul, a friend of Voltaire and a Freemason, was in the midst of the turmoil. While claiming to be an upholder of religion, this master of intrigue set about to destroy the Society of Jesus, zealous defenders of the Church against the ideas of the *philosophes.* His efforts were not confined to France, but extended to Portugal and Spain. In Portugal he conspired with the anticlerical Prime Minister, the Marquis of *Pombal, in spreading vicious and scandalous rumors about the Jesuits that resulted in the imprisonment and exile of members of the society. Using the same methods in Spain, Choiseul joined forces with Count d'Aranda, President of the Council of Castile, and they succeeded in the expulsion of the society in 1767. As a result of the Family Compact, the Jesuits suffered the same fate in the kingdom of Naples, and in 1773 the society was suppressed by *Clement XIV. Before then, however, Choiseul had himself become the victim of a conspiracy and had been sentenced to exile at Chanteloup, where he lived in great luxury.

Bibliography. É. F. DE CHOISEUL, *Mémoires,* 2 v. (Paris 1790). H. DANIEL-ROPS, *The Church in the Eighteenth Century,* tr. J. WARRINGTON (History of the Church 7; New York 1964). J. M. B. BINS DE SAINT-VICTOR, ed., *Documents historiques, critiques, apologétiques concernant la Compagnie de Jésus,* 3 v. (Paris 1827–30) v.1. J. LE ROND D'ALEMBERT, *An Account of the Destruction of the Jesuits in France* (London 1766). A. CARAYON, ed., *Charles III. et les Jésuites de ses états d'Europe et d'Amérique en 1767* (Paris 1868). G. MAUGRAS, *Le Duc et la Duchesse de Choiseul: Leur vie intime, leurs amis et leur temps,* 2 v. in 1 (Paris 1902); *La Disgrâce du Duc et de la Duchesse de Choiseul: La Vie à Chanteloup: Le retour à Paris: La Mort,* 2 v. in 1 (Paris 1903). M. BOUTRY, *Choiseul à Rome, 1754–57* (Paris 1895). S. J. DE CARVALHO E MELLO, *Pombal, Choiseul et d'Aranda: L'Intrigue des trois cabinets* (Paris 1830). A. BOURGUET, *Le Duc de Choiseul et l'Alliance Éspagnole* (Paris 1906).
Illustration credit: Archives Photographiques, Paris.

[A. N. HANSEN]

CHOISEUL DU PLESSIS PRASLIN, GILBERT DE, bishop; b. Paris 1613; d. Paris Dec. 31, 1689. He was a doctor at the Sorbonne by 1640; he was consecrated bishop of Comminges in 1644 then transferred to Tournai in 1671. Choiseul, a model pastor, visited every corner of his diocese, reformed his clergy, and founded many schools and seminaries. He showed a deep love for his flock by raising money to feed the poor during a famine and by ministering personally to victims of the plague. Choiseul was one of the first to champion the Jansenists of *Port-Royal against their critics both at Rome and at the court. He was one of 11 French bishops who petitioned the Pope "to allow this important dispute . . . to continue a little longer." One biographer claims that Choiseul gave Jansenist ideas an important foothold in the Diocese of Tournai, particularly among the clergy (F. Desmons, 372). Choiseul's sympathies for a sect condemned by Rome probably account also for his belligerent defense of the "Gallican Liberties." In his place Bishop Bossuet drafted the famous Articles of 1682 largely because Choiseul, the former head of the committee, had wanted to claim still greater autonomy for the French Church. Choiseul's important writings include *Memoires touchant la religion* (3 v. Paris 1681–85), *Lettre pastorale sur le culte de la Vierge* (Tournai 1907); *Les Psaumes, cantiques et hymnes de l'Église, traduit en français,* many editions of which are without place or date of publication.

Bibliography: M. H. LAURENT, DHGE 12:757–758. V. ZOLLINI, EncCatt 3:1562. R. METZ, LexThK² 2:1075–76. F. DESMONS, *Gilbert de Choiseul, évêque de Tournai, 1671–89* (Tournai 1907).

[J. Q. C. MACKRELL]

CHOLMOGORY, ABBEY OF, former Russian monastery dedicated to the Assumption of the Blessed Virgin, situated on one of the islands forming an arm of the Northern Dvina River about 70 miles from where it empties into the White Sea, in Archangel oblast, Russian S.F.S.R. in the archeparchy of Archangel. From the 14th century the site had been a trading center for merchants from *Novgorod, and in the 16th century it was frequented also by English merchants of the Moscow Company. About 1355 Ivan Ivanovich, Archbishop of Novgorod, stationed an agent there to collect the tithes. A monastery was situated there from about the same period, and the monks maintained themselves by trade in fish and salt. The town of Cholmogory developed independently of the monastery in the late

16th century. Almost nothing can be learned of the abbey's history because of present conditions. In 1691 the Transfiguration Cathedral was built nearby. The Russian poet Lomonosov (d. 1765) was born in Cholmogory.

Bibliography: *Bol'shaia sovetskaia entsiklopediia,* ed. V. V. Kuibysheva et al., 65 v. (Moscow 1927–47) 46:283. *Masarykův slovník naučný,* 7 v. (Prague 1925–33) 3:490.

[J. PAPIN]

CHOPIN, FRÉDÉRIC FRANÇOIS, romanticist composer; b. Zelazowa Wola (near Warsaw), Poland, Feb. 22, 1810; d. Paris, France, Oct. 17, 1849. He was the second of four talented children of Nicolas Chopin, a transplanted, vaguely Voltairean French schoolman, and Justyna Krzyzanowska, a Polish woman of refinement and piety. At age 7 Frédéric first played in public and had his first piece published—a polonaise set in type in the printshop of Visitation parish, where the boy later was organist. After piano training with A. Zwyny, he studied at Warsaw Conservatory under J. K. Elsner (1769–1854), a prolific composer who fostered the boy's unusual creative impulses. Following respectable successes as composer-recitalist in lesser cities, he settled (1831) in Paris, where he was lionized by French and *émigré* Polish nobility (while supporting himself by giving lessons to their daughters) and accepted as peer by the ranking literary and artistic spirits. Through one of these (F. *Liszt) he met and entered upon a liaison with the freethinking writer George Sand (Mme. Aurore Dudevant), in whose household he remained for the next 8 years, the arrangement being terminated by a sordid family quarrel. He died 2 years later, after receiving the last rites with great devotion (he had left the Church more through indifference than conviction). His body was buried in Père Lachaise cemetery, between the graves of *Bellini and *Cherubini.

Frédéric François Chopin, portrait by Eugène Delacroix, 1838, in the Musée du Louvre, Paris.

However sentimentalized his image in film and fiction, Chopin was a hard-working, tough-minded perfectionist whose very personality was shaped and limited by the pressure of his genius. His musical idiom partakes of the rhythms and melancholy (Lydian) mode of Polish folk music, the *bel canto* vocalisms he had heard in Warsaw opera productions, J. S. *Bach's counterpoint and *Mozart's formal clarity, the configurations of *Dušek, and the nocturne contour of the Irishman John Field. All such stimuli, however, were transformed by an act of intense parareligious self-discipline into a distinctive expression that revolutionized piano composition and performance, and in turn unleashed harmonic and melodic forces that were harnessed orchestrally by R. *Wagner and anticipated the edgeless sonorities of *Debussy, *Fauré, and 20th-century atonalists.

Bibliography: F. F. Chopin, *Selected Correspondence,* collected and annotated by B. E. Sydow, tr. and ed. A. Hedley (London 1962). M. J. E. Brown, *Chopin: An Index of His Works in Chronological Order* (New York 1960). A. Hedley, *Chopin* (New York 1949); Grove DMM 2:252–267. F. Liszt, *Frederic Chopin,* tr. E. N. Waters (New York 1963), probably the work of Carolyna von Sayn Wittgenstein. A. Boucourechliev, *Chopin: A Pictorial Biography,* tr. E. Hyams (New York 1963). W. Kahl, MusGG 2:1218–30. *La Revue musicale,* No. 121 (1931) and No. 229 (1955), Chopin numbers. *La rassegna musicale* (Turin, Oct. 1949), Chopin number. **Illustration credit:** Archives Photographiques, Paris.

[M. E. EVANS]

CHORBISHOP

The title given in the Orient to a bishop caring for people in the country. The rapid diffusion of Christianity in the first half of the 2d century "not only in the cities but also in the villages" (Pliny, *Ep. ad Traianum* 96) rendered necessary the "institution of bishops for the villages and countryside" (Clement *I ad Cor.* 42:4). Zoticus, bishop of the village of Comana in Phrygia *c.* 200, who excommunicated the Montanist Maximilla, is the first so named (Eusebius, *Hist. eccl.* 5:16); and the fact that this sect still had chorbishops in Phrygia in the 4th century (Sozomen, *Hist. eccl.* 7:19) lends credence to the belief that they existed in the 2d century when *Montanism began.

There are numerous mentions of chorbishops in the 3d century: in Bithynia, Asia, Phrygia, Antioch (Eusebius, *Hist. eccl* 7:30), Egypt, and Palestine (*Apost. Church Order* 16). In the religious peace that followed the persecution by the Roman Emperor *Decius, it was possible to centralize and subordinate the smaller bishoprics under the bishop of the civil metropolis of the province. There was considerable resistance, which left its mark in the canonical legislation of the 4th century (Nicaea I, can. 8; Laodicea, can. 57; Ancyra, can. 13; Antioch, can. 10; and Neocaesarea, can. 14, which cites the example of the subordination of the 70 Disciples).

Canonical institution was given to chorbishops by the bishop of the city (Antioch, can. 10), and they were called coadministrators (Neocaesarea, can. 14); they governed their territory with the bishop's supervision (Laodicea, can. 57), but they were confined to the villages and countryside (Antioch, can. 10). Their powers included the ordination of lectors, subdeacons and exorcists on their own authority, but of deacons and priests only with the consent of the bishop (Antioch, can. 10), which was to be obtained in writing (Ancyra, can. 13). *Basil of Ancyra demanded this even for subdeacons (can. 87). The care of the poor was particularly their office (Neocaesarea, can. 14). The institution was opposed (Ancyra, can. 89) because they were accused of not obeying the canons of the Fathers, and it was suggested that they be replaced by priests (Laodicea can. 57; Sardica can. 6).

In the 8th century chorbishops could not ordain even lectors without the bishop's consent (Nicaea II, can. 14), and in the 12th century the jurist *Balsamon judged it "senseless to speak of them since they were extinct" [*Syntagma* 3(1853)47]. Today the institution has completely disappeared in the Orthodox Churches. Among the united Chaldeans and Syrians, there is one per diocese, and he can ordain lectors and subdeacons. Among the Maronites, they serve as auxiliary bishops; among the Melchites, the term chorbishop is a purely honorary title.

In the West, there is no sign of a similar institution until the 8th century, when Pope *Zachary in a letter to Pepin (747) ordered their subordination to the diocesan bishop in accord with the Synod of Antioch (can. 10). On the Anglo-Saxon mission this system seems to have been an adaptation of the Irish institution of bishops attached to monasteries under the abbot, in which the bishop's sole function was spiritual. The abuse whereby bishops used a chorbishop as an auxiliary to perform his duties in his absence on secular affairs was opposed in the Carolingian reform (Synods of Paris, 829; Meaux, 845). While the system grew in the 9th century, it declined in the 10th and 11th and disappeared in the 12th century.

Bibliography: P. Linden, LexThK² 2:1080–81. E. Kirsten, ReallexAntChr 2:1105–14. H. Leclercq, DACL 3.1:1423–52. A. Coussa, EncCatt 4:545–547. F. Gillmann, *Das Institut der Chorbischöfe im Orient* (Munich 1903). T. Gottlob, *Der abendländische Chorepiskopat* (Bonn 1928). V. Fuchs, *Der Ordinationstitel . . .* (Bonn 1930). P. Joannou, Fonti CICO fasc. 9, v.2, Suppl. (Rome 1964), Index s.v. "Chorepiscopus."

[P. JOANNOU]

CHORISANTES, a fanatical sect of wandering men and women, so called because of the obscenely grotesque dance that characterized their religious frenzy. Dance madness was reported as early as the 9th century among certain monks and nuns of Syria, but in Europe the source was probably the old Germanic dances celebrating the summer solstice (*Sommersonnenwend-Tänze*), which in the Christian Era honored the nativity of John the Baptist (Sankti Johannis Chorea). Chorisantes (called variously *Dansatores, Dansers,* and *Tänzer*) appeared sporadically in the Rhineland and in the Low Countries from the 14th to 16th centuries. Their dance frenzy occurred usually in public places, near or in churches. Since they were regarded as being under *diabolical possession because of invalid Baptism or of Baptism administered by a priest living in concubinage, their cure was sought in *exorcism and in pilgrimages to churches of St. Vitus (hence, St. Vitus's dance).

Bibliography: *Annales Fossenses,* MGS 4:35. P. de Herenthals in É. Baluze, *Vitae paparum Avenionensium,* ed. G. Mollat, 4 v. (Paris 1914–27) 1:466–467. Radulph de Rivo, *Gesta pontificum Leodiensium* in *Gesta pontificum Tungrensium, Trajectensium, et Leodiensium,* ed. J. Chapeauville, 3 v. (Liège 1612–16) 3:19–22. J. F. K. Hecker, *The Dancing Mania of the Middle Ages,* tr. B. G. Babington (New York 1885). P. Frédéricq, *De secten der geselaars en der dansers in de Nederlanden* (Brussels 1899). G. Bareille, DTC 4.1:134–136.

[M. F. LAUGHLIN]

CHORON, ALEXANDRE ÉTIENNE, composer, theorist, and pedagogue; b. Caen (Normandy), France, Oct. 21, 1772; d. Paris, June 29, 1834. Passionately fond of music, mathematics, and philology from his boyhood and largely self-taught, he began in 1804 to edit and publish treatises and scores of Italian and German classic musicians as well as many of his own writings on musical theory and practice. From 1811 until the fall of Napoleon (1815), Choron reorganized training schools for church choirs and was director of official religious festivals. He was named director of the Paris Opera, and he reopened the conservatory but was forced to resign in 1817 for supporting too many new works by unknown composers. He next established the Institution Royale de Musique classique et religieuse but when deprived of government subsidy by the revolution of 1830, he closed this very successful rival to the conservatory and retired from public life (the school was later revived by L. Niedermeyer). Choron composed an unpublished opera, a Requiem, and various motets, including a *Stabat Mater.* Of greater interest are his numerous treatises, notably the *Dictionnaire historique des musiciens* (with F. J. Fayolle, 1810–1811), *Méthode concertante de musique à plusieurs parties* (1818), and *Méthode de plain-chant* (1818).

Bibliography: G. Chouquet, Grove DMM 2:277. E. Borrel, MusGG 2:1402–04. R. Dumesnil, *La Musique romantique française* (Paris 1944). Roland-Manuel v.2.

[R. W. LOWE]

CHRÉTIEN DE TROYES

French writer of romances (fl. *c.* 1170). Virtually nothing is known of his life. It is clear that he had some connection with the city of Troyes in Champagne; he dedicated his *Lancelot* to Marie, the Countess of Champagne, who married the Count most probably in or about 1159. This sets the earliest possible date for *Lancelot. Perceval* was dedicated to Philippe d'Alsace, the Count of Flanders, who died in 1191, and it was consequently written before that date. That is all that can be said of Chrétien's life with any degree of certainty.

In the prologue to his romance of *Cligés,* Chrétien gives us a list of his previous works, most of them now lost. He evidently started his brilliant literary career with a series of adaptations into French from Ovid's *Metamorphoses,* only one of which is extant. The *Philomena* episode inserted in the *Ovide moralisé* of the 14th century has been plausibly identified with one of Chrétien's adaptations. Most unfortunately, a tale about King Mark and Iseut la Blonde that antedated any Tristan text now extant, is also lost. The other major title listed is *Erec et Enide,* which has been preserved in seven manuscripts and some fragments. It is the first extant romance of King Arthur and the knights of the Round Table, and already shows the great narrative gifts that made Chrétien the acknowledged master of the courtly romance. Works not mentioned in the list in *Cligés*—and hence written later—are the romances of *Lancelot* or the *Knight of the Cart,* of *Yvain* or the *Knight of the Lion,* and of *Perceval* or the *Story of the Grail.*

The first four romances deal chiefly with the knightly adventures and courtly loves of their heroes. They are related with elegance, a refined subtlety that delighted aristocratic audiences, and a graceful mixture of gentle humor, realistic descriptions of court life, and fantastic and often supernatural adventures.

The Grail romance, unfinished at Chrétien's death, is the earliest extant account of a Grail quest. It was continued by several other writers and it is therefore impossible to judge how Chrétien would have finished it and how he would have explained the mysterious Grail itself, which exhibits no explicitly Christian or sacred character in Chrétien's own work.

Like all Chrétien's works, *Perceval* exerted great influence on other writers and was imitated in many other romances during the following century, both in France and in the rest of Western Europe.

See also ROMANCES, MEDIEVAL; ARTHURIAN LEGENDS; COURTLY LOVE; HOLY GRAIL, THE.

Bibliography: R. S. LOOMIS, *Arthurian Tradition and Chrétien de Troyes* (New York 1949). J. FRAPPIER, "Chrétien de Troyes," *Arthurian Literature in the Middle Ages,* ed. R. S. LOOMIS (Oxford 1959); *Chrétien de Troyes: L'Homme et l'oeuvre* (Paris 1957). J. MISRAHI, "More Light on the Chronology of Chrétien de Troyes," *Bulletin Bibliographique de la Société Internationale Arthurienne* 11 (1959) 89–120.

[J. MISRAHI]

CHRISMON, the Greek monogram or symbol of the name of Christ, appears in the early 3d century. The first dated use is 269. It takes many forms: ∗ (Chi and Iota), ☧ (Chi and Rho), ⳨ (Tau surmounted by Rho), but no rigorous chronology can be established for these variations. Forms later Latinized by adding a tail to the Rho (⳩) appear in Spain, Gaul, Italy, Africa, and even in Greece itself. First employed as an abbreviation, the chrismon was used by *Constantine I as a symbol on the *labarum, and, according to *Lactantius, on his soldiers' helmets and shields before the Battle of the Milvian Bridge (312). Constantine subsequently placed it on coins. Decorative forms of the chrismon appear in bas-reliefs, on lamps, rings, and seals. St. *John Chrysostom mentions its use in epistles (PG 62:364). During the Middle Ages it appeared at the beginning of charters; Merovingian scribes distorted it with flourishes. The imperial chancery used it until *c.* 1200. It appeared in papal documents frequently until the pontificate of *Leo IX (d. 1054); after the time of *Gregory VII (d. 1085) the chrismon was used only in private charters.

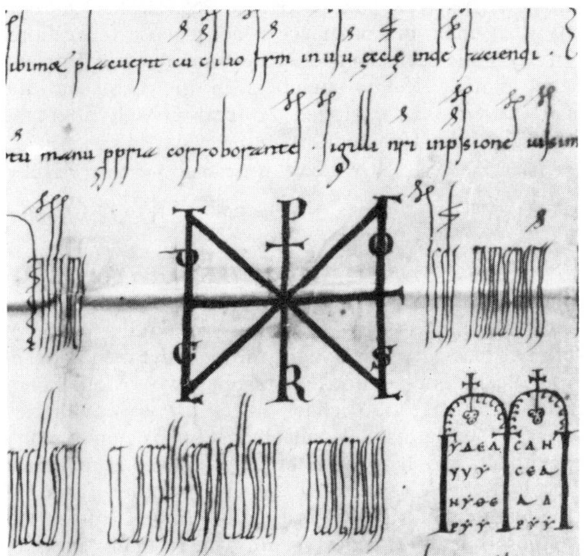

Monogram of Henry III of Germany on a document dated 1053. The chrismon is incorporated into the middle upright stroke of the elaborate imperial signature.

Bibliography: H. LECLERCQ, DACL 3.1:1481–1534. K. HONSELMANN, LexThK^{2} 2:1095. C. PAOLI, *Diplomatica,* ed. G. C. BASCAPÈ (Florence 1942). **Illustration credit:** Staatsarchiv Koblenz.

[C. M. AHERNE]

CHRIST, title of Jesus of Nazareth. The English word Christ is derived from the Latin *Christus* corresponding to the Greek Χριστός (anointed) that the Septuagint regularly used to translate the Hebrew word *māšîaḥ,* from which the word *Messiah is derived. In the OT the Israelite king was called *m^{e}šîaḥ yhwh,* "the anointed one of Yahweh" (*see* ANOINTING). In the last pre-Christian century the expected savior of the Jews, who was regarded as restoring the throne of David, was called simply *hammāšîaḥ,* "the Anointed One," the Messiah, or in Greek ὁ Χριστός. When the disciples of Jesus recognized Him as the promised savior, they proclaimed Him ὁ Χριστός, "the Christ" (Mk 8.29; Acts 5.42; 9.22; etc., where the article is as necessary in English as it is in Greek). However, when the Greek-speaking pagans began to be converted to Christianity, the Jewish concept of the Messiah meant little to them, and they understood the word Χριστός as one of the Savior's names, Christ—perhaps because it sounded practically the same as the personal name Χρηστός (good, kind). Therefore, in the NT Χριστός is often used without the article as the Savior's name, Christ, either alone (Rom 5.6, 8; 6.4, 9; etc.) or together with the name *Jesus, either in the form Christ Jesus (Acts 24.24; Rom 3.24; 6.3; etc.) or, especially, in the form Jesus Christ (Mk 1.1; Jn 1.17; Acts 2.38; Rom 1.4, 6, 8; etc.).

Bibliography: R. R. HAWTHORNE, "The Significance of the Name Christ," *Bibliotheca Sacra* 103 (1946) 215–222, 348–362, 453–463. S. V. MCCASLAND, "Christ Jesus," JBiblLit 65 (1946) 377–383. A. ROMEO, EncCatt 4:918–921. EncDictBibl 360.

[L. F. HARTMAN]

CHRIST THE KING, FEAST OF, celebration of the Savior's kingship on the last Sunday of October. It belongs to that class of feasts called idea-feasts, that is, it celebrates no specific event in the history of salvation but rather honors our Savior Himself under the title of king. Pius XI instituted this feast in 1925 to counteract the growing laicism, secularism, and atheism of his time. Against these errors this feast affirms the sovereignty and rule of Christ over persons, families, human society, the state, the whole universe. In particular the feast affirms the messianic kingship of Christ. Jesus is the king who has obtained His sovereignty through His blood. He is the Redeemer king. The original feast of Christ the King is that of the Ascension. On that day Jesus was exalted to the right hand of the Father and crowned with glory and honor. The October feast is only a duplication of that larger feast. For that reason the texts of the Feast of Christ the King are but an amplification of those used for Ascension Thursday. They deal with the same themes and present Christ in the language of the Apocalypse, which from beginning to

Christ as the exalted Lamb of God, one of the symbols of Christ the King, a panel from the "Ghent Altarpiece," by Jan and Hubert van Eyck, completed in 1432, and in the possession of the Church of Saint-Bavon, Ghent, Belgium.

end is a book of the triumph of the king of kings, the ascended Lord and the heavenly high priest.

Bibliography: PIUS XI, "Quas primas" (Encyclical, Dec. 11, 1925) ActApS 17 (1925) 593–610. W. DÜRIG, LexThK² 2:1130–31. P. OPPENHEIM, EncCatt 4:927. **Illustration credit:** Copyright A.C.L., Brussels.

[W. J. O'SHEA]

CHRISTADELPHIANS, or Brothers of Christ, a sect founded by Dr. John Thomas (1805–71), an English physician who came to the U.S. in 1832. At first he associated with the Campbellites (Disciples of Christ) but disagreed with them on several doctrinal points (*see* CAMPBELL, ALEXANDER; CHRISTIAN CHURCHES). He severed his ties with Campbellism in 1834. Between 1844 and 1847 Thomas developed his own theological system, which he maintained was that of primitive Christianity. Branding all existing churches as apostate, he won a few converts in the U.S., Canada, and England. The name Christadelphian was adopted during the Civil War.

Christadelphians reject the doctrine of the Trinity and the divinity of Jesus Christ. They deny eternal punishment and the existence of a personal devil. They believe that Christ will soon ascend David's throne in the Holy Land, gather the 12 tribes of Israel, and rule the world for 1,000 years. Baptism by immersion is considered the sole valid form. Only those who have heard and accepted what the sect considers divine truth will receive the gift of immortality; no others will be raised from the dead. Members of the sect try to disassociate themselves from the secular community; they do not serve in the armed forces, vote, seek public office, join labor unions, or indulge in wordly amusements. They are also opposed to smoking, divorce, and marrying outside of the sect.

Local congregations, called ecclesiae, follow a congregational polity. They employ no salaried clergy; each congregation elects its own "serving brethren" for 3-year terms. They handle all liturgical and administrative duties. Christadelphians usually meet for worship in private homes or rented halls. Local congregations hold a weekly communion service on Sunday. They emphasize the study of the Bible and sometimes sponsor public lectures to interest outsiders. The sect maintains no foreign missions, seminaries, or schools, except for a few summer Bible schools. Christadelphian congregations do not recognize an overall ecclesiastical authority; they may join other ecclesiae in loose federations. In 1964 the sect claimed 20,000 members in England and another 15,000 members in the U.S., but the Christadelphians exhibited no real growth after the middle of the 19th century.

Bibliography: B. R. WILSON, *Sects and Society* (Berkeley, Calif. 1961).

[W. J. WHALEN]

CHRISTE SANCTORUM DECUS ANGELORUM, an anonymous Latin hymn of five sapphic strophes addressed to Christ, in which the grace of eternal blessedness is sought through the mediation of the angels. The petitions in strophes two to four honor individual angels: Michael, angel of peace; Gabriel, angel of strength; and Raphael, angel-physician of man's health. In strophe five the grace of heaven is requested through the Virgin Mary. Julian lists four forms of the hymn: the original text found in three 11th-century manuscripts; the *Textus receptus;* the Roman *Breviary text; and that of the Roman Breviary appendix. The complete hymn is used at Lauds on May 8 and September 29. Strophes 1-3-5 and 1-4-5 are sung at Vespers and Matins on the feasts of the Archangels Gabriel (March 24) and Raphael (October 24), respectively.

Bibliography: J. STEVENSON, ed., *The Latin Hymns of the Anglo-Saxon Church* (Surtees Society 23; Durham 1851) 116. AnalHymn 50:197–198, for text. Julian DictHym 1:229–230; 2:1556. J. MEARNS, *Early Latin Hymnaries* (Cambridge, Eng. 1913) 21. M. BRITT, ed., *The Hymns of the Breviary and Missal* (new ed. New York 1948) 288–289. Connelly Hymns 194–195, for tr. Szövérffy AnnLatHymn 1:222, 225.

[M. I. J. ROUSSEAU]

CHRISTIAN OF PRUSSIA, Cistercian missionary and first bishop of Prussia; d. Poland, Dec. 4, 1245. Christian went to preach to the pagan Prussians from the Cistercian monastery in Poland. *Innocent III named him missionary bishop (1215), and he was consecrated in Rome. *Honorius III, who gave strong moral support to the Cistercian mission, gave Christian the privilege of a metropolitan and the right to erect episcopal sees and to consecrate bishops. He was thus at the center of the Cistercian missionary activity in Prussia. *Conrad of Masovia, who surrendered to him the Kulmerland as an independent territory, assisted him, and the *Knights of Dobrin (*Milites Christi*), at his instigation, fought the pagan Prussians. In 1230 Christian enfeoffed the Order of *Teutonic Knights of Kulmerland without prejudice to his episcopal rights, but the order did not respect Christian's rights. When he was captured by the Prussians in 1233, nothing was done to liberate him. His missionary aim, to convert the Prussians without destroying their national independence and to train a native clergy, was in total opposition to the desires of the Teutonic Knights, who wanted to subjugate and Germanize the Prussians. The Teutonic Knights therefore cut the Cistercians out of the mission and had it handed over by the Pope to the *Dominicans. When Christian succeeded in ransoming himself in the winter of 1239–40 he immediately resumed the fight for his rights, but without success. Shortly afterward he withdrew into a Polish Cistercian monastery. Though he became irascible in his old age, his aims were always pure and above reproach. His objective was to bring to the Prussians the "freedom of the children of God."

Bibliography: Zimmermann KalBen 3:393. M. TUMLER, *Der Deutsche Orden im Werden, Wachsen und Wirken bis 1400* (Vienna 1955). A. TRILLER, NDB 3:230. H. SCHMAUCH, LexThK[2] 2:1123–24. S. M. SZACHERSKA, *Opactwo cysterkie w Spetalu a Misja pruska* (Warsaw 1960). J. M. CANIVEZ, DHGE 12:772.

[C. SPAHR]

CHRISTIAN OF STABLO, or of Stavelot, Benedictine monk and exegete, one of the foremost among the lesser figures of the *Carolingian Renaissance; b. Burgundy, or Aquitania, first half of 9th century; d. Stablo (Stavelot), lower Lorraine (now in Belgium) after 880. He was one of the few scholars of his day who had a practiced knowledge of Greek. His only substantial work known today, however, is a commentary on St. Matthew (*c.* 865). Although addressed to beginners, it is interesting because of its careful explanation of the grammatical Biblical sense and its attempts to illustrate the text by topical allusions. A study of the commentary illumines the 9th century's methods of compiling scriptural expositions and of monastic teaching. (*See* EXEGESIS, MEDIEVAL.) Christian set forth the historical or literal meaning, rather than the allegorical, because he held that history was the foundation of the understanding of Scripture. The explanations of difficult passages are indicative of Christian's excellence as a teacher, independent spirit, and deep knowledge of the Bible. Very little has been written about Christian, and a critical edition of his commentary is needed to take the place of Migne's (PL 106:1259–1520) inaccurate edition. J. Lebon has located some of Christian's MSS, which should help to make a critical edition easier to prepare.

Bibliography: J. LEBON, RHE 9 (1908) 491–496. M. L. W. LAISTNER, "A Ninth Century Commentator on the Gospel of Matthew," HarvThRev 20 (1927) 129–149. C. SPICQ, *Esquisse d'une histoire de l'exégese latine au moyen âge* (Paris 1944) 49–51. Manitius 1:431–433. E. DUMMLER, SBBerlin 2 (1890) 935–952. F. DRESSLER, LexThK[2] 2:1124.

[J. J. MAHONEY]

CHRISTIAN (THE TERM). The term Christian appears but three times in the NT. According to Acts 11.26, "it was in Antioch that the disciples were first called 'Christians.'" In Acts 26.28 King Agrippa interrupts St. Paul's discourse with the ironic remark: "In a short while thou wouldst persuade me to become a Christian." And St. Peter, in 1 Pt 4.16, exhorts that if "one suffer as a Christian, let him not be ashamed, but let him glorify God under this name."

The Greek word Χριστιανός is a composite of the Greek title Χριστός and the Hellenized Latin suffix *-ianus* meaning "belonging to." Because of its mixed origin, the probability of its creation by Antiochean pagans, and St. Peter's allusion to the contempt surrounding it, many scholars conclude that the epithet was originally one of opprobrium. Such a conclusion, however, seems unwarranted because: (1) Latin suffixes were current in Greek and added to Greek words without opprobrious intent, e.g., Ἡρῳδιανός (*Herodian) and Καισαριανός (Caesarean), and (2) St. Luke's emphasis in Acts 11.26 was on the growth of the disciples, who were naturally designated Christians, i.e., partisans of Christ. It was only later, under Greco-Roman persecution, that the name Christian became the object of pagan hatred, while loyal Christians gloried in the title, so descriptive of their total commitment to the service of Christ.

Bibliography: E. J. BICKERMAN, "The Name of Christians," HarvThRev 42 (1949) 109–124. C. SPICQ, "Ce que signifie le titre de chrétien," *Studia Theologica* 15 (1961) 68–78. G. RICCIOTTI, *The Acts of the Apostles,* tr. L. E. BYRNE (Milwaukee 1958) 179–180, 375. EncDictBibl 360–361.

[W. F. DICHARRY]

CHRISTIAN AND MISSIONARY ALLIANCE, both a Protestant sect in the evangelical tradition and a worldwide missionary society that grew out of the work of the Rev. A. B. Simpson. A native of Canada, he served as a Presbyterian minister for 18 years, leaving the pulpit of a New York City church in 1881 to embark on an independent evangelistic program aimed at reaching the masses. Simpson at first preached in tents and halls and on street corners. In 1887 he organized twin societies at a convention in Old Orchard, Maine. The Christian Alliance emphasized home missions, while the Evangelical Missionary Alliance concentrated on the foreign field. The two associations were combined in 1897 to form the present Christian and Missionary Alliance. The founder died in 1919.

In continuing its policy of pioneering in foreign missionary fields where others have not gone, the Alliance sponsors 900 missionaries overseas, in addition to 1,600 pastors, evangelists, and church workers in North America. Only six U.S. Protestant denominations sponsor larger foreign mission programs than this small sect. Alliance missionaries preach and teach in more than 180 languages and have established self-sustaining and self-governing national churches in all its mission fields. In 1963 the Alliance began work in two new fields, Brazil and Taiwan, bringing to 24 the total of its mission fields overseas. The other fields are India, Guinea, Ivory Coast, Mali-Upper Volta, Congo, Gabon, Vietnam, Cambodia, Laos, Thailand, Colombia, Ecuador, Peru, Chile, Argentina, Hong Kong, Israel, the Arab lands, Japan, the Philippines, Indonesia, and West Irian. In North America, the sect directs home missionary efforts among Mexicans, Eskimos, Indians, Negroes, Jews, Puerto Ricans, and mountain people.

The theology of Alliance churches is conservative, and based on a literal interpretation of the Bible. The sect practices the anointing with oil for bodily healing and proclaims that Christ's Second Coming may be imminent (*see* PAROUSIA). Local congregations or branches, of which there are 1,200 in the U.S. and Canada, are identified as Alliance churches or sometimes as Alliance Gospel Tabernacles. These congregations contribute more than $4 million a year for foreign missionary work. Acceptance of Christ as "Savior, Sanctifier, Healer, and Coming King" is the basis for membership in the Alliance groups, as well as the test for persons volunteering for missionary careers. Congregations are organized with a minimum of denominational control, but adhere to a general constitution. Headquarters are in New York City. The Christian and Missionary Alliance operates three Bible colleges in the U.S. and one in Canada to train home and foreign workers. By 1963, membership in Alliance churches in North America had grown to 70,000, with an additional estimated 50,000 persons attending Alliance churches but designated as adherents rather than members. In its mission areas membership in national Alliance churches reached 140,000.

[W. J. WHALEN]

CHRISTIAN BROTHERS

The Institute of the Brothers of the Christian Schools (FSC), whose members are usually known as Christian Brothers, is a congregation of lay male religious begun by (St.) John Baptist de *La Salle about 1680 in Rheims, France, principally but not exclusively for the Christian education of the sons of the poor and of the working class.

Origin, Spirit, and Government. John Baptist de La Salle, born of a well-to-do family in Rheims, was ordained April 9, 1678. His pious youth and ordination were in no way an omen of his later service in education; he was led to his lifework imperceptibly and through unwelcome decisions. Once convinced that God had called him to the work, he gave his fortune to the poor and in 1682 took up residence with a group of schoolmasters who had been gathered in Rheims by Adrien Nyel, an energetic but inconstant founder of schools. In that year the schoolmasters took the name of Brothers of the Christian Schools. In 1684 De La Salle established his first novitiate, took the vow of obedience along with 12 brothers, and donned the habit of the community.

The 30 years that followed saw his institute spread to all parts of France, despite many disappointments and setbacks. Although he suffered from misunderstanding and opposition, and even from disloyalty, he never lost courage; and by the time John Baptist resigned as superior in 1717, his work was on a firm footing. His experience with the problems of education of the poor had convinced him that only in a religious congregation would teachers develop the courage and constancy needed to persevere in so difficult a labor. By degrees he formed his first coworkers into a congregation for which he later wrote a rule. His institute received legal recognition from Louis XV Sept. 24, 1724, and papal recognition in a bull of approbation from Benedict XIII Jan. 26, 1725.

As religious, the brothers aim first at their personal sanctification. They take the usual vows of poverty, chastity, and obedience, but they add a vow to persevere in their vocation and another to teach gratuitously. This last vow reflects De La Salle's concern to relate the religious life to the work of Christian education of the young. According to his thinking, such work has to be entirely disinterested, so that not only do the brothers receive no income for their teaching, but they are forbidden to accept any gifts from the students or their parents. To maintain themselves in such selfless service, the brothers require strong motivation. De La Salle understood this and therefore made the spirit of faith the chief spirit of his institute. This means that the brother does not allow himself to be guided by human views, but by the light of faith derived from the truths revealed in Holy Scripture. Accordingly, children in the classroom are not judged by appearance, by emotional likes or dislikes, not even by ability, but as individuals to be formed in Christ. Teaching is thus raised to the supernatural level; it is done primarily for God. This spirit leads the brother to make no distinction between the work of his personal sanctification and his work of teaching.

The government of the institute has remained basically the same since its early development. It is ruled by a superior general who is chosen for life by a general chapter. This body, which meets every 10 years, is composed of delegates, some of whom are elected, while the others participate by right of office. The chapter also chooses the assistants of the superior general. These, 12 in number, hold office for 10 years and generally reflect the ethnic and geographical groupings of the institute's membership. The basic governmental unit is the community, composed ordinarily of the brothers working in a given institution. Each community is headed by a director appointed by the superior general. Communities are grouped in districts (provinces) ruled by visitors, also appointed by the superior general. The motherhouse, located at different times in France, Italy, and Belgium, has been in Rome since 1936.

Growth and Apostolate. John Baptist's contribution to education was providing teachers who were trained to staff the schools that others would establish and support. He was ready to open institutions of any sort that would contribute, directly or indirectly, to the education of boys. He established teacher-training institutions, the first of their kind, to prepare young men to teach in the country districts. To reach boys who could not attend classes on school days he opened

Sunday schools, and in order to make his schools more attractive, he introduced the teaching of a suitable trade along with religion. Since the days of De La Salle, the Christian Brothers have directed elementary and high schools, boarding schools, colleges, agricultural schools, technical and trade schools, commercial schools, reform and penal institutions, and houses of retreat.

In 1700 De La Salle sent two brothers to establish a school in Rome. Only one of them, Brother Gabriel Drolin, remained with the task until he succeeded in 1705. John Baptist wanted to have his work established in Rome in order that it might be observed by the Holy See and ultimately given papal approval. He also wished to found a school near the Pope as an expression of his loyalty at a time when Jansenism, with its antipapal aspects, was rampant in France. The congregation grew rapidly, though almost entirely in France. At the death of its founder (1719) it had 27 houses, 274 brothers, and 9,000 pupils. By 1790 there were 123 houses, 920 brothers, and 36,000 pupils. In that year the French Revolutionary government imposed the oath of the *Civil Constitution of the clergy. Since the brothers refused to take the oath, they were driven from their schools, and in 1792 the institute was suppressed. Twenty brothers were thrown into prison, three were put to death, and one of them, Brother Solomon (Nicolas LeClercq, d. 1792), has been recognized as a martyr and beatified. By 1798 only 20 brothers, all of them in Italy, were officially wearing their habits and exercising their teaching functions.

Pius VI, recognizing the difficulties under which the institute was laboring, appointed in 1795 Brother Frumence, then in Rome, to act as superior general. Under his rule restoration was begun, and when he died in 1810, the brothers numbered 160 and their pupils 8,400. A great revival came under his successor, Brother Gerbaud. At his death in 1822 the brothers had increased to 950 in 310 schools with 50,000 students. Numerically the institute in 1822 was greater than it had been when the French Revolution broke out. It had also resumed its spread to other countries, opening a school in Belgium in 1816 and another on Réunion Island in the Indian Ocean in 1817. From this latter year is generally dated the missionary activities of the Christian Brothers, who have since spread throughout the world.

The growth during the generalate of Brother Philippe Bransiet (1838–74) was very rapid, the brothers increasing from 2,317 to 10,664, or slightly over 450 per cent, and the pupils from 143,800 to 396,100. During the 1850s the congregation spread to 10 additional countries. Thereafter, while the increase in the number of brothers remained steady, the growth in the number of students lagged. Hostile education laws in France were the major cause. This was especially so of the laicization law of July 7, 1904, that abolished teaching by religious congregations and thus led to the closing of 1,282 of the brothers' schools in France by 1908.

Yet France's loss brought gain to the rest of the world. From 1900 to 1910 fourteen new countries were added to those in which brothers were already teaching, while between 1904 and 1908 about 222 houses were founded in Europe, the Near East, North and South America, Africa, and Australia. Not until the 1950s did a similar expansion take place. In that decade the Christian Brothers arrived in 15 more countries, a figure unsurpassed by any other decade in their history. In 1950 the number of brothers engaged in teaching was approximately 14,600; by 1960 the figure was 16,337. Corresponding figures for their students were 436,866 in 1950 and 648,427 in 1960. The total personnel, obtained by adding 7,839 novices and prenovices to the number of professed brothers, was 24,176.

Political changes have reduced the number of countries, colonies, and dependencies in which brothers teach from a former record number of 90 to 77 in 1964. Nevertheless, great advances have been made, chiefly in Spain, where vocations increased notably after the Civil War of 1936, and in the U.S. The statistics show also that in 1964 there were about 2,700 brothers actively engaged in foreign mission work. Of these, approximately half were natives of the countries in which they taught.

Development in the U.S. The first Christian Brothers to teach in the U.S. labored in the parochial school at Ste. Genevieve, Mo., from 1819 to 1822. They had been sent from France in response to a request from Pius VII to whom Bp. Louis *Dubourg of New Orleans had appealed when his own request to Brother Gerbaud, the superior general, was refused. The first permanent institution in the U.S. was Calvert Hall College, established in Baltimore, Md., in 1845. At that time famine in Ireland and unsettled conditions in Germany were sending Catholics to the U.S. in such large numbers that the hierarchy besieged the superior general with requests for teaching brothers. The result was a quarter century of expansion unparalleled in the history of the Christian Brothers in the U.S. It was also a period of able leaders, among them Brothers Facile Rabut, Justin McMahon, Patrick Murphy, and Paulian Fanning.

When Brother Facile was appointed visitor of North America in 1848, there were 5 communities and 56 brothers on the continent. By 1873, when his responsibility for North America terminated, 5 districts had been created, 76 communities had been opened, and 900 brothers were teaching in more than 100 schools. Leadership and sacrifice made the last quarter of the 19th century also one of solid growth. By contrast, the years from 1900 to 1925, although they saw few losses, saw few gains. However, when high school education became the common education in the U.S.,

First Christian Brothers' school in the U.S., at Ste. Genevieve, Mo. (1819–22).

First permanent Christian Brothers' foundation in the U.S. (1845), Calvert Hall College (later St. Joseph's Academy), Baltimore, Md. Inset: the Brothers' original residence, formerly used by Bp. John Carroll.

the brothers entered this field with vigor and imagination. New leaders emerged, so that the years after 1925 were years of impressive increase in brothers, schools, and pupils; by 1965 there were 7 districts, with nearly 3,100 brothers in some 158 communities, teaching more than 96,000 students. Among their institutions of higher education are: *Christian Brothers College, *La Salle College, *Manhattan College, *St. Mary's College (Winona, Minn.), *St. Mary's College (St. Mary's, Calif.), *St. Michael's College (Santa Fe, N.Mex.), and *Lewis College.

Bibliography: W. J. BATTERSBY, *History of the Institute of the Brothers of the Christian Schools in the Eighteenth Century, 1719–1798* (London 1960); . . . *in the Nineteenth Century, 1800–1900,* 2 v. (London 1961–63). A. GABRIEL, *The Christian Brothers in the United States, 1848–1948* (New York 1948). G. RIGAULT, *Histoire générale de l'Institute des Frères des écoles chrétiennes,* 9 v. (Paris 1937–53); EncCatt 5:1709–11. M. DEMPSEY, *John Baptist de La Salle: His Life and His Institute* (Milwaukee 1940). **Illustration credits:** St. Mary's College, Winona, Minn.

[J. R. LANE]

CHRISTIAN BROTHERS COLLEGE

A men's college and technological institute located in Memphis, it is owned and conducted by Brothers of the Christian Schools of the St. Louis province in the U.S. (*see* CHRISTIAN BROTHERS). It was the first Catholic college founded in the state of Tennessee.

Origin and Development. At the request of Patrick A. *Feehan, Bishop of Nashville, Brother Maurelian, FSC, opened a school for boys in Memphis on Nov. 21, 1871. The building had been a Presbyterian school, called the Memphis Female College. In 1872 the state legislature of Tennessee transferred the 1854 charter of Memphis Female College to Christian Brothers College with the power "to confer such degrees as are usually conferred by similar Institutions of Learning." The institution, popularly known as CBC, conducted elementary, secondary, and collegiate units until World War I when, in 1915, the college division was suspended. The elementary grades were gradually dropped, the last in 1923. From 1923 until 1940, CBC operated as a 4-year high school at its original location.

In 1940, buildings on a new site in Memphis were dedicated. In addition to the high school, a junior college was operated from 1940 to 1943 and from 1946 to 1954. In 1953 a complete 4-year college program was reinstated and the first bachelor's degrees were awarded in May 1955.

The Southern Association of Colleges and Secondary Schools accredited the College in 1958. On Oct. 25, 1956, The Catholic University of America granted affiliation to Christian Brothers College as a senior college. It received constituent membership in the National Catholic Educational Association in 1957. It also became a member of the American Council on Education and the National Education Association. It was approved by the Veterans Administration for training under the G.I. Bill of Rights.

The college is administered through a board of trustees composed of the bishop of Nashville and the religious faculty. An advisory board consists of laymen. Chief administrative positions are those of president, dean, director of the scholasticate, deans of men and of the evening division, and heads of the academic departments. In 1963 the College faculty and staff comprised 22 brothers, 5 priests, and 26 laymen. The staff held 14 doctorates and 29 master's degrees. The College is financed mainly by income from tuition and fees and the contributed services of the Christian Brothers. Citywide fund drives in 1939 and 1963 have aided CBC significantly.

Organization. The institution is divided into a 4-year liberal arts and technological institute, an evening division, and a scholasticate in which trainees for the brothers receive their education. Major fields are: accounting; the sciences; civil, electrical, chemical, industrial, and mechanical engineering; English; marketing; and mathematics. The 29 laboratories include: biology (2), chemistry (5), computer center (1), electrical engineering (8), language laboratory (1), mechanical engineering (5), physics (4), and research (3). The B.S. degree is granted in all academic majors with the exception of English in which the B.A. is given. The College has awarded honorary doctorates. Prelaw, predental, premedical, preveterinarian, and prepharmaceutical courses are offered. The College library in 1964 had 42,000 volumes and received 325 periodicals.

Plans for an expanded curriculum include teacher training, which involves broadening the liberal arts division. The removal of the high school to a separate site on the outskirts of Memphis in 1965 provided for greater expansion of facilities. A development program provides for the registration of 1,200 students on the 45-acre campus. In the period 1963–64 the College enrolled nearly 800 students from 23 states and 12 foreign countries. About half of these students were boarders,

250 of them on campus. Stritch Hall housed 57 scholastics. Thirty per cent of the students were non-Catholic.

Bibliography: G. J. FLANIGEN, ed., *Catholicity in Tennessee* (Nashville 1937) 164–166. A. GABRIEL, *The Christian Brothers in the United States, 1848–1948* (New York 1948) 439–443. Brothers of the Christian Schools, *Mississippi Vista: The Brothers of the Christian Schools in the Mid-West, 1849–1949,* ed. H. GERARD (Winona 1948) 198–212. History and Records, Christian Brothers College Archives, Memphis.

[I. L. O'DONNELL]

CHRISTIAN CHARITY, SISTERS OF

Although founded in Germany in 1849 for the care of needy children, the Sisters of Christian Charity (SCC) now engage in every type of apostolic work, with teaching as their chief activity. They follow the Rule of St. Augustine and their own constitutions. Pauline von *Mallinckrodt, the daughter of a German nobleman, founded the congregation to care for the blind and neglected children of Paderborn. Within 20 years the activity of the growing community had spread to include elementary and secondary education in 16 European institutions. When Bismarck's May Laws forced religious educators to close their schools in Germany, Mother Pauline was able to send her religious to North and South America, in response to requests for teaching sisters. On May 4, 1873, a group of eight arrived in the harbor of New Orleans, La. In the autumn of the following year, a group of 12 made their way across the Andes by mule into Chile in South America. Subsequently the sisters established numerous foundations in the U.S., Argentina, Uruguay, Holland, and Italy.

Almost half the total number of Sisters of Christian Charity work in the U.S. in two provinces. The western province with its motherhouse and junior teaching college in Wilmette, Ill., conducts an orphanage and 38 schools in 8 states: Arkansas, Illinois, Iowa, Louisiana, Michigan, Minnesota, Missouri, and Ohio. It has likewise undertaken classes for the blind, the deaf, and the mentally retarded, and manages summer reading clinics and vacation schools. The eastern province administers 2 large hospitals and 40 schools in 7 states: Connecticut, Florida, Maryland, North Carolina, New Jersey, New York, and Pennsylvania. Its motherhouse and Assumption College (for sisters) are located in Mendham, N.J. Catechetical work continues to be the community's special apostolate in the U.S. Both provinces have established scholasticates to further the education of junior members. A sister destined for teaching or nursing must acquire a college degree before beginning her work; those who prefer domestic work receive vocational training.

Mother Pauline von Mallinckrodt.

In South America the community engages in nursing and in teaching both the poor and aristocratic classes. The government of Chile has decorated Sister M. Nomitia Schuecker in recognition of her outstanding contribution to the educational progress of that country. The Chilean province suffered a major setback when the earthquake of 1960 either damaged or totally destroyed 18 of its 25 foundations. In Europe the congregation has continued to work with the blind and has established institutions for the care of children, older girls, the sick, and the aged. The management of domestic science schools is a distinctive work of the sisters in Germany. Along with the Church, the German province suffered its share of Nazi persecution, and the destruction caused by two world wars.

Christian charity provides the particular rule and spirit of the community, following the example of the foundress. By reason of the congregation's second title, Daughters of the Blessed Virgin Mary of the Immaculate Conception, conferred in 1859 by Pius IX, the sisters consider special devotion to the Mother of God an obligation. From Mother Pauline the sisters have inherited also a tradition of love of the Holy Eucharist. The community numbered some 2,600 religious in 1964, located in 150 establishments in 7 countries. The general motherhouse is in Rome.

[R. WESLEY]

CHRISTIAN CHURCHES (DISCIPLES OF CHRIST)

The Disciples of Christ, together with the *Churches of Christ that derive from them, form the largest religious body of purely American origin (1964, about 1,780,000 members; Churches of Christ, 2,250,000). They are also the recognized leaders in promoting a noncreedal form of Christianity. Although the term Christians, as members of the Churches of Christ are called, is sometimes applied also to the Disciples, the latter are really a distinct denomination and their official name is Christian Churches, International Convention.

History. The founder of the Disciples of Christ, Thomas *Campbell, discouraged by the opposition his efforts met in Ireland, came to the U.S. in 1807, beginning his ministry in Philadelphia as a Presbyterian. Within 2 years he was resisted by the presbyteries, especially after his famous *Declaration and Address,* issued "to all that love our Lord Jesus Christ in all sincerity, throughout all the churches." Its main tenet was that the Church of Christ upon earth should be one, "essentially, intentionally and constitutionally," and consists of "all those in every place that profess their faith in Christ and obedience to him in all things according to the Scriptures." The constitution of this Church of Christ, said Campbell, is not a creedal statement or confession of faith but the New Testament itself. Sectarian churches have no right to impose on their members as articles of faith anything not expressly taught in the Bible. Even inferences or deductions from the New Testament are not to be held binding on the conscience of individuals unless they are accepted by the persons themselves. Just as in apostolic times "a manifest attachment to our Lord Jesus Christ in faith, holiness, and charity was the original criterion of Christian character," so in the united Church envisioned by Campbell, this alone should be "the foundation and cement of Christian unity." Campbell was joined by his son Alexander, who came to America (1809) to share and later carry on the work of his father. They organized the Christian Association of Washington, Pa. (1810), the first local church of the new denomination. Soon after a crisis arose on the manner of administering baptism. Deciding that the ordinance must be by immersion, father and son had themselves rebaptized by a Baptist minister. For 17 years the Christian Association operated as a branch of the *Baptists, until the younger Campbell's anticreedalism aroused a storm of protest.

Meanwhile the Campbellites were partially merged with another noncreedal group, called the Christians, who were founded by Barton Stone, a former Presbyterian minister. They combined forces at Lexington, Ky., in 1832. When the question of a new name arose, Stone preferred keeping "Christians," but Campbell favored "Disciples," with the result that today both titles are used. The local organization, however, is generally called a Christian Church or a Church of Christ. As members and churches multiplied, the need of organization was recognized and the first national convention was held at Cincinnati in 1849. The body flourished at home and abroad; by the end of the 19th century, the Disciples counted more than a million members and had missionaries in Asia and Africa. They even weathered the Civil War without division. A conservative group, however, gradually withdrew because of a conviction that missionary societies and instrumental music in public worship were alike unscriptural. These separatists became known as the Churches of Christ.

Belief and Practices. Although the Disciples profess to be nonconfessional, in practice they emphasize certain areas of faith and ritual that may be taken as representative. They believe that the Bible is the word of God, written by different persons somehow under the inspiration of the Holy Spirit. Yet they tend to equate this revelation with other forms of divine communication, including poetic insight and the light of natural genius. Unlike the Churches of Christ, the Disciples admit that the Church Universal is essentially invisible and that the visible Church exists in distinctive religious groups, such as the *Methodists, Baptists, and their own denomination. According to one of their spokesmen, to become a member of the Church invisible, it is necessary to have only an inner experience; but to enter the visible church, e.g., the Presbyterian, it is further required to have an outward expression and a new social attachment. The inner experience is to hear and believe the Gospel and to repent of sin, whereas the new social alignment is to become a member of the visible organization. Baptism is administered by immersion to those who have reached sufficient maturity to profess their faith in Christ the Savior and repent of their sins. The Lord's Supper is regularly given to the faithful under both forms, which may be either leavened or unleavened bread and either wine or grape juice.

Disciples of Christ at Sunday morning communion service. After prayers at the table, the deacons distribute the communion elements to the congregation.

There are two principal types of religious service, Morning Worship with the Lord's Supper, and Evening Worship without Communion. Ministers are urged to avoid elaborate worship programs. Emphasis should always be placed on simplicity. A standard order for Morning Worship begins with a hymn by the choir, during which the minister comes to the platform and takes charge of the function. Following the first hymn is the doxology, an invocation, another hymn, Scripture reading, and the communion hymn, which introduces the ceremony of the Lord's Supper. After communion is the offertory, during which prayers of self-oblation are said and contributions are made; then a sermon, benediction invoked upon the congregation, and a concluding choral response. Ritual differs in different communities, but recent efforts suggest a greater stress on the liturgy and more uniformity in the orders of worship.

While ministerial associations have been organized for mutual help and supervision, they have no authority among the Disciples of Christ, who are strictly congregational in their form of government. Local churches elect their own elders and deacons, followed by a ceremony of ordination if the officers are chosen for a perment term, to be ended by death or resignation. Many congregations choose their ministers for a limited term only, and the list of officials may be so arranged that one-third is elected each year. Although congregational in structure, the Disciples are fully organized as a denomination and grouped on three levels above the local church, into district and state conventions, and an international convention which meets annually as a representative of all the churches. The conventions on any level have only advisory power over the member bodies. More direct supervision is exercised through a number of boards, like the Board of Church Extension, whose purpose is to assist the churches to plan and finance their building projects; the Board of Higher Education, with 36 affiliated institutions including Texas Christian (Fort Worth), Butler (Indianapolis, Ind.), and Drake (Des Moines, Iowa) Universities, concerned with the education of youth in an atmosphere of Christian influence and the training of clergy; and the Christian Board of Publications, which services the local churches with religious literature and publishes a variety of books and periodicals.

Among the best known Disciples' publications is the *Christian Century*, originally founded (1894) as a rival to the denomination-minded *Christian Evangelist*. Its editorial policy favors a liberal approach to Christianity with a minimum of doctrine and ritual. In their opposition to ecclesiastical division, the editors have been prime movers in the American *ecumenical movement. They seek to implement the ideal of Alexander Campbell for a return to the Gospels without the encumbrance of confessional creeds.

Bibliography: B. A. ABBOTT, *The Disciples: An Interpretation* (St. Louis 1924). J. M. FLANAGAN, ed., *What We Believe* (rev. ed. St. Louis 1960). A. W. FORTUNE, *Adventuring with Disciple Pioneers* (St. Louis 1942). W. E. GARRISON and A. T. DEGROOT, *The Disciples of Christ: A History* (rev. ed. St. Louis 1958). H. E. SHORT, *Doctrine and Thought of the Disciples of Christ* (St. Louis 1951). **Illustration credit:** International Convention of Christian Churches, Indianapolis.

[J. A. HARDON]

CHRISTIAN DEMOCRACY

The term Christian Democracy originated in Italy at the end of the 19th century. It has been given different meanings at different times and places. In current use it refers to a range of movements—especially as organized in political parties and trade unions—that, inspired by Christian principles, pursue political or social aims for the sake of all the people whose interests touch each movement's sphere of action, and so far as possible with the participation and consent of all these people. Its inspiration may be Catholic, Protestant, or both at once. Christian Democratic movements are distinct from movements with primarily religious aims, such as those of *Catholic Action. Many of their leaders are trained in movements with religious purposes, and Christian Democratic movements refer for their ideas, usually explicitly, not only to practical experience but also to the official teaching of the Christian churches. However, their own aims are secular, and they belong to the area of life for which laymen have full and direct responsibility, subject only to the general teaching authority of the Church. Christian Democratic movements are also distinct from those movements, even if made up of Christians, that aim in any exclusive sense to promote the interests of a class, race, or nation, or to establish authoritarian forms of government or management. There can be and are Christian Democratic trade unions or employers' organizations or movements for national independence, and Christian Democrats accept and in fact stress the need for strong hierarchies of command. But they insist that the enforcement of authority and the pursuit of sectional aims are justified only as elements in an order designed to promote the common good and to maximize participation and consent. Although in current use the term Christian Democracy is applied only to movements, this is merely a matter of custom and practice. The term could well be extended to include the action of individuals who are inspired personally by Christian and democratic ideas and act on them through movements, such as the political parties or trade unions of Britain or the U.S., that do not as such claim any specifically Christian character. Neither of these forms of action can be said to be more Christian than the other. To choose one or the other or to switch between them is a matter of practical convenience and not of principle.

Doctrine. In their day-to-day practice Christian Democratic movements feel their way empirically. But most of them have also a basic charter or declaration of principles. Charters vary in detail according to the country, the type of movement, and the date at which each is drawn up, but they have a number of common features.

(1) Christian Democracy is personalistic, but not individualistic. Its central test for policy is the full, free, and dynamic development of individual personality. But this development is possible only through the effective organization of *society and socialization of the individual. The *person must accept solidarity with society and responsibility for its *common good.

(2) Christian Democracy is pluralist. Society is vital to individual development but must not be allowed to overwhelm it. For the sake of efficiency and personal welfare alike, the greatest possible scope must be left for personal initiative and the use of each individual's abilities. Decisions should be made at the lowest level at which they can be made efficiently. Government and management should be decentralized or, better, federal. Christian Democrats recognize the need for a strong state and strong international institutions; they have taken a leading part in the movements for federal unity in Europe and Latin America. One of their aims in decentralization is to increase the force with which ministers and civil servants govern by relieving them of detail that distracts them. But they stress particularly the role of smaller self-governing groups intermediate between the state and the individual and more within the individual's reach: the family; the small farm or business; the plant with an effective trade union and works council; the cooperative society; the self-governing social security fund; and the local government of the town, district, or region. So far as individuals themselves can make decisions efficiently, Christian Democrats insist that they should be free to do so. There should be political *democracy, freedom of *association, free choice of career, and free consumer choice. Each person should be free to hold his own religious and political beliefs and to express them within the limits of public order, alone or in concert with others. (*See* SUBSIDIARITY.)

(3) Christian Democracy is conservative but not traditionalist. The Christian Democratic movements are not particularly attached to the past. Many of them, especially those in developing countries and in the labor movement, call for sweeping and radical reforms. But they are aware of the importance of time and continuity for big achievements, and their normal approach is evolutionary. This does not exclude revolutionary action in extreme cases where democratic processes are blocked.

To be fully effective, political and social movements need a strategic doctrine at a level intermediate between basic principles and day-to-day tactics. This is a body of assumptions about the nature of the society in which each movement is working, its probable evolution for a generation or two ahead, the problems likely to prove important in the long run, and the solutions that, in the circumstances of the particular society, are most likely to work. It is at this level that Christian Democratic doctrine tends to be weakest. This fact is often concealed in the early days when movements are growing in response to particular needs in environments that largely determine what each movement has to do. But old and powerful Christian Democratic movements that have grown out of their early problems and could themselves control their environments often give the impression of having lost their strategic sense of direction. Their basic principles, though clear, are too remote to constitute a program. They react to their environments, often with great tactical skill, but do not always grasp the nature and evolution of these environments firmly enough to be able to dominate and transform them.

History and Current Strength. The rise of the Christian Democratic movements is one aspect of the effort of the Christian churches to grasp and surmount the problems of modern industrial society, which is increasingly dynamic, secular, popular, and unified on a national and a world scale. This effort began in a situation in which the churches' power to influence social events had largely been lost. By the mid-18th century, as Msgr. Philip Hughes has remarked, the Catholic Church was "more isolated from European life than at any time in its history" [*Popular History of the Church* (London 1949) 202]. Accordingly, in a first phase, lasting until about 1880, the action taken was chiefly defensive. Continental European Catholics and, to a lesser extent, Protestants dug in to defend the churches' own essential freedom against attacks by nationalists and secularists—freedom for the churches to manage their own internal affairs; freedom to teach; to extend, to found new institutions, and to play a part in secular fields most directly related to their work, such as education and social welfare. Democracy was spreading at that time, and in several countries the foundation of Christian Democratic political parties proved to be a useful way to defend church interests. By 1880 Holland had separate Protestant and Catholic parties; Germany, a Center party, formally interdenominational but in fact almost entirely Catholic; and Belgium and Switzerland, Catholic parties.

From the 1880s to World War II the general trend in European politics and social life was toward greater popular (or, under fascism and communism, pseudopopular) control and greater concern with social as apart from purely political issues. Christian Democracy developed in the same direction. The existing Christian Democratic parties acquired, after an internal struggle, strong "social" wings, more or less formally linked to the Christian labor movement. New parties founded in Italy and France had a markedly popular character from the start. Both old and new parties proved effective in attracting votes from a wider cross section of all classes than did parties of any other kind. Although Christian Democracy was suppressed by Mussolini in Italy and by Hitler in Germany and in German-occupied Europe, it was revived when their regimes fell. By the 1950s Christian Democratic parties were holding or had held majorities or near majorities in the parliaments of Holland, Belgium, Luxembourg, Germany, Austria, and Italy and had received substantial votes in France, Switzerland, and Norway. Christian trade unions and cooperatives—Catholic, Protestant, or interdenominational—were founded from 1880 onward all over Europe apart from Scandinavia and the British Isles and came to make up a significant part of the whole European labor movement. By the 1950s they constituted a majority of the labor movement in Holland and Flanders.

A variety of movements—employers, professional workers, youth, women, and adult-education—also grew up, but most of these had primarily religious aims and belonged to the sphere of Catholic Action (and parallel Protestant movements) rather than of Christian Democracy. At first there was much confusion between the two spheres, but between the two world wars the secular character of Christian Democratic movements and their right to independence of clerical control came to be recognized nearly everywhere. Clerical control disappeared, although a varying amount of clerical influence remains. The specifically religious and still more the denominational element in Christian Democratic movements has greatly diminished. Programs, although inspired by the teaching of the churches, are and must be justified in the light of political and social experience that non-Christians, too, can appreciate, and movements are open to all who support Christian Democratic programs irrespective of their personal beliefs.

Promising beginnings of Christian Democracy were cut short in Spain by the regime of General Franco and in Eastern Europe by communism, although in both cases Christian Democracy remains alive underground or in exile. In the early 1950s Christian Democracy was still chiefly a European movement, with its axis of greatest strength along the line of the Rhine from the North Sea to south of the Alps; it was a force in Belgium, Holland, and Luxembourg, eastern and northern France, western and southern Germany, and Austria, Switzerland, and parts of northern Italy. Subsequently there was a dramatic growth of Christian Democracy in Latin America. By the early 1960s Christian Democratic labor movements included perhaps 15 to 20 per cent of the organized workers in Latin America. Christian Democratic parties, though nowhere in a majority, had become influential in several countries, notably Chile, Peru, Venezuela, Brazil, and Uruguay. In a number of Latin American countries, as in Europe, Christian Democracy was driven underground or into exile by dictators of the right or the left. There was also a smaller but significant development of Christian Democracy in Africa and some development in Southeast Asia, particularly Vietnam. This wider international spread led in the 1950s and early 1960s to efforts, more effective in the case of the labor movements than of the political parties, to strengthen the machinery for international contact between the Christian Democratic movements.

The Challenge. The most fundamental question for the Christian Democratic movements in the early 1960s was whether, where, and how long they could avoid giving way to Christian Democracy in the other possible sense, more familiar in the English-speaking world, of Christians playing their part as individuals personally inspired by Christianity, in movements that, as such, claim no special Christian character. This issue was actively discussed in several of the Christian Democratic movements themselves, notably those in Holland and France, and in the labor movements.

The justification for separate Christian Democratic political or social movements may be of three kinds. (1) The conflicts most important for political and social action may follow the division of religious and philosophical beliefs. They may relate directly to fundamental beliefs, as with issues over education, sex, or Church and State. It may also happen that views on political or social strategy—for instance, the special stress laid by Christian Democrats on intermediate groups such as the family—though having no necessary connection with particular religions or philosophies, could in fact by historical accident become identified with them in a particular time and place. (2) Communications between Christians and other groups may be blocked and can be

GIRAUDON

"God Addressing Noe (left) and the Ark upon the Flood," detail of frescoes, *c.* 1100, in the church at Saint-Savin-sur-Gartempe, France.

opened only by force. Christians may have to organize to force a dialogue with others in the same way that trade unionists organize, not as an alternative to collective bargaining or consultation but in order to bring it about. (3) Christians may be capable of promoting their beliefs effectively in political and social life only if they are organized as a mass under such few leaders as are available. They may be too lacking in education and social skill to act effectively as individuals.

These three conditions are more likely to be found in countries in the first bewildering upheaval of industrialization, democratization, and educational advance than in those with more skill and experience in handling the problems of a modern industrial society, and with a maturer view of them. It is in fact at the stage of first upheaval that Christian Democratic movements have chiefly originated both in Europe and in Latin America. But it does not necessarily follow that advanced countries that already have Christian Democratic movements should abandon them. A working political and social structure cannot be created or changed overnight. It represents a heavy investment of time and effort. Even if it is not the structure most ideally suited to current conditions, it may not be worth the effort to replace it.

See also POLITICAL PARTIES, CATHOLIC; SOCIAL MOVEMENTS, CATHOLIC; CHRISTIAN TRADE UNIONS.

Bibliography: M. P. FOGARTY, *Christian Democracy in Western Europe, 1820–1953* (Notre Dame, Ind. 1957), with a full bibliography. For recent developments see *Boletin Informativo Demócrata Cristiano* (formerly *Información Democrática Cristiana*) published by the Christian Democratic Union of Central Europe. The International Federation of Christian Trade Unions publishes a bulletin *Labor* (Brussels 1956–).

[M. P. FOGARTY]

CHRISTIAN DOCTRINE, SISTERS OF OUR LADY OF (RCD), a congregation begun in 1908 by Marion Gurney (Mother Marianne of Jesus) in New York, N.Y., to assist pastors in teaching religion to public school students and adults. Miss Gurney, a convert from Anglicanism, was a graduate of Wellesley College. A pioneer social service director, she was cofounder of a catechetical normal training school at St. Rose's Settlement in New York City, and secretary of the city's first *Confraternity of Christian Doctrine at Good Counsel Church in 1902. The work of the congregation began in 1910 when Abp. John Farley invited the sisters to assist the underprivileged by providing cultural, educational, and recreational benefits. On Cherry Street they opened Madonna House, a settlement, nursery, and kindergarten. Volunteer and paid workers helped the sisters maintain a wide program of social services. The work of the congregation has since expanded to the Dioceses of Charleston, S.C.; Manchester, N.H.; and St. Augustine, Fla., where the sisters are engaged as catechists; census takers; and directors of nurseries, kindergartens, camps, and recreation-welfare centers. Membership in 1964 comprised 70 professed religious.

[M. C. BERRETTI]

CHRISTIAN DOCTRINE (NANCY), SISTERS OF, a religious congregation with papal approval (1886, 1929), founded in France *c.* 1700. The sisters, who take simple perpetual vows, are known also as Vatelottes, after their founder, Abbé Jean Baptiste Vatelot, who, together with three of his own sisters, opened a school for girls in his family home at Bruley, near Toul. From this institution the congregation gradually developed in France. During the French Revolution the religious adopted secular dress in order to continue their work; they later reorganized and established their motherhouse at Nancy (1804). New foundations were made throughout eastern France, and in Belgium (1833), Luxembourg (1840), Algeria (1841), Italy (1903), and Morocco (1911). After World War II the sisters opened missions in the Belgian Congo. In the early 1960s the nearly 2,000 members were located in about 250 houses, organized in four provinces. Under the direction of the superior general at Nancy, they were engaged primarily in the education of girls and in various forms of hospital and nursing activities.

Bibliography: U. MILLIEZ, *Catholicisme* 3:945–946.

[A. J. ENNIS]

CHRISTIAN EDUCATION, PAPAL TEACHING ON

The popes of the Middle Ages and the Renaissance fostered education in many ways: by chartering universities, sponsoring artists and scientists, and approving religious orders dedicated to teaching. However, it was only with the establishment of seminaries by the Council of Trent that they became responsible for the details of the educational system.

Nationalism and Education. With the rise of national systems of education in the late 17th and 18th centuries the problem of the relations between State and Church control of education became pressing. Through concordats, the Holy See attempted to protect Church control over seminaries, and then over religious schools for the laity. This struggle came to a climax in the 19th century in France and resulted in encyclical letters of Pope Leo XIII in which he spoke out clearly on the respective rights of the family, State, and Church in education. Leo initiated a fresh conception of the papacy, emphasizing the pope's role as teacher, and hence his responsibility for the whole process of education.

The nationalistic and laic governments of the 19th century conceived education as a means of preparing citizens indoctrinated with nationalistic ideals, and consequently tended to make education a state monopoly. The totalitarian governments of the 20th century have gone even farther and used education as a revolutionary instrument by which the whole life of the child is subordinated to a *mystique.*

Papal Encyclicals. Against this totalitarianism, Pope Pius XI wrote the encyclicals *The Christian Education of Youth* (1929), opposing the policies of fascism in Italy, and *Mit brennender Sorge* (1937), against those of national socialism in Germany. The former of these has been cited by Pope Pius XII and John XXIII as the classical expression of the Catholic theology of education. Pius XII elaborated its views in numerous allocutions, but it remains at present the most authoritative expression of papal teaching on the subject.

Pius XI and Education. In discussing the encyclical *The Christian Education of Youth,* it is important to recall its historical setting, which influenced its contents in two ways that are not always noted by Catholic writers. (1) The encyclical stresses the prior right of the family and of the Church over education but does not treat extensively of the educational rights of the State. It would seem that this aspect of the question now deserves greater attention. Plato, Aristotle, and St. Thomas Aquinas, to mention three great classical writers on the subject, all stressed the point that the primary function of civil government is educational. This does not mean that the State itself directly must operate the educational system, but that it has a primary duty to foster educational institutions. (2) It emphasizes the education of the whole man, and in particular moral and religious education, in order to show that the State as such cannot adequately fulfill this role. It does not, therefore, elaborate on the strictly intellectual aspect of education, either as to content or as to method. Consequently, it has sometimes been used as an excuse for an anti-intellectualistic and moralistic approach to education.

Leo XIII and Christian Wisdom. The specifically intellectual aspect of education, however, has not been neglected by modern popes. Again, it was Leo XIII who gave special attention to this phase of education. He saw clearly that educational planning must rest on the concept of Christian wisdom, that is, on a broad theology and philosophy, not on a mere indoctrination in an ideology or on merely eclectic or pragmatic foundations. At the end of the 19th century it was very difficult indeed to point out this Christian wisdom, since at that time theology was at low ebb and philosophy had long since broken up into a bewildering variety of personal systems, all of which were succumbing to the onslaught of *scientism. The materialistic and empiricist systems were openly antireligious, and Leo saw clearly that idealism, although apparently more favorable to religion, was fundamentally incompatible with basic Christian teachings on the Incarnation, the resurrection of the body, and the teachings of Vatican Council I on the relations of faith and reason.

Leo therefore proposed a return to a genuinely Christian tradition, rooted in the Biblical view of reality, enriched by the Church Fathers, who had assimilated Greek and Roman culture to that view, and given method and order by the scholastics. In his encyclical *Aeterni Patris* (1879) he chose St. Thomas Aquinas as the most representative master of this Catholic tradition. In 1893, in the encyclical *Providentissimus Deus,* he reemphasized the Biblical basis of Christian culture and used the Thomistic epistemology to effect a reconciliation between the doctrine of Biblical inspiration and the modern historical approach.

Thomism and Education. Subsequent popes reinforced this approval of the work of St. Thomas Aquinas as a fundamental norm of Catholic education. Neither Leo XIII nor his successors, however, intended this approval to exclude other systems of theology or philosophy from playing a legitimate role in Catholic education, and they insisted that the Thomistic synthesis could not fulfill the role they had assigned to it unless it was treated as a growing and developing system open to contemporary science and culture. It was to provide a common heritage on the basis of which Catholic education might make rapid progress.

Unfortunately, in practice Thomism was not always used in this way, and some of St. Thomas's most important educational insights were neglected. Following World War II a reaction set in against the rigidity in Catholic education, which some attributed to the existence of an official theology and philosophy. This gave rise to a demand for greater pluralism, openness, and dialogue in Catholic schools. The practical solution of this difficult problem, however, must take into account the wisdom of Leo XIII and of the other modern popes who insist on the value and fundamental unity of a Christian educational tradition.

[B. M. ASHLEY]

CHRISTIAN EDUCATION, RELIGIOUS OF (RCE), a congregation of sisters following the Rule of St. Augustine. They were founded in 1817 by Louis François Martin Lafosse (1772–1839) to work for the restoration of the Catholic faith in Échauffour, Normandy, a small parish ruined during the French Revolution. The community began with four religious who dedicated themselves to Christian education, especially in primary and secondary schools. Success at Échauffour and extension of the mission to neighboring parishes necessitated revision of the original constitutions. Subsequent petition for establishment as a papal institute was granted by Rome in 1893, and final approval of the constitutions came in 1931. Civic approbation of the work of the congregation, an early instance of which was the invitation of the government to found a teacher's college in France in 1838, encouraged steady expansion, but the hostile policies of a later anticlerical government (1903) caused withdrawal to houses already established in England (1889) and Belgium (1902).

In 1905 the sisters began their mission in the U.S. In Asheville, N.C., the sisters maintain St. Genevieve-of-the-Pines Academy (1908) and staff grammar schools in Hendersonville and West Asheville, N.C. In Massachusetts, Marycliff in Winchester (1913), and Jeanne d'Arc in Milton (1930), private academies for girls, and two parochial schools, St. Peter in Waltham (1910), and St. James in Arlington (1949), are under their direction. The novitiate for the U.S. (1926) and Lafosse Teacher Training College (1951) are located in Milton, Mass. To its 25 houses in France, Morocco, England, Ireland, and the U.S., the congregation added in 1958 2 mission schools in Dahomey, West Africa. Total membership in 1964 was about 500.

[A. M. MCNAMARA]

CHRISTIAN ENDEAVOR SOCIETY, an international, interdenominational Protestant youth organization founded by Rev. Francis Clark of the Williston Congregational Church, Portland, Maine, "to make young people more useful in the service of God and more efficient in church work thereby establishing them in their faith and the practise of the gospel." Clark, desiring to provide an avenue of expression for the religious life of young people and to give them an opportunity to perform tasks for the church, organized a local youth society, which was quickly duplicated in many Protestant congregations across the nation and beyond. An international and interdenominational organization was formed in 1885 called the United Society of Christian Endeavor, with Clark as its first president. In 1927 the official name was changed to the International Society of Christian Endeavor. By the 1960s the organization embraced thousands of local societies, representing 80 denominations in 50 countries.

The basic principles of the society are confession of Christ, service for Christ, loyalty to the Church, and Christian fellowship. Any Protestant youth organization that accepts these and adopts the name Christian Endeavor is admitted to all the privileges of the international society. Individuals are received into local societies on the basis of their commitment to the Endeavorer's pledge: "Trusting in the Lord Jesus Christ for strength, I promise Him I will strive to do whatever He would have me do." The local societies administer courses in religious training and leadership, provide for devotional meetings and social activities, and organize welfare and other Christian causes for their members. The international society holds conventions and conferences for youths of various denominations and nationalities, unites cooperating societies in interchurch programs, and joins with its constituent churches and other religious agencies in common enterprises for the Christian cause and human welfare. Headquarters for the international society (which had about 4 million members in 1964) was located in Boston, Mass., until 1946 when it moved to Columbus, Ohio.

[T. HORGAN]

CHRISTIAN FAMILY MOVEMENT, a specialized apostolic organization. Its basic unit is made up of five or six married couples, usually from the same parish. The couples meet in their homes and follow a program of discussion and action to educate and activate themselves as family units of the *lay apostolate. Their *social action is concerned with the communities of the layman's responsibility: family life, cultural life, political, economic, and international life. The couples act individually or with fellow members to affect some situation locally, nationally, or even internationally. The CFM groups are concerned not only with the betterment of their own family situations but also with the life of families everywhere. The origins of CFM were in a men's Catholic Action group started in Chicago in 1943 and transformed into a couples' organization in 1947. Two years later a national coordinating committee was formed for the exchange of ideas and experiences. Since then groups have been established in most of the dioceses of the U.S. and in Canada. Similar groups, often using the same program, have been developed in Latin America, Australia, New Zealand, the Philippines, Africa, and elsewhere. By 1963 there were more than 40,000 couples actively participating in the U.S. and Canada, and probably an equal number in similar groups in other countries. Group meetings prepared by one couple and the chaplain are usually held every 2 weeks. Each includes discussion of a Scriptural passage and a liturgical topic, and a longer social inquiry following the plan of "see, judge, and act" developed by the Young Christian Workers and commended by John XXIII in *Mater et Magistra.* The members of the group observe some particular phase of the life around them, discuss and judge whether it is fully human and Christian, and agree to take some simple action that will bring the situation into closer accord with Christian and human values. Each member is encouraged to articulate his thoughts in meetings, and the whole group profits from the collective experience. Each member is also supported morally and actually in actions that he could not or would not do alone. Annual programs and various publications, including the monthly bulletin *Act,* are prepared by the coordinating committee and issued from national headquarters in Chicago.

[P. AND P. CROWLEY]

CHRISTIAN LAW

According to the NT, God created man in and for Christ (Eph 1.3–14; Col 1.15–17), to take him up into His Trinitarian life (cf. Jn 17.20–24). With his nature, man received (Gn 2.17) his basic structure, norm of activity (ontological *natural law: Rom 2.14–15). Regenerated into a new creature (Gal 6.15; 2 Cor 5.17), he concretely tends to the beatific vision according to a new norm (ontological supernatural law) that incorporates the natural law. As a redeemed sinner, his march toward the end should be a "paschal ascent" following the Savior through the Cross to the Resurrection (Mt 16.24; Col 2.6; Heb 10.19–25). In anticipation of the incarnate "Way," Christ (Jn 14.6), God enlightened man's darkened conscience by a positive (Mosaic) law or economy, the revealed embodiment of a Divine "Way" (cf. Ps 118, 119). *See* LAW, MOSAIC. Not containing the *Word, it could not justify by its own works (Gal 2.16; Rom 3.28) or supply inner strength (Gal 3.21; Rom 7.16–24). Observed without *faith, it turned into a "letter" that kills (2 Cor 3.6–11; 1 Cor 15.56), into a prosecutor unveiling man's sinfulness (ἁμαρτία: Rom 3.20; 7.7) and thus became instrumental to transgression (παράβασις: Rom 4.15; Gal 3.19).

Christ, Man's Living Law. Christ both completes and terminates the economy of the law (Mt 5.17; Rom 10.4; Gal 3.25), for He is the Incarnate "Way" to all truth (Jn 14.6). From within (Jn 14.15–24; Rom 8.9–11; Gal 2.20; 1 Jn 5.11–13), Christ through His Spirit moves His members and guides them. By Himself and through His Spirit (Rom 8.2–4), *He is their living law* (St. Thomas, *In 8 Rom*), supplying the strength to observe it (Gal 5.16–25). Borne up by love (Rom 5.5; 1 Jn 5.3), the Christian as such does not feel compelled by exterior laws (Jas 1.25); he may not, indeed, transgress these, for he observes them eminently with the liberty and generosity of God's children (Gal 4.5–7; Rom 8.14–17). Qua Christian, man does not sin (Gal 5.16; 1 Jn 3.6, 9; 5.18); even, beyond strict obligation, he is invited to acts of supererogation (e.g., the counsels, cf. 1 Cor 7.7, 25–38); he is to tend to perfection (Mt 5.48; 19.21). In case he draws back from love, he is still compelled by the external law, which protects him from falling below a vital minimum of love (cf. 1 Tm 1.9; Gal 5.16–23). Jesus has been a "doctor" and lawgiver (cf. Mt 5–7; 11.29–30; 23.10); He has given His new commandments (Jn 15.12–17; 1 Jn 3.22). After Him, the Apostles too give precepts in their epistles. Christ's law (Gal 6.2; 1 Cor 9.21), however, constitutes man's very liberty in action, because it frees man from the slavery of any other (Gal 5.1, 13, 18; Rom 6.14).

Law of Charity. Basically the Christian law is the law of love (Mt 7.12; Mk 12.28–34; Rm 13.8–10; Gal 5.13–14; 1 Jn 4). Indeed, it canalizes man's tendency to the End loved as a good (ST 1a2ae, 1.3–8), and its driving force and its revealer—God in Christ—is love (1 Jn 4.8, 16). A real love proves and expresses itself in deeds (cf. Jn 14.15; 1 Jn 5.3): the acts of all the virtues, chiefly of fraternal charity (1 Jn 4.12, 20–21), mediate and determine specifically the basic tendency of love-charity in the various fields of moral activity (moral objects) and in the different active powers (subjective aspect, cf. ST 2a2ae, 23.8: *caritas . . . forma virtutum*). As for its content, the Christian law "fulfills" and elevates the structures—and the commandments—of the natural law, giving them their concrete, supernatural finality. It sets aside the precepts that are specifically Jewish (cf. Gal 2.14–21; 4.10–11; 6.12), creates a new hierarchy of moral values (Matthew 5), and adds the structures—and commandments—of the "new creation" (Trinitarian, sacramental, ecclesial). It leads directly to the following of Christ (Mt 16.24; 1 Cor 11.1). It is perceived by the reason elevated by faith and is lived in the Christian community (Acts 2.42–47; 4.32–35). In the Christian dispensation, explicit laws (canonical, civil, international) remain necessary; but their "letter" receives its meaning, inspiration, and obligation from the (individual and social) Christian dynamism proper to the members of Christ and springing from Christ Himself.

With the complete, divinized man for immediate criterion and with the God-Man for ultimate criterion, it judges of the morality of human laws according to absolute truth: above Caesar stands God and the Wisdom of His Word (cf. Prv 8.15).

See also AUTHORITY, ECCLESIASTICAL; CANON LAW; COMMANDMENTS, TEN; DISCIPLINE, ECCLESIASTICAL; FREEDOM, SPIRITUAL; HIERARCHY; JURISDICTION, POWER OF; KINGDOM OF CHRIST; KINGDOM OF GOD; LAW, DIVINE POSITIVE; OFFICE, ECCLESIASTICAL; SOCIETY (IN THEOLOGY).

Bibliography: P. BLÄSER, LexThK[2] 4:825–826. G. GILLEMAN, *The Primacy of Charity in Moral Theology,* tr. W. F. RYAN and A. VACHON (Westminster, Md. 1959) 253–279 and *passim.* E. HAMEL, "Loi naturelle et loi du Christ," *Sciences Ecclésiastiques* 10 (1958) 49–76. B. HÄRING, *The Law of Christ,* tr. E. G. KAISER, 3 v. (Westminster, Md. 1961) 1:227–285. S. LYONNET, "Liberté du Chrétien et loi de l'Esprit selon S. Paul," *Christus* (1954) 6–27; *Les Épîtres de saint Paul aux Galates, aux Romains* (BJ 38; 1953), annotations.

[G. A. GILLEMAN]

CHRISTIAN MOTHERS, ARCHCONFRATERNITY OF, originated in various parts of France, especially in Lille, when mothers began to gather to pray with and for one another and for their children, to discuss their problems, and to advise one another regarding the Christian rearing of their children. The movement gradually solidified, and on May 1, 1850, the first conference of Christian Mothers was held in Lille, under the leadership of Louise Josson de Bilhem, a court official. After the mothers received episcopal recognition for their growing organization, the society grew rapidly throughout France and neighboring countries. By 1963 there were six archconfraternities: Notre Dame de Sion Chapel, Paris (1850); San Agostino, Rome (1863); Church of St. Giles, Regensburg (1871); Church of St. Augustine, Pittsburgh, Pa. (1881); Church of St. Barbara, Cracow (1913); Abbatial Church of the Order of St. Benedict, Einsiedeln, Switzerland (1944).

The society was introduced into the U.S. by the Capuchin Friars and on Jan. 16, 1881, the Confraternity of Christian Mothers of St. Augustine Church, Pittsburgh, Pa., was raised to the rank of an archconfraternity with the right of affiliating other confraternities wherever the ordinary approved. Since 1881 over 2,900 confraternities have been affiliated with the Pittsburgh archconfraternity. The object of the confraternity is the home education and character formation of children by truly Christian mothers. It plans to unite by the observance of its rules and regulations all Christian women, married or widowed, with or without children, who are willing to assist each other to attain this purpose.

Bibliography: E. QUINN, *Archconfraternities, Archsodalities and Primary Unions with a Supplement on the Archconfraternity of Christian Mothers* (CUA CLS 421; Washington 1962).

[C. BULGER]

CHRISTIAN PHILOSOPHY

St. *Augustine was the first, it seems, to have employed the expression Christian philosophy to designate the teaching proposed to men by the Church and to distinguish it from the different wisdoms taught by the philosophers of antiquity. Before him, however, the term philosophy had been used by a number of Christian writers, ever since *Tatian, as a means of establishing contact with the speculative and practical thought that was widespread in the cultivated world in which the newborn Christianity developed. During the Middle Ages, the relationship between faith and reason was made more precise, to the extent that natural intelligence began to be seen by theologians as autonomous in the domain assigned to it by God. In modern times, philosophy claimed a growing independence, aiming at forming a body of doctrine as free from nonrational influences as possible and thus, in effect, opposing itself to the teaching of revelation. The relations between philosophy and Christianity have thus undergone changes in the course of time. It is, though, only since the 1930s that the notion of Christian philosophy has become an object of explicit discussion, albeit a discussion whose import has continually changed in keeping with the evolution of thought both inside and outside the Church. To comprehend the significance of the problem posed by the notion of Christian philosophy, it is thus important not to separate the theoretical point of view of past considerations from those that enter into the current debate. To do so is to risk either repeating general definitions, admitted by everyone, or giving only a concrete description of opposing positions in the 1960s. The exposition that follows reconsiders the essential definitions that explain a priori the difficulties contained in the idea of a Christian philosophy and makes as precise as possible the meaning of the current debate; it then proposes a clarification, in brief résumé, of the sense of the history of philosophy that is present within Christian revelation and a concluding summary of the significance of Christian philosophy in present and future thought.

Difficulties in the Notion. A complex concept expressed by the union of a substantive and an adjective is definable only if both terms have a precise and relatively fixed signification. If, on the contrary, one or other of the terms conveys different (and nonequivocal) meanings, certain problems necessarily pose themselves by reason of the variable relationships that ensue between the two terms and thereby affect the subject of the expression taken as a whole. Thus it is profitable to examine here each of the terms that compose the expression Christian philosophy and the problems that pose themselves a priori with respect to its subject.

Philosophy. By this word one may mean (1) any doctrine that proposes a *wisdom destined to conduct men toward their end by making known the origin and destination of all things, whether that wisdom be acquired naturally or revealed by God. Again, one may mean, more precisely, (2) an ensemble of truths discoverable by the human mind left to its own devices, without, however, excluding the influence of nonrational data. It is generally admitted that Greek philosophy, even when it ended in an encounter with Christianity—to which, in the persons of its last representatives, it opposed itself—had this conception of philosophical wisdom. Finally, one may mean, in a yet stricter sense, (3) a body of doctrine that possesses the coherence and certitude proper to the sciences, as these are understood in the modern sense. Philosophy, in such an understanding, would proceed from a simple and absolutely certain point of departure to draw out the entire sequence of its propositions in a necessary order. This conception has reigned since René *Descartes and dominates modern thought under the various forms of *rationalism and *positivism. The ideal of philosophy as a rigorous science adequately defines this conception of philosophical knowledge.

The Adjective Christian. Apart from the preceding distinctions concerning the substantive, there should be noted a diversity of meaning concerning the adjective Christian. This results from the manner in which the Catholic Church, on the one hand, and the disciples of Martin *Luther, on the other, conceive the relationship between nature and grace, granting the reality of sin and of its corruptive effects. On the one hand are the efforts at synthesis that Catholicism continually promotes by reason of its teaching concerning man's intelligence—an intelligence, it holds, that original sin was unable to alter substantially and that grace sustains and restores according to need. On the other is a tendency in Lutheran thought to divorce reason from grace, which is hostile to all that might resemble, proximately or remotely, an intrusion of nature into the order of salvation by faith.

The Problem. These reflections, summary though they be, allow one to eliminate at the outset two extreme positions, both negative, concerning the notion of Christian philosophy. The first, founded on the notion of philosophy in sense (3), rejects a priori—as contradictory to the true notion of philosophy—any influence that might be considered as properly Christian. The second, founded on the notion of Christian that implies a radical corruption of human nature by sin, rejects every pretension of natural intelligence, left to itself, to collaborate usefully in the discovery of the truth concerning God and the relationship of man with God. The Word of God alone, received in its purity and nudity, is the source of truth and of salvation.

One can pass rapidly over the notion of Christian philosophy founded on the concept of philosophy in sense (1). This offers no difficulty, since it signifies simply that the gospel, which contains the life and teaching of Jesus Christ, brings to man the only true doctrine of salvation and thus the only true wisdom, the only true philosophy, understood in a very broad sense.

There remain, then, philosophy in sense (2) and the concept of a relationship between the order of nature and grace that in no way rejects a priori—as threatening the purity of the gospel message—the notion that by his natural intelligence man can discover useful truths concerning both God, as Creator and End of the universe, and the natural foundations of human life, individual and collective, that grace elevates but does not destroy. Here the problem of Christian philosophy poses itself theoretically in the following manner. If one admits that there can exist a relationship between philosophy, as a work of human intelligence, and supernatural revelation, how is one to conceive any influence of revelation on philosophy without philosophy itself being transformed either (a) into a theology in the classical sense of the word, or (b) into a hybrid discipline composed of philosophy and data borrowed from faith (and tacitly guaranteed thereby), or (c) into a partial or total secularization, through transposition into abstract or scientific terms, of the concrete and historical account of the work of salvation accomplished by and in Jesus Christ? Does there even exist a choice among these three possibilities? Is it not necessary to exclude a priori any intermediary between theology properly so-called and speculations that simply subsume, in another mode, Christian data in their totality, as did G. W. F. *Hegel, or in their parts, as *existentialism and *personalism are accused of doing? Is a positive influence of revelation, faith aside, a *Christian* influence? If the answer is no, can one speak of "Christian influence" as anything more than that of the general climate of Western civilization? If the answer is yes, then what sort of symbiosis can be established between two modes of knowledge and of relationship to God that differ as much as do faith in the revealed word and a search for truth merely in function of natural evidence and certitude? The assent of supernatural faith and natural assent doubtless can coexist in one and the same mind, but one may identify them formally only by admitting a contradiction. If, therefore, one qualifies a philosophy as "Christian," even understood in sense (2), one must show that the epithet effectively qualifies the substantive without corrupting the essence of it.

Origins of the Current Debate. The simplest and most exact solution consists in saying that revelation exercises a control over philosophy that is negative and extrinsic, namely, by notifying a philosophy that may have come to a conclusion manifestly contrary to faith of its error. There then remains for philosophy the task of redoing its demonstrations and discovering the error. This solution implicitly presupposes the complete autonomy of the order of philosophical research and its extrinsic regulation by faith.

Gilson. Now, it is this solution that is questioned, indirectly, by the historical studies of É. Gilson concerned with Christian philosophy (*see* THOMISM, 3). Beginning with an examination of Cartesian thought, Gilson soon perceived that Descartes, far from constituting an absolute point of departure, could be understood only in continuity with medieval thought; for it was from this thought that he had inherited his vocabulary and a great number of his essential notions and major theses, notably in natural theology. Gilson's study of medieval thought went on to show, furthermore, that the latter was not simply a repetition of Greek thought, particularly that of Aristotle, but offered an original treatment of most of the main theses of *metaphysics, natural *theology, and *psychology. These novelties could be understood only in terms of the unquestionable influence that revelation exercised over the work of great theologians such as St. *Bonaventure and St. *Thomas Aquinas. A purely extrinsic regulation would not suffice to account for the facts such as they present themselves to the historian of Christian thought.

What Gilson wished to call to the attention of historians was the necessity of revising their concepts relative to the great periods in the history of Western philosophy. Instead of gaps between antiquity, the Middle Ages, the Renaissance, and modern times, he held for a real continuity that was disguised by arbitrary and false classifications. At the same time, he found himself placing in evidence the positive and intrinsic influence of Christian revelation, and this not only on the theologians of the Middle Ages but, through them, on the whole Western philosophical tradition. The latter differed profoundly from Greek thought, he argued, only because of transformations in the major themes of philosophy attributable to Christian influences during the centuries of medieval speculation.

This position could not but provoke a theoretical discussion concerning the notion of Christian philosophy, its a priori possibility, and whether or not it implied some type of contradiction. Those holding to the scholastic tradition, and notably those defending the doctrine of Aquinas, saw no intermediary possible between a pure philosophy and theology. They conceived philosophy as concerned with a completely independent order—as had been postulated by Descartes and those who followed him—with its own point of departure that would permit the construction of a coherent system, free from doubt as well as from nonrational or religious inspiration. They received the support of E. Bréhier (1876–1952), who, for reasons other than theirs but with the same concern for safeguarding the rational purity of philosophy, rejected the idea of a Christian philosophy as contradictory.

Maritain. J. Maritain, while maintaining the essential possibility of a pure philosophy, first proposed to distinguish this from philosophy's historical states. Later he came to formulate his thesis of a moral philosophy adequately understood, which he felt could be only Christian since it must be based on knowledge of the last end of man, an end that concretely is supernatural. (*See* THOMISM, 2.)

Blondel. The debate over Christian philosophy could not fail also to recall the passionate polemics that were incited after 1893 by the theses of M. *Blondel on action and on the relationship of philosophy to revelation. Also, Blondel intervened in the debate to reproach Gilson for perpetuating the equivocation against which Blondel had energetically fought in all his works. Blondel had been concerned over the impossibility of philosophy's understanding itself without discovering in its heart, in its own insufficiency, an appeal to a supernatural support. For him, philosophy is not simply controlled from without by revelation, nor is it simply to be utilized on occasion by the theologian as an instrument. It must vigorously seek, on its own ground, to do what it can for humanity, while recognizing that it must ultimately ask help from another order whose necessity it points out while admitting its gratuitous character. To let it be believed that philosophy can be sufficient of itself is to hold that the order of grace has no point of attachment in the human spirit, that nothing calls it or prepares for it, that the supernatural is introduced into nature as a foreign body into a living organism.

On the eve of World War II the situation was therefore as follows: first there were the majority of scholastic theologians, who defended a radical separation of philosophy and revelation and a conception of philosophy somewhat similar, if not identical, with that of the current rationalism; then there was Gilson, who no longer confined himself merely to the role of a historian; and finally there were Blondel and his sympathizers, for whom philosophy erred totally with respect to its true nature when it thought itself capable of closing in upon itself and of giving meaning to human life without reference to the supernatural order.

Later Factors. Since World War II the positions have been profoundly modified both by philosophers and by theologians, and the situation is still in flux.

Contemporary Philosophy. Under various influences, too many to describe in detail, a goodly number of philosophers have come to believe that the point of departure proposed by Descartes for philosophy, which has been taken up again and again by "system builders," is too utopian. When philosophers reflect sufficiently on the real conditions of philosophy, they find that it cannot begin with a pure subject (e.g., the *Cogito,* or a transcendental subject, of whatever nature this might be) or with a pure given, as does mathematics. Man's thought begins, and can only begin, with an initial situation that implies the presence and openness of his being, at all its levels, to a world that makes sense from the beginning, a sense that he never ceases to interrogate in order to discover its deepest meaning. Whether one speaks of "being in the world," or of the relationships of *Dasein* and *Sein,* or of "encompassing," or of contemporary interpersonal philosophies, this is always implied: it becomes actually impossible to dissociate this initial (and ultimate) datum from the human condition. To do so, one would have either to trace the subject back to a point of absolute zero, from which it is impossible to see how anything could come except by a kind of sleight of hand (as from the "nothingness" of J. P. Sartre); or else to posit an "in-itself," a datum as simple and inert as a point that remains eternally what it is when nothing is added from without; or else, finally, to trace man's being back to the divine condition of transcendental unity wherein the dignity of absolute subject and absolute object coincide.

The themes of philosophical faith, of objective participation, of something prior to predication such as myth, occupy a greater and greater place in contemporary philosophical literature. This is to say that, having abandoned the dream of being God, philosophers are turning more and more toward elucidating the real condition of the philosophical enterprise possible to man, such as it is seen to be when the illusions and mirages with which imagination and language continually cover it are dissipated. This work is a search for truth wherein the philosopher is led to reflect anew, on his own grounds, on a great number of metaphysical and anthropological problems to which revelation has also given answers that have transformed the perspectives of Western philosophy.

Contemporary Theology. Christian thought, on the other hand, has experienced a profound renewal through a return to its sources: Scripture, tradition (envisaged in all its amplitude and riches), and liturgy; and the development of Latin, Greek, and Oriental patristic thought, through the Middle Ages, to modern times. It is thus no longer possible to oppose the thought of Gilson or Blondel with the simple conception that appeared in the 1930s as the only possible view of philosophy and of its role in the immense effort pursued through almost 2 millenniums by Christians concerned with stating or defending the content of faith.

Historical Perspectives. The first result of all this research has been to make better understood the import of the debate begun in the 1930s. This debate actually was concerned only with an aspect of the effort that the Church has made since its beginnings and that it must pursue until the end of time, to present to men of different epochs, of different levels and types of culture, the message addressed to humanity by God in Jesus Christ. Since this message is the Word of God revealing supernatural mysteries, it is impossible that it not exercise a positive influence of transformation and elevation, both directly, on the conceptions and even the languages that are used to express it in a mode proper to each culture and epoch, and indirectly, on everything within a given mentality, individual or collective, that gravitates around revealed data as a center. There is thus room for theology, in the precise and classic sense of the word, which is the work pursued through the centuries to express more and more precisely (against heresies or possible false interpretations) and systematically (i.e., organized in the light of wisdom) the mysteries of salvation; and, apart from this, for other effects of the Church's effort, which are seen in the transformation and the progress achieved in solving the great philosophical problems that humanity posed for itself independently of Christianity. It is these latter effects that are principally discussed in the debate over Christian philosophy.

Leaving aside, even though they are important, the problems that have been raised concerning the passage of the revealed message from the Hebrew language and mentality to Greek and Latin cultures, the following historical survey treats the relation of that message to philosophy.

Attitude of Faith. The first attitude to be noted—after an early period of reserve, if not hostility, the echo of which is found periodically throughout the centuries—is that which utilizes philosophy as a discipline interior to faith with the intention of understanding, defining, or defending the content of faith. The philosophy first so utilized was *Platonism or, more precisely, *Neoplatonism in its various forms. By reducing all things to a transcendent principle and a universe of intelligible Forms, Platonism seemed to lend itself most naturally to the service expected of it, though not without making the faith run serious dangers or without undergoing, on its part, profound transformations. Philosophy interior to faith, during the first 10 centuries, may be characterized by its pastoral and monastic, i.e., basically religious, intention. It remained interior to a movement that proceeds from God's initial revelation to men back toward God, to whom the spirit of man returns guided by the Word Itself, but assimilated and, as it were, acclimated to the epoch and to the individuals at different levels of culture within it.

Scholarly Attitude. Despite the profound differences that separate the apologists, the Greek and Latin Fathers, St. Augustine, and St. Anselm, the ensemble constitute a period that is clearly distinct from *scholasticism, although not by the central attitude, which remained turned toward the comprehension and assimilation of Christian doctrine. In the earlier period, this assimilation was effected in a new style that was no longer immediately pastoral and contemplative, but scholarly and scientific, under the form of a dispute with an interlocutor, real or supposed, who was regarded as defending a contrary thesis. In the high scholastic period, especially through the influence of *Albert the Great and Thomas Aquinas, the philosophy of Aristotle came to replace that of Plato in theological teaching and to hold this position for a long time. Certainly, from the 13th century onward there begins to emerge, particularly with the masters of the faculties of arts, a purely philosophical thought—of which Latin *Averroism is the best-known representative, even though it has been necessary to reevaluate this movement in the light of recent studies. Besides, theologians themselves contributed as much as (or more than) members of the faculties of arts to transform and advance the great themes of philosophy, notably the metaphysics of being, natural theology, psychology, and moral science.

Rationalist Attitude. It is nonetheless beginning with Descartes that a conception of philosophy appears that views itself as built on its own foundations, as purely rational, and as proceeding along lines similar to those followed by mathematics. This it attempts through the construction of a system that relies on a natural certitude as solid as the *Cogito,* a system of which the philosopher is the architect without being personally involved therein. That such an enterprise, carried on by different means, was not in fact able to break the bonds that attached it to the overall structure of the culture fashioned by Christianity is easy to show. It was, nonetheless, an effort to form a philosophical thought detached from all nonrational influences.

Changing Attitude. The rationalist conception, popularized by C. *Wolff in university circles, came to be adopted by a number of scholastics beginning in the 19th century. Against this view rose philosophers who pointed out in various and somewhat opposed ways the fictitious character of a philosopher who is at once constructor and spectator. Such thinkers were led to place in evidence the true condition of man's confrontation with philosophical truth and to make philosophy resume the path toward an ultimate end that it followed, at least since Plato, until the dawn of the modern period. The relationship of such philosophers to Christianity has shown itself to be markedly different, i.e., either more positive or more brutally negative, than that of rationalism and its various developments.

Christian Attitude. From the end of the 19th century, nevertheless, Blondel undertook to construct a philosophy that would be Christian, not only indirectly through the effects, immediate or remote, of its use in theology, but directly and positively, as has been noted above. Developing Blondel's ideas further, M. Nédoncelle comes to this conclusion: "The fact that philosophy is not a matter of personal summons, and that it is always more or less detached from events and from the subject considered simply as such, shows that it cannot substitute for religion. Despite the elements which it has in common with religion, it has its own formally distinct object. For this reason alone, its language and that of Christian faith are not univocal. But since it can partially assimilate a supernatural message in a system of ideas, and since its autonomy is in no way diminished by grace, it is not obliged to fade away in face of Christianity as though its affirmations became erroneous in the presence of the divine Word or had no possible connection with revelation. Its duty is not to efface itself but to enter into this new order by its own free choice: and on this showing an intrinsically Christian metaphysic is possible, despite what so many believers and unbelievers maintain by a sort of tacit agreement which is too easy an escape from the problem for both parties" (151).

Concluding Summary. The expression Christian philosophy is thus applied in different contexts. There is, first, the fact of revelation's influence on philosophy—an undeniable influence, but one that is interpreted in various ways. It is necessary in any event to distinguish clearly the properly theological enterprise of faith's using philosophy in order the better to express itself and the influence that faith exercises in this way over philosophy and that goes beyond being a mere negative norm. There are, second, the efforts to form anew, within a civilization characterized as Christian, a philosophical order independent of Christian influence. This would constitute itself theoretically as if Christianity, in fact, did not exist: either by pretending to ignore it, or by trying to render it useless, or finally, by relegating it to another level of the intellectual life (with the secret intention, however, of meeting it again or of letting oneself be regulated negatively by it). There is, third and finally, the effort to form philosophies that, from the beginning, take into account the fact of Christianity no less than the existence of stars and planets. This would either form a system in which Christianity is reduced to the object of an abstract dialectic, or, alternatively, it would conduct its inquiry in a way that, without altering its natural character, opens philosophy to wait upon, or even to make appeal to, the order of grace.

Granted a formal distinction between the two orders of knowledge, natural and supernatural, that no Catholic philosopher would question, there remain different ways of conceiving the notion of Christian philosophy, a diversity that (at least for Catholic philosophers) depends in part on philosophers' opposed views of the nature of philosophy, but also on views that mutually complement, rather than completely exclude, one another.

See also EXISTENTIAL METAPHYSICS; THEOLOGY, NATURAL; GOD 5, 6.

Bibliography: For a complete survey of literature, see the Chronicles of BullThom 4 (1934–36) to the present. *Christian Philosophy and the Social Sciences* (ProcAmCathPhilAs 12; 1936). *The Role of the Christian Philosopher* (*ibid.*, 32; 1958). M. NÉDONCELLE, *Is there a Christian Philosophy?*, tr. I. TRETHOWAN (New York 1960). C. TRESMONTANT, *The Origins of Christian Philosophy*, tr. M. PONTIFEX (New York 1963). P. DELHAYE, *Medieval Christian Philosophy*, tr. S. J. TESTER (New York 1960). R. VANCOURT, *Pensée moderne et philosophie chrétienne* (Paris 1957), Eng. in prep. É. H. GILSON, *The Christian Philosophy of St. Thomas Aquinas*, tr. L. K. SHOOK (New York 1956). J. MARITAIN, *An Essay on Christian Philosophy*, tr. E. FLANNERY (New York 1955). A. C. PEGIS, *Christian Philosophy and Intellectual Freedom* (Milwaukee 1960).

[L. B. GEIGER]

CHRISTIAN REFORMED CHURCH, organized as a conference of protest in 1857, when two ministers and a group of laymen of the Reformed Church in America disagreed with the doctrines and policies of their church (*see* REFORMED CHURCHES IN NORTH AMERICA). They established the Holland Reformed Church, later known as the Christian Reformed Church, which in 1964 had more than 250,000 members.

The early growth of the Christian Reformed Church was erratic. Its first years were marked by schisms and defections; by 1863 there remained only three pastors for the entire church. Later growth came from immigration from Holland and from the affiliation of those opposed to *Freemasonry, which was tolerated by the Reformed Church in America. Others, who objected to what they held was doctrinal liberalism in the older church, joined the dissenters. Most members of the Christian Reformed Church come from Dutch backgrounds, but English has now replaced Dutch in worship in most of its 572 congregations. This church has continued to wage an active campaign against secret societies and forbids dual membership in the lodge and the church. It upholds classical Calvinist theology including an emphasis on predestination (*see* CALVINISM). The creedal standards are found in the *Heidelberg Catechism (1563), the Canons of Dort (1618–19), and the Belgic Confession (1561).

Through corporations of parents, members of this denomination support one of the largest Protestant school systems in the U.S. In 1964 their National Union of Christian Schools enrolled 50,000 pupils in 246 Christian elementary and high schools. Eight to 10 new schools were being opened each year. The church maintains Calvin College and Seminary in Grand Rapids, Mich., two junior colleges, 18 homes for the aged, and a publishing house.

Thirty classes, which meet every 4 to 6 months, form the basis of the church's government. The general synod, composed of two ministers and two laymen from each class, meets each year. The Christian Reformed Church carries on missionary activities among the American Indians, Jews, Negroes, and Chinese. It supports foreign missionaries in Japan, South America, Nigeria, and Formosa. The church has experienced a rapid growth in Canada, due largely to Dutch immigration to that country. [W. J. WHALEN]

CHRISTIAN SCHOOLS OF MERCY, SISTERS OF THE, or *Sorores Scholarum Christianorum a Misericordia* (SSC), a religious congregation with papal approval (1901, 1925), founded at Cherbourg, France, in 1807 by St. Marie Madeleine *Postel to promote Christian education. The congregation, whose members take simple perpetual vows, is governed by a superior general. The rule of St. John Baptist de *La Salle was substituted in 1837 for that of the foundress at the request of the local vicar-general. The foundress accepted it. The motherhouse is at Saint-Sauveur-le-Vicomte, Normandy, where the young community settled (1832). Despite initial setbacks, there were 150 members and 37 convents in 1846. The congregation spread from France to the Netherlands, England, Ireland, Italy, Indonesia, and the Congo. In 1862 four teachers took the habit and rule at Heiligenstadt, Eichsfeld, Germany. Since 1922 this has been an independent branch with its motherhouse at Heiligenstadt. The sisters are engaged mostly in teaching, but they also conduct orphanages, homes for the aged, and hostels, besides visiting the sick and the poor, nursing, and aiding in parishes. In 1964 there were about 1,100 members. The German branch had another 1,125 sisters in 111 houses.

Bibliography: G. GRENTE, *Une sainte normande* (Paris 1946). SISTER CALISTA, *Love Endureth All Things* (Cork 1953).

[W. J. BATTERSBY]

CHRISTIAN SCIENCE (CHURCH OF CHRIST, SCIENTIST)

A religious body founded in 1879 by Mary Baker *Eddy, whose discovery of what she named Christian Science resulted from a personal experience of prayer healing in 1866. Her *Science and Health with Key to the Scriptures,* the textbook of the Christian Science Church first published in 1875, described this experience. "I knew the Principle of all harmonious Mind-action to be God, and that cures were produced in primitive Christian healing by holy, uplifting faith; but I must know the Science of this healing, and I won my way to absolute conclusions through divine revelation, reason, and demonstration" (109).

Foundation and Growth. Mrs. Eddy did not at first expect to found a separate church or denomination, but hoped that other churches would take up the discovery and utilize it within their own systems. When they did not, she founded the Church of Christ, Scientist, at Boston, Mass., in 1879. Soon, groups of Christian Scientists sprang up in other places, and in 1892 Mrs. Eddy organized the Christian Science Mother Church, The First Church of Christ, Scientist, in Boston. Local churches throughout the world are regarded as branches of this church. Newspapers, magazines, and books attacked the new religion and its founder; it received hostile receptions in many communities. But its appeal of Christian healing made a deep impact on thousands, especially in the U.S. and other English-speaking countries, and also in western Europe, particularly Germany. In 1964 there were about 3,300 branch churches in 54 countries. Church policy forbids the publication of statistics on membership.

Teachings. Christian Science maintains that fundamental reality is spiritual, created by God and consistently good. Thus, man, as the image and likeness of God, has a birthright of harmony and perfection. The ills that beset humanity, such as sickness, sin, fear, death, and poverty, are not part of God's spiritual creation, but result from the failure of the human mind to understand and obey God perceptively. To the degree that humans do understand God and follow His precepts unswervingly, their lives are regenerated, they experience healing, and their thinking is spiritualized. The degree to which they may not be healed is a result of their limitations in understanding and loving God. Christian Science defines God not in superhuman or anthropomorphic terms, but as "the divine Principle of all that really is"; Biblical terms used directly or by implication for God, such as Life, Truth, Love, Soul, Spirit, Mind, were adopted by Mrs. Eddy. Her followers regard heaven and hell, not as localities, but as states of consciousness experienced by individuals in terms of their own spiritual progress or lack of it. The immortality of man's spiritual being is an emphatic teaching of Christian Science, while the experience of death is regarded as an illusion, not touching the real man who is spiritual.

The First Church of Christ, Scientist, in Boston, Mass.

Science and Health (497) summarized the following "religious tenets": "(1) As adherents of Truth, we take the inspired Word of the Bible as our sufficient guide to eternal Life. (2) We acknowledge and adore one supreme and infinite God. We acknowledge His Son, one Christ; the Holy Ghost or divine Comforter; and man in God's image and likeness. (3) We acknowledge God's forgiveness of sin in the destruction of sin and the spiritual understanding that casts out evil as unreal. But the belief in sin is punished so long as the belief lasts. (4) We acknowledge Jesus' atonement as the evidence of divine, efficacious Love, unfolding man's unity with God through Christ Jesus the Way-shower; and we acknowledge that man is saved through Christ, through Truth, Life, and Love as demonstrated by the Galilean Prophet in healing the sick and overcoming sin and death. (5) We acknowledge that the crucifixion of Jesus and his resurrection served to uplift faith to understand eternal Life, even the allness of Soul, Spirit, and the nothingness of matter. (6) And we solemnly promise to watch, and pray for that Mind to be in us which was also in Christ Jesus; to do unto others as we would have them do unto us; and to be merciful, just, and pure."

Organization, Services, and Publications. Mrs. Eddy's death in 1910 was a test of the plan of organization she had formulated in the Church Manual. It set up a five member self-perpetuating board of directors to transact the business of the Mother Church. Branch churches throughout the world are democratically self-governed. Since 1910 the movement has grown steadily, although not at a sensational rate.

There is no clergy or official prayer book, and the order of church service is simple, identical, and unceremonial. Sunday services are based on lesson-sermons, consisting of citations from the Bible and the Christian Science textbook. At the services these lesson-sermons, which have been studied in advance by church members, are read aloud by a "First and Second Reader," who are lay men or women elected for 3-year terms. Hymn singing from the Christian Science Hymnal, the Lord's Prayer in common, and silent prayer, are part of the order of service. A Sunday School is held for pupils up to 20 years of age. Wednesday evening meetings include readings from the Bible and *Science and Health,* and testimonies of healing or other spiritual experiences from members of the congregation.

Although there is no clergy, there are professional practitioners of Christian Science. These men and women, whose names are registered in the church's monthly publication, the *Christian Science Journal* (1883), carry on healing work and spiritual guidance through prayer as a full-time vocation. Moreover, all Christian Scientists try to use their understanding of God's infinite grace and His law for spiritual healing.

Main auditorium of the Extension of The First Church of Christ, Scientist.

There is no formal missionary work, but the church maintains a board of lectureship, whose members deliver public lectures on Christian Science throughout the world. Other publications include: the *Christian Science Quarterly,* which contains the lesson-sermons studied each week; the *Christian Science Sentinel,* a weekly first published in 1898, and the *Heralds of Christian Science,* of which a German edition was first published in 1903, and to which French, Norwegian, Swedish, Danish, English Braille, Dutch, Spanish, Portuguese, Italian, Indonesian, Japansese, and Greek editions have been added. In 1908, when Mrs. Eddy was in her 88th year, she directed the establishment of a daily newspaper, the *Christian Science Monitor.*

Bibliography: N. BEASLEY, *The Continuing Spirit* (New York 1956). M. B. EDDY, *Science and Health with Key to the Scriptures* (Boston 1908). D. JOHN, *The Christian Science Way of Life,* with *A Christian Scientist's Life* by E. D. CANHAM (Englewood Cliffs 1962). R. PEEL, *Christian Science: Its Encounter with American Culture* (New York 1958). C. P. SMITH, *Historical Sketches* (Boston 1941).

[E. D. CANHAM]

CHRISTIAN TRADE UNIONS

Originally denominational, Christian Trade Unions now admit to membership not only all Christians but also non-Christian workers who believe in God. Although there are affiliates of the International Federation of Christian Trade Unions (Confédération Internationale des Syndicats Chrétiens, CISC) in Canada, India, Indonesia, Viet Nam, Africa, and Latin America, more than 75 per cent of all members of that federation, as shown in the following table, are located on the European Continent. (The French abbreviation CISC is used hereafter to avoid confusion of the English abbreviation IFCTU with the abbreviation ICFTU, for the International Confederation of Free Trade Unions.)

DISTRIBUTION OF ALL CISC MEMBERS BY AREA*

Area	No. of members	Per cent
Europe	2,528,056	75.69
North America	102,186	3.06
Latin American Republics and Caribbean area	75,465	2.26
Africa	123,400	3.69
Asia	511,000	15.30
Total	3,340,107	100.00

*Generally, claimed membership data were used; in cases in which there was reason to believe that claimed membership figures were inflated and reliable estimates were available, estimated data were used.

SOURCES: For Europe, U.S. Department of Labor data (1965); for other areas, U.S. Department of Labor, *Directory of International Federation of Christian Trade Unions* (Washington 1963).

Problems of the Early Christian Movement. The Christian trade union movement was begun on the European Continent as a Christian—usually, a Catholic—response to the Socialist domination of the contemporary nonsectarian labor movement. Although the difficulties that it encountered differed from country to country, similar obstacles appeared in all countries. These included the problems experienced by the labor movement generally, such as legal restrictions, employer resistance, and worker apathy. The Catholic unions, however, were confronted with special difficulties. The Socialist unions looked upon them as a divisive force and often treated them with the contempt that U.S. unions reserved for company-sponsored representation plans a generation ago. Even more serious were the objections from influential circles within the Church that thought that militant associations of workingmen fostered class consciousness and that industrial organizations should be confined to groups composed of both employer and employees. The beginnings of the Catholic unions in Germany illustrate these difficulties.

Germany. Industrialization came late in Germany but, once begun, moved rapidly. Workingmen, long deprived both of the right to organize economic associations and of suffrage, and until the middle of the 19th century still limited in many areas in the right of free choice of occupation, lacked the organizations, the experience, and the rank-and-file leadership to cope with the problems that the rising tides of industrialization had brought upon them. This lack, however, the intellectuals with their ready-made programs of cosmic reform stood ready to remedy. The broad lines of labor activity became fixed when the Universal Workingmen's Association (Allgemeiner deutscher Arbeiterverein), created by Ferdinand Lassalle (1825–64), and the Social Democratic Labor party, led by August Bebel (1840–1913), united in 1875, 11 years after Lassalle's death, to form the Social Democratic party. This party, in its turn, fostered the growth of labor unions. These unions, however, in the view of the leaders of the new party, were to play a wholly subordinate role. Lassalle, accepting the iron law of wages as unchallenged truth, saw the welfare of the workingmen linked with a Socialist state and the cooperative productive associations that it would finance and maintain. The immediate goal of his program was universal suffrage; the ultimate goal, the Socialist state. In such a program there was no place for trade union activity. Karl *Marx, more realistic on this point than Lassalle, had insisted on the organization of labor unions, but he viewed them as vehicles for the transmission of socialism. Thus the goal of both groups, Lassallians and Marxists, who composed the new party was socialism. Their methods were predominantly political, and they sought not gradual and tangible gains for the workingman, but the ultimate transformation of the economic system. Their philosophies were materialistic and fundamentally anti-Christian.

An unpublished brochure by Bp. Wilhelm Emmanuel von Ketteler (1811–77) reflects the concern that these developments caused in Catholic circles:

> A great change has come over the labor movement since I wrote my first brochure: *Christianity and the Labor Question* [written 1863, published 1864]. By the fusion of the two parties which were then struggling for supremacy—a fusion effected at Gotha, 25 May, 1875, under the name of the Socialistic Labor Party and on the basis of a common platform—the old associations have not only gained in numbers and consistency, but have also in many respects altered their character completely. A movement national in character and confined almost exclusively to Germany has given place to one that embraces the workingmen of every land and is really and truly international; a movement whose chief aim was the realization of certain practical reforms for the amelioration of labor conditions has been succeeded by one that relegates practical reform proposals to the background and aims at the transformation of existing social conditions in regard to the acquisition and distribution of wealth and in the inauguration of the so-called "Socialistic era." Hence it would be unfair to apply to present conditions what I wrote in 1863. [*Kann ein katholischer Arbeiter Mitglied der sozialistischen Arbeiterpartei sein* in O. Pfülf, *Bishop von Ketteler* (3 v. Mainz 1899), tr. G. Metlake, *Christian Social Reform* (Philadelphia 1912) 226.]

He goes on to say:

> To insure any degree of real and lasting success every attempt to reorganize the laboring classes must be based on the following principles:
>
> (1) The desired organizations must be of *natural growth* (naturwüchsig), that is, they must grow out of the nature of things, out of the character of the people and its faith, as did the guilds of the Middle Ages.
>
> (2) They must have an *economic purpose* and not subserve the intrigues and idle dreams of politicians and the fanaticism of the enemies of religion. The Socialist Labor Party has avoided neither the one nor the other of these rocks. [*Ibid.* 230.]

Despite the widespread concern among Catholics about the rapid conversion of workingmen to socialism, Catholic trade unions were slow to develop. As a result of the work of Father Adolf Kolping (1813–65), there were 328 Catholic workingmen's clubs in 1865; but these associations, although aiding individual workingmen to acquire skills, were almost wholly moral and religious in orientation. In the years that followed the publication of Ketteler's *Christianity and the Labor Question* (1864), efforts were made to organize Catholic workers on economic lines and to go beyond the purely religious emphasis of the Kolping program; but the resulting *Vereine* stopped far short of trade union programs and were often characterized by considerable employer and clerical guidance.

One of the cardinal principles of the contemporary Catholic social thought was *solidarism, which emphasized the community of interests of employers and employees and contemplated the creation of corporations or orders that would unite in common groups the employers and employed in the same trades and industries. Unions, on the other hand, were class organizations and appeared to be in direct conflict with the Catholic program. As a result, there was but limited endorsement in Catholic circles of trade unions as such until the matter had been clarified by the publication of Leo XIII's *Rerum novarum* in 1891. In 1894 Father Franz Hitze (1851–1921) devised a set of principles for creating craft groups (*Fachabteilungen*) among existing workers' associations that would permit them to function much like trade unions. These craft branches of the *Arbeitervereine* had a remarkable growth, reaching a membership of about 626,000 in 1913.

From a trade union standpoint these *Vereine* had an obviously crucial defect. They admitted only Catholics to membership, whereas Catholics worked alongside non-Catholics as employees in the same establishments.

The idea of fostering Christian, rather than strictly Catholic or denominational, unions began to be discussed in both Catholic and Protestant circles in the Rhineland, and, in 1894, 398 delegates representing 157 organizations with a membership of 19,747 founded the Trade Union of Christian Miners for the District of Dortmund (Gewerkverein christlicher Bergleute für den Oberergamisbezirk Dortmund). Following this action the Christian trade union movement made considerable progress, achieving a membership of about 56,000 in 1899 and 350,000 in 1913. At the latter date the Christian unions in Germany had about one-seventh of the membership of the Socialist unions.

Catholic participation in interdenominational trade unions was not achieved without sharp controversy among Catholics. The action of the bishops in Prussia on Aug. 22, 1900, illustrates the strength of the opposition. In a joint pastoral letter they asserted that neutral unions were unnecessary and that the existing workers' associations were adequate for promoting the material as well as the spiritual needs of workingmen. In sending this pastoral to his clergy, Archbishop Nörber of Freiburg added that the word "Christian" in the context of Christian trade unions had a hollow ring. This opposition was ended by the letter of Pius X, *Singulari quadam,* to the German bishops in 1912. Interdenominational unions were to be tolerated where they already existed or in areas of mixed religious affiliations. The bishops, however, were responsible for seeing that participation in such unions did not endanger the Catholic formation of the workers and the workers themselves were obliged to join Catholic societies that would assure their spiritual and moral training.

Christian trade unions remained a minority element in the labor movement after World War I, but in cooperation with the *Center party were an important stabilizing and constructive force during the Weimar Republic. Like other trade unions they were wiped out by Hitler in the 1930s. Following the Allied victory in 1945, Catholics for several years participated in the unified labor movement; however, Christian unions were reestablished in the 1950s, and by 1965 had about 250,000 members, or about 4 per cent of the trade union membership of West Germany.

France. The formation both of Catholic and of Christian labor unions met objections among Catholics in France similar to those that had been encountered in

Germany. Nevertheless, a Catholic trade union had been established among white-collar workers in Paris by 1887 and before 1900 had begun to lose its purely denominational character. By 1919 Christian trade unionism had sufficiently developed to create the Confédération Française des Travailleurs Chrétiens (CFTC), with a membership of about 100,000. The movement, however, took on momentum after the establishment of the Catholic workers youth movement, the Jeunesse Ouvrière Chrétienne (JOC) in 1927. As former members of the JOC took their place in industry, they formed a corps of workers who were at the same time both militantly Catholic and union-minded. Opposition of CFTC leaders during World War II to the *syndicats uniques,* the official obligatory unions of the Vichy regime, and the part played by them in the Resistance, won the CFTC much respect among the working class in the postwar period; and it succeeded in winning members in the mining areas and in heavy industry, sectors where previously its influence had been unknown. It became the second most powerful of the three major labor groups in France. The U.S. Department of Labor data (*see* LABOR MOVEMENT, EUROPE) put membership of the Communist Confédération Générale du Travail at 900,000 in 1965; of the Socialist-inclined Force Ouvrière, at 425,000; and of the CFTC, at 600,000.

Belgium and Holland. Christian unionism in both Belgium and Holland is rooted in movements that antedate the 20th century, but its most significant growth occurred in the second quarter of the 20th century. In Belgium, membership in the Socialist trade unions in 1920 was 718,000; in Christian unions, 65,000. By 1930 the Socialist unions had declined to about 537,000, whereas the membership in Christian unions had risen to more than 200,000. In 1945 the Socialist unions had about 550,000; the Christian unions, about 350,000. In 1965 the Christian unions, with a membership of about 800,000, had about the same numerical strength as the Socialist unions.

In Holland the growth of Christian unionism followed a pattern similar to that of Belgium. The Netherlands Federation of Trade Unions, the traditional Socialist group, had in 1965 a membership of about 500,000. The Catholic Workers' movement (KAB), which grew rapidly in recent decades, had about 400,000; and a second group of Christian unions, a phenomenon peculiar to Holland, the Protestant Labor Federation (CNV), had 225,000. Thus membership in Christian unions exceeded that of the traditionally Socialist unions.

Italy. Although the beginnings of a Catholic workers' movement can be traced to the 19th century, Catholic trade unions began in the 20th century. Amintore Fanfani, a prominent Christian Democrat and prime minister of Italy during the 1950s and early 1960s, is quoted by Horowitz as saying that "the only political group which took to heart the workers' interests in Italy before 1900 was the Socialist Party. And once the Anarchist elements were beaten, the Republicans discredited—the Catholics remained apart—it can be said that the Socialists had the monopoly of the impulse and the guidance of the Italian labor movement" [D. L. Horowitz, *The Italian Labor Movement* (Harvard University Press Cambridge 1963) 95.] In 1910, the 374 Catholic trade union organizations had enrolled a membership of about 100,000. Of these organizations, two-thirds had been formed between 1901 and 1909, and only five dated from the 19th century. The slow manifestation of Catholic leadership in the labor movement resulted in part from the late industrialization of Italy. To a greater extent, however, it reflected on the part of those Catholics from whom leadership might have been forthcoming a preoccupation with the Roman Question, that is, with the peculiar relationship between the Church and the Italian government that resulted from the seizure of the Papal States. It also was a result of the slow recognition among Catholic leaders that the changing industrial situation called for autonomous worker organizations.

In 1918 a group of Catholic labor leaders, meeting in Rome, decided to form the Confederazione Italiana dei Lavoratori (CIL), a federation of Catholic inspiration but without confessional ties. This new organization experienced a short period of rapid growth, claiming a membership of about 1,250,000 in 1920. These gains had scarcely been realized when the Catholic unions, as well as their Socialist rivals, were threatened by the rising power of fascism. By 1926 the struggle had ended; the Fascist organizations had a legally guaranteed monopoly of labor representation.

Both as a result and as evidence of their common efforts in the Resistance during the Allied campaigns in Italy, representatives of the three major factions of Italian labor, the Socialists, the Communists, and the Christian Democrats, signed the Pact of Rome on June 3, 1944, which launched a unified labor movement, the Confederazione Generale Italiana del Lavoro (CGIL). By the terms of that agreement each of these three factions was to have equal representation in the administration of the new organization, irrespective of its numerical strength. At about the same time, however, Catholic Action organizations formed the Christian Associations of Italian Workers (Associazioni Christiane dei Lavorati Italiani, ACLI), which—although an educational, cultural, and recreational organization—had a geographical structure not unlike that of a labor organization, with its national, regional, and local officers and groups. Likewise, there was duplication of leadership and membership between the ACLI and the Catholic elements of CGIL.

Within a short time the Communists made clear their intention to dominate the CGIL. In October 1948 the Catholic groups withdrew and with the aid of the ACLI formed the Libera Confederazione Generale Italiana del Lavoro (LCGIL). Some months earlier the Socialist party, led by G. Saragat (Partito Socialista dei Lavorati Italiana PSLI), to be distinguished from the Partito Socialista Italiana (PSI), led by Pietro Nenni, who had been cooperating with the Communists, and Republican trade unions leaders had voted to abandon the CGIL. On June 4, 1948, the PSLI and the Republicans formed the Federazione Italiana del Lavoro (FIL). The FIL and the LCGIL united in April 1950 to form the nonconfessional but anti-Communist Confederazione Italiana Sindicati Lavoratori (CISL). In 1961 CISL had a membership somewhat less than 2 million, compared with a CGIL membership of about 2.5 million. Because the CISL, although enjoying Catholic support, is not a Christian union, its membership is not included in the table below.

International Federation of Christian Trade Unions. The CISC, to use the abbreviation of the French name of the federation, was founded at the Hague in 1920.

By its constitution it is pledged to promote a social order founded on Christian principles. From its earliest years, it has admitted both Catholic and Protestant unions, and many of its affiliates have for years admitted all Christians. The unions that had been formed in Asia and Africa by French, Belgian, and Netherland affiliates of CISC were composed chiefly of Moslems and Buddhists; and as they acquired independent status, CISC opened the way for their direct affiliation by agreeing to admit to membership all workers who believe in God. Many of these affiliates have substituted the word "believing" for "Christian" in their titles.

DISTRIBUTION OF CISC MEMBERSHIP IN EUROPE, 1965*

Country	No. of members	Per cent
Austria	110,000	4.35
Belgium	812,257	32.13
France	600,000	23.73
West Germany	233,000	9.22
Luxembourg	18,048	0.72
Malta	10,068	0.40
Netherlands	637,446	25.21
Switzerland	107,237	4.24
Total	2,528,056	100.00

*Generally, claimed membership data have been used. When there was reason to believe that claimed figures were inflated and reliable estimates were available, estimates have been used.
SOURCE: U.S. Department of Labor Data.

CISC has regional organizations for Africa, Europe, and Latin America. It cooperates with the International Confederation of Free Trade Unions in the Trade Union Advisory Committee of the Organization for Economic Cooperation and Development.

See also LABOR MOVEMENT (EUROPE), (CANADA), (LATIN AMERICA); SOCIALISM, III (CHRISTIAN SOCIALISM); CATHOLIC ACTION; CENTER PARTY.

Bibliography: U.S. Bureau of Internatl. Labor Affairs, *Directory of International Federation of Christian Trade Unions* (Washington 1963–). L. RIVA SANSEVERINO, *Il movimento sindacale cristiano dal 1850 al 1930* (Rome 1950). J. N. MOODY, ed., *Church and Society* (New York 1953). W. GALENSON, *Trade Union Democracy in Western Europe* (Berkeley, Calif. 1961); ed., *Comparative Labor Movements* (Englewood Cliffs, N.J. 1952). E. M. KASSALOW, ed., *National Labor Movements in the Postwar World* (Evanston, Ill. 1963). P. T. MOON, *The Labor Problem and the Social Catholic Movement in France* (New York 1921). G. JARLOT, "Christian Trade Unions: The European Scene," *Social Order* 9 (1959) 75–80, 108–116. J. B. DUROSELLE, *Les Débuts du catholicisme social en France, 1822–1870* (Paris 1951). M. EINAUDI and F. GOGUEL, *Christian Democracy in Italy and France* (Notre Dame, Ind. 1952). J. ZIRNHELD, *Cinquante années de syndicalisme chrétien* (Paris 1937). V. R. LORWIN, *The French Labor Movement* (Cambridge, Mass. 1954). M. DILL, "The Christian Trades Union Movement in Germany before World War I," *Review of Social Economy* 11 (1953) 70–86. D. L. HOROWITZ, *The Italian Labor Movement* (Cambridge, Mass. 1963). J. LA PALOMBARA, *The Italian Labor Movement: Problems and Prospects* (Ithaca, N.Y. 1957).

[L. C. BROWN]

CHRISTIAN UNITY, SECRETARIATE FOR PROMOTING

The organization of Vatican Council II that deals with the pastoral promotion of the ecumenical movement: *Secretariatus ad Christianorum Unitatem fovendam* (SPCU). Although its organization followed closely the pattern of the other conciliar commissions and secretariates, the purposes and activities of the SPCU necessitated a development of structure.

Institution. When John XXIII first announced his intention to convoke an "Ecumenical Council for the Universal Church" (Jan. 25, 1959), he stated that it would be "not only for the spiritual good and joy of the Christian People but also an invitation to the separated communities to seek again that unity for which so many souls are longing in these days throughout the world" [ActApS 51 (1959) 69]. In his motu proprio *Superno Dei nutu* (June 5, 1960), the same Pope instituted, among the preparatory conciliar commissions, the SPCU to enable "those who bear the name of Christians but are separated from this Apostolic See . . . to follow the work of the Council and to find more easily the path by which they may arrive at that unity for which Christ prayed" [ActApS 52 (1960) 436]. The new secretariate was seen immediately by Catholic and non-Catholic leaders as an active symbol of Pope John's loving concern to promote Christian unity. In August 1960 the Executive Committee of the *World Council of Churches stated that the creation of the SPCU was "an important development in the Roman Catholic Church. . . . It will no longer leave all initiative in this field [of ecumenical conversation] to individual Roman Catholics, but begin to speak and set itself in relation to other Churches and to ecumenical organizations" [*Ecumenical Review* (Oct. 1960) 46].

On June 6, 1960, John XXIII appointed Cardinal Augustin Bea (1881–), the German-born former rector of the Biblical Institute in Rome, to be the president of the SPCU. The appointed secretary was J. G. M. Willebrands (1909–), former representative of the hierarchy for ecumenical work in Holland and secretary of the International Catholic Conference on Ecumenical Questions. During the summer and early autumn of 1960 the first group of episcopal and clerical members and consultors were chosen, along with a permanent working staff in Rome. The offices, on the Via dei Corridori, opened in October 1960. During the conciliar preparations, there were six plenary sessions of the members and consultors (November 1960, February, April, and August 1961, November 1961, and March 1962). John XXIII, in January 1963, established two sections of the SPCU, one for the Eastern Churches separated from Rome, the other for the Churches issuing from the Reformation in the West; both sections are headed by an undersecretary.

Purpose. The immediate purpose of the SPCU directly concerned Vatican Council II. It was instituted to inform non-Catholic Christians of the work of the council; to receive and evaluate their wishes and suggestions relating to the council, and, if need be, to pass them on to the other commissions. In addition, from 1960 to 1962 it prepared five pastoral decrees: *On Ecumenism, On Religious Liberty, On the Jews, On the Necessity of Praying for Unity,* and *On the Word of God and Its Function in the Church.*

At the beginning of the first session of Vatican Council II (1962) the exact status of the SPCU was still ambiguous. It was the only preparatory commission that had not been dissolved, and, although it had prepared various schemas, it was not empowered to submit them directly to the council floor. On October 19, John XXIII raised the status of the SPCU to that of a conciliar commission with the same corresponding rights, privileges, and obligations. During the second session (Nov. 28, 1963) the number of episcopal members, then 18, was raised to 30, 8 elected by the council fathers, 4 appointed by Paul VI.

On Dec. 1, 1962, the council voted 2,068 to 36 in favor of a single document on church unity that would fuse the contents of the SPCU's ecumenism schema, the last chapter ("Unity of the Church") of the constitution on the Church, and the decree on the separated Churches of the East, prepared by the Commission for the Eastern Churches. The SPCU was the principal drafter of this final schema, *On Ecumenism.* It was promulgated on Nov. 22, 1964. John XXIII, implementing a conciliar vote, formed in November 1962 a mixed-commission of the SPCU and the Theological Commission with the task of redrafting the schema on divine revelation; the last chapter contains much of the SPCU's original draft on the pastoral role of the word of God. During the third session (1964), the draft on the Jews was incorporated, as chapter four, into the SPCU's enlarged schema, *On the Relation of the Church to the Non-Christian Religions.* This decree, along with those on divine revelation and on religious liberty, were promulgated at the fourth session (1965).

Through the SPCU, John XXIII and Paul VI invited the separated Churches of the East and the international councils and alliances of Protestant Churches to delegate official observers to the four sessions of the council. The observers were entitled to attend all the closed meetings of the general congregations, with no right, however, to speak or to vote. The SPCU held special sessions with the observers at least once a week, during which the council deliberations were discussed; critical observations were passed on to the respective conciliar drafting commissions. During the course of the four sessions 168 observers, including their substitutes, attended.

In response to many requests from the council fathers for more detailed guidelines for ecumenical action than those contained in the decree *On Ecumenism,* the SPCU began in March 1965 the drafting of such directives. The procedure was to issue a series of provisional guidelines on specific topics rather than to publish a comprehensive book of definitive directives.

The SPCU and Ecumenism. A larger and more general purpose of the SPCU, and one less directly concerned with Vatican II, is to study and evaluate the exact situation of the ecumenical movement throughout the world, to be a clearing house of information and guidance for local or national episcopal ecumenical commissions, and to represent the Holy See in the promotion of Christian unity.

The SPCU also acts as the liaison through which the Pope meets Christian leaders. The first of these meetings was between Geoffrey Fisher, Anglican Archbishop of Canterbury, and John XXIII in December 1960. Of particular historical importance was the fraternal meeting of Paul VI with Athenagoras, the Orthodox ecumenical patriarch, in Jerusalem (January 1964). The SPCU also chooses and authorizes official Roman Catholic observers to attend international church conferences (e.g., those of the Anglican Communion, the Lutheran World Federation, the Churches of Christ Disciples, and All-African Churches) and the main meetings of the World Council of Churches. The first group of observers with such credentials attended the third assembly of the World Council of Churches at New Delhi in November 1961.

Since May 1965 a Joint Working Group has been set up between the World Council of Churches and the Roman Catholic Church in order to explore officially the possibilities for greater mutual understanding and cooperation in study and action; the SPCU is the Catholic representative. A similar working group has been created, since August 1965, with the Lutheran World Federation. The SPCU envisages other such initiatives.

In his motu proprio *Finis concilio* (Jan. 3, 1966), Paul VI confirmed the SPCU as a permanent organ of the Holy See.

Bibliography: A. BEA, *The Unity of Christians,* ed. B. LEEMING (New York 1963) 157–192; *Unity in Freedom* (New York 1964) 160–209; "The Second Vatican Council and Non-Catholic Christians," in *Ecumenical Dialogue at Harvard,* ed. S. H. MILLER and G. E. WRIGHT (Cambridge, Mass. 1964) 40–67. T. F. STRANSKY, "The Vatican Council, 1962," *Wiseman Review* 236 (1962) 203–206; "The Council, the Secretariate and the Observers," *Ecumenist* 1 (Dec. 1962) 17–19; the extensive commentary on Vatican Council II, *Decree on Ecumenism* (pa. Glen Rock, N.J. 1965) 7–46.

[T. F. STRANSKY]

CHRISTIAN WAY OF LIFE, EARLY

In the Sermon on the Mount, Christ called His followers the salt of the earth and the light of the world (Mt 5.13–14); He admonished them to let their light shine among men by way of their good works (Mt 5.16). This admonition was preceded by the discourse on the *Beatitudes (Mt 5.3–12) and completed with a moral discourse (Mt 5.17–7.29). In the Gospels of Matthew and Mark, the eschatological atmosphere accompanying the call to repentance (*metanoia*) is stressed with the proclamation by John the Baptist that the kingdom of God is at hand (Mt 3.1–12; Mk 1.4–15). In Luke, the eschatological element is softened in favor of the history of salvation, in which conversion is offered to all through the apostolic preaching; and the promise of salvation is portrayed as realized in the Church (Lk 5.32; 15.7–10; Acts 7.38; 9.31).

Conversion and Metanoia. Conversion signifies a complete turnabout of mentality and a permanent, new way of life. The process of *metanoia* is described for the Jews in Acts (2.38–40; 3.19–21, 25–26) as the acknowledgment of their sinfulness, Baptism, remission of their sins, the gift of the Holy Spirit, their liberation, and participation in salvation. Paul speaks of the conversion of the Gentiles (*epistrephein*) as an opening of their eyes from the darkness to light, a turning from Satan to God, that they might receive the forgiveness of their sins and the call through faith among the saints (Acts 26.18).

In characterizing the way of life of the primitive Christians, the author of Acts says: "The multitude of believers had but one heart and one soul" (4.32). He describes the mutual charity exercised by the original Jerusalem community, in which the members sold their property and placed the price at the feet of the Apostles, who divided it among the members according to their need so that no one lacked anything among them (4.34). This idealized picture receives some support from the fact that the practice of a communal life is known to have been current among the *Qumram brethren and the Sadocites. *See* SADOC (ZADOK). It is likewise put into perspective by St. Paul's doctrine concerning the Church as the body of Christ, in which the members, though having different functions, formed part of one sole body (Rom 12.3–8; 1 Cor 12.12; Eph 2.20–22).

The Church at Jerusalem. Although in the beginning the Apostles and earliest converts continued to pray in the temple (Acts 2.46) and follow the Jewish ritual (3.1; 5.21), they gradually became aware of themselves as a separate community or church. The term church was applied first to the Church in Jerusalem (7.38), then extended to the Christian communities at Antioch (14.27) and at Caesarea (18.22). The Church at Jerusalem was directed by the elders under the guidance of James the Just, appointed by Peter, James, and John as *episcopus,* or bishop (Eusebius, *Hist. eccl.* 2.1.4), to whom Paul made a special visit during his stay at Jerusalem in 41 (Gal 1.18). While the widows, the poor, and the orphans among the convert Jews were cared for by the Jewish elders, the Apostles provided for the poor among the converts from Hellenism by ordaining seven deacons—Stephen, Philip, Prochorus, Nicanor, Timon, Parmenas, and the Antiochene Nicholas—thus freeing themselves for prayer and the ministry of the word.

The Lord's Day. The Jerusalem Christians assembled for prayer and the breaking of bread in their own homes (Acts 2.46), following the example of the assemblage of Apostles and Disciples awaiting the coming of the Holy Spirit in the *coenaculum,* or upper room (Acts 1.13). When Peter was released from prison, he found a large gathering at the home of Mary, the mother of John Mark, spending the night in prayer (12.12). Paul spoke to a group in the home of Lydia at Philippi (16.40) and celebrated the Eucharist at Troas on the third floor of a private home (20.9). He refers to the church in the house of Aquila and Priscilla at Rome and Ephesus (1 Cor 16.19), that of Nympha at Colossus (Col 4.15), and that of Gaius at Corinth (Rom 26.23). Besides daily gatherings for the breaking of bread and prayers of thanksgiving (Acts 2.46), the early Christians frequently spent the night of Saturday together in prayer after observing the Jewish Sabbath (Acts 20.7), gradually establishing the custom of keeping Sunday as the Lord's day (*kuriake* or *dominicum*). Acts describes the make-up of their meeting, which consisted of an instruction, the breaking of bread for the Eucharist (Acts 20.17) and the recitation of prayers (2.42). The instruction was called the didache or teaching, the exhortation or *paraklesis,* and the homily (Acts 14.22; 15.32; 20.11).

Postapostolic Documents. The Christian way of life consequent upon the apostolic preaching is described in a series of documents that appear at the turn of the 2d century. The epistle of *Clement I of Rome (*c.* 97) portrays the Church in sojourn at Corinth as a model of steadfast faith, sober and gentle piety, magnificent hospitality, and secure knowledge. Its members are praised for their obedience to God's commandments without care for rank or station, and for the respect they gave their rulers and elders. The young were trained to temperance; wives, to affectionate care for their husbands and household. All were content with the provisions Christ had made for them, and were happier in giving than in receiving. They meditated on the words of Christ, keeping His sufferings ever before their eyes. Under the outpouring of the Holy Spirit on the whole community, they experienced peace of soul, praying to God for forgiveness of inadvertent faults and vying with each other in behalf of the whole brotherhood. They mourned their shortcomings, judging their neighbors' faults their own. In virtuous citizenship, they fulfilled their duties in the fear of the Lord, whose precepts were engraved on the tablets of their hearts (*Epist. Clem.* 1, 2).

This idealized picture is offset by the history of the dissension that had broken out at Corinth and occasioned the Roman Church's letter; but the exhortations that accompany it reveal a consciousness of the Church as a strong organization whose line of authority descended from God through Christ and the Apostles to the elders of the fraternally united community (*ibid.* 42.1–5; 44.1–2). Despite the ravagings of "envy and jealousy, contention and contumacy" that accompany persecution, the letter insists on sanctification and justification, penance and conversion as leading to peace and order among men, as it characterizes God's creation of the cosmos (3.2–6.4; 13–14; 20.1–12).

Ignatius and Polycarp. According to *Ignatius of Antioch (d. *c.* 116), the true Christian imitated Christ in His passion, achieving a complete transformation of his way of life by regeneration in God and Christ though Baptism. This is expressed in the charity that begins with the gift of self in and to the community (*Epist. ad Eph.* 10.1–3; *Smyrn.* 6.2–7), and is perfected in the Church through a consciousness of unity with Christ and one another that proceeds from, and leads back to, the Trinity by way of the Eucharist, the symbol at once of immortality (*Eph.* 20.2) and the instrument of unity between the Christians in community and of communities within the Church. In concrete terms this is accomplished by loving care for "widows and orphans, the prisoner as well as the freedman, the hungry and thirsty" (*Smyrn.* 6.2).

The organization of the Church includes the bishop, who is the "living image of the invisible God" (*Mag.* 6.1; *Tral.* 3.1); the priests, "like the college of apostles surrounding Christ" (*Phil.* 4.1); and deacons, widows, and virgins (*Smyr.* 13.1). Finally, Ignatius asserts the prerogative of marriage for Christians, entered with the sanction of the bishop, that it may be in accord with the will of God; and he who can live in continence should do so without boasting (*Pol.* 5.1–2). This Ignatian doctrine is portrayed on a background of martyrdom, for death in and with Christ is the consummation of union with God that the Christian strives for in the practice of virtue (*Eph.* 11.1–2; *Rom.* 2.2).

To the Church at Philippi in mid-2d century, *Polycarp of Smyrna described the Christian way of life as essentially the imitation of Christ in his patience (*Epist. ad Phil.* 8.2; 9.1). Christians are to flee avarice and the love of money (2.2); and each in his station—husbands, wives, widows, deacons, and priests—must forgive injuries, practice kindness and moderation toward sinners, and pray for all, particularly rulers and magistrates (4–6). The priest in particular is described as "tenderhearted and merciful toward all, seeking the sheep who have gone astray, not neglecting widow or orphan or poor man . . . abstaining from anger, respect of persons, and unrighteous judgment, realizing that all are debtors because of sin" (6.1–3).

Hermas, Diognetus, and Justin. The practice of a moral way of life in imitation of Christ was supported by an eschatological conception of the Church that, according to the Shepherd of *Hermas, had been created before all things and was now, under the guise of a tower under construction, constituted at a time of special mercy in immediate preparation for the *parousia, or Second Coming of the Savior. The Shepherd as the angel of penance describes the Church of Rome toward the middle of the 2d century. It is a populous assembly with a large group of the rich and numerous poor, and among both classes are many who have relapsed into pagan ways, become blasphemers, heretics, propagandists of a false gnosis (*Sim.* 8.6–11). Hermas portrays hypocrites, ambitious clergymen, and dishonest deacons, as well as hospitable bishops, honest priests, martyrs, and the innocent. Along with a well-organized hierarchy, he speaks of itinerant apostles and teachers preaching under the inspiration of charismatic gifts; but the problem of their authenticity as faced in the Didache (11.1–12) seems all but solved (*Mand.* 10.11). For Hermas, it is moral perfection that leads to perfect knowledge (*gnosis*); hence faith without works is vain (14.4–5; 40.4; 90.2–3). The Christian is to keep the spirit of God intact within him, practicing continence, chastity in married life (29.1–11), justice and humility, while giving himself to works of supererogation (56.6–7).

In repelling the accusation of atheism and corruption brought against the Christians, the author of the letter to *Diognetus admits that they are persecuted by both the pagans and the Jews (5.11, 12, 16, 17); but he describes the injustice of this treatment since "Christians do not differ from other men in citizenship, in language, or in dress" (5.2). They are to be found in the Greek and barbarian cities, and conform to local usages as far as dress, food, and manner of life are concerned. They carry out all their duties as citizens. They marry like the rest of the world, but in procreating children, they do not abandon them; and although they partake of a common table, they do not share the same bed. While they pass their time on earth, they live as citizens of heaven; they obey the laws, love their enemies, and return good for evil. in a word "what the soul is to the body, Christians are to the world" (5.1–17; 6.1–10).

*Justin Martyr describes the Christian Sunday (*dies solis*) as the day on which those who live in towns or the country come together for a reading of the Gospels (*commentarii apostolorum*) or of the writings of the Prophets. When the reader stops, the bishop gives an exhortation stimulating the hearers to an imitation of what has been read. Afterward all rise and pray, after which the bishop blesses the bread and the wine and water with Eucharistic prayers, and those present communicate, sending the Sacrament to those absent through the deacons. The rich make an offering either directly or through the bishop, who cares for the widows and orphans, the sick and indigent, prisoners and strangers (*1 Apol.* 67). This bread and wine is not ordinary, and cannot be received except by those who believe and have been baptized in the remission of their sins and in the regeneration of Christ (*ibid.* 65).

Reorganization. Toward the end of the 2d century, Eusebius describes the status of the Church as in the course of a considerable reorganization (*Hist. eccl.* 3–4). In particular, he cites seven letters written by Bishop *Dionysius of Corinth, a contemporary of Pope Soter (166–175), to churches in Asia Minor, Crete, and Rome. In these "catholic epistles, useful to the whole church," Eusebius describes Dionysius as sending the Lacedemonians a catechesis of orthodoxy, devoted to peace and unity (4.23.2). He dispatched an exhortation to faith and conduct in keeping with the gospel to the Athenians (*ibid.*), blaming them for a falling off in fervor after the martyrdom of their bishop, Publius. In his letter to the Church of Nicomedia, he combatted the heresies of *Marcion and recalled the faithful to the rule of faith (*ibid.* 4). He praised the conduct of the Church at Gortyna in Crete for its great charity and Christian observance, making special mention of its bishop, Philip. He advised Bp. Palmas of Amastris in Pontus regarding marriage and continence, and suggested that he grant pardon to sinners, even to those returning from heresy.

Dionysius cautioned Bp. Pinytos of Cnossos that the burden of continence was not to be put on all the faithful as a necessity, and that he should have in mind the weakness of the majority. In return, Pinytos, though accepting the Corinthian's counsel, suggested that he should not hesitate to feed his flock with stronger doctrine, lest they grow into immature Christians. In replying to a letter from Pope Soter, Dionysius praised highly the generosity of the Roman Church, whose fervor had been preserved down to the "persecutions of our own times" (*ibid.* 9). He assured Soter that his letter was held in esteem, and records the fact that the letter of Clement I to the Corinthians was still being read in their Church. Finally, Dionysius warned against the falsifications of both the Scriptures and the letters of bishops.

Before the turn of the century, with Tertullian in Carthage, Clement in Alexandria, Lucian in Samosata, Irenaeus in Lyons, and Hippolytus in Rome, the testimony offered by the beginnings of a great Christian literature demonstrates the unity of faith in the diversity of liturgical practice, the problems in the discipline of penance and the instruction of catechumens, and the fervor and perseverence to martyrdom during the periods of persecution, all of which were characteristic of the Early Christian way of life.

Bibliography: Daniélou-Marrou ChrCent. J. Kleist, ed. and tr., *The Epistles of St. Clement of Rome and St. Ignatius of Antioch* (AncChrWr 1; 1946). P. T. Camelot, ed., *Ignace d'Antioche: Lettres* (SourcesChr 10; 3d ed. 1958), introd. H. I. Marrou, ed. and tr., *À Diognète* (*ibid.* 33; 1951) 118–207. Quasten Patr v.1–2. G. Bardy, *La Théologie de l'Église,* v.1 (Unam Sanctam 13; Paris 1945). F. X. Murphy, *Studia moralia,* v.1 (Rome 1963) 54–85. J. Dupont, *Les Problems du livres des Actes* (Louvain 1950). R. Michiels, EphemThLov 41 (1965) 42–78. V. Monachino, Greg 32 (1951) 5–49, 187–222. P. Carrington, *The Early Church,* 2 v. (Cambridge, Eng. 1957) v.1. Fliche-Martin v.1–2.

[F. X. MURPHY]

CHRISTIANA OF LUCCA, BL., virgin; b. Santa Croce sull' Arno, Italy, 1240; d. Santa Croce, Jan. 4, 1310 (feast, Feb. 18). She was born into a poor family and was baptized Oringa, although in later life she was popularly called Christiana, perhaps in tribute to the particular reverence she had for the state of virginity. She went into the service of a noble family at Lucca, from whom she took leave to go on pilgrimage to Monte Gargano and *Assisi. On her return to Santa Croce she founded a convent there in 1279, giving it the Rule of St. *Augustine. She was famed for her devotion to the Eucharist and the Blessed Virgin and was popularly acclaimed a saint. Her cult was affirmed by several popes and given official recognition in 1776.

Bibliography: EncCatt 4:894. ActSS Jan. 1 (1863) 650–662. M. BACIOCCHI DE PÉON, *La vergine Oringa* (Florence 1926). P. PACCHIANI, *La vergine santacrocese* (San Miniato 1939).

[J. L. GRASSI]

CHRISTIANITY AND HELLENISM

Hellenism is the ensemble of literary, philosophical, moral, and religious ideas that spread throughout the Mediterranean world from the time of Alexander the Great and constituted the foundation of Greco-Roman civilization. A. von Harnack popularised the view that Christianity, in seeking to penetrate this Greco-Roman world, failed to preserve its original purity and underwent a gradual Hellenization. But it is becoming increasingly clear from more recent studies and discoveries that the forms of Christian worship and the substance of Christian dogma all have their roots in the Jewish rather than the Hellenic culture of the 1st century world. There had to be Hellenization of some sort in order to make the new faith acceptable to the Hellenistic mind since Jew and Greek did not think alike (see 1 Cor 1.22). And the more learned converts to Christianity sought ways of putting their own schooling in Hellenism to work in the service of the gospel.

Ambivalence toward Hellenism. An uneasy ambivalence toward Hellenism is discernible from the 2d century, with Christian writers such as *Tatian (*Or.* 25, 31), Theophilus (*Ad Autol.* 2), Hermias, Tertullian (*De praesc.* 7; *De anima* 23) rejecting it as insidious and diabolical, and attributing any good elements in it to plagiarism from the Old Testament. However, *Justin Martyr, *Clement of Alexandria, *Origen, *Gregory of Nyssa, and *Methodius of Olympus followed *Philo Judaeus in regarding the Greek poets and philosophers as broken lights of Moses reflecting the truths already implicit in the Old Testament. The *Didascalia Apostolorum* wishes Christians to have nothing to do with pagan books since the Bible has all the secular as well as religious knowledge necessary: history, poetry, cosmology, and law. *Hippolytus of Rome also was ranged against Hellenism by Eusebius (*Hist. eccl.* 28.13), and *Epiphanius of Constantia listed it as one of the pre-Christian heresies. *Irenaeus of Lyons was impatient with it because it screened rather than illuminated the gospel.

Though some of the Fathers rejected Hellenism in theory, they were saturated with Greek philosophy and culture, and the influence of Greek rhetoric is marked in the majority of patristic writers, from *Melito of Sardes to Theodoret of Cyr, from Tertullian to Augustine. Tertullian asked: "What has Athens to do with Jerusalem?" (*De praescr.* 7, cf. *Apol.* 46; *De anima* 3); but his theology, ethics, and psychology are nonetheless heavily under Stoic influence, as is the *Octavius* of *Minucius Felix.

Eclecticism toward Hellenism. The eclecticism of the Fathers toward Hellenism can be seen in Justin's incorporation into his *Apology* of a Stoic, a Peripatetic, a Pythagorean, a Platonist, and finally a Christian who taught him the new "barbarian" philosophy. Justin, like many of the Apologists, insisted that Christianity is rational and should therefore be acceptable to the Greeks: "On some points we teach the same things as the poets and philosophers whom you honor" (*Apol.* 1.20). He resorted to the Platonizing-Stoic notion of the *logos spermatikos* to explain how everything true that Hellenism taught belonged to the Christians (*2 Apol.* 10.13). L. Bouyer remarks that "we should see in Justin not so much a Hellenization of Christianity as the Christianizing of Hellenism."

Clement of Alexandria, regarded as a true Hellenist, was widely read in Greek philosophy, mythology, and history and was eclectic in his tastes (*Strom.* 1.7.37, 6), but he had a strong predilection for "the truth-loving Plato" (*Strom.* 5.10). He saw Hellenism as a gift of God, one that does not make the truth of Christianity more cogent but provides a useful propaedeutic for it (*Strom.* 1.20.97).

The Origenist Tradition. Origen introduced the methodology of Greek philosophy into the study of Scripture, and he was less of a Stoic and more of a Platonist than Clement. *Gregory of Nyssa continued the Origenist tradition of interpreting Christianity in terms of Greek culture and Neoplatonist mystical language, but he was less liberal than Origen and probably less of a Hellenist than the other Cappadocians, *Basil of Caesarea and *Gregory of Nazianzus. Basil's Hellenism, especially the influence of Stoicism, is seen in his *In Hexaemeron.* His letter *To Young Men* insists on the value of the form of Greek literature as a useful propaedeutic for scriptural studies while rejecting its religious and moral content. An official, uncompromisingly hostile attitude to secular learning and outside philosophy (*philosophia exothen*) was fashionable with almost all of the Greek and Latin Fathers in spite of the fact that all of them were products of secular schools of rhetoric and philosophy. Even a Hellenist such as *Jerome condemned the *sordida dogmata* and *eloquentia* of the philosophers and was bothered at least in sleep by the incompatibility of being a Ciceronian and a Christian.

*Athanasius, too, was a disciple of Origen, but his chief concern was to uphold traditional Christianity against the danger of Hellenization posed by *Arianism. Like *Tertullian (*De anima* 3.23), he sensed that it was in heresies that Hellenism made its greatest inroads, and not in orthodoxy. Somewhat earlier *Eusebius of Caesarea employed his great classical erudition in his *Praeparatio evangelica* to prove the superiority of Judaism to paganism, while he refuted the works of Porphyry and Hierocles.

The exegetical school of *Antioch produced a succession of brilliant Hellenists, *Diodore of Tarsus, *Theodore of Mopsuestia, *John Chrysostom, and *Theodoret of Cyr. It was a Hellenism in the service of exegesis and apologetics, but it stemmed not so much from a wide knowledge of primary sources as from the *florilegia,* mainly of Aetius and Stobaeus.

Influence of Hellenism in the West. In the West, despite the decline in the study of Greek, almost all the great Christian writers, from Minucius Felix, *Cyprian, *Arnobius the Elder, *Lactantius, and Marius Victorinus to *Hilary, *Ambrose, Jerome, and Augustine, were all highly influenced by Hellenism. Stoicism, chiefly mediated through Cicero, and Platonism continued to be the dominant influences, though one may learn much about Epicureanism from Arnobius. Platonic terminology was employed by *Marius Victorinus and Augustine in elaborating a theology of the *Trinity; of a provident God, the Maker of the universe; and of the sensible world, which is but an image of an intelligible and divine world. Platonism was utilized also in the theology of the spirituality of the soul, superior to the body, and illuminated by God with an eternal destiny of rewards and punishments.

*Augustine's conviction that "truth is the Lord's no matter where it is found" (*Doctr. christ.* 11.18) made him more at ease with Hellenism than any of his predecessors. What St. Thomas said of him (ST 1.84.5) can be said about many of the Greek and Latin Fathers: "Whenever Augustine, who was imbued with the doctrines of the Platonists, found in their teaching anything consistent with faith, he adopted it; and those things which he found contrary to faith he amended." Thus Justin's conviction that "all that has ever in the whole human race been well said belongs to us Christians" (*2 Apol.* 13.4) led to the progressive Christianization of Hellenism.

Bibliography: C. TRESMONTANT, *La Métaphysique du christianisme et la naissance de la philosophie chrétienne* (Paris 1961). K. O. WEBER, *Origenes der Neuplatoniker* (Munich 1962). A. WIFSTRAND, *L'Église ancienne et la culture grecque* (Paris 1962). P. AUBIN, *Le Problème de la "conversion"* (Paris 1963). L. BOUYER, *The Spirituality of the New Testament and the Fathers,* tr. M. P. RYAN (New York 1964). P. T. CAMELOT, *Catholicisme* 5:588–592. A. MOMIGLIANO, ed., *The Conflict between Paganism and Christianity in the Fourth Century* (Oxford 1963). R. A. NORRIS, JR., *Manhood and Christ: A Study in the Christology of Theodore of Mopsuestia* (Oxford 1963). H. RAHNER, *Greek Myths and Christian Mystery,* tr. H. BATTERSHAW (New York 1963).

[T. P. HALTON]

CHRISTINA, QUEEN OF SWEDEN

Reigned Dec. 8, 1644 to June 1654; b. Stockholm, Dec. 8, 1626; d. Rome, April 19, 1689. Christina was the only child of *Gustavus Adolphus and Maria Eleanora of Brandenburg. When she was only 6, her father was killed in the *Thirty Years' War. Axel Oxenstierna was regent until she was of age. According to her father's orders, Christina was given the same education as a male heir. Her exceptional intellect led her into scholarly pursuits, and she later made the court a center for artists and scholars, including Hugo Grotius and René Descartes. On Dec. 8, 1644, she became queen and at first exercised a firm rule, worked for peace, encouraged commerce and industry, and opened schools. But she was unable to control the ambitious aristocracy and check the financial drain from the long war in Germany. Her inadequacy was compounded by a lack of interest in money matters and a liberality toward the nobility. Unwisely she augmented their number and granted them royal estates that had formerly provided income for the Crown. By 1648 Christina was already considering the possibility of abdication because of the instability of Sweden's politics, her desire for humanistic studies, and, after 1652, her interest in the Catholic faith. In June 1654, she abdicated in favor of her cousin Charles Gustavus, while reserving the right to an annual income and to her sovereignty and property. Christina went to Brussels, where she made a private confession of faith on Dec. 25, 1654. She was publicly received into the Church at Innsbruck on Nov. 3, 1655. There is no reason to doubt her sincerity in entering the Church, despite the French and Protestant rumors that questioned her motives. From Innsbruck she went to Rome to live permanently.

Queen Christina of Sweden, bust by Francesco Quieroli.

In Rome she shocked people by ignoring conventions in dress and manners, sometimes traveling in male attire. But she was admired for her intellectual acumen. In 1656 she founded the Roman Academy and continued to patronize artists and collect works of art and books. She was constantly in need of money. In 1656 and in 1657 she went to France, seeking the settlement of Swedish claims from the Thirty Years' War. While there she became involved in an abortive scheme to obtain the Neapolitan throne. When her income from Sweden ceased entirely in 1660, she returned to Sweden and demanded from the Diet a reconfirmation of the terms of her abdication and a recognition of her right to the crown if the new King, son of Charles Gustavus, died without issue. Christina made a second trip to Sweden in 1666 for similar financial reasons. Her authoritarian nature and nervous temperament sometimes strained relations between herself and the popes. She was critical, at times, of pious practices, but there is no proof of a weakening of faith. Through the influence of Cardinal Decio Azzolini her eccentricities were modified.

Bibliography: *Christine de Suède et le Cardinal Azzolino: Lettres inédites,* ed. C. N. D. BILDT (Paris 1899). W. H. GRAUERT, *Christina, Königin von Schweden und ihr Hof* (Bonn 1837–42). K. PFISTER, *Königin Christine* (Munich 1949). J. T. DE CASTELNAU, *Christine, reine de Suède, 1626–1689* (Paris 1944). Pastor 30, 31. W. GÖBELL, RGG³ 1:1736–37. S. SVAN, *Königin Christine von Schweden,* tr. from Swedish A. VON STRENECK (Frankfurt 1964). **Illustration credit:** Alinari-Art Reference Bureau.

[E. RENNER]

CHRISTINA OF HAMM, BL.; fl. 15th century, Westphalia, Germany (feast, June 22). According to W. Rolevinck in *Fasciculus temporum* (1482) 12 witnesses testified that a young girl named Stine, who had recently been baptized in 1464, had borne the stigmata (*see*

STIGMATIZATION) in her hands, feet, and side. She was honored with a popular cult. Her feast day was probably adopted from that of *Christina of Stommeln.

Bibliography: K. HONSELMANN, LexThK[2] 2:1129. A. SCHÜTTE, *Handbuch der deutschen Heiligen* (Cologne 1941) 88.

[M. G. MC NEIL]

CHRISTINA OF MARKYATE, recluse, daughter of Auti and Beatrix, gentlefolk of Huntingdon, England; d. *c.* 1155. As a child she took a private vow of virginity on a visit to the Abbey of *St. Albans. At the age of 16 she incurred the emnity of Ralph Flambard, Bishop of Durham and former Chancellor of England, by repulsing his immoral advances; in revenge he had her betrothed to one of his friends, Burhtred. Upon Christina's refusal to marry, her parents used flattery, ridicule, magic, and physical violence to force her hand. The Augustinian Prior of Huntingdon was induced to use his authority to change her mind, and on failing, he brought her before Bp. Robert Bloët of Lincoln, who at first decided in her favor but revoked his decision after a bribe. Encouraged by Ralph d'Escures, Archbishop of Canterbury, and abetted by the hermit Eadwine, Christina took refuge with Alwen, a recluse at Flamstead, where she stayed 2 years. A disagreement caused her to join Roger, a hermit at Caddington, with whom she stayed 4 years. On Roger's death, Archbishop *Thurstan of York wished to make her superior of a convent in York, but she settled at Markyate. There Abbot Geoffrey of St. Albans, where her brother Gregory was a monk, built a convent for her. She exercised a beneficent influence over the abbot and his community. She was celebrated for her prophetic insight and wonder-working, and was revered by King *Henry II and Pope *Adrian IV. For Adrian she made three miters and sandals. Her Psalter is preserved at Hildesheim.

Bibliography: *The Life of Christina of Markyate, a Twelfth Century Recluse,* ed. and tr. C. H. TALBOT (Oxford 1959). O. PÄCHT et al., *The St. Albans Psalter* (London 1960).

[C. H. TALBOT]

CHRISTINA OF SPOLETO, BL., widow, Augustinian; b. Augustina Camozzi at Porlezza on Lake Lugano, Switzerland, *c.* 1435; d. Spoleto, Italy, Feb. 13, 1456 (feast, Feb. 13). The daughter of a reputable physician, Augustina married and was widowed very young and then lived a worldly, disorderly life for several years. Converted, she entered the Third Order Regular of St. Augustine (*see* AUGUSTINIAN NUNS) at Verona, taking the name Christina. Her extremely penitential life forced Christina to change her residence frequently to remain unknown and to avoid veneration by others. Her remains, formerly in the church of S. Nicolò, now rest in S. Gregorio Maggiore, Spoleto. Gregory XVI confirmed her cult Sept. 6, 1834.

Bibliography: N. CONCETTI, "De beata Christina a Spoleto," *Analecta Augustiniana* 5 (1913–14) 457–465. W. HÜMPFNER, LexThK[2] 2:1129.

[M. G. MC NEIL]

CHRISTINA OF STOMMELN, BL., Beguine; b. Stommeln, near Cologne, 1242; d. there, Nov. 6, 1312 (feast, Nov. 6). At 13 she left her prosperous peasant family (Bruso), and became a *Beguine in Cologne. When her singular devotions and austerities disquieted her companions, she left the Beguine convent and returned to Stommeln. In 1267 she came under the direction of the Swedish Dominican Peter of Dacia (d. 1288), who kept a record of her experiences, the sensational nature of which has led some scholars to conjecture hallucinations or hysteria. Throughout her ordeals, however, Christina's firm faith and purity were evident. After the departure of Peter of Dacia in 1269, she corresponded with him through her parish priest, who added his own comments. Her relics were translated first to Niedeggen and then to Jülich, where they are still venerated. Pius X approved her cult in 1908.

Bibliography: ActSS June 5:231–387. Butler Th Attw 4:277–279. J. TORSY, LexThK[2] 2:1129.

[M. J. FINNEGAN]

CHRISTINE DE PISAN, one of the first women of French letters; b. Venice, Italy, 1364 or 1365; d. France, 1430?. Though born in Italy, she went to France in 1368 when her father, Thomas de Pisan of Bologna, an astrologer and physician (cf. Thorndike 3:611–27), became a member of the court of King Charles V, a patron of the arts. Christine grew up in a home of luxury and culture; not only was she well educated, for she studied Latin and "the sciences," but she was also surrounded by some of the better minds of her day. In 1379 she married Etienne de Castel, one of the royal secretaries. Charles V died in 1380 and her father lost his court position. Upon his death in 1385 and her husband's death in 1389, Christine was forced to take up writing as a profession to support herself and her 2 children. Writing on command, in prose or poetry, and often on banal subjects, she produced a hundred poems in French during the next 10 years, all evidencing a certain technical perfection and at times even a personal note, which was unusual in her day. She then turned to more serious work and produced over 15 longer pieces in prose or poetry, some protesting against contemporary medieval antifeminism, such as *Le Dit de la rose* (ed. Roy, v.2) and *La Cité des dames* (unpub.). Her *Le Livre des trois vertus* is a treatise on feminine education, while the prose *Lavision-Christine* (ed. Towner) is an encyclopedia of her mental equipment. Her *Faits et bonnes moeurs du roi Charles V* [ed. S. Solente (2 v. Paris 1936–41)], a biography of Charles, is her best historical piece. The *Mutacion de fortune* (unedited) most closely mirrors her philosophy of life. Some time after the Battle of Agincourt in 1415, Christine retired to the *Dominican convent of Poissy, where her daughter was a nun. After that she produced only the *Dittié a Jeanne d'Arc,* a poem saluting *Joan of Arc, in 1429. Widely read in Latin, Italian, and French literature, Christine may perhaps be best described as the first woman humanist in France.

Bibliography: *Verse Works,* ed. M. ROY, 3 v. (Paris 1886–96). M. J. PINET, *Christine de Pisan* (Paris 1927), for catalogue of works. M. L. TOWNER, ed., *Lavision-Christine* (Washington 1932), with introd. A. L. GABRIEL, "The Educational Ideas of C. de P.," JHistIdeas 16 (1955) 3–21. B. WOLEDGE, in *Fin du moyen âge et renaissance: Mélanges . . . offerts à Robert Guiette* (Antwerp 1961) 97–106. S. CIGADA, "Il tema arturiano del *Château Tournant;* Chaucer e C. de P.," StMed 3d ser., 2 (1961) 576–606.

[M. J. HAMILTON]

CHRISTMAS AND ITS CYCLE

The celebration of Christ's birth on December 25. The name is derived from the Old English *Cristes Maesse* or *Cristes-messe,* meaning the Mass of Christ. The cycle of Christmas includes related feasts beginning with Advent and ending on Candlemas.

History

The feast is first mentioned at the head of the *Depositio Martyrum* in the Roman Chronograph of 354 [ed. Valentini-Zucchetti (Vatican City 1942) 2:17]. Since the *Depositio* was composed in 336, Christmas in Rome can be dated back that far at least. It is not found, however, in the lists of feasts given by Tertullian (*De baptismo* 19; CSEL 20:217) and Origen (*Contra Celsum* 8.22; PG 11:1549).

Date. Inexplicable though it seems, the date of Christ's birth is not known. The Gospels indicate neither the day nor the month; and although Luke (2.1–3) sets the Nativity in a historical perspective, the year cannot be determined with exactitude. Modern scholarship favors the period 8 to 6 B.C. (*See* NATIVITY OF CHRIST.) Why, then, were December 25 and January 6 chosen for the celebration of the Lord's birth? Several theories are offered in explanation.

Some (John Chrysostom, B. Lamy; see Kellner, 143–145) actually believed December 25 was the birthday of Christ and tried to prove it by arguing from the conception of St. John the Baptist. Assuming, gratuitously, that Zachary was high priest and that the Day of Atonement fell on September 24, John would have been born on June 24 and Christ 6 months later, on December 25. This theory is now considered completely untenable.

L. Duchesne [*Christian Worship: Its Origin and Evolution* (5th ed. London 1949) 261–263] suggested that the date of Christmas was determined from March 25, the traditional date of the Crucifixion. Since fractional numbers have no place in symbolical systems, the ancients would have postulated a full number of years for the life of Christ. If He died on March 25, He must also have been conceived on this date and thus have been born 9 months later on December 25. More recently H. Engberding has tried, unsuccessfully, to defend a comparable position.

According to the hypothesis suggested by H. Usener, developed by B. Botte (*Les Origines*), and accepted by most scholars today, the birth of Christ was assigned the date of the winter solstice (December 25 in the Julian calendar, January 6 in the Egyptian), because on this day, as the sun began its return to northern skies, the pagan devotees of Mithra celebrated the *dies natalis Solis Invicti* (birthday of the invincible sun). On Dec. 25, 274, Aurelian had proclaimed the sun-god principal patron of the empire and dedicated a temple to him in the Campus Martius. Christmas originated at a time when the cult of the sun was particularly strong at Rome. This theory finds support in some of the Church Fathers' contrasting the birth of Christ and the winter solstice; indeed, from the beginning of the 3d century "Sun of Justice" appears as a title of Christ (Botte, *Les origines* 63). Though the substitution of Christmas for the pagan festival cannot be proved with certainty, it remains the most plausible explanation for the dating of Christmas.

Diffusion. The feast is found very early in North Africa. The oldest Christmas sermon extant was given by Optatus of Mileve in Numidia around 383 [pub. by A. Wilmart, "Un sermon de s. Optat pour la fête de Noël," RevScRel 2 (1922) 271–302]. The feast was known in Milan by the time of Ambrose (d. 397). The letter of Pope Siricius (384–399) to Himerius, Bishop of Tarragona (*Epist.* 1.2.3; PL 13:1134), proves that Christmas was observed in Spain before 384, while the earliest certain evidence of the feast in Gaul is found in the calendar of Perpetuus, Bishop of Tours from 461 to 491 (Gregory, *Hist. Francorum* 10.31.6; PL 71:566).

In the East the Feast of the Nativity was kept originally on January 6. Nevertheless, toward the end of the 4th century the Western feast of December 25 was admitted. The earliest testimony to an Eastern Feast of Christmas is a sermon of Basil (d. 379; *Homilia in s. Christi generationem,* PG 31:1457–76). On Dec. 25, 379 or 380, Gregory of Nazianzus preached a Christmas sermon in Constantinople (*In theophaniam oratio* 38; PG 36:311–334); he later referred to himself as the founder of the feast (*In sancta lumina oratio* 39.14; PG 36:349). It was known in Antioch between 386 and 388, for John Chrysostom preached about it (*In diem natalem Domini n. J. C.,* PG 49:351). Paul of Emesa gave a Nativity sermon at Alexandria in the presence of St. Cyril on Dec. 25, 432 (*De nativitate,* PG 77:1433–44). In Palestine, however, the birth of Christ was celebrated on January 6 until the middle of the 7th century, when December 25 was permanently accepted.

The Armenians alone never accepted December 25. Under pressure from Rome some of the Uniates in the 16th century accepted the Western feast, for which they simply duplicate the Mass and Office of January 6.

While opposition to the cult of the sun-god could explain the origin of Christmas in given localities, diffusion of the feast throughout the world, where it ran counter to the Eastern observance of January 6, must be attributed to the anti-Arian revival. Arianism was condemned at the Council of Nicaea in 325, and it was at that time that the feast appeared in Rome. The Arians would not have rejected the feast, which could have been interpreted to favor their position, if it had originated before their condemnation. The great anti-Arian Fathers of the East (the Cappadocians and John Chrysostom) seem to have been most influential in Eastern acceptance of Christmas.

Liturgy

The prolonged anti-Arian effort, and later the anti-Nestorian effort, also affected the contents of the feast. For Augustine, Christmas was a *memoria,* a commemoration of a historical event, not a mystery feast such as Easter. But 50 years later Leo the Great, who opposed the Arians and Manichaeans, spoke of Christmas as a mystery feast. Thus Christmas had become the liturgical celebration of the Mystery of the Incarnation (see Gaillard).

Three Masses. The Feast of Christmas has three proper Masses: at midnight, at dawn, and on the day itself. Though this polyliturgy is first mentioned by Gregory the Great (*Homil. 8 in evang.,* PL 76:1103), it must have existed earlier. However, the statement of the 6th-century Liber pontificalis (Duchesne LP 1:129) that Pope Telesphorus I (127–136) instituted the Mass at midnight cannot be true.

The earliest record of a Mass at midnight occurs in the diary of Etheria for January 6 (*Journal de voyage* 25; ed. H. Pétré, 202–204). In addition to this Mass celebrated at Bethlehem, another Mass was offered in the morning at the church on Calvary. This custom soon spread to Rome. Perhaps it was Sixtus III (d. 440) who introduced it, when after the Council of Ephesus he rebuilt the Liberian Basilica (St. Mary Major) with a replica of the grotto of Bethlehem behind the main altar. (Relics of the true crib were acquired in the 7th cen-

Fig. 1. The Grotto of the Nativity at Bethlehem. At the rear of the grotto, marked with a silver star, is the traditional site of Our Lord's birth.

tury, and in 1586 the entire reproduction was removed to the Sistine Chapel of the basilica.) The station for the Mass at midnight has always been at this altar of the *crib. The formulary is first found in the Gelasian Sacramentary (5–9; ed. K. Mohlberg, 7–8).

The Mass at dawn may also have been instituted in imitation of the liturgy of Palestine. Etheria describes a procession from Bethlehem back to Jerusalem with a synaxis at the Holy Sepulchre at dawn. Though it is not known whether a Mass followed (a folio is missing at this point), the Psalms repeated during the procession appear in the Gradual of the Roman Mass. The documents, beginning with the oldest Gregorian Sacramentaries (ed. K. Mohlberg, 2), list St. Anastasia as the station for this second Mass. In the 6th century the cult of the Byzantine martyr Anastasia was localized in this church, named either for its foundress or for the Anastasis in Jerusalem. Out of deference for the nearby Byzantine colony, the Pope celebrated Mass here at dawn on the feast of the martyr, December 25. The Mass was that of the saint, with a commemoration of Christmas. When the influence of Byzantium waned, the station was preserved and the Mass became one of Christmas with a commemoration of the martyr. From indirect evidence in the Gelasian Sacramentary, however, it has

Fig. 2. The Shrine of the Manger in the Grotto of the Nativity at Bethlehem.

been argued that the Christmas Mass antedates that of St. Anastasia.

The third Mass, the oldest and principal Mass, was celebrated in the Basilica of St. Peter. The station was transferred to St. Mary Major by Gregory VII (1073–85) to eliminate the inconvenience of repairing to St. Peter's after the earlier Masses (*Ordo Rom.* 11.17; PL 78:1032).

Originally the three Masses were stational and therefore celebrated only by the pope. But the polyliturgy spread with the Roman Sacramentaries to the titular churches of the city and then beyond Rome.

The Christmas Cycle. In the Leonine Sacramentary Christmas concludes the sanctoral cycle, but in the Würzburg Lectionary (7th century) it is found at the head of the temporal. Christmas had become the beginning of the liturgical year. Then, like Easter, it became the center of a cycle, with a period of preparation (*Advent), a vigil, an octave, and the related feasts of Epiphany and *Candlemas.

Vigil. The vigil of Christmas is found in the Würzburg Lectionary. Among the nine Christmas formularies of the Leonine Sacramentary, two are obviously for the vigil (ed. K. Mohlberg, 1240, 1253). Later books have a proper formulary. The present Mass is found in the Gregorian Sacramentary (ed. K. Mohlberg, 1).

Saints' Feasts. Since ancient times certain saints, called "Comites Christi" by Durandus (*Rationale divinorum off.* 7.42.1), have been commemorated on the days following December 25. They are mentioned by Gregory of Nyssa (*Oratio funebris in laudem fratris Basilii,* PG 46:789) and are found in all the Sacramentaries.

A Feast of St. Stephen on December 26 is mentioned by Gregory of Nyssa (*In sanctum Stephanum,* PG 46:701, 721), the *Breviarium Syriacum* [ed. B. Mariani (Rome 1956) 1:27], and the Calendar of Carthage (H. Leclercq, DACL 8.1:654). It is found in the Würzburg Lectionary and in the early Gregorian Sacramentaries. The Byzantine and Armenian rites, however, have the feast on December 27. The Leonine Sacramentary has it on August 3, but some of the texts (694, 696) contain explicit references to Christmas. Another (701) suggests that August 3 was the dedication of the Basilica of St. Stephen.

A Feast of St. John the Evangelist is found on December 27 in the Roman books, while many Oriental and Gallican books (e.g., *Breviarium Syriacum*) list SS. James and John. The Calendar of Carthage has St. John the Baptist with St. James, but this must be considered erroneous (DACL 8.1:645).

Eastern sources have a commemoration of SS. Peter and Paul on December 28 (*Breviarium Syriacum*) or of Peter with James and John on December 27 and Paul on December 28 (Gregory of Nyssa, *In laudem fratris Basilii,* PG 46:789). Because the feast of these two apostles was early fixed on June 29 in Rome, they are not commemorated after Christmas in the West.

A Feast of the Holy Innocents is found in most documents on December 28. Originally festive, under Gallican influence the commemoration acquired aspects of mourning (purple vestments, omission of *Te Deum, Gloria,* and *Alleluia*), all of which were suppressed in 1961.

The feasts of St. Thomas of Canterbury (d. 1170) on December 29 and of St. Sylvester on December 31 (in the Roman Chronograph of 354) were reduced to commemorations in 1961. A proper Mass for the Sunday after Christmas is first found in the 8th century.

Octave. January 1 has had at various times a Mass against pagan practices, a Mass of Our Lady, and a Mass of the octave of Christmas.

Oldest of these is the *Missa ad prohibendum ab idolis,* which bears witness to the survival of pagan practices (Righetti 2:42). St. Augustine (*Sermo* 198; PL 38: 1024–26) inveighed against such practices and exhorted the faithful to prayer and penance. The Second Council of Tours (567) and the Fifth Council of Toledo (633) ordered penance on this day [c.17 (Hefele-Leclercq 3:188); c.11 (*ibid.* 3:269)]. This Mass, however, fell into disuse in the 6th and 7th centuries. The Gregorian Sacramentary has preserved the Secret and Postcommunion, which are still in use today.

A Mass in honor of Our Lady on January 1 was also known at Rome (B. Botte, "La Première fête mariale . . ."). Such a commemoration at this time of the year is logical. The Byzantine and Syrian liturgies have a Feast of Our Lady on December 26. The Roman Mass, however, may have been inspired by local circumstances. The Mass may have originated as the dedication of S. Maria Antiqua, formerly the station on January 1. Or the pagan legend according to which a dragon devoured a vestal virgin on this spot in the Roman Forum each January 1 may have suggested a feast in honor of the Virgin who conquered the devil. The beautiful antiphons still used in the Office of this day were probably inherited from the Byzantine monks who once served S. Maria Antiqua. The formulary was *Vultum tuum,* the common of virgins, with proper orations and a Preface gleaned from a sermon of St. Augustine. At first the Gospel was from the same common (Mt 13.44–52); later the pericope Luke 2.21–32 was used. Though this Mass persisted in some places in the Middle Ages, it seems to have fallen into disuse as other feasts of Our Lady developed. According to Botte this Mass can be considered the oldest Marian feast in the Roman liturgy (*ibid.*).

The Gelasian and Gregorian Sacramentaries have a formulary "in octabas Domini." Originally the only reference to the Circumcision was in the Gospel, logically chosen from Luke 2.21–32. This pericope included also the Presentation until a proper feast of this event developed. The station, formerly at S. Maria ad Martyres, was transferred to S. Maria in Trastevere by Callistus II (1119–24). The Circumcision became the primary object of this day first in Spain, then in Gaul, and finally in Rome (Righetti 22:43). From the 15th century Roman books have the title "Feast of the Circumcision." The primitive title "Octave of the Nativity" was restored in 1961.

Holy Name. A Feast of the Holy Name is celebrated on the Sunday between January 1 and January 6 or, if either of these falls on Sunday, on January 2. Cult of the Holy Name was preached by St. John Capistran (d. 1456) and St. Bernardine of Siena (1380–1444). The feast was first celebrated at Camaiore in Italy in

(a)

(b)

(c)

Fig. 3. (a) Annunciation to the Shepherds, miniature accompanying the Propers for Christmas in a Sacramentary written at Mont-Saint-Michel in the 11th century (Morgan MS 641, fol. 2 v), (b) the Martyrdom of St. Stephen in the same manuscript (fol. 3 v), and (c) the miniature for the Feast of St. John the Evangelist (fol. 5).

1528. In 1721, at the behest of Charles VI, Innocent VIII extended it to the universal Church (Righetti 2:45).

Customs. In many countries the fast prescribed for Christmas Eve by Canon Law (CIC c.1252.2) is tempered by a festive meal in the evening. In 1966 Pope Paul VI issued new regulations limiting the days of fast and abstinence to Ash Wednesday and Good Friday.

The Feast of the Nativity is solemnly announced in the martyrology by a deacon. In some monastic Offices the genealogy of Christ (Mt 1.1–16) is read after the ninth lesson of Christmas Matins.

The Würzburg and Murbach Lectionaries have a prophecy from Isaias in each of the Christmas Masses. This usage has been preserved by some of the medieval rites (e.g., the Carmelite).

On the feast and during the octave a statue of the Infant may be placed over the altar (Sacred Cong. of Rites 3288, 3320). The use of the crib in church and home derives ultimately from the grotto in Bethlehem and its reproduction in St. Mary Major. The popular custom was introduced by St. Francis of Assisi in 1223.

The Christmas tree is derived, not from the pagan yule tree, but from the Paradise tree adorned with apples on December 24 in honor of Adam and Eve. The Christmas tree is found first at Strasbourg in 1605.

The term "carol," formerly designating a Christmas hymn of popular nature, is now used of all Christmas songs. The first Latin Christmas hymns date back to the 5th century. Popular carols originated in Italy under the influence of St. Francis of Assisi. Most of the well-known carols have been composed since mid-19th century. *See* CAROL.

Exchanging of gifts, so in harmony with the significance of Christmas, may have been influenced by a similar custom (*strenae*) among the pagans on January 1. Gifts are exchanged by the French on January 1, by the Spanish and Italians on January 6, and by other nationalities on December 25. In most parts of Europe it was the Christ Child who brought the gifts. After the Reformation the day itself was personified, and the figure of Father Christmas was later combined with St. Nicholas, the patron of children, to become Santa Claus. In Italy gifts are brought by the old woman Befana (from "Epiphany") and in Spain by the Three Kings.

See also MARY, BLESSED VIRGIN, ICONOGRAPHY OF; EPIPHANY, FEAST OF.

Bibliography: B. BOTTE, *Les Origines de la Noël et de l'Épiphanie* (Louvain 1932; repr. 1961). J. LEMARIÉ, *La Manifestation du Seigneur: La Liturgie de Noël et de l'Épiphanie* (Paris 1957). Miller FundLit 404–409. A. G. MARTIMORT, *L'Église en prière* (Tournai 1961) 727–738. Righetti 2:31–45. G. Löw, EncCatt 8:1667–73. J. A. JUNGMANN, *The Early Liturgy to the Time of Gregory the Great*, tr. F. A. BRUNNER (Notre Dame, Ind. 1959) 147–149, 266–277. A. BAUMSTARK, *Comparative Liturgy*, rev. B. BOTTE, tr. F. L. CROSS (Westminster, Md. 1958) 152–164. H. FRANK, "Frühgeschichte und Ursprung des römischen Weihnachtsfestes im Lichte neuer Forschung," ArchLiturgwiss 2 (1952) 1–24. H. ENGBERDING, "Der 25. Dezember als Tag der Feier der Geburt des Herrn," *ibid.* 25–43. J. FENDT, "Der heutige Stand der Forschung über

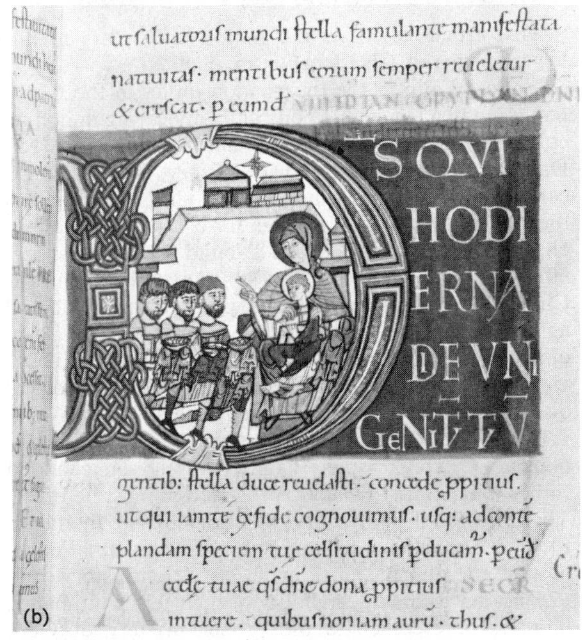

Fig. 4. Illuminated miniatures from the 11th-century Sacramentary from Mont-Saint-Michel (Morgan MS 641): (a) an Allegory of the Church surrounded by the infant martyrs, for the Feast of the Holy Innocents (fol. 6 r), (b) for the Feast of the Epiphany (fol. 9 r), and (c) for the Feast of the Presentation of Our Lord (fol. 18 r).

das Geburtsfest Jesu am 25. Dez. und über Epiphanias," ThLitZ 78 (1953) 1–10. F. J. DÖLGER, "Natalis Solis Invicti und das christliche Weihnachtsfest," *Antike und Christentum* 6 (1940–50) 23–30. A. STRITTMATTER, "Christmas and the Epiphany: Origins and Antecedents," *Thought* 17 (1942) 600–626. M. HIGGINS, "Note on the Purification and Date of the Nativity in Constantinople in 602," ArchLiturgwiss 2 (1952) 81–83. J. GAILLARD, "Noël: Memoria ou mystère?" *Maison-Dieu* 59 (1959) 37–59. G. HUDON, "Le Mystère de Noël dans le temps de l'Église d'après Saint Augustin," *ibid.* 60–84. J. LECLERCQ, "Aux origines du cycle de Noël," EphemLiturg 60 (1946) 7–26. B. BOTTE, "La Première fête mariale de la liturgie romaine," *ibid.* 47 (1933) 425–430. F. X. WEISER, *Handbook of Christian Feasts and Customs: The Year of the Lord in Liturgy and Folklore* (New York 1958). K. A. H. KELLNER, *Heortology* (St. Louis 1908). H. USENER, *Das Weihnachtsfest* (2d ed. Bonn 1911). **Illustration credit:** Fig. 3*a, b, c* and Fig. 4*a, b, c*, The Pierpont Morgan Library.

[C. SMITH]

CHRISTOCENTRISM

This article discusses the notion and refers to historical forms of Christocentrism.

Notion. Faith in the Incarnation unites in the Christian mind two tendencies constantly appearing in human culture: *theocentrism and *anthropocentrism (cf. Dawson. *Dynamics of World History,* index s.v. Incarnation). The sacred humanity of Christ is pivotal in the mystery that is God's design for creation (Ephesians ch. 1, etc.). In the new Adam is found the exemplar and efficacious principle of God's saving work. In this Christocentrism Catholic theologians are in substantial agreement. Discussion arises, however, concerning theological *methodology. St. Thomas Aquinas, whose view that the object ultimately specifying all theological discourse is the proper character of the divinity (ST 1a, 1.7) has been accepted by most theologians, notes the objection that Christian theology should be centered rather upon Christ (*ibid.*). A distinction must be made. The Christian mysteries may be studied in two manners: (1) insofar as they are revealed in the existential economy of the divine *missions, a *salvation history; and (2) insofar as the intelligibility of their terms ultimately involves a reference to the proper mystery of God, which transcends time. According to St. Thomas (*loc. cit.*), the second is the ultimate task of theology. But the first cannot be neglected in an adequate theology. It is evident that, since the Christ-event is the center of salvation history, the first must be Christocentric.

Another discussion has taken place concerning the centrality of the Christ-event in God's plan of creation. According to St. Thomas (ST 3a, 1.3) and most theologians, revelation indicates that in the present design of God the Incarnation is willed by God in view of Adam's fall, i.e., the Christ-event is the central event of a *saving* history. The Franciscan school, on the other hand, maintains as more probable the opinion that even in the present design the Incarnation is willed antecedently to any reference to the Fall, for the sake of Christ's cosmic primacy in itself (cf. Scotus, *Comm. oxon. in sent.* d. 7 q. 3, etc.).

Historical Review. In general, the Fathers' vision of salvation history gave their thought a Christocentric character. During the Middle Ages, while theology's concern with the analytical study of scholasticism increased, a new form of Christocentrism emerged, especially in the devotional life of the Church. It emphasized Christ's human existence, but in a manner that lost sight of the events of Christ's life as revelations of the mystery of salvation; and it tended more and more toward the naturalism that is so manifest in the religious art of the Renaissance. The Reformation movement's profoundly Christocentric emphasis must be seen, partly, as a reaction against the Renaissance's shallow appreciation of the Christ-event as the mystery of salvation. As the Church of the mid-20th century regains the patristic vision of the existential totality of salvation history, the program of renewal embraced by Vatican Council II (in particular with reference to the theology of the Church and of the liturgy) is notably Christocentric in character.

See also FIRSTBORN; FIRSTBORN OF EVERY CREATURE; INCARNATION, 3; JESUS CHRIST, III (SPECIAL QUESTIONS), 12; KINGDOM OF CHRIST.

Bibliography: H. KÜNG, LexThK² 2:1169–74. J. F. BONNEFOY, *Christ and the Cosmos,* tr. M. D. MEILACH (Paterson, N.J. 1965). C. H. DAWSON, *Dynamics of World History,* ed. J. J. MULLOY (New York 1956). Vatican Council II, *Constitution on the Sacred Liturgy; Dogmatic Constitution on the Church.*

[J. THORNHILL]

CHRISTOLOGICAL CONTROVERSY, EARLY

The disputes concerning the nature of Jesus Christ, true God and true man, that troubled the theological development of the early Church. Reflection on the nature of Christ was intimately connected with His soteriological activity and with His office or function as Lord (*Kyrios*). Paul, in Rom 1.3, had spoken of Christ as at once "according to the spirit" and "according to the flesh"; and the apostolic Fathers insisted that He was preexistent, unbegotten, and the head of creation. But there is little evidence for an interest in the manner in which the divine spirit and the human nature were joined together in Christ. Against the Gnostics and Ebionites, the apostolic Fathers insisted on a true divine spirit and a true body in Christ (Ignatius of Antioch, *Eph.* 3.2, 8.2; *Smyr.* 4.1), and Irenaeus considered the denial of this assertion heretical.

Apologists. In the 2d century the *Apologists insisted that Jesus Christ was the visible form of the divine Logos, a statement that made sense within the sphere of the popular Hellenistic philosophy. Whereas *Ignatius of Antioch had spoken of the historical Christ as the Logos through whom God had broken His eternal silence (*Mag.* 8.2), the Apologists identified the Logos with the preexistent cosmic principle of God's wisdom and power (1 Cor 1.24). Irenaeus, in conflict with the Gnostics, opposed their *Docetism with a theology of the *Incarnation, basing his thought on the tradition represented by Theophilus of Antioch, Justin Martyr, and Ignatius (*Eph.* 20.1). Irenaeus insisted that out of boundless love Jesus Christ became like unto men as a man so that He might fulfill in men that which He was Himself. This divinization of man required that Christ be at once true God and true man.

Tertullian. *Tertullian taught that the oneness of the Father and the Son required a oneness in substance that underlay the difference in persons in the Trinity. His corporeal concepts, tied in with time and quantity, however, involved his explanation in *Subordinationism; but his terminology regarding one Person in two substances, or natures, as well as the distinction of the three Persons in one substance in the Trinity, proved invaluable in the later Western Christological development. His intention was to combat *Monarchianism, which denied the diversity of Persons in the one God, as well as various forms of Adoptionism and Modalism. The Roman type of *Adoptionism that saw Christ raised to divinity in His Baptism was combated by the popes before 200; and *Callistus, with the condemnation of Sabellius, included a repudiation of the *Modalism of Noëtus and Praxeas in Asia Minor, who considered the three functions of the Father, Son, and Spirit in the history of salvation as mere manifestations or modes of the Godhead. This theory was rejected also by *Hippolytus of Rome. A further development of Modalism manifested itself in *Patripassianism, or the theory that if Father and Son were one in substance, the Father must have suffered for mankind.

Homoousios. Under the influence of the Neoplatonist teaching on the divine emanations, *Clement of Alexandria and *Origen considered Christ in His cosmic function and tended to explain the Savior as the head of creation; as seen from a worldly viewpoint, Christ was eternal and therefore divine, but from God's viewpoint, He was rather the first of all creation. Two further tendencies manifested themselves among the followers of Origen: *Gregory Thaumaturgus insisted on the oneness in nature of Son and Father; *Dionysius (Denis) of Alexandria, in opposing Libyan Modalism, asserted that Father and Son were of the same divine nature. Since the word *homoousios, or consubstantial, had been used by *Paul of Samosata in a Monarchian sense, it was looked upon with suspicion by the Alexandrians, and after 268 it was rejected also by the Antiochians. *Lucian of Antioch, influenced by Aristotelian logic and pursuing the conviction that the begotten Son could not be of the same being as the unbegotten Godhead, considered the Logos as joined to the divinity on a moral or even on an ethical principle. His pupil *Arius was condemned at the Council of *Nicaea I (325), where the doctrine that the Son was true God, of the same substance as the Father (homoousios), was clarified and the difference between creation out of nothing and the eternal generation of Persons in the Godhead was clearly recognized. In the politically dominated theological disputes of the next 40 years, *Athanasius of Alexandria played a leading part, insisting on the validity of the Nicene definition.

After the splintering of the Arianizing sects into Anomoean and Homoean groups (the Son is not like the Father; the Son is similar to the Father), Meletius of Antioch (*c.* 363) and the Cappadocian Fathers insisted on the consubstantiality of the three divine Persons, and by differentiating between *ousia* (substance) and *hypostasis* (person or individual) avoided the tendency to find subordination in the Trinity. *See* MELETIAN SCHISM. Under the influence of the Aristotelian concept of the unity of matter and form and in opposition to the Gnostic separation of Christ into the divine Savior and His earthly form, the *Apollinarists denied that Christ had a human soul, and *Eustathius of Antioch claimed that the divinity dwelt in the humanity in order to justify the concept of the *Logos-sarx* unity.

Nestorianism. The Antiochene theologians led by *Diodore of Tarsus rejected the Arian concept of the creation of the Logos, but maintained that a distinction had to be made between the flesh capable of suffering and the impassible Logos. *Theodore of Mopsuestia insisted that the Logos had assumed a complete manhood. Christ must have had a human soul, since His redemptive act as the God-man freed man's soul from sin, and He led man eventually through the Resurrection to a fulfillment of human nature that was based and modeled on His own human and divine experience. To emphasize this teaching, *Nestorius of Constantinople decided to call Mary the Mother of Christ rather than the *Theotokos, or Mother of God, in order to stress the validity of the true human nature.

In combating this manifestation of Nestorianism, *Cyril of Alexandria, on commission from Pope Celestine I, presided over the Council of *Ephesus (431) and condemned the teaching of Nestorius. But Cyril's extreme statement of the Alexandrian position in his 12 anathemas had to be modified by a letter of Union signed by himself and *John of Antioch in 433.

Monophysitism. Cyril held that the divine and human substance (or natures in an abstract sense) were complete and unconfused in Christ; they could be separated only in thought, by theoretical concepts, since the concrete Christ was the divine Logos incarnated as the God-man. Cyril's insistence that Christ had to be an individual was accepted in such literal fashion by *Eutyches that at the Synod of Constantinople (448) he was forced to admit that one nature resulted from the union of the divinity and humanity in Christ. This crude *Monophysitism was condemned at the Council of Chalcedon (451), where, in consequence of the teaching in the *Tome* of Pope *Leo I and the precise theological terminology achieved by a group of theologians including *Theodoret of Cyr, it was asserted that Christ was "of two natures without mixture, or confusion." This definition was rejected by Nestorius, who considered the distinction between *hypostasis* (person) and *ousia* (nature) as confused, and by the Monophysites, who said that to deny that Christ was of one nature led to a logical conclusion that there were two complete and therefore individual natures in the God-man.

With the condemnation of the *Three Chapters at the Council of *Constantinople II (553), the Chalcedonian definition took on its stabilized form early in Byzantine *theology. Cyril's doctrine that in Christ there is one nature (*mia physis*) was interpreted to mean that there is one individual or substantial being, and John the Grammarian clarified the fact that in the hypostatic unity the human nature is inalterably united to the divine Person. However, the founding of national churches in Egypt, Syria, and Armenia exaggerated the Monophysite position.

Monothelitism. The Emperor *Heraclius attempted to win back the Monophysites to unity by speaking of one energy or action in Christ, but this resulted in the controversies over *Monothelitism and Monergism. *Maximus the Confessor clarified these doctrines by insisting that in Christ there are two wills and two energies, representing, respectively, the fully coordinated divine and human natures. *John Damascene combined the dythelitism (two wills) doctrine with the Chalcedonian idea of the *enhypostasis,* or one Person with two natures, to reassert the Leonine teaching of the communication of idioms. This doctrine was used subsequently by the medieval *scholastic theologians in their teaching on the relations between the natures and person in Christ and on the relations of the natures with each other.

In the West, a new type of Adoptionism was discussed in 7th-century Spain, and was condemned by Charlemagne in several Carolingian synods. The later scholastics argued over the personality of Christ, and this problem has been resurrected in contemporary discussions concerning the ego of Christ. Protestant theology from Luther, Calvin, and Zwingli to Hegel, Strauss, Ritschl and M. Köhler has been more concerned with the religious, ethical, and historical implications of Christology than with the explanation of the union between the divine and human nature. Many contemporary non-Catholics accept some type of subordinationism in their Christological thinking.

See also SUBORDINATIONISM.

Bibliography: A. MICHEL, DTC, Tables générales 2:2642–45. Grill-Bacht Konz v.1–3. W. ELERT, *Der Ausgang der altkirchlichen Christologie* (Berlin 1957). R. V. SELLERS, *Two Ancient Christologies* (London 1940). B. M. XIBERTA Y ROQUETA, "Un conflicto entre dos Cristologias," MiscMercati 1:327–354. E. R. HARDY and C. C. RICHARDSON, eds., *Christology of the Later Fathers* (Philadelphia 1954). P. GALTIER, Greg (1959) 54–66. A. GRILLMEIER, "Der Neu-Chalkedonismus," HistJb 77 (1958) 151–166. B. SKARD, *Die Inkarnation* (Stuttgart 1958). G. WINGREN, *Man and the Incarnation,* tr. R. MACKENZIE (Philadelphia 1959). *Handbuch der Dogmengeschichte* 3.1, ed. M. SCHMAUS and A. GRILLMEIER (Freiburg 1965).

[F. X. MURPHY]

CHRISTOLOGY

The part of *dogmatic theology that studies the Person and attributes of Christ, and in particular the union in Him of divine and human natures. The study is motivated not by a merely theoretical but by a solidly practical interest. For the worship of Christ is the life of the Church. Consequently the Church has ever been under the necessity of explaining, both to its own faithful and to those without, how worship of Jesus, a man, can be combined with avowed and sincere monotheism.

In the unsystematic fashion characteristic of Sacred Scripture, the inspired authors of the New Testament had bequeathed to the primitive Christian community a double premise, viz, that Christ as a Person was indivisibly one and that He was simultaneously fully divine and fully human. The necessity of showing how these two affirmations could be held together in synthesis (the central problem of Christology) was not immediately felt. Confronted with the crude dissents of Ebionitism and Docetism, the Apostolic Fathers and the apologists simply repeated the gospel message either word for word or in carefully chosen equivalent terms. Their language of concrete and positive affirmation remains as a priceless witness to the vigor and clarity of faith in the subapostolic period.

Toward the close of the 2d century, a new group of thinkers, steeped in Greek philosophy, entered into the life of the Church and rapidly propelled Christology into its most decisive epoch. Later historians (e.g., A. von Harnack, O. Cullmann) profess to find at this juncture a major setback for authentic Christianity, charging that the Hellenic influence diverted faith from its true object and turned the Church down the path of sterile speculation. In rebuttal it can be shown (1) that the passionate theological debates that raged from the 3d to the 7th century could have been avoided only by a universal agreement to refrain from thinking about the central Figure of Christian worship and (2) that, given the right to think and the possibility of thinking incorrectly (a possibility that was repeatedly verified in fact), the Church was compelled to ponder ever more profoundly the gospel message in order to produce an apt reply to each freshly appearing heretical subtlety. The epoch opened in 318, when Arius published his daring conclusion that the Son was not God but merely a creature. There followed: Apollinarianism, which sought to mutilate the humanity of Christ by denying to Him a rational soul; Nestorianism, which beheld in the Incarnation a merely affective, quite extrinsic union between two persons, one divine and the other human; Monophysitism, which coupled belief in the one Person of Christ with the contention that He therefore possessed only one nature; and Monothelitism, which confessed two natures in Christ while denying Him two wills. To list those who struggled in the orthodox cause against these mischievous heresies would be to reproduce almost the entire roster of the Fathers of the Church. The outstanding champions, however, were St. Athanasius, St. Cyril of Alexandria, Pope St. Leo the Great, and St. Sophronius of Jerusalem. Under their respective leadership the Ecumenical Councils of Nicaea I (325), Ephesus (431), Chalcedon (451), and Constantinople III (680) fashioned the dogmatic definitions that to this day remain the clearest expression of the Church's faith in its Lord.

Medieval Christology strove to make explicit and to systematize the theological truths latent in the earlier dogmatic pronouncements. Christ's several kinds of knowledge, His possession of various types of grace, and the freedom of His human will received large attention. The attempt to interpret metaphysically the *hypostatic union aroused much dispute among the schools. These preoccupations of the medieval scholastic theologians formed the basis of Catholic works on Christology until very recently.

It cannot be said that this Christology commands the same allegiance among Catholic theologians today as heretofore. For the scholastic synthesis tends to portray a Christ not readily identifiable with the Christ of the New Testament that contemporary Biblical scholarship is in the process of discovering. One example of this unsettling discrepancy must here suffice. Arguing from what it considered an unassailable principle, yesterday's Christology refused to concede any real moral or psychic growth to Christ. It is difficult to reconcile this deduction with what seems to be a cardinal theme of the New Testament—the progressive realization by Jesus of His messianic destiny and His ever-deepening commitment to His role as savior of mankind. Generalizing from this and other instances, Catholic theologians are becoming more and more aware that a viable Christology cannot be separated from evangelical *soteriology and are attempting to devise a dogmatic theology concerning Christ that is more generously rooted in the primitive Biblical revelation.

See also JESUS CHRIST, II (IN DOGMATIC THEOLOGY); JESUS CHRIST, ARTICLES ON; THEOLOGY; THEOLOGY, HISTORY OF; THEOLOGY, INFLUENCE OF GREEK PHILOSOPHY ON.

Bibliography: DTC, Tables générales 2:2548–2655. A. MICHEL, DTC 7.2:1445–1539. A. GRILLMEIER, LexThK[2] 2:1156–66. G. SEVENSTER et al., RGG[3] 1:1745–89. W. SUNDAY, *Christologies Ancient and Modern* (New York 1910). H. M. RELTON, *Studies* *in Christian Doctrine* (New York 1960). H. M. DIEPEN, *Douze dialogues de christologie ancienne* (Rome 1960). K. RAHNER, "Current Problems in Christology," *Theological Investigations,* tr. C. ERNST, v.1 (Baltimore 1961) 149–200. T. E. CLARKE, "Some Aspects of Current Christology" in J. E. O'NEILL, ed., *The Encounter with God* (New York 1962) 33–58. B. LEEMING, "Reflections on English Christology" in Grill-Bacht Konz 3:695–718.

[J. J. WALSH]

CHRISTOPHER, ST., possibly a martyr, whose cult was widely spread in the East and West at an early date (feast, July 25). As early as 452 a church in Bithynia was dedicated in his honor. The Roman Martyrology states that a Christopher was martyred in Lycia under King Decius. According to the legendary *passio,* Christopher was called Reprobus before his baptism and was a Canaanite of great stature and strength. Legend states that when he discovered the devil's fear of Christ, he became a Christian. The story of Christopher's bearing the Christ child upon his shoulders while fording a river does not appear in the earliest accounts and is doubtless an accretion based upon the saint's name, "Christbearer." A drop of the martyr's blood was said to have healed a wound that the persecuting King suffered while attempting to execute Christopher. As a result of this miracle the King became a Christian. This gave rise to the popular medieval belief that anyone who looked upon the saint's image would be free from harm that day; hence the custom of putting up images of the saint opposite the church door. He is also the patron of travelers.

Bibliography: ActSS July 6:125–149. Amore et al., EncCatt 4:921–926. Butler Th Attw 3:184–187. B. KÖTTING, LexThK[2] 2:1167–68. **Illustration credit:** The Metropolitan Museum of Art, Gift of J. Pierpont Morgan, 1917.

[E. DAY]

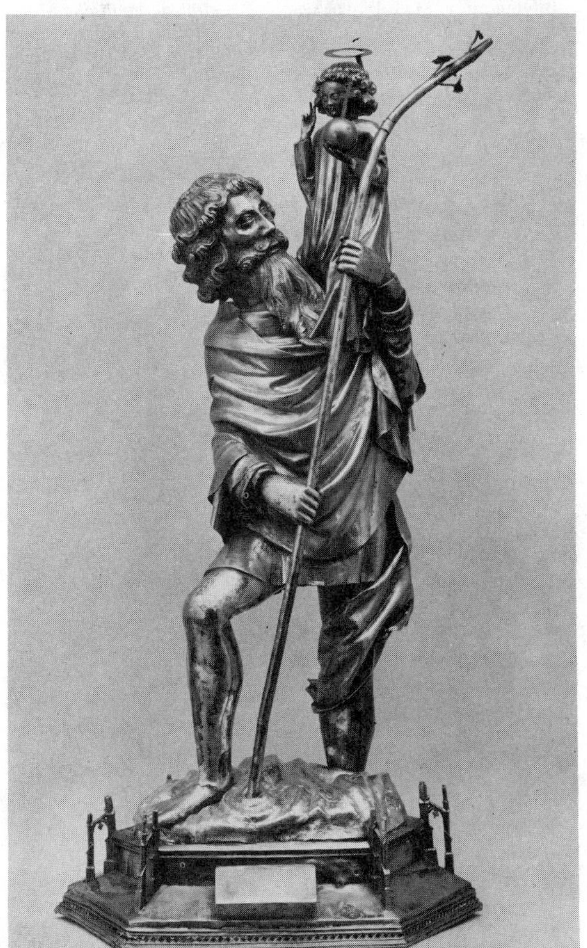

St. Christopher, 15th-century French silver-gilt statue.

CHRISTOPHER MACCASSOLI, BL., Franciscan; b. Milan, between 1415 and 1420; d. Vigevano, Italy, 1485 (feast, March 11). Born of a noble family, he joined the Franciscan Observants in 1435 and, after

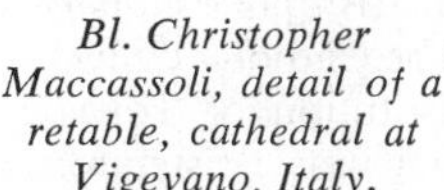

Bl. Christopher Maccassoli, detail of a retable, cathedral at Vigevano, Italy.

his ordination, was assigned to preaching. He was guardian of Abbiategrasso in 1477 and was transferred later to Vigevano, where he enlarged the friary and distinguished himself by his virtues. He was buried in the chapel of St. Bernardine in the Franciscan church. There a painting done in 1503 represents him with SS. Clare and Bernardine of Siena, before the Virgin and Child. *Aloysius Gonzaga attested to his holiness. His remains were discovered in 1588; in 1638 his name was inserted in the Franciscan martyrology. In 1717 the above-mentioned painting was placed over the main altar of the Franciscan church. The relics were relocated in 1743, and in 1810 the reliquary and painting were transferred to the cathedral. The diocesan process for his beatification continued from 1877 to 1884, and in 1890 Leo XIII permitted an Office and Mass to be celebrated in his honor in the Diocese of Vigevano and among the *Franciscans.

Bibliography: "Acta ordinis causae sanctorum ordinis nostri," *Acta Ordinis Minorum* 9 (1890) 117–119. P. M. SEVESI, *B. Cristoforo Macassoli* (Varese 1941). Butler Th Attw 1:563.

[J. CAMBELL]

CHRISTOPHER OF ROMANDIOLA, BL., companion of St. Francis, known also as Christopher of Cahors; b. Romandiola, Italy, *c.* 1172; d. Cahors, France, Oct. 31, 1272 (feast, Oct. 31). When *Francis of Assisi was passing through Romandiola in 1215, Christopher, a country parish priest, decided to become his disciple, and he was a member of the first group of *Franciscans sent to Aquitaine. The lives of these early Franciscan missionaries, who spent their time in prayer and the service of the sick and outcast, especially lepers, made a profound impression. They made many converts, and numerous houses were built for them. Christopher was a simple, devout man, not a preacher in the official sense of the word—*non erat* *officio praedicator*—and it seems certain that he was never minister provincial of the province of Aquitaine. He was present at the provincial chapter of Arles held in 1224 by John Bonnelli. The cult of Bl. Christopher was confirmed by Pope *Pius X in 1905.

Bibliography: L. DE CHERANCÉ, *Le Bx. Christophe de Cahors* (Paris 1907). A. BÉGUET, "Provincialat du Bx. Christophe de Cahors," ArchFrancHist 4 (1911) 619–621. *Vita e culto del B. Christoforo di Romagna* (Rome 1905). AnalFranc 3:161–173. W. FORSTER, LexThK[2] 2:1168–69. Butler Th Attw 4:200.

[T. C. CROWLEY]

CHRISTOPHER COLLEGE, a coeducational institution that offers a liberal arts and general education program leading to an associate of arts degree, is conducted by the Sisters of the Incarnate Word and Blessed Sacrament. The College was founded as Mary Immaculate Junior College in Corpus Christi, Tex., January 1958, but changed its name to Christopher College in August 1965. It is an affiliate of The Catholic University of America and a chartered institution of Texas.

Although the College was founded as a sister formation project to facilitate the education of the young sisters of the congregation, courses in the liberal arts have been made available to young men and women. Sisters of other congregations, assigned to teaching positions in and around Corpus Christi, also take advantage of the in-service courses offered. Programs of study include: theology, philosophy, history, English, Spanish, German, French, chemistry, biology, mathematics, and business.

The College is administered by the president, who is assisted by the dean-registrar, librarian, and counselors. In 1964 the teaching staff was composed of 1 priest, 4 laymen, and 5 sisters. Of these, 2 held doctorates, 2 were doctoral candidates, and the rest held master's degrees. Enrollment numbered 178 full-time and 33 part-time students in the regular session and 14 in the summer session. The library housed 8,000 volumes and received 127 periodicals.

[M. P. GUNNING]

CHRISTOPHERS, THE, founded in 1945 by James Keller, MM, is the name of a movement that attempts to stimulate people in all walks of life to accept personal responsibility for strengthening the great spheres of influence, especially those of government, education, labor-management relations, literature, and entertainment. It seeks to remind each follower of Christ that he has a mission from God to bring divine values into a fast-changing world. There are no membership lists, meetings, or dues. The movement is supported by voluntary donations. Persons are reached through the *Christopher News Notes,* sent free upon request to more than 1 million individuals eight times a year; through radio and television programs scheduled by more than 3,000 radio and television stations; through 23 Christopher books, among which are the titles *You Can Change the World, Government Is Your Business, Change the World from Your Parish,* and *How to Be a Leader;* through a syndicated column entitled "Three Minutes A Day" carried by 103 dailies; and through experimental leadership courses conducted at Christopher headquarters in New York City to inculcate basic leadership skills and Christlike motivation. The Christopher motto, "Better to light one candle than to curse the darkness," reflects St. Paul's admonition: "Be not overcome by evil, but overcome evil with good" (Rom 12.21).

[J. KELLER]

CHRISTUS, PETRUS, Flemish painter; b. Baerle, near Ghent, date unknown; d. Bruges, 1472 or 1473. Before being received as master in Bruges in 1444, Petrus was probably a pupil of Jan van *Eyck, whom he succeeded as leader of the Bruges school. He transformed the themes of Van Eyck into a more personal and homely language ("Exeter Madonna," 1450, Kaiser Friedrich Museum, Berlin). The influences of Dirk *Bouts, Roger van der *Weyden, and Robert *Campin are also to be seen in his religious works ("Nativity," *c.* 1440–50, National Gallery, Washington, D.C.; "Lamentation," Royal Museum, Brussels; "Nativity," Georges Wildenstein, N.Y.). His portraits are very human and show a deep psychological insight into character; they include: "Sir Edward Grymestone" (1486, Collection of Earl of Verulam, St. Albans); a portrait of a young lady (1470–71, Kaiser Friedrich Museum, Berlin); and a portrait of a Carthusian monk (1446, Metropolitan Museum, N.Y.). It does not seem improbable that Petrus may be the same person as the painter Piero di Burges, reported in Milan in 1457.

See also RENAISSANCE ART, 2.

Bibliography: M. J. FRIEDLÄNDER, *Die altniederländische Malerei,* 14 v. (Berlin 1924–37). Panofsky ENethPaint. E. PANOFSKY, in *Studies in Art and Literature for Belle da Costa,* ed. D. E. MINER (Princeton 1954) 102–108. **Illustration credit:** National Gallery of Art, Washington, D.C., Mellon Collection.

[P. H. HEFTING]

Petrus Christus, "The Nativity," panel, 51¼ by 38¼ in.

CHRODEGANG OF METZ, ST., bishop, who introduced Roman liturgy into the Frankish Church and wrote a rule for the common life of cathedral clergy; b. Hesbaye in Brabant, 712; d. Metz, March 6, 766 (feast, March 6). After being educated in the abbey school of *Saint-Trond, he went to the court of *Charles Martel and became his chancellor. He was consecrated bishop of *Metz in 742, but continued to hold his civil office under *Pepin III, Mayor of the Palace. In 748 Chrodegang founded the Benedictine Abbey of *Gorze. Later he founded the Abbey of *Lorsch. In 753 Pepin, now king of the *Franks, sent the bishop to Rome to offer refuge in France to Pope *Stephen II, who was besieged by the *Lombards. Stephen gave Chrodegang the personal title of archbishop and appointed him papal legate to the kingdom of the Franks. In this capacity Chrodegang presided over the meeting held at Quiercy-sur-Oise (754) and persuaded the Frankish lords to go to war against *Aistulf, the Lombard king, in order to win back the papal lands. He had a prominent voice also in all the reforming councils of the period, proving, during his 23-year episcopate, that he was the true successor to *Boniface as the reformer of the Frankish Church. Chrodegang was one of those responsible for the introduction of the *Roman rite and *Gregorian chant into the Frankish Church (*see* GALLICAN RITES). Apparently he observed the Roman practice on his early visit to Rome and sent chanters to learn it. The school of chant they established in Metz upon their return became widely known (*see* CAROLINGIAN REFORM).

Chrodegang formed the clergy of his cathedral church of St. Stephen into a community that lived in cloister. The rule he wrote for them was based on the *Benedictine Rule and consisted of a preface and 34 chapters. The clergy were to chant the Divine Office in common and to eat and sleep within the cloister. Every day a chapter of the rule was to be read in common, and from this the gathering itself began to be called "chapter." These canons regular did not take a vow of poverty. It is to the credit of Chrodegang's spiritual leadership that he could induce clergy, not bound by monastic vow, to undertake a quasi-monastic observance. Thus Chrodegang is one of the founders of the historic institution of Canons Regular (*see* CANONS, CHAPTER OF). His rule spread to other churches near Metz, and it was known in England and Italy—perhaps even in the Diocese of Rome.

Bibliography: CHRODEGANG OF METZ, *Regula canonicorum,* ed. W. SCHMITZ (Hanover 1889). MGS 2:267–268; 10:552–572. É MORHAIN, "Origine . . . de la *Regula canonicorum* de saint C.," *Miscellanea Pio Paschini,* 2 v. (Rome 1948–49) 1:173–185. G. HOCQUARD, *Catholicisme* 2:1094–96. J. C. DICKINSON, *The Origins of the Austin Canons* (London 1950). T. DE MOREMBERT, DHGE 12:781–784. M. VILLER, DictSpirAscMyst 2:877–878. Hauck 2:54–70.

[C. E. SHEEDY]

CHROMATIUS OF AQUILEIA, ST., 4th-century bishop and spiritual director; b. Aquileia?, date unknown; d. Aquileia, 407 (feast, Dec. 2). As a priest under Bishop Valerian of Aquileia (369–387), he was associated with the group of ascetics that included *Rufinus of Aquileia and St. *Jerome. Chromatius probably assisted at the anti-Arian Council of Aquileia (381) presided over by St. *Ambrose of Milan, who was also present at the election of Chromatius and consecrated him bishop in 387 or 388. Chromatius appealed to the Emperor Honorius in favor of St. *John Chrysostom when the latter was deposed at the Synod of the *Oak (403). Jerome dedicated his Latin translation of the Book of Solomon to Chromatius; Rufinus likewise dedicated his continuation of the Church history of Eusebius to him.

Chromatius intervened in the quarrel between the two former friends, counseling Rufinus not to respond to Jerome's attacks. Of Chromatius's *tractatus,* one on the Eight Beatitudes, seventeen on the Gospel of St. Matthew, and the *Prefatio orationis Dominicae* in the Gelasian Sacramentary have been preserved. R. Étaix has claimed eight further sermons on St. Matthew's Gospel preserved among the works of John Chrysostom for Chromatius, and J. Lemarié believes he has discovered a corpus of fragments that are the notes Chromatius collected before the compilation of his *tractatus* on St. Matthew.

Bibliography: CorpChrist 9 (1957) 371–447, ed. A. HOSTE, with bibliog. P. DE PUNIET, "Les Trois homélies catéchétiques du Sacramentaire Gélasien," RHE 5 (1904) 505–521; 6 (1905) 15–32, 304–318. P. PASCHINI, "Chromatius d'Aquilée et le commentaire Pseudo-Hiéronymien . . . ," RevBén 26 (1909) 469–475. R. ÉTAIX, "Tractatus in Matheum," *ibid.* 70 (1960) 469–503. J. LEMARIÉ, "Homélies inédites," *ibid.* 72 (1962) 201–277; 73 (1963) 100–107, 181–243; "Trois nouveaux témoins de l'homélie VIII et une homélie de Noël," *ibid.* 74 (1964) 147–155.

[G. ORLANDI]

CHROMOSOME

The most prominent feature of a cell viewed under the microscope is the nucleus, within which are found the chromosomes and *genes that govern the cell's activities and morphology. When a nucleus is stained with basic dyes a network of fine threads having coarse granules stands out. This is called the chromatin or the chromosomes in a diffuse state, a condition believed necessary since the nondividing cell is in its most active metabolic state. Chemical analysis of the chromatin material reveals the presence of four major components; deoxyribonucleic acid (DNA), ribonucleic acid (RNA), a basic protein or histone, and a high molecular weight protein. *See* NUCLEIC ACIDS (DNA, RNA). Typical amounts in chromosomes are: DNA, 40 per cent; RNA, 1 per cent; histones, 50 per cent; and other proteins, 8 per cent. In addition, there are some smaller molecules that may function in maintaining the structural integrity of the chromosome. It appears that some calcium compounds play such a role.

It is agreed that DNA is unique to chromosomes and that the amount of DNA per nucleus is essentially constant for each species although there may be considerable variation among the special tissues within the species. The basic proteins are histones and protamines, which are found in close association with DNA. Some variation exists in the amount and kinds present in different types of cells. Present in very small amounts is RNA, which is distributed also throughout the rest of the cell (especially, the nucleus, the nucleolus, and the microsomes). The chromosomes also contain some other proteins whose kinds depend upon the tissue being studied.

Almost without exception chromosomes are present in all organisms, but their presence in bacteria, blue-green algae, and viruses is not conclusively established. However, some bacteria and viruses are known not to contain DNA. In the nuclei of animals and plant cells the chromosomes float in a somewhat viscous fluid, the nuclear sap, and are enclosed by a nuclear membrane. In some organisms such as the sperm and egg of certain roundworms there is only a single chromosome; however, some insect secretory cells may contain as many as 20,000 chromosomes. Generally, all the cells of the same individual contain the same number of chromosomes, called the somatic or diploid number of that species; exceptions occur in the sex cells, or between the sexes, or members of the same species that may exhibit polyploidy. During the formation of sex cells in animals or the formation of pollen or ovules in plants, the chromosome number is reduced to one-half that of the diploid. This is known as the haploid number and is a result of meiosis. (*See* CELL DIVISION.)

In most species the chromosomes occur in homologous pairs. They are identified by their size and shape for each species. All the evidence from the classic experiments of G. *Mendel to present-day biochemical tests indicates that the chromosomes are the bearers of the hereditary materials. (*See* HEREDITY.)

Bibliography: F. H. C. CRICK, "The Structure of the Hereditary Material," *Scientific American* 191.4 (Oct. 1954) 54–61. J. H. TAYLOR, "The Duplication of Chromosomes," *ibid.* 198.6 (June 1958) 36–42. F. SCHRADER, *Mitosis* (2d ed. New York 1953). B. STRAUSS, *An Outline of Chemical Genetics* (Philadelphia 1960). C. P. SWANSON, *The Cell* (Englewood Cliffs, N.J. 1960).

[D. C. BRAUNGART]

CHRONICLER, BIBLICAL

The name given to the Biblical author who produced the historical corpus comprising the books of 1 and 2 Chronicles, Ezra, and Nehemia. These books give a religious history from the beginning of the world to the reforms of Nehemia and Ezra in the postexilic Jewish community. They set forth the reign of David as the ideal for which the restored theocratic state should again confidently strive, in view of God's promises through the Prophets and their partial fulfillment in the restoration of the Jewish community.

THE WORK AS A WHOLE

Originally this was copied as one literary work in the Hebrew textual tradition. Because of its size, however, it came to be written on two scrolls, with 1 and 2 Chronicles as one book on the first scroll, and Ezra and Nehemia as one book on the second. An unknown editor made the continuity of the scrolls evident by repeating the beginning of Ezra (Ezr 1.1–3a) at the end of Chronicles (2 Chr 36.22–23), thus also closing the latter on a happy note.

The greater bulk of the work in its Greek translation —the Greek alphabet wrote vowels as well as consonants, whereas ancient Hebrew wrote only consonants —led to a further division of the work into the four books of our present Bibles. This fourfold division passed from the Septuagint into the Vulgate and thence into the modern versions. It even made its way into the transmission of the Hebrew text, beginning with a manuscript dating from A.D. 1448.

Canonicity. Palestinian Jews placed the Chronicler's work at the end of the Writings, their third major division of the Bible. By a strange inversion of historical sequence, Ezra-Nehemia precedes the book(s) of Chronicles. This fact supports the supposition that Chronicles was accepted at a later period among the inspired books, perhaps because its matter was already found in a somewhat different form in the earlier books of Samuel and Kings. Chronicles seems to have won acceptance by NT times, however, at least if Jesus' allusion in Mt 23.35 to the deaths of Abel (Gn 4.8) and Zacharia (2 Chr 24.21–22) is to be taken as a reference to the first and last murders mentioned in the Scriptures and so to the whole sweep of the Jewish Bible. It is possible that the Chronicler's idealization of David and of the theocratic community may have influenced the Pharisees to accept Chronicles into the canon.

In the Septuagint and later translations, the four books appear in their normal order as supplements to, and continuation of, the earlier histories of Samuel and Kings.

Despite the variations of its position in the canon, the Chronicler's work has never been wanting from the canonical lists of Judaism and Christianity, if one excepts the earliest hesitation of the Syrian Church, which did not at first include 1 and 2 Chronicles in its translation of the Bible. The long history of acceptance of these books culminated in the declaration of the Council of Trent that they are among the books to be received by the faithful as "sacred and canonical" (Denz 1501–02).

Text and Versions. In general the Hebrew text of the Chronicler's work has been well preserved in transmission, despite the fact that many proper names and possibly some numbers have been garbled. The *Septuagint version is faithful to the traditional Hebrew text, sometimes so slavishly as to simply transliterate Hebrew words into Greek characters. Only the Old Latin version has value as an independent witness to the original text, since it is seemingly based on a Greek version that followed a Hebrew textual tradition other than the one represented in the Masoretic Text. The later versions—the *Vulgate, the Aramaic Targum, and the Syriac Peshitto—are less useful for textual criticism, the last named being sometimes a mere paraphrase of the Hebrew original.

Date of the Chronicler's Work. When they come to assigning dates for the Chronicler's work, authors vary widely, partly because they cannot agree on the work's unity of authorship. The most frequently accepted limits for the Chronicler's activity are the late 5th century B.C. (when the most recent events narrated took place) and the early years of Alexander's domination of Syria-Palestine, 333–323 B.C. (since these books show little Greek influence). Within these outer limits opinion fluctuates, although many scholars now favor a date near 400 B.C. for the work's appearance in its final form.

Other dates assigned may serve to illustrate the disagreements which exist: D. N. Freedman (441) says that the Chronicler, a monarchist, composed the basic work about 515 B.C. and that later a clericalist author added the Ezra-Nehemia memoirs (and certain other sections) to the work toward the end of the 5th century B.C. W. F. Albright (95) accepts a date shortly after 400 B.C. and sees Ezra himself as the Chronicler. A. M. Brunet (DBSuppl 6:1256) dates the work to the end of the 4th century B.C., about the time of Alexander the Great. C. C. Torrey, M. Noth, and R. H. Pfeiffer place the work well within the Greek period, Pfeiffer (580) dating it about 250 B.C.

Unity of Authorship and Identity of the Chronicler. Disagreement in dating the Chronicler is inevitably linked with disagreement over the literary unity of his work. However, strong arguments favor this unity. Not only does 2 Chr 36.22–23 repeat Ezr 1.1–3a, but the same spirit and themes can be found throughout the historiography. There is the same attachment throughout to the Jewish community and its legitimate civil and religious institutions; the same special love for the Temple and its cultic organization; the same special attention given to the lesser cultic ministers, particularly the Levites; the same concern for genealogies; and—perhaps the strongest argument of all—the same stylistic features of vocabulary, grammar, composition, and use of sources.

To these literary evidences of a single authorship can be added the traditional view of the rabbinic literature, the Church Fathers, and early commentators, who generally accepted these books as the work of one man, Ezra. The Babylonian Talmud says in fact (*Baba Bathra* 15a) that Ezra wrote his own book and the genealogies of Chronicles, beginning his own genealogy, which was completed by Nehemia. Suspect though it is in points, this testimony reflects the ancient view that the leading reformer of postexilic Judaism was largely responsible for the four Biblical books in question.

In modern times, J. W. Rothstein (1927), G. von Rad (1934), and A. C. Welch (1939), among others, have seen two strata (Deuteronomist and Priestly) in the Chronicler's work. K. Galling (1954) and D. N. Freedman (1961) have also seen successive editions in the work. But M. Noth (1943) and W. Rudolph (1955) have returned to the idea of a basic unity of authorship for the work as a whole, and W. F. Albright (95), basing his opinion in part on the observation of C. C. Torrey that the style and point of view of the Ezra memoirs are those of the entire work of the Chronicler, supports the earlier tradition that Ezra is indeed the author.

First and Second Chronicles

Although Chronicles was originally one work, it was first divided into two books in the Septuagint, a practice followed by subsequent versions and even by the Hebrew textual tradition since 1448.

Title. Palestinian Jews (and Hebrew printed Bibles) called these books (*sēper*) *dibrê hayyāmîm* [literally (the book of) the words of the days], a title idiomatically equivalent to "happenings of the times" or "annals." Greek-speaking Jews in their Septuagint (followed by the Vulgate and some modern editions) referred to these books by the name παραλειπόμενα (Paralipomenon), which Jerome (*Ep. 53, Ad Paulinum,* PL 22.548) and Theodoret (*Quaest. in libros Regum et Paralipomenon,* PG 80:801) understood as designating the books' content, "things omitted" (from previous Biblical histories). Some scholars, however, prefer to translate παραλειπόμενα as "things transmitted." J. P. Audet [JThSt 1 (1950) 154] proposes "things left aside" (for later translation from an Aramaic Targum).

The modern name for these books, "Chronicles," goes back to Jerome's *Prologus Galeatus* (PL 28:554), in which he writes of these books that they form a "χρονικόν [chronicle] of the whole of divine history." In his translation of the Bible M. Luther took up the term and called the books *Die Chronika,* and the name, thus popularized, is now generally accepted by the modern versions.

Contents of Chronicles. The Books of Chronicles have four clearly defined sections. (1) In 1 Chronicles ch. 1–9 a series of genealogies traces descent from Adam to the descendants of David and Solomon who were dwelling again in Jerusalem after the Edict of Cyrus in 538 B.C. (2) In 1 Chronicles ch. 10–29 the reign of *David, as it is described in his civil and religious organization of the kingdom, is idealized. (3) In 2 Chronicles ch. 1–9 the story of *Solomon emphasizes his wisdom, which is particularly evident in his building and dedicating the Temple at Jerusalem. (4) In 2 Chronicles ch. 10–36 an account is given of the successors of David and Solomon; but the rulers of the schismatic Northern Kingdom of Israel are ignored, and even of the kings of Juda only the three "good," i.e., reforming, kings—Josaphat (Jehoshaphat; *c.* 873–*c.* 849), *Ezechia (Hezekiah), and *Josia—are treated at length. The evil conduct of the other kings, the priests, and the people eventually brought about the destruction of Jerusalem and the nation (2 Chr 36.13–16). Here the story of Chronicles ends, to be completed by the Chronicler in Ezra-Nehemia.

Sources. In the composition of his work the Chronicler had recourse to many earlier writings, most of which he mentioned explicitly. Although he often adapted these documents to suit his own purposes, they still retained considerable historical value.

Biblical Sources. Among the sources used by the Chronicler are clearly some of the earlier books of the Bible, which he had in a form substantially identical with their present text. Although the Chronicler did not cite any of them by their known titles, he drew upon the following: (1) the Pentateuch (e.g., Gn 10.22–29 in 1 Chr 1.17–23), (2) Josue (e.g., Jos 19.1–8 in 1 Chr 4.28–33), (3) 1 and 2 Samuel (e.g., 1 Sm 31.1–13 in 1 Chr 10.1–12; 2 Sm 5.1–10 in 1 Chr 11.1–9), (4) 3 and 4 Kings (e.g., 3 Kgs 8.1–52 in 2 Chr 5.2–6.40; 4 Kgs 16.2–20 in 2 Chr 28.1–26), and (5) Psalms [e.g., Ps 104(105).1–15 in 1 Chr 16.8–22; Psalm 95(96) in 1 Chr 16.23–33; Ps 105(106). 1, 47–48 in 1 Chr 16.34–36)]. This list of OT citations is by no means complete.

Sources Explicitly Mentioned. Certain royal, prophetic, and other sources are mentioned in the Books of Chronicles.

The royal sources are: (1) The Book of the Kings of Israel and Juda (1 Chr 9.1; 2 Chr 27.7; 35.27; 36.8), (2) The Book of the Kings of Juda and Israel (2 Chr 25.26; 28.26; 32.32; 16.11), (3) The History of Jehu, the son of Hanani, which is inserted into the Book of the Kings of Israel (2 Chr 20.34), (4) The History of the Kings of Israel (2 Chr 33.18), and (5) The Midrash of the Book of Kings (2 Chr 24.27). Probably all these royal sources are in reality the same work.

The prophetic sources are: (1) The History of Samuel the Seer (1 Chr 29.29), (2) The History of Nathan the Prophet (1 Chr 29.29; 2 Chr 9.29), (3) The History of Gad the Seer (1 Chr 29.29), (4) The Prophecy of Ahijah the Shilonite (2 Chr 9.29), (5) The Visions of Iddo the Seer (2 Chr 9.29; 12.15), (6) The History of Semeia (Shemaiah) the Prophet (2 Chr 12.15), (7) The Midrash of the Prophet Iddo (2 Chr 13.22), (8) The History of Ozia (Uzziah) by the Prophet Isaia, the son of Amos (2 Chr 26.22), (9) The Vision of the Prophet Isaia, the son of Amos (2 Chr 32.32), and (10) The History of His [Manasseh's] Seers (2 Chr 33.19). Scholars dispute whether any, most, or all, of these sources belong to the same work that includes the royal sources.

Other sources are: (1) Family Records of Gad (1 Chr 5.17), (2) The Book of Chronicles of King David

(1 Chr 27.24), (3) David's Exact Specifications for the Temple and Its Furnishings (1 Chr 28.19), (4) The Prescriptions of David and Solomon for the Levites (2 Chr 35.4), and (5) Jeremia's Lamentation over Josia (2 Chr 35.25).

Use of the Sources. The manner in which the Chronicler used his sources can be seen from a comparison of his work with the earlier Biblical books. With his own specific purposes in mind he repeated, omitted, rewrote, shortened, and expanded his source materials. Some examples follow: (1) repetition, e.g., 1 Sm 31.1–13 in 1 Chr 10.1–12; (2) omissions, e.g., of David's troubles with Saul, his adultery with *Bethsabee (Bathsheba), and his murder of her husband; and of the revolt of Absalom and the dynastic intrigues at Solomon's accession; (3) rewriting of material, e.g., 2 Sm 24.1 in 1 Chr 21.1; (4) shortening, e.g., 4 Kgs 18.13–19.37 in 2 Chr 32.1–23; and (5) expansion, e.g., 4 Kgs 23.21–23 in 2 Chr 35.1–19.

Evaluation of the Sources. As in so many other matters affecting the Chronicler's work scholars differ in their assessing of his sources. It is evident that he knew and used the earlier Biblical books, from Genesis to Kings, and Psalms. Whether he used additional materials is in dispute. Torrey and Pfeiffer think that he probably did not. In the parts of his work that are not clearly derived from Biblical sources, they say, the spirit and language is that of the Chronicler himself, showing that these parts do not derive from other source materials. Torrey (*Ezra Studies* 223) even says that "there is no internal evidence, anywhere, of an intermediate source between our Old Testament books and the Chronicler." And he explains the numerous explicit references to source material as fabrication of the Chronicler in his need to "parade authorities." However, this argument based on stylistic and thematic consistency is not convincing if one considers that the Chronicler need not have reproduced his sources slavishly and that in fact he did not do so, even when he clearly drew from earlier Biblical books. Note, for instance, how 2 Chr 1.3–6 expands upon 3 Kgs 3.4.

More probably, then, as Brunet (DBSuppl 6:1241) and others maintain, the Chronicler's references point to one or more sources distinct from our canonical books. (Some even think that it was not the Biblical Books of Samuel and Kings that the Chronicler used, but their sources.) Finally, some authors reduce the Chronicler's non-Biblical sources to one, identified as the Midrash on the Book of Kings (2 Chr 24.27).

Historical Worth. The free use that the Chronicler makes of his sources has called into question the historical worth of his narrative. For example, in 2 Chr 13.3 the monstrous figures of 400,000 men in the army of Juda under Abia and of 800,000 men in the opposing army of Jeroboam I are obviously of no historical value; according to 2 Chr 8.1–2 Hiram, King of Tyre, gave to Solomon certain cities that were in reality given by Solomon to Hiram (3 Kgs 9.10); and David paid only 50 silver shekels for the threshing floor of Ornan (2 Sm 24.24), not 600 shekels of gold as stated in 1 Chr 21.25.

These and similar examples are best understood in the light of the Chronicler's chief interest—the theological significance of his material. It is this interest that leads him to exaggerate the size of the armies so that God's victory might be more striking. This same interest impels him to exalt Solomon by having Hiram give him the cities and to stress beyond its worth the value of the site purchased by David as the spot for his altar and eventually the Temple. Allowance must be made, then, for the Chronicler's handling of materials to achieve his theological purposes, but once this is done, the books of Chronicles become valuable historical references. In some instances, e.g., in 2 Chr 11.5–12, they preserve reliable historical details not available elsewhere.

EZRA-NEHEMIA

Like Chronicles, which they continue, these two books were originally one work and they first became separate works in the Septuagint. Even in the current Hebrew Bibles the Book of Nehemia follows the Book of Ezra on the same page with merely the usual paragraph division.

Titles. The first of the two books is named for the Priest-Scribe *Ezra, whose name (Heb. and Aram. *'ezrā'*, transcribed in Greek as 'Εζ[δ]ρας or 'Εσ[δ]ρα[ς]) means "help." In the Vulgate and some other Catholic Bibles the book is known also as 1 Esdras. The second book is named for *Nehemia (Heb. *nᵉḥemyâ*, transcribed in Greek as Νεεμίας), whose name means "Yahweh consoles." This work is known in the Vulgate and some other Catholic Bibles also as 2 Esdras.

In the Septuagint, the apocryphal book 'Εσδρας A, the Vulgate's 3 Esdras, precedes the canonical books of Ezra and Nehemia, which together constitute the Septuagint's 'Εσδρας B. The nomenclature is further complicated by the apocryphal *Apocalypse of Esdras,* which is known in the Vulgate as 4 Esdras. Finally, Protestant editions of the apocrypha refer to the Vulgate's 3 and 4 Esdras as 1 and 2 Esdras. *See* BIBLE, III (CANON), 4. The accompanying table shows the correspondences.

Hebrew	*Greek*	*Latin*
Ezra	'Εσδρας B, ch. 1–10	1 Esdras or Esdras (canonical)
Nehemia	'Εσδρας B, ch. 11–23	2 Esdras or Nehemias (canonical)
	'Εσδρας A	3 Esdras (apocryphal 1 Esdras)
		4 Esdras (apocryphal 2 Esdras)

Contents. In Ezra ch. 1–6 the story of the chosen people is continued where Chronicles left off. These chapters tell of the edict of restoration issued by Cyrus the Great in 538 B.C., of the first return under *Sassabasar, of early attempts to reconstruct the Temple, and of its final completion and dedication in the time of *Zorobabel and *Josue, son of Josedec. This leads to the story of Ezra's mission and his reforms as told in Ezra ch. 7–11. In Nehemia ch. 1–7 an account is given of the building of the walls and the city of Jerusalem by Nehemia. The rest of the Book of Nehemia (ch. 8–13) narrates the covenant concluded under Ezra's direction, gives census lists, and tells of the dedication of the city's wall and of Nehemia's reforms during his second administration of Juda.

Sources. The following materials were available to the Chronicler as he composed his work.

1. The Memoirs of Ezra (Ezr 7.27–9.15)
2. The Memoirs of Nehemia (Neh 1.1–7.5; 11.1–2; 12.27–13.31)
3. Aramaic documents
   a. A document in Ezr 4.7–23 embodying the protest of Rehum to Artaxerxes I, King of Persia,

about the rebuilding of Jerusalem's walls (Ezr 4.11–16) and the King's answer (Ezr 4.17–22)

b. A document in Ezr 4.24–6.18 that contains the letter of Thathanai to Darius I, King of Persia, about the rebuilding of the Temple at Jerusalem (Ezr 5.7–17) and the King's answer (Ezr 6.3–12)

c. The decree of Artaxerxes commissioning Ezra to reorganize Temple worship at Jerusalem (Ezr 7.12–26)

4. Official documents in Hebrew

a. Cyrus's edict of liberation of 538 B.C. (Ezr 1.2–4), which differs from the Aramaic form of the decree in Artaxerxes' letter to Thathanai (Ezr 6.3–5)

b. A list of those first returning from Babylon (Ezr 2.1–70; Neh 7.6–72)

c. A list of those returning with Ezra (Ezr 8.1–14)

d. A list of those promising to give up foreign wives (Ezr 10.18–44)

e. A list of those who helped repair the walls of Jerusalem (Neh 3.1–32)

f. A list of those signing the covenant agreement (Neh 10.1–28; the provisions of the pact are in Neh 10.29–40)

g. A list of the inhabitants of Jerusalem and vicinity in Nehemia's time (Neh 11.3–36)

h. Lists of priests and Levites (Neh 12.1–26).

Historical Worth. Since the Books of Ezra and Nehemia form the major source for the history of Juda in the postexilic period down to the late 5th century B.C., it is important to know whether, and to what extent, they are reliable.

Some scholars, such as Torrey and Pfeiffer, treat the Chronicler's documentation with skepticism. Others are more inclined to find his sources reliable. Admittedly, as in the Books of Chronicles, the author is motivated chiefly by theological interests. Consequently he gives a decidedly Jewish tone to Ezra's commission from Artaxerxes, in which the Mosaic Law is referred to as the "wisdom" of God (Ezr 8.25). The Chronicler's rewording may be seen also in the two accounts of Cyrus's edict of 538 B.C. (Ezr 1.2–4; 6.3–5). But fundamentally there is no adequate reason to impugn the basic authenticity of these or other documents that he employs.

Despite this confidence in the Chronicler's materials, however, it is not easy for the modern scholar to reconstruct the age about which the Chronicler writes, since the documentation in these books is obviously not in chronological order. Note, for example, how the patch that is Ezr 4.24 joins the later episode of Ezr 4.7–23 to the earlier situation in Ezr 5.1–6.22; logically (and chronologically) Ezr 5.1–6.22 should have followed Ezr 4.5.

But this is not the only disturbance of historical sequence. The order of Ezra's and Nehemia's ministries is another case in point. If the ministry of Ezra began in the 7th year of Artaxerxes I (465–424 B.C.), as Ezr 7.7 states, there would be no coordination between Ezra's ministry and that of Nehemia, contrary to Neh 8.9; 10.1. A date in the reign of Artaxerxes II (404–358 B.C.) would make him much later than Nehemia. A plausible solution—that the "7th year" of Artaxerxes in Ezr 7.7 should be read as the "37th year" of Artaxerxes I—resolves the difficulty and results in a Nehemia-Ezra sequence of activity.

Other historical difficulties remain to plague the interpreter, but in spite of them modern opinion favors the basic reliability of the Chronicler's work.

THE MESSAGE OF THE CHRONICLER

The Chronicler's major interest was in the history of the theocracy embodied in the Davidic dynasty and in the restored Jewish community of the postexilic period. The genealogies of 1 Chronicles ch. 1–9 are merely introductory, leading swiftly to David and his accomplishments.

Ideal Theocracy in the Davidic Dynasty. David's dynasty had proved to be, even before the Exile, the only legitimate one, the only one enjoying divine favor. And so the Chronicler ignored the history of the Northern Kingdom of Israel. Not all of David's descendants, however, proved worthy of him. In fact, only three—the reforming kings Josaphat (2 Chr 17.7–9; 19.4–11), Ezechia (2 Chronicles ch. 29–32), and Josia (2 Chr 34.1–33)—received favorable comment from the Chronicler. But even these three were not sufficient to ward off Yahweh's displeasure with His people, who had spurned the oracles of His Prophets (2 Chr 36.15–17; Neh 9.30). Chastened by the experience of the Exile, God's people returned to the Holy Land and rebuilt Jerusalem and its Temple. This return, which is described in Ezra-Nehemia, was the partial fulfillment of the prophetic promises (Jer 29.10 in 2 Chr 36.22 and Za 8.11–12 in Ezr 9.8, 13; Neh 9.31).

The Ideal Postexilic Community. Since the community had no Davidic ruler when the Chronicler wrote, it had to prepare for one by becoming the ideal community. This goal obliged it to a greater fidelity to God's word as contained in the Mosaic Law (Ezr 9.10–14) and to greater exactitude in worship. To inculcate this ideal of the perfect community, the Chronicler sought to legitimize the liturgical usages of his own day, and so he linked them to David (1 Chronicles ch. 23–29). Great importance was given also to Solomon's Temple and its ministers, particularly the Levites and the singers (2 Chr 5.11–13).

Thus constituted as a holy people, the Jews, who had been reduced to the service of a foreign king (Neh 9.36–37), turned in hopeful expectation to the next intervention of Yahweh their true King (Ezr 9.13; Neh 9.32).

Bibliography: A. M. BRUNET, "La Théologie du Chroniste: Théocratie et messianisme," *Sacra Pagina* 1 (1954) 384–397; DBSuppl 6:1220–61. A. LEFÈVRE, *ibid.* 6:393–424. R. H. PFEIFFER, InterDictBibl 1:572–580; 2:215–219. H. CAZELLES, *Catholicisme* 2:1098–1102; 4:428–434; *Les Livres des Chroniques* (2d ed. BJ; 1961). B. MARIANI, EncCatt 9:804–806. V. M. JACONO, *ibid.* 5:557–560. M. REHM, LexThK² 2:1184–85. H. SCHNEIDER, *ibid.* 3:1101–02; 7:868–869. K. GALLING, RGG³ 1:1803–06; 2: 694–697; 4:1396–98; *Die Bücher der Chronik, Esra, Nehemia* (Göttingen 1954). EncDictBibl 361–368. M. NOTH, *Überlieferungsgeschichtliche Studien I* (2d ed. Tübingen 1957). W. RUDOLPH, *Chronikbücher* (HAT ser.1, no.21; 1955). A. C. WELCH, *The Work of the Chronicler* (London 1939). C. C. TORREY, *Ezra Studies* (Chicago 1910); *The Chronicler's History of Israel* (New Haven 1954). W. F. ALBRIGHT, *The Biblical Period from Abraham to Ezra* (pa. New York 1963). D. N. FREEDMAN, "The Chronicler's Purpose," CathBiblQuart 23 (1961) 436–442. R. NORTH, "Theology of the Chronicler," JBiblLit 82 (1963) 369–381.

[N. J. MC ELENEY]

CHRONOGRAPHER OF 354. The designation given by T. Mommsen to the unknown compiler of a calendarlike reference work prepared for general use in Rome. The original compiler stopped at the year 354, but subsequently some additions brought it down to the year 496. Although the document is preserved only in fragments, scholars have succeeded in reconstructing almost completely this important source for the history of the ancient Church.

The contents of the work are: (1) a calendar in two parts, part 1 containing astronomical and astrological data, and part 2 a civil listing of pagan feasts and games, dates for the meetings of the Senate, and birthdays of the emperors. The calendar was composed by the calligrapher Furius Dionysius Philocalus (or Filocalus) and elaborately illustrated with miniatures. (2) Annals from the time of Caesar to the year 359 (added later by a copyist). (3) A list of the consuls from A.U.C. 245 to A.D. 354—the most complete list found in extant literary sources. (4) An Easter table from 312 to 411. (5) A list of the urban prefects at Rome for the years 254 to 354. (6) A *Depositio episcoporum* (list of the death dates of the popes from 254 to 352), and a *Depositio Martyrum* (list of Roman martyrs and martyrs venerated at Rome), the oldest extant martyrology. (7) A list of the bishops of Rome from St. Peter to Liberius—the earliest form of the Liber pontificalis. (8) Annals from the time of Caesar to 403, and from 455 to 496. (9) A world chronicle to the year 354, based on that of *Hippolytus of Rome. (10) A chronicle of the city of Rome to the death of the Emperor Licinius (324), written in 334 and closely connected with the world chronicle just mentioned. (11) A description of the 14 regions of the city of Rome.

The Emperor Constantine II, drawing in the Vatican MS of the Chronographer of 354 (Vat. Cod. Barber. XXXI, 39, fol. 13).

Bibliography: Editions. T. MOMMSEN, ed., MGAuctAnt 9.1 (1892) 13–196; *Gesammelte Schriften* 8 v. (Berlin 1905–13) 7:536–579. Studies. Bardenhewer 3:558–560. A. FERRUA, EncCatt 4:1007–09. O. SEECK, Pauly-Wiss RE 3.2 (1899) 2477–81. H. LECLERCQ, "Kalendaria," DACL 8.1:624–667; "Chronographe de 354," *ibid.* 3.1:1555–60. C. NORDENFALK, *Der Kalender vom Jahre 354 und die lateinische Buchmalerei des IV. Jahrhunderts* (Göteborg 1936). H. STERN, *Le Calendrier de 354: Étude sur son texte et sur ses illustrations* (Paris 1952). **Illustration credit:** Biblioteca Apostolica Vaticana.

[M. R. P. MC GUIRE]

CHRONOLOGY, ANCIENT

Chronology is the science that treats of the computation of time (Gr. χρόνος, time as seen in its duration or extent) by means of fixed periods, whereby the events of history can be dated. In general, the more ancient a historical event, the more difficult is its chronology. This article treats of the chronology of the following: (1) Egypt, (2) Mesopotamia, (3) the Old Testament, and (4) the New Testament.

1. EGYPT

According to the early history of *Manetho, Pharaonic Egyptian history is traditionally divided into 30 dynasties, starting with Menes, the traditional unifier of Upper and Lower Egypt and founder of the First Dynasty, and concluding with Nectanebo II in 343 B.C. To the Manethonian account a Thirty-first Dynasty of three Persian kings was added by a later chronographer. Modern scholarship normally divides these dynasties into the following 10 periods.

(1) The Archaic (Early Dynastic) Period (First and Second Dynasties, *c.* 3100–*c.* 2686 B.C.). (2) The Old Kingdom (Third to Sixth Dynasties, *c.* 2686–*c.* 2181 B.C.). (3) The First Intermediate Period (Seventh to Tenth Dynasties, *c.* 2181–*c.* 2040 B.C.). (4) The Middle Kingdom (Eleventh to Thirteenth Dynasties, *c.* 2133–1787 B.C.). (5) The Second Intermediate Period (Fourteenth to Seventeenth Dynasties, *c.* 1786–*c.* 1567 B.C.). (6) The New Kingdom (Eighteenth to Twentieth Dynasties, *c.* 1567–*c.* 1087 B.C.). (7) the Third Intermediate Period (Twenty-first to Twenty-third Dynasties, *c.* 1087–730 B.C.). (8) The Nubian Period (Twenty-fourth and Twenty-fifth Dynasties, 730–656 B.C.). (9) The Saite Period (Twenty-sixth Dynasty, 664–525 B.C.). (10) The Persian Period (Twenty-seventh to Thirty-first Dynasties, 525–332 B.C.).

Preceding this list, but not attested in Manetho, is the Predynastic Period, ending with Menes; while after the Manethonian account may be appended the period of the Greek rule of the *Ptolemies, established by Alexander in 332 B.C. and ended by Octavian after the Battle of Actium in 31 B.C.

The Manethonian dynasties each contain the names of the kings who comprised them, along with the total number of years each ruled. There are, however, errors in the list, and these must be corrected from other sources. First, it must be remembered that the Egyptians did not number their years successively as is done in modern chronology. The regnal years of each king were numbered, starting with the first regnal year of a given king and continuing until his death, then starting with the first regnal year of the new king, etc. A number of king lists from the Pharaonic age have been preserved that, like Manetho's, list the various kings of each dynasty in succession along with the total number of the years they reigned. The most important of these is the Royal Canon of Turin, which was composed in the Nineteenth Dynasty, in the reign of *Ramses II, and covered the period from the legendary dynasties of the gods until the end of the Second Intermediate Period. Two lists from the temples of Seti I and Ramses II at Abydos record 76 kings from Menes to Seti I of the Nineteenth Dynasty. A list from Karnak includes kings' names from Menes to *Thutmose III of the Eighteenth Dynasty, while a list from Sakkara covers the period from the sixth king of the First Dynasty until Ramses II. The Sakkara list and the two Abydos lists omit the Second Intermediate Period. The text of the Palermo Stone, dating from the Fifth Dynasty, is invaluable for the period from the late Predynastic Period until the Fifth Dynasty. The total of the reigns of the individual kings of these lists may be checked with the dated monuments of the individual reigns. Frequently the king lists do not take into account the coregency of a king with his successor or the concurrent existence of two or more dynasties, and an adjustment must be made. From the 7th regnal year of Sesostris III of the Twelfth Dynasty on, the over-all chronology of Egypt has been fixed with a reasonable degree of certainty by astronomical calculation, but for the periods preceding this, one must rely mainly on mathematical calculations from the king lists. Synchronisms with events recorded in external, non-Egyptian sources, e.g., the OT or the Assyrian and Hittite annals, and those derived from the archeological finds of dateable Egyptian objects in non-Egyptian contexts, and vice versa, help to flesh out the skeletal framework provided by Manetho and the king lists.

Bibliography: W. C. Hayes, et al., "Chronology: Egypt, Western Asia, and the Aegean Bronze Age," CAH² (1962) v.1, ch. 6. H. W. Helck, *Untersuchungen zu Manetho und den ägyptischen Königslisten* (Berlin 1956). R. W. Ehrich, ed., *Relative Chronologies in Old World Archeology* (Chicago 1954).

[A. R. SCHULMAN]

2. Mesopotamia

The very rich material for establishing the chronology of ancient Mesopotamia consists of king lists, lists of year names, eponym lists, chronicles, and royal inscriptions.

For their own chronological purposes the ancient Sumerian, Babylonian, and Assyrian scribes drew up lists of the various kings of the different dynasties, with the number of years each king reigned. There are five main lists of this nature. (1) The Sumerian King List. This begins with the mythical time "when kingship came down from heaven." After the Deluge the historical period begins to dawn, and the list mentions the cities that in the course of the centuries possessed the hegemony in Sumeria, with their dynasties, kings, and number of regnal years. The list was drawn up toward the end of the First Dynasty of Isin (*c.* 1733 B.C.). See T. Jacobsen, *The Sumerian King List* (Chicago 1939). (2) The List of the Dynasty of Larsa [see G. A. Barton, *The Royal Inscriptions of Sumer and Akkad* (New Haven 1929)]. (3) The Babylonian King List A + B, extending from the beginning of the First Dynasty of Babylon to the death of Kandalanu (627 B.C.); see Pritchard ANET 271–272. (4) The Assyrian King List from Chorsabad, preserved in two copies; see ArchOr 14 (1944) 367–369 and JNEastSt 13 (1954) 209–211. It likewise begins with the primordial period ("17 kings, tent dwellers") and reaches 746 B.C. Its continuation is given in the Babylonian Chronicle, beginning with 745 B.C., a Neo-Babylonian work, dated in the 22d year of Darius I (500 B.C.). (5) The so-called Synchronistic Table from Asshur; see Pritchard ANET 272–274. This arranges the approximately contemporaneous kings of Assyria and Babylon in parallel columns. Since there are still lacunae of considerable size for the Cassite period (*c.* 1530–*c.* 1170), it is still impossible to obtain fixed dates for this and for the preceding periods. Thus, for the 43-year reign of *Hammurabi, sixth king of the First Dynasty of Babylon, several dates have been proposed, the most probable being 1728–1686 B.C. (so W. F. Albright, F. Cornelius, R. de Vaux, et al.), although some still prefer 1792–1750 B.C. (so S. Smith, M. B. Rowton, et al.).

In the oldest period, business documents were seldom dated. But from the Dynasty of Akkad (*c.* 2370–*c.* 2230) on, each year received a name, usually from some important event that happened in the preceding year, e.g., "Shulgi became king," "Simurru was destroyed." This method of naming years was in use until the end of the First Dynasty of Babylon (*c.* 1531 B.C.). The year names, which were drawn up in lists since the Third Dynasty of Ur (*c.* 2060–*c.* 1950), offer the most valuable material for controlling the data of the king lists. (See ReallexAssyr 2:131–195.) From the Cassite period on, dating was done by regnal year.

In Assyria dating was done by eponyms, i.e., each year some man, usually a high official, was chosen to give his name to the year. So-called Eponym or Limmu (the Assyrian word) Lists were drawn up to show the sequence of the years. These have been preserved in unbroken sequence only for the period 909–648 B.C. Because of a recorded eclipse of the sun that occurred in 763 B.C., it is possible to obtain absolute dates for this whole period.

Babylonian King List A (cuneiform tablet 33332).

The so-called Babylonian Chronicle extends from the accession of Tiglath-Pileser III (745 B.C.) to that of Shamash-shumukin (668 B.C.) and offers a good summary of the historical events of this time (see F. Schmidtke, 90–97). The earlier period is treated in the so-called Synchronistic History (see F. Schmidtke, 84–89), extending from the time of Puzur-Asshur III (1490–67) to that of Adad-nirari (811–784). For the later period, see C. J. Gadd, *The Fall of Niniveh* (London 1923); S. Smith, *Babylonian Historical Texts* (London 1924); D. J. Wiseman, *Chronicles of Chaldean Kings,* 626–556 B.C. (London 1956).

The Royal Inscriptions offer further material for chronological purposes, especially where mention is made of earlier kings, e.g., the reference made by Shalmaneser I (*c.* 1265–*c.* 1236) to the various periods of numbered years between the different restorations that had been made in the past on the temple of the god Asshur [see D. D. Luckenbill, *Ancient Records of Assyria and Babylonia,* v.1 (Chicago 1926) par. 119].

See also MESOPOTAMIA, ANCIENT, 2.

Bibliography: F. K. GINZEL, *Handbuch der mathematischen und technischen Chronologie,* 3 v. (Leipzig 1906–14) 1:107–147. P. VAN DER MEER, *The Chronology of Ancient Western Asia and Egypt* (2d ed. Leiden 1955). F. SCHMIDTKE, *Der Aufbau der babylonischen Chronologie* (Münster 1952). R. A. PARKER and W. H. DUBBERSTEIN, *Babylonian Chronology, 626 B.C.–A.D. 75* (Providence 1956). E. F. CAMPBELL, JR., "The Ancient Near East: Chronological Bibliography and Charts," *The Bible and the Ancient Near East,* ed. G. E. WRIGHT (Garden City, N.Y. 1961) 214–224. W. C. HAYES et al., "Chronology," CAH. **Illustration credit:** Courtesy of the Trustees of the British Museum.

[F. SCHMIDTKE]

3. OLD TESTAMENT

Israel had no general era or method for reckoning the passing of the years valid for all the books of the OT. The Era of Creation that is now used by the Jews, with its starting point, the creation of man, in 3761 B.C. (so that A.D. 1966 is the year 5726–27 of this era), was first employed by them in the 11th century of the Christian Era when they took at face value all the seemingly chronological data of the Hebrew Bible, although the reckoning of a world era from creation goes back to Byzantine chronology, beginning in the 3d century, which, on the basis of the Septuagint data, puts creation at *c.* 5500 B.C. See V. Grumel, *Traité d'études Byzantines, I: La chronologie* (Paris 1958) 1–72. Actually, each of the main epochs of OT history has its own way of reckoning historical time.

Patriarchal Age. The epoch of the *Primeval Age in the Bible, i.e., the period of the antediluvian and postdiluvian Patriarchs, from Adam to Noe and from Noe to Abraham's father, Thare (*see* PATRIARCHS, BIBLICAL), has a pseudochronology based on the extremely high ages given to these Patriarchs (Gn 5.1–32; 11.10–26). But this is obviously an artificial, symbolic chronology of no historical value. For an interesting theory to explain the system on which it is based, see J. Schildenberger, *Vom Geheimnis des Gotteswortes* (Heidelberg 1950) 264–277.

The next epoch, that of the three patriarchal forefathers of the Israelites, Abraham, Isaac, and Jacob, is also lacking in direct chronological data. The relatively high ages given to these men are historically meaningless. Although Abraham may well have been more or less a contemporary of *Hammurabi, the attempt to identify the *Amraphel of Abraham's time (Gn 14.1–16) with Hammurabi (*c.* 1728–1686 or 1792–1750 B.C.) is now generally abandoned. However, the description of the Patriarchs' manner of life as given in Genesis ch. 12–36 fits in well with the conditions of Middle Bronze Age II (19th to 16th centuries B.C.) as these are known from modern Palestinian archeology. Even if the early Hebrews formed part of the *Habiri invasion of Canaan that is known from the *Amarna Letters of the 15th and 14th centuries B.C. and if there are some points of contact between their culture and that known from the *Nuzu (Nuzi) and *Ugarit document of these centuries, Abraham himself must be dated to a period older than this.

Exodus and Conquest of Canaan. Although the Exodus of the Israelites from Egypt and their covenant with Yahweh at Mt. Sinai form one of the most important events in their history, no true era was based on these events. The passages dating events in the wandering in the desert (Ex 16.1; 19.1; 40.17; Nm 1.1; 9.1; 10.11; 33.38; Dt 1.3) are all late, artificial reconstructions of the Pentateuchal *Priestly Writers. Equally artificial and useless for chronological purposes are the figures that give 480 years from the Exodus to Solomon's dedication of the Temple (3 Kgs 6.1) and 400 or 430 years for Israel's sojourn in Egypt, with or without the period of the Patriarchs added to it (Gn 15.13; Ex 12.40; Acts 7.6–7; Gal 3.17). On the other hand, the Biblical *genealogies know of only four generations between Jacob and Moses, or a period of about 100 years; but this may well be an equally artificial pattern. The events of this period in Israelite history can best be fitted into the framework of extra-Biblical history by putting the entrance of the sons of Jacob into Egypt in the time of the *Hyksos (*c.* 1700–1570 B.C.). The Pharao "who knew nothing of Joseph" (Ex 1.8) may then have been Amosis (*c.* 1570–45), who overthrew the Hyksos. The Pharao who made the Israelites work on the construction of the cities of *Phithom and *Rameses was almost certainly *Ramses II (1290–1224). Hence, if the Exodus is dated at *c.* 1270, the Israelite invasion of Canaan falls in the second half of the 13th century B.C., which fully agrees with the findings of archeology showing that many Canaanite cities were captured and destroyed at this time. (*See* MER-NE-PTAH.)

Period of the Judges and Early Monarchy. The *Deuteronomist who edited the stories of the Judges assigned 40, 80, and 20 years to the various oppressors and deliverers of Israel—obviously artificial numbers, which, if reckoned consecutively, would give too high a figure for this period. Probably some of the Judges functioned simultaneously. A span of about 200 years (*c.* 1220–1020) seems plausible for this period. Even the 40-year reigns given to Saul (Acts 12.31), David (3 Kgs 2.11), and Solomon (3 Kgs 11.42) are based on merely round numbers, although for David and Solomon they are approximately correct. A synchronism supplied by Josephus (*Ant.* 8.3.1; *Ap.* 1.126), according to which the 4th year of Solomon's reign (3 Kgs 6.37) was the 11th (or 12th) year of the reign of King Hiram of Tyre (see 3 Kgs 5.1–11), puts the accession of Solomon *c.* 961 B.C.

The Kingdoms of Israel and Juda. After the time of Solomon exact figures are given for the reigns of all the kings both of Israel and of Juda, together with a synchronism stating in what year of the reign of the ruler of one kingdom the ruler of the other kingdom began to reign. But often these figures are inconsistent, so that one must reckon (1) with the possibility of scribal errors, (2) with coregencies counted as part of full reigns, (3) with the question of including or excluding the accession year (the period from the coronation to the next New Year's Day) as part of the total regnal years, and (4) with the question of considering the first day of Nisan or the first day of Tishri as beginning the new year (*see* CALENDARS OF THE ANCIENT NEAR EAST).

The Egyptian and Assyro-Babylonian sources supply material for dating a few of the reigns of the kings of Juda or Israel with good probability or even certainty. *Sesac's invasion of Juda in the 5th year of *Roboam (3 Kgs 14.25) was probably *c.* 918 B.C., which would give *c.* 922–901 for the latter's reign. From the inscriptions of *Salmanasar III of Assyria it is known that *Achab of Israel and *Ben-Adad II of Damascus were in the coalition that fought the Assyrians in the battle of Qarqar in 853 B.C. (Pritchard ANET 279); allowing sufficient time for the subsequent war between Israel and Damascus in which Achab was killed (3 Kgs 22.1–37), one can date Achab's death and Ochozia's succession *c.* 850 B.C. The Black Obelisk of Salmanasar III shows Jehu of Israel paying tribute to the Assyrian King in 841 B.C. (Pritchard ANET 280–281), which makes this the latest possible year for the beginning of Jehu's reign. But the Biblical evidence makes 842 the earliest possible date for this. Therefore his accession year was certainly 842–841, a fixed, pivotal point for the whole chronology of the two Hebrew monarchies. This year also marks the last year of the reigns of Joram of Israel and Ochozia of Juda, since Jehu killed both these Kings when he usurped the throne of Israel (4 Kgs 9.24, 27). The fall of Samaria can be dated with certainty to 722–721, the last year of the reign of *Salmanasar V (4 Kgs 17.6) and the accession year of *Sargon II (Pritchard ANET 284–285). *Sennacherib records his siege of Jerusalem in 701, which was the 14th year of the reign of King *Ezechia of Juda (4 Kgs 18.13). The Babylonian Chronicle makes it certain that King *Josia of Juda lost his life in the battle of Mageddo in 609; that the Battle of Carchemis was fought in the accession year of *Nabuchodonosor, 605, which was the 4th year of the reign of King Joakim of Juda (Jer 25.1); that Jerusalem was first captured by the Babylonians on March 15–16, 597; and that this city was taken for the second time and destroyed by the Babylonians in the summer of 587, if the 11-year reign of King *Sedecia of Juda (4 Kgs 25.2) is reckoned from Nisan 597, or less probably in the summer of 586, if this reign is reckoned from Tishri 597.

Exilic and Postexilic Periods. The dates in Ezechiel (1.2; 33.21; 40.1) are reckoned from the first Babylonian capture of Jerusalem. The edict of *Cyrus in favor of the Jewish exiles can be dated with certainty to 538. Equally certain are the dates for the beginning (520: Ag 1.1–4; 2.1–4) and completion (516: Ezr 6.15) of the Temple of *Zorobabel in the reign of King *Darius I of Persia. Likewise certain is the date of *Nehemia's commission in the 20th year of the reign of King *Artaxerxes I, 445 B.C. (Neh 2.1–8), but there is a difficulty with dating *Ezra's return to Palestine in the 7th year of the reign of Artaxerxes I, 458 (Ezr 7.1–7), since the activity of Ezra seems to have been later than that of Nehemia. The numerous dates in 1 and 2 Machabees are complicated by the fact that apparently some of them are reckoned with the Seleucid Era beginning on Dios 1 (Oct. 7), 312 B.C., according to the Macedonian calendar, whereas others are reckoned with this era beginning on Nisan 1 (April 3), 311 B.C., according to the Babylonian calendar.

Bibliography: J. FINEGAN, *Handbook of Biblical Chronology* (Princeton 1964). A. JEPSEN and R. HANHART, "Untersuchungen zur israelitisch-jüdischen Chronologie," ZATWiss Beiheft 88 (1964). D. N. FREEDMAN, "Old Testament Chronology," *The Bible and the Ancient Near East,* ed. G. E. WRIGHT (Garden City, N.Y. 1961) 203–214. C. F. JEAN, "Chronology of the Old Testament," Robert-Tricot 107–122. W. F. ALBRIGHT, "The Chronology of the Divided Monarchy of Israel," BullAmSchOr Res 100 (1945) 16–22. C. SCHEDL, "Textkritische Bemerkungen zu den Synchronismen der Könige von Israel und Juda," VetTest 12 (1962) 88–119.

[F. SCHMIDTKE]

4. NEW TESTAMENT

The following chronological data for the life of Christ and the events of the apostolic age are given in the NT.

Birth of Christ. Jesus was born "in the days of King Herod" (Mt 2.1). *Herod the Great died in 4 B.C. The text of Lk 3.1, 23 (see below) prevents the placing of the birth of Christ long before that date. If allowance is made for the visit of the magi (see especially Mt 2.7, 16) and the flight into Egypt, the year 6 B.C. becomes a probable date for the birth of Christ.

Jesus was born during a universal census of the Roman Empire (Lk 2.1), while Quirinius was governor of Syria (2.2). There is no other historical reference to this census of Quirinius, but historical data concerning the career of Quirinius do not make it unlikely that he took up a census in Palestine *c.* 6 B.C. *See* CENSUS (IN THE BIBLE).

Beginning of Christ's Public Ministry. John the Baptist began to preach "in the fifteenth year of the reign of Tiberius Caesar" (Lk 3.1). Tiberius succeeded Augustus on the death of the latter on Aug. 19, A.D. 14, but for the previous 2 years Tiberius had been associated with Augustus as coregent. It is probable that the reign of Tiberius as referred to by Luke is to be reckoned from the death of Augustus, that the calculation is to be made according to the civil year in Syria (Palestine having been a dependency of Syria), and that the period between the death of Augustus and the beginning of the next civil year (October 1) is to be counted as the 1st year of Tiberius. Accordingly, the 15th year of Tiberius was Oct. 1, A.D. 27, to Oct. 1, A.D. 28.

Jesus began his ministry when he "was about thirty years of age" (Lk 3.23). Christ was born before 4 B.C. (see above). Consequently this verse implies that the ministry of Christ began shortly after the appearance of the Baptist. The same conclusion follows even more forcibly from Jn 2.20, where, on the occasion of the cleansing of the Temple, the Jews say, "Forty-six years has this temple been in building." The reconstruction of the Temple was begun in 20–19 B.C. If 46 full years are allowed, the cleansing of the Temple took place in A.D. 28.

Death of Christ. The Friday on which Christ died was the 14th day of the month of Nisan; the Passover, the 15th of Nisan, was Saturday (Jn 18.28; 19.14, 31). In the interval between A.D. 27 and 34, the 14th of Nisan fell on a Friday in 30 and 33. Since there are good reasons for holding that Christ's ministry began in 28 (see above) and since it is a good opinion that the ministry of Christ lasted about 2 years, A.D. 30 is the most likely year for the death of Christ. If so, the date was April 7.

The Synoptics seem to oppose the chronology of the Fourth Gospel. They apparently refer to the Last Supper as a paschal meal (Mt 26.17; Mk 14.12; Lk 22.7, 8, 15). Since the *Passover meal was eaten on the evening before the Feast of *Passover (actually the Passover day itself, since sunset began the new day), it seems that the Friday on which Jesus died could not be the 14th of Nisan. Various solutions have been proposed to solve this problem while leaving the chronology of the Fourth Gospel intact.

Apostolic Age. Absolute dates can be given for three events in Acts: the death of Herod Agrippa I (12.23) took place in A.D. 44; Junius Annaeus *Gallio, before whom Paul was brought on charges in Corinth (18.12), was proconsul in 51–52; Porcius *Festus succeeded Marcus Antonius *Felix (24.27) in 60. On the basis of these absolute dates, an approximate chronology can be given for the following events; Paul's conversion, A.D. 34; his visit to Peter at Jerusalem, 36 or 37; his first missionary journey, 47 to 49; Council of Jerusalem, 50; Paul's second journey, 50 to 52; third journey, 53 to 58; imprisonment at Caesarea, 58 to 60; beginning of imprisonment at Rome, 61.

Bibliography: J. FINEGAN, *Handbook of Biblical Chronology* (Princeton 1964). A. TRICOT, Robert-Tricot 2:123–146. J. BLINZLER, LexThK[2] 2:422–425. U. HOLZMEISTER, EncCatt 4:1014–20. J. LEBRETON, DBSuppl 4:970–975. F. PRAT, *ibid.* 1:1279–1304. EncDictBibl 1144–49; 1761–62.

[G. A. DENZER]

CHRONOLOGY, MEDIEVAL

The science of chronology, as it applies to the Middle Ages, treats of the method of reckoning time by year or era. This article discusses the subject in its Christian orientation as it applies to the East and to the West.

1. THE CHRISTIAN EAST

In addition to Olympiads, regnal years, consulates, and other civil and political eras that continued to be used as chronological indexes, the Christian East had its own methods of determining chronology, viz, according to world eras, particular eras, and cycles.

World Eras. These were formed on the basis of three factors: (1) the idea that the world would last 6 millenniums, corresponding to the 6 days of Genesis, the coming of Christ occurring in the middle of the 6th millennium; (2) the need to find a Friday coinciding with the paschal moon as a date for the Passion; (3) the belief that the paschal cycles of the moon must have a proleptic connection with Creation. Hence arose the various cycles and the various eras.

The Lunar Cycle of Anatolius and the World Era of Julius Africanus. *Anatolius of Laodicea established a 19-year lunar cycle, constructed on the new moon (*neomenia*) of the vernal equinox (March 22), beginning in 258, equivalent in the world era of *Julius Africanus (−5501; the minus signs indicates years before the birth of Christ) to 5759. By taking into account the precyclic year, which supposed 11 epacts from its beginning, the cycle through complete revolutions (303 × 19) rejoins the 1st year of the world era. In addition, the chronology of the Passion according to Africanus, *13 lunae,* March 23–31, is in agreement with the cycle of Anatolius for that same year (2d of the cycle).

The World Era of Alexandria. When the Alexandrines moved the equinox back to March 21, they changed the cycle by constructing it on the new moon of the first of the year (Thôth 1 = August 29). The inaugural year, 304, the 9th year of the cycle of Anatolius, was 8 years later than his. In the 5th century, Panodorus adapted a world era to this cycle: −5493, placing the Incarnation in 5494 (= 1) and the Passion in 5526 (= 34). Annianos, his rival, lowered it to −5492, fixing the Incarnation at March 25, 5501, and the Resurrection at March 25, 5534 (= 42), March 25 also being the day of Creation. This Alexandrine era was favored by ecclesiastical writers. Its year began on March 25, sometimes on September 1 on the occasion of the indiction.

Protobyzantine Era. Constantinople reformed its computation in 353 by adjusting the cycle according to the equinoctial *neomenia,* March 21. Accordingly, with the addition of the precyclic year, this cycle began 9 years earlier than that of Anatolius. The latter was to have begun again in 353; the new cycle, therefore, had its beginning in 344. The world era that followed was 8 years earlier than that of Africanus, therefore, −5509. The birth of Christ was placed at 5507 (= −3) and the Passion at 5540 (= 31). The year began March 21.

Byzantine Era. This was constructed by subtracting a year from the cycle and from the protobyzantine era to make these agree with the indiction. The era was therefore −5508. It made its first appearance in 630 with the computist Georgios, who nevertheless retained the Alexandrine chronology for Christ. This latter was finally abandoned and the Passion reestablished at the year 31 (5539 of the era). The year had its beginning on September 1.

Other World Eras. The Era of Malalas: −5965; birth of Christ: 5967 (= −2); Passion: 6000 (= 31). The Era of Abdisho (Nestorian): −5491; birth of Christ: 5490 (= −2). The Georgian Era: −5604, constructed on the basis of the protobyzantine cycle of 344.

Particular Eras. Era of Diocletian: 284, Thôth 1 (August 29). The years of the reign of this Emperor, first used to date Easter, were later used to fix the dates of documents and events. The Armenian Era (undetermined years)—July 11, 522; the Little Armenian Era (fixed years)—starting point, Aug. 11, 1084. The Era of the Ascension (used by *John Malalas and the *Chronicon paschale,* as well as by the Nestorian Syrians): beginning date, the year 31.

Cycles. (1) Lunar cycles (19 years) and Solar cycles (28 years), were used in synchronism. It is well to note whether the Alexandrine or Byzantine cycle is employed (see table in Grumel, 266–267). (2) Paschal cycles of 532 years, product of 19 × 28 (see Grumel): (*a*) The Georgian paschal cycle (532 years) was called *Kronikoni*—beginning, 781; it was constructed on the protobyzantine cycle of 344. (*b*) The Ethiopian paschal cycle was called the years of Mercy or of Grace—it began with the era of Diocletian, Aug. 29, 284. (3) *Indictions, which were periods of 15 years.

Bibliography: M. CHAINE, *La Chronologie des temps chrétiens de l'Égypte et de l'Ethiopie* (Paris 1925). V. GARDTHAUSEN, *Griechische Palaeographie,* 2 v. (2d ed. Leipzig 1911–13) v.2. F. K. GINZEL, *Handbuch der mathematischen und technischen Chronologie,* 3 v. (Leipzig 1906–14; repr. 1958) v.3. W. KUBITS-

CHEK, Pauly-Wiss RE 1.1 (1893) 606–652. L. KOEP, ReallexAnt Chr 3:52–60. D. LEBEDEV, "Iz istorii drevnich paschalnich ciklov," *Vizantiĭskiĭ vremennik,* ser. 1, v.18 (1911) 146–249. H. LIETZMANN, *Zeitrechnung der römischen Kaiserzeit, des Mittelalters und der Neuzeit für die Jahre 1–2000 nach Christus* (3d ed. Berlin 1956). E. MAHLER, *Chronologische Vergleichungs-Tabellen nebst einer Anleitung zu den Grundzügen der Chronologie* (Vienna 1888). A. MENTZ, *Beiträge zur Osterfestberechnung bei den Byzantinern* (Königsberg 1906). P. V. NEUGEBAUER, *Hilfstafeln zur technischen Chronologie* (Kiel 1937). F. RÜHL, *Chronologie des Mittelalters und der Neuzeit* (Berlin 1897). E. SCHWARTZ, *Christliche und jüdische Ostertafeln* (Berlin 1905); Pauly-Wiss RE 3.2 (1899) 2460–77. V. GRUMEL, *La Chronologie* (Paris 1958).

[V. GRUMEL]

2. THE WEST IN THE MIDDLE AGES

The solar calendar of approximately 365¼ days (12 months), which Julius Caesar introduced in 46 B.C., continued in use in the Middle Ages, remaining unchanged in fact until 1582 when it was revised by a commission appointed by Pope Gregory XIII (*see* CALENDAR REFORM).

Reckoning of Years. Throughout this period, however, various methods of reckoning years were employed: (1) Byzantine, counting from the year 5508 B.C. (creation); a method originated in the 7th century and used by the Greeks and the Orthodox Church until 1700. (2) Regnal Year, from the year of office of an authority, such as emperor, pope, king, or magistrate. (3) *Indiction, a fiscal reckoning of years from 312 (Constantine's triumph), which was widely used in chanceries, liturgical books, etc., at times in association with other reckonings. (4) Spanish, from 38 B.C., the date of the conquest of Spain by Augustus; it was used in Spain, Portugal, and Visigothic Gaul for most of the Middle Ages, but Catalonia abandoned it in favor of (5) in 1180. (5) Christian Era, the dating of years from the birth of Christ (*anno Domini, Incarnationis,* etc.), a usage that arose incidentally from the Easter *computus of *Dionysius Exiguus (526); its gradual adoption in Europe was due largely to Bede's *De ratione temporum* (725; PL 90:295–578).

The Beginning of the Year. For the beginning of the year itself various styles, generally based on major Christian festivals, were employed: (1) Byzantine (September 1), agreeing with the beginning of the Byzantine fiscal year (Indiction) and common outside of Byzantium in Byzantine parts of Italy, e.g., Bari. (2) Venetian (March 1), used at Venice until 1797. (3) Circumcision (January 1), corresponding to the beginning of the Roman and, since 1582, the modern civil year; it was widely used in Spain and Portugal and in several other places, e.g., Benevento. (5) Florentine Annunciation beginning with March 25 *after* the Nativity. The usage was introduced at Fleury about 1030 and thence spread to England and, in particular, to Florence; from *c.* 1145 to the end of the 17th century it was used consistently by the papal chancery. (5) Pisan Annunciation, beginning with March 25 *before* the Nativity; originating at Arles in the late 9th century, it spread to Burgundy and northern Italy, eventually becoming peculiar to Pisa. (6) Gallican or Easter, a reckoning from the movable feast of Easter (March 22–April 25), introduced in France by Philip II Augustus (1180–1223) and used also in parts of the Rhineland and in the Low Countries, e.g., at Liège until 1333. (7) Bedan or Nativity, dating from Christmas Day (December 25). It was used by Anglo-Saxon and Norman kings until *c.* 1220, by the Empire until *c.* 1245, by the papal chancery from 962 to 1088, and at various other places, e.g., at Liège and Louvain, from 1333.

Within each month the Julian fashion of numbering the days in one continuous series (Nones, Ides, Kalends) became quite common but never fully replaced the practice of reckoning by liturgical days: e.g., "in vigilia sancti Lucae" (October 17); "in Dominica *Dum clamarem*" (10th Sunday after Pentecost, so called from the opening words of the Introit); "This day is call'd the feast of Crispian" (October 25). Hence a handbook, such as that of Grotefend or Cappelli or Cheney, is indispensable.

Bibliography: *L'Art de vérifier les dates* . . ., 42 v. (Paris 1818–44). R. L. POOLE, *Medieval Reckonings of Time* (London 1918); *Studies in Chronology and History* (Oxford 1934). A. GIRY, *Manuel de diplomatique* (new ed. Paris 1925). A. CAPPELLI, *Cronologia, cronografia e calendario perpetuo* (2d ed. Milan 1930). H. GROTEFEND, *Taschenbuch der Zeitrechnung des deutschen Mittelalters und der Neuzeit,* ed. T. ULRICH (10th ed. Hanover, Ger. 1960). C. R. CHENEY, ed., *A Handbook of Dates for Students of English History* (London 1945; repr. 1961). J. AUGUSTI Y CASANOVAS et al., eds., *Manuel de cronología española y universal* (Madrid 1952).

[L. E. BOYLE]

CHRYSANTHUS AND DARIA, SS., martyrs; d. *c.* 300 (feast, Oct. 25). Their passion, probably written in Rome in the 6th or 7th century, is anachronistic and has little historical value. According to it, Chrysanthus was a rich young man from Alexandria who came to Rome and was baptized. Daria, a priestess of Minerva, was sent to him, but he converted her and they entered a continent marriage and converted many pagans, including the tribune Claudius and 62 soldiers who were martyred and buried in an abandoned aqueduct. For their apostolate Chrysanthus and Daria were buried alive in a sandpit on the Via Salaria. Christians visiting their tomb were sealed in on the orders of Numerianus (d. 284). Gregory of Tours, who knew of the last episode, said that Pope Damasus composed for the crypt an epitaph; this, however, has not been discovered. A later inscription for Chrysanthus and Daria says that their shrine was restored after the *Goths devastated it in 539. These martyrs seem to be genuine, but their stories appear to have been brought together because they were buried in the Via Salaria or because they were listed together in martyrologies. Oil from the lamps of the shrine was brought to the Frankish Queen Theodelinda. Chrysanthus and Daria appear in 6th-century mosaics in *Ravenna, and their tomb is mentioned in **Itineraria* of the 7th. In 844, their relics were brought to *Prüm and from there to Münstereifel where they are still venerated. The martyrologies list them on various dates.

Bibliography: P. ALLARD, DACL 3.1:1560–68. A. P. FRUTAZ, LexThK[2] 2:1192–93. J. DUBOIS, *Catholicisme* 2:1112–13.

[M. J. COSTELLOE]

CHRYSOBERGES, ANDREW, Byzantine Dominican scholar, archbishop of Rhodes; d. Famagusta, Cyprus, 1451. He was one of three Greek brothers who became Catholics and Dominicans under the influence of Demetrius *Cydones and the controversy over *Hesychasm. He is first mentioned in 1410 as professor of philosophy at the Dominican convent in Padua. At the Council of *Constance he joined the Greek ambassadors in persuading the conciliar fathers and Pope *Martin V of Greek readiness for union. On Feb. 12, 1418, he became master of theology, and between 1418 and 1425 he was in Constantinople and Caffa. On Feb. 12, 1420, he was made a member of the papal household, and on July 9, master of the Sacred Palace. In 1426 Pope Martin sent him to Constantinople with the Greek ambassadors returning from Rome to treat of union and appointed him vicar-general of the whole Societas Fratrum Peregrinantium et Unitorum. Chrysoberges returned to Rome before May 9, 1427, and in 1428–29 he was in Poland-Lithuania on a papal mission.

Although nominated bishop of Sutri (Feb. 23, 1429), he either refused or resigned the office. He acted for Martin V with the Greek envoys, who in 1430 drew up the agreement for a council of union in Italy that was in effect realized only at Ferrara-Florence in 1438. *Eugene IV made Chrysoberges archbishop of Rhodes on May 2, 1432, and sent him to Basel to mitigate that Council's conciliarism. *See* CONCILIARISM (HISTORY OF). He was unsuccessful but encouraged the papal party there and visited Emperor *Sigismund of Hungary on his return trip. At the Council of Florence he delivered the reply to Cardinal *Bessarion's opening eulogy, and spoke in the debate on purgatory and on the addition of the *filioque* to the Creed. After the promulgation of union, he visited his archdiocese, was sent to Cyprus to investigate Greek complaints of Latin intolerance (Nov. 5, 1441), and brought into the Church certain Chaldeans and Maronites, who later confirmed the union in Rome (Aug. 7, 1445). He was made archbishop of Nicosia (April 19, 1447) and apostolic legate for Cyprus and the Aegean Islands (July 30, 1447). A letter of his to Bessarion (*c.* 1437–38) has been preserved [E. Candal, ed., OrChrPer 4 (1938) 329–371], as has an unedited treatise to *Joseph of Methone against the encyclical of Mark *Eugenicus.

Bibliography: R. COULON, DHGE 2:1696–1700. Beck KTLBR 742–743. R. J. LOENERTZ, *Catholicisme* 2:1114–15; ArchFrPraed 9 (1939) 5–61. M. H. LAURENT, ÉchosOr 38 (1935) 414–438. J. GILL, *The Council of Florence* (Cambridge, Eng. 1959).

[J. GILL]

CHRYSOGONUS, ST., apparently suffered martyrdom *c.* 304 *ad Aquas Gradatas,* near Aquileia; venerated in northern Italy (feast, Nov. 24). His cult was brought to Rome, where his name was introduced into the Canon of the Mass. According to his legendary *Passio,* prefixed to that of St. *Anastasia, he was a Roman officer who became her spiritual father and continued to direct her by letter even after his imprisonment for the faith. He was beheaded under Diocletian in Aquileia. In Rome there is an early Christian church known as the *titulus Chrysogoni,* mentioned in an inscription of 521 and in the synods of Rome in 499 and 595. The legend of the saint apparently grew out of an attempt to identify the founder of the Roman church with the martyr of Aquileia.

Bibliography: V. L. KENNEDY, *The Saints of the Canon of the Mass* (Rome 1938). C. CECCHELLI, EncCatt 4:882–883. Butler Th Attw 4:418–419.

[M. J. COSTELLOE]

CHRYSOLORAS, MANUEL, Byzantine nobleman and humanist, founder of Greek studies in Renaissance Italy; b. Constantinople, *c.* 1350; d. April 15, 1415. He first appeared in Italy in 1393 on a mission for the Byzantine Emperor Manuel II, who was seeking aid for Byzantium against the Turkish menace. On his return to Italy in 1396 he was made professor of Greek at the *studium* of Florence. His teaching caused a sensation in the intellectual circles of Italy, and many of the leading humanists came to study with him. After about 3 years in Florence, he returned to Constantinople, where he remained until 1400, when once again he went to Italy. Chrysoloras remained in western Europe after this date, teaching at various times in Venice, Milan, Pavia, and Rome. A member of the secretariate of Popes Gregory XII and (antipope) John XXIII, he was sent by them on several missions to France, England, Spain, and Germany. Chrysoloras died while attending the Council of *Constance.

Before Chrysoloras, only a very few Westerners (notably *Petrarch) had attempted to study Greek. And, indeed, except for the Calabrian Greeks *Barlaam and Pilatus, there had been no really competent teacher of Greek available in the West until Chrysoloras's appearance in Florence. His translations of Homer and Plato's *Republic* into Latin, and the composition of his *Erotemata* (Greek grammar) were important instruments in the dissemination of Greek learning to the West.

However, his most important contribution may well have been the enthusiasm his teaching generated among Western humanists. Among his many pupils were *Filelfo, Pier *Vergerio, Leonardo *Bruni, and *Guarino da Verona, who later established his own humanist school of Ferrara. The activities of Manuel Chrysoloras, owing to the widespread influence of his many pupils, gave the study of Greek a tremendous impetus in the West. As Leonardo Bruni put it, rather exaggeratedly, his teaching in Florence marked the revival of a "language no Italian had understood for 700 years."

Bibliography: E. L. J. LEGRAND, *Bibliographie hellénique,* 4 v. (Paris 1885–1906; repr. Brussels 1963) 1:xix–xxx, still useful. G. CAMMELLI, *Manuele Crisolora,* v.1 of *I dotti bizantini e le origini dell'umanesimo* (Florence 1941–), most recent study. D. J. GEANAKOPLOS, *Greek Scholars in Venice: Studies in the Dissemination of Greek Learning from Byzantium to Western Europe* (Cambridge, Mass. 1962), on the dissemination of Greek learning via Byzantium.

[D. J. GEANAKOPLOS]

CHRYSOSTOM OF SAINT-LÔ, JOHN, Franciscan spiritual director and writer; b. Saint-Fremond, near Bayeux, France, 1594; d. Paris, March 26, 1646. He entered the Third Order Regular of St. Francis at the age of 16 and rapidly advanced to high positions within the order. In 1622 he was definitor of the province of France, in 1625 definitor general, in 1634 provincial of the province of France, and in 1640 provincial of the province of Saint-Yves. He was confessor to Marie de Médicis and Anne of Austria and was esteemed highly by Louis XIII and Cardinal Richelieu. Among Chrysostom's personal friends were St. Vincent de Paul, Jean Jacques Olier, and Charles de Condren. His writings were probably more extensive than the few short works that survive. These include *Divers traités spirituels et méditatifs* (Paris 1651), *Exercises de piété et de perfection* (Caen 1654), and *La Sainte désoccupation* (2d ed. Paris 1890). His greatest influence, however, was as a spiritual director, and as such he is remembered as a leading figure in French spirituality of the 17th century. He was the leading figure of the school of Norman mystics associated with the hermitage of Caen, and his disciples included St. John Eudes, Jean de Bernieres-

Louvigny, Marie de Vallées, Henri Boudon, and others notable in the history of spirituality.

Bibliography: H. Boudon, *L'Homme intérieur* (Paris 1684), also in *Oeuvres de Boudon,* ed. J. P. Migne (Paris 1856) 2:1127–1342. M. A. Souriau, *Deux mystiques normands au XVIIe siècle* (Paris 1913). G. Guillot, *Les Pères pénitents a St. Lô* (St. Lô 1914). R. Heurtevant, DictSpirAscMyst 2:881–885. É. Longpré, *Catholicisme* 2:1117–19.

[J. C. WILLKE]

CHTHONIC DIVINITIES, WORSHIP OF. This category of divinities in ancient Greek religion comprises the Earth (in Greek Χθών), or Gaia (Ge); the fertility goddesses who emanated from her, especially the Mother Goddesses of Asia Minor; and the dead, who often figure as spirits of fertility. S. Eitrem [*Opferritus und Voropfer der Griechen und Römer* (Christiania 1914)] attempted to show—and M. Nilsson concurred (1:135)—that the introductory ceremonies of the normal Greek sacrifice offered to the celestial gods indicated an important phenomenon. Inasmuch as the celestial divinities allowed themselves to be associated in the cult of the dead, they were very probably regarded as the dead with whom the spirits of the place were identified. This would mean that a remnant of the animistic-agrarian form of religion going back to pre-Greek culture was preserved as an essential element in the cult of the Olympian gods. At the stage of archaic Greek religion represented by Homer, the dead were mere wraiths who did not even have a cult. However, the employment of a cleft or fissure for channeling an offering in liquid form from the top of the grave or altar into the earth is confirmed by archeology for shaft graves of Mycenae and by the discovery of such altars in ancient Crete. Unquestionably, in ancient Crete and in the Minoan culture in general, the motherly earth was no longer viewed only as a vague personification or an abstractly conceived fertility power, the receiver of chthonic cult, but, on the contrary, as the Mistress of Life, active in the fruitful earth itself.

The close union also of the Olympian gods with an element that falls within the earthly sphere was especially striking not only in the case of the sea god, Poseidon, the Earth-Shaker, the husband of Dao (i.e., Demeter, the Earth-Goddess), but especially in the case of Hermes, the god of stone piles, who, perhaps even in his office as guide of the dead, was called Chthonios. Zeus himself was associated as Chthonios at Athens in certain sacrifices to Gaia, and was therefore the object of a chthonic cult in practice, although not perhaps by formal rite. The earliest children of Gaia, the Titans and Giants, had a continued life only in myth. The Titans conquered by Zeus were chthonic gods through their confinement, at first in Tartarus as a place of punishment and then, after their pardon by Zeus, through their abode in Elysium, the land of the dead on the rim of the earth. The worship of fertility demons frequently had an important place in the complex of cults of rural areas.

Bibliography: H. J. Rose, *Handbook of Greek Mythology* (6th ed. New York 1958) 17–101. Nilsson GeschGrRel v.1. U. von Wilamowitz-Moellendorff, *Der Glaube der Hellenen,* 2 v. (Berlin 1931–32) v.1. H. Schwabl, "Weltschöpfung," Pauly Wiss RE Suppl 9 (1962) 1433–1582, esp. 1440ff.

[K. PRÜMM]

CHUANG TZŬ, Chinese philosopher, contemporary of *Mencius, also known as Tschuang Tzŭ, Chuang-tze, Chuang-tse, Chou; b. *c.* 370; d. *c.* 285 B.C. Unlike Mencius, Chuang Tzŭ did not travel far to preach his doctrine; yet his fame reached the King of the state of Tch'ou, the largest of federal states in China at that time, who asked him to become his prime minister. Chuang Tzŭ declined the invitation, preferring to live simply in a small village and discuss philosophy with his disciples and friends. The Book of Chuang Tzŭ, written by his disciples, had 52 chapters, but only 33 are extant. His teachings on cosmology, ethics, and politics are similar to those of *Lao Tzŭ. He taught that all values are relative and that all extremes will eventually meet because they are really different aspects of the same unique reality. He developed a technique of dialectics that he used effectively in discussions. He analyzed the problem of knowledge in more detail than other philosophers of his time, but offered a solution that was subjectivist and agnostic. After Lao Tzŭ, Chuang Tzŭ was considered the great master of Taoist philosophy.

See also CHINESE PHILOSOPHY.

Bibliography: Chuang-tzŭ, *Chuang Tzŭ,* tr. H. A. Giles (2d ed. London 1926). Lao Tzŭ, *The Wisdom of Laotse,* ed. and tr. Lin, Yu-t'ang (New York 1948) with supplementary writings of Chuang Tzŭ. Fung, Yu-lan, *A Short History of Chinese Philosophy,* ed. D. Bodde (New York 1960) ch. 10.

[A. A. TSEU]

CHUNGKING, ARCHDIOCESE OF (CIOMCHIMENSIS), metropolitan see since 1946, in Szechwan (Ssu-ch'uan) province, central *China. Statistics for 1950, the latest available, showed the See of Chungking (Ch'ung-ch'ing), 135,135 square miles in area, to have 52 parishes, 85 secular priests, 6 men in 1 religious house, 114 women in 4 convents, and 38,000 Catholics in a population of 11 million. Its 7 suffragans, all created in 1946, had 274 priests, 196 sisters, and 122,000 Catholics in a population of 44 million; they were: Ch'eng-tu, K'ang-ting, Lo-shan (Kiating), Hsi-ch'ang (Ningyüan), Nan-ch'ung (Shunking), I-pin (Suifu), and Wan-hsien.

From *Macao, the Jesuits Ludovico *Buglio and Gabriel de Magalhaens arrived in Szechwan in 1640 but were expelled (1646–47). Another Jesuit arrived (1661) after Szechwan came under the administration of François *Pallu (1659). In 1690 the area was part of the Diocese of *Peking under the Portuguese *padroado, but in 1696 it became a vicariate under the *Paris Foreign Mission Society (1733), administering the Vicariates of Kweichow, Yünnan, and Hukwang. Outstanding missionaries were the Chinese priest Andrea Ly and Bishops Pottier (d. 1792), John de Saint-Martin, and Bl. Gabriel Dufresne (who convoked the "Synod of Szechwan" in 1803 and with many others died a martyr in Ch'eng-tu in 1815). In 1856 Szechwan was divided into northwest (Ch'eng-tu) and southeast vicariates. In 1860 the southeast vicariate was divided into a south vicariate (I-pin) and an eastern one (called Chungking in 1924), from which the Vicariate of Wan-hsien was detached in 1929. The See of K'ang-ting is the successor of the Vicariate of *Tibet, established in 1846.

Bibliography: *Annuaire de l'Église catholique en Chine* (Shanghai 1950). MissCattol 352–358. A. Pucci, EncCatt 3:1571–72.

[J. KRAHL]

CHUR, MONASTERY OF, former Premonstratensian abbey, Graubünden canton, Switzerland, Diocese of Chur (patron, St. Lucius). It is improbable that the Benedictine foundation dated from St. *Lucius, but possibly a small clerical community, living on the site, became Benedictine *c.* 800. Before 1149, Conrad of Biberegg, Bishop of Chur, committed the monastery to the *Premonstratensians from Roggenburg and relocated the nuns of the original double monastery at St. Hilary, not far from the abbey. Churwalden in the Engadine was a daughter house. In 1529, the abbot Theodul Schlegl was martyred by the Calvinists, and the abbey was suppressed in 1538. The community found refuge at Bendern in Liechtenstein. In 1624 Chur was restored, though most of its possessions were lost. Although legally it was once again an abbey *sui juris* by 1717, it remained practically a dependent house of Roggenburg. In 1806 the last abbot surrendered the monastery to the bishopric of Chur, which now uses the abbey as its diocesan seminary.

Bibliography: Hugo OrdPraemAn 2:103–112. Cottineau 1:831. Backmund MonPraem 1:68–70. M. H. VICAIRE and N. BACKMUND, DHGE 13:213–221. G. VASELLA, *St-Luziuskirche* (Munich 1955).

[N. BACKMUND]

CHURCH, ARTICLES ON

The principal articles concerning the Church as an institution are: CHURCH, I (IN THE BIBLE); CHURCH, II (THEOLOGY OF); CHURCH, HISTORY OF, I (EARLY); CHURCH, HISTORY OF, II (MEDIEVAL); CHURCH, HISTORY OF, III (EARLY MODERN: 1500–1789); CHURCH, HISTORY OF, IV (LATE MODERN: 1789–1965). For discussion of the theological discipline that concerns the Church, *see* ECCLESIOLOGY. Major areas of interest in ecclesiology, as well as minor areas, concepts, and even phrases used in ecclesiological investigation, are treated in individual articles. In the area of the dogmatic theology, ecclesiological topics are the most numerous: e.g., MYSTICAL BODY OF CHRIST; MYSTICI CORPORIS; SOCIETY (IN THEOLOGY); INCORPORATION IN CHRIST; MEMBERSHIP IN THE CHURCH; VOTUM; COMMUNION OF SAINTS; MARKS OF THE CHURCH (PROPERTIES); MIRACLE, MORAL; MIRACLE, MORAL (THE CHURCH); HIERARCHY; TEACHING AUTHORITY OF THE CHURCH (MAGISTERIUM); INFALLIBILITY.

[E. A. WEIS]

CHURCH, I (IN THE BIBLE)

The important considerations about the Church from a Biblical viewpoint are the original terms used for it, its adumbrations in the OT, the development of its notion in the NT, and a theological synthesis of the NT doctrine.

Original Terms. The English word church, like the German *Kirche,* is derived ultimately, through the Gothic, from the Greek τὸ κυριακόν, "thing or place pertaining to the Lord." The words for church in the Romance languages, such as French *église* and Italian *chièsa,* come from the Latin *ecclesia,* an exact transliteration of the Greek ἐκκλησία.

In the profane Greek ἐκκλησία designated an assembly of the people as a political force; it was used in this meaning in Acts 19.32, 39, 41; its meaning in 1 Cor 11.18 was colored by its profane signification. In the Septuagint (LXX) ἐκκλησία designated an assembly convoked for religious purposes [e.g., Dt 23.2–3; 3 Kgs 8.5, 14, 22; Ps 21(22).26]. It is used 81 times to translate the Hebrew term *qāhāl,* and 4 times derivatives of *qāhāl* [1 Sm 19.20, conjectured; Neh 5.7; Ps 25(26).12; 67(68).27]. *Qāhāl* was used in most cases to designate a religious assembly, a usage especially of the *Deuteronomists, the Biblical *Chronicler, and the Book of *Psalms. The word *qāhāl* was translated also by other words in the LXX, in particular by συναγωγή, which, however, more frequently translated *'ēdâ,* "a gathering." There is little doubt that both the assonance and the similarity in meaning of *qāhāl* and ἐκκλησία, "that which is called forth," influenced the translators who produced the LXX.

In the NT ἐκκλησία is found 61 times in the Pauline corpus (including Hebrews), 23 times in Acts, 20 times in Apocalypse, and 11 in the remaining books. The meaning in each case must be derived from the context.

It was altogether natural that Jesus, in establishing a new *covenant and hence a new people of God having continuity with the ancient one, would have designated this people with a Biblical name for a religious assembly; in Aramaic He would have used *'edtâ'* or *kᵉništâ',* (both translated into Greek as συναγωγή), or *qᵉhalâ',* in Greek ἐκκλησία. Only when the break between Christians and Jews became definitive did ἐκκλησία become a purely Christian term and συναγωγή (*synagogue) a Jewish term.

Adumbrations in the Old Testament. From its beginnings mankind was called to live in society (Gn 1.27; 2.18), to multiply itself, to subdue and to have dominion over the earth (Gn 1.28), and to live in familiarity with God (Gn 2.8–25). But sin was committed by man and broke this special relationship to God; yet God promised mercy to a sinful mankind (Genesis ch. 3). As a result of sin, men manifested hatred for one another (Gn 4.8; 6.11), showed inordinate pride (Gn 11.8–9), and lost familiarity with their Creator (Gn 3.8; 4.14).

The process of the formation of God's people commenced with the election of Abraham, which was sealed with a *bᵉrît,* "covenant." The covenant was renewed and made more particular with some of Abraham's descendants during the *Exodus from Egypt under Moses (Exodus ch. 19–24). The Israelites were not always faithful to God. This infidelity showed itself during the Exodus (Ex 32.1–6), notwithstanding God's special care of them (Exodus ch. 16–17), and more brazenly later on. Instead of being God's faithful spouse, Israel acted like an adulterous wife (Osee ch. 1–3; 9.1; Ezechiel ch. 16); it violated God's laws and belied the covenant (Is 1.2–9; 5.1–7). The Prophets often predicted that only a portion of the people, the faithful and holy *remnant of Israel, would be the beneficiary of the divine promises (Is 4.3; Am 3.12; 9.8–10; Jer 3.14–18). Then God would conclude a new covenant with His people (Jer 31.31–34; Ez 11.14–21). These two ideas, the faithful remnant and the new covenant, were reaffirmed during the centuries following the Babylonian Exile, and they nourished the messianic hopes of Israel (Is 54.9–10; Za 2.11–17; 9.7; Ag 1.12; 2.2–5; 1 Mc 2.49–64); they also held an important place in the teaching of the *Qumran community.

Development of the Concept in the New Testament. While the new and ultimate covenant was ratified by Jesus' death and Resurrection, and hence the Church began at that time, only gradually was the nature of the new community manifested as separate from Judaism and as having its own proper structure.

In the Acts of the Apostles. After the Ascension, the Apostles, whom Jesus had chosen and to whom He "had given commandments through the Holy Spirit" (Acts 1.2), together with the disciples, remained in

Fig. 1. The Church of the Circumcision, detail of a mosaic erected during the pontificate of Pope Celestine I (422–432) over the inner portal of the Church of S. Sabina at Rome.

Jerusalem awaiting the coming of the Spirit; they elected Matthias as successor of Judas Iscariot at the urging of Peter to fill out the number of the *Twelve (Acts 1.12–26). After the coming of the Spirit they began immediately to preach to the Jews and to baptize (Acts 2.4–41; 4.2), though they met opposition (Acts 4.1; 5.17–18; 9.1; 12.1–5). The first members of the Jerusalem church voluntarily shared their possessions (Acts 4.34–5.11). Gradually the Apostles assigned to other members of the community certain duties; the deacons were given charge of charitable works, preaching, and baptizing (Acts 6.1–6; 8.5, 12–13, 31–38). However, a certain type of *imposition of hands in order to receive the Holy Spirit was a work of the Apostles alone (Acts 8.14–18). "The communion of the *breaking of the bread" was a central rite (Acts 2.42, 46; 20.7, 11). At an early date non-Jews were admitted to the Church (Acts 10.44–48); outside of Palestine, especially at Antioch, the work also of proselytizing Gentiles met with success and it was at Antioch that "the disciples were first called Christians" (Acts 11.19–26). *See* CHRISTIAN (THE TERM). Jewish dietary laws and circumcision did not bind the converts from paganism (Acts 11.1–18), though minor restrictions were imposed on some churches by an Apostolic decision (Acts 15.23–29; *see* JERUSALEM, COUNCIL OF). With the conversion of Paul, a former persecutor of Christians, the tempo of proselytism among non-Jews was accelerated and the tensions between the Jewish and non-Jewish elements in the Church increased (Acts 15.1–2, 35; 21.20–25). However, the Apostles and their converts from Judaism, including Paul, continued to assist at the services in the Temple in Jerusalem (Acts 3.1; 5.42; 21.26). The preaching of the Apostles and other ministers centered on Jesus, who was crucified, was raised from the dead, was to reign as King over the new Israel (Acts 2.22–39; 13.16–41), and whose subjects would rise as Jesus had (Acts 23.6; 26.23). St. Luke's record of the expansion of the Church under the guidance of the Holy Spirit ceased when the good news had reached as far as Rome (Acts 1.8; 28.28–31).

In the Pauline Corpus. The content of Paul's letters should now be examined for their teaching about the Church. The Apostle of the Gentiles, more than any other NT author, gave his personal reflections on the Church's nature. In the vision on the road to Damascus he received the revelation of the mysterious identity between Christ and the Church (Acts 9.4–5) and his later experiences forced him to delve more deeply into this mystery.

According to Paul the universal Church was composed of various local churches whose members were "saints," chosen by God (1 Cor 1.2). There was authority in the Church: Peter (Gal 1.18; 2.6–14); the Twelve and Paul himself (1 Cor 15.1–11); Timothy, Titus, and the "bishops" [1 Tm 1.3–5; 3.2; Ti 1.7; Phil 1.1; Acts 20.28; *see* BISHOP (IN THE BIBLE)]; elders or *presbyters (Ti 1.5; 1 Tm 5.17); and *deacons (Phil 1.1). There were also those possessing various *charisms, among whom the Prophets had a special place; in their activity the charismatics were not to cause disorder (1 Cor 14.33, 40). The members of the Church lived in the expectation of the *Parousia of Jesus (1 Thes 1.10; 1 Cor 11.26) and the resurrection of the just (1 Thes 4.13–18; 1 Corinthians ch. 15), but the time of the Parousia was not known (1 Thes 5.1–3; 2 Thes 2.1–8). The communities were to live according to the traditions that Paul had passed on to them (1 Cor 11.2, 23–24; 15.1–3; Gal 1.6–10); the traditions were rooted in the life and teaching of Jesus (1 Cor 7.10; 11.23; 2 Cor 4.5) and concerned belief (1 Cor 15.1–4), rites such as baptism and the Lord's supper (Gal 3.26–27; Eph 4.5; 1 Cor 11.23–24), and ways of acting (1 Cor 7.10). Baptism united the believer to the dead and risen Lord Jesus (Rom 6.3–11); and the partaking of the bread effected unity (1 Cor 10.16–17). Baptism and the profession of faith went together (Gal 3.26–27); faith came from hearing and accepting the proclamation of Christ's word (Rom 10.17). *See* BAPTISM (IN THE BIBLE).

Paul described the Church as God's plantation, the growth of which depended upon God's aid (1 Cor 3.6–9), as God's building whose foundation was Christ (1 Cor 3.9–15), and as God's sanctuary (1 Cor 3.16). The Church was "the pillar and mainstay of truth" (1 Tm 3.15), a new creation (2 Cor 5.17; Gal 6.15), the spouse of Christ (2 Cor 11.2–3; Eph 5.22–33), the new covenant (1 Cor 11.25), and the kingdom of God's beloved Son (Col 1.13). The Church was made up of those who were in Christ, who were Christ's, and who were the body of Christ (1 Cor 10.16–17; 12.12; Rom 12.4–8).

The description of the Church as the *mystical body of Christ is considered by many to have been the most characteristic feature in Paul's consideration of the Church. There was a development in the Apostle's thought on this theme between the composition of 1 Corinthians (*c.* 57) and that of Colossians and Ephesians (*c.* 62). In the latter Epistles Christ was described as the head of His body (Col 1.18; Eph 5.22–24, 29–30) and the Church was called the plenitude of Christ's fullness (Eph 1.22–23), notions that were not explicitly noted in the earlier letters (1 Cor 6.15–17; 10.14–22; 12.12–31; Rom 12.4–8). The idea of the many united in the one of 1 Corinthians and Romans was conducive to the more developed idea of the body as Christ in His fullness. The Church's ministries were given by Christ "in order to perfect the saints for a work of ministry, for building up the body of Christ, until we all attain to the unity of the faith and of the deep knowledge of the Son of God, to perfect manhood, to the mature measure of the fullness of Christ" (Eph 4.11–13). The members of the Church were to be "imitators of God" (Eph 5.1) and were to "grow up in all things in . . . Christ" (Eph 4.15). Moved as they were by the Spirit to know and confess Jesus as the Christ (1 Cor 12.3), Christ's members shared in His powers, indeed in the very principle of His life (Col 2.19; Eph 4.15–16). The Apostles were in a special sense His ministers and the dispensers of His and God's mysteries (1 Cor 4.1).

Charity was to reign in the Church; as a concrete expression of this principle, Paul organized the collection on behalf of the Jerusalem church among the believers in the Greek territories (1 Cor 16.1–4; 2 Corinthians ch. 8–9; Rom 15.26–27). This was but one way of emphasizing the fact that the Church's members formed one people (Gal 3.24–29) who were children of the one God and Father (Eph 4.1–6); thus there were among them no human divisions but all were reconciled one to another (Eph 2.11–22), Greeks and barbarians, masters and slaves, men and women (1 Cor 12.13; Col 3.11). As Christ could not be divided, neither could the Church (1 Cor 1.12–13; 3.4). Yet there were sinners in the Church, some of whom were to be expelled, though the hope of pardon was not taken away (1 Corinthians ch. 5).

In the Synoptic Gospels. The first Gospel's teaching concerning the Church was for the most part contained within the teaching concerning the kingdom of heaven. It was to have modest beginnings (Mt 13.31–33) about which men would argue (Mt 13.37–43). Entrance into it was difficult (Mt 7.13–14; 11.12), since obedience and renouncement were necessary (Mt 7.21; 12.50). It was predicted in the OT (Mt 13.35). The wise and proud would not enter into the kingdom (Mt 5.3–10; 11.25; 13.10–15), but sinners and Gentiles would (Mt 8.10–12; 9.9–13; 21.28–32). The last point was treated at some length in the Gospel because of the need to solve the problem that the religious Jews had generally rejected the life and teachings of Jesus, although He was the authentic fulfillment of the OT. The solution was contained in the parables and lessons recalling Israel's former infidelity (Mt 20.1–16; 21.28–32, 33–46; 22.1–10). The OT foretold that many of the Jews would renounce their privileges because of their obstinacy (Mt 21.42; 23.34–39); the benefits would then be given to those who had a modicum of belief (Mt 5.3–12; 13.12; 25.29).

Alone among the evangelists Matthew used the word ἐκκλησία (Mt 16.18; 18.17). The three uses of the word show the communitarian interests of the evangelist and of the Judeo-Christian Church whose preoccupations he reflected; it was a Church aware that it was the new chosen people, the beginning on earth of the Kingdom of God. It therefore put particular insistence upon

Fig. 2. The Church of the Gentiles, detail of a mosaic erected during the pontificate of Pope Celestine I over the inner portal of the Church of S. Sabina at Rome.

Peter's role (Mt 16.16–18) and the duties of the sacred community's members (Matthew ch. 18). The new kingdom was inaugurated with the death and Resurrection of Jesus (Mt 27.50–53; 28.16–20); yet it would reach a milestone in its life with the fall of Jerusalem in A.D. 70 (Matthew ch. 24). The community was to be governed by the authority constituted by Jesus (Mt 16.16–18; 18.15–18); it was to have sacramental rites, baptism (Mt 28.19) and the Eucharist (Mt 26.26–29). Its authorities were to proclaim the teaching of Jesus to the whole world (Mt 28.20). While the Church was the kingdom of heaven on earth, inaugurated and ruled by Christ, the Church was not completely identical with the kingdom of the Father (cf. Mt 13.37–43 with 13.43 and 25.34). The concept of the Church presented in St. Mark's Gospel added nothing to the data found in Matthew.

The doctrine concerning the kingdom of God on earth in St. Luke's Gospel was the same as that found in the other two Synoptic Gospels, but more than they, Luke emphasized its universalistic characteristics (Lk 4.25–27; 24.47). While Matthew used the more Hebraic phrase "kingdom of heaven" as a title for the Church, Luke and Mark used "kingdom of God," a sign that their works were addressed primarily to non-Jewish elements within the Church.

In the Johannine Literature. In the theology of St. John, Jesus was King of a kingdom that was "not of this world" (Jn 18.36). The members of the kingdom were born, "not of blood, nor of the will of the flesh, nor of the will of men, but of God" (Jn 1.13; cf. 3.3–8; 1 Jn 2.29–3.1–2, 9; 4.7; 5.1, 4, 18); they were by belief *sons of God (Jn 1.12; 1 Jn 5.1). Their birth was through water and the Spirit (Jn 3.5). The Christian abided in Christ and in God (Jn 6.57; 15.4–7; 1

Jn 2.6, 24, 27–28; 3.6; 4.16). The Christian was to eat the flesh and drink the blood of Jesus (Jn 6.52–57). While emphasis certainly was given in the fourth Gospel to the relationship of the individual Christian to Jesus, the allegory of the Good Shepherd (Jn 10.1–18) and that of the Vine and the Branches (Jn 15.1–7) brought out the community aspects of John's teaching concerning believers. In the fourth Gospel the Apostles were given the power to forgive sins (Jn 20.22–23). Peter was constituted the shepherd of Jesus' flock (Jn 21.15–17), which should be universally one (Jn 10.16; 17.11). The Apostles would have the duty of carrying on the mission given by the Father to Jesus (Jn 20.21).

The suffering and ultimately triumphant Church was the main subject of the Apocalypse. The principal figures of the Church were the *woman clothed with sun and fighting with the dragon, Satan (Apocalypse ch. 12), and the Temple and its environs (Ap 11.1–13). Warnings against various communal sins and defects were given in the letters to the seven churches of Asia Minor (Ap 1.9–3.22).

In the Other NT Literature. According to the doctrine found in the Epistle to the Hebrews, Christians did not have on earth a permanent city but were to seek that which was to come (Heb 13.14), to which heavenly state each was called but which, to a certain degree, was already possessed (Heb 3.1; 6.4–5). The Christians' sole high priest was already in heaven interceding for them (Heb 5.1–10; 9.11–14). Christians were brothers one to another (Heb 3.1, 12), sanctified by Jesus into one brotherhood with Him (Heb 2.11–18); they were "partakers of Christ" (Heb 3.14), His house (Heb 3.6), and had been purified in His blood (Heb 9.18–28). Unlike the wandering Jews of the Exodus they were a caravan traveling in obedience toward the true, i.e., perfect, Promised Land (Heb 3.1–4.13).

In 1 Peter many figures were used to describe Christ and His Church: a cornerstone, a precious stone chosen by God, a spiritual house, "a holy priesthood, to offer spiritual sacrifices acceptable to God through Jesus Christ," "a chosen race, a royal priesthood, a holy nation, a purchased people" that should proclaim "the perfections of him who has called you out of darkness into his marvelous light," a people that had now obtained mercy (1 Pt 2.4–10). The "presbyters" were to "tend the flock of God, . . . governing not under constraint, but willingly" (1 Pt 5.1–2). Younger members of the Church were to be subject to the presbyters (5.5).

In 2 Peter the faithful were warned against false teachers and unsound interpreters of Sacred Scripture (2 Pt 2.1–3, 3.16); the Parousia would occur suddenly but it was now delayed for the Lord did not wish "that any should perish but that all should turn to repentance" (3.9).

According to Jude, the Church's members were the "called who have been loved in God the Father and preserved for Christ Jesus" (Jude 1.1); they were to be wary of false teachers.

According to James, the Church was made up of the poor who were "heirs of the kingdom which God has promised to those who love him" (Jas 2.5). There was, moreover, a special ritual for the sick that was reserved to the presbyters, who were to assemble and pray over the sick man, "anointing him with oil in the name of the Lord" (Jas 5.14–15). The prayer of faith would cure him and the Lord would raise him, and if he were guilty of sins, he would be forgiven. *See* ANOINTING OF THE SICK, I (THEOLOGY OF).

Theological Synthesis. The question of the essential characteristics of the Church has been a problem for theologians. What is the most complete single representation of the Church's reality, that, like Paul's gospel, may be said to be a "mystery that has been kept in silence from eternal ages but is . . . now made known to all the Gentiles" (Rom 16.25–26)? Indeed, the reality is so great that no synthesis of it can ever be perfect.

Many modern scholars believe that the synthesis should center around the notion of the Church as the new people of God. The concept of the new covenant, however, may be more fitting, for Israel as a people and a nation was brought into existence by a divinely given covenant (Genesis ch. 15; Exodus ch. 24), which found its fulfillment in the new covenant (Mt 26.28; Lk 22.19–20).

The Church as the People of the New Covenant. God redeemed His people from the power of sin and the devil (Eph 1.7; Col 1.13–14; Jn 12.31; 16.11), just as He redeemed the Israelites from exile in Egypt and later in Babylon. God remitted their sins (Mt 26.28), as He forgave the sins of the Israelites (Ex 34.7–9). He sanctified them (Heb 13.12; Ex 31.13) and gave them life (Jn 5.21, 24; Ex 3.7–10). He dwelt among His people in the person of Jesus (Jn 1.14), to an infinitely greater degree than He was with the ancient Israelites (Dt 4.7). He manifested His power and goodness to the members of both covenants (in the manna of the OT and in the Eucharist of the NT). God is the Father of His people (Is 63.16; Mt 5.48; 6.9).

According to the NT doctrine the Church was God's people, a precious possession (1 Pt 2.9), as Israel was God's special people (Ex 19.5). Israel was chosen by God (Dt 7.6), as were the members of the Church (Jn 15.16). Israel was a people set apart (Nm 23.9); the Church was a people in this world but not of it (Jn 15.19; 1 Cor 5.9–13). Israel was the sacred assembly of Yahweh; the Church was Christ's (Mt 16.18) and hence God's sacred assembly (1 Cor 1.2). Both Israel and the Church were regal and sacerdotal (Ex 19.6; 1 Pt 2.9). Israel, if faithful, was to have dominion over other nations (Dt 15.6); the members of the new Israel were to be judges of angels (1 Cor 6.3). Israel was the flock (Jer 13.17) and spouse of Yahweh (Os 2.17–25); the Church was the flock (Jn 10.1–13) and spouse of Jesus the Christ (Mt 9.15; 2 Cor 11.2). Both were holy (Ex 19.6; Col 3.12). The Israelites had obligations toward God (Exodus ch. 20–23); so did Christians (Matthew ch. 5–7; Jn 13.34; Romans ch. 12–15).

Moses had been the mediator of the old covenant (Ex 19.1–9); the new covenant had Jesus as mediator (Heb 5.1–10). Each covenant was inaugurated with a sacrifice (Ex 24.4–8; Gn 15.9–11; Jn 6.52; 19.30; Heb 9.15–28). Moses had been of a priestly family; Jesus was a priest according to the order of Melchisedec (Heb 6.20–7.3). The victims of the Mosaic covenant sacrifice had been dumb animals (Ex 24.5); Jesus as man was the sacrificial victim of the new covenant (Heb 10.10). Just as the Israelites had been commanded to recall their election, deliverance from Egypt, and the gift of the Holy Land by sacrificing their first fruits (Dt 26.5–10), so Christians were to commemorate their deliverance through Christ's death by celebrating the *Lord's Supper (1 Cor 11.23–27).

Fig. 3. The Procession of the Church to the Cross, full-page miniature in a late 10th-century Reichenau manuscript of the "Canticle of Canticles" in the Staatliche Bibliothek, Bamberg (MS Bibl. 22, fol. 4 v).

In contrast to the old covenant the new had but one sacrifice (Heb 9.11–15), which supplanted the multitude of sacrifices of the former (Heb 10.1–18) and was offered by the one and only high priest (Heb 5.1–10), who was eternally perfect priest (Heb 7.26–28) and mediator of the superior covenant (Heb 8.6–13). Jesus' unique sacrifice took away all sin, something not accomplished by the sacrifices of the OT period (Heb 10.11–18).

In the society effected by each covenant there was an initiating rite—circumcision for the old, especially after the Exile (Gn 17.9–14; 1 Mc 1.60–61), baptism for the new (Acts 2.38–41). In each covenant certain individuals were duly constituted authorities (Ex 3.7–12; 4.10–17; 18.13–27; Mt 16.16–18, etc.).

The Church as a Spiritual Community Established by Christ. Not everyone interprets the NT data concerning the Church in the same way. There are some Christians, for example, who deny that the Church was presented in the NT as a religious community ruled by properly constituted authorities who could dispense sacraments. Others deny that certain peculiarities of the nascent Church were to continue, e.g., the special office of Peter. Some Catholics consider that many of the charismatic offices were peculiar to the early years of the Church.

In contrast to the latter part of the 19th century, when many non-Catholics viewed the Church as merely a grouping together of various believers for mutual edification and for the giving of united testimony to nonbelievers, it is generally admitted by modern scholars that according to the NT the Church was something prior to the individual believer, who entered a Church that was already existing, having already been established by God through Jesus Christ. Thus according to the NT the most important factor was the relationship of the Church's members, not to one another, but to Jesus. The NT presented the Church as the presence of Christ among men, a presence that was to last until the end of the world. It was in and through the Church that God brought to completion the work of redemption announced first in the OT and realized in the life and person of Jesus.

Although some non-Catholic scholars still think that there existed a lapse of time between Jesus' life and the foundation of the Church and that Jesus merely proclaimed the nearness of the end, whereas the Christological and ecclesiological teaching found in the NT was a product of the community as such or of certain members of it, nevertheless a growing consensus of scholars holds that the NT doctrine of the Church originated in Jesus' lifetime and in His person. For the latter group, Jesus' teaching concerning the kingdom of God was indeed the starting point for later NT teaching regarding the Church, which was a legitimate deduction from Jesus' words and, under the guidance of the Spirit, the proper complement to them.

Much study is being devoted to the early development of the Church's organization. Examination of the *Pastoral Epistles (*c.* A.D. 65–67) already shows that the Church was in transition and on the way to taking on the form that it had in the 2d century.

Further Catholic studies of the understanding that the first generation believers had of their sacred community are necessary. It is clear that the expectation of the end played an important part in their thought (1 and 2 Thessalonians) and that they thought of themselves, to a great degree, as the messianic community (Matthew). But more attention should be given to the integrating of the present juridical aspects of the Church with its spiritual reality as the living mystery of the gospel (Rom 16.25–26); the NT data about the importance of God's word must be assimilated into present theology. The doctrine concerning God's word working in and through the Church would thus be elucidated. Studies concerning the nature of the *hierarchy, in its NT presentation, would be illuminating, even though the loose terminology of the NT makes this task difficult. The growing tendency to view the Apostolic Church as one that was in the process of growth and evolution should lead Catholics to understand more precisely the Church's development from its small beginnings in Jerusalem to its 2d-century characteristics. Finally, a theology of the charisms found mainly in 1 Corinthians ch. 12–14 should be developed.

The preoccupation with showing that the Church is an external society, hierarchically organized, which has characterized so much Catholic work since the Protestant Reformation, is no longer necessary, because the need for such an apologetics is not as great. Emphasis on the external aspect of the Church should no longer lead to a neglect of other important aspects of the Church and its members.

The Church did not come into existence in a cultural vacuum; it had to be intelligible to the men who joined its communion. Greater understanding of the NT Church will come, therefore, from a fuller knowledge of the milieu in which the NT was produced and of the cultural influences that affected its teaching. The Church's organization was influenced also by that of groups in the midst of which it was born and grew. Studies of the Palestinian culture and institutions in the last century B.C. and in the 1st Christian century are and will continue to be helpful, e.g., the already vast literature about the Qumran community, in which there is evidence that the organization of the nascent Church may have been patterned along the line of this sect or some similar group, although there are obvious essential differences.

Bibliography: EncDictBibl 376–385. A. MÉDEBIELLE, DBSuppl 2:487–691. K. L. SCHMIDT, Kittel ThW 3:502–539. L. CERFAUX, *The Church in the Theology of St. Paul,* tr. G. WEBB and A. WALKER (New York 1959). J. A. T. ROBINSON, *The Body: A Study in Pauline Theology* (London 1952). M. BLACK, *The Scrolls and Christian Origins* (New York 1961). *L'Église dans la Bible: Recherches de philosophie et de théologie publiées par les facultés S. J. de Montréal* (Studia 13; Bruges 1962). D. M. STANLEY, "Reflections on the Church in the N.T.," CathBibl Quart 25 (1963) 387–400. B. M. AHERN, "The Concept of the Church in Biblical Thought," ProcSocCathCollTeachSacrDoctr 7 (1961) 32–61. P. BENOIT, *Exégèse et théologie,* 2 v. (Paris 1961) 2:107–177, 232–317; "Qumrân et le NT," NTSt 7 (1960–61) 276–296. J. GNILKA, "Die Kirche des Matthäus und die Gemeinde von Qumran," BiblZ 7 (1963) 43–63. **Illustration credits:** Figs. 1 and 2, Alinari-Art Reference Bureau. Fig. 3, Hirmer Verlag München.

[J. J. O'ROURKE]

CHURCH, II (THEOLOGY OF)

In the total mystery of salvation the mystery of the Church is the meeting place where the lines of force of so many other mysteries—the divine missions, sin, Redemption, grace, Sacraments, Christian anthropology, eschatology—intersect and find a prime focus. In the Christian economy the mystery of the Church illustrates what Vatican Council I called "the connection of the mysteries one with another and with man's last end" (Denz 3016). The Church is God's handiwork, what

He has wrought and is doing in the mystery of public *salvation; it is at the same time the instrumentality through which God works to bring mankind the divine light and love that is salvation. The Church is a phenomenon with multiple and moving dimensions: human and divine, visible and invisible, juridical and mystical, immanent and transcendent, earthbound and destined for heaven. It is both means and end: both a sociosacramental instrumentality divinely qualified to work for the salvation of men and, at the same time, even in its pilgrim state, an anticipated realization in the obscurity of faith of the final glorious company of the heavenly Church. In this world the Church is neither wholly alien nor wholly at home; as the *Epistle to Diognetus* said of the early Christians: "Every foreign land is their home, and every home a foreign land" (ch. 5). The Church exists in this world as a saving sign raised up by God in the movement of human history to serve and to embody God's saving love in mankind; nonetheless it is a heavenly reality that hopefully and eagerly awaits the close of time and the achievement of sacred history to find its own full unfolding in glory.

In order to synthesize theologically the data of revelation touching on this "one complex reality" [Vatican II, *Lumen gentium* 8; ActsApS 57 (1965) 11] of the mystery of the Church, it is feasible to adopt various central themes, or a combination of themes. This article sets forth in a general way, without excluding or minimizing other modes of systematization, the theology of the Church centered on the Biblical and traditional theme of communion, *koinonia* (κοινωνία). The Church is in its deepest being the communion of life between the Father and mankind in His Son Jesus Christ, the Redeemer and glorious Lord of life, through the gift of their one Spirit of love. As a result of this primary communion, descending vertically from the initiative of the Father's love communicated to His Son in their one Spirit, there comes into being a lateral, or horizontal, communion among men who, as adoptive sons of the Father in Jesus Christ, the one true Son, are by that fact brothers one of another in the same community of life and love. The Church as a communion of life with the Father in Christ necessarily entails the Church as a communion of life with the brethren in the same Christ, in each instance through the Spirit, the common love of the Father and of the Son. It is in Jesus, the one and only Son made man, that the vertical communion in sonship and the horizontal communion in brotherhood meet and join in the mystery of the Church. The Church is a sacramental communication of the Father's love for man in Christ, involving "a destiny and an existence lived in communion with Christ and with one another in Christ" [V. Warnach "Kirche," *Bibeltheologisches Wörterbuch*, ed. J. B. Bauer (2d ed. Graz 1962) 2:710]. It is a communion of brotherhood with Christ in a sacramental faith and love, administered and directed by the episcopal order, which is itself a lesser communion of ministerial office and function, sacramentally established and commissioned by Christ to provide Himself and His work with a continuing vicarious presence in time and space. It is a community of life that requires all remaining history to develop and to achieve its full realization when, at the Second Coming, the Body of the Church wil rise in its total glory and will enter, escorted by its head, into the blessings of the Father, who will be "all in all" (1 Cor 15.28). The mystery of the Church in all its concentrated intensity is already fontally present in the glorified Christ from the first moment of His *Resurrection at Easter (see Heb 2.10; 5.9); the eschatological Church is the final unfolding of the abundant plenty of the Easter Christ in all His members in their totality as full communion forever with the Father.

In the unknown span of time between the two comings of Christ, before the final full renewal, it is the Christian brotherhood in its entirety, in both time and space, as one communion of life in the Spirit of Christ, that fulfills its spiritual itinerary. All that must be done in the Lord on the way of Christian history—the plenary worship of the Triune God, the endless warfare against sin and demoniac forces, the patient Christianization of the world, and the unfolding of the manifold riches of the love and truth of the glorious Lord—is gradually and perseveringly achieved, in the measure assigned in the economy of God, only in and with the whole brotherhood, of all ages and places, acting in concert in the one Spirit of Christ. To act as brother in the brotherhood in the Spirit of Christ is the style of life and the law of action of the Christian in the communion of the Church.

In Christian tradition the term communion came to comprise the whole range of this common life, from its subjects taken collectively and singly to their style and forms of concrete living, from its inmost spiritual principles to its varied social embodiments. Both the structures and the life are evoked by the term communion, although in the beginnings the stress lay rather on the interior principles of the common life.

New Testament. The Church is communion with the Father in Christ through the Gift of the Spirit.

Wellspring of the Church. The Church is the assembly of the Father, the Body of Christ and the temple of the Holy Spirit. In the Church men are enabled to share together in the most personal goods of the Triune God (2 Cor 13.13)—the gifts of the Father (Rom 12.3) and of the Son (Eph 4.7) and of the Spirit (Rom 12.11). The eternal council and compact of the Triune God lies at the origin of the Church (Eph 1.3–14). The Church's wellspring is the Father (Rom 11.36), who in unflawed love has sent His Son with the fullness of the Spirit to the sinful men of this fallen and estranged world (Rom 5.8; 8.32; 2 Cor 5.19; Gal 4.4–7; Eph 2.4–10; Ti 3.4–7; 1 Jn 4.9–16; Jn 3.16–17, 34–36; 6.58; 17.3, 18–25); it is the Father who has inspired His Son made man with the Spirit of love to save the world from sin, death, and the demon (Heb 9.14) and, as the glorious head of His Body the Church (Eph 1.22), to give all men in Himself and His Body "'access to the Father in the one Spirit" (Eph 2.18; see 2.19–22; Heb 10.19–20).

Visible Continuum of Christ's Mission. In establishing His Church, Christ, the while remaining wholly dependent on the loving designs of His Father (Jn 5.30; 6.38–40; 1 Cor 15.23–28), gave His own saving mission a visible continuum in history, a sociosacramental ministry in the Spirit (2 Cor 3.3, 8), charging His *Apostles to supply a vicarious and ministerial presence to His Person and His work, achieved once and for all (Heb 7.27; 9.26–28; 10.10) and ratified once and for all in His own Body-Person in its passage from death to a glorious life (Acts 2.33–36; Phil 2.9–11). Hence the eternal loving resolve of the Father to make men sharers in the divine life descends and takes body, ministerial and authentic, in the apostolic Church commissioned by Christ (Jn 20.21; 17.18; 15.9; Acts ch. 2). The Apostles trace their office and mission to the loving will of the Father embodied in the work of the incarnate Word (1 Cor 1.1; 2 Cor 1.1; Gal 1.1; Col 1.1). St. Paul is "by God's will an apostle of Jesus Christ" (Eph 1.1), and he is an Apostle in the power of Christ's Spirit (1 Thes 1.5; 1 Cor 2.4–5).

It is the role of the apostolic Church, as Christ's mandatary and the qualified servant of His word and work in the Spirit, to introduce men into the life of the Triune God, baptizing them in the name of the Father and of the Son and of the Holy Spirit (Mt 28.19). The entire existence of the Church, in this present age and until its final destiny in the next world, is suspended from, and caught up into, the movement of life that joins the Father and the Son in their personal love, the Spirit. The Church as means, i.e., as the instrumentality of the Father's love in Christ, exists in order to inaugurate and to sustain the divine life in men; and the Church as end, i.e., as the communion of the saints, is that life in its real beginnings here below, humble but victoriously hopeful. St. John writes: ". . . What we have seen and heard, we announce it to you in order that you may be in communion with us. As for our communion, it is with the Father and with His Son Jesus Christ" (1 Jn 1.3). That "we are in communion with one another" (1 Jn 1.7) is possible and true only because we are in communion with the Father and with His Son through the Gift of their one Spirit (1 Jn 4.13–16).

Pledge of the Spirit. The Son, commissioning His Apostles before His visible withdrawal from the world of men, pledges His own Spirit to them (Jn 16.7) and in them to the whole Church, as the Love of the Father and of Himself, under the formality of what St. Thomas Aquinas calls "the prime Gift" (ST 1a, 38.2) and "the Love transporting us into the heavenly world" (ST 3a, 57.1 ad 3). The very atmosphere or breath of the Church's life is the Spirit of love, making the life of the Church not intermittent reality but enduring existence, notwithstanding the abiding weakness of the men who are the human actors in the Church's pilgrimage. The supernatural world of the Church is in Christ and in His Spirit a kind of descent into time of the timeless life movement of the Triune God, catching the Body of the faithful up into the universe of the intradivine intimacy.

Having Part with Christ. If men are to share in the life of the Triune God, they must "have part with" (Jn 13.8) Jesus Christ, who is in the plenary sense the historical epiphany of the living God in the world of men (Jn 1.14; Heb 2.14–17; Col 2.17) and the total and fontal principle of the communion of men with the Father (Heb 2.10; 5.9; 6.20; 10.20; 1 Cor 15.20–23; 15.45–49; 2 Cor 1.19–22). The ecclesia of God the Father is the ecclesia of God in Jesus Christ (1 Thes 2.14). In the words of St. Thomas: ". . . In Christ spiritual good is not restricted or partial, but is absolutely entire, so that He is the entire good of the Church, nor is He together with others anything greater than He is by Himself" (ST 3a, suppl., 95.3 ad 4). Christ, the beloved Son and the *firstborn (Col 1.13, 15), has come from the Father to share with men His own plenary good, His divine life as Son, which He holds from the Father (Jn 1.16; 5.26; 6.57; 1 Jn 5.11–12), and thus to bring men into the family life of God as the adopted sons of the Father in Himself, the one Son (Gal 4.4–7; Rom 8.29–30). "God can be depended on, and it was He who called you to communion with His own Son, Jesus Christ our Lord" (1 Cor 1.9).

The reality of "having part with" Christ, of being "partners with Christ" (Heb 3.14), entails the most intimate association between the One who in love shares His sonship with men and the Many who in Him share in the one new life of adoptive sonship; moreover, it necessarily brings about the most close communion between all those who are fellow shareholders in "the common salvation" (Jude 3) of Jesus Christ the glorious Lord. This reality of communion commands a law of living, a style or deportment of life, incumbent on the Church as a whole and on each member singly. "The status of the new creature is defined as communion with God, thanks to Christ" [C. Spicq, *Dieu et l'Homme selon le N.T.* (Paris 1961) 216]; "the anthropology of the NT is a matter of *koinonia* with Christ" (*ibid.* 218), a *koinonia* that, centered in Christ, ascends to the Father through their Spirit and that reaches outward to embrace the totality of those who are one in the embodied communion of Christ's ecclesia. Stig Hanson, commenting on the parties and factions that plagued the Church of Corinth (see 1 Cor 1.10–13), says: ". . . Factions and ἐκκλησία are, in principle, contrasts. In the former case, it is the ego that is the main thought, in the latter, we. In a faction it is the individual who is the basic principle; the Church, on the other hand, aims at totality" [*The Unity of the Church in the NT: Colossians and Ephesians* (Uppsala 1946) 74]. The law of communion is the acting "We" of the brotherhood under God the Father in Christ through the Gift of their Spirit. "The identity of the Spirit of Christ in all the members of His Body, the Church, is what grounds and makes possible the Christian We" [H. Mühlen, *Der Heilige Geist als Person* (Münster in Westfalen 1963) 193].

This fraternal communion of brothers in Christ is realized in the Spirit only through the Sacraments of "our common faith" (Titus 1.4), i.e., through Baptism (Rom 6.4; Col 2.12; Eph 4.4–6), and supremely through the Eucharist, which is the most real communion with the dead and risen Christ and in Him with one another (1 Cor 10.17). At the altar of the Lord Christians are made in the full sense fellows of Christ, sharers in His passage from death to new life, and co-sharers with all who are their fellow communicants. Here is the primordial communication of all the blessings of the new covenant. "In this Sacrament the whole mystery of our salvation is contained" (St. Thomas, ST 3a, 83.4); "the Eucharist contains the Sacred in an absolute sense" (ST 3a, 73.1 ad 3). As the sacramental representation of the one sacrifice of the new covenant, it is the fullest presence and communication in Christ's body and blood of the Father's love in the Spirit for His people of the new alliance, and the surest and fullest anticipation of the heavenly banquet in the life to come (Jn 6.54; Mk 14.25).

Multiple Levels. Such a sharing in the life and destiny of the incarnate Son finds expression in St. Paul in a series of verbs compounded with σύν ("with") that scan the whole moving sweep of the Church's communion with Christ its head. These verbs delineate the content and the stages of the sharing of Christ's Church

Body and of His members in His passage from history to its term, from death to total glorious life in the Father. The σύν verbs mark the simultaneous multiple levels of the new life shared in Christ, its dynamism, and its movement and growth toward its final achievement when Christ will come to judge the living and the dead and to hand over the kingdom to His Father (Col 3.4; 1 Cor 15.24–28).

There is a dying and a living with Christ (Rom 6.8), a suffering with Christ (Rom 8.17), a crucifixion with Christ (Rom 6.6), a *burial with Christ (Rom 6.4; Col 2.12), a glorification with Christ (Rom 8.17), an inheritance with Christ (Rom 8.17), a reigning with Christ (2 Tm 2.12). Suffering with Christ is the necessary prelude and the sure pledge of the coming glory in Him (Phil 3.10–11; Rom 8.17; 1 Pt 4.13); in the communion of Christ's Body suffering is a fundamental law serving the upbuilding of the whole Body. "The 'We-for-Christ' (2 Cor 12.10; Phil 1.29; see Col 1.24) must match the 'Christ-for-us.' We must hold firmly that the saving function of the Church consists chiefly in representing and realizing a communion with the dying and rising Redeemer" (V. Warnach, "Liebe," *op. cit.* 2:810).

Role of the Spirit. Just as the Father's love has given His Son to the world of men, so too He "lavishes the Spirit" (Gal 3.5) on the Church in order that the Paraclete may bring to achievement the work of Christ in the Church Body of the Redeemer and in the world of men. "Who would deny," says St. Basil, "that the saving designs with respect to mankind which have been realized by our great God and Savior Jesus Christ in accord with the goodness of God are fulfilled by the grace of the Spirit?" (*De Spiritu Sancto* 16.39; PG 32:140) The Spirit is "the gift of God" (Acts 8.20; see Acts 2.38; Rom 5.5; Jn 14.16) of which men are made "partakers" (Heb 6.4) in order to become sharers in the sonship of Christ (Rom 8.14–17; Gal 4.6). It is the role of the Spirit to Christianize the Church and all its members, to make them fellows of Christ in His life and truth (1 Cor 12.13; Eph 2.22; Jn 15.26; 16.14–15; Phil 3.3), to keep the whole Church faithful to its origins in the historical Christ and to its destiny in the Christ to come, to hold the members of each and every age in a concert of loving service of the whole Body, to keep the Body one in Christ by communicating its varied graces and gifts to the good estate of the whole (1 Cor 12.7).

"Communion with Christ leads necessarily to communion with Christians, to communion of the members, one with another" (F. Hauck, KittelThW 3:807). See Phlm 17; 2 Cor 8.4; Rom 12.13; 15.26–27; Gal 6.6; Phil 1.7; 4.14–15; Heb 10.33; 13.16. Dependence on the love and life of Christ means interdependence in love on one another in Christ. The new life in Christ is not an isolated gift enclosed within a multitude of discrete selves; it lives only insofar as it is lived together in the one Spirit of love by all those who are partakers of the salvation of the new alliance (1 Cor 12.25; Rom 12.5; Eph 3.6; 4.25). The joint holding and sharing of the new life in Christ shows itself as a Christian grace, i.e., as an inward-outward grace. It is embodied in prayer and almsgiving, in compassion, sympathy, and heartfelt mutual assistance, in an interchange of the spiritual and temporal works of mercy, between Christian and Christian, between local Church and local Church, between the Jewish and gentile world in Christ. Fraternal love, the great gift of the Spirit (1 Cor 12.31–13.3), is, with its expansive and assimilative rhythm, the mark of communion in the Church (Jn 15.1–17; 1 Jn 3.14–18; 4.11–12; 4.19–21). C. H. Dodd writes of the NT *koinonia:* ". . . All the experiences and activities of the whole Church are in some sort communicated to the individual believer; and in turn the due activity of each part enables the Body to grow and build itself up (Eph 4.16)" [*The Johannine Epistles* (New York 1946) 7]. This lateral communion in its various forms is one that the Fathers and the scholastic theologians especially stressed.

Patristic Period. The Biblical theme of communion as applied to the Church in all the varied manifestations, sacramental and social, of its total moving life is a central theme of patristic thought, if not always verbally, at least in reality. See, e.g., L. Hertling, *Communio: Chiesa e papato nell'antichità cristiana* (Rome 1961); W. Elert, *Abendmahl und Kirchengemeinschaft in der alten Kirche hauptsächlich des Ostens* (Berlin 1954); J. Korbacher, "Die Kirche als Gemeinschaft," *Ausserhalb der Kirche kein Heil* (Munich 1963) 52–79; A. Demoustier, "L'Ontologie de l'église selon saint Cyprien," RechScRel 52 (1964) 554–588; M. Pellegrino, "Le Sens ecclésial du martyre," RevScRel 35 (1961) 151–175.

This article presents, without pressing too much considerations of chronology, certain selected aspects of patristic thought on the Church as communion.

Ecclesia Mater. Karl Delahaye has studied the use that the Fathers of the first 3 centuries made of the theme of the Church's motherhood to symbolize the role of the whole Church as the bearer of Christ's salvation to mankind [*Erneuerung der Seelsorgsformen aus der Sicht der frühen Patristik* (Freiburg 1958)], and in this careful investigation he has made clear the strong sense that the Fathers had of the entire Church Body as one communion of all the faithful in Christ, jointly sharing in Christ's light and life and jointly communicating Christ's truth and grace to men. Because "the Church is the great We of the faithful" (Delahaye, 135) in Christ and in His Spirit, then all the faithful together are enabled and required to serve in unison the handing on of the "common salvation" (Jude 3) to all.

The patristic imagery of the Church as mother strongly emphasizes "the responsibility of all the faithful for all others in the life of the community, their effective and genuine participation, their authentic and living collaboration in the duties of the community in the midst of this world" (Delahaye, 190). Every division of labor within the Church's total mediatorial activity has its meaning and justification only from within the total Church as the one communion of sanctification and sanctity. "Hierarchy and community, each in its own proper way, are the authorized and mandated bearers of the Church's pastoral activity; hence they are the subjects of that activity" (*ibid.* 191).

> . . . The early Church considers all the saints without exception as both subject and object of the Church's saving work. . . . The Church as mother is the communion of the saints, comprising all those who are joined to Christ in faith and Baptism. Since her motherhood is grounded on her inward mysterious union with Christ, then all who have entered into this communion with Christ share in the Church's motherhood. Under the aspect of her pastoral activity the Church as the communion of the saints is always at the same time a saving community. [*Ibid.* 142–143.]

God realizes His saving designs "toward all and with all. Hence all must take part in it and work together in communicating it" (*ibid.* 179).

In the imagery of the Church's maternity there is expressed the belief that God charges the whole Church, the structured communion of the saints and each member according to his role and gift, to work together in preserving and in communicating the treasures of life that they share in the one Spirit and that the one Spirit moves them to share with others. The whole Body of the Church is in its common life, to borrow a word that St. Ignatius of Antioch applied to the Church of Smyrna, ἁγιοφόρα, a fruitful "bearer of holy things" (*Smyrn.* introd.). For the Fathers the basic reason why the whole Church must act in concert in communicating the good news of Christ and the new life in Christ is the whole Church's ontological unity of life in Christ through communion in His one Spirit (see Delahaye, 149–150) and through communion in His Eucharistic body and blood. As Ignatius of Antioch wrote, "the union is both according to the Spirit and according to the flesh" (*Magn.* 13.2). Much later Pope Martin I (d. 655) expressed the thought in a letter to the Church of Carthage: "Whatever is ours is yours in accordance with our undivided sharing in the one Spirit" (*Epist.* 4; PL 87:147).

St. Augustine. It is appropriate to set forth in some detail certain reflections of St. Augustine on the mystery of the Church as a community of life with the Triune God and with the whole company of Christian believers in the same Trinity. Although not all of St. Augustine's speculations may be finally acceptable, still his vast achievement and perduring influence in the history of ecclesiology, particularly of the Western Church, warrant special consideration.

Discoursing on blasphemy against the Holy Spirit (see Mt 12.31), Augustine describes the Holy Spirit in the intra-Trinitarian life of God as "the community of the Father and of the Son" (*Serm.* 71.12.18; PL 38:454) and then continues:

> It is through that which is common to the Father and to the Son that they have wished us to have communion both with one another and with themselves; it is through that Gift which both have in common, i.e., through the Holy Spirit, God and the Gift of God, that they have wished to gather us together into one. [*Ibid.*]

The unity of communion within the Church is then the reflection of the communion of life within the Triune God, and in each case, although in vastly different ways, the communion is ascribed to the Holy Spirit, who is "the community of the Father and of the Son" and who "in His various workings [in the Church] is not another Spirit, different from Himself, but one and the same" (*Serm.* 71.16.26; PL 38:459–460). Referring to 1 Cor 12.11, St. Augustine writes that the Spirit is "the one who divides and apportions, but who is Himself undivided, because He is one and the same" (*Epist.* 187.6.20; PL 33:839). "To whom in the Trinity does communion in this society [the Church] pertain, if it is not to the Spirit who is common to the Father and to the Son?" (*Serm.* 71.18.29; PL 38:461). "He is the Spirit of the adoption of sons, in whom we cry 'Abba Father' " (*Serm.* 71.17.28; PL 38:460–461); "the society by which we are made the only Body of God's only Son is the Spirit's role" (*ibid.*)— "that society of the sons of God and of the members of Christ that is to exist in all nations" (*ibid.*).

> . . . The society of the unity of the Church of God, outside of which there is no forgiveness of sins, is, so to speak, the proper work of the Holy Spirit—the Father and the Son, to be sure, working together with Him—because the Holy Spirit Himself is in a certain sense the society of the Father and of the Son. [*Serm.* 71.20.33; PL 38:463.]

Fritz Hofmann says of the role of the Holy Spirit in the ecclesiology of St. Augustine: "*Donum, caritas,* and *communio* stand in the center of the *ecclesia Spiritus,* precisely because the Holy Spirit Himself is essentially *donum, caritas,* and *communio*" [*Der Kirchenbegriff des hl. Augustinus . . .* (Munich 1933) 136].

The Church as a mystery of communion in the Trinity comprises in the outreach of its love all those who are sharers in the same divine life. The vertical (descending-ascending) communion becomes indissolubly a comprehensive lateral communion of all the members of the Body of Christ in the one Spirit. St. Augustine expresses the indivisibility of the total communion in love in the following way:

> The sons of God are the Body of the one and only Son of God . . . . Therefore whoever loves the sons of God loves the Son of God, and whoever loves the Son of God loves the Father; nor can anyone love the Father unless he loves the Son; and whoever loves the Son also loves the sons of God.
>
> What sons of God? The members of the Son of God. It is through love that He becomes one of His own members, it is through love that He enters into the unity of the Body of Christ; and there will be only one Christ loving Himself. When the members love one another, the Body loves itself. . . . When you love the members of Christ, you love Christ; when you love Christ, you love the Son of God; when you love the Son of God, you love the Father too. Love then is indivisible. Choose to love one, and all the others follow your choice. [*In epist. Ioh.* 10.3; PL 35: 2055–56.]

Just as God Himself says to His sons, "Love itself makes me present to you" (*ibid.* 10.4; PL 35:2057), so too, although in an infinitely lesser way, each member of the Body in the communion of love that is the Church is present to all the others in the one Spirit of Christ, who gives to that communion in Himself as Gift the reality of its undivided love. In the Spirit of Christ each Christian is present to the whole Church, and the Church is present to each Christian.

Just as in the human body there are "different functions, but a common life" (*Serm.* 267.4.4; PL 38:1231), so too in the Church Body of Christ, by virtue of the one Spirit, "each one has his own role to enact, but all alike live together" (*ibid.*). "The services of the members are variously apportioned, but the one Spirit holds them all together" (*Serm.* 268.2; PL 38:1232). The Spirit, therefore, with "the holy and indivisible charity" (*Epist.* 98.5; CSEL 34.2:526) that He pours into the hearts of the saints, gives to the varied graces and gifts of the Body's many members a saving and serving presence to the whole Body.

> . . . The many gifts that are proper to each one are divided for the common good among all the members of Christ by the Gift that is the Holy Spirit. For not every one has all of them, but some have these and others those, although all have the Gift Himself by whom the gifts proper to each one are apportioned, i.e., the Holy Spirit. [*Trin.* 15.19.34; PL 42:1084.]

St. Augustine writes of "the showing forth of the Spirit in view of the common good" (1 Cor 12.7): "If you love unity, then whoever has anything in the unity of

Birth of the Church from the side of Christ, detail of a full-page miniature for the Book of Genesis is in a "Bible moralisée" composed at Paris, c. 1250, and now in the Austrian National Library at Vienna (Codex 1179). The participation of the Father (standing) and the Holy Ghost (dove-shaped flames) is also represented.

the Church, has it for you" (*In evang. Ioh.* 32.8; Corp Christ 36:304).

For St. Augustine, as for the Fathers in general, communion with Christ meant indissolubly communion with His Eucharistic body in His Church Body. "For St. Augustine the sacred mystery of the Eucharist stands sovereignly in the midpoint of the inner and outer life of the Church" (Hofmann, 390). "The Eucharist is the Sacrament of the Mystical Body itself joined with its head; the whole essence of the Church, which consists in the unity of the members one with another, in the unity of the Body with the head, and in the unity of the *totus Christus,* realized through the mediation of the God-Man, with God, is set forth in the Eucharist in a sacramental but real way" (Hofmann, 412). Alluding to 1 Cor 10.17, Augustine writes: "O Sacrament of mercy! O sign of unity! O bond of charity! Whoever wishes to live has both where he may live and the wherewithal he may live. Let him draw near and believe; let him be made one Body in order to be given life" (*In evang. Ioh.* 26.13; CorpChrist 36:266); "let them become the Body of Christ if they wish to live from the Spirit of Christ" (*ibid.*). Christ "wishes this food and drink to be understood as the common life of that Body and its members which is holy Church . . ." (*In evang. Ioh.* 26.15; CorpChrist 36:267). Not only is the Eucharist the supreme sacramental realization of the common life of the entire Church Body in its total unity; it is also the sacrifice of the entire Church Body in the sacrament of the Lord's saving Passion. In the Eucharist the Church Body of the Lord is made one sacrifice in and with the sacrificial death of the unique priest Jesus Christ.

> . . . The whole redeemed city, i.e., the congregation and society of the saints, is offered as a universal sacrifice to God through the great priest who offered Himself in the Passion for us that we might be the Body of so great a head . . . . This is the sacrifice of Christians: "the many, one Body in Christ." In the mystery of the altar so familiar to the faithful the Church celebrates that sacrifice wherein is made clear to the Church that it itself is offered in the very reality that it offers. [*Civ.* 10.6; CorpChrist 47:279.]

Christ "wished the sacrifice of the Church to be the daily sacrament [of His own sacrifice on the cross], and the Church, since it is the Body of the head, learns how to offer itself through Him" (*Civ.* 10.20; Corp Christ 47:294). The whole Church, one in a communion of sacrificial love that the Spirit keeps alive in its heart, offers itself and its works of charity and mercy in the sacrament of the Lord's Passion.

For St. Augustine's speculations on the theme of *ecclesia mater* or the communion of the saints as the strictly active factor in the saving and sanctifying activity of the Church, see Hofmann, 263–275; K. Adam, *Die kirchliche Sündenvergebung nach dem hl. Augustin* (Paderborn 1917) 99–113.

Patristic Orientations. Not only St. Augustine but the Fathers in general looked on the Church in its entirety and in all its local realizations as a common life centered in Christ and in His salvation. It is a communion of life that is the work of the numerically one and same Spirit of Christ, dwelling in Christ plenarily and in His Body derivatively; a fraternal communion of those who in the one Spirit live together a life of one faith, one hope, and one love; a sacramental communion that finds its supreme sign and realization in the center of the sacramental cult of the Church, i.e., the Eucharist, containing the one sacrifice of the new alliance and the one food of the new people on its pilgrimage; an active expansive communion communicating its new life to all those who are called to share in it; a moving dynamic communion that looks to the next world and to the "peace of the heavenly city," i.e., "the perfectly ordered and harmonious society of those who find their joy in God and in one another in God" (St. Augustine, *Civ.* 19.13; CorpChrist 48:679). In the early Church the We of Church communion had its first ground in the one faith, authoritatively professed in the "We believe" and "We confess" with which the doctrinal decrees of the synods so often began. Orthodoxy is "homodoxy," as St. Basil the Great says, speaking of "the communion of those who hold one and the same faith" (*Epist.* 28.3; PG 32:309). W. Elert writes of the Church as a communion in faith:

> The subject of the "We believe" is the Church . . . . The We begins with the Apostles and reaches without any break up to the present. The baptismal creed, the *regula fidei,* and dogma are professions of faith, and in their harmony there is expressed the unity of the Church as unanimity. [*Op. cit.* 53–54; see 62–63.]

Preaching on the anniversary of his elevation to the pontificate, St. Leo the Great said: "Beloved, in the unity of faith and Baptism we share an undivided common life . . .." (*Serm.* 4.1; PL 54:148). To give one or two further examples of the centrality of the Sacrament of the Eucharist in the patristic understanding of the Church as communion, St. Cyril of Alexandria writes:

> . . . we have been made one Body together [*σύσσωμοι*] in Christ, fed with the one flesh, and sealed unto unity with the one Holy Spirit, and since Christ is indivisible (for He has never been divided), we are all one in Him. . . . See how we all are one in Christ and in the Holy Spirit, both according to the Body and according to the Spirit. [*Dial. Trin.* 1; PG 75:697.]

And in an old Gallican commentary on the Creed, dating from the 6th or 7th century but reflecting much earlier convictions, one reads: "There is found holy communion with the Father and the Son and the Holy Spirit, where each Sunday all the faithful ought to communicate [see text in JThSt 21 (1920) 109].

In the mind of the Fathers the episcopal order with its authoritative mission and its special sacramental powers and graces exists to beget, sustain, and foster the Christian communion of the Church, in its totality and in its parts, with a fidelity to its Christian origins and to its final destiny of Christian plenitude (see Delahaye, 190–191; Hertling, 16–45). The hierarchical order is a ministry commissioned by Christ to serve the communion of Christian faith, and to ward off the disunion of heresy, by authoritatively handing on the message of faith; to serve the community of Christian charity, and to ward off the disunion of *schism, by guiding and orientating the varied expression of its common life of mutual dedication and service in the Lord; and above all to serve the community of sacramental life, wherein faith and love find their prime stay and embodiment, by administering the Eucharistic cult, by admitting to or denying Eucharistic communion (*see* EXCOMMUNICATION), and by administering the penitential procedures which issued in full Eucharistic communion (*see* PENANCE, SACRAMENT OF, 1). Hence the Church is a juridically ordered communion. St.

Cyprian speaks of those who "receive the Eucharist by right of communion" (*De dom. orat.* 18, CSEL 3.1:280; see *Epist.* 57.2, CSEL 3.2:652), a right of which the bishop was the judge. The local Church finds in its bishop, as the representative of Christ, the qualified center and criterion of its communion, competent to teach, to rule, and to sanctify (see St. Ignatius of Antioch, *Smyrn.* 8; *Eph.* 4). The whole Church has in the episcopal order with its Roman center the criterion of its total communion [*see* COUNCILS, GENERAL (ECUMENICAL), THEOLOGY OF]. Finally the prime bishop of Rome is the center of communion for the whole Church: St. Ambrose, writing to the Emperors Gratian, and Theodosius Valentinian, (381), affirms that from Rome "are spread abroad to all the Churches the rights of the communion that must be revered" (*Epist.* 11.4; PL 16:946). *See* HIERARCHY.

The ancient Church had no elaborate theory of communion; rather it was a sacramental reality lived from day to day in the ordered brotherhood of the whole believing Church and of its local realizations.

St. Thomas. "St. Thomas's whole teaching on the Church is to be divided into his teaching on the principles of the Church's being and life, on the organs of the Church's life, and on the realization of the Church's life" [M. Grabmann, *Die Lehre des heiligen Thomas von Aquin von der Kirche als Gotteswerk* (Regensburg 1903) 68]. In St. Thomas's ecclesiology the Church's life of grace, which is a sharing in the Trinitarian life, is necessarily a social life: "the principle of supernatural life, divine grace, is intrinsically characterized by a social tendency, a certain inclination toward communication" (*ibid.* 78). Hence St. Thomas writes: "In the spiritual life . . . we enjoy society not only with men but also with God" (*In 3 sent.* 37.2 sol. 2). At times St. Thomas describes the life of grace in a way that clearly signifies its social aspect, and, it is to be noted, in a context indicating that the Holy Spirit is the ultimate ground of the social orientation of the life of grace. For example, in a discussion of schism, which is a sin directly opposed to the unity of the Church as a communion in love, St. Thomas argues that schism offends against the Holy Spirit in the sense that it is "a spiteful hatred of fraternal grace . . . of the grace of God growing in the world" (ST 2a2ae, 14.2); schism means "hatred of the fraternal grace by which the members of the Church are joined together" (*ibid.* ad 4). The Christian brotherhood of grace that is the Church is directly attacked when the charity of the Spirit that moves men to live together as brothers in Christ, one of another, in the family of God the Father, is contemned and rejected.

Grabmann further notes that "just as the grace of Christ has within it a certain social tendency, a power of expansion, so too is it a characteristic of this grace to manifest itself, to incorporate itself, so to speak . . ." (*op. cit.* 91). In his treatise on the evangelical law (ST 1a2ae, 106–109), St. Thomas delineates the movement of the grace of the new testament as it embodies itself, socially and sacramentally, in the Church of the new testament. Everything in the Church, whose prime center of force and of life is the grace of the Spirit of Christ, is either an embodiment of the grace of the Spirit, or a disposition and a way toward this grace (see ST 1a2ae, 106.1; 108.1). Because "the grace of the Holy Spirit . . . is manifested in faith working through love" (ST 1a2ae, 108.1), and because "the new law, which is the law of liberty. . . comprises the moral precepts of the natural law, and the articles of faith and the Sacraments of grace" (*Quodl.* 4.8.2), the Church is an inward-outward communion of life in the grace of the Spirit, a communion realized through a living faith and through the Sacraments of faith (see ST 3a, 64.2 ad 3).

Power of the Spirit. St. Thomas assigns to the activity of the Holy Spirit a primordial role in the Church as one body of believers and worshipers who live together a common life, sociosacramental, in Christ with the Father. The Holy Spirit, who is immanently present in all the members, is "the ultimate and principal perfection of the whole Mystical Body" (*In 3 sent.* 13.2.2 sol. 2); "all the members of the Mystical Body have as their final ground of perfection the Holy Spirit, who is numerically one in all of them" (*ibid.* ad 1); ". . . in the spiritual life our every movement must come from the Spirit" (*In epist. ad Gal.* 5 lect. 7). "Just as the result of the mission of the Son was to lead to the Father, so the effect of the mission of the Holy Spirit is to lead the faithful to the Son" (*In Joann.* 14 lect. 6). "Through the Spirit we are united to Christ in a union of faith and of love and are made members of the Church" (*ibid.* 6 lect. 7); "there is in the Church an unbroken union [between Christ and His members] by reason of the Holy Spirit, who, numerically one and the same, fills and unites the whole Church" (*De ver.* 29.4). Christ "unites us one to another and to God through His Spirit, whom He gives to us" (*In epist. ad Rom.* 12 lect. 2).

Furthermore St. Thomas stresses the Spirit's primary role in the Church insofar as it is a lateral communion of member with member and with the whole Body, a presence in charity of one to another and to the whole, a reciprocal communication of life and service. Thus he speaks of "the power of the Holy Spirit who through the unity of love communicates the blessings of Christ's members with one another" (ST 3a, 82.6 ad 3; see 3a, 68.9 ad 2; *In 3 sent.* 25.1.2). "The diversity of roles and functions in the Church" (ST 2a2ae, 183.2), which is essential to the reality of the Church as a horizontal communion, does not "hamper the unity of the Church, which is achieved through unity of faith and love and mutual service" (*ibid.* ad 1), precisely because "the harmonious interplay of the various members in the Body of Christ is assured by the power of the Holy Spirit, who vivifies the Body of the Church" (*ibid.* ad 3). "A man falls away from this unity of the Spirit when he seeks what is exclusively his own" (*ibid.*). Hence it is the role of the indwelling Spirit in the power of His goodness (1) to dissipate the exclusiveness and partiality that disserves the good of the other and of the whole Body and (2) to move the member parts to seek their own good only in the whole and in the movement of the whole Body toward its final perfection.

Schism. In his treatment of the sin of schism, St. Thomas says that "schism is per se opposed to the unity of ecclesiastical love" (ST 2a2ae, 39.1 ad 3), a love "which does not simply unite one person with another in the spiritual bond of love, but also joins the whole Church in the unity of the Spirit" (ST 2a2ae, 39.1). One must consider two aspects of this unity of the whole Church in the Spirit of love, i.e., "the connection or communion of the members of the Church with one another; and . . . the relation of all the members of the Church to one head," the one head being "Christ, whose vicar in the Church is the supreme pontiff" (*ibid.*). "And hence they are called schismatics who refuse to obey the supreme pontiff, and who refuse to live a common life with the members of the Church subject to the pontiff" (*ibid.*). Here one sees how St. Thomas conceives the role of the hierarchy in the life of the Church as a communion with Christ and with one another in love in the Body of Christ. The hierarchical order is a ministerial, vicarious service of the sociosacramental common life in faith and love, under the headship of Christ and the quickening of the Spirit. "The ministers of the Church . . . [are] in a certain sense the instruments of that life-giving influence which the head exercises on His members" (ST 3a, suppl., 36.3 ad 2). One may cite here the passage in *C. graec.* (2.32) in which St. Thomas associates the roles of the Spirit and of the supreme pontiff in assimilating the Church to Christ its head.

> Christ Himself, the Son of God, dedicates His Church to His service and authentically seals it with the Holy Spirit as with His own mark and stamp . . .. And in like fashion the vicar of Christ, as a faithful servant, by his primacy and foresight keeps the whole Church subject to Christ.

Dependence on the Whole. It has often been noted (see Grabmann, 181) that Cajetan, commenting on St. Thomas's teaching on schism, has excellently elaborated on St. Thomas's doctrine on the Church's unity of communion, particularly as it is understood in the lateral or horizontal sense. Cajetan writes:

> . . . The faithful are moved by the Holy Spirit to the works of the spiritual life, i.e., to believe, to hope, and to love, to sanctify and to be sanctified, to obey and to command, to enlighten, etc. . . . in such a way that they do all these things as parts of one whole. . . . And therefore [the Spirit] moves each faithful to act inwardly and outwardly as part of the one whole and for the sake of the one whole and in accordance with that one whole. . . . And hence it is that . . . there is a connection of part to part in a congregation numerically one that is ruled first and chiefly by the Holy Spirit. [*In ST* 2a2ae, 39.1.]

This spiritual unity of the numerically one Church is an effect of charity because "it is through charity that the Holy Spirit moves each single faithful to wish to be part of the one catholic communion that He vivifies . . ." (*ibid.*). All the faithful according to Cajetan, whatever be their office or act, hierarchical or not, extraordinary or simple, act as parts in and of a totality, of a united whole numerically one; all, therefore, act in dependence on the whole, and all act in charity for the good estate of the whole. It must be noted that the dependence of the part on the whole is here one of communion, i.e., the part finds a measure, a perspective, an aid, and a finality in the existence and functioning of the whole.

Eucharist. Faithful to the patristic tradition, St. Thomas held in closest association, in the ontology of the Church, Eucharistic communion and ecclesiastical communion, with the sacramental body of Christ being the supreme sign and ground of the communion of the Mystical Body. "The universal spiritual good of the whole Church is contained substantially in the Sacrament of the Eucharist" (ST 3a, 65.3 ad 1; see 3a, 73.1 ad 3; 3a, 83.4). In ST 3a, 73.4 St. Thomas quotes the saying of St. John Damascene that the Eucharist "is called Communion, and truly is, because through it we communicate with Christ . . . and because through it we communicate with and are joined to one another" (*De fide orth.* 4.13; PG 94:1153). "The Eucharist is called the Sacrament of charity" (ST 3a, 73.3 ad 3; see 3a, 78.3 ad 6), an ecclesial charity that leads to a communion of life with the Father and with the brethren in Christ and head of the Body. "The Eucharist is the Sacrament of the Church's entire unity" (ST 3a, 83.4 ad 3); "the unity of the Mystical Body is the fruit of the true body received sacramentally" (ST 3a, 82.9 ad 2); "the effect of this Sacrament . . . is the union of the Christian people with Christ" (ST 3a, 74.6; see the Council of Florence, Denz 1320). What the scholastic theologians called the *res,* or reality, of this Sacrament, i.e., the ultimate grace effected, is "the Mystical Body of Christ, which is the society of the saints" (ST 3a, 80.4). The Eucharist is the Sacrament of the wayfaring Church on earth in its itinerary toward the heavenly Jerusalem, "the true Church, our mother toward which we are tending, the exemplar of the militant Church" (*In epist. ad Eph.* 3 lect. 3). "The Sacrament does not immediately lead us into glory, but it gives us the power to reach glory" (ST 3a, 79.2 ad 1); the tendency of the Eucharist is toward heaven and "the society of the saints where there will be peace and full and perfect unity" (*ibid. corp.*). The Eucharist is *the* Sacrament that forms and realizes the wayfaring Church as a communion of life in the Son with His Father and with His brethren, in the sense that it purifies the Church from sin, which is the root of separation from God and of segregation from the brethren, and that it conveys the fullest beginnings of the Christian life, both in soul and in body, which is communion. "In strict theology, the principal effect of the Eucharist is the upbuilding of the Church as *a communion of life*" [J. M. R. Tillard, *L'Eucharistie, Pâque de l'église* (Paris 1964) 231]—of the Church as a communion of Christian life in the conditions of this world and turned toward its full consummation as communion in the heavenly Church.

Modern Era. From the later Middle Ages until relatively modern times there is discernible in much theological writing a tendency to focus on the Church as the divinely authorized sociojuridic means of communicating Christ's salvation to men, without at the same time considering the Church so conceived in an intimate association with the reality of the Church as the whole company of the faithful and the communion of the saints. The symbiosis of the Church as means and the Church as finis, and the interplay of life and energies between the two in a total common life, did not often find a full and harmonious exposition. The defensive reaction to movements such as conciliarism, Protestantism, Gallicanism, Jansenism, and Febronianism conspired to put theological stress on the Church as the institutional means of salvation with its unique mission and powers and with its social stance of plenary independence over against the encroachment of the secular state.

Furthermore, during this period, the general absence of a separate treatise of dogmatic ecclesiology, as distinct from a canonicoapologetical treatment, did not favor the development of a rounded ecclesiology of communion. The doctrinal elements that were needed to come together to form a balanced dogmatic ecclesiology were studied in relative isolation from one another; hence, what was often lacking was "the connection of the mysteries one with another and with man's last end" (Denz 3016). For example, the mission of the Holy Spirit was not sharply related to the total Church, and in general pneumatology, apart from the inhabitation

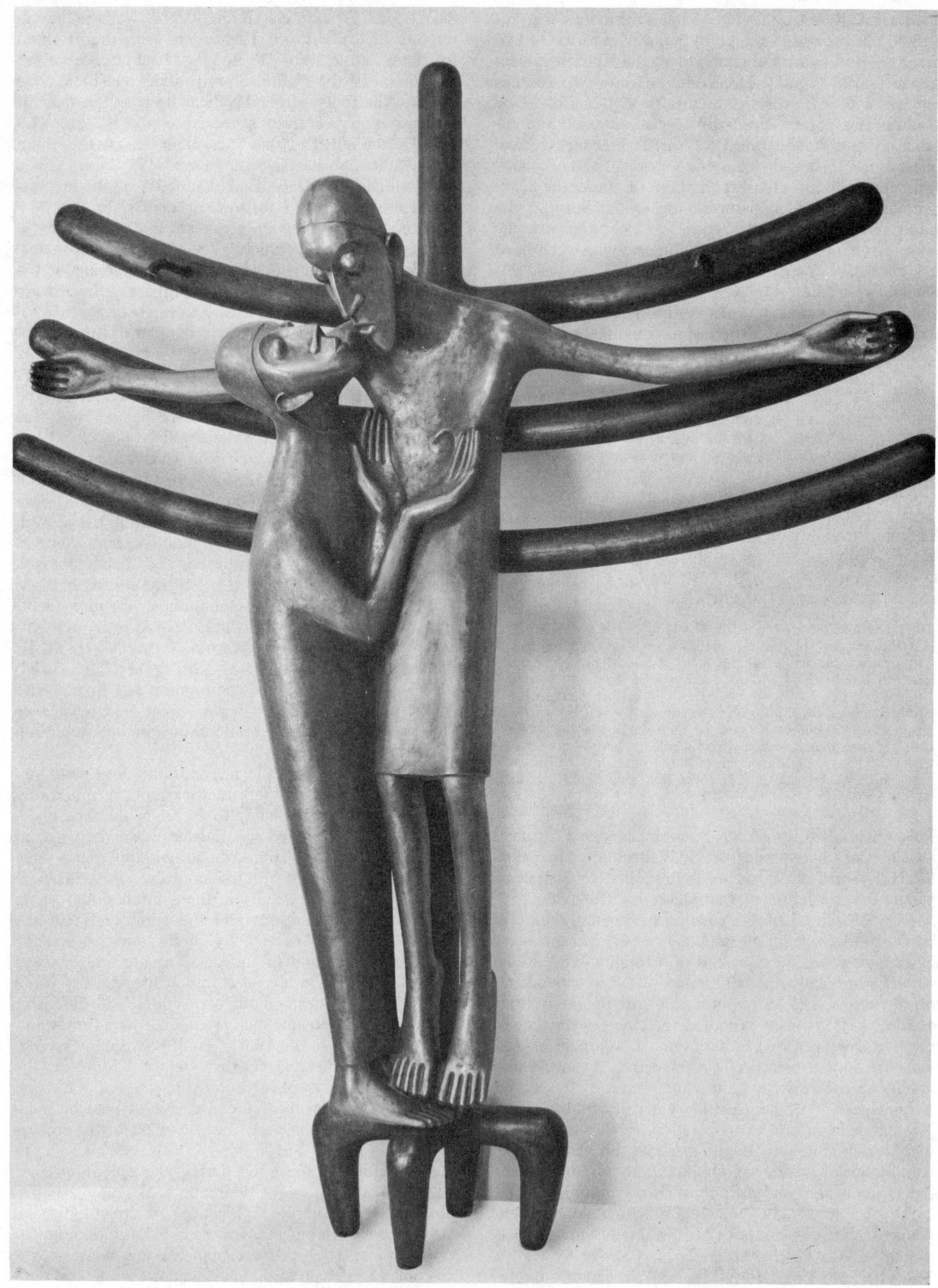

"Christ and the Church," bronze, by the German sculptor Toni Zenz, 1961, church of St. Marien, Oberhausen.

of the Spirit in the individual soul, was not much developed. The single Sacraments were not usually seen within the perspective of the total prime sacrament of the Church; and the Eucharist in particular was less attended to in its intimate relationship with the whole Church Body of Christ, as the sacramental sacrifice and the sacramental food of the whole Body on its pilgrimage to the heavenly Jerusalem. Hence a more clericalized and less genuinely popular liturgy was the result.

The ecclesial dimension of Christian anthropology was less emphasized than was desirable; as a result the individual Christian was less seen as one who believes, hopes, and loves in the one faith, hope, and love of the whole Church; and the call of all to sanctity in the one holy Church was less emphasized in favor of specialization in this field. Theological writing on the tradition, the apostolate, and the liturgical life of the Church did not sufficiently stress the responsibility and the participation of all the faithful, baptized and confirmed in Christ, in these aspects of the Church's total life. Moreover eschatology tended to be more individual than collective in its theological presentation.

The 19th Century. The beginnings in theology of a renewed consideration of the Church as a communion of supernatural life in Christ wherein all share and all should contribute their share were seen in the 19th century. Among the representatives of this newer direction must be mentioned J. A. *Möhler (1796–1838), whose brilliant work, at times unduly infected by the philosophical categories of a romantic vitalism, always tended to conceive the Church as a total living communion, "a communion in the Holy and of the saints" [*Die Einheit in der Kirche,* ed. J. R. Geiselmann (Cologne 1957) 315]. For an assessment of Möhler's development and achievement in this respect, see Geiselmann's commentaries in his edition of Möhler's works: *Die Einheit* 613–619 and *Symbolik* (Cologne 1961) 2:609–686. It is appropriate also to recall here the *De ecclesia Christi* (2 v. Regensburg 1853, 1856), which was the joint work of Carlo *Passaglia (1812–87) and Klemens *Schrader (1820–75); from this work, left unfinished, one may instance the authors' reflections on "the social charity" of the Church, i.e., on "the charity of communion, the charity of the Body, and the Christian communion of the Church" (lib. 3:412; see 411–418, 461, 574–575, 581–586), on the Trinitarian origin and destiny of this communion in love (lib. 3:418), and on the Sacraments as expression of this charity of communion (lib. 3:419). M. J. *Scheeben (1835–88) has much of lasting value on "the organic unity of the teaching body with the body of the faithful in the Catholic Church" (*Theologische Erkenntnislehre; Dogmatik* 1, §13, No. 168, see Nos. 168–186); Scheeben speaks in a way reminiscent of the early Fathers of "the whole Church . . . in the communion of the simple faithful as *mater fidei*" (*ibid.* No. 184). The lay theologian Friedrich Pilgram (1819–90) made the theme of communion the very center of his valuable, if complicated, study on the Church [*Physiologie der Kirche* (Mainz 1860)]. Finally there are the observations of Hermann *Schell (1850–1906) in his *Dogmatik* 3.1 (Paderborn 1892) 382–386, where the concept of the Church as a community of life with the Triune God and with one another in Christ is elaborated; as Schell says, "God does not separate and isolate, but associates and joins together in a living union, because He is triune" (386).

20th Century. The teaching of the modern popes on the sharing of the whole Church in the apostolate and in particular on the missionary role and spirit of the Church as compassing all the faithful without exception [see, e.g., Pius XII, *Fidei donum,* ActApS 49 (1957) 237–238] indicates clearly the participation of all the faithful in the total common life of the Church and in its major activities. Pius XII's encyclicals **Mystici corporis* (June 29, 1943) and *Mediator Dei* (Nov. 20, 1947) manifest an intensified sense of the whole Church as one worshiping and saving community in Christ through the Spirit. See, for instance, the definition of the liturgy in *Mediator Dei* (Denz 3841); and in *Mystici corporis* one reads: "We must all cooperate with Christ in this work of salvation—'all of us who from One and through One are saved and save' " [ActApS 35 (1943) 221].

Vatican II in its constitutions on the Church and on the sacred liturgy and in its decrees on the Eastern Catholic Churches and on ecumenism has given a notable impetus toward an ecclesiology of communion. For example, in the *Dogmatic Constitution on the Church* the mystery of the Church is presented as rooted in the Trinity [*Lumen gentium* 1–4; ActApS 57 (1965) 5–7]. The universal Church is "a people made one from the unity of the Father and of the Son and of the Holy Spirit"; a people "established by Christ as a communion of life, love, and truth"; one holy community, sacerdotal and prophetic, in which "all the faithful scattered throughout the world lead a common life with the rest in the Holy Spirit" and in which all "both labor and pray that the fullness of the world be transformed into the people of God, the Body of the Lord, and the temple of the Holy Spirit" [*ibid.* 4, 9, 13, 17; ActApS 57 (1965) 7, 13, 17, 21].

See also COMMUNION OF SAINTS; ECCLESIOLOGY; KINGDOM OF CHRIST; KINGDOM OF GOD; MISSIONS, DIVINE; MYSTICAL BODY OF CHRIST; SACRAMENT OF THE CHURCH; SACRAMENTS, ARTICLES ON; SOCIETY (IN THEOLOGY); TRINITY, HOLY; UNITY OF FAITH; UNITY OF THE CHURCH; CHURCH, ARTICLES ON.

Bibliography: DTC, Tables générales 1:1110–30. R. SCHNACKENBURG et al., LexThK[2] 6:167–186. J. SCHMID et al., Fries HbTh Grdbgr 1:790–822. G. W. H. LAMPE, ed., *A Patristic Greek Lexicon* (Oxford 1961–) fasc. 3, 762–764. M. J. LE GUILLOU, *Le Christ et l'église* (Paris 1963); *Mission et unité,* 2 v. (Paris 1960). J. HAMER, *L'Église est une communion* (Paris 1962). F. MALMBERG, *Ein Leib-Ein Geist,* tr. R. E. TORFS (Freiburg 1960). H. MÜHLEN, *Una mystica persona* (Munich 1964). H. SEESEMANN, *Der Begriff κοινωνία im Neuen Testament* (Giessen 1933). J. M. TILLARD, *L'Eucharistie, Pâque de l'église* (Paris 1963). **Illustration credits:** Fig. 1, Photo Archives, Maria-Laach. Fig. 2, Photo Archives–Das Münster.

[F. X. LAWLOR]

CHURCH, HISTORY OF, I (EARLY)

The Christian Church took its rise with Christ's commission to the Apostles: "Go out into the whole world and preach my gospel to every creature." The historical fulfillment of that command began on the first Pentecost when, as Christ had promised (Acts 1. 5), the Holy Spirit descended on the Apostles and disciples, and Peter preached to the "devout Jews from every nation . . . Parthians, Medes, Elamites, inhabitants of Mesopotamia, Judea, Cappadocia, Pontus, Asia, Phrygia, Pamphilia, Egypt, and the parts of

Libya about Cyrene, visitors from Rome, Jews also and proselytes, Cretans and Arabians" (Acts 2.5–11). Calling upon them to repent and be baptized in the name of Jesus Christ for the forgiveness of their sins (Acts 2.38), "he added that day about 3,000 souls" (Acts 2.41).

The idealization of the picture drawn by *Luke is not overdone. The primitive Christian community, although considered at first but another sect within the Jewish milieu, proved unique in its theological teaching, and more particularly in the zeal of its members, who served as witnesses to Christ "in all Judea and Samaria and even to the ends of the earth" (Acts 1.8). While Christianity arose in the milieu of the religious life of late Judaism, and at first manifested an enthusiastic piety and messianic character similar to that of such sects as the Damascus and Qumran communities, the Christian *kerygma* did not stop at the border of Judea, but penetrated the surrounding world that was unified and dominated by the Greek language and the Hellenic civilization.

Early Expansion. In Palestine, Greek was understood and used in business; among the Jews living in the Diaspora, it became their native tongue; and with the Greek language a world of concepts, categories of thought, metaphors, and subtle connotations entered late Jewish ideology. It was particularly to the Hellenized portion of the Jewish people that the first Christian preachers turned. After the martyrdom of Stephen, his fellow deacons, including Philip, Nikanor, Prochoros, Timon, Parmenas, and Nicolaos seem to have scattered through Palestine, Syria, and the East and begun the missionary activity of the next generation.

The new sect received the name of Christians (*Christianoi*) at Antioch (Acts 11.26), a Greek city; and after his conversion, Paul addressed himself in Greek to the Jews gathered in the synagogues in the principal cities of the Mediterranean world. *Paul was a thoroughly educated Jew, a Pharisee of the Pharisees in his own words, who in his travels addressed himself first to the Hellenized Jews, then to the Gentiles. Paul's powerful grasp of the central mystery of salvation in Christ, the Son of God, prevented the new religion from being infected by the Hellenistic mystery cults or from being absorbed into one of the Jewish or Gnostic sects. His theological insight was basic for the preservation of the mystery of redemption in and through the Church as the body of Christ.

There is little reliable evidence concerning the missionary travels of the Apostles; but by the year 65 the Christian message had penetrated into Syria, Asia Minor, Greece, and Rome. The movement was recognized, however imperfectly, by the Roman authorities, as is witnessed by *Tacitus (*Ann.* 15.44) and Suetonius (*Claud.* 29.1); and Christians were apparently blamed by the Emperor Nero for the burning of Rome. In the persecution that followed, Peter and Paul suffered martyrdom.

Doctrinal Development. The theological evolution that accompanied the spread of the Christian *kerygma* was greatly influenced by developments in the late Jewish apocalypses, apocrypha, and eschatological literature and has been characterized as Judeo-Christian, its original impetus having been given by the community at Jerusalem. It was also strongly marked by the liturgical writings of Qumran, the angelological and eschatological doctrines of several dynamic Jewish sects, and the dualism of the Essenes. However, the collections of the *Logia,* or sayings, of Jesus and the *Evangelia* quickly found their way into Greek, and the Christian writers of the apostolic age adopted the literary forms of the epistle and of the *praxeis* or acts in use among the secularist philosophers and their disciples. The next generation (*see* APOSTOLIC FATHERS) added other literary forms, adapting the diatribe, especially, to Christian use.

With the adaptation of literary forms there was an assimilation of methods of propaganda and manner of expression current mainly among the Cynics, Stoics, Pythagoreans, and Epicureans, who spread philosophical and religious tracts among the ordinary people. James, for example, in his Epistle, used the Orphic concept of "the wheel of birth" (3.6), and the Didache employed the Pythagorean device (also used by Hesiod) of the Two Ways in a moral context.

There was conflict between the Judaizers and Hellenists in the explanation and development of the Christian message, as is evident from the Pauline warnings against aberrations from the traditional faith given to him as to the other Apostles by Christ; this conflict is emphasized in the testimony of the Pseudo-Barnabas and the Clementine literature.

In Paul's first letter to Timothy there is an indication of the organization of the Church of Asia with a college of presbyters and a president bearing the title and office of *episcopus,* or bishop, and deacons. Some of the earliest Christian communities were seemingly monarchically organized, such as that under James in Jerusalem; but it is obvious that the faithful had a voice in the community life of prayer and witness to Christ, while the charismatic gifts of preaching, comforting the afflicted, and healing were held in great respect.

Clement I of Rome and Ignatius. By the turn of the 2d century, the Christian Church had emerged as a widespread entity united by a common faith and a communion of spiritual interests. The letter of the Church at Rome to the Church at Corinth, although predominantly a moral exhortation to unity and obedience, reveals a consciousness of the Church as a strong, clear, ecclesiastical organization whose line of authority descended from God through Christ and the Apostles to the elders of the fraternally united community (*Epist. Clem.* 42.1–5; 44.1–2). Utilizing the holiness code of the Old Testament synagogic teaching, it imposed a Christocentric theology of virtues on the Christian community advocating imitation of Christ in His patience and long suffering (13.2–4) and guaranteeing man's full deliverance in the resurrection (24–26). Though apparently written by *Clement I of Rome, the letter gives no direct evidence as to the structural organization of the Church in either Rome or Corinth.

In the letters of *Ignatius of Antioch (d. *c.* 116) to the Churches of Asia Minor and to Polycarp of Smyrna, a monarchical type of episcopal government prevails. Ignatius witnesses to a shift of spiritual interest from the Pauline preoccupation with Mosaic law and original justice, to the Greek concern about fate and the value of existence. While the Judaic influence seems to have persisted in the *Quartodeciman controversy centered in Asia Minor, in Rome and the Mediterranean cities there was a gradual development of theological consciousness that considered the Church a transcendent entity.

The Shepherd of *Hermas in the treatise on penance described the Roman Church as a fairly populous assembly (*c.* 140) containing a segment of the rich as well as numerous poor. Many in both classes had relapsed into pagan ways of blasphemy and idolatry; they are described as hypocrites in concert with ambitious clergymen and dishonest deacons. But the majority are referred to as hospitable bishops, zealous priests, martyrs, and the innocent. The Church itself is well organized, with a hierarchy of bishops, priests, and deacons. Considerable emphasis was placed on the achievement of *gnosis,* or a superior knowledge of the triune mystery, particularly in relation to Baptism and the Eucharist. This was a direct offshoot of the rabbinic preoccupation with the "marvelous and true mysteries" that the one God "reveals to the hearts of his servants" as expressed in the Qumran theology (DSD 11.3; 15–16; DSH 7.1–7).

Persecution. Tacitus described the Neronian persecution of the primitive Christians as due "not so much to their having set fire to the city, as to their hatred of the human race" (*Annal.* 15.44). This *odium humani generis* was equivalent to the Greeks' *misanthropia,* a charge originally leveled against the Jews (Diodorus, *Hist.* 24), and subsequently used against the Christians because of their particular customs and refusal to participate in Roman civic and religious rites. Josephus listed these accusations as the adoring of a donkey's head, ritual murder, and incest (*Contra Apion.* 79).

While the recognition of Christianity as a separate religion took place only gradually, there seems to have been a persecution under Domitian (81–96), apparently connected with messianic troubles and millenarianism, in which the senator Flavius Clemens was put to death for "atheism and Jewish practices" (Suetonius, *Domit.* 15) and Domitilla was exiled to Pandateria (Eusebius, *Hist. eccl.* 3.18.4). The letter of Clement I (1.1) speaks of the misfortunes of the Roman Church at this time, and the Apocalypse (1.9; 2.3–13) refers to the persecution of the Churches in Asia Minor.

Accusations. Whereas Paul had called for obedience to the imperial authorities, the Apocalypse registers hostility to the empire. This attitude is reflected also in the *Sibylline Oracles* and the *Ascension of Isaia.* Under Nerva, peace returned. Trajan (98–117), in reply to the Governor of Bithynia, Pliny the Younger, decided that Christians were not to be sought out; but when denounced as guilty of crimes (*flagitia*), they were to be condemned if they refused to abjure. He also cautioned, however, against false and anonymous denunciations, indicating that pressure for persecution came not so much from the government as from people who were intolerant of those bearing the name of Christians (*Epist.* 96.2–3). It is this decision, and not a governmental proscription, that was misinterpreted as indicating the existence of an *institutum Neronianum* by *Tertullian. The most famous martyr of this period was Ignatius of Antioch. Under Hadrian (117–138) the Christians enjoyed comparative peace; but during the reigns of Antoninus Pius and Marcus Aurelius, they were the object of attack by intellectuals such as Fronto (Min. Felix, *Octav.* 9.16; 31.1–2), Lucian (*Life of Peregrinus*), and Crescens the Cynic (fl. 152). Galen, who visited Rome in 162 and 166, accused the Christians of fanaticism and credulity; but the great indictment was launched by the philosopher *Celsus, who considered them charlatans and vagrants dangerous to the civic ideals of the Roman state. This was the basic accusation behind the persecutions.

The Apologists. By the mid-2d century, the new religion had attracted a number of educated men who used their literary competence in defending Christianity against the charges of atheism and idolatry, and began to assess the philosophical and moral thought of their contemporaries in the light of the Judeo-Christian teachings. They are known as the *apologists; but only a few of their writings have survived. They continued the catechetical approach of the older Apostles; this they combined with the propagandist methods of their contemporaries. *Justin Martyr (*c.* 100–160) supplied both Jewish and pagan audiences with a "rule of faith" and a description of the rites of Baptism and the Eucharist while encouraging a conversion from pagan immorality to the *Christian way of life. The *Letter to *Diognetus* described the divine economy of salvation and claimed that Christians in the empire differed in no way from their contemporaries in marriage and family life, in civic custom, and the observance of the laws; but they avoided idolatry, strove to serve as models of moral excellence, and prayed for the preservation of the empire.

Reorganization and Expansion. In the last decades of the 2d century, there was evidence (*c.* 180) of a great reorganization of the Church and its missionary and catechetical endeavors. Christian unity was emphasized by the Roman Church in its controversy with the Church of Asia Minor over the date of Easter, which continued from the reign of *Anicetus (154–166) to that of *Victor I (189–198). *Irenaeus of Lyons stated that Polycarp of Smyrna had visited Rome, but had failed to reach agreement on the question (Eusebius, *Hist. eccl.* 5.24.16). While Polycrates of Ephesus acknowledged the apostolic foundation of the Roman Church by Peter and Paul, he insisted that the customs of the Church in Asia had equal apostolic backing.

Synods and Unity. The practice of holding synods to settle ecclesiastical problems seems to have begun in Asia Minor in the middle of the 2d century and was apparently based on a precedent of civil practice. Evidence supplied by Dionysius of Corinth in his so-called Catholic Epistles displays the interchange of doctrinal and disciplinary interests between the Churches in Greece and Asia Minor. Testimony preserved by Eusebius (*Hist. eccl.* 5.25) indicates that the Churches of Palestine, Pontus, Osrhoene, and Gaul, in synods, registered their agreement with the decision of a Roman synod under Victor that Easter should be celebrated only on a Sunday. Finally Irenaeus gave a list of the popes from Peter to Eleutherius (174–189) and described the efforts made by the early heretics to obtain Roman sanction for their doctrines, while Tertullian claimed that communion with the Roman See was regarded as communion with the whole Church (*Adv. Prax.* 1). He was the first churchman to utilize the so-called Petrine text (Mt 16.18); yet the institution of the papacy had achieved a definitive form by the end of the 2d century: it was the center of unity. Rival claims to occupy the apostolic see by *Hippolytus (217–235) and *Novatian (251) were disallowed by the other Churches, and these men were considered antipopes.

In the dispute over the rebaptism of heretics that involved the Churches of North Africa and Rome after the Decian (251) and Valerian (257) persecutions, Cyprian of Carthage acknowledged that the primacy had been given to Peter, and he saw in the *cathedra* of Peter a source of unity, while he still claimed the independence of individual bishops as successors to the Apostles. Despite difficulties with Novatian, Pope Stephen (254–257) asserted the validity of the Roman practice, and although a synod at Carthage (256) upheld Cyprian, no attempt was made to sever communion with Rome.

Local Churches. By the 3d century there were flourishing Christian communities in Gaul at Lyons, Vienne, Marseilles, Arles, Toulouse, Paris, and Bordeaux. Cyprian of Carthage wrote to the Churches of León-Astorga and Mérida in Spain (*Epist.* 67) and mentioned the community at Saragossa. There were 19 bishops at the Synod of Elvira (*c.* 306). In Germany churches at Cologne, Trier, Metz, Mainz, and Strassburg have left testimony in archeological remains, and the spread of Christianity along the trade routes of the Danubian provinces of Rhaetia, Noricum, and Pannonia is attested by the martyrs of the Diocletian persecution. North Africa was clearly a well-established Christian center based on Carthage in the late 2d century, and the Church in Egypt had developed with its center at Alexandria in the same epoch.

In Asia Minor there were synods in Phrygia between 172 and 180 that dealt with the errors of *Montanism (Eusebius, *Hist. eccl.* 5.16), and the satirist Lucian complained of Christians in Pontus (*c.* 170: *Alexander* 25). *Armenia received Christian missionaries in the 3d century, and Antioch in western Syria had a Church of apostolic origin from which missionaries Christianized the East. The house-church at *Dura-Europos testifies to the presence of Christianity (3d century) in eastern Syria; and Edessa, modern Urfa, and Osrhoene were likewise early recipients of the gospel, though the stories of *Addai and Mari are legendary. *Tatian and Bardesanes preached there (*c.* 170); and the Christian message spread to Mesopotamia and Adiabene in Assyria, to Parthia and to Persia, particularly under King Sapor I (241–272). A synod at Bostra testified to Christianity in Arabia (*c.* 244), and there is evidence, however questionable, for its spread as far east as India.

Final Persecutions. The development of the Christian way of life and its expansion continued to meet grave difficulties from within because of doctrinal disputes, and from without, through sporadic outbursts of persecution. Under Marcus Aurelius (161–180), a Stoic philosopher, a series of physical calamities disturbed the empire in the form of famine, pestilence, and barbarian incursions. The people blamed them on the failure of the Christians to worship the pagan gods. A persecution broke out whose severity is indicated by the apologists Athenagoras, Melito, and Miltiades. Justin Martyr was put to death, apparently in Rome, with six companions; and a number of martyrs are recorded in Lyons (177), including Blandina, Photinus, and Ponticus (Eusebius, *Hist. eccl.* 5.1–2). A letter from the Church at Lyons to that at Vienne described the persecution. After a period of peace, Septimius Severus (193–211) put down a series of Jewish insurrections and turned against the Christians, particularly in Egypt, where Leonides, the father of Origen, was martyred, and in Carthage, the place of the martyrdom of Felicitas and *Perpetua (March 7, 203).

Caracalla (211–217) allowed his mother, Julia Domna, to propagate the mystery cults of the East, particularly sun worship, and Mithraism became an official cult of the army. This caused great difficulty for Christian soldiers and officials. Severus Alexander (222–235) showed clemency, influenced by his mother, Julia Mammaea, who heard Origen lecture at Antioch. But with Maximinus Thrax (237–238), Decius (249–251), and Valerian (253–260), systematic and severe persecutions of the Christians were carried out. Under *Diocletian (284–305) and *Galerius a final attempt was made to destroy Christianity at its roots. The effort was not supported by the elder Constantius I in Gaul and the West, and it failed.

Conversion of Constantine. While the nature and manner of Constantine's conversion is controverted, there is no question about the fact. With the Battle of the Milvian Bridge and the taking of Rome (313), Christianity was accepted as a legitimate religion and rapidly reached a favored status in the empire, although it was not the religion of the vast majority. Determined to use the religious factor as a unifying force within the state, Constantine evidently employed Bp. *Hosius of Córdoba as a counselor and accepted appeals in regard to the Donatist problems in North Africa. He instructed the Bishop of Rome, Miltiades (311–314), to hold a synod at the Lateran, followed by others at Arles (314) and elsewhere, to resolve the situation, and resorted to force only later. With the rise of *Arianism, he convoked the Council of *Nicaea I (325), which defined the doctrine of the homoousios or consubstantiality of the Father and the Son. Nicaea I determined also that in the ecclesiastical organization, the Sees of Rome, Alexandria, and Antioch held special status as patriarchal dioceses. Other sees, such as Carthage, Ephesus, Caesarea in Palestine, Caesarea in Cappadocia, Heraclea in Thrace, and Arles in Gaul also assumed metropolitan status for surrounding sees; and the general organization of the Church was patterned on that of the civil dioceses.

Constantine came to consider himself the providentially appointed guardian of the Church; Eusebius referred to him as an *Isapostolos* (the same as an Apostle). He started a vast building program in Rome that included the Vatican, Pauline, and Lateran Basilicas; in Jerusalem, evidently under the instigation of Helena; and at Antioch and Treves. Eventually he transferred the seat of his government to Byzantium, which he rebuilt as the Christian city of *Constantinople. His baptism on his deathbed by *Eusebius of Nicomedia, however, gave encouragement to the so-called semi-Arian bishops, and under the sons of Constantine turmoil marked theological disputes. There was a series of synods and counter synods that involved such champions of orthodoxy as *Athanasius of Alexandria, *Hilary of Poitiers, and Pope *Liberius in a sequence of painful exiles.

Basil of Caesarea died (379) just as the orthodox cause was about to succeed at the Council of *Constantinople I (381) under *Theodosius I (379–395), who made Christianity the official religion of the empire.

Pagan opposition had reached a final climax under *Julian the Apostate (361–363); but with the removal of the statue of Victory from the Senate, despite the protest of the pagan prefect Symmachus, and with the renunciation of the title *Pontifex Maximus* by Gratian (375–383), the power of the pagan priesthood was broken. Laws had to be passed to prevent the complete dismantling of the pagan temples.

Asceticism and Spirituality. The papacy of Damasus (366–384) and the close of the 4th century saw the rapid rise of a spiritual movement that affected men such as Jerome, Gregory of Nazianzus, Gregory of Nyssa, and Chromatius of Aquileia, and that received a definite ascetic and mystical advancement with the writings of *Evagrius Ponticus. *Monasticism had developed and spread quickly in Egypt, Syria, and Asia Minor, and was stimulated in Italy and Gaul particularly by Athanasius through his *Life of Anthony the Hermit.* Pilgrimages to the Holy Land and to Rome, with the development of the cult of the holy places and of the martyrs, took on enormous proportions and influenced the rise of a popular literature that paralleled the spiritual and theological writings of Ephraem of Edessa, John *Cassian, *Didymus the Blind, and *Epiphanius of Constantia (Salamis). The *Lausiac History of Palladius,* the *Apophthegmata Patrum,* the *Historia monachorum,* and the *Peregrinatio ad Loca sancta* of Aetheria, encouraged ascetical and monastic interests.

Patristic Theology. The conversion of Augustine brought a new theological development in the West that, particularly through Ambrose of Milan and Rufinus of Aquileia, had been closely dependent on the Eastern Fathers. Augustine dealt with *Pelagianism and *Donatism, as well as with the problems posed by the Trinity, truth, education, grace, marriage, virginity, and concupiscence. In the East, *John Chrysostom proved an indefatigable homilist, commenting on St. Paul and the whole of Scripture in a popular and practical fashion. *Jerome translated the Old Testament from Hebrew, provided a guide to the *hebraica veritas,* and utilized the works of Origen and Eusebius of Caesarea to put Scripture study, exegesis, and Christian literature on a firm basis. He encouraged an ascetical movement in Rome, and he became involved in the first phase of the Origenistic controversy that was precipitated by Epiphanius of Salamis. This occasioned difficulties between Jerome and Rufinus, as well as with Bp. John of Jerusalem, and eventually enabled *Theophilus of Alexandria to depose John Chrysostom from the See of Constantinople, at the Synod of the *Oak.

Two Theologies in the East. By the start of the 5th century, two principal theologies had emerged: that of Alexandria with its insistence on the divinity of Christ, and an allegorical interpretation of the Scriptures in the pursuit of man's divinization in Christ; and that of Antioch, devoted to a literal interpretation of Scripture and an insistence on man's perfection through the humanity of Christ in the Resurrection. The differences led to the *Christological controversies of the 5th and 6th centuries and the Councils of *Ephesus (431), *Chalcedon (451), and *Constantinople II (553), which made vigorous efforts to clarify the problems presented by the two natures and one person in Christ. These councils also proved occasions for the expression of the latent rivalries among the Sees of Alexandria, Antioch, and Constantinople. The preeminence of the latter had been asserted at Constantinople I (381) as based on its civil status as the new Rome; it was challenged at Ephesus (431) when *Cyril of Alexandria ousted *Nestorius of Constantinople as a heretic; and its validity was denied by *Leo I after Chalcedon. The interference of the emperors, particularly in the affairs of the Eastern Church, brought conflict with the patriarchs and a general if reluctant acknowledgment of the primacy of the bishop of Rome, to whom appeals in both doctrinal and disciplinary matters were regularly made.

Leo the Great. Pope Leo I (440–461) followed a tradition handed down at least from Siricius (384–399), through Innocent I (401–417), Celestine (422–432), and Sixtus III (432–440) in giving the Church's organization a legal determination. He felt himself the vicar of Christ in the person of Peter and entertained a "care for all the churches"; he made liturgical, moral, and doctrinal decisions for the East as well as the West. His *Tome to Flavian* helped clarify the Christological issue at Chalcedon, and in collaboration with Marcian and Pulcheria, then with Emperor Leo I (457–474), he attempted to stem the rise of *Monophysitism in Egypt and Syria. He defended Rome and Italy from the depredations of the *Huns under Attila, and the *Vandals under Gaiseric. In dealing with the emperors, he was conscious that he was a citizen of the empire; hence he deferred to their authority, yet felt that that same authority was entrusted to the civil ruler for the enhancement of the Christian religion. This issue was further clarified by Pope Gelasius I (492–496), who spoke of the "world as governed by two sovereignties, the papal authority and the imperial power that come from God, the supreme sovereign."

Monophysitism. With the rebellion of *Timothy Aelurus and Peter Mongus in Alexandria and Peter the Fuller in Antioch, Monophysitism gradually assumed a deep political as well as doctrinal and spiritual character. The great Monophysite teachers, such as *Severus of Antioch (512–518) and *Philoxenus of Mabbugh, were not actually heretics in doctrine since they followed Cyril of Alexandria literally. Their power came from their literary competence and the emphasis they placed on the spiritual doctrine of the divinization of man in Christ; they were aided by the persecution of the imperial government, which they used to influence the lower clergy, the monks, and the people.

The Emperor *Zeno issued his *Henoticon* (484) to clarify the Christological issue but merely succeeded in occasioning the *Acacian Schism between Rome and Constantinople. This was continued under Emperor Anastasius I (491–518) despite the efforts of Popes Anastasius II (496–498) and Symmachus (498–514) to achieve a reconciliation. The Roman intervention was complicated by the rise of the Ostrogothic kingdom of Italy under *Theodoric the Great and the rivalry of the Roman factions, one of whom elected Symmachus, while the anti-Byzantine party selected the deacon Laurentius and appealed to the Ostrogoths for support. Three synods in Rome (*c.* 502) settled the election in favor of Symmachus, and despite a campaign of calumny on the part of the Laurentians, Theodoric accepted Symmachus as the true pope.

Age of Justinian. In 518 *Justin I became emperor. He was Latin and Catholic, and with his nephew Justinian he made peace with Rome, condemned the Monophysite factions, and supported Pope Hormisdas

(514–523), whose decree condemning both *Eutyches and Nestorius and asserting the validity of Leo's *Tome* and the Council of Chalcedon was made the touchstone of orthodoxy. Pope John I (523–526) was dispatched to Constantinople by Theodoric as an emissary; but despite an honorable reception, his mission failed, and he was maltreated by the King on his return. The philosopher Boethius and his intimates were also put to death in an anti-Byzantine outbreak.

*Justinian I (527–565), a theologian and also an administrator, legislator, and autocrat, attempted to wipe out paganism and closed the University of Athens (529). He passed disabling legislation against Jews and heretics and attempted to introduce some Christian concepts into the Justinian code. At the suggestion of the deacon, later Pope Pelagius, he condemned Origenism (*see* ORIGEN AND ORIGENISM) as a possible solution to doctrinal troubles among the Palestinian monks. His close adviser Theodore Ascidas suggested the condemnation of the *Three Chapters as a countermeasure. Together with the Monophysite cause generally, Ascidas received the support of the Empress *Theodora (1), who appeared to counter her husband's religious policies while living an edifying private life with him.

In 532 Justinian called a colloquy of Severian Monophysite and orthodox bishops; he pursued a vigorous policy of suppression of apparent Nestorianism, attempted to appease the Monophysite monks with the Theopaschite formula, and finally brought Pope *Vigilius (532–555) to the capital and convoked the Council of Constantinople II (553), which redefined the Christological doctrine in what has been termed a Neochalcedonian fashion. The Pope refused to attend the council after suffering ignominious treatment; he had issued his own *Judicatum* or *Verdict on the Three Chapters* in 548; during the council he put out his *Constitutum,* which condemned the writings of the three incriminated theologians *prout sonant* (as they read) but refrained from condemning them in person. The council (7th session) condemned the Pope and separated itself from the *sedens* but not the *sedes* (the occupant, but not the See of Rome); and in December 553 the Emperor finally forced the aged Pope to accede to the condemnation of the Three Chapters with his *Constitutum II,* in which he repudiated his former stand.

On the death of Vigilius, to counter the theological rebellion of the Western bishops, Justinian selected Pelagius I (556–561) as pope despite his previous opposition to the council. Pelagius found the West in turmoil, supported in part by the *In Defense of the Three Chapters* of *Facundus of Hermiane and the exiled African bishops. Schisms broke out in Milan and Aquileia. Justinian had given Vigilius a Pragmatic Sanction for the adjustment of civil affairs in Italy; and the Pope became the protector of the population against tax gatherers, the depredations of the soldiery, and the Lombard invasions. In his last years, the Emperor favored the aphthartodocetic heresy attributed to *Julian of Halicarnassus. But his suppressive measure against the Monophysites had had little effect. They were countered by the organizational efforts of James *Baradai; and gradually Egypt and Syria became disaffected against the empire on both religious and nationalist issues.

In Gaul the conversion of *Clovis (481–511), under the influence of his wife, the Burgundian princess Clotilda, brought the whole nation into the Church (as *Avitus of Vienne remarked) and checked the spread of Arianism by the Ostrogoths. The tomb of St. Martin of Tours became a national pilgrimage center. Despite the interference of the kings in ecclesiastical affairs, more than 30 synods were held between 511 and 614. Among the more outstanding churchmen of this period were Remigius of Reims (d. 535), the great preacher *Caesarius of Arles (d. 542), *Germain of Paris (d. 576), and the historian *Gregory of Tours (d. 594), as well as the poet Venantius *Fortunatus of Poitiers (d. 601). The Gothic peoples, whose conversion had been effected by Bishop *Ulfilas and by his translation of the Bible into Gothic, were gradually brought over from forms of Arianism to Catholicism.

Britain had been evangelized early; but the invasions of the Angles, Saxons, and Celts brought back paganism except in small sections of Wales and Cornwall. Although Palladius had been sent to Ireland by Pope Celestine in 431, the conversion of the island was due to St. *Patrick, who had studied at Lérins and Auxerre and returned to Ireland *c.* 432. The Irish Church was organized on a monastic basis, and Irish monks set out from foundations such as that of St. *Comgall at Bangor to Scotland, England, Gaul, Germany, and Italy, where they became an important aid in the development of the Church in the 6th and succeeding centuries.

Pope *John III (561–574) made a strenuous effort to protect Rome and Naples from the Lombards, who had conquered Ravenna; and *Benedict I (575–579) had to wait a full year before receiving imperial confirmation of his election from Constantinople. His successor, *Pelagius II (579–590), turned to the Franks for protection against the Lombards and supported Leander of Seville when he converted King Reccared and the Arian *Visigoths to Catholicism.

Gregory the Great. *Benedict of Nursia had laid the foundations of Benedictine monasticism with his monastery at *Monte Cassino (*c.* 529) and evidently was encouraged by Pope *Agapetus (535–536) in the composing of his rule, which displays pedagogical wisdom and well-balanced asceticism in leading the monks to a perfect following of Christ. Benedictine monasticism received a great stimulus from *Gregory I the Great (590–604), who had served both as prefect of the city of Rome and as papal *apocrisiarius* in Constantinople before being elected pope. Despite war and pestilence brought to Italy through the depredations of the Lombards and the continued schism in Milan, he initiated a far-sighted program of reform. He reformed church music and the liturgy, and as his tombstone proclaimed, as the *Consul Dei,* he made efforts to bring the Germanic peoples closer to the papacy and sent Augustine of Canterbury and his companions as missionaries to the British Isles. He protested the use of the title Ecumenical Patriarch for the archbishop of Constantinople. His pastoral and exegetical writings helped to preserve a modicum of ecclesiastical culture for succeeding ages. His *Liber regulae pastoralis* was translated into Greek during his own lifetime and into Anglo-Saxon by Alfred the Great. His *Moralia* is a practical handbook of pastoral morality, in the form of a commentary on the Book of Job. His exegesis of the Gospels and of Ezechiel, as well as his *Dialogues* on the lives and miracles of the Italian saints, though replete with legends, filled a great ascetical and spiritual need; and his 848 letters contain a major portion of the history of his age. While *Cassiodorus (d. *c.* 580), at his retreat in Vivarium, Calabria, preserved theological and literary learning through his *Institutiones divinarum et saecularium lectionum* and his *Historia tripartita ecclesiastica,* Gregory, as the *servus servorum Dei,* created the moral, doctrinal, and pastoral atmosphere that prevailed in the early Middle Ages.

The first period of Church history came to a natural close with Gregory. The reasons for the rise and spread of the Christian Church have challenged the ingenuity and competence of historians, particularly in modern times; but the problem is impossible to solve without an acknowledgment of the intervention of divine providence in the course of human events; it is equally insolvable without a realization that the Church, while divine in its origin and objective, is governed by human beings whose perceptions and ambitions frequently trail far behind the grace and inspiration needed to give finality to the achievement of the kingdom of God on earth.

Bibliography: L. DUCHESNE, *Early History of the Christian Church,* 3 v. (London 1909–24); *L'Église au VIe siècle* (Paris 1925). Bihlmeyer-Tüchle v.1. Daniélou-Marrou ChrCent. K. BAUS, Jedin HbKirchgesch. Caspar v.1. T. G. JALLAND, *The Church and the Papacy* (SPCK; 1944). Fliche-Martin v.1–5. EUSEBIUS, *Hist. eccl.,* Eng. tr. H. J. LAWLOR and J. E. OULTON, 2 v. (SPCK; 1927–28). Tillemont. P. HUGHES, *A History of the Church,* 3 v. (rev. ed. New York 1947–49). P. CARRINGTON, *The Early Christian Church,* 2 v. (London 1957–60).

[F. X. MURPHY]

CHURCH, HISTORY OF, II (MEDIEVAL)

The history of the Western Church in the Middle Ages falls, as does the general history of Europe, into two main phases. In the first (600–1050), Catholic Christianity, hitherto a community within or coextensive with the Roman Empire, converted the new races that had overrun the ancient civilization. It was itself, however, hampered and pinioned by the imperfectly developed social and economic conditions of pagan and feudal Europe and remained only partially organized. In the second phase (1050–1500), the Church in all its organs and activities shared in the adolescence and maturity of medieval civilization; for almost 5 centuries Europe was a single cultural unit under a uniform religious organization that was dominated by the *papacy. Each of these two phases can be subdivided almost equally. In the first period, from the death of Gregory the Great (604) to the coronation of Charlemagne (800), the papacy slipped its allegiance to the Eastern emperor, only to fall under the shadow of the Frankish monarchy; and the initiative in missionary, devotional, and even theological matters passed to the newly converted peoples of the northwest of Europe. In the second period, from 800 to *c.* 1050, the Church was absorbed into feudal society and the papacy was powerless, first in the hands of the Roman faction and then under the control of the German monarchy. In the third, from the accession of Leo IX (1049) to the death of Boniface VIII (1303), the papacy asserted and developed its claim to supremacy in spiritual matters and endeavored, for a time with success, to regulate the politics of Europe as well. Concurrently, the flowering of medieval civilization presented a religious and Catholic culture in all its aspects, intellectual, artistic, and social. In the fourth period, from 1303 to the height of the Italian Renaissance, a series of catastrophes befell Europe and the papacy; a new spirit of nationalism divided the peoples; and a moral decline afflicted many of the institutions of the Church.

First Period: 603 to 800. *Gregory the Great stood on the threshold of the medieval centuries, looking back to the days when Church and Empire were coincident and looking forward to the time when the papacy would dominate the Western world. He was also the last pope for many centuries to impose his will and set his mark on western Europe outside Italy. He was followed by a long succession of short-lived, generally meritorious but mediocre popes who were hard pressed to maintain their ground in an Italy abandoned by imperial forces and a prey to the Lombard invaders. At the same time, they were called upon to defend the orthodox faith endangered both by old and new heresies and by that violence of Eastern emperors that culminated in the capture and subsequent death of Pope *Martin I. Gregory I, lacking imperial protection, had already taken over the civil and military administration of Rome, and during the next 50 years the pope came to control the various territories between Ravenna and Terracina, enfolding the nucleus of the patrimony of St. Peter, that came to be known as the *States of the Church and remained in being until 1870. The popes thus became, by accident and of necessity, temporal sovereigns of a small and vulnerable slice of territory with no natural frontiers. For more than 1,000 years this helped to give them status, independence, and financial support, though proving at the same time to be a source of political entanglement and temptation that distracted them from their essential purpose.

Meanwhile a series of theological issues in the Eastern Church, such as *Monothelitism and the controversy over *iconoclasm, joined with personal antagonisms in separating the Eastern and Western Churches, especially after the rise of Mohammed and the Islamic invasions. These, by reducing the Eastern Empire and by virtually eliminating the ancient patriarchates, united the emperor and the patriarch of Constantinople, often his creature, in hostility toward the claims of Rome. When at last (754) Pope *Stephen II, hard pressed by the *Lombards, appealed for help to the powerful King of the Franks, *Pepin III, a contact was made that led to a close alliance with the Frankish monarchy and the eventual coronation (800) of *Charlemagne as emperor and protector of the papacy.

Missionary Activity. During this same time, Christianity extended its frontiers. The mission of *Augustine of Canterbury to England spread slowly in Kent, Essex, and the Thames Valley, while the conversion of Northumberland and Mercia was due to *Aidan from Celtic *Iona and to *Cuthbert of Lindisfarne from beyond the Cheviots. The fusion of England's churches under Roman obedience at *Whitby, followed by the mission of Abp. *Theodore of Canterbury and the reorganization of the Church in England, ushered in the golden age of Northumbria and Wessex (*see* ENGLAND). During the same period, *Columban and his disciples and converts founded monasteries and preached the faith in eastern France and what is now Switzerland. More influential were the Anglo-Saxon missionaries of the early 8th century, *Willibrord, the apostle of Frisia (The Netherlands), and Wynfrith or St. *Boniface, the apostle of Germany, who, besides his labors and successes in Hesse, Württemberg, and Bavaria, where he reorganized the existing Christians, did much to rejuvenate the flagging Frankish Church. Willibrord, Boniface, and Boniface's relative *Willibald all visited Rome and worked under the direct instruction of popes. In consequence, the German and Frisian Churches and their derivatives stood, like the Anglo-Saxon Church, in direct relationship with Rome, a circumstance that was to be of greatest significance in the later history of the papacy. In time, missionaries from England and from Germany also went to the Scandinavian countries, which were not wholly Christianized until the 11th century. To the northeast of Italy the *Slavs of Moravia were converted in the late 9th century by the Byzantine brothers Constantine (*Cyril) and Methodius, working under papal patronage, though part of the territory evangelized by them later joined the *Orthodox Church. It was not until the 10th century that missionaries, preceding and accompanying the German pressure eastward, converted the Magyars and Poles, and not until the 12th and early 13th centuries that Poles and Germans together colonized and converted the tribes on the eastern shores of the Baltic.

Invasions. But there were losses to set against these gains. The armies of Islam, besides submerging the ancient Eastern churches and beating on the gates of Constantinople, overran the scattered Christian churches of North Africa and then conquered Visigothic *Spain, one of the most cultured communities of Christendom, in less than 3 years (711–713). Washing past the Pyrenees at either end, they were only halted (732) near Poitiers, 12 years after their armies in the East had been thrown back from the walls of Constantinople. Later, the Hungarians or Magyars swept across central Europe as far as the Elbe and Burgundy, while in the north the Scandinavian raids on Britain, Ireland, and the coasts of Frisia and France, beginning shortly before 800, continued for more than a century. During part of this age, European Christendom was confined to what was little more than a wide corridor extending from Italy to the British Isles.

Second Period: 800 to 1050. A period of reconstruction began under the Frankish monarchs, culminating in the long reign of *Charlemagne (768–814), who ultimately united almost all Continental Christians under his Empire. Protector of the pope and, as such, crowned emperor by the pope, Charlemagne continued and developed the regime of his predecessors as divinely ordained governor and administrator of the Church of God. He appointed bishops, settled liturgical affairs, and even pronounced upon theological issues, with the aid of a group of able clerics, among whom the Anglo-Saxon *Alcuin was preeminent. *Adoptionism, the question of *Iconoclasm and the *filioque controversy were all dealt with at *Aachen, though the papacy was recognized as the ultimate source of authority and orthodoxy. When Charlemagne died, his son *Louis I the Pious at first continued and even extended his control of the Church, but the division of the Empire and Louis's own faults and misfortunes allowed the bishops of the court, the heirs of the *Carolingian Reform, to assert their powers. For a generation they controlled the Continental Church north of the Alps, the scene being dominated by Abp. *Hincmar of Reims (845–888). It was the age of the *False Decretals, the predestinarian and *Eucharistic controversies, of *Paschasius Radbertus, *Rabanus Maurus and *Ratramnus, and also of *Gottschalk of Orbais and *John Scotus Erigena. A long series of complaisant and mediocre popes was broken by *Nicholas I (858–867), the greatest Pope between Gregory I and Leo IX. Nicholas, in his reestablishment of authority over the Frankish hierarchy, including Hincmar, in his steadfast refusal to countenance the divorce of Lothair II and in his treatment of the first phase of the *affaire* *Photius, asserted in exemplary fashion and maintained in practice the plenary supremacy of the Roman See. If Nicholas's firmness seems at times to have become intransigence, this is attributable to his secretary, the enigmatic *Anastasius the Librarian. His successor, *Adrian II, maintained his position, but the collapse of the Carolingian Empire in 885 and the eclipse of the papacy heralded an epoch of political anarchy and weakness, in which the papal office reached a degree of degradation without parallel in the history of the Church.

Monastic Centuries. The 5 centuries after 600 have been called monastic, in the sense that the higher intellectual, spiritual, missionary, and administrative life of the Church was largely in the hands of monks, who were by and large the only teachers and writers of the age. In the 7th century, Irish monachism was still active, both in the Celtic homelands and in Continental foundations such as Columban's *Luxeuil and *Bobbio; but the future lay with the traditional Mediterranean type of community, which gradually accepted the *Benedictine Rule to the exclusion of all others. The monasteries became large landowning establishments, particularly in the German lands, where they were often centers of colonization and missionary activity, as well as seats of bishoprics. Charlemagne and Louis the Pious attempted to impose uniformity of discipline and strict observance of the rule on all monks of the Empire under *Benedict of Aniane. But the organization was wanting, and the union dissolved; henceforth, however, all monks of France and Germany took St. Benedict as patron. The prevailing decadence that ensued was broken by the *Cluniac Reform (909), which gradually built up a vast and uniform congregation, strictly dependent on the abbot of Cluny.

Feudalization of the Church. The disappearance of the Carolingian Empire implied the final separation of France and Germany. In France decomposition into numerous feudal fiefs was rapid, and for 2 centuries the monarchy was in eclipse. In Germany the five (later six) great duchies came into being, one of the dukes being king of all. In 962 *Otto I the Saxon, known as Otto the Great, demanded and received the imperial crown from the Pope, who alone had the right to bestow it. For nearly a century the papacy, when not a pawn of Roman intrigue, was treated as a religious appanage of the monarchs of Germany. As emperors or kings, these rulers regarded the papacy as their supreme ecclesiastical benefice. This attitude reflected the practice of more than 2 centuries throughout Europe, the regime of the *proprietary church. During this period the old concept of the individual church as a corporation, with property and rights, and of the bishop as supporting and disposing of his clergy, had disappeared. The church was now a chattel, the parochial cure a benefice, and both were in the control of the lord, who appropriated much of the income and bestowed the office of priest, with its residual emoluments, on a clerk of his choice. Bishoprics and abbeys could be treated in the same way, while on the other hand bishops and even the papacy could own churches within or without the diocese of their title. Under such a regime the concept of a spiritual office was low. A church or a bishopric could be bought; a priest, tied by quasi-feudal obligations, might share the common rights of society, marry, or at least share domestic life with a consort and children and pass on his benefice to a son. Thus any program of reform demanded a chaste clergy and the canonical election of bishops without any payment for office.

Third Period: 1050 to 1303. The wind of reform began to blow in north Italy and in the monastic world. St. *Romuald and St. *John Gualbert, both Cluniac monks, founded strict new orders, the *Camaldolese and *Vallombrosans. *Peter Damian, a disciple of Romuald, was the fiercest preacher of reform. In France *William of Saint-Bénigne, a Cluniac, reformed houses in Burgundy, north Italy, and Normandy; and there were other centers in Flanders and Lorraine. Men from all these centers, particularly Lorraine, worked for a reform of the papacy, using the ancient Canon Law (including the False Decretals and other unauthentic pieces) to exalt the office. *Leo IX, a Lorrainer, appointed by Emperor Henry III in 1048, was the first pope of the new age. He traversed Germany and France, holding synods and deposing simoniacs, the first pope for 2 centuries to seize the reins firmly and to display papal authority in action throughout Europe. He was less well advised in his choice of the extremist Cardinal *Humbert of Silva Candida for the mission of 1054 to Constantinople, which led to the disastrous breach of relations that displayed, though it did not cause, the total lack of understanding between East and West. Leo's successors continued to press reform, and in 1059 a conciliar decree assigned the right of papal election to the cardinals (*see* PAPAL ELECTION DECREE). This circumvented royal control, but the crucial moment came in 1073 with the election of the archdeacon Hildebrand as *Gregory VII. The new Pope developed his control of the Church, sending legates, deciding episcopal elections, and holding synods, moving firmly against clerical unchastity and simony. He did more. From an intensive study of Canon Law, he extracted a program of papal supremacy that included papal unaccountability and the right to excommunicate and depose a king or emperor. This right he asserted in 1075 when Emperor *Henry IV was excommunicated and deposed for appointing a rival archbishop at Milan. Faced with rebellion and a rival, Henry appeared as a penitent at Canossa and was absolved by the Pope, who allowed spiritual duty to outweigh political wisdom. Henry vanquished his rival, whom the Pope supported, and was again excommunicated and deposed (1080). He created an antipope, however, and Gregory was driven into exile, dying at Salerno in 1085. The great issue between priesthood and kingship had been joined.

Gregory VII was one of the greatest of the popes. Basing himself soundly on traditional and papal action in the past, he drove principles to their extreme conclusions and acted fearlessly and drastically when justice seemed to him to demand it. He created the centralized, politically minded papacy of the later Middle Ages; indeed, the scope of papal action in the modern world derives from his exposition of traditional doctrine. Whether in both act and word he carried firmness into harshness and spiritual truth into political design will always be debated, but the papacy could not now retreat; his ideas and ideals (*see* GREGORIAN REFORM) inspired popes and bishops in the century that followed. Pope *Paschal II extended Gregorian practice; *Urban II seized the moral leadership of Europe by preaching the first *Crusade; and *Gelasius II, after a period of confusion, settled the *investiture struggle by the *Concordat of Worms (1122). Meanwhile, the reconquest of Spain, marked by the capture of Toledo (1085), added to Christendom a nation born of a crusade and reorganized by the papacy, a land that was soon to be a focus of new learning and thought.

12th Century. The 12th century saw the progress of Gregorian ideas throughout Europe. Canonical elections, clerical celibacy, legatine visitations and councils, appeals to Rome, papal protection of exempt religious houses, and assertions of the freedom of the Church were universal. The extraordinary development of intellectual activity and organizational ability throughout Europe and the emergence of numerous new and centralized religious orders accelerated the study and circulation of *Canon Law and perfected the ecclesiastical machinery of justice and administration at papal and diocesan level. It was then that the *cathedral chapter, the bishop's curia, the archdeaconry, and the rest were set up all over Europe. At the same time there was an unparalleled expansion of the canonical and monastic life. Large and small communities of the regular "black canons," or *Canons Regular of St. Augustine, appeared. Later the more monastic "white canons," or *Premonstratensians of St. *Norbert, covered northern and central Europe. The traditional Benedictine "black monks" and Cluniacs continued to increase, especially at the periphery of Christendom, while the new "white" *Cistercians, with their institute of lay brothers (*see* CONVERSI), enjoyed a vogue of spectactular proportions. The building of cathedrals, monasteries, and parish churches was equally remarkable. Beginning in France early in the 11th century, a new style of Romanesque architecture and sculpture was developed and spread to Spain, north Italy, south Germany, and later, in its distinctive Norman form, to England after the Conquest. Earlier buildings were torn down to make way for larger ones, and half way through the 12th century the common use of stone vaulting and the pointed arch led to the new Gothic style that, as the techniques of design and construction improved, created masterpieces such as the cathedrals of Chartres, Amiens, and Reims; of Canterbury, Durham, and Lincoln; of Bamberg; and of Seville. These have never been surpassed in majesty of appearance or beauty of appointments (*see* CHURCH ARCHITECTURE, 4, 5). *Manuscript illumination, the art par excellence of the cloister, reached a new height of achievement. This material and artistic expansion was matched by literary and devotional development. The output of sermons, treatises, commentaries, chronicles, biographies, and letters rose steeply, as may be seen by a glance at such collections as Migne's *Patrology*. Furthermore, quality matched quantity. Such writers as *Anselm of Canterbury, Peter *Abelard, *Bernard of Clairvaux, *John of Salisbury, *William of Malmesbury, *Otto of Freising, *Adam

Fig. 1. "Mater Ecclesia" buttressing the shelter of a group of clergy and a group of laymen, miniature on a late 11th-century Exultet Roll written and illuminated at Monte Cassino (Vat. Barb. lat. 592, detail).

of Saint-Victor, and a hundred others put *medieval Latin literature high among the achievements of European civilization. Though the "monastic centuries" ended *c.* 1150, it was the age that in great part "monachized" the sentiment and devotion of Western Christendom; i.e., monastic practices and ideals, such as liturgical elaborations, particular festivals, special psalmody, communal life, and vowed poverty, came to be applied to the secular clergy and even to devout lay folk, with the institution of lay brethren, oblates, and confraters. And the founding of a religious house became a good work beyond all others for a landowner.

These activities were accomplished by a society that, for its numbers, gave birth to an unexampled number of saints and edifying prelates. Popes such as Leo IX, Gregory VII, and Eugene III; bishops such as *Lanfranc, Anselm of Canterbury, *Ivo of Chartres, and Norbert at Magdeburg; monks and canons such as *Stephen Harding, Bernard of Clairvaux, *Aelred of Rievaulx, and *Gilbert of Sempringham; and women such as *Margaret, Queen of Scotland—all are names taken almost at random as representative of a great multitude. Especially outstanding among them was Bernard, who for 30 years was the spiritual director and *ombudsman* of the Church and the Doctor of his age; he was at once the last of the Fathers and the source of many elements in the devotional life of succeeding ages. No one in private place has ever held such a position of influence and esteem in the history of the Church.

The 12th century ended on a less buoyant note. The renaissance of letters was fading, the new religious orders had lost their first fervor, there were fewer men of genius and sanctity. There were internal clashes of authority and the beginnings of heresy in Italy and France. The cathedral schools were losing ground to the nascent universities, but *scholasticism had not yet unfolded its wings. The growing towns in Lombardy, Flanders, and south Germany were restless and uncared for. The papacy, at odds for years with *Frederick Barbarossa and his claims to Sicily, had become entangled in anti-imperial diplomacy.

Innocent III. Then at last, after a run of elderly, short-lived popes, the cardinals in 1198 chose the young Roman canonist who took the name of Pope *Innocent III. With extraordinary energy and breadth of view the new Pope picked up the threads of government and resolved to devote his pontificate to the Crusade, to the defeat of heresy, and to reform. To the control and reform of the Church as understood by Gregory VII,

Innocent added the supervision of Christendom and the claim to act and to rectify in the political sphere when justice or the good of nations demanded. In other words, the power and prestige of the papacy were in intention directed toward the purification of the Church and the well-being of the commonwealth. Innocent's unremitting work, seen in his correspondence and his decretals, was crowned by the Fourth *Lateran Council, the first Western council to rival the ancient gatherings in catholicity and scope. Touching every aspect and degree of Church life, it is notable above all as the first council to legislate for the general body of the faithful in its prescription of paschal Communion and annual parochial confession.

Nevertheless, Innocent had to deal with several difficult matters in which his success was incomplete: the growth of heresy, the Crusade, and German and English affairs. The heretical *Cathari in Languedoc and Toulouse demanded attention; and after the attempts of preachers had failed, the Pope launched a Crusade of northern French barons, who massacred and ravaged, replacing the papal project of peaceful settlement by military conquest (*see* LOUIS VIII, KING OF FRANCE). Innocent's Eastern *Crusade ended in the deplorable sack of Constantinople and the establishment of a *Latin Empire, which Innocent, in this too much a man of his age, rejoiced to see. In England, his stern action against the wayward and violent King John was hastily replaced by his support of the externally penitent King. In Germany, after more than one change of front, he supported the young King Frederick II, a child of sorrow for the papacy. In all these fields the Pope suffered a great disadvantage in conducting shifting politics at weeks' or months' distance from the scene of action, but in each, also, he misjudged the human agents concerned. Against these failures of policy, it is only fair to set his merit in having recognized the sanctity and value of *Francis of Assisi and St. *Dominic. His pontificate was the summit of the medieval papacy, and all too short.

Mendicant Orders. The foundation of the two first orders of friars did more than any political or conciliar action to rejuvenate the Church. Francis of Assisi, one of the most original and arresting personalities in European history, the harbinger of a new age with his emotional and aesthetic delicacy and his capacity for self-surrender, probably never wished to found the order that so exactly met the needs and aspirations of his day. Dominic, with a clear and more conventional aim and a genius for organization, supplied the framework later adopted by all the friars. It has been said, with some inaccuracy, that Francis made the Preachers friars while Dominic made the Minors an order. Both groups had a phenomenal success and inspired many imitators, of whom the *Carmelites, *Augustinians, and later the *Servites were the only bodies of European importance. As centralized, supranational institutes, at once favored and exploited by the papacy, they were a source of spiritual and missionary strength for the Church of the 13th century, to which each order gave a pope, a Doctor, and many notable bishops. Above all, the *laity of the cities and towns profited by their preaching and direction and, later, by the consequences of their theological wisdom.

13th Century. The century following Innocent III and the Fourth Lateran Council was the high summer of the medieval Church. Universal centralization, given depth by the legislation of the Council and the teaching of the new universities and administered by a hierarchy more competent and in general more zealous than at any previous epoch, brought about a new growth of religion at the parish level as well as in the cathedral towns and schools. Dioceses were now fully organized and parishes cared for, while in the material sphere churches were built and rebuilt on a scale and with a magnificence never to be surpassed. At the center, Innocent III was followed in the papacy by a series of able, mature lawyers who carried on and developed his program; but they were men of lesser genius and narrower vision, and it seemed to contemporaries that they monopolized power and exploited the Church. The appointment of bishops—removed from monarchs and restored to canonical electors by the Gregorians—was now claimed by the papacy in an increasing number of situations and finally in all cases by Urban V (1363). Election became a costly business for the bishop-elect. Similarly, *provision to benefices, great or small, throughout the Church, was increasingly claimed by or restricted to the pope: in 1265 Clement IV had asserted the principle that was gradually put into practice more and more. Papal provision, like papal appointment of bishops, brought cash as well as patronage to the Roman Curia, while bishops lost many of their assets as patrons and churches suffered from foreign or absentee incumbents. Above all, papal taxation, begun indirectly toward the end of the 12th century, increased rapidly and actual direct taxation began in 1199. Before the middle of the 13th century, first fruits on bishoprics (i.e., 1 year's revenue) and tenths on all clergy were regularly levied, in addition to the fees payable by exempt houses for particular favors and for costs in litigation. Under *Innocent IV this exploitation was accompanied by a rigorous use of all means of control and every source of revenue, such as legatine visitations and the visits of bishops (**ad limina*) to Rome. The pontificate of Innocent IV has been taken as the moment when the papacy first seemed to fleece rather than to feed its flock (*see* FINANCE, ECCLESIASTICAL).

In the realm of politics, Innocent IV used weapons of excommunication and interdict ruthlessly and methodically against *Frederick II, and the Pope was obeyed by most of the German bishops. The excommunication and deposition of the Emperor in 1245, followed by his death in 1250, are usually taken to mark the end of the long struggle and the victory of the papacy over the Empire, and they were also the principal business of the First Council of *Lyons in 1245.

The same epoch—the 13th century—saw the University of *Paris reach the height of its fame with a series of eminent doctors: *William of Auvergne, *Alexander of Hales, *Bonaventure, *Albert the Great, *Thomas Aquinas, *Robert Kilwardby, *John Peckham, and the enigmatic master of arts *Siger of Brabant. Their careers coincided with the final translation, reception, and criticism of the whole Aristotelian corpus by the theologians and with the appearance, under Siger, of heterodox integral Aristotelian teaching that provoked the Paris condemnations of 1270 and 1277. These marked the end or at least the suspension of the endeavor to make Aristotle the exclusive master of thought, though not before Aquinas had rethought the

Fig. 2. "Church Triumphant," 13th-century miniature by an unknown German artist.

Philosopher and produced a system of Christian philosophical and theological doctrine, and an answer to the old problem of clarifying the relationship of reason to revelation, of nature to grace.

The end of the 13th century was a period of harshness and embitterment. The campaign against heresy was now conducted by the *Inquisition, equipped with extraordinary powers and with the operating machinery of secret delation and examination assisted by torture, in which the accused was consistently at a legal disadvantage. The rivalry between the Preachers and the Minors (not yet called *Dominicans and *Franciscans), exacerbated by the condemnation of 1277, molded theological teaching into schools coincident with the various orders of friars. Within the Minors the tension between those who claimed to follow the rule and those who accepted the many papal interpretations and relaxations—alleviated for a time by the moderation and spiritual wisdom of St. Bonaventure—was now becoming a schism between Franciscan *Spirituals and *Franciscan Conventuals, while the wider tension between clerics and secular powers was moving from Germany to England and France, where strong monarchs and a mounting spirit of nationalism were resisting papal claims to tax and to provide. In the Roman Curia the small number of cardinals gave national and family feuds an undesirable influence, and several papal elections became long and bitter contests. An attempt to escape from these resulted in the strange election of an inexperienced hermit as Pope *Celestine V, and the confusion caused by his incompetence and resignation led to the election of Benedetto Gaetani as *Boniface VIII (1294–1303). With Boniface papal claims to supremacy in the political sphere rose to their highest point. Thwarted in his attempt to prevent the taxation of clergy by kings, he became involved in an exchange of threats with *Philip IV (the Fair) of France. The Pope claimed the right to supervise and condemn royal policies and acts, and if need be to excommunicate and depose. The King and his ministers retorted with charges of simony, immorality, and heresy, and threatened Boniface with a general council. The Pope's bull **Unam sanctam*, a masterly exposition of extreme papal claims, was followed by his temporary capture by *Nogaret at Anagni and his death a few months later.

Fourth Period: 1303 to 1500. Boniface's successor died after a brief pontificate, and the French archbishop of Bordeaux succeeded him as Pope *Clement V. Dominated by the French King, who demanded a posthumous trial of Boniface VIII, Clement temporized but yielded to Philip in suppressing the *Templars, whose wealth the King coveted and whose conviction was secured by calumny and barbarous torture. By his creation of numerous French cardinals, Clement also ensured a series of French popes and settled the papal court at Avignon in 1308, thus occasioning the *Avignon papacy. His successor, the septuagenarian *John XXII (1316–34), was the most remarkable pope of the century. A financial and administrative genius, he reorganized papal finances, greatly increasing the yield from direct taxation; he reformed the papal Curia and reshaped the diocesan pattern in France. Quarrelsome and obstinate, he forced the Emperor *Louis IV the Bavarian into hostility, thereby depriving the papacy of its Italian revenue and creating an asylum for those who were enemies of the Pope on other counts. These enemies included the bitter secularist *Marsilius of Padua; the creator of *Nominalism, *William of Ockham; and the rebellious minister general of the Franciscans, *Michael of Cesena, who refused to accept the Pope's condemnation of the teaching that Christ on earth owned no property. This opinion, passionately held by the Franciscan Spirituals and many other Franciscans, led them to accuse the Pope of heresy, a charge that was redoubled when John XXII gratuitously aired his opinion that souls, however pure, failed to enjoy the fullness of the *beatific vision immediately after death. This aberration was condemned by John's successor, *Benedict XII, a Cistercian, memorable for his reforming constitutions for monks and canons. The residence at Avignon did not end until *Gregory XI returned to Rome in 1377.

The "Babylonian Captivity" at Avignon has been the object of bitter invective from the days of the contemporary *Petrarch to our own. But during the past 50 years, opinion has changed. The worst charges of vicious living and subservience to the French monarchy cannot be maintained. The Avignon popes were on the whole respectable and personally devout and not without a care for the wider needs of the Church. Apart from the complaisance of Clement V, few of their failings can be directly attributed to their place of residence. On the other hand, there is no doubt that during the decades at Avignon the luxury and venality of the Curia became a scandal and that the financial exactions and centralization of administration became excessive. The sense that the papacy exploited the Church grew, with the added bitterness that the exploitation was for financial, not for high political, ends, while the French monopoly of places and power and the neglect of Roman interests, spiritual and temporal, undoubtedly angered contemporaries.

There were other aggravating circumstances in this period of discontent. The catastrophic *Black Death (1348–49) and the previous outbreak of the Hundred Years' War between England and France demoralized western Europe and accelerated its division into mutually hostile nations. At the same time, the intellectually disturbing effects of Nominalism and the ruthless attacks on the papacy and ecclesiastical government by Marsilius and Ockham provided a background of theory for political actions such as the English antipapal statutes of *provisors and *praemunire (1351, 1353).

Western Schism and Basel. The return of the papacy to Rome was followed within a few months by an unforeseeable disaster even more damaging to religion. This was the election in 1378 of two popes in succession by the same small body of factious cardinals; the *Western Schism had begun. Though Roman tradition and modern scholarship agree on the probable validity of the first election (of Pope *Urban VI), contemporaries had no means of arriving at certainty; within a few weeks each party was furnished with cardinals, a curia, and a palace (at Rome and at Avignon), and Europe split into two camps. France, the Iberian Peninsula, and Scotland were in one; the Empire, Hungary, the Netherlands, and England, in the other; Italy was divided. All attempts at a solution by means of resignation or conference failed; both papal lines were perpetuated, and an agreement by the cardinals of both parties to call a council at *Pisa in 1409 resulted in the election of a third and certainly illegitimate pope, or antipope, *John XXIII. Meanwhile, the opinion that only a general council could provide a solution for such a crisis was strengthened by arguments then gaining strength in academic circles at Paris, that such a council was a sovereign power superior to the pope (*see* CONCILIARISM). The vicious circle was at last broken by the Emperor *Sigismund, who persuaded John XXIII to convoke a council at *Constance (1414), which in course of time deposed him, accepted the resignation of the Roman pope, and declared the Avignon claimant deposed. Then a Colonna cardinal was elected (1417) pope as *Martin V. Previously, the Council had condemned and burned John Hus and passed the decree *Frequens,* which stated that a council should meet after 5 years, with decennial councils in perpetuity. Martin V successfully restored and improved the papal financial and administrative machinery and with equal success resisted reform of the papal Curia and its abuses. He yielded to opinion, however, by convoking another council, which he did not live to see. This Council, at *Basel, largely composed of academicians maintaining conciliar supremacy, successfully resolved the quarrel between Catholics and *Hussites in Bohemia, and passed several thoroughgoing decrees against papal reservation of benefices and Curial avarice. Pope *Eugene IV, a patient conservative, awaited his hour; and when the Eastern Emperor approached both him and the Council, asking for assistance and promising reunion, the Pope overbid the Council by transferring its sessions to Ferrara to meet Greek convenience. He was successful in achieving an artificial union with the Greeks at the succeeding Council of *Florence (1438–39), thereby securing the general esteem that the Council failed to diminish even after "deposing" him and electing an antipope. The gathering at Basel expired in 1449 and with it the "conciliar era," though threats of a council continued to alarm popes until the ghost was laid at Trent. It was symptomatic of the return to traditional forms of Church government that two eminent men, conciliarists in their early career, should become staunch papalists. *Nicholas of Cusa, who in his thought turned back to Neoplatonism, was one; the other, Cardinal Juan de *Torquemada, was a harbinger of the Thomist revival of the following century. Meanwhile, Eugene IV had skillfully made terms with the various governments and, by making some concessions, had retained far more power for the papacy than the nations at Basel had desired, with the single exception of France. There, the epoch had given birth to *Gallicanism, which transferred all powers of appointment and taxation from pope to king, while admitting the spiritual supremacy of Rome. This arrangement, reasserted in the *Pragmatic Sanction of Bourges (1439), was constantly at-

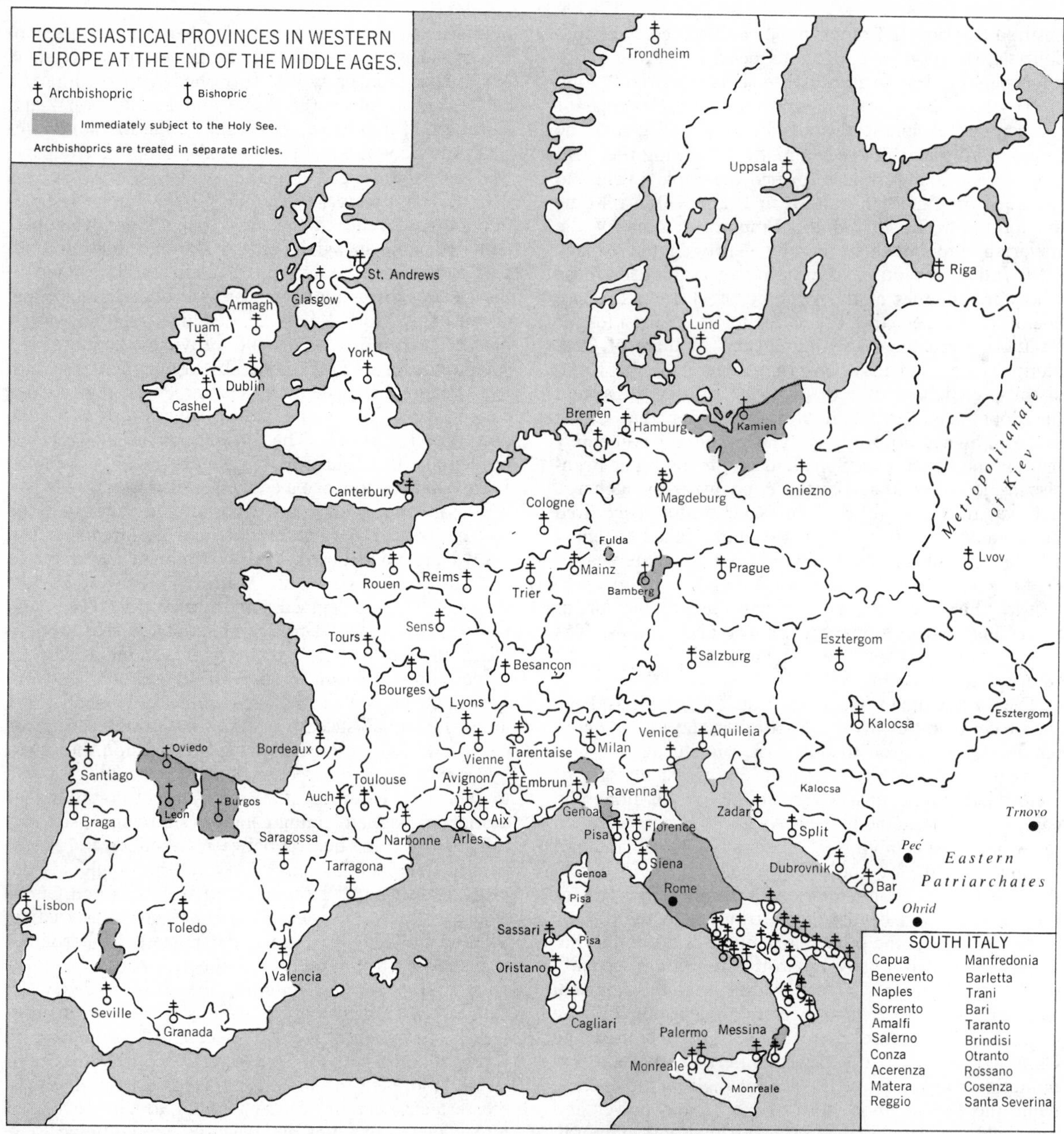

Fig. 3. Map of western Europe showing points of ecclesiastical interest at the end of the Middle Ages.

tacked by the papacy but remained the Magna Carta of Gallicanism for more than 3 centuries.

By mid-15th century conciliarism was dead, and the papacy had ostensibly recovered its status. The 40 years of unparalleled doubt and division had, however, done immense harm in lowering the spiritual prestige of the papal office and in calling into question its usefulness, its necessity, and its rights. Following hard upon the residence at Avignon, they did more than anything to prepare the ground for the great revolution of the 16th century.

Wyclif and Hus. Meanwhile, heresy had appeared again in a form that was to have only partial success in its early version but was to be absorbed later into the program of mature Protestantism. John *Wyclif, a leading realist philosopher at Oxford, turned to theology and found the Church in the invisible society of the predestined. He denied the transubstantiation of the Eucharistic elements; questioned the powers of pope, bishop, and priest; and took the Bible as the only rule of faith, preaching poverty and a married ministry. Censured and silenced by Abp. William *Courtenay, he died in communion with the Church; and his disciples, called *Lollards, were driven underground by persecution. By a strange turn of events, his teaching was carried to Bohemia (*Czechoslovakia), where it served as the basis and confirmation of the message of John *Hus, a popular preacher and national leader. Hus and his disciple *Jerome of Prague were condemned and burned at Constance. Their followers, who combined a puritan zeal with nationalist enthusiasm in a country that had recently risen to a notable place in European culture, rose in armed defense of their cause, of which reception of the Eucharist under both species was a shibboleth, giving them their name (*Utraquists). They successfully resisted a crusade of the Emperor Sigismund, and the Council of Basel was constrained to make a compromise in the Compacts of Prague, which in fact granted little save the optional use of the chalice. Such as it was, the arrangement gave the Hussites an uneasy place within the Catholic Church for almost a century. Though only partially successful and compounded of many elements, not all of them religious, the Hussite movement marked a point of no return. It was the first attempt of a professedly Christian body to break away from Rome in the later Middle Ages; and though it is difficult to establish direct contact between the Wyclif-Hus evangel and the first writings of Martin Luther, the identity of ideas between it and the fully developed program of the great Reformer is unmistakable.

Devotio Moderna. The period from 1300 to 1500 was not wholly one of discord and disaster. There were many notable instances of sanctity, with reformers such as *Bernardine of Siena and *Antoninus of Florence and women such as *Catherine of Siena, *Bridget and *Catherine of Sweden, and *Frances of Rome. Above all, it was an age of mystical experience and writing. The Dominican school of the Rhineland, originating with Meister *Eckhart and developed by *Tauler and *Henry Suso, lay behind the teaching of the great Flemish mystic, *Ruysbroeck, and in its main lines, wholly traditional in essence, though colored by Neoplatonic language, was to pass to Spain and become classical. The practical aspects of *Dominican spirituality served as food for countless families of devout women in Rhenish and Flemish convents. In England, joined to the traditional Bernardine-Victorine teaching, it appeared in the works of the unknown master of the **Cloud of Unknowing* and Walter *Hilton, while Richard *Rolle and the exquisite *Julian of Norwich stood apart as preachers of their own experience. How deeply religious faith still saturated all kinds of men may be seen in *Dante and *Petrarch in Italy, and in England in *Chaucer and his contemporaries William Langland (*see* PIERS PLOWMAN) and the poet of **Pearl.*

Still more extensive was the movement of the contemporary *Brethren of the Common Life, who owed their way of life to the inspiration of Gerard *Groote (1340–89) and whose spirit has been preserved for all subsequent generations by *Thomas à Kempis in his **Imitation of Christ*. The Brethren gave to generations of their countrymen a solid religious education, pure morals, and a simple devotion that anticipated the puritan sentiment of a later age; an orthodox faith with a minimum of speculation and liturgical display.

Renaissance. When the Council of Basel expired (1449), the papacy had entered a new phase; the brilliant and artistic activity of Italy was inspiring secular attitudes, and in Europe as a whole an age of authority and absolutism was about to begin. The Roman Curia and in particular the College of Cardinals, in which members of the leading families of Italy were dominant, shared to the full in the luxury and refinement of the age, while the popes entered into the shifting power politics of the day. In the past many popes had been diplomats and some had been warriors, but never before had the papacy stood in the forefront of European diplomacy in the guise of a secular power, the military ally or enemy of other states, a participant in the struggle for supremacy and territorial gain. In an age of individualism and *virtù,* a succession of pontiffs stood out as intensely human, egoistic sovereigns, who used their near relatives as faithful agents, and bought or rewarded their services with ecclesiastical as well as secular honors. The age from 1447 to 1550 was one of papal nepotism and patronage of the arts. Pope *Nicholas V was the first to harness the Italian *Renaissance to the papal chariot; henceforward for more than a century, Rome, which itself was poor in artistic talent, was the mecca of architects, sculptors, and painters, whose works remain for the world to visit in *St. Peter's Basilica, the *Sistine Chapel, and the galleries of the Vatican palace. The converted conciliarist and brilliant, if slightly raffish, literary genius Aeneas Sylvius (Pope *Pius II, 1458–64) was the quintessence of his age; he was also the last of the medieval popes in his valiant but unavailing attempt to rouse a crusade. His sucessors devoted their attention to war and alliances in Italy. *Sixtus IV, a Franciscan, lived (it was said) on war and advanced his disreputable nephews, clerical and lay, to further his policy; he also planned the decoration of the chapel that bears his name. Under his rule the papal court rivaled the splendors of Florence. Under *Innocent VIII, *Alexander VI, and *Julius II the papacy, outwardly magnificent and skillfully steered in the Italian maelstrom, countenanced around it a degree of wordly display and spiritual emptiness that contemporaries at once admired and deplored. For more than a century the cry for reform in head and members of the Church had been heard—and not least frequently in Italy itself, where the tragic career of *Savonarola had revealed so many of the religious, social, and political ills of the time.

Yet there were still many examples of sanctity in the century of *Joan of Arc, *Francis of Paola, and *Catherine of Genoa. In France and in England, at the end of the century, *Lefèvre d'Étaples and John *Colet were inaugurating the study of Pauline teaching and the human life of Christ that was to seem to many a new and truer basis of religion than a piety of indulgences and monastic observance. The critical scholarship that was beginning to reveal the Gospels and the early Church in a new light, the discoveries that had opened a new half-world, the diffusion of thought that printing was beginning to make possible—all this and much else, was heralding a new age; but in 1500 no one could have foreseen what shape reform would take, if indeed it were to come.

Bibliography: The whole period is covered by *Histoire de l'Église,* ed. originally A. FLICHE and V. MARTIN, now by J. B. DUROSELLE and E. JARRY (Paris 1935–) v.5–15. The sections by É. AMANN and A. FLICHE are particularly valuable. Of the older historians, A. HAUCK, *Kirchengeschichte Deutschlands,* 5 v. (8th ed. Berlin 1954), covers France to 900 and Germany and Central Europe to 1428 and is still unrivaled for breadth of scope and wealth of documentation. H. K. MANN, *The Lives of the Popes in the Early Middle Ages,* 18 v. (London 1902–32). G. MOLLAT, *Les Papes d'Avignon* (9th ed. Paris 1950), Eng. tr. J. LOVE (New York 1963). L. PASTOR, *History of the Popes,* tr. F. I. ANTROBUS et al., 40 v. (London 1936–61), various editions. M. CREIGHTON, *A History of the Papacy from the Great Schism to the Sack of Rome,* 6 v. (new ed. New York 1897), is still valuable. C. J. HEFELE, *Histoire des conciles,* ed. and tr. H. LECLERCQ, 10 v. (Paris 1907–13), 1911 has many useful notes.

Early Middle Ages. R. W. and A. J. CARLYLE, *A History of Mediaeval Political Theory in the West,* 6 v. (Edinburgh 1903–

36; repr. New York 1953). L. DUCHESNE, *Les Premiers temps de l'état pontifical* (3d ed. Paris 1912), Eng. tr. A. H. MATHEW (London 1908). Caspar. Latourette v.2. W. LEVISON, *England and the Continent in the Eighth Century* (Oxford 1946). F. DVORNIK, *The Making of Central and Eastern Europe* (London 1949). H. X. ARQUILLIÈRE, *L'Augustinisme politique* (2d ed. Paris 1955). W. ULLMANN, *The Growth of Papal Government in the Middle Ages* (2d ed. New York 1962).

Gregorian Reform. A. FLICHE, *La Réforme grégorienne,* 3 v. (Louvain 1924–37). Z. N. BROOKE, CMedH 5:51–166. Fournier-LeBras. J. P. WHITNEY, *Hildebrandine Essays* (Cambridge, Eng. 1932). H. X. ARQUILLIÈRE, *Saint Grégoire VII: Essai sur sa conception du pouvoir pontifical* (Paris 1934). StGreg.

12th Century. E. VACANDARD, *Vie de Saint Bernard,* 2 v. (Paris 1895; 3d ed. 1902). C. H. HASKINS, *The Renaissance of the Twelfth Century* (Cambridge, Mass. 1927; repr. 1933). G. PARÉ et al., *La Renaissance du XII*[e] *siècle: Les Écoles et l'enseignement* (Paris 1933). J. GUIRAUD, *Histoire de l'Inquisition au moyen-âge,* 2 v. (Paris 1935–38). H. RASHDALL, *The Universities of Europe in the Middle Ages,* ed. F. M. POWICKE and A. B. EMDEN, 3 v. (new ed. Oxford 1936). É. DE MOREAU, *Histoire de l'Église en Belgique* (2d ed. Brussels 1945–). J. F. LEMARIGNIER et al., *Institutions ecclésiastiques,* v.3 of *Histoire des institutions françaises au moyen-âge,* ed. F. LOT and R. FAWTIER (Paris 1957–). J. LECLERCQ et al., *Histoire de la spiritualité chrétienne,* v.2 (Paris 1961). H. C. LEA, *The Inquisition of the Middle Ages,* with introd. by W. ULLMANN (London 1963).

13th Century. A. LUCHAIRE, *Innocent III,* 6 v. (Paris 1906–08), a classic, but a political, not a religious study; supplement with Fliche-Martin v.10 (1950). H. GRUNDMANN, *Religiöse Bewegungen im Mittelalter* (2d ed. Hildesheim 1961); "Neue Beiträge zur Geschichte der religiösen Bewegungen im Mittelalter," *Archiv für Kulturgeschichte* 37 (1955) 129–182. G. BARRACLOUGH, *Papal Provisions* (Oxford 1935). M. H. VICAIRE, *Saint Dominic and His Times,* tr. K. POND (New York 1965).

14th Century. N. VALOIS, *La France et le grand schisme d'Occident,* 4 v. (Paris 1896–1902). J. HALLER, *Papsttum und Kirchenreform* (Berlin 1903). J. RIVIÈRE, *Le Problème de l'église et de l'état au temps de Philippe le Bel* (Paris 1926). W. E. LUNT, *Papal Revenues in the Middle Ages,* 2 v. (New York 1934); *Financial Relations of the Papacy with England,* 2 v. (Cambridge, Mass. 1939–62). B. TIERNEY, *Foundations of the Conciliar Theory* (Cambridge, Eng. 1955). G. DE LAGARDE, *La Naissance de l'esprit laïque au déclin du moyen-âge,* 5 v. (new ed. Louvain 1956–63).

15th Century. P. IMBART DE LA TOUR, *Les Origines de la Réforme,* 4 v. (Paris 1905–35) v.2, re-ed. Y. LANHERS (Melun 1946). N. VALOIS, *Le Pape et le Concile, 1418–1450,* 2 v. (Paris 1909). V. MARTIN, *Les Origines du gallicanisme,* 2 v. (Paris 1939). A. RENAUDET, *Préréforme et humanisme à Paris* (2d ed. Paris 1953). Jedin Trent v.1. J. LORTZ, *Die Reformation in Deutschland,* 2 v. (4th ed. Freiburg 1962), Fr. tr. (Paris 1956). J. GILL, *The Council of Florence* (Cambridge, Eng. 1959). **Illustration credits:** Fig. 1, Biblioteca Apostolica Vaticana. Fig. 2, National Gallery of Art, Washington, D.C., Rosenwald Collection.

[M. D. KNOWLES]

CHURCH, HISTORY OF, III (EARLY MODERN: 1500–1789)

In the early modern age, the Church faced the gravest crisis it had yet experienced in the West, the Protestant *Reformation. After suffering the loss of a considerable part of Europe, Catholicism managed by a great effort of self-reform to emerge strengthened and purified of many of the abuses that had in part caused and furthered *Protestantism. The new energies were used in answering the missionary challenges posed by Africa, Asia, and the Americas, in consolidating the position of the Church in those parts of Europe that had remained within the old unity, in quelling grave theological quarrels within its own fold, and in maintaining the Church's autonomy within absolutistic European states. Before the end of this period, the Church was faced with yet a new challenge, the rise of disbelief and secularism. The following survey will be divided into two periods: the first (1500–1648) will treat of the Protestant Reformation, the *Counter Reformation, Catholicism within the various European nations, and the missionary expansion of the Church; the second period (1648–1789) will treat of the internal theological problems and Church-State quarrels, and the situation of the Church throughout the world at the end of the *ancien régime.*

THE CHURCH, 1500 TO 1648

Although certain movements and currents of thought, while more prominent in one period, are common to both the first and the second period, the end of the *Thirty Years' War does mark in many respects a turning point in the history of the Church, for by 1648 both the Reformation and the Counter Reformation ceased to win any large number of new adherents.

Eve of the Reformation. The general situation of the Church on the eve of the Reformation was one of seeming great prestige and power but of internal apathy and hollowness. The cry for reform in head and members had not been satisfactorily heeded. The papacy had suffered a grievous loss of prestige in the period at Avignon and in the Great Schism. By 1500 the popes seemed to be more Renaissance princelings than spiritual fathers of Christendom. While, as rulers of an Italian state, they were necessarily concerned with the independence and government of their territories, the temptation to use the papacy to advance their families was too often overwhelming. In *Alexander VI (1462–1503), *Julius II (1503–13), and *Leo X (1513–21), the Church had successively at its head a man of immoral private life, a warrior, and a pleasure-seeker. The tone of the papal court may be judged by the attempt on the life of Leo X in 1517 in which some of his own cardinals were involved. The reputation of the Roman *Curia for rapaciousness at the expense of the Christian flock was of long standing. Absenteeism, pluralism, and lack of pastoral interest characterized the episcopacy in varying degrees; the same was true of other members of the upper clergy (e.g., the canons and the pastors of wealthy parishes). The lower clergy suffered above all from inadequate spiritual, intellectual, and moral formation, which often resulted in ignorance of even basic Christian doctrine and in the growth of concubinage. In the religious orders, despite the existence of some exemplary reformed cloisters, apathy and spiritual torpor appeared to be dominant. Although the devout Christian laity still followed their appointed leaders, the abuses and excessive privileges of the clergy were fostering an anticlericalism, which, while not new, was growing. A dessicated theology remote from pastoral concerns, an externalism in sacramental practice, and a proliferation of devotional practices often peripheral to the central message of Christianity were component parts of the spiritual malaise that gripped the Church. A spiritual hunger was felt—unconsciously by some, consciously by the more educated clerics and laymen—for the spiritual treasures of the Sacred Scriptures and for a theology and practice of the Sacraments centered upon their nature as signs of faith and sources of grace for the Christian community. The Reformers seemed to many to provide the answer to their longing for a deeply thought and lived Christianity. But when the new formulations denied or excluded part of divinely entrusted teaching, the Church could only reject those theses of Protestantism that it felt were a narrowing down or impoverishment of the riches of the Christian message. If the Reformers rediscovered

Religious divisions of Europe in the 17th century.

basic Christian principles hidden in what was without doubt a dry, decadent, and tired scholasticism, their formulations of these were outside the central stream of Christian tradition and were linked with denials of other doctrines and practices that formed an inseparable part of the inheritance of both the Eastern and the Western Churches.

The Reformation. The Reformation took four main forms: *Lutheranism, *Calvinism, Radicalism, and *Anglicanism.

Lutheranism. The Lutheran Reformation, which spread from Saxony throughout much of Germany and into the Scandinavian and Baltic lands, was the result of an Augustinian monk's struggle to find peace of soul for a conscience tortured by doubts about salvation. Martin *Luther, in his reading of St. Paul, felt that he had discovered the absolutely central truth of Christianity, viz, that God forgives man his sins or justifies him by faith alone without any other activity on man's part (*see* JUSTIFICATION, 3). In other words, only God is active in the process of salvation; man's only reply, which has bearing upon his salvation, is his faith in his Redeemer, Jesus Christ. Good works are the fruit of justification, but are of no avail to salvation. The exclusiveness of this formulation, which had necessarily to rule out free will, forced the Church to reject it. While the Lutheran churches in varying degrees conserved more of ancient practices than the Calvinist and Radical, other denials also made the Lutheran answer impossible for the Church to accept. The hierarchical constitution of the Church was rejected. All Christians were to be considered priests without distinction. Scripture alone was to be the rule of faith without an authoritative interpreter. The Sacraments were reduced to two, Baptism and the Eucharist, while both the sacrificial character of the Mass was denied and an already rejected theory of the Eucharistic presence was introduced, that of consubstantiation.

Calvinism. The Calvinist Reformation, which spread from Switzerland to France, the Low Countries, and parts of Germany, England, and Scotland, derived from the Lutheran and a somewhat more radical type of reform that had been taking place in certain southern German and especially Swiss cities. In Switzerland the chief early leader of this radical reform was *Zwingli in Zurich. John *Calvin, a Frenchman, who became the reformer of Geneva, accepted the cardinal doctrines of Luther: justification by faith alone and the all-sufficiency of Sacred Scripture, but he presented them in a more highly organized and systematic form and shifted the emphasis from the forgiveness of the sinning creature to the transcendency of the forgiving God. Calvinism required a far more austere way of life and worship than Lutheranism. The rejections of traditional Catholic doctrine were the same as those of Luther, while the rejection of traditional Catholic practices were more radical than those of Luther, who was willing to retain such of them as did not violate the doctrine of justification by faith alone. In one doctrinal respect, the manner of the Eucharistic presence, Calvinism differed irreconcilably from Lutheranism. While Luther steadfastly maintained the reality of Christ's presence in the Eucharist through consubstantiation, Calvin admitted only a presence of Christ in the believing communicant.

The Radical Reformation. The Radical Reformation is a term used to designate various sectarian movements that arose after the beginning of the Lutheran Reformation. No single doctrine characterized the adherents of the many, sometimes tiny, groups who are called radical, but rather they manifest a tendency to go farther than Lutheranism or Calvinism. The Low Countries, Germany, Bohemia, and Poland were the main centers. Three subjects especially interested the radical: the Eucharistic presence, which some interpreted as purely symbolic (*Sacramentarians); infant baptism, which some rejected (*Anabaptists or *Baptists); and the Incarnation, which some denied (*Socinians, *Unitarians). These movements, always small, were mostly suppressed by both Catholics and Protestants, but some few of them survived the Reformation era or were later revived.

Anglicanism. The Anglican Reformation, which was confined to the British Isles, differs in many respects from the Continental Reformation. In England, rather than a theological leader such as Luther or Calvin, it was more the monarch and parliament who defined the shape and form of the new ecclesiastical structure. Under *Henry VIII the English Church was separated from Rome, but Catholic practice and doctrine were retained almost without alteration. During the short reign of his son, Edward VI, liturgy and doctrine were, however, altered in a Protestant sense. Following the also brief reign of *Mary Tudor, during which the ties with Rome were restored, the definitive establishment of a church comprising both Catholic and Protestant elements was accomplished by and under *Elizabeth I. The uniqueness of Anglicanism lay in this attempt to synthesize Protestantism and much of the old Catholic tradition. Only the Anglican Church has, besides the confession of faith of the *Thirty-Nine Articles, a liturgical book, the Book of *Common Prayer, as the basis for its beliefs. The Prayer Book is essentially a combined Breviary, Missal, and ritual, retaining many Catholic practices but with Protestant elements, especially in connection with the Eucharist and the Eucharistic service. The Thirty-Nine Articles are an attempt to fuse Catholic and Protestant doctrines in formulations broad enough to be acceptable to both. The Eucharistic service of the Prayer Book eliminated reference to its sacrificial character. Those who wished a more profound Protestantization in the Calvinist sense eventually became known as *Puritans and managed briefly in the 17th century to gain political and ecclesiastical power. Those who wished to remain fully Catholic were reduced to a tiny persecuted minority compromised in their political allegiance by the futile attempt of *Pius V to depose Queen Elizabeth. By severing its link with Rome, the English Church broke communion with the Catholic Church.

Thus, despite the rich scriptural piety of the Lutherans and their warm devotion to their Savior, the profound awe before the transcendent God and the austere sobriety of life of the Calvinists, the traditionalism and sober piety of the Anglicans, and the commitment to a totally Christian life of some of the radical Protestants, the Church had necessarily to oppose Protestantism and to attempt to answer Protestant negations.

The Catholic Reaction. In the beginning the reply to Protestantism was a defensive reaction. Basic tenets of Lutheran doctrine were solemnly condemned by the papal bull *Exsurge, Domine* (1520). In the previous year the Universities of Cologne and Louvain had issued condemnations, as did the Sorbonne in 1521. In reply to the flood of Lutheran publications, scores of Catholic theologians entered the fray to publish refutations. The quality of these works was quite uneven. Luther and his followers had the advantage of promoting a new movement that promised a long-awaited reform. The Catholic theologians, none of whom had the theological and literary genius of Luther, seemed to be defending the *status quo.* Moreover, until the Council of *Trent, there was, at least on certain points, some confusion as to what was the traditional Catholic position. Nevertheless a great deal of preparatory work, which was later to prove valuable at Trent, was done by these theologians, not only in Germany but throughout Europe. In Germany there were such men as Johann *Eck, one of Luther's first and most passionate opponents; Johannes *Cochlaeus, responsible for a Catholic view of Luther enduring for centuries; the erudite Johannes Fabri of Vienna; the humanistic catechist Frederich *Nausea, and many others, especially among members of the religious orders. At Louvain, Luther, by his own admission, found his most powerful opponent in Jacobus *Latomus. Elsewhere in Europe also much was written against the new doctrines. In England, for example, ironically Henry VIII, as well as John *Fisher and Thomas *More, wrote against Luther. Out of hundreds only a few additional names can be mentioned, such as Alfonso de Castro (Spain), Josse *Clichtove (France), and Ambrose Catharinus (Italy). If the work of these men, often quite unappreciated in its time, in defending Catholic doctrine was flawed by anything, it was that they were speaking as individuals without the authority of the entire Church. Only an ecumenical council would at that time be heeded as speaking with the necessary authority, but such a council required convocation by the Pope. For too long, the papacy hesitated to call a council mainly because it feared a resurgence of *conciliarism.

The Convoking of a Council. After the brief pontificate of the last non-Italian pope, Adrian VI (1522–23), one of the rare high prelates to admit the responsibility of the Church for the rupture of religious unity, *Clement VII (1523–34) ascended the papal throne. An indecisive pope, his fear of conciliarism, of the Emperor *Charles V, and of a possible deposition because of his illegitimate birth caused him to refuse to summon the council that Christendom was clamoring for. His successor *Paul III (1534–49), while guilty of lavish *nepotism and not himself a reformer, nevertheless by his encouragement of reforms of the religious orders, by his nomination of reform-minded cardinals, and above all by successfully bringing the Council of Trent into being, effectively if belatedly placed the papacy behind the movement of Catholic reform.

It was not easy to convoke a council in a period of warfare between France and the Empire and of threatening war within the Empire itself. Attempts to convoke a council at Mantua and Vicenza failed. Moreover, in the 1540s the Emperor decided to attempt to seek his own religious agreement in Germany by means of theological conversations. These failed because the theological rift proved to be too deep. Moreover, political considerations were involved, and neither side seems really to have believed in the sincerity of the other. To Catholics, Protestants were obstinate formal heretics and the despoilers of the goods of the Church; to Protestants, Catholics were the defenders of corrupt doctrine and of entrenched abuses and interests. The meager, unwilling, brief, and fruitless appearance of Protestants at Trent in 1552 manifested their view that the demands for a free council on German soil had not been met. By a "free" council the Protestants meant one free of papal control. This demand could not be granted. Trent, however, the city where most of the council was held, was in fact part of the Empire. While the popes never appeared personally at the council, they presided through legates over its sessions, during which, it should be noted, debate was free.

The Council of Trent. The Council of Trent met in three periods separated by suspensions under three different popes. The first period (1545–48), under Paul III, produced the Catholic reply to the most profound doctrinal problem that the Reformers had raised, the manner of man's justification, along with decrees on the canonical Scriptures, the Vulgate, and original sin. It had been decided to treat reform and doctrine *pari passu* as a compromise to satisfy the curialist party, who wished to treat only of doctrine, and the imperialist party (that is, those bishops subject to the Emperor, whether German, Spanish, or Italian), who wished to treat only of reform. The latter feared to further alienate the Protestants. If the reform decrees at times were timid, it should be remembered that the papacy felt that the reform of the Curia was its prerogative. Moreover, what seemed to be abuses to some were viewed as legitimate exceptions to law by others. After treating the Sacraments in general, the Council was transferred to Bologna by the legates in 1547, partly because of an outbreak of a contagious fever at Trent and partly because of the desire of the papacy to have the council more under its control. Some of the imperialist bishops protested and refused to follow. Though the council discussed future decrees on the Sacraments at Bologna, no promulgations were made before it was suspended in 1549.

*Julius III (1550–55) reconvoked the Council of Trent for its second period (1551–52), during which decrees on the Sacraments were promulgated, including the Catholic doctrine on the manner of the Eucharistic presence. The outbreak of war in the Empire caused the suspension of the Council in 1552. After the 3-week reign of Pope Marcellus II (1555), the fiery, reform-minded *Paul IV (1555–59) succeeded to the papal throne. Wanting in moderation, jealous of papal power, and too ready to brand innocent men as heretics, he refused to summon the council back into session. After his fortunately brief reign, a pope favorable to reform through the council, *Pius IV (1559–64), was elected. Pius IV brought the last period of the council (1562–63) to a successful conclusion and confirmed its decrees. Through his extremely able legate, G. *Morone, the Council was enabled to surmount its final and most dangerous crisis, which had been brought about by the tensions between the curialist and imperialist parties, to whom were added also in this last session the French. Doctrinally, the most important decisions of these sessions concerned the sacrificial character of the Mass. From the standpoint of discipline the greatest achievement was the creation of a system of schools (seminaries) for the moral, intellectual, and spiritual formation of diocesan priests.

The Council of Trent furnished in the doctrinal order a much needed clarification of the divine economy of salvation in its decrees on original sin, justification, the Sacraments, and the Mass. A positive body of doctrine was thus created that would not only answer Protestant denials but also set the tone for Catholic theology, spirituality, and even culture for the succeeding centuries. If certain lines were drawn concerning Catholic belief, nevertheless the possibility of future discussions of doctrine even on the above-mentioned topics was not ruled out. The failure of the council to mention any of the Protestant Reformers by name has been taken to indicate that it did not wish to rule out the possibility of future conversations. The disciplinary reforms were somewhat disjointed in form and incomplete, but still a model of the ideal pastor, both bishop and priest, was provided, which would be imitated gradually but with increasing effectiveness. The institution of seminaries was of the highest importance in the achievement of this end.

Catholic Reform. Not all reform in the Church, however, was due to Trent. A movement of self-reform reaching back into the Middle Ages had been growing steadily even before the Reformation and without reference to it. It was especially concentrated in Spain and Italy. In Spain its early leaders were the Archbishop of Granada, Fernando de Talavera y Mendoza (1428–1507), and the Cardinal-Archbishop of Toledo, Francisco *Ximénez de Cisneros (1436–1517). In Italy, before and independently of the Reformation, groups of priests interested in self-reform and more zealous pastoral care had been arising here and there. Of this type was the Roman confraternity, the Oratory of *Divine Love, which was founded some years before the outbreak of the Reformation and which became a seed-bed of future Catholic reformers. Some of these groups developed into new societies of clerics regular, such as the *Theatines (1524), founded by St. Cajetan of Tiene and others, including the future Paul IV; the *Barnabites, founded by St. Antonio Maria Zaccaria (1530); and finally the *Somaschi, founded by St. Jerome Emiliani (1540). The important educational order of nuns, the *Ursulines, was founded by St. Angela Merici and approved by Paul III (1544). There were also a number of reforming bishops in Italy, of whom the most outstanding was Gian Matteo *Giberti of Verona (1495–1543). The number of reforming bishops grew after Trent.

The Jesuits. While the *Jesuits are often identified with the Counter Reformation, that is, the militant Catholicism of the post-Tridentine Church, their roots are fully in the earlier Catholic movement of self-reform. In fact, the spirituality and structure of the society were developed in complete independence of the struggle against Protestantism. Beginning as a group of pilgrims to the Holy Land gathered around Ignatius of Loyola as their leader, the first Jesuits had put themselves at the disposition of the Pope. After the pilgrimage had proved impossible and they had come into contact with the new clerics regular in northern Italy, a religious society called the Company of Jesus was developed by Ignatius and approved by Paul III in 1540. The originality of the new group did not consist only in its distinctive *Ignatian spirituality, with its emphasis on a considered commitment to Christ, or in the mobility of the society, with its revolutionary dispensation from Divine Office in choir. It was both the paramilitary character with which its soldier-founder endowed the society and, above all, the very close link between the order and the papacy that were new. The Jesuits were to be the spiritual soldiers of the papacy, tied by bonds of unquestioning obedience to the pope. Since the members were bound to observe poverty and not to seek ecclesiastical preferment, the papacy had at its disposal an increasingly vast international body of selfless supporters. When they defended the papacy they could not be accused of furthering their own personal interests—an accusation that had been raised, not always unjustly, against the curialists and others. Thus, in an age when the papacy was both denied and discredited, the Jesuits were an example of unselfish devotion to the primacy of Peter.

While the Jesuits, whose growth was extraordinary, began as part of the movement of Catholic internal reform, and while their widespread missionary activities were of great importance, they came soon to be associated with the Counter Reformation. In Germany St. Peter *Canisius (1521–97) through his diplomatic activity, his example and preaching, his catechisms, and above all through the foundation of colleges, aided immeasurably the revival of Catholicism there. In the face of the widespread decay of the universities, which until the second half of the 17th century did not flourish in Catholic countries as they had in medieval times (except briefly in Spain), the Jesuit school system was of great importance in maintaining to some degree the prestige of Catholic intellectual activity. But while the Jesuit colleges developed an estimable form of Christian humanism, though not without borrowing something from the similar tendencies of renaissance humanism and *Melanchthon, their openness to new subjects of study was timid. The higher education given by the Jesuits was exclusively for those entering the priesthood. The Catholic universities, perhaps recoiling from the fact that the Reformation had been in some measure the creation of academicians, remained closed to subjects of secular interests and either died of atrophy or became ultimately the secular universities of the modern world. Within this period then, until the advent of the teaching brothers, a high quality of teaching was not to be found in the universities but rather in the colleges of the Jesuits, in the houses of study of religious orders, and especially in the seminaries in France, which were highly successful in elevating the standards of the clergy.

Reforms in Religious Orders. In addition to completely new religious orders, the Catholic reform brought about a number of revivals in the older orders, which occasionally led to the foundation of new branches of congregations. A strict new congregation of the *Camaldolese Benedictines was founded by Paolo Giustiani (1476–1528). The generals of the *Augustinians, *Giles of Viterbo and especially Girolamo *Seripando, were both reformers of their order. The *Franciscans, the target of much pre-Reformation and Reformation satire, were hampered in their attempts to reform by fears of yet another split in the order, which was already divided into two branches—the Conventuals and the Observants. In a fresh attempt to return to the spirit of St. Francis, a third branch, the Capuchins, came into existence and thrived, despite the handicaps of a founder, Matteo da *Bascio (*ca.* 1495–1552), who left his new foundation, and of a fourth vicar-general, Bernadino *Ochino (1497–1564), who became a Protestant. The Capuchins were officially separated from the Conventuals in 1619. Under the aegis of *Teresa of Avila (1515–82), a new reformed branch of the *Carmelites, the Discalced, was formed both for women and for men [St. *John of the Cross (1542–91)]. Gradually reforms were brought about in the other orders.

Reforming Popes. The papacy of the period immediately after Trent produced three strong figures, *Pius V, *Gregory XIII, and *Sixtus V, who all aided in accelerating the rate of the centralization of Church government. This trend was not new, but it received additional force from the critical situation in which the Church found itself. Pius V (1566–72), the first saintly pope of the modern era, reformed the college of cardinals, the Curia, and the religious orders, and was also the first pope belonging completely to the age of the Counter Reformation. Such anachronistic gestures as the attempted deposition of Elizabeth I of England, however, were ultimately harmful. The milder Gregory XIII (1572–85) furthered the Jesuits, the missions, education (especially priestly), and both the Catholic internal reform and the Counter Reformation. To him the Gregorian calendar is due, and also an increase in the number of permanent papal diplomatic missions. The most important reorganization of the Curia, however, took place under Sixtus V (1585–90). In 1588 the cardinals were organized into 15 congregations, some concerned with the government of the papal states, others with the government of the entire Church. The Congregation of the Roman and Universal Inquisition (renamed Congregation for the *Doctrine of the Faith, 1965), which had originated in 1542 under Paul III as a commission of cardinals, achieved its final form at this time. New regulations for the *ad limina visits and reports of bishops, another step in the increasing centralization of the Church, were issued in this pontificate. Sixtus also effected a number of reforms in the papal states and may be called the father of Rome as a baroque city.

Papal Decline. The lesser figures who occupied the papal throne until the middle of the 17th century were characterized by their interest in the beautification of Rome and in the government of the papal states. Nepotism on the part of the popes themselves was not absent, nor were curial abuses. The longer reigns were those of *Clement VIII (1592–1605), *Paul V (1605–21), *Urban VIII (1623–44), and *Innocent X (1644–55). Just as the last major papal attempt to declare a monarch deposed had been unsuccessfully made under Pius V, so also under Paul V a last and equally ineffective attempt was made to place an entire state, Venice, under interdict. Further grave Church-State conflicts were soon to come, but even before them the political weakness of the papacy became more evident. Thus, Innocent X's protest against the religious provisions of the Peace of *Westphalia went unheard.

Outside the papal states in this period, the rest of Italy was also generally in political and economic decline, with part of the country under Spanish rule (Naples, Sicily, Milan, and Sardinia). Ecclesiastically, however, the decrees of Trent were accepted in the various states, and reforms were carried out both within the religious orders and by reforming bishops. One of the most striking of these last was Charles *Borromeo (1538–84), the reformer of the See of Milan. A nephew of Pius IV, he was one of the rare examples of a happy outcome of nepotism.

The Wars of Religion. If Italy remained in relative peace during the last half of the 16th and the first half of the 17th centuries, much of the rest of Europe was involved in the wars often called (somewhat incorrectly) the *wars of religion, including those in France, the revolt of the Spanish Netherlands, and the Thirty Years' War.

France. In France the wars of religion (1562–98) were really a series of eight small wars divided by truces and periods of peace. The principal and original cause was the struggle for and against Calvinism, but such motives as the dynastic question, the struggle between feudal conceptions of the monarchy and an absolutist, centralizing view, and foreign intervention come to play important roles also. With the acceptance of Catholicism by *Henry IV, the issuance of the Edict of *Nantes (1598) specifying the conditions for the coexistence in France of Protestant communities and Catholicism, and the peace with Spain (Vervins 1598), order was reestablished in France. The effect of the wars, however, was to put off the necessary internal Catholic reform. While the French government refused to accept officially the decrees of Trent, the doctrinal decrees were accepted by all without question. Despite the high degree of control over the Church that the Concordat of 1516 gave the French monarchy, many reforms were effected, especially through the influence of such saintly men as *Francis de Sales (1567–1622), Pierre de *Bérulle (1575–1629), Charles de *Condren (1588–1641), Jean Jacques *Olier (1608–41), John *Eudes (1601–80), and *Vincent de Paul (1581–1660). All of these fostered the moral, spiritual, and intellectual training of priests, especially through the new system of seminaries.

Revolt of the Spanish Netherlands. The revolt of the Spanish Netherlands is sometimes classed as a religious war between the Dutch, who were principally Calvinists, and Catholic Spain. The desire of the Dutch, however, to shake off the political and economic domination of a foreign power was equally important. In Spain itself the excessive control of the Church by the state in a period when the monarchy was entering a time of continual degeneration could scarcely encourage the religious revival that had begun with Ximenes. Spanish missionary activity, on the other hand, continued to flourish.

The Thirty Years' War. The third great religious war, the Thirty Years' War (1618–48), was fought principally on the territory of the Empire. While religious causes, especially the law that forbade the secularizing of ecclesiastical property, were not absent, political causes were or became the major factors. At the end of the war Catholic France was fighting with Lutheran Sweden against the Catholic Emperor. The Peace of Westphalia, so unsatisfactory to the papacy, marked the end of the Counter Reformation considered as an attempt to regain territories lost to Protestantism. It also marked the end of any large shifts of allegiance from one religious body to the other. When, somewhat later, the Electors of Saxony wished to be elected also Kings of Poland, they became Catholic, but their Saxon subjects remained Lutheran, and their Polish subjects remained Catholic.

Catholicism in the British Isles. In the British Isles the dwindling persecuted Catholic minority suffered not only because they refused to accept Anglicanism but also because they were accused of political disloyalty. Their lot was aggravated by the fact that England's chief foreign enemy was Catholic Spain. After the death of Elizabeth, under Mary Stuart's son *James I (1603–25), who had been raised a Protestant, the situation of Catholics did not improve, but their treatment under Charles I (1625–49) was slightly milder. The Civil War, however, brought in the Protector, Oliver *Cromwell, a much more determined opponent of Catholicism than the Tudor or Stuart monarchs. Catholics in Scotland, which was united to England in personal union from 1603, fared no better, but a small number survived as in England. In Ireland, completely under English rule from 1602, despite persecution under extremely severe penal laws, and apart from the plantations, almost the entire population remained faithful to Catholicism.

Catholicism in Eastern Europe. In Eastern Europe the Catholic reform was introduced gradually. The religious situation of Poland mirrored the confused political order, but under the aegis of Cardinal Stanislas *Hosius (1504–79) and the Jesuits, a strong Catholic revival took place toward the end of the 16th and the beginning of the 17th century. An important reunion of Eastern Christians, the Ruthenians, was effected by the Union of *Brest (1595–96) and also by the Union of Užhorod (1646). In Hungary the Catholic reform and Counter Reformation were fostered especially by Cardinal Peter *Pázmány (1570–1637).

Missionary Activity. The enthusiastic missionary activity of the 16th and 17th centuries was paralleled only by the preaching of the gospel in the first centuries. The impetus to this revived activity came from the explorations and discoveries that had begun in the 15th century. Of the newly discovered lands, or the hitherto scarcely known lands, including North and South America, the East and Far East, only Africa remained largely untouched by the missionaries, whose activities Rome began to coordinate (from 1622) under the Congregation for the *Propagation of the Faith. An essential difference between the evangelization of the Western and the Eastern worlds was the fact that in North and South America, the missionaries, mostly members of the new and old religious orders, accompanied Spanish and Portuguese conquerors and colonists, whereas in the East the missionaries, also chiefly from the religious orders, sought to evangelize old established civilizations. This occasioned two quite different methods. In the New World, the old existing civilizations were destroyed, and in most of South and Central America an Iberian cultural and ecclesiastical order was established. Thus the first see, *Santo Domingo, was established in 1511, and by 1582 there were 15 more. The missionaries fought with varying degrees of success to prevent the exploitation of the natives by their own countrymen. In *Paraguay, the Jesuits organized model communities (*reductions) of native Christians. Eventually governmental opposition and an excessive paternalism caused these experiments to fail. The greatest single weakness of the Spanish and Portuguese missionary effort in Central and South America was the failure to foresee early the need for a native clergy. Consequently, in the 18th century there was a dearth of clergy and a decline of missionary zeal, although evangelization did not cease completely (e.g., *California).

In the East and the Far East, the missionaries faced different problems. There, after the early heroic exploits of St. Francis *Xavier in India, China, and Japan, a number of missionaries, especially Matteo *Ricci, J. Adam *Schall, and Roberto de *Nobili, began to propose the adaptation of Christianity to certain of the cultural and intellectual features of the centuries-old civilizations of China and India. Other missionaries violently opposed such accommodations, and the problem was referred to Rome (*see* CHINESE RITES CONTROVERSY). For nearly a century it was debated until the last disapproval of adaptation was given by Rome in 1742. Interorder rivalries and national interests had envenomed the quarrels. Along with the already-noted decline of missionary fervor in the 18th century, the outcome of the rites controversy marked the virtual end of missionary activity in the East until the 19th century. The Philippines, a Spanish possession, however, presented an exception. The attempt to Christianize Japan had failed even before the rites controversy. There violent persecutions (1614–46) almost completely destroyed the missionaries' efforts, although small secret groups of Christians (Old Christians) continued on without priests. A final and lamentable result of the rites controversy was that it, along with the other grave theological dissensions, helped to discredit Christianity among the intellectual classes during the late 17th and the 18th century.

The European Church, 1648–1789

The history of the Church in the century and a half before the French Revolution is dominated by a series of dissensions on doctrinal matters within the Church, above all the quarrels over *Jansenism, *Quietism, and *Febronianism, and of dissensions between the papacy and the Catholic states, principally over *Gallicanism, *Josephinism, and the suppression of the *Jesuits. These quarrels contributed to the profoundly weakened state and seeming apathy of the Church at the end of the *ancien régime,* with whose fate its own seemed inexorably bound. It was not until the 19th and 20th centuries that the Church recovered its vigor both in thought and action.

Theology and Theological Quarrels. The trends and schools of theology from the 16th century on become exceedingly diverse. Whereas the medieval theologians had in the main been universal theologians, treating in their works of the whole of theology, later theologians became specialists in such recognized branches of theology as dogmatic or speculative, moral, ascetic, or positive. Although the traditional purely speculative method still was carried on by schoolmen such as *Báñez, *John of St. Thomas, and *Suárez, their efforts represented the work of theologians living to some degree in the past. The important new dimension in theology was the historical or positive theology, which derived from the methods of the humanists, such as *Erasmus. While an effort was made to integrate positive and speculative theology (e.g., Melchior *Cano), theology became quite fragmentized, and no theologian of the status of the great patristic and medieval theologians emerged to produce a new synthesis. The interest in historical theology had results important for the growth of the historical sciences both ecclesiastical and secular. In this regard, the work of the *Bollandists in hagiography and of the Benedictines of the Congregation of St. Maur are especially notable (*see* MAURISTS). In Biblical criticism, however, the work of Richard Simon, who was well ahead of his time, was condemned. Similarly, the condemnation of Galileo (*Galilei) implied a conflict between Christianity and science and had unfortunate consequences. The quarrel with Protestantism often brought forth only a defensive and negative theology; worse yet, internal theological quarrels exhausted the energies of the best theologians. These same quarrels were in no little part also responsible for the growth of disbelief and indifference to religion, which, in turn, presented new problems to the Church.

Jansenism. The gravest of these quarrels centered around the Augustinian doctrine of nature and grace and its practical applications. A theologian of Louvain, Cornelius *Jansen (1585–1638), and a French ecclesiastic, Jean *Duvergier de Hauranne (1581–1643), dreamed of a revival of patristic theology and practice beginning with the doctrine of grace. For them scholasticism and the humanistic theology of some Jesuit theologians were abhorrent, and Calvin had, in their view, grasped Augustine's teaching even if he expressed himself badly. Thus, Jansenism was in a sense a crypto-Calvinism. The Jansenists, however, never wished to leave the Church, but rather hoped to have their doctrine accepted by the Church or at least tolerated by it. This explains, in part, the persistence of Jansenism even into the 19th century. Jansen produced his great theoretical work of doctrine in the *Augustinus* (1640), published 2 years after his death.

Meanwhile, Duvergier de Hauranne, now abbot of Saint-Cyran, had spread enthusiasm for their views in France, especially into the large *Arnauld family, many of whom were or became religious and whose activities were centered around the Cistercian convents of Port-

Royal-des-Champs near Paris and *Port-Royal in Paris. Schools established by the Jansenists (*petites écoles*) fostered Jansenist doctrine, as well as new methods of pedagogy. Jansenism was almost immediately condemned by Rome, but the Jansenists, led by Antoine Arnauld (1612–94), refused to accept the condemnation as valid for what Jansen had actually taught and for what they actually held. An endless quarrel ensued about the right of the Church to judge and condemn error in a concrete case. The Jansenists admitted only a *de iure* right and denied that the condemned doctrine was *de facto* in Jansen's writings. A new leader, Pasquier *Quesnel (1634–1719), emerged toward the end of the 17th century. Repeated condemnations and harassments failed to drive Jansenism from the French Church, where it continued clandestinely until the 19th century. French Jansenism had always been more interested in the moral rigorism that seemed to follow from Jansen's thought rather than his doctrinal elaboration, and toward the end of its history Jansenism was more a symbol of protest against ecclesiastical and political authority than a theological doctrine. A still-existing schismatic church was founded as the result of the Jansenist quarrel at Utrecht in 1723 (*see* UTRECHT, SCHISM OF).

Quietism. The quarrel over Quietism was smaller and less grave than the Jansenist quarrel. The father of Quietism was a Spaniard resident in Italy, Miguel de *Molinos (1628–1717), although his thought was not entirely original. Molinos's *Spiritual Guide* (1675), translated into five languages, proposed a doctrine of total passivity in the face of divine action in the soul. Molinos was condemned and imprisoned, but similar ideas on the spiritual life were put forth by an unstable French woman, Mme. J. M. *Guyon. It was *Fénelon (later archbishop of Cambrai), however, who, having become Mme. Guyon's confessor, became the chief spokesman for Quietism in France. The touchstone of Quietism was the belief that the soul might reach such a state of pure love that not only would it be indifferent to its own perfections and the practices of virtue, but it might even cease to will its own salvation. This doctrine of the exclusive action of God on the soul has affinities with Luther's teaching, but Luther never drew the Quietist conclusions. Fénelon's doctrine, attacked by *Bossuet, was condemned by Rome in 1699. Although Fénelon submitted, he denied that he had preached the condemned teaching. Unlike Jansenism, Quietism died out immediately and completely. Both Jansenism and Quietism, however, indirectly encouraged the growth of disbelief by the public spectacles that had been made of doctrinal differences within the Church. As a result, even within the Church a certain mistrust of mystical tendencies became evident.

Febronianism. The dissatisfaction of some German ecclesiastics with papal centralization manifested itself in several ways in the 18th century. The most important of these was the work of an auxiliary bishop of Trèves, Johann Nikolaus von *Hontheim (1701–90). His work, published beginning in 1763 under the pseudonym of Febronius and often called simply the *Febronius*, foresaw a revival of conciliarism in an extreme form in which the papacy would be stripped of the powers that Hontheim claimed it had usurped. The *Febronius* was soon translated from Latin into other languages and achieved considerable popularity. It was condemned, and Hontheim retracted, but in a quite ambiguous manner. The work gave expression to the desire on the part of certain churchmen to be free from papal and curial control. In this it was not far removed from Gallicanism, which was, however, a political attempt to be free of these same controls.

Church-State Quarrels. This period witnessed a number of disagreements between the papacy and various Catholic states.

Gallicanism. The term Gallicanism is used to cover a number of theories of ecclesiastical government, all generally in various degrees hostile to or suspicious of Rome. All of these were present in France in the 17th century—from the purely ecclesiastical theories of authority vested in all the faithful or the clergy as a whole or the entire episcopate to political Gallicanism. The latter doctrine in its extreme form made the monarch in effect head of the Church in his country. In France it was the attempt by *Louis XIV to extend his powers over the Church, which led in the 1680s almost to schism. Louis, since about 1670, had been attempting to increase his already extensive regalian rights, both temporal and spiritual. Meeting some opposition, he inspired the calling of an extraordinary meeting of the general assembly of the clergy. While Bossuet's opening address on the unity of the Church was credited with avoiding a break with Rome, it was he who drew up the summary of Gallican doctrine called the Four Articles of 1682. Royal edict forced the acceptance of these on the French Church. For about 15 years the papacy refused to institute Louis's appointments to the French dioceses until a large number became vacant. Finally, concessions were made on both sides, but the monarchy gave up the prescribed acceptance of the Gallican Articles. Gallicanism, while partially defeated, did not, however, die out. The state church of the Revolution was the last attempt in France to give it concrete form.

Josephinism. Not unlike the policies of Louis XIV were those of the Hapsburg Emperor *Joseph II (1765–90) in his Austrian domains. Even his pious mother, *Maria Theresa, had, in fact, involved herself in strictly ecclesiastical matters. Moreover, due reforms were not effected by the ecclesiastical authorities themselves. In a certain sense, however, Joseph went further than Louis by attempting to make the Church a department of the state and above all by interfering in what were beyond question strictly ecclesiastical affairs, such as the curricula of seminaries, and even the liturgy. His attitude toward the Church was more than a little influenced by the *Enlightenment and enlightened despotism. An attempt by Pius VI in 1782 by a personal visit to Vienna to change the Emperor's views did not succeed. Joseph's brother Leopold, his successor briefly as emperor, attempted similar reforms in the Grand Duchy of Tuscany. The Jansenist Bishop S. *Ricci of Pistoia and Prato aided him, and a synod at Pistoia in 1786 drew up a list of reforms partly Jansenist, partly enlightened. The other Tuscan bishops refused, however, to follow Ricci.

While the failure to effect reforms was in part responsible for the lethargic situation of the Church in the Catholic countries in the 18th century, the method of reform proposed by the enlightened despots would have disastrously compromised the independence of the Church. The Constitutional Church of the French Revolution disintegrated when power was assumed by nonbelievers.

Suppression of the Jesuits. The most unhappy Church-State quarrel of the 18th century was the suppression of the Jesuits. Opposition to the Jesuits had arisen from many quarters—from the Jansenists, the Gallicans, and the thinkers and rulers of the Enlightenment. The Jesuits were accused, in most cases unjustly, of having acquired excessive power and wealth. They were, moreover, the religious society with the greatest loyalty to the papacy. They were suppressed by Portugal in 1759, France in 1764, and Spain in 1767, but the Catholic powers were not content until they obtained a complete suppression from Rome. This they succeeded in getting from *Clement XIV in 1773. Only in Russia did the society survive until its restoration in 1814.

The Papacy, 1648–1789. The political prestige of the papacy continued to decline in the period from 1648 to 1789. No longer were the popes arbiters in international disputes. Generally, in fact, they were excluded from the major international conferences. They failed also to supply the necessary leadership or to effect reforms in their own states. In the religious domain, on the other hand, they successfully resisted Jansenism and Quietism and restrained Gallicanism and Febronianism. In dealing with the enlightened despots and their followers, especially in the matter of the Jesuits, however, they failed. The most notable papal figures during this period were *Innocent XI (1676–89), *Benedict XIV (1740–58), and Pius VI (1775–99), who died a prisoner of the French.

Catholicism in Non-Catholic Lands. Generally speaking, the position of Catholics in Protestant lands improved somewhat during the 18th century. This was in part due to the Enlightenment with its ideal of tolerance. In the United Provinces, the existence of Catholics was tolerable although complicated by the Jansenist Church of Utrecht. In Scandinavia there were scarcely any Catholics except for a few, mostly foreigners, in Sweden. In Great Britain there was gradual progress toward greater toleration, but Catholics remained very few in number and still were not emancipated. Ireland also was beginning to progress toward emancipation (Relief Bill of 1778).

The Church Under the Old Regime. A brief survey of the situation of the Church in France on the eve of the Revolution offers a view of the virtues and failings of the Church in the Catholic lands. The struggle between Church and State had sunk from the level of the monarchy to quarrels between the Jansenist lawyers of the *Parlements* and the Church. The episcopacy, while not composed of unworthy men, was often nonresident and almost entirely drawn from the nobility. Most of the bishops were to leave France en masse when the Revolution threatened. The lower clergy, well-educated and often devoted, nevertheless resented their inability to rise in the ecclesiastical hierarchy. The monasteries had vast possessions but had experienced a sharp drop in vocations, and some were almost empty. The abuses of *commendation had continued. Among the laity, the educated classes were imbued with the spirit of the Enlightenment, and some had ceased to believe; the working classes, mostly still agrarian, remained for the most part attached to Catholicism.

Bibliography: Schottenloher. Jedin HbKirchgesch v.4, bibliog. Jedin Trent. CModH² v.2, 5, 7. Fliche-Martin v.16–19, bibliog. Pastor. J. LORTZ, *Die Reformation in Deutschland,* 2 v. (4th ed. Freiburg 1962). Hughes RE. J. T. MCNEILL, *The History and Character of Calvinism* (New York 1954). A. MARTIMORT, *Le Gallicanisme de Bossuet* (Paris 1953). J. ORCIBAL, *Les Origines du jansénisme,* 5 v. (Louvain 1947–62). G. SCHNÜRER, *Katholische Kirche und Kultur im Zeitalter des Barock* (Paderborn 1937); *Katholische Kirche und Kultur im 18. Jahrhundert* (Paderborn 1941). F. MAASS, ed., *Der Josephinismus: Quellen zu seiner Geschichte in Österreich, 1760–1850,* 5 v. (Fontes rerum Austriacarum II.71–75; Vienna 1951–61). Bihlmeyer-Tüchle, bibliog. Latourette v.3. H. TÜCHLE, *Reformation und Gegenreformation* (*Geschichte der Kirche* 3; Einsiedeln 1965). O. CHADWICK, *The Reformation* (The Pelican History of the Church 3; Baltimore 1964). G. R. CRAGG, *The Church and the Age of Reason: 1648–1789* (New York 1961; *ibid.* 4 in preparation). S. NEILL, *History of Christian Missions* (*ibid.* 6; 1964).

[W. S. BARRON]

CHURCH, HISTORY OF, IV (LATE MODERN: 1789–1965)

The Catholic Church has passed the most recent period of its life amid changes incomparably more numerous and diverse than human society has ever experienced in a similar span of time. These changes have been far-reaching in the political, social, and economic realms. Numerous branches of learning have advanced enormously. The natural sciences and technology have enjoyed unparalleled progress, immensely increasing man's knowledge of his environment and his control over it; this progress has continued at an accelerating rate. The industrial revolution, begun late in the 18th century in Great Britain, has spread over Western Europe and North America and over sections of other continents. The world's population has more than tripled and become urban and industrialized.

The impact of these transformations has varied widely in different sections of the world, but with the passage of time almost every corner of the earth has come to feel their force. Particularly strong has been the effect of these multitudinous developments on western Europe, for centuries Catholicism's main center. Directly or indirectly the Church has been much affected; it has found some external changes beneficial, others harmful. Western civilization, ever more secularized in its ideals and practices, has continued to drift farther and farther away from the Church that was largely instrumental in creating it and to which it had been intimately united for centuries. The problem of adjusting to the radically new conditions of civilization remains for the Church a major one. Never have the Church's enemies been as well organized, powerful, and determined. Throughout this entire period *persecutions have persisted, never more violent and destructive than in the 20th century. Despite this, indeed in good part because of it, the Church has become a more spiritual and more closely knit organization, under the unquestioned primacy of the popes. In civil society *nationalism swelled to ominous proportions; it has been extolled as a kind of religion, but its fruits have often been hatred and bloodshed. Ecclesiastical particularism, on the other hand, shrank to minimal proportions with the disappearance of Gallicanism, Febronianism, and Josephinism, which in the 18th century had been the bane of a Church that is of its nature one and universal. Inner threats to unity in the form of heresies and schisms were few and gained slender followings; they were not to be compared with the divisions of the 16th century. Religious indifferentism within the fold and leakage of individuals from it have, however, been sources of great concern. Counterbalancing these losses there have been great numerical gains as the Church spread to all corners of the world as the result of large-scale emigration from Catholic Europe and of unparalleled missionary activity.

The more important developments and the most characteristic trends are sketched here; no more is possible. Not all of these trends are universally applicable; the modern world is too complex. Church history no longer possesses the unity it had when it could confine itself to the Roman Empire, the limits of the early Church; or to western and central Europe, as in the Middle Ages. Into the 19th century, non-European sectors of the Church, mostly mission territories, were numerically of lesser importance, and their roles were minor. This has been decreasingly true, particularly of the Western Hemisphere. (For the ecclesiastical history of individual nations, see the articles on each country of the world.)

From 1789 to 1815. Relations between the spiritual and civil powers have provided a staple of ecclesiastical history since the Apostolic Age. This has been true also of the most recent age, although important changes in the nature of that relationship have appeared.

France has for centuries played a significant role in the Church's life, but never before or since has it monopolized the stage to the extent it did between the outbreak of the *French Revolution and the downfall of *Napoleon I. As a political and social upheaval, the Revolution was of major importance in world history; from the religious viewpoint it was scarcely of less moment for the Church, both in France and elsewhere. Fittingly, therefore, this event is selected as inaugurating a turning point in the Church's history. Enthusiastic support from the clerical members of the Estates-General was an important factor in the start of the Revolution. Quickly the Constitutional Assembly legislated the destruction of the *ancien régime,* one of whose main pillars was the Church. Nothing short of a revolution could have eradicated in so brief a spell the multitudinous abuses that had become deeply embedded in that venerable structure. The demolition process, insofar as it attacked the Church, involved many reprehensible actions, along with defensible ones. After abolishing clerical privileges, nationalizing Church properties, and suppressing religious orders, the Constitutional Assembly enacted the *Civil Constitution of the Clergy, which created a schism and split France religiously into two hostile camps. As time went on, leadership in the Revolution fell into the hands of men bitterly hostile to the Church, more intent on destroying than reforming it. An attempt was made to dechristianize the country by violent persecution, wholesale iconoclasm, reorganization of the calendar, imprisonment and deportation of the clergy, separation of Church and State, and propagation of a series of naturalistic, patriotic cults as substitutes for Christianity. As their crowning attack on religion, the revolutionists stripped Pope Pius VI of his temporal power, seized him, and marched him captive to southern France, where he died a prisoner.

Victorious Revolutionary armies swept into the Low Countries, Germany, Switzerland, and Italy, where they imposed the recent French innovations. Throughout the 19th century the aspirations of the Revolution kept spreading through Europe and the New World. The French Revolution afforded, then, a preview of what was in store for the Church. Reconciliation with the principles of 1789 posed for the Church a major problem that was not solved completely a century later. Even this span of years did not suffice to close the rift in French society opened during the revolutionary decade. The heirs of the great Revolution were the republicans, liberals, and anticlericals of the 19th century. Loyal Catholics tended to link democracy with godlessness; in good part their politics were conservative and monarchist. They resisted the *Ralliement and formed the backbone of *Action Française.

When Napoleon Bonaparte gained control of Revolutionary France, he turned it into a military dictatorship and an instrument of his boundless ambitions. After his military genius had subjected most of western Europe, he introduced into the conquered territories the ideology of the Revolution, whose devotee he claimed to be. Napoleon, a man of little or no Christian faith, utilized religion to promote his state policies. Since political considerations counseled the restoration of religious peace in France, he concluded with the Holy See the *Concordat of 1801, which regulated Church-State relations for a century, and which served as a model for numerous other concordats with other countries during the 19th century. Many of the benefits accorded to the Church by the Concordat of 1801 were withdrawn as soon as they were given, by Bonaparte's unilateral action in publishing the *Organic Articles. In Italy Napoleon arranged a concordat on similar terms. He was mainly responsible for the vast secularization of ecclesiastical territories in Germany. This impoverishment of the Church in Germany had the most melancholy results spiritually, economically, and intellectually, along with some unintended benefits. Had Napoleon attained his goals, Paris would have replaced Rome as the center of the Church and the pope would have become his chaplain. When the First Consul decided to become emperor, he humiliated Pius VII by forcing him to travel to Paris and then to attend the coronation ceremony in Notre Dame as a mere spectator, while the new Emperor broke with tradition and placed the crown on his own head. In retaliation for the Holy See's refusal to ally with France and to join the Continental Blockade, the Emperor seized the *States of the Church and held Pius VII captive (1809–14) until military reversals sent Bonaparte to exile in Elba.

Ecclesiastical Restoration. Following the Battle of Waterloo came a period of restoration for the Church, as well as for European governments. At the Congress of *Vienna, attended by Cardinal *Consalvi, the papal secretary of state, the victorious powers undertook to revive, as far as possible, the *ancien régime.* In their endeavor to stabilize conservative monarchical governments in power, they disposed of thrones and territories on the principle of legitimacy. Political considerations predominated; but the Church, particularly the papacy, became a major beneficiary. The statesmen at Vienna were well aware that the absolutist rulers who had weakened the Church in the 17th and 18th centuries had unwittingly undermined their own thrones in the process, as events after 1789 demonstrated. The conclusion was that throne and altar are best united. A much more benign attitude toward religion came into vogue. As a result, the allied powers that had watched unmoved when Pius VII was deprived of his temporal power and detained as a prisoner, decreed the return of most of the States of the Church. Not all the decisions at Vienna were of this tenor, to be sure. Catholic Belgium was united with Holland and subjected to the Protestant House of Orange. Most of Poland passed to Russia. German lay rulers, generally Protestants, were allowed to retain their recently acquired ecclesiastical principalities. Injurious as all this was to the Church locally, it worked to the ultimate advantage of the papacy.

In this changed atmosphere, Pius VII restored the Society of Jesus throughout the world in 1814, soon after his release from Fontainebleau; he was able to take this step without objection from the royal courts that had exerted strong pressure on Clement XIV to suppress the *Jesuits in 1773. The situation allowed the badly disrupted Church to reorganize itself in Europe and in the mission fields. It was very significant that the papacy, whose authority had been much weakened since the mid-17th century, took the lead in this process. From this point date the upswing in papal spiritual power, the pronounced trend toward centralization of ecclesiastical administrative power in Rome, and the unquestioned exercise of papal primacy of jurisdiction throughout the Church; these were among the most significant developments of the century. The *concordats and other less solemn agreements that were concluded by the Holy See were an important part of this reorganization.

Not surprisingly, the Church regarded the Restoration regime with favor, just as it had looked askance at the French Revolution and what it represented. The alliance of throne and altar had, however, serious disadvantages that became more apparent in succeeding decades. After 1815 the Church was identified in many minds with the reactionary Restoration; the reorganization of the States of the Church along the lines of the *ancien régime* did nothing to dispel this notion. *Metternich, the leading exponent of the political Restoration, hoped that this edifice would be an enduring one; yet revolutionary outbreaks in Latin America in the 1820s and in Europe in 1830 soon weakened its foundation. It could not withstand the explosions of nationalistic and constitutional furies of 1848, promoted by the liberals, to whom belonged the future.

Church and Liberalism. *Liberalism and its manifold relations with the Church provided main themes for 19th-century ecclesiastical history. Liberalism is a broad but vague term that defies precise definition; its connotations varied in different countries and in different decades. In general the liberal outlook favored a minimum of restrictions on individual liberty in private and public life and defended a maximum of freedom for the individual in his social, economic, and religious existence and in his relations to the state. This viewpoint was rooted in rationalism; it was based, therefore, on an ideology sharply at variance with the Catholic one. The liberals upheld the ideals of the French Revolution and abhorred those of the Restoration. The trend in the 19th century was toward constitutional regimes, popular sovereignty, broadening of the suffrage, complete religious liberty, equality for all citizens, abolition of established churches and of clerical privileges, separation of Church and State, and assumption by the government of functions formerly exercised by the Church. Thus the civil power came to claim control over marriage, charitable endeavors, public welfare, and education. The tendency was to view the Church as a society within the state, part of it and subject to it like other societies, inferior to the state even in the religious sphere. This trend found its strongest supporters among the liberals, who looked upon the Church's conservatism as a major obstacle to their victory. Religious and philosophical propositions fundamental to doctrinaire liberalism attracted the ire of the Church in the *Syllabus of Errors, **Quanta cura,* and other notable papal pronouncements (*see* CHURCH AND STATE).

A group of Catholic liberals (or democratic Catholics), particularly in France, quickly foresaw the perils to the Church in aligning itself with forces destined for proximate oblivion. Hugues Félicité de *Lamennais was the pioneer in seeking an accommodation with the new order developing out of the French Revolution. His program advocated freedom of education, of association, and of the press. Still more revolutionary to the Church of his day was his advocacy of complete religious liberty and complete separation of Church and State. Among his principal disciples, Lamennais counted *Gerbet, *Gousset, *Guéranger, *Lacordaire, *Montalembert, and *Rohrbacher. In some respects Lamennais was a man of accurate prophetic vision. Unfortunately he advanced his proposals in exaggerated fashion and mixed them with a good deal of unsound theology. The conservative *Gregory XVI solemnly condemned them in *Mirari vos* (1832) and *Singulari nos* (1834). In France the hierarchy and the majority of the laity sided with the Pope, and the cause of liberal Catholicism accordingly suffered a serious setback. But the Catholic pattern was not uniform everywhere. Thus, in Belgium, Catholics joined forces with liberals to win independence in 1830 and to draft a liberal constitution. Daniel *O'Connell, who led the successful struggle in Great Britain for Catholic *emancipation (1829), and who then started an unsuccessful drive to repeal Ireland's legislative union with England, represented a decidedly liberal outlook.

Liberals, drawing their strength mainly from the middle class, came to control several countries, particularly from mid-19th century to World War I. In Spain, Portugal, Italy, France, and Latin America their rule was hostile to the Church and characterized by *anticlericalism, sometimes of the most extreme type. In Germany, Austria, and Switzerland they supported the *Kulturkampf.

Political Organization of Catholics. A striking modern innovation has been the organization of Catholics for political purposes. The Catholic Association, started in Ireland by Daniel O'Connell to win emancipation, was a pioneer. With the growth of representative government and of political parties, along with the need for Catholics to band together to further their rights, Catholic political parties were formed in several western European countries, notably in Belgium, the Netherlands, France, Germany, Austria, Switzerland, and Italy. These groups were not always professedly confessional; this was true of the best known of them, the *Center party in Germany, which was succeeded after World War II by the Christian Democratic party. *Christian Democracy became more prominent after 1918. In France after 1945 the *Mouvement Républicaine Populaire became important (*see* POLITICAL PARTIES, CATHOLIC).

Political Developments Since 1918. Following World War I, a series of national and international political upheavals confronted the Church with new and delicate problems of the first magnitude to replace the ones associated with liberalism. Exaggerated nationalism was a major factor in the outbreak of two world conflicts a quarter of a century apart, separated by a great economic crisis, and followed by the division of the globe into two violently hostile ideological groups with an "iron curtain" between them and by the increasing importance and independence of non-Western peoples in Africa and Asia. Western Europe became less prominent in the Church, although the gradient of this descent by no means paralleled the steepness of the political, economic, and intellectual declines. Particularly significant was the rise of *fascism in Italy under Benito *Mussolini. This dictatorial regime laid to rest the Roman Question; yet it kept relations with the Holy See in a state of uneasy tension for 2 decades. *National Socialism, which came to power in 1933 under Adolf *Hitler, was much more hostile to religion ideologically and subjected the Church in Germany to severe persecution. More important for the Church in the long run has been the rise of socialism and communism.

Socialism and Communism. The spread of the industrial revolution, along with the shortcomings of prevailing liberalism, impelled the formulation of plans to reorganize society that were far more radical and sweeping than those propounded by the French Revolution. Progress in preventing and controlling diseases resulted in rapid *population increases. Technological innovations sped the multiplication of factories, one of the effects of which was *urbanization. To the industrial centers came hordes of poorly educated persons who settled in squalid slums. There the labor of men, women, and children was ruthlessly exploited by a greedy, selfish middle class, indifferent to the welfare of their employees and intent on accumulating for themselves maximum profits under a capitalistic system that favored fierce, open competition, minimal state control of bourgeois individualism, and slight governmental efforts at *social legislation. The disparity in wealth and political power between the minority who owned the means of production and the proletarian majority of wage earners was glaring and became ever more irritating. *Socialism arose as a solution to the evils connected with private *property. In general the Socialists aimed to improve society on the basis of public ownership of the means of production, but they differed widely among themselves in principles and, still more, in the application of them. In addition to contriving theories, Socialists became active in politics and in the labor movement. Socialist political parties rose to prominence in several European countries in the second half of the 19th century; they continued to be important in the 20th century.

Some Socialists were Christians, but very many of them ignored Christianity or attacked it. Neither Claude Henri de *Saint-Simon (1760–1825), the father of French socialism, nor his leading disciples considered themselves Christians. Pierre Proudhon (1809–65) assailed all religions, and Mikhail Bakunin (1814–76) preached atheism. *Communism evolved out of the theories of Karl *Marx (1818–83) and Friedrich *Engels (1820–95), as a completely materialistic and militantly atheistic system. Pius IX, Leo XIII, and succeeding popes on several occasions condemned the basic errors in socialism and communism. In return, both of these groups regarded the Church as their most stalwart foe and entered into bitter struggle against it. For huge numbers in the working class, socialism served as a substitute for Christianity or as a religion in itself; it caused large-scale defections from Catholicism and, even more, from Protestantism. After World War I, Communists gained control of the *Union of Soviet Socialist Republics. Subsequent to World War II, they came to rule several countries in Eastern Europe as well as China. Persecution of all religion, particularly of the Catholic religion, has been the usual aftermath of these victories. International communism is the most determined, most ruthless, most persevering, and best organized foe ever encountered by the Church.

Social Catholicism. Catholics recognized the implications of the French Revolution much more quickly than they did those of the industrial revolution. They became actively concerned about the political and religious aspects of liberalism long before they became fully aware of the novelty, magnitude, and complexity of the problems treated by economic liberalism. Socialism thereby gained a considerable headstart on Catholicism in attempting to solve the social question. After its beginnings in predominantly Protestant Great Britain late in the 18th century, the industrial revolution spread to the Continent, reaching different countries in different decades. The material distress and moral abandonment of the industrial proletariat became known quickly and roused sympathy and the desire to alleviate them. What was lacking at first was a satisfactory approach. Poverty was a problem older than Christianity. It was widely believed that the traditional method of private charity, applied on an enlarged scale, was the proper and sufficient solution. Only gradually did it become clear that *social justice as well as charity was involved and that structural changes in the social order were required. Before Catholics could be convinced of this, they had to divest themselves of the prevailing laissez-faire outlook that affected them, as it did the liberals. Eventually a program in conformity with Catholic teachings was framed and put into practice. By that time, unfortunately, the industrialized proletariat of western Europe had become in great part alienated from the Church. The dechristianization of this group was, as Pius XI labeled it, "the great scandal of the 19th century." There was also considerable lag in providing the new industrial suburbs with adequate pastoral care. The impoverishment of the Church after the secularizations of ecclesiastical properties explained to some extent the failure to build new churches. Inadequacy of vocations was partly responsible for the failure to allocate priests to working-class sections, but a redistribution of available personnel would have eased this pressing need. The result was that an entire generation or more passed its life out of contact with the Church. Valiant efforts were made later to regain them, but even the heroic sacrifices of the *worker priests met with partial success at best.

Catholics did not meet the problem simultaneously everywhere, nor were their responses the same in all lands. German Catholics were among the first to resolve the question, although the industrial revolution penetrated Germany after reaching France and Belgium. Adolf *Kolping and Bp. Wilhelm von *Ketteler acted as pioneers around mid-century, and the Center party was an early advocate of enlightened social legislation. As a result, German Catholics did not desert the Church en masse as did Protestant industrial workers, who flocked to the Social Democratic party and adopted its socialist, irreligious ideas. French Catholics, on the other hand, remained wedded to social conservatism, and French bishops and priests were slow in displaying interest in or comprehension of the problem; for some time they disapproved labor unions. Belgium also was tardy in meeting the new situation. The Church in Great Britain and the U.S. escaped the calamitous results visited upon France and Belgium, even though men of farsighted social vision, such as Cardinal *Manning of Westminster and Cardinal *Gibbons of Baltimore, were not common. (For social Catholicism in various countries, *see* SOCIAL MOVEMENTS, CATHOLIC; SOCIAL THOUGHT, CATHOLIC.)

Pius IX was preoccupied with liberalism's political and doctrinal aspects rather than with its evil social and economic consequences. In *Quanta cura,* however, he outlined the program that Leo XIII developed much more fully in **Rerum novarum* (1891), the first thorough papal pronouncement on the subject. With this famous encyclical, the papacy assumed the leadership in supplying the Catholic solution. Succeeding popes have on many occasions amplified Leo XIII's teachings and applied Catholic principles to new situations, most notably in the encyclicals **Quadragesimo anno* (1931) and **Mater et Magistra* (1961). *See* SOCIAL THOUGHT, PAPAL.

The Popes. To such an extent has the recent life of the Church centered in Rome that an understanding of the development of the papal office and of the course of papal history is essential for a comprehension of Church history. One of the most remarkable phenomena in the entire history of the Church is the rapid change in papal fortunes subsequent to 1815. After a period of declining prestige and effectiveness that extended from mid-17th century and reached its nadir in the misfortunes of Pius VI and Pius VII, the papacy took advantage of the changed external situation and asserted effectively its spiritual authority over the universal Church to a degree never before equaled. Once the stormy revolutionary era closed with Napoleon's downfall, authority tended to be centralized more and more in Rome. This trend, which became more pronounced after mid-century, reached its culmination in 1870 at *Vatican Council I, when the papal prerogatives of *primacy of jurisdiction and *infallibility were solemnly defined. Especially from the time of Pius IX, the popes have been active to an unprecedented extent in the exercise of their *teaching authority. Papal *temporal power, on the other hand, kept declining, until in 1870 it disappeared with the loss of the States of the Church. The *Lateran Pacts (1929) resurrected this power on a very limited scale when they solved the *Roman Question by creating the State of *Vatican City. (For the historical development of the papal office, *see* PAPACY.)

Following Pius VI (1775–99) and Pius VII (1800–23) came Leo XII (1823–29), Pius VIII (1829–30), Gregory XVI (1831–46), Pius IX (1846–78), Leo XIII (1878–1903), Pius X (1903–14), Benedict XV (1914–22), Pius XI (1922–39), Pius XII (1939–58), John XXIII (1958–63), and Paul VI (1963–). As a group the popes of the 19th and 20th centuries have been dedicated, industrious leaders, whose intellectual and spiritual qualifications were outstanding. (For the history of these pontificates, see the article on each pope.)

Clergy. Wide variations, quantitatively and qualitatively, can be observed in the inner, more important, phase of the Church's life in various parts of the world. On the whole there has been a decided improvement in the average caliber of the clergy, on whom depends to a great extent the religious quality of the laity. The loss of ecclesiastical wealth, clerical privileges, and lofty social status, along with the democratic spirit of the recent period, have changed for the better the character of the hierarchy; it has become more plebeian but more knowledgeable and more intent on fulfilling its duties as the shepherd of souls. The day has passed when the upper strata of society monopolized bishoprics, canonries, and other higher posts, which were too often esteemed as sinecures. Much more attention has focused on ameliorating and standardizing the intellectual and spiritual training of priests in *seminaries. The Holy See has made the *seminary system the object of continual solicitude and of watchful supervision (*see* DEUS SCIENTIARUM DOMINUS; SEMINARIES AND UNIVERSITIES, CONGREGATION OF). The result has been the formation of a body of priests throughout the world who are better educated and disciplined, more zealous and spiritual than in any previous age. Priests of the 20th century have been better prepared than their predecessors in the 19th century to meet the problems created by vast economic, social, and intellectual upheavals. Pastoral vision in the 19th century had too often been narrow, and pastoral methods adjusted themselves slowly to a rapidly changing society.

Religious Institutes. One of the most conspicuous indications of the restored vitality of the 19th-century Church was the extraordinary progress made by religious orders and congregations. Only the 13th century can be compared with the 19th in this respect. Yet the century opened very inauspiciously for religious. The age of the Enlightenment had been one of decline for the orders, whose most conspicuous loss came in 1773 with the suppression of the Jesuits. So much religious property was seized and so many orders were dissolved in whole or in part after 1789 that most institutes had to make a fresh start after 1815. Since then the growth of previously existing orders and of new foundations has been steady, despite several attempts by anticlericals to stunt it in Germany and in Latin countries, notably in France. Some older orders have never regained their former importance or numbers; others have succeeded in doing so only in the very recent past. Monastic orders, which were hardest hit by secularization, were the slowest to recover. Thus the Benedictines verged on extinction for a while, but after mid-19th century they began to prosper once more. The Dominicans and Capuchins diminished greatly in numbers until a reversal set in late in the 19th century. The Vincentians declined to a few hundred and then increased to about 6,000 by 1963. There were only a few dozen Christian Brothers left at the opening of the 19th century, but membership swelled to 18,000 in 1963. After Pius VII restored the Society of Jesus in 1814, it grew steadily to 36,000 in 1964. Older orders of women, such as the Ursulines, Visitation Nuns, and the Daughters of Charity of St. Paul, went through similar experiences.

Numerous new congregations appeared, more so in the 19th than in the 20th century. Most frequently they originated in France, Italy, or Spain, but much of the growth of the larger ones occurred outside these borders, even outside Europe. In the vast majority of cases these new institutes engaged in the active apostolate, predominantly in education, hospital work, and missionary endeavors. Several groups were founded explicitly for work in the missions. To an unprecedented extent, religious women traveled to foreign missions. The trend favored centralized, mobile, international organizations.

Among the new congregations for men, those that became best known include the Assumptionists, Blessed Sacrament Fathers, Claretians, Consolata Missionary Fathers, Divine Word Society, Holy Cross Congregation, Holy Ghost Fathers, Immaculate Heart of Mary Congregation (Scheut Fathers), La Salette Missionaries, Mariannhill Missionaries, Marianists, Marist Fathers, Montfort Fathers, Oblates of Mary Immaculate, Oblates of St. Francis de Sales, Sacred Hearts Missionaries (of Issoudun), Sacred Heart of Jesus Priests (of Saint-Quentin), Sacred Hearts Fathers, Salvatorians, Stigmatine Fathers, Verona Fathers, Viatorians, and Xaverian Missionary Fathers. The most phenomenal growth of all has been experienced by the foundations of St. John *Bosco, the Salesians and Salesian Sisters, whose more than 40,000 members have spread throughout the world.

Societies of men who live a common life without vows include the African Missions Society, Pallottines, Pontifical Institute for Foreign Missions, Precious Blood Society, and White Fathers. The Columban Fathers and St. Patrick's Missionary Society were founded in Ireland; the Mill Hill Missionaries, in England; and the Josephite Fathers, Maryknoll Missionaries, and Paulists, in the U.S. The Missionary Society of St. James the Apostle was the creation of Cardinal Richard Cushing of Boston.

Several congregations of brothers were founded. Among the more prominent ones are the Brothers of Christian Instruction of Ploërmel (La Mennais Brothers), Brothers of Christian Instruction of St. Gabriel, Charity Brothers, Immaculate Conception Brothers, Lourdes Brothers, Mercy Brothers, Our Lady Mother of Mercy Brothers, Sacred Heart Brothers, and Xaverian Brothers. The Marist Brothers grew to a membership exceeding 10,000. Ireland was the place of foundation of the Irish Christian Brothers, Patrician Brothers, and Presentation Brothers.

Congregations of women far exceeded those of men in the number of new foundations and in total membership. Women have come to constitute a higher percentage of all religious than in earlier centuries. The number of groups of Benedictine sisters alone is large; so are the numerous groups of Charity, Dominican, Franciscan, Good Shepherd, Notre Dame, Precious Blood, Providence, and Sacred Heart Sisters. The Society of the Sacred Heart, founded by St. Madeleine Sophie *Barat, became famous for its educational work. The School Sisters of Notre Dame blossomed into a much larger organization. The Little Sisters of the Poor have greatly endeared themselves by their care of the aged and impoverished. The Mercy Sisters, founded in Ireland by Mother Catherine *McAuley, is the largest ever established in the English-speaking world (see articles on each of the above congregations).

*Secular institutes represent a new direction in the religious life that has become more prominent in the mid-20th century.

Laity. *Leakage and dechristianization processes have drained large numbers of the faithful. The careful surveys of religious practice that have occasionally been made in mid-20th century have usually confirmed widely held opinions about the sizable, sometimes alarmingly high, percentage of nominal Catholics. Yet, the level of observance and devotion among the faithful laity seems to be higher than in the preceding period. Certainly the laity have become more prominent in the life of the Church, particularly in the present century. Since World War I this has been one of the most significant phenomena in the Church (*see* CATHOLIC ACTION; LAY APOSTOLATE; LAY MISSIONARIES). Much attention has been devoted to the lay state as a special vocation and to a type of spirituality best suited to this state (*see* LAITY, VOCATION OF; LAY SPIRITUALITY).

Catholic Organizations. The multiplication of flourishing Catholic organizations has been another striking feature of this period. Some have arisen to foster particular devotions, others to promote the Church's rights, to aid the poor and the sick, to cultivate social life, or to unite Catholic workers, tradesmen, professional persons, war veterans, students, teachers, colleges, hospitals, etc. Prominent among these associations are the *Holy Name Society, the *Legion of Mary, and the National Federation of *Sodalities of Our Lady. The vast expansion of missionary activity, which is nowadays dependent on private charity for material subsistence, has given great importance to mission aid societies, such as the Society for the *Propagation of the Faith, the *Pontifical Association of the Holy Childhood, and the *Missionary Union of the Clergy. Antoine Frédéric *Ozanam initiated the work of the Society of *St. Vincent de Paul, whose charitable undertakings have branched into numerous countries. (*See* CHARITY, WORKS OF; NATIONAL CONFERENCE OF CATHOLIC CHARITIES). *Pax Romana and the *Newman apostolate are intended for students and intellectuals. The *Görres-Gesellschaft fosters Catholic scholarship. Catholic political parties have been noted above. Catholics have formed their own labor unions (*see* CHRISTIAN TRADE UNIONS). In the U.S. there is the *National Catholic Educational Association, *National Catholic Rural Life Conference, *National Catholic Social Action Conference. *National Council of Catholic Men, *National Council of Catholic Women, *Christian Family Movement, and various Catholic *youth organizations. Leading fraternal organizations in the U.S. include the *Knights of Columbus, *Catholic Daughters of America, and *Daughters of Isabella. Other countries have Catholic organizations suited to their own needs and desires. The *National Catholic Welfare Conference coordinates the efforts of American Catholics to carry out the Church's social program.

Devotions. Traditional forms of piety did not vanish, but new trends and emphases appeared. *Jansenist piety, with its moral rigorism, gave way gradually to a more sentimental type of devotion, associated with Italian Catholicity, that stressed external practices and frequentation of the Sacraments. This interior transformation of Catholic inner life north of the Alps has been termed "the real triumph of ultramontanism," more so than the definition of papal infallibility. Late in the 19th century another trend developed and gained momentum in the following decades. Catholic spirituality became predominantly Christocentric in its orientation. Evidence of this appeared in the widespread devotion of the *Sacred Heart. The 19th century has been called "the century of the Sacred Heart," but this devotion still retained its popularity in the 20th century. Pius XI extended the feast of the Sacred Heart to the universal Church. Christocentric also are the devotion to the *Precious Blood and still more to the Eucharist, manifest in the common practice of perpetual *adoration, the development of *Eucharistic congresses and of frequent *Communion. Relaxation of the requirements for Eucharistic *fast served to increase this practice; but this modification was in line with the general trend observable in the laws concerning *fast and abstinence, *censures, and other disciplinary regulations.

Devotion to the Blessed Virgin Mary on a worldwide scale also was characteristic of the period (*see* MARY, BLESSED VIRGIN, DEVOTION TO). It was promoted by the solemn definitions of the doctrines of the *Immaculate Conception (1854) and the *Assumption of Mary (1950), and by progress in the study of *Mariology. As a result of the visions of St. Catherine *Labouré, devotion to the *miraculous medal gained many adherents. The apparitions to St. Bernadette *Soubirous has made *Lourdes one of the most frequented *shrines in the world. *Fátima and, to a lesser extent, *La Salette also have become goals of international *pilgrimages.

A third characteristic trend in recent lay piety has been its Biblical orientation. Relatively few Catholics in the 19th century read the Bible with any regularity, and the Modernist crisis early in the 20th century deterred ecclesiastical authorities from seeking to alter this situation. *Biblical theology has received more attention in recent decades. Catholic scholars have worked with greater freedom since the appearance of Pius XII's encyclical **Divino afflante Spiritu* (1943) and they have produced numerous scholarly works. The availability of good vernacular translations of the Sacred Scriptures and of worthwhile popular literature on the subject, as well as the urging of the hierarchy, have given great impetus to this movement (*see* BIBLE READING; BIBLE, IV; SPIRITUALITY, CONTEMPORARY).

The *liturgical movement progressed during the 19th century after the pioneer efforts of Dom *Guéranger, and in the following century it became one of the most impressive developments in the Church, one that promoted notably the role of the laity in liturgical services and that increased interest in the liturgy (*see* LITURGICAL PARTICIPATION; LITURGICAL REFORM).

Intellectual Life. The Church confronted an enormous task of ever-increasing magnitude in solving the religious problems posed by discoveries in the natural sciences and in many other fields of learning and by new directions in thought and letters. An explosion of discoveries in physics, chemistry, geology, astronomy, and biology vastly expanded knowledge about man's environment. These findings raised numerous questions about the *universe, *man, traditional religious beliefs, and the reconciliation of science with faith. So successful was the method of the natural sciences that many became convinced that that was the sole adequate method (*see* FAITH AND REASON; GOD AND MODERN SCIENCE; INTELLECTUAL LIFE; SCIENCE, ARTICLES ON; PHILOSOPHY OF SCIENCE; SCIENTISM; THEOLOGY AND SCIENCE). Enormously influential were the writings of Charles *Darwin on evolution, popularized by Thomas *Huxley; they were accepted enthusiastically by scientists and thinkers and came to be applied to widely diverse fields. Their impact on religion was great and for some time destructive (*see* EVOLUTION, HUMAN; EVOLUTION, ORGANIC). Scientific investigations into the workings of the mind by psychiatrists and psychologists resulted in great advances in the understanding of man, but they also led to mechanistic, deterministic views and supplied many with substitutes for Christianity (*see* PSYCHIATRY, ARTICLES ON; PSYCHOLOGY, ARTICLES ON; PSYCHOLOGISM; BEHAVIORISM).

Modern philosophers have been much interested in religion, and their writings have had a profound influence on theology, more on Protestant than on Catholic theology. Many leading thinkers ceased to believe in Christianity, and some were openly anti-Christian. Their philosophical systems differed widely among themselves, but they tended directly or indirectly to portray Christianity as irrelevant or harmful (*see* PHILOSOPHY, HISTORY OF, 4, 5; RELIGION, PHILOSOPHY OF; AGNOSTICISM; ATHEISM; RATIONALISM; EVOLUTIONISM; EXISTENTIALISM; HEGELIANISM; HUMANISM, SECULAR; IDEALISM; KANTIANISM; LOGICAL POSITIVISM; MATERIALISM; MECHANISM; MONISM; NATURALISM; PANTHEISM; POSITIVISM; DETERMINISM, PSYCHOLOGICAL; RELATIVISM; UTILITARIANISM).

The Bible was subjected to an enormous amount of critical attention, especially in Germany. Basic to the outlook of many of the more prominent critics was a denial of all supernatural faith and a habitual contesting of the truth of Sacred Scripture. The problem of the historical Jesus gave rise to dozens of theories. David *Strauss and Joseph Ernest *Renan, who published two of the best-known 19th-century lives of Christ, were sceptics and passed on to their readers their own disbelief in the Gospel narratives [*see* BIBLE, VI (EXEGESIS), 2]. Historical study of the origins and early development of the Church was another favorite field for scrutiny and resulted in a number of theories derogatory to Catholic claims. The comparative study of religion was a well-tilled field, but its products proved injurious, in many cases, to belief in Christianity as the sole road ordained by God for salvation (*see* RELIGION, COMPARATIVE STUDY OF). Literature served often to disseminate in wide circles these new ideologies, in the form of novels, plays, and poems impregnated with naturalistic outlooks and disdainful of Christian standards (*see* NATURALISM, LITERARY).

Catholic scholarship was for some decades ill-prepared to surmount these challenges. The closing of numerous Catholic universities, theological faculties, and monastic schools during the Revolutionary and Napoleonic periods and the disastrous infiltration of the Enlightenment and Kantian ideas into Catholic thought, even in seminaries, left Catholicism at a low intellectual ebb. Recovery was slow until mid-19th century; since then progress has been rapid and continuous. Signs of renewal became apparent first in France early in the 19th century, with the influential, if not profound, writings of François de *Chateaubriand, whose *Genius of Christianity* (1802) was a sensational success, and those of Joseph de *Maistre and Louis de *Bonald. *Apologetics was cultivated extensively, most notably toward mid-century by John Henry *Newman, Victor *Dechamps, and Jaime *Balmes. Church history, patrology, and the history of dogma also received much study at this time, especially in Germany, where Johann *Möhler, Johannes Ignaz von *Döllinger, and Carl von *Hefele were outstanding. German emphasis on historical theology caused tensions, however, with the theologians in Rome, who were traditionally attached to scholasticism.

The key problem of conciliating *faith and reason produced several solutions, not all of them acceptable. Thus *Hermesianism, as evolved by Georg *Hermes, *traditionalism, *ontologism, and the systems advocated by Franz von *Baader, Anton *Gunther, and Jakob *Frohschammer met official Roman disapproval. Vatican Council I supplied an impetus to ecclesiastical scholarship. The renewal of *scholasticism and *Thomism gained strong encouragement from Leo XIII in 1879 in his encyclical **Aeterni Patris* (*see* NEOSCHOLASTICISM AND NEOTHOMISM). When *Americanism, *Reformakatholizismus, and, more important, *Modernism appeared around the turn of the 20th century, the exercise of the papal magisterial power sufficed to quell them speedily. The same fate befell new theological trends in France after World War II subsequent to the publication of **Humani generis* (1950). Heterodox movements since 1789 that resulted in lasting group separations from the Church have been rare. Deutschkatholizismus, initiated by Johann *Ronge and Johann *Czerski, the *Old Catholics, the *Los-von-Rom movement, and the *Polish National Catholic Church were the most sizable schisms, but their followings were relatively limited even at the height of their popularity. Since 1918 Catholic ecclesiastical scholarship, centering in western Europe, has been very active and prominent and has moved out of the position of secondary rank it occupied earlier. The Catholic press has spread its influence throughout the world (*see* CATHOLIC PRESS, WORLD SURVEY).

Expansion. Emigration and missionary evangelization have, since 1789, established the Church in almost every corner of the globe and greatly increased its numbers. Millions of emigrants from Catholic countries in Europe have been the main factors in building the Church in the *United States, *Canada, *Australia, and *New Zealand; they have also augmented the Catholic populations converted earlier in *Latin America.

By 1789 the missions were in a sad state after a century of stagnation and decline, hastened by the heavy loss of personnel when the Jesuits were suppressed in 1773. During the next 4 decades and longer, this situation deteriorated further as the religious orders suffered dissolutions, confiscations, and diminution of numbers. It has been estimated that in 1800 the vast territories in both hemispheres entrusted to the Congregation for the *Propagation of the Faith (Propaganda), much more extensive then than in 1965, had only about 500 priests (about half of them natives), a few dozen sisters, and somewhere between 1,400,000 and 5,000,000 faithful. Not until the pontificate of Gregory XVI was it possible to begin improving matters. After 1878 progress was remarkable. So extraordinary have been the activity and accomplishments since then that these decades constitute one of the most flourishing periods in all mission history. No similar length of time has recorded anywhere near as many converts. Mainly responsible for this growth has been the revival of the religious orders. Gregory XVI, the leading mission pope of his century, and all his successors helped enormously by taking keen interest in the missions and by assuming a far more active leadership than their predecessors did or could (*see* PAPACY). The huge expenditures involved in evangelization have been met by the charitable contributions of the laity, who have carried the material burdens once assumed by the Catholic governments of Spain, Portugal, and France. External factors helped. Travel became easier and safer. China, Japan, and Siam reopened their doors to foreigners. Places such as inner Africa ceased to be inaccessible.

European colonial expansion was a mixed blessing. It ensured an ingress to missionaries and put a curb on warlike local potentates. But it did not stop all religious persecutions. Indeed a notable percentage of those moderns who have been given the honors of the altar earned them with their blood on the missions (*see* CHINA, MARTYRS OF; KOREA, MARTYRS OF; TONKIN, MARTYRS OF; UGANDA, MARTYRS OF). Almost all missionaries until the 20th century came from Europe; they suffered, not always without justification, from having their work regarded as merely one phase of European *colonialism. Their reluctance in some areas to prepare native clergies gave added substance to the charge; but their outlook was severely disapproved by Rome and has disappeared (*see* CLERGY, INDIGENOUS; SEMINARIES, MISSIONARY). With the multiplication of precise papal directives, the attention focused on mission science, and the improvements in special training given to missionaries, the proper function and activity of the missions came to be more perfectly understood and practiced (*see* MISSIONS, PAPAL LETTERS ON; MISSIONARY FORMATION; MISSIOLOGY; MEDICAL MISSIONS). Disadvantageous also to the missions was the tarnished image of Christianity furnished by the arrogance, greed, immorality, and religious indifference of many transplanted colonial officials, merchants, and adventurers. By mid-20th century European prestige had dimmed, and a blaze of anti-Europeanism had erupted, fed by rising nationalisms and demands for independence. Missionaries also faced serious competition. Protestants began to spread the gospel with great zeal and success in the 19th century (*see* MISSIONS, PROTESTANT). Islam has been a serious rival in Africa and elsewhere. Communism has permeated mission areas. In China, as in other lands where communism gained political mastery, Christian missionaries were persecuted and expelled.

Despite all this, statistics leave no doubt about the tremendous progress of the missions. By 1957 there were some 30,000 priests, 8,000 brothers, and 60,000 sisters—about half of them native—in the territories allotted to Propaganda alone, not counting the areas dependent on the Congregation for the *Oriental Church, the *Consistorial Congregation (in North Africa), or the Congregation for *Extraordinary Ecclesiastical Affairs (Portuguese possessions). There were also 4,000 native seminarians and 150,000 catechists and teachers. One in six of the 683 territories under Propaganda was confided to native bishops, a development that progressed rapidly under Pius XI and his successors. About 50 million Catholics inhabited mission lands. Nearly half of them were in Africa, the scene of the most spectacular gains, since the total in 1800 approximated 50,000, and in 1900, 500,000 (*see* MISSIONS, HISTORY OF; MISSIONS, CATHOLIC; AFRICA; ASIA; OCEANIA; and the articles on the individual countries in these regions).

Reunion. *Unity of faith and *unity of the Church are ideals toward which the Catholic Church must always strive. For centuries it has worked to mend the break with the *Orthodox Churches, and on a few occasions the attempts seemed to verge on success. Practical, as well as theological, considerations have heightened the urgency in the 20th century to promote these aims; they have resulted in a far greater readiness to engage in interfaith dialogue. Interfaith movements have become extremely prominent and well-received. Catholics and Anglicans utilized the *Malines Conversations (1921–26) to try to resolve their differences. By far the best-known recent attempt to restore all Christians to unity is the *ecumenical movement, in which Protestants have taken the initiative and worked most (*see* WORLD COUNCIL OF CHURCHES). Through the *Unitas Association, the *Una Sancta movement, and many other ventures, Catholics have demonstrated a growing spirit of cooperativeness. Many obstacles must be surmounted before the ultimate goal is approached, but the sincerity with which the task has been faced has already vastly improved the relations between religious bodies that were intolerant of one another in the not too distant past.

Conclusion. Numerically the Church has progressed both absolutely and relatively. The 130 or so million Catholics in 1789 had increased to about 545 million by 1961. This fourfold multiplication more than matched the tripling of world population from 900 million to the vicinity of 3 billion. Catholics came to constitute 18 per cent of the world's inhabitants instead of 14.5. During the 20th century, both Catholic and world populations have doubled; therefore the Catholic percentage has remained approximately the same since 1900. The 915 million Christians in 1961 represented 30 per cent of the world's population. Approximately 60 per cent of all Christians were Catholics. About 2 per cent of the Catholics, 11 million, belonged to the *Eastern Churches; the rest pertained to the *Latin rite. Europe, exclusive of Russia, held 44 per cent of all Catholics, and the Western Hemisphere about the same, with one-third of all Catholics in Latin America and one-tenth in North America (*see* STATISTICS OF RELIGIOUS BODIES).

Administratively the Catholic world in 1964 was divided into 11 residential patriarchal sees, 363 metropolitan sees, 52 archiepiscopal and 1,536 episcopal residential sees, 115 prelatures and abbeys *nullius,* 9 apostolic administrations, 130 vicariates and 100 prefectures apostolic, and 6 missions and districts *sui juris.*

The hierarchy then included 1,660 residential and 1,064 titular archbishops and bishops. In 1963 there were about 419,000 priests (280,000 diocesan; 139,000 religious). Religious women totaled about 1 million. Three-fourths of this multitude of priests and sisters belonged to Western Europe and North America. Even with the addition of 130,000 brothers and several 10s of thousands of secular and religious seminarians, female vocations far outnumbered male ones.

As the Church entered the last third of the 20th century, it confronted many problems of adjustment to internal stresses and to the world about it. Periodic renewal is necessary if the Church, as the Bride of Christ, is to remain ever young and fair despite 19 centuries of age (*see* REFORM IN THE CHURCH). *Aggiornamento* was the great opportunity and challenge; the chief instrument for carrying it to successful completion was *Vatican Council II.

Bibliography: Bibliographies. RHE, fullest bibliogs. For literature, esp. in Eng., see *Catholic Periodical Index* (New York-Haverford, Pa. 1930–). *Index to Religious Periodical Literature* (since 1949) (Princeton 1953–). *International Index to Periodicals* (New York 1907–). *Guide to Catholic Literature,* ed. W. ROMIG et al. (Detroit-Grosse Pointe, Mich.–Haverford, Pa. 1888–).

Longer histories. J. LEFLON, *La Crise révolutionnaire, 1789–1846* (Fliche-Martin 20; 1949). R. AUBERT, *Le Pontificat de Pie IX* (*ibid.* 21; 2d ed. 1964). H. DANIEL-ROPS, *History of the Church of Christ,* v.8 *The Church in an Age of Revolution: 1789–1870,* tr. J. WARRINGTON (New York 1965); v.9, Fr. only, *L'Église des révolutions: Un Combat pour Dieu* (Histoire de l'Église du Christ 6.2; Paris 1963). Latourette Christ19th-20th Cent. F. MOURRET, *A History of the Catholic Church,* tr. N. THOMPSON, 8 v. (St. Louis 1931–57) v.7 and 8 (1775–1878); v.9 (1878–1903), in Fr. only, *Histoire générale de l'Église* (Paris 1924). A. BOULENGER, *Histoire générale de l'Église,* v.8–9 (Paris 1943–50). G. KRÜGER, ed., *Handbuch der Kirchengeschichte,* 4 v. (Tübingen 1909–12), v.4 by H. STEPHAN and H. LEUBE, *Die Neuzeit* (2d ed. Tübingen 1931). F. J. MONTALBAN et al., *Historia de la Iglesia Católica,* v.4 (1648–1951) (BiblAut Crist 76; 1951). L. A. VEIT, *Die Kirche im Zeitalter des Individualismus 1648–1932,* 2 v. (Freiburg 1931–33).

Shorter histories. Bihlmeyer-Tüchle v.3, excellent bibliog. N. C. EBERHARDT, *Summary of Catholic History,* 2 v. (St. Louis 1961), v.2. J. LORTZ, *History of the Church,* ed. and tr. E. G. KAISER from 4th Ger. ed. (Milwaukee 1938); *Geschichte der Kirche in ideengeschichtlicher Betrachtung,* 2 v. (21st rev. and enl. ed. Münster 1962–64), v.2; also in 1-vol. ed. (1964). C. POULET, *A History of the Catholic Church,* tr. S. A. RAEMERS, 2 v. (4th ed. St. Louis 1934–35), v.2. W. GURIAN and M. A. FITZSIMONS, eds., *The Catholic Church in World Affairs* (Notre Dame, Ind. 1954). E. E. Y. HALES, *The Catholic Church in the Modern World* (New York 1958; pa. 1960). J. N. MOODY, ed., *Church and Society, 1789–1950* (New York 1953).

Papal history. Schmidlin. P. PASCHINI and V. MONACHINO, eds., *I papi nella storia,* 2 v. (Rome 1961), v.2.

Missions. Delacroix HistMissCath v.3–4. Latourette v.4–7. Mulders. A. FREITAG, *The Universe Atlas of the Christian World* (London 1963), tr. from Fr. H. EMMERICH, *Atlas missionum a Sacra Congregatione de Propaganda Fide dependentium* (Vatican City 1958).

Statistics. *Bilan du Monde.* AnnPont.

[J. F. BRODERICK]

CHURCH, SYMBOLS OF

The images of dwelling, garden, and woman, and their derivatives, are the most widely used symbols of the Church.

Basic Symbols. In the New Testament the image of the Church as a dwelling or building that is also a temple is exemplified in Eph 2.20–22: "You are built

Fig. 1. The Church as a vine growing out of a chalice, detail of an early Christian tomb mosaic in the museum at Sousse, Tunisia.

upon the foundation of the apostles and prophets with Christ Jesus himself as the chief corner stone. In him the whole structure is closely fitted together and grows into a temple holy in the Lord, in him you too are being built together into a dwelling place for God in the Spirit." The Church is represented by the larger metaphor of the city of God in Heb 12.22. In this city, which is the eschatological Jerusalem, the tree of life of the Garden or Paradise is found (Ap 22.1–2).

The symbol woman appears in the New Testament under the aspect of bride and of mother. The city is compared to a bride in Ap 21.2: "And I saw the holy city, New Jerusalem, coming down out of heaven from God, made ready as a bride adorned for her husband." The similitude of mother is applied to the heavenly Jerusalem in Gal 4.26. The fusion of these symbols, especially that of bride and groom, begins to take place in the Old Testament (Isaia ch. 61–62). The image of the Church as "body" has reference to the system of bridal symbolism; the Church is Christ's Body at the same time that she is His Bride, according to the principle that husband and wife are one flesh (Eph 5.23–32). *See* CHURCH, II (THEOLOGY OF).

In Christian antiquity these Biblical Church symbols were developed with poetic ingenuity through literary and pictorial images. In Hellenistic art, the vine had symbolized mystic union with a lifegiving deity. As an ornament in synagogues it represented Israel, God's vineyard, according to Is 5.1–7 (the vineyard song), Ez 19.1–14 (allegory of the vine branch), and Ps 79(80).9–19 (restoration of the Lord's vineyard). In the light of passages such as Jn 15.1–17 (Christ as true vine) and Mt 21.33–41 (parable of the vinedressers), Christian art saw the pre-Christian meaning of this symbol fulfilled in the Church. Related to the vine as Church symbols are the wreath, the fountain, and the tree of life.

Often appearing together with the vine and its related symbols is the figure of a woman in the early Christian attitude of prayer, the "orant." This image may stand for an individual member of the Church (living or departed), especially its most representative member, the Virgin Mary. The main concern, however, is with the use of the image to symbolize the whole concept of the Church. As soon as churches were built they became symbols of the Church as the community of the faithful "so gathered in God's house as to become God's House" (St. Augustine, PL 43:241). The symbolism of dwelling, garden, and woman was developed extensively in patristic literature. The Church was seen to be foreshadowed by Jerusalem and the Temple, Paradise and the garden of Ct 4.12 (the lover and his garden), and by the various figures of woman in the Bible, especially Mary to whom the Church is "most similar" (St. Augustine, PL 38:1064). The bridal symbolism gave rise to an extensive system of *ecclesiology that borrowed ideas from Hellenistic astrology and mysticism and presented the Church as moon (female) receiving light and life from Christ as sun (male).

Other Symbols. The ark as an image of the Church was sanctioned by 1 Pet 3.20, where Baptism is equated with the saving power of Noe's ark. The ship symbol is probably of independent origin, from the *Testamentum Nephtali* and Lk 5.3, where Christ teaches from the boat. The ark and the ship are sometimes contrasted and sometimes fused in another important system of

Fig. 2. Apocalyptic scene on one of the large panels of the 5th-century carved cypress doors of the church of Santa Sabina at Rome. The female figure being crowned by two Apostles in the bottom vignette is a personification of the Church, the holy city, the New Jerusalem, as a bride adorned for her husband, the whole scene being a graphic rendering of the events in Apocalypse (21.2).

Fig. 3. The Church as a ship with Christ crucified on the mast, miniature in a Breviary (Morgan MS 799, fol. 234 v) illuminated in Lombardy, third quarter of the 15th century.

early ecclesiology through which the cross (as "saving wood" and as mast of Peter's Bark) soon came to stand for the Church. Throughout the Middle Ages, Church symbolism inspired by elaborate allegorical interpretation of the Bible was translated into artistic forms. The development reached its climax in the medieval cathedral, which was conceived as a mirror of the universe in which "all things prefigure Christ and His Church" (Anastasius of Sinai, PG 89:894).

With the decline of the Middle Ages, Church allegories tended to become fanciful and didactic. For example, the Church was represented as a chariot drawn by the symbols of the Evangelists and by the Fathers of the Church. The symbol "woman" developed into allegorical representations of Mother Church with cross, banner, or crown, often contrasted with the Synagogue personified. A second area of great development was in Madonna pictures. Only in the East did the full meaning of the "orant" survive, especially in the iconography of the Ascension and in the type of Our Lady of the Sign. As God's dwelling, identified through garden symbols with Paradise, and through liturgical references with Jerusalem, Spouse, and Mother, the church building retained its symbolic meaning in the West, even during the centuries when theology lost touch with symbols. Within the framework of 20th-century Church renewal, traditional symbolism has provided a source of new insights into the nature of the Church. Contemporary church architecture, for example, has been affected by a reconsideration of the concept of "the Church incarnate."

For related illustrations, *see* CHURCH, I (IN THE BIBLE); CHURCH, II (THEOLOGY OF); CHURCH, HISTORY OF, II (MEDIEVAL).

Bibliography: Consult pertinent articles in H. LECLERCQ, DACL 15.2:1756–1811. ReallexAntChr. Künstle Ikonog. C. LEONARDI, *Ampelos: Il simbolo della vite nell'arte pagano e paleocristiana* (Rome 1947). W. LOWRIE, *Art in the Early Church* (New York 1947), illus. L. OUSPENSKY and W. LOSSKY, *The Meaning of Icons,* tr. G. E. H. PALMER and E. KADLOUBOVSKI (Boston 1956). R. BRUNET, DictSpirAscMyst 4:384–401. R. SCHWARZ, *The Church Incarnate: The Sacred Function of Christian Architecture,* tr. C. HARRIS (Chicago 1958). J. DANIÉLOU, *From Shadows to Reality: Studies in the Biblical Typology of the Fathers,* tr. W. HIBBERD (Westminster, Md. 1960); *Primitive Christian Symbols,* tr. D. ATTWATER (Baltimore 1964) P. S. MINEAR, *Images of the Church in the New Testament* (Philadelphia 1960). H. RAHNER, *Our Lady and the Church,* tr. S. BULLOUGH (New York 1961); *Symbole der Kirche, Die Ekklesiologie der Väter* (Salzburg 1964). Y. M. J. CONGAR, *The Mystery of the Temple,* tr. R. F. TREVETT (Westminster, Md. 1962). **Illustration credits:** Fig. 2, Leonard Von Matt. Fig. 1, German Archaeological Institute, Rome. Fig. 3, The Pierpont Morgan Library.

[D. WINZEN]

CHURCH AND STATE

This article presents in four parts a chronological survey of the relations between Church and State in Western civilization. The doctrinal aspects of these relations are treated more fully in other articles (*see* FREEDOM OF RELIGION), as are historical and legal aspects that have particular reference to the New World and especially to the U.S. *See* CHURCH AND STATE IN LATIN AMERICA; CHURCH AND STATE IN THE U.S. (LEGAL HISTORY); FREEDOM OF RELIGION, U.S. LAW OF.

THE CHURCH IN THE ROMAN EMPIRE

In the ancient Near East and the Mediterranean world religious and civil functions were inseparable. The state was supreme in the religious as well as in the civil sphere, and its subjects or citizens were normally required to participate in public worship. Nonconformance was regarded as a form of treason or sacrilege. When *Akhnaton made his Aton cult the official religion of Egypt, the worship of Amon was proscribed and the nonconforming priesthood of Amon was persecuted. Even in the Greek city-states, acceptance of the gods of the state and participation in the official cults were likewise prescribed. The famous trials of *Anaxagoras and *Socrates at Athens on the charge of impiety indicate that the most enlightened Greek state could demand religious conformity—although in these two instances religion was used as a pretext for attack by political enemies. However, it should be noted that *Plato assigned a central role to religion in the ideal state he described in the *Laws* and that he advocated the death penalty for persistent atheism.

The policy of ancient imperial states toward the religions of conquered peoples was, in general, based on toleration. The great Persian Kings *Cyrus and *Darius even aided the Jewish exiles to return from Babylonia and to reestablish the worship of Yahweh in Jerusalem. There were important exceptions, however, to the policy of toleration. The Assyrians, as is evident from their own records and from the Bible, tended to impose the worship of their militant god Ashur on conquered peoples, and *Antiochus IV, King of Syria, instituted a formal persecution against those Jews who would not conform to his program of Hellenization. Some centuries later, the Sassanid kings of the New Persian Empire persecuted Christians, Manichaeans, and all others who would not accept or participate in the official Zoroastrian religion of the state. In practice, the acceptance of the religion of the conqueror or the toleration of the religions of conquered peoples presented no serious problems to adherents of polytheism, as the conquered could incorporate the worship of foreign divinities—or even the worship of a divine king himself—into their own cults. The Jews, on the other hand, as the chosen people of Yahweh, were committed to His worship alone. Owing in part to the historical circumstances of their association with Rome from the days of *Judas Machabee and in part to the general Roman policy toward subject ethnic groups, the Jews were granted special immunities out of respect for their religious beliefs and practices. Above all, under the early Empire, they were freed from the obligation of participating in the imperial cult.

In summary, before the rise of Christianity, the official religion of a state was an essential and inseparable element in its structure and functioning. The problem of the relations of the religions of subject peoples and the ruling state had arisen, but in practice it was not a serious one except in the case of the Jews, whose uncompromising and exclusive monotheism constituted a unique phenomenon in a polytheistic world [*see* MONOTHEISM (IN THE BIBLE)]. The Romans never attempted to understand *Judaism; they tolerated it, but with restrictions against proselytism.

Primitive Christianity and the Roman State. In the Jewish conception of the state, the religious and the civil were inseparably combined. The Jewish state was a kind of religious community, a *theocracy, in which institutions and laws were religious in origin, being founded in Scripture and interpreted and applied according to the spirit of Scripture. Given this background, subjection to a foreign—and pagan—power was particularly difficult to endure. Hence the question put to Christ regarding the payment of tribute to Rome was motivated in part by a desire to impugn his Jewish patriotism and in part to expose him to a charge of disloyalty to Rome. His answer, "Render, therefore, to Caesar the things that are Caesar's, and to God the things that are God's" (Mk 12.17; see also Rom 13.7), marked the beginning of a new epoch in the history of the relations between religion and the state. For the first time, a formal distinction was made between the obligations owed to God and those owed to the state, with a clear declaration that man has the duty to fulfill the obligations owed to both. St. Paul's teachings on civil *authority and civil obedience merely applied concretely the principle enunciated by Our Lord. Subsequent Christian teachings, and their elaboration, on the relations of Church and State have necessarily been based on this same principle as their ultimate foundation.

The conflict between Christianity and the Roman state was occasioned by the nonparticipation of Christians generally in public and private life, and, above all, by their refusal to worship the emperor. The imperial cult had been instituted by *Augustus and was promoted by his successors as a means, strengthened and sanctioned by religion, for developing loyalty and unity throughout the *Roman Empire. When, about the middle of the 1st century A.D., the Roman authorities became aware that Christianity was not identical with Judaism and that increasing numbers of non-Jews were joining the new religion, Christians, like other non-Jewish citizens or subjects, were expected to participate in various aspects of Roman public and private life and, above all, in the imperial cult. The hope of an imminent Second Coming (*see* PAROUSIA), a strong spirit of *pacifism among some, and the general deep religious fervor of the first two or three generations of Christians were all factors in developing and maintaining an attitude of aloofness toward the life around them, but the main cause of this aloofness was paganism itself. Every aspect of public and private life was permeated with pagan rites and customs. It was practically impossible for a Christian to serve even as a petty magistrate without having to take an active part in pagan ceremonies, and military service required an oath to the divine emperor and worship of the imperial standards and other rites. It is against this background that one should interpret the statement of St. Paul that "our citizenship is in heaven" (Phil 3.20), and should understand the consolation that it offered to those who first heard it.

Sometime between the principates of *Nero and *Trajan, Christianity was condemned as a religion inimical to the state, and refusal to worship the emperor or to participate in official sacrifices was regarded as an act of treason against the state (see PERSECUTIONS). From this period to the Edict of *Galerius (311) and the agreement on religious policy reached by *Constantine and Licinius (the so-called Edict of *Milan of 313), Christianity was proscribed by the Roman state. In practice, however, there were long intervals in which the law against the Christians was not enforced, at least on a universal basis. The rank and file of Christians, although often attacked or ridiculed, were not officially persecuted, and some Christians occupied important posts in the imperial service.

Meanwhile, the Church grew steadily in numbers, especially in the East, and developed a complicated and strong hierarchical organization (*see* CHURCH, HISTORY OF, I; PAPACY, 1). It became a great sacred corporation, although one not recognized by the state, that was regarded as a menace to imperial unity as symbolized in the imperial cult and in other official acts of pagan public worship. The elaborately organized persecutions of *Decius and of *Diocletian and Galerius were directed especially against the leaders of the Church and ecclesiastical organization, with the hope that Christianity might be eliminated by destroying its higher and lower clergy. Despite the severities of the age of persecutions, Christian martyrs and apologists constantly maintained that they were loyal citizens and that they were bound by the precepts of their religion to render obedience to civil authority. They could and did pray *for* the emperor, but they could not pray *to* the emperor, because they had to reserve their worship for their Lord and Savior Jesus Christ, to whom the emperor himself belonged and from whom he derived his power (*Martyr. Polycarpi* 8.2; 9.2; 10.1; Tertullian, *Apol.* 4).

From Constantine to the Death of Theodosius the Great (A.D. 313–395). Constantine's extension of freedom of worship to Christians, which signified that Christianity was recognized officially as a *religio licita* beside paganism, was a revolutionary act that marked a great turning point in the history of the early Church and in universal history as well. By his legislation, Constantine continued to strengthen the position of Christianity. This policy was continued by his successors with the exception of *Julian, whose persecution of Christianity was brought to an abrupt end by his death. Finally, in the last quarter of the 4th century, *Theodosius the Great made Christianity the official religion of the Empire and suppressed public pagan worship.

The Relation of the Church to the Christian Empire. The Church had emerged triumphant from its long struggle with the pagan Roman state and its pagan emperors, but its precise relations with the Christian Empire and Christian emperors remained to be worked out. By the age of Constantine, the Church had become a highly organized universal sacred society, conscious of its divine origin and divine mission. As is clear from the writings of the ante-Nicene and post-Nicene Fathers, it regarded itself as the new *people of God and its leaders, the bishops, as the successors not only of the Apostles appointed by Christ to rule His Church, but also of their prototypes, the Prophets of the Old Testament, as spokesmen of God. The Church, accordingly, in keeping with its divine foundation and its concern with the things of God, considered itself supreme in the theological and spiritual sphere and as possessing its own rights and privileges within that sphere. On the other hand, and in keeping with the doctrine laid down by Christ Himself, it recognized fully the supremacy of the state and its rulers in political or civil affairs.

The Christian emperors inherited the lofty absolutism of their office from their pagan predecessors, who were supreme in religious affairs, as was symbolized by the title *pontifex maximus.* This title was relinquished by *Gratian only in A.D. 382. Constantine considered that he was emperor by divine election and that he not only had the duty to promote the new religion that he had adopted but also the right to interfere directly in religious affairs in the interest of imperial order and unity. Thus he took for granted that he could summon ecclesiastical councils and even suggest the actions that should be taken. In any event, he considered that it was his duty to put into effect, by force if necessary, conciliar decrees. In their joy at deliverance from persecution, the Christian bishops did not perceive that Constantine's handling of the Donatist affair was to be ominous for the future (*see* DONATISM). Their joy over the imperial support received at the Council of *Nicaea I, however, was soon ended when Constantine exiled *Athanasius, the great champion of orthodoxy, and favored the Arians.

From this time forward, it became clear that the emperor would be a defender of the faith, but that in practice this would mean the faith to which he himself subscribed. It became evident also that an emperor could and would regard himself as superior to all bishops, including the pope, in matters ecclesiastical. Arianism, in fact, owed much of its success to the official support it received from the Emperors *Constantius and *Valens and the Empress Justina, regent of her son *Valentinian II. Athanasius (for the second and third time), *Hilary of Poitiers, *Hosius of Córdoba, *Lucifer of Cagliari, *Eusebius of Vercelli, and Pope *Liberius were all exiled by Constantius, an ardent promoter of Arianism as the official religion of the state. Athanasius was exiled again by Julian the Apostate and by Valens.

Divergence between Eastern and Western Theories. Two main Christian attitudes or, rather, theories of the relations of Church and State began to take definite shape from the age of Constantine. In the West the idea of the two societies, the ecclesiastical and the civil, with their respective rights and privileges, was maintained and developed. In the East, *Eusebius of Caesarea advanced the view that as the Empire was becoming Christian the two societies were merging into a single Christian society with the emperor as its head. He thus laid the foundations for what has been called *caesaropapism in practice, if not in theory. It was only natural, accordingly, that the Germanic kings who were converted to Arian Christianity should regard themselves as heads of the Church in their realms. At Constantinople and in the Arian kingdoms, the Church thus became in many respects a department of government.

Despite the opposition of Athanasius and other Eastern Fathers to Eusebius's concept of the merging of the two societies and, above all, to the supremacy of the emperor in the field of religion, this concept received constant imperial support and elaboration until it culminated under *Justinian the Great, who regarded himself as "priest-emperor." In the West, St. *Ambrose was the first great and successful champion of the rights of the Church, and he defended these rights with the vehemence and courage of an Old Testament Prophet. He maintained that the Church has certain sacred and inviolable rights, that it possesses jurisdiction over all Christians, and that the state cannot exercise jurisdiction over strictly ecclesiastical affairs (see his *Enarr. in Ps.* 37.43; *Epist.* 21.4). In his *Sermon against Auxentius* (36), he declared that the emperor had no title more honorable than "son of the Church" and that "the emperor is within the Church and not over it" (*imperator enim intra Ecclesiam, non supra Ecclesiam est*). For the massacre of Thessalonica, he required the powerful Emperor Theodosius the Great to acknowledge his guilt publicly, thus demonstrating that the Church had the right and the duty to insist that even an emperor obey the Christian moral law.

From the Death of Theodosius to the Accession of Justinian (A.D. 395–527). Following the death of Theodosius, the two halves of the Empire remained separated until Justinian made the recovery of the West one of the major policies of his reign (his conquests in the West were largely temporary only). Beginning with the sack of Rome by Alaric (410), Roman authority in the West disintegrated steadily. The deposition of Romulus Augustus (476) marked the formal end of a Roman rule that for decades had been nominal only. Meanwhile, the bishops of the West, and especially the popes, developed the theory of the relations of Church and State much further; and they gave it the definitive form that became the inheritance of the Middle Ages.

St. *Augustine, in his various writings, but above all in his *De civitate Dei,* dealt in a comprehensive manner with the idea of the two societies. Unlike Eusebius, he emphasized their different character and their continued separation. Despite his fear regarding the dangers of interference by the state in religious affairs, he felt obliged, because of the violence of the Donatists, to call upon the imperial government for help. This action set a fateful precedent for the future.

In the period after Augustine, the popes, as Roman civil authority crumbled in the West, were forced to assume an increasingly important political role as the protectors and defenders of the Christian communities against the evils resulting from the Germanic invasions. At the same time, they had to defend the rights and the freedom of the Church in the East as well as in the West against the State-Church theory of the Byzantine emperors and Germanic Arian kings—and the application of the theory in practice. Popes *Leo the Great (440–461), *Simplicius (468–483), *Felix III (II) (483–492), *Gelasius I (492–496), and *Symmachus (498–514) were understandably deferential in the communications that they addressed to the Roman emperors at Constantinople, for in their civil capacity they were really subjects of these exalted rulers. However, they all showed an uncompromising firmness in maintaining the rights, freedom, and supremacy of the Church in the spiritual sphere.

The theory of the two powers was given its clearest and most definitive form by Gelasius in his letter to the Emperor Anastasius:

> There are two [powers], August Emperor, by which this world is chiefly governed. The two powers are the *auctoritas sacrata pontificum* and the *regalis potestas.* Of the two the charge of the priests [*sacerdotes*] is heavier, in that they have to render an account in the Divine judgment for even the kings of men. For you know, most gracious son, that, though you preside over humankind by virtue of your office, you bow your neck piously to those who are in charge of things divine and from them you ask the things of your salvation; and hence you realize that, in receiving the heavenly mysteries and making proper arrangement for them, you must in the order of religion submit yourself rather than control, and in those matters you are dependent on their judgment and do not desire them to be subject to your will. For if, as far as the sphere of civil order is concerned, the bishops themselves, recognizing that the imperial office has been conferred upon you by Divine disposition, obey your laws . . . with what zeal, I ask you, should you not obey those who are deputed to dispense the sacred mysteries? [Epist. 12.2; tr. Ziegler; see also *Tract.* 4.11.]

This exposition on the two powers served as the foundation for the medieval theological and political teaching on the two swords.

See also ARIANISM.

Bibliography: H. RAHNER, *Kirche und Staat im frühen Christentum: Dokumente aus acht Jahrhunderten und ihre Deutung* (Munich 1961); et al., "Kirche und Staat," StL 4:991–1050, esp. 991–997, 1005–16, and 1046–47, bibliog. Daniélou-Marrou Chr Cent v.1, ch. 7, 11, 14–19, 25–26, 31, 33. R. W. and A. J. CARLYLE, *A History of Mediaeval Political Theory in the West,* v.1, *The Second Century to the Ninth* (London 1927), esp. 81–193. K. F. MORRISON, "Rome and the City of God: An Essay on the Constitutional Relationships of Empire and Church in the Fourth Century," *Transactions of the American Philosophical Society,* NS 54.1 (1964) 3–55, with valuable bibliog., 53–54. E. CRANZ, "*De civitate Dei* XV, 2, and Augustine's Idea of Christian Society," *Speculum* 25 (1950) 215–225; "The Development of Augustine's Ideas on Society before the Donatist Controversy," HarvThRev 47 (1954) 255–316. P. R. L. BROWN, "St. Augustine's Attitude to Religious Coercion," *Journal of Roman Studies* 54 (1964) 106–116. A. K. ZIEGLER, "Pope Gelasius I and His Teaching on the Relation of Church and State," CathHist Rev 27 (1942) 3–28, a study of basic importance.

[M. R. P. MC GUIRE]

THE MIDDLE AGES

Both in practice and in theory, the relationship between Church and State did not remain static over the 1,000 years of the *Middle Ages but changed as social conditions, levels of learning, and traditions of thought also underwent change.

Early Middle Ages. It was the common assumption in the early Middle Ages that there was only one Christian society, one "congregation of the faithful," and the great problem was to balance the authority of the two chief offices, the princely office, or *regnum,* and the priestly office, or *sacerdotium,* which God had established to rule over it (*see* CHURCH, HISTORY OF, II; PAPACY, 2).

Developments in the East. In the medieval Eastern, or *Byzantine, Empire, where strong imperial rule was unbroken by invasions and where ancient, especially Hellenistic, traditions were congenial with ideas of a sacred kingship, the emperors exercised the dominance over both Church and State that gave rise to the term *caesaropapism. Emperor *Justinian I (517–565) expressly counted among his responsibilities "the dignity and honor of the clergy" and "the true doctrines of the Godhead" (CorpIurCivNov 6). To maintain the clergy's dignity and honor, the emperors set the qualifications for ordinations, created bishoprics and changed their boundaries and status, appointed and even forced the resignation of patriarchs, supervised the monasteries and corrected abuses that recurred within them. Concern for true doctrine led them to summon councils, supervise their proceedings, and enforce their decisions. *Zeno in his *Henotikon* (482), *Heraclius in his *Ekthesis* (638), and other emperors attempted to settle dogmatic disputes even without conciliar support. The Patriarch Antonius, writing between 1394 and 1397 to Prince Vasili I of Russia, maintained that the Christian emperors "from the beginning established and confirmed true religion" and that it was unthinkable and impossible to have a Church without an emperor. Not only Byzantium but also the Eastern peoples that learned from Byzantium accepted a similar princely tutelage over the Church. The Russian Primary Chronicle, for example, describes how the Prince of Kiev, Iaroslav the Wise (1016–54), built and endowed churches, appointed and supported priests, looked to their education and "bade them teach the people . . . and to go often into the churches."

This submissiveness in the East of the *sacerdotium* to the *regnum* permitted the prince to make free use of the wealth, administrative skills, and immense moral power of the Church; and this close cooperation was of inestimable value for harrassed peoples on Europe's frontier, struggling to survive against a barbarian sea. The priesthood in turn, largely freed from profane distractions, could devote itself to the sumptuous liturgy and rich mystical life characteristic of the Eastern churches. But submissiveness to princes also weakened contacts with sister churches and the universal Church, promoted a certain isolationism, facilitated schism, and compromised somewhat the prophetic liberty of the Church, in that it hampered it in its duty to denounce evil even when tolerated or perpetrated by princes. Czar Ivan the Terrible could murder a patriarch, and Peter the Great could abolish the office altogether, with impunity.

The Church in the West. In the Latin West, the relations between the princely and sacerdotal powers developed under very different conditions. Up to the 11th century the low cultural level of the West, not fully relieved even by the *Carolingian Renaissance in the 9th century, was not conducive to original speculation on the nature of Christian society. Those pre-Carolingian and Carolingian writers who touched on kingship—*Isidore of Seville, the unknown Irish author of the *De duodecim abusivis saeculi* (written probably between 630 and 650), Kathvulf (author of an address to Charlemagne), *Smaragdus of Saint-Mihiel, *Jonas of Orléans, *Sedulius Scotus and *Hincmar of Reims—attempted no profound analysis of the nature of royal authority, and their assumptions may be described as vaguely Gelasian: the king had a right to rule, but priests must advise him for his own spiritual welfare. The coronation of *Charlemagne (800) also brought a revival of royal pretensions to dominance over the Church. Charlemagne himself, in a letter to *Leo III, limited the pope's duties to praying "like Moses" for the emperor's victories, while he took charge of all other functions in the government of the Church, including the task of fortifying it "with the knowledge of the faith."

In the same period, amid a long-lasting vacuum of effective lay power, popes and bishops were developing a spirit of self-reliance and independence, as they exercised leadership not only in religious matters but in many secular affairs as well. *Gregory I (590–604), for example, had to arrange for the economic support and military security of Rome. In the early 8th century, *Gregory II and *Gregory III vigorously rejected the iconoclastic policies of the Byzantine Emperor *Leo III and denounced imperial interference in dogmatic questions. The *Donation of Constantine, a crude but effective forgery redacted probably about 750, was tantamount to a papal declaration of independence from Byzantine authority (Constantine had supposedly given the whole Western Empire to the pope), and offered justification for the momentous papal decision to seek a new champion in the Frankish monarch. The donation of the Frankish King *Pepin III, promised in 754 and completed in 756, further established the popes' claim to the temporal sovereignty over central Italy, the "patrimony of St. Peter," although throughout the Carolingian age the Frankish kings remained the effective rulers of the area.

Another expression of clerical independence were the Pseudo-Isidorian decretals, a collection of largely forged papal letters redacted probably between 847 and 852 in France and primarily intended to defend French bishops against mounting lay oppression (*see* FALSE DECRETALS). Pseudo-Isidore emphasized clerical immunities and papal authority, but he does not seem to have envisioned a true priestly or papal theocracy. More forceful than Pseudo-Isidore in expressing the supremacy of the *sacerdotium* and papacy was the strong-willed Pope *Nicholas I (858–867), whose letters contain, apparently for the first time, the unambiguous assertion that the emperor derived his power not directly from God but from the Church and priesthood.

The early Middle Ages thus developed a broad spectrum of opinion concerning the proper distribution of power in Christian society, but a full confrontation of opposing views did not occur until the 11th century, until the great quarrel between the papacy and the *Holy Roman Empire known as the *investiture struggle.

High Middle Ages. By the middle of the 11th century, a group of reformers, led by Cardinal *Humbert of Silva Candida, author of the highly influential *Libri III adversus simoniacos* (1054–58), by *Leo IX, *Nicholas II, and above all by the great Hildebrand, *Gregory VII, had concluded that lay domination over the Church, and in particular lay control of clerical appointments, was flooding the Church with unworthy prelates, undermining clerical morality, and placing in jeopardy the salvation of Christians. These reformers demanded a full "liberty of the Church," which implied not only freedom from lay interference in clerical elections but also the immunity of the clergy from the law, courts, discipline, and even taxes of lay rulers. Emperor *Henry IV (1056–1106) resisted this program, which would have emasculated his power, but he was excommunicated and deposed (1076) and was forced to do a humiliating penance at Canossa (1077). The Concordat of *Worms (1122) patched together a compromise with respect to clerical appointments, but left unresolved the fundamental issue as to who, pope or emperor, exercised supreme authority over the medieval Christian commonwealth, the *Respublica Christiana.*

The Papalists. The essence of Gregorian thought, which dominated papal policy for the rest of the Middle Ages, seems to have been this: the priesthood, responsible for guiding the individual Christian to personal reform, was also responsible for actively leading the Christian commonwealth to the reform of its public morals, customs, and even institutions. The papacy, through its universal authority, provided unity and direction in this work of regenerating Christian society. Kings had to follow the leadership of priests and to place their swords at their service; to oppose them was to merit reprimand, excommunication, and even deposition. Despite these exalted views of priestly leadership, it does not appear that Gregory VII was a true theocratic "monist," in the sense of maintaining that all authority derived from the priesthood. In his letters, Gregory expressed only an Augustinian disdain for the office and works of kings and no claim that the priesthood was the source of their power. *Manegold of Lautenbach, one of the ablest of Gregorian publicists, justified Gregory's deposition of Henry not because the pope could make and unmake emperors at will, but because Henry had violated a kind of *social contract made with his subjects and had in fact deposed himself.

From the investiture controversy to the *Avignon papacy (1305), the period of their maximum prestige and power, the popes continued to pursue, with some success, these Gregorian ideals. The theory of papal hegemony was also strengthened. St. *Bernard of Clairvaux, in a famous analogy, likened the priestly and regal power to the two swords mentioned in Lk 22.38 and held that both belonged to the Church and were to be employed in its service. The great development in the study of Canon Law, which the investiture controversy itself had stimulated, added a new precision, rigor, and systematic spirit to the papalist argument (*see* CANON LAW, HISTORY OF). Canonists—decretists from the 12th century and, still more, decretalists in the 13th—contended that the pope, as vicar of God, must necessarily include royal authority within his plenitude of power and that a Christian society with two heads would be some sort of monster. To these ideas the papal publicists *Giles of Rome (d. 1316) and *Augustine of Ancona

Emperor Otto III, enthroned and blessed by God and the Church, miniature in a Gospel Book presented to the Emperor, 1000, probably by an artist of Reichenau or the Court School, in the treasury of the Aachen cathedral.

(d. 1328) gave the most extreme expression, attributing to the pope dominion over all men, Christian and pagan, and ownership of all their possessions.

The popes of the epoch—notably *Innocent III, *Innocent IV, *Alexander IV, and *Boniface VIII—remained in their public utterances distinctly more restrained than their enthusiastic theorists. Innocent III (1198–1216), for example, though often expressing exalted views on papal power, also, in the decretal *Novit*, written in 1204 to *Philip II of France, disclaimed all intent of diminishing royal jurisdiction or of judging concerning fiefs. Even the bull **Unam sanctam* (1302) of Boniface VIII, the most famous papal pronouncement on Church-State relations in the Middle Ages, was essentially a summons to Christian unity through obedience to the pope, but the document, oddly anachronistic in the allegorical and imprecise arguments used, left vague the extent of the obedience demanded.

Historians still disagree as to whether these medieval popes really envisioned a kind of theocratic "world monarchy" under absolute papal power. Certainly the popes welcomed and echoed the sweeping claims of their supporters, but they were also realistic men. They seem to have used these grandiose speculations not to define the primary aims of papal policy, but as useful arguments in the achievement of the more limited and more practical goals of maintaining ecclesiastical liberty, Christian unity, and papal leadership in spiritually significant affairs.

Development of the Concept of the State. In the 12th and 13th centuries, the papacy faced an ever-stronger lay challenge to its hegemony from such powerful rulers as the Emperors *Frederick I and *Frederick II and the Kings *Henry II and *Edward I of England and *Philip IV of France. Moreover, the renewed study of Roman law in the 12th century and the recovery of Aristotle's *Politics* in the 13th contributed strongly to what some historians call an emergent "lay spirit." Roman law attributed an unlimited *sovereignty to a prince who drew his power directly from the community, and Aristotle located the basis for political authority in the very nature of man. In this creative period, medieval political thinkers were in fact fashioning the modern idea of the *state; establishing its autonomy; and, through their acute constitutional speculations, exploring the management of its power.

In the face of this naturalistic and lay challenge to the religious premises of all prior medieval political thought, *Thomas Aquinas, with characteristic prudence, attempted to defend in new terms the traditional Gelasian notion of a balance of spiritual and secular power. For Thomas, nature and the natural law established the autonomy of, but also limited, the sovereignty of princes. Revealed or divine law established the autonomy of, but also limited, the sovereignty of popes. God alone was truly sovereign, and both the natural and divine laws, and the State and Church they established, drew their authority from His sovereign will, from what Thomas calls the eternal law of the universe (*see* NATURAL LAW IN POLITICAL THOUGHT; POLITICAL THOUGHT, HISTORY OF).

Close to Thomas in his ideal of balance, but far more explicit in defending the autonomy of kings and rebuking papal pretensions to sovereignty over them, was *John of Paris, author of the *Tractatus de potestate regia et papali* (1302). The *De monarchia* of *Dante

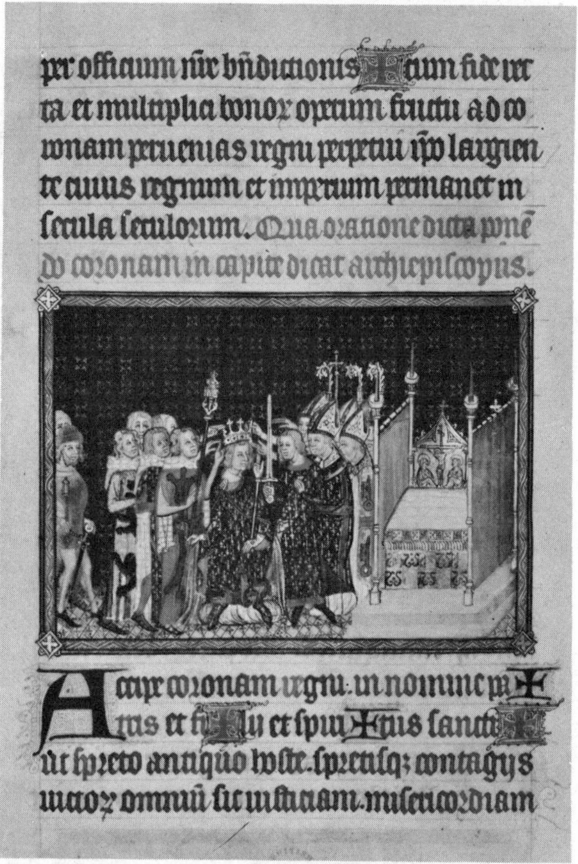

Spiritual and temporal peers holding the crown over the King's head at his coronation, miniature from the Coronation Book of Charles V of France, c. A.D. 1363 (Cotton MS Tiberius B. viii, fol. 59v).

Alighieri (written between 1310 and 1316) used Aristotelian naturalism to show the necessity of a universal empire and used Aristotelian logic to refute the allegorical use of scriptural figures (two swords, sun and moon, etc.) that papalists had enlisted to support their claims. Far more radical challenges to papal authority were presented by the Englishman *William of Ockham (d. 1349) and especially by *Marsilius of Padua, author of the *Defensor pacis* (1324). Marsilius, a true theoretical monist in that he conceded unlimited power to the community and to the prince who represented it, denied all substance to clerical authority and totally subjected priesthood and papacy to the prince's regulation, supervision, and discipline.

Late Middle Ages. The last 2 centuries of the Middle Ages were marked by the progressive disintegration of the medieval Christian commonwealth, brought about by the declining power and prestige of the papacy and the growing power of princes, who were able through their own enactments and through *concordats with the papacy to gain ever-wider powers over their territorial churches. Political thought in this period was occupied more by the argument over *conciliarism—concerning the relation of popes and general councils—than by questions of Church and State. But such conciliarist thinkers as *Conrad of Gelnhausen, *Henry Heinbuche of Langenstein, Francesco *Zabarella, Jean *Gerson, and *Nicholas of Cusa, in attempting to make the pope subject to the corporate community of the

Church, in conceding to the princes a position of prominence within that community, also contributed, if indirectly, to the growing lay power over territorial churches. More directly favoring state power was the great heretic John *Wyclif (d. 1384), who denied to the unregenerate clergy all rights of dominion and ownership and looked to the lay magistrate for leadership in reform.

The great medieval effort to build a commonwealth of Christian peoples and princes bound together by obedience to the pope and under his supreme guidance thus ended in failure. The popes themselves were perhaps too slow in recognizing that active world leadership carried grave risks of demeaning secular involvements and a degrading fiscalism and that many of their own ideals of social order and welfare could be achieved and were better achieved by the lay states that they had hoped to tutor. But that effort was not without value for the achievement in medieval Europe of a higher level of political order and an intensified political consciousness, and it also remains a rich and instructive chapter within the larger history of the Church's continuing quest to bear effective Christian witness within a complex and changing world.

See also SOCIAL THOUGHT, CATHOLIC, 3.

Bibliography: E. BARKER, *Social and Political Thought in Byzantium* (Oxford 1957). A. MICHEL, *Die Kaisermacht in der Ostkirche, 843–1204* (Darmstadt 1959). M. PACAUT, *La Théocratie: L'Église et le pouvoir au moyen âge* (Paris 1957). W. ULLMAN, *Medieval Papalism: The Political Theories of the Medieval Canonists* (London 1949); *The Growth of Papal Government in the Middle Ages* (2d ed. New York 1962). B. TIERNEY, *The Crisis of Church and State, 1050–1300* (Englewood Cliffs, N.J. 1964). G. TELLENBACH, *Church, State and Christian Society at the Time of the Investiture Contest,* tr. R. F. BENNETT (Oxford 1959). A. STICKLER, *Sacerdotium et regnum nei decretalisti e primi decretalisti* (Turin 1953). F. KEMPF, *Papsttum und Kaisertum bei Innocenz III* (Rome 1954). J. M. POWELL, *Innocent III, Vicar of Christ or Lord of the World?* (Boston, 1963).

[D. J. HERLIHY]

THE PERIOD OF CONFESSIONAL STATES

The monarchical consolidation of power in the nation-states of western Europe was achieved at the expense of the anachronistic claims of the papacy to temporal sovereignty. By the early 1500s, several princes, imbued with the secular philosophy of *Marsilius of Padua and Niccoló *Machiavelli, warred with the *States of the Church. Popes of the *Renaissance, as much secular as spiritual princes, engaged actively in diplomacy, sometimes compromising claims to temporal sovereignty in order to win allies. The *Holy Roman Empire was fraught with heresy, confederative tendencies, and *nationalism. Germans, Czechs, and Swiss resented Spanish and Italian interference. There were strong anticlerical traditions in England and France.

Momentous forces let loose by the *Crusades, the *Black Death, nascent *capitalism, overseas exploration, and the rise of the merchant-professional middle class played havoc with traditional political, social, and economic institutions. Great ecclesiastics were humbled by greater kings. Laymen often replaced bishops and abbots in government when the temporal claims of the papacy were opposed by nationalistic monarchs in struggles over lay investiture, ecclesiastical courts, clerical taxation, and similar issues. The prestige of the papacy had suffered through serious religious controversies from the Babylonian captivity to the rise of *conciliarism. Effective leadership and spirituality were lacking in some Renaissance popes and bishops. Reform movements of the 15th century fell short of the achievements of those of earlier periods. (*See* CHURCH, HISTORY OF, III; PAPACY, 3.)

Theories of the Reformers. Into this maelstrom the Protestant *Reformation injected disquieting ideas that attacked papal temporal and spiritual sovereignty. Certain secular princes supported the Reformers against the pope in order to realize private political aims. The effect of the Reformation, therefore, was to encourage nationalism and *absolutism through the removal of papal restraints and the emphasis on *Erastianism. Conversely, without help from antipapal princes, the Reformers probably could not have survived against the awesome papal weapons of *excommunication, *interdict, *Inquisition, and the *Index of Forbidden Books.

Luther. Martin *Luther was deeply concerned about the relation of Church and State, but he was inconsistent in his views. Strongly nationalistic, he resented Italian domination of the Church and Spanish interference in the Empire. Similar-minded German princes sustained him and promoted his doctrines. He originally advocated the separation of Church and State, holding that all authority originated with God and passed through Him to princes, whose power on earth was superior to ecclesiastical authority. Practical problems forced him to alter this theory, however. He condoned civil control over religion in connection with the Saxon visitation of 1527, arguing that the Elector's syndics should supervise preaching, suppress Catholicism, and punish schismatics such as the *Anabaptists. Luther also supported the Leagues of Torgau and Schmalkalden, which forcefully advanced his doctrines. He favored the aristocracy against the peasants in 1525, thereby supporting pragmatically the civil authorities and furthering *Lutheranism and German nationalism. He often stated theoretically that neither bishops nor princes should impose decrees or laws against the convictions of conscience, but he argued practically for theocratic absolutism. He denied papal supremacy and rejected episcopal authority as unscriptural. His advocacy of passive obedience to lawful temporal jurisdiction encouraged the 17th-century doctrine of the *divine right of kings.

Calvin. John *Calvin of Geneva also taught the strict separation of civil and ecclesiastical power but later found it impractical to enforce it except at the cost of impairing the success of his tenets. Calvin's *Institutes* (1535) illustrate how well trained he was in theology and law and how easily he made the transition from Genevan minister to dictatorial head of the theocratic city-state. He considered the function of civil government to be simply the preservation of law and the enforcement of religion and personal piety according to his doctrines. All civil offices were divinely ordained so that it was unlawful and immoral to rebel against the state unless the state violated God's will (as Calvin interpreted it). Accordingly, civil obedience was a moral duty; and civil disobedience against immoral princes, a right. Calvin's doctrine of jusitifiable rebellion through magistrates was employed by his followers in Holland, Scotland, England, and France during the next century. His politicoecclesiastical system operated as an aristocratic *theocracy headed by him and assisted by the consistory, composed of ministers and elders, which functioned as the coordinating body between magistrates and ministers. Although Calvin may have originally preached that Church and State were exclusive societies, the former admonishing citizens to moral and spiritual perfection and the latter enforcing uniformity by punishing sinners, in effect the temporal and ecclesiastical officers worked together to further *Calvinism.

Zwingli. Huldrych *Zwingli of Zurich, who wished to expel foreign influence and suppress aristocratic oligarchy, was a modern-day prophet-avenger. He hoped to establish divine law as revealed in Scriptures through the forcible implementation of civil authority. Each community or state, he said, should determine its religion and enforce it strictly through civil officers. Denying altogether the authority of the pope and bishops, Zwingli advocated the fullest cooperation between civil and ecclesiastical officers in ruling a government operated according to Christian precepts.

English Developments. Whereas Lutheranism and Calvinism were as much social and economic as religious movements, *Anglicanism was from the first almost entirely political. The long history of Anglo-papal controversy after the Conquest of 1066 culminated in *Henry VIII's Act of Supremacy (1534), severing the link between England and Rome by making him supreme head of the Church *in* England. Not until the Acts of Supremacy and Uniformity (1559) under *Elizabeth I, however, did Anglicanism become doctrinally the Church *of* England. The English Church and Parliament established an episcopalian ecclesiastical polity under the primacy of the monarch. Erastianism became a cardinal policy of Anglicanism, the crown-in-convocation ruling the Church. Puritanism, rooted in Calvinism, sprang up quickly. Most *Puritans accepted Episcopalianism, hoping, however, to increase lay participation in ecclesiastical affairs. Some separatist Puritans in England and Scotland favored *Presbyterianism with its kirk sessions, synods, and general assemblies; John *Knox and George *Buchanan in Scotland and Thomas *Cartwright in England were its chief theorists. Other separatists were *Congregationalists, advocating the doctrinal and governmental autonomy of each parish.

Caesaro-papism found its exponents and opponents in 17th-century England. The principal Anglican apologist was Richard *Hooker, who in *The Laws of Ecclesiastical Polity* (1594) defended episcopalianism against the incursions of Presbyterians. He favored monarchy that should be fully, albeit passively, obeyed. Divine-right monarchy, sanctioned directly by God (not by the pope, councils, or popular will) and invested with spiritual and temporal power flowered under the early Stuarts. Their struggles with Parliament were essentially constitutional (absolute versus mixed monarchy), but their quarrel was also vitally concerned with issues such as that of *fundamentalism versus *Arminianism. Many parliamentarians favored the governmental enforcement of "true religion"; others wanted a strict separation of Church and State. Thomas *Hobbes argued that absolute monarchy, sovereign in civil and ecclesiastical affairs, was the best form of government. Revolution against it was therefore unthinkable, and religious uniformity was preferable to sectarianism. John *Locke later maintained that separation of Church and State was essential and that religious toleration would develop from noninterference by the government, whose authority lay outside questions of conscience. Yet neither he nor Hobbes included Catholics among the tolerated because they were allegedly subject to external papal authority.

Catholic Response. The vehement attacks against hierocratic doctrine by the Reformers and their magisterial supporters demanded firm answers, but the Emperor *Charles V and the popes from *Paul III to *Pius IV differed over what the answers should be. Rome considered doctrinal issues vital, whereas Charles wished to promote Catholic-Protestant talks aimed at resolving political disunity. Charles had already compromised the Church's position in the Peace of *Augsburg (1529) and in concessions to Lutheran princes before Paul III convened the Council of *Trent (1545–63), which was in itself an admission that the pope alone could not solve the great issues. Charles disliked the choice of Trent as a site; and when the Council adjourned to Bologna in 1547, he prohibited Germans from going there. The Spaniards, remembering Spanish-papal disputes in Italy, were also unhappy. Meanwhile, Charles authorized unorthodox religious practices to placate the Reformers. Although the Council made no dogmatic pronouncement on papal infallibility, it did buttress papal authority by denying that princes could interfere with the Inquisition, excommunication, papal bulls, and ecclesiastical courts. Political problems involving the Holy See nevertheless arose soon afterward respecting England, Holland, and France. In addition, *Philip II of Spain accepted papal help to suppress the Dutch Calvinists and the Anglicans; the pope lost prestige when both ventures failed.

Gallicanism. *Gallicanism in France posed a serious problem from the 15th century to the *French Revolution. The clergy had fallen increasingly under monarchical control since the reign of *Philip IV (d. 1314), and caesaropapism became entrenched legally through the Pragmatic Sanction of Bourges (1438) and the Concordat of Bologna (1516), through which the king obtained the right to appoint hierarchs, subject only to *pro forma* papal approval. Naturally, *Francis I and his successors nominated hierarchs sympathetic to royal policy, whether or not it coincided with the interests of the Church. Gallicanism encouraged the evolution of a virtual French national Church dominated by the monarch, whose supervision of churchmen and Church property was coextensive with the degree of royal absolutism; this reached its apogee under *Louis XIV (d. 1715).

Political theorists about the turn of the 17th century avidly supported Gallicanism. Pierre *Pithou (d. 1596), for instance, argued that papal decrees had no force in France without the *placet* of the French bishops meeting in council. Edmond *Richer (d. 1633) maintained that the authority of ecumenical councils was superior to papal authority.

Theoretical Developments. About the same time two illustrious Catholic authors, the Jesuits Robert *Bellarmine (d. 1621) and Francisco *Suárez (d. 1617), upheld papal spiritual supremacy but denied the pope's right to interfere in temporal affairs. Bellarmine advocated the separation of Church and State and rejected the temporal power of the pope except to prevent the implementation of laws threatening the Church's rights or to depose heretical monarchs, but he later rescinded this view of the *potestas indirecta*. Suárez likewise made a distinction between papal temporal and spiritual jurisdiction, but he held it lawful for the pope to interfere in a state's religious policy because princes were subject to divine law, which superseded civil law. He also urged freedom of conscience, even for pagans and heretics.

Decline of Papal Power. Secular authorities no longer took papal temporal power seriously after the middle of the 17th century, and religious persecution waned. Princes dismissed, for instance, the Pope's objections to the Peace of *Westphalia in 1648. Persecution in the Empire and England became uncommon. *Henry IV (d. 1610), converted from Calvinism to Catholicism, issued the Edict of *Nantes (1598) in the hope of resolving the long struggle between Catholics and *Huguenots. *Richelieu and *Mazarin tolerated the Huguenots because they were important to the French economy, although they were attacked occasionally for political reasons. Louis XIV continued the lenient policy until 1685, when he revoked the edict, saddening *Innocent XI, who privately urged toleration by Louis and *James II of England. The persecution of Huguenots and Jansenists was a manifestation of divine-right absolutism aimed at regulating French life, though Louis also felt it his moral duty to suppress heresy. He frequently interfered in Church government even to the point of isolating French bishops from contact with Rome, espousing bizarre doctrines, and confiscating the revenues of vacant episcopal sees. In 1682, with Louis's approval, more than 70 French bishops rejected papal infallibility, reiterated Gallican liberties, and maintained that ecumenical councils had a higher order of authority than the pope.

The Age of Enlightenment. The ideas of the 18th-century *Enlightenment embodied a conception of a mechanistic universe regulated by immutable physical laws. *Rationalism, *Deism, and the *social contract theory of government gave a materialistic explanation of the origin of matter and of the political and social order that challenged the teachings of the Catholic Church and, indirectly, the authority of Christ's vicar. Since rationalist political theorists maintained that the state evolved from practical necessity and was dependent on popular will, the pope was excluded from any association with civil power.

Febronianism and Josephinism. It is surprising, however, that the principal opposition to the authority of the Holy See came not from the rationalists but from the Catholic exponents of *Febronianism and *Josephinism, two closely related theories that developed in Germany and Austria. Bishop John Nikolaus von *Hontheim of Trier (d. 1790), writing under the pseudonym Febronius, held that the popes had usurped primacy and were no more powerful than other bishops, a general Church council alone being authoritative. Moreover, neither papal nor conciliar decrees were binding in a country unless its ruler sanctioned them. Febronius recanted in 1778, but his ideas were widely adopted by German bishops, including the three ecclesiastical electors. At the Congress of *Ems (1786) these bishops demanded privileges of episcopal independence that infringed upon papal primacy, in effect emulating Gallicanism in what amounted to the government of a separate German Catholic Church. Febronianism and its Austrian counterpart, Josephinism, thrived during Prussia's and Austria's supremacy under *Frederick II (the Great) and *Maria Theresa. The Empress put the clergy and Church property under state control and rejected papal or episcopal decrees of which she disapproved. Her successor, *Joseph II, appointed bishops without papal approbation, altered diocesan boundaries, changed the liturgy and Church calendar, suppressed women's religious orders, and closed hundreds of convents. Leopold II of Tuscany, his brother, made similar changes.

The First Secular States: the U.S. and France. Secularization in the Enlightenment led in part to the creation of secular states in France and the U.S. Blaming the Church for evils that oppressed the lower classes, the French revolutionaries first confiscated Church property and later subordinated ecclesiastics to the state through the *Civil Constitution of the Clergy (1790). Many clergy, however, refused to acknowledge allegiance to what amounted to a French national Church in the face of *Pius VI's declaration that the Constitution was heretical and that he would excommunicate clergy who submitted to it. The Constitution therefore created schisms within France and between it and the papacy that were not healed until *Napoleon I, for political reasons, signed with *Pius VII the *Concordat of 1801.

Puritanism in America had admitted the close connection of ministerial and magisterial authority during the 17th century in the northern and mid-Atlantic colonies. But Congregationalism had found widespread support and the "saints" had gradually given ground. In most colonies the principle of Church and State separation had been commonly accepted by the mid-18th century so that, with the winning of American independence and the acceptance of the Constitution, there was no question that the separation principle was firmly established. The first American Catholic bishop, John *Carroll, and others that followed him supported the principle as well as religious toleration for all [*see* CHURCH AND STATE IN THE U.S. (LEGAL HISTORY)].

Bibliography: O. F. VON GIERKE, *Political Theories of the Middle Ages*, tr. F. W. MAITLAND (Cambridge, Eng. 1900; pa. Boston 1958). F. GAVIN, *Seven Centuries of the Problem of Church and State* (New York 1938) 68–128. C. C. ECKHARDT, *The Papacy and World Affairs as Reflected in the Secularization of Politics* (Chicago 1937). R. G. GETTELL, *History of Political Thought* (New York 1924), esp. ch. 6, 8–13, 18. F. MOURRET, *A History of the Catholic Church*, tr. N. THOMPSON, 8 v. (St. Louis 1930–57) v.6, 7, *passim*. C. POULET, *A History of the Catholic Church*, tr. from 4th Fr. ed. by S. A. RAEMERS, 2 v. (St. Louis 1934–35), v.2, *passim*. H. DANIEL-ROPS, *The Church in the Seventeenth Century*, tr. J. BUCKINGHAM (London 1963). C. D. CREMEANS, *The Reception of Calvinistic Thought in England* (Urbana, Ill. 1949). G. DONALDSON, *The Scottish Reformation* (Cambridge, Eng. 1960). J. T. ELLIS, *Perspectives in American Catholicism* (Baltimore 1963) 1–39. A. SIMPSON, *Puritanism in Old and New England* (Chicago 1955).

[M. J. HAVRAN]

CHURCH AND STATE SINCE 1789

Scholars are inclined to stress the relationships among the political movements of the late 18th century and to include them under a comprehensive title—the democratic revolution (*see* DEMOCRACY). In Europe and in North and South America these movements had a common element in the rejection of absolutist pretensions and hereditary privilege. There were similar demands for checks on executive power through popular representation, assertions of popular sovereignty and the natural *equality of man, and appeals to individual rights of conscience, speech, and assembly (*see* HUMAN RIGHTS).

Extension of Liberal Constitutionalism. If the proponents of change had a common base, they were faced with different situations. In England, the theory of *constitutionalism had already been accepted; there remained the tasks of extending *civil liberties to unpopular minorities such as Catholics and Jews and of broadening the base of political participation. On the Continent, entrenched institutions and social groups provided determined resistance that was only gradually overcome in the course of the 19th century. In the U.S. the social structure offered no such resistance to ideas and institutions that had been maturing during the colonial period.

Implicit in the constitutional theory was the distinction between the *state, with its specific centrally coordinated activities, and *society, with its manifold uncentralized relationships. The *Constitution of the U.S. made this distinction explicit in its concept of reserved and delegated powers and in its first 10 amendments. In Continental Europe there remained considerable ambiguity in this field both on the theoretical level, where a Rousseauist monism had some influence, and in the tendency of the state to continue the control of religion characteristic of the Old Regime. A clear example of the latter was the *Civil Constitution of the Clergy (1790).

In broadest terms the 18th-century political revolutions can be considered as efforts to reestablish constitutionalism, or the limitation of governmental authority by private right, in opposition to theories of obedience to the state that had developed since the Renaissance. Medieval precedents could be cited to justify such efforts. But when proposed in the 18th century, constitutionalism had to face the problem that the Protestant *Reformation had strengthened the tendency to consider a common religion as the necessary cement for a cohesive community structure. Various Christian churches had been established in many states through arrangements that afforded protection and support to a privileged religion over which the state exercised considerable control.

American Developments. As religion weakened as a social bond in the 18th century, "reason," "nature," and patriotism were appealed to as substitutes (*see* DEISM; NATIONALISM; RATIONALISM). When specific circumstances made religious pluralism necessary, it was accepted. Thus, a combination of Catholic leadership and a Protestant majority led to the *Toleration Acts in *Maryland (1639, 1649); the royal charter for *Rhode Island (1663) accepted the principle of religious liberty, though it was circumscribed in practice; and William *Penn's Frame of Government in *Pennsylvania (1682) made his colony the freest in religious matters. This trend toward separation of Church and State was greatly extended by the American Revolution: Thomas Jefferson authored *Virginia's Act for Establishing Religious Freedom (1786), which affirmed the neutrality of the state in matters of faith.

When the Bill of Rights was appended to the U.S. Constitution (1791), the opening words of the First Amendment declared: "Congress shall make no law respecting an establishment of religion, or prohibiting the free exercise thereof." The decisive factor in this solution was pragmatic: in no other way could the thirteen states, four of which had established churches and all of which had a mosaic of religious variations, be formed into a single nation. In only one other nation, *Belgium, was full religious liberty written into the constitution at the foundation of the state. There, as in the U.S., special circumstances made Catholics favorable to constitutional limitations on government and to freedom of religion.

Objections of Catholic Theorists. The doctrine of popular sovereignty associated with these developments met objection from Catholic theorists on the ground that it denied that God was the source of all authority. They also found disestablishment unpalatable on the premise that Church and State are independent societies, with the Church superior because of its end. Asserting the "indirect power" of the Church, they maintained that the state must support it when its aid is needed or when the temporal and spiritual converge (e.g., in education, marriage). With a variety of nuances this position continued to dominate Catholic thinking throughout the 19th century. The struggle to preserve the *States of the Church strengthened this position, for the *temporal power was incompatible with a theory of separation. Nor did the cause of separation recommend itself since many of its proponents wished to strip the Church of all public influence.

Theoretical objections, however, did not impede the gradual extension of liberal constitutionalism. On the practical level, circumstances determined the reaction of most Catholics to the disappearance of the confessional state. In areas where they were a minority, as in England, Canada, Australia, New Zealand, Scandinavia, Switzerland, the Netherlands, and in some German and eastern European states, Catholics welcomed any steps that extended religious freedom. The same attitude prevailed where Catholics were a majority but the governing power was non-Catholic, as in Ireland and Poland.

Attempts at Accommodation. Even where religious liberty conferred the greatest benefits, as in the U.S., few developed a consistent theory to explain their preference. Those who did so were mostly Europeans and were known as Liberal Catholics. Faced with the necessity of making some accommodation with reality, the majority accepted the formula of "thesis-hypothesis." The "thesis," or ideal, was asserted to be the situation in which civil society would recognize only the true religion and would value it as the foundation of public order; the "hypothesis" was applied to situations in which the Church would accept the actual circumstances of divided religious loyalty and would demand only the right to preach the gospel freely, to rule and guide the baptized, to organize private and public religious worship, and to possess property. Even the outstanding Liberal Félix *Dupanloup, Bishop of Orléans, appealed to this distinction to explain the apparent rigidity of the *Syllabus of Errors of *Pius IX (1864). The favorable response he drew from bishops in all countries testified to the popularity of this partial accommodation to the disappearance of the confessional state.

Use of Concordats. The proponents of indirect power and of the thesis-hypothesis formula had some difficulty in explaining the *concordats that became a prominent feature of ecclesiastical policy in the 19th century. Patterned on the arrangements made by *Napoleon I with

*Pius VII for France (1801) and Italy (1803), the concordats bound the Church and specific governments to mutual reciprocal obligations. Both in the negotiations and in the texts, these had the appearance of contractual engagements between sovereigns. They afforded no support to the assumption of superiority of the ecclesiastical power required by the thesis.

Liberal Catholics. The Liberal Catholics made a more explicit attempt to adjust to the condition in which the Church could no longer count on the coercive power of the state to support its mission. The term Liberal Catholic lacks precision; those whom it designates were not liberal in the sense that they raised the banner of personal autonomy against authority in institutionalized religion (*see* LIBERALISM). Nor were they genuinely philosophical in their approach to political problems. They began with the conviction that privilege was dead and that the Church could count only on the free assent of its members. They did not consider the passing of the confessional state a tragedy. They welcomed it as a boon that had already proved its worth in Belgium and the U.S. They were impressed by Daniel *O'Connell's use of the parliamentary process to gain Catholic *emancipation, and contrasted the advantages of religious liberty with the deadening dependence of the Church on arbitrary power in the old regimes.

Nearly everywhere their views met resistance, notably in Rome. Early Liberal Catholics, such as Félicité de *Lamennais, were strong advocates of papal power, which they viewed as a necessary counterweight to the national state's control of religion. But *Gregory XVI's *Mirari vos* (1832), and particularly the determination of *Pius IX to oppose all political forms that posed a threat to the continued existence of the Papal States, caused the Liberal Catholics to drift from the *ultramontanism that had been their hallmark. In the crisis leading to the disappearance of the temporal power, the term ultramontanist came to be applied to those supporters of the papal position who rejected all accommodation with representative institutions and individual liberties.

Growth of Catholic Institutions. While circumstances were adding to the difficulties of Catholics who wished to accept the new political order, there was a remarkable growth of Catholic institutions in democratic and liberal states. Conflicts over education led to the establishment of Catholic schools; interest in social questions increased the number of welfare institutions and stimulated the formation of Catholic workingman's associations; political conflicts, such as the *Kulturkampf in Bismarck's Germany, contributed to the strengthening of viable Catholic *political parties. Even dramatic breaks with tradition, such as the unilateral denunciation of the concordat by Republican France (1905), ultimately diverted Catholic energies into social and apostolic tasks. As decision-making in government broadened to include some participation by the majority of citizens, compacts with heads of states no longer provided sufficient guarantees for the vitality or even the safety of the Church. In this context, Catholic social organizations were to provide new methods of achieving the Church's mission. *See* SOCIAL MOVEMENTS, CATHOLIC.

Reorientation of Papal Policy. *Leo XIII did not provide a new theoretical basis for Church-State relations. But he did give a new approach to modern political problems. He made strenuous efforts to detach French Catholics from their loyalty to monarchical government (*Au milieu des sollicitudes*); he praised the religious situation in the U.S. (*Longinqua*); he emphasized the God-given gift of liberty of the human person (**Libertas*); and he declared that the people had the right to choose their rulers freely, though not to confer the right to rule (*Diuturnum*). *Pius X made no notable contribution in this field, though he did remove the *Roman Question from the arena of world politics and improved relations with Italy by modifying the **non expedit*. *Benedict XV removed the latter entirely and allowed Italian Catholics to form the Popolari party on a nonconfessional basis.

Threat of Totalitarianism. The immediate consequence of World War I was a great expansion of the areas in which the form of the state was democratic with constitutions guaranteeing civil rights and full freedom of worship. Benedict XV and *Pius XI entered into cordial relations with most of these and negotiated concordats that accepted religious pluralism. But the collapse of the Czarist regime had given birth to a Soviet totalitarian state that was avowedly hostile to religion (*see* COMMUNISM, INTERNATIONAL). The March on Rome (1922) established a Fascist state in Italy that became increasingly totalitarian (*see* FASCISM). In 1933 Hitler came to power in Germany and established a dictatorship incompatible with Christianity (*see* NATIONAL SOCIALISM). Dictatorships replaced democratic systems in several smaller states (*see* TOTALITARIANISM).

Pius XI made a determined effort to protect the rights of the Church with the *Lateran Pact and concordat with Mussolini (1929) and a concordat with Hitler (1933). But the principles of these regimes made it impossible for the Church to operate normally, and Pius XI condemned their basic tenets in *Non abbiamo bisogno* on Italian Fascism (1931), *Mit brennender sorge* against German National Socialism (1937), and **Divini Redemptoris* against atheistic Communism (1937). Troubles with other dictatorships underlined the relatively favorable position of the Church in the democracies.

Papal Teaching on Democracy and Freedom of Religion. This experience was reflected in the wartime messages of *Pius XII, especially that of Christmas 1944 (*Benignitas et humanitas*). In it the Pope rejected absolutism in all its forms. While insisting on the right of peoples to choose their form of government, the Pope noted that men "are demanding a system of government more consistent with the dignity and liberty of the citizen" [ActApS 37 (1945) 13]. The Church shared this interest and believed that man should be an active participant in social life. The Pope contrasted the *masses with a "people worthy of the name," free to hold opinions, to express them, and to use them for the common good. Later, in an address (*Ci riesce*) to the national convention of Italian jurists (1953), Pius XII maintained that in the new international community with states professing a variety of religions, false religions and moral error could be tolerated to promote the common good. The state is not bound to repress error in all circumstances; the common good is the decisive element.

A comprehensive statement on the historic issues of Church and State is found in *John XXIII's **Pacem in terris,* which was intended to be a guide for the 2d session of *Vatican Council II. Throughout the document, the distinction between society and the state is explicit. Equally clear is the right of conscience: "Every human being has the right to honor God according to the dictates of an upright conscience, and the right to profess his religion privately and publicly" (14). Error does not destroy human rights (158). Among essential human rights based on "the dignity of the human person" is "the right to take an active part in public affairs and to contribute one's part to the common good of the citizens" (26). This is not in conflict with the principle that "authority comes from God," which can be accommodated to democracy (52). Fundamentally, "every civil authority must take pains to promote the common good of all without preference for any single citizen or civic group" (56). The basic function of government is to preserve rights: "For to safeguard the inviolable rights of the human person and to facilitate the fulfillment of duties, should be the essential office of every public authority" (60). The description of the government that best corresponds to "the innate demands of human nature" (68–77) reads like a sketch of American democracy. Throughout, liberty becomes a basic norm of political life. (*See* SOCIAL THOUGHT, PAPAL.)

In the same year (1963), Cardinal Augustine Bea, SJ, in an address to the Italian Catholic jurists, used the encyclical to discuss "The Importance of Religious Liberty." Declaring that religious liberty was an inalienable right, he defined it as the exclusion of any restraint on the part of men or society, and the right to profess, proclaim, and propagate one's religious beliefs.

The teaching of Pope John had been foreshadowed by a number of European and American theologians who described the confessional state as the product of historical circumstances rather than an ideal toward which Catholics were bound to strive. Their work was assisted by a growing awareness of the vocation of the *laity in representing the Church in the temporal order and in the emphasis on autonomous bodies of laymen in *Catholic Action. John Courtney Murray, SJ attempted a restatement of the Gelasian formula. The Christian is both a child of God and a member of the human community as a citizen of the state. In each capacity he is endowed with a set of rights. Harmony between Church and State must be achieved in the human person. It is democratic man, conscious of his freedom and his social obligations, who must assure the primacy of the spiritual in human society. It is by his witness to the faith that the mission of the Church is furthered.

A declaration on religious freedom, submitted to the third (1964) session of Vatican Council II, repudiated all coercion in religious matters as contrary to the dignity of man. Although supported by an overwhelming majority of the fathers, it was postponed for final decision until the fourth session. *See* FREEDOM OF RELIGION.

Bibliography: H. A. ROMMEN, *The State in Catholic Thought* (St. Louis 1945); *The Natural Law,* tr. T. A. HANLEY (St. Louis 1947). D. A. BINCHY, *Church and State in Fascist Italy* (New York 1941). A. C. JEMOLO, *Church and State in Italy, 1850–1950,* tr. D. MOORE (Philadelphia 1960). J. N. MOODY, ed., *Church and Society* (New York 1953). J. C. MURRAY, *We Hold These Truths* (New York 1960). J. MARITAIN, *Man and the State* (Chicago 1951). L. STURZO, *Church and State,* tr. B. B. CARTER (London 1939; Notre Dame, Ind. 1962). J. N. MOODY and J. G. LAWLER, eds., *The Challenge of Mater et Magistra* (New York 1963). **Illustration credits:** Fig. 1, Foto Ann Bredol-Lepper, Germany. Fig. 2, Trustees of the British Museum.

[J. N. MOODY]

CHURCH AND STATE IN LATIN AMERICA

Relations between Church and State in Latin America since independence have varied from a privileged position for the Church, guaranteed by the State, to active persecution of it. In Portuguese as well as in Spanish America the tensions derived from the operation of royal patronage in the colonial period. (*See* PATRONATO REAL.) This had resulted in a union of Church and State under the comparatively stable Iberian monarchies and the identification of such a relationship with national sovereignty. The republican governments were conditioned by this heritage. Their solutions of the problem were unrealistic and often bordered on jungle warfare. The State at times tried to use the property and prestige of the Church as a support for the secular ends of government; at other times, anticlerical and positivistic, it crushed all public evidence of religion. Rarely did the effort at union come from the Church. Decades of struggle marked its effort to gain autonomy; tension and religious paralysis were the result. In Brazil the recovery proceeded with a measurable momentum. In sharp contrast, Mexican conflict heightened to the climax of acute persecution. Elsewhere, save for two volcanic interludes in Ecuador and Paraguay, pressure slowly lessened until some order came to prevail between a free Church and a self-sufficient State. This article discusses Church and State in (1) Mexico, (2) Spanish South America, and (3) Brazil.

1. MEXICO

Mexico came to independence as best educated, most populous, and most productive of the new Spanish American republics. It had an outstanding missionary history. All this was reversed for over a century.

The Constitution of 1824 provided for national patronage, but the clergy vetoed any continuation of the old Spanish system and made a serious effort to organize the hierarchy on independent lines. Then appeared the anticlericals, the Catholics who would use Church affiliation while stifling Catholic principles in public life. They had destroyed the independence of the Spanish Church. *Gómez Farías, an honest but callow ideologist, in the 1830s dismantled the entire Catholic school and university structure in the name of a new evangel presented by the recently identified Liberals. To weaken the public influence of religion, he forced through legislation that canonized the abandonment of religious vows, a measure called by Callcott, "indecent, repulsive, and sacrilegious." This politically inept administration suppressed the missions and seized the Pious Fund of the Californias. Forced loans from church properties were demanded to fortify the national treasury in default of a rational tax schedule. His work was the model for his successors.

Complications arose at the same time from another quarter, the *clericazo.* The hierarchy died out with the passing of Bishop Pérez in 1829. This was the climax of a series of events that made for a shortage of priests. Many died in the insurgent wars. Many others, without the normal direction of a diocesan, plunged into the full wave of politics, to the neglect of their flocks and the astonishment of the faithful. Such was Ramos Arizpe, sometime secretary of state, cofounder of the Masonic York Lodge, who championed the program set by Gómez Farías. Others simply laid aside the cassock. Men of this type effectively blocked a movement for reform begun by the new bishops of 1831, and this condition prevailed for many years. It meant confusion when the bishops tried to reach a stable agreement vis-à-vis a government alternately directed by the two Masonic Lodges, Scot and York. There was literally no authentic unity of direction to guide the faithful, despite the heroic efforts of clerics as devoted as Bishop Vásquez and Father Arrillaga, ably seconded by the great layman Lucas Alamán. The latter pointed out an issue that a united voice could have resolved, namely, the large number of clerical properties held in mortmain for centuries and therefore beyond the impact of any tax, a highly involved question, not yet really investigated in detail. At any rate the positivist intervention of the Juárez regime ended the matter in the Reformist Constitution of 1856.

The Juárez Reform. The coming of Juárez and the Plan de Ayutla meant a definite frontal attack on the Mexican Church, an intervention beyond all just bounds. Juárez brushed aside the work of the commission set up by Pius IX to readjust the titles to the mortmain lands. He espoused the Gómez Farías program and blessed it with the principles of Auguste Comte, whose first preachment denied the validity of the concept of divine revelation. The Constitution of 1856 was made by men most of whom were honorable in their professions but illogical in their thinking, overwhelmed with dismay at the results of bad government since the first presidency of Guadalupe Victoria. The parishes were deprived by law of the right to church buildings. Gabino Barreda, Comtean expert in education, was entrusted with the cabinet office in control of all schools, and he set out boldly to remake them on positivistic principles. A terrible civil war ensued, followed by the intervention of the French and the adventurer Maximilian. Victory went to the Juárist forces. The Constitution of 1856 was made official under his successor Lerdo de Tejada. By this time the Church had no legal existence in the country; there were no schools and no buildings for religious purposes that were not national property or owned by men with a double conscience. Lawyers could not discuss the two societies in terms of the same human law.

Juárez was a man who meant well, a child of the Mexico of Gómez Farías: implacable, silent, unforgiving, determined to establish his positivist utopia in Mexico. Instead, he left as an inheritance a monolithic political party. Since 1856 the PNR has ruled Mexico without challenge. Unhappily, party loyalty often superseded good intention and prevented a just balance of rights. The *Ley Lerdo* of his confidant authorized seizure and sale of both Church and Indian (*ejido*) properties. Many party men, nominal Catholics, followed the law and "denounced" millions of acres, got titles for party fidelity, and thus accentuated the land hunger that beckoned Indian leaders to warfare. Cold-hearted greed added to the imbalance of society. Widespread peonage followed during the 19th century.

Revolution in the 20th Century. Under the regime of Porfirio *Díaz, who professed obedience to the party and Constitution, independent Mexico enjoyed its longest period of peace, security, and prosperity. A breathing spell was given the Church. Under her direction, intensive reconstruction of public education took place. The clergy vigorously attacked the social problem and initiated important scholarship. Men felt that reason had returned to interpersonal relations, and the successor of Díaz, Francisco Madero, in 1911 won the presidency by a peaceful revolution. But he was soon assassinated, and there began 3 decades of savagery in public office. The names of Huerta, Morones, Obregón, Calles, Gil, and Lázaro Cárdenas stand out garishly during those times. The period opened with Carranza's Constitution of 1917, which provided, in article 3, that "No religious corporation, no minister of religion, will be allowed to open or direct establishments for private education." This was understood to affect only Catholics, who made up some 95 per cent of the people. Organized labor was then put under subsidy, the "lider" recognized as one quite willing to let his men suffer for a price. No Catholic might teach, and public institutions of learning practically excluded him from gaining a degree. No priest could say Mass without fear of a bullet, and the bullet often found those who attended and received Communion. The hierarchy were publicly denounced as traitors, evildoers, or more modernly "enemies of progress." Churches were closed, and the number of parish priests severely limited. Raids were made on catechism classes, sodality meetings, and study clubs as though they were dens of iniquity, as Calles charged. Finally the bishops, fearing a total destruction of the Church, called on the laity to save it. A young man of Chihuahua, José Antonio Urquiza, in 1937–39 formed a small group of courageous students to study tactics, devise an organization fit for the task, and go to work. Theirs was a remarkable piece of Catholic action. They formed an organization pledged not to kill but to remake their country on its best ideals. This Sinarquista Association numbered more than 1 million. A nonpolitical union, it publicly dramatized the cause and the way to win. Using the Communist tactic of boring from within, they Christianized labor, schools, and government offices. They marched and sang by the thousands; though the founder was assassinated, the members carried on. When Cárdenas became president, he modified many of the laws and reopened the churches. His successor, Avila Camacho, made his simple affirmation to a newsman: "Yo soy creyente!" (I believe in God!). And he added, "Mexico is a democracy and large enough to tolerate people of differing ideas." The spell was broken. In Monterrey a great new complex of industries and an outstanding Institute of Superior Studies began to show the capital how Mexico could be reborn. Since then the conditions for the Church's work have improved so far as to justify the view that the relation with government has almost reached permanent peace.

2. Spanish South America

These nine independent republics each have their own history. However, the circumstances in which they became independent set them off from Mexico and justify a unitary treatment of them. The events during the struggle for liberation from Spanish control influenced all their later history. In the development of societies historians recognize the effects of timing and of duration and in these see an explanation for the variation in the progress of Church-State relations in Mexico and in her southern neighbors. Mexico achieved independence in 1821 within a matter of months without firing an effective shot. Civil war, not secession, had characterized her previous fighting. But by 1821 South America had been engaged in continuous conflict with Spain for 11 years, and 3 more were to follow. Mexico thus remade its religious organization while at peace with foreigners. Internal tension carried no overtones of struggle for national security. South Americans faced serious problems in maintaining the Church while governments gave paramount attention to the issue of war. They had no such repose as did Mexico to spend on argument over the Church. Southern leaders, such as Belgrano, San Martín, and Bolívar, exerted every force to fortify patriotism with religion, an attitude confirmed by 14 years of battle. It carried through afterward so that postwar adjustment of the two interests entailed little rancor. Paradoxically, but understandably, this cordiality would make for later weakness, while the developing challenge in the north called forth in time strong faith and dedicated sacrifice. Materially, the Church in South America and the body of the clergy suffered immensely more harm in the destruction of war, resulting in the later impoverishment of clerical spirit and the lack of resistance to laymen who would overlord the Church.

Problem of Vacant Sees. An immediate issue was the royalist bishops, some of whom fell under suspicion on the grounds of loyalty to the new regimes. Lue y Riega of Buenos Aires felt the displeasure of the governing junta, and his movements were restricted to the environs of the capital. Others who were able simply packed off for Spain, thus settling their question of conscience. Many, though, remained on the spot, some like Rodríguez of Santiago, who rallied allegiance to Spain, and some like Coll y Prat of Caracas, who clearly sided with the insurgents. Filling the vacant sees soon presented larger difficulties. In default of diocesan discipline the university-trained clerics turned their minds to political matters. One example was Dean Funes of Córdoba, who, though a fine person, spent his thought and energy on juntas and *decretos* rather than on the Sacraments. Others, such as those of the monasteries whose superiors went home to Spain or out of office at the end of their terms, not infrequently took to street fighting for their party candidates in government.

But the question that overshadowed all others was the replacement of bishops who died in the period 1810 to 1831. No new appointees of Spain were accepted anywhere, while the Americans fought a life-and-death struggle for independence. This intransigence was absolute after 1814, the year when Ferdinand VII came to the crown, first swearing to uphold the Constitution of Cadiz (1812) and its antireligious clauses and then repudiating it. The 1810 attitude of "Our old king or none" had now changed to "None." Here one must note two factors: Spanish control of the seas, and the king's control over the American church. The former impeded communication with Rome. The latter made it futile. For, by papal grant of 1508, the king ruled religion as a feudal enclave. He had full power over the creation of all bishops in the empire. He was judge of all clerical actions and sovereign supervisor in the field of their economy. Appeal to Rome against him came to a dead end as he stopped all letters to the pope. To deepen the rift, the Holy Alliance threatened the papacy in case it listened to overseas petition on grounds of successful insurrection. Moreover, the pope always followed the policy of being last to void a concordat or treaty. This produced what the Argentines called the "great incommunication," and it continued until 1831. To make things more difficult, American leaders demanded residential bishops, and not those *in partibus,* to satisfy their nationalist spirit that grew strong during the wars.

Valiant efforts were made to break the blockade. Pius VII in 1822–23 sent Archbishop *Muzi with a delegation to La Plata and Chile to arrange immediate creation of bishops, but he was rebuffed when he could not name them as residential. Both countries ordered him to leave. On his way home he stopped at Rio de Janeiro long enough to lay the ground for a secret nunciature with power to name bishops. Archbishop Ostini in time headed this office and cooperated with Bolívar, who in 1827 sent assurance to Rome that Gran Colombia would gladly accept bishops under any title. The Gordian knot was cut definitely only in 1831, when the "Mexican Pope," Gregory XVI, announced that he would immediately recreate the Mexican hierarchy and all other American churches.

National Patronage. As the restoration of the hierarchy went forward, it coincided with a constitutional development of great importance, the establishment of national patronage throughout the southern Americas. The historic foundations of this idea in Spain, supposedly rejected *in toto* by the winning of independence, remained nevertheless in the *Weltanschaung* of the successor nations. While trying to cut every artery from Spain, they unwittingly fell into the trap of keeping the very institution that was most undemocratic of all the emblems of royal control. And it augured with certainty the future subjection of the Church to the political arm of society—and this with no consent whatsoever in Rome. When, in the year 1811, Archbishop Coll y Prat of Carcacas proclaimed the end of all Spanish patronage in America, he was speaking in hope rather than in deed, for the variations of war kept Spanish sovereignty alive in many places for years. Not until 1821 did Venezuela, through the battle of Carabobo, make good her freedom, and in that very year she proclaimed her possession of the *patronato nacional.*

Long before that, Argentine decision foreshadowed the simple beginnings of the national system. In 1816 Mariano Moreno, secretary of the junta of Buenos Aires, recorded this decision of the junta: "during the incommunication with Rome, the objectives of the *patronato* are cared for by the junta, in the same way as by the viceroys." Nor was the argument simply one of necessity. For centuries Argentine scholars had argued the innate presence of a royal patronage in the very essence of sovereign power. *Solórzano Pereira was an able and outspoken champion of the idea as early as 1653, and he still has followers on this point of law. The very duration and success of Spanish absolutism in the matter had been an everyday fact in colonial history. Rare was the appeal of a prelate sent directly to Rome, and the *pase regio* prevented what was indirect. Even the quinquennial visitations of bishops were stopped by the Laws of the Indies. It is, then, not surprising that patronal practice during war became law when peace arrived. Both history and national pride argued its justice, though a dispassionate eye might have discerned that the process begot a race of ecclesiastics who were subjected to the will of him who "made them" and that disloyalty to the head of the Church was built into the machinery.

Perhaps the clearest statement of the meaning of patronage as it was in use came from Juan Alberdi in his famous *Bases y puntos,* the treatise prepared for the post-Rosas Constituent Assembly at Santa Fe in 1852. Definitely religious in thought, he held nevertheless that the ecclesiastical polity of Argentina should serve political purposes, and that Church should be joined to State. Accordingly he outlined the presidential power in the matter. This should demand, first, that the archbishops, bishops, dignitaries, and prebends of cathedral churches should be selected from three lists of names prepared by the senate. Second, the president was to have the right of national patronage in regard to churches, benefices, and all ecclesiastical persons. He would then be empowered to grant or to refuse the *pase* to all bulls, briefs, or other papal documents, with the previous consent of the senate. Special legislation was required when these documents contained general or lasting dispositions. This policy reflected much of the practice that had been employed generally in all the states up to that time, and it became the rule for most of the countries in South and Central America. In it, and not in any Catholic demand for the protection of the Church, was the chief motive of the drive for "union of Church and State." Unhappily some clerics did hope for salvation in this union, but most were unwilling victims of the reality. Its blunting of their initiative is a patent factor. Exceptions to this rule are found only where constitutional reform provided complete religious freedom, as in Chile, Uruguay, Brazil, and Mexico. In Venezuela, as in Bolivia and Paraguay, the first rulers simply arrogated to themselves the apparatus of a *patronato nacional,* and they have retained it, although President Betancourt in 1963 asked and got Rome to terminate the practice. Ecuador had a difficult time in this question until *García Moreno (1821–75) came to the presidency. He bodily attacked the *patronato* as the central breeding-ground of widespread national corruption. The concordat of 1862 explicitly rejected any *patronato.*

Union of Church and State got a definite shock when, in the middle 19th century, an intellectual revolt swung many minds to embrace Positivism as the guide for law, administration, education, and literature. Metaphysics and theology were outlawed in the schools in the name of "science," by a people who were struggling to rid themselves of all past allegiance and enter a new era. It was the language of protest: "How can we come to be something other than what we were and are?" In itself the thought of futility, it led government to denigrate the Church as the staunch upholder of past values. Its spokesmen swarmed all over the literary arena, men such as *Sarmiento, Alberdi, *Lastarria, *Bello, Barros Arana, Amunategui, Vicuna Mackenna. In other countries it led to bloody war, in all to great hurt of a Church so tied to official desire and decision. A late exponent was Juan Perón, with his deliberately cultivated union of *descamisados* (workers) and soldiers, as anvil and hammer to bow the heads of their fellow citizens. The outspoken judgment of the Church in 1955 gave an opening to the right. Within a year, diplomas of Catholic schools for the first time in a century gave their graduates equal standing with those of governmental institutions.

This great change was due to some extent to the action of Leo XIII, who in 1899 summoned the important Latin American Council to Rome. For months they considered the effects of Positivism in a patronal society. Their 998 decrees, subscribed to under oath by 53 prelates on July 9, 1899, indicated the need for reform inside the Church and strenuous effort to turn the tide. The cause of labor finally provided a new field for this engagement and remade the whole position of the Church in the states of South America.

[W. E. SHIELS]

3. BRAZIL

Church and State were separated in Brazil in 1890 shortly after the proclamation of the republic. During the colonial and monarchical periods, relations between the two institutions were regulated by the norms of the Padroado. "In short," says a historian, "patronage consisted practically of the control of nominations of ecclesiastical authorities by the State and in the management by the latter of the finances of the Church."

Patronage under the Empire. The Constitution of the Empire, promulgated in 1824 "in name of the Holy Trinity," provided that the Catholic religion should continue "to be the religion of the Empire," other religions being permitted "with their private or domestic cult, in houses destined for that purpose but without outward signs of a church" (art. 5); those not professing "the religion of the State" would be ineligible for appointment as deputies (art. 95.3). Among the powers of the emperor was that of "appointing bishops and filling ecclesiastical benefices," as well as that of granting or denying approval to the decrees of the councils or to apostolic pronouncements or any other ecclesiastical constitutions. A concordat not having been signed, the situation was merely tolerated by the Holy See, while the Brazilian government more than once took advantage of the prerogatives of the Grand Master of the Order of Christ, which were refused by the Empire itself when the Holy See conferred the title on the Emperor. The Church enjoyed various privileges: the State maintained the bishops, supported the parochial clergy by means of allowances, and subsidized the seminaries; the Constitution, however, denied the right of voting to the religious and to those living in cloistered communities (art. 92.4) and subjected the properties of the Church to the laws of mortmain. The list of laws, decrees, pronouncements, and advices of temporal power on ecclesiastical matters was long. Thus, the conflicts between the two powers were frequent and, at times, serious.

The most serious of these clashes were the closing in 1855 of the novitiates of the religious congregations, having as an objective declared by the civil government the reform of the communities, and in 1874 the condemning to prison with hard labor of two bishops who had placed under interdict the brotherhoods in their dioceses that had refused to expel their associates who were Masons. During the minority of the second Emperor between 1833 and 1837, a regent of the Empire, Father Diogo Antônio *Feijó, had proposed the abolition of ecclesiastical celibacy and the separation from Rome of the Brazilian Church, provoking strong opposition from the episcopate. Regalism, which characterized the politics of the Brazilian Empire, always had the strong backing of Parliament, including the secular clergy who held seats there. Because of its conflict with the State, during the last two decades of the monarchical regime, the Church was violently attacked by the press, especially by members of Masonic lodges.

The Church under the Republic. The Republican regime, installed in 1889, immediately separated the Church from the State in Decree No. 119A, of Jan. 7, 1890, in which it prohibited the intervention of federal authority and of the federal states in religious matters, allowed the full liberty of cults, and abolished patronage. This was followed by decrees of the Provisional Government instituting civil marriage and secularizing cemeteries. In a collective pastoral letter dated March 19, 1890, the episcopate analyzed the situation, stated the doctrine of the Church on the relations with the State, denounced the threats to the Catholic faith and the spirit hostile to the Church in Brazil, which they said was "rigorous, disagreeable in its demands, incarnated in a powerful and dominant sect" (Masonry), but concluded confidently, affirming that the decree of separation assured "a certain amount of liberties which the Church had never had during the monarchy." The law of separation established that the subsidies of the seminaries would be maintained for 1 year and also, until their terms expired, the allowances, salaries, and gratuities of the canons, dignitaries, and other beneficiaries of the cathedrals, and of the permanent and removable vicars.

The new regime, however, diminished the liberty of the Church by declaring, in an Advice of March 31, 1891, that the personal properties and real estate of the regular orders could not be disposed of without permission from the government, the mortmain law of Dec. 9, 1830, remaining in effect. The episcopate, in addition to speaking in defense of the doctrine of union between Church and State, addressed a vigorous protest to the head of the Provisional Government against some of those measures and against provisions of the official plan for the Constitution of the Republic, which proposed the expulsion of the Jesuits, the prohibition of religious orders, the exclusion of religious teaching from public schools, the denial to priests of participation in the legislative assemblies, and the rupture of relations with the Holy See.

Complete Separation of Church and State. The Constitution, promulgated on Feb. 24, 1891, included the following provisions: (1) liberty of belief and worship; (2) civil marriage; (3) secularization of the cemeteries; (4) lay teaching in public schools; (5) prohibition of any subsidy from the State or any relationship of dependence or alliance between the State and any church, or of any interference with the practice of any religious cult; (6) taking of political rights away from any who exempted themselves from any civic duty for reasons of religious belief; and (7.) prohibition from voting and holding elective office to members of monastic orders, societies, congregations, or communities subjected to a vow of obedience, rule, or statute that would entail renunciation of individual liberty. The Positivists, who held office in the republican government and who strongly influenced public opinion through the Parliament, the press, and the institutions of higher education, played an important part in achieving these secularizing measures. But it is also certain that the complete liberty given to the Church in the Constitution was a victory for both Catholic and Positivist constituents. When the Constitution was amended in 1926, an article was inserted reestablishing diplomatic representation to the Holy See; these relations have not been interrupted.

Collaboration between Church and State. After the Revolution of 1930, when the Constitution of 1934 was voted "placing our trust in God," the regime of complete separation was replaced by a regime of collaboration. The restrictions on the political rights of the religious were suppressed; religious services on military expeditions, in hospitals, in penitentiaries and other official establishments were instituted without a burden on public finance or restraint or coercion of those involved. Postponement of military service was granted to students in ecclesiastical seminaries, and priests were classified as third-class reservists for service in a religious capacity. The celebration of religious rites in public cemeteries was permitted, and religious organizations were allowed to maintain private cemeteries under the condition that they not refuse burial when a secular cemetery was not available. Churches were exempted from taxes. Religious teaching, on an elective basis, was permitted in public schools, according to the religious beliefs of the student as indicated by his parents or guardians. Civil validity was given to religious marriage of any denomination if the marriage partners were qualified in accordance with civil law and the act was inscribed in the Civil Register.

A new principle, included in the Constitution of 1934—excluded from that of 1937 issued by the regime of Getúlio Vargas, but reestablished in that of 1946—was that the separation between Church and State would be maintained "without harm to reciprocal collaboration in favor of collective interest." The last Constitution introduced a second disposition according to which labor legislation recognized weekly rest on civil and religious holidays in accordance with local tradition and instituted religious services on a permanent basis, ministered by a Brazilian citizen, in the armed forces and in institutions of public support. The regime of collaboration in practice expresses itself in different forms, notably in full religious °autonomy and in reciprocal support of Church and State, even in regard to the varied denominations and religious cults.

[T. DE AZEVEDO]

Bibliography: Spanish America. J. L. MECHAM, *Church and State in Latin America* (Chapel Hill, N.C. 1934). J. BRAVO UGARTE, *Historia de México,* 4 v. (Mexico City 1941–59). M. CUEVAS, *Historia de la Iglesia en México,* 5 v. (5th ed. Mexico City 1946–47). A. RÍUS FACIUS, *Méjico cristero: Historia de la ACJM, 1925 a 1931* (Mexico City 1960). W. H. CALLCOTT, *Church and State in Mexico, 1822–1857* (Durham, N.C. 1926); *Liberalism in Mexico 1857–1929* (Stanford 1936). L. ZEA, *The Latin-American Mind,* tr. J. H. ABBOTT and L. DUNHAM (Norman, Okla. 1963). R. D. CARBIA, *La revolución de mayo y la iglesia* (Buenos Aires 1945).

Brazil. M. BARBOSA, *A igreja no Brasil* (Rio de Janeiro 1945). A. J. LACOMBE, "A igreja no Brasil colonial," *História geral da civilização brasileira,* ed. S. BUARQUE DE HOLLANDA (São Paulo 1960–) 1.2:51–75. W. J. COLEMAN, *First Apostolic Delegation in Rio de Janeiro and Its Influence in Spanish America, 1830–1840* (Washington 1950). M. C. THORNTON, *Church and Freemasonry in Brazil, 1872–1875* (Washington 1948).

CHURCH AND STATE IN THE U.S. (LEGAL HISTORY)

The U.S. law of *freedom of religion has evolved from many historical circumstances and often conflicting ideologies. The Church-State arrangements of the colonial period were to require a new pattern when full union was finally attained. By a process of legislation and judicial decisions, continual adjustments were made to accommodate the needs and to meet the demands of a nation becoming ever more pluralistic in religion. The study of Church and State in American law indicates that there is wide latitude for the solution of conflicts and problems still to come.

1. Colonial Period (1607–1776)

Church-State understandings in the U.S. had their origins in the Colonial period between 1607 and 1776. The law of this period reflected a growing spirit of freedom and grew out of the colonists' adjustment to New World opportunities. The colonists had always to reckon with the Church of England and the religious policy of the mother country. Great diversity came out of the experience in the three major regions, the Southern, Middle, and New England Colonies, which were to some extent distinct cultural groups. Certain legal landmarks in each of the colonies of these regions will be pointed out and an account taken of the forces behind them. Restrictions on dissenters from the varying versions of establishment had great implications even for Catholics, and these will be noted.

Virginia. The Church of England was officially maintained in Virginia from the very beginning. The 1606 Virginia Company Charter urged the colony to foster Christianity "according to the rites and doctrine of the Church of England." The Royal Charter of 1624 in the era of Abp. William *Laud carried forward the design of Anglicanism without regard for Dissenters. Novelties of doctrine were opposed and the assembly passed laws applying Canon Law. The colonial government regulated the building of chapels and appointment of ministers and ritual. It was in this environment that the first Lord Baltimore unsuccessfully attempted a settlement and saw the need of locating elsewhere. Catholics were soon disfranchised. Comprehensive legislation on these matters was passed in 1642.

The 17th century was marked by a successful move toward local vestry control of parishes. This involved conflict with the governor. Following the lead of a predecessor, William Berkeley insisted on examining credentials of ministers to make certain that they had the approval of the bishop of London. However, he won the power of presentation of ministers only in Jamestown; elsewhere parish vestries, in the hands of the planter gentry, controlled appointment.

Puritans were unable seriously to modify this order of things even during the Commonwealth period. When Berkeley returned as governor in 1661, he made further provisions for the enforcement of Anglican liturgy; legal illegitimacy was imputed to children of parents outside this rite of matrimony. Fines were levied on those failing to meet church obligations, and assessments were collected for support of the church. Quakers, Puritans, and Catholics were unwelcome during this era. Giles Brent, the wealthy Catholic planter, as an exception held a seat in the assembly.

The *Declaration of Rights of 1689 compelled Virginia to give legal status to congregations that were not strictly in the Anglican tradition. Huguenots and German Lutherans organized churches between 1700 and 1730 with legal incorporation. The Hanover Presbytery legally placed itself under the Philadelphia Synod. Dissenters in time established their churches in this manner, but their practice of having itinerant preachers created legal difficulties that had to be remedied by other legislation. Francis *Makemie first won a certificate to preach as a Presbyterian. In time itinerant preachers came to enjoy the same legal right, and Samuel Davies among Baptists played a leading role in widening practices of toleration when his appeal to the royal government was upheld.

Methodists and Baptists, however, experienced *de facto* intolerance at the hands of local officials. Instances of imprisonment for alleged disturbance of peace and verbal attacks on the Church of England shortly before the Revolution created a rallying point for opposition to establishment. General taxes on nonconformists for the support of the Church of England now became a major issue. The laity from within the Church indirectly supported this trend when they opposed what was called the "Parson's Cause." They resented the clergy's claim to greater income in the face of the losses from fluctuation in tobacco prices. They now became militant in the traditional cause against a resident bishop, who would claim more taxes and the very ecclesiastical power which the lay vestries had long retained. It was only with the Revolution, however, that the new form of the Protestant Episcopal Church brought what the laity wanted. Other denominations likewise had their remaining disabilities removed by this turn of events.

Carolinas. The Church of England was established in the Carolinas, even though dissenters soon constituted a majority of the inhabitants. The ecclesiastical law of England was applied by the Charter of 1663, and the lord proprietors soon made declarations in which religious freedom was promised. Charles II, however, gave them discretionary power in limiting it in the interest of the establishment and civil order.

The Fundamental Constitution of 1670, attributed to John *Locke, showed greater toleration while retaining establishment. All save atheists were allowed, although tax benefits went only to the Church of England. The freedom granted to non-Christians was intended to aid the conversion of the Indians. A law of 1696 specifically excluded Catholics from full citizenship and religious freedom. This occurred in a period of Quaker influence; a governor of that faith took office in 1694. As in Virginia, Protestant dissenters struggled for full freedom in the 18th century in the face of a more firmly established Church of England. The assembly began to supervise them strictly, and they were for a time disfranchised by a law of 1704. Assemblymen had to conform to the Anglican communion ritual. Dissenting ministers were not recognized and were excluded from congregations petitioning them. Joseph Boone, however, appealed successfully to the Crown and the Fundamental Constitution. Particularly in North Carolina, which became a separate colony in 1691, Quakers fought against the established church and the Vestry Act of 1704. It was some time before they were relieved of disabilities implied in oath requirements. Marriages before non-Anglican clergymen were not legal in North Carolina until 1766.

Georgia. The Charter of George II in 1732 assured all inhabitants except Catholics "a free exercise of Religion . . . ," and Quakers were allowed to substitute an affirmation for the usual oaths. The trustees in their "Design" encouraged European Protestant settlers and shortly offered material support to clergy who would minister to new communities. When the colony was put under direct royal control in 1752, formal establishment of the Church of England came about. Its parishes received support and stipends for their clergy.

Massachusetts. The founders of Massachusetts Bay brought with them the belief that the true church was the individual congregation. A group of such churches could, however, be viewed collectively as within the Church of England. The New Englanders, following the teaching of William Ames and in opposition to Thomas *Cartwright, rejected the idea that the congregation existed by authority of the Church of England.

A second principle produced what has been called a "Bible State," or theocracy in Massachusetts. The Hebraic concept of covenant as a relationship between the soul and God found legal application. Persons who enjoyed such a relationship were the only full citizens, or saints. Their status was verified by the elders of the local congregation. Such covenanted souls and congregations collectively formed a covenanted state. The civil magistrates and judges ruled as the counterpart of the congregation elders. While clergymen were not civil officials, they were their authentic guides in fashioning laws, which all assumed would conform to the Bible. Such godly magistrates were guardians both of public morals and church discipline. Because religious and civil authority both derived immediately from the rule of divine revelation in the Bible, the commonwealth was properly called a theocracy.

Using to advantage the vague language of the Massachusetts Bay Company Charter, the founders through the general court limited the control and full benefits to settlers "such as are members of some of the Churches. . . ." Four years later, in 1635, such churches had to be approved by the general court. Within 3 years assessments were levied for the support of these congregations. Fines were soon imposed for nonattendance, and in 1646 the Act Against Heresy listed punishments that would be meted out for denial of justification, immortality of the soul, and of other orthodox beliefs.

Adjustment of authority was made within this framework of law. The clergy as learned divines were earnestly consulted by all magistrates to see that the actions of the latter conformed to the directives of Holy Scripture. Nathaniel Ward wrote a code of laws for this purpose in 1641. Controversy over the manner of forming and approving true congregational churches led to the Cambridge Platform; and a general court act of 1651 put down the *Westminster Confession of Faith as a criterion of orthodoxy. Thus an aristocracy of magistrates and church elders was preserved by the balance of authority that these prescriptions established.

Judicial decisions fell harshly upon dissenters from these laws. The magistrates expelled Anne Hutchinson for the heresy of antinomianism and Roger *Williams for his notion of separation of Church and State. Quakers were executed when they defied decrees of expulsion, and the Salem witchcraft trials at the end of the 17th century were the result of this legal system. Catholics were singled out by specific laws as being even more unwelcome than Quakers. The Christmas festival was forbidden as a manifestation of popery.

Reaction against such harshness, the pressures of a growing secularization and religious diversity, forced concessions. The Half-Way Covenant as a law relaxed requirement for church membership and full citizenship. The strict rule of baptism for children only of parents in full communion no longer held. Forms of "communion in spirit" were applied as norms. Anglicans were increasingly receiving the Lord's Supper, and in time their churches were legally recognized. Yet Congregationalism combined with other sects in stopping the spread and influence of these churchmen lest an Anglican establishment be imposed on New England. The *Declaration of Rights of 1689 urged Massachusetts to extend freedom to all Christians except Catholics. Financial support of Congregationalism became the bone of contention. The Five Mile Act of 1727 allowed Anglicans to apply their assessment to one of their churches or ministers provided they were within that distance. The 18th century saw gradual extension of this practice even to the benefit of Anabaptists. Incidental inequities were a continual object of attack by Baptists, Presbyterians, and others through the Revolution.

The Plymouth settlement, founded before Massachusetts and joined to it in 1691, did not strive so strenuously for theocracy. The *Mayflower Compact made no specific provision for theocracy, although Puritans predominated in drafting it and applying it to civil life. Laws gave civil officials power to keep peace in the churches and promote attendance at worship without specifying any sect. Financial support of some clergy was enforced. In 1671 freemen came to be limited to those of orthodox belief. Quakers were unwelcome as were Catholics, and oaths created a problem for both groups.

Connecticut. New Haven, which was joined to Connecticut in 1662, was a pure theocracy. Under the leadership of John Davenport and the Fundamental Agreement of 1639, unorthodox views were suppressed. Those who were not Congregational Church members had to apply for a certificate if they would remain in the colony and then they were without full citizenship. All settlers were put under the government of magistrates who were pillars of the church. These men chose a governor who had a similar standing.

Connecticut was not so strict a theocracy. Thomas *Hooker, who formed its principles, disagreed with John Winthrop's aristocratic theory of magistracy. Church membership was not a requirement for citizenship. The assembly was therefore more open. The governor, possessed of less authority than in Massachusetts, was required to have church standing. The substance of theocracy was found in the authority of the assembly over church discipline. It chartered Congregational and all other churches, and in disputes it might sit as a quasi-ecclesiastical court. After 1656 Connecticut was guided by Massachusetts' Half-Way Covenant and its own Saybrooke Platform of 1708 in relaxing requirements for congregations and membership. Assessments of all for the support of the official Congregational Church prevailed throughout the period.

The religious homogeneity of Connecticut in the 17th century had minimized the difficulty of dissent, but this condition of homogeneity soon changed. However, Quakers once viewed as unwelcome now found some protection. A law of 1708 made further concessions to liberty when Anglican Churches were authorized. In the Act of 1727 to protect dissenters, one provision allowed Anglicans to apply their religious assessment to their own ministers and churches. After 1750 Presbyterians and others were given a similar benefit.

New Hampshire. When John Wheelwright was banished from Massachusetts, he successfully established the foundations of what would become in 1679 the independent colony of New Hampshire. The Agreement of 1639 put down no religious requirement for citizenship, officeholding, and voting. Massachusetts agreed to this and admitted New Hampshire delegates to its general court. At the same time New Hampshire early passed laws of assessment for the support of the clergy without specifying to what sect they must belong.

Beginning in 1680 steps were taken to make a royal colony of New Hampshire. Past practices continued. Except for a few intervals before 1700 the mother country effectively formed a policy that protected, and at times favored, the Church of England. Freedom of Protestants was decreed and dissenter churches were not opposed.

Rhode Island. The only truly radical departure from the prevailing conviction that Church and State should be united was made by Rhode Island. Roger *Williams, its founder and guiding genius, argued against Massachusetts laws within the framework of Calvinistic theology. Rhode Island's first charter contained only customary statements on religious freedom. A fundamental code was soon drawn up that denied civil magistrates authority over spiritual matters. Persons of all religious persuasions were granted citizenship, and no levy of taxes for the support of any church was permitted. In his oversimplified analysis the church must stand before the law as any other corporation, free of any complicated characteristics that might put it beyond the nation or with a purely spiritual existence. Williams's own adjustments of theory to practice were confined to the task of dealing with Quakers and others where freedom of conscience might disrupt public order. In 1662 Charles II approved the original charter. The 18th century saw departures from the full measure of toleration. In 1729 Roman Catholics were disfranchised. Jews were disbarred on religious grounds from public office.

New York. The 1638 Articles of Colonization made it clear that Dutch companies were responsible for promoting the Dutch Reformed Religion. This arrangement, however, never resulted in a very strict establishment, and dissenters were generally respected.

These conditions continued to a great extent when the Catholic Duke of York, later King James II, took over control with his laws of 1665. Liberty of conscience was specifically granted and the Catholic governor, Thomas *Dongan, reasserted more forcefully in 1683 the provision for religious freedom for Christians. An attempt was made in 1693 to compel appointment of Anglican ministers only, but these efforts failed. Dissenting congregations and their clergy were recognized. The Presbyterian Francis Mackemie and others were allowed to preach throughout the province.

Concessions were made to Quakers regarding oath-taking in 1734, but no concessions ever clearly freed Moravians. Catholics were specifically denied benefits of toleration, and instructions from the Crown and the governors reinforced this measure.

New Jersey. Both East and West Jersey came under the force of New York law between 1702 and 1738. Before this time official "Concessions" of the lord proprietors gave toleration to Scotch Presbyterians, Quakers, and Dutch Reformed; and in 1693 to other Christians, except Catholics. No full establishment was found after 1738, when New Jersey became a royal colony.

Pennsylvania. The proprietary form of colonial charter provided the foundation upon which Pennsylvania developed, free of an established religion. As an exercise of personal power Charles II repaid an old debt of money, services, and friendship to Admiral William *Penn through the admiral's son of the same name. Young William's deep involvement with the Quakers, who were laboring under legal disabilities, made it natural to seek in the charter issued to him in 1681 a remedy for his religious troubles. Its only reference to the Church of England was an assurance to its adherents that they might freely petition and receive preachers.

The year following the issue of the charter brought a fuller public statement of the colony's legal structure. In keeping with the "Holy Experiment" characterization he had given the colony, Penn's Frame of Government clearly acknowledged God as the author and end of society. Liberty was assured to any believer in Him. The Sabbath and Scriptures were to be honored. When Penn's first colonial assembly met, representatives saw fit to require that voters and officeholders profess Christianity. No reservations were made in reference to Roman Catholics (*see* PENN'S CHARTER OF LIBERTIES).

In 1693 William and Mary annulled all the Pennsylvania laws, but the colonial assembly immediately passed them anew. Apparently their legality needed to be established since the legality of Stuart provisions may have been questioned. Certainly the broad provision for freedom in Pennsylvania would have been narrowed if the *Declaration of Rights of 1689 had been applied to it. As it was, public worship, even by Roman Catholics, continued all through the Colonial period. Unlike practices in England, one need not take the oath of supremacy nor perform prescribed acts of worship in the Church of England.

The oath, however, was required in connection with voting and officeholding in Pennsylvania. William Penn failed in his own efforts to relieve Americans of this burden, particularly to the consciences of Quakers and Catholics. Under pressure, the first assembly passed in 1696 "A New Act of Settlement," which practically had the effect of excluding many Quakers and all Catholics from voting and holding public office. It was not until 1725 that Quakers obtained relief, when the Crown finally ceased to disallow action in their favor by the assembly. Benefits of this law were extended to other societies in 1743 and in 1772 to any person who objected to the practice of oaths. Oaths and declarations against Catholic doctrines were demanded of immigrants and do not seem to have been removed during the Colonial period, although they may not have been applied consistently.

Delaware. A Swedish Lutheran Church was established in the period before the Dutch attached the colony of Delaware to New Netherlands in 1663. Initially part of Pennsylvania when English rule began, it continued after 1701 as a separate colony to have a toleration similar to that in Pennsylvania. Oaths in particular were mitigated to the advantage of immigrants and others during the next 20 years. Church property rights were recognized. Neither benefits, however, came to Catholics.

Maryland. The Maryland Charter of 1634 freed George Calvert, First Lord Baltimore, and his colonists from requirements of the Church of England. The general references to religion in the charter and his own instructions secured freedom of conscience for all—probably including non-Christians. The Maryland *Toleration Act in the ordinance of 1639 made this freedom even more certain. The act of 1649 gave special force to the Christian's claim to toleration. This legislation was repealed in 1654 when the Puritans came to power, but was restored again when Cecil Calvert, Second Lord Baltimore, recovered full control as proprietor in 1660.

George Calvert had two legal controversies with the Jesuits during this early period of the colony. He refused to exempt laymen on church property from civil law and its courts. A Jesuit title to land received from Indians was successfully challenged, and legislation against mortmain followed.

An Act for the Establishment of the Protestant Religion was passed by the assembly following the overthrow of the Stuarts by William and Mary. Catholic proprietary government was thereafter illegal. In 1700 taxes for support of the Church of England were voted. Benedict Leonard Calvert won back proprietary rights after he had conformed to the Church of England in 1714.

The governor's powers of presentation and induction of clergy were a source of continual controversy. Attempts at obtaining a resident bishop, or a permanent commissary to supervise the clergy, failed. As late as 1769 the governor prevented the clergy of the Church of England from holding a convention to deal with their affairs.

While concessions to Quakers and other Protestants came in the 18th century, penalties continued to be imposed on Catholics. There was an Act to Prevent the Growth of Popery that ruled out public officeholding and public worship. Catholic immigrants found obstacles in coming to Maryland, and possession by a Catholic widow of children by a Protestant husband was declared unlawful.

Bibliography: H. S. SMITH et al., *American Christianity: An Historical Interpretation with Representative Documents,* 2 v. (New York 1960–63) 1:1–416. A. P. STOKES, *Church and State in the United States,* 3 v. (New York 1950) 1:151–358. S. H. COBB, *The Rise of Religious Liberty in America* (New York 1902). E. H. DAVIDSON, *The Establishment of the English Church in the Continental American Colonies* (Durham, N.C. 1936).

[T. O. HANLEY]

2. THE DISESTABLISHMENT PERIOD (1776–1834)

By the time of the American Revolution, physical persecution of religious dissenters had ended, and a measure of toleration existed. Yet 10 of the original 13 colonies—the exceptions were Rhode Island, Pennsylvania, and Delaware—continued to prefer and support one religion, over all others. The church that by law enjoyed that status was spoken of as the established church, or establishment, of that state. The erosion of the preferential position of the established church is traced from the Revolution to the mid-19th century when, for the first time in world history, Church and State were completely divorced.

No Federal Establishment. Before proceeding, it is important to note that there has never been a Federally established church. In the Articles of Confederation, there is only one reference to religion. Each state is guaranteed the assistance of its sister states if attacked "on account of religion." The Articles only maintained the status quo.

When the Constitutional Convention met in Philadelphia in 1787, the practical needs of the situation as much as the political and philosophical theories of the day demanded that only timid reference, if any, be made to religion. By 1789, the states were on their way to religious freedom. To interfere with this current by establishing a Federal church would have jeopardized the new Union. The New England colonies generally supported a Congregational Church, while the Middle Atlantic and southern colonies possessed Episcopal establishments. Even if the founding fathers had not believed in separation of Church and State, which church was to be established? The only way Episcopal and Congregational churches could federate with Presbyterians, Baptists, and smaller groups was on a basis of Church-State separation. Article 6, proscribing a religious test of office, was the offspring of this innocuous neutralism. European political states traditionally required their officers to follow the state religion. The American colonies were no exceptions. Almost all of them enacted some religious prerequisite to holding public office. Even though the new states had not yet effected disestablishment at home, they included Article 6 in the proposed Constitution. It read: "No religious test shall ever be required as a qualification to any office or public trust under the United States."

In the state conventions called to ratify the Constitution, a desire for even stronger guarantees of religious liberty was voiced by the delegates. Whether a state still retained its own establishment or not, its delegates announced the tenor of the times: the Federal government, if only to preclude encroachment on the privileges of the state establishment, should not establish Federal religion. The Federal government was not to be antagonistic to religion, but was rather to remain impartial in that matter and to attend to its civil business.

Responding to this public sentiment, the First Congress drafted a Bill of Rights, ratified by the states in 1791, which in part declared negatively that "Congress shall make no law respecting an establishment of religion, or prohibiting the free exercise thereof." Both Article 6 and the religious guarantees of the First Amendment applied only to the Federal government. [*Barron v. Mayor of Baltimore,* 7 Peters 243 (1833).] It was easier to breach centuries of history and bar a Federal religion where none yet existed than to dislodge existing establishments in the states. Thus the states of the Union that had not already done so were to spend the next half-century attaining this Federal standard of Church-State relationship. (*See* RELIGIOUS TEST FOR PUBLIC OFFICE; FREEDOM OF RELIGION.)

Reasons for Disestablishment. The states granted religious freedom of their own volition, since the Federal government was without jurisdiction over a state's internal affairs. [*Permoli v. New Orleans,* 3 How. 588 (1845).] The disestablishment of state churches was the result of several factors: (1) The argument voiced by establishment proponents that religion and ultimately the state would die out without the continued support of the government was rebutted dramatically by the growth of religion in the free soil of Rhode Island and Pennsylvania. (2) With the ease resulting from their wealth and legally secured position, the established churches had become stagnant and stilted, had obtained few converts, and lacked a fervent congregation that would energetically oppose disestablishment. (3) As immigration to the New World increased and the dissenting churches gained more converts, the established groups became the political minority. (4) And the Bill of Rights, even though legally inapplicable to the states, added impetus to the disestablishment process by emphasizing individual liberties. Catholic agitation during this period, while unequivocal, should not be overemphasized. At the time of the Constitutional Convention, less than 2 per cent of the churches in the U.S. were Catholic.

New England States. With the exception of Rhode Island, the New England states supported the Congregational Church and were more reluctant to disestablish than the states to the south.

Connecticut. Connecticut operated for more than 40 years after the Revolution under the royal charter of 1662, which designated the state church as the Congregational. Disestablishment was not achieved until 1818, after a long and bitter politico-religious struggle. Here, as in Massachusetts, the established Congregational ministry had retained tremendous political, social, and economic influence long after the Federal Constitution was ratified. With the Toleration Act of 1784, the first glimpse of disestablishment was visible. The act removed many disabilities, and established a "certificate" scheme whereby a dissenter was excused from contributing to the established church if he executed a paper declaring that he regularly attended a dissenting church. The dissenter might then pay his tax to his own body, but he was still required to support some one religion.

The political agitation was intense. Congregational members had always aligned themselves with the Federalist Party. The dissenters joined the liberal Jeffersonian Republican Party. As in all the New England states, the Baptists, both for reasons of religious belief and practical advantage, pressed the cause of separation. In 1816, compulsory church attendance was repealed. In 1817, Oliver Wolcott, a liberal coalition candidate, won the gubernatorial election, ending a Congregational monopoly of that post. A constitutional convention was called for the following year. After recognizing the individual's freedom to enjoy religious profession and worship, the new constitution declared that "no person shall be compelled to join or support, nor by law be classed with or associated to any congregation, church or religious association." The Methodists secured a charter for Wesleyan University in 1831, and the disestablishment was completed.

Massachusetts. Though not as slow as Connecticut in adopting a state constitution, Massachusetts was slower in bringing about a financial disestablishment of the Congregational Church. The state constitution of 1780 contained an important and inclusive Declaration of Rights (Moehlman, 40). But an abrupt and absolute break with the past was not conceivable, so the constitution went on to provide for the support of the Protestant ministry and for compulsory attendance at some religious instruction. The proposed constitutional amendment of 1820 to overturn these vestiges of the establishment was defeated by nearly 2 to 1. The end of the establishment did not come until 1833, when a comprehensive amendment to the constitution was ratified by an overwhelming vote (Moehlman, 67).

New Hampshire. The colonial attitude was akin to that of Massachusetts, since New Hampshire was a part of it until 1679. The Bill of Rights of 1784 acknowledged the right of conscience, but permitted the several towns of the state "to make adequate provision at their own expense, for the support and maintenance of public Protestant teachers of piety, religion, and morality." Protection of the law was extended only to Christians (Moehlman, 50). Legal status was granted the Baptists in 1804, the Universalists the following year, and the Methodists in 1807. The Toleration Act of 1819 retained the requisite that public teachers and public officials be Protestant, but it did abolish mandatory support for the establishment, thereby mollifying the dissenters. An amendment of 1877 decreed that "no person is disqualified to hold office by reason of his religious opinion."

Rhode Island. From the beginning, Rhode Island guaranteed religious freedom to all its citizens. The success of Roger Williams' "Lively Experiment" was a constant rebuke to those proponents of a union of Church and State who argued that one would collapse without the other. For a time a slight "blemish" appeared on Rhode Island's record of religious freedom. In some printed editions of its charter, Roman Catholics were excepted from the "liberty to choose and be chosen officers in the Colony." This restriction was foreign to the spirit of the colony, and both Thorning and Stokes argue that it was inserted without legislative authorization, possibly a result of a clerical error. It remained in the laws of Rhode Island until 1783. The constitution of 1842 guaranteed religious and civil liberties to all citizens (Moehlman, 72).

Middle Atlantic States. Unlike New England, there was never a firmly intrenched establishment in any of the Middle Atlantic states, though New York and New Jersey did favor the Church of England.

New York. In the years preceding the Revolution, the general policy of the New York government was to favor the established Church of England as much as possible without severely alienating dissenters. By the first state constitution, enacted in 1777, the Act of Establishment of 1683 was repealed (Moehlman, 48). "Religious profession and worship, without discrimination," were assured to all citizens. No religious test was prescribed for any state officer, with the exception that ministers of the gospel were denied the right to hold public office. Quakers were allowed to affirm an oath rather than swear to it, and they were permitted to substitute a money payment for military service. The first constitutional revision in 1821 did little to change the clauses regarding religion. The disability of public office was removed from the ministry in the amendment of 1846. In New York, the disestablished church was guaranteed at all times continuous possession of lands granted them during the establishment period, a reversal of the Virginia precedent.

New Jersey. Close political ties with liberal New York, plus the mild and tolerant spirit of the Quakers in the state legislature, leavened the whole course of New Jersey's attainment of religious freedom. The state's first constitution, adopted 2 days before the Declaration of Independence was announced, exempted all persons from mandatory attendance at religious services and the obligation of maintaining a church or ministry. Only Protestants, however, "were capable of being elected into any office of profit or trust, or being a member of either branch of the Legislature" (Moehlman, 48). This situation continued until 1844, when a new constitution was enacted granting civil liberties equally to all the citizenry (Moehlman, 72).

Pennsylvania. Under the enlightened William Penn, Pennsylvania grew without an establishment. His *Charter of Liberties and Privileges, granted in 1701, guaranteed freedom of worship to all theists and the right to hold office to all Christians. This liberal bent was continued in the Pennsylvania constitution of 1776, but the religious test of office found in the charter was retained. Each member of the house of representatives was required to attest before being seated: "I do believe in one God, the creator and governor of the universe, the rewarder of the good and punisher of the wicked. And I do acknowledge the Scriptures of the Old and New Testament to be by Divine inspiration." This admitted Roman Catholics to full rights and was in this respect more liberal than contemporaneous constitutions of its sister states. The reference to the New Testament was, of course, distasteful to the Jewish community in Philadelphia, and in 1783 they petitioned that it be dropped. This was done in 1790, but the test of belief in God was retained.

Delaware. Delaware gained independence from Pennsylvania in 1701, and taking its lead from its parent state, it never had an established church. Religious freedom, therefore, was always the rule; complete civil freedom was not so immediate. In its constitution of 1776, Delaware, like Pennsylvania, required an oath of all elected officials to provide that the state should be governed by orthodox Christians (Moehlman, 52). Contrariwise to Pennsylvania, however, Delaware abolished any religious test of office in 1792, completely separating the state from religion.

The South. All the southern states established the Church of England. The contrast between the conduct of Virginia and that of South Carolina during the Revolution is notable.

Maryland. The position of Roman Catholics in Maryland at the time of the Revolution was more secure than in the other colonies because of the strong Catholic influence in the early years of the colony and the weak position of the Maryland establishment, the Anglican Church.

The declaration of rights adopted as part of its new constitution of 1776 recognized that "all persons, professing the Christian religion are equally entitled to protection of their religious liberty." The Quakers, Dunkers, and Mennonites, opposed to taking judicial oaths, were allowed "to affirm" and were "admitted as witnesses in all criminal cases not capital." This was extended to capital cases in 1798. Charles Carroll of Carrollton, the Catholic patriot, was one of those voting in favor of the article authorizing the state legislature to "lay a general and equal tax, for the support of the Christian religion." Finally, a "declaration of a belief in the Christian religion" was required by the constitution for admission to any office of trust or profit (Moehlman, 41). The Jew and the freethinker were still under disabilities. There were only a few Jews in the state, and the legislature did not act to remove the restriction until 1826. The religious test of office, which has since been struck down by the U.S. Supreme Court *Torcaso v. Watkins,* 367 U.S. 488 (1961), was then unacceptable only to a small number of agnostics and atheists, since a declaration of belief in the existence of God was still necessary.

Virginia. Thomas Jefferson, James Madison, George Mason, the Baptists, and the Presbyterians united to disestablish the conservative Episcopalian Church of Virginia and to light the path to religious freedom in the U.S. The Declaration of Rights, passed 3 weeks before the Declaration of Independence, and the Bill for Establishing Religious Freedom combined to assure members of all faiths complete religious and civil liberties by 1785. This influenced immeasureably the course of the Federal and sister states' governments (*see* DISESTABLISHMENT IN VIRGINIA).

North Carolina. The Carolina Charter of 1663 specially recognized the Church of England, but it provided for a measure of toleration so long as nonconformity did not interfere with the civil authority. North Carolina was second only to Virginia in adopting a constitution, guaranteeing complete religious freedom (Moehlman, 44). The constitution restricted public office to those acknowledging "the being of God [and] the truth of the Protestant religion [and] the divine authority of the Old and New Testament," thereby excluding Roman Catholics and Jews. Clergymen were not permitted to hold office.

In 1835, at Raleigh, the word Protestant was changed to Christian in deference to the Roman Catholics. In fact, however, the Protestant requirement had not been enforced, for Thomas Burke, who became governor in 1781, and William Gaston, who was appointed to the North Carolina supreme court in 1833, were both Catholics. The Jewish disability was enforced, for there was little pressure to remove the bar since most of the Jewish population in the U.S. was found in the large cities to the north. The constitution of 1868 removed this last restriction to total religious freedom (Moehlman, 108).

South Carolina. South Carolina had established the Anglican Church. By the constitution of 1778, all theists were "freely tolerated," but that document further declared that "the Christian Protestant religion shall be deemed, and is hereby constituted . . . the established religion of this State." Despite the existence of a preferred religion, the dissenters' onerous task of supporting an establishment was removed. Only Protestants could hold public office. Any religious society holding property was permitted to retain it. This law was very beneficial to the Anglican Church, the prior establishment, since it had been the donee of much official largesse.

The state exercised a Connecticut-like control over religious activities. The election of a pastor or clergyman was prescribed by the constitution to be by majority vote of the congregation. The elected minister was further required to subscribe to a declaration anticipating his official and unofficial conduct during his tenure.

By the constitution of 1790, dissenters, previously only "tolerated," were guaranteed the "free exercise and enjoyment of religious profession and worship, without discrimination or preference." The Roman Catholics and other non-Protestant groups were enfranchised. The document was a drastic departure from the narrowly Protestant constitution of 12 years earlier (Moehlman, 45). By 1868, only those who denied the existence of a Supreme Being were ineligible to hold public office.

Georgia. The Georgia Charter of 1732 secured by James Oglethorpe stipulated that all office holders be Protestant, and "that all . . . persons, except papists, shall have a free exercise of religion." The derogatory term "papist" was deleted by the constitution of 1777 and freedom of worship was extended to all citizens. As was frequently the case, the clergy were unable to hold office. There was no religious test for voting, but the Protestant prerequisite of membership in the state legislature was retained. The 1789 constitution removed all religious restrictions upon service in public office. Thus Georgia from early times was provided with religious freedom.

In conclusion, though the Federal government was forbidden to establish a preferred religion, remnants of the state establishments existed well into the 19th century. For the first time in history, State and Church were independent of each other. The pace of disestablishment is notable, but more notable is the historic result.

Bibliography: P. W. Coons, *The Achievement of Religious Liberty in Connecticut* (New Haven 1936). J. De L. Ferguson, *The Relation of the State to Religion in New York and New Jersey During the Colonial Period* (New Brunswick, Conn. 1912). Leon Hühner, *The Struggle for Religious Liberty in North Carolina* (Baltimore 1907). J. C. Meyer, *Church and State in Massachusetts from 1740 to 1833* (Cleveland 1930). C. H. Moehlman, *The American Constitutions and Religion* (Berne, Ind. 1938). J. F. Thorning, *Religious Liberty in Transition* (Washington 1931). A. P. Stokes, *Church and State in the United States* (New York 1950). A. W. Werline, *Problems of Church and State in Maryland During the 17th and 18th Century* (South Lancaster, Mass. 1948).

[M. J. MULLANEY, JR.]

3. Period of Conflict (1834–1900)

The 19th century was an era of conflict on the religious front in the *United States of America. Resentment against immigrants brought forth American *nativism in the form of such movements as the *Ku Klux Klan and *Know-Nothingism. The amazing growth of the Catholic parochial system was a response to the problems of the era. *See* EDUCATION I (HISTORY OF), 9.

At the start of this period only a few effects of state establishment of religion still remained. The most obnoxious was the religious test for public office. In spite of the Federal and state guarantees of religious freedom, the churches in the 19th century encountered several new types of difficulty with the government. A proposed constitutional amendment (Blaine Amendment) that sought to deprive religious-affiliated schools of state financial aid had a lasting effect in many states. The Mormon Church and its practice of polygamy came under direct attack. A series of disputes reached the courts as a result of schisms that split the churches into warring factions. Religious practices in public schools were both approved and forbidden by the various state courts. Problems arose concerning the holding of church property and the incorporation of churches. Amid all this conflict there was, strangely enough, a 20-year period in which the U.S. and the Vatican had diplomatic relationship.

Religious Tests for Public Office. The founding fathers of the U.S. thought that a necessary prerequisite for securing the freedom of religion in this country was the inclusion in the constitution of a clause prohibiting any religious test as a requirement for holding public office. The proposal was made originally in 1787 at the Constitutional Convention by Charles Pinckney of South Carolina. There was considerable debate on the subject at the convention; but it was finally drafted into Article 6 of the U.S. Constitution, and passed easily, North Carolina being the only state that voted against it. Article 6 of the U.S. Constitution states that elected officials shall be bound by oath or affirmation to support the Constitution, and then continues, ". . . but no religious test shall ever be required as a qualification to any office or public trust under the United States."

Although this provision in the U.S. Constitution was almost unanimously approved by the original 13 states, they were very slow to incorporate similar provisions in their own state constitutions. Most of the states were still feeling the effects of religious establishment and consequently limited public office to those who professed the "Protestant religion," those who were "Christians," those who believed in the "Old and New Testament" and other such conditions. Five of the original states had provisions in their constitutions limiting holders of public office to those who professed a belief in the Protestant religion (Georgia, New Hampshire, New Jersey, North Carolina and South Carolina). Georgia was the first of the five to remove this requirement, in 1789, when its constitution was changed to read that no religious test for public office would be required. New Jersey and New Hampshire did not follow suit until 1844 and 1877 respectively. North Carolina changed "Protestant" to "Christian" in 1835, and in 1868, revised it to "belief in God." This requirement is still a part of the North Carolina constitution. South Carolina replaced the qualification "Protestant" by that of belief in a supreme being in 1868, and the law still exists. Maryland and Delaware originally required officeholders to be Christians. Delaware removed this restriction in 1792. Maryland changed the requirement to belief in God in 1826, and it held until 1961, when the U.S. Supreme Court declared it unconstitutional (*Torcaso v. Watkins* 367 U.S. 488). Pennsylvania early required a belief in both the Old and New Testaments, but it was changed in 1790 to "belief in God" and is still retained (1965). The slow pace at which the original states proceeded to remove religious tests can be attributed to the fact that they were free to retain or modify their laws of religious liberty as they chose.

However, the new states to gain admission to the Union had to have their constitutions approved by Congress, and Congress after the beginning of the 19th century required that states have adequate guarantees of religious freedom. Consequently only four states admitted to the Union after the original states have any kind of religious restriction for public officeholders (Arkansas, Mississippi, Tennessee, Texas). These four require officeholders to hold a belief in God or in a supreme being. As of 1965 the constitutions of these states still retain this requirement. Most of the states admitted to the Union during the 19th and the early 20th century have some specific constitutional provision forbidding any religious test for public office. Some, though not specifically referring to public office, forbid a religious test in guaranteeing civil or political rights to all. A few states have made no mention of a religious test in their constitutions.

By 1912, with the admission of the 48th state to the union, the states specifically prohibiting any religious test included Alabama, Arizona, Delaware, Georgia, Idaho, Illinois, Indiana, Iowa, Kansas, Louisiana, Maine, Minnesota, Missouri, Nebraska, New Hampshire, New Jersey, New Mexico, New York, Ohio, Oregon, Rhode Island, Utah, Vermont, Virginia, Washington, West Virginia, Wisconsin, and Wyoming. States forbidding a religious test to guarantee civil and/or political rights included Michigan, Montana, Oklahoma, and South Dakota. States whose constitutions made no mention of any form of religious test were California, Colorado, Connecticut, Florida, Kentucky, Nevada, and North Dakota. Those requiring a belief in God or a supreme being included Arkansas, Maryland, Mississippi, North Carolina, Pennsylvania, South Carolina, Tennessee, and Texas. One state, Massachusetts, obliges the people in choosing their officials to pay attention to principles of piety. (*See* RELIGIOUS TEST FOR PUBLIC OFFICE.)

The Blaine Amendment. On Dec. 14, 1875, James Gillespie Blaine, a congressman from Maine, presented a proposed amendment of the U.S. Constitution to the House of Representatives. The proposed amendment sought primarily to prevent the states from directly or indirectly devoting any public money or land to schools having any religious affiliation. As proposed, the amendment read:

> No state shall make any law respecting an establishment of religion, or prohibiting the free exercise thereof; and no religious test shall ever be required as a qualification to any office or public trust under any State. No public property, and no public revenue of nor any loan of credit by or under the authority of the United States, or any State, Territory, District or municipal corporation, shall be appropriated to, or made or used for, the support of any school, educational or other institution, under the control of any religious or anti-religious sect, organization, or denomination, or wherein the particular creed or tenets shall be read or taught in any school or institution supported in whole or in part by such revenue or loan of credit; and no such appropriation or loan of credit shall be made to any religious or anti-religious sect, organization or denomination, or to promote its interests or tenets. This article shall not be construed to prohibit the reading of the Bible in any school or institution, and it shall not have the effect to impair rights of property already vested. Congress shall have power, by appropriate legislation, to provide for the prevention and punishment of violation of this article.

The issue was debated in Congress, and discussion centered on the questions of states rights to determine their educational policies, and the privilege of a religious people to secure their teachings in schools attended by their children. The proposal failed to win the necessary two-thirds majority in the Senate and was never put to the states for ratification.

Since the amendment's original failure, it has been reintroduced 20 times; but only once was it reported on by the committee to which it was referred. Even this report recommended that the resolution should not be passed. But its effect has been felt in subsequent amendments or revisions of many state constitutions. Between 1877 and 1913, more than 30 state constitutions forbade financial aid to parochial schools. The provisions adopted vary greatly in detail. Some use the same language as the Blaine amendment; others say the same thing in different words. However, they all have the same purpose, of preventing the use of public school funds by private sectarian schools.

Only eight states had any constitutional provision on this matter before the Blaine amendment was introduced. These provisions were very limited in scope, usually prohibiting aid to theological and religious seminaries. The states were Wisconsin (1848), Michigan (1850), Indiana (1851), Oregon (1857), Minnesota (1857), Kansas (1858), Nebraska (1866), and Illinois (1870).

States that early responsed to the Blaine amendment and incorporated some similar provision in their own constitutions before 1880 included Pennsylvania (1873); Missouri, Alabama, and Nebraska (1875); Texas and Colorado (1876); Georgia, Minnesota, and New Hampshire (1877); California and Louisiana (1879); and Nevada (1880). Other states were to follow in the next 20 years: Florida (1885); Idaho, Montana, North Dakota, South Dakota, and Wyoming (1889); Mississippi and Kentucky (1890); New York (1894); South Carolinia and Utah (1895); and Delaware (1897). The three states admitted to the Union after 1900 joined in adopting similar provisions in their constitutions: Oklahoma (1907), New Mexico (1911), and Arizona (1912). Several states that have since 1900 adopted new constitutions have retained provisions on this matter that appeared in their earlier constitutions: New Hampshire, Louisiana, Massachusetts, and Alabama.

The articles on each state in this encyclopedia contain the provisions still in effect in each state. (*See* BLAINE AMENDMENT.)

The Mormon Church. In 1852 the Mormon Church decreed that the practice of polygamy was in accord with its doctrine. The practice, was permitted only to people of good moral character who could afford a large family. It was never widespread even among the Mormons. But opposition to it was strong. Many non-Mormons clamored for some type of legislation to suppress and prohibit the practice.

Congress responded in 1862 with the passage of the Anti-Polygamy Act (12 Stat. 501) making polygamy in any U.S. territory a crime, and prescribing a penalty of up to 5 years imprisonment for violations of the act. The law was difficult to enforce because it was hard to get evidence of plural marriages; the Mormon Temple officials secretly retained the records of such services. It was hard to get convictions also because the juries hearing the cases were often composed primarily of Mormons. One case of violation of the act did reach the U.S. Supreme Court [*Reynolds v. U.S.*, 98 U.S. 145 (1878)]. The Court upheld the conviction of Reynolds, reasoning that freedom of religion does not extend so far as to condone overt acts that may be disruptive of the social order.

In 1882 Congress passed the Edmunds Act (22 Stat. 30), making it a crime to cohabit with two women at once. To secure enforcement it was further provided that in a prosecution under this act no one could serve as a juror unless he swore that he never practiced polygamy or that he disapproved of such practice. The act also excluded polygamists from voting or holding public office in any territory. Prosecution under this law was much more successful than under the previous one.

Congress followed in 1887 with the Edmunds-Tucker Act (24 Stat. 635), which further restricted the privileges of people practicing polygamy. It permitted the vote only to those who would swear an oath against polygamy, and required all marriage ceremonies to be registered. It annulled laws that indirectly supported the practice, such as those affording inheritance rights to illegitimate children, laws limiting prosecution for adultery to cases in which there is a complaint by the wife, and laws that provided for elective judgeships in order to afford judicial support to the practice. This act also dissolved the corporation of the Mormon Church and seized all its property except that used for worship. Shortly after passage of this act the Mormon church officially disavowed polygamy and advised its members to abide by the laws of the U.S. in regard to it.

Shortly thereafter, in 1896, Utah was admitted to the Union with a constitutional provision forbidding the practice of polygamy. Four other Western states subsequently admitted to the Union also forbade the practice in their constitutions (Oklahoma, Idaho, Arizona, and New Mexico). *See* POLYGAMY, U.S. LAW OF.

Religious Practices in Public Schools. The 19th century saw the advent of the public school system in the U.S. under the leadership of Horace *Mann. Gradually, parochial schools of most denominations were absorbed into the public school system; the major exception was the Catholic school system. When parochial schools were merged with the public schools, there was not an immediate desecularization; religious practices and instruction were common in the early public schools. Since the Protestant religion was predominant at this time, most public schools incorporated the Protestant teaching in their curriculum. Catholics objected to this practice and accordingly thought it expedient to continue their own schools with their own religious instruction. *See* EDUCATION, I (HISTORY OF), 8.

Gradually antireligious and nonreligious elements of the population began to work for the discontinuance of religious instruction in the public schools, and they soon succeeded. Toward the end of the 19th century the public school system was conducted by the state, divorced from all church control, and given over exclusively to the dissemination of secular information.

Though public schools were no longer to be controlled by any religious factions, vestiges of sectarian influence still remained in many states. Many schools retained the practices of saying prayers, singing hymns, and reading the Bible.

The several court decisions in the 19th and early 20th centuries concerning the propriety of Bible reading in public schools had conflicting results; a minority of the decisions prohibited such practices. Wisconsin [*State v. School Dist. of Edgeton,* 44 N.W. 967 (1890)], Nebraska [*State v. Scheve,* 91 N.W. 846 (1902)], Illinois [*People v. Bd. of Educ.* 92 N.E. 251 (1910)], and Louisiana [*Herold v. Bd. of School Div.* (1915)] were the four states to disallow Bible reading in public schools. Illinois excluded the Bible entirely; Nebraska and Wisconsin barred it only so far as it was sectarian and not when it was used to teach moral ethics. Louisiana barred it as giving preference to Christians over Jews. Twelve other states in which the question reached the courts decided in favor of allowing the reading of the Bible; they were Colorado, Georgia, Iowa, Kansas, Kentucky, Maine, Massachusetts, Michigan, Minnesota, Ohio, Pennsylvania, and Texas.

Similar inconsistent results occurred when the courts were asked to decide whether the holding of religious services and Sunday schools in the public school buildings was proper. Some courts prohibited such use, stating that school buildings can be used only for educational purposes and thereby excluding religious services. Other courts upheld the decisions of the school officials in these matters, whether the school officials allowed or disallowed the use.

The propriety of the practice of employing Roman Catholic nuns as teachers in the public schools also came to the courts for determination. Objectors pointed out that the wearing of religious garb with crucifixes and rosaries had a sectarian influence on the education in such schools. Statutes forbidding the wearing of religious garb were upheld in both Pennsylvania [*Commonwealth v. Herr* (1910) 78 Atl. 68] and New York [*O'Connor v. Hendrick* (1906) 77 N.E. 612]. *See* PUBLIC SCHOOLS, RELIGIOUS GARB IN.

In the late 19th century, antireligious feelings concerning public schools brought pressure to bear on legislation. As a result, from 1876 to 1912 nine of the ten states admitted to the Union were required as a condition of admission to agree that provision be made for the establishment of public schools free from sectarian control. *See* PUBLIC SCHOOLS, RELIGIOUS PRACTICES IN.

Tenure of Church Property. Early in the 19th century most of the property of the Catholic Church was held or administered by lay trustees. This was the result of an interplay of several factors including Old World customs, Protestant influence, and practical necessity.

Since priests were scarce in the early colonies, small communities desiring to establish a church had to rely on traveling missionaries. The only practical method of caring for church property in the absence of priests was to entrust its care to the lay members of the church. Also, many of the early Catholics in the U.S. had come from continental Europe, where a similar lay trustee system worked well in a civil-law framework. Problems were to arise, however, under the new system of law in the U.S. Finally, since the Protestant sects were in a majority in the U.S. and since they were organized on a basis of lay control, the Catholics were inclined to trust in lay organization.

The lay trusteeship form of control of church property in the U.S. was the cause of great dissension and conflict within the Church for 50 years. Trustees attempted to secure a voice in spiritual affairs of the Church. Cases occurred in which they refused to accept the services of lawfully appointed priests and attempted to name priests of their choice. Often these differences resulted in civil court cases and occasionally went to Rome for settlement. (*See* TRUSTEEISM.)

In 1829 the First Provincial Council of Baltimore attempted to put an end to such internal disorders and dissension by decreeing that in the future no church could be built unless it were assigned to the bishop of the diocese in which it was to be built. The decree cited the ills of the trustee system and obviously meant to abolish this system in the future. It was immediately carried out.

Bishop as Absolute Owner. Under this system the bishop holds absolute title to the property and administers it in his individual name. This was a useful system for some time in that it proved better than the lay trustee system. However, certain difficulties arose in regard to the transfer of property at the death of the bishop, as well as in regard to improper use or disposition of the property by the bishop during his life. Attempts were made by the provincial councils of 1837, 1840, and 1843 to guarantee continuance of property in the church's hands by requiring the bishops holding title to make valid wills in favor of fellow bishops. Many courts aided the Church in this matter by declaring that the bishop mentioned in a conveyance held the property only as trustee for the members of the Church, even though no trust is expressed in the instrument. By virtue of this interpretation the property would not descend to the heirs of a bishop not having a will, nor could he dispose of it by will since the beneficiary of the trust would be the equitable owner. By the same token, under this interpretation, the property cannot be reached for satisfaction of a bishop's personal debts as it could were he the absolute title holder. An important case in which this result was reached was *Mannix v. Purcell* [46 Ohio St. 102 (1888)].

As a result of the troubles involved in this system, the Third Plenary Council (1884) decreed that the method of making the bishop the absolute owner of church property was to be used only as a last resort. On July 29, 1911, the Congregation of the Council forbade the method entirely.

Bishop as Trustee. Under this system of property ownership the legal title is vested in the trustee (bishop) and the equitable title is vested in the *cestui que trust* (members of the congregation). The bishop holds title for the benefit of the congregation. As legal owner of the property the bishop is free to administer it according to the canons of the Church. He can delegate control of the property to administrators while retaining the right of supervision over the administration. Other advantages of the system include the protection of the property of the Church. The property of the Church cannot be reached by creditors of the bishop, and neither is there a problem of testate or intestate succession since the members of the Church are the equitable owners.

Most courts have minimized the importance of the bishop as trustee and classify him as a passive, silent trustee with little power, thereby giving the members of the congregation considerable voice in deciding what use or disposition is to be made of the property. (See *Arts v. Guthrie* 37 N.W. 395.) This is the only objection to this form of church property ownership, and in recent times such interference by a congregation is rare.

Bishop as a Corporation Sole. Some states in the U.S. provide for a system of church property ownership called the corporation sole. By this system the bishop and his successors are incorporated by law and are afforded perpetuity. The corporation consists of one person, the bishop. At his death the corporation does not cease but is merely in abeyance until a successor is appointed, the successor then becoming the new corporation sole. The corporation sole holds absolute title to its property. The bishop, though he is the corporation, does not hold title. This means that the property does not descend to the bishop's heirs, nor can it be reached by the bishop's creditors. The property is transferred to the succeeding bishop.

This type of ownership existed in the colonial days wherever established religions existed, e.g., in Maine, Massachusetts, and Virginia. With the disappearance of the establishments, the corporation sole disappeared until the late 19th century, when a few states provided for it by statute. Other states have created quasi corporation soles through court decisions without legislation authority.

Corporation Aggregate. Two types of corporation aggregate appeared: the trustee corporation and the congregational corporation. The trustee corporation is an outgrowth of the lay trustee system. To remedy the faults inherent in the lay trustee system, churches sought special charters incorporating the trustees. Later most states provided for such incorporation in their general statutes. In this form of property ownership the legal title is vested in the incorporated trustees, and the equitable title is in the unincorporated society. Death of a trustee has no effect on the life of the corporation, and title to property after such a death is never in abeyance.

The congregational corporation is composed of all the members of the parish. Together they form a single legal entity. The title of property is vested in the body corporate. Officers are elected (often called trustees), but they do not hold title to the property. They merely are entrusted with the management of the business affairs of the corporation and as such are agents of the corporation. Their discretion is similar to that vested in the board of directors of an ordinary business corporation.

These types of aggregate corporations began to appear with regularity in the second half of the 19th century as various states passed laws permitting their establishment. Prior to this time religious societies were not allowed to be incorporated except by special charter. This system was criticized because favoritism to certain churches was becoming manifest.

Schisms and the Courts. A schism has been defined as a division or separation in a church or denomination of Christians occasioned by diversity of opinion [*Nelson v. Benson* 69 Ill. 29 (1873)]. Such schisms have occurred with considerable frequency in the history of the churches of the U.S., with comparatively few of them involving the Roman Catholic Church. Usually when a schism occurs a dispute arises concerning the property of the church. Both factions seek to have title to and use of the property. The resolution of such disputes has often been placed in the hands of the civil courts of the U.S. The courts have struggled with the difficult problems involved, the primary difficulty arising from the fact that solution depends on the type of church involved. The large number and variety of denominations with varying forms of government make it impossible to find a solution that is applicable to all such disputes.

A study of the case law in this area shows that courts of the several states have given uniform treatment to these problems according to the type of church involved. In the only U.S. Supreme Court decision on this matter, the Court summarizes the various types of cases that have occurred and classifies them according to three categories [*Watson v. Jones* 80 U.S. 679 (1871)].

Specific Trust. A type of controversy arises when a schism occurs in a church that holds property deeded to it with an express stipulation that it be used to spread some specific form of doctrine or belief. In such a case it is the duty of the court to see that the property is not diverted to any other than the specified use. The court has to decide which faction of the church still adheres to the tenets or beliefs specified in the deed. This solution will often depend on the type of church involved. Is the church totally independent of any higher form of government or is it part of a national church by which it is governed? If the church is totally independent, the court must decide for itself which faction is adhering to the specified beliefs. There is no higher church government to rely on. If the church is a part of a larger organization, the court enforces the decision of the highest tribunal of the church. Accepting this decision, the civil court has merely to decree that one faction is entitled to the use of the property according to the terms of the deed. This result will follow even if the recognized faction is a minority of the original local congregation

[*Wilson v. Pres. Church of John's Island* 2 Rich. Eq 192 (1846) S.C.].

Independent Congregation. Another type of controversy arises when a schism occurs in a religious congregation that owes no fealty to a higher authority or any other ecclesiastical association. The property that is the subject of the controversy has not been specifically entrusted. Such an organization is entirely independent and governs itself either by the will of a majority of its members or by such other local organism as the majority may have instituted for the purpose of ecclesiastical government. The rules to be followed in these cases are the ordinary principles governing voluntary associations. Whatever form of government is set up by the congregation must be followed. If the majority is to rule, the courts will abide by this, even if the majority has made a complete reversal from the doctrines to which it originally adhered. If certain officers are vested with control of the church, then whatever faction is headed by these officers will be entitled to the property. No inquiry may be made into the doctrine or beliefs of the various factions of the church. In *Shannon v. Frost* [3 B. Monro 253 (1842)], a Kentucky court showed its reluctance to interfere with the decision of the majority of an independent Baptist Church by stating: "The judicial eye cannot penetrate the will of the church for the forbidden purpose of vindicating the alleged wrongs of excised members." The court refused to allow the minority to use the house of worship, basing the decision on the decision of the majority. A Vermont court, in *Smith v. Nelson* [18 Vt. 511 (1846)], stated that in a review of church proceedings they cannot be treated differently from any other voluntary association.

In a 1903 Texas case involving a church of this type, the court correctly stated that the question of a higher church government cannot be a test, since the society is independent of all such higher ecclesiastical control, and can, by majority vote, conduct its government as it pleases (*Gibson v. Morris* 73 S.W. 85).

Associated Church. Another type of case, and the type under which most of the court cases seem to fit, is that of property normally acquired and intended for general use of a religious congregation that is itself part of a large and general organization of some religious denomination, with which it is more or less intimately connected by religious views and ecclesiastical government.

Most early cases were in agreement as to how disputes over property should be handled in such a case. Often a majority of a local congregation would attempt to break away from the general association and attempt to retain rights to its property. The courts recognized that although the dissenting group might be a majority of the local congregation, consideration must be given to the church government of the association of which the local congregation is a part.

A church originally formed as a branch of an associated church, subordinated to the government of that church, cannot break away from that form of government and discipline without losing the character or identity that confers rights to property [*Miller v. Gable* (1845) 2 Denio (NY) 492]. The portion of a church that separates itself from the old organization to form a new one cannot validly claim property belonging to the old organization if the old organization retains its original framework, tenets, and beliefs [*Gibson v. Armstrong* (1847) 46 Ken. 481]. Any majority of a local congregation that organizes resistance to the legitimate authority of its ecclesiastical superiors is not a true congregation and is not entitled to use of the church property [*Winebrenner v. Colder* (1862) 43 Pa. 244].

In a case in which a majority of a congregation withdrew from a presbytery of the Protestant church and denounced its teachings, the court held that the title to church property should remain with that portion of the congregation adhering to the tenets and discipline of the larger organization to whose use the property was originally dedicated. This is true even though the remaining faithful are a minority [*Ferraria v. Vascanelles* 23 Ill. Repts. 403 (1860)].

These cases indicate that a minority of a local Methodist Episcopal congregation that adheres to its conference or of a local Presbyterian Church that adheres to its presbytery is entitled to the property in such a dispute. It has likewise been decided that a Roman Catholic congregation that has placed itself under authority of its archbishop cannot divorce itself from such authority and still keep title to property acquired by it [*Dochkus v. Lithuanian Benefit Society of St. Anthony* (1903) 206 Pa. 25].

The Supreme Court case of *Watson v. Jones* (81 U.S. 679) involved a division in a local congregation in Kentucky, part of the Presbyterian Church. In deciding in favor of the group still recognized by the Protestant presbytery, the Court stated:

> In this class of cases we think the rule of action which should govern the civil courts, founded in a broad and sound view of the relations of church and state under our system of laws, and supported by a prepondering weight of judicial authority is, that, whenever the questions of discipline, or of faith, or ecclesiastical rule, custom, or law have been decided by the highest of these church judicatories to which the matter has been carried, the legal tribunals must accept such decisions as final, and as binding on them, in their application to the case before them.

The court based its decision on two principles. It feared that freedom of religion would be subverted if an aggrieved party could appeal to the secular courts after the church judicatory had decided against him. Second, the court reasoned that ecclesiastical courts and scholars were better equipped with the knowledge proper for deciding questions of this nature.

Generally speaking, U.S. civil courts have refused to hear cases concerning purely ecclesiastical matters; rather, they accept the holding of the ecclesiastical judicatories. Also, if a civil court should choose to hear such a case, it will only do so after the aggrieved person has exhausted all possible appeals in the particular church judicatory structure [*German Reformed Church v. Seibert* 3 Barr 282 Pa. (1846)]. *See* CHURCHES, LAW GOVERNING (U.S.).

Diplomatic Representation at the Vatican. Prior to 1846 there were a few isolated instances in which the idea was proposed that the U.S. send a diplomatic representative to the Vatican. However, in 1846 with the election of Pius IX to succeed Gregory XVI as pope, the idea gained new impetus since this election was greatly favored in the U.S.; Pius IX was considered a liberal who would strive for reforms and greater freedoms.

In June 1847 the American consul at Rome in a dispatch to the secretary of state proposed that formal diplomatic relations be established between the U.S. and the government of the Vatican. This proposal was made after high officials of the Vatican government and the Pope himself expressed the desire that such diplomatic relations be started.

In December 1847 Pres. James K. Polk in his message to Congress proposed the opening of such diplomatic relations, giving as reasons the political events occurring in the papal states and protection of U.S. commercial interests there. In Congress the proposal met with some opposition, but easily passed (137 to 15 in the House and 36 to 7 in the Senate). The opposition argued that under the U.S. Constitution the government could play no part in ecclesiastical matters and that the U.S. had no actual commercial interests to protect in the Vatican. Some feared that the President was making the proposal merely as a political move, to secure the vote of the Roman Catholic population.

With the passage of this proposal, Jacob T. Martin, a convert to Roman Catholicism, was named the first chargé d'affaires to the Vatican in 1848. Martin's instructions from the secretary of state read:

> There is one consideration which you ought always to keep in view in your intercourse with the Papal authorities. Most, if not all Governments which have Diplomatic Representatives at Rome are connected with the Pope as the head of the Catholic Church. In this respect the Government of the United States occupies an entirely different position. It possesses no power whatever over the question of religion. All denominations of Christians stand on the same footing in this country,—and every man enjoys the inestimable right of worshiping his God according to the dictates of his own conscience—Your efforts, therefore, will be devoted exclusively to the cultivation of the most friendly civil relations with the Papal Government, and to the extension of the commerce between the two countries. You will carefully avoid even the appearance of interfering in ecclesiastical questions, whether these relate to the United States or any other portion of the world. It might be proper, should you deem it advisable, to make these views known, on some suitable occasion, to the Papal Government; so that there may be no mistake or misunderstanding on this subject.

The diplomatic relationship thus created lasted for 20 years, until 1867. During these years six different chargés d'affaires represented the U.S. in the Papal States. There was no interruption of the friendly feelings that existed between the two governments. Most of the matters arising were unrelated episodes that called for no sustained policy on the part of either country. Some of the more important incidents that arose included the alleged recognition of the Southern Confederacy by the Vatican; the question of the status of Msgr. Cajeton Bedini, who came to the U.S. as apostolic delegate; the protection of Vatican property by the U.S. legation during Garibaldi's entrance into Rome; and the refusal of the Washington Monument Association in 1852 of a block of marble for the monument sent by the Pope.

The matter that caused the most concern and eventually the cessation of U.S. diplomatic representation at the Vatican revolved around the institution of Protestant services conducted for American citizens within the Vatican. Such worship apparently seemed to the papacy inconsistent with the idea of Rome as the center of the one, true, universal, Church. To enable the American chapel, set up outside the legation, to continue their Protestant services, the American minister in 1866 placed the arms of the American legation over the building used as a chapel. The American minister insisted that this arrangement was satisfactory to the papal authorities. Nevertheless, as a result of this difficulty, which had been greatly exaggerated, the Congress refused to appropriate money for continuance of the U.S. representative at the Vatican. Thus the mission ceased to exist without ever having been formally discontinued. No formal message of explanation was ever sent to the Vatican.

Bibliography: L. C. Feiertag, *American Public Opinion on the Diplomatic Relations between the U.S. and the Papal States, 1847–1867* (Washington 1933). L. F. Stock, *United States Ministers to the Papal States,* v.1 (Washington 1933). P. J. Dignan, *A History of the Legal Incorporation of Catholic Church Property in the U.S., 1784–1932* (Washington 1933). C. J. Bartlett, *The Tenure of Parochial Property in the U.S.* (CUA CLS 31; 1926). C. F. Zollmann, *American Church Law* (St. Paul 1933). A. P. Stokes, *Church and State in the U.S.,* 3 v. (New York 1950). J. J. McGrath, "Canon Law and American Church Law: A Comparative Study," *Jurist* 18 (1958) 260–278. R. A. Billington, *The Protestant Crusade, 1800–1860* (New York 1938).

[J. C. POLKING]

4. Search for Solution (1900–66)

The 1st Amendment to the U.S. Constitution provides in part that "Congress shall make no law respecting an establishment of religion or prohibiting the free exercise thereof." The 1st Amendment provided religious guarantees only against encroachment by the Federal government [*Barron v. Baltimore* 7 Peters 243 (1833); *see* FREEDOM OF RELIGION, U.S. LAW OF].

At the advent of the 20th century there existed few areas of interaction between the Federal government and religious activities. When the U.S. entered World War I in 1917, Congress enacted a draft law with exemptions from combat duty for *conscientious objectors. The exemption was attacked as a religious establishment but was upheld by the U.S. Supreme Court [*Arver v. U.S.,* 245 U.S. 366 (1918)]. After the war the Court interpreted the naturalization law to deny citizenship to aliens conscientiously opposed to bearing arms in defense of the country [*U.S. v. Schwimmer,* 279 U.S. 644 (1929); *U.S. v. Macintosh,* 283 U.S. 605 (1931)]. This statutory construction was abandoned in 1946 (*Girouard v. U.S.,* 328 U.S. 61).

Expansion of Federal interest in education after World War II brought new contacts between the national government and religious institutions. Congress enacted the Servicemen's Readjustment Acts (1944, 1952), the National School Lunch Act (1946), the National Defense Education Acts (1958, 1961, 1963), and the Higher Education Facilities Act (1963). To date no challenge to these programs involving aid to church-related schools and their students has reached the Supreme Court. (*See* FEDERAL AID TO EDUCATION; PRIVATE SCHOOL PUPILS, HEALTH AND WELFARE SERVICES FOR; PRIVATE SCHOOLS, GRANTS AND LOANS TO; SCHOLARSHIPS, GOVERNMENTAL; TAX EXEMPTION.)

14th Amendment. The *14th Amendment, adopted in 1868, has been construed to apply 1st Amendment protection to interactions between local governments and religious activities. The 14th Amendment expressly prohibits the states from depriving any person of life, liberty, or property without *due process of law. On the basis of the due process clause, the Supreme Court unanimously invalidated an Oregon statute requiring the attendance of all children of school age at public schools [*Pierce v. Society of Sisters,* 268 U.S. 510 (1925)]. The Court found the statute to be a denial of parental rights in education. In the same area and era, the Court upheld public provision of textbooks in secular subjects for pupils attending church-related schools [*Cochran v. Louisiana,* 281 U.S. 340 (1930)].

In 1940 the Court extended the protection of the 14th Amendment to guarantee religious freedom against state action (*Cantwell v. Connecticut,* 310 U.S. 296). In 1947 the Court completed the absorption of 1st Amendment freedoms into the 14th Amendment by incorporating the religious establishment clause (*Everson v. Board of Education,* 330 U.S. 1).

Freedom of Religious Exercise. Since 1940 the Supreme Court has weighed the individual's claim to religious freedom against the interest of the community in a variety of contexts.

Proselytizing. In *Cantwell v. Conn.* three Jehovah's Witnesses were convicted of violating a Connecticut statute that required solicitors for religious causes to be certified by a local official. The Court unanimously overturned the convictions and found the statute an unconstitutional abridgment of the defendants' rights to the free exercise of their religion. Speaking through Justice Roberts, the Court acknowledged that the *freedom to act* according to conscience is not absolutely guaranteed by the Constitution; the *freedom to believe* is absolutely guaranteed. The Court held the statute a prior restraint upon the exercise of religious liberty since a public official was entrusted with the power to determine whether a solicitor's cause was genuinely religious. In 1942 the Court upheld the right of a community to levy a tax on itinerant evangelists peddling religious tracts door-to-door but reversed the decision the next year (*Jones v. Opelika,* 316 U.S. 584; *Murdock v. Pennsylvania,* 319 U.S. 105). The Court concluded in the *Murdock* case that itinerant evangelists were engaged in a religious rather than commercial venture and that a license tax unrelated to the activities or revenues of the evangelists abridged the free exercise of their religious beliefs. The Court extended the *Murdock* principle to evangelists who made their living selling religious literature [*Follett v. Town of McCormick,* 321 U.S. 573 (1944)]. The Court also invalidated an ordinance against summoning occupants to the door for the distribution of religious literature [*Martin v. Struthers,* 319 U.S. 141 (1943)].

Although local communities may prohibit the distribution of commercial handbills on public streets, the Court accorded constitutional protection to handbills of religious nature that incidentally solicit funds and invite the purchase of books [*Jamison v. Texas,* 318 U.S. 413 (1943)]. The right of itinerant evangelists to distribute religious literature extends to company towns [*Marsh v. Alabama,* 326 U.S. 501 (1946)] and to Federal housing projects [*Tucker v. Texas,* 326 U.S. 517 (1946)], but not to private apartment houses [*Watchtower Bible and Tract Society v. Metropolitan Life Insurance Co.,* 79 N.E. 2d 433; *cert. denied* 335 U.S. 886 (1949)]. The Court has upheld the application to religious literature of a statute forbidding the sale by minors of religious papers or periodicals on public streets [*Prince v. Massachusetts,* 321 U.S. 158 (1944)]. Local authorities may also regulate parades by religious groups and charge license fees proportionate to the public expense incurred [*Cox v. New Hampshire,* 312 U.S. 569 (1941)]. The rights of free speech and free religious exercise do not extend to "fighting words" [*Chaplinsky v. New Hampshire,* 315 U.S. 568 (1941)]. *See* PROSELYTIZING, U.S. LAW OF.

In 1952 the Court upset an effort by the New York legislature to wrest control of church property from a Moscow-appointed patriarch [*Kedroff v. St. Nicholas Cathedral,* 344 U.S. 94 (1952)]. The Court found that the legislation regulating the appointment of Russian Orthodox clergy in New York invaded the freedom of religious exercise. *See* CHURCHES, LAW GOVERNING (U.S).

Flag Salute. A few weeks after the *Cantwell* decision, the Court decided the first flag-salute case [*Minersville School District v. Gobitis,* 310 U.S. 586 (1940)]. Justice Frankfurter, speaking for eight justices, upheld the constitutionality of a Pennsylvania law that required all public school pupils to salute the flag. The defendants, Jehovah's Witnesses, refused on religious grounds to permit their children to salute the flag and claimed that the statute infringed their freedom of religious exercise. Justice Frankfurter esteemed the promotion of national unity sufficient to warrant the action of the Pennsylvania Legislature. Only Chief Justice Stone argued that the cause of national unity was insufficient to coerce pupils to act against their consciences.

The *Gobitis* decision was much criticized, and 3 years later the Court reversed itself [*West Virginia State Board of Education v. Barnette,* 319 U.S. 624 (1943)]. Justice Jackson, speaking for a majority of six justices, declared that a West Virginia statute requiring the flag salute transcended constitutional limitations and invaded the spiritual sphere preserved by the 1st Amendment from all official control. To the *Barnette* majority, freedom of speech could be restricted only to prevent grave and immediate danger to paramount community interests. In this instance, lack of patriotism was not such a danger. (*See* PUBLIC SCHOOLS, FLAG SALUTE.)

Sunday Legislation. A recent and bitter controversy claiming the attention of the public and the Court was *Sunday legislation. Sabbatarians complained that they suffered adverse economic consequences if they obeyed the Sunday laws and observed the Sabbath according to the dictates of their conscience. In 1961 six justices upheld the constitutionality of these laws against the claim of Sabbatarians to exemption on the basis of the constitutional guarantee of religious freedom (*Braunfeld v. Brown,* 366 U.S. 599). Chief Justice Warren, speaking for the majority, conceded that the Sunday laws in dispute operated indirectly to make the practice of Sabbatarian beliefs more expensive, but he insisted that the laws were primarily designed to achieve legitimate secular goals. An exemption to Sabbatarians might adversely affect these goals in several ways: Sabbatarians might gain an economic advantage over competitors, complicate enforcement, inject a religious factor into the employment picture, and undermine the common day of rest. Justices Douglas, Brennan, and Stewart dissented. Justice Brennan reasoned that the free exercise of religion is a preferred freedom and, even indirectly, may be infringed only to prevent a grave and imminent danger of substantive evil; the mere convenience of having everyone rest on the same day could not justify Sunday laws that made Sabbatarian religious beliefs economically disadvantageous.

In 1963 seven justices held that a state may not constitutionally exclude from unemployment compensation a claimant who, for reasons of conscience, turned down a job involving suitable work on Saturday (*Sherbert v. Verner,* 374 U.S. 398). Justice Brennan, who spoke for five justices, found that South Carolina had no compelling interest to outweigh the injury done to the claimant's religious freedom. Justices Harlan and White, dissenting, argued that the decision singled out religiously motivated abstention from work for financial assistance but denied similar compensation to identical behavior differently motivated. With Justice Stewart of the majority, they held the decision inconsistent with the *Braunfeld* case. (*See* SHERBERT V. VERNER.)

Religious Establishment. By 1947, when the Supreme Court applied the 1st Amendment's prohibition of a religious establishment to the states, two developments in American education had brought local governments into new relations to religious activity: the growth of an increasingly nonreligious public school and the corresponding growth of private schools. Some parents sought religious instruction and exercises for their children in public schools; other parents sought public support for the cost of their children's secular education in private schools. The response of local governments to these desires was challenged, and most of the Court's decisions on the religious establishment clause have involved the issue of religion and education.

Public Transportation. The first case was **Everson v. School Board,* 330 U.S. 1 (1947). A township school board, acting in accordance with a New Jersey statute, reimbursed parents for money spent in sending children to parochial schools on local buses. A bare majority of the Court upheld the board's actions. Both the majority, speaking through Justice Black, and the minority, led by Justice Rutledge, agreed that the 1st Amendment's religious establishment clause absolutely forbade every form of governmental support to religious activity. They disagreed whether public transportation of parochial school pupils involved aid to religion. The majority held that the state's contribution of free transportation constituted a benefit to the welfare of the children rather than support of denominational institutions. The minority argued that public transportation enabled the children in a substantial way to gain religious education. (*See* PRIVATE SCHOOL PUPILS, PUBLIC TRANSPORTATION FOR.)

The central ambiguity of the *Everson* decision lay in the implicit conflict between the profession of "absolute" separation of Church and State and the acceptance of public transportation of parochial school children as a welfare measure. On the one hand, the majority thought the religious establishment clause a "wall" extensive enough to forbid support to any religious activity or institution; on the other, the Court found public transportation an aid to the individual child rather than the denominational school. This raised the question whether the Court would consider other forms of public assistance to pupils attending church-related schools compatible with the religious establishment clause on the basis of the child-benefit theory. Many constitutional authorities felt that the Court might have reached the same result more realistically by avoiding an attempt to make aid to religion and child benefit mutually exclusive and by suggesting instead the distinction between preference of religion and incidental aid to religiously oriented institutions fulfilling secular purposes. The *Everson* majority might have stressed the principle of governmental neutrality in matters of religion more successfully than the unrealistic formula of absolute separation of Church and State.

Released Time. One year later the Court faced the issue of released time for religious instruction in the public schools [**McCollum v. Board of Education,* 333 U.S. 203 (1948)]. The Champaign, Ill. school board permitted sectarian instruction in the local schools during school hours for children whose parents so requested. (*See* PUBLIC SCHOOL FACILITIES, PRIVATE USE OF.) The mother of a pupil who did not attend these classes objected to the program as an infringement of religious freedom and an establishment of religion. Speaking for the Court, Justice Black again affirmed the absolute separation of Church and State but concluded that the Illinois program was inconsistent with that standard. He complained of two features of the contested released-time program: the use of tax-supported public school buildings for the dissemination of religious doctrines and the use of the state's compulsory education machinery to provide pupils for the religion classes. It is difficult to reconcile the Court's objection in *McCollum* to the use of public school property for religious instruction with the availability of public parks to the orderly use of religious groups [*Niemotko v. Maryland,* 340 U.S. 268 (1951); *Fowler v. Rhode Island,* 345 U.S. 67 (1953)]. Critics of *McCollum* have also questioned whether compulsory education laws require that a child's formal schooling be exclusively secular. They suggest that the law requires only that a child secure formal schooling that includes the secular education specified as necessary to fulfill the duties of citizenship.

In a concurring opinion, Justice Frankfurter, joined by the other justices of the *Everson* minority, repeated his affirmation of the absolute separation of Church and State. He characterized the public school as a symbol of secular unity and deplored the divisive effect of sectarian instruction. To Justice Frankfurter, the released-time program put pressure upon school children to attend. Legal scholars suggested that Justice Frankfurter's failure to distinguish between state-sponsored religious instruction and that permitted at the request of parents reflected an inadequate appreciation of parental rights in education.

The sole dissenter was Justice Reed. He conceded that passing years had brought about the acceptance of a broader meaning to the religious establishment clause than the prohibition of a state church probably intended by the framers. But he would not accept a separation of Church and State so absolute as to prohibit the incidental benefits that religious bodies together with similarly situated groups obtain as a result of membership in organized society. Justice Reed pointed to areas in which the government cooperated with religious activities: tax exemption of church property; transportation, textbooks, and lunches for parochial school children at public expense; legislative chaplains; military chaplains; and public support of World War II veterans at church-related colleges. Justice Reed did not suggest, however, a constitutional standard to distinguish permissible from impermissible Church-State relations.

In 1952 the Court modified the *McCollum* decision by permitting a New York City program of released time for religious instruction off the public school premises (**Zorach v. Clauson,* 343 U.S. 306). Justice Douglas, speaking for a majority of six justices, denied that the 1st Amendment prescribed a separation of

Church and State in every respect. A state may recognize the religious nature of the American people and adjust the schedule of the public schools to meet sectarian needs. The majority rejected the contention that the New York program coerced public school pupils into religious instruction. Justices Black, Frankfurter, and Jackson dissented. They accused the majority of abandoning the standard of absolute separation of Church and State and saw no significant difference between the Illinois program invalidated in *McCollum* and the New York program sustained in *Zorach*. Justice Black again objected to the use of the state's compulsory education machinery, while Justices Frankfurter and Jackson were concerned with the coercive effects of the released-time program on students who did not attend the religious instruction classes. Most commentators have regarded the *McCollum* and *Zorach* decisions as fundamentally inconsistent. (*See* RELEASED TIME IN PUBLIC SCHOOLS.)

In 1961 the Court broke the silence of almost a decade on the establishment clause and upheld the Sunday laws of Maryland, Massachusetts, and Pennsylvania (*McGowan v. Maryland,* 366 U.S. 420). The Court refused to characterize the existing laws as establishments of the Christian religion and held economic and recreational goals to be the primary purpose of the legislation. Only Justice Douglas dissented from this view. In a separate opinion Justice Frankfurter attempted to clarify the general structure of the religious establishment clause. Conscious that the concerns of the state and those of religion perforce overlap, Justice Frankfurter suggested that the establishment clause prohibits both legislation whose primary purpose is religious and legislation furthering secular and religious ends by means unnecessary to the attainment of the secular end alone. Justice Frankfurter's analysis veered away from the formula of absolute separation and opened the way for the neutrality principle announced in the *Abington* decision.

Less than a month later, the Court unanimously struck down a Maryland statute that required all officeholders to declare their belief in the existence of God [*Torcaso v. Watkins,* 367 U.S. 488 (1961)]. Justice Black, speaking for the Court, reaffirmed and amplified the *Everson* definition of religious establishment as the basis for the decision. The Court held that Maryland had imposed a requirement that preferred belief over nonbelief. (*See* RELIGIOUS TEST FOR PUBLIC OFFICE.)

State Prescribed Prayer. No decision on the religious establishment clause aroused more opposition than the invalidation of the New York Regents' Prayer [*Engel v. Vitale,* 370 U.S. 421 (1962)]. The Court declared unconstitutional the Regents' recommendation that the following prayer be recited at the beginning of each school day: "Almighty God, we acknowledge our dependence upon Thee, and we beg Thy blessings upon us, our parents, our teachers, and our country." Speaking for the Court, Justice Black held that the state laws recommending the prayer violated the establishment clause because the prayer was composed by government officials as part of a government program designed to further religious beliefs. In a footnote the Justice dissociated the religious exercise involved in the New York program from patriotic or ceremonial occasions in which school children are officially encouraged to recite historical documents containing references to God or to sing officially espoused anthems including the composers' professions of faith in God. Justice Douglas, concurring separately, considered the vice of the New York program to consist in the financial aid given to the religious exercise. The sole dissenter, Justice Stewart, viewed the action of the school board as simply providing opportunity for pupils who wished to join in a brief prayer at the beginning of the school day.

Despite the storm over the *Engel* decision, the following June the Court struck down officially sponsored reading of the Bible and recitation of the Lord's Prayer at the beginning of the public school day [*School District of Abington Township v. Schempp,* 374 U.S. 203 (1963)]. Justice Clark, speaking for the Court, characterized Americans as a religious people but affirmed the absolute equality of belief and nonbelief before the law. He explained the test of neutrality in terms of the purpose and primary effect of the legislation; to withstand the strictures of the establishment clause, there must be a secular purpose and a primary effect that neither inhibits nor advances religion. Since Bible reading and recitation of the Lord's Prayer are religious exercises, the Court concluded that their requirement by the state violated the neutrality demanded by the establishment clause. By invoking the principle of neutrality, the Court transcended the unrealistic formula of absolute separation, recognized the overlapping concerns of religion and government, and suggested a norm to distinguish impermissible from permissible interaction. However, Justice Clark did not seek to distinguish state-sponsored from state-accommodated religious activities in the public school. He appeared to confine the place of religion exclusively to the individual, the home, and the church. In the view of many commentators, this reflects an inadequate consciousness of the primary role of parents in the education of their children.

Justices Douglas, Brennan, and Goldberg filed separate concurring opinions. Justice Douglas agreed with the Court that religious exercises under state auspices violated the neutrality required of the government but also insisted that they were unconstitutional because financed by public funds. Justice Brennan's notable concurrence reviewed the origins, judicial history, and problem areas of the religious establishment clause. He wrote that the state must be neutral in all matters of faith and neither favor nor inhibit religion, but neutrality would not forbid the application of secularly motivated legislation to alleviate burdens upon the free exercise of an individual's religious beliefs. Justice Brennan agreed with the majority that the state cannot sponsor religious exercises in the public school. He defended public support of military and penal chaplains, prayers before legislative bodies, nondevotional study of the Bible, tax exemptions for religious institutions, the accommodation of public welfare programs to Sabbatarian beliefs, and Sunday laws. Justice Goldberg, joined by Justice Harlan, also stressed the principle of neutrality and expressly acknowledged the propriety of military chaplains. Justice Stewart again registered the sole dissent. (*See* PUBLIC SCHOOLS, RELIGIOUS PRACTICES IN.)

Retrospect and Prospect. Seven major decisions of the U.S. Supreme Court since 1947, over the dissent or reservation of only two justices, have evolved the principle of governmental neutrality in matters of religion. Whatever the theory or practice in other periods of American history, the Court has concluded that harmony among citizens as partners in the democratic polity in our day requires the equality of Protestant, Catholic, Jewish, and secular humanist creeds before the law. But neutrality, which prohibits the preference of religion, should not be construed to bar governmental aid to religious institutions performing secular functions or governmental accommodation of religious activities where no preference is implied.

An understanding of the problems of religion and education depends on the recognition of both the absolute equality of all citizens in matters of belief and the primacy of parental rights in education. For the government to sponsor religious instruction or exercises would violate the equality of citizens and prefer religious belief over nonbelief. For the government to be unable to permit parents to choose a reasonable period of religious instruction for their children within public education on an elective basis or to support financially the choice of parents to educate their children in church-related schools would deny the primacy of parental rights and prefer nonbelief over religious belief.

Bibliography: For a general survey and interpretation of the 1st Amendment's religious guarantees, see P. B. KURLAND, *Religion and the Law of Church and State and the Supreme Court* (Chicago 1962). R. J. REGAN, *American Pluralism and the Catholic Conscience* (New York 1963). R. F. DRINAN, *Religion, the Courts, and Public Policy* (New York 1963). P. G. KAUPER, *Civil Liberties and the Constitution* (Ann Arbor 1962). J. C. MURRAY, *We Hold These Truths* (New York 1960) 45–78. L. PFEFFER, *Church, State, and Freedom* (Boston 1953).

Two valuable composite works are J. COGLEY, ed., *Religion in America* (New York 1958). Fund for the Republic, *Religion and the Free Society* (New York 1958).

On specific Church-State issues in education, see N. G. MCCLUSKEY, *Catholic Viewpoint on Education* (New York 1958; rev. ed. Image Bks. 1962). Fund for the Republic, *Religion and the Schools* (New York 1959). W. B. BALL, "The Constitutionality of the Inclusion of Church-Related Schools in Federal Aid to Education," *Georgetown Law Journal* 50 (1961) 397–455. R. J. REGAN, "The Dilemma of Religious Instruction and the Public Schools," *Catholic Lawyer* 10 (1964) 42–54, 82.

[R. J. REGAN]

CHURCH ARCHITECTURE

A vast array of literature surrounds the study of religious architecture, embracing a range of interests from archeology, anthropology, sociology, and aesthetics, to the evolution of consciousness and theology. This article, in 12 parts, attempts, in its introduction, to clarify those theoretical and technical aspects of religious architecture that are particularly relevant to its development; the succeeding sections present systematic summaries of the history of church architecture from the Early Christian period to the present day. The church architecture of certain cultures and periods is mentioned only briefly or omitted in these summaries where it has been more desirable to present them elsewhere. For extended treatment of specific areas and problems, *see* MISSIONARY ART; LATIN AMERICA, ART AND ARCHITECTURE IN; ARMENIAN ART; GEORGIAN LITERATURE AND ART; HUNGARIAN ART; CZECHOSLOVAKIAN ART; POLISH ART; YUGOSLAVIAN ART; CLUNIAC ART AND ARCHITECTURE; CISTERCIAN ART AND ARCHITECTURE. For special contemporary problems related to liturgy and church legislation, *see* LITURGICAL ART, 1, 2, 3, 5; ABSTRACT ART AND THE CHURCH. Articles on important architects and monuments may be referred to under their respective titles.

1. INTRODUCTION

In the following section five concomitants of architectural development are presented as an introduction to the subject; these are: (1) social and cultural considerations, (2) exigencies of ritual and function, (3) symbol and meaning in architectural conception, (4) technique and structural possibilities, and (5) concepts of form.

Social and Cultural Considerations. Church architecture services the worship of a community, and its construction depends on a patronage that utilizes the collective resources of the worshiping community. Consequently its artistic realization is not independent.

Social Aspect. Both the architect and church architecture in particular are bound to an immediate need of society. A church is not initiated by an architect's will to form but rather by a congregation's will to build. The creative act of the architect must recognize both the will and needs of his patrons. In modern times the most common social impediment to the production of a significant ecclesiastical structure occurs when a patron refuses to allow the architect to express the identity of the congregation in and through the architect's own will to form. Under such circumstances the architect is asked to relinquish his special abilities to create architectural form and instead act as a skillful transmitter of the congregation's collective will toward a form of established acceptability. This obstacle dominated 19th-century church architecture and was promoted by J. *Ruskin in his *Lamp of Obedience:* "We want no new style of architecture. . . . It does not matter one marble splinter whether we have an old or new architecture. . . . The forms of architecture already known to us are good enough and far better than any of us." The result of the 19th-century *Gothic revival was a church architecture of questionable artistic value.

The effort to make the architect's vision that of society reduces the educated artistic sensibility of the architect to a position of servitude to the less-educated sensibility of the congregation or pastor. The proper relationship between socio-cultural determination and architectural formation is one of mutual specification. One of the aphorisms about architecture is that "as we shape our buildings, likewise do our buildings shape us." Among significant churches of the 20th century that have helped to restructure society's view of acceptable religious architecture are F. L. *Wright's Unity Temple, A. *Perret's Le Raincy, Mies van der Rohe's Illinois Institute of Technology Chapel, and *Le Corbusier's Notre Dame du Haut (Ronchamp).

Cultural Aspect. This interdependency between architecture and society has led many to regard architecture as a mirror of man's cultural progress. For V. Hugo, for example, "Architecture is the book of human history . . . the handwriting of humanity." Monuments of religious architecture (all but synonymous with the general development of architecture for thousands of years) are most useful in tracing the origins, growth, and decline of various cultures in history. The validity of this measure rests on the assumption that a given culture has interrelated parallels in the development of its art, architecture, literature, economics, politics, philosophy, and theology. The effort to document these interrelationships has promoted some excellent though sometimes controversial studies. Among these are E. Panofsky's *Gothic Architecture and Scholasticism* (Latrobe 1951), which sheds new light on the relationship between medieval scholasticism and the visual articulation of Gothic structures, and V. Scully's *The Earth, the Temple and the Gods* (1962), which explores the influence of mythical cult and belief upon the location, orientation, and nature of Minoan, Mycenaean, and Greek temples. Cultural-architectural monographs are rare, and a definitive study of the cultural evolution of church structures has not as yet been written.

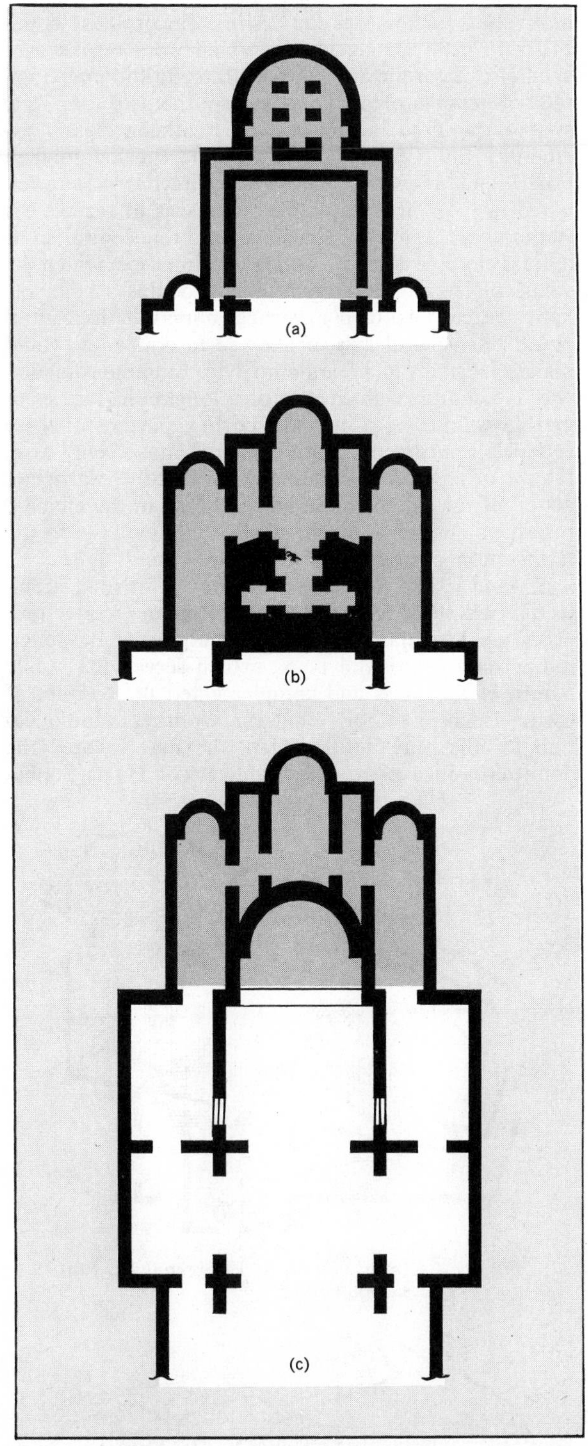

Fig. 1. St-Philibert-de-Grandlieu, development of the chevet: (a) first reconstruction, 826–829. (b) second reconstruction (lower crypt area), 840–847. (c) second reconstruction (upper nave area), showing devotional chapels arranged ladderwise or "enéchelon."

Exigencies of Ritual and Function. The questions that arise from the relating of ritual to church architecture are to what extent and how architectural form is, and ought to be, determined by liturgical function. Men of different periods have varied in their attitude toward this issue; in certain periods one finds a relatively high degree of ritual specification of form, such as in the Romanesque (Fig. 1) and in the baroque, whereas other periods show a low degree of ritual specification, as in churches of the Renaissance and 19th-century revivalism. The architectural significance of ecclesiastical structures is not necessarily dependent upon the degree of ritual determination; the Renaissance preference for centralized form promoted an architecture of merit, but its primary concern was not liturgical function. In some circumstances preoccupation with formalism produced conflicts with ritual use; the transept seating arrangement of H. H. *Richardson's Trinity Church is an example (Fig. 2).

Church architecture in the 20th century has actively addressed itself to the problem of ritual determination of form. The majority of mid-20th-century liturgical conferences on sacred art have supported the thesis that an adequate analysis of function accompanied by a genuine insight into sacred purpose will aid in the production of a significant church architecture. The idea is a vestige of the functionalist revolution that occurred in architectural thinking after the turn of the century. It emerged as a reaction against lingering public affection for outmoded revivalist styles and against the construction of churches that engaged naïve symbolic "shape-isms." Contemporary ritual functionalism is an attempt to liberate church architecture from traditional misconceptions of what churches ought to look like, and, in theory, it seeks to distinguish itself from older concepts of functionalism. The difference between the traditional Vitruvian notion of *utilitas* and the new notion of utility appears in the thesis that ritual accommodation is a sufficient aesthetic criterion for the production of a church structure. G. Santayana states this position for architecture in general: "Architecture . . . has all its forms suggested by practical demands. Use requires all our buildings to assume certain determinate forms." This view demands study of liturgy in order to avoid an erroneous conception of ritually determined form. It assumes that the ritually specified form carries the religious meaning of the building and is in itself symbolic. Although church form has always reflected functional patterns, older church structures depended upon mosaic, sculpture, and stained glass to provide religious symbolism. A. Aalto's church at Vuoksenniska, Imarta, Finland (1956–58), a good example of ritual functionalism, does not. It is starkly white and devoid of traditonal images; the uniqueness of its form is derived from a spatial interpretation of a sectioned seating arrangement in which each area forms a volume of its own by closure of folding doors (Figs. 3, 4). This church forsakes the traditional three-entry system common to the Latin-cross plan and provides five entry-ways, each giving access to a defined area; the front entry is used only when full congregational participation is intended, at which time the dynamics of the total space is experienced.

Ritual Functionalism and Typology. The seemingly permanent and immutable fundamental ways of orga-

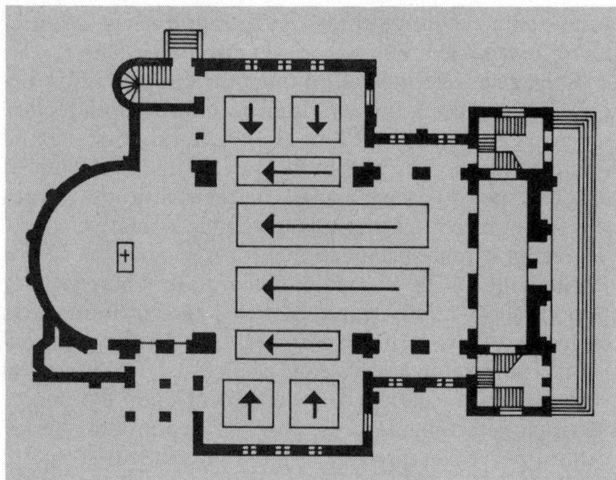

Fig. 2. H. H. Richardson, Trinity Church, Boston, 1872–77, illustrating a transept seating arrangement.

nizing ritual action are the general concern of ecclesiastical typology, which offers two systems of ritual arrangement: the one is the longitudinal plan in which the congregation forms a linear procession toward a terminally located sacred object (Fig. 5); the second is the centripetal plan in which the congregation groups around a centrally located sacred object (Fig. 6). Both types have conceptual value and have detemined architectural form for centuries.

The temple of Khonsu at Karnak utilized an impeded processional way (Fig. 7). Axial movement is suggested by symmetrical rows of columns, centrally placed doorways, and longitudinal arrangement of spaces. The processional way is impeded in its arrangement by the diminishment of size and light intensity of the chambers in the direction toward the sacred terminus. This arrangement was eminently suitable for the resident god Amon, who was physically unapproachable except by the most purified of mortals and for a caste system of worshipers who were restricted to their own specific areas. The basilica of St. Paul utilized a single spatial procession that was not impeded (Fig. 8): the church is a nave opening directly onto the terminal sanctuary; longitudinal movement is accentuated by the symmetrical rows of columns, the decoration of the clerestory walls, and the perspective view natural to such an arrangement; axial movement is direct and only slightly modulated by the visually restricting action of the triumphal arch. The basilica arrangement ritually reflects the oneness of the *ecclesia* and the public nature of Christ. The climax of processional movement in both Khonsu and St. Paul's occurs at the end of the longitudinal axis and also at the end of the architectural space.

The mastaba of Queen Merneith of Egypt utilizes the centripetal arrangement (Fig. 9): the central sarcophagus of the Queen was placed within a larger wood chamber around which a brick chamber was constructed; outside were the subsidiary graves of the court with the entire ensemble bounded by a wall. The design, best described as a "box-in-a-box," reflects the social-religious position of the Queen as sole inheritor of an after-life that the court wished to share. The centripetal arrangement of S. Costanza in Rome has the altar centrally located in a dome-covered chamber (Fig. 10); an ambulatory forms a dark lower periphery of space while the inner core explodes in light and in height, giving to the arrangement a hierarchy of impressions natural to centripetal schemes. In contrast to the longitudinal plan, the space of centripetal arrangements does not end at the terminal object but continues around it.

Although early civilizations tended to keep these two systems separate, their merging did occur with increasing frequency beginning with the Roman Empire. The motivation for this was the desire to incorporate domical centripetal arrangements, which were regarded as symbolic of cosmic authority, with the traditional longitudinal temple plan. To combine the two disparate systems required ingenuity. The Pantheon clearly exemplifies the combination (Fig. 11): the longitudinal processional movement began at a forecourt and terminated in the rear rotunda apse that was to receive the statue of the Emperor Hadrian; onto this central spine a great circular domed rotunda was imposed, which, by virtue of its geometric genesis and oculus as the sole light source, instituted a vertical climax at its central point; this vertical axis, if allowed to dominate, would make Hadrian's niche anticlimactic. But subordination was avoided through the use of a longitudinal series of marble roundels set into the portico pavement; these roundels reinforced the processional movement. Also, the use of an interior colonnade negated the centripetal action of the side niches, and the break in the entablature over Hadrian's niche gave visual emphasis to the termination of the longitudinal movement.

Summary of Christian Adaptation. Christian architecture was the direct heir to these Roman architectural practices. Christianity favored a merging of the longitudinal and centripetal plans, which served the public nature of the Mass and complemented the concept of Christ as Cosmocrator. While the West kept a predilection for the pure basilica plan, the East favored the domical-basilica plan. The architects of Hagia Sophia

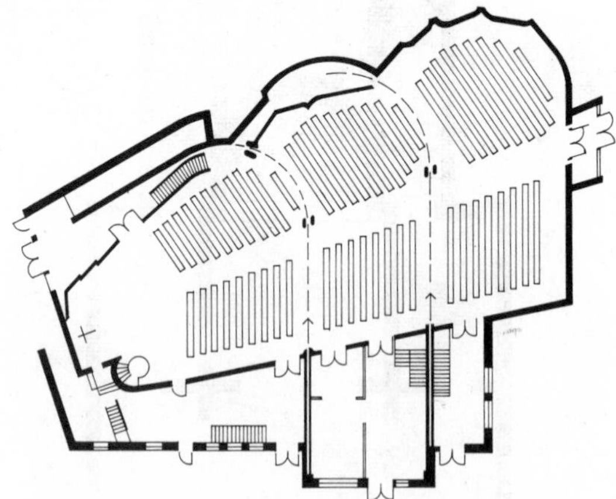

Fig. 3. A. Aalto, church at Vuoksenniska, Finland, 1956–58, plan.

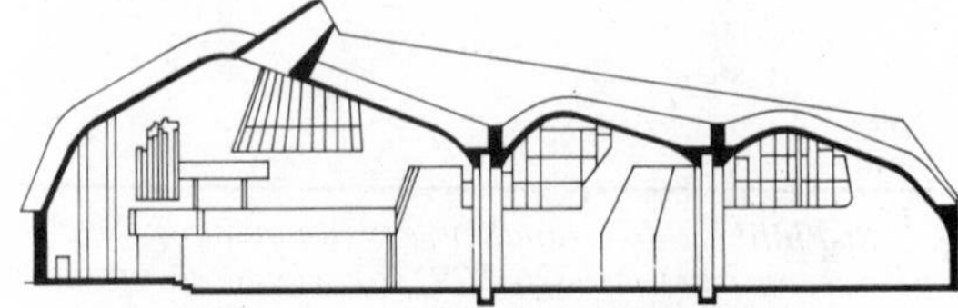

Fig. 4. Church at Vuoksenniska, section.

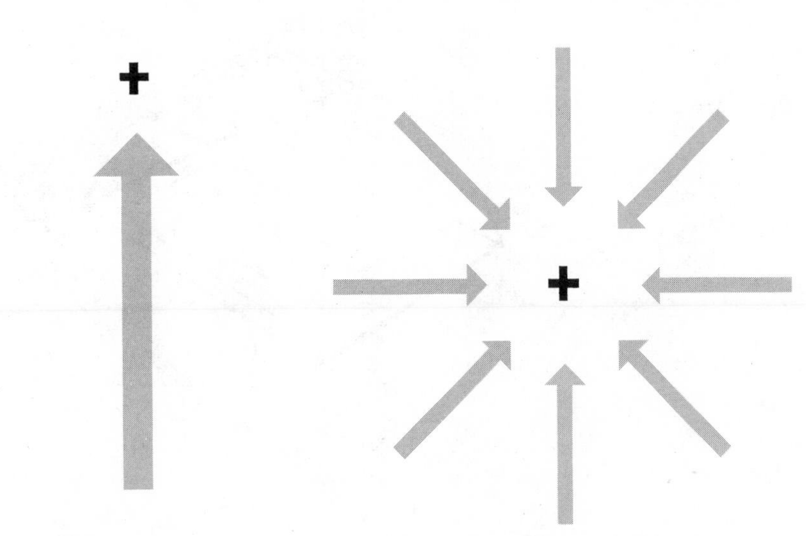

Fig. 5. Longitudinal plan type.

Fig. 6. Centripetal plan type.

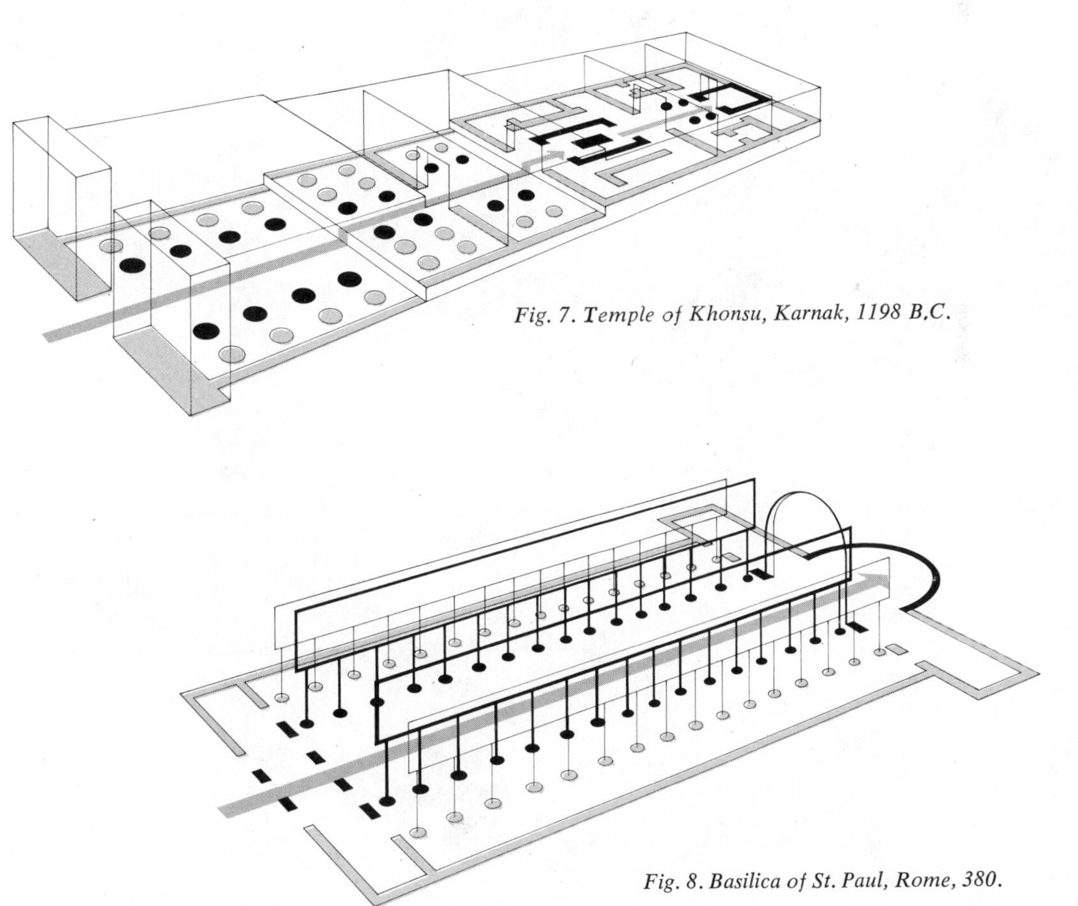

Fig. 7. Temple of Khonsu, Karnak, 1198 B.C.

Fig. 8. Basilica of St. Paul, Rome, 380.

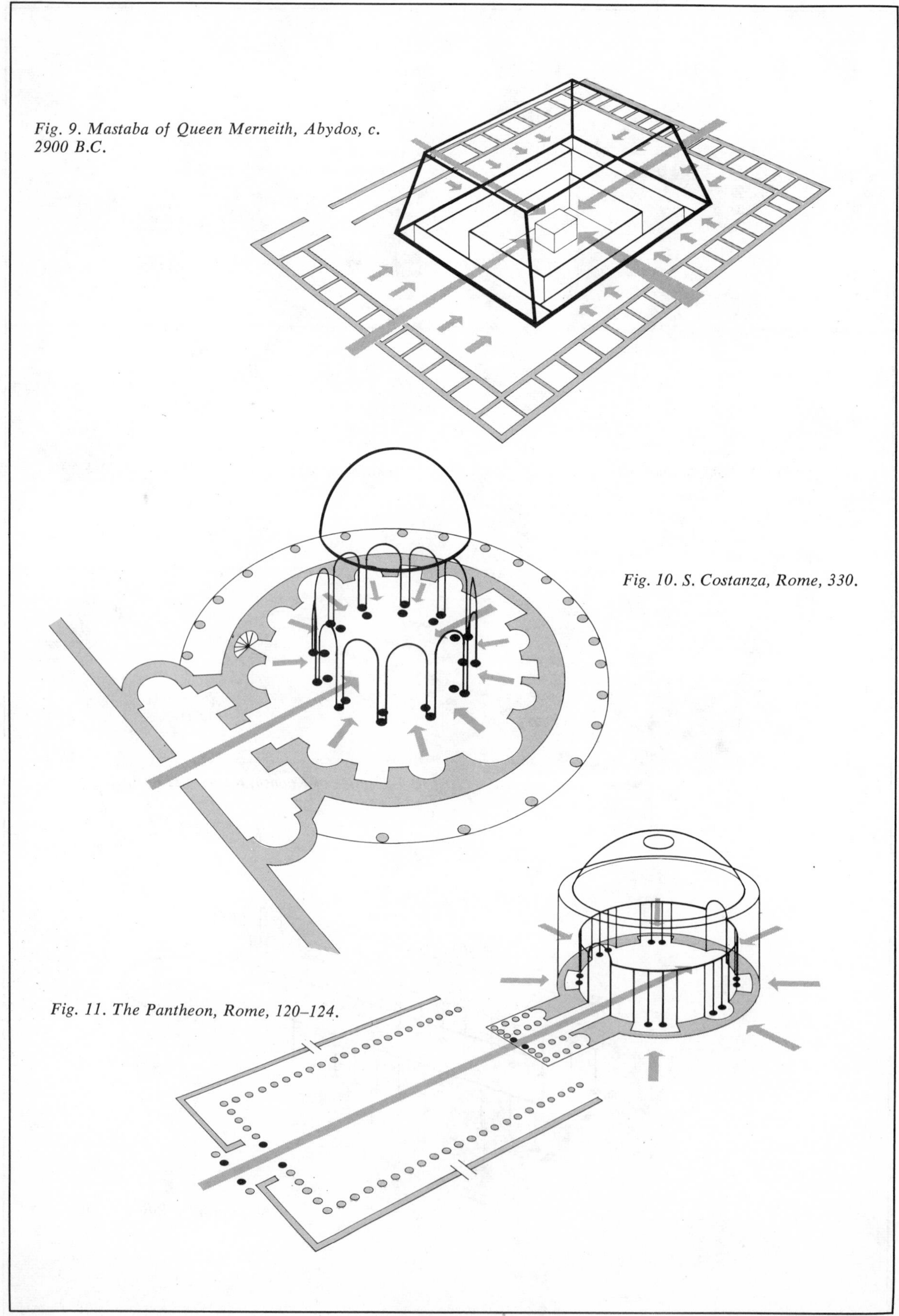

Fig. 9. Mastaba of Queen Merneith, Abydos, c. 2900 B.C.

Fig. 10. S. Costanza, Rome, 330.

Fig. 11. The Pantheon, Rome, 120–124.

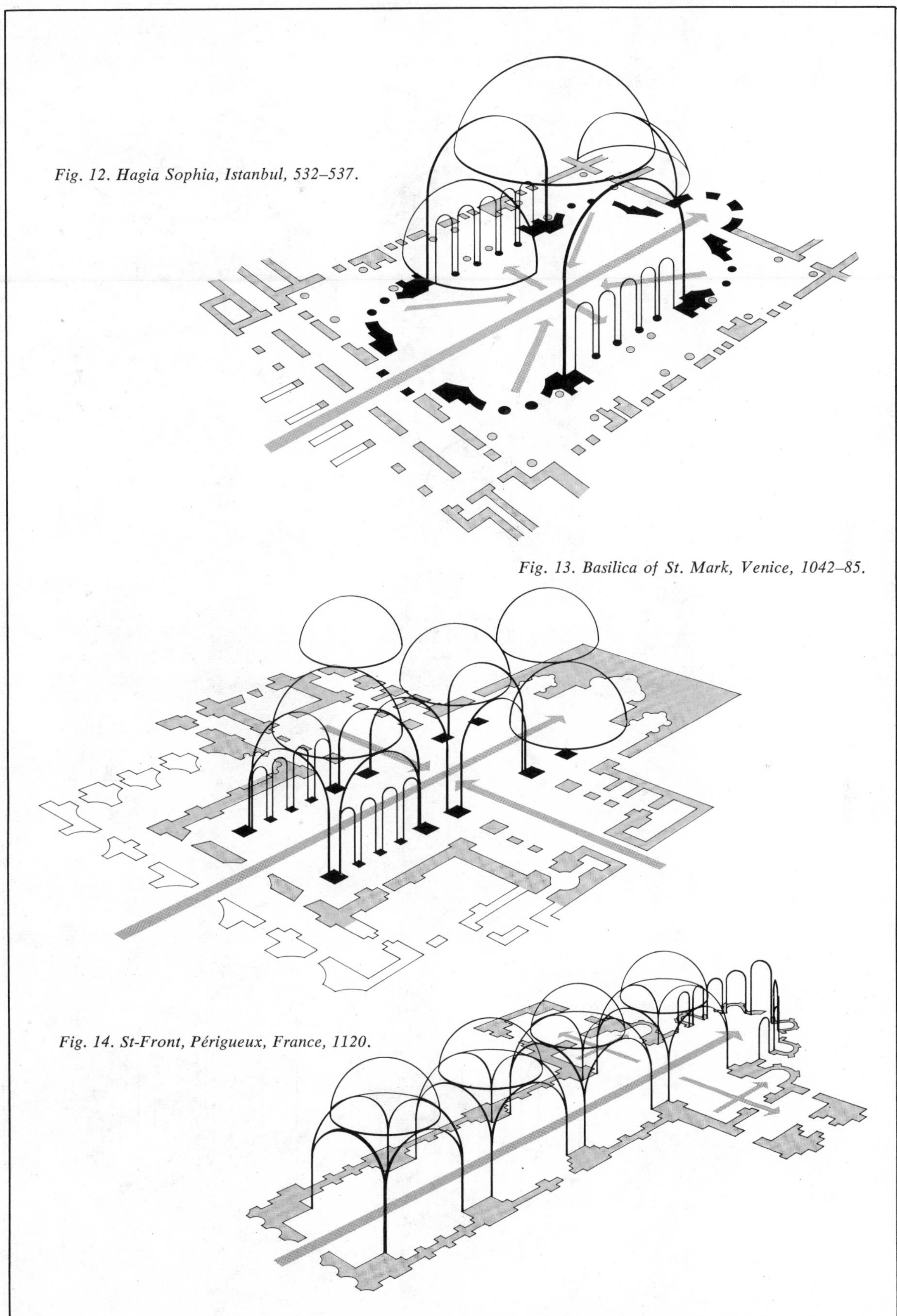

Fig. 12. *Hagia Sophia, Istanbul, 532–537.*

Fig. 13. *Basilica of St. Mark, Venice, 1042–85.*

Fig. 14. *St-Front, Périgueux, France, 1120.*

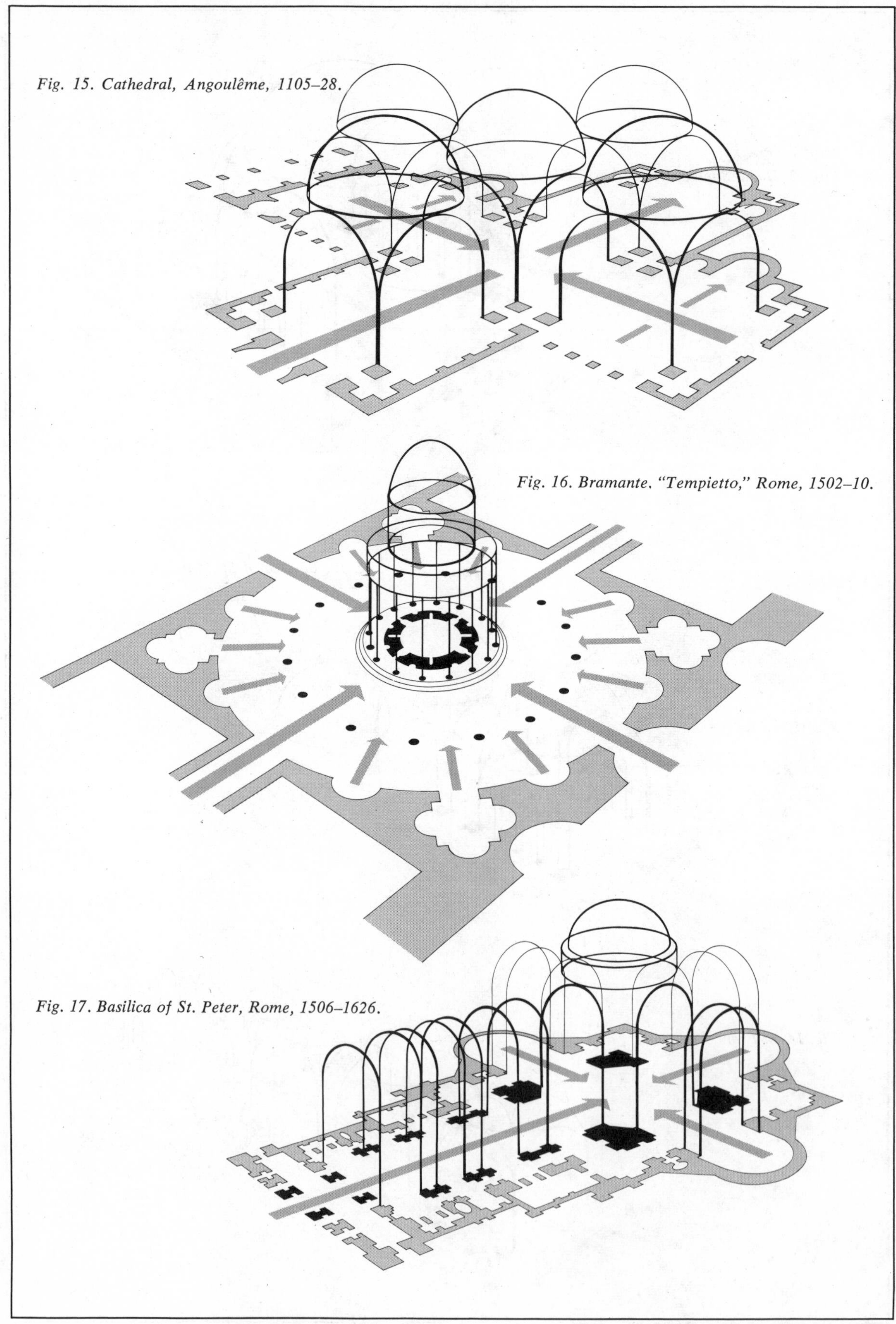

Fig. 15. Cathedral, Angoulême, 1105–28.

Fig. 16. Bramante. "Tempietto," Rome, 1502–10.

Fig. 17. Basilica of St. Peter, Rome, 1506–1626.

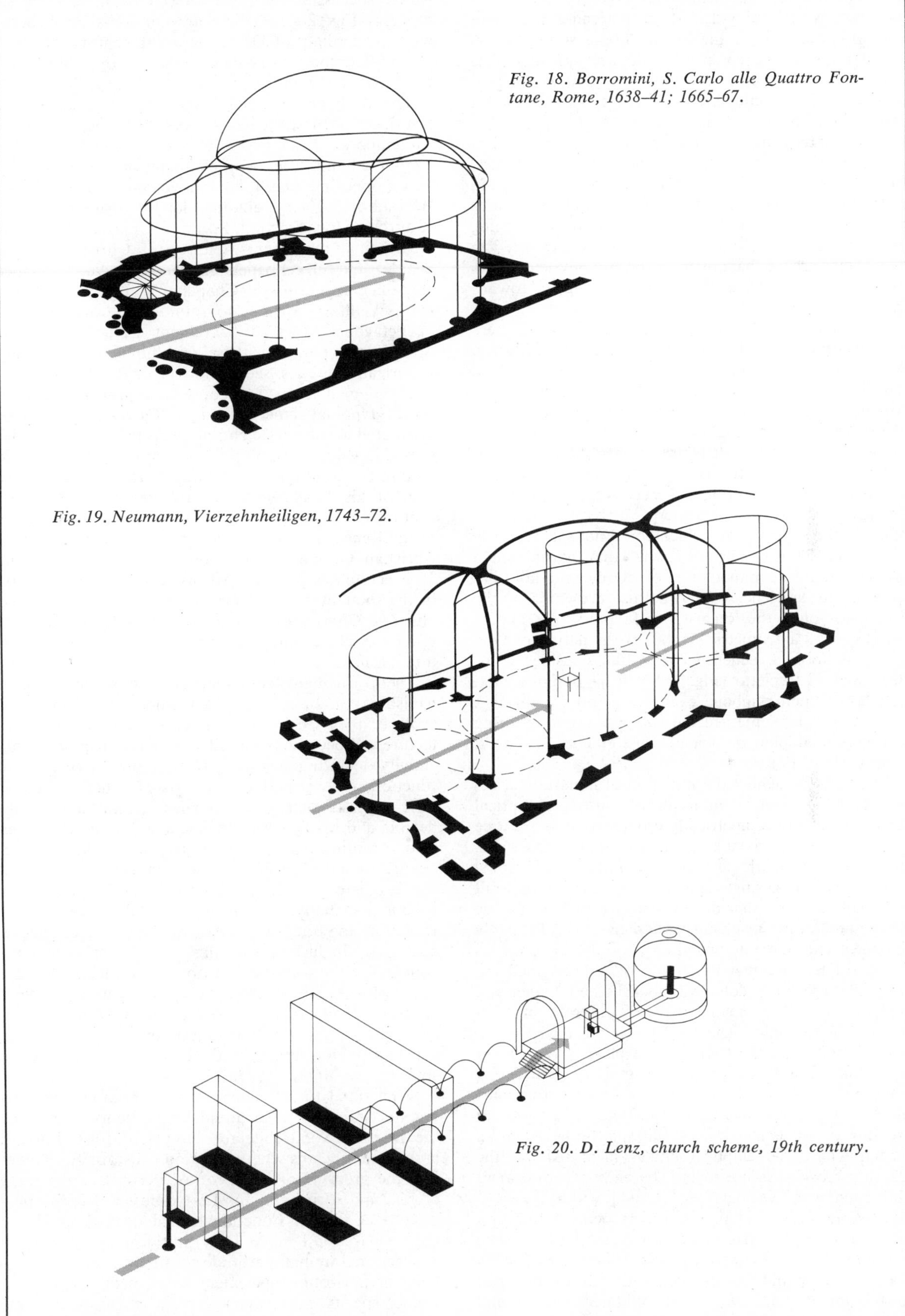

Fig. 18. Borromini, S. Carlo alle Quattro Fontane, Rome, 1638–41; 1665–67.

Fig. 19. Neumann, Vierzehnheiligen, 1743–72.

Fig. 20. D. Lenz, church scheme, 19th century.

in Istanbul (Fig. 12) achieved a real fusion of the two systems by placing the side nave arcades directly in line with the face of the central dome supports; the visual force of the complete structural system of the dome could not then be seen in a way that would promote the dome as climax. Furthermore, with the lateral extension of the nave under the dome curtailed and two half dome areas engaged with the central dome, a forced longitudinal movement toward the altar was successfully contrived. In St. Mark's, Venice (Fig. 13), in order to modulate the cruciform plan and its obvious crossing climax (and also to reduce the overwhelming presence of the five domes), the architects resorted to a one-story arcade that directs visual and physical movement longitudinally past the central crossing and toward the altar.

In the church of St-Front, Périgueux (Fig. 14), there is no modulation of the cruciform plan as at St. Mark's. As a result it is the crossing that becomes a climax, and the altar area is an anticlimax. The architects of the Angoulême cathedral (Fig. 15) simply placed a series of domes in longitudinal arrangement, thus preserving the identity of both systems in a rather simple fashion.

Dispute over the processional plan versus the centripetal plan occurred during the Renaissance. The traditionalists advocated the Latin-cross or basilica plan and opposed the central plan, which could not satisfactorily situate the altar in terms of what they considered a proper ritual accommodation of clergy and laity. In spite of the deficiencies for ritual use presented by the centripetal plan, the Renaissance favored it. Architectural form as a geometric symbol of the nature of God and man took precedence over ritual considerations. Bramante's Tempietto (Fig. 16) and his design for St. Peter's are such symbolic exercises in pure centrality. *Mannerism later merged the two systems by grafting a longitudinal plan onto a centripetal plan, as in St. Peter's (Fig. 17).

The baroque achieved a mutation of longitudinal action and centripetal action through use of elliptical forms, which are geometrically originated at two source points, thus giving axial extension to domical structures. Borromini's S. Carlo alle Quattro Fontane (Fig. 18) is conceived as a single spatial experience; here vault and walls are not kept distinct but are merged in one great undulating movement toward the altar. Probably the most extreme interpenetration of the systems occurred in B. *Neumann's church of Vierzehnheiligen (Fig. 19); the single dome was abolished altogether and replaced with three spatial ovals of different size disposed longitudinally. These ovals are engaged by two circular spaces at the transept; the plane arrangement is modulated by the ceiling arrangement of intersecting transverse ovals; each one provides a spatial forecourt immediately preceding the two altars. The transept crossing is not defined by a traditional dome but by a trough where the elliptical domes meet so that the transept crossing is not focal. The elliptical movement and counter movements are merged with the walls; when seen in conjunction with lavish rococo decoration and natural light system that fractures precise visual division of objects, Vierzehnheiligen becomes a complex and sensual spatial totality. The 19th century returned to the longitudinal type in its imitated Gothic and Romanesque churches. Churches showed a succession of styles beginning with the Egyptian restricted longitudinal plan and ending in a Renaissance central plan, which succession may be viewed as a single great process (Fig. 20). R. Schwarz considers this "sacred way" in the light of D. *Lenz's 19th-century efforts to recapitulate the history of salvation on the walls of the church (*The Church Incarnate,* 145–153).

The 20th century uses both the longitudinal and centripetal arrangements as equally valid ways to solve contemporary ritual needs. The desire to make churches communal and intimate in character has resulted in the use of opposing longitudinal movements (St. Clement's, Alexandria, Va.), elliptical-longitudinal movement (Church of Resurrection, St. Louis), partial centripetal-longitudinal movement (Church of Christ the King, Seattle), and full centripetal movement in various shaped containers from square (Chapel of St. James the Fisherman, Wellfleet, Mass.), to round (St. Louis Priory), or octagonal (Blessed Sacrament Church, Holyoke, Mass.); for plans of these and other contemporary American churches, see section 11 of this article.

Typology Theory. A theoretical approach to ecclesiastical typology emerged when Renaissance theorists attempted to categorize church plans in accordance with symbolic values. In 1547, for example, Serlio recorded nine basic variations of centripetal arrangements in the fifth of his *Five Books on Architecture*. Subsequent centuries produced commentaries debating the merits of the Renaissance system (central type) and the Early Christian–Gothic system (longitudinal type). In the 20th century, typology underwent major revitalization in the thought of the German architect R. *Schwarz. His *The Church Incarnate* presents a typology based upon a symbolic interpretation of the physiological nature of man.

There are many contemporary critics who seek to banish typology as a valid method of architectural analysis; they see in it the inherent danger that architecture will become regarded as a kind of suprapersonal activity operating according to rigid laws derived from functional, constructional, or visual schemes. Bruno Zevi suggests that "functionalism is not a rigid inflexible and mathematically calculable norm. . . . Even in confronting what would appear to be the most restrictive practical problems, the architect is not the tool of the type of building; he interprets and represents its functions spatially." The accuracy of this view is demonstrated by the brief account of the longitudinal and the centripetal in history showing that neither system accounts for the variation of forms in which they are contained. Although typology is a factor that cannot be overlooked since it provides a useful insight regarding basic configuration, it is of value only when constantly reinterpreted in the light of the architectural spirit of the times.

Strict ritual functionalism has not been endorsed by architects and critics as an adequate theory, since they see the essence of architecture elsewhere: for E. Lutyens architecture begins where function ends; for A. *Gaudí it is the ordering of light; for A. Perret it is the sense of line and form; and for Le Corbusier it is the play of volumes in light. Functionalism alone does not satisfy the love for design. At best, liturgical use suggests a proper programmatic attitude that may result in an intelligent horizontal placement of elements; of itself it cannot specify a necessary vertical extension of these elements, that is to say, the very quality and quantity of the spatial container. For the realizing of this, the architect must resort to his creative propensity to form (for ritual specification and instructions provided by Vatican Council II, *see* LITURGICAL ART, 2, 5).

Symbol and Meanings in Architectural Conception. The use of symbol or other modes of conceptualization may give to ritual utility visible form that is expressive of the supernatural. Symbolism, myth, analogies of proportion, light, number, or other factors might be employed in architectural conception. These influence the disposition of structure and are of particular importance in church architecture. Important modes of significative conceptualization that have influenced church architecture are presented here beginning with the pagan temple and briefly surveying influences up to the present day.

Symbol in Mythical Consciousness. The use of symbol is determined by the attitude that man's consciousness takes in response to reality. Various authors (E. *Cassirer, M. Eliade, H. Frankfort, G. van der Leeuw) observe that ancient civilizations and primitive peoples made use of a form of mental activity, called mythical, in which consciousness was wholly specified in the moment of confrontation with things; in both experience as well as expression myth is bound to the substantive (immediate impressions) and lacks the category of the abstract (mediate impressions). Mythical consciousness does not differentiate between concept and reality (the subjective and the objective), since things are accepted for what they are experienced as being. For mythical consciousness the sense of the sacred stems from the immediacy of object-enthrallment; things, whether animate or inanimate, that sufficiently stimulate the psyche of man beyond the normal experience of events might be regarded as having a life of their own and even as being sacred. The mythical mind does not separate what a thing is experienced as being from the place where it was experienced as being; both share in the same existential actuality. Thus space is not regarded abstractly but is comprehended by an emotional identification with it.

Sacred Place in Temple Architecture. For the mind of the primitive, the location-form-deity relationship is not arbitrary or referential but necessary and presentational. Mythical consciousness does not structure an architecture of mediate symbolism but structures the reality itself. Where the 20th-century mind sees representation, a myth tends to experience real identity; the architecture does not stand for sacredness but is identified with sacredness. C. Yavis's study of Greek altars documents the origins of certain cult localities as an evolution from immediate manifestation (momentary deification), to site deification, altar deification, and anthropomorphic image deification, until final enclosure by the temenos wall and construction of the temple. A similar evolution occurred in other civilizations: in Mesopotamia, as at Eridu, temples went through successive reconstructions layered on top of one another because that one specific locality was where the god was first revealed.

Myth does not determine space by objective measurement but by an emotional identification of a place with the sacred. H. Nissen observes that the Romans allocated space by divining the wills of the gods, and that once the lines were drawn, the space was immediately occupied by a god; not only was this true for the cosmos, but every articulated region, city, house, room, field, and vineyard had its own spirit who consequently gained an individuality and a specific name by which man could invoke him. The word temple means a space cut or marked out. The god Terminus occupied the boundary stones of Rome, and, at the festival of Terminalia, thresholds were crowned with garlands and sprinkled with sacrificial blood. The Greek propylon (entry gate) assumed the typological form common to temples because it was conceived as entrance to a temple inhabited by boundary gods. As locality participated in the location of the god, so too did architectural form. H. Frankfort observes that the Mesopotamian ziggurat is the cosmic mountain which connects earth to heaven and from which all life springs; R. Edwards discovers the pyramid form as being the primeval hill of creation upon which Atum-Ra sat when he made all things to appear out of the waters of chaos; V. Scully's and J. Lockyear's examinations of Greek and Egyptian temples, respectively, illustrate that the location-orientation of sacred structures is a necessary embodiment of a geophysical and astronomical identity of the deities.

Mythical consciousness regards architecture as an immediate symbol of the sacred; all things, from column to floor, have real identifications that go beyond utility. Architecture is not unique in this regard since myth constantly merges daily existence and ritual existence into a single homogeneous reality. The understanding of the full symbolic system of temple architecture requires a perception of myth's coalescence of all aspects of existence into a single mythical landscape or interconnected panorama. Immediate symbolism by nature is temporary and transitory and cannot be fully documented by history.

Myth does not exclude the rational but apparently precedes it. The growth of the rational (following the maturation of language, according to E. Cassirer) did not terminate myth; the mythical and the rational coexist in the development of culture as two modes of dealing with reality. Reason's liberation from myth occurred with the advent of Greek scientific philosophy. The philosophic search for a first principle, in the Aristotelian system, resolved itself into the two nonimagery (abstract) concepts of "matter" and "form." With the Greek philosophers the intellect gained force over myth—things became subject to logic in an appeal to reason. Greek architecture was quick to respond to the process of reason: the Doric, Ionic, and Corinthian columns underwent logical development according to a seemingly abstract idea or type; the temples reached an apogee in architectonics in their optical refinements and integral proportional systems. However, reason was unable to achieve a purely mediate symbolic architecture since the Greek religions were bound to myth.

The Christian Transformation. Christianity transformed the nature of sacred architecture for Western man. An important difference appears in the context of the Eucharistic celebration, which was not confined to a particular place. Mythical cult centers had been generally places of unique manifestations of the deity, and worship was bound to a specific locality. Christianity, however, has no one cult center restricted to locality (with the exception of certain shrines and fixed devotional places such as Lourdes). Unlike mythical sacredness, neither the locality nor the form of Christian architecture shares a real identity with Christ. Church architecture in Christianity was relatively free to develop a symbolic system of its own.

Medieval. Christian architecture did not immediately produce a system of meanings integrated with architectural form. In early centuries Christians adopted Roman forms of building, especially the basilica type, which was suitable for communal assembly; the celebration of the Eucharist and hearing the Gospels, wherever it might be, was in itself meaningful. Gradually painting, mosaic, and relief sculpture were employed as referential explicatives and signs of belief. These, however, did not radically affect the architectural conception. Elaborate philosophic and theological speculation eventually came to affect the very architectural conception in efforts to incorporate meanings into the structure.

Crucial for architecture was the Pythagorean-Platonic philosophy that saw number as immutable measure in all things. Pythagoras discovered that musical tones can be physically measured and that the musical consonances were determined by the ratios of small whole numbers. This occasioned the belief that audible-visual harmonics pervaded the cosmos. Plato added the clarification that cosmic order and harmony are contained in certain numbers (*Timaeus*). St. Augustine found support for this thesis in the Solomonic text "thou hast ordered all things in measure, number and weight" (Wis 11.20). In his *De Musica,* Augustine proposed that numerical ratios are but the echoes of the perfection of God. In music these ratios are audible; in architecture they are visible. The most admirable ratio is 1:1 since here the unity of relationship is equal and perfect; then came 1:2, 2:3, 3:4. Through the contemplation of the visible configurations of architecture, the mind is led to proportion, from proportion to number, and from number to the idea of God. This thesis of perfect ratio became the first purely mediate religious symbol in Western church architecture. Boethius agreed with Augustine that the artist can do his best only if he follows number and not intuition.

It appears that number symbolism did not have extensive architectural influence until the Gothic period. In the 12th century the school of Chartres fell heir to the Augustinian number system modified by the inclusion of Euclidian geometry through Arabic sources. Because *Thierry of Chartres insisted upon a geometric interpretation of the nature of God, his contemporaries accused him of changing theology into geometry. Others of the school (*William of Conches, *Abelard) attributed a mathematical action to God: the Holy Spirit ordered matter and the cosmos was regulated by ratios, and these ratios were best incorporated by man in architecture. God was regarded as divine Architect and Musician who gave to the cosmos its laws of harmonic proportion.

Concomitant with the emergence of number symbolism was light symbolism. St. Augustine found numerous Biblical references to light and proposed in the *City of God* that luminosity is the measure of the splendor of being. *Pseudo-Dionysius saw the world as one created, animated, and unified by a supraessential light. In his *Celestial Hierarchy* creation is described as an act of illumination; the beings (angels, men, rocks) emerge in a hierarchy corresponding to their amount of light. The notion of the cosmos as a procession of spheres leading to a luminous God was advanced by the 9th- and 10th-century Arabian philosophers Alkindi (al-*Kindī), *Alfarabi, and *Avicenna. In the 11th century, Alhazen discovered the laws of spherical light diffusion and optics. This led certain philosophers (e.g., *Avicebron) to attempt unification of a metaphysics of light-emanation with the physical laws of light-emanation. All these lines of thought came into the Western world along with the commentaries on Aristotle during the 11th and 12th centuries. (*See* TRANSLATION LITERATURE, LATIN INTO GREEK).

Meanwhile western Europe had maintained an unbroken continuity in its preoccupation with light. The writings of Pseudo-Dionysius were popular and played a critical role in the thought of Abbot Suger, who was instrumental in the reconstruction of the chevet of the Abbey of Saint-Denis as a light source: "Once the new rear part is joined to the part in front, the church shines with its middle part brightened for bright is that which is brightly coupled with the bright and bright is the noble edifice which is pervaded by the new light." *Robert Grosseteste (1175–1253), Bishop of Lincoln, sought to combine number symbolism and light symbolism. He saw in light the vehicle by which the traditional Aristotelian concepts of matter and form are united. Form, an ally of light, is a perfect unity and is represented by the number one; matter by the number two; the accord of form and matter by the number three; the composite itself by the number four. These numbers give rise to proportions that describe a being's nature, namely, 1:2, 1:3, 1:4, 2:3, 3:4, and will be the source of structuring harmony. In architecture it is the division of planes into these proportions that reveals the nature of divinity; man may then contemplate God through these harmonies. A good documentation of medieval number and light symbolism may be found in G. Lesser, *Gothic Cathedrals and Sacred Geometry,* and O. von Simpson, *The Gothic Cathedral.* The best available commentary concerning the scholastic attitude toward number, light, and aspects of the beautiful in its theological relationships is E. de Bruyne, *Études d'ésthétique médiévale.*

Renaissance. The Renaissance no less than the High Middle Ages looked to traditional number symbolism; L. B. *Alberti, A. *Palladio, and Serlio attempted to discover and express in mathematical ratios the visible-audible cosmic harmonics. For them the regulation of all parts of a church according to these ratios could manifest something of the nature of God. Man, made in the image of God, embodied the harmonies of the cosmos. This led to the use of the Vitruvian figure inscribed in a square and circle as the symbol of the geometric-mathematical proportion common to microcosm and macrocosm. The basilica plan was regarded as impure since its mathematical content did not correspond to ideal architectural form; instead the Renaissance favored the circle (central plan) in which geometric pattern generates the form with all its parts; this provides a most lucid, absolute, and immutable architecture. By the dividing and relating of all parts through measure, an architectural frame of reference was instituted by which man could contemplate the idea of an absolute and immutable God. R. Wittkower in *Architectural Principles in the Age of Humanism* explores in detail the Renaissance treatment of number-symbolism.

Number symbolism is based on a rationalized ideal expressed in mathematical terms that transcends the subjective and transitory nature of man. This classical system was disrupted by the mannerists, who saw man as subject to the chaos of his emotions more than to divine harmonics. This occasioned a shift of emphasis in religious symbolic patterns from the ideal world of God to the personal subjective world of man. The results were seen in secular works more than in major church structures (e.g., Palazzo del Tè). Mannerism is manifested in the illogical use of classical motifs as symbolic of earthly dissonance and opposed to divine consonance.

Baroque to Modern. The baroque merged classical geometry with the intense inner experience of man. Light and geometry were no longer the model for contemplating God; they became the experiential means of recognizing the existence of God and the reality of the Church through the activity of man's emotions. Architects forsook the purely architectonic symbolism of the Renaissance and depended more on the integration of iconography (in painting and sculpture) with architecture. This wedding of pictorial symbolism and architecture is well illustrated in Bernini's church of S. Andrea al Quirinale, Rome. The plan is worked out according to a series of intersecting circles of which the front courtyard segments extend outward; in the interior the geometric spaces are dynamic. The interior is divided into three distinct registers: the lower area, windowless, is executed in warm earth colors to symbolize the world of man; then the entablature separates earth from heaven and is the realm of sculptured angels who act as messengers of God; finally the dome, representing heaven, is executed in white and pervaded by light from the oculus in which the Holy Spirit (dove) floats. Man cannot contemplate this panorama disinterestedly. The way to heaven is by the purified flesh; the way is idealized in the white marble statue of St. Andrew that is placed so as to fracture the continuity of the entablature and thus join earth to heaven. The church is properly experienced only when the carefully calculated process of imagery and architecture are perceived. Baroque architecture in its classical phase employed a sophisticated literary type of representational symbolism in response to the teaching function of the reformed Church.

With the advent of the *rococo the engagement of subjective passions remained. With the exception of B. Neumann's brilliant geometric and psychological conception for the church of Vierzehnheiligen, few rococo churches illustrate an architectural symbolic system; meanings were carried by representational sculpture and painting.

The 17th and 18th centuries were periods of transition. With the rise of science the classical attitude toward cosmic harmonics quickly lost public favour; the dissemination of Cartesian rationalism shifted emphasis from universally valid rules of order to the authority of the perceiving subject. Architecture witnessed this transition in the argument that ensued over the laws of harmonic proportion. Certain architects, such as H. Wotton, P. de l'Orme, F. Blondel, and O. Scamozzi, maintained the soundness of mathematical ratios in architecture. Others, such as C. Perrault, T. Temanza, and G. Guarini, defended the eye of man as the important judge of proportion. As the classical system of world order and aesthetics was abandoned, so too was the classical system of number symbolism; church architecture could no longer promote an immutable measure in order to present the ideal nature of God.

In 18th-century neoclassicism, church architecture became the vehicle of an applied aesthetics derived from sources other than religion. In the 19th-century revivalisms, church architecture became a sign of religious sentiment for the past. Symbolism was firmly bound to literary association, as expounded by J. M. Neale and B. Webb (see bibliog.): "We enter. The triple breadth of Nave and Aisles, the triple height of Pier arch, Triforium, and Clerestory; the triple length of Choir Trancepts and Nave, again set forth the Holy Trinity. And what besides is there which does not tell of our Blessed Saviour? And that does not point out 'Him First' in the two-fold Western Door, 'Him Last' in the distant Altar: 'Him Midst,' in the great Rood: 'Him Without End' in the monogram carved on boss and corbel, in the Holy Lamb, in the Lion of the Tribe of Judah, in the Mystic Fish?" A. *Pugin held that redemption by the sacrifice of the cross was the visual basis for the form of Christian architecture.

20th Century. Symbolic determination of church architecture has been widely discussed in the 20th century. The postwar directives of the German bishops (1947) supported a literary architectural symbolism by suggesting that "the portals of the church, and especially the main portal, should by their impressive design suggest to the faithful the symbolism of church portals as representing the gates of heaven." This view has occasioned the construction of contemporary churches adopting a naïve type of symbolism, e.g., Harrison and Abramovitch's fish-shaped First Presbyterian Church at Stamford, Connecticut. With the advent of technology a church, more than any other type of building, offers the least programmatic restrictions and therefore the greatest opportunity for architects to explore pure forms. In order to temper the tendency toward whimsical symbolic forms, some architects have sought a guide to meaningful architectural symbolism in the nature of communal worship. S. Davis, for example, observes that "the church building is an image of the mystical body, and our churches should be fashioned in the likeness of the assembly and express its mystery." R. Schwarz, who greatly influenced postwar church building in Europe, noted: "Church architecture is not cosmic mythology—rather it is the representation of Christian life, a new embodiment of the spiritual. To build does not mean to solve mathematical problems nor to create pleasing spaces; it means to place great communal forms before God." The desire to give the church structure immediate symbolic expression by reference to the communal action of the mystical body has shifted the basis of church architecture away from programmed symbolism. Preprogrammed architectural symbolism becomes either referential (literary), as it did in the 19th century, or it becomes subject to rules of right making, as it did in the Renaissance. Today architects, artists, and theorists do not willingly accept a referential pictorial symbol or literary device in architectural conception in order to present some "content" (meanings). There has been a shift in artistic sensibility toward the immediate existential experience of the art image, which is seen in itself as symbol (e.g., the work of art that may not be representational). The symbol has become more an event than a representational form. This shift liberates symbolic context from the confinement of referential styles and allows the artist to exercise his creative intuition more fully. The quest for communal forms of architecture immediately significative of the mystical body of Christ and the search for aniconic (i.e., nonrepresentational) art forms suitably integrated in this architectural signification are signs of a new consciousness in the structuring of religious art (*see* ABSTRACT ART AND THE CHURCH).

Note on Multivalent Systems. Symbolism and meanings in architecture are usually multivalent. The Gothic style is a particularly fine example of a multiple meaning system in architecture; form followed symbol as much as function. Various studies have discovered the many symbolic modes at work. Besides the symbolism of number and light mentioned above, a number of other meanings are discoverable. É. Mâle, in *A Study in Medieval Iconography and Its Sources of Inspiration,* finds that symmetry was regarded as the expression of the mysterious inner harmony controlling the cosmos; he also explored the influence of the "Mirrors" of Vincent of Beauvais on the sculpture and stained glass program of many churches. E. Panofsky, in *Gothic Architecture and Scholasticism,* relates the articulation of cathedrals to the scholastic working habit, which is founded on the belief that the world is a unified, ordered, and indivisible hierarchy. In a different manner W. Worringer's *Form in Gothic* accounts for parallels between the sensual lucidity and the organic harmony of the Gothic "will to form" and scholastic transcendentalism. P. Fingesten's *Topographical and Anatomical Aspects of the Gothic Cathedral* traces the topography of Gothic cathedrals to ch. 21 of the Apocalypse and to the subsequent interpretation of the cathedral as a magic city upon a magic mountain; he also documents the commonly held view that the planar relationships of cathedrals are based upon the human body as observed in Vitruvius—"For without symmetry and proportion no temple can have a regular plan; that is, it must have an exact proportion worked out after the fashion of the members of a finely shaped body." He noted the recurrence of this concept in the observations of William Durandus (13th century): "The arrangement of a material church resembleth that of the human body: the chancel, or place where the altar is representeth the head: the transepts, the hands and arms, and the remainder, towards the west the rest of the body." He extended this notion to include the idea that the skeletal structure represents the womb and rib cage of Mary sheltering the Christ, which theory he bases on the anatomical discoveries of the times. P. Frankl presents an exhaustive study of the referential writings related to the Gothic in his monumental *Literary Sources of the Gothic.* The symbolic meanings of a particular period can be known only through a complete survey of the theological, mystical, and popular beliefs of the day, and a careful analysis of the source writings connected with individual monuments. The observations presented in this section have suggested some of the important known meanings manifest in ecclesiastical architecture.

Technique and Structural Abilities. Knowledge of the precise workings of structure took centuries to develop. The ancient civilizations approximated structure through practical experimentation; the posts and beams of ancient temples were often oversized in relation to their minimal necessary strength. The approximation of structural proportion through building experience continued well into the Gothic period; the height of the Beauvais Cathedral was finally determined by the point at which the structural system could no longer support the addition of stones without their falling. Traditional styles are often maintained because of the slow progress of man's awareness of structural potentials.

It is only since mid-19th century that a true science of structure has been developed. The determination of the precise nature of structural types through a theoretical analysis of their systems of stress critically transformed the character of church architecture. The contemporary architect has complete freedom in the creative planning of spatial containers that have not as yet been built but can be built with complete assurance of safety and stability. F. Candela's chapel of Las Lomas, Cuernavaca, Mexico, is a structurally derived shape whose form reflects its systems of stress; this type of structure was not possible *c.* 1850. Consequently the history of church architecture exhibits a polarity in the nature of its forms, which results principally from the cataclysmic emergence of scientific structures. The ancients exhibit a minimum number of forms with a maximum degree of refinements, whereas the moderns exhibit a maximum number of forms with a minimum degree of refinement. The evolution of church architecture has witnessed a change in attention from the detail of the form to that of the form itself.

Significance of Structure. Although structure is a major aspect in church architecture, it is not necessarily the vehicle of a church's significance. Building as a technique neither favors nor inhibits structural refinement; it is merely a means to enclosure. In certain periods technical inventiveness is integrally associated with the recognition of certain styles. This occurs in Roman, Gothic, late baroque, and the modern periods. In other periods architecture reached an apogee of development within preexisting structural techniques. This occurred in the Greek, Early Christian–Romanesque, Renaissance, and the classic baroque periods. Certain buildings gain a preeminence because of their structural avant-gardism. A partial list of examples would include the Great Pyramid, Hagia Sophia in Constantinople, Durham, Chartres, and Reims cathedrals, King's College Chapel, Brunelleschi's dome of the cathedral of Florence, Guarini's S. Lorenzo, Gaudí's Colonia Guëll Chapel, A. Perret's Le Raincy, O. Bartning's Stahlkirche, M. Breuer's abbey church of St. John the Baptist, O. Niemeyer's church of St. Francis, and F. Candela's church of La Virgen Milagrosa. Others derive their historic significance from refinements of space, materials, and traditional structural systems. Typical examples are Luxor Temple, the Pantheon, S. Apollinare Nuovo, St. Michael's at Hildesheim, Pazzi Chapel, S. Lorenzo Sacristy, S. Carlo alle Quattro Fontane, Vierzehnheiligen, Illinois Institute of Technology Chapel, church of Maria Königin, church of Santa Anna, and the chapel of Notre Dame du Haut.

Structural Determinism. The 20th century has been preoccupied with the nature of structure. The origin of this may be traced in part to the rationalism found in the writings of E. *Viollet-le-Duc. His work formed the immediate heritage of many early 20th-century structural innovators. A. Perret maintained that "structure is the mother tongue of the architect. . . . Anyone who hides structure deprives himself of architecture's only legitimate and beautiful ornament. Anyone who hides a pilaster commits an error; anyone who puts up a false one commits a crime." Church architecture is especially susceptible to structural exhibitionism since it is physically more flexible and less inhibiting than other structures. The physical demands of liturgy are not as rigid as are the functional demands of laboratories, schools, etc.; the adaptation of structure to churches permits a greater freedom of structural expression. Consequently structure is often given a leading role as expressive form. O. Niemeyer's, F. Candela's, and E. Torroja's imaginative use of thin-shell reinforced concrete has produced a rich vocabulary of forms that are of marked contrast to the traditional cubic shapes.

The forcefulness present in the unadorned pure structure has led many historians and critics to favor a technological viewpoint in the study of churches. Technical progress is viewed as artistic progress; technical significance, as artistic significance; technical history, as architectural history. Thus Gothic architecture is applauded for its general structural predilection, whereas the Renaissance loses favor for its lack of technical progress. This viewpoint is based on a misconception that identifies architectural significance with technical innovations. The science of structure contributes to technical methods of spatial qualification but of itself cannot determine the total reality of space. A. Raymond has pointed out that "the basis of design must be function and engineering; but function and engineering only is a brutality." The absolute insistence on macrostructure alone is bound to fail when faced with even the simplest nonstructural space-covering elements such as doors and windows. This is apparent in E. *Torroja's Pont de Suert Church and F. Candela's chapel of Nuestra Señora de la Soledad, which, although brilliantly conceived in regard to macrostructural purity, are naïve in their auxiliary attributes. Structural determinism archieves significance only when related to "the eternal and universal sense of line and form" (Perret). Moreover, the science of structures cannot of itself determine its forms or systems. Torroja, in *Philosophy of Structures,* declares that the birth of structural form is not rational but intuitive, and that mathematical calculations serve only to prove that what the creative intellect has imagined will, in fact, stand. Thus engineering is architecture not according to a predetermination by immutable laws of statics but according to its service to the architect's creation of form.

Use of Structure in Churches. Structure has been used in church architecture in four distinct ways. The first three are concerned with a relationship between structure as support and wall as enclosure. (1) The structure is actualized by the wall, and, while it may manifest itself in projections and decorations, it is the wall that carries primacy of visual importance. Renaissance architects were especially fond of this idea, which has been used throughout the history of Christian building. The term "mural wall system" describes wall systems of this type, which have surfaces suitable for painting, fresco, mosaic, and sculpture; it is seen in Early Christian architecture. (2) The structure becomes a visible skeleton that assumes primacy, in which case the wall enclosure must find a suitable subsidiary means of expression. The Gothic and modern periods are especially characterized by this approach. The term "baldachino" has been frequently used to describe such structures, but the term is limited since it refers properly to vaulting systems. (3) The structure is freed of the enclosing wall and forms a visual pattern that modulates the visual impression of the wall. The column in front of the wall is a well-known example of this. (4) Finally, structure in church architecture may be an "all-over" distribution of the wall itself. Such a system is proper to the 20th century, deriving from the new structural ability of shell construction. A shell construction is a working membrane that provides both structural strength and total space enclosure. In E. Torroja's church of the Ascension and O. Niemeyer's chapel of Las Lomas, wall, roof, and structural strength is the form itself. Certain architects (e.g., R. Schwarz) have regarded this method of construction as most perfect, since the whole structure is permeated by the same form.

Structure as Expression. Structure as a means of expression vacillates between the polarities of denial and assertion of supports. The denial of a sense of structure is evident in the solution of the ritual space of Hagia Sophia by way of a visual annihilation of the dome's structural supports. At times structural members become so excessively light that consciousness cannot grasp mass-support relationships; today this frequently occurs when baldachinos are hung with piano wire so that a great monolithic element appears to float without support, as in M. Breuer's abbey church of St. John (illustrated in section 11, below). Excessive cantilever also appears to be denied; the concept of dynamic balance intensified by modern prestressing techniques may also serve to frustrate natural psychophysiological responses.

The second pole is that of structural assertion. This tendency seeks to visually intensify the operation of structure as a visual element in churches. The structure is often overdesigned; joints thicken; pins and bolts are made larger than calculations warrant or more visible than their importance demands; materials are left brutally in their natural constructional stage (e.g., concrete that displays its framework as a surface presence). The priory of *St. Anselm (Tokyo), the church of St. Anthony the Abbot (Italy), the monastery of La Tourette (France), and a host of contemporary churches engage to some degree in constructional assertion; the emphasis is by far the most forceful in 20th-century church construction.

The contemporary search for positive structural expression is part of a general quest for technological honesty. The importance of this honesty in achieving genuine form has been stressed by many notable architects whose churches are witness to the force of their insights (e.g., A. Gaudí, A. Perret, O. Bartning, R. Schwarz).

Considerations on Form. The criteria considered above are subsumed in a larger search for formal laws that will determine the disposition of architectural elements in order to create the beautiful. By far the most prevalent concept in Western thought has been that the beauty of architecture is found in order. This sensibility was applied to all the arts, and is generally associated with the concept of God as a God of order. Classical theories of the beautiful in architecture are generally concerned with seeing the beautiful either in certain geometric forms or in numerical ratio; these fixed ratios and forms were considered eternally and absolutely beautiful. In classical architectural theory, beauty is a presentation to man's senses of a principle that is based on intellectual penetration rather than experiential response. In theories of architectural form from antiquity through the Renaissance the tendency was to identify beauty of form with an abstract conceptualization of harmonic order that can be objectified in an art work. *See* AESTHETICS; ART (PHILOSOPHY); ART, 3.

Transition from Classical Theory to Modern Theory. Extensive opposition to the classical manner appeared in the latter part of the 17th and in the 18th century in England. Beauty not found in order, or in certain geometric forms, emerged in English "Romantic" landscape architecture as a result of Europe's extended contact with the Orient. By 1720 the term picturesque, meaning a roughness or sudden variation joined to irregularity, was accepted as an art principle. The desire for unexpected visual stimulation in the landscape led to the use of Greek, Gothic, and Chinese structures; especially appropriate were church forms. The English philosophers of the mid-18th century found the source of much delight in the inner senses of man, which operate without the aid of reason in comprehending the beautiful. The result of their enquiry assumed two directions: some rejected classical canons; others modulated classical canons in accord with the new sensibility. Burke argued against reason and disputed the importance of proportion and order in accounting for the beautiful; for him beauty was a social quality connected with man's response in beholding the world of life around him. In contrast, Hutcheson proposed that beauty is found in a compound relationship between unity (order) and variety; Hogarth found in a precise serpentine line the physical basis of the beautiful object, and in variety, the principal attribute of beauty. Variety itself, especially in its purest of forms in the serpentine line, is a kind of invariable and presents aspects of the classical sensibility.

The 18th-century interest in variety and the response of man's inner senses did not lead to a revolution in church architecture. The classical sensibility dominated because of the authority issuing from the French taste during Boileau's period. This influence is seen in England in the styles of Inigo *Jones and Christopher *Wren. The practice of the arts, including architecture, was governed by the canons of correct taste (order, elegance, and grace). Sir J. *Reynolds, head of the British Academy, was able to incorporate the new sensibility with the old. He defended classical canons and introduced the new-found human element by using Hume's association of ideas to give a firm basis for the picturesque; he explicitly counted among the principles of architecture "that of affecting the imagination by means of association of ideas—thus we have naturally a veneration for antiquity; whatever building brings to our remembrance ancient customs and manners, such as the Castles of the Barons of Chivalry, is sure to give delight." Revivalism of any past style became a formal law of building and had great impact on church architecture for 2 centuries. The only pure style of architecture that emerged concurrently with the appearance of the picturesque was the French rococo. This style combined the classical manner with novel curvilinear formations. The rococo represents an intense but brief excursion away from the laws of antiquity. M. A. *Laugier's essay on Greek architecture, the archeological expeditions of Stuart and Revert, and Winckelmann's dictum that Greek art represents noble simplicity and quiet grandeur were witnesses to a resurgence of the classical canons of right making in the second half of the 18th century.

The 18th century introduced also the philosophy of the beautiful as a discipline separate from philosophy in general; Baumgarten named the science of aesthetics in his *Aesthetica* (1750). During the next 100 years in Germany a succession of thinkers (*Lessing, *Winckelmann, *Kant, *Goethe, *Schiller, *Fichte, *Schelling, *Hegel, *Schleiermacher, *Schopenhauer, *Nietzsche) struggled with the problems of aesthetics; interest centered on the role of the senses and of the emotions, the role of reason, the nature of the aesthetic object, the validity of rules of art, the freedom inherent in the creative process, and the relationship of society and the aesthetic object. Speculative aesthetics attempted to fabricate an idea of architecture from what it seems or ought to be within the wider frame of a particular aesthetic system.

German speculative aesthetics, which spread internationally, placed architectural theory in a compromising position. Architecture was not considered in its own nature, but rather as a residue of a larger speculative system. Church architecture, except for the symbolic-emotive connotations of its past styles, was considered even less. The result of a century of intense aesthetic thought was the placement of architecture in a dependent position between the classical mode (represented by Greek and Renaissance styles) and the Romantic mode (represented by Gothic, rococo, and medieval styles).

A transformation occurred *c.* 1870; the speculative school of aesthetics gave way to the scientific empirical method. G. *Fechner pioneered experimental aesthetics in 1876; rather than using a philosophic system to describe the facts, Fechner began with factual data in order to describe a system. In his researches and those that followed, the rise of the new sciences of physiology, psychiatry, psychology, biology, sociology, and ethnology furnished new material and diverse points of view from which facts could be compared and described. The empirical acceptance of reality influenced architectural theory. In the 20th century a number of formal considerations emerged as important in architectural developments; these provide a kind of phenomenology of architecture that greatly influenced church architecture in the postwar rebuilding.

Space. The concept of space as a primary attribute of architecture did not fully develop until the late 19th century. Renaissance theorists described architecture in terms of structure, form, and proportion. Certain authors, such as B. Zevi, have attempted to discover an implicit concept of space in the writings of Plato, Aristotle, Vitruvius, Alberti, Serlio, Michelangelo, and others, but this seems to be an overzealous attempt to discover space as a primary element in past architecture theory. The majority of historians attribute spatial consciousness first to the German art critics and aestheticians. Hegel referred to buildings in general as "limiting and enclosing a defined space" and to the Gothic in particular as "the concentration of essential soul-life which thus encloses itself in spatial relations." In particular the art studies of H. *Wölfflin were based upon spatial terminology, and it is probably through his followers that the idea became disseminated in the Western world. An awareness of the primacy of space became basic in the thought of many noted architects and critics soon after the turn of the century, and it has manifested itself consistently up to the present day; e.g.,

G. Scott (1914), O. Spengler (1918), L. Moholy-Nagy (1928), J. Focillon (1934), R. Schwarz (1938), and B. Zevi (1964).

The practical emergence of a spatially predicated architecture occurred after the turn of the century. Even before the spatial emphasis achieved any usable kind of conception, F. L. *Wright provided the first monumental work using it in the Unity Temple, Chicago, in 1906. Developed in complete isolation from the events of continental Europe, Wright's use of cantilevered balconies forming interpenetrating spaces made of him a native architectural prophet. Wright's observation that the interior space should be expressed on the exterior as the space enclosed, distinguishes him from his contemporaries, such as A. Perret, who followed a rationalistic logic of structures, or P. Behrens, who developed an expressionistic use of industrial materials characteristic of the new technology. Germany, the birthplace of spatial philosophy, was the first to acclaim the revolutionary significance of Wright. In 1908 H. Berlage said of Wright that "the art of the master-builder lies in this: the creation of space, not the sketching of façades." It was in Europe that Wright was received and it was there, between 1905 and 1930, that practical experiments in space continued. The cubists fractured objects in space; the futurists dynamically related objects in space; the purists placed geometric objects in space. Various artists probed architecture in their canvases: Mondrian painted a number of compositions called "façades" in a process of searching for equilibrium between horizontal and vertical; Malevich named several of his abstract rectangular works "architectonics"; the "Elementarists" or constructivists drew on the aesthetic potentials inherent in building techniques. In 1910 a monograph on F. L. Wright, published in Holland, led some historians to see a real connection between the spatial concern of the de Stijl group and the American master, but without sufficient documentation. The members of de Stijl explored aspects of pure space; for Mondrian, "space determination, and not space expression, is the pure plastic way to express the universal reality." The de Stijl group considered architecture to be a series of intersecting and overlapping planes, which, in certain relationships, could determine an infinitely discontinuous space of complete resolution. Their theory was put into practice immediately in Rietveld's Schroeder House and Mies van der Rohe's brick country houses of the 1920s, especially in his Barcelona Pavilion of 1929. This last work greatly influenced the spatial consciousness of architects the world over.

Church architecture resisted the advancement of spatial determination during those eventful years, and the appearance of the International Style in the 1930s partially interrupted the development of spatial consciousness. But in 1941, with the publication of S. Giedion's *Space, Time and Architecture* and the postwar rebuilding, space sensibility widened to international acceptance. Since then it has affected radically both the production and interpretation of architecture. In regard to it B. Zevi's *Architecture as Space* (1957) is very meaningful to a study of churches in history. Zevi's underlying theme is that the history of architecture is the history of the attending to the single space, and this particularly in relation to church structures, with the exception of the 20th century.

Time. Modern spatial awareness is radically different from that of antiquity since the dimension of time has become in the 20th century a conscious factor in architectural formation. Whereas Le Corbusier saw baroque space as theoretically fixed to a single position from which the spatial interpenetrations are best viewed, he found his own work making a new demand: movement in time is required to experience it since he observed that space is "the foot that walks, the eye that sees, the head that turns." According to S. Giedion, it is not relevant to view spatial structures such as *Ronchamp from a single viewpoint; the church is a hollowed out vessel in all directions so that no one cross-section or series of cross-sections reveals the spatial interpenetrations of interior and of exterior except through an experiential movement in time. Giedion, a major proponent of space-time consciousness, further demands that time does not simply refer to movement of the observer, but means a mode of consciousness. The conscious apprehension of space in time heightens perception of the process of life much as does the sensible apprehension of light and sound. Church architecture alive to spatial consciousness is a suitable container for the action of the *ecclesia* since it provides greater occasion for man to discover himself.

Mass, Enclosure, and Form. At its outer limits, architectural space is bounded by mass, or material enclosure, which presents a total configuration called form. Form gives to man objects and relationships; space gives to man only relationships. The former is easier to comprehend than the latter. In antiquity thinking about architectural form was largely object-directed. The laws of measure or proportion and the immutable relationships of geometry were the great discovery that the ancients objectified in architecture. In time the canons of form became a sort of dogma in architecture, and architecture became its life-sustaining vehicle. For the medievalists and humanists, formal measure and geometric proportion had meaning in the total spirit of their times; by the 19th century their doctrines of form had lost their relation to the world and had become little more than stylistic historical motifs. In the 20th century the power of form was regenerated by certain artists; meanings embodied in form were revitalized according to a new sensibility. Le Corbusier, who, along with A. Ozenfant, founded purism in 1918, advocated the reduction of all buildings to basic geometric shapes of cube, cylinder, square, etc., placed in space. For Le Corbusier, architecture was understood as "the wise, correct and magnificent play of volumes in light." His contemporary H. Luckhardt, echoing of Platonic formalism, said: "Pure form is that form which, detached from all that is decorative, is freely fashioned out of the basic elements of the straight line, curve and free form, and will serve the purpose of any expression—be it a religious building or a factory." These observations, *c.* 1915–25, were a reaction against the pseudo-architecture of the revivalisms and an enthusiasm for the machined products of the new industrial age.

Purism. The emergence of the *International Style marked the advent of 20th-century formalism. Although advocating volume as the first principle of architecture, its adherents conceived of architecture in terms of plane surfaces bounding a volume. Space was regarded as geometrically bounded. As a result the integrity of the geometric surface was to be maintained at all costs; smooth-faced stucco, glass, and polished metals were advocated. The highly regarded volume was the simple box made as open as possible through extensive glazing. In Mies van der Rohe, whose later philosophy (*c.* 1930) was expressed in the dictum that "the less is more," the International Style gained its greatest proponent. The governing principle of formal purism is that anything superfluous should be rejected from architecture, and that architectural expression should be sought in the fewest possible elements. Space became simply conceived as a cubic area bounded by glass walls articulated by a steel skeleton. Miesian philosophy is represented in his chapel at the Illinois Institute of Technology (for illustration, see section 11, below) and in his adherents' works, e.g., R. Jones' St. Patrick's, Oklahoma City, and P. Schweikher's First Universalist Church, Chicago.

Formal purism is characterized by simplicity of volume, linear austerity of exterior and interior walls, and precision in construction. This kind of architecture held virtual sway in America from *c.* 1945 to 1955, but since then it has declined. The application of the Miesian "universal space" to houses, office buildings, and churches may provide interesting technical and artistic solutions, but it is often inadequate for human functions. Its lack of flexibility and the inability to accommodate the variety of human needs, which it subordinates to a rectilinear geometry and abstraction, accounts for the weakening of its influence as a major architectural philosophy.

Plasticism. While the International Style ran its course, another style was developing under the influence of Le Corbusier. He attempted to manipulate a variety of forms in space to create a rich interplay among all the elements of architecture (form, mass, function) in dynamic balance. By the 1950s he was able to construct mature works in what has subsequently been called "plasticism" in architecture. Plasticism is generally understood as a quality of three-dimensional or volumetric relationships in contrast to two-dimensional or linear relationships. Although all architecture is three-dimensional as a form, it is only when elements are so disposed to make apparent the three-dimensional relationships between the elements that the term plasticity can be properly applied. To a large degree plasticity in architecture represents a method of giving to volume-mass relationships greater richness, diversity, and flexibility than the method advocated by the purists. Plasticity in architecture is not the unique possession of Le Corbusier; it was manifest in the works of A. Gaudí. Although many architects were showing plastic sensibility concurrently with Le Corbusier, it was Le Corbusier who brought plasticity into the main stream of modern architecture. Contemporary critics regard plasticity as potentially the most vital of all architectural tendencies and point to Le Corbusier's Notre Dame du Haut, Ronchamp, as tangible proof of "the fitness of plastic architecture to create the great symbols of our civilization, real landmarks of our time."

The conflict between advocates of space consciousness and those of plastic formalism is centered on the difference in their concepts of the function of mass. Some say mass should act as the reciprocal agent of space. Accordingly, the architectural exterior immediately signifies the interior and, in a sense, acts as a membrane between inside and outside space. Shell construction presents the apogee of this achievement. However, some deny that the exterior alone specifies interior space, but rather that it signifies the potential inherent in mass and its configurations. Thus R. Schwarz observed that the decisive point is whether "the boundary [enclosing structure] is the correct 'behavior' of the inside when it reaches the outside."

The Status Today. Obviously form and space are not the only considerations involved in church architecture; others are light, texture, sound, detail, construction, etc., any one of which may become a major factor in production or interpretation. As an art and as a working method, architecture does not attribute to any single one of these elements absolute primacy. Architecture succeeds only when elements are presented in suitable relations. In this regard E. Saarinen observed: "From an ashtray to a city plan everything is architecture. In working out a design you always keep thinking of the next largest thing; the ashtray in its relation to the table top; the chair in its relation to the room; the building in its relation to the city." This is the most meaningful formal consideration that can be applied to church architecture in 1965. Contemporary architecture theory does not recognize the existence of an autonomous manner of working that produces an independent style called "church architecture"; the architect's quest is to relate space, form, construction, function, and all other elements into meaningful patterns of relationships. The modern architect, schooled in space and form, structure and function, does not stress the object but relation. There is no law dictating suitable relationships except that found in the total configuration itself. He is hesitant to accept any law that claims to determine the suitability of relationships within a work before the fact of architectural creation.

Bibliography: For the history and theory of specific periods, see bibliog. following sections 2, 3, 4, etc. This bibliography presents: A select guide to handbooks and dictionaries on the subject and history of architecture in general; select histories of modern architecture in general (specialized studies on modern church architecture follow sections 10, 11, and 12); select literature relevant to theory, form, and interpretation of architecture.

General handbooks and dictionaries. For a useful guide to literature alphabetized by periods, see bibliog. in EncWA 1:693–710. E. E. VIOLLET-LE-DUC, *Dictionnaire raisonné de l'architecture française du XIe au XVIe siècle,* 10 v. (Paris 1858–68), illus., includes applied arts. J. BURCKHARDT and W. LÜBKE, *Geschichte der neueren Baukunst,* 10 v. (Stuttgart 1882–1927), illus. G. DEHIO and G. BEZOLD, *Die kirchliche Baukunst des Abendlandes,* 2 v. (Stuttgart 1887–1901, illus., atlas, bibliog. R. STURGIS, ed., *A Dictionary of Architecture and Building, Biographical, Historical, and Descriptive . . .,* 3 v. (New York 1901–02), illus., line dwgs., bibliog. F. M. SIMPSON, *A History of Architectural Development,* 5 v. (new ed. London 1954–), a new rev. ed. based on method and technique of the orig. ed. (1905–11). F. BENOIT, *L'Architecture . . .,* 4 v. (Paris 1911–34), antiquity and the East and West up to Gothic, indexes. G. WASMUTH, *Lexikon der Baukunst,* 5 v. (Berlin 1929–37), illus. with plates, portrs., maps, plans, diagr. Fletcher HistArch, illus. D. WARE and B. BEATTY, *A Short Dictionary of Architecture* (New York 1945). T. F. HAMLIN, *Architecture through the Ages* (rev. ed. New York 1953), useful 1-v. hist. J. E. GLOAG, *Guide to Western Architecture* (New York 1958), useful summary guide. *The Great Ages of World Architecture* (New York 1961–), series of concise monographs, select bibliog., each v. well illus.: W. L. MACDONALD, *Early Christian and Byzantine Architecture* (1962), H. SAALMAN, *Medieval* (1962), R. BRANNER, *Gothic* (1961), H. A. MILLON, *Baroque and Rococo* (1961), V. J. SCULLY, *Modern* (1961). N. PEVSNER, *An Outline of European Architecture* (7th ed. Baltimore 1963), illus., bibliog., useful concise history. H. R. HITCHCOCK, *World Architecture: An Illustrated History* (New York 1964). E. SHORT, *A History of Religious Architecture* (rev. ed. New York 1936).

General histories of modern architecture. B. ZEVI, *Storia dell' architettura moderna* (2d ed. Turin 1953), covers U.S. and Europe, illus., bibliog., useful indexing. A. WHITTICK, *European*

Architecture in the Twentieth Century, 2 v. (London 1950–53), illus., bibliog. H. R. HITCHCOCK, *Architecture: 19th and 20th Centuries* (2d ed. PelHArt Z15; 1963). J. JOEDICKE, *A History of Modern Architecture* (New York 1959). Hatje-Pehnt EncMod Arch, 1 v. illus.

Theory, form, and interpretation. P. ABRAHAM, *Viollet-le-Duc et le rationalisme médiéval* (Paris 1934). R. L. ACKOFF, *Aesthetics of the 20th Century Architecture* (Salt Lake City 1948). L. B. ALBERTI, *De re aedificatoria* (Florence 1485), Eng. *Ten Books on Architecture,* tr. J. LEONI (London 1955). G. BACHELARD, *Poetics of Space,* tr. M. JOLAS (New York 1964). R. BANHAM, *Theory and Design in the First Machine Age* (London 1959). A. BLUNT, *Artistic Theory in Italy, 1450–1600* (Oxford 1940; pa. 1950). C. F. BRAGDON, *Organic Architecture and the Language of Form* (Chicago 1917); *A Primer of Higher Space, the Fourth Dimension, to Which is Added Man the Square, a Higher Space Parable* (London 1939). E. DE BRUYNE, *Études d'esthétique médiéval,* 3 v. (Bruges 1946). E. CASSIRER, *The Philosophy of Symbolic Forms,* tr. R. MANHEIM, 3 v. (New Haven 1953–57), esp. v.2 *Mythical Thought.* S. CHERMAYEFF, "Structure and Aesthetic Experience," *Magazine of Art* 39 (1946). A. CHANG IH TIAO, *The Existence of Intangible Content in Architectonic Form Based upon the Practicality of Laotzu's Philosophy* (Princeton 1956). P. COLLINS, *Changing Ideals in Modern Architecture, 1750–1950* (London 1965); *Concrete: The Vision of a New Architecture: A Study of A. Perret and His Precursors* (New York 1959). R. A. CRAM, *Architecture in Its Relation to Civilization* (Boston 1918). T. H. CREIGHTON, ed., *Building for Modern Man* (Princeton 1949). D. DAVIDSON and H. ALDERSMITH, *The Great Pyramid: Its Divine Message* (London 1924; 1961). G. DURANDUS, *Symbolism of Churches and Church Ornaments* (Leeds 1843), with an introductory essay by J. M. NEALE and B. WEBB. I. E. S. EDWARDS, *Pyramids of Egypt* (London 1949). E. P. EVANS, *Animal Symbolism in Ecclesiastical Architecture* (London 1896). P. FINGESTEN, "Topographical and Anatomical Aspects of the Gothic Cathedral," JAesthArtCrit 20.1 (1961) 3–23. H. FRANKFORT et al., *The Intellectual Adventure of Ancient Man* (Chicago 1946). H. FRANKFORT, *Kingship and the Gods: A Study of Near Eastern Religion as the Integration of Society and Nature* (Chicago 1948). R. FRY, *Vision and Design* (London 1920). S. GIEDION, *The Eternal Present,* v.1 *The Beginnings of Art* (New York 1962), v.2 *The Beginnings of Architecture* (1964); *Space, Time and Architecture* (3d ed. New York 1956). W. GROPIUS, *Scope of Total Architecture* (London 1956). P. HAMMOND, ed., *Towards a Church Architecture* (London 1962). L. HAUTECOEUR, *Mystique et architecture: Symbolisme du cercle et de la coupole* (Paris 1954). J. HUDNUT, *Architecture and the Spirit of Man* (Cambridge, Mass. 1949). E. O. JAMES, *From Cave to Cathedral* (New York 1965). C. LE CORBUSIER, *Le Modulor: Essai sur une mesure harmonique* (Boulogne 1950); *Vers une architecture* (Paris 1924). G. LESSER, *Gothic Cathedrals and Sacred Geometry,* 2 v. (London 1957). W. R. LETHABY, *Architecture, Nature and Magic* (London 1956). É. MÂLE, *Religious Art in France, XIII Century: A Study in Mediaeval Iconography and Its Sources of Inspiration,* tr. D. NUSSEY (New York 1913); repr. as *The Gothic Image* (1958). R. D. MARTIENSSEN, *The Idea of Space in Greek Architecture* (Johannesburg 1956). P. A. MICHÉLIS, "Space-Time and Contemporary Architecture," *Journal of Aesthetics* 8 (1949–50). L. MOHOLY-NAGY, *The New Vision,* tr. D. M. HOFFMANN (4th ed. DocModArt 3; 1949). L. MUMFORD, *Art and Technics* (London 1952). R. NEUTRA, *Survival through Design* (New York 1954). H. NISSEN, *Das Templum* (Berlin 1869). N. PEVSNER, *Pioneers of Modern Design* (2d ed. New York 1949). S. PRENTICE, *The Heritage of the Cathedral* (New York 1936). W. N. PUGIN, *The True Principles of Pointed or Christian Architecture* (London 1841). F. R. S. RAGLAND, *The Temple and the House* (London 1964). H. READ, *Icon and Idea* (Cambridge, Mass. 1955). P. RUDOLF, "The Six Determinants of Architectural Form," *Architectural Record* 120 (Oct. 1956). J. RUSKIN, *The Seven Lamps of Architecture* (London 1849), and later eds. A. B. SAARINEN, ed., *Eero Saarinen on His Work* (New Haven 1962). E. SAARINEN, *Search for Form* (New York 1948). M. SALVADOR and R. HELLER, *Structure in Architecture* (Englewood Cliffs, N.J. 1963). P. H. SCHOLFIELD, *The Theory of Proportion in Architecture* (Cambridge, Eng. 1958). R. SCHWARZ, *The Church Incarnate,* tr. C. HARRIS (Chicago 1958). G. SCOTT, *The Architecture of Humanism: A Study in the History of Taste* (2d ed. London 1924). V. J. SCULLY, *The Earth, The Temple and the Gods* (New Haven 1962). R. K. SEASOLTZ, *The House of God* (New York 1963). S. SERLIO, *Regole generali di architettura sopra le cinque maniere degli edifici* (Venice 1537–51). C. SIEGEL, *Structure and Form in Modern Architecture* (New York 1962). E. B. SMITH, *Architectural Symbolism of Imperial Rome and the Middle Ages* (Princeton 1956); *The Dome: A Study in the History of Ideas* (Princeton 1950). L. H. SULLIVAN, *Kindergarten Chats* (rev. ed. New York 1947). P. THIRY et al., *Churches and Temples* (New York 1953). R. S. J. TYRWHITT, *Christian Art and Symbolism* (London 1872). H. WÖLFFLIN, *Renaissance and Baroque,* tr. K. SIMON from orig. Ger. ed. of 1888 (London 1964). W. WORRINGER, *Form in Gothic,* ed. and tr. H. READ (London 1927); rev. ed. New York 1964). F. L. WRIGHT, *The Future of Architecture* (New York 1953). VITRUVIUS POLLIO, *De architectura libri decem* (Leipzig 1899). C. G. YAVIS, *Greek Altars, Origins and Typology* (St. Louis 1949). B. ZEVI, *Architecture as Space* (New York 1957); *Towards an Organic Architecture* (London 1950).

[D. R. WALL]

2. EARLY CHRISTIAN

Spanning long centuries and distant provinces, Early Christian architecture embraces a lively variety of building types and styles, which gave direction to church architecture far into the Middle Ages and even beyond. The term "Early Christian" includes the architecture of the Church across the entire breadth of the Roman Empire, from earliest times down to the 6th century in the East, where it was supplanted by Byzantine, and down to the 9th century in the West, where it gradually gave way to Carolingian and then Romanesque styles of architecture.

Efforts to trace the origins of Early Christian architecture have demonstrated its dependence on many forms of late Roman building; elements of domestic architecture, business buildings, classical *heroa,* and imperial palace architecture were all clearly borrowed by the Christian architect. The earliest known Christian church, that of *Dura-Europos (*c.* 240), is no more than a traditional Roman home converted to church purposes. After the emancipation of the Church by Constantine, however, Christians required a more spa-

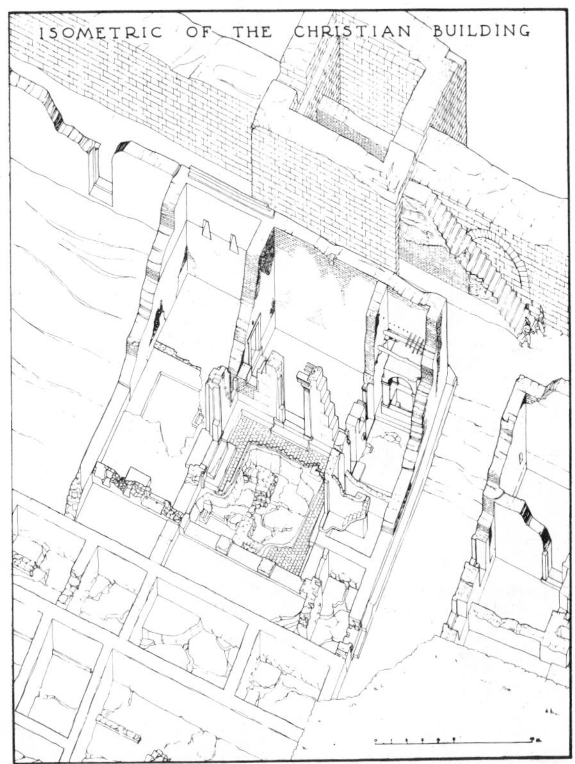

Fig. 21. Isometric drawing of the ruins of the 3d century Christian building at Dura-Europos.

cious building of greater dignity, and the basilica, or Roman business hall, was the logical choice. To Constantine himself belongs the credit for setting the pace by the grand series of basilicas he erected in Rome, in his newly founded Constantinople, and in the Holy Land.

Basilica. The Constantinian basilica consisted of a succession of contrasting spatial units along a strong horizontal, east-west axis. Entering from the street, one passed first into a rectangular courtyard surrounded by porticoes, with a fountain for washing in the center. Beyond this one entered the Eucharistic hall of the basilica proper, a timber-roofed construction consisting of a nave flanked by aisles and lighted by a clerestory above. There the long succession of columns carried the eye strongly to the sanctuary at the end of the nave, beyond which lay the apse housing the bishop's throne and the presbytery. If the basic elements were old, their Christian intent shaped them into a distinctive new style of architecture.

Made of brick, the Early Christian basilica presented a plain appearance on the exterior, contrasting sharply with the fine colonnades that surrounded pagan temples. Unlike the temple, the church was designed for the sake of its interior spaces where it housed the assembly of the faithful. The interior was therefore often richly furnished. The 4th-century mosaic exposed beneath the present cathedral of Aquileia features a profusion of vine decorations, medallions of the seasons, birds feeding, and sea motifs. Marble columns, ornate marble sanctuary barriers, mosaics in the apse, and coffered ceilings created an effect of splendor that for Eusebius was the perfect image of "the great temple which the Word, the great Creator of the universe, built throughout the whole world beneath the sun, forming again the spiritual image on earth of those vaults beyond the vaults of heaven" (*Eccl. hist.* 10.4.69).

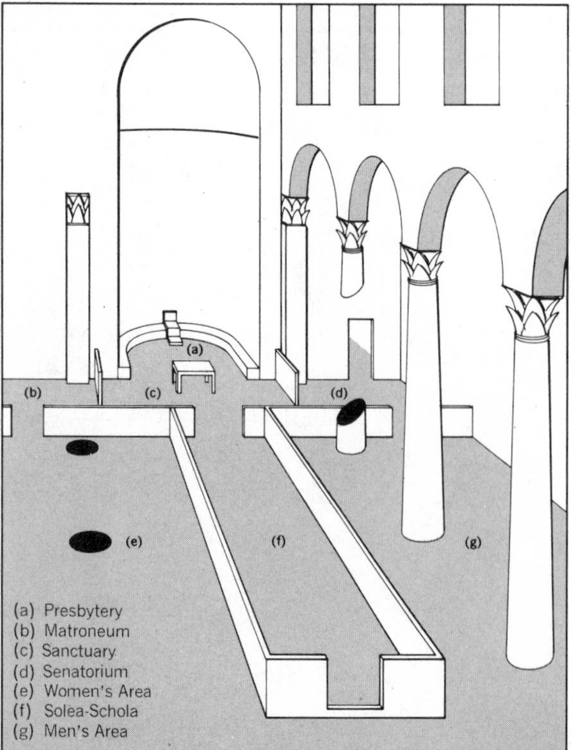

Fig. 22. Areas of the interior of a typical Early Christian basilica.

The Early Christian basilica was primarily a house for the liturgy. The long sweep of its colonnades enhanced the beauty of the elaborate liturgical processions —the entrance and exit of bishop and clergy and the processions of the faithful for Offertory and Communion. Chancel barriers marked off in simple, functional fashion distinct areas reserved for celebration of the Eucharist, for the lesser clergy and honor guards (*solea-schola*), and for the offering of gifts and receiving of Communion (*senatorium* and *matroneum*). Beyond the sanctuary lay the presbytery and throne, where the bishop presided at the fore-mass and where he stood to preach to his people. Add to this the lights, the banners, the vestments, the direct participation of the faithful in chant and procession, and the vision of the Early Christian architect begins to come to life.

The geographical spread of Early Christian architecture demonstrated the wide adaptability of the basilica. In the Latin province of Africa (the basilica of St. Cyprian outside Carthage, for example) it was used much the same as at Rome. The remains of the church show the plan with great clarity: the apse, from which Augustine is known to have preached, and the altar almost in the center of the nave. In Syria, on the other hand, altar and presbytery were reversed, though still retaining the fundamental basilica plan. The throne for the bishop and the benches for his clergy were located on a raised dais in the center of the nave; there the readings and instructions of the fore-mass took place in the midst of the community. The altar stood at the head of the church in the apse. Only further east in Mesopotamia, never solidly part of the Roman Empire, did the architect abandon basilica forms in favor of native temple plans.

In style too the Syrian architect reworked basilica forms with great imagination. Building in heavy stone blocks, he designed massive churches with powerful, squat arches, deeply carved architraves, and towered façades strangely foreshadowing the Romanesque. Syria, one of the liveliest centers of the early Church, was the home of some of the first great monastic complexes as men gathered from all sides to receive the spiritual direction of famous ascetics. Thus the monastery of Qalat Sem'an (*c.* 480) grew up at the site of St. Simeon's famous column near Aleppo.

Other Buildings. In addition to the basilica, the Church required other buildings of religious use, notably the *martyrium and *baptistery. The martyrium was a memorial shrine marking a holy site, whether it be the place of a martyr's burial (as at St. Peter's in Rome) or the place of some saving event (as at the holy places in Palestine). In distinction from the basilica, it was designed as a central-plan building, round, polygonal, or cruciform. Behind the basilica of Calvary, for example, stood the great rotunda of the Anastasis, centered on the spot of Our Lord's burial and Resurrection (*see* SEPULCHER, HOLY). Especially common at places of pilgrimage in the East, the martyrium was heir to the architectural traditions of pagan *heroa* and Jewish memorial shrines and became in turn the parent of the centralized vaulted designs of *Byzantine architecture.

In the West, on the other hand, the central-plan structure was reserved generally for baptisteries or mortuary buildings. It is significant that the most famous mar-

Fig. 23. Early Christian church architecture: (a) Ruins of the seven-aisled basilica of St. Cyprian near Carthage. (b) The basilica of St. Mary Major, Rome, 5th century with later additions and restoration, interior.

Fig. 24. Early Christian church architecture: (a) Hagios Georgios, Salonika, Greece, c. 310, altered in the 5th century, interior view looking northwest. Santa Sabina, Rome, 5th century, (b) interior view and (c) exterior.

Fig. 25. Santa Costanza, Rome, first half of the 4th century, view from the west.

tyrium in the West, the shrine of St. Peter, took the form rather of a transverse hall, or transept, at the end of the basilica, with an apse to mark the Apostle's grave. Thus whereas in the East the architect turned more and more to exploit the possibilities of a vertical, domed space, in the West the horizontal basilica space remained standard.

Though Byzantine architecture was not without some impact on Early Christian architecture in the West, these effects were more in furnishings than in structure. The ciborium over the altar and the ambos for reading seem to have come from the East in the 7th century; and in the 8th there was a notable increase in the use of images in reaction against *iconoclasm. Other developments modified the chancel arrangement during the same centuries. Provision for the veneration of relics directly beneath the altar required the raising of the sanctuary for the installation of *crypt and *confessio;* meanwhile, the increased sophistication of church music resulted in the augmenting of the choir space before the altar.

The enormous building activity of the 4th century all over the Mediterranean world was largely arrested, where not actually undone, in the West by the successive invasions of Visigoths and Vandals in the 5th century. And while the Eastern Empire proved stronger against the barbarian, it too suffered the destruction of the vast majority of its Early Christian monuments in the Arab invasions of the 7th century. Nevertheless, in the West, church architecture continued to follow Early Christian patterns far into the Middle Ages, and the churches of Rome proved especially influential in this respect. For it is to Rome that the pilgrim turned once Palestine had fallen to the Arabs, and in Rome he found a second Holy Land. In Rome stood the churches of SS. Peter and Paul, princes of the Apostles; St. Mary Major, with its shrine of the Nativity; Sta. Croce, with relics of the cross sent by St. Helena; and the Lateran, the pope's own basilica. Hence the architect's standard claim to fame in the Middle Ages is that he had built *more Romano,* after the pattern of the Early Christian churches of Rome.

See also ART, EARLY CHRISTIAN, 1, 2; ST. PETER'S BASILICA; CATACOMBS; BASILICA.

Bibliography: W. GERBER, *Altchristliche Kulturbauten Istriens und Dalmatiens* (Dresden 1912). H. C. BUTLER, *Early Churches in Syria: Fourth to Seventh Centuries,* ed. E. B. SMITH (Princeton 1929). R. KRAUTHEIMER, *Corpus Basilicarum Christianarum Romae* (Vatican City 1937–); "The Beginning of Early Christian Architecture," *Review of Religion* 3 (Jan. 1939) 127–148. J. W. CROWFOOT, *Early Churches in Palestine* (London 1941). M. ARMELLINI, *Le chiese di Roma dal secolo IV al XIX,* ed. C. CECCHELLI, 2 v. (new ed. Rome 1942). A. BERTHIER et al., *Les Vestiges du christianisme antique dans la Numidie centrale* (Algiers 1943). K. J. CONANT, *A Brief Commentary on Early Medieval Church Architecture* (Baltimore 1942). A. GRABAR, *Martyrium,* 3 v. (Paris 1943–46). J. LASSUS, *Sanctuairies chrétiens de Syrie* (Paris 1947). W. L. MACDONALD, *Early Christian and Byzantine Architecture* (New York 1962). G. A. SOTERIOU, "Hai palaiochristianikai basilikai tēs Hellados," *Archaiologikē Ephēmeris* (1929) 159–248. T. F. MATHEWS, "An Early Roman Chancel Arrangement and Its Liturgical Functions," RivArch Crist 38 (1962). **Illustration credits:** Fig. 21, Dura-Europos Publications, Yale University. Fig. 23*a,* J. Combier, Macon. Fig. 23*b,* Alinari-Art Reference Bureau. Figs. 24*a,* 24*b,* and 25, Hirmer Verlag München. Fig. 24*c,* Arthur O'Leary.

3. BYZANTINE

Although "Byzantine" is sometimes extended to include all the architecture of the Christian East from earliest times, it is more proper to restrict the term to the architectural style born of Justinian's empire in the 6th century. A style of great permanence, Byzantine architecture enjoyed nearly a millennium of living continuity and had periods of conspicuous creativity in the 6th century and again from the 9th to the 11th century. From its hub in the capital city of Constantinople it radiated over a wide area, following the spread of the Byzantine liturgy, with rich variations especially in Greece and Russia.

The complex history of Byzantine architecture revolves about a single architectural motif, the dome, and this principally in its religious use, though it had applications in civic and palace architecture as well. Once established, this motif was interpreted over and over in everchanging combinations. Precedent for the religious use of the dome was abundant in late Roman and Early Christian architecture. Particularly influential must have been the centrally planned baptisteries, martyria, and memorial buildings, such as S. Costanza in Rome, built as a tomb for Constantine's daughter, and the Anastasis Rotunda in Jerusalem. This latter circular building marked the site of Our Lord's Resurrection, the most important pilgrimage place in Christendom, and Emperor Justinian undertook its enlargement and restoration. But the Byzantine use of the dome quickly left all precedent behind and established a style that was quite new both in its aesthetic and in its technical accomplishment.

Early Works. The first masterworks of Byzantine architecture appear in Ravenna, the main stronghold of Justinian's rule in Italy. In S. Vitale (526–547; Fig. 27*c* and *d*) the essential themes of the new aesthetic are clearly enunciated. Basically the church consists of a central octagonal dome surrounded by an aisle and a gallery. But the classical ordering of spaces yields to a new fluidity. Each face of the octagonal core expands into the aisle and gallery in a semicircular apse with triple arcades on both levels. The main entrance, which is not on the axis but oblique, presents one with a complex view of overlapping and interpenetrating volumes. The controlled lighting on three levels lends a sense of unsubstantiality to the building, a feeling that is augmented by the handling of wall surfaces where varicolored marble, mosaic, and inlaid work mask the strength of the vaults and supporting members. Even the capitals are transformed, the classical plastic treatment of the acanthus giving way to a flat relief in which contrasts of light and shadow take precedence.

The use of the elevated dome at S. Vitale represents only one of a wide variety of early Byzantine plans. At SS. Sergius and Bacchus in Constantinople the octagonal central space was made to relate to a rectangular surrounding aisle, while at Hagia Eirene in the same city the central domed space was enlarged in an oval direction by large, major apses on the east and west. Elsewhere the dome unit itself might be multiplied, as at St. John of Ephesus, where a cross plan was crowned with a dome in the center and domes on each of the arms. In every case the architects of the 6th century strained the ancient Roman masonry techniques to accommodate a new spirit, a distinctive Byzantine aesthetic.

But in technique, too, the early Byzantine architect soon surpassed his Roman predecessor. Most important in this respect was the building of *Hagia Sophia (532–537; Fig. 28), where dome construction reached a triumph not approached again until the Renaissance. The architects not only chose to elevate a huge dome to unprecedented height (it spanned 103 feet, and its apex reached to about 163 feet), but they invented for its support the first large-scale use of pendentive vaults. The pendentive, a spherical triangular segment of vault, made a graceful transition from the circle of the dome above to the square of the piers below, carrying the weight of the dome more securely at the same time. Used only timidly in antiquity, it was now exploited to the full. The influence of Hagia Sophia on subsequent Byzantine architecture was decisive. As the principal church of the capital city it set a pattern for all the provinces. The central dome was thus established beyond question, and the Early Christian basilica type disappeared almost entirely from Byzantine architecture, except in Greece and Macedonia.

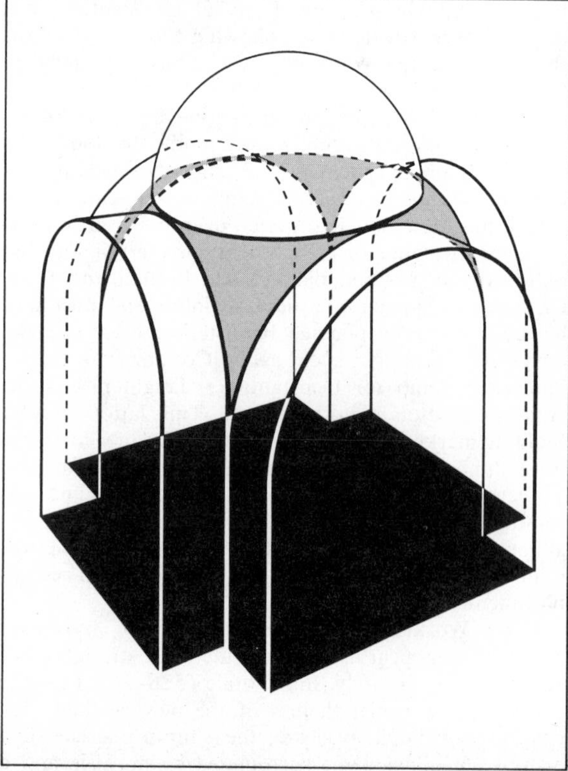

Fig. 26. A dome resting on pendentives (the shaded portion of the drawing).

Later Works. At the death of Justinian (565) his empire withered as fast as it had sprung up, and church architecture, always dependent on imperial patronage, likewise waned. To the east the Empire faced the threat of Islam; within, it suffered the turmoil of the iconoclast wars that destroyed many of the monuments of the first golden age (*see* ICONOCLASM). With the restoration of stability in the middle of the 9th century, however, a second golden age began, and a new church type emerged that was destined for a much more extensive diffusion than the earlier types. The new church type, pioneered in the now destroyed Nea Ecclesia (*c.* 860) and Pharos (*c.* 880) churches of Constantinople, was generally more modest in dimensions, monastic in orientation rather than imperial. It consisted of a barrel-vaulted cross inscribed in a rectangle, with a dome over the center generally elevated on a drum. Apses were multiplied on the eastern end, and minor domes multiplied in the angles between the arms of the cross. The overall effect was one of new elegance, with emphasis on the vertical line and the decorative detail.

On the exterior, the plain brick of the earlier style gave way to alternating bands of brick and stone and even tile, and the flat wall surfaces were enlivened with tall, narrow niches. On the interior, the victory of the orthodox acceptance of images over iconoclasm secured for the icon a role of great importance. The *regula,* or colonnade separating the sanctuary from the nave, was hung with icons and gradually transformed into an *iconostasis* (*see* ICON). At this time too the iconography of the interior took on a definitive system, arranging the divine hierarchy in descending importance from the image of Christ Pantocrator in the dome through choirs of angels, ranks of Patriarchs and Apostles, down to saints honored by feasts of the Church calendar in the lowest levels. Thus the entire fabric of the medieval church became a symbol of the whole supernatural cosmos. The church was "an earthly heaven in which the God of heaven lives and moves about, it contains in figure the crucifixion, burial and resurrection of Christ" (Pseudo-Germanus of Constantinople; PG 98:383).

Spread outside Byzantium. Although the Latin occupation of Constantinople (1204–58) terminated the second golden age of Byzantine architecture within the capital, the tradition had long since passed to the spiritual heirs of Constantinople. The nations of the Balkan peninsula and Russia were the principal beneficiaries, though nations farther east, such as Armenia, were sometimes indebted to the Byzantine. Greece preserved and enriched this architectural inheritance throughout the Middle Ages. The monastic centers of Daphni and Stiris in the 11th century, and later Athos and Mistra, built important original monuments. Characteristic of the Greek development, as seen in the church of the

Fig. 27. Byzantine church architecture: (a) Hagia Eirene, Istanbul, c. 532 and later, exterior view from the west. (b) SS. Sergius and Bacchus, 527–536, interior view from the west. (c) S. Vitale, Ravenna, consecrated 547, interior view looking toward the presbyterium. (d) S. Vitale, exterior view looking from the south.

Fig. 28. Hagia Sophia, Istanbul, by the architects Anthemius of Tralles and Isidorus of Miletus, view from the east. The minarets are late structures added by Moslem architects when the building was made into a mosque.

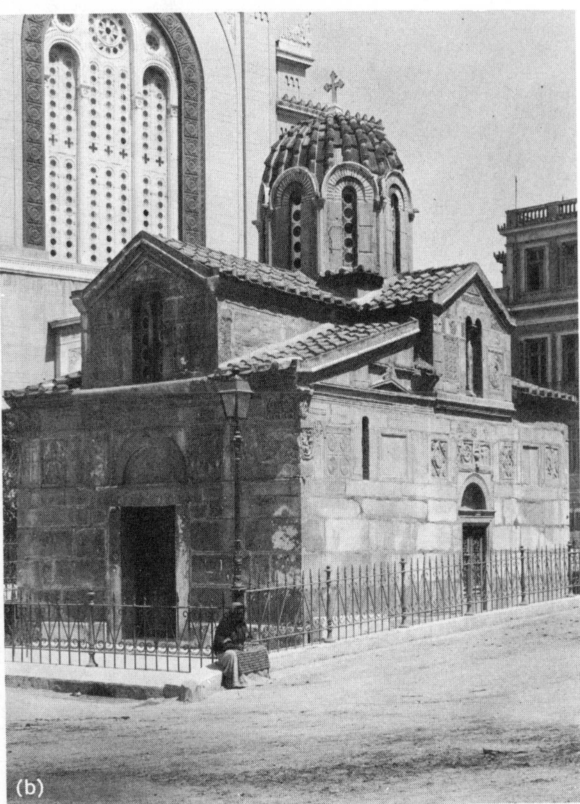

Fig. 29. Byzantine church architecture: (a) Church of the Assumption, Daphni, 11th century. (b) Hosios Eleutherios, "Little Metropole," Athens, 11th century. (c) Hosios Loukas, Stiris, interior looking southeast, 11th century.

Fig. 30. The cathedral of the Assumption, Vladimir, 1189.

Convent of the Assumption, Daphni, is the alternation of squared stone and brick, the fine masonry details, and the almost classical concern for the external proportions of the building (Fig. 29*a*).

The Russians too, after their conversion, looked to Constantinople as the parent church. As the story goes, it was the beauty of the liturgy at Hagia Sophia that first attracted to the faith Vladimir of Kiev, first Christian King of Russia (980–1015). His ambassadors related to him that "there is no such splendor or beauty anywhere on earth; we cannot describe it to you. Only this we know, that God dwells there among men and that their liturgy surpasses the worship of all other places." Byzantine architecture in Russia carries this kind of emotional overtone. Where the Bulgarians had elevated their domes on slender drums, the Russians both elevated and expanded their domes, developing eventually the picturesque onion shapes usually associated with Russia. The church was conceived as a compact grouping of vertical volumes capped by a cluster of shining domes. Later translating these forms into wooden structures in brilliant colors, the Russians succeeded in combining the Byzantine with the northern spirit.

Even in the West, Byzantine architecture has had considerable impact. The Mediterranean islands as far as Sicily, the monastery towns of southern Italy, and the great trading center of Venice are all rich in the Byzantine tradition. In Sicily, *Cefalù, Monreale, and Palermo are all important for their Byzantine mosaics. In Venice, the cathedral of *St. Mark borrowed from St. John of Ephesus the arrangement of several major domes distributed in a cross, whence this plan becomes part of the 12th-century tradition of Romanesque architecture in southern France.

See also CHURCH ARCHITECTURE, 2; HAGIA SOPHIA.

Bibliography: A. VAN MILLINGEN, *Byzantine Churches in Constantinople* (London 1912). G. MILLET, *L'École grecque dans l'architecture byzantine* (Paris 1916). O. M. DALTON, *East Christian Art* (Oxford 1925). E. H. SWIFT, *Hagia Sophia* (New York 1940). O. G. VON SIMSON, *Sacred Fortress* (Chicago 1948). G. H. HAMILTON, *The Art and Architecture of Russia* (PelHArt 26; 1954). J. A. HAMILTON, *Byzantine Architecture and Decoration* (2d ed. London 1956). G. DOWNEY, *Constantinople in the Age of Justinian* (Norman, Okla. 1960). W. L. MACDONALD, *Early Christian and Byzantine Architecture* (New York 1962). P. VERZONE, EncWA 2:758–785. R. KRAUTHEIMER, *Early Christian and Byzantine Architecture* (PelHArt; 1965). **Illustration credits:** Figs. 27 and 28, Hirmer Verlag München. Fig. 29*a*, Alinari-Art Reference Bureau. Fig. 29*c*, Jacqueline Lafontaine-Dosogne. Fig. 30, Society for Cultural Relations with the U.S.S.R., London.

[T. F. MATHEWS]

4. ROMANESQUE

Romanesque was the major medieval style in western European architecture from about 950 to 1150. Based on the principle of the Roman round arch, Romanesque architecture introduced to medieval church-building structural concepts of unprecedented monumental scale and originality. Its origins lay in the so-called proto-Romanesque structures of the preceding 2 centuries, notably in the imperial abbeys of the Carolingian renaissance and the Asturian and Mozarabic buildings of northern Spain. Since the most characteristic Romanesque monuments appeared between 1050 and 1150, the century from 950 to 1050 is generally regarded as a formative period.

From 950 to 1050. The adventuresome spirit that created the Romanesque style emerged in an atmosphere of general optimism in Western Christendom after the passing of the millennium. Within the newly stabilized framework of medieval culture, the character of Romanesque architecture was shaped by the pervasive influences of feudalism and monasticism. The decentralization of Europe into independent feudal states led to such a variety of distinctive regional idioms that some scholars prefer to define Romanesque as a group of related styles rather than a single style. However, through the powerful unifying force of monasticism, Romanesque became an international style, whose dissemination throughout western Europe was guaranteed by the arteries of communication opened by the great pilgrimages and the early *Crusades.

The builders of the abbey churches of the 11th and 12th centuries created a basic architectural vocabulary of compact masses animated by the vertical thrusts of exterior towers and interior vaults. These fortresslike structures tended to be conceived as additive complexes of quasi-independent components in an expanded basilica plan with ambulatory and radiating chapels. During its 2 centuries of experimentation with problems of structural articulation and vaulting techniques, Romanesque architecture produced a wide range of local variants within the framework of one international style.

Lombard-Catalan architecture, extending from northern Italy to French Catalonia and northern Spain, was one of the first Romanesque styles to concentrate on the practical problems of vaulting. Dominated by a basically utilitarian approach, the architecture of the Lombard-Catalan region developed in simple vaulted structures based on a direct revival of Roman techniques. The earliest and best-preserved buildings of the formative period, St-Martin-du-Canigou (1001–26) in the French Pyrenees and the Spanish pilgrimage church of Sta María at Ripoll (1020–38), are covered by heavy unribbed tunnel vaults carried on simple piers. Although their interior spaces were dark and crudely inarticulate, the exterior elevations were decorated with typical Lombard devices of delicate blind arcading. The mature phase of Lombard-Catalan architecture was reached with the introduction of domed-up, ribbed groin vaults in the nave of Sant'Ambrogio at Milan in the last quarter of the 11th century. These low, broad Milanese vaults, with their application of heavy ribs and alternating supports in compound piers, introduced a new structural articulation of the nave into double bays, but the cautious omission of clerestory windows resulted in a heavy, dark interior, characteristic of the Mediterranean area.

The later Romanesque architecture that developed in the wealthy Tuscan communes of central Italy was structurally more conservative, adopting only the decorative features of the northern Lombard style, while ignoring its innovations in vaulting. The 12th-century cathedral basilicas at Pisa and Lucca are distinguished chiefly by their ornate exterior overlay of marble veneers and decorative arcading.

In Germany the initial phase of Romanesque took the form of an ambitious Ottonian revival of *Carolingian architecture. The monastic foundations of Gernrode Abbey (*c.* 980) and St. Michael at Hildesheim (*c.* 1001–33) adopted the earlier double-ended plan with its western apse and multiple exterior towers. More concerned with aesthetic articulation than with technical problems, the builders of these early churches developed a system of alternating supports forming double bays in a nave still covered by a conservative, trussed timber ceiling. Under later Lombard influence, the 12th-century German cathedrals along the Rhine, e.g., Speyer, Mainz, and Worms, show groin vaulting applied to the nave and elaborate Lombard decorative motifs to the exterior walls.

From 1050 to 1150. The major developments of mature Romanesque architecture occurred in France. One of the most impressive and characteristic types appeared in the series of monumental abbey churches at Tours, Conques, *Limoges, and Toulouse, along the pilgrimage roads to *Santiago de Compostela in northwestern Spain. Modeled after the famous shrine of St. James (*c.* 1075–1150), the French pilgrimage church consisted of a huge Latin-cross plan, which included a spacious aisled transept and an elaborate ambulatory with radiating chapels to accommodate the cult of the relics. In its most typical example, St-Sernin at Toulouse, the dark, windowless nave is covered by a series of barrel vaults articulated by heavy transverse ribs and dynamically buttressed by quadrant vaults over the triforium gallery.

Under the patronage of the powerful Cluniac Order, the Burgundian churches of eastern France created one of the most original and experimental developments in Romanesque architecture. In its sophisticated efforts to solve the problem of admitting light to a vaulted interior, Burgundian architecture evolved a complex style that incorporated both Lombard and Norman influences. The nave of St-Philibert at Tournus (vaulted 1066–1120), which is covered by parallel, transverse barrel vaults carried by heavy cross walls springing directly from heavy masonry columns, is a typical example of the eccentric experimental direction of the Burgundian Romanesque style. At Vézelay, the church of La Madeleine (1104–32) illustrates the development of an equally radical vaulted nave in its application of ponderous, unribbed cross vaults over large oblong bays. The huge third abbey church at Cluny (1088–1130),

Fig. 31. The interior of the 11th- and 12th-century basilica of Sant'Ambrogio at Milan.

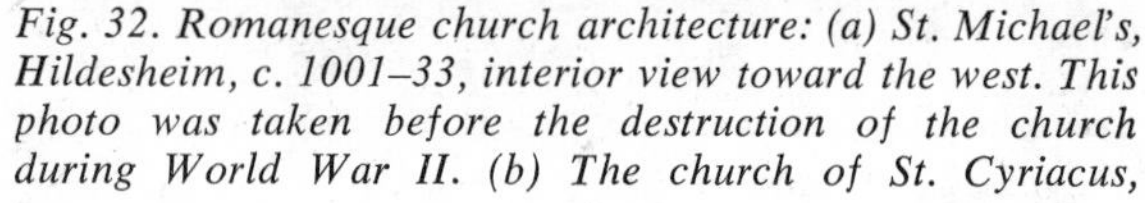

Fig. 32. Romanesque church architecture: (a) St. Michael's, Hildesheim, c. 1001–33, interior view toward the west. This photo was taken before the destruction of the church during World War II. (b) The church of St. Cyriacus, Gernrode, 958–1050, view from the northwest. (c) Main façade of the cathedral at Lund, 12th century. (d) Cathedral of San Rufino, Assisi, 11th century, a blending of Byzantine, Moorish, and Norman influences.

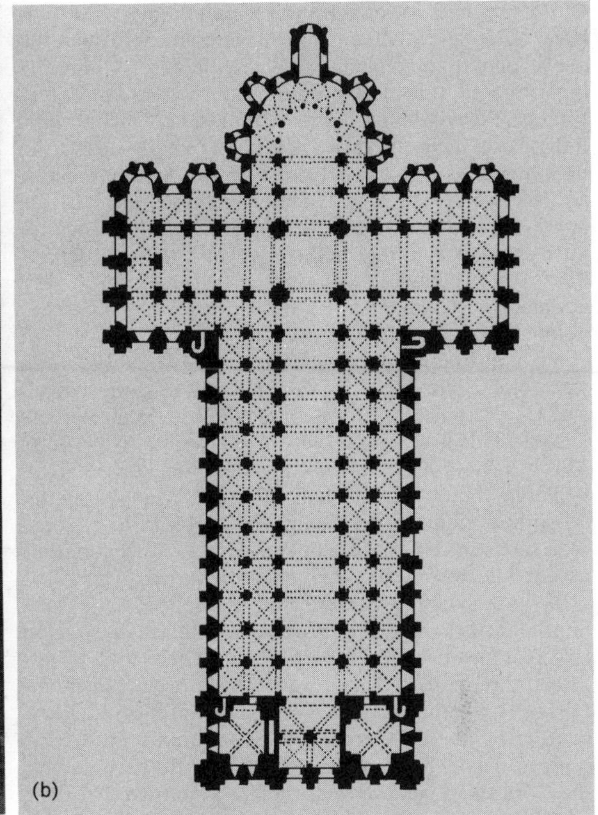

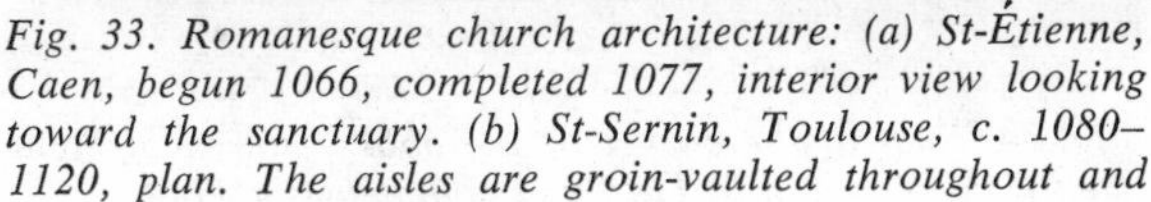

Fig. 33. Romanesque church architecture: (a) St-Étienne, Caen, begun 1066, completed 1077, interior view looking toward the sanctuary. (b) St-Sernin, Toulouse, c. 1080–1120, plan. The aisles are groin-vaulted throughout and are composed of square bays, which act as a module, or basic unit, for the composition of the dimensions of the building. (c) St-Sernin, exterior view from the south. (d) St-Sernin, interior view looking toward the altar.

with its double, towered transept, ambulatory with multiple radiating chapels and long covered narthex, was the chef-d'oeuvre of Romanesque architecture. Cluny III incorporated the most pronounced "half-Gothic" features of Burgundian style in the remarkably tall proportions of its nave, its thin, light barrel vaults buttressed by transverse ribs carried down into compound piers, and its use of the stilted, double-centered arch in the nave arcade. Following the Burgundian tendency to push Roman vaulting methods beyond their structural limits, the architect of St-Lazare at Autun (*c.* 1120–32) adopted the Cluniac stilted arch in a daring system of pointed barrel vaults over the nave.

Two distinctive types of Romanesque hall church were created in western France. In Poitou the barrel-vaulted churches of Notre-Dame-la-Grande at Poitiers (*c.* 1130–45) and St-Savin-sur-Gartempe (*c.* 1060–1115) have aisles and nave of almost the same height, while in Aquitaine the hall church developed under Byzantine influence as a single-nave structure covered by a series of domes on pendentives, e.g., the cathedrals at Angoulême (*c.* 1105–25) and at Périgueux (*c.* 1120).

Most conservative were the French Romanesque buildings of the southern provinces. The isolated region of Auvergne developed a unique feature in its high tower-like transept, e.g., Notre-Dame-du-Port at Clermont-Ferrand; whereas the 12th-century churches of Provence, St-Gilles-du-Gard and St-Trophime at Arles, preserved late Roman elements in the fluted columns, the Corinthian capitals, and the flat architraves of their façades.

The energetic Norman style, with its predilection for severe monumentality, logical articulation, and dynamic vertical momentum, produced the most progressive structural innovations in Romanesque vaulting. The Norman churches of the 11th century, e.g., Jumièges (1040–67) and St-Étienne at Caen (1066–77), adopted the conservative Ottonian timber-roofed nave divided into double bays by alternating piers with salient shafts rising through the whole height of the wall. With the application of low-sprung, sexpartite, ribbed vaults over the huge double bays in St-Étienne and Ste-Trinité at Caen (*c.* 1115), the structural function of the proto-Gothic rib was realized as a skeletal framework that could carry a lighter fabric of masonry in the vaults. Norman architecture was introduced in England by Edward the Confessor at Westminster and was established after the Conquest (1066) as a more massive, squared-off version of French Romanesque. While such English cathedrals as Durham (1093; 1128–33) applied heavy ribbed vaults to the nave, other Norman churches, e.g., Ely and Peterborough, retained timber coverings.

In the royal domain of the Île-de-France, the adoption and modification of the innovations of Norman proto-Gothic and the Burgundian "half-Gothic" Romanesque led to the creation of the first Gothic style in the abbey church of Saint-Denis (1137–44). Gothic then spread to the new town cathedrals of the later 12th century, while Romanesque survived in provincial examples well into the 13th century.

See also CATALAN ART; ROMANESQUE ART; CISTERCIAN ART AND ARCHITECTURE; CLUNIAC ART AND ARCHITECTURE.

Bibliography: K. J. CONANT, *Carolingian and Romanesque Architecture, 800–1200* (PelHArt Z13; 1959). H. SAALMAN, *Medieval Architecture: European Architecture 600–1200* (New York 1962). A. W. CLAPHAM, *Romanesque Architecture in Western Europe* (Oxford 1936). A. K. PORTER, *Medieval Architecture: Its Origins and Development* (New York 1909). R. C. DE LASTEYRIE DU SAILLANT, *L'Architecture religieuse en France à l'époque romane* (2d ed. Paris 1929). P. FRANKL, *Die frühmittelalterliche und romanische Baukunst* (Potsdam 1926). **Illustration credits:** Figs. 31 and 32*d*, Alinari-Art Reference Bureau. Fig. 32*a*, German Tourist Information Office. Fig. 32*b*, Marburg-Art Reference Bureau. Fig. 32*c*, The American-Swedish News Exchange. Fig. 33*a*, 33*c*, and 33*d*, Archives Photographiques, Paris.

[S. EDWARDS]

5. GOTHIC

A transition and change in construction systems, predominantly in ecclesiastical building, originated in northern France in the first half of the 12th century and produced the Gothic style of architecture that dominated Europe well into the 15th century (in some areas it was continued in the 16th century and even later). The Gothic style, developed first in monastic churches and the great cathedrals of northern France, was also adopted in the structuring of less ambitious parish churches. Although not confined to church architecture alone, it flourished and found its best expression in ecclesiastical building; its verticality did not lend itself easily to domestic building and its openness was not suitable for military architecture.

Gothic architecture is characterized by its ribbed vaulting, buttressing, and high piers. The weight and thrust of the vaulting is carried downward with the aid of extended (flying) buttresses, without needing heavy masonry walls (as in Romanesque). Hence the nave walls are an open skeletal frame free to receive large expanses of *stained glass. The exaggerated elongation of rising supporting members, which culminate in pointed arches, and the brilliant surfaces of light elevate the experience within to an otherworldliness where gravity seems overcome and natural light seems transformed. The exterior of Gothic structure achieves a similar transformation by disguising horizontals with steeply pointed elements and by multiplying vertical terminals with subtle gradations that fuse with the atmosphere.

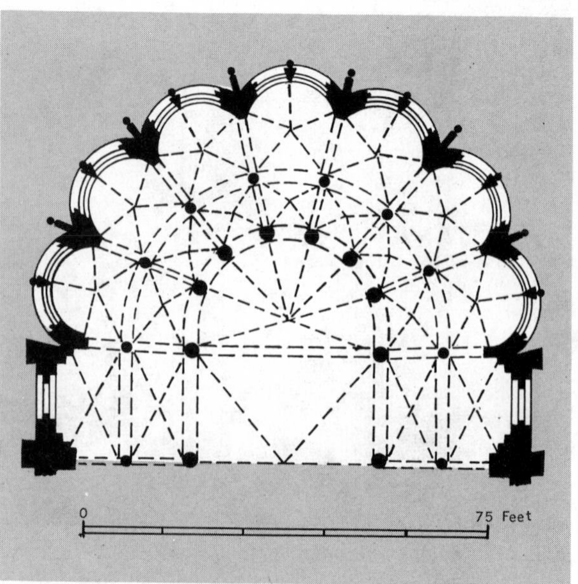

Fig. 34. Plan of the chevet of the abbey church of Saint-Denis, Paris, begun in 1140 and completed in 1144.

Theories on Gothic. Gothic ecclesiastical architecture has been viewed in many different and conflicting ways, none of them complete or perfectly accurate in itself. The French tend to be technical in their approach to the Gothic style (Eugène Emmanuel *Viollet-le-Duc, Camile Enlart). Germanic thought categorizes Gothic as a mystical expression of religious symbolism (Hans Sedlmayr) or of Neoplatonism (Hans Jantzen). The English view Gothic as a social manifestation of their own national character (A. N. W. *Pugin, John *Ruskin). Americans have been inclined to concentrate on developments of style (A. K. Porter, Robert Branner). Other writers have, of course, presented different views, linking religious experience with construction (Henry *Adams) or seeing in the perfection of Gothic architecture a parallel with medieval scholastic thought (Erwin Panofsky). *See* SCHOLASTICISM, 1, MEDIEVAL. But no workable, satisfactory, and definitive statement of the Gothic style of architecture has yet been advanced. Nor have the causes of its formation been fully explained, and it seems clear that no single point of view will suffice.

Some of the older, more blatantly unsatisfactory notions about the origin and meaning of Gothic architecture have, fortunately, long been abandoned. It is no longer accepted that the style began in the overlapping branches of Teutonic forests (Pseudo-Raphael Letter, between 1503 and 1510) or that it was Saracen in origin (Christopher Wren, 1713). But the very name "Gothic" betrays the derogatory connotations the style had for those Renaissance writers who first named it.

The "why" of the origin of Gothic architecture is not easily explained. Although the single-mindedness of a purely functional approach must be avoided, it seems equally unavoidable that the Gothic style originated amidst technical considerations. Over a given span, a pointed arch *is* more stable than a round arch. More important, because a pointed arch can be readily stilted by varying the point from which the arcs are swung, irregular spaces could be vaulted at uniform heights. The Île-de-France builders of the 1140s and 1150s were certainly aware of this. The rib vault, all too often seen simply as the *fons et origo* of the Gothic style, was unquestionably essential to it. The frankly insoluble problem is not whether the rib is a true supporting member whenever it appears in a vault, but what the medieval builder thought he was doing and why. And even if the Gothic style developed, as Paul Frankl maintains, from the vault downward, as designers attempted to give a visual unity from floor to keystone, it was a question of aesthetics no less than a question of construction.

But it must not be forgotten that aims, means, and results cannot be completely isolated one from another. The constructional means of voiding walls, however and for whatever reason achieved, made possible great areas of stained glass. The stories presented in these windows were exclusively nonstructural, ecclesiastical considerations, although the window plane itself formed a part of the wall. The mystical light of the Gothic church, so important at the very birth of the style, is perhaps more important to the character of the style than any number or combination of pointed arches. Because of the combined effect of the arches, the soaring shafts, the skeletal system of structure, the decorative moldings, the tracery screens, the finely cut sculpture, and the stained glass, one looking at Gothic architecture cannot help but repeat with Abbot *Suger (after Ovid, *Metamorphoses* 2.5), *materiam opusque superabat effectus.*

Origin and Development. Gothic architecture first appeared in the form of the chevet of Suger's *Benedictine abbey church at *Saint-Denis, outside Paris, between 1140 and 1144 (Figs. 34 and 36*a*). It was the effect, especially that of light, that was new or "Gothic" at Saint-Denis. Certain of the arch profiles came from the north, from Normandy, as did the concept of the rib vault, which made possible uniformly vaulted irregular spaces (Fig. 34). The idea of openness, of voiding the wall, probably came from Romanesque Normandy also (e.g., transept arms of Notre-Dame at Jumièges; La Trinité and Saint-Étienne at Caen). Pointed arches and a regular sequence of piers came from the south, from Romanesque Burgundy (e.g., Autun, *Cluny III, Paray-le-Monial). Thus it was the collocation of older Romanesque features in a new and ordered concept that gave rise to the Gothic style of architecture in the hitherto relatively barren Île-de-France.

The degree to which the new chevet at Saint-Denis, with its regularity of plan, spacious chapels, and flood of light, satisfied the general religious needs of the time as opposed merely to manifesting Suger's overt interest in light (see his *De Administratione* ch. 28) is apparent in the number of "copies" of the plan during the following decade (e.g., the cathedrals of Noyon and Senlis, the

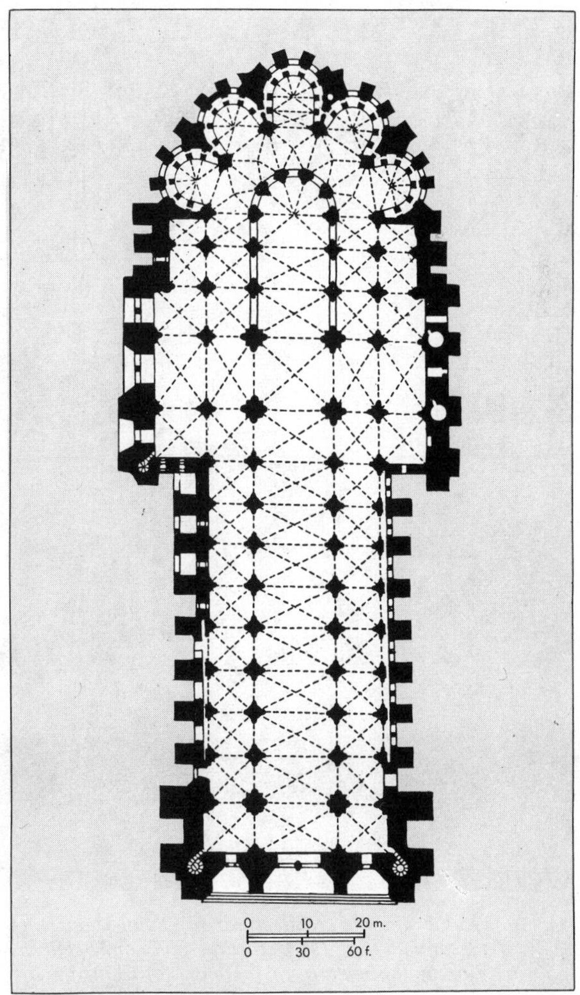

Fig. 35. Ground plan, cathedral at Reims, begun 1210.

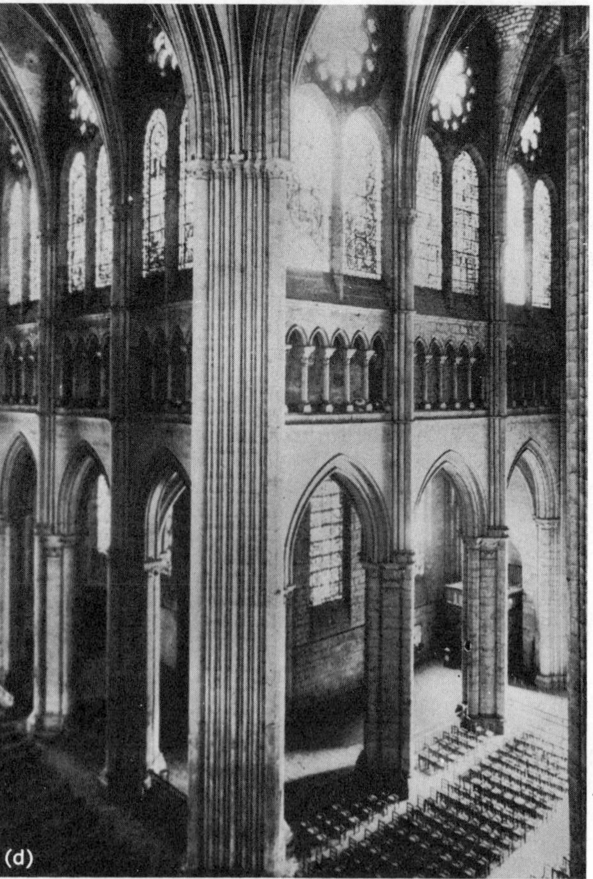

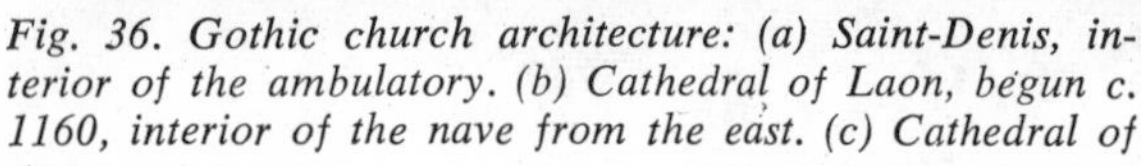

Fig. 36. Gothic church architecture: (a) Saint-Denis, interior of the ambulatory. (b) Cathedral of Laon, begun c. 1160, interior of the nave from the east. (c) Cathedral of Notre-Dame, Paris, begun between 1160 and 1163, view from the sanctuary gallery. (d) Cathedral of Chartres, begun 1194–95, interior at crossing.

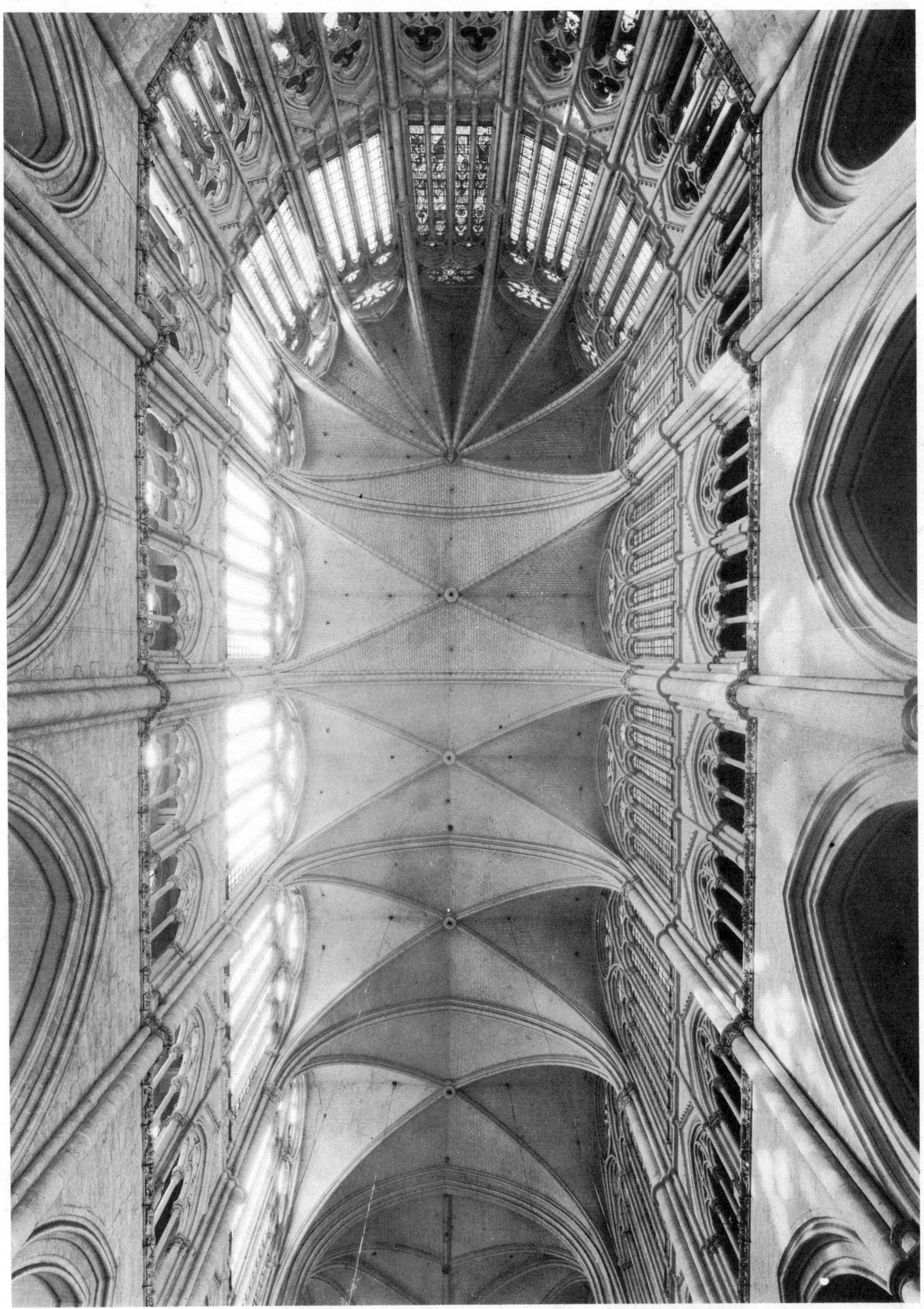

Fig. 37. The vaulting of the choir of the cathedral at Amiens, France. Begun in the early years of the 13th century and completed in 1287, this cathedral exhibits the culmination of the High Gothic style. This unusual view of the construction gives a good impression of the effect of height for which the architects strove.

abbey church of Saint-Germain-des-Prés). The problem of elevation was yet another matter, there being no readily available way to adapt older, heavier Romanesque schemes to meet the new desire for voided walls (light) and great height. During the second half of the 12th century a great number of experiments took place in the architecture of northern France. The result was a variety of buildings related by colossal size and four-part interior elevations—main arcade, vaulted tribune, triforium passage, and small clerestory (e.g., Saint-Remi at Reims, 1170–80; south transept arm of Soissons, 1176–90). There were, nonetheless, obvious differences of effect and appearance among these buildings. For example, Paris and Laon both were begun *c.* 1160, but the decorative plasticity of the latter contrasts sharply with the planar quality of the former (Fig. 36*b* and *c*).

Classic Gothic Plan. The solution of various problems, such as alternation of supports under six-part vaults and the logical codification of the desire for colossal buildings, came with the reconstruction of the cathedral of Chartres after a fire on June 9–10, 1194 (Fig. 36*d*). Here the first fully competent use of the flying buttress made possible an immense building with a simplified interior elevation of three stories, namely, main arcade, triforium passage, and gigantic clerestory (Fig. 36*c* and *d*). The regular vaulting system with one four-part nave bay vault for each four-part vault of the side aisle, the aisled transept arms, and the chevet with ambulatory and radiating chapels together formed what must be termed the "classic" Gothic plan, especially as it appeared completely regularized at Reims (begun after a fire, May 6, 1210; see Fig. 35). Space for pilgrims in great naves (Fig. 39*a*) and five or more radiating chapels for altars and relics—the plan was adopted for monastic use, e.g., Cistercian abbey church at Longpont, consecrated 1227—large areas of stained glass with the legends of the Church and its saints (Fig. 40), and complex exterior sculpture programs completed the High Gothic architectural ensemble (Fig. 38).

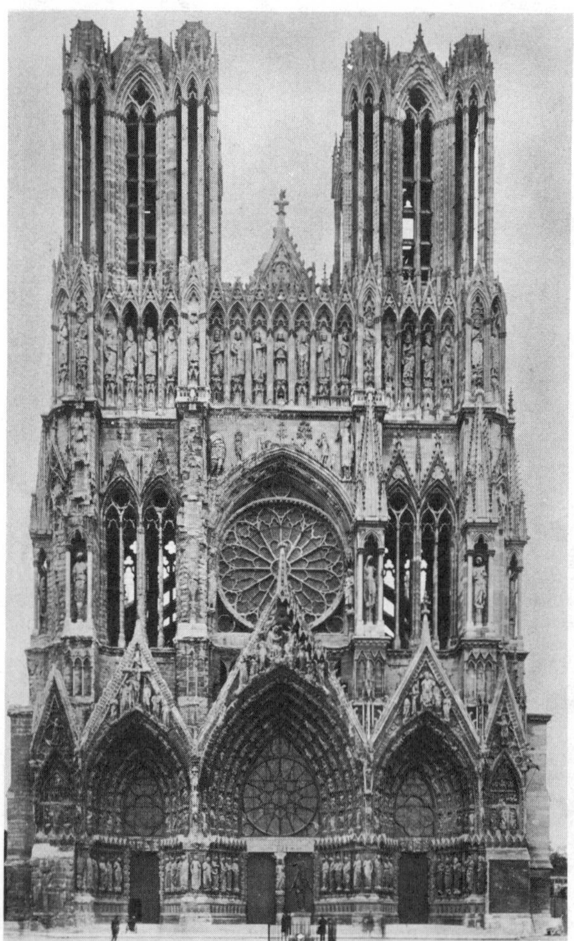

Fig. 38. The west façade of the cathedral at Reims, constructed c. 1230–1300.

Gothic outside France. Outside France before *c.* 1250, the Gothic style developed along individual, regional lines, and there seems to have been little interest in building strictly *in more francigeno*. England, despite the work of the Frenchman Guillaume de Sens at Canterbury in the 1170s, perfected a style emphasizing longitudinal rather than vertical fusion (e.g., Salisbury, begun 1220; see Fig. 39*a* and *b*) and coloristic, decorative effects (e.g., chevet at Lincoln, begun 1192). The flat chevets in England indicate the strong monastic orientation of the cathedrals in that country as well as the impact of the Cistercians.

In Italy, the Gothic style grew along very non-French lines. The large, open volume of such a building as the Dominican church of Santa Maria Novella in Florence (begun *c.* 1278) reflects the acoustical needs of a preaching order. The Gothic quality or character of this church lies mainly in the use of pointed arches, for the piers are purely Romanesque (Fig. 41*a*).

Germany and Spain, however, were much more receptive to French ideas and forms. The cathedral of Cologne (begun 1248) was modeled after those of Amiens and Beauvais and is extraordinarily French in character (Fig. 39*a* and *d*). By *c.* 1260 both León and Toledo in Spain had been influenced from France, the former by Reims (in plan) and Amiens (in elevation), the latter by Le Mans (mainly in plan and chevet buttressing system). However, it is both misleading and inaccurate to attempt to reduce the development of Gothic architecture in Europe after 1250 to expressions of French architecture, save in those special cases where a French architect can be isolated (e.g., Étienne de Bonneuil at the cathedral of Uppsala, Sweden, 1287). The appearance of *Hallenkirchen* in Germany (e.g., St. Martin at Landshut, begun 1387) owes nothing to France, despite earlier similar constructions in Poitou (e.g., Poitiers, begun 1162) and Anjou (e.g., hospital of Saint-Jean, Angers, 1170s).

Indeed, after the middle of the 13th century, French influence on the architecture of western Europe began to be less precise, the occasional mention of a church being built *in more francigeno* notwithstanding (e.g., Bruckhard von Hall, *c.* 1280, in reference to the then decade-old church at Wimpfen im Tal). In short, a desire for decorative effects began to overshadow interest in construction. Whether one chooses Hans Jantzen's term "the diaphanous wall" or Paul Frankl's notion of "surface texture," the effect is the same. The collapse in 1284 of the 156-foot-tall vaults of the chevet at Beauvais (begun 1225) cannot be blamed for a return to less ambitious buildings. The main problem posed by the Gothic system of construction, that of maintaining great vaulted areas with external flying buttresses, had been essentially solved at Amiens by 1250 and presented no

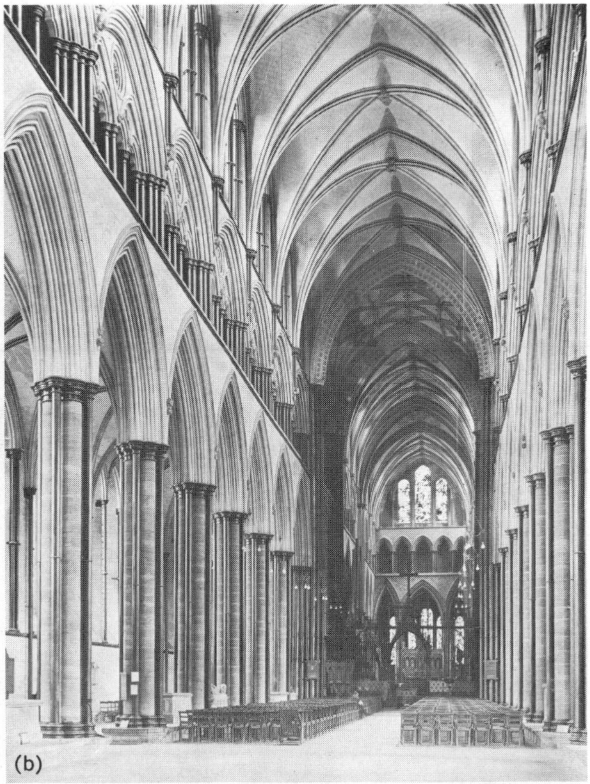

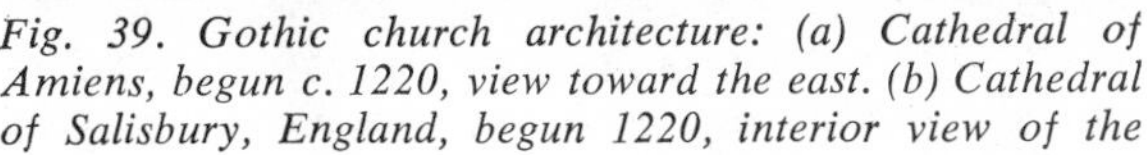

Fig. 39. Gothic church architecture: (a) Cathedral of Amiens, begun c. 1220, view toward the east. (b) Cathedral of Salisbury, England, begun 1220, interior view of the nave. (c) Westminster Abbey, London, interior of the Capitular Hall, built c. 1245–50. (d) Cathedral of Cologne, Germany, begun c. 1248, interior of nave.

Fig. 40. The interior of the upper chapel of the Sainte-Chapelle, Paris, looking toward the east. A two-level chapel, built by St. Louis to house relics of the Passion of Our Lord which had been brought to Paris by crusaders returning from the Holy Land, it is the most elegant of all the products of the Gothic architect.

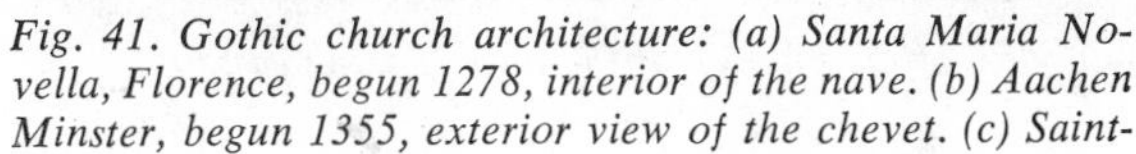
Fig. 41. Gothic church architecture: (a) Santa Maria Novella, Florence, begun 1278, interior of the nave. (b) Aachen Minster, begun 1355, exterior view of the chevet. (c) Saint-Maclou, Rouen, built 1500–14, west façade. (d) Sankt Martin, Landshut, Germany, begun 1387, interior view of the main aisle of the nave looking toward the east.

Fig. 42. King's College Chapel, Cambridge, England, begun 1446, view of the interior of the nave looking east.

new challenge to the builder after that time. In Paris, during the decade 1240–50, the appearance of small, elegant buildings such as Ste-Chapelle (consecrated 1248; Fig. 40) and the nave of Saint-Denis (begun 1243) reflect the stylistic interests of *Louis IX (the Saint) and his court. The voided walls of such French buildings as Saint-Urbain at Troyes (begun *c.* 1262), with screens of delicate tracery, together with the widespread use of the glazed triforium (e.g., nave of Saint-Denis; the chevet of Amiens, Fig. 39*a*) mark a new age in medieval architecture.

Save in Italy, there seems to have been a general interest throughout Europe in openness, in lightness, and in decorative effect—in extending the concept of plasticity to its utmost. This interest manifests itself in such widely scattered buildings as the cathedral of Prague (begun 1344; triforium level and clerestory after 1374), Aachen Minster (begun 1355; Fig. 41*b*), La Trinité at Vendôme, France (in the nave, begun 1306), and the reconstructed and redecorated chevet of Gloucester (begun 1337).

Flamboyant Gothic. The fantastic vaulting patterns of the late Gothic, especially the fan vaults of England (e.g., King's College Chapel, Cambridge, begun 1446; Fig. 42), spiral piers (e.g., chevet aisles, Brunswick, 1469), hanging keystones and pendent bosses (e.g., chapel of St. Catherine, Stephansdom, Vienna, begun 1340 or 1359), and complex tracery screens on façades (e.g., Saint-Maclou, Rouen, built 1500–14; Fig. 41*c*) all deny the clarity of earlier Gothic. But whether these architectural forms are termed flamboyant in France, *Sondergotik* in Germany, or Perpendicular in England, each in its own way was the ultimate statement of an experiment carried on from the very onset of the Gothic style.

One should not depreciate these late Gothic structures as decadent. They are among the finest expressions of the fertile medieval imagination. Rather, it remains to explain their rich fantasy of forms and effects. This cannot be done simply, but a parallel can at least be suggested with the growing inquisitiveness of the 14th- and 15th-century European mind and the ever-increasing preoccupation with the bizarre, as can be seen in the widespread popularity of the *danse macabre* (*see* DANCE OF DEATH) and the **Ars moriendi.*

Other Gothic Buildings. By comparison with the number of great cathedrals and abbey churches that have survived from the Gothic period, relatively few subsidiary structures such as cloisters, refectories, and hospitals (*hôtel-Dieu*) remain. However, such buildings as the hospital of Saint-Jean at Angers (1170s), the archiepiscopal chapel at Reims (*c.* 1210–15), the Synodal Hall at Sens (between 1222 and 1241, but overrestored), and the Capitular Hall at Westminster Abbey (*c.* 1245–50; Fig. 39*c*) demonstrate at least palely the wide variety of building types needed by the medieval Church and the inventiveness of the Gothic designer-builder in meeting this need.

Bibliography: Theoretical Studies. P. FRANKL, *The Gothic: Literary Sources and Interpretations through Eight Centuries* (Princeton 1960), the most comprehensive study of the subject; contains analyses, esp. those of H. JANTZEN from *Kunst der Gotik* (Hamburg 1957) Eng. *High Gothic,* tr. J. PALMES (New York 1962), H. SEDLMAYR from *Die Entstehung der Kathedrale* (Zurich 1950), E. PANOFSKY from *Gothic Architecture and Scholasticism* (Latrobe, Pa. 1951).

Surveys. R. BRANNER, *Gothic Architecture* (New York 1961), most current short survey. E. LAMBERT et al., EncWA 6:467–539, with extensive bibliog. 645–648. G. DEHIO and G. VON BEZOLD, *Die kirchliche Baukunst des Abendlandes,* 7 v. (Stuttgart 1897–1901), 2 v. text, 5 v. drawings. P. FRANKL, *Gothic Architecture,* tr. D. PEVSNER (PelHArt Z19; 1963), emphasizes the period after 1300. Some fine writing and thought is to be found in H. FOCILLON, *Art d'Occident* (Paris 1938), Eng. *The Art of the West in the Middle Ages,* ed. J. BONY, tr. D. KING, 2 v. (New York 1963).

France. E. E. VIOLLET-LE-DUC, *Dictionnaire raisonné de l'architecture française du XIe au XVIe siècle,* 10 v. (Paris 1854–68). R. C. DE LASTEYRIE DU SAILLANT, *L'Architecture religieuse en France à l'époque gothique,* 2 v. (Paris 1926–27). E. GALL, *Die Vorstufen in Nordfrankreich,* v.1 of *Die gotische Baukunst in Frankreich und Deutschland* (2d ed. Braunschweig 1955–). There exist some excellent monographs, e.g., C. SEYMOUR, *Notre-Dame of Noyon in the Twelfth Century* (New Haven 1939), but the studies of the Societé française d'Archéologie since 1834 in the *Congrès archéologique de France* and in the *Bulletin monumental* form the best general source of monograph studies on Fr. medieval architecture. A model regional study is R. BRANNER, *Burgundian Gothic Architecture* (London 1960).

England. F. BOND, *Gothic Architecture in England* (London 1905); *An introduction to English Church Architecture from the 11th to the 16th Century,* 2 v. (London 1913). G. F. WEBB, *Architecture in Britain: The Middle Ages* (PelHArt Z12; 1956). J. BONY, "French Influences on the Origins of English Gothic Architecture," *Journal of the Warburg and Courtauld Institutes* 12 (1949) 1–15.

Germany, Spain, and Italy. G. DEHIO, *Geschichte der deutschen Kunst,* 4 v. (Berlin 1923–34). L. TORRES BALBÁS, *Arquitectura gótica* (*Ars Hispaniae* 7; Madrid 1952). É. LAMBERT, *L'Art gothique en Espagne aux XIIe et XIIIe siècles* (Paris 1931). C. ENLART, *Origines françaises de l'architecture gothique en Italie* (Paris 1894).

Technical Studies. R. WILLIS, "On the Construction of the Vaults of the Middle Ages," *Transactions of the Royal Institute of British Architects* 1.2 (1842) 1–69. J. FITCHEN, *The Construction of Gothic Cathedrals* (New York 1961). E. LEFÈVRE-PONTALIS, "L'Origine des arcs-boutants," *Congrès archéologique de France* 82 (1919) 367–396. M. AUBERT, "Les Plus anciennes croisées d'ogives," *Bulletin monumental* 93 (1934) 5–67, 137–237; "La Construction au moyen âge," *ibid.* 119 (1961) 7–42. J. BILSON, "The Beginnings of Gothic Architecture," *Journal of the Royal Institute of British Architects,* ser. 3, v.6 (1898–99) 259–289, the Eng. viewpoint. The best studies of the architects themselves are L. F. SALZMAN, *Building in England, down to 1540* (New York 1952) 1–29; N. PEVSNER, "The Term *Architect* in the Middle Ages," *Speculum* 17 (1942) 549–562; and P. DU COLOMBIER, *Les Chantiers des cathédrales* (Paris 1953). **Illustration credits:** Fig. 36*a,* P. Devinoy. Figs. 36*b* and 41*c*, Archives Photographiques, Paris. Figs. 36*c*, 38, 39*a*, 39*d*, and 41*d*, Marburg-Art Reference Bureau. Fig. 36*d*, French Embassy Press and Information Division, New York. Fig. 37, Clarence Ward, Oberlin College. Fig. 39*b*, F. H. Crossley. Courtesy, University of London, Courtauld Institute of Art. Figs. 39*c* and 42, A. F. Kersting. Fig. 40, Giraudon. Fig. 41*a*, Alinari-Art Reference Bureau. Fig. 41*b*, Arthur O'Leary.

[C. F. BARNES, JR.]

6. RENAISSANCE

Renaissance architecture, so far as churches are concerned, began in Italy in the 1420s. It is generally accepted that a Renaissance church is not Gothic in style, but beyond this it is more difficult to establish agreement. Until recently, there tended to be a tacit assumption that the deliberate revival of the forms of imperial Roman architecture presupposed an abandonment of a specifically Christian architecture, which corresponded to Gothic forms. This argument was advanced, with great force, in mid-19th century by *Pugin and *Ruskin. It is, however, demonstrably false.

Brunelleschi. The first systematic attempts at a renaissance of Roman forms in architecture were made by *Brunelleschi and paralleled the revived interest in Latin letters displayed by his humanist contemporaries and predecessors. Brunelleschi's reputation was founded on the engineering feat of the dome of Florence Cathedral (*see* FLORENCE), which is a marriage between

Gothic vaulting and Roman domical forms. This was a special case; but Brunelleschi's two churches in Florence, S. Lorenzo and Sto Spirito, both dating from the 1430s and 1440s, were deliberately imitated from such Early Christian basilicas as S. Paolo in *Rome. The proportional system of Brunelleschi's churches is based on simple mathematical relationships, but their actual shapes, as well as the decorative forms used, are those of basilicas built in the Christian Roman Empire. Brunelleschi also built S. Maria degli Angeli in Florence, left unfinished in 1437. The shape of this church is that known as a central plan, that is, a regular geometrical figure rather than a cruciform shape. Here the shape is an octagon with a chapel on each of the eight sides. These shapes clearly recall those of the so-called Temple of Minerva Medica in Rome, so that once more the reference to antiquity is quite explicit. Brunelleschi thus revived the two main types of Early Christian churches: the large, Latin-cross basilica type,

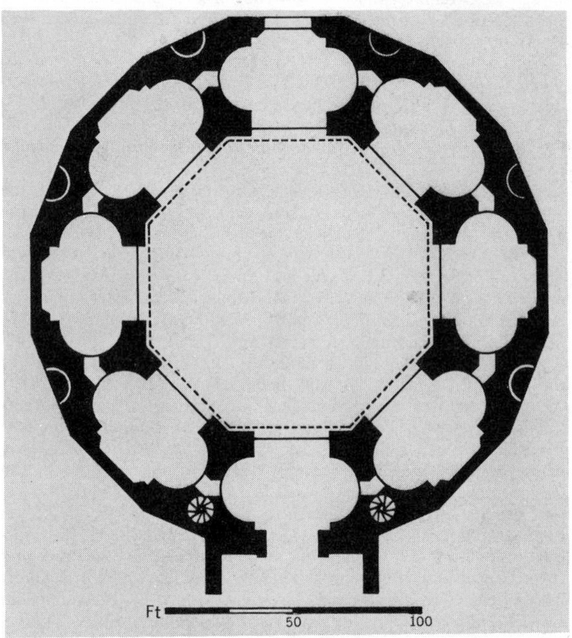

Fig. 43. Ground plan of S. Maria degli Angeli, Florence.

suitable for parish churches, and the smaller, centrally planned type that, in early Christian times, was normally reserved for baptisteries and commemorative buildings known as *martyria* (*see* MARTYRIUM).

Brunelleschi did not, so far as is known, formulate his theories explicitly; nor is there any other information about his views on church architecture. There is, however, a great deal of direct evidence in the form of writings by most of the major Italian architects of the 15th and 16th centuries, and their words make it quite clear that they regarded certain classical forms as specifically suited to the building of Christian temples (the use of *templum* for "church" is hardly evidence of paganism). It has been shown by Wittkower that the architectural forms employed between Brunelleschi's time and the Counter Reformation correspond to new, Platonic, theological ideas:

> The belief in the correspondence of microcosm and macrocosm, in the harmonic structure of the universe, in the comprehension of God through the mathematical sym-

Fig. 44. Renaissance church architecture: (a) Sto Spirito, Florence, Brunelleschi, 1436, from altar. (b) Sant'Andrea, Mantua, Alberti, 1470, view from entrance. (c) S. Biagio, Montepulciano, A. da Sangallo, interior.

Fig. 45. Interior of the Church of S. Giorgio Maggiore, Venice, designed by Palladio, view toward the sanctuary.

bols of centre, circle and sphere—all these closely related ideas which had their roots in antiquity and belonged to the undisputed tenets of mediaeval philosophy and theology, acquired new life in the Renaissance, and found visual expression in the Renaissance church. . . . For the men of the Renaissance this architecture with its strict geometry, the equipoise of its harmonic order, its formal serenity and, above all, with the sphere of the dome, echoed and at the same time revealed the perfection, omnipotence, truth and goodness of God. [Wittkower, 29.]

Alberti and Bramante. These ideas can be traced in the work of L. B. *Alberti, both in his treatise on architecture (written *c.* 1443–52) and in his two churches in Mantua. The earlier of these, S. Sebastiano, was designed about 1460 and is the earliest example of a Greek-cross plan, although one side has a porch that gives it a directional axis. This type of central plan can be traced back to the time of Constantine and, beyond that, to Roman tombs. In his second Mantuan church, Sant'Andrea, designed about 1470, Alberti repeated the Roman-basilica type used by Brunelleschi in Florence, but Alberti's forms are more classically Roman in spirit, and his church is covered by an enormous barrel vault of a purely antique type.

*Leonardo da Vinci never built anything, but he made many drawings of churches of the centrally planned type. At least three churches were actually built in this form at the end of the 15th and beginning of the 16th centuries: at Prato, where the church by Giuliano da *Sangallo is a combination of Brunelleschi's forms with the plan of Alberti's S. Sebastiano; and two others, at Todi and Montepulciano. These latter, together with Sant'Eligio in Rome, were all profoundly influenced by *Bramante (who had already built two churches in Milan), and specifically by Bramante's projects for the rebuilding of St. Peter's. There seems little doubt that the foundation medal, struck in 1506, represents St. Peter's as a Greek-cross building with a vast dome over it; and although this project was repeatedly modified, it proved an ideal form for several other churches, of which the most beautiful is S. Biagio at Montepulciano, begun by Antonio da Sangallo the Elder in 1518.

Bramante is said to have written a treatise, but it is not extant. Some idea of his theories can be gained, however, from the projects for St. Peter's and from the writings of Serlio, who was the pupil of a pupil of Bramante. Several other treatises give a good idea of the practice of Renaissance architects and of their view that the form of a building should be suited to its purpose. Serlio, for example, said that several shapes are possible for churches, but the circular (rather than the cruciform) is the most perfect: "Many and diverse forms of ancient and modern Temples are to be seen in all parts of Christendom . . . but because the circular form is the most perfect of them all I will commence with it" (prologue to book 5). The idea that Renaissance architects equated the ideals of symmetry, clarity, and harmony in church building with the perfections

Fig. 46. Martyrium, the so-called "Tempietto," in the courtyard of S. Pietro in Montorio, Rome, Bramante, 1502.

of God was most clearly stated by Palladio in his *Quattro Libri* of 1570, even though both his own churches in Venice were cruciform. In book 4 he said.

> We read that the men of Antiquity, in the building of their temples, set themselves to observe Decorum, which is one of the most beautiful elements of Architecture. And we, who know not false gods, in order to observe Decorum in the form of temples, will choose the most perfect and excellent, which is the circle; for it alone is simple, uniform, equal, strong, and adapted to its purpose. Thus, we should make our temples circular . . . most apt to demonstrate the Unity, the infinite Essence, the Uniformity and Justice of God.

It should be noted, however, that Palladio was born in 1508 and was thus 62 when his treatise was published. This was after the Council of Trent, which issued a decree on music in 1562 and on images in 1563, but made no special reference to architecture. The Counter Reformation ideals of church building were stated at length by Charles *Borromeo, in his *Instructiones Fabricae Ecclesiasticae* of 1577, in which he advocated the cruciform plan. *Palladio's theories reflect the early 16th century, the period now called the High Renaissance, about 1510 to 1520, rather than the Counter Reformation. The architectural ideals changed in accordance with theology; and in the 16th century it did not occur to anyone to condemn Palladio's architecture as pagan, as Ruskin did 300 years later.

Only a small number of churches were built in accordance with these ideals, and what should have been. the greatest of them all, Bramante's St. Peter's, was so profoundly modified that, in its present form, it is largely a baroque building (*see* ST. PETER'S BASILICA). Apart from churches already mentioned, there are some others, mostly small, in various Italian cities. *Vignola built Sant'Andrea in Via Flaminia and, far more important for later generations, Il Gesù, as the mother church of the Society of Jesus. Both are in Rome, as is the most beautiful of all centrally planned churches, the tiny *martyrium* built in 1502 by Bramante himself in the courtyard of S. Pietro in Montorio, on the spot that traditionally marks the place of St. Peter's martyrdom.

Bibliography: Sources. L. B. ALBERTI, *De re aedificatoria* (Florence 1485), Eng. *Ten Books on Architecture,* tr. J. LEONI (London 1955). S. SERLIO, *Regole generali di architettura . . .* (Venice 1537–51), and his later books, some pub. in France. Serlio was partly tr. into Eng. in 1611 but never completed. A. PALLADIO, *I quattro libri dell'architettura,* 4 v. in 1 (Venice 1570), Eng. *The Architecture of A. Palladio in Four Books,* tr. N. DUBOIS, 2 v. (3d ed. London 1742). All text translations are by P. Murray.

Literature. P. MURRAY, *The Architecture of the Italian Renaissance* (New York 1963), a general survey with bibliog. R. WITTKOWER, *Architectural Principles in the Age of Humanism* (3d ed. London 1962), most important modern work. G. SCOTT, *The Architecture of Humanism* (2d ed. London 1924), and later reprints. H. WÖLFFLIN, *Renaissance und Barock* (4th ed. Munich 1926), Eng. *Renaissance and Baroque,* tr. K. SIMON from the original Ger. ed. of 1888 (London 1964). **Illustration credits:** Figs. 44–46, Alinari-Art Reference Bureau.

[P. MURRAY]

7. BAROQUE

The formation of the baroque in church architecture took place in Rome toward the end of the 16th century; the diffusion of the baroque style followed in Italy during the 16th and 17th centuries, and finally it spread to France, Flanders, Spain, and the countries of central Europe.

Church architecture in the 17th and 18th centuries in western Europe is characterized, in Roman Catholic countries, by an integration of urban planning, architecture, sculpture, painting, and the decorative arts to a degree rivaled only, perhaps, by the Gothic. Acting to counter the effects of the Protestant Reformation, the reformatory orders of the 16th century restored to the Church confidence in the self-regenerative forces within Catholicism.

Artists and architects presented mysteries of the Church through interrelated illusionistic sensual displays that encouraged identification with the subject portrayed. The architect of the Renaissance, in contrast, due to the relation of the Renaissance to classical antiquity and Neo-platonic thought, approached the mysteries through mathematics and the intellect. As a result the ideas and forms of Renaissance architects, and those of painters and sculptors as well, remained more abstract, isolated, discrete, and independent.

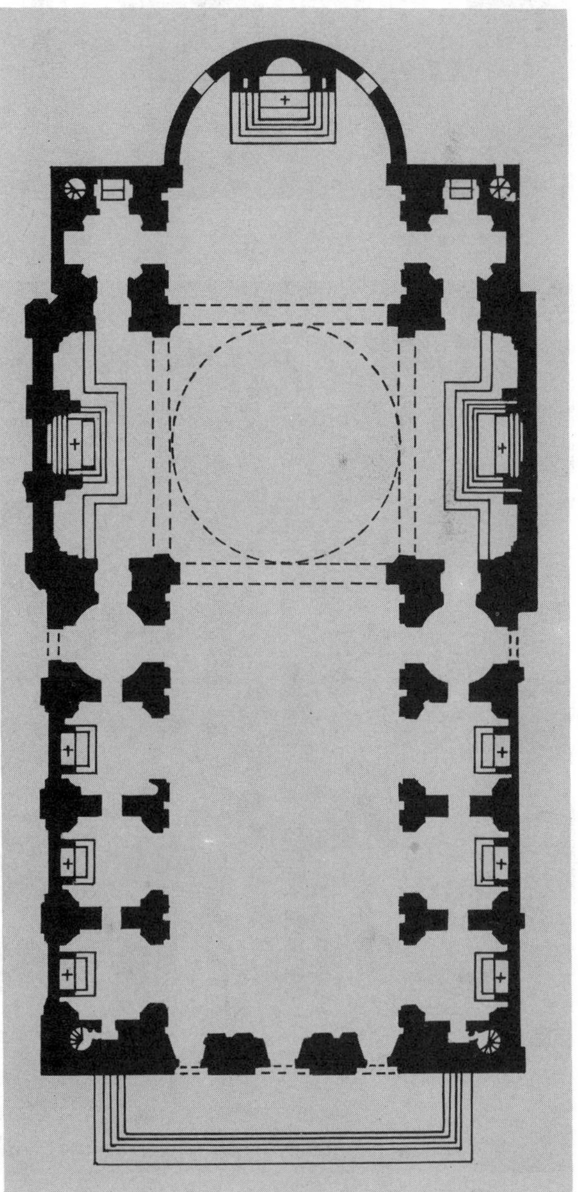

Fig. 47. Ground plan of the church of the Gesù, Rome.

(c)

Fig. 48. Baroque church architecture: (a) The Gesù, Rome, c. 1575–84. (b) The facade of S. Susanna, Rome, Carlo Maderno, 1597–1603. (c) St. Peter's, Rome, Carlo Maderno, 1607–14, view across the three aisles of the nave.

Development in Rome. The baroque began in Rome, where the Counter Reformation movements of the 16th century culminated in the building of a series of major longitudinal plan churches: the Gesù (1568) by the Jesuits; the Chiesa Nuova (1575) by followers of St. Philip Neri; and S. Andrea della Valle (1591) by the Theatines.

The plan of the Gesù with its wide nave, chapels but no side aisles, and short transepts provided an ideal preaching space. It was sufficiently successful for hundreds of churches with similar plans to be built in the succeeding century and a half and was probably responsible for the inclusion of a nave when St. Peter's was completed (1607–14) according to the designs of Carlo *Maderno (1556–1629).

Maderno. Maderno drew heavily on the works of his predecessor Giacomo della *Porta (1533–1602), who completed most of the projects Michelangelo left unfinished and was himself responsible for the façade of the Gesù and the plan and section of S. Andrea della Valle. Della Porta exploited both Michelangelo's emphasis on the vertical and his tendency to concentrate supporting members (in opposition to Renaissance horizontality and uniformly distributed supports). Della Porta, however, eliminated the conflicting elements that were the source of disturbing tensions and intriguing ambiguities in Michelangelo's work.

Maderno accepted Della Porta's interpretation of Michelangelo, but in addition he brought a richer play of mass and light and shadow to the otherwise planal surfaces of Roman architects and conceived architecture as part of a larger context. In individual buildings he included more plastic elements—half and fully round columns, the giant order, and more varied decorative sculptural features—and within a complex included more of the surroundings.

Maderno's new ideas can be first seen in the façade of S. Susanna (1597–1603), where he achieved dramatic emphasis on the central portal through (1) pilasters and columns arranged in a rhythmical sequence culminating at the central portal, (2) successive stepping forward of the wall surface toward the center increasing thereby the impression of mass of the wall, and (3) successive increase in size and relief of decorative detail from extremities to the central opening. Maderno also designed the buildings on either side of the church to make the façade become part of a much larger scheme—a focal point in an intentionally neutral setting.

In terms of urban design, Maderno was the first to develop some of the ideas implied by Domenico Fontana (1543–1607) and *Sixtus V (1585–90) when they planned straight avenues linking the major pilgrimage centers and culminating in centrally placed obelisks. For Fontana and Sixtus V the buildings lining the avenues were secondary; the circulation route and the foci, as they represented the pilgrimage centers, were essential. Maderno likewise conceived the church as part of an environment that included the background against which the church façade would be seen. After the initial successes of the baroque the city could no longer be thought of as a conglomerate of isolated churches, palaces, and other buildings but only as a formally and visually related whole.

In the nave of St. Peter's (1607–14) Maderno also altered the traditional Renaissance way of conceiving space and structure. In a Renaissance church (cf. S.

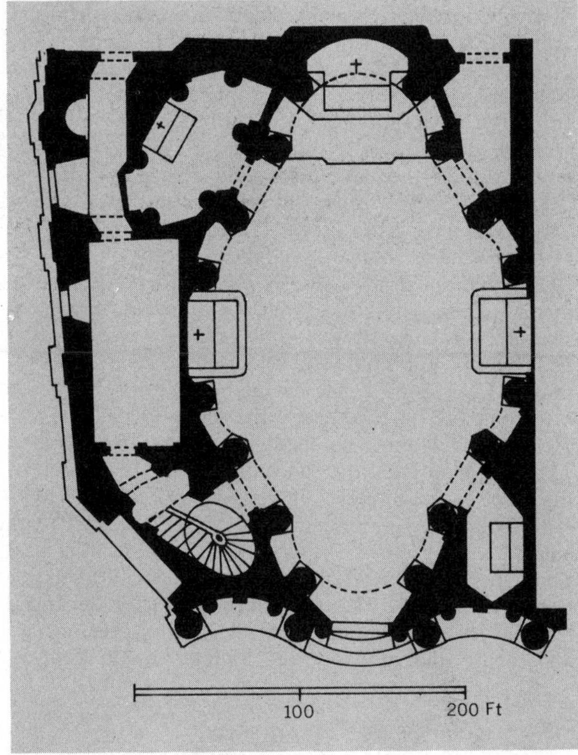

Fig. 49. Ground plan of S. Carlo alle Quattro Fontane.

Fig. 50. Interior of S. Carlo alle Quattro Fontane, Rome, by the architect Francesco Borromini, 1638–41. This small church, with its restless concave and convex surfaces, established the architect's fame in Italy and abroad.

Spirito, Florence, Brunelleschi; Sant'Andrea, Mantua, Alberti), structure served to define spatial units as discrete cells that, added together, composed the whole. Maderno, on the other hand, by widening and heightening the nave, admitting light through the vault and through domes in the side aisles, reducing the mass and width of the nave piers, and enlarging openings between chapels, sought to emphasize spatial unity across the nave from outer wall to outer wall, as well as from narthex to crossing and diagonally.

Borromini, Cortona, and Bernini. Maderno's achievements in the rhythmical manipulation of mass and spatial interaction for dramatic emphasis were continued by his pupil and successor, Francesco *Borromini (1599–1667), the painter-architect Pietro da *Cortona (1596–1669), and the sculptor, painter, and architect Giovanni Lorenzo *Bernini (1598–1680). These men initiated the full baroque. By 1640 each of the three had completed major works in Rome: Bernini—S. Bibiana reconstruction (1624–26), St. Peter's baldachino (1624–33); Cortona—SS. Martina and Luca (begun 1634); Borromini—S. Carlo alle Quattro Fontane (1638–41). Their achievements from the 1640s through the 1660s influenced all architecture in Italy and Sicily, and much of the architecture in France,

Fig. 51. Ground plan of S. Lorenzo, Turin.

Spain, and Belgium for the remainder of the century.

In accord with the precepts laid down by St. Charles *Borromeo in his *De fabrica ecclesiae,* the large Roman churches of the late 16th and the early 17th century were longitudinal cross-shaped plans serving to focus attention on the main altar. To Charles Borromeo the central plan was "less used by Christians than the longitudinal plan."

In contrast, in the full baroque there is a decisive return to the central plan, which, however, by treating the wall as an active sculptural surface, maintained and heightened the dramatic focus on the main altar: SS. Martina and Luca; S. Carlo alle Quattro Fontane; S. Ivo, Rome (Borromini, 1642–1650); S. Agnese, Rome (Borromini and Carlo Rainaldi, begun 1652); S. M. della Salute, Venice (Baldassare Longhena, begun 1631); S. M. Egiziaca, Naples (Cosimo Fanzago, 1651–1717); S. Tomaso di Villanova, Castel Gandolfo (Bernini, 1658–61); S. Andrea al Quirinale, Rome (Bernini, 1658–62); S. M. dell'Assunzione, Ariccia (Bernini, 1661–64); S. M. di Monte Santo, Rome (Rainaldi and Bernini, 1662–75); S. M. de'Miracoli, Rome (Rainaldi, 1662–79).

Diffusion in Italy and Other European Countries. The temporal power of the papacy declined in the last half of the 17th century, and with it Rome's artistic rule. By the end of the century Venice, Genoa, the Piedmont, and Naples became major artistic centers.

Guarino Guarini (1624–83), a Theatine priest who was a follower of Borromini working in Turin in the Piedmont, made the most significant contribution of the last half of the century when, in the SS. Sindone (1667–92) and S. Lorenzo (1666–79), he designed domes that admitted light through spaces left open between intersecting and superimposed arches.

In the early 18th century in Italy in the major centers two separate currents may be discerned. One is a classicizing continuation of the late baroque developing out of late Bernini and the Bernini school (for example, Carlo Fontana, 1634–1714); the other, a freer new current (the *rococo) developing most probably from Borromini, emphasizing skeletal structure, verticality, spatial unity, and abundance of light [for example, the late works of Filippo Juvarra (1678–1736) in Turin].

France. In France architecture of the 17th and 18th century has been labeled "classic" because of its greater dependence on both the principles of the High Renaissance and the architecture of Andrea *Palladio. Baroque classicism is a rational, reserved, and specifically French phenomenon that influenced most north European countries. French architects were not, however, insensitive to the discoveries of the Italian baroque and in restrained and subtle ways capitalized on the dramatic culmination that in both countries was achieved through subordination of parts to the whole, interactions and interpenetration of spaces, and vertical continuity of both structure and mass.

The baroque first appears in France in church buildings that reflect Italian precedent, such as the church of the Sorbonne, Paris, begun in 1635 by Jacques Lemercier (1580 or 85–1654), who studied in Rome from *c.* 1607 to 1614, and St. Paul–St. Louis, Paris, begun in 1627 by E. Martellange (1569–1641) and completed by François Derand (1588–1644). François *Mansart (1598–1666) was the unquestioned master of the mid-17th century in France. From his

Fig. 52. Baroque church architecture (at Paris): (a) The Val-de-Grâce, begun in 1645 by François Mansart and completed by Jacques Lemercier. (b) The Dôme des Invalides, by the architect Jules Hardouin Mansart, c. 1680–91.

earliest church (Ste. M. de la Visitation, begun 1632) to his unexecuted project for the Bourbon Mausoleum at Saint-Denis (1664) Mansart shows better than any of his contemporaries the spatial and structural unity of the baroque while both preserving and enhancing the scrupulous purity of the High Renaissance. Mansart's major church, the Val-de-Grâce (begun 1645 but completed later by Lemercier), best shows his cool, restrained, and precise interiors with crisp and finely detailed sculptural decoration executed completely in pale limestone.

The Dôme des Invalides, Paris (1680–91), by Jules Hardouin *Mansart (*c.* 1646–1708), is perhaps the best late 17th-century example exhibiting both a continued dependence on the High Renaissance central plan and a sophisticated integration of the spaces of the arms with the domed central space culminating in a frescoed double dome that is illuminated from hidden sources.

Flanders and Spain. Flemish architecture, due to its political ties with Spain and thereby to Italy, was more positively fluid and sensuous than in France and less dependent on the High Renaissance–Palladian tradition. Jacques Francart (1577–1651; Béguinage church, Malines, 1629) and Peter Huyssens (1577–1637; St. Charles Borromeo, Antwerp, 1615), in collaboration with the painter Peter Paul *Rubens (1577–1640), established an important center from which full baroque ideas were to flow in northern Europe. Notable mid-century examples include S. Michel, Louvain, 1650, by Willem Hesius and the Abbey of Averbode, 1662, by Jan van den Eynde.

Fig. 53. The church of the Abbey of Melk, designed by Jakob Prandtauer and begun in 1702.

Fig. 54. The ceiling of the main nave of the abbey church at Weingarten, Germany, with frescoes by Cosmas Damian Asam. This church, built between 1715 and 1723, is the largest religious structure of the baroque in Germany.

In Spain, as in Italy, the late baroque developed in two major directions, one free and curvilinear (e.g., SS. Justo y Pastor, Madrid, by Bonavia, 1739–46), indebted to Borromini and Guarini (who built the Theatine church in Lisbon), and the other a rectilinear version (e.g., cathedral, Saragossa, begun 1680, later altered), growing out of both the late 16th-century tradition in Spain and the influence of Bernini. However, there was in Spain a greater emphasis on dramatic spatial and light culminations and on surface texture. José Churriguera (1665–1725) gave his name to an entire style characterized by heavily ornate stucco decoration (Granada, Charterhouse, sacristy interior, 1742–47).

Central Europe. The unstable political situation reflected in the Thirty Years' War was followed by the threat of the expanding Ottoman Empire, and it was not until the Turks were crushed at Vienna in 1683 that energies could be devoted to rebuilding the country. The full baroque with an Italianate flavor appeared in central Europe after 1680, but it was not until the 18th century that independent work was produced. Chief among the late 17th-century architects were *Fischer von Erlach (1656–1723), Jakob Prandtauer (1660–1726), and Lukas von Hildebrandt (1668–1745). Fischer and Hildebrandt were court architects; Prandtauer's buildings were chiefly monastic. Particularly noteworthy are Fischer's Collegiate Church in Salzburg (1696) and the Karlskirche, Vienna (1716), Hildebrandt's Piaristen Church, Vienna (designed 1698), and Prandtauer's Abbey of *Melk (begun 1702).

Bibliography: General Histories. A. E. Brinckmann, *Die Baukunst des 17. und 18. Jahrhunderts in den romanischen Ländern* (Berlin 1915). V. Golzio, *Il seicento e il settecento* (Turin 1950). S. F. Kimball, *Creation of the Rococo* (Philadelphia 1943). H. A. Millon, *Baroque and Rococo Architecture* (New York 1961). W. Weisbach, *Die Kunst des Barock* (Berlin 1924).

Italy. R. Wittkower, *Art and Architecture in Italy, 1600–1750* (PelHArt Z16; 1958). A. Blunt, *Artistic Theory in Italy, 1450–1600* (Oxford 1940). C. Borromeo, *Arte sacra,* ed. and tr. C. Castiglioni and C. Marcora (Milan 1952). G. Delogu, *L'architettura italiana del seicento e del settecento* (Florence 1935). Fokker RomBarArt. É. Mâle, *L'Art religieux de la fin du XVIe siècle du XVIIe siècle et du XVIIIe siècle* (2d ed. Paris 1951). Pastor v.20–40. J. Weingartner, *Römische Barockkirchen* (Munich 1930).

France. R. T. Blomfield, *A History of French Architecture from the Reign of Charles VIII till the Death of Mazarin,* 2 v. (London 1911); *A History of French Architecture, 1661–1774,* 2 v. (London 1921). A. Blunt, *Art and Architecture in France, 1500–1700* (PelHArt Z4; 1953). L. Hautecoeur, *Histoire de l'architecture classique en France,* 7 v. in 9 (Paris 1943–57). P. Moisy, *Les Églises des Jésuits de l'ancienne assistance de France,* 2 v. (Rome 1958).

Spain and Portugal. G. Kubler and M. Soria, *Art and Architecture in Spain and Portugal and Their American Dominions, 1500–1800* (PelHArt Z17; 1959).

Central Europe. E. Hempel, *Baroque Art and Architecture in Central Europe* (Baltimore 1965). J. Bourke, *Baroque Churches of Central Europe* (London 1958). W. Hager, *Die Bauten des Deutschen Barocks* (Jena 1942). W. Hege and G. Barthel, *Barockkirchen in Altbayern und Schwaben* (Munich 1938; 3d ed. 1953). N. Lieb, *Barockkirchen zwischen Donau und Alpen* (Munich 1953). N. Powell, *From Baroque to Rococo* (New York 1959). H. Sedlmayr, *Österreichische Barockarchitektur 1690–1740* (Vienna 1930). M. Wackernagel, *Die Baukunst des 17. und 18. Jahrhunderts in den germanischen Ländern* (Berlin 1919).

Urban history. L. Mumford, *The City in History* (New York 1961). **Illustration credits:** Fig. 48*a*, Gabinetto Fotografico Nazionale, Rome. Figs. 48*b*, 48*c*, and 50, Alinari-Art Reference Bureau. Fig. 52, Archives Photographiques, Paris. Fig. 53, Austrian Information Service, New York City. Fig. 54, Leonard Von Matt.

[H. A. MILLON]

8. Eighteenth Century

European church building of the 18th century manifested those mutations of the classical theme, of both form and style, that had already been established in the high baroque of the 17th century. The dramatic, calculated manipulation of longitudinal and central church plans, the often daring disposition of interior space, the sweeping, formalized modeling of exterior form so characteristic of baroque construction formed a movement that flowed easily into the new century. Initially the unbaroque Palladianism of Italy continued strong in England, while France never quite deserted its formal classical structure. This century saw the mainstream of *baroque merge into the extravagance of *rococo, which, toward the end, was submerged by the rise of neoclassicism.

Although the 17th century had been one of much intellectual ferment and scientific inquiry, religion itself, despite those differences that disturbed its European community, had not been seriously challenged. In the new century, churches continued to be built—Palladian or Georgian in England, formally classical in France, and rococo in much of the rest of Europe, although there were exceptions to the general rule. The period of the Enlightenment in France preceded the antireligious storms of the end of the century.

Georgian. The life of Sir Christopher *Wren, perhaps the last great architect of the Renaissance tradition, spanned the turn of the century. In *St. Paul's Cathedral, London (1675–1710), and in his many smaller churches, he influenced the future development of the

Fig. 55. Lateral interior view of the Panthéon at Paris.

Fig. 56. Eighteenth-century church architecture: (a) St. Martin-in-the-Fields, London, James Gibbs, 1722–26. (b) Frauenkirche, Dresden, G. Bähr, 1726–40 (destroyed by aerial bombing during World War II). (c) Church of the Superga (Cathedral of San Giusto), Turin, Filippo Juvara, 1717–31. (d) St-Sulpice, Paris, J. N. Servandoni, 1733–49.

classical church in both England and America. These churches with their ingenious plans (often a combination of longitudinal and central types), their rich but simple detailing, and their superb towers and spires were eminently suitable to Protestant (Anglican) congregations of the Georgian era. Nicholas Hawksmoor (1661–1736), Thomas Archer (1668–1743), and James *Gibbs (1682–1764) continued the Wren theme in a succession of churches remarkable for a restrained interplay of baroque form and space and native English classicality allied with Palladianism.

The standard Georgian church, of which Gibbs's St. Martin-in-the-Fields, London (1722–26; Fig. 56*a*), is a typical example, usually has a columnar portico with tower and spire above, and it is most often based on a longitudinal plan; a galleried interior also is not uncommon. A good American example of the type is St. Michael's, Charleston, S.C. (1752–61). The Georgian church has been favored so long by public taste that it is still being erected today.

Rococo. The rococo style induced a general lightening of baroque pomp. Church buildings became more light, airy, and decorative, fluid in form and ambiguous in plan; they are ornamental and buoyant to the point of theatricality or fantasy. In France, where the style originated, rococo art was secular rather than ecclesiastical; and it may be seen best in Germany and Austria, where the new monastery and town churches demonstrated the almost pyrotechnical abilities of such architects as the brothers Asam and J. B. Neumann (1687–1772). The latter's church of Vierzehnheiligen (1743–72) in Franconia, florid and sinuous as it is, is like a splendid sonata, its flowing calculated melody based on subtle oval configurations of a longitudinal plan (Fig. 57*b*).

The Protestant Frauenkirche (1726–40) at Dresden (now destroyed) with its oval dome and central plan was a rather more restrained but equally sculpturesque rococo composition (Fig. 56*b*).

The rococo also flourished strongly in Spain and Portugal, notably in the work of José de Churriguera (1650–1725) and his followers; the Churrigueresque manner is characterized by an omnipresent rich ornamentation, encrusting and hiding the structure beneath it. The sacristy of the Cartuja (1727–64) at Granada and the façade of the cathedral of *Santiago de Compostela (1738–49) are good examples; here again construction is lost in thickets of florid ornament. The style was also popular in the New World, as in the sanctuary at Ocotlán, Mexico (*c.* 1745). Color is added to the polyphonic intricacy of the sculptured detail.

Italy had ceased to be an important architectural center, but the late baroque of that country was still vigorous enough to produce a fine domed church, the Superga (1717–31), near Turin, designed by Filippo Juvara (1676?–1736), which, although baroque in both composition and execution, has a certain grand simplicity of treatment that makes it one of the best of baroque churches (Fig. 56*c*). Although the Italian rococo is charming, as a rule its productions are in no way outstanding.

Neoclassicism. Contemporary with the Enlightenment, an architectural neoclassicism, characterized by a renewed interest in and a closer study of the arts of antiquity (especially those of ancient Greece), made

Fig. 57. Eighteenth-century church architecture: (a) Sacristy of the Cartuja, Granada, L. de Arevalo and M. Vasquez, 1727–64. (b) Interior of Vierzehnheiligen, J. B. Neumann, 1743–72. (c) The Panthéon (formerly the Church of Ste-Geneviève), Paris, J. G. Soufflot, 1755–92.

its appearance in France. Even before 1750, the rather severe façade of St-Sulpice in Paris, constructed (1733–49) after the design of J. N. Servandoni (1695–1766), prefigures the developing preoccupation with the past, while it graphically demonstrates the limited adherence of French architects to the baroque (Fig. 56*d*).

The church of Ste-Geneviève (1755–92) in Paris, secularized at the time of the Revolution and renamed the Panthéon, is perhaps the finest religious building of the century (Figs. 57*c*, 55). Its designer J. G. Soufflot (1713–80) was influenced by the new cult of antiquity, which demanded an architectural sobriety that was the very antithesis of the rococo. The Panthéon with its logical central plan and monumental Roman detail manifests certainly the spirit of the new movement, if not the letter. Soufflot was also sympathetic to English work since his dome has obviously been influenced by that of St. Paul's by Wren.

Soufflot also was acquainted with Gothic architecture, as is evident in the general lightness of construction of the Panthéon. In this final noble religious structure of the century, one may note how various were the sources that fed the broad neoclassical development that continued into the next century. Its dome sums up the grandest phase of 18th-century church building and also provides its epitaph. For the French Revolution, which took from Ste-Geneviève its ecclesiastical status, plunged all Europe into a turmoil hardly conducive to church building.

In conclusion, the age of the rococo was not a period of great religious buildings despite the presence of some admirable productions. The 18th-century church gives pleasure; it entertains the aesthetic sensibilities, if not the soul, but it rarely edifies or induces profound religious feeling.

Bibliography: S. Sitwell, *Southern Baroque Art* (London 1924). A. L. Mayer, "Liturgie und Barock," JbLiturgwiss 15 (1941) 67–154. S. F. Kimball, *The Creation of the Rococo* (Philadelphia 1943). L. Hautecoeur, *Histoire de l'architecture classique en France,* 5 v. in 7 (Paris 1943–57). M. Whiffen, *Stuart and Georgian Churches* (London 1948). P. Keleman, *Baroque and Rococo in Latin America* (New York 1951). S. P. Dorsey, *Early English Churches in America* (New York 1952). H. S. Morrison, *Early American Architecture* (New York 1952). J. N. Summerson, *Architecture in Britain 1530–1830* (4th ed. PelHArt Z3; 1963). R. Wittkower, *Art and Architecture in Italy, 1600–1750* (PelHArt Z16; 1958). G. Kubler and M. Soria, *Art and Architecture in Spain and Portugal and Their American Dominions, 1500–1800* (*ibid.* Z17; 1959). J. Bourke, *Baroque Churches of Central Europe* (2d ed. London 1962). N. Powell, *From Baroque to Rococo* (New York 1959). H. A. Millon, *Baroque and Rococo Architecture* (New York 1961). **Illustration credits:** Fig. 56*a*, The British Travel Association, New York City. Fig. 56*b* and 57*b*, Marburg-Art Reference Bureau. Fig. 56*c*, Alinari-Art Reference Bureau. Fig. 56*d*, 57*c*, and 55, Archives Photographiques, Paris. Fig. 57*a*, MAS, Barcelona.

[J. D. VAN TRUMP]

9. Nineteenth Century

The 19th century, which saw a series of profound changes in Western civilization, as well as its worldwide extension, was also a great church building age. Many churches were erected to serve the needs of the new urban centers created by the industrial revolution. Contemporary scientific thought was often no friend of religion, but numerous religious revivals—notably the Anglican and Roman Catholic in England—occurred during the period. The century evolved many building types to serve a vast new democratic population and yet remained faithful to the Church.

European architecture at the dawn of the new century was still largely classical, but this final broad deposit of the Renaissance tradition contained within itself strong currents moving outward to form new styles; a complex intermingling of innovations and revivals created a maze of stylistic trends. It was a century of unbridled architectural eclecticism.

The cultural romanticism that historically accompanied the democratic age threatened the classical traditions and eventually weakened them. A preoccupation with the medieval past, already manifested in 18th-century thought, increasingly informed the art and literature of the new century. In architecture the Romanesque and particularly the Gothic revivals were the result of this ferment, but styles remote in time or place—Indian, Chinese, or Japanese—also were favored by the romantics.

Greek Revival. The still-dominant classicism at the beginning of the century produced a full-fledged Greek revival that had generally run its course in Europe by 1830, although it did not lose favor in America until 1850. More Greco-Roman than Greek was the church of La Madeleine in Paris, built between 1806 and 1842, after the designs of Pierre Vignon (1763–1828). Originally intended to be a secular Temple de la Gloire, it was converted by Napoleon into a church—the Panthéon situation in reverse (see section 8, above).

The severe temple form of La Madeleine became fashionable also for churches elsewhere in Europe and in America; a rigorous adherence to Greek orders—especially the Doric—was generally maintained. Possibly the best Greek revival church in England is W. and W. H. Inwood's St. Pancras in London (1819–22)—a fine design based on the Erechtheion at Athens. In America also, Greek temple forms prevailed. Perhaps the most successful classical church of the new century in the U.S. was the domed Roman Catholic cathedral of the Assumption at Baltimore, which with the exception of the later added portico was built between 1805 and 1821 according to the design of B. H. *Latrobe (1764–1820). It bears some relation to the work of Sir John Soane in England. As the Greek revival waned, the classicists largely shifted their interest to the Renaissance, but classicism assumed a minor role in the later 19th century as a revived church "style."

Gothic Revival. The Gothic revival, unquestionably the most pervasive of the revival styles, had received considerable impetus in England from the Cambridge Camden (later the Ecclesiological) Society founded in 1839. Of considerable influence also was the work of A. C. and A. W. N. *Pugin, a father and son with a passion for the medieval past and vast knowledge of its Gothic ornament. The classicists did not give up without a struggle, but after the new Houses of Parliament (1840–*c.* 1865) were detailed by A. W. N. Pugin in the late Gothic and Tudor manner, the Gothic, if it did not entirely win the day, became a potent force in Western architecture. Although much used, the revived Gothic was not quite as important on the Continent as it was in England.

It was naturally adaptable to the building of churches and firmly lodged itself in all English-speaking countries. Moreover, it had a strong literary cast, as can be seen in the influence wielded by the *Ecclesiologist* (founded 1841), the magazine of the Ecclesiological Society, and the books written by many revivalist ar-

Fig. 58. Nineteenth-century church architecture: (a) La Madeleine, Paris, 1806–42, Pierre Vignon. (b) St. Pancras, London, 1819–22, W. and W. H. Inwood. (c) All Saints Church, London, 1849–59, William Butterfield.

Fig. 59. The interior of the church of Saint-Eugène, Paris, 1854–55, by the architect L. A. Boileau.

Fig. 60. The church of Sacré-Coeur, Paris, 1874–1900, by the architect Paul Abadie.

chitects. John *Ruskin (1819–1900) advanced his own Italianate version of the revival. The movement was aided in England by the revivals in both the Anglican and Roman Catholic religious bodies. As in the 14th and 15th centuries the Gothic again became an international style (*see* GOTHIC REVIVALISM).

The Gothic revival, through many mutations until its eventual disappearance about the time of World War II, interested a large number of architects. The Pugins reinforced their writing with their practice; they and the Ecclesiologists influenced a notable group of designers, of whom the most original was William Butterfield (1814–1900) and the most popular was Sir George Gilbert Scott (1811–78). The former's All Saints, Margaret Street, London (1849–59) manipulated the Gothic in a fresh if harsh manner, while the latter's Nicholaikirche at Hamburg (1845–63) was an impressive archeological project done with a contemporary flair.

Men of the century were devoted to the archeological restoration of medieval monuments. Eugène *Viollet-le-Duc (1814–79) and Sir G. G. Scott were famous for their activities in this field. During the course of the century many Gothic cathedrals and churches throughout Europe were restored and completed, a notable instance being Cologne Cathedral (1824–80). Meanwhile, on the side of modern technology, cast iron began to be used in churches, as at Saint-Eugène in Paris (1854–55) by L. A. Boileau (1812–96).

Romanesque Revival. A Romanesque revival paralleled the Gothic and produced a pre-Gothic style in which Byzantine and Renaissance elements were sometimes mixed. The new style was aptly christened by the Germans as the "Rundbogenstil." This round-arched style is to be found throughout much of Europe and in

Fig. 61. The interior of Westminster Cathedral, London, looking west along the nave, 1895–1903, J. F. Bentley.

Fig. 62. The Sagrada Familia, Barcelona, by the architect Antonio Gaudí, begun in 1884, and as yet unfinished.

surprising vernacular manifestations in America. Later in the century, the American architect H. H. *Richardson (1834–86) worked in a highly personal Romanesque manner; his best work is Trinity Church, Boston (1873–77), which recalls the Spanish lantern churches of the 12th century. Romanesque-Byzantine style characterized the Sacré-Coeur, Paris (begun in 1874 and largely finished by 1900), by Paul Abadie (1812–44), while London's Westminster Roman Catholic cathedral (1895–1903) by J. F. Bentley (1839–1902) is an impressive building in the Byzantine style.

In America, the two principal early practitioners in the Gothic style were Richard Upjohn (1802–78), whose Trinity Church, New York (1839–46), was inspired by English precedent, and James *Renwick, Jr. (1818–95), whose St. Patrick's Cathedral, New York (1858–79), was derived from French sources. The work of both architects was influential on church building in the U.S.

All the revival styles of the 19th century were continued well into the 20th century until they were replaced by the modern ideas following World War II. Perhaps the fantastic, highly original Gothic-derived church of the Sagrada Familia at Barcelona may be taken as the logical outcome of the Gothic revival. It was designed by Antonio *Gaudí (1852–1926), who took over its construction in 1884. It is still unfinished; but it is probably, as H. R. Hitchcock has said, the grandest ecclesiastical monument that was produced in the late 19th century.

Bibliography: A. C. Pugin, *Examples of Gothic Architecture,* 3 v. (2d ed. London 1838–40; repr. 1930–40). A. W. N. Pugin, *Contrasts: Or, a Parallel between the Noble Edifices of the Fourteenth and Fifteenth Centuries, and Similar Buildings of the Present Day, Showing the Decay of Taste* (London 1836); *An Apology for the Revival of Christian Architecture in England* (London 1843). J. Ruskin, *The Seven Lamps of Architecture* (London 1907; repr. 1932); *Stones of Venice,* ed. L. M. Phillips, 3 v. (New York 1921–27). C. L. Eastlake, *A History of the Gothic Revival* (London 1872). G. W. Shinn, *King's Handbook of Notable Episcopal Churches in the United States* (Boston 1889). K. M. Clark, *The Gothic Revival* (3d ed. New York 1962). B. F. L. Clarke, *Church Builders of the Nineteenth Century* (New York 1938). T. F. Hamlin, *Greek Revival Architecture in America* (New York 1944). D. R. Gwynn, *Lord Shrewsbury, Pugin and the Catholic Revival* (London 1946). G. W. O. Addleshaw and F. Etchells, *The Architectural Setting of Anglican Worship* (London 1948). H. M. Casson, *An Introduction to Victorian Architecture* (New York 1948). J. N. Summerson, *Heavenly Mansions* (New York 1950). R. Turnor, *Nineteenth Century Architecture in Britain* (London 1950). H. S. Goodhart-Rendel, *English Architecture since the Regency* (London 1953). H. R. Hitchcock, *Early Victorian Architecture in Britain,* 2 v. (New Haven 1954); *Architecture: Nineteenth and Twentieth Centuries* (2d ed. PelHArt; 1963). P. Ferriday, ed., *Victorian Architecture* (Philadelphia 1964). **Illustration credits:** Fig. 58*a,* French Embassy Press and Information Division, New York City. Figs. 58*b* and 58*c,* National Monuments Record, London. Fig. 59, Archives Photographiques, Paris. Fig. 60, Pan American Airways. Fig. 61, A. F. Kersting, London. Fig. 62, MAS, Barcelona.

[J. D. VAN TRUMP]

10. Contemporary European

Modern church architecture in Europe has been in the process of developing for a long time. Concepts of form, materials, and techniques, as well as cultural changes and growing liturgical awareness, have participated in this development. Whether the change in ecclesiastical architecture grows more significantly out of alterations in form and material or out of human intellectual, cultural, and spiritual aspirations is variously answered. Architecture in 20th-century Germany was a product of a liturgical and secular renewal, which elaborated in various stages a fresh concept of the Church and of the church building as an ecclesiastical edifice. It employed the most advanced stylistic resources and building techniques. These made possible a new breadth and centripetal articulation of the church interior. A surge of vitality and unprecedented structural ability combined with a rejuvenation of the liturgy.

Fig. 63. Interior of the Stahl Kirche (Evangelical) by the architect Otto Bartning. Erected in Cologne in 1928; it was destroyed by aerial bombing in 1943.

The new building materials (iron, concrete, glass) did not of themselves lead to a new church architecture: in France, Anatole de Baudot (1834–1915) had used reinforced concrete, but the new building materials remained at the outset simply a scaffolding for the traditional styles of architecture (St-Eugène, Paris, 1854, done in cast iron; St-Jean-de-Montmartre, 1894–1902, with moulded vaults). Open steel construction was used by Astruc in Notre-Dame du Travail in Paris (1899–1901), but it was not until 1920–24 that new stylistic use of these building materials was made. The advance occurred when Auguste *Perret designed Notre-Dame du Raincy near Paris, rightly termed the first stylistically modern church in Europe. The altar stands somewhat free on a raised stage, and steel columns support a concrete roof. The exterior walls have abstract light-absorbing ornamentation. Karl *Moser, inspired by the Raincy church, created the church of St. Antonius in Basel as early as 1927.

Unfinished concrete was then introduced as a stylistic element and was adopted and developed, despite many difficulties, by Hans Herkommer and Dominikus *Böhm in Germany. In 1928 Otto Bartning erected the first steel church (Evangelical) with stained glass in Cologne. The suitability of new building materials for sacred edifices remained a subject of controversy for a long time.

Contemporary European architecture began to develop during the period immediately prior to World War II; despite many problems, the liturgical movement gave birth to a new growth, especially in Germany. Since the war, church architecture has been given a deeper theological basis and has experienced a great renewal in every country of Europe.

Liturgical Movement. Opportunely, the liturgical movement, whose initial impulse had been given in the 19th century, had gathered momentum. It had gained impetus with the new Missal of the Benedictine Anselm Schott, who was interested as early as 1884 in the participation of the laity in the Mass. With the additional influence of Pius X, fresh vitality appeared in the liturgy after World War I. Six million Schott Missals had been printed by 1955. A new attitude and liturgical worship service had sprung up in French and Belgian monasteries, and the awakening extended into Germany as well as in such places as Maria Laach and Beuron.

A liturgical trend in church architecture can be detected from about 1910 in the work of Böhm. Even before World War I he had planned chapels to house the often neglected and meanly situated baptismal font, and he moved side altars as far from the principal sanctuary space as possible, to favor the main altar. During

Fig. 64. The Church of Sankt Engelbert, Cologne-Riehl, Germany, by the architect Dominikus Böhm, 1930.

World War I, together with the Benedictine-oriented architect Martin Weber, he drafted the first square church interior (1915). The church, which was to be built in Neu-Ulm, was to have apses for the side altars. The architects placed the baptismal font in the middle of the entrance hall, and brought the altar closer to the people on a raised, circular island. The bell tower on the side was incorporated into the design of the main structure.

Problems of Transition. Architectural forms and designs were strongly influenced by *Ravenna but modified by contemporary trends. German and Austrian architects (e.g., Otto Wagner) had begun to show concern for more space and a gradual abandonment of overloading. The progress represented by their plans and projects can be properly appreciated only when one reflects on the state of affairs that existed: in central Europe, neo-Gothic was considered to be the one proper form of architecture for sacred edifices. Accordingly, the Catholic cathedral of Cologne, the tower of a Protestant cathedral at Ulm, and the basilicas at Lourdes and Lisieux had all been finished in neo-Gothic style. In 1912 the Cologne hierarchy allowed only neo-Romanesque and neo-Gothic structures for ecclesiastical building. It was in 1927 that the Association for Christian Art in Cologne spoke out against the dominance of the old style, and even then it considered reinforced concrete a building material unsuitable for churches. As traditional styles lost popularity, new building materials developed their own potentialities and suggested new designs for churches. In the transitional period, Böhm developed the technique of laid-on hard wall plaster, especially in vaulting, and created the church of St. Engelbert, Cologne-Riehl, 1930. Reinforced concrete, steel, iron, and glass became legitimate building materials between 1925 and 1927. They rendered new ceiling solutions possible and reduced the structural confusion between supporting and space-enclosing elements, between wall and ceiling, thrust and load. The new wide interior with modern design and glass walls began to prevail. A new transparency was added to the breadth of the interior, materializing what Otto Wagner of Vienna had advocated as early as 1895. "Everything modern must correspond to the new material, to the demands of the present, if it is to suit modern man . . .."

In the midst of this transition stood Böhm (1880–1955). His first important designs were executed in 1922 for churches in Dettingen and Vaals (Holland). The latter design, for a Benedictine abbey church, places the tabernacle for the first time in the choir wall; the altar had on it only a cross and candles and was placed in a central location to accommodate the *circumstantes.* He designed also the St. John Baptist church in Neu-Ulm (1926), with its distinct baptismal chapel that influenced later building. After creating the design for Mainz-Bischofsheim (1926), he entered the "Opfergang" competition for the Frauenfriedenskirche in Frankfurt am Main. In this, the largest church architecture competition of the 20th century, Böhm won first prize among 650 competitors, although his design was never realized. His plan called for an enclosed space "with sheer presence" in which the community is led to the impressive place of sacrifice, emphasized by the lighting arrangement. The concept of the altar as central to the Mass had triumphed.

Growth in Germany. New church architecture prevailed in Germany more extensively than in other European countries prior to World War II. Advanced stylistic elements were demonstrated in the Corpus Christi Church in Aachen (1929–30), designed by Rudolf *Schwarz (1897–1961). He based his design on the ground plan of the Frankfurt design, on which he had worked as a collaborator with Böhm. The period from 1925 to 1927 was the moment of greatest innovation and stylistic power in German ecclesiastical architecture; churches were built in Bavaria with money that Cardinal Faulhaber had collected in the U.S. Such fruitful results were made possible by the earlier work of J. van Acken, by the liturgical movement, and by the renewal thought of a portion of the Christians in Germany after World War I. In 1927 *Der Verfall der kirchlichen Kunst* had been published in Germany. This work, by the Swiss artist A. *Cingria, had been published in French in 1917 as *La Decadence de l'art sacré*. It had been welcomed by P. Claudel, who expressed the hope for an encounter between creative imagination, joyous sensuous appeal, and Christianity. Pertinent as his insight was, it was dimmed in the general preoccupation with industrial development and natural science.

In Germany the questions of theology, ideals, form, and material continued to be the subjects of lively discussion. Serious reflection and a new religious attitude influenced architects of many European countries and others in America. Protestants also made intensive efforts to find a genuine church architecture: Otto Bartning was a leader in both his writing and designs. New ideas were being tried by Hans Döllgast, Hans Herkommer, Clemens Holzmeister, J. Krahn, Michael Kurz, Otto-Orlando Kurz, Alfons Leitl, Rudolph Schwarz, Hans Schwippert, and Thomas Wechs.

Meanwhile the liturgical movement received impetus from the abbeys of Maria Laach and Beuron, the Quickborn Youth Movement, and individuals such as R. Guardini, J. Jungmann, K. Kramp, and Bishop Landersdorfer. However, it was not unified and gave few direct impulses to church architecture. One feature that resulted from it, however, was a Christocentric emphasis in church plans in which the altar was detached from the choir wall and set on a raised "stage." As early as 1919, Weber and Böhm had proposed, without success, that altars be erected without tabernacles. Frankfurt am Main developed many remarkable churches after 1925. In the church of the Holy Spirit by Weber (1930), the altar was moved toward the middle of the church, so that it could be surrounded by the faithful, and the tabernacle was put onto a pillar. The trend in religious life and preaching was to accent essentials and to eliminate superfluities and accretions. Thus more attention was given to the altar, the font, and the confessional; side altars and statues of the saints were eliminated. The Stations of the Cross were assigned a less conspicuous place. The church was conceived as the spatial envelope for the altar, which is Christ, and not any longer the static site of the tabernacle.

Between 1927 and 1933 an impressive series of church designs emerged, such as those by Böhm for Leverkusen-Küppersteg, Hindenburg in Upper Saxony, München-Gladbach, Norderney, and Dülmen. Böhm also transferred the site of the choir, hitherto far off to

Fig. 65. Contemporary European church architecture (in Germany): (a and b) Exterior and interior, St. Michael's, Frankfurt, Rudolf Schwarz. (c) St. Andreas, Essen, Rudolf Schwarz. (d) Maria Königin, Saarbrücken, Rudolf Schwarz. (e) Holy Ghost Church, Essen-Katernberg, Gottfried Böhm. (f) St. Laurens Church, Cologne, Emil Steffann.

Fig. 66. The sanctuary of the church of Our Lady, Trier, renovated after World War II by Rudolf Schwarz.

one side in the west, to the chancel. His leading successor was Schwarz, who defended Böhm's ideas in lectures and writings; he proceeded to design interiors of imposing breadth and height. From 1933, the beginning of the Nazi regime, church architecture declined, and was throttled completely during World War II.

There followed a complete change in the European picture. Between 1933 and 1950, churches were built in Switzerland (chiefly in Basel, Lucerne, and Zurich), designed by Hermann Baur of Basel and F. Metzger of Zurich. These were more centralized churches that brought the congregation closer to the altar. Switzerland became the leader for the whole of Europe.

Church architecture experienced a revival after 1950, since many churches had been destroyed and the many new communities needed churches. Between 1950 and 1965, about 8,000 churches, Catholic and Protestant, were either built or remodeled, and others that had been slightly damaged were renovated. The number of gifted church architects grew to include A. von Branca, J. Elfinger, W. Groh, R. Jörg, W. Leonhardt, H. Lill, S. Oestreicher, and S. Ruf, in south Germany; Gottfried Böhm, J. Lehmbrock, F. Schaller, H. Schilling, J. Schürmann, E. Steffann, and R. Schwarz in north Germany. The centripetal church interior was cultivated most successfully by Hans Schädel of Würzburg.

A Deeper Theological Basis. The oppression of Christians from 1933 to 1945 had chastened and ennobled some of the Christian communities. Not only did they pray the Mass along with the priest, as had been the goal of efforts prior to 1933, but in addition the laity became more conscious of their status (1 Pt 2.5, 9; Apoc 1.6; 5.10; 20.6), and their concept of the Church was deepened. The altar was moved even further into the middle of the church, as it had been in primitive Christian worship; the faithful were grouped around the altar on all four sides; and, in the mystery of the Eucharist, stress was laid upon the commemorative sacrifice and the Consecration. Christology received less emphasis; more attention was directed to the Trinity and the entire economy of salvation embracing all of time to Judgment Day.

The long rectangular ground plan was almost completely supplanted by short rectangular, square, parabolic, rhomboidal, circular, polygonal, L-shaped, and T-shaped ground plans.

Unlike the basilicas of early Christian Churches, 20th-century structures developed on the basis of theological rather than secular considerations. Concepts of the relationship of the assembly to the altar have helped determine the planning of sanctuary and congregational space; the attempt has been to realize liturgical worship within the framework of expanded artistic possibilities.

In 1960 the character of the church building as a community assembly room began to be stressed. Since 1965 celebration of Mass facing the people has become general; the tabernacle has come to be housed more frequently in a chapel; and an area with ambo has been created for the liturgy of the Word. Often a slightly elevated seat is placed behind the altar for the priest. This new attitude, derived from the 1965 decrees of *Vatican II, was realized in the church of St. Helen, Munich, designed by Hansjakob Lill, the first church in this style since the council. Until about 1950–55, a strictly architectonic cubic interior with large flat surfaces had dominated modern church architecture; but after a few years, perhaps following the precedent of *Ronchamp, a tendency toward organic forms of spatial articulation began to be manifested. Walls and ceiling assumed a flexibility in flowing contours and a great variety of form and combination of materials. The danger arose that church architecture might degenerate into industrial art, and it stimulated discussion of a crisis in church architecture (1963–65). On the other hand, the freedom of articulation enabled remarkable structures to be erected, with the result that Catholic church architecture has attracted and challenged architects and has come to play a leading part in architecture as a whole. It has also engaged the interest of the decorative arts.

Austria. Because of financial difficulties and the strong hold of tradition, the development of a new church architecture in Austria had proceeded very slowly. Peter Behrens (1868–1940), summoned from Düsseldorf to Vienna, gave it its first impetus. Apart from a few churches by Holzmeister (b. 1886) and Robert Kramreiter (b. 1905), a disciple of Böhm, examples of new church architecture were few. Innovations began on a wide scale only around 1954, even though the liturgical movement had been promoted since 1922 by Canon Pius Parsch (Klosterneuburg). Notable buildings that have been designed include: the church of Christ the King (Gloggnitz, 1963) by C. Holzmeister; Klagenfurt seminary church by K. Holey; structures in Salzburg (1955) and Vienna (1957) by the Group 4 architects; a parish church (Neu-Arzl, Innsbruck, 1961) by J. Lackner; a structural steel church (Donawitz,

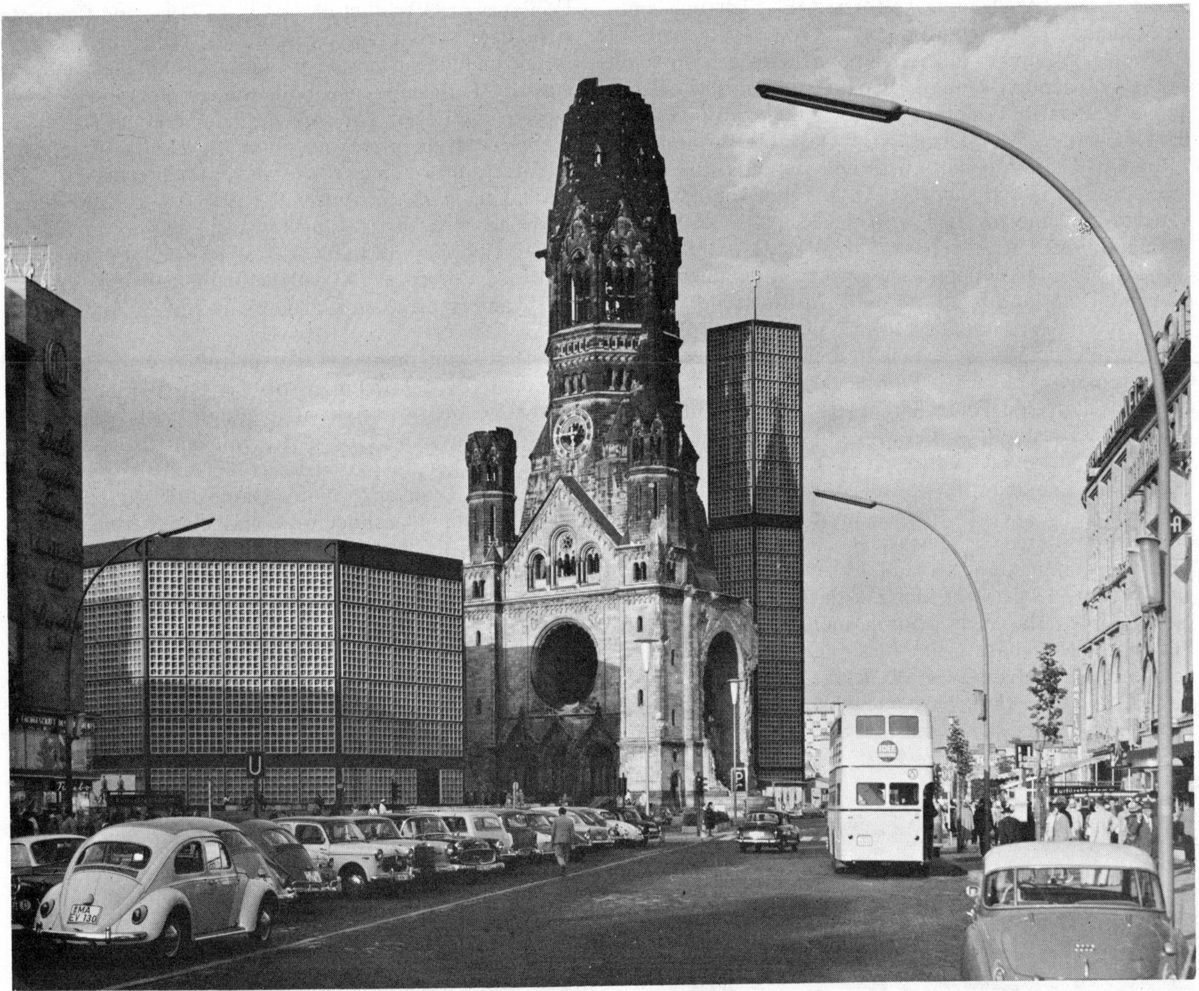

Fig. 67. The Kaiser Wilhelm Memorial Church, Breitscheidplatz, Berlin. The two new structures designed by the architect Egon Eiermann flank the ruins of the older church destroyed during bombing raids in World War II.

1954) by K. Lebwohl and K. Weber; Fatima Church (Graz, 1954) by G. Lippert; Holy Family Church (Kapfenberg-Hafendorf, 1963) by K. Schwanzer; and the chapel of Catholic University (Vienna, 1963) by O. Uhl. Notable work is being produced also by J. C. Gsteu, L. Hurschka, J. Krawina, H. Petermair, W. Schmutzer, and F. Zachhuber.

Italy. Italy was more tradition-bound than Austria, but new forces similar to those in Austria began to stir in 1954. The Bologna National Church Architecture Congress was held in 1955 and presided over by Cardinal Lercaro, a promoter of liturgy and art. In 1956 the Centro di Studio e Informazione per l'Architettura Sacra was founded, and a journal was initiated. A study center was established in Milan, where Cardinal Montini (later Pope Paul VI) promoted church building. Consequently, new Italian church architecture flourished in the industrial centers around Bologna and Milan, while Rome remained traditional. The 1957 competition for design of the shrine of the "Weeping Madonna" in Syracuse attracted a large number of talented architects, some of whom produced impressive designs. Church architecture in Italy moved forward aggressively; representative of its progress was the "highway church" of S. Giovanni a Campi Bisenzio, near Florence, designed by G. Michelucci.

The following Italian architects have been active in the promotion of new church building: E. Canino, P. Carbonara, E. del Debbio, R. Fagnoni, V. Fausto, I. Gardella, G. Gressleri, D. Jannicelli, C. Minniti, E. Montuori, P. Nervi, L. Passarelli, L. Quaroni, M. Righini, V. Rizzi, C. Santuccio, E. Summonte, G. Trebbi, G. Vaccaro, and V. Ziino.

Spain. In Spain the only commissions for new churches were those of Franciscans and especially Dominicans. But Madrid had in Miguel Fisac a leading architect, the first in Europe to promote "dynamic" church architecture, which was later carried forward in France by Le Corbusier and in Germany by Hans Schädel. The Dominican church of Alcobendas in Madrid, designed by Fisac, is impressive from the liturgical point of view. By 1965 there had been erected about 30 new churches, mostly rectangular in plan. The university church in Córdoba and the church of St. Rita in Madrid were both erected on a centripetal plan. Church architects in the 20th-century included: F. Alba, J. L. Fernández del Amo, M. Baldrich, F. Cavestany, Padre F. Coello de Portugal, F. Dampierre, J. García de Paredes, R. de la Hoz, L. Laorga, J. Masramon, J. R. Mijares, A. le Moragas Gallissa, D. Sánchez Puch, J. Puig Torne, M. de los Santos Francisco Robles, J. Saenz de Oiza, J. M. Sevra de Dalmases,

A. de la Sota, V. Temes, A. Teressa, E. *Torroja, and A. Vallejo.

France. A number of French painters toward the end of the 19th century (and more in the 20th century) were active leaders in Christian art: O. *Redon, P. *Puvis de Chavannes, M. *Denis, G. *Desvallières, and G. *Rouault. Church edifices with new building materials were erected in the suburbs of Paris, but the real advancement came in 1922 with the Raincy church designed by A. Perret (*see* RAINCY, NOTRE-DAME DU). Besides being revolutionary in concept, it included windows by Denis and sculpture by E. A. Bourdelle. Many new churches were built in France after World War I, though liturgical and architectural progress was slow. The architect Maurice Novarina designed the church of Notre-Dame de Toutes Graces at *Assy (1938–50). Though less aesthetic on the whole than the later chapel by H. *Matisse at *Vence, it is exceptional for its decorative elements; it was an effort, inspired by the Dominicans, especially P. *Couturier, to create a renaissance of sacred art. Jewish and other non-Catholic artists, including atheists and Communists, were engaged to produce works along with the Catholic artist G. Rouault. The Assy church includes work by P. *Bonnard, M. Chagall, F. *Léger, J. Lipchitz, J. Lurçat, and H. Matisse (see W. Rubin, *Modern Sacred Art and the Church of Assy,* New York 1961). Among Novarina's other structures are the parish church at Le Fayet (1939), that at Vongy (1938), and the more significant Sacred Heart Church at Audincourt (1952), which includes a mosaic façade and baptistery stained glass by J. Bazaine, and both stained glass and a choir tapestry by Léger. The stained glass here and elsewhere represented an improvement in the ability of modern architecture to engage the decorative artist [see D. Grosman, in *Das Münster* 9 (1958) 9–10]. Architecture had been progressing toward a climax in France for several years in the works of P. *Bellot: Our Lady of Peace, Suresnes, 1934; Benedictine convent, Vauves, 1935; and Immaculate Conception Church, Audincourt, 1935.

Fig. 68. Choir and sanctuary of the Dominican seminary church of St. Peter Martyr, Madrid, designed by the architect Miguel Fisac.

After 1939, many circular churches were designed, especially by G. H. Pingusson, for the worker parishes in the "Zone"; the first such designs were realized in Bouts, Corny, and Orsay. A significant thrust forward occurred when Le Corbusier completed the pilgrimage church at *Ronchamp (Notre-Dame du Haut, 1953–55). An astonishing architectural and engineering accomplishment was the ovoid Pius X Basilica at Lourdes (1956–58), designed by Le Donné, P. Vago, and P. Pinsard. New churches continued to be built in France after 1955 by G. Gillet, N. Kazis, R. Lecaisne, M. Lods, M. Marot, G. H. Pingusson, J. Rouquet, and G. Stoskopf and A. Biro.

Belgium and Holland. In Belgium, too, a new church architecture has made significant progress since about 1955. Designs for liturgical appurtenances and sacred vessels in particular have shown an interesting appropriateness. In regard to it, the Benedictine Abbey of St. Andrew, Bruges, publishes the journal, *Art d'Église.* In Holland the various Christian confessions have exercised an influence on new church styles, though not to the same extent as in Germany.

Bibliography: H. SCHNELL, *Zur Situation der christlichen Kunst der Gegenwart* (Munich 1962). X. VON HORNSTEIN, *St. Antonius, Basel* (Munich 1936). A. HOFF et al., *Dominikus Böhm* (Munich 1962). R. SCHWARZ, *The Church Incarnate: The Sacred Function of Christian Architecture,* tr. C. HARRIS (Chicago 1958); *Von der Bebauung der Erde* (Heidelberg 1949); *Kirchenbau* (Heidelberg 1960). J. VAN ACKEN, *Christozentrische Kirchenkunst* (2d ed. Gladbeck i. W. 1923). O. BARTNING, *Vom neuen Kirchbau* (Berlin 1919); *Vom Raum der Kirche* (Bramsche bei Osnabrück 1958). H. BAUR et al., *Kirchenbauten* (Zurich 1956). For modern Swiss church architecture, see the periodicals *Das Werk* (Winterthur 1914–) and *Das Münster.* R. HESS, *Neue kirchliche Kunst in der Schweiz* (Zurich 1962). For current reports on German, European, and other church architecture, see *Das Münster,* ed. H. SCHNELL (Munich 1947–), 6 issues yearly, well illus., the only German pub. in this field, with Eng., Fr., and Span. résumés. For up to 1937, see *Die christliche Kunst* (Munich 1904–37) and the yearbooks of the *Deutsche Gesellschaft für christliche Kunst* (Munich, to 1937, 1951–56). R. GROSCHE, "Überlegungen zur Theorie des Kirchenbaues," *Das Münster* 13 (1960) 344–349. H. SCHNELL, "Der neue Kirchenbau und die Konzilsberatungen," ThGlaube 53 (1963) 292–299; "Zur Konstitution des II. Vatikanischen Konzils über Liturgie und Kunst," *Das Münster* 17 (1964) 60–64. General surveys of German church architecture since 1948, in A. HENZE and T. FILTHAUT, *Contemporary Church Art,* ed. M. LAVANOUX, tr. C. HASTINGS (New Yorrk 1956), new ed. and illus. as *Neue kirchliche Kunst* (Recklinghausen 1958). R. JASPERT, ed., *Handbuch moderner Architektur* (Berlin 1957), with contributions by W. WEYRES on Catholic church architecture, and by G. LANGMAACK on Protestant. W. WEYRES, *Neue Kirchen im Erzbistum Köln 1945–56* (Düsseldorf 1957). W. WEYRES and O. BARTNING, eds., *Kirchen: Handbuch für den Kirchenbau* (Munich 1959), most comprehensive survey next to *Das Münster.* Exhibition catalogues by H. SCHNELL et al., *Arte liturgica in Germania: 1945–55* (Munich 1956); *Kirchenbau der Gegenwart in Deutschland* (Munich 1960). C. HOLZMEISTER, *Kirchenbau ewig neu* (Innsbruck 1951). R. KRAMREITER and P. PARSCH, *Neue Kirchendunst*

Fig. 69. Contemporary European church architecture: (a) Vuoksenniska Church (Lutheran), Vuoksenniska, Imatra, Finland, by Alvar Aalto. (b) Pilgrimage church of Notre-Dame du Haut, Ronchamp, France, Le Corbusier.

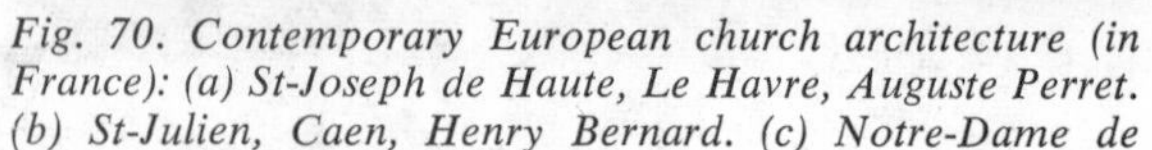

Fig. 70. Contemporary European church architecture (in France): (a) St-Joseph de Haute, Le Havre, Auguste Perret. (b) St-Julien, Caen, Henry Bernard. (c) Notre-Dame de Royan, Guillaume Gillet. (d) Maizières-les-Metz, Jean Rouquet. (e) Notre-Dame des Neiges, Mureaux, G. Stoskopf and A. Biro. (f) Sacré-Coeur, Mulhouse, Alsace, Le Donné.

im Geist der Liturgie (Vienna 1939). E. WIDDER, *Zeichen des Heils: Kirchenkunst der Gegenwart in Österreich* (Linz 1963). *Das Münster* 8.3–4 (1955), 17.7–8 (1964), special issues. *Der grosse Entschluss* (1946–), monthly, each issue contains a brief contribution by H. MUCK on contemporary Christian art. *Chiesa e quartiere* (Bologna 1957–), quarterly, ed. G. GRESLERI, esp. on northern Italy. *Dieci anni di archittetura sacra in Italia: 1945–1955,* ed. L. GHERARDI (Bologna 1956). *Fede e arte* (Rome 1953–), ed. G. FALLANI. *Cancelleria,* Vatican art journal. F. MORALES, *Arquitectura religiosa de Miguel Fisac* (Madrid 1960). Survey in A. FERNANDEZ ARENAS, *Iglesias nuevas en España* (Barcelona 1963), illus. *L'Art sacré* (1935–), monthly. *Art chrétien* (1934–), quarterly, illus. surveys of new churches in individual dioceses, with bibliogs. P. RÉGAMEY, *Religious Art in the Twentieth Century* (New York 1963). *Art d'Église* (Bruges 1927–), trimestrally, on Belgian and European Christian art. U. Hård af Segerstad, *Nya kyrkor i Skandinavien* (Stockholm 1962). Surveys on European Churches in F. PFAMMATER, *Betonkirchen* (Einsiedeln 1948). J. PICHARD, *Modern Church Architecture,* tr. E. CALLMANN (New York 1960). G. E. KIDDER-SMITH, *The New Churches of Europe* (New York 1964). *Christliche Kunst der Gegenwart* (Salzburg 1956–), biennial. **Illustration credits:** Fig. 64, Helga Schmidt-Glassner. Figs. 65 and 68, Courtesy, *Das Münster.* Figs. 67 and 69*a,* G. E. Kidder Smith. Fig. 69*b,* Ezra Stoller Associates. Fig. 70, Courtesy, *Art Chrétien.*

[H. SCHNELL]

11. AMERICAN

American church architecture may be discussed according to three main periods: colonial and missionary times, the 19th century, and the 20th century.

Colonial and Missionary Times. Church architecture in early America shows different influences in the three major areas of European settlement: Canada, which was settled by the French; the Southwest, colonized by the Spanish; and the Atlantic Coast, built up by the English. Gradually, in these sections, indigenous styles evolved.

Spanish Influence. The first Mass in the New World was celebrated in 1494; and as the colonists spread westward, missionary priests went also, building churches over a period of 300 years in Mexico and regions now known as Florida, Texas, New Mexico, Arizona, Kansas, and California. Influences in Mexico of Spanish baroque, Gothic, Aztec, and Miztec produced buildings of simple basilican form, with thick stone or adobe walls and rich interior decoration. The monastery church at Huejotzingo (1544–71) is an example, but by 1700 the mixture of indigenous styles had produced the flamboyant richness of churches such as Santo Domingo at San Cristobal las Casas, with domes, elaborately carved façade, and ornate interiors. In California, Arizona, and New Mexico, owing to the poverty of the people, the use of adobe for construction limited building to that of squat boxlike structures with low bell towers and roofs of thatch on poles, reflecting the building tradition of the Pueblo Indians. As Spanish baroque influence increased, forms became more elaborate and sanctuary walls more ornate; but there was no counterpart to the elaborate stone carving of Mexican churches. Thus began the mission styles whose later development included churches in California at Carmel, San Francisco (Mission Dolores), and San Juan Bautista; these are buildings with a long history of demolition and restoration, whose formal influence is still felt on the West Coast. (For further illustrations, *see* MISSIONS IN COLONIAL AMERICA, I, 4.)

French Influence. Missionaries in the New France built early churches of wood, stone, straw, and poles, from Quebec to the Great Lakes and southward; but by the 18th century they too had developed a style. It originated in the dependence on local materials and climate, in the building craft of Normandy, and in the architectural taste of the Île-de-France. A typical example is the small church of St. Laurent, Île d'Orleans (1708), with its Latin-cross plan, steeply pitched roof, low stone walls, roundheaded windows and doors, and a two-level wooden belfry. This development was attributable also to the efforts of the famed Bishop Laval of Quebec (1622–1708) and the architects Claude Baillief

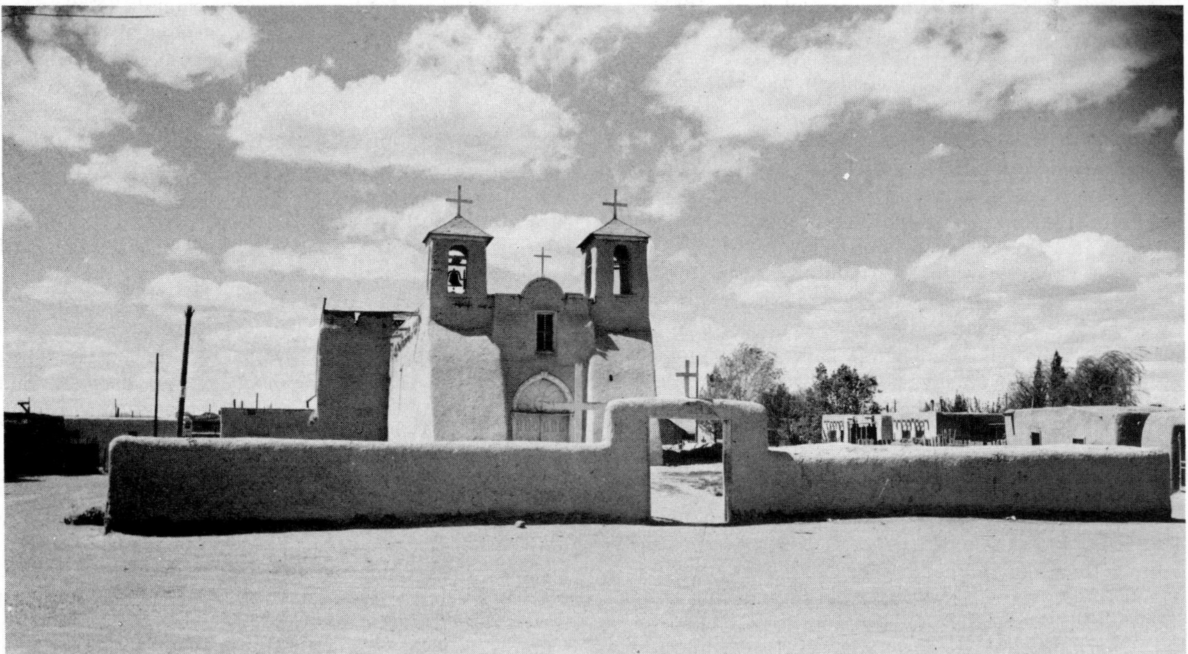

Fig. 71. The church of San Francisco de Ranchos de Taos, N.Mex., built 1805 to 1815, for the then-new Spanish settlement. Even though a 19th-century building, it reflects the ancient building style of the Pueblo Indians.

Fig. 72. St. Laurent Church, Île d'Orleans, Quebec, Canada, built 1708, now destroyed.

(1635–98) and Jean Baillargé (1726–1805). While New France was still a mission, Laval had many churches built, and from examples such as Lachenaie (1724) grew the restrained exteriors and exuberantly decorated interiors that became popular in 18th- and 19th-century Canada.

English Colonies along the Atlantic Coast. Catholics were few among the early settlers, most of whom were either Anglicans or dissenting Protestant sects seeking religious freedom. Their buildings reflected their differences in attitude and worship. The Anglicans, keeping a firm tie with the Eucharistic liturgy of the motherland, retained the English hierarchical plan with nave, rood-screen, chancel, choir, table, and lectern. The dissenters, on the other hand, gathered around the pulpit or lectern in an almost square space, emphasizing communal worship and the Word. Anglican churches, like those of England, were of stone or brick, with a bell tower as in St. Luke's, Smithfield, Va. (1682); but the meeting houses were usually clapboarded timber structures such as the Old Ship Meeting House at Hingham, Mass. (1681), generating a style identified only with America. Later the styles overlapped; St. Paul's, Wickford, R.I., was an Anglican meeting house, and the Old South Meeting House in Boston had a very English (Gibbsian) spire. The establishment of Maryland by Lord Baltimore (a convert to Catholicism) gave immigrant Catholics a base in the colonies, but the successive enactment and repeal of tolerance laws, with alternating freedom and oppression, gave this minority little opportunity for substantial church building. Survival was more urgent, and their first real contribution had to wait 150 years. James *Gibbs, in *A Book of Architecture* (1728), spread the formal ideas of English Georgian churches rapidly in North America. The carefully proportioned spires, classical portico, Palladian details, roundheaded windows, and ornate lightsome interiors inspired, among others, Christ Church, Philadelphia (Anglican, 1729–54); the First Baptist Meeting House, Providence, R.I. (1778); and the Anglican cathedral in Quebec (1804). The last mentioned was modeled on St. Martin-in-the-Fields, London, a contrast with the French Gothic tendencies of Catholics in New France.

The 19th Century. A wide range of stylistic directions flourished after the Revolution. Presidents Washington and Jefferson advocated use of classical Roman and Greek forms in architecture. Gibbs Georgian flourished in New England with the advent of design manuals such as carpenters' notebooks by Asher Benjamin and others. At mid-century the Gothic revival stimulated by the work of Augustus Welby *Pugin in England became the accepted ecclesiastical style. H. H. *Richardson countered this with a short-lived eclectic Romanesque period in Victorian times. Meanwhile the steel frame shaped Chicago's secular buildings away from the style of the church, and modern architecture and the skyscraper were born. Vast immigration increased the number of Catholics and the demand for churches. Great Catholic architects emerged.

In 1806 Bp. John Carroll consecrated Benjamin *Latrobe's Catholic cathedral at Baltimore, a classical building modeled on the Pantheon, and described by historian Henry Russell Hitchcock as the first masterpiece of American architecture. Bishop Carroll, choosing the most talented architect available, departed from Georgian precedent to develop a liturgical solution in which the choir formed a crescent behind the altar and the great dome united the people spatially with the priest. Many Catholic cathedrals followed with the rapid growth of the Church, and the early ones were decidedly neoclassical with occasional Georgian exceptions. Plans compromised between the architecture of the Anglican Church and the meeting house. The altar, sometimes placed against an end wall lacking even an apse, but clearly visible, reflected, perhaps, the desire for lay participation voiced by Bp. A. *Maréchal of Baltimore in 1822 and the earlier plea by John Carroll for use of the vernacular in the Mass (1778). Examples are at Bardstown, Ky., by John Rogers (1816); Old St. Louis Cathedral (1818) by Morton and Laveille; Letourneau's Old St. Peter's, Detroit (1841); and Henry Walters' St. Peter in Chains, Cincinnati (1845). But styles varied across the country, from Pedro Huizar's Mission San Jose in San Antonio, Tex. (1800; Spanish baroque), and the square wooden Russian church at Fort Ross, Calif. (1828), to the Egyptian revival of Minard Lafever's "Whalers' Church" at Sag Harbor, N.Y. (1844); from the "paste-board" Gothic of Notre Dame, Montreal, by James O'Donnell (1829) to the serene classical temple of the First Presbyterian Church at Princeton, N.J. (1836).

Maximilian *Godefroy's neo-Gothic chapel for St. Mary's Seminary in Baltimore (1806), contemporary

(a)

(b)

(c)

(d)

Fig. 73. American church architecture: (a) St. Luke's, Smithfield, Va., 1682. (b) Old Ship Meeting House, Hingham, Mass., 1681. (c) Christ Church, Philadelphia, 1729 to 1754. (d) Baptist Meeting House, Providence, R.I., 1778.

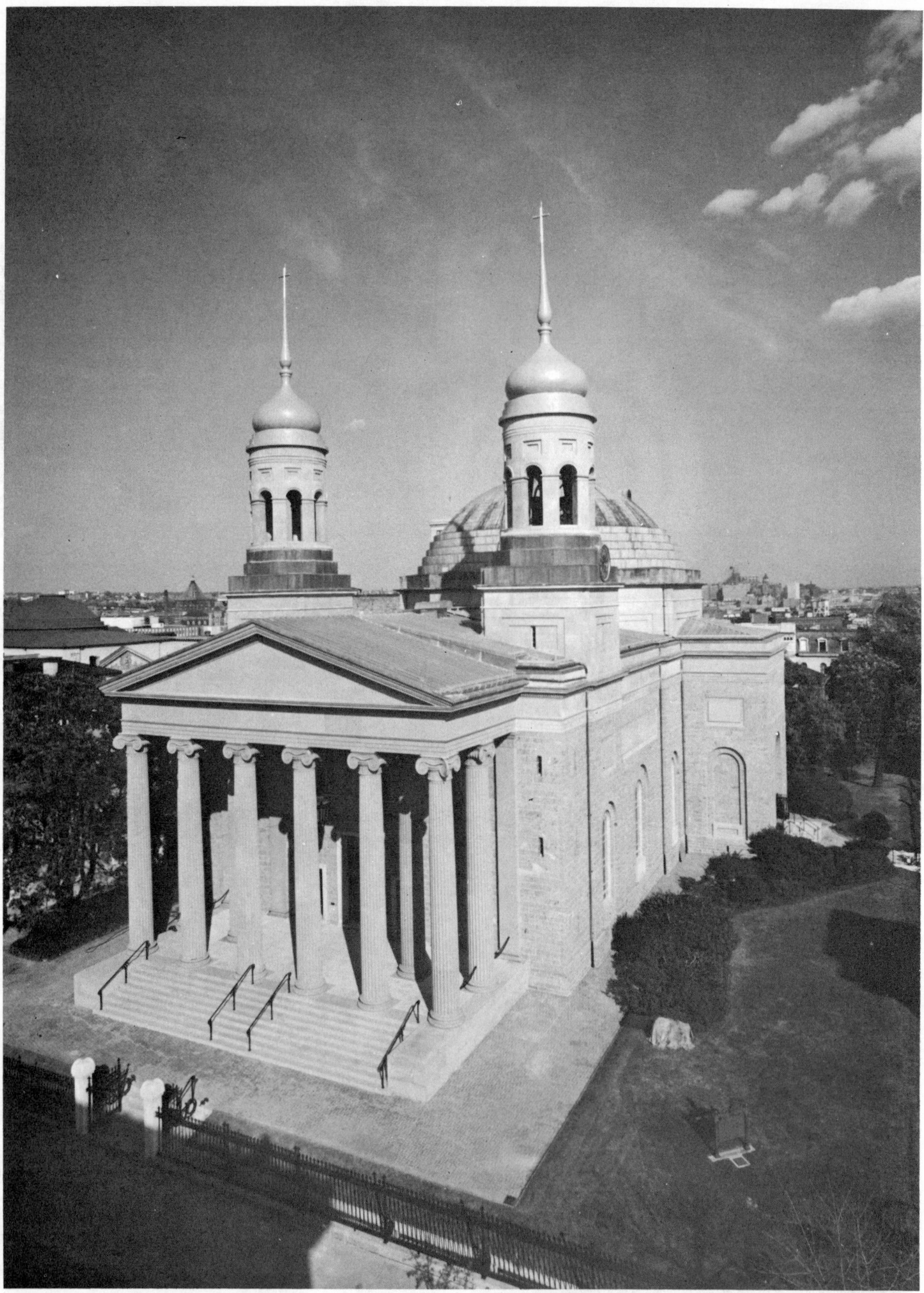

Fig. 74. Old cathedral (Basilica of the Assumption of the Blessed Virgin Mary), Baltimore, Benjamin Latrobe, 1806.

with Latrobe's great cathedral, was the small beginning of a great and widespread stylistic development. In 1846 Richard Upjohn's Anglican Trinity Church, and James Renwick's Grace Church, both in New York, established Gothic as the ecclesiastical style of the day, thus following the English example of Pugin; Upjohn's "rural architecture" provided models for Gothic chapels as far west as California. Further, the Oxford Movement in 1833 and the Cambridge ecclesiologists in 1841 in England stimulated a new interest in the richness of medieval liturgy. The first Catholic response was in SS. Peter and Paul, Brooklyn, N.Y. (1848), by Patrick *Keely, who designed hundreds of churches, including Holy Cross Cathedral, Boston (1867). In 1858 James Renwick built St. Patrick's, New York, perhaps the best of Catholic contributions. The ultimate leader of the movement was Ralph Adams *Cram, whose churches from 1890 to 1936, including St. Thomas (Episcopal), New York (1907), the chapel at West Point Military Academy (1907), and the redesign of St. John the Divine Cathedral, New York, illustrated his faith in English Perpendicular Gothic as the perfect frame for the liturgy. The soaring pinnacles and vaults of Gothic, with its long narrow nave, rood-screen, and deep chancel with the choir before the altar, became the symbol of High-Church building in America. Its influence was felt even in such structures as the Jewish temple in Cincinnati (1866).

The great H. H. Richardson established a rival Victorian trend in his neo-Romanesque Trinity Church at Boston (1873), which returned to the semicircular choir around the altar, and his Albany cathedral project of 1882, a trend that Cram denounced as being Low-Church but that many Catholic architects later followed. Toward the century's end, Catholic churches tended in many stylistic directions, Renaissance, Italianate, colonial revival, etc., perhaps because of two factors: (1) the great influx (5 million between 1815 and 1860) of Catholic immigrants of diverse nationalities demanded many new buildings in which expediency took precedence over liturgy or architecture; (2) the activities of nativist groups (Know-Nothings, etc.) in persecution of religious foreigners generated in the immigrants the desire to be accepted as established citizens and to conform, in architecture, to local fashion. Powerful architecture was readily seen as a status symbol.

The 20th Century. Frank Lloyd Wright's Unity Temple, Chicago (1906), can be considered America's first modern church, for it departed from axial planning and used nonderivative forms in poured concrete. The First Church of Christ Scientist, Berkeley, Calif. (1912), by Bernard Maybeck, despite Gothic elements, was avant-garde in its space arrangement, its hollow columns containing service ducts, and its creative use of industrial materials. Popular taste, however, had been affected by the neoclassical styles of the Chicago World's Fair (1893) and the plastic baroque of the San Diego exposition (1915), both of which added to the 19th-century stylistic heritage. Early 20th-century Catholic cathedrals were thus Gothic, Romanesque, Renaissance, Byzantine, baroque, and eclectic, the range including Halifax, Nova Scotia, by Cram; Seattle, Wash., by Maginnis and Walsh; St. Louis, Mo., by Barnett, Haynes, and Barnett; St. Paul, Minn., by Masqueray; and Los Angeles, Calif., by Maginnis and Walsh. The early Christian basilica inspired McKim, Mead, and

Fig. 75. First Presbyterian Church, Princeton, N.J., 1836.

White's Madison Square Presbyterian Church in New York City (1906) and St. John's Catholic Church at North Cambridge, Mass., by Maginnis and Walsh (1905).

The Early Liturgical Movement. A major factor in rescuing church building from the expensive romance with the past was a rising consciousness of the role of liturgy in community worship. The 1903 and 1905 encyclical letters of Pope St. Pius X encouraging greater lay participation in the Mass received little architectural response in America, except in a few remodeled churches of the Paulist Fathers. The later recognition of liturgical study and reform as the key to a new church architecture owes much to the work of the Benedictines at Collegeville, Minn., beginning with Dom Virgil *Michel, who in 1925 had studied new directions in Europe. The *Liturgical Arts Society, New York, founded in 1928, and the annual liturgical weeks, begun in Chicago in 1940, also helped to develop architecture that recognized the pastoral nature of the liturgy. In addition, the Immigration Bill of 1921 curtailed the influx of European Catholics and allowed the Church more time to reexamine its social, liturgical and architectural situation.

Early response among architects emphasized the visual primacy and accessibility of the altar and the elimination of excessive ornament, as in Barry Byrne's church of Christ the King, Tulsa, Okla. (1927), where the sanctuary projects into a short but wide, column-free nave. This contrasted with the monumentality of the National Shrine of the Immaculate Conception (1928–62) and the neo-Renaissance Trinity College chapel (1928), both by Maginnis and Walsh, in Washington, D.C.

Postwar Years. After World War II there was an urgent demand for churches. New techniques were tried, and experiments in form were launched by a host of talented young architects. Even in the war years, new directions emerged. The elimination of all touches of antiquarianism occurred in three new churches built in 1940 and 1941. Paul Thiry's church of Our Lady of the Lake, Seattle, Wash. (1941), and the *Saarinens' Tabernacle Church of Christ, Columbus, Ind. (1941), relied on an austere organization of light and proportions in modern structural materials. Even more radical was Paul Schweikher's Third Unitarian Church in Chicago (1940), a brick box whose formal origins were more secular than ecclesiastical. The latter fore-

AMERICAN
CHURCH
ARCHITECTURE

Fig. 76. American church architecture: (a) Trinity Church, New York, R. Upjohn, 1846. (b) Cathedral of the Holy Cross, Boston, P. C. Keely, 1867 to 1875, lithograph, 1871. (c) Trinity Church, Boston, H. H. Richardson, 1873.

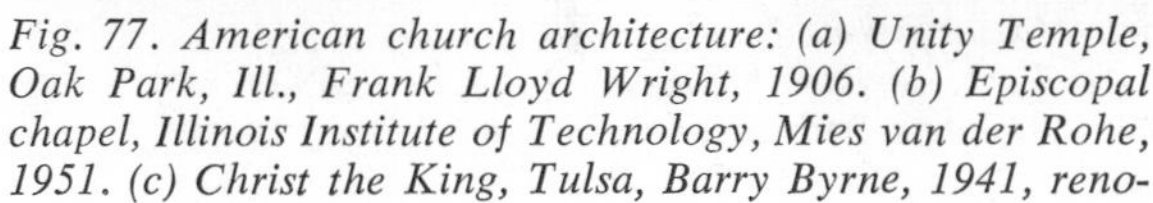

Fig. 77. American church architecture: (a) Unity Temple, Oak Park, Ill., Frank Lloyd Wright, 1906. (b) Episcopal chapel, Illinois Institute of Technology, Mies van der Rohe, 1951. (c) Christ the King, Tulsa, Barry Byrne, 1941, renovated 1964. (d) Church of the Resurrection, St. Louis, Murphy and Mackey, 1954. (e) St. Mark's, Burlington, Vt., Freeman, French, and Freeman, 1943. (f) St. Anthony's, Superior, Wis., Cerny Associates, 1960.

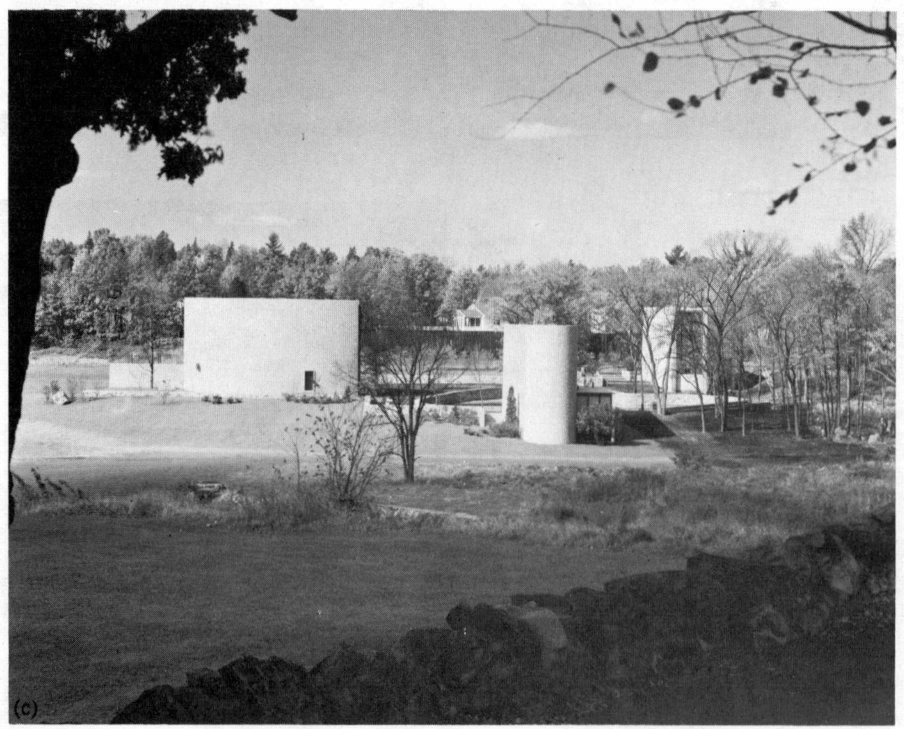

Fig. 78. American church architecture: (a) Chapel, Massachusetts Institute of Technology, Cambridge, Mass., Eero Saarinen, 1959. (b) U.S. Air Force Academy chapel, Colo., Walter Netsch, 1962. (c) Interfaith Center chapel complex, Brandeis University, Waltham, Mass., Harrison and Abramovitz, 1959.

shadowed sophisticated developments of the "rectangular box" church in Mies van der Rohe's serene Episcopal Chapel of brick, steel, and glass at the Illinois Institute of Technology, Chicago (1951); Schweikher's own First Universalist Church, Chicago (1956); and Ralph Rapson's Lutheran Chapel for the Deaf, St. Paul, Minn. (1961). Early attempts to ensure maximum lay participation resulted in St. Mark's, Burlington, Vt. (1943), by Freeman, French, and Freeman, a Greek-cross plan with seats on three sides of the altar, the choir on the fourth. A similar early attempt was St. Clement's (Episcopal), Alexandria, Va. (1947), by Joseph Saunders, which has seats on two sides of an axis linking the entry, font, altar, and pulpit. Fan-shaped plans focusing on the sanctuary were used in Joseph Murphy's Church of the Resurrection, St. Louis, Mo., (1954), Maynard Lyndon's Christian Science Church, Los Angeles, Calif. (1956), and Paul Thiry's semicircular church of Christ the King, Seattle, Wash. (1957). All of these exploited the plasticity and freedom of concrete construction. The altar was completely surrounded by seats in Olaf Hammarstrom's square wooden church (Episcopal, 1954) at Wellfleet, Mass., and in C. F. Wright's octagonal church of the Blessed Sacrament at Holyoke, Mass. (1954). Finally, the church became a circular tent at St. Peter's, Linda del Mar, Calif. (1962), by Mario Ciampi, and at the Benedictine priory church, St. Louis, Mo. (1963), by Hellmuth, Obata, and Kassabaum. The latter, a pyramid of parabolic shells, flooding the sanctuary with light, presents a new nonhistoricist symbolism, but poses visual and acoustic difficulties for preachers. New ways of enclosing worship space generated a new concern with formal symbolism. Frank Lloyd Wright's Unitarian church at Madison, Wis. (1951), had a roof modeled on "hands in the attitude of prayer." Barry Byrne's St. Francis Xavier Church at Kansas City, Mo. (1951), and the Stamford, Conn., Presbyterian Church by Max Abramovitz (1958) were shaped like the fish-symbol of the early Christians. Victor Lundy's church designs have been likened to "petals of a giant tropical wallflower" and a "bird about to take flight." Light, as a shaper of space, determined the sophisticated square geometry of Philip Johnson's synagogue at Port Chester, New York (1957), and Louis Kahn's magnificant Unitarian church at Rochester, N.Y. (1962). The desire for an atmosphere conducive to meditation produced Saarinen's small, cylindrical, brick chapel at Massachusetts Institute of Technology (1959). Form took precedence over liturgy in Walter Netsch's Air Force Academy chapel, Colo. (1962), where 150-foot spires of aluminum and stained glass enclose a long rectangular nave for Protestants, with Jewish and Catholic chapels beneath. In contrast to this, and earlier, was Max Abramovitz's Interfaith Center at Brandeis University, Waltham, Mass. (1959), where three concrete chapels almost similar in plan, grouped around a pool, emphasize at once the common and different aspects of three modes of worship.

Liturgical Renewal. The diverse forms of the 1950s gave way to more liturgy-conscious designs in the 1960s. A considerable amount of interdenominational study began, helped by the writings of Rudolf *Schwarz (Germany), Peter Hammond (England), and Father H. A. Reinhold (U.S.). The 1957 liturgical directives of the Catholic Archdiocese of Superior, Wis., modeled on a

Fig. 79. Benedictine priory church, St. Louis, Mo., Hellmuth, Obata, and Kassabaum, architects, 1962.

1947 publication by the bishops of Germany, raised new questions about liturgical planning in the light of modern theology and directly influenced the design of St. Anthony's, Superior (1960), by Thorsov and Cerny. There the concrete nave was short and wide; the choir stood beside the sanctuary; the pulpit became a simple lectern near the altar; and the font, symbolic of entrance, stood in an ample narthex, which also contained confessionals.

Liturgy was the chief determinant in the planning also of St. Patrick's, Oklahoma City (1960), by Robert Jones, where the glass-walled nave extends visually into a high surrounding concrete-walled atrium providing for overflow congregations. The influence of liturgy in planning is noticeable also in Pietro Belluschi's Episcopal church of the Redeemer, Baltimore, Md. (1960), an elegant cruciform wood structure, whose modern form has vague echoes of the Gothic; Belluschi's Benedictine priory at Portsmouth, R.I. (1962); and Robert Olwell's shallow-domed, circular Greek Orthodox church at Oakland, Calif. (1962).

In Canada, the church of St. Maurice, Duvernay, Quebec (1963), by Roger d'Astons, and the church of the Canadian Martyrs, St. Boniface, Manitoba (1962), by J. Gaboury, show innovation: the celebrant of the Mass faces the people, the choir is near the sanctuary, and there is a separate altar of reservation. St. Rose of Lima Church, Ste. Rose du Lac, Manitoba (1962), by Green, Blankenstein, and Russell, groups people on three sides of the altar in a small square space, an arrangement that follows the new trend in Europe.

Marcel Breuer's Benedictine abbey church at St. John's, Collegeville, Minn., the first modern church to rival the scale and majesty of the 19th-century neo-Gothic cathedrals, also grew from strictly liturgical considerations. Its vast folded-concrete structure encloses a sanctuary that visually unites the crescent choir with the congregation. The traditional communion rail is replaced by stations at the head of processional aisles; the ambos, central altar, and abbot's seat are all well

Fig. 80. The interior of the St. John's abbey church, Collegeville, Minn., Marcel Breuer, architect, 1962.

positioned to symbolize their liturgical roles. Church architecture in the early 1960s includes such widely contrasting types as the Episcopal and Catholic cathedrals in San Francisco. The neo-Norman Grace Cathedral (Episcopal), with its golden replica of Ghiberti's famous baptistery door in Florence and its altar now moved to a central position, was completed in 1964. Belluschi and Nervi's new Catholic cathedral has a diamond-shaped, column-free plan with central altar. Its great prestressed, marble-clad concrete roof-walls twist up to 180 feet in space to form a Greek-cross skylight. The San Francisco cathedral represents an approach far different from the long medieval plan (1954) for the new Baltimore Catholic cathedral by Maginnis and Walsh.

A research program in church architecture instituted by the American Institute of Architects in 1963 resulted in interfaith discussions by representatives of all faiths, on theology, liturgy, sociology, aesthetics, technology, and city planning and in the publication of clear descriptions of the liturgical structure of all participant churches. This exemplifies a new approach to church design, but the *Constitution on the Sacred Liturgy* issued by Vatican Council II has since become a prerequisite to the design of Catholic churches. The emphasis on the liturgy of the Word as a clearly defined part of the Mass, the clarification of the choir's role, the stress on the significance of Mass with the celebrant facing the people at Mass, and above all the pastoral and ecumenical overtones mark it as the single document that may ultimately lead to a clearly ordered 20th-century church architecture.

See also LITURGICAL ART; MONASTIC ART AND ARCHITECTURE.

Bibliography: H. S. MORRISON, *Early American Architecture* (New York 1952). W. ANDREWS, *Architecture, Ambition and Americans* (New York 1955; pa. New York 1964); *Architecture in America* (New York 1960). T. F. HAMLIN, *Greek Revival Architecture in America* (New York 1944); *Benjamin Henry Latrobe* (New York 1955). H. R. HITCHCOCK, *Architecture: 19th and 20th Centuries* (2d ed. PelHArt Z15; 1963); *Architecture*

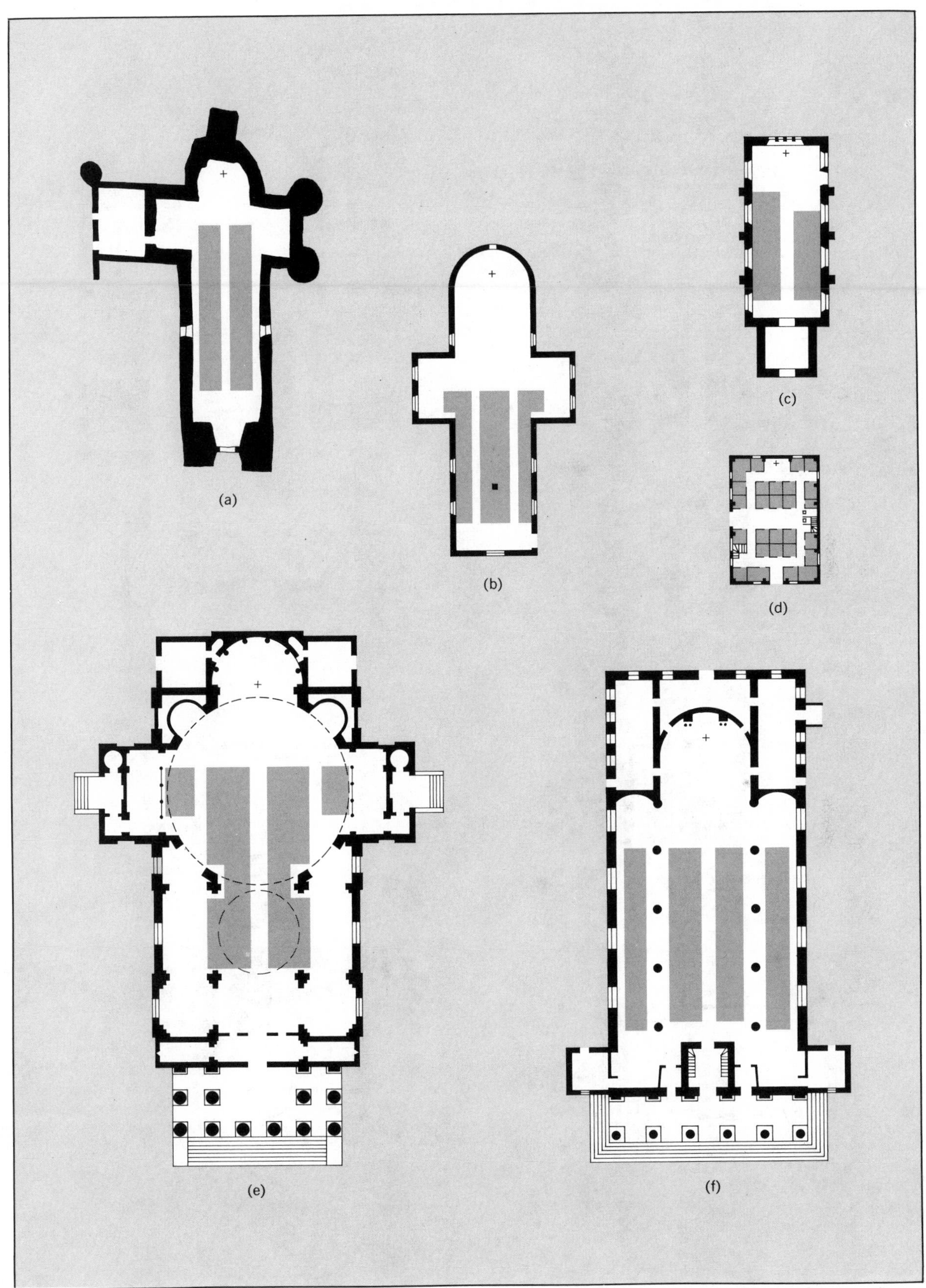

Fig. 81. American church architecture (comparative plans, all at the same scale): (a) San Francisco de Ranchos de Taos, N.Mex., 1805 to 1815. (b) St. Laurent, Île d'Orleans, 1708. (c) St. Luke's, Smithfield, Va., 1632. (d) St. Paul's, Wickford, R.I. (e) Assumption Basilica, Baltimore, 1806. (f) St. Joseph's Cathedral, Bardstown, Ky., 1816.

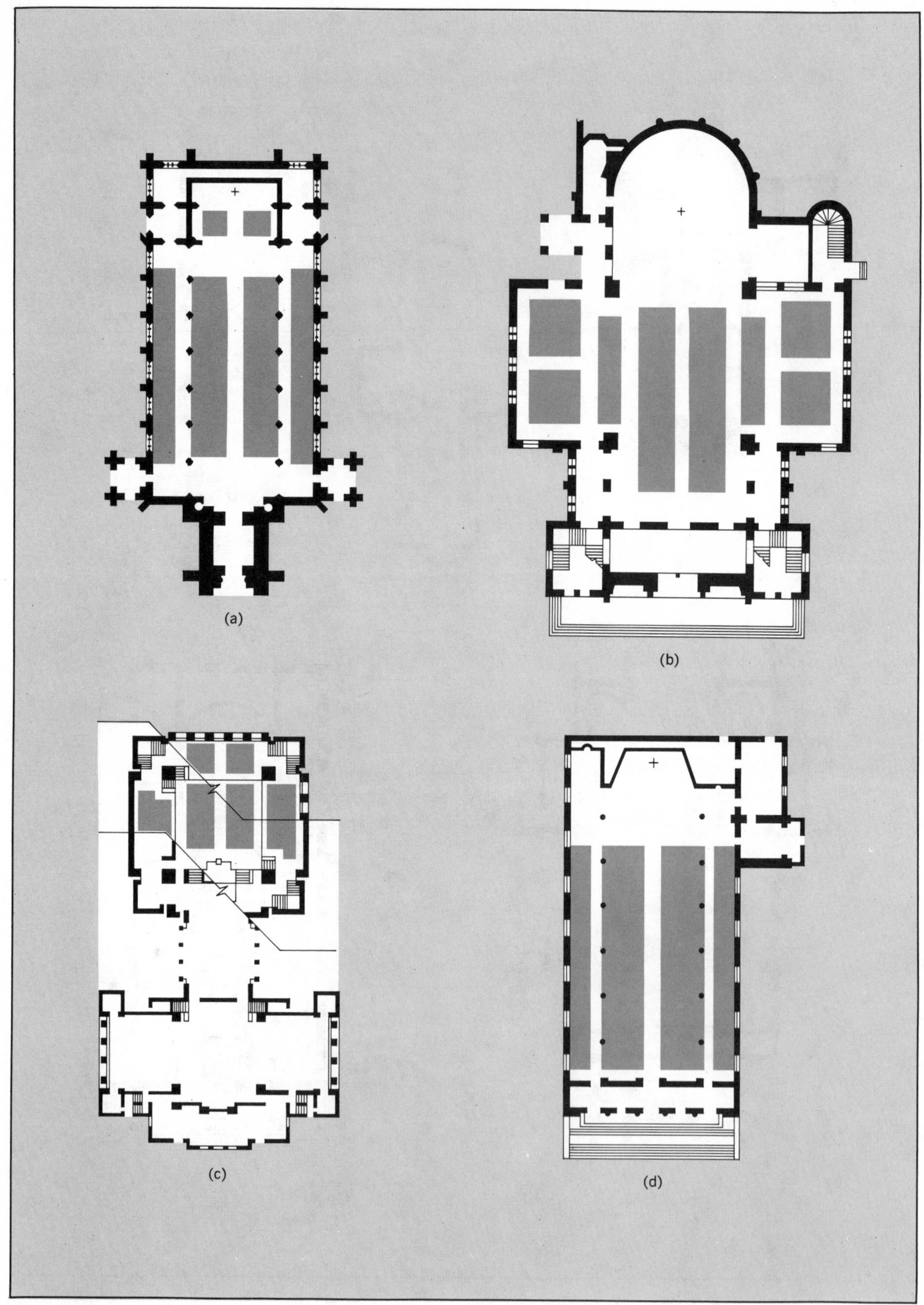

Fig. 82. American church architecture: (a) Trinity Church, New York City, 1846. (b) Trinity Church, Boston, 1873. (c) Unity Temple, Oak Park, Ill., 1906. (d) St. John's, North Cambridge, Mass., 1905.

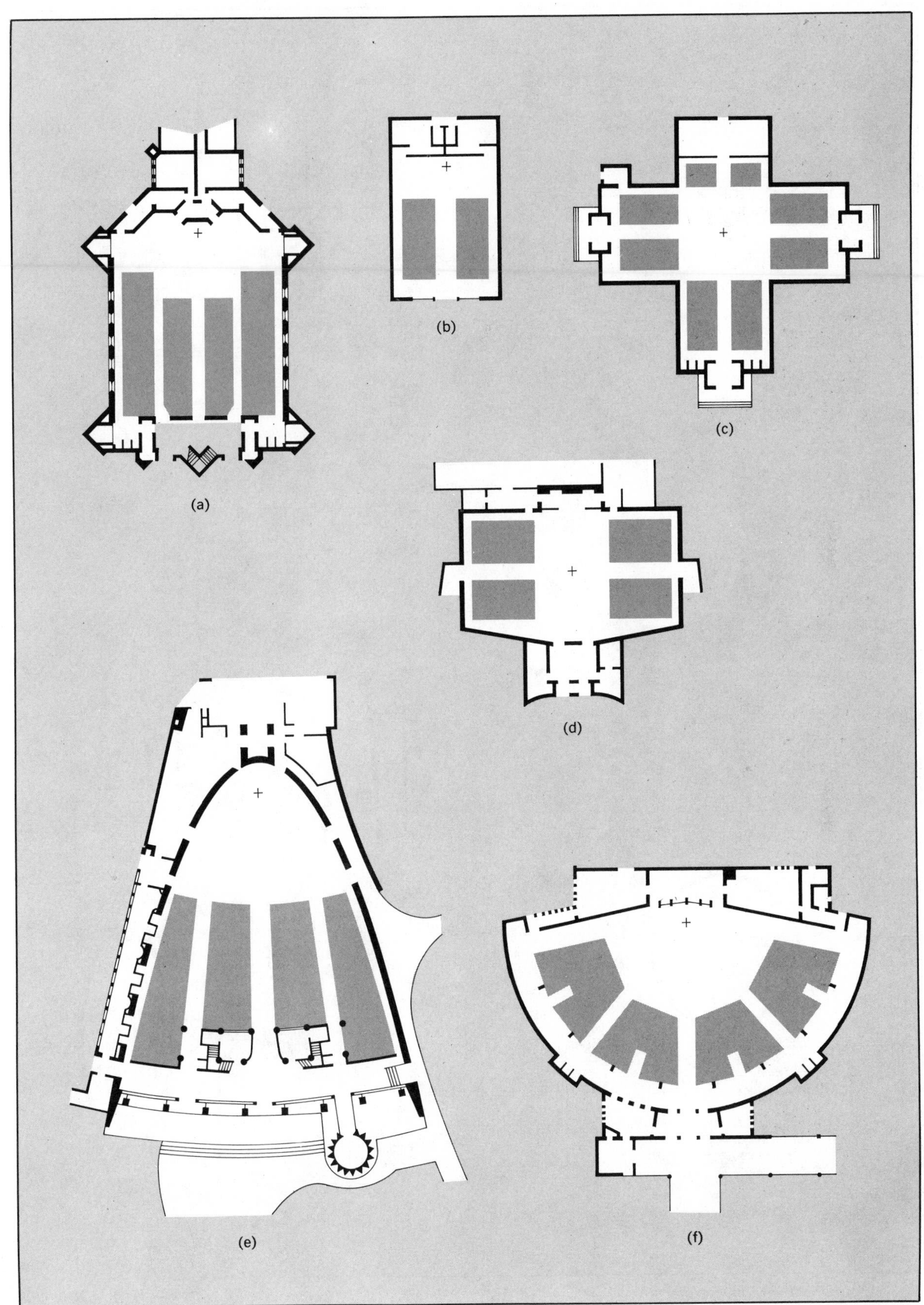

Fig. 83. American church architecture: (a) Christ the King, Tulsa, 1941. (b) Episcopal chapel, Illinois Institute of Technology, 1951. (c) St. Mark's, Burlington, Vt., 1943. (d) St. Clement's, Alexandria, Va., 1947. (e) Church of the Resurrection, St. Louis, 1954. (f) Christ the King, Seattle, Wash., 1954.

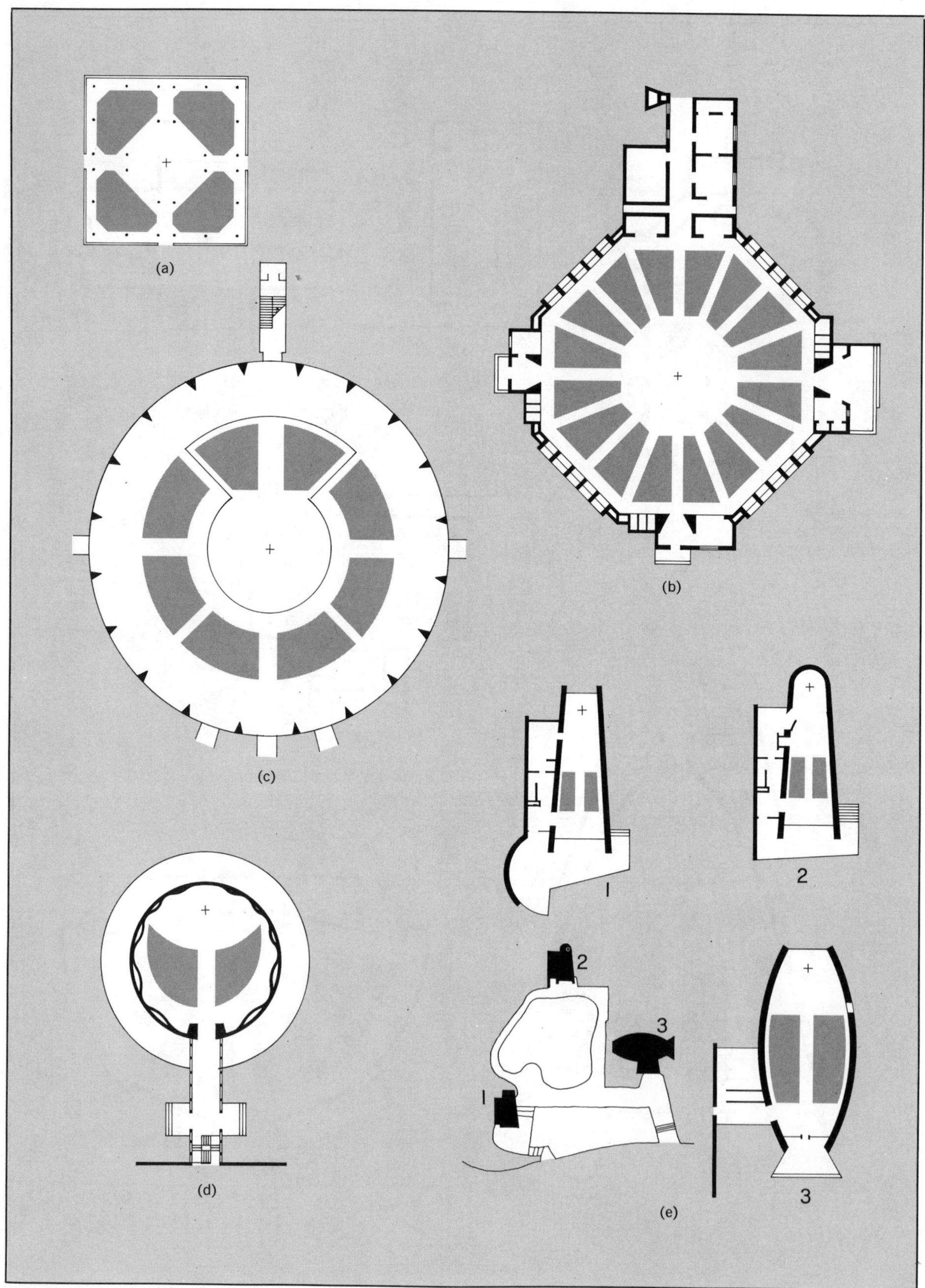

Fig. 84. American church architecture: (a) Chapel, Wellfleet, Mass. (b) Blessed Sacrament Church, Holyoke, Mass., 1954. (c) Benedictine priory, St. Louis, Mo., 1962. (d) Chapel, M.I.T., Cambridge, Mass., 1959. (e) Brandeis University Interfaith Center, Waltham, Mass., 1959—(1) Protestant chapel, (2) Catholic chapel, (3) synagogue.

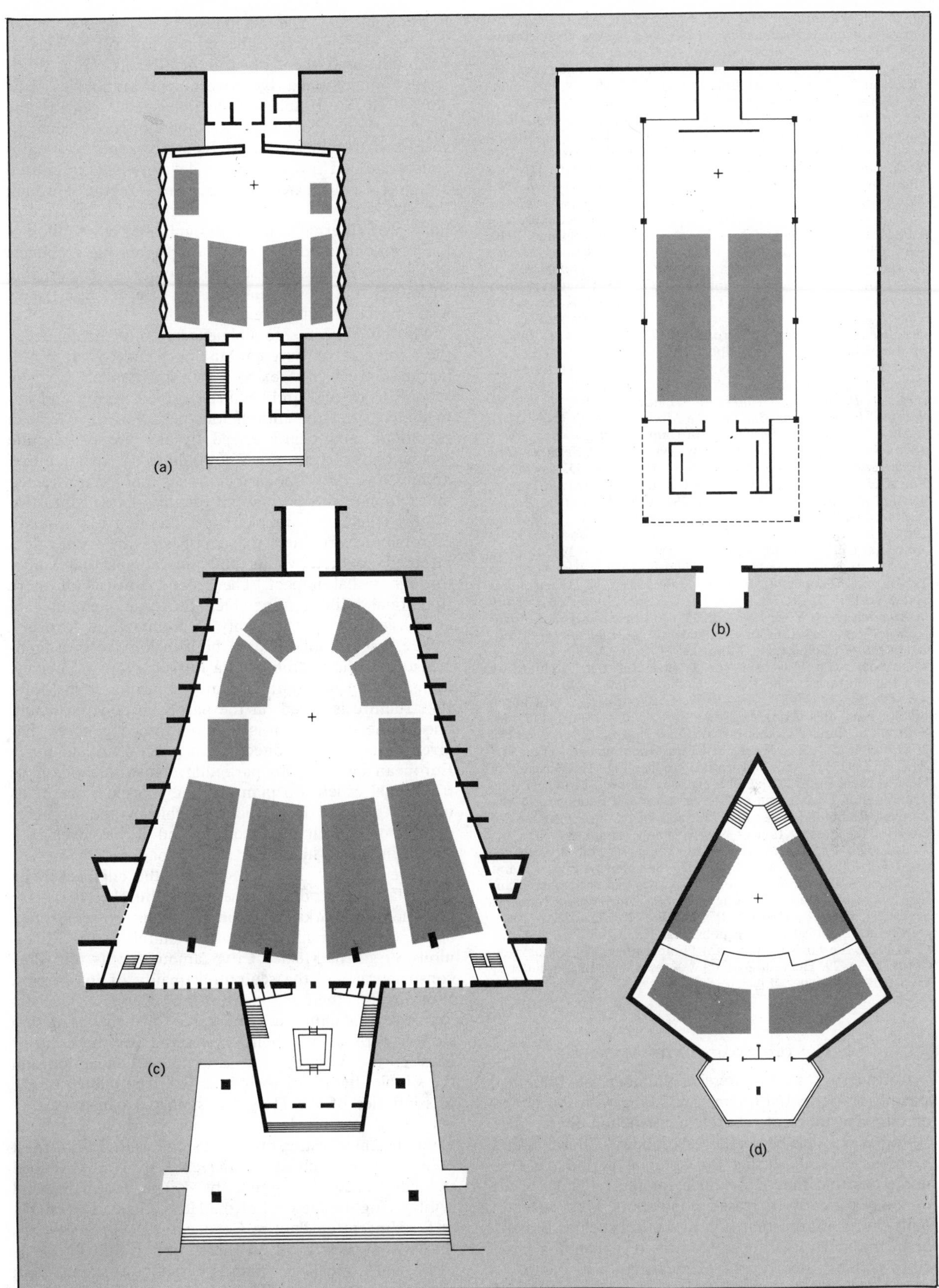

Fig. 85. American church architecture: (a) St. Anthony's Church, Superior, Wis., 1960. (b) St. Patrick's Church, Oklahoma City, 1960. (c) Church of St. John's Abbey, Collegeville, Minn., 1962. (d) Nuestra Señora de la Solodad Church, Coyoacán, Mexico, 1955 (for illustration of the last, see section 12 following.)

of H. H. Richardson and His Times (New York 1936). A. GOWANS, *Church Architecture in the New France* (New Brunswick 1955); *Looking at Architecture in Canada* (Toronto (1958). F. W. KERVICK, *Architects in America of Catholic Tradition* (Rutland, Vt. 1962). D. D. EGBERT and C. W. MOORE, "Religious Expression in American Architecture" in *Religious Perspectives in American Culture,* ed. J. W. SMITH and A. L. JAMISON (Religion in American Life 2; Princeton 1961) 361–411. A. CHRIST-JANER and M. M. FOLEY, *Modern Church Architecture* (New York 1962). K. BAER, *Architecture of the California Missions* (Berkeley, Calif. 1958). R. NEWCOMB, *Architecture of the Old Northwest Territory* (Chicago 1950); *Spanish-Colonial Architecture in the United States* (New York 1937). G. KUBLER, *The Religious Architecture of New Mexico* (Colorado Springs 1940; repr. Chicago 1962). J. A. BAIRD, *The Churches of Mexico* (Berkeley 1962). T. B. WHITE, ed., *Philadelphia Architecture in the 19th Century* (Philadelphia 1953). A. EMBURY, *Early American Churches* (Garden City, N.Y. 1914). R. K. SEASOLTZ, *The House of God* (New York 1963). R. TRAQUAIR, *The Old Architecture of Quebec* (Toronto 1947). A. GOWANS, *Images of American Living* (Philadelphia 1964). J. K. SHEAR, ed., *Religious Buildings for Today* (New York 1957). P. THIRY et al., *Churches and Temples* (New York 1953). W. H. HUNTER, *Century of Baltimore Architecture* (Baltimore 1957). W. W. WATKIN, *Planning and Building the Modern Church* (New York 1951). S. P. DORSEY, *Early English Churches in America, 1607–1807* (New York 1952). R. H. HOWLAND and E. P. SPENCER, *The Architecture of Baltimore* (Baltimore 1953). H. D. EBERLEIN, *The Architecture of Colonial America* (Boston 1915). P. DUELL, *Mission Architecture . . .* (Tucson 1919). M. SCHUYLER, *American Architecture,* ed. W. H. JORDY and R. COE, 2 v. (Cambridge 1961). R. A. CRAM, *My Life in Architecture* (Boston 1936); *American Church Building of Today* (New York 1929). B. F. L. CLARKE, *Anglican Cathedrals Outside the British Isles* (London 1958). R. C. BRODERICK, *Historic Churches of the United States* (New York 1958). H. W. ROSE, *The Colonial Houses of Worship in America* (New York 1963). P. HAMMOND, *Liturgy and Architecture* (New York 1961). Periodicals, etc. *Documents for Sacred Architecture* (Collegeville, Minn. 1957). LiturgA 1931– . C. D. MAGINNIS, "The Movement for a Vital Christian Architecture and the Obstacles: The Roman Catholic View," *Christian Art,* 4 v. (Boston 1907–08) 1:22–26. W. E. ANTHONY, "The Church of St. Paul the Apostle, New York," *ibid.* 3:101–117. M. SCHUYLER, "Italian Gothic in New York," *Architectural Record* 26 (1909) 46–54; "The Works of Cram, Goodhue and Ferguson," *ibid.* 29 (1911) 1–112. **Illustration credits:** Fig. 71, Museum of New Mexico. Fig. 72, McGill University Library, Montreal. Fig. 73*a,* Virginia Department of Conservation and Economic Development, Richmond. Figs. 73*b,* 73*d,* and 76*c,* Courtesy of the Society for the Preservation of New England Antiquities. Fig. 73*c,* Jules Schick. Fig. 76*a,* Wayne Andrews. Fig. 76*b,* Library of Congress. Fig. 77*a,* Alan Kimball. Fig. 77*c,* Ben Newby. Figs. 77*e* and 78*c,* Ezra Stoller Associates. Fig. 77*b,* Mies van der Rohe, architect; photo by Hedrich-Blessing. Fig. 77*d,* Murphy and Mackey, architects; photo by Hedrich-Blessing. Fig. 77*f,* The Cerny Associates, Inc., architects, Minneapolis. Fig. 78*a,* M.I.T. Fig. 78*b,* Mr. C. G. Coil, Stewart's Commercial Photographers, Inc., Colorado Springs. Fig. 79, Hellmuth, Obata & Kassabaum, Inc., architects; Gyo Obata, designer. Fig. 80, Shin Koyama.

[P. J. QUINN]

12. CONTEMPORARY LATIN AMERICAN

Considering the impressive number of buildings steadily rising in Latin America, along with the tempo of city development, church construction there since World War II has been relatively modest. Churches and monasteries built during the colonial period were so numerous that they still suffice for the religious needs of today's greatly increased population. Most recently built churches are situated in new cities such as Brasília or in the newly developed suburbs of expanding large cities such as Mexico City, Caracas, and São Paulo.

In contrast with the dynamism of modern civic and commercial structures, church architecture has remained somewhat conservative. The ecclesiastical hierarchy has been slow in adopting new architectural ideas and sometimes has openly expressed strong opposition to them. The two important advances in church architecture in Brazil, the church of St. Francis in Pampulha and the cathedral of Brasília (Fig. 89*e*), were commissioned by government authorities. The church of St. Francis, a distinguished work by the architect Oscar Niemeyer, was abandoned for some 10 years because the bishop of Belo Horizonte refused to consecrate it. However, recent developments in church architecture in Mexico have been encouraging. Through the support of men such as Sergio Méndez Arceo, Bishop of Cuernavaca, the designing of new buildings has been entrusted to a group of responsible architects and artists. The result is seen in a number of remarkable structures that have initiated a new life in Latin American church architecture.

Mexico. With the possible exception of the chapel of the Seminary of Foreign Missions, built by José Villagrán García in Mexico City, the typical Mexican school of art and architecture, formed during and immediately after the antireligious period of the Mexican revolution and characterized by the use of gigantic "social realist" murals, has not influenced recent church architecture. Most modern churches that have attracted international interest may be roughly divided into two groups reflecting parallel trends. The first is composed of romantic structures that emphasize the form of reinforced concrete vaults and aim at spiritual values through visual impact. The second consists of more functional buildings in which liturgical elements are emphasized by the simplicity of architectural forms.

The first Catholic church built in Mexico in a modern style is the church of "La Purísima" in Monterrey, designed in 1947 by the architect Enrique de la Mora. Its structure is based on the parabolic concrete vault, one of the typical forms that reinforced concrete has given to modern architecture in general and to many European churches in particular. Notwithstanding its traditional cruciform plan and the shortcomings of its interior design, this structure achieves the unprecedented in church architecture, and it has exerted a strong influence in Mexico and abroad.

More recently, De la Mora and the engineer Felix Candela have produced a series of churches that have become landmarks of modern architecture. Acting alone, Candela built in 1954 the church of the Miraculous Virgin in Mexico City, famous for its thin shell construction and the sculptural quality of its interior. Working together, De la Mora and Candela have designed several churches remarkable for their daring thin shell hyperbolic parabolic vaults and for the contrast between the lyricism of their aesthetic conception and the simple dignity of their interiors. The chapel of the Missionaries of the Holy Ghost in Coyoacán (1956) is covered by a single asymmetric hyperbolic parabolic vault elegantly resting on a lava stone wall. The farthest point of the vault is cantilevered over a V-shaped stained-glass wall designed by Kitzia Hofmann and symbolizing the Descent of the Holy Ghost. The chapel of St. Vincent de Paul in Coyoacán (1961) is perhaps the most successful of all the churches built by De la Mora and Candela. Its plan is basically a triangle with the altar in the center. The three points of the triangle, creating three naves intended for three categories of worshipers, are covered by gracious hyperbolic parabolic vaults supporting one another and separated by strips of abstract stained glass. Of a similar conception

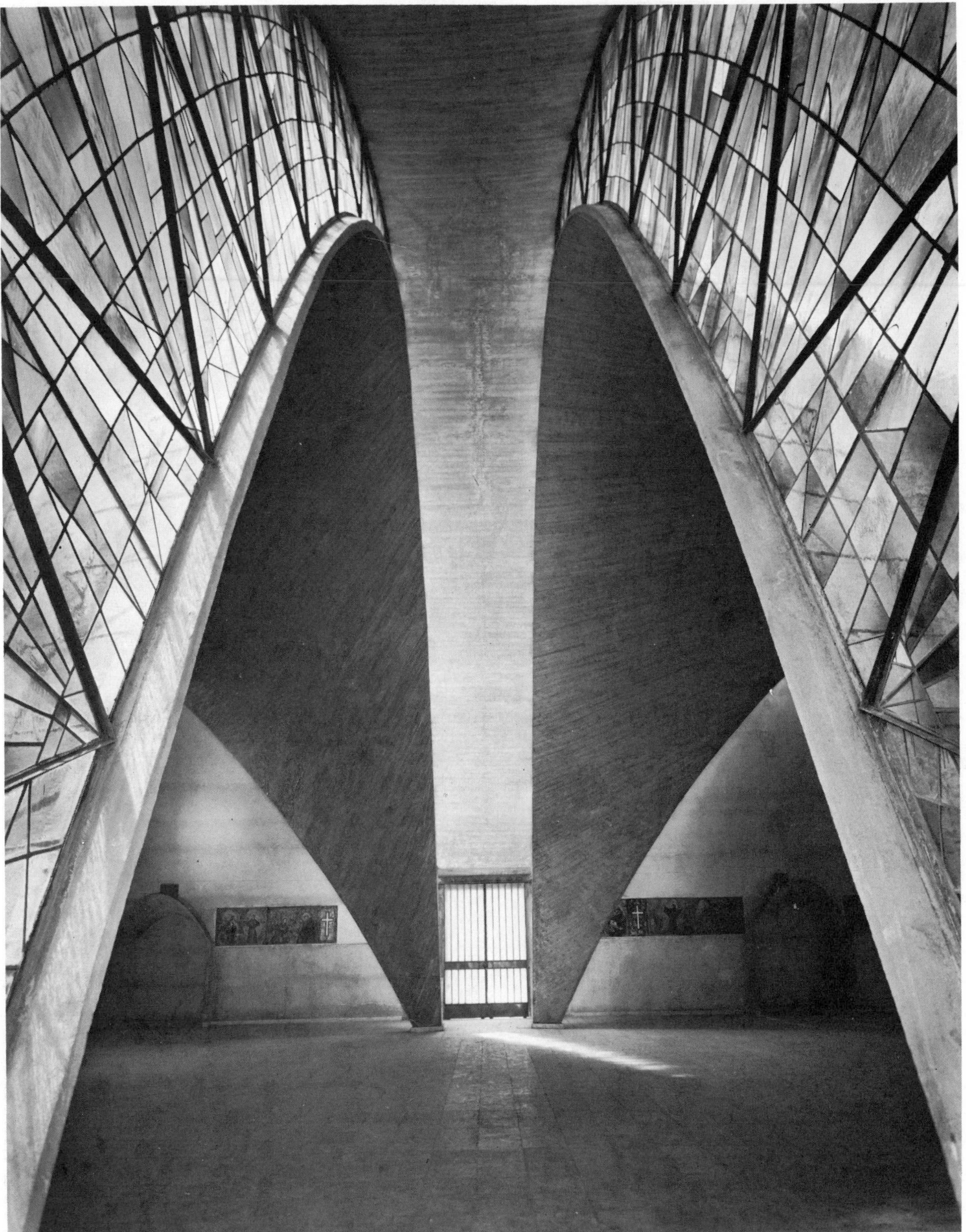

Fig. 86. Church of St. Anthony, F. Candela and E. de la Mora, Mexico City, 1961, interior, showing vaulting.

Fig. 87. The cathedral of Cuernavaca, Mexico, interior before restoration.

CHURCH ARCHITECTURE

Fig. 88. The sanctuary after restoration. This, one of the most noteworthy examples of American church interior renovation, was supervised by Ricardo de Robina, architect, in collaboration with Fray Gabriel (Chavez de la Mora), under the direction of Bp. Sergio Méndez Arceo.

Fig. 89. Contemporary Latin American church architecture: (a) St. Louis Betrán, Germán Samper G., Bogotá, Colombia. (b) St. Francis, Oscar Niemeyer, Pampulha, Brazil, 1943. (c) Chapel of the Gymnasio Moderno, Joyenal Moya Cárdenas, Bogotá, Colombia. (d) Chapel of the Missionaries of the Holy Ghost, F. Candela, engineer, Enrique de la Mora, architect, Coyoacán, D.F., Mexico, 1956. (e) Cathedral at Brasília (under construction), Oscar Niemeyer, architect. (f) Miraculous Virgin Church, Candela and De la Mora, Mexico City, 1954.

are the recent church of St. Anthony in Mexico City and of St. Joseph the Worker in Monterrey.

The thin shell vault system of construction has now been used by several architects engaged in church design and is exemplified by the outdoor chapel at Cuernavaca designed by Guillermo Rossell with the help of Candela. Other notable contemporary churches exhibit a more static and classical conception. The chapel of the Convent of the Capuchin Sisters of the Immaculate Heart of Mary, designed by the architect Luis Barragán and decorated by the artist Mathias Goeritz, remains one of the purest examples of modern church architecture in Mexico. Distinctively modern architecture characterizes also the church of St. Ignatius in Polanco (1963) by Juan Sordo Madaleno, the chapel of the Sanatorium of Zoquiapan (1954) by Venezuelan-born Israel Katzman, and the church of Our Lady of Peace in Guadalajara, by Ignacio Díaz Morales.

Great efforts are being made in Mexico toward the restoration of old churches and the elimination of statuary and decoration of dubious taste that have accumulated in the course of time. Colonial churches having spurious and extraneous features are thus restored to their original conception and completed, when necessary, with modern and functional liturgical elements contrasting with, but respecting and enhancing, the older forms. Ricardo de Robina, a Mexican architect known for his work in church architecture, has been responsible for unique restorations, among which are those of the church of St. Lawrence in Mexico City and the cathedral of Cuernavaca, carried out with the collaboration of Fray Gabriel (Chavez de la Mora), under the supervision of Bp. Sergio Méndez Arceo. The new works of art attempt to complement and continue the same spirit inherent in the old churches. The installation of modern abstract stained glass in restorations is an excellent example of the potential spiritual value in contemporary religious art. Of particular note are the windows designed by Mathias Goeritz with a wrought iron structural base for a number of restored churches including the cathedrals of Mexico City and Cuernavaca (*see* ABSTRACT ART AND THE CHURCH).

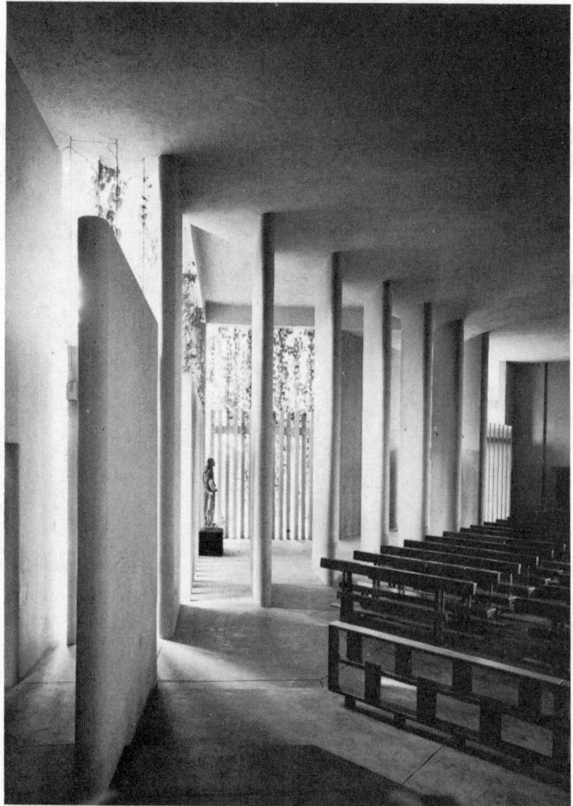

Fig. 90. Church of St. Martin de Porres, Henry Klumb, architect, Bayview, near San Juan, Puerto Rico, 1950.

Brazil. Brazilian architects, who have demonstrated their talent by developing an original architecture that has gained international recognition, have had little opportunity to deal with the problems of religious architecture. Among the relatively few new churches, only a very small number were entrusted to well-known architects. With the notable exception of the churches designed by Niemeyer, contemporary Brazilian church architecture is of little interest when compared with Brazilian architectural achievements in other fields.

The Church of St. Francis, built by Niemeyer in Pampulha in 1943, remains one of the most remarkable modern churches in the world. Here, for the first time, modern structural forms, completely freed from traditional methods of building, were used in the design of a religious edifice. The main vaults covering the nave and the sanctuary, and three secondary vaults containing the sacristy and its annexes, form a gracious rhythmic composition while expressing the plastic qualities of reinforced concrete. This church also made history in 20th-century sacred art, for it was here for the first time in Latin America that a major contemporary artist was invited to collaborate in the design of a religious building. Two major murals were executed for this church by the painter Candido Portinari. The reredos wall is entirely covered by a fresco executed in a strong expressionist manner representing Christ as the friend of the poor, the sick, and the erring. The exterior side of the rear wall bears a large mural depicting scenes from the life of St. Francis. Executed in the typically Brazilian blue and white glazed tiles (*azulejos*), it is probably the best work of Portinari in this medium. Other artists whose names are associated with this church include Alfredo Ceschiatti and Paulo Werneck.

The other major church designed by Niemeyer is the cathedral of Brasília, still under construction (1966). Structurally impressive and elegant, it is built on a circular plan with curved reinforced concrete members rising toward the sky and terminating in a symbolic crown. Access to this church is through an underground passage. The altar and sanctuary are located in the center of the circular nave. Two minor but interesting churches also built by the same architect in Brasília are the presidential chapel and the parish church of Our Lady of Fatima.

Colombia. No major movement of modern ecclesiastical art and architecture exists in Colombia. However, Colombian architects, who have proved their talent in excellent secular buildings, have also produced a few interesting modern churches. The most original, and also the earliest, is the chapel of the Gymnasio Moderno in Bogotá, designed by Joyenal Moya Cárdenas. The sanctuary is located in the center of a cruciform plan covered by elegant parabolic shell vaults of various heights, without any visible ties between them other

Fig. 91. The church of Del Carmen, Henry Klumb, architect, in the central plaza of Cataño, Puerto Rico, 1963.

than stained glass. The highest point and the most daring feature is a four-sided vault above the sanctuary entirely made of stained glass designed by the French artist Jean Barillet.

More recently, the architect Germán Samper G. built the church of St. Louis Beltran in Bogotá, a handsome structure combining the strong shapes of exposed reinforced concrete with the modest stucco walls of early Colombian colonial architecture. Among other small churches may be mentioned the chapel of the Hospital of Social Security, also in Bogotá. It is a small structure without much architectural distinction except for its interior and furnishings. These were designed entirely by a group of young architects and artists who united in an association for the integration of their arts.

Other Countries. Most other modern religious buildings in Latin America are isolated examples created by individualistic and talented architects. They represent neither a stated attitude on the part of the clergy nor a definite trend on the part of the architectural profession.

In Puerto Rico, Henry Klumb, a well-known architect and disciple of Frank Lloyd *Wright, has done some remarkable ecclesiastical work for the Dominican Fathers. His modest church of St. Martin de Porres, built in Bayview, near San Juan, in 1950, has attracted international attention for its adaptation to tropical climate, sensitive handling of natural light, and the creation of a devotional interior without any dramatic architectural effect. His church of Del Carmen, built in 1963, in the central plaza of Cataño, shows a masterly and playful treatment of architectural volumes in a small and difficult site. Now under construction in Hato Tejas is a Dominican seminary that will form the most interesting complex of ecclesiastical architecture in Puerto Rico.

In Argentina, two talented architects, Claudio Caveri and Eduardo Ellis, have created in the suburbs of Buenos Aires the modest but excellent parish church of Our Lady of Fatima. The plan is in the form of a cross with the nave floor sloping toward a central sanctuary covered by a pyramidal cupola. A low structure, without any ostentatious feature, it contains a humble atmosphere created by pure modern aesthetics combined with simple local construction materials such as stone and stucco.

In Uruguay, the architect Mario Payssé is at present (1965) completing a huge seminary for the Diocese of Montevideo, perhaps the largest of its kind to be built recently in Latin America. Payssé was selected by competition. His contemporary design tends to combine the expression of reinforced concrete structure with murals in the Uruguayan "Constructive Universalism" style and is consciously directed toward an integration of the arts.

In Venezuela, although modern architecture seems to be accepted, there are no large modern churches of any importance. The best work is to be seen in modest parish churches, such as the church of the housing development "23 de Enero" in Caracas, designed by Carlos Raúl Villanueva, a church in San Cristóbal and one in Maracaibo, designed, respectively, by Fruto Vivas and Jorge Castillo.

In Chile, ecclesiastical architecture has improved in mid-20th century. The chapel of the St. Ignatius school in Santiago is a clear architectural statement combined with contemporary sacred art. The ecclesiastical authorities of Santiago have built an excellent new seminary designed by the talented young architect Emilio

Duhart, but his very original plans for the chapel were rejected. This exemplifies a common difficulty for the creative architect whose work is often subject, in final judgment, to the unprofessional patron.

Bibliography: M. L. CETTO, *Modern Architecture in Mexico,* tr. D. Q. STEPHENSON (New York 1961). P. F. DAMAZ, *Art in Latin American Architecture* (New York 1963). C. FABER, *Candela, the Shell Builder* (New York 1963). H. R. HITCHCOCK, *Latin American Architecture since 1945* (New York 1955). H. E. MINDLIN, *Modern Architecture in Brazil* (New York 1956). S. PAPADAKI, ed., *The Work of Oscar Niemeyer* (New York 1950). **Illustration credits:** Fig. 86 and 89*d,* Guillermo Zamora. Fig. 89*a,* Germán Tellez. Fig. 89*b* and 89*e,* Marcel Gautherot. Fig. 89*c,* Annie Damaz. Fig. 89*f,* George Cserna. Fig. 90, J. Alex Langley. Fig. 91, Thomas Creighton.

[P. F. DAMAZ]

CHURCH MEMBERSHIP, U.S.

State articles in *The New Catholic Encyclopedia* each contain a graph indicating the distribution of major faiths within the state. These graphs are based on a series of 80 bulletins, *Churches and Church Membership in the United States,* published in 1956 by the National Council of Churches of Christ in the United States of America. Compiled by the National Council's Bureau of Research and Survey from data furnished in 1952 by 114 church bodies in 48 states and the District of Columbia, this report affords the most recent data available on church membership according to states. A series of Federal census reports on religious affiliation was issued in 1890, 1906, 1916, 1926, and 1936. No further volumes have appeared, and the Bureau of the Census, U.S. Department of Commerce, has abandoned inquiry concerning religious membership in response to protests that it contravenes the principle of separation of Church and State. Consequently, the only statistics available after 1936 are those maintained by individual church bodies and by centralized organizations. The *Yearbook of American Churches,* a publication of the National Council of Churches, offers membership totals for more than 200 churches, but these are national figures with no indication of state statistics. Diocesan totals appearing in the annual *Official Catholic Directory* supply quite accurate data on Roman Catholic membership. Jewish membership data must be taken from the *American Jewish Yearbook,* which makes a "culture count" rather than basing its figures on the rolls of local synagogues; the result is at best approximate and makes no distinction between Conservative, Reform, and Orthodox Judaism. The Church of Latter-Day Saints (Mormons) counts membership by "stakes" rather than by local churches. Mormon stakes, of which there were 277 in 1952, generally conform to county boundaries and are statistically useful in compiling state totals; the Mormons did not, however, report their considerable "mission" membership since it has no geographic basis.

Methodology. Interpretation of the graphs accompanying state articles should take note of the methods employed by the National Council of Churches in its survey and should make appropriate adjustments to compensate for the limitations of the study. The 114 participants were requested to furnish figures on membership and number of churches, which were then compiled and entered on IBM cards on a county by county basis. The cards were further processed by the Bureau of Applied Social Research of Columbia University, New York City. To aid the participants in the preparation of their returns, standardized definitions of key terminology were issued. The word "church" was regarded as any organized congregation that could be geographically located, thus embracing Methodist "preaching places." The National Council stated that "the counting was generally of regularly functioning, organized congregations with membership rolls and specific place of location." The term "church member" being variously defined by the churches, the National Council asked each participant to report according to its own criteria of membership. The resultant variety of standards seriously affects analysis of the graphs. Roman Catholic figures include all baptized persons regardless of age, as do Lutheran and Protestant Episcopal statistics. Mormons begin to include children in their data after they have reached the age of 8. Jewish membership includes all Jews in any community that has a congregation. Protestant membership customarily excludes children under 13, and in many cases counts only the adult baptized, the confirmed, or the communicant. A church that reports membership from infant baptism will show figures 30 per cent above a comparable institution reporting only adult confirmed members. Because the graphs in state articles indicate only absolute figures, with no adjustment made for such differences, it would be possible to alter proportions in states where Catholics, Mormons, Episcopalians, and Lutherans are not predominant. Texas, for example, where participating churches reported 2,400,000 members based only on confirmation, could by adding 30 per cent to this figure increase its proportion of church membership to population from 61.4 per cent to 72.1 per cent. As a region, the South in the 1952 survey had 18,823,261 Protestants among churches that numbered only confirmed persons as members. Comparable figures for the North Central states, after a 30 per cent adjustment, were 10,543,190; for the Northeastern states, 5,952,489; and for the West, 2,888,064. In evaluating the graphs, it is therefore most important to make allowances for membership definitions in Southern states; it is least important in the case of Western states. The National Council also supplied participants with a definition of the term "Protestant" by including in that category all U.S. religious bodies that were not Buddhist, Muslim, Jewish, Roman Catholic, Old Catholic, Polish National Catholic, or Eastern Orthodox. Of the 114 participants, 107 were thus classified as Protestant. Despite these definitions, which were superior to those employed in the 1936 census, a minor margin of error must be allowed for local inexperience in counting or for inability to adjust institutional statistical practice to the survey's requirements.

While some degree of error was unavoidable, the methods employed by the National Council were in several respects an improvement over those of the 1936 census. The census employed questionnaires sent to local church bodies as its means of gathering information. Although the questionnaire covered a broad spectrum of data that delved into such areas as the age of church members and the status of church finances, and although it reached loosely organized church bodies, it was less reliable than information secured by the National Council from the national headquarters of the various denominations. There was, moreover, an undetermined amount of failure to reply to the Federal questionnaire, and coverage was incomplete. The National Council achieved nearly total coverage of the 74,125,462 members reported in its survey, as against the 54,576,346 reported in 1936. The 1936 study had been deficient also in county analysis, one of the strengths of the 1952 study.

Limitations. Despite the merits of the National Council's survey, a number of limitations are to be observed. Some, perhaps all, were unavoidable. No statistics were available for the Church of Christ, Scientist, which has a regulation prohibiting "the numbering of people and reporting of such statistics for publication." Figures for Old Catholics, Polish National Catholics, and Eastern Orthodox were not statistically meaningful; they reported only 14,500 out of their 1952 membership of 2,720,739. The Churches of Christ were not included among the participants in the National Council's study, on the grounds that they lacked centralized records. Since their congregations numbered 1,500,000 members in 1953, this omission affects evaluation of the graphs for the Southeastern states, where most of their 16,000 churches were located. The major omission, however, was that of the five principal Negro churches in the South: the National Baptist Convention, U.S.A., Inc.; the National Baptist Convention of America; the African Methodist Episcopal Church; the African Methodist Episcopal Zion Church; and the Christian Methodist Episcopal Church. With a membership totaling 9,392,694 in 1952, these churches were unable to participate, and this tended to exclude much of the Negro population of the U.S. from the National Council's study. Some Negroes were certainly included in the membership totals of the 114 participants. Nevertheless, the National Council states that, "the absence of this very large block of members in the present study is its greatest single weakness," and warns that "this fact should be kept in mind in assessment of all findings in the course of this study." Lack of Negro coverage accounts for much of the 27 per cent gap between the 92,277,129 members reported by 251 churches in the 1953 *Yearbook of American Churches* and the 74,125,462 members reported in the National Council's survey. Some adjustments, only roughly accurate, can be made in the National Council's figures by subtracting the Negro population figures from the 1950 census and computing religious proportions accordingly. Regionally, Southern population can be lowered from 47,197,088 to 36,971,681. Northeastern figures drop from 39,477,986 to 37,459,804; North Central go from 44,460,762 to 42,232,886; and Western from 19,561,525 to 18,990,704. The effect of these alterations is to increase the national average of church membership from 49.2 per cent of population to 54.6 per cent. Most states are substantially affected by the change, with the most important differences occurring in the South. There church ratios increase from 42.2 per cent to 53.9 per cent, with Mississippi, South Carolina, Georgia, and Louisiana most affected. These adjusted ratios offer a more accurate picture of church membership than the absolute figures employed in the graphs, but they in turn distort by failing to discount Negroes reported by the participating churches.

If lack of Negro data is the weakest link in the National Council's statistical chain, Roman Catholic reporting is the strongest. An approach to complete accuracy was achieved, as the county totals for the survey indicated a national membership of 29,688,058 against 29,621,483 Catholics counted in the *Official Catholic Directory* for 1953. The discrepancy was attributable to the probable inclusion of some mission figures that should have been excluded. Data for the Catholic count was obtained from three sources: (1) a study of several Southern dioceses conducted by Rev. Maurice V. Shean of the Catholic Committee of the South; (2) chancery offices in 55 dioceses; and (3) a formula, based on the 1936 census, that employed population changes from 1930 to 1950 and diocesan membership changes since 1936. The progressive steps of the formula, which was devised by the Bureau of Research and Survey and was used in 52 dioceses, is presented here:

1. 1950 county population divided by 1930 county population equals percentage change in population.
2. Population change times 1936 Roman Catholic population equals the estimated increase in county Roman Catholic population.
3. Estimated increase plus 1936 Roman Catholic population equals estimated 1950 Roman Catholic population.
4. Total of estimates for all counties within the diocese equals estimated diocesan membership for 1950.
5. Diocesan total from 1953 *Official Catholic Directory* divided by estimated diocesan membership equals margin of error.
6. Estimated county Catholic population, plus margin of error times estimated county Catholic population equals actual county Roman Catholic population.

About 47 per cent of Catholic membership was estimated in this manner. While the margin of error varied from county to county, it was lowest where Catholics were numerous and highest where they were few. In any event, errors were balanced out so that county totals were equal to diocesan figures.

In addition to the precautions already observed, two other factors may be noted in the use of the graphs. One is that the material is to some extent dated, being more than a decade old in 1964. On the assumption that proportional distribution of faiths has not materially altered, some estimate of more recent church population can be obtained by employing population figures for 1962 and appropriately increasing the membership figures indicated by the graphs. The 1950 population figure used in the graphs was 150,697,631; by Aug. 1, 1962, the Bureau of Census estimated population at 186,847,000, an increase of 24 per cent. Thus the 74,125,462 membership reported in 1952 may be estimated for 1962 at 91,915,573. A similar procedure may be employed for each state. Second, it may be noted that the nature of the survey tends to give the lowest possible estimate of church membership. The use of unadjusted data, the omission of significant church bodies, the paucity of Negro statistics, and the participation of but 114 out of 251 churches all contribute to a pessimistic portrait of church strength. This may be contrasted with the results of the 1957 survey made by the Bureau of the Census. A sample survey testing religious preference, not actual church membership, suggested that 96 per cent of the population over 14 years of age had a preference for some religious institution. Only 4 million stated that they had no religion, as against 70 million who claimed to be Protestant, 30 million Catholic, and 4 million Jewish. Doubtless these figures are optimistic, but they suggest the need for upward adjustments in the raw data employed in the graphs. The ratio of church membership would be most reliably calculated by percentage increases on the basis of population growth, membership criteria, and Negro participation. These would raise the national ratio of church membership to population from 49.2 per cent to 61.1 per cent, still a most conservative estimate.

Analysis of Graphs. With the precautions described above, the state graphs permit meaningful conclusions concerning the distribution of faiths at national, regional, and state levels.

National Distribution. Nationally, the graphs show church membership at 49.2 per cent of population, with 26.1 per cent Protestant, 19.7 per cent Catholic, and 3.4 per cent Jewish. In 19 states the ratio of membership exceeds 50 per cent; Rhode Island leads with 75.7 per cent, Oregon is lowest with only 28.4 per cent. Among church members reported in the survey, 53 per cent were Protestant, 40 per cent Catholic, and 7 per cent Jewish. Methodists and Southern Baptists constituted 43 per cent of Protestant figures, and 91 per cent of the denominational total was reported by 14 church groups. There was a notable difference in the relative size of Catholic and Protestant churches. Over the nation, each Catholic church averaged 1,884 members, while the average for Protestant churches was 240. The Catholic average was highest in Rhode Island (3,282) and the Northeastern states (2,591), lowest in North Carolina (235) and the North Central states (1,354). Protestant averages went from a high of 601 in the District of Columbia and 293 in the Northeast to a low of 124 in Maine and 216 in the South. These figures indicate that even more distortion is produced by equating Catholic parishes with Protestant churches than by matching Catholic-Protestant membership totals. They further suggest that in most areas of the U.S. Protestants are faced with the problem of "overchurching," of providing an excessive number of churches in relation to population and the available number of "unchurched" persons not served by any faith. In 1952 there were 369 unchurched persons for each Protestant church in the nation. The problem is especially acute in rural communities, with an average of 244 unchurched; in metropolitan areas the figure rises to 681. The National Council viewed this situation as "resulting in uneconomical use of clerical manpower and congregational energy as well as church funds, and often creating unhealthy competition between religious groups."

Regional Distribution. From a regional point of view, most church members were located in the Northeast (31.9 per cent) and the North Central states (30.4 per cent), with 26.9 per cent in the South and 10.8 per cent in the West. Catholic membership was heavily concentrated in the Northeast (New England and the Middle Atlantic states), where 44.1 per cent of its members resided. Catholics were numerous also in the North Central region, with 30.6 per cent, but they were scattered in the South (12.8 per cent) and West (12.5 per cent). Protestant strength lay in the South (40.0 per cent), followed by the North Central (32.1 per cent), Northeast (18.1 per cent), and West (9.8 per cent). Relative to population, church membership was highest in New England (62.5 per cent), while Protestants did best in the West North Central region (36.2 per cent), and Catholics in New England (43.1 per cent). Protestant membership tended toward a regional denominational pattern. New England statistics revealed a high proportion of Congregational, Methodist, American Baptist, and Episcopalian members. The South was primarily Southern Baptist, Methodist, Presbyterian Church in the U.S., Disciples of Christ, and Protestant Episcopal. In the North Central states, the Evangelical Lutheran, Lutheran Church—Missouri Synod, Methodist, and Presbyterian Church in the U.S.A. predominated. Latter-Day Saints, Methodists, Presbyterians U.S.A., and Episcopalians were most numerous in the Western Mountain states, while Methodist, Presbyterian U.S.A., and Episcopalian appeared most frequently in the Pacific region. This concept of pattern extends from the regional down to the county level, where one church body can claim more than one-half the total church membership in more than 50 per cent of the nation's counties. Oregon, lacking any county where one religious group can claim a plurality, is an exception; but it is more than counterbalanced by the dominance of the Latter-Day Saints, who possess in excess of 90 per cent of church membership in all but three counties of Utah. Baptist strength is concentrated chiefly in the Southeast, where Baptists predominate in nearly all counties of North and South Carolina, Georgia, and Alabama. Lutheran superiority lies in the Middle Western states, especially North Dakota, Minnesota, and Wisconsin. Smaller denominations also follow a geographic pattern; the Disciples of Christ, for example, are most heavily concentrated in Kentucky, North Carolina, Virginia, and a few Middle Western states. Several of the largest denominations, however, are so widely distributed that they cannot be fixed on any regional basis. This is preeminently true of the Methodist Church, which is the most numerous Protestant denomination, yet dominates only the states of Maryland and Delaware. Episcopal, Congregational, and Presbyterian churches also follow a national pattern. While the Roman Catholic pattern is scattered over several regions, the Catholic lead in church membership in more than 50 per cent of counties can be attributed to Louisiana and Texas in the South, New Mexico and Arizona in the Mountain States, and California. In New England, Catholics are the most numerous in nearly every county in Massachusetts, New Hampshire, and Vermont, and every county in Connecticut and Rhode Island.

State Distribution. On the state level, the graphs reveal that church bodies are most numerous in populous states with large metropolitan areas. Such states as Illinois, Ohio, Indiana, Pennsylvania, and California reported more than 75 religious groups. Small states such as Nevada or Rhode Island had less than 30 church bodies, against a national average of 50.3. The nine Protestant churches that reported membership in excess of 1 million each, the Roman Catholic Church with 29,688,058 members, and the Jewish Congregations with 5,112,024, were distributed among the states in the following manner: the Methodist Church, with 8,790,025 members in the U.S., ranked among the four major denominations in all states, ranked first among Protestant churches in 17 states of the North, and second in 21 others, mostly in the South. Southern

Baptists, with 8,121,069 members, were found in most states outside the Northeast, but 91 per cent of its membership was in the South. The 2,544,320 members of the Protestant Episcopal Church were so well distributed that it topped the Protestant list only in Rhode Island, while appearing among the five leading denominations in 32 states and the District of Columbia. The Presbyterian Church in the U.S.A., with 2,448,249 members, was among the Protestant leaders in 27 states, but its strength lay in the states of New York, Pennsylvania, Ohio, and California. The United Lutheran Church was the most numerous Lutheran group with its 1,998,826 members concentrated in the East, notably in Pennsylvania where it dominates the Protestant list. The Disciples of Christ, International Convention, ranks as a rural church whose 1,836,014 members are found in practically every state; it was among the major Protestant churches in 22 states. The Lutheran Church—Missouri Synod, with 1,835,605 members, led the Protestants in Wisconsin and was a major factor in 15 states. The 1,528,846 members of the American Baptist Convention were located principally in Rhode Island, being completely absent from the lists in New Mexico and the Southern states. The 1,263,472 members of the Congregational Christian Churches were found in every state, and constituted the most numerous Protestant body in New Hampshire, Connecticut, Massachusetts, and Vermont. Jewish membership was almost exclusively urban and Eastern, with New York accounting for 50 per cent of the Jewish population. Roman Catholic membership was greatest, more than 2 million, in the states of New York, Massachusetts, Pennsylvania, Illinois, and California.

Although the state graphs do not afford information on rural-urban distribution of church membership, the National Council's survey developed patterns that can be briefly summarized. About 40 per cent of Protestants live in the fundamentally rural South, which had 31 per cent of U.S. population in 1952. Most (73 per cent) Southern Protestants belong to the Methodist (4 million) or Southern Baptist (7 million) churches, making their denominations more rural than urban. Among the several Lutheran churches, the United Lutherans show the greatest amount of urban concentration since they are numerous in the populous Northeast. The Evangelical Lutherans are the most rural of leading Protestant churches with their membership found mostly in the West North Central states. The Protestant Episcopal Church is the most urban Protestant faith. Jewish membership is everywhere urban; 99 per cent of California's 400,000 Jewish population, for example, lives in a metropolitan center. The Catholic Church is chiefly urban in the Northeast and North Central states, but it becomes more rural in Southern and Western states that were colonized by France or Spain.

Conclusion. Religious statistics available to church historians have left much to be desired. They have generally been inaccurate, sporadic, and unscientific. The colonial historian must often content himself with counting the number of churches and making educated guesses concerning membership. While the situation improved after 1800 and Federal census data was of some help after 1850, much more research remains to be done on denominational and county history in order to chart the progress of American churches with reliability. Equally necessary are future studies based on sound statistical principles similar to those developed by the National Council's survey.

Bibliography: W. ZELINSKY, "An Approach to the Religious Geography of the United States," *Annals of the Association of American Geographers* 51.2 (June 1961) 139–193 is the most recent effort to describe patterns of church membership. The best general work is E. S. GAUSTAD, *Historical Atlas of Religion in America* (New York 1962), which has extensive bibliog. An analysis of the 1926 Federal census may be found in C. L. FRY, *The U.S. Looks at Its Churches* (New York 1930). Earlier studies based on Federal data are F. A. WALKER, *Statistical Atlas of the United States . . . 1870* (Washington 1875). H. GANNETT, *Statistical Atlas of the United States* (Washington 1898). *Religious Bodies, 1906* (Washington 1910). A good general work is C. O. PAULLIN, *Atlas of the Historical Geography of the United States* (Washington 1932). For the colonial period the four volumes of F. L. WEIS, *The Colonial Clergy and the Colonial Churches* (Lancaster, Mass. 1936–55) are invaluable. Useful 19th-century works are R. BAIRD, *Religion in America* (New York 1856); *The Christian Retrospect and Register* (New York 1851). D. DORCHESTER, *Christianity in the United States* (New York 1888); *The Problem of Religious Progress* (New York 1900). Among denominational histories, C. C. GOSS, *Statistical History of the First Century of American Methodism* (New York 1866) and H. C. WEBER, *Presbyterian Statistics through One Hundred Years 1826–1926* (Philadelphia 1927) are representative, but see the denominational bibliog. in Gaustad. G. SHAUGHNESSY, *Has the Immigrant Kept the Faith? A Study of Immigration and Catholic Growth in the United States 1790–1920* (New York 1925) has become the standard work for Catholic statistics. The most recent work by a Catholic scholar is J. A. HARDON, *The Protestant Churches of America* (2d ed. Westminster, Md. 1963), part three of which is devoted to church statistics.

[J. L. MORRISON]

CHURCH (CHURCHES) OF GOD

At least 10 denominations in America are called Churches of God and, though juridically distinct, they reflect a common reaction against denominationalism in all its forms. The very name implies a profession of faith in God as the only founder of the Church and a protest against other "man-made" institutions.

There are two main forms of Church of God in the U.S., deriving either from the Holiness or the Pentecostal movements, and both tracing their ancestry to John *Wesley, the founder of *Methodism (*see* HOLINESS CHURCHES; PENTECOSTAL CHURCHES). In his original teaching, Wesley stressed the importance of rising above the level of justification by faith to a true conversion of spirit or sanctification by grace. The Churches of God have sought to give these Wesleyan principles organized expression; but unlike other Holiness or Pentecostal groups who are in the same tradition, they want to avoid anything savoring of a structured, authoritarian society and prefer to speak of themselves as a "reformation movement" among the various Christian bodies.

The three largest Churches of God account for almost 80 per cent of the American membership and are generally representative of the movement as a whole. One group calls itself simply the Church of God and has its headquarters in New York. It was founded in 1903 by A. J. Tomlinson, an American Bible Society salesman from North Carolina, and was headed by him until his death in 1943. As first conceived by Tomlinson, "There are no creeds connected with the Church of God, but only the Bible, rightly divided, with the New Testament as the only rule of faith and practice." Tomlinson's death was the signal for a chain of schisms that is still going on. He had designated his son Homer to succeed him, but the choice was opposed by a group of state overseers. Homer placed his younger brother Milton in charge. Shortly after, Homer was expelled from the church, whereupon he formed the New York group, which claims direct lineage from the elder Tomlinson. In 1964 this church reported a total of 71,606 members.

Two other groups, Church of God, Anderson, Ind., and Church of God, Cleveland, Tenn., had independent beginnings and no relation to Tomlinson's organization. The Anderson body was started in 1880 by Daniel S. Warner and several minister companions who "severed their connection with humanly-organized churches" and maintained that "Scriptural, all-sufficient standard for Christians is membership in the body of Christ alone." In January 1881 Warner published the first issue of the *Gospel Trumpet,* which later (1963) became *Vital Christianity,* to give the church a weekly journal that, more than anything else, has kept the denomination organized and flourishing, beyond that of other Churches of God. In 1964 inclusive membership totaled 145,241.

Like the Anderson group, the Church of God of Cleveland believes in the soul's personal encounter with God, but its emphasis is more extreme. It began in 1886 under the title Christian Union, was reorganized in 1902 as the Holiness Church, and in 1907 adopted its present name. Its total membership as reported in 1964 was 179,651. The *Church of God Evangel,* an inspirational weekly, serves to encourage the faithful to share their own conversion experience with others. Where the Indiana segment is more conservative, the Tennessee organization believes that the Holy Spirit manifests His presence in the soul through such extraordinary signs as the gift of tongues. *Revivalism is prominent and mission work in countries such as Brazil caters to those who want a strong emotional appeal in Christianity.

Even when they are well organized, as in Anderson, the Churches of God are strictly congregational in polity. The highest directing body is the General Assembly, which meets annually or biennially. Ritually they recognize baptism by immersion, the Lord's Supper as a memorial of Christ's Passion, and (among some) foot-washing as a divine ordinance. Ideally they are pacifist in their sentiments, oppose all secret societies, and abstain from alcoholic beverages.

The Churches of God may be described as anti-sectarian in their concept of Christianity, Wesleyan in their belief that divine grace offers the prospect of personal holiness, fundamentalist in theology, legalistic in the stress on external practices of morality (notably temperance), and charismatic in their expectation that the Holy Spirit will manifest His presence by extraordinary signs.

Bibliography: A. F. GRAY, *The Nature of the Church* (Anderson 1960). H. C. RICE, *Tell Me About the Church* (Anderson 1956). F. G. SMITH and K. JONES, *What the Bible Teaches* (Anderson 1960). J. W. V. SMITH, *Truth Marches On* (Anderson 1956). R. E. STERNER, *We Reach Our Hands in Fellowship* (Anderson 1960).

[J. A. HARDON]

CHURCH OF THE BRETHREN (DUNKERS)

Also known as German Baptists and, historically, as Taufer, Tunkers, Dompelaars, and Dunkards. The Brethren immerse the kneeling candidate for Baptism three times forward in the water; their popular name is derived from the German word *tunken* which means to dip or immerse.

The Brethren movement originated in 1708 at Schwarzenau, Germany, as part of the Pietistic-Anabaptist protest against the established Lutheran and Reformed churches (*see* PIETISM; ANABAPTISTS). Seeking less formalism and dogma and more warmth in religion, they emphasized study of the Bible and right living. Their leader, Alexander Mack, Sr. (1679–1735), was baptized by trine immersion and in turn baptized seven companions in the same manner. When the early Brethren were persecuted in their homeland, some fled to Holland and eventually to the Germantown area in Pennsylvania; others came directly from Germany to America. The first Dunkers came to American shores in 1719, and Mack himself arrived with additional families in 1729.

Until recently most brethren remained farmers; the largest concentration of adherents is still in Pennsylvania. They oppose participation in war, oaths, and secret societies. For many years the Brethren spoke only German and until around 1900 wore a distinctive, plain garb; the women were expected to wear veils in church. They reject all creeds and follow only the New Testament. Parts of the Old Testament are rejected since they uphold war, slavery, divorce, and the idea of revenge. Largest by far of the Brethren sects is the Church of the Brethren or Conservative Dunkers, which in 1964 reported 200,000 members in 1,072 churches in the U.S. and Canada. Another 20,000 Brethren belonged to overseas churches in India, Nigeria, Ecuador, and Puerto Rico. This church supports six colleges and a graduate school of theology. Its headquarters and publishing house are in Elgin, Ill. The Church of the Brethren has carried out extensive relief and rehabilitation work since World War II.

The church follows a theology similar to that of the mainstream Protestant denominations. Although it baptizes by trine immersion, it now receives into its fellowship Christians who have been baptized in other ways. It recognizes four ordinances: baptism, the Lord's Supper, anointing of the sick, and imposition of hands on Christian workers. The love feast, observed once or twice a year, includes an evening fellowship meal, the foot-washing rite, and communion; many congregations hold additional communion services at other times. Voting delegates from each congregation meet for the annual conference, the church's highest authority. This conference elects 25 members of the General Brotherhood Board, which directs the daily administrative work of the denomination. The church belongs to the National and World Councils of Churches.

Several smaller sects have grown out of the Brethren movement. A group of Brethren, objecting to certain traditions and to the church's alleged disinterest in education, left the parent body in 1882. They were known as Progressive Brethren. In 1939 these Progressive Brethren split into two informal groupings. The Brethren Church (Ashland, Ohio) prefers an Arminian to a Calvinist theology, and in 1964 claimed more than 18,000 members in 114 congregations (*see* ARMINIANISM). The National Fellowship of Brethren Churches, or Grace Brethren, favor *Calvinism and maintain headquarters at Winona Lake, Ind. It reported 25,355 members in 175 congregations. The Old German Baptist Brethren or Old Order Brethren objected to the liberalism of the other Brethren and established their own organization in 1881. They oppose missions, Sunday schools, a salaried ministry, and church-operated schools, and still wear plain garb. Most of the 4,100 Old German Baptist Brethren live in Ohio and Indiana.

Bibliography: H. A. KENT, *250 Years Conquering Frontiers: A History of the Brethren Church* (Winona Lake, Ind. 1958). F. MALLOTT, *Studies in Brethren History* (Elgin, Ill. 1954). J. E. MILLER, *The Story of Our Church* (rev. ed. Elgin, Ill. 1957). D. DURNBAUGH, comp. and tr., *European Origins of the Brethren* (Elgin, Ill. 1958).

[W. J. WHALEN]

CHURCH OF THE NAZARENE

One of the largest of the *holiness churches formed (1908) as a separate church by the union of several small pentecostal groups. Although most of these were originally Methodist congregations or missions founded under Methodist auspices, holiness evangelists of the Ohio Yearly Meeting of Friends were influential also in originating the Church of the Nazarene.

The principal bodies involved in the 1908 merger were the Church of the Nazarene, with headquarters at Los Angeles, Calif.; the Association of Pentecostal Churches of America, centered at Brooklyn, N.Y.; and the Pentecostal Mission of Nashville, Tenn. Missions to the unchurched in the slums of newly urbanized America were one of the first fruits of the holiness movement in this country. The Peoples' Evangelical Church at Providence, R.I., founded in 1887, became the nucleus for the Central Evangelical Holiness Association formed in 1890 of holiness missions in industrial towns in Massachusetts and Rhode Island. About the same time William Hoople and Charles BeVier established the Utica Avenue Tabernacle in Brooklyn, uniting first with other New York congregations and then with the New England group to form (1896) the Association of Pentecostal Churches. The years 1888 to 1894 saw the holiness advocates steadily losing ground in Methodism. Phineas Bresee, removed as presiding elder by Bp. John H. Vincent in 1892, established a mission at Peniel Hall, Los Angeles, in 1894. Further difficulties led to its separation from Methodism and the founding (1895) of the Church of the Nazarene. The Pentecostal Mission at Nashville, led by B. F. Haynes and J. O. McClurkan, began negotiations for union with the Church of the Nazarene in 1901. Other independent congregations in the South, including the New Testament Church of Christ formed by Robert L. Harris, and the Holiness Association of Texas, both originally Methodist, merged in 1905 to form the Holiness Church of Christ. In 1907 the Church of the Nazarene and the Brooklyn Association churches united and in 1908 union was completed with several small Southern bodies, including the Holiness Church of Christ. The Nashville group joined the others only in 1915 after protracted negotiations. The Middle West then became the scene of intense missionary work and rapid growth in membership. Differences over the meaning of baptism and other issues led to the secession of Seth C. Rees and a California congregation in 1917, and financial problems led to much greater centralization after 1923. The Church of the Nazarene established (1904) a Spanish-speaking mission in Los Angeles, the precursor of many home missions to minority groups. Its foreign mission work began in Africa (1907) and was extended to Mexico (1919) and Peru (1917) and later to most parts of the world.

The Church of the Nazarene is essentially a fundamentalist group in its theology. The original creedal statement drawn up at Los Angeles in 1895 stressed the Unity and Trinity of God, the inspiration and sufficiency of the Scriptures, man's fallen nature, Christ's atonement, the work of the Holy Spirit in conversion, and sanctification by faith. In the tradition of the holiness movement, Nazarene theologians have emphasized the crisis and process of sanctification, seeing it as an instantaneous experience, a second religious crisis after conversion, in which the Christian is cleansed from inner sin by the sanctifying baptism with the Holy Spirit. Nazarene services, whether "evangelistic" or "worship" services, are always open to demonstrations of praise or zeal; their ritual and sacramental observances are simple and allow for freedom of spirit. Although enthusiasm at times broke all bounds, the trend in the 1960s was against spontaneity in worship and in favor of a more formal service. In its tradition, the Church of the Nazarene is democratic. Congregations retain a large measure of independence, although its missionary, educational, and publishing activities have been centralized since 1911. In polity, as in worship, it is close to Methodism; its superintendents are similar to Methodist bishops. The Church of the Nazarene has always been opposed to use of liquor, tobacco, dancing, as well as various other kinds of worldliness and adornment.

Bibliography: C. T. CORBETT, *Our Pioneer Nazarenes* (Kansas City, Mo. 1958). T. L. SMITH, *Called unto Holiness* (Kansas City, Mo. 1962). W. PURSIKER, *Conflicting Concepts in Holiness* (Kansas City, Mo. 1958); *Exploring Our Christian Faith* (Kansas City, Mo. 1960).

[R. K. MAC MASTER]

CHURCH PROPERTY

The history of Church property is considered here according to the following periods: (1) the first 3 centuries (to 313); (2) the Christian Roman Empire (313–*c.* 500); (3) the Middle Ages (*c.* 500–1500); (4) the modern world (*c.* 1500 to the present).

First Three Centuries (to 313). To maintain its worship and its charitable activities, the Christian Church from its origins acquired, administered, and distributed property. Even before the death of Christ, the Apostles had accepted donations (Lk 8.3) and had kept a common purse (Jn 12.6). Christ Himself had directed His Apostles to be unstinting in their charity (Lk 6.29–30) and told them that they in turn could expect to be supported by those to whom they ministered (Mt 10.10; Lk 10.7). After Pentecost, the first converts at Jerusalem sold their possessions (Acts 2.45), gave the price to the Apostles, and "distribution was made to each according as anyone had need" (Acts 4.34–35). This passage was frequently cited with admiration by later ecclesiastical writers, but the communistic regimen it describes seems in fact to have been limited to the Church at Jerusalem. Christians at Antioch (Acts 11.29) and in the provinces of Galatia (1 Cor 16.1–2), Macedonia (2 Cor 8.1), and Achaia (2 Cor 9.2) evidently retained private means, as they were exhorted to be generous in giving help to their impoverished brethren at Jerusalem. The same passages, however, leave no doubt that the obligation to support their own and sister churches rested upon all Christians. Tertullian (*Apol.* 38), writing in 198, described how Christians often paid to their churches a regular voluntary tax (*stipes*) proportionate to their wealth. This *stipes* was probably analogous to the *qorbānîm* paid by Jews to their synagogues.

Ecclesiastical possessions initially consisted in movables—the sacred vessels used in worship, the liturgical oblations made by the faithful at the Christian services, and the charitable donations in kind and money to be distributed among the poor. Tertullian mentions an *arca,* or treasury, in which the community's valuables were kept.

It is uncertain when the churches first acquired real property. Christians seem to have worshipped in private homes and buried their dead in private cemeteries until about 200. In the *Life* (ch. 49) of Alexander Severus (d. 235), attributed to Lampridius and preserved in the *Augustan History,* a Christian community is mentioned as the collective owner of its place of worship. The edict of Emperor *Gallienus in 257–258 (Eusebius, *Hist. Eccl.* 7.13), ending a persecution of the Christians, stipulated that their cemeteries should be restored to them. In a discussion of Church property from the first half of the 3d century, *Origen (PG 13:1696–97) used technical terms—*dispensator,* or administrator, of real properties, *redditus* or ground rents—that make it almost certain that churches by then possessed income-producing lands. By the late 3d and early 4th centuries, similar references to ecclesiastical property became clearer and more numerous, leaving no doubt that the churches were landlords even before the conversion of the Emperor, *Constantine I.

The precise juridical title by which the often persecuted churches held their properties has long puzzled historians. In 1864 G. B. de *Rossi ingeniously suggested that the churches enjoyed the status of Roman funeral colleges (*collegia tenuiorum*), to which Roman law conceded the capacity to own property. Rossi's thesis has been much criticized, chiefly because the Christian churches greatly differed from the funeral colleges in their internal organization and purpose. Recent research, however, has tended to favor his interpretation. The Roman state, viewing the churches from the outside and having little accurate knowledge of their internal constitution and purposes, may well have considered them analogous to the familiar *collegia tenuiorum* and, between persecutions, conceded them a right to hold property. It is also likely that ecclesiastical possessions were assimilated to the sacred property, the *res sacrae et religiosae* of Roman law (Gaius, *Inst.* 2.2–9), which meant that they could not be alienated or restored to secular purposes.

The Apostles were initially responsible for the administration of ecclesiastical possessions of the Church of Jerusalem, though they appointed seven *deacons to relieve them of the burden (Acts 6.1–6). According to later sources, full authority over the possessions of each church fell to its bishop. *Justin Martyr (1 *Apol.* 67.12), writing about 150, described the "president" or bishop of the community as receiving and distributing the donations of the faithful. St. *Cyprian (*De Lapsis,* 6) condemned bishops who used Church property for their private interests. In other words, well before the conversion of Constantine, supreme and unrestricted authority over a church's property rested with its bishop, although his personal possessions were sharply differentiated from those of his church.

The Apostles and the bishops were aided in administering property by the deacons, already mentioned in Acts 6.9. The deacons had similar responsibilities according to the *Didache (A.D. 80–90; 15.1–2) and the writings of *Ignatius of Antioch (A.D. 110–117; *Ad Trallesios,* 2–3). The 4th-century *Legend* of St. *Lawrence, the deacon of the Church of Rome martyred in about 268, recounts how a pagan judge ordered the saint to produce the treasures he, as deacon, was known to possess (he foiled his persecutors by producing the Church's poor). By the 3d century, Origen mentioned a still more specialized officer: the *dispensator* or *oikonomos,* responsible for the administration of real property.

Donations and revenues maintained worship, supported Church officials, and aided the poor. St. Paul had insisted upon the right of those who ministered to churches to be supported by them (1 Cor 9.13–14), and widows too were to be maintained by the churches (1 Tm 6.3–18). Justin Martyr (1 *Apol.* 67) mentions as recipients of aid orphans, captives, travelers, and the poor.

No estimate can be given of the extent of Church property in this early period, but undoubtedly it remained small. Still, the fact that these often persecuted churches were able to acquire and manage property, maintain a budget, and support their religious and charitable services within a hostile social milieu is no small tribute to their dedication, energy, and precocious administrative skill.

Christian Roman Empire (313–c. 500). The so-called Edict of *Milan (313) and the official establishment (380) of the Christian Church within the Empire affected its property holdings in three ways. Ecclesiastical wealth, particularly in land, grew enormously. The historic patrimony of the Church, functioning as a major factor in economic and social history, must be considered the product of the 4th and 5th centuries. Church property also acquired a clarified, standardized, and privileged juridical status throughout the Empire. And the churches themselves developed more specialized and effective administrative offices and techniques in managing their enlarged endowments.

Through the generosity of the Christian emperors and the growing numbers of the faithful, the patrimonies of such ancient and honored churches as *Rome, *Alexandria, *Antioch, *Carthage, and *Milan soon reached prodigious size. The Roman church owned lands and estates scattered over the Mediterranean world from *Syria and *Egypt to *Gaul. On the other hand, churches in such newly Christianized areas as Gaul seem to have possessed only modest holdings. No estimate can yet be made as to the extent of ecclesiastical land. It undoubtedly varied among regions, but was substantial in its totality.

By the 5th century, the churches were also fully recognized as corporate persons before the law, able to acquire and manage property without impediments or restrictions. Their holdings were also privileged. The emperors of the early 4th century exempted them from the property tax (CodTheod 16.2.15), from the *annona* or grain requisition (CodTheod 11.1.1), and from the obligatory services or *corvées* known as the *munera sordida.* These and other privileges, many of which are preserved in Book 16 of the *Theodosian Code, served as a precedent and model for the Church's later claims to tax immunities and exemptions.

While the bishop's personal possessions were rigorously distinct from those of his church, he still exercised almost absolute control over his church's holdings.

He directly administered all ecclesiastical properties within his diocese and collected all the revenues from them. This almost modern system of financial administration—based upon a unified patrimony, single budget, and salaried clergy within each diocese—reflected the favorable economic conditions of the late Empire, notably the still lively commercial exchange and abundance of money.

Although he was the supreme administrator, the bishop was supposed to conform to a growing number of regulations set by councils, emperors, and popes, concerning his use of property. According to the Council of Antioch (ch. 24 and 25; A.D. 332–341), bishops were forbidden to alienate their church's holdings. In a famous decretal of 494, Pope *Gelasius I (*Ep.* 14.27) advised the bishops of Lucania to retain one-fourth of their revenues for themselves and to spend one-fourth for the clergy, one-fourth for buildings and one-fourth for charity (for *clerus, cultus,* and *caritas*). Churches in Gaul and *Spain followed slightly different formulas for allocating revenues, these having been defined by the councils of Agde (ch. 36; A.D. 506) and Braga (ch 7; A.D. 563). But churches everywhere devoted a substantial part of their revenues to social and charitable services, in fact completely relieving the state of responsibility for them. The social service of the churches has been and is one of the major justifications for ecclesiastical wealth.

Administrative offices also developed greatly under the Christian Empire. From the 4th century, the *archdeacon assumed the role of the bishop's chief lieutenant in property administration, and he continued to fulfill this function in the Middle Ages. Widely in the East and occasionally in the West, the *oikonomos* also served as property administrator. Another clerical official, the *defensor ecclesiae* is mentioned in 452 (CodTheod, *Novellae* of Valentinian, 35), and such "defenders" were still the chief administrators of the patrimony of the Roman Church under *Gregory I the Great (590–604); 14 of them are mentioned in his letters. Lay *defensores,* responsible for defending churches in lawsuits and suggestive of the later medieval *advocatus,* are cited in 407 (CodTheod 16.2.38) but disappear after 438; their historical importance is that they represent an early penetration of laymen into the ecclesiastical administration.

The 4th century witnessed also the first protests concerning ecclesiastical wealth. On moral and religious grounds, critics such as *Lucifer of Cagliari were already condemning the luxurious living of many clergymen. The pagan *Ammianus Marcellinus (*Rer. gest.* 27.3.14) similarly castigated clerical affluence. Even the Christian emperors, faced with mounting fiscal needs, curtailed some of the ecclesiastical tax exemptions in the 5th century (CodTheod 16.2.40; 5.3.6; CorpIurCivCod 1.2.11), though the privileged status of Church property was never fully abrogated. The age of the Christian Roman Empire, in other words, bequeathed to the Middle Ages not only a large and well administered ecclesiastical endowment, but also the tenacious social and moral problems connected with it.

Middle Ages (c. 500–c. 1500). The patrimony of the churches was profoundly affected by the new economic, social, political, and intellectual conditions of the Middle Ages, and in its turn it greatly influenced the course of medieval history. The decline of commercial exchange and the growing scarcity of money in the early Middle Ages no longer permitted the support of the clergy of each diocese through salaries paid by the bishop. Just as lay lords had to maintain their dependents through direct grants of land (fiefs), so the bishops from at least the early 6th century were distributing from their formerly unified patrimonies grants of land, called *beneficia* or *precaria.* The recipient of a *benefice enjoyed the usufruct, or income, from the property granted him; but he could not alienate it, and with his death it was supposed to revert to the bishop. The ecclesiastical patrimony also was divided through the need to establish and support rural churches as Christianity, originally urban, spread through the countryside. From about the 4th century in Italy and from the 5th in Africa, Gaul, and Spain, local churches were acquiring and holding their separate patrimonies. Like the benefice, the endowments of local churches remained under the bishop's supreme, if often remote, supervision.

From the 5th century too, monasteries held their own separate endowment. From the 7th century on, many of the great monasteries were able to obtain from kings, emperors, popes, and the bishops themselves partial or complete exemptions from episcopal supervision. From the 9th century, even the bishop's own cathedral clergy acquired a distinct endowment. The portion of the church's lands set aside for the support of the chapter was called a *mensa,* or table. The canons might keep it integral, living a common life by the income it provided; or they might divide it among themselves as separate prebends or livings. Exactly comparable to this separate table, and likewise dating from the early 9th century, were the portions, similarly called *mensae,* set aside from monastic patrimonies for the support of the monks (as distinct from the abbot). Similarly too, the monks might keep their *mensa* unified. But by the late Middle Ages the practice developed of providing separate livings for the great monastic officers (the obedientiaries) and even for the monks themselves. This clearly abusive practice was hard to reconcile with the Benedictine ideal of individual poverty.

Feudalism. An even more serious threat to episcopal authority was the extension, in the early Middle Ages, of the *proprietary church. This was a church owned by a layman (frequently its founder) who exercised a quasi-episcopal authority over it. He supervised and managed its endowment, appointed the priest who served in it, and often collected fees for the spiritual services performed. The proprietary or private church was once thought to be a specifically Germanic institution, but it is now recognized as common to Latins, Germans, and even Greeks, and is peculiarly a product of the economic and juridical conditions of the early Middle Ages.

The development of the tenurial system of *feudalism also confused ecclesiastical and lay property and often subordinated churches to laymen or lay interests. Bishops were inevitably drawn into the feudal hierarchy; they gave and received fiefs to such an extent that historians sometimes speak of a "feudalization" of the Church and its endowment in the early Middle Ages. Laymen also came to exercise extraordinary authority in the administration of supposedly ecclesiastical property. The lay *advocatus* or *avoué,* for example, of the Carolingian Age, acted as a kind of policeman upon ecclesiastical estates, defended the churches in lawsuits with outsiders, and often claimed exorbitant payments for his services.

Because so much of the ecclesiastical revenue was diverted to laymen, it is difficult to calculate exactly the extent of Church property in the Middle Ages, although a rough estimate can be made. In the age of the barbarian kingdoms (6th and 7th centuries), the churches and monasteries effectively owned—in the sense of claiming the major portion of rents—about 10 per cent of the land, and exercised a shadowy lordship over considerably more. Under the Carolingian rulers, Church property seems to have grown considerably, reaching 33 per cent, probably its peak, by the late 9th century. The chaos of the 10th century was accompanied by extensive pillaging of the Church's property, reducing it by the early 11th century to about 20 per cent. The great religious revival of the 11th century, climaxed in the *Gregorian Reform, effected a partial recovery, raising the percentage to about a quarter of Europe's cultivated lands. From the middle 12th century, the portion of ecclesiastical property became largely stabilized and even slightly declined, reflecting growing lay opposition to its continued growth and, perhaps, a cooling of ardor among the faithful. In the later Middle Ages after the *Black Death (1348) the increase of lay piety brought another increase, but *hospitals and confraternities (many of which remained under effective lay control), rather than churches or monasteries, benefited.

Successes and Failures. The history of ecclesiastical property is intimately connected with both the successes and failures of the medieval Church. Ecclesiastical estates made a major contribution to the economic growth of Europe, particularly in the early Middle Ages. In a barbarous and socially chaotic period, ecclesiastical managers were literate, disciplined, relatively enlightened, and able to take advantage of the administrative continuity and enlarged resources that community ownership made possible. Monks such as the *Cistercians were the great practitioners of farming in the Middle Ages. On the other hand, these same characteristics of ecclesiastical management—discipline, conservatism, rigidity, and engagement with other concerns—were to prove obstructive to economic progress in the more stable society and buoyant economy of later periods. Monasteries meanwhile served as early centers of credit in the countryside, and the military-religious order of the *Templars, founded in the course of the *Crusades, was a pioneer in banking. The history of medieval banking and taxation is in fact inextricable from the history of ecclesiastical *finance. Moreover, the Church's rich endowment alone provided for the medieval community its hospitals, orphanages, and social services. And it can never be forgotten that ecclesiastical wealth made possible those magnificent achievements of medieval culture—the *cathedrals, *universities, and systems of thought they engendered.

But ecclesiastical wealth also cast shadows over the moral and spiritual life of the medieval Church. There was acute maldistribution of ecclesiastical revenues; inadequate support for the lower clergy led many of them to exploit their sacramental powers for material profit; extravagant revenues went to the great prelates and abbots; and there was a growing institutional paralysis in the correcting of the balance. The splintering of the ecclesiastical endowment and the erosion of episcopal authority introduced chaos into property administration. Up to the 11th century, lay owners of private churches and lay overlords and vassals were chiefly responsible for diverting the revenues from the priests who served the people to other uses. The Gregorian Reform of the 11th century sought with no little success to free the Church from this pernicious lay domination. Meanwhile the private churches themselves survived. Many were acquired and retained by monasteries, which monopolized their revenues and appointed miserably paid vicars to serve in them. Laymen often retained rights of advowson or presentation over parochial churches, assuring them of a strong and not always beneficent influence over clerical appointments. Furthermore, by the late Middle Ages the practice was widespread of delivering monasteries and abbeys to laymen *in commendam;* the laymen were supposed to protect the interests of the commended institutions, but they often ruined them. The increase in the number of commended abbeys seemed a resuscitation of the private church, and the familiar evils associated with this were resuscitated too (*see* COMMENDATION).

While the Gregorian Reform curtailed without entirely eliminating direct lay control over the Church, episcopal supervision continued to be obstructed and ecclesiastical discipline threatened by the unrestrained growth of exempt monasteries, chantries, collegiate churches, and hospitals. Since the bishop was unable and often unwilling to maintain discipline, such characteristic abuses as pluralism (the simultaneous holding of several benefices) and absenteeism proliferated; income was thereby diverted from the support of the people's ministers to those who contributed nothing to their spiritual welfare.

Unfortunately, the growth of papal taxation must be recognized as a major factor in this breakdown of clerical discipline. To be sure, the medieval *papacy was slow to emerge as a financial power, and the amount of its revenues has often been grossly exaggerated. As late as the 12th century papal income from all over Europe seems to have amounted to a paltry 810 silver marks, whereas at the same time, Normandy and England together provided their common ruler 85,000 marks. Papal revenues on the eve of the Reformation amounted to only 450,000 ducats—well below the contemporary income of the Kingdom of Naples.

The Holy See, which assumed primary responsibility for financing the crusading movement while simultaneously pursuing a great-power policy in Europe, was for most of the Middle Ages severely strapped for funds. But rather than curtail its aspirations, it took to exploiting its spiritual authority for fiscal ends. The age of papal fiscalism was the period of the *Avignon papacy (1305–77), and its greatest architect was Pope *John XXII (1316–34). Papal taxation developed with extraordinary rapidity and complexity. The popes imposed a variety of claims whenever a benefice changed hands: the *spolia* or the inheritances of bishops who died intestate; vacancies or revenues from unoccupied benefices; *annates or common services, from a third to a half of the first year's revenue of a benefice; *expectancies or fees paid for appointment to benefices not yet vacant. Exemptions and dispensations from canonical obligations, chancery fees, *tithes, and traffic in *indulgences were exploited in unseemly fashion for revenue. Many of these claims the Holy See had to dispute or share with bishops and even kings, and given the difficulties of collection, only a small portion of the revenues ever reached Rome. But the mounting fiscalism weighed heavily upon the lower clergy, angered laymen who resented the flow of bullion to Rome, promoted an often virulent anti-clericalism, undermined episcopal authority, and disrupted ecclesiastical discipline.

The Critics. With growing abuses came growing criticisms. Such thoroughly orthodox writers as *Peter Damian in the 11th century, *Bernard of Clairvaux and *Peter Cantor in the 12th, *Dominic in the 13th and *Alvaro Pelayo in the 14th were unsparing in their denunciations of lax clerical morality associated with excessive clerical wealth. In the tradition of secular letters, the goliards (*see* GOLIARDIC POETRY) and other satirists of the 12th century, later humanists such as *Erasmus, pilloried the fiscal interests and devices of the Roman Curia. Ominously, ecclesiastical wealth attracted the violent strictures of heretics: the *Albigenses, *Waldenses, Franciscan *Spirituals, *Lollards, and *Hussites. John *Wyclif (d. 1384) categorically denied the Church's right to own property and called for the lay magistracy to secularize ecclesiastical holdings and reform the Church. His ideas anticipated by 150 years the essential program of the *Reformation.

Ominously too, the ever more powerful secular states of the late Middle Ages encroached upon Church property. The effort of *Philip IV to tax the clergy of France led directly to his famous dispute with Pope *Boniface VIII and the papal humiliation at Anagni (1303). By the late Middle Ages most of the powerful kings of Europe were able to extract "free gifts" from their clergy almost at will, to limit papal taxation within their frontiers, and to inhibit the export of specie to Rome. The popes had little choice but to enter into concordats with the lay rulers, as with *Francis I of France in 1516, and thus concede to the lay lords a practical supremacy over their territorial churches (*see* GALLICANISM). The Reformation, in its attack on ecclesiastical property and undermining of Church unity, only brought to a climax trends that had long been in evidence.

Modern World (c. 1500 to the Present). The history of Church property in the modern age is largely the account of a radical transformation in the Church's financial basis and fiscal administration. Much of this story concerns the progressive *secularization of Church property by the Protestant princes, enlightened despots, French revolutionists, and liberals of the 19th century. The Church itself, in the *Counter Reformation, attempted to correct the abuses and institutional paralysis that had bred such disasters. The common effort of the reforming popes of the 16th century, of the Council of *Trent, and of such model bishops as St. Charles *Borromeo of Milan was to restore the bishops' disciplinary authority over churches, religious institutions, and clerics within his diocese, and thus to correct the long-standing misuse of Church revenues. This aspect of the Catholic reformation enjoyed real success, but neither the reforming popes nor the Council of Trent was able to limit the baneful influence that the Catholic princes exerted over their territorial churches (*see* JOSEPHINISM; CHURCH AND STATE). By the 18th century, maldistribution of revenues, inadequate support of the lower clergy, a careerist and spiritually lukewarm upper clergy—the classical syndrome of abuses—had come again to disfigure the churches of the old regime and to invite the condemnations and secularizations of the revolutionary period.

The collapse of the old regime in the revolutionary and liberal epochs, the gradual emancipation of the churches from the tutelage of princes, even the secularization of their historic patrimonies, proved in many ways an unexpected blessing. The churches had to seek out a new basis for their economic support, and more and more the continuing donations of the faithful, rather than property, rents or obligatory tithes, have provided it. The Church in the U.S. probably provides the best example of the new fiscal basis of ecclesiastical life. The yearly budgets of some American dioceses, with gigantic educational and charitable as well as religious activities to support, run to tens of millions of dollars. While no exact figures are available, only a minute part of these huge operating revenues comes from rents or investments. The American churches have, to be sure, acquired large physical possessions in buildings and lands, but little additional revenue is provided by them. The Church in America could not live without the weekly freewill offerings of the faithful. It is not an exaggeration to say that the fiscal basis of the modern American Church, dependent as it is upon the continuing and free donations from the faithful, more nearly resembles that of the pre-Constantinian Church than that of the Middle Ages (*see* UNITED STATES OF AMERICA). That the Church should have become a great landlord in the medieval past is understandable. A bastion of organized social life in a tumultuous age, it had little choice but to assume the responsibilities of property management. Its stewardship was on the whole good, and civilization was served by it, but the role caused frequent and deep injury to its spiritual life. The modern Church, on the other hand, must rely for its support primarily upon the free donations, the good will and the love of its members, and this has proved a liberation.

Bibliography: Fliche-Martin (all volumes). J. GAUDEMET, *L'Église dans l'Empire romain* (Paris 1958). É. LESNE, *Histoire de la propriété ecclésiastique en France*, 6 v. (Lille 1910–43); *L'Origine des menses dans le temporel des églises et des monastères de France au IXe siècle* (Mémoires et travaux pub. par des professeurs des Facultés catholiques de Lille 7; Lille 1910). A. PÖSCHL, *Bischofsgut und Mensa episcopalis: Ein Beitrag zur Geschichte des kirchlichen Vermögensrechtes*, 3 v. (Bonn 1908–12). H. LECLERCQ, DACL 14.2:1906–24. G. KRÜGER, *Die Rechtsstellung der vorkonstantinischen Kirchen* (Stuttgart 1935). G. B. DE ROSSI, *La Roma sotterranea cristiana*, 3 v. (Rome 1864–77). G. G. COULTON, *Getting and Spending*, v.3 of *Five Centuries of Religion* (Cambridge, Eng. 1923–). D. HERLIHY, "Church Property on the European Continent, 701–1200," *Speculum* 36 (1961) 81–105. V. PFAFF, "Die Einnahmen der römischen Kurie am Ende des XII. Jhts.," *Vierteljahrsschrift für Sozial- und Wirtschaftsgeschichte* 40 (1953) 97–118. M. MONACO, *La situazione della Reverenda Camera Apostolica nell'anno 1525* (Rome 1960). H. J. BYRNE, "The Financial Structure of the Church in the United States," *The Catholic Church, U.S.A.*, ed. L. J. PUTZ (Chicago 1956) 93–108.

[D. HERLIHY]

CHURCH PROPERTY, ADMINISTRATION OF

According to the constitutional nature of the Church, the pope is the supreme administrator and dispenser of all ecclesiastical goods (CIC cc.101.1, 218, 1518). By right he may administer all property of any subordinate moral person in the Church. Moreover, in his capacity as supreme administrator he is not bound by the limitations imposed by ordinary and extraordinary acts necessary for the control and maintenance of property.

Although the pope has the right to administer both immediately and mediately the property of the universal Church and that of every moral person in the Church, he does not have the direct and complete dominion, that is, radical ownership, over all ecclesiastical property. Under the natural law each man is entitled to his own property, and this principle is applicable to moral persons too. Canon Law readily recognizes this, as is evident. It states that ownership of ecclesiastical goods belongs, under the supreme authority of the Apostolic See, to that person who acquires these same goods legitimately (CIC c.1499). The dominion belongs to the moral person, and it is the use only that is limited by the authority of the Apostolic See.

Eminent domain, or the right of the state to expropriate property for the common good, is universally recognized. The pope enjoys a similar right. Civil rulers are obliged by the natural law to make just compensation to the property owner. Some ecclesiastical authors teach that this applies equally to the pope, whereas others deny it. The latter argue that the pope is the vicar of Christ, and in this capacity he has vicarious power, at least indirectly, over all earthly goods. When the common good demands it, he can validly and lawfully expropriate property without compensation. The exercise of this act of expropriation flows ultimately from his vicarious power and not from the power of eminent domain. In practice, the papacy requires that just compensation be made to the moral person.

The exercise of the papal right to administer all property of any subordinate moral person is subject to a twofold limitation: first, ecclesiastical goods by their very nature are held in trust by ecclesiastical persons for religious and charitable purposes; and second, it is physically impossible for the pope to administer personally all these goods. The property of the Holy See is administered immediately by the cardinal camerlengo, especially when the papacy is vacant (CIC c.262). The possessions of other moral persons are administered indirectly by the Holy See, that is, through subordinate superiors whose activity is regulated by the general laws of the Church. Ordinarily the general laws allow much freedom for individual initiative, and they are supplemented by particular law.

Acting in the name of the pope, the Roman Curia exercises a supervisory authority over subordinate administrators. The Congregation of the Council has charge over the entire discipline of the secular clergy and the faithful and supervises the affairs of pastors, canons, pious sodalities, pious legacies and works, Mass stipends, benefices and offices, movable and immovable ecclesiastical goods, diocesan taxes, taxes of the episcopal curias, and similar affairs (CIC c.250).

The Congregation of Seminaries and Universities oversees the temporal administration of seminaries and universities, with due regard for the rights of the Congregation of the Propagation of the Faith in mission territories (CIC c.256).

When the temporal administration of ecclesiastical goods involves a controversy or negotiations between the Church and a civil government, the Council of Extraordinary Affairs is competent (CIC c.255).

Property Within a Diocese. The foundation for the authority of the local ordinary over ecclesiastical property is his jurisdictional power, the exercise of which is limited by the territory and the people assigned to him, as to each bishop, by the pope. In Church law the local ordinary has the duty of supervising the administration of all ecclesiastical goods in his territory, except those goods that have been removed from his jurisdiction (CIC c.1519.1). The term local ordinary includes the residential bishop, abbot, prelate nullius, vicar-general, apostolic administrator, vicar apostolic, prefect apostolic, and all those who temporarily succeed any of these persons in the government of the territory (CIC c.198.1).

The supervisory power of the local ordinary over secular parochial property (that is, property not owned by religious institutions) extends to: (1) all parish churches, even parochial churches that are united *pleno iure* to a religious community, unless a parochial church is owned by a religious community with strict property rights; (2) other parochial property, such as alms for parishoners, the school, and other buildings belonging to the parish; and (3) money donated to an individual religious or a religious house for the benefit of a parish or mission.

The local ordinary must exercise vigilance over certain religious property, such as the administration of religious dowries by major superiors in his territory, the administration of goods of diocesan institutes whose motherhouse is in his diocese, and the administration of the individual houses of diocesan religious in his territory.

Furthermore, the local ordinary must supervise the administration of nonparochial and nonreligious property. His watchful care extends to the administration of pious wills, pious foundations, property belonging to noncollegiate moral persons (hospitals, seminaries, orphanages, and the like), money given in trust to clerics or religious with the condition that it be used for a pious cause, and property of lay associations that have the status of a moral person, even when these associations are established in churches of exempt religious.

Immediate administrative power is wielded by the local ordinary over ecclesiastical property that is strictly diocesan, and all funds belonging to the diocesan seminary (CIC cc.1357, 1359); the *mensa episcopalis,* or property that constitutes specifically the episcopal benefice (CIC cc.1472–83); the property of the cathedral church; alms given for an unspecified charitable purpose; bequests contained in wills (provided that they are not left to a religious institute exempt from his administrative supervision, with the stipulation that they be for strictly internal purposes of the institute); revenue accruing from the establishment of pensions and from levying taxes; property of divided or extinct parishes; and property that the ordinary administers in virtue of a special title of administration, for example, when the conditions of legal prescriptions are verified (CIC cc.1508–12).

Every 5 years the local ordinary has the right and duty of making a visitation of all persons, places, and things within his diocese that are not exempt from his jurisdiction (CIC c.343). On such occasions he can demand an account of all acts of administration, inspect the books, and receive an auditor's report. Furthermore, he can compel ecclesiastical administrators to comply with the requirements of civil law in order to protect ecclesiastical property.

The Code exhorts the local ordinary to regulate local administration by means of diocesan statutes and instructions. At the same time he must observe the limitations placed upon him by the common law, acquired rights, legitimate customs, and other circumstances. The ordinary must respect the rights of the individual moral persons, such as parishes and orphanages, who retain the right to administer their own property. The physical persons who administer such property act in the name of the moral person. However, these administrators are subject to the vigilance and certain regulations of the local ordinary (CIC cc.485, 1182, 1476, 1491).

It is the mind of the Church that the local ordinary's function be primarily one of supervision and vigilance, and that the actual work of administration of ecclesiastical property be performed by his appointees. Hence, the common law requires that the ordinary have in his episcopal city a board of administrators. He is the president of the board and is assisted by two or more qualified members, who should be experts in civil law. The members of the board are appointed by the bishop, after he has conferred with his diocesan consultors, unless another mode has been legitimately established by special law or custom. Laymen are not excluded from membership on the diocesan council of administration (CIC c.1520.1). The members of the board must take an oath in the presence of the ordinary that they will properly perform the duties of their office (CIC c.1520.2).

In the more important administrative matters of the diocese, the bishop must consult with the board of administration. Ordinarily, their vote is only consultative, unless the common law or the charter of foundation states that it is deliberative. Among canonists there is a division of opinion as to the validity of acts performed by a bishop who does not seek the required consultative vote. It is solidly probable that a doubt of law exists in this matter, and hence his actions are valid even when he fails to seek a consultative vote (CIC cc.11, 105, 1520).

When neither the law nor the charter of foundation designates the administrators for goods that belong to a church or pious foundation, the local ordinary must appoint qualified men for 3 years. Whenever laymen share in the administration of ecclesiastical property, they must perform their work in the name of the Church. They are subject to inspection by the local ordinary, who may demand an accounting and prescribe the method of administration (CIC c.1521.1). Although a layman cannot be placed in sole control of the administration of ecclesiastical property, the law does not seem to demand more than the appointment of one cleric.

Because the pastor is the administrator of his parish, the common law does not require that the local ordinary appoint a committee to assist him in his work of administration. Frequently in the U.S. pastors are aided in their administration by two lay trustees. If the lay or clerical appointees participate in the administration of a church, they constitute together with the president (the ecclesiastical administrator) a church council of administration.

Before they assume office, the members of the church board of administration or pious foundation must: (1) take an oath before the local ordinary or *vicar forane* (rural dean) that they will faithfully carry out their administration; (2) make an accurate and specific inventory of immovable and precious movable goods and all other property (if they use an old inventory, they must indicate the goods lost or acquired in the interim, and the inventory must be signed by all the administrators); (3) place one copy in the archives of the administration and another in the diocesan archives. This inventory is to be kept current (CIC c.1522). All holders of benefices in the U.S. have been bound by similar obligation since the Third Plenary Council of Baltimore (ActDecrConcPlenBaltIII 276; CIC cc.1476, 1483).

If a bishop wishes to keep his personal furnishings separate from those of the diocese, he must draw up an authentic inventory of this personal property (CIC c.1299).

Duties of Administrators. All administrators, including pastors and lay trustees, must manifest the same degree of responsibility for ecclesiastical property under their charge, as does the conscientious head of a family. To guarantee that this will be done, the Code states that administrators shall: guard against any loss or damage; observe Canon and civil law and any special rules imposed by the founder, donor, or legitimate authority; collect the revenues and incomes of the property, keep them in a safe place, and spend them according to the intention of the founder or the specifications of pertinent regulations; invest the surplus revenue of the church, with the consent of the local ordinary, in a way which benefits the church; and keep proper records of receipts and expenditures and the documents and papers pertaining to the property rights of the church in the archives. Authentic copies are to be placed in the diocesan archives (CIC c.1523).

Moreover, the Third Plenary Council of Baltimore legislated that adequate fire insurance be carried and that the deeds to parish property be prepared by experts and deposited in the diocesan archives. The Council further decreed that the pastor or church committee must send an annual revision of the inventory of parochial property, including that of the cemetery, to the chancellor. A second copy of the inventory was ordered to be kept on the files of the parish or pious foundation and it was to be presented to the incoming administrator by his predecessor or by the rural dean (ActDecrConcPlenBaltIII 270, 276, 278, 282, 283).

Since the annual report is an integral part of good business practice, the Code directs all clerical and lay administrators to include in this report to the bishop an account of their administration of churches, canonically erected pious houses, and confraternities (CIC cc.690, 691, 1489).

Unless he obtains the written permission of the local ordinary, an administrator acts invalidly when he exceeds the limits of ordinary administration (CIC c.1527.1). Ordinary administration includes the collection of rents, debts, interests or dividends; the payment of debts and taxes; and whatever else is necessary for the ordinary maintenance of church property and personnel. Acts of alienation, the purchase of land, construction of new buildings, extensive repair of old ones, opening of a cemetery, investment of capital, establishment of a parochial institution, and the taking up of a special collection are considered extraordinary acts.

The Church does not consider itself liable for contracts made by ecclesiastical administrators without the permission of the competent superiors, when such contracts work to its disadvantage (CIC c.1527.2). In the U.S. churches and other ecclesiastical institutions are generally incorporated under the provisions of civil law. Ordinarily, the rules of Canon Law and the particular regulations drawn up by the bishop may be embodied in the by-laws of the corporation; thus, unauthorized contracts negotiated by ecclesiastical administrators are null and void before the civil law of the state.

Administrators who have expressly or tacitly accepted the responsibility of an office and later abandoned it on their own authority are held liable for any injury resulting from this action (CIC c.1528). It is evident that they have failed to make a reasonable effort to prevent harm to the Church. The office of administrator should lapse after a reasonable time or when the competent superior accepts the resignation or removes the officeholder.

Involvement in litigation by a church administrator is prohibited under the common law, unless the local ordinary has granted him permission to initiate a law suit or to act as a defendant to a suit in the name of the Church. In case of an emergency, at least the permission of the rural dean must be obtained, and the dean must inform the ordinary immediately about the permission given (CIC c.1526).

The Econome. The office of économe, as distinct from that of the diocesan administrator, exists in Latin law only when the see is vacant. The diocesan consultors must elect an économe, in addition to the spiritual administrator of the diocese (vicar capitular). Even in this case both offices may be united in one person (CIC cc.432, 433). From the moment that the local ordinary takes possession of his see, he becomes *ex officio* the économe of all ecclesiastical goods of the diocese. But in Oriental law the office of économe exists distinct from the position of local ordinary. However, the économe is still under the supervision of the ordinary. *See* ÉCONOME (CANON LAW).

This office flourished as early as the 4th century, and every bishop was obliged by canon 26 of the Council of Chalcedon (451) to have an économe. With the increase of Church property the office grew in prestige. Gradually, as the office of syncellus (vicar-general) developed, the office of économe diminished in stature, and finally the office of économe *sede plena* was eliminated by several Oriental groups.

The recent codification of Oriental law has restored the office of économe, and this action indicates a return to the Eastern tradition that the local ordinary should be relieved of the burden of temporal administration so that he can concentrate on his pastoral duties.

There is a patriarchal économe whose responsibility is the management of the temporal affairs of the patriarchate. He must be a cleric, and he is appointed and removed by the patriarch. Each year he submits a report to the permanent synod, and as least two synodal bishops must examine the report, audit the available funds, inspect the real estate, documents, and securities, and make recommendations for preserving and increasing the patriarchal patrimony (ClerSanc c.299).

Each eparchy (diocese) must have an économe. His qualifications are the same as those of the patriarchal économe, and the two offices can be united, with the consent of the permanent synod, in the patriarch's own eparchy. The eparchial économe has one or more clerical or lay associates.

Under the authority of the bishop, the eparchial économe administers the property of the eparchy, supervises the administration of the ecclesiastical property in the eparchy, and administers personally whatever property does not have an administrator designated by law. He renders an annual report, which is inspected by the bishop and at least one consultor (ClerSanc c.438). The bishop is forbidden to act as immediate administrator, although he may issue instructions and supervise or inspect the administration of the économe.

Bibliography: A. COULY, DDC 1:192–214. J. J. COMYNS, *Papal and Episcopal Administration of Church Property* (CUA CLS 147; Washington 1942). Abbo 2:1518–28. Bousc-Ellis 802–809. Woywod-Smith 2:1518–28. Pospishil PersOr 149, 190–207. J. E. MCMANUS, *The Administration of Temporal Goods in Religious Institutes* (CUA CLS 109; Washington 1937).

[W. J. NESSEL]

CHURCH PROPERTY, ALIENATION OF (CANON LAW)

Alienation is a contract transferring full dominium of property belonging to an ecclesiastical moral person of the Latin or Oriental Churches, so that ownership is lost and the property along with the proprietary title passes into the complete and pacific ownership and possession of another corporation or individual. This is alienation in the strict sense. It occurs in sale, donation, or exchange.

Alienation has also a wide sense, and occurs in mortgages, loans, leases, contracting debts and obligations, issuing bonds and debentures, entering annuity agreements, renouncing active easements, allowing passive easements, and any other transaction that may render the financial condition of the ecclesiastical moral person less secure.

Alienation affects nonperishable property whether movable or immovable (CIC c.1530.1; PostApost c.279.1) but only that portion termed "stable capital." Stable capital is any property that has become, at least by implicit designation of the superior, part of the corporation's capital or assets that are to be permanent or fixed, thus constituting its patrimony. In cases of doubt, real estate is presumed to be stable capital while money is presumed not to be.

Prerequisites. Before alienating, certain prerequisites are to be fulfilled—some necessary for lawfulness, others for validity. The Code requires a just cause (CIC c.1530.1n2; PostApost c.279.1n2) that can be (1) urgent necessity on the part of either the alienating corporation or some other moral or physical person, (2) evident advantage to the Church, or (3) piety, which includes performing some work of religion or the corporal or spiritual works of mercy. Without a just cause, the responsible persons are bound to restitution when the transaction harms the Church. No one but the Holy See can dispense from the need of a just cause.

An appraisal of the property to be alienated must be made by at least two experts, though not necessarily professionals. Their reports, filed separately or together, must be signed (CIC c.1530.1n1; PostApost cc.66.4, 279.1n1). The appraiser is never to consider the blessing or consecration of the property in determining its value (CIC c.1539.1; PostApost c.289.1). The qualifications of experts are judged by the superior, who may appoint them or others. Property may not be alienated for a lesser amount than that for which it was appraised (CIC c.1531.1; PostApost c.280.1).

Religious who petition permission to contract debts or obligations must submit a financial statement listing all previous debts and obligations on the same moral person. Otherwise the permission is invalid (CIC c.534.2; PostApost c.66.5). They must also submit detailed reports of (1) current assets and liabilities; (2) receipts and expenditures for enough years to estimate accurately the normal amounts; and (3) obligations not occurring under liabilities, such as guarantor, surety (apostolic delegate, letter, Nov. 13, 1936).

If property is divisible, the petition to alienate must inform the superior of any part or parts already alienated; otherwise the permission obtained is invalid (CIC c.1532.4; PostApost c.281.3) and subsequent alienation is invalid.

Permission. Depending on the kind of property or its value, permissions of certain superiors are required for the validity of alienation (CIC cc.534, 1281, 1530.1n3; PostApost cc.66, 279.1n3). Permission of the Holy See (*beneplacitum apostolicum*) is required to alienate:

1. Important or major relics, images of great value, and other relics and images held in great esteem by the people (CIC c.1281.1).
2. Offerings made in fulfillment of a vow (votive) at a famous shrine or altar (ActApS 11, 416–419, Jan. 14, 1922; ActApS 14, 160) and those made in memory of departed persons.
3. For Latins: every object classified as precious (CIC cc.534.1, 1532.1n1), i.e., worth more than 1,000 francs; and any object exceeding in value 30,000 lire or francs (CIC cc.534.1, 1532.1n2). For North and Central America the latter at present means $5,000 U.S.; for Canada, $5,000 Canadian; for Great Britain, £2,000 (Bouscaren, *Canon Law Digest* 4:392, 203).
4. For Orientals: any property including precious objects exceeding in value 60,000 francs in the patriarchates, 30,000 francs outside the patriarchates (PostApost cc.66.2n1, 281.1nn1,2). These sums were reduced by one-half on May 10, 1952 (ActApS 44, 632).

By the motu proprio *Pastorale munus* issued by Pope Paul VI on Nov. 30, 1963, the local ordinary may grant permission to alienate ecclesiastical goods up to that sum of money which the national or regional conference of bishops establishes. If the alienation involves a sum higher than this, the permission of the Holy See is needed. For lesser amounts permissions of ordinaries or religious superiors, or both, are required (cf. CIC cc.534.1, 1532.2, 3; PostApost cc.66.2nn2–4, 66.3, 281.1nn2, 3).

According to circumstances in each case, the ecclesiastical superior granting permission to alienate is required to use other precautions in order to avoid all loss to the Church (CIC c.1530.2; PostApost c.279.2), for example, requiring a mortgage or some other legally enforcible method of assuring payment when property is sold.

Alienation must occur at public auction or at least in a public manner, unless circumstances require otherwise, and the property must go to the highest bidder (CIC c.1531.2; PostApost c.280.2). Should it be to the definite advantage of the Church, the local ordinary would be empowered to transact the alienation less publicly or even secretly. If the highest bidder's ability to pay is in any way doubtful, a lower bidder may be selected in order to assure less risk to the Church.

To sell or lease immovable property to the administrator himself, or to his own relatives, a special permission of the local ordinary is required over and above his or the Holy See's permission to alienate. This added requirement extends to the relatives in the second degree of consanguinity or affinity in the Latin Church (CIC c.1540) and to the fourth degree of consanguinity or affinity in the Oriental Church (PostApost c.290) but is not necessary for validity.

All money received (after the expense of the transaction) from alienations must be invested carefully, securely, and advantageously so that the Church benefits (CIC c.1531.3; PostApost c.280.3). The Congregation of the Council (Dec. 17, 1951, ActApS 44, 44) has ruled that money realized from alienating $5,000 or more is to be invested only in acquiring immovable property for the benefit of the Church or of the corporation concerned. This procedure to date has not been required for religious by the Congregation of Religious.

The legitimate superior who permitted the contracting of a debt is to see that it is paid off as soon as possible and is to determine the annual rate of payment on the principal (CIC cc.536.5, 1538.1,2; PostApost cc.68.6, 288.1,2).

Illegal Alienation. Invalid alienations can be sanated only by the Holy See, since the Holy See alone is able to dispense from the required procedures and solemnities.

Those who are deliberately involved in alienation of ecclesiastical property without the required *beneplacitum apostolicum* are excommunicated (CIC c.2347n3). Other penalties are prescribed for invalid alienation of amounts not requiring the consent of the Holy See (CIC c.2347n1,2). These penalties are applicable only when it is alienation in the strict sense, and do not apply when it is alienation in the wide sense.

When alienation in the strict or wide sense is unlawful but valid, a suit for compensation may be entered against the alienator and his heirs (CIC c.1534.1; PostApost c.284.1). But when alienation is invalid, a suit to regain the property may be entered against anyone in possession. This suit may be entered by the one responsible for the invalid procedure, by his superior, by successors of either in office, and by any cleric attached to the Church corporation that held the property before alienating (CIC c.1534.1,2; PostApost c.284.1,2).

Alienations that are unlawful but completed in good faith are subject to the laws on prescription (CIC cc.1508–12; PostApost cc.246–250).

Bibliography: Abbo 2:1530–35, 1539. Bousc-Ellis 746, 779, 870. G. Vromant, *De bonis Ecclesiae temporalibus* (Louvain 1927). J. F. Cleary, *Canonical Limitations on the Alienation of Church Property* (CUA CLS 100; Washington 1936). E. L. Heston, *The Alienation of Church Property in the United States* (CUA CLS 132; Washington 1941); "The Element of Stable Capital in Temporal Administration," *Jurist* 2 (1942) 120–133. A. Larraona, "Commentarium Codicis," ComRel 13 (1932) 187–191, 353–358; 14 (1933) 41–44. J. B. Stenger, *The Mortgaging of Church Property* (CUA CLS 169; Washington 1942). *Dictionarium morale et canonicum* (Rome 1962–) v.1.

[J. B. STENGER]

CHURCH PROPERTY, CANON LAW OF

Church property includes corporeal or incorporeal things that belong either to the universal Church and to the Apostolic See or to some other moral person established in the Church (CIC c.1497.1; PostApost c.234.1). Corporeal Church property is either immovable, e.g., land, or movable, e.g., a chalice. Incorporeal property is exemplified by stocks or bonds. A distinction is made between sacred things, which are set apart for divine worship by consecration or blessing (e.g., a church); precious things of notable artistic, historical, or material value; and ordinary property (CIC c.1497.2; PostApost c.234.2).

History. From prehistoric times men have set aside, embellished and maintained special places for worship, and have supported men who would lead the worship. The records of Sumer and Egypt show that great temples, richly endowed, were built to house the gods of the city or kingdom and their high priests and assistants. The laws of Greece and Rome permitted certain gods, i.e., their temples with the groups that served there, to be recipients of gifts or to be named as heirs in wills. The property was considered *res sacra,* untouchable even by the testator's children, once it was dedicated to the temple. Moreover it was suggested, and Canon Law requires, that heirs should honor the pious intention of the donor even if the instrument failed for want of formalities (CIC c.1513.2; PostApost c.251.2). In return the temples and their priests helped the people in times of need.

With the coming of a supranational Church, temples were no longer the dwellings of the national gods and ministers were the interpreters of a supranational law rather than a code given for a particular nation. Men found difficulty in adapting to the new situation concepts that gave legal protection to religion.

At first the Roman Empire reacted by outlawing the new doctrine, and for 3 centuries the property of the Christian Church was held in whatever way was feasible. During lulls in the persecution property was acquired, and decisions, even imperial, were rendered in favor of the Christian Church's right to hold property. Thus, Alexander Severus (A.D. 235) awarded land to Christian claimants rather than to tavern-keepers, saying that it was better that a god be worshipped there in some way. Aurelian (A.D. 275) awarded the bishop's residence at Antioch to Domnus, recognized as lawfully entitled thereto by Italian bishops and the bishop of Rome, rather than to Paul of Samosata who had been condemned as a heretic. The Edict of Milan (A.D. 313) restored to the Christians not only those places where they had been accustomed to meet but also others that belonged to their corporate entity and that had been confiscated during the final persecution. Despite the anti-Christian laws the Church had acquired a considerable amount of property.

Constantine and his successors approved acquisitions of property by the Christian Church, which became the official church of the empire, and restricted the holdings of other groups. Justinian's Code reflects the attempt to adapt older Roman concepts to the new situation. It allows a testator to name as heir "Jesus Christ," i.e., the Christian Church in the place where the testator had his domicile (CorpIurCivCod 1.2.25). Approval was given also to sales of Church property to sustain life in times of famine (CorpIurCivCod 1.2.21). This was reminiscent of an earlier idea, which is mentioned above. Formerly god or temple had been named as heir, and the property of the temple, administered by the high priest, had been allowed to be used for worship, for the support of the priest and his assistants, and to provide help for the people in times of hardship. But the approval mentioned in CorpIurCivCod 1.2.21 does not furnish us with any clear idea of the theory of ownership applied to Church property in the period of Justinian.

The tribes that migrated into Western Europe at first treated the Christian Church as one of their conquered Roman subjects, so it continued to be governed by the rules contained in its own canons and in the legislation of Justinian. Upon their conversion to Christianity, following their penchant for concreteness, these Germanic peoples considered the altar and the ground on which it stood the property of the saint to whom it was dedicated. The rest of the church building and its grounds, as well as the rents, tithes, and other income by which it was supported, were considered iron appurtenances of that altar-ground.

With the decline of urban life in Western Europe in the early Middle Ages the bishops had to provide for those living outside the see city, as the bishops in the more populous Middle East had already done. While establishing parishes in the expanses of territory between cities in the West, they encountered a complication arising from feudal law. Not infrequently a nobleman built a church on his domains and required his serfs to attend and to contribute to it rather than to the parish church. The bishops at first could do little more than refuse to consecrate these patronal churches unless proper provision was made for their support and that of those who would serve there (CIC cc.1162.2, 1415). Only after a long struggle was the administration of such Church property reserved to the pastor acting under the supervision of the bishop (CIC cc.1476–78; PostApost cc.258, 261, 264.1).

In such a situation it was no longer feasible to have a single diocesan fund, administered by the bishop through his archdeacon, for the building and maintenance of the cathedral, for the support of the bishop and his assistant clergy, and for works of charity, spiritual or temporal. Separate funds had to be established for the support of individual parish churches, their pastors and assistants, their schools and other charities, with a *cathedraticum for the bishop acknowledging his jurisdiction over the parish (CIC c.1504; PostApost c.242).

The great abbeys that could afford protection to those living on their lands were given more and more farms on condition that the donors and their heirs could continue to live there as tenants of the abbeys.

By the 13th century the medieval canonists, more given to speculating on the theories behind the law than were the Roman jurists, had worked out the idea that each *benefice, whether diocese, parish, or canonry, was a separate legal entity. Therefore a fund, established as a legal entity, was set aside in perpetuity by competent ecclesiastical authority to provide a living for those who would perform certain services connected with the worship of God (CIC cc.1409–11; PostApost c.308). Similarly, endowments of hospitals, orphanages, and other pious works were treated as a trust to be applied according to the wishes of the settlor or testator (CIC cc.1489–90, 1544–51; PostApost cc.294–301). In addition to such nonmembership corporations or trusts there were membership corporations, chapters, abbeys, and other religious communities that held property (CIC cc.531–536; PostApost cc.63–68).

Despite occasional forced loans, e.g., to fight the invading Saracens in A.D. 732, and outright expropriations contrary to the canons (CIC cc.2345–47), gifts and bequests, together with careful management, increased the endowments of the churches, abbeys, and trust funds in the course of centuries.

To avoid improvident management, certain limits were placed upon alienation of such properties (CIC cc.1530–33, 1538; PostApost cc.66, 279–283, 288), requiring the administrators to justify their actions before undertaking to sell or give away (CIC cc.537, 1535; PostApost cc.69, 285) property that was intended for the benefit of the Christian community or the needy members thereof. Commercial interests developing in the 13th century found irksome the restraints on alienation, whether secular or ecclesiastical. Statutes of mortmain (dead hand) were adopted to limit the amount of land that could be given to the Church and thus taken out of the course of commerce.

When the unity of Western Christendom was broken up into national churches, those that were officially recognized continued, with the support of the state, to acquire, hold, and administer property. Those that were not official found themselves once more in the situation that had existed at the time of the Edict of Milan. They had to acquire, hold, and administer property in whatever way was possible under the laws of the particular country (CIC c.1520.1; PostApost c.263.1). Modern practice varies from the favoring of one religious group and the exclusion of all others, to the exclusion of all. In between there are various degrees of support or of exclusion of the right of a church to acquire, hold, and administer property.

Acquisition of Property. With variations as to each, then, the Church acquires property in many ways. One way is by gifts (CIC cc.1513.1, 2348; PostApost c.251.1). When given to a person in charge of a church, they are presumed to be intended for that church, unless the contrary is specified (CIC c.1536.1; PostApost c.286.1). Gifts cannot be refused without permission of the bishop (CIC c.1536.2–3; PostApost c.286.2–3). Once they are accepted they cannot be withdrawn simply because the one in charge of the church does not show sufficient gratitude (CIC c.1536.4; PostApost c.286.4).

Legacies, bequests, and devises in wills (CIC cc.1493, 1513–15; PostApost cc.251–253) are other means by which the Church acquires property. Again, dues and fees (CIC c.1410) are paid as being incidental to membership in the group served by the church or to the request for the performance of special services. Tithes and first fruits can be received (CIC c.1502; PostApost c.239) in areas where there are local rules or customs regarding them. Income from investments in land (CIC cc.1541–42; PostApost cc.291–292) or securities (CIC cc.1523n3–4, 1481, 533.1; PostApost cc.269n3–4, 65.1) is another source of property for the Church, its ministers, and its poor (CIC c.1473).

When entering certain religious orders of women it is customary for girls to bring dowries (CIC c.547.1–3; PostApost c.79.1–3). This money is invested (CIC c.549; PostApost c.81), with the consent of the bishop (CIC c.533.1–2; PostApost c.65.1–3), so that the income is available for their support. Hence the principal cannot be spent before the death of the religious, at which time it becomes property of the community (CIC c.548; PostApost c.80). Premature use of this principal incurs the penalty of loss of office by a superior who should spend it (CIC c.2412n1). Should a girl decide to leave the community, the principal of the dowry is returned to her (CIC c.551.1; PostApost c.83.1). *See* DOWRY, CANON LAW.

The Church can acquire property also by occupation, accession, *prescription, seat rents, bazaars, etc. The primary source, however, is collections, which are carefully regulated. Thus, private individuals, whether clergymen or laymen, are forbidden to collect money for any pious or ecclesiastical institute or purpose unless they have the permission, in writing, of the Apostolic See, the patriarch, or their own bishop or superior, and of the bishop of the diocese in which they wish to make such a collection (CIC c.1503; PostApost c.240.1).

Free-will Offerings. Certain religious orders have been approved as mendicant, i.e., living from alms given them. These groups can take up collections, with permission of their own superiors, if they are already established (CIC c.497) in a diocese. Although they are required to have the written permission of the bishops of neighboring dioceses to take up collections there, the bishops are not to deny or revoke such permission except for grave and urgent reasons, if the community cannot be supported by collecting only in the diocese where it is established (CIC c.621).

In order to take up a collection, members of religious congregations other than mendicants must have a particular concession from the Apostolic See, and unless that concession provides otherwise, the written permission of the patriarch and of the bishop of the diocese (CIC c.622.1; PostApost c.171.1n1–3, 171.2).

Members of a group established in a diocese by the bishop thereof must have his written permission to take up a collection. If they wish to collect outside that diocese, they must have the permission also of the bishop of the other diocese (CIC c.622.2; PostApost c.171.1n3, 171.2).

Bishops are not to give permission for such collections to the two groups last named, especially where mendicants are already established, unless they are clearly convinced of the true need of a group or pious work for which other provision cannot be made. The area, too, within which the collection is permitted is restricted (CIC c.622.3; PostApost c.171.4).

If someone from the Oriental rites wishes to take up a collection in territory of the Latin rite, or vice versa, he must have written permission of the Congregation for the Oriental Church and of the bishop or eparch who has jurisdiction over the territory (CIC c.622.4; Post Apost cc.171.1n4, 240.3).

Furthermore, superiors of religious communities are not to entrust the taking up of collections to any but professed members of their communities who are mature both in age and wisdom, especially when they are women. Never may superiors assign to this task those who are still in school (CIC c.623; PostApost c.172).

As to the methods to be used in taking up collections and the rules to be followed by the collectors, members of religious communities, whether men or women, must abide by the instructions of the Apostolic See (CIC c.624; PostApost c.173).

No association of lay persons is permitted to take up a collection unless its constitution and bylaws allow it, and necessity requires. Permission of the bishop must be obtained for both the collection and the manner of taking it up; the approval of both bishops is required if the collection is to be taken up outside the diocese in which the association has its headquarters (CIC c.691.3–4).

Ownership of Property. The ownership of the property acquired in any of these ways is, under the supreme jurisdiction of the Apostolic See, vested in that church, corporation, or trust that has lawfully acquired it (CIC c.1499.2; PostApost c.236.2). In addition, therefore, to the Apostolic See (which holds property for its own purposes), patriarchates, archdioceses, dioceses, eparchies, abbeys, and prelacies subject to no bishop (CIC c.319.1), and vicariates and prefectures apostolic (CIC c.293–294) have their own property. Similarly, parishes and other churches, e.g., shrines, hold property.

Chapters of canons who take care of divine services in cathedrals or other churches have property for the support of the group and of the individual members. Abbeys have property of their own and, if united in a monastic congregation, they have means for support of the superior of the congregation and his staff (CIC c.488n2; PostApost cc.11.1, 313.1). A religious community of pontifical right has a general house serving as headquarters for the entire community, where the general superior and his staff live and have their offices (CIC c.502; PostApost c.29); provincial houses (CIC c.488n6; PostApost c.314.4) take care of the needs of the provincial superior and his staff. Individual communities whose members serve some church or school usually have a separate residence (CIC cc.531, 536; PostApost cc.9.2, 16, 19.2, 68).

Religious communities, though chartered only within the limits of one or two dioceses, also have houses for their members (CIC c.488n3; PostApost c.17). Those also who live a community life without vows have houses of their own (CIC 676.1; PostApost c.227.1). While members of secular institutes may live in their own houses, they contribute to the support of a central house to which they can go for retreats or when they are ill or ready for retirement [*Provida Mater Ecclesia* (ActApS 38:114) Art. 2.1; Art. 3.4]. Associations of laymen, established in the Church (CIC c.686), possess property for their own purposes (CIC c.691); they are usually third orders, archconfraternities, confraternities, primary pious unions, or other pious unions (CIC c.701.1).

Nonmembership corporations or trusts, such as hospitals and orphanages, have their own property (CIC c.1489) to be used as the settlor or testator has indicated. He may specify the purpose, administration, use of income, and disposal, in case the institute should cease to exist (CIC c.1490.1). Moreover, such moral persons, as well as churches (CIC cc.1549.1, 1550; PostApost cc.299–300) may hold *pious foundations, i.e., property given them with the perpetual or long-term obligation to offer the Sacrifice of the Mass or perform certain other ecclesiastical functions or works of piety or charity (CIC c.1544; PostApost c.294).

If goods are given to a clergyman or a member of a religious community in trust for pious purposes, whether by gift *inter vivos* or by will, he must notify the bishop or superior of his trust and furnish an inventory of all such goods, movable or immovable, together with a list of obligations imposed. If the donor forbids this, he cannot accept the trust. The bishop must see that the entrusted goods are safely invested and he must watch over the execution of pious wills. If the property of a trust is given to a member of a religious community for the churches of the locality or diocese to help the people or for pious purposes there, the bishop of the diocese is to be notified and to supervise it; otherwise the superior of the religious community must do so (CIC c.1516; PostApost c.254).

When the territory served by a moral person is divided so that a part of it is united to some other, or a separate corporation or trust is established for the part separated, the common property that was intended for the benefit of the whole territory and the debts contracted for the whole territory are divided equitably between them by the ecclesiastical authority that has the right to make the division. In such division the wills of founders or settlors, acquired rights, and special rules whereby the corporation or trust is governed must be safeguarded (CIC cc.494.1, 1427.1, 1500; PostApost cc.15, 237).

If a church can no longer be used for divine worship and there is no way of restoring it, it can be turned over to other, but not to sordid, uses, and the bishop can transfer the obligations, income, and title of the parish, if it is a parish church, for another church (CIC c.1187).

If an ecclesiastical moral person ceases to exist, the property passes to the corporation or trust immediately superior, always safeguarding the wishes of founders or settlors, lawfully acquired rights, and the special rules whereby the extinct corporation or trust was governed (CIC c.1501; PostApost 238).

No religious community, once it is lawfully established, even if it consists of but one house, can be suppressed except by the Holy See. The right to dispose of the property is reserved to the Holy See, always safeguarding the will of those who donated it (CIC c.493; PostApost c.14).

If a confederation of monasteries ceases to exist, or is suppressed, the Apostolic See or the patriarch determines the disposition of the property (PostApost c.12.2–3). If a province ceases to exist, the determination of what to do with its property, safeguarding the requirements of justice and the will of the donors, pertains to the general chapter. Apart from the time of the chapter, if a decision is necessary, the general superior, with his council, decides (CIC c.494.2; PostApost c.15.2).

Right to Property. A fundamental right to acquire, retain, and administer temporal goods for the attainment of their own particular reasons for existing is asserted for the Catholic Church and the Apostolic See. It is free and independent of the civil authority. (CIC c.1495.1; PostApost c.232.1). Groups of churches, individual churches, and other corporations or trusts established by ecclesiastical authority have a similar right within the limits laid down by Canon Law (CIC c.1495.2; Post Apost cc.232.2, 235). The Church, independently of the civil power, can require from the faithful what is necessary for divine worship, for the proper support of its clergy and other workers, and for any of the reasons for which it exists (CIC c.1496; PostApost c.233). It can, therefore, acquire temporal things in all the ways in which other persons can when these are in accord with natural or positive law (CIC c.1499.1; PostApost c.236.1).

While the Church has ever preached a spirit of detachment from things of this world, it could not fulfill its reason for existing in the world if it did not have a certain amount of property. For instance, the Vicar of Christ has to have land and buildings where he and those who assist him can do their work for the universal Church, and means to keep up the property and support himself and his coworkers as well. The same is to be said of his brother bishops and their coworkers. Even in countries where the cathedral is also a parish church, supported by the parish, the bishop must have a residence and an office in which he can transact diocesan business. While his coworkers may reside in various parishes, they need space in a central building where their activities can be coordinated. In addition, there are certain works of religion, e.g., education of seminarians (CIC cc.1352–71) and of charity, e.g., provision for the infirm and aged, that exceed the capacities of the individual parishes and must be supported on a diocesan scale. These require land, buildings, furnishings, and maintenance, together with support for those who work there. For all these reasons the dioceses must possess property.

Since Mass is to be offered in a church or oratory that has been consecrated or blessed (CIC cc.822.1, 1165.1), not, ordinarily, out of doors (CIC c.1249) or in chapels, cemeteries, or private homes (CIC cc.1194–95), a parish must have land on which to build a church and rectory, and the funds to furnish (CIC cc.1296–1306) and maintain them as well as to support the pastor and assistants who serve there (CIC c.1162.2).

Support must be secured not only for the clergy but also for the sacristan, the organist, and those who work in the church or cemetery (CIC c.1185). Each parish should have a cemetery unless there is a single one established by the bishop for several parishes together (CIC c.1208.1). Church employees must be paid a living, family wage, which, as the Church teaches, is required in justice (CIC c.1524; PostApost c.272.1).

The parish needs land and a building for a school (CIC c.1379.1) and funds for its furnishings and maintenance if it is to provide the traditional spiritual works of mercy and education. It needs a house for the sisters teaching there, as well as funds to furnish and maintain it and to support the sisters.

Religious communities need houses if the members are to perform their functions in the Church. Similarly, charitable institutions must have buildings and income if they are to serve the people in time of need.

Hence the Church has condemned those who oppose all ownership of property, or Church ownership, or who give all power to the State of this regard.

Bibliography: Abbo 2:1495–1551. Woywod-Smith 2:1487–1544. Beste 1495–1551. Regatillo 2:277–335.

[T. O. MARTIN]

CHURCHES, CANON LAW OF

By the name "church" is understood a sacred building dedicated to divine worship, having the principal purpose of serving the faithful in the public exercise of divine worship (CIC c.1161). This definition distinguishes a church from *oratories which are defined as places destined for divine worship but not having the principal purpose of serving the faithful at large in the public exercise of their religion (CIC c.1188.1).

History. For the celebration of the Eucharist the first Christians usually assembled in the private homes of wealthy Christians. By the middle of the 3d century some of these homes had been converted into house-churches. With Constantine's victory over Maxentius in 312 and a rapid increase in the number of Christians, larger buildings became necessary for worship. During the 4th and 5th centuries a style of church architecture developed that became known by the name of the Latin basilica.

In the 5th and 6th centuries, the legislation of several councils introduced a distinction between churches and oratories. The term "church" was progressively limited to places of worship that enjoyed the rights of parishes. Places of worship constructed by private families or in monasteries were referred to as oratories and later as chapels. By the 9th century numerous councils had enacted legislation that obliged all the faithful to assist at Mass on Sundays and feast days in their parish churches.

The appearance, in the 13th century, of mendicant orders consecrated to the active life, threw into confusion the distinction between churches and oratories or chapels. The religious mendicants opened their chapels for the use of the faithful even on Sundays and holy days of obligation. In spite of the opposition of the secular clergy to this violation of their parochial rights, the obligation of assisting at Mass in the parish church was gradually abolished through contrary custom in many regions. In the 16th century Leo X, Pius V, and Clement VIII granted religious the privilege of admitting the faithful to their chapels for the purpose of fulfilling their Mass obligation. The Council of Trent mildly reminded the bishops to exhort their faithful to attend Mass in their parishes frequently, at least on Sundays and the greater feasts.

When the legislation governing churches, chapels, and oratories became for all practical purposes the same, the terms gradually lost their own meanings and were often used interchangeably. This confusion in terminology continued until the 19th century. At that time a question arose concerning the celebration of the feast day of the titular saint of a church. The rubrics imposed the obligation of celebrating the titular feast on churches, but not on oratories. In a reply given in 1855 and confirmed in 1899, the Sacred Congregation of Rites made the following distinction: "A church is built primarily for the public use of the faithful. A public chapel, on the other hand, even though it may have an entrance on a public street, is meant for the convenience of some family or community rather than for the free use of the faithful." These decrees were the source of the distinction between churches and oratories which we find in canon 1161 of the present Code of Canon Law.

Legislation. The most recent norms concerning churches are the directives laid down by the Vatican Council II. Article 128 of the Council's *Constitution on the Sacred Liturgy* directs that "there is to be an early revision of the ecclesiastical laws and statutes which govern the provision of material things involved in public worship. Any laws which seem less suited to the reformed liturgy are to be brought into harmony with it, or else abrogated; and any which are helpful are to be retained if already in force, or introduced where they are lacking." The Council gives explicit recognition to the principle of cultural adaptation: "The local bishops' conferences are empowered to adapt such things to the needs and customs of their different regions; this applies especially to the materials and styles of church furnishings and of sacred vestments."

The principles for the reform of church architecture and legislation date back to 1922 when a group of clergy, architects, and artists was formed in Germany to study the basic principles of modern church design. The group included Ildefons Herwegen, Abbot of the Benedictine monastery of Maria Laach, and Romano Guardini. Their work served to clarify the following principles: (1) The church building is the house of the Church, the *domus ecclesiae,* in the Biblical sense of that word; the house of the people who are themselves the temple of the living God, the habitation of the Spirit; a spiritual house built of living stones. It has no meaning apart from the community which it serves. Reduced to its bare essentials, it is a building to house a congregation gathered round an altar. (2) The church building is also the house of God, the *domus Dei.* If its primary function is to provide a convenient space for the people of God to celebrate the liturgy, it is also an embodiment, a visible manifestation, of what the Church is and believes. If the plan and structure of the church building are informed by a genuine understanding of the nature of the Christian community and its liturgy, the church will be a true image of the Mystical Body of Christ.

Bibliography: R. K. SEASOLTZ, *The House of God* (New York 1963). P. HAMMOND, *Liturgy and Architecture* (London 1960). Vatican Council, 2d, *The Constitution on the Sacred Liturgy,* commentary G. SLOYAN (Glen Rock, N.J. 1964) chs. 6, 7. H. WAGNON, DDC 5:171–211.

[J. ST. LEGER]

CHURCHES, DEDICATION OF

The consecration of a church is one of the most richly developed rites in the Catholic liturgy. Although the dedication of a church was unknown to primitive Christianity since there were no fixed places of worship, there are in the OT accounts of celebrations similar to the present rite of consecration. After the construction of the Temple at Jerusalem, Solomon gathered the Israelites together to witness the entrance of the Ark of the Covenant into the Holy of Holies (2 Chr 5–7). Likewise, when Judas Machabee regained Jerusalem from the hands of Antiochus IV, he reinaugurated the Temple worship with solemn sacrifice (1 Mc 4). On both occasions, the dedication of the Temple consisted not in a blessing or consecration, but rather in the celebration of worship within the edifice.

Dedication of a church and the burial of relics in the altar, detail of the ivory cover of the Sacramentary of Drogo of Metz (Paris, B. N., MS lat. 9428), c. 855.

History. The first recorded instance of the dedication of a Christian church edifice is that recounted by Eusebius (*Hist. Eccl.* 10.3) when he described the dedication of the basilica of Tyre in 314 under Constantine the Great. The church was dedicated simply by the celebration of Mass, without any additional ceremonies. In the 6th century Pope Vigilius mentioned in a letter to Profuturus of Braga a sprinkling of the edifice with water, but he insisted that a church is to be considered dedicated once Mass has been celebrated in it. In the same letter he mentioned the depositing of relics in the church, a practice that developed out of the custom of celebrating Mass over the tombs of martyrs (PL 69:18).

At the beginning of the Middle Ages, the Roman practices were fused with more solemn and symbolical Gallican rites, especially the anointings of the altar and walls of the church. Finally, William *Duranti the Elder reworked the ceremonial in his edition of the Pontifical that forms the basis for the present Roman Pontifical. Thus there developed an extraordinarily intricate and lengthy rite of dedication whose basic structure was obscured by the multiplicity of details.

Modern Rite. A thoroughly revised and simplified rite of dedication was included in the reformed edition of part 2 of the Roman Pontifical authorized by the Congregation of Rites on April 13, 1961. The present rite may be divided into four parts: (1) the lustration and taking possession, (2) the burial of the relics, (3) the consecration of the church and altar, (4) the Mass of dedication.

The lustration signifies the expulsion of every evil power from the house of God, which is set aside for worship alone. The bishop stands before the locked empty church and prays to the Trinity. He commences the lustration in front of the door and proceeds around the edifice as he sprinkles the walls with "Gregorian" water composed of salt, wine, ashes, and water. Psalm 86 is sung during the procession and is concluded with an oration. Next follows the entrance into the church by the bishop, clergy, and people. In response to the bishop's request that the door be opened, a deacon unlocks the door. During the procession into the church the Litany of the Saints is sung. The lustration of the interior of the church follows, and finally there is the lustration of the altar. The bishop then formally takes possession of the church. With his crosier he inscribes the Latin and Greek alphabets on the beam of a St. Andrew's cross that has been traced on the floor of the presbyterium, or nave, with sand or ashes. This is followed by a solemn prayer and a preface that speaks of the power of prayer in God's house.

The entombment of the relics consists of a procession with the relics and their entombment in the altar,

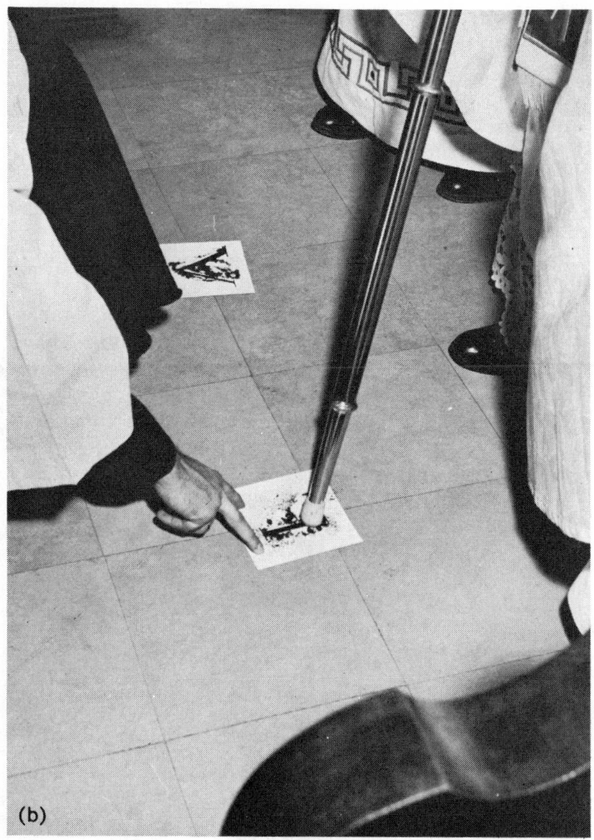

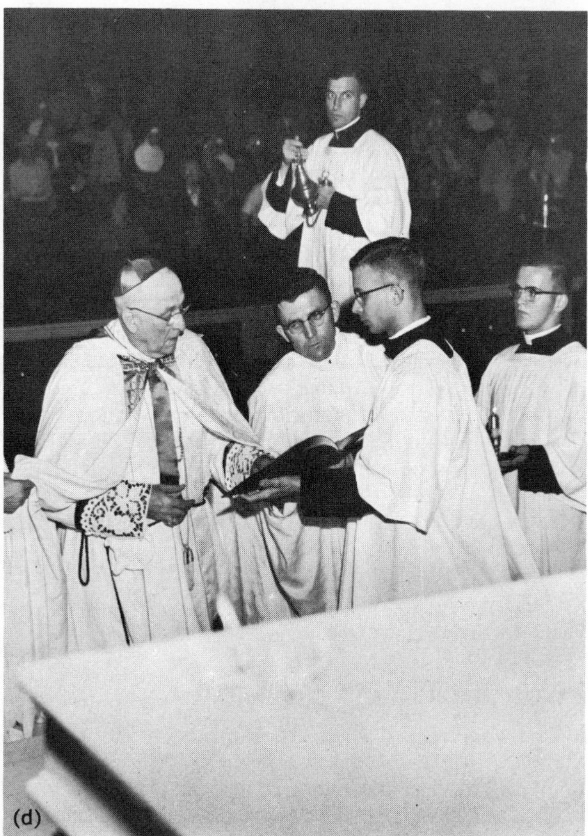

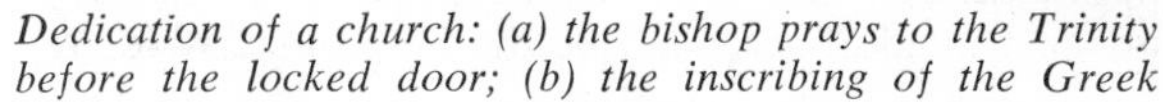

Dedication of a church: (a) the bishop prays to the Trinity before the locked door; (b) the inscribing of the Greek and Latin alphabets; (c) anointing of the wall with sacred chrism; (d) incense is burned on the altar.

accompanied by various antiphons. The rite concludes with an oration.

At 12 places along the walls of the church, which have been marked by consecration crosses, the bishop anoints the walls of the church with sacred chrism. These crosses symbolize the 12 Apostles, the foundation stones of the heavenly Jerusalem (Ap 21.14). Each cross is incensed, and a candle is lighted before each. When the bishop arrives at the church door, he anoints the door posts. The consecration of the church concludes with an oration.

The consecration of the altar follows. The altar table and supports are anointed while Psalm 44 is sung. Then the altar is incensed, and a symbolic sacrifice of incense is burned on it. The consecration of the altar is concluded by a solemn prayer and the consecratory Preface of the dedication. While Psalm 95 is chanted, the altar is prepared for Mass. The Mass concluding the dedication is normally celebrated by the bishop himself. The text is the proper Mass for the dedication of a church with a commemoration only of the patron of the church. (*See* ALTAR, 4.)

Legislation. Canon Law stipulates that the liturgy may not be celebrated in a new church until it has been dedicated either by solemn consecration or by the rite of simple blessing (CIC c.1165.1) contained in the Roman Ritual. However, cathedral, collegiate, conventual, and parochial churches are normally to be consecrated (c.1165.3); and only churches made of stone, brick, or reinforced concrete may be consecrated, whereas those made of wood or metal are blessed (c.1165.4). If the church is only blessed, the rite may be performed by the ordinary or any other priest with the permission of the ordinary (c.1166.2).

The consecration of a church is celebrated as a feast of the Lord for those who are attached to the church. Although the dedication may take place on any day, it should be held on a Sunday or feast day (c.1166.1). It is fitting that the consecrator and those who are associated with the church fast and abstain on the day before the dedication. The anniversary of the dedication of consecrated churches and the feast of the titular of churches that are consecrated or at least solemnly blessed are celebrated as first class feasts.

A church loses its consecration or blessing if it is entirely destroyed, if most of its walls collapse, or if it is converted to profane uses (c.1170). A church is violated if certain notorious criminal actions are performed within it. In such a case the church should be reconciled as soon as possible according to the rite contained in the Roman Pontifical.

Bibliography: P. DE PUNIET, DACL 4.1:374–405. J. LOEW, "The New Rite of Consecration," *Worship* 35 (1961) 527–536. "La Dédicace des églises," *Maison-Dieu* 70 (1962), special issue. R. W. L. MUNCEY, *History of the Consecration of Churches and Churchyards* (Cambridge, Eng. 1930). **Illustration credit:** Fig. 1. Photo Archives-Maria Laach.

[R. K. SEASOLTZ]

CHURCHES, LAW GOVERNING (U.S.)

The Federal and state governments in the United States recognize the absolute right of religious belief or nonbelief, and the right of freedom to practice religion, limited only by the health, morals, and peace of the community in question. In regard to the Federal government, the First Amendment of the Constitution provides that: "Congress shall make no law respecting an establishment of religion, or prohibiting the free exercise thereof . . .." This amendment has been judicially interpreted by the courts to guarantee to every person the absolute right to have any religious or nonreligious convictions whatsoever, and to express these convictions in action as long as the overt acts do not adversely affect the common good (*see* FREEDOM OF RELIGION, U.S. LAW OF). By 1833, all the states voluntarily followed the Federal policy by incorporating a neutral position toward religious belief or nonbelief and religious worship or nonworship in their constitutions.

A further guarantee of religious belief and practice in the area of the states came from two epoch-making decisions of the Supreme Court. In 1871, the case of *Watson v. Jones* [80 U.S. (13 Wall.) 679], held in effect that the court of appeals of Kentucky had no authority to rule that the General Assembly of the Presbyterian Church in the U.S. exceeded its jurisdiction in determining a church dispute. It stated (p. 728) that: "In this country the full and free right to entertain any religious belief, to practice any religious principle, and to teach any religious doctrine which does not violate the laws of morality and property, and which does not infringe personal rights, is conceded to all. . . ." It is significant that the holding in *Watson* was ". . . founded in a broad and sound view of the relations of church and state under our system of laws, and supported by a preponderating weight of judicial authority. . ." (727).

In 1940, the same court ruled in the case of *Cantwell v. Connecticut* (310 U.S. 296), that the First Amendment bound not only the Federal government, but also the states through the due process clause of the *Fourteenth Amendment, namely, ". . . nor shall any State deprive any person of life, liberty, or property, without due process of law. . . ." From then on, the U.S. Supreme Court has upheld religious freedom in the area of the states under the liberty clause of the Fourteenth Amendment, rather than under the general principles of the Anglo-American legal system, i.e., apparently, objective natural law, which had been the basis of the holding in the pioneer case of *Watson v. Jones* (*supra*).

Nonestablishment. Under the uniquely American doctrine of "separation of Church and State," neither the Federal government nor any state government may recognize the existence of any church or denomination as a matter of law. Recognition as a legal entity would give a privileged position to religion. But this is constitutionally forbidden. A legal entity is an artificial person before the law with rights and duties analogous to those of a natural person.

One historical exception, however, may be mentioned. The legal personality of the Roman Catholic Church was recognized by the U.S. in Cuba, the Philippines, and Puerto Rico in 1898 [*Ponce v. Roman Catholic Apostolic Church in Porto Rico,* 210 U.S. 296 (1908); *Santos v. Holy Roman Catholic and Apostolic Church, Parish of Tambobong, Phillippines,* 212 U.S. 463 (1909); and *Gonzalez v. Roman Catholic Archbishop of Manila,* 280 U.S. 1 (1929)]. Article VI of the Federal Constitution provides, among other things, that: "This Constitution and the Laws of the United States which shall be made in Pursuance thereof; and all Treaties made, or which shall be made, under the Authority of the United States, shall be the Supreme Law of the

Land. . . ." In 1898, the law made by the Treaty of Paris between Spain and the U.S. (30 U.S. Stat. at Large 1754) constituted the supreme law of the land. In this treaty, the executive branch of the U.S. government conceded the legal personality of the Catholic Church, and papal sovereignty, under international law in those territorial acquisitions that were formerly under Spanish dominion. From the very beginning of Spanish colonization after 1492, the legal personality of the Church, with unrestricted corporate rights, including ownership of property, had been acknowledged by a number of concordats entered into between Spain and the Papacy.

International law obliged the executive branch of the U.S. government to allow the continuation of the status quo in regard to the law of the Catholic Church in those Spanish possessions that were acquired in 1898. The treaty-making power in turn bound the U.S. Supreme Court to give effect to the action of the executive branch. It may be noted that the imposed obligations of international law ultimately rest on the authority of natural law. (*See* DIPLOMACY, PAPAL.)

Incorporation of Churches. Most of the states will allow any or all churches to achieve the advantages of legal personality by the formation of a corporation to act for the church in temporal matters. Since 1837, a distinction has been made between the congregation, the church, and the corporation [*Miller v. Baptist Church,* 16 N.J.L. 251 (1837)]. This distinction continues to exist [*Gray v. Good,* 89 N.E. 498 (Ind. 1909)]. The congregation is the visible group of persons who meet at stated intervals to worship God. But the members of the congregation are not necessarily the members of the church. Thus they may not accept all the tenets of the church, for example. But the church is the spiritual entity, resulting from those in the group in question who have church membership, profess the same basic religious faith, and are subject to the same ecclesiastical discipline through rules and regulations [*Hundley v. Collins,* 32 So. 575 (Ala. 1902)].

Since no church is recognized as a legal entity, it may not acquire, hold, or transfer property, borrow money, sue, or be sued. But special laws exist in all the states of the union, except Virginia and West Virginia, under which churches may incorporate for these purposes. By "church," in this connection, is meant a group of three or more persons who represent the ecclesiastical body in question, or who are its trustees.

Of course, it is not necessary for churches to incorporate. If they decide to do so, they may use either the special laws for church corporations, or the general laws for nonprofit corporations. The church corporation is not the church. It is rather a legal entity established to possess and administer property, and to perform various legal acts for the benefit of the religious society. In fact, the church and the church corporation are indissolubly connected, but in law, they are two absolutely separate and distinct entities (*Hundley v. Collins, supra*). Since freedom of religious worship is constitutionally guaranteed within the limits of right reason, any group of persons may join together to form a church without the authority of the state. But state authority is necessary to incorporate.

The corporation has no denominational character or ecclesiastical function. To some extent it is controlled by the state. It must comply with state laws in regard to its incorporation and continuance. These laws will be enforced by the state.

At first, the special church incorporation laws were not satisfactory, but they gradually improved. Generally speaking, they are adequate to accommodate the purposes of all types of churches, namely, congregational, synodal, and prelatial. The civil law has recognized the rights of these three types of churches to incorporate trustees or individual members, as a corporation aggregate, or, in the instance of the prelatial type, to incorporate the bishop as a corporation sole [*Mora v. Murphy,* 23 P. 63 (Calif. 1890)].

Moral Personality of Churches. All churches in the U.S. are regarded as voluntary associations of individuals. But a considerable evolution has taken place in the concept of the nature of church membership. In the first stage, the courts held that members were bound to their church by a contract that did not substantially differ from other contracts for business or pleasure [*Stebbins v. Jennings,* 27 Mass. (10 Pick.) 172 (1830); *Perry v. Tupper,* 74 N.C. 550 (1876); *Hundley v. Collins, supra*]. But in the second period, the Federal courts and a considerable number of state courts held that the relations of a member to his church are not contractual. According to *Nance v. Busby* [18 S.W. 874 (Tenn. 1892), at p. 879]: "No bond of contract, express or implied, connects him with his communion or determines his rights. Church relationship stands upon an altogether higher plane, and church membership is not to be compared to that resulting from connections with mere human associations for profit, pleasure, or culture." This view had earlier been expressed in *Watson v. Jones* (*supra*). In the *Nance* case, the court declared (p. 879): "We think that the effect of the judgment of this congregation, it being that of the only judicature known to such an independent church, is as great as if it was the decision of the last church judicature in a church more highly organized."

It was stated in *Watson v. Jones* (*supra*) that a church may have a governmental structure with a true juridical order, like the Roman Catholic and Presbyterian churches, or have no higher law-making power, like the Baptist and Congregational churches. If a church has a government structure, it may be of the prelatial or hierarchical type, with different echelons of superiors like the Catholic Church, or it may be of synodal type, with different levels of authoritative bodies or courts, as in the instance of the Presbyterian church. If a church lacks a juridical order, then it is held together wholly by spiritual and organizational means. It is for the particular church to decide the matter of its structure [*Klix v. Polish Roman Catholic St. Stanislaus Parish,* 118 S.W. 1171 (Mo. 1909)].

Watson v. Jones (*supra*) implicitly recognized that those churches which had true juridical orders were moral persons. It did this by admitting the independence of the decisions of those orders. These decisions were not subject to review by the civil courts. In this way, the existence of an ecclesiastical entity with a degree of permanence and continuity beyond its members was acknowledged.

But *Watson* did not recognize the moral personalities of churches of the congregational type. The Court stated: ". . . the rights of such bodies to the use of the property must be determined by the ordinary principles which govern voluntary associations" (*supra,* 725). Churches of the congregational type recognize no authority higher than that of the local church, and are in no way subject to the discipline or rule of any other body. Authority is moral and ecclesiastical, but not juridical.

But the moral personality of the individual church of the congregational type is recognized. It is regarded as an entity controlled by the majority vote of its members. Their decision is analogous to the formal decree of the tribunal of last recourse in highly organized types of churches (*Nance v. Busby, supra,* 879).

The existence of church groups also is recognized as a matter of fact, especially when legislatures are enacting, modifying, or abrogating laws that affect religion. Informal information may be obtained from such groups under such circumstances in order that the legislation may be as just and fair as possible since this is conducive to the good of society.

Spiritual Disputes. Civil courts will not interfere with the purely spiritual determinations of religious societies. They have no jurisdiction over such matters even though dissatisfied persons appeal for redress. They will not determine any controversy, therefore, that relates solely to ecclesiastical issues. Such issues would arise from questions of faith and morals, heresy, schism, excommunication, expulsion, denial of the sacraments, the appointment and dismissal of the clergy, and the like. The civil courts may challenge the jurisdiction of a church tribunal for fraud, but not the nonfraudulent decision of the highest ecclesiastical tribunal. Of course, civil courts will adjudicate the issue of whether a particular decision has actually been made by the lawful church tribunal in question.

It is now well settled that neither the Federal nor a state government has any authority to name or to remove any priest, rabbi, or minister of any religious denomination. Their appointment and removal are regarded as acts relating to the internal, spiritual affairs of the church, and hence are to be exclusively determined by the laws, customs, and regulations of the particular denomination [*Rector, Churchwardens, and Vestrymen v. Melish,* 146 N.E. 2d. 685 (N.Y. 1957); *Kedroff v. St. Nicholas Cathedral,* 344 U.S. 94 (1952)]. The state may not execute nor forbid action of the church against its priests or ministers.

The civil courts have no jurisdiction over the spiritual relationship that exists between a minister of the gospel and his congregation or his bishop. It has authority only over the temporal aspects of this relationship. Civil courts may not enforce the reciprocal duties between the congregation and the pastor which exist exclusively under church law. [See *Travers v. Abbey,* 58 S.W. 247 (Tenn. 1900).]

It is well settled that civil courts will not review decisions denying the sacraments to a church member, because the church tribunals are better judges of the ecclesiastical law than civil courts [*Carter v. Papineau,* 222 Mass. 464 (1916)]. Even persons who join an independent church voluntarily submit themselves to the arbitrary power of the majority, and tacitly agree to abide by the judgment of that majority, so that no civil court has jurisdiction to annul a decree of excommunication or a denial of the sacraments. It was held in *Shannon v. Frost* [42 Ky. 253 (1842)] that civil courts may not adjudicate the justice or injustice of such a decree. The only remedy is recourse to the ecclesiastical tribunals [*Grosvenor v. United Society of Believers,* 118 Mass. 78 (1875)]. The U.S. Supreme Court declared in *Watson v. Jones* (*supra* 727):

> . . . whenever the questions of discipline, or of faith, or ecclesiastical rule, custom, or law have been decided by the highest of these church judicatories to which the matter has been carried, the legal tribunals must accept such decisions as final, and as binding on them, in their application to the case before them.

Property Rights. Civil courts will assume jurisdiction over church disputes if civil or property rights are involved, but only to the extent necessary for the protection of these rights. Civil courts will intervene in a church dispute only to the extent necessary to protect these rights when they undertake to adjudicate such rights. Of course, it is for the civil courts to decide whether civil or property rights are involved in a particular dispute.

Sometimes ecclesiastical tribunals render a decision that affects civil rights or the disposition of property. Of course, the decisions of church tribunals that deal with property and legal rights do not have the force of a judgment for which execution or other legal implementation will issue. But civil courts consider ecclesiastical tribunals as legally constituted in their own sphere, with their own proper jurisdiction. Hence, it was held in *Elston v. Wilborn,* that:

> In the United States of America where Church and State are separate, the courts have steadily asserted their refusal to determine any controversy relating purely to ecclesiastical or spiritual features of a church or religious society. The courts intervene only to protect the temporal rights of such bodies, and to determine property rights. [*Elston* v. *Wilborn,* 186 S.W. 2d. 662 (Ark. 1945); see also *Ragsdall* v. *Church of Christ in Eldora,* 55 N.W. 2d. 539 (Iowa 1952).]

But there are two exceptions to the rule that the civil courts will not review church decisions. If the controversy arising out of an activity of a church or a decision of a church tribunal involves the civil or property rights of an individual, the civil courts will take jurisdiction. In such cases, however, these courts will decide the matter according to the internal laws of the particular church and the decisions of church tribunals of last resort. These become binding on the secular courts in determining whether basic civil or property rights have been violated. The second exception is that the civil courts will assume jurisdiction if there is fraud in the church determination.

When property and civil rights, therefore, depend upon an interpretation of the ecclesiastical law, the civil courts are bound to enforce the church law, as determined by the ecclesiastical tribunals. It was held in *Lamb v. Cain* (p. 21):

> From these considerations the rule in this country has become elementary that, when a civil right depends upon some matter pertaining to ecclesiastical affairs, the civil tribunal tries the right, and nothing more, taking the ecclesiastical decisions out of which the civil right has arisen as it finds them, and accepts such decisions as matters adjudicated by another legally constituted jurisdiction. [*Lamb v. Cain,* 29 N.E. 13 (Ind. 1891); see also *First Presbyterian Church of Lincoln v. First Cumberland Presbyterian Church of Lincoln,* 91 N.E. 761 (Ill. 1910).]

Schism. This is the most frequent cause of litigation concerning church property. A schism has been defined in American case law as a division or separation in a church or denomination caused by differences of opinion concerning matters of doctrine, faith, government, or discipline [*Holm v. Holm,* 51 N.W. 579 (Wis. 1892)]. Many causes may arise to create such a split in the membership with a resulting struggle for control of the church property. Most of the disputes that come into the courts in this connection relate to trespass.

The schism may be in a constituent part of a synodal or prelatial type of church, or in the final authority itself. Again, it may be in a local church of the non-associated type, i.e., congregational in structure, so that there is no higher authority than the majority of the particular church membership. The law varies as to the temporal result of a schism, depending on whether the church in question is of the congregational, presbyterian or prelatial type.

American civil law is more inclined to assume jurisdiction in cases of disputes concerning property in the instance of the prelatial or presbyterian type. If the schism originates in a constituent part of this type of church, i.e., at the bottom, it will be held that the majority of the congregation does not control the property against the majority of the entire church. The controversy will always be decided in favor of those who adhere to the doctrine professed by the congregation, and to the form of worship and practice, which existed when the ownership of the property began [*Britton v. Jackson,* 250 P. 763 (Ariz. 1926)].

In the case of *McAuley's Appeal* [77 Pa. 397 (1875)], it was decided that where a congregation holds its property as a constituent part of a particular religious denomination, it may not withdraw upon receiving an unfavorable decision from the higher church body to which it belongs, and claim the property [*Smith v. Pedigo,* 33 N.E. 777, *rehearing denied* 44 N.E. 363 (Ind. 1896)].

It has been held that the subordinate members of an ecclesiastical government may not sever their connection with the central organization without its consent [*Ferraria v. Vasconcelles,* 23 Ill. 456 (1860)]. It was brought out that the question is not whether either faction has a local majority, but whether its position is in accord with its own ecclesiastical law [*Sutter v. Trustees of the First Reformed Dutch Church,* 42 Pa. 503 (1862)].

Cases have held that the authority of the local majority in prelatial churches, such as the Roman Catholic and the Methodist Episcopal, is not determinative of the legal issue [*Dochkus v. Lithuanian Benefit Society of St. Anthony,* 206 Pa. 25, 55 Atl. 779 (1903)]. The same is true of the Presbyterian Church, which adheres to the decisions of its presbyters.

The controversy over property that arises will be decided, therefore, in favor of that party which represents the legitimate succession of the old united body. This is quite an easy matter in the case of schisms occurring in local congregations of the synodal or prelatial type. The property will be awarded to that part, whether majority or minority, which has adhered to the general body of which the congregation is an integral part.

But the problem is more difficult when the schism originates at the top rather than at the bottom, i.e., has driven a rift into the general body of a synodal or prelatial church. Since there is no superior body in such a case, the civil court must decide which of the two bodies before them has retained its identity with the body of which both at one time were parts. This necessarily involves an investigation into the faith and government, the laws and principles, the usages and customs that were accepted by the united body before the division. The property will be awarded to that part which acts in harmony with such norms, or comes closest to adherence to such norms [*Barton v. Fitzpatrick,* 65 So. 390 (Ala. 1914)]. The proof of church law and theological principles in civil courts is governed by the ordinary rules of evidence. An Oregon court has made clear that the distinction between canon law and religious creed is not important [*Philomath College v. Wyatt,* 31 P. 206 (Ore. 1892)]. When the schism develops at the top of a synodal or prelatial church, the process of adjudication is analogous to that followed in deciding problems that arise out of a schism in an independent congregation because in both kinds of schism, there is no spiritual superior except in the case of the Roman Catholic Church.

Property that belongs to an independent church will be awarded, generally speaking, in the case of schism, to that faction which constitutes a majority [*McBride v. Porter,* 17 Iowa 203 (1864)]. In this connection, a majority means more than one-half of those who vote in a particular election, not of those who might have voted, but did not do so. Since independent congregations are generally small democracies governed by a majority vote under a simple form of organization, such majority vote will often be the only criterion of which courts can take hold to decide the questions presented by a schism in such bodies [*Thomas v. Lewis,* 6 S.W. 2d. 255 (Ky. 1928)]. Absolute control of the property in question by a particular worshipping unit is more important than its connection with the main body in doctrinal or spiritual matters.

According to the civil courts, the religious liberty of the members of the church is not violated since they have the right to leave the church that has become objectionable to them. But they do not have the right to take the church property with them. The religious freedom clauses in the various state constitutions are not relevant in this connection.

A church may not be destroyed by the action of certain members. It has its own distinct quality of unity and the power of perpetuity, even though it is not a corporation or legal entity. Property is owned by this unity rather than by the members in their individual capacities.

The leading case in the field of schism is *Watson v. Jones* (*supra*). The schism resulted from a split in the Presbyterian Church over the slavery issue, shortly after the Civil War. The facts in the case were that the general assembly of the Presbyterian Church in the U.S. condemned the institution of slavery. This caused a schism. Each faction claimed title to the property of a local church in Kentucky. The supreme court of that state ruled that the general assembly, although it was the highest tribunal in the Presbyterian Church, had exceeded its jurisdiction in recognizing that the title to the property in question belonged to the antislavery faction.

Some of the parties to the litigation lived in Indiana. Because of the diversity of citizenship that existed, the case was properly brought to the Federal courts. The U.S. Supreme Court upheld the validity of the action of the general assembly.

The Watson case has been followed to the present day. Thus it was cited with approval in the important case of *Kedroff v. St. Nicholas Cathedral* [344 U.S. 94

(1952)]. This case resulted from a schism in the Russian Orthodox Church in the U.S. This was caused by the domination of the church in America by the patriarch in Moscow, who was suspected of being under the control of the Russian government. The schismatics prevailed upon the legislature of New York to pass special legislation providing that ". . . all the churches formerly administratively subject to the Moscow synod and patriarchate should for the future be governed by the ecclesiastical body and hierarchy of the American metropolitan district" (*supra,* 98, 99).

The plaintiff was a corporation created under New York law to acquire a cathedral for the Russian Orthodox Church in North America. It held legal title to St. Nicholas Cathedral in New York City. It sued the defendants in a New York state court. There were clergy appointed by the supreme authority in the Russian Orthodox Church. The court of appeals of New York decided for the plaintiff. But the U.S. Supreme Court reversed the decree on the basis of the liberty clause of the First Amendment of the Federal Constitution. This case confirmed a long line of precedent that the civil law may not interfere with the wholly internal and spiritual affairs of ecclesiastical, juridical orders in general, or with the appointment or removal of the clergy in particular. The court wrote:

> Ours is a government which by the "law of its being" allows no statute, state or national, that prohibits the free exercise of religion. There are occasions when civil courts must draw lines between the responsibilities of church and state for the disposition or use of property. Even in those cases when the property right follows as an incident from decisions of the church custom or law on ecclesiastical issues, the church rule controls. This under our Constitution necessarily follows in order that there may be free exercise of religion (*supra,* 120, 121).

The Christian Science Church has a hierarchical government. When the use of its name was denied to a local church, the civil court followed the Watson case and held itself bound by the decision of the highest judicatory of the Christian Science Church. The court wrote:

> Thus because the plaintiffs are the highest authority and adjudicatory of The Mother Church and her branch churches, this court should not disturb their interpretations of church law, from which they claim to derive the authority to grant or deny official church recognition to branch churches and the use of branch church nomenclature." [(*Watson v. Jones* was cited.) *Jandron v. Zuendel,* 139 Fed. Supp. 887, 889 (1955).]

Ministers. Property rights may be involved not only in instances of schism, but also in the area of services performed by a minister of the gospel. In congregational types of churches, it has been held that the relationship of a clergyman to his congregation is governed by the law of contracts, express or implied, but not by church law [*Tuigg v. Sheehan,* 101 Pa. 363 (1882)]. The relationship is governed by the general law of contracts, and hence an action for breach may be brought.

But in the prelatial type of church, no contract right exists between a priest and bishop, either before or after the priest has been assigned to his charge. Hence, a bishop is not liable for the salary of a priest who has been appointed by him. This is so because the relationship between priest and bishop is based on status, and not contract, although the status was voluntarily assumed. It is not the relationship of an employer and employee. [*Leahey v. Williams,* 6 N.E. 78 (Mass. 1886)].

Indeed a priest is without legal recourse for his salary against his congregation since he has no contract. But no civil action may be brought against a priest if he lays down his office even though he is subject to punishment under the canon law of his church. Nor may a congregation sue a bishop for removing his priests [*Wardens of the Church of St. Louis of New Orleans v. Blanc,* 8 Rob. La. 51 (1844); *Stack v. O'Hara,* 98 Pa. 213 (1881)]. A bishop is answerable only according to the law of his own church.

Under the Methodist form of religious organization, a clergyman may not recover his salary on the basis of *quantum meruit* because in that church ministers are not regarded as employees. Hence there can be no question as to the implication of a promise of compensation.

Conclusion. American civil law does not claim the right to create churches, or to invest them with spiritual power. Indeed it is not concerned with the origin or exercise of the ecclesiastical authority of the religious denomination in question. Membership in churches under American law is based principally upon the "higher plane" theory, and not contract. The law forbids the state to interfere in the internal life of any church. It provides an adequate means for the acquisition, possession, administration, and transfer of property through the legal device of trustees or corporations, who may act in the name of the church.

Bibliography: B. F. BROWN, *The Canonical Juristic Personality* (CUA CLS 39; Washington 1927); "The Notion of Canonical Auctoritas with Respect to Statute, Custom and Usage," American Society for Legal History, *Essays in Jurisprudence in Honor of Roscoe Pound,* ed. R. A. NEWMAN (Indianapolis 1962) 271–295. J. J. MCGRATH, "Canon Law and American Church Law," *Jurist* 18 (1958) 260–278; ed., *Church and State in American Law* (Milwaukee 1962). C. F. ZOLLMANN, *American Church Law* (St. Paul 1933).

[B. F. BROWN]

CHURCHES OF CHRIST

A body of churches that separated from the Disciples of Christ in 1906 and ever since have distinguished themselves as rigid constructionists in "restoring primitive Christianity." *See* CHRISTIAN CHURCHES (DISCIPLES OF CHRIST). The name Churches of Christ is loosely applied also to many of the older New England churches and to local units of the Disciples of Christ.

Alexander *Campbell, founder of the Disciples, had been a Baptist from 1812 to 1829, during which time he advocated certain conservative policies. These, later abandoned by him, were developed by a strong reactionary party among the Disciples. They were against open Communion and the use of "Reverend" in addressing the clergy. But their main grievance was the organization of missionary and other societies, which they construed as a form of denominationalism and a concession to authoritarianism. They objected also to installing organs in churches. After years of controversy in the pulpit and religious press, the conservatives estimated they had enough solidarity to separate from the main body. The government census for 1906 listed them for the first time as a distinct religious body, the Churches of Christ, with an estimated membership of 200,000 at the turn of the century. In 1964 they claimed a total of 2,250,000 members.

Doctrinally the Churches of Christ do not differ much from the Disciples, except that they discourage any semblance of imposed confessional creeds. Both believe that baptism should be administered by immersion and only to adults who have reached sufficient maturity to profess the faith and repent of their sins. The Lord's Supper is commonly held to be only a memorial of Christ's Passion and death, although the Christians, as they are called, more frequently recommend that unleavened bread and unfermented grape juice be used for Communion. As a rule, the Churches of Christ are more fundamentalist in their approach to the Scriptures and less tolerant of the *ecumenical movement.

The principal feature of the Churches of Christ, however, is their organizational structure. There is no juridical authority beyond the local congregation. The Christians maintain that denominations that are ruled by ecclesiastical forms of government are ignoring Christ the head of the Church and are assuming the right of self-government. This is held to be clearly against the Bible, which records that shortly before His Ascension, Christ declared that "all authority has been given to me in heaven and on earth." Since "Christ has all authority; therefore man has none." Unlike the Disciples who admit the existence and need of denominations, the Christians defend their own claim to being nondenominational. They further regard themselves as heirs of a new movement, which began in the 19th century, to restore the true church which had become lost to the multitudes "because of the doctrines of Catholicism and denominationalism." After the lapse of centuries, they believe, Thomas and Alexander Campbell rediscovered the fact that "faith in Jesus Christ as the Son of God is sufficient profession to entitle a man or woman to become a member of the Church of Christ."

As a result of their congregational independency, the Churches of Christ have no organization larger than the local church community. This has created the dilemma of how to operate the churches efficiently without some degree of unity, while remaining nondenominational in spite of some organization. In practice the problem is solved by permitting cooperative effort among the churches, but always short of being on a national scale. Moreover, books and periodicals from common publishing houses serve to unite the autonomous groups into a kind of federation.

Although the Churches of Christ have no national headquarters comparable to the Disciples, they have not been without a distinctive unity. Solidarity was first achieved and remains operative by their resistance to the "human innovations" of other religious bodies, in the form of set creeds, church officials above the parochial level, and ritual requirements for membership. They have been fairly consistent also in opposing musical instruments in churches, to such a degree that they are sometimes described as the "noninstrumental music" segment of the parent body. Their religious publications are labeled "unofficial," and their colleges are simply "nonsectarian." While large-scale missionary societies are forbidden because they are said to lack scriptural foundation, foreign missionaries are sponsored by individuals or local churches. Although adherents may be found throughout the U.S., they are concentrated in an arc that stretches from the middle Atlantic seaboard across Indiana down to Texas, and in the far West. Their weekly publication, *Gospel Advocate,* is one of the best known organs of nondenominational Christianity in the U.S.

Bibliography: B. BAXTER, *What is the Church of Christ?* (Nashville 1960). A. CAMPBELL, *The Christian System* (2d ed. Pittsburg 1839). B. W. STONE et al., *An Apology for Renouncing the Jurisdiction of the Synod of Kentucky . . .* (Lexington, Ky. 1804). T. CAMPBELL, *Declaration and Address of the Christian Association of Washington* (Washington, Pa. 1809). M. M. DAVIS, *How the Disciples Began and Grew,* (Cincinnati 1947). W. E. GARRISON and A. T. DEGROOT, *The Disciples of Christ: A History* (rev. ed. St. Louis 1958).

[J. A. HARDON]

CHYTRAEUS, DAVID (KOCHHAFE), Evangelical theologian and historian; b. Ingelfingen (Württemberg), Feb. 26, 1531; d. Rostock, June 25, 1600. His father, Matthäus (d. 1559), who was a pastor at Ingelfingen and Menzingen, sent him to Tübingen (1539) for his early schooling. Later Chytraeus went to Wittenberg (1544), Heidelberg (1547), and again to Wittenberg, where he was taught by Philipp Melanchthon. In 1548 he became a professor at the University of Rostock, teaching theology from 1561. Chytraeus was a productive author of theological works and also a gifted organizer. He drew up the statutes of the University of Rostock and other German universities after the pattern of reform in operation at Wittenberg. His opinions in theology were respected in Lutheran circles. He was called upon by the Evangelical Estates of Austria (1569) and of Steiermark (1574) to draw up new church statutes. From Wittenberg he published *Regulae vitae* (1555), *Praecepta rhetoricae inventionis* (1558), *De studio theologiae* (1562), *Regulae studiorum* (1572), and *De morte et vita aeterna* (1581). As a church historian he is renowned for his continuation of Albert Krantz's history, *Vandaliae et Saxoniae Alberti Crantzii continuatio . . .* (4 v. 1588–99).

Bibliography: O. KRABBE, *David Chyträus* (Rostock 1870): *Die Universität Rostock im 15. und 16. Jahrhundert* (Rostock 1854). Schottenloher 1:2877–94. E. WOLF, NDB 3:254–255. J. STABER, LexThK² 2:1200. G. LOESCHE (H. Liebing), RGG³ 1:1823.

[T. D. OLSEN]

CIASCA, AGOSTINO, Orientalist; b. Polignano a Mare, Italy, May 7, 1835; d. Rome, Feb. 6, 1902. His baptismal name was Pasquale; he received the name Agostino when he entered the Order of St. Augustine in 1856. He made his religious profession in March 1857 and was ordained in 1858. Ciasca was outstanding for his proficiency in Oriental languages, especially Arabic and Coptic. In 1866 he obtained the chair of Hebrew in the College of Propaganda. He assisted at the Vatican Council I as a theologian and as interpreter for the Oriental bishops. In 1879 he participated in a pontifical mission to Egypt and Syria. He examined and corrected the Syrian Breviary and acquired many important MSS, mostly Christian Arabic. In 1891 he was created titular archbishop of Larissa with the appointment to the office of prefect of the Vatican Secret Archives. He presided at the Ruthenian Synod of Lemburg in 1891. In 1892 he was named prosecretary and later secretary (1893) of the Congregation of the Propaganda, during which time he helped organize some Catholic missions to the Congo. He was elevated to the cardinalate June 19, 1899.

Among his scholarly contributions may be mentioned *Examen critico-apologeticum super constitutionem dog-*

maticam de Fide Catholica editam in sessione tertia SS. Oecumenici Concilii Vaticani (1872), *I papiri Copti del Museo Borgiano della S.C. de Propaganda Fide tradotti e commentati* (1881), his publication of a very ancient Coptic Version of the OT "Sacrorum Bibliorum Fragmenta Copto-Sahidica Musei Borgiani" (2 v. 1885–89), and his discovery and publication (1888) of a valuable Arabic version of the **Diatessaron* of Tatian.

Bibliography: D. A. PERINI, *Studio Bio-bibliografico sul Cardinale Agostino Ciasca* (Rome 1903); *Bibliographia Augustiniana,* 4 v. (Florence 1929–38) 1:229–231. A. PALMIERI, DTC 2.2:2472–73. G. HOFFMAN, LexThK² 2:1201. A. C. DE ROMANIS, EncCatt 3:1578–79.

[B. A. LAZOR]

CIBORIUM, a word of which the etymology is disputed, was the name given in early times to a pillared canopy, of Byzantine origin, erected over the altar. In the late Middle Ages it was applied to a small sacrament house with a gabled top in which the Blessed Sacrament was reserved. Finally, in the 16th century, it was used to designate the vessel in which the Blessed Sacrament was reserved for the Communion of the faithful. This vessel is but a developed form of the *pyx, which, in the 13th century, acquired a foot under the cylindrical container. At first the ciborium was small, containing but a few Hosts for the sick. After the Council of Trent Communion of the faithful became less infrequent, and was given from preconsecrated Hosts kept in the tabernacle. The ciborium then had to be made larger, and was given the shape of a cup, often with a conical lid. According to present law, it must be made from solid and good material, gold-plated inside; it must have a lid that is not hinged so that it can be removed completely. The ciborium is not a consecrated vessel; it requires only a blessing before it is first used.

Medieval ciborium of copper gilt with Champlevé enamel decoration, French, 14th century, height 14³⁄₁₆ inches.

Contemporary ciborium by Gilles Beaugrand, Inc., Montreal, silver and lapis lazuli, height 10¼ inches.

Bibliography: J. BRAUN, *Das christliche Altargerät* (Munich 1932). G. PODHRADSKY, *Lexikon der Liturgie* (Innsbruck 1962).
Illustration credit: Fig. 1, National Gallery of Art, Washington, D.C., Widener Collection.

[C. W. HOWELL]

CIBOT, PIERRE MARTIAL, Jesuit missionary and scientist; b. Limoges, Aug. 14, 1727; d. Peking, Aug. 8. 1780. He is noted chiefly for his many contributions to the memoirs composed by the missionaries in Peking and published under the title *Mémoires concernant l'histoire, les sciences, les arts, les moeurs, les usages etc. de Chinois* (16 v. Paris 1776–89). Cibot entered the Society of Jesus in 1743, and in 1758 he was sent to Peking, where he remained at the court until his death. A zealous missionary and an eager, intelligent student with wide scientific interests, he wrote on a great variety of subjects. Often accused of using his imagination too much in his writings and of sometimes being unreliable, he nevertheless contributed much interesting information on customs, institutions, trees, plants, etc., of China. His work on the chronology of the Chinese Empire was strongly assailed by learned contemporaries, but modern science has become somewhat favorable to his thesis.

Bibliography: Pfister 2:896–902, with detailed bibliog. A. DE BIL, DHGE 12:826. J. BRUCKER, DTC 2.2:2473. H. M. BROCK, CE 3:767–768. Sommervogel 2:1167–69.

[M. J. BARRY]

CICERO, MARCUS TULLIUS

Orator, statesman, and greatest man of letters of antiquity; b. Arpinum, Italy, Jan. 3, 106 B.C.; d. Formiae, Dec. 7, 43. He was of middle-class origin, and he received an excellent education at Rome that was completed by philosophical and rhetorical studies at Athens and Rhodes. He distinguished himself as an orator and served as quaestor in 75, as praetor in 66, and as consul in 63. His greatest political triumph was the unmasking and suppression of the conspiracy of Cataline. As an opponent of Caesar he was exiled in 58–57, but through Pompey's efforts he was able to return to Rome. In 51–50 he served as a governor of Cilicia. In the Civil War he supported Pompey and the Senate. Following the assassination of Caesar, he courageously defended the senatorial cause against Mark Antony. He perished as a victim, with the acquiescence of Octavian, of Antony's hatred.

Cicero was a man of peace, innately conservative in politics, who found himself deeply involved in the violence that marked the last years of the Republic. Owing to the preservation of most of his voluminous writings, especially of his letters, his life is better known than that of any other ancient personality, with the possible exception of St. *Augustine.

Cicero's chief extant works comprise orations, rhetorical compositions, and philosophical treatises, cast in the form of dialogues, and letters. His orations and letters, apart from their high literary place in oratory and epistolography, are invaluable sources for the history of the late Republic. His rhetorical works are primarily concerned with the theory of oratory and give precious information on the earlier Roman orators. His extant philosophical dialogues cover political theory and religion as well as philosophical themes as ordinarily understood. They are: *De Republica* (preserved only in part), *De legibus, Academica, De finibus bonorum et malorum, Tusculanae disputationes, De natura deorum, De divinatione, De senectute, De amicitia, Paradoxa Stoicorum,* and *De officiis.* His *De consolatione* and the *Hortensius,* which exercised such a great influence on the young Augustine, have been lost.

Cicero was not an original thinker, but as an eclectic he expounded in a beautiful literary style the basic ideas of the chief Greek schools of philosophy. In epistemology he followed the New Academy; in ethics, chiefly the Stoics. He rejected both the materialism of the Epicureans and the popular religious beliefs in the gods, but believed in a divine providence and the immortality of the soul. Cicero is the undisputed master of Latin prose style and the creator of Latin philosophical language. He was the first, for example, to employ such basic terms as *essentia, qualitas,* and *materia* in their philosophical sense.

Cicero's influence on subsequent Latin prose style was immediate and very significant because of his central place beside *Vergil in the ancient school tradition. Since the ancient Christian writers were trained chiefly in pagan schools, it is only natural that they should reflect Ciceronian influence in both thought and style. Cicero's treatment of Greco-Roman philosophy and religion furnished Christian apologists with arguments that were all the more effective because they were based on a universally acknowledged authority. *Minucius Felix, *Arnobius the Elder, and *Lactantius drew heavily on Cicero's *De natura deorum, De divinatione,* and other works. Lactantius, because of his indebtedness to Cicero for his content and style, has been called the "Christian Cicero."

St. *Ambrose's *De officiis* shows the obvious influence of Cicero in its title and in its division into three books, but in actual content it is much less dependent on its model than is usually assumed. St. *Jerome's dream and the style of his treatises and letters furnish ample testimony for his familiarity with the great Roman writer. The reading of the *Hortensius,* as already noted, marked a turning point in the life of the young Augustine. Later, Augustine found Cicero and Varro invaluable sources for his apologetic in the *De civitate Dei.* His definition of the pagan state, for example, is taken from Cicero. Book 4 of his *De doctrina Christiana,* a treatise on Christian rhetoric, is based essentially on Cicero's theory of rhetoric and education. *Boethius reflects Ciceronian influence in his style of writing rather than in his thought.

The influence of Cicero continued throughout the Middle Ages, but it was confined largely to the knowledge and use of a limited number of his philosophical works, his rhetorical treatise *De inventione,* and the *Auctor ad Herennium,* which was regarded as a Ciceronian production. Few scholars in the Middle Ages were as familiar with Cicero as *Lupus of Ferrières, *John of Salisbury, and *Peter of Blois. From the beginning of the Renaissance, with the recovery and study of his extant works, Cicero became the universally recognized, and for a time the exclusive, master of Latin prose style.

The cultivation of Ciceronian Latin in the European school tradition exercised a marked effect on the development of vernacular prose style in general. In the late 19th century Pope *Leo XIII gave Ciceronian Latin a basic place in his reform of papal chancery style; his own encyclicals, especially, and those of his successors exhibit the deliberate use of Ciceronian language and stylistic devices. Ciceronian thought exercised some influence throughout the modern period, but his influence in modern times has been primarily in the field of rhetorical theory and style.

Bibliography: G. C. Richards, OxClDict 188–191, with bibliog. K. Büchner, "M. Tullius Cicero, der Redner (29)," PaulyWiss RE 7A.1 (1939) 827–1274. C. Becker, ReallexAntChr 3:86–127, with bibliog. J. W. Duff, *A Literary History of Rome from the Origins to the Close of the Golden Age,* ed. A. M. Duff (3d ed. London 1953) 255–290, with bibliog. 501–503. Sandys, indices s.v. "Cicero." Manitius, indices s.v. "Cicero." G. Highet, *The Classical Tradition* (New York 1949), index s.v. "Cicero." R. R. Bolgar, *The Classical Heritage and Its Beneficiaries* (Cambridge, Eng. 1954), index s.v. "Cicero." H. Hagendahl, *Latin Fathers and the Classics* (Göteborg 1958), index s.v. "Cicero." M. Van de Bruwaine, *La Théologie de Cicéron* (Louvain 1937). T. A. Dorey, ed., *Cicero* (London 1965).

[M. R. P. MC GUIRE]

CICONIA, JOHANNES, Walloon musician and theorist of the *Ars nova;* b. Liège, Belgium, *c.* 1335–40; d. Padua, Italy, December 1411. In 1350 he was in Avignon, France, as favorite of Clement VI's niece, Alienor de Cominges-Turenne, and in 1358 he was in the employment of Cardinal *Albornoz, then papal legate for Italy, who granted him a canonry at Cesena and obtained one from Urban V at St. John the Evangelist, Liège, previously requested by Clement's niece. After Albornoz's death (1367) Ciconia returned to his native land and in 1372 took up his Liège canonry. Finally, in 1401, he returned to Padua as canon and precentor at St. John church. Trained in the French musical tradition, in both his own country and Avignon, he became acquainted early with Italian music, and his first works, Italian madrigals and ballatas, testify to his knowledge of the art of Jacopo da Bologna and the Lombard court composers. On returning to Liège, he wrote some Masses in the Avignon style, blending French structures with the allurements of Italian melody, with which his French songs are imbued. At Padua he composed Masses and motets for special occasions and at the end some ballatas in which archaisms mingle with the innovations of the musical dialectic that was to usher in the polyphony and resonances of the *quattrocento.* Ciconia's known works, all preserved in their original codices in Padua, Rome, Trent, and other cities, are: 4 madrigals and 11 ballatas on Italian texts; 2 French songs (virelay and ballade);

2 canons, one on a Latin text, the other, French; 11 Mass parts; and 13 motets. His five-book theoretical work, *Nova Musica,* has never been published.

Bibliography: Modern reprints of his music appear in Denkm TonkÖst 7, 14, and 61; *Polyphonia Sacra,* ed. C. VAN DEN BORREN (University Park, Pa. 1963). S. CLERCX[-LEJEUNE] *Johannes Ciconia: Un musicien liégeois et son temps,* 2 v. (Brussels 1960) bibliog. xi–xxii. H. BESSELER, MusGG 2:1423–34; "Johannes Ciconia, Begründer der Chorpolyphonie," *International Congress on Sacred Music, Proceedings 1950* (Rome 1952). E. DANNEMANN, Grove DMM 2:295–96. M. F. BUKOFZER, "The Beginnings of Choral Polyphony," *Studies in Medieval and Renaissance Music* (New York 1950) 176–189.

[S. CLERCX-LEJEUNE]

CIENFUEGOS, ÁLVARO, theologian; b. Anguerina, Spain, Feb. 27, 1657; d. Rome, Aug. 19, 1739. After studying philosophy in Salamanca, he entered the Society of Jesus in 1676 and studied theology in the same city. He taught philosophy at Compostela (1688–91) and theology at Salamanca.

Charles of Austria named Cienfuegos his envoy to Portugal and retained him as an advisor. At the end of the war of 1714, Charles VI, then Emperor, called him to Venice and in 1720 succeeded in having him named cardinal. In 1722 he was consecrated bishop of Catania and in 1724 archbishop of Monreal. Cienfuegos had to renounce his archbishopric when the Bourbons occupied the Kingdom of the two Sicilies. He was then given the See of Fünfkirchen by the Emperor (1735), although he continued to live in Rome as the Emperor's legate and held important posts in Roman congregations until his death.

As a theologian he was considered to have sharp and brilliant ingenuity. His principal theological works are: the *Aenigma Theologicum,* 2 v. (Vienna 1717), and the *Vita abscondita* (Rome 1728). The first, on the Trinity, does not give any new solutions, although the author appears to believe it does. Cienfuegos's doctrine on the Eucharist, contained in the second work, had more of a hearing. According to him, the sacramental Christ supernaturally exercises acts of the sensitive life, but immediately after the Consecration this activity is suspended until the mingling of the two species, which is a symbol of the Resurrection. The sacrificial immolation properly consists in this suspension. Communion really unites the faithful to the soul of Christ; even though the species are dissolved, the communicant is, like a motor, an instrument of the Word. Franzelin comments: "Certainly this opinion is so constructed that a cautious theologian would be frightened by its singularity" (*De Eucharistia,* th. 16).

Cienfuegos also wrote the *Heroica vida, virtudes y milagros dal grande San Francisco de Borja* (Madrid 1702). Although it is difficult reading, it is better documented than earlier biographies.

Bibliography: Sommervogel 2:1182–85. Hurter Nomencl 4:1020–26. H. DUTOUQUET, DTC 2:2511–13. A. PEREZ GOYENA, "Teólogos antifranceses en la Guerra de Sucesión," *Razón y Fe* 91.2 (1930) 326–338.

[J. M. DALMAU]

CIENFUEGOS, JOSÉ IGNACIO, Chilean bishop and enlightened reformer; b. 1762; d. Talca, 1845. He was ordained in 1785 and stationed in Talca until 1813. As a member of the education commission of the new national regime in Chile, he effected his most important action, the union of the Tridentine Seminary with the National Institute, the new foundation planned by the Creole junta. The consolidation of the seminary with the basic college for humanistic, philosophic, and scientific studies, intended for laymen, opened the way for the new enlightened and liberal ideas among future secular priests. The fusion of these institutions was characteristic of Josephinism, current throughout America during the period of independence (*see* LATIN AMERICA, CHURCH AND ENLIGHTENMENT IN).

Cienfuegos was banished to the Juan Fernandez Islands at the time of the Spanish reconquest, but returned in 1817, when independence was finally achieved. He was president of the Senate and on various occasions was governor of the bishopric of Santiago, owing to the confidence that the political heads of the new state had in him. In 1821, as plenipotentiary, he went to the Holy See and brought about the mission of Juan *Muzi to Chile; it failed and the legislative reforms of the Church were consolidated. Muzi accused Cienfuegos of usurping episcopal jurisdiction since Bp. *Rodríguez Zorrilla had been expelled by O'Higgins, but Cienfuegos went to Rome again in 1827 and succeeded in vindicating himself. Nevertheless, he had cooperated with the ecclesiastical reforms and proposed the selection of parish priests by the people in accord with the parochial tendencies then in vogue.

He became titular bishop of Rétimo in 1828 and bishop of Concepción in 1830. In 1837 he gave up his diocese and retired to Talca, where he died. Among his charitable works are his donations to the hospital and the Institute of Talca, and the foundation of a chair of theology. He published a *Catechism of Christian Doctrine* (Geneva 1829), with commentary, which shows the moral seriousness that characterized his pastoral work. Among the Chilean clergy he is the chief representative of the so-called Catholic Enlightenment.

Bibliography: L. F. PRIETO DEL RÍO, *Diccionario biográfico del clero secular de Chile* (Santiago de Chile 1922).

[M. GÓNGORA]

CIEPLAK, JAN, bishop; b. Dabrowa Górniczna, Poland, Aug. 17, 1857; d. Jersey City, N.J., Feb. 17, 1926. After his mother's death (1859), Cieplak was reared by his maternal grandmother and by two priests. In 1869 he entered the Gymnasium at Kielce, and in 1873 began to study for the priesthood in the Latin rite. He pursued higher studies in St. Petersburg (1878) and was ordained (1881). In 1882 he became professor at the Catholic academy in St. Petersburg. He was consecrated bishop of Evaria and appointed auxiliary bishop of *Mogilev (1908). After the Russian Revolution he became archbishop of Achrida and apostolic administrator of Mohilev in place of the imprisoned Archbishop Ropp (1919). Accused of conspiring with the papal nuncio in Warsaw, Cieplak was arrested as a counterrevolutionary and sentenced to death (1923). His sentence, however, was commuted through the intervention of the Holy See, the U.S. and British governments, and Edmund *Walsh, SJ. In 1924 Cieplak was transferred from Butyrki prison to Lubianka, and was soon after deposited penniless at the Latvian border. From Riga he went to Poland and then to Rome. In 1925 he began an extended tour of the U.S., where in the course of 3 months he visited 375 parishes and 800 institutions in 25 dioceses. He was named archbishop of Vilna (then in Poland), but died as he was preparing to go there. His cause for beatification has been introduced, and the *decretum super scripta* was issued in 1960.

Bibliography: F. DOMANSKI, *The Great Apostle of Russia: The Servant of God Archbishop John Baptist Cieplak* (Chicago 1953). J. LEDIT, *Archbishop Jan Baptist Cieplak* (Montreal 1963).

[J. PAPIN]

CILICIA OF THE ARMENIANS, PATRIARCHATE OF (CILICIAE ARMENORUM)

Catholic patriarchate of the *Armenian rite; in southeast *Turkey, also called Lesser *Armenia. It was reunited with Rome in 1742, moved to *Beirut (1749–1867) and *Istanbul (1867–1928), and is now located in Beirut, *Lebanon. Under the patriarchate are four Armenian archbishoprics, *Alep, Baghdad (or Babylon) formerly in *Mardin, Istanbul, and the patriarch's own See of Beirut (created in 1928). In 1963 Cilicia (Beirut) had 11 parishes, 28 secular and 7 religious priests (in 2 convents), 44 sisters in 7 convents, and 18,500 Catholics. The patriarchate derives from the episcopacy of St. *Gregory the Illuminator (315).

Cilicia, with its Cilician Gates, has long been a link between *Asia Minor and *Syria. It was under the *Hittites, the Persians (*c.* 500 B.C.), *Alexander the Great (333 B.C.), and Rome (103 B.C.), who rid its coast of pirates (62 B.C.) and made it part of the Diocese of the East (A.D. 297). Invaded by Arabs from 639 and retaken by the Byzantine *Nicephorus II Phocas (965), it became a principality under Armenians who had fled the *Seljuk Turks (1080). It was an ally of the Latin crusaders and became a kingdom (1199), which went to the Lusignans of *Cyprus (1342) and then fell to the *Mamelukes (1375). By 1522 Cilicia was part of the *Ottoman Empire.

St. *Paul was born in Tarsus, a capital of Cilicia and one of nine Cilician sees represented at the Council of Nicaea I (325). To the original two ecclesiastical provinces of Cilicia under the Patriarchate of *Antioch, Tarsus with 5 suffragans and Anazarbus with 9 suffragans, Seleucia with 23 suffragans was added in Constantine's time. *Mopsuestia also was an important city of Cilicia. Some 15 of the ancient sees of Cilicia still exist as titular sees. Remains of basilicas have been discovered in the region, which had early Christian martyrs.

Monophysitism divided Cilicia into *Jacobites and *Melchites, and the Arab conquest caused more harm to the Church there. Pope Gregory VII corresponded with the Armenian *catholicos Gregory II before the Crusades. *Leo II's coronation as king of Lesser Armenia by a papal legate (1199) restored unity with Rome until 1375. Latin crusaders had established Latin sees in Cilicia; and a Dominican organization worked for union with Rome from 1328 but had to be abandoned. Sis, capital of Cilicia to 1375, had a catholicos (1293–1441), who moved to Echmiadzin (part of Russia since 1828). Echmiadzin's position as head of the Armenian National Church, which still obtains, was eventually recognized by the dissident "catholicos" of Sis, who was acknowledged by Echmiadzin as a subordinate "patriarch." This Armenian Catholicos-Patriarch of Sis, who presided over 15 dioceses and 285,000 souls in 1914, fled Turkey (1921) by moving to Alep and Lebanon (1928). Several councils in Sis (1251, 1307, 1342) and Adana (1316) dealt with the matter of union with Rome. Sis was also the seat of a Jacobite bishop and, from 1292 to 1387, of the Jacobite patriarch.

In 1740 Abraham (Peter) Ardzivean, Catholic bishop of Alep, was elected Catholicos-Patriarch of Sis and in 1742 received the pallium in Rome; but he had to reside in Lebanon, as dissidents held Sis. Bzommar, outside Beirut, was the Catholic seat (1749–1867). The primatial archbishopric for Catholic Armenians established in Istanbul (1830) was united with the Patriarchate of Cilicia (1867) following a jurisdictional dispute over six new sees created in Turkey (1850), and the patriarch moved to Istanbul (1867–1928). Reorganization of the patriarchate (1928) after the persecution following World War I established the patriarch in Beirut. Cardinal Gregory Peter XV Agagianian (patriarch 1937–62) resigned the patriarchate in favor of his auxiliary bishop, Ignatius Peter XVI Batanian.

Bibliography: F. TOURNEBIZE, DHGE 4:290–391, esp. 338–344. E. JOSI, EncCatt 3:1610–12. M. OUDENRŸN, LexThK[2] 1: 869–872. O. VOLK, ibid. 6:144–146. OrientCatt 393–413. Ann Pont (1964) 6, 49.

[J. A. DEVENNY]

CIMABUE, GIOVANNI (CENNI DI PEPO),

Florentine painter active from around 1240 to about 1302. The sources provide very little information about him; he is mentioned as having served as a legal witness in Rome in 1272 and as having received payment for 94 days' work at Pisa in 1301. His fame in his own day, however, is attested by Dante in his *Divine Comedy* (*Purgatory* 11.94). Judging from those works that are attributed to him, Cimabue's style would appear to be

Giovanni Cimabue, "Madonna and Child with St. John the Baptist and St. Peter," 13½ by 9¾ inches.

fundamentally Byzantine. The only definitely authenticated work, however, the figure of St. John, which is part of a mosaic of the Deësis (1302) in the cathedral of Pisa, exhibits the more plastic style of the Roman school. Cimabue was capable also of an extraordinary emotional expressiveness, as in the frescoes in the upper and lower churches of San Francesco in Assisi (*c.* 1288–*c.* 1296). The "Crucifixion" especially, in the upper church, is intensely moving with its huge sagging body of Christ, weeping angels, and despairing mourners. Also attributed to Cimabue are a crucifix (1270–75) in the Church of San Domenico, Arezzo, a "Madonna with Angels" (1285–90) in the Uffizi, and a "Madonna Enthroned" (*c.* 1301–02) in the Louvre. Because of his heightened expressiveness and marked creative spirit, Cimabue may be considered as the first outstanding personality of western European painting.

Bibliography: Vasari 1:21–28. J. A. CROWE and G. B. CAVALCASELLE, *Early Christian Art,* v.1 of *A History of Painting in Italy,* 6 v. (2d ed. London 1903–14) 173–193. A. NICHOLSON, *Cimabue* (Princeton 1932). G. FRANCASTEL, "Cimabue," *Italian Painting: From the Byzantine Masters to the Renaissance,* tr. W. J. STRACHAN (New York 1956) 28–31. DeWald ItPaint 66–74. S. SAMEK-LUDOVICI, *Cimabue* (Milan 1956). **Illustration credit:** National Gallery of Art, Washington, D.C., Samuel H. Kress Collection.

[G. MC NEIL]

CIMAROSA, DOMENICO, composer best known for his comic operas; b. Aversa (near Naples), Dec. 17, 1749; d. Venice,. Jan. 11, 1801. He received his musical training at a Franciscan free school in Naples and then at the Conservatorio Santa Maria di Loreto (1761–72). His first opera, *Le Stravaganze del Conte,* was produced in 1772. Despite rivals in the field of Neapolitan opera (notably *Paisiello) Cimarosa was soon writing both comic and serious operas for various theaters throughout Italy. In 1787 he accepted an invitation to become chamber composer to Catherine II in St. Petersburg, but he left there in 1791 for the court of Leopold II in Vienna. There he wrote his best-known work, *Il Matrimonio segreto* (1792), a masterpiece of

Domenico Cimarosa.

genuine *buffo* style, which received 67 consecutive performances the following year in Naples. Cimarosa helped welcome French revolutionary troops into Naples in 1799; on the return of the Bourbons he was sentenced to death, then pardoned. Setting out again for Russia, he fell sick in Venice and died shortly after. In addition to 75 operas, he wrote many motets and concerted Masses, several oratorios, cantatas, and shorter vocal and instrumental compositions, all of them largely forgotten.

Bibliography: R. VITALE, *Domenico Cimarosa* (Aversa 1929). M. TIBALDI CHIESA, *Cimarosa e il suo tempo* (Milan 1939). Comitato nazionale per le celebrazioni cimarosiane 1949, *Per il bicentenario della nascita di Domenico Cimarosa,* ed. F. DE FILIPPIS (Aversa 1949). Grout HistOp. H. WIRTH, MusGG 2: 1442–49. Baker 294–295. **Illustration credit:** Museo Teatrale alla Scala.

[R. W. LOWE]

CIMMERIANS, an Indo-European-speaking people, possibly related to the Thraco-Phrygian peoples who first lived in South Russia before the 8th century B.C. Their origin and geographical extent, as well as their history, are unclear; but they migrated to Anatolia in the 7th century B.C. They are known in Assyrian sources as Gimirrai; in the Bible (Ez 38.6; see also Gn 10.2–3) as Gomer in Cappadocia; and in Armenian as Gamirk', meaning Cappadocia. They were first noted by the Greeks as living near Greek colonies in the Crimea, and they gave their name to the Cimmerian Bosphorus (later the Straits of Kerch). Homer in the *Odyssey* (11.11–13) mentions them as living in the dark north.

Herodotus (1.103 and 4.11–12) relates how the Cimmerians were driven from their South Russian homes by the Scythians, after which they invaded Media and Anatolia. The Cimmerian expansion to the east is confirmed by Assyrian cuneiform sources, which tell of their raids and their settlement northwest of Lake Van. Rusa I, King of Urartu, campaigned against the Cimmerians in their new home *c.* 716 B.C. The Assyrian King *Asarhaddon defeated a large group of them *c.* 679 B.C. in the country of the Mannai south of Lake Urmia. The role of the Cimmerians in the destruction of the kingdom of Urartu is uncertain, for the Scythians, according to Herodotus, followed the Cimmerians and seemingly absorbed those in the east. In the Akkadian version of the *Behistun Inscription of *Darius I, King of Persia, the Cimmerians are mentioned where the Old Persian and Elamite parallel versions have, instead, the Saka or Scythians. The Cimmerians in the east then vanish from the scene of history.

In Anatolia, however, the Cimmerians overran the kingdom of the Phrygians, probably destroying the city of Gordium. Then they invaded the district of *Lydia and captured *Sardis (Herodotus 1.15). The date of this conquest coincided with the death of the Lydian King Gyges, which was *c.* 652 B.C. The last half of the 7th century B.C. in Anatolia was a period of confusion, when Thracians were moving into Bithynia and elsewhere from the Balkans and the Armenians too were moving into their present homeland. The part played by the Cimmerians in the movements of these peoples is unknown, but apparently the Thracians were driven into the mountainous areas of Cappadocia, where their name persisted for many centuries. The wide geographical spread of the name Cimmerian may be the result of Greek and Near Eastern generalizations for all peoples of the steppes of South Russia. Cim-

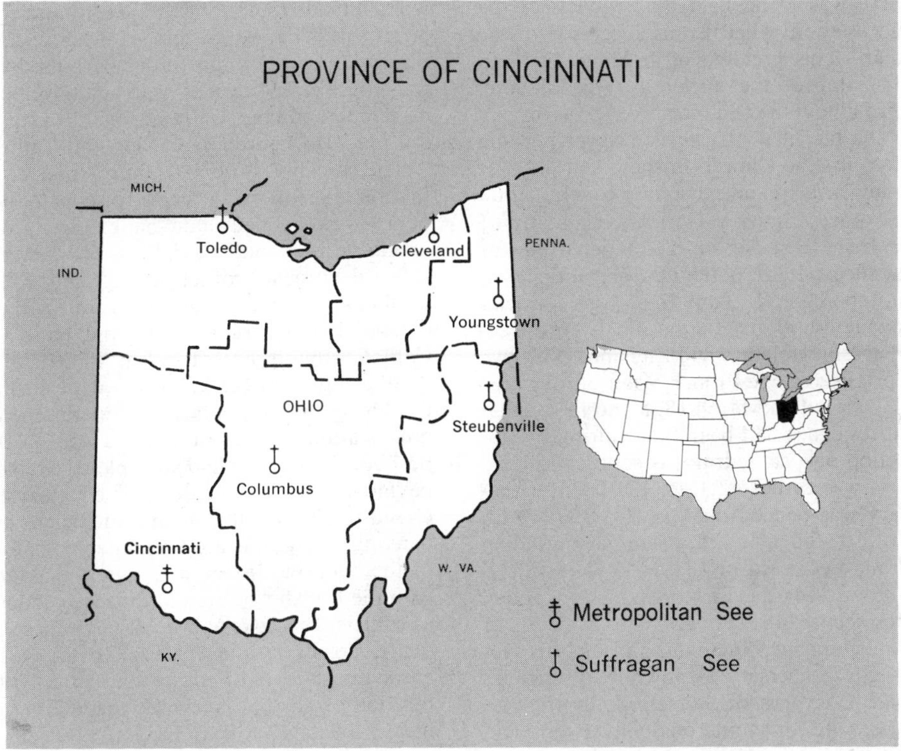

Province of Cincinnati comprising the Archdiocese of Cincinnati, known as the metropolitan see, and five dioceses called suffragan sees. The archbishop has metropolitan jurisdiction over the province.

merian may have been a generic name for all nomadic peoples of the north, as later Scythian and Hun.

Bibliography: C. F. LEHMANN-HAUPT, Pauly-Wiss RE 11.1 (1921) 397–434. J. A. H. POTRATZ, *Die Skythen in Südrussland* (Basel 1963) 85–96. B. B. PIOTROVSKII, *Vanskoe Tsarsto, Urartu* (Moscow 1959) 232–241.

[R. N. FRYE]

CINCINNATI, ARCHDIOCESE OF (CINCINNATENSIS)

Metropolitan see comprising 19 counties in southwest Ohio, an area of 8,543 square miles, with a population (1963) of 2,473,372, of whom 515,716 were Catholics; the diocese was created June 19, 1821; the archdiocese, July 19, 1850. The suffragan Sees of *Cleveland, *Columbus, *Steubenville, *Toledo, and *Youngstown were included in the territory of the original jurisdiction, which embraced the entire state of Ohio, and also Michigan and the Old Northwest, until they were withdrawn in 1833 by the erection of the Detroit diocese. In 1847 the northern part of Ohio was cut off to form the Diocese of Cleveland, and in 1868 the southeastern section was removed for the new See of Columbus. New dioceses were established in Toledo in 1910, Youngstown in 1943, and Steubenville in 1944.

Early History. Until 1785 when Cincinnati became part of the prefecture apostolic of the new republic, the territory was included in the immense Quebec diocese; with the creation of the Baltimore diocese in 1789 it became part of this first U.S. see. French missionaries undoubtedly accompanied expeditions to the area in the first half of the 18th century, but the first permanent settlement in Ohio was made in 1788, at Marietta, by colonists from Massachusetts. Two years later French Catholics settled at Gallipolis in southeastern Ohio where they were served for a few years by Peter Joseph Didier, OSB, until he left the colony in discouragement. The few Catholics scattered in Ohio were dependent upon the occasional missionary journeys of priests from Kentucky, and, after 1808, upon the ministrations of Edward *Fenwick, Dominican missionary and one of the founders of the first house of his order in the U.S. near Springfield, Ky.

Diocese. The needs of the increasing Catholic population in Ohio were recognized when on June 19, 1821, Pius VII decreed the erection of the Cincinnati diocese and the appointment of Fenwick as its first bishop.

Fenwick. The new bishop was consecrated by Bp. Benedict Flaget in St. Rose's Church, Washington County, Ky., on Jan. 13, 1822, and on March 23 took up residence in his see city where a small rented house served as the episcopal residence. Because his log church on the outskirts of the city was inaccessible at times, Fenwick purchased a lot on Sycamore between Sixth and Seventh Streets, where a new church was completed by December 1822. When this change of location caused controversy with the laymen who had built the original church, the bishop demanded transfer of the property title to himself. A later problem concerning the property acquired by Dominican priests working in Ohio and held in the name of the Dominican Order was settled when the Congregation of the Propagation of the Faith ordered a separation of diocesan and Dominican property. The agreement signed in 1828 provided that diocesan property was to be held by Fenwick in the name of the diocese and willed to his successor in the See of Cincinnati. This practice of holding diocesan property in the name of the bishop for the diocese, which spread throughout the Old Northwest, was largely responsible for the fact that *trusteeism never became a serious problem for the Church in these states.

To secure financial help and personnel for the 6,000 Catholics of his diocese, mostly German but many of them Swiss or Irish, Fenwick in 1823 departed for Europe. He was successful in obtaining substantial contributions from Pope Leo XII, from the Lyons Association of the Propagation of the Faith, and from collections made in Belgium, Holland, and England. With five recruits—four priests and one French Sister of Mercy—he returned to Cincinnati in March 1825 and found that a new episcopal residence had been built during his absence. Construction of a cathedral was soon completed and the structure was dedicated Dec. 17, 1826; a theological seminary was opened on May 11, 1829, with an enrollment of 10 students; and a seminary building was completed and dedicated in 1831.

While in Baltimore for the First Provincial Council (1829), Fenwick secured the services of four Sisters of Charity of Emmitsburg for Cincinnati and of four Dominican sisters for Somerset. Meanwhile, Fenwick's regular missionary journeys on horseback throughout his diocese had resulted in numerous conversions and the establishment of many parishes and missions. When this evoked bitterness from the Protestant press and pulpit, the *Catholic Telegraph,* a weekly newspaper, began publication in October 1831. On four occasions poor health and the exactions of his office led Fenwick to ask for a coadjutor. Before Rome acted favorably, he died in Wooster, Ohio, Sept. 26, 1832, while on a mission tour through Ohio and the Northwest.

Purcell. On May 12, 1833, Pope Gregory XVI named as second bishop of Cincinnati John Baptist *Purcell, president of Mt. St. Mary College, Emmitsburg, Md., who was consecrated in Baltimore on Oct. 13, 1833. Purcell attended the Second Provincial Council of Baltimore before traveling west to his diocese by stage and steamboat. After his installation on November 14 by Bishop Flaget, his first concern was to execute the will of his predecessor relative to the division of diocesan and Dominican property. Following negotiations with the Dominicans, 7 of the 16 churches in Ohio were named as diocesan, and 9 as Dominican property. The bishop lost no time in beginning the long series of annual missionary visitations for which his episcopate was noted, and which were responsible for a considerable part of the steady growth of Catholicism. His seven European trips between 1838 and 1869 helped to supply the vocational and financial needs of the diocese. A new cathedral on West Eighth Street, begun in 1841, was consecrated on Nov. 2, 1845, under the patronage of St. Peter in Chains.

Archdiocese. In 1850 Cincinnati was raised to the rank of metropolitan see and Archbishop Purcell received the pallium when he visited Rome (1851). During the controversy preceding the Civil War, the archdiocese observed an official silence. With the outbreak of war, Purcell and the *Catholic Telegraph* became strongly Unionist. The Catholic population supported Lincoln's administration and helped to supply the military needs of the North. Religious communities of women made their contribution in nursing service when Sisters of Charity, Sisters of Mercy, and Franciscan Sisters served as opportunity permitted, and a part of the House of Mercy was used as a hospital and prisoner-of-war cantonment. Catholic loyalty during the war years did much to overcome earlier anti-Catholic sentiment.

The so-called "Purcell failure" marred the otherwise favorable record of Purcell's episcopate. When the panic of 1837 weakened state banks, an informal banking operation was conducted from the cathedral by Father Edward Purcell, brother of the bishop. Their ignorance of financial matters and their mistrust of banks, increased by recurrent panics and bank failures, made Catholic immigrants turn in increasing numbers to "Father Purcell's Bank," where deposits mounted steadily during the 40 years of its operation. Following the great national panic of 1873, a run on the money deposited with Purcell had so depleted available funds that payments were suspended. When an examination disclosed the insolvent state and inefficient methods of the banking operation, an assignment of all the resources of the bank was made to Edward B. Mannix, together with the transfer of certain diocesan property estimated as sufficient to cover all liabilities. These proved inadequate, however, and from 1880 to 1905 legal action ensued in state and Federal courts until a final legal disposition of all the issues was made. To supplement the means available to pay creditors, voluntary donations were collected from priests and people of the archdiocese and from other dioceses throughout the U.S.

In addition to the loss and consequent hardships suffered by many poor depositors, this failure also resulted in the abandonment of the faith by many scandalized Catholics, temporary difficulty in effecting conversions to the Catholic faith, the closing of the seminary for a time, and the inability to promote the material growth of the diocese until the eve of World War I. As these troubles were developing, Bp. William H. *Elder of Natchez was appointed coadjutor, Jan. 3, 1880, with the right of succession to Purcell. The ill health and advanced age of Purcell led him to resign all administration to his coadjutor 3 years before his own death on July 4, 1883.

Elder. Repair of the harm resulting from the Purcell bank failure and a reorganization of the administration of the diocese constituted the major work of Elder's episcopate. Among the improvements were the establishment of a chancery, canonical courts, advisory bodies, and compulsory annual reports from ecclesiastical institutions. Age and physical infirmities led him to request a coadjutor, and on April 27, 1903, Rome appointed Henry J. Moeller, Bishop of Columbus, Ohio, coadjutor with right of succession.

Moeller. On Elder's death, Oct. 31, 1904, his coadjutor succeeded him. Moeller had been associated with the administrative structure of the archdiocese and continued the important work of reorganization. Recovery from the Purcell failure made possible the founding of new parishes as well as construction of a new major seminary; a hotel and a center for Catholic men, the Fenwick Club; and St. Rita's School for the Deaf. A diocesan bureau of Catholic Charities was organized, and national headquarters for Catholic Charities and the Catholic Students Mission Crusade were established in Cincinnati. At his death on Jan. 5, 1925, Moeller's work to improve the diocesan school system was well under way and included provisions for better training of teachers and the creation of central Catholic high schools.

McNicholas. On July 15, 1925, Bp. John T. *McNicholas of Duluth, Minn., was appointed to Cincinnati where the quarter-century of his episcopacy was marked by an extraordinary growth. Fifty new parishes were established and the number of priests working in the diocese almost doubled; mission chapels were constructed in rural areas and administered by seminary professors until they required parochial status; more than 100 diocesan priests were educated in extensive programs of graduate study in order to staff the diocesan agencies and educational institutions. The central high schools planned by his predecessor were expanded by McNicholas to 28. The need for organized youth activities on a diocesan basis led to the establishment of the Catholic Youth Organization (CYO) and the National Federation of Catholic College Students (NFCCS) under episcopal sponsorship, and the development of Fort Scott Camps. McNicholas led an unsuccessful movement of Ohio Catholics during the 1930s to obtain state aid for Catholic schools. The retreat movement for lay men and women was fostered by the establishment of diocesan and religious centers, with the result that thousands of Catholics became annual retreatants. An organized apostolate for the Negro was undertaken; 12 parishes were built for, or converted to, the work of this apostolate, and two high schools were established to meet its special needs. An archdiocesan confederation of Parent-Teachers Associations was formed in 1925. Because of the decay of the neighborhood in the basin of the city, St. Monica's became the cathedral in place of St. Peter in Chains (1937). The approach of the centenary of the archdiocese found McNicholas in poor health, and his death on April 22, 1950, prevented his celebration of this great event and of his 25th year as archbishop.

Alter. The appointment of Bp. Karl J. Alter of Toledo, Ohio, to Cincinnati was announced on June 20, 1950, and initiated a period of marked progress. Curtailment of building during the depression and war years had left a backlog of necessary ecclesiastical construction, which was further emphasized by the extraordinary growth in population during the same period. Alter directed a program embracing 350 archdiocesan and parochial projects costing $60 million. The most notable single work was the remodeling and reconstruction of the Cathedral of St. Peter in Chains and its reconstitution as the cathedral of the archdiocese. The restored cathedral was rededicated in November 1957, before the largest assemblage of the hierarchy and clergy in the history of the archdiocese. A second major project was the completion of St. Gregory preparatory seminary, in part made necessary by a fire that destroyed the south wing on the night of Good Friday, 1956. Four city-wide campaigns raised more than $13 million for new high schools. The fifth synod of the archdiocese in 1954 revised diocesan legislation in relation to Canon Law and contemporary conditions. The curia was reorganized and existing lay organizations were coordinated in archdiocesan councils of Catholic men, women, and youth.

Institutional Development. Diocesan synods were held on occasion from 1837 to 1954. Those of 1865, 1886, 1898, 1920, and 1954 are classified as formal synods, and codes of the legislation enacted have been published. Decrees affecting the development of the parochial system of education became patterns for similar legislation in other dioceses in the U.S. The provincial councils of 1855, 1858, 1861, 1882, and 1889 enacted legislation to secure conformity throughout the province in disciplinary or procedural concerns.

Altar, Cathedral of St. Peter in Chains, Cincinnati.

The archdiocese has had five auxiliary bishops: Sylvester H. Rosecrans (1862–68); Joseph H. Albers (1929–37), later bishop of Lansing, Mich.; George J. Rehring (1937–50), later bishop of Toledo, Ohio; Clarence G. Issenmann (1954–57), later bishop of Columbus, Ohio; and Paul F. Leibold (1958–).

The chancery and curia of the archdiocese have developed progressively, the preparation of personnel for these specialized offices having received particular attention from McNicholas and Alter.

The field of Catholic Charities has been extended to departmental agencies concerned with the guidance of youth, supervision of adoptive homes, cooperative programs with the juvenile and domestic relations courts, family service, unemployment service, a Catholic guidance clinic, a boy's service, and the care of displaced persons.

Educational Development. Even in the early missionary years of Cincinnati the objective was a school in every parish. This was realized to a considerable degree in the 16 parishes established during Fenwick's episcopate, and it became the common practice under Purcell to open church and school simultaneously. His success in bringing teaching communities to the archdiocese was one of the most significant factors in the developing parochial school system. The Sisters of Notre Dame de Namur began their work in 1840, the Franciscan Fathers and Brothers in 1844, the Ursulines in 1845, the

Brothers of Mary in 1849, the Sisters of Mercy in 1858, the Sisters of the Sacred Heart in 1869, the Franciscan Sisters in 1876, and the Sisters of Christian Charity in 1881. By the end of Purcell's episcopate, the parochial school system was so generally established that his successor, Elder, could promulgate regulations for compulsory attendance at Catholic schools. During the same period, schools were attached to orphanages and convents.

The need for control and organization at an archdiocesan level was fulfilled in 1906 by the establishment of an archdiocesan superintendent of schools. The first report from this office in 1908 listed 27,233 students in attendance in 110 schools; in 1963 there were 156 schools with a total of more than 76,000 students. By 1963, the archdiocese also had 33 high schools with a total enrollment of nearly 21,000.

A related development began with the establishment, in 1928, of the archdiocesan teachers college. Although primarily intended for teaching communities of sisters, the program attracted lay teachers, seminarians, and priests as well. The Athenaeum of Ohio, incorporated in 1928 with a board headed by the archbishop for the supervision of all Catholic colleges, seminaries, high schools, and other institutions of higher learning in the archdiocese, was reorganized in 1953. Its jurisdiction was limited to the two seminaries, including the college department of St. Gregory's minor seminary, and, on the graduate level, Mt. St. Mary's of the West seminary and the institute of Thomistic theology; and to the secondary schools. Undergraduate training of diocesan teachers was transferred to Our Lady of Cincinnati and Mt. St. Joseph colleges, and to Xavier University and the University of Dayton for graduate work. Nondiocesan institutions of higher learning in the archdiocese include *Xavier University conducted by Jesuits, the University of *Dayton under the Society of Mary, College of *Mt. St. Joseph on the Ohio under the Sisters of Charity, and *Our Lady of Cincinnati College conducted by the Sisters of Mercy.

Bibliography: E. A. CONNAUGHTON, *A History of Educational Legislation and Administration in the Archdiocese of Cincinnati* (Washington 1946). J. H. LAMOTT, *History of the Archdiocese of Cincinnati, 1821–1921* (New York 1921). V. F. O'DANIEL, *The Right Reverend Edward Dominic Fenwick, O.P., . . . First Bishop of Cincinnati* (Washington 1920). K. J. ALTER, *The Mind of an Archbishop: A Study of Man's Essential Relationship to God, Church, Country and Fellow Men,* ed. M. E. REARDON (Paterson 1960).

[A. STRITCH]

CINGRIA, ALEXANDRE, artist, pioneer in the modern renewal of sacred art; b. Geneva, March 22, 1879; d. Lausanne, Nov. 8, 1945. Of French and Italian descent by his father and Polish by his mother, Alexandre Cingria lived and worked almost exclusively in his beloved country, Switzerland. Cingria was a painter, a mosaic worker, a theater costume designer, and a stained glass artist. It was in this last capacity that he reached his highest achievement. In contrast to his contemporary Georges *Rouault in Paris, who was weighed down by the awfulness of sin, Cingria was exuberant with the joy of his faith, certain of final victory. His work displays a colorful and rhythmic character that is audacious both in subject and in conception.

In 1920 Cingria founded the Society of St. Luke, composed of a small group of forward-looking sculptors and painters, who often had to suffer the criticism of their fellow Catholics, but who happily were supported by Bishop Besson and other clergy such as Abbé Dussiller of the church of Notre Dame, Fribourg. Cingria's work contributed to Switzerland's role in establishing a more intelligent approach to sacred art in the 20th century. His early work can be seen at the church in Carouge, a small village just outside Geneva. Churches in Fribourg have the greatest number of his works; among the most important is "The Apparition of the Sacred Heart" in the church of Notre Dame. His latest window, completed in 1942, is in the University of Geneva: "Orpheus Charming the Beasts."

In his theater work Cingria designed costumes for Henri Gheon's *Pendu dépendu,* for René Morax's *Le Roi David* and *Judith,* and for É. Jaques-Dalcroze's *La Veillée.* He did colored illustrations for Shakespeare's *The Tempest,* produced in a luxurious edition of only 10 copies.

Bibliography: A. CINGRIA, *Décadence de l'art sacré* (new ed. Lausanne 1930). J. B. BOUVIER, *Alexandre Cingria* (Geneva 1944).

[J. U. MORRIS]

CINITES (KENITES), a nomadic tribe located chiefly in the eastern *Negeb, near the Gulf of 'Aqaba. Little is known with certainty of the Cinites, but their connections with the *Rechabites (1 Chr 2.55) indicate that they were a nomadic people. The Cinites (Heb. *qînîm* or collective *qenî*) were probably a clan of the *Madianites, to whom Moses fled after slaying the Egyptian (Ex 2.15) and to whom he was related by marriage (Ex 2.21; 3.1; *see* JETHRO). Hobab, the Cinite brother-in-law of Moses (Jgs 4.11), served as a guide to the Exodus party in their Sinai wanderings (Nm 10.29–32). Henceforth the Cinites were always on cordial terms with the Israelites (1 Sm 15.6). Although the statement in Jgs 1.16 seems to indicate that the Cinites entered the promised land from the east with the Israelites, this may be a later attempt to explain the inclusion of various Negeb Bedouins in the hegemony of Juda (1 Sm 27.10). Since the word Cinite is apparently connected with the Hebrew word *qayin,* meaning smith, the Cinites may have been itinerant smiths whose services would have been in great demand at the rich copper deposits in the *Araba (cf. Gn 4.22). Some scholars have suggested that it was from the Cinites that the divine name Yahweh and certain elements of Yahwism were mediated to Moses.

Bibliography: EncDictBibl 388. H. SCHNEIDER, LexThK[2] 6: 114. Abel GéogrPal 1:273. H. H. ROWLEY, *From Joseph to Joshua* (London 1950) 152–160 and *passim.*

[T. KARDONG]

CIRCUMCISION

The cutting off of the prepuce of the male. While there are instances of similar operations performed on females (e.g., the cutting off of the internal labia), the term circumcision is usually limited to males. Circumcision is a very ancient practice common to various peoples of primitive agriculture, but not among those of truly primitive culture. Among these peoples living in such disparate locales as Africa, America, and Australia, it seems to have been a rite connected in some way with puberty and the entrance into the adult or married state and probably related to fertility rites.

Its use by the Israelites is well known. Great emphasis was placed upon it as a sign of orthodoxy, especially in postexilic times. Allusions to this rite in the Bible confirm some of the primitive characteristics of this practice. The mention, for instance, in Ex 4.25; Jos 5.2 of flint knives used in the operation points to the antiquity of the practice. The enigmatic action of Moses' wife Sepphora and her reference to a "*spouse of blood" (Ex 4.25–26), as also the incident with the men of Sichem recorded in Gn 34.14–17, could refer to the connection of this rite with marriage.

The origin of the practice among the Israelites cannot be clearly determined. Some scholars are of the opinion that the Israelites received it from the Egyptians, since it was practiced in Egypt in the time of the Old Kingdom. Others disagree with this view, holding for a common source for both the Egyptians and the Israelites rather than a direct transmission. According to this view the Israelites would have accepted the practice from the Canaanites as they settled among them in Palestine. It would appear that these people did practice circumcision, since the Israelites refer to the Philistines as the uncircumcised (e.g., 1 Sm 14.6), but they never thus distinguish the other peoples with whom they were in contact in Palestine.

Whatever its origin, this rite had a special religious significance for the Israelites. It was practiced as a sign of the relationship with God stemming from the covenant made with Abraham. It is not clear just when the rite took on such a significance. The principal texts describing its origin with this significance all belong to the Pentateuchal *priestly writers (Gn 17.10–14; Ex 12.43–48; Lv 12.3). The fact that the practice does not appear in the other Israelite law codes suggests that this was a family ceremony adopted from the practices of the neighboring peoples. Probably in the beginning its connection with matrimonial rites was maintained, but gradually it received a more lofty religious significance, especially when the rite began to be administered immediately after birth rather than at puberty. Then, when the people found themselves in exile among those who did not practice such a rite, circumcision would have become the distinctive mark of the man who belonged both to Israel and to Yahweh.

The metaphorical usage of the concept of circumcision seems to strengthen the hypothesis that circumcision in Israel was connected with the rite of marriage. In such places as Dt 10.16; 30.6; Jer 4.4; 6.10; 9.25; Lv 26.41; Ex 6.12, 30, reference is made to "uncircumcised" lips, heart, and ears as organs that do not fulfill their function; they can do so only when they are, metaphorically speaking, circumcised.

Toward the end of the OT period, circumcision occupied a very important place in the religious life of the people. *Antiochus IV Epiphanes energetically opposed the practice with cruel punishments (1 Mc 1.63–64; 2 Mc 6.10), and to cling to this rite was the test of Jewish faith.

The early Christians, too, had difficulty with the practice of circumcision within the context of the controversy over the necessity for Gentile converts to observe the prescriptions of the Mosaic Law. St. Paul clearly saw the error of attributing any efficacy to such practices since it would mitigate the universality of the salvific effect on Christ's sacrifice (Gal 5.6; 6.15). Those who urged such requirements he called "enemies of the cross of Christ" (Phil 3.18).

In modern-day Judaism circumcision is still practiced by both Orthodox and Reform elements. The male infants are circumcised on the 8th day after birth, even if it is a Sabbath or Day of Atonement. Among the Orthodox the rite is carried out by a functionary called a mohel (circumciser). The Reform Jews allow the rite to be performed by a physician; contrary to the practice of the Orthodox, they do not require it for adult proselytes.

See also CIRCUMCISION OF OUR LORD.

Bibliography: De Vaux AncIsr 46–48. EncDictBibl 389–390. J. SCHMID, LexThK² 2:289–291. G. STANO, EncCatt 3:1701–07. F. R. LEHMANN and K. GALLING, RGG³ 1:1090–91. S. H. BLANK and M. JOSEPH, UnivJewishEnc 3:211–216.

[S. M. POLAN]

CIRCUMCISION OF OUR LORD. Christ's circumcision is briefly described in Lk 2.21: "And when eight days were fulfilled for his circumcision, his name was called Jesus, the name given him by the angel before he was conceived in the womb."

In the 1st century the Jews did not bring their children to the Temple or to the synagogue for the rite of circumcision; it was performed in the midst of the assembled family at home with great ceremony. It was at this time that the child was given his name. It seems that the circumcision of Christ took place in Bethlehem, because of the obligation imposed on the Jews by sacerdotal prescription to have their sons circumcised on

"The Circumcision of Our Lord," painting, c. 1500, by the Italian artist Marco Marziale (active 1493–1507).

the 8th day after birth; this obligation was so strict that it superseded the ordinance of the Sabbath rest. Only when a child was so weak that the operation would endanger his life could the ceremony be postponed. Since the father of the household usually was the minister of circumcision, it would seem that St. Joseph performed this ceremony for Christ. The prescriptions of the law mentioned in Gn 17.12 and Lv 12.3 were followed, since there is no other indication in the Gospels of any specific divine command to Mary and Joseph. The Gospel stresses that the newly born Savior of the world is the appointed heir of the promises made to Abraham, and that this is confirmed by the rite of circumcision; on this same occasion He is given the name Jesus to indicate His role as Savior.

The practice of administering circumcision on the 8th day after birth, and not as a puberty rite, specified the act among the Jews as a religious rite. It was thus more easily recognized as the religious act by which the child became a member of the people of God and heir of the messianic promises made to Abraham. In St. Luke's mind in describing the circumcision of Christ, since salvation is from the Jews, the Savior of the world must be the descendant of Abraham. It is through faith in Christ, who was Himself circumcised, that the new Israel is grafted on to the root of Abraham, and therefore the physical circumcision has become unnecessary (Gal 5.6; 6.15).

See also CIRCUMCISION.

Bibliography: H. LESÊTRE, DB 2.1:772–780. J. LEBRETON, DBSuppl 4:980. F. CABROL, DACL 3.2:1717–28. EncDictBibl 389–390. X. LÉON-DUFOUR, ed., *Vocabulaire de théologie biblique* (Paris 1962) 134–135. **Illustration credit:** Reproduced by courtesy of the Trustees, National Gallery, London.

[R. L. FOLEY]

CIRCUMINCESSION

This article briefly considers first the positive foundations of the doctrine and then its theological formulation.

Positive Foundations. By the term circumincession theology understands the mutual immanence and penetration of the three Divine *Persons. *Circuminsessio* (*circum-in-sedere:* to sit around) stresses rather the passive, somewhat static aspect of the doctrine, whereas *circumincessio* (*circum-incedere:* to go, to move around) looks at it from the dynamic angle of movement. The earliest usage was of a corresponding Greek word, περιχώρησις, by St. Gregory of Nazianzus (middle of 4th century), not in a Trinitarian but in a Christological context, to signify the mutual immanence of the two natures in Christ (*Epist.* 101; PG 37:182). *See* PERICHORESIS, CHRISTOLOGICAL. In its present Trinitarian meaning it was first used by St. John Damascene in the 8th century (*De fide orth.* 1.8; PG 94:829). However, the doctrine itself has deep roots in Scripture: ". . . believe in the works, that you may know and believe that the Father is in me and I in the Father" (Jn 10.38; 14.11; 17.21). These three Johannine texts have traditionally been understood by Catholic (J. Knabenbauer, A. Wikenhauser, J. Leal) and Protestant (C. Barret, W. Hendriksen) exegetes in the sense of a mutual divine immanence between Father and Son. Explicit scriptural basis for the mutual penetration of the Holy Spirit and the other two Persons is lacking. (1 Cor 2.10, often quoted, is inconclusive.)

Formulation. St. Thomas (ST 1a, 42.5) admirably synthesizing the two conceptions, Latin and Greek, explains circumincession by the unicity of the divine nature (Latin) as well as by the very origin of the Persons (Greek).

The divine nature, numerically one, is conceived by Latin theology as the common ground (in its theory with a certain unavoidable logical priority over the Persons) where Father, Son, and Holy Spirit meet. All three are necessarily linked by the common bond of the only divine essence, which is equally possessed by all three. Besides this unity of nature, there is a perfect fusion of personal rational activities: the three Persons cannot but think, decide, and act together, with all these divine acts flowing down the very same channel of the divine nature.

The Greek background is different: less static, more vital and dynamic. For a Greek the primary datum is not nature but Person, throbbing with life, communicable life. Each Divine Person is irresistibly drawn, by the very constitution of His being, to the other two. Branded in the very depths of each one of them is a necessary outward impulse, a centrifugal force, urging Him to give Himself fully to the other two, to pour Himself out into the divine receptacle of the other two. It is a "reciprocal irruption" (Cyril of Alex., *In Jo.* 1.5; PG 73:81), or unceasing circulation of life. Thus, each Person being necessarily in the other two, unity is achieved not so much on account of the unicity of a single passive nature but rather because of this irresistible impulse in each Person, which mightily draws them to one another.

One has here two different explanations, substantially identical, yet rich and colorful in their variety, of the same divine circumincession. Probably the best formulation of this mysterious reality is that given in the West by the 11th Council of Toledo (675), which, with an unmistakable oriental ring, teaches that the mutual relations, binding the Persons and referring them to one another, are the deepest root of the doctrine (Denz 532). In the beatific vision "it will be granted to the eyes of the human mind, strengthened by the light of glory, to contemplate the Father, the Son, and the Holy Spirit in an utterly ineffable manner, to assist throughout eternity at the processions of the Divine Persons, and to rejoice with a happiness like to that with which the holy and undivided Trinity is happy" (Pius XII MysCorp 80).

See also TRINITY, HOLY, ARTICLES ON; NATURE; PERSON (IN THEOLOGY); PROCESSIONS, TRINITARIAN; RELATIONS, TRINITARIAN.

Bibliography: A. CHOLLET, DTC 2.2:2527–32. M. SCHMAUS, LexThK[2] 8:274–276. T. DE RÉGNON, *Études de théologie positive sur la Sainte Trinité,* 4 v. (Paris 1892–98). A. DENEFFE, "Perichoresis, circumincessio, circuminsessio," ZKathTh 47 (1923) 497–532. L. PRESTIGE, "περιχωρέω and περιχώρησις in the Fathers," JThSt 29 (1928) 242–252.

[A. M. BERMEJO]

CIRCUMSTANCES, MORAL

A human act is moral insofar as it is subject to reason. That which specifies a human action as morally good or bad is whatever makes an action to be the kind of act that it is, and this is determined by the object of the act. The object of a moral act is that to which the action tends by its very nature. For example, the object of murder is the taking of the life of an innocent person. It is the object, so understood, that primarily specifies an action as morally good or bad. This moral object makes the action to be good or bad as such.

No action, however, is performed in the abstract. Every human act in the concrete order is done under particular circumstances. Circumstances may therefore affect the morality of an action and add something to the moral quality that it has by reason of its object. The latter concerns the abstract nature of the act, that is, what kind of action it is morally, while the circumstances concern the individuality of the action, that is, the act as it exists here and now. But since many individuating conditions or circumstances are involved in any human action, we must restrict circumstances to those that have a moral bearing on the action. For example, the action of murder is by its object morally evil; the circumstance of using a dagger is relevant whereas the circumstance of the murderer's wearing a necktie is not. A moral circumstance, therefore, is an individuating condition that, though it is something over and beyond the nature of the action itself, nevertheless modifies in some real way the moral quality of the act.

Aristotle first treated moral circumstances in an explicit manner, in the context of ignorance: an agent's ignorance of this or that circumstance could introduce an involuntary aspect into a given action and, to the extent that it does, it lessens responsibility (*Eth. Nic.* 111a 3–8). St. Thomas Aquinas, taking Cicero into account as well as Aristotle, treated moral circumstances in terms of seven questions that can be asked about a moral action, and noted which circumstances are the most important (ST 1a2ae, 7.3–4).

Classification of Circumstances. Some circumstances affect the very doing of the action. *When* the action takes place refers to the relevance this or that period of time has in the performance of an act, e.g., whether it is done by day or night, during war or peace, and so on. *Where* the action takes place can affect its morality; murder in a cathedral adds an additional moral evil to murder itself. *How* the action occurs concerns the manner in which the action is carried out, e.g., a person saves the life of another by acting with courage.

Other circumstances relate to causes that bring about the action. *Why* the action takes place refers to the motive or purpose a person has in performing an action; it is the extrinsic end for which the action is done. *Who* is doing the action refers to the agent himself who performs the act, and this circumstance is significant when some quality of his person affects the moral character of what he does. *By what means* the action is carried out refers to the instrumental moral cause used to accomplish the action; it makes a difference, for example, whether a murderer chooses a painful means to commit his crime.

Another circumstance concerns the effect of the action with regard primarily to its *quantitative* aspect. Stealing is an action morally wrong by its object; stealing a large amount of money is a circumstance aggravating the malice of the act.

Moral Consequences of Circumstances. It is clear that circumstances add varying degrees of moral good and evil to a voluntary act to the extent that a person is aware of them. The primary and essential morality of a human action, however, is taken from the object and not from any of the circumstances. The moral kind of an act cannot be changed by any circumstance attending its performance. The taking of the life of an innocent person is murder and as such is morally evil; accompanying circumstances will not alter this primary specification. However, granted the primary moral worth of the action, circumstances may clearly contribute additional morality to it. Sometimes circumstances affect the morality of the action only in degree, that is, they increase or diminish its goodness or malice. Stealing is bad by object; stealing a rare object increases the malice of the action but it adds no additional kind of evil to the act. Giving money for a charitable cause is a good action in itself; giving a large amount that one can afford increases the goodness of the action.

Sometimes circumstances add a new kind of morality to an act. In the example of murder in a cathedral, the evil action of murder, through circumstance of place, involves the profanation of a consecrated place of worship and hence the additional evil of sacrilege. However, it is the circumstance of end, the purpose in doing the act, that matters most in this regard and, indeed, is the most important circumstance of all precisely because it can, more than any other circumstance, add a new moral quality to an action. The motive an agent has can change an act morally good by object into a morally evil act. Telling the truth is a morally good action by object, but to tell the truth about someone with the intention of injuring him turns an action still good by object into a bad one. However, the reverse effect does not occur, namely, that a good intention should turn an act evil by object into one that is morally good. The reason for this is that the morality of an act is based essentially on its specification by its object. No motive the agent has in mind, regardless of how noble it may be, can change what is essentially evil into something good. In a word, no end or motive, no matter how good, can morally justify an essentially evil means; for example, one cannot use murder, morally evil by object, as a means to any end, no matter how good.

Bibliography: THOMAS AQUINAS, ST 1a2ae, 18. D. M. PRÜMMER, *Manuale theologiae moralis*, ed. E. M. MÜNCH, 3 v. (10th ed. Barcelona 1945–46) 1:75–86. J. A. OESTERLE, *Ethics: The Introduction to Moral Science* (Englewood Cliffs, N.J. 1957) 103–110.

[J. A. OESTERLE]

CISNEROS, GARCÍA DE, Benedictine abbot of the abbey of *Montserrat, monastic reformer, and ascetical writer; b. Cisneros, Diocese of Léon (Castile), 1455 or 1456; d. Montserrat, Nov. 27, 1510. Cousin of Cardinal Francisco *Ximénez and only son of a poor but proud nobleman, García early gave up the possibility of social privilege to enter the austere Castilian monastery of San Benito de Valladolid in 1475. Chosen as subprior in 1488, he played a prominent role in Valladolid's efforts to centralize and reform monastic observance in the newly united Spain of Ferdinand and Isabella. When called to initiate the observance of Valladolid in the Catalan monastery, shrine of Our Lady of Montserrat, he found himself favoring the independence of that monastery and accepted papal permission to become its abbot for life. He succeeded in winning Valladolid's recognition of his adaptations for the venerable pilgrimage center. In 1500 he published *Directorio de las horas canónicas* (Directory of the Canonical

Hours) for community prayer at Montserrat; the *Constitutions* of 1501 established the monastery's character and observances for the next 2 centuries. His most famous work (also 1500), *Ejercitatorio de la vida espiritual* (Exercises for the Spiritual Life), is a skillful compilation drawn from Devotio Moderna sources and intended for both monks and pilgrims (such as St. Ignatius would be in 1522) as a practical, systematic guide toward contemplation. He was an important link between medieval, monastic piety and the psychological, analytical systems of St. Ignatius of Loyola and the Spanish mystics later in the century.

Bibliography: *Obras completas,* ed. C. BARAUT (Montserrat 1965), bibliog. E. A. PEERS, *Studies of the Spanish Mystics,* v.2 (London 1930; repr. 1960) 3–37, 401–407. G. COLOMBÁS, *Un reformador benedictino en tiempo de los reyes católicos: García Jiménez de Cisneros, abad de Montserrat* (*Scripta et documenta* 5; Montserrat 1955), biog. and bibliog.

[P. EDWARDS]

CISON (KISHON), a narrow river bed in northern Palestine that runs along the northeastern side of Mt. Carmel and empties into the Mediterranean Sea near modern Haifa. It is called a wadi (Heb. *naḥal*) in the Bible, though for most of its course it lies in a wide, flat valley. The Cison formed part of the boundary of the tribe of Zabulon (Jos 19.11). It was at the Cison that Sisara, leader of a Canaanite coalition, was defeated in one of the crucial battles of the Israelite conquest of the land [Jgs 4.12–16; 5.19–22; Ps 82(83).10]. The poetic account of the battle in Jgs 5.19–22 (*see* DEBORA, CANTICLE OF) tells that the victory was made possible by the overflowing of the Cison; this is confirmed by 4.15, where it is said that Sisara had to abandon his chariot and flee on foot. It was at the Cison, too, that the prophets of Baal were put to death after failing to meet Elia's challenge (3 Kgs 18.40).

Bibliography: EncDictBibl 390–391. Abel GéogrPal 1:467–469. A. LEGENDRE, DB 2.1:781–786. L. PICARD, "Zur Geologie der Kischon-Ebene," ZDeutschPalVer 51 (1928) 5–72.

[G. H. GUYOT]

CISTERCIAN ART AND ARCHITECTURE

The Cistercians occupy an important place in the history of art primarily because of their architecture. They excelled also in manuscript illumination and stained glass, but the few surviving specimens of these types of work pale when compared with the immense array of monasteries they constructed during the 12th and 13th centuries all over Europe and even in Cyprus and Syria.

Architecture. The Cistercian buildings, and especially their churches, were distinguished by structural simplicity and lack of ornamentation, which were the result of the principles laid down by the founders of *Cîteaux as the basis of their reform of the order. As Étienne Gilson pointed out, "Cistercian architecture forms an integral part of Cistercian spirituality and cannot be separated from it." The aim of the Cistercian reform was a return to the full observance of the Rule of St. Benedict, which over the centuries had changed and slackened, particularly with regard to simplicity and poverty. The Cistercians desired to be poor with Christ, who was poor. As a result they decided to reject everything that might imply luxury or diminish poverty, whether in divine worship, clothing, or food. In their architecture they renounced stone bell towers, paintings, and sculpture for their churches, feeling that these might distract the religious from their prayer and meditation. All this was vigorously expressed by St. Bernard in the famous *Apologia* addressed to his friend *William, a Benedictine abbot of Saint-Thierry, near Reims. In this essay, which reads like a pamphlet, the saint protested against the extravagant splendor of the Cluny churches, their excessive size, their sumptuous decoration, and especially the ornamentation of the capitals in both the cloisters and the churches. He admitted that the representation of scenes from the Bible or the lives of the saints can serve for the instruction and edification of the faithful; "but," he said, "of what use is that for men vowed to poverty, for monks, for spiritual men?" He went on to add the following well-known passage: "What are these ridiculous monsters, this deformed beauty and this beautiful deformity, doing in the cloisters under the eyes of monks occupied by their reading? What are these filthy apes, ferocious lions, monstrous centaurs doing there? . . . Good God! Even if one is not ashamed of these stupidities, one should at least regret the expenditure of money they involve."

The noble and austere architecture that is so esteemed by the Cistercians sprang from their rules and the *Apologia* of St. Bernard. After a long period of fidelity to the Roman architectural style, their master workmen adopted the Gothic style and contributed to its expansion all over Europe, where numerous examples of their work are still to be found everywhere. To name some of the most typical churches: in France, Fontenay, *Le Thoronet and Silvacane; in Germany, *Eberbach and *Ebrach; in England, *Fountains and *Rievaulx; in Austria, *Heiligenkreuz; in Belgium, *Villers; in Spain, Poblet and Santes Creus; in Italy, *Fossanova and Casamari; in Poland, Mogila and Wachock; in Portugal, *Alcobaça; in Sweden, Varnhem; and in Switzerland, Bonmont and *Hauterive. Ultimately even the Cistercians succumbed to the malady of building immense churches decorated with sculpture and painting. When baroque art became the rage, in Germany, Austria, and Switzerland they went so far as to reconstruct their monasteries in accordance with the taste of the times, or they simply added rococo decoration to already existing buildings. All of this was a far cry from the architecture of the first Cistercians, which, as Henri Focillon said, "is still an ancient witness to a very great spiritual revolution."

Manuscript Illumination. The oldest manuscripts from the scriptorium of Cîteaux are filled with ornamented letters and illumination work of a high artistic level, as in a copy of the Bible that was begun under the direction of Stephen Harding during the first years of the foundation and completed in 1109, and the *Moralia in Job* of St. Gregory the Great, which dates from 1111. But a short time later, *c.* 1150 and under the influence of St. Bernard, a decree of the general chapter ruled that only one color was to be used for the initial letters. The copyists then devoted all their care to the quality of the parchment used, to the outline of the letters, and to the arrangement of the text on the page, the only ornamentation being the beautiful initial letters in monochrome. Nothing was allowed to interfere with the beautiful arrangement of the calligraphy. Soon, however, the prohibitive rule was forgotten and illuminations reappeared.

Fig. 1. Cistercian architecture: (a) Fontenay, nave and choir of the abbey church. (b) Le Thoronet, north aisle of the abbey church. (c) Silvacane, south aisle of the abbey church from the nave. (d) Sénanque, cloister and church.

Fig. 2. Thirteenth-century white glass window in the church at Obazine Abbey.

Fig. 3. Frontispiece to "Moralia in Job" executed at Cîteaux in 1111 (Dijon MS 168, fol. 4v).

CISTERCIAN ART AND ARCHITECTURE

Fig. 4. Tree of Jesse in a commentary on Isaia (Dijon MS 129, fol. 4v).

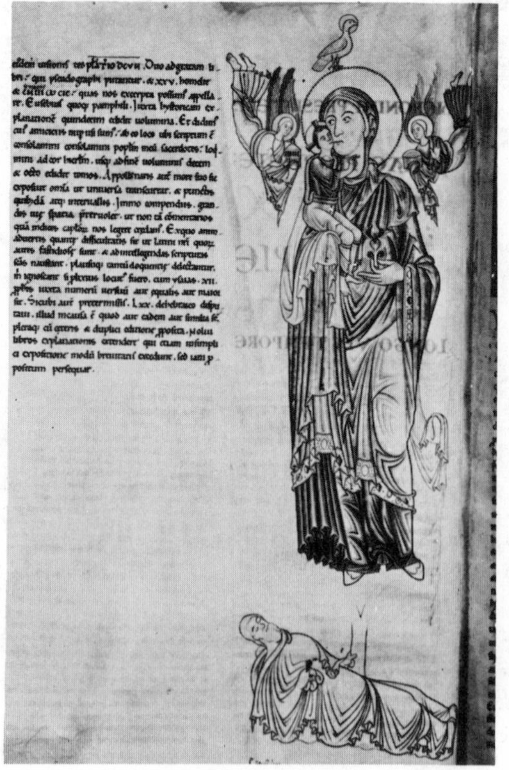

Stained Glass. A statute of the general chapter decreed that the windows should be of clear glass, without either cross or color. The Cistercian master glassworkers then hit upon the idea of tracing all sorts of foliated scrolls, rosettes, interlacing designs and arabesques on the glass with the lead in which the glass was set. Very beautiful effects were produced by this technique. Unfortunately, very few specimens of this type of glasswork have survived. The finest are to be found in France in the churches of Bénisson-Dieu in the Diocese of Lyon, of *Obazine in the Diocese of Tulle, and of Bonlieu in the Diocese of Limoges. However, at the end of the 13th century the Cistercians came to employ representational windows.

Bibliography: General. M. A. Dimier, *Recueil de plans d'églises cisterciennes,* 2 v. (Paris 1949), v.1, text; v.2, plates. F. van der Meer, *Atlas de l'ordre cistercien des origines jusqu'à la Révolution française, avec une introduction aux images cisterciennes* (Amsterdam 1965). M. Aubert, *L'Architecture cistercienne en France,* 2 v. (2d ed. Paris 1947). M. A. Dimier and J. Porcher, *L'Art cistercien, France* (La Pierre-qui-Vire 1962). H. P. Eydoux, *L'Architecture des églises cisterciennes d'Allemagne* (Paris 1952); "L'Abbatiale de Moreruela et l'architecture des églises cisterciennes d'Espagne," *Cîteaux in de Nederlanden* 5 (1954) 173–207. J. Bilson, "The Architecture of the Cistercians, with Special Reference to Some of Their Earlier Churches in England," *Archaeological Journal* 66 (1909) 185–280. P. Clemen and C. Gurlitt, *Die Klosterbauten der Cistercienser in Belgien* (Berlin 1916). L. Fraccaro de Longhi, *L'architettura delle chiese cistercensi italiane* (Milan 1958).

Illumination. C. Oursel, *Minatures cisterciennes, 1109–1134* (Mâcon 1960), 40 color pl. L. Bonnay, "Église d'Obazine (Corrèze): Vitraux du XIIe siècle," *Bulletin scientifique et archéologique de la Corrèze* 2 (1879) 199–211, 4 diagrams. **Illustration credits:** Figs. 1*a,* 1*c,* 1*d,* and 2, Photo Zodiaque. Fig. 1*b,* Photo Franceschi-Zodiaque. Figs. 3 and 4, Bibliothèque Municipale, Dijon.

[M. A. DIMIER]

CISTERCIAN NUNS

Under this title are included several groups of cloistered nuns who, in their history and tradition, are associated with the *Cistercians. The first Cistercian monastery for women was organized at Tart, near *Cîteaux, *c.* 1120. Other foundations followed throughout Europe; many were Benedictine convents that adopted the Cistercian reform. In the beginning the monks had rejected any legal relationship with the nuns. A century later Cîteaux incorporated a group of convents, although most remained under diocesan jurisdiction. The incorporated convents were subject to the Cistercian general chapter and were directed by neighboring abbots who assigned chaplains and furnished occasional economic assistance. The convent of Helfta (1258), Eisleben, Saxony, under Abbess Gertrude of Hackeborn (1251–92), developed a rich mystical tradition, represented by St. *Gertrude (the Great) and *Mechtild of Magdeburg. Cîteaux's continuing reluctance to assume full responsibility occasioned the emergence of several prominent convents as organizers and leaders of other communities. Thus, Tart in the 13th century headed a group of 18 convents and convoked annual chapters for the abbesses. About the same time a similar and still more extensive Spanish organization was controlled by the royal Abbey of Las Huelgas, near Burgos, founded (1187) by King Alfonso VIII of Castile (1158–1214).

The Hundred Years' War, the Reformation, and subsequent secularization and warfare destroyed hundreds of convents. Surviving ones often abandoned their rural isolation and sought permanent refuge within walled cities. The 17th century witnessed a number of local reforms; many of these reformed nuns adopted the name Bernardines. Famous among the Cistercian convents of that period was *Port-Royal, outside Paris. It was reformed by Angélique *Arnauld and became a stronghold of *Jansenism under the influence of the Abbé de Saint-Cyran (*see* DUVERGIER DE HAURANNE, JEAN). A later reform movement, that of the Trappistines, began during the period of the French Revolution when Dom Augustin established (1796) the convent La Sainte Volonté de Dieu near Riédra, Switzerland. In the 19th century, when the revived Cistercian Order found itself divided into Strict and Common Observances, both groups of monks renewed their associations with many Cistercian convents. The nuns of both observances lead cloistered and contemplative lives.

Cistercian Nuns of the Common Observance. Known also as Cistercians of the Original Observance or as Bernardines, the *Sacer Ordo monialium Cisterciensium* (SOCist) had, in 1964, 83 convents, only 9 of which were under the full jurisdiction of the Cistercian general chapter. These 9 were located in Switzerland, Germany, and Austria. The remaining convents were under episcopal jurisdiction, save for their internal monastic life, which was guided by the male branch of the order. The largest unit was in Spain and was divided into two congregations: The Federation of Cistercian Nuns of the Regular Observance of St. Bernard, with 26 convents under the abbess of Las Huelgas; and the Federation of Cistercian Nuns in Spain, with 20 convents, directed by the abbess of Valdoncella (Barcelona). The Swiss convent of Frauenthal established St. Ida's Convent near Prairie du Sac, Wis., in 1957. There were 10 professed religious there in 1964.

Cistercian Nuns of the Strict Observance. Known also as Trappistines, the *Ordo monialium Cisterciensium strictioris observantiae* (OCSO) numbered some 2,000 nuns in 40 convents (1964), of which 13 were in France, 7 in Spain, and 4 each in Belgium and Japan; the others were in Germany, England, Ireland, Holland, Italy, Switzerland, Republic of the Congo, Dahomey, and the U.S. Mount St. Mary's Abbey, Wrentham, Mass., founded in 1949, had 58 professed members, and the Abbey of Our Lady of the Mississippi, Dubuque, Iowa, had 13 professed religious.

Bibliography: A. J. Luddy, *The Cistercian Nuns* (Dublin 1931). Y. Estienne, *Les Trappistines cisterciennes de la stricte observance* (Paris 1937). J. Bouton, "L'Établissement des moniales cisterciennes," *XXIVe Congrès de l'Assoc. Bourguignonne des Sociétés savantes* (Dijon 1953) 37–70. E. G. Krenig, "Mittelalterliche Frauenklöster nach den Konstitutionen von Cîteaux," AnalOCist 10 (1954) 1–105. Heimbucher 1:356–362, 373.

[L. J. LEKAI]

CISTERCIANS

The Order of Cîteaux (SOCist), a Roman Catholic monastic order based on the Rule of St. Benedict, originated in 1098, and was named after the first establishment, Cîteaux, in Burgundy, France (Lat. *Cistercium*).

History

Cîteaux was founded by (St.) *Robert of Molesme (d. 1111). As Benedictine abbot of *Molesme he had failed to achieve real monastic reform, so he left that abbey with 21 of his adherents, and in 1098 founded

*Cîteaux in a wooded wilderness, near Dijon. The purpose of the new establishment was the instituting of a life of poverty, simplicity, and eremitical solitude, under the guidance of the Rule of St. Benedict in its strictest interpretation. Such a program was no novelty at the end of the 11th century, but Cîteaux found itself exposed to the hostile criticism of neighboring monasteries. In July 1099, through the intervention of higher ecclesiastical authority, Molesme enforced the return of Robert; (St.) Alberic (1099–1109) succeeded him at Cîteaux. In 1100, Pope Paschal II approved the new foundation and placed Cîteaux under papal protection. According to tradition, it was under Alberic that the monks adopted their distinctive white or gray habit under a black scapular; hence the popular name, White Monks.

After Alberic's death the Englishman (St.) *Stephen Harding, an organizer of broad vision and experience, was elected abbot (1109–33). Although there were still many problems to be solved, a sound program and able leadership assured the survival of Cîteaux. The first regulations, passed either under Alberic or Stephen, revealed Cîteaux's uniqueness, for unlike other reformed Benedictine houses, the statutes rejected all feudal revenues, and based the monastic economy on the manual labor of the monks themselves, assisted by lay brothers. Other measures simplified the overgrown monastic liturgy then customary in Benedictine houses, and prescribed austere simplicity both in church vestments and in church furnishings.

Expansion. As early as 1113, a small band of monks was ready to leave Cîteaux for the foundation of her first "daughter," La Ferté. Yet, the dramatic growth and extraordinary popularity of the order was due to (St.) *Bernard, who in 1113, with about 30 companions, applied for admission at Cîteaux. It was his example and magnetic personality that drew thousands of others to Cîteaux, and to the rapidly multiplying new establishments. La Ferté was followed by the foundation of *Pontigny in 1114, and in 1115 Bernard became the founder and first abbot of *Clairvaux. It was largely through Bernard's international fame that the order spread with unprecedented rapidity throughout foreign lands as well as France. In 1120, Cistercians founded their first establishment in Italy, in 1123 they settled in Germany, in 1128 in England, in 1130 in Austria, in 1132 in Spain, and foundations in all other countries of Western Christendom followed. Bernard was personally responsible for the organization of 65 new houses in France and abroad. At his death in 1153, the order possessed more than 300 monasteries, and toward the end of the same century the number exceeded 500. The rise of the *mendicant orders reduced monastic vocations considerably, but growth continued at a slower pace until, before the Reformation, there were 742 Cistercian houses, with 246 abbeys in France alone. At the peak of

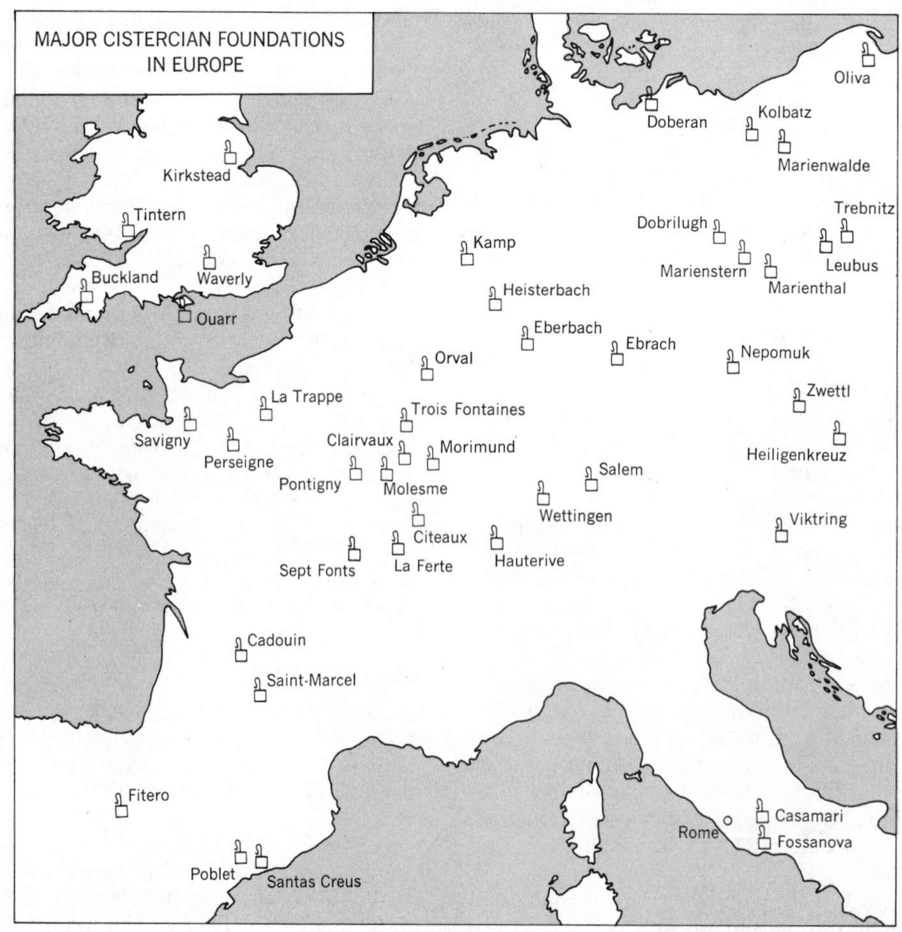

Fig. 1. Map showing the early Cistercian foundations in Europe.

Fig. 2. Our Lady of Spring Bank, Okauchee, Wis. First Cistercian foundation in the U.S., 1928.

their popularity, the monastic population of many abbeys amounted to several hundred, although these figures included a large number of lay brothers.

As another result of Bernard's example, the order gradually became involved in activities beyond the scope of a purely contemplative life. Abbots served as papal diplomats, others combated Albigensian heretics, participated in the Crusades, and served as missionaries in Eastern Europe and in the Baltic lands. Cistercians were responsible for the organization of several military orders in Spain. The greatest of them, *Calatrava, was founded in 1158, and, in spiritual matters, was under the control of the Abbey of *Morimond. An increasing number of monks were engaged in pastoral activities, and by the 16th century most houses took care of the spiritual needs of the surrounding population. All this was a departure from the original ideals of Cîteaux, although each incident occurred as a response to a particular contemporary need, or as an act of obedience to higher authorities.

Decline. The decline of the order, well in evidence in the 15th century, was caused not so much by external engagements nor by the impact of the Renaissance, as by outside intervention originating during the Avignon papacy. The right of monastic communities to elect their abbots was superseded by a commendatory system (*see* COMMENDATION), in which abbots were appointed either by the pope or by secular rulers. Such appointees were not members of the order but usually secular prelates who received the title for other than monastic virtues. Commendatory abbots rarely lived in their monasteries and were concerned mostly with the collection of abbatial revenues. The result was devastating. Lacking the guidance and control of their abbots, the communities became impoverished, discipline deteriorated, churches and monasteries became dilapidated, and eventually many houses were virtually deserted. The damage was particularly severe in Italy and France, where by the end of the 16th century nearly all abbeys were *in commendam*. The subsequent religious and civil wars of the Reformation era threatened the order with annihilation. Within a few decades Cistercians disappeared in England and Scotland, in the Scandinavian countries, and in the greater part of Germany. Meanwhile, the central administration of the order broke down and each abbey struggled alone for bare survival.

Reform. Nevertheless, the 16th century witnessed vigorous attempts at reform, which, in the absence of initiative from Cîteaux, originated on a local or regional basis and resulted in the formation of more or less independent congregations, each differing in customs and discipline. One such reform was that of the *Feuillants, initiated by Jean de la *Barrière (1544–1600), abbot of Les Feuillants in France. The congregation united a number of monasteries in France and Italy, was approved in 1586 by Sixtus V, and became entirely independent; it was noted for extraordinary severity of discipline. The Feuillants, however, failed to survive the French Revolution. Still more significant was the reform of the Strict Observance, for it resulted in a permanent schism within the order. This movement combined the efforts of several reformed communities in France early in the 17th century, and aimed at the restoration of the initial discipline of Cîteaux. The reform was spreading on a voluntary basis when, between 1623 and 1635, Cardinal François de La Rochefoucauld (1558–1645), as visitor of the order, repeatedly attempted to enforce the same discipline over all houses in France. His violent measures encountered embittered resistance on the part of the reluctant Common Observance. The same method was adopted by Cardinal Armand *Richelieu, who in 1635, enforced his own election as abbot of Cîteaux. At

Fig. 3. Paschal II approving the Cistercian Order. Woodcut printed (1491) at Dijon, France, by Peter Metlinger.

the time of his death (1642) only 30 monasteries belonged to the reform, but by the end of the same century the Strict Observance was followed in 60 houses. Because of its leaders' Gallican bent the Strict Observance received no support from the papacy; instead, a more moderate reform of the Common Observance was launched by Alexander VII in 1666.

Although the *Enlightenment undermined the foundations of monasticism, the fatal blow was struck in 1791 by the French revolutionary government. In that year all Cistercian establishments in France were dissolved and later, in the wake of Napoleon's armies, nearly all abbeys were secularized elsewhere in Europe. The end of the revolutionary area found only a dozen surviving houses, scattered throughout the Hapsburg Empire.

La Trappe. After the Bourbon restoration, the Strict Observance was successfully revived by former members of La Trappe, hence their popular name, *Trappists. The Common Observance was reorganized in Italy under papal auspices, and having made considerable gains elsewhere, by 1891, numbered 30 monasteries with nearly 1,000 monks. During the 19th century the difference between the two observances became more pronounced. The Trappists insisted on a strictly contemplative life according to the interpretation of the reformer of La Trappe, the Abbé Armand-Jean de Rance (1626–1700), while the Common Observance assumed an increasing load of teaching and pastoral duties. The final break took place in 1892, when the Trappist congregation became independent as the Order of Cistercians of the Strict Observance (OCSO), while the Common Observance has been known as the Sacred Order of Cistercians (SOCist).

Growth in the 20th Century. The growth of both groups continued in the 20th century, and establishments were made in nearly every Christian land. The end of World War II found Eastern and Central Europe under Communist control. The satellite governments, with the exception of the Polish, suppressed all Cistercian houses, among them the most populous congregation of the order, the Hungarian. In 1963, the Sacred Order of Cistercians had a total membership of about 1,600 in 66 monasteries divided into 10 congregations (provinces). They maintained 21 houses in Italy; 10 in Austria; 5 each in France, Brazil, and Vietnam; 4 in Poland; 3 each in Germany and the U.S.; 2 in Belgium; and one house in Holland, Switzerland, Spain, Yugoslavia, Canada, Bolivia, Ethiopia, and Eritrea.

U.S. Foundations. The first house of the Sacred Order of Cistercians in the U.S., Our Lady of Spring Bank, in Okauchee, Wis., was founded in 1928 by Austrian monks. The same group added to its possessions in 1935 a small residence, Our Lady of Gerowvall, in Paulding, Miss. In 1955 refugees from Hungary established Our Lady of Dallas monastery near Dallas, Tex. The latter is a teaching community, furnishing a part of the faculty of the diocesan University of Dallas.

Constitution

The founders of Cîteaux had no intention of establishing a new order. It was called, in its early years, simply the "New Monastery," one among many reformed communities, all following, more or less closely, the Rule of St. Benedict. The peculiar significance of Cîteaux lay in the fact that in a time of crisis, when the great *Cluny had lost much of its luster, and Oriental ideas had infiltrated the Western monastic world, the New Monastery reaffirmed in uncompromising terms the authority of the *Benedictine Rule. The problem of a distinct central organization, i.e., the foundation of an order, emerged only when Cîteaux had established her first daughter houses.

Charta Caritatis. The document aiming at the maintenance of uniform customs and discipline for all houses, known as the *Charta Caritatis* or Charter of Charity, was the work of Stephen Harding. The precise date of its composition, and the exact nature of the text has been a much debated question. Undoubtedly, during the course of the 12th century, the initial document was repeatedly revised and modified before it reached its final form. An early version of the charter, approved by Pope Callixtus II in 1119, already had incorporated the basic concept of the Cistercian constitution. It represented a compromise between the isolated independence of the earliest Benedictine houses, and the excessive centralization of the congregation of Cluny. While insisting on uniformity of liturgy and discipline, the charter granted extensive autonomy to individual establishments under the surveillance of the abbot responsible for the foundation, who was expected to visit such affiliations annually. The abbot of Cîteaux claimed no jurisdiction over the whole order. Both legislative and judicial power was entrusted to the general chapter composed of all abbots, meeting annually at Cîteaux. The abbot of Cîteaux convoked the chapter and presided over the gathering, but except for the direct affiliations of Cîteaux, he could act only as an agent of the chapter. Cîteaux itself was subject to annual visitation, made jointly by the abbots of her first four daughters, La Ferté, Pontigny, Clairvaux, and Morimond, the so-called protoabbots. In time of material need, mutual assistance was decreed.

Modifications. The first major modification of the Charter of Charity occurred in 1265, when Pope Clement IV issued the apostolic constitution *Parvus Fons.* This document, in an attempt to curb the influence of the protoabbots and to expedite the proceedings of the chapters, created an advisory council of 25 abbots, the *definitorium.* However, as the attendance at the general chapters decreased, this advisory council came to exercise a decisive influence over the chapters. Another papal constitution, the *Fulgens Sicut Stella,* issued in 1335 by the Cistercian Benedict XII, further modified the charter. It decreed the formal scholastic education of young monks, and put fiscal administration on a business basis. The turbulent era shortly before and after the Reformation witnessed the breakdown of central administration. Independent reform congregations refused to obey orders from Cîteaux and, especially in Italy and Spain, adopted mendicant customs and discipline, remaining Cistercian in name only. For the same reason, chapters were no longer held annually. Nicholas Boucherat I (1571–84), Abbot of Cîteaux, in an attempt to fill the gap, assumed the title of abbot general. The same title has been used by all his successors, although the abbot's legal position has not been altered.

During the course of the 17th century, central control was reestablished over France, Belgium, the German-speaking countries, and Poland. Even the Strict

Observance had to submit to Cîteaux's authority. In 1666, a new constitution by Pope Alexander VII, *In Suprema,* enforced a moderate reform of uniform discipline that remained in effect until the French Revolution. After the dissolution of Cîteaux in 1791, attempts to restore the unity of the scattered remains of the order were fruitless until 1869, when a general chapter finally initiated an effective reorganization. The modern Cistercian constitution calls for chapters in every fifth year, while in the chapterless years the *definitorium* holds meetings. The abbot general, considered the legal heir of the abbot of Cîteaux, is elected for life by the general chapter, and resides in Rome. The abbey of Cîteaux was successfully revived by the Trappists in 1898, but their abbot general, too, resides in Rome.

Cultural Contributions

The basis of Cistercian piety was the Rule of St. Benedict, but the greatest contribution of Bernard and his school to medieval spirituality was the revival of a mysticism having the sacred humanity of Christ and the Blessed Virgin as its center of devotion. The most eminent of Bernard's followers were *William of Saint-Thierry (d. 1148), *Guerric of Igny (d. 1157), St. *Aelred of Rievaulx (d. 1167), *Isaac of Stella (d. 1169), *Gilbert of Hoyland (d. 1172), and later *Adam of Perseigne (d. 1221).

Letters. Early Cistercian monastic training did not emphasize education. Those, however, who had received their education before entering the order continued their literary activity. Stephen Harding (d. 1134) composed a lucid and well-documented history of early Cîteaux, the *Exordium Parvum.* Otto of Freising (d. 1158) was certainly the greatest historian of his century. Toward the end of the 12th century, Conrad of Eberbach compiled a collection of Cistercian legends, the *Exordium Magnum.* Caesar of Heisterbach (d. 1240) was responsible for an even more popular book of similar nature, the *Dialogus Miraculorum.* *Scholasticism was eventually adopted under the influence of the mendicants. A general house of studies in Paris, the Bernardinum, founded in 1245, was followed by a number of other colleges elsewhere. Teaching in secondary schools became the profession of several communities in Austria and Hungary, when under governmental pressure they took over abandoned Jesuit schools after the suppression of the Society of Jesus in 1773.

Arts. The characteristic mark of early Cistercian art was austere simplicity (*see* CISTERCIAN ART AND ARCHITECTURE). The best preserved example of this style is Fontenay in France. By the middle of the 13th century the rules of simplicity were much relaxed. Royaumont near Paris, Fountains and *Rievaulx in England, and *Melrose in Scotland, are only a few examples of many splendid monuments of the most elaborate Gothic. The Renaissance added little to the existing monastic plants, but the era of Baroque was characterized by a feverish building activity, especially in Southern Germany and Austria. The history of economy praises Cistercians as the most accomplished agriculturists of the Middle Ages. Their spectacular achievements in clearing forests and reclaiming waste land, however, were results not of revolutionary techniques, but rather of the intelligent employment of hundreds of lay brothers under central direction. In the middle of the 13th century the sharply declining number of lay brother vocations ended the era of Cistercian prosperity.

Bibliography: Sources. P. GUIGNARD, *Les Monuments primitifs de la règle cistercienne* (Dijon 1878). H. SÉJALON, *Nomasticon cisterciense, editio nova* (Solesmes 1892). J. CANIVEZ, *Statuta Capitulorum Generalium Ordinis Cisterciensis, ab anno 1116 ad annum 1786,* 8 v. (Louvain 1933–41). J. TURK, *Cistercii Statuta Antiquissima* (Rome 1949). B. GRIESSER, *Exordium Magnum Cisterciense* (Rome 1961). B. LUCET, *La Codification cistercienne de 1202 et son évolution ultérieure* (Rome 1964).

General. L. JANAUSCHEK, *Origines Cistercienses,* v. 1 (Vienna 1877). H. ROSE, *Die Baukunst der Cistercienser* (Munich 1916). G. MÜLLER, *Vom Cistercienser Orden* (Bregenz (1927). M. AUBERT, *L'Architecture cistercienne en France,* 2 v. (Paris 1943). A. DIMIER, *Recueil de plans d'églises cisterciennes,* 2 v. (Paris 1949). J. B. MAHN, *L'Ordre cistercien et son gouvernement, des origines au milieu du XIIIe siècle* (new ed. Paris 1951). J. CANIVEZ, DHGE 12:852–997. *Menologium Cisterciense* (Westmalle 1952). L. J. LEKAI, *The White Monks* (Okauchee, Wis. 1953). A. A. KING, *Cîteaux and Her Elder Daughters* (London 1954). C. BOCK, *Les Codifications du droit cistercien* (Westmalle 1955). L. BOUYER, *The Cistercian Heritage,* tr. E. A. LIVINGSTONE (Westminster, Md. 1958). V. HERMANS, *Commentarium cisterciense historico-practicum in Codicis Canones de Religiosis* (Rome 1961). A. DIMIER and J. PORCHER, *L'Art cistercien* (Abbaye Ste-Marie de la Pierre-Qui-Vire 1962). H. DANIEL-ROPS, *Bernard of Clairvaux,* tr. E. ABBOTT (New York 1964).

The following periodicals are dedicated exclusively to Cistercian history and spirituality: *Cistercienser-Chronik* (1889–). *Collectanea Ordinis Cisterciensium Reformatorum* (1934–). *Analecta Sacri Ordinis Cisterciensis* (1945–). *Cîteaux. Commentarii cistercienses* (Belgium 1950–).

For further bibliography see: Chevalier TB 1:721–722. Heimbucher 1:330–356. Cottineau 1:787–790. **Illustration credit:** Fig. 2, Jon-Mille Studio. Fig. 3, Library of Congress, Rosenwald Collection.

[L. J. LEKAI]

CISTERCIANS (RITE)

The Cistercians have a manner of celebrating the liturgy proper to their order. This article will discuss their form of the Divine Office and Mass.

Divine Office. The Cistercian Office is basically that of the Rule of St. Benedict. Before the founding of Cîteaux this Office had become so overlaid with additional psalms, little offices, litanies, processions, and commemorations that the monks were spending the greater part of their day in choir and had little or no time for manual labor. In the first half of the 12th century the Cistercians swept aside these accretions and boasted of having returned to the balanced monastic day that St. Benedict had intended. Yet the second half of the century witnessed the same process of elaboration of the choral service. First an office of the dead was to be said in choir on most days, then a daily office of Our Lady; processions were multiplied, and common commemorations introduced. Only in the 20th century was this process brought to halt and measures taken to return to the Office as it stands in the Holy Rule. Today a visitor to a Cistercian monastery finds the Office executed almost exactly as prescribed in the Rule.

On ferial days Vigils (Matins) has 2 nocturns, each with 6 psalms, the first nocturn containing either 3 lessons or 1 short lesson. On Sundays and feasts there are 3 nocturns, the first 2 each containing 6 psalms and 4 lessons, the third having 3 canticles and 4 lessons. Lauds and the Little Hours are similar in structure to those of the Roman rite. Vespers has only four psalms, and these are always ferial, that is, they do not vary for feasts. Compline begins with a 15-minute reading in the cloister, contains Psalms 4, 90, and 133 every day, and lacks the familiar Confiteor, Nunc Dimittis, and *In Manus Tuas* of the Roman rite. Proper to the Cistercians are a commemoration of Our Lady before the hours, and the well-known Cistercian *Salve Regina* after Compline.

Mass. Since the Rule of St. Benedict did not give detailed instructions for the celebration of Mass, the first Cistercians seem simply to have taken the rite of the ecclesiastical province of Lyons in which they were first situated, together with some Cluniac usages from Molesmes. In their desire for uniformity they made this rite obligatory for all houses, no matter where located. The early Cistercian Mass was characterized by simplicity. There were two grades of high Mass: the Sunday-feast-day Mass with deacon and subdeacon, and the ferial-day Mass with only one sacred minister, either a deacon or a subdeacon. The dalmatic and tunic were not worn. Incense was used on Sundays and feasts, only at the Offertory. There were no acolytes, merely a server who came up from the choir when needed. Holy Communion was still being distributed at that time under both species, and the profound bow had not yet given way to the genuflection. Later centuries saw progressive embellishment in the form of added candles, incense, dalmatic and tunic, pontifical Masses, and a greater variety of chants. When at the end of the 16th century Pius V published his reformed Roman Missal, the ancient religious orders, although not required to adopt it, were invited to do so. The Cistercians, after much internal dissension, finally accepted the rubrics of the new Missal. That is why at the present day there is little difference between a Cistercian Mass and one of the Roman rite. Yet the Cistercian high Mass can still be seen with only a deacon. The kiss of peace is given to communicants at both their high Mass and low. Two, four, or six candles are used at high Mass according to the rank of the feast.

Bibliography: R. TRILHE, DACL 3.2:1779–1811. J. M. CANIVEZ, DHGE 12:852–997. P. GUIGNARD, *Les Monuments primitifs de la règle cistercienne* (Dijon 1878). H. SÉJALON, ed., *Nomasticon cistercienne* (new ed. Solesmes 1892). A. MALET, *La Liturgie cistercienne* (Westmalle 1921). A. A. KING, *Liturgies of the Religious Orders* (Milwaukee 1955) 62–156. L. J. LEKAI, *The White Monks* (Okauchee, Wis. 1953) 171–186. L. SHEPPARD, *The Mass in the West* (Twentieth Century Encyclopedia of Catholicism 111; New York 1962).

[T. BOYD]

CÎTEAUX, ABBEY OF

Chief abbey of the Cistercian Order, founded in 1098 in the Diocese of Chalon-sur-Saône (today the Diocese of Dijon), 23 kilometers south of Dijon, Burgundy, France. The Latin variants of the abbey's name are *Novum monasterium, Cisterium, Cistellum.* The first monks came from the Benedictine abbey of *Molesme with their abbot, *Robert of Molesme, in order to observe the *Benedictine Rule in its primitive simplicity. Land was donated by Raynard, Viscount of Beaune; Eudes I, Duke of Burgundy, was the great benefactor of Cîteaux. In 1099 Abbot Robert returned to Molesme but was succeeded by Alberic (1099–1109), who received from Pope Paschal II approbation of the *Instituta monachorum cisterciensium de Molismo venientium.* Under Alberic's successor, *Stephen Harding (1109–33), the abbey experienced some difficult years at first because it was impoverished and lacked recruits, but in 1112 *Bernard of Clairvaux entered Cîteaux with his 30 companions. As early as 1113 the Abbey of *La Ferté was founded; in 1114, *Pontigny; in 1115, the Abbeys of *Clairvaux and *Morimond. In 1119 Pope Callistus II approved the *Charta caritatis,* once attributed to Stephen Harding. It is the fundamental document of the order of Cîteaux, calling for autonomy of each abbey, annual canonical *visitation, and an annual general chapter at Cîteaux, which chapter was to be the supreme authority in the order. The abbey grew prosperous; the domain was large, and the monks and **conversi* (lay brothers) cultivated many granges. At the death of Abbot Stephen (1134), the *Cistercians had 75 abbeys spread throughout every country of Europe.

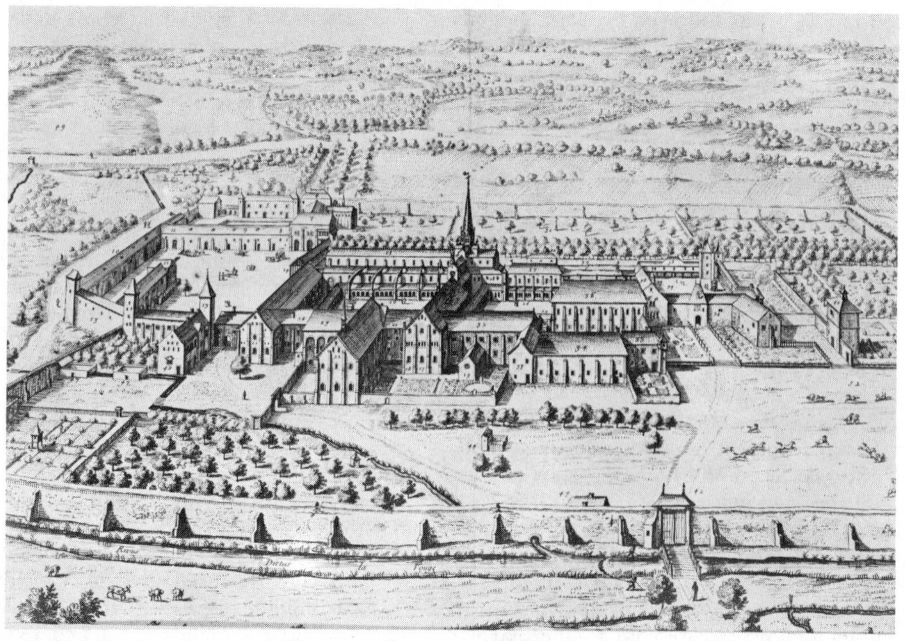

The Abbey of Cîteaux, from a 17th-century engraving.

The first three abbots were entered in the Cistercian menology as "blessed." In 1164 conflict erupted between Cîteaux and its first four daughter abbeys. A bull of Pope Clement IV, *Parvus fons* (1265), ended the quarrel by modifying the constitution. During the 14th century the abbey was hard hit by the *Black Death and the Hundred Years' War: in 1360, 1364, and 1392 the religious had to seek refuge in Dijon. Then *commendation resulted in relaxation of spiritual life as well as in financial difficulties. The *Western Schism caused a division within the order, and it became apparent that reform was necessary. In 1589 and 1595, during the *Wars of Religion, the abbey was pillaged and burned. It was no longer possible for the annual chapter to meet, and a period of decadence followed. Abbot Nicolas Boucherat (1605–25) visited the abbeys to reform them, but his ideas was accepted by only a few: *Orval, Clairvaux, La Charmoye, and Châtillon. As a result a conflict that lasted 40 years erupted between the reformed abbeys and those that had rejected reform (*see* TRAPPISTS). In 1636 Cîteaux was plundered by imperial troops. During the French Revolution (1791) the abbey was sold, and the surviving 12th-century buildings were destroyed. In 1841 Arthur Young, a disciple of F. Fourier, established a phalanstery at Cîteaux, and in 1846 the Abbé Joseph Rey opened a school for juvenile delinquents. In 1898 the reformed Cistercians repurchased the Abbey, and since that time they have occupied the large residence, constructed in 1772 by Lenoir le Romain, the first building of the grandiose plan that was interrupted by the French Revolution.

Bibliography: Sources. WILLIAM OF MALMESBURY, *Gesta regum anglorum* 4:334–337, in PL 179:1286–90. ORDERICUS VITALIS, *Historia ecclesiastica* 3.8.25, in PL 188:640–642. C. HENRIQUEZ, *Regula, constitutiones et privilegia ordinis cisterciensis* (Antwerp 1630). P. GUIGNARD, *Les Monuments primitifs de la règle cistercienne* (Dijon 1878). J. M. CANIVEZ, ed., *Statuta capitulorum generalium ordinis cisterciensis,* 8 v. (Louvain 1933–41). B. GRIESSER, *Exordium Magnum Cisterciense* (Rome 1961). J. MARILIER, *Chartes et documents concernant l'abbaye de Cîteaux, 1098–1182* (Rome 1961). Literature. Cottineau 1:787–790. Beaunier, *Abbayes et prieurés de l'ancienne France,* ed. J. M. BESSE, v.12 (Paris 1941) 306–308. J. B. MAHN, *L'Ordre Cistercien et son gouvernement, des origines au milieu du XIII*[e] *siècle, 1098–1265* (new ed. Paris 1951). M. A. DIMIER, *Recueil de plans d'églises cisterciennes,* 2 v. (Paris 1949) 1:99. J. M. CANIVEZ, DHGE 12:852–874. L. J. LEKAI, *The White Monks* (Okauchee, Wis. 1953). A. A. KING, *Cîteaux and Her Elder Daughters* (London 1954). J. WINANDY, "Les Origines de Cîteaux et les travaux de M. Lefèvre," RevBén 67 (1957) 49–76. J. B. VAN DAMME, "Autour des origines cisterciennes," CollO CistR 20 (1958) 37–60, 153–168, 374–390; 21 (1959) 70–86, 137–156. C. OURSEL, *Miniatures cisterciennes* (Mâcon 1960).
Illustration credit: Musée Archéologique de Dijon.

[M. A. DIMIER]

CITIZENS FOR DECENT LITERATURE (CDL), a nonprofit corporation, organized and operated exclusively for scientific, literary, and educational purposes. It acts as a medium for accumulation and dissemination of information pertinent to the problem of obscenity in printed matter, motion pictures, and other mass media; it aims to eliminate obscene literature through education of the community on the nature and extent of the problem; and to cooperate with legal enforcement of the nation's obscenity laws. Though inaugurated by the concern of a Catholic lawyer, Charles H. Keating, Jr., it is nonsectarian. In the CDL educational program, members of its speaker's bureau employ four half-hour educational films that dramatize the obscenity problem.

The movement began in 1956 as an association of 12 Cincinnati business and professional men with families, and was incorporated in December 1958. Its members surveyed newsstand publications and, enlisting popular support through the speakers' bureau, asked for enforcement of the obscenity laws. Successful prosecutions in Ohio were widely publicized and encouraged other communities to take similar action. In 1962 CDL units throughout the nation commenced consolidation with the Ohio corporation to form a national CDL with headquarters in Cincinnati. In 1963 CDL launched a monthly newsletter, *The National Decency Reporter.* In 1965 a full-time attorney was employed to provide legal assistance to local units and to assist in the preparation of *amicus curiae* briefs. A CDL youth group was formed in Cincinnati in 1959 under the guidance of adult CDL counselors; it has had a national growth parallel to that of the adult group.

[J. J. CLANCY]

CITIZENS FOR EDUCATIONAL FREEDOM (CEF), is a nonprofit, nonsectarian, nonpartisan organization dedicated to obtaining for students in private and independent schools government financial support equal to that given those attending public schools. CEF was founded in St. Louis in 1959 by a group of citizens aroused by the inequities of the proposed Murray-Metcalf bill, under which funds raised on the basis of every school-age child in every U.S. school would be used for state schools only. It was incorporated under the laws of the State of Missouri in 1961.

CEF's slogan, "a fair share for every child," sums up the program's underlying principles, the first of which is that parents have the primary and inalienable right to educate their children and to choose the kind of school in which they are to be educated. Under the theory that every citizen is entitled to a free education, CEF holds that parents who, for reasons of conscience or other motives, elect to send their children to independent schools should not be penalized by being deprived of the educational benefits accruing from state or Federal taxes and suggests that aid be given by a system of tax rebates or by grants. CEF also advocates such contingent benefits for independent schools as teacher tuition loans and the grants currently enjoyed by the public schools and asks that any law passed to confer benefits on government schools be extended to private schools.

By a campaign of speeches and letters members make their position known to the public and to their political representatives in particular. CEF claims credit for a change in the climate of public opinion as well as for substantial political success evidenced by the 1963–64 provisions of the National Defense Education Act (1958) that extended some of its previously restricted benefits to independent schools. CEF played a major role in bringing about the passage of a school bus law in Michigan that made it mandatory for local communities to provide bus service for children in both public and independent schools. It was responsible in 1965 for the adoption of the school bus law in Pennsylvania requiring the transportation of private school pupils on publicly owned buses over existing routes, and in Missouri it helped to have the state extend special services to handicapped children of parochial and independent schools. CEF publishes a monthly newspaper, *Freedom in Education,* under the editorship of Vincent P. Corley.

In 1965 CEF had 408 chapters divided into 14 state federations, with Missouri, Ohio, Pennsylvania, and New York in the lead. Membership, which may be individual or joint, numbers 50,000. Executive offices are in Washington, D.C. The board of trustees is composed of prominent persons of all faiths; among them in 1965 were Virgil Blum, SJ, Rep. Hugh Carey of New York, and William H. Conley, president of *Sacred Heart University, Bridgeport, Conn.

[M. H. WAGNER]

CITIZENSHIP

Citizenship is the legal link that binds man to the national *state. The individual receives guaranteed rights, privileges, and protection in return for his allegiance and obligations. Political and civil rights are not always conferred by citizenship; full political participation may be withheld for such reasons as each state may establish. Because of conflicting legal systems, some persons may possess dual citizenship and others may be stateless. Although leading international lawyers use the terms citizenship and nationality synonymously, "the word *nationality* . . . has a broader meaning than the word *citizenship*. Likewise the terms *citizen* and *national* are frequently used interchangeably. . . . The term *national* includes a citizen as well as a person, who though not a citizen, owes permanent allegiance to the state and is entitled to its protection" (Hackworth, 3:1–2). It has long been a principle of the law of nations that aliens may be denied admission to a country and that entrance may be under such conditions as the receiving state may establish. Aliens have a duty to observe the law while they are in the foreign land.

History of Concept. Varying meanings have been given citizenship in different times and places. In ancient Athens the family, government, and religion were united in the concept. Only a fraction of the population held citizenship; natives of other cities, slaves, and women were ineligible. The obligations of the Athenian to his city-state were many: he served as a soldier, took his turn at administration and jury service, and participated in the assembly. For many of these civic responsibilities the choice was by lot.

The Romans, unlike the Greeks, gradually extended membership in the body politic to their neighbors and later to the whole Empire. When the high mortality during the Punic Wars changed the character of the army, men received citizenship upon enrollment instead of after 20 years of service. Manumission of slaves was curbed since the state was making gifts to citizens. Conflicts over citizenship were recurrent from the time of the Gracci in the Republic until the time of the Empire. A status known as *civitas sine suffragio* granted civil rights but withheld political rights; later, to ensure minority control, the newly enfranchised were allowed to vote in only 8 of the 35 districts. In 212 A.D. the Emperor Caracalla issued the *Constitutio Antoniniana,* which gave citizenship to most of the Empire's freemen. The Greek notion of membership in a direct democracy had been abandoned for a legal status and for individual allegiance to the emperor.

After the fall of Rome, individual citizenship fell into disuse, but the theory was preserved by the Church and *Roman law. *Feudalism precluded wide participation in governmental affairs, but the rise of the towns gave freedom to city residents, including serfs who took refuge in the cities. Because of their wealth, city dwellers became a third force with the clergy and nobles in the French Estates General and the British Parliament. In the age of *absolutism, individuals became subjects of the king. It was the American and French Revolutions that gave a new meaning to citizenship. The egalitarian spirit of the latter exalted the civic virtues, and *citoyen* became a title of honor, while popular sovereignty replaced the belief that man was a subject (*see* EQUALITY).

Laws of Citizenship. For the majority of individuals today, citizenship is determined by birth. Under *jus soli* (law of the soil) citizenship is given persons born within the territorial limits of the state; *jus sanguinis* (law of blood) holds the citizenship of the parents to be the determining factor. No state follows either system exclusively. A second method of acquiring citizenship is by naturalization. After satisfying the legal requirements, the alien applies to a court, administrative body, or legislature, renounces his former allegiance, and takes an oath to support the state. In a few cases an individual may be naturalized solely by residence in a territory, by marriage, or through election. A woman losing her nationality by marriage may regain it with a change of her marital status and compliance with statutory requirements. When territory is ceded in a peace treaty or by purchase, the inhabitants may acquire a new nationality. In former times cession automatically changed citizenship, but since the past century many treaties permit the individual to elect his citizenship.

Many countries provide for the loss of citizenship by those joining the armed forces of another nation. Other states cancel citizenship of those considered politically untrustworthy, of men who emigrate to avoid military service, and of persons living abroad for prolonged periods. Some nations permit a person with dual nationality to renounce one citizenship and choose the other, but other states refuse to recognize expatriation.

Dual or multiple nationality may occur in several ways. Children of citizens or former citizens of states following *jus sanguinis* may acquire a second nationality by birth in a country that observes *jus soli.* A third nationality can be acquired by marriage. Persons of double citizenship have found their position desperate; Japanese-American dual citizens were inducted into the Japanese army in World War II only to face treason charges by the U.S. at the end of the war. Had they refused to serve Japan they would also have been accused of treason. There is no accepted international law on this subject, and a person with dual citizenship is subject to the law of both jurisdictions.

Anyone who loses citizenship is stateless. Since World War I the League of Nations and the United Nations have sought to mitigate the disabilities of statelessness. Despite resolutions declaring that everyone should have a nationality (Declaration of Human Rights of the UN General Assembly, 1948), the plight of the stateless remains very real.

U.S. Practice. The word *citizen* appears several times in the Constitution of the U.S., but it was not defined, and the question of priority of state or national citizenship was unsettled for years. In *Dred Scott v. Sanford* [19 Howard 393 (1857)] the U.S. Supreme Court held state citizenship to be a requirement for national citizenship, but this was changed by the 14th Amendment

(1868). By this enactment "all persons born or naturalized in the United States and subject to the jurisdiction thereof, are citizens of the United States and the states wherein they reside." Since then *jus soli* has been the main rule. In the leading case of *U.S. v. Wong Kim Ark* [169 U.S. 649 (1898)], the high court held that a child born in the U.S. was a citizen even if his parents were ineligible. The court excluded four classes of persons: those born to foreign diplomats or sovereigns; children born to Indians living in tribes; persons born to enemy nations occupying U.S. territory; and individuals born on foreign public vessels in American waters. Since 1802 Congress has granted citizenship to children born overseas to American parents. For many years the U.S. followed an inconsistent policy; the common-law rule of perpetual allegiance was observed while simultaneously objection was raised, especially during the War of 1812, to English observance of this rule. The first naturalization law was passed in 1790, and since 1868 the U.S. has insisted that expatriation is a natural and inherent right. The Bancroft Treaties (1868) led to a series of bilateral conventions respecting emigration and expatriation. Under the Immigration and Nationality Act of 1952 (66 Stat. 163), the most recent codification of U.S. statutes on naturalization, no person can be denied naturalization because of race. Denaturalization can occur when a person secures naturalization through fraud, and this process has been employed against Communists and criminals.

See also CITIZENSHIP EDUCATION; PUBLIC LIFE, OBLIGATIONS OF.

Bibliography: *The Constitution of the United States of America,* ed. E. S. CORWIN (Washington 1953) 254–261, 963–965. G. H. HACKWORTH, *Digest of International Law,* 8 v. (Washington 1940–44) 3:1–420.

[A. MARLOW]

CITIZENSHIP EDUCATION

At whatever level, government is the organ of the body politic, whose responsibility it is to secure the temporal common good of its members. Since the attainment of that goal depends on the physical, intellectual, and moral qualities of the citizens, most governments require that schools, both public and private, make direct efforts to help their students develop in all of these ways. It is this feature of the schools' work that people ordinarily have in mind when they speak of citizenship education.

The programs involved are too varied to be individually described or evaluated. All require some degree of physical education and health instruction, include laws compelling attendance at school to a definite age, and involve governmental efforts to maintain and improve academic standards. Specific required courses, such as those in national history and in government, have the twofold purpose of instructing the student concerning the development of his own nation and the operation of its political institutions, and of arousing in him loyalty to those institutions. Many colleges and universities offer military instruction leading to commissioned rank in either the active or reserve armed services.

Because students are also citizens, government should exercise jurisdiction over schools. The extent of that jurisdiction, however, should be limited, for the school is directly the auxiliary of the family rather than of the state, and moreover has a real though limited autonomy of its own. Thus, government may require the teaching of national history; but the student, who is a man before he is a citizen, has the right to insist that history be taught accurately rather than as a species of official propaganda. In a democracy, as in any form of political organization, the good citizen must first be the good man, who is responsible, informed, and as politically mature as possible. The state that aims first at making the citizen may really want only a parody, the conveniently obedient servant of an authoritarian government. The school that, even though voluntarily and within a democratic society, espouses the same primary aim, risks leaving largely undone the work of intellectual formation which is its specific though not exclusive reason for existence.

Since civic life is both essential and difficult, there must be citizenship education, and schools should take part in that process. What they can best do, however, will be limited by their nature and purpose. They should demand of their students responsible conduct and the highest intellectual achievement of which they are capable, thus preparing them to subordinate their individual advantage to the common good and to reason competently about complex issues. To fulfill their obligations in citizenship education, school officials must respect the human dignity and rights of all students. Schools themselves, insofar as it is possible, should impart a common body of knowledge that will form the basis for the communication of ideas and the preservation of the political community. In this way they will best contribute their limited share to citizenship education.

Bibliography: G. JOHNSON and R. J. SLAVIN, *Better Men for Better Times* (Washington 1943). J. MARITAIN, *Education at the Crossroads* (New Haven 1943). PIUS XI, "Divini illius magistri" (encyclical, Dec. 31, 1929) ActApS 22 (1930) 49–86, Eng. *The Christian Education of Youth* (New York 1936).

[H. JOHNSTON]

CIUDAD BOLÍVAR, ARCHDIOCESE OF (CIVITATIS BOLIVARENSIS), created a diocese in 1790 (called first the diocese of Guayana); raised to an archdiocese in 1958. In 1964 this Venezue-

The city of Ciudad Bolívar, showing the cathedral.

lan ecclesiastical province had three suffragan sees: Barcelona (1954), Cumaná (1922), and Maturín (1958).

Until 1790 the vast eastern and southern territories of this archdiocese were under the jurisdiction of the Diocese of Puerto Rico and were visited by the bishops from there on several occasions. On becoming a diocese, it was first suffragan to Santo Domingo and after 1803 to Caracas. It has had 11 bishops and 1 archbishop. The first bishop, Francisco de Ibarra, was the only native Venezuelan raised to the episcopate during Spanish rule. He became the archbishop of Caracas. The second bishop, José A. Mohedano, had previously been the pastor in the village of Chacao, east of the valley of Caracas, where he had introduced the cultivation of coffee. Prominent as a public figure, writer, preacher, and legislator was Bp. Mariano de Talavera y Garcés (1829–42), the author of *Apuntes de historia eclesiástica de Venezuela.* In the Diocese of Cumaná is the beautiful island of

1964 STATISTICS

Area	Population	Catholics (per cent)	Parishes	Clergy	
				Sec.	Reg.
Ciudad Bolívar	213,543	89	16	16	25
Barcelona	382,002	98	25	23	13
Cumaná	491,484	99	28	29	13
Maturín	246,217	98	12	12	7

Margarita, on which is the shrine of the Blessed Virgin, the Virgen del Valle, patroness of eastern Venezuela and especially of mariners and fishermen. In 1964 the ecclesiastical province had 54 schools, instructing over

The Church of the Virgen del Valle at El Valle del Espíritu Santo, on the island of Margarita, Venezuela.

10,000 students; 57 students were in the seminaries. Members of male religious orders numbered about 66 and about 250 sisters of various congregations were serving in the area.

Bibliography: J. M. GUEVARA CARRERA, *Apuntes para la historia de la diócesis de Guayana* (Ciudad Bolívar 1930). I. ALONSO et al., *La Iglesia en Venezuela y Ecuador* (Madrid 1962). **Illustration credits:** Embassy of Venezuela, Information Service, Washington, D.C.

[P. P. BARNOLA]

CIVEZZA, MARCELLINO DA, Franciscan missiologist and historian of the 19th century; b. Civezza, Italy, May 29, 1822; d. Leghorn, 1906. Although his family name was Ranise, he commonly used the name of his native Ligurian village. He entered the Franciscan Order in 1831 and was ordained in 1845. Very early, Civezza manifested a gift for research and writing. In 1856 the general of the Franciscan Order, Bernardino de Montefranco, commanded Civezza to write a history of the Franciscan missions. The first five volumes, with the title *Storia universale delle missioni francescane,* appeared in rapid order between 1857 and 1861. Then the series lagged. In 1875 the then general of the Franciscan Order, Bernardino de Portogruaro, not only insisted that Civezza complete his history of the missions but also made it possible for him to spend several years visiting the main libraries and archives of Europe and arranged to have friars in America, especially Ubaldo Pandolfi, send him needed documents and maps. Volume six was published in 1881 and the last volume, nine, in 1895. In all, Civezza published more than 100 works besides innumerable magazine articles. Most of these are of ephemeral value, but his source studies on the life of St. Francis were epoch-making, while *Saggio di bibliografia geografica, storica, etnografica sanfrancescana* (Prato 1879), *Il romano pontificato nella storia d'Italia* (3 v., Florence, 1886–87), and his studies on the life of Dante have permanent value. Most important is his history of the Franciscan missions from the time of St. Francis to modern times, a survey of magnificent proportions, even though it has occasional weaknesses because preliminary monographic studies were not available.

Bibliography: R. PRATESI, "Il P. Marcellino da Civezza, O. F. M.: Vita e scritti," ArchFrancHist 43 (1950) 243–334.

[L. G. CANEDO]

CIVIL CONSTITUTION OF THE CLERGY

An organic law adopted by the Constituent Assembly (July 12, 1790) to impose a new organization on the Church in France. It began a serious conflict between the *French Revolution and the Catholic Church.

Genesis of the Law. When the Estates-General met in 1789, it was generally recognized in France that civil administrative reorganization and ecclesiastical reform were needed. Ambition to recast the political constitution necessarily implied modification of the Church's status; for under the ancien régime, Church and State were so intimately bound that one could not be touched without disturbing the other.

The Constituent Assembly voted abolition of the privileges of the nobles and clergy (Aug. 4, 1789); seizure of ecclesiastical possessions to balance the government's financial deficit (Nov. 2); and suppression of religious houses, or at least the release of religious from their vows (February 1790). These first measures introduced such profound changes in the traditional structure of the Church that other steps had to be taken to prevent shackling the exercise of religion and alarming the people. The Revolution, morever, needed the support of the *curés* known as "patriots." It envisioned, therefore, supplying a religious foundation for the moral unity of the nation. An Ecclesiastical Committee, appointed (Aug. 20, 1789) by the *Constituante,* presented 9 months later a plan to reorganize the French Church.

This plan was not inspired by the antireligious ideas of the *Enlightenment, save perhaps in its tacit provision to suppress the religious congregations. It proceeded in places from the theses of *Richer and from the *Jansenism in vogue among the lower clergy and the legal profession. It reflected, above all, the defiance of *Gallicanism toward Rome and the resolve of the Jacobins to submit the religion of the nation exclusively to State authority. Here the assembly members were copying the royal absolutism that they sought to overthrow. The new constitution was termed civil because, according to its authors, it dealt only with matters pertaining to temporal power. The Constituent Assembly considered it beneath its dignity to consult in advance the views of the clergy or to negotiate with the Holy See. During the long, bitter discussion (May 29–July 12) and in numerous controversial writings, Catholic deputies tried vainly to have their colleagues seek papal assent, without which the law would be unacceptable. *Pius VI hoped that at least the King would refuse to acquiesce in the vote of the Assembly. *Louis XVI, however, approved the Constitution (Aug. 24) to avoid worse troubles.

Contents of the Law. The Civil Constitution was a document of considerable length, in four sections that dealt with: (1) ecclesiastical offices, (2) appointments to benefices, (3) payment of ministers of religion, and (4) obligations of ecclesiastics as public functionaries.

Ecclesiastical boundaries were drawn to coincide with the new administrative divisions, with one diocese per *département,* one parish for 6,000 souls. This reduced the number of dioceses from 135 to 85, grouped in 10 metropolitan districts. The sole ecclesiastical functionaries recognized were bishops, pastors (*curés*), and curates (*vicaires*). The law suppressed chapters and ignored religious congregations, which later laws were to destroy.

Bishops and pastors had to be elected by the populace, with voting power restricted to "active" citizens, Catholics and non-Catholics, who paid the required taxes. A newly elected bishop did not need to solicit from the pope even his spiritual investiture; but he was required to seek canonical investiture from the first or oldest bishop of the metropolitan district (*métropole*). Bishops were to administer dioceses with a council of *vicaires.*

Ecclesiastical functionaries of the Catholic religion alone were to be paid by the State, since the clergy no longer possessed landed properties after nationalization. They had to provide religious services gratuitously and remain in residence unless authorized to absent themselves from their posts.

Defenders of the legislation emphasized during the debates that the Civil Constitution left to Catholicism the dignity of being the national religion, with other "religious opinions" granted mere tolerance; also that it ended grave abuses and restored certain usages of the primitive Church. But adversaries objected that the Holy See would never accept a modification of ecclesiastical boundaries drawn up unilaterally, an elective procedure that permitted Protestants and unbelievers to choose Catholic bishops and pastors, or the separation introduced between bishops and the Pope, who alone could give to a bishop his episcopal character and his jurisdiction over a diocese.

The Civil Constitution was, therefore, doubly vicious in that it was imposed on Catholics and severed the unity between Pope and bishops that is essential to the Catholic religion. French bishops were unanimous, save for *Loménie de Brienne, *Talleyrand-Périgord, and five others, in censoring very firmly the principles of the Constitution and in proclaiming their attachment to the successor of St. Peter. After 8 months of delays and consultations, Pius VI published two briefs (March 10 and April 13, 1791) condemning the law outright and forbidding the faithful to participate in its application.

Results. Before the papal condemnation, the Assembly had put into effect a law concerning which it wanted no compromise. It proved this by enjoining (Nov. 27, 1790) all bishops, pastors, and functionary priests to take an oath of fidelity to the Civil Constitution under pain of deposition. To replace those refusing to take the oath (the refractory clergy or nonjurors), the Assembly also expedited the election of new bishops, commonly termed constitutional bishops or jurors, but stigmatized by the Pope as schismatics and intruders.

Clergy and faithful divided into two rival Churches. The Constitutional Church, the sole legal one, stood for the State; the Refractory Church, the sole orthodox one, sided with the papacy. Their forces were in balance. On one side were the clergy whose patriotism and attachment to their parishioners impelled them to submit to the law. They represented more than one-third of the clergy and enjoyed the support of the public authorities. On the other side were those clergy faithful to Roman orthodoxy, numbering all but three of the bishops in charge of dioceses and a majority of the priests. At first this latter group was not prominent, but it grew stronger when the judgments of the Holy See on the affairs of France became known.

This division caused discord and then civil war; to a large extent it modified the course of the Revolution. The Pope, almost the entire French episcopate, many priests, and religious men and women turned against the Revolution, which was accused of seeking to subvert the Church. The revolutionary assemblies, especially the Legislative Assembly, accused the refractory clergy of accepting aristocrats and foreigners as accomplices. According to a decree of Nov. 20, 1791, ecclesiastics who had not taken the oath were "suspect of revolt against the law" and against the Fatherland, and should be deported. At least 30,000 ecclesiastics fled or were driven from France. Those who remained in the country, particularly after the outbreak of war between revolutionary France and the rest of Europe, risked life as well as liberty. Henceforth the Catholic clergy, whose support was responsible for the first successes of the Revolution, joined the front rank of its adversaries. Religious difficulties complicated all the political crises confronting the Convention and the Directory during the period.

The Constitutional Church succeeded in establishing itself and for 3 years strove, after a fashion, to replace the Catholic Church amid populations attached to the traditional religion. For a number of reasons the attempt proved vain. Revolutionary governments abandoned the constitutionals. Under the terror the dechristianizers attacked all clerics, jurors and nonjurors alike, and all cults. Then on Feb. 21, 1795, the Thermidorian Convention adopted a regime separating the State from the Churches, thereby abandoning the Civil Constitution.

Internal decadence infected the Constitutional Church, which counted dubious, ambitious, or corrupt elements. *Grégoire and other of its bishops showed dauntless courage and undeniable integrity at the height of persecution; but Bishop *Gobel of Paris and numerous others defected, seriously harming their cause. Catholics in France very often demonstrated their favor for the refractory "good priests" in preference to the jurors. Outside France, Catholics manifested solidarity with the **émigré* clergy faithful to orthodoxy.

*Napoleon, as First Consul, showed himself eager to reestablish religious peace as a necessary preliminary to domestic concord. As a result, he signed with *Pius VII the *Concordat of 1801, which implied a rejection of the Civil Constitution and resulted eventually in the submission to the Holy See of the last Constitutionals.

Bibliography: Sources. J. H. STEWART, *A Documentary Survey of the French Revolution* (New York 1951), contains an Eng. tr. of the Civil Constitution, the papal condemnation, *Charitas,* and other closely related documents.

Literature. L. SCIOUT, *Histoire de la Constitution civile du clergé,* 4 v. (Paris 1872–81). A. MATHIEZ, *Rome et le clergé français sous la Constituante* (Paris 1911). C. CONSTANTIN, DTC 3.2:1537–1604. A. LATREILLE, *L'Église catholique et la Révolution française,* 2 v. (Paris 1946–50). J. LEFLON, *La Crise révolutionnaire 1789–1846* (Fliche-Martin 20; 1949). L. CARRET, DDC 4:429–453.

[A. LATREILLE]

CIVIL LAW, MORAL OBLIGATION OF

Civil law, as a general principle, obliges in conscience; but the exact nature of the obligation depends on the various kinds of laws, laws that simply command or forbid, laws that render contrary acts void or rescindable, etc. Since the 13th century some theologians have upheld the so-called penal law theory, according to which certain civil laws oblige in conscience not regarding the determined action but merely regarding the penalty imposed for violating the law.

The General Principle. Scripture attests to the general principle that civil law obliges in conscience. St. Paul is most explicit: "Let everyone be subject to the higher authorities, for there exists no authority except from God, and those who exist have been appointed by God. Therefore he who resists the authority, resists the ordinance of God; and they that resist bring on themselves condemnation. . . . For it is God's minister. . . . Wherefore you must needs be subject, not only because of the wrath, but also for conscience' sake" (Rom 13.1–7). St. Peter expresses the same teaching: "Be subject to every human creature for God's sake, whether to the king as supreme, or to governors as sent through him for vengeance on evil doers and for the praise of the good. For such is the will of God, that by doing good you should put to silence the ignorance of foolish men" (1 Pt 2.13–15).

The Fathers and theologians echo the teaching of Scripture. The social encyclicals of Leo XIII [*Diuturnum,* ActSSed 14 (1881) 3–14, and *Immortale Dei,* ActSSed 18 (1885) 161–180] and the *Pacem in terris* of John XXIII emphasize the moral obligation of civil law. John XXIII declared that "human society can be neither well-ordered nor prosperous without the presence of those who, invested with legal authority, preserve its institutions and do all that is necessary to sponsor actively the interests of all its members. And they derive their authority from God. . . . Governmental authority, therefore, is a postulate of the moral order and derives from God" (46, 51).

Theological arguments in support of this position are deduced from the very nature of civil society, the common good, and human law. Authority secures the common good of civil society, which is a natural means necessary for the individual to achieve his end. The civil law is merely an extension of the natural law in particular circumstances, for it establishes what is necessary or useful for the common good.

Purely Penal Laws. The distinguishing characteristic of the purely penal law, despite varied explanations and definitions, is the absence of moral obligation except with regard to the penalty imposed. The notion of penal law apparently appeared for the first time in the prologue of the Dominican Constitutions of 1236.

Henry of Ghent (d. 1293) was the first theologian to apply the concept of penal law to civil laws. Subsequent theologians such as Angelo Carletti di Chivasso, Alfonso de Castro, F. Suárez, and C. Billuart accepted and amplified the notion of penal law. However, all these theologians, as most theologians until the 19th century, classify a law as purely penal by reason of its verbal form and not its content. A purely penal law, according to the older moralists, is one that does not command or prohibit something but merely imposes a penalty on one who does or omits something, e.g., whoever does this shall pay a penalty.

Although modern theologians agree in defining a penal law as one that binds only to the penalty even though a particular act is commanded or forbidden, they disagree about the exact nature of a purely penal law. (1) The theory of moral disjunctive obligation maintains that the subject is free to choose an obligation in conscience either with regard to the act or with regard to the penalty. (2) The theory of a conditional moral obligation recognizes a purely juridical obligation with regard to the act; but if the juridical obligation is not fulfilled, there is a moral obligation to submit to the penalty. (3) The theory of juridical obligation denies any moral obligation both with regard to the act and the penalty. The moral obligation of sustaining the penalty comes from the natural law obligation of not resisting public authority.

The specific arguments proposed in favor of the penal law theory are: a custom existing in favor of purely penal laws, the common estimation of prudent men, the power of the legislator to bind with less than a moral obligation if he can still safeguard the common good and attain the end of society, the existence of a purely juridical fault, the expressed or implied will of the legislator of not obliging in conscience, and the fact that modern legislators frequently have no regard for an obligation in conscience.

The arguments proposed in defense of the purely penal law theory can be reduced to two generic foundations: (1) an attempt to save the ordinary citizen from being overburdened with numerous laws obliging in conscience, many of which are even unjust, and (2) the nature of positive law according to which the obligation depends primarily on the will of the legislator.

In the theological literature outside the manuals there has been a reaction against the purely penal law theory. Such a theory is not needed to ensure the practical goal of saving the citizen from being overburdened with many, and even unjust, laws. Today political conditions are different, especially in the democratic societies in which there are fewer unjust laws than under the older absolute forms of government. The application of the principle that unjust laws do not oblige, in addition to the prudent use of excusing causes and the virtue of *epikeia, can accomplish the same practical results as the purely penal law theory.

The theoretical justification of purely penal laws seems to many contemporary theologians to put too much stress on the will of the legislator. A more Thomistic approach, as opposed to the Suarezian emphasis on the will of the legislator, derives the moral obligation from the nature of human law itself and not the will of the legislator. The human legislator positively establishes the order necessary or useful for the common good. This ordering for the sake of the common good effects the consciences of the members of the society because they are bound by the very nature of society to work for the common good. The existence of the law depends on the will of the legislator, but its obliging characteristic stems from the very fact that law is an ordering for the sake of the common good. Likewise, the purely penal law theory does not seem to correspond completely with the teaching of Scripture and the magisterium of the Church.

The penal law theory tends to take civil, political, and social life outside the scope of conscience and religion. Today, more than ever, Christian witness and life in the world demand the penetration of religion into all spheres of life and existence. On the other hand, the prudent use of excusing causes and epikeia help form mature Christians who in their daily living can work better for the Christianization of the world.

Bibliography: M. Herron, *The Binding Force of Civil Laws* (Paterson 1958). T. E. Davitt, *The Nature of Law* (St. Louis 1951). J. R. Connery, "Should We Scrap the Purely Penal Law?" AmEcclRev 129 (1953) 244–253. L. Riley et al., "The Problem of Penal Law," CathThSoc 10 (1955) 259–284. E. T. Dunn, "In Defense of the Penal Law," ThSt 18 (1957) 41–59. A. Janssen, "De lege mere poenali," *Ius pontificium* 4 (1924) 119–127, 187–201; 5 (1925) 24–32. G. Renard, *La Théorie des leges mere poenales* (Paris 1929). V. Vangheluwe, "De lege mere poenali," EphemThLov 16 (1939) 383–429. G. Pace, *Le leggi mere penali* (Turin 1948). J. Tonneau, "Les lois purement pénales et la morale d'obligation," RevScPhilTh 36 (1952) 30–51. E. González, "¿Obliga en conciencia la ley civil?" *Ciencia tomista* 84 (1957) 641–647. F. López y López, "¿Leyes meramente penales?" *Burgense* 1 (1960) 205–232. I. Fuchs, "Auctoritas Dei in auctoritate civili," PeriodicaMorCanLiturg 52 (1963) 3–18.

[C. E. CURRAN]

CIVIL LIBERTIES

In the most comprehensive sense, civil liberties constitute that broad and changing body of substantive liberties and procedural safeguards that Justice Benjamin Cardozo once referred to as "of the essence of a scheme of ordered liberty" [*Palko v. Connecticut,* 302 U.S. 319 (1937)]. This vast complexus is customarily differentiated according to the nature of the freedoms guaranteed or the obstructions to their free enjoyment. Constitutional liberties are protected against government in the interest of individual freedom. *Civil rights give rise to reciprocal obligations enforceable against private persons. These in turn admit of two categories. The first category comprises all those private rights recognized in the law of torts, contract, and property and protected also by criminal law, as well as the further specification and extension of these rights by legislation, e.g., in rights to be secure against bodily assault, to be free to enter into contracts and to have them enforced, and to deny trespass on private property. Such rights generally have their origin in *common law or statute; and any individual, without regard to group identity, may assert them against infringement by government or by private action. In the second category are political liberties and rights ensuring freedom to participate in the political processes of government and in the privileges of citizenship, e.g., the franchise, eligibility for public office, the freedom of speech and press to criticize governmental activities and the conduct of public officials, the right of the people peaceably to assemble, and the right to petition government for the redress of grievances. *Human rights are such as are guaranteed to all without regard to citizenship, e.g., the requirements of due process of law in the administration of justice in court proceedings, the right to be unmolested in person and property. Depending on the context of reference, constitutional, political, and human rights and liberties may also be denoted as civil liberties or civil rights.

Moral and Legal Foundations

The basic documents of the American Union, the *Declaration of Independence and the *Constitution of the U.S., are explicit with reference to the moral and legal bases of civil liberties.

Moral Basis. The ultimate moral foundations on which the inviolability of the human personality is predicated in American constitutional law are the Hebraic-Christian beliefs and natural-law doctrines that hold, in the words of the Declaration,

> that all men are created equal, that they are endowed by their Creator with certain unalienable Rights, that among these are Life, Liberty, and the pursuit of Happiness.—That to secure these rights, Governments are instituted among Men, deriving their just powers from the consent of the governed,—That whenever any Form of Government becomes destructive of these ends, it is the Right of the People to alter or to abolish it, and to institute new Government, laying its foundations on such principles and organizing its powers in such form, as to them shall seem most likely to effect their Safety and Happiness.

So prevalent among the colonists were the philosophical convictions thus expressed that Thomas Jefferson could write to Henry Lee 50 years after the event that the Declaration was "intended to be an expression of the American mind" and that "all its authority rests then on the harmonizing sentiments of the day" [*Writings* (Washington, D.C. 1903) 118]. *See* POLITICAL THOUGHT, AMERICAN.

Legal Sources. The dominant theme of the Constitutional Convention was that a national government limited by a written constitution to specific enumerated powers delegated by the people, and structured by the division of functions, separation of powers, and checks and balances, would be legally incompetent and practically unable to make encroachments on basic human rights and liberties that were beyond the reach of governmental authority. Nonetheless, the framers of the Constitution set down in the original organic act certain guarantees of civil liberties, namely, protection against suspension of the writ of habeas corpus (Art. 1, sec. 9), prohibition of bills of attainder or ex post facto laws by Congress (Art. 1, sec. 9) or by the states (Art. 1, sec. 10), the ban on religious tests as a qualification for public office (Art. 6), the requirement of trial by jury (Art. 3, sec. 2), restrictions on convictions for treason (Art. 3, sec. 3), and the guarantee to the citizens of each state of all privileges and immunities of citizens in the several states (Art. 4, sec. 2).

During the public debates in the state ratifying conventions, it became evident that adoption of the Constitution by some states would be on the condition that specific guarantees of liberties against Federal encroachment would be added. At the insistence of Roger Sherman of Connecticut the celebrated Bill of Rights was appended to the Constitution in the form of amendments, so as to emphasize the insertion of these guarantees as express and deliberate limitations on Federal power, something that might not have been accomplished by incorporating them in the body of the document, as James Madison had proposed. More than 20 specific provisions may be singled out in the first eight amendments. The First Amendment guarantees freedom of speech, press, assembly, and religion. The Second and Third Amendments on the right of the people to keep and bear arms and on the quartering of soldiers in private homes are significant mainly for disclosing certain deeply felt necessities and grievances of the new nation. The Fourth to Eighth Amendments have to do in great part with procedural protections in criminal trials, with other provisions on the right to privacy, and with government compensation for the taking of private property for public use. The 10th Amendment is simply declaratory of an existing constitutional arrangement on the division and delegation of powers to the Federal and state governments by the people. The Ninth Amendment, which provides that the enumeration of rights in the Constitution shall not be construed to deny or disparage others retained by the people suggests that basic human rights are broader than those specifically guaranteed and, by implication, these rights are no less inviolable against government encroachment.

Despite the reliance of Alexander Hamilton on the restriction of governmental powers in a written constitution, and the contention of the constitutional historian William W. Crosskey that the addition of the Bill of Rights was unnecessary and was actually intended to allay the fears aroused by the opponents of centralized national sovereignty (*Politics and the Constitution in the History of the United States,* Chicago 1953), the significance of these amendments for the constitutional development of civil rights and liberties is beyond doubt, especially since the U.S. Supreme Court has made them applicable to the states through the 14th Amendment.

CLASSIFICATION

The whole aggregate of substantive and procedural civil rights and liberties can be divided into two categories on the basis of their origin. The basic distinction is between those rights and liberties that are protected by the language of the 14th Amendment against infringement or denial by the states and those Federally created rights and liberties that owe their origin to explicit or inferred provisions of the Constitution or to congressional enactment. This basic distinction between "protected" and "Federally created constitutional liberties" has great bearing in determining the proper agency, state or Federal, for the effective guarantee of their free exercise. The role of Congress in the area of "protected" rights and liberties is limited to authorizing corrective devices whereby the judicial and executive branches of government can ensure the unhampered enjoyment of civil liberties. Congress has a broader function in regard to Federally created rights and liberties by reason of its constitutionally endowed powers to originate these rights and to prescribe means of enforcement (see 14th Amendment, sec. 5). In this creative legislative role the actions of Congress are further strengthened by the interpretative and enforcement functions of the courts. To the Department of Justice of the executive branch falls the responsibility of the general enforcement of the laws of the U.S. as well as such specific functions committed to it by congressional authorization.

Protected Rights and Liberties. The 14th Amendment enjoins, "nor shall any State deprive any person of life, liberty, or property without due process of law, nor deny to any person within its jurisdiction the equal protection of the laws" (sec. 1). The Supreme Court in the *Civils Rights Cases,* 109 U.S. 3 (1883), found unconstitutional the Civil Rights Act of 1875 prohibiting racial discrimination in inns, public conveyances, and places of amusement; the Congress, it ruled, was not empowered under the 14th Amendment to enact positive legislation with respect to civil rights and to secure equality in the enjoyment of rights as against interference by private persons, but only to enforce these provisions against state action (sec. 5). Thus, since the enforcement power conferred is only corrective, Congress is not authorized to enact positive legislation governing private action in public facilities not owned or operated by a state government. Because of the precision of this ruling the constitutionality of Federal civil rights legislation may have to rest on both the 14th Amendment and the interstate commerce clause, on the supposition that discriminatory practices in privately owned public accommodations entail in some responsible way state complicity, or that the denial of these services affects substantially interstate commerce, which Congress has the constitutional power to regulate. The Federal government may also discourage discriminatory racial practices indirectly by withholding funds from local community projects.

Because the Court construed narrowly the 14th Amendment's grant of power to Congress to embrace no more than remedial and corrective legislation, the task of giving positive content and meaning to the "due process" and "equal protection" clauses of this amendment has devolved on the judiciary. It is what the Supreme Court says is required by due process and equal protection that constitutes these protected rights against state impairment. In addition to what the Court declares these protected rights to be as restraints on state action, the Court has also read into the meaning of "liberty" in the 14th Amendment elements of the Bill of Rights so that the incorporated liberty has become an identical limitation on state and Federal power.

Application to States. Although the history of the drafting and adoption of the Bill of Rights gives strong evidence that it was intended to restrict only the Federal government, in only two amendments is a limitation specifically directed against the national government, namely, in the First Amendment, which by its wording is made applicable only to Congress, and in one clause of the Seventh Amendment that stipulates that "no fact tried by a jury, shall be otherwise reexamined in any Court of the United States, than according to the rules of the common law." The limitation was settled beyond doubt in a unanimous opinion written by Chief Justice John Marshall in *Barron v. Baltimore,* 7 Pet. 243 (1833), in which the Court ruled that general provisions of the Constitution, including guarantees of the Bill of Rights, apply only to the Federal government. Arguing from history and textual interpretation, Marshall pointed out that whenever the organic act intended to reach state action it did so by explicit reference; e.g., sec. 9 and 10 of Art. 1 both contain series of prohibitions on legislative action, but in section 9 these are expressed in general language, whereas in section 10 all the prohibitions imposed on the states are mentioned specifically. "Whenever the Constitutional provision was meant to affect the states," Marshall concluded, "words are employed which directly express that intent. . . . These amendments contain no expression indicating an intention to apply them to the state governments."

Although the adoption of the 14th Amendment did not affect the *Barron* ruling, it provided the legal instrumentality by which the Court could incorporate certain specifics of the first eight amendments into the meaning of "liberty" under the 14th Amendment and, accordingly, guarantee the identical rights protected against Federal encroachment equally against state interference. This judicial process of incorporation began in *Gitlow v. New York,* 268 U.S. 652 (1925), when the Court said that for "present purposes we may and do assume that freedom of speech and of the press—which are protected by the First Amendment from abridgment by Congress—are among the fundamental personal rights and 'liberties' protected by the due process clause of the Fourteenth Amendment from impairment by the states." Later decisions added religion [*Hamilton v. Regents of the University of California,* 293 U.S. 245 (1934), and *Cantwell v. Connecticut,* 310 U.S. 296 (1940)] and assembly and petition [*De Jonge v. Oregon,* 229 U.S. 353 (1937)]. The right of a criminally accused person to the benefit of counsel in capital cases was upheld in *Powell v. Alabama,* 287 U.S. 45 (1932). In *Gideon v. Wainwright,* 372 U.S. 335 (1963), this assurance was extended to all types of criminal cases. In *Mapp v. Ohio,* 367 U.S. 643 (1961), the Court added to the "included" rights the freedom from unreasonable search and seizure of the Fourth Amendment; in *Robinson v. California,* 370 U.S. 660 (1962), it added the prohibition against cruel and unusual punishments of the Eighth Amendment. On June 15, 1964, the Court overruled the precedent established in *Twining v. New Jersey,* 211 U.S. 78 (1908), when it held that the privilege of the Fifth Amendment applied in state as well as in Federal proceedings. The Federal standard of mere claim of liability to self-incrimination thus supersedes the general standard of state laws, according to which a mere claim of self-incrimination without explanation was regarded as insufficient and trial judges could determine whether there was reasonable ground to apprehend danger of criminal liability from compelled testimony. Another precedent was overruled on the same day when the Court held that a grant of immunity by either state or Federal government in order to compel testimony would preclude prosecutional action by the other as well (on the basis of the testimony given).

Fundamental Liberties. A distinction may be drawn between two sorts of rights and liberties that the Court has incorporated into the clauses of the 14th Amendment. Certain liberties are said to be "fundamental" and "basic" [cf. *Near v. Minnesota,* 283 U.S. 697 (1931)], so that they inhere in the concept of ordered liberty enunciated in *Palko v. Connecticut* and are equally restrictive of Federal and state action. These "fundamental" rights and liberties may coincide with their equivalent legal formulation in the Bill of Rights, as in the case of the First Amendment liberties, but as fundamental liberties they do not owe their origin to the Federal Constitution; among these are trial by jury in controversies in which $21 is at stake (Seventh Amendment) and criminal accusation on a presentment or indictment of a grand jury (Fifth Amendment). There is a substantial difference between the First Amendment freedoms that are incorporated in the 14th Amendment against state action by judicial construction and those liberties that are incorporated in the 14th Amendment because they are fundamental freedoms, basic and implicit in the concept of ordered liberty, although they may also coincide with First Amendment liberties. Although both sorts are operative upon the states, the manner of judicial determination differs in each case. The First Amendment freedoms enjoy a preferred status or, according to a minority of justices, an absolute status. Any law infringing upon these liberties is initially viewed by the Court with presumptive invalidity that only grave reasons of national security and public order may overcome under the "clear and present danger" norm. Fundamental freedoms rest solely on the due process clause of the 14th Amendment and, conceived as related to ordered liberty, are subject to the reasonable exercise of police power in the legitimate requirements of public order. In litigation on fundamental liberties the Court will either defer to legislative determination or weigh in a balance of interests the private claim of constitutional liberty against the gravity of national security under the "reasonable man" theory of judicial review.

Usually, however, the incorporation theory has reference to the absorption of specifics of the Bill of Rights into the clauses of the 14th Amendment. Within the Court, justices have divided by the narrowest of margins on the question whether the inclusion of Bill of Rights liberties and guarantees is only partial or total. In *Adamson v. California,* 332 U.S. 46 (1947), the Court, relying on the Twining and Palko decisions, held through Justice Stanley Reed that "the due process clause of the Fourteenth Amendment does not draw all the rights of the federal Bill of Rights under its protection." Justice Felix Frankfurter, in a concurring opinion, maintained that the 14th Amendment does not apply to the states "a shorthand summary of the first eight amendments, but rather protects from invasion by the States through the due process clause only those basic freedoms which are implicit in the concept of ordered liberty" and such as are in accordance with "those canons of decency and fairness which express the notions of justice of English-speaking peoples." At times the Court, independently of the incorporation process by which a universal application is affirmed, will rule in an *ad hoc* instance with sole reliance on due process that in a particular set of circumstances the requirements of essential justice or fairness have not been met. Thus, long before the Gideon case (1963), the Court held in *Powell v. Alabama* (1932) that "in a capital case, where the defendant is unable to employ counsel, and is incapable adequately of making his own defense because of ignorance, feeblemindedness, illiteracy, or the like, it is the duty of the court, whether requested or not, to assign counsel for him as a necessary requisite of due process of law." The actual holding was limited to the specific facts of the case without relating the due process clause of the 14th Amendment to the 6th Amendment. The continuing expansion of "fundamental" rights that correspond with those enumerated in the Bill of Rights, together with the gradual absorption of the formally defined liberties and guarantees of the Bill of Rights into the clauses of the 14th Amendment, may bring about an almost total parallelism just short of those specifics of the Bill of Rights for which state laws may have alternate or even superior provisions, as in requirements for a jury trial in civil suits or in the manner of criminal indictment.

Judicial Standards for Civil Liberties Litigation. Certain rights, such as the franchise and trial by jury, are specific in kind and in the manner of their enjoyment cannot conceivably pose any threat to the rights of others and to the legitimate and reasonable exercise of police power. But First Amendment freedoms of religion, press, speech, and assembly admit a variety of expression that under certain circumstances and conditions may pose a grave challenge to the just requirements of national security and public order. The Constitution does not forbid Congress to abridge speech, press, etc.; rather, it denies to Congress the power to abridge the freedom of speech, etc. The Court has at different times formulated diverse canons of construction with which to mark off the area of inviolable freedom and the legitimate and reasonable functioning of police power.

The theory that prevailed in the trials brought under the Alien and Sedition Acts (1798) was taken from the English common law carried over into American law by way of Blackstone's *Commentaries*. It defined freedom of expression as freedom from previous restraint from a licensing power but with liability to punishment for the very fact of adverse criticism of the government and of its officers. Although the expiration of these two repressive statutes by their own terms kept them from an adjudication by the Supreme Court, the common-law freedom from previous restraint subject to the punitive consequences of the law received occasional affirmation well into the 1930s. In *Patterson v. Colorado,* 205 U.S. 454 (1907), Justice Oliver Wendell Holmes, better known for the "clear and present danger" test he developed years later, held that "the main purpose of such constitutional provisions (the First Amendment) is to 'prevent all such *previous restraints* upon publications as had been practiced by other governments,' and they do not prevent the subsequent punishment of such as may be deemed contrary to the public welfare." Not until *Grosjean v. American Press Co.,* 297 U.S. 233 (1936), did the Court abandon the narrow construction that the freedom consisted only in immunity from previous censorship.

In the meantime the Court forged another test with which to distinguish legitimate freedoms of speech and press from license. It had applied the "reasonable tendency" rule in World War I espionage cases that involved either pamphlets or foreign-language newspapers critical of the war effort and in the State Criminal Syndicalism Act cases of the 1920s. In these instances the Court looked to the reasonable tendency of the acts done to influence or bring about the effects and consequences forbidden by law. While this test held sway a new norm, the "clear and present danger" test, was formulated by Holmes in *Schenck v. United States,* 249 U.S. 47 (1919):

> The question in every case is whether the words used are used in such circumstances and are of such a nature as to create a clear and present danger that will bring about the substantive evils that Congress has a right to prevent. It is a question of proximity and degree. When a nation is at war many things that might be said in time of peace are such a hindrance to its effort that their utterance will not be endured so long as men fight and that no court could regard them as protected by any constitutional right.

When Chief Justice Charles Evans Hughes, in *Near v. Minnesota* (1931), revitalized the "no previous restraint" theory in its broader meaning, disengaged from summary consequences of law for adverse criticism, it prevailed during the decade of the 1930s in place of the "bad tendency" theory of the 1920s and of the "clear and present danger" theory. The Holmesian norm finally achieved majority status in the 1940s. It was extended beyond cases involving national security to uphold picketing; to strike down statutes and municipal ordinances that interfered with the activities of the Jehovah's Witnesses; to contempt of court cases, state and Federal, that arose from public criticism about the conduct of pending trials; and even to defend the right to make provocative public utterances, critical and contemptuous of the creed of casual auditors.

The alarming successes of the Communist worldwide conspiracy brought about a substantial modification of the "clear and present danger" test in *Dennis v. United States,* 341 U.S. 494 (1951), when the Court adopted the formula that Justice Learned Hand had used in the Court of Appeals: "Whether the gravity of the evil, discounted by its improbability, justifies such invasion of free speech as is necessary to avoid the danger." The substitution of "probability" for "remoteness" seemed to require something more than "reasonable tendency" but something less than a "clear and present danger." This rephrasing of the concept of danger to be weighed was not used subsequently as a rule of decision by a plurality or majority of the Court. In the early 1960s, when an apparent conflict arose between the First Amendment freedoms of belief, expression, and association and congressional investigatory powers and legislation on subversive activities and membership, a narrowly divided Court resorted to the norm of "balancing of interest." The restrictions that governmental regulations imposed on the entire freedom of individual action were weighed against the value to the public of the ends that the regulations were intended to achieve.

Each of these judicial canons of construction presupposes a concept of the status of the freedoms in question and an attitude toward legislative findings. Absolutists such as Justice Hugo Black insist on a strict literal acceptance of the First Amendment prohibition so that Congress may not under any circumstances impinge upon the unrestricted or absolute enjoyment of these liberties. A modified version of the absolutist position is to exclude from the definition of a protected freedom certain types of self-expression. In the Roth and Albert cases (1957) the Court ruled that obscene publications are not the type of self-expression protected by the free press guarantees of the First Amendment. At times the Court has given a preferred status to these liberties so that any law restricting them is viewed with presumptive invalidity and government has had the burden of justifying before the Court the restrictive regulation on grounds of "clear and present danger" or by a show of substantive and grave danger. The "reasonable man" theory that is employed usually in a balancing of private versus public interest generally defers to legislative determinations. By the early 1960s the Court was inclined to approach First Amendment issues by considering them as questions of evidence rather than as requiring decision on constitutional grounds. In *Garner v. Louisiana,* 368 U.S. 157 (1961), a "sit-in" case, the Court chose to rest its decision on whether the petitioners' convictions were justified by evidence "which would support a finding that the petitioners' acts caused a disturbance of the peace." All these diverse canons of construction on First Amendment freedoms seem ultimately to involve some sort of balancing of interests, the difference in approach being prompted by an appraisal of contemporary social conditions.

Federal Rights and Liberties. In addition to the "protected" rights guaranteed against state impairment by the 14th Amendment, there is the category of Federally established constitutional rights and liberties. These originate either in the Constitution or in Federal legislation and treaties. They are protected by the Federal government not only against encroachment by Federal and state governments but also against interference by private persons. These Federally created rights and liberties may be said to be incident to national citizenship. As guarantees against private obstruction, they are considered as civil rights; as against governmental infringement they are called civil liberties. Since they originate formally in the Constitution or owe their existence to the constitutional powers of the Federal government, its laws and treaties, they are generally called constitutional liberties. Although there has been no complete official enumeration of them, a listing of many may be found in a Federal court of appeals case, *Brewer v. Hoxie,* 238 F. 2d 91 (1956).

Originating in the Constitution. Specifically designated in the Constitution are the right to vote for congressmen (Art. 1, sec. 2) and senators (17th Amendment). Qualified Federal electors are those who become eligible electors under state law subject, however, to constitutional prohibitions against exclusion based on race (15th Amendment) or sex (19th Amendment) and to the requirements of the equal protection clause of the 14th Amendment. Because of their distinctly Federal character, Congress may take appropriate measures to protect these rights against state and private hindrance [*United States v. Classic,* 313 U.S. 299 (1941)]. Congress also has the power expressly granted to it by the Constitution to "make or alter" regulations on the "Times, Places and Manner of holding Elections" for Federal officers (Art. 1 sec. 4).

Federal rights that constitute the privileges and immunities of national citizenship are the right to interstate travel; the right of access to the Federal government and its officers; the right to protection by Federal officers against violence in the enjoyment of the decrees of a Federal court, in testifying before a Federal tribunal, and in fulfilling the duties of a Federal office to which one has been lawfully elected; and the right of the people peaceably to assemble to petition Congress for a redress of grievances. It is a matter of judicial determination to affirm what rights and liberties are among the privileges and immunities of Federal citizenship.

Originating in Federal Legislation and Treaties. Federal rights that are a product of congressional legislation embrace three categories.

First, by virtue of its sumptuary legislative power over Federal territories Congress may legislate against discriminatory practices in employment, public facilities, and privately owned public accommodations and impose criminal and civil sanctions for noncompliance [*District of Columbia v. John R. Thompson Co.,* 346 U.S. 100 (1953)].

Second, by its power to regulate interstate commerce Congress has enacted the National Labor Relations Act, establishing the statutory right of collective bargaining, and rights to strike and picket within limits set by Congress (29 U.S.C.A. secs. 141 *et seq.* 18 U.S.C.A., sec. 610), and the Federal Communications Act (47 U.S.C.A. sec. 605), defining the rights to secrecy and privacy of the mails and electronic communications and immunity against the use of unlawfully intercepted communications in Federal court proceedings. Congressional statutes forbid interstate carriers to discriminate in their services for reasons of race or color or to enforce regulations of these statutes that prescribe racial segregation [49 U.S.C.A., secs. 216 (d) and 316 (d)]. On the basis of these statutes the Supreme Court in *Boynton v. Virginia,* 364 U.S. 454 (1960), forbade restauranteurs who service interstate passengers from discriminating against Negroes. On a broad interpretation of interstate commerce in conjunction with the 14th Amendment, Congress enacted the Civil Rights Act of 1964 to bar racial discrimination in employment and in use of public facilities and of privately owned accommodations on the ground that certain discriminatory practices bear a substantive impact on interstate commerce that Congress has the power to regulate.

Third, there is the spending power of Congress exercised for the promotion of civil rights by withdrawing or denying Federal funds for the construction of both public and private housing, schools, or hospitals where business enterprises or communities persist in racially discriminatory practices. Similar provisions may be stipulated in government contracts with private industries. The Federal denial of these fiscal benefits is to be distinguished from the corrective power that the 14th Amendment confers on the Congress for the enforcement of the due process and equal protection clauses. Civil liberties and rights that originate in congressional legislation have their own statutory remedies and sanctions. A manufacturer, for example, whose products are engaged in interstate commerce and who practices racial discrimination in employment contrary to congressional legislation may be subject to criminal sanctions for violating the act, may be liable to civil damages, may be restrained by an injunctive remedy, or may be held to an administrative hearing for determination of the unfair labor practices.

The difference between the "protected" rights and the Federally created rights differentiates the role of Congress in relation to these liberties. In regard to the "protected" rights Congress is limited by the narrow interpretation of the 14th Amendment in the *Civil Rights Cases*. Its function is broader, however, when it exercises one of its several constitutionally granted substantive powers to legislate positively in the creation of rights and liberties and thereby establish a Federal cause of action in favor of persons injured by private individuals as well as by state action through the abridgment of Federally created constitutional rights.

Enforcement

All three branches of government necessarily participate in the enforcement of civil liberties. Also, some private organizations, such as the American Civil Liberties Union, are devoted specifically to the cause of civil liberties.

Judicial. The principal instrumentality by which the judiciary ensures the independence of its own judicial process and the carrying out of its decisions is the exercise of the Federal equity power to issue restraining orders or injunctions and court decrees commanding that an action be done. It is a very effective remedial device, since it can be issued without delay and it subjects persons guilty of violating court decrees to summary contempt procedure and to fines and imprisonment or both without a jury trial. Progress against the obstructive tactics of state officials in defiance of the school desegregation ruling was made principally through the employment of the injunctive power. It also has the advantage of reaching private individuals, whose obstructive tactics are not subject as are state actions to the equal protection clause of the 14th Amendment, on the grounds that they are thereby interfering with Federal court orders or with the enjoyment of Federally created rights based on Federal court decrees [*Kasper v. Brittain,* 245 F. 2d (6th Cir. 1957)]. Consequently, intimidations, threats, and physical and economic reprisals by private individuals to keep citizens from the free exercise of their civil liberties—e.g., by registering and voting in Federal elections or attending a public school integrated by a local school board with the sanction of a Federal court decree—may be enjoined to desist and so be brought within range of the contempt power of the Federal courts. Where massive resistance to court decrees renders the regular officers of the court, the marshals, incapable of enforcing the court orders, statutory law empowers the President to use Federal troops in order to remove obstructions to the carrying out of the decree of the Federal court (Sec. 333, 10 U.S.C.A.).

The most creative action of the judiciary in the cause of civil liberties has been the practical consequence of its narrow construction of the 14th Amendment in the *Civil Rights Cases*. The judiciary thereby assumed the principal role of determining the essential content of due process and equal protection of the 14th Amendment and of the rights they embrace. In this creative function, the Court has defined the rights of the accused in state criminal proceedings, the guarantee of counsel in capital cases, the selection of impartial juries, admissible evidence, and, above all, the momentous ruling on equal protection in the school desegregation cases. To these must be added the elements of the Bill of Rights incorporated into the "liberty" of the 14th Amendment as well as the designation of fundamental human rights operative with equal and identical restriction on state as well as on Federal governmental power.

Legislative. Congress possesses vast reservoirs of substantive powers for the protection and creation of civil liberties and rights. The 14th Amendment confers on Congress the power to enact corrective legislation against state denial of civil liberties and, in addition, the Constitution delegates to Congress several independent legislative powers that may be directly or indirectly employed for the promotion of civil liberties and rights—power over interstate commerce, the spending power, and sumptuary legislative powers over Federal territories.

Until 1957 the constitutional history of congressional legislation on civil rights and liberties had been almost wholly a record of frustration and ineffectiveness. The Civil Rights Act of 1866 that became law over the veto of Pres. Andrew Johnson provided in part:

> That all persons born in the United States and not subject to any foreign power, excluding Indians not taxed, are hereby declared to be citizens of the United States, and such citizens, of every race and color, without regard to any previous condition of slavery or involuntary servitude except as a punishment for crime whereof the party shall have been duly convicted, shall have the same right, in every State and Territory in the United States, to make and enforce contracts, to sue, be parties, and give evidence, to inherit, purchase, lease, sell, hold, and convey real and personal property, and to full and equal benefit of all laws and proceedings for the security of person and property, as is enjoyed by white citizens, and shall be subject to like punishment, pains and penalties, and to none other, any law, statute, ordinance, regulation, or custom to the contrary notwithstanding. [Act of April 9, 1866, 14 Stat. 27.]

Serious doubts raised about the constitutionality of this act led to the adoption of the 14th Amendment in 1868. It defined citizenship and enjoined the states from abridging the privileges or immunities of citizens of the U.S.; depriving any persons of life, liberty, or property without due process of the law; or denying any person equal protection of the laws. The 15th Amendment of 1870 declared that the right of citizens of the U.S. to vote shall not be denied or abridged by the U.S. or by any state on account of race, color, or previous condition of servitude.

Enforcement Acts. In 1870 Congress passed the First Enforcement Act (Act of May 31, 1870, 16 Stat. 140) in order to implement the 14th and 15th Amendments. It declared that all citizens of the U.S. who are otherwise entitled to vote in any state election, municipality, or other subdivision shall be entitled to vote without distinction of race, color, or previous condition of servitude. State prerequisites for voting were to apply to all citizens with equal opportunity. Persons hindering, obstructing, or exercising control over qualified electors in the exercise of their franchise were made subject to fine, imprisonment, or both. Violators were to be prosecuted in the courts of the U.S. and all Federal officials were to cooperate in the enforcement of the law. On Feb. 28, 1871, Congress passed the Second Enforcement Act. It provided that supervisors of elections were to be appointed by Federal courts so that any interference with the discharge of their duties constituted a Federal offense. Elections and supervisors and their work were placed under the jurisdiction of the Federal courts (16 Stat. 433). On April 20, 1871, Congress passed the Third Enforcement Act (17 Stat. 13) generally known as the "Ku Klux Act" because sections of it were directed against the clandestine activities of secret societies such as the Klan.

When the disputed presidential election of 1876 was resolved in favor of Republican Rutherford B. Hayes by the close vote of eight to seven on strict party lines in a special electoral commission, the acceptance of this decision by Southern Democrats was made contingent on the promise that Federal troops would be withdrawn from the South and that a Southerner would be appointed to the cabinet. The withdrawal of the last Federal troops from the South in 1877 was the start of a succession of reversals that rendered the newly adopted constitutional amendments and congressional statutes wholly incapable of any effective implementation and enforcement. In 1880 Congress enacted legislation that forbade the employment of military forces in elections (Act of May 4, 1880, 21 Stat. 113), and in 1894 it repealed those portions of the First Enforcement Act that required qualifications to be equal for all persons, obliged election officials to receive the vote of all qualified electors, and provided punishment for any person found guilty of obstructing the exercise of the franchise. Congress also repealed the provisions of the Second Enforcement Act that stipulated the conditions and manner under which Federal elections were to be supervised.

Of the remaining legislation, two important sections of the Third Enforcement Act that have since been incorporated under title 18 of the U.S. Criminal Code have been sustained by the Supreme Court. Section 241 provides a fine of up to $5,000 and imprisonment of up to 10 years or both for a conspiracy by two or more persons to "injure, oppress, threaten or intimidate any citizen in the free exercise or enjoyment of any right or privilege secured to him by the Constitution or laws of the United States, or because of his having so exercised the same." Under this section, private persons who are guilty of infraction of Federally created rights, including the rights of citizenship, can be punished. On June 26, 1964, agents of the Federal Bureau of Investigation arrested three men in Mississippi for violating this section by interfering with the right to engage in voter-registration activities. The other criminal statute, sect. 242, provides a $1,000 fine or 1 year in prison, or both, for any person who acting "under color of any law, statute, ordinance, regulation, or custom, wilfully subjects any inhabitant of any State, Territory, or District to the deprivation of any rights, privileges, or immunities secured or protected by the Constitution or laws of the United States." "Under color of law" means not only action exercised by virtue of the authority of public office [*Ex parte Virginia,* 100 U.S. 339 (1880)] but also "misuse of power, possessed by virtue of state law and made possible only because the wrongdoer is clothed with the authority of state law" (*United States v. Classic*). A state police officer could be indicted under sec. 242 for causing the death of a prisoner in his custody even if his action was totally lawless and in violation of state law [*Screws v. United States,* 325 U.S. 91 (1945)].

Parallel to these two criminal action statutes are two civil suit statutes. Section 1985 of title 42 allows a damage suit against two or more persons who deprive or conspire to deprive "any person or class of persons of the equal protection of the laws, or of equal privileges and immunities under the laws." This statute incongruously sets remedial damage action against private persons for obstructing the equal protection of laws, which according to the Court's interpretation of the 14th Amendment are restraints only on state activities. Section 1983 of title 42 provides for civil suits against state officers by making them liable to monetary damages for "unlawful law enforcement," such as officially enforcing segregation ordinances and practices in public schools, buses, and parks. These criminal and civil liability statutes have not proved very effective in the guarantee of either "protected" or Federally created "secured rights." The prospects of an adverse verdict from a local jury in some communities have not been such as to discourage seriously further violations of civil liberties. Monetary compensation does not correct the actual denial of a liberty and ordinarily the financial assets of a state officer scarcely allow more than a nominal award.

Civil Rights Act of 1875. The Civil Rights Act of 1875 declared that all persons within the jurisdiction of the U.S. "shall be entitled to the full and equal enjoyment of the accommodations, advantages, facilities and privileges of inns, public conveyances on land and water, theatres, and other places of public amusement; subject only to the conditions and limitations established by law and applicable alike to citizens of every race and color, regardless of any previous condition of servitude" (Act of March 1, 1875, 18 Stat. 335). In its historic decision declaring this act unconstitutional, the Court, as already noted, restricted Congress to appropriate legislation to enforce the prohibitions that sec. 1 placed on the states, thus limiting the enforcement power to a corrective, remedial function and denying to Congress the role of defining in positive terms the content of individual rights that the states were prohibited to deny.

Civil Rights Act of 1957. Impetus for the Civil Rights Act of 1957 (71 Stat. 634) gathered momentum as a consequence of the *Segregation Cases* of 1954. The act authorized the Federal government to bring civil suits in its own name to obtain injunctive relief in order to protect the right to vote from hindrance. While this relieved the offended person from the expense of litigation, it also effectively brought within the reach of Federal contempt proceedings registration officials who persisted in discriminatory practices. The use of the criminal contempt power as an instrument for enforcing an equitable decree is intended to eliminate frustrating delays by avoiding a jury trial, with the exception, however, that in the event of a conviction exceeding a fine of $300 or a jail sentence of 40 days, the defendant is entitled to a trial *de novo* before a jury (42 U.S.C.A. sec. 1995). The Federal district courts were given jurisdiction over these civil proceedings without first requiring recourse to state remedies. The civil rights section of the Department of Justice was granted the statutory status of a new division with the appointment of an assistant attorney general. The act established a civil rights commission, the first of its kind in American history (42 U.S.C.A. sec. 1975) with powers of subpoena to investigate allegations of denials of civil rights, to gather information, and to make reports and recommendations on needed legislation. In *Hannah v. Larche,* 363 U.S. 420 (1960), the Supreme Court upheld the commission's power to conduct hearings on the basis of information given by secret informers without disclosing their names. However, the effectiveness of the 1957 act was seriously impaired by the new evasive tactics of resigning state registrars and the unavailability of registration and voting records to Federal inspectors.

Civil Rights Act of 1960. By the Civil Rights Act of 1960 (74 Stat. 86) Congress provided that discriminatory practices of registrars would be deemed also acts of the state, which might therefore be enjoined as a party defendant. In the event of the resignation of a registrar, the proceeding may still be instituted against the state. Voting records are required to be preserved for 22 months following an election, and the attorney general has the right of inspection and copying in order to determine whether a suit should be instituted. Federal district courts are authorized to appoint Federal voting referees to weigh the complaints of qualified electors alleging that they were prevented from registration and voting. If the referee reports to the court the existence of obstructive tactics, the court may then issue a decree ordering that the qualified elector be permitted to vote. Defiance of the decree is punishable as contempt of court (74 Stat. 86). By this new device of court-appointed voting referees, the Federal government entered into a process normally under state control. In a number of litigations, the constitutionality of "interpretation tests" of state constitutions that some prospective voters had to pass to the satisfaction of registrars were successfully challenged in Federal district courts.

Civil Rights Act of 1964. In 1964 Congress enacted another Civil Rights Act (78 Stat. 241), wherein it extended the reach of Federal power by granting to the attorney general authority to initiate suits in areas other than voting, to request trials before a statutory three-judge Federal court in order to avoid the prejudiced rulings of sectionally minded judges, and to approve of summary criminal contempt proceedings without trial by jury under certain prescribed limits.

Title 1, on voting, was intended to remove the arbitrary obstacles placed in the way of Negro voting applicants and to hasten the process of judicial remedies. It prohibits registrars from applying different standards to white and Negro citizens. It strikes at the arbitrary literacy and law interpretation tests Negroes were required to pass to the discretionary satisfaction of the registrars by making a sixth-grade education a rebuttable presumption of literacy. No one is to suffer disqualification because of inconsequential errors on the forms. By provision of the Third Enforcement Act of 1871 (42 U.S.A. sec. 1983), aggrieved individuals could institute civil damage suits against state officers for depriving them of their constitutional rights of sec. 131. The Civil Rights Act of 1957 authorized the Federal government to bring civil suits in its own name to obtain injunctive relief when any person is denied or threatened in his right to vote, since many were unable to support the financial cost of protracted litigation. Section 601 of the Civil Rights Act of 1960 authorized Federal district courts to ascertain on request of the attorney general whether deprivation of voting is pursuant to a pattern or practice, and also the use of Federal court-appointed voting referees to receive applications from prospective voters who claim to have been denied free and equal opportunity to register and vote. If the referee reports to the court that the complaint of the prospective elector is proved, then the court will issue a decree ordering that the qualified voter be permitted to vote, thus relieving him of the personal responsibility of initiating civil suit himself. Refusal to honor the decree is punishable as contempt of court. Reflecting the endeavor of Congress to further expedite the judicial remedies, title 1 of the Civil Rights Act of 1964 permits the attorney general to apply to the courts for relief wherever a pattern of discrimination exists, and allows him or the defendant state officials to request trial by a three-judge court—of whom one must be a circuit judge—with precedence for voting cases on the calendar. In the absence of an established pattern of discrimination, the aggrieved person must sue for his rights.

Title 2 of the act of 1964 bans discrimination and refusal of service on ground of race, color, religion, or national origin in privately owned public accommodations, such as, hotels, motels, restaurants, gasoline stations, and places of amusement if their operation affects interstate commerce or if their discriminatory practices are supported by state action. Excluded are beauty parlors and owner-occupied rooming houses with no more than five rooms. When there has been an attempted or actual deprivation of these rights, civil action for preventive relief may be instituted by the aggrieved person and the court may in its discretion permit the attorney general to intervene if the case is of general public importance. Waiting periods are required before instituting a private suit in a Federal court to permit states with antidiscrimination laws to settle the issue or to allow the Federal community relations service to bring about voluntary compliance in states without such laws. Further, the attorney general is empowered to initiate suits promptly without a waiting period (as in private suits) only when he finds patterns or practices of resistance without first receiving complaints as is required under the titles for public facilities and public schools. This title does not permit the attorney general to file suits on behalf of individuals as he is permitted to do for citizens who are unable to sue effectively under the titles for public facilities and public schools. The attorney general may also request trial by a three-judge court.

Title 3 requires that no one may be denied, on the ground of race, color, religion, or national origin, equal utilization of any publicly owned or operated facilities other than public schools, such as parks, swimming pools, and libraries. Whereas formerly the aggrieved person had to sue for his own rights, the attorney general is permitted to initiate suits on behalf of the aggrieved but only after receiving a written complaint from one whom he judges unable to sue effectively.

Under title 4 the attorney general is empowered to institute suits to compel desegregation in public schools under the same conditions as in title 3. Furthermore, the Federal government is authorized to provide limited financial and technical aid to school districts to assist in the process of desegregation. This title specifically excludes correction of racial imbalance in public schools by compulsory busing of pupils.

Title 5 extended the life of the civil rights commission to Jan. 1, 1968.

Title 6 declares that no person shall be subjected to racial discrimination "under any program or activity receiving federal financial assistance." It directs Federal agencies in charge of certain programs, not including Federal insurance activities, to take definite steps to eliminate existing discriminatory practices and if necessary, as a last resort, to terminate aid to the culpable local institution or community. Any final decision to stop Federal funds is made subject to judicial review.

Title 7 established an equal employment opportunity commission with authority to investigate complaints of discrimination by employers or unions with 100 or more employees or members in the first year the act was effective, this number to be reduced over a 4-year transitional period to 25 or more. The attorney general is authorized to sue in the Federal courts if he believes any person or group is engaged in a pattern or practice of resistance to the title and the offending employer or union cannot be persuaded to end discrimination voluntarily. He is also empowered to ask for trial by a three-judge court.

Title 8 directs the census bureau to ascertain the number of persons eligible to vote in areas designated by the civil rights commission. Such information might be used to enforce the provision of the 14th Amendment that states that discriminate in voting shall lose seats in the House of Representatives.

Title 9 was intended to cope with the frustration felt by defendants in state criminal trials who have, on a show of jeopardy to their civil rights in state tribunals, been allowed to remove their cases to the Federal courts, with the result, more often than not, that lower Federal judges have remanded these cases back to the state courts and the decisions to remand have been held unappealable. Title 9 also allows appellate review of such orders.

Title 10 established in the U.S. Department of Commerce a community relations service to mediate racial disputes.

Title 11 guarantees jury trials for criminal contempt under any part of the act except Title 1 and provides that the statute shall not invalidate state laws with consistent purposes and that it shall not impair any existing power of Federal officials.

The Civil Rights Acts of 1957, 1960, and 1964, and other measures such as the Voting Rights Act of 1965, disclose amply what a large reservoir of diverse substantive powers Congress possesses not only for legislating remedial and corrective measures for the guarantee of the unhampered exercise of "protected" rights and liberties, but also for the exercise of a positive function of creating Federal rights and liberties with adequate and effective enforcement procedures against both private and public impairment. The Voting Rights Act of 1965 condemns poll taxes in state and local elections, instructs the attorney general to move in the courts to invalidate discriminatory poll taxes, provides Federal machinery for registration of Negroes in Southern states, and extends the presumption of literacy to persons whose native tongue is not English but who have had at least six grades in an "American flag school" (e.g., Puerto Ricans).

Executive. The role of the executive in relation to civil rights and liberties is, apart from moral leadership and in the recommendation and promotion of congressional legislation for their advancement, to ensure the independence of court proceedings and the carrying out of their decrees, even to the extent, as a last resort, of summoning armed forces to ensure freedom of judicial action and compliance (Sec. 333, 10 U.S.C.A.). The Department of Justice is invested with the power to initiate criminal actions under sections 241 and 242 of the criminal code, title 18; and under the terms of the Civil Rights Acts of 1957, 1960, and 1964 it is also authorized to institute civil suits in its own name to obtain injunctive relief to enforce the provisions of these laws and to intervene in certain specified instances.

American Civil Liberties Union. A number of private organizations have dedicated themselves to the cause of civil rights and liberties. Some, such as the National Association for the Advancement of Colored People, have labored for the protection of individual rights against denials based on race, color, religion, or national origin. The American Civil Liberties Union (ACLU) has had from its establishment a broader range of rights and activities to defend. Since its foundation in 1917 by Roger Baldwin, it has come to the support of the rights of conscience and self-expression of others against antievolution laws and Federal antisedition statutes, and it has supported the right of labor to organize, to bargain collectively, and to strike. On First Amendment liberties, it tends to favor unrestricted freedom of expression, opposing the Smith Act of 1940, the Federal loyalty programs, and laws against obscene literature as threats to civil liberties. It has upheld conscientious objectors to military service and to flag saluting and has fought against zoning laws excluding religious institutions from residential areas. On the relations of Church and State it has committed itself unequivocally to total neutrality, toward the elimination of any religious exercise or manifestation in public schools—prayer, Bible reading, crêches, religious festivities—and to the denial of any aid in any form to church-related schools. It disagrees with and hopes for the reversal of the decision in *Everson v. Board of Education,* 330 U.S. 1 (1947), which upheld free bus transportation to pupils of parochial schools, and the ruling in *Zorach v. Clauson,* 343 U.S. 306 (1952), allowing released time off school premises for religious instructions. The ACLU has an admirable record in fighting for the elimination of segregation in travel, housing, employment, and schooling. Some of its more significant achievements have been in the enlargement of the rights of the accused in court proceedings and of witnesses before congressional investigatory committees, and of the protection that should be accorded aliens. The ACLU has fought for civil rights and civil liberties without reference to group identity.

See also CATHOLIC COUNCIL ON CIVIL LIBERTIES; CIVIL RIGHTS; FREEDOM, POLITICAL; HUMAN RIGHTS.

Bibliography: W. M. BEANEY, *The Right to Counsel in American Courts* (Ann Arbor 1955). *The Constitution of the United States of America,* ed. E. S. CORWIN (Washington 1953). D. FELLMAN, *The Constitutional Right of Association* (Chicago 1963); *The Defendant's Rights* (New York 1958). E. G. HUDON, *Freedom of Speech and Press in America* (Washington 1963). P. G. KAUPER, *Civil Liberties and the Constitution* (Ann Arbor 1962). C. B. SWISHER, *American Constitutional Development* (2d ed. Boston 1954). U. S. Commission on Civil Rights, *Freedom to the Free, Century of Emancipation 1863–1963: A Report to the President* (Washington 1963).

[J. F. COSTANZO]

CIVIL RIGHTS

Although there is no clear, universally recognized distinction between *civil liberties and civil rights, a practical distinction in common use categorizes as civil liberties those freedoms that may be asserted against the exercise of governmental power, and as civil rights those freedoms that may be asserted against private individuals or groups. Civil rights in this sense are guaranteed by the 13th, 14th, and 15th Amendments to the *Constitution of the U.S.; by other provisions of the Constitution insofar as judicial interpretation has found them applicable; and by acts of Congress, state legislatures, and municipalities. Civil rights laws, as they are known popularly, prohibit discrimination by public officials and private individuals on grounds of race, color, creed, national origin, and sometimes sex and age, in such varied spheres as voting, jury panels, employment, education, housing, health services, and public accommodations. This article presents the historical background of such legislation; for further discussion, *see* CIVIL RIGHTS, U.S. LAW OF.

Origins of the Problem. The problem of securing the rights of a minority group has never given way to a quick or easy solution and has frequently been complicated by differences in color. *Equality, like freedom, involves a relationship. If every man attempts to be free, every freedom-seeking man becomes in some way an obstacle in the path of someone else's freedom. Historically, freedom has been dependent on power. But as political power has become broadly based, freedom has become more widely distributed. With this democratization of power, however, there has arisen a new problem in the determination of freedom. As much of the history of the U.S. during the 18th and 19th centuries shows, *democracy in America resulted in an unequal division of freedom, allowing superior freedom to the majority who were Protestants in religion and white in race. But this period of equal distribution of freedom has been rapidly drawing to a close. (*See* FREEDOM, POLITICAL.)

The measure of equality has increasingly become the standard for settling disputes over freedom. By equality is meant not the principle that all men are in fact equal, but the principle that men should treat one another in religious and racial affairs as though they were equal. It has taken centuries to develop this principle for settling conflicts, and it has taken form more by necessity than by desire. Whenever men have had the power to enforce their views, they have revealed their attitudes of superiority. Puritans were reluctant to grant equality to Quakers; Protestants, to Catholics; Christians, to Jews; and whites, to Negroes. But immigration to America produced religious and racial diversity, and democracy gave each new generation the power to challenge the unequal distribution of freedom and the claimed superiorities of older Americans.

Because the English colonies were composed of people of different national origins (English, French, Dutch, Spanish, German), different religions (Anglican, Puritan, Quaker, Methodist, Baptist, Presbyterian, Roman Catholic, Jewish), and different racial groups (American Indian, Negro, and white), it was inevitable that civil rights should assume an important place in the history of the U.S. Among the early settlers there were no interminable debates over segregation in education or housing or about the right to vote. But the arrival of each new group raised the question of how to solve the differences between the new group and old. Always the decision was made to make adjustments to each other's cultural, religious, and racial differences. (*See* MINORITIES IN THE U.S.)

Racism and Slavery in Early America. The American settlers of the 17th century made one of the most important decisions in American history when they permitted the growth of what has become cultural and social *pluralism. Of course, there was ill feeling and misunderstanding, and there were attacks by one group upon another; but in early America a heterogeneous society developed without significant challenge. There were differences between whites, Indians, and Negroes; but these differences were handled in such a way as not to threaten the experiment then under way. Since most settlers regarded Indians as natural enemies, the latter remained outside the problem of assimilation and adjustment. The status of the Negro was settled for the time by the institution of *slavery. When John Locke wrote into the constitution of Carolina that the status of slaves would not be changed by their becoming Christians, this meant that Negroes would not acquire rights by becoming civilized or Christianized. *See* NEGROES IN THE U.S., I (HISTORY OF).

When the "self-evident" truth that all men were created equal was proclaimed in the *Declaration of Independence, there were approximately 500,000 slaves in America. But the Declaration was silent on the question of slavery and the slave trade, and this silence made it difficult for later Americans to find precedent for their insistence on the universal application of the rights of man. Even so, the implications of the Declaration were so powerful that the defenders of slavery found it necessary to deny the self-evident truths. Thomas Cooper of South Carolina spoke for many defenders of slavery when he said, "We talk a great deal of nonsense about the rights of man. We say that man is born free, and equal to every other man. Nothing can be more untrue: no human being ever was, now is or ever will be born free" ["Slavery," *Southern Literary Journal* (Charleston 1835) 1.188].

The Constitution of the U.S. gave protection to property rights but provided for no protection for the personal liberties of the individual. The Bill of Rights, however, secured to the individual immunity against certain actions by the Federal government. In 1807 Congress enacted the legislation that legally ended the importation of slaves. This action was not prompted by regard for the rights of man. It was motivated primarily by the fear and danger that Negroes, who constituted some 19 per cent of the population at the time (the highest ratio of Negroes to whites that has ever existed in the country) would become so numerous as to upset the safe ratio of the races and create a social peril and probably a military menace.

*Prejudice against Negroes was so strong early in the 19th century that, in addition to the prohibition of the further importation of slaves into the country, many of the northern states passed laws against the immigration of free Negroes, while in the South removal from the state was often a condition of emancipation. White Americans, unable to eliminate racial diversity, were confronted with the alternatives of racial equality or white supremacy. They chose the latter. In 1855 an English traveler in the U.S., William Chambers, was quoted as having observed, "There seems, in short, to be a fixed notion throughout the whole of the States, whether slave or free, that the colored is by nature a subordinate race; and that, in no circumstances, can it be considered equal to the white" [*De Bow's Review* 18 (1855) 449].

Thus the theory of *racism—that Negroes were subhuman and consequently not entitled to the rights enjoyed by human beings—was used to give legitimacy to the superior condition of whites and the subordinate condition of Negroes. This theory was a fundamental part of the slavery controversy and remained a fundamental part of the later segregation controversy. The white citizen's councils of the mid-20th century have used the same themes the defenders of slavery used more than a century before. The concept of white supremacy later identified with the South, however, was by no means confined to the South. There was a national assumption of white supremacy in the U.S. in the 19th century. Even Abraham Lincoln subscribed to it in his debate with Senator Douglas at Peoria, Ill., Oct. 16, 1854; contemplating the equality of Negroes with whites, he declared, "My own feelings will not admit of this; and if mine would, we well know that those of the great mass of white people will not. Whether this feeling accords with justice and sound judgment, is not the sole question, if indeed it is any part of it. A universal feeling, whether well or ill-founded, cannot be safely disregarded. We can not, then, make them equals" [*Collected Works* (New Brunswick, N.J. 1953) 256].

Civil Rights Amendments and Legislation. Until the outbreak of the Civil War, the question of rights, civil and otherwise, agitated and divided the public mind. In the effort to extend man's inalienable rights, there were attempts to broaden the franchise, establish free public education, grant certain rights to women, and protect labor. But it was in the struggle against slavery that the sense of injustice had its greatest manifestation. The abolitionists and others who fought slavery contended that it weakened the nation and endangered the liberties and rights of all men. And although Lincoln as president regarded the Civil War as a war to save the Union, it was also a struggle to abolish slavery and broaden the concept of civil rights.

The Civil War emphatically settled the question of human slavery, but it did not settle the question of how the "unalienable" rights of 1776 were to be secured for all Americans, nor did it basically alter the general acceptance of white supremacy. There were, however, significant constitutional changes. The 13th Amendment (1865) abolished slavery; the 14th amendment (1868) conferred citizenship and equal protection of the law upon Negroes; and the 15th Amendment (1870) prohibited the denial of suffrage "on account of race, color, or previous condition of servitude." For a brief period during Radical Reconstruction the Negro did enjoy some rights. He could vote and hold office, and he did not suffer the severe economic and social discrimination that was to come later with Jim Crow legislation. But the efforts of the Radicals to establish racial equality and civil rights for the freedmen were defeated not only by resistance in the South, but also by inadequate support in the North. In fact, in three important areas—the military service, the new public schools, and the churches—Reconstruction actually fostered segregation. Withdrawal of Negroes from churches, however, was voluntary.

Each of the new constitutional amendments gave Congress the power "to enforce this article by appropriate legislation," and Congress proceeded to do just that. The Civil Rights Act of 1866 bestowed citizenship upon the Negro (this was necessary because of the Dred Scott decision of 1857) and sought to secure the same privileges and immunities for the Negro as were enjoyed by whites. The Enforcement Acts of 1870 and 1871 gave Federal protection to the Negro's right to vote, and the Ku Klux Klan act of 1871 made it a Federal offense to conspire to deprive Negroes of the equal protection of the law. The Civil Rights Act of 1875 undertook to secure to the Negro "full and equal enjoyment of the accommodations, facilities, and privileges of inns, public conveyances on land or water, theaters, and other places of public amusement," as well as the right to serve on juries.

Victory of White Supremacy. But certain developments in the last quarter of the 19th century undercut the efforts to establish racial equality and civil rights for Negroes. The removal of the Federal troops from the South by Pres. Rutherford B. Hayes in 1877 meant the abandonment of the Southern Negro to the custody of Southern whites on the promise that they would protect his constitutional rights. When the promise was ignored and the Negro's rights violated, little protest was heard from his former Northern champions. Congress, which had enacted three constitutional amendments and several enforcement acts to protect the Negro, gave up and turned the "Negro problem" over to the South. It made no difference to the Negro whether the Republicans or Democrats were in power. Both parties made hypocritical statements about equality and constitutional rights but neither did anything to implement them.

Postwar Accommodations. Many Northerners also desired reconciliation between North and South; and since the Negro was the symbol of sectional antagonism, they frequently deplored agitation in his behalf and adopted a more indulgent attitude toward the South's racial policies. The "hope and assurance of the South," according to Henry Grady of the Atlanta *Constitution,* was "the clear and unmistakable domination of the white race, dominating not through violence, not through party alliance, but through the integrity of its own vote and the largeness of its sympathy and justice through which it shall compel the support of the better classes of the colored race" (speech at Dallas, Tex., Oct. 27, 1888).

There was, too, an important shift in leadership among Negroes themselves that helped to encourage white assaults on the Negro. Negro opinion had long ceased to be a deterrent to white aggression. But the dominant position of Booker T. Washington among American Negroes from 1895 until his death in 1915 helped to encourage an impression of submissiveness. Washington proposed that for the time the Negro should forgo agitation not only for the vote, but for social equality as well, and devote his efforts to achieving economic security and independence. This idea won the enthusiastic support of the white community, and with that support Washington was able to fix the pattern of race relations for most of his lifetime. Most Negroes also accepted Washington's strategy, although a later generation rejected it as too passive.

Judicial Sanction. The Negro was also abandoned by the courts. Practically every important Supreme Court decision after 1877 that affected the Negro somehow "nullified or curtailed" his rights. The Court drastically curtailed the powers of the Federal government to intervene in the states to protect the rights of Negroes, and to all intents and purposes nullified the 14th and 15th Amendments as they affected the Negro. In the *Civil Rights Cases,* 109 U.S. 3 (1883), the Court declared the Civil Rights Act of 1875 unconstitutional on the grounds that the 14th Amendment was binding on states, not on individuals, and that Congress had no authority to pass general legislation on the subject. This ruling virtually ended Federal attempts to protect the Negro against discrimination by private persons, and the Civil Rights Act of 1875 was the last congressional Civil Rights legislation for 82 years.

The Court treated the 15th Amendment in the same way. In *U.S. v. Cruikshank,* 92 U.S. 542 (1876), and *U.S. v. Reese,* 92 U.S. 214 (1876), the Court found that this amendment did not confer the right to vote on any one and that Congress did not have authority to protect the right to vote generally, but only where the right was denied by the state, and on grounds of race or color. Accordingly, sections of the Enforcement Act of 1870 were declared unconstitutional in that they provided penalties for hindering a person in voting in any way. In 1894 Congress repealed the entire law and enacted no further legislation on the subject until 1957.

Finally in two decisions that were handed down in the 1890s, the Supreme Court paved the way for the curtailment of Negro rights, disfranchisement, and a system of segregation. In *Plessy v. Ferguson,* 163 U.S. 537 (1896), the Court formally accepted the doctrine that "legislation is powerless to eradicate racial instincts" and decided that even in places of public accommodation such as railroads and, by implication, schools, segregation was legal so long as "separate but equal" facilities were provided. In this manner the Court laid down the "separate but equal" rule in defense of segregation that was to be the law of the land until 1954. In the case of *Williams v. Mississippi,* 170 U.S. 213 (1898), the Supreme Court completed the opening of the legal road to disfranchisement by giving its approval to the Mississippi plan for depriving Negroes of the vote.

Northern Acceptance. Most Northerners supported the government and the Court in their attitude toward Negroes. Press opinion of the decision in the *Civil Rights Cases* was nearly all favorable. In news stories, papers presented a stereotyped, derogatory picture of Negroes, no matter what the actual circumstances. In the pages of such high quality and influential magazines as *Harper's, Scribner's, Century,* the *North American Review,* and the *Atlantic Monthly,* in the closing decades of the 19th century, can be found all the themes of white supremacy. The Negro was generally pictured as innately inferior and shiftless. Even educated, intelligent Northerners believed the Negro inferior. A historian has concluded, "At the beginning of the twentieth century what is now called second-class citizenship for Negroes was accepted by presidents, the Supreme Court, Congress, organized labor, the General Federation of Women's Clubs—indeed by the vast majority of Americans, North and South, and by the 'leader' of the Negro race" [Rayford W. Logan, *The Negro in American Life and Thought; The Nadir 1877–1901* (New York 1954) ix–x].

Thus, within a generation the nation had repudiated or abandoned its Civil War promises of Negro rights and racial equality. Civil rights for Negroes had become a dead letter; disfranchisement enjoyed Federal approval and support; "separate but equal" was the law of the land; and racism was a national creed, not a regional view. In short, there was by 1900 a merging of Southern and national racial outlooks, and there was a general acceptance in the country of white supremacy. This situation lasted, without serious disturbances, for almost 4 decades into the 20th century. It might have lasted for an even longer period of time had there not been a vast shift in Negro population, beginning about the time of World War I, that was accelerated by World War II. The attendant shift in attitudes in the country gained impetus from the rise of Africa in world politics and the consequent American effort to win allies among the emerging nations.

Rise of the Civil Rights Movement. Despite the reform movement of the Progressive era, progressivism was for whites only; in the South, the typical reformer came to power on a platform designed to deprive the Negro of his vote. President Woodrow Wilson's New Freedom allowed segregation and the downgrading and dismissal of Negro employees in Washington bureaus. Wilson himself defended segregation in the Federal government as "distinctly to the advantage of the colored people themselves" [quoted in A. Link, *Wilson: The New Freedom* (Princeton 1956) 251]. In the years that followed World War I, racism was strong in all parts of the country. Race riots and lynchings swept across the nation. The new Ku Klux Klan, which reached its pinnacle in the mid-1920s, attracted a larger following outside the South than within. Although tension between the two races eased during the 1930s and although there were some gains for the Negro during the New Deal, segregation remained basically unchallenged. Segregationists could still be New Dealers in good standing almost as readily as those who had been accepted as good Wilsonians. The paradoxical combination of racism and progressivism was still generally respectable in politics.

Federal Action. In the 1940s, however, there was a barrage of agitation for Negro rights and a flood of demands and denunciations descending upon the South from the North. World War II awakened Americans from their appalling apathy in regard to racial discrimination. Nazi anti-Semitism and atrocities in the name of Nordic supremacy caused a revulsion against racist theory. The global struggle for power after the war had its effect. For the first time in their history, Americans became concerned about how Africans regarded the American treatment of Negroes. Likewise, the exodus of Negroes from the South brought them into political significance in the North and awakened whites there to the existence of a problem that many hitherto had regarded as being a problem that was peculiar to the South.

The combination of these events caused Pres. Franklin D. Roosevelt to act. In 1939 the civil rights section was created in the Department of Justice. Two years later, Roosevelt established the Fair Employment Practices Committee (FEPC) by executive order. In 1943 another executive order required "no discrimination" clauses in defense contracts. After the war Pres. Harry S. Truman established by executive order in 1946 the President's Committee on Civil Rights. In its report in 1947, the Committee recommended antilynching and anti–poll-tax laws, a permanent FEPC, a strengthening of the civil rights section of the justice department, and the use of the Federal Bureau of Investigation in cases involving violations of civil rights. Although Truman asked Congress every year to enact such laws, he was unable to bypass the threat of a Southern filibuster in the Senate. But in 1948 he courageously ordered the end of segregation in government departments and in the armed forces, and began the practice of having the justice department aid private parties in civil rights cases.

Role of the U.S. Supreme Court. In the meantime, the U.S. Supreme Court, with a general change of personnel and outlook, began an assault on its traditional racially restrictive rulings. In 1941 segregation in Pullman cars was outlawed, and before the end of the 1940s most forms of segregation in interstate transportation were declared illegal. In 1944 the white primary election was prohibited. Thus, many of the traditional forms of legal restrictions began to topple, but the important bottleneck—equal educational opportunity—remained. This was finally opened when the Supreme Court in a unanimous decision in the case of *Brown v. Board of Education of Topeka,* 347 U.S. 483 (1954), invalidated the "separate but equal" doctrine of *Plessy v. Ferguson* by asserting that "separate educational facilities are inherently unequal" and that "segregation in public education" denied the Negro pupils "equal protection of the law."

Civil Rights Acts. Other civil rights gains were made during the presidency of Dwight D. Eisenhower. He ordered the end of segregation on Federal naval bases and similar installations, completing the integration of the armed forces that had started under Roosevelt and Truman. He insisted that civilian officials of the government also respect the principle of racial equality in their employment policies, and he directed the District of Columbia's Board of Commissioners to begin enforcing integration in public places. He helped to maneuver through Congress the Civil Rights Act of 1957, the first Federal legislation in the field since 1875. The act created a temporary Federal Civil Rights Commission to investigate denials of civil rights and make recommendations for further legislation, and it authorized Federal district courts to issue injunctions against interference with the right to vote. The Civil Rights Act of 1960 went further by authorizing the Federal courts to appoint referees to enroll qualified voters in districts where local officials were found to be systematically excluding Negroes.

Under Pres. John F. Kennedy the use of executive power in the field of civil rights was increased. The Department of Justice began to assist in the enrollment of Negro voters in the South. A new committee on equal employment opportunity took more vigorous action than its predecessors to open up jobs for Negroes in firms holding government contracts. In 1962 segregation in Federally assisted housing was banned by executive order.

Yet Negroes still found themselves being treated as second-class citizens 100 years after the Civil War. They lost patience with the slow and sporadic action in civil rights, and in the North and West as well as in the South began to protest and even rebel against local laws and customs. They took direct action through boycotts, sit-ins at lunch counters, and freedom marches and freedom rides to protest discrimination. The National Association for the Advancement of Colored People became more active, and new organizations such as Martin Luther King's Southern Christian Leadership Conference and the Congress of Racial Equality attracted thousands of new recruits. Negroes wanted stronger civil rights legislation, more and better jobs, better housing, and equal and integrated education. They confronted the nation with what, some observers said, amounted to a Negro revolution.

President Kennedy responded to this situation by sponsoring a stronger civil rights bill. In June 1963 he sent a special message to Congress pressing for new legislation that would give the attorney general authority to initiate suits for school integration; that would outlaw segregation in nearly all places of public accommodation, including theaters, hotels, and restaurants; and that would aid Negroes in obtaining jobs. As it was passed in 1964, during Pres. Lyndon B. Johnson's administration, the Civil Rights Act extended the life of the Civil Rights Commission, created a community relations service to assist communities and individuals in resolving problems of discrimination in places of public accommodation, including hotels, motels, inns, restaurants, cafeterias, lunch counters, soda fountains, theaters, concert halls, sports arenas, and gas stations. The act also created an equal employment opportunity commission to assist local groups in eliminating job discrimination, make technical studies on the subject, and offer conciliation service when requested by employees.

See also CIVIL LIBERTIES; CIVIL RIGHTS, U.S. LAW OF; HUMAN RIGHTS; NEGROES IN THE U.S.

Bibliography: M. BERGER, *Equality by Statute: Legal Controls over Group Discrimination* (New York 1952). O. K. FRAENKEL, *The Supreme Court and Civil Liberties: How the Court Has Protected the Bill of Rights* (2d ed. Dobbs Ferry, N.Y. 1963). J. H. FRANKLIN, *From Slavery to Freedom* (rev. ed. New York 1956). M. R. KONVITZ and T. LESKES, *A Century of Civil Rights* (New York 1961). M. R. KONVITZ, *The Constitution and Civil Rights* (New York 1962). R. LOGAN, *The Negro in American Life and Thought: The Nadir, 1877–1901* (New York 1954). U.S. Commission on Civil Rights, *Freedom to the Free: A Report to the President* (Washington 1963). C. V. WOODWARD, *The Strange Career of Jim Crow* (new ed. New York 1957).

[V. P. DE SANTIS]

CIVIL RIGHTS, U.S. LAW OF

A civil right has been defined as a right that appertains to a person by virtue of his citizenship, a right accorded to every member of a distinct community or nation. In the U.S., in popular conception, civil rights laws are considered those that define and protect the legal and political rights of persons of minority racial, ethnic, and religious groups, particularly the Negro.

Bases of Civil Rights Law. The authority of the Federal government to enact civil rights laws is derived principally from the 13th, 14th, and 15th Amendments to the Constitution. Other constitutional powers are, however, sometimes utilized, including the 5th Amendment, the commerce clause, and the war powers. The 13th Amendment prohibits slavery and involuntary servitude. The 14th defines U.S. citizenship, protects the rights, privileges, and immunities of citizens against abridgment by the state, and requires states to afford to all persons due process and equal protection of the law. The 15th forbids both state and Federal governments to deny any person the right to vote because of race, color, or previous condition of servitude. All three amendments vest in Congress power of enforcement by appropriate legislation.

Early Congressional Action. Post–Civil War Congresses adopted a series of seven civil rights laws in the period 1866 to 1875 to implement the amendments. Among the objectives sought by Congress were to guarantee equal legal rights to the recently freed slaves, to protect their right to vote, to defend them from violence, and to require that they be given equal access to places of public accommodation, such as inns, public carriers, and theaters. These objectives were largely thwarted by nonenforcement, adverse decisions of the Supreme Court, and state legislation imposing rigid segregation.

Certain decisions of the Supreme Court aided in the imposition of racial segregation. Two crucial decisions were rendered in *Civil Rights Cases,* 109 U.S. 3 (1883), and *Plessy v. Ferguson,* 163 U.S. 537 (1896). In the former the Court held that the 14th Amendment applied only to state, not private, action; and it declared unconstitutional the law requiring equal access to places of public accommodation. In the latter it held that it was not unreasonable for a state to require separate facilities on public carriers for different racial groups. It thus opened the doors for a flood of state and local laws requiring "separate but equal" treatment for Negroes in all types of facilities, public and private.

Favorable Action. Some civil rights protections survived judicial review. The requirement of jury selection free from discrimination was affirmed in *Ex parte Virginia,* 100 U.S. 339 (1880); in *Yick Wo v. Hopkins,* 118 U.S. 356 (1886), equal application of laws to all racial groups was required. After the beginning of the 20th century the Federal government—through its judicial, then later its executive and legislative branches —reversed the anti–civil rights trend.

Judicial Action. The negative attitude of the Supreme Court toward civil rights slowly shifted until by the 1950s the Court became recognized as a bastion for the protection of the rights of minorities. In implementing the 15th Amendment, the Court declared unconstitutional the "grandfather clause," under which Negroes were prevented from voting by strict literacy requirements whereas whites were exempted if they were descendants of persons who had voted prior to adoption of the 15th Amendment, *Guinn v. U.S.,* 238 U.S. 347 (1915). It found unconstitutional primary elections restricted to white persons in *Nixon v. Herndon,* 273 U.S. 536 (1927), and *Nixon v. Condon,* 286 U.S. 73 (1932), and other restrictive practices. Under the 14th Amendment the Court held to be unconstitutional residential zoning laws based on race, *Buchanan v. Warley,* 245 U.S. 60 (1917); and it held unenforceable real estate covenants prohibiting transfers of property to persons of specified racial groups, *Shelley v. Kraemer,* 334 U.S. 1 (1948). It consistently reversed criminal convictions when juries were selected under a racially exclusive or discriminatory pattern. In *Moore v. Dempsey,* 261 U.S. 86 (1923), it reversed convictions obtained where public passions, based on race of the defendants, precluded a fair trial. Acting under the Interstate Commerce Act and the commerce clause of the Constitution, the Court prohibited segregated seating in interstate carriers, segregated dining cars, and segregated facilities in terminals.

Undoubtedly the greatest legal assault made on governmentally supported segregation was through cases involving public education. A series of cases brought to the Supreme Court began with *Missouri ex rel Gaines v. Canada,* 305 U.S. 337 (1938), in which the Court held that it was a denial of equal protection of the law to require a student to accept a scholarship out of the state, and culminated in the historic decision in *Brown v. Board of Education,* 347 U.S. 483 (1954), in which the Court found racially segregated public education to be inherently unequal. The following year it ordered an end to the practice of segregation in public education "with all deliberate speed." The principle of the *Brown* case was applied to other governmentally operated or regulated institutions and facilities, including parks, swimming pools, and other recreational facilities, libraries, museums, hospitals, courtrooms, cafeterias, public conveyances, etc. In *Johnson v. Virginia,* 373 U.S. 61 (1963), the court in a *per curiam* opinion said: ". . . it is no longer open to question that a State may not constitutionally require segregation of public facilities." Thus was laid to rest the doctrine of "separate but equal."

In addition to overruling in fact, if not in words, the *Plessy* case, the Supreme Court considerably muted the effect of the *Civil Rights Cases* by its treatment of the concept of state action. Among its decisions are those holding the following subject to the 14th Amendment: a privately owned "company town," *Marsh v. Alabama,* 326 U.S. 501 (1946); a private school whose trustees are governmentally appointed, *Pennsylvania v. Board of Directors,* 353 U.S. 230 (1957); and a privately operated restaurant on state-owned property, *Burton v. Wilmington Parking Authority,* 365 U.S. 715 (1961). In refusing certiorari, the Supreme Court left standing an appeals court ruling that private hospitals that had received financial assistance pursuant to a Federal-state plan of grants must not discriminate. This decision could affect a large number of private institutions assisted by the Federal or state governments. In a series of "sit-in" cases the Supreme Court has held that private discrimination in places of public accommodation cannot be enforced if in any way influenced by state or local law, police action, or the statements of public officials. At the opening of the 1964–65 term of the Court it was still undetermined whether arrests and convictions for trespass or other offenses based on defiance of privately ordered segregation are prohibited by the 14th Amendment.

While not equating equal protection of the law with due process under the 5th Amendment, the Supreme Court has on occasion held that the 5th Amendment requires no less of the Federal government than the 14th does of the state. The chief example of this is *Bolling v. Sharpe,* 347 U.S. 497 (1954), a companion to the *Brown* case, in which school segregation in the District of Columbia was held unconstitutional.

Executive Action. There was ample precedent for executive action for civil rights in the Emancipation Proclamation, under which President Abraham Lincoln freed the slaves in the Confederate States through the exercise of his war powers. It was not until World War II, however, that another president acted decisively to advance the cause of civil rights. Franklin D. Roosevelt in 1941 issued an executive order prohibiting employment discrimination in defense industries. President Harry S. Truman ordered equality of opportunity in the armed services and in government employment; President Dwight D. Eisenhower, in employment practices of those contracting with the government; and President John F. Kennedy, in most housing projects assisted by the Federal government. In 1939 the Department of Justice established a unit to enforce latent civil rights criminal laws, especially 18 U.S.C. 241 and 242, protecting civil rights against conspiracies and persons acting under cover of law.

Congressional Action. After 1875 the Congress took no substantial affirmative civil rights action until 1957. In that year it passed a law that gave the attorney general authority to file suits to protect the right to vote and established a Commission on Civil Rights and a Civil Rights Division in the Department of Justice. Congress again acted in 1960, making some minor changes in the enforcement of voting laws and bringing some types of bombings and transportation of explosives under Federal jurisdiction, to control "hate" bombings.

The most comprehensive legislative action of the 20th century was the enactment of the Civil Rights Act of 1964. The principal features of this act were: the prohibition of discrimination based on race, color, religion, and national origin in most places of public accommodation; similar prohibitions, plus discrimination based on sex in employment practices; grants of authority to the attorney general to institute civil rights cases involving public education and public facilities and to intervene in others; requirements that all Federal funds be spent without discrimination; and establishment of an Equal Employment Opportunity Commission and Community Relations Service to encourage voluntary solutions of employment and community problems arising out of discrimination. Enforcement of provisions of the act are by civil injunctive suits brought by the attorney general or individuals.

In the first tests of the act, the Supreme Court upheld the constitutionality of the public accommodations title in *Heart of Atlanta Motel v. U.S.* and *Katzenbach v. McClung,* and held that the act abated prosecutions for "sit-ins" in places covered by the act, even if these occurred prior to the passage of the act, in *Hamm v. Rock Hill.*

Problems of Enforcement. Many of the problems of enforcement of Federal civil rights law are inherent in the U.S. Federal system. The lack of a general police power in the Federal government has limited its effectiveness in preventing or punishing lynchings, race riots, and other forms of violence. The reliance on court enforcement is accompanied by necessary delays required by legal procedures and proceedings. The rules of Congress have often prevented legislative action even when a majority in both houses favored civil rights legislation. The constitutional requirement that voting qualifications be established by the states has prevented a major enlargement of the franchise that could bring reform through the normal democratic procedures.

See also CIVIL LIBERTIES.

Bibliography: J. GREENBERG, *Race Relations and American Law* (New York 1959). J. K. JAVITS, *Discrimination: U.S.A.* (New York 1960; rev. ed. 1962). U.S. Commission on Civil Rights, *Freedom to the Free: A Report to the President* (Washington 1963). C. V. WOODWARD, *The Strange Career of Jim Crow* (new ed. New York 1957).

[J. F. POHLHAUS]

CLAIRVAUX, ABBEY OF, former *Cistercian abbey founded in 1115 as the third daughter abbey of *Cîteaux, in the Diocese of Langres (now the Diocese of Troyes) in the Aube Valley near Bar-sur-Aube, Champagne, France (Latin, *Claravallis*). Its first abbot was *Bernard of Clairvaux, and the first religious were, for the most part, relatives who had entered Cîteaux with Bernard. Land for the abbey was donated by his cousin, Josbert of La Ferté. The abbey prospered rapidly. Its property was increased by donations and acquisitions and included as many as 12 granges and two wine cellars. Meanwhile Bernard attracted numerous recruits, and Clairvaux, which numbered as many as 700 residents, was soon able to found other abbeys: Trois-Fontaines in Champagne in 1118; Fontenay in Burgundy in 1119, Foigny in Thiérache in 1121; and Igny in Champagne. In 38 years Bernard founded 68 abbeys, which in turn founded others; by the end of the 15th century there were 350 abbeys descending from Clairvaux. Bernard assembled an important library and placed much emphasis on studies. The writings—particularly sermons—of several monks of Clairvaux have been preserved, namely, those of *Geoffrey of Clairvaux, *Guerric of Igny, Gilbert of Hoyland, and Henry of Clairvaux. In 1244, abbot

Stephen de *Lexinton founded the college of St. Bernard near the University of Paris.

Clairvaux became a school for sanctity. One of its monks became Pope *Eugene III, 12 were made cardinals, more the 30 became bishops, and many were abbots. Although Clairvaux escaped commendatory abbots, it nevertheless experienced a period of decline and financial difficulty during the 15th and 16th centuries. In 1615, Abbot Denis Largentier reformed the abbey, introducing the Strict Observance, but this was abandoned by his nephew and successor, Claude Largentier. During the French Revolution, the abbey was sold, and in 1808 it was converted into the central prison. None of the buildings erected by Bernard remains. The structure used by the conversi, dating from the end of the 12th century, still stands, but all other existing buildings were constructed during the 18th century. The abbey church was destroyed between 1812 and 1819.

Bibliography: Sources. *Chronicon Clarevallense* in PL 185: 1247–52. J. WAQUET, *Recueil des chartes de l'abbaye de Clairvaux*, fasc. 1 (Troyes 1950). J. M. CANIVEZ, ed., *Statuta capitulorum generalium ordinis cisterciensis*, 8 v. (Louvain 1933–41). Literature. A. WILMART, "L'Ancienne bibliothèque de Clairvaux," CollOCistR 11 (1949) 101–127, 301–319. Cottineau 1:799–800. BEAUNIER, *Abbayes et prieurés de l'ancienne France*, ed. J. M. L. BESSE, 12 v. (Paris 1905–41) 12:308–344. J. M. CANIVEZ, DHGE 12:1050–61. M: A. DIMIER, *Recueil de plans d'églises cisterciennes Grignan*, 2 v. (Paris 1949) 1:100–101; *Saint Bernard, pêcheur de Dieu* (Paris 1953); "Saint Bernard, Fondateur de monastères," CollOCistR 15 (1953) 45–60, 130–139; 16 (1954) 122–128, 192–203. A. A. KING, *Cîteaux and Her Elder Daughters* (London 1954) 207–328.

[M. A. DIMIER]

CLAIRVOYANCE, SPIRITUAL

An intellectual occult phenomenon in which a person is able to sense, feel, or know something about a person or thing or is able to receive or send knowledge to a person at a distance of time or space without using any ordinary medium of communication. It remains to be seen whether or not there is a natural explanation for certain types of clairvoyance, whether by means of some type of *extrasensory perception, a kind of wave that radiates from brain to brain, or some occult energy or force that emanates from one soul to another. Since clairvoyance has been manifested by persons under the influence of the devil, by canonized saints, and by persons suffering from pathological states, this phenomenon may proceed from diabolical, supernatural, or natural causes as yet unknown. If it is irrevocably established that a type of clairvoyance, such as the reading of hearts and minds, is a true miracle, then neither the devil nor a purely natural cause could be offered as an explanation.

Under the general name of clairvoyance other special phenomena may be listed. *Telepathy is the sensation or knowledge of something at a distance or the communication of knowledge at a distance, with no known means of communication intervening. There has been no positive and certain explanation of its cause. Telesthesia is the ability to see, sometimes as in a vision, events or persons who are at a great distance; it is recorded of *Swedenborg, who claimed to have seen in his mind's eye the burning of Göteborg. Cryptoscopy is the ability to read a letter enclosed in its envelope, to read a book without opening the cover, or to see what is happening on the other side of a wall or closed door. This feat is said to have occurred in the strange case of Mollie Fancher, born in Brooklyn, N.Y., in 1848 (Thurston, 294–325).

Psychometry is a kind of retrospective clairvoyance in which a person can witness or relive events that have happened in the past, sometimes centuries ago. Such clairvoyance was claimed for Bridey Murphy and for the Misses Moberly and Jourdain [cf. C. A. E. Moberly and E. F. Jourdain, *An Adventure*, ed. Joan Evans (New York 1955)]. Occult divination or second sight is the ability to see clearly and often in detail some event that will happen in the future, sometimes in a manner similar to a prophetic vision. The reading of hearts is a special insight by which one individual is able to know the secrets of another person, even when the second person is unwilling that those secrets be known. St. John Vianney is an outstanding example of this phenomenon among the saints. Hierognosis is the ability to recognize immediately either holiness or evil in any person, place, or thing. This phenomenon, like true reading of hearts, transcends the natural order and cannot be explained by natural or diabolical causes. It was manifested in the lives of Catherine Emmerich and SS. Catherine of Siena and Frances of Rome.

Bibliography: H. THURSTON, *The Physical Phenomena of Mysticism*, ed. J. H. CREHAN (Chicago 1952). Z. ARADI, *The Book of Miracles* (New York 1956). J. G. ARINTERO, *The Mystical Evolution in the Development and Vitality of the Church*, tr. J. AUMANN, 2 v. (St. Louis 1949–51). A. F. POULAIN, *The Graces of Interior Prayer*, tr. L. L. YORKE SMITH (St. Louis 1950). J. MARÉCHAL, *Studies in the Psychology of the Mystics*, tr. A. THOROLD (London 1927). R. OMEZ, *Psychical Phenomena*, tr. R. HAYNES (New York 1958).

[J. AUMANN]

CLARA, JERÓNIMO EMILIANO, Argentine defender of the rights of the Church; b. Villa del Rosario, province of Córdoba, Nov. 12, 1827; d. Córdoba, Dec. 29, 1892. He was ordained in 1850 and was a parish priest, chaplain, canon, archdeacon of the cathedral of Córdoba; vice rector at the Colegio of Monserrat; rector of the seminary in that same city; and capitular vicar *in sede vacante* in 1883 and 1884. In 1877 he founded the Institute of Daughters of Mary Immaculate, which still exists. In 1883 and 1884 he was the

Jerónimo Emiliano Clara.

most intrepid and determined opponent of the antireligious laws promulgated in Buenos Aires to destroy the influence of the Church, expressing his position in pastoral letters against secular education and civil matrimony. Córdoba society supported Clara wholeheartedly and followed his example. Some professors of the University of Córdoba supported their pastor so forcefully that they were dismissed from their posts. Among them were Rafael García Montaña, Nicéforo Castellano, and Nicolás Berrotarán. The government urged the ecclesiastical cabildo of Córdoba to oust Clara from the post of capitular vicar, but the request was denied. He was then taken prisoner by order of the national government and was kept imprisoned until Juan C. Tissera took possession of the See of Córdoba in December 1884. In Salta, Bp. Buenaventura Rizo Patron emulated Clara's example, and other foreign vicars did the same.

Bibliography: F. COMPANY, *El Vicario Clara: Sus ideales, sus trabajos, su lucha* (Buenos Aires 1955).

[G. FURLONG]

CLARE OF ASSISI, ST., foundress of the Poor Clares; b. *Assisi, Italy, 1194; d. San Damiano near Assisi, Aug. 11, 1253. She was a descendant of the noble family Di Favarone; her conversion took place under the influence of *Francis of Assisi in 1211. Having escaped from her parental home, she received the habit from Francis (March 18–19, 1212) in the Church of the *Portiuncula. Her example was soon followed by her sister *Agnes of Assisi. Both lived at San Damiano, where later their mother, *Ortolana, and their sister Beatrice also entered. In 1215–16 *Innocent III granted Clare the privilege of taking the vow of poverty. After many difficulties, her own rule was approved (Aug. 9, 1253). From 1224 or 1225 until her death she was almost constantly sick and confined to bed. Her devotion to the Holy Eucharist freed her convent and the city of Assisi from the Saracens in 1240 and 1241 (she did not personally carry the Blessed Sacrament). Her spiritual life was strongly influenced by the doctrine of the Mystical Body of Christ. Her remains, still incorrupt, were first interred in the Church of S. Giorgio; on Oct. 3, 1260, they were transferred to S. Chiara in Assisi. She was canonized Aug. 15, 1255; Clare is venerated as the patroness of good weather and of television, and her intercession is sought in childbirth and in cases of eye disease. Her special feasts among the Poor Clares are September 23, the *Inventio* of her body (1850), and October 3, the *Translatio*. In iconography she is pictured with a book (the rule), lily, crucifix, ciborium, or monstrance.

"The Death of St. Clare," by the master of Heiligenkreuz, Franco-Austrian School, early 15th century.

Bibliography: Sources. THOMAS OF CELANO, "Legenda S.C.," ActSS Aug. 2:739–768; also ed. F. PENNACCHI (Assisi 1910). Canonization process, ed. Z. LAZZERI, ArchFrancHist 13 (1920) 403–507. Works. *Seraphicae legislationis textus originales* (Quaracchi 1897) 49–75, 273–280. W. W. SETON, ArchFranc Hist 7 (1914) 189–190; 17 (1924) 509–519. All sources in E. GRAU, *Leben und Schriften der heiligen Klara von Assisi* (Franziskanische Quellenschriften 3; 3d ed. Werl, W. Ger. 1960), Eng. tr. (St. Bonaventure, N.Y. 1953).

Literature. CollFranc 27–28 (1957–58) 819–838. M. FASSBINDER, "Untersuchungen über die Quellen zum Leben der heiligen Klara," FranzStud 23 (1936) 296–335. A. FORTINI, "Nuove notizie intorno a S. Chiara," ArchFrancHist 46 (1953) 3–43. FranzStud 35 (1953) 145–384, special ed. *S. Chiara d'Assisi 1253–1953* (Perugia 1954). Biographies. M. BEAUFRETON (4th ed. Paris 1925). P. BARGELLINI (Florence 1952). F. CASOLINI (3d rev. ed. Assisi 1954). E. SCHNEIDER (Paris 1959). Englebert-Brady-Brown (bibliography, 1939–63). **Illustration credit:** National Gallery of Art, Washington, D.C., Samuel H. Kress Collection.

[L. HARDICK]

CLARE GAMBACORTA, BL., widow, Dominican reformer; b. Pisa, 1362; d. Pisa, April 17, 1419 (feast, April 17). At birth she was named Tora; she was the daughter of Pietro Gambacorta, ruler of Pisa (1369–93), and the sister of (Bl.) *Peter of Pisa. At the age of 12 she accepted a political marriage, but was widowed at 15. Urged by (St.) *Catherine of Siena to abandon secular life, she joined the *Poor Clares the next year, receiving the name Clare. She was immediately removed by her family and imprisoned. Released by her father after 5 months, she was allowed to join the *Dominicans and was free eventually to found a community of strict observance. In 1382, she and five companions established the convent of S. Domenico in Pisa. Her virtues attracted vocations of quality, won the affection of Pisans, and, together with her insistent pleadings, influenced the reform of the Dominican Order. Clare's father and two brothers were killed in an uprising in 1393; one of them met death at the door of the monastery when, to protect the nuns, she had to refuse him refuge. She heroically pardoned the murderers. A special fragrance, noted on her person in life, was observed at her death and renewed, 13 years later, when her body was exhumed, at which time her tongue was found incorrupt. Pius VIII approved her cult in 1830. Clare's spirit as well as her fidelity to the strict observance still mark the community she founded.

Bibliography: Archives, Monastero S. Domenico, Pisa. N. ZUCCHELLI, *La B. Chiara Gambacorta* (Pisa 1914). D. TONCELLI, *La. B. Chiara Gambacorta* (Pisa 1920). M. E. MURPHY, *Blessed Clara Gambacorta* (Fribourg 1928). Butler Th Attw 2:117–119. T. MCGLYNN, *This is Clara of Pisa* (Pisa 1962).

[T. MCGLYNN]

CLARE OF MONTEFALCO, ST., Augustinian; b. Montefalco (Umbria), *c.* 1275; d. there, Aug. 17, 1308 (feast, Aug. 17). Clare, perhaps as a secular tertiary, for a time followed the Franciscan Rule (*see* THIRD ORDER), but from 1290 on she was a member of her sister's Augustinian (*see* AUGUSTINIAN NUNS) convent at Montefalco. In 1291 she succeeded this sister, Joan, as abbess. She preserved her community from a current quietism, being herself much given to penitential works. Her prayer, notably when centered on the Passion, often took the form of ecstasy. She enjoyed the gift of counsel and a power of miracles. Her body is preserved intact; the dissected heart is said to display formations resembling the instruments of the Passion. She was beatified in 1742 and canonized in 1881.

Bibliography: BERENGARIUS DONADEI, *Vita Sancte Clare de Cruce* (*c.* 1309), ed. first by M. FALOCI PULIGNANI in *Archivo storico per le Marche e l'Umbria* 1 (1884) 557–625; 2 (1885) 193–266, and more recently by A. SEMENZA (Rome 1944). ActSS Aug. 3:676–688. M. FALOCI PULIGNANI, *Miscellanea Francescana* 14 (1913) 129–152. A. N. MERLIN, *Une Grande mystique ignorée* (Paris 1930). E. A. FORAN, *Life of St. Clare of the Cross* (Oconomowoc, Wis. 1954). L. OLIGER, *De secta Spiritus libertatis in Umbria saec. XIV* (Rome 1943), *passim.* P. DEBONGNIE, DHGE 12:1037.

[J. E. BRESNAHAN]

CLARE OF RIMINI, BL., Franciscan tertiary, mystic; b. Rimini, Italy, 1262 or 1282; d. Rimini, Feb. 10, 1320 or 1346 (feast, Feb. 10). Born of the wealthy Agolanti(?) family, Clare married young and lived scandalously until at the age of 34 she received the grace of conversion. She then joined the Franciscan *Third Order and after the death of her second husband gave herself to rigorous penance, prayer, and the service of the poor. Living with several companions near the *Poor Clare convent, which she had established, she observed the Rule of St. *Clare of Assisi but without enclosure, in order not to hinder her works of charity. Her mystical experiences, to which her iconography sometimes refers, centered on the Passion and the wounded side and heart of Christ. Although Pius VI confirmed her cult (1784), her feast is not in the Franciscan calendar.

Bibliography: Wadding Ann 7:394–400. LÉON DE CLARY, *Lives of the Saints and Blessed of the Three Orders of St. Francis,* 4 v. (Taunton, Eng. 1885–87). Butler Th Attw 1:297–298.

[M. F. LAUGHLIN]

CLARENBAUD OF ARRAS

French scholastic, representative of the school of Chartres; fl. 1130 to 1170. He studied at Paris under *Hugh of Saint-Victor and Thierry of Chartres probably in the late 1130s. From at least 1152 until 1156 he was provost of the church of Arras. "Summoned" to direct the schools by Walter II of Mortagne, Bishop of Laon from 1155 to 1174, he went to Laon, probably in 1160. He did not teach there for long, but returned to Arras, where he was made archdeacon by Andrew, Bishop of Arras (1161–73). He is known to have been alive in the 1170s, for he possessed some relics of St. Thomas *Becket, who died in 1170.

Although Clarenbaud taught philosophy, he is best known for his theological writings. Many monks turned to him, complaining that they were unable to understand the commentary on Boethius's *De Trinitate* written by *Gilbert de la Porrée. At their repeated and "sacred requests" he agreed to write a commentary of his own, relying mainly on the lectures of his two "venerable teachers." In his lucid and polished commentary on *De Trinitate,* he severely criticized *Abelard and Gilbert de la Porrée. He accused Abelard of *Sabellianism and claimed that he had read "many childish, ridiculous and damnable things" in Abelard's *Theologia* (*De Trin.* 1.38). More frequently he criticized Gilbert not only for errors and heresies, but also for a deliberately involved and obscure style. He strongly rejected Gilbert's assertion that the divine persons "differ by number," and admitted only a certain "otherness" among the persons (*De Trin.* 3.35–36).

At a later date Clarenbaud wrote a commentary on the third of Boethius's tracts, *De hebdomadibus,* and a *Tractatulus* on the opening chapter of Genesis. In all his writings he relied heavily on Thierry of Chartres without simply plagiarizing him. In addition to a polished style and lucid presentation of doctrine, Clarenbaud's writings reveal a vast knowledge of Christian and non-Christian literature.

Since for Clarenbaud ignorance of creation leads to heresies, he carefully analyzed the notion of creation as a transition from nonbeing to being. The first movement of created being marks the beginning of time. Creatures are composed of primeval matter and seminal causes. Primeval matter is absolute potency (*possibilitas absoluta*), itself formless, containing every nature in a possible state. A seminal cause is a hidden power implanted by God in the four elements. Only God, or "Absolute Necessity," can operate on primeval matter, giving it forms that determine the nature of "defined potency" (*possibilitas definita*). From Absolute Necessity descends "the necessity of combination or concatenation" (*necessitas concatenationis*). Thus all things existed in the divine wisdom in undeveloped simplicity. They unfold and descend from the eternally One in a predetermined order and are, as it were, produced in concatenated and interwoven steps. He points out that St. *Augustine and *Pythagoras present the same doctrine in different terms.

Bibliography: N. M. HARING, *Life and Works of Clarembald of Arras* (Studies and Texts 10; Toronto 1965). W. JANSEN, *Der Kommentar des Clarenbaldus von Arras zu Boethius 'De Trinitate'* (Breslauer Studien zur historischen Theologie 8; Breslau 1926) 26–105. Gilson HistChrPhil 149–150, 623. A. TOGNOLO, EncFil 1:1074.

[N. M. HARING]

CLARENDON, CONSTITUTIONS OF, a list of allegedly ancestral customs put forward by King *Henry II of England in January 1164 at a council held near Salisbury. Relations between the King and Abp. Thomas Becket had been strained by Becket's refusal to hand over for punishment by the King "criminous clerks" convicted in the church courts. Instead, Becket proposed degradation to the lay state which would render them in the future liable to trial by the royal courts. Henry, at a council at Westminster (1163), required the bishops to swear to observe the ancient customs of the kingdom in this and other matters. They demurred, but Becket finally agreed, commanding the others to follow. The King at Clarendon insisted upon solemn submission to written provisions. Of these, six clauses were innocuous. Six others clearly ran counter to Canon Law: clauses 6 and 8 forbade clergy to leave the country or appeal to Rome without royal permission; clauses 5, 6, and 10 limited the bishops' powers of excommunication; and clause 12 regulated the royal control of episcopal elections. Four others defined in the King's favor questions of jurisdiction, including the punishment of criminous clerks. Historians agree that as a whole the constitutions were a fair statement of royal practice under *Henry I, but that several clauses were incompatible with the freedom of the Church as defined by current Canon Law. On the issue of criminous clerks, opinion is divided as to both the canonical validity and the practical justification of the Archbishop's claim, which was subsequently upheld by Pope *Alexander III. The Archbishop yielded; his subsequent remorse and resistance are recorded elsewhere.

See also BECKET, THOMAS, ST.

Bibliography: Text. W. STUBBS, *Select Charters* (Oxford 1929) 163–167. *English Historical Documents,* ed. D. C. DOUGLAS (New York 1953–) 2:718–722. A. L. POOLE, *From Domesday Book to Magna Carta* (Oxford 1955) 205–207. H. G. RICHARDSON and G. O. SAYLES, *The Governance of Medieval England* (Edinburgh 1963) 303–318.

[M. D. KNOWLES]

CLARENI, a group of radical Franciscan *Spirituals, cofounded by the Franciscans Peter of Macerata and Peter of Fossombrone when the former obtained from Pope *Celestine V an authorization (1294) for his group to separate from the Franciscan Order and become hermits, or *Celestines, directly under the Rule of St. Francis. Macerata was thereafter called Liberato; his associate, *Angelus Clarenus. When *Boniface VIII annulled Celestine's concession on April 8, 1295, this group of Celestines or more properly, Clareni, moved to Achaia for 2 years and then to southern Thessaly and finally had to return to Italy *c.* 1304. Upon the death of Liberato (1307), Angelus succeeded as head of the group, which was at first settled along the banks of the Chiarino River. When the bull *Sancta Romana* of *John XXII (Dec. 30, 1317) refused autonomy to any of the groups that it called *Fraticelli (including the Clareni) —in an attempt to preserve the unity of the *Franciscans—the Clareni reluctantly joined the main group of (Benedictine) Celestines and moved to the Subiaco area. In 1334, alarmed by the Roman *inquisition investigating the extremism of the Clareni, Angelus moved to Basilicata, Italy, where he died (1337). But the Clareni, then located in several places throughout Italy, refused to disband, even in the face of inquisitorial proceedings, the death of Angelus, and the confirmation of their suppression (1341). Their life continued to be difficult; e.g., at the end of the 14th century Florence framed laws to expel them from the city.

At a time difficult to pinpoint, there appeared the *Societas pauperum hermitarum quondam fr. Angeli de Clarino,* an orthodox Congregation of Clareni under episcopal jurisdiction. This group obtained a bull from Boniface IX (1389–1404), confirming its orthodoxy, and thus ending its persecution. The Clareni of St. Maria de Valle Ceraso, near Treia, were recognized as orthodox in 1437 and 1439; a bull of Eugene IV did the same for those of Narni (1446); and a year later a bull of Nicholas V cleared the name of the Clareni in nine dioceses of central Italy. In 1473 Sixtus IV subordinated them to the Franciscan minister general, and in 1475 they were exempted from episcopal jurisdiction. In September 1483 their chapter adopted the Franciscan rule, but the Clareni remained a separate Franciscan family under their own vicar. Their Roman residence was San Geronimo (1473–1524), then San Bartolomeo on the Island. United to the Franciscan Observants in 1512, they formed a separate province of San Geronimo (1518–36) and of San Bartolomeo (1536–68), when the rites and statutes of the Clareni were abolished, and the group finally merged with the Observants.

Bibliography: D. L. DOUIE, *The Nature and the Effect of the Heresy of the Fraticelli* (Manchester, Eng. 1932). A. GHINATO, EncCatt 11:1151–3.

[J. CAMBELL]

CLARET, ANTHONY MARY, ST., archbishop, founder of the Claretians; b. Sallent, Spain, Dec. 23, 1807; d. Frontfroid, France, Oct. 24, 1870 (feast Oct. 23). A weaver's son, he worked in his youth as a weaver and a designer in the textile mills of Barcelona. In 1835 he was ordained for the Diocese of Vich, and after 1840 he became one of Spain's most popular preachers. In his preaching he centered everything on devotion to the Eucharist and the Immaculate Heart of Mary. He founded a congregation of preachers called the Sons of the Immaculate Heart of Mary (*see* CLARETIANS). In 1850 he was appointed to the much-neglected Archdiocese of Santiago in Cuba. Immediately he set about reforming the seminary and his clergy and began extensive visitations of his vast territory. His greatest efforts were directed against the widespread concubinage and illegitimacy on the island. He also encouraged sound farming methods and credit unions among the poor so as to create material conditions favorable to a good Christian family life. In 1857 he returned to Spain to become the confessor of Queen Isabella II. The frequent royal tours of the country afforded him an occasion to resume his earlier preaching. Claret was also impressed by the power of the popular press. In Catalonia and at Madrid, he founded societies to publish and distribute free Catholic literature, much of which he himself had written. His position at the royal court excited the suspicion and hostility of the anticlerical liberals, and consequently he became the victim of vicious calumny in the radical press. During the revolution of 1868 Claret, forced to leave Spain, went to Rome where he participated in Vatican Council I. On May 31, 1870, he spoke before the Council in defense of papal infallibility. Claret died at the Cistercian Monastery of Frontfroid, France. He was beatified by Pius XI on Feb. 25, 1934, and canonized by Pius XII on May 7, 1950.

St. Anthony Mary Claret.

Bibliography: A. M. CLARET, *Escritos autobiográficos y espirituales* (Madrid 1959); *Autobiography of Blessed Anthony Mary Claret,* tr. L. J. MOORE (Compton, Calif. 1945). C. FERNÁNDEZ, *El Beato Padre Antonio María Claret* (Madrid 1941). F. ROYER, *St. Anthony Claret* (New York 1957). D. SARGENT, *Assignments of Antonio Claret* (New York 1948). **Illustration credit:** Library of Congress.

[T. P. JOYCE]

CLARET DE LA TOUCHE, LOUISE, Visitandine and mystic; b. Saint-Germain-en-Laye, March 15, 1868; d. Vische, May 14, 1915. Her health was fragile. At 11 she made a vow of virginity, and on Nov. 20, 1890, entered the Visitation at Romans. While there were no sensible visions recorded in her life, she experienced many mystical graces. These are difficult to isolate in character because she recorded them as they occurred from day to day and no synthesis has yet been made of them.

In 1902 she records that Christ said to her: "Margaret Mary showed my heart to the world; you will show it to priests." About 1913 opposition arose to her promulgation of this message and as a result she was detached from her community. Under the authority of Monsignor Filipello, she made a new foundation at Vische in March 1914, which, while following the rule of the Visitation, practiced greater exterior austerity and recited the full office. This community is now known as Bethany of the Sacred Heart and sponsors L'Alliance Sacerdotale, which encourages priests to study and imitate the mercy of the Sacred Heart. In 1933 an informative process was opened by the bishop of Ivrée.

Bibliography: *Messagère de l'amour infini: Mère Louise Marguerite Claret de la Touche* (Paris 1937), an anonymous work with a preface by R. P. HÉRIS.

[J. VERBILLION]

CLARETIANS

Missionary Sons of the Immaculate Heart of Mary, *Cordis Mariae Filii* (CMF), a religious congregation of simple vows founded in 1849 by (St.) Anthony Mary *Claret in Vich, Spain, for the apostolate of preaching.

Foundation and Development. When anticlericalism in Spain after 1835 led to the suppression of all but a few Dominican and Franciscan monasteries, a group of diocesan clergy in Catalonia, led by Anthony Claret, took up the work of the suppressed religious, who had had almost exclusive charge of catechizing and popular preaching. Claret realized that the necessity of forming a community in which the preachers could practice the evangelical counsels and the common life without formally professing religious vows or even promises, at that time prohibited by law. Thus he and five young Catalan diocesan priests formed the first community on July 16, 1849, at the diocesan seminary of Vich.

The community, left without a written rule when Claret was appointed archbishop of Santiago, Cuba, in 1850, had a difficult time for the next few years. Confusion arose as to the founder's purpose in establishing the association, and as new members entered, much of the earlier missionary zeal and fervor waned. In 1857, at the insistence of José Xifré, who became the second superior general (1857–99), Claret drew up a constitution of 15 chapters that became the core of the Claretian rule; in it the active apostolate of preaching is emphasized. In 1859 the constitutions were approved by the Spanish government; the following year they received the decree of praise from the Holy See.

At first only priests were admitted into the community after a year of probation. They were bound neither by vows nor promises and were free to leave without formality at any time. After the general chapter of 1862, however, all members were required to pronounce private vows of obedience, chastity, and poverty in a public ceremony after a year of novitiate. At the same time they were to make an oath of perseverance in the community and promise not to accept any honor outside the community without the express permission of the superiors or the command of the Holy See. The revised constitutions received the definitive approbation and confirmation of Pius IX, May 8, 1870. The community was also raised to the status of a religious congregation and all members were required to make a public profession of simple vows. After the constitutions were revised in accordance with the new Code of Canon Law, Pius XI solemnly approved them on July 16, 1924.

Apostolate. The earliest work of the Claretians was to continue the popular preaching begun by Claret. This preaching had always centered on devotion to the Holy Eucharist and to the Immaculate Heart of Mary. After 1862 the apostolate of the Claretians was extended to include teaching in diocesan seminaries and the direction of parishes. By the time of their founder's death (1870), Claretians had been sent to their first foreign mission in North Africa. In 1885 the vicariate of Fernando Po, in Spanish Guinea (Africa), was entrusted to the Claretians. In 1963 they had missions in Spanish and Portuguese Guinea, Colombia, Panama, China, the Philippine Islands, and Japan. In the field of scholarship, Claretians have distinguished themselves especially for their studies in the Canon Law for religious and in Mariology. In 1920 a quarterly dealing with canonical questions related to the religious life, *Commentarium pro Religiosis,* was founded at Rome. In 1951 another journal, *Ephemerides Mariologicae,* was initiated by the general government of the congregation to further Marian studies. By 1963 the Claretians numbered about 3,600 and were established in 25 countries. They were divided into 16 provinces, 7 vice-provinces, and two missions directly under the general government. The general chapter constitutes the supreme governing body and meets every 12 years.

U.S. Foundations. The Claretians were first invited to the U.S. in 1902 to preach to the Spanish-speaking in Brownsville, Tex.; from there they soon spread to San Antonio, Tex., and Los Angeles, Calif. To them Bp. John Forest entrusted his Cathedral of San Fernando in San Antonio, and from this center they spread out through central Texas, preaching and founding parishes and missions for the Spanish-speaking. In 1907 the Claretians were established at San Fernando Mission, Los Angeles, but the following year they transferred to San Gabriel Mission. In the earliest years the Claretians confined their labors almost exclusively to the Spanish-speaking of Texas, Arizona, and California. In 1922 when there were nine American communities, the general government separated them from the Mexican province and formed an independent American province. In 1926 a major and minor seminary was begun at Compton, Calif.

In 1925 the Claretians went to Chicago, Ill., where they erected the National Shrine of St. Jude, and in 1929 the League of St. Jude, to foster devotion to the Apostle. The league also fosters vocations and supports Claretian seminaries; it publishes two Catholic monthlies of general interest, *U.S. Catholic* and *Today,* and a devotional magazine, *Immaculate Heart Crusader.* In 1932 a special branch of the league was added for the

Chicago Police Department. The Police League, a religious organization ministering to the special needs of policemen and placing them under the protection of St. Jude, had about 9,200 members (1963), with a branch in Kankakee, Ill. This Claretian initiative led other cities, such as Milwaukee, Wis., Indianapolis, Ind., and Grand Rapids, Mich., to adopt St. Jude as patron of their Catholic police organizations, though they are not affiliated with the Claretian League.

In 1926 Rev. Joseph Maiztegui, a consultor on the government of the American province, was appointed vicar apostolic of Darien, Panama, which was made dependent on the American province for its missionaries. From the U.S., missions were established in the Philippine Islands (1947) and in Japan (1951). In 1963 American Claretians were serving in the missions of Panama, Japan, and the Philippine Islands. In 1954 the American province of the Claretians was divided into the Eastern province, centered in Chicago and having jurisdiction over two communities in Canada; and the Western province, centered in Los Angeles. In 1963 these had about 275 professed religious and novices. They served 18 parishes in 12 cities and directed 1 high school for boys.

Bibliography: A. M. CLARET, *Escritos autobiográficos* (Madrid 1959). M. AGUILAR, *Historia de la Congregación de Misioneros Hijos del Immaculado Corazón de María,* 2 v. (Barcelona 1901).

[T. P. JOYCE]

CLARITUS, BL., monastic founder; b. Florence, Italy, *c.* 1300; d. convent of Chiarito, Florence, May 25, 1348 (feast, May 6). He was a member of the noble Voglia family, and although he had received orders, he married. After a miraculous answer to an appeal to St. Zenobius (early 5th-century bishop of Florence), he returned to the clerical state, founding *c.* 1343 the convent of Chiarito (Regina Coeli), where his wife, Nicolosia, became a nun. He prescribed the Rule of St. *Augustine for the community and devoted himself to ministering to its needs until his death. His tomb, in the convent, and his crucifix, also on display there, were objects of popular veneration. Pope *Leo XI, while he was still archbishop of Florence, recognized the cult of Claritus. His body is now in the church of the Dominican sisters, Al Sodo (in Florence-Castello).

Bibliography: ActSS May 6:160–164. *Bollettino storico Agostiniano* 1 (1924) 15–20. R. VAN DOREN, DHGE 12:1068. Mercati-Pelzer DE 1:637. W. HUMPFNER, LexThK[2] 2:1215.

[B. J. COMASKEY]

CLARKE, MARY FRANCES, MOTHER, foundress of the Sisters of Charity of the Blessed Virgin Mary, and of Clarke College, Dubuque, Iowa; b. Dublin, Ireland, March 2, 1803; d. Dubuque, Dec. 4, 1887. She was the daughter of Cornelius and Catherine (Hyland) Clarke. Mary and three young Irish girls arrived as missionary teachers in Philadelphia, Pa., in 1833. After meeting with Rev. Terence J. Donaghoe, her lifelong mentor, she founded her order in November 1833. Bishop John Hughes requested Mother Clarke to settle in the New York diocese; but since it was already well staffed, she responded instead to requests by Bp. Jean Mathias Pierre Loras and Pierre De Smet, SJ, to serve the Diocese of Dubuque. Her sisters, the first in Iowa, were transferred to Dubuque in 1843; and Donaghoe, director of the order, was made diocesan vicar-general. After the death of Donaghoe in 1869, Mother Clarke made application for pontifical status, and a decree of final approbation was issued in 1885. She died after governing for 54 years, leaving schools that were pioneers in the late-19th-century movement for women's colleges.

Mother Mary Frances Clarke.

Bibliography: M. L. DORAN, *In the Early Days: Annals, 1833–87* (St. Louis 1925).

[M. ST. V. BERRY]

CLARKE, SAMUEL, English philosopher and divine; b. Norwich, Oct. 11, 1675; d. Leicester, May 17, 1729. Educated at Caius College, Cambridge, he became an ardent disciple of Isaac *Newton. In 1697 he published a Latin translation of Rohault's *Traité de Physique,* an established textbook of Cartesian physics, adding notes to explain the ideas of Newton's *Principia.* In 1706 he published a Latin translation of Newton's *Optics.* His correspondence with G. W. *Leibniz apart, his most important work is the two sets of Boyle lectures he delivered in 1704 and 1705, published together (1719) under the title *A Discourse concerning the Being and Attributes of God, the Obligation of Natural Religion, and the Truth and Certainty of the Christian Revelation. . . .* In natural theology he used a method "as near mathematical as the nature of such a discourse would allow." His proofs of the existence of God were well known in 18th-century England and were treated by D. *Hume as the standard ones. When Leibniz criticized some of Newton's ideas—about space and his mechanistic physics—for the theological and philosophical conclusions he saw in them, Clarke defended his master and published the correspondence in *A Collection of Papers which passed between the late Learned Mr Leibnitz and Dr Clarke relating to the Principles of Natural Philosophy and Religion* (1717). Clarke wrote also a number of theological works, notably, *The Scripture Doctrine of the Trinity* (1712), for which he was severely criticized on account of his Arian and Latitudinarian ideas. He ranks among the foremost rationalist theologians of the time.

See also BRITISH MORALISTS.

Bibliography: *Works,* 4 v. (London 1738–42) preface, B. HOADLY. *The Clarke-Leibniz Correspondence,* ed. H. G. ALEXANDER (New York 1956). L. STEPHENS, DNB 4:443–446. M. A.

HOSKIN, "Mining All Within: Clarke's Notes to Rohault's *Traité de Physique*," *The Dignity of Science*, ed. J. A. WEISHEIPL (Washington 1961) 217–227.

[E. A. SILLEM]

CLARKE, WILLIAM NEWTON, Baptist theologian; b. Cazenovia, N.Y., Dec. 2, 1841; d. Deland, Fla., Jan. 14, 1912. He received his A.B. (1861) from Madison University (now Colgate, Hamilton, N.Y.) and graduated 2 years later from Colgate Theological Seminary. While pastor at Newton Center, Mass., he made a study of the doctrine of the Atonement that led him to abandon the traditional theological interpretations. After 11 years at Newton he became pastor of the Olivet Baptist Church, Montreal, Canada, where he wrote his *Commentary on Mark* (1881). Two years later an accident, followed by several subsequent injuries, left him in poor health and forced him to curtail his pastoral work. He accepted the chair of New Testament interpretation at the Baptist Theological School, Toronto, Canada, and in 1890 was elected Joslin Professor of Christian Theology at Colgate Seminary. In 1898 he published his *Outline of Christian Theology,* in which he sought to interpret theology by substituting a combination of a historical approach to the Scriptures and an experiential knowledge of the world for traditional theological terms. Hence his theology is singular and personal. He relied heavily on the Bible, but only as interpreted by his own religious experience. His writings are serene and nonbelligerent, possibly because his first book appeared when he was 57 years old. While avoiding the controversies of his day, he dissented from current orthodoxy by emphasizing the need for a vital and transforming Christian experience. Among his books are *Can I believe in God the Father?* (1899), *What Shall We Think of Christianity?* (1899), *The Use of Scripture in Theology* (1905), and *The Ideal of Jesus* (1911).

Bibliography: S. MATHEWS, "In Memoriam: William Newton Clarke," *American Journal of Theology* 16 (July 1912) 444–449.

[E. DELANEY]

CLARKE COLLEGE. A 4-year liberal arts college for women located in Dubuque, Iowa, the institution began as St. Mary's Female Academy in 1843, 3 years before Iowa became a state. Acting upon the invitation of Bp. Jean Mathias P. Loras, The Sisters of Charity of the Blessed Virgin Mary in that year came from Philadelphia to establish their first convent school west of the Mississippi. Three years later, the school was moved to the prairie a few miles west of Dubuque where it was known as St. Joseph Academy. In 1859 it was returned to the city, where in 1879 it moved to its 60-acre campus. At that time, it was known as Mt. St. Joseph College. In 1928 the name was changed to Clarke College. Its permanent charter was issued in 1901.

The archbishop of Dubuque is chancellor of the college. The board of trustees is made up of 7 community officials and the college president; a lay advisory board is supplemented by a development council of over 100 business and professional men, alumnae, and parents of past and present students. In 1964 the faculty was composed of 5 priests, 65 sisters, and 21 laymen. Among the staff there were more than 30 with doctorates and 54 with master's degrees. The College has a moderate endowment, supplemented by the contributed services of the religious.

Its facilities include a 36-unit language laboratory, a planetarium, the campus broadcasting radio station (CLRK), the Clarke College Radio Kitchen, and a theater. The campus library in 1964 housed about 57,229 volumes and received 355 periodicals. Among student publications are a bimonthly newspaper and a literary magazine, the *Labarum*.

Clarke offers a 4-year program in the liberal arts, and provides a major in each of 15 departments leading to the bachelor's degree. Courses offered include the liberal arts and sciences, economics, modern languages, sociology, psychology, and home economics. Distinctive programs are advanced placement, the honors program, an honor system in student government, and optional study abroad. Under this junior-year-abroad program, introduced in 1956 in cooperation with the Institute of European Studies, students have studied in Madrid, Vienna, Paris, Rome, and in various Latin-American universities.

Enrollment has doubled every 25 years; in 1964 there were 773 full-time and 111 part-time students. A 1963 summer session enrolled 498. The percentage of alumnae attending graduate schools began to rise sharply in the 1950s. About half of each graduating class enters the teaching profession.

Clarke is fully accredited by the North Central Association of Colleges and Secondary Schools, by the National Council for Accreditation of Teacher Education, and the Iowa State Department of Public Instruction. It is affiliated with The Catholic University of America and is a corporate member of the American Association of University Women.

Bibliography: Sisters of Charity, *In the Early Days: Annals, 1833–87* (St. Louis 1912). Dubuque County, Iowa, *The History of Dubuque County, Iowa* (Chicago 1880).

[M. A. MULHOLLAND]

CLARUS, ST., abbot; b. near Vienne, in Dauphiné, France, beginning of the 7th century; d. *c.* 660 (feast, Jan. 1). He became a monk at Saint-Ferréol, then abbot of Saint-Marcel (*c.* 625). His virtues gained for him the admiration of Cadeoldus, Bishop of Vienne, who charged him with the spiritual direction of the hermits at Sainte-Blandine. The ancient cult of Clarus was confirmed by Pius X in 1903. He is the patron saint of tailors.

Bibliography: BHL 1:1825. DCB 1:548–549. M. BLANC, *Vie et le culte de s. Claire,* 2 v. (Toulon 1898). Baudot-Chaussin 1:15. R. AIGRAIN, *Catholicisme* 2:1160. W. BÖHNE, LexThK[2] 2:1216. R. VAN DOREN, DHGE 12:1030.

[B. F. SCHERER]

CLAUDE LORRAIN, one of the great painters of ideal landscape; b. Claude Gellée, in Champagne (Lorraine), 1600; d. Rome, Nov. 23, 1682. In 1613, or within a few years after, Claude journeyed to Rome, where he found employment with Agostino Tassi, a decorative frescoist who became his principal master. He remained with Tassi until 1625, when he went back to his native land for a brief period, returning in 1627 to settle down in Rome for the rest of his life. The original inspiration for Claude's art seems to have been derived from many sources: the mannerist style of Tassi; an interest in the effects of early morning, noonday, or evening light; the poems of Vergil; and even the preserved fragments of Roman landscape frescoes. The influences of Paul Brill and *Elsheimer are also evident in his paintings, although transformed into a more poetical spirit. Claude's style underwent a change in the 1660s toward a more asymmetrical and open composition in which the human figure in the landscape is accorded even less prominence than heretofore ("Perseus and the Medusa," 1674).

As a careful and diligent craftsman, Claude kept a record of 195 of his paintings in four books of drawings known collectively as the *Liber Veritatis.* In the history of 17th century French painting, his importance is second only to that of *Poussin.

Bibliography: L. CARACCIOLO, *Liber Veritatis di Claudio Gellée,* 3 v. (Rome 1915). W. FRIEDLAENDER, *Claude Lorrain* (Berlin 1921). A. BLUM, *Les Eaux fortes de Claude Gellée* (Paris 1922). P. COURTHION, *Claude Gellée* (Paris 1932). T. HETZER, *Claude Lorrain* (Frankfurt 1947). M. RÖTHLISBERGER, *Claude Lorrain* (New Haven 1961).

[T. BUSER]

CLAUDEL, PAUL LOUIS CHARLES MARIE

French poet and dramatist; b. Villeneuve-sur-Fère-en-Tardenois (Champagne), Aug. 6, 1868; d. Paris, Feb. 23, 1955. He was not, as is commonly thought, of the peasantry of Champagne. His family, originally from the Vosges and Ile-de-France, were in public administration on his father's side; his mother came from one of those rural middle-class families, the Cerveaux, whose rise in status was promoted by the Revolution of 1789. The Cerveaux, who are important in the Claudelian psychology, are reflected in Toussaint Turelure, the principal character in *L'Otage* (1910) and *Pain dur* (1914). But if Paul Claudel was not "un paysan" (for his diplomatic career kept him constantly away from his native heath), he was nonetheless marked by his home region, even to its accent: that famous manner of grinding out his words between his teeth.

Roots and Early Formation. This background was important with respect both to his poetic genius and to his spiritual attitude, two qualities strongly bound together. The soil of Champagne, its rustic tales, and the local history and family tradition fed the imagination of the dramatic poet, and their influence is especially notable in one of his masterpieces, *L'Annonce faite à Marie* (1912). But it was particularly in the house at Villeneuve, the site of his vacations—although the family moved when he was 2 to Bar-le-Duc, where his father had been named to a new post—that the "child perched among the apples" in the top of an old tree discovered the world and foresaw, yearned for, a connection among all things, a complete meaning, "a catholic order." It was there also that at the age of 13 he witnessed the death of his maternal grandfather Cerveaux, a doctor, so ravaged by cancer that he died suffering hallucinations. With Villeneuve as its center, the family moved about as the father received various assignments, and the child passed from one school to another. The Claudels and the Cerveaux were Catholic by tradition and there were several priests in the family, but the family maintained a respectful indifference. Young Paul received only as much religious instruction as was needed to prepare him for his first Communion (1880) and he soon abandoned all religious observances. He was 14 when his mother and the three children, at the insistence of the eldest daughter Camille, who was to become the very talented pupil (and a victim of the mental cruelty) of the sculptor *Rodin, took up residence in Paris. Paul Claudel entered the lycée Louis-le-Grand, where he won a first prize in oratory and, on that occasion, was "kissed on the brow" by *Renan. There he came under the influence of, and accepted as a disheartening reality, a philosophy that placed absolute confidence in science, at that time authoritative and triumphant. He spoke later of the "sad Eighties," of the "materialistic prison," and of "the state of suffocation and despair" he experienced as a student (1889) at L'Ecole de droit et des sciences politiques de Paris. For although the dogmatism of "science" seemed indisputable to young Claudel, there still remained within him the overpowering need to satisfy the urge he had experienced from earliest youth—to understand the "why" of life.

Literary and Religious Stirrings. In June 1886, after having been introduced to great literature—Aeschylus, Dante, Shakespeare—by his sister Camille, he read in a magazine first *Les Illuminations* and then *Une Saison en enfer* by Arthur *Rimbaud. In his own words, this was a "capital event," because the works of a "miserable poet" revealed to him that, in spite of the dominant philosophy, the universe was not a machine, obedient to the "laws" of nature, but that a limitless realm of the spiritual—in truth, of the supernatural—was a reality. In this frame of mind he went to Notre Dame de Paris for the Christmas services of the same year. In the famous story of his conversion he called his attitude "superlative dilettantism." He followed the high Mass with but moderate interest; he went again the next afternoon to hear Vespers. It was then, "near the second pillar by the entrance to the choir, on the night, in the direction of the Sacristy," that dilettantism dissolved in grace: "In one instant my heart was touched, and I believed." A 4-year struggle followed; the faith was there, but so were the convictions of his ingrained philosophy, intact and irreconcilable. On that first evening the convert opened a Bible belonging to his sister Camille and chanced upon a chapter in the Book of Wisdom. That voice "so sweet and so uncompromising" engaged him in a colloquy that lasted until his death. Some serious reading—Pascal, Bossuet, *The Imitation of Christ,* Aristotle, St. Thomas—contributed to the complete cleansing of his spirit: "I was before Thee as a fighter who yields." The final victory for God was won on Christmas Day in 1890 when Paul Claudel made his second Communion.

Paul Claudel.

One cannot neglect these preliminaries, however anecdotal they may seem, because they set the course, simultaneously and organically, for a long life and prodigious work.

Full Religious Transformation. In the interval between the first touch of grace in 1886 and the decisive "capitulation" of 1890, Claudel wrote a play, a work of genius—making allowances for the fumblings of a 20-year-old author—and particularly indicative of his fundamental need: *Tête d'or*. He had already produced *Premiers vers* and had had a close association with *Mallarmé, with whose pure aestheticism he was not satisfied. But with *Tête d'or,* "a drama of the conquest of the earth," about a hunger for power that collides with the mystery of death, he found his own voice: "Here am I—foolish, ignorant—an inexperienced man before the unknown! O being, young and fresh! Who are you? What are you doing?" This question by the first person on stage, Cébès, and the inability of his friend Simon Agnel, nicknamed "tête d'or" because of his flaming locks, to reply to it, express the duality and the confusion of the young Claudel, and, at the same time, give us a clue to the continuous unfolding of Claudel's poetic and catholic creation and its fundamental unity.

This unfolding can be called a "development"—as Claudel said of the Church—following his experiences of the inner life. He has been accused—and not always without reason, on the artistic level—of repeatedly turning his works to the ends of moral enlightenment. From *La Jeune fille Violaine* (1892) to the final *L'Annonce faite à Marie* (1948) on the theme of sacrifice, one can count five versions of the same drama. There are two versions of *Tête d'or;* there were two versions also of *La Ville* (1890), its sequel, a work concerned with the temptations of a "paradise on earth"; and two of *L'Échange* (1894), a conflict between the desire for freedom, represented by an American actress, and the "passion for service," represented by a woman who was sold to a trader by her husband. There are also two versions of *Père humilié,* the last book of the trilogy that includes *L'Otage* and *Le Pain dur,* in which the upstart Toussaint Turelure forces marriage on the aristocratic Sygne de Coufontaine in exchange for the liberty of Pope Pius VII; and *Protée,* a lyric farce. And there are three versions of *Partage de midi* (1905), an echo of a serious emotional upset, of which the two versions of *Soulier de satin* (1921), truly the Claudelian "whole," became the amplified orchestration and the idealized transformation.

Claudel's veritable obsession to revise his work was motivated at first by the necessity for self-enlightenment, for reworking the first spontaneous creation into a perspective that would lend it a sense of the supernatural and the providential. But his conviction that he was bound to use his gifts as an apostolate and to channel them toward moral enlightenment is not a sufficient explanation for the extent to which he felt compelled to revise.

In this respect, another keystone in Claudel's thought and art, a gauge of the mutual fructification of poetry and the faith within him, is to be found in his *L'Art poétique* (1907). The two treatises of which it is made up, *De la Connaissance de temps* and *De la Co-naissance au monde et de soi-même,* are based on the argument of Holy Writ that "things visible are only for the purpose of leading us to an understanding of things invisible." Accordingly, by analogy and metaphor, the poetic word echoes the divine word, permits the deciphering and ordering of the "holy truth," and becomes a religious act. No less than his dramatic works, the lyrics of Claudel, especially *Cinq grandes odes* (1910) and *La Cantate à trois voix* (1911), thus have some of the characteristics of a glimpse of the cosmos rendered intelligible through the vision of faith. And yet both are firmly planted in the soil, not only through their concrete language and their "native tang," but also by all Claudel put there from his own experience: his taste for violent adventure, for extreme hazard, for the "savage mystic." This aspect of Claudel's psychology contrasts strikingly with his exemplary and fruitful career as a diplomat.

Public Career. Claudel took first place (1870) in a course on foreign affairs, and after some time in L'École des Langues Orientales in Paris he made his diplomatic debut as French vice-consul in New York (1893), then served as acting consul at Boston (1894). He was later assigned to China—Shanghai, Foochow, Peking, Tientsin—until 1908. These were among his most productive years, the years of *Connaissance de l'est* (1900). He kept both irons in the fire—his diplomatic duties and his literary productivity—without diverting a single hour from the former to the benefit of the latter. Furthermore, he feared that his poetry might be injurious to his public career and published his work quietly, almost confidentially. He was recognized as a genius at once, but he long remained well known only to the literary coterie. In the course of a sojourn in France, in 1900, he made retreats at the Abbeys of Solesmes and Ligugé, but he felt himself "mysteriously rejected" (*Partage de midi* carries some evidence of this). In 1905 he married Reine Sainte-Marie Perrin, who bore him five children. He was consul at Prague (1908), consul-general at Frankfort (1911) and Hamburg (1913), *chargé* of the Economic Mission at Rome, minister plenipotentiary to Brazil (1917) and to Copenhagen (1919), and ambassador to Japan (1922), to Washington (1927), and to Brussels (1933). After retirement (1935), he divided his residence between the chateau at Brangues (Isère) and Paris, where he died, full of years, work, and honors. A most unusual honor was accorded when a reading of his poetry was given by the artists of the Théâtre Hébertot de Paris before Pius XII, with Claudel present, on April 29, 1950.

Claudel's recognition by the general public was long delayed; his theatrical successes date only from World War II, and his election to the French Academy, from 1946. But his influence on the elite goes back a long way, and the most recalcitrant (foremost among them André Gide) toward the severity of Claudel's Catholicism have acclaimed, and still acclaim, the imposing work that stands as witness of that Catholicism.

In addition to the works cited above, at least the following must be mentioned: For the theater, *le Livre de Christophe Colomb* (1933), *Jeanne au bûcher* (1939); for poetry, *Corona benignitatis anni Dei* (1915), *Ode jubilaire pour le sixième centenaire de la mort de Dante* (1919), *Cent phrases pour éventails* (1942); for prose, *Le Chemin de la Croix* (1915), *Correspondance avec Jacques Rivière* (1926), *Positions et propositions,* 2 v. (1928–34), *Conversations dans le*

Loir-et-Cher (1929), *Introduction à L'Apocalypse* (1946), *L'Oeil écoute* (1946), and *Correspondance avec André Gide* (1949).

Bibliography: *Oeuvres complètes,* ed. R. MALLET et al. (Paris 1950–), the first 9 v. ed. under direction of Claudel, 23 v. pub. to 1964. J. RIVIÈRE, "Paul Claudel, poète chrétien," *Études* 3 (Paris 1911) 61–129. F. DE MIOMANDRE, *Claudel et Suarès* (Brussels 1907). J. DE TONQUÉDEC, *L'Oeuvre de Paul Claudel* (Paris 1917). P. LASSERRE, *Les Chapelles littéraires* (Paris 1920). E. SAINTE-MARIE PERRIN, *Introduction à l'oeuvre de Paul Claudel* (Paris 1926). F. LEFÈVRE, *Les Sources de Paul Claudel* (Paris 1927). J. BENOIST-MÉCHIN and G. BLAIZOT, *Bibliographie des oeuvres de Paul Claudel* (Paris 1931). P. PETIT, "Bibliographie claudélienne," VieIntell (Dec. 1931–Feb. 1932). J. MADAULE, *Le Génie de Paul Claudel* (Paris 1933); *Le Drame de Paul Claudel* (Paris 1936). E. FRICHE, *Études claudéliennes* (Porrentruy, Switz. 1943). C. CHONEZ, *Introduction à Paul Claudel* (Paris 1947). F. MAURIAC, *Répose à Paul Claudel* (Paris 1947). L. BARJON, *Paul Claudel* (Paris 1953). S. FUMET, *Claudel* (Paris 1958). P. A. LESORT, *Paul Claudel par lui-même* (Paris 1963). G. C. RAWLINSON, *Recent French Tendencies from Renan to Claudel* (London 1917). F. CASNATI, *Paul Claudel e i suoi drammi* (Como 1921). H. HATZFELD, *Paul Claudel und Romain Roland* (Munich 1921). E. R. CURTIUS, *Die literarischen Wegbereiter des neuen Frankreichs* (Potsdam 1923); *Französischer Geist im zwanzigsten Jahrhundert* (Bern 1952). R. GROSCHE, *Paul Claudel* (Hellerau, Ger. 1930). H. DIECKMAN, *Die Kunstanschauung Paul Claudels* (Munich 1931). E. FRANCIA, *Paul Claudel* (Brescia 1947). M. RYAN, *Introduction to Paul Claudel* (Westminster, Md. 1951). J. VILA SELMA, *André Gide y Paul Claudel frente a frente* (Madrid 1952). H. U. VON BALTHASAR, epilogue to Claudel's *Der seidene Schuh* (Salzburg 1959). **Illustration credit:** French Embassy, Press and Information Division, New York.

[L. ESTANG]

CLAUDIANUS MAMERTUS, Gallic writer of the 5th century; b. Lyon; d. *c.* 474. A monk and a priest, he collaborated with his brother, Saint Mamertus, Bishop of Vienne. His principal work, *De statu animae,* is dedicated to his friend *Sidonius Apollinaris. It is a refutation of *Faustus of Riez and his theory of the corporeal soul. Book 1 establishes the spirituality of the soul on a rational basis; book 2 makes an appeal to the arguments of authorities: the Greek and Latin philosophers, the Fathers of the Church, and the Bible; book 3 refutes the arguments of Faustus. Though a hymn and a lectionary are lost, Mamertus's letters to the rhetor Sapaudus and to Sidonius Apollinaris have been preserved; none of the poems attributed to him were his. Mamertus was formed by the ancient thought, particularly that of Plato and Neoplatonism. He seems also to have reflected Augustinian views and to have influenced the early scholastics and Descartes.

Bibliography: *Opera,* ed. A. ENGELBRECHT (CSEL 11; 1885). F. BOEMER, *Der lateinische Neuplatonismus und Neupythagoreismus und Claudius Mamertus* (Leipzig 1936). A. JÜLICHER, Pauly-Wiss RE (1899) 2660–61. J. MADOZ, ed., *Liciniano de Carthagena* (Madrid 1948) 35–53. P. COURCELLE, *Les Lettres grecques en occident* (rev. ed. Paris 1948) 223–235. W. SCHMID, ReallexAnt Chr 3:169–179. N. K. CHADWICK, *Poetry and Letters in Early Christian Gaul* (London 1955) 207–210. É. AMANN, DTC 9.2: 1809–11.

[P. ROCHE]

CLAUDIUS CLAUDIANUS, with Ausonius his contemporary, the last of the great poets of Roman antiquity in the pagan tradition. He was born or grew up in Alexandria and was of Greek or Oriental origin. Greek was his native tongue but he acquired such an excellent knowledge of Latin that he was able to produce his chief literary compositions in that language. He spent the years 395–404 in Italy. His poetry may be classified under three heads: political panegyric and invective, mythological poems, and short pieces. The first group includes his panegyrics on the consulship of Anicius Probinus and Anicius Olybrius, on the consulship of Honorius, and on the consulship of Stilicho, his invectives against Rufinus and Eutropius, and his Fescennine poem on the marriage of Honorius. In the mythological field, his most elaborate, but unfinished, effort is his *Rape of Proserpine.* His shorter poems are miscellaneous pieces that remind one of *Statius. It is possible that he wrote a Christian poem, *De Salvatore.* At best he was a nominal Christian, though Augustine (*Civ.* 5.26) and Orosius (*Adv. paganos* 7.35) both regarded him as a pagan. While Claudianus may be called a poet-rhetorician, there are many passages in his works that justify his claim to second rank greatness. He enjoyed the highest renown in his own age. An inscription on the pedestal of a statue erected in his honor in the Roman Forum of Trajan calls him *praegloriosissimus poetarum* (Dessau ILS 2949).

Bibliography: Raby SecLP 87–97. SchHosKrüg GeschRL 4.2: 3–32. *Claudian,* tr. M. PLATNAUER, 2 v. (LoebClLib; 1922).

[M. R. P. MC GUIRE]

CLAUDIUS OF CONDAT, ST., bishop and abbot; b. possibly Franche-Comte, early 7th century; d. Condat, France, June 6, 696 (feast, June 6). The accounts of his life are largely legendary, but it appears that he was already well advanced in years and had introduced the *Benedictine Rule at Condat as abbot before he was called to serve as bishop of *Besançon. Several years before his death he resigned his see and retired to the monastic life at Condat. He was later mistakenly identified by *Ordericus with another Claudius of Besançon, who was present at the councils of Epao (517) and Lyons (529). After his death the abbey was dedicated to his memory, and in 1213 the monks discovered his remains. The church became a place of pilgrimage for the local inhabitants, but the relics were lost during the French Revolution.

Bibliography: ActSS June 1:634–696. BHL 1:1840–47. R. VAN DOREN, DHGE 12:1072. H. W. HERRMANN, LexThK[2] 2: 1219. G. BARDY, *Catholicisme* 2:1171–72. Zimmermann KalBen 2:279–281.

[P. BLECKER]

CLAUDIUS OF TURIN, bishop and exegete; b. probably near Seo de Urgel, Spain; d. Turin, Italy, toward the end of 827. He received his education among the clerics of Felix of Urgel, one of the main figures of the Adoptionist heresy (*see* ADOPTIONISM). Toward the end of the 8th century he went to Lyons, attracted by the reputation of the school of *Leidradus. There he received most of his theological and scriptural formation. He became a priest in the court of *Louis the Pious in Aquitaine, and when the latter became emperor, Claudius followed him to Aachen. His teaching in the schools of both cities gave him material for his numerous Biblical commentaries. In 817 or 818 he was elevated to the bishopric of Turin. As bishop he attacked the cult of images, as can be seen in his *Liber de imaginibus,* long attributed to *Agobard of Lyons; an *Excerptum* of this work is preserved. It was on this excerpt that his opponents *Dungal and *Jonas of Orléans based their attacks against him. Claudius's *Biblical commentaries belong to the collectanea type: they constitute true Biblical **catenae.* He contributed to the formation of this type of commentary, which was generally followed in Carolingian and later medieval times.

His commentaries are: Genesis (808 or 811), a Chronicle (814), Matthew (815), Galatians (815), Ephesians-Philippians (816), Romans (812–820), 1 and 2 Corinthians (820), Exodus (821), Numbers (823 or sometime before—lost), Leviticus (823), Ruth-Kings-Questions on Kings (824), and Josue-Judges (825–826). He probably prepared commentaries on all of the Pauline Epistles, but none of the introductory letters are known to be extant. Many of his works are unedited and some are attributed to other authors: Genesis and Kings, for example, appears as pseudo-*Eucherius of Lyons. The following commentaries attributed to *Atto of Vercelli certainly belong to Claudius: Colossians, Titus, Philemon, and Hebrews. The homilies found in various Breviaries and dictionaries under Claudius's name are extracts from his exegetical works.

Bibliography: PL 104:199–250, 615–928; 50:893–1208; 105: 459–464; 134:609–644, 699–834. MGEp 4:586–613. Stegmüller RB 2:no. 1949–75. J. B. Hablitzel, HistJb 27 (1906) 74–85; 38 (1917) 539–548. Manitius 1:390–396. G. Boffitto, "Il codice Vallicelliano C 3," *Atti Acc. Sc. Torino* 33 (1898) 250–285. E. Riggenbach in *Forschungen z. Geschichte d. neutestamentlichen Kanons u. d. altkirchl. Literatur,* v.8.1, ed. T. Zahn (Leipzig 1907). A. Souter, *The Earliest Latin Commentaries on the Epistles of St. Paul* (Oxford 1927). P. Bellet, "Claudio de Turín, autor de los comentarios *In Genesim et Regum* del Pseudo Euquerio," *Estudios biblicos* 9 (1950) 209–223; in *Colligere fragmenta: Festschrift Alban Dold* (Beuron 1952) 140–143; "El *Liber de imaginibus sanctorum,* bajo el nombre de Agobardo de Lyon, obra de Claudio de Turín," AnalSacTarracon 26 (1953) 151–194. A. Bigelmair, LexThK² 2:1220.

[P. BELLET]

CLAUDIUS AND COMPANIONS, SS., Asterius, Neon, Domnina, and Theonilla, saints and martyrs of Aegaeae in Cilicia in 285; commemorated in the Western *Martyrologies on August 23 and in the Greek *Synaxaries on October 30 and January 27. Two late Latin recensions of their acts are still extant; both of them are different in detail from the two abbreviated accounts of their martyrdom in the Synaxary of Constantinople and the Menology of Basil. According to the Latin texts, "three brothers and two women with an infant" were brought before Lysias, the governor of the province. After the interrogation, torture, and condemnation of Claudius, Asterius, and Neon, Domnina was stripped and beaten to death. Theonilla was cruelly tortured and slain by having burning coals heaped on her stomach. Neither the Synaxary of Constantinople nor the Menology of Basil mention Domnina. This fact and the incongruities in the second part of the Latin acts led Pio Franchi de' Cavalieri to suspect that the deaths of the two women were later added by two different hands to explain what had happened to them. Nothing is said about the child. If the accounts of the martyrdom of the women belong to the original protocol, the child must have been Domnina's since Theonilla declares that she has been a widow for 23 years.

Bibliography: C. van Hulst, EncCatt 3:1797. P. Franchi de' Cavalieri, "Su gli atti dei SS. Claudio, Asterio e Neone," *Note Agiografiche* 5 (StT 27; 1915) 107–126.

[M. J. COSTELLOE]

CLAUSIUS, RUDOLF JULIUS EMANUEL, physicist, known for his work in thermodynamics; b. Köslin, Prussia, Jan. 2, 1822; d. Bonn, Aug. 24, 1888. Clausius was educated at the Stettin gymnasium and the Universities of Berlin and Halle, where he was graduated in 1848. After 5 years as professor of physics at the Royal Artillery and Engineering School, Berlin, he received, in 1855, professorships at both the university and the Polytechnic Institutes in Zürich. In 1867 he became professor of physics at the university at Würzburg and 2 years later he moved to the university at Bonn where he remained for the rest of his life.

By the time Clausius received his first professorship, in Berlin in 1850, he had published half a dozen scientific papers concerned with the scattering of light by the atmosphere. In 1850 he published his most famous paper in the *Annalen der Physik und Chemie,* "Ueber die bewegende Kraft der Wärme und die Gesetze welche sich daraus für die Wärmelehre selbst ableiten lassen" (On the Moving Force of Heat and the Laws Regarding the Nature of Heat Itself Which Are Deducible Therefrom). In this important paper he enunciated the principle that came to be known as the second law of thermodynamics: "heat will not flow, of its own accord, from one object to another hotter one," the first law being, "energy cannot be created or destroyed." The combination of these two principles opened the way to the development of thermodynamics in the late 19th century. Clausius himself applied thermodynamical theory to an analysis of the operation of the steam engine. He invented the term *entropy for what he called the "transformation content" of an object. His studies on the kinetic theory of gases established that theory as a portion of mathematical physics.

[D. H. D. ROLLER]

CLAVER, PETER, ST., Jesuit missionary, called the Saint of the Slaves; b. Verdu, Spain, 1580; d. Cartagena, Colombia, 1654. Very little is known of his early years. He entered the Society of Jesus in 1602. In 1605, while studying for his degree in philosophy in the San Sion College of Mallorca, he was befriended by Alfonso Rodriguez, who encouraged him in his apos-

St. Peter Claver, 17th-century woodcut, the first published portrait of the saint.

tolic zeal and in his later missionary work in the New World. He continued his theological studies in Barcelona until 1610, when he was sent to Cartagena, which was then a very important port of entry to the Indies, teeming with merchants and slave traders. In Cartagena he met Alonso de Sandoval, who was deeply concerned with helping the slaves who, captured in Africa, were landed in America chained together in misery and fear of the unknown. Two important books by Sandoval are fundamental to any knowledge of the fate of African slaves in the Indies. The first, and less known, was published in 1627, *Naturaleza, policía sagrada y profana, costumbres, ritos y supersticiones de todos los Etíopes.* The second, published in 1641, was *De instauranda aethiopum salute.* Sandoval's indignation was soon shared by Claver.

In 1616 Claver was sent to Bogotá, where he was the first member of the Society of Jesus to be ordained. After Sandoval's transfer to another mission, Claver returned to Cartagena, probably on the recommendation of Sandoval, who must have early recognized his zeal and compassion. Claver was not only a missionary but a doctor and teacher. He greeted the incoming slave ships with his small host of interpreters. Carrying on high the holy cross, he went into the infested holds where during the long voyages epidemics and despair had taken their toll. Braving the horrible odors, the sickly atmosphere, and anxiety, Claver not only brought these slaves spiritual comfort but cured their sores, bandaged their wounds, and sometimes carried the disabled ones on his own shoulders. He first befriended the so-called savages, winning their confidence before starting on their catechization. He converted more than 300,000 by 1615.

During his lifetime he was already considered a saint. The stories of his miracles were passed from place to place through that mysterious primitive form of communication known only to those kept in bondage. In his last years Claver suffered a paralysis that kept him at the mercy of a surly slave who vented on him his resentment and evil nature. While suffering all these trials in Christian resignation, he learned that his friend Alfonso Rodriguez was being considered for canonization and in 1639 he learned of Urban VIII's bull condemning slave traffic. Claver was canonized in 1888 by Pope Leo XIII.

Bibliography: A. VALTIERRA, *Peter Claver: Saint of the Slaves* (Westminster, Md. 1960).

[H. VIVAS SALAS]

CLAVIGERO, FRANCISCO JAVIER, Mexican Jesuit teacher and scholar, best known for writing the first popular work on the Aztecs; b. Veracruz, Mexico, Sept. 9, 1731; d. Bologna, Italy, April 2, 1787. Clavigero spent his earliest years in the Mixteca, the western part of the modern state of Oaxaca, where his father was royal agent. In February 1748 he entered the Society of Jesus in Puebla. He was ordained in October 1754. Late in 1756 he was sent to Mexico City to teach the Indians at San Gregorio's, an Indian school adjoining the famed Jesuit school of St. Peter and St. Paul. Here he deepened his enthusiasm for pre-Columbian Mexican history. In March 1762 Clavigero was transferred to another Indian school in Puebla, where he remained until appointed professor of philosophy at Morelia in the summer of 1763. Heeding the call of the Jesuit general to modernize the curriculum of studies in the Jesuit schools, he taught courses in the new physics of Isaac Newton. In so doing he won lasting fame as a pioneer in the intellectual reform of 18th-century Mexico. When the Jesuits were banished from the Spanish Empire in June 1767, Clavigero went to Bologna and at first occupied his leisure hours in the study of Aztec civilization. He was distressed by the misinformation European books contained about the Americas in general and Mexico in particular. He determined to refute these errors by portraying Mexico as it really was. The result was the *Ancient History of Mexico* (1780–81), which for its systematic arrangement, clear style, and sympathetic interest in Aztec civilization was praised by historians and won him international renown. His work strongly influenced the study of Aztec civilization for many decades, and it is still held in high repute, despite shortcomings and the fact that much progress has been made in Aztec studies since Clavigero's time. He also wrote a *History of [Lower] California* (1789). After the suppression of the Jesuits in 1773, Clavigero spent the rest of his life as a diocesan priest in Bologna.

Bibliography: E. J. BURRUS, "Jesuit Exiles: Precursors of Mexican Independence," *Mid America* 36 (1954) 161–175. J. LE RIVEREND BRUSONE, "La historia antigua del padre Francisco Javier Clavijero," in *Estudios de historiografía de la Nueva España,* by H. DÍAZ THOMAS et al. (Mexico City 1945).

[C. E. RONAN]

CLAVIUS, CHRISTOPHER, Jesuit mathematician and astronomer, and one of the principal collaborators in the Gregorian calendar reform (1577–82); b. Bamberg, 1537?; d. Rome, Feb. 6, 1612. He entered the Jesuit Order in 1555, studied at Coimbra under

Christopher Clavius, 18th-century engraving.

P. *Nunes, and taught mathematics at the Collegio Romano from 1565.

In addition to his defense and explanation of the calendar, *Novi calendarii romani apologia* . . . (Rome 1595), Clavius wrote on all branches of mathematics. He is noted for his pedagogical skill, rather than as a creative mathematician. His *Euclides Elementorum* . . . (1574 and many later editions), with its detailed commentaries and supplementary material, became the standard text in the schools. The first six books were translated into Chinese under the direction of his student Matteo *Ricci. His *Opera Mathematica* (5 v. Mainz 1611–12) contains, among other works, his practical arithmetic (first pub. 1583), practical geometry (1604), algebra (1608), and commentaries on the sphere of *John de Sacrobosco (1570) and Theodosius (1586).

Clavius corresponded with the leading scholars of the day, and his letters confirming Galileo's discoveries with the telescope were very influential.

Bibliography: Sommervogel 2:1212–24. E. LAMALLE, NDB 3:279. J. E. HOFMANN, *Geschichte der Mathematik* v.1 (1953). E. C. PHILLIPS, "The Correspondence of Father Christopher Clavius, S.J.," ArchHistSocJesu 8 (1939) 193–222.

[J. B. EASTON]

CLAVUS, CLAUDIUS (NICHOLAS NIGER), a Danish cartographer, known also as Claudius Claussøn Swart, Nicolaus Niger, Claudius Niger, Nicolaus Gothus, Claudius Cymbricus; b. Sept. 14, 1388; d. after 1424. Clavus was educated in a Cistercian monastery and may have been an ecclesiastic. He is known chiefly for the first scientific extension of *Ptolemy. He prepared two charts with lines of latitude and longitude that were the earliest maps to include northern Europe, Greenland, and Iceland in their correct geographical positions. The first of his two charts, often reproduced with Clavus's accompanying description, is contained in the Ptolemy codex (Cod. lat. 441), now in the Nancy city library; it was completed before 1427 for Cardinal Guillaume *Fillastre. Later, Clavus prepared a second and better map, the original of which is lost. However, the chart was reproduced in the late 15th century by German cartographers; it influenced cartographic incunabula and was copied and used until the 18th century. The descriptive text originally accompanying the second map, but not found until the late 19th century, indicates that Clavus probably witnessed the destruction by the Eskimo of the eastern settlement of Greenland, "the last Norse colony in America."

Bibliography: A. A. BJÖRNBO and C. S. PETERSEN, *Der Däne C. C. Swart, der älteste Kartograph des Nordens, der erste Ptolemäus-Epigon der Renaissance* (Innsbruck 1909). F. NANSEN, *In Northern Mists: Arctic Explorations in Early Times,* 2 v. (New York 1911) 2:248–276. Sarton 3:1155. L. BAGROW, *History of Cartography,* ed. R. E. SKELTON, tr. D. L. PAISEY (Cambridge, Mass. 1964).

[T. C. HERNDON]

CLAYMOND, JOHN, early English humanist; b. Frampton, Lincolnshire, England, *c.* 1468; d. Nov. 19, 1537. He entered Magdalen College, *Oxford, in 1484 and was elected a fellow in 1488. At that time he met Richard *Foxe, who, on becoming bishop of Durham, invited Claymond to teach Latin in his diocese and gave him the vicarage of Norton in 1498. Claymond was ordained in 1499 and became a doctor of theology in 1510. A modest pluralist, he owed most of his preferments to Foxe. When Foxe, as visitor of Magdalen, removed its president, Claymond was elected to succeed him (1507). In 1517 Foxe, as founder, appointed Claymond the first president of Corpus Christi College, Oxford. Though both men were natives of south Lincolnshire, their principal bond was an interest in the revival of classical learning, or *humanism. Claymond corresponded with *Erasmus and belonged to the same literary circle as Thomas *More and Cuthbert *Tunstall. He prepared but did not publish commentaries on Pliny's *Natural History* and was highly esteemed for the breadth of his reading. His library, now in Corpus Christi Library, is formed mainly of printed Greek and Latin texts, with the classics and the Fathers evenly balanced. This reflects the founder's aim for Corpus Christi, i.e., the promotion of classical learning and of theological teaching based on patristic studies. Claymond was renowned for his piety and generosity; he was a benefactor to Brasenose, Corpus Christi, and Magdalen Colleges.

Bibliography: A. WOOD, *Athenae Oxonienses,* ed. P. BLISS, 5 v. (London 1813–20) 1:104–106. T. FOWLER, *Corpus Christi* (London 1898) 1–55. Emden 1:428–430.

[R. L. STOREY]

CLEMEN, CARL, Lutheran theologian and historian of religions; b. Sommerfeld (near Leipzig), March 30, 1865; d. Bonn, July 8, 1940. After a long period of teaching at Halle (1892–1910), he was professor of the history of religions at Bonn from 1910 until his death. He was a pioneer in the application of the principles and methods of the school of comparative religion to the study of the New Testament and the origins of Christianity. While recognizing the original character of Christianity, he stressed the importance of studying it in the whole context of the civilization in which it developed. He gradually extended his researches over a wide field of ancient religion in general. Among his chief works are *Die Entstehung des N.T.* (2d ed. Leipzig 1926), *Religionsgeschichtliche Erklärung des N.T.* (2d ed. Giessen 1924), *Religionsgeschichte Europas* (2 v. Heidelberg 1926–31) and *Urgeschichtliche Religion* (Bonn 1932). He was an editor or collaborator in two important works, *Die Religionen der Erde* (Munich 1927) and *Fontes historiae religionum* (7 fascicles, Bonn 1920–36).

Bibliography: N. TURCHI, EncCatt 3:1806. F. LENGSFELD, LexThK[2] 2:1221. H. H. SCHREY, NDB 3:280.

[G. SANDERS]

CLEMENCEAU, GEORGES BENJAMIN, French statesman; b. Mouilleron-en-Pareds (Vendée), France, Sept. 28, 1841; d. Paris, Nov. 24, 1929. After studying medicine at Nantes and the University of Paris, he received his degree (1865) and went to the U.S. (1865) where he traveled widely and sent numerous newspaper dispatches to *Le Temps* to supplement his income. Before returning to France, he married Mary Plummer in a civil ceremony (June 1869). The Franco-Prussian war (1870–71) and its aftermath launched Clemenceau on his public career. His elective offices over 5 decades saw him mayor of the 18th arrondissement of Paris; deputy from the department of the Seine to the National Assembly (1871); member and president of the Paris municipal council (1871–76); member of the Chamber of Deputies; senator; cabinet minister and twice premier of France. As a leader of the Radical party from the beginning of the

Georges Benjamin Clemenceau.

Third Republic, Clemenceau established a reputation as a destroyer of ministries, and earned as a nickname "The Tiger." His attacks on government policies and public figures appeared in the newspapers that he founded or for which he wrote: *La Justice, L'Aurore, L'Homme libre,* and *L'Homme enchaîné.* His articles rallied the supporters of *Dreyfus; condemned *Combes for permitting his minister of war to utilize *Freemasonry to ferret out anti-Republicans among the army officers; prodded the government during World War I; and bitterly condemned the pacifists. Clemenceau was an atheist, a supporter of *anticlericalism, *laicism, and complete separation of Church and State. As premier (1906–09, 1917–20) he disappointed many of his followers. He alienated labor and socialist leaders during his first ministry, when he seemed to champion vested interests. During his war ministry, he ran roughshod over all opposition to the war effort, assuming almost dictatorial control. Following the war the fanatically nationalistic, proud, iron-willed premier fought savagely to realize French war aims, firmly convinced that France must become as strong as possible in a world torn by national rivalries. As the foe of Woodrow Wilson, he had great influence on the terms of the Versailles Treaty. His opposition to reopening diplomatic relations with the Vatican was instrumental in terminating his second premiership. Defeat in his bid for the presidency of France, due mainly to strong Catholic opposition, ended his public career (1920). Many of his numerous publications were written during his retirement.

Bibliography: G. MICHON, *Clemenceau* (Paris 1931). J. J. H. MORDOCQ, *Clemenceau au soir de sa vie, 1920–29,* 2 v. (Paris 1933); *Clemenceau* (Paris 1939). G. BRUUN, *Clemenceau* (Cambridge, Mass. 1943). J. H. JACKSON, *Clemenceau and the Third Republic* (New York 1948). Lecanuet ÉglFrance. L. CAPÉRAN, *L'Invasion laïque: De l'avènement de Combes au vote de la séparation* (Paris 1935); *Histoire contemporaine de la laïcité française,* 3 v. (Paris 1957–61). Dansette. E. KORDT, StL 2:488–491. **Illustration credit:** French Embassy, Press and Information Division, New York City.

[D. R. PENN]

CLEMENCY, a virtue whose act is to moderate punishment. In a spirit of leniency it would lessen *punishment as far as the demands of justice permit. Clemency does not seek to mitigate punishment contrary to the order of justice or the dictates of right reason. Rather, considering the circumstances of fact, person, manner, place, etc., it judges that right reason does not require the guilty one to be punished as severely as the words of the law or custom would otherwise demand. To be good, the act must proceed from a virtuous motive. The mitigation of punishment because of sentimental considerations, fear, or bribery would not be an act of clemency, except in material sense.

Clemency is related to severity as *epikeia is to legal justice. But it differs from epikeia. In the latter there is a diminution of penalty because it is supposed that the mind of the legislator did not intend the severity expressed in the words of the law to be applied to a given case; this is probable where there are notably extenuating circumstances. Clemency, however, brings about the diminution because the one whose duty it is to impose the penalty has a certain tenderness or consideration toward the offender and is therefore unwilling to inflict punishment to the full extent of his authority.

Clemency and mildness are the same as far as the virtue of temperance moderates the feelings and their external expression; but in spite of a certain affinity, they differ, clemency being a virtue proper to superiors while mildness is something that should be common to all. Cruelty, which is a savage readiness to inflict punishment, is the direct opposite of clemency.

Bibliography: THOMAS AQUINAS, ST 2a2ae, 157.4. H. D. NOBLE, DictSpirAscMyst 2.1:944–947. L. DESBRUS, DTC 3.1:45–47.

[W. HERBST]

CLEMENS WENZESLAUS, archbishop of Trier, Duke of Saxony; b. Hubertusberg Castle, Saxony, Sept. 28, 1739; d. Marktoberdorf, Swabia, July 27, 1812. He was the youngest son of Friedrich August II, King of Poland and Elector of Saxony. Clemens first pursued a military career, but after a serious illness (1761) deserted it for an ecclesiastical one. Because of his noble rank, his advance in the Church was rapid. He was prince-bishop of Freising and Regensburg (1763–68), coadjutor (1764) and then bishop (1768) of Augsburg. In 1768 he became archbishop and elector of Trier, the last to hold these two offices. In addition he was coadjutor (1772) and prince provost (1778) of Ellwangen. Clemens Wenzeslaus possessed laudable priestly qualities, and with the help of influential advisers he inaugurated reforms in monastic and devotional life, and sought to improve primary and secondary schools. His reforms were those advocated by the leaders of the *Enlightenment who aimed to improve the Church. Clemens forced Johann von *Hontheim, his auxiliary bishop, to retract the writings he had published under the pseudonymn Febronius; yet the archbishop participated in the Congress of *Ems. He was adverse to extreme views and represented a moderate *episcopalism. Ferdinand von Duminique, his minister after 1782, utilized his family ties in gaining for Trier the support of France and Austria. The financial and economic policies of Clemens promoted the prosperity of his subjects. In 1794 he fled from the armies of the French Revolution to Augsburg.

Bibliography: H. RAAB, *Clemens Wenzeslaus von Sachsen und seine Zeit (1739–1812)* (Freiburg 1962–); LexThK² 2:1231. L. JUST, NDB 3:282–283.

[V. CONZEMIUS]

CLEMENS NON PAPA, JACOBUS, Renaissance composer; b. Ypres, Flanders, *c.* 1510; d. Dixmuide?, *c.* 1555. In 1544, then a priest, he was appointed choirmaster at St. Donatien, Bruges, but was dismissed the following year. Writers in the 17th century place his activity at Antwerp, Ypres, and finally Dixmuide, where he is said to have died. His final work, the motet *Hic est vere martir,* was copied in 1555, and it is likely that death interrupted composition of his *Souterliedekens* (Little Psalter Songs), completed and published by Susato (Antwerp 1556). A lament on his death by Jakob *Vaet appeared in 1558. He was published under the name Jacques Clément until he began using Clemens non Papa in 1546—to distinguish himself, so it is thought, from an Ypres poet, Jacobus Papa. His works include 15 Masses, 231 motets, many French and Flemish songs, and *Souterliedekens,* three-part settings of the Psalms in Flemish, employing popular tunes of the day. His clear and expressive style influenced such composers as Orlando di *Lasso.

Bibliography: *Opera omnia,* ed. K. P. BERNET KEMPERS (Corp MensMus 4; 1951–), 21 v. planned. K. P. BERNET KEMPERS, *Jacobus Clemens non Papa und seine Motetten* (Augsburg 1929); MusGG 2:1476–80. "Zum Todesjahr des Clemens non Papa," *Karl Gustav Fellerer zum 60 Geburtstag,* ed. H. DRUX et al. (Studien zur Musikgeschichte des Rheinlandes 2; Cologne 1962). E. LOWINSKY, *Secret Chromatic Art in the Netherlands Motet,* tr. C. BUCHMAN (New York 1946). Reese MusR.

[M. PICKER]

CLEMENT I, POPE, ST.

Pontificate, 92? to 101 (feast, Nov. 23). Accurate biographical data on Clement of Rome are meager. His identity with the Clement mentioned in Phil 4.3 or with the consul Titus Flavius Clemens, put to death for his faith by Emperor Domitian, is conjectural. There is no extant evidence to support the view that he was a convert from Judaism. Due to divergent notices in such early Christian writers as *Tertullian (*De Praescriptione* 32) and *Irenaeus (*Adv. Haer.* 3.3.3), and because of Epiphanius's efforts (*Panarion* 27.6) to reconcile the conflicting data, Clement's traditional third place (following Linus and Cletus) in the list of Peter's successors is not certain. His pontificate is usually assigned to the last decade of the 1st century. Accounts of his martyrdom are legendary, based on the *Passio S. Clementis,* written in either the 4th or 5th century.

First Epistle. In spite of biographical uncertainties, Clement of Rome is an important Apostolic Father whose eminence is founded on the *First Epistle of Clement to the Corinthians.* The text of the Epistle nowhere claims Clement as its author; it states merely that the Church of Rome is writing to the Church of Corinth. This too is the opinion of Irenaeus (*loc. cit.*), who notes that during the episcopacy of Clement the Church of Rome wrote a most fitting letter to the Church of Corinth. Eusebius (*Hist. Eccl.* 4.23.11) quotes a letter written by *Dionysius, Bishop of Corinth, to Pope Soter shortly after the middle of the 2d century that clearly links the sending of the Epistle with Clement. His name has thus been associated with the letter since early Christian antiquity and its authenticity is not questioned. The letter was considered inspired, and was read in many churches of the subapostolic era. It has long been studied for evidence of the sojourn and martyrdom of Peter and Paul in Rome, for its dogmatic and juridical contents (the distinction between clergy and laity, the illicitness of depriving duly appointed officials of their office), and for references to the moral code and liturgy of the early Church in Rome.

Historical Background. The historical background of the Epistle is still in need of clarification. The ancient Greek city of *Corinth was destroyed in 146 B.C. by the Romans, who executed the men and sold the women and children into slavery. The Corinth mentioned in Clement's letter is Laus Julia Corinthiensis founded *c.* 44 B.C. as an urban colony by a large population of Roman freedmen and veterans. Its importance as the seat of the administration of the Roman province of Achaia and as a commercial center attracted large numbers of Greeks, Jews, and other peoples. In the course of his second missionary journey, St. Paul founded a flourishing Christian community there. Even during his lifetime strife and factions, among other disorders, caused serious problems for the community (1 Cor 1.11–16). Apparently, similar conditions developed in the days of Clement during the last decade of the 1st century.

Structure. In structure, the Epistle consists of an introduction (1–3), two main sections (4–36 and 37–61), and a brief conclusion (62–65). After calling attention to the once flourishing Christian community, Clement deplores the present factions and exhorts the community to penance, piety, humility, and hospitality,

Pope St. Clement I celebrating Mass, detail of an 11th-century fresco in the subterranean basilica of St. Clement, Rome.

Pope Clement II, detail of the 13th-century figure, by sculptors of the school of Bamberg, placed over the Pope's tomb in the cathedral at Bamberg.

adding numerous quotations and examples from Scripture to each admonition. After reminding the Corinthians of the harmony in all creation and of God's goodness and omnipotence he ends the first section with remarks on the resurrection and judgment and an exhortation to faith and good works. Stoic thought is an element in this doctrine, which, however, may have come from the OT *Sapiential books.

The second main section deals directly with the quarrel in the local Church. God requires order and obedience from all creatures, consequently obedience and discipline are necessary in the Church. Just as there were definite offices and duties established by God in the Old Law, so too Christ chose Apostles, who in turn appointed bishops and deacons to continue His work. The contentious elements among the Corinthians are exhorted to do penance as well as to be submissive.

The conclusion summarizes the exhortations and expresses the hope that the envoys who delivered the letter will return with the good news that peace has been reestablished. There is no evidence that the Church of Corinth appealed to the Church of Rome for an authoritative decision, nor does the tone of the Epistle indicate that it is an official reply to a situation formally presented for action and solution. In fact, the letter clearly states that it gives counsel (58.2) and is making a request (59.2).

Salutation. The salutation of the Epistle, "The Church of God which sojourns in Rome to the Church of God which sojourns in Corinth," echoes in its very wording the preoccupation of the subapostolic age with the imminence of the *Parousia, the second coming of Christ as judge. In a spirit of fraternal solidarity, the Church in Rome appeals to the Christian community in Corinth to restore peace and harmony, using language that is hortatory rather than peremptory. The frequent use of the hortatory subjunctive (70 times in contexts that include both Romans and Corinthians) compared with the limited use of the imperative (in 24 contexts, exclusive of scriptural quotations and appeals for divine help) lends support to this view. Only three of the imperatives are directed to those responsible for the factions, and five to the whole community: "accept our advice, send back our messengers, take up the epistle of blessed Paul, see how wonderful is charity, learn to be submissive, consider who they are who have perverted you." The remaining contexts in which the imperatives occur refer to obligations incumbent upon Christians without reference to conditions in Corinth.

The so-called *Second Epistle of Clement to the Corinthians* is not a letter, but rather a homily, written perhaps at Corinth by an unknown author, probably near the middle of the 2d century.

Bibliography: T. LENSCHAU, Pauly-Wiss RE Suppl. 4 (1924) 1033–34. H. CAMPENHAUSEN, *Kirchliches Amt und geistliche Vollmacht* (Tübingen 1953). E. MOLLAND, RGG[3] 1:1836–38. A. STUIBER, ReallexAntChr 3:188–197; LexThK[2] 2:1222–23. Altaner 99–103. Quasten Patr 1:42–58. W. W. JAEGER, *Early Christianity and Greek Paideia* (Cambridge, Mass. 1961). Jedin HbKirchgesch 1:164, 173, 178–179. C. ANDRESEN, ReallexAnt Chr 6:111–113. **Illustration credit:** Alinari-Art Reference Bureau.

[H. DRESSLER]

CLEMENT II, POPE, Dec. 24, 1046, to Oct. 9, 1047; b. Suidger (the surname "von Mayendorff" was added in the 16th century for no apparent reason); d. near Pesaro. Suidger, of noble Saxon stock, first occurs in the records as a canon of the cathedral of Halberstadt. As chaplain in 1032 he accompanied his provost Herman, who had been made archbishop of Hamburg-Bremen. After Herman's death Suidger became chaplain at the imperial court. Following a canonically proper election King *Henry III named him bishop of *Bamberg (consecrated Dec. 28, 1040). After Henry's removal of the antipope Sylvester III and of *Gregory VI, at the Synod of Sutri and Rome, Suidger, the king's faithful protégé, was named pope with the acclamation of the clergy and the people. He was enthroned as Clement II, Dec. 25, 1046. His first official act was the imperial coronation of Henry III and his wife, Agnes. As early as the Roman Synod of January 1047, Clement issued sharp condemnations of the practice of simony, introducing at Rome a series of reforms that had previously been initiated in Germany. But his reign lasted only 9 months and 16 days. During a journey to the north he died in the monastery of St. Thomas. Recent investigation has shown that the cause of his sudden death was probably lead poisoning. His body was taken immediately to Bamberg (he had retained title to the diocese during his pontificate) and was entombed in the choir of St. Peter in the cathedral. The tomb was opened in 1942 and it was possible to salvage the pontifical vestments, which have now been restored. They comprise a valuable part of the treasures of the Bamberg cathedral. (For illustration, see preceding page.)

Bibliography: Jaffé L 1:525–528. E. v. GUTTENBERG, *Regesten der Bischöfe von Bamberg* (Würzburg 1932) 99–108; E. v. GUTTENBERG, ed., *Das Bistum Bamberg,* v.1.1 of *Die Bistümer der Kirchenprovinz Mainz* (Germania Sacra 2; Berlin 1937). K. HAUCK, "Zum Tode Papst Clemens II," *Jahrbuch für fränkische Landesforschung* 19 (1959) 265–274. S. MÜLLER-CHRISTENSEM, *Das Grab des Papstes Clemens II. im Dom zu Bamberg. Mit einer Studie zur Lebensgeschichte des Papstes von Alex. von Reitzenstein* (Munich 1960). Haller 2:280–285, 574–577. R. FOREVILLE, DHGE 12:1093–96. **Illustration credit:** Landesamt für Denkmalpflege, Munich.

[F. DRESSLER]

CLEMENT III, POPE, Dec. 19, 1187, to March 1191; b. Paolo Scolari at Rome, date unknown. *Saladin had captured Jerusalem in October 1187, and Clement's first concern was to rally Europe to a new *Crusade. Peace in Europe was necessary first. The long-standing dispute with the Romans was settled, and Clement was finally in Rome in February 1188. He won the Emperor *Frederick I Barbarossa to the crusade, but lived to share the discouragement at Frederick's death in Asia Minor in 1190. He also endeavored to enroll warring France and England in the armed pilgrimage to the East. He declared an indulgence for participants; others were to contribute the Saladin tithe. Emphasizing the religious character of the crusade, Clement forbade all luxuries of diet and dress to the crusaders. His efforts for peace were finally successful, and *Richard I the Lion Hearted and *Philip II Augustus of France set sail for the Holy Land (1190). The death of William II of Sicily, the Pope's vassal, threatened the peace. Fearing for the independence of a papacy surrounded by the territories of the new Emperor, *Henry VI, Clement supported Henry's rival in Sicily, Tancred. However, Clement agreed to crown Henry, who then led a powerful army into Italy. Before he reached Rome, Clement had died. The Pope continued the work of the medieval reformation, especially in the areas of matrimonial law and the organization of missionary dioceses, and freed the Scottish Church from the jurisdiction of the metropolitan of *York. (Illus., preceding page.)

Bibliography: Jaffé L 2:535–576, 770. PL 204:1275–1506. Mann 10:341–382. R. FOREVILLE, DHGE 12:1096–1109. Seppelt 3:304–309. G. SCHWAIGER, LexThK[2] 2:1223–24.

[J. R. SOMMERFELDT]

CLEMENT IV, POPE, Feb. 5, 1265, to Nov. 29, 1268; b. Guy Fulcodi, Saint-Gilles (Rhône), toward the end of the 12th century. Guy was a lawyer in the service of the counts of Toulouse and a consultant of King *Louis IX. After the death of his wife (*c.* 1256), he was ordained and served as archdeacon of Le Puy. His advancement in the Church was meteoric: he became bishop of Le Puy Oct. 19, 1257; archbishop of Narbonne, 1259; cardinal bishop of Sabina, 1261; and papal legate to England, Wales, and Ireland. He was elected pope at Perugia—*in absentia.* During much of his pontificate Clement, in collaboration with France, participated in the political affairs of Italy and Germany. He abetted the cause of *Manfred's antagonist, Charles of *Anjou, the brother of St. Louis. In a bull (Nov. 4, 1265) Clement confirmed Charles in the Kingdom of Sicily. The Angevin was crowned in St. Peter's (1266) by cardinals appointed by the Pope. Moreover, Clement helped considerably in the financing of Charles's expedition against Manfred who was defeated at Benevento and slain Feb. 26, 1266. Clement and Charles disagreed over the King's failure to fulfill the agreement made at his coronation. On several occasions Clement upbraided him for his rapacity, greed, and the cruelty that he exercised toward his new subjects.

Clement IV, tomb effigy, in San Francesco, Viterbo.

Difficulty again arose in the Kingdom of Sicily when Conradin, the son of *Conrad IV, was persuaded to invade Italy and assert his hereditary claims. Clement, not wishing to have another Hohenstaufen neighbor, sent letters to Abp. Wernher of Cologne and to other ecclesiastical princes in Germany, excommunicating all who would abet Conradin's candidacy for the vacant ecclesiastical princes in Germany, excommunicating in April 1267. In Lombardy and Sicily, Ghibellines rose in Conradin's support, but the problem was decided in favor of the Angevins when Charles defeated and captured Conradin in 1268 (*see* GUELFS AND GHIBELLINES). Ghibelline resistance collapsed, and savage reprisals culminated in the execution of Conradin. Clement actively supported the "crusade" in Prussia, Livonia, and Courland. He also vigorously assisted *Alfonso X of Castile against the Moors of Spain and Africa. Although often criticized for his centralizing and financial policies, particularly his extension of the usage of reserving benefices to the Holy See, Clement was primarily concerned in lessening the influence of local nobles and kings in the important matter of the appointment of bishops.

Bibliography: E. JORDAN, *Les Registres de Clement IV* (Paris 1904). Potthast Reg 2:1542–1650. J. HEIDEMANN, *Papst Clemens IV: Das Vorleben des Papstes und sein Legationregister* (Münster 1903). E. HORN, "Le Rôle politique de Clement IV," *Compte rendu de l'Académie des sciences morales et politiques* (1925) 273–300. Mann 15. C. NICOLAS, *Un Pape Saint-Gillois: Clément IV dans le monde et dans l'Église* (Nimes 1910). Haller 4:314–359, 451–464. **Illustration credit:** Leonard Von Matt.

[J. J. SMITH]

CLEMENT V, POPE

Pontificate, June 5, 1305, to April 20, 1314; b. Bertrand de Got, in the Bordelais, *c.* 1260; d. Roquemaure, Comtat Venaissin. Having studied Canon Law in Orléans and Bologna, he became bishop of Comminges in March 1295 and archbishop of Bordeaux in December 1299. He was elected pope at Perugia in 1305 by cardinals who were split into partisans and opponents of *Boniface VIII. His election, the result of compromise, was nonetheless a patent triumph for the anti-Bonifatians, maneuvered by King *Philip IV the Fair of France, in whose presence Clement was crowned at Lyons on Nov. 14, 1305.

French influence was later to become more manifest: Clement chose to live in France, in various places, notably at Poitiers (1307–08). He immediately created 10 new cardinals (one Englishman, nine Frenchmen), thus putting the Italians in a minority in the sacred college. Subsequent promotions—not unblemished by nepotism—were to make this French preponderance overwhelming. Affable but impressionable, unable to refuse any request, Clement showered favors on his relatives and his Gascon compatriots who invaded the papal administration, to the great scandal of the Italians (Dante). In his relations with Philip, Clement at times acted firmly as the defender of the rights of the Church, then appearing deplorably weak, the victim of sheer lassitude (he suffered from cancer). In the main, the King dominated Clement by his strong personality. Philip pushed tenaciously to gain a decision in the trial of Boniface VIII that would be favorable to his own royal person; Clement continued to procrastinate, but

Pope Clement V, detail of an early 14th-century fresco by Taddeo Gaddi in the Dominican convent of Santa Maria Novella, Florence.

finally (April 1311) arrived at a verdict that cleared the King entirely, conditionally absolved *Nogaret, but did not entirely besmirch the memory of Boniface. Clement canonized Pope *Celestine V in 1313.

In the affair of the Knights *Templars, however, Philip had his way, despite the temporizing of the Pope. Since the spring of 1307 Philip had insisted that Clement investigate the Templars and suppress the order; the mass arrests of the knights and the blackmail practiced by the King and his spokesmen irritated the Pope. But Clement was caught in the meshes of the King's intrigue and his "independence" soon proved to be a mockery. The legal examination of the case was already completed when the Council of *Vienne, convoked by Clement to decide the affair of the Templars, opened in October 1311. In the face of the renewed royal interference, Clement abolished the order (April 3, 1312).

Clement's solicitude for the other sovereigns of Europe prompted him to offer help and advice and his good offices in arbitrating their disputes. But his pontificate was marked throughout by growing tax demands (*annates) and a persistent interference in the granting of *benefices (reservation), the latter evoking protests in England (Parliament of Carlisle, 1307). Clement's authoritarianism was notable; under his impetus, centralization gained ground, and the Curia profited. The constitution *Pastoralis cura,* the ultimate in theocratic thinking, proclaimed the superiority of the Holy See over the Empire. From March 1309 Clement lived in the *Venaissin, which was papal territory, or at *Avignon, which belonged to the king of Naples, his vassal. This did not mean that he had abandoned the idea of returning to Rome; but his indifferent health and the unfavorable situation in Italy (i.e., the failure of papal arbitration between the Tuscan factions; Venetian designs on Ferrara, a papal city, involving a war between the papacy and Venice; the blustering descent of Emperor *Henry VII for coronation; Roman instability; blunders and exactions of French papal officials sent into Italy) gave him only too much encouragement to stay north of the Alps, an unfortunate example for his successors. Clement did nothing to curb *heresy; the *Inquisition remained inactive, and Clement's constitution *Multorum querela* was an effort to reduce its arbitrary power. He showed himself favorable to education, founding the University of Perugia (1307) and creating chairs for the teaching of Asiatic languages for mission work at the suggestion of Raymond *Lull. An eminent canon lawyer, he published bk. 7 of the Decretals, the **Clementinae.*

See also AVIGNON PAPACY.

Bibliography: Regestum Clementis papae V, 9 v. in 8 (Rome 1885–92). *Tables des registres de Clément V,* ed. Y. LANHERS and C. VOGEL, 2 v. (Paris 1948–57). É. BALUZE, *Vitae paparum Avenionensium,* ed. G. MOLLAT, 4 v. (Paris 1914–27). G. MOLLAT, *The Popes at Avignon, 1305–1378,* tr. J. LOVE (New York 1963). W. OTTE, *Der historische Wert der alten Biographieen des Papstes Clemens V.* (Breslau 1902). H. FINKE, *Papsttum und Untergang des Templerordens,* 2 v. (Münster 1907). G. LIZERAND, *Clément V et Philippe le Bel* (Paris 1911). E. MÜLLER, *Das Konzil von Vienne, 1311–1312 . . .* (Münster 1934). E. R. LABANDE, "Clément V et le Poitou," *Bulletin de la Société des Antiquaires de l'Ouest et des musées de Poitiers,* 4th ser., 4 (1957) 11–33, 83–109. J. BERNARD, "Le Népotisme de Clément V et ses complaisances pour la Gascogne," *Annales du Midi* 61 (1949) 369–411. Y. RENOUARD, "Edouard II et Clément V d'après les rôles gascons," *ibid.* 67 (1955) 119–141. R. GAIGNARD, "Le Gouvernement pontifical au travail. L'Exemple des dernières années du règne de Clément V . . .," *ibid.* 72 (1960) 169–214. **Illustration credit:** Alinari-Art Reference Bureau.

[E. R. LABANDE]

CLEMENT VI, POPE

Pontificate, May 7, 1342, to Dec. 6, 1352; b. Pierre Roger, Corrèze, France, *c.* 1291; d. Avignon. A Benedictine of *Chaise-Dieu since 1301, he received a doctorate in theology before becoming abbot of *Fécamp and Chaise-Dieu. He was bishop of Arras (1328), archbishop of Sens (1329) and of Rouen (1330), and cardinal priest (1338). His learning, eloquence, amiable manner, and diplomatic skill won him the favor of King Philip VI of France and Pope *John XXII. Having been elected successor to Pope *Benedict XII, he was crowned May 19, 1342, at Avignon (*see* AVIGNON PAPACY).

During his pontificate the Church became markedly centralized. In 1344 he decreed that all churches, dignities, offices, and ecclesiastical *benefices were subject to papal *provision. The bishops objected but to no avail. *Edward III of England retaliated in 1345 by seizing all benefices in his country held by foreigners. Philip VI followed his example in 1347, and the Pope's remonstrances resulted only in an exception being made for cardinals, the curialists, and the Pope's official family. By contrast, there were almost no difficulties in Aragon over the conferring of benefices. Conflicts there with Pedro IV centered upon the seizure of the estates of deceased bishops and the exercise of ecclesiastical jurisdiction. But in the political arena, the kingdom of Majorca was reunited to the crown despite Clement's objections. Clement opposed the Franciscan *Spirituals.

In spite of his diplomatic skill, Clement never succeeded in ending the hostilities of the Hundred Years' War. Likewise, in Italy he had only disappointments, e.g., the revolution in Rome of *Cola di Rienzi, the regicide of the husband of Jeanne I of Sicily. Within the Empire, Clement ended the long quarrel between the Church and Emperor *Louis IV of Bavaria by depos-

Silver coin of Pope Clement VI, Vatican Library.

ing him and favoring the election of *Charles IV of Luxembourg as emperor (1347).

Clement was buried at Chaise-Dieu where his tomb still remains. Political enemies, especially *Petrarch, vilified his memory, reproaching him for the ostentatious pomp of his court, which was the most sophisticated court of the day. The incriminations against his moral conduct are unfounded.

Bibliography: Sources. CLEMENT VI, *Lettres closes, patentes et curiales se rapportant à la France*, ed. E. DÉPREZ et al. (Paris 1901–); *Lettres . . . intéressant les pays autres que la France*, ed. E. DÉPREZ and G. MOLLAT (Paris 1960–). É. BALUZE, *Vitae paparum Avenionensium*, ed. G. MOLLAT, 4 v. (Paris 1914–27). G. MOLLAT, *The Popes at Avignon, 1305–1378*, tr. J. LOVE (New York 1963); *Comptes rendus des séances de l'Académie des inscriptions et belles-lettres* (1957) 412–419; *Mélanges d'archéologie et d'histoire* 71 (1959) 377–380; *ibid.* 73 (1961) 375–389; *Journal des savants* (1959) 16–27; *ibid.* (1963) 191–195; *ibid.* (1960) 122–129; RHE 55 (1960) 5–24. A. PÉLISSIER, *Clement VI le Magnifique, premier pape limousin* (Brive, France 1951). R. J. LOENERTZ, "Ambassadeurs grecs auprès du pape C. VI," OrChrPer 19 (1953) 178–196. H. S. OFFLER, "A Political *Collatio* of Pope C. VI, O.S.B.," RevBén 65 (1955) 126–144. A. H. BURNE, *The Crecy War* (New York 1955). F. GIUNTA, "Sulla politica orientale di C. VI," *Studi di storia medievale e moderna in onore di ettore Rota*, ed. P. VACCARI, and P. F. PALUMBO (Rome 1958) 149–162. **Illustration credit:** Leonard Von Matt.

[G. MOLLAT]

CLEMENT VII, POPE

Pontificate, Nov. 19, 1523, to Sept. 25, 1534; b. Giulio de'Medici, Florence, May 26, 1478; d. Rome. He was the illegitimate son of Giuliano de'Medici and Antonia del Cittadino, member of the Gorini family. Giulio, born a month after the Pazzi conspiracy, in which his father was slain, was raised by his grandfather, Lorenzo de' *Medici (the Magnificent), Florentine merchant prince and statesman. After Lorenzo's death (1492) Giulio remained with the family. During the period of Medici exile (1494–1512) he visited several European cities with his cousins Giuliano and Giovanni, and then took up residence in Rome.

Ecclesiastical Offices. On May 9, 1513, Giulio was appointed archbishop of Florence by his cousin Giovanni, who had become *Leo X 2 months before. Because of the impediment of illegitimacy, he was granted a dispensation *super defectu natalium*. On September 22 of that same year he was raised to the cardinalate, after a document was published stipulating that his parents had been betrothed *per sponsalia de praesenti* and declaring him legitimate. He was appointed vice chancellor, March 9, 1517, and was chiefly responsible for determining the political policies of the Pope. He was active at the later session of the Fifth Lateran Council (1512–17) and was the first to apply the new decrees in his own diocese of Florence. In 1515 he was present at the meeting of Leo X and *Charles V at Bologna. At the death of Leo X (1521) he came to Rome, and though at first a strong candidate for the papal throne, he lost the election to *Adrian VI.

Troubled Pontificate. In a conclave that lasted 6 weeks (Oct. 8 to Nov. 19, 1523) Giulio was chosen to succeed Adrian VI. He faced the problems of curtailing the progress of the Protestant revolt, the political rivalries of *Francis I, King of France, and the young Emperor Charles V, the question of the annulment of the marriage of *Henry VIII, King of England, and the need of general Church reform.

Pope Clement VII, portrait by Sebastiano del Piombo in the Gallerie Nazionale di Capodimonte, Naples.

Lutheran Movement. Shortly after his accession, Clement sent Lorenzo *Campeggio as papal legate to the Diet of Nuremberg (1524) to assure the Emperor that he supported the Edict of Worms (1521). He conferred with Charles V on means of conciliating the Lutherans but opposed calling a general council of the Church, which the Emperor favored. Clement met the Emperor twice at Bologna for discussion, but could never agree on the means of solving the Lutheran question, so that at the end of his pontificate the issue was greater than ever.

Hapsburg-Valois Rivalry. The contest between Francis I and Charles V to dominate Europe included the control of Italy. Clement attempted to maintain a *status quo* that would prevent the success of either one. He supported the imperialist cause that ended in the Battle of Pavia, Feb. 24, 1525, where the Spanish commanders, the Constable de Bourbon and the Marquis de Pescara, defeated the French and took Francis I as a prisoner to Madrid. In the Treaty of Madrid (Jan. 14, 1526) Francis surrendered his claims in Italy. On May 22, 1526, Clement entered the League of Cognac with Francis I, the Sforza of Milan, Florence, and Venice to check the growing power of Charles. This led to the humiliation of the sack of Rome by mutinous imperial mercenary forces (1527) and the virtual imprisonment of Clement in the *Castel Sant'Angelo for more than 7 months. Upon his release he fled to Orvieto, and then to Viterbo, and reentered Rome on Oct. 6, 1528. In a period of peace Charles received the imperial crown from Clement in Bologna, Feb. 24, 1530. In February 1532 Clement again met the Emperor at Bologna to discuss the formation of a league of Italian states. In October 1533 Clement met with Francis I at Marseilles, where he officiated at the marriage of his niece, Catherine de Médicis, and the King's son (later Henry II, 1547 to 1559). In these interviews he failed to reconcile the two rulers.

The Marriage of Henry VIII. In 1527 Henry VIII requested an annulment of his 18-year-old marriage to *Catherine of Aragon, alleging his scruples over its validity. Clement, mindful that Catherine was the aunt of Charles V, his captor, and hoping that the King's interest in Anne Boleyn would wane, adopted a policy of delay. He sent Lorenzo Campeggio to London to act as co-legate with Cardinal Thomas *Wolsey in the inquiries, with instructions to keep the proceedings from solution. Not until March 23, 1534, did the papal tribunal declare the validity of Henry's marriage to Catherine. Meanwhile, the King had married Anne (1533), and his parliament had begun its series of acts that effected the schism. *See* REFORMATION, PROTESTANT (IN THE BRITISH ISLES).

Church Reform. Clement was hindered from serious consideration of the pressing need for reform. The first 5 years of his reign were filled with the Hapsburg-Valois wars and the threatening developments of Lutheranism. The last 6 years were troubled by the increased seriousness of the Protestant revolt, the opposition of Francis I to a general council, and the rapid development of the events of Henry VIII's attempted annulment toward a complete break with Rome. Motions toward reform, however, were already under way in the activities of the Oratory of *Divine Love in northern Italy and the appearance of future religious founders: Cajetan (Gaetano da Thiene) and Gian Pietro Carafa (Paul IV, 1555–59, Theatines), Jerome Emiliani (Somaschi), Anthony Zaccaria (Barnabites), Matteo di Bassi (Capuchins), Ignatius of Loyola (Jesuits), Angela Merici (Ursulines), and others. Clement's successor approved these groups and inaugurated the Council of Trent.

Clement was a patron of the arts and encouraged such artists as Raphael and Sebastiano del Piombo. He commissioned Michelangelo to prepare tombs for two members of his family. His own tomb is in the church of S. Maria sopra Minerva in Rome. The tomb was made by Baccio Bandinelli; the statue of Clement, by Giovanni di Baccio Bigio.

The verdict of history on the pontificate of Clement has not been favorable. Clement's weakness and indecision, which contributed to the growth of the Protestant revolt, are accentuated by the position of his reign between those of two reform popes, Adrian VI and Paul III.

Bibliography: H. M. VAUGHAN, *The Medici Popes* (New York 1908). P. CRABITES, *Clement VII and Henry VIII* (London 1936). Hughes RE v.1. BullRom 6:26–172. H. M. FÉRET, *Catholicisme* 2:1191–93. P. BALAN, *Clemente VII e l'Italia dé suoi tempi* (Milan 1887). Pastor v.9–10. R. MOLS, DHGE 12:1175–1244, bibliog. Fliche-Martin v.17. H. HEMMER, DTC 3.1:72–76. H. LUTZ, LexThK[2] 2:1226. E. P. RODOCANACHI, . . . *Les Pontificats d'Adrien VI et de Clément VII* (Paris 1933). G. B. PICOTTI, EncCatt 3:1821–27. **Illustration credit:** Alinari-Art Reference Bureau.

[W. J. STEINER]

CLEMENT VII, ANTIPOPE

Pontificate, Sept. 20, 1378, to Sept. 16, 1394; b. Robert of Geneva, at Geneva, 1342; d. Avignon. He had been bishop of Thérouanne (1361) and of Cambrai (1368), and, as cardinal (1371), the legate in Italy of the last Pope of the *Avignon papacy, Gregory XI. When the cardinals assembled at Fondi nullified the election of the irascible Bartolomeo Prignano (*Urban VI), they elected Robert, who took the name Pope Clement VII (September 1376). The Italian cardinals attended but did not participate in this much-disputed election that marked the beginning of the *Western Schism. Displacing Urban by force of arms was out of the question after Clement's troops were quickly defeated. Clement retired to Naples where he was in favor with the queen, but the populace there made it expedient for him to leave Italy, and he went to Avignon (June 1379). In France, Charles V had temporarily adopted a neutral stand toward the rival papal claimants, but after reading the dossier concerning the election at Fondi, he sided with Clement (November 1379). Brittany followed France's lead and supported Clement, as did Arras, Cambrai, Thérouanne, and Tournai. England held to Urban VI, as did those areas under English influence, i.e., Guienne and Aquitaine, Flanders, Utrecht, and Liège. The king of Castile sent ambassadors to conduct an inquest into the disputed elections and then declared adherence to Clement (May 1381). The kings of Aragon and Navarre followed suit; Portugal remained with Urban. Ireland was divided, but the Urbanists triumphed. In Scotland, politics dictated rallying to the pope recognized by her ally France. Within the Empire the Emperor rejected the validity of the Fondi election, but many princes and cities believed it authentic, although the followers of Urban were in the majority. In spite of Clement's active effort, he failed to convince Hungary, Poland, Denmark, or Scandinavia of the truth of his claim. In Italy, the queen of Sicily was coerced into adherence to Urban, but she broke with him (October 1379) following intrigues between him and enemies who sought to dethrone her. Throughout the rest of Italy, Urban's irascibility brought him disappointment and vexation. Without formally backing Clement, Bologna and Florence nonetheless maintained relations with him. In the Orient, Paul II, King of Cyprus, followed Clement. On Corfu, in Albania, and in the Pelopponesus, Clement was favored; Genoa and Venice neutralized his influence.

Contemporaries deplored the Schism. Some felt that a general council should be called to end it. But neither Clement, nor Urban, nor the cardinals would give their consent to this remedy, for it raised the question of who would actually convoke such a council as well as the allied problem of *conciliarism. Clement remained convinced of the legitimacy of the Fondi election. Despite the efforts of individuals, such as Catherine of Siena, and of the University of Paris, no solution of the Schism was in sight when Clement died at Avignon, to be succeeded by Antipope *Benedict XIII.

Bibliography: G. MOLLAT, DHGE 12:1174–75, lists sources extensively. Pastor 1:134–174. Seppelt 4:172, 196, 198–209, 211, 216–219, 222–223. For additional bibliog. *see* WESTERN SCHISM.
Illustration credit: The Pierpont Morgan Library, New York City.

[G. MOLLAT]

A detail of the opening section of the bull of Pope Urban VI, excommunicating the Antipope Clement VII, dated Feb. 13, 1383. This copy is an official transcript.

CLEMENT VIII, POPE

Pontificate Jan. 30, 1592, to March 5, 1605; b. Ippolito Aldobrandini, Fano, Italy, Feb. 24, 1536. Of an old and distinguished Florentine family, the fourth son of Silvestro *Aldobrandini and Lisa Deti, Ippolito studed law at Padua, Perugia, and Bologna, where he received the doctorate. Under Pius V, a family benefactor, he became consistorial advocate in 1568, and auditor of the Rota in 1570. Rapidly promoted under Sixtus V, he became datary, and in December 1585 he was made cardinal priest of the titular church of St. Pancratius. In January 1586 he became grand penitentiary. His public prominence was furthered when, as legate extraordinary, he successfully mediated the dispute over the Polish throne to the satisfaction of both King Sigismund III and Emperor Rudolf II. During three conclaves, from 1590 to 1591, he received support, but he was elected in 1592 when the influence of Philip II in papal elections had begun to wane.

A lifetime friend of St. Philip Neri, Clement was known for his high moral integrity and devout character, as well as for industry and attention to detail. As pope he was an example of kindliness and charity in his frequent visits to Roman churches and his care for the poor, sick, and imprisoned; in his legislation he aimed at improving conditions within the papal territories. With true piety and pastoral zeal he worked tirelessly for the improvement of the Church, for the spiritual growth, and for the removal of abuses and scandals.

Of primary importance was Clement's enlightened policy regarding the Church in France. He reversed the former pro-Spanish policy of the papacy in the *Wars of Religion by absolving *Henry IV and recognizing him as legitimate king in France. This reconciliation was followed by papal toleration of the Edict of *Nantes (1598) and the implementation of the Tridentine decrees that brought about the rejuvenation of the French Church. Henry's support in 1597 allowed Clement to claim successfully, against the opposition of Spain and the Empire, that the Duchy of Ferrara had devolved to papal jurisdiction after the death of Duke Alphonso II

Monument of Pope Clement VIII by sculptors of the Milanese school in the Basilica of S. Maria Maggiore, Rome.

without legitimate heir. Moreover, Clement was able to bring about peace between France and Spain in 1598 and also between France and Savoy.

Clement also attempted to improve the situation of the English Catholics. While dealing with the *archpriest controversy and internal disputes within the English mission, he supported and strengthened the English colleges on the Continent and established the Scottish college in Rome. His hopes for reconciliation with the English court proved futile. Although James VI of Scotland had seemed amenable to a settlement with the papacy, after his succession to the English throne was secured, James proved recalcitrant.

Clement assisted the work of St. Francis de Sales in Geneva and furthered Catholic reform in Poland and Germany. He received the reunion of the metropolitan of Kiev and a number of Ruthenian bishops in 1595 following the Union of *Brest. Clement failed in his efforts to inaugurate an effective league of Christian princes against the Ottoman Turks, but he furthered the foreign missions by establishing central commissions whose work anticipated that of the Congregation for the Propagation of the Faith.

In a series of decrees he promoted the reform of religious houses and the fidelity of bishops and clergy to the dictates of Trent. He ordered a new and corrected edition of the Vulgate, and also new editions of the Pontifical (1596), the Ceremonial (1600), the Breviary (1602), and the Missal (1604). He raised to the cardinalate Cesare Baronius, Robert Bellarmine, Francesco Tarugi, Francisco de Toledo, Silvio Antoniano, and his two nephews Cinzio and Pietro Aldobrandini. His excellent choice of advisers more than compensated for his sometime lack of force and decisiveness.

During Clement's reign a serious theological controversy arose over Luis de *Molina's theory of the efficacy of divine grace. Confronted by a heated dispute between the Jesuits and the Dominicans, Clement established a commission to investigate the problem, the famous *Congregatio de Auxiliis. While Clement personally presided at the debates before the commission, he refrained from pronouncement, and the matter was settled only after his death.

His remains rest in the Basilica of S. Maria Maggiore under a monument erected by the Borghese family.

Bibliography: Pastor v.23 and 34. BullRom v.9–11. R. Mols, DHGE 12:1249–97. J. de la Servière, DTC 3.1:76–86. A. F. Artaud de Montor, *The Lives and Times of the Popes,* ed. and tr. C. Artaud de Montor, 10 v. (New York 1910–11) 5:221–260. **Illustration credit:** Alinari-Art Reference Bureau.

[J. C. WILLKE]

CLEMENT IX, POPE, June 20, 1667, to Dec. 9, 1669; b. Giulio Rospigliosi, Pistoia, Jan. 28, 1600. He came of an ancient family from Lombardy. He studied first at Rome with the Jesuits, then at the University of Pisa. A man of talents, Rospigliosi was not only the author of verses, but also a successful playwright. His dramas on religious themes, influenced by Calderón, were quite successful. Through the favor of Urban VIII he rose from referendary (1632) to become nuncio to Spain (1644–53) and titular archbishop of Tarsus.

Pope Clement IX, portrait by the Italian artist Carlo Maratti (1625–1713).

Alexander VII made him his secretary of state (1657) and cardinal priest of S. Sisto. The two chief problems of his pontificate were the stubborn Jansenists and the oncoming Ottomans. Four Jansenist bishops—Caulet de Pamiers, Buzenvol de Beauvais, Pavillon d'Alet, Henri Arnauld d'Angers—had refused to give their acceptance to the formulary of Alexander VII (1665), and these were supported by many others. They had written pastorals that had been condemned and in general had showed themselves recalcitrant. The French authorities, alarmed over the possibility of schism, persuaded the four bishops to sign their acceptance of Alexander's bull. Clement, "more generous than the father of the prodigal son," allowed them to do this without any explicit retraction of their pastoral letters. The bishops signed, with reservations carefully kept from the Pope, and an uneasy peace (*Pax Clementina*) settled on France. Since the Jansenists had deceived the Pope, the peace was not lasting. (*See* JANSENISM; HERESY, HISTORY OF.)

The Ottomans, who had been attacking Crete since 1645, were engaged in reducing Candia, the last Christian stronghold on that island kingdom. Clement did everything to help the beleaguered Venetians. He failed to secure the aid of Louis XIV and in sadness learned that Candia had fallen on Sept. 5, 1669. Clement was a good shepherd. He reduced taxes and was charitable to the poor, solicitous for the spiritual welfare of his flock, and interested in missionary expansion. He was kind to Christina of Sweden, who returned to Rome after an absence of more than 2 years in her homeland. During his reign he canonized Mary Magdalene de'Pazzi and Peter of Alcantara, and declared Rose of Lima blessed.

Bibliography: Pastor 31:314–430. A. F. ARTAUD DE MONTOR, *The Lives and Times of the Popes,* 10 v. (New York 1910–11) 6:106–115. Brémond 4:241–242. N. J. ABERCROMBIE, *The Origins of Jansenism* (Oxford 1936). BullRom 17:512–839. G. SORANZO, EncCatt 3:1830–31. R. MOLS, DHGE 12:1297–1313, with bibliog. J. DE LA SERVIÈRE, DTC 3:86–94, with bibliog. R. CHALUMEAU, *Catholicisme* 2:1195. **Illustration credit:** The Metropolitan Museum of Art, gift of Archer M. Huntington, 1891.

[J. S. BRUSHER]

CLEMENT X, POPE

CLEMENT X, POPE, April 29, 1670 to July 22, 1676; b. Emilio Bonaventura Altieri, Rome, July 13, 1590. He came of a family of ancient Roman nobility. He obtained a doctorate in law in 1611 and worked for a time with John Baptist Pamfili (later Innocent X). At the urging of his elder brother, John Baptist, he became a cleric and in 1623 served as auditor to Lancellotti in the nunciature in Poland. On his return to Italy in 1627, Emilio replaced his brother as bishop of Camerino. Innocent X in 1644 appointed him nuncio to Naples, where his diplomatic acumen was tested during the revolution of Tommaso Aniello in 1647. In 1652 he returned to his see, and 2 years later by appointment of Alexander VII he became secretary of the Congregation of Bishops and Regulars and a consultor of the Inquisition. Clement IX made him superintendent of the Exchequer and, a month before his death, raised him to the cardinalate. In the next conclave, prolonged by a conflict of interests among the Spanish and French cardinals for more than 4 months, Emilio was elected at the age of 80. He adopted Cardinal Paluzzi degli Albertoni as cardinal nephew and entrusted him with administration to an excess that irritated Romans.

During his reign of 6 years, Clement brought order to papal finances, took great interest in agricultural conditions, assembled a special congregation for Polish affairs, and regulated by his decree of June 21, 1670, the relationship between bishops and religious orders.

Pope Clement X, statue by Ercole Ferrata (1610–1685) in St. Peter's Basilica, Rome.

He canonized Cajetan, Philip Benitius, Francis Borgia, Louis Bertrand, and Rose of Lima, and beatified Pius V, John of the Cross, and the martyrs of Gorkom in Holland. His most conspicuous foreign policies centered on resistance to *Louis XIV's demands on the *regale* (royal right to revenues of vacant sees), pressed by Cardinal César d'Estrees (*see* GALLICANISM), and his large financial aid to Poland in its struggle against Turkish invasion. He celebrated the Holy Year 1675 and is remembered in Rome for the erection of the Palazzo Altieri, the fountains in the piazza of St. Peter, and the statues on the bridge of Sant' Angelo.

Bibliography: Pastor 31:431–508. Seppelt v.5. J. DE LA SERVIÈRE, DTC 3:94–98. R. MOLS, DHGE 12:1313–26. G. HANOTAUX, *Recueil des Instructions Données aux Ambassadeurs et Ministres de France,* 3 v. (Paris 1888–). BullRom 18. **Illustration credit:** Alinari-Art Reference Bureau.

[S. V. RAMGE]

CLEMENT XI, POPE

Pontificate, Nov. 23, 1700, to March 19, 1721; b. Giovanni Francesco Albani, Urbino, Italy, July 23, 1649. Of a noble Umbrian family, he was educated at the Roman College, where he became so expert in the classics that he was admitted into the famed Academy of Queen Christina of Sweden. The study of theology and law followed, and at the age of 28 he became associated with the Papal Curia as governor of Rieti and, later, of the Sabine province, and Orvieto. In 1687 he was appointed secretary of briefs and in 1690 created cardinal deacon. He was ordained in September 1700. When more senior candidates in the conclave of 1700 proved unacceptable, Cardinal Albani, only 51 and

Pope Clement XI, portrait by the 18th-century Italian artist Carlo Maratta, now in the collection of the Villa Albani at Rome.

highly regarded by all for his virtuous life and his experience in government, was elected pope after 46 days of deliberation.

European Diplomacy. It was his misfortune to reign while the prestige of the papacy was diminishing in the political life of Europe. The chief European powers were at war during much of his pontificate. Neutrality was most difficult, since almost every decision Clement made in international affairs was challenged by one of the monarchs involved. Shortly after his election, he approved the selection of the French Philip of Anjou as king of Spain, but when the Austrians invaded the Papal States and threatened Rome in 1709, Clement was forced to favor the cause of the Austrian Hapsburg claimant to the Spanish throne. In the proceedings of the Treaty of Utrecht (1713), not only was the Pope ignored, but one of the papal dominions, Sicily, was transferred to Savoy. Similarly, the treaty opposed the Pope by granting the title of king of Prussia to the elector of Brandenburg and by discounting the claims of the son of James II to the English throne. On the other hand, Clement was successful in a project that gave him great consolation—the arousing of Spain and Austria to take defensive measures against the Turks.

Church-State Relations. No less complicated were Clement's problems in Church-State relations, with Spain after Philip V was rejected and with France during the closing years of Louis XIV's rule and the Regency period. Some historians have felt that the Pope lacked vigor and decisiveness in handling the major problems that confronted him. He seems to have been timorous by nature; he loved peace and harmony, and hence was slow to press for immediate solutions. He was, however, realistic enough to appreciate the fact that the power of the papacy was waning, and therefore persuasion and negotiation were more necessary. Thus he wrestled for years with the Jansenist-Gallican party in France and showed extraordinary patience with the highly controversial archbishop of Paris, Cardinal Louis de *Noailles. In condemnation of *Jansenism he issued the bulls *Vineam Domini* (1705) and *Unigenitus* (1713), the latter being a detailed study of the doctrine of the Jansenist Pasquier *Quesnel. *Unigenitus* proved to be a source of contention in France for the next 30 years, but eventually it was accepted as official policy in Church and State. Equally controversial was Clement's decision in the *Chinese rites controversy, when he curtailed the use of local Chinese customs in the Jesuit missions. The decision was reached after lengthy discussions in commissions and after long study by the Pope himself. Furthermore, the implementation of the new policy by his representatives in China lacked discretion and was the cause of severe tensions in the missions.

The foreign missions were close to Clement's heart, a mark of his burning desire to further the Church's interests. He encouraged especially missionary work in northern Germany and in the Philippine Islands, and he promoted new missionary colleges in Rome. His pastoral concern for the clergy and faithful was felt more directly in Rome and in the papal dominions. He encouraged bishops to reside in their sees and recommended to all the clergy the annual retreat, and in particular the Spiritual Exercises of St. Ignatius. His generosity to the poor was exemplary. And with all his administrative duties, he remained a scholar, striving always to enlarge the collections of the Vatican Library and to preserve the cultural treasures of Rome. Clement composed the Breviary Office in honor of St. Joseph. His letters, briefs, and homilies were collected and published by his nephew, Cardinal Annibale *Albani (2 v. Rome 1729).

Bibliography: Pastor v. 33. Fliche-Martin v. 19.1–2. L. NINA, *Le Finánze pontificie sotto Clemente XI* (Milan 1928). A. ALDOBRANDINI, *La guerra di successione di Spagna negli stati dell'Alta Italia dal 1702 al 1705 e la politica di Clemente XI dal carteggio di Mons* (Rome 1931). P. DALLA TORRE, EncCatt 3: 1832–33. A. CORNARO, LexThK[2] 2:1227–28. **Illustration credit:** Alinari-Art Reference Bureau.

[C. B. O'KEEFE]

CLEMENT XII, POPE

Pontificate July 12, 1730, to Feb. 6, 1740; b. Lorenzo Corsini, Florence, April 7, 1652. His family was influential in Florence for centuries and included in its record the 14th-century Bishop of Fiesole, St. *Andrew Corsini. After studies at the Roman College Lorenzo proceeded to the University of Pisa to study law. Upon the death of his father, he then gave up his rights of inheritance and entered the service of the Church, where his merit was recognized. Corsini became in turn titular bishop of Nicomedia (1691), nuncio to Vienna (1691), governor of the *Castel Sant' Angelo (1696), cardinal deacon of S. Susanna (1706), and later cardinal priest of S. Pietro in Vincoli and cardinal bishop of Frascati. Already as a cardinal, Corsini became known as a patron of art and scholarship. Corsini's long experience in church administration and his excellent life brought him to the papacy. At 79 he was experienced and wise, but he suffered much from gout and poor eyesight, which deteriorated to the point of blindness in 1732. In spite of his physical debility Clement proved to be a

Pope Clement XII, monument by the 18th-century sculptor Giovanni Battista Maini, basilica of St. John Lateran.

vigorous leader, showing good executive judgment in his choice of capable officials. He sentenced the venal Cardinal Niccolò Coscia, who had abused the confidence of his predecessor, Benedict XIII, to 10 years' imprisonment. Among the measures Clement took to improve the bad state of finances in the papal kingdom was the restoration of the state lottery, which had been suppressed by Benedict XIII. With the money brought in by his many financial measures Clement was able to spend considerable sums to alleviate the distress of areas afflicted by natural disaster, as well as carry out a building program that included the erection of the famous Fontana di Trevi and improvements of the venerable basilica of St. John Lateran. He also established a papal printing press.

His dealings with foreign powers were troubled. When Antonio Farnese, Duke of Parma and Piacenza, died in 1731 without a son, Don Carlos, son of King Philip V of Spain, claimed the duchies and took them over without regard for the Pope's suzerainty. Clement protested in vain and maintained an attitude of prudent neutrality in the war in which Don Carlos also drove the Austrians out of Sicily.

Clement continued the policy of his predecessors with regard to the Jansenists. He demanded full submission to Clement XI's bull **Unigenitus* (1713). In this matter he had the satisfaction of receiving the submission of the Benedictine Congregation of St. Maur (*see* MAURISTS). While Jansenism was dying, other movements were growing in this 4th decade of the 18th century. The Freemasons, who were making great progress throughout Europe, founded lodges in Italy during Clement's pontificate. In 1738 Clement condemned *Freemasonry and forbade Catholics to belong to Masonic lodges under pain of excommunication. In the bull *In Eminenti* the Pope expressed his reasons: the Freemasons are men of all sects and any religion, bound together by natural morality; this bond is secret with a secrecy bound by oath and enforced with exaggerated penalties.

Perhaps Clement's greatest glory was his unceasing interest in missionary activity. He began by helping missionary seminaries. He founded a seminary for training priests of the Greek rite at Ullano in southern Italy. He helped the Maronites of Lebanon by sending the distinguished Lebanese scholar and Vatican librarian, Joseph *Assemani, to preside over a national synod. He sent Franciscans to Abyssinia to work for the union of that kingdom with the Holy See. In the Far East he continued the policy of his predecessors in opposing the so-called Chinese and Malabar rites.

In the interests of justice, Clement overruled his representative at Ancona, the once powerful and famous minister of Spain, Cardinal Giulio *Alberoni, who in 1739 annexed the small republic of San Marino to the Papal States. Clement heeded the protests of the mountain folk and restored their freedom.

Bibliography: Pastor 34:301–510. A. F. ARTAUD DE MONTOR, *The Lives and Times of the Popes,* 10 v. (New York 1910–11) 6:246–268. BullRom v.23–24. P. DALLA TORRE, EncCatt 3:1833–34. J. DE LA SERVIÈRE, DTC 3.1:111–115. R. MOLS, DHGE 12: 1361–81, bibliog. R. CHALUMEAU, *Catholicisme* 2:1197. **Illustration credit:** Alinari-Art Reference Bureau.

[J. S. BRUSHER]

CLEMENT XIII, POPE

Pontificate, July 6, 1758, to Feb. 2, 1769; b. Carlo della Torre Rezzonico, Venice, March 7, 1693. His family, which originated at Como in central Italy, emigrated to Genoa and then to Venice (1640), where the family name was inscribed in the Golden Book of nobility (1687).

Ecclesiastical Career. Carlo was educated in humanities and philosophy at the Jesuit college at Bologna, and received his doctorate in theology and Canon Law at the University of Padua; in 1714 he entered the Accademia ecclesiastica at Rome to prepare for a career of diplomacy. Two years later he was ordained, began service as a prothonotary, and was immediately appointed by Clement XI as governor of Rieti, then as governor of Fano (1721). Benedict XIII called him to Rome (1725) as a member of the Consulta, and after 4 years selected him as an auditor of the Rota for Venice. His diligence in this office is reflected in the *Decisiones S. Rotae Romanae coram R. P. D. Carolo Rezzonico,* 3 v. (Rome 1759). He was created a cardinal deacon by Clement XII (Dec. 20, 1737) with the title of S. Niccolò in Carcere (changed to cardinal priest of S. Maria in Ara Coeli, then to S. Marco), and on March 11, 1743, he succeeded Pietro Ottoboni in the See of Padua; his consecration was performed by Benedict XIV in the church of the SS. Apostoli. His interest in the improvement of his clergy made his episcopate imitative of those of Charles Borromeo and Gregory Barbarigo. The latter, his predecessor in the bishopric of Padua (1667–97), was a relative through his mother, Vittoria Barbarigo; Gregory was beatified by Clement, Sept. 20, 1761. Rezzonico held a synod (1746) and spent large sums of his own wealth in enlarging and improving the seminary. At Padua he was regarded as *il santo,* and at Rome diplomatic agents wrote of his conscientiousness, candor, affability, benev-

Pope Clement XIII, by the 18th-century German artist Anton Raphael Mengs, oil on canvas, 52⅞ by 38 inches.

olence, and generosity, although some commented on his *talento mediocre.*

Papal Election. The conclave of 53 days that brought the tiara to Rezzonico opened on May 15, 1758, and became an electoral contest among the *Anziani* (elders), the imperialists, the supporters of the Bourbons, and the *Zelanti,* who sought a candidate who would bring vigor to the office. A deadlock resulting from the *exclusiva* used by the Bourbon party against Cardinal Cavalchini ended when Cardinal Spinelli, leader of the *Zelanti,* and the imperial Cardinal Roth of Constance proposed Rezzonico as a compromise candidate; his name was 14th on the list of those acceptable to Vienna. Surprised and humbled before the high office, Clement faced the problems inherited from his predecessor, Benedict XIV. One urgent problem was the anti-Romanism in the attitudes of the rulers of the states of Europe, which expressed itself in the *Febronianism of Johann Nikolaus von *Hontheim and the deism of the *Encyclopedists. Its particular expression, however, was the "family pact" of the Bourbon courts of France, Spain, Naples, and Parma to destroy the Jesuits, who were at a high point in their influence with 23,000 members, 800 residences, 700 colleges, and 270 missions.

The Jesuit Question. The extinction of the Jesuits became the *affaire célèbre* that harassed the new pontiff, who, inclined to timidity and indecision, relied upon his curial advisers: first, Cardinals Spinelli and the Secretary of State, Alberico Archinto, both inimical to the society, then Cardinal Luigi Torrigiani, successor to Archinto (1758) and a strong defender of the Jesuits. Clement's nephew, Carlo Rezzonico, created a cardinal, Oct. 2, 1758, had neither skill nor interest in diplomacy.

Portugal. The reign of Joseph I (1750–77) was dominated by his chief minister, Sebastião José de Carvalho e Mello, Marquis of *Pombal, who saw the Jesuits as an obstacle to his plans for strengthening the monarchy and exploiting the colonies. Under Benedict XIV he had accused them of opposing the Hispano-Portuguese Treaty (Jan. 8, 1750) that partitioned Paraguay, of organizing the natives for rebellion, and of practicing illicit trade (including slaves) at Maranhão and Gran Pará. On Sept. 20, 1757, he dismissed Jesuit confessors from court and obtained from Benedict the appointment of Cardinal Francesco Saldanha as visitor of Jesuit houses. When the King was wounded by gunshot (Sept. 3, 1758) while returning with his valet, Texeiras, from the house of the Marchioness Teresa da Távora, the Jesuits were included in accusations made at the trial proceedings that sent José Mascarenhas, Duke of Aviero, the Marquis da Távora, and members of his family and household to a cruel execution for treason and regicide (Jan. 12, 1759). By royal edict (Jan. 19) Jesuits were confined to their houses, their property declared confiscated, and a list of their transgressions in the colonies (*Relacão abreviada*) was sent to Rome and circulated. Clement's brief of August 18, appealing for canonical procedures in the handling of the Jesuits, and his two subsequent letters were rejected as "unauthorized." On September 17 the deportation of approximately 1,100 Jesuits to Civitavecchia began; there they found refuge and kindness from the Pope. Two hundred and fifty other Jesuits (superiors and foreigners) were imprisoned in the subterranean dungeons of São Juliao, São Jorge, and Belem until the death of Joseph (1777), when 60 survivors were freed. Diplomatic relations were severed when the papal nuncio Filippo *Acciaioli was expelled, and the Portuguese ambassador Almada was recalled from Rome (July 7, 1760). The break was made more dramatic when the Jesuit Gabriel *Malagrida, already indicted in the Távora trial, was declared a heretic by the Inquisition, strangled, and burned in a solemn auto-da-fé (Sept. 21, 1761); Clement regarded him as a martyr.

France. The unwise speculation of the procurator of the mission of Martinique, Antoine de La Valette (1709–67), brought the Jesuits of the Paris province to bankruptcy and also to the attention of Parlement, which in May, 1761, examined the constitutions of the society, and advocated a vicar-general for the Jesuits of France, appointed by the Crown and independent of the generalate in Rome. The Parlement also compiled the *Extraits des assertions dangereuses et pernicieuses,* where passages from Jesuit writings, often quoted with inaccuracy or invented, were used to prove the society a menace to the state. Louis XV, at the behest of Clement, consulted the Assembly of the French Clergy (December 1761): 45 bishops against 6 approved the constitutions as they were; of the others, the Jansenist bishop FitzJames of Soissons asked for the suppression of the Jesuits; 27 absent bishops voted favorably on the constitutions. The King, fearful of Parlement and influenced by his mistress, Mme. de Pompadour, and her adviser, Étienne François de *Choiseul, ignored the votes of the bishops and petitioned Rome for a special vicar-general, but was refused. On this occasion Clement remarked to Lorenzo *Ricci, the Jesuit general, "Sint ut sunt aut non sint" (Let them be as they are or not be). His appeal to the King was without effect, and in a final *arrêt* of the Paris Parlement (Aug. 6, 1762), the society was suppressed and declared "nonexistent" by Louis in November 1764. In protest Clement wrote a solemn bull, *Apostolicum pascendi munus* (Jan. 9, 1765), restating papal approval of the Jesuits, praising their achievements, and declaring this affront to the society to be equally an affront to the Church.

Spain, Naples, and Parma. Charles III (1759–88), regarded as an enlightened despot and the greatest of the Spanish Bourbons, was at first apparently friendly to the Jesuits, though surrounded by ministers who sought their destruction. Among these ministers were the Irishman Richard Wall, Minister of Foreign Affairs; his successor, Marqués de Grimaldi (1763); Manuel de Roda y Arrieta, Minister of Justice; Pedro Campomanés, fiscal; Count Pedro Pablo Aranda, president of the Council of Castile; and José Moniño (Count Florida Blanca), ambassador to Rome. Moreover Charles still received the advice of Bernardo *Tanucci, who had been his chief minister when he was King of Naples (1738–59), and now served his son, King Ferdinand IV. The queen mother, Elizabeth Farnese, stayed their influence on the King, but after her death (July 10, 1766) Charles was led to accept the Jesuits as the authors of pamphlets urging insurrection, as conspirators for his deposition on the grounds of illegitimate birth, and as the principal opponents to the canonization of Ven. Juan de *Palafox y Mendoza, Bishop of Mexico (d. 1659), whose cause Charles favored. In a session of the Extraordinary Council of Jan. 29, 1767, the Jesuits were declared instigators of rebellion and by a royal decree (February 27) were banished from Spain and its colonies. In a letter to Clement (March 31) Charles announced that the reasons for his action were locked in the royal breast; Clement's reply urging clemency and justice was unheeded. On the night of April 2–3 Jesuits were expelled from their houses and hustled into ships to sail to Civitavecchia; their property was voided to the state, and a yearly pension of 100 pesetas, to be forfeited upon leaving the Papal States, was promised to each member of the society. Because of the diplomatic indignity of this act and the impossibility of settling so great a number of exiles (5,100 Jesuits would converge from the ports of Spain; 2,600 of all nationalities from the colonies), the Pope's officials refused their embarkation. Under Joseph *Pignatelli's leadership, the Jesuits settled in Corsica until 1768 when they were received into the Papal States and the cities of northern Italy.

Charles's edict was duplicated in the other countries controlled by the Spanish Bourbons. In the name of the young King Ferdinand IV of Naples (1759–1825) the regent Tanucci forbade the reading of the *Apostolicum pascendi munus,* and on Feb. 8, 1768, issued the decree of expulsion; 1,400 Jesuits were marched over the frontier into the Papal States. Pinto de Fonseca, Grandmaster of the Knights of Malta, a feudatory of Naples, expelled 20 Jesuits from the island, April 23, 1768. On Jan. 16, 1768, François du Tillot, Marquis of Fellino and chief minister of Duke Ferdinand of Parma, Piacenza, and Guastalla (1765–1802), ordered a commission to investigate monastic charters. Clement, as traditional suzerain of the Duchy of Parma, protested in a brief known as the *Monitorium,* which was rejected, and on February 8 in retaliation 170 Jesuits were exiled. The Bourbon courts supported Parma; France occupied Avignon and Venaissin; Naples invaded Pontecorvo and Benevento. The crisis reached its summit when in January of the next year the ambassadors of France, Spain, and Naples placed a formal demand for the suppression of the society. To forestall action, Clement called a special consistory to decide the fate of the Jesuits, but the day before its scheduled meeting (February 3), an apoplectic stroke ended his trials.

Pastor and Patron. The pastoral interest that won him praise as bishop of Padua marked his government of Rome and the Papal States. During the great drought of 1763 and 1764 Clement instituted a *monte dell' abbondanza,* bought grain and oil, and built shelters for the thousands who crowded into Rome; he also attempted to drain the Pontine marshes, but was unsuccessful (1762). In his name the Holy Office condemned the *Histoire du peuple de Dieu . . .* by the Jesuit Isaac Joseph Berruyer (Dec. 2, 1758), *Encyclopédie* by Denis *Diderot et al. (Sept. 3, 1759), *De l'Esprit* by Claude Adrien Helvétius (Jan. 31, 1759; in that year it was condemned also by the Sorbonne and publicly burned), *Exposition de la doctrine chrétienne . . .* by François Philippe Mésenguy (1677–1763), called the "Second Quesnel" (June 14, 1761), *Emile ou Traité de l'Éducation* by Jean Jacques *Rousseau (Sept. 9, 1762; condemned also by Parlement), and *De statu ecclesiae et legitima potestate Romani pontificis* by Febronius (Feb. 27, 1764).

Arts and scholarship were favored during this pontificate. The completion of the Villa Albani was entrusted to Niccolò Savi (1763), and of the Fontana di Trevi to Giuseppe Pannini (1762). The painters Anton Raphael Mengs (1728–79) and Giovanni *Piranesi received Clement's patronage, although they shared the dismay of artists when Clement ordered coverings for the "indecent" statues of antiquity in the Villa Albani and Vatican and commissioned Stefano Pozzi to paint over the nudities of the frescoes in the Sistine Chapel. St. Paul's-Outside-the-Walls, the Quirinal Palace, and the Castel Gandolfo were adorned. The *Vatican Library was enriched with Oriental MSS, many formerly owned by the Assemani; the *Illyricum sacrum,* 8 v. (1751–90) by Daniele *Farlati, SJ, and the *Inscriptiones romanae infimi aevi* of Pier Luigi Galletti, OSB, 3 v. (1760) had his support; and Giuseppe *Garampi, prefect of the Archives, was sent twice (1761, 1764) to Germany on diplomatic missions and was appointed secretary of the ciphers (1766).

Clement advanced the devotion to the Sacred Heart by granting a Mass and Office for Poland, as requested by King Augustus III, and for the Archconfraternity of the Sacred Heart in Rome (Jan. 26, 1765). The Immaculate Conception was declared the principal patronal feast for Spain (Nov. 8, 1760) and the title "mater immaculata" was added to the litanies; the Preface of the Trinity was ordered for all Sunday Masses. On the anniversary of his coronation (Aug. 16, 1767) Clement canonized *Joseph Calasanctius, *Joseph Cupertino, Jerome *Emiliani, Jane Frances de *Chantal, *John Cantius, and *Serafino of Ascoli. He beatified the Trinitarian Simon de Rojas (May 19, 1766) and the Capuchin *Bernard of Corleone (April 29, 1768), and declared many venerable.

Bibliography: BullRomCon, v.3. G. X. DE RAVIGNAN, *Clément XIII et Clément XIV* (2d ed. Paris 1856). Pastor 36, 37. J. SARRAILH, *L'Espagne éclairée de la seconde moitié du XVIIIe siècle* (Paris 1954). F. ROUSSEAU, *Le Règne de Charles III d'Espagne, 1759–1788,* 2 v. (Paris 1907). A. FERRER DEL RÍO, *Historia del reinado de Carlos III en España,* 4 v. (Madrid 1856). M. DANVILA Y COLLADO, *Reinado de Carlos III,* 6 v. (Madrid 1890–96). J. L. D'AZEVEDO, *O Marquêz de Pombal e a sua época* (2d ed. Lisbon 1922). O. BUSCH, "Pombal und die Jesuiten," StimZeit 164 (1958–59) 466–470. M. CHEKE, *Dictator of Portugal: A Life of the Marquis of Pombal, 1699–1782* (London 1938); *The Cardinal de Bernis* (New York 1959). L. DOLLOT, *Bernis et Choiseul* (Paris 1941). S. J. DE CARVALHO E MELLO, *Pombal, Choiseul et d'Aranda: L'Intrigue des trois cabinets* (Paris 1830). C. LO SORDO, *Tanucci e la Reggenza al tempo di Ferdinando IV* (Bari 1912). S. F. SMITH, "The Suppression of the Society of Jesus," *Month* 99 (1902) 113–130, 346–368, 497–517, 626–650; 100 (1902) 20–34, 126–152, 258–273. E. ROTA, *Le origini del Risorgimento, 1700–1800,* 2 v. (2d ed. Milan 1948). E. DAMMIG, *Il movimento giansenista a Roma nella seconda metà del secolo XVIII* (StTest 119; 1945). Koch JesLex 991–993. R. MOLS, DHGE 12:1381–1410, bibliog. J. DE LA SERVIÈRE, DTC 3.1:115–124. H. RAAB, LexThK[2] 2:1229. I. DANIELE, EncCatt 3:1834–36.
Illustration credit: Samuel H. Kress Collection, Isaac Delgado Museum of Art, New Orleans, La.

[E. D. MC SHANE]

CLEMENT XIV, POPE

Pontificate, May 19, 1769, to Sept. 22, 1774; b. Giovanni Vincenzo Antonio Ganganelli, at Sant' Arcangelo, near Rimini (Legation of Ravenna), Oct. 31, 1705. His father, Lorenzo, was a surgeon; his mother, Angela Serafina, was a descendant of the distinguished family of Mazza in Pesaro. After his education with the Jesuits at Rimini and the Piarists at Urbino, Ganganelli entered the novitiate of the Conventual Franciscans at Mondaino (May 1723), taking Lorenzo as his name in religion; he was solemnly professed on May 18, 1724. At the completion of his studies at the College of St. Bonaventure in Rome, he received a doctorate in theology (1731) and taught philosophy and theology at the convents of Ascoli, Milan, and Bologna. In May 1740 he was appointed rector of St. Bonaventure's through the recommendation of a Jesuit to Cardinal Annibale Albani, patron of the college. At Milan he printed a theological defense (*Diatriba theologica,* 1743) with a dedication to St. Ignatius of Loyola and a foreword of praise for the Society of Jesus. He was chosen first consultor of the Holy Office (1746), and twice (1753, 1759) refused the nomination to the generalship of his order. On Sept. 24, 1759, Clement XIII created him a cardinal with the title of S. Lorenzo in Panisperna (later changed to SS. Apostoli), calling him a Jesuit in the clothes of a Franciscan. It has been claimed that he was recommended to Clement either by Lorenzo Ricci, the Jesuit general, because of his avowed esteem for Jesuits, or by Cardinal Giuseppe Spinelli because of Ganganelli's concealed dislike for "Gesuitismo." Throughout the 9 years before his elevation to the papacy, Ganganelli's manner was devout, frugal, unostentatious, and impenetrable. A reserve and fear of being influenced in his judgments made him usually reluctant to declare his mind. By some diplomats this was regarded as a sign of astuteness and keen wit, by others, as a mark of insincerity and deceit, e.g., Bernardo *Tanucci, who remarked that Ganganelli rode keeping his feet in two stirrups ("tiene li piede sulle due staffe"). That he was already veering toward the Bourbon courts appears in his opposition to the pro-Jesuit policies of the papal secretary of state Cardinal Luigi Torrigiani; in his defense of the Bourbon Duke Ferdinand of Parma's stand against the *Monitorium* of Clement XIII (1768); and in his intimacy with Manuel de Roda y Arrieta, the anti-Jesuit Spanish minister.

The Conclave of 1769. The conciliation of Portugal, 9 years in virtual schism, and of the Bourbon courts of France, Spain, Naples, and Parma, who had demanded the suppression of the Jesuits at the end of the reign of Clement XIII, was the issue of this conclave, which opened solemnly on February 15. The 43 electors split into three parties: the *Zelanti,* pro-Jesuit and advocating a strong stand against the Powers; the Crown Cardinals, seeing the peace of the Church possible only through the sacrifice of the Jesuits; and the Indifferents or Undeclared. The requirements of strict secrecy and seclusion set down in the bulls of Julius II (*Cum tam divino,* Jan. 14, 1505), Pius IV (*In eligendis,* Oct. 9, 1562), Gregory XV (*Aeterni Patris,* Nov. 15, 1621), and Clement XII (*Apostolatus officium,* Oct. 5, 1732) were transgressed. Cardinals François de *Bernis, Paul d'Albert Lynes, and Domenico Orsini d'Aragona were in open and frequent communication with the French ambassador Marquis d'Aubeterre and the Spanish ambassador Abp. Thomas Azpuru. They were instructed to use the *exclusiva* against all "unenlightened" candidates. In a list sent to the courts, the cardinals were divided into classes and judged as very good, good, bad, and very bad. Ganganelli, the only regular cleric in the conclave, was placed in the first class, and rated "good" (Spain), "very good" (Choiseul), and "there are letters which say he is a Jesuit" (Tanucci). In the conclave Ganganelli "trimmed his sails to the wind" on the question of the Jesuits. On one occasion he remarked that there should be no more thought of abolishing the Society of Jesus "than of overturning St. Peter's." Yet when asked his opinion on its possible suppression he said that if the precepts of Canon Law were observed, it was possible, even profitable. The idea of a written or oral promise to suppress the society as a condition for election was proposed by D'Aubeterre and Azpuru, and again by the Spanish Cardinal Francisco de Solis when he arrived at the conclave (April 27), but it was rejected. The claim that Ganganelli made such a simoniacal bargain is unproved and held by no historian except Crétineau-Joly. When the crown candidate, Antonio Sersale, Archbishop of Naples, failed to win the support of the *Zelanti,* attention moved to Ganganelli, who was elected with only one opposing vote (his own, which was cast for Cardinal Carlo Rezzonico) on May 19. The Bourbons rejoiced; Charles III of Spain called the election a miracle worked by St. Francis and Ven. Juan de *Palafox y Mendoza.

Peace by Concession. The inscription on the first medal struck by Clement, *Fiat pax in virtute tua,* revealed his eagerness to come to terms with secular powers. To the "exemplary Catholic Charles III," he wrote (Nov. 30, 1769) an acknowledgment of his indebtedness and devotion and promised that there would be "shortly a plan for the complete dissolution of the society." He also appointed the former nuncio to Madrid, Opizio Pallavicini, to be his secretary of state, and reintroduced the process of beatification for Juan de Palafox. A settlement with Portugal came with the appointment (Nov. 26, 1769) of a nuncio, Innocenzo Conti, pleasing to the Marquis of *Pombal; a red hat for Pombal's brother, Paulo de Carvalho e Mendoza, who died (Jan. 17, 1770) 3 days before the announcement of this honor (Clement gave it to another of the minister's favorites, João Cosme da Cunha, Bishop of Evora); and the confirmation of eight of Pombal's episcopal nominations. The reading of the bull *In coena Domini* (so called because from 1364 it was published annually at Rome on Maundy Thursday, and cited reserved censures), which had been used by Clement XIII to announce the excommunication of Duke Ferdinand of Parma (1768), was omitted in 1770, and dropped completely after 1774. He further pleased the Duke by granting a dispensation for his marriage to his cousin Amelia, daughter of Empress Maria Theresa. In a letter to Louis XV, written in French, Clement promised that the Jesuit matter would be terminated "avec satisfaction reciproque" (October 1769).

Suppression of the Jesuits. Clement delayed decisive action regarding the Jesuits for 4 years. He met the formal petition for their extinction, made by the courts of Portugal, Spain, and France (July 22, 1769) with alternative proposals such as a complete reform of the society, or its gradual dissolution by allowing no election of a general after the death of Lorenzo *Ricci, but he finally yielded before the unrelenting harassment of Cardinal de Bernis and José Moniño, who succeeded Azpuru as Spanish ambassador (July 4, 1772). As preliminary steps, documents were gathered for a motu proprio, and a program to diminish the prestige of the Jesuits in Rome and the Papal States was begun. Bishops were advised to withhold their permission to preach or hear confessions; Jesuits were removed from their colleges in Frascati, Macerata, Modena, Bologna, Ferrara, Ravenna; a visitation of the Irish College and the Roman Seminary was entrusted to Cardinal Marefoschi, of the Jesuit houses in Bologna to Cardinal Malvezzi; Jesuit exiles from Portugal were deprived of the pensions granted by Clement XIII. On December 13, after renewed threats of schism and attempts to bribe his only confidant, the Conventual friar Bontempi, the Pope appointed Francesco Saverio Zelada, titular bishop of Petra, to collaborate with Moniño in the preparation of the brief of suppression. The resulting document, *Dominus ac Redemptor,* was signed by Clement on June 9, 1773 (though dated July 21). Already more than half of the members of the society were exiled; this brief extinguished the remaining 11,000 Jesuits, 266 colleges, 103 seminaries, and 88 residences. On September 23, Ricci was imprisoned for questioning in the Castel Sant'Angelo together with his assistants of Spain, Italy, Portugal, Germany, and Poland.

The Brief "Dominus ac Redemptor." The reception of this brief was varied. Festivities were ordered in Lisbon, but there was disappointment in France and Spain that the document was not a solemn bull. Maria Theresa accepted it regretfully and allowed Jesuits to remain in their houses as secular priests; Frederick II of Prussia and Catherine II of Russia forbade its promulgation, thereby insuring the survival of the society. At the end of the pontificate of Clement XIII, the territories of Avignon and Venaissin had been taken by the French, and Pontecorvo and Benevento invaded by Naples; these were now returned to papal jurisdiction.

In the brief, Clement proclaims his duty in the interest of peace to sacrifice things most dear to himself. Just as past pontiffs had suppressed the Templars (1312), the Humiliati (1571), the Reformed Conventuals (1626), the Order of SS. Ambrose and Barnabas (1643), the Order of St. Basil of Armenia (1650), and the Jesuati (1668), so he had examined the Society of Jesus and found that at its birth seeds of strife and jealousy germinated within it, and against other orders, the secular clergy, and princes. Since it could no longer be fruitful or useful and hindered the peace of the Church, he, for the reasons given, and for others "reserved in our heart," dissolved, suppressed, extinguished, and abolished the said society. The members "whom We love with a paternal love" were thus free from the weight of oppression. Novices were to be released; scholastics were permitted to remain in their houses for a year, and being liberated from their vows might embrace a new state of life; priests might enter other religious orders or place themselves under the jurisdiction of a bishop. All appeals or attempts to defend the society were prohibited. It is to be noted that the brief does not condemn the constitutions of the order, nor any specified member, nor the orthodoxy of any Jesuit doctrine (BullRomCon 4:619–629). According to a letter of June 29, 1774, Clement retracted *Dominus ac Redemptor* and instructed his confessor to transmit it to the next pope (Pius VI). The letter is found in P. P. Wolf, *Allgemeine Geschichte der Jesuiten . . .*, 4 v. (Zurich 1789–92) v.3, but its authenticity is still disputed.

Other Affairs. During the long struggle over the Jesuit question, Clement received Marc Simeon, Patriarch of the Nestorians, and six of his bishops into union with Rome (1771); condemned Abbé Jean Martin de Prades's abridgment of Claude Fleury's *Histoire ecclesiastique* (March 1, 1770), the philosophical works of Julien Offray de La Mettrie (Feb. 15, 1770), and some lesser works of Voltaire (Nov. 29, 1771); favored the Carmel of Saint-Denis after it received Louise of France (Thérèse de Saint Augustin), daughter of Louis XV (1770); and brought new hope for Catholic emancipation in England by abandoning the support of the exiled Stuarts and negotiating with William Henry, Duke of Gloucester, brother of King George III, for the appointment of Giovanni Battista Caprara as papal nuncio (1772). He patronized the arts and letters by commissioning Raphael Mengs to decorate the Vatican Museum, by acquiring antiquities for the Museo Clementino, by increasing the papal coin collection, by encouraging literati, and by decorating the 14-year-old prodigy Mozart with the order of the Golden Spur (1770). Clement canonized no one, but he beatified Francesco Caracciolo (June 4, 1769) and Paolo Burali of Arezzo (May 13, 1772); he confirmed the cultus (not solemn beatification) of Antonio Primaldi and his 840 companions executed at the capture of Otranto by the Ottomans (1480), of Tommaso Bellaci (d. 1447), of Bonaventura of Potenza (d. 1711), of Giuliana Puricelli (of Busto Arsizio, d. 1501), of Bernhard von Baden (d. 1458), of Giovanni Scopelli (of Reggio Emelia, d. *c.* 1491), and of Giovanni Bottegoni (of Bastone, d. 1240); and he declared the heroicity of the virtues of the Oratorians Giovanni Battista Villani and Antonio Grassi, of John of St. William, of Charles of Sezze, and of Pedro de Betancur, founder of the Bethlehemites of Guatemala. Clement had a deep regard for St. Paul of the Cross and reconfirmed the rule of the Passionists in *Supremi apostolatus* (Nov. 15, 1769) and approved the rule of the Passionist nuns (Feb. 9, 1771).

The last year of Clement's life was one of depression, fear of assassination, and torment caused by a scorbutic skin ailment. After his death the rapid decomposition of the body, which required that the face be covered with a mask for the solemn exequies at St. Peter's, fortified rumors of poison. An autopsy by Clement's physicians, Natale Saliceti and Pasquale Adinolfi, indicated death from natural causes; more recent medical interpretations of their reports ascribe death to edema and possible gastric carcinoma.

Clement's policy of appeasement and his ambiguous behavior have brought a generally adverse judgment to his pontificate and little praise to himself. In Pastor's *Lives* (published posthumously) he is called "one of the weakest and most unhappy of the long line of popes, and yet one most deserving of sympathy, for though filled with the best intentions he failed in almost everything, being quite unfitted to deal with the extraordinarily difficult situation" (38:550; for the debate over this volume, see bibliog.).

Bibliography: BullRomCon v.4. *Clementis XIV . . . epistolae et brevia selectiora . . .*, ed. A. THEINER (Paris 1852). *Lettere interesanti del pontefice Clemente XIV Ganganelli*, ed. L. A. CARACCIOLI, 5 v. (Venice 1776–79), Fr. tr., 2 v. (Paris 1776), interpolated and untrustworthy; Eng. tr., 2 v. (London 1777). *Lettere, bolle e discorsi di Ganganelli*, ed. C. FREDIANI (Florence 1845). G. C. CORDARA, *De suis ac suorum rebus . . . usque ad occasum Societatis Jesu commentarii . . .*, ed. G. ALBERTOTTI and A. FAGGIOTTO (Miscellanea di storia italiana, ser. 3, v.22; Turin 1933); *De suppressione Societatis Jesu commentarii*, ed. G. ALBERTOTTI (Padua 1925), extracts and comments in J. J. I. VON DÖLLINGER, *Beiträge zur politischen, kirchlichen und Kultur-Geschichte der 6 letzten Jahrhunderte*, 3 v. (Regensburg 1862–82) 3:1–74. J. CRÉTINEAU-JOLY, *Clément XIV et les Jésuites* (Paris 1847); *Le Pape Clément XIV: Lettre au Père Augustin Theiner* (Paris 1853). A. THEINER, *Geschichte des Pontificats Clemens XIV*, 2 v. (Leipzig-Paris 1853), favorable to Clement. I. DE RÉCALDE, *Le Bref "Dominus ac Redemptor"* (Paris 1920), hostile to Jesuits. F. MASSON, *Le Cardinal de Bernis depuis son ministère, 1758–1794* (Paris 1884). S. F. SMITH, "The Suppression of the Society of Jesus," *Month* 100 (1902) 517–536, 581–591; 101 (1903) 48–61, 179–197, 259–277, 383–403, 498–516, 604–623; 102 (1903) 46–63, 170–184. F. BERTOLINI, *Clemente XIV e la soppressione dei gesuiti* (Rome 1886). A. GALLASSI, "La malattia e morte di Clemente XIV," *Revista di storia delle scienze* 48 (1950) 153–165. L. GUALINO, *Storia medica dei romani pontefici* (Turin 1934) 69–97, 109–113. A. VON REUMONT, *Ganganelli, Papst Clement XIV, seine Briefe und seine Zeit* (Berlin 1847). P. DUDON, "De la suppression de la Compagnie de Jésus, 1758–1773," RevQuestHist 132 (1938) 75–107. Pastor v.38. For dispute between the Conventual Franciscans and the Jesuits over the documents used by Pastor, see L. CICCHITTO, "Il Pontefice Clemente XIV . . . della *Storia dei Papi* di L. von Pastor," *Miscellanea Francescana* 34 (1934) 198–231. P. LETURIA, "Ancora intorno al 'Clemente XIV' del Barone von Pastor," CivCatt (Nov. 3, 1934) 225–240. E. ROSA, "Intorno al Pontificato di Clemente XIV . . .," CivCatt (Jan. 5, 1935) 17–35. G. KRATZ and P. LETURIA, *Intorno al "Clemente XIV" del Barone von Pastor* (Rome 1935). E. PRÉCLIN, DHGE 12:1411–23. H. RAAB, LexThK[2] 2:1229–30. P. PASCHINI, EncCatt 3:1836–41. R. CHALUMEAU, *Catholicisme* 2:1199–1200. Koch JesLex 994–996. S. SOLERO, Mercati-Pelzer DE 1:649–650. J. DE LA SERVIÈRE, DTC 3.1:124–134.

[E. D. MC SHANE]

CLEMENT OF ALEXANDRIA

Titus Flavius Clemens, 3d-century Father of the Church, after *Origen, the principal representative of the early theological School of *Alexandria.

Life. Of the two traditions for Clement's birthplace extant in Epiphanius's time, modern authors prefer Athens, even though Clement spent most of his life in Alexandria. Clement, a convert to Christianity, traveled extensively to seek instruction from famous Christian teachers, until he came to Egypt. There he attached himself to one whom Eusebius (*Hist. eccl.* 5.11.2) assumed to be *Pantaenus, the earliest of the Alexandrian teachers known to us and one of Origen's masters.

Eusebius (*Hist. eccl.* 6.6) asserts that Clement succeeded Pantaenus as head of the catechetical School of Alexandria, and places Origen among Clement's disciples. But modern historians offer serious objections to these assertions. As J. Munck observes, the Christian instruction given by Clement probably never had an official character, but remained a private enterprise, in keeping with the pedagogic practice of other philosophers in those days. Such institutions ended when their founders ceased teaching. The fact that Origen never cites Clement in his writings is a reason for doubting that he had studied under Clement, despite their obvious intellectual affinity.

Clement's activities in Alexandria were interrupted by the persecution of Septimius Severus in 202 or 203, and he left Egypt apparently never to return. About 211 Alexander, Bishop of Cappadocia, sent a priest named Clement with a letter to the Church of Antioch: "I am sending you, my lords and brothers, this letter through the intermediary of Clement, the blessed priest, an esteemed and virtuous man whom you already know. His presence here, through the providence and vigilance of the Master, has strengthened and enhanced the Church of the Lord" (Eusebius, *Hist. eccl.* 6.11.6). It is possible that this refers to Clement of Alexandria, for Bishop Alexander was his friend and admirer, and Clement had dedicated one of his works to him (*Hist. eccl.* 6.13.3). In a letter addressed to Origen in 215 or 216, the same Alexander, having meanwhile become bishop of Jerusalem, mentions some deceased teachers, including Pantaenus and "holy Clement who has been my master and has helped me," thus giving rise to the conjecture that Clement had taken refuge in Cappadocia and that he was dead by the time Alexander wrote to Origen.

Eusebius is apparently relying on the letter from Alexander to the Church at Antioch when he designates Clement as a priest in his *Chronicle* (ed. Helm, GCS 24.211.1), but a passage in the *Paedagogus* (1.6.37) often cited to prove Clement's priesthood can no longer be advanced after O. Stählin's textual correction (GSC 12.112.17).

Writings. Clement was a cultured Greek philosopher and scholar, though his erudition was often secondhand; a Christian apologist and exegete; a theologian and mystic. His open mind and enthusiasm are reflected in a varied literary output, original and daring in content, refined and elegant in style. The absence of method and synthesis in his work was often calculated, but it disconcerts the modern reader.

Protrepticus, following the meaning of the word, is an "exhortation" to conversion and an apology for Christianity, addressed to pagans. The work reveals close links with the earlier Christian apologetic, whose terms and types of argument Clement uses, but with a personal touch and uncommon warmth. Clement criticizes Greek religion (he supplies valuable details on the "mysteries") and Greek philosophical doctrines about God (ch. 2–5). He maintains that the best philosophers and poets of old had caught glimpses of the truth (ch. 6–7); but this truth is revealed through the Hebrew prophets and above all by the Logos, who calls men to faith and conversion, and whose role in the world Clement extols in remarkable language (ch. 8–12).

Paedagogus, a sequel to the *Protrepticus,* is addressed to the baptized. Clement portrays Christ the Educator as He trains the Christian in a moral way of life. Book 1 presents the pedagogy of the Word and introduces the reader to a thoroughly evangelical spirituality that stamps the ethics of Clement with a truly Christian character. Books 2 and 3 form a treatise on practical morality, and describe in detail the Christians' daily life, mixing together moral precepts and rules of decency and hygiene. This combination of Christian casuistry and etiquette parallels Stoic literature and employs long excerpts borrowed from Musonius, the teacher of *Epictetus. The Stoic influence gives a highly rational character to Clement's presentation of morality: man must follow "nature" or "reason" (*logos*), which for Clement meant at the same time following the divine Logos.

After the "exhortation" to conversion and moral "pedagogy" at the outset of the *Paedagogus,* Clement calls attention to a third stage in the action of the Logos: doctrinal instruction. Historians debate whether Clement had contemplated a trilogy that would add a dogmatic work to the *Protrepticus* and *Paedagogus* and whether the *Stromata* should be considered an imperfect attempt in this direction.

Stromata (tapestries—a term used for a work of very free composition comparable to an anthology or miscellany), in eight books, is the most important of Clement's extant writings, and is a veritable mine of ideas, but it defies analysis. The absence of a plan and the deliberate obscurity of style make for difficult reading. Certain principal themes dominate the whole: the relations between Christianity and *Hellenism, and between faith and philosophy; the elaboration of a Christian gnosis to confront the "false gnosis"; and the search for ways to know God and achieve union with Him. The only definite chronological indication is that Book 1 was written after the death of the Emperor Commodus in 192 (cf. *Strom.* 1.21.139–147).

Quis dives salvetur? (What rich man will be saved?), a homily, is a delicately expressive commentary on Mk 10.17–31. *Eclogae Propheticae,* exegetical notes, and the *Excerpta ex Theodoto,* annotated extracts from Gnostic writings, are collections of materials assembled by Clement in preparation for further work. Of other writings only fragments survive, especially in the case of the *Hypotyposes,* a long exegetical work on the Old and New Testaments.

Doctrine. In his *Stromata* Clement deals extensively with the problem of the relation of Christianity to Greek culture and philosophy. In Christian thought he opened an optimistic and liberal approach to secular knowledge, laying the foundations for a Christian humanism and introducing philosophy to its role as "the servant of theology." He considered Plato the best of philosophers (1.42.1); but far from being a confirmed Platonist, Clement exemplifies the eclecticism of his time. If Platonism serves to clarify his conception of man's union with God, it is Stoicism that permeates his ethic. He admits that by philosophy he means "what each of the different schools has said that is good" (1.37.6). As such, philosophy is a gift of God (1.37.1); it is partial but nonetheless real truth (6.83.2). It forms a propaedeutic to faith for the unbeliever (1.28.1; 7.20.2; cf. 1.28.3), a useful exercise for the believer (1.20.2), and a necessary aid to a deeper scientific penetration of the faith (1.35.2). Still, faith can spring up in a soul and lead it to salvation without philosophy (*ibid.* 2 and 4).

Clement affirms the autonomy and transcendence of faith and Christian truth. On occasion he goes back to the less fortunate themes of the older Christian apologetic, which claimed that the truths known by the pagan philosophers had been "stolen" by lesser angels or borrowed from the Bible, and thus he insists on the "barbarian" origin of Greek philosophy (1.66–1.81; 148).

The influence of Greek philosophy contributed greatly to the intellectualist tendency of Clement's ethic and spirituality, and to his desire to fashion an authentically Christian gnosis. Knowledge and contemplation are in the foreground of the spiritual life: the perfect Christian is a gnostic. But Clement dissociates himself sharply from unorthodox *Gnosticism. Every Christian is, in a real sense, perfect from the moment of his Baptism (*Paed.* 1.25–31). Gnosis is not in conflict with faith, but is faith's perfection and flowering: "Gnosis is faithful, and faith is gnostic" (*Strom.* 2.16.2; cf. 5.1.3). "Faith, to all intents and purposes, is a condensed gnosis of essential truths, but gnosis is the strong and solid demonstration of the truths accepted by faith . . . leading to an unshakable certainty and a scientific understanding" (*ibid.* 7.57.3). In opposition to the Gnostics, and while clearly underlining the role and necessity of grace (*ibid.* 2.5.4–5; 3.57.2), Clement insists that free choice is a condition of salvation (*ibid.* 2.115.2). Likewise the Platonic dualism that crops up sometimes in his spirituality does not prevent him from defending the essential goodness of the body, worldly goods, and marriage.

On the other hand, Clement draws closer to the Gnostics when he introduces into the Christian gnosis the knowledge of revelations secretly transmitted from the time of the Apostles or hidden in Scripture under symbols discoverable only by an allegorizing exegesis whose method he derives from *Philo Judaeus. This esotericism sometimes leads the author of the *Stromata* to place the favored Christian who is a gnostic in opposition to a mere believer.

Völker, however, has clearly shown that Clement's gnosis is as much an ethic as an intellectual quest. It leads to the ἀπάθεια, apathy (*Strom.* 6.71–79) and the ἀγάπη or love (*ibid.* 7.57.4) that assimilate and unite the soul to God. By thus sketching the states of mystical ascent and by orienting his spiritual doctrine toward contemplation, Clement, together with Philo and Origen, exercised a profound influence on the whole of Greco-Christian spirituality.

Clement's contribution to speculative theology is of minor importance; at times it is unfortunate, as when he seems to favor a kind of *docetism. Only occasionally in his theology does he mention the place of the Church (*Strom.* 7.89; 7.107), Baptism (*Paed.* 1.26), and the Eucharist (*ibid.* 42–43) in the process of salvation. But he witnesses to what might be termed a pastoral approach to theology in the 3d century that was actual and effective. He depicts the life of the intelligent Christian family in its ascent toward union with God. For this reason, too, his contribution to the development of Christian thought is far from negligible.

Bibliography: Quasten Patr 2:5–36. J. MUNCK, *Untersuchungen über Klemens von Alexandria* (Stuttgart 1933). M. SPANNEUT, *Le Stoïcisme des Pères de l'Église* (Paris 1957). E. F. OSBORN, *The Philosophy of Clement of Alexandria* (Cambridge, Eng. 1957). F. QUATEMBER, *Die christliche Lebenshaltung des Klemens von Alexandrien nach seinem Paedogogus* (Vienna 1945). C. MONDÉSERT, *Clément d'Alexandrie: Introduction à l'étude de sa pensée religieuse à partir de l'Écriture* (Paris 1944). P. T. CAMELOT, *Foi et Gnose: Introduction à l'étude de la connaissance mystique chez Clément d'Alexandrie* (Paris, 1945). W. VÖLKER, *Der wahre Gnostiker nach Clemens Alexandrinus* (TU 57; 1952), with important bibliog.

[M. SPANNEUT]

CLEMENT THE BULGARIAN, ST., or Clement of Ochrida, bishop of Velitsa (probably near Ochrida, Yugoslavia); b. Macedonia; d. Ochrida, July 27, 916 (feast, Gregorian, July 17; Julian, July 27). He was a pupil of SS. *Cyril and Methodius, whom he accompanied on their mission to Moravia. Expelled from Moravia under the pressure of the German bishops after Methodius's death in 885, he found refuge, along with many colleagues, among the *Bulgars. He was sent to Devol in western Bulgaria (now Albania), where he established a mission and school, and in 893 or 894 he was consecrated bishop of Velitsa. He is buried in the monastery of St. Panteleimon at Ochrida, which he founded. He founded also three churches, which still survive. Clement was one of the fathers of Slavonic literature; his works include liturgical texts translated from the Greek, homilies and lives of saints, and probably the surviving Life and Encomium of St. Cyril. Not all are yet published.

Bibliography: THEOPHYLACT OF OCHRID, *Vita* in PG 126:1194–1240. L. N. TUNNICKIJ, *Monumenta ad SS. Cyrilli et Methodii successorum vitas resque gestas pertinentia* I (Zagorsk 1918); *Svjatoj Kliment episkop Slověnskij* (Zagorsk 1913). I. SNEGAROV, *Bŭlgarskijat pŭrvoučitel ' Sv. Kliment Okhridski* (Sofia 1927). V. STEFANIC, DHGE 12:1086–87. A. MILEV, *Teofilakt Ohridski, Žitie na Kliment Ohridski* (Sofia 1955) 33–88. F. DVORNIK, *Les Slaves, Byzance et Rome au IX siècle* (Paris 1926). F. GRIVEC, *Konstantin und Method: Lehrer der Slaven* (Wiesbaden 1960).

[R. BROWNING]

CLEMENT OF IRELAND, ST., Irish grammarian and master of the palace school under *Charlemagne and *Louis I the Pious; b. Ireland, mid-8th century; d. on the Continent, after 828 (feast, March 20). He was probably at the Carolingian court before 796 when *Alcuin became abbot of Saint-Martin's, Tours, and Clement succeeded him as head of the *palace school. Irish influence on the studies there was attacked by *Theodulf of Orléans, Alcuin, and *Einhard, but Clement retained his position at least till 826, when he was present at court at the baptism of the Danish King Harold. Modestus of Fulda and the future emperor, *Lothair I, were among Clement's pupils. An entry in a *Würzburg necrology—*IV Kal. Junii Clementis Magistri Palatini*—suggests that he may have died there on pilgrimage to the tomb of St. *Kilian of Würzburg. Clement wrote (*c.* 817–20) an *Ars grammatica,* dedicated to Lothair, which is valuable for its extensive quotations from earlier authors. It contains three parts: *De philosophia* (the grammatical part proper), *De metris,* and *De barbarismo;* the entire text was first published in *Philologus* (Supplementband 20; 1928).

Bibliography: R. L. POOLE, DNB 4:487–488. Manitius 1:456–458. Kenney 1:531–549. M. CAPPUYNS, DHGE 12:1430.

[T. Ó FIAICH]

CLEMENT, CAESAR, priest of the English Mission; place and date of birth unknown; d. Aug. 28, 1626. He was the grandson of John *Clement and the illegitimate son of Thomas Clement. He sought admission into the English College at Rome in February 1578, but was refused as too young. He was admitted in September 1579, took the missionary oath in 1584, and was ordained in December of the following year. It is not known at which Italian university or when he received the D.D. He was sent to England at the end of 1587 but no record of his life there exists. He is next heard of as Dean of St. Guddule's, Brussels, and as vicar-general of the Spanish army in the Netherlands. He was greatly attached to his aunt, Margaret Clement, Prioress of St. Ursula's convent, Louvain, from 1570, whom he aided in the foundation of St. Monica's Convent, Louvain, in 1609. In 1612 he was commissioned by Rome to accompany Robert Chambers in the visitation of Douai College so as to settle the administrational disturbances there. There is no account of his later years.

Bibliography: DNB 4:448. DictEngCath 1:496.

[E. E. REYNOLDS]

CLEMENT, JOHN, protégé of St. Thomas *More and president of the College of Physicians, London; year of birth unknown; d. Mechlin, Flanders, July 1, 1572. He went to St. Paul's School, London, and then entered the household of Sir Thomas More. He is the "John Clement, my boy" of More's *Utopia.* In 1516 he was in the service of Cardinal *Wolsey and 3 years later was at Cardinal College, Oxford, as reader in rhetoric and Greek. He left for Italy in 1520 to study medicine, earning his M.D. at Siena in 1525. About 1526 he married Margaret Giggs, the learned foster sister of Margaret More (*Roper). On Feb. 1, 1528, Clement was admitted to the College of Physicians; became president in 1544, and later royal physician. He was sent to attend Wolsey after his fall, and was consulted on *Fisher's illness in the Tower. Both Clement and his wife took the oath to the Succession. Margaret brought help to the starving Carthusians in Newgate Prison in May 1537 until prevented. The Act of Uniformity of 1548 drove the Clements into exile at Louvain where they remained until the accession of Mary Tudor (*see* UNIFORMITY, ACTS OF). Clement was active in his profession until the religious policy of Elizabeth sent him into exile again in 1562. He practised as a doctor first at Louvain and then at Mechlin, where Margaret died on July 6, 1570; both were buried in St. Rumbold's Church.

Bibliography: DNB 4:489.

[E. E. REYNOLDS]

CLEMENT, VINCENT, churchman, diplomat; b. Valencia, Aragon; d. by March 1475. A Spaniard, he entered the diplomatic service of the English crown about 1439 when he became a naturalized Englishman. Oxford granted him a doctorate in theology in 1441. Up to 1460 he served frequently as *Henry VI's proctor at the Roman Curia, and acted there also for *Humphrey, Duke of Gloucester, and several English prelates and religious houses. Between 1462 and 1468 Edward IV of England and John II of Aragon employed him as a confidential agent in their negotiations. He was frequently collector for the apostolic *camera in England (1450–69), although for a time removed by Pope Pius II for unworthy conduct. A greedy and acquisitive man, he soon became a notorious pluralist, holding benefices in Aragon, Normandy, and England simultaneously. In addition to holding many rectories and prebends, he was chancellor and then treasurer of Lichfield cathedral (1447–75), archdeacon of Wiltshire (1457–64), and archdeacon of Winchester from 1459 and of Huntingdon from 1464 until his death. A man of some classical culture, he corresponded with Piero del Monte, Thomas *Bekynton, and other humanists, and introduced many neoclassical writings into England.

Bibliography: Emden 1:432–433. R. WEISS, *Humanism in England during the 15th Century* (2d ed. Oxford 1957), *passim.*

[C. D. ROSS]

CLEMENTINAE, the accepted title of the authentic collection of legislation of Pope Clement V (1305–14) and of the Council of Vienne (1311–12), which was promulgated by John XXII in 1317. In the troubled period after the deaths of Boniface VIII (1303) and Benedict XI (1304), Clement had issued a number of important decretals, some of which were presented for approval at the last session of Vienne (May 6, 1312). This collection was enlarged afterward by the inclusion of the legislation of the Council and of at least two later constitutions of Clement (*Romani principes* and *Pastoralis cura,* both after Aug. 24, 1313); it was published, possibly as Liber Septimus, at a consistory in Monteux (Carpentras, southern France) on March 21, 1314. Promulgation in the usual manner (i.e., by sending copies to certain universities, principally Bologna) was interrupted by Clement's death on April 20, although the bull of promulgation, *Cum nuper,* had been drawn up, if not sent out. It was left to John XXII, his successor after a 3-year vacancy, to complete the formal procedure of promulgation on Oct. 25, 1317.

John in his bull does not use the title Liber Septimus; indeed, the great decretalist *Joannes Andreae, when writing in 1326 what was to become the **Glossa ordinaria,* refused the title to the work on the grounds that a proper Liber Septimus should include all decretals appearing after the *Liber Sextus of 1298: he preferred *Constitutiones Clementis V* or *Clementinae.* With the exception of one decretal of Boniface VIII (*Super cathedram*), which had been abrogated by Benedict XI and restored by Vienne (CorpIurCanClem 3.7.2), and of one of Urban IV also reinstated at Vienne (CorpIur CanClem 3.16), all the legislation in the *Clementinae* appears as *Clemens V in concilio Viennensi* in most manuscripts. How much is Clementine in origin, as distinct from conciliar, is not at all clear; just as Clement's legislation previous to the Council certainly was approved there, so also he may have had a mandate to issue other constitutions afterward as though they were issued from the Council.

Unlike the Decretals of *Gregory IX and the Liber Sextus, the *Clementinae* were not exclusive, and did not abrogate all other legislation between 1298 (Sext) and 1317. Divided along the lines of the Decretals and Sext into 5 books, 52 titles, and 106 chapters, they are cited accordingly, thus: CorpIurCanClem 3.7.2. Commentaries appeared as early as 1319 with the *apparatus* of *William of Mont Lauzun, followed by an *apparatus* of Gesselin de Cassanges (1323) and glosses by Joannes Andreae (1326), etc. There are a number of printed editions of the Clementines, notably that in the official **Corpus Iuris Canonici* of 1582; the latter is repeated, with critical notes, in the edition of A. Friedberg (Leipzig 1881).

Bibliography: F. EHRLE, "Aus den Acten des Vienner Concils," Denifle-Ehrle Arch 4 (1888) 439–464. G. MOLLAT, DDC 4:635–640. E. MÜLLER, *Das Konzil von Vienne, 1311–1312* (Münster 1934) 396–408, 671–706. Schulte 2:45–50. Stickler 264–268.

[L. E. BOYLE]

CLENOCK, MAURICE (CLYNNOG), first rector of the English College, Rome; b. Caernarvonshire, Wales, *c.* 1525; drowned at sea, 1580 or 1581. He earned the D.D. and B.C.L. degrees at Oxford, where he lectured in civil law. Later he was almoner and secretary to Cardinal Reginald Pole, and chancellor of the prerogative court at Canterbury. He was nominated to the See of Bangor in 1558, but the death of Mary Tudor prevented his consecration. He retired in exile to Louvain, where he studied theology and advocated the restoration of English Catholicism by foreign military intervention. At Milan in 1558 he published a book of Christian doctrine in Welsh, entitled *Athravaeth Gristnogavl.* In 1565 and from 1576 to 1577 he was warden of the Hospice for exiled English dons in Rome and was closely concerned with the negotiations that transformed it into a seminary. He became its first rector but was dismissed in 1579 through the appeals of the English students to the Pope, who alleged his partiality for Welshmen. The seminary was then entrusted to the Society of Jesus.

Bibliography: *Dictionary of Welsh Biography* (London 1959) 78–80. DictEngCath 1:501–505.

[J. M. CLEARY]

CLEOPAS, one of the two disciples to whom Christ appeared on the road to *Emmaus after His Resurrection (Lk 24.18). Except for his part in the account of the Resurrection appearance found in Lk 24.13–35, nothing is known with certainty of this disciple, for the name does not recur in the NT. However, the Greek name Cleopas (Κλεοπᾶς, a shortened form of Κλεόπατρος) may have been used as a substitute for Clopas (Κλωπᾶς), probably an Aramaic name of uncertain meaning (cf. the *qlwp'* found at *Palmyra). If the equivalence of the two names is accepted, the way is opened for the identification of the Cleopas named by St. Luke with the Clopas who was the husband (or possibly, though less likely, the father) of one of the Marys present at the Crucifixion in St. John's account (19.25), though there is no positive basis for such identification. If the enumeration "his [Jesus'] mother and his mother's sister, Mary of Clopas [Μαρία ἡ τοῦ Κλωπᾶ], and Mary Magdalene" (Jn 19.25) is to be taken as identifying Mary of Clopas with "his mother's sister," Clopas and Mary, his wife, would be related to Jesus and Mary. Such an identification is possible only if "sister" is taken in the broad Semitic sense of a female relative; otherwise is would entail the unlikely supposition of two sisters named Mary. Tradition has sometimes identified Clopas with Alphaeus, the father of James (Mt 10.3; Mk 3.18; Lk 6.15; Acts 1.13), but there is no sure basis for this. *See* JAMES (SON OF ALPHAEUS), ST.

Bibliography: EncDictBibl 395. E. JACQUIER, DB 1.1:418–419. F. PRAT, *Jesus Christ: His Life, His Teaching, and His Work,* tr. J. J. HEENAN, 2 v. (Milwaukee 1950) 1:132–138, 500–510.

[J. A. LEFRANÇOIS]

CLÉRAMBAULT, LOUIS NICOLAS, organist and composer of the classical style; b. Paris, Dec. 19, 1676; d. Paris, Oct. 26, 1749. After having studied composition with J. B. Moreau and organ with André Raison, he followed Raison as organist at the church of Saint-Jacques. In 1714 he succeeded Nivers, whom he had already assisted for about 10 years, as choirmaster and organist of the Royal School of St. Cyr, and was also for a time organist of Saint-Sulpice in Paris. He may be considered as the last master in the classical French organ tradition. In addition to his harpsichord and organ literature, he composed a Latin oratorio, *Histoire de la femme adultère;* motets and pastorales for St. Cyr; and more important, ballets and cantatas for the Jesuit College of Louis-le-Grand (*see* JESUIT DRAMA), the court of Versailles, and the Paris Opéra. He was largely responsible, together with Morin, for adapting to French taste the Italian cantata, as well as the sonata for strings and *continuo* in the style of Corelli.

See also ORGAN MUSIC.

Bibliography: L. N. CLÉRAMBAULT, *L'Amour piqué par une abeille,* ed. C. BORDES (Paris 1919), *Orphée* and other chamber cantatas and motets also ed. C. BORDES; *Premier livre d'orgue* v.3 of *Archives des maîtres de l'orgue,* ed. F. A. GUILMANT and A. PIRRO, 9 v. (Paris 1898–1909) see also foreword to v.3 by A. PIRRO. A. PIRRO, *Les Clavecinistes* (Paris 1924). R. GIRARDON, MusGG 2:1496–1502.

[R. W. LOWE]

CLERGY, INDIGENOUS

In areas where mission work is carried on by foreigners, the development of a native clergy sooner or later becomes desirable. The specific object of mission work consists in establishing the Church on an indigenous basis in those parts of the world where this has not yet been accomplished.

Pius XI, addressing the heads of missions in *Rerum ecclesiae,* writes: "Let Us recall to your attention how important it is that you build up an indigenous clergy. If you do not work with all your might to accomplish this, We maintain that your apostolate will not only be crippled, but it will become an obstacle and an impediment to the establishment and organization of the Church in those countries . . ." (ActApS 18:73–74). He continues: "It is necessary to supply your territories with as many indigenous priests as shall suffice to extend by themselves alone the boundaries of Christianity, and to govern the community of the faithful of their own nation without having to depend upon the help of outside clergy" (*ibid.,* 76).

The Church may be well established long before the inhabitants of a country are converted. In general, it is the Asiatic clergy who must spread the gospel in Asia, and the African clergy who must Christianize Africa. One of the missionaries' tasks is that of organizing an indigenous clergy.

The Church has, from the beginning, commanded those working among pagan peoples to select from their early converts suitable candidates for the priesthood. The natives should be given, as early as possible, spiritual leaders from their own soil, who have advantages over foreigners in dealing with their own people.

Missionaries have never been available in sufficient numbers to supply the needs of the newly won communities and to continue to carry on the work of conversion with full vigor at the same time. Hence, where the foreign missionaries do not concern themselves with the training of indigenous helpers in good time, they sooner or later become so tied up with parish work among their new Christian communities, that they cannot go farther afield to continue their work among the pagans.

The countries, whence most missionaries come, are themselves in need of more priests for the work to be done at home. There has been a decline in the number of priestly vocations since World War II. These countries can hardly be asked to send more than a small portion of their priests to mission territories. These few cannot possibly suffice to meet the need in the missions of the Church.

Furthermore, people of a different race, culture, and civilization find it difficult to confide in strangers who do not understand their language, their customs, their culture, their needs and aspirations, especially if the strangers fail to adapt themselves to the native mentality and way of life. This is especially true if they find fault with everything they encounter, and try to introduce indiscriminate changes and innovations in the native way of life (*see* ADAPTATION, MISSIONARY).

Indigenous priests, on the other hand, find it easy to communicate with their countrymen, being conversant and in sympathy with their customs, mentality, tastes, needs and aspirations. Better than any other, the indigenous priest knows what means to employ to persuade and convince them. Because there is less fear or suspicion of him, he can often find entrance where a foreign priest would not be admitted.

In times of war, persecution, political upheaval, or acute nationalism, the foreign missionary finds his stay precarious, if not impossible, and may face death, imprisonment, or expulsion; whereas the indigenous priest may escape suspicion; or, if he is forced to disguise himself or to go into hiding, he is not so easily discovered. An indigenous clergy, spread like a network throughout the threatened territory, could well save the local Church from extinction in such circumstances.

If the foreign missionaries in China had, from the start, formed an indigenous clergy, there might have been 70 million Catholics in China in 1950 instead of a mere 7 million. A larger number would almost certainly have had a much better chance of survival behind the Bamboo Curtain than the present number has; China might even have escaped Communist domination altogether.

It appears that the missionaries of the early Church established mission churches from city to city and from country to country, training the local Christians to carry on what they had begun, even in areas where the natives were on a low culture level. The Apostles preached the Gospel and appointed presbyters (bishops) from city to city (Acts 14.23; Ti 1.5–7), and so did their successors. It was only from the 16th century on that the missionaries deviated from the traditional practice. Rome did not sponsor this deviation, as the repeated letters of the popes, the Propaganda, and the mission encyclicals of Leo XIII, Benedict XV, Pius XI, Pius XII, and John XXIII clearly show.

The deviation was due to many conditions. One was the interference of Spain and Portugal, whose governments and missionaries did not favor granting Holy Orders to aborigines, mestizos, and mulattos in the vast, newly discovered territories allotted to them by the "padroado" until the natives should have reached a culture level approximating their own. There was a general lack of understanding of the good qualities of natives from a low cultural level, and a misconception of the cultural values of the high pagan civilizations of India and China, along with a gross lack of empathy with the natives. An exaggerated nationalism on the part of many missionaries was partly responsible, too, since it led to disregard of the national aspirations and feelings of their charges. The long outmoded educational program for indigenous clerical candidates left them wholly unprepared for leadership. Hence, the complaint of Benedict XV: "It is sad to think that there are still countries where the Catholic Faith has been preached for several centuries, but where you will find no indigenous clergy, except of an inferior quality; that there are nations, deeply penetrated by the light of the Faith, that . . . have reached such a degree of civilization as to possess men distinguished in every department of secular knowledge, . . . and have as yet been able to yield neither bishops to rule them, nor priests to direct them" (*Maximum illud,* ActApS 11:445–446).

Even the strongly worded apostolic letter *Maximum illud,* just quoted, was not heeded generally in mission circles until it was confirmed by the encyclical *Rerum ecclesiae* of Piux XI in 1926, and the startling consecration, by the Pope himself, of six Chinese bishops in the same year.

Bibliography: J. LECLERCQ, *Thunder in the Distance: The Life of Père Lebbe,* tr. G. LAMB (New York 1958), for deviational policy in China. J. BECKMANN, *Der einheimische Klerus in Geschichte und Gegenwart* (Beckenried, Switz. 1950). L. J. LUZBETAK, *The Church and Cultures: An Applied Anthropology for the Religious Worker* (Techny, Ill. 1963) 104–108. A. LEE, *De formatione cleri localis in missionibus* (Rome 1958).

[P. WEYLAND]

CLERICAL DRESS (CANON LAW)

For the first 3 centuries of the Christian era clerics used no special dress when engaged in divine services. About the beginning of the 4th century, a distinction began to be made between the everyday wear of the clergy and the vestments used by them in sacred functions. SS. Athanasius (295–373), Jerome (*c.* 342–420), and John Chrysostom (*c.* 345–407), among others, made mention in their writings of special garb to be used by clerics in the performance of liturgical actions. This is especially true with reference to the orarion, or primitive stole. Councils of the same and succeeding periods, e.g., the Council of Laodicea, 343 to 381, referred quite often to a special clerical vesture for use in sacred functions.

History. Special clerical dress for use outside the sanctuary did not exist much before the 6th century. The garb worn by clerics was the old Roman dress, i.e., a tunic without sleeves (*collobium*) and a long white coat with sleeves (*dalmatica* or *tunica manicata et talaris*). For several centuries there was no other evident distinction observed between the ordinary apparel of the cleric and the layman save that inherent in the fact that the former was more constrained to wear that which was more modest and grave, and becoming his state in life. It seems that the use of a specific clerical dress in daily wear came about as a result of the fact that the clergy gradually came to be composed chiefly of philosophers and ascetics, men who all along had worn a distinctive garb, the pallium. Prior to the early 6th century various members of the clergy had tried without success to introduce the pallium as a specific garb for clerics in place of the birrus, the common tunic worn by members of the secular clergy and by Christians generally.

Even as to the color of the garb, centuries passed before any definite regulations were laid down. The Council of Trent (1545–63) required merely that "clerics always wear a dress conformable to their order, that by the propriety of their outward apparel they may show forth the inward uprightness of their morals" (sess. 14, *de ref.*, c.6). Nothing was mentioned about the color. Reliable authors state that black has been the color of the cleric's garb only since the 17th century. In the Byzantine Catholic rites, the subrhason (cassock) may be of any color; the rhason, worn over it in public, must be black. Pope Sixtus V (1585–90) called the dress demanded by the Council of Trent the *vestis talaris* or cassock. From his time onward clerics were obliged to wear the cassock at all times as their distinctive dress. By approved custom, however, the interpretation prevailed that what was prescribed by Pope Sixtus was the wearing of the cassock at least for sacred and public functions.

Third Council of Baltimore. In the U.S. the Third Plenary Council of Baltimore (1884) decreed that clerics were to wear the Roman collar and cassock at home and in the church, while outside the house they were to wear the Roman collar together with a coat of black or somber color, the length of which reached to the knees. This prescription has never been revoked, but from the very beginning it has been interpreted to mean that clerics should conform to the style adopted by conservative laymen. There now exists a custom contrary to the law. The Code itself merely states that all clerics must wear an appropriate ecclesiastical garb that is in accord with the legitimate customs of the region and the prescriptions of the local ordinary. They need not wear the tonsure in those countries where custom directs otherwise (CIC c.136.1; ClerSanc c.77.1).

Deprivation. While all clerics have the right and the obligation to wear a distinctive clerical dress, they may be deprived of that right, either for a time or perpetually because of scandalous and incorrigible conduct (CIC cc.2298nn9,11, 2300, 2304). This deprivation carries with it the prohibition of exercising any ecclesiastical ministry and the deprivation of the clerical privileges while it lasts. This vindicative penalty may be inflicted on any cleric in major orders exclusive of the pope. The use of special procedural norms is mandatory in cases involving bishops, cardinals, and apostolic legates. Both forms of the penalty ordinarily require a judicial process for their infliction—temporary deprivation requires one judge and perpetual deprivation requires a collegiate tribunal of five judges. In cases of factual notoriety, the penalty can be inflicted by way of extrajudicial precept.

Bibliography: J. Bingham, *The Antiquities of the Christian Church,* 2 v. (London 1856). H. J. McCloud, *Clerical Dress and Insignia of the Roman Catholic Church* (Milwaukee 1948). J. A. Shields, *Deprivation of the Clerical Garb* (CUA CLS 334; Washington 1958).

[J. A. SHIELDS]

CLERICAL STATE (CANON LAW)

The clerical state in the Catholic Church is that part of the hierarchical society in which all the members are dedicated to the divine ministry and have received at least first tonsure. The word cleric comes from the Greek word *kleros* and means "lot," "portion," or "heritage." Since the 2d century the word cleric has been the common name applied to those who, according to St. Jerome, "belong to that body of men who are the portion of God and at the same time have God Himself as their lot." The clerical state exists in the Catholic Church by divine institution. Therefore the distinction between clerics, who participate in the powers of order and jurisdiction, and the laity, who do not, is of divine origin. However, not all the orders in the clerical state are of divine institution.

In the Latin rite a man is admitted into the clerical state by receiving first tonsure. The tonsure is not an order in itself, but rather a rite preliminary to orders. It was introduced into the Church about the 8th century and consists in a partial shearing of the hair from the head of the candidate for Holy Orders. The first tonsure is conferred by a bishop. It is privately renewed from time to time in those places where the common law makes the habitual wearing of the tonsure obligatory for all clerics.

In the Oriental Church tonsure is not mentioned as the sacred rite by which a person is received into the clerical state. The genuine tradition of the Oriental Church has no set rite of reception into the clergy that is not at the same time an order. Each Oriental rite determines for itself what sacred rite will be used to assign men to the sacred ministry.

Hierarchy. All the members of the clerical state do not belong to the same rank. There is a *hierarchy among them, some being subordinated to others. By divine institution, the hierarchy of Orders consists of bishops, priests, and ministers; as regards jurisdiction, it consists of the supreme pontificate and the subordinate episcopate; other grades have been added to these by ecclesiastical institution (CIC c.108). The hierarchy is the totality of the powers vested in the Church, and these powers are divided into the power of Orders and power of *jurisdiction. The power of Orders is the power to sanctify the faithful by sacred rites; the power of jurisdiction is the power to govern the faithful for the attainment of the supernatural end for which the Church is established.

The hierarchy of Orders consists of a series of eight degrees: doorkeeper, exorcist, lector, acolyte, subdiaconate, diaconate, priesthood, and episcopate. The last four degrees are called major, or sacred, orders; the others, minor orders. Only the last three are held with certainty to be of divine origin and to constitute the Sacrament of Holy Orders; the other degrees are of ecclesiastical institution. The hierarchy or jurisdiction also has many degrees, two of which are of divine institution, the primacy of the pope and the episcopate. All the other degrees, e.g., vicar apostolic, prefect apostolic, patriarch, are of ecclesiastical institution. Those who are received into the hierarchy of the Church are not accepted by the consent or at the call of the people or of the secular power, but are constituted in the degrees of the power of Orders by sacred ordination. In the hierarchy of jurisdiction the person in the highest office of all, the pope, receives jurisdiction by the divine law itself after a legitimate election has been held and the person elected has freely accepted it. All the other degrees of jurisdiction are by canonical appointment (CIC c.109).

Incardination. Incardination is the affiliation of a secular cleric to his diocese. It is also the canonical act by which a cleric is attached to a diocese and made subject to its ordinary. Each cleric must belong either to some diocese or to some religious organization, and no recognition may be extended to vagrant clerics. By reception of the first tonsure, a cleric is ascribed to—or as it is called, incardinated in—the diocese for the service of which he was promoted (CIC c.111). This *incardination to a diocese or affiliation to a religious community was recognized from the earliest centuries of the Church, and bishops were not permitted to ordain any cleric except for a definite service in his territory. During the Middle Ages there were a considerable number of unattached clerics; this led the Council of Trent to decree that "no one hereafter be ordained who is not attached to the Church or pious place for whose necessity he is received."

The bishop of the diocese where a candidate has a canonical domicile is the bishop who has the right to promote the candidate to the clerical rank. It is presumed he will ordain only as many as the diocese can use. If he has more candidates than he can use in his own diocese, a bishop may ordain these men with the understanding that they will be transferred to a diocese that has a shortage of clergy. This arrangement is made before the ordination. After the ordination the candidate is excardinated, or separated, from the first diocese and then incardinated into the second one. This is explicit incardination. Implicit incardination occurs when the ordinary of one diocese gives to a cleric of another diocese a benefice, such as a parish, which requires permanent residence in the diocese. Before he can accept the benefice the cleric must obtain the written consent of his own proper ordinary. Another case of implicit incardination is found in canon 641. If a bishop accepts a secularized religious in major orders for a 3-year trial, he may prolong the period of probation for a second period of 3 years; but if he does not dismiss the former religious before the second period has elapsed, the latter is automatically incardinated.

Rights of Clerics. Even though the clerical state exists in the Catholic Church by divine institution, there is no attempt to ascribe all of the rights and privileges of clerics to the natural or divine law. However, the clerical state is superior to the lay state, and this superiority is made manifest through the rights and privileges of clerics that trace their origin to the centuries when the Church Christianized the nations of Europe. Today very few countries in the world recognize all the rights and privileges of clerics.

The rights of clerics are certain general capacities that are exclusive to clerics. The Code of Canon Law states these rights very briefly in canon 118: clerics alone are capable of obtaining the power of Orders or of ecclesiastical jurisdiction and of holding ecclesiastical benefices and pensions. These are rights in the strict sense, not mere privileges. These rights are reserved to the clergy because the divine organization of the Church enjoys the peculiarity that ecclesiastical power is granted only to those chosen by Christ. Hence whatever pertains to the hierarchical power can be conveyed only to those who belong to the hierarchy. It follows logically that clerics are the only ones who have the right to receive ecclesiastical benefices and pensions since they are directly connected with a spiritual office that only clerics are capable of obtaining.

The power of the pope, however, is not taken away by CIC c.118, and he can by way of exception grant benefices and pensions even to laymen. Subordinate superiors, however, would act invalidly if on their own authority they granted benefices or pensions to a lay person. Religious, unless they are also clerics, do not share in these rights.

Privileges of Clerics. All the privileges of clerics belong to them by virtue of their state and remain as long as they are not forfeited by the loss of that state or by virtue of the penal law. Lay religious and novices also possess these privileges.

Privilege of the Canon. All the faithful owe reverence to clerics according to their various grades and offices and they commit a sacrilege if they do a real injury to a cleric (CIC c.119). Most of this canon dates back to the Second Lateran Council, 1139. The violent acts perpetrated by Arnold of Brescia and his followers against priests and religious led the Council to repeat and summarize previous synodal acts of Reims and Pisa. The injury must be a real injury, not just words, and the person who commits the injury must have intended it and also have known that the victim was a cleric. In the penal section of the Code there are a number of different penalties that are decreed for those who perpetrate any injury against a cleric, and the penalties vary with the grade and office of the person attacked (CIC c.2343).

Privilege of the Forum. All lawsuits against clerics, both civil and criminal, must come before an ecclesiastical court, unless other provisions have been made between Church and civil authorities. Cardinals, legates of the Holy See, bishops, and supreme heads of religious organizations approved by the Holy See may not be sued in the secular courts in matters relating to their offices without permission of the Apostolic See. The ordinary of the place must give his permission before any cleric may be sued in the secular court. The ordinary, however, should not refuse such permission without a just and serious reason, especially when the plaintiff is a lay person and even more so when the bishop has vainly endeavored to effect a friendly settlement between the parties (CIC c.120).

Privilege of Personal Immunity. All clerics are immune from military service and from other functions and public civil affairs that are alien to the clerical state (CIC c.121). As regards military service, the practice in the U.S. has been to recognize this immunity at least in part. The Selective Service Act of 1940 provides that ordained ministers of religion must register, but they are not called to service. The Code does not specify what functions and offices are incompatible with or alien to the clerical state. The bishop of the diocese must determine this according to local custom and practice. However, certain kinds of employment are specifically forbidden to clerics by CIC cc.139, 142.

Privilege of Competency. Clerics are protected by this privilege from being reduced to absolute poverty. Even though the creditors have a just debt to collect, clerics shall not be deprived of what is necessary for their adequate support according to the prudent judgment of the ecclesiastical judge. They remain under the obligation to satisfy their creditors as soon as possible (CIC c.122).

The Code of Oriental Canon Law adds a new privilege to the list of privileges just mentioned. The hierarch shall see to it that a sum of money is set aside in his eparchy for granting pensions in order to be able to support pastors and other secular clerics of the eparchy who have become incapable of discharging their duties on account of impaired health (ClerSanc c.59).

The privileges just enumerated belong primarily to the clerical state. They cannot be waived by private agreement. They are lost by a cleric reduced to the lay state or by a cleric who has been perpetually deprived of clerical garb.

Obligations of Clerics. The special rights, privileges, and dignities that clerics enjoy in the clerical state impose on these clerics a special obligation to lead a holy life. The Code demands that clerics live both interiorly and exteriorly a holier life than lay people and that they must excel them in giving the example of virtue and good deeds (CIC c.124). Canons 125 to 144 of the Code enumerate the positive and negative obligations common to the clerical state; and unless it appears otherwise from the content, these same canons apply also to religious, including novices, and to members of communities without vows.

Piety. The local ordinary must see to it that all the clergy go frequently to confession and that they devote some time daily to meditation, visit the Blessed Sacrament, say the rosary, and examine their conscience. Also all secular priests must make a retreat at least every 3d year, for a period of time to be determined by their own ordinary in a pious or religious house designated by him; and no priest is exempt from this obligation except in a particular case for a just cause and with the express permission of his ordinary (CIC c.126). Religious and seminarians must make a spiritual retreat every year. A very important obligation in this area is the recitation of the Breviary. All clerics who are in the major orders are bound to recite the canonical Hours daily according to approved liturgical books.

Obedience. All clerics, but especially priests, are bound by a special obligation to show reverence and obedience each to his own ordinary. This obligation arises from their incardination in their diocese and the special promise of obedience every cleric makes to his ordinary in the ordination ceremony. The obligation of obedience includes whatever is already obligatory by either the common or the particular law and whatever is lawfully imposed by precept, even beyond the law, for the good of the Church.

Clerics must accept and faithfully discharge any function assigned to them by their ordinary as often and as long as, in the judgment of the ordinary, the needs of the Church require it, unless they are prevented from doing so by a lawful impediment (CIC c.128). Therefore clerics are obliged to accept any assignment, such as teaching or chancery work, even though it is not strictly clerical by nature, if the ordinary of the diocese demands this and there is no lawful impediment to excuse them.

Studies after Ordination. One of the most important obligations clerics have is to continue the study of the sacred sciences after ordination. They should continue their studies also in the so-called profane sciences such as literature, law, history, and the natural sciences. To encourage these studies all priests, even those with a parochial or canonical benefice, must undergo an examination every year for 3 years following ordination in the various matters included in the sacred sciences. Moreover, several times throughout the year clerical conferences must be held in the diocese to promote knowledge and piety among the clergy (CIC c.131).

Celibacy and Chastity. Clerics who are in major orders are prevented from marrying and are so bound to observe chastity that if they sin against it they are guilty also of sacrilege. Minor clerics can contract marriage, but they fall *ipso iure* from the clerical state (CIC c.132). Besides being obliged to abstain from all acts of impurity, clerics must not have in their houses or associate habitually with women who might be objects of suspicion. To help them observe the laws of celibacy and chastity clerics are urged to observe the common life, that is, living together and sharing a common table.

In the Oriental Church candidates who are to be ordained as married men must enter into marriage before the reception of the subdiaconate. Subdeacons and all clerics ordained to major orders are forbidden to marry to the extent that according to law they become incapable of contracting marriage (ClerSanc c.70). *See* CELIBACY, CANON LAW OF.

Life and Conduct. All clerics are bound to conduct themselves in public as well as in private in a way that is proper to their state in life. Therefore clerics are bound to wear a clerical garb according to the legitimate local customs and the regulations of the ordinary. The hair is to be dressed in a simple style.

Clerics must abstain completely from all activities that are unbecoming to their state. These include indecorous occupation, habitual gambling for money, carrying weapons, and habitual hunting. Clerics are forbidden also to attend spectacles, dances, and pageants that are unbecoming or at which it would be scandalous for a cleric to be present. They are prohibited from conducting business or trade either personally or through agents, either for their own benefit or that of other persons. In the case of necessity of the cleric himself or his family, the ordinary can dispense a cleric from this last obligation.

Even though they have no residential benefice or office, clerics must not absent themselves from their diocese for any notable time without at least the presumed permission of their ordinary (CIC c.143).

Bibliography: Abbo. Woywod-Smith. M. CONTE A CORONATA, *Institutiones iuris canonici*, 4 v. (4th ed. Turin 1950–56). Bousc-Ellis. M. RAMSTEIN, *A Manual of Canon Law* (Hoboken 1948). C. A. BACHOFEN (C. AUGUSTINE), *A Commentary on the New Code of Canon Law*, 8 v. (St. Louis 1918–31). Pospishil PersOr. H. A. AYRINHAC, *General Legislation in the New Code of Canon Law* (New York 1923).

[J. KELLIHER]

CLERICALISM

Since the Middle Ages the adjective clerical has designated that which relates to clerics and the clergy. In the 19th century the French and Italians created a noun out of the term and imparted to it a new meaning whereby clerical signified a Catholic, cleric or lay, who with more or less success defended the rights of the Church, particularly those of the pope as temporal sovereign. Enemies of the Church and defenders of Italian unity attributed to these clericals a system, which *c.* 1865 they labelled clericalism. The aim of this system, it was claimed, was to make civil governments on the national and local levels submit to the desires of popes, bishops, and priests. English journalists adopted the neologism *c.* 1883; but anti-Roman polemics had previously enriched its vocabulary with terms almost synonymous, such as priestdom, priestcraft, priest-ridden, monkish, and popery. Subsequent decades enlarged the connotations of clericalism, so that it served to designate every excessive intervention of a religion in public affairs, or every attempt at domination over a state by a religion. Attention will be confined here to the clericalism attributed wrongly or rightly to the Church by anticlericals and by Catholics themselves.

For anticlericals, clericalism has proved a useful word for polemical purposes. Under the pretext of remedying an abuse, anticlericals have often attacked the Church. One phrase has become famous: "Le cléricalisme, voilà l'ennemi!" (Clericalism! That is the enemy). Léon *Gambetta, who coined it (May 4, 1877), claimed to be citing his friend Peyrat. Peyrat did not, however, use precisely these words, but: "Le catholicisme, c'est là l'ennemi!" [L. Capéran, *Histoire contemporaine de la laïcité française* 3 v. (Paris 1957) 1:60, 63]. In the Chamber of Deputies in 1901 René Viviani denied that there could be a difference between the most sincere Catholic and the clerical. Politicians pretended that they wanted to single out, not good pastors or their flocks, but *Jesuits, the *Congregation, the Vatican (understood as a foreign power), and international religious congregations accumulating properties in mortmain.

Catholics, on the other hand, were not astonished that the Church was the object of persecution. The success of a persecution utilizing such an equivocal notion did, however, move Catholics to a self-examination. In their reaction against an invasion of laicism they questioned whether or not the successors of Gregory VII had gone too far; whether the revocation of the Edict of *Nantes (1685), so widely acclaimed by the French hierarchy, had not been an injustice; whether in defense of its immunities a well-protected clergy had not cloaked its egotism; whether many clerics were not dreaming about a new Constantine who would facilitate their ministerial work; whether the French clergy had not been too complaisant toward *Napoleon III, who was so adroit in making use of them; whether it was important religiously to prefer a monarchical to a republican regime; and whether pastors did not display too pronounced a tendency to act like "parish captains." In brief, clericalism has existed in the past and continues to exist. Even if it disappears, the tendency expressed by it will very likely endure.

See also ANTICLERICALISM; LAICISM.

Bibliography: J. LECLER, *The Two Sovereignties* (New York 1952), tr. from Fr.; *Catholicisme* 2:1235–39. F. MÉJAN, *La Laïcité de l'État* (Cahiers laïques 32; Paris 1956). C. A. WHITTUCK, Hastings ERE 3:689–693.

[C. BERTHELOT DU CHESNAY]

CLERICIS LAICOS, constitution of *Boniface VIII (Feb. 24, 1296), whereby, under sentence of excommunication reserved to the Apostolic See, ecclesiastics were forbidden to pay taxes, under any pretext, to lay rulers without express leave of the pope, and whereby lay authorities were enjoined from imposing and receiving such taxes and from seizing goods deposited in churches. The constitution, defended by Boniface as a reaffirmation of existing canons (CorpIur Can X 3.49.4, 7), with the addition of penalties against transgressors, was the result of clerical complaints, in particular from the lower clergy of England, against the financial exactions of *Edward I and *Philip IV the Fair. Its promulgation caused serious problems between Boniface and Philip and strained relations between the English clergy, especially Abp. *Robert of Winchelsea and Edward. Ultimately the constitution was a failure. Benedict XI modified it; Clement V revoked it.

Bibliography: G. DIGARD et al., eds., *Les Registres de Boniface VIII,* 4 v. (Paris 1884–1939) 1:584–585, No. 1567. T. S. R. BOASE, *Boniface VIII* (London 1933).

[E. J. SMYTH]

CLERK, JOHN, Henrician bishop of Bath and Wells; b. place and date unknown; d. St. Botolph's, Aldgate, Jan. 3, 1541. He took his B.A. at Cambridge in 1499 and his M.A. in 1502. He later took a doctor's degree in law at Bologna. He received rapid preferment and in 1519 became archdeacon of Colchester, then dean of Windsor, a judge in Star Chamber, Thomas Wolsey's chaplain, and dean of the King's chapel. In 1521 he was sent as ambassador to Rome and presented Henry VIII's *The Defense of the Seven Sacraments,* prefaced by an "Oratio" of his own, to Leo X. On Leo's death Clerk was employed to further Wolsey's aspirations to the papal throne, but he could not get enough support. He was unsuccessful again 2 years later on the death of Adrian VI. In 1523 Clerk was nominated bishop of Bath and Wells. Three years later he was sent to France to attempt to negotiate a marriage between Francis I and Princess Mary Tudor. The following year he was in Rome, and in 1529 he was a counselor for Queen Catherine in the divorce proceedings. His last task was that of appeasing the Duke of Cleves after Henry's farcical marriage with the Duke's daughter, Anne. On his return trip he fell sick at Dunkirk and died a few months later in England.

Bibliography: W. HUNT, DNB 4:495–496. S. H. CASSAN, *Lives of the Bishops of Bath and Wells,* 2 v. (London 1829). Hughes RE.

[M. M. CURTIS]

CLERKS REGULAR OF THE MOTHER OF GOD

A religious order, *Ordo Clericorum Regularium Matris Dei* (CRMD, OMD), whose members are known also as Religious of the Mother of God, or Leonardini. It was founded by St. John *Leonardi in the church of the Madonna of the Rose, Lucca, Italy, Sept. 1, 1573, to combat Protestantism and to promote the Counter Reformation as advocated by the Council of Trent. In accordance with the founder's wish, members have charge of parishes, preach, teach Christian

The sanctuary of S. Maria in Campitelli, Rome, mother church of the Clerks Regular of the Mother of God.

doctrine to youths, direct Catholic organizations, promote devotion to the Eucharist and to the Blessed Virgin, and perform a variety of other pastoral works. Members were called Reformed Priests of the Blessed Virgin until 1580, when the founder transferred their headquarters to the church of S. Maria Corteorlandini. When Bp. Alessandro Guidiccioni approved the institute canonically (1583), it took the name Congregation of Secular Clerics of the Blessed Virgin. Clement VIII gave it papal approbation in 1595.

Despite opposition from Protestants and from the leaders of the Republic of Lucca, who claimed to detect in the new organization religious and political dangers to the state, the infant congregation survived and prospered. In 1601 St. John Leonardi established in Rome the convent of S. Maria in Portico (now Campitelli). The first general chapter there (1603) elected Leonardi superior general for life, and approved the constitution elaborated by him during the preceding 3 decades. Clement VIII approved this constitution in 1604. In 1621 Gregory XV designated the institute a religious order with solemn vows, and with all the privileges of other orders. The Leonardi united in 1614 with the *Piarists at the urging of Cardinal Giustiniani, but the two groups separated in 1617 because the pastoral nature of the former proved incompatible with the scholastic character of the latter. From this time Leonardi's institute took the definitive name of Clerks Regular of the Mother of God.

As the order spread in Italy from Lucca to Genoa, Milan, Rome, southern Italy, and Sicily, it flourished. In Lucca its school produced the leading citizens of the upper and middle classes. The Leonardini were active in all forms of the apostolate and in literary movements. Among the outstanding members of the order were Ippolito Marracci (d. 1675), author of about 100 works on the Immaculate Conception, and his brother Ludovico (d. 1700), an Arabic scholar; Bartolomeo Beverini (d. 1686), theologian, historian, and man of letters; Massimiliano Dezza (d. 1704), preacher at the court of Vienna; Sebastiano Paoli (d. 1751), orator and man of letters; and Giovanni *Mansi (d. 1779), theologian.

Suppressions in the Napoleonic period and in the late 19th century by the Italian government practically destroyed the order, which had no houses outside Italy. Throughout the 19th century the order continued to lead a precarious existence. Conditions became more promising around 1925, when Giuseppe Tosto was superior general. In 1964 the order had 100 priests. In Italy there were 11 houses, 3 apostolic schools, a novitiate, and a theological school; in France 2 houses; and in Chile 3 parishes and an apostolic school. The Church has officially recognized the sanctity of the founder, canonized in 1938, and of his first two companions, Giambattista Cioni and Cesare Franciotti, who have received the title of Venerable.

Bibliography: F. FERRAIRONI, *Tre Secoli di storia dell'Ordine Religioso della Madre di Dio* (Rome 1939). V. PASCUCCI, *S. Giovanni Leonardi* (Rome 1963). Heimbucher 2:113–114.

[P. PIERONI]

CLERMONT-TONNERRE, ANNE ANTOINE JULES DE, cardinal, archbishop of *Toulouse; b. Paris, Jan. 1, 1749; d. Toulouse, Feb. 21, 1830. He was born into an illustrious family, studied at the Seminary of Saint-Sulpice and received a doctorate from the Sorbonne. In 1774 he became vicar-general of the archdiocese of Besançon, and in 1781 bishop of Châlons-sur-Marne. He was elected a deputy to the Estates General (1789). Upon refusing the oath of loyalty to the *Civil Constitution of the Clergy, he went into exile (1791) in Belgium and Germany. After the *Concordat of 1801, he resigned his see and returned to retirement in France. *Louis XVIII named him a peer of France (1814). Since his former see was not reestablished, Clermont-Tonnerre was promoted to that of Toulouse (1820), and to the cardinalate (1822). In his diocese he restored discipline, reorganized seminaries, founded a missionary society, published a Ritual, and fought for the restoration of all the Church's rights. Notably he opposed the regulations on minor seminaries (1828). He attended the 1829 conclave in Rome, despite a serious accident on the way there, which led ultimately to his death.

Bibliography: É. FRANCESCHINI, DictBiogFranc 8:1515–16. C. LAPLATTE, DHGE 12:319–322. G. CAYRE, *Histoire des évêques et archevêques de Toulouse* (Toulouse 1873). *L'Épiscopat français depuis le Concordat jusqu'à la Séparation (1802–1905)* (Paris 1907).

[R. LIMOUZIN-LAMOTHE]

CLERVAUX, ABBEY OF, in the Congregation of France, dedicated to SS. Maurice and *Maurus; founded in *Luxembourg (1909–10) by monks of *Saint-Maur-sur-Loire (Glanfeuil), who left France to avoid the laws of exception. The neo-Romanesque buildings were raised with the aid of the Coëtlosquet family. So fast did the abbey grow that Pius XI asked it to accept the foundation of St. Jerome in Rome (1933), for the revision of the Vulgate Bible. Expelled from Clervaux by Nazis (1941), the monks returned to their ruined abbey in 1947. In 1965 Clervaux had 83 monks (16 in Rome). The publications of the abbey include several editions of a Missal in French. Some of the monks devote themselves to an ecumenical apostolate, especially in Scandinavia, Pius X having established in Clervaux an association of prayers for the union of Christians of Nordic lands.

Bibliography: ActApS 2 (1910) 187–189; 26 (1934) 85–87. Cottineau 1:808. R. GAZEAU, *Catholicisme* 2:1247. M. SAHLER, *Les Abbayes en Belgique, Pays-Bas et Luxembourg* (Auch 1949). Kapsner BenBibl 2:197.

[R. GRÉGOIRE]

CLEVELAND, DIOCESE OF (CLEVELANDENSIS)

Suffragan of the metropolitan See of Cincinnati. It comprises the eight counties of Ashland, Cuyahoga, Geauga, Lake, Lorain, Medina, Summit, and Wayne in north central Ohio, an area of 3,414 square miles, with a total population (1963) of 2,754,820. Of these 834,367 were Catholics largely of German, Irish, Bohemian, Hungarian, Slovak, Polish, Slovenian, and Italian extraction. The diocese, which was established in 1847, embraced the third of the state north of 40°41′, but a subsequent agreement with Cincinnati, ratified in 1868 by the Holy See, adjusted the boundary to respect county lines; the 33 counties were reduced to 8 by the establishment of the Diocese of Toledo, 1910; and Youngstown, 1943.

Early History. Early Catholicity in northern Ohio is associated with the work of Father Edward *Fenwick and other Dominicans who ministered to the scattered Catholics there between 1817 and 1842. In 1834 the newly arrived Redemptorists were assigned to care for the German immigrants in the area, and in 1844 they were succeeded by the Precious Blood Fathers. Numbers of the secular clergy likewise labored in the area, laying the foundations for future congregations. Between 1822 and 1847 northern Ohio was part of the Cincinnati diocese, whose second bishop, John Purcell, petitioned Rome in 1846 for a division of his jurisdiction then comprising the entire state. Pius IX responded on April 23, 1847, cutting off the northern part of the state for the new Cleveland diocese and naming Louis Amadeus Rappe as first bishop.

Diocese 1847–1908. The new bishop, a 46-year old French-born missionary in the Toledo area, was consecrated on Oct. 10, 1847, and a week later took possession of St. Mary on the Flats, the only church in the diocese. Within five years a cathedral was completed and on Nov. 7, 1852, dedicated to St. John the Evangelist. During Rappe's administration parishes, schools, charitable institutions, convents, and a seminary were established; numerous religious orders including the Society of Mary and the Franciscan Fathers, Sisters of the Holy Humility of Mary, Sisters of the Good Shepherd, Ursulines, and Little Sisters of the Poor were introduced into the diocese and a new group, the Sisters of Charity of St. Augustine, was founded. Diocesan synods were held in 1848, 1852, 1854, 1857, and 1868. In August 1870 Rappe resigned, going to New England where he worked as a missionary among the French until his death on Sept. 8, 1877. He was buried in the Cleveland cathedral.

St. John's Cathedral, Cathedral Square, Cleveland.

The second bishop, Richard *Gilmour, was a Scotch convert from Presbyterianism who had served as missionary in Kentucky, Virginia, and Ohio until his consecration as the ordinary for Cleveland on April 14, 1872. His administration was marked by an increase in the number of churches to 233 and the setting up of a chancery office. In 1872 and 1882 synods were held whose provisions anticipated the decrees of the Third Council of Baltimore, 1884. Sisters of St. Joseph and of Notre Dame arrived to help staff the expanding school system. The Jesuit College of St. Ignatius (John Carroll University) was founded in 1886, and four new hospitals were opened. A diocesan newspaper, the *Catholic Universe,* was established in 1874; it combined with the *Bulletin* in 1926. The Catholic Central Association was also formed in 1874 for the defense of Catholic interests against a growing nativism.

Following the death of Gilmour on April 13, 1891, Ignatius Horstmann, chancellor of the Philadelphia archdiocese, was appointed Cleveland's third bishop and consecrated in Philadelphia on Feb. 25, 1892. Noteworthy in his episcopate were the founding of the Cleveland Apostolate, a group of diocesan priests who worked among non-Catholics until 1920; and the appointment, on his request, of an auxiliary bishop for the growing foreign population, especially of the Slavic races, in the diocese. Joseph *Koudelka, pastor of St. Michael's church, Cleveland, was consecrated Feb. 25, 1908, the first auxiliary bishop of special jurisdiction in the U.S. By 1897, the golden jubilee year of the diocese, numerous grade and high schools had been added to the diocesan system. Horstmann died suddenly of a heart attack on May 13, 1908, while making a visitation of Canton, Ohio.

After 1908. John Patrick Farrelly, spiritual director of the North American College, Rome, was consecrated the fourth bishop of Cleveland on May 1, 1909, in the chapel of that college. Within the year his diocese was divided, separating 16 western counties to create the Toledo diocese on April 15, 1910. Churches, schools, and hospitals multiplied under his direction; Catholic Charities Corporation was organized to support the charitable work of the diocese; and a larger use was made of native priests in bilingual congregations. Following Farrelly's death on Feb. 12, 1921, Bp. Joseph *Schrembs of Toledo was appointed fifth bishop of Cleveland on June 16, 1921, and installed there on September 8.

At Schrembs's request, Eire, Richland, and Huron counties in the western part of the diocese were transferred from the jurisdiction of Cleveland to that of Toledo in 1922. Under his direction various administrative changes improved the efficiency of the chancery offices and other agencies of the diocese. Our Lady of the Lake seminary was built, numerous primary and secondary schools were opened, and in 1928 a diocesan Sisters' College was established. Then, in 1948, a graduate program in education and a baccalaureate program in nursing were added and the name changed to St. John College. Ursuline College and Notre Dame College, liberal arts colleges for women, were both authorized in 1922. The same year the Benedictine Fathers established a monastery and 9 years later the Blessed Sacrament Fathers opened a seminary. The Sisters of St. Joseph of the Third Order of St. Francis established a provincialate in 1926 as did the Dominican Sisters in 1929. Additional arrivals included the Sisters of St. Joseph of St. Mark, 1926; Incarnate Word, 1927; and Vincentian Sisters of Charity, 1928. In 1939 Schrembs was given the title of archbishop as a personal honor, thereafter ruling as archbishop-bishop of Cleveland until his death on Nov. 2, 1945. A coadjutor, Bp. Edward F. Hoban of Rockford, Ill., had been named in November 1942; he accordingly became Cleveland's sixth bishop Nov. 2, 1945. On July 23, 1951, he received the personal title of archbishop.

During Hoban's administration, Bishop Rappe's cathedral was rebuilt and consecrated Sept. 6, 1948, new parishes were erected especially in the suburban areas, and educational and charitable facilities were expanded. Borromeo Seminary opened with a 4-year secondary school and 4-year college program. By 1963 there were 225 parishes and 4 missions in the diocese, 872 priests, 4 Catholic colleges with a combined enrollment of 5,371, 23,440 students in 35 Catholic secondary schools, 112,730 students in 191 Catholic elementary schools, and a total of 4,153 teachers in the diocese. In October 1964 Bp. Clarence G. Issenmann of Columbus was transferred to Cleveland as coadjutor with right of succession.

Bibliography: M. J. HYNES, *History of the Diocese of Cleveland 1847–1952* (Cleveland 1953). G. F. HOUCK and M. W. CARR, *A History of Catholicity in Northern Ohio and in the Diocese of Cleveland from 1749 to December 31, 1900,* 2 v. (Cleveland 1903). U.S. Work Progress Administration, *Roman Catholic Church: Parishes of the Catholic Church, Diocese of Cleveland* (Cleveland 1942). **Illustration credit:** Catholic Universe Bulletin.

[L. P. CAHILL]

CLICHTOVE, JOSSE, theologian; b. Nieuwpoort in Flanders (now in Belgium), *c.* 1472; d. Chartres, Sept. 22, 1543. He studied first in Louvain and then in Paris, where he obtained a doctorate in theology in 1506. Until 1518 Clichtove taught in Paris at the College of Navarre and at the Sorbonne, and at the same time he was mentor for various persons. Among his last pupils was Bp. Louis Gillard, who influenced his master's career by naming him his personal theologian first at Tournai (1519–21) and then finally at Chartres in 1526. His published works cover three fields: literature, philosophy, and theology. Clichtove, a former student of J. *Lefèvre d'Étaples, later became his collaborator. He propagated the ideas of humanist circles and wrote commentaries on treatises of eloquence and style as well as on many of Aristotle's books. Among his theological works worthy of note are his editions of the commentaries of Cyril of Alexandria, John Damascene, and the Pseudo-Dionysius, and the works of St. Bernard and Hugh of Saint-Victor. As early as 1520 Clichtove severed relations with his former humanist friends and fought against the reformers. He participated in the Sorbonne writings against Luther, and published *Antilutherus* (Paris 1524) and *De Sacramento Eucharistiae contra Oecolampadium* (Paris 1527).

Bibliography: H. M. FÉRET, *Catholicisme* 2:1248–49. A. CLERVAL, DTC 3.1:236–243. F. X. BANTLE, LexThK[2] 2:1234–35.

[C. DUMONT]

CLIFFORD, RICHARD, civil servant, bishop of London; d. Aug. 20, 1421. No firm evidence survives concerning his parentage and education. He was not styled master before 1397 or regularly afterward, and this scholastic title may have been used in error or as a compliment. Most authorities assert Clifford's descent from the baronial house of Westmorland; his father may have been the Lollard courtier Sir Lewis Clifford. As a retainer of the Black Prince and his wife, Lewis could have introduced his son to King *Richard II. Richard Clifford was known as a "king's clerk" from 1380, when he received the first of numerous benefices. He was one of the royal chaplains arrested by the Lords Appellant in 1388 but was soon released. He was appointed keeper of the great wardrobe (1390) and keeper of the privy seal (1397), an office he retained even after Richard II's deposition.

In 1400 the new King, Henry IV, refused to allow Clifford's *provision to the See of Bath and Wells but did assent to his transfer to that of *Worcester (1401) and to his translation to the See of *London (1407). Clifford had resigned the privy seal soon after his consecration as bishop and thereafter took little part in secular government except for an embassy to Germany (1402). He was one of the episcopal assessors at Sir John *Oldcastle's trial as a Lollard heretic (1413). He served in Henry V's embassy to the Council of *Constance and was its spokesman, favoring the election of Pope *Martin V. The unsupported statement of Thomas *Walsingham in his *Historia Anglicana* (RollsS 2:320) that Clifford himself was considered as a candidate for the papacy is hard to credit in view of his comparatively undistinguished career. He was buried in St. Paul's, London.

Bibliography: T. A. ARCHER, DNB 4:525–526. Emden 1:440–441.

[R. L. STOREY]

CLIMATIC CHANGE

During the long span of geologic time great and widespread changes on the surface of the earth have been caused by variations in climate. Effects of such variations have been both direct and indirect. Climatic variations and the resultant changes in vegetation affect the manner and rate of rock weathering, the soil forming processes, and the effectiveness of the erosive agents. Plant, animal, and human migrations have been occasioned by climatic changes.

Effects. The great Ice Age of the Pleistocene epoch began about 1 million years ago. Climatic conditions during and since the glacial age are deduced from glacial deposits, buried soil horizons, buried forest beds, pollen-bearing horizons in peat bogs, abandoned shorelines, animal skeletons, and even remains of human settlements. The instrumental record, which for most of the world is less than 100 years, by itself is inconclusive, but when it is correlated with other data, short-term trends are indicated. (*See* ISOTOPES, 3.) Conditions prior to the Pleistocene can only be inferred. There are indications, however, of more than one ice age in pre-Cambrian time, and glaciers were widespread in the southern hemisphere immediately preceding and during the early Permian period.

The Pleistocene Ice Age was not one of unrelieved cold. Four distinct glacial periods were interrupted by three interglacial intervals that were as warm or warmer than the present. Evidence from cores of deep sea sediments indicates that the chilling and warming effect of the glacial and interglacial intervals was worldwide.

During the Pleistocene epoch atmospheric circulation was essentially similar to that of today. The upper mid-latitudes were 10° to 15°F colder than the present, while the tropics were only 2° or 3°F colder. The build-up of cold anticyclonic air masses in high latitudes resulted in an equatorward shift of the zonal wind systems. Because of this and because of the steeper temperature gradient between the tropics and the mid-latitudes, the latter were much stormier than at present. Thus a cooler and wetter climate made possible the development and spread of continental ice sheets.

The shift of the zonal wind systems compressed the subtropical high pressure centers, and a much more humid climate prevailed in areas that are now semiarid or arid. The Mediterranean basin was more humid, and two large lakes, Lahontan and Bonneville, developed in the presently arid intermontane section of the U.S. Tropical deserts persisted, but were reduced in size. The equatorial regions also were more humid, and lakes in East Africa expanded into extensive bodies of water now indicated by abandoned shorelines.

At the height of the interglacial stages temperatures in the mid-latitudes were probably as much as 10°F warmer that at present; equatorial regions were only slightly warmer, but polar regions were markedly warmer.

Climatic conditions during postglacial times have been marked by variations in both temperature and precipitation. The most complete picture has been worked out for Europe, and scattered evidence from other parts of the world show parallel conditions. A remarkably warm, humid climate, 5°F warmer than the present, prevailed in Europe from 5600 to 2500 B.C. This so-called "Atlantic Climatic Optimum" was followed by a cooler, drier climate with periodic droughts until about 500 B.C. From then until the advent of the Christian Era a cold, wet climate prevailed. Glaciers advanced, transalpine travel was suspended, and rising water levels forced abandonment of lakeshore villages.

By the beginning of the Christian Era the climate was similar to that of the present. A milder climate prevailed during the Viking period, but the time from 1550 to 1850 was mainly one of glacial advance. The earlier part of this span is known as "the Little Ice Age" in Europe, where mountain settlements were displaced by advancing glaciers. Since 1850 glaciers generally have been retreating. In the 1930s the shrinkage was very rapid, but since 1950 the trend seems to have been arrested.

Causes. Several theories have been proposed to explain the lower temperatures of the Pleistocene era, but none fit all the known facts. To account for the warm interglacial intervals, inference of some cyclical temperature change is necessary. It has been suggested that glaciers develop during periods of reduced solar radiation, but since humidity varies with temperature, it also has been suggested that low solar radiation would cause cool, dry periods and high solar radiation hot, dry periods. Therefore, a cool, wet glacial period would occur during the transition from one extreme to another.

There is also a correlation between short-term variations in the number of sunspots and ultraviolet radiation. High sunspot activity corresponds with high ultraviolet radiation, which in turn correlates with atmospheric pressure conditions conducive to hot, dry weather in northern mid-latitudes. Analogous long term correlations of the instrumental record and known conditions of existing glaciers with sunspots since 1750 appear significant. From this H. C. Willet has postulated that low sunspot activity induces an expansion of the polar high-pressure areas, pushing the zonal wind belts equatorward and giving cool, stormy weather in mid-latitudes.

Whether the extremes of long-term variation in either quantity or quality of solar radiation are great enough to induce a glacial climate is uncertain. However, when these variations occur in conjunction with some other condition, such as crustal uplift, the resultant cooling might be sufficient.

Widespread crustal uplifts culminated at the beginning of the Pleistocene epoch. As a result, the land stood higher than it had for many millions of years. Significantly, all centers of glaciation were located in one of these newly uplifted areas. Perhaps uplift reduced temperatures and induced precipitation sufficiently to permit glaciers to develop and spread to adjacent lowlands. However, uplift alone would not account for the alternate cooling and warming of the Pleistocene.

Carbon dioxide in the atmosphere has an effect on the absorption of both terrestrial and solar radiation. It has been postulated that if the present volume of carbon dioxide in the atmosphere were reduced by 50 per cent the average surface temperatures would be reduced 7°F. It also has been suggested that increased quantities of volcanic dust or cosmic matter in the atmosphere would decrease temperatures by reflecting solar radiation back into space. However, evidence that the air had unusual amounts of dust in the Pleistocene is lacking.

Transfer of heat from equatorial regions to polar regions is accomplished by atmospheric and oceanic circulation. During the Pleistocene glacial stages, oceanic circulation across submarine sills was inhibited by a drop in sea level of some 300 feet. However, this would have been a perpetuating rather than a causal factor. The theory of continental drift suggests that the continents are not fixed and have shifted positions since they were formed. Consequently, when parts of a drifting continent extend into high latitude they become glaciated. Other theories, which have not won wide support, involve either a shifting of the earth's geographic poles or eccentricity in the earth's orbit around the sun.

Effect of Glaciation. Effects of post-Pleistocene climatic variation have been relatively minor compared to those resulting from widespread continental glaciation. Recent effects have consisted mostly of plant and animal migrations. During the Pleistocene about 30 per cent of the land was covered by ice at one time or another as compared to 10 per cent today. The two major centers of advance were Labrador and Scandinavia. Minor ice caps over Greenland and the British Isles merged with their larger neighbors. Highland areas, some of them even in low latitudes, also experienced extensive glaciation.

The effect of widespread glaciation was both direct and indirect. Areas over which the ice spread were scoured and gouged and then veneered with erosional debris when the ice melted. Preglacial relief and drainage were altered. Beyond the ice margins, melt waters laid down stratified deposits of sand and gravel. Winter winds sweeping down off the ice across these sands raised clouds of dust that later sifted down over bordering lands. These aeolian deposits, called loess, now form some of the world's best soils.

During the glacial stages so much water was locked in ice that sea level dropped about 300 feet below the present level, causing steams to erode their channels to new base levels. The weight of thousands of feet of ice depressed underlying lands. Waning glaciers subsequently released melt water, and sea level rose accordingly. Coral reefs grew upward to match new levels. Released from the weight of the ice, depressed portions of continents slowly rose as evidenced by warped and elevated abandoned shorelines. If all the glacial ice in the world today were to melt, sea level would rise at least 100 feet to former interglacial levels.

Bibliography: J. K. CHARLESWORTH, *The Quarternary Era* (New York 1957). R. F. FLINT, *Glacial and Pleistocene Geology* (New York 1957). C. E. P. BROOKS, "Geological and Historical Aspects of Climatic Change," *Compendium of Meteorology*, ed. T. F. MALONE (Boston 1951) 1004–18. H. SHAPLEY, ed., *Climatic Change: Evidence, Causes and Effects* (Cambridge, Mass. 1953).

[K. J. BERTRAND]

CLIMENT, JOSÉ, Spanish bishop, distinguished for charitable and educational work; b. Castellon de la Plana (Valencia), May 11, 1706; d. same town, Nov. 28, 1781. His parents were humble farmers who gave him a sound religious education. He received a doctorate in theology at the University of Valencia, where he later taught philosophy. For several years he was a parish priest at the Church of San Bartolomé and a beneficiary of the Cathedral of Valencia, and also served as a member of the Cortes. In 1766, he was consecrated bishop of Barcelona. He used his income to build primary schools, to establish a Chair "De Locis Theologicis" at the University of Valencia, to maintain a cemetery, and to help the poor. In 1775, after 9 arduous years of episcopal activity, he resigned his see, refused appointment to the See of Malaga and returned to his native city. There he founded the institution of "San Vicente Ferrer" for orphans. Bishop Climent was one of the most celebrated preachers of his time. His writings on pastoral and theological subjects are found in *Coleccion de las obras del ilustrisimo Señor D. José Climent* (Madrid 1788).

Bibliography: J. A. BALBÁS, *Castellonenses Ilustres* (Castellon 1883).

[S. A. JANTO]

CLINICAL PSYCHOLOGY

The branch of practical or applied *psychology concerned with the assessment and attempted rectifying of psychological abnormality. Thus it may be regarded as applied *abnormal psychology. It is the area of psychology most familiar to the general public, who often erroneously consider it representative of psychology in general. Because of its concern with the abnormal, clinical psychology is sometimes confused with *psychiatry, the medical specialty dealing with the diagnosis and treatment of mental illness. The fact that the fully qualified clinical psychologist holds a Ph.D. degree, which entitles him to be called doctor, has done nothing to lessen this confusion.

It is generally recognized, however, that the clinical psychologist is not trained in medicine and cannot presume to use medical techniques in the assessment and attempted modification of human behavior. What is not so well recognized is that the psychiatrist's medical training as such does not equip him to assess or modify behavior psychologically; that the psychiatrist may have had little or no education in scientific psychology; and that his employment of psychological techniques, e.g., psychodiagnosis and *psychotherapy, is not necessarily based on either medical or psychological science. Where mental aberration is known to be due to physical causes—as in brain damage or in toxic psychosis—or where its treatment may require medication or other physical intervention, e.g., tranquilizers or shock treatment, there is no doubt of the primacy of the physician's responsibility. But where there is no evidence of physical etiology, or where the method of treatment is psychological or psychosocial, the medical man is no more competent than such professionals as social workers and clinical psychologists.

A fully qualified clinical psychologist holds the diploma of the American Board of Examiners in Professional Psychology. This requires a Ph.D. in the field (which includes at least 1 year's supervised internship in a psychological service center such as a mental hospital, a child guidance clinic, or a community mental health agency) and 4 years of postdoctoral clinical experience. Most typically the professional training and experience of the clinical psychologist are interdisciplinary, involving collaboration with physicians, correction officers, hospital administrators, and others concerned with the understanding and management of the defective or deviant. Frequently the clinical psychologist is the middle member of a mental hygiene team consisting of psychiatrist, psychologist, and psychiatric social worker. Though traditionally viewed as inferior in prestige to the psychiatrist on the team (and accordingly paid less), the clinical psychologist has begun to insist that, in virtue of his comparable period of education and experience and his superior training in the research methods of behavioral science and the techniques of psychometric assessment (testing), he be regarded as at least equal to the psychiatrically trained medical doctor. Nevertheless, the tension that this insistence has generated has not prevented the great majority of individual psychiatrists and clinical psychologists from working together effectively.

Though the behavior deviations and deficiencies with which clinical psychology is concerned are only a small part of the subject matter of psychology, and though clinical formulations are hardly representative of psychology at its scientific best, it is clinical psychology that has contributed most to the development of psychology as a profession by bringing the psychologist out of the classroom and the laboratory and demanding that he deal professionally with the real problems of troubled people. Unlike the psychiatrist, the psychologist was not accustomed to assume professional responsibility for the well-being of his clients. In this respect he had (and still has) much to learn from interprofessional cooperation with physicians, especially psychiatrists, and social workers.

Historical Development. The first child guidance clinic in the U.S. was begun by the psychologist Lightner Witmer at the University of Pennsylvania in 1896, but clinical psychology as a profession developed slowly until World War II. Although by the 1930s many mental hospitals, mental hygiene clinics, and child guidance agencies employed psychologists to work with psychiatrists and social workers in the assessment and treatment of deviants and defectives, the status and role of the psychologist were restricted. The "applied" psychologist seldom had training beyond the master's degree, and his functions were confined largely to testing intelligence and coordinating the efforts of educational specialists with the treatment program established by the psychiatrist. His activities were directed rather narrowly by the clinic supervisor—always a physician and usually a psychiatrist—and his status was not much above that of medical assistant or laboratory technician.

World War II effected many changes in the clinical psychologist's position. Many psychologists were commissioned in the armed services because millions of men had to be evaluated psychometrically in a very short time. Intelligence *measurement was a primary aspect of this evaluation; the army general classification test, developed by psychologists, became a principal determinant of eligibility for officer candidate school; the measurement of mechanical, linguistic, and other aptitudes was important in assigning men to pilot training, strategic services, communications, etc. The contribution of psychology in these areas transformed the pilot training program, for example, from a hit-or-miss affair in which more than half of those selected "washed out" of pilot school to an efficient program in which only a small percentage of those scoring high on the pilot aptitude battery failed to complete training. Moreover, it became increasingly clear that emotional factors and aspects of *personality having little relation to general or specific aptitudes were crucial in determining suitability for military service. Of 15 million men examined at induction centers between 1940 and 1945, almost 2 million were rejected for neuropsychiatric (i.e., psychological) abnormalities. Of the 10 million accepted for service, more than 600,000 were discharged for disabilities that were psychological or psychosocial rather than physiological. Many hundreds of thousands more were temporarily disabled psychologically but were evaluated as able to return to duty after a period of rest and, in some cases, treatment, The volume of psychodiagnostic and minimal psychotherapeutic effort required to process these cases was far beyond the capacity of the military psychiatric staff. Consequently, psychologists who had been commissioned as "personnel selection officers" were pressed into service as clinical psychologists, i.e., as psychodiagnosticians and psychotherapists. And hundreds of psychologists were soon to be needed for neuropsychiatric cases being admitted into Veterans Administration hospitals.

To meet such needs, doctoral training programs in clinical psychology were established in American universities, and in 1947 the American Board of Examiners in Professional Psychology was incorporated to evaluate the qualifications of individuals principally in the field of clinical psychology, but also in industrial and counseling psychology. In 1965 more than 60 universities offered doctoral programs in clinical psychology approved by the American Psychological Association (APA), and more than 100 others offered master's degrees in clinical or related psychological services, such as school psychology, child guidance, and counseling. Of the almost 25,000 psychologists belonging to the APA, 37 per cent regarded themselves as principally clinical psychologists, and the division of clinical psychology was by far the largest division of the APA. In 1965, indeed, there were over 8,000 clinical psychologists in the APA, whereas in 1940 the total APA membership was less than 700.

This enormously rapid growth has not been without its pains and problems. The demand that psychology "do something" to help people has seemed at times to take precedence over the scientific need for understanding and to occasion hurried applications of poorly validated methods of assessment and behavior modification, so that clinical psychology cannot altogether escape the charge, first leveled at psychiatry, of being the application of a science that has not yet been invented. Some clinical psychologists seem impatient of the painstaking slowness of the scientific method and indifferent or even hostile toward research, while some academic psychologists, particularly those of experimental orientation, may regard clinical psychology as popularized science (if not science fiction) and view its practitioners as professionals without scientific interest or competence.

Catholics in Clinical Psychology. The negative attitude of many Catholics toward clinical psychology has been conditioned partly by reservations toward psychiatry with its Freudian sexual associations and partly by suspicion of the *determinism so often voiced by social and behavioral scientists. Such attitudes have become rare, however, since the foundation in the late 1940s of the *American Catholic Psychological Association and the *Guild of Catholic Psychiatrists, whose publications have done much to make clear that a psychodynamic approach to human motivation, especially aberrant motivation, does not, however much it may owe to Freud and psychoanalysis, necessarily imply a Freudian pansexualism or antireligious attitude. Many Catholic psychologists, philosophical and empirical, have argued tellingly that the determinism of *behaviorism is methodological rather than metaphysical, and that the group predictions and collective generalizations of psychology do not nullify free will. Moreover, and most importantly from the standpoint of clinical psychology, it seems that the very effort to counsel another human person presupposes the ability of that person to harness emotion to rational purposes, to inhibit impulse in the light of understanding, and in some measure to guide future conduct by his own intelligent choice. Psychotherapy, in short, implies rather than denies free will.

In the 1890s, under Msgr. E. A. *Pace, The Catholic University of America had one of the pioneer departments of clinical psychology; and, under Father T. V. Moore, this department was the first in the U.S. to offer systematic training in clinical psychology as part of its regular program. In 1916 Moore, a psychiatrist as well as a psychologist, founded a child guidance clinic connected with the University that provided psychology students with practical training in a psychiatric setting. But until 1959 his was the only Catholic department in the U.S. offering an APA-approved doctorate in clinical psychology; Loyola University, Chicago, and Fordham University have since received APA approval. In addition, some Catholic universities offer either doctorates in general psychology (e.g., St. John's University), not-yet-approved clinical doctorates (e.g., the University of Portland, Ore.), or clinically oriented master's degrees (e.g., the University of Detroit, Marquette University, De Paul University).

In Europe, the University of Louvain has been a center of psychological research, both theoretical and applied, since the early 1900s, and renowned for the experimental investigations of its leading figure, A. Michotte. Even wider-ranging were the researches at the University of the Sacred Heart in Milan undertaken by the physician-psychologist-priest A. *Gemelli. R. Dalbiez in France and J. Nuttin in Belgium are among the psychotherapists and clinical theorists who have contributed notably to reconciling the psychodynamic and Christian views of man, but nowhere in Europe has there been developed the kind of doctoral training program in clinical psychology that has become the accepted mode in the U.S. The clinician as scientist-practitioner appears to be a uniquely American ideal, seldom even approached outside the U.S. and Canada.

Evaluation. But this is an ideal, many would say, honored more in the breach than in the observance. In actuality, they argue, clinical psychologists tend to become dedicated either toward practice or toward research and criticism, but seldom toward both. Part of the difficulty may be temperamental: the helpmeet orientation and the critical research orientation are not easily reconciled in the same person. More fundamental perhaps is the objection that experimental methods have been developed chiefly to deal with artificially isolated part-functions and the behavioral signs of elementary cognitive processes such as may be found in lower organisms, rather than with the human being in his uniquely individual yet pervasively social complexity, as the clinical psychologist finds him. Even statistical techniques, important as they are for psychological measurement and prediction, are designed primarily to deal with group phenomena, group averages and dispersions, group norms, and the reliability of group differences. The individual, the proper concern of the clinical psychologist, can be treated statistically only indirectly and relative to the group. Thus the psychologist who is saturated with experimental and statistical methodology may find little in the clinical area to which his methods can be readily applied, while the perceptive clinician, concerned with understanding and helping the disturbed individual, can find little in established scientific methodology to help him and must rely on intuitive and phenomenological, rather than experimental and statistical, methods. The conflict is not irreconcilable, however, for experimental and statistical techniques can be adapted to deal with the complexities of human individual and social interaction, as the social psychologists have demonstrated in their analyses of *group dynamics, prejudice, and cognitive dissonance. Moreover, clinically interested psychometricians such as J. Zubin, P. E. Meehl, and H. J. A. Rimoldi have developed statistical techniques for analyzing the unique patterns and complexities within the individual (*see* PSYCHOMETRICS).

What seems to be needed in the scientific training of clinical psychologists is not less rigorous but more relevant experimental and quantitative methods; more training in human development and social learning and less perhaps in sensory psychology and animal conditioning. A doctrinaire adherence to Freudian sexual instinct theory has been a deterrent to developing a critical scientific and research orientation in clinical psychology, as it has in American psychiatry. In such concepts as ego-defense mechanisms and unconscious motivation Freud made the greatest contribution of any single person to the analysis of abnormal behavior, but in his obsessive preoccupation with the vicissitudes of infantile sexuality as the single and sovereign explanation of all adult motivation, normal and abnormal, he belongs more to the tradition of literary mythology than to scientific psychology. Clinical psychology has turned to Freud partly in imitation of psychiatry but also because general psychology had failed to develop an empirically meaningful and coherent general theory of human *motivation, *learning, and development. One can discern the beginnings of such a theory, however, in the work of R. Woodworth, G. Allport, C. Rogers, H. Harlow, H. McCurdy, and H. Mowrer, C. Curran, and J. Nuttin.

Though the 20th century has not produced an outstanding Catholic theorist in scientific psychology, Catholics have been in the forefront of those demanding from general psychology a more adequate and pertinent image of man. At the same time, Catholic institutions in the U.S. have shown an increasing interest in the application of psychology. Psychological screening of candidates for the religious life, using clinical devices such as the Rorschach Technique, the Thematic Apperception Test, and the Minnesota Multiphasic Personality Inventory, has become almost routine; an increasing number of Catholic universities offer degrees in psychology; and clinical services provided under Catholic auspices in child guidance, education and training of the retarded, vocational and marital counseling, and in the rehabilitation of the delinquent and the psychotic have shown an enormous proliferation since World War II. Thus the opportunities for Catholics in clinical psychology, whether under Catholic or secular auspices, are unlimited.

See also PSYCHOLOGY; COUNSELING; INDUSTRIAL PSYCHOLOGY; METHODOLOGY (PSYCHOLOGY); PSYCHOLOGICAL TESTING.

Bibliography: W. A. Hunt, *The Clinical Psychologist* (Springfield, Ill. 1956). R. I. Watson, "A Brief History of Clinical Psychology," PsychBull 50 (1953) 321–346. N. D. Sundberg and L. E. Tyler, *Clinical Psychology* (New York 1962). W. B. Webb, ed., *The Profession of Psychology* (New York 1962). J. R. Braun, comp. of articles from the official house organ of the APA, the *American Psychologist,* under the title *Clinical Psychology in Transition* (Cleveland 1961). H. Misiak and V. Staudt, *Catholics in Psychology* (New York 1954). *Newsletter* of the American Catholic Psychological Association, Fordham U., New York. R. J. McCall, "On the Nature of Psychology," *Journal of Clinical Psychology* 20 (1964) 311–325. *Catholic Psychological Record,* ed. A. A. Schneiders (New York 1963–) v.2, 3. *The Catholic Counselor,* ed. N. Pallone (New York 1956–). *Newsletter* of the National Catholic Guidance Conference, Mt. Mary College (Milwaukee, Wis. April 1952), mimeo.

[R. J. MC CALL]

CLITHEROW, MARGARET, BL.

The "pearl of York," English martyr; b. *c.* 1556; d. March 25, 1586 (feast, March 25). Her father, Thomas Middleton, was a prosperous chandler and sheriff of York. He died soon after his term of office (1564–65). In 1571 Margaret married John Clitherow, a rich and prominent butcher in York. Margaret had been brought up a Protestant; but John, although he conformed to the new faith, belonged to a Catholic family and had a brother who was a priest. Two or three years after her marriage, Margaret became a Catholic, although her husband, by then a chamberlain of York, was necessarily becoming more resolute in his Protestantism. By this time the Clitherows had two children, Henry and Anne; their third child, William, was born in prison during one of Margaret's internments for her faith. After her release she returned to her home, The Shambles, and her duties, looking after the butcher's shop and teaching her children. (She had taught herself to read in prison.) Soon, however, she decided that she was no longer qualified to teach her elder son, so she sent him abroad to Douai for a Catholic education and employed a tutor, Mr. Stapleton, for her two other children and those of her Catholic neighbors. Her husband turned a blind eye to this and to her other more dangerous practice of harboring priests.

Margaret, however, was becoming known as a fearless and outspoken Catholic. The government, perturbed by the persistence of the old faith in Yorkshire, urged the Council of the North to take strong measures and make an example of the leading Catholics. On March 10, 1586, the Council summoned John Clitherow to explain his son's absence abroad. While John was testifying, they sent a search party to his house. Stapleton escaped; there were no signs of priest, vestments, or chalices. The Clitherow children revealed nothing when questioned, but a Flemish boy was frightened into betraying where the vestments were hidden. Margaret and her household were arrested. Charged with harboring priests and attending Mass, Margaret refused to plead, saying, "Having made no offence, I need no trial." Had she pleaded, her own children might have been forced to give evidence against her, and this she was determined to prevent. The punishment for refusing to plead was *peine forte et dure,* and reluctantly Judge Clinch pronounced it: "You must . . . be stripped naked, laid down, your back upon the ground and as much weight laid up on you as you are able to bear and so to continue for three days . . . and on the third day to be pressed to death." Margaret was not allowed to see her children again. In prison she sewed a loose shift, for she was determined not to die naked. On March 25 the sentence was carried out. She died within a quarter of an hour, but her body was left for six hours in the press.

Bibliography: A contemporary memoir by her confessor, John Mush, appears in J. MORRIS, ed., *The Troubles of Our Catholic Forefathers Related by Themselves,* 3 v. (London 1872–77) 333–440. Butler Th Attw 1:679–682. M. T. MONRO, *Blessed Margaret Clitherow* (New York 1947). DictEngCath 1:517–519.

[G. FITZ HERBERT]

CLODION (CLAUDE MICHEL), sculptor; b. Nancy, Dec. 20, 1738; d. Paris, March 29, 1814. He won the Prix de Rome for sculpture in 1759. He spent his early career from 1762 to 1771 in Rome making numerous small terra-cotta groups, chiefly of fauns and nymphs and other such sensuous subjects. The large marbles he made of the same subjects, like the small, display the extreme *rococo refinement of the *baroque. In 1774 he sulptured a marble St. Cecilia for the Rouen cathedral, and in 1779 he completed his most famous work, a seated statue of Montesquieu, at the Institut, Paris. An excess of Republican virtue after the French Revolution nearly ruined Clodion, but he adapted to neoclassicism and executed reliefs for the Vendôme Column and the Arc du Carrousel, both in Paris.

Bibliography: H. THIRION, *Les Adam et Clodion* (Paris 1885). H. STEIN, Thieme-Becker 7:110–111. J. HOLDERBAUM, EncWA 3:697–698.

[T. BUSER]

CLOISTER, CANONICAL RULES FOR

Cloister, from the Latin *claustrum* meaning bar, signifies that part of a religious house, as well as gardens and recreational areas, reserved for the exclusive use of the religious. Always excluded from the enclosure are the church (or oratory) and its sacristy, guest quarters, and parlors or public offices (CIC c.597.2; Post Apost c.140.2). In the formal sense, cloister denotes the body of laws governing egress and ingress to the enclosure. Both in the Latin and Oriental Churches the law of enclosure is obligatory in all lawfully established religious houses. If these have an annexed building for resident students or for other works proper to the institute an area subject to the law of enclosure must be reserved for the exclusive use of the religious (CIC c.599.1; PostApost c.142.1).

Monks and Religious Orders of Men. With the exception of the wives of heads of state or of federated states, and the women in their entourage, entry within the precincts of the cloister is forbidden to females of whatever age, status, or condition (CIC c.598; Post Apost c.141.1). In the Latin Church dispensation from this norm is reserved to the Holy See. According to the Oriental law, the major superiors of the institute, for a grave cause, can dispense, providing the woman is accompanied by two discreet monks (PostApost c.141.2).

Nuns and Religious Orders of Women. In the Latin Church the Pontifical or Papal Cloister was observed in all monasteries of nuns, either in its major form when the nuns take solemn vows and lead an exclusively contemplative life; or in the form of minor enclosure when a notable number of the nuns, even though bound by solemn vows, regularly engage in some compatible apostolic activity, or by special permission of the Holy See take simple vows but lead only a contemplative life (apostolic constitution *Sponsa Christi,* 3 n 2; 3 nn 2, 3). However, Vatican Council II decreed that, while Papal Cloister should be maintained in the case of nuns engaged exclusively in the contemplative life, it must be adjusted to conditions of time and place and obsolete practices be suppressed. Nuns engaged in apostolic work outside the convent should be exempted from Papal Cloister to enable them better to fulfill their duties. Nevertheless, cloister must be maintained according to the prescriptions of their constitutions (*Decree on the Adaptation and Renewal of the Religious Life,* 16).

The law forbids entry to persons regardless of status, condition, sex, or age. Exception, however, is made for ecclesiastical or religious authorities at the time of canonical visitation, for authorized priests to administer the Sacraments of Penance and Holy Eucharist to the sick and to provide for the sacramental needs of those in danger of death, and, where it is the custom, for the interment of the deceased. Ingress is permitted also to cardinals, to the head of state and of federated states and their wives, together with their entourage, to doctors, surgeons, craftsmen, and to others whose services are generally needed and who have been approved by the local ordinary (CIC c.600; Instruction of the Congregation for Religious *Inter cetera,* n 27a).

Residential bishops, vicars and prefects apostolic, permanent administrators apostolic and abbots and prelates nullius, for just reasons, enjoy the right of ingress in the monasteries within their jurisdiction; and for a just and grave cause may grant this permission to others (motu proprio *Pastorale Munus,* n 34). Where the Minor Papal Cloister is observed, those in whose favor the apostolate is exercised as well as all persons who have a reasonable interest in or connection with the work itself or in those for whom the nuns labor may enter those parts of the monastery reserved for the apostolate (*Inter cetera,* nn 53–56).

Even though the nuns are bound to remain perpetually within the pontifical enclosure, they may leave when threatened by imminent death or other grave harm arising from any cause whatsoever, such as from fire, flood, earthquake, or military attack. Moreover, they may go out from the cloister when there is an urgent need for medical or surgical treatment or when contagious disease constitutes a threat to the entire community (*Inter cetera,* nn 20, 21). For a just and grave cause, residential bishops and other local ordinaries mentioned above may authorize egress for the nuns for as long a time as required (*Pastorale Munus,* n 34). Nuns of the Minor Cloister engaged in the apostolate can be permitted egress from the monastery by the superior when the work of the apostolate so demands, or to prepare for it, or to conduct business related to the particular apostolic activity (*Inter cetera,* nn 50b, 51).

The law of the Oriental Church does not admit of a distinction between a major and minor cloister, and the nuns are subject to the strict law of enclosure forbidding their egress and excluding from entry all members of the opposite sex of whatever age, status, or condition (PostApost c.143.1). For a grave reason a patriarch may dispense from the law for those monasteries within his patriarchate and the local hierarch for those in his territory (PostApost c.143.2). However, the law admits of exceptions for those ecclesiastical and civil dignitaries, sacramental ministers, and necessary personnel mentioned above in relation to the nuns of the Latin Church and it grants more ample right of ingress to patriarchs and archbishops. Providing they pertain to his rite, the patriarch and his entourage may enter a monastery of nuns anywhere; and an archbishop enjoys right of ingress in all monasteries within the territory of his archbishopric (PostApost c.143.1n1). In addition, local hierarchs may enter the enclosure not only at the time of canonical visitation, but whenever pastoral care requires (PostApost c.143.1n2). Nuns who have made either major or minor profession of vows may not leave the cloister except for a grave cause and with the permission of the local hierarch, but when necessity urges and there is no time for recourse, permission may be presumed (PostApost c.145).

Congregations of Religious Men and Women. In institutes of both men and women whose members take simple vows (in the Latin Church) or make minor profession (in the Oriental Church), the law of enclosure is obligatory. Entry within the enclosure is forbidden to members of the opposite sex, excepting the ecclesiastical and civil dignitaries, sacramental ministers, and necessary personnel referred to above. However, the religious superiors for a just and reasonable cause may authorize entry for those normally excluded (CIC c.604.1; PostApost c.150.1; 314.2); and egress of the religious is governed by the particular constitutions or statutes of the institute (CIC c.606.1; PostApost 152.1).

Custody and Violation of the Cloister. Primarily it is the duty of religious superiors to see to it that the laws of the enclosure are observed; and all to whom this custody is entrusted must guard against abuses that would be detrimental to religious spirit and discipline (CIC cc.605, 606.1; PostApost cc.151, 152.1). Apart from the demands of the apostolate exercised under religious obedience, superiors ordinarily may not permit their subjects to live outside of a house of the institute; but for a just cause they may grant permission for as brief a time as possible. Except for reasons of study, religious of the Latin Church require the permission of the Holy See for an absence from their religious house of more than 6 months. Among the Orientals such authorization can be granted by the patriarch, or outside the patriarchate by the president of a monastic confederation or the superior general of an institute (CIC c.606.2; Post Apost c.152.2).

Nuns of the Latin Church unlawfully leaving the monastery following profession, anyone unlawfully entering the parts of the monastery reserved for the use of the nuns, and anyone introducing or admitting such persons incur automatically an excommunication reserved simply to the Holy See. If the violator is a cleric, he is liable to suspension by his ordinary (CIC c.2342.1.3). In the case of the minor cloister, nuns who, without permission, enter those parts of the monastery set aside for apostolic work are liable to punishment by the superior or local ordinary; others who unlawfully enter these precincts may be punished by the local ordinary (*Inter cetera,* nn 61a, 63). There are no penalties established in Canon Law for either religious or others who violate the law of enclosure observed in the houses of congregations. However, for grave reasons in special circumstances the local ordinary can enforce the observance by means of censure, except in the case of exempt clerical institutes (CIC c.604.3).

The uniform law for religious of the Oriental Church grants to the local hierarch the right to penalize, even by censure, all who violate the enclosure of nuns. Moreover, if the nuns are subject to a male religious superior, he also may impose penalties upon delinquents (Post Apost c.147). With regard to the houses of religious congregations, the local hierarch enjoys the same right of enforcement as mentioned above for the Latin ordinary (PostApost c.150.3).

Bibliography: J. Creusen, DDC 3:891–907. Bousc-O'Connor 4:220–237; 3:222–248a. L. Fanfani and O'Rourke, *Canon Law for Religious Women* (Dubuque, Iowa 1961). C. Pujol, *De Religiosis Orientalibus* (Rome 1957). T Schäfer, *De Religiosis ad normam Codicis iuris canonici* (4th ed rev. Rome 1947).

[W. B. RYAN]

CLONMACNOIS, MONASTERY OF, former monastic foundation in County Offaly, Ireland (Gaelic, Clúain moccu Nois). St. Ciarán (or Kieran) founded it in 545; it was exceeded in influence only by *Armagh, and it in turn outshone Armagh in learning and sanctity. Its *paruchia* extended over about half of Ireland, and students flocked there, even from abroad. From its scriptorium came some of the most valuable manuscripts Ireland possesses: *Chronicon Scotorum, Annals of Tigernach,* Rawlinson B 502, and *Lebor na hUidre.* It successfully resisted domination by secular princes, and in the 8th and 9th centuries it was a reforming influence in a period of general decline. In the 10th century its abbots began to exercise episcopal jurisdiction, thus originating the Diocese of Clonmacnois. Referred to as the Westminster Abbey of Ireland (with countless royal tombs), it invited marauding attacks from its beginnings until its final razing at the hands of the English in 1552. Some idea of the magnitude of this monastic city may still be gained from the surviving ruins: 2 round towers, 8 churches, 3 large sculptured *Irish crosses, a castle, and over 200 inscribed tombstones, all of which have been the subjects of an imposing list of studies.

Bibliography: J. R. GARSTIN, "On the Identification of a Bronze Shoe-shaped Object as Part of the Head of an Ancient Irish Crozier," *Proceedings of the Royal Irish Academy* ser. 2, 1 (1879) 261–264. *Clonmacnois, Kings County,* extract from the 75th annual report of the Commissioners of Public Works in Ireland (Dublin 1906–07). Kenney 1:376–383. R. A. MACALISTER, "Story of Clonmacnois," *Proceedings of the Belfast Natural History and Philosophical Society* ser. 2, 1 (1935–40) 9–11. F. O. BRIAIN, DHGE 13:10–14. J. RYAN, "The Abbatial Succession at Clonmacnois," *Essays and Studies Presented to Professor Eoin MacNeill,* ed. J. RYAN (Dublin 1940) 490–507. E. H. L. SEXTON, *Descriptive and Bibliographical List of Irish Figure Sculptures of the Early Christian Period* (Portland, Maine 1946) 101–114. H. G. LEASK, *Irish Churches and Monastic Buildings,* 3 v. (Dundalk, Ire. 1955–60). **Illustration credit:** Commissioners of Public Works in Ireland.

[C. MC GRATH]

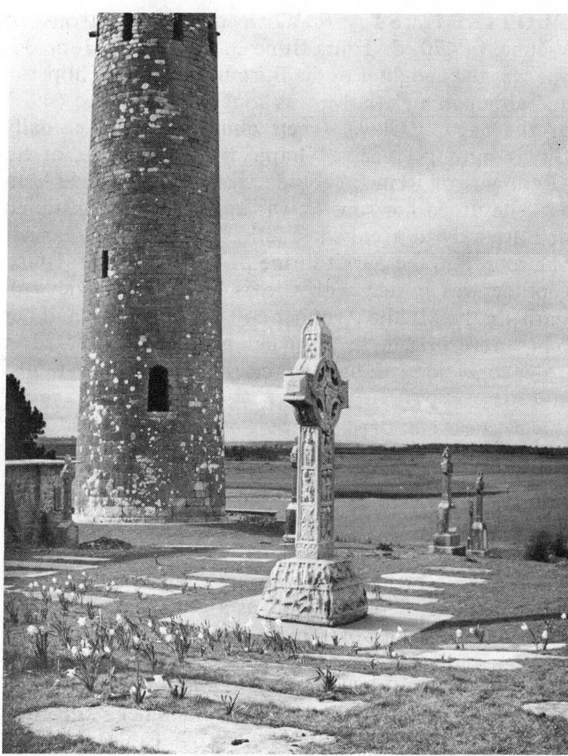

One of the round towers and the cross of the Scriptures at the site of the monastery of Clonmacnois, Ireland.

CLORIVIÈRE, JOSEPH PIERRE PICOT DE, soldier, priest; b. Brittany, France, Nov. 4, 1768; d. Washington, D.C., Sept. 29, 1826. He was the son of Michel Alain Picot and Renée Jeanne Roche, and for many years was called simply Joseph Picot de Limoëlan. He studied at the College of Rennes and the Royal Military School in Paris. He was assigned to the Régiment d'Angoulême, but resigned his commission early in 1791 and from then until 1799 was associated with the counterrevolutionists, taking an active part in the abortive plot to assassinate Napoleon on Dec. 24, 1800. He escaped to Savannah, Ga., and henceforth was known as Joseph Picot de Clorivière. In 1808 he entered St. Mary's Seminary in Baltimore; he was ordained Aug. 1, 1812. Charleston, S.C., with many refugees from Santo Domingo, needed a French priest, and he was sent there to assist Simon Felix *Gallagher. In 1814 he went to France, and on his return to Charleston he found that Gallagher and the vestry of the church had replaced him with another priest and would not honor his appointment from Abp. John Carroll. Archbishops Carroll, Leonard Neale, and Ambrose Maréchal in turn upheld him against the trustees and interdicted the church. To restore peace, Maréchal sent Benedict Fenwick, SJ, to Charleston in 1818, and Clorivière was appointed chaplain at the Visitation Convent in Georgetown, Washington, D.C. He also helped in founding St. Joseph's School in the District of Columbia. He was generous to the Visitation Convent and is considered its second founder.

Bibliography: D. H. DARRAH, *Conspiracy in Paris: The Strange Career of Joseph Picot de Limöelan* (New York 1953). P. K. GUILDAY, *The Life and Times of John England,* 2 v. (New York 1927). G. P. and R. H. LATHROP, *A Story of Courage: Annals of the Georgetown Convent of the Visitation of the Blessed Virgin Mary* (Cambridge, Mass. 1895). R. C. MADDEN, *Joseph Pierre Picot de Limoëlan de Clorivière* (Master's diss. unpub. CUA, Washington 1938).

[R. C. MADDEN]

CLOSED SHOP, a form of union security, incorporated in a collective bargaining agreement, under which only union members may be hired. It was outlawed in the U.S. by the Taft-Hartley Act (1947). It tended to persist, however, in the construction, printing, maritime, and entertainment industries because of such special hiring circumstances as skill requirements or the transient nature of employment. In 1959 the Landrum-Griffin Act relegalized it in effect in the construction industry, subject to the general Taft-Hartley provision that discharge from employment for nonmembership is permissible only when the latter results from the worker's refusal to tender regular dues and initiation fees. The closed shop should be distinguished particularly from the more common "union shop," under which union membership does not become a condition of employment until a certain period after hiring, usually 30 days.

See also COLLECTIVE BARGAINING (U.S.); OPEN SHOP; UNION SHOP.

[D. J. WHITE]

CLOTILDE, ST., Frankish queen; b. Lyons or Vienne, *c.* 470; d. Tours, June 3, 545 (feast, June 3). She was the daughter of the Burgundian King Chilperic, and although a Catholic, was sought in marriage (492) by the pagan *Clovis. Their children, and eventually Clovis himself, received Baptism at the hands of St. *Remigius of Reims. Clotilde was widowed in 511. In 523 she urged her sons to war against King Sigismund of Burgundy to avenge her father's death years earlier. She retired to the burial shrine of St. *Martin of Tours. Clotilde was buried with Clovis at St. *Geneviève in Paris. In the Middle Ages her cult was extensive and her relics were prized. In 1793 her body was cremated in order to avoid profanation, and the ashes were retained at Paris.

Bibliography: F. OPPENHEIMER, *Frankish Themes and Problems* (London 1952). J. M. WALLACE-HADRILL, *The Long-Haired Kings* (London 1962). G. BARDY, *Catholicisme* 2:1259–60. A. DUMAS, DictBiogFranc 9:34–35.

[R. H. SCHMANDT]

CLOUD, ST., known also as Chlodovald; d. Sept. 7?, 560 (feast, Sept. 7). He was a grandson of *Clovis and youngest son of Chlodomer, King of Orléans. Clovis's widow *Clotilde reared the three sons of Chlodomer after he was killed in an attack on the Burgundian kingdom (524). To acquire Chlodomer's kingdom, his brothers Childebert I and Chlothar I murdered two nephews, but Cloud escaped and voluntarily renounced royalty by entering religion. He led an edifying life, founded a monastery at Novigentum near Paris, and died a priest. Miracles occurred at his tomb, and by 811 his foundation was known as Saint-Cloud.

Bibliography: Sources. ActSS Sept. 3:91–101. BHL 1732–34. GREGORIUS TURONENSIS, *Historiarum libri,* 3:6, 18, ed. B. KRUSCH and W. LEVISON, MGSrerMer 1:101–103, 117–120. *Vita sancti Chlodovaldi,* ed. B. KRUSCH, *ibid.* 2:349–357. Literature. O. M. DALTON, ed. and tr., *The History of the Franks by Gregory of Tours,* 2 v. (Oxford 1927) 1:98–100. A. DUMAS, DHGE 13:22.

[W. GOFFART]

CLOUD OF UNKNOWING. Of unknown authorship, it is generally considered the greatest spiritual classic to issue from the mystical movement of the 14th century in England. It is a treatise on the contemplative life written for the instruction of a disciple who has already passed through the preparatory stages of discursive prayer and now finds himself in a state of deprivation and darkness, "as it were a cloud of unknowing." The *Cloud* is evidently the work of a priest and theologian at home in both patristic thought and contemporary controversy and speculation. He stresses the primacy of the will (as the faculty for loving) over intellect in the work of contemplation: "By love He may be gotten and holden; but by thought neither." He synthesizes with masterly skill traditional doctrine (especially of the Dionysian and Victorine line) and argues with the closely reasoned thought characteristic of Thomistic theology. His skill in working scriptural language and images into the very texture of his prose is a feature of his markedly original and forceful prose style. Manuscript evidence assigns the *Cloud* to the late 14th century and to an East Midland dialect.

Bibliography: P. HODGSON, ed., *The Cloud of Unknowing and The Book of Privy Counselling* (EEngTSoc 218; London 1944); ed., *Deonise hid Diuinite and Other Treatises* (EEngTSoc 231; London 1955); "Walter Hilton and 'The Cloud of Unknowing': A Problem of Authorship Reconsidered," *Modern Language Review* 50 (1955) 395–406. J. MCCANN, ed., *The Cloud of Unknowing* (London 1952). E. UNDERHILL, ed., *A Book of Contemplation, the Which Is Called The Cloud of Unknowing* (London 1946). D. KNOWLES, *The English Mystical Tradition* (New York 1961). C. PEPLER, *The English Religious Heritage* (St. Louis 1958).

[M. E. EATON]

CLOUET, JEAN AND FRANÇOIS, court painters, father and son, who created the French Renaissance portrait style. Jean (Janet); b. Low Countries?, *c.* 1485; d. Paris?, *c.* 1540. His work is characterized by a linearity tempered, especially in later years, by a modeling derived from *Leonardo. The disputed Louvre "Francis I" (*c.* 1523) and the Metropolitan Museum "Guillaume Budé" (*c.* 1535) represent his principal paintings. Numerous portrait drawings in three-crayon technique exist also, and display the unusual vitality and verisimilitude that distinguish his style. The portrait drawing as a work in itself quickly became a collector's item in 16th century France, and is apparently a French invention (perhaps Jean's).

François, also called Janet, b. Tours, *c.* 1515; d. Paris, 1572. Besides many drawings attributable to him there are, among his documented works, two autograph paintings, "Pierre Quthe" (1562, Louvre) and "Diane de Poitiers" (*c.* 1550, National Gallery, Washington, D.C.). His drawing style, although much in debt to Jean, differs in being sharper and far more detailed, lacking Jean's freer touch and fuller modeling. Of the two, Jean seems more the Renaissance artist; François, more the mannerist.

See also RENAISSANCE ART.

Bibliography: I. ADLER, "Die Clouet," *Jahrbuch der Kunsthistorischen Sammlungen in Wien,* NS 3 (1929) 201–246, extensive bibliog. A. CHÂTELET and J. THUILLIER, *French Painting*

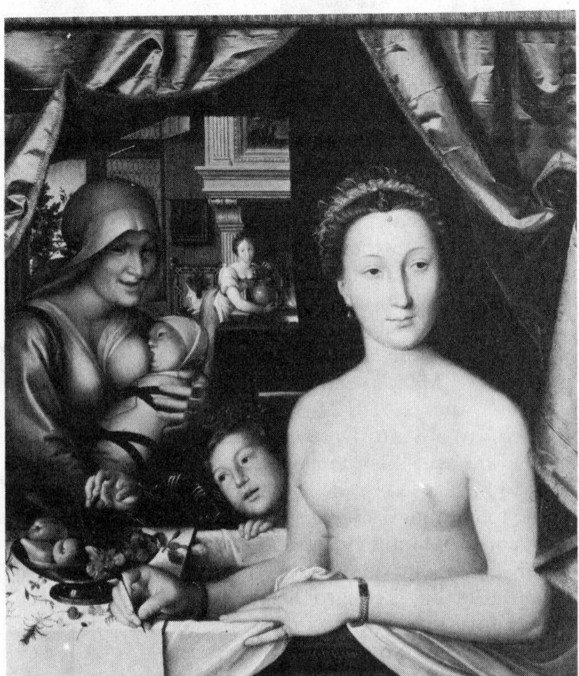

François Clouet, "Diane de Poitiers," panel, 36¼ by 32 in.

from Fouquet to Poussin, tr. S. GILBERT (Cleveland 1963) 121–136, *passim*. L. DIMIER, Thieme-Becker 6:116–120. **Illustration credit:** National Gallery of Art, Washington, D.C., Samuel H. Kress Collection.

[O. A. RAND]

CLOVIS I, KING OF THE FRANKS. (Chlodovech, Ludovicus); b. Tournai, 465; reigned 481–511; the real founder of the Merovingian state. The son of Childeric I and Basina, at the age of 15 he attained the kingship of the Salian and other Franks around Tournai. A barbarian, shrewd, ruthless, and opportunistic, his success was due to military strength and a willingness to employ brute force to solve any problem. With some trouble Clovis united the many petty tribes of the Frankish confederacy into a single, strong state. He achieved this by himself murdering or having murdered other Frankish kinglets: Ragnachar of Cambrai, Chararic, Cloderic of Cologne, and "many other kings" whom *Gregory of Tours does not name. In 486 Clovis began his brilliant expansionist policy by defeating Syagrius, an independent Roman governor, at Soissons. On his eastern border the Alamanni threatened the Franks with an expansion into Alsace. Clovis marched against them (496?, 503?, or 506?) and in a single battle at Tolbiac broke their power. Some Alamanni immediately accepted him as king. He then defeated the Visigoths, who controlled Gaul south of the Loire and most of Spain, but were rent by dissension. After temporizing with Alaric II, Clovis declared war in 507, personally slew Alaric at Vouillé, and captured Toulouse and Bordeaux. All Visigothic land in Gaul except Septimania passed to Clovis. His one significant failure was his inability to subdue the Arian Burgundians who were inhabitants of the Rhône-Saône region.

"Baptism of Clovis" by the "Master of St. Gilles."

Clovis's conversion to orthodox Catholicism rather than Arianism was of great importance. His motives are not known. His Catholic wife Clotilde influenced him, but legend attributes his decision to divine aid at the battle of Tolbiac. He must have seen political advantages in his conversion. With the consent of the Franks, who followed him into the Church, he allowed St. *Remigius of Reims to baptize him, probably at Reims shortly after Tolbiac. His new faith served him against the Arian Visigoths and guaranteed the permanence and stability of the Merovingian state. It won invaluable episcopal support and put the Church's authority at the king's disposal. The first national synod, at Orléans in 511, summoned and directed by Clovis, accepted royal domination. His government combined Germanic elements with the traditional Roman administration. He received from Emperor Anastasius the honorary titles of consul and patrician. He promulgated the *Lex Salica* as the Frankish law code *c.* 508. Four sons survived him: Theuderic (born of a concubine) and Clotilde's children—Chlodomer, Childebert I, and Chlothar I. His sister Albofled married Theodoric the Ostrogoth. *See* THEODORIC THE GREAT.

Bibliography: F. OPPENHEIMER, *Frankish Themes and Problems* (London 1952). J. M. WALLACE-HADRILL, *The Long-haired Kings* (New York 1962). G. BARDY, *Catholicisme* 2:1264–66. E. EWIG, LexThK[2] 2:1073. A. DUMAS, DictBiogFran 9:44–48. **Illustration credit:** National Gallery of Art, Washington, D.C., Samuel H. Kress Collection.

[R. H. SCHMANDT]

CLUNIAC ART AND ARCHITECTURE

During the 250 years after their foundation, the monastic houses of Cluny became the most important and widespread in Europe, comprising some 1,450 priories and some 10,000 monks in England and on the Continent as far east as Poland. Very active in the arts, the Cluniacs were responsible for bringing to fruition the Romanesque style, especially in France. The practicing of St. *Benedict's precept of prayer and work (*ora et labora*) virtually guaranteed the order great church and cloister architecture. Music was essential also; *Odo, a former precentor at Tours and the first great abbot at Cluny (927–949), firmly established the inseparable musical and spiritual traditions of the Cluniacs (*see* CLUNIAC REFORM). *Peter the Venerable, the last great 12th-century abbot at Cluny (1122–57), gave an intellectual and artistic interpretation to *labora:* "It is more noble to set one's hand to the pen than to the plow, to trace divine letters upon the page than furrows upon the fields." It was during his abbacy that Cluniac art reached its zenith.

Architecture. The most important single Cluniac manifestation of Romanesque style was the great church of SS. Peter and Paul constructed at Cluny under Abbots *Hugh of Cluny (1049–1109) and Peter the Venerable between its official founding, Sept. 30, 1088, and its formal dedication by Pope Innocent II, Oct. 25, 1130. Work continued until about 1450 on the western towers, long after Cluniac power had diminished. The church itself was destroyed, save for the south arm of the western transept, between 1798 and 1823. Cluny III, so termed in contradistinction to two earlier churches of the 10th century that it superseded, was

Fig. 1. "The Third Tone of Plainsong," capital from the chevet of Cluny, now in the Musée Ochier, Cluny.

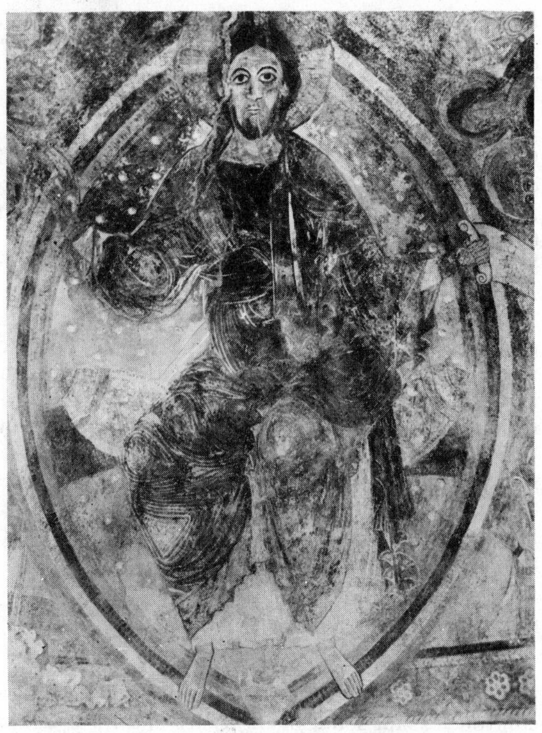

Fig. 2. "Christ in Glory," fresco, c. 1100, in the chapel of St. Hugh of Cluny, Berzé-la-Ville.

CLUNIAC ART AND ARCHITECTURE

Fig. 3. "Christ in Glory," tympanum, c. 1130, of the church of Saint-Pierre, in Carennac, France.

the largest church in Europe save St. Peter's in Rome and was the principal expression of Benedictine Romanesque monastic architecture.

Built on the plan of a double-armed archiepiscopal cross, Cluny III was over 600 feet in length, including a Gothic narthex completed about 1225, and reached an interior vaulted height of 100 feet for the first time in medieval architecture. This feat duly impressed a chronicler in 1120, who wrote, ". . . and suddenly [as one enters the nave] a giant basilica surges up . . .." As capital church of the Cluniac congregation of Benedictines, Cluny III was able to hold all the monks of the order; in 1132 there were 1,212 monks assembled in procession in the church. Medieval visitors were no less impressed by its workmanship than by its size; later visitors were equally awed by its total effect: "If you see its majesty a hundred times, you are overwhelmed on each occasion" (Mabillon, 1682).

The *chevet* of the great church had five isolated chapels radiating from an ambulatory, a distinguishing feature of later Cluniac Romanesque architecture. It is seen in Saint-Étienne at Nevers, consecrated 1097, and Paray-le-Monial, 1104, each of which has three chapels. But at Cluny concentration focused on the great altar whose top is preserved in the Musée Ochier, Cluny, and from which for nearly 700 years song and incense rose daily to the large "Christ in Glory" fresco in the apse. This painting is now destroyed, but a contemporary reflection may be seen in Abbot Hugh's chapel in the Cluniac grange at nearby Berzé-la-Ville (*c.* 1100). The mosaic floors with images of the saints led past two transepts (a rare feature for the time), each with lateral chapels, to the great five-aisled nave. The central nave aisle, 33 feet wide and 100 feet high under its pointed, ribbed barrel vault (part of which collapsed in 1125 but was rebuilt by 1130), was flanked by compound piers 8 feet in diameter. It consisted of a main arcade, a false triforium having no lateral passage in the wall, and a clerestory. The pointed arches used at Cluny III for the first time on such a scale in medieval architecture may have reflected, as did the cusping of the triforium arcade, Islamic influences from Spain, one of whose monarchs, Alfonso el Bravo (d. 1109), was married to Hugh's niece Constance and contributed annually 200 ounces of gold to the abbey. The basic concept, however, was neither Spanish nor Islamic. The architects of Cluny III were Gunzo, a retired abbot of Baume, who served as designer (*μηχιανίκος*), and Hérzelo, a former canon of Liège, who served as builder (*ἀρχιτέκτων*). As K. J. Conant has demonstrated, the design was based on several systems of musical numbers, notably the Pythagorean series of 2, 3, 4, 6, 8, 9, and 12. Further, since Gunzo is known to have been a musician (*psalmista praecipuus*), it is not impossible that the design should have been related to *Gregorian chant, an essential part of Cluniac ritual and one demanding vaulted churches for acoustical reasons.

A number of buildings reflect the interior disposition of Cluny III, especially the nave of Autun cathedral (*c.* 1125) and the Cluniac priory churches of Paray-le-Monial and La Charité-sur-Loire (consecrated 1107), but there never existed a Cluniac school of architecture in the sense that Cistercian churches of the 12th century unquestionably relate to a single concept. *See* CISTERCIAN ART AND ARCHITECTURE. Cluniac influence may account for the general uniformity found in the great churches of the pilgrimage roads, such as Sainte-Foi at Conques and Saint-Martial at Limoges, the latter a Cluniac dependency; but, despite discernible interdependent relationships and groupings among the some 325 Cluniac churches remaining at least in part (for example, the *en échelon* apse plan of Cluny II and Payerne, Switzerland, after 1050), Conant is correct in saying that the "Cluniacs were more zealous for uniformity in customs, discipline, and liturgy than in architecture."

Sculpture. Cluniac sculpture developed from manuscript illustrations, the expected source in an intellectual order. St. Benedict's Rule required each monk to read one book during Lent, and the library at Cluny possessed some 570 volumes in the 12th century. Nowhere is the relationship between manuscript illustration and sculpture more clearly seen than by comparing the cloister plaques at Moissac (*c.* 1100) with manuscripts known to have been at the Cluniac abbey. However, the most artistically complete treatment of iconographic themes is to be found at Cluny III itself. The now-destroyed "Christ in Glory" with symbols of the *Evangelists of the central west tympanum (carved *c.* 1115; destroyed 1810) was "painted like a manuscript page" and was the first large sculptural expression of this theme, the forerunner of many such portals extending in time well into the Gothic period (Carennac, *c.* 1130; Charlieu porch, *c.* 1145; Last Judgment at Beaulieu, *c.* 1135; central narthex tympanum at Vézelay, by 1135).

Cluniac capitals were often Corinthianesque in form, especially after 1090, and the order found place also for such Islamic motifs as pointed arches (Cluny III; Paray-le-Monial; Vézelay) and cusping (Cluny III; La Charité-sur-Loire; Chalais, *c.* 1150). Cluny did not, then, invent Romanesque themes or inaugurate stylistic features, but it did give the former a coherency and the latter a fullness that neither had previously.

This consummate combining of theme and style is most evident in the ambulatory capitals surviving from the *chevet* of Cluny III, consecrated Oct. 25, 1095, by Pope Urban II (Musée Ochier, Cluny). The illustrated themes provided the first important series of allegorical capitals in Romanesque art. Inspired by the writings of Radulphus Glaber, they included the four seasons, the cardinal virtues, the four trees (a new subject), and the four rivers of paradise. Two capitals from the ambulatory represented the eight tones of the chant; they indicate a link between Cluniac liturgy and art. These personifications of the musical tones, based on a late 11th-century *tonarius* manuscript from Saint-Martial at Limoges (Paris, Bibl. Nat., MS lat. 1118), are among the finest of all early Romanesque capitals and demonstrate fully how the Cluniacs gave sculptural substance to musical and allegorical themes.

St. *Bernard of Clairvaux (d. 1153) disliked Cluniac "ostentatiousness" in art, but even he acknowledged its "endless varieties of forms . . . fashioned with marvelous subtlety of art" (*Apologia ad Guillelmum, c.* 1125). Through the enrichment of decoration with meaningful and systematic symbolism, the Cluniacs made one of their most important contributions to the development of medieval art.

Bibliography: J. EVANS, *The Romanesque Architecture of the Order of Cluny* (Cambridge, Eng. 1938); *Cluniac Art of the Romanesque Period* (Cambridge, Eng. 1950), the two best gen. introds. to Cluniac art and architecture, with extensive bibliogs.

K. J. CONANT, "Mediaeval Academy Excavations at Cluny, VIII: Final Stages of the Project," *Speculum* 29 (1954) 1–43, author's many earlier *Speculum* articles are cited on p.1; "New Results in the Study of Cluny Monastery," *Journal of the Soc. of Archi-tect. Hist.* 16 (Oct. 1957) 3–11; "Mediaeval Academy Excavations at Cluny, IX: Systematic Dimensions in the Buildings," *Speculum* 38 (1963) 1–45, good illus.; *Carolingian and Romanesque Architecture, 800 to 1200* (PelHArt Z13; 1959). M. AUBERT, "Église abbatiale de Cluny," *Congrès archéologique de France* 98 (1935) 503–522, a good description, but dating of the sculpture too late. F. DESHOULIÈRES, "Le Rôle de Cluny," *Bulletin monumental* 94 (1945) 413–434, indicates the specific Cluniac contributions of Romanesque architecture. **Illustration credit:** Archives Photographiques, Paris.

[C. F. BARNES, JR.]

CLUNIAC REFORM

One of the most significant monastic movements of the high Middle Ages. It is necessary first of all to clarify the notion of "Cluny" and of the reform movement that sprang from it. Cluny as such is a mere abstraction, given different meanings at various times and places. If the reform is limited to the period extending from its foundation (909) to the death of St. *Hugh of Cluny (1109), it denotes a monastic evolution (expressed by the various successive Customaries), and an administrative evolution brought on by rapid territorial expansion. The reform was centered in one place: the Abbey of *Cluny. It is a mistake to attribute to the Order of Cluny or to the Abbey of Cluny the reforming activity carried out by the great abbots of Cluny as individuals, and the reverse also is true.

History of the Reform. The Abbey of Cluny was not founded as a reforming agency. Originally, Cluniac monasticism drew its inspiration from the Rule of St. Benedict and the legislation of *Benedict of Aniane. Because of specific historical circumstances, alien to the mentality of its founders, Cluny rapidly became the center of a vast movement of reform that continued until the 12th century. The popes and feudal authorities alike entrusted to the abbots of Cluny the reform of

older monasteries and the foundation of new houses. There is, however, no trace of a "will to power" prejudicial to contemporary monastic congregations independent of the Cluniac movement. Following G. Tellenbach, J. Leclercq has noted that the influence of the Cluniacs, first in Aquitaine and later over a wider area, was the result of a flexible method of adaptation to various feudal milieus and to concrete circumstances at various monasteries, which interested princes and lay lords in monastic reform and reduced to a minimum the obstacle that political frontiers might have created. The spread of the Cluniac reform was spontaneous in most instances. Cluny did not try to gain possession of churches belonging to laymen. This fact is worth noting, since the feudal Church had fallen into lay hands. Beginning with *Odo of Cluny (d. 949), the expansion of the Cluniac Order accelerated, and Cluny benefited from the changing conditions in feudal society. Enjoying temporal immunity from the time of its foundation, it received canonical exemption only in 931 (Bull of John XI), and exemption from episcopal authority, *c.* 998–999 (Gregory V granting the privilege confirmed and clarified by John XIX in 1027; later by his successors, notably Gregory VII). The monasteries attached to Cluny enjoyed the same temporal and spiritual independence, except in certain specific cases such as those of Saint-Martin-des-Champs and *Saint-Bertin. Henceforth Cluniac monasteries were the property of the Apostolic See, which defended and protected them in jurisdictional conflicts, notably those instigated by the bishops of Mâcon, in whose territory Cluny was situated. The strong organizing personalities of *Odilo and Hugh assured a certain juridical unity among the monasteries, but the ties of each community varied from strict subjection to simple affiliation or mere adoption of the Cluniac Customary (which did not necessarily imply juridical dependence). This unity consisted in a federation, independent of sectionalism and of political and territorial structures, lay and ecclesiastic. Its members (abbeys and priories with their dependencies) were united to a central authority, the abbot of Cluny, by bonds of varying degrees of closeness and according to a meticulously ordered hierarchy.

Nature of the Reform. The Cluniac reform, without deviating from its initial purpose, dedicated itself also to tasks of the temporal and political order. The abbots, especially Odo, Odilo, and Hugh, gave to this objective the loyal support of personal service and moral influence, without loss of independence. This is evidenced in the diplomatic missions they carried out on behalf of German emperors, Capetian kings, and popes, notably during the *investiture struggle. And yet the trust in Cluny engendered in the world's great leaders did not hinder its human and spiritual influence, of which there are abundant contemporary records.

The Cluniac reform consisted first of all in the establishment of a monasticism based on *Consuetudines,* to which *Statuta* were later added. Only secondarily did it lend support to the renovation undertaken by ecclesiastical and lay authorities regarding simony and unworthy clerics; and in so doing it promoted an effective and general recognition of papal supremacy. The Order of Cluny was never a specialized entity organized to combat the decadence of the Church or to withstand the Empire, even when Cluniac monks became popes, cardinals, and bishops. Other movements of reform received their inspiration from Cluny. Suffice it to cite the *Ordo monasterii sancti Benigni* of Dijon, organized before 1069, which was based literally on the Customaries of *Bernard (*c.* 1070) and Udalric (*c.* 1080–83). The *Ordo* of Dijon was later adopted at *Fécamp, as well as at *Fruttuaria, which introduced its reform into Germany.

The End of Reform. After more than 2 centuries of unparalleled expansion, Cluniac monasticism was weakened in part by its internal structure and by the order's excessive expansion, temporal power, and the absence of a centralized governing body. It has been calculated that at the height of its development the order had 1,184 houses, situated in several provinces. *Peter the Venerable (d. 1157) understood the need for adaptation required by economic and social change; and at successive general chapters statutes were passed. But in the same era the new order of Cîteaux seemed to be a return to Cluny's primitive simplicity; and with the rapid development of the *Cistercian movement, the Cluniac reform came to an end. In the centuries that followed, Cluny itself was in need of reform.

Bibliography: G. DE VALOUS, DHGE 13:35–178. J. LECLERCQ, "Pour une histoire de la vie à Cluny," RHE 57 (1962) 385–408, 783–812. G. SCHREIBER, "Gregor VII, Cluny, Cîteaux, Prémontré zur Eigenkirche, Parochie, Seelsorge," ZSavRGKan 34 (1947) 31–171. K. HALLINGER, *Gorze-Kluny,* 2 v. (Rome 1950–51). J. WOLLASCH et al., *Neue Forschungen über Cluny und die Cluniacenser,* ed. G. TELLENBACH (Freiburg 1959). C. VIOLANTE, "Il monachesimo cluniacense di fronte al mondo politico ed ecclesiastico (secoli X e XI)," *Spiritualità cluniacense* (Todi 1960) 153–242. J. F. LEMARIGNIER, "Les Institutions ecclésiastiques en France de la fin du Xe au milieu du XIIe siècle," *Institutions ecclésiastiques,* v.3 of *Histoire des institutions françaises au moyen âge,* ed. F. LOT and R. FAWTIER (Paris 1957–62).

[R. GRÉGOIRE]

CLUNY, ABBEY OF

A Benedictine abbey of primary importance in the reform of the Church in the Middle Ages, located in the Rhone Valley (Burgundy), Diocese of Mâcon, department of Saône-et-Loire.

Foundation and Buildings. On Sept. 2, 909, Duke William of Aquitaine offered Bl. *Berno the territory of Cluny on which he planned to build a monastery under the patronage of SS. Peter and Paul and which he exempted from all temporal authority except that of the Holy See. The successive stages of the buildings at Cluny have been the subject of intensive study by K. J. Conant. Berno replaced the original oratory with a church begun in 910 (Cluny I); this church, razed by *Majolus, was replaced by Cluny II, which was dedicated in 981. The monastery was rebuilt by *Odilo. Under *Hugh, Cluny III was an immense church completed *c.* 1113, and dedicated by *Innocent II in 1130. Its main altar had been consecrated by *Urban II in 1095. This sumptuous basilica influenced the Romanesque architecture of Burgundy (*Paray-le-Monial, etc.) and the monumental sculpture of France and Spain in the 12th century. Six centuries later, during the tenure of Frederick Jerome de la Rochefoucauld (1747–57), the monastery was partially replaced by structures still in existence. The old basilica was almost totally destroyed from 1798 to 1823.

Abbots and Monks. The list of abbots has been carefully established by G. de Valous [DHGE 13 (1956) 40–135]. Several of these had a hand in the making of medieval Europe. *Odo of Cluny (927–942), Berno's

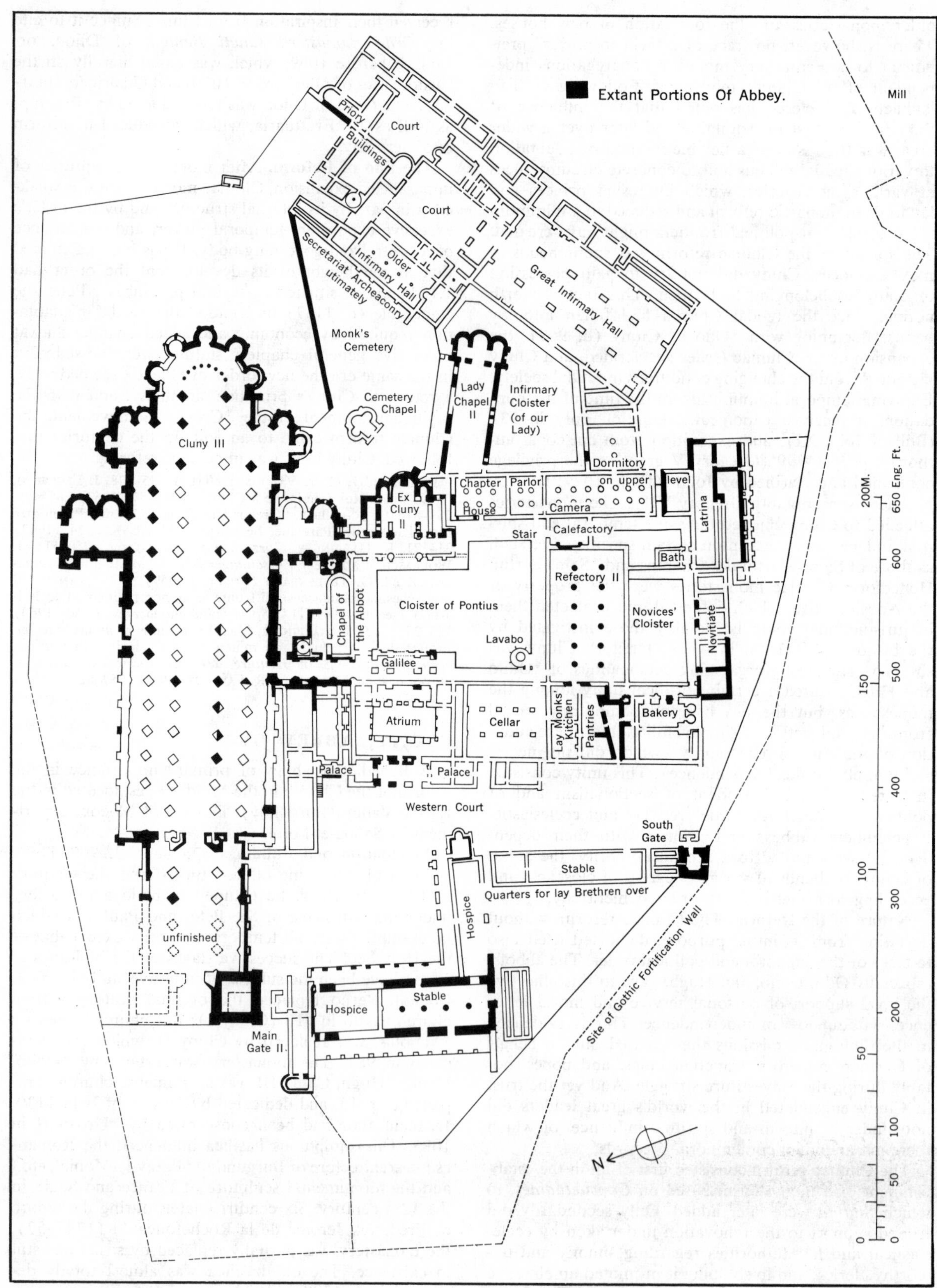

The Abbey of Cluny as it looked c. 1157, with indications of certain later additions.

successor, was the first of a series of abbots who during 2 centuries enabled Cluny to play its important role. Majolus (948–994), Odilo (994–1049), and Hugh (1049–1109) were saints who epitomized the Cluniac ideal. Besides being counselors to the German emperors and diplomats in the service of popes and kings, the abbots of Cluny strove to create an authentic monastic spirit in their concern for the interests of the Church and the needs of the time. Many monasteries introduced internal reforms and adopted Cluniac customs; priories were founded and gradually united by the adoption of common observance in essential matters. Together these formed an *Ordo cluniacensis,* which progressively became an order (i.e., a grouping of monasteries under the sole authority of the abbot of Cluny) under Odilo, Hugh, and their successors (*see* CLUNIAC REFORM). Until the 12th century, the growth of the Cluniac properties was rapid. Cluniac "provinces" were established in France, Germany, England, Italy, and Spain, totaling 1,184 houses at the peak of the order's development (beginning of 12th century). Enjoying canonical exemption and temporal immunity, they were subject only to the Apostolic See.

Under Pons de Melgueil (1109–22) a less glorious period began, even though the prestige of Cluny remained great. *Peter the Venerable (1122–57) engaged in a series of animated discussions with *Bernard of Clairvaux concerning Cluniac observance. Despite the fact that the statutes were reformed in 1132, the vitality of Cluny diminished, especially because of difficult economic conditions. Subsequent abbots, chosen often from the great feudal families (Clermont, Anjou, Alsace, etc.), engaged in national or local struggles, and at the end of the 13th century, the order became completely national and French. Unfortunately the popes, with a view to remedying the deplorable state of the Curia's finances, conceded Cluniac priories *in commendam,* and certain abbots preferred to reside in Avignon rather than at Cluny. Jean de Bourbon (1456–85) was the last regular abbot. The commendatory abbots left a part of the government in the hands of vicars-general, but Cluny declined rapidly despite efforts at reform, especially in the 17th century. The order was divided into the Old Observance and the Strict Observance. On Feb. 19, 1790, Cluny came to an end juridically. The number of monks living in the Abbey of Cluny varied. There were 76 at the time of Odilo's election (994); more than 400 at the beginning of the 12th century; 140 during the abbacy of Eymard Gouffier (1518–28); 72 in 1635; and 36 in 1725.

Legislation and Observance. At the time Cluny's foundation, Berno introduced the usages of Baume, i.e., the Rule of St. *Benedict as adapted by the legislation of *Benedict of Aniane (*see* BENEDICTINE RULE). At the beginning of the 11th century, the first customary appeared. It was a liturgical directory founded on usage, not on law. Several redactions, even for Cluny itself, are known. Under Abbot Odilo: the *Antiquiores consuetudines (B), c.* 1000 to 1015; and the *Consuetudines Farfenses, c.* 1030 to 1049. During the tenure of Hugh: the *Consuetudines Bernardi, c.* 1070; and the *Consuetudines Udalrici, c.* 1080 to 1083. The *Consuetudines* are descriptive rather than regulatory and do not contain the entire observance. When the needs of the order demanded, as they did during the terms of Peter the Venerable (1132) and Jean de Bourbon (1458), the *Statuta* were revised. Religious observance varied during the 8 centuries of the abbey's existence. The daughter abbeys, moreover, were not required to follow the same observances as Cluny, for the customary was essentially flexible and devoid of legalism.

Cluny, the remaining transept of the medieval church.

Cultural and Liturgical Life. Cluny's influence was not the result merely of the strong personalities of its abbots. Its monastic spirit was due to the hundreds of monks who generously consented to live the Cluniac observance of prayer and work, and whom Callistus II, in 1120, called "the mirror of monastic observance in modern times" (PL 180:1164 D). The cultural and artistic activity of Cluny surpassed that of all other monastic centers, with the exception of *Monte Cassino (*see* CLUNIAC ART AND ARCHITECTURE). Texts cited by J. Leclercq show that Cluny joined a profound spirituality with broad culture. The library had 570 volumes in the 12th century; and Cluniac writings reveal essentially Biblical, patristic, and historical orientation, which attached importance to the authors of classical antiquity.

The primacy of the liturgy in Cluniac observance did not impede individual work and private prayer. Most of the additional liturgical offices that brought on Cluny the accusation of "ritualism" had accumulated prior to Cluny. The customaries and statutes provided for many mitigations and dispensations (especially with regard to the monks entrusted with conventual functions). The weekly liturgy was essentially the same as that of the Rule of St. Benedict, with various supplements and with an amount of solemnity measured by the importance of a feast. The temporal and sanctoral cycles were related to the Roman rite, with local and monastic usages. A long and sometimes exhausting liturgy seems not to have excluded an air of joy and contentment.

Bibliography: Cottineau 1:816–825, with bibliog. K. J. CONANT, "Mediaeval Academy Excavations at Cluny, VIII: Final Stages of the Project," *Speculum* 29 (1954) 1–43; "Mediaeval Academy Excavations at Cluny, IX: Systematic Dimensions in the Buildings," *ibid.* 38 (1963) 1–45; "New Results in the Study of Cluny Monastery," *Journal of the Soc. of Architect. Hist.* 16 (Oct. 1957) 3–11; "Measurements and Proportions of the Great Church at Cluny," *Beiträge zu Kunstgeschichte und Archäologie des Frühmittelalters* 22 (1960) 230–238. P. SCHMITZ, "La Liturgie de Cluny," *Spiritualità cluniacense* (Todi 1960) 83–99. J. LECLERCQ, "Spiritualité et culture à Cluny," *ibid.* 101–151, with bibliog.; *Aux Sources de la spiri-*

tualité occidentale (Paris 1964). K. HALLINGER, ed., *Corpus consuetudinum monasticarum* (Siegburg 1963–), ed. of Cluniac customaries. For additional bibliog., *see* CLUNIAC REFORM. **Illustration credits:** Fig. 1, Courtesy, Kenneth J. Conant, Mediaeval Academy of America. Fig. 2, French Embassy, Press and Information Division, New York City.

[R. GRÉGOIRE]

COADY, MOSES MICHAEL, educator; b. East Margaree, Nova Scotia, Canada, Jan. 3, 1882; d. Antigonish, Nova Scotia, July 28, 1959. He was the son of Michael J. and Sara Jane (Tompkins) Coady. After studying at St. Francis Xavier University, Antigonish, where he received his B.A. in 1905, he went to Rome and began studies for the priesthood at the Urban College there, later receiving the Ph.D. (1907) and D.D. (1910) degrees. He was ordained in Rome (1910); on returning to Canada, he taught in St. Francis Xavier High School and University (1910–25) and was professor of education at St. Francis Xavier University (1925–28). He later studied education at The Catholic University of America, Washington, D.C., and in 1928 became the first director of St. Francis Xavier University's extension department. In 1927 he was appointed by the federal government to organize maritime shore fishermen into cooperatives. In his capacity as director of the extension department he launched a highly successful program of adult education among the fishermen and promoted cooperatives and credit unions, all of which improved the economic conditions of the fishermen of the Maritime Provinces. In recognition of his work in the *Antigonish Movement, he was the recipient of numerous awards and was raised to the dignity of domestic prelate (1946) by Pius XII. He served as president of the Canadian Association for Adult Education from 1949 to 1951. His book, *Masters of Their Own Destiny* (New York 1939), is an account of the Antigonish Movement through economic cooperation. It had three editions and was translated into French (Gardenville, P.Q., 1948).

Moses Michael Coady.

Illustration credit: St. Francis Xavier University, Antigonish, Nova Scotia.

[J. T. FLYNN]

COAKLEY, THOMAS FRANCIS, educator; b. Pittsburgh, Pa., Feb. 20, 1880; d. there, March 5, 1951. He was the son of Thomas and Agnes (Quinn) Coakley. He attended St. Brigid's elementary school and completed his secondary and college education at Holy Ghost College (later Duquesne University), in Pittsburgh, graduating in 1903. As a young man he was employed as a clerk with the Pennsylvania Railroad, and during college he worked as a secretary with various companies. In 1903 he was sent to study at the North American College and the College of the Propaganda in Rome. He was ordained in Rome on May 25, 1908, after receiving the doctorate in theology. Upon returning to Pittsburgh, he was assigned as an assistant at St. Paul's Cathedral, and in 1918 was appointed secretary to Bp. J. F. Regis Canevin and assistant director of diocesan charities. During World War I he served as a chaplain in France and was later assistant senior chaplain with the army of occupation in Germany. In 1920 he returned to Pittsburgh as pastor of St. Patrick's parish; 3 years later he became pastor of Sacred Heart parish, Pittsburgh, where he remained until his death. He dedicated Sacred Heart Church in 1926 and was also responsible for a modern grade school and a girls' high school. He was one of the founders and first director of De Paul Institute for deaf and speech-defective children. His articles on education and other subjects appeared in Catholic newspapers, and he was a prolific pamphleteer.

[J. B. MC DOWELL]

COBO, BERNABÉ, Jesuit natural scientist and historian; b. Lopera, Jaén, Spain, Nov. 26, 1580; d. Lima, Oct. 9, 1657. He sailed as an adventurer to the Indies in 1595, and the following year was in Santo Domingo, from which he reached Lima in December 1598. He studied there at the Jesuit College of San Martín and entered the Society of Jesus on Oct. 14, 1601. After having completed his ecclesiastical studies in Lima and Cuzco, he went to Juli (Department of Puno, Peru). He made his profession on May 16, 1622. His travels took him through Bolivia and all the regions of Peru, and from 1629 to 1642 he visited Central America and Mexico on study trips. His greatest work was the *Historia del Nuevo Mundo*, a study of the geography, astronomy, meteorology, mineralogy, botany, and zoology of the Indies, especially of the regions he had visited. It included information on the Indians: their ethnology, civil and religious history, and architecture; and also on the accomplishments of the Spaniards, especially in Lima. Cobo, gifted with a talent that was more than speculative, was a keen observer with a fine scientific awareness augmented by wide reading and personal experience; he made himself independent of the physical science of his day and created the school of Indianologist naturalists.

Bibliography: *Obras*, ed. F. MATEOS, 2 v. (Madrid 1956). M. GONZÁLEZ DE LA ROSA, "El padre Bernabé Cobo," *Monografías históricas sobre la ciudad de Lima,* 2 v. (Lima 1935) 1:vii–xxii.

[A. DE EGAÑA]

COCHLAEUS, JOHANNES (JOHANN DOBENECK), priest, humanist, theologian, and opponent of Luther; b. Wendelstein, near Nuremberg, 1479; d. Breslau, Jan. 10, 1552. He came of peasant origin. He studied humanism first at Nuremberg and then more intensively at the University of Cologne (1504–07) with Ulrich Von *Hutten. As rector of the Latin school of St. Lawrence in Nuremberg (1510–15), he published noted textbooks and improved methods of instruction. He studied law at Bologna (1515–17), took a degree in scholastic theology at Ferrara in 1517, although he preferred the humanist method, and was ordained while in Rome (1517–19). At Frankfurt in 1520 he entered the reformation controversies, granting need of reform and trying, with Girolamo *Aleandro, to reconcile Martin *Luther. When Luther spurned debate, Cochlaeus began to write the first of his many polemical tracts, to which Luther answered but once. In his nearly 200 writings Cochlaeus was always zealous and often persuasive, but too frequently his learning was inadequate or clouded with invective. Such was his *Commentaria de actis et scriptis Martini Lutheri* (1549), long famous among Catholics but now discredited. Valuable for reference is his *Historia Hussitarum XII libri* (1549). Some of his works ended on the Index, because of his *argumentum ad absurdum* against "Scripture alone." He gave his services to Cardinal *Albrecht of Brandenburg (1526) and became chaplain and secretary to Duke *George of Saxony from 1528 to 1539. With them he attended the famous diets and helped refute the *Augsburg Confession (1530).

Bibliography: M. SPAHN, *Johannes Cochlaeus* (Berlin 1898), a catalogue of his works. H. JEDIN, *Des Johannes Cochlaeus Streitschrift De libero arbitrio hominis* (Breslau 1927). A. HERTE, *Das Katholische Lutherbild im Bann der Lutherkommentare des Cochlaeus,* 3 v. (Münster 1943). R. BÄUMER, LexThK² 2:1243–44. H. LIEBING, RGG³ 1:1842.

[J. T. GRAHAM]

COCKRAN, WILLIAM BOURKE, U.S. congressman; b. Sligo, Ireland, Feb. 28, 1854; d. Washington, D.C., March 1, 1923. He was the son of Martin and Harriet (Knight) Cockran. After his education at the Marist Brothers' school in Lille, France, and in Irish seminaries, he immigrated (1871) to New York. There he taught at a Catholic girls' academy and served as principal of a Tuckahoe, N.Y., public school before turning to the study of law. He was admitted to the New York bar in 1876 and practiced in Mount Vernon, N.Y. After moving to New York City, where he joined Tammany Hall, he gained national attention at the Democratic national convention of 1884 with a speech opposing the candidacy of Grover Cleveland.

Cockran was elected to Congress in 1886, 1890, and 1892, but broke with Tammany in 1894. As a supporter of the gold standard, he campaigned in 1896 for William McKinley against William Jennings Bryan. By 1900 his opposition to Republican imperialism influenced his return to the Democratic party, and he was again elected to Congress in 1904. After serving as grand sachem of Tammany Hall for 3 years, he left the Democrats and campaigned for Theodore Roosevelt in 1912. Subsequently, Cockran rejoined the Democratic party and at the 1920 national convention placed Alfred E. Smith in nomination. He returned to Congress that year and was reelected in 1922, serving in the House until his sudden death.

Cockran defended the interests of organized labor, participated as a moderate in the Irish movement in America, opposed Prohibition, and resisted restrictions upon immigration and naturalization. He was an adviser to three New York archbishops, a member of the Third Order of St. Francis, and founder of the New York Perpetual Adoration Society. In 1916 he was made a knight commander of the Order of St. Gregory the Great. He was married three times: in 1879 to Mary Elizabeth Jackson, who died in childbirth the following year; in 1888, to Rhoda Elizabeth Mack, who died in 1895; and in 1906, to Anne Louise Ide, who survived him.

Bibliography: J. MCGURRIN, *Bourke Cockran: A Free Lance in American Politics* (New York 1948). A. KENNEDY, *American Orator: Bourke Cockran, His Life and Politics* (New York 1948).

[E. M. MC NULTY]

COCLICO, ADRIANUS PETIT, Renaissance composer and theorist; b. Flanders, *c.* 1500; d. Copenhagen, 1562. Little is known about his early life; although he claimed to have been a pontifical chapel singer, bishop, pope's confessor, musician in the courts of France and England, and student of *Desprez, none of this can be proved. His first known activity is as a student in Wittenberg in 1545; by then he was a Protestant. For the remainder of his life he wandered from town to town, teaching, studying, and composing, with no permanent position. His most active period was *c.* 1552 in Nuremberg, where he published a collection of motets, the *Musica Reservata* (available in modern transcription, Lippstadt 1958), and his theoretical treatise *Compendium musices* (facsimile, Kassel 1954). Coclico, a better theorist than composer, stressed the relation of music and poetry, giving highest place to poet-composers who understood both the demands of prosody and the ways music could reinforce emotional meanings of words.

Bibliography: M. VAN CREVEL, *Adrianus Petit Coclico* (The Hague 1940). E. LOWINSKY, *Secret Chromatic Art in the Netherlands Motet,* tr. C. BUCHMAN (New York 1946). B. MEIER, "The Musica Reservata of Adrianus Petit Coclico," MusDisc 10 (1956) 67–105. Reese MusR.

[A. SEAY]

COCURRICULUM IN CATHOLIC HIGHER EDUCATION

The sum of organized activities, not part of a regular classroom experience but contingent on the total curriculum, such as interscholastic and intramural athletics, clubs, student government, lecture programs, and assemblies. Cocurriculum replaces the term extracurriculum, so long in use in U.S. higher education. Developed after World War I in non-Catholic universities, the term has found general usage in Catholic colleges and universities. Historically, Catholic higher education has always endeavored to develop the whole man through spiritual, physical, and social activities allied to the academic curriculum.

Historical Background. In 19th-century U.S. Catholic institutions cocurricular programs centered around such activities as oratory, debate, and literary sessions, with the debate or oratory society the oldest student organization in most Catholic colleges. Since this was a period of intense political interest and activity on local, state, and national levels, students, no doubt with few outside amusements to distract them, became deeply involved in college-sponsored oratorical and political societies in which they could test their debating skills. Journalism, although narrowly technical, also offered some outlet for self-expression through the medium of religious or academic bulletins and announcements. Shortly before the Civil War, although not associated with it, most colleges had military drill companies that were generally well trained and a source of personal pride. Interest in drill companies persisted until about the 1900s. Literary and drama groups also flourished before the Civil War, and before their absorption into the academic curriculum, modern languages, mainly French, Spanish, and German, were often taught as cocurricular activities.

After the Civil War, athletic events became a part of the campus scene, and most common sports were played. Baseball soon became popular. In the 1880s intercollegiate contests were allowed. In the early 20th century, football began its rise in Catholic colleges with the contribution to modern football of the forward pass, developed at St. Louis University in 1906. Public awareness of this innovation in football came when Charles E. Dorais used the play, passing to Knute Kenneth Rockne in the University of Notre Dame victory over Army in 1913. Notre Dame and the University of San Francisco fielded excellent post-World War II teams, but many older schools dropped football during and after the War. The growth of professional football, high costs, and a realization that intercollegiate football had become an extracurricular activity rather than a cocurricular activity led to its demise.

Basketball took over where football declined and almost every Catholic coeducational, men or women's college has a team active on the intercollegiate scene.

Since World War II Catholic colleges have increased physical education facilities and intramural programs and have opened to more students a complete physical development program. Compared with the programs of residential institutions, the lack of land has hindered intramural activity on urban campuses. The development of urban renewal programs, however, and the relocation of city campuses have somewhat compensated for this limitation.

Religious and Academic Activities. Religious activities are as old as the colleges themselves, and the Sodality of the Blessed Virgin, the Apostleship of Prayer, the Acolythical Society, the Confraternity of Christian Doctrine, and the League of the Sacred Heart are found on almost every campus. The literary, drama, speech, and debate activities are the core of cocurricular activities, but yearbooks, campus student newspapers, and other student publications are also widely represented.

Honor Societies. Catholic colleges were slow to obtain chapters of national honor societies. The first Phi Beta Kappa Catholic chapter was not chartered until 1938 at St. Catherine's College, St. Paul, Minn. Three other Catholic institutions hold Phi Beta Kappa charters: The Catholic University of America, Washington, D.C.; Fordham University, New York, N.Y.; and Georgetown University, Washington, D.C. Since the 1950s increasing numbers of Catholic schools are seeking charters for honor societies from the various fields of academic discipline.

Professional Societies. Professional fraternities and sororities, which appeared in Catholic medical schools as early as the 1890s, flourish in Catholic colleges of medicine, law, commerce, and engineering. The first recognized social fraternity, Magi Fraternity, was founded at the University of Detroit, Mich., in 1916 and is still in existence (1964). National fraternities and sororities, both social and professional, appeared on Catholic campuses shortly before World War II, and by 1963, 29 Catholic colleges had approved their establishment. Few of these groups own fraternity houses, however, although a fraternity or sorority on a Catholic campus helps to forge closer ties between commuter students and the school.

Trends. In the 1950s the advent of modern space technology, scientific interest, and increased academic demands on students' time caused social and cocurricular activities to shift their course. Although many colleges had more than 100 such groups before 1955 their number has since considerably declined. A growing social awareness on the part of students has given a new direction to cocurricular affairs with consequent attraction for activities closely related to the curriculum, to social issues, and community affairs. Common on a Catholic campus of the 1960s are groups such as the Young Republicans, Young Americans for Freedom, Young Democrats, Student Chapter of the National Association for the Advancement of Colored People (NAACP), Human Relations Club, International Relations Club, International Students Club, Young Christian Students, National Federation of Catholic College Students (NFCCS) and similar social-issue groups. Academic clubs and student chapters of national professional societies are growing rapidly, and students exhibit greater interest in awards, honors, and honor societies.

Much of this is reflected in student governments that tend to demand more of a share, not only in the traditional social and athletic programs, but also in the formation of daily campus culture and in the various administrative, academic, and religious operations. With this demand there has appeared a new trend toward responsibility among students created by an awareness of off-campus social issues. The development of student-faculty relations and a growing sensitivity to social problems tend to correlate and bring a meaningful college and university cocurriculum into greater cooperation with daily life in the community, state, nation, and world at large.

Bibliography: C. A. SCHOENFIELD, *The University and Its Publics* (New York 1954). H. C. HAND, *Campus Activities* (New York 1938). K. H. MUELLER, *Student Personnel Work in Higher Education* (Boston 1961). E. G. WILLIAMSON, *Student Personnel Services in Colleges and Universities* (New York 1961); "The Extracurriculum and General Education," *General Education,* 51st Yearbook, NatSocStEd pt. 1 (Chicago 1952). E. FRIEDSON, ed., *Student Government, Student Leaders and the American College* (Philadelphia 1955). W. R. BAIRD, *Manual of American College Fraternities,* ed. J. ROBSON (17th ed. Menasha, Wis. 1963).

[T. A. EMMET, JR.]

CODDE, PIETER (CODDAEUS), archbishop of Sebaste *in partibus,* seventh vicar apostolic of the Dutch Mission; b. Amsterdam, Nov. 27, 1648; d. Utrecht, Dec. 18, 1710. He came of an aristocratic family; he pursued his studies at Malines and Louvain. In Paris he joined the Congregation of the Oratory before he was ordained in 1672. He became the vicar-general of Utrecht in 1683 and succeeded Johannes van Neercassel as vicar apostolic 5 years later. In 1689 he was consecrated archbishop of Sebaste. The Jesuits of the mission and some secular priests stigmatized his doctrine and practices as Jansenistic. At Rome in 1701 Codde wrote three statements in his defense *Declaratio, Responsiones, De morte Christi pro omnibus,* but 3 years later he was condemned by a decree of the Inquisition and deprived of spiritual jurisdiction. He furthermore refused to sign the anti-Jansenistic formula of Alexander VII without restriction. This question of Jansenism occasioned the schism of Utrecht in 1723. Some friends attempted to persuade Codde that the Pope had exceeded his rights, but he refused to reassume the exercise of his functions, while at the same time he persevered in his protests against his dismissal from office.

Bibliography: P. Polman, ed., *Romeinse Bronnen,* v.3, 4 (The Hague 1952, 1955). L. J. Rogier, *Geschiedenis van het Katholicisme in Noord-Nederland,* 2 v. (Amsterdam 1945–46) 2:268–348. A. C. de Veer, DHGE 13:184–188.

[P. POLMAN]

CODE OF CANON LAW (CODEX IURIS CANONICI)

Canon Law, deriving its name from the Greek κανών, a rule or norm, is the whole body of laws by which the Church of Christ is governed. Some of these laws are of divine origin, from the natural or the divine positive law, and are merely presented and authentically interpreted by the Church; others are ecclesiastical in the strict sense, enacted by ecclesiastical authority. These latter may be universal, enacted for the whole Latin Church by the pope or an ecumenical council, or particular, decreed by a particular council, a local ordinary, or a religious superior or chapter. The Code of Canon Law contains only universal laws, but makes provision also for particular ones.

Historical Background. Three periods may be distinguished in the historical development of Canon Law before the promulgation (1918) of the Code: (1) from apostolic times to the time of Gratian (1140–50), (2) from Gratian to the Council of Trent (1545–63), (3) from the Council of Trent to the Code.

From very early times Peter, and the bishops of Rome as his successors in the primacy, carried on ecclesiastical government by settling certain points of general discipline. Other bishops made particular regulations for their own territory; and some of these, by passing from one church to another, eventually gained universal recognition and so became part of the general law. After the Edict of Constantine in 313 the Church became free to develop her own organization.

The First Council of Nicaea in 325 and the other ecumenical councils up to the tenth (the Second Lateran in 1139, about the time of Gratian), though occupied with matters of faith, also enacted some disciplinary legislation for the whole Church. Meanwhile, customs and particular regulations continued to attain the stature of universal laws, in some cases through general acceptance. It was difficult to know which of the laws currently accepted were genuine, and still more difficult to discover whether they had been revoked either expressly or because they could not be reconciled with laws that came later.

By the middle of the 12th century, Canon Law was in a state of utter confusion. The time was ripe for the most notable of all the efforts made before the Code to bring order out of chaos. This was the work of the Camaldolese monk Gratian, whose unofficial compilation, well named *Concordantia discordantium canonum* —a concordance of discordant canons—became known as Gratian's Decree and was for centuries the best-known book of Canon Law (*see* GRATIAN, DECRETUM OF). Five distinct collections of later laws were eventually added, which together with Gratian's Decree constituted the **Corpus Iuris Canonici.* But even this proved inadequate to the growth of the Church.

Neither the Council of Trent nor the First Vatican Council (1869–70) was able to undertake a general codification, though the need for it was constantly increasing. Some partial reforms, however, were attended with success. Pius IX clarified the law regarding censures by the constitution *Apostolicae Sedis* of Oct. 12, 1869, and Leo XIII in the constitution *Officiorum* of Jan. 25, 1897, promulgated a complete piece of legislation on the previous censure and prohibition of books. But as for ecclesiastical law in general, it was at the beginning of the 20th century in such a state of doubt and disorder that Benedict XV in the apostolic constitution *Providentissima Mater* of May 27, 1917, promulgating the finished new Code, could say of the antecedent confusion: "Canonical enactments had so increased in number and were so disconnected and scattered that many of them were unknown not only to the people but to many of the experts themselves." To clear away this debris of the previous 700 years was the firm resolve of Pius X, announced in the encyclical of March 19, 1904, beginning with the appropriate words, *"Arduum sane munus"* (an arduous task indeed).

Making of the Code. The process of codification followed this general order: A commission of cardinals was appointed, the Pope acting as chairman and Pietro Gasparri, afterward named cardinal, as secretary. Archbishops throughout the world were invited to confer with their suffragans and to send in their suggestions. When a tentative draft was finished it was submitted to the expert canonists acting as consultors, and also to all bishops and others who were entitled to attend a general council. Their comments were discussed repeatedly, and the text was finally adopted. The work went on for about 13 years without being interrupted even by World War I. The Code was promulgated on Pentecost, May 27, 1917, to become effective on the following Pentecost, May 19, 1918. A few canons were declared effective at once.

Physical Make-up. The actual legislation of the Code is contained in successive canons numbered from 1 to 2414 and in nine documents, later reduced to six, printed after the canons and sometimes referred to in them. The canons are divided systematically into five books: I, General Norms; II, Persons; III, Things; IV, Procedure; and V, Crimes and Penalties. The books are further subdivided into parts, and sometimes into sections, titles and chapters. The preface by Cardinal Gasparri, the footnotes or references to former laws, which are printed in some editions of the Code as aids to historical study, and the alphabetical index at the end, are not parts of the Code but merely accessory aids without the authority of law. But the analytical index at the beginning is authentic and can furnish a basis for canonical argument.

The scope of two of the five books is sufficiently indicated in their titles: Book IV, Procedure, and Book V, Crimes and Penalties. Book II, Persons, is subdivided into three parts: clerics, religious, and the laity. The part on clerics, after treating of clerics in general, defines and describes the offices of the entire graded body of clerics, from the Roman pontiff down to pastors, parochial vicars, and rectors of churches. The part on religious deals in great detail with institutes of both men and women, not only those of a strictly religious character but others also, such as the so-called societies of common life, which approach the religious ideal without realizing it completely. On the secular institutes, authentically defined only in 1947, the Code itself is necessarily silent. The title of part three, the laity, is really a misnomer. Only 2 of its 44 canons deal with the laity as such; the rest are concerned with associations of the faithful, which may include also clerics and religious. The apostolate of the laity, which has since become so prominent in the mind of the Church, is not directly mentioned. Book III, with the noncommittal title of Things, is very comprehensive. It includes the Sacraments, sacred places (churches, chapels, altars, cemeteries), sacred times (holy days of obligation, days of fast and abstinence), divine worship, the teaching office of the Church, benefices, and ecclesiastical property.

Application and Effect. Book I, General Norms, is juridically the most important part of the Code, defining its scope and laying down principles governing its application and effects. Except in a few cases, the Code applies only to Latin, not to Oriental Catholics; the Oriental Church has its own Code. *See* ORIENTAL CODES (CANON LAW). As for non-Catholic Christians, since Baptism of water is the door to the Church (CIC c.87), all validly baptized persons, even though separated from Rome, are subject to the obligations of the law unless exempted, as they are, for example, from observing the juridical form of marriage when both parties are non-Catholics (CIC c.1099.2).

Preexisting laws, general or particular, if contrary to the Code, are revoked. So are all general laws, even though not contrary to the Code, unless they are implicitly or explicitly mentioned. Custom under definite conditions is declared a source of unwritten law for the future; but antecedent customs are preserved only if they are not contrary to the new law. If they are contrary to it, certain ones are expressly reprobated and so completely extinguished. Others may be tolerated only under rather severe conditions, viz, centenary duration and the judgment of the ordinary that they cannot prudently be removed. Finally, this first book gives general norms for the computation of time, for rescripts (replies in writing from ecclesiastical authorities), privileges, and dispensations.

Benedict XV in the motu proprio of Sept. 15, 1917, established a pontifical Commission for the Authentic Interpretation of the *Code of Canon Law. At the same time he provided for the stability of the Code by decreeing that if any new canons should eventually become necessary, they should be drawn up by this same Commission and inserted in the Code in such a way as not to interfere with the consecutive numbering of the canons. A new canon was to be designated with the same number as the preceding canon and the addition of *bis* or *ter,* "so that no canon of the Code should ever lose its place, nor the series of numbered canons be in any way confused." This admirable provision has never been put into practice because no new canons have been formally enacted in this way. Nevertheless there have been many and important changes in the Code of Canon Law since 1918.

Changes in the Law. The limitations of space forbid any attempt to enumerate all these changes. It is possible only to indicate some of the principal ones and to call attention to the variety of forms in which this new legislation has come. Some of these changes have been effected by the pope's directly ordering an explicit revision of the text of the canons themselves.

Pius XII by a motu proprio of Aug. 1, 1948, ordered that canon 1099.2 be altered by expunging a lengthy clause exempting children of non-Catholics, baptized in the Catholic Church but raised from infancy without any Catholic instruction, from observing the juridical form of marriage. The same supreme authority, by a motu proprio of Dec. 25, 1953, expunged from canon 2319.1n1, the words *"contra praescriptum canonis 1063.1,"* which were being wrongly interpreted as excusing from the penalty of excommunication Catholics who attempted marriage before a non-Catholic minister, provided they had not beforehand or did not afterward contract a valid marriage before the Church. By another motu proprio of Pius XII, of Dec. 16, 1947, the faculties for confession granted by canon 883 to priests on an ocean voyage were extended under the same conditions to priests traveling by air. John XXIII directly altered canon 231 regarding the number of cardinals and canon 240 concerning the privileges of cardinal deacons. He also directly reorganized the government of the suburbicarian sees.

Document I in the original edition of the Code, concerning the conclave and the election of the pope, has been repeatedly amended, the latest changes being decreed by John XXIII in the motu proprio *Summi Pontificis electio* of Sept. 5, 1962.

In many other cases no precise textual change has been decreed, but pontifical documents of the highest authority make it obviously necessary that certain canons be deleted, supplemented, or amended, because the law is now different from the provisions that they contain. This is true, for example, of the canons on the eucharistic fast, the time of Mass, the papal cloister of monastic nuns, the competence of the Congregations for the Oriental Church and for Religious and that of the Consistorial Congregation, the fast on the vigil of Christmas, the reception of Holy Communion during Holy Week, and other matters. The changes above mentioned have resulted from documents of the Roman pontiffs (encyclicals, apostolic constitutions, motu proprio letters).

Almost equal authority attaches to instructions and decrees issued by the Congregations with the approval or express confirmation of the Holy Father. According to the motu proprio of Benedict XV of Sept. 15, 1917, establishing the Code Commission, the Congregations were not thereafter to issue any new general decrees. Nevertheless many of their instructions and decrees are of general application and contain new regulations and prescriptions that are neither explicit nor implicit in the Code. These are recognized as obligatory when approved by the pope and promulgated. Under these conditions it is difficult in practice to distinguish their binding force from that of laws formally enacted. A few examples may illustrate this. The Congregation of the Council has established a number of new excommunications *latae sententiae,* transferred the obligation of fast and abstinence from the vigil of the Assumption to the vigil of the Immaculate Conception, and issued regulations for clerics attending secular universities, priests teaching in public schools, and priests on vacation outside their proper dioceses. The Congregation of the Sacraments has legalized the administration of Confirmation by pastors to persons in danger of death when the bishop is not available, and has supplemented the canons on matrimonial procedure by several detailed instructions. The Consistorial Congregation has regulated the migration of clerics. Both this Congregation and that for Religious have several times readjusted the limit-values set down by the Code beyond which permission for the alienation of church property must be obtained from the Holy See. The Holy Office has proscribed certain consultations of *radiaesthesia* by clerics and religious and also has forbidden them to practice psychoanalysis or to consult psychoanalysts unless their ordinary permits it for a grave reason. The Sacred Penitentiary with the approval of the Holy Father has enlarged the power of certain prelates to grant various indulgences.

The authentic interpretations of the canons made by the Code Commission constitute a class by themselves. If formally promulgated they have the force of law (CIC c.17.2). They have been very numerous, particularly in the earlier years after the promulgation of the Code. Through these replies many doubts inherent in the text of the canons have been clarified, sometimes in the direction of greater liberty. For example, the designation of the place for the hearing of confessions of religious women by the occasional confessor has been progressively extended by replies of the Commission. Likewise the condition that "the ordinary cannot be reached," which is required for the use of certain special faculties, has been declared to be fulfilled provided he can be reached only by telegraph or telephone. The concept of affinity as an impediment to marriage has been freed from an obscurity resulting from its imperfect definition in canon 97.1. The definition of a putative marriage (c.1015.4) has been restricted by a declaration that in order to be considered putative the marriage must be celebrated before the Church.

Actual Plans for Revision. It is evident that the Code of Canon Law has for some time needed to be at least brought up to date. On Jan. 25, 1959, Pope John XXIII announced three great forthcoming events: the Roman Synod, Vatican Council II, and the revision of the Code of Canon Law. This last, he said, was to "accompany and crown" the work of the other two. He used the word *aggiornamento,* which means a bringing up to date rather than a complete recasting. In later public pronouncements he frequently referred to the great work of revising the Code, which would take place, he said, after the promulgation of the complete Oriental Code. The deliberations of the Council reveal in what sense the preparation of the new Code can "accompany" the sessions. The lines traced by the Council under the guidance of the Holy Spirit must necessarily influence the molding of the new Code. The law of the Church must reflect and express the reawakened spirit of the Church.

But despite its need of amendment the Code of 1918 must continue to be recognized as a magnificent achievement, a veritable landmark in the history of the Church. Its deficiencies are for the most part but the necessary consequence of the growth of the Church in a half-century of unparalleled world history. John XXIII on March 28, 1963, shortly before his death, announced the appointment of a commission of cardinals headed by Cardinal Pietro Ciriaci and including Cardinal Giovanni Battista Montini, then Archbishop of Milan, to which he entrusted the work of revising the Code of Canon Law. This "much desired and eagerly awaited event," to use the Pope's own words, has passed beyond the realm of conjecture. The young and vigorous Church has outgrown her juridical vesture of 1918, but a new one, better-fitting and made of the same durable fiber, is assured.

Bibliography: Pius XII, *Voluistis, praeclari viri* (Allocution April 29, 1952 ActApS 44 (1952) 371–377. P. Gasparri, "Preface," *The Code of Canon Law* (Rome 1948) xxi–xliii. Abbo 1:xiii–xx. Beste 38–40. Bousc–O'Connor. J. Abbo, "The Revision of the Code," *Jurist* 20 (1960) 371–397. O. Cassola, "De iure poenali codicis canonico emendando," *Apollinaris* 32 (1959) 240–259. D. Staffa, "Imperfezione e lacune del primo libro del codice di diritto canonico," *Apollinaris* 33 (1960) 45–73.

[T. L. BOUSCAREN]

CODE OF CANON LAW, COMMISSION FOR THE AUTHENTIC INTERPRETATION OF

A commission of cardinals established by Benedict XV, Sept. 15, 1917, to give authentic interpretations of the *Code of Canon Law (Codex Iuris Canonici). Its purpose was to ensure the stability of the Code against two principal dangers: "uncertain opinions and conjectures of private persons regarding the true meaning of the canons, and the frequent enactment of various new laws," either of which could produce obscurity and doubt concerning the true meaning of the law.

The Commission consists of a number of cardinals, chosen by the pope, one of whom is designated as president; canonists from both branches of the clergy as consultors; and a secretary.

It has the exclusive right to interpret authentically the canons of the Code, upon consultation, however, in matters of greater moment, with that congregation within whose special province lies the matter that is proposed for decision. Its interpretations have the force of law, and fall under three types: those merely declaratory, the law being already clear; those resolving doubts or obscurities inherent in the text; and those restricting or extending the scope of the law (CIC c.17.2). These last two types of replies are equivalent to new legislation and accordingly are not retroactive and require promulgation. The replies of the Commission do not need the approval of the pope, but are in fact shown to him before being communicated or published.

Replies are given only to questions presented by or in the name of ordinaries or major superiors of religious institutes (*see* ORDINARIES, ECCLESIASTICAL). Any question that is either of minor importance or not very difficult can be resolved by the president of the Commission alone [ActApS 11 (1919) 480, n.1]. The opinions of some of the consultors are usually asked but are never published. The form of the replies is often brief: e.g., "In the affirmative to the first part, in the negative to the second." But the reply may also abandon the form of the questions and give the sense of the canon in different words. Many of the replies are not published in the *Acta Apostolicae Sedis* (and hence not promulgated) but must be culled from various canonical reviews.

For the Oriental Code, there is no specific commission for interpretation; authentic interpretations are given by the commission appointed for drawing up the Oriental Code.

Bibliography: C. Lefebvre, DDC 6:665–667. A. Cicognani, *Commentarium ad librum primum Codicis iuris canonici* (2d ed. Rome 1939) 260–272. Michiels Norm 1:495–499. A. Brems, "De interpretatione authentica CIC per pontificiam commissionem," *Jus Pontificium* 15 (1935) 161–190, 298–313; 16 (1936) 78–105, 217–256.

[T. L. BOUSCAREN]

CODETERMINATION

In its broadest sense, refers to an industrial relations system in which the workers have some voice in management (Ger., *Mitbestimmung,* or *Mitbestimmungsrecht;* Fr., *cogestion*). More specifically, it consists of equal partnership of employers and employees in the operation of a business enterprise. The broad spectrum between these two definitions includes the following plans or programs: Pope Pius XI's recommendation of partnership contracts, in *Quadragesimo Anno;* various plans in the Netherlands, France, Canada, and some Latin American countries whereby workers share in management decisions; United States programs of union-management cooperation; consultative boards representing the workers in some of England's nationalized industries; the German drive for full codetermination; miscellaneous programs of worker representation in the Communist-dominated countries of Yugoslavia, Poland, and Czechoslovakia; and the appeal of Pope John XXIII in *Mater et Magistra* (1961) for a greater share in ownership by workers in enterprises that retain a large portion of earnings.

Origin. There is little agreement regarding the origin of codetermination. Some regard the German drive for *Mitbestimmung* in the 1950s as a unique development. Others regard it as having begun in the German Works Councils under the Weimar Republic in the period after World War I. Broadly speaking, the desire of workers to have some voice in management decisions affecting their job security is probably as old as trade unionism itself. Even in the United States, where union leaders have shown little interest in codetermination of the German variety, union representatives at the labor-management conference convoked by President Truman in 1945 refused to accept the management proposal that the conference begin by listing certain unassailable "management prerogatives" that would be removed from the ambit of collective bargaining.

Codetermination in Germany. During the period of allied occupation of Germany following World War II, the occupying authorities (notably the British) in certain highly industrialized German states permitted the passage of laws calling for full equality of representation for workers on boards of directors in the pivotal industries of coal and steel.

The West German Federal Republic was established May 24, 1949, under the chancellorship of Konrad Adenauer, and Germany passed out of allied control.

In the autumn of 1949 a German Catholic social convention, the *Katholikentag,* meeting in Bochum (Ruhr), declared solemnly that codetermination was a "natural right in the order willed by God."

Despite the fact that Pius XII in a series of addresses and allocutions denied the existence of a "natural right" to codetermination, the DGB (the German Federation of Labor), sensing strong Catholic support, conducted an active lobby for a federal statute on codetermination. Such a law was passed May 21, 1951.

The Codetermination Law of 1951 applied only to firms in the coal and steel industries. It contained two main provisions: (1) parity representation for workers on the board of directors, and (2) the election of a labor director (*Arbeitsdirektor*) to the 3-man management board, which includes also a production manager and a sales manager. Actually, there were 11 members on the Boards of Directors. Labor and management each selected 5 men and the 11th was chosen by these 10. If they failed to agree, the complicated method of selecting the "odd man" favored the management members of the board. This meant, in effect, that workers were to enjoy representation on the boards of directors because they were partners in production, and not on the basis of stock ownership, as in the United States.

Emboldened by this initial success, the DGB attempted to secure an extension of codetermination to other industries. They scored a partial success in the Works Constitution Law of 1952. On the one hand, the new law was extended to all German industries, excepting only state and federal employees. On the other hand, worker representation on the boards of directors was limited to one-third of the board membership.

The Representation of Public Servants Act was passed in 1955. It extended codetermination to all officials; salaried employees, and workers employed by the federal government; by public corporations, institutions, and foundations; and by the federal courts.

The final step in the German codetermination movement came in August 1956 with the passage of a law extending it to holding companies in the coal and steel industries.

Papal Position. It might almost be said that Pius XI anticipated the German drive toward codetermination by 20 years. In the encyclical *Quadragesimo Anno* (par. 64 and 65) he contrasted the wage contract and certain forms of partnership contracts, and indicated specifically that workers might become "sharers in ownership or management or participate in some fashion in the profits received." Since 1931 Catholic social scientists have taken a keen interest in the development of these partnership forms. Profit sharing has long been espoused. Interest in various forms of comanagement has been awakened in the period since World War II.

Pius XII got into the center of the codetermination discussion after the Bochum *Katholikentag,* Aug. 31 to Sept. 2, 1949. His Holiness issued statements touching on the subject on several occasions: May 7, 1949, to Catholic employers; June 3, 1950, to the International Congress of Social Studies; July 7, 1950, to the 39th Social Week (*Semaine Sociale*) in Dijon, France; Sept. 14, 1952, to the Austrian *Katholikentag* in Vienna; and in his Christmas message of Dec. 24, 1952. The general thrust of these statements was twofold. On the one hand, he denied the existence of a "natural right" to codetermination, pointing out that such matters are properly governed by state or federal statutes determining the form of business organization in various countries. As long as these private (positive) law enactments do not contravene natural rights of man they are to prevail within the prescribed jurisdiction of the particular statute. On the other hand, Pius XII approved of voluntary partnership arrangements whose purpose was to give fuller scope for developing the personality of the workingman by giving him a sense of participation in the affairs of his company.

Pope John XXIII went further than any of his predecessors in specifying circumstances under which workers should become sharers in ownership, and thus *a fortiori,* in the management of firms in which they work. In *Mater et Magistra* (par. 75) he stated, "We must notice . . . the system of self-financing adopted in many countries by large, or comparatively large firms. Because these companies are financing replacement and plant expansion out of their own profits, they grow at a very rapid rate. In such cases we believe that the workers should be allocated shares in the firms for which they work, especially when they are paid no more than a minimum wage."

Conclusions. Some studies were undertaken in the 1950s to determine how codetermination was actually working out in Germany. Several tentative conclusions were reached: (1) Voting on economic matters within the Board of Directors never found board members split evenly along "party lines," half on the labor side and half on the management side. There was much consensus in decisions. (2) The workers interviewed experienced a sense of genuine participation in reaching decisions of importance to all. They believed their status to have been enhanced. (3) Management judged it, too, had gained, in that the drive for socialization of the steel industry had been checked, and possibly even averted. (4) There was continued dissatisfaction among the members of the DGB because the type of codetermination in the coal and steel industries was not extended to the rest of the economy. (5) There was little pressure to extend the German type of codetermination to other countries.

Bibliography: J. NEWMAN, *Co-responsibility in Industry* (Westminster 1955). A. SHUCHMAN, *Codetermination: Labor's Middle Way in Germany* (Washington 1957). "Codetermination," Am CathSocRev 14 (1953) 66–83. See also the series of articles appearing in *Industrial and Labor Relations Review* v.5–12 (1951–59) and in *Monthly Labor Review* v.73–83 (1951–60).

[E. A. KURTH]

CODRINGTON, THOMAS, preacher to James II; place and date of birth unknown; d. Saint-Germain, France, 1691?. He was probably the son of Edward Codrington of Sutton Mandeville, Wiltshire, England, who was presented for recusancy (1645 and 1669), together with his sons, Bonaventure and Thomas, secular priests who worked in England. He was educated at Douai, where he was ordained and became a prominent professor of humanities. Later, having been invited to Rome, he there became chaplain and secretary to Cardinal Philip *Howard. In July 1684 he returned to England, and he became one of the preachers in ordinary and chaplains to James, Duke of York, later King James II. In Rome he had joined a German institute of secular priests. John Morgan and he were appointed procurators to introduce the community into England. The rule was published in 1697, but elicited much opposition and was attacked by the Rev. John Sargeant in "A Letter to our worthy Brethren of the new Institute." This opposition proved fatal to the institute, which was ordered suppressed by Bishop Giffard in 1703. Codrington was preacher to James II at £60 per annum during his reign and followed him into exile at Saint-Germain, France.

Bibliography: *The Victoria History of the County of Wiltshire,* ed. R. B. PUGH and E. CRITTALL (London 1953) v.3, for the Codrington family. T. COOPER, DNB 4:666. DictEngCath 1:520–522.

[H. S. REINMUTH, JR.]

COEDUCATION

In a wide sense, a variety of educational practices and programs in which both sexes are educated together; in a narrow sense, an identical educational curriculum for both sexes in the same institution, i.e., the same classes, teachers, textbooks, and methods. Coeducation implies, in theory or in practice, an opposition to the age-old custom of educating the sexes separately. It is sometimes distinguished from "coordinate" or "coinstitutional" education, inclusive terms for practical arrangements or institutional systems devised to permit separate classes and distinctive curriculums for each sex in the same educational institution or, in the case of higher education, separate colleges for men and women in the same university.

Historical Background. Educational practices generally reflect prevailing cultural patterns and attitudes. In a long tradition reaching back to classical antiquity, all Western societies rigidly separated the sexes in social and economic life. Major political and intellectual functions were reserved for men, while tasks concerning domestic economy and the rearing of children were relegated to women. As a result, except for universal elementary education introduced into Protestant countries after the Reformation, educational opportunities for women were nonexistent. During the period of the industrial revolution these assumptions began to be effectively challenged. The employment of women in factories and outside the home, and their gradual gaining of a degree of leisure time and economic independence in the ensuing economic revolution, profoundly altered women's social status in the Western world. Social and economic changes of this magnitude, necessarily involving educational changes, brought about widespread demands for the rights of girls and women to equal educational opportunities. Recognition of this right, first in public opinion and second in law, gradually followed in one country after another. Since available schools were boys' schools, this demand for educational opportunity was in many specific instances a demand for coeducation. Hence, by the latter part of the 18th and early part of the 19th century the factor of coeducation as a practical movement, as a novel experiment, or as a controversial theoretical topic, began to make an impact on dominant educational viewpoints. Coeducation is thus a modern phenomenon linked to the growth of educational opportunities for women, which, in turn, are a reflection of the economic and social changes in the 20th century.

In the U.S. European countries tend to interpret equality of educational opportunity for women as an opportunity for girls and young women to pursue academic courses similar to those offered to boys and young men. Generally, a coeducational pattern to achieve this has not been deemed essential. In the U.S., on the contrary, coeducational practices developed so rapidly and so widely that some dictionaries state that the term "coeducation" originated in the U.S. In America, as in Europe, the first schools were for boys. In the colonial period, if girls received any formal education at all, it came from the "dame schools" or from private tutors. After the American Revolution, elementary schools were gradually opened to girls. As the high schools developed in the 1820s and 1830s they too were gradually opened to girls, but general acceptance of the need for secondary education for girls did not secure wide acceptance until the 1850s. *See* EDUCATION I (HISTORY OF), 7, 8, 9. Although practical considerations, primarily economic and administrative, were instrumental in setting coeducational patterns for this growth, no widespread objections were raised as to the desirability of coeducation during elementary school years, and the practice became almost universal in all elementary schools throughout the country. Since discussion about coeducation has been chiefly focused on the adolescent years, however, it is usually only at the level of secondary education that some division of opinion exists. In practice, public high schools in all states tend to be coeducational. Many independent schools and academies, on the other hand, have retained noncoeducational patterns, although some have introduced systems of coordinate education. Some independent schools, particularly day schools, are coeducational (*see* INDEPENDENT SCHOOLS). Catholic high schools and academies tend to follow these independent school practices, although new experimental, cooperative programs with public high schools, e.g., *shared-time programs, may alter existing practices.

Outside the U.S. Although coeducation can be said to be a characteristic feature of public high school education in the U.S., such is not the case in western Europe, French-speaking Canada, and South America. Secondary education in these countries, reflecting different national and cultural characteristics, presents a wide spectrum of educational practices. At one end of this spectrum, predominant opinion and public policy in the Romance countries does not favor coeducation at all. At the other end, the Soviet Union espouses a deliberate policy of coeducation from the elementary school through the university. In between, various practices exist, some experimental, some matters of public policy. In Austria, Belgium, Eire, Germany, and Greece public opinion is against coeducation in the secondary schools. England has both separate and coeducational programs. Some of the *Laender* in postwar Germany have been experimenting with coeducational community schools, the *Gemeinschaftschulen.* Poland has a substantial percentage of coeducational secondary schools. In Holland and Yugoslavia the majority of secondary schools are coeducational.

Higher Education for Women. In the provision of educational opportunities for women in the field of higher education, the U.S. was something of a pioneer. The impetus came from several sources: increasing demands for better prepared teachers in elementary and secondary schools, new industrial and technological needs, the passage of the Morrill Act of 1862 that stimulated the growth of the state universities whose doors soon opened to the daughters as well as the sons of taxpayers, and the organized efforts of women themselves. Some of these early educational opportunities were coeducational. Oberlin College, Ohio, opened as the first coeducational college in 1833. Antioch College, Yellow Springs, Ohio, followed in 1853. Although these early efforts suffered sharp popular attacks and not a few college presidents were opposed to coeducation in principle, college enrollments on a coeducational basis moved forward substantially. This was particularly true in the land-grant colleges of the Middle West. The University of Wisconsin (Madison) and the University of Iowa (Ames) admitted women in the 1860s, and the Universities of Michigan (Ann Arbor), Maine (Orono), and Cornell University (Ithaca, N.Y.) became coeducational in the 1870s. While the state universities in the West and Middle West continued this movement toward coeducation in the decades that followed, Eastern colleges and universities tended to maintain separate programs for men and women. Many private women's colleges were formed in this period, some of them under Catholic auspices. Fourteen non-Catholic colleges were opened before 1860, 15 more by 1880, and by 1900 an additional 27. This represented the peak period of growth for this group. Catholic women's colleges, several of which were founded in the late 19th and early 20th centuries, reached their peak period of growth from 1921 to 1940 when an average of two such institutions opened each year. They account for approximately one-half of the currently existing women's colleges. Catholic and non-Catholic women's colleges enroll somewhat less than 10 per cent of the total 4-year college student population.

Decline of Men's and Women's Colleges. Public universities, colleges, and the most rapidly growing segment of American higher education, the 2-year public community colleges, have developed, on the contrary, almost entirely along coeducational lines. This has been accompanied by a decline in private, liberal arts colleges for men, and since 1930, a decline in the non-Catholic private women's colleges. Many of these institutions have become coeducational or coordinate colleges. Since many graduate schools of high quality now admit women freely, it can be said that graduate work had become characteristically coeducational throughout American universities. For the academic year 1964 to 1965, the overall ratio of women to men students in all categories of U.S. higher education (opening enrollment, all institutions, 5,320,294) was roughly 2 to 3. Women enrollments were highest proportionally in teacher-training programs, lowest in advanced graduate work.

Causes. The milieu in which these developments took place was conducive to the spread of coeducation in America. A pervading democratic ideology assumed equality of opportunity for every citizen. This was accompanied by popular demand for increased governmental responsibility to ensure education of all the nation's children. The fact that separate schools for boys and girls were more expensive to build and operate than coeducational ones was a circumstantial reality that buttressed prevailing assumptions and accelerated the movement. Among the causes operating in higher education to explain the shift to coeducational institutions, two stand out. Vastly increased numbers of young people, many from lower socioeconomic groups, began to find that at least 2 years of education beyond high school was now a vocational necessity. The only practical way to achieve this was to attend a 2-year or a 4-year college, almost all coeducational, within commuting range of their homes. A second cause is a clearly marked preference of increasing numbers of students, particularly women students, to attend coeducational colleges.

Objections. Although many so-called facts used in past arguments against higher education for women have been reduced to quaint terms in the history of education, e.g., exacting intellectual requirements of secondary and higher education are injurious to young women's health, not all the old issues and arguments for or against coeducation have been closed out. Those issues that remain open meaningfully focus on the level of secondary education, since no dispute has arisen as to the feasibility of coeducation up to the time of adolescence. Critics have mounted various arguments against coeducation: (1) in physical and vocational education the needs of each sex differ so much that identical education is precluded and curriculum planning rendered more difficult; (2) the differing sensitivities involved in the teaching of such courses as biology and psychology make classroom instruction in mixed classes less effective; (3) moral problems are created through the free association of adolescents in U.S. high schools; (4) since girls mature more rapidly than boys, the competition is uneven and is frequently a discouraging factor to boys; (5) coeducation prevents the adequent development of certain qualities, some of them intangible, associated with feminity in young women and manliness in young men; (6) social activities in coeducational schools start too early and are too intense, thereby adversely affecting serious interest and sense of purpose in study; (7) boys do better when taught by men during their adolescent years, and girls, when taught by women; and (8) because of feminine influence, large coeducational universities have become training schools for husbands.

Advantages. Those favoring coeducation have advanced contrary arguments: (1) coeducation is more economical, an important factor in an era of rapidly rising educational costs; (2) it promotes a democratic and healthy interchange between the sexes resulting in more informally realistic relationships; (3) education, as a preparation for life, must provide opportunities for young men and young women to involve themselves in the community of interests and cooperative efforts now characteristic of social and economic life; (4) the moral tone of coeducational institutions, generally speaking, is better than that in noncoeducational schools; (5) those who work and play together in responsibly supervised educational programs "run better in the harness of married life"; (6) girls bring to the class a beneficial, civilizing effect not present when boys are educated separately; (7) coeducation does not necessarily mean identical education in all aspects of the curriculum, and in most high schools a variety of separate courses are open to each sex to advance characteristic or special talents and life purposes.

In Catholic Institutions. Catholic parochial schools in the U.S. have developed almost entirely along coeducational lines at the elementary level. Catholic secondary schools have in general followed coinstitutional and to a lesser extent coeducational patterns, although a good number of academies and preparatory schools provide separate programs for young women or young men. Colleges and universities under Catholic auspices are either coeducational, particularly in professional or graduate schools and in large institutions in urban centers, or traditional men's colleges and women's colleges. Some coordinate women's undergraduate colleges have been established as part of universities traditionally open to men only.

Encyclicals and Canon Law. The educational concern of the Church in matters of moral and spiritual welfare has not only been shown by the creation and support by U.S. Catholics of a major educational enterprise, but has also been manifested in certain papal encyclicals and Vatican documents issued over the years relative to educational matters (*see* CHRISTIAN EDUCATION, PAPAL TEACHING ON). Specific developments in different countries posing a danger to faith or morals usually provided the occasion. For instance, the encyclicals by Pius IX, Leo XIII, and Pius XI treated of laicism, false naturalism, and atheistic communism. In 1929 Pius XI issued his encyclical "On the Christian Education of Youth" (*Divini Illius Magistri*), stating, "false also and harmful to Christian education is the so-called method of 'coeducation'," particularly "when founded upon naturalism and the denial of original sin." Upon the invitation of Pius XII, the Congregation of the Religious convened a plenary, mixed meeting to study the question and on Dec. 8, 1957, issued an instruction on the subject. This stated that "coeducation in its true concept cannot in itself be approved in general," but "if mixed Catholic schools . . . are administered with certain precautions, even coeducation according to the norm of the encyclical *Divini Illius Magistri* can be tolerated." The instruction also made it clear that "the question of coeducation is dealt with here only insofar as it concerns high school education. It does not apply to universities or to elementary schools. Ordinaries have the faculty of deciding the age when boys and girls can be educated in such schools."

One out of two Catholic children is accommodated in a Catholic parochial school, and one out of three in a Catholic high school in the U.S. Catholic college students in ever-increasing numbers and in significant proportions are attending public universities and colleges. Catholic teachers are employed in vast numbers throughout the public school system of the U.S., and Catholic professors serve their fellow religionists in public universities and private colleges that are not related to the Church. Coeducation is thus a fact of life in U.S., and consequently attempts to apply broad theoretical formulations such as the 1957 instruction to the practical situation have been difficult. Similarly, CIC, c.1374, which forbids attendance of Catholic children at non-Catholic or mixed schools, has been unenforceable. Some Catholics have taken the position that leaving the choice of a school to the well-formed and properly instructed consciences of the Catholic people would give non-Catholics in a pluralistic society a better impression of the Catholic Church's true attitude toward education.

Practical Adaptation. Whether or not the convergence of sex roles in U.S. education has gone far enough or too far, it has been characteristic in an action-oriented American society to treat such issues in practical terms. One result has been that all types of schools have increasingly made provision for individual differences, aptitudes, and talents. The continuing evaluation and experimentation that has been part of this process has in recent years occasionally produced warnings that the uncritical acceptance of any educational practice, even as popular a one as that which minimizes or ignores sex-related differences, is in itself poor educational method. On the other hand, the relevancy of canonically formulated propositions characteristic of the theory-oriented European tradition, has also been questioned in terms of an educational method that attempts to fit the most appropriate curriculum to the needs of a unique individual under the best available circumstances. For U.S. Catholics coping with such issues, deep-running trends within Catholicism toward renewal and updating brought to the surface by Vatican Council II give promise of producing methodological changes that should facilitate the discussion and resolution of such educational issues that pertain to coeducation.

Bibliography: B. M. FRISON, *Coeducation in Catholic Schools: A Commentary on the Instruction on Coeducation* (pa. Boston 1959), Latin text in *Commentarium pro religiosis* 37 (1958) 274–282. M. NEWCOMER, *A Century of Higher Education for American Women* (New York 1959). A. H. DORN, "Administrative Patterns in the Constitutional High School," *Catholic School*

Journal 60 (Nov. 1960) 37–41. Pius XI, "Divini Illius Magistri" (On the Catholic Education of Youth, New York 1936).

[D. F. KENNY]

COEFFETEAU, NICOLAS, theologian; b. Chateau-du-Loir, 1574; d. Paris, April 21, 1623. He joined the Dominican Order in 1588. After receiving his doctorate in theology at Paris (1590), he taught theology, was prior, and served as regent of studies at the Priory of St. Jacques in the same city for 9 years. He was also vicar of the French congregation of his order. In 1608 Henry IV chose him as court preacher. Paul V named Coeffeteau coadjutor bishop of Metz in 1617, and he was designated bishop of Marseilles in 1621. In all these capacities he proved himself a staunch defender of the faith against Calvinism. He was a prolific writer, so much so that he is considered one of the creators of French prose. Chief among his works are: *Merveilles de la saincte eucharistie* (Paris 1606), *Defense de la saincte eucharistie et présence réelle du Corps de Jésus Christ* (Paris 1607), *Pro sacra monarchia ecclesiae* (Paris 1623), and *Tableau des passions humaines* (Paris 1620).

Bibliography: Quétif-Échard 2.1:434–435. Hurter Nomencl 3:715–718. R. COULON, DTC 3.1:267–271. H. M. FÉRET, *Catholicisme* 2:1278–79.

[J. H. MILLER]

COELLO, CLAUDIO, painter widely regarded as the last great master of the 17th-century school of Madrid; b. Madrid, 1642; d. Madrid, April 20, 1693. He was apprenticed by his father, a Portuguese bronzeworker, to Francisco Rizi (1608–85). Professional association with Juan Carreño de Miranda (1614–85) and Jose Jiménez Donoso (1628–90) brought him closer to the Spanish court and to Italian fashions. In 1683 he was named royal painter, and *pintor de cámara* in 1686. His most important work is "La Sagrada Forma" (1685–90), a monumental altarpiece for the *Escorial sacristy. As in a mirror the altarpiece depicts the scene in the sacristy in 1684 when a Communion wafer, once desecrated by *Zwingli's adherents in Holland, was blessed in the presence of Charles II and his court during a Mass of thanksgiving for the liberation of Vienna from the Ottoman threat. Other great paintings include frescoes in the Toledo cathedral vestry (with Donoso, 1671) and in the Mantería church, Zaragoza (1682); the "Triumph of St. Augustine" (1664) and "Madonna between Saints and Theological Virtues" (1669), both now in the Prado, Madrid; and the "Stoning of St. Stephen" (1692, S. Esteban, Salamanca).

See also BAROQUE ART.

Bibliography: J. A. GAYA NUÑO, *Claudio Coello* (Madrid 1957). G. KUBLER and M. SORIA, *Art and Architecture in Spain and Portugal and Their American Dominions, 1500–1800* (Pel HArt Z17; 1959). O. F. L. HAGEN, *Patterns and Principles of Spanish Art* (Madison 1943). Mayer HistPintEsp 496–505, *passim.* **Illustration credit:** MAS, Barcelona.

[G. KUBLER]

Claudio Coello, "La Sagrada Forma," altarpiece in the sacristy of the Escorial at Madrid.

COFFEY, JAMES VINCENT, jurist; b. New York City, Dec. 14, 1846; d. San Francisco, Calif., Jan. 15, 1919. He was the son of James and Catherine Coffey. After admission to the California bar in 1869, Coffey spent the next 6 years practicing law and writing editorials for the *San Francisco Examiner,* which then supported the Democratic party. He won public attention and served from 1875 to 1878 in the state assembly, where he advocated regulation of streetcar fares. In 1882 he began a 37-year career as a judge of the San Francisco superior court. As chief of its probate department, he adjudicated over a half billion dollars in estates, including those of the principal railroad, mine, and land owners of the West. His practice of correlating an attorney's fees with the value of an estate reduced expense and marked an innovation in probate action. His judicial opinions gave definitive interpretation to holographic wills, testamentary trusts, undue influence, and expert testimony. His rulings were published in *Reports of Decisions in Probate* (1894–1916), a six-volume work popularly known as *Coffey's Probate Reports.* It is a compendium of probate law extensively cited by the legal profession in California.

[M. MC DEVITT]

COFFIN, EDWARD, Jesuit controversialist; b. Exeter, 1570 or 1571; d. Saint-Omer, France, April 17, 1626. He entered the English College, Rome, in 1588, was ordained in Rome (1593), and was sent to England (1594); he joined the Society of Jesus (1598) while on the mission. On his way to make his novitiate in Flanders he was captured by the Dutch near Antwerp and sent back to England as a prisoner. He spent the next 5 years in jail, but on the accession of James I (1603) he was released and exiled. For nearly 20 years he was confessor at the English College, Rome. Near the end of his life he set out again for the English mission but got no farther than Saint-Omer. He wrote a number of books, including several controversial works against the English Protestants. He edited and contributed a lengthy introduction to Robert *Persons' posthumous reply to William Barlow, Bishop of Lincoln, *A Discussion of the Answere of M. William Barlow, 1612.*

Bibliography: T. COOPER, DNB 4:671–672. CathRecSoc v.37. Sommervogel 2:1270–71. DictEngCath 1:522–523.

[A. F. ALLISON]

COGITATIVE POWER

The cogitative power (or sense) is a power of knowledge that acts in a roundabout, discursive way. The name is borrowed from the Latin *vis cogitativa,* which in turn refers to *cogitatio*—rational, or discursive, thought in contrast to *intuition, *certitude, and immediate knowledge. This power is also less commonly called the *discursive power. It plays a role in human knowledge similar to that of the *estimative power in brute animals.

History of the Notion. The first distinctive use of the term was that proposed by *Avicenna. He developed a notion of distinct powers of knowledge that are distinguished from one another by their formal objects. On this basis, he distinguished the following "internal senses," *common sense, phantasy, *imagination or cogitative power, *memory, and reminiscence (*Liber canonis* 1.1.6.5; *De anima* 1.5; 2.1; 4.1, 3). The cogitative power was distinguished from the other powers by its manner of acting in the composition and separation of images.

A different theory was evolved by *Averroës. He regarded Avicenna's theory as not founded on the Aristotelian text, and referred the knowledge of good and evil to *nature and imagination (*Destructio Destructionum,* disp. 2). He held that *intellect and sense are distinguished completely, but also that the internal *senses approach intellect to some extent. The external senses grasp the object according to external accidents as presented here and now. The imagination grasps the same object, according to its permanent qualities, as abstracted from the here and now. The cogitative grasps the object as a particular *substance, abstracting from the accidents. Finally, the intellect grasps the universal substance, abstracting from all particularity (*Collegit,* 2.20; *In 3 anim.* comm. 6, 7, 20, 33, 57).

Since Avicenna's *De anima* was the first work to make these notions known to the Latin West, his version of the internal senses was first adopted by such authors as *Alexander of Hales, *John of La Rochelle, and St. *Bonaventure. However, St. *Albert the Great also made use of Averroës.

St. *Thomas Aquinas adopted most of the basic ideas of Avicenna concerning the internal senses, but also considered the explanations and criticisms of Averroës. Notable are St. Thomas's refusal to accept the real distinction between the phantasy and imagination, and his transfer of the term cogitative to the human estimative; in both of these considerations he seems to have been influenced by Averroës. Basically, his reason for asserting that man possesses this cogitative power is that he learns concrete good and evil by a kind of comparison of many individual instances (ST 1a, 78.4). St. Thomas himself made only brief references to the evidence for this. Contemporary thinkers, such as Rudolf *Allers, adduce material both from the slow and uncertain way in which an individual learns, and from the relativity of human opinions about good and evil, as shown, for example, by anthropologists.

Existence and Nature. Some philosophers have professed to find the notion of the cogitative difficult if not contradictory. Knowledge of good, it is said, is knowledge of a relation, and only intellect can know a relation. A first and immediate answer is accepted by all Thomists. For "to know good" is quite different from knowing goodness. The cogitative knows a concrete good; it cannot know goodness and relation as abstract and universal (John of St. Thomas, *Curs. phil.* 3:260–65).

For this reason, the knowledge or judgment of the cogitative cannot be called free except by denomination, in the sense of "free in its cause, not in itself." For, as is commonly held by Thomists, only a power that can grasp its formal object as such in *abstraction is able to reflect on its own act and on itself.

Exclusively in Man. First, then, the cogitative power can be found only in man. Secondly, its special mode of operation is due to the fact that it is a sense power of a rational nature, that is, under some influence from reason (ST 1a, 78.4). In general, all Thomists accept this position.

Moreover, an influence implies some kind of causality. There is the order of formal causality, and in this way, the *quiddity of the cogitative power is ordered to the quiddity of the intellect. Then, too, there is the order of *final causality, according to which the cogitative power subserves the purposes of intellect and will. So much is agreed on by all Thomists. It is in the order of *efficient causality that differences arise. Most Thomists, and E. Hugon would here be typical, hold that there is a permanent influence of intellect upon the cogitative as power, prior to activity. Others regard this proffered explanation as obscure. They hold that an efficient influence can be found only in the act of the cogitative.

Impressed Species. Another question often raised, also from a systematic viewpoint, is the way that the cogitative is put into act. According to the general Thomistic theory of cognitive powers, such a power cannot be put into act except through an intrinsic inherent determination, called the "impressed species" (*see* SPECIES, INTENTIONAL). Apart from minor variations, Thomists generally explain the impressed species of the cogitative thus: An external sensation (or an act of the imagination) is joined with the act of *consciousness to impress a particular determination upon the cogitative. By the external sense (or imagination) an object is made present; by the *central sense, the knowing subject is cognitively present. The simultaneous impression of these two acts upon the cogitative provides the concrete relation, which is judged good or evil partly by the very nature of the power, partly by reason and *experience.

Acts of the Cogitative. It is clear that in the very beginning of human life, one cannot act from prior experience. Thus, if there are any evaluative judgments at this level, they must be of a purely sensory nature. In this sense man has an estimative power. But as a child gains some experiences, he can begin to relate and compare. In the beginning he cannot do this actively, but can only accept those instances of good and evil that occur in his environment. Because a baby's environment is mostly a human one, the learning of sensory good and evil is rational—that is, at first with the rationality of the family and the culture, and only considerably later with the person's own rationality.

Experience gradually leads to complex memories. Memory depends on attention, and at this early stage this can be only what appeals to *appetite. Thus the cogitative power is actively involved with the construction of elaborated phantasms from which the intellect in time draws its concepts and forms its judgments and reasonings (*see* KNOWLEDGE, PROCESS OF). In this account, the cogitative power is associated with the formation of phantasms according to its nature as evaluative.

Some Thomists, among whom A. da Castronovo would be typical, offer a different account of the functioning of the cogitative power, basing this on St. Thomas's commentary on Aristotle's *De anima.* There St. Thomas follows Averroës in stating that the cogitative power knows "an individual as standing under a common nature" (*In 2 de anim.* 13, 398). Many interpret this text, possibly in the light of a tradition stemming from the dubious *De principio individuationis,* to mean that the cogitative power comes to know individuals, and to recognize that they have a common nature. Thus it prepares for the intellect a *phantasm of a number of individuals from which the intellect can legitimately abstract a common nature because it is already known to be there. This knowledge is possible because of the previously mentioned influence of the intellect upon the cogitative power as power.

Cogitative as Particular Reason. From one point of view, all human action is a doing (*agere*) and as such falls under the virtue of *prudence. One of the tasks of prudence is to judge about an action insofar as that action has a relation to the agent himself and his interior attitudes. In this connection judgments are made about what is suitable and reasonable. This "particular reason" is just what the cogitative power grasps, and so the power itself is sometimes called "particular reason." The intellect directs the cogitative power to make such concrete evaluations as here and now, for this man, express a general *value judgment. Since the operations of principal and *instrumental causality are one action (though the causes are two), the action of intellect and cogitative power in the particular evaluation are also one action of judging (*In 6 eth.* 4, 7, 9; ST 2a2ae, 47.3 and ad 3).

From still another point of view, the universal knowledge and the particular sense cognition are comparable as form and matter-form composite. In other words, the principle must be particularized and embodied in a concrete judgment of good and evil.

These considerations point out a way in which we can understand how the judgment of the cogitative is what it is—a discursive judgment of human good or evil—by its union with the intellect of man. For the matter-form unity of two acts into one composite activity explains why that single activity shows aspects of reason on the one hand (discursiveness, direct relation to the universal, some transcendence of the order of mere sense pleasure and even utility), and on the other shows aspects of sense (particularity, concreteness, contingence).

See also SENSES; SENSATION; ESTIMATIVE POWER; FACULTIES OF THE SOUL.

Bibliography: M. A. GAFFNEY, *Psychology of the Interior Senses* (St. Louis 1942). G. P. KLUBERTANZ, *The Discursive Power: Sources and Doctrine of the Vis Cogitativa According to St. Thomas Aquinas* (St. Louis 1952). J. PEGHAIRE, "A Forgotten Sense, the Cogitative, According to St. Thomas Aquinas," ModSchoolm 20 (1943) 123–140, 210–229. R. ALLERS, "The Vis Cogitativa and Evaluation," NewSchol 15 (1941) 195–221. A. DE CASTRONOVO, "La cogitativa in S. Tommaso," *Doctor Communis* 12 (1959) 99–244. C. FABRO, "Knowledge and Perception in Aristotelic-Thomistic Psychology," NewSchol 12 (1938) 337–365. R. HAIN, "De vi cogitativa et de instinctu hominis," RevUnOttawa 3.2 (1933) 41–62. T. V. MOORE, "The Scholastic Theory of Perception," NewSchol 7 (1933) 222–238. H. A. WOLFSON, "The Internal Senses in Latin, Arabic, and Hebrew Philosophic Texts," HarvThRev 28 (1935) 69–133.

[G. P. KLUBERTANZ]

COGOLLUDO, DIEGO LÓPEZ DE, Franciscan missionary and author; b. and d. dates unknown. He joined the Franciscan Order in 1629 at his native city, Alcala de Henares, Spain. In 1634 he arrived in Yucatán, where he learned Maya from Juan Coronel, then served in various pueblos, and taught philosophy and theology at Mérida. He was elected provincial in 1663 and probably died before the end of his 3-year term. His *Historia de Yucatán,* written during 1647–56 and published posthumously by Francisco de Ayeta, treats of both civil and religious matters and includes data on native religion and custom. In addition to using the works of others, including Bernal Díaz, Herrera, Torquemada, Las Casas, Remesal, Lizana, Sánchez de Aguilar, and Cárdenas Valencia, Cogolludo consulted the documents preserved in the governmental and Franciscan archives of Yucatán and, when possible, the private papers of prominent citizens. He had not, however, access to Landa's *Relación* or the *Relaciones de Yucatán.* His failure to meet modern standards of historical scholarship in the use of his sources is an inevitable reflection of the outlook and standards of his time. Although he could be naively credulous, he displayed, on occassion, fine critical sense. The enduring value of Cogolludo's work rests on the success of his efforts to collect and preserve much valuable historical material.

Bibliography: D. L. DE COGOLLUDO, *Historia de Yucatán,* 2 v. (5th ed. Mexico City 1957), prologue by J. I. RUBIO MAÑÉ. E. B. ADAMS, *A Bio-Bibliography of Franciscan Authors in Colonial Central America* (Washington 1953).

[E. B. ADAMS]

COHEN, HERMANN (AUGUSTINE MARY OF THE BLESSED SACRAMENT), Jewish convert who became a Carmelite priest after a career as a pianist; b. Hamburg, Germany, Nov. 10, 1820; d. Berlin, Jan. 20, 1870. As a child prodigy, he was brought to Paris by his mother at the age of 11 and became a student of Franz Liszt. He grew up in the artists' circle in Paris and was a special protégé of Georges Sand; he soon gave piano recitals and concerts of his own. Until he was 27 Cohen led an irresponsible artist's life, traveling throughout Europe and gambling. While playing the organ in the church of Saint-Valère in Paris as a favor to a friend, he experienced during Benediction of the Blessed Sacrament a sudden desire to change his life and become a Catholic. Two years later he entered the Discalced Carmelite novitiate at Le Broussey near Bordeaux and was ordained after 4 years. He became a renowned preacher in France, and when he returned to Paris for the first time his opening statement in the pulpit of Saint-Sulpice was: "My first words from this Christian pulpit must be words of repentance for the scandals I once committed in this city." He founded the Carmelite desert at Tarasteix at the foot of the Pyrenees and led the first group of Carmelites to return to London since the Reformation. When the Franco-Prussian War broke out it became politically difficult for him to remain in France, and he returned to Berlin where he died of smallpox in the prison camp of Spandau while ministering to the prisoners.

Bibliography: C. Sylvain, *Life of the Reverend Father Hermann,* tr. F. Raymond-Barker (New York 1925). Élisée de la Nativité, *Catholicisme* 5:662–663.

[P. T. ROHRBACH]

COIMBRA, UNIVERSITY OF

A Portuguese university of medieval origin under the jurisdiction of the ministry of higher education. Founded in 1290 by King Dinis, the University of Coimbra is among the oldest European universities in the world. It was originally established in Lisbon, where it remained until 1308. Subsequent years, however, found the University shifting back and forth between Coimbra and Lisbon, as circumstances demanded: 1308 to 1338, Coimbra; 1338 to 1354, Lisbon; 1354 to 1377, Coimbra; 1377 to 1537, Lisbon. In 1537 the University was permanently established in Coimbra. These continual changes were not unusual in a period when educational installations and equipment were naturally still rudimentary. Although another university was founded in Évora in 1559 under Jesuit direction and continued in operation until 1759, it lacked Faculties of Medicine, and Civil and Canon Law, leaving Coimbra the center of Portuguese cultural life until the 20th century, when the Universities of Lisbon and Oporto were founded in 1911.

Early History. Until 1290 education in Portugal had been limited to the primary and secondary levels offered in parish, *monastic, and *cathedral schools. Famous among the monastic schools were the Cistercian monastery of Alcobaça and the Augustinian monastery of Santa Cruz de Coimbra, whose pupil Fernando de Bulhões, later known as St. Anthony, became a Doctor of the Church. Previous to this time Portuguese students in pursuit of higher learning were obliged to go either to the University of *Bologna in Italy, *Paris in France, or *Salamanca in Spain. To avoid the inconveniences of travel abroad, King Dinis founded the first Portuguese university, which Pope Nicholas IV confirmed, granting the new institution, among other privileges, the *ius ubique docendi* and ecclesiastical immunity.

The University was composed of four Faculties: Medicine, Civil Law, Canon Law, and Arts, which included the trivium and the quadrivium. There was no Faculty of Theology, which the Church, with the intention of preserving unity of faith, reserved to the University of Paris. Doctors and lawyers, however, could now be educated in their own country, a fact that led to their increase in number and to an educational self-sufficiency that the University has preserved throughout the centuries.

As a cultural center, in the 14th century the University probably devoted time to the study of astronomy, thus preparing the way for the geographical discoveries for which Portugal is renowned. In the 15th century Prince Henry, famous leader of the maritime enterprises, became the protector of the University, now

A courtyard of the University of Coimbra, Portugal.

deeply committed to the study of mathematics. It was not until the 15th century that theology was introduced into the course of studies.

When in 1537 King John III established the University permanently in Coimbra, he undertook a complete reform of studies, not sparing any effort to place the University of Coimbra among the most famous institutions of the Renaissance. The professors included both outstanding Portuguese and foreign scholars, among them the Portuguese mathematician Pedro Nunes and the Spaniards Martin Azpilcueta, a famous canonist, and the learned anatomist Guevara. Erasmus also was invited to the University. Among the students who have left their names to posterity is Luis de Camões, author of the *Lusíadas,* the Portuguese national epic. King John III initiated the foundation of the Coimbra University colleges, the majority of which belonged to religious orders, to enable their members to attend the University. These colleges increased in number until in 1834, when religious orders were suppressed in Portugal, they totaled 23. To this day the buildings are used for various purposes and contribute in large part to Coimbra's architectural distinction as a university city.

Decline and Restoration. The early period of University splendor, enhanced by King John III's protection, was followed by one of decline, to which two major factors contributed: (1) Spanish domination toward the end of the 16th century, which came to an end in 1640 with the restoration of independence; and (2) the subsequent period of political conflict, in which both students and professors took part and which terminated with the peace of 1668. Despite the unrest, however, the University had its notable professors, among them the well-known Jesuit scholastic philosopher Francisco *Suárez. The University's greatest decline, in comparison with other European universities, was noted in mathematics and experimental sciences. This was remedied, however, by the large-scale reform undertaken in 1772 by the Marques de Pombal, minister to King Joseph I.

Pombal's reform was preceded by the expulsion from Portugal of the Jesuits, who since 1555 had influenced or directed University education. The reform, which had the support of the founder of the Oratorians, Philip *Neri, among other things substituted St. Augustine for Aristotle, qualitative for quantitative physics, and created the Faculty of Mathematics and the Faculty of Philosophy, the latter including natural history, experimental physics, and chemistry. It relegated metaphysics to the background and provided for properly equipped facilities in line with the new educational orientation, e.g., the observatory for astronomy and the botanical gardens, both of which are still worthy of admiration. The Faculty of Theology continued to function until early in the 20th century, when it was replaced by the Faculty of Letters.

The University of Coimbra in 1965 was composed of the Faculties of Letters, Medicine, Law, and Sciences and the School of Pharmacy. Both the Faculties of Letters and of Sciences comprise various divisions or institutes that confer their own degrees. All Faculties grant the licentiate and the doctorate. During the summer the Faculty of Letters offers a course in Portuguese language and culture for foreigners. The teaching staff in 1964–65 included 240 professors and about 450 lecturers, instructors, and administrative personnel. Student enrollment totaled 7,000 men and women of all faiths. The main library housed 1,200,000 bound volumes and 5,000 manuscripts. In addition each faculty, as well as the School of Pharmacy, with its respective institutes maintains its own specialized library. Outstanding among these are the Juridical Institute (Faculty of Law); the Botanical Institute (Faculty of Sciences); the Dr. António de Vasconcelos Institute of Historical Research; and the Jorge Faria Drama Library (Faculty of Letters). Instruction is carried on through lectures, discussion, laboratory experiments, and seminars.

The University is financed in part by the state and in part by students' fees. Both the state and private agencies, particularly the Gulbenkian Foundation, provide scholarships for those who meet certain requirements.

Publications. Among the University's many publications are *Revista da Universidade de Coimbra, Boletim da Biblioteca da Universidade de Coimbra, Biblos, Revista Portuguesa de Filologia, Revista Portuguesa de História, Revista de História Literária de Portugal, Humanitas, Brasília, Boletim da Faculdade de Direito, Folia Anatomica Universitatis Conimbrigensis, Arquivos do Instituto de Anatomia Patológica da Universidade de Coimbra, Revista da Faculdade de Ciências, Memórias e Notícias Publicações do Museu Mineralógico e Geológico da Universidade de Coimbra, Memórias e Estudos do Museu Zoológico da Universidade de Coimbra, Boletim da Sociedade Broteriana, Memórias da Sociedade Broteriana, and Boletim da Escola de Farmácia.* A very important reference work is the *Acta Universitatis Conimbrigensis,* with an annual supplement.

The University of Coimbra for centuries has maintained the unity of Portuguese culture through the educational services rendered not only to metropolitan Portugal and its insular and ultramarine dependencies but also to Brazil. No longer the sole Portuguese institution of higher learning, it serves as a guide and inspiration to younger institutions that draw on its centuries of experience in the world of letters.

Bibliography: H. RASHDALL, *The Universities of Europe in the Middle Ages,* ed. F. M. POWICKE and A. B. EMDEN, 3 v. (new ed. Oxford 1936). M. BRANDÃO and M. LOPES D'ALMEIDA, *A Universidade de Coimbra: Esbôço da sua História* (Coimbra, Port. 1937). **Illustration credit:** Casa de Portugal.

[S. DIAS ARNAUT]

COINAGE, ANCIENT (IN PALESTINE)

Coins (planchets of gold, silver, bronze, etc., bearing the impression of an official mark which guarantees their weight and fineness, *see* NUMISMATICS) circulated in Palestine shortly after coinage first gained acceptance in Western Asia. The periods of principal interest for Palestinian coinage are the Persian, Hellenistic, and Roman periods; in this article, a final section will treat of the coins mentioned in the Bible.

Origins and Persian Period. The oldest coins, which began circulating in western Asia Minor in the 7th century B.C., never reached Palestine. Darius Hystaspis (521–486 B.C.) introduced into Persia a coinage consisting mainly of gold coins, the famous darics, and silver coins known as *σίγλοι.* Although they probably came into use also in Persian-dominated Palestine, where large groups of Jews had returned following the permit granted by Cyrus, they have never been found there. Actually, the oldest coin found so far in Palestine seems to be a piece dug up at Balāta (Shechem), belonging either to Thasos or Northern Macedonia, struck *c.* 500 B.C. In addition to the imperial Persian coinage, not only was a limited provincial currency in use, but also the miniature Philisto-Arabian coinage, probably minted at Gaza. Moreover, occasional specimens prove that Greek 5th- and especially 4th-century coins, as well as the pre-Alexandrine coinage of the cities on the Phoenician coast, circulated in Palestine. A limited number of coins of this period are known that give in Hebrew letters the name of the province, *yᵉhûd,* or of a Jewish fiscal officer; aside from such distinguishing features, they are otherwise not remarkable.

Hellenistic Period. The conquest of the Middle East by Alexander the Great brought about a change in currency everywhere. Of the 20 chief mints of Alexandrine coinage, one was established in Palestine (at Accho). The battle of Ipsus (301 B.C.) brought Palestine under Ptolemaic rule, which was followed a century later by Seleucid domination. The continuous struggle between Ptolemies and Seleucids is well reflected in the output of the Palestinian and Phoenician mints. The decline of the Seleucid reign sparked the revival of local autonomous mints, including a Jewish mint, and a decree by Antiochus VII (1 Mc 15.2–9) permitted Simon the Machabee "to coin money for his country with his own stamp." Recent research, however, has made it clear that the silver shekels and the bronze coins of "year 4," formerly attributed to Simon, belong to the First Revolt of the Jews against Rome about 200 years later. Jewish coinage began with the bronze coins of John Hyrcanus I (135–104 B.C.), although, according to the latest study, many coins formerly ascribed to him belong to John Hyrcanus II in the subsequent period. Only bronze coins were minted by the Hasmonaeans, notably by Alexander Jannaeus (103–76 B.C.), who called himself "King Alexander" rather than high priest, on many of the coins issued during his reign.

Ancient Coinage of Palestine. (a) Coin of John Hyrcanus. (b) "Shekel of Israel" from the 2d year of the First Revolt, A.D. *67. (c) Bronze coin of Alexander Jannaeus. (d) Bronze coin of Herod the Great. (e) Silver shekel of the Second Revolt. All coins are here reproduced larger than actual size.*

Roman Period. Following the conquest of Palestine by Pompey in 63 B.C., Roman coins came into use there, parallel with the last of the Hasmonaean bronzes and the products in Hellenistic style from nearby Eastern Mediterranean mints for silver and gold. The Herodian bronze coinage, from Herod the Great (37–4 B.C.) to Agrippa II (A.D. 50–100), is easily identified. It is not a continuous series, because the deposition of Archelaus by the Romans in A.D. 6 and his replacement by a Procurator occasioned the issue of the so-called Procurator-coins, local bronze issues from Caesarea first minted under Augustus and continued under Tiberius, Claudius, and Nero.

Jewish Coinage of the Two Revolts. The First Revolt (66–70) was marked by the issue of the famous silver shekels, dated year 1 through 5; half-shekels, year 1 through 4, and various bronze coins dated year 2, 3, or 4. This self-consistent series of independent Jewish coins has been properly understood only since about 1940, and earlier descriptions of it are confused. The Roman victory over the Jews was celebrated by a series of so-called *Iudea Capta* coins, known under Vespasian, Titus (with Greek inscriptions), and Domitian (with Latin inscriptions). Most of them were issued at Rome, but some were struck in Palestine itself. The Second Revolt (132–135) brought the greatest development of autonomous Jewish coinage, the variety of types surpassing that of all previous periods. As they were generally overstruck on Roman imperial or provincial silver and local bronze coins (mostly of Ascalon and Gaza), the issuance of these coins during the Second Revolt is established beyond a doubt.

Roman Colonial Issues. Besides the Roman, Herodian, Procurator, and possibly Hasmonaean coins, many others from the mints of Antioch and Tyre were in circulation in Palestine during the lifetime of Our Lord. Palestinian city-coins did not play an important role at this time, as the only mints in operation were at Ascalon and Gaza, besides the two Phoenician mints of Dora and Ptolemais-Accho and, in Transjordan, Gadara. Some Nabataean coinage may have found its way to Palestine, although only the bronze coins of Aretas IV (with Shaqilath) are frequently found there.

From the 2d half of the 1st century through the 1st half of the 3d century, however, local Syro-Palestinian coinage saw its greatest development. From the historical, cultural, and artistic viewpoints, this constitutes the most interesting period of Palestinian numismatics. In Judaea, the chief mints were Colonia Aelia Capitolina (Jerusalem), Ascalon, and Gaza. Raphia was of minor importance, and only sporadic issues were produced at Anthedon, Eboda, Eleutheropolis, and Nicopolis. Besides that of Caesarea on the coast, there was an important mint at Neapolis in Samaria. A considerable number of coins was struck at Nysa-Scythopolis and Sebaste, and short-lived mints operated at Antipatris, Diospolis, and Joppa. In Galilee, only two mints struck coins, Sepporis-Diocaesarea and Tiberias; coins ascribed to Dabora are misread pieces of Joppa. In the Trachonitis, mints were established at Caesarea Philippi and Gaba.

The two Phoenician mints inside Palestine were at Dora and Ptolemais-Accho. In the Decapolis and the province of Arabia, the most important mints were those of Bostra, Gadara, and Philadephia (Ammān), with a limited production at Abila, Adraa, Antiochia ad Hippum, Canatha, Capitolias, Dium, Gerasa, Madaba, Pella, Petra, Philippopolis, and Rabbathmoba. There were isolated issues, under Elagabal only, at Esbus and Charachmoba (Kerak). With the cessation of the local mints, the classical period of Palestinian coinage came to an end. Imperial mints never operated in Palestine, either during the remaining centuries of the Roman Empire or during the Byzantine period.

Coins in the Bible. In the OT, specific references to coined money are very scarce. *Dark*[e]*mōn,* occurring in postexilic texts, is the Hebrew form of Greek genitive plural δραχμῶν, standing for either drachma, or, possibly, daric. Drachmas are mentioned in 2 Mc 4.19; 10.20; 12.43. The frequently mentioned shekel is a weight, not a coin. In the NT the silver coins mentioned are the denarius, drachma, didrachma, stater, and shekels.

Denarius. A Roman silver coin worth 16 as. During the lifetime of Our Lord most of the silver currency consisted of denarii and Tyrian shekels. The well-known "coin of the tribute" occurring in Mt 22.19–21; Mk 12.15; Lk 20.14, was most probably a denarius of the then reigning emperor Tiberius.

Drachma. A Greek silver coin, known in a large number of currency systems. It occurs in Lk 15.8–9 (the lost drachma), but contemporary drachmas did not exist. It may be just another name for the denarius, which had the same value, or, if indeed a drachma was meant, it may be that some drachmas of previous times were still in circulation.

Didrachma. A Greek silver coin, equal to two drachmas, mentioned in Mt 17.24. There were no contemporary didrachmas; those from the provincial mints at Antioch and Caesarea in Cappadocia are too late to be taken into consideration. The most likely similar Biblical coin is the half-shekel from Tyre.

Stater. An ancient Greek denomination both for gold and silver. Mentioned in Mt 17.27 (the only text where the word occurs), the stater was found in the mouth of the fish and meant as a payment for both Jesus and St. Peter, hence probably a shekel of Tyre or a tetradrachmon of Antioch.

Pieces of Silver. These coins mentioned in Mt 26.15; 27.3–5 (the 30 coins given to Judas), were certainly neither the thick Jewish shekels nor the Roman denarii (though the opinion that the latter coins were given is reflected in the Roman Breviary). They must have been Tyrian shekels, since the payment was made from the temple treasury, which accepted by preference (and hence, paid in) Tyrian silver money; the same applies to Mt 28.12. In Acts 19.19, τὸ ἀργύριον stands for either Roman denarii (in the Vulgate) or drachmas from Ephesus or Caesarea in Cappadocia.

Bronze Coins. Of bronze coins, three Roman denominations occur: as, in Mt 10.29 and Lk 12.6, worth one-sixteenth of a denarius; quadrans, a quarter of an as, in Mt 5.26 and Mt 12.42; dupondius, a double-as, in Lk 12.6 (Vulgate only). The as and dupondius referred to may be either the coins from the imperial mints or, more probably, provincial coins from Antioch. The quadrans, which was never struck in the Antioch series under the early emperors, was struck under Augustus at Rome and Lugdunum. The *minutum* or λεπτόν, in Mk 12.42 and Lk 12.59; 21.2, better known as the (widow's) mite, is difficult to determine. It is said to be equal to half a *quadrans* (Mk 12.42) and is probably the same as the *pruta* of the Mishnah. It may also be a small Procurator, Herodian, or even Hasmonaean coin. In fact, the smallest Palestinian coins are the so-called "imitations" of Alexander Jannaeus.

Bibliography: A. Reifenberg, *Ancient Jewish Coins* (2d ed. Jerusalem 1947). G. F. Hill, *Catalogue of the Greek Coins of Palestine* (London 1914). F. de Saulcy, *Numismatique de la Terre Sainte* (Paris 1874). *Corpus Nummorum Palaestinensium,* pub. Israel Numismatic Society (Tel Aviv 1956–). L. Kadman, *Coins of Aelia Capitolina* (1956); *Coins of Caesarea Maritima* (1957); *Coins of Ptolemais-Akko* (1961). J. Babelon, DBSuppl 5:1346–75, with extensive bibliog. A. Spijkerman and J. Starcky, "Un Nouveau lot de monnaies palestiniennes," Rev Bibl 65 (1958) 568–584. H. Seyrig, "Temples, cultes et souvenirs historiques de la Décapole," *Syria* 36 (1959) 60–78. A. Kindler and J. Meyshan, *The Dating and Meaning of Ancient Jewish Coins and Symbols* (Tel Aviv 1958). L. Kadman, *The Coins of the Jewish War 67–73 C.E* (Tel Aviv 1960). B. Kanael, "The Beginning of the Maccabaean Coinage," IsrEplorJ 1 (1950–51) 170–175; "Ancient Jewish Coins and Their Historical Importance," BiblArchaeol 26 (1963) 37–62. **Illustration credits:** American Numismatics Society, New York.

[A. SPIJKERMAN]

COLA DI RIENZO

Roman revolutionary; b. Rome, Italy, 1313 or 1314; d. Campidoglio Palace, Rome, Oct. 8, 1354. He was born into humble surroundings (an anonymous contemporary biographer says that his father, Lorenzo, was a tavernkeeper and his mother a washerwoman and water carrier) and was orphaned at an early age. Until he was 20 years old he lived at Anagni, and in 1333 or 1334 he returned to Rome. There he devoted himself to the study of the classics and of Roman antiquities; he also began to study law. In 1343 he was sent to Avignon by the popular government of the 13 *boni homines* to inform Pope *Clement VI of the pitiable state of the city and beg him to declare 1350 a *Holy Year. The personality and eloquence of the Roman politician greatly impressed the Pope, who named him a notary of the papal camera in Rome on April 13, 1344. While at Avignon he met *Petrarch and found in him a man who shared his own ideals. In 1344 he returned, not without difficulty, to Rome and there began his public career. He created a sensation by the allegorical images and messianic tone of his speeches, set against the background of a continued deterioration of affairs in the city. Supported by the popular elements of the city, as well as by the gentry and the wealthy merchants, he staged a *coup d'état* on Pentecost Sunday, May 20, 1347. Rienzo assumed broad governmental powers and proclaimed new ordinances intended to restore the material and spiritual well-being of the city, reduce the privileged position of the nobility, and guarantee security and justice for all classes of the population. He applied himself with decision to implementing this program, took the title of tribune, and surrounded himself with a sumptuous and often ludicrous ceremonial that, together with the fantastic claims he then began to make, tended to aggrevate the political situation in Rome and to increase the opposition of its citizens. A series of contretemps embittered his relations with the Pope and the Roman townspeople, until he was forced (December 15) to resign and withdraw to *Castel Sant' Angelo.

Pursued by the papal authorities, he sought refuge in 1348 among the hermits of Maiella near Mt. Merrone. Incited by his reading and conversations with the sense of an almost prophetic mission, he traveled to the court of Emperor *Charles IV in Prague (July 1350), but was imprisoned as an excommunicate. In 1352 he was transferred to Avignon and subjected to a lengthy trial by the *Inquisition, which ended in his absolution and liberation. *Innocent VI decided to use Rienzo in preparing the ground for Cardinal *Albornoz in his efforts to reestablish papal authority at Rome, for he could hold the lower classes in check and lead the opposition to the nobility. On Aug. 1, 1354, at the head of an army of mercenaries, Rienzo entered Rome amid wild acclaim, bearing the title of senator conferred on him by the papal legate. A series of unpopular and arbitrary acts, however, together with violence and extortion that were associated with his rule, turned the people against him and he was killed in the course of a popular riot. The personality of Cola di Rienzo is a controversial subject even today, and varying and sometimes contradictory interpretations of his career make it difficult to judge its precise significance.

Bibliography: COLA DI RIENZO, *Briefwechsel . . .* , ed. K. BURDACH and P. PIUR, 5 v. in 6 (Berlin 1912–29). *La vita di Cola di Rienzo,* ed. A. M. GHISALBERTI (Florence 1928). P. PIUR, *Cola di Rienzo* (Vienna 1931). F. PAPENCORDT, *Cola di Rienzo und seine Zeit* (Hamburg 1841). F. A. GREGOROVIUS, *History of the City of Rome in the Middle Ages,* tr. from 4th Ger. ed. by A. HAMILTON, 8 v. in 13 (London 1894–1902). R. MORGHEN, *Cola di Rienzo, senatore, 1354,* ed. L. GATTO (Rome 1956). E. DUPRÉ THESEIDER, *Roma dal comune di popolo alla signoria pontificia, 1252–1377* (Bologna 1952); *I papi di Avignone, e la questione romana* (Florence 1939). H. VIELSTEDT, *Cola di Rienzo: Die Geschichte des Volkstribunen* (Berlin 1936). G. VINAY, "Cola di Rienzo e la crisi dell'universalismo medievale," *Convivium* NS 2 (1948) 96–107. M. PETROCCHI, EncCatt 3:1941–43.

[M. MONACO]

COLBERT, JEAN BAPTISTE, minister of Louis XIV, financial reformer, and organizer; b. Reims, Aug. 29, 1619; d. Paris, Sept. 6, 1683. He was the Jesuit educated son of a merchant draper of Reims. He entered the employ of Cardinal Jules Mazarin and provided evidence at the start of Louis XIV's reign that contributed to the disgrace of the Superintendent of Finances, Nicolas Fouquet, and to his own advancement. His many titles, controller general of finances, minister of marine, superintendent of buildings, among others, barely suggest the great range of his activities. It is to Colbert primarily that we owe the refreshing spirit of reform that characterizes the first two decades of the Sun King's personal rule. "We are not in the reign of little things," Colbert wrote. He was a fervent crusader for a prosperous France. Because his plans infringed on powerful vested interests, they never attracted a deserved popular support. He is best remembered for perfecting the economic system known as mercantilism until it became generally synonymous with his name. Years before his death, Colbert fell out of the King's favor and died in semidisgrace, a lonely, defeated, and intensely unpopular man.

In matters of religion, Colbert consistently subordinated religion to political and economic policies. A firm mercantilist, he was convinced of the necessity for reducing the number of religious in France on the grounds of their unproductivity. He brought tension to Franco-Roman relations in the 1660's by advocating the raising of the minimum age for taking religious vows, reducing

Jean Baptiste Colbert, by Claude Le Fèbvre, Versailles.

the number of holy days, and curtailing the establishment of new religious orders. In contrast to his own religious indifferentism are his numerous close relatives who rose to prominence in the Church: Michel Colbert (1633–1702), abbot general of the Premonstratensians; Jacques Nicolas Colbert (1655–1707), Archbishop of Rouen; Charles Joachim Colbert (1667–1738), Bishop of Montpellier and one of the staunchest opponents of the bull **Unigenitus*.

Bibliography: J. B. COLBERT, *Lettres, instructions et mémoires,* ed. P. CLÉMENT, 7 v. (Paris 1861–73). C. W. COLE, *Colbert and a Century of French Mercantilism,* (2 v. New York 1939). C. FARRÈRE, *Jean Baptiste Colbert* (Paris 1954). C. BOUREL DE LA RONCIÈRE, *Un Grand ministre de la marine* (Paris 1919).
Illustration credit: Archives Photographiques, Paris.

[L. L. BERNARD]

COLE, HENRY, confessor of the faith; b. Godshill, Isle of Wight, *c.* 1500; d. Fleet Prison, February 1580. He was educated at Winchester College and New College, Oxford, and received a bachelor of civil law degree on March 3, 1530. He traveled abroad, residing mainly at Padua. Upon acknowledging Henry VIII head of the church in England, he received several ecclesiastical prebends. After he became doctor of civil law (Oxford 1540) he was elected (1542) warden of New College and rector of Newton Longueville, Buckinghamshire. As an ardent reformer during the reign of Edward VI, he later regretted this and between 1548–51 gradually resigned all his preferments. At Queen Mary's accession he publicly adhered to Roman Catholicism and was appointed archdeacon of Ely in 1553, and canon of Westminster and provost of Eton College in 1554. Cole was chosen by the Queen to preach the sermon before the execution of Thomas Cranmer (1556). He was a delegate of Cardinal Pole for the visitation of Oxford

(1556), was elected dean of St. Paul's and judge of the Archiepiscopal Court of Audience (1557). Cardinal Pole appointed him executor of his will. Under Elizabeth Cole was one of eight leading Catholics appointed to take part in the disputation at Westminster in 1559. He was heavily fined for his defense of the faith and deprived of all his preferments. He was committed to the Tower on May 20, 1560, but was transferred to the Fleet in June. Here he died, after nearly 20 years imprisonment.

Bibliography: DictEngCath 1:529–532. H. TOOTELL, *Dodd's Church History of England,* ed. M. A. TIERNEY, 5 v. (London 1839–43) v.2, 3. A. à WOOD, *Athenae Oxonienses,* ed. P. BLISS, 5 v. (London 1813–20) v.1. Hughes RE.

[J. D. HANLON]

COLEMAN, EDWARD, BL., controversialist, intrigant, and victim of the Popish Plot; b. Suffolk, sometime before 1650; d. Tyburn, London, Dec. 3, 1678. Coleman, a Puritan and a Cambridge graduate, became a Catholic about 1670, certainly before 1673, and shortly thereafter assumed the office of secretary to Mary of Modena, wife of James, Duke of York and the King's brother. In this capacity Coleman engaged in frequent correspondence with civil and ecclesiastical authorities at the French court, concerning aid for a Catholic revival in England under the leadership of the newly converted Duke of York, and conducted able polemical exchanges with Edward Stillingfleet and Gilbert Burnet. When in September 1678 Titus Oates made his revelation of a "popish plot," Coleman confidently accepted arrest and interrogation (*see* OATES PLOT). To the arraignment of high treason, on the testimony of Oates and William Bedloe that he had conspired with a French Jesuit, several Irish cutthroats, and the royal physician, to murder the King and foment rebellion against Parliament, he replied that he had indeed discussed foreign subsidies for influencing parliamentary elections and reinstating the Duke of York in the Admiralty, but that none of this corresponded to the perjured charges made against him. He was nevertheless found guilty and executed as a traitor.

Bibliography: DictEngCath 1:532–536. For a résumé of Oates's charges see H. FOLEY, ed., *Records of the English Province of the Society of Jesus,* 7 v. (London 1877–82) 5.1: 97–109. D. OGG, *England in the Reign of Charles II,* 2 v. (Oxford 1934). J. W. EBSWORTH, DNB 4:744–745.

[R. I. BRADLEY]

COLEMAN, WALTER, poet; b. Cannock, Staffordshire, date unknown; d. London, England, 1645. Coleman (Colman) was certainly the younger son of Walter Coleman (b. *c.* 1566) and his wife, Dorothy, of Cannock, Staffordshire, a community whose 400 inhabitants were described in 1604 as virtually all Catholic. He entered the English College, Douai, Sept. 19, 1616. Later he was educated in France. He went back to England for a time, but returned to Douai, where he entered the English Franciscans of the Strict Observance in 1625, receiving the religious name Christopher à Santa Clara. He was sent to England as a missionary and imprisoned, probably in late 1627, but later released. He spent several more years as a missionary and was then rearrested, imprisoned at length, and finally brought to trial at the Old Bailey with six other priests in December 1641. He was sentenced to death, but Charles I, at the behest of the French ambassador, commuted the sentence; Coleman was returned to prison at Newgate, where he died after a lengthy illness. In 1633 he published a poem in 262 stanzas, entitled *La Dance Machabre,* or *Death's Duell,* a rare work that has been virtually unnoticed by literary historians; its dedication to Queen Henrietta Maria is in French.

Bibliography: *The Victoria History of the County of Stafford,* ed. L. M. MIDGLEY (London 1959), for references to the Coleman family. E. H. BURTON and T. L. WILLIAMS, eds., *The Douay College Diaries* (CathRecSoc 10; 1911). T. COOPER, DNB 4:852. DictEngCath 1:536–538.

[H. S. REINMUTH, JR.]

COLERIDGE, HENRY JAMES, editor and writer; b. Ottery St. Mary, Devonshire, Sept. 20, 1822; d. Roehampton, April 13, 1893. He was a great-nephew of Samuel Taylor Coleridge; the son of John Taylor Coleridge, a judge of the Queen's Bench; and the brother of Lord Coleridge, the Lord Chief Justice of England. After attending Eton, he followed J. H. Newman's footsteps at Oxford as a scholar of Trinity College who became a Fellow at Oriel. He took Anglican orders in 1848 and was one of the cofounders of the *Guardian,* the organ of the High Church party. One of the second generation of the Tractarians (*see* TRACTARIANISM), he was refused appointment as tutor at Oriel because of his devotion to Newman, just after Newman was received into the Church. Coleridge himself was received in 1852, went to Rome, where he studied for the priesthood at the Accademia dei Nobili, and was ordained (1856). The following year he entered the Jesuit novitiate at Roehampton; his superiors quickly availed themselves of his exceptional talent, and in 1865 he was appointed editor of the recently founded (1864) *Month.* During the 16 years of his editorship, the journal became a leading Catholic publication. He was also editor of the *Messenger* (1877–81). He was a thorough scholar, and in order to raise the level of Catholic education, he founded the Quarterly Series, to which he contributed, among other works, *The Public Life of Our Lord* (1872), *The Life and Letters of St. Francis Xavier* (1872), *The Life and Letters of St. Teresa* (1881–88), and *The Story of the Gospels Harmonized for Meditation* (1884). In all he wrote some 20 books. Always an ardent student of the New Testament, he devoted himself to this interest in his later years, even after his health broke in 1890. He spent the last 2 years of his life, a period of great suffering, at the novitiate where he had begun his Jesuit life.

Bibliography: J. PATTERSON and R. F. CLARKE in *Month* (1893) 153–181.

[D. WOODRUFF]

COLERIDGE, SAMUEL TAYLOR

Poet, philosopher, critic, seminal thinker; b. Ottery St. Mary, Devon, Oct. 20, 1772; d. Highgate, London, July 25, 1834. He was the youngest son and ninth child of Rev. John Coleridge, vicar of Ottery and master of the grammar school there, by his second wife, Anne (nee Bowdon). While studying at Christ's Hospital (1782–91), the young Coleridge was known as an eccentric but gregarious virtuoso, and formed an important friendship with Charles Lamb (1775–1834).

Career and Works. Coleridge entered Jesus College, Cambridge (1792), as exhibitioner and sizar; but after a brilliant and tempestuous beginning, he joined the Dragoons (1793). After release from military service, he met (June 1794) his future brother-in-law Robert

Southey (1774–1843); he never seriously resumed his university career. In Bristol in 1795 Coleridge and Southey sought unsuccessfully the means to found an ideal community in the U.S. In the same year he married Sarah Fricker, by whom he had four children. At that time Coleridge began to establish his reputation as a poet and journalist. He met Unitarian intellectuals and for a time intended to become a Unitarian minister, but by 1802 the Trinitarian doctrine had become the basis for his theological reflections.

Coleridge settled at Nether Stowey, Somerset, in 1796 and was joined in 1797 by William and Dorothy (1771–1855) Wordsworth. In 1796 and in 1797 Coleridge had published collections of his poems. In 1798 his poetic gifts flowered in *The Rime of the Ancient Mariner* and *Kubla Khan,* in some of his other contributions to the volume *Lyrical Ballads,* which he published jointly with *Wordsworth, and in his "conversation poems." His visit to Germany in 1798–99 enabled him to master the German language and gave him his first acquaintance with Immanuel *Kant and German philosophy. In 1800 he moved to Keswick, Cumberland, to be near the Wordsworths and Sara Hutchinson (1775–1835). In April 1804, hoping to halt the deterioration of his health and escape from marital unhappiness, he went to the Mediterranean, where for a time he was private secretary to the governor of Malta, and then acting public secretary. He also traveled in Sicily and Italy. Coleridge returned to England in July 1806—ill, addicted to opium, estranged from his wife, uncertain of his future—relying upon the Wordsworths for comfort and direction. At Grasmere he wrote his periodical, *The Friend* (1809–10, 28 numbers). His alienation from the Wordsworths, which had been deepening since 1807, was never repaired after 1812. Coleridge was in London and Bristol from 1811 to early 1815, working intermittently as a journalist and lecturer; he was in poor health and spirits, and was looked after by new friends, until he finally resolved to break his drug addiction.

The renewal of Coleridge's powers was marked by his collection of poems, *Sibylline Leaves,* and his *Biographia Literaria* of 1815. In April 1816 he took up residence with Dr. James Gillman in Highgate, London, where he remained until his death. Coleridge's early Highgate years were his most prolific: in 1816 he produced the *Christabel* volume and *The Statesman's Manual;* in 1817, the second *Lay Sermon, Biographia Literaria,* and *Sibylline Leaves;* in 1818, *On Method,* a much-enlarged *Friend,* and two pamphlets on the factory children; and in 1818–19, an important series of literary lectures and the *Philosophical Lectures* (ed. K. Coburn, 1949). Coleridge never completed his philosophical-theological *opus maximum,* and published only two more books, *Aids to Reflection* (1825) and *Church and State* (1830), but he issued collective editions of his poems in three volumes (1828, 1829, 1834).

Coleridge's daughter and his nephew H. N. Coleridge (1798–1843) prepared new editions of his work after his death, and collected and edited much of his unpublished writings. The work of accurate editing, long deferred by the difficulties of the task, should be fulfilled with the edition of the *Notebooks* (ed. K. Coburn, 4 v. New York and London 1957, 1962; 11 v. planned), *Collected Letters* (ed. E. L. Griggs, 4 v. Oxford 1956, 1959; 6 v. planned), and the *Collected Coleridge* (K. Coburn, gen. ed; 4 v. New York 1966; about 23 v. planned).

Samuel Taylor Coleridge, portrait by P. Vandyke, 1795.

His Influence. Coleridge's poetry at its best is characterized by sensitive craftsmanship, a symbolic rather than descriptive thrust, and a way of making myth out of his interior life and the actual world. The strength of his criticism arises from his acute introspective understanding of the psychology and ontology of poetry. Imagination, a way of mind that he distinguished sharply from fancy, is the supreme realizing activity in which a person becomes unified. His *Biographia Literaria,* though allusive and difficult, laid the foundations for the complex critical revolution of the 20th century; Coleridge's splendid critique of Wordsworth's unique genius has not been superseded; and the fragmentary records of his Shakespeare lectures have been influential.

Coleridge's philosophy has Platonic and Kantian origins, but transcends both in establishing an organic (or dynamic or polar) framework in which he sees life as the interpenetration of opposites. J. S. *Mill regarded Coleridge and *Bentham as "the two great seminal minds of England in their age," and recognized that in all his thinking Coleridge "expresses the revolt of the human mind against the philosophy of the 18th century," i.e., mechanical *materialism. Unity was always Coleridge's theme; and life, his guiding analogy. In the absence of a central philosophical work from Coleridge, his reputation and influence as philosopher and theologian depend on scattered passages in his various writings and on the recollection of his lectures and conversation. His philosophy has a strong ethical bias: "My metaphysics are merely the referring of the mind to its own consciousness for truths indispensable to its own happiness." Reason and understanding correspond in the ethical field to imagination and fancy in the poetical, and faith is "the personal realization of the reason by its union with the will." An admirer of the *Caroline divines and *Cambridge Platonists, he was familiar also with the work of Johann Eichhorn (1752–1827) and F. D. E. *Schleiermacher, as well as that of the contemporary English Biblical scholars; he greeted with enthusiasm the emerging historical and anthropological analysis of the Bible (*see* BIBLE, VI). In the posthumously published *Confessions of an Inquiring Spirit* (1840) he sought, in an age of "Bibliolatry," to establish the invulnerability of the Bible, not by avoiding criticism, but by insisting on broader and deeper understanding of Scripture. He had an important influence on the New England transcendentalists (*see* TRANSCENDENTALISM, LITERARY); and his theological influence in England is acknowledged by Thomas Arnold (1795–1842), Thomas *Carlyle, J. C. Hare (1795–1855), F. D. *Maurice, and John Henry *Newman, among others.

Bibliography: *Complete Works,* ed. W. G. T. SHEED, 7 v. (2d ed. New York 1884), crabbed and incomplete; *Inquiring Spirit,* ed. K. COBURN (New York 1951), best gen. introd. to his thought; *Poetical Works,* ed. J. D. CAMPBELL (New York 1903), ed. E. H. COLERIDGE (Oxford 1912), standard but needs revision; *Biographia Literaria,* ed. J. SHAWCROSS, 2 v. (Oxford 1907), useful nn., but text superseded by the Everyman ed. by G. WATSON (New York 1956). J. D. CAMPBELL, *Samuel Taylor Coleridge: A Narrative of the Events of His Life* (New York 1894), the best biog. E. K. CHAMBERS, *Samuel Taylor Coleridge: A Biographical Study* (Oxford 1938), useful. Bateson CBEL v.3, 5, best cumulative bibliog. J. H. MUIRHEAD, *Coleridge as Philosopher* (New York 1930). C. R. SANDERS, *Coleridge and the Broad Church Movement* (Durham, N.C. 1942). B. WILLEY, *Nineteenth Century Studies* (New York 1949). A. H. HOUSE, *Coleridge* (New York 1953). J. D. BOULGER, *Coleridge as a Religious Thinker* (New York 1961). **Illustration credit:** National Portrait Gallery, London.

[G. WHALLEY]

COLET, JOHN

Dean of St. Paul's, major figure in early Tudor humanism; b. London, 1467?; d. Sept. 16, 1519. He was the son of Sir Henry Colet, enormously wealthy and twice Lord Mayor of London; he was the only one of 11 sons and as many daughters to survive childhood. Educated probably at St. Anthony's School, London,

John Colet.

and Magdalen College, Oxford, he may have begun Greek with *Grocyn and *Linacre, who had just returned from their Italian studies. Doubtless stimulated by their accounts of Italian *humanism, Colet went to Italy in 1493 and there studied Canon and Civil Law, Greek, philosophy, and Sacred Scriptures. He did not meet *Ficino but did correspond with him (Jayne), and the work of Ficino, *Pico della Mirandola, and other Italian *Neoplatonists was a strong influence on his own thought. He apparently returned to Oxford about 1496 and resumed his studies for the degree of doctor of divinity (which he probably received in 1504); between 1496 and 1499 he was ordained, carried further his philosophical and scriptural studies, and wrote commentaries. In 1499 he met *Erasmus, and the two greatly influenced each other. In 1509 he became Dean of *St. Paul's, London.

Soon after his return from Italy he lectured on the Epistles of St. Paul at Oxford; the lectures on I Corinthians made a very strong impact because of their new stress on Paul and their concern with Paul's writings in the context of early Christianity. Colet's interest, then, was moral and historical, not allegorical or speculative. In these lectures, fortunately extant, "Paul and Colet together have much to say about fifteenth-century evils" (Harbison), and here were "the roots of Colet's later famous sermons as Dean of St. Paul's castigating clerical abuses and advocating a Christian pacifism" (*see* PREACHING, I). Though he published very little (like others of his generation of humanists, such as Grocyn and Linacre), Colet communicated through his conversation and correspondence, and one can see the power of his influence upon friends like Erasmus and Thomas *More, and perhaps also on *Tyndale, who is likely to have heard him at Oxford and in London. And, finally, his foundation of St. Paul's School the year before his death enabled him to build a living memorial of many of his educational ideals, a memorial that played a significant role in the development of Tudor education (*see* EDUCATION, I, 4). About 1510 Colet wrote a Latin grammar—his accidence (*Aeditio*) for the syntax by William *Lily—and this work was frequently reprinted both separately and as part of what was popularly known as Lily's grammar. The later official textbook of Henry VIII, compiled after Lily's death, built upon not only Colet and Erasmus but also Melanchthon and others.

His untimely death was a great loss to Tudor England, for Colet, by virtue of his prestige and the weight of his integrity, might have modified some of the events of the 1520s and 1530s. His would have been a vigorous theological mind to give support to Bp. John *Fisher, whom a Spanish theologian remarked as the one English prelate competent in theology.

See also ENGLISH LITERATURE, 3.

Bibliography: Works, ed. and tr. J. H. LUPTON, 5 v. (London 1867–76). F. SEEBOHM, *The Oxford Reformers . . .* (3d ed. London 1887). J. H. LUPTON, *A Life of John Colet* (new ed. London 1909; repr. Hamden, Conn. 1961). D. ERASMUS, *Opus epistolarum,* ed. P. S. ALLEN et al., 12 v. (Oxford 1906–58) 4:1211; *The Epistles of Erasmus . . .,* ed. and tr. F. M. NICHOLS, 3 v. (New York 1901–18; repr. 1962). P. A. DUHAMEL, "The Oxford Lectures of John Colet," JHistIdeas 14 (1953) 493–510. E. H. HARBISON, *The Christian Scholar in the Age of the Reformation* (New York 1956). E. W. HUNT, *Dean Colet and His Theology* (London 1956). V. J. FLYNN, "The Grammatical Writings of William Lily, ?1468–?1523," *Papers of the Bibliographical Society of America* 37 (1943) 85–113. For the full story of Lily's Latin grammar and that of Henry VIII see C. G. ALLEN in *The Library,* 5th ser. 9 (1954) 85–100; 14 (1959) 49–53. P. B. O'KELLY, *John Colet's Commentary on I Cor.* (Doctoral diss. unpub. Harvard U. 1960). L. MILES, *John Colet and the Platonic Tradition* (La Salle, Ill. 1961), largely superseded by JAYNE. C. S. MEYER, "John Colet's Significance for the English Reformation," *Concordia Theological Monthly* 34 (1963) 410–418; *John Colet Bibliog.* (privately printed; Concordia Seminary, St. Louis, Mo. 1963). S. R. JAYNE, *John Colet and Marsilio Ficino* (Oxford 1963). Emden 1:462–464.

[R. J. SCHOECK]

COLETTE, ST., foundress of Colettine Poor Clares; b. Nicolette Boylet (or Boellet) at Calcye, near *Corbie, Jan. 13, 1381; d. Ghent, March 6, 1447 (feast, March 6). Born in answer to her parents' prayer, she lived a life marked by the unusual. At 21 she became a recluse, after three unsuccessful attempts at the religious life, and for several years lived in rigorous penance. During this time her mission to reform the *Poor Clares was made clear to her. She sought permission from antipope *Benedict XIII, at Avignon, who received her into the Second Order of St. Francis, dispensed her from a novitiate, and appointed her abbess general. In 1408, with the help of Bl. Henry de la Baume, she began the work of restoring the primitive Rule of St. Clare (1253), imposing absolute poverty and perpetual fast. Many existing convents of the Urbanist Clares were reformed and some 20 new ones established during her lifetime. In 1412 the *Franciscan Conventuals in northern France and Belgium established a reformed branch called Coletans. Never numerous, they were suppressed in 1517. Iconography shows Colette as an abbess, barefooted, usually with a lamb at her feet. She was canonized in 1807.

Bibliography: ActSS March 1:531–626. UBALD D'ALENÇON, ed., *Les Vies de sainte Colette Boylet de Corbie . . . écrites par ses contemporains . . .* (Paris 1911). F. IMLE, *Die hl. C.* (Munich 1916). Q. VAN ALPHEN, "De hl. C. van Corbie," *Franciscaansch Leven* 20 (1937) 156–166, 212–222; 21 (1938) 292–301; 22 (1939) 198–208. A. P. SCHIMBERG, *Tall in Paradise* (Francestown, N.H. 1947). M. FRANCIS, *Walled in Light* (New York 1959). Butler Th Attw 1:506–508. S. ROISIN, DHGE 13:238–246.

[M. F. LAUGHLIN]

COLETTE, GABRIELLE SIDONIE, French novelist; b. Saint-Sauveur-en-Puissaye (Yonne), France, Jan. 28, 1873; d. Paris, April 3, 1954. In 1893, after her early education (highly romanticized in the *Claudine* series), she married Henri Gauthier-Villars. He urged her to write about her childhood in Burgundy and thus the *Claudine* series came into being. The first four books (1900–03) were signed with his pseudonym, Willy. After being divorced in 1907, Colette turned to the music hall in order to earn a living. In 1912, she married the baron Henri de Jouvenal whom she later divorced. From this union was born in 1913 a daughter who lives in Colette's stories under the charming Provençal name of Bel-Gazou. During World War I, Colette spent some time in Italy and wrote articles and chronicles that won the praise of both Gide and Proust. Two short novels, *Chéri* (1920) and *Le Blé en herbe* (1923), revealed her unique talents. In 1935 she became Mme. Maurice Goudeket.

Of such prominent woman writers of this century as Anne de Noailles, Marie Noël, Simone de Beauvoir, and Simone Weil, Colette is probably the most widely read. Drawing largely on her childhood, during which she had been taught by a wise mother to be sensitive to natural beauty, Colette, though reticent about herself, consistently revealed various aspects of her life. The *Claudine* series depicts her early life, and the Sido and Bel-Gazou episodes give us intimate glimpses of her mother, whom she adored, and of her child, equally

Gabrielle Sidonie Colette.

dear to her. Vignettes of the stage, backstage, and dressing-rooms are caught in *La Vagabonde* (1910) and *L'Envers du music-hall* (1913). The world of courtesans is given vitality in *Chéri, La Fin de Chéri* (1926), and *Gigi* (1945). Colette's work is essentially sensuous; religious matters and social problems hardly entered her thought. She used war and politics as peripheral material, but her concern was only with men and animals; at times, she even seemed to prefer the company of animals. The human heart in the throes of love is her other great contribution to the literature of her times. Whether it be adolescent love (*Le Blé en herbe*), jealousy (*Duo,* 1934; *La Chatte,* 1933), a woman abandoned by a younger love (*Chéri; La Fin de Chéri,* 1926), or the problems of love (*La Naissance du jour,* 1928), Colette explored all of them sensitively and sensually. Hers was a humanism of natural wisdom, compounded of pity for humanity, respect for the human person, a deep love of beauty, and a refusal to acknowledge the vulgar. She was president of the Académie Goncourt, grand officer of the Legion of Honor, and a member of the Royal Academy of Belgium.

Bibliography: *Colette, par elle-même,* ed. G. BEAUMONT and A. PARINAUD (Paris 1951). M. CROSLAND, *Madame Colette: A Provincial in Paris* (London 1953). M. DAVIES, *Colette* (New York 1961). M. GOUDEKET, *Près de Colette* (Paris 1956). M. LE HARDOUIN, *Colette* (Paris 1956). E. MARKS, *Colette* (New Brunswick, N.J. 1960). T. MAULNIER, *Introduction à Colette* (Paris 1954). P. TRAHARD, *L'Art de Colette* (Paris 1941). **Illustration credit:** French Embassy Press and Information Division, New York City.

[J. D. GAUTHIER]

COLGAN, JOHN

Irish Franciscan hagiographer; b. Priest-town, near Carndonagh, County Donegal, *c.* 1592; d. St. Anthony's College, Louvain, Jan. 15, 1658. There is no definite information about his early years. He left Ireland for Spain or Belgium about 1612, and having done courses in philosophy and theology, was ordained about 1618. He entered the Franciscan Order at St. Anthony's College, Louvain, on April 26, 1620. A letter in Irish written by Colgan on Dec. 26, 1628, leaves the impression that he had at that time been teaching for a period in

John Colgan, detail of a 17th-century fresco by Father Emmanuel di Como in St. Isidore's College, Rome.

Germany and indicates that he was being transferred to Mainz as lector of theology.

Sometime before June 1634 he returned to St. Anthony's College, Louvain, where he was appointed lector in theology and master of novices. He also joined wholeheartedly in a scheme, which was then under way at St. Anthony's College, for the collection and publication of manuscript material dealing with the ecclesiastical history of Ireland and the lives of the Irish saints. This scheme grew out of a meeting between two Irish Franciscans, Hugh Ward and Patrick Fleming, and an Irish secular priest, Thomas Messingham, at Paris in 1623. Messingham was preparing a volume on the lives of the Irish saints, and Ward and Fleming decided to join with him in the project. The agreement reached with Messingham fell through, and Ward and Fleming continued on their own. It was their intention to gather, at St. Anthony's College, copies of the lives of the Irish saints to be found in the libraries of Europe, and Ward sent Brother Michael O'Clery to Ireland in 1626 to make copies of the material in the old books there. Many other Irish Franciscans took an active part in the work, and there is evidence to show that in 1628 Colgan was already interested in the project since he was then inquiring about documents that could be copied from libraries in Central Europe. Patrick Fleming was killed in Bohemia in 1631, and 4 years later Hugh Ward died. It fell to Colgan to direct the historical publications that they had had in mind. He set about his task by putting the finishing touches to Ward's work and by preparing for the printers manuscripts and copies of manuscripts that had been brought together at Louvain. He sought out new material; and if there was no biography available for some particular saint, Colgan compiled one from various scattered references.

Although he applied himself diligently to the task of preparing the lives of Irish saints for publication, poor health and lack of sufficient money thwarted his efforts. However, in 1645 he succeeded in having the first volume of the *Acta Sanctorum* published at Louvain; it contained the lives of Irish saints whose feastdays fell in January, February, and March. A generous grant of money from Hugh O'Reilly, Archbishop of Armagh, covered the cost of printing. In 1647 appeared his *Triadis Thaumaturgae Acta,* containing the lives of SS. Patrick, Brigid, and Colmcille. Archbishop Thomas Fleming of Dublin met the expenses of this volume. Both volumes were illustrated with copious notes and valuable appendices.

In 1651 Colgan had been appointed commissary of the three Irish Franciscan colleges at Louvain, Prague, and Vielun (Poland), but because of failing health he found it necessary to ask his superiors to relieve him of this office in February 1652. In 1655 he published at Antwerp a book of about 200 pages dealing with the life, writings, and fatherland of John Duns Scotus. He was an ardent defender of the Irish birth of Scotus. At the time of his death Colgan had a third volume on the Irish saints in an advanced stage of preparation; it contained the lives of those saints whose feastdays fell in the months of April, May, and June, but the necessary financial support to have it printed was not forthcoming. It was his intention to publish seven or eight folio volumes in all, and three of these were to be devoted to the Irish apostolate abroad.

Bibliography: T. O'Donnell, ed., *Father John Colgan, 1592–1658: Essays in Commemoration of the Third Centenary of His Death* (Dublin 1959). B. Jennings, *Michael O Cléirigh, Chief of the Four Masters, and His Associates* (Dublin 1936). J. Ware, *The History and Antiquities of Ireland . . . with the History of the Writers of Ireland,* ed. W. Harris, 2 v. in 1 (Dublin 1764) 140–141. L. Bieler, "John Colgan as Editor," FrancStudies 8 (1946) 1–24. F. Ó Briain, DHGE 13:247. **Illustration credit:** Foto Pino, Rome.

[C. GIBLIN]

COLIGNY, GASPARD DE

Admiral of France and Huguenot leader, known as "Admiral of Châtillon"; b. Châtillon-sur-Loing, Feb. 16, 1519; d. Paris, Aug. 24, 1572. He was the third son of Gaspard de Coligny (1470?–1522), marshal of France. Coligny gained early military repute in the wars of Francis I in Flanders and was wounded at Montmédy (1542) and Binche (1543); he fought also in Italy at the battle of Cérisoles (1544). Henry II made him colonel-general of infantry (1547), admiral of France (1552), and governor of Paris and Ile-de-France. In 1550 he negotiated the Anglo-French agreement over Boulogne. Coligny distinguished himself at the battle of Renty (1554) and at Saint-Quentin, where he was besieged by the Spaniards (1557), who captured him. He remained their prisoner until the Peace of Cateau-Cambrésis (1559). While in captivity Coligny embraced Protestantism and henceforth gave himself to the Huguenot cause. With *Louis I Condé he became the joint leader of the Huguenot party (1560) and played a prominent role at the Colloquy of Poissy (1561). Coligny shared the command of the Huguenot army

The three brothers Coligny: Cardinal Odet de Chatillon, Gaspard, and the Maréchal d'Ancelot. Drawing by an unknown 16th-century artist of the French school, in the Bibliothèque Nationale, Paris. The drawing must have been done after the cardinal renounced the cardinalate to become a member of the Huguenot church.

with Condé; after the latter's death (May 13, 1569) he became commander in chief. The admiral, defeated at Dreux (December 1562), Saint-Denis (October 1567), Jarnac (May 1569), and Moncontour (October 1569), was victorious at Hondau (February 1568) and at La Roche-l'Abeille (June 1569), where he defeated Gaspard de Saulx de Tavannes. Later, Henry de Navarre joined him as leader of the party. In August 1570 Coligny concluded a favorable peace at Saint-Germain. Convinced of the futility of religious wars, he appeared at court at Blois (September 1571), intent on preserving and strengthening the Huguenot party and hoping to cooperate with the royal camp. As he was wary of the Spanish danger, he planned to frustrate Spain's expansionist ambitions, and won King Charles IX over to his side. An expedition to help the uprising of William of Orange in the Netherlands was being secretly prepared and Coligny sent the Duke of Genlis and François de La Noue to support the uprising and called for a mobilization in Picardy. The King hesitated to reveal his position and finished by repudiating the action of Genlis. Catherine, fearing Huguenot reaction, ordered Maurevel to assassinate Coligny. (*See* CATHERINE DE MÉDICIS.) On Aug. 22, 1572, the admiral was wounded by two shots fired by Maurevel (known also as Louviers de Maurevert) from an arquebus. Charles IX visited the wounded leader, reassured him, and promised an inquiry and revenge. Yet in the early hours of August 24, when the Massacre of *St. Bartholomew's Day began, Coligny was killed by Swiss soldiers, who were led by Besme (Jean Yanowitz) and who were under the command of Duke Henry de *Guise.

Coligny showed remarkable ability, as chief of the Huguenot forces, in repeatedly saving his army from disaster. A courageous soldier but only a mediocre general, he was a skillful diplomatist who valued political victories higher than military glory. He was a leader of considerable imagination whose vision extended beyond the religious and military spheres. His interests included reform of the system of justice and of the national finances, as well as colonial expansion (he promoted emigration to the New World where he established Huguenot colonies in 1562 and 1564). He was reputed to have a truly noble character and to be zealous and unselfish. In his complete devotion to the *Huguenot cause, he was hailed as a hero by its adherents and was depicted as such in romantic literature.

Bibliography: A. W. WHITEHEAD, *Gaspard de Coligny* (London 1904). J. DELABORDE, *Gaspard de Coligny, l'amiral de France,* 3 v. (Paris 1879–82). C. MERKI, *L'Amiral de Coligny* (Paris 1909). K. MANOURY, *Die Schlachten Colignys 1562–1570,* v.1 of *Das Kriegswesen der Hugenotten 1562–1598* (Berlin 1957–). H. NOGUÈRES, *The Massacre of Saint Bartholomew,* tr. C. E. ENGEL (London 1962). P. BREZZI, EncCatt 3:1946. J. JORDAN, LexThK[2] 3:2. **Illustration credit:** Archives Photographiques, Paris.

[W. J. STANKIEWICZ]

COLIN, FREDERIC LOUIS, missionary, founder of the Canadian College in Rome; b. Lignières, France, Jan. 14, 1835; d. Montreal, Canada, Nov. 27, 1902. Although admitted to the École Normale Supérieure of Paris, he entered the Sulpician seminary of Issy (1855) and was ordained in Paris Dec. 17, 1859. He was sent to Montreal (1862), where he served as missionary, curate, and professor and director of the major seminary. From 1881 until his death he was superior of the Sulpicians in Canada. He distinguished himself in the field of education, founding the philosophy seminary in Montreal (1892), and playing a major part in establishing what later became the University of Montreal (1876). At the suggestion of Cardinal Edward H. Howard, Colin organized and founded the Canadian College in Rome, where the first students were enrolled in 1888.

Bibliography: H. GAUTHIER, *Sulpitiana* (Montreal 1926).

[J. LANGIS]

COLIN, JEAN CLAUDE MARIE, VEN., founder of the *Marist Fathers and *Marist Sisters; b. Saint-Bonnet-le-Troncy, near Lyons, France, Aug. 7, 1790; d. La Neylière (Rhône), Nov. 15, 1875. During his boyhood his ambition was to lead a religious life as a solitary. He was ordained (1816) after studies in the seminary at Lyons, where he became interested in the plan for a society of Mary promoted by a fellow seminarian, Jean Claude Courveille. On the day after his ordination he and 11 others signed a promise to strive for the creation of this society. In 1817 Colin and Jean Marie Chavoin founded the Marist Sisters. While working as assistant to his brother Pierre in Cerdon (Ain), Colin composed the first rule of the Marist Fathers and received from Pius VII in 1822 a letter encouraging him to proceed with the formation of this congregation. When Colin was assigned to the Diocese of Belley, restored in 1822, the bishop placed him in charge of the missionary Marists of the diocese (1825–29) and head of the minor seminary (1829–45). Aspirant Marist priests elected Colin superior (1830). After the Holy See approved the congregation (1836) subsequent to Colin's acceptance of Western Oceania as a mission, Colin became superior general (1836–54). As head of the institute he promoted mission and educational works at home and sent more than 100 missionaries to the Pacific area. Colin revealed enterprise and prudence as superior general and in his dealings with ecclesiastical and civil officials in Oceania he displayed diplomatic talent. By 1854 the Marists had 280 priests and brothers. Upon completing his term as superior general Colin spent his remaining years at La Neylière, where he completed the final text of the congregation's constitutions (1869), which were approved by Rome (1873). The decree introducing his cause for beatification was issued in 1908, and the decree on the validity of his process in 1926.

Bibliography: *Le Très Révérend Père Colin,* 6 v. Lyon 1895–98). P. MULSANT, *Le Vénérable Père Jean-Claude Colin* (Paris 1925); *L'Âme du vénérable Père Colin* (Lyons 1933). J. BONNEFOUX, DictSpirAscMyst 2:1078–85. J. COSTE and G. LESSARD, eds., *Origines maristes, 1786–1836,* 4 v. (Rome 1960–66).

[S. W. HOSIE]

COLL Y PRAT, NARCISO, archbishop of Caracas, Venezuela, during the War of Independence; b. Cornellá de Ter, Gerona, Spain, 1754; d. Madrid, Dec. 28, 1822. He was a doctor of law, both civil and Canon; professor at the University of Cervera, Spain; and member of the Academy of Fine Arts of Barcelona.

Narciso Coll y Prat.

He took possession of the archbishopric of Caracas on July 31, 1810; just as there had been established a new political regime that would proclaim absolute independence from Spain the next year. That independence cost long years of warfare, during which Republicans and Royalists were alternately in power. In addition to the calamities of war, a terrible earthquake destroyed large parts of cities and towns. In Caracas alone more than 10,000 persons died, almost a third of the population. In the face of the misery and helplessness of the populace, the archbishop showed extraordinary charity. As a Spaniard and appointee of the King, he was loyal to the Spanish authorities; but he also showed respect and obedience to the republican authorities. Above all, with the authorities of either, he always tried to be a good pastor, preventing cruelty, interceding in behalf of those persecuted by either faction, and helping those in need, while at the same time maintaining religious services, religious discipline, and the piety of the faithful. Bolívar recognized the virtues of the archbishop and therefore retained him in his position. On the other hand, the Spanish authorities considered Coll lax in his behavior toward the Republicans, and he was recalled by the King. On Dec. 8, 1816, he returned to Spain to answer the charges of disloyalty made by the Spanish leader Morillo. To justify himself, he wrote two extensive *Memoriales,* to which he attached numerous supporting documents. In 1822 he was appointed bishop of Palencia, Spain, but he died without assuming the office.

Bibliography: N. COLL Y PRAT, *Memoriales sobre la independencia de Venezuela* (Caracas 1960). P. LETURIA, *Relaciones entre la Santa Sede e Hispanoamérica,* 3 v. (AnalGreg 101–103; 1959–60). N. E. NAVARRO, *Anales eclesiásticos Venezolanos* (2d ed. Caracas 1951).

[P. P. BARNOLA]

COLLATIO, a term having several meanings in ecclesiastical contexts, especially the following: (1) The light meal permitted on days of fasting in addition to the full meal (CIC c.2151). (2) The lives of the Fathers, especially as arranged for public reading in monastic establishments of the Middle Ages; a usage deriving, perhaps, from the *Collationes Patrum* of John *Cassian. (3) A sermon or exposition of a passage from Scripture, the religious rule, or a patristic writing, common in houses of friars in the 13th and 14th centuries (e.g., the *Collationes in Hexaemeron* of St. *Bonaventure); sometimes only an outline or plan is meant. (4) In some 13th-century scholastic circles, the inductive stage of philosophical investigation. (5) In Canon Law, the second and most essential of the three stages in the provision of an ecclesiastical office or benefice (*see* BENEFICES, CANON LAW OF), the first and third of which are presentation and institution. In this sense a collation is the act of conferring an ecclesiastical benefice or office (*collatio tituli*) on a designated person or presentee, whether by right of ordinary jurisdiction (e.g., a bishop) or of a prerogative arising out of a lawful title, custom, or privilege, e.g., patronage (*see* PATRONAGE, CANON LAW OF; CIC cc.1431–47).

Bibliography: J. LECLERCQ, "Recherches sur l'anciens sermons monastiques," *Revue Mabillon* 36 (1946) 1–14. J. G. BOUGEROL, *Introduction à l'étude de Saint Bonaventure* (Paris 1962) 178–192. M. D. CHENU, "Notes de lexicographie philosophique médiévale," RevScPhilTh 16 (1927) 435–446. Regatillo (6th ed. Santander 1961) 1:228–245. G. BARRACLOUGH, *Papal Provisions* (Oxford 1935); "Praxis Beneficiorum," ZSavRGKan 27 (1938) 94–134. G. MOLLAT, DDC 2:413–431. N. DEL RE, Mercati-Pelzer DE 1:663. Cross ODCC 310. A. STURM, LexThK² 3:3.

[L. E. BOYLE]

COLLECTIONS DURING MASS

A term referring to the practice in Catholic churches of gathering money contributions during Mass. This custom has a complicated history.

History. From earliest times money has been given by the faithful (e.g., Acts 4.34; 6.1; 11.29; 1 Cor 9.8; 2 Thes 3.8). Even though it may well have been collected when the faithful were at Mass, there is no evidence that the collection was during the course of the Mass. The purpose of the collection was to supply the needs of the clergy (in justice) and the poor (in charity). Hence the nature, manner, and purpose of these collections were all extraliturgical; they had no intrinsic connection with the sacrifice of the Mass.

From about the 4th century bread, wine, and other requisites for the Mass were given by the faithful. The collection was usually taken by means of an Offertory procession during Mass; its purpose was to supply the needs of the altar (worship). It is true that the amounts contributed often exceeded the immediate needs, and that the surplus went to the clergy and the poor; yet its immediate purpose was the needs of the altar. Hence its nature, manner, and purpose were all *liturgical;* it had an intrinsic connection with the sacrifice of the Mass.

From about the 11th century some of the faithful presented money instead of bread and wine. By the time unleavened bread had completely supplanted leavened bread, money gifts had generally supplanted gifts in kind (apart from a few special exceptions like the consecration of bishops and the canonization of saints). Moreover, the offertory procession had been dropped and was replaced by taking up a collection. Hence the matter and manner of the gift-giving changed; yet its purpose remained as before. Money, indeed, is not material for sacrifice, and the passing round of a plate or basket is not a ritual action; yet it may be argued that because it is taken up during Mass and intended primarily for the needs of the altar (worship), this collection has an intrinsic connection with the sacrifice. It should not be classed with the extraliturgical money collections of the early Church (concerned with justice and charity), but with the *liturgical* gift-giving of the medieval Church (concerned with worship). This money collection, by its circumstances and primary purpose, has acquired a liturgical significance and may be said to be a part of the Mass.

Significance. Often it is said that such money is a "gift to God," a symbol of the donor's self-giving in sacrifice. This idea has a basis of truth, but must not be exaggerated in a way that would eliminate the mediatorship of the Church. It would be more accurate to say that the layman gives money "to the Church" (rather than "to God") in order that the Church may transmute his gift into the materials needed for the sacrifice. The bread and wine in turn are consecrated into the victim of the sacrifice (Christ's body and blood). Then the layman, through and with the priest, offers the divine victim to the Father and thereby offers himself as included in Christ by reason of his membership in the Mystical Body. Strictly speaking, it is not the layman's money that is offered in sacrifice, not even the bread and wine his money buys; the only victim of the sacrifice of the Mass is Christ. This is the truth that has to be safeguarded by taking care not to misinterpret the Offertory or the collection of money that is made during it.

See also OFFERTORY.

Bibliography: Miller FundLit 268–270. A. CLARK, "The Function of the Offertory Rite in the Mass," EphemLiturg 64 (1950) 309–344. J. A. JUNGMANN, *The Mass of the Roman Rite* (New York 1959) 315–326. Righetti 3:180–183.

[C. W. HOWELL]

COLLECTIVE BARGAINING (U.S.)

Collective bargaining is the process of negotiating terms and conditions of employment between a worker organization and an employer organization. When the employers bargain through an association, it becomes collective on both sides. The process includes as well the administration of the agreement by the parties in the day-to-day conduct of the enterprise.

Background. In the mid-1960s there were about 150,000 collective bargaining agreements in force in the U.S., covering just short of 17 million employees organized into about 180 national unions and an undetermined number of local unions. The national unions varied in size from the Teamsters and Automobile Workers (more than 1 million members) to small but powerful organizations such as the Pattern Makers' League. About 15 million trade unionists were blue-collar workers. Although union membership has dropped slightly in recent years because blue-collar employment in organized industries has fallen off and the unions have made only small headway in organizing white-collar workers and plants located in the South, unions continue to be a dominant force in the skilled trades and in the largest enterprises in the country. A 1962 presidential executive order establishing three forms of recognition for employee organizations in Federal employment spurred hopes for greater organization there.

Most of the union contracts in the country cover but one company and a limited number of workers. In 1961, however, about 8 million workers came under 1,733 contracts, each covering 1,000 or more workers. Approximately half of these contracts covered more than one employer. Multiemployer bargaining has been traditional in such industries as mining, construction, trucking, longshoring, maritime and retail trade. It is the exception in manufacturing. Unions there, however, have sought quite successfully through "pattern bargaining" to establish similar terms among competing firms by individual agreements as economic pressures and the unions' natural interest in the "standard rate" favored such uniformity. Bargaining has tended to be conducted by local unions in local product markets, such as construction, and by national unions in national product markets, such as coal mining.

Job Consciousness of American Unions. American trade unions came to favor collective bargaining, rather than political action and efforts for broad social reform, as their method of improving the lot of American workers because the unions developed as job-conscious rather than class-conscious institutions. This in turn was due to factors inherent in the American environment, such as the early development of manhood suffrage and political democracy, the abundance of economic opportunity in a growing nation, the prevailing individualistic philosophy, the early failure of trade union efforts at political action and broad social reform because of public antipathy and division among the workers themselves, and the secularly rising productivity of the American economy, which made possible significant gains through collective bargaining.

The force of these environmental factors was clearly perceived by Samuel Gompers, the first president of the American Federation of Labor (AFL), founded in 1886. He laid down the principles that autonomous national unions should each have exclusive jurisdiction to organize their respective "job territory" and should seek gains through collective bargaining. Organization of the skilled into strong craft unions was to be the primary objective. Ties among the national unions were to be loose, with the AFL concentrating on supervising jurisdictional lines and on seeking legislation favorable to collective bargaining by "rewarding its friends and punishing its enemies" in political life rather than by any attempt at such independent political action as sponsorship of a labor party. Although since the 1930s American unions have intensified their lobbying and other political activities for the attainment and improvement of government-run social programs, collective bargaining has remained their focal activity.

Craft Basis of First Unions. The 1930s are a dividing line in the development of trade unionism and collective bargaining. Before that the unions tended to limit their own influence by concentrating on organization on a craft basis mainly among the skilled, except for the mining industry. They met with fierce employer opposition. Strikes, boycotts, and picketing were severely restrained by labor injunctions issued freely by the courts until their use was drastically curtailed by the Norris-La-Guardia Act of 1932. *See* LABOR LAW (U.S.). Membership arose from fewer than 1 million just before 1900 to a temporary peak of 5 million at the close of World War I and dropped to 3 million in 1930. Except for the 1920 peak, the unions never included more than 10 per cent of the nonagricultural work force. Organization was concentrated in the construction, clothing, railroad, printing, and coal-mining industries.

Growth of Industrial Unions. A number of factors led to the surge of trade unionism and collective bargaining to national prominence in the 1930s. The chaos of the great Depression and the increased mechanization and concentration of industry, on the one hand, stimulated the interest of the nation's millions of mass-production workers in becoming organized and, on the other hand, generated public sympathy for such efforts. The passage of the National Labor Relations Act (Wagner Act) of 1935 greatly assisted the process of organization. It made encouragement of the practice and procedures of collective bargaining the national policy. It provided election procedures to facilitate self-organization. It forbade interference by employers with workers' rights to organize. The formation of the Congress of Industrial Organizations (CIO) after 1935 stimulated efforts to organize on an industrial basis. In rapid succession the rubber, steel, auto, and electrical industries became effectively organized. Union membership rose from fewer than 3 million in 1933 to nearly 9 million in 1940. It expanded further to about 15 million in 1946 under the stimulus of favorable labor-market conditions during World War II. Since the war unions have represented just less than one-third of the nation's nonagricultural work force—they are a vast and influential minority.

Collective Bargaining Process. For collective bargaining to occur, the workers must first be organized and have a bargaining agent.

Acquiring Status as Bargaining Agent. Until the Wagner Act the predominantly craft unions each employed the organizational strike in the face of employer opposition in an effort to organize its jurisdiction, that is, its craft as defined by the AFL. The Wagner Act stressed self-organization and gave the National Labor Relations Board (NLRB) the power in each case to determine the appropriate collective bargaining unit, to hold elections, and to certify as the bargaining agent the union receiving the majority employee vote. Organization by election largely displaced organization on the picket line. The NLRB, not the organizing union, designated the appropriate collective bargaining unit.

The extent and the composition of the unit for representation obviously affected a given union's chances of winning an election; it also affected the subsequent bargaining and its results. Quite often, different work groups, unions, and the employer involved have sought the unit that each deemed most favorable to it, e.g., craft, plant, company, or industry. In general, under the Wagner Act, the Taft-Hartley Act of 1947, and the Landrum-Griffin Act of 1959 [*see* LABOR LAW (U.S.)], the NLRB has tried to resolve conflicts by establishing the unit that would implement orderly and stable collective bargaining. For example, in the basic steel industry the NLRB has barred narrow craft units because of the integrated nature of the production process.

Negotiating the Agreement. Once the NLRB has certified a union, the law requires the employer to bargain with it since it is the exclusive representative of *all* the employees in the unit. The process of negotiating involves strategy, proposals and counterproposals, occasional threats, sometimes a strike, compromise, and agreement. The typical contract is reduced to writing and is effective for 1, 2, or occasionally 3 years. As a rule, the contract must be ratified by a vote of the membership. Agreement is facilitated when experienced negotiators have adequate authority to make a settlement, when both sides avoid seriously miscalculating each other's strength, genuinely want to reach agreement, and are willing to settle on terms that do not threaten the basic security of the other party. The possibility of a strike works to induce agreement in the large majority of cases, as most of the thousands of agreements negotiated annually are made without a strike. Moreover, strike activity has declined in recent years as collective bargaining relationships have matured. Strikes are still significant, however; and when they occur in an essential industry, they present one of the most difficult problems in industrial relations.

Collective bargaining negotiators often employ the technique of the "big demand." Accordingly each side is in a position to make concessions as it comes to discover through the bargaining process what probably can be achieved. Items withdrawn or set aside often become important in subsequent negotiations. Moreover, the big-demand technique saves each organization, and especially the union, from having to turn down proposals that may stem from a special sector in its own camp. Instead, such proposals just die in the bargaining process. Some concerns, however, notably General Electric Company, have tried to get away from the big-demand technique. Instead, such companies painstakingly research the collective bargaining scene, especially the attitudes of their own employees, and they listen to the union's demands. They then make an offer they are convinced will be accepted and adhere to it. Where this technique has worked, as it has at General Electric, some critics charge that the bargaining process is being thwarted. Whether or not that is true in any given case, it is still a fact that the presence and degree of forcefulness of the union are important factors influencing the company's conduct, and the terms of settlement are no doubt quite different from what the company would choose to do in the union's absence.

The collective bargain differs from an individual bargain in many respects. In both cases the parties are seeking favorable terms, but in collective bargaining they must finally agree, even if the agreement is reached only after a strike, because neither is in a position to operate the enterprise without the other and both depend on it. Again, an individual bargain may be casual and transient, but the collective bargain is an incident in the continuing relationship between the parties. Therefore, both parties must negotiate with an eye to the effect of the resultant bargain on their future relationship. Finally, the collective bargaining agreement is not like a contract to deliver a certain number of tons of pig iron at a certain price by a certain date. Rather, it is an agreement on terms and conditions of employment under which work will be performed. Performance of the work is a voluntary act fundamentally within the control of the worker, not the union or employer. On the other hand, the employer, within economic limits, usually sets the number of employment opportunities. Not only do these conditions suggest that for good results both sides must regard the agreement as basically fair and workable, but they suggest also that what occurs in the day-to-day plant relationship is as important a part of collective bargaining as the negotiations themselves.

Administration of the Agreement. The agreement is the law of industrial relations in the bargaining unit that it applies to. It is not self-administering. Normally it incorporates a grievance procedure, through which questions of contract interpretation or alleged violation may be reviewed and resolved. Grievances may spring from such circumstances as a charge that the management violated the agreement in disciplining an employee; or two sections of the agreement may appear to be in conflict; or the agreement may be unclear or incomplete. The grievance procedure typically has several levels, so that successively higher authorities on each side may jointly review and try to settle the issue. A grievance that goes through all of these steps and remains unresolved usually then goes before an arbitration tribunal for disposition, a process described later.

The grievance procedure has many advantages. It substitutes industrial jurisprudence for work stoppages and permits the evolution of a substantial body of common law. It shows up problems the parties need to consider in subsequent negotiations. It uncovers trouble spots. It facilitates vertical communications. It may, however, serve as an instrument of warfare when dissatisfied employees flood it with real or fancied grievances.

Collective Bargaining Patterns. Collective bargaining relationships vary from outright conflict at one extreme to positive cooperation at the other. A relationship often starts out as belligerent and evolves gradually through passive acceptance to accommodation as the bargaining process matures. A few go on to full cooperation.

A landmark study by S. H. Slichter, J. J. Healy, and E. R. Livernash of Harvard University, *The Impact of Collective Bargaining on Management* (1960), has shown that collective bargaining since 1940 has narrowed management's discretion, stimulated the development of management by policy, and led firms to develop staff organization to administer rules and to coordinate the efforts of staff specialists and operating officials. The study found also that collective bargaining has shown great diversity depending on the policies of particular unions and managements, and the technological and economic environment; but despite such diversity, there has been a growth in accommodation in day-to-day relations. The study noted that the growing tendency for management to propose contract changes and the increasing use of facts to resolve issues and uncover what each party really wants are the two most outstanding changes in collective bargaining negotiations over the period studied. The conclusion drawn from the investigation was that collective bargaining is one of the nation's most successful economic institutions.

Bargaining Power. Collective bargaining is both a power relationship and a problem-solving process. Many attempts have been made to define and measure bargaining power, but the results have not been definitive. Sources of bargaining power may be identified, however. One is the relative skill of the negotiators not only at the bargaining table but also in getting their respective constituencies to adopt the stance most favorable to success. This is especially important for union representatives, who must maintain membership militancy for bargaining purposes while keeping a climate in which the membership will accept a reasonable settlement that may fall short on some counts. All elements considered, however, probably minimum advantage accrues to either side from superior negotiating skill, as the representatives on both sides usually are quite skillful or they would not last.

Certain objective forces are more important in determining bargaining power. For example, a union's bargaining power in any given set of negotiations depends on the extent to which competing firms are organized; the extent and character of competition in the product market; the elasticity of demand for the product and whether it is increasing or decreasing; whether general business conditions are favorable or unfavorable; whether machinery can be easily substituted for labor; and the proportion of total costs constituted by labor costs. When the above factors were most favorable, it is estimated that some strong unions have been able to raise the wages of their members by perhaps 10 to 15 per cent above what the wages might otherwise have been.

Some critics maintain that union bargaining power raises wages and decreases employment in organized sectors and that this causes unemployment and depressed wages in other sectors. They also say collective bargaining produces inflation by increasing wages faster than productivity. They would apply the antitrust laws to break up unions and weaken them. These contentions are rebutted by supporters of collective bargaining, who insist that union pressures for higher wages can force management to become more efficient. They say that any tendencies for union power to produce uneconomic settlements can best be met by strengthening employer bargaining arrangements, such as that of bargaining on an association basis, and by a more vigorous enforcement of the antitrust laws to promote improved competition in product markets. To date, the effect of collective bargaining on the price level has been quite moderate, but the discovery of ways to reduce the tendency for collective bargaining to produce higher prices, while preserving free collective bargaining, is one of the great challenges of this era.

Collective bargaining is more than a mere power relationship, however. Where the relationship has become reasonably mature and stable, it can silhouette problems, such as a chaotic wage structure or inadequate job security, and it can also provide a vehicle for rationally attacking them. For example, labor and management in the basic steel industry in 1946, after years of discussion, study, and bargaining, agreed on a simplified, stable industrial wage structure embodying job-evaluation principles. Again, unions and managements in some industries in recent years have established joint study committees to work on complex issues during the contract term so that they may not be an obstacle to agreement in the "crisis" atmosphere that often surrounds negotiations for a new contract. Thus mature bargaining can eliminate irrational conflict and generate mutually beneficial solutions. There is, however, no panacea. Even with the best of goodwill and understanding, occasions occur when intractable issues cause negotiations to break down. This is one of the unavoidable costs of free collective bargaining.

Content of the Agreement. As they have evolved, collectively bargained agreements have come to include provisions covering such areas as the following: (1) the contract's scope, purpose, and duration, no-strike clause, and grievance procedure; (2) union and management rights, including union recognition, security, provision for deduction of union dues, and management-rights clauses; (3) allocation and maintenance of job opportunities, including provisions on hiring, transfer, promotion, layoff, and reemployment and the effect of seniority on these; (4) the scheduling of work, working conditions, health and safety, and, on occasion, work speeds and production methods; (5) compensation, including the wage structure and its administration, the method of payment, and "fringe benefits," such as paid holidays, paid vacations, severance pay, insurance, health, welfare, pension, and supplementary unemployment benefit plans.

These so-called fringe benefits have grown so rapidly that the designation is no longer appropriate. Surveys by the U.S. Chamber of Commerce show that the cost of such wage supplements in 91 companies rose from 14.6 per cent of the payroll in 1947 to 26.4 per cent in 1961. These findings refer to large concerns, so that the figures reported are probably high for the country as a whole, but they show that wage supplements have continued to grow substantially.

The increase in negotiated health, welfare, and pension programs has been especially marked. Health and insurance plans covered but 4 per cent of organized workers in 1945; by 1960 they covered 78 per cent, or 14 million employees. Pension plan coverage rose from 11 per cent of organized employees in 1947 to 60 per cent in 1960. The available evidence indicates that these benefits have spread further and faster than they would have in the absence of collective bargaining.

Widening Scope of Bargaining. The scope of bargaining has been a continuing issue in recent years.

At the President's Labor-Management Conference in 1945, union representatives readily agreed that "the functions and responsibility of management must be preserved if business and industry is to be efficient, progressive and provide more good jobs." They would not agree, however, "to build a fence around the rights and responsibilities of management on the one hand and the unions on the other." They maintained that experience showed that "with the growth of mutual understanding the responsibilities of one of the parties today may well become the joint responsibility of both parties tomorrow." Management representatives, on the other hand, wanted to classify certain functions, such as production and finance, as exclusively management prerogatives. Some personnel functions they were willing to leave open to review by agreed-upon grievance procedures. Agreement in this area proved to be impossible.

In the ensuing years union pressures, buttressed by favorable NLRB and court decisions, considerably expanded the area of bargaining. Retirement and pension plans (1947), health and insurance plans (1949), stock bonuses (1951), stock purchase plans (1956), plant relocation (1957), closing a plant (1961), and contracting out work (1962) were held by the NLRB to be matters on which the employer must bargain under the Taft-Hartley Act. The Supreme Court in 1960 held that a railroad must not abolish jobs without bargaining on the matter. And it held in 1964 that, when one firm absorbs another, the successor employer may be required to arbitrate with a union under a contract between that union and the firm absorbed. One circuit court ruled that seniority rights "vest" in the employees covered by a union contract so that even after expiration of that contract these rights must be honored by the employer at a new plant opened in a different geographical area to replace the old one where the contract had been in force.

Decisions such as these—even though they may shift somewhat with changes in NLRB membership and occasional second thoughts by the courts—foreshadow a constant shrinkage in the matters management may decide independently. They imply that further expansion of collective bargaining can mean that unions will impose outside, negative-type controls on business decisions without any increase in union responsibility for the enterprise; for ultimate decision and responsibility still rest with management. Since the process of production has to be essentially cooperative because neither labor nor management can accomplish much without the other, as Pope Leo XIII stressed long ago, and since responsibility for service to the community rests as much with the employees as with management, the challenge to dynamic collective bargaining is to create a system that will go beyond the increasing of negative restrictions on management and give the organized work force an opportunity to assume some responsibility for the enterprise and its relation to the economy. This has been accomplished through informal consultation in many firms and through formal union-management cooperation in a limited number of others. The success of these efforts shows that such arrangements do not disrupt the unified authority required for success in the management function. The further development of such arrangements is the frontier of modern collective bargaining.

Labor Contract. As seen earlier, the labor contract is an agreement about terms under which work will be performed.

A complicated legal structure has grown up around the labor contract in the U.S. For example, violation of a labor agreement by a union or an employer is subject to a suit for damages. The employer, the union, or individual employees may sue under section 301 of the Taft-Hartley Act for enforcement of the labor contract. Many states also have labor boards with powers calculated to enforce the collective bargaining agreement. *See* LABOR LAW (U.S.).

The vast majority of labor contracts in the U.S. is self-enforcing, however, because private, voluntary arbitration is the final step of the grievance procedure in more than 90 per cent of all labor agreements.

Although such arrangements were adopted early in the 20th century in the clothing industry and spread to some other contracts before 1940, they became widespread during World War II when the War Labor Board adopted the policy of requiring provision for grievance arbitration in those contracts submitted to it. This policy was endorsed by the 1945 President's Labor-Management Conference. Arbitration has the great value of promoting development of an industrial jurisprudence as an alternative to work stoppages as a method of resolving disputes that arise during the term of a collective bargaining agreement.

Grievance arbitration differs essentially from contract arbitration. The former is intended to resolve issues concerning rights under an existing contract; the latter deals with matters of interest, that is, with the question of what provisions shall go into a contract. Contract arbitration, either voluntary (by agreement of the parties) or compulsory (dictated by the government or some outside authority), is little favored or used in the U.S. Voluntary contract arbitration, however, has been used in a few industries, such as local transit. The most notable example of compulsory contract arbitration occurred in 1963, when it was ordered by an unprecedented Act of Congress on two issues in the railroad industry work-rules dispute.

Grievance arbitration is wholly a creation of the parties. They jointly determine the nature of the tribunal, the statement of the issue, and the selection of the arbitrator. The commonest arrangements are either for a single neutral person to be chosen jointly to hear and decide the dispute or for a board made up of equal representation from each side plus a jointly chosen neutral to serve as the tribunal. The arrangement usually is ad hoc, with the neutral arbitrator being chosen as each case arises; an agreement, however, may name an arbitrator to serve for its term. The parties may recruit their own neutrals, or they may obtain them from panels of qualified arbitrators maintained by agencies such as the American Arbitration Association or the Federal Mediation and Conciliation Service. Most commonly the parties share equally the arbitration fees and expenses. The arbitration profession has its own association, the National Academy of Arbitrators, founded in 1947.

In the usual arbitration case the parties give to the arbitration tribunal a statement of the issue in dispute, and the tribunal receives evidence in an informal hearing. Its subsequent decision is accompanied by an explanatory opinion.

The agreement to arbitrate and the resulting award are both enforceable in the courts. Indeed, Supreme Court rulings since 1960 have consigned virtually all issues raised under collective bargaining agreements to determination by arbitrators rather than by the courts. The NLRB as well has adopted the policy generally of deferring to the arbitrator's award in matters where the jurisdiction of the arbitrator under the labor contract and of the Board under Federal law overlaps.

Union Security. More than 80 per cent of all collective bargaining agreements make some provision for union security. The strongest form is the closed shop, which provides that only union members may be hired. The most common is the union shop, which requires a worker, as a condition of his continued employment, to become a union member within a certain period after being hired, usually 30 days. Less common are maintenance-of-membership clauses that make union membership voluntary but require the worker who joins a union to remain a member for the duration of the contract. Still somewhat rare is the agency shop, in which the worker who refuses to join the union must pay it a fee, usually equivalent to union dues, as a contribution toward the cost of collective bargaining representation.

The closed shop has been traditional in the skilled trades and in such casual occupations as longshoring, but it was outlawed by the Taft-Hartley Act in 1947. The arrangement tended to persist, however, in such industries as building construction, printing, maritime, and entertainment because of special hiring conditions, such as skill requirements or the indefinite tenure of employment. Partially in recognition of such factors, the Landrum-Griffin Act in effect relegalized the closed shop in the construction industry.

The union shop is legal under the Taft-Hartley Act and the Railway Labor Act, which covers the railroad and air transport industries. But both laws provide that a worker may be discharged for nonmembership in a union only if the latter is due to the worker's failure to tender regular dues and initiation fees. The Taft-Hartley Act provides also for deauthorization, under certain circumstances, of union shops through elections conducted by the NLRB. It specifies also that where any state has adopted a law forbidding the union shop, the state law is to prevail. Such laws have been adopted by 19 states, containing about 15 per cent of the nation's industrial employment. Indiana, a highly industrialized state, repealed its law in 1965.

In effect, these state laws enforce the open shop; that is, they specify that employment is to depend in no way on union membership. Their proponents call the laws right-to-work laws, though the statutes guarantee work to no one. Unions label them right-to-wreck laws. Available research indicates the laws thus far have had little practical effect.

Ethical and practical aspects of the union shop and legislation related to it have been much debated. Its opponents often overlook the fact that the legal union shop today is only a dues-maintenance shop. It does not require union membership in any real sense. It requires, rather, a *quid-pro-quo* to support the bargaining service that, under the law, a union must provide for all members in the bargaining unit. Moreover, in its present form the union shop is hardly any greater invasion of individual freedom than the legal requirement that lawyers be members of an integrated bar. On the other hand, unions must have considerable power before they can successfully negotiate the union shop; so it seems unlikely that they would perish without it. Again, there can be an issue of political freedom under the union shop where dues are spent for ideological or political purposes against a member's wishes. But the remedy for that would appear to be even stricter segregation by law of funds intended for political purposes, rather than to ban the union shop.

In practical terms, the position one takes on the union shop depends on whether one believes strong, stable unions are desirable, because the union shop makes a union less vulnerable to attack by a rival union or the employer. As Slichter pointed out, the union shop contributes to stable industrial relations, for a secure union can be more reasonable, especially about such matters as promotion and layoff, where it must discriminate among workers in the bargaining unit. The Catholic Church in its papal encyclicals and pronouncements has consistently defended the right of workers to form unions. Many see in this position an implied approval of the union shop where it is not abused. In any event, it is inconsistent to demand that unions be "responsible" and, at the same time, by denying them the union shop, to deprive them of the security that would permit responsible group action.

Predatory Unionism. Predatory practices such as racketeering and general financial dishonesty have been the exception in American unions. Such practices as extortion, the sale of "labor peace," and robbery of union or welfare funds have occurred, however, where over-intense competition for customers or jobs has provided a hospitable economic climate, as in local building construction, trucking, and on the docks of New York and New Jersey. "Cooperative" laxity in law enforcement, collusion with corrupt politicians, employers' willingness to "pay off," however reluctant, and the apathy of members have also been contributing factors to dishonesty within the unions.

Racketeering is not an inevitable result of trade unionism. Unions and their members are its victims, not its beneficiaries. The problem is one of law enforcement; of achieving better ethical standards in business, labor and politics; and of remedying underlying economic conditions that foster corruption.

Racketeering and predatory union practices have always been illegal, but in 1959 Congress passed the Landrum-Griffin Act, which, by establishing reporting requirements and providing heavy penalties for extortion and financial malfeasance, brought the power of the Federal government to bear against corruption in labor unions and labor relations. The nation's leading labor federation, the AFL-CIO, pledged in its 1955 constitution "to protect the labor movement from any and all corrupt influences." It has adopted six codes of ethical practice and has expelled several unions, including the Teamsters, for corruption. The expulsion of the Teamsters, however, failed to bring the desired change in top leadership and showed that the labor movement's powers for self-reform are limited. Nevertheless, the AFL-CIO codes of ethical practice set an auspicious tone and reflected the basic integrity of American trade unionism as a whole.

Union Democracy. By many tests American trade unions are democratic organizations. Their constitutions are democratic. Their policies, although usually determined by the leadership, are designed to promote the interests of the rank and file. They generally respect the equal right of admission to membership, although some have been slow to drop the "color bar" and then only under heavy outside pressure. Competition for local union office has been considerable.

The key issue in trade union government, however, is its disciplinary policies and practices. Unions need strong, stable leadership to bargain successfully, meet employer opposition, avoid chaotic and disruptive factionalism, and resist occasional rival union attacks. Consequently, with the exception of the long-standing two-party system in the Typographical Union, unions have had one-party political systems, with national officers holding long tenure. Since there is no independent judiciary incorporated into the union, opportunity for legitimate opposition and protection of dissenting members from arbitrary treatment must be provided.

This need was recognized by the AFL-CIO ethical practices codes previously mentioned. They provided minimum standards for the conducting of union elections and for disciplinary procedures. Unfortunately, only three national unions, the Upholsterers, the Packinghouse Workers, and the Automobile Workers have provided for independent review of internal disciplinary actions. The United Automobile Workers Public Review Board, established in 1957, consists of leading professional people from outside the union. The board is available to review decisions of the union's international executive board, and when it finds that a worker's membership rights have been violated, it can wipe out any penalties he faces. Through 1963 the board had overruled the union's decision in about one-fourth of the cases reviewed.

Union members have long been able to sue at common law to protect their rights. More important now, however, are the protective provisions of the Landrum-Griffin Act. That Act aims also at promoting broader membership participation and influence in union government. *See* LABOR LAW (U.S.). A real problem is how to effect these gains in union democracy while avoiding the more frequent strikes and uneconomic collective bargaining settlements that might be precipitated by politically motivated, ill-informed dissident groups within the union. This requires a more sophisticated and active participation in union affairs than the members have taken in the past; it also points up the value of attractive, sound educational programs for the rank and file.

Growth of New Forms of Property Rights. In recent years collective bargaining has significantly enlarged the rights attached to seniority and employment.

For some time seniority, or length of service, has been the principal factor in determining employment rights on the occasion of a reduction in the work force. It has also become a critical determinant of rights under pension, severance-pay, extended-vacation, and supplementary-unemployment-benefit arrangements. Moreover, the Sugar Workers and other unions have negotiated guaranteed work opportunities for employees who meet certain length-of-service requirements. The Railroad Telegraphers have bargained for limitations on the rate at which the railroads might eliminate telegrapher positions. The West Coast Longshoremen and the Pacific Maritime Association agreed in 1961 on payments by employers of $5 million annually for 5 years into a fund to compensate workers for displacement by labor-saving devices.

Arbitrators, the NLRB, and the courts have broadened the meaning of employment rights. A number of arbitration awards have held that firms may not contract out work as long as any of their own employees are in layoff status or where transferring the work to the outside firms would result in a layoff of some of their own employees. And these awards were made in the interpretation of labor agreements that lacked specific provisions barring or limiting the employer's right to contract out work. The NLRB had ruled that employers must bargain about contracting out work, and the Supreme Court had held that a railroad must bargain about the proposed abolition of telegrapher positions.

In the railroad and airline industries public opinion and government intervention have led to settlements that enhance employment rights by cushioning the impact of technological change on workers. The settlement of the railroad work-rules dispute that lasted from 1959 to 1964 illustrates this trend. Two crucial issues were finally settled by compulsory arbitration under a special Act of Congress. Other issues were settled through the mediation of an emergency board appointed by the president of the U.S. That board in its mediation efforts was guided by the recommendations of an earlier tripartite railroad commission that had been appointed by the President. In its report the commission had recommended a substantial, but gradual, reduction in the number of workers; it, however, had recommended generous severance payments and retraining allowances for shorter-service employees, and guaranteed employment for employees with longer service. In the airline industry the reduction in the size of crews in the cockpit from four to three on jet-driven airplanes was worked out on the basis of recommendations of emergency boards appointed by the President. These boards recommended that displaced pilots and flight engineers be protected against loss of pay for 4 years and that the airlines give the engineers flight training to help them qualify as pilots.

Although it is impossible to predict trends it is clear that, as the result of collective bargaining, public recommendations in key disputes, and certain arbitration awards, employment and seniority are being given greater meaning, have increased value, and must be considered as a form of nontransferrable property.

See also LABOR ARBITRATION AND MEDIATION; CODETERMINATION; INDUSTRY, HUMAN RELATIONS IN; LABOR MOVEMENT (CANADA); LABOR MOVEMENT (EUROPE); LABOR MOVEMENT (LATIN AMERICA); LABOR MOVEMENT (U.S.); LABOR LAW (U.S.); PROFIT SHARING; RIGHT-TO-WORK LEGISLATION; STRIKE; CHRISTIAN TRADE UNIONS; UNION-MANAGEMENT COOPERATION; WAGES; WORKER EDUCATION IN THE U.S.

Bibliography: E. W. BAKKE, *Mutual Survival: The Goal of Unions and Management* (New York 1947). E. W. BAKKE et al., *Unions, Management and the Public* (2d ed. New York 1960). J. BARBASH, *Labor's Grass Roots: A Study of the Local Union* (New York 1961). J. A. BIERNE, *New Horizons for American Labor* (Washington 1962). G. A. BRIEFS, "Compulsory Unionism," *Review of Social Economy* 18 (1960) 60–77. L. C. BROWN, "Right to Work Laws and the Freedom of the Union," *ibid.* 51–59; "The Shifting Distribution of the Rights to Manage," Industrial Relations Research Association, *Proceedings 1948* (Madison 1949) 132–144. J. HERLING, "Record of Collective Bargaining in the Last 25 Years," *ibid. 1962* (1963) 186–201. W. L. HORVITZ, "The ILWU-PMA Mechanization and Modernization Agreement: An Experiment in Industrial Relations," *ibid. 1963* (1964) 22–33. R. A. SMITH, "Government Intervention in the Substantive Areas of Collective Bargaining," *ibid. 1962,* 237–241. *Health Insurance and Pension Plan Coverage in Union Contracts, Late*

1960 (Bureau of Labor Statistics, Report 228; Washington 1962). N. W. CHAMBERLAIN, *Collective Bargaining* (New York 1951); *The Union Challenge to Management Control* (New York 1948). M. K. CHANDLER, *Management Rights and Union Interests* (New York 1964). J. R. COMMONS, *Legal Foundations of Capitalism* (Madison 1957). J. T. DUNLOP and J. J. HEALY, *Collective Bargaining* (rev. ed. Homewood, Ill. 1953); *Industrial Relations Systems* (New York 1958); *Wage Determination under Trade Unions* (New York 1950). W. GALENSON, *Trade Union Democracy in Western Europe* (Berkeley 1962); ed., *Labor and Economic Development* (New York 1959); ed., *Comparative Labor Movements* (Englewood Cliffs, N.J. 1952). General Motors Corp., *Sixteen Years of Progress through Collective Bargaining* (Detroit 1964). C. S. GOLDEN and V. D. PARKER, eds., *Causes of Industrial Peace under Collective Bargaining* (New York 1955). W. GOMBERG, "On Work Rules and Work Practices Problems," *Labor Law Journal* 12 (1961) 643–654. P. G. MARSHALL, "Enforcing the Labor Contract," *ibid.* 14 (1963) 353–358. C. O. GREGORY, *Labor and the Law* (2d ed. New York 1961), with suppl. F. H. HARBISON and J. R. COLEMAN, *Goals and Strategy in Collective Bargaining* (New York 1951). P. P. HARBRECHT, *Pension Funds and Economic Power* (New York 1959). J. B. S. HARDMAN, ed., *American Labor Dynamics* (New York 1928). Institute of Social Order, St. Louis U., *Social Orientations* (Chicago 1954). Labor Study Group, *The Public Interest in National Labor Policy* (New York 1961). T. KENNEDY, *Automation Funds and the Displaced Worker* (Cambridge, Mass. 1962). C. KERR, *Unions and Union Leaders of Their Own Choosing* (New York 1958). C. KERR et al., *Industrialism and Industrial Man* (Cambridge, Mass. 1960). A. KORNHAUSER et al., eds., *Industrial Conflict* (New York 1954). W. M. LEISERSON, *American Trade Union Democracy* (New York 1959). F. G. LESIEUR, ed., *The Scanlon Plan* (New York 1958). R. A. LESTER, *As Unions Mature* (Princeton 1958). C. E. LINDBLOM, *Unions and Capitalism* (New Haven 1949). B. L. MASSE, *Justice for All* (Milwaukee 1964). F. MEYERS, *"Right to Work" in Practice: A Report to the Fund for the Republic* (New York 1959). H. R. NORTHRUP and G. F. BLOOM, *Government and Labor . . .* (Homewood, Ill. 1963). H. L. NUNN, *Partners in Production* (Englewood Cliffs, N.J. 1961). S. R. PERLMAN, *A Theory of the Labor Movement* (New York 1959). P. J. W. PIGORS and C. A. MYERS, *Personnel Administration* (New York 1961). T. V. PURCELL, *The Worker Speaks His Mind on Company and Union* (Cambridge, Mass. 1953). *Report of the Presidential Railroad Commission* (Washington 1962). A. REES, *The Economics of Trade Unions* (Chicago 1962). L. G. REYNOLDS, *Labor Economics and Labor Relations* (4th ed. Englewood Cliffs, N.J. 1964). B. M. SELEKMAN et al., *Problems in Labor Relations* (2d ed. New York 1958). J. SHISTER et al., *Public Policy and Collective Bargaining* (New York 1962). G. P. SHULTZ and J. R. COLEMAN, eds., *Labor Problems: Cases and Readings* (2d ed. New York 1959). S. H. SLICHTER, *The Challenge of Industrial Relations . . .* (Ithaca, N.Y. 1947). S. H. SLICHTER et al., *The Impact of Collective Bargaining on Management* (Washington 1960). G. G. SOMERS, et al., eds., *Adjusting to Technological Change* (New York 1963). J. W. STIEBER, *The Steel Industry Wage Structure* (Cambridge, Mass. 1959). M. STONE, *Labor-Management Contracts at Work* (New York 1961). P. SULTAN, *Right to Work Laws* (Los Angeles 1958). P. TAFT, *The Structure and Government of Labor Unions* (Cambridge, Mass. 1954); *The A. F. of L. in the Time of Gompers* (New York 1957). G. W. TAYLOR, *Government Regulation of Industrial Relations* (Englewood Cliffs, N.J. 1948). Amer. Assembly, *Wages, Prices, Profits and Productivity . . .* (New York 1960). *The President's National Labor-Management Conference November 5–30, 1945* (Dept. of Labor, Division of Labor Standards Bulletin 77; Washington 1946). L. ULMAN, *The Rise of the National Trade Union* (Cambridge, Mass. 1955). *A Guide to Labor Management Relations in the United States* (Bureau of Labor Statistics Bulletin 1225; Washington 1958). Chamber of Commerce of the U.S. of A., *Fringe Benefits: 1961* (Washington 1962). K. O. WARNER, ed., *Management Relations with Organized Public Employees* (Chicago 1963). S. and B. WEBB, *Industrial Democracy*, 2 v. (London 1897). A. R. WEBER, ed., *The Structure of Collective Bargaining* (Glencoe, Ill. 1961). W. F. WHYTE, *Pattern for Industrial Peace* (New York 1951). "Worker Security in a Changing Economy" *Monthly Labor Review* 86 (1963) 611–764, a special issue in honor of the 50th Anniversary of the U.S. Dept. of Labor. W. S. WOYTINSKY et al., *Employment and Wages in the United States* (New York 1953). D. M. WRIGHT, ed., *The Impact of the Union* (New York 1951).

[D. J. WHITE]

COLLECTIVE RESPONSIBILITY

In the ancient Semitic world, collective responsibility was often practiced in its cruder forms; and, as part of a common heritage, it became a significant basis for society and law in the world of the OT. With the insight gained from revelation and experience, the concept of collective responsibility was refined; and this was effected especially by due recognition of individual responsibility. In the NT it is explicitly revealed that the principle of the solidarity of the human race, an instance of collective responsibility, stands at the center of the economy of salvation.

This article will treat in order: the common Semitic attitude of collective responsibility; instances of collective responsibility in the OT, the growth of the concept of individual responsibility in the OT, and, finally, the solidarity of the human race in salvation history.

Common Semitic Attitude. In the ancient Near East, a man was looked upon more as a member of his social group than as an individual person. This was due especially to the fact that in nomadic communities the tribe's fight for subsistence bound its members so closely together that each member was filled with the same community spirit. The ideas, engendered by such community spirit, when applied to criminal law, held a man responsible for the deeds of another of his group, particularly of his family. Perhaps the best example of this was the law of blood vengeance. In the Code of Hammurabi there are noteworthy examples: "If a man struck another man's daughter and caused her to have a miscarriage . . . if she died, they shall put his daughter to death" (209–210); "If a builder built a house for a man but did not make his work strong and as a result the house collapsed . . . if this cause the death of the son of the owner of the house, they shall put to death the son of the builder" (229–230); "If a man held another man's son as pledge for a debt and the son dies from beating or abuse, they shall put to death the son of the distrainer" (115–116).

Primitive notions about collective responsibility were slow in changing. Even in postexilic times the popular idea that the presence of a great sinner on a ship endangered all the travelers was commonly accepted (Jon 1.7); and among the Medes and Persians it was customary for the children to be punished for the sins of their parents (Dn 6.25; Est 9.10, 14). That such primitive notions were still current in Christ's time is seen in the narrative about the man born blind (Jn 9.2).

Collective Responsibility in OT. In the OT there are many examples where God punishes or rewards a group for the acts of one individual. The sin of Adam is most noteworthy. Although the OT does not explicitly teach the doctrine of *original sin, it does teach a certain solidarity with Adam; all men share in punishment for Adam's sin. Implicit in the punishment of Cain is the punishment of his offspring (Gn 4.13–14). The curse brought forth by the shameless behavior of Ham falls on his son Canaan (Gn 9.18–27). Because of the unwilling fault of Pharao, his whole house is struck (Gn 12.15–20). Their wives and children share in the punishment of Dathan and Abiram (Nm 16.27). The family of Achan, though they did not share in his sinful violation of the ban, shared his punishment (Jos 22.20). In the Book of Judges it is in accordance with the idea of collective responsibility that the stereotyped formula of sin, punishment, repentance, and liberation sums up current history. In Exodus 20.5 the punishment of children for their parents' violation of the First Commandment is threatened: "I the Lord, your God, am a jealous God, inflicting punishment for their fathers' wickedness on the children of those who hate me down to the third and fourth generation; but bestowing mercy on the children of those who love me and keep my commandments" (Ex 20.5–6; see also 34.7; Nm 14.18; Dt 5.9).

As stated in the passage just quoted from Ex 20.6, God blesses the descendants of a virtuous individual for many generations. There are many instances of this: Noe's family shares his salvation in the ark (Gn 7.1); Lot's family accompanies him out of Sodom (Gn 19.12); and, the descendants of Caleb share in his blessings in the land (Dt 1.36). If 10 just men could have been found in Sodom and Gomorra, God would have spared the city (Gn 18.22–32).

The covenant relationship to God, whereby the Israelites stood as one body before God, i.e., as a church (*qāhāl*), made the people all the more conscious of collective responsibility. Until the time of the Exile, the Israelite considered his reward or punishment from God not so much a response from God to his individual actions, but as common participation in the response given by God to the whole people.

Individual Responsibility. Yet, the correct understanding of collective responsibility does not exclude a strong feeling of individual responsibility; indeed, some of the oldest stories in the OT show clearly that God punished or rewarded the individual as an individual for his deeds. There are many punitive laws in the Pentateuch based on the principle of individual responsibility. In Dt 24.16 (dealing with human, not with divine justice as in Ex 20.5), there is a protest against the punishment of the children for their parents' sins: "Every one shall die for his own sin."

But it was the preaching of the Prophets that emphasized individual responsibility, thus correcting the cruder notions of collective responsibility common to their world. During the Exile the inherited view whereby children suffer full punishment for the sins of their parents began to be questioned. The older theology had been synthesized into a proverb: "Fathers have eaten green grapes, thus their children's teeth are on edge" (Ez 18.2). Ezechiel, in response, answers that any sinner can be saved, if he does penance, and that if "Noe, Daniel, and Job were in it [the land], as I live, says the Lord God, I swear that they could save neither son nor daughter; they would save only themselves by their virtue" (14.20). Thus Ezechiel becomes the champion and, so to say, the theorist of individual responsibility. A similar reaction against the more primitive notions of collective responsibility is found in Jer 31.30 (though perhaps not written by him, but a later addition based on Ez 18.2): "Through his own fault only shall anyone die: the teeth of him who eats the unripe grapes shall be set on edge" (see also Prv 24.12; Sir 16.14).

Solidarity in Economy of Salvation. Considering the Exile experience in the light of collective responsibility, it is not surprising that the concept of vicarious suffering of the future Messiah, based on the principle of solidarity, should be explicitly expounded in the *Servant of the Lord oracles (Is 52.13–53.12). Yet for Pauline theology in the NT, although the role of Christ as the Servant of the Lord was recognized (Phil 2.7), the central OT text used for explaining the reality of human solidarity in Christ's redemption was the fall of Adam (see Rom 5.12–19; 1 Cor 15.22). For the Christian religion, the whole of theology ultimately is summed up in the intervention of two persons: the one (Adam) in whom all men fell, and the other (Jesus Christ) in whom alone man can be saved. The NT, insisting on a solidarity with the risen Christ through personal faith, satisfies both the demand of individual retribution and the law of human solidarity in sin and salvation (see Rom 5.19; 1 Cor 15.21–22; Eph 4.25; 1 Cor 12.26; etc.).

See also RETRIBUTION.

Bibliography: L. V. A. BOURGEOIS, . . . *Solidarité* (3d ed. Paris 1902). J. LAROCHE, *La Rétribution sous l'ancienne alliance* (Cahors 1904). H. BÜCKERS, "Kollektiv und individualvergeltung im Alten Testament," ThGlaube 25 (1933) 273–286. H. W. ROBINSON, "The Hebrew Conception of Corporate Personality," Beih ATWiss 66 (1936) 49–62. EncDictBibl 2032–36.

[M. RODRÍGUEZ]

COLLECTIVISM

Generally defined by reference to individualism, collectivism is taken to be its opposite. Its basic assumption is that the activity of some secular grouping is superior in value to any individual or personal action. In its milder forms, it is simply a special emphasis on the importance of group action as such. In its virulent, totalitarian forms it attributes absolute value to the activity of the specific secular grouping in terms of which everything is ultimately to be judged. In these latter cases, the human person is reduced to the status of a mere part of the group; the transcendental good, true, and beautiful become immanent attributes of the collectivity that is in process of realizing itself.

Aristotle had discerned the dilemma underlying the conflict between individualism and collectivism long before the emergence of the terms (*Pol.* 1260b 27–1264b 25). The depth of the tension inherent in the traditional formulations of the problem can be seen clearly by a comparison of two sentences of St. Thomas Aquinas: "Since the individual man is a part of the community, each one, in all that he is and has, belongs to the community" (ST 1a2ae, 96.4). "A man is not ordained to the political community by virtue of all that he is and has; hence it is not fitting that all of his actions be considered worthy of praise or blame with respect to the political community; but all that a man is, and can, and has must be ordained to God" (ST 1a2ae, 21.4 ad 3). (*See* COMMON GOOD; COMMUNITY; SOCIETY; SUBSIDIARITY.)

Historically, military threats to a society have tended to emphasize the status of a man as part of the social whole. Whenever that emphasis has come to dominate the vision of society, a militaristic form of collectivism has been realized. However, the chief impetus to the elaboration of collectivist thought and action, and to the rise of totalitarianism, has been the reaction against the atomization of society by modern individualism. It was in opposition to the extreme economic *individualism of the laissez-faire economists of the 18th and 19th centuries that several varieties of *socialism arose. They emphasized the social or collective aspects of production, distribution, and exchange, as well as the political context within which economic activity takes place. In Marxian communism (*see* COMMUNISM, INTERNATIONAL, I), the economic and political activity of the proletariat becomes the sole standard of good, and replaces the salvific mission acknowledged by Christianity as belonging to Christ Jesus.

Against the extreme political individualism of radical, liberal, democratic ideology progessively elaborated since the 18th century, there have arisen varieties of statist or racial collectivism. Mussolini's *fascism, for example, attributed to the state absolute and salvific functions analogous to those assigned to the proletariat by Marxism. Under *National Socialism in Germany, the race of supermen being developed was to take the place of God, the Creator and Ruler of the world.

A number of attempts to restate a middle position, taking modern phenomena into account, have been elaborated under the names of *distributism and *personalism.

Bibliography: H. ARENDT, *The Origins of Totalitarianism* (New York 1951). N. A. BERDÎAEV, *Slavery and Freedom*, tr. R. M. FRENCH (New York 1944). W. Y. ELLIOTT, *The Pragmatic Revolt in Politics: Syndicalism, Fascism, and the Constitutional State* (New York 1928). F. A. VON HAYEK, ed., *Collectivist Economic Planning* (London 1935). J. MARITAIN, *The Person and the Common Good*, tr. J. J. FITZGERALD (New York 1947). J. MESSNER, *Social Ethics*, tr. J. J. DOHERTY (St. Louis 1949). J. A. SCHUMPETER, *Capitalism, Socialism and Democracy* (3d ed. New York 1950).

[E. A. GOERNER]

COLLEGE

In its broadest sense (Lat. *collegium;* O.F., *collège;* Sp. *colegio;* It. *collegio*) "an organized society of persons performing certain common functions and possessing special rights and privileges; a body of colleagues, guild fellowship, association" (*New English Dictionary,* Oxford 1888), e.g., College of Cardinals, College of Surgeons, electoral college. In a more specific sense, a college is (1) an institution of higher education, usually offering only a curriculum in the liberal arts and sciences, and empowered to confer degrees, or in junior colleges, associate titles; (2) a major division of a university (usually of arts and sciences), especially one requiring for admission no study beyond the completion of secondary education; (3) an institution of secondary education, a usage common in Europe and in Latin American countries, but rare in the U.S.; (4) the building or buildings housing a college (*Dictionary of Education,* New York 1959).

Historical Development. College, as an institution, has undergone various phases of development.

Secular and Religious Medieval Colleges. The rise of colleges was closely linked with the rise of medieval universities. *See* EDUCATION, I (HISTORY OF), 3. As students began to congregate at the new centers of learning in the 12th century, towns were unprepared to accommodate the sudden population growth, and the housing problem became acute. Since the average age of students beginning the arts course was 15 or 16, parents and clergy, fearing for their moral life in the atmosphere of growing university centers, called for some system of board and lodging where the young students would be supervised. Monasticism, in fact, had already provided an example of ordered life, which it seemed wise to imitate, with its regular hours for prayer, study, class, and sleep, and a superior or chaplain to guide students in their daily life and spiritual problems (*see* MONASTIC SCHOOLS). Thus the first colleges founded at Paris were residence halls for students who attended classes at the university. Religious orders—Franciscans, Dominicans, Benedictines, and Augustinians—later constructed the same type of college for their scholastics or seminarians. In time instructions were gradually introduced into the colleges, but the granting of a degree was still reserved to the university.

Historically, the first college was founded at the University of *Paris. Others followed rapidly with 20 French colleges founded in the 13th century, 54 in the 14th century, and 12 in the 15th. In England also, colleges answered the need for residence halls; Dominicans established a hall at Oxford in 1220, and the Franciscans in 1224 (*see* OXFORD, UNIVERSITY OF; CAMBRIDGE, UNIVERSITY OF). Other societies founded 4 English colleges in the 13th century, 12 in the 14th, and 9 in the 15th. Merton College, founded by Walter de Merton in 1250, began a trend in England for colleges to assume functions usually reserved to universities. In 1379 at Winchester, Bp. William Wykeham founded the first college outside the university complex where students received instruction in grammar and literature before going to study at New College, Oxford. Winchester inaugurated the movement to establish colleges geographically and legally independent of a university. Thus by the middle of the 14th century colleges had evolved from a university residence hall to an institution imparting instruction.

Colleges built on the Continent followed the French model that reserved traditional corporate and educational powers to the university. In Italy benefactors endowed one college in the 13th century, 10 in the 14th, and 5 in the 15th (*see* BOLOGNA, UNIVERSITY OF; PADUA, UNIVERSITY OF; PAVIA, UNIVERSITY OF; ROME, UNIVERSITY OF). Spain listed two foundations, both in the 14th century (*see* ALCALÁ, UNIVERSITY OF; SALAMANCA, UNIVERSITY OF). The Germanies had 9 colleges endowed in the 14th century and 7 in the 15th (*see* COLOGNE, UNIVERSITY OF; MUNICH, UNIVERSITY OF; TÜBINGEN, UNIVERSITY OF).

American Colleges. Although the colleges founded in colonial America along the eastern seaboard followed in large part the plan established by the English universities, Oxford and Cambridge, they differed in one main respect: they were from the beginning independently chartered, degree-granting institutions rather than residences affiliated with a university. Harvard (1636), Cambridge, Mass., was modeled on Emmanuel College, Cambridge, England, where many of the founders and supporters had been educated, and granted its first degrees in 1642. William and Mary College (1693), Williamsburg, Va., followed Queen's College, Oxford, and conferred its first degrees in 1700. Yale (1701), New Haven, Conn., followed lines somewhat similar to those of Harvard and granted its first degrees in 1702. These and subsequent colonial colleges were founded "to supply the publicke with fit Instruments principally for the work of the ministry" with the exception of the College of Philadelphia (1755), Pa., whose founders, in the spirit of Benjamin Franklin, ruled out sectarianism. With the founding of the College of New Jersey (Princeton, 1746), King's College (Columbia, 1754), the College of Rhode Island (Brown, 1764), Queen's College (Rutgers, 1766), and Dartmouth College (1769), by 1776 the American colonists had established nine degree-granting independent colleges. Paradoxically, however, in the reorganization of higher education in the period 1870 to 1890, all these early colleges ceded their educational supremacy to the emerging university. *See* HIGHER EDUCATION (U.S.).

Influence of Medieval Colleges on Modern Educational Institutions. The medieval college, like the medieval university, still influences contemporary higher education. The custom of prelates, nobility, statesmen, businessmen, alumni, and guilds or unions constructing or endowing colleges continues in our building fund campaigns, foundation grants, and private endowments. Scholarships to needy and superior students had their counterpart in early European and American colonial colleges, and faculty salaries are an extension of the special provisions made at medieval colleges to pay senior scholars or fellows for their tutoring. The academic dress of special color and material worn to identify a medieval college still brightens modern convocations (*see* ACADEMIC DRESS). Compulsory attendance at chapel, though disappearing on the American scene, originated in the Middle Ages when colleges and universities were for the most part church affiliated. The contemporary revolt against strict disciplinary regulations and *in loco parentis* supervision recalls medieval town and gown conflicts and students' perennial struggle for autonomy. Although *academic degrees were not granted by medieval colleges, the practice adopted in American colleges originated in the medieval universities with which the European colleges were affiliated. In a word, speaking of contemporary institutions of higher learning, one can say *nil novi sub sole,* but rather only variations of customs adapted to time and place.

Bibliography: H. RASHDALL, *The Universities of Europe in the Middle Ages,* ed. F. M. POWICKE and A. B. EMDEN, 3 v. (new ed. Oxford 1936). L. J. DALY, *The Medieval University, 1200–1400* (New York 1961). L. THORNDIKE, *University Records and Life in the Middle Ages* (New York 1944). A. L. GÁBRIEL, "The College System in the Fourteenth Century Universities," *The Forward Movement of the Fourteenth Century,* ed. F. L. UTLEY (Columbus, Ohio 1961); *Student Life in Ave Maria College, Mediaeval Paris* (Notre Dame, Ind. 1955). J. BRUBACHER and W. RUDY, *Higher Education in Transition: An American History, 1636–1956* (New York 1958).

[E. G. RYAN]

COLLÈGE DE FRANCE

An institution of higher learning and research in Paris, founded in 1530 by Francis I, King of France.

Early History. When the end came to Francis I on March 31, 1544, he could face death satisfied. He had bequeathed to France a college that, throughout the years and into the 20th century, despite numerous difficulties, was to promote and assure the advance of all branches of knowledge with the greatest respect for the human mind. The first stone of the royal college that became the Collège de France was laid only on Aug. 6, 1610, by *Louis XIII, then age 9.

At the end of the 15th century, Frenchmen such as Guillaume Fichet, Robert *Gaguin, and *Lefèvre d'Étaples had enthusiastically embraced the ideals of Italian *humanism. In the early 16th century the study of Greek and Hebrew began with the work of Jerome Aléandre and François Tossard. The humanistic movement attracted scholars to the College of Cambrai, where the King established chairs of Latin, Greek, and Hebrew. The French humanists soon saw a need for a new institution, wherein the masters and the program would escape the control of theologians, who from the time of Charlemagne had presided over the destinies of teaching in France. Their efforts eventually led to the foundation of the Collège de France, by *Francis I.

Francis was raised in a milieu where belles-lettres were highly esteemed. His sister Marguerite de Navarre was herself a person of deep culture and independent spirit. Francis was the ideal sovereign to realize the project elaborated by his friends and counselors, the "three Williams": Guillaume *Budé, the humanist scholar; Guillaume Petit, the King's confessor and "the lawyer of all the men of letters"; and Guillaume Cop, Francis' doctor.

A letter from Budé to *Erasmus (early 1517) mentioned the project and invited him to join the new institution. Erasmus refused on the ground that he did not wish to alienate "the goodness, and the liberality of the king" (Charles V). His refusal profoundly disappointed Francis, who nevertheless renewed the offer some years later, but without success.

Petit, who had suggested inviting Erasmus, and Étienne Poncher, Archbishop of Paris, who conducted the negotiations with the famous humanist, counseled the King to appoint the scholar Agostino Giustiniani, Bishop of Nebbio, "quinque linguarum interpres," to the chair of Hebrew and Greek. But war intervened, and only after the Treaty of Cambrai (1529) did Budé remind the King of his promise to "found a school, a nursery, as it were, of scholars."

Francis had not forgotten. He had even tried an experiment at Milan in 1520, under the care of Lascaris, to prepare professors of Greek, and his visit to the University of Alcalá during his captivity in Spain had increased his desire to establish in France a college that would eclipse all others. In March 1530 Francis signed a decree establishing royal lecturers, and he charged his secretary and *lecteur ordinaire,* J. Colin of Auxerre, to attend to its execution. That same year two chairs of Greek were established, one occupied by Pierre Danès (succeeded by J. Strazel, 1535, and J. Dorat, 1556), the other by J. Toussaint (succeeded by Turnebe, 1547, *Ramus, 1551, and Denis, 1560). Two chairs in Hebrew also were established, for A. Guidacerius and F. *Vatable. Their success was so great that a third chair was created in 1531, for P. Paradis. Latin chairs were set up somewhat later. In 1534 the famous scholar B. *Latomus commenced his course in Latin eloquence. The chairs of Oriental languages (G. Postel, 1538) and of Latin and Greek philosophy (F. de Vocomercato, 1542) followed. As early as 1530 Oronce Fine held the chair of mathematics, and in 1542 Vidius inaugurated that of medicine, which was doubled in 1768, awaiting the establishment of the chair of surgery in 1582. Between 1539 and 1544 F. Vatable had published his Hebrew Bible, and following Danés and Toussaint, P. Ramus in 1551 had gathered around his chair hundreds of French and foreign auditors who were initiated not only into the reading and translation of such writers as Vergil and Cicero but also became versed in all the problems of Greek and Latin antiquity.

It remained to give the college "built on men," a body worthy of its "soul" in order to guarantee its existence and its autonomy. Unfortunately the Collège had to wait until the end of the 18th century to be adequately lodged. Even then the building was a far cry from the palace dreamed of, but in default of museums, formal gardens, and porticos, it had established chairs in Syrian (1692), Persian and Chinese

(1714), and Turkish (1768), and had added botany and natural history to medicine (1773) and had replaced pharmacy with chemistry.

During the Revolution the Collège, which for a while was subject to the Sorbonne (1772–92), encountered new difficulties. Indeed, its ideal of liberty and independence could only flatter the new masters—*Mirabeau, *Condorcet, Daunou, *Chaptal—who successively came to its defense. Nationalized by the Convention, under the empire the Collège became part of the University of France. After a period of silence and dispersion, however, it regained its early vigor and independence. In 1814 the Collège founded a chair in the Iranian language under A. L. Chézy, J. P. Abel-Rémussat taught Chinese language and literature, and in 1831 the archeologist J. Champollion introduced Egyptology. Later the Collège de France introduced the classics and other non-Oriental languages. In 1840 the Collège welcomed the Polish exile A. Mickiewicz to whom it entrusted the chair in the language and literature of Central Europe, while assigning to Edgar Quint German literature. With these professors, however, politics entered the Collège. Their chairs, like that of the historian J. Michelet, became tribunes and their courses, which turned into speeches, provoked violent reactions. The authorities were disturbed and, despite the courageous resistance of the assembly of professors, the government in 1851 removed the three culprits. Some years later, the literary historian and critic, C. A. de Sainte-Beuve, for similar reasons had to resign his chair (1854), and in 1862 the Orientalist E. Renan was dismissed from the Collège that both had considered "the asylum of discussion and free enquiry."

Later Development. After this period of unrest the Collège embarked on a period of calm during which new methods and subjects were introduced. Henceforth experience and objectivity gained ascendancy over eloquence. History and philosophy progressed under V. Duruy and P. Meyer, and with Renan's return, Oriental studies regained their place. In 1874 J. Oppert initiated a chair in Assyriology; in 1880 the history of religions was introduced, and Claude Bernard and Claude Louis Berhelot founded chairs in modern physiology and organic chemistry.

The administrators of the Collège de France have succeeded one another with amazing continuity, an interesting fact that no doubt explains the fidelity of the Collège de France to its founders' principles and the development of its orientation. Under royalty the administrator ex officio was the chief almoner to the king of France, and history can only rejoice that occupying this post were such men as Duchatel, the Cardinal of Lorraine, Jacques Amyot, and Cardinal du Perron. After 1800, however, and for more than 50 years, Orientalists presided over the destiny of the Collège de France, e.g., Silvestre de Sacy, Letronne, Stanislas Julien, and Renan. Finally, for almost half a century the administrators have been medievalists, e.g., Gaston Paris, Joseph Bédier, Edmond Faral, who was succeeded (1965) by Marcel Bataillon, an outstanding example of Erasmian culture and wisdom.

Science and Research. One should not conclude that the Collège de France has sacrificed sciences to humanism. Faithful to its motto, *Docet omnia,* its 50 chairs in science still prove that its mission is indeed, as Renan remarked, to serve science "in the process of beginning." While Lucien Febvre lectures on modern civilization and Louis Massignon conducts research in the history and philosophy of Islam, following in A. Ampère's footsteps are such scientists and scholars as P. Langevin and I. Joliot-Curie. For the former the chair of mineral chemistry became the chair of chemistry and nuclear physics, which the latter with F. Perrin divided into atomic and molecular physics and Leprince Ringuet into nuclear physics. In medicine E. Bernard was succeeded by C. E. Brown-Séquard and A. d'Arsonval who prepared the way for researchers such as R. Leriche and (1965) B. Halpern.

Thus the College, which in 1770 with its 19 chairs had already attracted the attention of all learned Europe, in 1965 had 50 chairs divided into three sections: mathematical, physical, and natural science; philosophy and social science; and history, philology, and archeology. A large part of the institution's success derives no doubt from its independence, which, although financially only relative, is total on the educational level. The council of professors freely decides which chairs to introduce and which ones to eliminate. Thus in 1934 the scientist Frédéric Joliot replaced an Indianist. This same council submits to the ministry of education the nomination of professors who are chosen not because of their degrees (P. Valéry and M. Roques did not have doctorates) but because of their research. The enlightened advice of the academy is naturally sought, but only in rare cases has the ministry or academy failed to follow the recommendation of the council of professors.

Each professor is obliged to give 20 to 30 lectures in public courses, which are attended by very different public audiences. It is, however, in the silence of the libraries and laboratories that they pursue the research that each professor directs according to his choice.

Besides the general library each section has a special library reserved for the professors. Certain sections, which have been endowed with valuable donations, are well provided with books and periodicals. But since the teaching of the Collège de France is dedicated to the service of science "in the process of becoming," other equipment than the libraries is necessary. Besides the archeological missions where indefatigable research is pursued among the ruins of history, the Collège de France has specialized laboratories throughout France and abroad: in Pic du Midi for cosmic physics, at Saclay, for atomic and molecular physics, at Concarneau for general biochemistry, for which there are also laboratories in the Zoological Park in Naples, Italy.

In addition, in many instances the professors of the Collège de France work in collaboration with foreign foundations and institutions such as Dumbarton Oaks, in Washington, D.C., and the Cini Foundation in Venice, Italy. Mathematicians are in communication with the Rice Institute of Berkeley, Calif., and the Institute for Advanced Study at Princeton, N.J., while the social-anthropological laboratory is largely assisted by the international foundation of the Wenner Gren Foundation for Anthropological Research in New York.

It must not be forgotten that if the French state furnishes three-fourths of the Collège budget, the rest is completed by revenues from various French and foreign foundations, the most important of which are the Mrs. Bostwich-Voronof endowment and that given in memory of Mrs. Winnareta Singer, Princess of Polignac. In this way the Collège de France has continued its work for man and truth overseas and outside its own borders for more than 4 centuries. It could not better serve humanism and its motto *Docet omnia* and thus fulfill the words of Terence, *Humani nihil a me alienum puto*.

Bibliography: C. P. GOUJET, *Mémoire historique et littéraire sur le collège royal de France*, 3 v. (Paris 1758). A. J. M. LE FRANC, *Histoire du Collège de France depuis ses origines jusqu'à la fin du premier Empire* (Paris 1893). S. D'IRSAY, *Histoire des universités* 2 v. (Paris 1933–35) v.1. H. RASHDALL, *The Universities of Europe in the Middle Ages*, ed. F. M. POWICKE and A. B. EMDEN, 3 v. (new ed. Oxford 1936).

[R. MARCEL]

COLLEGE MISERICORDIA, a 4-year liberal arts college for women, College Misericordia is conducted by the Sisters of Mercy of the Union in the United States. The College was founded in 1924 by the Wilkes-Barre foundation of the Sisters of Mercy on a 100-acre campus in Dallas, Pa. It is accredited by the Middle States Association of Colleges and Secondary Schools and the National Association of Schools of Music. Chartered by the Commonwealth of Pennsylvania Jan. 31, 1927, it is recognized by the Pennsylvania State Council of Education, the Pennsylvania Board of Law Examiners, and the Board of Regents of the University of the State of New York. It is affiliated with The Catholic University of America and with the Trinity College of Music, London, England. A state reciprocity contract provides that Misericordia graduates of the baccalaureate program in elementary education are eligible for teacher certification in the New England and Middle Atlantic States.

The College is governed by a board of trustees consisting of both religious and lay members. In 1964 the faculty included 13 priests, 55 sisters, and 47 laymen, who held 11 doctoral, 2 professional, and 52 master's degrees. Student enrollment totaled 1,322, with an additional 453 students in the summer session. The library offered a collection of 45,000 volumes, 410 current magazines, and 12 daily and weekly newspapers.

The College offers a liberal arts curriculum with philosophy and theology as its core. It grants the following degrees: B.A.; Mus.B.; and B.S. in science, secretarial science, home economics, nursing, nursing education, and elementary education.

In cooperation with the University of Scranton, the College offers graduate studies in history, English, and education leading to the M.A. or M.S. degree. In October 1961, in order to meet rising educational demands, College Misericordia initiated an educational and guidance institute in Wilkes-Barre, Pa., to help young students develop their academic potential in preparation for college and future careers. In 1962, College Misericordia and King's College, Wilkes-Barre, arranged a cooperative extension program for undergraduate students.

Since the laying of the cornerstone on Sept. 24, 1922, the physical growth of the College has progressed steadily. McAuley Hall was opened as a student residence, April 1930, and building wings were added at intervals between then and 1957. Between 1959 and 1963, the College provided facilities for increased enrollment of residents by purchasing six residences on the fringe of the campus. In September 1963, the Merrick Student Center and Alumnae Hall were completed. In addition to the 17 buildings occupied by the College, the Provincial House of the Sisters of Mercy, the Novitiate, and the House of Studies for young sisters are also located on the College campus.

[M. J. KELLY]

COLLEGES AND SEMINARIES, ROMAN

The institutions established in Rome at the instance of the popes for the formation of non-Roman diocesan clergy, with the purpose of strengthening the unity of the Church around the papacy. Their students are selected by the bishops of their respective dioceses and pursue their studies under the direction of the Holy See. This article deals only with those institutions properly so-called and not with the seminaries or colleges of the religious orders and congregations.

Americano del Nord, Pontificio Collegio. The North American College was founded by Pope Pius IX on Dec. 8, 1859, for the seminarists of the U.S., and declared a pontifical college by Leo XIII on Oct. 25, 1884. Its students attend the Gregorian University. In 1948 Pope Pius XII transferred the college from the control of the Congregation of Propaganda to the American hierarchy, and it is usually directed by a bishop as rector. Having been originally established in the Palazzo Orsini on the Via del Umiltà in the center of the city, the college was closed in 1940 and reopened in 1948. It was transferred to a new building on the Via del Gianicolo 14 overlooking the Vatican in 1953, and the old building is used for priest graduate students.

Armeno, Pontificio Collegio. The first attempt to found a college for the Armenians goes back to Pope Gregory XIII in the 16th century, and a second attempt was made by Pius IX in 1867. The erection of the present college was the work of Leo XIII (March 1, 1883). It is located on the Salita S. Nicolà da Tolentino 17 and its students attend the Gregorian University.

Beda, Pontificio Collegio. The Beda, founded by Pope Pius IX in 1852 as a part of the English College, was separated from the latter in 1917 and is reserved for students who decide to study for the priesthood at a later age (the minimum age is 24 years). Those students who cannot follow the university courses in philosophy and theology are given special courses in the college itself. A new building was erected in 1963 on the Viale San Paolo 18, close to the basilica of St. Paul-outside-the-Walls.

Belga, Pontificio Collegio. The Belgian College, founded by Pope Gregory XVI in 1844 for the seminarists of the six dioceses of Belgium, is located on the Via del Quirinale 26.

Canadese, Pontificio Collegio. The Canadian College was founded on Nov. 11, 1888, by Pope Leo XIII, was declared a pontifical institute by Pius XI on May 6, 1932, and has only student priests engaged in graduate work. It is situated on the Via Quattro Fontane 117.

Capranicense, Almo Collegio. The Capranica, established by Cardinal Domenico Capranica in 1457, is the oldest of the Roman colleges. It was reformed by Alexander VII, closed in 1778 upon the formation of the Roman Republic, but reopened in 1807 by Pius VII. The college is on the Piazza Capranica 98. Students attend the Gregorian University and by disposition of

Benedict XV are employed in liturgical services in the basilica of S. Maria Maggiore.

Etiopico, Pontificio Collegio. The origin of the Ethiopian monastery at Rome can be traced to the 15th century, when Pope Sixtus IV confided to Ethiopian monks the church of S. Stefano, which was located behind the old basilica of St. Peter and called then St. Stephen of the Moors. Because of a lack of Ethiopians, in 1731 the monastery was opened also to the Copts. The death of the last rector of the Ethiopian College, George Galabadda, in 1845 brought about the cession of the monastery to the Trinitarians, who remained there until Benedict XV decided to use the college for the formation of Ethiopian secular clergy, on Oct. 1, 1919. Pius XI constructed a new building in the Vatican Gardens with the constitution *Curis ac Laboribus* of Feb. 12, 1930, made it a pontifical college and confided it to the governance of the Capuchins. Its students attend the Pontificia Università Urbaniana (Propaganda).

Filippino, Pontificio Collegio-Seminario. The Philippine College was erected on June 29, 1961, by Pope John XXIII. It is located on the Via Aurelia 490.

Francese, Pontificio Seminario. The French College was founded on Oct. 2, 1853. It was approved by Pope Pius IX on July 14, 1859, and given its rules (*regolamento*) on May 24, 1867. It is located on the Via di S. Chiara 42.

Germanico-Ungarico, Pontificio Collegio. The German College began on Aug. 31, 1552, under Pope Julius III at the suggestion of (St.) Ignatius Loyola for the formation of priests to work in Germany and nearby countries to counteract the Protestant Reformation. Between 1574 and 1798 it occupied a site next to the church of S. Apollinare. In 1580 it was united to the Hungarian College, obtaining also the church of S. Stefano Rotondo on the Coelian Hill. Closed in 1798 with the suppression of the Society of Jesus and the formation of the Roman Republic, it was reopened near the church of the Gesù in 1818. Its present location on the Via S. Nicolò da Tolentino 13 dates from 1940 to 1944, but the College was reorganized on Oct. 28, 1952. It is under the direction of the Jesuits, and its students attend the Gregorian University.

Greco, Pontificio Collegio. The Greek College was erected by Pope Gregory XIII on Jan. 13, 1577, and received its first rule in 1583 from Cardinal Giulio Antonio Santoro, who confided it to the direction of the Jesuits in 1591. It occupied three different sites until 1803, when it was closed for lack of funds. It was reopened in 1845, reformed by Leo XIII in 1897 and confided to the direction of the Benedictines. It is on the Via del Babuino 149, and its students attend the Pontificia Università di S. Tommaso (the Angelicum).

Inglese, Venerabile Collegio. The origins of the English College go back to a hospice for English pilgrims constructed in 1362 on the Via Monserrato to accommodate the many pilgrims coming to Rome from England. When the hospice was closed in the late 16th century, Pope Gregory XIII instituted a seminary on the spot for English students (April 23, 1578). The Jesuits had the direction of the college until the suppression of the society in 1773. Although it was closed with the other colleges in 1798 by the Roman Republic, it was reopened in 1818 and given to the direction of the English secular clergy. Its students attend the Gregorian University.

Irlandese, Pontificio Collegio. The reason for the formation of an Irish College goes back to the English laws forbidding the education of a Catholic clergy in Ireland in the 16th and 17th centuries. In 1625 the Irish bishops requested Pope Urban VIII for the foundation of an Irish College in Rome, and Cardinal Ludovico Ludovisi constructed one at his own expense (1628), confiding its direction to the Franciscans, from whom it passed to the Jesuits until 1772. It was closed in 1798 and reconstituted on Feb. 14, 1826, then confided to the direction of the Irish secular clergy. It occupied various sites until in 1926 it was finally established on the Via dei SS. Quattro 7, near the church of that name. Its students attend the Lateran University.

Lituano "di S. Casimiro." The foundation of the Lithuanian College was decided on by the Lithuanian bishops in exile in 1945, and it was canonically established by Pope Pius XII with the bull *Humana sic ferunt* (May 1, 1948). It is on the Via Casal Monferrato 20 and its students attend the Gregorian University and the Lateran University.

Lombardo dei SS. Ambrogio e Carlo, Pontificio Seminario. The Lombard College was founded in 1863 for priests and seminarians from the province of Lombardy in northern Italy, and reestablished in 1920. It now occupies a new building on the Via Aurelia 172. Its students attend the Lateran University.

Maronita, Collegio. The Maronite College was started as a hospice for pilgrims by Pope Gregory XIII in 1581 in the Trastevere section of Rome. Three years later (July 11, 1584) that Pontiff changed it into a seminary, and Cardinal Antonio Caraffa confided it to the direction of the Jesuits, who cared for it until the suppression of the society in 1773. Thereafter the college went through grave difficulties and was closed for several decades until Leo XIII ordered its restoration and transfer to the Via di Porta Pinciana 14 (Nov. 30, 1891). Pope Benedict XV gave it its final ordination (Oct. 10, 1920), and Pope Pius XI returned it to the care of the Jesuits. It was closed during World War II and reopened in 1949. Its students attend the Gregorian University.

Nepomuceno, Pontificio Collegio. The institution, which was originally called the Bohemian College, was begun by Pope Leo XIII in 1884; it was located on the Via Sistina in 1890 and became a pontifical college on January 1 of that year. Its present location is on the Via Concordia 1. It was called the Bohemian College until 1919, when it was opened to students from Moravia and Slovakia. When reorganized by Pope Pius XI on April 23, 1930, the college was given the name of Nepomuceno in honor of the martyr St. John Nepomucene. Its students attend the Lateran University.

Olandese Pio XI, Pontificio Collegio. The Dutch College, inaugurated by Pope Pius XI on Oct. 26, 1930, is reserved for young priests who have come to Rome for graduate studies. It is located on the Via Ercole Rosa 1 and its students attend various universities in Rome.

Pio Brasiliano, Pontificio Collegio. The Brazilian College is fairly new. Until the 19th century Brazilian students received their formation in the Collegio Pio Latino Americano, but, with the increase in Brazilian dioceses, to overcome the difficulty of language (since the Brazilians speak Portuguese) Pope Pius XI ordered the foundation of the new college in 1934 for Brazilian clerics. It is now housed on the Via Aurelia 527. The direction is confided to the Jesuits, and its students attend the Gregorian University.

Pio Latino Americano, Pontificio Collegio. Pius IX formed the Latin American College in 1858 and it was elevated to the dignity of pontifical college by Pope Pius X. It is reserved for South American students who speak Spanish. It is on the Via Aurelia 511 and is under the direction of the Jesuits. Its students attend the Gregorian University.

Pio Romeno, Pontificio Collegio. The Rumanian College, authorized by Pope Pius XI on May 12, 1930, is on the Passeggiata del Gianicolo 5 overlooking Vatican City. It is under the governance of the secular clergy, and its students attend the Pontificia Università Urbaniana (Propaganda).

Polacco, Pontificio Collegio. Pius IX established the Polish College on March 9, 1866. The building for it on the Piazza Remuria 2-A was secured in 1947–48 with the assistance of Polish Americans. In 1949 the college was confided to the Jesuits, and its students attend the Gregorian University. The graduate house (Pontificio Istituto Ecclesiastico Polacco) is situated on the Via Pietro Cavallini 38.

Portoghese, Pontificio Collegio. The Portuguese College, initiated by Pope Leo XIII on Oct. 20, 1900, for the students of Portugal and its overseas colonies, stands on the Via del Banco di S. Spirito 12. Its students attend the Gregorian University.

Romano, Pontificio Seminario. The Roman Seminary, established by Pope Pius IV in 1565 for the students of the Diocese of Rome, includes the major seminary at the Lateran, located on the Piazza San Giovanni in Laterano 4; the minor seminary in the Vatican, on the Viale Vaticano 42; and the pontifical Roman seminary for law students, which was founded by Pope Benedict XV in 1920, located at the Piazza S. Apollinare 49.

Russo di S. Teresa del Bambino Gesù, Pontificio Collegio. The Russian College was erected for students destined for the apostolate among the Russians by Pope Pius XI on August 15, 1929. It stands on the Via Carlo Cattaneo 2, near the basilica of S. Maria Maggiore. It is under the direction of the Jesuits, and its students attend the Gregorian University.

Ruteno di S. Giosafat, Pontificio Collegio. The Ruthenian College was inaugurated by Pope Leo XIII on Dec. 18, 1897, for students from the Ukraine. It is under the direction of the Basilian Fathers. It is located on the Passegiata del Gianicolo 7 overlooking Vatican City; its students attend the Pontificia Università Urbaniana (Propaganda).

Emigrazione Italiana, Pontificio Collegio dei Sacerdoti per la. The college was founded on March 19, 1914, and opened at the direction of Pope Benedict XV on Jan. 6, 1920, for the education of priests to assist Italian emigrants. It is on the Via della Scrofa 70.

S. Giovanni Damasceno Istituto. Pius XII planned the College of St. John Damascene, which opened on Dec. 4, 1940, on the Passeggiata del Gianicolo 5 overlooking Vatican City; it houses students doing graduate work in preparation for the mission in the East.

S. Girolamo Degli Illirici, Collegio. The College of St. Jerome of the Illyrians was founded by Pope Leo XIII on Aug. 1, 1901, on the Via Tomacelli 132. It was opened by Pope Pius X in 1911 for Croatian priests doing graduate study, and was closed in 1915 and reopened in 1924.

S. Maria del Lago, Collegio. Cardinal George Mundelein, archbishop of Chicago, founded the St. Mary of the Lake College in 1935 on the Via Sardegna 44 to accommodate priests from the Archdiocese of Chicago engaged in graduate studies.

S. Pietro Apostolo, Collegio. The College of St. Peter the Apostle, authorized by the Congregation of the Propaganda on Jan. 18, 1947, shelters priests from missionary territories who have come to Rome for graduate study. It is on the Viale delle Mura Aurelie 4.

Scozzese, Pontificio Collegio. The Scotch College originated with Pope Clement VIII on Dec. 5, 1600, for the formation of secular clergy for the dioceses of Scotland. It was confided to the care of the Jesuits in 1615 and turned over to the secular clergy in 1820. It was closed between 1798 and 1820 and again during World War II (1940–46). It is now situated at the Villa Scozzese in Marino near Lake Albano, and its students attend the Gregorian University.

Sloveno, Collegio. The Slovene College, erected for Slovene students by Pope John XXIII on Nov. 22, 1960, is at Via dei Colli 8. It is directed by Jesuits.

Spagnolo, Pontificio Collegio-Convitto. The Pontifical Spanish Resident-College originated on April 1, 1892, was confirmed by Leo XIII on Oct. 25, 1893, and was declared a pontifical college in 1904. The graduate house stands on the Via S. Apollinare 8, whereas the seminary is at Via di Torre Rossa 2, and its students attend the Gregorian University.

Teutonico di S. Maria dell'Anima, Pontificio Istituto. On the Via della Pace 20 stands the Pontifical German College of S. Maria dell'Anima which was established in 1859 for 30 priests from the dioceses of Austria and Germany doing graduate work in preparation for positions in the chancellaries of their respective dioceses.

Teutonico di S. Maria in Camposanto, Collegio. Priests of German nationality coming from the ancient territories of the Holy Roman Empire are accommodated in the German College of S. Maria in Camposanto, begun by Pius IX on Nov. 21, 1876. They are engaged mainly in archeological and Church history research. The college is likewise the Roman center of the Görresgesellschaft, whose members are engaged in the publication of the sources for the Council of Trent. It is on the Via della Sagrestia 17.

Ungherese, Pontificio Istituto Ecclesiastico. The Hungarian College dates from July 16, 1940, when Pope Pius XII established it for Hungarian priests doing graduate work in Rome. It is situated on the Via Giulia 1.

Urbano di Propaganda Fide, Pontificio Collegio. The Pontifical Urban College of the Propagation of the Faith was founded by Pope Urban VIII on Aug. 1, 1627, with the bull *Immortalis Dei* and was intended for the formation of seminarians coming from the dioceses under the jurisdiction of the Congregation of the Propaganda; it had a varied history before being closed from 1798 to 1817. Its present site on the Via Urbano VIII 16 on the Gianicolo Hill overlooking the Vatican was determined by Pope Pius XI, who personally inaugurated its opening on April 24, 1931. It is under the direction of the secular clergy, and its students attend the Pontificia Università Urbaniana (Propaganda).

Bibliography: M. G. O'CONNOR et al., EncCatt 3:1952–63. AnnPont (1964) 1060–64.

[F. CHIOVARO]

COLLEGES AND UNIVERSITIES, GOVERNMENT CONTRACTS WITH

Expenditures by the Federal government for scientific research and development have increased enormously since 1940. The unique capability of colleges and universities for performance of scientific work has resulted in increased involvement by these institutions as recipients of government funds. This, in turn, has raised questions as to the appropriateness of such participation, particularly by private institutions of higher learning.

Federally sponsored research and development at institutions of higher education may have the simple objective of enlarging knowledge in some general area, the exact approach and coverage falling within the discretion of the institution selected to perform the work. This is the method often used when basic research is involved. On the other hand, the objective may be highly specific and allow the institution almost no discretion in the performance of the work. This method is used chiefly where applied research and development are involved.

History. Federal support of scientific research and development at educational institutions is nothing new. Following the establishment of state land-grant colleges under the terms of the Morrill Act of 1862, the Hatch Act enacted in 1887 provided for Federal support of agricultural experimental stations at these colleges. Subsequent legislation has continued and enlarged the scope of these activities. During World War I the National Research Council, which was supported partially with Federal funds, financed research at universities. Under the authority of the National Academy of Science Act of 1863, the National Research Council was made a permanent organization by executive order in 1918.

During World War II colleges and universities moved into a position of prominence with respect to federally supported scientific research and development. Many contracts for such work were awarded to academic institutions by the Office of Scientific Research and Development, and funds were appropriated by Congress for the establishment of large research centers at universities, such as the radiation laboratory at the Massachusetts Institute of Technology. In 1944, the Public Health Service Act made possible the support of research in medicine and related fields by Federal funds.

During the postwar period, the role of colleges and universities in federally sponsored research and development has continued to grow. The legislation establishing the Office of Naval Research in 1946 expressly provided for contracts and grants to educational institutions. An amendment to the Atomic Energy Act in 1956 permits contracts and grants to educational, charitable, and other eleemosynary institutions for activities related to the atomic energy program. The Armed Services Procurement Act of 1947, as amended, recognizes the role of academic institutions in scientific research and development affecting national defense, and supplemental legislation enacted in 1952 confers specific contracting authority in these areas.

By far the most important postwar legislation affecting colleges and universities in their relation to Federal procurement agencies consists of the National Science Foundation Act of 1950 and Public Law 85–934 enacted in 1958. The former act enabled the National Science Foundation to contract and make grants for basic scientific research with educational institutions as well as with other organizations without regard to the normal requirements for formal advertising and other formalities related to government contracting. The latter law gave to each Federal agency having authority to contract for basic scientific research with nonprofit institutions of higher education, and other nonprofit organizations whose primary purpose is scientific research, the authority to make grants for similar purposes to these same institutions. This power also includes authority to turn over to the institution involved property purchased with grant or contract funds.

It is significant that the words "basic scientific research" are used in both of these statutes. There is no exact definition as to what constitutes basic scientific research, and experience has demonstrated that what is one man's basic research may be another man's "applied" research or "development." Since a grant or contract for scientific research between a government agency and a college or university invariably represents a desire on the part of each that such work be undertaken, the question whether the research to be performed is truly basic is not likely to arise between the parties to the undertaking. The comptroller general could raise this issue under his power to determine whether government funds have been used in accordance with statute. Public Law 85–934 does nothing but confer authority to make grants on agencies that have existing authority to contract for basic scientific research. The major Federal agencies vested with this authority include: the National Science Foundation, Department of Agriculture, Department of Health, Education and Welfare (National Institutes of Health and Public Health Service), Atomic Energy Commission, Department of Defense (including Army, Navy, Air Force and Defense Supply Agency), National Aeronautics and Space Administration, Department of Labor, Department of the Interior, Department of Commerce, and the Veterans Administration. Certain other Federal agencies have statutory authority to contract for basic research, and thus by the authority of Public Law 85–934 can make grants, but they do not customarily enter into contracts or make grants to colleges and universities.

Scientific research and development have assumed the proportions of big business in recent years and two-thirds of all funds used for these purposes come from the Federal government. In the calendar year 1963, nearly $15 billion has been budgeted by various Federal agencies for research and development, and about $1.5 billion of this will go to colleges and universities in the form of contracts and grants. Most of this scientific activity will be in the natural sciences, but a growing share is being allocated to research in the social sciences.

Contracts. The conventional method by which an educational institution performs services for the government is through a contract. As long as the government agency is acting within the scope of its authority and responsibilities, there is no constitutional limitation on its power to enter into contracts with institutes of higher education for scientific research and development. The authority of the government to contract in order to meet its needs is a power inherent in sovereignty. For example, there is no doubt that the Office of Scientific Research and Development had authority, even in the absence of statute, to contract with colleges and universities for research and development related to the prosecution of World War II. Nevertheless, contracting for research and development is a very specialized activity and a Federal agency will not ordinarily assume that it has such authority in the absence of a specific enabling statute.

A contract is not an instrument of largess and consequently there is no justification for the assumption that the government is giving anything away when it enters into a contract for scientific research and development with an educational institution. Such an undertaking is strictly a business proposition with each contracting party owing a specific duty to the other. It seems clear that the government can contract with any organization without the inference of giving aid being legitimately raised.

For the purposes of scientific research and development, the contract is not always the best means of achieving the desired objectives. A contract with a Federal agency is a complex, formal document and must adhere to many requirements that are imposed by statute and regulation. In addition, it may not be possible to spell out the objectives of scientific research with sufficient definiteness to permit the use of the contract device. In order to relieve this problem, the use of the grant has become increasingly significant.

Grants. By the use of grants, Federal funds and property can be turned over to nonprofit educational institutions either without restriction or in return for the institution's undertaking to use the grant for a stated purpose or objective. If an objective is specified, it is not a condition of the grant that the objective be achieved or even that the best effort be used. The grant can be made by means of a simple written statement, and there are no restrictions on the manner in which grant funds can be expended, unless a specific restriction is expressed by Congress in making the appropriation or by the agency making the grant.

Although authorities differ on this point, it does not appear technically sound to consider a grant as a form of contract. To do so would unduly restrict the scope of the grant device. Grants may, however, have some of the attributes of contracts. For instance, while it is clear that a grant can be revoked by the grantor, the grantee should be able to recover any funds properly expended in reliance on the grant prior to notice of its revocation.

In contrast to the power to contract, the authority of Federal agencies to make grants can be conferred only by statute. The grantee usually renders some services to the grantor in return for the grant, but by the very nature of a grant, this *quid pro quo* is not a requirement. It is thus possible to view a grant as bestowing Federal aid—either in the form of money or property—on the grantee. When the grantee is a church-supported or church-controlled college or university, the question of possible conflict with the provisions of the First Amendment arises. Actually the assistance provided to educational institutions by grants is far less direct than would be a program providing for Federal support of academic building construction or payment of faculty salaries. Federal assistance through grants is more analogous to the type of aid afforded nonprofit and charitable organizations by tax exemption, the assistance to hospital construction provided by the Hill-Burton Act of 1946, or low-interest loans for construction of housing. In any event, since virtually all the legislation permitting grants to colleges and universities specifies that they can be made to nonprofit public and private institutions of higher learning, it is obvious that Congress anticipated that some of the grants would be made to institutions having some degree of religious affiliation. The fact that nearly all private educational institutions were founded under church sponsorship, and that many still continue under it, could not have escaped legislative notice. No case has been found in which a grant has been challenged as a violation of the First Amendment. As a practical matter, such a challenge would be technically difficult since neither an ordinary taxpayer nor another educational institution would likely have standing to sue. This problem is further minimized by existing regulations concerning grants that require high-level review and approval of the purposes of such grants.

Administrative Problems. Contracts and grants to colleges and universities for scientific research and development are not always an unmixed blessing. While they may sometimes permit an institution to expand and strengthen one or more of its academic departments, severe problems may arise when a contract or grant comes to an end, if there has been a more rapid increase in personnel than the institution can absorb in the long run. Overcommitment to Federal contracts and grants by academic institutions may also be at the expense of their teaching obligations and independent research programs. These problems can be alleviated to some extent by the use of the separate research center device, but this in turn requires a large outlay of Federal funds for capital plant and equipment, a step that may be neither necessary nor desirable under given circumstances. One continuing problem for colleges and universities that have received grants for scientific research and development has been recovery of indirect costs attributable to the work sponsored by such grants. Most agencies are limited by statute as to the share of a grant that can be applied to indirect expenses such as admininstrative costs, building usage, and library expense. Current statutes limit the payment of indirect expenses to between 15 and 20 per cent of the total grant, which often means that such a grant becomes a cost-sharing proposition for the receiving institution, an eventuality not usually provided for in its budgeting.

As long as Federal expenditures for scientific research and development continue to increase, the participation in such activities by colleges and universities will probably increase. On the horizon, however, is increased competition for Federal funds from noneducational, nonprofit institutions that devote their entire resources to research and development, and from government laboratories that are ever increasing in resources.

See also PRIVATE SCHOOLS, GRANTS AND LOANS TO.

Bibliography: D. K. PRICE, *Government and Science* (New York 1954). G. GLOCKLER, "The Contractual Versus the Grant Approach to Basic Research Activities," *Federal Bar Journal* 17 (1957) 265–284. J. W. WHELAN, "Public Law 85–934: New Federal Support for Basic Scientific Research," *Journal of Public Law* 8 (1959) 462–498. U.S. National Science Foundation, *Government-University Relationships in Federally Sponsored Scientific Research and Development* (2d ed., Washington 1958). U.S. Navy Dept. Office of General Counsel, *Navy Contract Law* (Navexos P-1995; 2d ed. Washington 1959) ch. 8. A. M. RIVLIN, *The Role of the Federal Government in Financing Higher Education* (Washington 1961). H. ORLANS, *The Effects of Federal Programs on Higher Education* (Washington 1962). R. D. CALKINS, *Government Support of Higher Education* (Washington 1960).

[H. C. PETROWITZ]

COLLIER, PETER FENELON, pioneer U.S. Catholic subscription book and magazine publisher; b. Myshall, Ireland, Dec. 12, 1849; d. New York City, April 24, 1909; son of Robert C. and Catherine (Fenelon) Collier. Coming to the U.S. in 1866, the family settled in Dayton, Ohio, where Peter worked in the railroad shops. In 1868 he entered the seminary of the Cincinnati Archdiocese but soon left and moved to New York City. There he worked as a book salesman for the Catholic publishing firm of J. and D. *Sadlier and later as a salesman for the firm of P. J. *Kenedy. In 1875, with a capital of $300, he set up his own firm, which quickly achieved success in selling Catholic and Irish-national books for small monthly payments. He then branched out into general reference publishing.

Encouraged by the success of his book business and to promote it further, Collier began in 1888 a magazine, *Once A Week,* which had an initial sale of 50,000 copies and grew to 200,000 in 2 years. In 1895 the name was changed to *Collier's Weekly,* which at the time of its demise in December 1956 had more than 4 million subscribers. As the "father of the subscription book industry," Collier first brought the works of standard authors, encyclopedias, and reference books to the average family. After his death the business was continued by his son Robert, who died in 1918; the following year the controlling interest in the Collier company was taken over by the Crowell Publishing Company, and in 1939 the name was changed to the Crowell-Collier Publishing Company.

[J. F. CARROLL]

COLLINS, DOMINIC, Irish martyr; b. Youghal, Ireland, 1567; d. Cork, Oct. 29, 1602. He was born of a noble family, and his brother was mayor of Youghal in 1600. Dominic went to France in 1586 and served as a soldier for Philip Emmanuel of Lorraine, who made him commander of cavalry. He served in the Spanish army from 1594 until 1598 when he entered the Society of Jesus. After his profession as a lay brother in 1601 he was chosen as companion to Father James Archer, who was then about to return to Ireland. Dominic sailed there in the Spanish fleet in 1602. He was at Dunboy during the siege, not as a combatant, but as one concerned with the spiritual and temporal needs of the besieged, who chose him to treat for terms with the English. Taken prisoner, he was offered his liberty on condition of the renouncing of his faith and swearing allegiance to Elizabeth I. He was hanged, apparently without trial. All contemporary accounts state that he died at Cork. Such details as disemboweling and quartering are found only in later (Jesuit) sources.

Bibliography: Archives (unpublished) of the Society of Jesus, Rome. E. HOGAN, *Distinguished Irishmen of the Sixteenth and Seventeenth Centuries* (London 1894).

[F. FINEGAN]

COLLIUS, FRANCESCO (COLLIO), theologian; b. Milan, exact date not known; d. Milan, 1640. He entered the Milanese congregation of the Oblates of St. Charles, and later served as grand penitentiary for the Diocese of Milan. Three authentic works are ascribed to him: *Conclusiones in sacra theologia numero MCLXV una cum variorum doctorum opinionibus* (Milan 1609), *De sanguine Christi libri quinque in quibus de illius natura, effusionibus ac miraculis copiose disseritur* (Cologne 1612; Milan 1617), and the *De animabus paganorum* (Milan 1622). The last work manifests the author's preoccupation with the problem of whether the souls of well-known Biblical and pagan personages of antiquity have attained salvation.

Bibliography: B. HEURTEBIZE, DTC 3.1:369.

[G. M. GRABKA]

COLLOREDO, HIERONYMUS, Prince archbishop of Salzburg; b. Vienna, May 31, 1732; d. there May 20, 1812. This second son of Prince Rudolph Joseph studied at the Collegium Germanicum at Rome, became a canon of the cathedral at Salzburg (1747), prior of Kremsier in Moravia (1761), bishop of Gurk (1762), and after a drawn-out election prince bishop

Hieronymous Colloredo.

of Salzburg (1772). His main interest was his principality, whose well-being he sought to promote in every way. He raised the level of elementary education, patronized literary and artistic efforts, summoned German professors, and sent young noblemen to foreign universities. In Church history, however, he made a place for himself not as secular ruler but as the prince archbishop of enlightened ideas. The program he developed in his famous pastoral letter of May 29, 1782, met with complete approval by Emperor Joseph II and was translated into French and Italian. His reforms were aimed at a simple Christianity, purified of all incidentals and externals. They failed partly through opposition from conservative classes, but mostly because they were effected in haste and without sympathetic understanding of the mentality of the people. Colloredo did not vie for popular favor and even in exile sought to protect his episcopal rights as against the Emperor. He was buried in St. Stephen's Cathedral.

Bibliography: J. C. ALLMAYER-BECK, NDB 3:327–328. J. MACK, *Die Reform- und Aufklärungsbestrebungen unter Colloredo,* (Munich 1912). J. SCHÖTTL, *Kirchliche Reformen des Salzburger Erzbischofs Hieronymus v. Colloredo im Zeitalter der Aufklärung* (Hirschenhausen 1939). E. WOLF, RGG[3] 1:1851. F. LOIDL, LexThK[2] 3:5–6.

[F. MAASS]

COLMAN, SS., five Irish saints of the 6th and 7th centuries.

Colman of Cloyne, bishop, patron of Diocese of Cloyne, Ireland; b. 530 (Annals of Inisfallen); d. 606 (feast, Nov. 26). A bard, he was a late vocation to the priesthood. His life centered in County Cork, where he founded his principal church at Cloyne, with another important foundation at Kilmaclenine.

Colman of Dromore, bishop, patron of Diocese of Dromore, Ireland, early 6th century (feast, June 7). He is one of the early important but obscure Irish saints. His life and work centered in County Down. He appears to have studied under St. Caylan at Nendrum on Strangford Lough, and may have founded his church at Dromore *c.* 514. Devotion to Colman spread to Scotland and Wales, where several churches were dedicated to him.

Colman Elo (Eala) of Lynally, monastic founder; b. County Tyrone, Ireland, *c.* 555; d. 611 (Annals of Ulster) or 613 (Annals of Inisfallen); feast, Sept. 26. His principal monastery was at Lynally, County Offaly. He was a friend of *Columba of Iona and stayed at *Iona on one of his visits to Scotland. Several Scottish churches were dedicated in his honor.

Colman of Lindisfarne, third Irish bishop-abbot of *Lindisfarne, England; d. *c.* 670 (feast, Feb. 18, also noted for Aug. 8). Colman opposed the anti-Celtic decisions of the Synod of *Whitby in 664. Hence he and the Irish monks and some of the English monks left Lindisfarne for *Iona, and then for the island of Inishbofin off the west coast of Ireland. From there, the English monks founded Mayo abbey on the Irish mainland.

Colman Macduach, patron of Diocese of Kilmacduagh, Ireland; b. Kiltartan, County Clare, 7th century (feast, Oct. 29). Having studied on the Aran Islands, he lived as a hermit in the Burren district of the Irish mainland opposite these islands. Later he founded a great monastery at Kilmacduagh, but in his old age he returned to the Burren hills to found Oughtmama.

Bibliography: Of Cloyne. J. C., "St. Colman of Cloyne," *Journal of the Cork Historical and Archaeological Society* 16 (1910) 132–142. Butler Th Attw 4:419. Of Dromore. ActSS June 2:24–29. Butler Th Attw 2:493–494. Kenney 466. Elo. Kenney 400. C. PLUMMER, *Bethada náem nÉrenn,* 2 v. (Oxford 1922) 1:168–182; 2:162–176; comp., *Vitae sanctorum Hiberniae,* 2 v. (Oxford 1910) 1:258–273. F. Ó BRIAIN, DHGE 13:257–258. Butler Th Attw 3:654. Of Lindisfarne. BEDE, *Eccl. Hist.* 3.25, 26; 4.4. Kenney 463–464. F. O BRIAIN, DHGE 13:256. D. D. C. POCHIN MOULD, The Irish Saints (Dublin 1964) 89–90. Butler Th Attw 1:369–370. Cross ODCC 312. Macduach. J. FAHEY, *The History and Antiquities of the Diocese of Kilmacduagh* (Dublin 1893). Kenney 456. Butler Th Attw 4:218.

[D. D. C. POCHIN MOULD]

COLMAR, JOSEPH LUDWIG, German bishop; b. Strasbourg, June 22, 1760; d. Mainz, Dec. 15, 1818. He was the son of an eminent Greek scholar and professor of languages. After ordination (1783) Colmar taught history and Greek in the Gymnasium at Strasbourg. He remained in the city during the French Revolution, but his refusal to subscribe to the oath supporting the *Civil Constitution of the Clergy required him to carry out his zealous pastoral works under various disguises amid danger of arrest. He was a preacher in the cathedral at Strasbourg from 1799 until 1802, when he was made bishop of *Mainz. By his labors and personal example he restored religious life among clergy and laity after the ravages of the Revolution. In 1804 he established a seminary. He obtained from Napoleon I the restitution of the cathedrals in Mainz and Speyer, which had been destined for destruction. Colmar's accomplishments as an administrator, pastor, preacher, and theologian rank him as outstanding in the reorganization and restoration of Catholic life in the Rhineland. Seven volumes of his sermons have been published, besides various spiritual works.

Bibliography: J. WIRTH, *Monseigneur Colmar, évêque de Mayence 1760–1818* (Paris 1906). C. LAPLATTE, DHGE 13:272–274. L. LENHART, LexThK[2] 3:7.

[E. J. DUNNE]

COLOGNE

City in west central Germany, North Rhineland–Westphalia, on both sides of the Rhine River, with 836,000 inhabitants (1963). It is the seat of many offices, industries, and services (especially banks and insurance), and, because of the vicinity of Bonn, capital of the German Federal Republic, the residence of many diplomatic representatives. It is also a cultural center, with a university, three advanced schools, historical buildings, and outstanding museums, as well as the seat of the most important German archbishopric (*Coloniensis*), whose history, as that of the city, dates from Roman times.

The City. The son-in-law of Emperor Augustus, M. Vipsanius Agrippa, settled the Ubii, from the right bank of the Rhine, between the Rhine and the Maas. The *oppidum Ubiorum* with its military camp and colony of veterans (*c.* 12 B.C.) was to become, with its shrines (*ara Ubiorum*), the capital of *Germania;* but, after the Roman defeat in the Teutoburg Forest (A.D. 9), the frontier *oppidum* remained. Thanks to Agrippina the Younger, who was born there and became the wife of Emperor Claudius, it obtained the city privileges (A.D. 50); and, thereafter called *Colonia Claudia Ara Agrippinensis,* it was the capital of *Germania inferior,* with many buildings, a glass and pottery industry, and (from the 4th century) Christian churches. Constantine built the first permanent bridge across the Rhine there.

Under the Franks (from *c.* 400) Cologne became a royal residence, soon famous for its many churches. Under Charlemagne it was the point from which Saxony was conquered and evangelized. In the division of the Carolingian Empire (843) it went to the Middle Kingdom (Lotharingia); when Lotharingia was divided (870), Cologne went to the East Frankish kingdom, later the German Empire.

The Ottonians and the archbishop rulers of the city favored its development as a trade center, and it had expanded several times by 1200. From *c.* 1100 the burghers struggled for independence of the archbishop and in 1288 won complete freedom. Thereafter the archbishops resided in Bonn, and Cologne became a free imperial city. In 1396 the burghers drew up a democratic constitution. From the 11th to the 16th century, Cologne, the largest and richest city of the empire, had a thriving trade with Scandinavia, Poland, and Russia, as well as with Flanders and England. It was a leading city in the *Hanseatic League.

Riches encouraged achievements in art, especially ecclesiastical. Through its possession of relics of the Three Magi (from 1164), Cologne became a major pilgrimage center. The city seal of 1150, the oldest in Germany, bears the inscription *Sancta Colonia Sanctae Romanae Ecclesiae Fidelis Filia.* Even after the departure of the archbishop, Cologne remained the seat of diocesan administration and the most important ecclesiastical center of Germany. In the city were the

Fig. 1. Cologne, Church of the Apostles, built in the late 12th and the 13th centuries.

cathedral domain and those of 10 collegiate churches and 3 Benedictine abbeys, besides 19 parishes and cloisters of most religious orders. The *studia generalia* of Dominicans and Franciscans prepared the way for the university of 1388 (see below). The city vigorously prevented inroads of the Reformation, banning Lutheranism until 1794. At the end of the 16th century began a gradual decline, following the opening of new routes for world trade and religious and political changes in Germany. Cologne remained a medieval city until *c.* 1800; in the face of new ideas the traditionalist burghers remained passive. The archbishop elector resided elsewhere, and there was no baroque prince to fashion changes.

After conquest by France (1794–1814), Cologne was incorporated in Protestant *Prussia, little to the city's liking. A steady growth began *c.* 1850, attributable primarily to local forces, and Cologne became the economic and cultural center of west Germany, the crossroads of European transport routes, and the center of political and social Catholicism. Large-scale expansion and building took place under Mayor Konrad Adenauer (1917–33). In 1933 Cologne was the third largest German city, 75 per cent of whose 750,000 residents were Catholic. In the last Reichstag election (March 1933) *Hitler received less than 30 per cent of the votes.

In World War II, Cologne was especially hard hit. From May 1942 to March 1945 methodical Allied bombing completely destroyed the inner city, doing irreparable ruin to one of Europe's most beautiful cities and claiming 25,000 lives. Most of the people fled, but in May 1945 some 40,000 still lived in the ruins. One church out of 104 was undamaged. Rebuilding of a modern city has proceeded apace, and Cologne's position has been regained. The influx of refugees from East Germany has altered religious statistics. In 1963 Catholics numbered 65 per cent, Lutherans 29 per cent.

The Archbishopric. Christian origins date from *c.* 200. The first historically known bishop, Maternus, attended the Councils of Rome (313) and Arles (314). The see survived the Frankish conquest, but to *c.* 600 the episcopal list has many gaps. *Cunibert (623–*c.* 660) raised Cologne's status. Pope Zacharias gave St. *Boniface Cologne as a metropolitanate (745); but the Frankish episcopacy and nobility thwarted the plan, fearing for their independence, and *Mainz was chosen instead.

Under Charlemagne the metropolitan system of Germany developed. Cologne became a metropolitanate (785) with the suffragans *Liège, *Utrecht, and the new Saxon sees of *Münster, *Osnabrück, Minden, and for a while *Bremen. The borders of the vast archbishopric (23 deaneries and in Westphalia on the Rhine, Ruhr, and Wupper Rivers) and of the ecclesiastical province were almost unchanged through the Middle Ages. Utrecht became an archdiocese and several deaneries went to the new See of Roermond in 1559. Protestant Minden was suppressed as a see in 1648. From the 12th century the archbishop yielded authority to the 10 archdeacons (provosts and deans freely elected by their respective chapters). Four of them especially, the cathedral provost of Cologne and the provosts of Bonn, Xanten, and Soest, won jurisdictional rights that survived the centralizing tendencies of the Council of Trent.

The list of great medieval prelates begins with *Bruno I (953–965), brother and collaborator of Otto I the Great, who as duke of Lotharingia first united episcopal and secular authority. His successors developed a principality whose borders partly coincided with those of the archdiocese. From the 11th century the archbishops were archchancellors of the Italian part of the empire. They also won the right to crown German kings and belonged to the influential electors of the king; the Golden Bull of Charles IV (1356) made them definitely part of the privileged group of seven electors.

*Heribert (999–1021) was the friend and chancellor of Otto III. Pilgrim (1021–36), Herman II (1036–56), and *Anno II (1056–75, for a while viceregent of the empire) sponsored church and cloister reform. Instead of royal nomination, election by the cathedral chapter (most of whom belonged to the Rhenish nobility) determined episcopal appointment after the Concordat of Worms (1122); from the 13th century, 8 of 24 canonries were reserved for clergy of bourgeois origin. Imperial influence continued to be strong, however. Frederick I Barbarossa had two of his chancellors archbishops, the talented *Rainald of Dassel (1156–67), who conceived and directed the antipapal imperial policy of the Emperor, and Philip of Heinsberg (1167–91), who acquired the duchy of Westphalia. In following years the emperor's power waned. Even Cologne's archbishops (except *Engelbert, 1216–25, viceregent of the empire) followed a predominantly territorial policy; the fall of the Hohenstaufen encouraged the archbishops, especially Conrad of Hochstaden (1238–61), to consolidate a large state in northwest Germany. But a coalition of neighboring princes, allied with the city of Cologne, brought their plan to naught (1288). The constitution of the Electorate (1463) conceded some rule to the cathedral chapter, counts, knights, and cities. Hermann V von Wied (1515–47), a good sovereign, favored the Reformation and so met opposition from his chapter, the university, and the city of Cologne; he resigned under pressure from the Emperor. Gebhard *Truchsess von Waldburg (1577–83) became Lutheran and sought to make the archbishopric a secular electorate. In the "War of Cologne" the Emperor and his allies assured the continuation of Catholicism in northwest Germany and a Catholic majority in the college of electors.

When Duke Ernst of Bavaria became archbishop (1583–1612), he began a series of Wittelsbach electors, who while protecting the Church used their position on the Rhine to further Wittelsbach policies. Ernst and his successors, Ferdinand (1612–50), Maximilian Heinrich (1650–88), Joseph Clemens (1688–1723), and Clemens August (1723–61), also held several neighboring bishoprics. They devoted themselves mostly to politics and art (baroque churches and castles). Only Ferdinand, who took a personal interest in reform and the revival of Church life, was a distinguished ecclesiastic. Spiritual administration was in the hands of good auxiliary bishops and general vicars.

Maximilian Friedrich von Königsegg-Rothenfels (1761–84) supported the *Enlightenment and in the Nuntiature Controversy defended his episcopal rights against the centralization of Rome. Maximilian Franz of Austria, youngest son of Maria Theresa and last Elector of Cologne (1781–1801), who favored the same course, took part in the anticurial *Ems Congress (1786). He was also an outstanding prelate and regent, surpassing most of his predecessors in conscientiousness and zeal. When the French invaded (1794), he fled to the right bank of the Rhine.

The part of the see on the left bank of the Rhine became French and was placed under the Diocese of *Aachen founded by Napoleon (1801); church goods were secularized. On the right bank, where the episcopal administration of Cologne continued, the secularization of 1803, which initiated the end of the *Holy Roman Empire, took place.

After French domination, the archbishopric of Cologne was restored (1821), with Prussian consent. But it had been reduced in area, and had as suffragans Münster, *Paderborn, and *Trier. The Prussian regime's mistrust of Catholics led to strained relations, but it lessened after 1840, under Frederick William IV. The prudent Ferdinand August von *Spiegel (1824–36) reorganized the archdiocese, dividing it into 44 deaneries. His many accomplishments were clouded by his indulgence in the question of mixed marriages (*see* COLOGNE, MIXED MARRIAGE DISPUTE IN), which laid the basis for the arrest of his successor, Clemens August von *Droste zu Vischering (1835–45). Johannes von *Geissel (1846–64), cardinal in 1850, made gains for Church freedom and Catholic organizations. In 1848 he presided at the first conference of all German bishops in Würzburg, and in 1860 held a provincial council. Paulus *Melchers (1866–85), opponent of papal infallibility at *Vatican Council I, headed Prussian bishops in the *Kulturkampf, was arrested (1874) and in exile in the Netherlands from 1876. In 1885 he resigned, in the interest of a settlement, and became a cardinal in the Roman Curia (d. 1895). Philipp Krementz (1885–99), cardinal in 1893, repaired the damage of the Kulturkampf.

Most of the industrial area of the Ruhr, Rhine, and Wupper lay in the Archdiocese of Cologne. Population migration and concentration in the large cities posed serious problems of pastoral care. Associations developed with success; the most important Catholic organizations in all Germany (trade unions, Borromeo societies, the association for Catholic Germany (Volksverein), and the mission center) had headquarters in the archdiocese, as did interdenominational Christian trade unions, which Abp. Antonius Fischer (1902–12) defended against integrationist attempts. Centers of pastoral care were established for immigrant Polish workers in the Ruhr. Karl Joseph Schulte (1920–41), cardinal in 1921, who fostered scholarship and modern techniques in pastoral care, was a confirmed opponent of National Socialism; he died during a bombing raid. The Prussian Concordat (1929) introduced changes in ecclesiastical organization. The extensive archdiocese of 3,500,000 Catholics ceded 29 deaneries with 1,000,000 Catholics to the new See of Aachen in 1930. Paderborn became an archbishopric. As suffragans Cologne has had since then Aachen, Limburg, Münster, Osnabrück, Trier, and (since 1957) Essen. Joseph Frings (1942–), cardinal in 1946, was a wise advocate for the German people before the victorious powers after World War II. He sponsored modern art in reconstruction, founded Misereor and Adveniat for the Church and the suffering people of Asia and South America, and was a prudent leader of the reform group at *Vatican Council II.

Fig. 2. The main façade of the Gothic cathedral of Cologne. The foundation stone was laid in 1248 and consecration took place in 1322, but the structure was not completed until 1880.

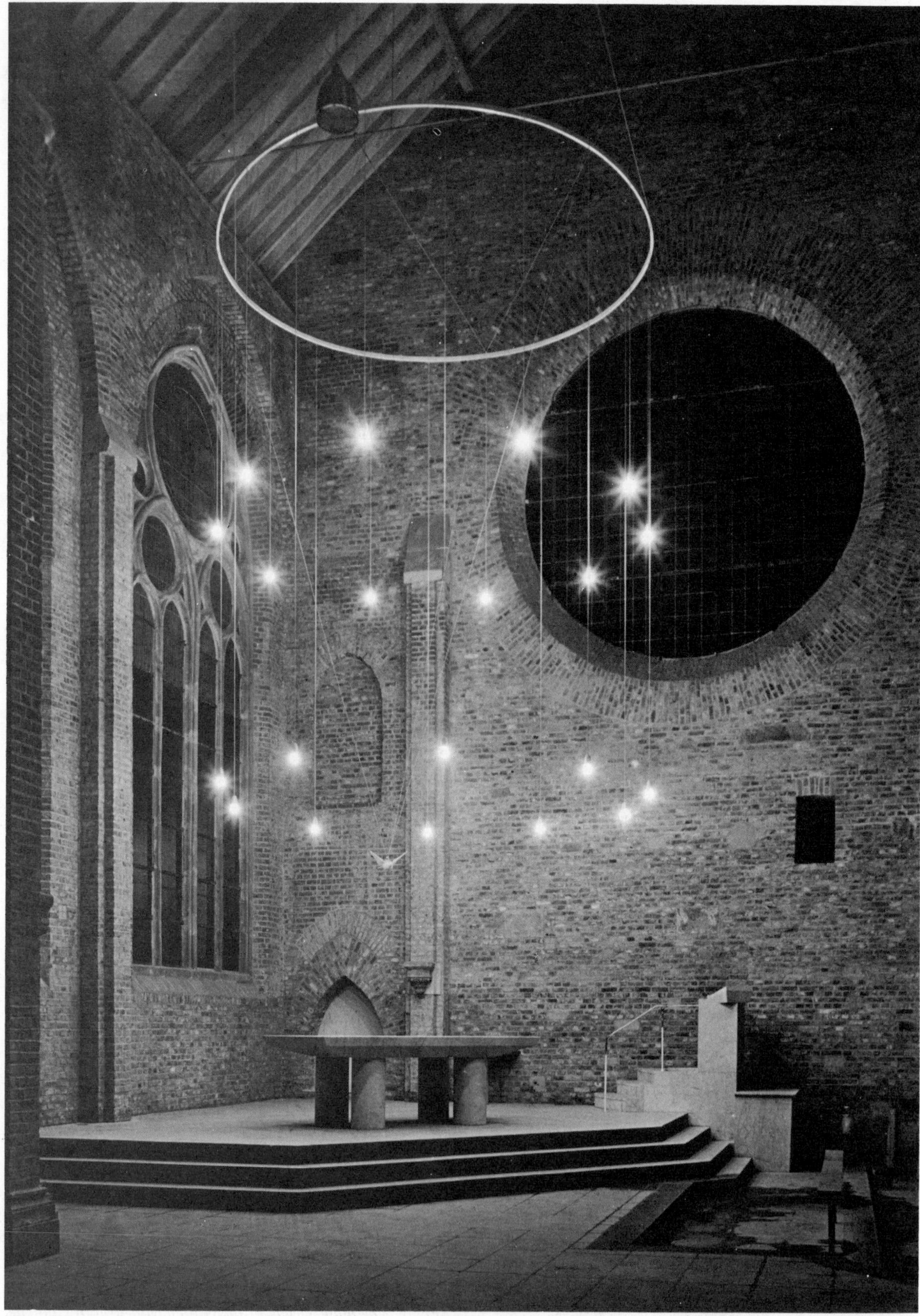

Fig. 3. Cologne, sanctuary of the Franciscan church, rebuilt by the architect Emil Steffann in the 1950s.

In 1957 part of the archdiocese went to the new See of Essen. In 1963 the See of Cologne had 1,658 secular and 676 religious priests, 1,398 men in 69 religious houses, 7,346 women in 391 convents, and 2,520,000 Catholics in a population of 4,740,000; it is 2,387 square miles in area.

Art. From Roman and early Christian times there survive many burial monuments, high quality glass, a mosaic of Dionysius (*c.* 200), and remains of the city wall. St. *Ursula and St. Gereon date from cemetery edifices over tombs of the martyrs; St. Gereon was an oval monument. St. Kunibert and St. Maria im Kapitol (7th century) were built in Frankish times. Recent excavations reveal a 6th-century church under the cathedral, with some of the richest tombs of Frankish princes.

From late Carolingian days come large church edifices, which were later copied. Excavations beneath the Gothic cathedral show that the earlier cathedral (to 870) was the first large German church with two transepts. St. Pantaleon (*c.* 980) had a wider nave with monumental work on the west side. St. Maria im Kapitol (mid-11th-century, as is St. Georg) had a round three-apse choir damaged in World War II. The *Gero cross in the cathedral (*c.* 970) is the first German monumental sculpture. From the same period and later come pieces of smaller sculpture, ivory carvings, and MS illumination, showing Byzantine influence.

The artistic peak was reached with late Romanesque in which most of the churches of Cologne were built (*c.* 1150–*c.* 1250). Classical proportions and colors, three-apse choirs, the marked division of inner and outer walls, and rich detail mark the style of this period. Exuberant later forms reflect the characteristic joy of the style: the choir (*c.* 1190) and decagon (1219–27) of St. Gereon; the choir (to 1172) of Great St. Martin; the west part (1188) of St. Georg; St. Cecilia (1160–70); the restoration and new choir of Holy Apostles (1200–20); St. Andreas (after 1200); St. Kunibert (1200–47); the new choir of St. Severin (to 1237); and the Overstolzenhaus and gates of the city fortress (early 13th century). Of the same high quality are the sculpture (figures in St. Maria im Kapitol) and painting (frescoes in St. Maria Lyskirchen *c.* 1250 and glass paintings in St. Kunibert *c.* 1230). Especially precious is the goldwork, influenced by that of the Maas, in the costly shrines for relics; the most famous is that of the Three Magi (1180–1220), the largest sarcophagus in Europe, with goldwork, whose classical figures anticipate the sculpture of Gothic cathedrals. Other masterpieces are the shrines of SS. Heribert, Maurinus, Albinus, Aetherius, and Anno and many smaller reliquaries and liturgical vessels.

The most important Gothic structure is the cathedral, dedicated to St. Peter and the Blessed Virgin, which brought the school of north French cathedrals to completion. It is a five-nave basilica with a three-nave transept, a three-story design with high walls broken by pillars and large windows, which was begun in 1248; the choir was consecrated in 1322. Construction, discontinued in the 16th century, was completed in the 19th century after Romanticists rediscovered Gothic and Cologne's cathedral was seen as a national German monument. Other Gothic churches are the Franciscan Church (13th century), St. Ursula (choir 1287), the Church of the Brothers of St. Anthony (1384), the Carthusian Church (1393), and St. Andreas (choir 1420); and among secular edifices, the Hansa hall (1360) and the tower (*c.* 1410) of the town hall, and Gürzenich banqueting palace (1437–44). Many statues and paintings, especially anguished Crucifixions and loving Madonnas, show the influence of mysticism. After 1350, Cologne's art became more statuesque and corporeal.

Glass paintings and frescoes of the cathedral were the first work of the Cologne school of painting, the longest-lived of any German school (*c.* 1300–*c.* 1530), of a constantly high quality. It was distinguished by lyrical lines, light and bright colors, and pious thoughtful themes. Although open to outside influences, the school stuck to its own tradition. Of the masters of the 15th century, only Stephen *Lochner (d. 1451) is known (thanks to Dürer); Lochner was the artist of the altar of Cologne's patron saints in the cathedral. Others are known by their most important works: the master of the Veronica, the master of the Life of Mary, the master of the Holy Family, etc. Barthel Bruyn (d. 1555), the last of the Cologne school, committed himself freely to Renaissance ways.

Other works of the Renaissance, influenced from the Netherlands, are the vestibule of the town hall (1567–71) and the choir screens in St. Pantaleon and St. Maria im Kapitol (1502–23).

Cologne had few outstanding baroque buildings: the Jesuit Church of the Assumption (1618–27) with strong traces of Gothic; St. Maria on Schnurgasse (1643–1716); and several secular buildings, few of which have survived. The sculpture of J. F. Helmont was destroyed in World War II. Baroque goldwork was of high quality: the Engelbert shrine in the cathedral (1633), monstrances, chalices, reliquaries, and rich vestments.

The destruction of Cologne's art began after secularization (1803), when many churches were wrecked. The worst came in World War II. Although almost all churches were damaged, many have been restored; movable objects survived the war best. Many works, dispersed following secularization, came into museums: Darmstadt, Munich, Nürnberg, and London. Of the works left in Cologne, many are in churches and others are in city museums: Roman-Germanic Museum, Schnütgen Museum (medieval sculpture and objects), Wallraf-Richartz Museum (Cologne school of painting; also important Dutch works, German and French masters of the 19th century, and a large modern collection), and the museum of applied arts. The archiepiscopal museum contains church art from the Middle Ages to the baroque age.

Many churches have been built since the 1930s and especially since 1945. They are all oriented to the liturgy, with altar and congregation brought together. The space and disposition of buildings and furnishings are symbolic of their liturgical functions (*see* CHURCH ARCHITECTURE, 10).

Bibliography: General. *Kunstdenkmäler der Rheinprovinz,* ed. P. CLEMEN, 6–7 (Düsseldorf 1906–38). *Handbuch des Erzbistums Köln* (25th ed. Cologne 1958). *Regesten der Erzbischöfe von Köln,* ed. R. KNIPPING et al (Bonn 1902–61). Periodicals. *Annalen des Historischen Vereins für den Niederrhein* (1855–). *Jahrbuch des Kölnischen Geschichtsvereins* (1913–). *Kölner Domblatt* (1948–).

Studies. M. BRAUBACH, *Kurköln* (Münster 1949); *Kurfürst Maximilian Franz* (Vienna 1961). H. SCHMITZ, *Colonia Claudia Ara Agrippinensium* (Cologne 1956); *Rheinische Kirchen im Wiederaufbau,* ed. W. NEUSS (München-Gladbach 1951). *Studien zur Kölner Kirchengeschichte,* ed. the Archiepiscopal historical archives (1952–), 8 v. to date. A. STELZMANN, *Illustrierte Geschichte der Stadt Köln* (Cologne 1958). *Geschichte des Erzbistums Köln* v.1 ed. W. NEUSS and F. W. OEDIGER (Cologne 1964). H. REINERS, *Die Kölner Malerschule* (München-Gladbach 1925). H. VOGTS, *Köln im Spiegel seiner Kunst* (Cologne 1950). A. VERBEEK, *Kölner Kirchen* (Cologne 1959). H. SCHNITZLER, *Rheinische Schatzkammer,* 2 v. (Düsseldorf 1957–59). H. RODE, *Kunstführer Köln* (2d ed. Cologne 1963). R. HAASS et al., Lex ThK[2] 6:383–396. A. FRANZEN, DHGE 13:275–311. AnnPont (1965) 218–219. W. LIPGENS, *Ferdinand August Graf Spiegel und das Verhältnis von Kirche und Staat 1789–1835,* 2 v. (Münster 1965). **Illustration credits:** Fig. 1, Rheinisches Bildarchiv, Cologne. Fig. 2, Arthur O'Leary. Fig. 3, Courtesy of the architect.

[R. LILL]

COLOGNE, MIXED MARRIAGE DISPUTE IN

The Cologne dispute, which found its external climax in the arrest of Abp. Clemens von *Droste zu Vischering of Cologne (Nov. 20, 1837), was the first great controversy over the liberation of the Catholic Church in Germany from state tutelage. Its immediate occasion was the mixed marriage question and the teaching of Georg *Hermes, professor of theology at the University of Bonn. The deeper causes were the opposition between the ecclesiastical policy of Prussia, which since the secularization of the Catholic Church in Germany and the end of the Holy Roman Empire (1806) had forced the Church into a largely dependent relationship, and the movement for Church freedom, supported principally by the lower clergy and the laity. This movement had been gaining strength since the 1820s. Prussia's policy was similar to that of the other German states.

When Prussia applied its legislation on mixed marriages to the Catholic regions in the Rhineland and Westphalia that had been acquired in 1815, great discontent resulted. In his brief of March 25, 1830, Pius VIII went to great lengths to accommodate Prussia by permitting priests to render passive assistance at mixed marriages that did not have the guarantees customarily required by the Church, but the government of Frederick William III wanted more. After giving considerable counterpledges, it induced Abp. Ferdinand von *Spiegel of Cologne to sign a secret agreement (June 19, 1834) that made solemn consecration of mixed marriages possible even in cases in which the non-Catholic party refused to allow the children to be educated as Catholics. The three suffragan bishops of Cologne gave their assent. One of them, Joseph von Hommer of Trier, recanted before his death (November 1836) and informed the Roman Curia of the arrangement. At first the Curia was content with a diplomatic protest. Many priests and laymen, however, disapproved of the complaisance of the bishops; their complaints were disseminated in the press outside Prussia.

Hermes made the first attempt to reconcile Catholic theology with German idealist philosophy, but his doctrine was condemned by Gregory XVI for its rationalist tendencies (Sept. 26, 1835). The papal decree was not fully implemented in Prussia because the government supported the Hermesian professors. When Droste became archbishop of Cologne in 1836, he at once took sharp, and in part illegal, measures against the Hermesians on the Catholic Theology Faculty at the University of Bonn. As a champion of the seminaries and an opponent of training candidates for the priesthood in universities, he wanted also to strike at the Faculty as such. When the professors turned to the state for help, the archbishop was soon in grave difficulty.

In the spring of 1837 Droste took up the mixed-marriage question, in which the government was clearly in the wrong, and demanded an exact observance of the papal brief of 1830. Neither promises nor threats could change him. Thereupon the government had him arrested on the false charge of engaging in revolutionary activities. Gregory XVI defended Droste and solemnly protested against this act of violence in his allocution of Dec. 10, 1837. The bishops of Münster and Paderborn then renounced the convention of 1834. When Abp. Martin von *Dunin of Gnesen and Posen demanded in 1838 that the Church's law concerning mixed marriage be respected, he too was arrested.

It was not so much the arrest of the rigid, unpopular Droste as the press reaction to the movement for Church freedom that stirred up the Catholics and helped them attain a common conviction on Church policy. The greatest effect was achieved by Johann von *Görres, who in his polemic masterpiece *Athanasius* (January 1838) supported Droste, demanded freedom for the Church, and denounced the police-state principles of the Prussian bureaucracy. Numerous other polemical works followed and so aroused public opinion that, for the first time in 19th-century German history, it became a significant factor in establishing government policy. Settlement of the conflict took place only under Frederick William IV (1840–61), who desired the close cooperation of the state with both the Catholic and Lutheran Churches. Dunin returned to his see. Droste was released from custody and received a personal apology from the King; but at Prussia's request the Pope assigned the administration of his archbishopric to his coadjutor, Johannes von *Geissel (September 1841). In a simultaneous agreement with Rome, the government left the handling of the mixed-marriage question to the bishops and granted other important concessions. Thus the *placet* was abolished. Bishops were permitted unrestricted communications with the pope. Selections of bishops were to be free, except that the king could strike undesirable names from the list of candidates. Also it was agreed to set up a section for Catholic affairs in the ministry of education. With this settlement there began in Prussia a period of peace in matters of ecclesiastical policy that lasted until the *Kulturkampf. After the Cologne conflict the group that supported Church freedom and close ties to Rome assumed more and more the leadership of German Catholicism.

Bibliography: G. GOYAU, *L'Allemagne religieuse: Le Catholicisme, 1800–48,* 2 v. (Paris 1905) 2:142–201. H. SCHRÖRS, *Die Kölner Wirren: Studien zu ihrer Geschichte* (Berlin 1927). H. BASTGEN, *Forschungen und Quellen zur Kirchenpolitik Gregors XVI,* 2 v. in 1 (Paderborn 1929); *Die Verhandlungen zwischen dem Berliner Hof und dem Hl. Stuhl über die konfessionell gemischten Ehen* (Paderborn 1936). J. GRISAR, "Die Allokution Gregors XVI vom 10. Dez. 1837" in *Gregorio XVI Miscellanea Commemorativa,* 2 v. (Rome 1948) 2:441–560; "Das Kölner Ereignis nach den Berichten italienischer Diplomaten," HistJB 74 (1955) 727–739. A. THOMAS, "Bischoff Hommer von Trier und seine Stellung zu Mischehenfrage," TrierThZ 58 (1949) 76–90, 358–373. F. SCHNABEL, *Deutsche Geschichte im 19. Jahrhundert,* v.4 (3d ed. Freiburg 1955) 106–164. R. LILL, *Die Beilegung der Kölner Wirren 1840–1842* (Düsseldorf 1962). E. HEGEL, LexThK[2] 6:394–395. W. LIPGENS, *Ferdinand August Graf Spiegel und das Verhältnis von Kirche und Staat 1789–1835,* 2 v. (Münster 1965).

[R. LILL]

COLOGNE, SCHOOL OF. Prior to the Council of Trent a group of Catholic theologians known as the school of Cologne developed a theory of double justice designed to bridge the gap between the reformers and the Church. A. *Pigge, J. Gropper, and G. *Seripando had much in common in their presentation of this unorthodox doctrine. Although Gasparo *Contarini came into contact with the school merely by attempting to clarify the issues raised by it, he nonetheless came under its influence.

Pigge distorted the traditional teaching on original sin and treated justification in a corresponding way by ascribing to man the vicarious justice of Christ. Gropper, putting Pigge's statements into a systematized framework, placed them before the Ratisbon Conference of 1541, convinced that the members would recognize in them a suitable basis for discussion with the Protestants. When Gropper's document was rejected, the Augustinian Seripando defended both men from accusations of heresy.

Then Seripando formulated their thought for the Council of Trent. Because he failed to distinguish concupiscence from original sin, while he admitted the intrinsic character of sanctifying grace, he yet maintained that only when God applies exteriorly to the soul the merits of Jesus can a man become truly a child of God. In his turn, Contarini spoke indiscriminately of "iustitia nobis donata et imputata," inclining subtilely toward a doctrine of double perfection by attributing the efficient causality of justification to the Holy Spirit.

Despite the sincerity of the efforts of these theologians, they missed their mark by projecting an Ockamism channeled to them through the voluntarism of Biel. The lengthy investigation of their views at Trent, however, indicates the esteem in which they were held by their peers. The Tridentine declaration that sanctifying grace is the only formal cause of man's justice put an end to the theory of double justice.

See also IMPUTATION OF JUSTICE AND MERIT; JUSTICE, DOUBLE; JUSTICE OF MEN; JUSTIFICATION; GRACE, ARTICLES ON.

Bibliography: J. RIVIÈRE, DTC 8.2:2182–84. B. HEURTEBIZE, DTC 3.2:1615–16. A. HUMBERT DTC 6.2:1880–85. É. AMANN, DTC 12.2:2094–2104. J. MERCIER, DTC 14.2:1923–40. H. RONDET, *Gratia Christi* (Paris 1948) 244–258, 261, 263. R. W. GLEASON, *Grace* (New York 1962) 94–95, 213–218.

[K. HARGROVE]

COLOGNE, UNIVERSITY OF

An autonomous institution of medieval origin, under the jurisdiction of the ministry of education, and financially maintained by the State of North Rhine-Westphalia, Germany.

When founded by Urban VI in 1388, at the instance of the town council, existing conditions were favorable to its growth: Urban's subordinates, prevented by the *Western Schism from studying in Paris, flocked to Cologne; Heidelberg professors (*magistri artium*), fleeing from the plague, offered their services to the nascent university; and lecturing on the rights of the Empire and Rome could be pursued without interference. Furthermore, the four mendicant orders—Carmelites, Dominicans, Franciscans, and Augustinians—had already established *studia generalia* in Cologne. They incorporated the *studia,* drew up a university charter, and elected a rector. The president of the University was the cathedral provost, who was represented by a vice president, one of the *magistri artium*. The head of the administration was the rector, who was elected by the professors. He was assisted by the beadle, who functioned as emissary and secretary, and by the benefactors and the board of advisers (the University's Privileges and Finances). The deans of the Faculties (Art, Theology, Law, and Medicine) were bound by their own statutes. Since the University did not have a central building, the schools were scattered throughout the city, the students living in *collegia* (student hostels), according to the *leges collegii,* under the direction of a regent and a vice regent. After enrollment, the advancement of the students (as well as that of the mendicants whose goal was the doctoral degree) was regulated by statutes modeled after those in use at the University of *Paris.

To provide endowments for professors, various popes, notably Boniface IX (1394), Eugene IV (after 1430), and Paul IV (1559), set aside numerous church benefices and grants, some of which imposed the obligation to teach. Grants were also made available for students in financial need. By 1540 the University of Cologne, from which originated foundations at Louvain, Belgium (1526); Trier (1453) and Mainz (1476), Germany; and Copenhagen, Denmark (1479), ranked third in enrollment among German universities.

The institution's intellectual impact was evident in the large enrollment of foreign students, its copious writings, and the stand taken in the critical issues of the times. The University was represented at the Councils of *Basel and *Constance and was involved in the controversy regarding the authority of council and pope. It sided with those in favor of reform, although otherwise maintaining a neutral position (with the exception of the Franciscan, Heinrich of Werl, who upheld papal primacy); and opposed the *via moderna* of *William of Ockham, thereby consciously defending the *via antiqua* in the spirit of the great scholastics. In the Reformation and Counter Reformation, as well as during the "Age of Enlightenment," the University was a stronghold of the Catholic faith. However, Cologne's position was opposed and greatly weakened by the foundation of an Academy at Bonn in 1771 and the subsequent establishment of the University of Bonn in 1786. Unable to withstand its vigorous rival, the University of Cologne gradually lost ground and was finally suppressed under the French occupation in 1798.

In 1919, however, Konrad Adenauer and the citizens of Cologne succeeded in reestablishing the University, which consists of five Faculties: Economics and Social Science; Law; Medicine (including dentistry); Philosophy (including liberal arts, education, and musicology); and Mathematics and Natural Sciences, and the Institute of Physical Education, in addition to about 120 institutes, seminars, and clinics attached to the various Faculties. The University grants master's and doctoral degrees.

The University is governed by a board of trustees and the senate. In 1964 the faculty numbered 338 full-time and 124 part-time professors holding higher degrees. Enrollments totaled 14,824 students, of whom 1,137 were foreigners. The library housed 971,457 volumes.

Bibliography: H. RASHDALL, *The Universities of Europe in the Middle Ages,* ed. F. M. POWICKE and A. B. EMDEN, 3 v. (new ed. Oxford 1936). S. D'IRSAY, *Histoire des universités françaises* *et étrangères des origines à nos jours,* 2 v. (Paris 1933–35). S. CLASEN, "Walram von Siegburg, O.F.M. und seine Doktorpromotion an der Kölner Universität (1430–1435)," ArchFrancHist 44 (1951) 257–317; 45 (1952) 72–126, 323–396. G. M. LÖHR, *Die theologischen Disputationem und Promotionen an der Universität Köln im ausgehenden 15. Jahrhunderts* (Leipzig 1926).

[S. CLASEN]

COLOMAN, ST., Irish pilgrim; b. Ireland, late 10th century; d. Stockerau, near Vienna, Austria, July 17, 1012 (feast, Oct. 13). He may have been the son of Maolsheachlainn II, High-King of *Ireland (980–1002 and 1014–22). While traveling secretly as a pilgrim to the Holy Land, he was arrested as a spy on July 16, 1012, and after being tortured was hanged on the following day. Subsequently, many miracles were reported where his body had been buried and on Oct. 13, 1014, Margrave Henry I had it transferred to *Melk, where he now rests in the Benedictine abbey church. Throughout Austria, Hungary, and southern Germany scores of churches are dedicated to him, and he is invoked as protector of farm animals and patron of marriageable girls. Several villages in Austria and Germany also bear his name. Iconographically he is shown with pilgrim staff and a rope or withe about his neck. He is one of the patrons of Austria, but was superseded as national patron by St. *Leopold III in 1663.

Bibliography: Sources. ActSS Oct. 6:357–362; Suppl., 13 Oct.:149–152. MGS 4:674–681. Literature. J. URWALEK, *Der königliche Pilger St. Colomann* (Vienna 1880). BHL 1:1881–82. C. JUHAIZ, *S. Koloman der einstige Schutzpatron Niederösterreichs* (Linz 1916). L. GOUGAUD, *Les Saints irlandais hors d'Irlande* (Louvain 1936) 47–50. F. O. BRIAIN, DHGE 13:256–257. I. HÖSL, LexThK² 3:7–8.

[T. Ó FIAICH]

COLOMBIA

The present Republic of Colombia has had various names. During the colonial period, it was called the New Kingdom of Granada. In the Congress of Angostura (1819) it received the name of Colombia, and included Venezuela and Ecuador. When Gran Colombia was dissolved in 1831, the state took the name of New Granada until 1858, when it became Confederación Granadina. From 1863 to 1886, it was the United States of Colombia, and from then on, simply Colombia. It has coastlines on the two oceans and its land borders Venezuela and Brazil on the east, Ecuador and Peru on the south, and Panama on the northwest. It has an area of 439,829 square miles and, in 1964, had a population of approximately 17 million; in area it is the third largest country in South America. The capital is Bogotá, which has more than 1,500,000 inhabitants.

Colombia is exceptionally rich in minerals: gold, of which the republic is the largest producer in South America; silver; platinum, in the production of which Colombia stands fifth in the world; emeralds, of which it has practically a world monopoly. There are huge deposits of rock salt and of coal. Deposits of hydrocarbons are very rich. Iron deposits abound (Paz de Río), and there are appreciable copper reserves. The variety of climates favors the cultivation of many agricultural products: coffee, which is one of the bases of national economy; bananas; tobacco; cotton; sugar cane; and other products. Cattleraising improved in quality and quantity in mid-20th century. Since the 1920s industrial production has both increased and improved.

Although the opinions of ethnologists do not agree, the racial groups of Colombia are divided approximately as follows; natives, 2 per cent; Negroes, 4 per cent; mulattoes and zambos, 22 per cent; mestizos, 46 per cent; and whites, 26 per cent. The most important European stock has been the Spanish throughout the country's history.

Early Christianization. The Catholic Church penetrated into the New Kingdom of Granada with the first discoveries. Missionary work began with reducing natives to community life in planned settlements. The missionary was concerned with stimulating new industries, perfecting existing ones, opening roads for commerce, importing tools, and bringing in trained craftsmen who would teach new trades to the Indians. He erected the church in which the neophytes congregated morning and afternoon; he built the hospital and school in which they received the rudiments of reading, writing, arithmetic, chant, and above all Christian doctrine. (*See* MISSIONS IN COLONIAL AMERICA, I.) A duty of the Church from the earliest times was the defense of the natives, who were many times mistreated and exploited without mercy by encomenderos without conscience.

This enormous apostolic burden was carried with special dedication by the religious orders and by the secular clergy. Franciscans, Dominicans, Augustinians, Jesuits, and Capuchins carried the faith to the most remote parts of the country.

In the middle of the 17th century there was already an exuberant religious life: a metropolitan seat with three suffragan dioceses, numerous parishes and doctrines, appropriate canonical legislation emanating from synods and provincial councils, a numerous clergy in convents and seminaries. Idolatry was almost completely uprooted, and thousands of natives were converted and instructed in the Catholic faith.

Among the most important missionary figures of colonial times were St. Louis *Bertrand and St. Peter *Claver, the apostle of the Negroes; the Augustinian Francisco Romero, author of *Llanto Sagrado* (1693); the Jesuits Alonso de Sandoval (1576–1652), José Gumilla (1686–1750), and Juan Ribero (1681–1736).

Diocesan Organization. During the 16th century, the first dioceses in the territory of present-day Colombia were erected: Santa Marta, Jan. 10, 1534; Cartagena, April 24, 1534; Popayán, Sept. 1, 1546; and Santafé de Bogotá, March 22, 1564. The first bishop of Santa Marta chosen by the King of Spain was Alonso de Tobes, of the Colegio de San Bartolomé in Salamanca. When his appointment was confirmed in Rome, he had been dead for more than 2 weeks, so it was Dominican Tomás Toro who held the seat of Cartagena for the first time (1534–36). Juan del Valle, a great defender of the Indians, was the first bishop of Popayán. The Franciscan Juan de los Barrios was bishop of Santa Marta and first archbishop of Santafé de Bogotá. Among the archbishops who directed the metropolitan see in colonial times were: Juan de los Barrios, who called the first synod (1556) and founded the first hospital (1564); Luis *Zapata de Cárdenas; Bartolomé Lobo Guerrero (1599–1608), who founded the Colegio Seminario de San Bartolomé in 1605, which later, after many vicissitudes, became the present Seminario Conciliar of San José; Hernando Arias de Ugarte, born in Santafé de Bogotá, who governed the archdiocese from 1619 to 1624, then was transferred to the metropolitan See of

Prefecture Apostolic of San Andrés and Providencia Islands
82°
81°
13°
San Andrés y Providencia
4: 5800
12°
10°
75°
70°
Riohacha
8: 68,632
Santa Marta
25: 390,000
Barranquilla
39: 585,000
CARTAGENA
51: 668,000
Valledupar
15: 177,818
PANAMA
VENEZUELA
Montería
24: 360,000
San Jorge
22: 215,000
Bertrania
4: 25,000
Prelacy Nullius
Ocaña
27: 248,000
Cúcuta
21: 243,000
Barranca Bermeja
21: 214,000
NUEVA PAMPLONA
24: 133,909
Bucaramanga
46: 404,120
Arauca
8:
Santa Rosa de Osos
72: 346,706
Antioquia
20: 210,500
Socorro y San Gil
56: 364,569
MEDELLÍN
128: 1,000,000
Quibdó
8: 67,000
Sonsón
27: 345,000
Duitama
42: 382,000
Casanare
10: 51,000
Vichada
3: 1,830
Jericó
28: 305,000
MANIZALES
51: 699,000
Zipaquirá
40: 289,351
Tunja
84: 538,924
Pereira
44: 500,000
Istmina
13: 27,950
Facatativá
32: 292,000
Armenia
16: 345,000
BOGOTÁ
118: 1,480,000
Cartago
30: 370,000
Girardot
42: 357,000
Ibagué
45: 500,000
Espinal
26: 312,000
Villavicencio
21: 235,000
Buenaventura
5: 84,000
Cali
55: 894,891
Palmira
36: 440,000
Tierradentro
3: 39,350
Guapi
4: 49,800
POPAYÁN
64: 475,000
Garzón
49: 375,000
Tumaco
10: 169,500
Florencia
4: 89,500
Pasto
62: 483,047
Sibundoy
11: 52,124
Mitú
8: 4,500
EQUATOR
BRAZIL
ECUADOR
PERU
Leticia
3: 14,000
0
100
200
Miles
Ecclesiastical Colombia, 1964
1,609 Parishes: 15,928,821 Catholics
Archbishopric
Ecclesiastical Provinces
Bishopric
Diocesan Borders
Vicariate Apostolic
Prefecture Apostolic

Fig. 1. The ecclesiastical divisions of the Republic of Colombia in 1964.

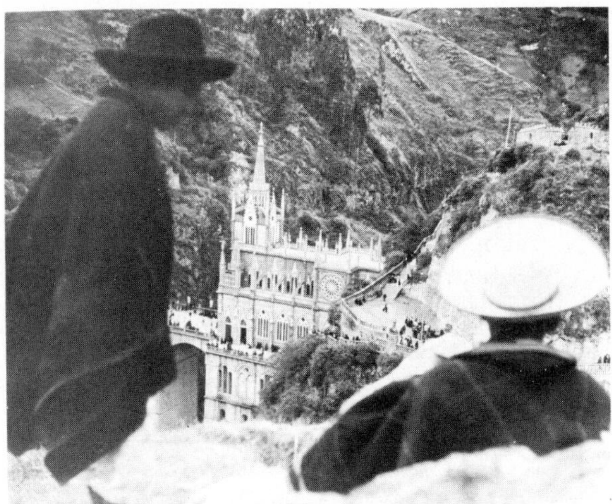

Fig. 2. The Santuario de las Lajas, built in a gorge of the mountains near Pasto, Colombia.

Charcas, and who convoked the first provincial council in 1625; and the Dominican Cristóbal de Torres (1635–54), who founded in 1653 the Colegio Mayor de Nuestra Señora del Rosario, which still exists. Among the bishops of Cartagena was Dionisio de *Sanctis (1574–78), author of the first Indian catechism. In the Diocese of Popayán, at the side of the first bishop, Juan del Valle, one of the most interesting figures among the prelates of his time, was the Augustinian Agustín de la Coruña, a man of great virtue and saintliness.

Obstacles to the Spread of Christianity. Many obstacles were encountered in the propagation of the faith in Colombia. The doctrine itself, although it satisfies the aspirations of human nature, is nevertheless too elevated above human reason to be understood by all, and so very difficult for those simple minds for which any truth of an elevated nature becomes an incomprehensible mystery. Christian morality conflicted with Indian customs, vices, and excesses. Further, the preaching of the gospel among the natives found serious resistance among the caciques and witch doctors on the one hand and, on the other, among the Spaniards, who with their cruelties and mistreatments contradicted the doctrine they claimed to profess. There were rivalries among the religious orders prejudicial to the preaching of the gospel and interference of civil authorities in purely ecclesiastical matters because of the ecclesiastical patronage.

Great difficulty was presented by the linguistic diversity among the Indians. When the missionary succeeded in mastering one language with much effort, he saw, unhappily, that it served for communication with only a small number of natives. The missionary had the backing of the Crown for his penetration into the area, but he used, above all, purely spiritual arms: the preaching of doctrine and good example. Some have insisted that the Christian religion propagated itself in America by force of arms. Nothing is more contrary to the facts. Synods and councils stressed the necessity of freedom in receiving Baptism. Thus in the New Kingdom certain tribes refused to receive the doctrine at first and only later became Christians.

Religious Orders. The first attempts at Franciscan evangelization date from 1508; they were established formally in 1550 with the erection of the Custody of San Juan Bautista. The first Dominicans arrived in 1529; they founded a convent in Cartagena in 1549 and one the following year in Santafé. The Mercedarians established a convent in Cali in 1537. The Augustinian Hermits erected a convent in Santafé in 1575 and in 1597 organized the province of Nuestra Señora de la Gracia. The Jesuits came with Archbishop Lobo Guerrero. They opened schools in Cartagena in 1603 and in Santafé the following year. In 1605 they took charge of the seminary founded by the archbishop. The Jesuit province was erected in 1610. At the end of the 16th century the Hospitallers of St. John of God erected their first house, and at the beginning of the 17th century the Augustinian Recollects arrived. The religious or various orders were dedicated above all to missionary work. The first religious were Europeans, largely Spaniards, but gradually Creoles and even natives entered the orders. In 1960 there were more than 35 religious communities of men in the country, with 514 houses, 1,755 priests, and 1,771 lay brothers.

The first convent of nuns in Colombia, Santa Clara, was founded in 1573; the Franciscan Conceptionists arrived in 1583; the Discalced Carmelites in 1606; the Order of Santa Inés de Montepulciano in 1645; the Recollect Tertiaries of St. Augustine in 1739; and the Order of the Company of Our Lady (La Enseñanza) in 1783. The religious of La Enseñanza established the first school for women in New Granada. Others dedicated themselves to the contemplative life. They found vocations among the daughters of Spaniards and among Creoles and Indians. In the 1960s there were more than 90 female religious communities with 14,000 nuns who worked in all areas of the apostolate. (*See* RELIGIOUS ORDERS OF WOMEN IN COLONIAL SPANISH AMERICA.)

Composition of the Clergy. The bishops of colonial times were mainly Spaniards; a few were Creoles; and none were Indians. The whites were freely admitted to the priesthood and to the religious life, as were some mestizos. Indians were admitted in the religious houses as lay brothers, and the Indian women were admitted into the female communities. Archbishop Zapata de Cárdenas ordained the first natives in Santafé.

When Bishop Barrios arrived in Santafé (1553), he found far too few clergy to minister effectively to the extensive diocese. He asked Spain for help, but at his death there were still no more than 50 religious and 20 members of the secular clergy, almost all Spaniards. In 1563 the Dominican fathers established a professorship of Latin in the convent of Santafé, where a few Creoles prepared for the priesthood. Archbishop Barrios ordained the first Creole and the first mestizo of New Granada. In 1573 Zapata de Cárdenas encountered a serious shortage of clergy even though the Dominicans already had a chair of art and theology. Conferring orders on the Saturdays of the four ember days, Zapata ordained a number of Creoles and mestizos over the protests of local authorities, priests, and the regular clergy. He also founded, in 1582, the first seminary of Santafé, one of the first in America, San Luis de Tolosa. This seminary was of short duration but of great importance in the ecclesiastical history of the country. From the 20 priests that Zapata had on his arrival at Santafé, the number increased to 93 during his 10 years of administration.

Fig. 3. View of the city of Cartagena, Colombia, from the tower of the church of St. Peter Claver.

There are no statistics on the number of priests in each century of Spanish domination. It can be supposed, with reason, that the number increased in time until the needs of the huge territory of New Granada were met. A help in this was the opening of the Colegio Seminario de San Bartolomé in 1605. In the 17th century, a seminary in Popayán was opened and in the following century, those in Cartagena and Santa María. In 1964 there was a shortage of clergy, the various causes of which were being carefully studied in order to arrive at a solution to this common problem in Latin America.

Charitable Institutions. From the 16th century on the Church had founded hospitals and asylums. To the first archbishop of Santafé, Juan de los Barrios, the city owes its first hospital, which began operation in 1564 in his house. After a century of service it was entrusted to the Hospitallers of St. John of God. It is known today as the Hortúa.

In the instructions written by Archbishop Zapata de Cárdenas in 1576 for the use of the clergy, he stated that the clergy should establish in the Indian towns a house for the sick close to the church, where natives could be attended in their illnesses. For the maintenance of the hospitals, farms were to be worked and the profits used to support the ill and the nurses. The Indians were to contribute chickens or other birds. Two Indian nurses were to be provided to prepare the food and care for the patients. Homes for the aged, widows, and orphans were also to be founded. Rodrigo Enríquez de Andrade, the physician of Archbishop Torres, established the first chair of medicine in the Colegio Seminario de San Bartolomé (1636). The Hospitallers practiced medicine, some under the title of "protomédicos." In 1802 Miguel de Isla founded a chair of medicine in the Colegio del Rosario (1802). The Jesuits established the first pharmacy in Santafé. The clergy and the religious gave great service during epidemics and public calamities.

Education. Educational institutions of colonial times were intimately tied to the Church. The *doctrineros* in their chapels and the friars in their convents furthered cultural advancement. In the hands of the Church rested the educational mission, supported by the throne. Seminaries, convents, and universities were run by the Church. The Colegio Seminario de San Bartolomé and the Colegio Mayor de Nuestra Señora del Rosario were founded by two archbishops of Santafé. The Colegio de la Enseñanza (1783) was founded for the education of women. In these educational centers, instruction was given mainly to the children of Spaniards, but also to Creoles and even to Indians. The Botanical Expedition founded by the archbishop-viceroy Antonio *Caballero y Góngora in 1783 had as director the learned priest José Celestino *Mutis and had the technical assistance of various priests.

The first press was introduced in the country by the Jesuits and printed mainly catechisms and small books of devotion. The first-known printed item was dated 1738. Culture revolved around the schools, seminaries, and universities, where groups of writers were formed who gave glory to the Church in colonial times. Priests and religious wrote the first chronicles of conquest and colonization, cultivated the sacred science, became outstanding in the humanities, and were poets, dramatists, and noted orators.

The Church in the 19th and 20th Centuries. For the role of the Church in the independence movement, *see* LATIN AMERICA, CHURCH AND INDEPENDENCE IN. After independence, the state believed itself to be heir to patronage (law of 1824), but this was never acknowledged by the Holy See. At first the government tried to establish diplomatic relations with the Holy See, but in 1853 the separation of Church and State was sanctioned and the persecution of the Church began. In 1887 and 1892 the concordats prevailing today were negotiated. The president of the republic can intervene in two ways in the appointment of bishops: in

Fig. 4. Entrance to a subterranean church carved from a mountain of rock salt at Zipaquirá, Colombia.

recommending candidates to the Holy See or in vetoing for civil or political reasons those chosen for appointments.

During the colonial period the Church acquired great wealth from legacies, foundations, and chaplaincies, which it used for religious services and the support of convents. In the 19th century the properties were confiscated by the state and passed into the hands of individuals. Today the Church has no wealth. In compensation for the confiscated properties, the state appropriates an annual sum for the Church.

In Colombia the most famous center of pilgrimage is the sanctuary of Nuestra Señora de Chiquinquira, where a statue of Our Lady, miraculously renovated in the 16th century, is venerated. All social classes participate in this devotion, which attracts people from neighboring countries as well.

The Catholic Church, in addition to being the dominant religion, is influential in cultural and social areas in Colombia. In 1964 it had a vigorous hierarchy with 8 archdioceses, 26 dioceses, 10 apostolic vicariates, and 7 prefectures apostolic.

Bibliography: J. M. GROOT, *Historia eclesiástica y civil de la Nueva Granada,* 5 v. (2d ed. Bogotá 1889–93). M. G. ROMERO, *Fray Juan de los Barrios y la evangelización del Nuevo Reino de Granada* (Bogotá 1960). A. LEE LOPEZ, "Clero indígena en el arzobispado de Santa Fé en el siglo XVI," *Boletín de historia y antigüedades* 50 (1963) 1–86. J. A. SALAZAR, *Los estudios eclesiásticos superiores en el Nuevo Reino de Granada, 1563–1810* (Madrid 1946). **Illustration credits:** Figs. 2 and 4, Pan American Union, Washington, D.C.

[M. G. ROMERO]

COLOMBO, MATTEO REALDO, anatomist; b. Cremona, Italy, early 16th century; d. Rome, 1559. He followed his father in the study of pharmacy, but his interest soon turned to medicine. *Vesalius was his teacher and his friend. In 1544 he succeeded Vesalius as teacher of anatomy at the University of Padua. About a year later he was at the University of Pisa when Pope Paul IV summoned him to Rome where he remained the rest of his life. His outstanding work, "Dell' Anatomia," (*De re anatomica libri XV*) was published at Venice in the year of his death, decorated with a frontispiece by Veronese. This work places him among those who made significant contributions to the discovery of the circulation of the blood. Colombo erroneously assigned to the liver the most important function in the circulation of the blood and to the veins that of carrying the nutritious blood through the body, according to the idea of the ancients. Nevertheless he indicated in his work the fundamental mechanism of the heart's action, that of the cardiac valves and of pulmonary circulation.

Bibliography: *Dizionario letterario Bompiani degli autori,* 3 v. (Milan 1956).

[G. ABETTI]

COLOMBO IN CEYLON, ARCHDIOCESE OF (COLUMBENSIS IN CEYLON), metropolitan see since 1886, on the west coast of the island of *Ceylon, of which Colombo is the capital. In 1963 the see had 80 parishes, 75 native secular priests, 126 religious priests (mostly Oblates of Mary Immaculate, who have care of the see), and 395,000 Catholics in a population of 2,232,000; it is 1,540 square miles in area. Its five suffragans, which had 137 parishes, 303 priests, 1,053 sisters, and 357,000 Catholics in a population of 6 million, were: Chilaw (created in 1939), Galle (1893), Jaffna (1886), Kandy (1886), and Trincomalee (1893).

Missions flourished in Colombo, first evangelized by Portuguese Franciscans in 1517, from the time of St. Francis *Xavier to the Dutch conquest *c.* 1650. The English succeeded the Dutch in 1796 and brought religious liberty. Part of the See of *Goa (1534) and of Cochin (1558), Ceylon became a vicariate with its seat in Colombo (1834). In 1845 the vicariate was divided between Colombo and Jaffna. In 1883 Kandy was detached from Colombo, which, exempt of Goa in 1884, became an archbishopric with the establishment of the Indian hierarchy (1886). In 1939 Chilaw was detached from Colombo. Bishop Bonjean (1883–93), who built the seminary in 1883, gave a vigorous impulse to Catholic life, directing missionaries, furthering the formation of a native clergy, and building schools. The decision of the Synod of Colombo (1887) to emphasize the apostolate among Buddhists (70 per cent of the population) produced few results. In 1960 there were 301 Catholic schools (English and Sinhalese or Tamil) and a university college. As a result of a Buddhist campaign beginning in 1956, 277 of the 301 Catholic schools were nationalized and non-Ceylonese nuns had to leave the hospitals in 1961.

Bibliography: *Catholic Directory of Ceylon* (last complete issue 1958). MissCattol 252–257. AnnPont (1964) 116.

[R. BOUDENS]

COLONIALISM

The term ordinarily used to denote both a situation in which one political entity exercises direct political control over part of the world not contiguous to it, and any movement or set of ideas designed to bring about or to justify such a relationship. Domination of overseas areas without the acquisition of *de facto* sovereignty over them or the expansion of a nation's political system over contiguous areas (although sometimes referred to as colonialism) are relationships best considered as variants of *imperialism.

The historical prototype from which the phenomenon of colonialism gets its name is the practice of the Greek city states of sending excess population abroad to areas where new city states composed of Greek inhabitants were established, largely independent of the mother city. Modern colonialism differs fundamentally from its Greek prototype; it is an aspect of the expansion of European civilization and political power over the whole world that began in the 15th century and has since assumed a variety of forms.

Types. Modern colonies can be divided into three types: (1) the settlements of Europeans in overseas areas where, demographically, they overwhelmed the indigenous inhabitants (e.g., the U.S., Canada, Australia, New Zealand, and most of Latin America); (2) areas politically controlled by Europeans but primarily inhabited by indigenous populations, in which Europeans were always a small, essentially transient minority devoted primarily to political and economic administration and religious work (e.g., India, Indonesia, Indo-China, and most of Africa); and (3) areas where a minority of Europeans not only exercised political control over an indigenous majority but settled permanently among them in substantial numbers (e.g., Algeria,

Kenya, Southern Rhodesia, the Republic of South Africa, and Angola).

History. Motivations for colonialism have varied with the particular colonial powers involved and the periods in history in which the colonization took place. Originally the motivation was largely economic, springing from the desire—especially strong in the Iberian powers—to find new sources of the precious metals that the prevailing *mercantilism made the basis of economic strength, the desire to acquire trading stations, and the desire for plantations that could produce certain kinds of agricultural products without the loss of foreign exchange (another desideratum of mercantilism). This latter motivation was especially strong among the English. Closely linked with economic motives were religious ones; zeal for spreading the true faith among the heathens was especially important among the Catholic powers. *See* MISSIONS, HISTORY OF (GENERAL). British expansion in Africa during the 19th century was occasioned largely by the humanitarian motive of suppressing the slave trade.

At this time, too, considerations of political power loomed larger as a motive for acquiring colonies. Colonies were areas in which surplus populations loyal to the mother nation could allegedly flourish, forming a manpower reserve; colonies were a source of national prestige (a strong motivation for the new states of Germany and Italy); they were important elements in international strategic planning, and colonial expansion played a part in maintaining the delicate European balance of power. Also, according to the English economist J. A. Hobson, expanding *capitalism needed new sources of raw materials, new markets, and new areas for investments, preferably under the political control of the capitalist power itself. Finally, in the late 19th century the missionary impetus, which continued to be an important factor, was supplemented by a secularized version that held modern industrial civilization to be so inherently superior to any other that the West had an obligation to dominate, and where possible to populate, the rest of the world and to work for the cultural assimilation of nonwhite races. The British poet Rudyard Kipling wrote of the civilizing of the allegedly backward races as a "white man's burden" to be carried throughout the world, and leading social Darwinists and their political epigoni, such as Cecil Rhodes and Theodore Roosevelt, held it essential that the Teutonic races should dominate the earth and find additional living space upon it.

Movements Toward Independence. Colonialism of the type in which the European settlers—arriving in temperate and thinly inhabited lands—soon controlled the lands and became a majority of the population, presented few moral or political problems. Theologians such as Bartolomé de *Las Casas insisted that the Indians of the New World were true human beings with corresponding rights; thus, although they were oppressed to the point of extinction in some areas under Iberian domination, they were never hunted for sport as were the Bushmen of Australia. No one contested the right of the technologically advanced and incidentally Christian nations to dispossess and rule the native inhabitants, and—save in a few places in Latin America—the indigenous inhabitants never had the demographic strength to reassert themselves politically. Therefore, in these areas, the struggle against rule by the colonizing power was carried on by the white settler communities. The U.S. won its independence from Britain as a result of a revolution in the 18th century; Latin America won its freedom from Spain and Portugal during the 19th. Areas of English settlement overseas, such as Canada, Australia, New Zealand, and South Africa, gradually attained sovereign status in the late 19th and early 20th centuries.

Extension of Control over Indigenous Majorities. While the areas inhabited predominantly by white descendants of European settlers were winning their independence, partly on the ground that their European racial and cultural backgrounds entitled them to it, the second type of colonialism, involving white political control over indigenous majorities, was being extended, along with its variant in which large numbers of Europeans settled on the land alongside the indigenous peoples. Each colonial power had differing and mixed motivations in seeking control of such areas, and each therefore developed different forms of political domination.

British Policies. British motivations were primarily economic and focused on the short run, with strong emphasis on free trade and *laissez faire*. The British preferred to rule whenever possible through local indigenous political agents (especially in parts of Africa), largely because it was cheaper. In most British colonies and protectorates missionaries (mainly Protestant) were encouraged to spread both religion and education, but despite such policies as Macaulay's, which made English the language of the educated in India, the British never seriously sought to assimilate non-European inhabitants culturally. Where European settler communities were important, they were allowed a limited amount of self-government on a gradually increasing basis as exigencies demanded. It was assumed by the British—as by all colonial powers save the Americans—that the colonial relationship would continue into the indefinite future, so that no attempt was made to prepare the indigenous inhabitants for any political participation beyond limited local self-government.

French Policies. Convinced that their civilization represented the quintessence of human culture and that it was accessible to all human beings given proper tutelage, the French invested large amounts of money in their colonies in the attempt—in many cases successful—to create African and Asian Frenchmen. Colonial rule in the French empire was more rationalized, more centralized, and more direct than in the British. The status of the missions in French colonies varied depending on the degree of anticlericalism of the government in power at home, although generally colonial administrators were less anticlerical than their metropolitan superiors. The government's desire for Gallicanization of the native inhabitants gave an advantage to Catholic missions, which were more capable of preaching and teaching in French than were the Protestant.

Policies of other European Powers. Belgian colonialism in the Congo sought to build up the region economically while repressing it politically, to create a black petty bourgeoisie prior to some far distant day when limited political rights might be given the inhabitants. The Catholic missions, which enjoyed a favored status, were partners in this enterprise. Portuguese overseas territories, on the other hand, became in theory integral parts of Portugal. Although hindered partly by limited economic resources, attempts were made to assimilate the local inhabitants culturally and Catholic missions played a large role in these attempts. The overwhelming majority of native inhabitants, however, were not citizens but subjects with a lower legal status. Dutch colonialism—concentrated in the East Indies—sought to maintain political control for economic reasons. No serious large scale attempt was made to Westernize local cultures, and missionary activity was not generally encouraged.

U.S. Policy. The colonial policy of the U.S. was largely *ad hoc.* Attempts to modernize the Philippines and Puerto Rico, formerly controlled by Spain, led to clashes with locally dominant Catholic elements. Other American colonial possessions (the term is for various reasons not accepted in American terminology) either have been incorporated in the U.S. or are extremely small and of little intrinsic importance. The Philippines was given its independence following World War II. Puerto Rico has a constitutionally anomalous status as an "associated commonwealth."

Ethical Problems. Observers differ as to the ethical merits of colonialism. In areas where the colonized are a majority but large numbers of Europeans are permanent residents, settler populations are often accused of exploiting those among whom they settle, of taking the best land, and of enjoying special privileges. Their supporters, however, argue that the economic activity they dominate is largely the result of their own presence, that their preeminence is only a recognition of the special role their capital and talents play in the society, and that their presence results in a better life for all. Since these settlers assume that the majority's resentment of them would lead to their despoliation in case of self-rule, they seek to retain political control, sometimes against the wishes of the colonial power, thus denying the moral validity of the principle of political *equality.

In the more usual case of the domination of the indigenous inhabitants by those who make no pretense of being members of a local community, supporters of colonialism hold that colonial rule has maintained law and order (including suppression of the slave trade and other inhuman practices), supplied the potential for a higher living standard through establishment of a modern economy and modern educational facilities, and offered opportunities to become acculturated to Western civilization, including Christianity. Opponents argue that there is economic exploitation under colonialism, that the destruction of indigenous cultures has been psychologically and morally demeaning, and, above all, that any rule by a person or group not of one's free choosing is an affront to human dignity.

Although not overlooking the many benefits bestowed by colonialism, Catholic thought has increasingly tended to stress the equality of the human personality that colonial rule explicitly or implicitly denies. In the encyclical *Pacem in terris* John XXIII condemned the idea that some peoples or cultures were so inherently superior to others that they had the right to rule over them (para. 88, 89, 92); he noted with approval that national independence was becoming universal (para. 42, 43).

Ethical considerations aside, the relationship of Christianity to colonialism has been, in practical terms, an equivocal one. Were it not for the colonial period, Christianity would not have spread to and become dominant in North and South America, Australia, the Philippines, and South Africa; nor would it have gained the strong foothold it presently has in India, Vietnam, and sub-Saharan Africa. Colonialism made possible the extension of Christian missionary activity to areas where otherwise it could not have been safely carried on. The prestige attaching to Christianity as the religion of the colonizers and the hunger for the education offered by the mission schools led many indigenous groups to embrace Christianity in large numbers. Now that colonialism is in retreat throughout the world, Christianity is meeting increased hostility as an alien religion imposed from without; nationalism and the reassertion of local cultures are now impeding its further spread. The Christian churches' response has been to accelerate the growth of a native clergy, to devolve ecclesiastical jurisdiction to the native clergy as soon as possible, and to allow more flexibility and creativity in fusing local cultural traditions with the Christian religion, thus reducing the artificial identity of Christianity with Western cultural forms.

Nationalism. Anticolonial *nationalism has arisen in almost every area subject to colonial rule. In part it has been spurred by the economic and educational advances made possible by colonialism and by the democratic political ideas espoused if not practiced by the colonial powers. The weakness of the colonial powers following World War II, the proclamations on behalf of freedom and self-determination by the democratic nations during the war, the spread of anticolonial sentiment within the Western nations themselves, the existence of the United Nations, and the ideological struggle with communism combined to create a climate favorable to anticolonialism. After World War II almost all the colonies of Britain, France, the Netherlands, and Belgium gained their independence, sometimes with bloodshed but usually without. All that remain are a few small colonies of doubtful economic and political viability, Portugal's African possessions and the white-dominated colony of Rhodesia.

Yet political independence did not lessen the dependence of former colonies on outside economic and military assistance. This led to Communist-encouraged claims by nationalist groups that, under the trappings of independence, "neocolonialism" enables the former colonial powers to maintain their dominance. Partly in order to prove that they were in fact independent agents, the former colonial territories usually adopted a posture of "neutralism" or "nonalignment" in world affairs, eschewing military ties with the major powers, striving to maintain economic and political relations with both Western and Communist nations, and seeking with limited success to act as a "third force" in the UN and in world affairs generally.

Although the remnants of the old colonial empires remained, the mid-20th century was an era in which the domination of the world by Europe—of which colonialism was a major expression—came to an end and in which new forms of relationship—cultural and religious as well as political and economic—were being developed in a decentralized and pluralistic world community.

Bibliography: S. C. EASTON, *The Rise and Fall of Western Colonialism* (New York 1964). R. EMERSON, *From Empire to Nation* (Cambridge, Mass. 1960). P. T. MOON, *Imperialism and*

World Politics (New York 1926). R. STRAUSZ-HUPÉ and H. W. HAZARD, eds., *The Idea of Colonialism* (New York 1958). A. G. KELLER, *Colonization* (Boston 1908). J. A. HOBSON, *Imperialism: A Study* (3d ed. London 1938). J. P. PLAMENATZ, *On Alien Rule and Self-Government* (New York 1960). D. O. MANNONI, *Prospero and Caliban* (New York 1956). R. DELAVIGNETTE, *Christianity and Colonialism* (New York 1964).

[V. C. FERKISS]

COLONNA

Powerful family of Rome from the Middle Ages to the 20th century. The history of the family from 1100 to 1562 was that of the Colonna-led Ghibelline struggle against the papacy, the Orsini, and other Guelf families. This article provides some general observations to establish a historical setting, a comparison of the Colonna and Orsini families, a description of the Ghibelline-Guelf conflict, and a history of the family after 1562.

Historical Context. When the Colonna began opposing the papacy in the 12th century, *feudalism was a major institution, with emphasis on land and family loyalty. The nobles had their own armies, made war and peace, and held court to decide the innocence or guilt of their people. Ambitious, energetic nobles sought wealth and power by acquiring more land. Another method of achieving wealth was by obtaining higher offices in the Church, and it became common practice to have younger sons become churchmen. Such appointees reflected the influences of the time. Some were inspiring religious leaders, others were interested in the new learning of the Renaissance. *Cardinals were not always ordained; they served as administrators in the *States of the Church, performing services that laymen supply today.

Powerful nobles could, and sometimes did, challenge a ruler. There was, however, an important difference in *Rome, resulting from the dual role of the *papacy during the medieval period in both spiritual and temporal affairs and the difficulty of separating the two roles. The Colonna and other Ghibelline families did not oppose the pope as a religious ruler; they objected to his temporal power or his being a sovereign in civil affairs. There had been an attempt to revive the civil competence of the Roman Senate, but in 1188 ecclesiastical jurisdiction was established over the Senate. However, in the 13th century more nobles became senators, and the Senate was no longer ecclesiastically dominated. Yet the Ghibellines could still arouse the people to revolt with the cry, "The People and Colonna." (*See* GUELFS AND GHIBELLINES.)

Colonna-Orsini. More than 100 years ago G. *Moroni pointed out (14:278; 49:146) that the Colonna family always had its own interests as well as the emperor's at heart; the *Orsini, in turn, thought of their family as well as of the papacy. Both families had property in Rome and in the countryside. Their first houses in Rome were like fortresses, guarded by their men. Both first possessed a few villages, then in the 13th century a dozen or more with one village becoming the chief family seat, e.g., Palestrina for the Colonna. Both families produced about the same number of cardinals over the years, but the Orsini possessed the greater number before 1562. In the 16th century both acquired the special honor of having the head of the family at papal functions with the title "prince in attendance at the papal throne."

The Colonna struggle for power was not one of slow even gains or of long periods of success. After a victory came defeat. Houses in Rome were destroyed or seized, villages were captured, absence from Rome was often necessary. But the Colonna returned, rebuilt, and again became influential.

Ghibelline-Guelf Conflict. From 1100 until the modern era that began in 1562 the Ghibelline-Guelf conflict passed through six periods.

From 1100 to 1200. The ancestors of the Colonna were the *Tusculani. *Pietro de Colonna* (1064–1118?) was the first member to use this name. Writers differ about the origin of the name. It may have derived from his possible home in the district of Rome near Trajan's Column or in the village of Colonna, 16 miles from Rome. Early in the 12th century he tried to capture Cave, which belonged to the papacy. In defeat he lost two villages. About 1167 the Colonna, assisted by troops belonging to *Frederick I Barbarossa, defeated the Romans near Monte Porzio. After 1168 the Orsini and *Savelli destroyed the Colonna and Conti houses in Rome. In 1191 the Romans destroyed Tuscolo. The first cardinal in the family, the Benedictine *Giovanni,* created 1192 or 1193 (d. *c.* 1214), served as legate in several countries.

From 1200 to 1288. The Colonna family was stronger in the 13th than in the 12th century, having three branches: Palestrina, Gallicano, and Gelazzano. In Rome it had fortified the mausoleum of Augustus and dominated the district near the church of the Holy Apostles. *Giovanni,* created cardinal in 1212 (d. 1244), was legate to the Holy Land during the Fifth *Crusade. He brought back a part of the column at which Christ was scourged and placed it in his titular church, St. Praxedes, where it may still be seen. Changing sides, he became a supporter of Emperor *Frederick II against the Pope. While the Holy See was vacant (1241–43), Senator Matteo Russo Orsini defeated the Colonna and captured their stronghold, the mausoleum. For more than 30 years the Colonna seemed unimportant. Then they won recognition from Pope *Nicholas III, an Orsini, who created *Giacomo* cardinal in 1278 (d. 1318) as a kind of peace offering between the two families.

From 1288 to 1298. It might be said that Pope *Nicholas IV (1288–92), who had been bishop of Palestrina, adopted the Colonna, so much did he favor them. He made *Pietro* a cardinal in 1288 (d. 1326). For the first time the family had two members in the college of cardinals. During a rebellion in 1290 the people called *Sciarra Colonna* (d. 1329) their Caesar. Alarmed at such power, Pope *Boniface VIII, a Guelf of the *Gaetani family, decided to restrict it. In the altercation that followed, family feeling bound Cardinal Giacomo to his nephews Sciarra, *Stefano* (d. after 1347), and Cardinal Pietro, rather than to the Pope. When Stefano's men seized the papal treasury as it was being brought from Anagni to Rome, Boniface insisted on its restoration and the cession of the towns of Palestrina, Colonna, and Zagarolo. The cardinals agreed about the treasury but refused to give up the property. Excommunications and war followed. With Orsini support, Palestrina was captured. The Colonna fled. Eventually they reached France. There the new Pope, *Clement V, reinstated the Colonna cardinals, and they remained in *Avignon until their deaths.

The heraldic charge of the Colonna family, a column, incorporated into the coat of arms of Pope Martin V, detail of the pope's funeral monument by Simone di Giovanni Ghini (c. 1406–91) in St. John Lateran, Rome.

Cardinal Giacomo's sister, Bl. **Margaret Colonna,* belonged to the *Poor Clares and was venerated for centuries after her death in 1290. She is representative of the religious members of her family—the monks, abbots, and bishops, who are less well known than the cardinals and the aggressive members.

From 1303 to 1417. In 1303 Sciarra returned to Rome with King *Philip IV of France's representative, *Nogaret. Their violent treatment of Boniface VIII probably hastened his death. Stefano supported Emperor *Henry VII when he went to Rome in 1312, but he then changed to the side of the papacy and opposed Emperor *Louis IV the Bavarian's coronation in Rome. Sciarra, however, supported Louis and was at his coronation in St. Peter's, 1328; Sciarra then left Rome and died in exile. Pope *John XXII rewarded Stefano by making his son *Giovanni* cardinal in 1327 (d. 1348), the only Colonna churchman created cardinal during the *Avignon papacy (1305–78). Cardinal Giovanni proved an able judge in civil cases; he was a learned man and a friend of *Petrarch. The Colonnas fought bravely against *Cola di Rienzo, several members of the family being killed. After Rienzo's death, they helped to restore order in Rome. An example of Colonna generosity was shown at the time of the *Black Death, when the Romans toiled up the Capitoline Hill to St. Mary in Aracoeli to pray for the end of the plague. Cardinal Giovanni Colonna arranged for the building of the first steps up the Capitoline Hill (1348), the only public construction in Rome between 1305 and 1378.

Among the learned Colonna was **Giles* of Rome (d. 1316), an *Augustinian who studied under Thomas Aquinas and became the general of the order in 1292. Some writers state that Boniface VIII created him a cardinal in 1302, but there was no public announcement.

Three Colonna cardinals were created during the *Western Schism: *Agapito* (d. 1380), who had served as nuncio to Emperor *Charles IV and peace envoy to Castile and Portugal, was created cardinal in 1378 along with his brother *Stefano* (d. 1379), and *Oddo,* later Pope *Martin V, became cardinal in 1405.

From 1417 to 1500. Pope Martin V (1417–31) increased the power and wealth of his family by giving it property, especially Paliano, which became the seat of an important branch. Queen Joanna II of Naples bestowed fiefs on Martin's two brothers. In 1426 Martin created his nephew *Prospero* cardinal (d. 1463), but he withheld the announcement until 1430. When Martin V died, Cardinal Prospero and his brothers tried to keep a part of the treasury, but the new Pope, *Eugene IV, made them give it up. The Colonna rebelled in 1434, forcing the Pope to leave Rome. In a second rebellion in 1437, however, the Orsini and others defeated the Colonna and destroyed Palestrina. Cardinal Prospero was excommunicated and exiled, though Pope *Nicholas V later absolved and reinstated him. Prospero's Ghibelline politics were only one of his interests; another was his appreciation of learning. During the last 3 years of the reign of Pope *Sixtus IV (1471–84), there was another Colonna-papacy conflict. The Orsini supported Girolamo *Riario, the Pope's nephew, and the Colonna opposed him. The Colonna suffered reverses and defeat: the imprisonment of *Giovanni,* who had been created cardinal in 1480 (d. 1508); the imprisonment of *Lorenzo,* during which he died or was killed; the confiscation of the Colonna palace, the loss of villages, and banishment. After the death of Pope Sixtus the Roman people rose against Riario and welcomed the return of the Colonna. The position of the family was shown when King *Charles VIII of France went to Rome on his way to Naples in 1495. *Prospero* (d. 1523) and *Fabrizio* (d. 1520) Colonna, great generals, rode in the cavalcade that received the King. Cardinal Giovanni was one of five cardinals who were admitted to his audiences.

From 1500 to 1562. In 1501 Cesare *Borgia defeated the Colonna; confiscations and exile followed. Pope *Julius II (1503–13) sought to conciliate the Colonna by restoring their palace and other possessions, marrying his niece to a Colonna, and bestowing on the head of the family the honor of being the "prince in attendance at the papal throne." Such acts did not satisfy

Pompeo Colonna (d. 1532), who had been forced to become a churchman by his family. When Julius was seriously ill in 1511, Pompeo gathered his supporters on the Capitoline to plot against the temporal power of the papacy. The Pope's recovery, however, prevented any action. Pope *Leo X created Pompeo a cardinal in 1517. The cardinal and *Ascanio Colonna* (d. 1559) displayed their position and wealth by a lavish entertainment given when Pope *Clement VII spent the night in their palace after making his official visit to St. John Lateran in 1523. Clement appointed Pompeo vice chancellor, but the cardinal continued to favor the Empire; e.g., he gave a banquet to celebrate the imperial victory over France at Pavia in 1525. To punish the Pope for making a treaty against Emperor *Charles V, the cardinal, together with *Vespasiano* and Ascanio Colonna, sacked the Vatican in 1526. The cardinal was not with the invaders in the siege of Rome, 1527. When he saw the resulting sad state of Rome, he showed compassion for the Pope and other persons, many of whom he took into his chancellery palace. In 1530 he became viceroy of Naples.

Marco Antonio II (d. 1584), Ascanio's son, fought the family's last battles against the papacy. Pope *Paul IV (1555–59) resented the control of Naples by Spain and the independence of Roman nobles. His restrictions on the nobles and their reaction led him to demand surrender of the Orsini and Colonna castles. The Orsini complied; the Colonna did not and fled to Naples. Their estates were declared forfeited and given to the Pope's eldest nephew in May 1556. In September the Duke of Alba, the Spanish general, and Marco Antonio began to march toward Rome. Their victories and nearness to Rome by July 1557 led to a negotiated peace. Spain insisted that all Colonna possessions be restored. All were returned except Paliano, which was not ceded until 1562. The year 1562 marked the end of the long Colonna-papacy struggle, which dated back to 1100. The decline of feudalism, the weakening of the imperial idea with the rise of the national states, and the preoccupation of the new states in other affairs—hence the lack of support for the Ghibellines in Italy—all made the old struggle meaningless.

Modern Era. In 1562 a new period began for the Colonna. Less than 13 years after Marco Antonio's march against the papacy, Pope *Pius V asked him (1570) to command the papal fleet in the war against the Turks. He immediately set to work to prepare the galleys. When the Pope made an alliance with Venice and Spain, Don Juan became the general of the expedition and Marco Antonio lieutenant. The latter's part in the Battle of *Lepanto (1571) made him a hero, and, against his wishes, he was awarded a triumphal march in Rome.

The large number of Colonna cardinals after 1562 indicates the high favor the family enjoyed with the papacy after that time: during 462 years of enmity (1100–1562) there had been 11 Colonna cardinals; in only 241 years of good relations (1562–1803, the death of the last cardinal) there were 12 Colonna cardinals, and there were often two of them sitting at the same time in the college of cardinals. The 16th- and 17th-century Colonna cardinals were: (1) *Marco Antonio IV,* cardinal 1565 (d. 1597), the nephew of Marco Antonio of Lepanto fame, an excellent administrator as archbishop of Taranto and Salerno, who attended the Council of *Trent, was appointed head of the Commission on the Vulgate, and became librarian at the Vatican; (2) *Ascanio,* cardinal 1586 (d. 1608), son of Marco Antonio of Lepanto, who won esteem because of his character and knowledge and served as viceroy of Catalonia; (3) *Girolamo,* cardinal 1628 (d. 1666), an excellent administrator of the Diocese of Bologna, who represented the King of Spain in Rome and spent his last years in Spain; and (4) *Federico Baldeschi,* cardinal 1673 (d. 1691), who was adopted by the Colonna family in order to have a cardinal. During the 18th century, Colonna cardinals were: (5) *Carlo,* cardinal 1706 (d. 1739); (6) *Prospero,* cardinal 1739 (d. 1743); (7) *Girolamo,* cardinal 1743 (d. 1763); and (8) *Prospero,* cardinal 1743 (d. 1765); (9) *Marco Antonio,* cardinal 1759 (d. 1803), the nephew of Cardinal Girolamo, who fulfilled his duties so well that he was a model for both lay and ecclesiastical princes; (10) *Antonio Branciforte,* cardinal 1766 (d. 1783), son of a Sicilian noble, nuncio to France and Venice; (11) *Pietro Pamphili,* cardinal 1766 (d. 1780), grandson of Olimpia Pamphili, brother of Cardinal Marco Antonio, nuncio to France; (12) *Niccolò Colonna di Stigliano,* cardinal 1785 (d. 1796), of Neapolitan nobility, nuncio to Spain.

After 1562 two popes, Sixtus V and Gregory XVI, confirmed the honor—shared only by the Orsini and Colonna—of being officially in attendance at papal functions. Protests came from the Savelli, the Conti, and in 1623 from the conservators, but to no avail. The honor or right has continued to be exercised into the 20th century.

In the 17th century the Colonna sold several of their properties, including Palestrina, to other Roman families. The present palace in Rome near the church of the Holy Apostles dates back to the 17th and 18th centuries, and a portion stands on the site of the palace built by Martin V in the early 15th century and of houses from a still earlier period. There is reason to believe that the family has lived in this district for 7 centuries, and perhaps longer.

See also COLONNA, VITTORIA.

Bibliography: P. LITTA et al., *Famiglie celebri italiane,* 14 v. (Milan 1819–1923) v.4. Moroni 4:61–62; 14:277–310; 55:233–243, for "Principe assistente al soglio pontificio." Pastor 1:282–328; 4:379–384; 5:229–231, 247–248, 451–455; 6:103–104; 9: 275–341, 367–461; 14:90–174; 18:369–434. P. COLONNA, *I Colonna* (Rome 1927). L. CÀLLARI, *I palazzi di Roma* (3d ed. Rome 1944). P. PASCHINI, EncCatt 4:14–21; *I Colonna* (Rome 1955). G. MOLLAT et al., DHGE 13:328–340. H. K. WEINERT and F. BOCK, LexThK² 3:8–12. **Illustration credit:** Anderson-Art Reference Bureau.

[M. L. SHAY]

COLONNA, GIOVANNI PAOLO, composer of baroque church music, cantatas, and operas; b. Bologna, Italy, June 16, 1637; d. Bologna, Nov. 28, 1695. The son of the organ-builder and organist Antonio di Stefano Colonna, he studied organ with Agostino Filipuzzi in Bologna. Later, in Rome he learned counterpoint and composition from *Carissimi, *Abbatini, and *Benevoli while serving as organist at San Apollinare. In 1659 he was named organist in the church of San Petronio, Bologna, succeeding to the post of choirmaster in 1674, and retaining it to his death. He was also a distinguished teacher, was elected president of the Accademia Filarmonica for four terms, and saw publication of 11 volumes of his music. Among his compositions there are large-scale polychoral settings of Masses and Psalms, and works for a smaller number of voices accompanied by instruments in *concertato* style. Six of his oratorios have been preserved in MS, but his four operas are lost.

Bibliography: A. LOEWENBERG, Grove DMM 2:381. R. PAOLI, MusGG 2:1565–66. There is no complete ed. of his works.

[R. STEINER]

COLONNA, VITTORIA, poet; b. Marino, near Rome, 1490; d. Rome, Feb. 27, 1547. In 1509 she married Ferrante d'Avalos, Marquis of Pescara. After his death (1525) from wounds received fighting for the Emperor at the battle of Pavia, she passionately celebrated his memory in verses that won her contemporary renown but are now less admired; they are mostly sonnets in the Petrarchan tradition of Christianized Platonism. Very devout and deeply concerned for the reform of the Church, Vittoria divided the rest of her life between religious seclusion in various convents (at Orvieto, Viterbo, and Rome) and the cultivation of friendships with people—churchmen, scholars, and artists—who shared her own spiritual aspirations. She actively supported the Franciscan Capuchin reform and, until his apostasy, was in touch with Bernadino *Ochino; she knew Cardinals Reginald *Pole and Gasparo *Contarini and various members of the circle of Juan de *Valdés. During her stay at Viterbo (1541–44), she was drawn most into contact with Pole and other Catholic reformers who were trying to continue Contarini's efforts to find a *via media* between Catholic teaching on grace and the Lutheran position (*see* JUSTICE, DOUBLE). Her purely religious poetry (the *Rime spirituali*) belongs to these later years. Her most famous friendship, however, was with *Michelangelo, who celebrated her beauty, both physical and spiritual, in many poems similar to her own in their Christian-Platonist inspiration, though far more powerful and intense. She was a minor poet, but she has an honorable place in the history of Italian spirituality.

Vittoria Colonna, reproduced from a facsimile of a chalk drawing by Michelangelo.

Bibliography: Works. V. COLONNA, *Le Rime,* ed. P. E. VISCONTI (Rome 1840); *Carteggio,* ed. E. FERRERO and G. MÜLLER, suppl. D. TORDI (2d ed. Turin 1892). L. BALDACCI, ed., *Lirici del Cinquecento* (Florence 1957). Studies. G. TOFFANIN, *Il Cinquecento* (4th ed. Milan 1950). "V. C.," *Italia francescana,* ser. 2., 22 (1947) 1–134. **Illustration credit:** Library of Congress.

[K. FOSTER]

COLOR

Variously defined as the *quality in things sensed by sight or the sense impression resulting from a variety of factors including the spectral composition of light, the reflecting and absorbing characteristics of objects, and the structure of the eye. This article considers only the physics of color and some philosophical problems associated with it; for a treatment of color from the viewpoint of psychology, *see* SENSATION.

Physics. Physicists normally speak of color in terms of the portion of the electromagnetic spectrum that is capable of affecting the human eye, viz, those wavelengths lying between 0.00007 and 0.00004 cm. *See* ELECTROMAGNETIC RADIATION; WAVES (PHYSICS). When light of a particular wavelength impinges upon the eye, it is sensed as a particular color; e.g., wavelengths at the upper end of the visible range are seen as red, those at the shorter end as violet. In an experiment performed in 1666, Isaac *Newton demonstrated that what may be referred to as white light is a mixture of electromagnetic waves of various wavelengths that can be separated by a prism. He showed that sunlight is composed of light of wavelengths distributed continuously throughout the visible range. Later studies have shown that the relative distribution of wavelengths depends on the light source. Thus the ordinary incandescent lamp provides a continuous distribution of wavelengths of varying intensity, whereas a sodium discharge lamp does not, since it emits only the discrete wavelengths associated with the spectrum of sodium (*see* ATOMIC THEORY). Newton further demonstrated that, by suitably recombining the light dispersed by one prism with another prism, white light again results. White light also is produced when the electromagnetic waves of complementary colors are superposed. Some colors can be reproduced by a suitable combination of two other colors, and all hues can be reproduced by suitably recombining the additive primaries of red, blue, and green.

The color perceived in objects results from the transmitting, reflecting, and scattering properties of their surfaces as well as from the character of the light illuminating them. No object reflects any one color totally; in fact, all bodies seem to reflect and absorb different colors in varying amounts. What is perceived as color by the eye is thus the result of a complex spectrum of transmitted, reflected, and scattered light. A transparent body that theoretically absorbs everything but green wavelengths appears green when viewed toward a source of white light or when seen by the light reflected from it. A gold object, as is well known, appears yellowish when viewed in sunlight; and yet white light, when seen through thin films of gold, appears green. Again, when illuminated only by red and green wavelengths, gold appears black since it absorbs these two wavelengths. One may thus state that, as a general principle, an object will be invisible unless it is capable of transmitting, reflecting, scattering, or absorbing light in the visible region of the spectrum.

Several other phenomena may be mentioned as affecting the color perceived in objects. Thus soap bubbles and oil films may appear colored because of multiple reflections that occur between their surfaces and produce interference effects. Some objects absorb light of one wavelength and emit light of a longer wavelength; the color thus perceived is spoken of as arising from fluorescence. The blue of the sky results from the selective scattering of the blue component of sunlight by particles in the atmosphere.

The hue and brilliance of a colored object is the result of the spectral distribution of the light received by the eye. Just as the electromagnetic waves of the primary colors may be recombined to reproduce all hues, so the primary pigments of red, yellow, and blue can be combined to produce all natural hues in the color of objects. The latter are called subtractive primaries to distinguish them from the former, or additive, primaries.

Philosophy. To simplify the treatment of their subject, most physicists refer to color as a property of light waves and thus by-pass the question that must be answered by the philosopher who advocates *realism, as opposed to *phenomenalism or *sensism, as a theory of knowledge, viz, how is color present in the objects of ordinary experience? An answer to this question may be given in terms of causal analysis of the way color is present in the surfaces of bodies, with particular reference to its efficient, material, and formal causes. (For a simpler example of causal analysis as applied to a sensible quality, *see* SOUND.)

Color is directly sensible to sight, just as sound is sensed by hearing and heat by touch. The efficient causes that render color existent and visible are twofold: one remote and the other proximate. The remote agent is electromagnetic radiation, which results from acceleration or deceleration of electric charges. The proximate active cause of color is the light source, which is usually a type of transducer within which the electrons are being accelerated or decelerated. This acceleration or deceleration might result when atoms collide with other atoms or when a free electron or other charged particle is acted upon by an electrical or magnetic field. The rays that are emitted in the process are not themselves colored, at least not in the same sense that surfaces are colored, but they have the ability to make visibly colored any surface containing this color at least virtually.

The material cause, or proper subject in which color is found, is a surface capable of selectively scattering and reflecting some particular wavelength distribution to the eye. In classical physics the capacity of a surface to absorb and reflect incident radiation is explained by the existence within the medium of electric oscillators. From the viewpoint of quantum mechanics one would say that there exists a system of energy levels, and an atomic or molecular system is raised to a higher energy level when light impinges on the surface. If radiation of the same or nearly the same frequency impinges on the surface, these oscillators absorb and reradiate it. If the density of oscillators is sufficiently high, the net result is that a large portion of the light is reradiated in the direction away from the surface. This selective radiation of light by the surface is what accounts for its color manifestation.

The formal cause of color, in line with this explanation, is the actualization of such a capacity or ability in the molecules of the body being illuminated. When this potency is actualized, the body is actually colored and is so seen by the eye. In view of the special relationship between color manifestation and the incident light illuminating a body, one cannot strictly specify the color of an object without reference to the light under which it is viewed, or the background against which it is seen. Similarly, if one questions whether colors exist in darkness or in the interiors of objects, answers can only be given in terms of the distinctions just indicated between the formal and material cause of color. Thus, colors do not formally exist in darkness or in the interior of bodies, because there they lack the light by which they become actually visible. They are present materially, however, when the structure of matter is such that it is capable of reflecting to the eye rays in the visible portion of the spectrum, should the object be illuminated by a proper light source.

From this analysis, it may be seen that there need be no conflict between the views of color proposed by physicists and those proposed by philosophers. The problems that commonly arise are mainly terminological, as when a physicist so defines color as to exclude the possibility of its existing in objects or when a philosopher speaks of color as an invariant property of objects without mentioning the many factors that affect what may actually be seen by the eye. When both concentrate on the objective correlate of what is subjectively sensed as color, however, their realism finds common ground and they are in substantial agreement as to the way in which objects may be said to be colored.

See also SENSE KNOWLEDGE; SENSIBLES.

Bibliography: D. B. JUDD, *Color in Business, Science, and Industry* (New York 1952). H. HELSON, "Color and Seeing," *Illuminating Engineering* 50.6 (1955) 271–278. W. A. WALLACE, "The Measurement and Definition of Sensible Qualities," New Schol 39 (1965) 1–25.

[W. S. RODNEY; W. A. WALLACE]

COLORADO

One of the Rocky Mountain States in the western U.S., bounded on the east by Kansas and Nebraska, on the north by Nebraska and Wyoming, on the west by Utah, and on the south by New Mexico and Oklahoma. The eastern half of the state consists of rolling plains and farm land with flat irrigated portions. The western half is mountainous, crisscrossed by ranges of the Rocky Mountains.

History. Archeologists have found evidence of human habitation in the area some 20,000 years ago. The cliff dwellings at Mesa Verde in southwestern Colorado were inhabited between 1000 and 1300 A.D. Spanish explorers and missionaries traversed the southern and western part of the state in the 16th century. In the 17th century French fur traders penetrated to the mountain areas, and France claimed the land east of the mountains. This section was transferred to the U.S. by the Louisiana Purchase (1803). American explorers Z. M. Pike (1806), S. H. Long (1820), and J. C. Fremont (1848) led expeditions into the state, naming some of the peaks. In 1821 the western part of Colorado became Mexican territory. This section was ceded

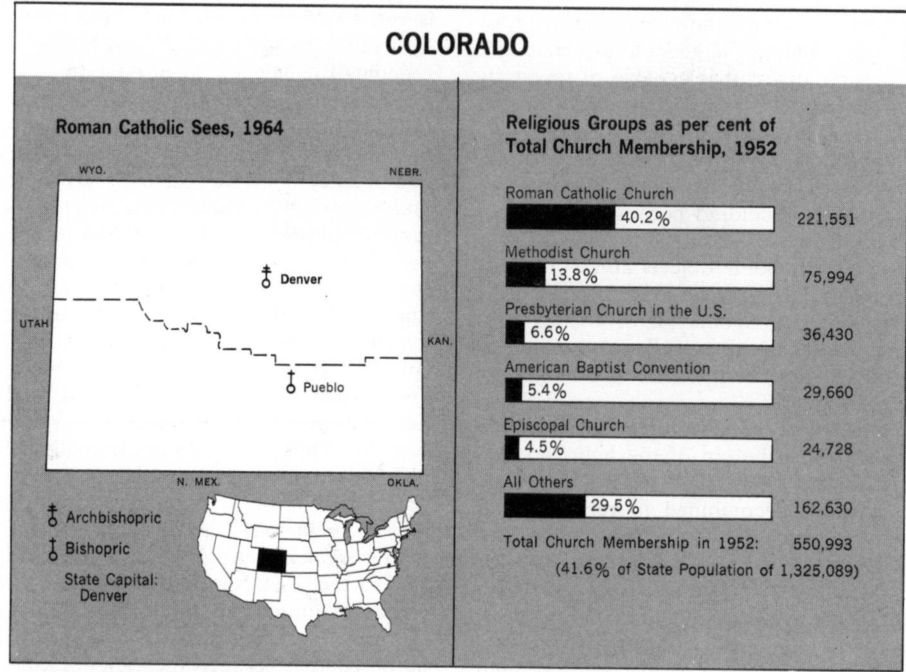

Church-membership statistics were compiled by the Bureau of Research and Survey of the National Council of the Churches of Christ in the U.S.A.

to the U.S. in 1848. The gold rush of 1859 brought thousands of prospectors to the area. Congress established the Colorado territory in 1861. The steady growth of population and the establishment of towns to serve the mining region, as well as the building of railroads and the settlement of farming communities, led to the admittance of Colorado to the Union in 1876.

Spanish Franciscans established missions in the southern and western part of the state in the 18th century. When Mexican rule superseded Spanish, the Franciscans were replaced by Mexican diocesan clergy. After the acquisition of the territory by the U.S., the southern Colorado missions were served by priests from New Mexico. The area north of the Arkansas River and east of the mountains was included in the Vicariate Apostolic of Kansas. After a visit to the gold mining camps in 1860, Bp. J. P. Miège of Leavenworth, Kans., advised that the Colorado area be transferred to the Diocese of Santa Fe, N.Mex. Accordingly, Bp. J. P. Lamy sent two priests, J. P. *Machebeuf and J. B. Raverdy, to the region. These priests served Denver and the mining towns for more than 25 years, building churches in Denver, Central City, Trinidad, Golden, Walsenburg, and Colorado Springs. In 1868 the area was established as a vicariate apostolic; it became the Diocese of *Denver in 1887 and was raised to an archdiocese in 1941, when the southern part of the state was detached to form the Diocese of *Pueblo. In the total state population of 1,325,089 in 1952, Catholics constituted 16.3 per cent; Protestants, 23.6 per cent; Jews, 1.3 per cent; and all others, 58.8 per cent (*see* CHURCH MEMBERSHIP, U.S.). In 1964 Catholics numbered 349,149 of the total state population of 1,747,937.

Education. The first Catholic school in Colorado was started by Machebeuf in 1863. In 1864 three Sisters of Loretto arrived from Santa Fe to found St. Mary's Academy and subsequently to teach in the Cathedral School for boys. In 1870 the Sisters of Charity of Cincinnati, Ohio, opened St. Joseph's Academy in Trinidad and staffed the public school there. The Jesuits established Sacred Heart (later Regis) College in 1883. Loretto Academy, founded in 1891, became Loretto Heights College in 1918. St. Thomas Seminary began the training of diocesan priests in 1907. In 1964 the Catholic educational system comprised 3 seminaries, 2 senior colleges (1,882 students), 20 high schools (7,156 students), and 90 elementary schools (29,695 students), with an additional 62,371 students receiving religious instruction.

Church-State Relations. References to and provisions affecting religion are incorporated in the state constitution and in acts of the legislature and the judiciary.

Constitution. Colorado is governed by the Constitution of 1876, as amended. The preamble invokes "profound reverence for the Supreme Ruler of the Universe."

Religious freedom is guaranteed, "but the liberty of conscience hereby secured shall not be construed to dispense with oaths or affirmations, excuse acts of licentiousness or justify practices inconsistent with the good order, peace or safety of the state." No person has to attend or support any place of worship or denomination, and no preference shall be given by law to any religion (art. 2, sec. 4).

Public funds shall not be used to aid "any church or sectarian society, or any sectarian purpose, or to help support or sustain any school, academy, seminary, college, university or other literary or scientific institution, controlled by any church or sectarian denomination whatsoever; nor shall any grant or donation of land, money or personal property ever be made by the state, or any such public corporation, to any church, or for any sectarian purpose" (art. 9, sec. 7).

Religious tests as a condition of admission into public educational institutions are forbidden "and no teacher or student of any such institution shall ever be required to attend or participate in any religious service whatever. No sectarian tenets or doctrine shall ever be taught in the public schools" (art. 9, sec. 8).

"Property, real and personal, that is used solely and exclusively for religious worship, for schools or for strictly charitable purposes, also cemeteries not used or held for private or corporate profit, shall be exempt from taxation, unless otherwise provided by general law" (art. 10, sec. 5).

Every member of the general assembly and every civil officer, except such inferior offcers as may be exempt by law, must take an oath or affirmation of office (art. 12, sec. 7, 8).

Marriage and Divorce. Marriages of men and women under 16 are forbidden except in certain cases of pregnancy. The consent of a parent or guardian is needed for men under 21 and women under 18. A license and blood test are required. Certain public officials and clergy may perform the ceremony. Common-law marriages are recognized.

Marriages are void if either party is bound by a prior subsisting marriage; if the parties are related by blood in any degree of the direct line, and up to but not including first cousins. Marriages may be annulled on the following grounds: fraud or duress; if either party is under 18; if the marriage is contracted as a jest, upon a dare, or while intoxicated; if one of the parties is incapable of performing the sex act in marriage or mentally incapable of consent. An action for a voidable marriage must be brought within 1 year of the discovery of the conditions. Any child born of a void or voidable marriage is deemed legitimate.

The grounds for absolute divorce are: impotency at marriage or resulting from immoral conduct after marriage; adultery; desertion for 1 year; cruelty; failure to support for 1 year; habitual drunkenness or drug addiction for 1 year; conviction of a felony; insanity for 3 years before the action (adjudicated insanity with party obtaining the divorce still liable for support); if parties who by force of the decree of a court of record of any state, territory, or U.S. possession have lived apart for 3 years or more prior to the action. Actions for divorce, annulment, or separate maintenance may be tried by a jury on demand. Either party may remarry after the final decree of divorce. *See* MARRIAGE, U.S. LAW OF; DIVORCE (U.S. LAW OF).

Abortion, Birth Control, Sterilization. The law forbids *abortion unless it is necessary to save the life of the mother. Persons who administer or cause to be administered or taken, any such poisonous substance, or liquid, or use or cause to be used any instrument of whatsoever kind, with the intention to procure the miscarriage of any woman with child may be fined up to $1,000 and imprisoned up to 3 years. In 1964 existing restrictions against *birth control were being eased by the removal of prohibitions against the sale of contraceptives (*see* ANOVULANTS; CONTRACEPTION). There are no references to sterilization in the state code.

Property and Taxation. Religious societies and charities may incorporate under the nonprofit corporation statute. The property of such congregations, parishes, or missions vests in the corporation; two or more members are elected as directors or trustees, whose power and duties are in keeping with the usages, customs, rules, and regulations of such congregation, church, or society.

The real and personal property of religious societies and charities that is used solely and exclusively for religious or charitable purposes is exempt from general taxation up to the amount of $6,000. There is no mortmain statute and no fund-raising statute.

Prisons and Reformatories. Equal privileges are given to clergymen of all religious denominations to impart religious instructions to inmates of industrial schools for boys. Reasonable times and places must be provided where such instruction may be given and open to all who may choose to attend. There must be a chaplain at the state reformatory and at the penitentiary. All regular officiating ministers of the gospel are authorized to visit the penitentiary at their pleasure.

Holidays and Sunday Observance. Christmas and New Year's Day, Labor Day, election day, Thanksgiving Day, any day appointed by the president or governor as a day of fast, prayer, or thanksgiving, February 22, May 30, July 4, and November 11 are legal holidays. When a holiday falls on Sunday, the next day is observed as a holiday. It is unlawful to carry on the business of barbering on Sunday in any first- or second-class city. It is unlawful for a manufacturer or wholesaler to make any delivery of malt, vinous, or spiritous liquors on Sunday, Memorial Day, Independence Day, Thanksgiving, Labor Day, or general election day.

Morality, Public Health, and Safety. No state condones polygamy. A Colorado law forbids the disturbance of religious services. It is unlawful for any person having the care or custody of any child willfully to cause or permit the life of such child to be endangered or the health of such child to be injured or willfully to cause or permit such child to be placed in such a situation that its life or health may be endangered. The chapter on the Department of Public Health states that "nothing in this article shall authorize the state department of public health to impose any mode of treatment inconsistent with the religious faith or belief of any person." The same applies to county and district boards, provided that sanitary and quarantine laws, rules, and regulations are complied with by such persons. In 1911 in *Smith v. People,* 117 Pac. 612, the court held that the accused fell under the statute prohibiting the practice of medicine without a license. Furthermore, the court stated that the statute did not interfere with religious liberty and the accused was not entitled to heal disease for hire under a religious guise.

Various Constitutional Freedoms. A city ordinance prohibiting solicitors from entering residences without the owners' or occupants' request or invitation, for the purpose of soliciting orders for the sale of goods, was held unconstitutional as denying freedom of speech and press to ministers of religious sects preaching the gospel and offering to take subscriptions for religious publications or selling them from door to door (*Donley v. City of Colorado Springs,* 40 F. Supp 15).

An ordinance prohibiting the use of loudspeakers as a means of attracting a crowd when applied without discrimination was found not unconstitutional; it was judged not to invade the defendant's freedom of speech and religion when applied to prevent the defendant minister from using a loudspeaker on city streets, where the ordinance was not dependent for its enforcement upon the whim of any individual [*Hamilton v. City of Montrose,* 124 P (2) 757].

Bibliography: L. R. and A. W. HAFEN, *Colorado* (Denver 1943). W. H. JONES, *The History of Catholic Education in the State of Colorado* (Washington 1955). W. O'RYAN and T. H. MALONE, *History of the Catholic Church in Colorado* (Denver 1889). *Statutes of Colorado, Revised, 1963* (Denver 1964). *Colorado Digest, 1864 to Date* (St. Paul, Minn. 1937–).

[E. M. GOODROW]

COLORS, LITURGICAL. All Church vesture achieves its effect by its cut, color, and texture. Color appeals most quickly to the emotions, and the proper use of it can help priest and people to feel the mood and spirit of a particular feast day. In the main, the colors of the spectrum may be associated with two moods: the warm, active, and exciting qualities of red and the cool, passive, and calming qualities of blue, violet, and green. Because of these associations, it is not surprising that a color sequence proper to particular feasts of the Church year became the subject of ecclesiastical legislation.

The first such legislation known is that of the 12th-century crusaders written for their Church at Jerusalem. Innocent III (A.D. 1198–1216) was careful to prescribe five colors for use in the Roman rite: white, red, green, black, and violet (*De Sacro Altaris Mysterio* 1.65). These are known as the liturgical colors. Although the directive is precise about what colors are to be used, it leaves the choice of shades of these colors to the vestment maker. Any red or green can be termed liturgical, provided that the shade of red or green has not been pushed so close to its neighbor in the spectrum that its own basic color has changed.

The rules given to us by Innocent III are observed commonly today. White is worn on feasts of Our Lord, Our Lady, confessors, and virgins, and on the Sundays during paschal time. Red is used for Pentecost and the feasts of Apostles and martyrs. Violet is used in Advent and Lent and the vigils of certain feasts. Green is used for the Sundays after Epiphany and Pentecost and black is worn at Masses for the dead and for part of the service on Good Friday.

From the 13th century, rose has been worn on the third Sunday in Advent and on the fourth Sunday in Lent. During the 19th century, permission to use blue was given to the Church in Spain for the feast of the Immaculate Conception; it may not be used elsewhere.

Bibliography: A. FLÜELER, *Paramente* (2d ed. enl. Zürich 1955). W. H. HOPE and E. G. ATCHLEY, *Liturgical Colors* (SPCK; London 1918). Eisenhofer Lit 145–146. T. SCHNITZLER, LexThK[2] 4:23–24. H. LECLERCQ, DACL 3.2:2999–3004.

[M. MC CANCE]

COLOSSAE, the oldest of the three major cities (with Laodicea and Hierapolis) in the Lycus Valley, in the southwestern part of ancient Phrygia. It was mentioned by both Herodotus and Xenophon. Although it was on one of the routes from *Antioch in Pisidia to *Ephesus, it does not seem that Paul visited the Christian community there (Col. 1.6–8). It had been evangelized by the Colossian Epaphras (Col 1.6–8; 4.12–13). Jewish, Greek, and ancient Phrygian elements composed the population; the Christians were mainly of Gentile origin. The city was abandoned in the 8th century, and the site has not yet been excavated.

Bibliography: S. E. JOHNSON, "Laodicea and Its Neighbors," BiblArchaeol 13 (1950) 1–18. T. DA CASTEL SAN PIETRO, EncCatt 4:23–24. H. LECLERCQ, DACL 3.2:2339–42. EncDictBibl 407–408.

[E. H. MALY]

COLOSSIANS, EPISTLE TO THE

Letter of St. Paul directed to the Christians of *Colossae, a town in the Lycus Valley of ancient Phrygia, a little more than 100 miles inland from Ephesus. They were of Gentile origin for the most part and had been brought into the faith by Epaphras (Col 1.7), a convert of Paul and a native of Colossae. Paul seems not to have visited the Colossian community personally, since he would likely have mentioned it in the letter.

Time and Place of Composition. The letter was written while Paul was a prisoner (4.3, 18), apparently at the same time the Epistle to *Philemon was written. The majority opinion still favors the period of Paul's Roman imprisonment in the early 60s. The next most serious claim is for an unrecorded imprisonment at Ephesus in the middle 50s. (For details, *see* CAPTIVITY EPISTLES.)

Authenticity. Since the rise of literary criticism there has been a strong current of scholarly opinion opposed to the Pauline authorship of Colossians, either because of the literary relationship to the Epistle to the *Ephesians, which was considered non-Pauline, or because of the developed thought of the Epistle that supposed a late theological development in the Church at Colossae. These arguments have carried less weight in recent years. Even the theory that Colossians was later edited by the unknown author of Ephesians has won few adherents, mainly because of the literary unity of Colossians. With some notable exceptions (e.g., R. Bultmann, E. Käsemann), scholars favor Pauline authorship.

Occasion. Among the false doctrinal tendencies that were being manifested among the Colossian Christians were an undue concern for the angelic order (2.15, 18), a misleading emphasis on the Mosaic Law and on ascetical practices (2.16–23), and an apparent conviction of special knowledge (2.8, 18). Epaphras must have told Paul of these incipient abuses, and the Apostle decided to write immediately before they got out of hand. Epaphras evidently was not returning at that moment (4.12), so Paul gave the letter to one *Tychicus (4.7–8). In this way he was able to provide, at the same time, a companion for *Onesimus, a slave who was returning to his master, Philemon, after his conversion to Christianity (4.9).

The precise situation to which Paul addressed himself in the letter is not easy to determine. As already mentioned, the Colossian Christians seem to have been converts from paganism. This is borne out by the references, both direct and indirect, to their former Gentile status (1.12–13, 27; 2.13), by the mention of vices that were more proper to paganism than to Judaism (3.5–7), and by the general failure to make use of arguments from the OT. However, the frequent mention of Judaizing tendencies must also be accounted for (*see* JUDAIZERS). The dietary and cultic scruples described in 2.16–17, 20–21 must have at least a partially Jewish background.

To explain these apparent inconsistencies, it is assumed that Judaizing elements in Asia Minor had made their influence felt among the Christian communities. It is known that the Jewish population in Asia Minor had grown ever since the Hellenistic conquest. It is clear, too, from the experience of Paul as recorded in Acts that, while many of these Jews accepted Christianity, there was a decided tendency among them to resist the abandonment of any of their Judaistic practices. It is suggested by some that there existed, especially in this area, a syncretistic Judaism that had been influenced by the philosophy and mysticism of a Hellenized Asia Minor. Such a Jewish heterodoxy would account for the type of speculation, asceticism, and mysticism attacked in Colossians. Specific Gnostic elements, such as characterized later groups, are not present here, and the possible Gnosticizing tendency (2.8, 18) can be explained on the basis of similar tendencies found in both Jewish and Gentile circles even before this time (*see* GNOSIS, CHRISTIAN).

Doctrine. In response to these dangers Paul presented some profound statements, which can be summed up under three headings: (1) Christ, (2) the Church, and (3) the Christian.

Christ. It is generally accepted that the most significant statement about Christ is found in 1.15–20; no higher Christology is found anywhere in the NT. Preexistence, equality with the Father, a cosmic dimension both in creation and in Redemption through Him, and absolute superiority over all creatures—these are all boldly stated of Jesus Christ. To sum up and to explain all this, Paul referred to the πλήρωμα (fullness) that God has made to dwell in Him (1.19). Its meaning is much discussed. Many scholars see Christ as containing within Himself everything that God is. Others see it rather in relation to the universe, so that Christ possesses the fullness of any excellence found in it. Because of this fullness Christ is the perfect mediator between God and man.

The absolute superiority of Christ over the angels (1.16) is such that He has despoiled them of any power they may have had over man before this (through the regime of the Law) and has made their inferiority to Himself publicly manifest (2.15). The point is so emphasized by Paul that it must have been occasioned by some doctrinal deviation. In relation to His Church Christ is the "head," an attribute that is His in the order of time by reason of His being "the firstborn from the dead" (1.18) and in the order of grace by reason of His reconciliation of all things to Himself (1.20).

The Church. In this Epistle the Church, too, takes on new dimensions. It refers here, as in Ephesians, not only to the local gathering of Christians (4.16) but primarily to the universal Church, which is more clearly seen to be organically connected with Christ; He is now, for the first time, explicitly called its head, and the Church is His body (1.18, 24). The realism of the assertion has been emphasized in recent exegesis. This is not a figure of speech used by Paul, nor does it signify merely a social entity, in which case the Church would be merely a body of "Christians" who are named after Christ. It is the body of Christ inasmuch as its members are united through Baptism to the physical but resurrected body of Christ and as a consequence are really His own members.

The Christian. The connatural emergent of this theology of Christ and the Church is the meaning it has for the Christian. Here, too, the Epistle offers profound insights. Central is the Christian's relation to Christ already mentioned. The assimilation to Christ is described here in a way that recalls Rom 6.3–11; the Christian repeats sacramentally in Baptism the saving acts of Christ (Col 2.12). For this reason it can be said that he receives of the fullness of Christ (2.10). So real is this resulting union that Paul could say that he is filling up in the flesh of his body "what is lacking of the sufferings of Christ" (1.24); it is Christ who is suffering in him. The realism of the Apostle's thought has resulted in expressions that pose many difficulties for the commentators.

Paul emphasized that all of this is possible only through the saving work of Christ. It was His body, subjected to that state in which sinful man finds himself, that was the place where reconciliation of mankind was effected through death (1.22). For if the Christian does die to sin and rise to life, it is because he dies, is buried, and rises "with Christ," i.e., as joined to Him (2.12). When God brought His Son to life, He brought the Christian along with Him (2.13). Once this is understood, then it is evident how useless are those practices that presume to possess within themselves the power to save (2.16–23). Only the intensity of Paul's convictions regarding the salvific work of Christ explains the intensity of his attack on these imperfect or humanly devised practices, including a false asceticism (2.20–22). This does not mean that he condemned all asceticism or mortification. In almost the same breath that he attacked the erroneous practices he also encouraged a life of mortification that is "in Christ" (3.5). Here Christians meet once again the familiar tension between the indicative and the imperative in the Christian life, between "you have put on Christ" and "put on Christ." In Baptism a renovation has already taken place, a complete incorporation into the resurrected Christ. It is now for the Christian to live in accord with this new life, to "strip off the old man with his deeds, and put on the new" (3.9–10; see also 2.11).

Specific ethical recommendations are made toward the close of the letter, no doubt occasioned by particular circumstances in the Colossian community. Especially encouraged is the proper Christian attitude of wives and husbands, children and parents to one another (3.18–21). But receiving more than the usual attention is the attitude of slaves and masters to one another (3.22–4.1). Perhaps this was occasioned by the presence of Onesimus, the slave of Philemon. At any rate, Paul seized the occasion to introduce some Christian elements into a social system that of its nature was incompatible with Christianity but that obviously could not be wiped out in a single day. Only a gradual change of attitude properly motivated would effectively bring that about. Paul here made his contribution to the effort.

Bibliography: J. GEWIESS, LexThK^{2} 6:400–401. T. DA CASTEL SAN PIETRO, EncCatt 4:24–27. E. KÄSEMANN and W. WERBECK, RGG^{3} 3:1727–28. EncDictBibl 408–410. Commentaries. T. K. ABBOT (Edinburgh 1897; 2d rev. ed. 1909; repr. 1954). J. B. LIGHTFOOT (London 1865). E. F. SCOTT (London 1930; 8th ed. 1952). C. F. D. MOULE (Cambridge, Eng. 1957). J. HUBY (12th ed. Paris 1946). C. MASSON (Paris 1950). E. LOHMEYER (Göttingen 1930). M. MEINERTZ (4th ed. Bonn 1931). K. STAAB (Ratisbon 1950). M. DIBELIUS and H. GREEVEN (3d ed. Tübingen

1953). J. Knox, "Philemon and the Authenticity of Colossians," JRelig 18 (1938) 144–160. For additional bibliography, *see* CAPTIVITY EPISTLES.

[E. H. MALY]

The east face of the so-called "Cross of Saints Patrick and Columba," Kells, County Meath, Ireland. The early 9th-century sculpture is so named because of the inscription on the base that mentions both these saints.

COLUMBA OF IONA, ST., Irish ascetic and monastic founder; b. Gartan, Donegal *c.* 521; d. Iona, June 9, 597 (feast, June 9). Columba, of the royal O'Neill dynasty, was educated at Clonard under St. Finnian, and at Glasnevin near Dublin. He was ordained in 551 and established a monastery at Derry. In 563 he migrated to the island of Iona (Hy) and established a monastic center for missions among the Picts and Northumbrians, as well as for scholarly pursuit. He apparently visited the Irish mainland on one or two occasions, and in the Assembly of Druim-Cetta (575) he acted as a peacemaker. He is credited with the authorship of poems in both Latin (*Altus Prosator*) and early Gaelic. The "cathach" psalter, the oldest known MS of the Gallican Psalter, may be in his handwriting. Columba left no written rule, but his *Vita* by *Adamnan of Iona gives a description of the manner of life of the monks.

Bibliography: L. Bieler, LexThK² 6:403. Adamnan of Iona, *Life of Columba,* ed. and tr. A. O. and M. O. Anderson (New York 1962). Kenney 1:422–442. **Illustration credit:** Commissioners of Public Works in Ireland.

[J. RYAN]

COLUMBA OF RIETI, BL., patroness of Perugia; b. Angelella Guadagnoli, Rieti, Feb. 2, 1467; d. Perugia, May 20, 1501 (feast, May 20). Her name was changed to Columba when a dove flew over the font at her christening. Refusing the marriage arranged by her parents, she made a vow of virginity and entered upon a solitary life. At the age of 19, having become a Dominican tertiary, she left her seclusion, journeying to Viterbo, Narni, Foligno, and eventually to turbulent Perugia, where she founded the convent of St. Catherine (1490). Civil rulers and members of the hierarchy came to consult her; her influence as a peacemaker was remarkable. She practiced severe penances and endured painful illnesses and calumnies. She was particularly devoted to St. *Catherine of Siena. When Columba was dying, the civil magistrates came to visit her, and the expenses of her funeral were defrayed by the city of Perugia. Her cult was confirmed in 1627.

Bibliography: *Année Dominicaine,* 23 v. (Lyons 1883–1909) May 2:527–544. M. D. de Ganay, *Les Bienheureuses Dominicaines* (4th ed. Paris 1924) 305–354. R. Frascisco, Mercati-Pelzer DE 1:668. Butler ThAttw 2:359–361. A. Walz, LexThK² 3:13.

[M. J. FINNEGAN]

COLUMBA AND POMPOSA, SS., virgin martyrs; b. Córdoba *c.* 830 and *c.* 840; d. Córdoba, Sept. 17 and 19, 853 (feasts, Sept. 17 and 19). Columba and her sister built the double monastery of Tabanos, from which came several of the first martyrs of *Córdoba. Columba was martyred after she confessed Christ and denounced the prophet Mohammed before the Moslem authorities. Christians recovered her relics from the Guadalquivir River and buried them in a basilica outside Córdoba. *Eulogius makes of her vita an exemplum of the virtues practiced in the monastic life. The youthful Pomposa slipped out of a monastery built by her parents and repeated Columba's words before the cadi. She was slain immediately. Her body also was recovered from the river and buried at the feet of Columba. Both were included in the Roman martyrology in 1583.

Bibliography: Eulogius, *Memoriale sanctorum* 3.10, 11 in PL 115:806–813. E. P. Colbert, *The Martyrs of Córdoba, 850–859* (Washington 1962).

[E. P. COLBERT]

COLUMBAN, ST., also Columbanus or Columba the Younger, Irish monk, abbot of *Luxeuil and *Bobbio; b. Leinster, Ireland, *c.* 543; d. Bobbio, Nov. 23, 615 (feast in the Roman Martyrology, Nov. 21). Columbanus studied at the school of St. Sinell (a disciple of St. Finnian of Clonard) at Cleenish in Lough Erne and entered the monastery and school of St. Comgall at *Bangor, where sanctity and scholarship were combined. In 591, after 30 years of teaching during which he composed a commentary on the Psalter and poems for his students, he was sent by St. Comgall with 12 companions to do missionary work on the continent of Europe. Invited by the Merovingian King Childebert he settled in Burgundy and founded three monasteries, Annegray, Luxeuil, and Fontaines, whence there originated some 200 monastic foundations for which he composed a *Regula monachorum* and a *Regula coenobialis.* Vigorously attacking the degenerate local clergy, the immoral court, and undesirable local customs, he introduced the strict Irish system of Penance, contributing two *Penitentials himself. He had difficulty with the local bishops over the date for celebrating Easter (*see* EASTER CONTROVERSY) and wrote to Pope *Gregory I for support, using the term *totius Europae* for the first time to express the Irish concept of the West as a Christian cultural unit. Expelled from *Burgundy by King Theuderic whom he censured for living in concubinage, Columbanus passed through Neustria at the request of King Clothar and settled near Zurich whence he was driven out by the local population for his attack on paganism. He crossed the Alps and founded a monastery at Bobbio in Italy; from there his influence spread all over Europe, although his successors mitigated some of the rigors of Irish *monasticism with Benedictine elements. His letters, rules, and poetry form part of the great tradition of Irish Latin literature and had a lasting effect on the culture of the Middle Ages. His body is buried in a crypt of the Church of St. Columbanus at Bobbio.

Bibliography: *S. Columbani Opera,* ed. G. S. M. WALKER (*Scriptores Latini Hiberniae* 2; Dublin 1957). JONAS OF BOBBIO, *Vita sancti Columbani,* ed. B. KRUSCH (MGSrerGerm 35; 1905). M. M. DUBOIS, *Saint Columban* (Paris 1950). J. O'CARROLL, tr., "The Chronology of St. Columban," IrTheolQ 24 (1957) 76–95. F. MACMANUS, *Saint Columban* (New York 1962). L. BIELER and D. A. BINCHY, eds., *The Irish Penitentials* (*Scriptores Latini Hiberniae* 5; Dublin 1963). Kenney 1:186–205.

[J. RYAN]

COLUMBAN FATHERS

St. Columban's Foreign Mission Society (SSC), popularly known as Columban Fathers, originated in Ireland in October 1916. An influential committee, organized by the missionary Edward J. *Galvin and Rev. John Blowick, a Maynooth professor, requested the Irish hierarchy to approve the foundation of a seminary to train secular priests as missionaries for China; the bishops authorized the project, and Benedict XV approved it. The seminary (major) was opened January 1918, at Dalgan Park, Galway; in March it was placed under the protection of the Congregation for the Propagation of the Faith. On June 29, 1918, 17 priests took the oath of membership in this new society which chose St. *Columban, Irish missionary (d. 615), as its patron. It became a pontifical society in 1924.

At the invitation of Abp. Jeremiah Harty, the Columban Fathers established their first house in the U.S. at Omaha, Nebr., on Dec. 14, 1918. Four years later, the first seminary (major) was dedicated at Bellevue, Nebr. In 1924 a minor seminary was opened at Silver Creek, N.Y., and in 1933, a novitiate, at Bristol, R.I. A second minor seminary was established in Boston, Mass., in 1945; later this became a college, which in 1963 was transferred to Oconomowoc, Wis. The major seminary was transferred from Omaha to Boston in 1953. There were 156 Columban priests and 214 seminarians in the U.S. in 1963, staffing houses in Boston, Mass.; New York City and Buffalo, N.Y.; Philadelphia, Pa.; Chicago, Ill.; St. Paul, Minn.; Denver, Colo.; Houston, Tex.; and San Francisco, Los Angeles, and San Diego, Calif.

In 1920, two Columban Fathers went to Australia, where a year later Abp. Daniel Mannix of Melbourne blessed the first Columban house in his archdiocese. A major seminary was established in the Archdiocese of Sydney, and a novitiate in the Archdiocese of Melbourne. The general headquarters of the society are located at Navan, Ireland. The procurator general resides at Collegio San Colombano, Rome. Headquarters in the U.S. are at St. Columbans, Nebr., and in Australia, at North Essendon, Victoria. In 1963 Columban priests numbered 856, of whom 509 served 223 parishes and 431 stations in China, the Philippines, Korea, Burma, Japan, the Fiji Islands, and the countries of South America.

In China the first area assigned to the Columban Fathers (1920) was Hanyang, where Galvin became first vicar apostolic in 1927, and bishop in 1946. The Communists expelled the bishop and the missionaries in 1952. In 1928 the society received a district in Kiangsi province, then the headquarters of the Communists. Father Patrick Cleary was consecrated the first bishop of Nancheng, Kiangsi, in 1939. When communism triumphed in China, at least 90 Columban Fathers were forced to depart from their mission stations where there were almost 56,000 Chinese Catholics.

In 1929 Columban Fathers went to the Philippines in response to an appeal from Archbishop O'Doherty of Manila. In 1963 there were 203 Columbans serving in 85 parishes in various dioceses throughout the Islands. In these, 102 Catholic schools provided education for 39,139 students. Two Columban Fathers were made prelates ordinary in the Philippines: Bp. Patrick Cronin of Ozamis and Bp. Henry Byrne of Iba. Nine Columbans have charge of Student Catholic Action in Manila.

Columbans, stationed in Korea since 1933, totaled 103 in 1963. Among those giving outstanding service there were Msgr. Patrick Brennan (of Chicago), Prefect of Kwangju, who was killed in the Taejon massacre in September 1950; his successor, Abp. Harold Henry (of Northfield, Minn.), who built a major seminary for 200 students of 4 southern dioceses of Korea; and Bp. Thomas Quinlan, survivor of the Korean War "death march" and Ordinary of Chunchon.

Columban Father John Howe was consecrated in 1961 as first bishop of Myitkyina, Bhamo, Burma, where members of the society have been working since 1936. In South America, 29 priests were sent to Lima, Peru, and Santiago, Chile; 20 additional volunteers were gathered when, in December 1960, the Holy See requested that the Columbans be empowered to recruit Irish and English diocesan priests for South America.

Bibliography: Archives, St. Columbans, Nebr. P. CROSBIE, *March Till They Die* (Westminster, Md. 1956). R. REILLY, *Christ's Exile: Life of Bishop Edward J. Galvin* (Dublin 1958). B. T. SMYTH, ed., *But Not Conquered* (Westminster, Md. 1958). F. HERLIHY, *Now Welcome Summer* (Dublin 1948).

[D. A. BOLAND]

COLUMBUS, CHRISTOPHER

Italian, Cristoforo Colombo and Spanish, Cristóbal Colón, seaman, chartmaker, navigator, discoverer of America; b. Genoa, Italy, Sept.–Oct. 1451; d. Valladolid, Spain, May 20, 1506. Christopher, Bartholomew, and Diego, sons of Domenico Colombo and his wife, Susanna Fontanarossa, became wool carders but not master weavers like their father and grandfathers. Christopher went to sea at 14, without schooling. His will of 1498 refers to Genoa as "that noble and powerful city by the sea." Throughout life, Columbus attempted to emulate St. Christopher, "the Christ bearer." Ardent in religious devotion, he desired to spread the Christian faith more than he wished for personal glory, wealth, and distinction. He had rare ability to acquire knowledge through observation and experience; he demonstrated superlative competence as a seaman and navigator during his four famous voyages. Little is known of his life prior to 1486. He served in a Genoese privateer; he made one or more voyages to Chios in the Aegean Sea. He survived the sinking of a ship in battle, off Cape St. Vincent, Portugal, Aug. 13, 1476. Although

Christopher Columbus, 16th-century Flemish engraving, possibly based upon an actual portrait.

wounded, he seized a large oar and used it for partial support in swimming to the Portuguese coast. After being cared for in the Genoese colony of Lisbon, he became a chartmaker with his brother Bartholomew. He made a voyage to Iceland, and visited Galway, Ireland. Castilian Spanish was the language of the educated in Portugal when the Columbus brothers were establishing themselves as chartmakers. The writings of Christopher are in Castilian with Portuguese spellings, or in Latin learned after he began to think in Spanish. As an agent for Genoese merchants he visited Genoa and lived in Madeira for a time. In command of a merchant vessel, he made at least one voyage to equatorial west Africa. He married Doña Felipa Perestrello e Moniz, whose brother held the hereditary captaincy of the island of Porto Santo, near Madeira. Their son Diego was born *c.* 1480. She died before Columbus went to Spain and was buried in the Moniz family chapel in Lisbon's church of the Carmo.

The Indies. Portugal led Europe in sea exploration and a chartmaker in Lisbon could be familiar with Portuguese progress. Christopher studied geography, and three of his books have been preserved: *Imago Mundi* by *Peter of Ailly of Cambrai, written *c.* 1410, printed *c.* 1480; *Historia Rerum Ubique Gestarum* by Aeneas Sylvius Piccolomini (*Pius II, 1458–64) written 1440, printed 1477; and the Far Eastern travels of *Marco Polo, also in Latin. Both brothers read and reread these books. Christopher made some 2,000 marginal notes and filled the blank pages at the ends of the volumes. He conceived the idea of sailing westward to Asia. The "Fixed Idea" of Columbus was based on faith in his own ability as a seaman-navigator, combined with a gross underestimate of the distance involved. The size of the earth had been debated for 1800 years. According to *Ptolemy (A.D. 145) the distance from Cape St. Vincent to easternmost China spanned 180° or halfway around the globe. Enthusiasm helped Columbus to prefer the earlier estimate of Marinus of Tyre, viz, 225°. The Venetian traveler Marco Polo placed China and Japan farther east. Columbus argued that a degree on the Equator measured 45.2 nautical miles, the smallest estimate ever made. Columbus obtained partial support from P. *Toscanelli of Florence in 1481, when the latter estimated that Japan was only 3,000 miles west of the Canary Islands. Christopher calculated that 2,400 miles was the distance, and placed the coast of Japan in the longitude of San Juan, Puerto Rico. He asked the King of Portugal to send him westward to Asia, but Portuguese geographers advised that the voyage would require fully 100 days.

Preparations for the Voyage. Unsuccessful in his effort to engage the support of King John II of Portugal, Columbus sought help elsewhere.

Columbus in Spain. Upon arriving at Palos from Portugal in 1485, Christopher left his son Diego with the Franciscan friars at La Rabida. Bartholomew continued chartmaking in Lisbon. The head of the Franciscans in Seville, Antonio de Marchena (*see* PÉREZ, JUAN), was favorably impressed by the ideas of Columbus, and the latter was able to explain them to Queen *Isabella at Córdoba, in May 1486. At that time the sovereigns were engaged in war against the Moorish Kingdom of Granada.

Columbus at Salamanca. Twice in Spain, and once in Portugal, royal commissions considered the advisability of financing an expedition for Columbus. Father Hernando de Talavera, later archbishop of Granada, headed the best known commission, December 1486, in Salamanca. It should be remembered that there was no accurate way to determine longitude prior to 1765. In 1486, neither the size of the earth nor the longitude of Japan was known. The commission reported that the earth was considerably larger than Columbus believed, that the distance to Japan was far greater than he estimated, and that available ships could not carry sufficient food and water for a voyage of that length. On these three points the commission was correct, but the members were favorably impressed by the dignity and earnestness of Columbus himself. The consensus in Spain then was that a degree on the equator measured 55.9 nautical miles; an underestimate of about 6.83 per cent in the size of the earth. By contrast, Columbus underestimated by about 24.67 per cent.

The popular "Columbus Myth" describes the Salamanca meeting as an attempt by Columbus to convince university professors, mostly churchmen, that the earth is round. The University of Salamanca was not involved. Spain had no capital at that time, and the royal commission met in that city because the court was there. The shape of the earth was not in question. Ever since men first built ships and put out from land it had been known that the earth is a sphere. The masts and spars of an approaching vessel appear over the horizon before the hull is seen. In heading away, a ship goes "hull down" before the masts disappear. Vessels often pass each other "hull down" at sea. Lookouts go to the masthead to see objects not visible from the deck. This explains the use of fires on headlands or lights on towers as aids to navigation. Lighthouses were in use for 2,100 years before the meeting at Salamanca.

Delays. The report of the Talavera Commission was delayed, and Columbus wrote King John II of Portugal. He was invited to return there, and he wrote in his copy of *Imago Mundi* that he was in Lisbon in December 1488 when Bartholomew *Dias returned after discovering the Cape of Good Hope. With the route to India around Africa thus open to him, the King of Portugal lost interest in Columbus's idea. Columbus probably supported himself by selling books and charts in Seville. Bartholomew Columbus failed to interest King *Henry VII of England in 1489. Although unsuccessful also in France, Bartholomew was retained at Fontainbleau as a chartmaker by the King's sister, Anne de Beaujeu, until he learned of his brother's discovery. Christopher suffered genuine distress after the unfavorable report of the Commission. Determined to go to France, he traveled first to La Rabida. Father Juan Pérez wrote to Queen Isabella and secured for Christopher another summons to court. His proposals were considered again, and referred to the Royal Council of Castile. Immediately after Columbus marched in the triumphal procession entering Granada on Jan. 2, 1492, his plan was rejected.

Queen Isabella's Decision. On the day that Christopher left court, one of King *Ferdinand V of Castile's Aragonese advisers, Luis de Santangel, persuaded Isabella to reconsider. Columbus was recalled and had another interview with Isabella. She won her husband's approval. Santangel argued that the enterprise required little risk while offering great possibilities. Probably the character of Columbus won for him the support of the Queen and of many able men. The Franciscan Father Juan Pérez assisted in making the agreements with the crown.

The First Voyage. With a total of 90 men embarked, the ship *Santa Maria* and the caravels *Pinta* and *Nina* sailed from Palos on Friday, Aug. 3, 1492. They departed the Canary Islands on September 9. With favorable weather and winds, they were beyond the position where land was expected on October 10, and the crew complained. Columbus promised to turn back if land was not sighted in 2 or 3 days. San Salvador Island was discovered on Oct. 12, 1492; latitude 24° 00′ north, longitude 74° 30′ west; 33 days and 3,066 nautical miles from the Canaries. After exploring northeastern Cuba, Columbus crossed the Windward Passage to the north shore of Hispaniola, where the *Santa Maria* was wrecked on Christmas morning. Forty men were left in a fort on shore called "Navidad." With a number of Indians and some gold, Columbus started his return passage in the *Nina,* from Samana Bay on Jan. 16, 1493. Heading northeast, Columbus weathered severe storms, stopped in the Azores, and was driven into Lisbon. After calling on the King of Portugal, Columbus reached Palos a few hours ahead of the *Pinta* on March 15, 1493.

News of the discovery spread rapidly in Spain and Italy, slowly elsewhere. Columbus visited the court at Barcelona, was ordered to prepare another expedition, and was confirmed in the title Admiral of the Ocean Sea. While recognizing his discovery, many educated men doubted that he had reached the Indies in 33 days from the Canaries.

Second Voyage. The second departure was on Oct. 13, 1493. A high mountainous island sighted Sunday, November 3 was named Dominica. Skirting the Leeward Islands, inside the Caribbean, via the Mona Passage, all 17 vessels reached Navidad safely on November 28. Columbus was shocked by the discovery that all of the garrison were dead, and influenced by the necessity of returning ships to Spain, he hastily chose for the new town of "Isabela" a site that lacked natural advantages. A better anchorage was available 20 miles east at Puerto Plata. Throughout the first voyage crews had been healthy, but hard work, exposure to mosquitos, rain, and strange diets made 300 men ill soon after work began at Isabela. Medicaments were exhausted; the doctor worn out. Columbus was not an experienced administrator; his errors were repeated, however, by the English in Virginia a century later, and by other colonizers. Columbus explored part of the southern coast of Cuba in May, circled Jamaica, and returned along the southern coast of Hispaniola, reaching Isabela on Sept. 29, 1494. His brother Bartholomew had arrived, and there was a letter from the sovereigns suggesting that he return to Spain to advise them. Although suffering from arthritis, Columbus remained while discontent increased in the colony. He sailed March 10, and reached Cadiz June 11, 1496.

The islands discovered by Columbus in the West Indies, woodcut in "De insulis nuper inuentis," printed in Basel in 1494 by Johann Bergman de Olpe. This book was the second publication of Columbus's letter of March 15, 1493, in which he announced his discoveries. Although the woodcut is a stylized view of the islands (which here bear the names Fernanda, Ysabella, Saluatorie, Hyspana, and Conceptionis Marie), it is of the greatest importance as the first printed representation of the New World.

Third Voyage. Departure was from the Cape Verde Islands July 4, 1498. Sighting Trinidad July 31, the admiral entered the Gulf of Paria, where he recognized that the volume of fresh water proved that the land to the South and West was part of a continent. Worried about conditions in Hispaniola, Columbus failed to seek the pearl fisheries after learning of them and seeing some pearls. Instead he left the coast near Margarita Island, heading for the colony. With the hope of improving matters, the admiral asked for a chief justice from Spain. Francisco de Bobadilla arrived while Christopher and Bartholomew were absent from Santo Domingo City; he listened to the malcontents and sent the brothers home in chains without hearing them. The sovereigns released Columbus, but King Ferdinand was preoccupied with diplomacy and did not study the colonial problem.

Fourth Voyage. This departure was from the Canaries May 26, 1502. Reaching Martinique June 15, the admiral headed for Santo Domingo with the hope of exchanging his flagship for a better vessel. Columbus recognized that a hurricane was imminent, asked for shelter in the Ozama River, suggested that all vessels be held in port until the storm passed. Disregarding the warning, 25 ships sailed; 20 ships and 500 men were lost. Denied shelter, the admiral rode out the storm at sea. He then spent 9 months exploring the coast of Central America from Honduras to a point about 125 miles east of Porto Bello. He suffered from malaria, and bad weather, tropical rain, sickness, and difficulties with the Indians affected all hands. Shipworms damaged the hulls of his vessels, and he was forced to run them aground in Saint Ann's Bay, Jamaica. Diego Méndez crossed to Cape Tiburon against wind and current, and made his way to Governor Ovando, but Ovando left the admiral and his men marooned for 370 days. Bartholomew and the admiral's younger son, Ferdinand, were on this voyage. Nearly half the men mutinied, and mistreated the Indians, and the latter almost ceased to supply food. Columbus knew that a total eclipse of the moon was expected on the night of Feb. 29, 1504. Summoning the Indian chiefs to a conference, the admiral told them that the God of the Christians would make a sign with the moon to show his disapproval of their failure to supply food to the stranded white men. The eclipse was persuasive. Rescued June 29, he reached Spain Nov. 7, 1504, a few weeks before Isabella's death, and died 2 years later. His remains rest in the cathedral of Santo Domingo City. Those of his son Don Diego, the second Admiral of the Ocean Sea, are in the cathedral of Seville. The will of Columbus commended the family, including Beatriz Enríquez de Harana, mother of Ferdinand (b. 1488), to Diego's benevolence.

Achievements of Columbus. In the most famous voyages of modern history Columbus set an example for Europe, raising standards as a seaman, as a navigator, and as an explorer. Before the development of celestial navigation he demonstrated a degree of skill in "dead reckoning" that would be highly creditable to the best navigators of the 1960s. He exhibited outstanding practical seamanship in fair weather and during storms. Although he had spent only a few years in the Caribbean area, his observations of weather conditions enabled him to predict an impending hurricane. He gave Spain an empire and extended Christian civilization. As an administrator he made mistakes, but few men have done better under similar primitive conditions in colonization.

Bibliography: J. WINSOR, *Christopher Columbus* (5th ed. Boston 1892); ed., *Narrative and Critical History of America,* 8 v. (Boston 1884–89) 2:1-128. R. Academia de la historia, Madrid, *Bibliografía Colombina: Enumeración de libros y documentos concernientes a Cristóbal Colón y sus viajes* (Madrid 1892). *Raccolta di documenti e studi pubblicati dalla R. Commissione Colombiana,* 14 v. (Rome 1892–94). J. B. THACHER, *Christopher Columbus: His Life, His Work, His Remains,* 3 v. (New York 1903–04). F. COLÓN, *The Life of the Admiral Christopher Columbus,* ed. and tr. B. KEEN (New Brunswick, N.J. 1959). S. E. MORISON, *Admiral of the Ocean Sea: A Life of Christopher Columbus,* 2 v. (Boston 1942); *Christopher Columbus, Mariner* (Boston 1955); ed. and tr., *Journals and Other Documents on the Life and Voyages of Christopher Columbus* (New York 1963). A. BALLESTEROS Y BERETTA, *Cristóbal Colón y el descubrimiento de América,* 2 v. (Barcelona 1945). L. HANKE, *Bartolomé de las Casas* (Philadelphia 1952). *Studi Colombiana,* 3 v. (Genoa 1952). C. SANZ, *Bibliotheca Americana vetustissima: Ultimas adiciones,* 2 v. (Madrid 1960). **Illustration credit:** Fig. 1. National Gallery of Art, Washington, D.C., Rosenwald Collection. Fig. 2. John Work Garrett Library, Johns Hopkins University, Baltimore, Md.; photo courtesy Walters Gallery.

[J. B. HEFFERNAN]

COLUMBUS, DIOCESE OF (COLUMBENSIS)

Suffragan of the metropolitan See of Cincinnati, comprising 23 counties in central Ohio, an area of 11,310 square miles. The area's Catholic origins go back to 1818, when a group of laborers on the National Road and a few German farmers began to worship at St. Joseph's, Somerset, Ohio. This mission was attended by the Dominican fathers, who prior to 1833 traveled to Columbus to hold services there in the Paul Pry house on Water Street. In 1866 the Second Plenary Council of Baltimore recommended the erection of a diocese at Columbus, and on March 3, 1868, "that part of the State of Ohio south of north latitude 40° 41′ and between the Ohio River on the east and the Scioto River on the west, together with the counties of Franklin, Delaware, and Morrow," was so erected. The first ordinary, Sylvester H. Rosecrans, had been auxiliary of Cincinnati since March 25, 1862, and a convert to the faith since 1845. The population of the see city was 30,000; the diocese had 40,000 Catholics attending 40 churches, 3 of which were in Columbus. By 1868 the Academy (later College) of *St. Mary of the Springs was established, and 3 years later St. Aloysius Seminary was begun, only to close after 5 or 6 years, having trained 15 for the priesthood. Rosecrans died Oct. 21,

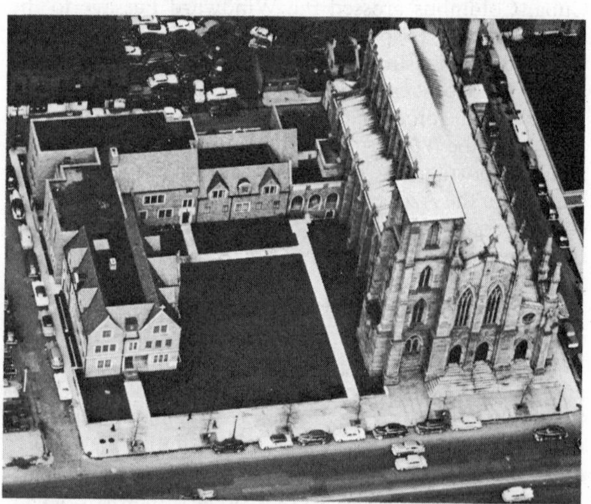

St. Joseph's Cathedral, Columbus, Ohio, completed in 1878, with chancery office and cathedral rectory (1949).

1878, the day after he dedicated St. Joseph's Cathedral, erected during his episcopacy.

John A. Watterson, President of Mt. St. Mary's College in Emmitsburg, Md., was appointed second bishop and consecrated Aug. 8, 1880. He discharged the cathedral debt and added to the extent and value of cathedral property. In 1894 Josephinum College, Worthington, was opened under Rev. Joseph Jessing as a seminary for German-speaking priests in the U.S.

After Watterson's death in 1899, the former chancellor of the Archdiocese of Cincinnati, Henry Moeller, was consecrated as the new bishop of Columbus Aug. 25, 1900. He assumed a diocesan debt of $200,000, which was prorated to the various parishes and paid by them in 3 years. Moeller was then named coadjutor of Cincinnati, and Pius X appointed James J. Hartley, pastor of Holy Name Church in Steubenville, Ohio, as fourth bishop of Columbus. He was consecrated Feb. 25, 1904, and administered the diocese for 40 years. Under his leadership St. Charles Seminary was founded in 1923 and developed on its present site in 1925. In 1941 Edward Hettinger was appointed his auxiliary and consecrated Feb. 24, 1942. Two years later Hartley died and his successor, Michael Ready, was consecrated in Washington, D.C., Dec. 14, 1944. A capable administrator, he directed the postwar building program in the Columbus area, establishing 18 new parishes, 9 elementary schools, and 5 high schools in little more than a decade. During his tenure the Catholic Welfare Bureau was also established. He died May 2, 1957, and Bp. Clarence G. Issenmann, then auxiliary bishop of Cincinnati, assumed charge of the diocese Dec. 5, 1957, until his transfer (1964) to Cleveland, Ohio. In January 1965 Bp. John J. Carberry of Lafayette, Ind., was named seventh ordinary of Columbus. By 1964 Catholics numbered more than 170,370 in a total population of about 1,674,000, and were organized in 106 parishes and 15 missions, served by 316 priests, of whom 87 were religious. Also working in the diocese were 18 brothers and 1,100 sisters, who helped to staff its 1 college, 25 high and 66 elementary schools, 6 general hospitals, 3 schools for nurses, 2 orphanages, and 2 homes for the aged.

Bibliography: *Archives, Diocese of Columbus.* J. J. HARTLEY, ed., *The Diocese of Columbus: History of Fifty Years, 1868–1918* (Columbus 1918); *History of Diocese of Columbus, 1918–43* (Columbus 1943).

[R. A. BONNELL]